August 12–16, 2012
Beijing, China

Association for
Computing Machinery

Advancing Computing as a Science & Profession

KDD'12 Vol. 2 of 2

The 18th ACM SIGKDD International Conference on

Knowledge Discovery and DataMining

Sponsored by:

KDD.org and ACM SIGMOD

Supported by:

Huawei, Baidu, Aliyun.com, Facebook, EMC², Elsevier, PayPal of Ebay, SAS, IBM Research, Opera Solutions, Soso, SAP, Microsoft, Google, Greenplum, Nokia Research Center, Deloitte, Adobe, Media6Degrees, NSF, CityGrid.com, HP, CRC Press, Springer, Zementis, Technicolor, and Morgan & Claypool Publishers

Association for
Computing Machinery

Advancing Computing as a Science & Profession

The Association for Computing Machinery
2 Penn Plaza, Suite 701
New York, New York 10121-0701

ISBN: 978-1-4503-1462-6 (Digital)

ISBN: 978-1-4503-1947-8 (Print Vol.2)

Additional copies may be ordered prepaid from:

ACM Order Department
PO Box 30777
New York, NY 10087-0777, USA

Phone: 1-800-342-6626 (USA and Canada)
+1-212-626-0500 (Global)
Fax: +1-212-944-1318
E-mail: acmhelp@acm.org
Hours of Operation: 8:30 am – 4:30 pm ET

ACM Order Number: 618122

Printed in the USA

General Chairs' Welcome Message

KDD-2012, the 18th ACM SIGKDD International Conference on Knowledge Discovery and Data Mining, is being held in Beijing, China, on August 12--16, 2012. KDD is the leading international forum for the exchange of research results and practical experience in the field of knowledge discovery and data mining. As we enter the era of Big Data, there is an increasing need to share our innovative ideas and state-of-the-art solutions on knowledge-discovery and data mining from multiple perspectives, ranging from academic research to industrial applications, from scientific discovery to health services. This volume highlights a snapshot of the developments in this rapidly developing field.

The KDD-2012 technical program features four parallel research tracks, an industrial / government track, and an industry practice expo (IPE), an Asia-pacific Track (APT) and a new KDD Summer School. The APT is specifically designed to take advantage of the fact that this KDD is held in Asia, by inviting a sample of top Asia-pacific researchers to present their data mining projects. We hope this new track will enable the KDD community to learn more on the developments in Asia-pacific region. The KDD Summer School allows students attending the conference to take advantage of availability of the many KDD experts at one location. The courses in the summer school will introduce two of the hot topics in KDD today: `Mining of Complex Data' and `Large Scale Data Mining'.

The KDD 2012 program also features keynotes from leaders of KDD research and practice, 20 workshops, 7 tutorials and one panel. The 2012 KDD Cup competition focuses on microblogging and Web search advertising problems from Tencent, China's Internet and social media giant, which also represent the largest KDD CUP data sets ever. Dozens of technical demonstrations and exhibits from vendors and other organizations underscore the conference's dual role as the leading industry and academic forum to discuss the advances in this field of research and applications.

The call for papers attracted 755 research papers and 113 industrial and government submissions from around the world. Each paper was independently reviewed by three members of the program committee for originality, significance, technical quality, and clarity of presentation. In the end, the program committee accepted 133 papers into the research track, representing an acceptance rate of 17.6%. The industry and government track of the conference accepted 30 papers into the program, representing an acceptance rate of 26.5%.

From the conference, we can see that the KDD community is continuing to be vibrant and growing, and KDD innovations remain very strong and have very high quality. The resulting program is notable for its diversity and vitality. With the exciting program as our backdrop, we certainly hope this conference will become a new starting point, where research and development on data science and data mining, and research and development on Big data analytics, will continue to flourish.

Qiang Yang
KDD2012 General Chair
HKUST, Hong Kong, China

Dou Shen
KDD2012 Associate General Chair
CityGrid Media, Seattle, WA, USA

Research Track Program Chairs' Welcome Message

The KDD conference has seen remarkable growth since its origins as an IJCAI workshop in Detroit in 1989, evolving into a full-fledged research conference in 1995, underscoring the important role data mining as a field has played in extracting knowledge and actionable insights from vast troves of data that is being generated in the digital world around us. This year we received a record 755 submissions to the research program, from which 133 papers were accepted, for an aggregate acceptance rate of 17.6% (quite similar to recent years).

Among the academic conferences, the KDD conference has typically more of an emphasis on research motivated by real-world applications. It is important to keep in mind that it is this synergy of research in areas like algorithms, computational geometry, database, graph theory, machine learning, natural language processing, statistics, visualization and many others when applied to problems arising in diverse fields such as web, medicine, climatology, marketing that drives our field forward, makes it vibrant and fun – who would know that ideas in computational geometry can be adapted to construct fast algorithms to improve online advertising and movie recommendations?

The breadth of topics covered in this year's research program is truly comprehensive, including social networks, privacy, text mining, predictive modeling, time-series forecasting, spatial data analysis, geometry, and more. We are very fortunate to have 4 world-class keynote speakers this year spanning industry and academia, providing inspirational talks on cutting-edge techniques and issues in web mining, information networks, statistical inference for big data, and social computing.

The process of whittling down the initial 734 submissions to the final set of 133 accepted papers required the coordination and time of a large number of willing volunteers. The program committee (PC) consisted of over 350 reviewers (PC members) and 50 senior PC members. In the first phase each submitted paper was automatically assigned to 3 reviewers (after a bidding process). Once the reviews from each of the 3 reviewers were completed, the program chairs rejected papers that did not receive much support from any of the reviewers. We rejected 259 papers at this stage. Special care was taken to minimize the error of rejecting a potentially good paper at this stage. The papers that survived the first phase were assigned to the senior PC members based on their bids, they had the option of initiating a discussion for any of their papers, e.g., if there was significant divergence in scores among reviewers, or if a paper was on the borderline of being accepted. Following the discussion phase, the senior PC members provided a recommendation score and a detailed meta-review for each paper. In the final phase, we (the program chairs) analyzed all of this information, starting with the obvious accept and reject decisions, and then gradually focusing in more detail on the papers near the borderline, seeking additional reviews and input from the PC and senior PC members where appropriate. We also initiated a shepherding phase with 15 papers having the opportunity of fixing mild issues we thought would be possible to address before they can be accepted. 13 of them were accepted after thorough revisions. Finally, it is quite likely that in hindsight some worthy papers may have been rejected as part of this process - these errors are an unfortunate reality of modern computer science conferences, and hard to avoid when a very large number of decisions have to be made over a short time span based on a subjective reviewing process. Nevertheless, we, the PC chairs, are responsible for those unfortunate errors and welcome suggestions on the matter.

We conclude with some well-deserved words of thanks to the large supporting cast. We thank all authors for submitting their research to KDD 2012. We are extremely grateful to the PC members and senior PC members for volunteering their time to help in the reviewing process. Diligent peer review is an essential cornerstone for research progress - we thank you all for the many detailed and conscientious reviews that were generated. Last year's program chairs, Joydeep Ghosh and Padhraic Symth, were generous in providing us with advice and expertise based on lessons learned in 2011. We would also like to convey our sincere thanks to the staff who run the Microsoft CMT system - they were more than willing to answer questions and help us at all times during the submission, reviewing, and decision process. And finally we would like to thank all of our colleagues on the KDD 2012 organization committee who were a pleasure to work with and without whom we would not have such a wonderful conference.

Let the 18th ACM SIGKDD conference begin - we hope you enjoy it!

Deepak Agarwal and Jian Pei
ACM SIGKDD 2012 Program Chairs

Asia Pacific Track Chairs' Welcome

It is our great honor to introduce the ***Asia Pacific Track*** at the 2012 ACM KDD conference. The Asia Pacific track features invited talks from leading data mining research groups located in the Asia Pacific region. We believe that this opportunity for the KDD community to hear directly from these experts will stimulate new research ideas and cross-continent collaborations.

In the last decade, universities and research laboratories in the Asia-Pacific region have made significant progress and contribution to the KDD research. Taking the advantage of the opportunity that KDD 2012 is held in Beijing, China, the conference features a new program of Asia-Pacific Track. The purpose of the Track is to promote KDD research achievements and to elevate the attention and momentum of the KDD research in this region. The program features invited speeches on KDD research results and projects in universities and industrial laboratories in this region. Recommended by a program committee consisting of Tu-Bao Ho, Jianyong Wang, Hiroshi Motoda, and Zhihua Zhou, it is our delight to invite the following 12 distinguished researchers to speak in the Asia Pacific Track.

1. Ming-Syan Chen, National Taiwan University
2. Paul Compton, University of New South Wales
3. Geoff Holmes, University of Waikato
4. Masaru Kitsuregawa, University of Tokyo
5. Cuiping Li, Renmin University
6. Deyi Li, Chinese Academy of Engineering
7. Jianzhong Li, Harbin Institute of Technology
8. Zhongzhi Shi, Chinese Academy of Sciences
9. Gordon Sun, Tencent
10. Naonori Ueda, NTT Communication Lab
11. Bo Zhang, Tsinghua University
12. Aoying Zhou, Eastern Normal University

We would like to thank all of our speakers for accepting our invitation to present their work at the KDD conference. We warmly welcome you to the Asia Pacific Track and hope that you will enjoy it.

David Cheung and Wei Wang
Asia Pacific Track Co- Chairs

Foreword to the KDD 2012 Industry Practice Expo

We warmly welcome you to the second year of the Industry Practice Expo (IPE) track at the KDD 2012 conference. The IPE features invited talks from leading experts who have developed and deployed large-scale data mining applications and systems in their respective fields that generated measurable and meaningful impact. The IPE aspires to bridge the gap between academia and industrial practice by bringing forth key trends, significant insights, and best practices. It complements the two well-established KDD tracks, Research and Industry/Government, which continue to feature the latest advances in the field via peer-reviewed publications. We trust that this opportunity for the KDD community to hear directly from industry pioneers will inspire new advances and broader inter-disciplinary collaboration between the academic researchers and their industry counterparts.

Last year's inaugural IPE was a huge success. The talks were well received and it was fascinating to hear about the numerous discussions between the speakers and attendees during the breaks. An important feedback from the attendees was that IPE should focus on technical talks and avoid talks that are purely marketing or promotional in nature. We have worked hard with our speakers for 2012 to achieve this right balance between business context and technical depth in the IPE talks.

In this year's IPE, we present to you renowned experts from around the world, from whose talks we hope will you will learn and take key ideas back to your respective professional activities. Featured topics at the IPE include large national scale projects on credit scoring and tax compliance, and real-world predictive analytics applications in decision management systems, e-commerce, semantic search, and telecommunications. Social media sites like LinkedIn, Facebook, and Twitter have taken the world by storm. We will hear about the key lessons learned in developing successful recommendation systems that power many interesting applications on these social media sites. Large-scale machine learning algorithms are an integral part of many successful data mining systems. One of the leading developers of industry strength machine learning software will share his experiences in building robust software that is now being used widely across the world. We are fortunate to have such a diverse panel of speakers be part of the IPE and would like to take this opportunity to thank them for their participation.

It has been a great pleasure to work with the IPE advisory comprising of Chid Apte, Usama Fayyad, Gregory Piatetsky-Shapiro, Ted Senator, Ramasamy Uthurusamy, Qiang Yang, and Michael Zeller. We thank them for their advice and support throughout the search for candidate speakers. We would also like to express our heartfelt gratitude to Michelle Chambers who was one of the speakers at the inaugural IPE in 2011. Michelle recommended several speakers and worked closely with us as we discussed the KDD opportunity with them.

We warmly welcome you to the KDD 2012 Industry Practice Expo and hope that you will enjoy it. Your suggestions and comments are very welcome.

Best regards,

Rajesh Parekh and Ying Li

Industry Practice Expo Track co-chairs

Foreword to the Industry & Government Track

The 2012 Industry & Government Track continued the direction that was implemented in 2010 and 2011 by clearly focusing on three areas of applied KDD work that are the sources of value to industrial and government organizations: (1) deployed applications, (2) knowledge discoveries, and (3) emerging applications. These areas build on the results of KDD research by applying the results of such research to enable the construction of novel and useful applications, the discovery of novel, interesting and useful knowledge, and the extension and application of research results to specific real world problems of interest. Papers were solicited and reviewed in these three areas:

- Deployed KDD systems that are providing real value to industry, government, or other organizations or professions. These deployed systems could support ongoing knowledge discovery or could be applications that employ discovered knowledge, or some combination of the two.
- Discoveries of knowledge with demonstrable value to industry, government, or other users (e.g., scientific or medical professionals). This knowledge must be "externally validated" as interesting and useful; it cannot simply be a model that has better performance on some traditional KDD metric such as accuracy or area under the curve.
- Emerging applications and technology that provide insight relevant to the above value propositions. These emerging applications must have clear user interest and support to distinguish them from KDD research papers, or they must provide insight into issues and factors that affect the successful use of KDD technology and methods. Papers that describe infrastructure that enables the large-scale deployment of KDD techniques also are in this area.

Industry & Government Track papers not only document and recognize significant accomplishments in these three areas, but also provide feedback to KDD researchers about needs, constraints, and applicability of KDD algorithms, methods and techniques in the real world. Our emphasis was on papers that advance the understanding of practical, applied, or pragmatic issues related to the use of KDD technologies in industry and government settings and highlight new research challenges arising from attempts to create such real KDD applications. We encouraged potential authors to address these issues and challenges in the Call for Papers and the accompanying Author Instructions http://www.kdd.org/kdd2012/author_instructions_industry.shtml

Our review process began with a validation by the reviewers that the authors correctly classified their paper's area – to ensure that the paper was reviewed according to the applicable criteria for that area – and a check that all required elements for that area were addressed in the paper. These required elements were:

- Deployed KDD case studies describe deployed projects with measurable benefits that include KDD technology. These papers must clearly describe the industry or government problem that is solved, the overall architecture of the deployed system, the data sources used, the reasons for the choices of particular KDD technologies, how KDD technologies solved the problem, the particular KDD process embodied by the deployed application, the use and payoff of the application, the costs to develop the application, the maintenance plan, and the number and types of users.
- Papers that describe discoveries of knowledge must clearly state what data sources and background knowledge were used, what data mining algorithms were tried, what overall KDD process was used, what the new discovered knowledge is, how the new knowledge was

validated, and what the value to the industry or government is of such newly discovered knowledge. Note that this category is intended for significant discoveries of domain knowledge that were enabled by KDD technologies and processes, and not for reporting of KDD research results.

- Emerging application and technology papers discuss prototype applications, tools for focused domains or tasks, useful techniques or methods, useful system architectures, scalability enablers, tool evaluations, or integration of KDD with other technologies. Such papers must clearly explain the requirements arising from the particular industry or government setting for which the application is being developed and from the particular databases on which the application is based. These papers must also identify how the emerging solution is using KDD technologies to address these requirements, the deployment plan, and the evaluation methodology and metrics for the emerging application. Pragmatic issues and considerations include important practical and research considerations, approaches, and architectures that enable successful applications. This category may include comparative evaluations of different KDD technologies for particular application problems. Preferences will be given to papers whose insights may generalize to other domains or problems. Product advertisements will not be accepted.

Specific review criteria included:

- Value/Payoff: What are the measurable benefits of the deployed application, the value of the newly discovered knowledge, or the generalizable insights from the emerging application?
- Cost: What is the cost/effort of the reported project? (To develop and maintain the application or to discover the new knowledge)
- External Significance: Is there clear evidence that the application problem being addressed and the KDD solution matters to an identified external set of users?
- External Validity: Is the knowledge discovered/used by the application externally validated? (This can be demonstrated by its use by a business, government, or profession; by publication in a peer-reviewed domain journal, or other means)
- Does the paper thoroughly describe the data sources and background knowledge used?
- Does the paper thoroughly describe the selection, use, appropriateness and effectiveness of the KDD technologies and/or data mining algorithms?
- Does the paper describe the KDD process enabled by the application or used to discover knowledge?
- Novelty/Originality: Does the work apply KDD technology to a new problem? Does it develop or apply a new type of KDD technology to an existing problem? Does it apply KDD technology to achieve a better result than with previous technology?
- Technical soundness: Does the paper show an accurate understanding of KDD research and technology? Does it identify relevant past work? Does it appropriately match techniques to problem characteristics?
- Evaluation: Is the reported work carefully evaluated? Is it statistically sound? Are the results compared to appropriate baselines? To other approaches and solutions? To previously reported work? Are its claims supported?
- Deployment/Use: Is there clear evidence that the application is deployed or on a path to deployment, or that the discovered knowledge will be used?

- Clarity: Is the paper written clearly? Is it organized logically? Are there sufficient figures and tables to illustrate its main points? Is it accessible to readers without specialized domain knowledge? Is it accessible to readers from different technical specialties and application domains?
- Does the paper contain insights or results that will generalize or apply to other domains or is it specialized to a particular domain?
- Will the paper be accessible to non-specialists in the particular domain?

Overall, the Program Committee reviewed 113 papers, representing an over 50% increase in submissions as compared to 2011 which clearly indicates the increased interest in data mining across Industry and Government. We accepted 30 papers, of which 8 describe deployed applications, 5 knowledge discoveries, and 17 emerging applications. The application areas cover a broad range, including finance, security, internet, text mining, science, public health, retail, mobile computing, and social networks, showing the many different fields to which KDD is being applied and adding value.

We hope you find these papers interesting and look forward to continued improvements in the use of KDD techniques to provide real value to industry and government.

Michael Zeller
Zementis, Inc.

Hui Xiong
Rutgers, the State University of New Jersey

KDD 2012 Industry & Government Track Program Chairs

Table of Contents

Organizers List xxv

KDD'12 Senior Program Committee Members xxvii

KDD12 Research Track Program Committee xxviii

KDD'12 Industry & Government Track Program Committee Members xxxi

KDD'12 Research Track External Reviewers xxxii

ACM SIGKDD KDD 2012 Sponsors & Supporters xxxv

Keynote Addresses

- **Nine Real Hard Problems We'd Like You to Solve** 1
  Robin Li *(Baidu, Inc)*
- **Mining Heterogeneous Information Networks: The Next Frontier** 2
  Jiawei Han *(University of Illinois at Urbana-Champaign)*
- **Divide-and-Conquer and Statistical Inference for Big Data** 4
  Michael I. Jordan *(University of California, Berkeley)*
- **Experiments in Social Computation (and the Data They Generate)** 5
  Michael Kearns *(University of Pennsylvania)*

Research Session A1: PageRank and Social Networks

- **Rise and Fall Patterns of Information Diffusion: Model and Implications** 6
  Yasuko Matsubara *(Kyoto University)*, Yasushi Sakurai *(NTT Communication Science Labs)*,
  B. Aditya Prakash *(Carnegie Mellon University)*, Lei Li *(University of California, Berkeley)*,
  Christos Faloutsos *(Carnegie Mellon University)*
- **Efficient Personalized PageRank with Accuracy Assurance** 15
  Yasuhiro Fujiwara, Makoto Nakatsuji, Takeshi Yamamuro, Hiroaki Shiokawa, Makoto Onizuka
  (NTT Softweare Innovation Center)
- **PageRank on an Evolving Graph** 24
  Bahman Bahmani *(Stanford University)*, Ravi Kumar *(Yahoo! Research)*, Mohammad Mahdian *(Google, Inc.)*,
  Eli Upfal *(Brown University)*
- **Information Diffusion and External Influence in Networks** 33
  Seth Myers, Chenguang Zhu, Jure Leskovec *(Stanford University)*
- **The Missing Models: A Data-Driven Approach for Learning How Networks Grow** 42
  Rob Patro, Geet Duggal, Emre Sefer, Hao Wang, Darya Filippova, Carl Kingsford *(University of Maryland)*

Research Session A2: Pattern Mining

- **Finding Minimum Representative Pattern Sets** 51
  Guimei Liu, Haojun Zhang, Limsoon Wong *(National University of Singapore)*
- **Mining Emerging Patterns by Streaming Feature Selection** 60
  Kui Yu *(Hefei University of Technology & University of Massachusetts, Boston)*,
  Wei Ding, Dan A. Simovici *(University of Massachusetts, Boston)*,
  Xindong Wu *(Hefei University of Technology & University of Vermont)*
- **Linear Space Direct Pattern Sampling Using Coupling from the Past** 69
  Mario Boley *(Fraunhofer IAIS and University of Bonn)*, Sandy Moens *(University of Antwerp)*,
  Thomas Gärtner *(Fraunhofer IAIS and University of Bonn)*

- **Mining Top-K High Utility Itemsets** 78
  Cheng Wei Wu, Bai-En Shie *(National Cheng Kung University)*, Philip S. Yu *(University of Illinois at Chicago)*, Vincent S. Tseng *(National Cheng Kung University)*
- **Sampling Minimal Frequent Boolean (DNF) Patterns** 87
  Geng Li, Mohammed J. Zaki *(Rensselaer Polytechnic Institute)*

Research Session A3: Probabilistic Models

- **The Contextual Focused Topic Model** 96
  Xu Chen, Mingyuan Zhou, Lawrence Carin *(Duke University)*
- **Practical Collapsed Variational Bayes Inference for Hierarchical Dirichlet Process** 105
  Issei Sato *(The University of Tokyo)*, Kenichi Kurihara *(Google)*, Hiroshi Nakagawa *(The University of Tokyo)*
- **Overlapping Decomposition for Causal Graphical Modeling** 114
  Lei Han, Guojie Song *(Peking University)*, Gao Cong *(Nanyang Technological University)*, Kunqing Xie *(Peking University)*
- **TM-LDA: Efficient Online Modeling of Latent Topic Transitions in Social Media** 123
  Yu Wang, Eugene Agichtein, Michele Benzi *(Emory University)*
- **Multi-View Clustering Using Mixture Models in Subspace Projections** 132
  Stephan Günnemann, Ines Färber, Thomas Seidl *(RWTH Aachen University)*

Research Session A4: Supervised Learning

- **A Simple Methodology for Soft Cost-Sensitive Classification** 141
  Te-Kang Jan, Da-Wei Wang *(Academia Sinica)*, Chi-Hung Lin, Hsuan-Tien Lin *(National Taiwan University)*
- **Intelligible Models for Classification and Regression** 150
  Yin Lou *(Cornell University)*, Rich Caruana *(Microsoft Corporation)*, Johannes Gehrke *(Cornell University)*
- **NASA: Achieving Lower Regrets and Faster Rates via Adaptive Stepsizes** 159
  Hua Ouyang, Alexander Gray *(Georgia Institute of Technology)*
- **Learning in Non-Stationary Environments with Class Imbalance** 168
  Thomas Ryan Hoens, Nitesh V. Chawla *(University of Notre Dame)*
- **Linear Support Vector Machines Via Dual Cached Loops** 177
  Shin Matsushima *(The University of Tokyo)*, S. V. N. Vishwanathan *(Purdue University)*, Alexander J. Smola *(Yahoo! Research)*

Industry/Govt Track A5: Mobile Computing

Session Chair: Yu Zheng

- **Discovering Regions of Different Functions in a City Using Human Mobility and POIs** ... 186
  Jing Yuan, Yu Zheng, Xing Xie *(Microsoft Research Asia)*
- **Constructing Popular Routes from Uncertain Trajectories** 195
  Ling-Yin Wei *(National Chiao Tung University)*, Yu Zheng *(Microsoft Research Asia)*, Wen-Chih Peng *(National Chiao Tung University)*
- **GetJar Mobile Application Recommendations with Very Sparse Datasets** 204
  Kent Shi, Kamal Ali *(GetJar Inc.)*
- **Differentially Private Transit Data Publication: A Case Study on the Montreal Transportation System** 213
  Rui Chen, Benjamin C. M. Fung, Bipin C. Desai *(Concordia University)*, Nériah M. Sossou *(Société de transport de Montréal)*

Asia-Pacific Track A6: Session 1

- **Interaction and Collective Intelligence in Internet Computing** 222
  Deyi Li *(Chinese Academy of Engineering)*
- **Building an Engine for Big Data** 223
  Masaru Kitsuregawa *(University of Tokyo)*

- **A New Challenge of Information Processing Under the 21st Century** 224
  Bo Zhang *(Tsinghua University)*
- **Developing Data Mining Applications** 225
  Geoff Holmes *(University of Waikato)*

Research Session B1: Social Opinions

- **Learning from Crowds in the Presence of Schools of Thought** 226
  Yuandong Tian *(Carnegie Mellon University)*, Jun Zhu *(Tsinghua University)*
- **Social Sampling** 235
  Anirban Dasgupta, Ravi Kumar, D. Sivakumar *(Yahoo! Research)*
- **From User Comments to On-Line Conversations** 244
  Chunyan Wang *(Stanford University)*, Mao Ye, Bernardo A. Huberman *(HP Labs)*
- **eTrust: Understanding Trust Evolution in an Online World** 253
  Jiliang Tang, Huiji Gao, Huan Liu *(Arizona State University)*, Atish Das Sarma *(eBay Inc.)*

Research Session B2: Time Series

- **Searching and Mining Trillions of Time Series Subsequences Under Dynamic Time Warping** 262
  Thanawin Rakthanmanon, Bilson Campana, Abdullah Mueen *(University of California, Riverside)*, Gustavo Batista *(University of São Paulo)*, Brandon Westover *(Brigham and Women's Hospital)*, Qiang Zhu, Jesin Zakaria, Eamonn Keogh *(University of California, Riverside)*
- **Fast Mining and Forecasting of Complex Time-Stamped Events** 271
  Yasuko Matsubara *(Kyoto University)*, Yasushi Sakurai *(NTT Communication Science Labs)*, Christos Faloutsos *(Carnegie Mellon University)*, Tomoharu Iwata *(NTT Communication Science Labs)*, Masatoshi Yoshikawa *(Kyoto University)*
- **Mining Recent Temporal Patterns for Event Detection in Multivariate Time Series Data** 280
  Iyad Batal *(University of Pittsburgh)*, Dmitriy Fradkin *(Siemens Corporate Research)*, James Harrison *(University of Virginia)*, Fabian Moerchen *(Siemens Corporate Research)*, Milos Hauskrecht *(University of Pittsburgh)*
- **A Shapelet Transform for Time Series Classification** 289
  Jason Lines, Luke M. Davis, Jon Hills, Anthony Bagnall *(University of East Anglia)*

Research Session B3: Matrices and Tensors

- **Accelerated Singular Value Thresholding for Matrix Completion** 298
  Yao Hu, Debing Zhang *(Zhejiang University)*, Jun Liu *(Siemens Corporate Research)*, Jieping Ye *(Arizona State University)*, Xiaofei He *(Zhejiang University)*
- **Fast Bregman Divergence NMF Using Taylor Expansion and Coordinate Descent** 307
  Liangda Li, Guy Lebanon, Haesun Park *(Georgia Institute of Technology)*
- **GigaTensor: Scaling Tensor Analysis Up by 100 Times - Algorithms and Discoveries** 316
  U Kang, Evangelos Papalexakis, Abhay Harpale, Christos Faloutsos *(Carnegie Mellon University)*
- **Active Learning for Online Bayesian Matrix Factorization** 325
  Jorge Silva, Lawrence Carin *(Duke University)*

Research Session B4: Unsupervised Learning

- **A Sparsity-Inducing Formulation for Evolutionary Co-Clustering** 334
  Shuiwang Ji, Wenlu Zhang *(Old Dominion University)*, Jun Liu *(Siemens Corporate Research)*
- **Detecting Changes of Clustering Structures Using Normalized Maximum Likelihood Coding** 343
  So Hirai, Kenji Yamanishi *(The University of Tokyo)*

- **Subspace Correlation Clustering: Finding Locally Correlated Dimensions in Subspace Projections of the Data** 352
  Stephan Günnemann, Ines Färber, Kittipat Virochsiri, Thomas Seidl *(RWTH Aachen University)*
- **Dependency Clustering Across Measurement Scales** 361
  Claudia Plant *(Florida State University)*

Industry/Govt Track B5: Social Network Analysis

Session Chair: Amol Ghoting

- **A Framework for Summarizing and Analyzing Twitter Feeds** 370
  Xintian Yang *(The Ohio State University)*, Amol Ghoting *(IBM Thomas J. Watson Research Center)*, Yiye Ruan, Srinivasan Parthasarathy *(The Ohio State University)*
- **Entity-Centric Topic-Oriented Opinion Summarization in Twitter** 379
  Xinfan Meng *(Peking University)*, Furu Wei, Xiaohua Liu, Ming Zhou *(Microsoft Research Asia)*, Sujian Li, Houfeng Wang *(Peking University)*
- **Community Discovery and Profiling with Social Messages** 388
  Wenjun Zhou *(University of Tennessee)*, Hongxia Jin *(IBM Research - Almaden)*, Yan Liu *(University of Southern California)*
- **Finding Trending Local Topics in Search Queries for Personalization of a Recommendation System** 397
  Ziad Al Bawab, George H. Mills, Jean-Francois Crespo *(Yahoo! Labs)*

Industrial Practice Expo B6: Session 1

- **China's National Personal Credit Scoring System: A Real-Life Intelligent Knowledge Application** 406
  Yong Shi *(Chinese Academy of Sciences / China Data Technology)*
- **Maximizing Return and Minimizing Cost with the Right Decision Management Systems** 407
  Rich Holada *(IBM)*

Research Session C1: Social and Web Mining Applications

- **Efficient and Domain-Invariant Competitor Mining** 408
  Theodoros Lappas *(Boston University)*, George Valkanas, Dimitrios Gunopulos *(University of Athens)*
- **Discriminative Clustering for Market Segmentation** 417
  Peter Haider *(University of Potsdam)*, Luca Chiarandini *(Universitat Pompeu Fabra)*, Ulf Brefeld *(University of Bonn)*
- **Interacting Viruses in Networks: Can Both Survive?** 426
  Alex Beutel, B. Aditya Prakash, Roni Rosenfeld, Christos Faloutsos *(Carnegie Mellon University)*
- **Aggregating Web Offers to Determine Product Prices** 435
  Rakesh Agrawal, Samuel Ieong *(Microsoft Research)*

Research Session C2: Event Mining

- **Mining Event Periodicity from Incomplete Observations** 444
  Zhenhui Li, Jingjing Wang, Jiawei Han *(University of Illinois at Urbana-Champaign)*
- **Towards Heterogeneous Temporal Clinical Event Pattern Discovery: A Convolutional Approach** 453
  Fei Wang, Noah Lee, Jianying Hu, Jimeng Sun, Shahram Ebadollahi *(IBM T.J. Watson Research Center)*
- **The Long and the Short of It: Summarising Event Sequences with Serial Episodes** 462
  Nikolaj Tatti, Jilles Vreeken *(University of Antwerp)*
- **Efficient Event Pattern Matching with Match Windows** 471
  Bruno Cadonna, Johann Gamper *(Free University of Bozen-Bolzano)*, Michael H. Böhlen *(University of Zurich)*

Research Session C3: Matrix Approximation

- **Optimal Exact Least Squares Rank Minimization** 480
  Shuo Xiang *(Arizona State University)*, Yunzhang Zhu, Xiaotong Shen *(University of Minnesota)*, Jieping Ye *(Arizona State University)*
- **Large-Scale Distributed Non-Negative Sparse Coding and Sparse Dictionary Learning** 489
  Vikas Sindhwani, Amol Ghoting *(IBM T.J. Watson Research Center)*
- **Learning Binary Codes for Collaborative Filtering** 498
  Ke Zhou, Hongyuan Zha *(Georgia Institute of Technology)*
- **Low Rank Modeling of Signed Networks** 507
  Cho-Jui Hsieh, Kai-Yang Chiang, Inderjit S. Dhillon *(University of Texas at Austin)*

Research Session C4: Supervised Learning with Multivariate Data

- **A Structural Cluster Kernel for Learning on Graphs** 516
  Madeleine Seeland *(Technische Universität München)*, Andreas Karwath, Stefan Kramer *(Johannes Gutenberg-Universität Mainz)*
- **Multi-Label Hypothesis Reuse** 525
  Sheng-Jun Huang, Yang Yu, Zhi-Hua Zhou *(Nanjing University)*
- **Rank-Loss Support Instance Machines for MIML Instance Annotation** 534
  Forrest Briggs, Xiaoli Z. Fern, Raviv Raich *(Oregon State Univeristy)*
- **Inductive Multi-Task Learning with Multiple View Data** 543
  Jintao Zhang, Jun Huan *(University of Kansas)*

Industry/Govt Track C5: Web Applications

Session Chair: Enhong Chen

- **Scalable Misbehavior Detection in Online Video Chat Services** 552
  Xinyu Xing *(Georgia Institute of Technology)*, Yu-li Liang *(University of Colorado at Boulder)*, Sui Huang *(Ohio State University)*, Hanqiang Cheng *(McGill University)*, Richard Han, Qin Lv *(University of Colorado at Boulder)*, Xue Liu *(McGill University)*, Shivakant Mishra *(University of Colorado at Boulder)*, Yi Zhu *(Tsinghua University)*
- **Keyword-Propagation-Based Information Enriching and Noise Removal for Web News Videos** 561
  Jun Zhang, Xiaoming Fan, Jianyong Wang, Lizhu Zhou *(Tsinghua University)*
- **Harnessing the Wisdom of the Crowds for Accurate Web Page Clipping** 570
  Lei Zhang *(University of Science and Technology of China & HP Labs China)*, Linpeng Tang *(Shanghai Jiao Tong University & HP Labs China)*, Ping Luo *(HP Labs China)*, Enhong Chen *(University of Science and Technology of China)*, Limei Jiao, Min Wang *(HP Labs China)*, Guiquan Liu *(University of Science and Technology of China)*
- **Bootstrapped Language Identification for Multi-Site Internet Domains** 579
  Uwe F. Mayer *(eBay Research Labs)*

Industrial Practice Expo C6: Session 2

- **Semantic Search and a New Moore's Law Effect in Knowledge Engineering** 586
  Wei-Ying Ma *(Microsoft Research Asia)*
- **Key Lessons Learned Building Recommender Systems for Large-Scale Social Networks** 587
  Christian Posse *(LinkedIn Inc.)*

Research Session A1: Community Mining

- **Magnet Community Identification on Social Networks** 588
  Guan Wang, Yuchen Zhao, Xiaoxiao Shi *(University of Illinois at Chicago)*, Philip S. Yu *(University of Illinois at Chicago & King Abdulaziz University)*

- **Vertex Neighborhoods, Low Conductance Cuts, and Good Seeds for Local Community Methods** 597
  David F. Gleich *(Purdue University)*, C. Seshadhri *(Sandia National Laboratories)*
- **Overlapping Community Detection via Bounded Nonnegative Matrix Tri-Factorization** 606
  Yu Zhang, Dit-Yan Yeung *(Hong Kong University of Science and Technology)*
- **DEMON: A Local-First Discovery Method for Overlapping Communities** 615
  Michele Coscia *(CID - Harvard Kennedy School)*, Giulio Rossetti *(University of Pisa)*,
  Fosca Giannotti *(KDDLab ISTI-CNR)*, Dino Pedreschi *(University of Pisa)*
- **On the Separability of Structural Classes of Communities** 624
  Bruno Abrahao, Sucheta Soundarajan, John Hopcroft, Robert Kleinberg *(Cornell University)*

Research Session A2: Sequential and Spatio-temporal Patterns

- **Discovering Lag Intervals for Temporal Dependencies** 633
  Liang Tang, Tao Li *(Florida International University)*, Larisa Shwartz *(IBM T.J. Watson Research Center)*
- **Testing the Significance of Spatio-Temporal Teleconnection Patterns** 642
  Jaya Kawale, Snigdhansu Chatterjee, Dominick Ormsby, Karsten Steinhaeuser, Stefan Liess, Vipin Kumar
  (University of Minnesota)
- **SeqiBloc: Mining Multi-time Spanning Blockmodels in Dynamic Graphs** 651
  Jeffrey Chan, Wei Liu, Christopher Leckie, James Bailey, Kotagiri Ramamohanarao *(University of Melbourne)*
- **USpan: An Efficient Algorithm for Mining High Utility Sequential Patterns** 660
  Junfu Yin, Zhigang Zheng, Longbing Cao *(University of Technology, Sydney)*
- **Mining Large-Scale, Sparse GPS Traces for Map Inference: Comparison of Approaches** 669
  Xuemei Liu *(Shanghai Jiao Tong University)*, James Biagioni, Jakob Eriksson *(University of Illinois at Chicago)*,
  Yin Wang, George Forman *(Hewlett-Packard Labs)*, Yanmin Zhu *(Shanghai Jiao Tong University)*

Research Session A3: Personalization and Recommendation

- **Transparent User Models for Personalization** 678
  Khalid El-Arini *(Carnegie Mellon University)*, Ulrich Paquet *(Microsoft Research)*,
  Ralf Herbrich *(Facebook, Inc.)*, Jurgen Van Gael *(Rangespan Ltd.)*,
  Blaise Agüera y Arcas *(Microsoft Corporation)*
- **Estimating Entity Importance via Counting Set Covers** 687
  Aristides Gionis *(Yahoo! Research)*, Theodoros Lappas, Evimaria Terzi *(Boston University)*
- **ComSoc: Adaptive Transfer of User Behaviors Over Composite Social Network** 696
  Erheng Zhong *(Hong Kong University of Science and Technology)*, Wei Fan *(IBM T.J. Watson Research Center)*,
  Junwei Wang, Lei Xiao, Yong Li *(Tencent Inc.)*
- **Online Learning to Diversify from Implicit Feedback** 705
  Karthik Raman, Pannaga Shivaswamy, Thorsten Joachims *(Cornell University)*
- **Playlist Prediction via Metric Embedding** 714
  Shuo Chen, Joshua L. Moore *(Cornell University)*, Douglas Turnbull *(Ithaca College)*,
  Thorsten Joachims *(Cornell University)*

Research Session A4: Supervised Learning with Auxilliary Information

- **Parallel Field Ranking** 723
  Ming Ji *(University of Illinois at Urbana-Champaign)*, Binbin Lin, Xiaofei He, Deng Cai *(Zhejiang University)*,
  Jiawei Han *(University of Illinois at Urbana-Champaign)*
- **Semi-Supervised Learning with Mixed Knowledge Information** 732
  Fanhua Shang, L. C. Jiao *(Xidian University)*, Fei Wang *(IBM T. J. Watson Research Center)*
- **Batch Mode Active Sampling Based on Marginal Probability Distribution Matching** 741
  Rita Chattopadhyay, Zheng Wang *(Arizona State University)*, Wei Fan *(IBM T. J. Watson Research Center)*,
  Ian Davidson *(University of California, Davis)*, Sethuraman Panchanathan, Jieping Ye *(Arizona State University)*

- **SPG-GMKL: Generalized Multiple Kernel Learning with a Million Kernels** 750
  Ashesh Jain *(Indian Institute of Technology Delhi)*, S. V. N. Vishwanathan *(Purdue University)*, Manik Varma *(Microsoft Research India)*
- **Efficient Evaluation of Large Sequence Kernels** 759
  Pavel P. Kuksa *(NEC Laboratories America, Inc.)*, Vladimir Pavlovic *(Rutgers University)*

Industry/Govt Track A5: Computational Advertising

Session Chair: Ron Kohavi

- **Estimating Conversion Rate in Display Advertising from Past Performance Data** 768
  Kuang-chih Lee, Burkay Orten, Ali Dasdan, Wentong Li *(Turn Inc.)*
- **Multimedia Features for Click Prediction of New Ads in Display Advertising** 777
  Haibin Cheng, Roelof van Zwol *(Yahoo! Labs)*, Javad Azimi *(Oregon State University)*, Eren Manavoglu, Ruofei Zhang, Yang Zhou, Vidhya Navalpakkam *(Yahoo! Labs)*
- **Trustworthy Online Controlled Experiments: Five Puzzling Outcomes Explained** 786
  Ron Kohavi, Alex Deng, Brian Frasca, Roger Longbotham, Toby Walker, Ya Xu *(Microsoft)*
- **Position-Normalized Click Prediction in Search Advertising** 795
  Ye Chen, Tak W. Yan *(Microsoft Corporation)*
- **Bid Optimizing and Inventory Scoring in Targeted Online Advertising** 804
  Claudia Perlich, Brian Dalessandro, Rod Hook, Ori Stitelman, Troy Raeder *(Media6Degrees)*, Foster Provost *(NYU Stern School of Business)*

Asia-Pacific Track A6: Session 2

- **Algorithms for Mining Uncertain Graph Data** 813
  Jianzhong Li *(Harbin Institute of Technology)*
- **Experience with Discovering Knowledge by Acquiring It** 814
  Paul Compton *(University of New South Wales)*
- **Bayesian Relational Data Analysis** 815
  Naonori Ueda *(NTT Communication Lab)*
- **Cross-Media Knowledge Discovery** 816
  Zhongzhi Shi *(Chinese Academy of Sciences)*

Author Index 817

Research Session B1: Review, Discussion, and Q & A

- **Review Spam Detection via Temporal Pattern Discovery** 823
  Sihong Xie, Guan Wang, Shuyang Lin *(University of Illinois at Chicago)*, Philip S. Yu *(University of Illinois at Chicago & King Abdulaziz University)*
- **Selecting a Characteristic Set of Reviews** 832
  Theodoros Lappas, Mark Crovella, Evimaria Terzi *(Boston University)*
- **Mining Contentions from Discussions and Debates** 841
  Arjun Mukherjee, Bing Liu *(University of Illinois at Chicago)*
- **Discovering Value from Community Activity on Focused Question Answering Sites: A Case Study of Stack Overflow** 850
  Ashton Anderson *(Stanford University)*, Daniel Huttenlocher, Jon Kleinberg *(Cornell University)*, Jure Leskovec *(Stanford University)*

Research Session B2: Outlier and Intrusion Detection

- **Integrating Community Matching and Outlier Detection for Mining Evolutionary Community Outliers** 859
  Manish Gupta *(University of Illinois at Urbana-Champaign)*, Jing Gao *(State Universityof New York, Buffalo)*, Yizhou Sun, Jiawei Han *(University of Illinois at Urbana-Champaign)*

- **Different Slopes for Different Folks: Mining for Exceptional Regression Models with Cook's Distance** 868
  Wouter Duivesteijn *(LIACS, Leiden University)*, Ad Feelders *(ICS, Utrecht University)*, Arno Knobbe *(LIACS, Leiden University)*
- **A Near-Linear Time Approximation Algorithm for Angle-based Outlier Detection in High-dimensional Data** 877
  Ninh Pham, Rasmus Pagh *(IT University of Copenhagen)*
- **Intrusion as (Anti)social Communication: Characterization and Detection** 886
  Qi Ding, Natallia Katenka *(Boston University)*, Paul Barford *(University of Wisconsin - Madison)*, Eric Kolaczyk, Mark Crovella *(Boston University)*

Research Session B3: Feature Selection

- **Robust Multi-Task Feature Learning** 895
  Pinghua Gong *(Tsinghua University)*, Jieping Ye *(Arizona State University)*, Changshui Zhang *(Tsinghua University)*
- **Unsupervised Feature Selection for Linked Social Media Data** 904
  Jiliang Tang, Huan Liu *(Arizona State University)*
- **Model Mining for Robust Feature Selection** 913
  Adam Woznica, Phong Nguyen *(University of Geneva)*, Alexandros Kalousis *(University of Applied Sciences)*
- **Feature Grouping and Selection Over an Undirected Graph** 922
  Sen Yang, Lei Yuan, Ying-Cheng Lai, Xiaotong Shen, Peter Wonka, Jieping Ye *(Arizona State University)*

Research Session B4: Nearest Neighbors

- **Maximum Inner-Product Search Using Cone Trees** 931
  Parikshit Ram, Alexander G. Gray *(Georgia Institute of Technology)*
- **A Probabilistic Model for Multimodal Hash Function Learning** 940
  Yi Zhen, Dit-Yan Yeung *(Hong Kong University of Science and Technology)*
- **On Socio-Spatial Group Query for Location-Based Social Networks** 949
  De-Nian Yang *(Academia Sinica)*, Chih-Ya Shen *(National Taiwan University)*, Wang-Chien Lee *(The Pennsylvania State University)*, Ming-Syan Chen *(National Taiwan University)*
- **Random Forests for Metric Learning with Implicit Pairwise Position Dependence** 958
  Caiming Xiong, David Johnson, Ran Xu, Jason J. Corso *(SUNY at Buffalo)*

Industry/Govt Track B5: Business Intelligence

Session Chair: Sreenivas Gollapudi

- **Empowering Authors to Diagnose Comprehension Burden in Textbooks** 967
  Rakesh Agrawal *(Microsoft Research)*, Sunandan Chakraborty *(New York University)*, Sreenivas Gollapudi, Anitha Kannan, Krishnaram Kenthapadi *(Microsoft Research)*
- **Coupled Behavior Analysis for Capturing Coupling Relationships in Group-based Market Manipulations** 976
  Yin Song, Longbing Cao *(University of Technology Sydney)*, Xindong Wu *(Heifei University of Technology & University of Vermont)*, Gang Wei, Wu Ye *(Shanghai Stock Exchange)*, Wei Ding *(University of Massachusetts Boston)*
- **HySAD: A Semi-Supervised Hybrid Shilling Attack Detector for Trustworthy Product Recommendation** 985
  Zhiang Wu *(Nanjing University of Finance and Economics)*, Junjie Wu *(Beihang University)*, Jie Cao *(Nanjing University of Finance and Economics)*, Dacheng Tao *(University of Technology, Sydney)*
- **Following the Electrons: Methods for Power Management in Commercial Buildings** 994
  Gowtham Bellala, Manish Marwah, Martin Arlitt, Geoff Lyon, Cullen Bash *(Hewlett Packard Laboratories)*

Industrial Practice Expo B6: Session 3

- **Ensembles and Model Delivery for Tax Compliance** 1003
  Graham Williams *(Australian Taxation Office)*
- **Leveraging Predictive Modeling to Reduce Signal Theft in a Multi-Service Organization Environment** 1004
  Seymour Douglas *(Deloitte Financial Advisory Services)*

Research Session C1: Team, Trends, and Social Profiling

- **Capacitated Team Formation Problem on Social Networks** 1005
  Samik Datta, Anirban Majumder *(Bell Labs, Bangalore)*, KVM Naidu *(Walmart Labs, Bangalore)*
- **Finding Trendsetters in Information Networks** 1014
  Diego Saez-Trumper *(Universitat Pompeu Fabra)*,
  Giovanni Comarela, Virgílio Almeida *(Universidade Federal de Minas Gerais)*,
  Ricardo Baeza-Yates *(Yahoo! Research)*, Fabrício Benevenuto *(Universidade Federal de Ouro Preto)*
- **Towards Social User Profiling: Unified and Discriminative Influence Model for Inferring Home Locations** 1023
  Rui Li, Shengjie Wang, Hongbo Deng, Rui Wang *(University of Illinois at Urbana-Champaign)*,
  Kevin Chen-Chuan Chang *(University of Illinois at Urbana-Champaign & Illinois at Singapore)*
- **Event-Based Social Networks: Linking the Online and Offline Social Worlds** 1032
  Xingjie Liu *(The Pennsylvania State University)*, Qi He, Yuanyuan Tian *(IBM Almaden Research Center)*,
  Wang-Chien Lee *(The Pennsylvania State University)*, John McPherson *(IBM Almaden Research Center)*,
  Jiawei Han *(University of Illinois at Urbana-Champaign)*

Research Session C2: Privacy

- **Differential Identifiability** 1041
  Jaewoo Lee, Chris Clifton *(Purdue University)*
- **Anonymizing Set-Valued Data by Nonreciprocal Recoding** 1050
  Mingqiang Xue *(National University of Singapore)*, Panagiotis Karras *(Rutgers University)*,
  Chedy Raïssi *(INRIA)*, Jaideep Vaidya *(Rutgers University)*, Kian-Lee Tan *(National University of Singapore)*
- **Adversarial Support Vector Machine Learning** 1059
  Yan Zhou, Murat Kantarcioglu, Bhavani Thuraisingham *(University of Texas at Dallas)*,
  Bowei Xi *(Purdue University)*

Research Session C3: Supervised Learning Applications

- **Web Image Prediction Using Multivariate Point Processes** 1068
  Gunhee Kim *(Carnegie Mellon University)*, Li Fei-Fei *(Stanford University)*,
  Eric P. Xing *(Carnegie Mellon University)*
- **Transductive Multi-label Ensemble Classification for Protein Function Prediction** 1077
  Guoxian Yu *(South China University of Technology)*,
  Carlotta Domeniconi, Huzefa Rangwala *(George Mason University)*,
  Guoji Zhang, Zhiwen Yu *(South China University of Technology)*
- **Multi-Domain Active Learning for Text Classification** 1086
  Lianghao Li, Xiaoming Jin *(Tsinghua University)*, Sinno Jialin Pan *(Institute for Infocomm Research, Singapore)*,
  Jian-Tao Sun *(Microsoft Research Asia)*
- **Modeling Disease Progression via Fused Sparse Group Lasso** 1095
  Jiayu Zhou, Jun Liu *(Arizona State University)*,
  Vaibhav A. Narayan *(Johnson & Johnson Pharmaceutical Research & Development, LLC)*,
  Jieping Ye *(The Biodesign Institute & Arizona State University)*

Research Session C4: Information Extraction

- **Open Domain Event Extraction from Twitter** 1104
  Alan Ritter, Mausam, Oren Etzioni *(University of Washington)*, Sam Clark *(Decide, Inc.)*

- **Stratified K-Means Clustering Over a Deep Web Data Source** 1113
  Tantan Liu, Gagan Agrawal *(The Ohio State University)*
- **Metro Maps of Science** 1122
  Dafna Shahaf, Carlos Guestrin *(Carnegie Mellon University)*, Eric Horvitz *(Microsoft Research)*
- **Active Sampling for Entity Matching** 1131
  Kedar Bellare, Suresh Iyengar *(Yahoo! Labs)*, Aditya Parameswaran *(Stanford University)*,
  Vibhor Rastogi *(Yahoo! Research)*

Industry/Govt Track C5: Medical Informatics

Session Chair: Jimeng Sun

- **An Integrated Data Mining Approach to Real-time Clinical Monitoring and Deterioration Warning** 1140
  Yi Mao, Wenlin Chen, Yixin Chen, Chenyang Lu, Marin Kollef, Thomas C. Bailey
  (Washington University in St. Louis)
- **Multi-Source Learning for Joint Analysis of Incomplete Multi-Modality Neuroimaging Data** 1149
  Lei Yuan, Yalin Wang *(Arizona State University)*, Paul M. Thompson *(University of California, Los Angeles)*,
  Vaibhav A. Narayan *(Johnson & Johnson Pharmaceutical Research & Development, LLC)*,
  Jieping Ye *(Arizona State University)*
- **RainMon: An Integrated Approach to Mining Bursty Timeseries Monitoring Data** 1158
  Ilari Shafer, Kai Ren, Vishnu Naresh Boddeti, Yoshihisa Abe, Gregory R. Ganger, Christos Faloutsos
  (Carnegie Mellon University)
- **SympGraph: A Framework for Mining Clinical Notes Through Symptom Relation Graphs** 1167
  Parikshit Sondhi *(University of Illinois at Urbana Champaign)*,
  imeng Sun, Hanghang Tong *(IBM T.J. Watson Research Center)*,
  ChengXiang Zhai *(University of Illinois at Urbana Champaign)*

Industrial Practice Expo C6: Session 4

- **Experiences and Lessons in Developing Industry-Strength Machine Learning and Data Mining Software** 1176
  Chih-Jen Lin *(National Taiwan University & eBay Research Laboratories)*

Research Session A1: Ads and Video Recommendation

- **Joint Optimization of Bid and Budget Allocation in Sponsored Search** 1177
  Weinan Zhang *(Shanghai Jiao Tong University)*, Ying Zhang *(Nankai University)*,
  Bin Gao *(Microsoft Research Asia)*, Yong Yu *(Shanghai Jiao Tong University)*,
  Xiaojie Yuan *(Nankai University)*, Tie-Yan Liu *(Microsoft Research Asia)*
- **The Untold Story of the Clones: Content-Agnostic Factors That Impact YouTube Video Popularity** 1186
  Youmna Borghol *(NICTA & University of New South Wales)*, Sebastien Ardon *(NICTA)*,
  Niklas Carlsson *(Linköping University)*, Derek Eager *(University of Saskatchewan)*, Anirban Mahanti *(NICTA)*
- **SHALE: An Efficient Algorithm for Allocation of Guaranteed Display Advertising** 1195
  Vijay Bharadwaj *(Netflix)*, Peiji Chen, Wenjing Ma, Chandrashekhar Nagarajan *(Yahoo! Labs)*,
  John Tomlin *(opTomax Solutions)*, Sergei Vassilvitskii *(Google)*, Erik Vee *(Facebook)*, Jian Yang *(Yahoo! Labs)*
- **Factoring Past Exposure in Display Advertising Targeting** 1204
  Neha Gupta *(University of Maryland, College Park)*,
  Abhimanyu Das, Sandeep Pandey, Vijay K. Narayanan *(Yahoo! Research)*
- **Online Allocation of Display Ads with Smooth Delivery** 1213
  Anand Bhalgat *(University of Pennsylvania)*, Jon Feldman, Vahab Mirrokni *(Google Inc.)*

Research Session A2: Graph Mining

- **Streaming Graph Partitioning for Large Distributed Graphs** 1222
  Isabelle Stanton *(University of California, Berkeley)*, Gabriel Kliot *(Microsoft Research)*

- **RolX: Structural Role Extraction & Mining in Large Graphs** 1231
  Keith Henderson, Brian Gallagher *(Lawrence Livermore National Laboratory)*,
  Tina Eliassi-Rad *(Rutgers University)*, Hanghang Tong *(IBM T.J.Watson Research Center)*,
  Sugato Basu *(Google Research)*,
  Leman Akoglu, Danai Koutra, Christos Faloutsos, Lei Li *(Carnegie Mellon University)*
- **Fast Algorithms for Maximal Clique Enumeration with Limited Memory** 1240
  James Cheng *(Nanyang Technological University)*, Linhong Zhu *(Institute for Infocomm Research)*,
  Yiping Ke *(Institute of High Performance Computing)*, Shumo Chu *(Nanyang Technological University)*
- **Summarization-based Mining Bipartite Graphs** 1249
  Jing Feng, Xiao He, Bettina Konte, Christian Böhm *(University of Munich)*,
  Claudia Plant *(Florida State University)*
- **Mining Coherent Subgraphs in Multi-Layer Graphs with Edge Labels** 1258
  Brigitte Boden, Stephan Günnemann, Holger Hoffmann, Thomas Seidl *(RWTH Aachen University)*

Research Session A3: Recommendation

- **Circle-Based Recommendation in Online Social Networks** 1267
  Xiwang Yang *(Polytechnic Institute of NYU)*, Harald Steck *(Bell Labs, Alcatel-Lucent)*,
  Yong Liu *(Polytechnic Institute of NYU)*
- **Incorporating Heterogeneous Information for Personalized Tag Recommendation in Social Tagging Systems** 1276
  Wei Feng, Jianyong Wang *(Tsinghua University)*
- **Cross-domain Collaboration Recommendation** 1285
  Jie Tang, Sen Wu *(Tsinghua University)*, Jimeng Sun *(IBM TJ Watson Research Center)*,
  Hang Su *(Tsinghua University)*
- **RecMax: Exploiting Recommender Systems for Fun and Profit** 1294
  Amit Goyal, Laks V. S. Lakshmanan *(University of British Columbia)*
- **Learning Personal + Social Latent Factor Model for Social Recommendation** 1303
  Yelong Shen, Ruoming Jin *(Kent State University)*

Research Session A4: Clustering

- **Two Approaches to Understanding When Constraints Help Clustering** 1312
  Ian Davidson *(University of California, Davis)*
- **Chromatic Correlation Clustering** 1321
  Francesco Bonchi, Aristides Gionis, Francesco Gullo, Antti Ukkonen *(Yahoo! Research - Spain)*
- **Locally-Scaled Spectral Clustering Using Empty Region Graphs** 1330
  Carlos D. Correa, Peter Lindstrom *(Lawrence Livermore National Laboratory)*
- **Active Spectral Clustering via Iterative Uncertainty Reduction** 1339
  Fabian L. Wauthier *(University of California, Berkeley)*, Nebojsa Jojic *(Microsoft Research)*,
  Michael I. Jordan *(University of California, Berkeley)*
- **Integrating Meta-Path Selection with User-Guided Object Clustering in Heterogeneous Information Networks** 1348
  Yizhou Sun, Brandon Norick, Jiawei Han *(University of Illinois at Urbana-Champaign)*,
  Xifeng Yan *(University of California at Santa Barbara)*, Philip S. Yu *(University of Illinois at Chicago)*,
  Xiao Yu *(University of Illinois at Urbana-Champaign)*

Industry/Govt Track A5: Intelligent Systems

Session Chair: Brian Dalessandro

- **Design Principles of Massive, Robust Prediction Systems** 1357
  Troy Raeder, Ori Stitelman, Brian Dalessandro, Claudia Perlich *(M6D Research)*,
  Foster Provost *(New York University and M6D Research)*
- **PatentMiner: Topic-driven Patent Analysis and Mining** 1366
  Jie Tang, Bo Wang, Yang Yang, Po Hu, Yanting Zhao, Xinyu Yan, Bo Gao, Minlie Huang *(Tsinghua University)*,
  Peng Xu, Weichang Li, Adam K. Usadi *(ExxonMobil Research and Engineering Company)*

- **Storytelling in Entity Networks to Support Intelligence Analysts** 1375
  M. Shahriar Hossain, Patrick Butler *(Virginia Tech)*, Arnold P. Boedihardjo *(U. S. Army Corps of Engineers)*, Naren Ramakrishnan *(Virginia Tech)*
- **A Framework for Robust Discovery of Entity Synonyms** 1384
  Kaushik Chakrabarti, Surajit Chaudhuri, Tao Cheng *(Microsoft Research)*, Dong Xin *(Google)*
- **SmartDispatch: Enabling Efficient Ticket Dispatch in an IT Service Environment** 1393
  Shivali Agarwal, Renuka Sindhgatta, Bikram Sengupta *(IBM Research)*

Asia-Pacific Track A6: Session 3

- **Social Media Data Analysis for Revealing Collective Behaviors** 1402
  Aoying Zhou, Weining Qian, Haixin Ma *(Eastern China Normal University)*
- **Information Processing in Social Networks** 1403
  Ming-Syan Chen *(National Taiwan University)*
- **Understanding Users' Satisfaction for Search Engine Evaluation** 1404
  Gordon Sun *(Tencent Technology)*
- **Similarity Search in Real World Networks** 1405
  Cuiping Li *(Renmin University)*

Research Session B1: Keywords and Documents

- **Large-Scale Learning of Word Relatedness with Constraints** 1406
  Guy Halawi *(Tel Aviv University)*, Gideon Dror, Evgeniy Gabrilovich, Yehuda Koren *(Yahoo! Research)*
- **Latent Association Analysis of Document Pairs** 1415
  Gengxin Miao, Ziyu Guan, Louise Moser, Xifeng Yan *(University of California, Santa Barbara)*, Shu Tao, Nikos Anerousis, Jimeng Sun *(IBM T.J. Watson Research Center)*
- **LIEGE: Link Entities in Web Lists with Knowledge Base** 1424
  Wei Shen, Jianyong Wang *(Tsinghua University)*, Ping Luo, Min Wang *(HP Labs China)*
- **Automatic Taxonomy Construction from Keywords** 1433
  Xueqing Liu *(Microsoft Research Asia & Tsinghua University)*, Yangqiu Song, Shixia Liu, Haixun Wang *(Microsoft Research Asia)*

Research Session B2: Patterns

- **An Enhanced Relevance Criterion for More Concise Supervised Pattern Discovery** 1442
  Henrik Großkreutz *(Fraunhofer IAIS)*, Daniel Paurat *(University of Bonn)*, Stefan Rueping *(Fraunhofer IAIS)*
- **Efficient Frequent Item Counting in Multi-Core Hardware** 1451
  Pratanu Roy, Jens Teubner, Gustavo Alonso *(ETH Zurich)*
- **On Nested Palindromes in Clickstream Data** 1460
  Michel Speiser *(IBM Research - Zurich & ETH Zurich)*, Gianluca Antonini, Abderrahim Labbi *(IBM Research - Zurich)*, Juliana Sutanto *(ETH Zurich)*

Research Session B3: Spatial and Pattern Recognition

- **Mining Discriminative Components with Low-Rank and Sparsity Constraints for Face Recognition** 1469
  Qiang Zhang, Baoxin Li *(Arizona State University)*
- **Fast Algorithms for Comprehensive N-point Correlation Estimates** 1478
  William B. March *(Georgia Institute of Technology)*, Andrew J. Connolly *(University of Washington)*, Alexander G. Gray *(Georgia Institute of Technology)*
- **On "One of the Few" Objects** 1487
  You Wu, Pankaj K. Agarwal *(Duke University)*, Chengkai Li *(The University of Texas at Arlington)*, Jun Yang *(Duke University)*, Cong Yu *(Google Research)*

Demonstration Track

- **BC-PDM: Data Mining, Social Network Analysis and Text Mining System Based on Cloud Computing** ... 1496
  Le Yu, Jian Zheng, Bin Wu, Bai Wang, Chongwei Shen, Long Qian, Renbo Zhang
  (Beijing University of Posts and Telecommunication)
- **Query-Driven Discovery of Semantically Similar Substructures in Heterogeneous Networks** ... 1500
  Xiao Yu, Yizhou Sun, Peixiang Zhao, Jiawei Han *(University of Illinois at Urbana-Champaign)*
- **DAGger: Clustering Correlated Uncertain Data (to predict asset failure in energy networks)** ... 1504
  Dan Olteanu, Sebastiaan J. van Schaik *(University of Oxford)*
- **UFIMT: An Uncertain Frequent Itemset Mining Toolbox** ... 1508
  Yongxin Tong, Lei Chen *(The Hong Kong University of Science and Technology)*,
  Philip S. Yu *(University of Illinois at Chicago)*
- **Visual Exploration of Collaboration Networks Based on Graph Degeneracy** ... 1512
  Christos Giatsidis, Klaus Berberich *(École Polytechnique)*, Dimitrios M. Thilikos *(University of Athens)*,
  Michalis Vazirgiannis *(Athens University of Economics and Business)*
- **TourViz: Interactive Visualization of Connection Pathways in Large Graphs** ... 1516
  Duen Horng (Polo) Chau, Leman Akoglu *(Carnegie Mellon University)*, Jilles Vreeken *(University of Antwerp)*,
  Hanghang Tong *(IBM T.J. Watson Research)*, Christos Faloutsos *(Carnegie Mellon University)*
- **D-INDEX: A Web Environment for Analyzing Dependences Among Scientific Collaborators** ... 1520
  Claudio Schifanella, Luigi Di Caro *(Università di Torino)*,
  Mario Cataldi, Marie-Aude Aufaure *(École Centrale Paris)*
- **Information Propagation Game: A Tool to Acquire Human Playing Data for Multi-Player Influence Maximization on Social Networks** ... 1524
  Hung-Hsuan Chen *(The Pennsylvania State University)*,
  Yan-Bin Ciou, Shou-De Lin *(National Taiwan University)*
- **MoodLens: an Emoticon-Based Sentiment Analysis System for Chinese Tweets** ... 1528
  Jichang Zhao, Li Dong, Junjie Wu, Ke Xu *(Beihang University)*
- **Intelligent Advertising Framework for Digital Signage** ... 1532
  Phil Tian, Addicam V. Sanjay, Kunapareddy Chiranjeevi, Shahzad Malik Malik *(Intel Corporation)*
- **AssocExplorer: An Association Rule Visualization System for Exploratory Data Analysis** ... 1536
  Guimei Liu, Andre Suchitra, Haojun Zhang *(National University of Singapore)*,
  Mengling Feng, See-Kiong Ng *(Institute for Infocomm Research)*,
  Limsoon Wong *(National University of Singapore)*
- **GeoSearch: Georeferenced Video Retrieval System** ... 1540
  Youngwoo Kim, Jinha Kim, Hwanjo Yu *(Pohang University of Science and Technology)*
- **Siren: An Interactive Tool for Mining and Visualizing Geospatial Redescriptions** ... 1544
  Esther Galbrun *(University of Helsinki)*, Pauli Miettinen *(Max Planck Institute for Informatics)*
- **Navigating Information Facets on Twitter (NIF-T)** ... 1548
  Shamanth Kumar, Fred Morstatter, Grant Marshall, Huan Liu *(Arizona State University)*,
  Ullas Nambiar *(IBM Research Lab India)*
- **HeteRecom: A Semantic-Based Recommendation System in Heterogeneous Networks** ... 1552
  Chuan Shi, Chong Zhou *(Beijing University of Posts and Telecommunications)*,
  Xiangnan Kong *(University of Illinois at Chicago)*,
  Philip S. Yu *(University of Illinois at Chicago & King Abdulaziz University)*,
  Gang Liu, Bai Wang *(Beijing University of Posts and Telecommunications)*
- **VOXSUP: A Social Engagement Framework** ... 1556
  Yusheng Xie, Daniel Honbo *(Voxsup, Inc.)*,
  Kunpeng Zhang, Yu Cheng, Ankit Agrawal *(Northwestern University)*, Alok Choudhary *(Voxsup, Inc.)*

- **A System for Extracting Top-K Lists from the Web** 1560
  Zhixian Zhang, Kenny Q. Zhu *(Shanghai Jiao Tong University)*, Haixun Wang *(Microsoft Research Asia)*
- **EventSearch: A System for Event Discovery and Retrieval on Multi-Type Historical Data** 1564
  Dongdong Shan, Wayne Xin Zhao, Rishan Chen, Baihan Shu, Ziqi Wang, Junjie Yao, Hongfei Yan, Xiaoming Li *(Peking University)*
- **EvaPlanner: An Evacuation Planner with Social-Based Flocking Kinetics** 1568
  Cheng-Te Li, Shou-De Lin *(National Taiwan University)*
- **PubMed Search and Exploration with Real-Time Semantic Network Construction** 1572
  Jinoh Oh, Taehoon Kim, Sun Park, Hwanjo Yu *(Pohang University of Science and Technology)*

Author Index 1576

KDD 2012 Conference Organization

General Chair: Qiang Yang *(Hong Kong University of Science and Technology)*

Honorary Conference Chairs: Lu Ruqian *(Institute of Mathematics, CAS)*
Bo Zhang *(Tsinghua University)*

Advisory Committee Chair: Deyi Li *(Chinese Academy of Engineering)*

Program Chairs: Deepak Agarwal *(LinkedIn)*
Jian Pei *(Simon Fraser University)*

Associate General Chair: Dou Shen *(CityGrid Media)*

Industry & Government Track Chairs: Michael Zeller *(Zementis)*
Hui Xiong *(Rutgers)*

Industry Practice Expo Chairs: Ying Li *(Concurix Corporation)*
Rajesh Parekh *(Groupon)*

Asia Pacific Track Chairs: David Wai-Lok Cheung *(University of Hong Kong)*
Wei Wang *(University of North Carolina at Chapel Hill)*

Workshop Chairs: Zhi-Hua Zhou *(Nanjing University)*
Sofus A. Macskassy *(Information Sciences Institute / USC)*

Tutorial Chairs: Jennifer Neville *(Purdue University)*
Yehuda Koren *(Google)*

Local Arrangements Chairs: Jie Tang *(Tsinghua University)*
Lei Zhang *(Web Search & Mining Group Microsoft Research Asia)*
Chao Liu *(Tencent Inc.)*

Exhibit and Demo Chairs: Tie-Yan Liu *(Microsoft Research Asia)*
Jian-Tau Sun *(Machine Learning group, Microsoft Research Asia)*
Natasha Balac *(University of California, San Diego)*

Industrial Liaison Chairs: Haixun Wang *(Microsoft Research Asia)*
Haifeng Wang *(Baidu)*

KDD Best Paper Awards Chairs: Ke Wang *(Simon Fraser University)*
Rich Caruana *(Microsoft Research)*

SIGKDD 2012 Awards Chair: Ramasamy Uthurusamy *(General Motors Corp.)*

KDD Cup Chairs: Brian Dalessandro *(Media6Degrees)*
Claudia Perlich *(Media6Degrees)*
Gordon Sun *(Tencent Inc.)*
Yading Yue *(Tencent Inc.)*

KDD Summer School: Maosong Sun *(Tsinghua University)*
Du Xiaoyong *(Renmin University of China)*
Hang Li *(Microsoft Research Asia)*

Media Chairs: Ming Hua *(Facebook Inc.)*
Jianyong Wang *(Tsinghua University)*
Rayid Ghani *(Accenture Technology Labs)*
Emilia Palaveeva *(Yantra PR)*

Panel Chairs: Raghu Ramakrishnan *(Microsoft)*
Charles X. Ling *(University of Western Ontario)*

Poster Chairs: Yan Liu *(University of Southern California)*
Ping Luo *(HP Labs)*

Publications Chairs: Alexandru Niculescu-Mizil *(NEC Laboratories America)*
Jingrui He *(IBM T.J. Watson Research Center)*

Registration Chair: Xingquan Zhu *(University of Technology Sydney)*

Social Network Chairs: Ron Bekkerman *(LinkedIn)*
Qiaozhu Mei *(University of Michigan)*

Sponsorship Chairs: Balaji Krishnapuram *(Siemens Medical Solutions USA)*
Shiqiang Yang *(Tsinghua University)*
Peng Cui *(Tsinghua University)*

Student Awards Chairs: Jimeng Sun *(IBM T.J. Watson Research Center)*
Jennifer G. Dy *(Northeastern University)*

Student Volunteer Chairs: Juanzi Li *(Tsinghua University)*
Min-Ling Zhang *(Southeast University)*

Treasurer: Raymond Chi-Wing Wong *(Hong Kong University of Science and Technology)*

Video Chairs: Steven C.H. Hoi *(Nanyang Technological University)*
Shou-de Lin *(National Taiwan University)*

Web Masters: Weike Pan *(Hong Kong University of Science and Technology)*
Guang-Tong Zhou *(Simon Fraser University)*
Xiao Meng *(Simon Fraser University)*

KDD'12 Senior Program Committee Members

Naoki Abe, *IBM*
Rakesh Agrawal, *Microsoft Research*
James Bailey, *The University of Melbourne*
Soumen Chakrabarti, *IIT Mumbai*
Bee-Chung Chen, *Yahoo! Research*
Diane Cook, *Washington State University*
Ian Davidson, *University of California, Davis*
Inderjit Dhillon, *University of Texas, Austin*
Charles Elkan, *University of California, San Diego*
Martin Ester, *Simon Fraser University*
Johannes Gehrke, *Cornell University*
Lise Getoor, *University of Maryland*
Joydeep Ghosh, *University of Texas, Austin*
Bart Goethals, *University of Antwerp*
Dimitrios Gunopulos, *University of Athens*
Jiawei Han, *University of Illinois at Urbana-Champaign*
David Jensen, *University of Massachussets, Amherst*
Christopher Jermaine, *Rice University*
Benjamin Kao, *The University of Hong Kong*
George Karypis, *University of Minnesota*
Sathiya Keethi, *Yahoo!*
Eamonn Keogh, *University of California, Riverside*
Ravi Kumar, *Yahoo! Research*
Laks Lakshmanan, *The University of British Columbia*
Jure Leskovec, *Stanford University*
Hang Li, *Microsoft Research*
Michael Mahoney, *Stanford University*
Nikos Mamoulis, *The University of Hong Kong*
David Mimno, *Princeton University*
Raymond Ng, *The University of British Columbia*
Zai-qing Nie, *Microsoft Research*
Srinivasan Parthasarathy, *The Ohio State University*
Daryl Pregibon, *Google Research*
Saharon Rosset, *Tel Aviv University*
Joerg Sander, *The University of Alberta*
Sunita Sarawagi, *IIT Bombay*
Alex Smola, *Yahoo! Research*
Ramakrishnan Srikant, *Google*
Dacheng Tao, *University of Technology, Sydney*
Andrew Tomkins, *Google Research*
Suresh Venkatsubramanian, *University of Utah*
Jianyong Wang, *Tsinghua University*
Wei Wang, *University of North Carolina at Chapel*
Ji-rong Wen, *Microsoft Research*
Xifeng Yan, *University of California, Santa Barbara*
Jeffrey Yu, *The Chinese University of Hong Kong*
Philip Yu, *University of Illinois at Chicago*
Mohammed Zaki, *Rensselaer Polytechnic Institute*
Changshui Zhang, *Tsinghua University*
Zhi-Hua Zhou, *Nanjing University*

KDD'12 Research Track Program Committee

James Abello, *DIMACS/Rutgers*
Foto Afrati, *National Technical University of Athens*
Charu Aggarwal, *IBM Research Watson*
Eugene Agichtein, *Emory University*
Christoforos Anagnostopoulos, *University of Cambridge*
Arthur Asuncion, *Google*
Sitaram Asur, *HP Research Labs*
Vassilis Athitsos, *University of Texas at Arlington*
Gustavo Batista, *University of Sao Paulo - USP*
Roberto Bayardo, *Google*
Tanya Berger-Wolf, *University of Illinois, Chicago*
Michael Berthold, *KNIME*
Kanishka Bhaduri, *NASA*
Mikhail Bilenko, *Microsoft Research*
Francesco Bonchi, *Yahoo! Research*
Gavin Brown, *University Manchester*
Deng Cai, *Zhengjian University, China*
Toon Calders, *Technische Universiteit Eindhoven*
Ricardo Campello, *University of Sao Paulo*
Ed Chang, *Google*
Jonathan Chang, *Facebook*
Kevin Chang, *University of Illinois at Urbana-Champaign*
Nitesh Chawla, *University of Notre Dame*
Sanjay Chawla, *University of Sydney*
Lei Chen, *Hong Kong University of Science and Technology*
Ming-Syan Chen, *NTU*
Weizhu Chen, *Microsoft*
Xuewen Chen, *University of Kansas*
Ye Chen, *Microsoft*
Yixin Chen, *Washington University in St Louis*
Zheng Chen, *Microsoft Research*
Zhiyuan Chen, *UMBC*
Hong Cheng, *Chinese University of Hong Kong*
James Cheng, *Nanyang Technological University*
David Cheung, *University of Hong Kong*
Wei Chu, *Microsoft*
Gao Cong, *Nanyang Technological University*
Alfredo Cuzzocrea, *University of Calabria*
Gautam Das, *University of Texas at Arlington*
Anirban Dasgupta, *Yahoo Research*
Umesh Dayal, *HP Labs*
Laura Dietz, *Max Planck Institute and University of Massachusetts Amherst*
Carlotta Domeniconi, *George Mason University*
Guozhu Dong, *Wright State University*
Zhicheng Dou, *Microsoft Research Asia*
Artur Dubrawski, *Carnegie Mellon University*
Murat Dundar, *Indiana University-Purdue University Indianapolis*
Saso Dzeroski, *Jozef Stefan Institute*
Tina Eliassi-Rad, *Rutgers University*
Andrew Fast, *Elder Research*
Ada Fu, *Chinese University of Hong Kong*
Johannes Furnkranz, *TU, Darmstadt*
Joao Gama, *University of Porto*
Jing Gao, *Univ. of Buffalo*
Rainer Gemulla, *Max-Planck Institute*
Amol Ghoting, *IBM TJ Watson Research Center*
C. Lee Giles, *Penn State University*
Aristides Gionis, *Yahoo! Research*
Aris Gkoulalas-Divanis, *IBM Research - Zurich*
Sharad Goel, *Yahoo! Research*
Michaela Goetz, *Twitter*
Rahul Gupta, *Google Research*
Qi He, *IBM Almaden Research Center*
Tin Kam Ho, *AT&T Bell Labs*
Ming Hua, *Facebook*
Jun Huan, *University of Kansas*
Jian Huang, *Google*
Jimmy Huang, *York University*
Shuiwang Ji, *Old Dominion University*
Yan Jia, *National University of Defense Technology*
Daxin Jiang, *Microsoft*
Rong Jin, *Michigan State University*
Ruoming Jin, *Kent State University*
Xiaoming Jin, *Tsinghua University*
Panos Kalnis, *KAUST*
Anitha Kannan, *Microsoft Research*
Panagiotis Karras, *Rutgers Business School*
Latifur Khan, *University of Texas at Dallas*
Daniel Kifer, *Penn State University*
Irwin King, *The Chinese University of Hong Kong*
George Kollios, *Boston University*
Nick Koudas, *University of Toronto and Sysomos Inc*
Akhil Kumar, *Penn State University*
Diane Lambert, *Google Research*

Thodoros Lappas, *Boston University*
Dongwon Lee, *Penn State University*
Hongrae Lee, *Google Research*
Mong Li Lee, *NUS*
Ronny Lempel, *Yahoo! Research*
Carson Leung, *University of Manitoba*
Guoliang Li, *Tsinghua University*
Jinyan Li, *University of Technology Sydney*
Jiuyong Li, *University of South Australia*
Lihong Li, *Yahoo! Research*
Ee Peng Lim, *Singapore Management University*
Chih Jen Lin, *National Taiwan University*
Jessica Lin, *George Mason University*
Xuemin Lin, *University of New South Wales*
Charles Ling, *University of Western Ontario*
Bing Liu, *University of Illinois at Chicago*
Chao Liu, *Microsoft Research*
Huan Liu, *Arizona State*
Jun Liu, *Siemens Corporate Research at Princeton*
Tie-Yan Liu, *Microsoft Research*
Yan Liu, *University of Southern California*
Eric Lo, *The Hong Kong Polytechnic University*
Stefano Lonardi, *University of California, Riverside*
Aurelie Lozano, *IBM Research*
Chang-Tien Lu, *Virginia Tech*
Jiebo Luo, *University of Rochester*
Shiqian Ma, *Columbia University*
Mohammad Mahdian, *Google*
Cecilia Mascolo, *University of Cambridge*
Prem Melville, *IBM TJ Watson Research Center*
Aditya Menon, *University of California, San Diego*
Donald Metzler, *University of Southern California*
George Michailidis, *University of Michigan*
Abdullah Mueen, *Microsoft Research*
S. Muthu Muthukrishnan, *Rutgers*
Olfa Nasraoui, *University of Louisville*
Jennifer Neville, *Purdue University*
David Newman, *University of California, Irvine*
Siegfried Nijssen, *Katholieke Universiteit Leuven*
Tim Oates, *University of Maryland Baltimore County*
Sandeep Pandey, *Yahoo! Research*
Spiros Papadimitriou, *IBM*
Panagiotis Papapetrou, *Aalto University*
Laurence Park, *University of Western Sydney*
Stott Parker, *UCLA*
Dino Pedreschi, *KDD Lab, University of Pisa, Italy*
Bernhard Pfahringer, *University of Waikato*
Jeff Phillips, *University of Utah*
Claudia Plant, *Florida State University*
John Platt, *Microsoft Research*
Kunal Punera, *Yahoo! Research*
Chedy Raissi, *INRIA*
Daniel Ramage, *Stanford University*
Naren Ramakrishnan, *Virginia Tech*
Louiqa Raschid, *University of Maryland*
Parisa Rashidi, *University of Florida*
Rajeev Rastogi, *Yahoo! Labs*
Chandan Reddy, *Wayne State*
Matthias Renz, *Ludwig-Maximilians-Universitat Munchen*
Matthew Richardson, *Microsoft Research*
Mirek Riedewald, *Northeastern University*
Venu Satuluri, *Ohio State University*
Thomas Seidl, *RWTH Aachen*
Sundararajan Sellamanickam, *Yahoo! Labs, Bangalore*
Jialie Shen, *Singapore Management University*
Kyuseok Shim, *Seoul National University*
Luo Si, *Purdue*
Vikas Sindhwani, *IBM Research-Watson*
Ambuj Singh, *University of California, Santa Barbara*
D. Sivakumar, *Yahoo! Research*
Myra Spiliopoulou, *Otto-von-Guericke-Universitaet Magdeburg*
Rohini Srihari, *University at Buffalo, State University of New York*
Michael Steinbach, *University of Minnesota*
Nick Street, *University of Iowa*
Jimeng Sun, *IBM TJ Watson Research Center*
Pang-Ning Tan, *Michigan State University*
Jie Tang, *Tsinghua University, China*
Yufei Tao, *Chinese University of Hong Kong*
Shirish Tatikonda, *IBM Almaden Research Center*
Manolis Terrovitis, *IMIS, Athena, Greece*
Evimaria Terzi, *Boston University*
Alex Thomo, *University of Victoria*
Hanghang Tong, *IBM Research*
Vincent Tseng, *National Cheng Kung University*
Leong Hou U, *University of Macau*
Duygu Ucar, *Stanford University*
Antti Ukkonen, *Yahoo! Research*
Lyle Ungar, *University of Pennsylvania*
Jaideep Vaidya, *Rutgers Univ.*

KDD'12 Industry & Government Track Program Committee Members

Dean Abbott, *Abbott Analytics*
John Akred, *Accenture*
Michael Berthold, *KNIME*
Kanishka Bhaduri, *NASA*
Eric Bloedorn, *MITRE - USA*
Rainer Burkhardt, *JgenCy*
Longbing Cao, *University of Technology Sydney*
Huanhuan Cao, *Nokia Research Center*
Haifeng Chen, *NEC Research Lab*
Enhong Chen, *University of Science and Technology of China*
James Cox, *SAS*
Kamalika Das, *NASA Ames Research Center*
Chao Deng, *China Mobile*
Wei Ding, *University of Massachusetts Boston*
David Duling, *SAS*
Wei Fan, *IBM Research*
Nancy Grady, *Science Applications International Corporation*
Simon Gyorgy, *Mayo Clinic*
Jianying Hu, *IBM T.J. Watson Research Center*
Ming Hua, *Facebook*
Sergei Israilev, *Jabiru Ventures*
Daxin Jiang, *Microsoft*
Bin Jiang, *Facebook*
Hongxia Jin, *IBM Research*
Yu Kai, *Baidu, Inc.*
Mei Kobayashi, *IBM Research Lab (Tokyo)*
Rui Kuang, *University of Minnesota*
Mohit Kumar, *Accenture*
Rick Lawrence, *IBM Research-Watson*
Aleksandar Lazarevic, *Travelers*
Christoph Lingenfelder, *IBM*
Nathan Nan Liu, *Hong Kong UST*
Fei Liu, *Bosch Research*
Jiebo Luo, *University of Rochester*
Ping Luo, *HP Lab*
Gideon Mann, *Google*
Manish Marwah, *HP Labs*
Gabor Melli, *VigLink*
Theodore Omtzigt, *Stillwater Supercomputing*
Gaurav Pandey, *Mount Sinai School of Medicine*
Mark Plutowski, *Flipboard*
Karl Rexer, *Rexer Analytics*
Mark Richards, *ISO*
Neal Rothleder, *MITRE*
Ramendra Sahoo, *Citi*
D Sculley, *Google*
Ted Senator, *SAIC*
Abhishek Sharma, *NEC Research Lab*
Ali Shaykhian, *NASA*
Manas Somaiya, *eBay*
Jacob Spoelstra, *Opera Solutions*
Jian-Tao Sun, *Microsoft Research*
AC Surendran, *Microsoft*
Arun Swami, *Google*
Shu Tao, *IBM Research*
Wayne Thompson, *SAS*
Hanghang Tong, *IBM Research*
Ramasamy Uthurusamy, *GM*
Peter van der Putten, *Pegasystems & Leiden University*
Ranga Vatsavai, *Oak Ridge National Labs*
Andrew Veal, *Government Communications HQ, UK*
Dave Vennergrund, *Delta Solutions and Technologies, Inc.*
Fei Wang, *IBM Research*
Stefan Weber, *Siemens AG*
Zhen Wen, *IBM Research*
Junjie Wu, *Beihang University*
Xing Xie, *Microsoft Research Asia*
Jiangang Yu, *Microsoft*
Kai Yu, *NEC Laboratories America*
Ruofei Zhang, *Yahoo Labs*
Zheng Zhao, *SAS*
Yu Zheng, *Microsoft*
Zijian Zheng, *Microsoft*
Zhaohui Zheng, *Yahoo!*
Scott Zoldi, *FICO*

KDD'12 Research Track External Reviewers

Mohammad-Ali Abbasi
Jaafar Ben Abdallah
Artur Abdullin
Zubin Abraham
Ferit Akova
Darko Aleksovski
Can Altinigneli
Saeed Amizadeh
Rajul Anand
Sam Anzaroot
Gowtham Atlure
Gowtham Atluri
Anton Bakalov
Lakshika Balasuriya
Honhji Bao
Iyad Batal
Christian Beecks
Gabriel Bender
Thomas Bernecker
Kasturi Bhattacharjee
Jinbo Bi
Hoda Bidkhori
Sam Blasiak
Brigitte Boden
Petko Bogdanov
Ivan Brugere
Fahrettin Cakir
Xin Cao
Lei Cen
Yashu Chamber
Kung-Hua Chang
Xi Chen
Chen Cheng
Si-Chi Chin
Byron Choi
Shumo Chu
Prakash Mandayam Comar
Michele Coscia
Aaron Crandall
Andrew Cron
Bruno Crémilleux
Decheng Dai
Kamalika Das
Mahashweta Das
Ritendra Datta
Elnaz Delpisheh
Sanjoy Dey
Arman Didandeh
Ivica Dimitrovski
Martin Dimkovski
Wenkui Ding
Anton Dries
Lian Duan
Denisa Duma
Narayanan Edakunni
Dora Erdos
Ines Faerber
James Faghmous
S M Faisal
Hadi Fanaee
Lujun Fang
Zheng Fang
Gang Fang
Hongliang Fei
Zhuo Feng
Jing Feng
Carlos Ferreira
Neil Fore
Sergej Fries
Glenn Fung
Stanislav Funiak
Bin Gao
Chuancong Gao
Huiji Gao
Priyanka Garg
Liang Ge
Rossetti Giulio
Rafael Giusti
Olga Gkountouna
Sebastian Goebl
Behzad Golshan
naiyang Guan
Ziyu Guan
Francesco Gullo
Pritam Gundecha
Tias Guns
Fan Guo
Chetan Gupta
Stephan Günnemann
Habiba
MohammadTaghi HajiAghayi
Yue Han
Qian Han
Hyoil Han
Elena Harris
Marwan Hassani
Basheer Hawwash
Xiao He
Di He
Jingrui He
Eric Heim
Minh Hoang
Thanh Lam Hoang
Ryan Hoens
Yuan Hong
Dzung Hong
Xia Hu
Weishu Hu
Yifan Hu
Xin Huang
Dino Ienco
Elena Ikonomovska
Allison Irvine
Anca Ivanescu
Arun Iyer
Ruoyi Jiang
Mehdi Kargar
Shiva Kasiviswanathan
Jaya Kawale
Rohan Khade
Mohammad Khoshneshin
Younghoon Kim
Woo-Cheol Kim
Hyun-Woo Kim
Steffen Kirchhoff
Arno Knobbe
Dragi Kocev
Bettina Konte
Parisa Kordjamshidi
Petr Kosina
NgaiMeng Kou
Philipp Kranen

Hardy Kremer
Georg Krempl
Peer Kröger
Da Kuang
Brian Kulis
Arjun Kumar
Shamanth Kumar
Choudur Lakshminarayan
Diane Lambert
Sean Landman
Nick Larusso
Chao-Hui Lee
Jeonghoon Lee
Victor Lee
Yuhong Lee
Matthijs Van Leeuwen
Jian Li
Ming Li
Wu-Jun Li
Nan Li
Yingming Li
Xiao Li
Fangtao Li
LongJie Li
Baichuan Li
John Liagouris
Shou-de Lin
Guang Ling
Lin Liu
Yi Liu
Haibin Liu
Sitong Liu
Lei Liu
Nathan Liu
Bo Liu
Steven Loscalzo
Grigorios Loukides
Cécile Low-Kam
Eric Hsueh-Chan Lu
Yan Luo
Kathy Macropol
Gjorgji Madjarov
Das Mahashweta
Son T. Mai
Julien Mairal
Charalampos Mavroforakis
Kyle McQuisten
Aranyak Mehta
Iñigo Mendialdua
Jun Miao
Pauli Miettinen
Iris Miliaraki
Darakhshan Mir
Seyed Mirebrahim
Varun Mithal
Samaneh Moghaddam
Anna Monreale
Gianmarco De Francisci Morales
Fred Morstatter
Vinod Nair
Abbas Nayebi
Vincenzo Nicosia
Johannes Niedermayer
Sadegh Nobari
Eirini Ntoutsi
Laurie O'Connor
Omar Odibat
Marcia Oliveira
Jeffrey Junfeng Pan
Pance Panov
Vanja Paunic
Diego Pennacchioli
Marc Plantevit
Michael Plavinski
Yevgeniy Podolyan
Anton Polishko
Miao Qiao
Tao Qin
Lu Qin
Nguyen Quang
Brian Quanz
Alain Rakotomamonjy
Sayan Ranu
Vikas Raykar
Mike Rechenthin
Rabbany K. Reihaneh
Matt Revelle
Elaine Ribeiro
Carlos Rojas
Giulio Rossetti
Senjuti Basu Roy
Yiye Ruan
Brian Ruttenberg
Senay Yasar Saglam
Tanwistha Saha
Ankan Saha
Shaghayegh Sahebi
Esin Saka
Hamman Samuel
Thomas Sandholm
Cicero Nogueira dos Santos
Tamas Sarlos
Christoph Sawade
Hassan Sayyadi
James Schaffer
Leander Schietgat
Johannes Schneider
Erich Schubert
Matthias Schubert
Yu-Keng Shih
Diego Furtado Silva
Michael Simpson
Ayush Singhal
Nick Skapura
Ivica Slavkov
Yangqiu Song
Vinicius Mourao Alves de Souza
Sargur Srihari
Daniela Stojanova
Ja-Hwung Su
Amarnag Subramanya
Fabian Suchanek
Aixin Sun
Khaled Ahsan Talukder
Syed K. Tanbeer
Jiliang Tang
Chayant Tantipathananandh
Vahid Taslimi
Maryam Tavafi
Yasushi Terazono
Saravanan Thirumuruganathan
Brian Thompson
Ryota Tomioka
Aneta Trajanov
Roberto Trasarti
Pucktada Treeratpituk
Honglei Tu
Vladimir Vacic
Thanasis Vergoulis
Davide Verzotto
Krishnamurthy Viswanathan

Peter Wackersreuther
Jiannan Wang
Qifan Wang
Taifeng Wang
Wenjun Wang
Wen Wang
Ye Wang
Xufei Wang
Jia Wang
Guan Wang
Robert Wright
Huanhuan Wu
Shanchan Wu
Leting Wu
shiming Xiang
Guang Xiang
Chenyan Xiong
Yi Xu
Zhiqiang Xu
Jianpeng Xu
Hui Yan
Haiqin Yang
Tao Yang
Sen Yang
Jaewon Yang
Ming Yang
Yiyang Yang
Chen Yang
Wen Yao
Jihang Ye
Zheng Ye
Beta Chi-Lap Yip
Man Lung Yiu
Shengkang Yu
Xiaofeng Yu
Guoxian Yu
Yintao Yu
Xiao Yu
Jun ZHANG
Zhihua ZHang
Reza Zafarani
Jesin Zakaria
Bernard Zenko
Mingyang Zhang
Yuchen Zhang
Zhihua Zhang
Yang Zhang
Wenjie Zhang
Peng Zhang
Chenyi Zhang
Min-Ling Zhang
Jiashu Zhao
Xueyi Zhao
Kang Zhao
Chao Zhou
Qin Zhou
Zhuojie Zhou
Ke Zhou
Zhe Zhu
Morteza Zihayat
Max Zimmermann
Albrecht Zimmermann
Bo Zong
Haitao Zou
Andreas Züfle

ACM SIGKDD KDD 2012 Sponsors & Supporters

Sponsors:

KDD.org — ACM Special Interest Group on Knowledge Discovery and Data Mining

ACM SIGMOD

Supporters

HUAWEI

SOSO 搜搜

Baidu 百度

SAP

阿里云 aliyun.com

Microsoft

facebook

Google

EMC²

Greenplum

ELSEVIER

Nokia Research Center

PayPal of ebY

Deloitte.

sas

Adobe

IBM Research

m6d media6degrees

OPERA SOLUTIONS

NSF

Review Spam Detection via Temporal Pattern Discovery

Sihong Xie[†] Guan Wang[†] Shuyang Lin[†] Philip S. Yu[†‡]
[†] Department of Computer Science, University of Illinois at Chicago, Chicago, IL
[‡] Computer Science Department, King Abdulaziz University, Jeddah, Saudi Arabia
{sxie6, gwang26, slin38, psyu}@uic.edu

ABSTRACT

Online reviews play a crucial role in today's electronic commerce. It is desirable for a customer to read reviews of products or stores before making the decision of what or from where to buy. Due to the pervasive spam reviews, customers can be misled to buy low-quality products, while decent stores can be defamed by malicious reviews. We observe that, in reality, a great portion (> 90% in the data we study) of the reviewers write only one review (singleton review). These reviews are so enormous in number that they can almost determine a store's rating and impression. However, existing methods did not examine this larger part of the reviews. Are most of these singleton reviews truthful ones? If not, how to detect spam reviews in singleton reviews? We call this problem *singleton review spam detection*.

To address this problem, we observe that the normal reviewers' arrival pattern is stable and uncorrelated to their rating pattern temporally. In contrast, spam attacks are usually bursty and either positively or negatively correlated to the rating. Thus, we propose to detect such attacks via unusually correlated temporal patterns. We identify and construct multidimensional time series based on aggregate statistics, in order to depict and mine such correlations. In this way, the singleton review spam detection problem is mapped to a abnormally correlated pattern detection problem. We propose a hierarchical algorithm to robustly detect the time windows where such attacks are likely to have happened. The algorithm also pinpoints such windows in different time resolutions to facilitate faster human inspection. Experimental results show that the proposed method is effective in detecting singleton review attacks. We discover that singleton review is a significant source of spam reviews and largely affects the ratings of online stores.

Categories and Subject Descriptors

H.2.8 [**Database Applications**]: Data Mining

KDD'12, August 12–16, 2012, Beijing, China.

General Terms

Algorithms, Experimentation

Keywords

Review spam, time series, adversarial data mining

1. INTRODUCTION

Online reviews and ratings about products and stores are essential parts in today's electronic commerce where they provide helpful information for potential customers. A product or store with a decent rating and a high proportion of positive reviews will attract more customers and larger amount of business, while a couple of negative reviews/ratings could substantially harm the reputation, leading to financial losses. Since there is no rule governing online reviews and ratings, some product providers or retailers are leveraging such public media to defame competitors and promote themselves unfairly, or even to cover the truth disclosed by genuine reviews. For example, suppose a customer finds the delivery service of a certain store unacceptably slow, she then writes a review about the fact and gives it a low rating on a review website. This review and rating present a unfavourable impression of the store to potential customers, who might choose other stores after reading that review. In order to avoid the drainage of business caused by this negative yet truthful review, the store could employ or entice a group of people to write undeserving positive reviews about the delivery service. Similarly, the store could also ask these people to write unfavorable reviews about its competitors, from which the store would like to distract customers. These hired reviewers are called spammers and the reviews they write are called spam reviews. In order to protect customers, honest online stores and the whole electronic commerce environment, it is desirable to detect spam reviews and take proper measures.

Previous works propose to use features of review contents and reviewers' behaviors [5, 10, 11, 1] or graph connecting reviewers, stores and reviews [6], to detect spam reviews. These methods work best in the situations where spammers write many reviews (see related work). In reality, however, most reviewers write only one review. For example, 68% of the reviewers write a single review in the Amazon review dataset studied in [10], and this percentage is 90% in the dataset we study here. If a review is the only review a reviewer has written, we call it a *singleton review* (SR for short). In fact, as we shall see later, the SR definition can be generalized to cover reviewers with a few reviews, not necessarily just one. One question is: are most of these SRs honest reviews? The answer is probably not, due to the *nature* of spam attacks. For a store to rapidly raise its fame and rating (resp. defame others) it is desirable to have spammers post plenty of favorable (resp. unfavorable) reviews about it (resp. its competitors) in a short time. Usually a spammer would not post many reviews with similar ratings for a store under the same name. Instead, he would rather write spam reviews under different names to avoid being caught. This spamming strategy brings a large number of SR. Most of the statistics adopted by previous works would not work on such singleton reviews. For example, the mean and standard deviation of ratings given by a reviewer [5] become meaningless if this reviewer has written only one review; in the rule or frequent pattern based detection method [11], singleton reviews are also ignored due to their low significance.

In the present paper, we focus on singleton review (SR) spam attack detection, and "spammer" refers to "SR spammer" if not otherwise specified. According to the above observations, we propose a novel approach that maps the SR spam detection problem to a abnoramlly correlated temporal pattern detection problem. The proposed algorithm is based on multi-scale multidimensional time series anomaly detection. In particular, we construct statistics whose joint anomaly could be a strong indicator of SR spam attacks. The identified statistics includes the average rating, the total number of reviews, and the ratio of singleton reviews among all reviews. We collect these statistics from ratings and reviews for each store to build the multidimensional time series, base on which we develop an SR spam detection model. We combine temporal curve fitting and LCS (Longest Common Sub-sequence) algorithms to find out abnormal sections in each dimension of the time series. We then devise a ranking-based algorithm to consolidate the anomalies in all dimensions to find out temporally correlated abnormal sections. Furthermore, since short term fluctuations are common in the constructed time series, we start with a larger time window (e.g. 2 months) to smooth out such noisy changes of the time series, so that any significant abnormal pattern can be detected robustly, therefore reducing false positive rate. After any singleton review attack is detected, we scale down the window size, so that the exact abnormal points become more obvious and one can quickly locate the suspicious reviews.

This paper makes the following contributions:

- We identify and formulate the singleton spam review detection problem, which has not been addressed in previous works. This problem is important yet difficult to solve, as we will point out in Section 2.
- We develop a new principle for SR spam detection based on the observation that the arrival pattern of SR tends to be bursty (Section 3.1) and temporally correlated to the rating. We identify multiple temporal statistics of reviews to support detection based on this principle. Instead of following traditional approaches, which consider the reviews as a static collection of documents, here we take a new approach of treating them as a series of events.
- We propose a hierarchical detection criterion to detect SR spam attacks robustly and accurately. This feature is especially useful for online review website quality and trust monitoring.
- We find the number of singleton spam reviews to far exceed the number of other types of spam reviews identified in the literature.

2. MOTIVATION OF SINGLETON REVIEW SPAM DETECTION

In the data studied here and in [10], we can observe that the reviewers who write only one review (a singleton review) dominate the body of reviewers. The sheer number of these reviews implies that the rating of a store or product, and potentially the customers' choices can be greatly manipulated by these reviews. This property make SR particularly attractive to spammers. Despite the significance of detecting SR spams, no existing work has addressed this problem. Indeed, detecting SR spams can be challenging. If a reviewer has written only one review, simply looking at this singleton review reveals little information about the true intention behind it, so it is hard for machines or even human beings to draw a conclusion. For example, in the experiment, we find that one reviewer said "For the few times that I've contacted customer service via phone, email, or chat, the person has always been helpful and gone out of his/her way." At a first glance, this is a normal review talking about customer service. Since it is the only review the reviewer has written, existing spam detection algorithms will simply ignore this review. Even for human beings, it is extremely difficult to tell if this is a spam review or not. However, if we look at the aggregate reviewers' behaviors in a temporal way, we can find that this review was written in a period when there was a burst of SRs and the rating of the store went up dramatically. It is abnormal for the number of reviews, the ratio of SR and the store rating to be temporally correlated, this review is pretty suspicious.

In particular, spammers have to write many positive (or negative) reviews in a short time, otherwise, the spammers are not effective in promoting or defaming a store or product. However, if a spammer posts his reviews quickly under the same name, he can be easily detected by checking the duration between two consecutive reviews with similar rating from a single person. So writing spam reviews under different names is a safer way. Based on the above reasoning, we make the following conjectures on SR spam attacks. When such an attack occurs in a certain period, there tends to be a sharp increase in the number reviews and the ratio of SRs, together with an increase (or decrease) in the average rating. Therefore, we can transform the SR spam detection problem to abnormally correlated temporal pattern detection in a multidimensional time series consisting of the above three indices. Note that spammers may want to evade the proposed method by writing more than one but not too many reviews. For these spammers, we can easily modify the algorithm to catch them (see Section 3.2.1) and we focus on the detecting SR spams. In the next section, we make several assumptions about reviewers' arrival patterns, which define a necessary condition of SR spam attacks.

3. SINGLETON REVIEW SPAM DETECTION MODEL

3.1 The Model of Reviewer Behavior

It is the difference in spammers' and genuine reviewers' behaviors that motivates the proposed algorithm. We show

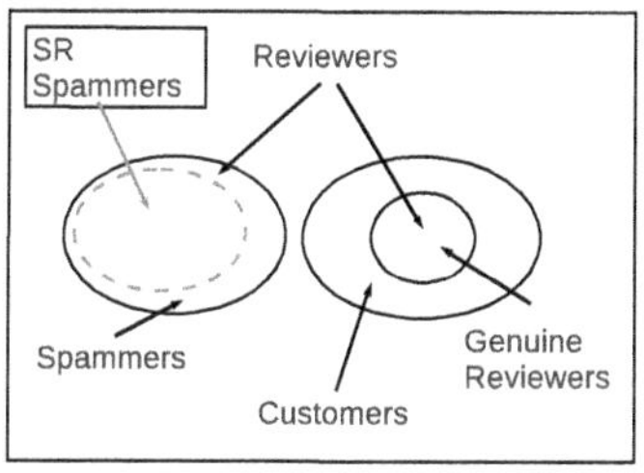

Figure 1: Relationship of Spammers, Reviewers and Customers

the relationship of reviewers, customers, spammers and SR spammers in Figure 1. Note that the areas do not reflect the actual number of groups of people. On one hand, we define a reviewer as a name under which at least one review is written. A customer is a person who has shopping experience with at least one store, and becomes a reviewer if he/she contributes a review. On the other hand, there are two categories of spammers, namely, SR spammers and other spammers. We assume a customer cannot be a spammer (the customer set does not intersect the spammer set in Figure 1). Indeed, though it is possible for a store to entice its customers to write favorable reviews for it, the store has to take the risks of the disclosing of such dishonesty to the public by its customers and harming the store's reputation. Instead, a store is more willing to hire dedicated spammers. Also, a spammer might later become a customer and write a genuine review, but our aim here is to detect *any* spamming activities, instead of telling spammers from customers. Therefore, we assume that a customer cannot be a spammer.

We make certain assumptions of reviewers' behaviors, divided into two phases: the arrival and writing phase. In the arrival phase, a customer buys something from a store or a spammer is hired or enticed by a store to write fake reviews. The writing phase is when a reviewer writes a review. There are mainly three patterns of arrival phase behaviors: normal arrival, promotion/sale event arrival, and spam attack pattern. First, the normal arrival pattern can be modeled by a homogeneous Poisson process with a fixed rate λ. A Poisson process is a set of random variables $\{N(t) : t \geq 0\}$ satisfying the following properties [9]:

- $\Pr\{N(t+h) - N(t) = 1 | N(t) = n\} = \lambda h + o(h)$ as $h \to 0$, for $n = 0, 1, \ldots$
- $\Pr\{N(t+h) - N(t) = 0 | N(t) = n\} = 1 - \lambda h + o(h)$ as $h \to 0$
- $N(0) = 0$

where $N(t)$ is the number of arrivals up to time t. λ is a constant controlling the intensity of arrivals, with a larger λ indicating more arrivals in a unit of time. Second, it is possible for a store to promote their products over a period and therefore increase the traffic of customers and reviews. We model this arrival pattern using a non-homogeneous Poisson process, with the rate parameter being a function of time $\lambda(t)$. Third, the spam attack arrival pattern is pretty much like that in the promotion mode, since a large number of spammers would be hired or enticed by the store.

In the writing phase, we model the writing behaviors of normal reviewers and spammers. First, in order to get the rewards offered by the store that tries to commit SR spam attacks, spammers tend to write spam reviews in a hurry, and there is seldom a delay in posting spam reviews. Therefore, we assume that the time when a spammer writes a review is the same as the time she arrives, and the spam reviews' arrival pattern is the same as spammers' arrival pattern, a bursty one. Second, for genuine reviewers, we claim that there are some random factors associated with the delays in posting their reviews after their shopping experiences, by the following reasons. A genuine reviewer seldom writes a review right after she shops with a store. Instead, most of them would write their reviews after receiving and trying out the products for some time. Therefore, one random factor is the time spent on delivery, this factor depends on how a customer and a store choose the way of delivery, the traffic and logistic conditions and so on. Another random factor is the time spent on tryouts, which depends on customers' personal behaviors. The randomness associated with the delay in a genuine reviewer's posting a review smoothes out the arrival intensity of reviews, even in a promotion event. In orther words, their reviews are less likely to concentrate in a short period and causing bursty peaks.

According to the above analysis, a spam attack tends to create a burst on the review arrival process, which is distinct from the normal and even promotion review arrivals. Nonetheless, as fluctuations in the volume of reviews do exist, bursty patterns in review arrival do not necessarily imply SR spam attacks. Observe that spammers are brought together to bring up or down the rating of a store, the ratings of spam reviews are more likely to correlate with these reviews' arrivals. In contrast, because genuine reviewers' opinions about a store vary wildly, depending on their satisfaction with speed of delivery, quality of products and customer services, etc. If we average the ratings of genuine reviews in a certain period of reasonable length, the positive and negative ratings will cancel out each other, therefore, the average ratings should be stable over time and independent of genuine reviews' arrivals. In summary, we should look at the joint abnormal patterns in review arrival and rating to detect such attacks more robustly.

3.2 A Correlated Temporal Anomalies Discovery based Approach

According to the above assumptions, we propose an SR spam detection approach based on correlated abnormal patterns discovery in multidimensional time series. To raise or lower the rating of a store safely and rapidly, spammers tend to post a large number of reviews with a high or low rating under different names. If there is a sharp increase in the volume of (singleton) reviews with rating increases or decreases dramatically at the same time, it is highly likely that the rating is manipulated by the newly arrived reviews. Therefore, detection by exploiting the correlation between ratings and volume of (singleton) reviews is more robust compared to using any single time series. In the paper, we will focus on the case where the rating goes up dramatically. The case with rating going down dramatically can be similarly modelled.

In the remaining of this section, we first describe how to construct multidimensional time series capturing reviewers' behaviors (Section 3.2.1). Then in Section 3.2.2 we describe algorithms to detect correlated anomalies in all three time series. Lastly, in Section 3.2.3, we describe the proposed hierarchical framework for robust SR spam detection.

3.2.1 Time Series Construction

The detection approach is based on time series of the number of reviews, average ratings and the ratio of singleton reviews. The data we study here is a set of reviews with texts and ratings posted for different stores on a review website in a certain time period. To construct these time series, we discard text information and keep the posting time and ratings of the reviews. This is reasonable as there exist other spam detection algorithms utilizing text information, so they are complementary methods to the proposed algorithm. The resulting data can be seen in this way: each store s has a series of ratings sorted in ascending order of posting time.

$$R(s) = \{r_1, \ldots, r_{n_s}\}$$

$$TS(s) = \{ts_1, \ldots, ts_{n_s}\}$$

where n_s is the number of reviews for store s, and ts_i is the time stamp when r_i is written, $ts_i \leq ts_j$ for all $1 \leq i < j \leq n_s$. After choosing the time windows size (denoted by Δt), the time interval under investigation (denoted by $I = [t_0, t_0 + T]$) can be divided into $N = T/\Delta t$ consecutive time windows or sub-intervals. Each time window is of length Δt and contains reviews posted during that time window. Let I_n denote the n-th time window, so

$$I_n = [t_0 + (n-1)\Delta t, t_0 + n\Delta t], \qquad I = \bigcup_{n=1}^{N} I_n$$

Given a time window I_n, we compute the average rating f_1, the number of reviews f_2, and the ratio of singleton reviews f_3. Formally,

$$f_1(I_n) = \sum_{ts_j \in I_n} r_j / f_2(I_n)$$

$$f_2(I_n) = |\{r_j : ts_j \in I_n\}|$$

$$f_3(I_n) = |\{r_j : ts_j \in I_n, r_j \text{ comes from an SR}\}| / f_2(I_n)$$

where $|A|$ denotes the cardinality of the set A. Given a store s, time interval $I = [t_0, t_0 + T]$ and time window size Δt, these aggregate functions represent a three dimensional time series and can be collectively represented by

$$F_s(I, \Delta t) = \begin{bmatrix} f_1(1) & \ldots & f_1(N) \\ f_2(1) & \ldots & f_2(N) \\ f_3(1) & \ldots & f_3(N) \end{bmatrix}_s$$

where $f_i(n)$ is a shorthand for $f_i(I_n)$, $i = 1, 2, 3$. In the following, we drop the index on stores and let $F(I, \Delta t)$ denote the time series constructed for a certain store. The way we construct these time series can be generalized to handle spammers who write just a few reviews with similar ratings. We can simply treat all the reviews as SR by ignoring reviewers' ids, then the way we construct these time series still makes sense and the proposed algorithm can detect SR attacks (see next section).

3.2.2 Correlated Abnormal Patterns Detection in Multidimensional Time Series

Given the three time series of a store, we would like to find out correlated abnormal blocks on all three series. In other words, these blocks should simultaneously present sudden increases in rating, ratio of singleton reviews and the number of reviews. Here we focus on the singleton review detection methodology based on burst detection algorithms. Instead of inventing a novel burst detection algorithm, which is not the focus in this paper, we use a three-step approach for the detection. First, on each dimension, we employ a Bayesian change point detection algorithm [4] to fit curves using the time series (other curve fitting algorithms will do the job, too). As an example, we plot the time series along with the fitted curves in Figure 2. We then apply a simple template matching algorithm to the fitted curves to detect bursty patterns. Lastly, a sliding window finds out the blocks in time series corresponding to a joint burst in all dimensions of the time series. In the above example, a joint burst is highlighted by the red box in Figure 2.

Assuming that we have obtained the fitted curves, we describe in what follows the last two steps in details, for the curve fitting algorithm, please refer to [4]. Let $C = \{\mathbf{c}_1, \mathbf{c}_2, \mathbf{c}_3\}$ be the fitted curves of the three dimensions of a time series. All curves have the same length (number of samples), which is also defined as the length of C. First, we want to detect sudden increases in each of the three curves separately. Based on the description of the arrival process in Section 3.1, this can be transformed to the problem of template matching. We use a step function-like template to represent a sudden rise in values

$$\mathbf{v} = \{-0.5, -0.5, 0.5, 0.5, 0.5\}$$

Note that one can use other values for $\mathbf{v}$ so long as it represents a sharp increase temporally. If a block on a fitted curve $\mathbf{c} = \{c_1, \ldots, c_n\} \in C$ is found to "match" this template well, then we find an anomaly of interest on the curve. One can obtain all blocks of $\mathbf{c}$ by sliding a window through $\mathbf{c}$, and all points falling into the window form a block which is denoted by

$$\mathbf{b} = \{c_{i_1}, \ldots, c_{i_5}\}$$

where $1 \leq i_k \leq n$ for $k = 1, \ldots, 5$ and $i_k + 1 = i_{k+1}$ for $k = 1, \ldots, 4$. Note that the length of a block is chosen to have the same length as the template. We use a modified longest common substring (LCS) for matching [13] between $\mathbf{v}$ and $\mathbf{b}$. In general, suppose we want to find the degree of match between two sequences $\mathbf{z}^1 = \{z_1^1, \ldots, z_n^1\}$ and $\mathbf{z}^2 = \{z_1^2, \ldots, z_n^2\}$. Without loss of generality, one can think of $\mathbf{z}^1$ as $\mathbf{v}$ and $\mathbf{z}^2$ as $\mathbf{b}$. In the modified LCS, how well two sequences match each other is measured by the number of points in one sequence matching those in the other sequence. By a "match" between two points, we mean the absolute difference between the values of two points is less than a given threshold ϵ. The modified LCS algorithm uses the following dynamic programming formula to find out how many matches occur between $\mathbf{z}^1$ and $\mathbf{z}^2$, for $0 \leq i, j \leq n$ and $|i - j| \leq 1$:

$$M(i,j) = \begin{cases} 0, & \text{if } i \text{ or } j = 0 \\ 1 + M(i-1, j-1), & \text{if } |z_i^1 - z_j^2| < \epsilon \\ \max\{M(i-1, j), \\ \qquad M(i, j-1)\}, & \text{otherwise} \end{cases}$$

where $M(i,j)$ records the number of matches between subsequences $\{z_1^1, \ldots, z_i^1\}$ and $\{z_1^2, \ldots, z_j^2\}$. The constraint $|i - j| \leq 1$ makes sure that, $z_i^1 \in \mathbf{z}^1$ is not matched to a point $z_j^2 \in \mathbf{z}^2$ far away from the position of z_i^1.

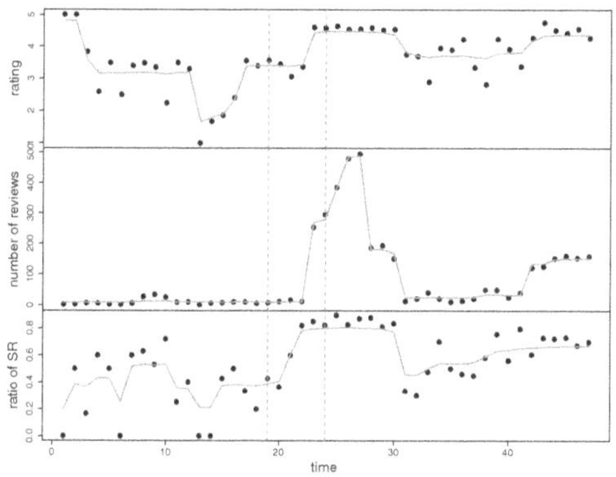

Figure 2: Bursty Patterns Detected in Store 24779

Algorithm 1 Bursts Detection in Single Time Series (**BD-STS**)

Input: fitted curve $\mathbf{c}$, template $\mathbf{v}$
Output: top k ranked periods with bursty pattern
m = length of $\mathbf{c}$.
n = length of $\mathbf{v}$.
for $i = 1 \to m - n + 1$ **do**
  Normalize $\mathbf{c}[i : i + n - 1]$.
  $factor = range(\mathbf{c}[i : i + n - 1])$.
  $s[i]$=LCS($\mathbf{c}[i : i + n - 1]$, $\mathbf{v}$) $\times$ $factor$.
end for
return Periods corresponding to top k values in s.

Algorithm 1 describes bursty pattern detection in a single time series. For each block $\mathbf{b}$ on a fitted curve $\mathbf{c}$, we first normalize it. Then the modified LCS procedure described above finds out the number of matches between the template and the normalized block $\mathbf{b}$. By this step, we can find out, in the time series, the locations corresponding to bursty patterns. Taking the degree of burst into account, the number of matches in each block is multiplied by the range of values in that block (the one before normalization), such that greater bursts will be ranked higher.

Algorithm 2 Correlated Abnormal Patterns Detection in Multidimensional Time Series (**CAPD-MDTS**)

Input: Multidimensional curves C
Output: Periods when correlated anomalies appear
for each dimension $\mathbf{c}_i$ **do**
  Time points of burst L_i=**BD-STS**($\mathbf{c}_i$)
end for
n = length of C, w = time frame length (set to 5)
$S = \emptyset$ // set of periods to return
for $b = 1 \to n - w + 1$ **do**
  $S = S \cup \{[b, b + w - 1]\}$ if $|\{x \in L_i : i = 1, 2, 3, x \in [b, b + w - 1]\}| == 3$
end for
return S

After we obtain a list time points corresponding to the top k bursts in each of the dimensions, we need to find out the time windows corresponding to joint increases in all three dimensions. By the first step, we know in each dimension the time when the bursty patterns appear, along with their intensities of burst. In the experiments, we take the top 5 time points. Then we slide a window of a certain size over the time axis. At each point, we find out how many top ranked locations in all dimensions are in the time frame specified by the current time window. A time window is reported if all three dimensions have bursty patterns falling into the window. These steps are formally described in Algorithm 2.

A running example based on the review data is shown in Figure 2. The length of the time window in time series construction is chosen to be 60 days. This example is also discussed in more detail in the experiment section. Each dimension of the time series is plotted in dark points (upper box - rating, middle box - number of reviews, lower box - ratio of singleton review). The solid lines are the fitted curves (to be discussed in the next subsection). We use red vertical dash lines to highlight one of the suspicious blocks detected in time series by the proposed approach. The significant joint bursty pattern locates in $\{19 \to 24\}$ (from Oct 13, 2005 to Sep 12, 2006), as enclosed by the pair of vertical lines. The three curves all go up in this interval.

3.2.3 A Hierarchical Framework for Robust Singleton Review Spam Detection

Given the review records of a store, one can construct multiple time series using different time window sizes (resolutions). If the window size is set too small, the general trend of a time series would be buried in a large number of fluctuations, which might cause high false positive rate. Therefore, we propose a hierarchical framework, which incorporates Algorithm 2 to robustly detect SR spam attacks. We summarize this hierarchical SR spam detection algorithm in Algorithm 3. We first smooth out short-term fluctuations using a larger window (lower resolution). Then we fit curves using these time series and use Algorithm 2 (**CAPD-MDTS**) to detect any suspicious periods with correlated abnormal patterns, which indicate the high likelihood of SR spam attacks. A smaller window size (higher resolution) can be used to reveal more details (e.g. the exact time of the burst). This is accomplished by constructing new time series with a higher resolution on the detected periods, and detecting any finer suspicious period. This process continues until one reaches the desired resolution such that the time of SR spam attacks can be easily pinpointed.

Algorithm 3 Multi-Scale Spam Detection Algorithm

Input: Reviews data of a store, initial window size Δt, time span I when all reviews are collected.
Output: Detected time intervals of spam activities.
Initialize time interval set $S_0 = \{I\}$. Scale $\ell = 0$.
while Δt not small enough **do**
  $\ell = \ell + 1$, $S_\ell = \emptyset$.
  for Each time interval $I \in S_{\ell-1}$ **do**
    Construct time series $F(I, \Delta t)$.
    Fit a curve for each dimension of $F(I, \Delta t)$.
    Sample the curves to obtain clean time series C.
    $S_\ell = S_\ell \cup$ **CAPD-MDTS**(C).
  end for
  Decrease window size Δt,
end while
return S_ℓ

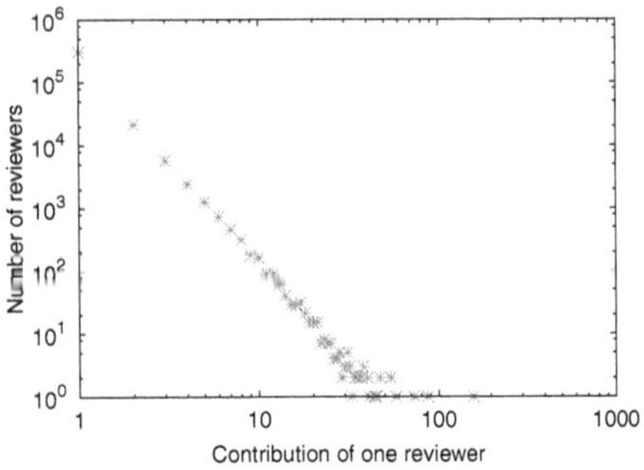

Figure 3: Contributions of reviewers

4. EXPERIMENTS

In this section, we first describe the dataset we use, then we give a couple of case studies to provide evidences of spamming activities caught by the proposed method.

4.1 Review Data Description

The review data we use in the experiments is a snapshot of a review website (`www.resellerratings.com`) on Oct 6th, 2010 [1]. It contains 408,469 reviews written by 343,629 reviewers (identified by their IDs on the website) for 25,034 stores. 310,499 reviewers (> 90%) wrote only one reviews and about 76% (310,499/408,469) of the reviews are SRs. The distribution of the number reviewers writing a number of reviews is plotted in logarithm scale in Figure 3. As we can see, the relation between these two quantities roughly follows the power distribution. This is also observed in [10]. The main body of the data consists of reviews, along with information about stores and reviewers. For each review we keep the following information: its rating (ranging from 1 to 5), the posting date and whether it is an SR.

4.2 Human Evaluation

In this section, we report the experimental results of human evaluation of the detected suspicious stores and reviews. We employ three human evaluators in this experiment.

4.2.1 Suspicious Store Detection

One way to use the algorithm is to run it against the reviews for a store to detect any singleton spam attack. We focus on stores with large number of SRs, so in the evaluation we select top 53 stores, each of which has more than 1,000 reviews. We ask human evaluators to read the reviews from all 53 stores and make decisions regarding the suspiciousness of these stores. If two or more evaluators vote a store as being likely to have committed an SR spam attack, we tag it to be a likely dishonest store. According to the human evaluation, there are a total of 29 stores having at least two votes. Out of the 53 stores, the proposed algorithm labels 36 ones as suspicious stores and the rest as normal ones. Out of the 36 detected ones, 22 stores have at least two votes for being suspicious. The proposed algorithm misses 7 suspicious ones. The recall is 75.86% (22/29), indicating that the proposed algorithm can catch most of the stores involved in SR spam attack. The precision is 61.11% (22/36). Though this precision looks a bit low, since our goal is to identify suspicious stores for human experts to investigate further, the proposed approach only enlarges the suspicious set moderately with a decent recall.

[1]Thanks to Keith Nowicki

Table 1: Human evaluation results on stores

	Evaluator 1	Evaluator 2	Evaluator 3
Evaluator 1	17	14	16
Evaluator 2	-	20	19
Evaluator 3	-	-	24

Table 2: Human evaluation results on reviews

	Evaluator 1	Evaluator 2	Evaluator 3
Evaluator 1	59	20	28
Evaluator 2	-	41	38
Evaluator 3	-	-	72

Table 1 shows the agreement between evaluators when evaluating the detected stores. The numbers on the diagonal show how many stores each evaluator considers as dishonest. For example, evaluator 1 regards 17 out of 53 stores as suspicious ones. The off-diagonal numbers give how many stores that both evaluators in that row and column identify as dishonest stores. For example, the number on the intersection of Evaluator 1 and Evaluator 2 means that both evaluators 1 and 2 agree upon 14 stores that are suspicious stores. In any case, there are 26 stores at least one of the evaluators regarding it to be suspicious. Comparing the off-diagonal numbers with the diagonal numbers shows the limitation of the content-based approaches. Even human evaluators examining the contents cannot reach agreement a lot of the times as these cases are often very subtle.

4.2.2 Singleton Reviews on a Detected Store

We also ask three human evaluators to examine 147 reviews contained in the detected time window of burst given in the first case study (see next section). Each review is given a score (0-negative, 0.5-possibly, 1-positive) indicating the degree of being regarded as a spam review by each evaluator. Lastly, for each review, the scores from three evaluators are added up to get the final score. Among the 147 reviews, 43 reviews (38 are SR) have final score at least 2, and 12 reviews (11 are SR) have final score equal to 3. This indicates that lots of spam identified are indeed SR and the proposed algorithm can locate the period when SR are more likely to happen.

On the other hand, we can also use similar evaluation technique as in Table 1. Table 2 shows the results of human evaluation on spam reviews. Evaluator 1 tags 59 out of 147 reviews as spam reviews, while the other two regard 41 and 72 reviews as spam reviews, respectively. There are 98 reviews that at least one of the evaluators regard as spam. Similarly, the numbers off the diagonal show the agreement between evaluators. Again, this table shows that it is not easy for human beings to reach agreements on whether a review is an SR spam, and content-based methods will be less effective in the detection of this kind of spams.

4.3 Spam Detection Case Study

In this section, we closely study the evidences of SR attacks committed by several stores.

4.3.1 First Case Study

The results of running the proposed multidimensional multi-scale detection algorithm on the reviews of a store (id=24811)

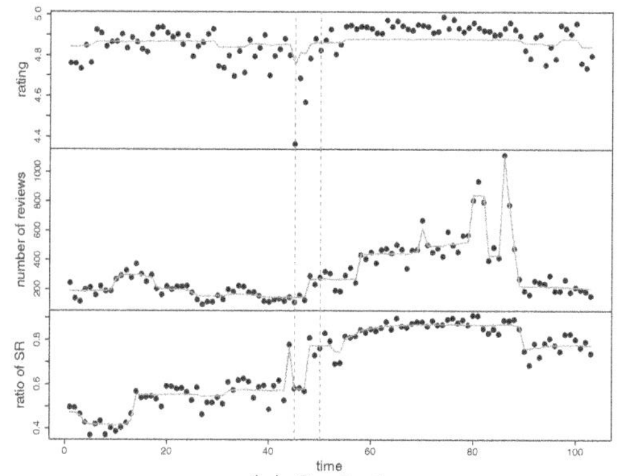

(a) Scale 1

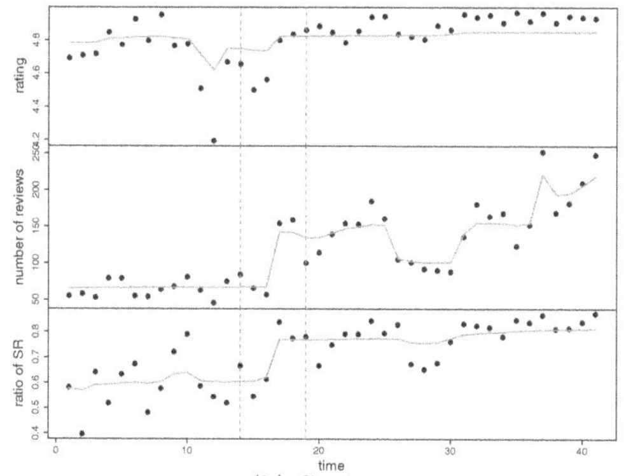

(b) Scale 2

Figure 4: Anomaly detection on multi-scale multi-dimensional time series

are shown in Figure 4. The multidimensional time series in the first subfigure (Figure 4(a)) is produced using a larger time window (30 days) with review data from Apr 2002 and to Aug 2010. The format of this figure is the same as that of Figure 2. In this higher level of detection, we find a sharp increase in $\{45 \rightarrow 50\}$, which corresponds to the time interval from Oct 30, 2005 to Mar 30, 2006. Notice the burst occurs in a two-month period. We construct another 3-dimensional time series from the review data in the detected time window to find more details of the burst. With the window size set to 15 days, we run the detection algorithm again. The block $\{14 \rightarrow 19\}$ (from Dec 17, 2005 to Mar 3, 2006) with suspicious activities are found and highlighted in Figure 4(b). Note that this detected time window is smaller than the previous one. In this time interval, the number of singleton reviews increases from 57 to 154, the rating goes up from 4.56 to 4.79, and the ratio of singleton reviews goes up from 61% to 83%. These all happen in a two-weeks period. It looks like the ratings were bolstered by the sudden increase of singleton reviews.

However, one might still not be convinced that there are probably spams activities in the detected time intervals. We provide further evidences by analyzing the review contents. Note that looking for these evidences is *not* part of the proposed algorithm, which only uses the reviewers' behaviors for detection. This is only for the purpose of validation. We find out that around the time when the bursts in all three dimensions are detected, the phrases "customer service" and

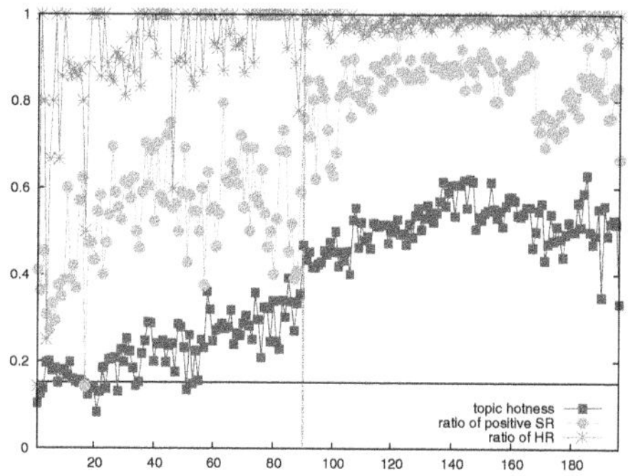

Figure 5: Topic Hotness Trend

"customer support" are unusually frequent among the SRs. Such correlation indicates that there could be spammers giving undeserving high ratings to "customer service" of that store. Next we study this correlation quantatively.

When constructing multidimensional time series, we divide the time from Apr 2002 to Aug 2010 into intervals of two weeks. For each interval, we calculate the "hotness" of the topic "customer service". The "hotness" of a topic is the ratio of reviews about that topic to all reviews in a certain period. If a review contains one of the phrases "customer service" and "customer support", we consider it to be related to that topic. In Figure 5, we show the trend of the hotness of the topic in the blue curve with solid squares. One can see that there is a burst of topic hotness occurs at time 90 (Feb 06, 2006, indicated by the dashed line). Note that this burst occurs in a two-week long period with the hotness goes up from 35% to 46%. Also, note that the time of this burst coincides with that of the burst detected in the multidimensional time series by the proposed algorithm. This makes the detected time interval look suspicious. The black horizontal solid line shows the topic hotness calculated from all reviews except those from the store being investigated. We can see that, on average, less than 16% of the reviews mentions the phrases. This number is calculated using 376,758 reviews out of the total 408,470 reviews, so it well represents reviewers' general interests of this topic. By comparison, we can see that the hotness within this store is twice as high as the average level. This is unlikely in normal business, since it is quite hard to gain the recognition of "customer service" from real customers in two weeks. After that time, the topic hotness keeps going up and is far higher than the average level. In particular, one out of two reviews is talking about "customer service" on average.

Besides "topic hotness", we consider two other reviewer behaviors. The green curve with solid circles shows the ratio of singleton 5 star reviews to the topic-related reviews. We can see that from the time Feb 06, 2006 on, this ratio is rather high, namely, more than 80% of the singleton reviews are related to "customer service". We can conclude that the burst and hotness of the topic is supported by the burst and high volume of singleton reviews. Lastly, the red curve with stars gives the ratio of reviews which are written by "hurry reviewers" (HR) to the singleton 5 star reviews. We define an HR to be a reviewer who writes a review on the same day she registers her id. From the figure, one can tell that, from Feb 06, 2006 on, a high percentage (over 90%) of 5 star singleton reviews about "customer service" are produced by

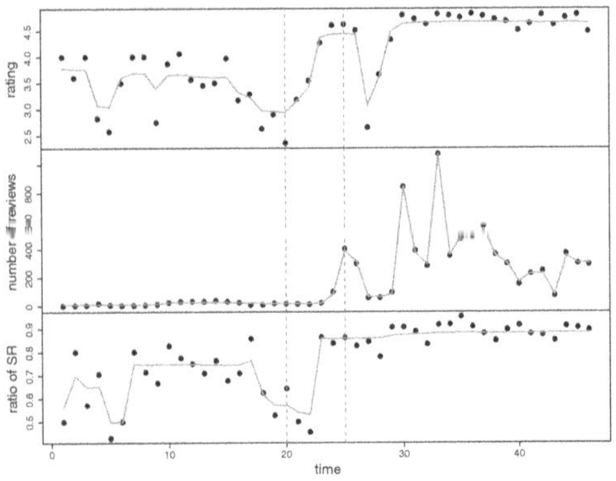

Figure 6: Bursty Patterns Detected in Store 24938

"hurry reviewers". Since at least for those who registered in 2005 never write another review in the following 5 years, this is quite dubious. As a way of validation, we read reviews of the store in the period of topic hotness burst. We found a reviewer once disclosed the fact that the store emailed her for a favorable rating. The reviewer had an unpleasant experience with that store and got customer service only after she low-rated it on the review website.

4.3.2 *Second Case Study*

When we try to investigate a store *meritline* with high SR spams identified by the proposed algorithm, we find out it also operates under another name *cdrdvdrmedia*. Hence this case of spamming is quite interesting. The following facts support this observation: first, the addresses of the two companies are the same[23]. Second, on the review website we are studying, *meritline* is an alien of *cdrdvdrmedia*. Third, according to a domain analysis website, these two stores have the same Google analytics account[4]. Lastly, one reviewer says the package and receipt she received were from *meritline* though she shopped with *cdrdvdrmedia*[5]. We perform the proposed multidimensional times series analysis on the reviews for meritline. Figure 2 (Section 3.2) shows the time interval when an SR spam attack is likely to have happened. *cdrdvdrmedia* sells the same set of products as *meritline* does, but with a much lower rating. There are only 48 reviews in near 8 years (from Aug-2002 to Jan-2010). The average rating of the store is only 3.06 and people are talking about credit card problems, low-quality products and customer service. Therefore, the high volume of reviews and good rating for *meritline* are quite suspicious.

4.3.3 *Third Case Study*

We find another store (*supermediastore*) which is likely involved in singleton review spamming. The multidimensional time series for the store and the detected bursty patterns are shown in Figure 6. This store is probably owned by the same owner as *meritline* and *cdrdvdrmedia*. This is supported by at least two forum posts[6]. We also find an interesting review[7] telling that the reviewer was cheated by *supermediastore* when it tried to entice her into spamming. The reviewer once received an email from the store about writing a review for it. In return, the reviewer would receive a "gift", which she never receive. This is a direct evidence that this store is hiring/enticing people to write favorable reviews. This review is written during the time when there is a burst of singleton reviews.

5. RELATED WORK

There is few existing algorithm specifically designed for singleton review spams detection. In [12], the authors consider singleton review spams in their data collecting process. They "artificially" construct singleton review spams for evaluation, while in this paper, the singleton review spams occur in a real-world dataset. Therefore, the singleton reviews they construct don't exhibit the temporal features that real-world singleton review spams should have. In [15], the authors attempt to detect hotels which are more likely to be involved in spamming. They construct several features, based on which two ranking algorithms detect the most suspicious hotels. Their method is not comparable with the one we proposed, because their method is supervised (they need to know if certain positive reviews are shill reviews reacting to negative reviews). As their method provides a ranking list of hotels, one will not be able to tell how many hotels need further inspection, while the proposed method gives a list of suspicious stores for further human evaluation.

Another work considers reviewers' behaviors by introducing a social graph connecting reviewers, their reviews and stores [6]. They discover the reinforcement relations of reviewers' trustiness, reviews' honesty, and stores' reliability. They use such relations to discover suspicious spammers. However, their method is unable to handle singleton reviews, because SRs have insufficient information in the constructed graph to infer their trustiness. Another work [5] uses reviewers' behaviors as indicators of spamming. The features include multiple similar rating on a single product, similarity between reviews written by a single reviewer, etc. One will not be able to compute these features for SRs.

The works [1, 2] study group spammers. They first use frequent pattern mining to find groups of reviewers who frequently write reviews together. Then in [1], they construct features to find the most likely groups of spammers, or in [2], construct a graph modeling the relations between groups of spammers, spammers and products for group spammer ranking. These methods are novel in detecting a new form of spam activity. Yet they still do not address the singleton review spam problem, because only groups of reviewers who write reviews together at least 3 times will be considered as candidate groups. Similarly, the rule-based algorithm for unexpected review activities detection proposed in [11] would also fail, because during the rule discovery step, SRs will be pruned due to the support threshold.

Earlier works on spam detection mainly rely on review similarities to construct features for spam reviews. For ex-

[2]`www.cdrdvdrmedia.com/contact-us.html`

[3]`www.la.bbb.org/business-reviews/General-Merchandise-Retail-By-Internet/Meritline-in-City-of-Industry-CA-13135057`

[4]`domaintraker.com/meritline.com`

[5]`www.resellerratings.com/store/view/CDRDVDRMEDIA_17/page/1`, see username "sableman"

[6]`forum.doom9.org/archive/index.php/t-36023.html` and `forum.videohelp.com/threads/143262-Meritline-Very-Disappointed`

[7]`www.resellerratings.com/store/view/Supermediastore/page/895`, see the review from the ID "defile"/

ample, the work in [10] categorizes spam reviews into three types: untruthful opinions; reviews on brands only; non-reviews. To detect these different types of spams, they use simple duplicate detection, feature construction and logistic regression. There are some drawbacks. First, it needs to collect a considerable amount of spam reviews manually. This is time consuming, even if it only looks at those reviews which are obviously spams. Second, it only deals with a small portion of all the reviews (neither the duplicated nor the manually labeled reviews represent a large enough fraction of the reviews). Finally, it does not address the singleton reviews spam problem, for example, the reviewers' centric features again rely heavily on the basis that a reviewer posts more than one review.

There are researches on multidimensional or multivariate time series anomaly detection [16, 7, 3]. However, we cannot directly apply these methods to the singleton spam detection problem. The methods in [3, 7] are designed for general abnormal pattern mining in multidimension time series, and [16] proposes to search all subspaces of all attributes in a relation (in the database sense), where the subspaces reported contain anomaly. We focus on detecting correlated abnormal patterns in all three dimensions, while a general detection algorithm will produce many abnormal patterns irrelevant to the problem in this paper, and therefore increase false positive rate.

Regarding burst detection, there are some excellent related works [8, 14, 4]. The work in this paper is not directly comparable to any general burst detection or curve fitting algorithm for the following reasons: first, the algorithm we propose is a general framework, which can incorporate any burst detection algorithm. Second, the problem we study in this paper is not merely a burst detection problem in time series, since we are not given the time series. Instead, we need to model the behaviors of reviewers and construct the time series. Also we need to identify the way in which abnormal patterns are uniquely correlated.

6. CONCLUSION

This paper studies the problem of singleton review spam detection, which is both difficult and important to solve. We transform this problem to a temporal pattern discovery problem. We identify three aggregate statistics which are indicative of this type of spam attack, then we construct a multidimensional time series using these statistics. We design a multi-scale anomaly detection algorithm on multi-dimensional time series based on curve fitting. Experimental results show that the proposed algorithm is effective in detecting singleton review spams.

7. ACKNOWLEDGEMENTS

This work is supported in part by NSF through grants IIS-0905215, IIS-0914934, CNS-1115234, DBI-0960443 and OISE-1129076, US Department of Army through grant W911NF-12-1-0066, and Google Mobile 2014 Program.

8. REFERENCES

[1] Mukherjee A, Liu B, Wang J, Glance N, and Jindal N. Detecting group review spam. WWW '11.

[2] Mukherjee A, Liu B, and Glance N. Spotting fake reviewer groups in consumer reviews. WWW '12.

[3] Vahdatpour A and Sarrafzadeh M. Unsupervised discovery of abnormal activity occurrences in multi-dimensional time series, with applications in wearable systems. In *SDM'10*.

[4] Chandra E and John W. E. bcp: An R Package for Performing a Bayesian Analysis of Change Point Problems. *Journal of Statistical Software*, 2007.

[5] Lim E-P, Nguyen V-A, Jindal N, Liu B, and Lauw H W. Detecting product review spammers using rating behaviors. CIKM '10.

[6] Wang G, Xie S, Liu B, and S.Yu P. Identify online store review spammers via social review graph. In *ICDM'11*.

[7] Cheng H, Tan P, Potter C, and A. Klooster S. Detection and characterization of anomalies in multivariate time series. In *SDM'09*.

[8] Jon K. Bursty and hierarchical structure in streams. KDD '02.

[9] S. Karlin and H. M. Taylor. *A First Course in Stochastic Processes*. Academic Press, 2 edition, 1975.

[10] Jindal N and Liu B. Opinion spam and analysis. WSDM '08.

[11] Jindal N, Liu B, and Lim E-P. Finding unusual review patterns using unexpected rules. CIKM '10.

[12] M Ott, Y Choi, C Cardie, and J. T. Hancock. Finding deceptive opinion spam by any stretch of the imagination. HLT '11.

[13] Michail V, Marios H, Dimitrios G, and Eamonn K. Indexing multi-dimensional time-series with support for multiple distance measures. KDD '03.

[14] Michail V, Christopher M, Zografoula V, and Dimitrios G. Identifying similarities, periodicities and bursts for online search queries. SIGMOD '04.

[15] G Wu, D Greene, and P Cunningham. Merging multiple criteria to identify suspicious reviews. RecSys '10.

[16] Li X and Han J. Mining approximate top-k subspace anomalies in multi-dimensional time-series data. In *VLDB'07*.

Selecting a Characteristic Set of Reviews

Theodoros Lappas
Boston University
tlappas@cs.bu.edu

Mark Crovella
Boston University
crovella@cs.bu.edu

Evimaria Terzi
Boston University
evimaria@cs.bu.edu

ABSTRACT

Online reviews provide consumers with valuable information that guides their decisions on a variety of fronts: from entertainment and shopping to medical services. Although the proliferation of online reviews gives insights about different aspects of a product, it can also prove a serious drawback: consumers cannot and will not read thousands of reviews before making a purchase decision. This need to extract useful information from large review corpora has spawned considerable prior work, but so far all have drawbacks. Review *summarization* (generating statistical descriptions of review sets) sacrifices the immediacy and narrative structure of reviews. Likewise, review *selection* (identifying a subset of 'helpful' or 'important' reviews) leads to redundant or non-representative summaries. In this paper, we fill the gap between existing review-summarization and review-selection methods by selecting a small subset of reviews that together preserve the statistical properties of the entire review corpus. We formalize this task as a combinatorial optimization problem and show that it NP-hard both to solve and approximate. We also design effective algorithms that prove to work well in practice. Our experiments with real review corpora on different types of products demonstrate the utility of our methods, and our user studies indicate that our methods provide a better summary than prior approaches.

Categories and Subject Descriptors

H.3.3 [**Information Search and Retrieval**]: Selection Process; H.2.8 [**Database Management**]: Database applications—*Data Mining*

Keywords

customer reviews, review selection, reviews

1. INTRODUCTION

One of the most significant developments in consumer shopping in recent years has been the explosive proliferation of online reviews. This reflects the great utility and trust that individuals ascribe to first-person reviews of products and services, particularly when those reviews come from actual past customers. It also reflects the fact that reviews are often highly detailed: reviews routinely cover many different aspects of a single product, allowing the reader to compile a very thorough picture of the strengths and weaknesses of any given product. Because of the utility and impact of reviews, major e-commerce sites have adopted them as a standard feature (e.g., `Amazon.com`), and a number of popular websites have emerged whose main goal is simply hosting online reviews (e.g., `Yelp.com`).

The immense value of online reviews has led to a vast body of reviews for individual items. For example, Amazon has more than 32,000 reviews for its Kindle e-reader, and there are individual restaurants in Yelp that have more than 100,000 reviews. Having a large number of reviews on the same product is desirable, since a large review-corpus is more likely to provide insights about different aspects of the item at hand. In addition, a large number of reviews increases the reader's confidence in the opinions they express.

However, the vast body of reviews for individual items is also a serious drawback. Consumers can not and will not read thousands of reviews before making a purchase decision. When a body of reviews is massive, its sheer size can prevent readers from extracting its useful information. A number of researchers have therefore begun to look for methods to extract the useful information contained in large review corpora, into a form that users can absorb more easily, despite having limited time or limited screen space.

For example, a significant amount of work has been devoted to the development of *review-summarization* methods [5, 20, 14, 15, 18]. The goal of these approaches is to create a summary of a review corpus that is both compact and representative of the opinions it contains. These summaries are statistical in nature, recording the number of positive and negative opinions that are expressed on each of the item's features. However, the drawback of such summaries is that they lack the immediacy and narrative structure of reviews as written by real users. This sacrifices one of the primary benefits of online reviews: the ability to appreciate the first-person experience of a previous buyer.

In response to this drawback of statistical summaries, another set of methods seek to summarize a review corpus using a subset of 'important' reviews. These important reviews are ultimately the ones shown to the user. For example, there exists a considerable amount of work in the area of *review ranking* [4, 7, 9, 10, 11, 17, 19]. Those approaches first produce a score for each review. They then show the top-k highest-scoring reviews to the user. However, these methods also suffer from a serious drawback: they do not seek coverage over the range of features that are important to users, and can therefore be highly redundant. For example, all the top reviews of a new camera may be highly informative about its long-range zoom ability, but mention nothing about how easy it is to use or carry. In other words, by evaluating each review separately, these approaches fail to consider the *complementarity* among reviews.

Hence, a number of recent efforts has focused on the problem of *review selection based on feature coverage*. For example, Lappas and Gunopulos [8] select a subset of reviews that collectively comment upon of *all* the features of the product at hand. Similarly, Tsaparas *et al.* [16] select a set of reviews that collectively provide both the negative and the positive aspects of each commented feature. While these methods do diversify the reported set of reviews, they fail to accurately capture the *proportion* of opinions (both positive and negative) in the underlying collection. For example, the summary constructed by method in [16] will always contain at least one positive and at least one negative opinion on each feature, even if one kind of opinion is significantly more common in the reviews of the underlying collection.

In this paper, we fill the gap between existing methods for review summarization and selection, by providing a subset of reviews that collectively present a statistically accurate summary of the entire review collection. More specifically, we preserve the integrity, coherence, and immediacy of actual reviews by providing users with a subset of reviews written by real previous customers. At the same time, we also ensure that the selected set of reviews preserves the statistics of the underlying corpus with respect to the positive and negative opinions expressed for different features. On a high level, the problem that we address in this paper is the following: "Given a corpus of Reviews $\mathcal{R}$ on item, find a small subset $\mathcal{S} \subseteq \mathcal{R}$ of reviews that accurately capture the proportion of opinions of the item's features." To the best of our knowledge, we are the first to formally define and study this problem, which we call the CHARACTERISTIC-REVIEW SELECTION problem.

In our work, we provide a formalization and thorough analysis of the problem, and identify and overcome the challenges that arise in efficiently finding its solution. We present novel algorithmic techniques, and show that they are effective through a rigorous evaluation. We show that our methods can accurately represent large review corpora, using only a small subset of reviews (e.g., from 5 to 20 reviews). Finally, we confirm the utility of the reported sets through a user study in which actual users judge the relative value of our approaches compared to the state of the art.

In addition to our main contribution of formalizing and solving the CHARACTERISTIC-REVIEW SELECTION problem, we also address an important precursor problem. A statistical summary is only meaningful if the distribution of positive and negative opinions in the corpus is stable at the time the summary is formed. If the state is unstable or immature, then the reported set could also be misleading. Taking this into consideration, we include an analysis of real review corpora in our experiments, and explore how the allotment of opinions in such corpora changes through time. Our analysis provides valuable insight on the converge of opinions, and allows us to identify when a body of reviews is sufficiently stable so as to serve as the basis of an informative summary.

Roadmap: The rest of the paper is organized as follows. First, we review related work in Section 2. We formally define our problem in Section 3, and in Section 4 we describe our algorithms for solving it. In Section 5, we present a thorough experimental evaluation of our methods. We conclude the paper in Section 6.

2. RELATED WORK

The goal of our work is to select a characteristic subset of reviews from a given corpus, in order to provide users with a compact and representative source of information. Although – to the best of our knowledge – the exact problem formulation we are proposing has not been considered before, our work clearly has ties with existing work in the domains of review summarization and review selection.

Review Selection: A recent line of work has addressed the problem of selecting a subset of reviews from a given corpus. Lappas and Gunopulos [8] proposed the selection of a set that represents the *majority opinion* on each feature. The drawback of this approach is that it overlooks the minority opinion, regardless of how significant it is. In a follow-up work, Tsaparas *et al.* [16] adopted an alternative formulation: given an upper bound on the number of the selected reviews, their goal is to select the set of reviews that covers as many features as possible. In their work, a feature is considered covered if the reported set includes at least one positive and at least one negative opinion on it. The shortcoming of this formulation is that it disregards the ratio of the number of positive and negative opinions on a feature. Thus, the reported set can be misleading to the user, who cannot use this set to deduce the actual proportion of positive and negative opinions across product features. The set of characteristic reviews reported by our methods does not have such drawbacks, since our goal is to accurately emulate the opinion distribution in the underlying corpus.

Review Summarization: Our work has ties to the extensive research devoted to review summarization. The problem of summarization was essentially introduced by Hu and Liu [5], who proposed a method for opinion-extraction, and applied the mined knowledge to create a statistical summary that informs the user of the number of positive and negative opinions in the corpus. A similar approach to the problem was taken by Zhang *et al.* [20]. In that work, the authors focused on the review domain, enriching their summary with opinionated sentences from the corpus. Instead of reporting the number of positive and negative opinions, Meng and Wang [14] report the terms that are used to characterize each feature (e.g. "small" or "expensive"). Another extension is proposed by Shimada *et al.* [15], who enrich the produced summary with objective information on the item, mined from web sources (i.e. Wikipedia). Finally, Liu *et al.* [9] explore ways to filter out low-quality reviews, in order to prevent them from corrupting the produced summary.

While the proposed approaches use statistical findings and isolated snippets to represent the given corpus, our own formulation asks for the selection of a characteristic set of actual reviews. We consider reviews as cohesive linguistic constructs, which provide users with an intuitive and user-friendly representation of the corpus. Nonetheless, in the context of a review-hosting website, our selection paradigm can be easily complemented by a corresponding statistical summary, in order to provide users with the maximum amount of information.

Review Quality and Ranking A significant amount of work has been devoted to evaluating different aspects of review quality [1, 11, 17]. These methods assign a quality score to every review, which is then used for ranking the reviews. The most prolific line of work in this field has focused on finding ways to emulate the user-assigned helpfulness votes that are present in review-hosting websites [19, 10, 7, 19, 4]. The main shortcoming of these approaches is that they evaluate the quality of each review separately. Hence, they completely dismiss the potential of reviews to complement each other and cover as many of the item's features as possible. High-quality reviews can still be redundant, reiterating the same opinions on the same features, and thus conveying no additional information to the user. Our selection paradigm overcomes such shortcomings, by considering the complementarity among reviews. Nonetheless, our methodology is fully compatible with quality-evaluation techniques, which can be used to filter out substandard reviews.

3. PROBLEM DEFINITION

In this section, we describe the notational conventions that we will use throughout the paper. We also provide a formal definition of the CHARACTERISTIC-REVIEW SELECTION problem and discuss its computational complexity.

3.1 Preliminaries

We use $\mathcal{R}$ to denote the collection of n reviews of the item of interest. We also assume that every item is associated with a set of z features $\{f_1, \ldots, f_z\}$. One should think of the features as the characteristics of the item that reviewers comment upon. For example, the features of a restaurant may be the `food quality`, `ambiance`, `service`, and so forth. A typical review only comments on a subset of these features, express either positive or negative opinions. In fact, the same review may have a positive opinion about one feature and a negative opinion about another. Hence, in order to describe the opinions that appear in reviews, we form the set of binarized feature opinions, which we refer to simply as the *opinions* of the item. That is, for each feature f_i, there are two possible opinions: positive and negative. Hence, the opinion vector of a item has cardinality $m = 2z$; we denote it by $A = \{a_1, \ldots, a_m\}$.

Throughout the paper, we assume that features and opinions can be automatically extracted. There are a number of methods for this task. In our experiments, we use the method by Ding *et al.* [2]. Therefore, every review $R \in \mathcal{R}$ can be represented as a subset of opinions from A; we say that R *covers* all the opinions that appear in R.

Given a collection of reviews $\mathcal{S} \subseteq \mathcal{R}$, we use $\pi(\mathcal{S})$ to denote the m-dimensional vector of that represents the fraction of the reviews in $\mathcal{S}$ that cover each opinion. That is, $\pi(\mathcal{S}, i)$ denotes the fraction of reviews in $\mathcal{S}$ that cover opinion a_i. We refer to $\pi(\mathcal{S})$ as the *opinion vector* of $\mathcal{S}$.

In addition to the opinion vector, we also use the notion of a *target vector* τ. The target vector is also defined over the set of opinions in A and, thus, it is also an m-dimensional vector. We quantify the closeness between two vectors π and τ using the L_2^2 norm of their difference. We denote this by

$$D(\pi, \tau) := L_2^2(\pi - \tau) = \sum_{i=1}^{m} (\pi(i) - \tau(i))^2 .$$

Given a set of reviews $\mathcal{S}$ and a target vector τ we call the value of $D(\pi(\mathcal{S}), \tau)$ the *error* of the collection $\mathcal{S}$.

3.2 The CRS problem

Given a collection of reviews $\mathcal{R}$ about a item and a target vector τ, our high-level goal is to select a subset of reviews $\mathcal{S} \subseteq \mathcal{R}$ such that $D(\pi(\mathcal{S}), \tau)$ is small. At the same time, we also want the subset $\mathcal{S}$ to consist of a small number of reviews. The encoding of these two goals is incorporated in the following problem definition.

PROBLEM 1 (CHARACTERISTIC-REVIEW SELECTION (CRS)). *Given a collection of reviews $\mathcal{R}$, a target vector τ and an integer number k, find $\mathcal{S} \subseteq \mathcal{R}$ such that $|\mathcal{S}| \le k$ and $D(\pi(\mathcal{S}), \tau)$ is minimized.*

Problem 1 would be trivial if all the reviews contained at most one opinion. Without such unrealistic restrictions, however, the problem is hard. Specifically, our analysis below demonstrates that the CRS problem is not only NP-hard, but it is also NP-hard to approximate. In order to see this, lets consider the decision version of the problem which is defined as follows: Given a collection of reviews $\mathcal{R}$, and real number L and integer K does there exist a subset $\mathcal{S} \subseteq \mathcal{R}$ with $|\mathcal{S}| \le k$ and $D(\pi(\mathcal{S}), \tau) \le d$? We call this decision version of the problem DECISION-CRS. The following lemma shows that this problem is NP-complete.

LEMMA 1. *The* DECISION-CRS *problem is NP-complete.*

PROOF. We will reduce and instance of X3C (EXACT COVER BY 3 SETS) [3] to DECISION-CRS. An instance of X3C consists of a universe of n items U and a set of sets $\mathcal{C} = \{C_1, \ldots, C_M\}$ where $|C_i| = 3$ for every $i = 1, \ldots, M$ and $C_i \subseteq U$. Given integer K, the decision version of the problem asks whether there exists a subset $\mathcal{C}' \subseteq \mathcal{C}$ such that $|\mathcal{C}'| = K$, U and every element in U is covered by exactly one set in C'.

We transform an instance of X3C to an instance of DECISION-CRS by setting the set of opinions A to be the universe U. In this case, every set $C_i \in \mathcal{C}$ is represented by a review $R_i \in \mathcal{R}$; review R_i covers opinion $a_j \in A$ if set C_i contains the j-th element of U. To complete the instance of the DECISION-CRS problem, we set the target vector τ to consist of n dimensions all equal to $1/K$, and we also set $k = K$ and $d = 0$. Then, it is easy to see that the answer to the X3C decision problem is "yes" if and only if there exists a solution to the instance of the DECISION-CRS problem, which we created above. □

By the fact that we used X3C for our reduction, we can show that the problem is NP-hard even if all the reviews of the collection have exactly three opinions. Another immediate corollary of Lemma 1 is the following.

COROLLARY 1. *The* CRS *problems is NP-hard and NP-hard to approximate. That is, it is NP-hard to find a polynomial - time approximation algorithm for the* CRS *problem.*

PROOF. We will prove the hardness of approximation of the CRS problem by contradiction. Assume that there exists an α-approximation algorithm for the CRS problem. Then if $\mathcal{S}^*$ is the optimal solution to the problem and $\mathcal{S}^A$ is the solution output by this approximation algorithm, it will hold that $D(\pi(\mathcal{S}^A), \tau) \leq \alpha D(\pi(\mathcal{S}^*), \tau)$. If such an approximation algorithm exists, then this algorithm can be used to decide decision instances of the CRS problem for which $d = 0$. However, this contradicts the proof of Lemma 1, which indicates that these problems are also NP-hard. Thus, such an approximation algorithm does not exist. □

So far, we have discussed the CRS problem for an arbitrary target vector τ. For a collection of reviews $\mathcal{R}$, the most natural instantiation of the target vector is the *mean opinion vector*, denoted by $\pi(\mathcal{R})$. Figure 1 shows an example of a review corpus and the optimal characteristic subset that minimizes $D(\pi, \pi(\mathcal{R}))$. The corpus consists of 6 reviews $R_1, R_2, R_4, R_4, R_5, R_6$. These reviews comment on 3 distinct features f_1, f_2, f_3. A plus (resp. minus) denotes a positive (resp. negative) opinion on the feature. For example, review R_1 expressed positive opinions on features f_1 and f_2 and a negative opinion on feature f_3. In this example, the mean opinion vector corresponding to the included opinions $f_1^+, f_1^-, f_2^+, f_2^-, f_3^+, f_3^-$ is $\pi(\mathcal{R}) = (4/6, 2/6, 4/6, 0/6, 2/6, 4/6)$. We observe that the opinion vector of the selected characteristic set $\{R_4, R_5, R_6\}$ is identical: $(2/3, 1/3, 2/3, 0/3, 1/3, 2/3)$. Therefore, this set is optimal with respect to the objective function, when the target is the mean vector.

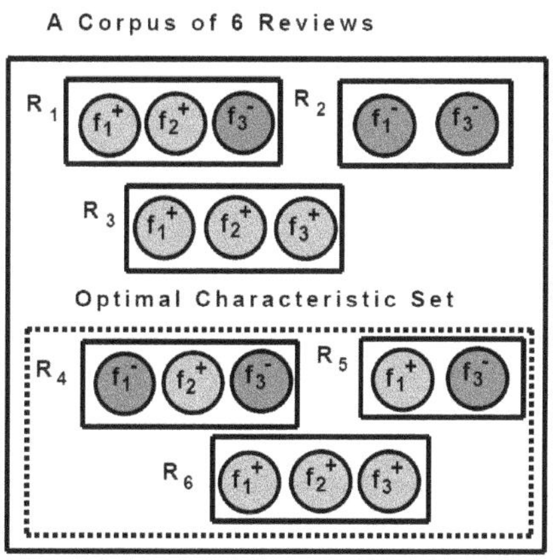

Figure 1: An example of a review corpus and the optimal characteristic set that minimizes $D(\pi, \pi(\mathcal{R}))$, where $\pi(\mathcal{R})$ is the mean opinion vector.

This instantiation of the target vector – and the CRS problem – corresponds to a very natural geometric problem: Given a set of points in m-dimensional space, select a subset of them of size k whose centroid approximates the centroid of the collection as well as possible. In the case of CRS the m-dimensional vectors are also binary, but the general problem where vectors lie in $\mathbb{R}^m$ is also interesting and – to the best of our knowledge – unexplored. Another natural target vector is the distribution of features in $\mathcal{R}$. However, one can observe that this is actually a simple rescaling of the mean opinion vector $\pi(\mathcal{R})$. Although in all our experiments we use $\pi(\mathcal{R})$ as our target vector, we note that alternative instantiations may also arise in practice. For example, when the goal is to provide personalized sets of characteristic reviews, then one may choose to approximate a specially-selected set of reviews (e.g. reviews written by reviewers with similar preferences as the interested user). Hence, in such cases the target vector would be tuned by the characteristics of the particular user.

4. ALGORITHMS

Although the CRS problem is NP-hard and NP-hard to approximate, our experiments with real datasets demonstrate that, in practice, there exist heuristics that work extremely well. We describe such heuristics below. With the exception of `Random` (described in Section 4.3), all our heuristics work for arbitrary target vectors τ.

4.1 The `Greedy` algorithm

The `Greedy` algorithm is an iterative algorithm for CRS. At every iteration t, the algorithm picks one review R to form subset $\mathcal{S}^t$. The review R is picked so that the distance $D\left(\pi\left(\mathcal{S}^{t-1} \cup \{R\}\right), \tau\right)$ is minimized. The pseudocode of the `Greedy` algorithm is shown in Algorithm 1.

Algorithm 1 The `Greedy` algorithm

Input: $\mathcal{R}$, target vector τ and integer k
Output: $\mathcal{S} \subseteq \mathcal{R}$, $|\mathcal{S}| = k$
1: $\mathcal{S} = \emptyset$
2: **for** $i = 1 \ldots k$ **do**
3: $\quad R = \arg\min_{R' \in \mathcal{R}} D(\tau, \pi(\mathcal{S} \cup \{R'\}))$
4: $\quad \mathcal{S} = \mathcal{S} \cup \{R\}$
5: $\quad \mathcal{R} = \mathcal{R} \setminus \{R\}$
6: **end for**
7: return $\mathcal{S}$

For a collection $\mathcal{R}$ of n reviews, the running time of `Greedy` is $O(knT_D)$, where T_D is the time required to compute the distance D required in line 3 of Algorithm 1. In our case, T_D requires $O(m)$ time, and therefore the running time of `Greedy` is $O(knm)$.

4.2 The `Integer-Regression` algorithm

The `Integer-Regression` algorithm finds the set of k characteristic reviews by first solving a continuous version of the CRS problem, and then transforming the obtained continuous solution into the closest discrete one. This is a well known strategy that has been shown to be effective for combinatorial optimization problems.

To describe the `Integer-Regression` algorithm, we use matrix notation. We start with the $m \times n$ binary matrix $\mathbf{R}$ in which entry $\mathbf{R}_{ij} = 1$ iff opinion a_i appears in review R_j. The CHARACTERISTIC-REVIEW SELECTION problem can then be restated as: find a 0-1 vector $\mathbf{s}$ such that $D(\mathbf{Rs}, \tau)$ is minimized, and $\mathbf{s}$ contains at most k 1s. The fact that $\min_{\mathbf{s}} D(\mathbf{Rs}, \tau)$ has the form of a linear regression is what inspires our approach.

In reality, $\mathbf{R}$ can contain duplicate columns; these are irrelevant for regression, so we remove them to form $\tilde{\mathbf{R}}$ having size $m \times n'$ and consisting of distinct columns. However, duplicate columns in $\mathbf{R}$ correspond to distinct reviews that may be useful in approximating τ; hence we keep track of the number of such duplicate columns by remembering for each column i of $\tilde{\mathbf{R}}$ its *multiplicity* c_i in $\mathbf{R}$.

The `Integer-Regression` algorithm works in two steps, which are repeated for all values from 1 to k:

For $\ell = 1$ to k

Step 1: Form a nonnegative real-valued vector $\mathbf{x}$ such that $D(\tau, \tilde{\mathbf{R}}\mathbf{x})$ is small, and the number of nonzero elements of $\mathbf{x}$ is not larger than ℓ.

Step 2: Form a nonnegative integer-valued vector $\tilde{\mathbf{s}}$ representing k reviews that together approximate $\mathbf{x}$ in distribution. That is, find $\tilde{\mathbf{s}}$ such that $\forall i$, $\tilde{\mathbf{s}}_i \leq c_i$, $||\tilde{\mathbf{s}}||_1 \leq k$, and $||\frac{\tilde{\mathbf{s}}}{||\tilde{\mathbf{s}}||_1} - \frac{\mathbf{x}}{||\mathbf{x}||_1}||_1$ is minimized.

Step 1 solves a regression problem, with the constraint that the solution has no more than ℓ positive coefficients. In statistics, regression with this sort of constraint is referred to as a *subset selection* problem; in signal processing it is called *sparse signal reconstruction.* We adopt an algorithm from signal processing for this step, namely NONNEGATIVE ORTHOGONAL MATCHING PURSUIT (`NOMP`) [12, 13]. However, a variety of algorithms are known for this problem, and we expect that our general approach can make use of other algorithms as well. `NOMP` works iteratively; at each iteration t, it greedily selects the (not-yet selected) column from $\tilde{\mathbf{R}}$ that has the largest dot-product with the residual of the target vector τ. Then, the corresponding coefficients $\mathbf{x}^t$ are computed via least-squares, and a new residual is computed as $\tau - \tilde{\mathbf{R}}\mathbf{x}^t$.

Step 1 returns a nonnegative real-valued vector $\mathbf{x}$ such that $D(\tau, \tilde{\mathbf{R}}\mathbf{x})$ is minimized. Intuitively, the entries of $\mathbf{x}$ encode the "proportions" of each column of $\tilde{\mathbf{R}}$ that are needed in order to accurately approximate the target vector τ. The vector $\mathbf{x}$ is real-valued, and does not take into account the multiplicity of reviews c_i. Hence, $\mathbf{x}$ cannot be used directly as a solution to the CRS problem; instead, we use $\mathbf{x}$ to guide us to an actual set of reviews from the original collection $\mathcal{R}$. Accordingly, we transform the proportions of reviews encoded in $\mathbf{x}$ into integer values in $\tilde{\mathbf{s}}$ such that $||\tilde{\mathbf{s}}||_1 = k$ and for every element $\tilde{\mathbf{s}}_i$ of $\tilde{\mathbf{s}}$ it is guaranteed that $\tilde{\mathbf{s}}_i \leq c_i$ (i.e., each column in $\tilde{\mathbf{R}}$ cannot be used more times than its multiplicity in $\mathbf{R}$). This translation from proportions to integers is accomplished in **Step 2** of the algorithm.

The reason that we perform these steps for $\ell = 1, ..., k$ is that a trade-off exists between the sparsity of $\mathbf{x}$ and the hard limit k on the total number of reviews. When ℓ is small (say, 1) then it is difficult to find an $\mathbf{x}$ such that τ is well approximated by $\tilde{\mathbf{R}}\mathbf{x}$; after all, $\mathbf{x}$ can only have ℓ nonzero elements. On the other hand, when ℓ is large (say, k) then it is difficult to approximate the real-valued $\mathbf{x}$ with k integer-valued reviews. Intuitively, we expect the best value of ℓ to be somewhere in between 1 and k; in practice, we simply test all values of ℓ between 1 and k.

As we have already discussed, **Step 2** constructs the closest possible discrete approximation to the output of **Step 1**. The problem can expressed as follows: Let the number of nonzero elements in $\mathbf{x}$ be p. Given the nonnegative real vector $\mathbf{v} \in \mathbb{R}^p$ having $||\mathbf{v}||_1 = 1$, and a set of integers $c_1, c_2, ..., c_p$, output a nonnegative integer vector $\tilde{\mathbf{s}} \in \mathbb{R}^p$ such that $\forall i$ $\tilde{s}_i \leq c_i$ and $||\frac{\tilde{\mathbf{s}}}{||\tilde{\mathbf{s}}||_1} - \mathbf{v}||_1$ is minimized.

We use an efficient algorithm to solve the above problem in $O(Cp)$ time, where $C = \sum_{i=1}^{p} c_i$. The basic idea is 'conditioning' on the sum of $\tilde{\mathbf{s}}$ elements, i.e., $||\tilde{\mathbf{s}}||_1$. That is, we augment the problem with the requirement that $||\tilde{\mathbf{s}}||_1 = N$. We can solve this efficiently as follows. First, we observe that the $\tilde{\mathbf{s}}$ that minimizes $||\frac{\tilde{\mathbf{s}}}{||\tilde{\mathbf{s}}||_1} - \mathbf{v}||_1$ also minimizes $||\tilde{\mathbf{s}} - N\mathbf{v}||_1$. Next, we set aside the constraints c_i and solve the unconstrained problem. For that, let $U = \sum_{i=1}^{p} \lceil N\mathbf{v}_i \rceil$ and $L = \sum_{i=1}^{p} \lfloor N\mathbf{v}_i \rfloor$. If $N \leq L$ (resp. $N \geq U$) then the solution is to set each $\tilde{\mathbf{s}}_i$ value below (resp. above) the corresponding value of $N\mathbf{v}_i$. If $L < N < U$, then compute $X = N - L$. Let the set $\mathcal{L}$ be the elements of $\mathbf{v}$ having the X largest values of $N\mathbf{v}_i - \lfloor N\mathbf{v}_i \rfloor$. For elements $i \in \mathcal{L}$, set $\tilde{\mathbf{s}}_i = \lceil N\mathbf{v}_i \rceil$. For the other elements, set $\tilde{\mathbf{s}}_i = \lfloor N\mathbf{v}_i \rfloor$. In order to solve the constraint version of the problem, we first fix $\tilde{\mathbf{s}}_i = c_i$ for all entries i such that $c_i < N\mathbf{v}_i$. Then, we solve the unconstrained version of the problem for the remaining elements. For any given N, this yields the optimal $\tilde{\mathbf{s}}$ in $O(p)$ time. Since the maximum allowable value of $||\tilde{\mathbf{s}}||_1$ given the constraints is C, we only need to run this algorithm for each $N \in 1, ..., C$ to find the optimal value of $\tilde{\mathbf{s}}$.

The computational complexity of **Step 1** of the `Integer-Regression` algorithm requires $O(k^3)$ in general. However, since `NOMP` works column-wise, incremental algorithms exist that lower the complexity of the regression to $O(k^2)$. Combined with the outer loop over k, this brings the overall complexity to $O(k^3)$. Thus, for small values of k that are most appropriate for review summaries, the running time of this step is negligible. As we have already discussed, the running time of **Step 2** is $O(Cp)$. As $C = O(n)$ and $p = O(k)$ the worst-case running time of this step is $O(nk)$. For the very small values of k that we consider in practice, the running time of this step is almost linear in n.

4.3 The `Random` algorithm

When the target vector τ is the mean opinion vector of the collection of reviews $\mathcal{R}$ (denoted by $\pi(\mathcal{R})$) we have the following observation.

OBSERVATION 1. *A random sample $\mathcal{S}$ of $\mathcal{R}$ of size k guarantees that* $D(\pi(\mathcal{R}), \pi(\mathcal{S})) = 0$ on expectation.

In other words, for a random sample of reviews $\mathcal{S}$, $\pi(\mathcal{S})$ is an unbiased estimator of $\pi(\mathcal{R})$. However, the algorithm that randomly samples k reviews from $\mathcal{R}$, which we call `Random`, performs poorly in practice. This is because its results have high variance, which also leads to higher error. In order to reduce the variance, we also propose an iterative version of `Random` – which we call `Iterative-Random`. The `Iterative-Random` selects a reasonably large number of random samples from $\mathcal{R}$ and reports the one with the best valuation of the objective function of the CRS problem.

5. EXPERIMENTS

Here, we present a thorough experimental evaluation of our methodology using review corpora from Amazon. In all our experiments, we use the mean opinion vector of the underlying collection of reviews as our target vector

We start our experimental evaluation in Section 5.2, where we present a study of the convergence of the opinion vectors of different corpora. We then evaluate the performance of the different algorithms with respect to the objective function of CRS in Section 5.3. We conclude our experimental study in Section 5.4, by presenting a user study that demonstrates the appeal of our summaries to real users.

5.1 Datasets

In our experiments, we use six different datasets of reviews from Amazon.com. The data was extracted from the collection of reviews introduced by Jindal and Liu [6]. This collection, crawled in June 2006, covers a wide range of different product from Amazon.com. It includes 5.8 million reviews, 2.14 million reviewers and 6.7 million products. For our own experiments we extract six datasets from six different domains: MP3 players, Digital Cameras, Coffee Makers, Printers, Books, and Vacuum Cleaners. We refer to these as `MP3`, `CAM`, `COF`, `PRINT`, `BOOK` and `VAC`. These datasets include reviews on 238, 233, 40, 112, 11447, and 62 different items, respectively. The mainstream nature and popularity of these domains ensures the availability of sizable review corpora. Other than that, our methods do not benefit from this selection. For the `BOOK` dataset, we purposefully avoided introducing any further constraints on the genre or type of the book. Our goal was to evaluate our algorithms in the context of a very large dataset of ambiguous items that typically encourage subjective reviews.

For our experiments, we extracted the opinions expressed in a review using the method proposed by Ding *et al.* [2]. Recall that an opinion is defined as the mapping of a feature (e.g. the lens of a digital camera) to a positive or negative polarity. While the method of Ding *et al.* worked well in practice, our framework is compatible with any method for opinion extraction.

5.2 Convergence of opinion vectors

The CRS problem asks for a set for a set of reviews that respect the opinion vector $\pi(\mathcal{R})$ of the underlying corpus. Such a set would only be informative and depictive of the reviewed item's true qualities, if the target opinion vector has converged to a stable state. On the other hand, if the arrival of new reviews causes big variations to the opinion vector, then the resulting set can be misleading.The goal of this section is to experimentally explore whether such variations appear in practice.

In order to study this for a corpus $\mathcal{R}$ on a particular item, we proceed as follows. First, we sort the reviews in ascending order of their submission date and set a checkpoint every 10 reviews. Using a checkpoint attached to a calendar unit (e.g. monthly or weekly) was not desirable since, for most corpora, the number of included reviews varies greatly across units. As we saw in our experiments, setting checkpoints every 10 reviews results in batches that include opinions on at least 90% of the item's features. Further, 10 is the number of reviews that is typically included in a single webpage of a review-hosting site (e.g. `Amazon.com`), since it is big enough to provided sufficient information, and small enough to respect the users' attention span.

Therefore, for a corpus with T checkpoints and $t \in \{1, \ldots, T\}$ we use $\mathcal{R}_t$ to denote the set of the $10t$ oldest reviews in the corpus. We measure the variation between the opinion vectors of $\mathcal{R}_{t-1}$ and $\mathcal{R}_t$ by measuring

$$D_t = D\left(\pi(\mathcal{R}_{t-1}), \pi(\mathcal{R}_t)\right).$$

Given a sequence of T such measurements and a threshold d, we say that an item is *converged* with respect to d, if there exists a t such that $D_t \leq d$. If, in addition to the above, we also observe that for every $t' \geq t$ $D'_t \leq d$, then we say that the item is *strongly converged.* Therefore, the opinion vector of strongly-converged items shows little or no variation after a particular checkpoint. Finally, we refer to items that are converged but not strongly converged as *relapsed* items.

For a given item with corpus $\mathcal{R}$, and T measurements $D_1, \ldots, D_T$, we study the following questions: (a) Do the D_t values decrease as t increases? (b) How long does it take for a corpus converge? (c) How often do items relapse? Next, we address these questions and present the corresponding experimental findings.

Figure 2(a) shows the average D_t values across all items as a function of the checkpoint t. The figure validates our intuition that as the size of a corpus increases, the D_t values decrease. For the plot, we use $T = 25$ for all items, since the D_t values for $t > 25$ are almost zero. The plot demonstrates that the opinion vectors of all corpora show little variation as time progresses. Starting from a maximum value around 0.3, the average D_t value drops fast with t and for $t = 25$, it becomes almost zero.

To gain additional insight, we study the percentage of items that have relapsed at least once. The results for different values of the threshold $d \in \{0.025, 0.05, 0.1, 0.2, 0.4\}$ are shown in in Figure 2(b). In order to properly interpret these results, we need to know the percentage of converged items per threshold; this percentage is shown in Figure 2(c). Figure 2(b) clearly demonstrates that only a minuscule percentage of items relapse. Therefore, most of the items are actually strongly converged. The significance of this finding is enhanced even further by its applicability across all datasets, despite the fact that they correspond to different types of products. Figure 2(c) shows the percentage of converged items for different values of d. For threshold values $d = 0.025$ and $d = 0.05$, the percentage of converged items ranges from 1% (`CAM`-0.025) to 33% (`MP3`-0.05). This variance demonstrates that, for small values of d, the convergence results are domain-specific. However, as d increases (e.g., $d = 0.4$), the percentage of converged items is equal or very close to 100% for all datasets.

Overall, our analysis demonstrates that the opinion vectors of review corpora converge as new reviews are added. In addition, we discovered that the vast majority of the items in our collections are strongly converged.

5.3 Comparison of the selection algorithms

In this section we evaluate the solutions reported by the `Greedy`, `Integer-Regression` and `Iterative-Random` algorithms for the CRS problem.

Randomization testing: We start our evaluation by performing the following randomization experiment. For each corpus $\mathcal{R}$ in our collection we use algorithm `Alg`[1] to extract a set of k characteristic reviews $\mathcal{S}_{\texttt{Alg}}$. Then, we evaluate the error of this set, i.e., $D_{\texttt{Alg}} = D(\pi(\mathcal{S}_{\texttt{Alg}}), \pi(\mathcal{R}))$. We compare the value $D_{\texttt{Alg}}$ with the corresponding error of a random set of k reviews $D_{\texttt{R}}$. After considering $N = 1000$ such random sets, we report the empirical p-value of algorithm `Alg` to be the fraction of times for which the random set exhibited a smaller error than the set reported by `Alg`. Formally, such an empirical p-value is computed as follows:

$$p_{\texttt{Alg}} = \frac{1}{N}\sum_{i=1}^{N}\mathbb{I}(D_{\texttt{Alg}} < D_i).$$

In the above equation, D_i corresponds to the error of the i-th random sample and $\mathbb{I}(D_{\texttt{Alg}}, D_i)$ is an indicator variable that takes value 1 if the error of the set reported by `Alg` is less than the error reported by the error of the i-th ran-

[1] `Alg` can be any of the three `Iterative-Random`, `Greedy` or `Integer-Regression` algorithms.

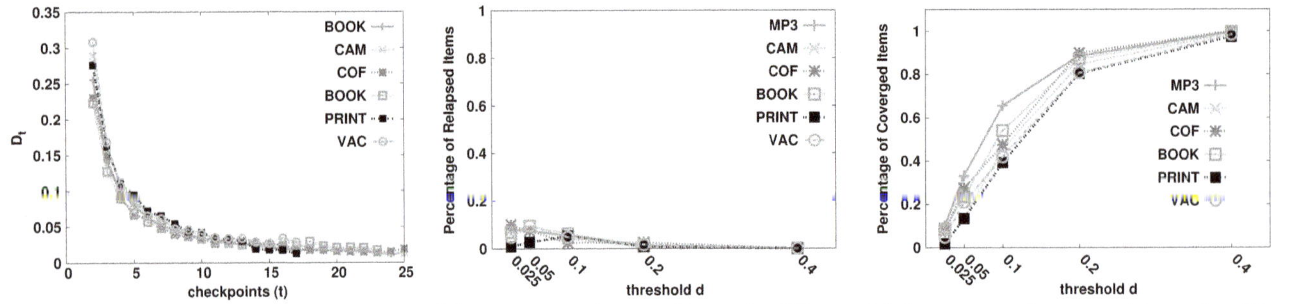

(a) Average D_t values across items for values of t in $\{1, \ldots, 25\}$.

(b) Percentage of relapsed items for different thresholds d.

(c) Percentage of converged items for different threshold values d.

Figure 2: Convergence experiments.

dom sample of k reviews. Small values of $p_{\texttt{Alg}}$ are desirable, as they indicate that `Alg` has a very low probability of outperformed by a random set of k reviews from $\mathcal{R}$. The empirical p-values for the `Greedy`, `Integer-Regression` and `Iterative-Random` algorithms as a function of k are shown in Table 1. The values reported in the table are averages over all the corpora of every dataset.

Table 1: Average empirical p-values for the solutions reported by `Greedy`, `Integer-Regression` and `Iterative-Random` for all datasets; average is taken over all items of a dataset.

	$k=5$	$k=10$	$k=15$	$k=20$
MP3				
Greedy	0.0	0.0	0.0	0.0
Integer-Regression	0.04	0.01	0.01	0.0
Iterative-Random	0.03	0.0	0.0	0.0
CAM				
Greedy	0.1	0.01	0.0	0.0
Integer-Regression	0.09	0.01	0.0	0.0
Iterative-Random	0.03	0.0	0.0	0.0
COF				
Greedy	0.14	0.0	0.0	0.0
Integer-Regression	0.9	0.0	0.0	0.0
Iterative-Random	0.06	0.0	0.0	0.0
BOOK				
Greedy	0.3	0.03	0.01	0.0
Integer-Regression	0.27	0.05	0.02	0.0
Iterative-Random	0.3	0.05	0.013	0.0
PRINT				
Greedy	0.13	0.02	0.01	0.0
Integer-Regression	0.07	0.0	0.0	0.0
Iterative-Random	0.05	0.0	0.0	0.0
VAC				
Greedy	0.07	0.014	0.0	0.0
Integer-Regression	0.8	0.01	0.0	0.0
Iterative-Random	0.05	0.0	0.0	0.0

We observe that the empirical p-values obtained for all our algorithms are either zero or close to zero. Therefore, the low-error solutions obtained by our algorithms cannot be attributed to randomness. For all datasets, the highest p-values are observed for $k = 5$. This trend is particularly pronounced in the `BOOK` dataset. This indicates that, for this dataset, it was more challenging for the algorithms to select a characteristic set with such a small size. This can be attributed to the ambiguity of the domain, which is less entertaining to objective judgments. Such ambiguity may lead to a more diverse opinion vector (i.e. with multiple positive and negative opinions per feature), and makes it more challenging to find a very small characteristic set of reviews. Nonetheless, the results show that the empirical p-values drop sharply as k increases. In fact, they reach zero or (near-zero) value for all datasets when $k \geq 15$.

Error values: The actual error values of the solutions reported by `Greedy`, `Integer-Regression` and `Iterative-Random` as a function of k are also shown in Table 2. Again the reported values are averages over all corpora in each dataset. The standard deviations within every dataset (not shown in the table) are values in the range $[0, 0.05]$ for all algorithms, datasets and values of k. The error values indicate all three algorithms achieve low errors that are reduced to near-zero as k is increased. Further, `Greedy` and `Integer-Regression` have a consistent advantage over `Iterative-Random`, in terms of both the absolute error values, and their ability to utilize larger values of k; observe that, for larger values of k, both `Greedy` and `Integer-Regression` achieve lower errors than `Iterative-Random`.

Error ratios: In order to further investigate the relationship between `Greedy`, `Integer-Regression` and `Iterative-Random`, we also conduct the following experiment. First, we collapse all the items from all six datasets into a single collection. For each value of k and each item, we compute $E_{\texttt{G}}$ (resp. $E_{\texttt{IR}}$) as the ratio of the error of the solution reported by `Greedy` (resp. `Integer-Regression`) to the error of the solution reported by `Iterative-Random`. We refer to both $E_{\texttt{G}}$ and $E_{\texttt{IR}}$ as the *error ratios*. Figure 3 shows the average values of these ratios for different values of k; the average is taken over all items. The results demonstrate that both ratios are consistently less than 1, indicating that both `Greedy` and `Integer-Regression` achieve less error than `Iterative-Random`. In fact, as the value of k increases the values of both ratios drop. This indicates that the advantage of `Greedy` and `Integer-Regression` becomes more pronounced as the value of k increases. Another observation is that `Integer-Regression` slightly outperforms `Greedy`, especially for larger values of k. This demonstrates that this algorithm is better at utilizing the flexibility of large values of k than `Greedy`, which simply extends the solution that it has obtained for smaller values of k.

Table 2: **Average error of the solutions reported by** `Greedy`**,** `Integer-Regression` **and** `Iterative-Random` **for all datasets; the average is taken over all items of a dataset.**

	$k = 5$	$k = 10$	$k = 15$	$k = 20$
MP3				
Greedy	0.22	0.12	0.09	0.07
Integer-Regression	0.28	0.16	0.11	0.09
Iterative-Random	0.36	0.25	0.2	0.17
CAM				
Greedy	0.25	0.14	0.1	0.08
Integer-Regression	0.24	0.13	0.08	0.06
Iterative-Random	0.27	0.18	0.14	0.12
COF				
Greedy	0.22	0.13	0.1	0.07
Integer-Regression	0.23	0.12	0.08	0.06
Iterative-Random	0.23	0.15	0.12	0.11
BOOK				
Greedy	0.18	0.1	0.07	0.06
Integer-Regression	0.18	0.09	0.06	0.05
Iterative-Random	0.18	0.12	0.1	0.08
PRINT				
Greedy	0.24	0.14	0.1	0.09
Integer-Regression	0.23	0.13	0.09	0.07
Iterative-Random	0.25	0.17	0.14	0.12
VAC				
Greedy	0.28	0.16	0.12	0.1
Integer-Regression	0.26	0.14	0.09	0.07
Iterative-Random	0.29	0.2	0.16	0.13

5.4 User study

The goal of our user study is to demonstrate that the set of reviews reported by our methods is more appealing to the average user than the current state-of-the-art. To achieve this, we we randomly select 10 items from the `MP3` dataset. For the 10 review corpora that correspond to these items, we select representative sets of reviews by using three approaches: `Helpfulness`, `GroupCover`, and our own `Integer-Regression` algorithm. The first one ranks the review by the standard *helpfulness* measure that is implemented as a feature in major review hosting-sites such as `Yelp.com` or `Amazon.com`; we obtain the helpfulness scores of the reviews of our corpora while crawling. The second is the review-selection method proposed by Tsaparas *et al.* [16]. This method tries to maximize the number of features for which there is at least one positive *and* one negative opinion in the reported set. We use the `Integer-Regression` algorithm to represent our own selection paradigm, since it was shown to outperform the other algorithms in our other experiments, and is the one that gave the least-error solutions.

For each of the 10 items, we use the above three methods to select a set of 5 reviews. We chose to select no more than 5 reviews, to ensure that the human annotators would be able to complete the task in a reasonable amount of time. We asked the human annotators to rank the three sets from best (score 1) to worst (score 3). The criterion for the ranking was how well each set represents the entire corpus of reviews on the item. Clearly, it was impossible for the annotators to process the tens or even hundreds of reviews of the entire review corpus in order to make a decision. Thus,

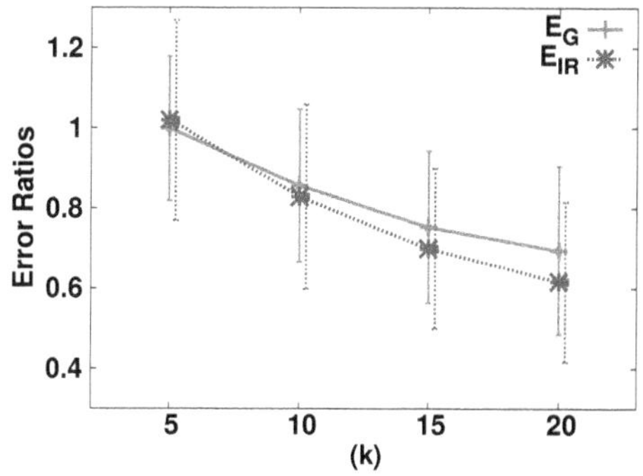

Figure 3: Average error ratios E_G and E_{IR} for $k \in \{5, 10, 15, 20\}$. The reported ratios are averages over all items in the union of all six datasets.

for each item, the annotator was shown the total number of positive and negative opinions expressed on each feature (*Price, Sound Quality, Battery Life, Connectivity, Design, Screen, Menu* and *Radio*) in the entire corpus. We also provided annotators with the original link to the review corpus on Amazon's website. In this way, we provided them with all the necessary information needed to determine their rankings. To conduct our survey, we created a HIT (Human Intelligence Task) on Amazon's Mechanical Turks platform. We hired 40 annotators to work on our HIT. The sets were shown in a randomized order to the annotators, who were thus oblivious to which set correspond to each approach.

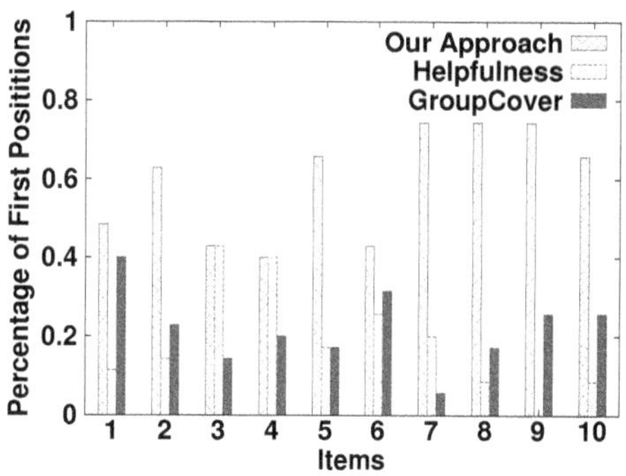

Figure 4: User study: percentage of rankings for which different methods were ranked first by the human annotators.

Figure 4 shows, for each of the 10 items, the percentage of workers that chose the set reported by each approach as the best one (i.e. ranked as 1). The results illustrate that the human subjects had a clear preference to the sets reported by our approach. A high percentage of the annotators consistently reported our approach as the best one, leading to percentages as high as 77%. In fact, our set was selected as the best for all items, with the exception of items 3 and 4 (for which our approach was tied with helpfulness).

Figure 5 shows the average rank assigned to each approach, for each of the 10 items. Recall that lower values are desirable (since smaller ranks indicate higher preference of users to the results of a method). This plot illustrates that our approach outperforms the two baselines. Items 3 and 4 are the only exceptions. For these, the reviews selected us-

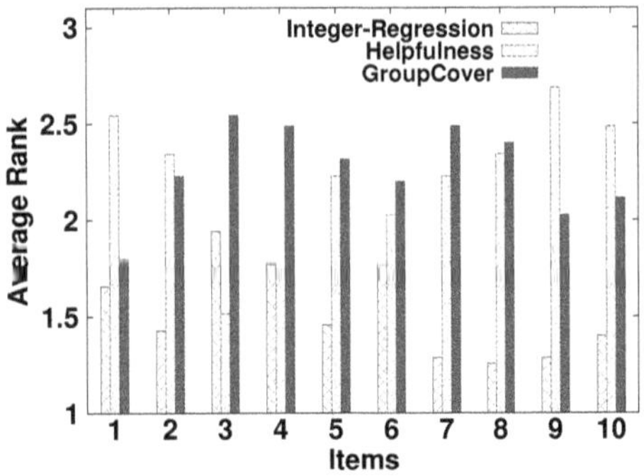

Figure 5: User study: average ranking of different methods as ranked by human annotators.

ing the helpfulness scores were ranked slightly higher than ours. For all the other items, the average ranking achieved by our method was significantly lower than that of `Helpfulness` and `GroupCover`. In conclusion, the results of the user study demonstrate the validity and superiority of our selection paradigm, when compared to existing ranking criteria and state-of-the-art review-selection methods.

6. CONCLUSIONS

In this paper we introduced the problem of selecting a characteristic set of reviews from a given corpus. Our selection paradigm is a significant improvement over previous relevant work, since it is the first to ask for a set that respects the *proportion* of opinions on each feature (both positive and negative), as observed in the underlying corpus. We formally define the CHARACTERISTIC-REVIEW SELECTION problem and prove that it is NP-hard both to solve and approximate. We propose three heuristic algorithms for selecting a characteristic review set, which we evaluate on a wide range of review datasets from different domains. The results indicate that our algorithms are consistently able to find a compact set of reviews that yields a highly accurate approximation of the set of opinions in the corpus. To demonstrate that our problem definition and solution is an important improvement over previous efforts, we perform a user study using the Amazon Mechanical Turks platform. The study reveals that users consistently prefer the set of reviews selected by our methods, as opposed to those selected by previous state-of-the-art methods. Our work can be easily incorporated into any review-hosting website, in order to provide users with a compact set of real reviews, that accurately represents the opinions expressed in the entire corpus.

Acknowledgments

This research was supported by gifts from Microsoft, Yahoo! and Google, by the NSF award #1017529, and by the NSF grants CNS-0905565, CNS-1018266, CNS-1012910, and CNS-1117039.

7. REFERENCES

[1] S. Baccianella, A. Esuli, and F. Sebastiani. Multi-facet rating of product reviews. In *Proceedings of the 31th European Conference on IR Research on Advances in Information Retrieval*, ECIR '09, pages 461–472, Berlin, Heidelberg, 2009. Springer-Verlag.

[2] X. Ding, B. Liu, and P. S. Yu. A holistic lexicon-based approach to opinion mining. In *Proceedings of the international conference on Web search and web data mining*, WSDM '08, pages 231–240, New York, NY, USA, 2008. ACM.

[3] M. Garey and D. Johnson. *Computers and Intractability: A Guide to the Theory of NP-Completeness.* 1979.

[4] A. Ghose and P. G. Ipeirotis. Designing novel review ranking systems: predicting the usefulness and impact of reviews. In *ICEC '07*, pages 303–310. ACM, 2007.

[5] M. Hu and B. Liu. Mining and summarizing customer reviews. In *Proceedings of the ACM SIGKDD Conference on Knowledge Discovery and Data Mining (KDD)*, pages 168–177, 2004.

[6] N. Jindal and B. Liu. Opinion spam and analysis. In *WSDM, year = 2008, pages = 219–230, publisher = ACM Press.*

[7] S.-M. Kim, P. Pantel, T. Chklovski, and M. Pennacchiotti. Automatically assessing review helpfulness. In *EMNLP*, pages 423–430, 2006.

[8] T. Lappas and D. Gunopulos. Efficient confident search in large review corpora. In *ECML/PKDD (2)*, pages 195–210, 2010.

[9] J. Liu, Y. Cao, C.-Y. Lin, Y. Huang, and M. Zhou. Low-quality product review detection in opinion summarization. In *EMNLP-CoNLL*, pages 334–342, 2007. Poster paper.

[10] Y. Liu, X. Huang, A. An, and X. Yu. Modeling and predicting the helpfulness of online reviews. In *ICDM*, pages 443–452, 2008.

[11] Y. Lu, P. Tsaparas, A. Ntoulas, and L. Polanyi. Exploiting social context for review quality prediction. In *WWW*, 2010.

[12] S. Mallat. *A Wavelet Tour of Signal Processing.* Academic Press, 1999.

[13] S. Mallat, G. Davis, and Z. Zhang. Adaptive time-frequency decompositions. *SPIE Journal of Optical Engineering*, pages 2183–2191, 1994.

[14] X. Meng and H. Wang. Mining user reviews: from specification to summarization. In *ACL/AFNLP (Short Papers)*, pages 177–180, 2009.

[15] K. Shimada, R. Tadano, and T. Endo. Multi-aspects review summarization with objective information. *Procedia - Social and Behavioral Sciences*, 27(0):140 – 149, 2011.

[16] P. Tsaparas, A. Ntoulas, and E. Terzi. Selecting a comprehensive set of reviews. In *KDD*, 2011.

[17] O. Tsur and A. Rappoport. Revrank: a fully unsupervised algorithm for selecting the most helpful book reviews. In *ICWSM*, 2009.

[18] J. Zhan, H. T. Loh, and Y. Liu. Gather customer concerns from online product reviews: A text summarization approach. *Expert Systems with Applications*, 36(2, Part 1):2107 – 2115, 2009.

[19] Z. Zhang and B. Varadarajan. Utility scoring of product reviews. In *CIKM*, pages 51–57. ACM, 2006.

[20] L. Zhuang, F. Jing, X. Zhu, and L. Zhang. Movie review mining and summarization. In *CIKM*, 2006.

Mining Contentions from Discussions and Debates

Arjun Mukherjee and Bing Liu
Department of Computer Science
University of Illinois at Chicago
arjun4787@gmail.com, liub@cs.uic.edu

ABSTRACT

Social media has become a major source of information for many applications. Numerous techniques have been proposed to analyze network structures and text contents. In this paper, we focus on fine-grained mining of contentions in discussion/debate forums. Contentions are perhaps the most important feature of forums that discuss social, political and religious issues. Our goal is to discover contention and agreement indicator expressions, and contention points or topics both at the discussion collection level and also at each individual post level. To the best of our knowledge, limited work has been done on such detailed analysis. This paper proposes three models to solve the problem, which not only model both contention/agreement expressions and discussion topics, but also, more importantly, model the intrinsic nature of discussions/debates, i.e., interactions among discussants or debaters and topic sharing among posts through quoting and replying relations. Evaluation results using real-life discussion/debate posts from several domains demonstrate the effectiveness of the proposed models.

Categories and Subject Descriptors

H.2.8 [Database Management]: Database Applications – *Data mining*; H.3.1 [Information Storage and Retrieval]: Content Analysis and Indexing.

General Terms

Algorithms, Experimentation

Keywords

Contention Analysis, Debates, Discussions, Social Media

1. INTRODUCTION

Social media such as reviews, blogs, comments, discussions and debates contain valuable information that can be used for many applications. The essence of such media is that it enables people from anywhere in the world to express their views and to discuss any issue of interest in online communities. A large part of such discussions is about social, political and religious issues. On such issues, there are often heated discussions/debates, i.e., people argue and agree or disagree with one another. In this paper, we model this form of interactive social media. Given a set of discussion/debate posts, we aim to perform the following tasks:

1. Discover expressions that people often use to express contention (e.g., "*I disagree*", "*you make no sense*") and agreement (e.g., "*I agree*", "*I think you're right*"). We collectively call them *CA-expressions*.
2. Determine contentious topics. First discover discussion topics in the whole collection, and then for each contentious post, discover the contention points (or topics).

KDD'12, August 12–16, 2012, Beijing, China.

Although there is a large body of literature on social media analysis such as social network analysis [14], sentiment analysis [27, 34], and grouping people into different camps [1, 32, 40, 42], to the best of our knowledge, limited research has been done on the fine-grained analysis of discussion/debate forums as proposed in this paper. This problem is important because a large part of social media is about discussions/debates of contentious issues, and discovering such issues is useful for many applications. For example, in a political election, contentious issues often separate voters into different camps and determine their political orientations. It is thus important for political candidates to know such issues. For contentious social topics, it is crucial for government agencies to be aware of them so that they can address the problems. Even for consumer products/services, contentions about them can be used to identify different types of customers and to make effective marketing and business decisions.

In this paper, we use statistical modeling to perform the aforementioned tasks. Three new models are proposed. The first model, called JTE (Joint Topic-Expression model), jointly models both discussion topics and CA-expressions. It provides a general framework for discovering discussion topics and CA-expressions simultaneously. Its generative process separates topics and CA-expressions by using maximum-entropy priors to guide the separation. However, this model does not consider a key characteristic of discussions/debates, i.e., authors quote or mention the claims/views of other authors and express contention or agreement on those claims/views. That is, there are interactions among authors and topics through the reply-to relation, which is a salient feature of discussion/debate forums. We then extend the JTE model and propose two novel and more advanced models JTE-R and JTE-P which model the interactions of authors and topics in two different ways, based on reply-to relations and author-pair structures respectively.

Works related to ours are quite different both in application and in modeling. On application, the closely related work to ours is the finding of different camps of people in discussions/debates [1, 32, 40, 42]. This thread of research, however, does not discover CA-expressions or contention points, which are the objectives of this work. From a modeling point of view, our work is related to topic modeling in general and joint modeling of topics and certain other information in particular. Topic models are a principled way of mining topics from large text collections. There have been many extensions [5, 7, 13, 29, 35, 43] to the initial models, LDA (Latent Dirichlet Allocation) [4] and pLSA (Probabilistic latent semantic analysis) [20]. However, these models mine only topics, which are insufficient for our problem. In recent years, researchers have also proposed joint models of topics and sentiments [21, 26, 30, 47]. Our JTE model is related to these joint models. However, these models treat documents/posts independently, which fail to capture author and topic interactions in discussions/debates, i.e., authors reply to and quote each other's claims/views and express contentions or agreements. Due to such interactions, posts are clearly not independent of one another. The proposed JTE-R and JTE-P models capture such interactions. The detailed comparison with these models and other related work appears in §5.

The proposed models are evaluated both qualitatively and quantitatively using a large number of real-life discussion/debate posts from four domains. Experimental results show that the two

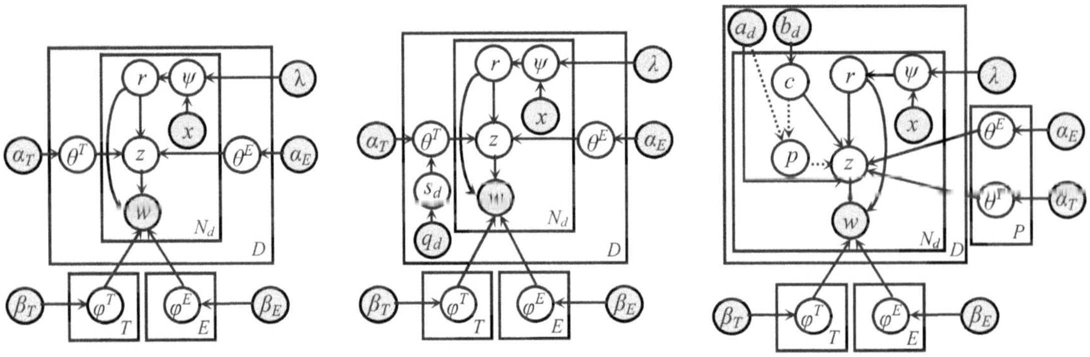

Figure 1: Graphical Models: Plate notations of JTE, JTE-R, JTE-P models. Shaded and unshaded variables indicate observed and latent variables respectively. Note that the pair variable p in the JTE-P model is introduced for derivational convenience and thus its causalities are shown by dotted arrows.

advanced models (JTE-R and JTE-P) outperform the base JTE model significantly, which indicate that the proposed interaction modeling is effective. Experiments using statistical metrics such as perplexity and KL-Divergence also demonstrate that the interaction models fit the discussion/debate data better and can discover more distinctive topics and CA-expressions.

2. JTE MODEL

This section presents the proposed JTE (Joint Topic Expression) model which lays the ground work for jointly modeling topics and CA-expressions. The JTE model belongs to the family of generative models for text where words and phrases (n-grams) are viewed as random variables, and a document is viewed as a bag of n-grams and each n-gram (word/phrase) takes one value from a predefined vocabulary. We use up to 4-grams, i.e., n = 1, 2, 3, 4, in this work. Note that topics in most topic models like LDA are usually unigram distributions over words and assume words to be exchangeable at the word level. Arguably, this offers a great computational advantage over more complex models taking word order into account for discovering significant n-grams [44, 45]. Yet there exist other works which try to *post-process* discovered topical unigrams to form multi-word phrases using relevance [46] and likelihood [6] scores. However, our goal in this work is to enhance the expressiveness of our JTE model (rather than modeling n-gram word order) by considering n-grams and preserving the advantages of exchangeable modeling. Thus, we consider both words and phrases as our vocabulary (more details in §4.1). For notational convenience, from now on we use *terms* to denote both *words* (unigrams) and *phrases* (n-grams). Since we are dealing with large corpora, for computational reasons, we only consider terms which appeared at least 30 times in the corpus[1]. We denote the entries in our vocabulary by $v_{1...V}$, where V is the number of unique terms in the vocabulary. The entire corpus (document collection) of study is comprised of $d_{1...D}$ documents. A document (e.g., discussion post) d is represented as a vector of terms $\boldsymbol{w_d}$ with N_d entries. W is the set of all observed terms in the corpus with cardinality, $|W| = \sum_d N_d$. The JTE model is motivated by the joint occurrence of CA-expression types (*contention* and *agreement*) and topics in discussion posts. A typical discussion/debate post mentions a few topics (using semantically related topical terms) and expresses some viewpoints with one or more CA-expression types (using semantically related contention and/or agreement expressions). This observation motivates the generative process of our model where documents (posts) are represented as random mixtures of latent topics and CA-expression types. Each topic or CA-expression type is characterized by a distribution over terms. Assume we have t = 1,…, T topics and e = 1,…, E expression types in our corpus. Note that in our case of discussion/debate forums, based on reading various posts, we hypothesize that E = 2 as in such forums, we mostly find two expression types: contention and agreement (which we also statistically validate in §4.4.1). However, the proposed JTE and other models are general and can be used with any number of expression types. Let $\psi_{d,j}$ denote the probability of $w_{d,j}$ being a topical term with $r_{d,j} \in \{\hat{t}, \hat{e}\}$ denoting the binary indicator variable (topic or CA-expression) for the jth term of d, $w_{d,j}$. $z_{d,j}$ denotes the appropriate topic or CA-expression type index to which $w_{d,j}$ belongs. We parameterize multinomials over topics using a matrix $\Theta^T_{D\times T}$ whose elements $\theta^T_{d,t}$ signify the probability of document d exhibiting topic t. For simplicity of notation, we will drop the latter subscript (t in this case) when convenient and use θ^T_d to stand for the dth row of Θ^T. Similarly, we define multinomials over CA-expression types using a matrix $\Theta^E_{D\times E}$. The multinomials over terms associated with each topic are parameterized by a matrix $\Phi^T_{T\times V}$, whose elements $\varphi^T_{t,v}$ denote the probability of generating v from topic t. Likewise, multinomials over terms associated with each CA-expression type are parameterized by a matrix $\Phi^E_{E\times V}$. We now define the generative process of JTE (see Figure 1(a) for plate notation).

1. For each CA-expression type e, draw $\varphi^E_e \sim Dir(\beta_E)$
2. For each topic t, draw $\varphi^T_t \sim Dir(\beta_T)$
3. For each forum discussion post $d \in \{1 ... D\}$:
   i. Draw $\theta^E_d \sim Dir(\alpha_E)$
   ii. Draw $\theta^T_d \sim Dir(\alpha_T)$
   iii. For each term $w_{d,j}$, $j \in \{1 ... N_d\}$:
      a. Set $\psi_{d,j} \leftarrow MaxEnt(\overrightarrow{x_{d,j}}; \lambda)$
      b. Draw $r_{d,j} \sim Bernoulli(\psi_{d,j})$
      c. if ($r_{d,j} = \hat{e}$) // $w_{d,j}$ is a CA-expression term
         Draw $z_{d,j} \sim Mult(\theta^E_d)$
         else // $r_{d,j} = \hat{t}$, $w_{d,j}$ is a topical term
         Draw $z_{d,j} \sim Mult(\theta^T_d)$
      d. Emit $w_{d,j} \sim Mult(\varphi^{r_{d,j}}_{z_{d,j}})$

We use Maximum Entropy (Max-Ent) model to set $\psi_{d,j}$. The Max-Ent parameters can be learned from a small number of labeled topical and CA-expression terms which can serve as good priors. The idea is motivated by the following observation: topical and CA-expression terms usually play different syntactic roles in a sentence. Topical terms (e.g. "U.S. senate", "sea level", "marriage", "income tax") tend to be noun and noun phrases while CA-expression terms ("I refute", "how can you say", "probably agree") usually contain pronouns, verbs, wh-determiners, and modals. In order to utilize the part-of-speech (POS) tag information, we place $\psi_{d,j}$ (the prior over the indicator variable $r_{d,j}$) in the word plate (see Figure 1 (a)) and draw it from a Max-Ent model conditioned on the observed feature vector $\overrightarrow{x_{d,j}}$ associated with $w_{d,j}$ and the learned Max-Ent parameters λ (see §

[1] This is reasonable as our corpus contains about 100,000 documents (see §4). It is unlikely for a term with frequency less than 30 to show up as a top topical or CA-expression term.

4.1). $\overrightarrow{x_{d,j}}$ can encode arbitrary contextual features that may be discriminative. In this work, we encode both lexical and POS features of the previous, current and next POS tags/lexemes of the term $w_{d,j}$. Specifically, the feature vector, $\overrightarrow{x_{d,j}} = [POS_{w_{d,j}-1}, POS_{w_{d,j}}, POS_{w_{d,j}+1}, w_{d,j} - 1, w_{d,j}, w_{d,j} + 1]$. For phrasal terms ($n$-grams), all POS tags and lexemes of $w_{d,j}$ are considered as features. To learn the JTE model from data, exact inference is not possible. We thus resort to approximate inference using collapsed Gibbs sampling [18]. We first derive the joint distribution below and then the Gibbs sampler.

To derive the joint distribution, we factor the joint according to the conditional distributions (causalities) governed by the Bayesian network of the proposed generative model.

$$P(W,Z,R) = P(W|Z,R) \times P(Z|R) \times P(R) \quad (1)$$

Since we employ a collapsed Gibbs sampler, we integrate out θ and φ and obtain the joint as follows.

$$P(W,Z,R) = \left[\prod_{t=1}^{T} \frac{B(n_t^{TV}+\beta_T)}{B(\beta_T)} \times \prod_{e=1}^{E} \frac{B(n_e^{EV}+\beta_E)}{B(\beta_E)}\right] \times \left[\prod_{d=1}^{D}\left(\frac{B(n_d^{DT}+\alpha_T)}{B(\alpha_T)} \times \frac{B(n_d^{DE}+\alpha_E)}{B(\alpha_E)}\right)\right] \times \left[\prod_{d=1}^{D}\prod_{j=1}^{N_d} p(r_{d,j}|\psi_{d,j})\right] \quad (2)$$

where $p(r_{d,j}|\psi_{d,j}) = (\psi_{d,j,\hat{t}})^{u}(\psi_{d,j,\hat{e}})^{1-u}$; $u = \begin{cases} 1, r_{d,j} = \hat{t} \\ 0, r_{d,j} = \hat{e} \end{cases}$ and the outcome probabilities of the Max-Ent model are given by:

$$\psi_{d,j,\hat{t}} = p(y = \hat{t}|x_{d,j});\ \psi_{d,j,\hat{e}} = p(y = \hat{e}|x_{d,j});$$

$$p(y|x_{d,j}) = \frac{\exp(\sum_{i=1}^{n} \lambda_i f_i(x_{d,j},y))}{\sum_{y\in\{\hat{t},\hat{e}\}} \exp(\sum_{i=1}^{n} \lambda_i f_i(x_{d,j},y))}$$

$\lambda_{1...n}$ are the parameters of the learned Max-Ent model corresponding to the n binary feature functions $f_{1...n}$ from Max-Ent. $n_{t,v}^{TV}$ and $n_{e,v}^{EV}$ denote the number of times term v was assigned to topic t and expression type e respectively. $B(\cdot)$ is the multinomial Beta function $B(\vec{x}) = \frac{\prod_{i=1}^{\dim(\vec{x})} \Gamma(x_i)}{\Gamma(\sum_{i=1}^{\dim(\vec{x})} x_i)}$. $n_{d,t}^{DT}$ and $n_{d,e}^{DE}$ denote the number of terms in document d that were assigned to topic t and CA-expression type e respectively. n_t^{TV}, n_e^{EV}, n_d^{DT}, and n_d^{DE} denote the corresponding row vectors.

We use Gibbs sampling for posterior inference. Gibbs sampling is a form of Markov chain Monte Carlo (MCMC) method where a Markov chain is constructed to have a particular stationary distribution. In our case, we want to construct a Markov chain which converges to the posterior distribution over R and Z conditioned on the observed data. We only need to sample z and r as we use collapsed Gibbs sampling and the dependencies of θ and φ have already been integrated out analytically in the joint. Denoting the random variables $\{w,z,r\}$ by singular subscripts $\{w_k, z_k, r_k\}$, $k_{1...K}$, $K = \sum_d N_d$, a single iteration consists of performing the following sampling:

$$p(z_k = t, r_k = \hat{t}|Z_{\neg k}, W_{\neg k}, R_{\neg k}, w_k = v) \propto \frac{n_{d,t}^{DT}{}_{\neg k} + \alpha_T}{n_{d,(\cdot)}^{DT}{}_{\neg k} + T\alpha_T} \frac{n_{t,v}^{TV}{}_{\neg k} + \beta_T}{n_{t,(\cdot)}^{TV}{}_{\neg k} + V\beta_T} \times \frac{\exp(\sum_{i=1}^{n} \lambda_i f_i(x_{d,j},\hat{t}))}{\sum_{y\in\{\hat{t},\hat{e}\}} \exp(\sum_{i=1}^{n} \lambda_i f_i(x_{d,j},y))} \quad (3)$$

$$p(z_k = e, r_k = \hat{e}|Z_{\neg k}, W_{\neg k}, R_{\neg k}, w_k = v) \propto \frac{n_{d,e}^{DE}{}_{\neg k} + \alpha_E}{n_{d,(\cdot)}^{DE}{}_{\neg k} + E\alpha_E} \times \frac{n_{e,v}^{EV}{}_{\neg k} + \beta_E}{n_{e,(\cdot)}^{EV}{}_{\neg k} + V\beta_E} \times \frac{\exp(\sum_{i=1}^{n} \lambda_i f_i(x_{d,j},\hat{e}))}{\sum_{y\in\{\hat{t},\hat{e}\}} \exp(\sum_{i=1}^{n} \lambda_i f_i(x_{d,j},y))} \quad (4)$$

where $k = (d,j)$ denotes the jth term of document d and the subscript $\neg k$ denotes assignments excluding the term at k. Omission of a latter index denoted by $(\cdot)$ represents the marginalized sum over the latter index. The conditional probabilities in (3) and (4) were derived by applying the chain rule on the joint distribution. We employ a blocked sampler where we sample r and z jointly, as this improves convergence and reduces autocorrelation of the Gibbs sampler [37].

3. JTE-R and JTE-P MODELS

We now augment the JTE model to encode two kinds of interactions (topic and author) in discussion/debate forums.

3.1 JTE-R: Encoding Reply Relations

We first improve JTE by encoding the reply-to relations as authors usually reply to each other's viewpoints by explicitly mentioning the user name using @name, and/or by quoting others' posts. For easy presentation, we refer both cases by *quoting* from now on. Considering the reply-to relation, we call the new model JTE-R (Figure 1 (b)). This model is based on the following observation:

Observation: Whenever a post d replies to the viewpoints in some other posts by quoting them, d and the posts quoted by d should have similar topic distributions.

This observation indicates that the JTE-R model needs to depart from typical topic models where there is usually no topical interaction among documents, i.e., documents are treated as being independent of one another. Let q_d be the set of posts quoted by post d. Clearly, q_d is observed[2]. In order to encode this "reply-to" relation into our model, the key challenge is to somehow constrain the topic distribution of d, θ_d^T to be similar to the topic distributions of posts in q_d. Specifically, it is how to constrain θ_d^T to be similar to $\theta_{\acute{d}}^T$, where $\acute{d} \in q_d$ (i.e., constraining topic assignments to documents) during inference while the topic distributions of both θ_d^T and $\theta_{\acute{d}}^T$, $\acute{d} \in q_d$ are latent and unknown *apriori*. Note that this situation is very different from that in [2] where it constrains word assignments to topics *apriori* knowing that some words are semantically related and probably should belong to the same topic. To solve our problem, we propose a novel solution, which exploits the following salient features of the Dirichlet distribution:

1. Since $\theta_d^T \sim Dir(\alpha_T)$, we have $\sum_t \theta_{d,t}^T = 1$. Thus, it suffices that θ_d^T can act as a base measure for Dirichlet distributions of the same order.
2. Also, the expected probability mass associated with each dimension of the Dirichlet distribution is proportional to the corresponding component of its base measure[3].

Thus, to constrain a post d's topic distribution to be similar to the posts whom it replies/quotes (i.e. posts in q_d), we now need functional base measures as it is the base measure that governs the expected mass associated with each topical dimension in θ_d^T. One way to employ functional base measures is to draw $\theta_d^T \sim Dir(\alpha_T \boldsymbol{s_d})$, where $\boldsymbol{s_d} = \sum_{d' \in q_d} \theta_{d'}^T / |q_d|$ (the expected topical distribution of posts in q_d). For posts which do not quote any other post, we simply draw $\theta_d^T \sim Dir(\alpha_T)$. For such a topic model with functional Dirichlet base measures, the sampling distribution is more complicated. Specifically, the document-topic distribution, θ_d^T is no longer a simple predictive distribution, i.e., when sampling z_n^d, the implication of each quoted document related to d by reply-to relations and their topic assignments must be considered because the sampling distribution for z_n^d in document d must consider its effect on the joint probability of the entire model. Unfortunately, this too can be computationally expensive for large corpora (like ours). To circumvent this issue, we can hierarchically sample documents based on reply-to relation network using sequential Monte Carlo [9], or approximate the true Gibbs sampling distribution by updating the original smoothing parameter (α_T) to reflect the expected topic distributions of quoted documents ($s_{d,t}\alpha_T$), where $s_{d,t}$ is the tth component of the base measure, s_d which is computed at runtime during sampling. We take the latter approach (see Eq. (5)). Experiments show that this

[2] We crawled the ids of posts quoted by each post.

[3] Taking moments on $(X_1 \ldots X_n) \sim Dir(\alpha_1 \ldots \alpha_n)$, we get $E[X_i] = \frac{\alpha_i}{\Sigma\alpha_i}$. Thus, $E[X_i] \propto \alpha_i$

approximation performs well empirically. The approximate Gibbs distribution for JTE-R while sampling $z_n^d = t$ is given by:

$$p(z_k = t, r_k = \hat{t} | Z_{\neg k}, W_{\neg k}, R_{\neg k}, w_k = v) \propto \frac{n_{d,t_{\neg k}}^{DT} + s_{d,t}\alpha_T}{\sum_{t=1}^{T}\left(n_{d,t_{\neg k}}^{DT} + s_{d,t}\alpha_T\right)} \frac{n_{t,v_{\neg k}}^{TV} + \beta_T}{n_{t,(\cdot)_{\neg k}}^{TV} + V\beta_T} \times \frac{\exp(\sum_{i=1}^{n}\lambda_i f_i(x_{d,j}, \hat{t}))}{\sum_{y \in \{\hat{t},\hat{e}\}}\exp(\sum_{i=1}^{n}\lambda_i f_i(x_{d,j}, y))} \quad (5)$$

3.2 JTE-P: Encoding Pair Structures

JTE-R builds over JTE by encoding reply-to relations to constrain a post to have similar topic distributions to those it quotes. An alternative strategy is to make θ^T and θ^E author-pair specific. The idea is motivated by the following observation.

Observation: When authors reply to others' viewpoints (by @name or quoting other authors' posts), they typically direct their own topical viewpoints with contentious or agreeing expressions to those authors. Such exchanges can go back and forth between pairs of authors. The discussion topics and CA-expressions emitted are thus caused by the author-pairs' topical interests and their nature of interactions.

Let a_d be the author of a post d, and $b_d = [b_{1 \ldots n}]$ be the list of *target authors* (we will also call them *targets* for short) to whom a_d replies to or quotes in d. The pairs of the form $p = (a_d, c)$, $c \in b_d$ essentially shapes both the topics and CA-expressions emitted in d as contention or agreement on topical viewpoints are almost always directed towards certain target authors. For example, if c claims something, a_d quotes the claim in his post d and then contends/agrees by emitting CA-expressions like "you have no clue", "yes, I agree", "I don't think," etc. Clearly, this pair structure is a crucial feature of discussions/debate forums. Each pair has its unique and shared topical interests and interaction nature (contention or agreement). Thus, it is appropriate to condition θ^T and θ^E over author-pairs. We will see in §4.4.1 that this model fits the discussion data better. Standard topic models do not consider this key piece of information. Although there are extensions to consider authors [37], persona [31] and interest [24], none of them are suitable for considering the pair structure.

We extend the JTE model to incorporate the pair structure. We call the new model JTE-P, which conditions the multinomial distributions over topics and CA-expression types (θ^T, θ^E) on authors and targets as pairs rather than on documents as in JTE and JTE-R. In its generative process, for each post, the author a_d and the set of targets b_d are observed. To generate each term $w_{d,j}$, a target, $c \sim Uni(b_d)$, is chosen at uniform from b_d forming a pair $p = (a_d, c)$. Then, depending on the switch variable $r_{d,j}$, a topic or an expression type index z is chosen from a multinomial over topic distribution θ_p^T or CA-expression type distribution θ_p^E, where the subscript p denotes the fact that the distributions are specific to the author-target pair p which shape topics and CA-expressions. Finally, the term is emitted by sampling from topic or CA-expression specific multinomial distribution $\varphi_{z_{d,j}}^{r_{d,j}}$.

The graphical model in plate notation corresponding to the above process is shown in Figure 1 (c). Clearly, in JTE-P, the discovery of topics and CA-expressions are guided by the pair structure of reply-to relations in which the collection of posts was generated. For posterior inference, we again use Gibbs sampling. Note that as a_d is observed, sampling c is equivalent to sampling the pair $p = (a_d, c)$. Its Gibbs sampler is given by:

$$p(z_k = t, p_k = p, r_k = \hat{t} | \ldots, w_k = v) \propto \frac{1}{|b_d|} \times \frac{n_{p,t_{\neg k}}^{PT} + \alpha_T}{n_{p,(\cdot)_{\neg k}}^{PT} + T\alpha_T} \times \frac{n_{t,v_{\neg k}}^{TV} + \beta_T}{n_{t,(\cdot)_{\neg k}}^{TV} + V\beta_T} \times \frac{\exp(\sum_{i=1}^{n}\lambda_i f_i(x_{d,j}, \hat{t}))}{\sum_{y \in \{\hat{t},\hat{e}\}}\exp(\sum_{i=1}^{n}\lambda_i f_i(x_{d,j}, y))} \quad (6)$$

$$p(z_k = e, p_k = p, r_k = \hat{e} | \ldots, w_k = v) \propto \frac{1}{|b_d|} \times \frac{n_{p,e_{\neg k}}^{PE} + \alpha_E}{n_{p,(\cdot)_{\neg k}}^{PE} + E\alpha_E} \times \frac{n_{e,v_{\neg k}}^{EV} + \beta_E}{n_{e,(\cdot)_{\neg k}}^{EV} + V\beta_E} \times \frac{\exp(\sum_{i=1}^{n}\lambda_i f_i(x_{d,j}, \hat{e}))}{\sum_{y \in \{\hat{t},\hat{e}\}}\exp(\sum_{i=1}^{n}\lambda_i f_i(x_{d,j}, y))} \quad (7)$$

where $n_{p,t}^{PT}$ and $n_{p,e}^{PE}$ denote the number of times the pair p was assigned to topic t and expression type e respectively. As JTE-P assumes that each pair has a specific topic and expression distribution, we see that Eq. (6, 7) shares topics and expression types across pairs. It is also worthwhile to note that given A authors, there are $\binom{A}{2}$ possible pairs. However, the actual number of pairs (i.e., where the authors have communicated at least once) is much less than $\binom{A}{2}$. Our experimental data consists of 1824 authors and 7684 actual pairs. Hence we are only modeling 7684 pairs instead of $\binom{1824}{2} \approx 4$ million pairs.[4]

4. EXPERIMENTS

We now evaluate the proposed models and compare with baselines. We first qualitatively show the CA-expressions and topics discovered by the models. We then evaluate the models quantitatively based on the two objectives of this work:

i) Discovering contention and agreement expressions (or CA-expressions).
ii) Finding contention points or topics in each contentious post.

Experiments are also conducted on statistical metrics such as perplexity and KL-Divergence. They show that the interaction models (JTE-R and JTE-P) fit the discussion/debate data better and find more distinctive topics and CA-expressions than JTE.

For our experiments, we used debate/discussion posts from Volconvo[5]. The forum is divided into various domains: Politics, Religion, Society, Science, etc. Each domain consists of multiple threads. Each thread has a set of posts. For each post, we extracted the post id, author, time, domain, ids of all posts to which it replies/quotes, and the post content. In all, we extracted 26137, 34986, 22354 and 16525 posts from Politics, Religion, Society and Science domains respectively. Our final data consists of 5978357 tokens, 1824 authors with an average of 346 words per post, and 7684 author-target pairs.

4.1 Topic and CA-expression Discovery

To set the background for our quantitative evaluation of the two tasks in the next two sub-sections, we first show the topics and the CA-expressions discovered by our models, and also compare them with topics found by LDA [4] and its variant SLDA (sentence-LDA) [21]. We choose LDA as it is the best-known topic model. We use SLDA as it constrains words in a sentence to be generated from a single topic [21]. Since CA-expressions may appear with topics in the same sentence, we want to see how it performs in mining topics and CA-expressions although SLDA is unable to separate topical terms and CA-expressions.

For all our experiments here and the subsequent ones, the hyper-parameters for LDA and SLDA were set to the heuristic values $\alpha = 50/T$, $\beta = 0.1$ as suggested in [18]. Similarly, for the proposed models, we set $\alpha_T = 50/T$, $\alpha_E = 50/E$, $\beta_T = \beta_E = 0.1$. To learn the Max-Ent parameters λ, we randomly sampled 500 terms from our corpus appearing at least 50 times[6] and labeled them as topical (372) or CA-expressions (128) and used the corresponding feature vector of each term (in the context of posts where it

[4] Note that in modeling pair interactions, JTE-P conditions topic and CA-expression emission over debating pairs. The model could be made further fine-grained by modeling topic specific interaction of authors by incorporating some ideas in [16, 37] While this approach is richer, it calls for more complex inference. We will study these possibilities in the future. We thank one anonymous reviewer for this suggestion.

[5] http://www.volconvo.com/forums/forum.php

[6] A minimum frequency count of 50 ensures that the training data is reasonably representative of the corpus.

(a) JTE

t_1: Spirituality	t_2: Burka/Veil	t_3: Homo-sexuality	t_4: Evolution of Life	t_5: 9/11 Attacks	t_6:Theism/Atheism	t_7: Global warming	t_8: Vegetarianism	t_9: IRS/Taxes	t_{10}: U.S. Politics
spirituality	burka	marriage	evolution	9/11	god	earth	animals	tax	vote
life	burqa	gay	species	september 11	belief	co2	meat	government	president
soul	suffering	couples	theory	terrorism	**existence**	warming	egg	irs	democrats
wrong	hijab	straight	dna	**fox**	atheist	weather	beef	state	politics
self	women	homosexuality	humans	news	**evidence**	pollution	slaughter	money	electoral
death	islam	trans	homo sapiens	terror attacks	faith	global warming	kill	pay	us government
karma	conceals	individual right	darwin's theory	plane	irrational	floods	life	federal	obama
suffering	**death**	gay marriages	life	cia	jesus	ice	diet	state taxes	**policy**
afterlife	tyranny	heterosexual	intelligence	conspiracy theory	supreme being	nuclear waste	meat industry	services	elections
self realization	terrorism	legal	mendel's theory	al qaeda	creationism	sea level	vegan	social security	senate
mortal	muslim bigots	**law**	human dna	bin laden	big bang	climate change	vegetables	income tax	libertarian
self knowledge	sexist	sex	theory of evolution	bush	omnipotent	arctic ice	meat consumption	budget	left wing

(b) LDA

t_1: Spirituality	t_2: Burka/Veil	t_3: Homo-sexuality	t_4: Evolution of Life	t_5: 9/11 Attacks	t_6:Theism/Atheism	t_7: Global warming	t_8: Vegetarianism	t_9: IRS/Taxes	t_{10}: U.S. Politics
life	burka	gay	life	9/11	god	earth	kill	tax	vote
evil	**man**	couples	**god**	laden	religion	planet	meat	pay	electoral
live	women	straight	evolution	bush	jesus	ice	animal	agent	obama
knowledge	immoral	sex	**religion**	terror	**desire**	weather	cow	income	house
purpose	muslim	dating	intelligence	dead	**bang**	warming	egg	revenue	political
values	islam	family	human	**twin**	faith	floods	cooking	us	american
natural	sadistic	**funny**	beings	plane	life	level	**earth**	irs	democrats
existence	terrorism	trans	theory	obl	man	change	diet	american	party
goal	bigot	love	sea	**new**	adam	**clean**	milk	**draft**	bill
self	sexist	children	biology	crash	exists	polar	**fur**	fund	bush
sex	**beautiful**	**law**	earth	tower	**being**	climate	**herbivorous**	funding	senate
spirit	conceals	**ancient**	dna	**york**	omnipotent	**waste**	vegan	state	presidential

(c) SLDA

t_1: Spirituality	t_2: Burka/Veil	t_3: Homo-sexuality	t_4: Evolution of Life	t_5: 9/11 Attacks	t_6:Theism/Atheism	t_7: Global warming	t_8: Vegetarianism	t_9: IRS/Taxes	t_{10}: U.S. Politics
life	burka	gay	life	9/11	god	planet	kill	tax	vote
evil	muslim	couples	theory	laden	religion	ice	meat	pay	electoral
spirit	hijab	dating	evolution	plane	theist	earth	chicken	income	senate
knowledge	women	sex	**homo**	*nonsense*	life	level	egg	*valid*	house
values	*incorrect*	**cannot**	earth	terror	islam	*agree*	beef	state	*correct*
agree	bigot	family	human	bush	**cannot**	change	**fur**	irs	american
existence	sexist	*disagree*	**argument**	*incorrect*	belief	floods	diet	*agree*	democrats
live	terrorism	**don't**	sea	crash	**argument**	**point**	**claim**	**think**	*definitely*
correct	burqa	trans	biology	obl	adam	arctic	milk	us	bush
don't	**man**	children	*prove*	*bogus*	creationism	polar	*disagree*	revenue	elections
goal	*nonsense*	**funny**	dna	cia	**your**	*indeed*	**strength**	budget	obama
purpose	**beautiful**	**law**	darwin	tower	jesus	**clean**	cow	**draft**	*disagree*

Table 1: Top terms of 10 topics discovered by JTE (a), LDA (b), and SLDA (c). Red (**bold**) denotes errors and *blue* (*italics*) denotes contention/agreement terms.

occurs) to train the Max-Ent model. We set the number of topics, T = 100 and the number of CA-expression types, E = 2 (contention and agreement) as in discussion/debate forums, there are usually two expression types (This hypothesis is further statistically validated in §4.4.1).

Due to space constraints, we are unable to list the topics discovered by all proposed models. As JTE is the basic model (others build over it) and is also closest to LDA and SLDA, we compare the top terms for 10 topics discovered by JTE, LDA and SLDA in Table 1. The top topical terms by other models are not so different. However, we will evaluate all the proposed models quantitatively later using the task of identifying topics (or "points") of contention in each contentious post, which is one of our objectives. From Table 1, we can still observe that JTE is quite effective at discovering topics. Its topical terms are more specific and contain fewer semantic clustering errors (marked red in bold) than LDA and SLDA. For example, owing to the generative process of JTE, it is able to cluster phrases like "homo sapiens", "darwin's theory," and "theory of evolution" in t_4 (Evolution of Life), which makes the topic more specific.

It is important to note that both LDA and SLDA cannot separate topics and CA-expressions because they find only topics. That is why we need joint modeling of topics and CA-expressions. We can see that the topics of SLDA do contain some CA-expressions (marked blue in italics) because SLDA constrains all words in a sentence to be generated from a single topic [21]. Since CA-expressions can co-occur with topical words in a sentence, they are clustered with topics, which is undesirable. Our proposed models solve this problem based on the joint model formulations.

Next we look at the discovered CA-expressions. We first list some top CA-expressions found by JTE in Table 2 for qualitative inspection. Since CA-expressions found by JTE-R and JTE-P were quite similar to those of JTE among the top 30 terms, they are omitted here. However, all three models are quantitatively evaluated in the next sub-section. From Table 2, we see that JTE can discover and cluster many correct CA-expressions, e.g., "I disagree," "I refute" and "completely disagree" in contention; and "I accept," "I agree," and "you're correct" in agreement. It additionally discovers more distinctive expressions beyond those observed in the training data of Max-Ent. For example, we find phrases like "I don't buy your", "I really doubt", "can you prove", "you fail to", and "you have no clue" being clustered in contention and phrases like "valid point", "rightly said", "I do support", and "very well put" clustered in agreement. These newly discovered phrases are marked *blue* (in italics) in Table 2.

Lastly, we note that CA-expressions of JTE do contain some errors marked **red** (in bold). However, this is a common issue with

I, disagree, **don't**, I don't, **claim**, **you**, oppose, **debate**, I disagree, **argument**, reject, I reject, I refute, **your**, I refuse, doubt, nonsense, *I contest*, dispute, **I think**, completely disagree, don't accept, don't agree, *your claim isn't*, incorrect, *hogwash*, ridiculous, *I would disagree*, false, *I don't buy your*, **really**, *I really doubt*, your nonsense, **true**, *can you prove*, argument fails, *you fail to*, **sense**, your assertions, *bullshit*, *sheer nonsense*, **cannot**, *doesn't make sense*, why do you, *you have no clue*, *how can you say*, *do you even*, absolute nonsense, *contradict yourself*, absolutely not, *you don't understand*, ...

(a) JTE Contention expressions, $\Phi^E_{Contention}$

agree, **I**, correct, yes, true, **do**, accept, **you**, I agree, right, **indeed**, indeed correct, I accept, **claim**, **your**, **point**, are right, **don't**, valid, *I concede*, *is valid*, **your claim**, *you are right*, **not really**, *would agree*, **might**, *agree completely*, **very**, yes indeed, **mean**, you're correct, **completely**, *valid point*, **argument**, proves, *do accept*, support, **said**, agree with you, *I do support*, *rightly said*, **personally**, absolutely, *completely agree*, well put, *very true*, *well said*, *personally agree*, **doesn't necessarily**, exactly, *very well put*, absolutely correct, **probably**, *kudos*, acknowledge, *point taken*, *partially agree*, agree entirely, ...

(b) JTE Agreement expressions, $\Phi^E_{Agreement}$

Table 2: Top terms (comma delimited) of two expression types of the JTE model. Red (**bold**) terms denote possible errors. *Blue* (*italics*) terms are newly discovered; rest (black) were used in Max-Ent training.

n	JTE				JTE-R				JTE-P			
	C		A		C		A		C		A	
	@50	@100	@50	@100	@50	@100	@50	@100	@50	@100	@50	@100
100	0.60	0.61	0.58	0.62	0.62	0.63	0.60	0.62	0.62	0.64	0.68	0.64
200	0.64	0.63	0.62	0.61	0.66	0.65	0.66	0.65	0.64	0.67	0.70	0.66
300	0.68	0.67	0.64	0.63	0.70	0.71	0.70	0.67	0.68	0.73	0.76	0.68
400	0.72	0.71	0.70	0.65	0.74	0.76	0.76	0.70	0.76	0.77	0.78	0.71
500	0.74	0.75	0.74	0.68	0.78	0.79	0.80	0.71	0.82	0.81	0.80	0.73

Table 3: p@50, 100 for Contention (C), Agreement (A) of various models across different numbers (n) of terms in the labeled sets used for Max-Ent training.

all unsupervised topic models for text and the reason is that the objective function of topic models does not always correlate well with human judgments [11]. In our case, the issue is mainly due to unigram CA-expressions like "I", "your", "do", etc., which by itself do not signify contention or agreement but show up due to higher frequencies in the corpus. There are also phrase errors like "doesn't necessarily", "not really", etc. A plausible approach to deal with this is to discover significant *n*-grams based on multi-way contingency tables and statistical tests along with linguistic clues to pre-process and filter such terms. These issues are worth investigating and we defer them to our future work.

4.2 CA-expression Evaluation

We now quantitatively evaluate the discovered CA-expressions by all three proposed models in three ways. We first evaluate them directly and then evaluate them indirectly through a classification task. Lastly, we examine the sensitivity of the performance with respect to the amount of labeled data. In this case, we do not have an external baseline method as existing joint topic models cannot discover CA-expressions (See §5). However, we will show that the interaction models, JTE-R and JTE-P, are superior to JTE.

4.2.1 Evaluation of CA-expression Rankings

Since CA-expressions (according to top terms in Φ^E) produced by JTE, JTE-R, and JTE-P are rankings, we evaluate them using *precision @ n (p@n)*, which gives the precision at different rank positions. This measure is commonly used to evaluate a ranking when the number of correct items is unknown, which is our case. For computing *p@n*, we also investigated multi-rater agreement. Three judges independently labeled the top *n* terms as correct or incorrect for Contention and Agreement. Then, we marked a term to be correct if all the judges deemed it so which was then used to compute *p@n*. Multi-rater agreement using Fleiss kappa was greater than 0.80 for all *p@n*, which imply perfect agreement. This is understandable because one can almost certainly make out whether a term expresses contention, agreement or none.

Figure 2 shows the precisions of contention and agreement expressions for the top 50, 100, 150, 200 positions (i.e., *p@* 50, 100, 150, 200) in the two rankings. We observe that both JTE-R and JTE-P are much better than JTE. JTE-P produces the best results. We believe the reason is that JTE-P's expression models being pair specific (θ_p^E) can capture CA-expressions better as contention/agreement expressed by an author is almost always directed to some other authors forming author-pairs.

4.2.2 Contention/Agreement Post Classification

We now use the task of classifying a post as being contentious or agreeing to evaluate the discovered CA-expressions. This classification task is also interesting in its own right. However, we should note that our purpose here is not to find the best classifier to classify posts but to indirectly show that the discovered CA-expressions are of high quality as they help to perform the classification better than the standard word *n*-grams and part-of-speech (POS) *n*-gram features for text classification.

To perform this experiment, we randomly sampled 1000 posts from our database and asked our human judges (3 graduate students well versed in English) to classify each of those posts as *contentious*, *agreeing*, or *other*. Judges were made to work in isolation to prevent bias. We then labeled a post as contentious or agreeing if all judges deemed it so. In this way, 532 posts were classified as contentious, 405 as agreeing. We inspected the rest 63 posts which had disagreements. We found that 18 of them were the first posts of threads. We removed them as the first posts of threads usually start the discussions and do not express agreement or contention. For the remaining 45 of them, 13 posts were partly contentious and partly agreeing (e.g., "*Although I doubt your claim, I agree with your point that…*"), and the rest were mostly statements of views without contention or agreement. Since the number of these posts is small (only 45), we did not use them in classification. That is, we considered two mutually exclusive classes (contentious and agreeing) for post classification. We also conducted a labeling agreement study of our judges using Fleiss multi-rater kappa and obtained $\kappa_{Fleiss} = 0.87$ which shows perfect agreement among the judges according to the scale[7] provided in [25]. This high agreement is not unnatural because by reading a post one can almost certainly make out whether it is overall contentious or agreeing.

For supervised learning, a challenging issue is the choice of features. Word and POS *n*-grams are traditional features. We now compare such features with CA-expressions discovered by the proposed models. We used the top 1000 (contention and agreement) terms from the CA-expression rankings as features. Using classification learning algorithms, we compare a learner trained on all word and POS *n*-grams with those trained on CA-expressions induced by our models. We used SVM, Naïve Bayes (NB), and Logistic Regression (LR). For SVM, we used SVM^{light} (http://svmlight.joachims.org) and for NB and LR, we used the WEKA implementations (http://www.cs.waikato.ac.nz/ml/weka). For SVM, we tried linear, RBF, polynomial and sigmoid kernels, but linear kernel performed the best and hence we only report the results of SVM using linear kernel. Linear kernel has also been shown very effective for text classification by many researchers, e.g., [22]. Table 4 reports the accuracy results. Accuracy is appropriate here as the two classes are not skewed and we are interested in both classes. All results were obtained through 10-fold cross-validation. As the major advantage of CA-expressions arise from dimensionality reduction and feature selection, we also compared with two state-of-the-art feature selection schemes: Information Gain (IG) and Chi-Square test (χ^2). We can observe that SVM performed the best among all learners. The accuracy dramatically increases with CA-expression (Φ^E) features. JTE, JTE-R, and JTE-P progressively improve the accuracy beyond those obtained by traditional *n*-gram features. JTE-P performed the best. Feature selection schemes also improved performance but the proposed models outperform feature selection schemes as well. All accuracy improvements are significant ($p<0.001$) using a two tailed *t*-test over 10-fold CV. This clearly shows that CA-expressions are of high quality. We also experimented with different numbers of top CA-expressions as features to see how they affect the accuracy results (Figure 3). Here only SVM results are reported as it performed best. We observe in Figure 3 that when the number of CA-expressions reaches about 1000, the classification accuracies start to level-off for all models.

In fact, for JTE and JTE-R, since we know the per post distribution of CA-expression type (θ_d^E), we can also classify a post directly without supervised learning. For each post, if the probability mass associated with type contention is higher than that of agreement, it is classified as a contentious post else an agreeing post. The accuracies using this scheme are: JTE: 74.9%, JTE-R: 75.9%, which are respectable. It is understandable they are lower than supervised methods because supervised learning uses a large number of features. Note that JTE-P cannot be used directly here as its CA-expression types are conditioned over author pairs (θ_p^E) rather than documents (θ_p^E) as in JTE and JTE-R.

4.2.3 Effect of Labeled Term Set Size

Having evaluated CA-expressions, we now examine the sensitivity of model performance with respect to the amount of labeled data. In Table 3, we report the *p@*50, 100 values for all models across contention and agreement on different sizes of labeled term sets used for learning the Max-Ent λ parameters. We see that with more labeled terms, the results improve which is intuitive as more

[7] No agreement ($\kappa<0$), slight agreement ($0 < \kappa \leq 0.2$), fair agreement ($0.2 < \kappa \leq 0.4$), moderate agreement ($0.4 < \kappa \leq 0.6$), substantial agreement ($0.6 < \kappa \leq 0.8$), and almost perfect agreement for $0.8 < \kappa \leq 1.0$.

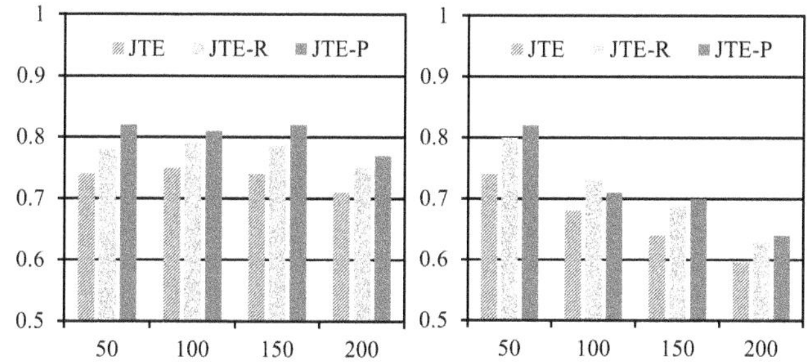

Figure 2: Precision @ top 50, 100, 150, 200 rank positions for Contention (left) and Agreement (right) expressions discovered by various methods.

Features	SVM	NB	LR
W+POS 1-gram	69.37	68.20	68.84
W+POS 1-2 gram	70.33	68.94	69.90
W+POS, 1-3 gram	70.86	69.16	70.44
W+POS, 1-4 gram	70.97	69.26	70.54
W+POS, 1-4 gram + IG	75.67	74.01	75.34
W+POS, 1-4 gram + χ^2	76.21	75.11	76.09
CA-Expr. Φ^E, JTE	80.79	78.55	79.30
CA-Expr. Φ^E, JTE-R	82.18	79.19	80.15
CA-Expr. Φ^E, M-JTE-P	83.88	79.30	81.43

Table 4: Accuracies of post classification: different learners and feature settings. The improvements of our models are significant (p<0.001) over two tailed t-test across 10-fold cross validation.

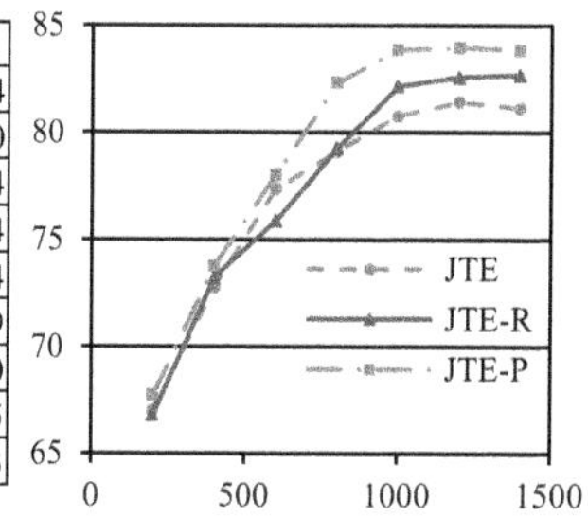

Figure 3: 10-fold CV accuracy of SVM for post classification versus the number of top expressions of Φ^E across all proposed models.

D	Φ^E + Noun/Noun Phrase						JTE						JTE-R						JTE-P					
	J_1			J_2			J_1			J_2			J_1			J_2			J_1			J_2		
	P	R	F_1	P	R	F_1	P	R	F_1	P	R	F_1	P	R	F_1	P	R	F_1	P	R	F_1	P	R	F_1
D1	0.60	0.70	0.65	0.55	0.62	0.58	0.75	0.79	0.77	0.68	0.74	0.71	0.78	0.82	0.80	0.74	0.75	0.74	0.79	0.84	0.81	0.74	0.76	0.75
D2	0.61	0.68	0.64	0.57	0.61	0.59	0.74	0.77	0.75	0.67	0.70	0.68	0.76	0.80	0.78	0.70	0.70	0.70	0.77	0.82	0.79	0.70	0.72	0.71
D3	0.62	0.69	0.65	0.54	0.60	0.57	0.73	0.80	0.76	0.65	0.67	0.66	0.77	0.81	0.79	0.71	0.69	0.70	0.77	0.84	0.80	0.72	0.70	0.71
D4	0.63	0.71	0.67	0.53	0.58	0.55	0.72	0.81	0.76	0.63	0.71	0.67	0.74	0.83	0.78	0.67	0.72	0.69	0.73	0.82	0.77	0.68	0.72	0.69
Avg.	0.62	0.70	0.65	0.55	0.60	0.57	0.74	0.79	0.76	0.66	0.71	0.68	0.76	0.82	0.79	0.71	0.72	0.71	0.77	0.83	0.79	0.71	0.73	0.72

Table 5: Evaluation of topics or "points" of contention expressed in posts. For each method, we report the precision (P) and recall (R) for discovering points of contention in posts belonging to a particular domain. The experiments were performed on four domains D1: Politics, D2: Religion, D3: Society, D4: Science. The precision and recall for each domain are the average precision and recall over 125 posts in that domain.

Statistical significance: Differences between Nearest Noun Phrase and JTE for both judges (J_1, J_2) across all domains were significant at 98% confidence level (p<0.02). Differences among JTE, JTE-R and JTE-P for both judges (J_1, J_2) across all domains were significant at 95% confidence level (p<0.05). A two tailed t-test was used for testing significance.

labeled data will result in more accurate Max-Ent estimates. We used 500 labeled terms in all our experiments.

4.3 Discovering Points of Contention

We now turn to the task of automatically discovering points of contention in contentious posts. By "points", we mean the topical terms on which the contention has been expressed. We employ the JTE and JTE-R models in the following manner using estimated θ_d^T. Note that JTE-P cannot be directly used for this task because it has θ^T placed in the author pair plate so its topics are pair specific (θ_p^T) rather than post specific. However, since we know the posterior topic assignments of z_n^d, we can get a posterior estimate of θ_d^T for JTE-P using $\theta_{d,t}^T = \frac{|\{j|z_j^d=t,1\le j\le N_d\}|}{|\{j|r_{d,j}=\hat{t},1\le j\le N_d\}|}$.

Given a contentious post d, we first select the top k topics that are mentioned in d according to its topic distribution, θ_d^T. Let T_d denote the set of these top k topics in d. Then, for each contentious expression $e \in d \cap \varphi_{Contention}^E$, we emit the topical terms of topics in T_d which appear within a word window of v from e in d. More precisely, we emit the set $H = \{w|w \in d \cap \varphi_t^T, t \in T_d, |posi(w) - posi(e)| \le v\}$, where $posi(\cdot)$ returns the position index of the word/phrase in a document d. To compute the intersection $w \in d \cap \varphi_t^T$, we need a threshold. This is so because the Dirichlet distribution has a smoothing effect which assigns some non-zero probability mass to every term in the vocabulary for each topic t. So for computing the intersection, we considered only terms in φ_t^T which have $p(v|t) = \varphi_{t,v}^T > 0.001$ as probability masses lower than 0.001 are more due to the smoothing effect of the Dirichlet distribution than true correlation. In an actual application, the values for k and v can be set according to the user's need. In this experiment, we use $k = 3$ and $v = 5$, which are reasonable because a post normally does not talk about many topics (k), and the contention points (topical terms) appear close to the contentious expressions.

For comparison, we also designed a baseline. For each contentious expression $e \in d \cap \varphi_{Contention}^E$, we emit the nouns and noun phrases within the same window v as the points of contention in d. This baseline is reasonable because topical terms are usually nouns and noun phrases and are near contentious expressions. But we should note that this baseline cannot standalone as it has to rely on the expression models Φ^E of JTE-P.

Next, to evaluate the performance of these methods in discovering points of contention, we randomly selected 125 contentious posts from each domain in our dataset and employed the aforementioned methods on the posts to discover the points of contention in each post. Then we asked two human judges (graduate students fluent in English) to manually judge the results produced by each method for each post. We asked them to report the precision (% of terms discovered by a method which are indeed valid points of contention in a post) and recall (% of all valid points of contention which were discovered) for each post. In Table 5, we report the average precision and recall for 125 posts in each domain by the two human judges J_1 and J_2 for different methods. Since this judging task is subjective, the differences in the results from the two judges are not surprising. We observe that across all domains, JTE, JTE-R and JTE-P progressively improve performance over the baseline. Note that it is difficult to compute agreement of two judges using kappa because although the models identify topic terms (which are the same for both judges), the judges also identify additional terms (for recall calculation) which are not found by the models.

4.4 Statistical Experiments

We now compare the proposed models across statistical metrics: perplexity and KL-Divergence.

4.4.1 Perplexity

To measure the ability of JTE, JTE-R and JTE-P to act as good "generative" models, we computed the test-set (see below) perplexity under estimated parameters and also compared with the resulting values of LDA and SLDA models.

Perplexity, widely used in the statistical language modeling community to assess the predictive power of a model, is algebraically equivalent to the inverse of the geometric mean per-word likelihood. A lower perplexity score indicates a better generalization performance. As perplexity monotonically

Iteration	LDA	SLDA	JTE	JTE (E=3)	JTE (E=4)	JTE-R	JTE-P
1000	1795	1745	1475	1489	1497	1467	1442
2000	1684	1568	1381	1397	1423	1343	1326
3000	1575	1474	1318	1331	1348	1273	1257
4000	1561	1421	1248	1266	1278	1223	1208

(a) Perplexity vs. Gibbs Iteration

KL-Div.	LDA	SLDA	JTE	JTE-R	JTE-P
Θ^T	3.4	3.3	9.2	9.9	13.0
Θ^E	-	-	14.1	15.1	17.8
Φ^T	16.8	17.7	20.1	21.8	22.2
Φ^E	-	-	10.9	11.3	11.8

(b) Avg. KL-Div. between models

Table 6: (a) Perplexity comparison of models across Gibbs iterations. The number of topics and CA-expression types were fixed at T = 100, E = 2. All differences are statistically significant (p<0.001) over two tailed t-test across samples from different chains for each group. (b) Average KL-Divergence of topics and CA-expressions, $D_{KL}(\varphi_z||\varphi_{\acute{z}})$ and per document distributions of topics and CA-expressions, $D_{KL}(\theta_d||\theta_{\acute{d}})$. For JTE-P we report the average per pair distributions of topics and CA-expressions $D_{KL}(\theta_p||\theta_{\acute{p}})$. All differences are significant (p<0.01) over two tailed t-test.

decreases with increase in log-likelihood (by definition), it implies that lower perplexity is better since higher log-likelihood on training data means that the model "fits" the data better and a higher log-likelihood on the test set implies that the model can "explain" the unseen data better. Thus, lower perplexity implies that the words are "less surprising" to the model. In our experiments we used 15% of our data (in §4) as our held out test set. As JTE-P requires pair structures, for proper comparison across all models, the corpus was restricted to posts which have at least one quotation. This is reasonable as quoting/replying is an integral part of debates/discussions and we found that about 77% of all posts have quoted/replied-to at least one other post (this count excludes the first posts of threads as they start the discussions and usually have nobody to quote/reply-to). The perplexity (PPX) of JTE given the learned model parameters Φ^T, Φ^E and the state of the Markov chain $\mu = \{\vec{z}, \vec{r}, \vec{w}\}$ is given by:

$$PPX = exp\left[-\frac{1}{\widetilde{W}}\sum_{\tilde{d}=1}^{D_{test}}\frac{1}{S}\sum_{s=1}^{S} logP(\tilde{d}|\mu^s)\right] \quad (8)$$

where $\widetilde{W}$ denotes the total number of terms in D_{test}. To obtain a better estimate, we average the per-word log-likelihood over S different chains. μ^s denotes the Markov state corresponding to chain s. From the generative process of JTE, we get:

$$logP(\tilde{d}|\mu^s) = \sum_{v=1}^{V}\left(n_{\tilde{d}}^{v}\log\left(\sum_{t=1}^{T}\varphi_{t,v}^{s}\theta_{\tilde{d},t}^{s} + \sum_{e=1}^{E}\varphi_{e,v}^{s}\theta_{\tilde{d},e}^{s}\right)\right) \quad (9)$$

where $n_{\tilde{d}}^{v}$ denotes the number of times term $v \in V$ occurred in $\tilde{d} \in D_{test}$ and $\theta_{\tilde{d},t}^{s}$ and $\theta_{\tilde{d},e}^{s}$ are estimated by querying the model according to the query sampler. In a similar way, the perplexities of the other three models can also be derived.

We compare model perplexities across Gibbs iterations with T = 100 and E = 2 in Table 6 (a). We note the following observations: i) *Noise Reduction*: The proposed models attain significantly (see caption of Table 6(a)) lower perplexities with fewer iterations than LDA and SLDA showing that the new models fit the debate/discussion forum data better and clustering using the new framework contains less noise. This improvement is attributed to the capabilities of the framework to separate and account for CA-expressions using Φ^E. ii) *The number of CA-expression types*, E: In §2 and 4, we hypothesized that for discussions/debates we mostly have two expression types: contention and agreement. To test this hypothesis, we ran JTE with E > 2 (Table 6(a), columns 5, 6). We find that the test-set perplexity slightly increases (than E = 2) showing performance degradation. It is interesting to note that the number of CA-expression types E impacts perplexity differently than the number of topics T (as the decrease in perplexity usually slows in inverse proportions with increase in the number of topics [4]). We also tried increasing E to 5, 10, etc. However, the performance deteriorated with increase in model perplexity. This result supports our prior hypothesis of E = 2 in debate forums.

4.4.2 *KL-Divergence*

Another important measure for topic models is topic distinctiveness [24]. Here, we want to assess how distinctive the discovered topics and CA-expressions are. To measure topic and CA-expression distinctiveness, we computed the average topic and CA-expression distribution (φ_z^T and φ_z^E) separations between all pairs of latent topics and CA-expression types. To measure separations, we choose KL-Divergence as our metric as suggested in [24]. Clearly, for more distinctive topic and CA-expression discovery, it is desirable to have higher average KL-Divergence. Table 6(b) shows the comparison results. Again, as JTE-P requires pair structures, for proper comparison, all models were run on the restricted corpus where posts have at least one quotation. We observe that topics discovered by the new models are more distinctive than LDA and SLDA. For both topics and CA-expressions, JTE-R performed better than JTE showing that reply relations are highly beneficial. JTE-P with pair structures performed the best. Table 6(b) also reports the average separations of per document distribution of topics and expressions (θ_d^T and θ_d^E). For models JTE and JTE-R, having higher average KL-Divergence for Θ^T and Θ^E implies that documents are well separated based on the estimated topics and two CA-expression types exhibited. We see that both JTE and JTE-R obtain higher average KL-Divergence for Θ^T than LDA and SLDA. Such separations are particularly useful when topic models are used for performing retrieval [19].

Lastly, we look at the average per pair separation of topics and CA-expressions for JTE-P. Clearly, the KL-Divergence values indicate good separations. This information may be further used to mine contending author-pairs or classify these pairs according to interests, i.e., the posterior on θ_p^E can be used to make predictions on the interaction nature of any two authors. However, these are beyond the scope of this paper. We will study them in future.

5. RELATED WORK

Although limited research has been done on fine-grained mining of contentions in discussion/debate forums, there are several general research areas that are related to our work.

Sentiment analysis: Sentiment analysis mines positive and negative opinions from text [27,34]. Agreement and contention are different concepts. Sentiments are mainly indicated by sentiment words (e.g., *great*, *good*, *bad*, and *poor*), while contention and agreement are indicated by CA-expressions. Sentiment analysis approaches are thus not directly applicable to our tasks and we also need to discover CA-expressions. However, from a modeling perspective, there exist several joint sentiment and topic models which are related to our work and are discussed below. Other related works in sentiment analysis include pro-con classification [3], contradictions [23, 36], attitude [38] and negotiations [39].

Topic models: Topic models such as Latent Dirichlet Allocation (LDA) [4] have been shown effective in mining topics in large text collections. There have been many extensions to correlated [5], supervised [7], multi-grain [43] and sequential [13] topic models. In the context of our JTE-R model, constraining document-topic distributions of a post d to be similar to its quoted posts in q_d is related to topic modeling with network structure [12, 17, 28, 33] where for each pair of documents, a binary link variable is conditioned on their contents. This requires sampling all D^2 links which can be computationally very expensive for large corpora. Chang and Blei [10] improved the efficiency by treating non-links as hidden. In [40], links were assumed to be fixed and topics were conditioned on both the document itself and other linked documents. [29] used a network regularization approach to ensure topics of neighboring documents in a network are similar. This work is based on pLSA [20] and EM rather than LDA and Gibbs sampling. Our approach is simpler. However, all these existing models are mainly used to find topics for corpus exploration. When applied to discussion/debate forums, they are unable to discover contentious topics and CA-expressions at the same time.

There have also been attempts to jointly model both topics and opinions in sentiment analysis. For example, the ME-LDA model [47] added a sentence plate and used maximum-entropy to separate topics and sentiment terms. [26] added a sentiment variable to LDA and conditioned topics over sentiments. The TSM model [30] encodes positive, negative and neutral sentiment variables and a background word variable to separate topical words from background words. In the ASUM model [21], for each sentence a sentiment is chosen over a multinomial, and a topic is chosen conditioned on the sentiment. However, contention and agreeing expressions are emitted differently. Unlike sentiments and topics which are mostly emitted in the same sentence, contention and agreeing expressions often interleave with users' topical viewpoints and may not be in the same sentence. Most importantly, JTE-R and JTE-P can capture the key characteristics of discussions: topic and author interactions, using reply relations and pair structures. Existing joint models are unable to use them.

Support/oppose classification: There have been works aimed at putting debate authors into support/oppose camps. In [15], conversations are classified into agree, disagree, backchannel and other classes. In [1], the reply network was used to classify discussion participants into camps. In [32], a rule-based approach first classifies replies into contention and agreement classes, and max-cut then classifies authors into opposite camps. None of these works, however, mines CA-expressions or contentious topics.

Stances in online debates: In [40], an unsupervised classification method was proposed to recognize stances in debates. In [42], speaker stances were mined using a SVM classifier. In [8], collective classification techniques were employed. Clearly, our work is different as these existing classification methods do not mine CA-expressions or points of contention in each post.

6. CONCLUSIONS

This paper proposed the task of mining contentions in discussion/debate forums, and presented three new models as a principled way to jointly model and mine topics and linguistic expressions indicating agreements and contentions considering topic and author interactions. Existing models are unable to perform these tasks. Specifically, a joint model (JTE) of topics and CA-expressions was first proposed, which was then improved by encoding two key features of discussions or debates, i.e., topical interactions (using reply-to relations) and author interactions (through pair structures), which yielded the JTE-R and JTE-P models. Experimental results showed that the proposed models outperformed baselines for our tasks: i) discovering topics and CA-expressions; and ii) for each contentious post, discovering the contention points or topics. Statistical experiments of perplexity and KL-Divergence were also conducted. They showed that the proposed models fit the data better and discover more distinctive topics and CA-expressions. In all experiments, the interaction models JTE-R and JTE-P consistently gave better results.

7. ACKNOWLEDGMENT

This work is supported in part by National Science Foundation (NSF) under grant no. IIS-1111092.

8. REFERENCES

[1] Agarwal, R. Rajagopalan, S. Srikant, R. Xu. Y. Mining newsgroups using networks arising from social behavior. *WWW*. 2003.

[2] Andrzejewski, D., Zhu, X., Craven, M. Incorporating domain knowledge into topic modeling via Dirichlet forest priors. *ICML*. 2009.

[3] Awadallah, R., Ramanath, M. and Weikum, G. Language-model-based pro/con classification of political text. *SIGIR*. 2010.

[4] Blei, D., Ng, A., Jordan,M. Latent Dirichlet Allocation. *JMLR*. 2003.

[5] Blei, D. and Lafferty, J. D. Correlated topic models. *NIPS*. 2006.

[6] Blei, D. and Lafferty J. Visualizing topics with multi-word expressions. Tech. Report. 2009. arXiv:0907.1013v1.

[7] Blei, D. and McAuliffe, J. Supervised topic models. *NIPS*. 2007.

[8] Burfoot, C., Bird, S., Baldwin, T. Collective Classification of Congressional Floor-Debate Transcripts. *ACL*. 2011.

[9] Canini, K., Shi, L., Griffiths, T. 2009. Online inference of topics with latent Dirichlet allocation. AISTATS. 2009.

[10] Chang, J. and Blei, D. Relational Topic Models for Document Networks. *AISTATS*. 2009.

[11] Chang, J., Boyd-Graber, J., Wang, C. Gerrish, S. Blei, D. Reading tea leaves: How humans interpret topic models. *NIPS*. 2009.

[12] Daume III, H. Markov random topic fields. *ACL-IJCNLP* 2009.

[13] Du, L., Buntine, W. L. and Jin, H. Sequential Latent Dirichlet Allocation: Discover Underlying Topic Structures within a Document. *ICDM*. 2010.

[14] Easley D. and Kleinberg. J. Networks, Crowds, and Markets: Reasoning About a Highly Connected World. Cambridge, 2010.

[15] Galley, M., McKeown, K., Hirschberg, J., Shriberg, E. Identifying agreement and disagreement in conversational speech: Use of Bayesian networks to model pragmatic dependencies. *ACL*. 2004.

[16] Gerrish, S. and Blei, D. A Language-based Approach to Measuring Scholarly Impact. *ICML*. 2010.

[17] Griber, A., Rosen-Zvi, M., Weiss, Y. Latent Topic Models for Hypertext. *UAI* 2008.

[18] Griffiths, T. and Steyvers, M. Finding scientific topics. *PNAS*. 2004.

[19] Heinrich, G. Parameter estimation for text analysis. Tech. Rep. 2005.

[20] Hofmann, T. Probabilistic Latent Semantic Analysis. *UAI*. 1999.

[21] Jo, Y. and Oh, A. Aspect and sentiment unification model for online review analysis. *WSDM*. 2011.

[22] Joachims, T. (1998) Text categorization with support vector machines: Learning with many relevant features.. *ECML*, 1998.

[23] Kawahara, D., Inui, K. and Kurohashi, S. Identifying contradictory and contrastive relations between statements to outline web information on a given topic. *COLING*. 2010.

[24] Kawamae, N. Latent interest-topic model. *CIKM*. 2010.

[25] Landis, J. R. and Koch, G. G. The measurement of observer agreement for categorical data. *Biometrics*, 33, 159-174, 1977.

[26] Lin, C. and He, Y. Joint sentiment/topic model for sentiment analysis. *CIKM*. 2009.

[27] Liu, B. Sentiment analysis and opinion mining. *Morgan & Claypool Publishers*, 2012.

[28] Liu, Y., Niculescu-Mizil, A., Gryc, W. Topic-Link LDA: Joint Models of Topic and Author Community. *ICML*. 2009.

[29] Mei, Q., Cai, D., Zhang, D., Zhai, C. Topic modeling with network regularization. *WWW*. 2008.

[30] Mei, Q. Ling, X., Wondra, M., Su, H. and Zhai, C. Topic sentiment mixture: modeling facets and opinions in weblogs. *WWW*. 2007.

[31] Mimno, D. and McCallum, A. Expertise modeling for matching papers with reviewers. *KDD*. 2007.

[32] Murakami A., and Raymond, R. Support or Oppose? Classifying Positions in Online Debates from Reply Activities and Opinion Expressions. *COLING*, 2010.

[33] Nallapati, R., Ahmed, A., Xing, E., Cohen, W. Joint Latent Topic Models for Text and Citations. *KDD*. 2008.

[34] Pang, B. and Lee, L. Opinion mining and sentiment analysis. *Foundations and Trends in Information Retrieval*. 2008.

[35] Ramage, D., Hall, D., Nallapati, R. and Manning, C. Labeled LDA: A supervised topic model for credit attribution in multi-labeled corpora. *EMNLP*. 2009.

[36] Ritter, A., Downey, D., Soderland, S. and Etzioni, O. It's a contradiction — No, it's not: A case study using functional relation. EMNLP. 2008.

[37] Rosen-Zvi, M., Griffiths, T., Steyvers, M., and Smith, P. The author-topic model for authors and documents. *UAI*. 2004.

[38] Sauper, C. Haghighi, A. and Barzilay, R. Content models with attitude. *ACL*, 2011.

[39] Sokolova, M., and Szpakowicz, S. Language Patterns in the Learning of Strategies from Negotiation Texts. CAI, 2006.

[40] Somasundaran, S., Wiebe, J. Recognizing stances in online debates. *ACL-IJCNLP*. 2009.

[41] Sun, C., Gao, B., Cao, Z., Li, H. HTM: A Topic Model for Hypertexts. *EMNLP*. 2008.

[42] Thomas, M., Pang, B., and Lee, L. Get out the vote: Determining support or opposition from Congressional floor-debate transcripts. *EMNLP*. 2006.

[43] Titov, I. and McDonald, R. Modeling online reviews with multi-grain topic models. *WWW*. 2008.

[44] Wallach, H. Topic modeling: Beyond bag of words. *ICML*. 2006.

[45] Wang, X., McCallum, A., Wei, X. Topical n-grams: phrase and topic discovery, with an application to information retrieval. *ICDM*. 2007.

[46] Zhao, X., Jiang, J., He, J., Song, Y., Achanauparp, P., Lim, E., Li, X. Topical Keyphrase Extraction from Twitter ACL-HLT. 2011.

[47] Zhao, X., Jiang, J. Yan, H., Li, X. Jointly modeling aspects and opinions with a MaxEnt-LDA hybrid. *EMNLP*. 2010.

Discovering Value from Community Activity on Focused Question Answering Sites: A Case Study of Stack Overflow

Ashton Anderson
Stanford University
ashton@cs.stanford.edu

Daniel Huttenlocher
Cornell University

Jon Kleinberg
Cornell University

{dph, kleinber}@cs.cornell.edu

Jure Leskovec
Stanford University
jure@cs.stanford.edu

ABSTRACT

Question answering (Q&A) websites are now large repositories of valuable knowledge. While most Q&A sites were initially aimed at providing useful answers to the question asker, there has been a marked shift towards question answering as a community-driven knowledge creation process whose end product can be of enduring value to a broad audience. As part of this shift, specific expertise and deep knowledge of the subject at hand have become increasingly important, and many Q&A sites employ voting and reputation mechanisms as centerpieces of their design to help users identify the trustworthiness and accuracy of the content.

To better understand this shift in focus from one-off answers to a group knowledge-creation process, we consider a question together with its entire set of corresponding answers as our fundamental unit of analysis, in contrast with the focus on individual question-answer pairs that characterized previous work. Our investigation considers the dynamics of the community activity that shapes the set of answers, both how answers and voters arrive over time and how this influences the eventual outcome. For example, we observe significant assortativity in the reputations of co-answerers, relationships between reputation and answer speed, and that the probability of an answer being chosen as the best one strongly depends on temporal characteristics of answer arrivals. We then show that our understanding of such properties is naturally applicable to predicting several important quantities, including the long-term value of the question and its answers, as well as whether a question requires a better answer. Finally, we discuss the implications of these results for the design of Q&A sites.

Categories and Subject Descriptors: H.3.4 [**Information Storage and Retrieval**]: Systems and Software.
General Terms: Experimentation, Human Factors.
Keywords: Question-answering, reputation, value prediction.

1. INTRODUCTION

Question-answering sites — in which people pose questions to a community of Internet users — have evolved steadily over the past half-decade. One direction this evolution has taken is the development and maturation of sites such as Stack Overflow and Quora built around focused communities in which a significant fraction of the participants have deep expertise in the domain area. One consequence of this trend is that the content on these question-answering sites increasingly has lasting value: since questions and answers are saved on the site and often prominently ranked via search engines, people in the future who may not even be a priori aware of the site can be directed to the information there. Thus, rather than viewing each answer principally in terms of the immediate information need of the question-asker, the focus in recent years has broadened to further include the potential long-lasting value to people in the future who might have a similar question.

Given these developments, there is a clear opportunity to add value for both the producers and consumers of information on these sites by developing techniques that can analyze and extract valuable information from the community dynamics taking place. For consumers of information, there is the potential to identify and highlight questions of lasting value as soon as possible after they have appeared on the site, so that users can be directed to them. For producers of information — experts who are able to answer difficult questions on the site — there is the potential to identify questions that have not yet been successfully answered, so as to highlight them for increased attention.

A number of interesting lines of recent work have pursued related issues through a focus on the question-answer pair as a basic unit of analysis. Recent work in information retrieval, for example, has proposed methods by which high-quality question-answer pairs can be extracted and hence used for people who have the same (or similar) questions [15].

A systemic view of question-answering sites. Here we develop an alternate approach for extracting information from the activity on question-answering sites. Rather than considering free-standing question-answer pairs, we consider questions together with their set of corresponding answers. There are two aspects to this view — one at the question level, and another at the full site level.

First, as questions on these sites become more complex, single questions often generate multiple good answers produced by different experts who explore distinct aspects of the problem. As one of many prototypical examples, a question like "How do you format a JSON date in jQuery?" on Stack Overflow generates multiple useful responses; the answerers and subsequent commenters then differentiate among the several approaches and debate their relative merits. In this respect, the full set of answers constitutes an investigation of issues relevant to the original question that would be lost if any one of the answers — even a very good one — were viewed in isolation. Thus, when one talks about the creation of long-lasting value on a site like Stack Overflow, we claim that it is the question as well as all the corresponding answers that *together* bring long-lasting value to the site.

KDD'12, August 12–16, 2012, Beijing, China.

Second, in order to understand whether the question has been sufficiently answered, there is useful information residing in the community dynamics that govern the site as a whole — the reputation mechanism on a site like Stack Overflow both provides information about levels of community involvement, as well as provides incentives for effective contributions and good behavior. As we will see, properties such as reputation and community involvement also serve as correlates for further forms of behavior, including the dynamics of how users arrive to answer new questions that are posed, and how their answers receive approval or disapproval from the community.

Overview of Results. To make progress on the issues discussed above, we formulate two concrete tasks that capture the potential applications of this type of analysis for users of question-answering sites. The first task, motivated by the goals of information consumers on these sites, is the *prediction of long-lasting value*: given the activity on a question within a short interval after it was posed, can we tell whether it will continue to draw attention long into the future? The second task, motivated by the potential to elicit further contributions from experts, is the *prediction of whether a question has been sufficiently answered*: given the answers to a question so far, and the activity around the question, can we tell whether the needs of the question-asker have been met yet?

We develop approaches to these tasks using data from Stack Overflow, which is an ideal domain for considering these issues for several reasons. The first is due to its scale and adoption; it is one of the most successful focused question-answering sites on the web, and has a very active user community in which more than 90% of the questions posed receive an answer that is formally accepted by the question-asker. But beyond the activity on the site itself, Stack Overflow has played a major role in shaping the current paradigm for on-line question-answering, as more than 80 other Q&A sites have adopted the same basic platform. For our purposes, what is important is that Stack Overflow exhibits a set of basic properties that are now present in a wide range of focused Q&A sites: complex questions on a focused domain, active engagement by its users, and a substantial number of experts.

In order to address our two basic tasks on Stack Overflow, we begin by identifying sources of latent information in the community activity on the site that can be used for analysis. There is a rich pattern of behavior on Stack Overflow that generates such information: for each question on Stack Overflow, the answers (as well as the question itself) can receive positive and negative votes from members of the community, signaling evaluations of quality; independently of this, the user who posed the question may at any point decide to *accept* one of the answers. All of these contribute to a user's numerical *reputation score* on the site. Meanwhile, the question itself acquires attention from users other than its answerers, as people vote on the question and the answers, and arrive to view it from outside the site.

From our analysis of these processes, we identify two important but subtle principles that help drive the process of question-answering in this domain. These principles provide an organizing framework as well as specific features for our approach to the two tasks we have defined. The first principle is that the wide range of expertise levels lead to a kind of aggregate sequencing of the contributed answers to a question, with the most expert users generally moving first. Thus, although there is no explicit structure on the site that formalizes this dynamic, we can think of users as conceptually organized into a kind of latent "pyramid," with expert users at the top; a question enters at the top of the pyramid, where it is first considered by the elites, after which it progressively filters down through the reputation levels if it remains unanswered. This mental image is a simplification, but it is a useful guide for thinking about how expertise, answer speed, and content quality inter-relate.

The second principle we identify is that a higher activity level around a question not only signals the potential interest in the question, but in aggregate it also tends to benefit *all* the answerers of the question, in terms of the evaluation and reputation increases they receive. Thus, although a question-asker can only formally accept one of the answers, it is too simple a view to consider the multiple answers as existing in a state of pure competition. Rather, high activity tends to correspond to the presence of multiple answers that receive endorsement from the community more broadly, and hence hints at the type of lasting value we are seeking.

Following our discussion of the evidence for these two principles, we show that features based on this view lead to performance on our two tasks that improves significantly on natural baselines. More precisely, for predicting whether a question will have long-lasting value, we find that features of the answer arrival dynamics within as little as an hour after the question is posed can be effective at predicting whether the number of pageviews to the question will be high or low *a year later*. Our formulation of these features is motivated by the latent expertise pyramid discussed above. Moreover, we find that the number of answers to the question, and related measures, are particularly powerful features for this task, reinforcing our premise that questions on a site such as Stack Overflow acquire greater value when they attract a diverse set of answers.

For our second task, identifying questions that have not been resolved to the satisfaction of the question-asker, we establish a way of evaluating our predictions by making use of instances in which the questioner returns to offer a "bounty" for a better answer to the question. Here too we find that features based on the underlying community processes can lead to effective prediction; on the other hand, it is interesting that the actual speed of answer arrival is much less informative for this task.

Overall, our goal is to contribute to a broader investigation of this perspective on question-answering sites, and our performance on these tasks suggests that features arising from the community dynamics on a site such as Stack Overflow can provide important information beyond simply considering individual question-answer pairs.

2. RELATED WORK

Community question answering websites have been studied from several different perspectives. The first is the study of user communities, where research has investigated users, their interests and motivation for contribution [1, 19, 4]. Insights from such studies informed the design of network-based ranking algorithms for identifying users with high expertise [10, 17, 25, 26].

The second is the perspective of information retrieval where a question is viewed as a "query" and answers could be thought of as "results" [15, 8, 16, 2, 9]. One goal of this line of work is to take a question with multiple answers and extract the answer of best quality or the answer that is most related to a particular search query. This can be viewed as an attempt to "declutter" the question-answering pages by focusing on one "best" answer for each question. The exact problem is often formalized as a classification task of trying to predict whether a single given answer is of high quality (under various notions of quality [21]) with respect to a particular question. In our work, however, we recognize that users get significant benefit from good answers produced by diverse experts. In this respect the full set of answers constitutes a discussion of competing approaches that would be lost if any one of the answers were viewed in isolation. Models of question answering communities as zero-sum two-sided markets of question askers and answers have

Users	440K (198K questioners, 71K answerers)
Questions	1M (69% with accepted answer)
Answers	2.8M (26% marked as accepted)
Votes	7.6M (93% positive)
Favorites	775K actions on 318K questions

Table 1: Statistics of the Stack Overflow dataset.

also emerged [11] with the goal of explaining the dynamics and stability of Q&A communities.

Broadly related to our prediction tasks of long-term question value and question hardness is the work on novelty and popularity of online content [24, 20, 22], which is wrapped up with the broader theme of the role of search engines in online content discovery [6]. Another more distantly related line of work is on deliberation, voting and explicit user feedback in online communities [5, 12, 14]. While this line of work mainly seeks to predict user voting behaviors [3, 7, 13], our work attempts to identify early community-based indicators of question and answer quality.

Lastly, the Stack Overflow and the related Math Overflow question answering communities have been studied in the past for correlating user reputation and the perceived answer quality [23]. Recently, Oktay et al. studied the dynamics of Stack Overflow answerer arrivals [18] with a focus on demonstrating the use of several quasi-experimental designs to establish causal relationships in social media. Their observation relevant for our work here is that even after the best answer has been identified by the question asker, answers to the question keep arriving. In the light of our findings here this can be interpreted as an effort by the Stack Overflow community to provide answers that go beyond the current information need of the question asker.

3. DATASET DESCRIPTION

General question answering sites such as Yahoo! Answers, Quora, and others support many different types of interaction: expertise sharing, discussion, everyday advice, and moral support [1]. On the other hand, focused Q&A sites, like Stack Overflow, the programming-related Q&A site we study, differ from these broad interest sites in that all questions are meant to be objective and factually answerable – most subjective questions are frowned upon by the Stack Overflow community. Stack Overflow questions are generally hard, in the sense that relatively few people can provide a sufficient answer. Deep expertise and domain knowledge is thus often essential to providing a good answer. As mentioned in the introduction, this type of focused Q&A model has been extremely successful.

Stack Overflow's success is largely due to the engaged and active user community that collaboratively manages the site. Content is heavily curated by the community; for example, duplicate questions are quickly flagged as such and merged with existing questions, and posts considered to be unhelpful (unrelated answers, commentary on other answers, etc.) are removed. As a result of this self-regulation, content on Stack Overflow tends to be of very high quality. We obtained a complete trace of all the actions on the Stack Overflow website between its inception on July 31, 2008 and December 31, 2010. The data is publicly available off the Stack Overflow site and the basic statistics are shown in Table 1.

There is a rich set of actions a user can perform on Stack Overflow, which grows as a user builds up reputation on the site. The most basic actions are asking and answering questions. Both questions and answers can be upvoted or downvoted by other users. The basic mode of viewing content is from the *question page*, which lists a given question along with all the answers to the question and their respective votes. The vote score on an answer, the difference between the number of updates and downvotes it receives, determines the relative ordering in which it is displayed on the question page. The questioner can select an answer as the *accepted answer* at any point in time, indicating that it was the "best" answer to his/her question. Users may comment on other questions and answers and also vote on the comments. Any user may mark a question as a *favorite*, bookmarking it for future reference.

Action	Reputation change
Answer is upvoted	+10
Answer is downvoted	-2 (-1 to voter)
Answer is accepted	+15 (+2 to acceptor)
Question is upvoted	+5
Question is downvoted	-2 (-1 to voter)
Answer wins bounty	+bounty amount
Offer bounty	-bounty amount
Answer marked as spam	-100

Table 2: Stack Overflow's reputation system.

The reputation system on Stack Overflow is designed incentivize users to produce high-quality content and to be generally engaged with the site. Table 2 shows how reputation is gained and lost. Some actions have effects on two users' reputations, *e.g.* if user A downvotes an answer by user B, then B loses 2 reputation points and A loses 1. The ability to vote on answers is not granted to new users, but is earned relatively quickly, requiring 15 points for the right to upvote and 125 for the right to downvote. A user also has the ability to offer a *bounty* on their question if they want to provide an additional incentives for good answers. The questioner funds the award with their own reputation (it must be between 50 and 500 reputation points). A bounty can be offered only after two days have elapsed since the question was asked, and a bounty period of 1 week begins. At any time the questioner may decide to award the bounty to one of the answers.

4. DESCRIPTION OF TASKS

We first introduce the two prediction tasks that motivate our analyses. Both are drawn from practical problems that occur naturally on Q&A sites: the first is predicting the long-term interest and value of a question page; the second is predicting whether a question has been sufficiently answered or not. In both cases, we describe quantitative proxies for these properties that we use in prediction.

Our primary goal in formulating these tasks is to use them as an analysis framework, assessing how the information about community processes can be used to determine value on Q&A sites. As such, they are structured to explore relative performance gains from different types of information, rather than for optimizing raw performance per se.

4.1 Predicting long-term value of a question

As we discussed in the introduction, Q&A sites have increasingly shifted from revolving around satisfying the questioner's information need to building up repositories of useful knowledge about a given question. Thus, predicting which question pages have lasting value and garner a lot of attention — as well as understanding which properties are associated with lasting value — is of central interest to maintainers of a question answering community. Question pages that show early signs of long-term value could be displayed more prominently on the site or could be recommended to experts to contribute answers. The insights we derive in the next section can provide effective approaches for this task.

First, we note that surprisingly good performance on this task is possible due to the fact that the time scales on which social processes for each question occur are in fact a bit complex: the typical question has a "fast" phase when it acquires answers and votes, and a "slow" phase in which members of the community indicate its longer-term value — both by visiting the question page and through the mechanism of *favoriting*. The majority of answers and votes on both questions and answers occur within the first day after the question is asked (and the median *response time*, how long it takes for a question to be first answered, is just 12 minutes across Stack Overflow's entire history).

However, we find strong evidence that, although most of the votes and answers arrive within a day of the question creation, question pages are of lasting value: for example, only 37% of favorites on a question arrive within the same time frame. After this initial period, favorites accumulate extremely gradually over time. This is consistent with a two-phase view of the lifecycle of a question page — first there is a "construction" phase, when most of the answering and voting (signaling of quality) take place, after which follows a long period of existence in mostly static form as a potentially valuable public resource to future would-be questioners.

4.2 Predicting whether a question has been sufficiently answered

Our second task forms a natural complement to the first: whereas before we aim to predict the long-lasting value of the question, now we try to tell if a question has been satisfactorily answered or not. This would be obviously useful on Q&A sites: attention could be directed towards currently unsatisfactory question pages to help turn them into useful resources.

On Stack Overflow, a questioner can decide to offer a reputation award (a *bounty*) on her question. If this happens, it is safe to assume that the question has not been answered to the questioner's satisfaction yet — otherwise she would not spend her reputation points on the bounty. On the other hand, if the questioner accepts an existing answer, we can say that the questioner is satisfied. In this task, we consider predicting if a bounty will be offered on a question or if the questioner will accept an existing answer.

Now that we've introduced our motivating tasks, predicting two complementary properties of questions, we explore the various community processes that lead to the creation of question pages. After this exploration, we will show that the information we derive from these processes helps us accurately predict both properties.

5. COMMUNITY DYNAMICS OF QUESTION ANSWERING

The Stack Overflow community responds to questions in two main ways: by answering them, and by voting on the answers and the question. We observe these two processes, answering and voting, as occurring simultaneously. In this section, we investigate some of the basic principles that govern these community processes at work. We group this analysis into two parts, corresponding to the answering and voting processes, respectively: (1) the ways in which reputation interacts with the arrival of users to answer a given question; and (2) the consequences of a question's overall level of activity. In these two parts, we identify some basic and recurring phenomena that will be useful when we develop techniques for our prediction tasks in the following section.

5.1 A Reputation Pyramid

There is an incentive to answer questions quickly on Stack Overflow, since many question-askers will accept the first answer that they deem satisfactory, thereby conferring reputation on the answerer. Hence, we expect to see that the higher a user's reputation, the faster he or she answers questions.

In Figure 1 we examine how median answerer reputation varies with the time-rank of an answer for questions with a fixed number of answers. We find that the highest-reputation answerers do usually occur earlier in the time-ordering of answers on a question.

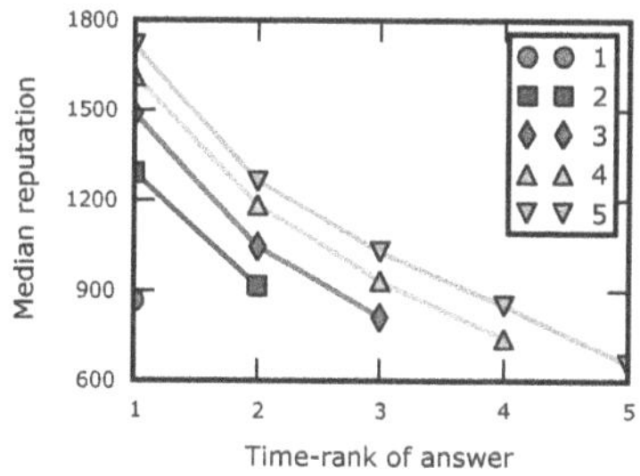

Figure 1: Median reputation versus answer time-rank. Questions with a total of 1 to 5 answers plotted (one curve each). High reputation users tend to answer early.

Reputation clearly decreases with increasing rank within a question, which is evidence of a direct relationship between reputation and answer speed.

Instead of the time-order of answers, we can also consider wall-clock time — how fast users of various reputation levels respond to questions. Here we find the same relationship: the higher the reputation, the quicker the user is to reply to a question. The typical (i.e. modal) response time is approximately the same — around 5 minutes — for all levels of reputation; the main difference is that high-reputation users hit this target of 5 minutes on a much larger fraction of the questions they answer.

These results suggest the conceptual picture mentioned in the introduction, in which users are organized in a *reputation pyramid*, with the highest-reputation users at the top and the lowest-reputation users at the bottom. A question enters the system at the top of the pyramid, where it is first considered by the highest-reputation users, then progressively percolates down through the reputation levels if it remains unanswered. This is a simplified picture of answering dynamics, but it is a useful conceptual picture for thinking about how answer speed, reputation, and content quality inter-relate. We stress that we are not claiming such an explicit vertical organizational structure exists on Stack Overflow; rather we are pointing out that many of the patterns we observe in this section are consistent with this picture of implicit behavior. For example, it helps explain the finding shown in Figure 2: the longer a question goes unanswered, the more likely it is that no satisfactory answer will be given (i.e. no answer will be accepted). Our picture of a question descending downward through reputation layers suggests this effect may at least partially be due to lower-reputation users becoming disproportionately likely to give a first answer the longer the question goes unanswered. The fact that lower reputation users give lower-quality answers on average (as measured in votes from other users) could then contribute to the observed relationship. We note that there could well be other factors contributing to the effect seen in Figure 2, including the fact that questions on which the first answer is slow to arrive may be more difficult or more idiosyncratic. These results suggest that high-value questions tend to be answered quickly and by high-reputation users, trends that we'll exploit in our prediction tasks.

These connections between reputation and answer speed show that the incentives arising from Stack Overflow's reputation system are producing behavior beneficial to the site. High-reputation users achieve their reputations largely by answering questions quickly and correctly, and presumably gain utility by doing so. From the questioner's perspective, the order in which answerers usually answer questions (high to low reputation) is ideal, since the questioner's expected time to receive a good answer is minimized.

Homophily by reputation. We observe that all reputation levels gain the majority of their reputation from receiving upvotes on

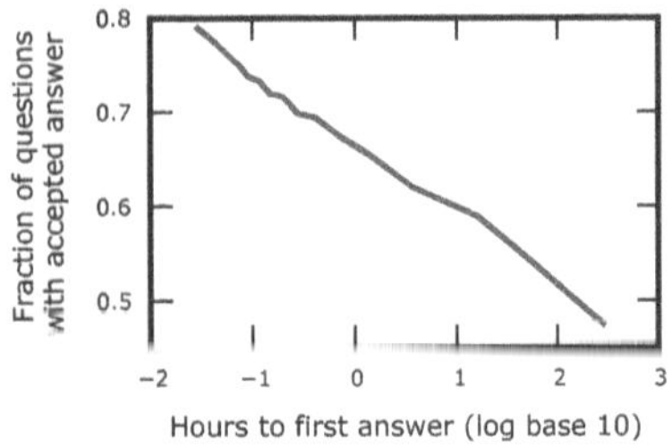

Figure 2: Fraction of questions with the accepted answer as a function of the time for the first answer to arrive. The longer the wait to get the first answer, the less likely it is for any answer to be eventually accepted.

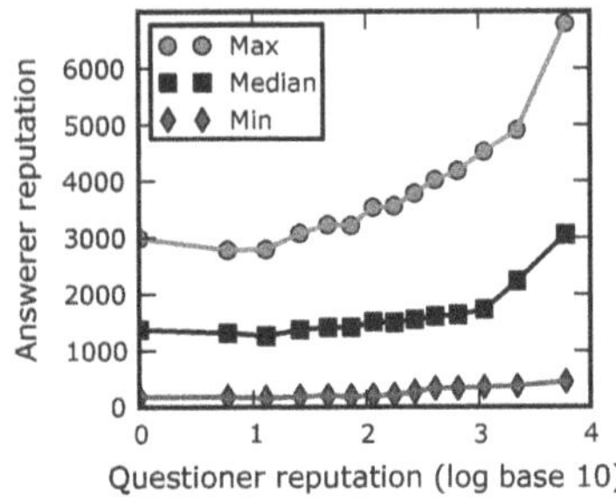

Figure 3: Max/median/min answerer reputation as a function of the questioner reputation.

their answers. This highlights an interesting fact about Stack Overflow: users who have attained upper-tier reputations are generally "answer-dominant": they gain the bulk of their reputation from answering others' questions well, and do not ask many questions of their own. Also, we see that the "elites", those users who have achieved over 100K reputation, gain significantly more of their reputation from their answers being accepted than other reputations levels, and correspondingly less from receiving upvotes (plot not shown due to space constraints). This fact about elites, however, appears to be largely due to an idiosyncrasy of the reputation system on Stack Overflow: once users gain 200 points in a day, they can only gain more from either having their answers selected or winning bounties. Since only the highest-reputation users hit this daily cap on a regular basis, we see a shift in the source of their reputation from upvotes to having answers accepted.

Having established that high-reputation users tend to gain most of their reputation from answering questions, one can ask whether there is any further stratification in *which* questions the high-reputation users answer. For example, one might have conjectured that there is a hierarchy of questioners and answerers, with high-status answerers reserving their efforts for questions from high-status questioners. But we do not see strong evidence for such a hierarchy; for example, Figure 3 shows that except at the highest levels of reputation, the median reputation of a question's answerer depends very little on the reputation of the user asking the question, and the maximum reputation among the answerers increases only weakly in the questioner's reputation. Thus, the real picture seems to be that high-reputation users are fairly omnivorous in the questions they answer.[1]

Although there isn't a strong connection between the questioner and answerer reputations, there could still be correlations between the reputations of answerers who answer the same questions. Indeed, our mental picture of a question floating down through different reputation levels suggests this might be the case — and we now show that it is.

A first approach to doing this is to compute the correlation coefficient between the reputations of co-answerers — pairs of users who answer the same question. To determine whether the correlation coefficient is indicative of homophily by reputation (i.e. the tendency of users with similar reputations to answer the same question) we compare it to the correlation coefficient for reputations of co-answerers in a randomized baseline. For this baseline, we consider the bipartite graph formed by questions on one side and answerers on the other, and with a link between a question Q_i and an answerer A_j if A_j answered Q_i. We then randomly rewire the bipartite graph while preserving the degrees on the left and right; this gives us our randomized baseline pattern of co-answering. The correlation coefficient between the reputations of the real co-answerers is 0.11 and the correlation coefficient between the reputations of the co-answerers in the randomized baseline is 0.031 (we use reputations on a log scale). This calculation shows that answerers with similar reputations are much more likely to answer the same question than would be expected by random chance given the distributions of answers by reputation. Thus, it seems that answerers in a given reputation level are attracted to the same sorts of questions, and that the source of this attraction is not the reputation of the questioner (due to Figure 3).

This previous calculation ignores the time-ordering in which the answers arrive. We now carry out a computation to answer the following question: What are the characteristics of *ordered* reputations on questions? Let r_i denote the reputation of the answerer who authors the i-th answer to arrive. Our question is: when a user with reputation r_1 first answers a question, what is then the conditional distribution over reputations of the second answerer (provided there is a second answerer)? In Figure 4 we show this conditional distribution, subtracted from the overall distribution of r_2 for the full population restricted to the set of response times in the figure (we restricted to questions where first answer comes in 6 minutes after the question). As the figures show, when the first answerer has high reputation, then high reputations are overrepresented in the population of second answerers; and correspondingly, when the first answerer has low reputation, the second answer has an elevated chance of having low reputation as well. Thus, this provides another indication of homophily by reputation among the answerers of a question. This is another phenomenon that provides useful information for the tasks we introduced in Section 4.

Interleaved processes of question answering and voting. Recall our observation from the beginning of this section about answers and the votes they receive, that one should think of the arrival of answers and votes as simultaneous. We find that they are in fact interleaving — both accumulate during the initial "fast" phase after a question is posed. The effect of this can be seen in Figure 5(a), which shows the reputation gained by an answer when it is the i-th answer to arrive out of k total answers. The linear decrease in i and the fact that the line is shifted upward for larger k can both be explained by the fact that answers and votes are arriving in an interleaved fashion: this means that earlier answers have more time to receive votes (hence the linear decrease in i), and as k grows, it means that the arrival process goes on longer, resulting in more votes for all answers.

There are some other aspects of this arrival process that stand largely as open questions, however. For example, we see in Figure 5(b) that the fraction of positive votes for the i-th answer out of k *increases* with i. (Note that all the fractions are very close to 1, so this is a distinction involving small differences.) There are

[1]Indeed, this may be almost by necessity: if relatively few high-reputation users ask questions, then one cannot acquire a very high reputation by restricting one's activities to questions from this subset.

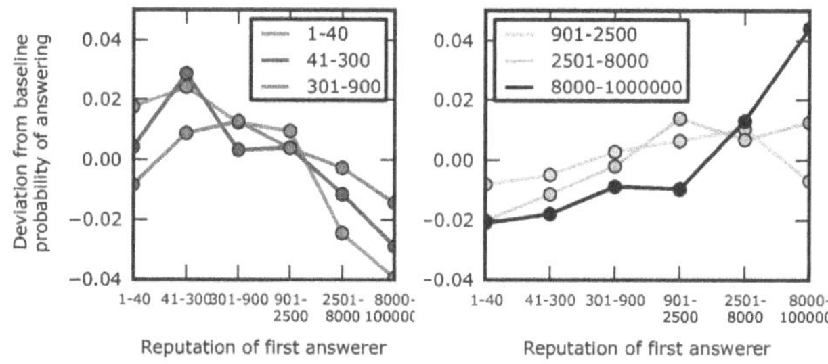

Figure 4: Each curve shows how, given the reputation of the second answerer on a two-answer question, the likelihood of answering second deviates from a uniform baseline as a function of the reputation of the first answerer. The curves on the left (showing the bottom three reputation levels) slope downward, indicating lower reputation levels are more likely to answer questions second if the first answerer also has low reputation; and the curves on the right (showing the top three reputation levels) slope upward, illustrating an analogous homophily by reputation effect.

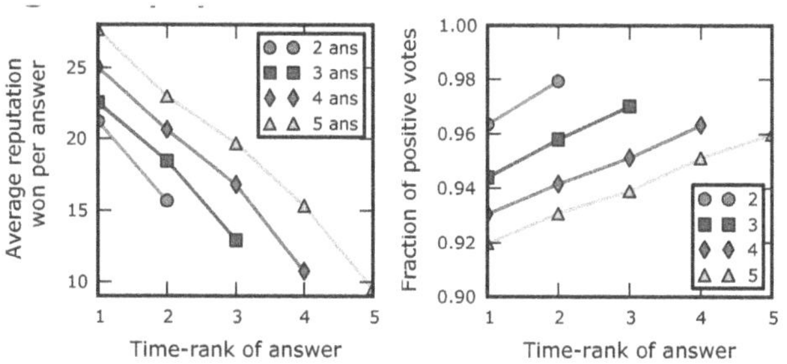

Figure 5: (left) Average reputation points won, (right) Fraction of positive votes on a answer as a function of answer-rank i when the total of k were given to the question.

several possible conjectures for this increasing behavior; for example, the fact that early answers receive negative votes may be the reason that the user posing the question allows answers to continue accumulating before accepting one of them.

5.2 The Activity Level of a Question

In the previous section we analyzed various aspects of the answer arrival process, and how our model of the reputation pyramid explains many of the phenomena we observe. Now we turn our attention to the other interleaved community process on questions: voting. Specifically, we consider the level of activity on a question, and its consequences for how both the answers and the question itself are evaluated by the community. Interestingly, when a question receives many answers, all the answerers benefit in terms of reputation gained, and the question receives more favorites over time. Thus, instead of viewing the answers as competing with one another for the community's limited attention, it appears that an essentially opposite view is more apt, and one in keeping with a central premise of the paper — that heightened activity around a question leads to greater value.

Higher activity produces benefits. As we previously discussed, questions on Stack Overflow are supposed to be answerable factually and objectively (if they're not, then they're marked as a "Community Wiki" question and actions on them do not count towards one's reputation score). This creates an incentive to answer quickly, since it is likely that the first correct answer may well be accepted. (Of course, as highlighted in the introduction, there are better and worse ways to give a factual answer — being grounded in fact is

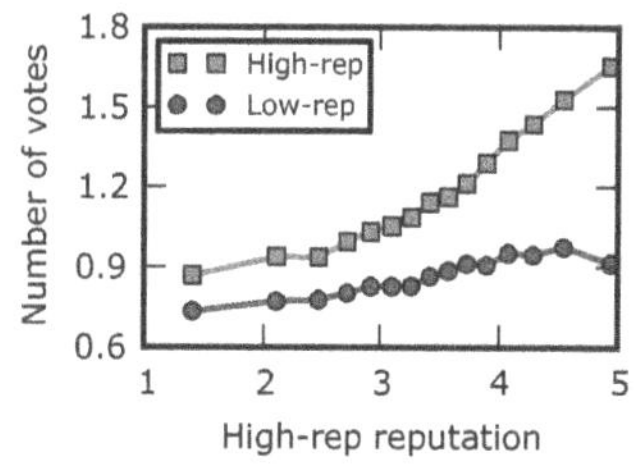

Figure 6: Average number of votes per answer for both answerers on a 2-answer question as a function of the higher answerer reputation. Lower reputation fixed between 75-125. High reputation plotted on a logarithmic (base 10) scale.

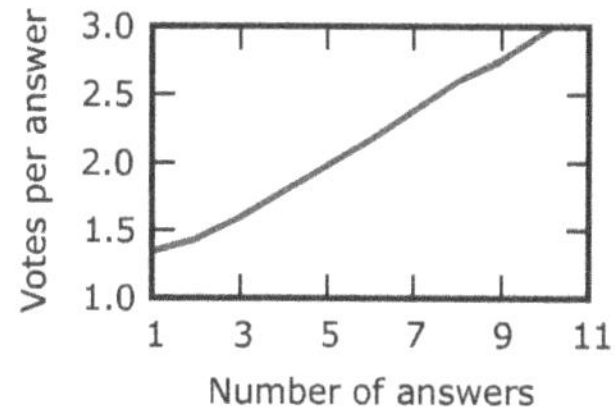

Figure 7: Number of votes per answer as a function of the number of answers on the question.

not the only prerequisite for being a good answer). However, this raises an interesting question: Does this mean that answers compete with each other for votes — that answers act as players in a zero-sum game? Or is it that answers are judged more by their inherent quality than in relation with the other answers to the question? Or perhaps there is some other phenomenon at work.

We answer this question with the following experiment. Let r_i denote the reputation of the i-th answerer, as before, and let v_i denote the vote score of the i-th answer. We now fix r_2 and observe how v_2 varies as a function of r_1. If the "competition" theory is correct, then we would expect v_2 to drop as r_1 is increased, since higher-reputation users are more likely to produce the correct answer quickly. If answers are judged by their inherent quality alone, we would expect v_2 to stay roughly the same. We show the relationship in Figure 6. Surprisingly, v_2 goes *up* as r_1 is increased. Clearly the answers are not playing a zero-sum game. We observe this effect because questions with high-reputation users participating receive more attention than average. As r_1 increases, both $v_1/(v_1 + v_2)$ and v_2 increase. This means the high-reputation user increasingly "wins" the question on a relative scale (as measured in the share of the votes), but the lower-reputation user still gains on an absolute scale (by gaining more votes).

Next, we examine how the number of votes per answer varies with the number of answers on the question. Again, if the first theory (that answers compete for votes) is correct, then we would expect that the number of votes per answer decreases with the number of answers since more answers are competing to be the best. As can be seen in Figure 7, the opposite is again true: the more answers there are, the higher the votes-to-answers ratio. This is primarily due to the fact that questions with many answers receive a large amount of attention. Still, the fact that answers on question with many answers get more votes on average than votes with fewer "competitors" reinforces the point that answering and voting on Stack Overflow is not a zero-sum game. Even if answers compete for "individual" votes, we've seen that the increased attention on your answer both from having higher-reputation competitors and from having more competitors more than makes up for any competition between answers.

Finally, we show that questions with more answers are also viewed as more valuable by the community over the long time scale dur-

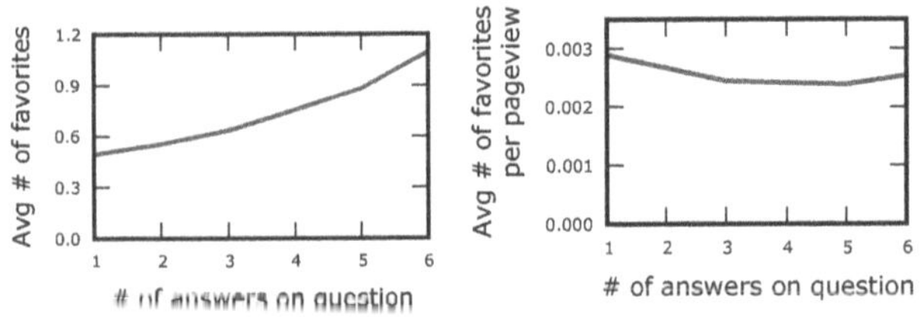

Figure 8: (Left) Number of question favorites plotted against the number of answers over all questions where the maximum answer vote score is 5. (Right) Same plot normalized by pageviews.

ing which the question is favorited. In Figure 8 we consider questions in which we fix the evaluation of the "best" answer — that is, we look at questions in which the highest-voted answer always received exactly five votes. Given a best answer of fixed quality, does it help to have additional answers? Figure 8 shows that the number of users favoriting the question indeed increases monotonically in the number of answers.

Again, this increase seems largely due to the increased activity around a question — though it is worth noting that this is increased activity in a highly generalized sense, since the favoriting is occurring over a significant time period, long after the burst of answering and voting on the question has subsided. In Figure 8 we see that the probability a user chooses to favorite a question they are viewing remains roughly constant with the number of answers. Thus, the correct way to view this may be as follows: having more answers increases the number of viewers of the question in the long term, and it does so with no downside in the *rate* of favoriting — each given user is still equally likely to favorite the question.

This again fits closely with a central theme of the introduction. Rather than viewing multiple answers to a question as a form of "clutter" that needs to be cleaned up, we see here that questions with multiple answers produce benefits in the form of increased attention, and they do this without suffering any loss in the chance that a reader of the question will choose it as a favorite.

6. PREDICTION TASKS

The previous section presented a set of principles governing the community process of question-answering on Stack Overflow. Now we show that this new understanding is directly applicable to the two prediction tasks introduced in Section 4. First we introduce the features that our analyses suggest would be helpful for the tasks.

Features used for learning. Overall, we explore four different classes of features (27 features in all) describing static and dynamic properties of the answering process to a given question. Note that the actual models we present in this section will not necessarily include all the features. Our aim here is to illustrate the space of features that arise from our findings in the previous sections. We then focus on building explanatory models using only the most essential features. The full set of features we consider is as follows:

- **Questioner features** (S_A), 4 features total: questioner reputation, # of questioner's questions and answers, questioner's percentage of accepted answers on their previous questions.
- **Activity and Q/A quality measures** (S_B), 8 features total: # of favorites, # of page views, # positive and negative votes on question, # of answers, maximum answerer reputation, highest answer score, reputation of answerer who wrote highest-scoring answer,
- **Community process features** (S_C), 8 features total: average answerer reputation, median answerer reputation, fraction of sum of answerer reputations contributed by max answerer reputation, sum of answerer reputations, length of answer by highest-reputation answerer, # of comments on answer by highest-reputation answerer, length of highest-scoring answer, # of comments on highest-scoring answer.
- **Temporal process features** (S_D), 7 features total: average time between answers, median time between answers, minimum time between answers, time-rank of highest-scoring answer, wall-clock time elapsed between question creation and highest-scoring answer, time-rank of answer by highest-reputation answerer, wall-clock time elapsed between question creation and answer by highest-reputation answerer.

6.1 Predicting long-lasting value

Recall from Section 4.1 that our first task is to predict long-lasting value of a question together with its answers.

Experimental setup. We use the number of pageviews of a question with its answers in a given time-frame as our measure of the amount of attention the question receives and thus as a proxy of its long-term value. The number of times the question was favorited would be an alternate proxy for value; however, we consider the number of pageviews (after controlling for question age) to be a better choice for several reasons: the number of pageviews is a large and robust number, whereas the number of favorites is quite sparse for most questions, and hence a noisy indicator of the community's reaction to the question. Moreover, only registered users can favorite a question, whereas the full Internet population contributes to its pageviews — hence the latter measure is consistent with our goal of viewing the question with its answers as having value that transcends the question-answering community itself.

To control for the age of the question and Stack Overflow's ever-increasing popularity, we restrict our attention to questions created in the same month and predict the number of pageviews one year later. We only consider questions in which the first answer arrives within an hour after the question was asked (otherwise the question almost certainly doesn't receive a lot of attention). We formulate the task of predicting pageviews as a binary classification task[2], and report our performance on two setups: in the first case, the response variable is whether the question's number of pageviews is in the bottom or top quartile of the questions in our controlled sample (thus excluding the middle half of the dataset), and in the second case the response variable is whether the question's number of pageviews is in the bottom or top half of the questions (thus using the entire dataset). The full dataset consists of 28,722 examples, and our dataset is balanced (the response variable is split 50-50) in both cases by construction.

Since the practical application of this task would be to predict question quality early on in a question's lifetime, we perform this task using only the information available up to a given amount time after the question is asked. The time-frames we consider are 1, 3, 24, and 72 hours after the question is posted[3].

We performed feature selection and found a core set of 8 features that we use in this task: questioner reputation (log scale), # of questions the questioner has asked (log scale), # of answers on the question, sum of scores on answers to question, # of comments on highest-reputation answerer, and 3 features of the highest-scoring answer: length, # of comments on it, and how long after question creation it was written. We call this set S_8.

[2]Formulating this task as a regression problem puts too much emphasis on predicting the exact number of pageviews, and detracts from the main object of interest to a Q&A site operator: whether a page will be of high or low value in the long run.

[3]Another interesting feature is the number of pageviews in this short time-frame; however, we do not have access to such data.

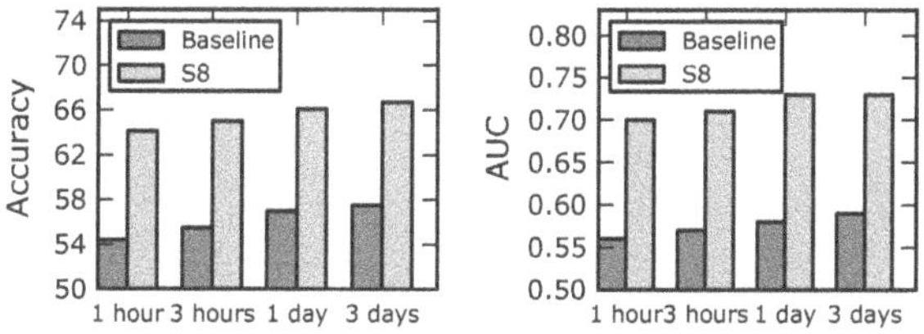

(a) Predicting top quartile vs. bottom quartile

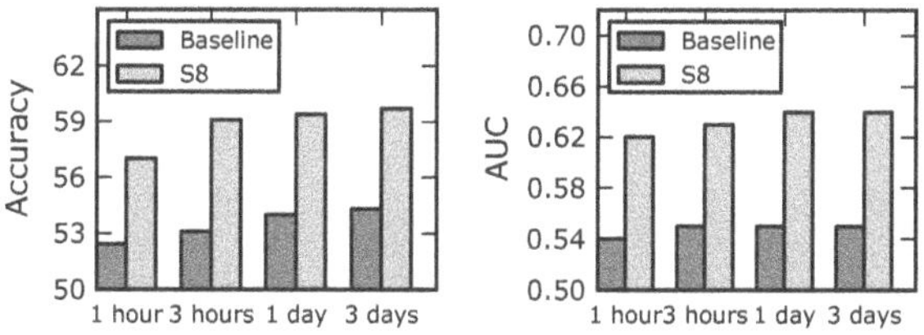

(b) Predicting top half vs. bottom half

Figure 9: Results of pageview prediction. Notice strong absolute and also relative performance of our method. (left) Accuracy, (right) Area under ROC curve.

We standardize all the features. For interpretability and ease of comparison, we use a logistic regression classifier, perform 10-fold cross validation and report classification accuracy and the area under the ROC curve (AUC).

To establish a baseline set of features we notice that on Stack Overflow there are two main mechanisms by which users can directly evaluate a question's quality: they can upvote or downvote it, and they can mark it as a favorite. Since these are ways Stack Overflow directly asks users about question quality, they should be strong predictors on this task. Therefore, we compare our features against these two "crowd-sourced" features: # of favorites on the question, # of positive minus negative votes on the question.

Experimental results. Figure 9a gives the results of the prediction task with the top-vs-bottom quartile setup. Surprisingly, the baseline only gives less than 5% improvement in accuracy over random guessing 1 hour after the question was asked.[4] This means that the number of votes and the favorites, which are two direct signals of question interestingness and value from the Stack Overflow user community, only slightly improves over random guessing. Extending the time window to 3 days — after which most answers, votes, and a large fraction of favorites have arrived (see Section 5) — only improves this to a 7.5% accuracy gain over random guessing. However, the community process and dynamics features (S_8) inspired by our previous analyses double the improvement to 9-10% in accuracy and 14-15 AUC points in each time frame. We achieve 0.70 AUC using the S_8 features available in the hour after the question was asked; the baseline only scores 0.56 AUC in the same time frame. Figure 9b shows that the results are similar when we don't exclude the middle half of examples, except that the absolute performance levels drop since the output variable is inherently noisier (i.e. differentiating between the 52nd and 48th percentiles is harder than differentiating between the 77th and 23rd percentiles).

To fully appreciate the result we emphasize that we are extracting features available only 1 hour after the question was asked and are predicting question pageviews 1 year in the future. We find it remarkable that only after a single hour there is already enough signal to predict the long-term question-page value, and that much of

[4]One way to reconcile this weak improvement with the clear relationship between pageviews and favoriting is to recall the point made earlier that favorites are quite sparse, and so fail to provide information about many questions.

Feature	Coefficient
Number of answers	+0.61
Sum of answer scores	+0.47
# of questioner's questions (log scale)	-0.46
Length of highest-scoring answer	+0.38
Questioner's reputation (log scale)	+0.31
Time for highest-scoring answer to arrive	+0.22
# comments on highest-scoring answer	+0.19
# comments on highest-reputation answerer's answer	+0.17

Table 3: Relative importance of features for predicting long-lasting value of the question.

this signal comes from community features beyond simply looking at direct evaluations of the question.

Incorporating the rich contextual information found on the question page significantly helps predict eventual question attention and quality – even over directly asking Stack Overflow users. The relative importance of the S_8 features (aside from those included in the baseline) is listed in Table 3.

The single most important feature is the number of answers. This is already a strong indication that considering all of the answers instead of just one is helpful. Since the baseline knows the number of votes and favorites, this isn't purely an attention effect. The second-most informative feature provides another variation on our central theme of multiple good answers providing value over and above the best answer: the sum of the answer scores is more informative than any single feature of the highest-scoring answer. Interestingly, the effect of community interaction in the form of comments on answers also has significant predictive power. The fact that the time for the highest-scoring answer to arrive has a significant positive coefficient (meaning the *longer* it takes to arrive, the better the eventual question quality) is intriguing, and perhaps related to Figure 5, which shows that later answers get positive votes at a slightly higher rate. These results show that our findings in Section 5 significantly help predict the long-term value of question pages.

6.2 Predicting whether the question has been sufficiently answered

We now show that these same features also help on our second task: predicting if a question has been satisfactorily answered.

Experimental setup. Every question that eventually has a bounty offered on it (a "bounty question") has some number k of answers on it at the moment when the bounty is offered. Let B_k be the set of bounty questions with k answers prior to when the bounty is offered, and let A_k denote the set of non-bounty questions for which exactly k answers arrive before the questioner decides to accept one of them (and in which the questioner had less reputation points than required offer a bounty). Our classification task is then to use the information on a question page with k answers to predict whether it is a member of A_k or B_k. Since bounty questions are quite rare (there are 13K of them in total), we take a random sample of questions from A_k so that our dataset is balanced. We performed this prediction task for different values of k and the results were all qualitatively similar. We report our results for $k = 3$.

In contrast to the previous task, there is no natural baseline to compare to since Stack Overflow lacks a direct mechanism by which the user community could explicitly express that a question has not been satisfactorily answered thus far. Thus, instead of arbitrarily choosing certain features to act as a baseline, we study the performance of the four feature classes described at the outset.

Features used for learning. We again started with our full feature set $S_A \cup S_B \cup S_C \cup S_D$, and since we are given the exact number of answers so far (k), we also considered few additional features. Specifically, we computed the individual # of positive and negative vote counts for each answer (added to S_C), answerer reputations of

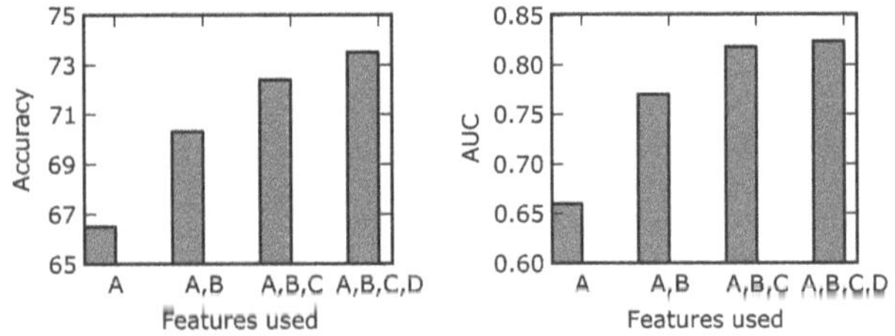

Figure 10: Results of bounty prediction. (left) Accuracy, (right) Area under the ROC curve.

each answer (added to S_C), and time between the answers (added to S_D) as additional features.

After conducting feature selection, we reduced our features to a smaller set of 18 features: 3 from S_A (questioner reputation, # of questioner's questions, and # of questioner's answers), 5 from S_B (# favorites on question, maximum answer score, maximum answerer reputation, and positive and negative question votes, 6 from S_C (average answerer reputation, # positive votes on last answer, # negative votes on 2nd answer, length of highest-scoring answer, length of answer given by highest-reputation answerer, and # comments on highest-scoring answer), and 4 from S_D: average time difference between answers, time difference between last 2 answers, time-rank of highest-scoring answer, and time-rank of answer by highest-reputation answerer. We add a prime to the names of the feature sets (*e.g.*, S'_A) to denote the subsets we chose.

Experimental results. The results for $k = 3$ are reported in Figure 10. Notice that the properties of the questioner on their own (S'_A) have good predictive power because high-reputation questioners can more easily afford to offer a reputation bounty. The page activity and question and answer quality measures (S'_B) are also useful predictors, as expected. But adding features incorporated from our study of the community processes governing Stack Overflow (S'_C and S'_D) gives a gain of nearly 5 AUC points over S'_A and S'_B. Again, we see that taking into account the rich interaction on the question page improves performance over even strong categories of features.

7. CONCLUSION

As question-answering sites grow in complexity, with more involved questions that are increasingly addressed by multiple experts, it becomes useful to think not just in terms of a "best" answer to a question but in terms of a set of answers and the community processes that produce them. We have seen how Stack Overflow, a site that exemplifies these aspects of question-answering, has a rich temporal structure that we have been able to use to identify important properties of a question together with its corresponding set of answers—specifically which questions and their answers are likely to be of lasting value, and which ones are in need of additional help from the community.

Our goal in this paper has been to start exploring the foundations for reasoning about community processes in question-answering. We anticipate that further analysis could potentially suggest richer ways of assessing expertise among users, identify a more intricate spectrum of genres among the questions that appear, and quantify more fully the role that incentives and competition play within a community as it answers questions.

Acknowledgements. We thank Stack Overflow for providing their data. This research has been supported in part by NSF CNS-1010921, IIS-1016909, IIS-1149837, IIS-1159679, IIS-0910664, CCF-0910940, and IIS-1016099, a Google Research Grant, a Yahoo Research Alliance Grant, the Albert Yu & Mary Bechmann Foundation, Boeing, Allyes, Samsung, Yahoo, an Alfred P. Sloan Fellowship, and a Microsoft Faculty Fellowship.

8. REFERENCES

[1] L. A. Adamic, J. Zhang, E. Bakshy, and M. S. Ackerman. Knowledge sharing and Yahoo Answers: everyone knows something. *WWW*, 2008.

[2] E. Agichtein, Y. Liu, and J. Bian. Modeling information-seeker satisfaction in community question answering. *ACM Trans. Knowl. Discov. Data*, 3(2009).

[3] A. Anderson, D. Huttenlocher, J. Kleinberg, and J. Leskovec. Effects of user similarity in social media. *WSDM*, 2012.

[4] C. Aperjis, B. A. Huberman, and F. Wu. Human speed-accuracy tradeoffs in search. *HICSS*, 2011.

[5] C. Danescu-Niculescu-Mizil, G. Kossinets, J. Kleinberg, L. Lee. How opinions are received by online communities: a case study on Amazon.com helpfulness votes. *WWW*, 2009.

[6] S. Fortunato, A. Flammini, F. Menczer, A. Vespignani. Topical interests and the mitigation of search engine bias. *Proc. Natl. Acad. Sci. USA*, 103(34):12684–12689, 2006.

[7] R. Guha, R. Kumar, P. Raghavan, and A. Tomkins. Propagation of trust and distrust. *WWW*, 2004.

[8] F. M. Harper, D. Raban, S. Rafaeli, and J. A. Konstan. Predictors of answer quality in online Q&A sites. *CHI*, 2008.

[9] J. Jeon, W. Croft, J. Lee, S. Park. A framework to predict the quality of answers with non-textual features. *SIGIR*, 2006.

[10] P. Jurczyk E. Agichtein. Discovering authorities in question answer communities by using link analysis. *CIKM*, 2007.

[11] R. Kumar, Y. Lifshits, and A. Tomkins. Evolution of two-sided markets. *WSDM*, 2010.

[12] J. Leskovec, D. Huttenlocher, J. Kleinberg. Governance in social media: A case study of the Wikipedia promotion process. *ICWSM*, 2010.

[13] J. Leskovec, D. Huttenlocher, J. Kleinberg. Predicting positive and negative links in online social networks. *WWW*, 2010.

[14] J. Leskovec, D. Huttenlocher, and J. Kleinberg. Signed networks in social media. *CHI*, 2010.

[15] Q. Liu, E. Agichtein, G. Dror, E. Gabrilovich, Y. Maarek, D. Pelleg, I. Szpektor. Predicting web searcher satisfaction with existing community-based answers. *SIGIR*, 2011.

[16] Y. Liu, J. Bian, E. Agichtein. Predicting information seeker satisfaction in community question answering. *SIGIR*, 2008.

[17] K. K. Nam, M. S. Ackerman, and L. A. Adamic. Questions in, knowledge in?: A study of naver's question answering community. *CHI*, 2009.

[18] H. Oktay, B. J. Taylor, and D. Jensen. Causal discovery in social media using Quasi-Experimental designs. *SIGKDD Wkshp Soc. Media Analytics*, 2010.

[19] J. Preece, B. Nonnecke, D. Andrews. The top five reasons for lurking: Improving community experiences for everyone. *Computers in Human Behavior*, 20(2004).

[20] J. Ratkiewicz, S. Fortunato, A. Flammini, F. Menczer, A. Vespignani. Characterizing and modeling the dynamics of online popularity. *Phys. Rev. Lett.*, 105(2010).

[21] C. Shah, J. Pomerantz. Evaluating and predicting answer quality in community QA. *SIGIR*, 2010.

[22] G. Szabo and B. A. Huberman. Predicting the popularity of online content. *CACM*, 53(2010).

[23] Y. R. Tausczik and J. W. Pennebaker. Predicting the perceived quality of online mathematics contributions from users' reputations. *CHI*, 2011.

[24] F. Wu and B. A. Huberman. Novelty and collective attention. *Proc. Natl. Acad. Sci.*, 104(45):17599–17601, Nov. 2007.

[25] J. Yang, L. Adamic, M. Ackerman. Crowdsourcing and knowledge sharing: Strategic user behavior on taskcn. *EC*, 2008.

[26] J. Zhang, M. Ackerman, L. Adamic. Expertise networks in online communities: Structure and algorithms. *WWW*, 2007.

Integrating Community Matching and Outlier Detection for Mining Evolutionary Community Outliers

Manish Gupta
University of Illinois at Urbana-Champaign
gupta58@illinois.edu

Jing Gao
State Univ. of New York at Buffalo
jing@buffalo.edu

Yizhou Sun
University of Illinois at Urbana-Champaign
sun22@illinois.edu

Jiawei Han
University of Illinois at Urbana-Champaign
hanj@illinois.edu

ABSTRACT

Temporal datasets, in which data evolves continuously, exist in a wide variety of applications, and identifying anomalous or outlying objects from temporal datasets is an important and challenging task. Different from traditional outlier detection, which detects objects that have quite different behavior compared with the other objects, temporal outlier detection tries to identify objects that have different *evolutionary behavior* compared with other objects. Usually objects form multiple communities, and most of the objects belonging to the same community follow similar patterns of evolution. However, there are some objects which evolve in a very different way relative to other community members, and we define such objects as *evolutionary community outliers*. This definition represents a novel type of outliers considering both temporal dimension and community patterns. We investigate the problem of identifying evolutionary community outliers given the discovered communities from two snapshots of an evolving dataset. To tackle the challenges of community evolution and outlier detection, we propose an integrated optimization framework which conducts outlier-aware community matching across snapshots and identification of evolutionary outliers in a tightly coupled way. A coordinate descent algorithm is proposed to improve community matching and outlier detection performance iteratively. Experimental results on both synthetic and real datasets show that the proposed approach is highly effective in discovering interesting evolutionary community outliers.

Categories and Subject Descriptors

H.1.0 [**Information Systems**]: Models and Principles; H.4.m [**Information Systems Applications**]: Miscellaneous

General Terms

Algorithms, Experimentation

Keywords

community matching, evolutionary community outliers, anomaly detection, ECOutlier, temporal outliers

1. INTRODUCTION

For a large number of applications, systems can be modeled as temporal datasets. Each snapshot in such a temporal dataset could describe the attributes of a collection of objects or a network of connected objects. For example, consider a database of employees in a company. Each employee can be associated with a large number of temporal attributes like salary, address, telephone number, designation, etc. As another example, consider co-authorship networks like DBLP where each author node is associated with temporal data and links. In daily life, various kinds of records like credit, personnel, financial, judicial, medical, etc. are all temporal. Given a snapshot of such a temporal dataset, analysts often perform clustering of objects with the goal of determining intrinsic grouping of objects in an unsupervised manner. We can refer to each group as a *community.* By analyzing a pair of snapshots from such a temporal dataset, we can observe that these communities evolve, often contracting, expanding, splitting or merging with each other. Most of the objects within a community follow similar evolution trends and their average defines the evolution trend of the community. However, evolutionary behavior of certain objects is quite different from the average evolutionary behavior of its community. Our goal is to detect such anomalous objects as *Evolutionary Community Outliers* (or *ECOutliers*) given a pair of snapshots from a temporal dataset.

***ECOutlier* Examples**

ECOutliers are interesting because they evolve against the trend, and often times they prove to be trend-setters. Interesting examples of *ECOutliers* can be commonly observed in real-life scenarios. We list a few below.

- A stockbroker who suddenly changes his portfolio and starts investing in another sector against his historical investments even when other similar stockbrokers continue to invest in the same old sector.
- Conglomerate diversification, e.g., "Walt Disney" moved from producing animated movies to construction of theme parks and vacation properties.

Case Studies

Now let us study two specific cases in detail.

Computer Science Research Evolution. An *ECOutlier* author may change his research area across time while others in his community continue to research in the same area. For example, consider the two snapshots 1997 and 1998 when Soumen Chakrabarti changed his research area from "Parallel Systems" (characterized by work in ICALP, PLDI, SPAA) to "Data and Information Systems" (characterized by work in VLDB, SIGMOD). In a bibliographic network, a conference may change the sub-topics it deals with while other conferences in the area continue to focus on the same subtopics. For example, in 2010, there were 13 papers in CIKM about personalization, while none of the other IR conferences like WWW, WSDM, SIGIR or ECIR focused so much on personalization in that year.

Employee Promotion. Suppose we have collected the communication frequencies among employees in a company. Also, each employee has temporal attributes like salary, designation, location, etc. We can identify the natural communities based on their attribute values and communication links. Across two snapshots of this small company, say only one employee E gets promoted from a developer two levels up to a team lead. Also, E's salary increases, and his communication pattern changes because he starts communicating more with managers. Due to change in links and the associated data, the community membership of E changes too. As E has behavior (community membership) changes much different from other members in his original community, he can be considered as an *ECOutlier.* E can be detected by identifying and comparing the communities of the two snapshots.

Existing Work

Here we briefly mention the difference between this work and existing outlier detection techniques. More discussions can be found in Section 2. (1) *Single-snapshot outlier detection*: Distance-based [22, 30] and density-based [7, 24] methods have been proposed but they work on only single snapshot data and hence cannot detect temporal changes. (2) *Temporal outlier detection*: Traditional time series literature [13] defines two types of outliers (Type I/additive and Type II/innovative) based on the data associated with an individual object across time, ignoring the community aspect completely. (3) *Stream outlier detection*: Recent work on outlier detection on data streams has focused on distance-based local outliers [29] or on graph outliers [4], while we focus on outliers in the community context. In general, existing work ignores time or community information in outlier detection, and thus the outliers detected traditionally are not evolutionary community outliers as proposed in this paper.

Integrated Framework

Evolutionary community outliers are objects that do not follow the evolutionary trend compared with other objects in the same community. Therefore, one natural way to identify such *ECOutliers* is to detect objects which change their community belongingness against the trend across time. However, community discovery is an unsupervised procedure, so communities discovered at different snapshots may not match with each other. Moreover, communities evolve too, and thus communities must be matched across snapshots. *ECOutliers* can be detected with high accuracy if the community matching across two snapshots is of high quality. However, community matching suffers from the presence of *ECOutliers* itself. Outliers are objects that defy the trend, and the trend must be obtained from community matching. Therefore, community matching and outlier detection cannot be separated. This motivates us to present an integrated framework which models outlier detection and community matching as a joint optimization problem. As we will show in Section 5, such an integrated approach is much more effective compared to a two-stage approach, which detects outliers after community matching is done.

Brief Overview of ECOutlier Detection

Consider a temporal dataset represented by the snapshot series X_1, X_2, ..., X_T. In this paper, we focus on the problem of detecting evolutionary outliers from any of the two snapshots X_i and X_j. Given community detection results on all pairs of snapshots, evolutionary outliers across multiple snapshots can be easily defined based on simple post-processing. For the sake of simplicity, let us denote the pair of snapshots as X_1 and X_2. Latent community discovery on X_1 (or X_2) leads to a matrix $\boldsymbol{P}$ (or $\boldsymbol{Q}$). Each element of $\boldsymbol{P}$ (or $\boldsymbol{Q}$) denotes the probability with which a particular object belongs to a particular community in snapshot X_1 (or X_2). Next, one needs to match a particular community in X_1 to one or more communities in X_2. Note that community mismatch happens due to permutation of community labels and community evolution. Such matching should try to minimize the distance between the matrices $\boldsymbol{P}$ and $\boldsymbol{Q}$. To ignore the effect of *ECOutliers* from such an optimization, the distance function should appropriately discount the matrix entries ((object, community) pairs) corresponding to outliers, thereby also learning an outlierness score for every (object, community) pair. Hence, we formulate the problem as an optimization problem over both outlierness degree and community correspondence. Community matching and outlier detection are improved through iterative updating procedures, and upon convergence, meaningful outliers are output.

Summary

We make the following contributions in this paper:

- We introduce the notion of Evolutionary Community Outliers *ECOutliers*. To the best of our knowledge, this is the first work on detecting evolutionary outliers considering both time and community information.
- We formulate the problem using an integrated optimization framework and develop an iterative algorithm that performs community matching and evolutionary outlier detection simultaneously.
- We show the interesting and meaningful outliers detected from multiple real and synthetic datasets.

Our paper is organized as follows. We discuss related work in Section 2. In Section 3, we define the *ECOutlier* detection problem, and present the optimization framework and solution. In Section 4, we present analysis and discussions related to the algorithm. We discuss experimental setup and results with detailed insights in Section 5. The paper is summarized in Section 6.

2. RELATED WORK

Our work is related to the areas of community matching and outlier detection.

Community Matching: The problem of community matching appears mainly when multiple different clusterings need to be integrated into a single clustering. Community mismatch happens because of 'label switching' or 'genuine multimodularity' [20]. Community matching (consensus clustering) can be done in a hard or a soft way. Hard community matching can be performed by selecting the best matching pair of communities one by one, avoiding conflict with already selected pairs [10, 11] or using greedy algorithms like CLUMPP [20]. Soft community matching can be done so as to minimize the distance between the two matrices [27]. In computer vision, community matching has been

Notation	Meaning
o	Index for objects
i	Index for a community in X_1
j	Index for a community in X_2
N	Number of objects
K_1	Number of communities in X_1
K_2	Number of communities in X_2
$\boldsymbol{P}^{N\times K_1} = [p_{oi}]$	Belongingness matrix for snapshot X_1
$\boldsymbol{Q}^{N\times K_2} = [q_{oj}]$	Belongingness matrix for snapshot X_2
$\boldsymbol{S}^{K_1\times K_2} = [s_{ij}]$	Correspondence matrix
$\boldsymbol{A}^{N\times K_2} = [a_{oj}]$	Outlierness matrix
μ	Estimated sum of outlierness

Table 1: Table of Notations

done by using cluster features like position, intensity, shape and average gray-scale difference [23], and degree of match between surrounding clusters [28]. Words-based communities could be matched using TF-IDF similarity [9]. Different from these studies, we introduce a new soft community matching technique which is evolutionary-outlier-aware.

Outlier Detection: Outlier (or anomaly) detection is a very broad field and has been studied in the context of a large number of application domains. Chandola et al. [8] and Hodge et al. [18] provide extensive overview of outlier detection techniques. Four main types of outliers studied in literature are point outliers, contextual outliers, collective outliers and evolutionary outliers. A variety of supervised, semi-supervised and unsupervised techniques have been used for outlier detection. These include mixture of models [12], neural networks, stat profiling using histograms, SVMs [19], rule based systems, parametric stat modeling, non-parametric stat modeling, bayesian networks, etc. The problem studied in this paper has connections with distance-based outlier detection algorithms [21] in the sense that we are trying to search outliers in a space with community change trends as dimensions. Outliers have been discovered in high-dimensional data [2], uncertain data [3], stream data [4], network data [15] and time series data [13]. Recently, there has been significant interest in detecting outliers in evolving datasets [16, 17], but none of them explores the outliers with respect to communities in a general evolving dataset.

Trajectory outlier detection and community tracking methods [5, 26] (1) usually work well for *longer* time series (unlike two timestamps in our setting), (2) and need crisp correspondence among clusters across timestamps. Also, often such methods cannot model link dependencies between objects (e.g. in networks) in the same timestamp. Such techniques usually use Markov models, which could lead to expensive computation or approximate solutions; our method provides high accuracy in time linear in the number of objects.

3. ECOUTLIER DETECTION APPROACH

In this section, we will present our integrated framework for *ECOutlier* detection. Let us start by first introducing the notations. We represent a matrix using the notation $\boldsymbol{B}$. We use $\vec{b_{i\cdot}}$ and $\vec{b_{\cdot j}}$ to represent the ith row and j^{th} column of $\boldsymbol{B}$ respectively. We will represent the $(i,j)^{th}$ element of the matrix $\boldsymbol{B}$ using b_{ij}. Given two vectors $\vec{a}$ and $\vec{b}$, we will use $\vec{a} \cdot \vec{b}$ to denote their dot product. Table 1 shows the important notations that we use in this paper. Next, we use these notations to define our problem.

3.1 Problem Definition

We start with an introduction to some basic concepts.

Community

A community is a probabilistic collection of similar objects, such that similarity between objects within the community is higher than the similarity between objects in different communities. For example, a research area is a community in a co-authorship network. We will use K_1 and K_2 to denote the number of communities in the two snapshots respectively.

Belongingness Matrix

Each entry in the belongingness matrix corresponds to the probability with which an object o belongs to a community i. The rows of the matrix correspond to objects while the columns correspond to communities. Let us denote the belongingness matrices for the N objects in X_1 and X_2 by $\boldsymbol{P}$ and $\boldsymbol{Q}$ respectively. Thus, $\boldsymbol{P} \in [0,1]^{N\times K_1}$, $\boldsymbol{Q} \in [0,1]^{N\times K_2}$, $\sum_{i=1}^{K_1} p_{oi} = 1$ and $\sum_{j=1}^{K_2} q_{oj} = 1$ for every object o.

Correspondence Matrix

We propose to use a soft matching of communities across snapshots. Soft correspondence means that a community of a given clustering corresponds to every community in another clustering with different weights. Hence, the match between two clusterings may be formulated as a matrix called as the correspondence matrix $\boldsymbol{S}^{K_1\times K_2}$. Also, $\sum_{j=1}^{K_2} s_{ij} = 1$ $(\forall i = 1 \ldots K_1)$.

Outlierness Matrix

We denote the outlierness matrix by $\boldsymbol{A}^{N\times K_2}$. a_{oj} represents the outlierness score for the (object, community) entry (o,j).

Evolutionary Community Outlier

An (object, community) pair (o,j) is an *ECOutlier* if change in p_{oi} to q_{oj} is quite different from the average change trend for community i in X_1 and j in X_2. An object can be considered as an outlier if the change in its probability distribution with respect to community belongingness is quite different from that of its X_1 community members.

Evolutionary Community Outlier Detection Problem

Given two snapshots ($\boldsymbol{P}$ and $\boldsymbol{Q}$), our problem is to estimate $\boldsymbol{S}$ and $\boldsymbol{A}$ and thereby derive *ECOutliers* with respect to the two snapshots.

To perform community matching between the matrices $\boldsymbol{P}$ and $\boldsymbol{Q}$, one needs to estimate a correspondence matrix $\boldsymbol{S}^{K_1\times K_2}$ such that the distance (sum of entrywise squared differences) between the matrices $\boldsymbol{Q}$ and $\boldsymbol{P} \times \boldsymbol{S}$ is minimized. However, such an approach will perform biased community matching if we take into account the contribution from outlier entries too, when estimating the correpondence matrix $\boldsymbol{S}$. For higher quality matching, one needs to ignore evolutionary outlier entries. Hence, we need to incorporate the outlierness score matrix $\boldsymbol{A}$ into community matching. In the remainder of this section, we will develop an integrated approach to compute $\boldsymbol{S}$ and $\boldsymbol{A}$.

3.2 Integrated Framework

Let μ be the estimated sum of outlierness in the snapshot. Then, we can incorporate the outlierness score into the community matching formulation as shown in Eqs. 1 to 5. We will discuss the estimation of μ in Section 3.5.

In the objective function (Eq. 1), $\boldsymbol{S}$ and $\boldsymbol{A}$ are the variables to be learned. $(q_{oj} - \vec{p_{o\cdot}} \cdot \vec{s_{\cdot j}})^2$ denotes the squared error incurred in community matching and $\log\left(\frac{1}{a_{oj}}\right)$ determines the outlier weight associated with the $(o,j)^{th}$ entry. Note that even if there were no outliers, there would still be some matching error, because each object evolves somewhat differently from the community averages. However, outliers that evolve very differently from community averages are penalized using a higher a_{oj} value. Using $\log\left(\frac{1}{a_{oj}}\right)$ in the objective function allows us to smooth out outlierness values. The log function makes sure that the weights for individual entry matching across snapshots lie within a small range. The more anomalous a particular (object, community) entry (o, j) is, the higher will be the value of a_{oj} and so $\log\left(\frac{1}{a_{oj}}\right)$ will be lower. This would mean that lower weight will be associated with the $(o, j)^{th}$ outlier entry when performing community matching. While there could be other ways of formulating the objective function, we use this particular formulation for ease of computation.

$$\min_{\boldsymbol{S},\boldsymbol{A}} \sum_{o=1}^{N}\sum_{j=1}^{K_2} \log\left(\frac{1}{a_{oj}}\right)(q_{oj} - \vec{p_{o\cdot}} \cdot \vec{s_{\cdot j}})^2 \quad (1)$$

subject to the following conditions

$$s_{ij} \geq 0 \quad \forall i = 1 \ldots K_1, \forall j = 1 \ldots K_2 \quad (2)$$

$$\sum_{j=1}^{K_2} s_{ij} = 1 \quad \forall i = 1 \ldots K_1 \quad (3)$$

$$1 \geq a_{oj} \geq 0 \quad \forall o = 1 \ldots N, \forall j = 1 \ldots K_2 \quad (4)$$

$$\sum_{o=1}^{N}\sum_{j=1}^{K_2} a_{oj} \leq \mu \quad (5)$$

Total Amount of Outlierness

If the total amount of outlierness is unbounded, one can simply mark all entries as outliers and then there will be no useful community matching. This corresponds to the trivial solution of setting all $\boldsymbol{A}$ elements to very high values, for the optimization (Eq. 1). Hence, we need to put in a constraint based on how many outliers we expect. Note that normal entries have small a_{oj} values, while outlier entries have large a_{oj} values. Thus, we would like to bound the total sum of all a_{oj} values to be within a maximum level of outlierness we expect in the snapshot. This can be achieved using the constraint $\sum_{o=1}^{N}\sum_{j=1}^{K_2} a_{oj} \leq \mu$ (Eq. 5). We replace it by an equality constraint to simplify computation. In fact, the semantic meanings of outlierness scores will not change by this action because we only care about the relative ranking of the scores. Essentially the equality claims that there is a certain level of outlierness in the entire snapshot. We will show later how we can estimate μ.

The objective function can be minimized (local minimum) by alternately optimizing one of $\boldsymbol{S}$ and $\boldsymbol{A}$ while fixing the other. Next, we will derive iterative update rules for the correspondence entry (s_{ij}) and the outlierness scores (a_{oj}). Using the method of Lagrangian Multipliers, we can rewrite the problem as follows. Here, β_i and γ are Lagrangian variables.

$$\min_{\boldsymbol{S},\boldsymbol{A}} \ f = \sum_{o=1}^{N}\sum_{j=1}^{K_2} \log\left(\frac{1}{a_{oj}}\right)(q_{oj} - \vec{p_{o\cdot}} \cdot \vec{s_{\cdot j}})^2$$
$$+ \sum_{i=1}^{K_1} \beta_i \left[\sum_{j=1}^{K_2} s_{ij} - 1\right] + \gamma \left[\sum_{o=1}^{N}\sum_{j=1}^{K_2} a_{oj} - \mu\right] \quad (6)$$

subject to the following conditions

$$s_{ij} \geq 0 \quad \forall i = 1 \ldots K_1, \forall j = 1 \ldots K_2 \quad (7)$$

$$1 \geq a_{oj} \geq 0 \quad \forall o = 1 \ldots N, \forall j = 1 \ldots K_2 \quad (8)$$

3.3 Derivation of Update Rules

Taking the partial derivative of Eq. 6 with respect to a particular a_{oj} and setting it to 0, we obtain the following.

$$a_{oj} = \frac{(q_{oj} - \vec{p_{o\cdot}} \cdot \vec{s_{\cdot j}})^2}{\gamma} \quad \textit{and} \quad \sum_{o=1}^{N}\sum_{j=1}^{K_2} \frac{(q_{oj} - \vec{p_{o\cdot}} \cdot \vec{s_{\cdot j}})^2}{\mu} = \gamma \quad (9)$$

This gives us the update rule for a_{oj} as follows.

$$a_{oj} = \frac{(q_{oj} - \vec{p_{o\cdot}} \cdot \vec{s_{\cdot j}})^2 \mu}{\sum_{o'=1}^{N}\sum_{j'=1}^{K_2} (q_{o'j'} - \vec{p_{o'\cdot}} \cdot \vec{s_{\cdot j'}})^2} \quad (10)$$

The numerator $(q_{oj} - \vec{p_{o\cdot}} \cdot \vec{s_{\cdot j}})^2$ represents the squared error for the $(o, j)^{th}$ entry, which represents the error incurred by matching the community detection results between two snapshots on the oth object with respect to the j-th community in $\boldsymbol{Q}$. The denominator in Eq. 10 represents the overall error across all the entries in matrix $\boldsymbol{Q}$, given a particular $\boldsymbol{S}$, which serves as a normalization factor. Intuitively, we assign a higher outlierness score to objects and communities that incur higher community matching error, while objects that are matched well with respect to certain communities across two snapshots are considered normal and thus receive lower outlierness score.

Now, we will obtain the update rule for s_{ij}. Taking partial derivative of f with respect to s_{ij}, we obtain the following.

$$\sum_{o'=1}^{N} \left[2\log\left(\frac{1}{a_{o'j}}\right)(q_{o'j} - \vec{p_{o'\cdot}} \cdot \vec{s_{\cdot j}})(-p_{o'i})\right] + \beta_i = 0 \quad (11)$$

After some algebraic simplifications, we obtain the following update rule for s_{ij}.

$$s_{ij} = \frac{\sum_{o'=1}^{N} 2\log\left(\frac{1}{a_{o'j}}\right) p_{o'i}\left[q_{o'j} - \sum_{k=1, k\neq i}^{K_1} p_{o'k} s_{kj}\right] - \beta_i}{\sum_{o'=1}^{N} 2\log\left(\frac{1}{a_{o'j}}\right) p_{o'i}^2} \quad (12)$$

The intuition behind Eq. 12 is as follows. Our goal is to compute s_{ij} when other elements of the matrix $\boldsymbol{S}$ are fixed. s_{ij} involves matching of all objects with respect to the ith column of $\boldsymbol{P}$ and the jth column of $\boldsymbol{Q}$. Contributions from each object o' are weighted by $\log\left(\frac{1}{a_{o'j}}\right)$ such that highly outlying objects contribute little to matching. Fixing other elements of $\boldsymbol{S}$, $\left[q_{o'j} - \sum_{k=1, k\neq i}^{K_1} p_{o'k} s_{kj}\right]$ represents the part of $q_{o'j}$ that needs to be explained by $p_{o'i}s_{ij}$. β_i and the denominator of Eq. 12 are used to make sure that $\sum_j s_{ij} = 1$. β_i's can now be computed easily using Eq. 12 and the constraints $\sum_{j=1}^{K_2} s_{ij} = 1$ ($\forall i = 1 \ldots K_1$). This value of β_i can then be substituted back in Eq. 12 to obtain the update rule for s_{ij}.

3.4 Interpretation of *S* and *A*

$\boldsymbol{S}$ captures the average evolution trend for the communities in the two snapshots. It also captures the permutation effect when matching two clusterings. s_{ij} represents the degree to which the community i in snapshot X_1 contributes to the community j in snapshot X_2. Thus, s_{ij} averages the evolution/match across all the objects belonging to i in X_1 and j in X_2. If a community i splits into two parts j_1 and j_2, s_{ij_1} and s_{ij_2} will have non-zero values. Similar to this split case, s_{ij} can be used to represent community merges, community expansion, community shrinking and a mix of such scenarios. Apart, a community i may die out with all s_{ij}'s set to 0. Similarly, $\boldsymbol{S}$ can also capture birth of new communities.

Now, if there are evolutionary outliers, they will possess values quite different from the average. For example, when

Algorithm 1 OneStageμ Outlier Detection Algorithm

Input: $\boldsymbol{P}$, $\boldsymbol{Q}$
Output: Estimates of $\boldsymbol{S}$ and $\boldsymbol{A}$
1: Initialize μ to 1
2: Initialize all $s_{ij} \Leftarrow \frac{1}{K_2}$ and all $a_{oj} \Leftarrow \frac{1}{NK_2}$.
3: **while** NOT converged **do**
4: Update $\boldsymbol{A}$ using Eq. 10 (Outlier Detection Step).
5: Update $\boldsymbol{S}$ using Eq. 12 (Community Matching Step).
6: **end while**
7: $\mu \Leftarrow \frac{\sum_{o'=1}^{N} \sum_{j'=1}^{K_2} (q_{o'j'} - \vec{p_{o'.}} \cdot \vec{s_{.j'}})^2}{\max_{o,j}(q_{oj}^2)}$
8: Repeat Steps 2 to 6.

s_{ij}=1, community i in X_1 gets merged with, or is renamed as community j in X_2. However, an outlier will have most of its mass moving from community i in X_1 to communities other than j in X_2. Presence of such outliers can affect the computation of s_{ij} itself because outliers can lead to significantly different average values. In our formulation, a weight is given to an object o when computing the community evolution values for community j, which is a function of a_{oj}. For normal (object, community), a_{oj} should be low, while for outlying (object, community), a_{oj} should be high. $\boldsymbol{A}$ is designed to capture such evolutionary outlierness.

3.5 Estimation of Overall Outlierness μ

Note that μ indicates the total sum of outlier scores (in Eq. 5). If we set μ to 1, a_{oj} is expected to be quite small for most of the (o, j) entries. There are N objects and K_2 communities, and thus the matching error of one entry is much smaller than the total squared sum of errors. The consequence is that the difference between a_{oj} is also small and it is hard to judge whether an object is an outlier or not based on a_{oj}. Techniques that transform and interpret outlierness scores [25] might help solve this problem. However, another problem is that a small μ causes overfitting of $\boldsymbol{S}$ to the outlier entries, when performing community matching. Hence, we would like to have μ as high as possible without violating constraints in the optimization. μ is upper-bounded by the combination of Eq. 10 and the constraint $a_{oj} \leq 1$. Therefore, we propose the following two-pass procedure to set μ. In the first pass, the overall snapshot outlierness μ is initialized to 1. After the first pass, μ is estimated as the ratio of overall error to the maximum entry value, as shown in Line 7 of Algorithm 1. The algorithm then uses this estimated μ for the second pass. Since μ increases compared to the first pass, a_{oj} values are relatively large. This reduces the overfitting of $\boldsymbol{S}$ to the outlier entries. Hence, matching for non-outlier entries improves, and so outlier detection improves too. Also, due to relaxation in matching, the overall error, i.e., the denominator in Eq. 10 is higher than the overall error in the first pass, and thus the value of a_{oj} remains ≤ 1, ensuring that the constraint is not violated.

Algorithm 1 summarizes the proposed *ECOutlier* detection algorithm. We name it *OneStageμ* to distinguish it from several baselines we evaluated, which will be discussed in detail in Section 5. "OneStage" indicates that the proposed method conducts outlier detection and community matching together, and μ is used to represent the two-pass procedure that estimates μ. As can be seen, the proposed method iteratively learns both parameters representing the outlierness scores (a_{oj}) and the community correspondence values (s_{ij}). At every iteration, a_{oj} values are first updated assuming all s_{ij} are fixed, and then s_{ij} values are sequentially updated based on the values of all a_{oj} and s_{ij} from other entries. The algorithm terminates when the change in the value of the objective function is less than a threshold ϵ.

4. ANALYSIS AND DISCUSSIONS

In this section, we analyze the convergence property and time complexity of the proposed *ECOutlier* detection method. We also discuss several important issues in implementing the method.

Convergence

LEMMA 4.1. *Algorithm 1 converges and the final solution is a stationary point of the optimization problem presented in Eqs. 1 to 5.*

PROOF. As stated in [6, p. 267-271], a block coordinate descent algorithm converges to a stationary point if the function achieves minimum at each step with respect to the set of working variables when the values of other variables are fixed. To prove this, we first check the convexity of the function. We notice that the constraints (Eqs. 2 to 5) are all linear. When we consider $\boldsymbol{S}$ as constant, the optimization function is a linear combination of negative log of a_{oj}'s. As $\log(\frac{1}{a_{oj}})$ is convex, its linear combination is also convex. When $\boldsymbol{A}$ is fixed and s_{ij}'s are updated sequentially, the objective function can be written as a quadratic function in s_{ij}. Since p_{ij} are all positive, it can be derived that the function is convex in each s_{ij}. As the function to be minimized is convex at each step, setting derivatives with respect to the working variables to zero will give unique minimum. Hence, Algorithm 1 is guaranteed to converge. □

Computational Complexity

Recall that N is the number of objects, K_1 and K_2 are the number of communities in the two snapshots respectively. Sum of all error values in Eq. 10 can be computed once for all a_{oj}'s in $O(NK_1K_2)$ time. Then, computation of each a_{oj} takes $O(K_1)$ time. $\boldsymbol{S}$ consists of K_1K_2 entries. When computing $\boldsymbol{S}$, at every iteration, for each s_{ij}, one needs to use Eq. 12 which is $O(NK_1)$ itself. Thus, computational complexity of the *OneStageμ* Algorithm is $O(NK_1^2K_2I)$ where I is the number of iterations. As can be seen, the running time is linear with respect to the number of objects. Usually the number of communities is small, and thus the proposed method scales well to large data sets.

Identifying Outliers

Algorithm 1 allows us to obtain outlierness scores for every (object, community) pair, given two snapshots of a temporal dataset. These scores are useful to identify interesting objects that are outliers with respect to a particular community. One could also aggregate such outlierness scores in a variety of ways to obtain the outlierness score for an object across all communities. Different aggregation functions could be used; weighted sum of scores or maximum (object, community) entry corresponding to an object may be a good choice, depending on the application. Also, when reporting top outlier objects in the snapshot one may want to consider the overall activity of the object along with its outlierness score. For example, an author publishing 50 papers in a snapshot with a relatively lower level of outlierness may still be more interesting than an author publishing only 5 papers but with a relatively higher level of outlierness.

Initialization

We initialize all a_{oj} values to $\frac{1}{NK_2}$, i.e., we begin by considering all entries to be equally anomalous. We initialize all s_{ij} entries to $\frac{1}{K_2}$, i.e., we assume that each community in snapshot X_2 evolves equally from each of the communities in snapshot X_1.

Series of Snapshots

In this paper, we focused on finding *ECOutliers* given a pair of snapshots. However, it is quite natural to extend our approach given a series of snapshots. We can perform community matching and outlier detection across every pair of consecutive snapshots, using the proposed module. Also, when the evolution is gentle, one can smooth out community matching over several consecutive snapshots. This can help in improving the community matching accuracy, thereby also improving the outlier detection.

5. EXPERIMENTS

Evaluation of outlier detection algorithms is quite difficult due to lack of ground truth. We perform experiments on multiple synthetic datasets, each of which simulates real scenarios. We will evaluate outlier detection accuracy of the proposed algorithm based on outliers injected in synthetic datasets. We evaluate the results on real datasets using case studies. We perform comprehensive analysis of objects to justify the top few outliers returned by the proposed algorithm. The code and the data sets are available at: `http://blitzprecision.cs.uiuc.edu/ECOutlier`

5.1 Baselines

We compare the proposed algorithm with three baseline methods: *OneStage (1S)*, *TwoStage (2S)* and *NearestNeighbor (NN)*. As discussed, our method is named as *OneStageμ (1Sμ)* because it integrates outlier detection and community matching, and μ is estimated using a two-pass procedure. The baseline methods are explained as follows.

OneStage (1S): *1S* is the one pass version of *1Sμ* (Steps 1 to 6 of Algorithm 1), in which total outlier score μ is set to 1. Thus, comparison with *1S* will help us understand improvement in accuracy by improved estimation of μ.

TwoStage (2S): Outliers are obtained by looking at the top values in $\boldsymbol{Q} - \boldsymbol{P} \times \boldsymbol{S}$ where $\boldsymbol{S}$ is computed by matching $\boldsymbol{P}$ and $\boldsymbol{Q}$. Comparison with *2S* will help us understand which method is better – performing outlier detection after community matching (*2S*) or doing them in an integrated way (*1Sμ*).

NearestNeighbor (NN): For every object o, we find its k-Nearest Neighbors set, $NN_{X_1}(o)$, in $\boldsymbol{P}$ using the KDTree implementation in Java-ML [1]. Recall that $\boldsymbol{P}$ and $\boldsymbol{Q}$ are the belongingness matrices for snapshots X_1 and X_2. We exclude the object o from $NN_{X_1}(o)$. The outlierness score for (object, community) pairs (o, j) can then be computed as $a_{oj} = \left| q_{oj} - \frac{\sum_{o' \in NN_{X_1}(o)} q_{o'j}}{|NN_{X_1}(o)|} \right|$. Note that this means that an outlier entry (o, j) has a high score if $q_{o,j}$ (i.e., belongingness of object o to community j in the second snapshot) is quite different from the average belongingness of its X_1 nearest neighbors to the same community j in X_2. *NN* seems to follow the exact definition of *ECOutliers* and so one would expect it to get high accuracy but we will discuss later on why it fails to perform better than other methods.

5.2 Synthetic Datasets

Dataset Generation

We generate a variety of synthetic datasets to capture different spatial cases of evolution (Figs. 1 and 2). For each dataset, the figures show two snapshots. In each snapshot, we generate multiple clusters, each of which represents a community. Each cluster is modeled using a 2D Gaussian distribution, and evolution is modeled by changing the means and the variances of the Gaussians. For example, to model contraction (expansion) of a cluster, we reduce (increase) the standard deviation of the corresponding cluster (the first two plots in Fig. 1). *NoEvolution* is represented by Plots 3 and 4 in Fig. 1. Plots 5 and 6 in Fig. 1 show the case of *Merge* where top four clusters merge to form one big cluster, and *Split* is shown in the last two plots in Fig. 1 where the upper cluster splits into four small clusters. We model a mix of cluster evolution in Fig. 2, which consists of cluster expansion, contraction, merging and splitting. Thus, we try to incorporate all forms of possible cluster evolution in our synthetic datasets. The circles represent 2σ boundary for the cluster Gaussian. For each cluster, we generate a set of N/K_1 points, each of which is sampled from the cluster Gaussian. For each of the N points, we obtain p_{oj} and q_{oj} as the probability with which the point can be generated from its cluster's Gaussian distribution. Using $\boldsymbol{P}$ and $\boldsymbol{Q}$, we obtain $\boldsymbol{S}$ as the community matching matrix in absence of any outlierness. $\boldsymbol{S}$ captures evolution without the effect of outliers.

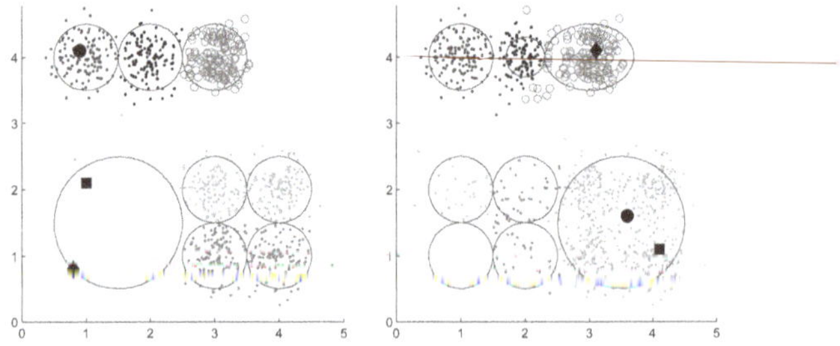

Figure 2: *SynMix* Dataset (X_1 and X_2)

Next, we inject outliers as follows. First we set an outlierness factor Ψ and choose a random set of objects, R with $N \times \Psi$ objects. For each object o in R, we swap the $q_{oj_{min}}$ and $q_{oj_{max}}$ values where j_{min} and j_{max} are the communities with the min and the max q_{oj} values. Thus, we inject two outliers per object in R. Finally, we set $a_{oj} = (q_{oj} - \vec{p_{o\cdot}} \cdot \vec{s_{\cdot j}})^2$. For each of the datasets, for X_2, we show the top three outliers (using different black filled shapes) discovered by *OneStageμ*. We show their original positions in X_1 and their new positions in X_2.

Results on Synthetic Datasets

We experiment using a variety of different settings. For each setting, we perform 100 experiments and report the mean values. We fix the threshold ϵ for convergence to 10^{-6}. We vary the number of objects as 1000, 5000 and 10000. We vary the percentage of outliers injected into the dataset as 1%, 2%, 5% and 10%. Using these settings, we compare the actual outlier objects with the top outliers returned by various algorithms. For each algorithm, we show the precision of outlier detection with respect to the ranking of outliers. The results of the three baselines and the proposed method are shown in Fig. 3 for *SynMix* dataset (10000 objects, Ψ=10%). Note that the proposed algorithm (*1Sμ*) outperforms the others in finding the top few outliers most precisely. The area under this curve (AUC) is a good measure of the effectiveness of the algorithm in identifying the outliers. We report the AUC values in Table 2 (Average variances are .0012 for *NN*, .0021 for *2S*, .0017 for *1S*, and .0005

N	Ψ (%)	SynContractExpand				SynNoEvolution				SynMerge				SynSplit				SynMix			
		NN	2S	1S	1Sμ	NN	2S	1S	1Sμ	NN	2S	1S	1Sμ	NN	2S	1S	1Sμ	NN	2S	1S	1Sμ
1000	1	.755	.947	**.966**	**.966**	.832	.791	.853	**.965**	.720	.774	.835	**.926**	.786	.918	.929	**.931**	.606	.891	.904	**.925**
	2	.729	.920	.948	**.957**	.812	.733	.789	**.961**	.702	.715	.781	**.908**	.779	.865	.920	**.924**	.675	.823	.860	**.915**
	5	.710	.853	.913	**.956**	.726	.712	.752	**.928**	.645	.654	.719	**.849**	.697	.799	.891	**.920**	.631	.770	.817	**.920**
	10	.619	.766	.833	**.960**	.657	.684	.706	**.881**	.580	.617	.656	**.801**	.630	.749	.832	**.918**	.594	.730	.776	**.917**
5000	1	.778	.945	**.970**	**.970**	.938	.793	.848	**.971**	.713	.762	.801	**.928**	.796	.913	**.942**	**.942**	.691	.881	.895	**.918**
	2	.756	.930	.947	**.961**	.864	.772	.815	**.962**	.677	.752	.791	**.903**	.768	.885	.938	**.940**	.646	.862	.876	**.919**
	5	.689	.901	.929	**.964**	.742	.750	.779	**.941**	.626	.698	.749	**.827**	.689	.806	.913	**.924**	.608	.831	.860	**.921**
	10	.622	.778	.829	**.964**	.656	.730	.747	**.912**	.579	.643	.679	**.795**	.624	.762	.834	**.929**	.593	.783	.824	**.919**
10000	1	.769	.949	.973	**.974**	.926	.807	.856	**.974**	.707	.788	.817	**.933**	.789	.938	.955	**.960**	.665	.882	.897	**.921**
	2	.752	.937	.949	**.963**	.851	.788	.828	**.964**	.681	.762	.796	**.898**	.758	.898	.948	**.951**	.670	.869	.881	**.916**
	5	.695	.900	.930	**.964**	.738	.763	.788	**.951**	.627	.719	.756	**.826**	.683	.807	.914	**.922**	.604	.847	.871	**.919**
	10	.622	.771	.825	**.965**	.660	.753	.769	**.926**	.583	.645	.681	**.795**	.621	.769	.827	**.934**	.584	.812	.845	**.917**

Table 2: Syn Dataset AUC (*NN=NearestNeighbor, 2S=TwoStage, 1S=OneStage, 1Sμ=OneStageμ*)

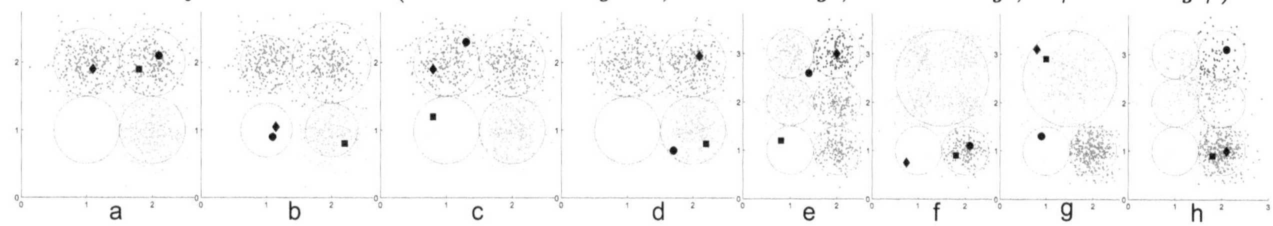

Figure 1: Two Snapshots (X_1 & X_2) each for *SynContractExpand* (a→b), *SynNoEvolution* (c→d), *SynMerge* (e→f), *SynSplit* Datasets (g→h)

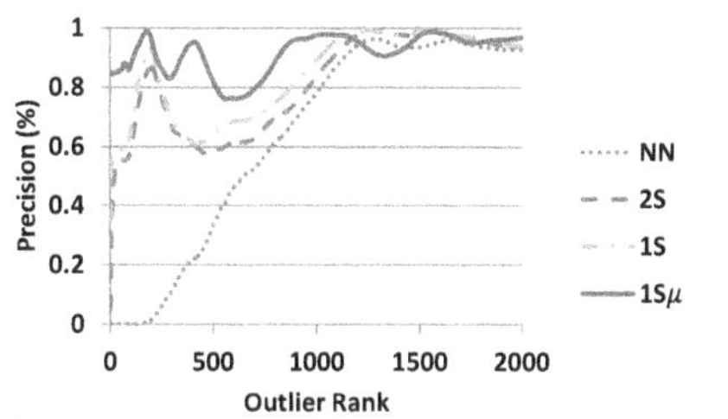

Figure 3: Precision for SynMix (*NN=NearestNeighbor, 2S=TwoStage, 1S= OneStage, 1Sμ=OneStageμ*)

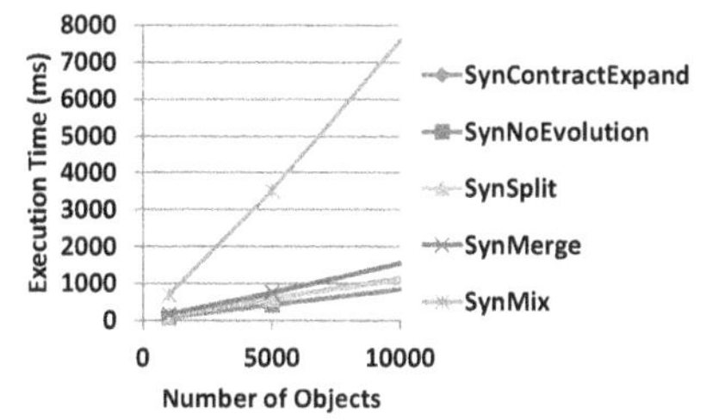

Figure 4: Running Times (ms) for *OneStageμ* (Scalability with Increasing Dataset Size)

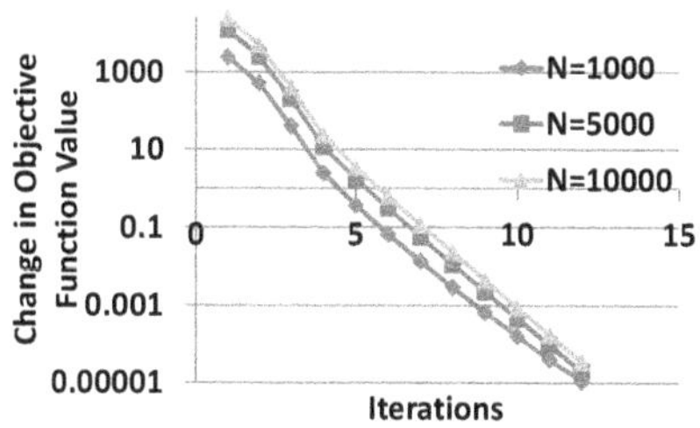

Figure 5: Convergence of OneStageμ Algorithm

for *1Sμ*). For *NearestNeighbors*, we tried k=5, 10, 50 and 100. We found the best AUC at k=10 and hence report the values for k=10. As the table shows, the proposed algorithm outperforms all the other algorithms for all the settings by a wide margin (sometimes as high as 30% better than the *TwoStage* method). *NearestNeighbors* performs fairly well for *SynNoEvolution* but not for other datasets. This is because it does not consider evolution and assumes that the set of nearest neighbors does not change across the snapshots. In contrast, the proposed algorithm detects outliers in the context of community evolution.

5.3 Real Datasets

Dataset Generation

We perform experiments using three real datasets: *IMDB*, *DBLP* and *Four Area* (subset of *DBLP*). We use *iTopicModel* [31] to perform community detection on the dataset since it uses both data and link information. It outputs the belongingness matrix $\boldsymbol{P}^{N\times K_1}$ ($\boldsymbol{Q}^{N\times K_2}$) for the snapshot X_1 (X_2).

IMDB: We consider the co-starring graph (edge weight = co-starring frequency) created using actors who acted in at least 5 movies per snapshot. The two snapshots correspond to the years '06-'07 (15337 actors) and '08-'09 (13142 actors). Sets of genres of movies in which the actor acted constitutes the data associated with an actor. After community detection, we retain only those actors (6609) that are present in both snapshots. We consider number of communities as $K_1 = K_2 = 5$.

DBLP: We consider the co-authorship graph (edge weight = co-authorship frequency) created using publications in the top 1500 conferences by authors, each of which published ≥ 10 papers per snapshot. The two snapshots correspond to the years '06-'07 (4784 authors) and '08-'09 (5633 authors). Sets of related conferences constitute the data associated with an author. After community detection, we retain only those authors (2666) that are present in both snapshots. We consider number of communities as $K_1 = K_2 = 5$. Similar to the author network, we also create a network of conferences (edge weight = #authors publishing at both conferences) where the words in paper titles constitute the data associated with each conference. 920 conferences are present in both snapshots and again, we set $K_1 = K_2 = 5$.

Four Area: This is a subset of DBLP for the four areas of data mining (DM), databases (DB), information retrieval (IR) and machine learning (ML). It consists of papers from 20 conferences (5 per area). For details, read [14]. We obtain two snapshots corresponding to the years '01-'04 (601 authors) and '05-'08 (1206 authors). We build the co-authorship network similar to the one for *DBLP*. $K_1 = K_2 = 4$, and 374 authors are present in both snapshots.

Results on Real Datasets

Here, we discuss case studies obtained from these datasets.

Conference	Sim_1	Sim_2	Sim_3	Sim_4
ANTS	0.55	0.16	0.14	0.08
TLCA	0.60	0.53	0.14	0.08
INFOS	0.83	0.75	0.10	0.22
Sigite Conf.	0.66	0.33	0.11	0.27
Gil Jahrestagung	0.77	0.81	0.08	0.31

Table 3: Analysis of Top Outlier Conferences ($1S\mu$)

***IMDB*: Top two outlier actors returned by *OneStageμ* are discussed below.

1. Kelly Carlson (I): In X_1, she did many Sport, Thriller and Action movies, while in X_2 she switched to Drama, Music, Reality-TV. Most of her top ten closest collaborators in X_1 still do Documentary, Thriller, Action in X_2. Few of her co-stars collaborate with her in the second time snapshot. Also, her X_1 neighbors used to do Sport, Comedy, Documentary, Action while her X_2 neighbors do Drama, Documentary, Thriller, Music. Thus, clearly she changed her community from Sports, Thriller, Action genres to Drama, Music genres.

2. Josh Brolin: In X_1, he did a lot of Thriller, Drama, Crime and Mystery movies. In X_2, he acted in a lot of Documentary, Comedy, History, Music movies. Not only did he change his genres completely, but also not many other actors show such a change in the type of their movies. This is why, in X_2, his genres are quite different from that of his X_1 nearest neighbors. Hence, clearly he is an outlier.

***DBLP* (Authors Network):** We will discuss about the top two authors which are detected as evolutionary community outliers.

1. Georgios B. Giannakis. In X_1, his publications were mainly in CISS, ICC, GLOBECOM, INFOCOM. In X_2, he published in completely different conferences: ICASSP, ICRA. We looked at the conferences at which his X_1 community members published in X_2. This set of conferences (GLOBECOM, ICC, CISS, INFOCOM) is completely different from the set of conferences at which he published in X_2, but much similar to his own published venues in X_1.

2. Vassilios Peristeras. In X_1, his publications were mainly in HICSS, ICEGOV, IEEE SCC, EDOCW, CSREA, etc. In X_2, he published in completely different conferences: WSKS, ICSC, OTM, ICDIM, SAC. We looked at the conferences at which his X_1 community members published in X_2. This set of conferences (HICSS, ISI, ICEGOV, etc.) is completely different from the set of conferences at which he published in X_2, but much similar to his own conferences in X_1. This clearly justifies him to be a community outlier.

***DBLP* (Conf Network):** Table 3 shows the top five conferences returned as outliers by *OneStageμ*. We performed some analysis and hence list four measures in Table 3: similarity between top 20 words (we removed most frequent 100 words from dataset) for the conference across the snapshots, similarity in top 20 words between the conference at X_2 and its ten closest X_1 community members, similarity in neighbor conferences across the two snapshots, similarity in the words shared by the neighbors in the first snapshot and neighbors in the second snapshot.

As the table shows, each of the conferences have very low similarity for at least one of the measures, justifying their detection as *ECOutliers*. For comparison with the baseline, we present the top five conferences returned as outliers returned by *TwoStage* in Table 4. As one can clearly see, the similarity values in Table 4 are much higher compared to Table 3. Thus, the outliers returned by *TwoStage* are not as good as the outliers returned by the proposed algorithm.

Conference	Sim_1	Sim_2	Sim_3	Sim_4
ESEC SIGSOFT FSE	0.26	0.71	0.72	0.70
ISORC	0.64	0.66	0.75	0.74
Communications in Computing	0.16	0.57	0.58	0.70
ICDE Workshops	0.27	0.65	0.74	0.78
HICSS	0.78	0.60	0.83	0.79

Table 4: Analysis of Top Outlier Conferences ($2S$)

***Four Area* (Authors Network):** In this dataset, we observe a trend of people moving from ML community to DM community. Also, many authors often publish in both DB and IR. For this dataset, we will discuss two outliers returned by *OneStageμ*, who behave quite different from these trends.

1. Jérôme Lang. For this author, most of his community members moved from logical reasoning and related areas to other areas like DM and IR but he stays in AI field. He published 5 and 11 papers in the two snapshots respectively. Words in the titles of his papers are mainly "logic, planning, representation, action, uncertainty, propositional". We looked at the words which his X_1 community members (other authors having similar word distributions) use in X_2. The top words were "data, retrieval, xml, web, learning, mining". This clearly shows that his community members moved from logical reasoning to other areas while Jérôme decided to stay in the area, opposed to the trend. While he continued to publish in pure ML and AI conferences, his community members publish in a lot of IR and DM conferences in X_2.

2. Georg Gottlob. Generally the observed trend is that ML authors move to other related areas like DM and IR. Sometimes, some DM authors publish in ML conferences. But Georg has been a DB author in X_1, who started publishing in ML community in X_2. In X_1, he published frequently in PODS, VLDB, ICDE. In X_2, apart from PODS, he published heavily in IJCAI and AAAI. His set of collaborators also changed by a large extent across the two snapshots. A lot of his X_2 collaborators publish in ML conferences.

5.4 Running Time and Convergence

The experiments were run on a Linux machine with 4 Intel Xeon CPUs with 2.67GHz each. The code was implemented in Java. Fig. 4 shows the execution time for *OneStageμ* on different synthetic datasets in ms. Note that the algorithm is linear in the number of objects. These times are averaged across 100 runs of the algorithm. On an average *OneStageμ* needed ~13 iterations per pass to converge on both real and synthetic datasets. Fig. 5 shows the change in the objective function value with iterations for the *SynMix* dataset for different number of objects, using a log-linear plot. The figure shows that *OneStageμ* converges fairly quickly.

6. CONCLUSIONS

We introduced the notion of evolutionary outliers with respect to latent evolving communities, i.e., *ECOutliers*. Such outliers represent the objects which disobey the common evolutionary trend among the majority of the objects in a community. The challenge is that both community evolution patterns and outliers are unknown. Outliers should be derived based on community matching across different snapshots, but need to be ignored when conducting community matching. We proposed an optimization framework which integrates community matching and outlier detection. The objective function is to minimize community matching error, in which the contributions from outlier objects are weighed lower. An iterative algorithm *OneStageμ* is developed to solve the optimization problem, which improves community matching and *ECOutlier* detection gradually. Experiments on a series of synthetic data show the proposed algorithm's capability of detecting outliers under various types of community evolution. Case studies on *DBLP*, *IMDB* and *Four Area* datasets reveal some interesting and meaningful evolutionary outliers. Although the proposed algorithm focuses on two snapshots, it can detect both short-term and long-term trends and outliers, as snapshots can consist of short or long intervals. Moreover, it can be extended to handle multiple snapshots.

7. ACKNOWLEDGEMENTS

We thank Vinod Vydiswaran and anonymous KDD reviewers for discussions and insightful comments. Research was sponsored in part by the Cyber Security project (W911NF-11-2-0086) of U.S. Army Research Laboratory, NSF IIS-0905215, and U.S. Air Force Office of Scientific Research MURI award FA9550-08-1-0265. The views and conclusions contained in this document are those of the authors and should not be interpreted as representing the official policies, either expressed or implied, of the Army Research Laboratory or the U.S. Government. The U.S. Government is authorized to reproduce and distribute reprints for Government purposes notwithstanding any copyright notation here on.

8. REFERENCES

[1] T. Abeel, Y. Van de Peer, and Y. Saeys. Java-ML: A Machine Learning Library. *Journal of Machine Learning Research*, 10:931–934, Jun 2009.

[2] C. C. Aggarwal and P. S. Yu. Outlier Detection for High Dimensional Data. *SIGMOD Records*, 30:37–46, May 2001.

[3] C. C. Aggarwal and P. S. Yu. Outlier Detection with Uncertain Data. In *Proc. of the SIAM Intl. Conf. on Data Mining (SDM)*, 483–493, 2008.

[4] C. C. Aggarwal, Y. Zhao, and P. S. Yu. Outlier Detection in Graph Streams. In *Proc. of the* 27th *Intl. Conf. on Data Engineering (ICDE)*, 399–409. 2011.

[5] J. Alon, S. Sclaroff, G. Kollios, and V. Pavlovic. Discovering Clusters in Motion Time-Series Data. In *Proc. of the IEEE Conf. on Computer Vision and Pattern Recognition (CVPR)*, Volume 1, 375–381. IEEE Computer Society, 2003.

[6] D. P. Bertsekas. *Non-Linear Programming (2nd Edition)*. Athena Scientific, 1999.

[7] M. M. Breunig, H.-P. Kriegel, R. T. Ng, and J. Sander. LOF: Identifying Density-Based Local Outliers. In *Proc. of the 2000 ACM SIGMOD Intl. Conf. on Management of Data (SIGMOD)*, 93–104. ACM, 2000.

[8] V. Chandola, A. Banerjee, and V. Kumar. Anomaly Detection: A Survey. *ACM Surveys*, 41(3), 2009.

[9] W. W. Cohen and J. Richman. Learning to Match and Cluster Large High-Dimensional Data Sets for Data Integration. In *Proc. of the* 8th *ACM SIGKDD Intl. Conf. on Knowledge Discovery and Data Mining (SIGKDD)*, 475–480. ACM, 2002.

[10] E. Dimitriadou, A. Weingessel, and K. Hornik. Voting-Merging: An Ensemble Method for Clustering. In *Proc. of the Intl. Conf. on Artificial Neural Networks (ICANN)*, 217–224. Springer, 2001.

[11] S. Dudoit and J. Fridlyand. Bagging to Improve the Accuracy of a Clustering Procedure. *Bioinformatics*, 19(9):1090–1099, 2003.

[12] E. Eskin. Anomaly Detection over Noisy Data using Learned Probability Distributions. In *Proc. of the 17th Intl. Conf. on Machine Learning (ICML)*, 255–262. Morgan Kaufmann Publishers Inc., 2000.

[13] A. J. Fox. Outliers in Time Series. *Journal of the Royal Statistical Society. Series B (Methodological)*, 34(3):350–363, 1972.

[14] J. Gao, F. Liang, W. Fan, Y. Sun, and J. Han. Graph-based Consensus Maximization among Multiple Supervised and Unsupervised Models. In *Proc. of the* 23rd *Annual Conf. on Neural Information Processing Systems (NIPS)*, 585–593. Curran Associates, Inc., 2009.

[15] J. Gao, F. Liang, W. Fan, C. Wang, Y. Sun, and J. Han. On Community Outliers and their Efficient Detection in Information Networks. In *Proc. of the* 16th *ACM SIGKDD Intl. Conf. on Knowledge Discovery and Data Mining (SIGKDD)*, 813–822, 2010.

[16] Y. Ge, H. Xiong, Z. Zhou, H. Ozdemir, J. Yu, and K. C. Lee. Top-Eye: Top-K Evolving Trajectory Outlier Detection. In *Proc. of the* 19th *ACM Conf. on Information and Knowledge Management (CIKM)*, 1733–1736, 2010.

[17] A. Ghoting, M. E. Otey, and S. Parthasarathy. LOADED: Link-Based Outlier and Anomaly Detection in Evolving Data Sets. In *Proc. of the* 4th *IEEE Intl. Conf. on Data Mining (ICDM)*, 387–390, 2004.

[18] V. J. Hodge and J. Austin. A Survey of Outlier Detection Methodologies. *AI Review*, 22(2):85–126, 2004.

[19] W. Hu, Y. Liao, and V. R. Vemuri. Robust Anomaly Detection Using Support Vector Machines. In *Proc. of the Intl. Conf. on Machine Learning (ICML)*, 282–289. Morgan Kaufmann Publishers Inc, 2003.

[20] M. Jakobsson and N. A. Rosenberg. CLUMPP: A Cluster Matching and Permutation Program for Dealing with Label Switching and Multimodality in Analysis of Population Structure. *Bioinformatics*, 23:1801–1806, Jul 2007.

[21] E. M. Knorr and R. T. Ng. Algorithms for Mining Distance-Based Outliers in Large Datasets. In *Proc. of the* 24th *Intl. Conf. on Very Large Data Bases (VLDB)*, 392–403. Morgan Kaufmann, 1998.

[22] E. M. Knorr, R. T. Ng, and V. Tucakov. Distance-Based Outliers: Algorithms and Applications. *The VLDB Journal*, 8:237–253, Feb 2000.

[23] D. Kottke and Y. Sun. Motion Estimation Via Cluster Matching. *IEEE Transactions on Pattern Analysis and Machine Intelligence*, 16:1128–1132, 1994.

[24] H.-P. Kriegel, P. Kröger, E. Schubert, and A. Zimek. LoOP: Local Outlier Probabilities. In *Proc. of the* 18th *ACM Conf. on Information and Knowledge Management (CIKM)*, 1649–1652. ACM, 2009.

[25] H.-P. Kriegel, P. Kröger, E. Schubert, and A. Zimek. Interpreting and Unifying Outlier Scores. In *Proc. of the* 11th *SIAM Intl. Conf. on Data Mining (SDM)*, 13–24. SIAM / Omnipress, 2011.

[26] J.-G. Lee, J. Han, and X. Li. Trajectory Outlier Detection: A Partition-and-Detect Framework. In *Proc. of the* 24th *Intl. Conf. on Data Engineering (ICDE)*, 140–149. IEEE Computer Society, 2008.

[27] B. Long, Z. M. Zhang, and P. S. Yu. Combining Multiple Clusterings by Soft Correspondence. In *Proc. of the* 5th *IEEE Intl. Conf. on Data Mining (ICDM)*, 282–289. IEEE Computer Society, 2005.

[28] M. J. Miller, A. D. Olson, and S. S. Thorgeirsson. Computer Analysis of Two-Dimensional Gels: Automatic Matching. *ElectroPhoresis*, 5(5):297–303, 1984.

[29] D. Pokrajac, A. Lazarevic, and L. J. Latecki. Incremental Local Outlier Detection for Data Streams. In *IEEE Symposium on Computational Intelligence and Data Mining (CIDM)*, 504–515. IEEE, Apr 2007.

[30] S. Ramaswamy, R. Rastogi, and K. Shim. Efficient Algorithms for Mining Outliers from Large Data Sets. *SIGMOD Records*, 29:427–438, May 2000.

[31] Y. Sun, J. Han, J. Gao, and Y. Yu. iTopicModel: Information Network-Integrated Topic Modeling. In *Proc. of the* 9th *IEEE Intl. Conf. on Data Mining (ICDM)*, 493–502. IEEE Computer Society, 2009.

Different Slopes for Different Folks

Mining for Exceptional Regression Models with Cook's Distance

Wouter Duivesteijn
LIACS, Leiden University
The Netherlands
wouterd@liacs.nl

Ad Feelders
ICS, Utrecht University
The Netherlands
ad@cs.uu.nl

Arno Knobbe
LIACS, Leiden University
The Netherlands
knobbe@liacs.nl

ABSTRACT

Exceptional Model Mining (EMM) is an exploratory data analysis technique that can be regarded as a generalization of subgroup discovery. In EMM we look for subgroups of the data for which a model fitted to the subgroup differs substantially from the same model fitted to the entire dataset. In this paper we develop methods to mine for exceptional regression models. We propose a measure for the exceptionality of regression models (Cook's distance), and explore the possibilities to avoid having to fit the regression model to each candidate subgroup. The algorithm is evaluated on a number of real life datasets. These datasets are also used to illustrate the results of the algorithm. We find interesting subgroups with deviating models on datasets from several different domains. We also show that under certain circumstances one can forego fitting regression models on up to 40% of the subgroups, and these 40% are the relatively expensive regression models to compute.

Categories and Subject Descriptors

H.2.8 [**Database Management**]: Database Applications—*Data mining*

Keywords

Subgroup Discovery, Exceptional Model Mining, Linear Regression, Cook's Distance

1. INTRODUCTION

Exceptional Model Mining (EMM) [16, 8] is an exploratory data analysis technique that can be regarded as a generalization of subgroup discovery. In subgroup discovery the aim is to find subgroups of the data for which the distribution of a single target variable deviates from its distribution in the entire dataset. In EMM we look for subgroups for which a model fitted to the subgroup differs substantially from the same model fitted to the entire dataset. This is a general framework which can be used for different purposes, depending on the type of model that is fitted, and how one measures the difference between models. In this paper we focus on the "work horse" of data analysis: linear regression models.

Let us consider an example to illustrate why the results of such an analysis might be of interest. The economic *law of demand* states that (all else equal) if the price of a product increases, the demand for the product will decrease. In a regression model this would result in a negative slope when we regress demand on price. However, under specific conditions, people tend to buy more of a product when the price increases [13]. Hence, for those exceptional cases, we would get a positive slope of the regression line. This idea was first published in 1895 [17]. Over one hundred years later, in 2008, this so-called *Giffen behavior* was for the first time observed in a field experiment [13]. In certain theoretically induced subsets (the poor, but not too poor) of households in Hunan, China, demand for rice rose when the price increased. The algorithm we propose is able to find such an exceptional subgroup in the data automatically.

Testing whether the regression coefficients for two groups are different is in fact common practice in applied regression analysis. One common way of doing this is through the use of dummy (i.e. binary) variables. Consider for example the problem of predicting house prices. Suppose we know for each house its selling price, lot size and whether or not it has air conditioning. To test whether the effect of lot size on selling price is different for houses with and without air conditioning, one could estimate the model

$$\text{Price} = \beta_0 + \beta_1 \times \text{Lot Size} + \beta_2 \times \text{Airco} \times \text{Lot Size}, \quad (1)$$

where Airco=1 if the house has air conditioning and Airco=0 otherwise. If we consider these two cases separately we see that the regression equation becomes

$$\text{Price} = \beta_0 + \beta_1 \times \text{Lot Size},$$

if Airco=0, and

$$\text{Price} = \beta_0 + (\beta_1 + \beta_2) \times \text{Lot Size},$$

if Airco=1. Hence, to test whether these two groups of houses have different slopes, we can test whether the coefficient estimate of β_2 in model (1) is significant. In this setup we have to decide in advance for which groups we want to test whether they have different slopes in the regression.

The algorithm presented in this paper can be regarded as a way of automatically finding the subgroups for which the slopes are substantially different. The subgroup description can be more complex than the simple condition in the above example: it can be a conjunction of conditions on categorical and numeric variables as is common in subgroup discovery. The fact that many textbooks on applied regression analysis (see for example chapter 10 of [14]) devote considerable attention to the problem of *testing* whether two regressions (for different subgroups of the data) are different, underlines the relevance of such questions in practical data analysis and motivates our work. Essentially we embed an old regression technique in a new Exceptional Model Mining setting, to automate a traditional regression problem.

This paper is organized as follows. In Section 2 we introduce some notation, discuss the basic EMM framework, and present the combination of EMM and linear regression models. In Section 3 we propose a quality measure for the exceptionality of subgroups, which measures the distance between the coefficient vector of the global model, and the coefficient vector of the subgroup model. In this section we also consider possibilities to limit the number of models that have to be fitted on subgroups, by using bounds that can be computed quite easily from the data and the global model. In Section 4 we discuss the extent to which we can prune the search space, while in Section 5 we illustrate the application of our algorithm by analyzing a number of publicly available real life datasets. Finally, Section 6 concludes.

2. PRELIMINARIES

Throughout this paper, we assume a dataset $\mathcal{D}$ to be a bag of N *records* $r \in \mathcal{D}$ of the form

$$r = \{a_1, \ldots, a_k, x_1, \ldots, x_{p-1}, y\}$$

where k is a positive integer and p is an integer such that $p \geq 2$. We call $a_1, \ldots, a_k$ the *attributes* of r, and $x_1, \ldots, x_{p-1}, y$ the *targets* of r. Each target is assumed to be numeric, while the attributes are taken from an unrestricted domain $\mathcal{A}$. The requirement that the x_i are numeric may seem very restrictive, but in fact nominal variables can be handled in the usual way by creating "dummy" (binary) variables. We refer to the ith record by r^i.

For our definition of subgroups we need to define *patterns*. These are functions $P : \mathcal{A} \to \{0, 1\}$. A pattern P *covers* a data point r^i if and only if $P(a^i) = 1$.

Definition (Subgroup). A *subgroup* corresponding to a pattern P is the bag of data points $G_P \subseteq \mathcal{D}$ that P covers:

$$G_P = \left\{ r^i \in \mathcal{D} \,\middle|\, P\left(a^i\right) = 1 \right\}$$

From now on we omit the P if no confusion can arise, and refer to a subgroup as G.

In order to objectively evaluate a candidate pattern in a given dataset, we need to define a *quality measure*. For each pattern P in the pattern language $\mathcal{P}$, this function measures how interesting the model is that we induce on G_P.

Definition (Quality Measure). A *quality measure* is a function $\varphi_{\mathcal{D}} : \mathcal{P} \to \mathbb{R}$ that assigns a unique numeric value to a pattern P, given a dataset $\mathcal{D}$.

2.1 EMM revisited

Exceptional Model Mining [16, 8] is a data mining framework that can be seen as a generalization of the Subgroup Discovery (SD) framework. SD strives to find patterns that satisfy certain user-specified constraints. Usually these constraints include lower bounds on the quality of the pattern ($\varphi(P) \geq lb_1$) and size of the induced subgroup ($|G_P| \geq lb_2$). More constraints may be imposed as the question at hand requires; domain experts may for instance request an upper bound on the complexity of the pattern. Most common SD algorithms traverse[1] the search space of candidate patterns in a general-to-specific way: they treat the space as a lattice whose structure is defined by a *refinement operator* $\rho : \mathcal{P} \to 2^{\mathcal{P}}$. This operator determines how patterns can be extended into more complex patterns by atomic additions. Most applications (including ours) assume ρ to be a *specialization operator*: $\forall\ P_s \in \rho(P_g)\ :\ P_g \succeq P_s$ (i.e. P_s is more specialized than P_g). The algorithm results in a ranked list of patterns (or the corresponding subgroups) that satisfy the user-defined constraints.

In traditional SD there is only a single target variable. Hence, the typical quality measure contains a component indicating how different the distribution over the target variable in the subgroup is, compared to its distribution in the whole dataset. Since unusual distributions are easily achieved in small subsets of the dataset, the typical quality measure also contains a component indicating the size of the subgroup. Thus, whether a pattern is deemed interesting depends on both its exceptionality and the size of the corresponding subgroup.

EMM can be seen as an extension of SD. Rather than the regular single target variable, EMM uses a more complex target concept. For each subgroup under consideration, we induce a model on the targets. Then quality measures are defined that indicate how exceptional the model fitted on the targets in the subgroup is, compared to the model fitted on the targets in the whole dataset. For example, [16] proposes quality measures for correlation models, a simple linear regression model, and classification models.

In the EMM setting, usually the *beam search* strategy is chosen, which performs a level-wise search. On each level, the best w patterns according to our quality measure φ are selected, and refined to create the candidate patterns for the next level. The search is constrained by an upper bound on the complexity of the pattern and a lower bound on the support of the corresponding subgroup. This search strategy combines the advantages of a greedy method with those of the implicit parallel search: as on each level w alternatives are considered, the search process is less likely to end up in a local optimum than a pure greedy approach, but the selection of the w best patterns at each level keeps the process focused and thus more tractable.

There are Subgroup Discovery techniques that exhaustively explore the search space. These however usually either compel the attributes to be nominal [9, 15] or impose an anti-monotonicity constraint on the quality measure [11]. Since we do not want such restrictions on the attributes or the quality measure, we employ heuristic search.

[1] we consider the exact search strategy to be a parameter of the algorithm

2.2 Linear Regression Model

The previous section introduced Exceptional Model Mining in its general form. In this paper, however, we are concerned with one particular instance: the linear regression model:

$$Y = X\beta + \varepsilon$$

where Y is the $N \times 1$ vector of y-values from our dataset, X is the $N \times p$ full rank matrix of which the first column consists of N times the value 1 and column $i+1$ contains the x_i-values from our dataset, β is the unknown $p \times 1$ vector consisting of the regression parameters, and ε is the $N \times 1$ vector of randomly distributed errors such that $\mathbb{E}(\varepsilon) = 0$ and $\mathrm{Var}(\varepsilon) = \sigma^2 I$. Of course, I denotes the $N \times N$ identity matrix.

Given an *estimate* of the vector β, denoted $\hat{\beta}$, one can compute the vector of *fitted values* $\hat{Y}$. These quantities can be used to assess the appropriateness of the fitted model, by looking at the *residuals* $e = Y - \hat{Y}$. We will estimate β with the ordinary least squares method, which minimizes the sum of squared residuals. This leads to the estimate:

$$\hat{\beta} = \left(X^\top X\right)^{-1} X^\top Y$$

After computing the vector of fitted values, we find that we can now write the corresponding residual vector as:

$$e = (e_i) = Y - \hat{Y} = \left(I - X\left(X^\top X\right)^{-1} X^\top\right) Y$$

We will denote a part of this equation by V:

$$V = (v_{ij}) = X\left(X^\top X\right)^{-1} X^\top$$

This matrix was dubbed the *hat matrix* by John W. Tukey, since $\hat{Y} = VY$, i.e. the hat matrix transforms Y into $\hat{Y}$ [12].

2.3 Regression meets EMM

To mine for exceptional regression models, we have to come up with a good quality measure. It stands to reason that this quality measure should quantify the difference between the coefficient vector $\hat{\beta}$ estimated on the dataset, and the vector $\hat{\beta}^G$ estimated on the subgroup. One could for example use the squared Euclidian distance

$$(\hat{\beta}^G - \hat{\beta})^\top (\hat{\beta}^G - \hat{\beta}) = \sum_{i=1}^{p} (\hat{\beta}_i^G - \hat{\beta}_i)^2 \tag{2}$$

to measure the quality of subgroup G. One can argue that in many applications we are not really interested in the influence of all variables on y, but just in the influence of one, or a small subset, of them. The other variables are merely included in the regression to obtain good estimates of the coefficients we are interested in. This can be easily accommodated by summing over the subset of interest in Equation (2), were one so inclined.

As Equation (2) suggests, to compute the quality of a subgroup we have to fit a model on it in order to obtain the estimates $\hat{\beta}^G$. Since one has to evaluate many subgroups, this can be computationally quite demanding. Therefore, it is of some interest to determine whether such explicit computation can be avoided or limited.

In the next section we propose a more sophisticated quality measure for exceptional regression models, and look at the possibilities of limiting explicit model fitting on subgroups.

3. COOK'S DISTANCE

In the previous section, we suggested the squared Euclidian distance between estimated coefficient vectors as a quality measure. The disadvantage of this measure is that it ignores the variance of the estimator $\hat{\beta}$, and the covariances between $\hat{\beta}_i$ and $\hat{\beta}_j$. For example, if $\hat{\beta}_i$ has a large variance compared to $\hat{\beta}_j$, then a given change in $\hat{\beta}_i$ should contribute less to the overall quality than the same change in $\hat{\beta}_j$, because the change in $\hat{\beta}_i$ is more likely to be caused by random variation. This suggest that

$$(\hat{\beta}^G - \hat{\beta})^\top [\mathrm{Cov}(\hat{\beta})]^{-1} (\hat{\beta}^G - \hat{\beta})$$

might be a better distance measure than the normal Euclidian distance. In fact this expression is equivalent to Cook's distance up to a constant scale factor. R. Dennis Cook originally introduced his distance [3] in 1977 for determining the contribution of single records to $\hat{\beta}$. In this section we discuss this distance measure in detail.

3.1 Cook's distance for single observations

Recall that the least squares estimate of β is

$$\hat{\beta} = \left(X^\top X\right)^{-1} X^\top Y.$$

The corresponding residual vector becomes

$$e = Y - \hat{Y} = Y - X\hat{\beta} = (I - V)Y,$$

where V is the hat matrix defined in Section 2.2. The covariance matrices of $\hat{Y}$ and e, respectively, are

$$\mathrm{Var}\left(\hat{Y}\right) = V\sigma^2, \qquad \mathrm{Var}(e) = (I - V)\sigma^2$$

Finally, Cook states that according to normal theory [10], the $(1-\alpha) \times 100\%$ confidence ellipsoid for the unknown vector, β, is given by the set of all vectors β^* satisfying

$$\frac{\left(\beta^* - \hat{\beta}\right)^\top [\widehat{\mathrm{Cov}}(\hat{\beta})]^{-1} \left(\beta^* - \hat{\beta}\right)}{p} =$$

$$\frac{\left(\beta^* - \hat{\beta}\right)^\top X^\top X \left(\beta^* - \hat{\beta}\right)}{ps^2} \leq F(p, N-p, 1-\alpha)$$

where

$$s^2 = \frac{e^\top e}{N-p}, \qquad \widehat{\mathrm{Cov}}(\hat{\beta}) = s^2 \left(X^\top X\right)^{-1}$$

and $F(p, N-p, 1-\alpha)$ is the $1-\alpha$ probability point of the central F-distribution with p and $N-p$ degrees of freedom. Here, s^2 is the unbiased estimator for σ^2.

Now the stage has been set to determine the degree of influence of single records. Suppose we want to know how record r^i influences $\hat{\beta}$. Then one could naturally compute the least squares estimate for β with the record removed from the dataset. Let us denote this estimate by $\hat{\beta}_{(i)}$. We can adapt the confidence ellipsoid as an easily interpretable measure of the distance between $\hat{\beta}_{(i)}$ and $\hat{\beta}$. Hence, *Cook's distance* is defined as:

$$D_i = \frac{\left(\hat{\beta}_{(i)} - \hat{\beta}\right)^\top X^\top X \left(\hat{\beta}_{(i)} - \hat{\beta}\right)}{ps^2} \tag{3}$$

Suppose for example that for a certain record r^i we find that $D_i \approx F(p, N-p, 0.5)$. Then removing r^i moves the

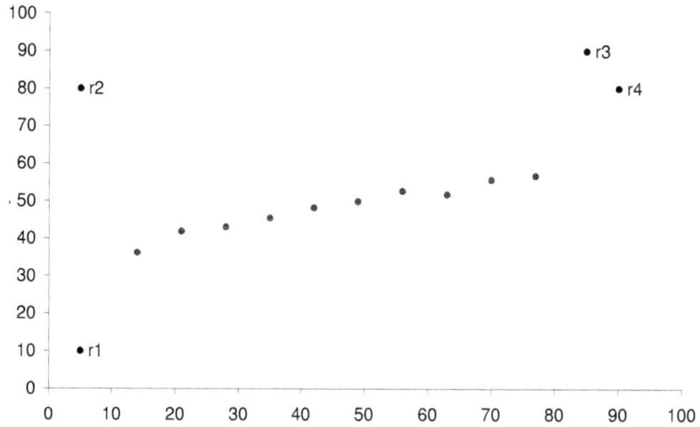

Figure 1: Records r^1 and r^2 are individually influential, but not jointly. Conversely, r^3 and r^4 are jointly influential, but not individually.

least squares estimate to the edge of the 50% confidence region for β based on $\hat{\beta}$.

Bingham [2] showed that Equation (3) can be rewritten in the form

$$D_i = \frac{\left(\hat{Y}_{(i)} - \hat{Y}\right)^\top \left(\hat{Y}_{(i)} - \hat{Y}\right)}{ps^2}$$

which suggests that apart from the scale factor ps^2, D_i is the ordinary squared Euclidean distance that the fitted vector moves when r^i is removed from the dataset.

Cook's distance would not be particularly useful if one really would have to compute $\hat{\beta}_{(i)}$ for each record in the dataset. However, Cook shows [3] that under some mild assumptions D_i can be rewritten as

$$D_i = \frac{t_i^2}{p} \cdot \frac{\text{Var}\left(\hat{Y}_i\right)}{\text{Var}\left(e_i\right)} \tag{4}$$

where t_i is the studentized residual of the ith record. These quantities all relate to the full dataset. Clearly t_i is a measure of how well r^i can be considered an outlier from the assumed model. The ratio of variances measures the relative sensitivity of $\hat{\beta}$ to potential outliers at each data point. Combining these factors hence produces a measure of the impact of any single point on the least squares estimate.

3.2 Cook's distance for multiple observations

Whenever we want to compute the influence of deleting several points simultaneously, as is the case in EMM, one cannot simply use Equation (3) and sum over all records concerned. We will illustrate why with a simple constructed example [4]. Consider linear regression on the dataset from Figure 1. Suppose that we consider removing records r^1 and r^2 from the dataset. If we would remove either of these records, this will have a rather large influence on the slope of the resulting regression line, hence according to Equation (3) both D_1 and D_2 will be large. However, when we remove both records from the dataset, the influences of the records will cancel each other out, and the slope of the regression line will barely change at all: r^1 and r^2 are not *jointly influential*. On the contrary, when removing either record r^3 or r^4 from the dataset, the slope of the regression line will barely change, hence according to Equation (3) both D_3 and D_4 are small. However, their joint influence is quite large: removing both records from the dataset will significantly influence the slope of the regression line.

Hence, we cannot give a reliable measure for the joint influence of a set of records by aggregating over values of D_i. Therefore, Cook and Weisberg extended Cook's distance to cope with deleting multiple records simultaneously [4]. Let I be a vector of indices that specify the m records to be deleted. From now on, we let the subscript (I) denote "with the m cases indexed by I deleted", while the subscript I without parentheses denotes "with only the m cases indexed by I remaining". The only notation that deviates from this rule of thumb is the definition of Cook's distance, which is easily extended to multiple observations:

$$D_I = \frac{\left(\hat{\beta}_{(I)} - \hat{\beta}\right)^\top X^\top X \left(\hat{\beta}_{(I)} - \hat{\beta}\right)}{ps^2} \tag{5}$$

and its geometric interpretation is identical to the geometrical interpretation of D_i. Any subset that has a large joint influence on the estimation of β corresponds to a large D_I.

The fact that the definition of Cook's distance does not follow the notational rule of thumb can be very confusing. We choose to retain the definition in this form to make our work compatible with previously released papers and books. However, it is important to stress the notational anomaly: whenever we write D_I, Cook's distance is computed for the case where the records indexed by I are *deleted*. Whenever we write *anything else* with a subscript I, it is computed for the case where the records indexed by I are *retained*, and all other records are deleted.

Unfortunately, unlike in the case where we deleted only one record, D_I cannot simply be rewritten in a form resembling Equation (4). Hence we need another solution to the problem that computing $\hat{\beta}_{(I)}$ for each candidate subgroup is computationally very expensive.

The upper bounds for Cook's distance are derived [5, pp. 136] by rewriting the numerator of the right hand side of Equation (5) in terms of e_I and V_I. Then the spectral decomposition of V_I is used, rewriting the sub-matrix of the hat matrix in terms of its eigenvalues and eigenvectors. We denote those eigenvalues by $\lambda_1, \ldots, \lambda_m$, and can assume without loss of generality that $0 \leq \lambda_1 \leq \ldots \leq \lambda_m \leq 1$. Notice that if the last inequality is not strict, i.e. $\lambda_m = 1$, then removing the records indexed by I would lead to a rank deficient model, and we cannot properly perform the linear regression. Finally, a proper approximation for these λ_i is required; Cook proposes to use $\text{tr}(V_I)$ here, but notes that this is only a good approximation under the condition that $\text{tr}(V_I) < 1$. Assuming that this condition holds, we can bound D_I by:

$$D_I \leq \frac{\text{tr}(V_I)}{(1 - \text{tr}(V_I))^2} \cdot \frac{\sum_{i \in I} e_i^2}{ps^2} \tag{6}$$

Unfortunately, this bound is potentially different for each I. Cook also gives bounds that hold for all subsets I of a fixed size m. When we fix m and let I vary over all such subsets, we can either use $R^2 = \max_I \left(\sum_{i \in I} e_i^2\right)$, which turns Equation (6) into:

$$D_I \leq \frac{\text{tr}(V_I)}{(1 - \text{tr}(V_I))^2} \cdot \frac{R^2}{ps^2} \tag{7}$$

or we could use $T = \max_I \left(\sum_{i \in I} v_{ii}\right)$, which turns Equation (6) into:

$$D_I \leq \frac{T}{(1-T)^2} \cdot \frac{\sum_{i \in I} e_i^2}{ps^2} \tag{8}$$

Both simplifications R^2 and T can be combined to turn Equation (6) into:

$$D_I \leq \frac{T}{(1-T)^2} \cdot \frac{R^2}{ps^2} \tag{9}$$

Rather obviously, there are relations between the bounds, i.e. (6) $\leq$ (7) $\leq$ (9) and (6) $\leq$ (8) $\leq$ (9).

3.3 Subsets of $\hat{\beta}$

For practical purposes one might not be interested in computing Cook's distance based on the entire parameter vector $\hat{\beta}$. For instance, one might be interested in the influence records have on the regression coefficient corresponding to one particular attribute, while excluding the intercept and other coefficients from the evaluation. To this end, Cook and Weisberg [5] introduce the zero/one-matrix Z, with dimensions $q \times p$, where q is the number of elements of $\hat{\beta}$ that we are interested in (hence $q \leq p$). The matrix Z is defined in such a way that $\psi = Z\beta$ are the coefficients of interest. Hence, if we are interested in the last q elements of $\hat{\beta}$, Z will start from the left with $p - q$ columns containing all zeroes, followed by a $q \times q$ identity matrix ($Z = (\mathbf{0}, \mathbf{I_q})$).

When using this transformation, Cook's distance (Equation (5)) becomes:

$$D_I^{\psi} = \frac{\left(\hat{\beta}_{(I)} - \hat{\beta}\right)^\top Z^\top \left(Z \left(X^\top X\right)^{-1} Z^\top\right)^{-1} Z \left(\hat{\beta}_{(I)} - \hat{\beta}\right)}{qs^2}$$

One can show that $qD_I^{\psi} \leq pD_I$ for all I, hence one can make all bounds (6)–(9) relevant for D_I^{ψ} by multiplying them by the factor $\frac{p}{q}$.

3.4 Cook's distance in EMM

Since Cook's distance is invariant to changes in scale of the variables involved [3], it would make an excellent quality measure for use in EMM:

Definition (φ_{Cook}). Let G_P be a subgroup. Its *quality according to Cook's distance* is given by:

$$\varphi_{\text{Cook}}(G_P) = D_I^{\psi}, \text{ where } I = \left\{ i \middle| r^i \in \mathcal{D}, P\left(a^i\right) = 0 \right\}$$

Hence, Cook's distance of a subgroup is the distance bridged when the records that are not covered by the subgroup are simultaneously discarded. This definition seems a bit convoluted; it is constructed in such a way that the notational anomaly discussed in Section 3.2 is repaired: whenever we write $\varphi_{\text{Cook}}(G_p)$, Cook's distance is computed for the case where the records belonging to the subgroup G_p are *retained*.

3.5 Pruning with Cook's bounds

Whenever one has the possibility to enumerate all candidate subgroups for mining with Cook's distance, the bounds (6)–(9) can be used for pruning. In combination with the beam search strategy, we propose to do this in the following way.

Per search level, we determine the number of subgroups S we are interested in retaining. We enumerate all candidate subgroups in descending ordered according to one of the bounds. Then we consider the subgroups in this order.

For each subgroup, we compute the bounds in order of decreasing ease of computation, i.e. first bound (9), then bound (8), then bound (7), and finally bound (6). We check whether any of these bounds has a value that is lower than Cook's distance for the Sth best evaluated subgroup so far. If so, we know that Cook's distance for this new subgroup can not enter the top-S, since the bound is an upper bound for Cook's distance. Hence we can skip computing Cook's distance for this subgroup, which saves us the computation of a relatively expensive regression. If none of the bounds help us out, we compute Cook's distance for the new subgroup.

Dataset	N	k	p
Ames Housing	2930	77	3
Auction	1225	3	7
EAEF	2714	32	3
Giffen Behavior	1254	6	16
PC486	6259	3	7
Wine	5000	6	4

Table 1: Some elementary properties of the datasets. N is the total number of records, k is the number of attributes that can be used to define subgroups, and p is the number of coefficients in the fitted regression model.

4. BOUND BEHAVIOR AND PRUNING

Table 1 lists the datasets we have used in the experiments. All datasets are publicly available. The Giffen behavior dataset[2] was used for a study that claimed to provide the first real-world evidence of Giffen behavior, i.e. an upward sloping demand curve [13]. The EAEF dataset[3] was analyzed in [7]. The Wine data was analyzed in [6], and is available from the data archive of the Journal of Applied Econometrics[4]. The Ames Housing data is available from the Journal of Statistics Education data archive[5]. Finally, the PC486 data and the Auction data were analyzed in [19] and [18] respectively, and are both available from the data archive of the Journal of Applied Econometrics.

To illustrate what can reasonably be expected from pruning with the bounds, we simulated their behavior on random subgroups of the EAEF dataset. For each possible subgroup size, we drew a random sample of the data with that size. Then we computed the values of the bounds for these subgroups, when fitting the model

$$\text{Earnings} = \beta_0 + \beta_1 \times \text{YrsOfSchool}$$

The results can be found in Figure 2. The figure depicts the subgroup size on the x-axis (linear scale), and the values of the bounds on the y-axis (logarithmic scale).

[2]The data can be downloaded from: www.aeaweb.org/articles.php?doi=10.1257/aer.98.4.1553

[3]The data can be obtained from www.oxfordtextbooks.co.uk/orc/dougherty4e/

[4]http://econ.queensu.ca/jae/

[5]http://www.amstat.org/publications/jse/jse_data_archive.htm

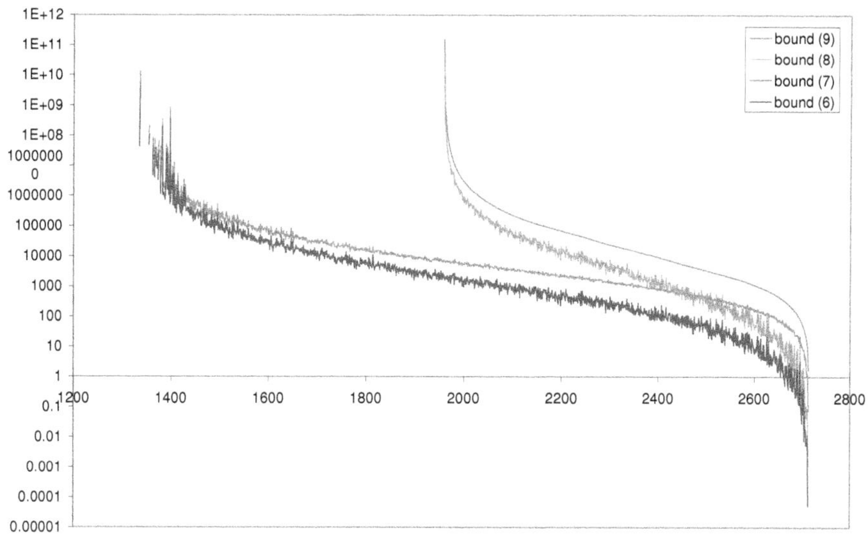

Figure 2: Bound values (logarithmic scale) for random subgroups of different sizes on the EAEF dataset. Fitted model: Earnings = $\beta_0 + \beta_1 \times$ YrsOfSchool.

The EAEF dataset has 2714 records, so when a subgroup approaches this size it will correspond to deleting very few records, and as one would expect Cook's distance becomes very small, as do the bounds. Furthermore, one notices that the bound quality lines do not extend all the way to subgroup size 0. This is caused by limitations in the approximations used in the bounds. As we mentioned in Section 3.2, the bounds are only good approximations whenever $\mathrm{tr}(V_I) < 1$. When this constraint is not satisfied, the bounds cannot be computed. For bounds (8) and (9), the quantity T is used as an estimate for $\mathrm{tr}(V_I)$, but this too only makes sense when $T < 1$, or else the bounds cannot be computed.

The practical upshot is that for subgroups smaller than 1960 records, bounds (8) and (9) cannot be computed. For subgroups smaller than roughly 1250 records, this also holds for bounds (6) and (7). When viewed as a percentage of the number of records in the datasets, we find that these borders are roughly the same over all datasets: bounds (6) and (7) can only be computed when the subgroup contains at least 50% of the records, and bounds (8) and (9) only when the subgroup contains at least 75% of the records. We also find that the more complex the model we fit, the further these thresholds move towards larger percentages.

The bounds can not be computed for at least half of the subgroups we consider, and the bound values tend to increase enormously just before these threshold values are reached. However, the bounds are computable for the largest subgroups, and the computation of the hat matrix is quadratic in the subgroup size. Hence whenever we can prune a subgroup, it always takes a relatively expensive regression computation out of the total runtime.

4.1 Empirical bound evaluation

To empirically see how the bounds perform, we performed a depth-1 subgroup discovery run on each dataset, with the goal to find the top-1 subgroup. When numeric attributes were used to generate candidate subgroups, we split them into 12 equal-sized bins. We discarded any subgroup that covered less than 100 records, since we consider these too small to be considered interesting from a statistical point of view. For each bound we counted how often it was computed, and how often it caused a subgroup to be pruned.

The results can be found in Table 2. This table features the datasets, dataset characteristics, number of times every bound is computed, number of subgroups pruned with every bound, fraction of candidate subgroups for which at least one bound was computable, and fraction of candidate subgroups that were pruned. Notice that there is a strong dependency between the "Bound computed" and "Subgroups pruned" columns: in the Ames Housing dataset we can compute bound (9) for 196 subgroups, of which we can prune 155, so only 41 subgroups remain for which we compute bound (8). However, the number of subgroups for which we compute bound (7) is larger, since the condition under which this bound is computable is less strict than the condition for bound (8) and (9). Of the 228 subgroups for which we compute bound (7) we can prune 191, leaving 37 subgroups for which we compute bound (6).

As we indicated in the previous section, the fraction of subgroups for which we can compute the bounds is strongly dependent on the complexity of the fitted model. As we can see from the table, in the datasets for which $3 \leq p \leq 4$ we can compute bounds for over 40% of the subgroups, in the datasets for which $p = 7$ we can compute bounds for $33 - 35$% of the subgroups, and in the dataset for which $p = 16$ we can compute bounds for just 1% of the subgroups. This dependency becomes somewhat less direct when we look at the percentage of subgroups we can actually prune, since this is relatively low for the EAEF dataset on which we fit a relatively simple model. However, apart from this one dataset, we still see a strong relation between model simplicity and pruning success.

Since we are rarely interested in only the one best-performing subgroup, we replicate these experiments with the goal to find the top-50 subgroups. Since we need to have considered at least 50 subgroups before we can make sure others

Dataset	N	$\|\mathcal{C}\|$	p	Bounds computed				Subgroups pruned				$\frac{\|\text{bounded } \mathcal{C}\|}{\|\mathcal{C}\|}$	$\frac{\|\text{pruned } \mathcal{C}\|}{\|\mathcal{C}\|}$
				(9)	(8)	(7)	(6)	(9)	(8)	(7)	(6)		
Ames Housing	2930	980	3	196	41	228	37	155	28	191	11	0.419	0.393
Auction	1225	40	7	5	0	9	5	5	0	4	0	0.350	0.225
EAEF	2714	204	3	35	29	68	68	6	9	0	21	0.407	0.176
Giffen Behavior	1254	100	16	1	1	1	1	0	0	0	1	0.010	0.010
PC486	6950	6	7	0	0	2	1	0	0	1	0	0.333	0.167
Wine	5000	56	4	2	2	26	20	0	0	6	11	0.464	0.304

Table 2: Pruning results for depth-1 EMM runs, when looking for the top-1 subgroup. N **is the total number of records,** $\mathcal{C}$ **is the set of candidate subgroups considered, and** p **is the number of coefficients in the fitted regression model.**

Dataset	N	$\|\mathcal{C}\|$	p	Bounds computed				Subgroups pruned				$\frac{\|\text{bounded } \mathcal{C}\|}{\|\mathcal{C}\|}$	$\frac{\|\text{pruned } \mathcal{C}\|}{\|\mathcal{C}\|}$
				(9)	(8)	(7)	(6)	(9)	(8)	(7)	(6)		
Ames Housing	2930	980	3	196	125	272	122	71	68	150	44	0.419	0.340
EAEF	2714	204	3	35	34	77	77	1	5	0	11	0.407	0.083

Table 3: Pruning results for depth-1 EMM runs, when looking for the top-50 subgroups.

will not enter the top-50 based on their bounds, we know in advance that there will be little or no pruning possible for the Auction, PC486, and Wine datasets. We also expect to gain little information from the Giffen Behavior dataset, hence Table 3 encompasses the results of these experiments on merely the Ames Housing and EAEF dataset. Notice that the fraction of subgroups we can prune on the Ames Housing dataset has only decreased slightly, while the fraction of subgroups we can prune on the EAEF dataset is cut in half.

We repeated all these experiments with depth-2 subgroup discovery runs with beam width 10. We find that in these experiments, we can barely compute bounds for any level-2 subgroups, let alone prune subgroups. This is caused by the fact that level-2 subgroups are refinements of well-scoring level-1 subgroups, which are usually relatively small. Well-scoring level-1 subgroups almost never cover more than 50% of the records, hence their refinements also almost never do so. Fortunately, that also means that the regression computations for these subgroups is relatively cheap.

5. ILLUSTRATIVE RESULTS

In this section we give a number of examples of the types of results that can be obtained with our algorithm. The reader should keep in mind that this type of analysis should normally be performed in collaboration with a subject area expert who could aid in the interpretation of the results.

5.1 Giffen Behavior Data

This dataset was used for a study that claimed to provide the first real-world evidence of Giffen behavior, i.e. an upward sloping demand curve [13]. As common sense suggests, the demand for a product will usually decrease as its price increases. According to economic textbooks, there are circumstances however, for which we should expect to see an upward sloping demand curve. The common example is that of poor families that spend most of their income on a relatively inexpensive staple food (e.g. rice or wheat) and a small part on a more expensive type of food (e.g. meat). If the price of the staple food rises, people can no longer afford to supplement their diet with the more expensive food, and must consume more of the staple food.

The dataset we analyze was collected in different counties in the Chinese province Hunan, where rice is the staple food. The price changes were brought about by giving vouchers to randomly selected households to subsidize their purchase of rice. The global model estimated in [13] is:

$$\begin{aligned}\%\Delta\text{staple}_{i,t} &= \alpha + \beta\%\Delta p_{i,t} + \sum \gamma\%\Delta Z_{i,t} + \\ &+ \sum \delta\text{County} \times \text{Time}_{i,t} + \Delta\varepsilon_{i,t},\end{aligned}$$

where $\%\Delta\text{staple}_{i,t}$ denotes the percent change in household i's consumption of rice, $\%\Delta p_{i,t}$ is the percent change in the price of rice due to the subsidy (negative for $t = 2$ and positive for $t = 3$), and $\%\Delta Z_{i,t}$ is a vector of percent changes in other control variables including income and household size. County $\times$ Time denotes a set of dummy variables included to control for any county-level factors that change over time. For each household, two changes are observed: the change between periods 2 and 1 ($t = 2$), capturing the effect of giving the subsidy; and the change between periods 3 and 2 ($t = 3$) capturing the effect of removing the subsidy. For further details about the design of the study and the estimation strategy, we refer to [13].

The coefficient of primary interest is β. If $\beta > 0$ we observe Giffen behavior. The other variables are included in the model to control for other possible influences on demand, so that the effect of price can be reliably estimated. Therefore it makes sense to restrict our quality measure to the coefficient β, that is, the quality of a subgroup is proportional to the absolute difference between $\hat{\beta}$ and $\hat{\beta}^G$.

The authors of [13] suggest that for the extremely poor, one might not observe Giffen behavior, because they consumed rice almost exclusively anyway, and therefore have no other possibility than buying less of it in case of a price increase. The Initial Staple Calorie Share (ISCS) was also measured in the study, and the hypothesis is that families with a high value for this variable do not display Giffen behavior. The authors of [13] tried different manually selected thresholds on ISCS; for example, for the subgroup of households with ISCS > 0.8, indeed it is observed that $\hat{\beta} = -0.585$ (no Giffen behavior) whereas for ISCS ≤ 0.8 they get $\hat{\beta} = 0.466$ (Giffen behavior).

We analyzed this dataset with ISCS as one of the variables on which the subgroups could be defined. At depth 1, the best subgroup we found was ISCS ≥ 0.87 with $\hat{\beta} = -0.96$ (against $\hat{\beta} = 0.22$ for the complete dataset). The size of this subgroup is $n = 106$. This confirms the conclusion that Giffen behavior does not occur for families that almost exclusively consume rice anyway. This conclusion can also be reached by defining subgroups on *income per capita* rather than ISCS. Particularly illustrative examples are the 4th-ranked subgroup: Income per Capita ≤ 64.67, with a slope of -0.41, and the 6th-ranked subgroup: Income per Capita ≥ 803.75, with a slope of 0.79 (strong Giffen behavior).

5.2 EAEF Data

This dataset has been extracted from the National Longitudinal Survey of Youth 1979-(NLSY79). It contains information about hourly earnings of men and women, and information about, among others, their education. For more details, we refer to Appendix B of [7]. We fit a model relating years of schooling and years of work experience to earnings. The model fitted on the complete dataset is:

$$\text{Earnings} = -29.15 + 2.78 \times \text{YrsOfSchool} + 0.63 \times \text{YrsWorkExp}$$

All coefficients in this model are significant at $\alpha = 0.01$, and R^2 is approximately equal to 20%.

The 4th ranked subgroup we found was COLLBARG = 1, meaning that the pay was set by collective bargaining. The fitted model for this subgroup of size $n = 533$ is:

$$\text{Earnings} = -8.93 + 1.57 \times \text{YrsOfSchool} + 0.43 \times \text{YrsWorkExp}$$

This suggests that for this group an extra year of schooling on average leads to an increase of just \$1.57 in hourly earnings, compared to \$2.78 for the whole dataset. The same is true for the influence of an extra year of work experience: just \$0.43 for the collective bargaining subgroup, against \$0.63 in the complete dataset. This is consistent with the finding that unions tend to equalize the income distribution, especially between skilled and unskilled workers [1].

5.3 Wine Data

This dataset was analyzed in [6]. It is composed of 9600 observations derived from 10 years (1991-2000) of tasting ratings reported in the Wine Spectator Magazine (online version) for California and Washington red wines. Our analysis uses a random sample of size 5000 from the original data. For a detailed description of the data we refer to [6]. The global model is

$$\text{Price} = -186.61 - 0.0002 \times \text{Cases} + 2.35 \times \text{Score} + 5.51 \times \text{Age},$$

where *Price* is the retail price suggested by the winery, *Score* is the score from the Wine Spectator, *Age* is the years of aging before commercialization, and *Cases* is the number of cases produced (in thousands). All coefficients are significant at $\alpha = 0.01$, and R^2 is approximately equal to 31%. Furthermore, all coefficients have the sign that one would expect based on common sense.

The most deviating subgroup is *Variety = Non-varietal* (alternatives are Pinot noir, Cabernet, Merlot, Zinfandel and Syrah). The regression model for this subgroup is:

$$\text{Price} = -341.92 - 0.0004 \times \text{Cases} + 4.16 \times \text{Score} + 7.22 \times \text{Age}$$

Non-varietal actually means that multiple varieties of grapes are used, and on average these wines are more expensive than the single-variety wines (average price of \$44,16 against \$28,89). People buying those more expensive wines tend to be better informed (e.g. read Wine Spectator Magazine) than the average buyer. This explains to a certain extent why the price of those more expensive wines is more sensitive to its score and age: they have more critical buyers.

5.4 Ames Housing Data

This dataset contains information from the Ames Assessor's Office used in computing assessed values for individual residential properties sold in Ames, Iowa from 2006 to 2010. It consists of 2930 observations on 82 variables. The global model is

$$\text{Price} = -108225.05 + 1.93 \times \text{Lot Area} + 44201.87 \times \text{Quality},$$

where *Price* is the sales price of the house in dollars, *Lot Area* is the lot size in square feet, and *Quality* rates the overall material and finish of the house on a scale from 1 to 10. All coefficients are significant at $\alpha = 0.01$, and R^2 is about 67%.

By far the most deviating subgroup we find is where the building type is a *townhouse inside unit*:

$$\text{Price} = -17674.20 + 24.62 \times \text{Lot Area} + 15786.88 \times \text{Quality}$$

The size of this subgroup is $n = 101$, and the R^2 of the model fitted to this subgroup is about 71%. The dependence of price on lot area is much stronger for town houses, whereas the dependence of price on overall quality is less strong than in general. In an attempt to explain this pattern, we note that the average lot area of town houses (2353 square feet) is much smaller than the overall average (10148 square feet) which is largely determined by the predominant building type *single family detached*. Furthermore, it stands to reason that for townhouses a larger part of the lot area is actually occupied by the house itself than for the single family detached houses. This is consistent with a much stronger dependence of their price on the lot area.

6. CONCLUSIONS

In this paper, we have proposed to use Cook's distance in an Exceptional Model Mining setting. This allows us to find subgroups of the data, for which a regression model fitted on certain dedicated target variables is substantially different from that model for the whole dataset. The use of Cook's distance has two large benefits.

On the one hand, Cook's distance has some desirable properties. It is invariant under changes in the scale of a variable, and it explicitly takes the covariance matrix of $\hat{\beta}$ into account. Hence when using Cook's distance we need not worry whether the outcome of the EMM algorithm is influenced by the scale ones attributes happen to arrive in (attributes need not be normalised), or the interactions that happen to be present between the regression parameters.

On the other hand, there are some theoretical upper bounds on Cook's distance, that can be computed without actually performing the relatively expensive regression computations. As we have seen, these bounds can only be computed under certain constraints, which correspond to the subgroup covering at least 50% of the records. On the one hand, this means that we can compute the bounds for relatively few subgroups, but on the other hand, whenever we can prune a subgroup, we always prune a relatively expensive regression computation, since the computational complexity is quadratic in the subgroup size. In future research, we would like to develop bounds for Cook's distance that can be computed for subgroups with small coverage as well.

As we have seen in Section 4, the fraction of subgroups that can be pruned is strongly dependent on the complexity of the regression model we fit. We have seen some datasets (Ames Housing and Wine) for which the model complexities are modest, on which we can prune almost 40% and 30% of the subgroups, respectively. On datasets for which the model complexities are mediocre, we can still prune approximately 20%, and on the dataset for which the model complexity is high, we can prune only 1%.

In Section 5 we have discussed some illustrative examples of subgroups found on datasets from different domains. The models fitted on these subgroups are discussed. These examples show the versatility of the problems which EMM with Cook's distance can solve.

We discussed in Section 3.2 how the joint influence of records makes Cook's distance for single observations theoretically unsuitable for use in a setting where multiple observations are removed simultaneously. However, it may very well be that this problem is not that serious on real-life datasets. Hence, in future research, we would like to see whether we can use Cook's distance for single observations as a proxy for Cook's distance for multiple observations, for instance by summing over D_i for all $i \in I$.

Also in future work, we would like to explore whether we can improve pruning for complex models. Often one is not interested in the influence of all model coefficients, and in Section 3.3 we have seen an adaptation of Cook's distance such that it is evaluated on a subset of the coefficients. We also gave a way to modify the bounds accordingly, but this is done in a rather blunt way. We plan to study whether more sophisticated bounds can be derived, with which we can prune more subgroups.

Finally, this paper was motivated by the Giffen behavior example, in which coefficients not only substantially change in magnitude, but additionally change in sign. Such sign changes can be found on other datasets as well, and the subgroups to which such models are fitted are usually among the most striking subgroups we can find. In future work, we would like to develop a quality measure that explicitly seeks for such sign changes.

Acknowledgments

This research is financially supported by the Netherlands Organisation for Scientific Research (NWO) under project number 612.065.822 (Exceptional Model Mining).

7. REFERENCES

[1] T. Aidt and Z. Tzannatos, Unions and Collective Bargaining, The World Bank, 2002.

[2] C. Bingham, Some identities useful in the analysis of residuals from linear regression, technical report no. 300, School of Statistics, University of Minnesota, St. Paul, 1977.

[3] R. D. Cook, Detection of Influential Observation in Linear Regression, Technometrics 19(1), pp. 15–18, 1977.

[4] R. D. Cook, S. Weisberg, Characterizations of an Empirical Influence Function for Detecting Influential Cases in Regression, Technometrics 22(4), pp. 495–508, 1980.

[5] R. D. Cook, S. Weisberg, Residuals and Influence in Regression, Chapman & Hall, London, 1982.

[6] M. Costanigro, R. C. Mittelhammer, J. J. McCluskey, Estimating Class-Specific Parametric Models under Class Uncertainty: Local Polynomial Regression Clustering in an Hedonic Analysis of Wine Markets, Journal of Applied Econometrics 24, pp. 1117–1135, 2009.

[7] C. Dougherty, Introduction to Econometrics (4th edition), Oxford University Press, 2011.

[8] W. Duivesteijn, A. Knobbe, A. Feelders, M. van Leeuwen, Subgroup Discovery meets Bayesian networks – an Exceptional Model Mining approach, Proc. ICDM, pp. 158–167, 2010.

[9] J. Friedman, N. Fisher, Bump-Hunting in High-Dimensional Data, Statistics and Computing 9(2), pp. 123–143, 1999.

[10] J. F. Gentleman, M. B. Wilk, Detecting outliers II: Supplementing the direct analysis of residuals, Biometrics 31, pp. 387–410, 1975.

[11] H. Grosskreutz, S. Rüping, On Subgroup Discovery in Numerical Domains, Data Mining and Knowledge Discovery 19(2), pp. 210–226, 2009.

[12] D. C. Hoaglin, R. Welsh, The hat matrix in regression and ANOVA, American Statistician 32, pp. 17–22, 1978.

[13] R. T. Jensen, N. H. Miller, Giffen Behavior and Subsistence Consumption, American Economic Review 98(4), pp. 1553–1577, 2008.

[14] G. G. Judge, R. C. Hill, W. E. Griffiths, H. Lütkepohl, T.-C. Lee, Introduction to the Theory and Practice of Econometrics (2nd ed.), Wiley, 1988.

[15] W. Klösgen, Subgroup Discovery, Handbook of Data Mining and Knowledge Discovery, ch. 16.3, Oxford University Press, New York, 2002.

[16] D. Leman, A. Feelders, A. J. Knobbe, Exceptional Model Mining, Proc. ECML/PKDD (2) 2008, LNCS, volume 5212, pp. 1–16, Springer, Heidelberg.

[17] A. Marshall, Principles of Economics, MacMillan and co., 1895.

[18] L. Rezende, Econometrics of Auctions by Least Squares, Journal of Applied Econometrics 23, pp. 925–948, 2008.

[19] T. Stengos, E. Zacharias, Intertemporal Pricing and Price Discrimination: A Semiparametric Hedonic Analysis of the Personal Computer Market, Journal of Applied Econometrics 21, pp. 371–386, 2006.

A Near-linear Time Approximation Algorithm for Angle-based Outlier Detection in High-dimensional Data

Ninh Pham
IT University of Copenhagen
Copenhagen, Denmark
ndap@itu.dk

Rasmus Pagh
IT University of Copenhagen
Copenhagen, Denmark
pagh@itu.dk

ABSTRACT

Outlier mining in d-dimensional point sets is a fundamental and well studied data mining task due to its variety of applications. Most such applications arise in high-dimensional domains. A bottleneck of existing approaches is that implicit or explicit assessments on concepts of distance or nearest neighbor are deteriorated in high-dimensional data. Following up on the work of Kriegel et al. (KDD '08), we investigate the use of *angle-based outlier factor* in mining high-dimensional outliers. While their algorithm runs in cubic time (with a quadratic time heuristic), we propose a novel random projection-based technique that is able to estimate the angle-based outlier factor for all data points in time near-linear in the size of the data. Also, our approach is suitable to be performed in parallel environment to achieve a parallel speedup. We introduce a theoretical analysis of the quality of approximation to guarantee the reliability of our estimation algorithm. The empirical experiments on synthetic and real world data sets demonstrate that our approach is efficient and scalable to very large high-dimensional data sets.

Categories and Subject Descriptors

H.2.8 [**Database Management**]: Database Applications—*Data mining*

General Terms

Algorithms

Keywords

outlier detection, high-dimensional, angle-based, random projection, AMS Sketch

1. INTRODUCTION

Outlier mining is a fundamental and well studied data mining task due to the variety of domain applications, such as fraud detection for credit cards, intrusion detection in network traffic, and anomaly motion detection in surveillance video, etc. Detecting outliers is to identify the objects that considerably deviate from the general distribution of the data. Such the objects may be seen as suspicious objects due to the different mechanism of generation. For example, consider the problem of fraud detection for credit cards and the data set containing the card owners' transactions. The transaction records consist of usage profiles of each customer corresponding the purchasing behavior. The purchasing behavior of customer usually changes when the credit card is stolen. The abnormal purchasing patterns may be reflected in transaction records that contain high payments, high rate of purchase or the orders comprising large numbers of duplicate items, etc.

Most such applications arise in very high-dimensional domains. For instance, the credit card data set contains transaction records described by over 100 attributes [21]. To detect anomalous motion trajectories in surveillance videos, we have to deal with very high representational dimensionality of pixel features of sequential video frames [16]. Because of the notorious "curse of dimensionality", most proposed approaches so far which are explicitly or implicitly based on the assessment of differences in Euclidean distance metric between objects in full-dimensional space do not work efficiently. Traditional algorithms to detect distance-based outliers [13, 19] or density-based outliers [6, 18] suffer from the high computational complexity for high-dimensional nearest neighbor search. In addition, the higher the dimensionality is, the poorer the discrimination between the nearest and the farthest neighbor becomes [1]. That leads to a situation where most of the objects in the data set appear likely to be outliers based on the evaluation on their neighborhood using concepts like distance or nearest neighbor in high-dimensional space.

In KDD 2008, Kriegel et al. [14] proposed a novel outlier ranking approach based on the variance of the angles between an object and all other pairs of objects. This approach, named Angle-based Outlier Detection (ABOD), evaluates the degree of outlierness of each object on the assessment of the broadness of its angle spectrum. The smaller the angle spectrum of a object to other pairs of objects is, the more likely it is an outlier. Because "*angles are more stable than distances in high-dimensional space*" [15], this approach does not substantially deteriorate in high-dimensional data. In spite of many advantages of alleviating the effects of the "curse of dimensionality" and being a parameter-free measure, the time complexity taken to compute ABOD is significant with $O(dn^3)$ for a data set of n objects in d-dimensional

KDD'12, August 12–16, 2012, Beijing, China.

space. To avoid the cubic time complexity, the authors also proposed heuristic approximation variants of ABOD for efficient computations. These approximations, however, still rely on nearest neighbors and require high computational complexity with $O(dn^2)$ used in sequential search for neighbors. Moreover, there is no analysis to guarantee the accuracy of these approximations.

In this paper, we develop a near-linear time algorithm to approximate the variance of angles for each data object. Our proposed approach works in $O(n \log n(d + \log n))$ time for a data set of size n in d-dimensional space, and outputs an unbiased estimator of variance of angles for each object. The main technical insight is the combination between random hyperplane projections [11, 7] and AMS Sketch on product domains [12, 5], which enables us to reduce the computational complexity from cubic time complexity in the naïve approach to near-linear time complexity in the approximation solution. Another advantage of our algorithm is the suitability for parallel processing. In fact, we can achieve a nearly linear (in the number of processors used) parallel speedup of running time. We give a theoretical analysis of the quality of approximation to guarantee the reliability of our estimation algorithm. The empirical experiments on real world and synthetic data sets demonstrate that our approach is efficient and scalable to very large high-dimensional data.

The organization of the paper is as follows. In Section 2, we briefly review related work. The algorithm description including preliminaries and the proposed approach is presented in Section 3. Section 4 introduces the analysis of the accuracy of our approach. In Section 5, we show experimental evaluations of our proposed approach with synthetic and real world data sets. Finally, we make some conclusions about our work in Section 6.

2. RELATED WORK

A good outlier measure is the key aspect for achieving effectiveness and efficiency when managing the outlier mining tasks. A great number of outlier measures have been proposed, including global and local outlier models. Global outlier models typically take the complete database into account while local outlier models only consider a restricted surrounding neighborhood of each data object.

Knorr and Ng [13] proposed a simple and intuitive distance-based definition of outlier as an earliest global outlier model in the context of databases. The outliers with respect to parameter k and λ are the objects that have less than k neighbors within distance λ. A variant of the distance-based notion is proposed in [19]. This approach takes the distance of a object to its kth nearest neighbor as its outlier score and retrieve the top m objects having the highest outlier scores as the top m outliers. The distance-based approaches are based on the assumption, that the lower density region that the data object is in, the more likely it is an outlier. The basic algorithm to detect such distance-based outliers is the nested loop algorithm [19] that simply computes the distance between each object and its kth nearest neighbor and retrieve top m objects with the maximum k^{th} nearest neighbor distances. To avoid the quadratic worst case complexity of nested loop algorithm, several key optimizations are proposed in the literature. Such optimizations can be classified based on the different pruning strategies, such as the approximate nearest neighbor search [19], data partitioning strategies [19] and data ranking strategies [4, 10, 20]. Although these optimizations may improve performance, they scale poorly and are therefore inefficient as the dimensionality or the data size increases, and objects become increasingly sparse [2].

While global models take the complete database into account and detect outliers based on the distances to their neighbors, local density-based models evaluate the degree of outlierness of each object based on the local density of its neighborhood. In many applications, local outlier models give many advantages such as the ability to detect both global and local outliers with different densities and providing the boundary between normal and abnormal behaviors [6]. The approaches in this category assign to each object a local outlier factor as the outlierness degree based on the local density of its k-nearest neighbors [6] or the multi-granularity deviation of its ϵ-neighborhood [18]. In fact, these approaches implicitly rely on finding nearest neighbors for every object and typically use indexing data structures to improve the performance. Therefore, they are unsuitable for the requirements in mining high-dimensional outliers.

Due to the fact that the measures like distance or nearest neighbor may not be qualitatively meaningful in high-dimensional space, recent approaches focus on subspace projections for outlier ranking [2, 17]. In other words, these approaches take a subset of attributes of objects as subspaces into account. However, these approaches suffer from the difficulty of choosing meaningful subspaces [2] or the exponential time complexity in the data dimensionality [17]. As mentioned above, Kriegel at al. [14] proposed a robust angle-based measure to detect high-dimensional outliers. This approach evaluates the degree of outlierness of each data object on the assessment of the variance of angles between itself and other pairs of objects. The smaller the variance of angles between a object to the residual objects is, the more likely it is outlier. Because the angle spectrum between objects is more stable than distances as the dimensionality increases [15], this measure does not substantially deteriorate in high-dimensional data. However, the naïve and approximation approaches suffer from the high computational complexity with cubic time and quadratic time, respectively.

3. ALGORITHM DESCRIPTION

3.1 Angle-based outlier detection (ABOD)

As elaborated above, using concepts like distance or nearest neighbor for mining outlier patterns in high-dimensional data is unsuitable. A novel approach based on the variance of angles between pairs of data points is proposed to alleviate the effects of "curse of dimensionality" [14]. Figure 1 shows the variance of angles for the three kinds of points. Notice that the border and inner points of the cluster have very large variance of angles whereas this value is much smaller for the outliers. In other words, the smaller the angle variance of a point to the residual points is, the more likely it is an outlier. This is because the points inside the cluster are surrounded by other points in all possible directions while the points outside the cluster are positioned in particular directions. Therefore, we use the variance of angles (VOA) as the outlier factor to evaluate the degree of outlierness of each point of the data set. The proposed approaches in [14] do not deal directly with the variance of angles but variance of cosine of angles weighted by the corresponding distances of the points instead. We argue that the weighting factors are

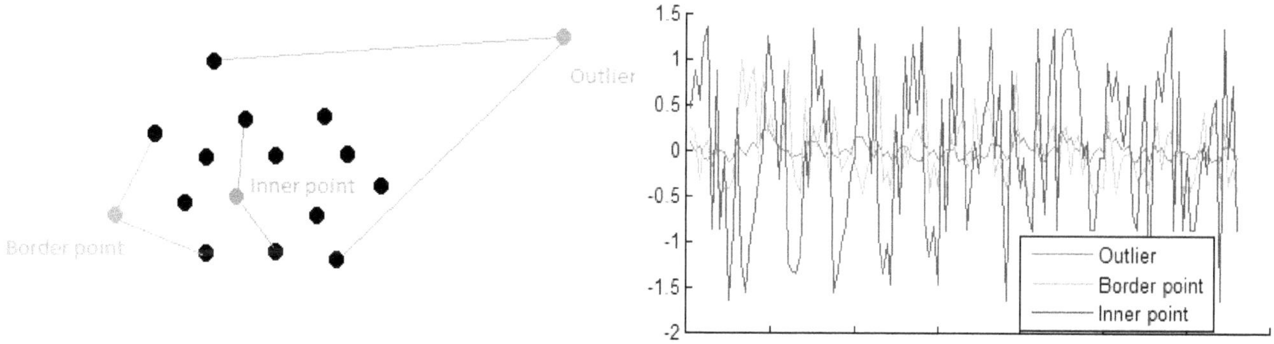

Figure 1: The variance of angles for different kinds of points.

less and less meaningful in high-dimensional data due to the "curse of dimensionality". We expect the outlier rankings based on the variance of cosine spectrum with or without weighting factors and the variance of angle spectrum are likely similar in high-dimensional data. We therefore formulate the angle-based outlier factor using the variance of angles as follows:

DEFINITION 1. *Given a point set $S \subseteq \mathbf{R}^d$, $|S| = n$ and a point $p \in S$. For a random pair of different points $a, b \in S \setminus \{p\}$, let Θ_{apb} denote the angle between the difference vectors $a - p$ and $b - p$. The angle-based outlier factor VOA(p) is the variance of Θ_{apb}:*

$$VOA(p) = \mathbf{Var}[\Theta_{apb}] = MOA_2(p) - (MOA_1(p))^2$$

where MOA_2 and MOA_1 are defined as follows:

$$MOA_2(p) = \frac{\sum_{\substack{a,b \in S\setminus\{p\} \\ a \neq b}} \Theta^2_{apb}}{\frac{1}{2}(n-1)(n-2)}; MOA_1(p) = \frac{\sum_{\substack{a,b \in S\setminus\{p\} \\ a \neq b}} \Theta_{apb}}{\frac{1}{2}(n-1)(n-2)}$$

It is obvious that the VOA measure is entirely free of parameters and therefore is suitable for unsupervised outlier detection methods. The naïve ABOD algorithm computes the VOA for each point of the data set and return the top m points having the smallest VOA as outliers. However, the time complexity of the naïve algorithm is in $O(dn^3)$. The cubic computational complexity means that it will be very difficult to mine outliers in very large data sets.

3.2 Technical Overview

The general idea of our approach is to efficiently compute an unbiased estimator of the variance of the angles for each point of the data set. In other words, the expected value of our estimate is equal to the variance of angles and we show that it is concentrated around its expected value. These estimated values are then used to rank the points. The top m points having the smallest variances of angles are retrieved as top m outliers of the data set.

In order to estimate the variance of angles between a point and all other pairs of points, we first project the data set on the hyperplanes orthogonal to random vectors whose coordinates are independently chosen from the standard normal distribution $\mathbf{N}(0, 1)$. Based on the partitions of the data set after projection, we are able to estimate the unbiased mean of angles for each point. We then approximate the second moment and derive its variance by using the AMS Sketches to summarize the frequency moments of the points projected on the random hyperplanes. The combination between random hyperplane projections and AMS Sketches on product domains enables us to reduce the computational complexity to $O(n \log n(d + \log n))$ time. In the following we start with some basic notions of random hyperplane projection and AMS Sketch, then propose our approach to estimate the variance of angles for each point of the data set.

3.3 Preliminaries

3.3.1 Random Hyperplane Projection

Following Charikar [7], we take random vectors $r_1, \ldots, r_t \in \mathbf{R}^d$ such that each coordinate is chosen independently from the standard normal distribution $\mathbf{N}(0, 1)$.

For $i = 1, \ldots, t$ and points $a, b, p \in S$ consider the independent random variables

$$X^{(i)}_{apb} = \begin{cases} 1 & \text{if } a \cdot r_i < p \cdot r_i < b \cdot r_i \\ 0 & \text{otherwise} \end{cases}$$

For a vector r_i we see that $X^{(i)}_{apb} = 1$ only if the vectors $a - p$ and $b - p$ are on different sides of the hyperplane orthogonal to r_i, and in addition $(a-p) \cdot r_i < 0$. The probability that this happens is proportional to Θ_{apb}, as exploited in the seminal papers of Goemans and Williamson [11] and Charikar [7]. More precisely we have:

LEMMA 2. *For all a, b, p, i, $\Pr[X^{(i)}_{apb} = 1] = \Theta_{apb}/(2\pi)$.*

Note that we also have $\Pr[X^{(i)}_{bpa} = 1] = \Theta_{apb}/(2\pi)$ due to symmetry [11]. By using t random vectors r_i, we are able to boost the accuracy of the estimator of Θ_{apb}. In particular, we have $\Theta_{apb} = \frac{2\pi}{t}\sum_{i=1}^{t} X^{(i)}_{apb}$. The analysis of accuracy for random projections will be presented in the Section 4.

3.3.2 AMS Sketch

Alon at al. [3] described and analyzed a sketching approach, called AMS Sketch, to estimate the second frequency moment of a high-dimensional vector.

LEMMA 3. *Given a high-dimensional vector $w_1, \cdots, w_q$, take a 4-wise independent vector $s \in \{\pm 1\}^q$. The AMS Sketch is the value $\mathbf{Z} = \sum_{i=1}^{q} s_i w_i$. Define $\mathbf{Y} = \mathbf{Z}^2$ then $\mathbf{E}[\mathbf{Y}] = \sum_{i=1}^{q} w_i^2$ and $\mathbf{Var}[\mathbf{Y}] \leq 2(\mathbf{E}[\mathbf{Y}])^2$.*

Recently, Indyk and McGregor [12], and Braverman et al. [5] have considered AMS Sketches with two different 4-wise independent vectors for outer product. In this case, we view the matrix as vector of matrix elements.

LEMMA 4. *Given two different 4-wise independent vectors $s^1, s^2 \in \{\pm 1\}^q$. The AMS Sketch of an outer product (uv), where by definition $(uv)_{ij} = u_i v_j$, is:*

$$\mathbf{Z} = \sum_{(i,j)\in|q|\times|q|} s_i^1 s_j^2 (uv)_{ij} = \left(\sum_{i=1}^{q} s_i^1 u_i\right)\left(\sum_{j=1}^{q} s_j^2 v_j\right)$$

Define $\mathbf{Y} = \mathbf{Z}^2$ then $\mathbf{E}[\mathbf{Y}] = \sum_{ij}(u_i v_j)^2$ or squared Frobenius norm of the outer product (uv) and $\mathbf{Var}[\mathbf{Y}] \le 8(\mathbf{E}[\mathbf{Y}])^2$.

That is, the AMS sketch of the outer product is simply the product of the AMS sketches of the two vectors (using different 4-wise independent random vectors).

3.4 Approximate ABOD

To avoid the cubic time complexity, we propose a near-linear time algorithm to estimate the variance of angles for each data point based on random hyperplane projections.

3.4.1 First Moment Estimator

Given a random vector r_i and a point $p \in S$, we estimate $MOA_1(p)$ using Lemma 2 as follows:

$$F_1(p) = \frac{2}{(n-1)(n-2)}\left(2\pi \sum_{\substack{a,b\in S\setminus\{p\}\\ a\neq b}} \mathbf{E}[X_{apb}^{(i)}]\right)$$

$$= \frac{2\pi}{(n-1)(n-2)} \sum_{\substack{a,b\in S\setminus\{p\}\\ a\neq b}} \left(\mathbf{E}[X_{apb}^{(i)}] + \mathbf{E}[X_{bpa}^{(i)}]\right)$$

$$= \frac{2\pi}{(n-1)(n-2)} |\mathbf{L}_p^{(i)}||\mathbf{R}_p^{(i)}|$$

where the sets $\mathbf{L}_p^{(i)} = \{x \in S\setminus\{p\} \mid x \cdot r_i < p \cdot r_i\}$ and $\mathbf{R}_p^{(i)} = \{x \in S\setminus\{p\} \mid x \cdot r_i > p \cdot r_i\}$ consist of the points on each side of p under the random projection.

Note that this value is an unbiased estimator of mean of angles between the point p and the other pairs of points. We boost the accuracy of the estimation by using t random projections. We therefore have the more accurate unbiased estimator of $MOA_1(p)$:

$$F_1(p) = \frac{2\pi}{t(n-1)(n-2)} \sum_{i=1}^{t} |\mathbf{L}_p^{(i)}||\mathbf{R}_p^{(i)}| \qquad (1)$$

3.4.2 Second Moment Estimator

Since estimation of the second moment is more complicated, we first present the general idea by considering a less efficient approach and then propose an efficient algorithm to compute the unbiased second moment estimator. Focus on a single point p, suppose that we fix an arbitrary ordering of the set $S\setminus\{p\}$ as $x_1, x_2, \cdots, x_{n-1}$. For each projection using the random vector r_i, we take the two vectors $u_i, v_i \in \{0,1\}^{n-1}$ such that their k^{th} coordinate corresponds to the kth point of the set $S\setminus\{p\}$. The kth coordinate of u_i (or v_i) is 1 if the kth point of the set locates on the left (or right) partition, and 0, otherwise. We consider the matrix $\mathbf{P} = \sum_{i=1}^{t}(u_i v_i)$ where $(u_i v_i)$ is the outer product of u_i and v_i. Note that all diagonal elements of $\mathbf{P}$ are 0. Consider any pair of points $a, b \in S\setminus\{p\}$ where $a = x_i$ and $b = x_j$, it is clear that $\mathbf{P}_{ij}$ is the number of times that a locates on the left side and b locates on the right side after t projections. We can therefore estimate Θ_{apb}^2, the squared angle between p and a, b based on the element $\mathbf{P}_{ij}$ of the matrix $\mathbf{P}$.

$$\mathbf{P}_{ij}^2 = \left(\sum_{i=1}^{t} X_{apb}^{(i)}\right)^2 = \sum_{i=1}^{t}\left(X_{apb}^{(i)}\right)^2 + 2\sum_{\substack{i,j=1\\ i\neq j}}^{t} X_{apb}^{(i)} X_{apb}^{(j)}$$

$$\mathbf{E}[\mathbf{P}_{ij}^2] = \sum_{i=1}^{t} \mathbf{E}[(X_{apb}^{(i)})^2] + 2\sum_{\substack{i,j=1\\ i\neq j}}^{t} \mathbf{E}[X_{apb}^{(i)}]\mathbf{E}[X_{apb}^{(j)}]$$

$$= t\frac{\Theta_{apb}}{2\pi} + t(t-1)\left(\frac{\Theta_{apb}}{2\pi}\right)^2$$

So we have the unbiased estimator:

$$\Theta_{apb}^2 = \frac{(2\pi)^2}{t(t-1)}\left(\mathbf{E}[\mathbf{P}_{ij}^2] - \frac{t}{2\pi}\Theta_{apb}\right)$$

Therefore, we can compute $MOA_2(p)$ based on all elements of $\mathbf{P}$ as follows:

$$MOA_2(p) = \frac{2}{(n-1)(n-2)} \sum_{\substack{a,b\in S\setminus\{p\}\\ a\neq b}} \Theta_{apb}^2$$

$$= \frac{1}{(n-1)(n-2)} \sum_{\substack{a,b\in S\setminus\{p\}\\ a\neq b}} (\Theta_{apb}^2 + \Theta_{bpa}^2)$$

$$= \frac{4\pi^2}{t(t-1)(n-1)(n-2)}\left(\sum_{i=1}^{n-1}\sum_{j=1}^{n-1} \mathbf{E}[\mathbf{P}_{ij}^2] - \frac{t}{\pi}\sum_{\substack{a,b\in S\setminus\{p\}\\ a\neq b}} \Theta_{apb}\right)$$

$$= \frac{4\pi^2}{t(t-1)(n-1)(n-2)}\left(\mathbf{E}[\|\mathbf{P}\|_F^2] - \frac{t(n-1)(n-2)}{2\pi} MOA_1(p)\right)$$

$$= \frac{4\pi^2}{t(t-1)(n-1)(n-2)}\mathbf{E}[\|\mathbf{P}\|_F^2] - \frac{2\pi}{t-1} MOA_1(p)$$

From the equation above, we can estimate $MOA_2(p)$:

$$F_2'(p) = \frac{4\pi^2}{t(t-1)(n-1)(n-2)} \|\mathbf{P}\|_F^2 - \frac{2\pi}{t-1} F_1(p) \qquad (2)$$

However, the squared Frobenius norm $\|\mathbf{P}\|_F^2$ will not be computed exactly, since we do not know how to achieve this in less than quadratic time. Instead, it will be estimated using AMS Sketches on product domains. Let $AMS(\mathbf{L}_p^{(i)})$ and $AMS(\mathbf{R}_p^{(i)})$ be the AMS Sketches of the vectors u_i and v_i (using different 4-wise independent random vectors), respectively. Due to linearity the sketch of sum of distributions is equal to the sum of sketches of the distributions, so:

$$\|\mathbf{P}\|_F^2 = \left(\sum_{i=1}^{t} AMS(\mathbf{L}_p^{(i)}) AMS(\mathbf{R}_p^{(i)})\right)^2$$

We therefore derive the second moment estimator $F_2(p)$:

$$F_2(p) = \frac{4\pi^2\left(\sum_{i=1}^{t} AMS(\mathbf{L}_p^{(i)}) AMS(\mathbf{R}_p^{(i)})\right)^2}{t(t-1)(n-1)(n-2)} - \frac{2\pi F_1(p)}{t-1} \qquad (3)$$

3.4.3 Algorithm

Based on the estimators of $MOA_1(p)$, and $MOA_2(p)$ for any point p described above, we introduce FastVOA, a near-linear time algorithm to estimate the variance of angles for all points of the data set. The pseudo-code in Algorithm 1 shows how FastVOA works.

At first, we project the data set S on the hyperplanes orthogonal to random projection vectors (Algorithm 2). *RandomProjection()* returns a data structure $\mathcal{L}$ containing the

Algorithm 1 FastVOA(S, t, s_1, s_2)

Ensure: Return the variance estimator for all points

1: $\mathcal{L} \leftarrow RandomProjection(S, t)$
2: $F1 \leftarrow FirstMomentEstimator(\mathcal{L}, t, n)$
3: **for** $i = 1 \rightarrow s_2$ **do**
4: $\quad \mathbf{Y}_i \leftarrow \sum_{j=1}^{s_1} (FrobeniusNorm(\mathcal{L}, t, n))^2 / s_1$
5: **end for**
6: $F2 \leftarrow median\{\mathbf{Y}_1, \cdots, \mathbf{Y}_{s_2}\}$
7: $\mathbf{Var} \leftarrow [0]^n$
8: **for** $j = 1 \rightarrow n$ **do**
9: $\quad F2[j] = \frac{4\pi^2}{t(t-1)(n-1)(n-2)} F2[j] - \frac{2\pi F1[j]}{t-1}$
10: $\quad \mathbf{Var}[j] = F2[j] - (F1[j])^2$
11: **end for**
12: **return** $\mathbf{Var}$

Algorithm 2 RandomProjection(S, t)

Ensure: Return a list $\mathcal{L} = L_1 L_2 \cdots L_t$ where L_i is a list of points ordered by their dot product with r_i

$\mathcal{L} \leftarrow \emptyset$
for $i = 1 \rightarrow t$ **do**
$\quad$ Generate a random vector r_i whose coordinates are independently chosen from $\mathbf{N}(0, 1)$
$\quad$ Let L_i be an empty list containing pairs of point ID and its dot product with r_i
$\quad$ **for** $j = 1 \rightarrow n$ **do**
$\qquad$ Insert $(x_j, x_j \cdot r_i)$ into the list L_i
$\quad$ **end for**
$\quad$ Sort L_i based on the dot product order
$\quad$ Insert L_i into $\mathcal{L}$
end for
return $\mathcal{L}$

information of the partitions of S under t random projections. Using $\mathcal{L}$, we are able to efficiently identify the values $|L_p^{(i)}|$ and $|R_p^{(i)}|$ corresponding to each point p and r_i. The pseudo-code in Algorithm 3 computes the first moment estimator for each point. Similarly, we also make use of $\mathcal{L}$ to compute the Frobenius norm $\|\mathbf{P}\|_F$ for each point p in Algorithm 4. To boost the accuracy of the AMS Sketches, we have to repeat the computation of *FrobeniusNorm()* $s_1 s_2$ times, and output $F2$ as the median of s_2 random variables $\mathbf{Y}_1, \cdots, \mathbf{Y}_{s_2}$, each being the average of s_1 values (lines 3 - 6). After that, the second moment estimator and variance value for each point are computed in lines 9 - 10.

3.4.4 Computational Complexity and Parallelization

It is clear that the computational complexity of FastVOA depends on Algorithms 2 - 4. We note that Algorithm 2 takes $O(tn(d + \log n))$ time in computing dot products and sorting for all points while both Algorithm 3 and 4 run in $O(tn)$ time. Since we have to repeat the Algorithm 4 in $s_1 s_2$ times, the total running time is $O(tn(d + \log n + s_1 s_2))$. To guarantee the accuracy of FastVOA, we have to choose $t = O(\log n)$ and $s_1 s_2$ sufficiently large to boost the accuracy of estimation as analyzed later in Section 4. Therefore, the running time is dominated by the AMS Sketch computational time. That means FastVOA runs in $O(s_1 s_2 n \log n)$ time.

It is worth noting that Algorithms 2 - 4 use the **for** loop with t random vectors that performs the same independent operations for each random vector. Therefore, we can simply parallelize this loop in these three algorithms to achieve a nearly linear (in the number of processors used) speedup.

Algorithm 3 FirstMomentEstimator$(\mathcal{L}, t, n)$

Ensure: Return the first moment estimator for all points

$F1 \leftarrow [0]^n$
for $i = 1 \rightarrow t$ **do**
$\quad C_l \leftarrow [0]^n, C_r \leftarrow [0]^n$
$\quad L_i \leftarrow \mathcal{L}[i]$
$\quad$ **for** $j = 1 \rightarrow n$ **do**
$\qquad idx = L_i[j].pointID$
$\qquad C_l[idx] = j - 1$
$\qquad C_r[idx] = n - 1 - C_l[idx]$
$\quad$ **end for**
$\quad$ **for** $j = 1 \rightarrow n$ **do**
$\qquad F1[j] = F1[j] + C_l[j]C_r[j]$
$\quad$ **end for**
end for
return $\frac{2\pi}{t(n-1)(n-2)} F1$

Algorithm 4 FrobeniusNorm$(\mathcal{L}, t, n)$

Ensure: Return $\|\mathbf{P}\|_F$ for each point p

$F2 \leftarrow [0]^n$
Initialize 4-wise independent vectors $S_l[n]$, $S_r[n]$ whose entries are in $\{\pm 1\}$ with equal probability
for $i = 1 \rightarrow t$ **do**
$\quad AMS_l \leftarrow [0]^n, AMS_r \leftarrow [0]^n$
$\quad L_i \leftarrow \mathcal{L}[i]$
$\quad$ **for** $j = 2 \rightarrow n$ **do**
$\qquad idx1 = L_i[j].pointID$
$\qquad idx2 = L_i[j-1].pointID$
$\qquad AMS_l[idx1] = AMS_l[idx2] + S_l[idx2]$
$\quad$ **end for**
$\quad$ **for** $j = n - 1 \rightarrow 1$ **do**
$\qquad idx1 = L_i[j].pointID$
$\qquad idx2 = L_i[j+1].pointID$
$\qquad AMS_r[idx1] = AMS_r[idx2] + S_r[idx2]$
$\quad$ **end for**
$\quad$ **for** $j = 1 \rightarrow n$ **do**
$\qquad F2[j] = F2[j] + AMS_l[j]AMS_r[j]$
$\quad$ **end for**
end for
return $F2$

4. ERROR ANALYSIS

It has already been argued that our estimators are unbiased, i.e., produce the right first and second moments in expectation: $\mathbf{E}[F_1(p)] = MOA_1(p)$ and $\mathbf{E}[F_2(p)] = MOA_2(p)$.

In this section we analyze the precision, showing bounds on the number of random projections and AMS sketches needed to achieve a given precision ε. This will imply that the variance is estimated within an additive error of $O(\varepsilon)$. For $MOA_1(p)$ we get this directly with high probability, whereas for $MOA_2(p)$ the basic success probability of the estimator $F_2(p)$ is only 3/4. However, by repeating the second moment estimation procedure $s_2 = O(\log(1/\delta))$ times and taking the median outlier score for each point, the success probability can be magnified to $1 - \delta$, for any $\delta > 0$ as argued in [3].

We will use the following version of the Chernoff bound from [8, Theorem 1.1]:

LEMMA 5. *Let* $Y = \sum_{i=1}^{t} Y^{(i)}$ *be a sum of independent random variables with values in* $[0;1]$. *For any* $\Delta > 0$,

$$\Pr[|Y - \mathbf{E}[Y]| > \Delta] \leq 2e^{-2\Delta^2/t} .$$

First moment estimator.

Consider the probability (over choice of vectors $r_1,\ldots,r_t$) that $F_1(p)$ deviates from $MOA_1(p)$ by more than ε. Splitting the sum $F_1(p)t/\pi$ into t terms we can apply Lemma 5. Then we get that its deviation from the mean exceeds $\varepsilon t/\pi$ with probability at most $2e^{-2(\varepsilon t/\pi)^2/t}$. If we choose $t > \varepsilon^{-2}\pi^2 \ln(n)$ this probability is at most $2/n^2$. So the probability that all of n first moment estimators have error at most ε is $1 - O(1/n)$.

Second moment estimator.

Next, consider the probability (again over choice of vectors $r_1, \ldots, r_t$) that the first version of the second moment estimator, $F_2'(p)$, deviates from its expectation by more than ε, given that $F_1(p)$ deviates by at most ε from its expectation. Looking at (2) we see that this happens when $||\mathbf{P}||_F^2$ deviates from its expectation by at least $\binom{n-1}{2}\binom{t}{2}\varepsilon/\pi^2$. Thus, it suffices to show that each squared entry $\mathbf{P}_{ij}^2$ deviates by at most $\frac{1}{4}\varepsilon t^2/\pi^2$ from its expectation with high probability. Recall that $\mathbf{P}_{ij} = \sum_{k=1}^{t} X_{x_i,x_j}^{(k)}$, a sum of independent indicator random variables, which means that Lemma 5 applies. For $t > 16\varepsilon^{-2}\pi^4 \ln(n)$ we get that $\mathbf{P}_{ij}$ deviates from its expectation by at most $\frac{1}{4}\varepsilon t/\pi^2$ with probability $1 - O(1/n^2)$. Since $\mathbf{P}_{ij} \leq t$ this implies that $\mathbf{P}_{ij}^2$ deviates by at most $\frac{1}{4}\varepsilon t^2/\pi^2$, as desired. The total error for $F_2'(p)$, accounting for all $2\binom{n-1}{2}$ entries of $\mathbf{P}$, is therefore bounded by ε with probability $1 - O(1/n^2)$.

Finally, we should account for the error caused by the use of AMS sketches in the final estimator $F_2(p)$, equation (3). By Lemma 4 the variance of the estimator is bounded by $8MOA_2(p)^2$. Taking the average of s_1 sketches the variance is reduced to at most $\frac{8MOA_2(p)^2}{s_1}$. By applying Chebychev's inequality, the probability that $F_2(p)$ deviates by $\frac{\varepsilon}{\pi^2}MOA_2(p)$ from its expectation of $MOA_2(p)$ is at most:

$$\frac{8MOA_2(p)^2/s_1}{(MOA_2(p)\varepsilon/(\pi^2))^2} = \frac{8\pi^4}{s_1\varepsilon^2} .$$

For $s_1 > 32\pi^4/\varepsilon^2$ this is less than 1/4. It is simple to verify that this deviation corresponds to a deviation for $F_2(p)$ of 2ε. As stated above, the failure probability is reduced exponentially by repeating the estimation s_2 times.

5. EXPERIMENTS

We implemented all algorithms in C++ and conducted experiments in a 2.67 GHz core i7 Windows platform with 3GB of RAM on both synthetic and real world data sets.

5.1 Data sets

For the sake of fair comparison, we made use of the same synthetic data generation process as ABOD approaches [14]. We generated a Gaussian mixture including 5 equally weighted clusters having random means and variances as normal points and employed a uniform distribution in full-dimensional space as the outliers. For each synthetic data set, we generated 10 outliers which are independent on the Gaussian mixture. We evaluated the performance of all algorithms on synthetic data sets with varying sizes and dimensions.

For the real world high-dimensional data sets, we picked three data sets (Isolet, Multiple Features and Optical Digits) designed for classification and machine learning tasks from UCI machine learning repository [9]. Isolet contains the pronunciation data of 26 letters of the alphabet while Multiple Features and Optical Digits consist of the data of handwritten numerals ('0' - '9'). For each data set, we picked all data points from some classes having common behaviors as normal points and 10 data points from another class as outliers. For instance, we picked points of classes C, D, and E of Isolet that share the "e" sound as normal points and 10 points from class Y as outliers. Similarly, we picked points of classes 6 and 9 of Multiple Features, classes 3 and 9 of Optical Digits as normal points because of the similar shapes and 10 points of class 0 as outliers. It is worth noting that there are some outliers that probably locate on the region covered by inliers. Therefore, we are not able to isolate exactly all outliers. Instead, we expect our algorithms to rank all outliers into sufficiently high positions.

5.2 Accuracy of Estimation

This subsection presents the accuracy experiments to evaluate the reliability of our estimation algorithm. As analysis in the Section 4, the estimators $F_1(p)$, $F_2'(p)$, and $F_2(p)$ for any point p of the data set can deviate from their expectations by more than ϵ with probability at most δ by using a sufficiently large number of random projections $t = O(\log n)$ and AMS Sketches $s_1 s_2$. Note that $F_2(p)$ is the second moment estimator using AMS Sketch while $F_2'(p)$ is based on only random projections. At first, we carried out experiments to measure the accuracy of estimators based on only random projections. We measured the deviation error ϵ of $F_1(p)$ and $F_2'(p)$ from their expectations with error probability $\delta = 0.1$. We took t in ranges [100, 1,000] and conducted experiments on 2 synthetic data sets having 1,000 points on 50 and 100 dimensions, namely Syn50 and Syn100, as well as the three real world data sets, namely Isolet, Mfeat and Digit. Figures 2.a and 2.b display the deviation error (ϵ) from expectation of the estimators $F_1(p)$ and $F_2'(p)$ with error probability $\delta = 0.1$. Using these two estimators, we derived the variance estimator and measured its deviation from expectation with $\delta = 0.1$, as shown in Figure 2.c. Although the theoretical analysis requires a sufficiently large number of random projections t to achieve the small ϵ, the results on 5 data sets surprisingly show that with a rather small t, we are able to estimate exactly the variance of angles for all points. With $t = 600$, 90% number of points of 5 data sets have the first moment, the second moment and the derived variance estimators deviating from their expectations at most 0.035, 0.08 and 0.015 respectively. When t increases to 1,000, 90% of points of 5 data sets have the variance estimator deviate from its expectation by at most 0.01. Therefore, for such data sets having large difference between VOA of outliers and VOA of border points, the use of random projections to estimate VOA can achieve good performance on detecting outliers.

To quantify the error due to the AMS Sketches, we measured the error probability δ of the variance estimator us-

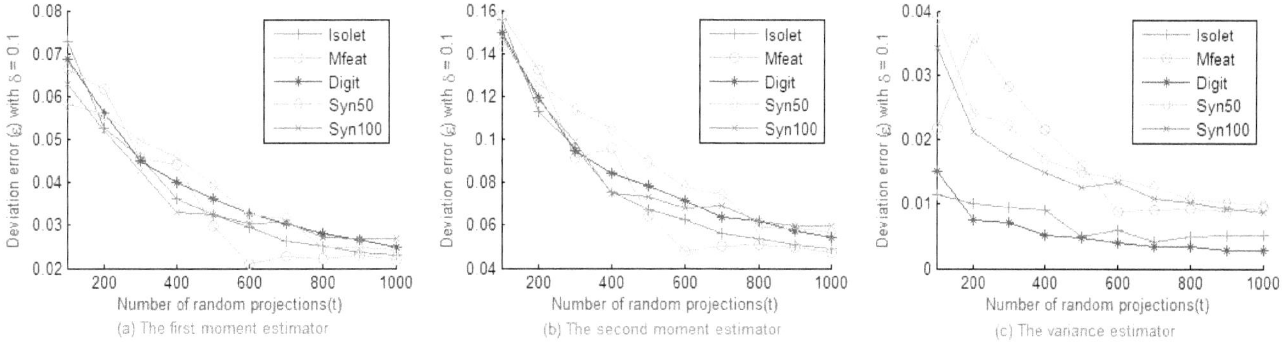

Figure 2: Deviation error of random projection estimators on 5 data sets.

ing AMS Sketches and fixing parameters $t = 1,000, s_1 = 7,200, s_2 = 50, \epsilon = 0.1$ on all data sets. Concretely, we computed the number of points p of the data set such that its variance estimator by using AMS Sketch deviates by more than $\epsilon VOA(p)$ from its expectation $VOA(p)$. Table 1 presents the error probability of variance estimators on 5 data sets.

Table 1: Error probability of variance estimator using AMS Sketch on 5 data sets

Isolet	Mfeat	Digit	Syn50	Syn100
0.75	0.19	0.35	0.04	0.03

It is clear that the two synthetic data sets obtain very small errors while the real world data sets take rather large errors, especially on Isolet. This is because the variance estimator of all points of the data set may be underestimated or overestimated by using AMS Sketch. To guarantee the capability of our approximation approach on detecting outliers, we analyzed the accuracy of outlier ranking between the brute force algorithm called SimpleVOA and the approximate algorithm FastVOA. The accuracy of outlier ranking is defined as $\frac{|A \cap B|}{m}$ where A and B are the top m positions retrieved by SimpleVOA and FastVOA algorithms, respectively. Figure 3 shows the accuracy of outlier ranking between SimpleVOA and FastVOA where m is in ranges 10 - 100.

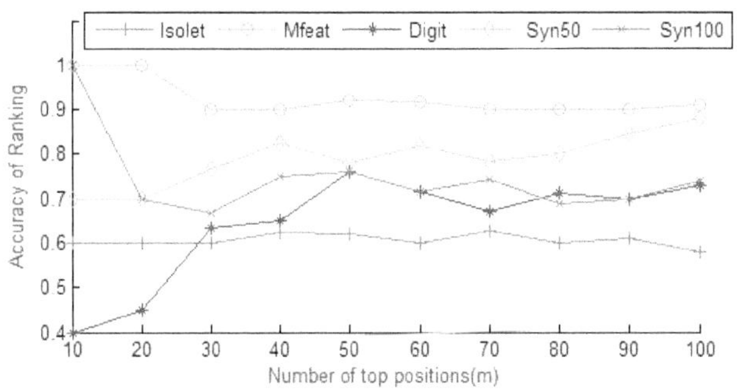

Figure 3: The accuracy of outlier ranking between SimpleVOA and FastVOA on 5 data sets.

The results of outlier ranking indicate that FastVOA provided a rather high accurate ranking on all data sets. While 2 synthetic data sets and Multiple Feature show a highly accurate ranking for all ranges of top positions, the other data sets offered a medium accurate ranking when $m < 30$ but more accurate when $m > 40$. Although the use of AMS Sketch may lead to underestimate or overestimate of the variance estimator, FastVOA still introduces good performance on ranking data points based on VOA.

5.3 Effectiveness

It is obvious that our approaches are dealing directly with the variance of angles (VOA) while the approaches in [14] compute the variance of cosine of angles weighted by distances (ABOF). This subsection demonstrates experiments to measure the effectiveness of both measures on detecting outliers. For each measure, we compared the quality of outlier ranking provided by brute force (SimpleVOA and ABOD) and approximation algorithms (FastVOA and FastABOD). For the sake of fair comparison, we used the precision-recall graph to evaluate the capability of each algorithm to retrieve the most likely outliers. The precision is the number of retrieved points that are indeed outliers. For each precision level, we measured the recall as the percentage of the number of outliers in the retrieved set.

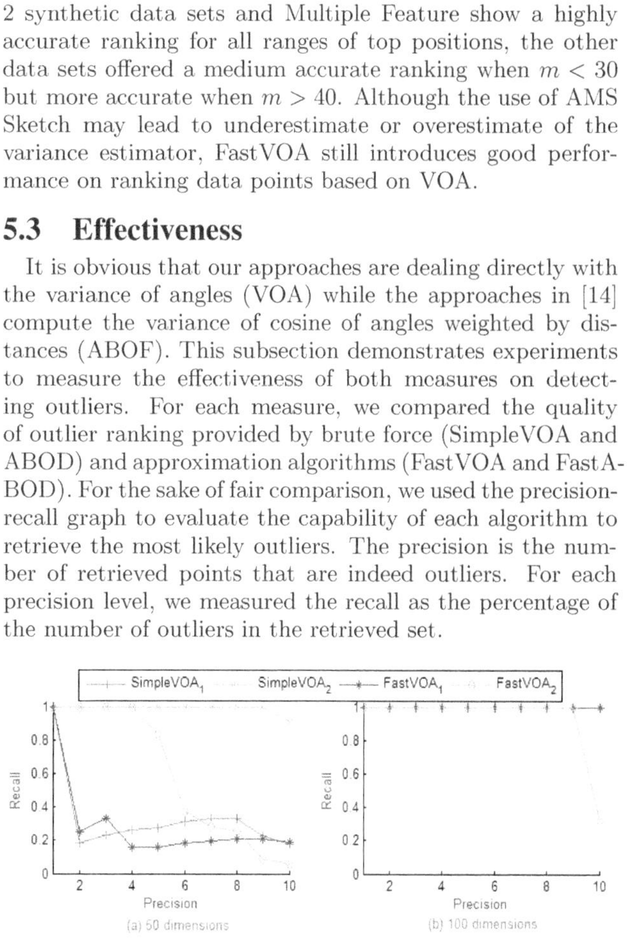

Figure 4: Precision-Recall Graph for 4 synthetic data sets. Each graph describes the behavior on 1,000 and 5,000 points.

For synthetic data sets, we generated 4 data sets with varying sizes of 1,000 and 5,000 points and dimensions of 50 and 100. We observed that the differences of VOA between outliers and border points on synthetic data sets become large when the size increases. Therefore, we adjusted the parameter settings for FastVOA on synthetic data sets of size 5,000 points to reduce the time complexity. In particular, we determined $t = 100$, $s_1 = 1600$, $s_2 = 10$. We

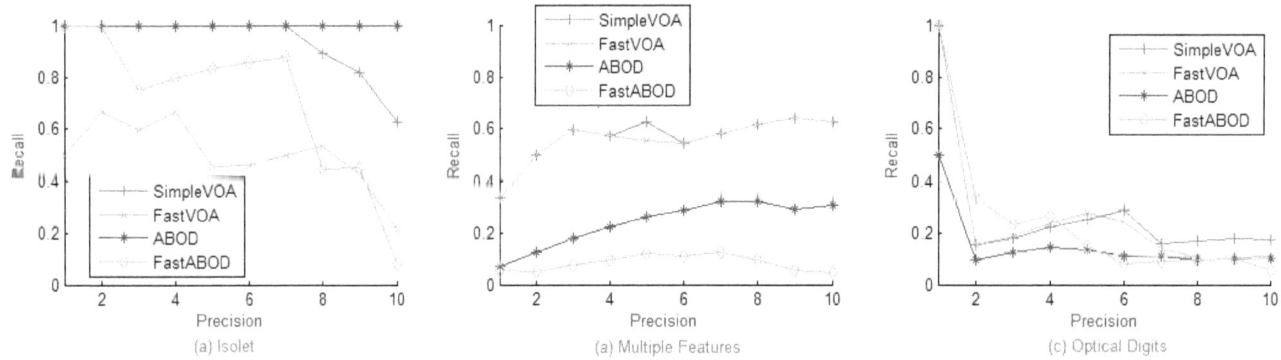

Figure 5: Precision-Recall Graph for 3 real world data sets.

kept the same parameter setting as Section 5.2 for the other data sets. The sample size of FastABOD is chosen as $0.1n$ as [14]. Let us note that both ABOD and FastABOD offered perfect results on 4 synthetic data sets. That means all 10 outliers were ranked into the top 10 positions. Therefore, we did not show the results of ABOD and FastABOD on synthetic data sets. Figure 4 depicts the precision-recall graph for synthetic data sets. Figure 4.a shows the results of brute force (SimpleVOA_1 and SimpleVOA_2) and approximation algorithms (FastVOA_1 and FastVOA_2) on the 2 data sets of 50 dimensions and varying sizes of 1,000 and 5,000 points. In the medium dimensionality of 50, VOA did not work well in the small data set size but achieved almost perfect performance in the large data set by ranking all 10 outliers between top 11 retrieved points. It is clear that the better performance of SimpleVOA leads to the better performance of FastVOA. Results of 2 synthetic data sets with 100 dimensions are displayed in Figure 4.b. Since the effect of weighting factors in ABOF is not meaningful in high-dimensional data, SimpleVOA and FastVOA show competitive results with ABOD and FastABOD with almost perfect performance.

Figure 5 shows the observed precision-recall graphs for 3 real world data sets. On Isolet, SimpleVOA and ABOD offered almost perfect performance by ranking 10 outliers in top 10 and top 16 positions, respectively. FastABOD provided better outlier ranking than FastVOA on detecting 7 outliers in top 10 positions. However, on ranking all 10 outliers, both of them did not work well for large recall levels. Both SimpleVOA and FastVOA performed rather well on Multiple Features by ranking all outliers on the top 16 positions while both ABOD and FastABOD performed very badly. All approaches had difficulties to detect outliers on Optical Digits. However, the VOA based approaches clearly offered better results than the ABOF based ones.

5.4 Efficiency

This section compares the running time of 3 algorithms, namely FastVOA, LB_ABOD and FastABOD on large high-dimensional data sets. In fact, there are very few large real world data sets where the outliers are identified exactly in advance. Therefore, we decided to evaluate the efficiency of these 3 approaches on synthetic data sets. We carried out experiments measuring the CPU time of each approach on data sets with varying both size and dimensions in ranges 10,000 - 100,000 points and 100 - 1,000 respectively.

It is clear that both LB_ABOD and FastABOD run in $O(dn^2)$ time while the running time of FastVOA depends on the parameters t, s_1, s_2. As mentioned in Section 5.3, we can use rather small parameter settings for FastVOA in very large high-dimensional synthetic data sets without reducing the accuracy. Therefore, we set $t = 100$, $s_1 = 1600$, $s_2 = 10$ for FastVOA and the sample size of FastABOF chosen as $0.1n$. Let us note that the value $0.1n$ becomes rather large when the data set size increases. In contrast, FastVOA only needs rather small number of random projections and the AMS Sketch sizes. As analysis in the Section 3.4.4, the total running time of FastVOA is $O(tn(d + \log n + s_1 s_2))$. With the choice of parameters above, the total running time of FastVOA is still dominated by the computation time of AMS Sketches with $O(ts_1 s_2 n)$ time.

Figure 6.a shows the CPU time in (ms) of FastVOA, LB_ABOD and FastABOD for data sets having 100 dimensions and sizes of 10,000 - 100,000 points while Figure 6.b displays the CPU time in (ms) for data sets having size of 20,000 points and dimensions in 100 - 1,000. It is clear that the running time of FastVOA is linear time in the size of data set and independent on number of dimensions. In contrast, both LB_ABOD and FastABOD run in quadratic time in the size of data set and linear time in number of dimensions.

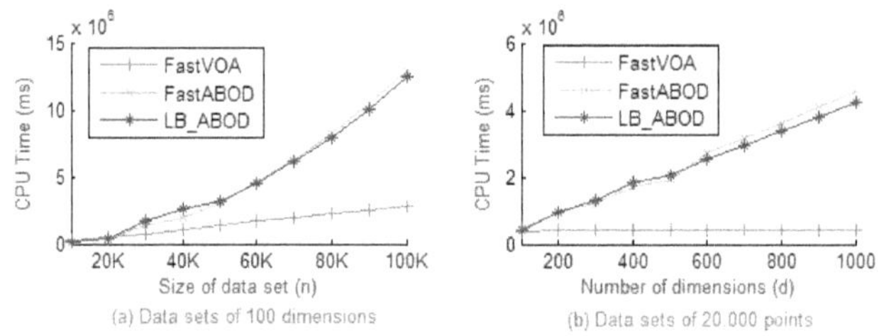

Figure 6: Comparison of CPU time of FastVOA, FastABOD and LB_ABOD.

We conclude the efficiency evaluation of FastVOA by illustrating its suitability for parallel processing. We made use of Open Multi-Processing API (OpenMP) supporting multi-platform shared memory multiprocessing programming in C++ to parallelize the **for** loop of random projection vectors in Algorithms 2 - 4 of Section 3.4.3. We measured the parallel speedup when running on 4 processors of Core i7 machine. Table 2 illustrates a nearly linear parallel speedup of FastVOA (in the number of processors used) on synthetic data sets with size of 10,000 points on 100 dimensions.

Table 2: Parallel speedup of FastVOA

Number of processors	1	2	4
Speedup	1	2.3	3.7

6. CONCLUSION

In this paper, we introduced a random projection-based algorithm to approximate the variance of angles between pairs of points of the data set, a robust outlier score to detect high-dimensional outlier patterns. By combining random projections and AMS Sketches on product domains, our approximation algorithm runs in near-linear time in the size of data set and is suited for parallel processing. We presented a theoretical analysis of the quality of approximation to guarantee the reliability of our estimation algorithm. The empirical experiments on synthetic and real world data sets demonstrate the scalability, effectiveness and efficiency of our approach on detecting outliers in very large high-dimensional data sets.

7. ACKNOWLEDGMENTS

We deeply thank Dr. M. Schubert for his released synthetic data generator and useful comments about ABOD. We also thank T. L. Hoang for useful discussion in the early stage of this work.

8. REFERENCES

[1] C. C. Aggarwal, A. Hinneburg, and D. A. Keim. On the surprising behavior of distance metrics in high dimensional spaces. In *Proceedings of ICDT'01*, pages 420–434, 2001.

[2] C. C. Aggarwal and P. S. Yu. Outlier detection for high dimensional data. In *Proceedings of SIGMOD'01*, pages 37–46, 2001.

[3] N. Alon, Y. Matias, and M. Szegedy. The space complexity of approximating the frequency moments. *Journal of Computer and System Sciences*, 58(1):137–147, 1999.

[4] S. D. Bay and M. Schwabacher. Mining distance-based outliers in near linear time with randomization and a simple pruning rule. In *Proceedings of KDD'03*, pages 29–38, 2003.

[5] V. Braverman, K.-M. Chung, Z. Liu, M. Mitzenmacher, and R. Ostrovsky. Ams without 4-wise independence on product domains. In *Proceedings of STACS'10*, pages 119–130, 2008.

[6] M. M. Breunig, H.-P. Kriegel, R. T. Ng, and J. Sander. Lof: Identifying density-based local outliers. In *Proceedings of SIGMOD'00*, pages 93–104, 2000.

[7] M. Charikar. Similarity estimation techniques from rounding algorithms. In *Proceedings of STOC'02*, pages 380–388, 2002.

[8] D. P. Dubhashi and A. Panconesi. *Concentration of Measure for the Analysis of Randomized Algorithms.* Cambridge University Press, 2009.

[9] A. Frank and A. Asuncion. UCI machine learning repository, 2010.

[10] A. Ghoting, S. Parthasarathy, and M. E. Otey. Fast mining of distance-based outliers in high-dimensional datasets. *Data Mining and Knowledge Discovery*, 16(3):349–364, 2008.

[11] M. X. Goemans and D. P. Williamson. Improved approximation algorithms for maximum cut and satisfiability problems using semidefinite programming. *Journal of the ACM*, 42(6):1115–1145, 1995.

[12] P. Indyk and A. McGregor. Declaring independence via the sketching of sketches. In *Proceedings of SODA'08*, pages 737–745, 2008.

[13] E. M. Knorr and R. T. Ng. Algorithms for mining distance-based outliers in large datasets. In *Proceedings of VLDB'98*, pages 392–403, 1998.

[14] H.-P. Kriegel, M. Schubert, and A. Zimek. Angle-based outlier detection in high-dimensional data. In *Proceedings KDD'08*, pages 444–452, 2008.

[15] H.-P. Kriegel, M. Schubert, and A. Zimek. Outlier detection techniques. In *Tutorial at KDD'10*, 2010.

[16] V. Mahadevan, W. Li, V. Bhalodia, and N. Vasconcelos. Anomaly detection in crowded scenes. In *Proceedings of CVPR'10*, pages 1975–1981, 2010.

[17] E. Müller, M. Schiffer, and T. Seidl. Statistical selection of relevant subspace projections for outlier ranking. In *Proceedings of ICDE'11*, pages 434–445, 2011.

[18] S. Papadimitriou, H. Kitagawa, P. B. Gibbons, and C. Faloutsos. Loci: Fast outlier detection using the local correlation integral. In *Proceedings of ICDE'03*, pages 315–326, 2003.

[19] S. Ramaswamy, R. Rastogi, and K. Shim. Efficient algorithms for mining outliers from large data sets. In *Proceedings of SIGMOD'00*, pages 427–438, 2000.

[20] Y. Wang, S. Parthasarathy, and S. Tatikonda. Locality sensitive outlier detection: A ranking driven approach. In *Proceedings of ICDE'11*, pages 410–421, 2011.

[21] R. Wheeler and J. S. Aitken. Multiple algorithms for fraud detection. *Knowledge Based Systems*, 13(2-3):93–99, 2000.

Intrusion as (Anti)social Communication: Characterization and Detection

Qi Ding
Boston University
qiding@math.bu.edu

Natallia Katenka
Boston University
nkatenka@math.bu.edu

Paul Barford
University of Wisconsin
pb@cs.wisc.edu

Eric Kolaczyk
Boston University
kolaczyk@math.bu.edu

Mark Crovella
Boston Univeristy
crovella@cs.bu.edu

ABSTRACT

A reasonable definition of intrusion is: entering a community to which one does not belong. This suggests that in a network, intrusion attempts may be detected by looking for communication that does not respect community boundaries. In this paper, we examine the utility of this concept for identifying malicious network sources. In particular, our goal is to explore whether this concept allows a core-network operator using flow data to augment signature-based systems located at network edges. We show that simple measures of communities can be defined for flow data that allow a remarkably effective level of intrusion detection simply by looking for flows that do not respect those communities. We validate our approach using labeled intrusion attempt data collected at a large number of edge networks. Our results suggest that community-based methods can offer an important additional dimension for intrusion detection systems.

Categories and Subject Descriptors:

C.2.3 [**Network Operations**]: Network Monitoring, C.4 [**Performance of Systems**]: Modeling Techniques, E.1 [**Data**]: Data Structures

General Terms:

Algorithms, Design, Experimentation, Measurement, Security

Keywords:

Intrusion detection, Social graphs

1. INTRODUCTION

Network-based intrusion detection and prevention systems (IDS/IPS) play a significant role in protecting IT assets from malicious attacks. Nonetheless, it has been known for some time that attackers can often easily defeat IDS/IPS systems [19]. The difficulty of on-going identification of new vulnerabilities coupled with the explosion in diversity of malware makes it virtually impossible to keep standard signature-based intrusion detection and prevention systems [16, 18] configured with rule sets that protect against previously-unseen attacks. This inherent challenge speaks directly to the need for complementary methods for network-based attack detection.

Anomaly-based network attack detection offers a compelling alternative to signature-based methods. The conceptual framework for network anomaly detection depends on defining characteristics of traffic that are considered "normal," and labeling as anomalous the traffic that deviates significantly from normality. In this way anomaly detectors have the potential to identify unanticipated or previously unseen attacks that would otherwise be invisible to signature-based detectors.

Despite their appeal, there are significant barriers to the practical use of anomaly-based detectors in IT security infrastructures. In particular, anomaly detection relies on formulating a robust definition of normality that sharply separates wanted from unwanted traffic. This has proven to be difficult in the past, in particular for detection systems that consider only simple features such as traffic volume [17]. Thus, we argue that new, creative methods for defining the "essence" of normal behavior are required in order to begin to realize the promise of anomaly detection. In this paper we examine the utility of one such definition for the specific problem of intrusion detection.

We start from the hypothesis that intrusion is *entering a community to which one does not belong.* The advantage of this starting point for intrusion detection is that it is rooted in a community-centric essence of normality. That is, rather than defining intrusion in terms of locations in physical space (where normality is harder to characterize), this hypothesis defines intrusion in terms of locations in social space, where normality often has well-understood properties. In fact, different network applications have clearly-identifiable communication patterns (*e.g.,* P2P systems), and these patterns can reflect the social behavior of users [8].

To connect our hypothesis to network traffic, we consider whether communication patterns between end hosts (identified by IP address) as evidenced in network flow data can form the basis for community detection, and whether the resulting communities form an effective basis for intrusion detection. A standard representation of communication patterns in network traffic is the bipartite graph, in which traffic sources and traffic destinations form the two vertex sets, and directed edges denote traffic flow from sources to destinations. In addition to this standard view, we explore the utility of a simpler graph representation in which vertices correspond only to traffic sources. This simpler representation admits a number of variants that differ in their level of detail.

Armed with this range of representational choices, we examine the characteristics of graph nodes using `netflow` data collected from a large European ISP. We use firewall and IDS/IPS logs pro-

KDD'12, August 12–16, 2012, Beijing, China.

vided by Dshield.org [22] to identify malicious nodes in our data corpus. We show that malicious nodes do indeed exhibit distinctive properties across a range of graph representations. We begin by considering the use of cardinality [9] as a tool to identify malicious nodes. We show that, while cardinality can identify some malicious nodes, it misses the majority of malicious nodes. Furthermore, it is clear that a detector based on high cardinality is easily overcome by attacks that keep the number of outgoing connections below a normal-seeming threshold.

Therefore, we go beyond the simple cardinality measure to examine features that are more specific to communication that disregards community boundaries – *i.e.,* metrics of antisocial behavior. This definition is critical in the security context because it significantly increases the difficulty of obviation by an attacker whose connection behavior is inconsistent with the community. We propose a simple proxy for a node that seems to disregard communities in our graphs: the *cut-vertex*. We show that, in our data, cut-vertices are very likely to be malicious. Unfortunately, the condition of being a cut-vertex is a fragile one, and depends strongly on the density of communication and the degree of sampling present in the underlying data. As the volume of data analyzed increases, cut-vertices become hidden.

This motivates us to generalize and make robust the concept of a cut-vertex using concepts from the social networking literature. We hypothesize that natural extensions of the cut-vertex concept can be based on local clustering coefficient and betweenness centrality. In fact, we show that low local clustering coeffecient and high betweenness centrality are strongly associated with malicious sources in certain graph representations. We explore these metrics by considering their application to our set of different network representations, from simple to detailed.

Our results evaluate the relative utility of different graph representations, and of different metrics on those graphs, for capturing antisocial behavior as it relates to network intrusion. We show that clustering is a particularly useful metric in this regard, while the proper choice of graph representation (simple versus detailed) is less crucial. Our results show that the proper choice of graph and metric allows us to detect a large fraction of malicious sources, even among those sources that are low-degree and therefore undetectable using traditional methods. Taken in total, these results are strongly suggestive that community-based analysis can shed significant light on the nature of malicious traffic sources.

2. DATA

In our study we use `netflow` data collected from a large European ISP. We focus on traffic collected at one router over a range of days from May 1, 2007 to May 14, 2007. For our examples, results are often for a single day (May 1) only; for the full evaluation of our methods, results are given for the period spanning all 14 days.

An important aspect of our work is that all of our `netflow` data is based on 1/1000 packet sampling. This level of packet sampling is typical of a large ISP, and we consider it a requirement of practical intrusion detection methods to be effective despite the information loss dictated by low sampling rates. For example, a single day's traffic (May 1) consists of 29,585 sources sending 2,033,520 flows to 185,145 destinations.

In any study of proposed intrusion detection methods, validation is both crucial and problematic. Traffic containing known, labeled intrusion attempts is rare or else severely outdated [12]. Hence we take a novel approach to identifying intruders in our data. We obtain from the SANS Institute the DShield logs for each day covered by our data [22]. DShield collects firewall and intrusion detection system logs from over 1700 networks world wide. The logs provide a summary of malicious and unwanted activity in each of the provider's networks. Each log entry includes, among other information, the unobfuscated source IP address of the packet that triggered the entry. DShield logs have been used in a number of prior studies of global malicious activity [23, 2].

For each day's traffic, we identify those traffic sources that also attempted an intrusion as recorded by DShield (we call these *DShield sources*). While not all of the traffic from DShield sources is sure to be intrusion attempts, we show in Section 4 that the vast majority shows characteristics suggestive of intrusion. Thus we make the approximation that if a source appears in DShield, its activity in our traffic data on the same day is malicious. While this is far from a perfect form of ground truth, we believe that inaccuracies are not likely to strongly influence our final results. This is because our primary results concern the comparison of detection methods (rather than absolute detection rates).

For example, in our May 1 data, 329 sources recorded in DShield logs also appear in our traffic. Note however that these 329 sources sent out 392,723 distinct flows to 66,618 distinct destinations. This sort of activity is highly suggestive of intrusion attempts. We provide more detailed evidence of the malicious nature of DShield sources in Section 4.

3. NETWORK REPRESENTATIONS

To begin, we note that our motivating hypothesis – *i.e.,* that intrusion is entering a community to which one does not belong – requires us to identify when one 'belongs' (and when one does not 'belong') to a 'community.' Both of these terms are relational in nature, and so it is natural to employ network-based representations of our data for our work. Generally speaking, any choice of network representation needs to be made carefully and can be expected to influence the level of success one achieves with high-level tasks utilizing such networks (*e.g.,* [13, Ch 3]). For that reason, one of the goals of our study is to examine certain alternatives in choice of network representation and understand the implications of this choice on our ability to detect intrusions.

We begin by defining a standard bipartite graph representation of communication patterns in computer network traffic. Specifically, let $G_B = (V, U, E_B)$, where vertices $v \in V$ represent source IPs (srcIP), vertices $u \in U$ represent destination IPs (dstIP), and edges $\{v, u\} \in E_B$ represent data flows from sources v to destinations u. In constructing such a graph G_B from data, we assign a vertex $v \in V$ for every unique IP address that played a role as a source, and a vertex $u \in U$ for every unique IP address that played a role as a destination. We assign an edge $\{v, u\}$ to E_B if and only if there is a flow in our data from v to u. In principle, multiple edges arise when there are several flows between address pairs. However, we find it convenient in what follows to simplify this structure by assigning edge weights equal to the multiplicity of an edge.

Figure 1 shows an illustration of such a graph G_B, consisting of a small connected component extracted from our data. There are 10 source nodes (*i.e.,* nodes 1 through 10), 4 destination nodes (*i.e.,* nodes a through d), and 13 edges, corresponding to 25 flows, with weights ranging from 1 to 4. Note that sources share destinations to varying extents. For example, sources $1, 2, 3$, and 10 all talk only to destination a, while sources 4 and 6 talk only to destination c. This pattern suggests some common purpose to the traffic in each of the two subsets of corresponding flows, and hence suggests in turn that some notion of 'community' may apply to these two sets of sources. In contrast, while source 9 also talks to destination a and source 7 also talks to destination c, they each talk as well to destination b. This observation suggests that, while sources 7 and 9 participate in the communities defined around destinations a and

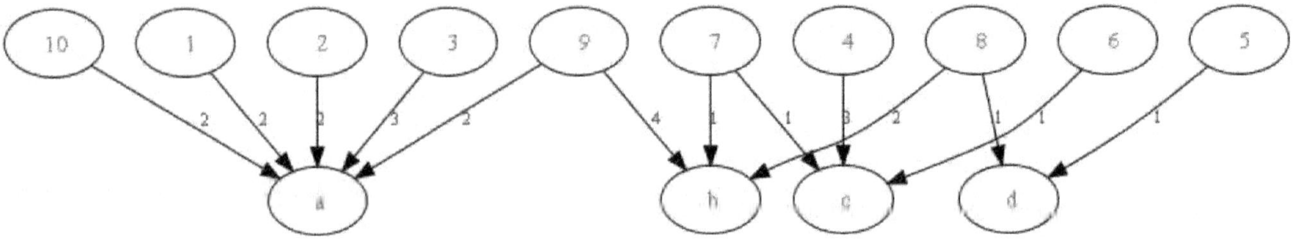

Figure 1: Bipartite graph representation of network flow traffic.

c, they do not necessarily belong to those communities. Hence, we say that their role is both 'social' and 'anti-social' in nature. It is this behavior that we hypothesize may usefully be associated with intrusion.

While G_B is a standard representation of network traffic, it is difficult to analyze for antisocial behavior because nodes in G_B are not all of the same type: some are traffic sources, and some are traffic destinations. Since our focus is on identifying sources of malicious traffic, a natural way to simplify the problem is to consider graphs in which vertices correspond only to sources. These networks are essentially reductions of the bipartite graph G_B. These reductions may be defined in a number of alternative ways, and the alternatives can vary in detail. We consider two such alternatives in this study.

The first is a standard one-mode projection of G_B, in the form of an undirected graph $G_P = (V, E_P)$, where nodes v_i and v_j are connected if and only if they share at least one common destination. The one-mode projection of the bipartite graph in Figure 1 is shown in Figure 2. Note that under this representation the types of 'communities' we identified, *i.e.,* source nodes that all communicate with a common destination, exhibit a distinct topological structure in G_P, in the form of cliques. For example, nodes $1,2,3,9$, and 10 form a five-clique, while nodes $4,6$, and 7 form a three-clique. Note too that nodes 7 and 9, which we identified as exhibiting an example of antisocial behavior, stand out clearly as being both members of their respective cliques and, at the same time, connected by a single edge to each other's cliques.

This edge is an example of a *bridge*, in that its removal increases the number of components in the graph. Similarly, these two vertices are examples of a *cut-vertex*. These two complementary notions are popular in the social network literature (*e.g.,* [6, Sec 7.3]), where they are used, among other things in the study of diffusion of information. Here we maintain that, if cliques in our network G_P capture the traffic common to Internet communities sufficiently well, and if bridges and cut-vertices capture antisocial behavior on the fringe of these communities, then this illustration suggests that identification of communities and the bridges/cut-vertices between them may be used to detect source IPs sending intrusive traffic.

A potential drawback of the one-mode projection G_P as a source-based view of the communication underlying our network flow data is the loss of certain information. For example, regardless of whether two source nodes send traffic to a single common destination or 100 common destinations, only a single edge will be placed between them in G_P. Furthermore, it can be argued that the notion of communication in a community being determined solely by sending traffic to a common destination is rather limited, and that real communication is decidedly more nuanced. For example, if sources v_1 and v_2 both send traffic to destination a, and v_2 and another source v_3 both send traffic to a different destination b, it may be that all of v_1, v_2 and v_3 belong to the same community. In other words, what is important in determining source-based communities may be a sense of how similar a set of sources are to each other in the bipartite communication graph G_B.

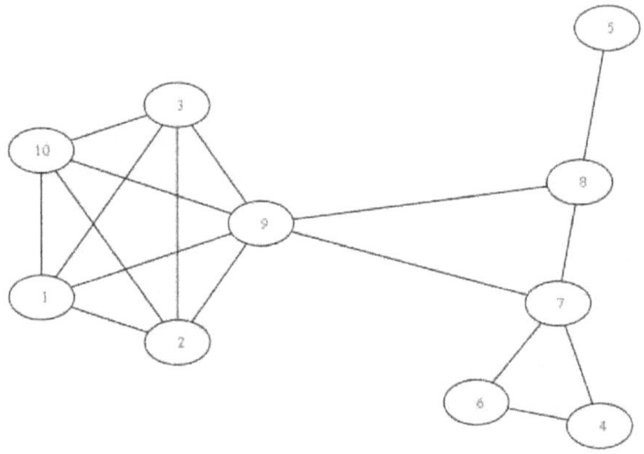

Figure 2: One-mode projection.

4. CHARACTERIZING MALICIOUS SOURCES

A number of previous studies have examined how the properties of communication graphs can be used to identify malicious sources. The main approach taken to date has been to simply observe that malicious sources often send traffic to many other nodes, and so candidates for detection are 'high cardinality' nodes – in the language of the previous section, those with high out-degree in G_B [9, 11, 3, 8].

Unfortunately, attackers now routinely seek to scan or probe without raising cardinality alerts, and detection based on source out-degree has to be tuned quite carefully [10]. We can observe this effect in our data. Figure 3 shows the histogram of the base-10 log of out-degree for all of the Dshield sources in our May 1 dataset. The figure shows that malicious sources have out-degrees spanning a vast range; while some sources send to thousands of destinations, many send to only hundreds or tens of destinations.

To illustrate the problem this causes for degree-based detectors, we evaluated the performance of a degree-based detector on our data. Such a detector is configured by choosing the false alarm rate that is considered tolerable by the operator. We chose false alarm rates of 5% and 2.5%; these are in practice quite high, but doing so presents the detection ability of the degree-based method in the best possible light.

Nonetheless, even when high false alarm rates are tolerated, the degree-based detector fails to detect a significant fraction of the malicous sources. The thresholds for degree-based detection at false alarm rates of 5% and 2.5% are shown in Figure 3. For each threshold, sources to the right of the line are those that would be detected. The figure shows that much more than half (64% and 79%) of the malicious sources go undetected using the degree-based method.

This observation motivates our interest in developing detection methods that complement pure cardinality-based approaches. That is, we seek methods that can identify potential attackers despite the fact that the attacker does not send a large number of probes in the observation period (and so does not have high out-degree).

To that end, we turn to the notion of antisocial communication as a potentially more sophisticated indicator of network intrusion. To do so, we need to define metrics that can identify antisocial nodes within the graphs G_P and G_W defined in the previous section. In the remainder of this section we present such metrics. Then, in the next section, we will show simple detection algorithms based on these metrics that are remarkably accurate in identifying malicious sources among those sources that are *not* high-cardinality hosts.

To illustrate the metrics we define, in this section we use flow data from just the first of our 14 days (*i.e.,* May 1st, 2007). In addition, for reasons of computational efficiency, we use a subset of the network flow data for that day, based on the set of all flows sent from a simple random sample of size 10K selected from those source IP addresses active that day in our dataset. The flows obtained in this manner induced a corresponding sampling of destination IP addresses. Completing our sampled source and destination lists with those destinations and sources obtained in the original stage that also acted as sources and destinations, respectively, we are left with a subset of the data whose bipartite graph representation $G_B = (V, U, E_B)$ has $|V| = 10,897$, $|U| = 53,877$, and $|E_B| = 879,010$. From this we then created the binary and weighted one-mode projections of G_B, *i.e.,* $G_P = (V, E_P)$ and $G_W = (V, E_W)$, respectively; where $|V| = 10,897$ (being the same set V defining G_B) and $|E_P| = |E_W| = 766,680$. The results below for these graphs are representative of what we observed over multiple simulation trials, over multiple days, as we discuss later, in Section 5.

Importantly, for our purposes, among the 10,897 sources in our networks G_B, G_P, and G_W, 182 were identified as malicious by examination of the DShield logs of that day. In what follows in this section, we focus on the challenge of characterizing these malicious source IPs given only the basic information on which IPs sent flows to which others. We explore three classes of techniques, based on ideas of community detection, cut-vertices, and local graph structure, respectively. The lessons we learn from this characterization study then lead naturally to the detection algorithms we present later in Section 5.

4.1 Community Detection

Our notion of (anti)social behavior in the source-based social networks defined in the previous section, and the reliance of this notion on 'communities' in those networks, suggests the relevance of so-called community detection methods from the social network literature in developing detection algorithms. There are many such methods of this sort. All of them essentially take as input a graph topology and they output a partitioning of the graph into subsets of nodes, for which nodes within subsets are more heavily linked than nodes between subsets. See [13, Ch 4.3.3] and references therein, for example.

A popular method in this area is that of Newman, Clauset and Moore [4], based on the concept of modularity. This method, as with others like it, attempts to optimize a certain complexity score (called the 'modularity') to produce as parsimonious a partition of the graph as possible. For illustration, we applied this algorithm to the largest connected component of the one-mode projection source graph G_P, consisting of 8480 source nodes (out of the 10,897 sources in the full graph) and the edges among them. Among these 8480 nodes, 161 of those are DShield sources (the other 24 DShield sources are represented as singleton nodes in the full graph). The algorithm found an optimal clustering with a total of 68 clusters (or 'communities'), the size and number of which are summarized in Table 1.

Table 1: Summary of clusters produced by standard community detection, as applied to the largest connected component of G_P.

Size of Cluster	# of Clusters	# of DShields
6784	1	158
986	1	1
8 to 243	10	0
≤ 7	56	2
Total	68	161

Unfortunately, the partitioning of our subgraph into these communities, relative to the distribution of the 161 malicious DShield source nodes, does little to reveal the latter in any obvious fashion, since 158 of these DShield source IPs are contained within the largest cluster. See Table 1. Hence, this particular method of defining 'communities' does little to distinguish the DShield sources from those communities upon which they intrude. In fact, this result is not entirely surprising, since it has been found that the maximum modularity partition suffers from a so-called 'resolution limit', in which it tends to fail to extract clusters smaller than a certain size, due to the particular manner in which the degree distribution of the underlying graph enters into the criterion function being optimized. See [7], for example.

4.2 Cut-Vertices

The problem with the standard community detection approach in this setting is that, in seeking a highly parsimonious partitioning, it is not operating at a sufficiently fine scale. While we could, of course, choose to explore partitions of the graph resulting from non-optimal choices of the objective function (*i.e.,* modularity), it is not clear how best to do so once optimality is left behind. Alternatively, therefore, we implemented a type of simple, bottom-up iterative pruning algorithm, which proved to be decidedly more powerful in isolating malicious nodes.

Specifically, and recalling the importance of cut-vertices in our illustrations of Section 3, as prototypical examples of how a node might participate in communication in (anti)social ways, we implemented a simple recursive seach-and-prune strategy for greedily finding such cut-vertices. Starting again with the largest connected component of the one-mode projection source graph G_P, we used a standard max-flow/min-cut algorithm to identify all cut-vertices in that component. These vertices were then removed, the act of which, by definition, broke the component into at least two separate connected components. We then took the larger of these connected components and repeated the process just described. This series of steps was iterated until we reached a largest connected component in which no further cut-vertices are found. This component had 4633 nodes, just over 50% the size of that in the first stage of the algorithm (i.e., 8480).

Note that at each stage of the algorithm, until convergence, the act of pruning induces additional cut-vertices, which in some sense

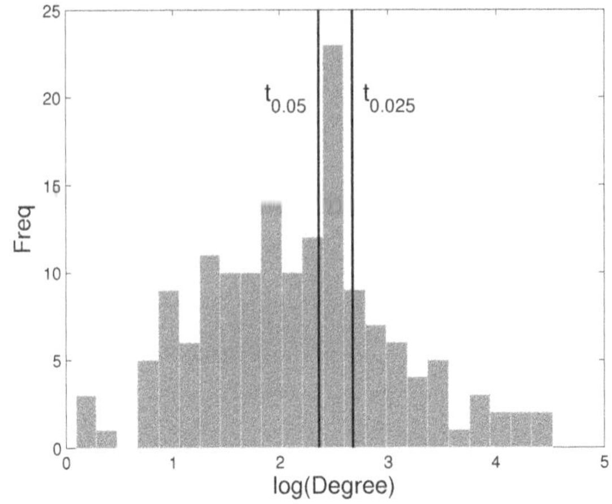

Figure 3: Distribution of base-10 log of Dshield source out-degrees.

therefore were 'nearly' cut-vertices at the previous iteration. So our algorithm can be viewed as a 'quick-and-dirty' way of discovering nodes where the notion of cut-vertex is applied in an increasingly robust manner. The output of our algorithm is a list of 1303 nodes. In examining this list, we find that 86 are DShield sources, *i.e.*, the proportion of Dshield sources among cut-vertices is about 6.6% . While this percentage may not seem large in itself, this is likely due in no small part to the greedy nature of our algorithm (*i.e.*, recall that at each iteration we work only on the largest connected component emerging from the component analyzed at the previous iteration). Importantly, however, a cross-validation study shows that this number is highly significant. Specifically, using the same network G_P, we randomly assigned the 161 labels of 'DShield' to arbitrary nodes in this graph and applied our algorithm. This process was repeated 100 times. The average proportion of pseudo-DShield nodes discovered over the 100 trials of this simulation was 1.66%, with a 95% confidence interval of (1.06%, 2.27%). These results suggest that DShield source IPs are highly enriched among cut-vertices.

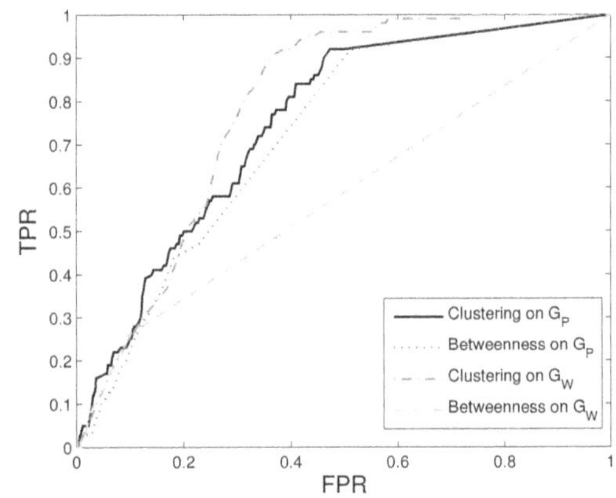

Figure 4: Detection accuracy for Day 1.

5. DETECTING MALICIOUS SOURCES

With an ability to distinguish between DShield and non-DShield nodes, we now demonstrate the use of clustering and betweenness on our source graphs for detection. We present first the results for the analysis of a single day of traffic, in detail, and then a summary of results for the same analysis over fourteen consecutive days of traffic.

The previous section showed that a sizeable fraction of malicious hosts can not be detected by simple degree-based methods. Hence, in all our analyses below, we focus only on detection of those nodes that can *not* be detected by degree-based methods. That is, we eliminate from our validation sets all those nodes having degree greater than the threshold shown in Figure 3 for the 5% false alarm rate.

It is important to recognize that high-degree malicious sources are easily detected using the antisocial metrics, because they communicate with so many unrelated communities. Hence, restricting our attention only to low-degree nodes makes our detection problem much harder, and focuses on a set of sources that are not detectable using standard (degree-based) methods.

5.1 Analysis of Day 1 Traffic

Our proposed intrusion detection system is simple and intuitive, in that it entails just the thresholding of the clustering and betweenness metrics introduced in the previous section in our characterization of malicious sources. To evaluate this approach, we do the following. Given a graph G_P or G_W, constructed from a set of network flow data as described in Section 3, we calculate the clustering and betweenness values for all vertices in our validation set (*i.e.*, those not detected by a standard degree-based method, at 5% false alarm rate). These values are then compared to a threshold, across the appropriate range of thresholds, with a node being declared malicious if its clustering coefficient (betweenness centrality) is below (above) that threshold. Receiver operating characteristic (ROC) curves and the area under the curve (AUC) are used summarize performance.

To begin to understand the relative power of the two metrics (clustering and betweenness) and the two graph representations (the projection G_P and the weighted projection G_W), we present detection results in Figure 4. This receiver operating characteristic (ROC) plot shows the tradeoff between false alarm rate (on the x

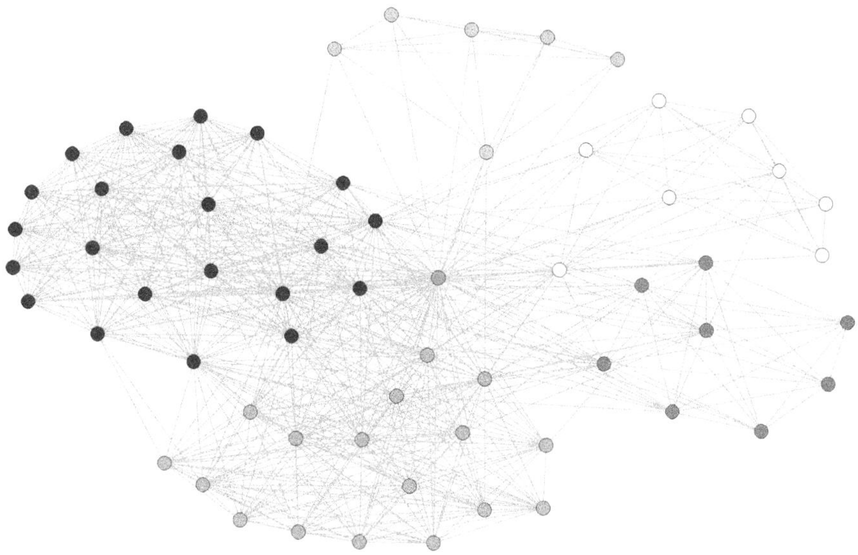

Figure 5: Visualization of DShield neighborhood comprised of 62 nodes.

axis) and detection rate (on the y axis) for the four combinations of metric and graph representation.

Overall, the figure shows that detection ability of the antisocial method for these difficult-to-detect sources is quite good. It also highlights distinctions among the approaches. The area under the curve (AUC) for these ROC curves, a single-number summary of accuracy, is higher for clustering than betweenness in both the binary graph G_P (i.e., 0.75 versus 0.724) and the weighted graph G_W (*i.e.,* 0.787 versus 0.581). These numbers – particularly the AUC of 0.787 for clustering on the weighted projection source graph G_W – are quite encouraging, and point strongly to the utility of our use of social structures here.

To illustrate the nature of the antisocial communication detectable using these methods, we chose an arbitrary DShield source. We then extracted from the source graph G_P the so-called 'egocentric' subgraph associated with this source, consisting of the source node, its 62 neighboring nodes, and those edges to and among these neighbors. Figure 5 shows a representation of the subgraph thus obtained. The Dshield node is depicted in the middle of what can be seen to be five natural clusters, indicated by different colors, identified using a standard community detection algorithm. The Dshield node was placed in its own cluster by the algorithm. The overall structure of the subgraph is consistent with our notion of (anti)social behaviour in the source-based social networks: the malicious source node is clearly 'entering' communities to which it does not 'belong.'

5.2 Analysis of 14-day Traffic

In order to verify the robustness of the 1-day results in Section 5.1 for our proposed intrusion detection system, we analyzed all fourteen days of the data described in Section 2. For each day, we repeated 10 times the process described in Section 4, wherein each time we generated a random bipartite graph G_B from $10K$ randomly sampled source vertices and constructed the corresponding source projections G_P and G_W. For each such pair of projection graphs, we calculated the local clustering and betweenness values

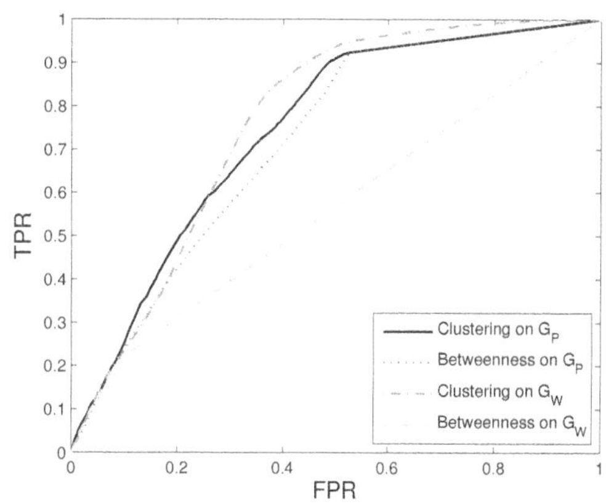

Figure 6: Average ROC curves summarizing detection accuracy over 14 days.

for all sources in components of size at least three (*i.e.,* we dropped all singletons and dyads from our analysis).

In Figure 6 we show the average of the resulting ROC curves, over the 140 samples drawn over the 14 days. And in Table 2 we show the average corresponding AUC values, and their associated standard errors. We see that for clustering and betweenness on both G_P and G_W, the average AUC over 14 days is nearly identical to what we saw for the first day. Particularly, on G_P, the average is essentially the same for both clustering (*i.e.,* 0.75 for Day 1 versus 0.744 for 14 days) and betweenness (*i.e.,* 0.724 for Day 1 versus 0.718 for 14 days); and on G_W, the average clustering (i.e., 0.787 versus 0.7625) and betweenness (*i.e.,* 0.581 versus 0.562) are also comparable. This suggests a good level of robustness of our results, on average, to the choice of day.

These results also lend support to the conclusion that the clustering metric provides much better discriminatory power than the

Table 2: Summary of AUC for Detection over 14 Days.

	Mean(AUC)	SE(AUC)
Clustering on G_P	0.7440	0.0103
Betweenness on G_P	0.7180	0.0084
Clustering on G_W	0.7625	0.0080
Betweenness on G_W	0.5621	0.0034

betweenness metric. On the other hand, the emerging picture is that the weighted graph G_W, despite its more nuanced view of antisocial communication (*i.e.*, through the incorporation of information on multiple flows between source-destination pairs), does not offer a significant improvement in detection accuracy over the simpler, unweighed G_P.

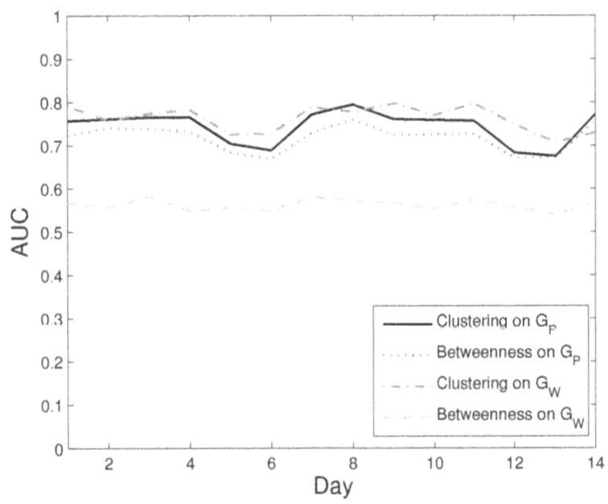

Figure 7: AUC as a function of day, over 14 days.

A slightly more refined picture emerges in examining Figure 7, where we show the daily average AUC for each of the four detection methods, with the averages here computed over the 10 sampled flow datasets each day. The associated standard errors (not shown) are on the order of at most 0.03 in all cases. We see that the relative performance of each of the four methods is quite stable with respect to each other over this two-week period. Somewhat interestingly, the performance of the topmost scoring method, based on clustering on G_P,while largely constant over the two weeks, clearly degrades slightly in two places, which correspond to weekends (*i.e.*, May 5-6 and 12-13). The other three methods appear to be affected to much lesser extents, or not at all, by the weekend. It is unclear what may be causing this differentiation in relative performance.

6. RELATED WORK

As mentioned already, our work is informed by recent studies showing that distinctive, community-based graph structures are evident in normal network traffic [8]. We use these structures to motivate our search for intruders as hosts that do not respect such community boundaries.

A number of other efforts have used properties of the graphs induced by flow records to detect malicious traffic. The notion that malicious hosts have high degree in the bipartite flow graph has motivated algorithms for identifying such "high cardinality" or "superspreader" nodes [9, 11]. However, these approaches rely only on node degree and do not incorporate any notion of graph structures reflecting social properties (*e.g.*, clustering or betweenness). The significant number of malicious hosts in our data that are not "superspreaders" was illustrated in Section 4. The authors in [3] also investigate a graph-based method for intrusion detection. However, their focus is on identifying large scale patterns such as worm outbreaks and their approach is rule-based. Likewise, the authors in [21] consider the same problem and apply simple rules to identify intrusion between clusters of nodes. As with the high-degree heuristic, these methods are not based on social properties

In our work we start from a definition of normality that incorporates social interactions. Other work has considered intrusion detection based on a simpler definition of normality: namely, normality is simply what is common or frequent. This leads to the problem of identifying unusual substructures in graphs [15, 5]. The drawback to this approach is that attacks must be rare in order to be recognized as anomalous. Further, the particular methods used are highly sensitive to noise, which is a significant drawback when applied to sampled flow data.

The work in [14] is focused on worm detection, but has some similarity to our work in that historical communication patterns are used to define communities for each host. However the approach taken is rigid and not based on known properties of social networks, but rather on defining normal communication as that which has happened in the past.

In this paper we build our most detailed view of community-based similarity using *the cosine similarity measure*. Other work has looked at different definitions of community-based similarity for bipartite graphs. For example, [20] defines a similarity-based neighborhood of a particular node by using a random walk with restarts at the node. Our work required a similarity measure between pairs of nodes.

7. DISCUSSION

As discussed in the Introduction, signature-based intrusion detection systems are quickly outdated, which has spurred interest on identifying characteristics of normal traffic that are violated by intrusions. Of course, no single characteristic is sufficient for this purpose. While attention has focused on high cardinality hosts, we show that this characteristic alone cannot reliably detect intrusions.

Accordingly, our focus is on new characteristics that can be exploited in the context of a multi-faceted or multi-filter intrusion detection system, to augment approaches based on cardinality and other metrics. Our hypothesis is that communities are exposed in communication graphs, and that community structure can be exploited for intrusion detection. Our results (in particular, showing high AUC values – as high as 79%) show that indeed, communication that consistently crosses community boundaries is often evidence of intrusion. Another point discussed in the Introduction is that validated intrusion data is rare and quickly outdated. In this study we have used logs from the DShield database to identify hosts that are malicious, which is of course only an approximation to ground truth. However, one result of this approximation is that our stated results may be somewhat pessimistic — there may be many malicious sources that are in fact detected by our methods but are not labeled as such because they do not appear in DShield logs. Indeed, there is some evidence that this is the case. For example, in our single-day dataset, we find that 3.1% of detections that are labelled as DShield sources send to destination port 0. This is not surprising, as port 0 is a common attack target. However, we also find that 1.6% of the detections that are not labelled as DShield sources also send to port 0. This is in contrast to the negatives (sources that are not detections), in which only 0.6% send to port 0. The fact that there is a higher tendency to exhibit this characteristic of malicious behavior among even the non-DShield detections as compared to the negatives suggests that our methods may in fact be performing better than our results indicate.

The limitation of DShield data as a definition of ground truth led us to explore other ways of identifying malicious sources. To this end, we also analyzed a corpus of honeynet logs provided by the Internet Motion Sensor (IMS) project at the University of Michigan [1] collected over the same period in 2007 as the flow logs. The IMS honeynet monitors a large portion of a /8 address space, and report non-spoofed source IP addresses that sent packets to the honeynet. Similar to Dshield, those sources are typically considered to be malicious, but the nature of the data is complementary: DShield is based on signature detection, while the IMS data collects traffic to dark space. Our results using this data were consistent with our DShield results. In particular, the clustering metric applied to G_P showed best performance overall, with a relatively high AUC value (0.63) suggesting that socially-based analysis is effective for detecting these sorts of malicious sources as well.

8. CONCLUSION

This paper evaluates a variety of ways of representing and measuring the social information contained in network flow data, and shows how to identify traffic sources that engage in (anti)social behavior — that is, communication that does not respect community structure.

We find that traditional approaches to community identification (*e.g.,* based on modularity) operate at too coarse a level to be useful for this problem. In contrast, a more useful approach is a local one, based on the idea of a cut-vertex. We show that one can make the notion of cut-vertex more robust, in our context of intrusion detection, by using metrics from the social network literature: clustering and betweenness. We find that clustering provides a more effective detector of antisocial behavior than does betweenness, but that the added complexity of the weighted graph G_W does not deliver a corresponding improvement in detection ability over its simpler cousin G_P. We also show that the use of social properties is more powerful than the use of source degree (cardinality), in the sense that it allows detection of malicious low-degree sources that can not be detected by the degree-based detector.

Having identified appropriate graph representations and appropriate socially-oriented metrics, we form and evaluate a detection system for malicious sources. Despite the fact that the resulting system operates on flow data (without signature inspection), we show that the resulting system effectively detects the vast majority of sources that the DShield logs identify (using signatures). This holds promise for the use of socially-based methods on data from core networks where many more flows are visible than at network edges (where most intrusion detection systems operate).

Acknowledgements

We are grateful to Johannes Ullrich and the SANS Institute (`www.sans.org`) for making DShield logs available to us for the purposes of this study. We also thank Michael Bailey and the IMS project members at the University of Michigan for making their honeynet data available to us.

This work was supported in part by NSF grants CNS-0831427, CNS-0905186, CNS-1018266, CNS-1012910, and CNS-1117039. Any opinions, findings, conclusions or other recommendations expressed in this material are those of the authors and do not necessarily reflect the view of the NSF. Partial support was also provided by ONR award N000140910654.

9. REFERENCES

[1] M. Bailey, E. Cooke, F. Jahanian, J. Nazario, and D. Watson. The Internet Motion Sensor: A Distributed Blackhole Monitoring System. In *Proceedings of the Network And Distributed Security Symposium*, San Diego, CA, January 2005.

[2] P. Barford, R. Nowak, R. Willett, and V. Yegneswaran. Toward a Model for Sources of Internet Background Radiation. In *Proceedings of the Passive and Active Measurement Conference*, Adelaide, Australia, March 2006.

[3] S. Cheung, R. Crawford, M. Dilger, J. Frank, J. Hoagland, K. Levitt, J. Rowe, S. Staniford-Chen, R. Yip, and D. Zerkle. The Design of GrIDS: A Graph-Based Intrusion Detection System. UC Davis Technical Report CSE-99-2, 1999.

[4] A. Clauset, MEJ Newman, and C. Moore. Finding community structure in very large networks. *Physical Review E*, 70(6):66111, 2004.

[5] G. Cormode, F. Korn, S. Muthukrishnan, and Y. Wu. On signatures for communications graphs. In *Proceedings of ICDE*, Cancun, Mexico, April 2008.

[6] W. de Nooy, A. Mrvar, and V. Batagelj. *Exploratory Social Network Analysis with Pajek.* Cambridge University Press, New York, 2005.

[7] Benjamin H. Good, Yves A. de Montjoye, and Aaron Clauset. Performance of modularity maximization in practical contexts. *Physical Review E*, 81(4):046106+, April 2010.

[8] Y. Jin, E. Sharafuddin, and Z. Zhang. Unveiling core network-wide communication patterns through application traffic activity graph decomposition. In *Proceedings of ACM SIGMETRICS*, Seattle, WA, June 2009.

[9] Yu Jin, Jin Cao, Aiyou Chen, Tian Bu, and Zhi-Li Zhang. Identifying high cardinality Internet hosts. In *Proceedings of IEEE INFOCOM*, Rio de Janeiro, Brazil, April 2009.

[10] J. Jung, V. Paxson, A. Berger, and H. Balakrishnan. Fast Portscan Detection Using Sequential Hypothesis Testing. In *IEEE Symposium on Security and Privacy 2004*, Oakland, CA, May 2004.

[11] N. Kamiyama, T. Mori, and R. Kawahara. Simple and adaptive identification of superspreaders by flow sampling. In *Proceedings of IEEE INFOCOM*, Anchorage, AK, April 2007.

[12] KDD Cup data. `http://kdd.ics.uci.edu/databases/kddcup99/kddcup99.html`, August 1999.

[13] Eric D. Kolaczyk. *Statistical Analysis of Network Data: Methods and Models.* Springer, New York, 2009.

[14] P. McDaniel, S. Sen, O. Spatscheck, J. van der Merwe, B. Aiello, and C. Kalmanek. Enterprise security: A community of interest based approach. In *Proceedings of NDSS*, San Diego, CA, February 2006.

[15] C. Noble and D. Cook. Graph-based anomaly detection. In *Proceedings of SIGKDD*, Washington, DC, August 2003.

[16] V. Paxson. Bro: A system for detecting network intruders in real-time. *Computer Networks, (Special Issue on Intrusion Detection)*, 31(23-24):2435–2463, December 1999.

[17] H. Ringberg, A. Soule, J. Rexford, and C. Diot. Sensitivity of pca for traffic anomaly detection. In *Proceedings of ACM SIGMETRICS*, San Diego, CA, June 2007.

[18] M. Roesch. Snort – lightweight intrusion detection for networks. In *Proceedings of the Usenix LISA Conference*, Seattle, WA, November 1999.

[19] S. Rubin, S. Jha, and B. Miller. Automatic generation and analysis of nids attacks. In *Proceedings of Annual Computer Security Applications Conference (ACSAC)*, Tucson, AZ, December 2004.

[20] J. Sun, H. Qu, D. Chakrabarti, and C. Faloutsos. Relevance search and anomaly detection in bipartite graphs. *Proceedings of SIGKDD Explorations Special Issue on Link Mining*, 7(2), 2005.

[21] J. Tolle and O. Niggemann. Supporting Intrusion Detection by Graph Clustering and Graph Drawing. In *Proceedings of the Symposium on Recent Advances in Intrusion Detection*, Toulouse, France, October 2000.

[22] J. Ullrich. The Dshield Project. http://www.sans.org, 2010.

[23] V. Yegneswaran, P. Barford, and J. Ullrich. Internet Intrusions: Global Characteristics and Prevalence. In *Proceedings of ACM SIGMETRICS*, San Diego, CA, June 2003.

Robust Multi-Task Feature Learning

Pinghua Gong[†], Jieping Ye[‡], Changshui Zhang[†]
[†]State Key Laboratory on Intelligent Technology and Systems
[†]Tsinghua National Laboratory for Information Science and Technology (TNList)
[†]Department of Automation, Tsinghua University, Beijing 100084, China
[‡]Computer Science and Engineering, Center for Evolutionary Medicine and Informatics,
[‡]The Biodesign Institute, Arizona State University, Tempe, AZ 85287
[†]{gph08@mails, zcs@mail}.tsinghua.edu.cn, [‡]Jieping.Ye@asu.edu

ABSTRACT

Multi-task learning (MTL) aims to improve the performance of multiple related tasks by exploiting the intrinsic relationships among them. Recently, multi-task feature learning algorithms have received increasing attention and they have been successfully applied to many applications involving high-dimensional data. However, they assume that all tasks share a common set of features, which is too restrictive and may not hold in real-world applications, since outlier tasks often exist. In this paper, we propose a Robust Multi-Task Feature Learning algorithm (rMTFL) which simultaneously captures a common set of features among relevant tasks and identifies outlier tasks. Specifically, we decompose the weight (model) matrix for all tasks into two components. We impose the well-known group Lasso penalty on row groups of the first component for capturing the shared features among relevant tasks. To simultaneously identify the outlier tasks, we impose the same group Lasso penalty but on column groups of the second component. We propose to employ the accelerated gradient descent to efficiently solve the optimization problem in rMTFL, and show that the proposed algorithm is scalable to large-size problems. In addition, we provide a detailed theoretical analysis on the proposed rMTFL formulation. Specifically, we present a theoretical bound to measure how well our proposed rMTFL approximates the true evaluation, and provide bounds to measure the error between the estimated weights of rMTFL and the underlying true weights. Moreover, by assuming that the underlying true weights are above the noise level, we present a sound theoretical result to show how to obtain the underlying true shared features and outlier tasks (sparsity patterns). Empirical studies on both synthetic and real-world data demonstrate that our proposed rMTFL is capable of simultaneously capturing shared features among tasks and identifying outlier tasks.

Categories and Subject Descriptors

H.2.8 [**Database Management**]: Database Applications—*Data Mining*

General Terms

Algorithm

Keywords

Multi-task learning, feature selection, outlier tasks detection

1. INTRODUCTION

Multi-task learning [8] aims to improve the performance of multiple related tasks by utilizing the intrinsic relationships among these tasks. Multi-task learning has been applied successfully in a wide range of applications including object recognition [8], speech recognition [28], handwritten digits recognition [30] and disease progression prediction [44]. A critical ingredient in these applications is how to model the shared structures among tasks. Existing algorithms can be broadly classified into two categories: explicit parameter sharing and implicit structure sharing.

Under explicit parameter sharing, all the tasks explicitly share some common parameters; examples include hidden units in neural networks [8, 5], prior in hierarchical Bayesian models [4, 31, 36, 38], parameters of Gaussian process [18], feature mapping matrix [1], classification weight [11] and similarity metric [28, 40]. On the contrary, algorithms under implicit structure sharing do not explicitly impose all tasks to share certain parameters, but they implicitly capture some common structures; for example, the algorithms in [29, 24] constrain all tasks to share a common low rank subspace and the algorithms in [27, 2, 23, 19, 22, 17, 35, 41] constrain all tasks to share a common set of features.

One key assumption of the above multi-task learning algorithms for both categories is that all tasks are related to each other by the presumed structures. However, this may not hold in real-world applications, as outlier tasks often exist. Thus, simply assuming that all tasks share a certain structure may degrade the performance. This motivates the development of several recent multi-task learning algorithms for discovering the inherent relationship among tasks. For example, some multi-task learning algorithms [32, 34, 14, 42, 16] cluster the given tasks into different groups and impose the tasks in the same groups to share a certain common structure. Multi-task learning algorithms with a composite regularization [15, 9, 10] have been proposed to capture different types of relationships using regularization.

In this paper, we consider the multi-task learning setting where the relevant tasks share a common set of features while outlier tasks exist. We propose a Robust Multi-Task Feature Learning algorithm (rMTFL) which simultaneously captures the shared features among relevant tasks and detects outlier tasks. Specifically, we decompose the weight matrix W consisting of the prediction models of all tasks into the sum of two components P and Q. We employ the well-known group Lasso penalty on row groups of P such that the relevant tasks capture a common set of features. In addition, we employ the same group Lasso penalty but on column groups of Q to simultaneously identify the outlier tasks. The main contributions of this paper include:

(1) We propose a Robust Multi-Task Feature Learning formulation (rMTFL) which simultaneously captures a common set of features among relevant tasks and identifies outlier tasks. We propose to employ accelerated gradient descent to efficiently solve the optimization problem involved in rMTFL, and show that the proposed algorithm is scalable to large-size problems.

(2) We present a theoretical bound to measure how well rMTFL can approximate the underlying true evaluation, and give bounds to measure the error between the weights estimated from rMTFL and the underlying true weights. Moreover, by assuming that the underlying true weights are above the noise level, we present a sound theoretical result to show how we can obtain the underlying true shared features and outlier tasks (sparsity patterns).

(3) We perform empirical studies using both synthetic and real-world data. Our experiments demonstrate the efficiency of the proposed algorithm. Results also demonstrate the effectiveness of rMTFL for capturing shared features among tasks and identifying outlier tasks simultaneously.

Organization: The remainder of this paper is organized as follows: In Section 2, we introduce our proposed rMTFL formulation. In Section 3, we present the proposed optimization algorithm for rMTFL. In Section 4, we provide a detailed theoretical analysis on rMTFL. In Section 5, we discuss related work. Experimental results are presented in Section 6 and we conclude the paper in Section 7.

Notations: Scalars, vectors, matrices and sets are denoted by lower case letters, bold face lower case letters, capital letters and calligraphic capital letters, respectively. x_i and x_{ij} denote the i-th entry of a vector $\mathbf{x}$ and the (i,j)-th entry of a matrix X. $\mathbf{x}^i$ ($\mathbf{x}_i$) denotes the i-th row (column) of a matrix X. $X^{\mathcal{J}}$ denotes a submatrix composed of the rows of X indexed by $\mathcal{J}$. $x_{jk}^{(i)}$ and $\mathbf{x}_j^{(i)}$ denote the (j,k)-th entry and the j-th column of a matrix X_i. Euclidean and Frobenius norms are denoted by $\|\cdot\|$ and $\|\cdot\|_F$. $\ell_{p,q}$-norm of a matrix X is defined as $\|X\|_{p,q} = \left(\sum_i \left((\sum_j x_{ij}^q)^{1/q}\right)^p\right)^{1/p}$ and the inner product of X and Y is denoted by $\langle X, Y\rangle$. $\mathbb{N}_m$ is defined as the set $\{1,\cdots,m\}$ and $N(\mu,\sigma^2)$ denotes a normal distribution with mean μ and standard deviation σ.

2. THE PROPOSED FORMULATION

Assume that we are given m learning tasks associated with the training data $\{(X_1,\mathbf{y}_1),\cdots,(X_m,\mathbf{y}_m)\}$, where $X_i \in \mathbb{R}^{d\times n_i}$ is the data matrix of the i-th task with each column as a sample; $\mathbf{y}_i \in \mathbb{R}^{n_i}$ is the response of the i-th task (y_i has continuous values for regression and discrete values for classification); d is the data dimensionality; n_i is the number of samples for the i-th task. The data has been normalized such that the (j,k)-th entry of X_i denoted as $x_{jk}^{(i)}$ satisfies

$$\sum_{k=1}^{n_i} \left(x_{jk}^{(i)}\right)^2 = 1, \forall j \in \mathbb{N}_d. \tag{1}$$

We consider learning a linear function

$$y_{ji} \approx f_i\left(\mathbf{x}_j^{(i)}\right) = \left(\mathbf{x}_j^{(i)}\right)^T \mathbf{w}_i, i \in \mathbb{N}_m, j \in \mathbb{N}_{n_i}$$

for each task and decomposing the weight matrix $W = [\mathbf{w}_1,\cdots,\mathbf{w}_m] \in \mathbb{R}^{d\times m}$ into the sum of two components P and Q (Please refer to Figure 1 for illustration). We make use of different regularization terms on P and Q to exploit relationships among tasks. Formally, our rMTFL model is formulated as:

$$\min_{W,P,Q} \sum_{i=1}^{m} \frac{1}{mn_i} \left\|X_i^T\mathbf{w}_i - \mathbf{y}_i\right\|^2 + \lambda_1\|P\|_{1,2} + \lambda_2\left\|Q^T\right\|_{1,2},$$
$$s.t.\ W = P + Q, \tag{2}$$

where the first regularization term on P captures the shared features among tasks and the second term on Q discovers the outlier tasks; λ_1 and λ_2 are nonnegative parameters to control these two terms. Specifically, the first regularization term is based on the well-known group Lasso penalty on row groups of P which restricts the rows of the optimal solution $P^\star$ to consist of all zero or nonzero elements [2]. Thus, all related tasks should select a common set of features. However, the assumption that all tasks share the same set of features may not hold in real applications, as outlier tasks often exist. To address this issue, we introduce the second regularization term based on the same group Lasso penalty but on column groups of Q to discover these outlier tasks. Similarly, the columns of the optimal solution $Q^\star$ consist of all zero or nonzero elements, with the nonzero columns corresponding to outlier tasks. Intuitively, if the i-th column of $Q^\star$ is nonzero, then the i-th column of $W^\star$ is also nonzero, thus the i-th task does not share a common set of features with other tasks, identified as an outlier task; meanwhile, for the remaining tasks corresponding to the zero columns of $Q^\star$, they share a common set of features captured by the nonzero rows of $P^\star$ (see Figure 1).

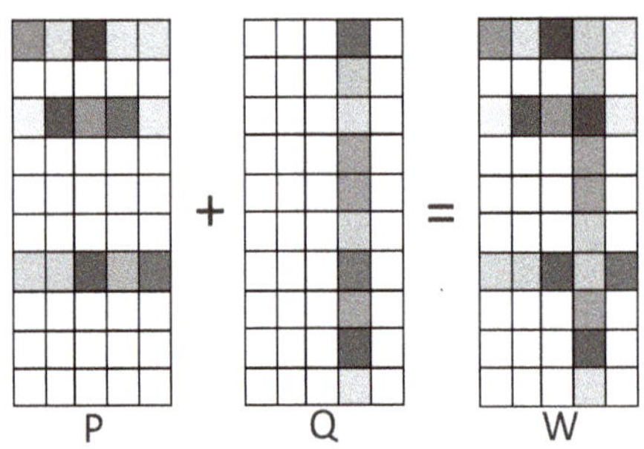

Figure 1: Illustration of weight matrix decomposition for rMTFL, where squares with white background denote zero entries. There are 5 tasks, where the fourth task is an outlier task. Please refer to the text for detailed explanation.

3. OPTIMIZATION ALGORITHM

In this section, we show how to solve the rMTFL formulation in Eq. (2) efficiently. Denote

$$l(P,Q) = \sum_{i=1}^{m} \frac{1}{mn_i} \left\| X_i^T(\mathbf{p}_i + \mathbf{q}_i) - \mathbf{y}_i \right\|^2,$$
$$r(P,Q) = \lambda_1 \|P\|_{1,2} + \lambda_2 \left\| Q^T \right\|_{1,2}, \tag{3}$$

where $l(P,Q)$ is the empirical loss function and $r(P,Q)$ is the regularization term. We note that the objective function in Eq. (2) is a composite function of a differential term $l(P,Q)$ and a non-differential term $r(P,Q)$. Denote

$$T_{R,S,\eta}(P,Q) = l(R,S) + \left\langle \frac{\partial l(R,S)}{\partial R}, P - R \right\rangle + \frac{\eta}{2}\|P-R\|_F^2$$
$$+ \left\langle \frac{\partial l(R,S)}{\partial S}, Q - S \right\rangle + \frac{\eta}{2}\|Q-S\|_F^2, \tag{4}$$

which is the first order Taylor expansion of $l(P,Q)$ at (R,S), with the squared Euclidean distance between (P,Q) and (R,S) as the regularization term. The traditional gradient descent algorithm obtains the solution at the k-th iteration ($k \geq 1$) by $(P^k, Q^k) = \arg\min_{P,Q} T_{P^{k-1},Q^{k-1},\eta_k}(P,Q) + r(P,Q)$ with a proper step size η_k. Here we propose to employ the accelerated gradient descent [25, 26] to solve the optimization problem, which generates the solution at the k-th iteration ($k \geq 1$) by computing the following proximal operator [20, 19, 21, 12, 37, 3]:

$$(P^k, Q^k) = \arg\min_{P,Q} T_{R^k,S^k,\eta_k}(P,Q) + r(P,Q), \tag{5}$$

where $R^1 = P^0, S^1 = Q^0$ and $R^{k+1} = P^k + \alpha_k(P^k - P^{k-1}), S^{k+1} = Q^k + \alpha_k(Q^k - Q^{k-1})$ for $k \geq 1$; η_k ($k \geq 1$) is set by finding the smallest nonnegative integer m_k such that with $\eta_k = 2^{m_k}\eta_{k-1}$:

$$l(P^k, Q^k) \leq T_{R^k,S^k,\eta_k}(P^k, Q^k). \tag{6}$$

We note that (R^{k+1}, S^{k+1}) is in fact a linear combination of (P^k, Q^k) and (P^{k-1}, Q^{k-1}). The coefficient α_k plays an important role in the convergence of the algorithm. As suggested by [6], we set $\alpha_k = (t_{k-1} - 1)/t_k$, where $t_0 = 1$ and $t_k = \left(1 + \sqrt{t_{k-1}^2 + 1}\right)/2$ for $k \geq 1$. According to the theoretical analysis in [6], we present the following convergence result for rMTFL:

THEOREM 1. *Let (P^k, Q^k) be generated by Eq. (5) with a properly chosen η_k satisfying Eq. (6). Then for any $k \geq 1$,*

$$f(P^k, Q^k) - f(P^\star, Q^\star) = O\left(\frac{1}{k^2}\right), \tag{7}$$

where $f(\cdot,\cdot)$ and $(P^\star, Q^\star)$ are respectively the objective function and the optimal solution in Eq. (2).

3.1 Implementation details

There are two issues that remain to be addressed: how to compute the proximal operator in Eq. (5) and how to select a proper initial value η_0.

Due to the decomposable property of Eq. (5), we can cast Eq. (5) into the following two separate proximal operator problems:

$$P^k = \arg\min_P \frac{1}{2}\left\| P - \left(R^k - \frac{1}{\eta_k}\nabla_R l(R^k, S^k)\right)\right\|_F^2 + \frac{\lambda_1}{\eta_k}\|P\|_{1,2}$$
$$Q^k = \arg\min_Q \frac{1}{2}\left\| Q - \left(S^k - \frac{1}{\eta_k}\nabla_S l(R^k, S^k)\right)\right\|_F^2 + \frac{\lambda_2}{\eta_k}\left\|Q^T\right\|_{1,2}$$

where $\nabla_R l(R^k, S^k)$ and $\nabla_S l(R^k, S^k)$ are the partial derivatives of $l(R,S)$ with respect to S and R at (R^k, S^k). The above proximal operator problems admit closed form solutions with time complexity of $O(dm)$ [19]:

$$\left(\mathbf{p}^{(k)}\right)^i = \max\left(0, 1 - \frac{\lambda_1}{\eta_k \|(\mathbf{u}^{(k)})^i\|}\right)\left(\mathbf{u}^{(k)}\right)^i, \ \forall i \in \mathbb{N}_d,$$
$$\mathbf{q}_j^{(k)} = \max\left(0, 1 - \frac{\lambda_2}{\eta_k \left\|\mathbf{v}_j^{(k)}\right\|}\right)\mathbf{v}_j^{(k)}, \ \forall j \in \mathbb{N}_m,$$

where $U^k = R^k - \frac{1}{\eta_k}\nabla_R l(R^k, S^k), V^k = S^k - \frac{1}{\eta_k}\nabla_S l(R^k, S^k)$; $\left(\mathbf{u}^{(k)}\right)^i$ and $\mathbf{v}_j^{(k)}$ denote the i-th row of U^k and the j-th column of V^k, respectively.

An appropriate choice for η_0 is the Lipschitz constant L of the gradient of $l(P,Q)$. However, the Lipschitz constant L is unknown and calculating it is computationally expensive. Next, we show how to estimate its lower and upper bounds. Denote by $D \in \mathbb{R}^{dm \times (\sum_{i=1}^m n_i)}$ a block diagonal matrix with $\sqrt{\frac{2}{mn_i}}X_i$ ($i \in \mathbb{N}_m$) as the i-th block. Then the Lipschitz constant L is just the squared maximum singular value of D. According to matrix norm properties [13], we can bound L as follows:

$$\min\left(\frac{\|D\|_{\infty,1}^2}{\sum_{i=1}^m n_i}, \frac{\left\|D^T\right\|_{\infty,1}^2}{dm}\right) \leq L \leq \|D\|_{\infty,1}\left\|D^T\right\|_{\infty,1}. \tag{8}$$

We note that D is a block diagonal matrix and it is sparse when m (the number of tasks) is large, which makes the bounds of L very tight. If we set η_0 as the upper bound of L, then we do not need line search, because when $\eta_k \geq L$, Eq. (6) is always satisfied [6]. Otherwise, line search is necessary. Although setting η_0 as the upper bound of L can eliminate line search, it may increase the outer iterative steps. On the contrary, it leads to a smaller outer iterative steps by setting η_0 as the lower bound of L. In our experiments, we use the lower bound of L to initialize η.

4. THEORETICAL ANALYSIS

4.1 Basic Assumption

We assume that the responses are given by a linear model plus Gaussian noise[1], i.e.,

$$y_{ji} = f_i^\star\left(\mathbf{x}_j^{(i)}\right) + \delta_{ji} = \left(\mathbf{x}_j^{(i)}\right)^T \mathbf{w}_i^\star + \delta_{ji}, i \in \mathbb{N}_m, j \in \mathbb{N}_n, \tag{9}$$

where $W^\star$ is the true weight matrix decomposed as the sum of two underlying true components $P^\star$ and $Q^\star$:

$$W^\star = [\mathbf{w}_1^\star, \cdots, \mathbf{w}_m^\star] = P^\star + Q^\star \in \mathbb{R}^{d \times m}; \tag{10}$$

[1]For notation simplicity, we assume that the number of training samples of all tasks are the same. However, the following theoretical analysis can be easily extended to the case with different training sample sizes for different tasks.

$$X_i = \left[\mathbf{x}_1^{(i)}, \cdots, \mathbf{x}_n^{(i)}\right]^T \in \mathbb{R}^{d \times n}, \mathbf{y}_i = [y_{1i}, \cdots, y_{ni}]^T \in \mathbb{R}^n \tag{11}$$

are respectively the training data and responses of the i-th task;

$$\boldsymbol{\delta}_i = [\delta_{1i}, \cdots, \delta_{ni}]^T \in \mathbb{R}^n, \delta_{ji} \sim N(0, \sigma^2), i \in \mathbb{N}_m, j \in \mathbb{N}_n \tag{12}$$

$$\mathbf{f}_i^\star = X_i^T \mathbf{w}_i^\star = \left[f_i^\star\left(\mathbf{x}_1^{(i)}\right), \cdots, f_i^\star\left(\mathbf{x}_n^{(i)}\right)\right]^T \in \mathbb{R}^n \tag{13}$$

are the i.i.d. normal noise and the true evaluation, respectively. Thus, we have

$$\mathbf{y}_i = \mathbf{f}_i^\star + \boldsymbol{\delta}_i, \; i \in \mathbb{N}_m. \tag{14}$$

We also define

$$\mathcal{J}(P) = \{i \mid \mathbf{p}^i \neq \mathbf{0}\}, \; \mathcal{J}_\perp(P) = \{i \mid \mathbf{p}^i = \mathbf{0}\} \tag{15}$$

as the index sets for the nonzero and zero rows of P.

4.2 Theoretical Bounds

The following theorem provides a key property of the optimal solution of Eq. (2), which is critical for our subsequent theoretical analysis:

THEOREM 2. *Let $(\hat{P}, \hat{Q})$ be an optimal solution of Eq. (2) for $m \geq 2$ and $n, d \geq 1$. Let X_i and $\mathbf{y}_i$ be defined in Eq. (11); let $\boldsymbol{\delta}_i$ and $\mathbf{f}_i^\star$ be defined in Eq. (12) and Eq. (13), respectively. We assume that the data is normalized as in Eq. (1). Choose the regularization parameters λ_1 and λ_2 as*

$$\lambda_1, \lambda_2 \geq \alpha, \; \alpha = \frac{2\sigma}{mn}\sqrt{dm + t}, \tag{16}$$

where t is a positive scalar. Then with probability of at least $1 - \exp\left(-\frac{1}{2}\left(t - dm \log\left(1 + \frac{t}{dm}\right)\right)\right)$, for any $P, Q \in \mathbb{R}^{d \times m}$, we have

$$\sum_{i=1}^{m} \frac{1}{mn}\left\|X_i^T(\hat{\mathbf{p}}_i + \hat{\mathbf{q}}_i) - \mathbf{f}_i^\star\right\|^2 \leq \sum_{i=1}^{m} \frac{1}{mn}\left\|X_i^T(\mathbf{p}_i + \mathbf{q}_i) - \mathbf{f}_i^\star\right\|^2 + 2\lambda_1\left\|(\hat{P} - P)^{\mathcal{J}(P)}\right\|_{1,2} + 2\lambda_2\left\|(\hat{Q}^T - Q^T)^{\mathcal{J}(Q^T)}\right\|_{1,2}. \tag{17}$$

Based on Theorem 2, we present some performance bounds of our rMTFL model in Eq. (2). We first introduce some notations to unclutter the equations. Let $X \in \mathbb{R}^{dm \times mn}$ be a block diagonal matrix with $X_i \in \mathbb{R}^{d \times n}$ ($i \in \mathbb{N}_m$) as the i-th block. Define a vectorization operator 'vec' over an arbitrary matrix $A \in \mathbb{R}^{d \times m}$ such that $\text{vec}(A) = [\mathbf{a}_1^T, \cdots, \mathbf{a}_m^T]^T$. Then, Eq. (17) can be rewritten as

$$\frac{1}{mn}\left\|X^T\text{vec}(\hat{P} + \hat{Q}) - \text{vec}(F^\star)\right\|^2 \leq \frac{1}{mn}\left\|X^T\text{vec}(P + Q) - \text{vec}(F^\star)\right\|^2 + 2\lambda_1\left\|(\hat{P} - P)^{\mathcal{J}(P)}\right\|_{1,2} + 2\lambda_2\left\|(\hat{Q}^T - Q^T)^{\mathcal{J}(Q^T)}\right\|_{1,2}, \tag{18}$$

where $F^\star = [\mathbf{f}_1^\star, \cdots, \mathbf{f}_m^\star] \in \mathbb{R}^{n \times m}$. Next, we make the following assumption about the training data and the weight matrix, which generalizes the restricted eigenvalue assumption in [7].

ASSUMPTION 1. *For a matrix pair $\Gamma_P \in \mathbb{R}^{d \times m}$ and $\Gamma_Q \in \mathbb{R}^{d \times m}$, let r and c ($1 \leq r \leq d, 1 \leq c \leq m$) be the upper bounds of $|\mathcal{J}(P^\star)|$ and $|\mathcal{J}(Q^{\star T})|$, respectively, and let β_1 and β_2 be positive scalars. We assume that there exist positive scalars $\kappa_1(r)$ and $\kappa_2(c)$ such that*

$$\kappa_1(r) = \min_{\Gamma_P, \Gamma_Q \in \mathcal{R}(r,c)} \frac{\left\|X^T\text{vec}(\Gamma_P + \Gamma_Q)\right\|}{\sqrt{mn}\left\|(\Gamma_P)^{\mathcal{J}(P)}\right\|_F} \tag{19}$$

$$\kappa_2(c) = \min_{\Gamma_P, \Gamma_Q \in \mathcal{R}(r,c)} \frac{\left\|X^T\text{vec}(\Gamma_P + \Gamma_Q)\right\|}{\sqrt{mn}\left\|(\Gamma_Q^T)^{\mathcal{J}(Q^T)}\right\|_F}, \tag{20}$$

where the set $\mathcal{R}(r, c)$ is defined as

$$\mathcal{R}(r,c) = \Big\{\Gamma_P, \Gamma_Q \in \mathbb{R}^{d \times m} \mid \Gamma_P \neq 0, \Gamma_Q \neq 0, |\mathcal{J}(P)| \leq r, \left|\mathcal{J}(Q^T)\right| \leq c, \left\|(\Gamma_P)^{\mathcal{J}_\perp(P)}\right\|_{1,2} \leq \beta_1\left\|(\Gamma_P)^{\mathcal{J}(P)}\right\|_{1,2}, \left\|(\Gamma_Q^T)^{\mathcal{J}_\perp(Q^T)}\right\|_{1,2} \leq \beta_2\left\|\left(\Gamma_Q^T\right)^{\mathcal{J}(Q^T)}\right\|_{1,2}\Big\},$$

$\mathcal{J}(\cdot)$ is defined in Eq. (15) and $|\mathcal{J}|$ denotes the number of elements in the set $\mathcal{J}$.

Note that Assumption 1 is related to the restricted eigenvalue assumption which is a critical condition in [7]. Some previous studies on multi-task learning [22, 10] also make use of similar assumptions. Our main theoretical result is summarized in the following theorem for performance bounds.

THEOREM 3. *Let $(\hat{P}, \hat{Q})$ be an optimal solution of Eq. (2) for $m \geq 2$ and $n, d \geq 1$ and take the regularization parameters λ_1 and λ_2 as in Eq. (16). Then under Assumption 1, the following results hold with probability of at least $1 - \exp\left(-\frac{1}{2}\left(t - dm\log\left(1 + \frac{t}{dm}\right)\right)\right)$ ($t > 0$):*

$$\frac{1}{mn}\left\|X^T\text{vec}(\hat{P} + \hat{Q}) - \text{vec}(F^\star)\right\|^2 \leq \left(\frac{2\lambda_1\sqrt{r}}{\kappa_1(r)} + \frac{2\lambda_2\sqrt{c}}{\kappa_2(c)}\right)^2, \tag{21}$$

$$\left\|\hat{P} - P^\star\right\|_{1,2} \leq \frac{(\beta_1 + 1)\sqrt{r}}{\kappa_1(r)}\left(\frac{2\lambda_1\sqrt{r}}{\kappa_1(r)} + \frac{2\lambda_2\sqrt{c}}{\kappa_2(c)}\right), \tag{22}$$

$$\left\|\hat{Q}^T - Q^{\star T}\right\|_{1,2} \leq \frac{(\beta_2 + 1)\sqrt{c}}{\kappa_2(c)}\left(\frac{2\lambda_1\sqrt{r}}{\kappa_1(r)} + \frac{2\lambda_2\sqrt{c}}{\kappa_2(c)}\right). \tag{23}$$

If in addition, the following conditions hold:

$$\min_{j \in \mathcal{J}(P^\star)}\left\|(\mathbf{p}^\star)^j\right\| > \frac{2(\beta_1 + 1)\sqrt{r}}{\kappa_1(r)}\left(\frac{2\lambda_1\sqrt{r}}{\kappa_1(r)} + \frac{2\lambda_2\sqrt{c}}{\kappa_2(c)}\right), \tag{24}$$

$$\min_{j \in \mathcal{J}(Q^{\star T})}\|(\mathbf{q}^\star)_j\| > \frac{2(\beta_2 + 1)\sqrt{c}}{\kappa_2(c)}\left(\frac{2\lambda_1\sqrt{r}}{\kappa_1(r)} + \frac{2\lambda_2\sqrt{c}}{\kappa_2(c)}\right), \tag{25}$$

then with the same probability, the following two sets

$$\hat{\mathcal{J}}_1 = \left\{j \mid \left\|\hat{\mathbf{p}}^j\right\| > \frac{(\beta_1 + 1)\sqrt{r}}{\kappa_1(r)}\left(\frac{2\lambda_1\sqrt{r}}{\kappa_1(r)} + \frac{2\lambda_2\sqrt{c}}{\kappa_2(c)}\right)\right\}, \tag{26}$$

$$\hat{\mathcal{J}}_2 = \left\{j \mid \|\hat{\mathbf{q}}_j\| > \frac{(\beta_2 + 1)\sqrt{c}}{\kappa_2(c)}\left(\frac{2\lambda_1\sqrt{r}}{\kappa_1(r)} + \frac{2\lambda_2\sqrt{c}}{\kappa_2(c)}\right)\right\} \tag{27}$$

estimate the true sparsity pattern $\mathcal{J}(P^\star)$ and $\mathcal{J}(Q^{\star T})$, re-

spectively. That is,

$$\hat{\mathcal{J}}_1 = \mathcal{J}(P^\star), \tag{28}$$

$$\hat{\mathcal{J}}_2 = \mathcal{J}(Q^{\star T}). \tag{29}$$

Theorem 3 provides important theoretical guarantee for rMTFL. Specifically, these bounds not only measure how well our rMTFL model can approximate the true evaluation values defined in Eq. (9) [Eq. (21)], but also measure how well our rMTFL model can approximate the true weight matrices ($P^\star, Q^\star, W^\star = P^\star + Q^\star$) [Eq. (22) and Eq. (23)]. Moreover, under the assumption that the underlying true weights are above the noise level [Eq. (24) and Eq. (24)], we can also estimate the true sparsity patterns (i.e., $\mathcal{J}(P^\star), \mathcal{J}(Q^{\star T})$) with high probability [Eq. (26) and Eq. (27)].

5. RELATED WORK

Previous studies in [15, 9, 10] also decompose the weight matrix into two components; rMTFL differs from these work in several aspects:

(1) rMTFL employs different regularization terms from the algorithms in [15, 9, 10]. The regularization terms in rMTFL not only have intuitive explanations for feature selection and outlier tasks detection (see Figure 1 and detailed explanation in Section 2), but also have sound theoretical guarantee (see Section 4).

(2) rMTFL has the mechanism of detecting outlier tasks, unlike the algorithms in [15, 9]. Although the algorithm in [10] has the ability to detect the outlier, it focuses on capturing the low rank structure among tasks, while rMTFL has advantages on high dimensional multi-task feature learning problems. Specifically, in terms of the evaluation performance, the main difference between our Theorem 2 and Lemma 4.3 in [10] is that the bound of rMTFL is based on $\|(\hat{P} - P)^{\mathcal{J}(P)}\|_{1,2}$, while the bound of RMTL in [10] is based on $\|\mathcal{Q}(\hat{L}-L)\|_{\mathrm{tr}}$. In practical multi-task learning problems, the dimensionality is often high and the underlying selected features are few, that is, the number of elements in $\mathcal{J}(P)$ can be small, which indicates that $\|(\hat{P} - P)^{\mathcal{J}(P)}\|_{1,2}$ is small, leading to a tight bound in Theorem 2. However, in the scenario of a large number of tasks, the relevant tasks may share a low rank subspace, resulting in a small value of $\|\mathcal{Q}(\hat{L} - L)\|_{\mathrm{tr}}$. Therefore, rMTFL has an advantage of identifying a few shared features for high dimensional data, while RMTL in [10] focuses on discovering low rank subspace among a large number of tasks. Our experimental results in Section 6.4 demonstrate that rMTFL outperforms RMTL in the high dimensional scenario, and RMTL is preferred when the number of tasks is large but the dimensionality is low.

(3) Unlike the analysis in [10], we provide theoretical bounds to measure the error between the estimated weights of rMTFL and the underlying true weights. Moreover, we have theoretically shown under what conditions we can obtain the underlying true shared features and outlier tasks (sparsity patterns). In addition, both Theorem 2 and Theorem 3 work with probability of at least $1-\exp\left(-\frac{1}{2}\left(t - dm\log\left(1 + \frac{t}{dm}\right)\right)\right)$ which is higher than $1 - m\exp\left(-\frac{1}{2}\left(t - d\log\left(1 + \frac{t}{d}\right)\right)\right)$ presented in Lemma 4.3 and Theorem 4.1 of [10].

(4) Each step of the optimization method in [10] involves SVD operation with a time complexity of $O(\min(d^2m, m^2d))$, thus it does not scale to large-size problems (e.g., the number of tasks and the dimensionality are large). As we show in Section 3.1, the optimization method of rMTFL has a much lower time complexity of $O(dm)$ and hence can be applied to large-size problems.

6. EXPERIMENTS

6.1 Competing Algorithms and Data Sets

Competing Algorithms: We compare our rMTFL algorithm on multi-task regression problems with seven representative algorithms: ridge multi-task regression (ridge), ℓ_1-norm multi-task regression (lasso), trace-norm multi-task regression (trace), $\ell_{1,2}$-norm multi-task regression (L1,2), dirty model multi-task regression (DirtyMTL) [15], sparse structures and low rank multi-task regression (SLR) [9] and robust multi-task regression (RMTL) [10]. All eight algorithms employ a quadratic loss function. Matlab codes of the rMTFL algorithm are available online [43].

Synthetic data: The synthetic data is generated as follows: we set the number of tasks $m = 30$ and each task has $n_i = 200$ samples in $d = 200$ dimension; each entry of the data matrix $X_i \in \mathbb{R}^{d\times n_i} (i \in \mathbb{N}_m)$ is sampled from the distribution $N(0, 25)$ and it is normalized such that Eq. (1) is satisfied; each entry of the ground truth weight matrices $P \in \mathbb{R}^{d\times m}$ and $Q \in \mathbb{R}^{d\times m}$ is generated from the distribution $N(0, 64)$; we set the first 160 rows of P and the first 20 columns of Q as zero vectors; the elements of the noise vector $\boldsymbol{\delta}_i \in \mathbb{R}^{n_i} (i \in \mathbb{N}_m)$ are sampled from the distribution $N(0, 1)$; the response $\mathbf{y}_i \in \mathbb{R}^{n_i} (i \in \mathbb{N}_m)$ is computed via $\mathbf{y}_i = X_i^T(P + Q) + \boldsymbol{\delta}_i$. Under this setting, we have constructed 20 related tasks and 10 outlier tasks.

Real-world Data: We adopt two data sets for our multitask regression evaluation: School data[2] and MRI data.

The School data set is from the Inner London Education Authority (ILEA), consisting of examination records of 15362 students (samples) from 139 secondary schools in years 1985, 1986 and 1987. Each sample is represented by 27 binary attributes which include year, gender, examination score, etc., plus 1 bias attribute (In our experiments, the bias attribute is not used). The response (target) is the examination score. So we have 139 tasks with each task corresponding to one school.

The MRI data set is from the ANDI database. It contains MRI data of 675 patients preprocessed using FreeSurfer[3]. The MRI data include 306 features which can be categorized into 5 types: cortical thickness average, cortical thickness standard deviation, volume of cortical parcellation, volume of white matter parcellation, and surface area. The response (target) is the Mini Mental State Examination (MMSE) score coming from 6 different time points: M06, M12, M18, M24, M36, and M48. We remove the samples which fail the MRI quality controls and with missing entries. After the preprocessing above, we have 6 tasks with each task corresponding to a time point and the sample sizes corresponding to 6 tasks are 648, 642, 293, 569, 389 and 87, respectively.

6.2 Experimental Setting

In our experiments, we terminate all the algorithms when the relative change of the two consecutive objective func-

[2] `http://www.cs.ucl.ac.uk/staff/a.argyriou/code/`
[3] `www.loni.ucla.edu/ADNI/`

Table 1: **Comparison of eight multi-task regression algorithms on the MRI data set in terms of averaged nMSE and aMSE.**

measure	traning ratio	ridge	lasso	trace	L1,2	DirtyMTL	SLR	RMTL	rMTFL
nMSE	0.15	0.9494	0.6469	0.6889	0.6445	0.6355	0.6905	0.6930	**0.5743**
	0.20	0.9355	0.6242	0.6629	0.6555	0.6231	0.6648	0.6557	**0.5700**
	0.25	0.9151	0.6015	0.6230	0.6446	0.6082	0.6244	0.6239	**0.5498**
aMSE	0.15	0.0270	0.0188	0.0195	0.0184	0.0177	0.0196	0.0196	**0.0168**
	0.20	0.0262	0.0177	0.0184	0.0184	0.0172	0.0185	0.0182	**0.0163**
	0.25	0.0255	0.0170	0.0171	0.0181	0.0167	0.0171	0.0171	**0.0157**

Table 2: **Comparison of eight multi-task regression algorithms on the School data set in terms of averaged nMSE and aMSE.**

measure	traning ratio	ridge	lasso	trace	L1,2	DirtyMTL	SLR	RMTL	rMTFL
nMSE	0.16	1.2325	1.0457	0.7829	0.9236	0.8989	0.7812	**0.7804**	0.8628
	0.24	1.0734	0.9441	**0.7606**	0.9017	0.8413	0.7608	0.7613	0.8173
	0.32	0.9996	0.8875	0.7506	0.8972	0.8019	0.7507	**0.7504**	0.7874
aMSE	0.16	0.3154	0.2735	0.2048	0.2395	0.2358	0.2044	**0.2041**	0.2252
	0.24	0.2773	0.2469	**0.1993**	0.2341	0.2203	0.1993	0.1995	0.2135
	0.32	0.2580	0.2312	0.1958	0.2316	0.2088	0.1958	**0.1958**	0.2049

tion values is less than 10^{-5}. We randomly split the samples (both synthetic and real-world data sets) from each task into training and test samples with different training ratios. We evaluate eight multi-task regression algorithms on the test data set, using normalized mean squared error (nMSE) and averaged means squared error (aMSE) as the regression performance measures [39, 10, 42]. For each training ratio, both nMSE and aMSE are averaged over 10 random splittings of training and test sets. All parameters of the eight algorithms are tuned via 3-fold cross validation.

6.3 Synthetic Data Experiments

We set the training ratio of synthetic data generated in Section 6.1 as 20% and 30%, respectively. Experimental results (averaged nMSE and aMSE) are shown in Figure 2. We observe that rMTFL outperforms all the other competing algorithms, which demonstrates the effectiveness of rMTFL for high dimensional problems with outlier tasks.

6.3.1 Illustration of Outlier Tasks Detection

Next, we further demonstrate the outlier tasks detection capability of rMTFL. We firstly generate another synthetic data set following the same procedure in Section 6.1, except that each task has $n_i = 20$ samples. Then, we set $\lambda_1 = 2\sqrt{dm+t}/\sum_{i=1}^{m} n_i, \lambda_2 = 6\sqrt{dm+t}/\sum_{i=1}^{m} n_i, t = 10^{-10}$ and run rMTFL on this synthetic data until the relative change of the two consecutive objective function values is less than 10^{-5}. Figure 3 shows the results of P and Q obtained by rMTFL. Specifically, there are 164 zero rows in P and 21 zero columns in Q. These results demonstrate the capability of rMTFL in simultaneously capturing the shared features among tasks (the nonzero rows of P) and discovering outlier tasks (the nonzero columns of Q).

6.3.2 Scalability Studies on rMTFL

We conduct scalability studies on two algorithms which are capable of identifying outlier tasks: rMTFL and RMTL [10], when the dimension and the number of tasks increase. We firstly fix $m = 20$ and let the dimension d increase as $\{50^i\}, i = 0, \cdots, 5$. Then we run rMTFL and RMTL on the synthetic data generated following the same procedure in Section 6.1. The computational time (CPU time) vs. dimension plot is shown in the left subfigure of Figure 4.

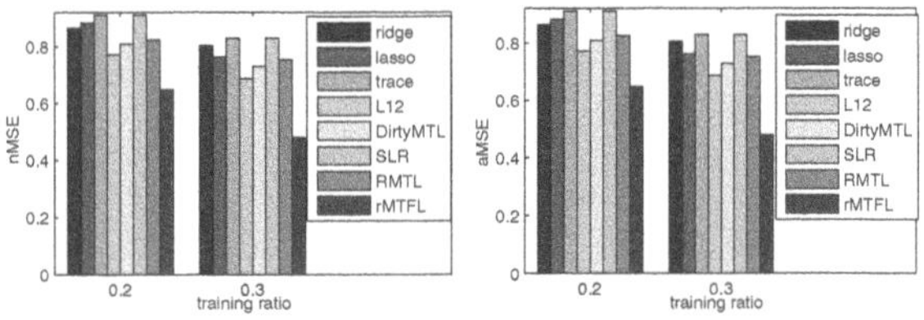

Figure 2: Averaged test error (nMSE and aMSE) vs. training ratio for synthetic data.

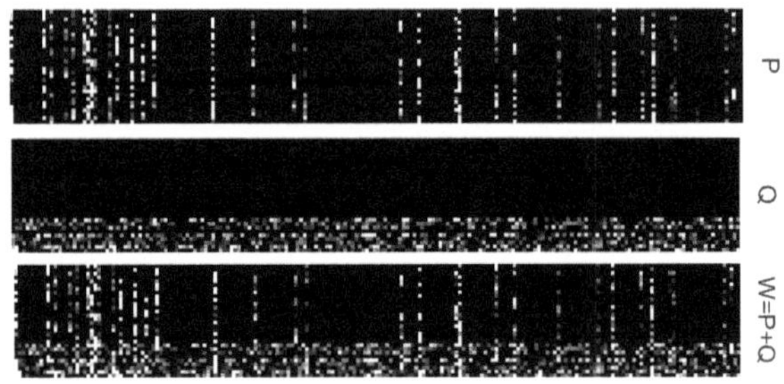

Figure 3: Figures of P, Q and $W = P + Q$ generated from rMTFL on the synthetic data. Black points correspond to zero entries. Note that the figures are clockwise rotated 90 degrees.

Similarly, we fix $d = 100$ and let the number of tasks m increase as $\{10^i\}, i = 0, \cdots, 5$. Then we run rMTFL and RMTL and show the computational time (CPU time) vs. the number of tasks plot as in the right subfigure of Figure 4. We observe that, the CPU time of both rMTFL and RMTL increases when the dimension d (or the number of tasks m) increases. However, the CPU time of RMTL increases significantly faster than rMTFL. Because the SVD computation with a time complexity of $O(\min(d^2m, m^2d))$ involved at each step of RMTL is computationally much more expensive than the computation of the $\ell_{1,2}$-norm proximal operator with a time complexity of $O(dm)$ involved at each step of rMTFL. This demonstrates the superior scalability of rMTFL over RMTL.

6.4 Real-world Data Experiments

For the School data set, we respectively set the training ratio as 16%, 24%, 32%, and for the MRI data set, we respectively set the training ratio as 15%, 20%, 25%. Table 1 and

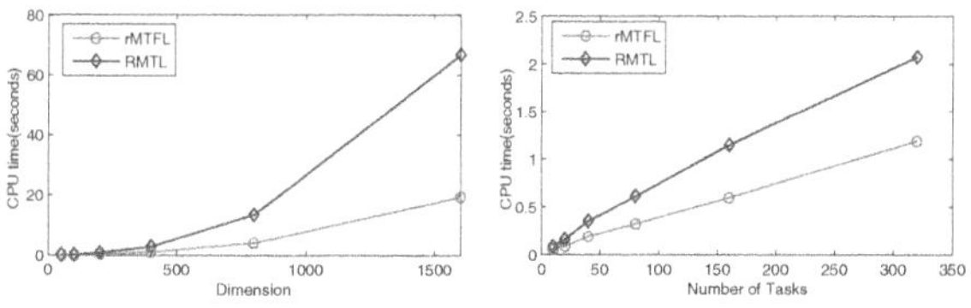

Figure 4: CPU time vs. dimension (left) and number of tasks (right) plots for rMTFL and RMTL. The CPU time is averaged over 10 independent runs.

Table 2 show the experimental results in terms of averaged nMSE and aMSE.

From these results, we have the following observations: (1) rMTFL outperforms all the other algorithms on the MRI data set. This may be due to the fact that for the MRI data set, the dimension ($d = 306$) is high especially when compared with the number of tasks ($m = 6$). (2) For the School data set, the multi-task learning algorithms based on trace norm (low rank) regularization (trace, SLR, RMTL) outperform the multi-task learning algorithms based on $\ell_{1,q}$-norm (feature selection) regularization (lasso, L1,2, DirtyMTL, rMTFL). This may be due to the fact that the number of tasks ($m = 139$) of the School data set is larger compared with dimension ($d = 27$). In this case, restricting all tasks to share a low rank subspace is more reasonable than restricting all tasks to share a few common features. (3) On both data sets, the performance of rMTFL is the best among the feature selection based multi-task learning algorithms (lasso, L1,2, DirtyMTL, rMTFL). This may be due to rMTFL's capability of simultaneously discovering the shared features and identifying outlier tasks.

6.4.1 *Outlier Tasks Detection*

The proposed rMTFL algorithm is capable of capturing the shared features among tasks and detecting outlier tasks. We next evaluate the outlier tasks detection performance on the MRI data set. Firstly, we run rMTFL on the whole MRI data set and observe that the fourth task is identified as an outlier task. Then, we remove the fourth task, obtaining a new multi-task regression problem with the remaining 5 tasks. Finally, we run $\ell_{1,2}$-norm multi-task regression on this 'clean' multi-task regression problem. We call this two-stage procedure as 2S-rMTFL. The test errors (nMSE and aMSE) on the MRI data set are shown in Figure 5. We can clearly see that after removing the outlier tasks, 2S-rMTFL outperforms L1,2 and rMTFL, which demonstrates the effectiveness of rMTFL in detecting outlier tasks.

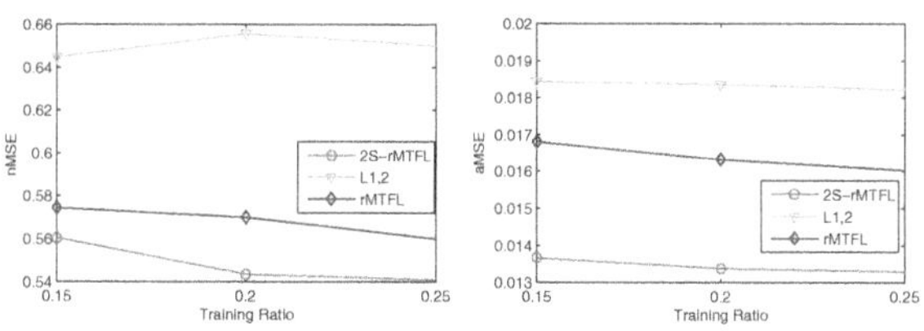

Figure 5: Test errors (nMSE and aMSE) on the MRI data set. See the texts for more details.

7. CONCLUSIONS

In this paper, we propose a Robust Multi-Task Feature Learning algorithm (rMTFL) to simultaneously capture the shared features among multiple related tasks and detect outlier tasks. We analyze the theoretical properties of rMTFL. Our analysis shows how well rMTFL can approximate the true evaluation, and measure how well rMTFL can approximate the underlying true weights. Moreover, we show that rMTFL can obtain the true sparsity patterns if the underlying true weights are above the noise level. In addition, the optimization problem involved in rMTFL can be solved efficiently, and rMTFL scales to large-size problems. In the future work, we will extend our rMTFL algorithm to multi-task learning problems with general loss functions and apply rMTFL to other real-world applications.

Acknowledgements

This work is supported in part by NSFC (Grant No. 60835002, 61075004 and 91120301), NIH (R01 LM010730) and NSF (IIS-0953662, CCF-1025177).

8. REFERENCES

[1] R. Ando and T. Zhang. A framework for learning predictive structures from multiple tasks and unlabeled data. *JMLR*, 6:1817–1853, 2005.

[2] A. Argyriou, T. Evgeniou, and M. Pontil. Convex multi-task feature learning. *Machine Learning*, 73(3):243–272, 2008.

[3] F. Bach, R. Jenatton, J. Mairal, and G. Obozinski. Optimization with sparsity-inducing penalties. *Arxiv preprint arXiv:1108.0775*, 2011.

[4] B. Bakker and T. Heskes. Task clustering and gating for bayesian multitask learning. *JMLR*, 4:83–99, 2003.

[5] J. Baxter. A model of inductive bias learning. *Journal of Artificial Intelligence Research*, 12:149–198, 2000.

[6] A. Beck and M. Teboulle. A fast iterative shrinkage-thresholding algorithm for linear inverse problems. *SIAM Journal on Imaging Sciences*, 2(1):183–202, 2009.

[7] P. Bickel, Y. Ritov, and A. Tsybakov. Simultaneous analysis of lasso and dantzig selector. *The Annals of Statistics*, 37(4):1705–1732, 2009.

[8] R. Caruana. Multitask learning. *Machine Learning*, 28(1):41–75, 1997.

[9] J. Chen, J. Liu, and J. Ye. Learning incoherent sparse and low-rank patterns from multiple tasks. In *SIGKDD*, pages 1179–1188, 2010.

[10] J. Chen, J. Zhou, and J. Ye. Integrating low-rank and group-sparse structures for robust multi-task learning. In *SIGKDD*, pages 42–50, 2011.

[11] T. Evgeniou and M. Pontil. Regularized multi–task learning. In *SIGKDD*, pages 109–117, 2004.

[12] P. Gong, K. Gai, and C. Zhang. Efficient euclidean projections via piecewise root finding and its application in gradient projection. *Neurocomputing*, pages 2754–2766, 2011.

[13] R. Horn and C. Johnson. *Matrix analysis*. Cambridge University Press, 1990.

[14] L. Jacob, F. Bach, and J. Vert. Clustered multi-task learning: A convex formulation. *NIPS*, 2008.

[15] A. Jalali, P. Ravikumar, S. Sanghavi, and C. Ruan. A dirty model for multi-task learning. *NIPS*, 2010.

[16] Z. Kang, K. Grauman, and F. Sha. Learning with whom to share in multi-task feature learning. In *ICML*, 2011.

[17] S. Kim and E. Xing. Tree-guided group lasso for multi-task regression with structured sparsity. In *ICML*, 2009.

[18] N. Lawrence and J. Platt. Learning to learn with the informative vector machine. In *ICML*, 2004.

[19] J. Liu, S. Ji, and J. Ye. Multi-task feature learning via efficient $\ell_{2,1}$-norm minimization. In *UAI*, pages 339–348, 2009.

[20] J. Liu, S. Ji, and J. Ye. Slep: Sparse learning with efficient projections. *Arizona State University*, 2009.

[21] J. Liu, L. Yuan, and J. Ye. An efficient algorithm for a class of fused lasso problems. In *SIGKDD*, pages 323–332, 2010.

[22] K. Lounici, M. Pontil, A. Tsybakov, and S. Van De Geer. Taking advantage of sparsity in multi-task learning. In *COLT*, 2009.

[23] S. Negahban and M. Wainwright. Joint support recovery under high-dimensional scaling: Benefits and perils of $\ell_{1,\infty}$-regularization. *NIPS*, 21, 2008.

[24] S. Negahban and M. Wainwright. Estimation of (near) low-rank matrices with noise and high-dimensional scaling. *The Annals of Statistics*, 39(2):1069–1097, 2011.

[25] Y. Nesterov. *Introductory lectures on convex optimization: A basic course.* Springer Netherlands, 2004.

[26] Y. Nesterov. Gradient methods for minimizing composite objective function. *Center for Operations Research and Econometrics (CORE), Catholic University of Louvain, Tech. Rep*, 76, 2007.

[27] G. Obozinski, B. Taskar, and M. Jordan. Multi-task feature selection. *Statistics Department, UC Berkeley, Tech. Rep*, 2006.

[28] S. Parameswaran and K. Weinberger. Large margin multi-task metric learning. *NIPS*, 23:1867–1875, 2010.

[29] T. Pong, P. Tseng, S. Ji, and J. Ye. Trace norm regularization: Reformulations, algorithms, and multi-task learning. *SIAM Journal on Optimization*, 20(6):3465–3489, 2010.

[30] N. Quadrianto, A. Smola, T. Caetano, S. Vishwanathan, and J. Petterson. Multitask learning without label correspondences. *NIPS*, 2010.

[31] A. Schwaighofer, V. Tresp, and K. Yu. Learning gaussian process kernels via hierarchical bayes. *NIPS*, 17:1209–1216, 2005.

[32] S. Thrun and J. O'Sullivan. Discovering structure in multiple learning tasks: The tc algorithm. In *ICML*, pages 489–497, 1996.

[33] D. Wallace. Bounds on normal approximations to student's and the chi-square distributions. *The Annals of Mathematical Statistics*, pages 1121–1130, 1959.

[34] Y. Xue, X. Liao, L. Carin, and B. Krishnapuram. Multi-task learning for classification with dirichlet process priors. *JMLR*, 8:35–63, 2007.

[35] X. Yang, S. Kim, and E. Xing. Heterogeneous multitask learning with joint sparsity constraints. *NIPS*, 23, 2009.

[36] K. Yu, V. Tresp, and A. Schwaighofer. Learning gaussian processes from multiple tasks. In *ICML*, pages 1012–1019, 2005.

[37] L. Yuan, J. Liu, and J. Ye. Efficient methods for overlapping group lasso. *NIPS*, 2011.

[38] J. Zhang, Z. Ghahramani, and Y. Yang. Learning multiple related tasks using latent independent component analysis. *NIPS*, 18:1585–1592, 2006.

[39] Y. Zhang and D. Yeung. Multi-task learning using generalized t process. In *AISTATS*, 2010.

[40] Y. Zhang and D. Yeung. Transfer metric learning by learning task relationships. In *SIGKDD*, pages 1199–1208, 2010.

[41] Y. Zhang, D. Yeung, and Q. Xu. Probabilistic multi-task feature selection. *NIPS*, 2010.

[42] J. Zhou, J. Chen, and J. Ye. Clustered multi-task learning via alternating structure optimization. *NIPS*, 2011.

[43] J. Zhou, J. Chen, and J. Ye. *MALSAR: Multi-tAsk Learning via StructurAl Regularization.* Arizona State University, 2012.

[44] J. Zhou, L. Yuan, J. Liu, and J. Ye. A multi-task learning formulation for predicting disease progression. In *SIGKDD*, pages 814–822, 2011.

APPENDIX

To prove the theorems presented in Section 4.2, we first provide some basic lemmas and then give the detailed proof.

LEMMA 1. *For any matrix pair $P, \hat{P} \in \mathbb{R}^{d \times m}$, we have the following inequality:*

$$\left\|\hat{P} - P\right\|_{1,2} + \|P\|_{1,2} - \left\|\hat{P}\right\|_{1,2} \leq 2\left\|(\hat{P} - P)^{\mathcal{J}(P)}\right\|_{1,2}, \tag{30}$$

PROOF. According to Eq. (15), we have

$$P^{\mathcal{J}_\perp(P)} = 0, \quad \left\|(\hat{P} - P)^{\mathcal{J}_\perp(P)}\right\|_{1,2} = \left\|\hat{P}^{\mathcal{J}_\perp(P)}\right\|_{1,2}.$$

It follows that

$$\begin{aligned} &\left\|(\hat{P} - P)^{\mathcal{J}_\perp(P)}\right\|_{1,2} + \|P\|_{1,2} - \left\|\hat{P}\right\|_{1,2} \\ &= \left\|\hat{P}^{\mathcal{J}_\perp(P)}\right\|_{1,2} + \|P\|_{1,2} - \left\|\hat{P}\right\|_{1,2} \\ &\leq \left\|(\hat{P} - P)^{\mathcal{J}(P)}\right\|_{1,2} \end{aligned} \tag{31}$$

We note that $\left\|\hat{P} - P\right\|_{1,2} = \left\|(\hat{P} - P)^{\mathcal{J}(P)}\right\|_{1,2} + \left\|(\hat{P} - P)^{\mathcal{J}_\perp(P)}\right\|_{1,2}$ Substituting Eq. (31) into Eq. (30), we verify Lemma 1. □

LEMMA 2. *Let δ_i be I.I.D. random variables with $\delta_i \sim N(0, \sigma^2), i \in \mathbb{N}_n$ and $\sum_{i=1}^n \alpha_i^2 = 1$. Then we have*

$$v = \frac{1}{\sigma} \sum_{i=1}^{n} \alpha_i \delta_i$$

is a standard normal random variable, i.e., $v \sim N(0, 1)$.

PROOF. Since δ_i are I.I.D. random variables with $\delta_i \sim N(0, \sigma^2), i \in \mathbb{N}_n$, v must be a normal random variable. Next, we need to show that the mean ($\mathbb{E}$) and variance ($\mathbb{V}$) of v are respectively 0 and 1, as given below:

$$\mathbb{E}(v) = \mathbb{E}\left(\frac{1}{\sigma} \sum_{i=1}^{n} \alpha_i \delta_i\right) = \frac{1}{\sigma} \sum_{i=1}^{n} \alpha_i \mathbb{E}(\delta_i) = 0,$$

$$\mathbb{V}(v) = \mathbb{E}\left(v^2\right) = \frac{1}{\sigma^2} \sum_{i=1}^{n} \alpha_i^2 \mathbb{E}(\delta_i^2) = 1.$$

□

LEMMA 3. *Let $\chi^2(d)$ be a chi-squared random variable with d degrees of freedom. Then, the following holds:*

$$\Pr\left(\chi^2(d) \geq d + t\right) \leq \exp\left(-\frac{1}{2}\left(t - d \log\left(1 + \frac{t}{d}\right)\right)\right), t > 0.$$

PROOF. By the Wallace inequality [33], we obtain

$$\Pr\left(\chi^2(d) \geq d + t\right) \leq \Pr\left(N > z(t)\right), t > 0, \tag{32}$$

where N is a standard normal random variable and $z(t) = \sqrt{t - d \log(1 + \frac{t}{d})}$. Lemma 3 follows directly from Eq. (32) and inequality $\Pr\left(N \geq z(t)\right) \leq \exp\left(-\frac{z(t)^2}{2}\right)$. □

Proof of Theorem 2:

PROOF. Since $(\hat{P}, \hat{Q})$ is an optimal solution of Eq. (2), the following holds for any P and Q:

$$\sum_{i=1}^{m} \frac{1}{mn} \left\|X_i^T(\hat{\mathbf{p}}_i + \hat{\mathbf{q}}_i) - \mathbf{y}_i\right\|^2 \leq \sum_{i=1}^{m} \frac{1}{mn} \left\|X_i^T(\mathbf{p}_i + \mathbf{q}_i) - \mathbf{y}_i\right\|^2$$
$$+ \lambda_1 \left(\|P\|_{1,2} - \left\|\hat{P}\right\|_{1,2}\right) + \lambda_2 \left(\left\|Q^T\right\|_{1,2} - \left\|\hat{Q}^T\right\|_{1,2}\right).$$

Substituting Eq. (14) into the above inequality, we have

$$\sum_{i=1}^{m} \frac{1}{mn} \left\| X_i^T(\hat{\mathbf{p}}_i + \hat{\mathbf{q}}_i) - \mathbf{f}_i^\star \right\|^2 \leq \sum_{i=1}^{m} \frac{1}{mn} \left\| X_i^T(\mathbf{p}_i + \mathbf{q}_i) - \mathbf{f}_i^\star \right\|^2$$
$$+ \lambda_1 \left(\|P\|_{1,2} - \left\|\hat{P}\right\|_{1,2} \right) + \lambda_2 \left(\left\|Q^T\right\|_{1,2} - \left\|\hat{Q}^T\right\|_{1,2} \right)$$
$$+ \frac{2}{mn} \left\langle Z, \hat{P} - P \right\rangle + \frac{2}{mn} \left\langle Z, \hat{Q} - Q \right\rangle, \tag{33}$$

where $Z = [X_1\boldsymbol{\delta}_1, \cdots, X_m\boldsymbol{\delta}_m] \in \mathbb{R}^{d\times m}$ with its (j,i)-th entry given by

$$z_{ji} = \mathbf{x}_j^{(i)}\boldsymbol{\delta}_i = \sum_{k=1}^{n} x_{jk}^{(i)}\delta_{ki}, i \in \mathbb{N}_m, j \in \mathbb{N}_d, \tag{34}$$

and $x_{jk}^{(i)}$ denotes the (j,k)-th entry of data matrix X_i for the i-th task. It follows from Eq. (1) that

$$v_{ji} = \frac{1}{\sigma} z_{ji} = \frac{1}{\sigma} \sum_{k=1}^{n} x_{jk}^{(i)}\delta_{ki} \ (i \in \mathbb{N}_m, j \in \mathbb{N}_d) \tag{35}$$

are i.i.d. standard normal random variables (see Lemma 2), i.e., $v_{ji} \sim N(0,1)$. Thus,

$$u = \sum_{j=1}^{d}\sum_{i=1}^{m} v_{ji}^2 = \frac{1}{\sigma^2}\|Z\|_F^2$$

is a chi-squared random variable with dm degrees of freedom, and it follows from Lemma 3:

$$\Pr\left(\frac{2}{mn}\|Z\|_F \geq \alpha\right) = \Pr\left(u \geq \frac{\alpha^2 n^2 m^2}{4}\right)$$
$$\leq \exp\left(-\frac{1}{2}\left(t - dm\log\left(1 + \frac{t}{dm}\right)\right)\right) \ (t > 0),$$

which is equivalent to the following:

$$\Pr\left(\frac{2}{mn}\|Z\|_F \leq \alpha\right) \geq 1 - \exp\left(-\frac{1}{2}\left(t - dm\log\left(1 + \frac{t}{dm}\right)\right)\right). \tag{36}$$

Under the event in Eq. (36), we bound $\frac{2}{mn}\langle Z, \hat{P} - P\rangle$ as

$$\frac{2}{mn}\left\langle Z, \hat{P} - P\right\rangle \leq \frac{2}{mn}\|Z\|_F \left\|\hat{P} - P\right\|_F$$
$$\leq \alpha \left\|\hat{P} - P\right\|_F \leq \alpha \left\|\hat{P} - P\right\|_{1,2}. \tag{37}$$

Similarly, under the event in Eq. (36), we have

$$\frac{2}{mn}\left\langle Z, \hat{Q} - Q\right\rangle \leq \frac{2}{mn}\|Z\|_F \left\|\hat{Q} - Q\right\|_F$$
$$\leq \alpha \left\|\hat{Q} - Q\right\|_F \leq \alpha \left\|\hat{Q}^T - Q^T\right\|_{1,2}. \tag{38}$$

Combine Eq. (33), Eq. (37), Eq. (38) and Lemma 1, we verify Theorem 2. □

Proof of Theorem 3:

PROOF. Let $\Gamma_P = \hat{P} - P$, $\Gamma_Q = \hat{Q} - Q$. Setting $P = P^\star$, $Q = Q^\star$, $P^\star$ and $Q^\star$ are the true weight matrices in Eq. (10), we have $X^T\text{vec}(P + Q) = X^T\text{vec}(P^\star + Q^\star) = \text{vec}(F^\star)$. Following Eq. (18), we obtain

$$\frac{1}{mn}\left\|X^T\text{vec}(\hat{P} + \hat{Q}) - \text{vec}(F^\star)\right\|^2 \leq 2\lambda_1 \left\|(\hat{P} - P^\star)^{\mathcal{J}(P^\star)}\right\|_{1,2}$$
$$+ 2\lambda_2 \left\|(\hat{Q}^T - Q^{\star T})^{\mathcal{J}(Q^{\star T})}\right\|_{1,2}. \tag{39}$$

Under Assumption 1, we have

$$\left\|(\hat{P} - P^\star)^{\mathcal{J}(P^\star)}\right\|_{1,2} \leq \sqrt{r}\left\|(\hat{P} - P^\star)^{\mathcal{J}(P^\star)}\right\|_F$$
$$\leq \frac{\sqrt{r}}{\kappa_1(r)\sqrt{mn}}\left\|X^T\text{vec}(\hat{P} + \hat{Q}) - \text{vec}(F^\star)\right\|, \tag{40}$$
$$\left\|(\hat{Q}^T - Q^{\star T})^{\mathcal{J}(Q^{\star T})}\right\|_{1,2} \leq \sqrt{c}\left\|(\hat{Q}^T - Q^{\star T})^{\mathcal{J}(Q^{\star T})}\right\|_F$$
$$\leq \frac{\sqrt{c}}{\kappa_2(c)\sqrt{mn}}\left\|X^T\text{vec}(\hat{P} + \hat{Q}) - \text{vec}(F^\star)\right\|. \tag{41}$$

Substituting Eq. (40) and Eq. (41) into Eq. (39), we obtain

$$\left\|X^T\text{vec}(\hat{P} + \hat{Q}) - \text{vec}(F^\star)\right\| \leq \sqrt{mn}\left(\frac{2\lambda_1\sqrt{r}}{\kappa_1(r)} + \frac{2\lambda_2\sqrt{c}}{\kappa_2(c)}\right),$$

which directly leads to Eq. (21).

Following Assumption 1, we have

$$\left\|(\Gamma_P)^{\mathcal{J}_\perp(P^\star)}\right\|_{1,2} \leq \beta_1 \left\|(\Gamma_P)^{\mathcal{J}(P^\star)}\right\|_{1,2},$$
$$\left\|(\Gamma_Q^T)^{\mathcal{J}_\perp(Q^{\star T})}\right\|_{1,2} \leq \beta_2 \left\|(\Gamma_Q^T)^{\mathcal{J}(Q^{\star T})}\right\|_{1,2},$$

which imply that

$$\left\|\hat{P} - P^\star\right\|_{1,2} \leq (\beta_1 + 1)\left\|(\hat{P} - P^\star)^{\mathcal{J}(P^\star)}\right\|_{1,2}, \tag{42}$$
$$\left\|\hat{Q}^T - Q^{\star T}\right\|_{1,2} \leq (\beta_2 + 1)\left\|(\hat{Q}^T - Q^{\star T})^{\mathcal{J}(Q^{\star T})}\right\|_{1,2}. \tag{43}$$

Substituting Eq. (42) and Eq. (43)) into Eq. (40) and Eq. (41), and considering Eq. (21), we can easily verify Eq. (22) and Eq. (23).

To prove Eq. (28), we need to show the following two:

$$(a)\ \forall j \in \hat{\mathcal{J}}_1 \Rightarrow j \in \mathcal{J}(P^\star), \tag{44}$$
$$(b)\ \forall j \in \mathcal{J}(P^\star) \Rightarrow j \in \hat{\mathcal{J}}_1. \tag{45}$$

We first prove (a) by contradiction. Assume there exists a j_1 such that $j_1 \in \hat{\mathcal{J}}_1, j_1 \notin \mathcal{J}(P^\star)$. Then according to the definitions of $\hat{\mathcal{J}}_1$ and $\mathcal{J}(P^\star)$, we have

$$\left\|\hat{\mathbf{p}}^{j_1} - (\mathbf{p}^\star)^{j_1}\right\| = \left\|\hat{\mathbf{p}}^{j_1}\right\| > \frac{(\beta_1 + 1)\sqrt{r}}{\kappa_1(r)}\left(\frac{2\lambda_1\sqrt{r}}{\kappa_1(r)} + \frac{2\lambda_2\sqrt{c}}{\kappa_2(c)}\right),$$

which contradicts with the following fact:

$$\left\|\hat{P} - P^\star\right\|_{\infty,2} \leq \left\|\hat{P} - P^\star\right\|_{1,2}$$
$$\leq \frac{(\beta_1 + 1)\sqrt{r}}{\kappa_1(r)}\left(\frac{2\lambda_1\sqrt{r}}{\kappa_1(r)} + \frac{2\lambda_2\sqrt{c}}{\kappa_2(c)}\right). \tag{46}$$

We thus verify (a). Similarly, if we assume there exists a j_2 such that $j_2 \in \mathcal{J}(P^\star), j_2 \notin \hat{\mathcal{J}}_1$, then using the condition in Eq. (24) and the definition of $\hat{\mathcal{J}}_1$ in Eq. (26), we have

$$\left\|\hat{\mathbf{p}}^{j_2} - (\mathbf{p}^\star)^{j_2}\right\| \geq \left\|(\mathbf{p}^\star)^{j_2}\right\| - \left\|\hat{\mathbf{p}}^{j_2}\right\|$$
$$> \frac{(\beta_1 + 1)\sqrt{r}}{\kappa_1(r)}\left(\frac{2\lambda_1\sqrt{r}}{\kappa_1(r)} + \frac{2\lambda_2\sqrt{c}}{\kappa_2(c)}\right),$$

which contradicts with Eq. (46), thus (b) holds. Combining (a) and (b), we verify Eq. (28). Similarly, we can prove Eq. (29). □

Unsupervised Feature Selection for Linked Social Media Data

Jiliang Tang
Computer Science and Engineering
Arizona State University
Tempe, AZ 85281
{Jiliang.Tang}@asu.edu

Huan Liu
Computer Science and Engineering
Arizona State University
Tempe, AZ 85281
{Huan.Liu}@asu.edu

ABSTRACT

The prevalent use of social media produces mountains of unlabeled, high-dimensional data. Feature selection has been shown effective in dealing with high-dimensional data for efficient data mining. Feature selection for unlabeled data remains a challenging task due to the absence of label information by which the feature relevance can be assessed. The unique characteristics of social media data further complicate the already challenging problem of unsupervised feature selection, (e.g., part of social media data is linked, which makes invalid the independent and identically distributed assumption), bringing about new challenges to traditional unsupervised feature selection algorithms. In this paper, we study the differences between social media data and traditional attribute-value data, investigate if the relations revealed in linked data can be used to help select relevant features, and propose a novel unsupervised feature selection framework, LUFS, for linked social media data. We perform experiments with real-world social media datasets to evaluate the effectiveness of the proposed framework and probe the working of its key components.

Categories and Subject Descriptors

I.5.2 [**Pattern Recognition**]: Design Methodology—*Feature evaluation and Selection*

General Terms

Algorithms, Theory

Keywords

Unsupervised Feature Selection, Linked Social Media Data, Pseudo-class Label

1. INTRODUCTION

The myriads of social media services such as Facebook and Twitter are available that allow people to communicate and express themselves conveniently and effortlessly. The pervasive use of social media produces massive data at an unprecedented speed. For example, 200 million tweets are posted per day[1]; 3,000 photos are uploaded per minute to Flickr[2]; and the number of Facebook users has increased from 100 million in 2008 to 800 million in 2011[3]. The massive and high-dimensional social media data poses new challenges to data mining tasks such as classification and clustering. One traditional and effective approach to handle high-dimensional data is *feature selection* [7, 18]. Feature selection aims to select relevant features from the high-dimensional data for a compact and accurate data representation. It can alleviate the curse of dimensionality, speed up the learning process, and improve the generalization capability of a learning model [16, 19].

According to whether the training data is labeled or unlabeled, feature selection algorithms can be roughly divided into *supervised* and *unsupervised* feature selection. It is time-consuming and costly to obtain labeled data. Given the scale of social media data, we propose to study unsupervised feature selection. Unsupervised feature selection is particularly difficult due to the absence of class labels for feature relevance assessment [3]. Social media data adds further challenges to feature selection. Most existing feature selection algorithms work with "flat" attribute-value data which is typically assumed to be independent and identically distributed (*i.i.d.*). However, the *i.i.d.* assumption does not hold for social media data since it is inherently linked. Figure 1 shows a simple example of linked data in social media and its two data representations. Figure 1(a) shows 8 linked instances (u_1 to u_8). These instances usually form groups and instances within groups have more connections than instances between groups [31]. For example, u_1 has more connections to $\{u_2, u_3, u_4\}$ than $\{u_5, u_6, u_7, u_8\}$. Figure 1(b) is a conventional representation of attribute-value data: rows are instances and columns are features. For linked data, except for the conventional representation, there is link information between instances as shown in Figure 1(c).

Linked data in social media presents both challenges and opportunities for unsupervised feature selection. In this work, we investigate: (1) *how to exploit and model the relations among data instances*, and (2) *how to take advantage of these relations for feature selection using unlabeled data.* One key difference between supervised and unsupervised fea-

KDD'12, August 12–16, 2012, Beijing, China.

[1]http://techcrunch.com/2011/06/30/twitter-3200-million-tweets/
[2]http://www.flickr.com/
[3]http://en.wikipedia.org/wiki/Facebook

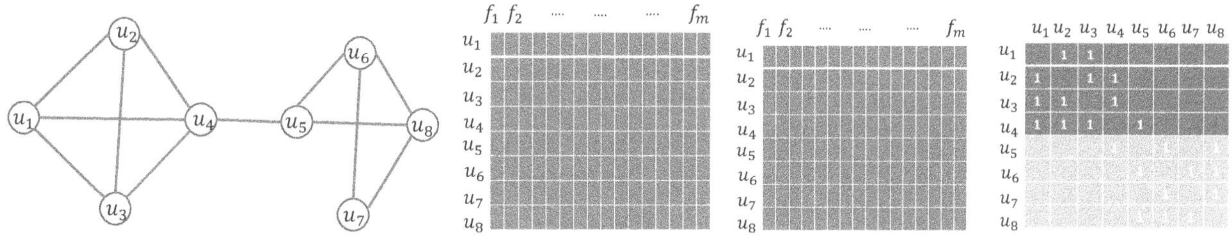

(a) Linked Users (b) Attribute-Value Data (c) Attribute-Value and Linked Data

Figure 1: A Simple Example of Linked Social Media Data

ture selection is the availability of label information. If we change our perspective and consider label information as a sort of constraints in the learning space, we can turn both types of feature selection to a problem with the same intrinsic property: selecting features to be consistent with some constraints [35]. In supervised learning, label information plays the role of constraint. Without labels, other alternative constraints are proposed, such as data variance and separability, for unsupervised learning [27, 7, 4, 14, 35, 3]. However, most of them evaluate the importance of feature individually and neglect the feature correlation [36, 34].

In our attempt to address the challenges of unsupervised feature selection for linked social media data, we propose a novel framework of Linked Unsupervised Feature Selection (LUFS). Our main contributions are summarized below:

- Employing social dimensions to exploit relations among linked data instances in groups and enable a concise mathematical model of these relations;
- Introducing the concept of pseudo-class labels to develop alternative constraints for unsupervised feature selection using linked data;
- Proposing a novel unsupervised feature selection framework, LUFS, for linked data in social media to exploit linked information in selecting features;
- Evaluating LUFS extensively using datasets from real-world social media websites to understanding the working of LUFS.

The rest of this paper is organized as follows. We formally define the problem of unsupervised feature selection for linked data in social media in Section 2; introduce our new framework of unsupervised feature selection, LUFS in Section 3, including social dimension regularization, optimization, and convergence analysis; present empirical evaluation with discussion in Section 4 and the related work in Section 5; and conclude this work in Section 6.

2. PROBLEM STATEMENT

In this paper, scalars are denoted by lower-case letters $(a, b, \ldots; \alpha, \beta, \ldots)$, vectors are written as lower-case bolded letters $(\mathbf{a}, \mathbf{b}, \ldots)$, and matrices correspond to boldfaced upper-case letters $(\mathbf{A}, \mathbf{B}, \ldots)$.

Let $\mathbf{u} = \{u_1, u_2, \ldots, u_n\}$ be the set of linked data (e.g., u_1 to u_8 in Figure 1) where n is the number of data instances and $\mathbf{f} = \{f_1, f_2, \ldots, f_m\}$ be the set of features where m is the number of features. Let $\mathbf{X} = (\mathbf{x}_1, \mathbf{x}_2, \ldots, \mathbf{x}_n) \in \mathbb{R}^{m\times n}$ be the conventional representation of $\mathbf{u}$ w.r.t . $\mathbf{f}$ where $\mathbf{x}_i(j)$ is the frequency of f_j used by u_i (e.g., Figure 1(b)). We assume that the data, $\mathbf{X}$, is centered, that is, $\sum_{i=1}^{n} \mathbf{x}_i = 0$, which can be realized as $\mathbf{X} = \mathbf{XP}$ where $\mathbf{P} = \mathbf{I}_n - \frac{1}{n}\mathbf{1}_n\mathbf{1}_n^\top$.

For social media data, there also exist connections among its data instances. Let $\mathbf{R} \in \mathbb{R}^{n\times n}$ denote their connections where $\mathbf{R}(i,j) = 1$ if u_i and u_j are linked, otherwise zero (e.g., the right subgraph in Figure 1(c)). In our work, we assume that the relationships among data instances form an undirected graph, i.e., $\mathbf{R} = \mathbf{R}^\top$.

With the above notations defined, the problem of *unsupervised feature selection for linked data* can be stated as: given n linked data instances, its conventional representation $\mathbf{X}$, its link representation $\mathbf{R}$, develop a method f, which can select a subset of relevant features $\mathbf{f}'$ from $\mathbf{f}$ by utilizing both $\mathbf{X}$ and $\mathbf{R}$ for these n linked instances, formally stated as,

$$f : \{\mathbf{f}; \mathbf{X}, \mathbf{R}\} \rightarrow \{\mathbf{f}'\}. \quad (1)$$

The above is substantially different from the traditional task of unsupervised feature selection, formally defined as,

$$f : \{\mathbf{f}; \mathbf{X}\} \rightarrow \{\mathbf{f}'\}. \quad (2)$$

3. UNSUPERVISED FEATURE SELECTION

Set $\mathbf{s} = \pi(\overbrace{0, \ldots, 0}^{m-k}, \overbrace{1, \ldots, 1}^{k})$ where $\pi(\cdot)$ is the permutation function and k is the number of features to select where $\mathbf{s}_i = 1$ indicates that the i-th feature is selected. The original data can be represented as $\mathrm{diag}(\mathbf{s})\mathbf{X}$ with k selected features, where $\mathrm{diag}(\mathbf{s})$ is a diagonal matrix. The difficulty faced with unsupervised feature selection is due to lack of class labels. Hence, we introduce the concept of pseudo-class label to guide unsupervised learning. We assume that there is a mapping matrix $\mathbf{W} \in \mathbb{R}^{m\times c}$, which assigns each data point with a pseudo-class label where c is the number of pseudo-class labels. The pseudo-class label indicator matrix is $\mathbf{Y} = \mathbf{W}^\top \mathrm{diag}(\mathbf{s})\mathbf{X} \in \mathbb{R}^{c\times n}$. Each column of $\mathbf{Y}$ has only one nonzero entity, i.e., $\|\mathbf{Y}(:, i)\|_0 = 1$ where $\|\cdot\|_0$ is the vector zero norm, counting the number of nonzero elements in the vector. Since $\mathbf{X}$ is centered, it is easy to verify that $\mathbf{Y}$ is also centered,

$$\sum_{i=1}^{n} \mathbf{y}_i = \sum_{i=1}^{n} (\mathbf{W}^\top \mathrm{diag}(\mathbf{s})\mathbf{x}_i) = (\mathbf{W}^\top \mathrm{diag}(\mathbf{s})) \sum_{i=1}^{n} \mathbf{x}_i = 0. \quad (3)$$

As shown above, both supervised and unsupervised learning tasks aim to solve the same problem: selecting features consistent with given constraints. In the supervised setting, pseudo-class label information is tantamount to the provided label information; in the unsupervised setting, we seek pseudo-class label information from linked social media data. We discuss technical details of the proposed framework LUFS in the following subsection.

3.1 Social Dimensions for Linked Data

First, we embark on dealing with linked data. In [30], social dimension is introduced as a means to integrate the interdependency among linked data and attribute-value data. Instances from different social dimensions are dissimilar while instances in the same social dimension are similar. Flattening linked data with social dimensions, traditional classification methods such as SVM obtain better performance for relational learning [30].

Social dimension extraction is a well-studied problem by social network analysis community [24, 11, 30]. In our work, we adopt a widely used algorithm, i.e., Modularity Maximization [24], which can formulated as:

$$\max_{\mathbf{H}^\top\mathbf{H}=\mathbf{I}} \quad Tr(\mathbf{H}^\top\mathbf{M}\mathbf{H}) \tag{4}$$

where $\mathbf{H} \in \mathbb{R}^{K\times n}$ is the social dimension indicator matrix, K is the number of social dimensions, and $\mathbf{M}$ is the modularity matrix defined as:

$$\mathbf{M} = \mathbf{R} - \frac{\mathbf{d}\mathbf{d}^\top}{2n} \tag{5}$$

where $\mathbf{d}$ is a degree vector, and $\mathbf{d}_i$ is the degree of u_i.

The standard K-means algorithm is performed to obtain the discrete-valued social dimension assignment, $\mathbf{H}(i,j) = 1$, if u_j is in the i-th dimension, and $\mathbf{H}(i,j) = 0$, otherwise.

Recall the simple example of linked data in Figure 1, we can extract two social dimensions, i.e, $\{u_1, u_2, u_3, u_4\}$ and $\{u_5, u_6, u_7, u_8\}$. From Figure 1, we can observe that instances in the same social dimension have more connections. The discrete-valued social dimension indicator matrix, $\mathbf{H}$, is:

$$\mathbf{H} = \begin{pmatrix} 1 & 1 & 1 & 1 & 0 & 0 & 0 & 0 \\ 0 & 0 & 0 & 0 & 1 & 1 & 1 & 1 \end{pmatrix}$$

Since social dimensions represent a type of user affiliations, inspired by Linear Discriminant Analysis, we define three matrices: within, between, and total social dimension scatter matrixes $\mathbf{S}_w$, $\mathbf{S}_b$, and $\mathbf{S}_t$ as follows:

$$\begin{aligned} \mathbf{S}_w &= \mathbf{Y}\mathbf{Y}^\top - \mathbf{Y}\mathbf{F}\mathbf{F}^\top\mathbf{Y}^\top, \\ \mathbf{S}_b &= \mathbf{Y}\mathbf{F}\mathbf{F}^\top\mathbf{Y}^\top, \\ \mathbf{S}_t &= \mathbf{Y}\mathbf{Y}^\top, \end{aligned} \tag{6}$$

where $\mathbf{F}$ is the weighted social dimension indicator matrix, which can be obtained from $\mathbf{H}$ as below,

$$\mathbf{F} = \mathbf{H}(\mathbf{H}^\top\mathbf{H})^{-\frac{1}{2}}, \tag{7}$$

where the j-th column of $\mathbf{F}$ is given by

$$F_j = \frac{(0,\ldots,0,\overbrace{1,\ldots,1}^{h_j},0,\ldots,0)}{\sqrt{h_j}}. \tag{8}$$

where h_j is the number of instances in the j-th social dimension.

Instances in the same social dimension are similar and instances from different social dimensions are dissimilar. We can obtain a constraint from link information, **social dimension regularization**, to model the relations among linked instances, via the following maximization problem,

$$\max_{\mathbf{W}} Tr\big((\mathbf{S}_t)^{-1}\mathbf{S}_b\big). \tag{9}$$

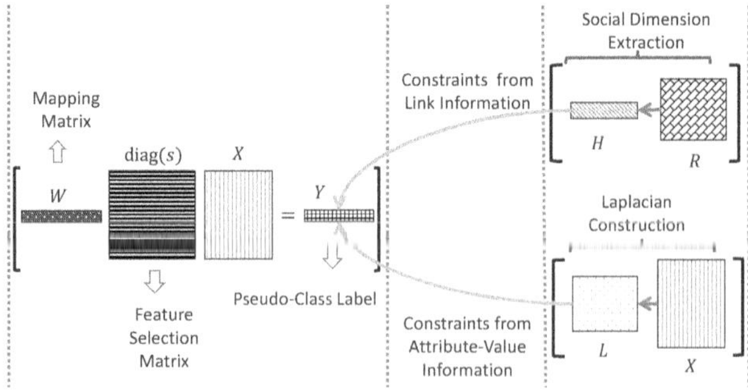

Figure 2: Illustration of the LUFS Framework

3.2 A Framework - LUFS

To take advantage of information from attribute-value part, i.e., $\mathbf{X}$, similar data instances should have similar labels. According to spectral analysis [22], the constraint from attribute-value part can be formulated as the following minimization problem,

$$\min \quad Tr(\mathbf{Y}\mathbf{L}\mathbf{Y}^\top) \tag{10}$$

where $\mathbf{L} = \mathbf{D} - \mathbf{S}$ is a laplacian matrix and $\mathbf{D}$ is a diagonal matrix with its elements defined as $\mathbf{D}(i,i) = \sum_{j=1}^{n} \mathbf{S}(i,j)$. $\mathbf{S} \in \mathbb{R}^{n\times n}$ denotes the similarity matrix based on $\mathbf{X}$, obtained through a RBF kernel as,

$$\mathbf{S}(i,j) = e^{-\frac{\|\mathbf{x}_i - \mathbf{x}_j\|^2}{\sigma^2}}. \tag{11}$$

By introducing the concept of *pseudo-class labels*, constraints from both link information and unlabeled attribute-value data are ready for unsupervised feature selection. Our framework of linked unsupervised feature selection, LUFS, is conceptually shown in Figure 2 with our solutions to the two challenges (need to take into account of linked data and lack of labels): extracting constraints from both linked and attribute-value data, and then constructing pseudo-class labels through social dimension extraction and spectral analysis. Thus, our proposed framework, LUFS, is equivalent to solving the following optimization problem,

$$\begin{aligned} \min_{\mathbf{W},\mathbf{s}} \quad & Tr(\mathbf{Y}\mathbf{L}\mathbf{Y}^\top) - \alpha Tr\big((\mathbf{S}_t)^{-1}\mathbf{S}_b\big), \\ s.t. \quad & \mathbf{s} \in \{0,1\}^n, \ \mathbf{s}^\top\mathbf{1}_n = k, \\ & \|\mathbf{Y}(:,i)\|_0 = 1, \ \ 1 \le i \le n. \end{aligned} \tag{12}$$

The problem in Eq. (12) is difficult to solve due to the two constraints. To make the problem solvable, we use some widely used relaxation methods. First, according to common relaxation for label indicator matrix [22], the constraint on $\mathbf{Y}$ is relaxed to orthogonality, i.e., $\mathbf{Y}\mathbf{Y}^\top = \mathbf{I}_c$.

With this relaxation, $\mathbf{S}_t$ in social dimension regularization is an identity matrix and $Tr(\mathbf{Y}\mathbf{Y}^\top) = c$ is a constant. Social dimension regularization can be rewritten as,

$$\min Tr(\mathbf{Y}\mathbf{Y}^\top) - Tr(\mathbf{Y}\mathbf{F}\mathbf{F}^\top\mathbf{Y}^\top). \tag{13}$$

the reason for adding the constant in social dimension regularization will be explained later. With this relaxation, Eq. (12) can be relaxed to,

$$\begin{aligned}\min Tr(\mathbf{Y}\mathbf{L}\mathbf{Y}^\top) + \alpha Tr(\mathbf{Y}\mathbf{Y}^\top - \mathbf{Y}\mathbf{F}\mathbf{F}^\top\mathbf{Y}^\top)\\ s.t.\quad \mathbf{s} \in \{0,1\}^n,\ \mathbf{s}^\top\mathbf{1}_n = k,\\ \mathbf{Y}\mathbf{Y}^\top = \mathbf{I}_c,\end{aligned} \tag{14}$$

The constraint on $\mathbf{s}$ makes Eq. (14) mixed integer programming [2], which is still difficult to solve. We observe that that diag($\mathbf{s}$) and $\mathbf{W}$ is as the form of diag($\mathbf{s}$)$\mathbf{W}$ in Eq. (14). Since $\mathbf{s}$ is a binary vector and $m - k$ rows of the diag($\mathbf{s}$) are all zeros, diag($\mathbf{s}$)$\mathbf{W}$ is a matrix where the elements of many rows are all zeros. This motivates us to absorb the diag($\mathbf{s}$) into $\mathbf{W}$, $\mathbf{W}$ = diag($\mathbf{s}$)$\mathbf{W}$, and add $\ell_{2,1}$ norm on $\mathbf{W}$ to achieve feature selection as,

$$\begin{aligned}\min_{\mathbf{W}}\quad & Tr(\mathbf{W}^\top\mathbf{X}\mathbf{L}\mathbf{X}^\top\mathbf{W}) + \beta\|\mathbf{W}\|_{2,1}\\ & + \alpha Tr(\mathbf{W}^\top\mathbf{X}(\mathbf{I}_n - \mathbf{F}\mathbf{F}^\top)\mathbf{X}^\top\mathbf{W})\\ s.t.\quad & \mathbf{W}^\top(\mathbf{X}\mathbf{X}^\top + \lambda\mathbf{I})\mathbf{W} = \mathbf{I}_c,\end{aligned} \tag{15}$$

where $\lambda\mathbf{I}$ is added to make $(\mathbf{X}\mathbf{X}^\top + \lambda\mathbf{I})$ nonsingular. $\|\mathbf{W}\|_{2,1}$, controls the capacity of $\|\mathbf{W}\|$ and also ensures that $\|\mathbf{W}\|$ is sparse in rows, making it particularly suitable for feature selection. $\|\mathbf{W}\|_{2,1}$ is the $\ell_{2,1}$-norm of $\|\mathbf{W}\|$ defined as [5],

$$\|\mathbf{W}\|_{2,1} = \sum_{i=1}^{m}\sqrt{\sum_{j=1}^{k}\mathbf{W}^2(i,j)} = \sum_{i=1}^{m}\|\mathbf{W}(i,:)\|_2. \tag{16}$$

Lemma 1. Assume $\mathbf{E} \in \mathbb{R}^{n\times m}$ is a matrix with orthonormal columns, that is, $\mathbf{E}^\top\mathbf{E} = \mathbf{I}_m$, then $\mathbf{I}_n - \mathbf{E}\mathbf{E}^\top$ is a symmetric and positive semidefinite matrix.

PROOF. It is easy to verify that $\mathbf{I}_n - \mathbf{E}\mathbf{E}^\top$ is a symmetric matrix since $(\mathbf{I}_n - \mathbf{E}\mathbf{E}^\top)^\top = \mathbf{I}_n - \mathbf{E}\mathbf{E}^\top$.

Let $\mathbf{E} = \mathbf{U}\Sigma\mathbf{V}^\top$ be the Singular Value Decomposition (SVD) of $\mathbf{E}$, where $\mathbf{U} \in \mathbb{R}^{n\times n}$ and $\mathbf{V} \in \mathbb{R}^{m\times m}$ are orthogonal. $\Sigma = \text{diag}(\sigma_1, \ldots, \sigma_m, 0, \ldots, 0)$ is diagonal where $\sigma_1 \geq \sigma_2 \geq \ldots \geq \sigma_m \geq 0$. Then we have,

$$\begin{aligned}\mathbf{E}^\top\mathbf{E} = \mathbf{I}_m \Rightarrow \mathbf{V}\Sigma^\top\Sigma\mathbf{V}^\top = \mathbf{V}\mathbf{V}^\top\\ \Rightarrow 1 \geq \sigma_1 \geq \sigma_2 \geq \ldots \geq \sigma_m \geq 0.\end{aligned} \tag{17}$$

Then,

$$\mathbf{I}_n - \mathbf{E}\mathbf{E}^\top = \mathbf{U}(\mathbf{I}_n - \Sigma\Sigma^\top)\mathbf{U}^\top. \tag{18}$$

Since $(\mathbf{I}_n - \Sigma\Sigma^\top)$ is a diagonal matrix and the diagonal elements are all nonnegative, $(\mathbf{I}_n - \Sigma\Sigma^\top)$ is a positive semidefinite matrix. Thus $\mathbf{U}(\mathbf{I}_n - \Sigma\Sigma^\top)\mathbf{U}^\top$ is a semidefinite matrix, which completes the proof. □

The importance of Lemma 1 is two-fold. First, it explains why we need a constant on the social dimension regularization. Adding the constant can guarantee the convexity of the objective function in Eq. (15). Second, it paves the way for the following theorem for LUFS.

THEOREM 1. *Eq. (15) can be converted into the following optimization problem,*

$$\begin{aligned}\min_{\mathbf{W}}\quad & f(\mathbf{W}) = Tr(\mathbf{W}^\top\mathbf{A}\mathbf{W}) + \beta\|\mathbf{W}\|_{2,1},\\ s.t.\quad & \mathbf{W}^\top\mathbf{B}\mathbf{W} = \mathbf{I}_c,\end{aligned} \tag{19}$$

where $\mathbf{A}$ *is a symmetric and positive semidefinite matrix and* $\mathbf{B}$ *is a symmetric and positive matrix.*

PROOF. It suffices to show how to construct a symmetric and positive semidefinite matrix $\mathbf{A}$ and a symmetric and positive matrix $\mathbf{B}$ from Eq. (15).

We construct $\mathbf{B} = \mathbf{X}\mathbf{X}^\top + \lambda\mathbf{I}$. It is easy to check that $\mathbf{B}$ is symmetric and positive when $\lambda \neq 0$ and then the constraint in Eq. (15) is converted into the one in Eq. (19).

We construct $\mathbf{A} = \mathbf{X}\mathbf{L}\mathbf{X}^\top + \alpha\mathbf{X}(\mathbf{I}_n - \mathbf{F}\mathbf{F}^\top)\mathbf{X}^\top$ and then the objective function in Eq. (15) is converted into the one in Eq. (19). According to Lemma 1, $(\mathbf{I}_n - \mathbf{F}\mathbf{F}^\top)$ is symmetric and positive semidefinite; and according to the definition of Laplacian matrix, $\mathbf{X}\mathbf{L}\mathbf{X}^\top$ is symmetric and positive semidefinite. Thus, $\mathbf{A}$ is symmetric and positive semidefinite, which completes the proof. □

3.3 Optimization Algorithm for LUFS

In recent years, many methods have been proposed to solve the $\ell_{2,1}$-norm minimization problem [21, 25, 34]. However, our problem is different from these existing ones due to the orthogonal constraint in Eq. (19). Hence, we propose the following algorithm, as shown in Algorithm 1, to optimize the problem in Eq. (19).

Algorithm 1 LUFS

Input: $\{\mathbf{X}, \mathbf{R}, \alpha, \beta, \lambda, c, K, k\}$
Output: k most relevant features

1: Obtain the social dimension indicator matrix $\mathbf{H}$
2: Set $\mathbf{F} = \mathbf{H}(\mathbf{H}^\top\mathbf{H})^{-\frac{1}{2}}$
3: Construct $\mathbf{S}$ through Eq. (11)
4: Set $\mathbf{L} = \mathbf{D} - \mathbf{S}$
5: Set $\mathbf{A} = \mathbf{X}\mathbf{L}\mathbf{X}^\top + \alpha\mathbf{X}(\mathbf{I}_n - \mathbf{F}\mathbf{F}^\top)\mathbf{X}^\top$
6: Set $\mathbf{B} = \mathbf{X}\mathbf{X}^\top + \lambda\mathbf{I}$
7: Set $t = 0$ and initialize $\mathbf{D}_0$ as an identity matrix
8: **while** Not convergent **do**
9: Set $\mathbf{C}_t = \mathbf{B}^{-1}(\mathbf{A} + \beta\mathbf{D}_t)$
10: Set $\mathbf{W}_t = [q_1, \ldots, q_c]$ where $q_1, \ldots, q_c$ are the eigenvectors of $\mathbf{C}_t$ corresponding to the first c smallest eigenvalues
11: Update the diagonal matrix $\mathbf{D}_{t+1}$, where the i-th diagonal element is $\frac{1}{2\|\mathbf{W}_t(i,:)\|_2}$;
12: Set $t = t + 1$
13: **end while**
14: Sort each feature according to $\|\mathbf{W}(i,:)\|_2$ in **descending** order and select the top-k ranked ones;

In Algorithm 1, social dimension extraction and weighted social dimension indicator construction are from line 1 to line 2. The iterative algorithm to optimize Eq. (19) is presented from line 8 to line 13. The convergence analysis of the algorithm starts with the following two lemmas.

Lemma 2. $\mathbf{A} \in \mathbb{R}^{m\times m}$ is symmetric and positive semidefinite and $\mathbf{B} \in \mathbb{R}^{m\times m}$ is symmetric and positive. If $\mathbf{W} \in \mathbb{R}^{m\times c}$ solves the following minimization problem:

$$\begin{aligned}\min_{\mathbf{W}}\quad & Tr(\mathbf{W}^\top\mathbf{A}\mathbf{W}),\\ s.t.\quad & \mathbf{W}^\top\mathbf{B}\mathbf{W} = \mathbf{I}_c,\end{aligned} \tag{20}$$

then $\mathbf{W}$ consists of the eigenvectors of $\mathbf{B}^{-1}\mathbf{A}$ corresponding to the c smallest eigenvalues.

PROOF. The lemma can be easily obtained through *Ky Fan Theorem* [15]. □

Lemma 3. The following inequality holds if $\mathbf{w}_t^i|_{i=1}^r$ are non-zero vectors, where r is an arbitrary number.

$$\sum_i \|\mathbf{w}_{t+1}^i\|_2 - \sum_i \frac{\|\mathbf{w}_{t+1}^i\|_2}{2\|\mathbf{w}_t^i\|_2} \leq \sum_i \|\mathbf{w}_t^i\|_2 - \sum_i \frac{\|\mathbf{w}_t^i\|_2^2}{2\|\mathbf{w}_t^i\|_2}. \quad (21)$$

PROOF. The detailed proof can be found in our previous work [29]. □

With the above two lemmas, we develop the following theorem regarding the convergence of Algorithm 1.

THEOREM 2. *At each iteration of Algorithm 1, the value of the objective function in Eq. (19) monotonically decreases.*

PROOF. According to Lemma 2, $\mathbf{W}_{t+1}$ in line 9 of Algorithm 1 is the solution to the following problem,

$$\mathbf{W}_{t+1} = \min_{\mathbf{W}^\top \mathbf{B}\mathbf{W}=\mathbf{I}} Tr\big(\mathbf{W}^\top(\mathbf{A}+\beta\mathbf{D}_t)\mathbf{W}\big), \quad (22)$$

which indicates that,

$$Tr\big(\mathbf{W}_{t+1}^\top(\mathbf{A}+\beta\mathbf{D}_t)\mathbf{W}_{t+1}\big) \leq Tr\big(\mathbf{W}_t^\top(\mathbf{A}+\beta\mathbf{D}_t)\mathbf{W}_t\big).$$

Then we have the following inequality,

$$Tr(\mathbf{W}_{t+1}^\top \mathbf{A}\mathbf{W}_{t+1}) + \beta\sum_i \|\mathbf{W}_{t+1}(i,:)\|_2 - \beta\Big(\sum_i \|\mathbf{W}_{t+1}(i,:)\|_2 - \sum_i \frac{\|\mathbf{W}_{t+1}(i,:)\|_2^2}{2\|\mathbf{W}_t(i,:)\|_2}\Big)$$
$$\leq Tr(\mathbf{W}_t^\top \mathbf{A}\mathbf{W}_t) + \beta\sum_i \|\mathbf{W}_t(i,:)\|_2 - \beta\Big(\sum_i \|\mathbf{W}_t(i,:)\|_2 - \sum_i \frac{\|\mathbf{W}_t(i,:)\|_2^2}{2\|\mathbf{W}_t(i,:)\|_2}\Big)$$

According to the lemma 3, we can obtain,

$$f(\mathbf{W}_{t+1}) \leq f(\mathbf{W}_t), \quad (23)$$

which completes the proof. □

According to Theorem 2, Algorithm 1 converges to the optimal $\mathbf{W}$ for the problem in Eq. (19).

4. EXPERIMENTS AND DISCUSSION

In this section, we present experiment details to verify the effectiveness of the proposed framework, LUFS. After introducing real-world social media datasets, we first evaluate the quality of selected features in terms of clustering performance, then study the effects of parameters on performance and finally further verify the constraint extracted from link information by social dimension.

4.1 Datasets, Baseline Methods, and Metrics

We collect two datasets from real-world social media websites, i.e., BlogCatalog[4] and Flickr[5], which are the subsets of two public available datasets used in [31] to uncover overlapping groups in social media. Some statistics of the datasets are shown in Table 1.

Table 1: Statistics of the Datasets

	BlogCatalog	Flickr
Size	5,198	7,575
# of Features	8,189	12,047
# of Classes	6	9
# of Links	27,965	47,344
# Ave Degree	5.38	6.25

LUFS is compared with the following three unsupervised feature selection algorithms,

- UDFS [34] selects features in batch mode by simultaneously exploiting discriminative information and feature correlation.
- Laplacian Score [14] evaluates the importance of a feature through its power of locality preservation.
- SPEC [35] selects features using spectral regression.

Following the existing evaluation practice for unsupervised feature selection, we assess LUFS in terms of clustering performance. We vary the numbers of selected features as $\{200, 300, 400, 500, 600, 700, 800, 900, 1000\}$. Each feature selection algorithm is first performed to select features, then K-means clustering is performed based on the selected features. Since K-means often converges to local minima, we repeat each experiment 20 times and report the average performance.

The clustering quality is evaluated by two commonly used metrics, *accuracy* and *normalized mutual information* (NMI)[6]. Denoting $l(c_i)$ as the label of cluster c_i, $l(d_j)$ as the predicted label of the j-th document, the accuracy is defined as:

$$Accuracy = \frac{1}{n}\sum_{i=1}^{K}\sum_{j=1}^{n}\delta(l(c_i), l(d_j)), \quad (24)$$

where $\delta(x,y)$ is the delta function that its value is 1 if $x=y$ and 0 otherwise.

Given two clusterings C and C', the mutual information $MI(C,C')$ is defined as:

$$MI(C,C') = \sum_{c_i\in C, c'_j\in C'} p(c_i,c'_j)\log_2\frac{p(c_i,c'_j)}{p(c_i)p(c'_j)}, \quad (25)$$

and NMI is defined by

$$NMI(C,C') = \frac{MI(C,C')}{\max(H(C),H(C'))}, \quad (26)$$

where $H(C)$ and $H(C')$ represent the entropies of clusterings C and C', respectively. Larger NMI values represent better clustering qualities.

4.2 Quality of Selected Features

In this subsection, we compare the quality of features selected by different algorithms using performance metrics given above. Conventionally, the parameters in feature selection algorithms are tuned via cross-validation. More discussion is given in Section 4.3. The resulting parameter values for LUFS are: $\{\alpha=0.1, \beta=0.1, K=70, c=9\}$ for Flickr while $\{\alpha=0.1, \beta=0.1, K=10, c=6\}$ for BlogCatalog. λ is used to make $(\mathbf{X}\mathbf{X}^\top+\lambda\mathbf{I})$ nonsingular and according to empirical experience, we set λ to 0.01 in both

[4]http://www.blogcatalog.com
[5]http://www.flickr.com/

[6]We use the source code from http://www.zjucadcg.cn/dengcai/Data/Clustering.html.

datasets. The comparison results of Flickr and BlogCatalog are shown in Tables 2 and 3, respectively. Note that the clustering performance with all features (i.e., without feature selection) is reported in the last columns.

We observe the performance change with the numbers of selected features: it increases, reaches the peak, and then decreases. For example, LUFS achieves its peak values when the number of selected features are 500 and 300 for Flickr and BlogCatalog, respectively. The clustering performance with as few as 200 features is better than that with all features. For instances, LUFS obtains 10.51% and 18.68% relative improvement in terms of accuracy for Flickr and BlogCatalog, respectively. These results demonstrate that the number of features can be significantly reduced without performance deterioration.

LapScore obtains comparable results with SPEC on both datasets. Most of time, UDFS outperforms both LapScore and SPEC, which is consistent with the results reported in [34]. LapScore and SPEC analyze features separately and select features one after another, which may omit the possible correlation between different features. While UDFS selects features in a batch mode and considers feature correlation. These observations support the conclusion in [3, 36, 34]: it is recommended to analyze data features jointly for feature selection.

We observe that LUFS consistently outperforms these baseline methods on both datasets. For example, LUFS gains up to 19.82% and 11.44% relative improvement in terms of accuracy in Flickr and BlogCatalog, respectively. All baseline methods are based on the data *i.i.d.* assumption, which is not valid due to linked data in social media; and LUFS explicitly takes advantage of link information through social dimension regularization. We also note that with the increasing number of features, the improvement progressively decreases. Usually, LUFS achieves its best results sooner than baseline methods do. For example, LUFS achieves its best results in terms of accuracy in Flickr when 500 features are selected compared to 900 features for baseline methods.

4.3 Parameter Selection

In addition to determining the number of selected features (which remains an open problem [34]), LUFS has four important parameters: the number of pseudo-class labels (c), the number of social dimensions (K), α (controlling social dimension regularization) and β (controlling $\ell_{2,1}$-norm regularization). Hence, we study the effect of each of the four parameters (c, K, α, or β) by fixing the other 3 to see how the performance of LUFS varies with the number of selected features. The processes of parameter selection for Flickr and for BlogCatalog are similar and we present the details for Flickr to save space. Examples of experimental results are presented next.

The number of pseudo-class labels c is varied from 2 to 20 with an incremental step of 1 while setting $\{\alpha = 0.1, \beta = 0.1, K = 70\}$. The performance variation w.r.t. c and the number of features is depicted in Figure 3. Most of the time, the clustering performance first increases rapidly, reaches its best performance and decreases as c increases. This observation can be used to guide the determination of the optimal number of c for LUFS. Note that when c varies from 5 to 11, the clustering performance is not sensitive to c, especially when the number of selected feature is large.

Fixing $c = 9$, $\alpha = 0.1$ and $\beta = 0.1$, we vary the number of social dimensions from 10 to 100 with an incremental step of 10 and the performance variation w.r.t. the number of social dimensions and the number of features is demonstrated in Figure 4. Most of the time, with the increasing number of social dimensions, the performance first increases, reaches its peak value and degrades. This pattern can be used to determine the optimal number of social dimensions for LUFS.

Fixing $c = 9$, $K = 70$ and $\beta = 0.1$, we vary α as $\{1e{-}6, 1e{-}3, 1e{-}2, 0.1, 0.3, 0.5, 0.7, 1\}$. The performance variation w.r.t. α and the number of features is depicted in Figure 5. The performance first increases and most of time, the peak values for both accuracy and NMI are achieved when $\alpha = 0.1$, indicating the importance of social dimension regularization for LUFS. After $\alpha = 0.5$, the performance is dramatically degraded, suggesting that only link information is not enough for LUFS.

To study how β and the number of features affect the performance, we vary β as $\{1e{-}6, 1e{-}3, 1e{-}2, 0.1, 0.3, 0.5, 0.7, 1\}$ and set $c = 9$, $K = 70$ and $\beta = 0.1$. The results are shown in Figure 6. We observe that the performance improves as β changes from 1e−3 to 1e−2 and from 1e−2 to 0.1. These results demonstrate the capability of the $\ell_{2,1}$-norm for feature selection.

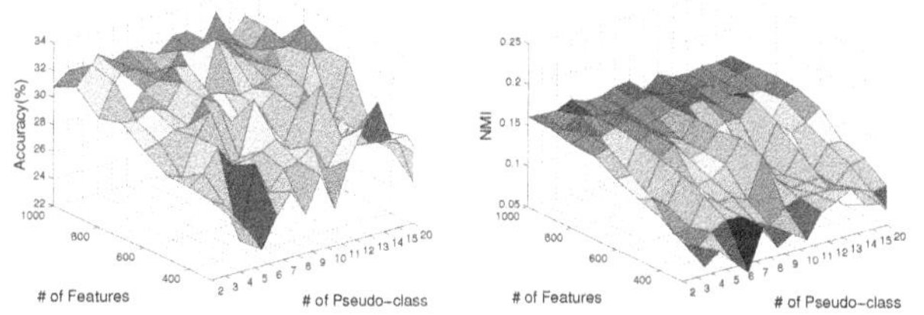

(a) Accuracy (b) NMI

Figure 3: Number of Pseudo-class Labels vs Number of Features

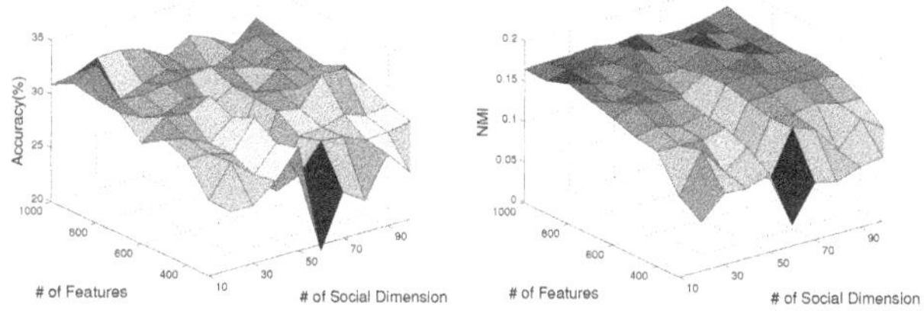

(a) Accuracy (b) NMI

Figure 4: Number of Social Dimension vs Number of Features

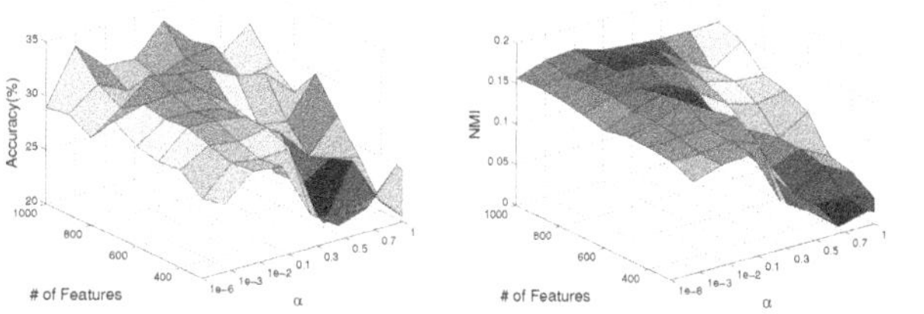

(a) Accuracy (b) NMI

Figure 5: α vs Number of Features

Table 2: Clustering Performance with Different Feature Selection Algorithms in Flickr

Accuracy										
	200	300	400	500	600	700	800	900	1000	12047
UDFS	26.29	26.41	27.02	27.29	27.55	27.95	28.41	31.07	30.79	25.49
LapScore	25.56	25.79	25.98	26.00	26.00	26.00	26.54	30.90	30.73	25.49
SPEC	26.29	26.29	26.29	26.29	26.29	26.29	26.30	26.35	[illegible]	25.49
LUFS	29.19	29.51	29.90	32.70	30.41	31.17	30.48	31.79	31.17	25.49
NMI										
	200	300	400	500	600	700	800	900	1000	12047
UDFS	0.0361	0.0409	0.0702	0.0761	0.0811	0.0921	0.1062	0.1110	0.1200	0.0296
LapScore	0.0302	0.0555	0.0691	0.0709	0.0662	0.0630	0.0694	0.0816	0.1056	0.0296
SPEC	0.0361	0.0361	0.0361	0.0361	0.0361	0.0361	0.0361	0.0361	0.0559	0.0296
LUFS	0.0951	0.1026	0.1489	0.1601	0.1582	0.1701	0.1614	0.1681	0.1596	0.0296

Table 3: Clustering Performance with Different Feature Selection Algorithms in BlogCatalog

Accuracy										
	200	300	400	500	600	700	800	900	1000	8189
UDFS	41.16	51.86	49.28	49.01	47.96	47.31	46.98	46.98	45.36	38.65
LapScore	41.07	49.83	48.93	48.59	47.75	46.84	46.69	46.76	45.09	38.65
SPEC	40.33	51.16	48.55	48.66	47.43	46.93	46.73	46.60	45.54	38.65
LUFS	45.87	55.70	52.72	51.41	50.93	50.68	50.35	48.95	47.20	38.65
NMI										
	200	300	400	500	600	700	800	900	1000	8189
UDFS	0.1842	0.1807	0.1789	0.1764	0.1741	0.1725	0.1744	0.1702	0.1673	0.1540
LapScore	0.1328	0.1755	0.1707	0.1746	0.1753	0.1757	0.1730	0.1675	0.1615	0.1540
SPEC	0.1819	0.1789	0.1768	0.1726	0.1765	0.1688	0.1742	0.1675	0.1654	0.1540
LUFS	0.2149	0.2121	0.2026	0.2040	0.2016	0.2014	0.1994	0.1927	0.1891	0.1540

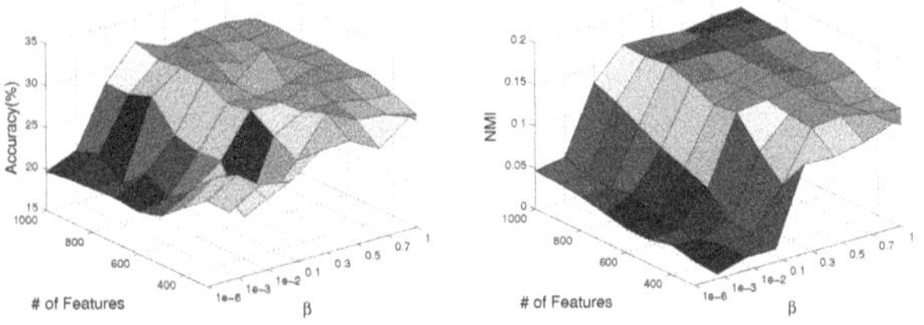

(a) Accuracy (b) NMI

Figure 6: β vs Number of Features

Among the these four parameters of LUFS, β is most sensitive, the number of pseudo-class labels, the number of social dimensions and α are not so.

4.4 Probing Further

A key contribution of LUFS to the performance improvement is to employ social dimensions extracted from linked data. Hence, we would like to probe further why the use of social dimensions works. One way is to investigate whether instances in the same social dimension are similar and instances from different social dimensions are dissimilar.

Let $\mathbf{z} = \{z_1, z_2, \ldots, z_K\}$ be the K social dimensions given by the social dimension extraction algorithm, i.e., Modularity Maximization [24] here, with sizes of $\{n_1, n_2, \ldots, n_K\}$ where n_i is number of instances in the i-th social dimension and $\sum_i n_i = n$. To create reference groups in comparison with social dimensions, we also randomly divide these n instances into K groups with sizes of $\{n_1, n_2, \ldots, n_K\}$. Let $\mathbf{z}' = \{z'_1, z'_2, \ldots, z'_K\}$ be the set of these randomly formed groups with sizes of $\{n_1, n_2, \ldots, n_K\}$ and then each group in $\mathbf{z}'$ (e.g., z'_i) corresponds to a social dimension in $\mathbf{z}$ (e.g., z_i). The label information is used earlier in assessing clustering performance. We use it again here. Let $\mathbf{Y}'$ be the class label indicator matrix. We center $\mathbf{Y}'$ as: $\mathbf{Y}' = \mathbf{Y}'\mathbf{P}$. Two distance metrics are defined: D_{within} and $D_{between}$ for within- and between-social dimension distance. D_{within} and $D_{between}$ can be obtained from within social dimension scatter matrix $\mathbf{S}_w$ and between social dimension scatter matrix $\mathbf{S}_b$, respectively,

$$D_{within} = Tr(\mathbf{S}_w), \quad D_{between} = Tr(\mathbf{S}_b). \qquad (27)$$

For each specific number of social dimensions, K, we calculate D_{within} and $D_{between}$ for $\mathbf{z}$ and $\mathbf{z}'$. Varying K from 2 to 100 with an incremental step of 1, we obtain 99 pairs of D_{within} and 99 pairs of $D_{between}$. The results for Flickr and BlogCatalog are shown in Figure 7.

D_{within} and $D_{between}$ change much faster for social dimensions, comparing with groups of random assignment. Moreover, D_{within} of a social dimension is much smaller than that of a random assignment group, thus, instances in the same social dimension are of similar labels. $D_{between}$ of a social dimension is much larger than that of a random assignment group, indicating that instances from different social dimensions are dissimilar.

We also perform a two-sample t-test on these pairs of D_{within} of $\mathbf{z}$ and $\mathbf{z}'$ at significant level 0.001. The null hypothesis, H_0, is that there is no different between these pairs; the alternative hypothesis, H_1, is that D_{within} of a social dimension is less than that of the corresponding random assignment group. The t-test results, p-values, are 6.0397e−060 and 8.2406e−083 on Flicker and BlogCatalog,

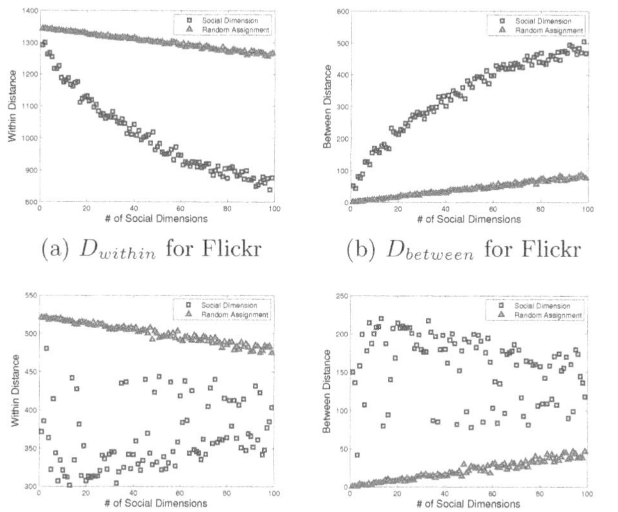

(a) D_{within} for Flickr (b) $D_{between}$ for Flickr

(c) D_{within} for BlogCatalog (d) $D_{between}$ for BlogCatalog

Figure 7: Within and Between Distance Achieved by Social Dimension and Random Assignment

respectively. Hence, there is strong evidence to reject the null hypothesis. We conduct a similar test for the pairs of $D_{between}$, and there is strong evidence to support that $D_{between}$ of a social dimension is significantly larger than that of its counterpart, a random assignment group. The evidence from both figures and t-test confirms the positive impact of the constraint from link information via social dimensions.

5. RELATED WORK

Traditionally, feature selection algorithms can be either supervised or unsupervised [7, 20] based on the training data being labeled or unlabeled.

Supervised feature selection methods [20] can be broadly categorized into the *wrapper* models [8, 17] and the *filter* models [13, 26]. The wrapper model uses the predictive accuracy of a predetermined learning algorithm to determine the quality of selected features. These methods can be egregiously expensive to run for data with a large number of features [6, 12]. The filter model separates feature selection from classifier learning so that the bias of a learning algorithm does not interact with the bias of a feature selection algorithm. It relies on measures of the general characteristics of the training data such as distance, consistency, dependency, information, and correlation [13]. Many researchers paid great attention to developing unsupervised feature selection [32, 14, 4]. Unsupervised feature selection [14, 7, 35] is a less constrained search problem without class labels, depending on clustering quality measures [10, 9], and can eventuate many equally valid feature subsets. With high-dimensional data, it is likely to find many sets of features that seem equally good without considering additional constraints. Another key difficulty is how to objectively measure the results of feature selection. A wrapper model is proposed in [7] to use a clustering algorithm in evaluating the quality of feature selection.

Recently, sparsity regularization, such as the $\ell_{2,1}$-norm of a matrix [5], in dimensionality reduction has been widely investigated and applied to feature selection including multi-task feature selection [1, 21], robust joint $\ell_{2,1}$-Norms [25], spectral feature selection [35], discriminative unsupervised feature selection [34]. Through sparsity regularization, feature selection can be embedded in the learning process.

The first attempt to select features on social media data is LinkedFS [29], a supervised algorithm. Various relations (coPost, coFollowing, coFollowed and Following) are extracted following social correlation theories [23]. LinkedFS significantly improves the performance of feature selection by incorporating these relations into feature selection. However, LinkedFS and LUFS are distinctively different. First, LinkedFS is formally stated as: $f : \{\mathbf{f}; \mathbf{X}, \mathbf{Y}\} \to \{\mathbf{f}'\}$ where $\mathbf{Y}$ contains the label information, while LUFS is a unsupervised feature selection algorithm. Second, LinkedFS exploits relations individually while LUFS employs relations as groups via social dimensions.

6. CONCLUSION

Linked data in social media presents new challenges to traditional feature selection algorithms, which assume the data instances to be independent and identically distributed. In this paper, we propose a novel unsupervised feature selection framework, LUFS, for linked data in social media. We utilize a recent developed concept of social dimensions from social network analysis to extract relations among linked data as groups, and define social dimension regularization inspired by Linear Discriminant Analysis to mathematically model these relations. We then propose the concept of pseudo-class labels to develop a new unsupervised feature selection framework by ensuring that instances in a social dimension are similar, and otherwise dissimilar. Experimental results on two datasets from real-world social media websites show that the proposed method can effectively exploit link information in comparison with the state-of-the-art unsupervised feature selection methods.

In social media networks, the availability of various link formation can lead to networks with relationships of different strengths [33, 28], which means that weak links and strong links are often mixed together. We plan to incorporate tie strength prediction into LUFS to further exploit link information. Also we believe that the concept of pseudo-class label introduced in the paper is a powerful means to effectively constrain the learning space of unsupervised feature selection and can be extended to different applications without labeled data but additional information.

Acknowledgments

The work is, in part, supported by ARO (#025071) and NSF (#0812551).

7. REFERENCES

[1] A. Argyriou, T. Evgeniou, and M. Pontil. Multi-task feature learning. *NIPS*, 19:41, 2007.

[2] S. Boyd and L. Vandenberghe. *Convex optimization.* Cambridge Univ Pr, 2004.

[3] D. Cai, C. Zhang, and X. He. Unsupervised feature selection for multi-cluster data. In *KDD*, pages 333–342. ACM, 2010.

[4] C. Constantinopoulos, M. Titsias, and A. Likas. Bayesian feature and model selection for gaussian mixture models. *TPAMI*, pages 1013–1018, 2006.

[5] C. Ding, D. Zhou, X. He, and H. Zha. R 1-pca: rotational invariant l 1-norm principal component analysis for robust subspace factorization. In *Proceedings of the 23rd international conference on Machine learning*, pages 281–288. ACM, 2006.

[6] R. Duda, P. Hart, D. Stork, et al. *Pattern classification*, volume 2. wiley New York, 2001.

[7] J. Dy and C. Brodley. Feature selection for unsupervised learning. *Journal of Machine Learning Research*, 5:845–889, 2004.

[8] J. G. Dy and C. E. Brodley. Feature subset selection and order identification for unsupervised learning. In *Proceedings of the Seventeenth International Conference on Machine Learning*, pages 247–254, 2000.

[9] J. G. Dy and C. E. Brodley. Visualization and interactive feature selection for unsupervised data. In *KDD*, pages 360–364, 2000.

[10] J. G. Dy, C. E. Brodley, A. C. Kak, L. S. Broderick, and A. M. Aisen. Unsupervised feature selection applied to content-based retrieval of lung images. *IEEE Transactions on Pattern Analysis and Machine Intelligence*, 25(3):373–378, 2003.

[11] E. Erosheva, S. Fienberg, and J. Lafferty. Mixed-membership models of scientific publications. *Proceedings of the National Academy of Sciences of the United States of America*, 101(Suppl 1):5220, 2004.

[12] I. Guyon, J. Weston, S. Barnhill, and V. Vapnik. Gene selection for cancer classification using support vector machines. *Machine learning*, 46(1):389–422, 2002.

[13] M. Hall. Correlation-based feature selection for discrete and numeric class machine learning. In *Proceedings of Seventeenth International Conference on Machine Learning (ICML-00)*. Morgan Kaufmann Publishers, 2000.

[14] X. He, D. Cai, and P. Niyogi. Laplacian score for feature selection. *NIPS*, 18:507, 2006.

[15] R. Horn and C. Johnson. *Matrix analysis*. Cambridge Univ Pr, 1990.

[16] G. John, R. Kohavi, and K. Pfleger. Irrelevant feature and the subset selection problem. In W. Cohen and H. H., editors, *Machine Learning: Proceedings of the Eleventh International Conference*, pages 121–129, New Brunswick, N.J., 1994. Rutgers University.

[17] Y. Kim, W. Street, and F. Menczer. Feature selection for unsupervised learning via evolutionary search. In *KDD*, pages 365–369, 2000.

[18] H. Liu and H. Motoda. *Computational methods of feature selection*. Chapman & Hall, 2008.

[19] H. Liu and L. Yu. Toward integrating feature selection algorithms for classification and clustering. *IEEE Transactions on Knowledge and Data Engineering*, 17(4):491, 2005.

[20] H. Liu and L. Yu. Toward integrating feature selection algorithms for classification and clustering. *IEEE Trans. on Knowledge and Data Engineering*, 17(3):1–12, 2005.

[21] J. Liu, S. Ji, and J. Ye. Multi-task feature learning via efficient l 2, 1-norm minimization. In *Proceedings of the Twenty-Fifth Conference on Uncertainty in Artificial Intelligence*, pages 339–348. AUAI Press, 2009.

[22] U. Luxburg. A tutorial on spectral clustering. *Statistics and Computing*, 17(4):395–416, 2007.

[23] P. Marsden and N. Friedkin. Network studies of social influence. *Sociological Methods and Research*, 22(1):127–151, 1993.

[24] M. E. J. Newman and M. Girvan. Finding and evaluating community structure in networks. *Physical review E*, 69(2):26113, 2004.

[25] F. Nie, H. Huang, X. Cai, and C. Ding. Efficient and robust feature selection via joint l21-norms minimization. NIPS, 2010.

[26] H. Peng, F. Long, and C. Ding. Feature selection based on mutual information: criteria of max-dependency, max-relevance, and min-redundancy. *IEEE Transactions on pattern analysis and machine intelligence*, pages 1226–1238, 2005.

[27] V. Roth and T. Lange. Feature selection in clustering problems. *NIPS*, 16:473–480, 2004.

[28] J. Tang, H. Gao, and H. Liu. mtrust: Discerning multi-faceted trust in a connected world. In *The ACM international conference on Web search and data mining*, 2012.

[29] J. Tang and H. Liu. Feature selection with linked data in social media. In *SIAM International Conference on Data Mining*, 2012.

[30] L. Tang and H. Liu. Relational learning via latent social dimensions. In *KDD*, pages 817–826. ACM, 2009.

[31] X. Wang, L. Tang, H. Gao, and H. Liu. Discovering overlapping groups in social media. In *2010 IEEE International Conference on Data Mining*, pages 569–578. IEEE, 2010.

[32] L. Wolf and A. Shashua. Feature selection for unsupervised and supervised inference: the emergence of sparsity in a weighted-based approach. *Journal of Machine Learning Research*, 6:1855–1887, 2005.

[33] R. Xiang, J. Neville, and M. Rogati. Modeling relationship strength in online social networks. In *Proceedings of the 19th international conference on World wide web*, pages 981–990. ACM, 2010.

[34] Y. Yang, H. Shen, Z. Ma, Z. Huang, and X. Zhou. L21-norm regularized discriminative feature selection for unsupervised learning. In *Proceedings of the Twenty-Second International Joint Conference on Artificial Intelligence*, 2011.

[35] Z. Zhao and H. Liu. Spectral feature selection for supervised and unsupervised learning. In *Proceedings of the 24th international conference on Machine learning*, pages 1151–1157. ACM, 2007.

[36] Z. Zhao, L. Wang, and H. Liu. Efficient spectral feature selection with minimum redundancy. In *Proceedings of the Twenty-4th AAAI Conference on Artificial Intelligence (AAAI)*, 2010.

Model Mining for Robust Feature Selection

Adam Woznica
University of Geneva
Department of Computer Science
7, route de Drize
Battelle - building A
1227 Carouge, Switzerland
Adam.Woznica@unige.ch

Phong Nguyen
University of Geneva
Department of Computer Science
7, route de Drize
Battelle - building A
1227 Carouge, Switzerland
Phong.Nguyen@unige.ch

Alexandros Kalousis
University Of Applied Sciences
School of Management
Department of Business Informatics
7, route de Drize
Battelle - building F
1227 Carouge, Switzerland
Alexandros.Kalousis@hesge.ch

ABSTRACT

A common problem with most of the feature selection methods is that they often produce feature sets–models–that are not stable with respect to slight variations in the training data. Different authors tried to improve the feature selection stability using ensemble methods which aggregate different feature sets into a single model. However, the existing ensemble feature selection methods suffer from two main shortcomings: (i) the aggregation treats the features independently and does not account for their interactions, and (ii) a single feature set is returned, nevertheless, in various applications there might be more than one feature sets, potentially redundant, with similar information content. In this work we address these two limitations. We present a general framework in which we mine over different feature models produced from a given dataset in order to extract patterns over the models. We use these patterns to derive more complex feature model aggregation strategies that account for feature interactions, and identify core and distinct feature models. We conduct an extensive experimental evaluation of the proposed framework where we demonstrate its effectiveness over a number of high-dimensional problems from the fields of biology and text-mining.

Categories and Subject Descriptors

I.5.2 [**Pattern Recognition**]: Design Methodology—*Feature evaluation and selection*

General Terms

Algorithms, Performance, Experimentation

Keywords

feature selection, stability, model mining, high-dimensional data, classification

1. INTRODUCTION

High-dimensional datasets are becoming more and more abundant in the field of data mining. A traditional approach of tackling the high-dimensional learning problems is based on the application of feature selection methods to select a set of features–feature models–as small as possible that accurately describe the learning examples.

A common problem with most of the feature selection methods is that they often produce feature models that are not stable (or robust) with respect to slight variations in the training set. This can be problematic when we want to identify a handful of features which are important for the given mining problem and present them to the domain experts together with quantifiable evidence of their robustness and stability. A typical application domain in which the stability and robustness of the selected features are of paramount importance is biology. The analysis of biological samples using high-throughput technologies produces learning instances of very high dimensionality, tens of thousands or even hundreds of thousands. Very often this high dimensionality is coupled with a limited number of samples. In such cases, the low stability of the selected features, often coupled with their weak discriminatory power, raises questions about the scientific significance of these discoveries [10, 9].

We can identify two sources of feature model instability. The first is a high level of feature redundancy (a situation that is very typical in biological problems); this can make the feature selection methods to produce unstable feature sets simply because they can select different features among the redundant features. In such cases very different feature sets can be equivalent predictors of some outcome because they describe different aspects of the same phenomenon. The second major cause of instability is the "underspecification" in the sample space with respect to the feature dimensionality, a problem often described as the High Dimensionality Small Sample Size (HDSSS) problem. In the HDSSS setting we do not have adequate statistics, and very often slight variations in the training data can produce radical changes in the feature models. For example, it was shown in [6] that for typical biological problems at least one order of magnitude more training instances are needed to reach an acceptable level of feature stability. However, the HDSSS problem is here to stay since sample availability is often limited due to unsurpassable practical constrains, while our ability to measure different variables is ever increasing.

A common approach to derive more robust feature sets is

to use ensemble feature selection over bootstrap samples [18, 1, 9]. More specifically, the feature selection algorithm we want to "stabilize" is applied on a number of random subsamples of the training data, and the different outputs are subsequently aggregated to produce a new, hopefully more stable, feature set. Almost all the existing algorithms focus on feature selection methods that produce feature rankings (or feature scores that can be trivially converted to rankings) and output an aggregated ranking, based on which the desired number of features can be finally selected. The existing aggregation strategies are most often based on the averaging of the individual rankings [18, 1], or the (soft) frequency of selection of individual attributes [15, 16, 9]. A common characteristic of all these methods is that they treat the features independently and do not consider feature interactions. Moreover, from the existing literature there is no consensus of whether the aggregated feature sets, in addition to the boosted stability, also bring an improvement in terms of predictive performance.

Although the existing approaches based on ensemble feature selection are conceptually simple and were shown to give rise to more stable feature sets they have two main limitations. First, as already mentioned, the aggregation operators are usually based on simple averaging techniques that consider attributes independently, and as such they often generate "artificial" structures that would not have been produced by the original feature selection method. For example average feature ranks produced over the models of a sparsity-imposed algorithm, such as LASSO, most likely do not correspond to any output of that algorithm [21]. In general, for feature models whose elements are generated independently from each other, such as the ones obtained by univariate feature selection methods, the standard techniques based on simple averaging are expected to be appropriate. In cases where the components of the feature selection models are not independent, a typical example of these are models produced by multivariate feature selection methods, the simple strategies might not be sufficient, and other techniques that account for feature interactions is needed.

The second limitation is that the existing aggregation techniques return a unique feature model. Nevertheless, in problems with high levels of redundancy it might very well be the case that there are more than one feature sets, redundant between them, with similar information content. In such situations the domain experts might prefer the identification of *a number of alternative feature models*, all of which describe different aspects of the same problem.

In this work we address these limitations and present a general framework in which we mine over feature models to extract feature patterns that we will use to derive more stable feature models and to identify distinct but equivalent, in terms of predictive behavior, feature models. We define aggregation operators over the feature models which we exploit to aggregate and summarize the different feature models. The model aggregation operators we formalize range from the simplest strategies that treat attributes independently, to the more complex ones that are structure-preserving and account for feature interactions. We perform an in-depth empirical study where we evaluate our framework on a number of biological and text mining datasets where we demonstrate the effectiveness of our approach.

The remainder of this paper is organized as follows. In Section 2 we present the feature model mining framework. In Section 3 we present the experimental setup that we will use evaluate our framework, and in Section 4 we present the experimental results. In Section 5 we review the related work, and we summarize our work in Section 6.

2. FEATURE MODEL MINING

In this section we present a general framework for feature model mining and describe a number of mining methods that operate over feature models. Our goal is to improve the stability and robustness of the feature selection as well as to provide the means to identify alternative feature selection models of equal quality.

We will first introduce some notation. Let $\mathcal{D} = \{(\boldsymbol{x}_1, y_1), \ldots, (\boldsymbol{x}_n, y_n)\}$ be a labeled dataset, where $\boldsymbol{x}_i \in \mathbb{R}^p$ is the i-th instance and $y_i \in \mathbf{Y}$ its class label. Feature selection identifies the most important features so that instances can be represented in a lower dimensional space without a significant loss of discriminatory power; most often, the number of desired features m is controlled by the user. Following the ideas that appeared recently in ensemble feature selection [18, 9] we generate b *base feature models* from b bootstrap subsamples of D using a given feature selection method. These base models will become the target of the feature model mining that we will present soon. Feature selection models come roughly in the following three flavors:

- feature weightings: $\boldsymbol{w} = (w_1, \ldots, w_p)^T$, $w_l \in \mathbb{R}$,
- feature rankings: $\boldsymbol{r} = (r_1, \ldots, r_p)^T$, $r_l \in \mathbb{N}^+$ (we assume that the values of r_l can be non-unique),
- feature subsets: $\boldsymbol{s} = (s_1, \ldots, s_p)^T$, $s_l \in \{0, 1\}$, with 0 and 1 indicating absence and presence of a feature.

In this work, we focus on the $\boldsymbol{r}$ and $\boldsymbol{s}$ representations; the output of a feature selection method that produces feature weightings can be always converted to a ranking.[1] We denote by $\mathcal{R} = \{\boldsymbol{r}_1, \ldots, \boldsymbol{r}_b\}$ and $\mathcal{S} = \{\boldsymbol{s}_1, \ldots, \boldsymbol{s}_b\}$ the feature rankings and subsets produced from the b bootstrap subsamples of the given dataset by the application of a given feature selection method. We will present a number of unsupervised feature model mining operators f which operate over $\mathcal{R}$ or $\mathcal{S}$, in fact most of the methods that we will present will work with the $\mathcal{S}$ representation. The different operators will aggregate the base feature models, while taking into account the feature model structures and systematically identify alternative feature models. By feature model structures here we mean the specific combinations of features, reflecting feature interactions and dependencies, that different feature selection algorithms are able to uncover according to their underlying learning bias. The signature of the feature model mining operators will be:

$$f \; : \; \mathcal{F} \longrightarrow \{\boldsymbol{s}'_i\}_{i=1}^k$$

where $\mathcal{F}$ is either $\mathcal{R}$ or $\mathcal{S}$, and k is a user specified parameter that defines the number of alternative feature models. We classify the operators to two groups according to the aggregation strategy they follow. In the first group, *Single Model Aggregation*, we have strategies that aggregate the different base feature models into a single model, i.e. $k = 1$. In the second group, *Multiple Model Aggregation*, we have strategies that produce a number of distinct models.

[1] [2] argues against directly aggregating weights–scores $\boldsymbol{w}_i$, especially those that correspond to p-values of univariate statistical tests.

2.1 Single Model Aggregation Strategies

We will start with a description of the first group which is the one that contains most of the proposed strategies. We separate the strategies of this group to different categories with respect to how they construct their final model, in terms of the model components of the base feature models, and how close is the final solution they produce to those that the feature selection algorithm would have generated.

Univariate Strategies.

In this category we have just two strategies *avgRank* and *mostFreq*, that produce the final model by looking at the individual feature scores, obtained either from their ranks or from their frequencies. More precisely, in *avgRank* [18, 1, 2, 9] the $score_l$ of the lth feature is the average of its rankings, i.e. $score_l = \sum_{i=1}^{b} r_{il}$. In *mostFreq* [15, 16, 9] we consider the frequency of the features that appear in $\mathcal{S}$, i.e. $score_l = \sum_{i=1}^{b} s_{il}$. In both cases, the final set of m features is selected according to their $score_l$. These two strategies make no effort what so ever to capture feature model structures since they treat the features independently. If one used a univariate feature selection to generate the base feature sets this is no problem, since no such structure exists. However, if the base feature sets have been produced by a multivariate feature selection algorithm, then it is probable that the final feature set will not reflect particular feature combinations that have been found informative by the feature selection algorithm since these aggregation strategies do not consider longer structures.

Model Component Combination Strategies.

Here we consider strategies that search for frequent itemsets over the different base feature sets, and then establish the union of the most frequent itemsets, until the number of distinct features in the union reaches m, i.e. the desired feature cardinality. One can think this strategy as the combination of frequent "model fragments" in to a final single feature model.

To limit the number of returned frequent itemsets, which depending on the dataset and the feature selection method can render the method computationally infeasible, we only focus on the frequent *maximal* [3] and *closed* [20] itemsets, giving respectively rise to the *maxApr* and *closedApr* strategies. An itemset is closed if no superset has the same support, and maximal if no superset is frequent. We note that for a given support threshold we have FMI $\subseteq$ FCI $\subseteq$ FI, where FCI, FMI and FI are respectively the set of all the frequent closed, all the frequent maximal, and all the frequent itemsets. The elements in FCI that are not in FMI necessarily have non-lower support with respect to those of FMI, and hence are in general shorter than those of FMI. Additionally, the elements in FCI are more redundant (as measured by the average number of items they share) than the elements of FMI. Both *maxApr* and *closedApr* can be seen as an extension of *mostFreq*; in the latter method the cardinality of the returned itemsets is trivially restricted to one and the threshold is specified not on the minimum support but on the number of returned itemsets.

Exact Structure Preservation Strategies.

In this category we have a number of strategies which select in a principled manner one of the base feature models, namely the most representative one. Clearly, the solutions fully reflect the learning bias of the feature selection algorithm that generate the base feature sets. The different approaches rely on different combinations of frequent itemset discovery and clustering techniques.

The simplest strategy of this category is *mostRep*. Here, the final feature model is simply the median model of the set of base models S. We use the median instead of the average because the former preserves the model structure since the median is actually an element of the underlying set. The underlying assumption of the *mostRep* strategy is that there is a meaningful median element over S. This is a valid assumption only if the feature models form a single unimodal cluster. However, in general we cannot assume that S has such unimodal structure. We thus introduce the *largeMed* strategy which uses the k-medoid clustering algorithm and the average silhouette criterion [12] to determine the best number of clusters and returns as the final feature model the medoid of the largest cluster. As before we rely in k-medoids instead of k-means because the averaging process does not necessarily preserve the feature model structures discovered by the feature selection algorithm. In this category we have two more strategies, *medMaxApr* and *medClosedApr*, which can be seen as the counterparts of *maxApr* and *closedApr* that preserve exactly the feature model structure of the feature selection algorithm. Both of them define IS_{top} as the set that contains the frequent feature sets with the top support. Then, they determine all base feature models that are supersets of at least one element of the IS_{top}, and constitute the S' set of base feature models. The final feature model is the median feature set of S'. In that sense these two strategies try to find the most representative base feature set using as initial seeds the most frequent feature itemsets.

Overall, what we have in the single model aggregation strategies is a spectrum of different approaches which are distinguished according to the degree to which they respect the structure of the original base feature models and the bias of the feature selection algorithm that produced them. At the lower end we have the Univariate Strategies (*US*) which completely ignore these using an univariate approach to select the features that will be included in the final feature model. In the middle of the spectrum we have the Model Component Combination Strategies (*MCCS*) which detect frequent model fragments–subsets of the base feature sets–that appear frequently within the base feature sets and produce the final model by bringing together these model fragments. Finally, we have at the higher end the Exact Structure Preservation Strategies (*ESPS*) that output as a final model one of the base feature sets of S; the methods of this group differ on how they select the prototypical feature set. The simplest method returns just the median of S, followed by the method that returns the median of the largest cluster, to the most complicated that return the median of the base feature sets that are supersets of the most frequent itemsets.

2.2 Multiple Model Aggregation Strategies

The aggregation strategies of this group take as input the base feature models and produce as output k different feature models. The simplest strategy of the group, *allMed*, applies the k-medoid clustering algorithm on set of the base feature models S and returns the medoid of each cluster. Clearly, the cardinality of the k feature models is dictated by that of the base feature models, so if it is m for the latter, it will also be m for the former. In addition to the clustering-based approach we also have two of frequent pattern-based approaches. The first one, *allClosedApr*, produces as output k feature models that correspond to the k highest support frequent closed itemsets.[2] Unlike *allMed* here we do not have control over the cardinality of the aggregated feature sets. It might very well be the case that this cardinality will be quite low since we are selecting the top frequent itemsets; depending on the dataset and the value of k the most frequent itemsets can easily consist of only single items—features. In order to be able to better control the cardinality of the final feature sets we derive an alternative of this strategy which we name *medClosedApr*. Here instead of simply returning as feature sets directly the top k itemsets we first get all the base feature models from S that contain the itemset(s) with the highest support, and return the corresponding k medoids. Like that each aggregated feature model will now have as many features as the base feature models.

3. EXPERIMENTS

In this section we investigate the behavior and performance of the different model aggregation strategies presented in Section 2. We have two suites of experiments dealing with the single and multiple model aggregation strategies.

We start with the single model aggregation strategies and evaluate them, over a panel of datasets and feature selection methods, both in terms of the stability of the aggregate feature models that they produce as well as in terms of the classification error they result to when these models are passed to a number of classification algorithms. Concretely, given a feature selection algorithm we generate b base feature models which will then be aggregated into a single one by each one of the different aggregation strategies. On each one of the aggregated models we train a classifier using a given classification algorithm. One of the primary goals of these experiments is to see whether the model aggregation strategies that account for the base feature model structures can bring an improvement over the univariate aggregation strategies.

In the second suite of experiments we examine the behavior of the multiple model aggregation strategies. We evaluate them with respect to a number of dimensions, namely the diversity of the multiple feature models they produce, the average errors of classifiers trained on them using some given classification algorithm, as well as the prediction agreement of the produced classifiers. What we want to examine is whether using the multiple model aggregation strategies we can produce very diverse feature models, i.e. feature models that deliver different descriptions of the classification problem, which give rise to accurate classifiers, i.e. the feature models are discriminatory, and that are "semantically similar", i.e. deliver the same predictions when they are asked to classify the same instance.

We set the cardinality of the base and the aggregate feature models m to 20. We performed additional experiments with different values of this parameter; however, these results reveal similar trends. We set the number of bootstrap samples b to 150. We implemented feature aggregation and performance computation (Section 3.1) using the R language.

3.1 Performance Measures

Stability Estimation.

To estimate the stability of feature models produced by a feature selection algorithm, or by a single model aggregation strategy coupled with a given feature selection algorithm, we compare the feature models generated over a number of variations of the input dataset. In this study we opted for N-fold stratified cross-validation (CV) with N = 10, resulting in a set of N feature sets $\mathcal{S}' = \{\boldsymbol{s}_1, \ldots, \boldsymbol{s}_N\}$. The different feature models are cross-compared and the average similarity sim_{avg} is computed:

$$sim_{avg}(\mathcal{S}') = \frac{2\sum_{1 \le i < j \le N} sim(\boldsymbol{s}_i, \boldsymbol{s}_j)}{N(N-1)} \quad (1)$$

where $sim(\cdot, \cdot)$ is a similarity measure between two feature models. In this work we follow [11] and define $sim(\boldsymbol{s}_i, \boldsymbol{s}_j) = \frac{|\boldsymbol{f}_i \cap \boldsymbol{f}_j|}{|\boldsymbol{f}_i \cup \boldsymbol{f}_j|}$, where $\boldsymbol{f}_i$ is a set of identifiers of selected features from $\boldsymbol{s}_i$ and $|\cdot|$ denotes the set cardinality. The sim measure takes values in $[0, 1]$, zero when there is no overlap and one when the two sets are identical, and allows comparisons also between feature sets of different cardinalities. We also note that the performance measure (1) will be also used in the second set of experiments to measure the diversity of the feature models generated by methods from Section 2.2; in this case $sim(\cdot, \cdot)$ will correspond to the average similarity between all the k feature models.

Error Estimation.

As already mentioned, to asses the predictive performance of a feature model aggregation method we estimate the error of a classification algorithm trained over the feature model produced by the given aggregation method. We estimate this performance measure using exactly the same fold separation as the one in the 10-fold CV used in the stability estimation.

Predictive Agreement Estimation.

To quantify the predictive agreement of two classification models c_1 and c_2 trained over the same input dataset but using different feature sets we measure the percentage of identical predictions over some test dataset $\mathcal{D}' = \{\boldsymbol{x}'_1, \ldots, \boldsymbol{x}'_l\}$. Concretely, we compute $agree(c_1, c_2, \mathcal{D}') = \frac{\sum_{1 \le i \le l} \delta(c_1(\boldsymbol{x}'_i), c_2(\boldsymbol{x}'_i))}{l}$ where $c_{\{1|2\}}(\boldsymbol{x}'_i)$ is the classification label assigned to the instance $\boldsymbol{x}'_i$ by the $c_{\{1|2\}}$ model; and $\delta(a, b) = 1$ if $a = b$, and 0 otherwise. The overall agreement of the k models produced by a multiple model aggregation strategy is then given by:

$$agree(\mathcal{D}') = \frac{2\sum_{1 \le i < j \le k} agree(c_i, c_j, \mathcal{D}')}{k(k-1)} \quad (2)$$

The final agreement estimation is the average of (2) over the 10-CV folds (again, we have exactly the same folds as in the error and stability estimation).

Statistical Significance and Methods Ranking.

We control the statistical differences of the errors of two methods using the McNemar's test, and the paired T-test for

[2] We also defined and experimented with a similar strategy obtained using the concepts of frequent maximal itemsets; however, its behavior was similar to that of *allClosedApr*.

the stability and prediction agreement; for all of them we set the significance level to 0.05. To acquire a better picture of the relative performances of the different methods we establish a ranking schema for each one of the performance measures based on the results of the pairwise comparisons. More precisely, if one method is significantly better than another one, it is credited with one point; if there is no significant difference then both are credited with 0.5 points; finally, if it is significantly worse it is credited with zero points. Clearly, the more points one method scores the higher its ranking will be. If we compare n different methods then the maximum number of points that one can obtain is $n-1$ if it is significantly better than all the other methods; if there is no significant difference then each will get $(n-1)/2$ points.

3.2 Datasets

We experiment with high-dimensional data from three application domains: proteomics, genomics and text mining. The proteomics datasets, *ovarian*, *prostate*, and *stroke*, are mass spectrometry datasets. The genomics datasets, *leukemia*, *nervous*, *colon*, are DNA-microarray datasets. The text mining datasets, *disease*, *alt*ernative, describe classifications of sentences to relevant or non-relevant to given topics; features are word frequencies. The references to these datasets are in [11]. In Table 1 we give a short description of them.

3.3 Feature Selection and Classification Algorithms

To create the base feature models we will use the following feature selection methods: *Information Gain (IG)*, *Chi-Square (CHI)* [5], *Symmetrical Uncertainty (SYM)* [5], *ReliefF (RELIEF)* [17], *SVMRFE* [7], *SVMONE* and *Correlation Based Feature Selection (CFS)* [8]. The first three methods are *univariate* feature selection methods; the remaining are *multivariate* methods that are in principle able to detect and exploit feature interactions. *RELIEF* delivers a weighting of the features by computing distances among each of the training instances and their 10-nearest neighbors, and estimating the contribution of each feature in these distances. *SVMRFE* is based on repetitive applications of linear *SVM* where the P% lowest ranked features are eliminated at each iteration. The ranks of the features are based on the order in which they are eliminated and the weights assigned to them by the linear *SVM*. In our experiments we set P to 10% and the complexity parameter C of the linear *SVM* to 0.5. We also included a simple linear support vector machine (*SVMONE*) which is equivalent to *SVMRFE* with a single iteration. *CFS* evaluates the worth of a subset of attributes by considering the individual predictive ability of each feature along with the degree of redundancy between them. Subsets of features that are highly correlated with the class while having low inter-correlation are preferred. We note that *CFS* is the only method in this study which automatically determines the appropriate feature cardinality and hence we do not control for the m parameter. We used the WEKA implementation of these algorithms.

Since, as we mentioned, feature selection and feature model aggregation methods do not deliver classification models we had to use classification algorithms in order to train from their results classification models that we can use to estimate the discriminatory power of the feature models that they produce. We have chosen the classification algorithms in such a manner that they represent distinct learning paradigms. We experiment with *Decision Tree (J48)*, *SVM* and *1NN* learning algorithms. We used the WEKA implementation of the algorithms; we set the parameters to default values, except for the C parameter of *SVM* which was set to 0.5.

Table 1: Statistics on the datasets. n, p and c denote respectively the number of training instances, data dimensionality and the number of classes.

Datasets	n	p	c
prostate	322	390	2
ovarian	253	385	2
stroke	208	172	2
leukemia	72	7129	2
colon	62	2000	2
nervous	60	7129	2
alt	4157	2112	2
disease	3237	2376	2

4. RESULTS

We will first experiment with and study the performance of the different single model aggregation strategies, and then that of the multiple model aggregation strategies.

4.1 Single Model Aggregation Strategies

Each one of the single model aggregation operators was applied on the b base feature models produced by each one of the seven different feature selection algorithms over a given dataset. The resulting aggregated feature models were subsequently passed to the three classification algorithms in order to have an estimate of their discriminatory power. The results over the different classification algorithms do not differ considerably so we will present only those of the *SVM*. We fix a feature selection algorithm and we rank the different aggregation operators with respect to the predictive error of the *SVM* models produced over their respective aggregated feature models, and with respect to the stability of their aggregated feature models. Ranking is done as described previously according to the points accumulated in terms of the significant wins and losses. Since for a given feature selection method we are comparing eight aggregation operators, plus one baseline which is the plain application of the given feature selection method (*nobagg*), the maximum number of points that one operator can score for a given dataset, if it is significantly better than all the rest, is eight; if there is no difference then everybody will all get four points.

In Table 2 we give these error and stability ranks for each aggregation operator averaged over all the different datasets with which we experimented. In this table the upper value in each cell is the error-based rank of the aggregation operator (indicated by the row) for the given feature selection algorithm (indicated in the column header); the bottom value is the respective stability rank. Clearly, error takes precedence over stability; a very high stability rank is useless if it is accompanied with a very low error rank.

Examining the averaged ranks (the last column of Table 2) we see that the best method in terms of its average error rank is *closedApr* that scores 5.6 points, followed by *maxApr* with 5.0 points, and *mostFreq* with 4.9; the latter has exactly the same number of points—rank—as the baseline method,

Table 2: Average prediction error & stability scores of the *single model aggregation operators* over all datasets when *SVM* is used as the classification algorithm. In each cell the upper value is the average error score of the model mining operator given in the row, over the different model mining operators, for the feature selection algorithm specified in the column header; the lower value is the respective stability score. The final column gives the respective averages for each model mining operator over the different feature selection algorithms. The larger the values the higher the rank of the method, the top rank per column is indicated in bold.

		Univariate Feature Selection			Multivariate Feature Selection				
		IG	*CHI*	*SYM*	*RELIEF*	*SVMONE*	*SVMRFE*	*CFS*	Avg
	nobagg	5.9	6.0	4.4	4.8	4.6	5.0	4.0	4.9
		6.1	**6.4**	5.8	5.9	4.3	3.7	4.7	5.3
US	*avgRank*	**6.1**	5.0	5.4	3.4	5.5	4.0	1.5	4.4
		7.2	6.2	**6.7**	5.6	6.1	**6.8**	4.8	6.2
	mostFreq	4.9	5.4	5.1	4.3	4.5	4.6	5.5	4.9
		5.9	6.3	6.4	**6.3**	**6.8**	6.7	**6.9**	**6.5**
MCCS	*maxApr*	4.9	4.8	4.6	4.6	5.2	5.2	5.8	5.0
		4.8	4.9	4.6	5.1	6.2	5.6	6.1	5.3
	closedApr	5.1	**6.4**	**6.1**	4.9	5.1	**5.8**	**6.1**	**5.6**
		5.8	6.0	6.3	6.0	6.6	6.7	6.5	6.3
ESPS	*medMaxApr*	0.9	0.9	0.9	1.5	1.0	1.1	2.3	1.2
		2.1	2.4	2.0	2.3	1.9	2.3	2.2	2.2
	medClosedApr	1.8	1.8	1.7	2.1	1.5	1.8	3.2	2.0
		2.1	2.0	2.0	2.2	1.9	2.1	2.2	2.1
	largeMed	3.5	3.1	4.4	5.0	2.6	3.5	4.5	3.8
		0.2	0.0	0.0	0.0	0.0	0.0	0.2	0.1
	mostRep	3.0	2.8	3.4	**5.4**	**5.9**	5.0	3.1	4.1
		1.9	1.8	2.2	2.6	2.1	2.1	2.4	2.2

nobagg. Essentially, the two strategies that manage to improve the predictive performance over the baseline are the two strategies that combine model components. When it comes to the average stability rank, the top ranked aggregation operator is the *mostFreq* with 6.5 points, closely followed by *closedApr* with 6.3 points, and *avgRank* with 6.2 points; all three methods are better than the baseline in terms of the stability which scores 5.3 points. The four remaining aggregation operators, *medMaxApr, medClosedApr, largeMed* and *mostRep*, do not seem to bring any improvement neither with respect to error nor to stability compared to the baseline method. Note that all of them are exact structure preservation operators, i.e. they return as the final feature model one of the b base feature models.

The difference in the performance, both in terms of error and stability, of *closedApr* and *maxApr* is puzzling since the two methods follow the same principle to produce the final feature set, i.e. the combination of frequent feature model components. Their only difference is that the first makes use of frequent closed itemsets, while the latter relies on frequent maximal itemsets. In order to try to understand this difference, we took a look at the number of top itemsets that each of the two methods needs to combine, in order to reach the desired number of m selected features, as well as the average size and support of these itemsets. In Table 3 we give the results for the *alt* dataset; however, the patterns that we will right away describe are the same over the different datasets. First, observe that the average itemset cardinality of the two methods is very similar: around 12 and 13 for the univariate feature selection methods, six to seven for the multivariate feature selection methods, and four to five for the *CFS* feature selection method. This difference between the univariate and multivariate methods is logical given the fact that univariate feature selection methods do not model for feature interactions and select a number individual (likely redundant) features with a similar (and potentially high) support from the b samples of the data; consequently, the combinations of these individual features will also have a high support. On the other hand, the multivariate methods exploit feature interactions and hence the selected subsets of features will have a lower support and will be shorter in length. The difference in support of frequent itemsets between these two classes of feature selection methods can be observed in Table 3. The lowest average itemset cardinality for *CFS* could be explained by the fact in this algorithm we do not control for resulting feature cardinalities.

When we now look at the average number of itemsets that need to be merged in order to arrive at the desired number of features we see that *maxApr* gets there with much less itemsets, on average 20% of that *closedApr* needs. Thus, the itemsets produced by *maxApr* are much more diverse in terms of the features they contain compared to those of *closedApr*, which, as already mentioned in Section 2.1, is expected given that the itemsets produced by *closedApr* include those produced by *maxApr*. In the former method the itemsets are variants around a core set of features which explains why it needs so many more itemsets to get to the desired number of features. This also gives us a hint on why there is a difference in performance between *closedApr* and *maxApr*: the former method aggregates shorter and more general core sets of features with a higher support, while *maxApr* aggregates longer sets of features that are placed "lower" in the apriori lattice, but which are nevertheless overly specific and do not "generalize" well. The last column in Table 3 demonstrates the lower average support of itemsets produced by *maxApr* in comparison with *closedApr*.

Overall, the two univariate aggregation operators achieve an important improvement over the baseline in terms of the stability of the final feature model they produce; however, their predictive performance is the same, *mostFreq*, or even worse, *avgRank*, than the baseline. The operator that achieves the best predictive performance is *closedApr*;

Table 3: **Averages of: number of frequent itemsets required to attain m distinct features, itemsets size, and support, for the *alt* dataset.**

FS	# ItemSets	Size	Support
	maxApr		
IG	12.50±3.10	13.91±0.35	0.38±0.08
CHI	12.30±3.02	14.18±0.35	0.41±0.04
SYM	16.80±4.47	13.78±0.38	0.35±0.05
RELIEF	32.20±8.61	7.49±0.57	0.37±0.03
SVMONE	68.90±32.06	7.26±0.39	0.21±0.06
SVMRFE	44.40±9.62	6.22±0.24	0.18±0.01
CFS	31.10±6.62	4.73±0.40	0.17±0.01
	closedApr		
IG	60.90±19.62	12.92±0.35	0.52±0.07
CHI	64.00±26.60	13.18±0.32	0.56±0.04
SYM	159.30±58.51	12.22±0.42	0.51±0.05
RELIEF	118.40±31.16	6.66±0.57	0.46±0.03
SVMONE	220.70±107.08	6.63±0.34	0.30±0.06
SVMRFE	106.20±41.25	5.82±0.23	0.26±0.01
CFS	164.20±31.34	3.91±0.27	0.28±0.01

its score is better than the baseline, and in addition it has the second best stability score very close to the best. So, overall it comes as the best strategy for feature model aggregation. Remember here that *closedApr* works by combining frequent model fragments into a single model, while the two univariate approaches examine each feature on its own. While the univariate approach can improve the stability, it fails to improve the predictive performance. For the latter capturing larger model structures seems to be more important. The performance of the operators that preserve exactly the feature model structure by picking one of the original base models is quite disappointing. All of them are worse than the baseline method. Among them the ones that combine frequent itemsets and then find the medoids, *medMaxApr* and *medClosedApr*, have the worse performance. The two clustering medoid variants, *largeMed* and *mostRep*, fair a bit better, namely in terms of error, however their stability is equally low. The low stability of the exact structure preserving variants can be explained by the fact that actually they do not perform any kind of aggregation, but try to select among the base models the most representative one, however, by doing so the chances that there will be a larger overlap over the different final models are reduced.

We will now drill further down to the results given in Table 2 in order to get an idea of how the different model aggregation strategies fair with respect to the two distinct feature selection paradigms that we have here, namely univariate and multivariate. While the univariate aggregation strategy *avgRank* seems to have the strongest advantage in the case of univariate feature selection algorithm IG, this advantage is not persistent over the other two univariate feature selection algorithms, CHI and SYM. On the same time the *mostFreq* operator, while similar in spirit to *avgRank*, does not perform particularly well with the univariate feature selection algorithms; for IG and CHI it has a performance that is worse than the baseline with respect to both error and stability. The *closedApr* performance with CHI and SYM is quite good both in terms of error as well as stability. When we examine the four multivariate feature selection algorithms we see that *mostFreq* has an excellent stability performance with all of them, it is ranked top in three of the four. However, in terms of predictive performance it is quite poor, for three out of the four feature selection algorithms it is actually worse than the baseline. The *closedApr* has also a stability performance that is similar to that of *mostFreq*, however, in addition it also has a very good error performance, being better than the baseline method in all four multivariate feature selection algorithms, and the best in two of them.

Overall, while univariate feature aggregation strategies can improve the feature selection stability they fail to deliver similar gains in terms of the predictive performance, compared to the baseline method with no aggregation. Exploiting the feature model structure information, as it is done by the model component combination strategies, can improve not only the stability but also the predictive performance. However, what is important in the latter category is how these model components are discovered, as it is evident by the strong advantage of *closedApr* compared to *maxApr*.

4.2 Multiple Model Aggregation Strategies

We now turn to the experimentation with the multiple model aggregation strategies. We will examine the k multiple models that each strategy computes with respect to the accuracy they achieve, the agreement of their predictions, and their model similarity, i.e. the average number of features they have in common. We want to describe the degree to which we can have different feature models of good predictive performance, that produce similar predictions, and have a relatively small feature overlap. The eventual goal is to provide the domain experts with a more global picture of the mechanism that underlines the training data, than what they would have obtained with a single feature set.

As in the first suite of experiments we evaluate each model aggregation strategy with each one of the seven feature selection algorithms. Subsequently, on each one of the feature models that a given aggregation strategy will output for a given feature selection algorithm, we train a classifier using a given classification algorithm. We report the prediction agreement of the resulting classifiers, computed by (2), their average accuracy, and the average feature model similarity, computed by (1). We estimate these quantities using 10-fold CV. We present the results for all three classification algorithms that we used. For all the model aggregation strategies we set the number of different models to $k = 10$. We performed additional experiments with different values of this parameter; however, these results reveal similar trends. For each model aggregation strategy and classification algorithm we highlight the feature selection algorithm that achieves the top rank according to the statistical significance tests over the different performance measures.

The results for the *leukemia* dataset are given in Table 4 (for other datasets similar trends hold). First, we notice that the multiple models generated by *allClosedApr* are of lower predictive performance, as measured by the average classification error, in comparison with the models obtained by the clustering-based *allMed* strategy; the classification error for *allClosedApr* is on average three times higher than for *allMed*. As already noted in Section 2, this is a result of the fact that unlike *allMed*, in *allClosedApr* we do not control for the cardinality of the aggregated feature sets. In the examined dataset this cardinality is low which naturally leads to low discriminatory power of the feature models; in fact, most of the top frequent itemsets are of cardinality just

Table 4: Average and standard deviation of error and prediction agreement of classifiers trained on the $k = 10$ multiple models produced on the *leukemia* dataset by each one of the *multiple model aggregation strategies* over the different feature selection algorithms. Additionally, average feature model similarity over the k models of each model aggregation strategy and feature selection algorithm. We highlight the top ranked results for each strategy and classifier, for each performance measure.

FS	*J48*		*SVM*		*1NN*		
	agreement	error	agreement	error	agreement	error	similarity
				allMed			
IG	**0.97±0.04**	**0.14±0.08**	**0.98±0.03**	0.06±0.07	**0.93±0.06**	0.08±0.06	0.31±0.03
CHI	**0.97±0.05**	**0.14±0.08**	**0.98±0.02**	0.07±0.08	**0.94±0.05**	0.08±0.06	0.33±0.05
SYM	**0.98±0.04**	**0.15±0.09**	**0.98±0.02**	0.06±0.07	**0.94±0.05**	0.07±0.06	0.45±0.03
RELIEF	0.95±0.04	**0.13±0.09**	**0.97±0.05**	0.06±0.07	**0.94±0.06**	0.08±0.07	0.34±0.04
SVMONE	0.88±0.09	**0.12±0.09**	**0.97±0.03**	0.06±0.07	**0.95±0.05**	0.08±0.06	0.28±0.04
SVMRFE	0.92±0.07	**0.12±0.06**	**0.98±0.02**	**0.03±0.05**	**0.95±0.04**	**0.05±0.05**	0.21±0.03
CFS	0.91±0.03	**0.13±0.08**	0.93±0.04	0.07±0.05	**0.91±0.08**	0.07±0.06	**0.14±0.01**
				allClosedApr			
IG	0.87±0.06	**0.12±0.07**	0.87±0.05	**0.17±0.07**	0.89±0.05	**0.11±0.05**	0.20±0.05
CHI	0.87±0.06	**0.11±0.07**	0.87±0.05	0.18±0.07	0.89±0.05	**0.10±0.05**	0.19±0.06
SYM	**0.92±0.06**	**0.12±0.06**	**0.89±0.06**	0.16±0.09	**0.92±0.07**	**0.10±0.06**	0.29±0.16
RELIEF	0.84±0.10	**0.13±0.08**	0.84±0.08	**0.16±0.06**	0.84±0.09	**0.13±0.08**	0.23±0.07
SVMONE	0.79±0.10	**0.16±0.09**	0.81±0.06	0.20±0.06	0.78±0.11	0.16±0.08	0.20±0.05
SVMRFE	0.81±0.11	**0.13±0.08**	0.82±0.05	0.22±0.05	0.81±0.10	**0.12±0.07**	**0.16±0.05**
CFS	0.84±0.06	**0.12±0.06**	0.86±0.05	0.21±0.06	0.84±0.08	**0.11±0.06**	**0.15±0.03**
				medClosedApr			
IG	**0.97±0.04**	0.15±0.08	**0.98±0.03**	0.06±0.07	0.94±0.06	0.08±0.06	0.32±0.04
CHI	**0.97±0.05**	0.14±0.08	**0.98±0.03**	0.06±0.07	**0.95±0.05**	0.07±0.06	0.33±0.03
SYM	**0.98±0.04**	0.15±0.09	**0.98±0.02**	0.06±0.07	0.94±0.05	0.07±0.06	0.45±0.03
RELIEF	0.95±0.04	0.14±0.09	**0.97±0.05**	0.06±0.07	0.95±0.06	0.08±0.07	0.34±0.04
SVMONE	0.89±0.08	0.13±0.10	**0.97±0.03**	0.06±0.07	0.96±0.04	0.07±0.07	0.28±0.04
SVMRFE	0.92±0.06	**0.11±0.07**	**0.98±0.02**	**0.03±0.05**	0.96±0.04	**0.05±0.05**	0.21±0.03
CFS	0.91±0.04	0.13±0.08	0.93±0.04	0.07±0.05	0.91±0.08	0.07±0.07	**0.14±0.01**

one. The low cardinalities of the resulting multiple models in *allClosedApr* have also a direct effect of the prediction agreement and the average model similarity, which are consistently lower than it is the case for *allMed*. The second observation is that the performance of *medClosedApr*, as measured by the three evaluation metrics, is very similar to that of *allMed*. This a consequence of the fact that a number ($k = 10$) of (frequent closed) itemsets with highest support is contained in a large fraction of base feature models, and hence the input the k-medoids algorithm in both *allMed* and *medClosedApr* is similar, resulting in similar medoids generated by these strategies. Finally, we note the good performance of *SVM* coupled with *allMed* with respect to both agreement and error, and an acceptable level of model similarity. In particular coupling *allMed*, *SVM* and *SVMRFE*, it is possible to generate quite diverse feature signatures (average model similarity of 0.21) which nevertheless give rise to powerful (classification error of 0.03) and "semantically similar" (prediction agreement of 0.98) models. The classification error of *SVM* coupled with *allMed* is not statistically different compared to the corresponding baselines in which we only do standard feature selection and classification (these results are not reported in Table 4).

5. RELATED WORK

The traditional approach to stabilize feature selection algorithms in learning problems with redundant features focuses on selecting relevant and non-redundant feature subsets in a pre-processing step; examples include CFS and Markov blankets. [19] addressed the redundancy problem by grouping correlated features together and treating these groups as the entities over which feature selection will take place; this work was refined in [14]. A related idea was proposed in [21] where the authors identified the problem of instability of LASSO for problems with high feature correlations, and proposed a regularization technique based on mixing different norms ("elastic nets"). All these approaches return a unique set of features. However, in many applications, as argued in this paper, it is more beneficial to be able to identify alternative but equivalent solution sets.

The main difference between the methods from [19, 14, 21] and our framework is that the former consider, explicitly or implicitly, groups of redundant features, which are included or excluded from the model simultaneously, whereas we aim at explicitly providing domain experts with groups of features that account for different aspects of a problem at hand. Moreover, the approaches from [19, 14, 21] consider specific notions of feature redundancy (e.g. the linear correlation in [19]), whereas our framework is more flexible as the notion of redundancy varies and depends on the feature selection algorithms (it is the linear correlation only for *CFS*). Finally, the previous works select the individual subsets within a specialized feature selection algorithm (e.g. regression regularized with the mixed norms [21]), while we identify the different solutions a-posteriori, based on sets of features which can be generated by using virtually any feature selection method.

As already mentioned, in the context of ensemble feature selection, the most popular methods are univariate aggregation strategies. Two more complex exceptions were presented in [4] and [13], both aggregating elements of $\mathcal{R}$. The former method is inspired by the well known PageRank algorithm and can be seen as a direct extension of *mostFreq* where all the *pairs* of top ranked features are considered, and the appearances of the different pairwise feature relationships (feature a ranked before feature b, or vice versa) are counted. These counts give rise to the corresponding frequencies, based on which the final aggregate ranking of attributes is generated. Our aggregation strategies based on frequent itemsets are considerably more general as they can account for higher-order feature interactions (see Table 3). The method from [13] is similar to *mostRep* as it looks for a feature model whose *weighted distance* to all the input models is minimal; the returned ranking does not necessarily appear in the set of input transactions. The authors consider two different distance measures over rankings and weight the elements by various performance measures. In this study we have shown that the single model aggregation strategies based on clustering do not fare well in comparison with the other proposed strategies. We also note that the methods from [4, 13] give rise to an aggregate ranking only for the most discriminating features.

6. CONCLUSION

In this paper we presented a general framework in which we mine over different feature models produced from a given dataset in order to extract patterns over the models. We use these patterns to derive more complex feature model aggregation strategies that account for feature interactions, and identify core and distinct feature models.

We empirically examined our framework on a number of high-dimensional datasets. The empirical evidence suggests that our framework is effective in comparison with the existing aggregation techniques. We demonstrated that the existing univariate aggregation techniques, although appropriate in many cases, are not the best solutions overall. While univariate feature aggregation strategies can improve the feature selection stability they fail to deliver similar gains in terms of the predictive performance, compared to the baseline method with no aggregation. Exploiting the feature model structure information, as it is done by the model component combination strategies, can improve not only the stability but also the predictive performance. What is however important is how these model components are discovered, as it is evident by the strong advantage of *closedApr* compared to *maxApr*. We also observed the poor performance of the operators that preserve exactly the feature model structure by picking one of the original base models. Overall, we recommend the *closedApr* aggregation strategy that provides a good compromise between the stability and predictive performances. When it now comes to the multiple models aggregation strategies we demonstrated that it is possible to construct distinct feature models of good predictive performance, that produce similar predictions, and have a relatively small feature overlap. Such diverse and yet equivalent feature models describe different aspects of the same problem, and hence provide domain experts with a more global picture of the mechanism under study. We recommend the *allMed* technique that is based on the k-medoids clustering algorithm and hence easy to implement.

7. ACKNOWLEDGMENTS

This work was partially funded by the European Commission through EU projects DebugIT (FP7-217139) and e-LICO (FP7-231519). The support from the COST Action BM072 ("Urine and Kidney Proteomics") is also gratefully acknowledged.

8. REFERENCES

[1] T. Abeel et al. Robust biomarker identification for cancer diagnosis with ensemble feature selection methods. *Bioinformatics*, 26:392–398, 2010.

[2] A.-L. Boulesteix and M. Slawski. Stability and aggregation of ranked gene lists. *Briefings in Bioinformatics*, 10:556–568, 2009.

[3] D. Burdick, M. Calimlim, and J. Gehrke. Mafia: A maximal frequent itemset algorithm for transactional databases. In *ICDE*, 2001.

[4] R. P. DeConde et al. Combining results of microarray experiments: A rank aggregation approach. *Stat. Appl. Genet. Molec. Biol.*, 5(1), 2006.

[5] R. Duda, P. Hart, and D. Stork. *Pattern Classification and Scene Analysis*. John Willey and Sons, 2001.

[6] L. Ein-Dor et al. Thousands of samples are needed to generate a robust gene list for predicting outcome in cancer. *PNAS*, 103(15):5923–8, 2006.

[7] I. Guyon, J. Weston, S. Barnhill, and V. Vapnik. Gene selection for cancer classification using support vector machines. *Mach. Learn.*, 46:389–422, March 2002.

[8] M. A. Hall. *Correlation-based Feature Subset Selection for Machine Learning*. PhD thesis, University of Waikato, 1998.

[9] A.-C. Haury, P. Gestraud, and J.-P. Vert. The influence of feature selection methods on accuracy, stability and interpretability of molecular signatures. 2011.

[10] J. P. Ioannidis. Microarrays and molecular research: noise discovery? *Lancet*, 365(9458):454–5, 2005.

[11] A. Kalousis, J. Prados, and M. Hilario. Stability of feature selection algorithms: a study on high-dimensional spaces. *Knowl. Inf. Syst.*, 12:95–116, May 2007.

[12] L. Kaufman and P. J. Rousseeuw. *Finding Groups in Data: An Introduction to Cluster Analysis*. Wiley-Interscience, 1990.

[13] S. Lin and J. Ding. Integration of ranked lists via cross entropy monte carlo with applications to mrna and microrna studies. *Biometrics*, 65(1):9–18, 2009.

[14] S. Loscalzo, L. Yu, and C. Ding. Consensus group stable feature selection. In *KDD*, 2009.

[15] M. S. Pepe et al. Selecting differentially expressed genes from microarray experiments. *Biometrics*, 59(1):133–142, 2003.

[16] X. Qiu, Y. Xiao, A. Gordon, and A. Yakovlev. Assessing stability of gene selection in microarray data analysis. *BMC Bioinformatics*, 7(1), 2006.

[17] M. Robnik-Šikonja and I. Kononenko. Theoretical and empirical analysis of relieff and rrelieff. *Mach. Learn.*, 53:23–69, October 2003.

[18] Y. Saeys, T. Abeel, and Y. Van de Peer. Robust feature selection using ensemble feature selection techniques. In *PKDD*, 2008.

[19] L. Yu, C. Ding, and S. Loscalzo. Stable feature selection via dense feature groups. In *KDD*, 2008.

[20] M. J. Zaki. Generating non-redundant association rules. In *KDD*, 2000.

[21] H. Zou and T. Hastie. Regularization and variable selection via the elastic net. *J R Stat Soc Series B*, 67(2):301–320, 2005.

Feature Grouping and Selection Over an Undirected Graph

Sen Yang[1], Lei Yuan[1,2], Ying-Cheng Lai[3], Xiaotong Shen[4], Peter Wonka[1], Jieping Ye[1,2]
[1]Computer Science and Engineering, [3]Electrical Engineering,
[2]Center for Evolutionary Medicine and Informatics, The Biodesign Institute,
Arizona State University, Tempe, AZ 85287, USA
{senyang, lei.yuan, ying-cheng.lai, peter.wonka, jieping.ye}@asu.edu
[4]School of Statistics, University of Minnesota, Minneapolis, MN 55455, USA
xshen@stat.umn.edu

ABSTRACT

High-dimensional regression/classification continues to be an important and challenging problem, especially when features are highly correlated. Feature selection, combined with additional structure information on the features has been considered to be promising in promoting regression/classification performance. Graph-guided fused lasso (GFlasso) has recently been proposed to facilitate feature selection and graph structure exploitation, when features exhibit certain graph structures. However, the formulation in GFlasso relies on pairwise sample correlations to perform feature grouping, which could introduce additional estimation bias. In this paper, we propose three new feature grouping and selection methods to resolve this issue. The first method employs a convex function to penalize the pairwise l_∞ norm of connected regression/classification coefficients, achieving simultaneous feature grouping and selection. The second method improves the first one by utilizing a non-convex function to reduce the estimation bias. The third one is the extension of the second method using a truncated l_1 regularization to further reduce the estimation bias. The proposed methods combine feature grouping and feature selection to enhance estimation accuracy. We employ the alternating direction method of multipliers (ADMM) and difference of convex functions (DC) programming to solve the proposed formulations. Our experimental results on synthetic data and two real datasets demonstrate the effectiveness of the proposed methods.

Categories and Subject Descriptors

H.2.8 [**Database Management**]: Database Applications - Data Mining

General Terms

Algorithms

Keywords

Feature grouping, feature selection, undirected graph, l_1 regularization, regression, classification

1. INTRODUCTION

High-dimensional regression/classification is challenging due to the *curse of dimensionality*. Lasso [18] and its various extensions, which can simultaneously perform feature selection and regression/classification, have received increasing attention in this situation. However, in the presence of highly correlated features lasso tends to only select one of those features resulting in suboptimal performance [27]. Several methods have been proposed to address this issue in the literature. Shen and Ye [15] introduce an adaptive model selection procedure that corrects the estimation bias through a data-driven penalty based on generalized degrees of freedom. The Elastic Net [27] uses an additional l_2 regularizer to encourage highly correlated features to stay together. However, these methods do not incorporate prior knowledge into the regression/classification process, which is critical in many applications. As an example, many biological studies have suggested that genes tend to work in groups according to their biological functions, and there are some regulatory relationships between genes [10]. This biological knowledge can be represented as a graph, where the nodes represent the genes, and the edges imply the regulatory relationships between genes. Therefore, we want to study how estimation accuracy can be improved using dependency information encoded as a graph.

Given feature grouping information, the group lasso [1, 7, 22, 11] yields a solution with grouped sparsity using l_1/l_2 penalty. The orignal group lasso does not consider the overlaps between groups. Zhao et al. [24] extend the group lasso to the case of overlapping groups. Jacob et al. [7] introduce a new penalty function leading to a grouped sparse solution with overlapping groups. Yuan et al. [21] propose an efficient method to solve the overlapping group lasso. Other extensions of group lasso with tree structured regularization include [11, 8]. Prior works have demonstrated the benefit of using feature grouping information for high-dimensional regression/classification. However, these methods need the feature groups to be pre-specified. In other words, they only utilize the grouping information to obtain solutions with grouped sparsity, but lack the capability of identifying groups.

There are also a number of existing methods for feature grouping. Fused lasso [19] introduces an l_1 regularization method for estimating subgroups in a certain serial order, but pre-ordering features is required before using fused lasso. A study about parameter estimation of the fused lasso can be found in [12]; Shen et al. [13] propose a non-convex method to select all possible homogenous subgroups, but it fails to obtain sparse solutions. OSCAR [2] employs an l_1 regularizer and a pairwise l_∞ regularizer to perform feature selection and automatic feature grouping. Li and Li [10] suggest a grouping penalty using a Laplacian matrix to force the coefficients to be similar, which can be considered as a graph version of the Elastic Net. When the Laplacian matrix is an identity matrix, Laplacian lasso [10, 5] is identical to the Elastic Net. GFlasso employs an l_1 regularization over a graph, which penalizes the difference $|\beta_i - \text{sign}(r_{ij})\beta_j|$, to encourage the coefficients β_i, β_j for features i, j connected by an edge in the graph to be similar when $r_{ij} > 0$, but dissimilar when $r_{ij} < 0$, where r_{ij} is the sample correlation between two features [9]. Although these grouping penalties can improve the performance, they would introduce additional estimation bias due to strict convexity of the penalties or due to possible graph misspecification. For example, additional bias may occur when the signs of coefficients for two features connected by an edge in the graph are different in Laplacian lasso [10, 5], or when the sign of r_{ij} is inaccurate in GFlasso [9].

In this paper, we focus on simultaneous estimation of grouping and sparseness structures over a given undirected graph. Features tend to be grouped when they are connected by an edge in a graph. When features are connected by an edge in a graph, the absolute values of the model coefficients for these two features should be similar or identical. We propose one convex and two non-convex penalties to encourage both sparsity and equality of absolute values of coefficients for connected features. The convex penalty includes a pairwise l_∞ regularizer over a graph. The first non-convex penalty improves the convex penalty by penalizing the difference of absolute values of coefficients for connected features. The other one is the extension of the first non-convex penalty using a truncated l_1 regularization to further reduce the estimation bias. These penalties are designed to resolve the aforementioned issues of Laplacian lasso and GFlasso. The non-convex penalties shrink only small differences in absolute values so that estimation bias can be reduced; several recent works analyze their theoretical properties [26, 14]. Through ADMM and DC programming, we develop computational methods to solve the proposed formulations. The proposed methods can combine the benefit of feature selection and that of feature grouping to improve regression/classification performance. Due to the equality of absolute values of coefficients, the model complexity of the learned model can be reduced. We have performed experiments on synthetic data and two real datasets. The results demonstrate the effectiveness of the proposed methods.

The rest of the paper is organized as follows. We introduce the proposed convex method in Section 2, and the two proposed non-convex methods in Section 3. Experimental results are given in Section 4. We conclude the paper in Section 5.

2. A CONVEX FORMULATION

Consider a linear model in which response y_i depends on a vector of p features:

$$\mathbf{y} = \mathbf{X}\boldsymbol{\beta} + \boldsymbol{\varepsilon}, \tag{1}$$

where $\boldsymbol{\beta} \in \mathbb{R}^p$ is a vector of coefficients, $\mathbf{X} \in \mathbb{R}^{n\times p}$ is the data matrix, and $\boldsymbol{\varepsilon}$ is random noise. Given an undirected graph, we try to build a prediction model (regression or classification) incorporating the graph structure information to estimate the nonzero coefficients of $\boldsymbol{\beta}$ and to identify the feature groups when the number of features p is larger than the sample size n. Let (N, E) be the given undirected graph, where $N = \{1, 2, \ldots, p\}$ is a set of nodes, and E is the set of edges. Node i corresponds to feature $\mathbf{x}_i$. If nodes i and j are connected by an edge in E, then features $\mathbf{x}_i$ and $\mathbf{x}_j$ tend to be grouped. The formulation of graph OSCAR (GOSCAR) is given by

$$\min_{\boldsymbol{\beta}} \frac{1}{2}\|\mathbf{y} - \mathbf{X}\boldsymbol{\beta}\|^2 + \lambda_1\|\boldsymbol{\beta}\|_1 + \lambda_2 \sum_{(i,j)\in E} \max\{|\beta_i|, |\beta_j|\} \tag{2}$$

where λ_1, λ_2 are regularization parameters. We use a pairwise l_∞ regularizer to encourage the coefficients to be equal [2], but we only put grouping constraints over the nodes connected over the given graph. The l_1 regularizer encourages sparseness. The pairwise l_∞ regularizer puts more penalty on the larger coefficients. Note that $\max\{|\beta_i|, |\beta_j|\}$ can be decomposed as

$$\max\{|\beta_i|, |\beta_j|\} = \frac{1}{2}(|\beta_i + \beta_j| + |\beta_i - \beta_j|).$$

$\frac{1}{2}(|\beta_i + \beta_j| + |\beta_i - \beta_j|)$ can be represented by

$$|\mathbf{u}^T\boldsymbol{\beta}| + |\mathbf{v}^T\boldsymbol{\beta}|,$$

where $\mathbf{u}, \mathbf{v}$ are sparse vectors, each with only two non-zero entries $u_i = u_j = \frac{1}{2}$, $v_i = -v_j = \frac{1}{2}$. Thus Eq. (2) can be rewritten in a matrix form as

$$\min_{\boldsymbol{\beta}} \frac{1}{2}\|\mathbf{y} - \mathbf{X}\boldsymbol{\beta}\|^2 + \lambda_1\|\boldsymbol{\beta}\|_1 + \lambda_2\|\mathbf{T}\boldsymbol{\beta}\|_1, \tag{3}$$

where $\mathbf{T}$ is a sparse matrix constructed from the edge set E.

The proposed formulation is closely related to OSCAR [2]. The penalty of OSCAR is $\lambda_1\|\boldsymbol{\beta}\|_1 + \lambda_2 \sum_{i<j} \max\{|\beta_i|, |\beta_j|\}$. The l_1 regularizer leads to a sparse solution, and the l_∞ regularizer encourages the coefficients to be equal. OSCAR can be efficiently solved by accelerated gradient methods, whose key projection can be solved by a simple iterative group merging algorithm [25]. However, OSCAR assumes each node is connected to all the other nodes, which is not sufficient for many applications. Note that OSCAR is a special case of GOSCAR when the graph is complete. GOSCAR, incorporating an arbitrary undirected graph, is much more challenging to solve.

2.1 Algorithm

We propose to solve GOSCAR using the alternating direction method of multipliers (ADMM) [3]. ADMM decomposes a large global problem into a series of smaller local subproblems and coordinates the local solutions to identify the globally optimal solution. ADMM attempts to combine the benefits of dual decomposition and augmented Lagrangian methods for constrained optimization [3]. The problem solved by ADMM takes the form of

$$\begin{aligned} &\min\nolimits_{\mathbf{x},\mathbf{z}} f(\mathbf{x}) + g(\mathbf{z}) \\ &s.t.\ \mathbf{A}\mathbf{x} + \mathbf{B}\mathbf{z} = \mathbf{c}. \end{aligned}$$

ADMM uses a variant of the augmented Lagrangian method and reformulates the problem as follows:

$$L_\rho(\mathbf{x}, \mathbf{z}, \boldsymbol{\mu}) = f(\mathbf{x}) + g(\mathbf{z}) + \boldsymbol{\mu}^T(\mathbf{A}\mathbf{x} + \mathbf{B}\mathbf{z} - \mathbf{c}) + \frac{\rho}{2}\|\mathbf{A}\mathbf{x} + \mathbf{B}\mathbf{z} - \mathbf{c}\|^2,$$

with $\boldsymbol{\mu}$ being the augmented Lagrangian multiplier, and ρ being the non-negative dual update step length. ADMM solves this problem by iteratively minimizing $L_\rho(\mathbf{x}, \mathbf{z}, \boldsymbol{\mu})$ over $\mathbf{x}$, $\mathbf{z}$, and $\boldsymbol{\mu}$. The update rule for ADMM is given by

$$\begin{aligned}\mathbf{x}^{k+1} &:= \arg\min_{\mathbf{x}} L_\rho(\mathbf{x}, \mathbf{z}^k, \boldsymbol{\mu}^k),\\ \mathbf{z}^{k+1} &:= \arg\min_{\mathbf{z}} L_\rho(\mathbf{x}^{k+1}, \mathbf{z}, \boldsymbol{\mu}^k),\\ \boldsymbol{\mu}^{k+1} &:= \boldsymbol{\mu}^k + \rho(\mathbf{A}\mathbf{x}^{k+1} + \mathbf{B}\mathbf{z}^{k+1} - \mathbf{c}).\end{aligned}$$

Consider the unconstrained optimization problem in Eq. (3), which is equivalent to the following constrained optimization problem:

$$\begin{aligned}&\min_{\boldsymbol{\beta},\mathbf{q},\mathbf{p}} \tfrac{1}{2}\|\mathbf{y} - \mathbf{X}\boldsymbol{\beta}\|^2 + \lambda_1\|\mathbf{q}\|_1 + \lambda_2\|\mathbf{p}\|_1\\ &s.t. \quad \boldsymbol{\beta} - \mathbf{q} = \mathbf{0},\ \mathbf{T}\boldsymbol{\beta} - \mathbf{p} = \mathbf{0},\end{aligned} \tag{4}$$

where $\mathbf{q}, \mathbf{p}$ are slack variables. Eq. (4) can then be solved by ADMM. The augmented Lagrangian is

$$\begin{aligned}L_\rho(\boldsymbol{\beta}, \mathbf{q}, \mathbf{p}, \boldsymbol{\mu}, \boldsymbol{\upsilon}) &= \tfrac{1}{2}\|\mathbf{y} - \mathbf{X}\boldsymbol{\beta}\|^2 + \lambda_1\|\mathbf{q}\|_1 + \lambda_2\|\mathbf{p}\|_1\\ &+ \boldsymbol{\mu}^T(\boldsymbol{\beta} - \mathbf{q}) + \boldsymbol{\upsilon}^T(\mathbf{T}\boldsymbol{\beta} - \mathbf{p}) + \tfrac{\rho}{2}\|\boldsymbol{\beta} - \mathbf{q}\|^2 + \tfrac{\rho}{2}\|\mathbf{T}\boldsymbol{\beta} - \mathbf{p}\|^2,\end{aligned}$$

where $\boldsymbol{\mu}, \boldsymbol{\upsilon}$ are augmented Lagrangian multipliers.

Update $\boldsymbol{\beta}$: In the $(k+1)$-th iteration, $\boldsymbol{\beta}^{k+1}$ can be updated by minimizing L_ρ with $\mathbf{q}, \mathbf{p}, \boldsymbol{\mu}, \boldsymbol{\upsilon}$ fixed:

$$\begin{aligned}\boldsymbol{\beta}^{k+1} &= \arg\min_{\boldsymbol{\beta}} \tfrac{1}{2}\|\mathbf{y} - \mathbf{X}\boldsymbol{\beta}\|^2 + (\boldsymbol{\mu}^k + \mathbf{T}^T\boldsymbol{\upsilon}^k)^T\boldsymbol{\beta}\\ &+ \tfrac{\rho}{2}\|\boldsymbol{\beta} - \mathbf{q}^k\|^2 + \tfrac{\rho}{2}\|\mathbf{T}\boldsymbol{\beta} - \mathbf{p}^k\|^2.\end{aligned} \tag{5}$$

The above optimization problem is quadratic. The optimal solution is given by $\boldsymbol{\beta}^{k+1} = \mathbf{F}^{-1}\mathbf{b}^k$, where

$$\begin{aligned}\mathbf{F} &= \mathbf{X}^T\mathbf{X} + \rho(\mathbf{I} + \mathbf{T}^T\mathbf{T}),\\ \mathbf{b}^k &= \mathbf{X}^T\mathbf{y} - \boldsymbol{\mu}^k - \mathbf{T}^T\boldsymbol{\upsilon}^k + \rho\mathbf{T}^T\mathbf{p}^k + \rho\mathbf{q}^k.\end{aligned}$$

The computation of $\boldsymbol{\beta}^{k+1}$ involves solving a linear system, which is the most time-consuming part in the whole algorithm. To compute $\boldsymbol{\beta}^{k+1}$ efficiently, we compute the Cholesky factorization of $\mathbf{F}$ at the beginning of the algorithm:

$$\mathbf{F} = \mathbf{R}^T\mathbf{R}.$$

Note that $\mathbf{F}$ is a constant and positive definite matrix. Using the Cholesky factorization we only need to solve the following two linear systems at each iteration:

$$\mathbf{R}^T\hat{\boldsymbol{\beta}} = \mathbf{b}^k,\ \ \mathbf{R}\boldsymbol{\beta} = \hat{\boldsymbol{\beta}}. \tag{6}$$

Since $\mathbf{R}$ is an upper triangular matrix, solving these two linear systems is very efficient.

Update q: $\mathbf{q}^{k+1}$ can be obtained by solving

$$\mathbf{q}^{k+1} = \arg\min_{\mathbf{q}} \frac{\rho}{2}\|\mathbf{q} - \boldsymbol{\beta}^{k+1}\|^2 + \lambda_1\|\mathbf{q}\|_1 - (\boldsymbol{\mu}^k)^T\mathbf{q}$$

which is equivalent to the following problem:

$$\mathbf{q}^{k+1} = \arg\min_{\mathbf{q}} \frac{1}{2}\|\mathbf{q} - \boldsymbol{\beta}^{k+1} - \frac{1}{\rho}\boldsymbol{\mu}^k\|^2 + \frac{\lambda_1}{\rho}\|\mathbf{q}\|_1 \tag{7}$$

Eq. (7) has a closed-form solution, known as *soft-thresholding*:

$$\mathbf{q}^{k+1} = S_{\lambda_1/\rho}(\boldsymbol{\beta}^{k+1} + \frac{1}{\rho}\boldsymbol{\mu}^k), \tag{8}$$

where the *soft-thresholding operator* is defined as:

$$S_\lambda(x) = \text{sign}(x)\max(|x| - \lambda, 0).$$

Update p: Similar to updating $\mathbf{q}$, $\mathbf{p}^{k+1}$ can also be obtained by *soft-thresholding*:

$$\mathbf{p}_i^{k+1} = S_{\lambda_2/\rho}(\mathbf{T}\boldsymbol{\beta}^{k+1} + \frac{1}{\rho}\boldsymbol{\upsilon}^k). \tag{9}$$

Update $\boldsymbol{\mu}, \boldsymbol{\upsilon}$:

$$\begin{aligned}\boldsymbol{\mu}^{k+1} &= \boldsymbol{\mu}^k + \rho(\boldsymbol{\beta}^{k+1} - \mathbf{q}^{k+1}),\\ \boldsymbol{\upsilon}^{k+1} &= \boldsymbol{\upsilon}^k + \rho(\mathbf{T}\boldsymbol{\beta}^{k+1} - \mathbf{p}^{k+1}).\end{aligned} \tag{10}$$

A summary of GOSCAR is shown in Algorithm 1.

Algorithm 1: The GOSCAR algorithm

Input: $\mathbf{X}, \mathbf{y}, E, \lambda_1, \lambda_2, \rho$
Output: $\boldsymbol{\beta}$
Initialization: $\mathbf{p}^0 \leftarrow \mathbf{0}, \mathbf{q}^0 \leftarrow \mathbf{0}, \boldsymbol{\mu}^0 \leftarrow \mathbf{0}, \boldsymbol{\upsilon}^0 \leftarrow \mathbf{0}$;
Compute the Cholesky factorization of $\mathbf{F}$;
do
  Compute $\boldsymbol{\beta}^{k+1}$ according to Eq. (6).
  Compute $\mathbf{q}^{k+1}$ according to Eq. (8).
  Compute $\mathbf{p}^{k+1}$ according to Eq. (9).
  Compute $\boldsymbol{\mu}^{k+1}, \boldsymbol{\upsilon}^{k+1}$ according to Eq. (10).
Until *Convergence*;
return $\boldsymbol{\beta}$;

In Algorithm 1, the Cholesky factorization only needs to be computed once, and each iteration involves solving one linear system and two soft-thresholding operations. The time complexity of the soft-thresholding operation in Eq. (8) is $O(p)$. The other one in Eq. (9) involves a matrix-vector multiplication. Due to the sparsity of $\mathbf{T}$, its time complexity is $O(n_e)$, where n_e is the number of edges. Solving the linear system involves computing $\mathbf{b}^k$ and solving Eq. (6), whose total time complexity is $O(p(p+n) + n_e)$. Thus the time complexity of each iteration is $O(p(p+n) + n_e)$.

3. TWO NON-CONVEX FORMULATIONS

The grouping penalty of GOSCAR overcomes the limitation of Laplacian lasso that the different signs of coefficients can introduce additional penalty. However, under the l_∞ regularizer, even if $|\beta_i|$ and $|\beta_j|$ are close to each other, the penalty on this pair may still be large due to the property of the max operator, resulting in the coefficient β_i or β_j being over penalized. The additional penalty would result in biased estimation, especially for large coefficient, as in the lasso case [18]. Another related grouping penalty is GFlasso, $|\beta_i - \text{sign}(r_{ij})\beta_j|$, where r_{ij} is the pairwise sample correlation. GFlasso relies on the pairwise sample correlation to decide whether β_i and β_j are enforced to be close or not. When the pairwise sample correlation wrongly estimates the sign between β_i and β_j, an additional penalty on β_i and β_j would occur, introducing estimation bias. This motivates our non-convex grouping penalty, $||\beta_i| - |\beta_j||$, that shrinks only small differences in absolutes values. As a result, estimation bias is reduced as compared to these convex grouping penalties. The proposed non-convex methods perform well even when the graph is wrongly specified, unlike GFlasso. Note that the proposed non-convex grouping penalty does not assume the sign of an edge is given; it only relies on the graph structure.

3.1 Non-Convex Formulation I: ncFGS

The proposed non-convex formulation (ncFGS) solves the following optimization problem:

$$\min_{\boldsymbol{\beta}} f(\boldsymbol{\beta}) = \frac{1}{2}\|\mathbf{y} - \mathbf{X}\boldsymbol{\beta}\|^2 + \lambda_1\|\boldsymbol{\beta}\|_1 + \lambda_2 \sum_{(i,j)\in E} ||\beta_i| - |\beta_j||, \tag{11}$$

where the grouping penalty $\sum_{(i,j)\in E} ||\beta_i| - |\beta_j||$ controls only magnitudes of differences of coefficients ignoring their signs over the graph. Through the l_1 regularizer and grouping penalty, simultaneous feature grouping and selection are performed, where only large coefficients as well as pairwise differences are shrunk.

A computational method for the non-convex optimization in Eq. (11) is through DC programming. We will first give a brief review of DC programming.

A particular DC program on $\mathbb{R}^p$ takes the form of

$$f(\boldsymbol{\beta}) = f_1(\boldsymbol{\beta}) - f_2(\boldsymbol{\beta})$$

with $f_1(\boldsymbol{\beta})$ and $f_2(\boldsymbol{\beta})$ being convex on $\mathbb{R}^p$. Algorithms to solve DC programming based on the duality and local optimality conditions have been introduced in [17]. Due to their local characteristic and the non-convexity of DC programming, these algorithms cannot guarantee the computed solution to be globally optimal. In general, these DC algorithms converge to a local solution, but some researchers observed that they converge quite often to a global one [16].

To apply DC programming to our problem we need to decompose the objective function into the difference of two convex functions. We propose to use:

$$\begin{aligned} f_1(\boldsymbol{\beta}) &= \tfrac{1}{2}\|\mathbf{y} - \mathbf{X}\boldsymbol{\beta}\|^2 + \lambda_1\|\boldsymbol{\beta}\|_1 + \lambda_2 \textstyle\sum_{(i,j)\in E}(|\beta_i + \beta_j| \\ &\quad + |\beta_i - \beta_j|), \\ f_2(\boldsymbol{\beta}) &= \lambda_2 \textstyle\sum_{(i,j)\in E}(|\beta_i| + |\beta_j|). \end{aligned}$$

The above DC decomposition is based on the following identity: $||\beta_i| - |\beta_j|| = |\beta_i + \beta_j| + |\beta_i - \beta_j| - (|\beta_i| + |\beta_j|)$. Note that both $f_1(\boldsymbol{\beta})$ and $f_2(\boldsymbol{\beta})$ are convex functions.

Denote $f_2^k(\boldsymbol{\beta}) = f_2(\boldsymbol{\beta}^k) + \langle \boldsymbol{\beta} - \boldsymbol{\beta}^k, \partial f_2(\boldsymbol{\beta}^k)\rangle$ as the affine minorization of $f_2(\boldsymbol{\beta})$, where $\langle \cdot, \cdot \rangle$ is the inner product. Then DC programming solves Eq. (11) by iteratively solving a sub-problem as follows:

$$\min_{\beta} f_1(\boldsymbol{\beta}) - f_2^k(\boldsymbol{\beta}). \tag{12}$$

Since $\langle \boldsymbol{\beta}^k, \partial f_2(\boldsymbol{\beta}^k)\rangle$ is constant, Eq. (12) can be rewritten as

$$\min_{\boldsymbol{\beta}} f_1(\boldsymbol{\beta}) - \langle \boldsymbol{\beta}, \partial f_2(\boldsymbol{\beta}^k)\rangle. \tag{13}$$

Let $\mathbf{c}^k = \partial f_2(\boldsymbol{\beta}^k)$. Note that

$$c_i^k = \lambda_2 d_i \mathrm{sign}(\beta_i^k)\mathbb{I}(\beta_i^k \neq 0), \tag{14}$$

where d_i is the degree of node i, and $\mathbb{I}(\cdot)$ is the indicator function. Hence, the formulation in Eq. (13) is

$$\begin{aligned} \min_{\boldsymbol{\beta}} & \tfrac{1}{2}\|\mathbf{y} - \mathbf{X}\boldsymbol{\beta}\|^2 + \lambda_1\|\boldsymbol{\beta}\|_1 - (\mathbf{c}^k)^T\boldsymbol{\beta} \\ & + \lambda_2 \textstyle\sum_{(i,j)\in E}(|\beta_i + \beta_j| + |\beta_i - \beta_j|), \end{aligned} \tag{15}$$

which is convex. Note that the only differences between the problems in Eq. (2) and Eq. (15) are the linear term $(\mathbf{c}^k)^T\boldsymbol{\beta}$ and the second regularization parameter. Similar to GOSCAR, we can solve Eq. (15) using ADMM, which is equivalent to the following optimization problem:

$$\begin{aligned} \min_{\boldsymbol{\beta},\mathbf{q},\mathbf{p}} & \tfrac{1}{2}\|\mathbf{y} - \mathbf{X}\boldsymbol{\beta}\|^2 - (\mathbf{c}^k)^T\boldsymbol{\beta} + \lambda_1\|\mathbf{q}\|_1 + 2\lambda_2\|\mathbf{p}\|_1 \\ s.t \ & \boldsymbol{\beta} - \mathbf{q} = \mathbf{0}, \ \mathbf{T}\boldsymbol{\beta} - \mathbf{p} = \mathbf{0}. \end{aligned} \tag{16}$$

There is an additional linear term $(\mathbf{c}^k)^T\boldsymbol{\beta}$ in updating $\boldsymbol{\beta}$ compared to Algorithm 1. Hence, we can use Algorithm 1 to solve Eq. (15) with a small change in updating $\boldsymbol{\beta}$:

$$\mathbf{F}\boldsymbol{\beta} - \mathbf{b}^s - \mathbf{c}^k = 0.$$

where s represents the iteration number in Algorithm 1.

The key steps of ncFGS are shown in Algorithm 2.

Algorithm 2: The ncFGS algorithm

Input: $\mathbf{X}, \mathbf{y}, E, \lambda_1, \lambda_2, \epsilon$
Output: $\boldsymbol{\beta}$
Initialization: $\boldsymbol{\beta}^0 \leftarrow \mathbf{0}$;
while $f(\boldsymbol{\beta}^k) - f(\boldsymbol{\beta}^{k+1}) > \epsilon$ **do**
  Compute $\mathbf{c}^k$ according to Eq. (14).
  Compute $\boldsymbol{\beta}^{k+1}$ using Algorithm 1 with $\mathbf{c}^k$ and $\lambda_1, 2\lambda_2$ as regularization parameters.
end
return $\boldsymbol{\beta}$;

3.2 Non-Convex Formulation II: ncTFGS

It is known that the bias of lasso is due to the looseness of convex relaxation of l_0 regularization. The truncated l_1 regularizer, a non-convex regularizer close to the l_0 regularizer, has been proposed to resolve the bias issue [23]. The truncated l_1 regularizer can recover the exact set of nonzero coefficients under a weaker condition, and has a smaller upper error bound than lasso [23]. Therefore, we propose a truncated grouping penalty to further reduce the estimation bias. The proposed formulation based on the truncated grouping penalty is

$$\min_{\boldsymbol{\beta}} f_T(\boldsymbol{\beta}) = \tfrac{1}{2}\|\mathbf{y} - \mathbf{X}\boldsymbol{\beta}\|^2 + \lambda_1 p_1(\boldsymbol{\beta}) + \lambda_2 p_2(\boldsymbol{\beta}) \tag{17}$$

where

$$\begin{aligned} p_1(\boldsymbol{\beta}) &= \textstyle\sum_i J_\tau(|\beta_i|), \\ p_2(\boldsymbol{\beta}) &= \textstyle\sum_{(i,j)\in E} J_\tau(||\beta_i| - |\beta_j||), \end{aligned}$$

and $J_\tau(x) = \min(\frac{x}{\tau}, 1)$ is the truncated l_1 regularizer, a surrogate of the l_0 function; τ is a non-negative tuning parameter. Figure 1 shows the difference between l_0 norm, l_1 norm and $J_\tau(|x|)$. When $\tau \to 0$, $J_\tau(|x|)$ is equivalent to the l_0 norm given by the number of nonzero entries of a vector. When $\tau \geq |x|$, $\tau J_\tau(|x|)$ is equivalent to the l_1 norm of x.

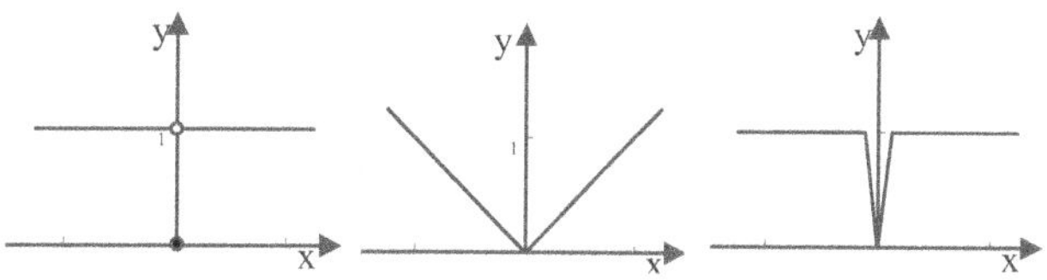

Figure 1: Example for l_0 norm (left), l_1 norm (middle), and $J_\tau(|x|)$ with $\tau = \frac{1}{8}$ (right).

Note that $J_\tau(||\beta_i| - |\beta_j||)$ can be decomposed as

$$\begin{aligned} J_\tau(||\beta_i| - |\beta_j||) &= \tfrac{1}{\tau}(|\beta_i + \beta_j| + |\beta_i - \beta_j|) \\ &\quad - \tfrac{1}{\tau}\max(2|\beta_i| - \tau, 2|\beta_j| - \tau, |\beta_i| + |\beta_j|), \end{aligned}$$

and a DC decomposition of $J_\tau(|\beta_i|)$ is

$$J_\tau(|\beta_i|) = \frac{1}{\tau}|\beta_i| - \frac{1}{\tau}\max(|\beta_i| - \tau, 0).$$

Hence, the DC decomposition of $f_T(\boldsymbol{\beta})$ can be written as

$$f_T(\boldsymbol{\beta}) = f_{T,1}(\boldsymbol{\beta}) - f_{T,2}(\boldsymbol{\beta}),$$

where

$$f_{T,1}(\boldsymbol{\beta}) = \frac{1}{2}\|\mathbf{y} - \mathbf{X}\boldsymbol{\beta}\|^2 + \frac{\lambda_1}{\tau}\|\boldsymbol{\beta}\|_1 + \frac{\lambda_2}{\tau}\sum_{(i,j)\in E}(|\beta_i + \beta_j| + |\beta_i - \beta_j|),$$
$$f_{T,2}(\boldsymbol{\beta}) = \frac{\lambda_1}{\tau}\sum_i \max(|\beta_i| - \tau, 0) + \frac{\lambda_2}{\tau}\sum_{(i,j)\in E}\max(2|\beta_i| - \tau, 2|\beta_j| - \tau, |\beta_i| + |\beta_j|).$$

Let $\mathbf{c}_T^k = \partial f_{T,2}(\boldsymbol{\beta}^k)$ be the subgradient of $f_{T,2}$ in the $(k+1)$-th iteration. We have

$$c_{T,i}^k = \text{sign}(\beta_i^k)\big(\frac{\lambda_1}{\tau}\mathbb{I}(|\beta_i^k| > \tau) + \frac{\lambda_2}{\tau}\sum_{j:(i,j)\in E} (2\mathbb{I}(|\beta_j^k| < |\beta_i^k| - \tau) + \mathbb{I}(||\beta_i^k| - |\beta_j^k|| < \tau))\big). \quad (18)$$

Then the subproblem of ncTFGS is

$$\min_{\boldsymbol{\beta}} \frac{1}{2}\|\mathbf{y} - \mathbf{X}\boldsymbol{\beta}\|^2 + \frac{\lambda_1}{\tau}\|\boldsymbol{\beta}\|_1 - (\mathbf{c}_T^k)^T\boldsymbol{\beta} + \frac{\lambda_2}{\tau}\sum_{(i,j)\in E}(|\beta_i + \beta_j| + |\beta_i - \beta_j|), \quad (19)$$

which can be solved using Algorithm 1 as in ncFGS.

The key steps of ncTFGS are summarized in Algorithm 3.

Algorithm 3: The ncTFGS algorithm

Input: $\mathbf{X}, \mathbf{y}, E, \lambda_1, \lambda_2, \tau, \epsilon$
Output: $\boldsymbol{\beta}$
Initialization: $\boldsymbol{\beta}^0 \leftarrow \mathbf{0}$;
while $f(\boldsymbol{\beta}^k) - f(\boldsymbol{\beta}^{k+1}) > \epsilon$ **do**
  Compute $\mathbf{c}_T^k$ according to Eq. (18).
  Compute $\boldsymbol{\beta}^{k+1}$ using Algorithm 1 with $\mathbf{c}_T^k$ and $\frac{\lambda_1}{\tau}, \frac{2\lambda_2}{\tau}$ as regularization parameters.
end
return $\boldsymbol{\beta}$;

---

ncTFGS is an extension of ncFGS. When $\tau \geq |\beta_i|, \forall i$, ncTFGS with regularization parameters $\tau\lambda_1$ and $\tau\lambda_2$ is identical to ncFGS (see Figure 3). ncFGS and ncTFGS have the same time complexity. The subproblems of ncFGS and ncTFGS are solved by Algorithm 1. In our experiments, we observed ncFGS and ncTFGS usually converge in less than 10 iterations.

4. NUMERICAL RESULTS

We examine the performance of the proposed methods and compare them against lasso, GFlasso, and OSCAR on synthetic datasets and two real datasets: FDG-PET images[1] and Breast Cancer[2]. The experiments are performed on a PC with dual-core Intel 3.0GHz CPU and 4GB memory. The code is written in MATLAB. The algorithms and their associated penalties are:

- Lasso: $\lambda_1\|\boldsymbol{\beta}\|_1$;
- OSCAR: $\lambda_1\|\boldsymbol{\beta}\|_1 + \lambda_2\sum_{i<j}\max\{|\beta_i|, |\beta_j|\}$;
- GFlasso: $\lambda_1\|\boldsymbol{\beta}\|_1 + \lambda_2\sum_{(i,j)\in E}|\beta_i - \text{sign}(r_{ij})\beta_j|$;
- GOSCAR: $\lambda_1\|\boldsymbol{\beta}\|_1 + \lambda_2\sum_{(i,j)\in E}\max\{|\beta_i|, |\beta_j|\}$;
- ncFGS: $\lambda_1\|\boldsymbol{\beta}\|_1 + \lambda_2\sum_{(i,j)\in E}||\beta_i| - |\beta_j||$;
- ncTFGS: $\lambda_1\sum_i J_\tau(|\beta_i|) + \lambda_2\sum_{(i,j)\in E}J_\tau(||\beta_i| - |\beta_j||)$;

[1]http://adni.loni.ucla.edu/
[2]http://cbio.ensmp.fr/~jvert/publi/

4.1 Efficiency

To evaluate the efficiency of the proposed methods, we conduct experiments on a synthetic dataset with a sample size of 100 and dimensions varying from 100 to 3000. The regression model is $\mathbf{y} = \mathbf{X}\boldsymbol{\beta} + \boldsymbol{\varepsilon}$, where $\mathbf{X} \sim \mathcal{N}(0, \mathbf{I}_{p\times p})$, $\beta_i \sim \mathcal{N}(0, 1)$, and $\varepsilon_i \sim \mathcal{N}(0, 0.01^2)$. The graph is randomly generated. The number of edges n_e varies from 100 to 3000. The regularization parameters are set as $\lambda_1 = \lambda_2 = 0.8\max\{|\beta_i|\}$ with n_e fixed. Since the graph size affects the penalty, λ_1 and λ_2 are scaled by $\frac{1}{n_e}$ to avoid trivial solutions with dimension p fixed. The average computational time based on 30 repetitions is reported in Figure 2. As can be seen in Figure 2, GOSCAR can achieve 1e-4 precision in less than 10s when the dimension and the number of edges are 1000. The computational time of ncTFGS is about 7 times higher than that of GOSCAR in this experiment. The computational time of ncFGS is the same as that of ncTFGS when $\tau = 100$, and very close to that of ncTFGS when $\tau = 0.15$. We can also observe that the proposed methods scale very well to the number of edges. The computational time of the proposed method increases less than 4 times when the number of edges increases from 100 to 3000. It is not surprising because the time complexity of each iteration in Algorithm 1 is linear with respect to n_e, and the sparsity of $\mathbf{T}$ makes the algorithm much more efficient. The increase of dimension is more costly than that of the number of edges, as the complexity of each iteration is quadratic with respect to p.

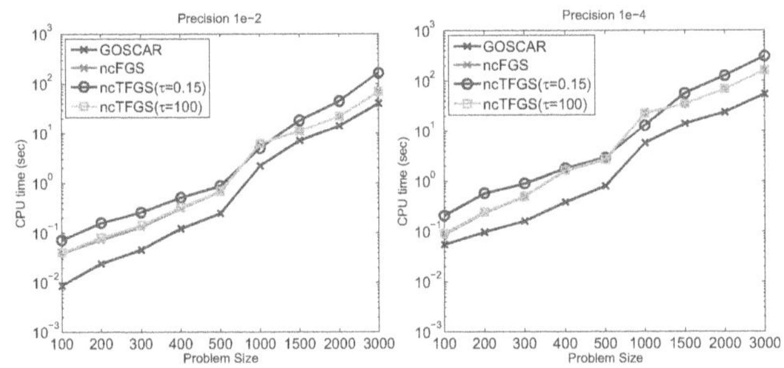

(a) The number of edges is fixed to 1000.

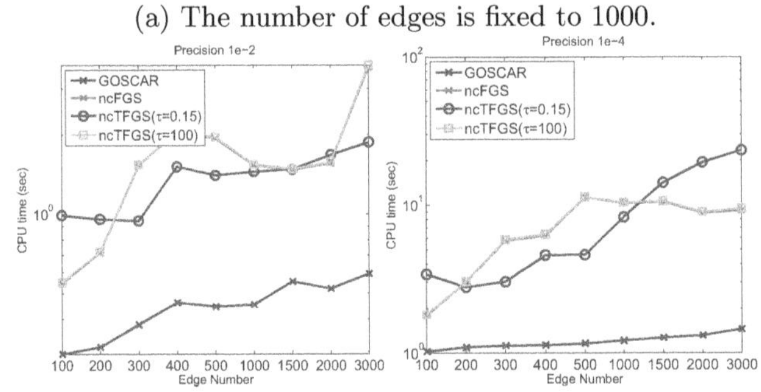

(b) The dimension is fixed to 500.

Figure 2: Comparison of GOSCAR, ncFGS, ncTFGS ($\tau = 0.15$), and ncTFGS ($\tau = 100$) in terms of computation time with different dimensions, precisions and the numbers of edges (in seconds and in logarithmic scale).

4.2 Simulations

We use five synthetic problems that have been commonly used in the sparse learning literature [2, 10] to compare the performance of different methods. The data is generated from the regression model $\mathbf{y} = \mathbf{X}\boldsymbol{\beta} + \boldsymbol{\varepsilon},\ \ \varepsilon_i \sim \mathcal{N}(0, \sigma^2)$. The five problems are given by:

1. $n = 100,\ p = 40$, and $\sigma = 2, 5, 10$. The true parameter is given by

$$\boldsymbol{\beta} = (\underbrace{0, \ldots, 0}_{10}, \underbrace{2, \ldots, 2}_{10}, \underbrace{0, \ldots, 0}_{10}, \underbrace{2, \ldots, 2}_{10})^T.$$

$\mathbf{X} \sim \mathcal{N}(\mathbf{0}, \mathbf{S}_{p\times p})$ with $s_{ii} = 1, \forall i$ and $s_{ij} = 0.5$ for $i \neq j$.

2. $n = 50,\ p = 40,\ \boldsymbol{\beta} = (\underbrace{3, \ldots, 3}_{15}, \underbrace{0, \ldots, 0}_{25})^T$, and $\sigma = 2, 5, 10$. The features are generated as

$$\begin{array}{ll} \mathbf{x}_i = Z_1 + \varepsilon_i^x,\ Z_1 \sim \mathcal{N}(0,1), & i = 1, \ldots, 5 \\ \mathbf{x}_i = Z_2 + \varepsilon_i^x,\ Z_2 \sim \mathcal{N}(0,1), & i = 6, \ldots, 10 \\ \mathbf{x}_i = Z_3 + \varepsilon_i^x,\ Z_3 \sim \mathcal{N}(0,1), & i = 11, \ldots, 15 \\ \mathbf{x}_i \sim \mathcal{N}(0,1)\ \ i = 16, \ldots, 40 & \end{array}$$

with $\varepsilon_i^x \sim \mathcal{N}(0, 0.16)$, and $\mathbf{X} = [\mathbf{x}_1, \ldots, \mathbf{x}_{40}]$.

3. Consider a regulatory gene network [10], where an entire network consists of n_{TF} subnetworks, each with one transcription factor (TF) and its 10 regulatory target genes. The data for each subnetwork can be generated as $\mathbf{X}_i^{TF} \sim \mathcal{N}(0, \mathbf{S}_{11\times 11})$ with $s_{ii} = 1, s_{1i} = s_{i1} = 0.7, \forall i, i \neq 1$ and $s_{ij} = 0$ for $i \neq j, j \neq 1, i \neq 1$. Then $\mathbf{X} = [\mathbf{X}_1^{TF}, \ldots, \mathbf{X}_{n_{TF}}^{TF}],\ n = 100,\ p = 110$, and $\sigma = 5$. The true parameters are

$$\boldsymbol{\beta} = (\underbrace{\frac{5}{\sqrt{11}}, \ldots, \frac{5}{\sqrt{11}}}_{11}, \underbrace{\frac{-3}{\sqrt{11}}, \ldots, \frac{-3}{\sqrt{11}}}_{11}, \underbrace{0, \ldots, 0}_{p-22})^T.$$

4. Same as 3 except that

$$\boldsymbol{\beta} = (5, \underbrace{\frac{5}{\sqrt{10}}, \ldots, \frac{5}{\sqrt{10}}}_{10}, -3, \underbrace{\frac{-3}{\sqrt{10}}, \ldots, \frac{-3}{\sqrt{10}}}_{10}, \underbrace{0, \ldots, 0}_{p-22})^T$$

5. Same as 3 except that

$$\boldsymbol{\beta} = (5, \underbrace{\frac{5}{\sqrt{10}}, \ldots, \frac{5}{\sqrt{10}}}_{10}, -5, \underbrace{\frac{-5}{\sqrt{10}}, \ldots, \frac{-5}{\sqrt{10}}}_{10},$$
$$3, \underbrace{\frac{3}{\sqrt{10}}, \ldots, \frac{3}{\sqrt{10}}}_{10}, -3, \underbrace{\frac{-3}{\sqrt{10}}, \ldots, \frac{-3}{\sqrt{10}}}_{10} \underbrace{0, \ldots, 0}_{p-44})^T$$

We assume that the features in the same group are connected in a graph, and those in different groups are not connected. We use MSE to measure the performance of estimation of $\boldsymbol{\beta}$, which is defined as

$$MSE(\boldsymbol{\beta}) = (\boldsymbol{\beta} - \boldsymbol{\beta}^*)^T \mathbf{X}^T \mathbf{X} (\boldsymbol{\beta} - \boldsymbol{\beta}^*).$$

For feature grouping and selection, we introduce two separate metrics to measure the accuracy of feature grouping and selection. Denote $I_i, i = 0, 1, 2, \ldots, K$ as the index of different groups, where I_0 is the index of zero coefficients. Then the metric for feature selection is defined as

$$s_0 = \frac{\sum_{i \in I_0} \mathbb{I}(\beta_i = 0) + \sum_{i \notin I_0} \mathbb{I}(\beta_i \neq 0)}{p},$$

and the metric for feature grouping is defined as

$$s = \frac{\sum_{i=1}^K s_i + s_0}{K+1},$$

where

$$s_i = \frac{\sum_{i \neq j, i, j \in I_i} \mathbb{I}(|\beta_i| = |\beta_j|) + \sum_{i \neq j, i \in I_i, j \notin I_i} \mathbb{I}(|\beta_i| \neq |\beta_j|)}{|I_i|(p-1)}.$$

s_i measures the grouping accuracy of group i under the assumption that the absolute values of entries in the same group should be the same, but different from those in different groups. s_0 measures the accuracy of feature selection. It is clear that $0 \leq s_0, s_i, s \leq 1$.

For each dataset, we generate n samples for training, as well as n samples for testing. To make the synthetic datasets more challenging, we first randomly select $\lfloor n/2 \rfloor$ coefficients, and change their signs, as well as those of the corresponding features. Denote $\tilde{\boldsymbol{\beta}}$ and $\tilde{\mathbf{X}}$ as the coefficients and features after changing signs. Then $\tilde{\beta}_i = -\beta_i,\ \tilde{\mathbf{x}}_i = -\mathbf{x}_i$, if the i-th coefficient is selected; otherwise, $\tilde{\beta}_i = \beta_i,\ \tilde{\mathbf{x}}_i = \mathbf{x}_i$. So that $\tilde{\mathbf{X}}\tilde{\boldsymbol{\beta}} = \mathbf{X}\boldsymbol{\beta}$. We apply different approaches on $\tilde{\mathbf{X}}$. The covariance matrix of $\mathbf{X}$ is used in GFlasso to simulate the graph misspecification. The results of $\boldsymbol{\beta}$ converted from $\tilde{\boldsymbol{\beta}}$ are reported.

Figure 3 shows that ncFGS obtains the same results as ncTFGS on dataset 1 with $\sigma = 2$ when τ is larger than $|\beta_i|$. The regularization parameters are $\tau\lambda_1$ and $\tau\lambda_2$ for ncTFGS, and λ_1 and λ_2 for ncFGS. Figure 4 shows the average nonzero coefficients obtained on dataset 1 with $\sigma = 2$. As can be seen in Figure 4, GOSCAR, ncFGS, and ncTFGS are able to utilize the graph information, and achieve good parameter estimation. Although GFlasso can use the graph information, it performs worse than GOSCAR, ncFGS, and ncTFGS due to the graph misspecification.

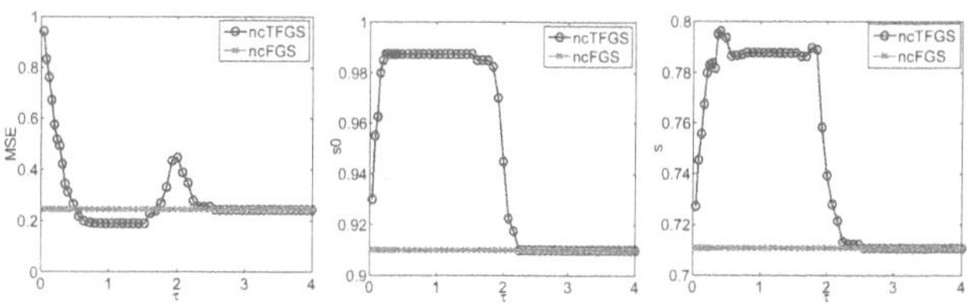

Figure 3: MSEs (left), s_0 (middle), and s (right) of ncFGS and ncTFGS on dataset 1 for fixed λ_1 and λ_2. The regularization parameters for ncTFGS are $\tau\lambda_1$ and $\tau\lambda_2$. τ ranges from 0.04 to 4.

The performance in terms of MSEs averaged over 30 simulations is shown in Table 1. As indicated in Table 1, among existing methods (Lasso, GFlasso, OSCAR), GFlasso is the best, except in the two cases where OSCAR is better. GOSCAR is better than the best existing method in all cases except for two, and ncFGS and ncTFGS outperform all the other methods.

Table 2 shows the results in terms of accuracy of feature grouping and selection. Since Lasso does not perform feature grouping, we only report the results of the other five methods: OSCAR, GFlasso, GOSCAR, ncFGS, and ncTFGS. Table 2 shows that ncFGS and ncTFGS achieve higher accuracy than other methods.

Table 3 shows the comparison of feature selection alone ($\lambda_2 = 0$), feature grouping alone ($\lambda_1 = 0$), and simultaneous feature grouping and selection using ncTFGS. From

Table 1: **Comparison of performance in terms of MSEs and estimated standard deviations (in parentheses) for different methods based on 30 simulations on different synthetic datasets.**

Datasets	Lasso	OSCAR	GFlasso	GOSCAR	ncFGS	ncTFGS
Data1 ($\sigma = 2$)	1.807(0.331)	1.441(0.318)	1.080(0.276)	0.315(0.157)	0.123(0.075)	**0.116(0.075)**
Data1 ($\sigma = 5$)	5.294(0.983)	5.328(1.080)	3.480(1.072)	1.262(0.764)	0.356(0.395)	**0.356(0.395)**
Data1 ($\sigma = 10$)	12.628(3.931)	13.880(4.031)	13.411(4.540)	6.061(4.022)	1.963(1.600)	**1.958(1.593)**
Data2 ($\sigma = 2$)	1.308(0.435)	1.084(0.439)	0.623(0.250)	0.291(0.208)	0.226(0.175)	**0.223(0.135)**
Data2 ($\sigma = 5$)	4.907(1.496)	4.868(1.625)	2.538(0.656)	0.781(0.598)	0.721(0.532)	**0.705(0.535)**
Data2 ($\sigma = 10$)	18.175(6.611)	18.353(6.611)	6.930(2.858)	4.601(2.623)	4.232(2.561)	**4.196(2.577)**
Data3 ($\sigma = 5$)	5.163(1.708)	4.503(1.677)	4.236(1.476)	3.336(1.725)	0.349(0.282)	**0.348(0.283)**
Data4 ($\sigma = 5$)	7.664(2.502)	7.167(2.492)	7.516(2.441)	7.527(2.434)	5.097(0.780)	**4.943(0.764)**
Data5 ($\sigma = 5$)	9.893(1.965)	7.907(2.194)	9.622(2.025)	9.810(2.068)	7.684(1.1191)	**7.601(1.038)**

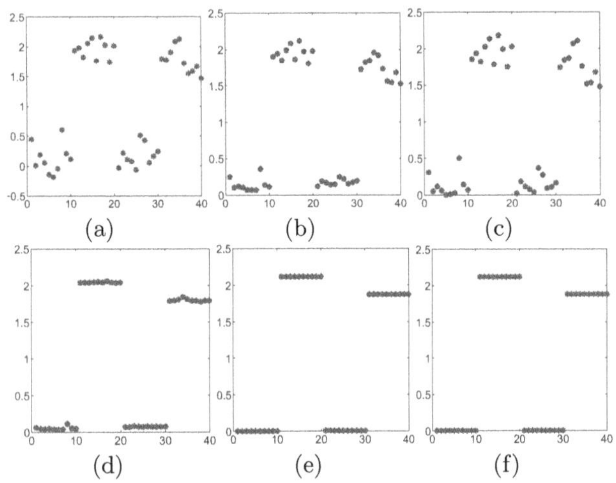

Figure 4: The average nonzero coefficients obtained on dataset 1 with $\sigma = 2$: (a) Lasso; (b) GFlasso; (c) OSCAR; (d) GOSCAR; (e); ncFGS; (f) ncTGS

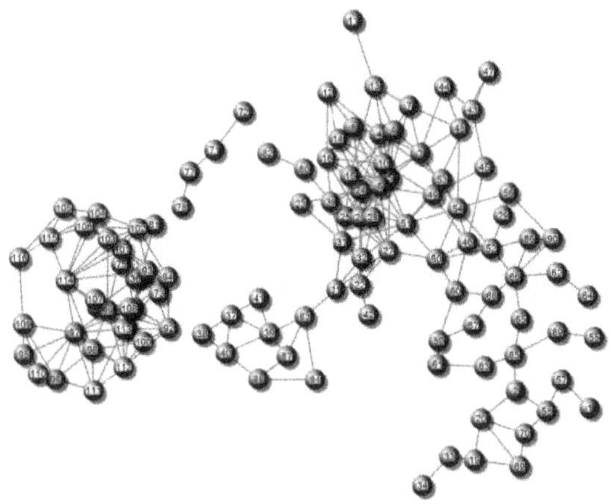

Figure 5: Subgraphs of the graph built by SICE on FDG-PET dataset, which consists of 265 edges.

Table 3, we can observe that simultaneous feature grouping and selection outperforms either feature grouping or feature selection, demonstrating the benefit of joint feature grouping and selection in the proposed non-convex method.

4.3 Real Data

We conduct experiments on two real datasets: FDG-PET and Breast Cancer. The metrics to measure the performance of different algorithms include accuracy (acc.), sensitivity (sen.), specificity (spe.), degrees of freedom (dof.), and the number of nonzero coefficients (nonzero coeff.). The dof. of lasso is the number of nonzero coefficients [18]. For the algorithms capable of feature grouping, we use the same definition of dof. in [2], which is the number of estimated groups.

4.3.1 FDG-PET

In this experiment, we use FDG-PET 3D images from 74 Alzheimer's disease (AD), 172 mild cognitive impairment (MCI), and 81 normal control (NC) subjects downloaded from the Alzheimer's disease neuroimaging initiative (ADNI) database. The different regions of whole brain volume can be represented by 116 anatomical volumes of interest (AVOI), defined by Automated Anatomical Labeling (AAL) [20]. Then we extracted data from each of the 116 AVOIs, and derived average of each AVOI for each subject.

In our study, we compare different methods in distinguishing AD and NC subjects, which is a two-class classification problem over a dataset with 155 samples and 116 features. The dataset is randomly split into two subset, one training set consisting of 104 samples, and one testing set consisting of the remaining 51 samples. The tuning of the parameter is achieved by 5-fold cross validation. Sparse inverse covariance estimation (SICE) has been recognized as an effective tool for identifying the structure of the inverse covariance matrix. We use SICE developed in [6] to model the connectivity of brain regions. Figure 5 shows sample subgraphs built by SICE consisting of 115 nodes and 265 edges.

The results based on 20 replications are shown in Table 4. From Table 4, we can see that ncTFGS achieves more accurate classification while obtaining smaller degrees of freedom. ncFGS and GOSCAR achieve similar classification, while ncFGS selects more features than GOSCAR.

Figure 6 shows the comparison of accuracy with either λ_1 or λ_2 fixed. The λ_1 and λ_2 values range from 1e-4 to 100. As we can see, the performance of ncTFGS is slightly better than that of the other competitors. Since the regularization parameters of subproblems in ncTFGS are $\frac{\lambda_1}{\tau}$ and $\frac{2\lambda_2}{\tau}$, the solution of ncTFGS is more sparse than those of other competitors when λ_1 and λ_2 are large and τ is small ($\tau = 0.15$ in this case).

4.3.2 Breast Cancer

We conduct experiments on the breast cancer dataset, which consists of gene expression data for 8141 genes in 295

Table 2: **Accuracy of feature grouping and selection based on 30 simulations for five feature grouping methods: the first row for each dataset corresponds to the accuracy of feature selection; the second row corresponds to the accuracy of feature grouping. The numbers in parentheses are the standard deviations.**

Datasets	OSCAR	GFlasso	GOSCAR	ncFGS	ncTFGS
Data1 ($\sigma = 2$)	0.675(0.098)	0.553(0.064)	0.513(0.036)	0.983(0.063)	**1.000(0.000)**
	0.708(0.021)	0.709(0.017)	0.702(0.009)	0.994(0.022)	**1.000(0.000)**
Data1 ($\sigma = 5$)	0.565(0.084)	0.502(0.009)	0.585(0.085)	**1.000(0.000)**	**1.000(0.000)**
	0.691(0.011)	0.709(0.016)	0.708(0.017)	**1.000(0.000)**	**1.000(0.000)**
Data1 ($\sigma = 10$)	0.532(0.069)	0.568(0.088)	0.577(0.061)	0.983(0.063)	**1.000(0.000)**
	0.675(0.031)	0.725(0.022)	0.708(0.020)	0.994(0.022)	**0.999(0.001)**
Data2 ($\sigma = 2$)	0.739(0.108)	0.544(0.272)	**1.000(0.000)**	0.958(0.159)	0.958(0.159)
	0.625(0.052)	0.823(0.029)	0.837(0.014)	0.831(0.052)	**0.846(0.041)**
Data2 ($\sigma = 5$)	0.763(0.114)	0.717(0.275)	**0.999(0.005)**	0.979(0.114)	0.975(0.115)
	0.650(0.066)	0.741(0.062)	0.833(0.011)	**0.845(0.030)**	0.842(0.037)
Data2 ($\sigma = 10$)	0.726(0.101)	0.818(0.149)	0.993(0.024)	**1.000(0.000)**	**1.000(0.000)**
	0.597(0.058)	0.680(0.049)	0.829(0.025)	0.851(0.015)	**0.856(0.014)**
Data3 ($\sigma = 5$)	0.886(0.135)	0.736(0.103)	0.382(0.084)	0.992(0.026)	**0.996(0.014)**
	0.841(0.056)	0.739(0.041)	0.689(0.013)	**0.995(0.017)**	0.978(0.028)
Data4 ($\sigma = 5$)	0.875(0.033)	0.881(0.026)	0.882(0.037)	0.796(0.245)	**0.950(0.012)**
	0.834(0.030)	0.805(0.035)	0.805(0.036)	**0.895(0.114)**	0.890(0.074)
Data5 ($\sigma = 5$)	0.760(0.203)	0.802(0.153)	0.861(0.051)	0.881(0.174)	**0.894(0.132)**
	0.858(0.031)	0.821(0.037)	0.805(0.037)	**0.920(0.056)**	0.919(0.057)

Table 4: **Comparison of classification accuracy, sensitivity, specificity, degrees of freedom, and the number of nonzero coefficients averaged over 20 replications for different methods on FDG-PET dataset.**

Metrics	Lasso	OSCAR	GFlasso	GOSCAR	ncFGS	ncTFGS
acc.	0.886(0.026)	0.891(0.026)	0.901(0.029)	0.909(0.026)	0.909(0.031)	**0.920(0.024)**
sen.	0.870(0.041)	0.876(0.038)	0.904(0.038)	0.909(0.041)	0.915(0.043)	**0.933(0.047)**
pec.	0.913(0.0446)	**0.917(0.050)**	0.902(0.046)	0.915(0.046)	0.908(0.047)	0.915(0.052)
dof.	22.150	29.150	24.350	21.300	31.250	**18.250**
nonzero coeff.	22.150	38.000	41.900	24.250	37.350	**19.350**

Table 3: **Comparison of feature selection alone (FS), feature grouping alone (FG), and simultaneous feature grouping and feature selection (Both). The average results based on 30 replications of three datasets with $\sigma = 5$: Data3 (top), Data4 (middle), and Data5 (bottom) are reported. The numbers in parentheses are the standard deviations.**

Meth.	MSE	s_0	s
FG	2.774(0.967)	0.252(0.156)	0.696(0.006)
FS	6.005(1.410)	0.945(0.012)	0.773(0.037)
Both	**0.348(0.283)**	**0.996(0.014)**	**0.978(0.028)**
FG	9.4930(1.810)	0.613(0.115)	0.770(0.038)
FS	6.437(1.803)	0.947(0.016)	0.782(0.046)
Both	**4.944(0.764)**	**0.951(0.166)**	**0.890(0.074)**
FG	10.830(2.161)	0.434(0.043)	0.847(0.014)
FS	10.276(1.438)	0.891(0.018)	0.768(0.026)
Both	**7.601(1.038)**	**0.894(0.132)**	**0.919(0.057)**

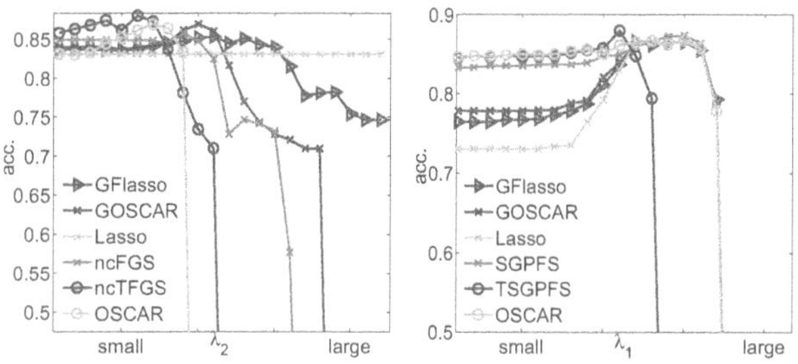

(a) λ_1 fixed (b) λ_2 fixed

Figure 6: Comparison of accuracies for various methods with λ_1 fixed (left) and λ_2 fixed (right) on FDT-PET dataset.

breast cancer tumors (78 metastatic and 217 non-metastatic). The network described in [4] is used as the input graph in this experiment. Figure 7 shows a subgraph consisting of 80 nodes of the used graph. We restrict our analysis to the 566 genes most correlated to the output, but also connected in the graph. 2/3 data is randomly chosen as training data, and the remaining 1/3 data is used as testing data. The tuning parameter is estimated by 5-fold cross validation. Table 5 shows the results averaged over 30 replications. As indicated in Table 5, GOSCAR, ncFGS and ncTFGS outperform the other three methods, and ncTFGS achieves the best performance.

5. CONCLUSION

In this paper, we consider simultaneous feature grouping and selection over a given undirected graph. We propose one convex and two non-convex penalties to encourage both sparsity and equality of absolute values of coefficients for features connected in the graph. We employ ADMM and DC programming to solve the proposed formulations. Numerical experiments on synthetic and real data demonstrate the effectiveness of the proposed methods. Our results also demonstrate the benefit of simultaneous feature grouping and feature selection through the proposed non-convex

Table 5: **Comparison of classification accuracy, sensitivity, specificity, degrees of freedom, and the number of nonzero coefficients averaged over 30 replications for various methods on Breast Cancer dataset.**

Metrics	Lasso	OSCAR	GFlasso	GOSCAR	ncFGS	ncTFGS
acc.	0.739(0.054)	0.755(0.055)	0.771(0.050)	0.783(0.042)	0.779(0.041)	**0.790(0.036)**
sen.	0.707(0.056)	0.720(0.060)	0.749(0.060)	0.755(0.050)	0.755(0.055)	**0.762(0.044)**
pec.	0.794(0.071)	0.810(0.068)	0.805(0.056)	0.827(0.061)	0.819(0.058)	**0.834(0.060)**
dof.	239.267	165.633	108.633	70.267	57.233	**45.600**
nonzero coeff.	239.267	243.867	144.867	140.667	**79.833**	116.567

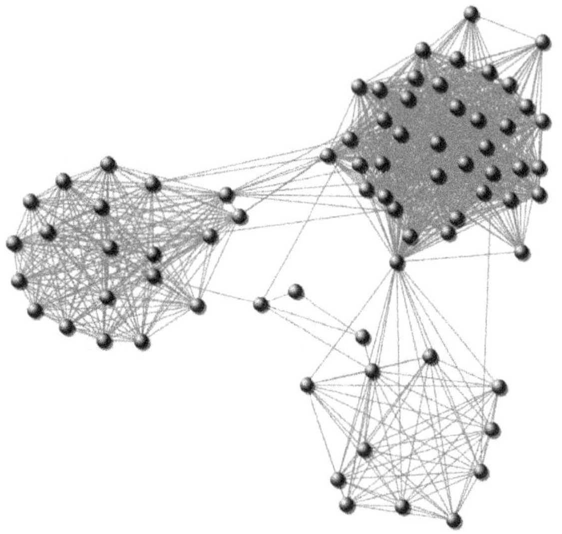

Figure 7: A subgraph of the network in Breast Cancer dataset [4]. The subgraph consists of 80 nodes.

methods. In this paper, we focus on undirected graphs. A possible future direction is to extend the formulations to directed graphs. In addition, we plan to study the generalization performance of the proposed formulations.

Acknowledgments

This work was supported in part by NSF (IIS-0953662, MCB-1026710, CCF-1025177, DMS-0906616) and NIH (R01LM010 730, 2R01GM081535-01, R01HL105397).

6. REFERENCES

[1] F. Bach, G. Lanckriet, and M. Jordan. Multiple kernel learning, conic duality, and the SMO algorithm. In *ICML*, 2004.

[2] H. Bondell and B. Reich. Simultaneous regression shrinkage, variable selection, and supervised clustering of predictors with oscar. *Biometrics*, 64(1):115–123, 2008.

[3] S. Boyd, N. Parikh, E. Chu, B. Peleato, and J. Eckstein. *Distributed optimization and statistical learning via the alternating direction method of multipliers*. 2011.

[4] H. Chuang, E. Lee, Y. Liu, D. Lee, and T. Ideker. Network-based classification of breast cancer metastasis. *Molecular systems biology*, 3(1), 2007.

[5] H. Fei, B. Quanz, and J. Huan. Regularization and feature selection for networked features. In *CIKM*, pages 1893–1896, 2010.

[6] S. Huang, J. Li, L. Sun, J. Liu, T. Wu, K. Chen, A. Fleisher, E. Reiman, and J. Ye. Learning brain connectivity of Alzheimer's disease from neuroimaging data. *NIPS*, 22:808–816, 2009.

[7] L. Jacob, G. Obozinski, and J. Vert. Group lasso with overlap and graph lasso. In *ICML*, pages 433–440, 2009.

[8] R. Jenatton, J. Mairal, G. Obozinski, and F. Bach. Proximal methods for sparse hierarchical dictionary learning. In *ICML*, 2010.

[9] S. Kim and E. Xing. Statistical estimation of correlated genome associations to a quantitative trait network. *PLoS genetics*, 5(8):e1000587, 2009.

[10] C. Li and H. Li. Network-constrained regularization and variable selection for analysis of genomic data. *Bioinformatics*, 24(9):1175–1182, 2008.

[11] J. Liu and J. Ye. Moreau-Yosida regularization for grouped tree structure learning. *NIPS*, 2010.

[12] A. Rinaldo. Properties and refinements of the fused lasso. *The Annals of Statistics*, 37(5B):2922–2952, 2009.

[13] X. Shen and H. Huang. Grouping pursuit through a regularization solution surface. *Journal of the American Statistical Association*, 105(490):727–739, 2010.

[14] X. Shen, H. Huang, and W. Pan. Simultaneous supervised clustering and feature selection over a graph. *Submitted.*

[15] X. Shen and J. Ye. Adaptive model selection. *Journal of the American Statistical Association*, 97(457):210–221, 2002.

[16] P. Tao and L. An. Convex analysis approach to DC programming: Theory, algorithms and applications. *Acta Math. Vietnam*, 22(1):289–355, 1997.

[17] P. Tao and S. El Bernoussi. Duality in DC (difference of convex functions) optimization. subgradient methods. *Trends in Mathematical Optimization*, 84:277–293, 1988.

[18] R. Tibshirani. Regression shrinkage and selection via the lasso. *Journal of the Royal Statistical Society. Series B*, pages 267–288, 1996.

[19] R. Tibshirani, M. Saunders, S. Rosset, J. Zhu, and K. Knight. Sparsity and smoothness via the fused lasso. *Journal of the Royal Statistical Society: Series B*, 67(1):91–108, 2005.

[20] N. Tzourio-Mazoyer, B. Landeau, D. Papathanassiou, F. Crivello, O. Etard, N. Delcroix, B. Mazoyer, and M. Joliot. Automated anatomical labeling of activations in SPM using a macroscopic anatomical parcellation of the MNI MRI single-subject brain. *Neuroimage*, 15(1):273–289, 2002.

[21] L. Yuan, J. Liu, and J. Ye. Efficient methods for overlapping group lasso. *NIPS*, 2011.

[22] M. Yuan and Y. Lin. Model selection and estimation in regression with grouped variables. *Journal of the Royal Statistical Society: Series B*, 68(1):49–67, 2006.

[23] T. Zhang. Multi-stage convex relaxation for feature selection. *stat*, 1050:3, 2011.

[24] P. Zhao, G. Rocha, and B. Yu. The composite absolute penalties family for grouped and hierarchical variable selection. *The Annals of Statistics*, 37(6A):3468–3497, 2009.

[25] L. Zhong and J. Kwok. Efficient sparse modeling with automatic feature grouping. *ICML*, 2011.

[26] Y. Zhu, X. Shen, and W. Pan. Simultaneous grouping pursuit and feature selection in regression over an undirected graph. *Submitted.*

[27] H. Zou and T. Hastie. Regularization and variable selection via the elastic net. *Journal of the Royal Statistical Society: Series B*, 67(2):301–320, 2005.

Maximum Inner-Product Search Using Cone Trees

Parikshit Ram
School of Computational Science & Engineering
Georgia Institute of Technology
p.ram@gatech.edu

Alexander G. Gray
School of Computational Science & Engineering
Georgia Institute of Technology
agray@cc.gatech.edu

ABSTRACT

The problem of efficiently finding the best match for a query in a given set with respect to the Euclidean distance or the cosine similarity has been extensively studied. However, the closely related problem of efficiently finding the best match with respect to the inner-product has never been explored in the general setting to the best of our knowledge. In this paper we consider this problem and contrast it with the previous problems considered. First, we propose a general branch-and-bound algorithm based on a (single) tree data structure. Subsequently, we present a dual-tree algorithm for the case where there are multiple queries. Our proposed branch-and-bound algorithms are based on novel inner-product bounds. Finally we present a new data structure, the cone tree, for increasing the efficiency of the dual-tree algorithm. We evaluate our proposed algorithms on a variety of data sets from various applications, and exhibit up to five orders of magnitude improvement in query time over the naive search technique in some cases.

Categories and Subject Descriptors

E.1 [**Data Structures**]: Trees; G.4 [**Mathematical Software**]: Algorithm design and analysis; H.2.8 [**Database Management**]: Database Applications—*Data mining*; H.3.3 [**Information Storage and Retrieval**]: Information Search and Retrieval—*Search process*

General Terms

Algorithms, Design

Keywords

Metric trees, cone trees, dual-tree branch-and-bound

1. INTRODUCTION

In this paper, we consider the problem of efficiently finding the best match for a query from a given set of points with respect to the inner-product similarity. We focus on improving the efficiency of this search. Formally, we consider the following problem:

Maximum inner-product search. For a given set of N points $S \subset \mathbb{R}^D$ and a query $q \in \mathbb{R}^D$, efficiently find a point $p \in S$ such that:

$$\langle q, p \rangle = \max_{r \in S} \langle q, r \rangle. \quad (1)$$

At first glance, this problem appears to be very similar to much existing work in literature. Efficiently finding the best match with respect to the Euclidean (or more generally L_p) distance is the widely studied problem of fast nearest-neighbor search in metric spaces [9]. Efficient retrieval of the best match with respect to the cosine similarity has been researched in the field of text mining and information retrieval [1]. But as we will explain in the next section, the maximum inner-product search is not only different from these aforementioned tasks, but also arguably harder.

1.1 Applications

An obvious application of maximum inner-product search stems out of the widely successful matrix-factorization framework in recommender system challenges like the "Netflix prize" [22, 21, 2]. The matrix-factorization results in accurate representation of the available data in terms of user vectors and items vectors (examples for items would be movies or music). In this setting, the preference of a user for an item is the inner-product between the corresponding user's vector and the item's vector[1]. The retrieval of recommendations for a user is equivalent to maximum inner-product search with the user as the query and the items as the reference set. Linear scan of the items are usually employed to find the best recommendations. An efficient search algorithm would make the retrieval of recommendations in the matrix-factorization framework scalable to larger systems.

The usual document retrieval tasks use the cosine similarity to match documents. However, in certain settings [11], the documents are represented as (not necessarily normalized) vectors and the inner-product between these vectors represent their mutual similarity. In this case, unless the vectors are normalized to have the same length, document matching using the cosine similarity [1] might make the algorithm scalable at the cost of returning inaccurate solutions since the inner-product is not the same as the cosine similarity (we will discuss this further in Section 2).

There is a similar problem known as the the max-kernel operation: for a given set of points S and a query q and a kernel function $\mathcal{K}(\cdot, \cdot)$, the task is to find the point $p \in S$ with the maximum value of $\mathcal{K}(q, p)$ over the set S. This

[1]The preference is actually the inner-product between the user and the item vector plus a item bias term. But this can be reduced to an inner-product by appending the user vector with 1 and the item vector with the item bias.

problem is widely used in maximum-a-posteriori inference [20] in machine learning, and for image matching [23] in computer vision. If the kernel function can be explicitly represented in the form a function $\varphi(\cdot)$ such that $\mathcal{K}(q,p) = \langle \varphi(q), \varphi(r) \rangle$, then this problem reduces to maximum inner-product search after all the points in the set S and the query q is transformed into the φ-space.

1.2 This Paper

In this paper, we propose two tree-based branch-and-bound algorithms along with a new data structure to solve this problem. In Section 2, we contrast this problem to the more familiar problems of nearest-neighbor search in metric spaces and best matches with respect to the cosine similarity. In Section 3, we propose a simple branch-and-bound algorithm using existing ball tree data structure [28] and a novel bound. In the following section (Section 4), we address the situation where there are multiple queries on the same set of points and propose a dual-tree branch-and-bound algorithm. In Section 5, we present a new data structure, the*cone trees*, to index the queries for the dual-tree algorithm. These structures take advantage of novel inner-product bounds which are tighter than those that can be achieved with traditional ball trees. The proposed algorithms are evaluated for their efficiency over a variety of data sets in Section 6. Section 7 demonstrates how the proposed algorithms can be applied to the max-kernel operation with general kernel functions without any explicit representation of the points in the φ-space. In the final section, we provide our conclusions along with possible future directions for this work.

2. MAXIMUM INNER-PRODUCT SEARCH

Numerous techniques exists for nearest-neighbor search in Euclidean metric space (see surveys like [9]). Large scale best matching algorithms have also been developed for the cosine-similarity measure [1], with a lot of focus on text data. The problem of nearest-neighbor search (in metric space) has been solved approximately with the widely popular *locality-sensitive hashing* (LSH) [14, 18]. LSH has been extended to other forms of similarity functions (as opposed to the distance as a dissimilarity function) like the cosine similarity [7][2]. The approximate max-kernel operations can also be solved efficiently with LSH under certain conditions on the kernel function. Dimension reduction [30] and dual-tree algorithms [20] have also been used to solve the approximate max-kernel operation efficiently.

2.1 How is maximum inner-product search different from existing problems?

Here we explain why the maximum inner-product search is different from these existing search problems. Hence techniques applied to these problems (like LSH) cannot be directly applied to this problem.

Nearest-neighbor search in Euclidean space. This involves finding a point $p \in S$ for a query q such that:

$$\begin{aligned} p &= \arg\min_{r \in S} \|q - r\|_2^2 = \arg\max_{r \in S} \left(\langle q, r \rangle - \frac{\|r\|_2^2}{2} \right) \\ &\neq \arg\max_{r \in S} \langle q, r \rangle \text{ (unless } \|r\|_2^2 = k \ \forall\ r \in S). \end{aligned}$$

[2] An important thing to note here is that the similarity function used in Charikar et.al.[7] is not exactly the cosine-similarity. The distance between two points p and q was measured by θ/π, where θ is the angle made the two points at the origin, making the similarity function $\left(1 - \frac{\theta}{\pi}\right)$. This similarity function has a direct correspondence to the cosine similarity.

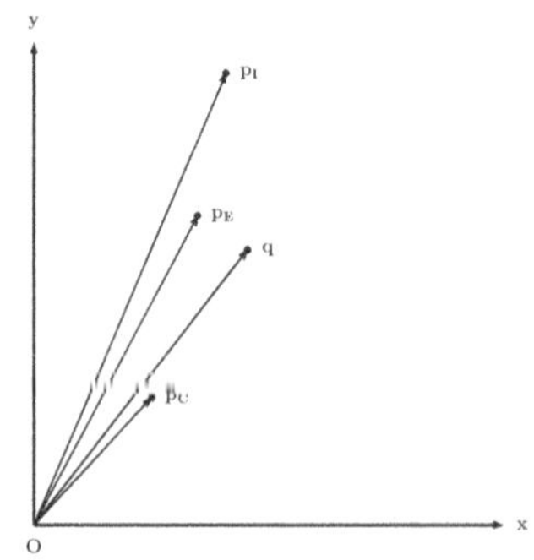

Figure 1: Best matches: For a given query q, p_C, p_E and p_I denote the different best match candidates with respect to the cosine similarity, the Euclidean distance and the inner-product respectively.

Hence, if the norms of all the points in S are normalized to have the same length, then maximum inner-product search is equivalent to nearest-neighbor search in Euclidean metric space. However, without this restriction, the two problems can have potentially very different answers (figure 2).

Best-matching with cosine similarity. This constitutes finding a point $p \in S$ for a query q such that

$$\begin{aligned} p &= \arg\max_{r \in S} \frac{\langle q, r \rangle}{\|q\| \, \|r\|} = \arg\max_{r \in S} \frac{\langle q, r \rangle}{\|r\|} \\ &\neq \arg\max_{r \in S} \langle q, r \rangle \text{ (unless } \|r\| = k \ \forall\ r \in S). \end{aligned}$$

The best match with cosine similarity gives the maximum inner-product only if all the points in the set S are normalized to the same length (counter example in figure 2).

Locality-sensitive hashing. LSH has been applied to a wide variety of similarity functions. LSH involves constructing hashing functions such that each hash function h satisfies the following for any pair of points $r, p \in S$:

$$\Pr[h(r) = h(p)] = \text{sim}(r, p), \quad (2)$$

where $\text{sim}(r,p) \in [0,1]$ is the similarity function of interest. For our situation, we can normalize our data set such that $\forall\ r \in S, \|r\| \leq 1$[3], and assume that the all the data is in the first quadrant (so that none of the inner-products go below zero). In that case, $\text{sim}(r,p) = \langle r, p \rangle \in [0,1]$ is a valid similarity function of interest.

It is known that for any similarity function to admit a locality sensitive hash function family (as defined in equation 2), the distance function $\mathbf{d}(r,p) = 1 - \text{sim}(r,p)$ must satisfy the triangle inequality (Lemma 1 in [7]). However, the distance function $\mathbf{d}(r,p) = 1 - \langle r, p \rangle$ does not satisfy the triangle inequality (even when all the points are restricted to the first quadrant)[4]. So LSH cannot be applied to the inner product similarity function even when all the data lies in the first quadrant (which is quite a restrictive condition).

Efficient max-kernel operation. Various techniques have been proposed to solve this problem efficiently. For kernel functions with very high (possibly infinite) dimensional explicit representations, Rahimi, et.al., 2007 [30], propose a technique to transform these high-dimensional representa-

[3] This normalization is different than the normalization mentioned earlier where all the points were normalized to have the same length. Here the lengths are normalized to be less than equal to one, but not equal to each other.

[4] Counter example: Let $x, y, z \in S$ be points such that $\|x\| = \|y\| = \|z\| = 1$, and angles made between x & y, y & z and z & x at the origin be $(\frac{\pi}{4} - 0.1)$, $\frac{\pi}{4}$ and $(\frac{\pi}{2} - 0.3)$ respectively. The triangle inequality, $\mathbf{d}(x,y) + \mathbf{d}(y,z) \geq \mathbf{d}(z,x)$, does not hold for $d(\cdot,\cdot) = 1 - \langle \cdot, \cdot \rangle$. $\mathbf{d}(x,y) = 0.23$, $\mathbf{d}(y,z) = 0.29$ & $\mathbf{d}(z,x) = 0.70$.

tions into lower-dimensions while still approximately preserving the inner-product to improve scalability. However, the final search still involves a linear scan over the set of points for the maximum inner-product or a fast nearest-neighbor search under the assumption that finding the nearest-neighbor is equivalent to maximizing the inner-product. For translation invariant kernels[5], a tree-based recursive algorithm has been shown to scale to large sets [20]. However, it is not clear how this algorithm can be extended to the general class of kernels. LSH is widely used for image matching in computer vision [23], but only for kernel functions that admit a locality sensitive hashing function [7]. Hence, none of the existing techniques can be directly applied to maximum inner-product search without introducing inaccurate results or limiting assumptions.

2.2 Why is maximum inner-product search possibly harder?

Inner-products lack a very basic property of generally used similarity functions – coincidence. For example, the Euclidean distance of a point to itself is 0; the cosine similarity of a point to itself is 1. The inner-product of a point $x \in S$ to itself is $\|x\|^2$, which may be high or low depending on the value of the $\|x\|$. Additionally, there can possibly be many other points $y \in S$ such that $\langle y, x \rangle > \|x\|^2$.

Efficient nearest neighbor search methods typically rely heavily on these properties (triangle inequality and coincidence) to achieve their efficiency. Hence, without any added assumptions, this problem of maximum inner-product search is inherently harder than the previously dealt similar problems. This is possibly the reason why there is no existing work for this problem in its general form, to our knowledge.

2.3 Why try trees?

Trees have been widely used for nearest-neighbor search [13, 4, 29, 8, 32]. Being widely used approach in the nearest neighbor case, we believe it is instructive to review them before considering the maximum inner-product search case.

For exact nearest-neighbor searches, trees can yield great accelerations in anywhere from low- to high-dimensional data, as long as there is low intrinsic dimensionality [4, 10]. Trees can also be easily adapted to the approximate case, with error guarantees of various sorts. These include approximation in the sense of *rank*, i.e. if the actual best match may not be returned, trees can be used in a way that guarantees that the result is, say, in the top 10 best matches [32] – rather than provide a guarantee in terms of potentially less meaningful abstract quantities such as distances (as is provided by LSH; it is not clear how to extend LSH to provide rank guarantees). This would appear to make particular sense in many applications such as recommendations. Trees can also be used for another kind of approximate search setting which can be important in practical applications, in which the best possible match is found given a user-defined time limit. This kind of approximation is possible for tree-based branch-and-bound algorithms because they are incremental algorithms. This is not possible with something like LSH – LSH provides theoretical error bounds, but there is no way of ensuring the error constraint *during* the search. Another important advantage of trees is that the trees require a single construction – the branch-and-bound algorithm adapts for the different levels of approximate and/or time limitations. Hashing techniques require multiple hashes for different levels of approximation. The usual norm is to pre-hash for multiple values of approximation. Trees can also be constructed by learning from the data using techniques from machine learning [6, 25] to provide better accuracy and efficiency.

The significant advantages of the tree-based approach for the nearest-neighbor setting motivate the question of whether they can be brought to the maximum inner-product case.

[5]Kernel functions $\mathcal{K}(p, q)$ which are dependent only the (Euclidean) distance between the points p and q are considered translation invariant kernels. The Gaussian RBF kernel is such a translation invariant kernel function.

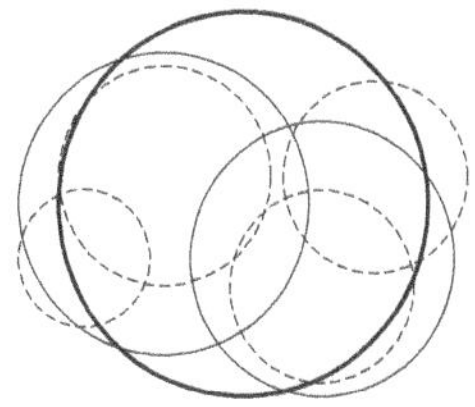

Figure 2: Ball trees

Algorithm 1 MakeBallTreeSplit(Data S)

Pick a random point $\mathbf{x} \in S$
$A \leftarrow \arg\max_{\mathbf{x}' \in S} \|\mathbf{x} - \mathbf{x}'\|_2^2$
$B \leftarrow \arg\max_{\mathbf{x}' \in S} \|A - \mathbf{x}'\|_2^2$
return (A, B)

Algorithm 2 MakeBallTree(Set of items S)

Input – Set S
Output – Tree T
$T.S \leftarrow S$ *//The set of points in node T*
$T.\mu \leftarrow \text{mean}(S)$ *//The center of the ball around T.S*
$T.R \leftarrow \max_{p \in S} \|p - T.\mu\|_2^2$ *//The radius of the ball around T.S*
if $|S| \leq N_0$ **then**
  return T
else
  $(A, B) \leftarrow$ MakeBallTreeSplit(S)
  $S_l \leftarrow \{p \in S \colon \|p - A\|_2^2 \leq \|p - B\|_2^2\}$; $S_r \leftarrow S \setminus S_l$
  T.lc $\leftarrow$ MakeBallTree(S_l) *//Left child*
  T.rc $\leftarrow$ MakeBallTree(S_r) *//Right child*
  return T
end if

Figure 3: Ball tree Construction

3. TREE-BASED SEARCH

Ball trees [29, 28] are binary space-partitioning trees that have been widely used for the task of indexing data sets. Every node in the tree represents a set of points and each node is indexed with a center and a ball enclosing all the points in the node. The set of point at a node is divided into two disjoint sets which form the child nodes, partitioning the space into (possibly overlapping) hyper-spheres. The tree is built hierarchically and a node is made a leaf if it contains a set of points of size below a threshold value N_0.

3.1 Tree construction

We use a simple ball tree construction heuristic that approximately picks a pair of pivot points which are farthest apart from each other [28], and splits the data by assigning the points to their closest pivot. The intuition behind this heuristic is that these two points might lie in the principal direction. The splitting and the recursive tree construction algorithm is presented in Algorithms 1 & 2 for completeness.

3.2 Branch-and-bound algorithm

Ball trees are widely used for the task of nearest neighbor search and are known to be fairly scalable to moderately high dimensions [28, 26]. The search usually employs

Algorithm 3 LinearSearch(Query q, Reference Set S)

for each $p \in S$ **do**
  if $\langle q, p\rangle > q.\lambda$ **then**
    $q.\text{bm} \leftarrow p$
    $q.\lambda \leftarrow \langle q, p\rangle$
  end if
end for

Algorithm 4 TreeSearch(Query q, Tree Node T)

if $q.\lambda < \mathbf{MIP}(q, T)$ **then**
  if *isLeaf*(T) **then**
    LinearSearch(q, $T.S$)
  else
    $I_l \leftarrow \mathbf{MIP}(q, T.\text{lc})$; $I_r \leftarrow \mathbf{MIP}(q, T.\text{rc})$;
    if $I_l \leq I_r$ **then**
      TreeSearch(q, T.rc); TreeSearch(q, T.lc);
    else
      TreeSearch(q, T.lc); TreeSearch(q, T.rc);
    end if
  end if
end if

Algorithm 5 ExactMIP(Query set V, Reference Set S)

$T \leftarrow$ MakeBallTree(S)
for each $q \in V$ **do**
  $q.\text{bm} \leftarrow \emptyset$; *//The current max-inner-product candidate*
  $q.\lambda \leftarrow -\infty$; *//The current highest inner-product*
  TreeSearch(q, T);
  return q.bm;
end for

Figure 4: Single-tree Search: See text for details

the depth-first branch-and-bound algorithm – a query is answered by traversing the tree in a depth-first manner by first going down the node closer to the query and bounding the minimum possible distance to the other branch with the triangle-inequality. If this bound is greater than the distance to the current neighbor candidate for the query, the branch is removed from computation.

An analogous greedy depth-first algorithm can be used for maximum inner-product search. But instead of traversing down the node closer to the query, the choice is made on the basis of the maximum possible inner-product between the query and any potential point from the node. The recursive depth-first branch and bound algorithm is presented in Algorithm 4. The search algorithm for a query (q) begins at the root of the tree (Alg. 5). At each step, the algorithm is at a tree node (T). It checks if the maximum possible inner-product between the query and any point in the node, $\mathbf{MIP}(q, T)$, is any better than the current best-match for the query (q.bm). If the check fails, this branch of the tree is not explored any more. Otherwise, the algorithm recursively traverses the tree, exploring the branch with the better potential candidates in a depth-first manner. If the node is a leaf, the algorithm just finds the best-match within the leaf with a linear search (Alg. 3). This algorithm ensures that the exact solution (i.e., the maximum inner-product) is returned by the end of the algorithm.

3.2.1 Bounding maximum inner-product with a ball

We present an novel analytical upper bound for the maximum possible inner product of a given point (in this case, the query q) with points in a ball. It is important to note that the information about the ball is limited to its center and its radius. For the rest of this section, we use the notation $\|\cdot\|$ to denote the $\|\cdot\|_2$.

THEOREM 3.1. *Given a ball $\mathcal{B}_{p_0}^{R_p}$ of points centered at p_0 with radius R_p and (query) point q, the maximum possible inner product between the point q and the ball $\mathcal{B}_{p_0}^{R_p}$ is bounded from above by:*

$$\max_{p \in \mathcal{B}_{p_0}^{R_p}} \langle q, p\rangle \leq \langle q, p_0\rangle + R_p \|q\| . \quad (3)$$

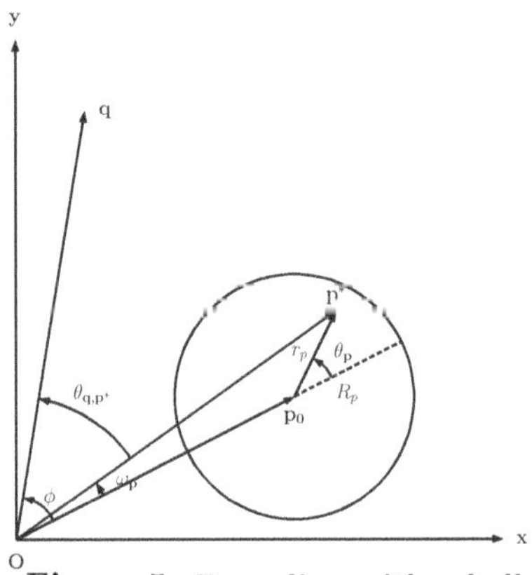

Figure 5: Bounding with a ball

PROOF. Suppose that p^* is the best possible match in the ball $\mathcal{B}_{p_0}^{R_p}$ for the query q and r_p be the Euclidean distance between the ball center p_0 and p^* (by definition, $r_p \leq R_p$). Let θ_p be the angle between the vector $\vec{p_0}$ and the vector $\vec{p_0 p^*}$, ϕ and ω_p be the angles made at the origin between the vector $\vec{p_0}$ and vectors $\vec{q}$ and $\vec{p^*}$ respectively (see figure 5). The length of p^* in terms of p_0 and θ_p is:

$$\|p^*\| = \sqrt{(\|p_0\| + r_p \cos\theta_p)^2 + (r_p \sin\theta_p)^2}. \quad (4)$$

The angle ω_p can be expressed in terms of p_0 and θ_p as:

$$\cos\omega_p = \frac{\|p_0\| + r_p \cos\theta_p}{\|p^*\|}, \sin\omega_p = \frac{r_p \sin\theta_p}{\|p^*\|}. \quad (5)$$

Let θ_{q,p^*} be the angle between the vectors $\vec{q}$ and $\vec{p^*}$. With the triangle inequality of angles, we have:

$$|\theta_{q,p^*}| \geq |\phi - \omega_p|.$$

Assuming that the angles lie in the range $[-\pi, \pi]$ (instead of the usual $[0, 2\pi]$), we get:

$$\cos\theta_{q,p^*} \leq \cos(\phi - \omega_p). \quad (6)$$

Using this inequality we obtain the following bound for the highest possible inner-product between q and any $p \in \mathcal{B}_{p_0}^{R_p}$:

$$\max_{p \in \mathcal{B}_{p_0}^{R_p}} \langle q, p\rangle = \langle q, p^*\rangle (\text{by assumption}) = \|q\| \, \|p^*\| \cos\theta_{q,p^*}$$

By equations 4, 5 & 6, we have

$$\begin{aligned} \max_{p \in \mathcal{B}_{p_0}^{R_p}} \langle q, p\rangle &\leq \|q\| \, \|p^*\| \cos(\phi - \omega_p) \\ &= \|q\| \left(\cos\phi(\|p_0\| + r_p \cos\theta_p) + \sin\phi(r_p \sin\theta_p)\right) \\ &\leq \|q\| \max_{\theta_p} \left(\cos\phi(\|p_0\| + r_p \cos\theta_p) + \sin\phi(r_p \sin\theta_p)\right) \\ &= \|q\| \left(\cos\phi(\|p_0\| + r_p \cos\phi) + \sin\phi(r_p \sin\phi)\right) \\ &\leq \|q\| \left(\cos\phi(\|p_0\| + R_p \cos\phi) + \sin\phi(R_p \sin\phi)\right). \end{aligned}$$

The third inequality comes from the definition of maximum. The following equality comes from maximizing over θ_p. This gives us the optimal value of $\theta_p = \phi$. The final inequality is comes from the fact that $r_p \leq R_p$. Simplifying the final inequality gives us equation 3. $\square$

For the tree-search algorithm (Alg. 4), we set the maximum possible inner-product between q and a tree node T as

$$\mathbf{MIP}(q, T) = \langle q, T.\mu\rangle + T.R \, \|q\| .$$

This upper bound can be computed in almost the same time required for a single inner-product (since the norms of the queries can be pre-computed before searching the tree).

4. DUAL-TREE BASED SEARCH

For a set of queries, the tree can be traversed separately for each query. However, if the set of queries is very large, a common technique to improve efficiency of querying is to index the queries in the form of a tree as well. The search is performed by traversing both trees simultaneously using the *dual-tree* algorithm [15]. The basic idea is to amortize the cost of tree-traversal for a set of similar queries. The dual-tree algorithms have been applied to different tree-based algorithms like nearest-neighbor search [15] and kernel density estimation [16] with theoretical runtime guarantees [31].

4.1 Dual-tree branch-and-bound algorithm

The generic dual-tree algorithm is presented in Alg. 6. Similar to the Alg. 4, the algorithm traverses down the tree on the reference set S (*RTree*). However, the algorithm also traverses down the tree on the set V of queries (*QTree*), resulting in a four-way recursion. At each step, the algorithm is at a QTree node Q and a RTree node T. For every Q, the value $Q.\lambda$ denotes the minimum inner-product between any query in Q and its current best-match candidate. If this value is greater than the maximum possible inner product, $\mathbf{MIP}(Q, T)$, between any query in Q and any reference point in T, this part of the recursion is no longer explored. When the algorithm is at the leaf level of both the trees, it obtains the best-matches for each query in the QTree leaf by doing a linear scan over the RTree leaf.

We explore two ways of indexing the queries – (1) indexing the queries using the ball-tree (*MakeQueryTree* in Alg.7 is Alg. 2) (2) indexing the queries using a novel data structure, the *cone-tree* (*MakeQueryTree* in Alg.7 is Alg. 9). In the following subsection, we derive expressions for $\mathbf{MIP}(Q, T)$ for the ball-tree. The expressions for the cone-tree is presented in section 5.

4.2 Using ball trees

In this subsection, we provide inner-product bounds between two balls with the following theorem:

THEOREM 4.1. *Given two balls $\mathcal{B}_{p_0}^{R_p}$ and $\mathcal{B}_{q_0}^{R_q}$ centered at p_0 and q_0 with radius R_p and R_q respectively, the maximum possible inner-product with any pair of points $p \in \mathcal{B}_{p_0}^{R_p}$ and $q \in \mathcal{B}_{q_0}^{R_q}$ is bounded from above by:*

$$\langle q_0, p_0\rangle + R_q R_p + \|q_0\| R_p + \|p_0\| R_q. \quad (7)$$

PROOF. Consider the pair of point (p^*, q^*), $p^* \in B_{p_0}^{R_p}$, $q^* \in B_{q_0}^{R_q}$ be such that

$$\langle q^*, p^*\rangle = \max_{p \in B_{p_0}^{R_p}, q \in B_{q_0}^{R_q}} \langle q, p\rangle. \quad (8)$$

Let θ_p be the angle $\vec{p_0}$ makes with the vector $\vec{p_0 p^*}$, and θ_q be the corresponding angle in the query ball. Let ω_p be the angle between the vectors $\vec{p_0}$ and $\vec{p^*}$ and ω_q be the angle between the vectors $\vec{q_0}$ and $\vec{q^*}$. Let r_p be the distance between p_0 and p^*, r_q be the distance between q_0 and q^*. Let ϕ be the angle made between p_0 and q_0 at the origin.

Some facts for the ball $\mathcal{B}_{p_0}^{R_p}$ (the facts are analogous for the ball $\mathcal{B}_{q_0}^{R_q}$):

$$\|p^*\| = \sqrt{\|p_0\|^2 + r_p^2 + 2\|p_0\| r_p \cos\theta_p},$$

$$\cos\omega_p = \frac{\|p_0\| + r_p\cos\theta_p}{\|p^*\|}, \sin\omega_p = \frac{r_p \sin\theta_p}{\|p^*\|}.$$

Using the triangle inequality of the angles, we know that:

$$|\theta_{q^*,p^*}| \geq |\phi - (\omega_p + \omega_q)|,$$

giving us the following:

$$\langle q^*, p^*\rangle = \|p^*\| \|q^*\| \cos(\phi - (\omega_p + \omega_q)). \quad (9)$$

Algorithm 6 DualSearch(QTree Node Q, RTree Node T)

```
if Q.λ < MIP(Q,T) then
  if isLeaf(T) & isLeaf(Q) then
    for each q ∈ Q.S do
      LinearSearch(q, T.S)
    end for
    Q.λ ← min_{q∈Q.S} q.λ
  else if isLeaf(T) then
    DualSearch(Q.lc, T); DualSearch(Q.rc, T);
    Q.λ ← min{Q.lc.λ, Q.rc.λ}
  else if isLeaf(Q) then
    I_l ← MIP(Q, T.lc); I_r ← MIP(Q, T.rc);
    if I_l ≤ I_r then
      DualSearch(Q, T.rc); DualSearch(Q, T.lc);
    else
      DualSearch(Q, T.lc); DualSearch(Q, T.rc);
    end if
  else
    I_l ← MIP(Q.lc, T.lc); I_r ← MIP(Q.lc, T.rc);
    if I_l ≤ I_r then
      DualSearch(Q.lc, T.rc); DualSearch(Q.lc, T.lc);
    else
      DualSearch(Q.lc, T.lc); DualSearch(Q.lc, T.rc);
    end if
    I_l ← MIP(Q.rc, T.lc); I_r ← MIP(Q.rc, T.rc);
    if I_l ≤ I_r then
      DualSearch(Q.rc, T.rc); DualSearch(Q.rc, T.lc);
    else
      DualSearch(Q.rc, T.lc); DualSearch(Q.rc, T.rc);
    end if
    Q.λ ← min{Q.lc.λ, Q.rc.λ}
  end if
end if
```

Algorithm 7 ExactMIPDT(Query Set V, Reference Set S)

```
T ← MakeBallTree(S)
Q ← MakeQueryTree(V)
∀ trees nodes Q' in the tree Q, Q'.λ ← −∞;
∀ queries q ∈ V, q.bm ← ∅, q.λ ← −∞;
DualSearch(Q, T);
∀ queries q ∈ V, return q.bm;
```

Figure 6: Dual-tree Search: See text for details.

Replacing ω_p and ω_q with θ_p and θ_q by using the aforementioned equalities (similar to the techniques in proof for theorem 3.1), we have:

$$\begin{aligned}
\langle q^*, p^*\rangle &= \langle q_0, p_0\rangle + r_p r_q \cos(\phi - (\theta_p + \theta_q)) \\
&\quad + r_p \|q_0\| \cos(\phi - \theta_p) + r_q \|p_0\| \cos(\phi - \theta_q) \\
&\leq \max_{\theta_p, \theta_q} \langle q_0, p_0\rangle + r_p r_q \cos(\phi - (\theta_p + \theta_q)) \\
&\quad + r_p \|q_0\| \cos(\phi - \theta_p) + r_q \|p_0\| \cos(\phi - \theta_q) \\
&\leq \max_{r_p, r_q} \langle q_0, p_0\rangle + r_p r_q + r_q \|p_0\| + r_p \|q_0\| \\
&\leq \langle q_0, p_0\rangle + R_p R_q + R_q \|p_0\| + R_p \|q_0\|,
\end{aligned}$$

where the first inequality comes from the definition of max. The second inequality follows from $\cos(\cdot) \leq 1$ and the final inequality comes from the fact that $r_p \leq R_p$, $r_q \leq R_q$. □

For the dual-tree search algorithm (Alg. 6), the maximum-possible inner-product between two tree nodes Q and T is:

$$\mathbf{MIP}(Q, T) = \langle q_0, p_0\rangle + R_p R_q + R_q \|p_0\| + R_p \|q_0\|.$$

It is interesting to note that this upper bound bound reduces to the bound in theorem 3.1 when the ball containing the queries is reduced to a single point, implying $R_q = 0$.

5. CONE TREES

In equation 1, the point p, where the maximum is achieved, is independent of the norm $||q||$ of the query q. Let $\theta_{q,r}$ be the angle between the q and r at the origin, then the task

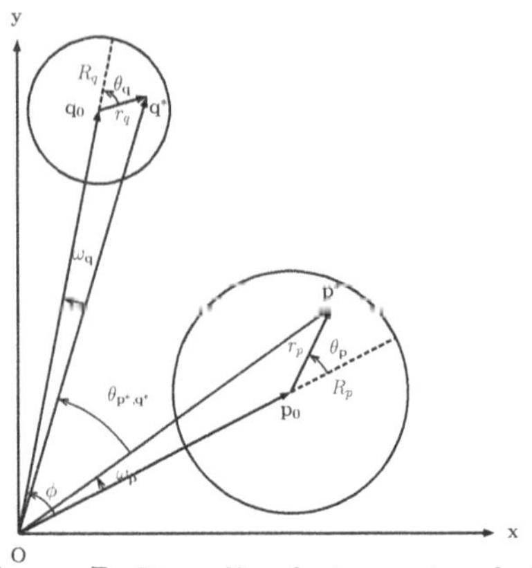

Figure 7: Bounding between two balls.

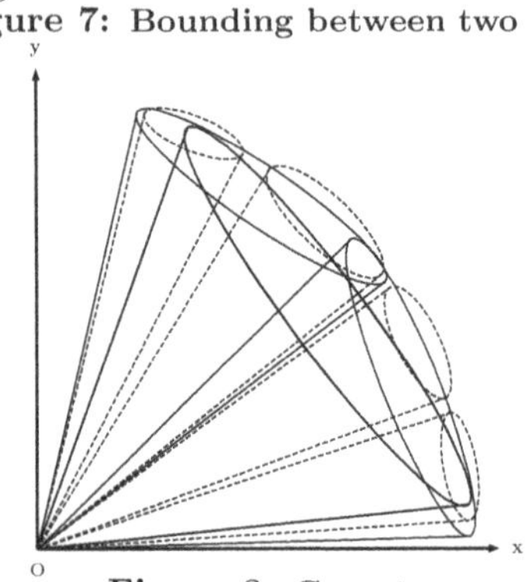

Figure 8: Cone tree

of maximum inner-product search is equivalent to finding a point $p \in S$ such that:

$$p = \arg\max_{r \in S} \|r\| \cos\theta_{q,r}. \quad (10)$$

This implies that only the directions of the queries affect the solution. Balls provide bounds on the inner-product since they bound the norm of the vector as well as the direction. Since the norms do not matter for the queries, indexing them in balls is not required (and hence bounding their norms) is not necessary. Only the range of their directions need to be bounded. For this reason, we propose the indexing of the queries on the basis of their direction (from the origin) to form a *cone tree* (figure 8). The queries are hierarchically indexed as (possibly overlapping) open cones. Each cone is represented by a vector, which corresponds to its axis, and an angle, which corresponds to its aperture[6].

5.1 Cone tree construction

The cone tree construction is very similar to the ball tree construction. The only difference is the use of cosine similarity instead of the Euclidean distances for the task of splitting (pseudo-code in Figure 8).

5.2 Cone-ball bound

Since the norms of the queries do not affect the solution in equation 10, we assume that all the queries have unit norm.

THEOREM 5.1. *Given a ball $\mathcal{B}_{p_0}^{R_p}$ of points centered at p_0 with radius R_p and a cone $\mathcal{C}_{q_0}^{\omega_q}$ of queries (normalized to length 1) with the axis of the cone q_0 and aperture of $2\omega_q \geq 0$, the maximum possible inner-product between any pair of points $p \in \mathcal{B}_{p_0}^{R_p}$, $q \in \mathcal{C}_{q_0}^{\omega_q}$ is bounded from above by:*

$$\|p_0\| \cos(\{|\phi| - \omega_q\}_+) + R_p, \quad (11)$$

where ϕ is the angle made between p_0 and q_0 at the origin and the function $\{x\}_+ = \max\{x, 0\}$.

[6]The aperture of the cone is twice the angle made between the axis and the perimeter of the cone.

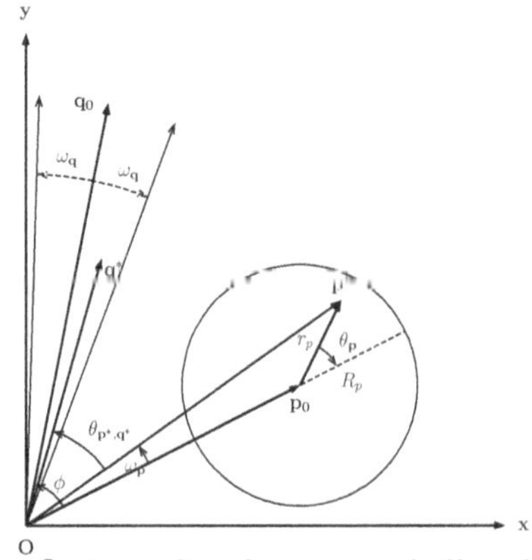

Figure 9: Bounding between a ball and a cone

Algorithm 8 MakeConeTreeSplit(Data Q)

```
Pick a random point x ∈ Q
A ← arg min_{x'∈S} cos θ_{x,x'}
B ← arg min_{x'∈S} cos θ_{A,x'}
return (A, B).
```

Algorithm 9 MakeConeTree(Set of items S)

```
Input - Set S
Output - Tree T
T.S ← S                        //The set of points in node T
T.μ ← mean(S)                  //The axis of the cone around T.S
T.C ← min_{p∈S} cos θ_{T.μ,p}  //The cosine of the aperture of the cone
if |S| ≤ N0 then
  return T
else
  (A, B) ← MakeConeTreeSplit(S)
  S_l ← {p ∈ S: cos θ_{A,p} > cos θ_{B,p}}; S_r ← S \ S_l
  T.lc ← MakeConeTree(S_l)     //Left child
  T.rc ← MakeConeTree(S_r)     //Right child
  return T
end if
```

Figure 10: Cone tree Construction

PROOF. There are two cases to consider here:
(i) $|\phi| < \omega_q$
(ii) $|\phi| \geq \omega_q$

For case (i), the center p_0 of the ball $\mathcal{B}_{p_0}^{R_p}$ lies within the cone $\mathcal{C}_{q_0}^{\omega_q}$, implying that

$$\max_{q \in \mathcal{C}_{q_0}^{\omega_q}, p \in \mathcal{B}_{p_0}^{R_p}} \|p\| \cos\theta_{q,p} \leq \|p_0\| + R_p. \quad (12)$$

since there could be some query $q^* \in \mathcal{C}_{q_0}^{\omega_q}$ which is in the same direction as p_0, giving the maximum possible inner-product.

For case (ii), let us assume that $\phi \geq 0$ without loss of generality. Then $\phi \geq \omega_q$. Continuing with the similar notation as in theorem 3.1 & 4.1 for the best pair of points (q^*, p^*) as well as the notation from figure 9, we can say that

$$|\theta_{p^*,q^*}| \geq |\phi - \omega_q - \omega_p| \quad (13)$$

Since ω_q is fixed, we can say that

$$\max_{q \in C_{q_0}^{\omega_q}, p \in B_{p_0}^{R_p}} \|p\| \cos\theta_{q,p} \leq \|p^*\| \cos\theta_{q^*,p^*} \text{ (by def.)}$$

$$\leq \|p^*\| \cos(\phi - \omega_q - \omega_p). (14)$$

Expressing $\|p^*\|$ and ω_p in terms of $\|p_0\|, r_p$ and θ_p, and then subsequently maximizing over θ_p and using the fact that $r_p \leq R_p$, we get that

$$\max_{q \in C_{q_0}^{\omega_q}, p \in B_{p_0}^{R_p}} \|p\| \cos\theta_{q,p} \leq \|p_0\| \cos(\phi - \omega_q) + R_p. \quad (15)$$

Combining case (i) and (ii), we obtain equation 11. □

Dataset	Dimensions	Reference set	Query Set
Bio	74	210,409	75,000
Corel	32	27,749	10,000
Covertype	55	431,012	150,000
LCDM	3	10,777,216	6,000,000
LiveJournal	25,327	121,625	100,000
MNIST	786	60,000	10,000
MovieLens	51	3,706	6,040
Netflix	51	17,770	480,189
OptDigits	64	1,347	450
Pall7	7	100,841	100,841
Physics	78	112,500	37,500
PSF	2	3,056,092	3,056,092
SJ2	2	50,000	50,000
U-Random	20	700,000	300,000
Y!-Music	51	624,961	1,000,990

Table 1: Datasets used for evaluation

6. EXPERIMENTS AND RESULTS

In this section, we evaluate the efficiency of algorithms 5(SB – single ball tree) & 7. For the dual-tree algorithm, we use the two variations – (i) the set of queries indexed as a ball tree (DBB – dual ball-ball), (ii) the set of queries indexed as a cone tree (DBC – dual ball-cone). We compare our proposed algorithms to the linear search presented in Alg. 3 (LS – linear search). We report the speedup[7] of the proposed algorithms over linear search. For the trees, the leaf size N_0 can be selected by cross-validation. However, for our experiments, we choose a ad hoc value of $N_0 = 20$ for all datasets to demonstrate the gain in efficiency without any expensive cross-validation.

Datasets. We use a variety of datasets from different fields of data mining. We use the following collaborative filtering datasets: MovieLens [17], Netflix [3] and the Yahoo! Music [12] datasets. For text data, we use the LiveJournal blog moods data set [19]. We also use the MNIST digits dataset [24] for evaluation. Three astronomy datasets, LCDM [27], PSF and SJ2, are also considered. A synthetic data set (U-Rand) of uniformly random points in 20 dimensions is used. The rest of the datasets are widely used machine learning data sets from the UCI machine learning repository [5]. The details of the dataset sizes are presented in Table 1[8].

Tree construction times. The tree-building procedure is extremely efficient. We present the tree construction times in table 6 and contrast them with the runtime of the linear search algorithm. In the last column, we present the ratio of the tree construction times with the runtimes of Alg. 3. For the single ball and dual ball-ball algorithm, the tree construction involves building one and two ball trees respectively. For the dual ball-cone algorithm, the queries are normalized to have unit length for convenience[9]. Following the query normalization, two trees are built. The time required for query normalization is included in the construction time. This accounts for the significant difference between construction times for the dual ball-ball and the dual ball-cone algorithm.

The numbers in the last column of table 6 (R) show how small the construction times are with respect to the actual linear search. The highest ratio is 0.15 for the OptDigits

Dataset	SB	DBB	DBC	LS	R(%)
Bio	4.3	5.7	10.6	4,028	0.25
Corel	0.2	0.27	0.66	43	1.5
Covertype	5.5	7.2	14.8	14,885	0.1
LCDM	36.7	56.46	99.3	1,984,200	0.005
LiveJournal	2223	4073	4745	517,194	0.92
MNIST	8.06	9.1	11.38	817	1.5
MovieLens	0.03	0.08	0.27	4.62	6
Netflix	0.2	8.27	33.5	1,878	1.7
OptDigits	0.01	0.012	0.022	0.135	15
Pall7	0.26	0.52	1.4	364	0.4
Physics	2.33	3.0	5.8	1,114	0.5
PSF	9.06	18.1	34.95	282,514	0.01
SJ2	0.1	0.2	0.46	75	0.6
U-Rand	4.94	6.9	15.64	26,586	0.6
Y! Music	9.72	28.85	112.5	137,306	0.08

Table 2: Tree construction time (in seconds) contrasted with the linear search time (in seconds).

Dataset	SB	DBB	DBC
Bio	7,059.62	6.55	273.52
Corel	14.27	17.38	7.68
Covertype	927.51	10.05	773.34
LCDM	29,526	1,327	101,950
LiveJournal	8.36	1.59	15.45
MNIST	2.61	2.22	2.5
MovieLens	2.23	1.36	1.67
Netflix	1.98	1.92	1.84
OptDigits	1.13	1.10	1.10
Pall7	1,020	23.14	2,285
Physics	4.93	4.0	4.08
PSF	61,502	96,570	125,800
SJ2	544	190	767
U-Rand	3.76	3.18	3.28
Y!-Music	2.11	2.09	2.16

Table 3: Speedups over linear search for $k = 1$

dataset. This implies that any speedup over 1.18 at search time is enough to compensate for the tree construction time. For most of the datasets, this ratio is much lower. Moreover, this tree building cost is a one time cost. Once the tree is built, it can be used for searching the dataset multiple times.

Search efficiency. The speedups over linear search are presented in Table 6. Overall, the speedup numbers vary from as low as 1.13 for the OptDigits dataset to over 10^5 (4 orders of magnitude) for the LCDM and the PSF dataset. An important thing to note here is that for datasets with low speedup (below an order of magnitude) with the single ball tree algorithm, the speedup numbers for all three algorithms were pretty low and fairly comparable. However, even a speedup of 2 is pretty significant in terms of absolute times. For example, for the Yahoo! music dataset, a search speedup of mere 2 with a tree construction time of 120 seconds gives a saving of 19 hours of computation time. For most datasets with a high value of speedup for single ball tree algorithm, the speedups for the dual-tree algorithms are also very high.

There are three important things to note here. Firstly, the dual-tree algorithms (Alg. 7) do not perform very well if the single-tree algorithms (Alg. 5) does not have a high speedup. This is mostly because the tree is unable to find tight bounds and hence has to travel every branch. The dual-tree scheme loosens the bound to amortize the traversal cost over multiple queries. But if the bounds are bad for algorithm 5, the bounds for the dual-tree are much worse. Hence, the dual-tree algorithm does not show any significant speedup. Secondly, the dual-tree algorithm (especially dual ball-cone) starts outperforming the single-tree algorithm sig-

[7]Speedup is defined as the ratio of the time taken by the linear search and the time taken by the evaluated algorithm.

[8]For the collaborative filtering datasets, the references (the items) and the queries (the users) are clearly defined. We randomly split the datasets into queries (V) and references (S) for the rest.

[9]This is because the query norms do not affect the answers.

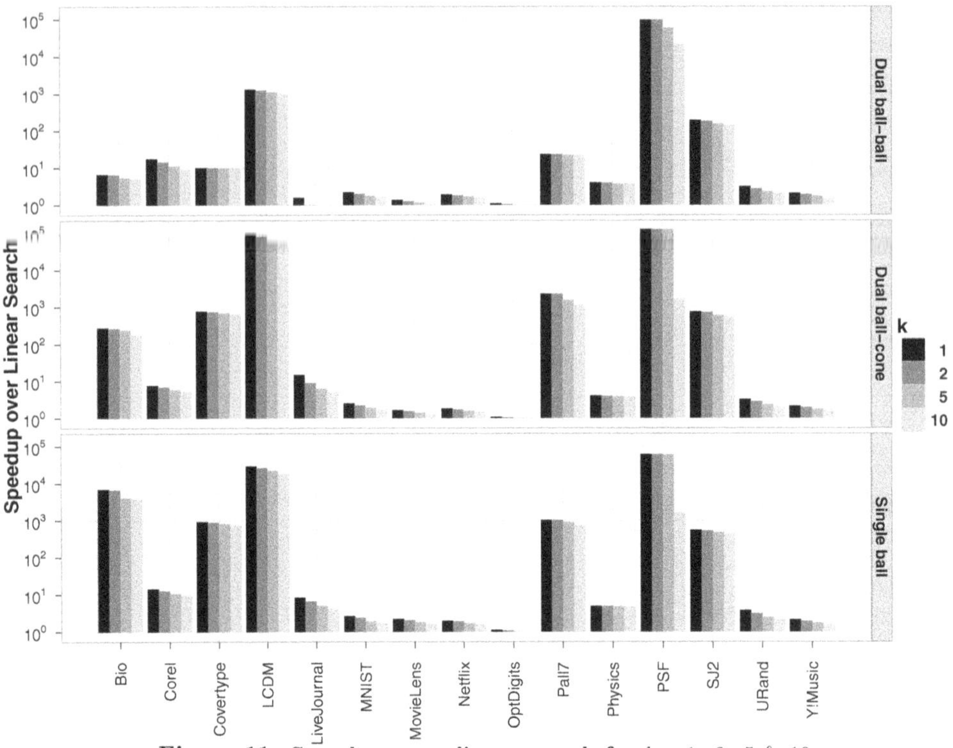

Figure 11: Speedups over linear search for $k = 1,\ 2,\ 5\ \&\ 10$.

nificantly when the set of queries is really large. This is a usual behavior for dual-tree algorithms. The query set has to be large enough for the gains from the amortization of query traversal of the reference tree (*RTree*) to outweigh the computational cost of traversing the query-tree (*QTree*) itself. Finally, the dual-tree algorithm with ball trees for the query set is generally significantly slower than the dual-tree with a cone tree for the queries. There are possibly two possible reasons for that – (i) The cones provide a tighter indexing of the queries than balls. A single cone can be used to index points in multiple balls which lie in the same direction but have varying norms. (ii) The upper bound for $\mathbf{MIP}(Q, T)$ in equation 10 is fairly loose.

We also consider the general problem of obtaining the points in the set S with the k highest inner-product with the query q. This is analogous to the k-nearest neighbor search problem. We present the speedups of our algorithms over linear search for $k = 1,\ 2,\ 5\ \&\ 10$ in figure 11.

7. MAX-KERNEL OPERATION WITH GENERAL KERNEL FUNCTIONS

In this section, we provide some discussion of how the proposed algorithms might be applied in an inner-product space without the explicit representation of the points in the inner-product space. The inner-products are defined by a kernel function $\mathcal{K}(q,p) = \langle \varphi(q), \varphi(p) \rangle$.

The tree construction has to be modified to work in the inner-product space. For a tree node T with the set of point $T.S$, the mean in φ-space is defined as $\mu = \frac{1}{|T.S|}\sum_{p \in T.S} \varphi(p)$. However, μ might not have an explicit representation, but it is possible to compute inner products with μ as follows:

$$\langle \mu, \varphi(q) \rangle = \frac{1}{|T.S|} \sum_{p \in T.S} \mathcal{K}(q,p).$$

However, this computation is possibly very expensive during search time. Hence we propose picking the point in the φ-space which is closest to the mean μ as the new center. So the new center p_c is given by:

$$p_c = \arg\min_{r \in T.S} \mathcal{K}(r,r) - \frac{2}{|T.S|} \sum_{r' \in T.S} \mathcal{K}(r', r). \qquad (16)$$

This operation is quadratic in computation time, but is done at the preprocessing phase to provide efficiency during the search phase. Given this new center p_c, the radius R_p of the ball enclosing the set $T.S$ in φ-space is given by:

$$R_p^2 = \max_{r \in T.S} \mathcal{K}(p_c, p_c) + \mathcal{K}(r,r) - 2\mathcal{K}(r, p_c). \qquad (17)$$

With these definitions for the center and the radius, a ball tree can be built in any φ-space using Algorithm 2. Given a ball in φ-space, the equation 3 in theorem 3.1 becomes:

$$\mathbf{MIP}(q, T) = \mathcal{K}(q, p_c) + R_p\sqrt{\mathcal{K}(q,q)}. \qquad (18)$$

Computing this upper bound is equivalent to a single kernel function evaluation ($\mathcal{K}(q,q)$ be pre-computed before searching the tree). Using this upper bound, the tree-search algorithm (Alg. 5) can be performed in any φ-space. We will evaluate this method in the longer version of the paper.

Using the same principles, the dual-tree algorithm (Alg. 7) can also be applied to any φ-space. For the dual-tree with ball-tree for the queries, the upper bound (eq. 7) on the maximum inner-product between queries in node Q and points in node T in theorem 4.1 is modified to:

$$\mathcal{K}(q_c, p_c) + R_p R_q + R_p\sqrt{\mathcal{K}(q_c, q_c)} + R_q\sqrt{\mathcal{K}(p_c, p_c)}, \qquad (19)$$

where p_c and q_c are the chosen ball centers in the φ-space with radius R_p and R_q respectively.

For queries indexed in a cone-tree, the central axis of the cone can be the point in the φ-space making the smallest angle with the mean of the set in the φ-space. Since the queries are supposed to be normalized in the φ-space, for a query tree node Q, the mean of the set $Q.S$ is supposed to be $\mu = \frac{1}{|Q.S|}\sum_{q \in Q.S} \frac{\varphi(q)}{\|\varphi(q)\|}$. So the new central axis q_c of the cone is given by:

$$q_c = \arg\max_{q \in Q.S} \frac{\sum_{q' \in Q.S} \frac{\mathcal{K}(q', q)}{\sqrt{\mathcal{K}(q', q')}}}{\sqrt{\mathcal{K}(r,r)}}. \qquad (20)$$

Again, this computation is quadratic in the size of the dataset, but provides efficiency during search time. The cosine of half the aperture of the cone is now given by:

$$\cos \omega_q = \min_{q \in Q.S} \frac{\mathcal{K}(q_c, q)}{\sqrt{\mathcal{K}(q_c, q_c)\mathcal{K}(q, q)}}. \quad (21)$$

The upper bound in theorem 5.1 for a cone-tree node Q of queries and a ball-tree node T of reference points becomes:

$$\sqrt{\mathcal{K}(p_c, p_c)} \cos(\{|\phi| - \omega_q\}_+) + R_p, \quad (22)$$

where ϕ is defined as:

$$\cos \phi = \frac{\mathcal{K}(p_c, q_c)}{\sqrt{\mathcal{K}(q_c, q_c)\mathcal{K}(p_c, p_c)}}.$$

This bound is very efficient to compute as it only requires a single kernel function evaluation (the terms $\mathcal{K}(p_c, p_c)$ and $\mathcal{K}(q_c, q_c)$ can be pre-computed and stored in the trees).

8. CONCLUSION

We consider the general problem of maximum inner-product search and present three novel methods to solve this problem efficiently. We use the tree data structure and present a branch-and-bound algorithm for maximum inner-product search. We also present a dual tree algorithm for multiple queries. We evaluate the proposed algorithms with a variety of datasets and exhibit their computational efficiency.

A theoretical analyses of these proposed algorithms would give us a better understanding of the computational efficiency of these algorithms. A rigorous analysis of the runtime for our algorithm would be part of our future work.

9. REFERENCES

[1] R. Bayardo, Y. Ma, and R. Srikant. Scaling Up All Pairs Similarity Search. In *Proceedings of the 16th Intl. Conf. on World Wide Web*, 2007.

[2] R. M. Bell and Y. Koren. Lessons from the Netflix Prize Challenge. *SIGKDD Explor. Newsl.*, 2007.

[3] J. Bennett and S. Lanning. The Netflix Prize. In *Proc. KDD Cup and Workshop*, 2007.

[4] A. Beygelzimer, S. Kakade, and J. Langford. Cover Trees for Nearest Neighbor. *Proceedings of the 23rd Intl. Conf. on Machine Learning*, 2006.

[5] C. L. Blake and C. J. Merz. UCI Machine Learning Repository. http://archive.ics.uci.edu/ml/, 1998.

[6] L. Cayton and S. Dasgupta. A Learning Framework for Nearest Neighbor Search. *Advances in Neural Info. Proc. Systems 20*, 2007.

[7] M. S. Charikar. Similarity Estimation Techniques from Rounding Algorithms. In *Proceedings of the 34th annual ACM Symp. on Theory of Comp.*, 2002.

[8] P. Ciaccia and M. Patella. PAC Nearest Neighbor Queries: Approximate and Controlled Search in High-dimensional and Metric spaces. *Proceedings of 16th Intl. Conf. on Data Engineering*, 2000.

[9] K. Clarkson. Nearest-neighbor Searching and Metric Space Dimensions. *Nearest-Neighbor Methods for Learning and Vision: Theory and Practice*, 2006.

[10] S. Dasgupta and Y. Freund. Random projection trees and low dimensional manifolds. In *Proceedings of the 40th annual ACM Symp. on Theory of Comp.*, 2008.

[11] S. C. Deerwester, S. T. Dumais, T. K. Landauer, G. W. Furnas, and R. A. Harshman. Indexing by Latent Semantic Analysis. *Journal of the American Society of Info. Science*, 1990.

[12] G. Dror, N. Koenigstein, Y. Koren, and M. Weimer. The Yahoo! Music Dataset and KDD-Cup'11. *Journal Of Machine Learning Research*, 2011.

[13] J. H. Freidman, J. L. Bentley, and R. A. Finkel. An Algorithm for Finding Best Matches in Logarithmic Expected Time. *ACM Trans. Math. Softw.*, 1977.

[14] A. Gionis, P. Indyk, and R. Motwani. Similarity Search in High Dimensions via Hashing. *Proceedings of the 25th Intl. Conf. on Very Large Data Bases*, 1999.

[15] A. G. Gray and A. W. Moore. '*N*-Body' Problems in Statistical Learning. In *Advances in Neural Info. Proc. Systems 13*, 2000.

[16] A. G. Gray and A. W. Moore. Nonparametric Density Estimation: Toward Computational Tractability. In *SIAM Data Mining*, 2003.

[17] GroupLens. MovieLens dataset.

[18] P. Indyk and R. Motwani. Approximate Nearest Neighbors: Towards Removing the Curse of Dimensionality. In *Proceedings of the 30th annual ACM Symp. on Theory of Comp.*, 1998.

[19] S. Kim, F. Li, G. Lebanon, and I. Essa. Beyond Sentiment: The Manifold of Human Emotions. *Arxiv preprint* arXiv:1202.1568, 2011.

[20] M. Klaas, D. Lang, and N. de Freitas. Fast Maximum-a-posteriori Inference in Monte Carlo State Spaces. In *Artificial Intelligence and Statistics*, 2005.

[21] Y. Koren. The BellKor solution to the Netflix Grand Prize. 2009.

[22] Y. Koren, R. M. Bell, and C. Volinsky. Matrix Factorization Techniques for Recommender Systems. *IEEE Computer*, 2009.

[23] B. Kulis and K. Grauman. Kernelized Locality-sensitive Hashing for Scalable Image Search. In *IEEE 12th Intl. Conf. on Computer Vision*, 2009.

[24] Y. LeCun. MNIST dataset, 2000. http://yann.lecun.com/exdb/mnist/.

[25] Z. Li, H. Ning, L. Cao, T. Zhang, Y. Gong, and T. S. Huang. Learning to Search Efficiently in High Dimensions. In *Advances in Neural Info. Proc. Systems 24*. 2011.

[26] T. Liu, A. W. Moore, A. G. Gray, and K. Yang. An Investigation of Practical Approximate Nearest Neighbor Algorithms. In *Advances in Neural Info. Proc. Systems 17*, 2005.

[27] R. Lupton, J. Gunn, Z. Ivezic, G. Knapp, S. Kent, and N. Yasuda. The SDSS Imaging Pipelines. *Arxiv preprint astro-ph/0101420*, 2001.

[28] S. M. Omohundro. Five Balltree Construction Algorithms. Technical report, International Computer Science Institute, December 1989.

[29] F. P. Preparata and M. I. Shamos. *Computational Geometry: An Introduction*. Springer, 1985.

[30] A. Rahimi and B. Recht. Random Features for Large-scale Kernel Machines. *Advances in Neural Info. Proc. Systems 20*, 2007.

[31] P. Ram, D. Lee, W. March, and A. Gray. Linear-time Algorithms for Pairwise Statistical Problems. In *Advances in Neural Info. Proc. Systems 22*. 2009.

[32] P. Ram, D. Lee, H. Ouyang, and A. G. Gray. Rank-Approximate Nearest Neighbor Search: Retaining Meaning and Speed in High Dimensions. In *Advances in Neural Info. Proc. Systems 22*. 2009.

A Probabilistic Model for Multimodal Hash Function Learning

Yi Zhen and Dit-Yan Yeung
Department of Computer Science and Engineering
Hong Kong University of Science and Technology
Hong Kong, China
{yzhen,dyyeung}@cse.ust.hk

ABSTRACT

In recent years, both hashing-based similarity search and multimodal similarity search have aroused much research interest in the data mining and other communities. While hashing-based similarity search seeks to address the scalability issue, multimodal similarity search deals with applications in which data of multiple modalities are available. In this paper, our goal is to address both issues simultaneously. We propose a probabilistic model, called *multimodal latent binary embedding* (MLBE), to learn hash functions from multimodal data automatically. MLBE regards the binary latent factors as hash codes in a common Hamming space. Given data from multiple modalities, we devise an efficient algorithm for the learning of binary latent factors which corresponds to hash function learning. Experimental validation of MLBE has been conducted using both synthetic data and two realistic data sets. Experimental results show that MLBE compares favorably with two state-of-the-art models.

Categories and Subject Descriptors

H.3 [**Information Storage and Retrieval**]: Information Search and Retrieval; H.4 [**Information Systems Applications**]: Miscellaneous; G.3 [**Mathematics of Computing**]: Probability and Statistics—*Probabilistic algorithms*

Keywords

Hash Function Learning, Binary Latent Factor Models, Multimodal Similarity Search, Metric Learning

1. INTRODUCTION

Similarity search, *a.k.a.* nearest neighbor search, is a fundamental problem in many data mining, database, and information retrieval applications [1, 34]. Given a query document[1], the similarity search problem can be regarded as finding one or more nearest neighbors of the query from a database according to some similarity measure chosen.

There are two challenging issues to address in similarity search, namely, the scalability and task-specificity issues [1, 33]. The scalability issue addresses the challenge when the database searched is of very large scale, possibly containing millions or even billions of documents. As for the task-specificity issue, the concern is that the similarity measure used should not be a generic one, but it should be specific to the application at hand to ensure that the nearest neighbors found are relevant.

Two major approaches have been proposed to address the scalability issue. One approach employs tree-based methods to organize data using data structures based on trees [3, 11]. The other approach uses hashing-based methods to map documents into bins such that collisions in the hash table reflect nearest neighbor relationships [12, 10, 9]. Although tree-based methods work well on low-dimensional data, they can easily degenerate into brute-force search as the data dimensionality increases. This limitation makes tree-based methods unappealing for real applications in which high dimensionality is commonly encountered. On the contrary, hashing-based methods can index data with compact binary codes and hence can perform very fast search without suffering from the curse of dimensionality.

The most well-known hashing-based methods belong to the locality-sensitive hashing (LSH) family [5, 17, 7, 2], in which hash functions are constructed (but not learned) based on random projections or permutations. Due to their simplicity and effectiveness, LSH algorithms have been successfully applied to many applications [19, 37, 42]. However, they often generate very long codes mainly due to their data independence nature. In other words, the hash functions are designed for some standard similarity measures which may not suit the application at hand. This is an example of the task-specificity issue in similarity search.

To address the two issues mentioned above, some research attempts in the past few years pursue a data-dependent approach by applying machine learning techniques to learn the hash functions from data automatically. We refer to this new direction as hash function learning (HFL).

To the best of our knowledge, Shakhnarovich *et al.* [35] made the first attempt to learn hash functions using a well-known machine learning algorithm, namely, a boosting algorithm [32]. Later, a method called semantic hashing [31] was proposed based on stacked restricted Boltzmann ma-

[1]In this paper, we use the term 'document' in a generic sense to refer to data from any modality, such as text, image, audio or even their combinations.

KDD'12, August 12–16, 2012, Beijing, China.

chines (RBMs) [16]. Using a large image database consisting of millions of images [36], it has been demonstrated that these two methods are much more effective than LSH. In a subsequent method called spectral hashing [40], a metric learning approach is used and the hash codes are found by spectral decomposition. Although spectral hashing is faster and more effective than the previous two methods, it takes a restrictive and unrealistic assumption that the data are uniformly distributed in a hyper-rectangle. Several new methods have since been proposed to relax this restrictive assumption, such as self-taught hashing [44], binary reconstructive embeddings [18], distribution matching [22], and shift-invariant kernel hashing [29]. Compared to spectral hashing, they have shown superior performance. Some more recent HFL methods focus on hashing in several special and important settings, including kernelized hashing [26, 14, 27], semi-supervised hashing [38, 39, 23], composite hashing [43], and active hashing [45].

Most existing HFL methods can only be applied to unimodal data. However, for a growing number of applications, it is also common to conduct similarity search on multimodal data with data belonging to multiple modalities. For example, given an image about a historic event, one may want to find some text articles that describe the event in detail. As a result, developing multimodal HFL methods is a very worthwhile research direction to explore. Up to now, however, only very few such attempts have been made [6, 20].

In this paper, we study hashing-based similarity search in the context of multimodal data. We propose a probabilistic latent factor model, called *multimodal latent binary embedding* (MLBE), to learn hash functions from multimodal data automatically. As a generative model, the hash codes are binary latent factors in a common Hamming space which determine the generation of both intra-modality and inter-modality similarities as observed either directly or indirectly. Given data from multiple modalities, we devise an efficient algorithm for learning the binary latent factors based on *maximum a posteriori* (MAP) estimation. Compared to its counterparts [6, 20], MLBE can:

(a) be interpreted easily in a principled manner;

(b) be extended easily;

(c) avoid overfitting via parameter learning;

(d) support efficient learning algorithms.

The remainder of this paper is organized as follows. Section 2 briefly introduces some recent related work. Section 3 presents our model and the learning algorithm. Experimental validation of MLBE conducted using both synthetic data and two realistic data sets is presented in Section 4. Finally, Section 5 concludes the paper.

2. RELATED WORK

Our work bears some resemblance to metric learning which aims at learning similarity or distance measures from data [41]. Such data-dependent similarity measures are generally more effective than their data-independent counterparts. Although a lot of research has been conducted on metric learning, multimodal metric learning is still largely unexplored even though multimodal data are commonly found in many applications. Some recent efforts have been made on non-hashing-based methods [21, 28]. Compared with hashing-based methods, these methods do not have the merits of low storage requirement and high search speed.

To the best of our knowledge, Bronstein *et al.* proposed the first hashing-based model, called cross-modal similarity sensitive hashing (CMSSH) thereafter, for multimodal similarity search [6]. Specifically, given a set of similar and dissimilar point pairs, CMSSH constructs two groups of linear hash functions (for the bimodal case) such that, with high probability, the Hamming distance after mapping is small for similar points and large for dissimilar points. In their formulation, each hash function (for one bit) can be obtained by solving a singular value decomposition (SVD) problem and the hash functions are learned sequentially in a standard boosting manner. However, CMSSH ignores the intra-modality relational information which could be very useful [40].

Recently, Kumar *et al.* extended spectral hashing [40] to the multi-view case, leading to a method called cross-view hashing (CVH) [20]. The objective of CVH is to minimize the inter-view and intra-view Hamming distances for similar points and maximize those for dissimilar points. The optimization problem is relaxed to several generalized eigenvalue problems which can be solved by off-the-shelf methods.

Both CMSSH and CVH have archieved successes in several applications but they also have some apparent limitations. First, both models can only deal with vectorial data which may not be available in some applications. Besides, they both involve eigendecomposition operations which may be very costly especially when the data dimensionality is high. Furthermore, CMSSH has been developed for shape retrieval and medical image alignment applications and CVH for people search applications in the natural language processing area. These applications are very different from those studied in this paper.

Our work is also related to binary latent factor models [25, 15] but there exist some significant differences. First, the binary latent factors in MLBE are used as hash codes for multimodal similarity search, while the latent factors in [25, 15] are treated as cluster membership indicators which are used for clustering and link prediction applications. Moreover, the model formulations are very different. In MLBE, the prior distributions on the binary latent factors are simple Bernoulli distributions, but in [25, 15], the priors on the binary latent factors are Indian buffet processes [13]. Furthermore, from a matrix factorization point of view, MLBE simultaneously factorizes multiple matrices but the method in [25] factorizes only one matrix.

3. MULTIMODAL LATENT BINARY EMBEDDING

We present MLBE in detail in this section. We use boldface uppercase and lowercase letters to denote matrices and vectors, respectively. For a matrix $\mathbf{A}$, its (i, j)th element is denoted by A_{ij}.

3.1 Model Formulation

For simplicity of our presentation, we focus exclusively on the bimodal case in this paper, but it is very easy to extend MLBE for more than two modalities. As a running example, we assume that the data come from two modalities $\mathcal{X}$ and

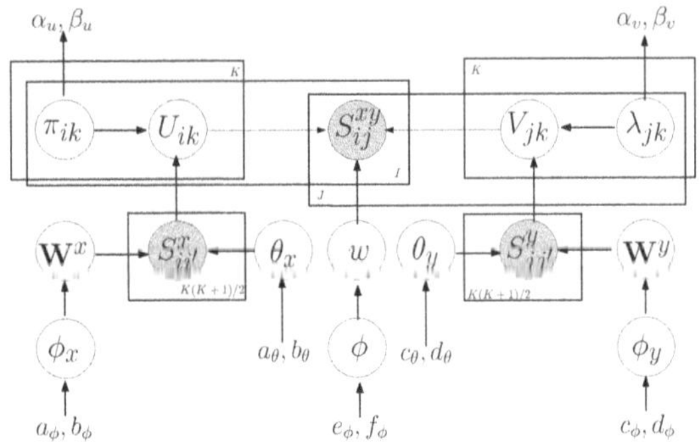

Figure 1: Graphical model representation of MLBE

$\mathcal{Y}$ corresponding to the image modality and text modality, respectively.

The observations in MLBE are intra-modality and inter-modality similarities. Specifically, there are two symmetric intra-modality similarity matrices $\mathbf{S}^x \in \mathbb{R}^{I\times I}$ and $\mathbf{S}^y \in \mathbb{R}^{J\times J}$, where I and J denote the number of data points in modality $\mathcal{X}$ and that in modality $\mathcal{Y}$, respectively. In case the observed data are only available in the form of feature vectors, different ways can be used to convert them into similarity matrices. For the image data $\mathcal{X}$, the similarities in $\mathbf{S}^x$ could be computed from the corresponding Euclidean distances between feature vectors. For the text data $\mathcal{Y}$, the similarities in $\mathbf{S}^y$ could be the cosine similarities between bag-of-words representations.

In addition, there is an inter-modality similarity matrix $\mathbf{S}^{xy} \in \{1,0\}^{I\times J}$, where 1 and 0 denote similar and dissimilar relationships, respectively, between the corresponding entities. Note that it is common to specify cross-modal similarities this way, because it is very difficult if not impossible to specify real-valued cross-modal similarities objectively. The binary similarity values in $\mathbf{S}^{xy}$ can often be determined based on their semantics. Take multimedia retrieval for example, if an image and a text article are both for the same historic event, their similarity will be set to 1. Otherwise, their similarity will be 0.

Our probabilistic generative model has latent variables represented by several matrices. First, there are two sets of binary latent factors, $\mathbf{U} \in \{+1,-1\}^{I\times K}$ for $\mathcal{X}$ and $\mathbf{V} \in \{+1,-1\}^{J\times K}$ for $\mathcal{Y}$, where each row in $\mathbf{U}$ or $\mathbf{V}$ corresponds to one data point and can be interpreted as the hash code of that point. In addition, there are two intra-modality weighting matrices, $\mathbf{W}^x \in \mathbb{R}^{K\times K}$ for $\mathcal{X}$ and $\mathbf{W}^y \in \mathbb{R}^{K\times K}$ for $\mathcal{Y}$, and an inter-modality weighting variable $w > 0$. The basic assumption of MLBE is that the observed intra-modality and inter-modality similarities are generated from the binary latent factors, intra-modality weighting matrices and inter-modality weighting variable. Note that the real-valued weighting matrices and weighting variable are needed for generating the similarities because the values in the latent factors $\mathbf{U}$ and $\mathbf{V}$ are discrete.

The graphical model representation of MLBE is depicted in Figure 1, in which shaded nodes are used for observed variables and empty ones for latent variables as well as parameters which are also defined as random variables. The others are hyperparameters, which will be denoted collectively by Ω in the sequel for notational convenience.

We first consider the likelihood functions of MLBE. Given $\mathbf{U},\mathbf{V},\mathbf{W}^x,\mathbf{W}^y,\theta_x$ and θ_y, the conditional probability density functions of the intra-modality similarity matrices $\mathbf{S}^x$ and $\mathbf{S}^y$ are defined as

$$p(\mathbf{S}^x \mid \mathbf{U},\mathbf{W}^x,\theta_x) = \prod_{i=1}^{I}\prod_{i'=1}^{I}\mathcal{N}(S_{ii'}^x \mid \mathbf{u}_i^T\mathbf{W}^x\mathbf{u}_{i'}, \frac{1}{\theta_x}),$$

$$p(\mathbf{S}^y \mid \mathbf{V},\mathbf{W}^y,\theta_y) = \prod_{j=1}^{J}\prod_{j'=1}^{J}\mathcal{N}(S_{jj'}^y \mid \mathbf{v}_j^T\mathbf{W}^y\mathbf{v}_{j'}, \frac{1}{\theta_y}),$$

where $\mathbf{u}_i$ and $\mathbf{u}_{i'}$ denote the ith and i'th rows of $\mathbf{U}$, $\mathbf{v}_i$ and $\mathbf{v}_{j'}$ denote the jth and j'th rows of $\mathbf{V}$, and $\mathcal{N}(x \mid \mu,\sigma^2)$ is the probability density function of the univariate Gaussian distribution with mean μ and variance σ^2.

Given $\mathbf{U},\mathbf{V}$ and w, the conditional probability mass function of the inter-modality similarity matrix $\mathbf{S}^{xy}$ is given by

$$p(\mathbf{S}^{xy} \mid \mathbf{U},\mathbf{V},w) = \prod_{i=1}^{I}\prod_{j=1}^{J}\left[\text{Bern}(S_{ij}^{xy} \mid \gamma(w\mathbf{u}_i^T\mathbf{v}_j))\right]^{O_{ij}},$$

where $\text{Bern}(x \mid \mu)$ is the probability mass function of the Bernoulli distribution with parameter μ, O_{ij} is an indicator variable which is equal to 1 if S_{ij}^{xy} is observed and 0 otherwise, and $\gamma(x) = 1/(1+\exp(-x))$ is the logistic sigmoid function to ensure that the parameter μ of the Bernoulli distribution is in the range $(0,1)$.

To complete the model formulation, we also need to define prior distributions on the latent variables and hyperprior distributions on the parameters. For the matrix $\mathbf{U}$, we impose a prior independently and identically on each element of $\mathbf{U}$ as follows:[2]

$$p(U_{ik} \mid \pi_{ik}) = \text{Bern}(U_{ik} \mid \pi_{ik}),$$
$$p(\pi_{ik} \mid \alpha_u,\beta_u) = \text{Beta}(\pi_{ik} \mid \alpha_u,\beta_u),$$

where $\text{Beta}(\mu \mid a,b)$ is the probability density function of the beta distribution with hyperparameters a and b. This particular choice is mainly due to the computational advantage of using conjugate distributions so that we can integrate out π_{ik}, as a form of Bayesian averaging, to give the following prior distribution on $\mathbf{U}$:

$$p(\mathbf{U} \mid \alpha_u,\beta_u) = \prod_{i=1}^{I}\prod_{k=1}^{K}\text{Bern}(U_{ik} \mid \frac{\alpha_u}{\alpha_u+\beta_u}).$$

Similarly, we define the prior distribution on $\mathbf{V}$ as:

$$p(\mathbf{V} \mid \alpha_v,\beta_v) = \prod_{j=1}^{J}\prod_{k=1}^{K}\text{Bern}(V_{jk} \mid \frac{\alpha_v}{\alpha_v+\beta_v}).$$

For the weighting matrices $\mathbf{W}^x$ and $\mathbf{W}^y$, we impose Gaussian prior distributions on them:

$$p(\mathbf{W}^x \mid \phi_x) = \prod_{k=1}^{K}\prod_{d=k}^{K}\mathcal{N}(W_{kd}^x \mid 0, \frac{1}{\phi_x}),$$

$$p(\mathbf{W}^y \mid \phi_y) = \prod_{k=1}^{K}\prod_{d=k}^{K}\mathcal{N}(W_{kd}^y \mid 0, \frac{1}{\phi_y}).$$

The weighting variable w has to be strictly positive to enforce a positive relationship between the inner product

[2]Conventionally, the Bernoulli distribution is defined for discrete random variables which take the value 1 for success and 0 for failure. Here, the discrete random variables take values from $\{-1,+1\}$ instead assuming an implicit linear mapping from $\{0,1\}$.

of two hash codes and the inter-modality similarity. So we impose the half-normal prior distribution on w:

$$p(w \mid \phi) = \mathcal{HN}(w \mid \phi) = e^{-\frac{\phi}{2}w^2}\sqrt{\frac{2\phi}{\pi}}.$$

Because the parameters $\theta_x, \theta_y, \phi_x, \phi_y$ and ϕ are all random variables, we also impose hyperprior distributions on them. The gamma distribution is used for all these distributions:

$$\begin{aligned}
p(\theta_x \mid a_\theta, b_\theta) &= \text{Gam}(\theta_x \mid a_\theta, b_\theta),\\
p(\theta_y \mid c_\theta, d_\theta) &= \text{Gam}(\theta_y \mid c_\theta, d_\theta),\\
p(\phi_x \mid a_\phi, b_\phi) &= \text{Gam}(\phi_x \mid a_\phi, b_\phi),\\
p(\phi_y \mid c_\phi, d_\phi) &= \text{Gam}(\phi_y \mid c_\phi, d_\phi),\\
p(\phi \mid e_\phi, f_\phi) &= \text{Gam}(\phi \mid e_\phi, f_\phi),
\end{aligned}$$

where $\text{Gam}(\tau \mid a, b) = \frac{1}{\Gamma(a)} b^a \tau^{a-1} e^{-b\tau}$ denotes the probability density function of the gamma distribution with hyperparameters a and b, and $\Gamma(\cdot)$ is the gamma function.

3.2 Learning

With the probabilistic graphical model formulated in the previous subsection, we can now devise an algorithm to learn the binary latent factors $\mathbf{U}$ and $\mathbf{V}$ which give the hash codes we need. A fully Bayesian approach would infer the posterior distributions of $\mathbf{U}$ and $\mathbf{V}$, possibly using some sampling techniques. However, such methods are often computationally demanding. For computational efficiency, we devise an efficient alternating learning algorithm in this paper based on MAP estimation.

We first update U_{ik} while fixing all other variables. To find the MAP estimate of U_{ik}, we define a loss function with respect to U_{ik} in Definition 3.1:

DEFINITION 3.1.

$$\begin{aligned}
\mathcal{L}_{ik} = &-\frac{\theta_x}{2}\sum_{l\neq i}^{I}\left[\left(S^x_{il} - \mathbf{u}_l^T\mathbf{W}^x\mathbf{u}_i^+\right)^2 - \left(S^x_{il} - \mathbf{u}_l^T\mathbf{W}^x\mathbf{u}_i^-\right)^2\right]\\
&-\frac{\theta_x}{2}\left[\left(S^x_{ii} - \mathbf{u}_i^{+T}\mathbf{W}^x\mathbf{u}_i^+\right)^2 - \left(S^x_{ii} - \mathbf{u}_i^{-T}\mathbf{W}^x\mathbf{u}_i^-\right)^2\right]\\
&+\sum_{j=1}^{J} O_{ij}\left[S^{xy}_{ij}\log\frac{\rho^+_{ij}}{\rho^-_{ij}} + (1 - S^{xy}_{ij})\log\frac{1-\rho^+_{ij}}{1-\rho^-_{ij}}\right] + \log\frac{\alpha_u}{\beta_u},
\end{aligned}$$

where $\mathbf{u}_i^+$ is the ith row of $\mathbf{U}$ with $U_{ik} = 1$, $\mathbf{u}_i^-$ is the ith row of $\mathbf{U}$ with $U_{ik} = -1$, $\rho^+_{ij} = \gamma(w\mathbf{v}_j^T\mathbf{u}_i^+)$, and $\rho^-_{ij} = \gamma(w\mathbf{v}_j^T\mathbf{u}_i^-)$.

With $\mathcal{L}_{ik}$, we can state the following theorem:

THEOREM 3.1. *The MAP solution of U_{ik} is equal to 1 if $\mathcal{L}_{ik} \geq 0$ and -1 otherwise.*

The proof of Theorem 3.1 can be found in Appendix A.1.

Similarly, we have Definition 3.2 and Theorem 3.2 for the MAP estimation of $\mathbf{V}$. The proof of Theorem 3.2 is similar and so it is omitted in the paper due to page limitations.

DEFINITION 3.2.

$$\begin{aligned}
\mathcal{Q}_{jl} = &-\frac{\theta_y}{2}\sum_{l\neq j}^{J}\left[\left(S^y_{jl} - \mathbf{v}_l^T\mathbf{W}^y\mathbf{v}_j^+\right)^2 - \left(S^y_{jl} - \mathbf{v}_l^T\mathbf{W}^y\mathbf{v}_j^-\right)^2\right]\\
&-\frac{\theta_y}{2}\left[\left(S^y_{jj} - \mathbf{v}_j^{+T}\mathbf{W}^y\mathbf{v}_j^+\right)^2 - \left(S^y_{jj} - \mathbf{v}_j^{-T}\mathbf{W}^y\mathbf{v}_j^-\right)^2\right]\\
&+\sum_{i=1}^{I} O_{ij}\left[S^{xy}_{ij}\log\frac{\lambda^+_{ij}}{\lambda^-_{ij}} + (1 - S^{xy}_{ij})\log\frac{1-\lambda^+_{ij}}{1-\lambda^-_{ij}}\right] + \log\frac{\alpha_v}{\beta_v},
\end{aligned}$$

where $\mathbf{v}_j^+$ is the jth row of $\mathbf{V}$ with $V_{jk} = 1$, $\mathbf{v}_j^-$ is the jth row of $\mathbf{V}$ with $V_{jk} = -1$, $\lambda^+_{ij} = \gamma(w\mathbf{u}_i^T\mathbf{v}_j^+)$, and $\lambda^-_{ij} = \gamma(w\mathbf{u}_i^T\mathbf{v}_i^-)$.

THEOREM 3.2. *The MAP solution of V_{ik} is equal to 1 if $\mathcal{Q}_{jl} \geq 0$ and -1 otherwise.*

With $\mathbf{U}, \phi_x$ and θ_x fixed, we can compute the MAP estimate of $\mathbf{W}^x$ using Theorem 3.3 below. The proof is in Appendix A.2.

THEOREM 3.3. *The MAP solution of $\mathbf{W}^x$ is*

$$\mathbf{w}^x = \left(\mathbf{A}^T\mathbf{M}_2\mathbf{A} + \frac{\phi_x}{\theta_x}\mathbf{M}_1\right)^{-1}\mathbf{A}^T\mathbf{M}_2\mathbf{s}^x,$$

where $\mathbf{w}^x$ is a K^2-dimensional column vector taken in a columnwise manner from $\mathbf{W}^x$, $\mathbf{s}^x$ is an I^2-dimensional column vector taken in a columnwise manner from $\mathbf{S}^x$, $\mathbf{A} = \mathbf{U}\otimes\mathbf{U}$, $\mathbf{M}_1$ is a diagonal matrix with each diagonal entry equal to 1 if it is the linear index of the upper-right portion of $\mathbf{W}^x$ and 0 otherwise, and $\mathbf{M}_2$ is similarly defined but with a different size which is determined by $\mathbf{S}^x$.

Similarly, we have Theorem 3.4 for $\mathbf{W}^y$.

THEOREM 3.4. *The MAP solution of $\mathbf{W}^y$ is*

$$\mathbf{w}^y = \left(\mathbf{B}^T\tilde{\mathbf{M}}_2\mathbf{B} + \frac{\phi_y}{\theta_y}\mathbf{M}_1\right)^{-1}\mathbf{B}^T\tilde{\mathbf{M}}_2\mathbf{s}^y,$$

where $\mathbf{w}^y, \mathbf{s}^y, \mathbf{B}$ and $\tilde{\mathbf{M}}_2$ are also defined similarly.

To obtain the MAP estimate of w, we minimize the negative log posterior $p(w \mid \mathbf{U}, \mathbf{V}, \mathbf{S}^{xy}, \phi)$, which is equivalent to the following objective function:

$$\begin{aligned}
\mathcal{L}_w = &\frac{\phi}{2}w^2\\
&-\sum_{i=1}^{I}\sum_{j=1}^{J}\left\{O_{ij}\left[S^{xy}_{ij}\log\lambda_{ij} + \left(1 - S^{xy}_{ij}\right)\log\left(1-\lambda_{ij}\right)\right]\right\},
\end{aligned}$$

where $\lambda_{ij} = \gamma\left(w\mathbf{u}_i^T\mathbf{v}_j\right)$.

Although the objective function is convex with respect to w, there is no closed-form solution. Nevertheless, due to its convexity, we can obtain the global minimum easily using a gradient descent algorithm. The gradient can be evaluated as follows:

$$\begin{aligned}
\nabla w = &\phi\cdot w \qquad (1)\\
&-\sum_{i=1}^{I}\sum_{j=1}^{J}\left\{O_{ij}\left[S^{xy}_{ij}\left(1-\lambda_{ij}\right)\mathbf{u}_i^T\mathbf{v}_j - \left(1 - S^{xy}_{ij}\right)\lambda_{ij}\mathbf{u}_i^T\mathbf{v}_j\right]\right\}.
\end{aligned}$$

As for the parameters, closed-form solutions exist for their MAP estimates which are summarized in the following theorem.

THEOREM 3.5. *The MAP estimates of $\theta_x, \theta_y, \phi_x, \phi_y$ and ϕ are:*

$$\theta_x = \frac{I(I+1) + 4(a_\theta - 1)}{4b_\theta + 2\sum_{i=1}^{I}\sum_{i'=i}^{I}\left(S^x_{ii'} - \mathbf{u}_i^T \mathbf{W}^x \mathbf{u}_{i'}\right)^2}, \tag{2}$$

$$\theta_y = \frac{J(J+1) + 4(c_\theta - 1)}{4d_\theta + 2\sum_{j=1}^{J}\sum_{j'=j}^{J}\left(S^y_{jj'} - \mathbf{v}_j^T \mathbf{W}^y \mathbf{v}_{j'}\right)^2}, \tag{3}$$

$$\phi_x = \frac{K(K+1) + 4(a_\phi - 1)}{4b_\phi + 2\sum_{k=1}^{K}\sum_{d=k}^{K}(W^x_{kd})^2}, \tag{4}$$

$$\phi_y = \frac{K(K+1) + 4(c_\phi - 1)}{4d_\phi + 2\sum_{k=1}^{K}\sum_{d=k}^{K}(W^y_{kd})^2}, \tag{5}$$

$$\phi = \frac{2e_\phi - 1}{2f_\phi + w^2}. \tag{6}$$

Theorem 3.5 can be proved easily. Briefly speaking, we first find the posterior distribution of each parameter and then compute the optimal value by setting its derivative to zero. Details of the proof are omitted here.

To summarize, the learning algorithm of MLBE is presented in Algorithm 1.

Algorithm 1: Learning algorithm of MLBE

Input : $\mathbf{S}^x$, $\mathbf{S}^y$, $\mathbf{S}^{xy}$ – similarity matrices
$\mathbf{O}$ – observation indicator variables for $\mathbf{S}^{xy}$
K – number of hash functions
Ω – hyperparameters

begin
Initialize all the latent variables and parameters except $\mathbf{W}^x, \mathbf{W}^y$;
while *not converged* **do**
Update $\mathbf{W}^x$ using Theorem 3.3;
Update ϕ_x using Equation (4);
Update each element of $\mathbf{U}$ using Theorem 3.1;
Update θ_x using Equation (2);
Update $\mathbf{W}^y$ using Theorem 3.4;
Update ϕ_y using Equation (5);
Update each element of $\mathbf{V}$ using Theorem 3.2;
Update θ_y using Equation (3);
Update w by gradient descent using Equation (1);
Update ϕ using Equation (6).
end

3.3 Out-of-Sample Extension

Algorithm 1 tells us how to learn the hash functions for the observed bimodal data based on their intra-modality and inter-modality similarities. However, the hash codes can only be computed this way for the training data. In many applications, after learning the hash functions, it is necessary to obtain the hash codes for out-of-sample data points as well. One naive approach would be to incorporate the out-of-sample points into the original training set and then learn the hash functions from scratch. However, this approach is computationally unappealing due to its high computational cost especially when the training set is large.

In this subsection, we propose a simple yet very effective method for finding the hash codes of out-of-sample points. The method is based on a simple and natural assumption that the latent variables and parameters for the training data can be fixed while computing the hash codes for the out-of-sample points.

Specifically, we first train the MLBE model using some training data selected from both modalities.[3] Using the latent variables and parameters learned from the training points, we can find the hash codes for the out-of-sample points by applying Theorem 3.1 or Theorem 3.2. For illustration, Algorithm 2 shows how to compute the hash code for an out-of-sample point $\mathbf{x}^*$ from modality $\mathcal{X}$ using the latent variables and parameters learned from two training sets $\hat{\mathcal{X}}$ and $\hat{\mathcal{Y}}$. It is worth noting that the hash code for each out-of-sample point can be computed independently. The implication is that the algorithm is highly parallelizable, making it potentially applicable to very large data sets. The same can also be done to out-of-sample points from the other modality with some straightforward modifications.

Algorithm 2: Algorithm for out-of-sample extension

Input : $\hat{\mathbf{S}}^x$ – intra-modality similarities for $\mathbf{x}^*$ and $\hat{\mathcal{X}}$
$\hat{\mathbf{S}}^{xy}$ – inter-modality similarities for $\mathbf{x}^*$ and $\hat{\mathcal{Y}}$
$\hat{\mathbf{U}}, \hat{\mathbf{V}}, \hat{\mathbf{W}}^x, \hat{w}, \hat{\theta}_x$ – learned variables
α_u, β_u – hyperparameters

begin
Initialize $\mathbf{u}^*$;
while *not converged* **do**
Update each element of $\mathbf{u}^*$ using Theorem 3.1.
end

3.4 Complexity Analysis

The computational cost of the learning algorithm is mainly spent on updating $\mathbf{U}, \mathbf{V}, \mathbf{W}^x, \mathbf{W}^y$ and w.

The complexity of updating an entry U_{ik} is $O(IK^2 + JK)$, which grows linearly with the number of points in each modality. Updating $\mathbf{W}^x$ requires inverting a $K^2 \times K^2$ matrix. Since K is usually very small, this step can be performed efficiently. The complexity of evaluating the gradient ∇w is linear in the number of observations of the inter-modality similarities. We note that the complexity can be greatly reduced if the similarity matrices are sparse, which is often the case in real applications.

4. EXPERIMENTS

We first present an illustrative example on synthetic data in Section 4.1. It is then followed by experiments on two publicly available real-world data sets. Section 4.2 presents the experimental settings and then Sections 4.3 and 4.4 present the results. The code and data can be downloaded at `http://www.cse.ust.hk/~dyyeung/code/mlbe/`.

4.1 Illustration on Synthetic Data

There are four groups of data points with each group consisting of 50 points. We associate each group with one of four hash codes, namely, $[1, 1, -1, -1]$, $[-1, -1, 1, 1]$, $[1, -1, 1, -1]$ and $[-1, 1, -1, 1]$, and use a 200×4 matrix $\mathbf{H}$ to denote the hash codes of all 200 points. We generate $\mathbf{W}^x$ and $\mathbf{W}^y$ from $\mathcal{N}(\cdot \mid 1, 0.01)$ and $\mathcal{N}(\cdot \mid 5, 0.01)$, respectively.

[3]We do not make any assumption on how the training data are selected. They may be selected randomly for simplicity or carefully based on how representative they are. Random selection is used in our experiments.

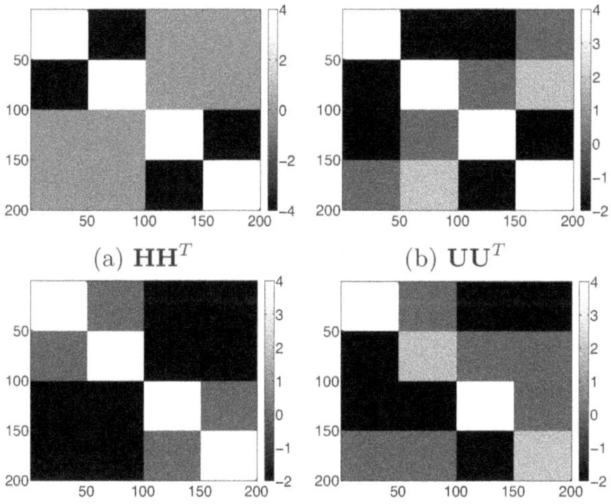

(a) $\mathbf{HH}^T$ (b) $\mathbf{UU}^T$ (c) $\mathbf{VV}^T$ (d) $\mathbf{UV}^T$

Figure 2: Illustration of MLBE

Based on the latent representation, we generate the similarity matrices $\mathbf{S}^x$ and $\mathbf{S}^y$ using $\mathcal{N}(S^x_{il} \mid \mathbf{h}_i^T \mathbf{W}^x \mathbf{h}_l, 0.01)$ and $\mathcal{N}(S^y_{jl} \mid \mathbf{h}_i^T \mathbf{W}^y \mathbf{h}_l, 0.01)$, respectively. Moreover, we set $S^{xy}_{ij} = 1$ if $\mathbf{h}_i = \mathbf{h}_j$ and $S^{xy}_{ij} = 0$ otherwise, assuming that all entries in $\mathbf{S}^{xy}$ are observed, i.e., $O_{ij} = 1, \forall i, j$.

Based on the similarities generated, we train MLBE to obtain the hash codes $\mathbf{U}$ and $\mathbf{V}$. Because the bits of the hash codes are interchangeable, it is more appropriate to use inner products of the hash codes to illustrate the similarity structures, as shown in Figure 2. Note that the whiter the area is, the more similar the points involved are. Figure 2(a) depicts the ground-truth similarity structure, Figure 2(b) and 2(c) show the learned intra-modality similarity structure for each modality, and Figure 2(d) shows the learned inter-modality similarity structure. As we can see, the whiter areas in the last three subfigures are in the same locations as those in Figure 2(a). In other words, both the intra-modality and inter-modality similarity structures revealed by the learned hash codes are very close to the ground truth, showing the effectiveness of MLBE.

4.2 Experimental Settings

We have conducted several comparative experiments on two real-world data sets, which are, to the best of our knowledge, the largest publicly available multimodal data sets that are fully paired and labeled. Both data sets are bimodal with the image and text modalities but the feature representations are different. Each data set is partitioned into a database set and a separate query set.

We compare MLBE with CMSSH[4] and CVH[5] on two common cross-modal retrieval tasks. Specifically, we use a text query to retrieve similar images from the image database and use an image query to retrieve similar texts from the text database. Since the data sets are fully labeled, meaning that each document (image or text) has one or more semantic labels, it is convenient to use these labels to decide the ground-truth neighbors.

We use *mean Average Precision* (mAP) as the performance measure. Given a query and a set of R retrieved documents, the *Average Precision* (AP) is defined as

$$\mathrm{AP} = \frac{1}{L} \sum_{r=1}^{R} P(r)\, \delta(r),$$

where L is the number of true neighbors in the retrieved set, $P(r)$ denotes the precision of the top r retrieved documents, and $\delta(r) = 1$ if the rth retrieved document is a true neighbor and $\delta(r) = 0$ otherwise. We then average the AP values over all the queries in the query set to obtain the mAP measure. The larger the mAP, the better the performance. In the experiments, we set $R = 50$.

We also report two types of performance curves, namely, *precision-recall* curve and *recall* curve. Given a query set and a database, both curves can be obtained by varying the Hamming radius of the retrieved points and evaluating the precision, recall and number of retrieved points accordingly.

For MLBE, the intra-modality similarity matrices are computed based on the feature vectors. We first compute the Euclidean distance d between two feature vectors and then transform it into a similarity measure $s = e^{-d^2/2\sigma^2}$, where the parameter σ^2 is fixed to 1 for both data sets. The inter-modality similarity matrices are simply determined by the class labels. Since MLBE is not sensitive to the hyperparameters, we simply set all of them to 1. Besides, we initialize $\mathbf{U}$ and $\mathbf{V}$ using the results of CVH, set the initial values of $\theta_x, \theta_y, \phi_x, \phi_y$ to 0.01, and use a fixed learning rate 10^{-4} for updating w.

In all the experiments, the size of the training set, which is randomly selected from the database set for each modality, is set to 300 and only 0.1% of the randomly selected entries of $\mathbf{S}^{xy}$ are observed.[6] To be fair, all three models are trained on the same training set.

4.3 Results on Wiki Data Set

The Wiki data set is generated from a group of 2,866 Wikipedia documents provided by [30]. Each document is an image-text pair and is labeled with exactly one of 10 semantic classes. The images are represented by 128-dimensional SIFT [24] feature vectors. The text articles are represented by the probability distributions over 10 topics, which are derived from a latent Dirichlet allocation (LDA) model [4]. We use 80% of the data as the database set and the remaining 20% to form the query set.

The mAP values for MLBE and the two baselines are reported in Table 1. The *precision-recall* curves and *recall* curves for the three methods are plotted in Figure 3.

Table 1: mAP comparison on Wiki

Task	Method	Code Length		
		$K = 8$	$K = 16$	$K = 24$
Image Query vs. Text Database	MLBE	**0.3810**	**0.2561**	**0.1915**
	CVH	0.2592	0.2190	0.1767
	CMSSH	0.2438	0.2014	0.1757
Text Query vs. Image Database	MLBE	**0.4955**	**0.3209**	0.2143
	CVH	0.3474	0.3094	**0.2576**
	CMSSH	0.2044	0.2286	0.2256

We can see that MLBE significantly outperforms CVH and CMSSH when the code length is small. As the code

[4]The implementation is kindly provided by the authors.

[5]Because the code is not publicly available, we implemented the method ourselves.

[6]We have tried larger training sets, e.g., of sizes 500 and 1,000, in our experiments but there is no significant performance improvement. So we omit the results due to space limitations.

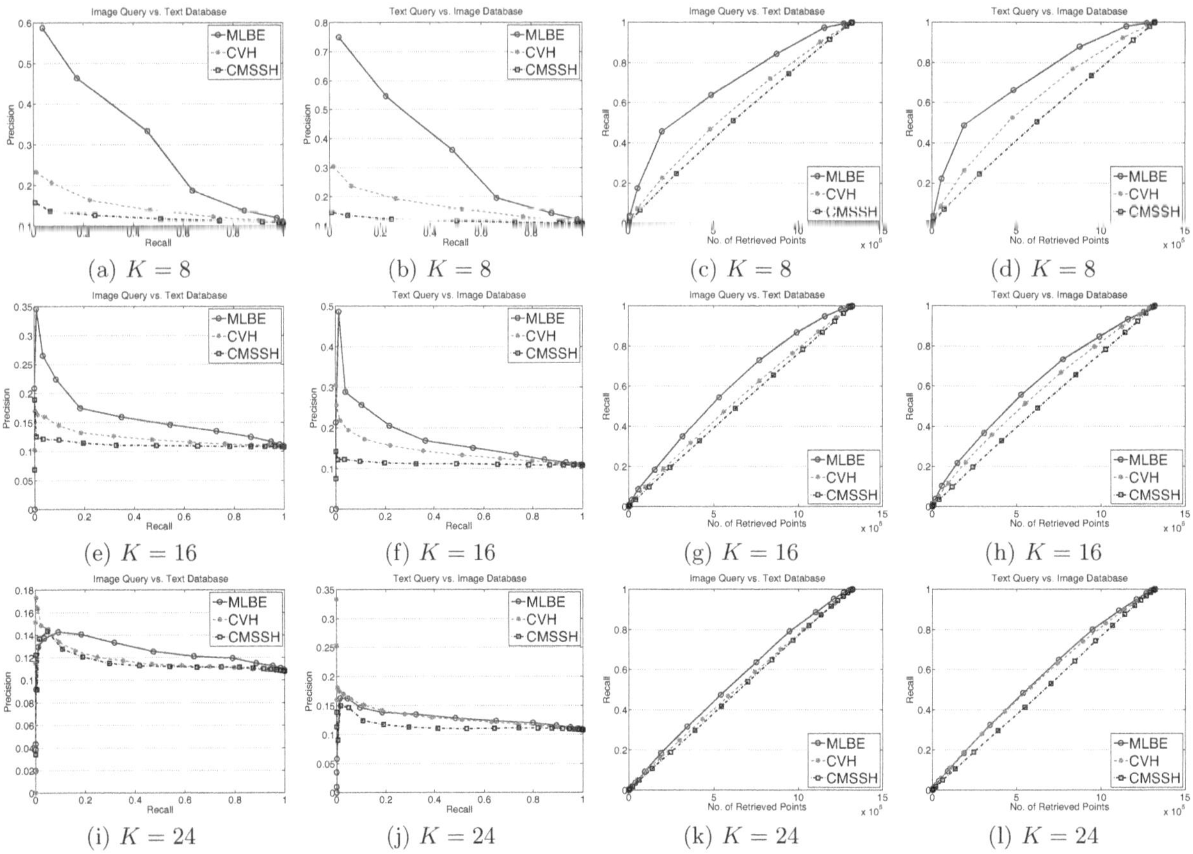

Figure 3: Precision-recall curves and recall curves on Wiki

length increases, the performance gap gets smaller. We conjecture that MLBE may get trapped in local minima during the learning process when the code length is too large.

Besides, we observe that as the code length increases, the performance of all three methods degrades. We note that this phenomenon has also been observed in [38, 23]. A possible reason is that the learned models will be farther from the optimal solutions when the code length gets larger.

4.4 Results on Flickr Data Set

The Flickr data set consists of 186,577 image-tag pairs, which are pruned from the NUS dataset [8] by keeping the pairs that belong to one of the 10 largest classes. Each pair is annotated by at least one of 10 labels. The image features are 500-dimensional SIFT features and the text features are 1000-dimensional vectors obtained by performing PCA on the original tag occurrence features. We use 99% of the data as the database set and the remaining 1% to form the query set.

Table 2: mAP comparison on Flickr

Task	Method	Code Length		
		$K = 8$	$K = 16$	$K = 24$
Image Query vs. Text Database	MLBE	**0.6322**	**0.6608**	0.5104
	CVH	0.5361	0.4871	0.4605
	CMSSH	0.5155	0.5333	**0.5150**
Text Query vs. Image Database	MLBE	**0.5626**	**0.5970**	0.4296
	CVH	0.5260	0.4856	**0.4553**
	CMSSH	0.5093	0.4594	0.4053

The mAP results are reported in Table 2. Similar to the results on Wiki, we observe that MLBE outperforms its counterparts by a large margin when the code length is small.

The corresponding *precision-recall* curves and *recall* curves are plotted in Figure 4. We note that MLBE has the best overall performance.

5. CONCLUSIONS

In this paper, we have presented a novel probabilistic model for multimodal hash function learning. As a latent factor model, the model regards the binary latent factors as hash codes and hence maps data points from multiple modalities to a common Hamming space in a principled manner. Although finding exact posterior distributions of the latent factors is intractable, we have devised an efficient alternating learning algorithm based on MAP estimation. Experimental results show that MLBE compares favorably with two state-of-the-art models.

For our future research, we will go beyond the point estimation approach presented in this paper to explore a more Bayesian treatment based on variational inference for enhanced robustness. We would also like to extend MLBE to determine the code length K automatically from data. This is an important yet largely unaddressed issue in existing methods. Besides, we also plan to apply MLBE to other tasks such as multimodal medical image registration.

6. ACKNOWLEDGMENTS

This research has been supported by General Research Fund 621310 from the Research Grants Council of Hong Kong.

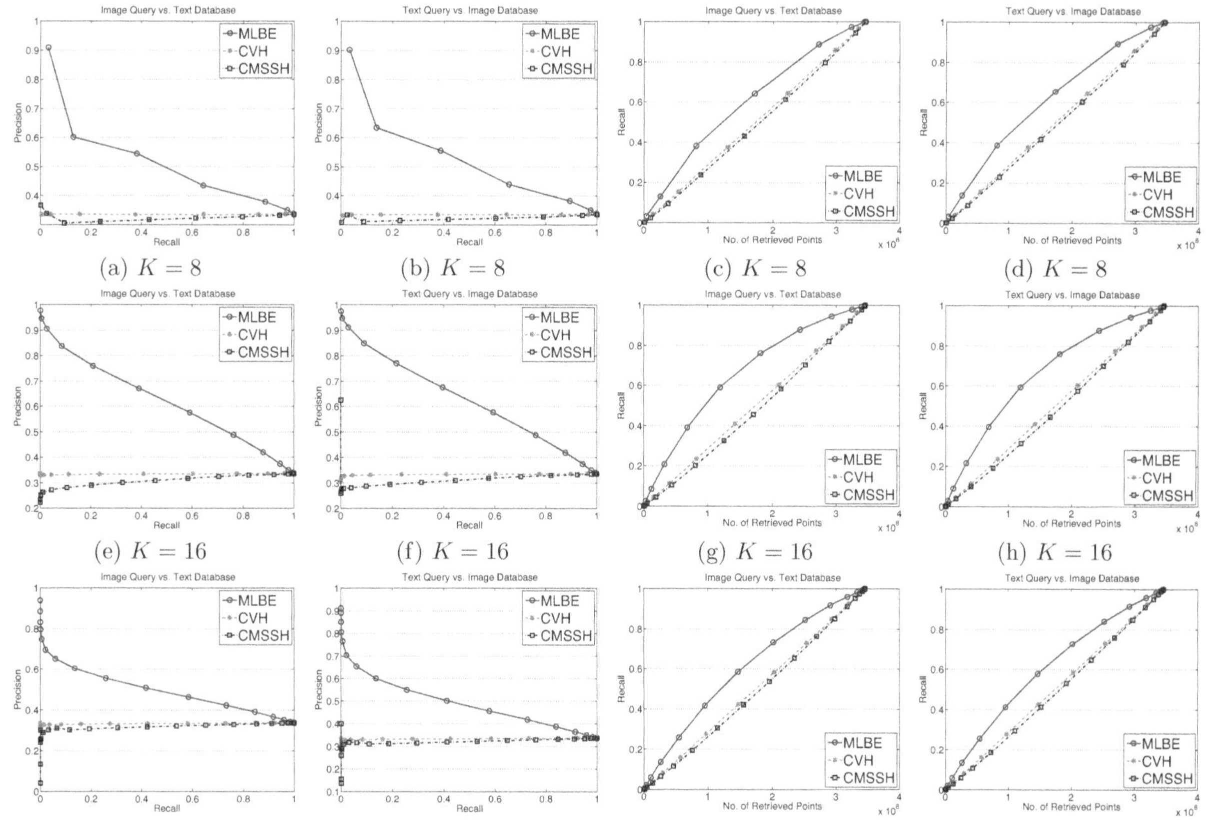

(a) $K = 8$ (b) $K = 8$ (c) $K = 8$ (d) $K = 8$

(e) $K = 16$ (f) $K = 16$ (g) $K = 16$ (h) $K = 16$

(i) $K = 24$ (j) $K = 24$ (k) $K = 24$ (l) $K = 24$

Figure 4: Precision-recall curves and recall curves on Flickr

7. REFERENCES

[1] A. Andoni. *Nearest Neighbor Search: the Old, the New, and the Impossible*. PhD thesis, Massachusetts Institute of Technology, 2009.

[2] A. Andoni and P. Indyk. Near-optimal hashing algorithms for approximate nearest neighbor in high dimensions. *Communications of the ACM*, 51(1):117–122, 2008.

[3] S. Arya, D. M. Mount, N. S. Netanyahu, R. Silverman, and A. Y. Wu. An optimal algorithm for approximate nearest neighbor searching in fixed dimensions. *Journal of the ACM*, 45(6):891–923, 1998.

[4] D. M. Blei, A. Y. Ng, and M. I. Jordan. Latent Dirichlet allocation. *Journal of Machine Learning Research*, 3:993–1022, 2003.

[5] A. Z. Broder, M. Charikar, A. M. Frieze, and M. Mitzenmacher. Min-wise independent permutations. In *STOC*, 1998.

[6] M. M. Bronstein, A. M. Bronstein, F. Michel, and N. Paragios. Data fusion through cross-modality metric learning using similarity-sensitive hashing. In *CVPR*, 2010.

[7] M. Charikar. Similarity estimation techniques from rounding algorithms. In *STOC*, 2002.

[8] T.-S. Chua, J. Tang, R. Hong, H. Li, Z. Luo, and Y.-T. Zheng. NUS-WIDE: A real-world web image database from National University of Singapore. In *CIVR*, 2009.

[9] A. Dasgupta, R. Kumar, and T. Sarlos. Fast locality-sensitive hashing. In *KDD*, 2011.

[10] K. Eshghi and S. Rajaram. Locality sensitive hash functions based on concomitant rank order statistics. In *KDD*, 2008.

[11] J. H. Friedman, J. L. Bentley, and R. A. Finkel. An algorithm for finding best matches in logarithmic expected time. *ACM Transactions on Mathematical Software*, 3(3):209–226, 1977.

[12] A. Gionis, P. Indyk, and R. Motwani. Similarity search in high dimensions via hashing. In *VLDB*, 1999.

[13] T. L. Griffiths and Z. Ghahramani. Infinite latent feature models and the Indian buffet process. In *NIPS 18*, 2005.

[14] J. He, W. Liu, and S.-F. Chang. Scalable similarity search with optimized kernel hashing. In *KDD*, 2010.

[15] K. A. Heller and Z. Ghahramani. A nonparametric Bayesian approach to modeling overlapping clusters. In *AISTATS*, 2007.

[16] G. E. Hinton and R. Salakhutdinov. Reducing the dimensionality of data with neural networks. *Science*, 313(5786):504–509, 2006.

[17] P. Indyk and R. Motwani. Approximate nearest neighbors: Towards removing the curse of dimensionality. In *STOC*, 1998.

[18] B. Kulis and T. Darrell. Learning to hash with binary reconstructive embeddings. In *NIPS 22*, 2009.

[19] B. Kulis and K. Grauman. Kernelized locality-sensitive hashing for scalable image search. In *ICCV*, 2009.

[20] S. Kumar and R. Udupa. Learning hash functions for cross-view similarity search. In *IJCAI*, 2011.

[21] D. Lee, M. Hofmann, F. Steinke, Y. Altun, N. D. Cahill, and B. Schölkopf. Learning similarity measure

for multi-modal 3D image registration. In *CVPR*, 2009.
[22] R.-S. Lin, D. A. Ross, and J. Yagnik. SPEC hashing: Similarity preserving algorithm for entropy-based coding. In *CVPR*, 2010.
[23] W. Liu, J. Wang, S. Kumar, and S.-F. Chang. Hashing with graphs. In *ICML*, 2011.
[24] D. G. Lowe. Distinctive image features from scale-invariant keypoints. *International Journal of Computer Vision*, 60(2):91–110, 2004.
[25] E. Meeds, Z. Ghahramani, R. Neal, and S. T. Roweis. Modeling dyadic data with binary latent factors. In *NIPS 19*, 2006.
[26] Y. Mu, J. Shen, and S. Yan. Weakly-supervised hashing in kernel space. In *CVPR*, 2010.
[27] M. Norouzi and D. J. Fleet. Minimal loss hashing for compact binary codes. In *ICML*, 2011.
[28] N. Quadrianto and C. H. Lampert. Learning multi-view neighborhood preserving projections. In *ICML*, 2011.
[29] M. Raginsky and S. Lazebnik. Locality-sensitive binary codes from shift-invariant kernels. In *NIPS 22*, 2009.
[30] N. Rasiwasia, J. Costa Pereira, E. Coviello, G. Doyle, G. R. Lanckriet, R. Levy, and N. Vasconcelos. A new approach to cross-modal multimedia retrieval. In *ACM MM*, 2010.
[31] R. Salakhutdinov and G. E. Hinton. Semantic hashing. In *SIGIR Workshop on Information Retrieval and Applications of Graphical Models*, 2007.
[32] R. E. Schapire. A brief introduction to Boosting. In *IJCAI*, 1999.
[33] G. Shakhnarovich. *Learning Task-Specific Similarity*. PhD thesis, Massachusetts Institute of Technology, 2005.
[34] G. Shakhnarovich, T. Darrell, and P. Indyk, editors. *Nearest-Neighbor Methods in Learning and Vision: Theory and Practice*. MIT Press, March 2006.
[35] G. Shakhnarovich, P. Viola, and T. Darrell. Fast pose estimation with parameter-sensitive hashing. In *ICCV*, 2003.
[36] A. Torralba, R. Fergus, and Y. Weiss. Small codes and large image databases for recognition. In *CVPR*, 2008.
[37] F. Ture, T. Elsayed, and J. Lin. No free lunch: Brute force vs. locality-sensitive hashing for cross-lingual pairwise similarity. In *SIGIR*, 2011.
[38] J. Wang, S. Kumar, and S.-F. Chang. Semi-supervised hashing for scalable image retrieval. In *CVPR*, 2010.
[39] J. Wang, S. Kumar, and S.-F. Chang. Sequential projection learning for hashing with compact codes. In *ICML*, 2010.
[40] Y. Weiss, A. Torralba, and R. Fergus. Spectral hashing. In *NIPS 21*, 2008.
[41] E. P. Xing, A. Y. Ng, M. I. Jordan, and S. Russell. Distance metric learning with application to clustering with side-information. In *NIPS 15*, 2002.
[42] H. Xu, J. Wang, Z. Li, G. Zeng, S. Li, and N. Yu. Complementary hashing for approximate nearest neighbor search. In *ICCV*, 2011.
[43] D. Zhang, F. Wang, and L. Si. Composite hashing with multiple information sources. In *SIGIR*, 2011.
[44] D. Zhang, J. Wang, D. Cai, and J. Lu. Self-taught hashing for fast similarity search. In *SIGIR*, 2010.
[45] Y. Zhen and D.-Y. Yeung. Active hashing and its application to image and text retrieval. *Data Mining and Knowledge Discovery*, To appear.

APPENDIX

A. PROOF OF THEOREMS

A.1 Proof of Theorem 3.1

To obtain the MAP solution of U_{ik}, it suffices to compare the following two posterior probabilities:

$$p_+ = \Pr(U_{ik} = 1 \mid U_{-ik}, \mathbf{V}, \mathbf{W}^x, w, \mathbf{S}^x, \mathbf{S}^{xy}, \theta_x),$$
$$p_- = \Pr(U_{ik} = -1 \mid U_{-ik}, \mathbf{V}, \mathbf{W}^x, w, \mathbf{S}^x, \mathbf{S}^{xy}, \theta_x).$$

Specifically, we compute the log ratio of the two probabilities, which is larger than or equal to zero if $p_+ \geq p_-$ and smaller than zero otherwise. The log ratio can be evaluated as follows:

$$\begin{aligned}
&\log \frac{\Pr(U_{ik} = 1 \mid U_{-ik}, \mathbf{V}, \mathbf{W}^x, w, \mathbf{S}^x, \mathbf{S}^{xy}, \theta_x)}{\Pr(U_{ik} = -1 \mid U_{-ik}, \mathbf{V}, \mathbf{W}^x, w\mathbf{S}^x, \mathbf{S}^{xy}, \theta_x)} \\
=& \log \frac{\Pr(\mathbf{S}^x \mid U_{ik} = 1, U_{-ik}, \mathbf{W}^x, \theta_x)}{\Pr(\mathbf{S}^x \mid U_{ik} = -1, U_{-ik}, \mathbf{W}^x, \theta_x)} \\
&+ \log \frac{\Pr(\mathbf{S}^{xy} \mid U_{ik} = 1, U_{-ik}, w, \mathbf{V})}{\Pr(\mathbf{S}^{xy} \mid U_{ik} = -1, U_{-ik}, w, \mathbf{V})} \\
&+ \log \frac{\Pr(U_{ik} = 1 \mid \alpha_u, \beta_u)}{\Pr(U_{ik} = -1 \mid \alpha_u, \beta_u)} \\
=& -\frac{\theta_x}{2} \sum_{l \neq i}^{I} \left[\left(S_{il} - \mathbf{u}_l^T \mathbf{W}^x \mathbf{u}_i^+\right)^2 - \left(S_{il} - \mathbf{u}_l^T \mathbf{W}^x \mathbf{u}_i^-\right)^2 \right] \\
&- \frac{\theta_x}{2} \left[\left(S_{ii} - \mathbf{u}_i^{+T} \mathbf{W}^x \mathbf{u}_i^+\right)^2 - \left(S_{ii} - \mathbf{u}_i^{-T} \mathbf{W}^x \mathbf{u}_i^-\right)^2 \right] \\
&+ \sum_{j=1}^{J} O_{ij} \left[S_{ij}^{xy} \log \frac{\rho_{ij}^+}{\rho_{ij}^-} + (1 - S_{ij}^{xy}) \log \frac{1 - \rho_{ij}^+}{1 - \rho_{ij}^-} \right] + \log \frac{\alpha_u}{\beta_u},
\end{aligned}$$

where U_{-ik} denotes all the elements in $\mathbf{U}$ except U_{ik}. The log ratio thus computed gives exactly $\mathcal{L}_{ik}$. This completes the proof.

A.2 Proof of Theorem 3.3

The negative log of the posterior distribution of $\mathbf{W}^x$ can be written as:

$$\begin{aligned}
&- \log p(\mathbf{W}^x \mid \mathbf{S}^x, \mathbf{U}, \theta_x, \phi_x) \qquad (7) \\
=& - \log P(\mathbf{W}^x \mid \phi_x) - \log P(\mathbf{S}^x \mid \mathbf{U}, \mathbf{W}^x, \theta_x) + \tilde{C} \\
=& \frac{\phi_x}{2} \sum_{k=1}^{K} \sum_{d=k}^{K} (W_{kd}^x)^2 + \frac{\theta_x}{2} \sum_{i=1}^{I} \sum_{i'=i}^{I} \left(S_{ii'}^x - \mathbf{u}_i^T \mathbf{W}^x \mathbf{u}_{i'}\right)^2 + \tilde{C} \\
=& \frac{\phi_x}{2} \mathbf{w}^{xT} \mathbf{M}_1 \mathbf{w}^x + \frac{\theta_x}{2} (\mathbf{s}^x - \mathbf{A}\mathbf{w}^x)^T \mathbf{M}_2 (\mathbf{s}^x - \mathbf{A}\mathbf{w}^x) + \tilde{C} \\
=& \frac{1}{2} \mathbf{w}^{xT} \left(\theta_x \mathbf{A}^T \mathbf{M}_2 \mathbf{A} + \phi_x \mathbf{M}_1\right) \mathbf{w}^x - \theta_x \mathbf{s}^{xT} \mathbf{M}_2 \mathbf{A} \mathbf{w}^x + \tilde{C},
\end{aligned}$$

where $\tilde{C}$ is a constant term independent of $\mathbf{W}^x$.

Setting the derivative of Equation (7) to zero, we get

$$\mathbf{w}^x = \left(\mathbf{A}^T \mathbf{M}_2 \mathbf{A} + \frac{\phi_x}{\theta_x} \mathbf{M}_1\right)^{-1} \mathbf{A}^T \mathbf{M}_2 \mathbf{s}^x.$$

This completes the proof.

On Socio-Spatial Group Query for Location-Based Social Networks

De-Nian Yang
Academia Sinica
Taipei, Taiwan
dnyang@iis.sinica.edu.tw

Chih-Ya Shen
National Taiwan Univ.
Taipei, Taiwan
chihya@arbor.ee.ntu.edu.tw

Wang-Chien Lee
The Penn State Univ.
State College, PA, USA
wlee@cse.psu.edu

Ming-Syan Chen
National Taiwan Univ.
Taipei, Taiwan
mschen@cc.ee.ntu.edu.tw

ABSTRACT

Challenges faced in organizing impromptu activities are the requirements of making timely invitations in accordance with the locations of candidate attendees and the social relationship among them. It is desirable to find a group of attendees close to a rally point and ensure that the selected attendees have a good social relationship to create a good atmosphere in the activity. Therefore, this paper proposes Socio-Spatial Group Query (SSGQ) to select a group of nearby attendees with tight social relation. Efficient processing of SSGQ is very challenging due to the tradeoff in the spatial and social domains. We show that the problem is NP-hard via a proof and design an efficient algorithm SSGSelect, which includes effective pruning techniques to reduce the running time for finding the optimal solution. We also propose a new index structure, Social R-Tree to further improve the efficiency. User study and experimental results demonstrate that SSGSelect significantly outperforms manual coordination in both solution quality and efficiency.

Categories and Subject Descriptors

H.2.4 [**Systems**]: Query processing

General Terms

Algorithms

Keywords

Query Processing, Spatial Indexing, Social Networks

1. INTRODUCTION

With the emergence of GPS-enabled mobile devices and Web 2.0 technology, mobile users can easily capture and upload their own locations to various location-based social networking (LBSN) applications, such as Loopt, Geomium, Buddy Beacon, FindMe, Facebook Place, BrightKite, Meetup, and Google Map. All these LBSN applications allow users to share their location information with friends and thus, as we envisage, may potentially enable instant organization of impromptu activities, e.g., having a dinner with friends nearby. However, with today's technology, the selection of invitees for these events still requires significant *manual* coordination. In this work, we aim to develop new techniques for an impromptu activity planning service to alleviate this effort.

Due to the inherited nature as an LBSN application, such an impromptu activity planning service needs to consider the following *spatial* and *social* factors: i) the selected friends need to be close enough to a rally point in order to minimize the waiting time for an activity; and ii) the selected friends need to have a good social relationship to create a good atmosphere in the activity. In other words, challenges faced in organizing impromptu activities lie in meeting the requirements of making *timely* invitations in accordance with the *locations* of candidate invitees and the *social* relationship among them. Notice that friends located nearby may not have tight social relationships with each other, while close friends may not happen to located near an intended rally point. Moreover, when the number of intended invitees increases, the invitation process becomes more complicated and thereby too tedious to coordinate manually. Therefore, efficient search algorithms that automatically suggest the most suitable attendees for an activity is a mandate for the impromptu activity planning service.

As the first step towards the aforementioned impromptu activity planning service, we propose a new query, namely *Socio-Spatial Group Query (SSGQ)*, aiming to find a set of most suitable candidates for a planned activity by taking into account certain spatial and social constraints. In this work, we assume that the service provider has access to the social connectivity of its users and their locations.[1] Thus, given a social graph consisting of socially connected users and their (published) locations, an SSGQ, specified a rally point q, the number of activity invitees p, and the average number of unfamiliar people an invitee may have k, returns a set of p invitees from the social graph of the activity initiator such that the average spatial distance for each invitee to the rally point is minimized. It is worth noting that the query incorporates a social constraint (denoted by k), to govern the unfamiliarity between invitees. Each attendee on average can have no social relationship with at most k other invitees. With a proper setting of k, the tightness of social relationships among invitees (and hopefully activity atmosphere) are ensured. As such, the SSGQ can facilitate

KDD'12, August 12–16, 2012, Beijing, China.

[1]The privacy issues on the locations and social connectivity of users are very important but out of scope of this study. A simple way is to allow each user to specify a friend list and time intervals, such that only the query issued from the friends in the list during those intervals can access the location information and social connectivity of the user.

users to organize different kinds of activities based on both the specified spatial and social conditions.

Note that SSGQ can be generalized for supporting other spatial/social relevant planning services that do not require a specific initiator. For example, when an user queries a nearby restaurant using a mobile device, an SSGQ may be issued to automatically recommend a group of socially close friends near the restaurant. Moreover, location-based advertisements can leverage SSGQ to a group of friends for a preferred restaurant in order to push mobile coupon, which is beneficial to both customers and restaurants.[2] Finally, the SSGQ is particularly useful for coordinating search and rescue operations in some scenarios of emergency and disasters, such as earthquakes and tsunamis. As social relationship, e.g., previous co-working experiences of the searchers, and spatial factor, e.g., distance for searchers to reach the disaster area, are important for success of rescue operations, the SSGQ can be employed to obtain the most suitable searchers.

The problem of processing SSGQ efficiently is challenging due to the tradeoff in the spatial distance and the social relationships. A simple strategy for processing SSGQ is to enumerate all possible groups of p invitees, eliminate those that do not satisfy the social constraints, and then return the group with minimal total spatial distance. This approach needs to evaluate C_p^f candidate groups, where f is the total number of candidate attendees, in the solution space and thus is not desirable. Note that, as we will show later, the problem of processing SSGQ is NP-hard. Nevertheless, due to the importance of spatial and social factors considered in SSGQ, we exploit the spatial and social constraints specified in SSGQ while forming the candidate groups to alleviate the processing cost. Our idea is to expand the solution space in a systematical way such that we can efficiently find the solution without examining all candidate groups in details. In other words, we incrementally select the invitees by giving priority to those (a) who are located close to the rally point and (b) who are close friends. Finding a group of friends who best meet both conditions of (a) and (b) is not trivial. An algorithm that prioritizes on (a) is inclined to generate candidate groups with small total spatial distance quickly but it does not always come up with a solution that satisfies the familiarity constraint, especially those activities specified with a small k. On the other hand, an algorithm that prioritizes on (b) may quickly find a group of friends who know each other very well but do not easily satisfy the minimum total spatial distance. In other words, the challenge in finding optimal SSGQ answer comes from the dilemma of (1) reducing the total spatial distance[3] and (2) ensuring that the solution satisfying the familiarity constraint.

Specifically, in this paper, we first prove that SSGQ is an NP-hard problem but, fortunately, while the problem is very challenging, it is still tractable since the size of p is relatively small in most impromptu activities. Therefore, to efficiently process this query, we design a new algorithm, called *SSGSelect*, to find the optimal solution. We design various strategies, Distance Ordering, Socio-Spatial Ordering, Distance Pruning, and Familiarity Pruning, to effectively reduce the processing time. During the selection of each attendee, we address both the spatial distance and social connectivity of the attendee, together with the characteristics of the social network for other candidate attendees that have not been considered, in order to prune unnecessary search space and find the optimal solution efficiently.

The above strategies incrementally consider and examine each candidate attendee. A potential approach to further improve the efficiency is to select multiple candidate attendees jointly, because the optimal solution can be constructed with fewer iterations. When an attendee close to the rally point is chosen, nearby candidate attendees are potential to be good candidates for joint selection due to their smaller spatial distances to the rally point. Nearby candidate attendees can be efficiently identified by leveraging the spatial index structure, such as R-Tree, since they are usually located in the same Minimum Bounding Rectangle (MBR) of R-Tree. Nevertheless, choosing *all* candidate attendees in the same MBR may not be able to generate a solution following the familiarity constraint with k since the social connectivity among them is not carefully examined. To effectively tackle this issue, we propose Social R-Tree (SR-Tree), which incorporates and summarizes the social information for the candidate attendees in an MBR. In SR-Tree, all candidate attendees in each MBR are indexed into multiple social clusters with different social densities to support SSGQ with different k.

With the proposed SR-Tree, SSGSelect is enhanced by a new strategy, Joint Insertion, which chooses multiple candidate attendees simultaneously to reduce the number of required iterations for finding the optimal solution. We implement SSGSelect in Facebook and conduct user study on 206 people. The contributions of this paper are summarized as follows.

- We formulate a useful query for social networking application, namely, SSGQ, to obtain the optimal set of attendees. SSGQ can be used to plan for various types of activities by specifying the familiarity constraint k. We prove that the problem is NP-hard.
- To efficiently process SSGQ, we propose SSGSelect with various strategies, including Distance Ordering, Socio-Spatial Ordering, Distance Pruning, and Familiarity Pruning, for finding the optimal solution. In addition, we design a new index structure, named SR-Tree, together with Joint Insertion, to simultaneously select multiple nodes at each iteration for finding the optimal solution in smaller time.
- We implement SSGSelect in Facebook and conduct an user study with 206 people. The results demonstrate that SSGSelect significantly outperforms manual coordination in both solution quality and efficiency.

The rest of this paper is summarized as follows. Section 2 introduces the related works. Section 3 formulates SSGQ and prove that it is NP-hard. We design algorithm SSGSelect in Section 4 and enhance it with the proposed SR-Tree in Section 5. Results of the user study and experiments are shown in Section 6, and we conclude this paper in Section 7.

2. RELATED WORK

Some LBSN applications, e.g., Meetup, have been developed for activity coordination. However, an activity initiator still needs to specify candidate attendees of the activity. This is undesirable because social familiarity is not

[2]Notice that location-based advertisement and social network-based advertisements have been exploited by websites, such as Google Map and Livingsocial.com. However, the two aspects have not been considered in an integrated fashion.

[3]Reducing the maximum spatial distance of an attendee is an alternative. This paper proposes to minimize the total spatial distance because many social activities can begin or warm up when most attendees arrives, and a few distant attendees are allowed to arrive late.

ensured, while the waiting time is not minimized, either. Manual assignment of candidate attendees is tedious and time-consuming for the initiator, especially for a large activity. Thus, SSGQ is very useful for such sites which recommends suitable attendees with efficient query processing.

In recent works, several researches on finding groups of socially connected members, e.g., team formation [2][3], community search [4], and Social-Temporal Group Query [7], have been reported in the literature. Nevertheless, their research context and objectives are totally different from our study that explores both the spatial and social dimensions in finding a group for impromptu activity planning. Specifically, team formation [2][3] finds a group of experts with the required skills, while aiming to minimize the communications cost between these experts. Community search [4] finds a compact community that contains particular members, aiming to minimize the total degree in the community. Social-Temporal Group Query [7] checks the available times of attendees to find the group with the most suitable activity time. To the best knowledge of the authors, researches on finding groups that consider constraints in both the spatial and social dimensions have not appeared. In contrast, our work examines the inter-play in both social and spatial dimensions, with an objective to find a group of mutually familiar attendees such that the total spatial distance to a rally point is minimized. As mentioned, we envisage that our research result can be employed in various LBSN applications for group recommendation.

Relevant to our work, spatial queries for selecting a set of spatial points, aiming to minimize the total spatial distance, have been proposed for various scenarios [5, 6, 8, 9]. However, in these works, the (social) connectivity among the spatial points is not considered. Specifically, given two sets of points P and Q, together with the number of points to be selected k, Group Nearest Neighbor Query [5] finds a set of k points in P such that the total spatial distance of the points to all points in Q is minimized. On the other hand, for a line segment and a set of points, Continuous Nearest Neighbor Search [6] returns the nearest neighbor of each point on the line segment, while the Continuous Visible Nearest Neighbor Queries [8] extends Continuous Nearest Neighbor Search [6] by incorporating the obstacles in the problem design, which may affect the visibility or distance between two points and lead to different results. Meanwhile, Continuous Obstructed Nearest Neighbor Query [9] retrieves the nearest neighbor with regard to the obstructed distance, i.e., the shortest path without crossing any obstacle. Therefore, the above-mentioned queries focus only on the spatial dimension and thereby are not applicable to our scenario of LBSN applications.

3. PROBLEM FORMULATION

Given a social graph $G = (V, E)$, where each vertex $v \in V$ is a candidate attendee with a location l_v, and any two mutually acquainted vertices u and v are connected by an edge $e_{u,v}$. A Socio-Spatial Group Query $SSGQ(p, q, k)$ finds a set F of p vertices from G where the total spatial distance from the vertices in F to the rally point q, i.e., $\sum_{v \in F} d_{v,q}$, is minimized and each vertex on average can share no edge with at most k other vertices in F.

Notice that the three parameters in an SSGQ, i.e., p, q, and k, determine the size of the answer group, spatial constraint, and social constraint of the query, respectively, and thus have significant implications regarding the processing strategy. First, as the size of group p increases, the solution space (which consists of all candidate groups) rapidly grows. Indeed, we prove that processing SSGQ is an NP-hard problem but, fortunately, while the problem is very challenging, it is still tractable since the size of p is relatively small in most cases. Second, the position of q hints that candidate invitees located close to q should be considered with priority as the search criteria aims to minimize the total spatial distance from members of the group to q. Finally, k dictates the tightness of social relationship among members of the group. A small k in SSGQ results in a group of mutually familiar invitees, while a larger k allows more unfamiliarity within the returned group of invitees. The spatial and social constraints can be employed for early pruning of unqualified candidate groups.

In this paper, we aim to develop efficient query processing algorithms for SSGQ with a new index structure, Social R-Tree. Moreover, we also devise several access ordering and pruning strategies to effectively reduce the computation time. In the next section, we design an efficient query processing algorithm by pruning unqualified candidate groups.

In the following, we first prove the hardness result.

THEOREM 1. *SSGQ is NP-hard.*

PROOF. We prove that SSGQ is NP-hard with the reduction from p-clique. Decision problem p-clique is given a graph G_c to find whether the graph contains a clique, i.e., a complete graph with an edge connecting every two vertices, with p vertices. In SSGQ, we let $G = G_c$, $k = 0$, and $d_{v,q} = 1$ for every vertex $v \in V$. We first prove the necessary condition. If G_c contains a p-clique, there must exist a group with the same vertices in the p-clique such that every person has social relations with all the other attendees of the group, and the total spatial distance is p. We then prove the sufficient condition. If G in SSGQ contains a group with the size as p and k as 0, G_c in problem p-clique must contain a solution with size p, too. The theorem follows. □

4. ALGORITHM DESIGN FOR SSGQ

In this section, we propose Algorithm SSGSelect to find the optimal solution for SSGQ. To guide an efficient exploration of the search space, we design effective strategies to selection new attendees and prune unnecessary search space. Later in Section 5, equipped with SR-Tree, SSGSelect is enhanced by Joint Insert to select multiple attendees at each iteration. Specifically, let S_I and S_R denote the intermediate solution set and the remaining set of candidate attendees, respectively. Initially, S_I is empty, and S_R is V. At each iteration afterward, we select a vertex from S_R to S_I. When S_I includes p vertices and follows the familiarity constraint, S_I is regarded as a feasible solution. Afterward, to improve the feasible solution, our algorithm backtracks to the previous iteration and previous S_I for choosing another vertex from S_R to S_I, while a branch-and-bound tree is maintained to keep track of the exploration process for backtracking.

The selection of the vertex from S_R into S_I at each iteration is critical. It is essential to avoid choosing a vertex that will lead to a large increment of the spatial distance. With this important factor in mind, Distance Ordering selects a vertex with a small spatial distance to the rally point q. To further consider the social connectivity, Socio-Spatial Ordering extends Distance Ordering by jointly considering the spatial and social domains. On the other hand, to trim unnecessary search space, Distance Pruning effectively avoids unnecessary exploration of S_R that will not lead to a better solution, by examining the sum of the current total spatial distance from S_I to q and the lower bound of the distance increment in selecting any vertex from S_R. In addition to

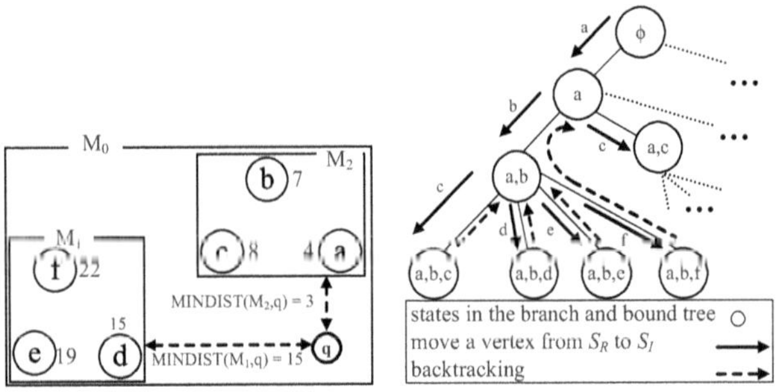

(a) (b)

Figure 1: Example of Distance Ordering and Branch-and-Bound Search.

the above spatial domain, Familiarity Pruning examines social connectiviy of the vertices in S_R and stops choosing any vertex from S_R if eventually it is not able to generate any feasible solution following the familiarity constraint.

Notice that SSGSelect is able to find the optimal solution because Distance Pruning only removes unqualified solutions (the solutions with larger total spatial distances to q), and Familiarity Pruning only trims infeasible solutions (the solutions that do not follow the familiarity constraints). The optimal solution does not belong the above two categories. Moreover, with Socio-Spatial Ordering, SSGSelect exploits both the spatial and social domain information to guide an efficient search for the optimal solution.

4.1 Distance Ordering

At each iteration, Distance Ordering selects the vertex with the minimum spatial distance to q, to minimize the increment of the total spatial distance for S_I. Naturally, a straightforward approach is to sort all vertices in G before the algorithm starts. However, this approach is not scalable for a large social network and is very computation intensive because q is allowed be different for every SSGQ. In contrast, a more efficient approach is leveraging a spatial index structure, such as R-Tree, and its distance browsing strategy [10] with a priority queue for vertex selection. Each element in the priority queue is either a vertex or a Minimum Bounding Rectangle (MBR). The distance of a vertex is its spatial distance to q, while the distance of an MBR M is the $MINDIST(M, q)$, which denotes the minimum distance between q and the border of M [1]. Finding the vertex with the minimum distance can be achieved by iteratively extracting the first element of the priority queue. Initially, the priority queue contains only the root MBR of R-Tree. When the extracted element is an MBR, we traverse the R-Tree and insert all its child MBRs into the priority queue. Therefore, the first extracted vertex from the queue is the one with the minimum distance to q.

For example, Figure 1(a) shows six vertices in an R-Tree, where q denotes the rally point. Assume that $MINDIST$ to q for MBRs M_0, M_1 and M_2 are 0, 15 and 3, respectively, and the actual distances of the vertices to q are marked besides each vertex. Initially, the priority queue contains only $\{M_0\}$. Afterward, we extract M_0 and insert M_1 and M_2 into priority queue. Now the first element of the priority queue is M_2 because $MINDIST(M_2, q) < MINDIST(M_1, q)$. Then, M_2 is popped from the priority queue with its children vertices a, b and c inserted. Now the elements in the priority queue are $\{a, b, c, M_1\}$. Therefore, Distance Ordering first selects and adds a to S_I because its spatial distance to q is the smallest one.

Figure 1(b) illustrates a part of the branch-and-bound tree with $p = 3$, where Distance Ordering iteratively moves the vertex with the minimum distance to q from in S_R to S_I. Notice that S_R is $\{c, d, e, f\}$ during the first visit of the state with $S_I = \{a, b\}$, and c is then selected and added to S_I to create a leaf node with $S_I = \{a, b, c\}$ with $p = 3$ in Figure 1(b). Since the number of vertices in S_I is sufficient for p, Algorithm SSGSelect backtracks from $S_I = \{a, b, c\}$ to $S_I = \{a, b\}$, and S_R now becomes $\{d, e, f\}$ since vertex c was just considered. Similarly, when backtracked from $S_I = \{a, b, d\}$ to $S_I = \{a, b\}$, S_R becomes $\{e, f\}$ since both c and d has been explored.

4.2 Socio-Spatial Ordering

With R-Tree, we demonstrated that Distance Ordering can efficiently select the vertex for S_I to minimize the increment of the total spatial distance to q, i.e., the objective value, at each iteration. Nevertheless, it is also desirable that the selected vertex has good social connectivity to other vertices in S_I in order to follow the familiarity constraint. To incorporate this key factor, Socio-Spatial Ordering enhances Distance Ordering by considering both the spatial distance and social connectivity during the selection of a vertex from S_R to S_I. Intuitively, when a vertex is extracted from the priority queue, we select the vertex and add it to S_I only when the vertex satisfies *Intra-Familiarity Condition*. This condition ensures that S_I together with the selected vertex leads to a mutually familiar group of attendees specified by k. If the vertex does not follow the condition, we extract and examine the next vertex from the priority queue. Therefore, both spatial and social factors are captured in Socio-Spatial Ordering.

To ensure that each selected vertex v has good social connectivity to the vertices in S_I, a simple approach is to restrict that v can be selected only when the number of edges between v and the vertices in S_I exceeds a given threshold. With a larger threshold, a candidate attendee that is familiar with more attendees in S_I is inclined to be chosen, such that it is easier for any solution growing from S_I to satisfy the familiarity constraint. Nevertheless, the connectivity of S_I is not examined during the selection of a vertex in the above approach. Intuitively, if S_I is already a mutually familiar group, it is expected that choosing a vertex v with fewer edges connecting S_I is more proper if it can minimize the total spatial distance. In addition, whether the connectivity of S_I is sufficient depends on k, which can be different in every SSGQ. Therefore, it is desirable to incorporate the connectivity of the vertices in S_I and parameter k during the selection of a vertex from S_R to S_I at each iteration. With the above observations in mind, we propose the following condition for Socio-Spatial Ordering.

Intra-Familiarity Condition (IFC). When a vertex v is extracted from the priority queue, we select the vertex and add it from S_R to S_I only when the vertex satisfies Intra-Familiarity Condition. To effectively consider the social domain, this condition first assumes that v is added to S_I and then examines whether the social connectivity of the new group $S_I \cup \{v\}$ is sufficient according to the criterion k. Specifically, let $F(S_I \cup \{v\})$ denote the *intra-familiarity* of the group,

$$F(S_I \cup \{v\}) = \frac{1}{|S_I \cup \{v\}|} \sum_{v \in S_I \cup \{v\}} |N_v|,$$

where N_v is the set of neighbors of v in $S_I \cup \{v\}$. For every attendee in $S_I \cup \{v\}$, intra-familiarity represents the average number of acquainted attendees in $S_I \cup \{v\}$. Vertex v is allowed to be selected and added to S_I if it satisfies IFC specified as follows,

$$F(S_I \cup \{v\}) \geq |S_I \cup \{v\}| - \frac{\widehat{k}\left(|S_I \cup \{v\}|\right)}{p-1} - 1,$$

where $\widehat{k}$ here is a filtering parameter and set as k initially. Intuitively, when $k = p - 1$, the activity allows all attendees to be mutually unfamiliar, and Distance Order in this case is the best strategy. In fact, IFC in this situation becomes $F(S_I \cup \{v\}) \geq -1$, and Socio-Spatial Ordering here is identical to Distance Order. In another extreme case with $k = 0$, IFC becomes $F(S_I \cup \{v\}) \geq |S_I \cup \{v\}| - 1$, and each attendee in $S_I \cup \{v\}$ needs to be acquainted with all the others in $S_I \cup \{v\}$.

It is worth noting that IFC incorporates a filtering parameter $\widehat{k}$, instead of including k directly, in order to properly handle other cases with $0 < k < p - 1$. When $k = 0$, if no vertex from S_R can satisfy IFC, it is not necessary to add any vertex v from S_R to S_I because every solution growing from $S_I \cup \{v\}$ cannot follow the familiarity constraint. When $k > 0$, it is worth noting that if no vertex from S_R can satisfy IFC, it does not imply that every solution growing from $S_I \cup \{v\}$ does not have sufficient social connectivity. In contrast, it is possible to find a vertex v in S_R and a solution growing from $S_I \cup \{v\}$ following the familiarity constraint, when other vertices added later bring a sufficient number of edges to the solution. Therefore, for any SSGQ with $k > 0$, Socio-Spatial Ordering sets $\widehat{k}$ as k initially and increases $\widehat{k}$ if no vertex from S_R can satisfy IFC, until at least one vertex follows IFC and is able to be selected for S_I. In other words, IFC first maintains a high criterion for social connectivity by setting $\widehat{k}$ as k, in order to prioritize a vertex leading to sufficient social connectivity. If no vertex from S_R can satisfy such a high criterion, IFC increases $\widehat{k}$ to avoid filtering out any feasible solution, and any vertex in S_R that did not satisfy IFC previously will be examined later with a large $\widehat{k}$.

At each iteration, the vertex chosen by Distance Ordering and Socio-Spatial Ordering may be different. The following example demonstrates that the result obtained by Distance Ordering enjoys a smaller total social distance but does not follow the familiarity constraint. For the six vertices in Figure 1(a) with the corresponding social graph in 2(a), where $p = 3$ and $k = 0$, the exploration of Socio-Spatial Ordering is shown as the thick line in Figure 2(b). In this example, at the beginning $\widehat{k} = 0$ and $S_I = \phi$, since a is the vertex with the minimum spatial distance to q and $F(\phi \cup \{a\}) = \frac{0}{1} \geq 1 - 1 - \frac{0 \cdot 1}{2}$ satisfies IFC, Socio-Spatial Ordering moves vertex a from S_R to S_I first and let $S_I = \{a\}$. However, $F(S_I \cup \{b\}) = \frac{0}{2} < 2 - 1 - \frac{0 \cdot 2}{2}$, which does not satisfy IFC. Therefore, Socio-Spatial Ordering examines vertex c and finds $F(S_I \cup \{c\}) = \frac{1}{2} \cdot 2 = 1 \geq 2 - 1 - \frac{0 \cdot 2}{2}$, which satisfies IFC. Therefore, vertex c is moved into S_I and now we have $S_I = \{a, c\}$. We then try to expand S_I by checking IFC with vertex d. $F(S_I \cup \{d\}) = \frac{1}{3} \cdot 6 = 2 \geq 3 - 1 - \frac{0 \cdot 3}{2}$. Therefore, d is moved to S_I, and $S_I = \{a, c, d\}$ now is a feasible solution. By contrast, Distance Ordering first selects vertex b as shown in the dashed-line in Figure 2(b) and then sequentially constructs four states $\{a, b, c\}$, $\{a, b, d\}$, $\{a, b, e\}$ and $\{a, b, f\}$ in the branch-and-bound tree. Unfortunately all of them cannot follow the familiarity constraint. Therefore, this example illustrates that it is desirable to jointly consider spatial and social domain in order to find a feasible solution for SSGSelect earlier, because this feasible solution is a key factor for the pruning strategy in the next subsection.

4.3 Distance Pruning

It is expected that Socio-Spatial Ordering can acquire the first feasible solution, which follows the familiarity constraint, prior to Distance Ordering because social connectivity is examined during the selection of vertices. With the first feasible solution and its total spatial distance D as a criterion, SSGSelect is able to prune unnecessary search space, in which the total spatial distance of any solution is no better than D. Moreover, to further improving the pruning capability, SSGSelect updates D when a better feasible solution is obtained afterward. As shown in our experimental results in Section 6, pruning of unnecessary search space can significantly reduce the time to find the optimal solution.

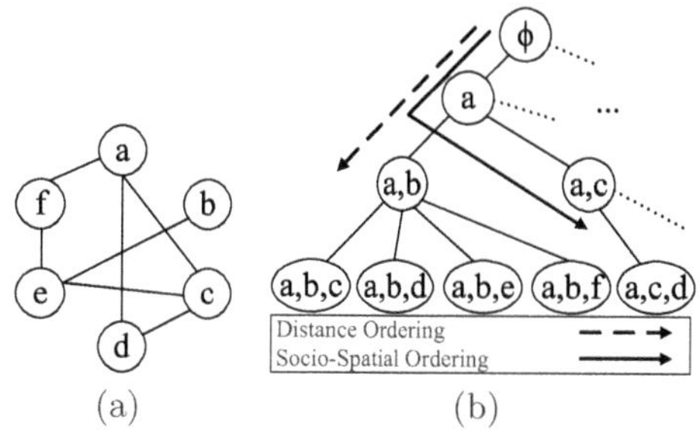

Figure 2: Example of Socio-Spatial Ordering.

For any intermediate solution S_I, there are $p - |S_I|$ vertices required to be selected from S_R to S_I. Apparently, further processing of S_I is unnecessary if choosing the $p - |S_I|$ vertices with the smallest spatial distances to q is not able to generate a solution better than D. Nevertheless, finding the $p - |S_I|$ vertices with the smallest spatial distances for every S_R in the branch-and-bound tree is inclined to incur more delay, especially for a large p. Therefore, Distance Pruning identifies a lower bound and stops processing S_I when the following condition holds,

$$\sum\nolimits_{u \in S_I} d_{u,q} + (p - |S_I|) d_{v_{\min},q} \geq D,$$

where the first term is the total spatial distance from the vertices in S_I to q. For S_R, only the vertex $v_{\min}$ with the smallest spatial distance to q is accessed here, and $(p - |S_I|) d_{v_{\min},q}$ represents a lower bound on the total spatial distance for the above $p - |S_I|$ vertices in S_R. Distance Pruning is computationally efficient since vertex $v_{\min}$ can be extracting from the priority queue in Section 4.1. On the other hand, if the first element of the priority queue is an MBR, Distance Pruning is specified as follows,

$$\sum\nolimits_{v \in S_I} d_{v,q} + (p - |S_I|) MINDIST(M, q) \geq D,$$

where $MINDIST(M, q)$ is the minimum distance between q and the border of M. Thus, the spatial distance of every vertex in M must be no smaller than $MINDIST(M, q)$. That is, $MINDIST(M, q) \leq v_{\min}$, and $(p - |S_I|) MINDIST(M, q)$ is a lower bound on the total spatial distance of the above $p - |S_I|$ vertices in S_R.

Consider an example with $p = 3$ with the spatial locations and social graph shown in Figure 1(a) and 2(a), respectively. After a feasible solution $\{a, c, d\}$ is explored, its total spatial distance 27 is assigned to D. When SSGSelect considers $S_I = \{a, b\}$ and $S_R = \{e, f\}$, since $\sum_{u \in S_I} d_{u,q} + (p - |S_I|) d_{v_{\min},q} = 11 + 1 \cdot 19 = 30 > 27$, Distance Pruning removes states $\{a, b, e\}$ and $\{a, b, f\}$, stops processing $S_I = \{a, b\}$, and backtracks to the previous state accordingly.

4.4 Familiarity Pruning

Distance Pruning trims the search space by stopping processing S_I and backtracks to the previous state in the branch-and-bound tree, when the total spatial distance from each vertex in S_R to q is too large to generate a solution better than the current feasible solution D in hand. In contrast, Familiarity Pruning examines the social connectivity of all possible solutions growing from S_I. Familiarity Pruning stops processing S_I and backtracks to the previous state if every possible solution growing from S_I via the exploration of S_R is not able to satisfy the familiarity constraint.

The challenge of designing a pruning strategy in social domain lies in various social connectivity allowed to appear in all possible solutions. It is expensive to examine each possible solution according to the familiarity constraint. Therefore, to efficiently prune unnecessary search space, Familiarity Pruning derives an upper bound on the social closeness of every possible solution growing from S_R. If the upper bound indicates that each attendee on average is acquainted with fewer than $p-k-1$ other attendees, every possible solution is not able to follow the familiarity constraint.

Specifically, the edges in any solution growing from S_I can be divided into three categories: 1) the set of edges E_I connecting any two vertices in S_I, 2) the edges of edges E_R connecting any two vertices selected from S_R, and 3) the set of edges E_{IR} connecting any two vertices in S_I and the vertices selected from S_R. Apparently, $|E_I|$ is $\frac{1}{2}\sum_{v\in S_I}|N_v^I|$, where N_v^I is the set of acquainted neighbors of v in S_I. Since the selected vertices in S_R is not clear now, a good way is to find an upper bound on $|E_R|$, i.e., $\frac{1}{2}(p-|S_I|)\max_{v\in S_R}|N_v^R|$, where N_v^R is the set of acquainted neighbors of v in S_R. It is an upper bound because the vertex with the maximum degree in S_R is identified, and $(p-|S_I|)$ vertices are selected from S_R. Similarly, an upper bound on $|E_{IR}|$ is $\sum_{v\in S_I}|InterEdge(v)|$, where $InterEdge(v)$ is the set of edges connecting v in S_I to any vertices in S_R.

Notice that the number of edges in a feasible solution is half of the degree sum of all the vertices in the solution, where the degree of a vertex represents the number of acquainted neighbors in the solution. Therefore, with the above three categories of edges, Familiarity Pruning stops processing S_I when the following condition holds,

$$\frac{1}{p}\left[\sum_{v\in S_I}|N_v^I| + (p-|S_I|)\max_{v\in S_R}|N_v^R| \right.$$
$$\left. +2\cdot\sum_{v\in S_I}|InterEdge(v)|\right]$$
$$< \quad (p-k-1),$$

where the left-hand-side is an upper bound on the average number of attendees acquainted to each person in any feasible solution growing from S_I. In the above condition, each attendee on average is acquainted with fewer than $p-k-1$ other attendees. Familiarity Pruning stops processing S_I and backtracks to the previous state if every possible solution growing from S_I via the exploration of S_R is not able to satisfy the familiarity constraint.

For the social graph in Figure 2(a) with $p=3$, $k=0$, if $S_I=\{b,d\}$ and $S_R=\{e,f\}$, Familiarity Pruning stops processing S_I because $\frac{1}{3}(0+1\cdot 1+2\cdot 1)=1<(3-0-1)=2$. In other words, moving any vertex from S_R to S_I will never generate a feasible solution following the familiarity constraint.

5. ENHANCED STRATEGY FOR SSGQ

The above strategies efficiently select and examine each candidate attendee. A potential approach to further improve the efficiency is to select multiple candidate attendees jointly, because the optimal solution can be constructed with

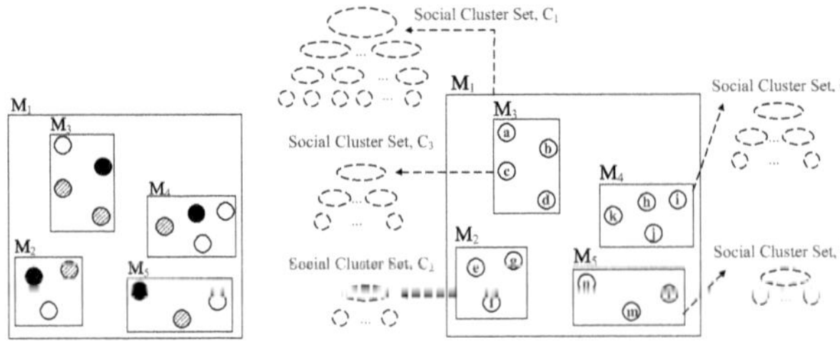

(a) (b)

Figure 3: Illustrations of SR-Tree.

fewer iterations. When an attendee close to the rally point is chosen, nearby candidate attendees in the same MBR of R-Tree are also potential to be good candidates for joint selection due to their smaller spatial distances to the rally point. Nevertheless, jointly selecting *all* candidate attendees in the same MBR may not be able to generate a solution following the familiarity constraint since the social connectivity among them is not examined. To effectively tackle this issue, we propose Social R-Tree (SR-Tree), in which candidate attendees in each MBR are indexed into multiple social clusters with different social connectivity to support SSGQ with different k. Equipped with SR-Tree, SSGQ reduces the number of iterations required to find the optimal solution with a new strategy, named Joint Insertion, which selects multiple vertices jointly at each iteration for S_I to grow faster.

5.1 Social R-Tree

In section 4.1, the feature of hierarchical MBRs in R-Tree enables SSGQ to efficiently extract the vertex with the smallest spatial distance to q. It is expected that the vertices in the same MBR are spatially closer to each other. Nevertheless, each vertex may not be familiar with all the others in the same MBR. For example, Figure 3(a) illustrates that only the vertices with the same color are acquainted with each other, and inserting all the vertices in M_1 to S_I is potential to be too aggressive to generate a solution satisfying the familiarity constraint. On the other hand, choosing a group of mutually acquainted vertices is not efficient, especially for a large k, since more vertices in the same MBR can be selected jointly. Thus, it is desirable to identify *social clusters* with different connectivity in order to consider various SSGQ with different k possibly specified by users.

In the following, we propose SR-Tree by finding a set of social clusters C_i for each MBR M_i of R-Tree, as shown in Figure 3(b). C_i for each MBR M_i is constructed in a bottom-up manner. We iteratively combine small social clusters in a lower level to large social cluster in the higher level in Figure 5. At the bottom level (level 0), each cluster is a single vertex. Multiple clusters in level i are combined to generate a new cluster in level $i+1$, while each cluster in level i is allowed to participate in multiple clusters in level $i+1$. For example, cluster $\{a\}$ at level 0 in Figure 5 appears in $\{a,b\}$ and $\{a,d\}$ in level 1. We tailor the social clusters for SSGQ according to the following three requirements.

(1) **Cross MBR Requirement.** To avoid generating duplicated clusters in multiple MBRs, each cluster c must span at least two child MBRs of the current MBR M_i, since a cluster spanning only one child MBR can be generated when we consider the child MBR. Figure 5 shows an example, where clusters $\{a,c\}$, $\{a,e\}$, $\{b,d\}$, $\{b,f\}$, $\{c,e\}$ and $\{d,f\}$ are not generated since the vertices in each of them are located within the same MBR.

(2) **Social Connectivity Requirement.** This require-

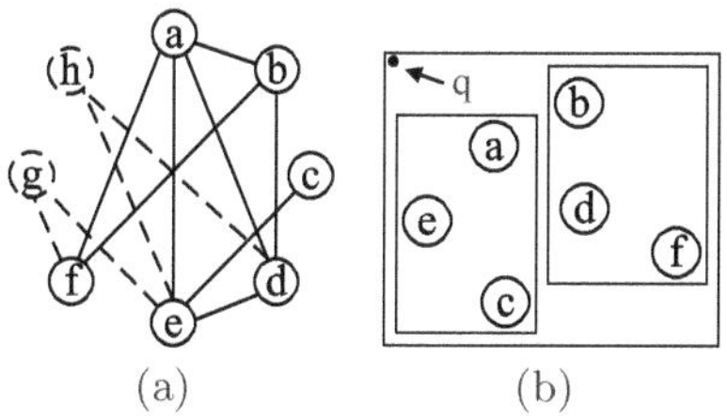

Figure 4: Example of a social network and the corresponding MBRs.

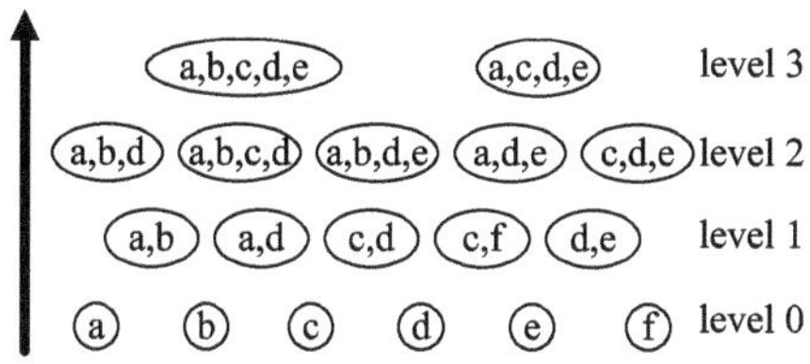

Figure 5: Hierarchically constructing the set of social cluster C_i for MBR M_i.

ment specifies the minimum social connectivity allowed for each generated cluster c. By lowering this requirement, more social clusters can be generated at the cost of more memory consumption. To strike a good balance between efficiency and memory requirement, a good way is referring to parameters k and p appearing in the past SSGQ history. Let P_S denote the average $\frac{k}{p}$ specified in SSGQ of the history. For each vertex v in c, P_S represents the percentage of vertices in c with no edge connecting to v. Therefore, Social Connectivity Requirement specifies that on average each vertex in a social cluster is allowed to share no edge with at most $\lceil |c|\, P_S \rceil$ other vertices in c. Here the ceiling function is adopted such that small social clusters are easier to be generated and then combined to large clusters. Consider an example with the social graph in Figure 4(a) and the corresponding MBRs in Figure 4(b), where vertices g and h are not located in these MBRs. When $P_S = 0.3$, cluster $\{a, b, c\}$ cannot be created in level 1 of Figure 5, because each vertex on average shares no edge with $\frac{4}{3}$ other vertices and exceeds $\lceil |c|\, P_S \rceil = 1$. Similarly, clusters $\{a, c, d\}$, $\{a, c, d, f\}$ and $\{c, d, f\}$ do not have sufficient social connectivity to be created.

(3) **Spatial Distance Requirement.** To avoid the case that the vertices of a social cluster is distributed diversely in a large MBR, it is necessary to limit the spatial distribution of a cluster, and Spatial Distance Requirement ensures that the average distance from a vertex to the *geometric median* of c must not exceed a threshold T_d. Given the coordinates (x_j, y_j) of each vertex v_j in c, the coordinates (x_m, y_m) of the geometric median m is $(x_m, y_m) = \arg\min_{(x'_m, y'_m)} \sum_{v_j \in c} \sqrt{(x'_m - x_j)^2 + (y'_m - y_j)^2}$. The geometric median is regarded as a spatial index in SR-Tree and plays an important role in Join Insertion to prioritize the selection of a social cluster. In Figure 5, cluster $\{e, f\}$ cannot appear in level 1 if T_d is identical to the distance from a to b.

5.2 Joint Insertion

To improve the efficiency of SSGSelect, Joint Insertion selects a social cluster with multiple vertices and moves them from S_R to S_I. A Joint Insertion operation can be regarded as a shortcut in the branch-and-bound tree, such that a good feasible solution D can be acquired earlier for Distance Pruning to remove unnecessary vertices that are not able to generate a better solution. Therefore, equipped with SR-Tree and Joint Insertion, SSGSelect can find the optimal solution with smaller time.

Table 1: $d_{m,q}$ and corresponding actual average spatial distance to q.

	$\{a,b\}$	$\{a,b,d,e\}$	$\{a,b,c,d,e\}$	$\{a,d\}$
$d_{m,q}$	9.6	10	11.2	11.3
$\sum_{v \in c} \frac{d_{v,q}}{\lvert c \rvert}$	9.8	10.8	11.7	11.8

Similar to Socio-Spatial Ordering, since it is desirable to choose a dense social cluster with a small average spatial distance to q, both the social and spatial domains are examined during the selection of a social cluster. Nevertheless, with only the spatial location of each vertex in c, it is expensive for a large cluster to find the average distance to q, because the spatial distance from each vertex to q specified at this query needs to be first calculated and then summed up on-line, while q is allowed to be different in each SSGQ. Therefore, Joint Insertion leverages the geometric median m in Section 5.1, which can be computed off-line and utilized for each query, and regards $d_{m,q}$ as the estimation of the average spatial distance from c to q. Note that Joint Insertion does not consider any cluster with $|S_I| + |c| > p$ or $S_I \cap c \neq \varnothing$. The reason is that the geometric median of c in the case with $S_I \cap c \neq \varnothing$ cannot correctly estimate the average spatial distance for the vertices to be jointly inserted, since some of them is already in S_I.

The social clusters are sorted according to the spatial distance from the geometric median of each cluster to q. Similar to Socio-Spatial Ordering, the first social cluster that satisfies Intra-Familiarity Condition (IFC) in Section 4.2 is selected and inserted to S_I, while IFC here examines $S_I \cup c$, instead of $S_I \cup \{v\}$.

Consider an example with the social graph and the corresponding MBRs in Figure 4, where $S_I = \{g, h\}$, $p = 6$, $k = 3$ and the rally point q is shown in Figure 4(b). Assume the total spatial distance from S_I to q is 13, and Table 1 lists the clusters with $d_{m,q}$, together with their corresponding actual average spatial distance to q. Joint Insertion first finds out that $\{a, b\}$ cannot be moved to S_I because it does not satisfy IFC with $\widehat{k} = 3$, i.e., $F(S_I \cup \{a, b\}) = \frac{1}{4} \cdot 2 = 0.5 < 4 - 1 - \frac{3 \cdot 4}{5}$. We then consider the intra-familiarity of $\{a, b, d, e\}$, $F(S_I \cup \{a, b, d, e\}) = \frac{1}{6} \cdot 16 \geq 6 - 1 - \frac{3 \cdot 6}{5}$, which satisfies IFC. Therefore, Joint Insertion simultaneously moves a, b, d, and e from S_R to S_I at one iteration, which produces a feasible solution with the total spatial distance as $13 + 10.8 \cdot 4 = 56.2$.

Join Insertion of c to S_I represents a shortcut in the branch-and-bound tree to efficiently find a feasible solution for Distance Pruning. After finding the feasible solution, SSGSelect backtracks along the original shortcut back to S_I and explores the search space in the same way described in Section 4 afterward. It is worth noting that some vertices in c needs to be considered again in order to construct another feasible solution with those vertices, S_I, and other vertices not appearing in $S_I \cup c$, to ensure that SSGSelect is able to find the optimal solution eventually.

6. EXPERIMENTAL RESULTS

6.1 Experiment Setup

We implement SSGSelect in Facebook. Figure 6(a) shows the input page of SSGQ to specify p, k, and the coordinate of q, which is captured by clicking a location in the map. The result of SSGSelect is displayed in Figure 6(b) with the names of the selected attendees and their locations. We

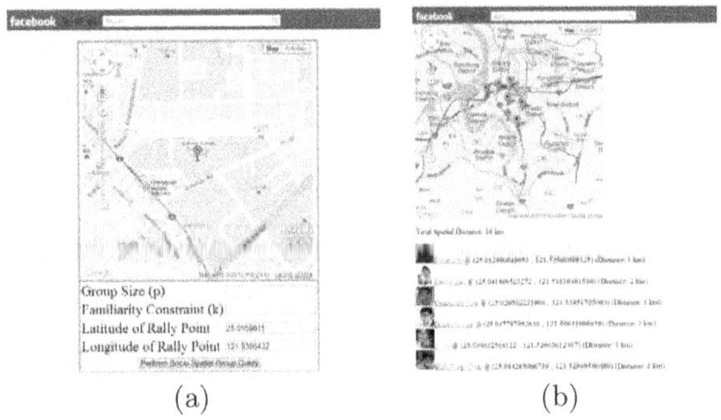

Figure 6: Implementation of SSGQ in Facebook.

invite 206 people from various communities, e.g., schools, government, and business to join our user study, which compares the solution quality and the time to answer SSGQ by manual coordination and SSGSelect. Each of them answers 24 SSGQ problems with the social graphs extracted from their social networks in Facebook, together with their spatial locations sampling from their Facebook Checkin records shared to the user study. The 24 problems span various p and network sizes. Different k are assigned in the first 12 problems, while k is not specified in the other 12 problems, to let each user freely select p people for finding out the familiarity preferred by each person in activities with different p. In addition to the real dataset *DataSet_FB* from the 206 people, we evaluate the performance and the solution quality of SSGSelect on a large real dataset, *DataSet_Large*, which is obtained by crawling Foursquare [11], one of the most representative LBSNs, for a month. *DataSet_Large* contains both the social and spatial information of 153577 individuals. The rally point q is assigned randomly, and we measure 50 samples in each scenario. Our algorithm is implemented in an IBM 3650 server with Linux Ubuntu 4.2.4, two Quadcore Intel X5450 3.0 GHz CPUs, and 8 GB RAM.

To evaluate the effectiveness of the proposed strategies in SSGSelect, three additional algorithms, Baseline, SSGSelectNoJI, and SSGHeuri(i) are evaluated here. Baseline is a brute-force algorithm that enumerates every possible solution. SSGSelectNoJI is identical to SSGSelect with SR-Tree and Joint Insertion removed. SSGHeuri(i) is a heuristic algorithm used for *DataSet_Large* and outputs the i-th feasible solution obtained by SSGSelect.

6.2 User Study

Figures 7(a)-(f) compare manual coordination and SSGSelect to answer SSGQ in the user study. Figure 7(a) compares the time to find the solutions in different scenarios. The result indicates that SSGQ is challenging for manual coordination, especially for a large network size. In contrast, SSGSelect obtains the optimal solution with less than 1 second. Figure 7(b) with $p = 5$ and $k = 3$ demonstrates that the solutions from manual coordination lead to larger spatial distance and thereby are not optimal. With a larger network size, i.e., more friends nearby, it is easier to find a group of attendees with a smaller total spatial distance to q. In addition, the solution quality in Figure 7(c) shows that even in $p = 5$, each solution obtained by manual coordination is not guaranteed to follow the familiarity constraint, according to the correctness rate shown in Figure 7(c), because it is very challenging for each person to jointly minimize the total spatial distance and ensure the familiarity constraint, and the correctness rate drops dramatically as the network size increases.

In Figures 7(d) and (e), we let each user freely select p

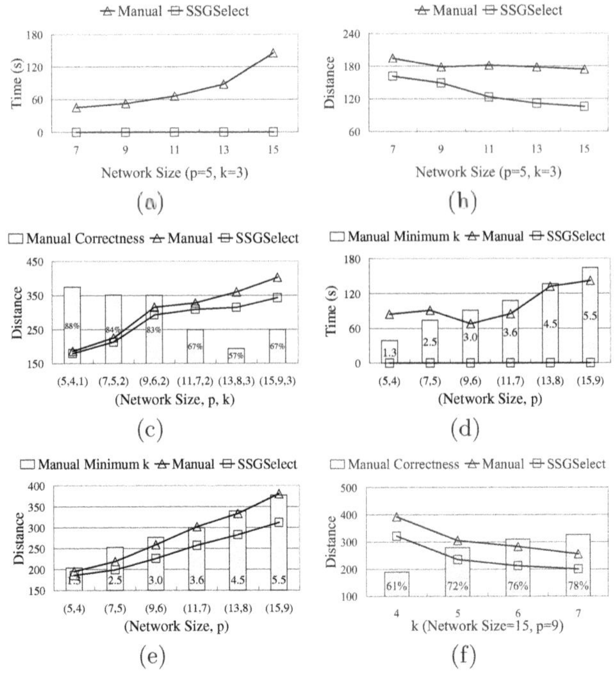

Figure 7: Results of user study.

people to find out the familiarity preferred by each person in activities with different p. The minimum k here represents the smallest k for each solution to follow the familiarity constraint. With this parameter extracted from the manual solution, we regard it as an input parameter for a SSGQ in the same social network, and the results demonstrate that SSGSelect can find a better solution following the same k with smaller time. In other words, even when an user does not specify k, it is possible to analyze the previous manual coordination results and find out a suitable k for the user, such that SSGSelect is able to find the optimal solutions in each query afterward.

Figure 7(f) with network size as 15 and p as 9 compares the results of different k. As k decreases, the correctness rate of manual coordination drops because it becomes more difficult for an user to find a tighter social group with the same number of attendees. Moreover, the solution obtained by manual coordination is still worse than the solution of SSGSelect even with a loose requirement on social connectivity, i.e., a large k.

6.3 Performance Evaluation

Figures 8(a)-(b) evaluate the efficiency of different algorithms on *DataSet_FB*. Figure 8(a) compares the execution time of the four algorithms with different network sizes. Since the search space of Baseline is enormous, Baseline is unable to return a solution within 12 hours when the network size is larger than 50. Therefore, there is only a single node for Baseline in Figure 8(a). On the other hand, with Socio-Spatial Ordering, Distance Pruning, and Familiarity Pruning, SSGSelect and SSGSelectNoJI both return the optimal solution in much smaller time. Furthermore, SSGSelect enhanced by SR-Tree and Joint Insertion outperforms SSGSelectNoJI because it can find feasible solutions in a shorter time for Distance Pruning to remove unnecessary search space earlier. Figure 8(b) compares the number of explored states in the branching-and-bound tree required to find a feasible solution of SSGSelect and SSGSelectNoJI.

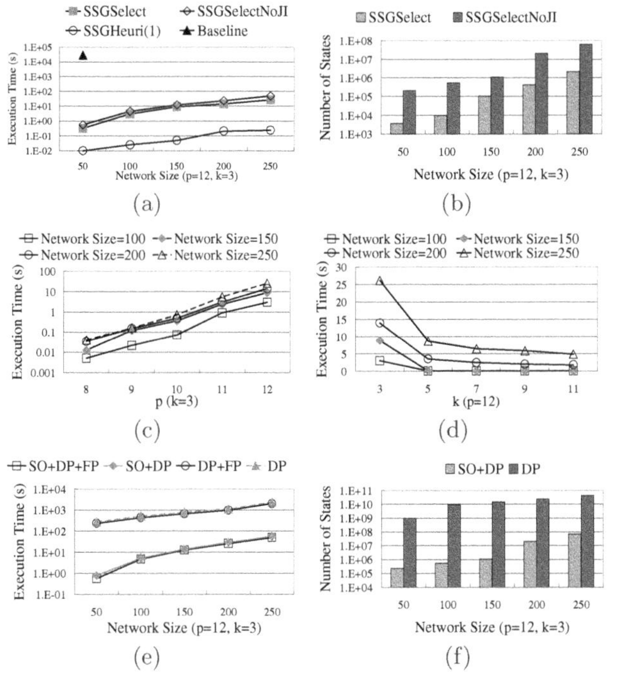

Figure 8: Experimental results on *DataSet_FB*.

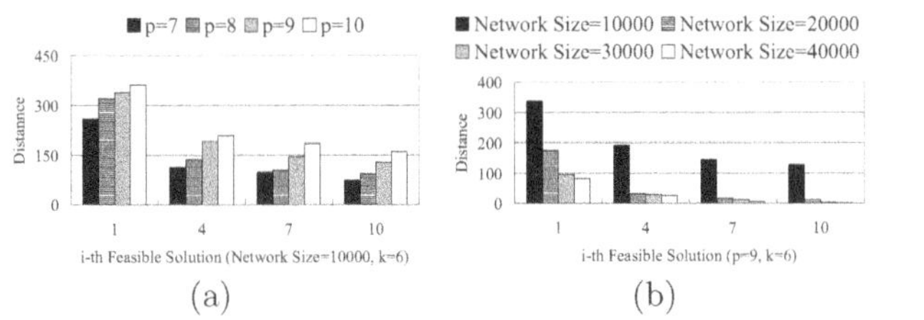

Figure 9: Experimental results on *DataSet_Large*.

It demonstrates that SSGSelect only needs 2% of the states in SSGSelectNoJI to find a feasible solution.

In addition to the network size, we compare SSGSelect with different p and k in Figures 8(c) and (d). Figure 8(c) indicates that the execution time increases as p grows, because SSGSelect in this case needs to explore a larger search space to find the optimal solution. On the other hand, Figure 8(d) shows that a larger k leads to a smaller execution time because it becomes easier to obtain feasible solutions for Distance Pruning to trim the search space. Figures 8(e) and (f) analyze the proposed strategies in Section 4. The result indicates that Socio-Spatial Ordering (SO) plays a crucial role to reduce the execution time for at least 40 times. This is because Socio-Spatial Ordering considers both spatial and social domains and thereby is able to guide the efficient search of the feasible solutions and optimal solution with fewer states explored in the branch-and-bound tree, as shown in Figure 8(f).

Figure 9 shows the solution quality of SSGHeuri(i) on the real dataset, *DataSet_Large*. Figure 9(a) demonstrates that the solution converges quickly as i increases, and SSGHeuri(i) can obtain good solutions within the first few feasible solutions. In Figure 9(b), we compare the i-th feasible solutions with different network sizes. The distances decrease when the network size grows since it is expected that a larger network includes more candidate nodes with smaller spatial distances.

7. CONCLUSION AND FUTURE WORK

To the best of our knowledge, there is no real system and existing work in the literature that addresses the issues of automatic activity planning based on social and spatial relationship of activity attendees. In this paper, we define a useful query, namely, SSGQ, to obtain the optimal set of attendees. We show that the problem is NP-hard and devise an efficient algorithm, namely, SSGSelect to process SSGQ. Various strategies, including Distance Ordering, Socio-Spatial Ordering, Distance Pruning, and Familiarity Pruning are explored to prune unnecessary search space and obtain the optimal solution efficiently. Moreover, with SR-Tree and Joint Insert, SSGSelect is improved and requires a smaller time to find the optimal solution. The algorithm is implemented in Facebook, and our user study demonstrates that the proposed algorithm significantly outperforms manual coordination in both solution quality and efficiency.

User study also brings useful suggestions to further enrich SSGQ as our future work. For example, since each candidate attendee is associated with multiple attributes in Facebook, such as age, gender, interest, company name, etc, those attributes can be specified as the input parameters for SSGQ to first filter unsuitable candidate attendees. A more interesting extension is to allow each user to specify the minimum number of attendees with each attribute value required to be selected, such as ensuring an activity with the same number of male and female attendees when considering the gender attribute. Some users also suggest us to integrate the proposed query processing system with automatically delivery of invitation messages and navigation instructions.

8. REFERENCES

[1] N. Roussopoulos, S. Kelley and F. Vincent. Nearest Neighbor Queries. *SIGMOD*, 1995.

[2] T. Lappas, K. Liu, and E. Terzi. Finding a Team of Experts in Social Networks. *KDD*, 2009.

[3] C.-T. Li and M.-K. Shan. Team Formation for Generalized Tasks in Expertise Social Networks. *SocialCom*, 2010.

[4] M. Sozio and A. Gionis. The Community-Search Problem and How to Plan a Successful Cocktail Party. *KDD*, 2010.

[5] D. Papadias, Q. Shen, Y. Tao and K. Mouratidis. Group Nearest Neighbor Queries. *ICDE*, 2004.

[6] Y. Tao, D. Papadias and Q. Shen. Continuous Nearest Neighbor Search. *VLDB*, 2002.

[7] D.-N. Yang, Y.-L. Chen, W.-C. Lee and M.-S. Chen. On Social-Temporal Group Query with Acquaintance Constraint. *VLDB*, 2011.

[8] Y. Gao, B. Zheng, W.-C. Lee, G. Chen. Continuous Visible Nearest Neighbor Queries. *EDBT*, 2009.

[9] Y. Gao and B. Zheng. Continuous Obstructed Nearest Neighbor Queries in Spatial Databases. *SIGMOD*, 2009.

[10] G. Hjaltason and H. Samet. Distance Browsing in Spatial Databases. *TODS*, 1999.

[11] M. Ye, P. Yin, W.-C. Lee and D.-L. Lee. Exploiting Geographical Influence for Collaborative Point-of-Interest Recommendation. *SIGIR*, 2011.

Random Forests for Metric Learning with Implicit Pairwise Position Dependence

Caiming Xiong
Department of Computer Science and Engineering
SUNY at Buffalo
cxiong@buffalo.edu

David Johnson
Department of Computer Science and Engineering
SUNY at Buffalo
davidjoh@buffalo.edu

Ran Xu
Department of Computer Science and Engineering
SUNY at Buffalo
rxu2@buffalo.edu

Jason J. Corso
Department of Computer Science and Engineering,
SUNY at Buffalo,
jcorso@buffalo.edu

ABSTRACT

Metric learning makes it plausible to learn semantically meaningful distances for complex distributions of data using label or pairwise constraint information. However, to date, most metric learning methods are based on a single Mahalanobis metric, which cannot handle heterogeneous data well. Those that learn multiple metrics throughout the feature space have demonstrated superior accuracy, but at a severe cost to computational efficiency. Here, we adopt a new angle on the metric learning problem and learn a single metric that is able to implicitly adapt its distance function throughout the feature space. This metric adaptation is accomplished by using a random forest-based classifier to underpin the distance function and incorporate both absolute pairwise position and standard relative position into the representation. We have implemented and tested our method against state of the art global and multi-metric methods on a variety of data sets. Overall, the proposed method outperforms both types of method in terms of accuracy (consistently ranked first) and is an order of magnitude faster than state of the art multi-metric methods (16x faster in the worst case).

Categories and Subject Descriptors

H.2.8 [**Database Management**]: Database Applications—*data mining*; I.5.1 [**Computing Methodologies**]: Pattern Recognition—*models*

General Terms

Algorithms

Keywords

Metric learning, random forests, pairwise constraints

1. INTRODUCTION

Although the Euclidean distance is a simple and convenient metric, it is often not an accurate representation of the underlying shape of the data [11]. Such a representation is crucial in many real-world applications [5,31], such as object classification [10, 12], text document retrieval [16, 26], data clustering [29] and face verification [8, 20], and methods that learn a distance metric from training data have hence been widely studied in recent years. We present a new angle on the metric learning problem based on random forests [1,6] as the underlying distance representation.[1] The emphasis of our work is the capability to incorporate the absolute position of point pairs in the input space without requiring a separate metric per instance or exemplar. In doing so, our method, called random forest distance (RFD), is able to adapt to the underlying shape of the data by varying the metric based on the *position* of sample pairs in the feature space while maintaining the efficiency of a single metric. In some sense, our method achieves a middle-ground between the two main classes of existing methods—single, global distance functions and multi-metric sets of distance functions—overcoming the limitations of both (see Figure 1 for an illustrative example). We next elaborate upon these comparisons.

The metric learning literature has been dominated by methods that learn a global Mahalanobis metric, with representative methods [3, 9, 14, 21, 24, 25, 28, 30]. In brief, given a set of pairwise constraints (either by sampling from label data, or collecting side information in the semi-supervised case), indicating pairs of points that should or should not be grouped (i.e., have small or large distance, respectively), the goal is to find the appropriate linear transformation of the data to best satisfy these constraints. One such method [30] minimizes the distance between positively-linked points subject to the constraint that negatively-linked points are separated, but requires solving a computationaly expensive semidefinite programming problem. Relevant Component

[1]An early version of this manuscript has been released on arXiv, article id:1201.0610

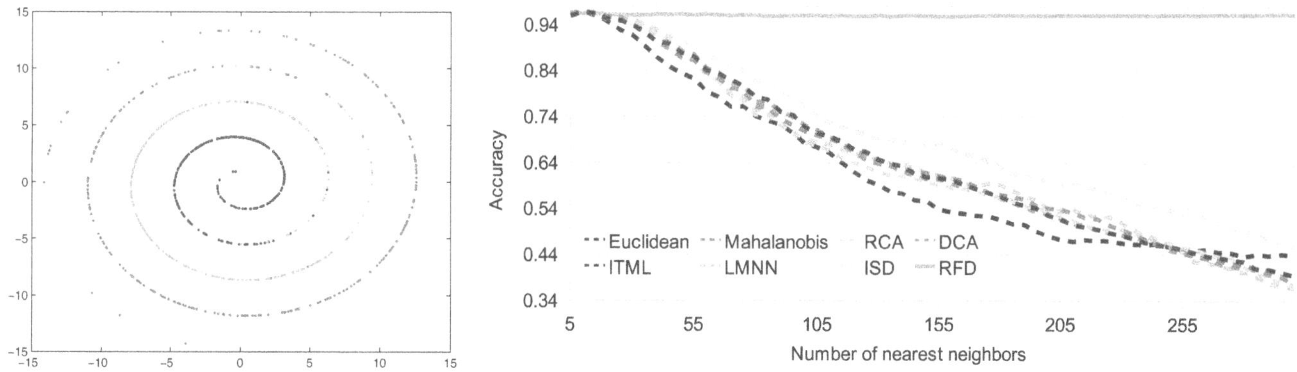

Figure 1: An example using a classic swiss roll data set comparing both global and position-specific Mahalanobis-based methods with our proposed method, RFD. All methods, including the baseline Euclidean, perform well at low K-values due to local linearity. However, as K increases and the global nonlinearity of the data becomes important, the monolithic methods' inability to incorporate position information causes their performance to degrade until it is little better than chance. The position-specific ISD method performs somewhat better, but even with a Mahalanobis matrix at every point it is unable to capture the globally nonlinear relations between points. Our method, by comparison, shows no degradation as K increases. (3 classes, 900 samples, validated using K-nearest neighbor classification, with varying K)

Analysis (RCA) [3] learns a linear Mahalanobis transformation to satisfy a set of positive constraints. Discriminant Component Analysis (DCA) [14] extends RCA by exploring negative constraints. ITML [9] minimizes the LogDet divergence under positive and negative linear constraints, and LMNN [24, 28] learns a distance metric through the maximum margin framework. Nguyen et al. [21] formulate metric learning as a quadratic semidefinite programming problem with local neighborhood constraints and linear time complexity in the original feature space. More recently, researchers have begun developing fast algorithms that can work in an online manner, such as POLA [23], MLCL [13] and LEGO [15].

These global methods learn a single Mahalanobis metric using the relative position of point pairs:

$$\text{Dist}(\mathbf{x}_i, \mathbf{x}_j) = (\mathbf{x}_i - \mathbf{x}_j)^\mathsf{T}\mathbf{W}(\mathbf{x}_i - \mathbf{x}_j) \tag{1}$$

Although the resulting single metric is efficient, it is limited in its capacity to capture the shape of complex data(see Figure 1 as example). In contrast, a second class, called multi-metric methods [11, 12, 29], distributes distance metrics throughout the input space; in the limit, they estimate a distance metric per instance or exemplar, e.g. [11,12] for the case of Mahalanobis metrics. Zhan et al. [32] extend [11] by propagating metrics learned on training exemplars to learn a metric matrix for each unlabeled point as well. However, these point-based multi-metric methods all suffer from high time and space complexity due to the need to learn and store $\mathbf{O}(N)$ d by d metric matrices. Wu et al. [29] learns a Bregman distance function which does not need to store the metric matrices for each data points, but it needs to take $\mathbf{O}(N)$ time to calculate the distance of single pair of points which is impractical for large scale data sets. A more efficient approach to this second class is to divide the data into subsets and learn a metric for each subset [2, 27]. However, these methods have strong assumptions in generating these subsets; for example, [2] learns at most one metric per category, forfeiting the possibility that different samples within a category may require different metrics.

We propose a metric learning method that is able to achieve both the efficiency of the global methods and specificity of the multi-metric methods. Our method, the random forest distance (RFD), transforms the metric learning problem into a binary classification problem and uses random forests as the underlying representation [1, 4, 6, 17]. In this general form, we are able to incorporate the position of samples implicitly into the metric and yet maintain a single and efficient global metric. To that end, we use a novel point-pair mapping function that encodes both the position of the points relative to each other and their absolute position within the feature space. Our experimental analyses demonstrate the importance of incorporating position information into the metric (Section 3).

We use the random forest as the underlying representation for several reasons. First, the output of the random forest algorithm is a simple "yes" or "no" vote from each tree in the forest. In our case, "no" votes correspond to positively constrained training data, and "yes" votes correspond to negatively constrained training data. The number of yes votes, then, is effectively a distance function, representing the relative resemblance of a point pair to pairs that are known to be dissimilar versus pairs that are known to be similar. Second, random forests are efficient and scale well, and have been shown to be one of the most powerful and scalable supervised methods for handling high-dimensional data [7]—in contrast to instance-specific multi-metric methods [11, 12], the storage requirement of our method is independent of the size of the input data set. Our experimental results indicate RFD is at least 16 times faster than the state of the art multi-metric method. Third, because random forests are non-parametric, they make minimal assumptions about the shape and patterning of the data [6], affording a flexible model that is inherently nonlinear. In the next section, we describe the new RFD method in more detail, followed by a thorough comparison to the state of the art in Section 3.

2. RANDOM FOREST DISTANCE: IMPLICITLY POSITION-DEPENDENT METRIC LEARNING

Our random forest-based approach is inspired by several other recent advances in metric learning [2,23] that reformulate the metric learning problem into a classification problem. However, where these approaches restricted the form of the learned distance function to a Mahalanobis matrix, thus precluding the use of position information, we adopt a more general formulation of the classification problem that removes this restriction.

Given the instance set $X = \{\mathbf{x}_1, \mathbf{x}_2, \cdots, \mathbf{x}_N\}$, each $\mathbf{x}_i \in \mathbb{R}^m$ is a vector of m features. Taking a geometric interpretation of each $\mathbf{x}_i$, we consider $\mathbf{x}_i$ the *position* of sample i in the space $\mathbb{R}^m$. The value of this interpretation will become clear throughout the paper as the learned metric will implicitly vary over $\mathbb{R}^m$, which allows it to adapt the learned metric based on local structure in a manner similar to the instance-specific multi-metric methods, e.g., [11]. Denote two pairwise constraint sets: a must-link constraint set $S = \{(\mathbf{x}_i, \mathbf{x}_j) | \mathbf{x}_i \text{ and } \mathbf{x}_j \text{ are similar}\}$ and a cannot-link constraint set $D = \{(\mathbf{x}_i, \mathbf{x}_j) | \mathbf{x}_i \text{ and } \mathbf{x}_j \text{ are dissimilar}\}$. For any constraint $(\mathbf{x}_i, \mathbf{x}_j)$, denote y_{ij} as the ideal distance between $\mathbf{x}_i$ and $\mathbf{x}_j$. If $(\mathbf{x}_i, \mathbf{x}_j) \in S$, then the distance $y_{ij} = 0$, otherwise, their distance $y_{ij} = 1$. Therefore, we seek a function $\text{Dist}(\cdot,\cdot)$ from an appropriate function space H:

$$\text{Dist}(\cdot,\cdot)^* = \underset{\text{Dist}(\cdot,\cdot)\in H}{\text{argmin}} \frac{1}{|S \cup D|} \sum_{(\mathbf{x}_i, \mathbf{x}_j) \in S \cup D} l(\text{Dist}(\mathbf{x}_i, \mathbf{x}_j), y_{ij}) \ , \tag{2}$$

where $l(\cdot)$ is some loss function that will be specified by the specific classifier chosen. In our random forests case, we minimize expected loss, as in many classification problems. So consider $\text{Dist}(\cdot,\cdot)$ to be a binary classifier for the classes 0 and 1. For flexibility, we redefine the problem as $\text{Dist}(\mathbf{x}_i, \mathbf{x}_j) = F(\phi(\mathbf{x}_i, \mathbf{x}_j))$, where $F(\cdot)$ is some classification model, and $\phi(\mathbf{x}_i, \mathbf{x}_j)$ is a mapping function that maps the pair $(\mathbf{x}_i, \mathbf{x}_j)$ to a feature vector that will serve as input for the classifier function F. To train F, we transform each constraint pair using the mapping function $\{(\mathbf{x}_i, \mathbf{x}_j), y_{ij}\} \rightarrow \{\phi(\mathbf{x}_i, \mathbf{x}_j), y_{ij}\}$ and submit the resulting set of vectors and labels as training data. We next describe the feature mapping function ϕ.

2.1 Mapping function for implicitly position-dependent metric learning

In actuality, all metric learning methods implicitly employ a mapping function $\phi(\mathbf{x}_i, \mathbf{x}_j)$. Standard Mahalanobis-based methods all learn a (positive semidefinite) metric matrix $\mathbf{W}$, and a distance function of the form $\text{Dist}(\mathbf{x}_i, \mathbf{x}_j) = (\mathbf{x}_i - \mathbf{x}_j)^{\mathsf{T}} \mathbf{W} (\mathbf{x}_i - \mathbf{x}_j)$, which can be reformulated as $\text{Dist}(\mathbf{x}_i, \mathbf{x}_j) = \vec{[\mathbf{W}]}^{\mathsf{T}} \vec{[}(\mathbf{x}_i - \mathbf{x}_j)(\mathbf{x}_i - \mathbf{x}_j)^{\mathsf{T}}]$, where $\vec{[\cdot]}$ denotes vectorization or *flattening* of a matrix. Mahalanobis-based methods can thus be viewed as using the mapping function $\phi(\mathbf{x}_i, \mathbf{x}_j) = \vec{[}(\mathbf{x}_i - \mathbf{x}_j)(\mathbf{x}_i - \mathbf{x}_j)^{\mathsf{T}}]$. This function encodes only relative position information, and adapting it to include absolute position information yields significant theoretical problems for Mahalanobis methods based on global weights (see Section 2.2).

However, our formulation affords a more general mapping function:

$$\phi(\mathbf{x}_i, \mathbf{x}_j) = \begin{bmatrix} \mathbf{u}(\mathbf{x}_i, \mathbf{x}_j) \\ \mathbf{v}(\mathbf{x}_i, \mathbf{x}_j) \end{bmatrix} = \begin{bmatrix} |\mathbf{x}_i - \mathbf{x}_j| \\ \frac{1}{2}(\mathbf{x}_i + \mathbf{x}_j) \end{bmatrix} \ , \tag{3}$$

which considers both the relative location of the samples $\mathbf{u}$ as well as their absolute position $\mathbf{v}$. The output feature vector is the concatenation of these two and in $\mathbb{R}^{2m}$.

The relative location $\mathbf{u}$ represents the same information as the Mahalanobis mapping function. Note that we take the absolute value of $\mathbf{u}$ to enforce symmetry within the learned metric. The primary difference between our mapping function and that of previous methods is thus the information contained in $\mathbf{v}$—the mean of the two point vectors. These features localize each mapped pair to a region of the space, which allows our method to adapt to heterogeneous distributions of data. It is for this reason that we consider our learned metric to be implicitly position-dependent. Note the earlier methods that learn position-based metrics, i.e. the methods that learn a metric per instance such as [11], incorporate absolute position of each instance only, whereas we incorporate the absolute position of each instance pair, which adds additional modeling versatility.

We note that alternate encodings of the position information are possible but have shortcomings. For example, we could choose to simply concatenate the position of the two points rather than average them, but this approach raises the issue of ordering the points. Using $\mathbf{v} = \begin{bmatrix} \mathbf{x}_i^{\mathsf{T}} & \mathbf{x}_j^{\mathsf{T}} \end{bmatrix}^{\mathsf{T}}$ would again yield a nonsymmetric feature, and an arbitrary ordering rule would not guarantee meaningful feature comparisons. The usefulness of position information varies depending on the data set. For data that is largely linear and homogenous, including $\mathbf{v}$ will only add noise to the features, and could worsen the accuracy. In our experiments, we find that for many real data sets (and particularly for more difficult data sets) the inclusion of $\mathbf{v}$ significantly improves the performance of the metric (see Section 3).

2.2 Why not Mahalanobis?

Before investigating the use of wholly new metric representations, it is reasonable to consider the use of absolute position information in a traditional Mahalanobis or Mahalanobis-like metric based on global weights. Here we show that such a formulation has immediate theoretical shortcomings.

Assume there exists a Mahalanobis metric $M > 0$ utilizing our position-embedded mapping function. Consider that $M = \begin{bmatrix} M_{uu} & M_{uv} \\ M_{vu} & M_{vv} \end{bmatrix}$. Since $M > 0$, we know $M_{uu} > 0$ and $M_{vv} > 0$.

Now, for any two points $\mathbf{x}_i$ and $\mathbf{x}_j$ such that $\mathbf{x}_i = k \cdot \mathbf{x}_j$ where k is a scalar, let us build two pairs $(\mathbf{x}_i, \mathbf{x}_i)$ and $(\mathbf{x}_j, \mathbf{x}_j)$. Obviously the distance between each of these point pairs should be small, so the difference between these two distances should also be small:

$$\begin{aligned} Dist(\mathbf{x}_i, \mathbf{x}_i) - Dist(\mathbf{x}_j, \mathbf{x}_j) = & \begin{bmatrix} \mathbf{u}(\mathbf{x}_i, \mathbf{x}_i) \\ \mathbf{v}(\mathbf{x}_i, \mathbf{x}_i) \end{bmatrix}^T \cdot M \cdot \begin{bmatrix} \mathbf{u}(\mathbf{x}_i, \mathbf{x}_i) \\ \mathbf{v}(\mathbf{x}_i, \mathbf{x}_i) \end{bmatrix} \\ & - \begin{bmatrix} \mathbf{u}(\mathbf{x}_j, \mathbf{x}_j) \\ \mathbf{v}(\mathbf{x}_j, \mathbf{x}_j) \end{bmatrix}^T \cdot M \cdot \begin{bmatrix} \mathbf{u}(\mathbf{x}_j, \mathbf{x}_j) \\ \mathbf{v}(\mathbf{x}_j, \mathbf{x}_j) \end{bmatrix} \end{aligned}$$

Since $\mathbf{u}(\mathbf{x}_i, \mathbf{x}_i) = \mathbf{u}(\mathbf{x}_j, \mathbf{x}_j) = 0$,

Table 1: UCI data sets used for KNN-classification testing

Dataset	Size	Dim.	No. Classes	Dataset	Size	Dim.	No. Classes
Balance	625	4	3	Iris	150	4	3
BUPA Liver Disorders	345	6	2	Pima Indians Diabetes	768	8	2
Breast Cancer	699	10	2	Wine	178	13	3
Image Segmentation	2310	19	7	Sonar	208	60	2
Semeion Handwritten Digits	1593	256	10	Multiple Features Handwritten Digits	2000	649	10

$$Dist(\mathbf{x}_i, \mathbf{x}_i) - Dist(\mathbf{x}_j, \mathbf{x}_j) = \mathbf{v}(\mathbf{x}_i, \mathbf{x}_i)^T M_{vv} \mathbf{v}(\mathbf{x}_i, \mathbf{x}_i) - \mathbf{v}(\mathbf{x}_j, \mathbf{x}_j)^T M_{vv} \mathbf{v}(\mathbf{x}_j, \mathbf{x}_j)$$

Since $\mathbf{x}_i = k \cdot \mathbf{x}_j$,

$$Dist(\mathbf{x}_i, \mathbf{x}_i) - Dist(\mathbf{x}_j, \mathbf{x}_j) = (k^2 - 1)(\mathbf{v}(\mathbf{x}_j, \mathbf{x}_j))^T M_{vv} (\mathbf{v}(\mathbf{x}_j, \mathbf{x}_j))$$

Thus, as $k \to +\infty$, $Dist(\mathbf{x}_i, \mathbf{x}_i) - Dist(\mathbf{x}_j, \mathbf{x}_j) \to +\infty$.

This is a nonsensical result, and clearly undesirable in a metric. For this reason, traditional Mahalanobis formulations based on global covariance weights are not suitable for use with our position-sensitive mapping function, and we thus pursue alternative distance representations.

2.3 Random forests for metric learning

Random forests are well studied in the machine learning literature and we do not describe them in any detail; the interested reader is directed to [1, 6]. In brief, a random forest is a set of T decision trees $\{f_t\}_{t=1}^T$ operating on a common feature space, in our case $\mathbb{R}^{2m}$. To evaluate a point-pair $(\mathbf{x}_i, \mathbf{x}_j)$, each tree independently classifies the sample (based on the leaf node at which the point-pair arrives) as similar or dissimilar (0 or 1, respectively) and the forest averages them, essentially regressing a distance measure on the point-pair:

$$\text{Dist}(\mathbf{x}_i, \mathbf{x}_j) = F(\phi(\mathbf{x}_i, \mathbf{x}_j)) = \frac{1}{T} \sum_{t=1}^{T} f_t(\phi(\mathbf{x}_i, \mathbf{x}_j)) \ , \quad (4)$$

where $f_t(\cdot)$ is the classification output of tree t.

It has been found empirically that random forests scale well with increasing dimensionality, compared with other classification methods [7], and, as a decision tree-based method, they are inherently nonlinear. Hence, our use of them in RFD as a regression algorithm allows for a more scalable and more flexible metric than is possible using Mahalanobis methods. Moreover, the incorporation of position information into this classification function (as described in Section 2.1) allows the metric to implicitly adapt to different regions over the feature space. In other words, when a decision tree in the random forest selects a node split based on a value of the absolute position $\mathbf{v}$ sub-vector (see Eq. 3), then all evaluation in the sub-tree is *localized* to a specific half-space of $\mathbb{R}^m$. Subsequent splits on elements of $\mathbf{v}$ further refine the sub-space of emphasis $\mathbb{R}^m$. Indeed, each path through a decision tree in the random forest is localized to a particular (possibly overlapping) sub-space.

The RFD is not technically a *metric* but rather a *pseudosemimetric*. Although RFD can easily be shown to be non-negative and symmetric, it does not satisfy the triangle inequality (i.e., $\text{Dist}(\mathbf{x}_1, \mathbf{x}_2) \leq \text{Dist}(\mathbf{x}_1, \mathbf{x}_3) + \text{Dist}(\mathbf{x}_2, \mathbf{x}_3)$) or the implication that $\text{Dist}(\mathbf{x}_1, \mathbf{x}_2) = 0 \implies \mathbf{x}_1 = \mathbf{x}_2$, sometimes called identity of indiscernibles. It is straightforward to construct examples for both of these cases. Although this point may appear problematic, it is not uncommon in the metric learning literature. For example, by necessity, no metric whose distance function varies across the feature space can guarantee the triangle inequality is satisfied. [11, 12] similarly cannot satisfy the triangle inequality. Our method *must* violate the triangle inequality in order to fulfill our original objective of producing a metric that incorporates position data. Moreover, our extensive experimental results demonstrate the capability of RFD as a distance (Section 3).

2.4 Theoretic analysis of RFD performance

For simplicity, we assume that the classes of must-link and cannot-link are balanced $|S| == |D|$. For the case of a single random decision tree, we suppose each leaf has a true probabilistic margin γ with a total of C training pairs that reach the leaf during the training process. Thus, a fraction $\frac{1}{2} + \gamma$ of C training pairs belongs to one class (e.g. must-link pair constraints), and a fraction $\frac{1}{2} - \gamma$ of them belong to the other class (e.g. cannot-link pair constraints). We denote a leaf as a must-link leaf if a majority of the training pairs in the leaf are must-link, and likewise denote it a cannot-link leaf if the majority of pairs are cannot-link. According to [19], it is straightforward to show that the probability that must-link pair will end up in a must-link leaf during testing is $\frac{1}{2} + \gamma$, and similarly for cannot-link pairs.

For the purposes of establishing error bounds, we can relax RFD to a binary classification algorithm that discriminates between must-link and cannot-link pairs. We do this by employing an *evidence voting* [22] procedure, wherein we drop a test pair through the T learned random decision trees and take the mode of the $C \cdot T$ training pairs stored in the leaves reached by the testing pair as a classification result. Given this setup, we can establish an upper bound on pair classification error in RFD:

PROPOSITION 1. *The probability of pair classification error in RFD* $P(\epsilon)_{RFD}$ *is* $\leq \exp(-8CT\gamma^4)$.

PROOF. Details in [22]. □

Computational complexity Since all trees are generated independently, we can build these trees in parallel. Thus the major computational cost for our method is the generation of single tree based on training data. For building single tree, it takes $\mathcal{O}(n \log n)$ time. And the learning processes of nodes from the same depth of one tree are also independent, so we can use the parallel computing technique for learning the nodes of same depth of tree to make our method more efficient.

3. EXPERIMENTS AND ANALYSIS

In this section, we present a set of experiments comparing our method to state of the art metric learning techniques on both a range of UCI data sets (Table 1) and an image data set taken from the Corel database. To substantiate our claim of computational efficiency, we also provide an analysis of running time efficiency relative to an existing position-dependent metric learning method. We also include results illustrating the effect of varying forest sizes on our algorithm's accuracy.

For the UCI data sets, we compare performance at the **K**-nearest neighbor classification task against both standard Mahalanobis methods and point-based position-dependent methods.[2]

[2]We note that previous work has established a connection between random forests and nearest neighbor analysis [18], but this relationship does not apply to RFD. In RFD, the "points" within the forest are actually point pairs, and thus

For the former, we test K-NN classification accuracy at a range of $\mathbf{K}$-values (as in Figure 1), while the latter relies on results published by other methods' authors, and thus uses a fixed $\mathbf{K}$. For the image data set, we measure accuracy at $\mathbf{K}$-NN retrieval, rather than $\mathbf{K}$-NN classification. We compare our results to several Mahalanobis methods.

The following is an overview of the primary experimental findings to be covered in the following sections.

1. RFD has the best overall performance on ten UCI data sets ranging from 4 to 649 dimensions against four state of the art and two baseline global Mahalanobis-based methods (Figure 2 and Table 2).
2. RFD has comparable or superior accuracy to state of the art position-specific methods (Table 3).
3. RFD is 16 to 85 times faster than the state of the art position-specific method (Table 4).
4. RFD outperforms the state of the art in nine out of ten categories in the benchmark Corel image retrieval problem (Figure 4).

3.1 Comparison with global Mahalanobis metric learning methods

We first compare our method to a set of state of the art Mahalanobis metric learning methods: RCA [3], DCA [14], Information-Theoretic Metric Learning (ITML) [9] and distance metric learning for large-margin nearest neighbor classification (LMNN) [24, 28]. For our method, we test using the full feature mapping including relative position data, $\mathbf{u}$, and absolute pairwise position data, $\mathbf{v}$, (RFD (+P)) as well as with only relative position data, $\mathbf{u}$, (RFD (−P)). To provide a baseline, we also show results using both the Euclidean distance and a heuristic Mahalanobis metric, where the $\mathbf{W}$ used is simply the covariance matrix for the data. All algorithm code was obtained from authors' websites, for which we are indebted (*our code is available, as well*).

We test each algorithm on a number of standard small to medium scale UCI data sets (see Table 1). All algorithms are trained using 1000 positive and 1000 negative constraints per class, with the exceptions of RCA, which used only the 1000 positive constraints and LMNN, which used the full label set to actively select a (generally much larger) set of constraints. In each case, we set the number of trees used by our method to 400 (*see Section 3.2 for a discussion of the effect of varying forest sizes*).

Testing is performed using 5-fold cross validation on the $\mathbf{K}$ nearest-neighbor classification task. In each fold, metric constraints, as well as neighbors used for classification, are drawn only from the training data. Rather than selecting a single $\mathbf{K}$-value for this task, we test with varying $\mathbf{K}$s, increasing in increments of 5 up to the maximum possible value for each data set (i.e. the number of elements in the smallest class). By varying $\mathbf{K}$ in this way, we are able to gain some insight into each method's ability to capture the global variation in a data set. When $\mathbf{K}$ is small, most of the identified neighbors lie within a small local region surrounding the query point, enabling linear metrics to perform fairly well even on globally nonlinear data by taking advantage of local linearity. However, as $\mathbf{K}$ increases, local linearity becomes less practical, and the quality of the metric's representation of the global structure of the data is exposed. Though the accuracy results at higher $\mathbf{K}$ values do not have strong implications for each method's efficacy for the specific task of $\mathbf{K}$-NN classification (where an ideal $\mathbf{K}$ value can just be selected by cross-validation), they do indicate overall metric performance, and are highly relevant to other tasks, such as retrieval.

Figure 2 shows the accuracy plots for ten UCI datasets. RFD is consistently near the top performers on these various data sets. In the lower dimension case (Iris), most methods perform well, and RFD without position information outperforms RFD with position information (this is the sole data set in which this occurs), which we attribute to the limited data set size (150 samples) and the position information acting as a distractor in this small and highly linear case. In all other cases, the RFD with absolute position information significantly outperforms RFD without it. In many of the more difficult cases (Diabetes, Segmentation, Sonar), RFD with position information significantly outperforms the field. This result is suggestive that RFD can scale well with increasing dimensionality, which is consistent with the findings from the literature that random forests are one of the most robust classification methods for high-dimensional data [7].

Table 2 provides a summary statistic of the methods by computing the mean-rank (lower better) over the ten data sets at varying $\mathbf{K}$-values. For all but one value of $\mathbf{K}$, RFD with absolute position information has the best mean rank of all the methods (and for the off-case, it is ranked second). RFD without absolute position information performs comparatively poorer, underscoring the utility of the absolute position information. In summary, the results in Table 2 show that RFD is consistently able to outperform the state of the art in global metric learning methods on various benchmark problems.

3.2 Varying forest size

One question that must be addressed when using RFD is how many trees must or should be learned in order to obtain good performance. Increasing the size of the forest increases computation and space requirements, and past a certain point yields little or no improvement and may possibly over-train. It is beyond the scope of this paper to provide a full answer as to how many trees are needed in RFD, but we have made some observations.

First, the addition of absolute position information noticeably increases the benefit that may be obtained from additional trees (see Figure 3). This result is unsurprising, considering the increased size of the feature vector, as well as the increased degree of fine-tuning possible for a metric that can vary from region to region. Second, in our experiments we observe significant improvements in accuracy up to about 100 trees, even without position information, and would recommend this as a reasonable minimum value. Intuition suggests that larger constraint-sets and more complex data distributions may require larger forests, but these two points have not yet been thoroughly explored by our group.

3.3 Comparison with position-specific multi-metric methods

We compare our method to three multi-metric methods that incorporate absolute position (by way of instance-specific metrics): FSM, FSSM and ISD. FSM [11] learns an instance-specific distance for each labeled example. FSSM [12] is an extension of FSM that enforces global consistency and comparability among the different instance-specific metrics. ISD [32] first learns instance-specific distance metrics for each labeled data point, then uses metric propagation to generate instance-specific metrics for unlabeled points as well.

We again use the ten UCI data sets, but under the same conditions used by these methods' authors. Accuracy is measured on the $\mathbf{K}$-NN task ($\mathbf{K}$=11) with three-fold cross validation. The parameters of the compared methods are set as suggested in [32]. Our RFD method chooses 1% of the available positive constraints and 1% of the available negative constraints, and constructs a random forest with 1000 trees. We report the average result of ten different runs on each data set, with random partitions of training/testing data generated each time (see Table 3). These results show that our RFD method yields performance better than or comparable to state of the art explicit multi-metric learning methods. Additionally, because we only learn one distance function and random forests are an inherently efficient technique, our method offers significantly better computational efficiency than these instance-specific approaches (see Table 4)—between 16 to 85 times faster than ISD.

The comparable level of accuracy is not surprising. While our method is a single metric in form, in practice its implicit position-dependence allows it to act like a multi-metric system. Notably, because our method learns using the position of each point-pair rather than each point, it can potentially encode up to n^2 implicit

potential nearest neighbors identified via the forest would represent similar pair constraints, rather than similar data elements.

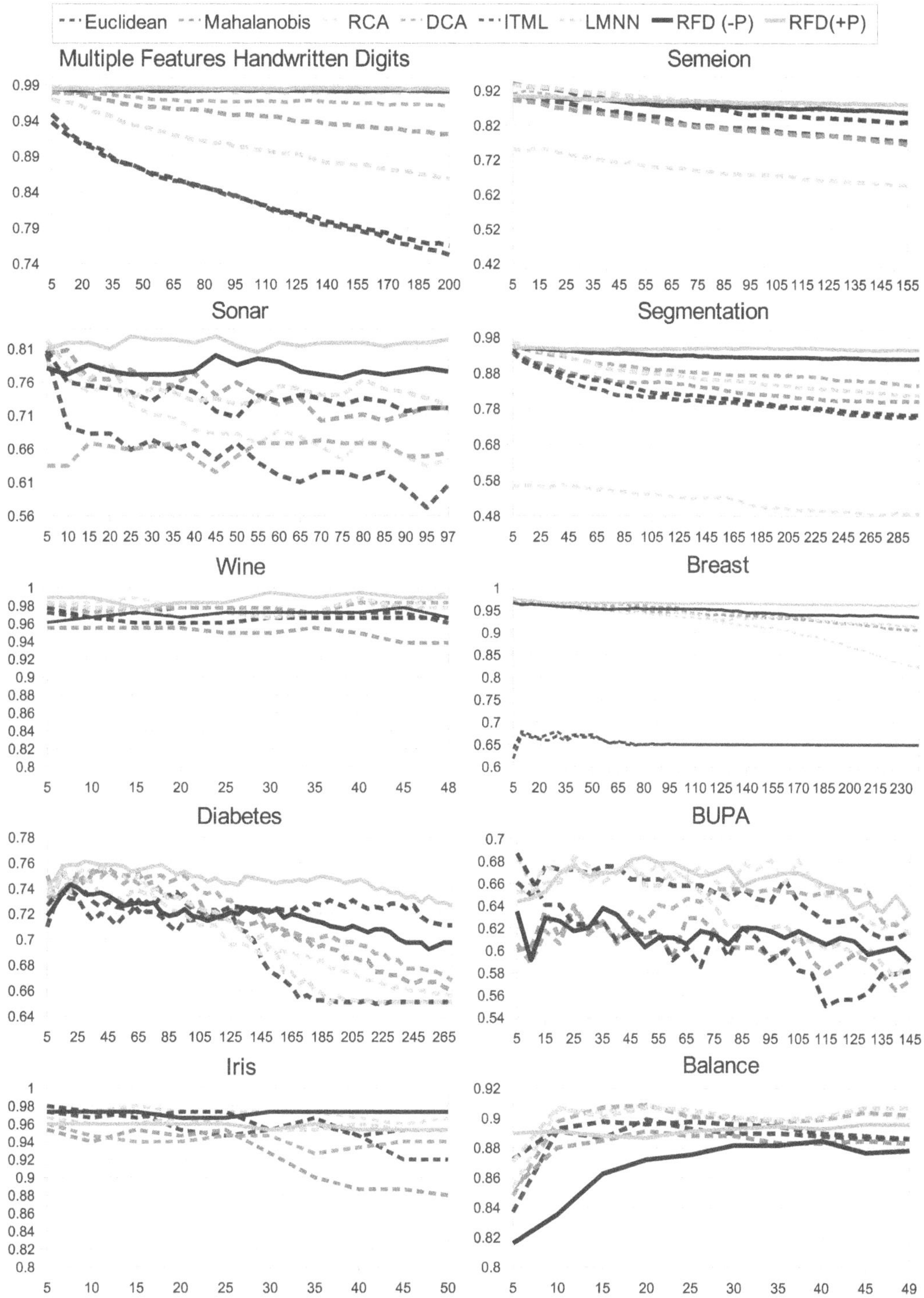

Figure 2: K-nearest neighbor classification results with varying K values of RFD versus assorted global Mahalanobis methods on 10 UCI data sets . Plots show K-nearest neighbor K-value versus accuracy. Note in particular the segmentation and breast datasets, where RFD shows little or no degradation over increasing distances, while other methods steadily decline in accuracy. Also note that the inclusion of position information in the RFD yields higher performance on all but the low-dimensional and highly linear iris dataset.

Table 2: Mean K-nearest neighbor classification accuracy ranking on 10 UCI data sets at varying K values (lower rank is better). The mean ranking is shown in each table cell as well as the corresponding overall rank, in parentheses. As expected, Euclidean distance nearly always has the worst rank. RFD with absolute position information attains the best rank in nearly all cases, and the relative performance of both RFD methods improves as K increases.

k value	Euclid	Mahal	RCA	DCA	ITML	LMNN	RFD (−P)	RFD (+P)
5	5.8 (8)	5.7 (7)	4.3 (4)	4.8 (5)	3.9 (3)	3.2 (2)	5.4 (6)	**2.9 (1)**
10	6.1 (8)	5.6 (7)	3.7 (3)	4.6 (4)	4.8 (5)	**2.9 (1)**	5.1 (6)	3.2 (2)
15	5.7 (8)	5.4 (6)	3.9 (3)	4.7 (5)	5.6 (7)	3.1 (2)	4.6 (4)	**3 (1)**
20	5.6 (8)	5.4 (7)	3.8 (3)	5.2 (5)	5.3 (6)	3.7 (2)	4.5 (4)	**2.5 (1)**
25	6.1 (8)	5.3 (6)	4 (3)	4.5 (4)	5.4 (7)	3.4 (2)	4.8 (5)	**2.5 (1)**
30	5.8 (7)	5.9 (8)	4.5 (5)	4.3 (3)	5.3 (6)	3.5 (2)	4.3 (3)	**2.4 (1)**
35	5.8 (8)	5.4 (6)	4.3 (4)	4.9 (5)	5.5 (7)	4 (3)	3.8 (2)	**2.3 (1)**
45	6.6 (8)	5.5 (6)	4.4 (4)	4.4 (4)	5.9 (7)	3.3 (2)	4.1 (3)	**1.8 (1)**
Max	6.5 (8)	6.1 (7)	5.1 (5)	3.7 (3)	5.5 (6)	3.7 (3)	3.5 (2)	**1.9 (1)**

position-specific metrics, rather than the $\mathbf{O}(n)$ learned by existing position-dependent methods, which learn a single metric per instance/position. RFD is a stronger way to learn a position-dependent metric, because even explicit multi-metric methods will fail over global distances in cases where a single (Mahalanobis) metric cannot capture the relationship between its associated point and every other point in the data.

Table 3: Comparison of test error (mean ± STD) for position-dependent metric learning methods. The best performance on each data set is shown in bold. We note that our method yields the best accuracy on 3 out of 5 data sets tested, and is within 1% of the best on the remaining 2.

Dataset	RFD	ISD L1	ISD L2	FSM	FSSM
Balance	.120±.024	**.114±.013**	.116±.014	0.134±.020	0.143±.013
Diabetes	**.241±.028**	.287±.019	.269±.023	.342±.050	.322±.232
Breast(Scaled)	**.030±.011**	.0.31±.010	**.030±.010**	.102±.041	.112±.029
German	.277±.039	.277±.015	**.274±.013**	.275±.021	0.275±.060
Haberman	**.273±.029**	.277±.029	**.273±.025**	.276±.032	.276±.029

Table 4: Run-time comparison of ISD and RFD (with position information, using 1000 trees) across several UCI data sets. All times are in seconds. Results were obtained by performing 5-fold cross validation and averaging the time for each fold. *Note that ISD is multithreading across 12 cores, while our implementation of RFD is fully sequential.

Dataset	ISD Time*	RFD Time	ISD:RFD Ratio
Iris	34.6	2.1	16.4
Balance	620.3	11.2	55.3
Breast (scaled)	657.4	7.8	84.6
Diabetes	849.5	14.7	57.8

3.4 Retrieval on the Corel image data set

We also evaluate our method's performance on the challenging image retrieval task because this task differs from **K**-NN classification by emphasizing the accuracy of individual pairwise distances rather than broad patterns. For this task, we use an image data set taken from the Corel image database. We select ten image categories of varying types (cats, roses, mountains, etc.—the classes and images are similar to those used by Hoi et al. to validate DCA [14]), each with a clear semantic meaning. Each class contains 100 images, for a total of 1000 images in the data set.

For each image, we extract a 36-dimensional low-level feature vector comprising color, shape and texture. For color, we extract mean, variance and skewness in each HSV color channel, and thus obtain 9 color features. For shape, we employ a Canny edge detector and construct an 18-dimensional edge direction histogram for the image. For texture, we apply Discrete Wavelet Transformation (DWT) to graylevel versions of original RGB images. A Daubechies-4 wavelet filter is applied to perform 3-level decomposition, and mean, variance and mode of each of the 3 levels are extracted as a 9-dimensional texture feature.

We compare three state of the art algorithms and a Euclidean distance baseline: ITML, DCA, and our RFD method (with absolute position information). Since retrieval problem is different from classification problem, there is no label for each point, only have labels for pairs such as must-link or cannot-link. But in the training process of LMNN, it needs the class label for each training points. Therefore we did not use the LMNN in the retrieval experiments.

For ITML, we vary the parameter γ from 10^{-4} to 10^{4} and choose the best (10^{-3}). For each method, we generate 1% of the available positive constraints and 1% of the available negative constraints (as proposed in [14]). For RFD, we construct a random forest with 1500 trees. Using five-fold cross validation, we retrieve the 20 nearest neighbors of each image under each metric. Accuracy is determined by counting the fraction of the retrieved images that are the same class as the image that retrieved them. We repeat this experiment 10 times with differing random folds and report the average results in Figure 4. RFD clearly outperforms the other methods tested, achieving the best accuracy on all but the cougar category. Also note that ITML performs roughly on par with or worse than the baseline on 7 classes, and DCA on 5, while RFD fails only on 1, indicating again that RFD provides a better global distance measure than current state of the art approaches, and is less likely to sacrifice performance in one region in order to gain it in another.

4. CONCLUSION

In this paper, we have proposed a new angle on the metric learning problem utilizing random forests. Our method, called random forest distance (RFD), incorporates conventional relative position information as well as absolute position of point pairs into the learned metric, and hence implicitly adapts the positon-based metric through the feature space. Our evaluation has demonstrated the capability of RFD, which attains the best overall performance in terms of accuracy and speed on a variety of benchmarks.

There are immediate directions of further inquiry that have been paved with this paper. First, RFD further demonstrates

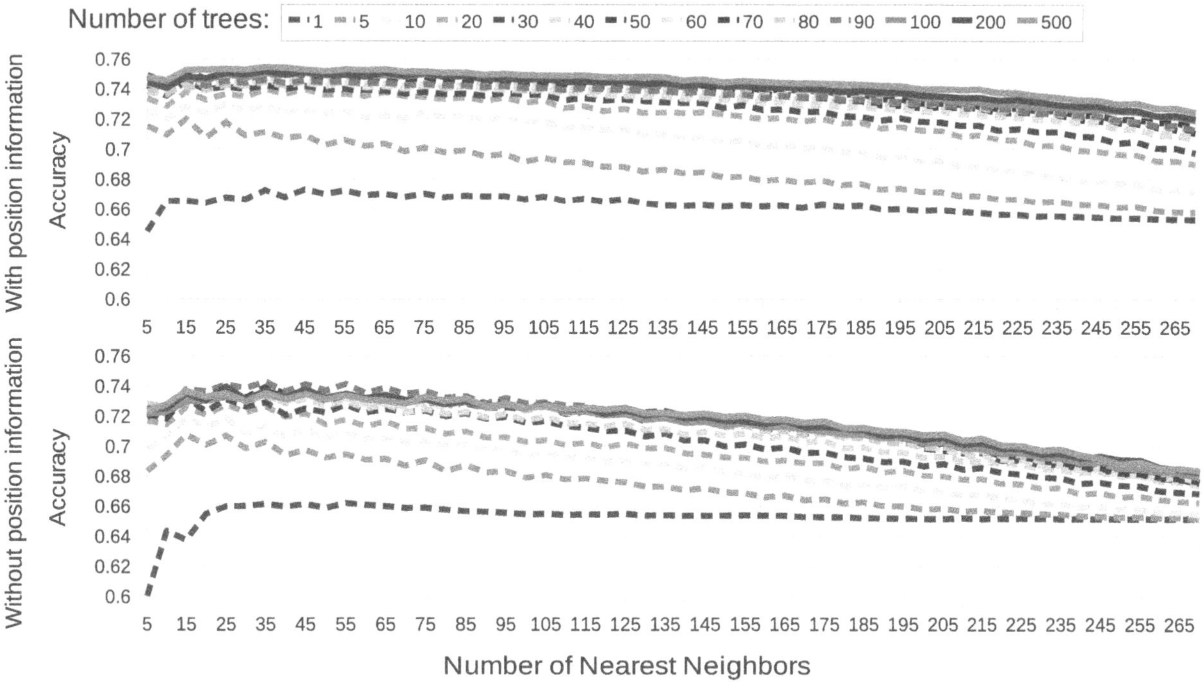

Figure 3: Effect of forest size on RFD performance on the UCI diabetes data set. Results were obtained by averaging results from 10 runs, each using 5-fold cross validation. Both with and without position information, increasing forest size yields notable improvements in accuracy up to about 100 trees. If no position information is included, then additional trees beyond this point provide modest gains at best. With position information, larger forests do appear to allow more fine-tuning, and can produce noticable improvements up to at least 500 trees.

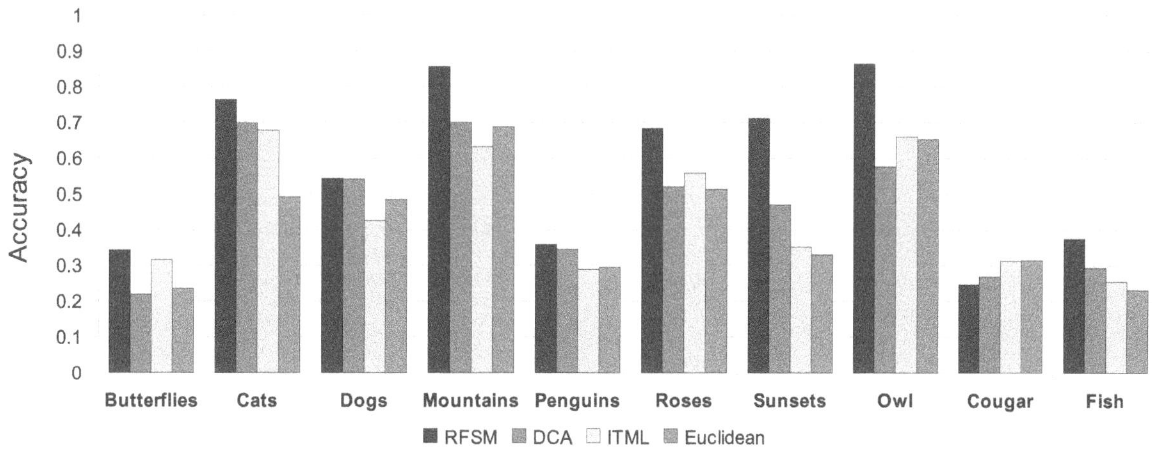

Figure 4: Average retrieval precision on top 20 nearest neighbors of images in the Corel data set. RFD outperforms DCA, ITML and the baseline Euclidean measure on all but one category.

the capability of classification methods as a foundation for metric learning. Similar feature mapping functions and other underlying forms for the distance function need to be investigated. Second, the usefulness of absolute pairwise position information is clear from our work—a good indication of the need for multiple metrics. Open questions remain about other representations for position information as well as the use of position in other metric forms. We are also investigating the use of RFD on larger-scale, more diverse data sets like the MIT SUN image classification data set.

5. ACKNOWLEDGEMENT

This work was partially supported by the National Science Foundation CAREER grant (IIS-0845282), the Army Research Office (W911NF-11-1-0090), DARPA CSSG (HR0011-09-1-0022 and D11AP00245). Disclaimer: The views and conclusions contained herein are those of the authors and should not be interpreted as necessarily representing the official policies or endorsements, either expressed or implied, of DARPA, ARO, NSF or the U.S. Government.

6. REFERENCES

[1] Y. Amit and D. Geman. Shape quantization and recognition with randomized trees. *Neural computation*, 9(7):1545–1588, 1997.

[2] B. Babenko, S. Branson, and S. Belongie. Similarity metrics for categorization: from monolithic to category specific. In *International Conference on Computer Vision*, pages 293–300, 2009.

[3] A. Bar-Hillel, T. Hertz, N. Shental, and D. Weinshall. Learning distance functions using equivalence relations. In *International Conference on Machine Learning*, volume 20, page 11, 2003.

[4] G. Biau and L. Devroye. On the layered nearest neighbour estimate, the bagged nearest neighbour estimate and the random forest method in regression and classification. *Journal of Multivariate Analysis*, 101(10):2499–2518, 2010.

[5] O. Boiman, E. Shechtman, and M. Irani. In defense of nearest-neighbor based image classification. In *Computer Vision and Pattern Recognition. IEEE Conference on*, pages 1–8. IEEE, 2008.

[6] L. Breiman. Random forests. *Machine learning*, 45(1):5–32, 2001.

[7] R. Caruana and A. Niculescu-Mizil. An empircal comparison of supervised learning algorithms. In *International Conference on Machine Learning*, 2006.

[8] S. Chopra, R. Hadsell, and Y. LeCun. Learning a similarity metric discriminatively, with application to face verification. In *Computer Vision and Pattern Recognition*, volume 1, pages 539–546. IEEE, 2005.

[9] J. Davis, B. Kulis, P. Jain, S. Sra, and I. Dhillon. Information-theoretic metric learning. In *International Conference on Machine Learning*, pages 209–216, 2007.

[10] M. Fink. Object classification from a single example utilizing class relevance metrics. In *Advances in Neural Information Processing Systems*, volume 17, page 449. The MIT Press, 2004.

[11] A. Frome, Y. Singer, and J. Malik. Image retrieval and classification using local distance functions. *Advances in Neural Information Processing Systems*, 19:417, 2006.

[12] A. Frome, Y. Singer, F. Sha, and J. Malik. Learning globally-consistent local distance functions for shape-based image retrieval and classification. In *International Conference on Computer Vision*, pages 1–8. IEEE, 2007.

[13] A. Globerson and S. Roweis. Metric learning by collapsing classes. *Advances in Neural Information Processing Systems*, 18:451, 2006.

[14] S. Hoi, W. Liu, M. Lyu, and W. Ma. Learning distance metrics with contextual constraints for image retrieval. In *Computer Vision and Pattern Recognition*, volume 2, pages 2072–2078. IEEE, 2006.

[15] P. Jain, B. Kulis, and K. Grauman. Fast image search for learned metrics. *Computer Vision and Pattern Recognition*, 2008.

[16] G. Lebanon. Metric learning for text documents. *Transactions Pattern Analysis and Machine Intelligence*, pages 497–508, 2006.

[17] C. Leistner, A. Saffari, J. Santner, and H. Bischof. Semi-supervised random forests. In *Computer Vision, 2009 IEEE 12th International Conference on*, pages 506–513. IEEE.

[18] Y. Lin and Y. Jeon. Random forests and adaptive nearest neighbors. *Journal of the American Statistical Association*, 101(474):578–590, 2006.

[19] G. Martinez-Munoz, N. Larios, E. Mortensen, W. Zhang, A. Yamamuro, R. Paasch, N. Payet, D. Lytle, L. Shapiro, S. Todorovic, et al. Dictionary-free categorization of very similar objects via stacked evidence trees. In *Computer Vision and Pattern Recognition, 2009. CVPR 2009. IEEE Conference on*, pages 549–556. IEEE, 2009.

[20] H. Nguyen and L. Bai. Cosine similarity metric learning for face verification. *Asian Conference on Computer Vision*, pages 709–720, 2010.

[21] N. Nguyen and Y. Guo. Metric Learning: A Support Vector Approach. *ECML PKDD*, pages 125–136, 2008.

[22] N. Payet and S. Todorovic. (rf) 2 — random forest random field. Advanced in Neural Information Processing Systems, 2010.

[23] S. Shalev-Shwartz, Y. Singer, and A. Ng. Online and batch learning of pseudo-metrics. In *International Conference on Machine Learning*, page 94. ACM, 2004.

[24] C. Shen, J. Kim, and L. Wang. Scalable Large-Margin Mahalanobis Distance Metric Learning. *Neural Networks, IEEE Transactions on*, 21(9):1524–1530, 2010.

[25] Y. Shi, Y. Noh, F. Sha, and D. Lee. Learning discriminative metrics via generative models and kernel learning. *Arxiv preprint arXiv:1109.3940*, 2011.

[26] J. Wang, S. Wu, H. Vu, and G. Li. Text document clustering with metric learning. In *Proceeding of the 33rd international ACM SIGIR conference on Research and development in information retrieval*, pages 783–784. ACM, 2010.

[27] K. Weinberger and L. Saul. Fast solvers and efficient implementations for distance metric learning. In *International Conference on Machine Learning*, pages 1160–1167. ACM, 2008.

[28] K. Weinberger and L. Saul. Distance metric learning for large margin nearest neighbor classification. *The Journal of Machine Learning Research*, 10:207–244, 2009.

[29] L. Wu, R. Jin, S. Hoi, J. Zhu, and N. Yu. Learning bregman distance functions and its application for semi-supervised clustering. *Advances in Neural Information Processing Systems*, 22:2089–2097, 2009.

[30] E. Xing, A. Ng, M. Jordan, and S. Russell. Distance metric learning with application to clustering with side-information. *Advances in Neural Information Processing Systems*, pages 521–528, 2003.

[31] W. Yang, Y. Wang, and G. Mori. Learning transferable distance functions for human action recognition. *Machine Learning for Vision-Based Motion Analysis*, pages 349–370, 2011.

[32] D. Zhan, M. Li, Y. Li, and Z. Zhou. Learning instance specific distances using metric propagation. In *Proceedings of the 26th Annual International Conference on Machine Learning*, pages 1225–1232. ACM, 2009.

Empowering Authors to Diagnose Comprehension Burden in Textbooks

Rakesh Agrawal Sunandan Chakraborty* Sreenivas Gollapudi Anitha Kannan
Krishnaram Kenthapadi
Search Labs, Microsoft Research
Mountain View, CA, USA

ABSTRACT

Good textbooks are organized in a systematically progressive fashion so that students acquire new knowledge and learn new concepts based on known items of information. We provide a diagnostic tool for quantitatively assessing the comprehension burden that a textbook imposes on the reader due to non-sequential presentation of concepts. We present a formal definition of comprehension burden and propose an algorithmic approach for computing it. We apply the tool to a corpus of high school textbooks from India and empirically examine its effectiveness in helping authors identify sections of textbooks that can benefit from reorganizing the material presented.

Categories and Subject Descriptors

H.3 [**Information Storage and Retrieval**]: Information Search and Retrieval

General Terms

Algorithms, Experimentation, Human Factors

Keywords

Data Mining, Knowledge Discovery, Education, Textbooks, Diagnostic Tool for Authors, Comprehension Burden, Concepts

1. INTRODUCTION

Education is known to be a key determinant of economic growth and prosperity [19, 41]. While the issues in devising a high-quality educational system are multi-faceted and complex, textbooks are acknowledged to be the educational input most consistently associated with gains in student learning [36]. Textbooks are the primary conduits for delivering content knowledge to the students and the teachers base their lesson plans primarily on the material given in textbooks [14].

Considerable research has gone into investigating what makes for good textbooks [11, 15, 20, 27, 40]. There has also been work on designing ideal textbook and guidelines and checklists have been proposed for assessing the quality of a textbook [5, 8, 31]. Most education researchers concur that the good textbooks are organized in a systematically progressive fashion so that students acquire new knowledge and learn new concepts based on known items of information [4, 23, 31]. Unfortunately, many textbooks suffer from what Harriet Tyson-Bernstein calls the "mentioning" problem [35] that causes concepts to be encountered before they have been adequately explained and forces students to randomly "knock around" in the book [8]. Indeed, the extensive survey in [6] reports a number of empirical studies in which learning from textbooks was successfully improved by rewriting the text to enhance comprehension.

We propose a diagnostic tool for authors to enable them to mine the content of a textbook to quantitatively assess the comprehension burden that a particular organization of the textbook can impose on the reader due to non-sequential presentation of concepts. A textbook with large comprehension burden makes it harder for the reader to understand the textbook material. We introduce the notion of comprehension burden, present a formal definition, and provide an algorithmic approach for computing it. We evaluate the proposed methodology over a corpus of Indian textbooks that demonstrates its effectiveness for identifying sections of textbooks that can benefit from reorganizing the material presented.

The layout of the rest of the paper is as follows. We begin with a discussion of related work in §2. We present key properties followed in well-written textbooks and provide a formal definition of comprehension burden based on these properties in §3. We also describe the algorithm for computing the comprehension burden in this section. We present the experimental results in §4 and conclude with a summary and directions for future work in §5.

2. RELATED WORK

The question of what factors influence understandability of a text has intrigued researchers for a long time. An early comprehensive investigation, dating back to 1935 [16], identified two principal sets of factors. The first set pertains to individual differences amongst readers, such as levels of intellectual capacity, reading skills, attitudes and goals, previous experiences, and personal interests and tastes. The

*Currently at New York University; work done during internship at Microsoft Research.

KDD'12, August 12–16, 2012, Beijing, China.

second set relates to the readability of the material, which in turn depends on format (page layout, appearance, etc.), organization (headings, indexes, flow, etc.), style (linguistic structural elements, tone of the writer, etc.), and content (theme, nature of the subject matter, etc.). Much of the readability research has focused on the style category because of perceived relative importance of stylistic variables and the fact that stylistic variables are easier to operationalize [18].

We refer the reader to the survey in [12] for overview of readability research. Sherman is considered to be the first to use statistical analysis for analyzing readability in 1890's. By counting average sentence length, he showed how sentence-length averages had shortened over time [32]. The first readability formula, a weighted index of vocabulary complexity, is attributed to the work of Lively and Pressley in 1923 [24]. Since then over two hundred formulas have been developed for measuring the difficulty of reading. Some popular formulas include Flesch Reading Ease Score, Flesch-Kincaid Grade Level, Dale-Chall Grade Level, Gunning Fog Index, SMOG Index, Coleman-Liau Index, and Automated Readability Index. The readability formulas have come under criticism because of their purported low validity from the perspective of psycholinguistic theories [7] and there have been efforts to develop new approaches for predicting reading difficulty, for example, by using statistical language modeling techniques and linguistic features [10, 22] and by devising domain-specific readability measures [42]. While this body of readability research can be used to assess the reading complexity of a piece of text in isolation, our focus is on studying the organization and presentation of concepts in the entire textbook.

In linguistics, cohesion refers to connections between sentences, whereas coherence refers to the connectedness of the ideas [39]. Cohesion provides a sense of flow from sentence to sentence and the principle of cohesion states that one must start a sentence with old information and end it with new information. The principle of coherence states that to make a series of individual sentences into a coherent passage, one must focus the topics of those sentences on a limited number of concepts. Discourse parsing techniques are used to build a structural representation of a text which reflects the semantic relationships among basic textual units [17, 25, 29, 33]. We build upon these ideas in our definition of comprehension burden, where we focus on flow from concept to concept.

The cognitive load theory proposes that poorly designed instructional materials place cognitive overload on learners as working memory is limited. This cognitive overload impairs schema acquisition, later resulting in a lower performance [26, 28]. The theory distinguishes between three types of load: intrinsic, extraneous and germane. Intrinsic load is a function of the complexity of the content rather than instructional design. Extraneous load on the other hand is not inherent within the content, but depends on how the instructional designer has structured and presented information. Intrinsic and extraneous loads are additive. Germane load is the remaining free capacity in working memory that may be directed toward schema acquisition. Thus, a well-designed book increases the learning capacity of a learner. We make use of these ideas in abstracting the properties of well-written books.

In [2], a probabilistic decision model has been proposed for identifying those sections of a textbook that are not well-written. The decision model is based on the syntactic complexity of the writing and the notion of the dispersion of key concepts mentioned in the section. However, each section is treated independently and the flow of writing across different sections is not taken into account. By contrast, the focus of the present paper is on determining whether the entire textbook is organized in a systematically progressive fashion.

3. COMPREHENSION BURDEN

We begin by enunciating properties of well-written textbooks abstracted from education literature. We then describe our model of a textbook and how a poorly written book can impose comprehension burden on the reader. Finally, after introducing some notations used in the paper, we formally define comprehension burden of a textbook.

3.1 Properties of Well-written Textbooks

3.1.1 Organization into Focused Sections

PROPERTY 3.1 (FOCUS). *Each section in a well-written textbook explains very few concepts.*

3.1.2 A Key Section for Every Concept

PROPERTY 3.2 (UNITY). *For each concept in a well-written textbook, there is a unique section that best explains the concept.*

The properties of FOCUS and UNITY are rooted in the following notion: a text that is more unified and addresses a single purpose results in better comprehension [4, 8, 16, 23, 39]. The cognitive load theory also proposes that intrinsic load may be reduced by dividing an instruction into smaller pieces and that if learners process the individual elements of instruction serially, rather than simultaneously, they are able to process the instruction more efficiently [9, 30]. In fact, Alfred North Whitehead admonished way back in 1917: "What you teach, teach thoroughly, seizing on the few general ideas which illuminate the whole, and persistently marshalling subsidiary facts around them" [38].

3.1.3 Sequential Presentation of Concepts

PROPERTY 3.3 (SEQUENTIALITY). *Concepts in a well-written textbook are discussed in a sequential fashion, that is, a concept is adequately explained prior to occurrences of this concept or any related concept.*

This property stems from the following insights: (a) good textbooks should be organized in a systematically progressive fashion [4, 31] (b) a well-designed book can reduce extraneous cognitive load and thus increase the learning capacity of a student [26, 28].

3.1.4 Prioritization of Concepts

PROPERTY 3.4 (PRIORITIZATION). *In a well-written textbook, the tie for precedence in presentation between two mutually related concepts is broken in favor of the more significant of the two.*

Although a well-written textbook strives to present the concepts in a sequential fashion, two mutually related concepts may vie to have precedence in the order of their presentation. A good book will break the tie in favor of the concept that is more significant [23].

3.2 Origin of Comprehension Burden

Although textbooks are typically organized into chapters which are subdivided into logical sections, for the purposes of this paper, we find it sufficient to model a textbook simply as a sequence of sections. Assume that the textbook has been written in such a way that each section *explains* one or very few concepts, that is, each of these concepts is discussed in depth (Property 3.1). But a section can also *mention* other concepts, that is, each of these concepts is referenced but not explained in detail. For each concept, there is a key section in the book that best explains it (Property 3.2). Thus a reader who has gone through the key section corresponding to a concept has comprehended the concept, while a reader who has not yet read the key section has a vague comprehension of the concept. A concept could be related to other concepts, and hence significant for understanding other concepts.

A textbook imposes comprehension burden on the reader if the concepts are not presented in a sequential fashion. In particular, for a concept c, an occurrence of a related concept d in a section preceding the key section for c imposes comprehension burden on the reader since the reader has not comprehended c yet and hence faces difficulty in understanding d. Note that d could be same as c, in which case the comprehension burden is imposed on the reader who encounters a mention of c in an earlier section whereas c has been explained properly in a later section (Property 3.3).

Suppose the reader encounters d in section i prior to explanation of c in its key section k_c. The more significant the explanation of c in the section k_c is for understanding other concepts in the book, the greater chance the reader cannot understand d in section i without thoroughly understanding c and hence larger the comprehension burden on the reader while reading section i. Further, the more significant d in section i is for understanding other concepts in the book, the larger is the comprehension burden since the reader may not be able to follow subsequent material that is based on the discussion of d in section i (Property 3.4).

For illustration, consider a book consisting of three sections, each of which contains three mutually related concepts, c_1, c_2 and c_3. UNITY demands that each concept has a unique key section where it is explained. FOCUS requires that a section explains very few concepts. Assume that a section can be the key section for only one concept. Suppose that c_1 is the most significant and c_3 is the least significant of the three. PRIORITIZATION implies that the author will explain c_1 in section 1, followed by c_2 in section 2, and finally c_3 in section 3. Concept c_1 obeys SEQUENTIALITY but not the other two. Its mention in any of the later sections does not incur comprehension burden as the reader has by now comprehended it. A mention of c_2 in section 1 will incur comprehension burden as it is explained only in section 2. However, its mention in section 3 will not incur comprehension burden. Similarly, any mention of c_3 in a section earlier than section 3 will incur comprehension burden.

As the above example demonstrates, there is a trade-off to be made since the properties interact with each other. In the extreme, a book that consists of a single long section violates FOCUS completely while satisfying the other three. Clearly, this organization is not acceptable. Typically the author faces the task of explaining certain mutually related concepts in a book. As all of them cannot be presented in the same section due to the requirement of FOCUS, SEQUENTIALITY needs to be violated and hence comprehension burden cannot be entirely avoided. However, different organizations can result in different amounts of comprehension burden, which points to the necessity of being able to quantify the comprehension burden due to a given organization of a textbook. We assume that the author first tries to satisfy FOCUS and UNITY as much as possible.

S	Set of sections in a given textbook
C	Set of concepts in a given textbook
$R(c)$	Set of concepts related to concept c
k_c	Key section for concept c
$\lambda(c,i)$	Significance score of concept c in section i
$\psi((d,i) \leftarrow c)$	Comprehension burden for concept d in section i attributed to concept c
$\psi(d \leftarrow c)$	Comprehension burden for concept d attributed to concept c
$\Psi(c)$	Comprehension burden attributed to concept c
$\tilde{\Psi}(i)$	Comprehension burden of section i
$\mathcal{B}$	Comprehension burden of the textbook

Table 1: Notations

3.3 Notations

Before formally defining comprehension burden, we introduce some notations. Let $S = \{1, 2, \ldots, n\}$ denote the set of sections in a given textbook. Let C denote the set of concepts in the book. For each concept $c \in C$, let k_c denote the key section for understanding the concept. For each concept $c \in C$, denote the set of concepts related to it by $R(c)$. Note that $R(c)$ includes c. Let $\lambda(c,i)$ denote the significance score of concept c in section i for understanding other concepts in the entire book.

Let $d \in R(c)$ be a concept related to c. We denote by $\psi((d,i) \leftarrow c)$ the comprehension burden imposed on the reader while reading about d in section i due to c being necessary for understanding d but c being explained in a later section in the book. We say that $\psi((d,i) \leftarrow c)$ is the comprehension burden for concept d in section i attributed to concept c. Similarly, denote the comprehension burden for concept d attributed to concept c over all sections by $\psi(d \leftarrow c)$, the comprehension burden on all concepts attributed to concept c by $\Psi(c)$, the comprehension burden of section i by $\tilde{\Psi}(i)$, and the total comprehension burden of the textbook by $\mathcal{B}$. Table 1 summarizes key notations.

3.4 Definition of Comprehension Burden

We now present the formal definition of comprehension burden for a given textbook, assuming that the book satisfies the FOCUS and UNITY properties.

DEFINITION 3.5. *1. Given a concept $c \in C$ with key section k_c, and a concept $d \in R(c)$ occurring in section i, define the* comprehension burden for concept d in section i attributed to concept c *as*

$$\psi((d,i) \leftarrow c) := \begin{cases} f(\lambda(d,i), \lambda(c,k_c)) & \text{if } i < k_c \\ 0 & \text{if } i \geq k_c, \end{cases}$$

where f is a monotonically increasing function in two variables satisfying $f(x,y) < f(y,x)$ whenever $x > y$.

2. *Given a concept $c \in C$ and a concept $d \in R(c)$, define the* comprehension burden for concept d attributed to concept c *as*

$$\psi(d \leftarrow c) := \sum_{i \in S} \psi((d,i) \leftarrow c).$$

3. *Define the* comprehension burden attributed to concept $c \in C$ *as*

$$\Psi(c) := \sum_{d \in R(c)} \psi(d \leftarrow c).$$

4. *Define the* comprehension burden of section $i \in S$ *as*

$$\tilde{\Psi}(i) := \sum_{d \text{ occurring in section } i} \; \sum_{c:\, d \in R(c)} \psi((d,i) \leftarrow c).$$

5. *Define the* comprehension burden of the textbook *as*

$$\mathcal{B} := \sum_{c \in C} \Psi(c) = \sum_{i \in S} \tilde{\Psi}(i).$$

3.4.1 Explanation of the Definition

The key aspect of Definition 3.5 is to quantify $\psi((d,i) \leftarrow c)$. Occurrence of d in k_c or a section following it does not impose any comprehension burden on the reader since the reader would have understood c before encountering d, and hence $\psi((d,i) \leftarrow c)$ is non-zero only when $i < k_c$. See Fig. 1 for an illustration.

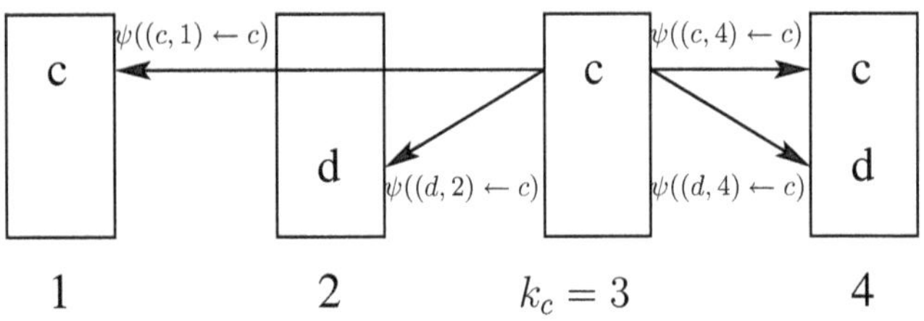

Figure 1: Illustration of comprehension burden: Concept c is explained in section 3 ($k_c = 3$) and is also mentioned in sections 1 and 4. A related concept d occurs in sections 2 and 4. As c is explained in section 3, the reader incurs comprehension burden when reading about c in section 1 ($\psi((c,1) \leftarrow c) > 0$) and about d in section 2 ($\psi((d,2) \leftarrow c) > 0$), but not in section 4 when encountering c and d ($\psi((c,4) \leftarrow c) = \psi((d,4) \leftarrow c) = 0$).

Burden $\psi((d,i) \leftarrow c)$ depends monotonically on the significance score of concept d in section i and the significance score of concept c in section k_c, and has been expressed as a monotonically increasing function $f(\lambda(d,i), \lambda(c,k_c))$. As the reader incurs comprehension burden every time she encounters an occurrence of d in a section prior to k_c, we sum $\psi((d,i) \leftarrow c)$ over all sections to obtain $\psi(d \leftarrow c)$. The comprehension burden attributed to concept c, $\Psi(c)$ is obtained by summing $\psi(d \leftarrow c)$ over all concepts related to c. The comprehension burden of section i, $\tilde{\Psi}(i)$ is obtained by summing $\psi((d,i) \leftarrow c)$ over all concepts that d is related to and then over all concepts in section i. The comprehension burden of the textbook is obtained by summing the comprehension burden attributed to each concept, or equivalently by summing the comprehension burden of each section.

3.4.2 Characterization of f

The requirement on f in Definition 3.5 stems from PRIORITIZATION property.

CLAIM 3.6. PRIORITIZATION *implies that $f(x,y) < f(y,x)$ whenever $x > y$.*

PROOF. Consider two organizations of a book differing in just the order of presentation of two mutually related concepts c and d. In the first version, c is explained in section i with significance score λ_c and d is explained in a later section j with significance score λ_d, where $\lambda_c > \lambda_d$. In the second version, the positions of c and d are interchanged. The first version obeys PRIORITIZATION while the second violates it. Hence the second version should impose larger comprehension burden on the reader. For the first version, $\psi(d \leftarrow c) = 0$ and $\psi(c \leftarrow d) = f(\lambda_c, \lambda_d)$ so that the total comprehension burden is $f(\lambda_c, \lambda_d)$. Similarly the total comprehension burden for the second version is $f(\lambda_d, \lambda_c)$. Thus, the requirement is that $f(\lambda_c, \lambda_d) < f(\lambda_d, \lambda_c)$ whenever $\lambda_c > \lambda_d$. In other words, f should satisfy $f(x,y) < f(y,x)$ whenever $x > y$. □

We next show that a broad category of simple functions can satisfy the above requirement.

CLAIM 3.7. *Suppose f is defined as the product of two univariate functions on either input: $f(x,y) = g(x) \cdot h(y)$. Then the characterization of f in Definition 3.5 is satisfied if $g(.)$ and $h(.)$ are monotonically increasing functions and $h(x)/g(x)$ is also a monotonically increasing function.*

The claim follows since (a) g and h are monotonically increasing $\Rightarrow$ f is monotonically increasing (b) $x > y \Rightarrow h(y)/g(y) < h(x)/g(x) \Rightarrow f(x,y) < f(y,x)$. Stated differently, the requirement above is that $h(.)$ grows faster than $g(.)$, or equivalently the significance score of concept c in section k_c is weighed more than the significance score of concept d in the earlier section i in the computation of $\psi((d,i) \leftarrow c)$. For example, $g(x) = 1$ and $h(x) = x$ is a valid choice that takes only $\lambda(c,k_c)$ into account, ignoring $\lambda(d,i)$.

3.4.3 Generalization of Comprehension Burden Definition

1. We use summation to define $\Psi(c)$ and $\mathcal{B}$, but in general, any function that is dominated by summation can be used instead since different concepts may be related and the marginal comprehension burden due to an additional concept could be less than the comprehension burden due to this concept in isolation.

2. Suppose the book does not satisfy UNITY, so that the explanation of a concept is spread across multiple sections. Then the burden $\psi((d,i) \leftarrow c)$ depends on the explanation of c not covered in sections up to i, and can be obtained by taking into account the significance score of concept d in section i and the significance scores of concept c in sections following i, that is, $\psi((d,i) \leftarrow c) := \sum_{j>i} f(\lambda(d,i), \lambda(c,j))$.

3. FOCUS does not figure in the definition of comprehension burden. The extent to which a textbook follows FOCUS can be measured by computing the average number of concepts to be explained in a section (closer to 1 is better) and the deviation of the number of concepts explained in each section from this average.

3.5 Computing Comprehension Burden

Computation of comprehension burden of a textbook using Definition 3.5 requires the following inputs: (i) concepts in the book, (ii) relationship between concepts, (iii) the significance score for each concept in each section, and (iv) the key section for every concept. We describe next the computation of each of these inputs.

3.5.1 Concepts

Following [3, 21], we define concept phrases to be terminological noun phrases. We first form a candidate set of phrases using linguistic patterns, with the help of a part-of-speech tagger [34]. We adopt the pattern A^*N^+, where A refers to an adjective and N a noun, which was found to be particularly effective in identifying concept phrases. Examples of phrases satisfying this pattern include 'cumulative distribution function', 'fiscal policy', and 'electromagnetic radiation'. The initial set of phrases is further refined by exploiting complementary signals from different sources. First, WordNet [13], a lexical database is used to correct errors made by the part-of-speech tagger. Next, both malformed phrases and very common phrases are eliminated, based on the probabilities of occurrences of these phrases on the Web, obtained using Microsoft Web N-gram Service [37]. The reason for eliminating common phrases is that they would be already well understood.

3.5.2 Relationship between Concepts

We first attempted to induce relationships between concepts by mapping concept phrases to Wikipedia articles and use the link structure between the Wikipedia articles to infer relationship between concepts. We discovered the following issues. Many Wikipedia articles have asymmetric hyperlink structure, plausibly due the encyclopedic nature of Wikipedia: there are relatively less links from articles on specialized topics to articles on more general topics. For instance, the Wikipedia article titled 'Gaussian surface' mentions 'electric field' 11 times but does not have a link to the latter. Furthermore, while Wikipedia provides good coverage for universal subjects like Physics and Mathematics, it has inadequate coverage for concepts related to locale-dependent subjects such as History.

We, therefore, derive the relationship between concepts directly from textbooks using co-occurrence. More precisely, we defined $R(c)$ to be the set of concepts (including c) that co-occur with c in at least e sections such that both c and the co-occurring concept c' occur within a window of size l in each of these e sections. The requirements of co-occurrence in multiple sections and co-occurrence within a window size ensure that we only consider concept pairs that are significantly related to each other. Our implementation sets $e = 2$ and $l = 500$ words.

3.5.3 Significance Scores

The significance score $\lambda(c, i)$ is a measure of how significant is the description of concept c in section i for understanding other concepts in the book. One possible approach would be to define the significance score in terms of the relative frequency of the concept phrase in the section, for example, $\lambda(c, i) := (freq(c, i))/(\sum_{1 \leq i \leq n} \sum_{c \in C} freq(c, i))$. A problem with such a definition is that it does not differentiate between two concept phrases c_1 and c_2 with the same frequency in a given section. However, concept c_1 may be related to many concepts that occur in other sections in the book and hence more significant for understanding the entire book, while c_2 may be relevant only for the current section. We, therefore, define the significance score of a concept phrase in a section taking into account: (a) how frequent is the concept in the section, and (b) how many concepts are related to it.

DEFINITION 3.8. *The significance score of a concept c in section i is defined as*

$$\lambda(c, i) := \pi(freq(c, i), |R(c)|),$$

where π is a monotonically increasing function in two variables.

Our implementation instantiates function π as $\pi(freq(c, i), |R(c)|) := freq(c, i) \cdot |R(c)|$. This choice has the interpretation that the significance score of a concept in a section is proportional to its frequency in the section as well as the number of concepts related to it.

3.5.4 Key Sections

We use the intuition that the key section for a concept will have high significance score for that concept. Thus, we algorithmically obtain the key section for a concept by comparing its significance scores in different sections. For each concept $c \in C$, we set the key section for c to be

$$k_c := \arg \max_{1 \leq i \leq n} \lambda(c, i).$$

With the significance score defined as in Definition 3.8, this choice is equivalent to selecting the section where the concept is most frequent.

We remark that multiple alternatives exist for computing the above inputs and our model of comprehension burden can admit multiple such choices. For example, the significance score computation can benefit by including anaphoric references to a concept when computing its frequency in a section.

4. FROM THEORY TO PRACTICE

We next present a diagnostic tool we have built based on the notions just introduced that allows an author to understand the sources of comprehension burden in a textbook. This tool helps authors accomplish the following goals:
(1) identify and investigate sections with large burden, and
(2) identify and probe concepts that impose large burden.

4.1 Corpus

We studied the characteristics of our tool over a corpus of Indian high school textbooks published by the National Council of Educational Research and Training (NCERT). We selected this corpus because millions of students study from these books every year and these books were readily available online. We applied the tool to eleven books from grades IX–XII, covering four broad subject areas: Sciences, Social Sciences, Commerce, and Mathematics. In [1], we

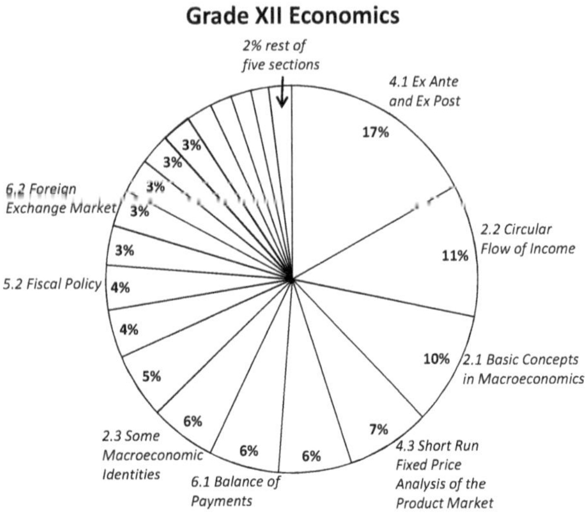

Figure 2: Textbook overview page, with sections listed in the decreasing order of burden. The number within a slice indicates percentage of total burden for the corresponding section. Names of some of the sections have been omitted for clarity.

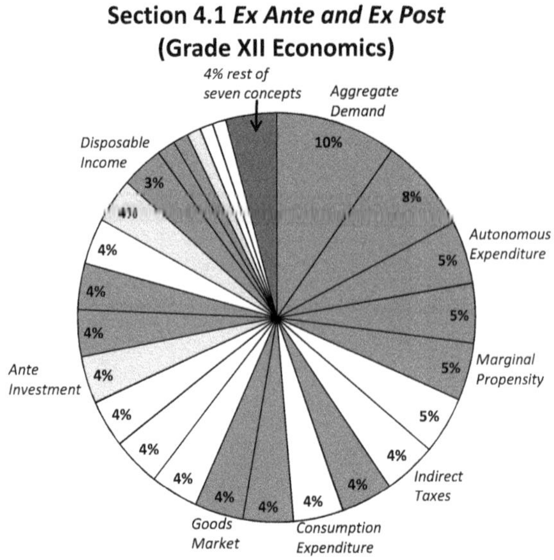

Figure 3: Section page. Concepts occurring in the section are shown in the decreasing order of their burden. Further, concepts that are explained in the section have light gray background color, concepts that are mentioned but explained in a later section have dark gray background, and concepts that are mentioned but have been explained earlier have white background. Names of some of the concepts have been omitted for clarity.

described how to quantify the properties in §3.1 and measured the extent to which these properties are followed in the above books. Here our focus is on measuring the comprehension burden in these books.

In applying the tool, we instantiate function f as $f(\lambda(d,i), \lambda(c,k_c)) := \lambda(c,k_c)$ for computing comprehension burden. This choice satisfies the characterization of f in Definition 3.5 and has the interpretation that the comprehension burden for concept d in section i attributed to c is proportional to the significance of c in its key section.

4.2 Diagnostic Tool

4.2.1 Burden of Sections

The author of a textbook might like to first determine sections where the readers incur large comprehension burden, so that she can prioritize such sections for revision. Hence our tool presents to the author an overview of the book with the sections ordered in the decreasing order of burden. Figure 2 illustrates this page for Grade XII Economics book. From this page, the author can observe that though this book consists of twenty five sections, 75% of the burden arises from just ten sections. Further, Section 4.1 titled "Ex Ante and Ex Post" has the largest burden.

Having identified a section with large burden, the author might next like to understand why the reader incurs large burden in the section. For this purpose, our tool allows navigation to a page created for each section. Figure 3 shows this page for the section, "Ex Ante and Ex Post". This page lists the concepts occurring in the section in the decreasing order of their burden. This page also helps the author to determine whether each of these concepts is *explained* or *mentioned* in the section, and for a concept that is mentioned, whether it has been explained in an earlier section or a later section. Thus, the author can identify those concepts that are mentioned in the section prior to their explanation in the book. For such a concept, the author may choose to include greater explanation in the current section or an earlier section where it occurs. The author can observe that the section "Ex Ante and Ex Post" contains a large number of distinct concepts, of which only a small fraction is explained in this section. About half of the remaining have been explained in earlier sections but the remaining half are explained in later sections. Moreover, 75% of the burden for the section arises from half of the concepts.

Next the author may want to drill down to understand what causes burden for each of these concepts. For this purpose, our tool permits navigation to a separate page dedicated to each concept occurring in the section. This page provides the distribution of the significance score of the concept across different sections in the book. It also shows the related concepts needed for understanding this concept, in the decreasing order of burden they impose on this concept. Figure 4 shows the page for the concept 'aggregate demand', which has the largest burden in the section, "Ex Ante and Ex Post". The author learns that this concept is mentioned in this section, prior to its explanation in a later section. Furthermore, the author sees that the large burden for 'aggregate demand' is caused by the presence of many related concepts (such as 'exchange rate', 'final goods' and 'government spending') that are explained only in later sections.

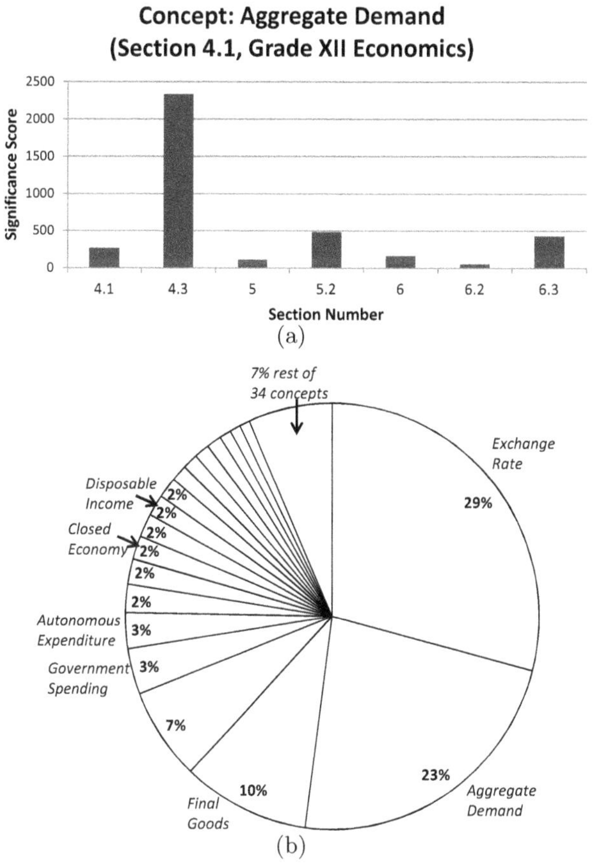

Figure 4: Concept page for a section. (a) The distribution of significance scores of the concept 'aggregate demand' across different sections is shown. (b) Related concepts are shown in the decreasing order of burden they impose on the concept 'aggregate demand' in the section "Ex Ante and Ex Post".

4.2.2 *Burden Attributed to Concepts*

The author may also examine the book along an orthogonal dimension by investigating concepts that impose large burden across the book. Such diagnosis is beneficial since the author may choose to include a glossary of such concepts. For this purpose, our tool presents an analysis of the book with respect to concepts present in the book, ordered in the decreasing order of burden imposed by them. Figure 5 shows this analysis for Grade XII Economics book. The author can see that concepts such as 'aggregate demand', 'exchange rate' and 'final goods' impose the largest burden on the reader, accounting for nearly 55% of the total burden in the book. Moreover, 80% of the burden is attributed to just 10% of the concepts.

For a high burden concept, the author might like to understand its impact on related concepts. This information might help the author decide whether this concept should be explained in an early section in the book. Hence our tool lets the author navigate to a page for each concept, which lists the burden imposed by this concept on its related concepts. Figure 6 illustrates this page for the concept 'aggregate demand'. By probing into concepts related to this concept and their distribution across sections, the author can infer that the burden can be reduced by explaining 'aggregate demand' in a section prior to occurrences of many of its related concepts.

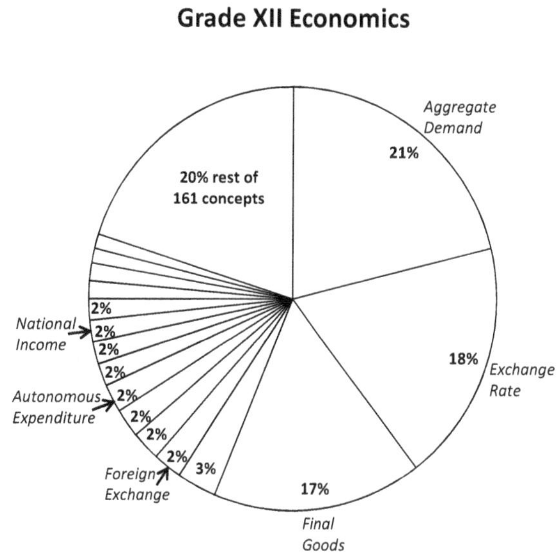

Figure 5: Textbook overview page, with concepts listed in the decreasing order of burden imposed.

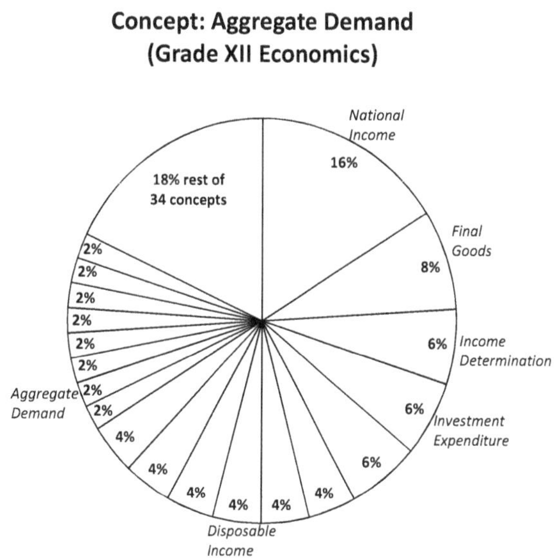

Figure 6: Concept page for the book. Burden imposed by the concept 'aggregate demand' on its related concepts is shown.

4.2.3 *Differences between Books*

We next present some comparative observations from applying our tool to books belonging to three different subjects: Grade XII Economics, Grade X Science, and Grade XII History. These books also had different organizational structure. Figure 7 gives a statistical overview of the sec-

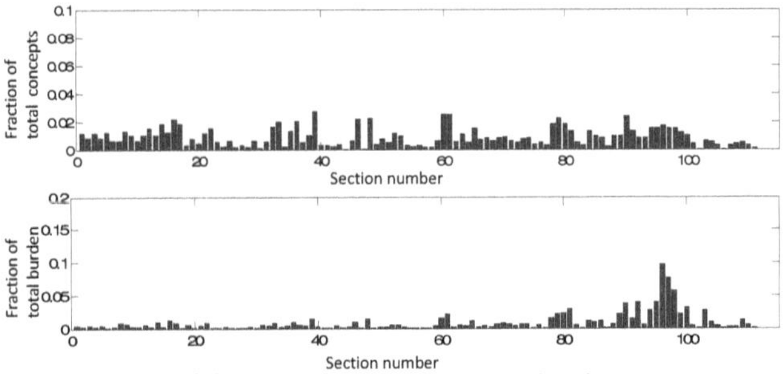

(a) Grade XII History textbook

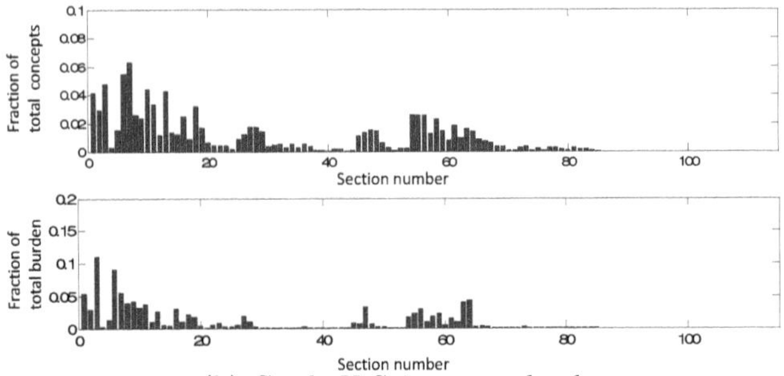

(b) Grade X Science textbook

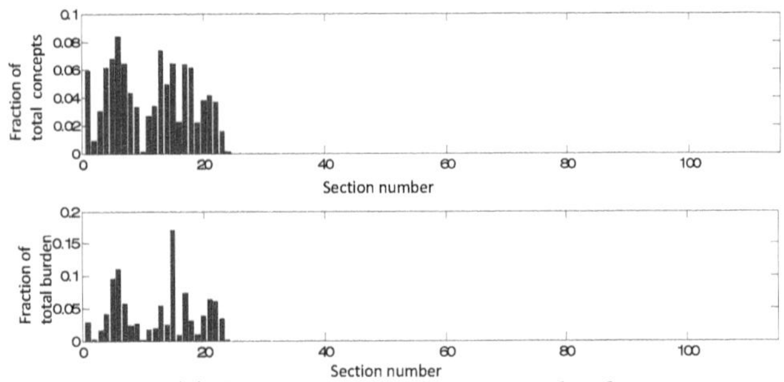

(c) Grade XII Economics textbook

Figure 7: Characteristics of different books.

tions in these books. It shows the distribution of burden across different sections in a book, as well as the distribution of the number of concepts across different book sections. Note that the X-axis refers to the section number (ordered over the entire book) and that these books have different number of sections.

Grade XII History book consists of chapters covering different periods of Indian history, ranging from 3000BC to the 20th century. Our manual inspection revealed that the last few chapters in this book pertain to interrelated topics such as British rule and Indian freedom struggle, while the chapters in the initial two thirds of the book mostly discuss disjoint time periods, and hence disjoint concepts. As a result, the burden for this book arises from very few sections occurring in the last few chapters.

Grade X Science book consists of independent modules, corresponding to Biology, Chemistry, Physics, and Environmental Sciences in that order. However certain concepts such as 'electric current' and 'carbon dioxide' are shared across modules, and are mentioned in the Biology module prior to their explanation in later parts of the book. Moreover, sections in the Biology module contain a large number of concepts. Consequently, the burden is concentrated in the initial part of the book.

By contrast, Grade XII Economics book pertains to the single theme of macroeconomics, with different sections sharing related concepts, and hence the burden is spread out across more sections. We also observe that sections with large burden tend to have a large number of concepts.

5. CONCLUSIONS AND FUTURE WORK

This paper represents our attempt to expand the scope of data mining by considering a new application area – mining textbooks for identifying sections and concepts that can benefit from reorganizing the material presented. Towards this goal, we introduced the notion of comprehension burden, presented a rigorous definition as well as an algorithm for computing it, and provided a diagnostic tool for authors to quantitatively assess the burden that a textbook imposes on the reader due to non-sequential presentation of concepts. We applied the tool to a corpus of high school textbooks, currently in active use in India. Using the tool, we were able to isolate high-burden sections and concepts.

The work presented here can be extended along several dimensions. One particularly important direction is to incorporate the background knowledge of the reader in the definition and computation of comprehension burden. For instance, consider a textbook designed for a course in Physics for which an introductory course covering basic ideas from different sciences is prerequisite. In such a book, it is reasonable for the author to presume that a mention of Newton's laws without explaining them will not impose comprehension burden, but this assumption is invalid for Einstein's theory of relativity. Similarly, authors may correctly mention concepts perceived to be part of the common knowledge of the target readers without explaining them. How should comprehension burden factor in such general knowledge? Another important direction is to explore the use of deeper text analysis to differentiate between bad mentions and mentions where the author has provided key idea and supplemented it with a reference to the section where the idea has been discussed in depth. It will also be interesting to investigate connections between comprehension burden and notions from cognitive psychology such as cognitive load and schema acquisition.

An obstacle we faced in our work was the lack of an established evaluation methodology for studying the performance of the proposed techniques. Ensuring objectivity and consistency across judges in the user studies are some challenges to be addressed in designing a direct measurement. Discounting externality and removing bias are some challenges to be addressed in designing an indirect measurement such as comparison of performance scores of students using good and bad versions of the same book. Designing sound evaluation methodology is fodder for rich future research.

6. REFERENCES

[1] R. Agrawal, S. Chakraborty, S. Gollapudi, A. Kannan, and K. Kenthapadi. Quality of textbooks: An empirical study. In *ACM DEV*, 2012.

[2] R. Agrawal, S. Gollapudi, A. Kannan, and K. Kenthapadi. Identifying enrichment candidates in textbooks. In *WWW*, 2011.

[3] R. Agrawal, S. Gollapudi, K. Kenthapadi, N. Srivastava, and R. Velu. Enriching textbooks through data mining. In *ACM DEV*, 2010.

[4] B. B. Armbruster and T. H. Anderson. Content area textbooks. Technical report, Reading Education Report No. 23, BBN, 1981.

[5] B. B. Armbruster and T. H. Anderson. Producing considerate expository text: Or easy reading is damned hard writing. Technical report, Reading Education Report No. 46, BBN, 1984.

[6] B. K. Britton, A. Woodward, and M. R. Binkley. *Learning from Textbooks: Theory and Practice.* Routledge, 1993.

[7] B. Bruce, A. Rubin, and K. Starr. Why readability formulas fail. *IEEE Transactions on Professional Communication*, PC-24, 1981.

[8] M. Chambliss and R. Calfee. *Textbooks for Learning: Nurturing Children's Minds.* Wiley-Blackwell, 1998.

[9] R. Clark, F. Nguyen, and J. Sweller. *Efficiency in learning: Evidence-based guidelines to manage cognitive load.* Pfeiffer, 2006.

[10] K. Collins-Thompson and J. P. Callan. A language modeling approach to predicting reading difficulty. In *HLT-NAACL*, 2004.

[11] E. K. Dishner. *Reading in the Content Areas: Improving Classroom Instruction.* Kendall/Hunt, 1992.

[12] W. DuBay. *The principles of readability.* Impact Information, 2004.

[13] C. Fellbaum. *WordNet: An electronic lexical database.* MIT Press, 1998.

[14] J. Gillies and J. Quijada. Opportunity to learn: A high impact strategy for improving educational outcomes in developing countries. *USAID Educational Quality Improvement Program (EQUIP2)*, 2008.

[15] S. R. Goldman. Learning from text: Reflections on the past and suggestions for the future. *Discourse Processes*, 23, 1997.

[16] W. Gray and B. Leary. *What makes a book readable.* University of Chicago Press, 1935.

[17] B. Grosz and C. Sidner. Attention, intentions, and the structure of discourse. *Computational linguistics*, 12(3), 1986.

[18] R. Guillemette. Predicting readability of data processing written materials. *ACM SIGMIS Database*, 18(4), 1987.

[19] E. A. Hanushek and L. Woessmann. The role of education quality for economic growth. *Policy Research Department Working Paper 4122, World Bank*, 2007.

[20] E. B. Johnsen. *Textbooks in the Kaleidoscope: A Critical Survey of Literature and Research on Educational Texts.* Scandinavian University Press, 1992.

[21] J. S. Justeson and S. M. Katz. Technical terminology: Some linguistic properties and an algorithm for indentification in text. *Natural Language Engineering*, 1(1), 1995.

[22] R. Kate, X. Luo, S. Patwardhan, M. Franz, R. Florian, R. Mooney, S. Roukos, and C. Welty. Learning to predict readability using diverse linguistic features. In *COLING*, 2010.

[23] D. Kieras and C. Dechert. Rules for comprehensible technical prose: A survey of the psycholinguistic literature. Technical Report TR-85/ONR-21, University of Michigan, 1985.

[24] B. Lively and S. Pressey. A method for measuring the vocabulary burden of textbooks. *Educational Administration and Supervision*, 9(73), 1923.

[25] D. Marcu. *The theory and practice of discourse parsing and summarization.* MIT Press, 2000.

[26] F. Paas, A. Renkl, and J. Sweller. Cognitive load theory and instructional design: Recent developments. *Educational Psychologist*, 38(1), 2003.

[27] J. M. Pawlowski, K. C. Barker, and T. Okamoto. Quality research for learning, education, and training. *Reading & Writing Quarterly*, 10(2), 2007.

[28] J. Plass, R. Moreno, and R. Brünken. *Cognitive load theory.* Cambridge University Press, 2010.

[29] L. Polanyi and R. Scha. A syntactic approach to discourse semantics. In *COLING*, 1984.

[30] E. Pollock, P. Chandler, and J. Sweller. Assimilating complex information. *Learning and Instruction*, 12(1), 2002.

[31] R. Seguin. The elaboration of school textbooks. Technical report, ED-90/WS-24, UNESCO, 1989.

[32] L. Sherman. *Analytics of literature: A manual for the objective study of English prose and poetry.* Ginn and Company, 1893.

[33] S. A. Thompson and W. C. Mann. Rhetorical structure theory: A framework for the analysis of texts. *IPRA Papers in Pragmatics*, 1(1), 1987.

[34] K. Toutanova, D. Klein, C. D. Manning, and Y. Singer. Feature-rich part-of-speech tagging with a cyclic dependency network. In *NAACL-HLT*, 2003.

[35] H. Tyson-Bernstein. A conspiracy of good intentions: America's textbook fiasco. Technical report, Council for Basic Education, Washington, 1989.

[36] A. Verspoor and K. B. Wu. Textbooks and educational development. Technical report, World Bank, 1990.

[37] K. Wang, C. Thrasher, E. Viegas, X. Li, and P. Hsu. An overview of Microsoft Web N-gram corpus and applications. In *NAACL-HLT*, 2010.

[38] A. N. Whitehead. The organisation of thought. *Proceedings of the Aristotelian Society*, 17, 1916–17.

[39] S. Witte and L. Faigley. Coherence, cohesion, and writing quality. *College Composition and Communication*, 32(2), 1981.

[40] A. Woodward, D. L. Elliott, and C. Nagel. *Textbooks in School and Society: An Annotated Bibliography and Guide to Research.* Garland, 1988.

[41] World-Bank. *Knowledge for Development: World Development Report: 1998/99.* Oxford University Press, 1999.

[42] J. Zhao and M. Kan. Domain-specific iterative readability computation. In *ACM JCDL*, 2010.

Coupled Behavior Analysis for Capturing Coupling Relationships in Group-based Market Manipulations

Yin Song*
Faculty of Engineering and IT,
University of Technology,
Sydney

Longbing Cao
Faculty of Engineering and IT,
University of Technology,
Sydney
longbing.cao@uts.edu.au

Xindong Wu†
Hefei University of Technology,
China;
University of Vermont,
Burlington

Gang Wei
Department of Research
Centre,
Shanghai Stock Exchange
weigang@sse.com.cn

Wu Ye
Department of Research
Centre,
Shanghai Stock Exchange
yewu@sse.com.cn

Wei Ding
Department of Computer
Science, University of
Massachusetts Boston
ding@cs.umb.edu

ABSTRACT

In stock markets, an emerging challenge for surveillance is that a group of hidden manipulators collaborate with each other to manipulate the price movement of securities. Recently, the coupled hidden Markov model (CHMM)-based *coupled behavior analysis* (CBA) has been proposed to consider the coupling relationships in the above group-based behaviors for manipulation detection. From the modeling perspective, however, this requires overall aggregation of the behavioral data to cater for the CHMM modeling, which does not differentiate the coupling relationships presented in different forms within the aggregated behaviors and degrade the capability for further anomaly detection. Thus, this paper suggests a general CBA framework for detecting *group-based market manipulation* by capturing more comprehensive couplings and proposes two variant implementations, which are *hybrid coupling* (HC)-based and *hierarchical grouping* (HG)-based respectively. The proposed framework consists of three stages. The first stage, *qualitative* analysis, generates possible qualitative coupling relationships between behaviors with or without domain knowledge. In the second stage, *quantitative* representation of coupled behaviors is learned via proper methods. For the third stage, anomaly detection algorithms are proposed to cater for different application scenarios. Experimental results on data from a major Asian stock market show that the proposed framework outperforms the CHMM-based analysis in terms of detecting abnormal collaborative market manipulations. Additionally, the two different implementations are compared with their effectiveness for different application scenarios.

*Email: yin.song@student.uts.edu.au.
†Corresponding author (xwu@uvm.edu).

KDD'12, August 12–16, 2012, Beijing, China.

Categories and Subject Descriptors

H.2.8 [**Information Systems**]: Database applications—*Data Mining*

General Terms

Algorithms, Economics, Security

Keywords

Coupled behavior analysis, anomaly detection, market manipulation, coupled hidden Markov model, hierarchical clustering, relational learning

1. INTRODUCTION

For many decades, human behavior analysis has been extensively investigated in many fields, such as social and behavioral sciences [5, 13] and computer science [10]. For simplicity, 'behavior' in this paper is used as a synonym of 'human behavior', which refers to an action from a human and usually interacts with behaviors of his/her own and of other actors [3]. 'Coupled' in this paper refers to actors and their behaviors having certain relationships which are not independent. The interactions within an actor are referred to as intra-coupled relationships (interchangeable with 'intra-couplings') while inter-coupled relationships (interchangeable with 'inter-couplings') are between behaviors of different actors [3]. Taking the couplings into account is critical for a deep understanding of group behaviors in many real-life scenarios. For instance, in stock markets, investors' trading behaviors are not isolated but affected by each other, which is caused by the supply-and-demand nature of the markets. Most of existing research efforts on behavior studies, however, focus mainly on individual behaviors [4]. A comprehensive analysis of intra and inter-coupled relationships is beyond current individual behavior analysis techniques, to the best of our knowledge. In addition, the intra- and inter- couplings between behaviors are usually implicit or hidden, making it even more challenging to define, model and analyze the coupling relationships among behaviors in a group.

One useful application of considering these intra and inter-couplings is to detect abnormal coupled behaviors in stock markets [4]. As mentioned before, the behaviors of investors are inherently coupled with each other. Meanwhile, on some trading days, some investors (termed as 'manipulators') may intentionally arrange trading behaviors for the purpose of exceptionally high profit, which is not allowed by the corresponding regulations and could bring great losses to other investors. Any financial market regulators are keen to effectively detect these coupled trading behaviors and discover such manipulations. As initial attempts for this purpose, the CHMM-based CBA [4] suggests a method to implicitly represent the couplings in statistical models, such as CHMM [2]. It regards all the actors as a whole group, aggregates their behaviors for each time interval and analyzes the aggregated behaviors based on a CHMM. This is feasible to some extent but has some limitations: e.g., segmentation and aggregation of the behaviors may lose important coupling information within these aggregated behaviors, which may further deteriorate the performance of anomaly detection. In other words, capturing richer couplings for coupled behavior analysis may enhance the capability of detecting manipulations. Motivated by this, this paper proposes a general CBA framework to capture richer coupling relationships between behaviors, which is further used to detect anomalies in group-based behaviors. By capturing more comprehensive couplings between the behaviors, better anomaly detection performance is expected.

The main contributions of this paper are summarized as follows.

- We extend the group-based CBA to a general framework to cater for more flexible and comprehensive analysis of coupled behaviors, which is expected to have better capability to detect abnormal behaviors. To achieve this, two stages: *qualitative* analysis (for reducing the possible coupled relationships space) and *quantitative* analysis (for proper numerical modeling of the couplings) are proposed to efficiently model the underlying rich coupling relationships in the behaviors.

- Two variant implementation approaches are proposed to model more comprehensive couplings. One is data-driven, which learns the coupled relationships directly from the data and the other is domain-driven, which integrates some domain knowledge for learning the couplings. These two approaches are useful for different application scenarios when domain knowledge is unavailable or available.

- The proposed framework has been tested on a real-world data set from a major Asian stock market to detect collaborative manipulations in stock markets, covering around 550,000 tick-based transactions on 388 valid trading days. We test different technical significance of the identified suspicious manipulations against the benchmark of miscellaneous alerts fired on the real-time transactions. The results show the advantages of our proposed framework compared to the previous CHMM-based framework. More specifically, the two proposed approaches are compared to reach the conclusion that they are superior to the CHMM-based CBA framework in different application settings.

The remainder of this paper is organized as follows. Section 2 describes the proposed general CBA framework. Then the hybrid coupling-based implementation of the proposed framework is described in Section 3, when assuming there is no domain knowledge of the coupling relationships. Section 4 describes another variant of the proposed framework based on a hierarchical grouping representation, when some domain knowledge is available. Section 5 reports the experimental results while conclusions are drawn and future work is discussed in Section 6.

2. CBA FOR GROUP-BASED MANIPULATION DETECTION

The proposed framework consists of three key stages: *qualitative* analysis, which converts the transactional data to proper representations and provides a flexible coupling structure for the next-stage quantitative coupling relationships modeling; *quantitative* analysis, which characterizes the coupled behaviors by learning the corresponding model and is helpful for further analysis; and anomaly detection, which is the final stage of checking whether or not the new coupled behaviors are abnormal. The following sections describe how the proposed framework works, which is depicted in Figure 1.

2.1 Qualitative Analysis

Here we first briefly review the concept of *coupled behaviors*. Suppose there are I actors, and an actor i undertakes m_i behaviors $\mathbf{b_{i1}}, \mathbf{b_{i2}}, \cdots, \mathbf{b_{im_i}}$. Each actor i's j^{th} behavior $\mathbf{b_{ij}}$ is associated with a behavioral type $T(\mathbf{b_{ij}}) = t_{\mathbf{b_{ij}}}$ (e.g., buy, sell and trade.). Each behavioral type $t \in T$ has a number of associated properties $\mathbf{P^t} = (P_1^t, P_2^t, \cdots, P_n^t)$($n$ may vary for different t value). Thus, each behavior $\mathbf{b_{ij}}$ is associated with a set of behavioral property value (a vector) $(p_1^{t_{\mathbf{b_{ij}}}}, \cdots, p_n^{t_{\mathbf{b_{ij}}}})$ (e.g., price and volume) determined by its behavioral type $t_{\mathbf{b_{ij}}}$. A *behavior feature matrix* $FM(\mathbf{b})$ for all actors for a specific period of time can be then represented as follows [3]:

$$FM(\mathbf{b}) = \begin{pmatrix} \mathbf{b_{11}} & \mathbf{b_{11}} & \cdots & \mathbf{b_{1m_{max}}} \\ \mathbf{b_{21}} & \mathbf{b_{21}} & \cdots & \mathbf{b_{2m_{max}}} \\ \vdots & \vdots & \ddots & \vdots \\ \mathbf{b_{I1}} & \mathbf{b_{I1}} & \cdots & \mathbf{b_{Im_{max}}} \end{pmatrix}. \quad (1)$$

where $m_{\max} = \max\{m_1, m_2, \ldots, m_I\}$, and for each actor i, if $m_i < m_{\max}$ the corresponding element $b_{ij}(m_i < j \leq m_{\max})$ is defined as $\emptyset$, which means no action taken. Thus, the *intra-couplings* are reflected by the relationship between elements within one row of the above matrix, whereas the relationships between elements of different rows indicate the *inter-couplings*. Actor i's behaviors $\mathbf{b_{ij}}$ are intra-coupled with other behaviors of the same actor in terms of the corresponding function $\theta_k^i(\cdot)(1 < j \leq m_i, k \neq j)$ and inter-coupled with other actors' behaviors in terms of the corresponding function $\eta_k^i(\cdot)(1 < k \leq I, k \neq i)$, with non-determinism.

The behavior feature matrix defined in Equation 1 represents a group of behaviors that are coupled for analysis. To consider the coupled relationships, the space for analyzing the couplings of these behaviors is almost infinite. For a

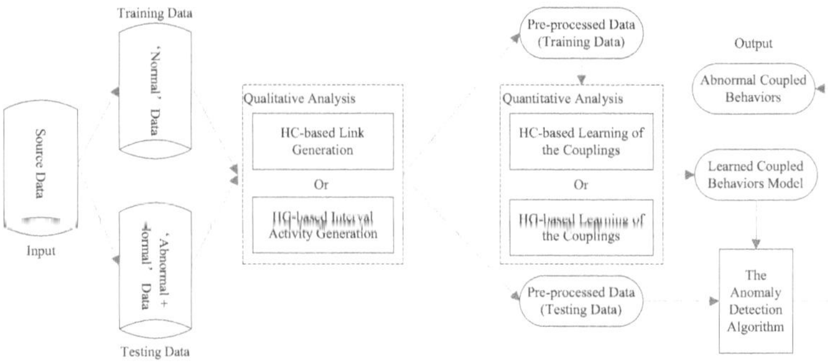

Figure 1: The Workflow of the Proposed Framework.

behavior $\mathbf{b_j}$ among n coupled behaviors, it can be coupled to any one of the remaining $n-1$ behaviors and the corresponding search space is $O(C_{n-1}^1) = O(n-1)$. Generally, if it is considered to be coupled to any k, $1 \leq k \leq n-1$, the possible search space can be $O(C_{n-1}^k) = O(\frac{(n-1)!}{k!\,(n-1-k)!})$. Thus, the sum of the above search space could be $O(2^{n-1})$, which means the computational complexity is exponential to the increase of the number of coupled behaviors. This is intractable when the number of coupled behaviors is large. To avoid this, the CHMM-based framework aggregates all the behaviors within time intervals and considers to model the couplings between these interval aggregated activities. The above approach may lose important coupling information within these aggregated behaviors, which may be useful for further anomaly detection. In this paper, to enrich the modeling capability of the CBA framework, we propose to integrate *qualitative* analysis into the CBA framework. To achieve this, two different strategies are designed, which are further discussed in Section 3 and Section 4. The former implementation is designed for the settings with no prior domain knowledge about the coupling relationships. Then we assume hybrid couplings exist between the behaviors, which means behaviors are associated with each other in a complicated structure of multiple different coupling relationships [3]. By contrast, when some domain knowledge is known about the couplings, the latter implementation is adopted. In this paper, we consider the hierarchical coupling structure [3], which means behaviors are coupled with each other in a hierarchical structure (determined by the corresponding grouping structure of the actors). All the above considerations are advantageous compared to the CHMM-framework because the possible coupled relationships we consider here are more comprehensive.

2.2 Quantitative Analysis

After the *qualitative* analysis of the coupled behaviors, the possible coupling relationships between behaviors are expanded and efficiently constrained, compared to the CHMM-based framework. Then how to quantitatively model the couplings becomes the key point and we solve it by modeling the autocorrelations that exist in coupled behaviors. More formally, for a set of coupled behaviors $\mathbf{b}$, there could be possible coupled relationships $(\theta(\cdot), \eta(\cdot))$; Then the autocorrelation for coupled behaviors with respect to one behavioral attribute P can be defined as follows:

DEFINITION 1 (COUPLED AUTOCORRELATION). *It measures the dependence among the values of a behavioral variable $P \in \mathbf{P^t}$ defined on the coupled behavior pairs $(\theta(\cdot), \eta(\cdot))$. Given a set of coupled behavior pairs $(\theta(\cdot), \eta(\cdot))$, the autocorrelation of a continuous variable can be calculated as:*

$$ca = \frac{\sum_{i_1,j_1,i_2,j_2 s.t.(b_{i_1j_1},b_{i_2j_2})\in(\theta(\cdot),\eta(\cdot))}(p_{i_1j_1}-\bar{P})(p_{i_2j_2}-\bar{P})}{\sum_{i s.t. i,j s.t. b_{ij}\in(\theta(\cdot),\eta(\cdot))}(p_{ij}-\bar{P})^2}$$

Motivated by the considerations of the coupled autocorrelations for *quantitative* analysis, different strategies are proposed for different variant CBA frameworks to efficiently consider these coupled autocorrelations for modeling the coupled behaviors.

2.3 Anomaly Detection Techniques

To determine whether the new coupled behaviors $\mathbf{b^k}$ are normal or abnormal, we choose to calculate the likelihood given the observations of the coupled behaviors based on the established normal model M. The higher the likelihood of the coupled behaviors $\mathbf{b^k}$, the more likely $\mathbf{b^k}$ conforms to be normal. The following two sections will describe two variant implementations for the general framework proposed in this section.

3. THE HC-BASED FRAMEWORK

When there is no prior knowledge of how the behaviors are coupled, to comprehensively capture the couplings with reasonable search space is challenging. In addition, to avoid the loss of coupling information of aggregating all the behaviors within time intervals, we alternatively consider the possible hybrid couplings within the behaviors. To achieve this, we use links to indicate possible coupled relationships that are suggested by some of the qualitative behavioral properties of the behaviors, which can be seen as *qualitative* analysis. This is advantageous compared to the CHMM-framework because we do not forcedly aggregate the behaviors within one time intervals and makes it possible to consider the couplings between them. Then the remaining behavioral properties can be defined as quantitative properties and used for learning the coupling relationships between the behaviors from the perspective of *quantitative* analysis. The formal definition of two such properties is as follows.

DEFINITION 2 (QUALITATIVE PROPERTY). *A qualitative property $R \in \mathbf{P}$ refers to the behavioral property which is used to generate the possible underlying coupling relationships between behaviors, usually user-defined.*

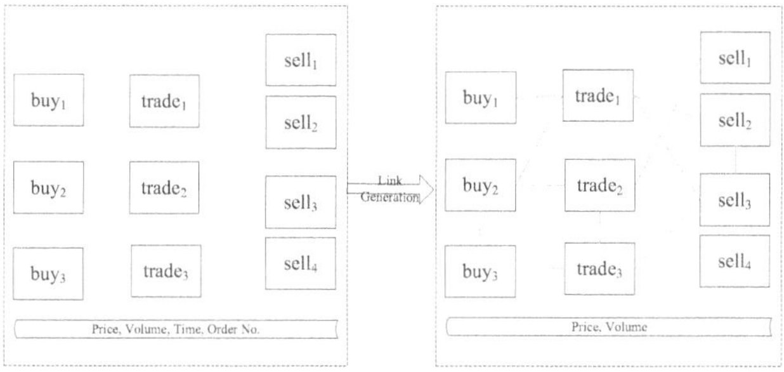

Figure 2: An Example of Qualitative Analysis.

DEFINITION 3 (QUANTITATIVE PROPERTY). *An quantitative property $A \in \mathbf{P}$ refers to the behavioral property which is used to learn the coupling relationships between behaviors.*

3.1 Qualitative Analysis: Link Generation

Based on the qualitative properties, Algorithm 1 describes the procedure to generate links according to the qualitative properties. In Algorithm 1, steps 2 to 8 form an inner loop process to generate links between behaviors which have the same values as the qualitative property and steps 1 to 9 form an outer loop process to generate the corresponding links for the behaviors according to every reference property. A toy example of the link generation process is shown in Figure 2, which transforms the raw behaviors[1] in the left to the linked behaviors in the right. To be more specific, in Figure 2, the behavioral properties of 'buy', 'sell' and 'trade' behaviors are: 'Price', 'Volume', 'Time' and 'Order No.'. The qualitative properties used are 'Time' and 'Order No.' while the quantitative properties used are 'Price' and 'Volume' after the link generation. Then a group of coupled behaviors can be represented by a typed attributed graph $G_B = (V_B, E_B)$. The nodes V_B represent behaviors (e.g., $buy_i(1 \leq i \leq 3)$, $sell_i(1 \leq i \leq 4)$ and $trade_i(1 \leq i \leq 3)$) and the edges E_B represent potential coupled relations among the behaviors (e.g., the edges in Figure 2).

Algorithm 1 The Link Generation Algorithm

Input: A Group of Behaviors $\{\mathbf{b_i}\}$,
A Set of Qualitative Properties $\{R_j\}$,
Output: A Set of Generated Links $\{l\}$.
1: $\{l\} \rightarrow \emptyset$
2: **for all** R_j in the set of qualitative properties **do**
3: **for all** values r_{jk} of the qualitative property R_j **do**
4: **if** exists $R_j^{b_m} == r_{jk}$ **then**
5: Add links $\{l_n\}$ between the behaviors $\{b_m\}$
6: $\{l\} \rightarrow \{l_n\} \cup \{l\}$
7: **end if**
8: **end for**
9: **end for**

3.2 Quantitative Analysis: Modeling Coupled Behaviors via Relational Learning

After obtaining the graph structure of the coupled behaviors, we explore the learning of couplings between the behaviors in a numerical form. For a *quantitative* model to describe the coupling relationships, we choose to learn the joint probability distribution of these behaviors' attributes considering their coupled autocorrelations. Exact learning of this joint probability is very computationally intensive and we adopt an approximate approach by learning a set of conditional prolixity distributions (CPDs) [12]. For each quantitative behavioral property $A \in \mathbf{A}$ we try to learn the probability distribution of its values conditioned on other possible coupled behaviors' behavioral attribute values (i.e., the CPD of A). Consequently, we approximate the joint probability distribution of the coupled behaviors with a set of CPDs. For this purpose, we introduce relational dependency network (RDN) [12], to model the joint probability distribution of the coupled behaviors since its key idea is based on a set of CPDs.

[1]Each behavior here refers to a transaction record.

3.2.1 Approximating the Joint Probability Distribution

The RDN learning algorithm uses pseudo-likelihood techniques [12] to efficiently approximate the joint probability distribution. Unlike relational Bayesian network (RBN) [8] and relational Markov network (RMN) [14], it learns conditional distributions independently, rather than jointly, using local conditional probability models, such as Relational Bayesian Classifiers (RBCs). For example, considering the coupled behaviors in Figure 2, for each behavioral property of these coupled behaviors, the RDN learns a CPD model and obtain a set of CPD models. The joint probability distribution model is formed by the integration of these models, which becomes the quantitative model of coupled behaviors. The next section describes how to learn these CPDs.

3.2.2 Modeling of the CPDs

In consequence, in order to model the coupled behaviors, we could estimate a set of the CPDs of the quantitative behavioral properties conditioned on other possible coupled behaviors' behavioral attribute values, and underline which coupled autocorrelations between behaviors are considered. To learn the CPD is challenging because of two issues: each quantitative behavioral attribute instance could be conditioned on different linked behaviors' behavioral property values (e.g., heterogeneous structure of links and various behavioral property types) and the linked behaviors to consider could be limitless. To cater for the second issue, we must determine how much should be modeled for the CPD of each quantitative behavioral attribute instance. For computational simplicity, we may only consider two related behavior links from the target behaviors for modeling the CPD. The whole graph can then be decomposed into subgraphs according to each quantitative behavior property and this could be done by the visual query language QGraph [1]. A toy example can be seen in Figure 3(a) and the quantitative behavioral property A is one of the property of 'trade' behaviors ($trade_1$ and $trade_2$ in Figure 2). Then $trade_1$ and $trade_2$ are transformed to two subgraphs with consideration of coupled behaviors 1-link away (we could consider n-link ($n \geq 1$), but we only depict the 1-link situation for simplicity).

After that, the aforementioned first issue can be solved by "flatten" the subgraphs into propositional instances consisting of relational features $RF_1, RF_2, \cdots, RF_n$ and the quantitative behavioral property A. Here we choose RBCs to generate the relational features for simplicity and efficiency.

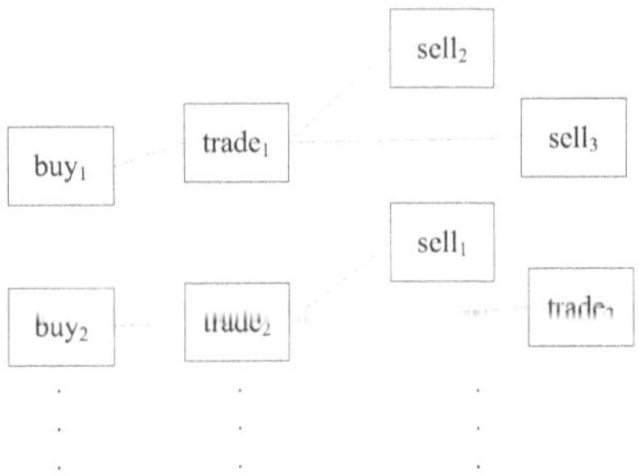

(a) An Example of the Subgraphs for Coupled Behaviors

	A	RF_1	RF_2	$\cdots$	RF_n
$trade_1$	x_1	rf_{11}	rf_{21}	$\cdots$	rf_{n1}
$trade_2$	x_2	rf_{12}	rf_{22}	$\cdots$	rf_{n2}
$\vdots$	$\vdots$	$\vdots$	$\vdots$	$\vdots$	$\vdots$

(b) An Example of the Relational Features for Coupled Behaviors

Figure 3: An Example of the "Flattened" Propositional Coupled Behavioral Data

The relational features for one quantitative behavioral attribute are the linked behaviors' attributes and each attribute contains multiple sets of values within the subgraph; for example, considering the quantitative property A of the 'trade' behaviors as in Figure 3. The RBC considers all the attributes associated with the linked behaviors 'buy', 'sell' and 'trade' and treats them as independent relational features $RF_1, \cdots, RF_n$. For any specific instance of RF_i $(1 \leq i \leq n)$, for example rf_{i1} is a multi-set of values $rf_{i11}, \cdots, rf_{i1m}$ and these values are assumed to be independently drawn from $p(RF_1|A)$. Then $p(RF_1|A)$ can be estimated by counting the frequency of the values in all the multi-set instances of RF_1 and similar estimation can be done on $p(RF_2|A), \cdots, p(RF_n|A)$. The CPD $p(A|RF_1, \cdots, RF_n)$ can be estimated as

$$\alpha p(A)p(RF_1|A)p(RF_2|A)\cdots p(RF_n|A) \quad (2)$$

where α is the normalized constant [12]. For example, with respect to the quantitative property A, the coupled behaviors in Figure 3(a) can be transformed into Table 3(b) by generating the relational features $RF_1, \cdots, RF_n$. CPD_A for A then becomes $p(A|RF_1, RF_2, \cdots, RF_n)$ and the joint probability distribution of coupled behaviors becomes $p(\mathbf{b}) = \prod_{A \in \mathbf{A}} CPD_A$, which model the coupled behaviors.

3.3 Efficient Abnormal Coupled Behavior Detection

Training on a set of coupled behaviors ($\{\mathbf{b^i}\}$) is computationally intensive and the coupling relationships in some $\{\mathbf{b^i}\}$ may be similar. Thus, in order to relief the computational complexity and modeling efficiency, we propose a match pursuit [11] like algorithm to only pick up a subset of coupled behaviors to model.

Matching pursuit [11] is a type of numerical technique widely used in signal processing. Informally speaking, the basic idea is to find the best representation of a signal using a subset of elements provided by a dictionary D. Similarly, our aim is to find the best representation of a subset of coupled behaviors among all groups of coupled behaviors. As described in Algorithm 2, step 1 initializes the dictionary D to all the set of training coupled behaviors. Then steps 2 to 11 choose the most representative groups of coupled behaviors and train a set of models $M_i (1 \leq i \leq n)$. Finally, steps 12 to 20 detect the anomaly based on the set of models. The training computational complexity is very intensive when the number of coupled behaviors increase and our proposed algorithm efficiently choose a small set of representative ones, which improves the efficiency of the learning process.

Algorithm 2 Matching Pursuit-like Anomaly Detection

Input: A Training set $\{\mathbf{b^i}\}$ $(1 \leq i \leq N)$,
A Testing set $\{\mathbf{b^k}\}$ $(1 \leq k \leq M)$,
Two Threshold Th_0, Th_1.
Output: An anomaly set $\mathcal{A}$.
1: $n \leftarrow 1$,
$D \leftarrow \{\mathbf{b^1}, \mathbf{b^2}, \cdots, \mathbf{b^N}\}$
2: **repeat**
3: Train one M_n model on the first training sample (sorted by temporal attributes, such as date.) chosen from D.
4: **for all** $\mathbf{b^d}$ $(1 \leq d \leq N)$ in D **do**
5: Compute the likelihood of $\mathbf{b^d}$ given the model M_n: $p(\mathbf{b^d}|M_n)$.
6: **if** $p(\mathbf{b^d}|M_n) > Th_1$ **then**
7: Delete $\mathbf{b^d}$ from D
8: **end if**
9: **end for**
10: $n \leftarrow n + 1$
11: **until** stop condition (e.g., $D = \emptyset$)
12: **for all** $\mathbf{b^k}$ in the Testing set **do**
13: **for** $i = 1 \rightarrow n$ **do**
14: Compute the likelihood of $\mathbf{b^k}$ given the model M_i: $p(\mathbf{b^k}|M_i)$
15: **end for**
16: $D_k = \max\{p(\mathbf{b^k}|M_i)\}$ $(1 \leq i \leq n)$
17: **if** $D_k < Th_0$ **then**
18: $\mathbf{b^k} \rightarrow \mathcal{A}$
19: **end if**
20: **end for**

4. THE HIERARCHICAL GROUPING-BASED FRAMEWORK

Sometimes, some prior domain knowledge is known about the possible coupling relationships among behaviors of some investors. This provides a possible method to explore couplings between behaviors of actors within certain subgroups (at a local level), rather than taking the whole population as a group (at a global level). Such analysis of behaviors is crucial for capturing more comprehensive couplings existing in behaviors, which may be helpful to further detecting abnormal coupled behaviors. As mentioned before, the CHMM-based CBA framework may fail to explore some detailed information of the couplings between behaviors, due to the aggregation of all the actors' behaviors, which makes the modeling relatively coarse and in turn may render it less capable to detect abnormal coupled behaviors. For this purpose, with the presence of some useful domain knowledge, we propose the corresponding hierarchical grouping-based CBA framework below.

The *qualitative* analysis stage is to partition the whole investor population according to prior domain knowledge so that the couplings between the behaviors in the resultant sub-groups will be modeled more precisely. We define these groups as 'Particle Groups'. Performing CBA on behaviors of these particle groups can lead to more precise modeling of local interaction characteristics within local groups than directly on the global population. However, dividing actors into particle groups only cater for the couplings between behaviors within each particle group, it does not necessarily consider the couplings between behaviors from different particle groups. To cater for between-group couplings, we further propose a hierarchical clustering-based algorithm to merge those relevant particle groups into larger groups until finally into one super-group. Through this manner, the couplings between behaviors from different particle groups are expected to be captured. Then in the *quantitative* analysis stage, the coupled relationships in different group levels are also modeled. This hierarchical grouping strategy captures behavior interactions at different group levels, therefore is more effective to capture the more comprehensive couplings within the coupled behaviors, which makes it possible for detecting abnormal couplings more accurately. In the next sections, we illustrate the details of this variant framework for the general CBA.

4.1 Qualitative Analysis: Domain Knowledge-driven Initial Grouping

In stock markets, investors may be intentionally or unintentionally grouped. Based on domain knowledge, stock market surveillance experts often create rules according to their judgement and group investors who are likely to cooperate to have manipulative behaviors. As a result, an empirical blacklist is often generated for further monitoring. Such domain knowledge is very helpful for our initial understanding of investors grouping. We model the normal couplings in each group of investor behaviors, and build initial corresponding particle groups. This initial grouping of the investors aims to divide them into small particle groups so that the most likely coupled investors form into particle groups with similar coupled relationships. We define the result of these groups as particle groups.

DEFINITION 4 (PARTICLE GROUPS). *The particle groups, which are represented by* $\{PG_j\}$ $(1 \le j \le N)$ *are the partitioning result of actors* $\{A_i\}$ $(1 \le i \le I)$ *by the rule* $R(\cdot)$ *made by domain experts:*

$$R(\cdot)|\{A_1, A_2, \cdots, A_I\} \rightarrow \{PG_1, PG_2, \cdots, PG_N\}. \quad (3)$$

This *qualitative* analysis stage is domain knowledge driven and any useful information related to investors can be utilized to group the investors. In this paper, except for trading record data, there is no additional information available about the investors. Domain knowledge experts advise us to consider the average ordering/trading volume of a trading day for each investor as an initial grouping rule. Based on such information and related domain knowledge, investors are grouped as if they have similar ordering/trading volume of a security. Because the abnormal collaborative behaviors are more likely to happen in these predefined groups, it is reasonable to model the normal couplings within the groups and use the model to check the anomaly. By dividing the actors into particle groups and performing CBA on them separately, we can avoid the influence of roughly analyzing all the investors as a whole group, which may weaken the performance of the modeling. According to [4], we can convert the behavioral data for each particle group into three behavioral sequences, the 'buy', 'sell' and 'trade' sequence, in terms of the trading behavior types. For a particle group, we can transfer the trading records related to them into three coupled sequences. Further, in order to fit the behavior sequences to CHMM observation sequences for modeling, we also convert them to interval activities to reflect the characteristic of behaviors within the particle group during a period, similar to [4]. This makes modeling the couplings within these particle groups possible. However, this mechanism of dividing actors into particle groups can only describe the couplings between behaviors within each particle group, while it may omit the couplings between behaviors from different particle groups.

To overcome this, we not only model the behavioral couplings within particle groups but also merge the particle groups into larger groups and consider the coupled relationships in different group levels. To do this, we further define the distance/similarity measure based on the coupling patterns of the two particle groups. Because of the variety and dynamics of coupled behaviors, we merge those groups having most similar coupling patterns first and then join the remaining groups progressively into a super hierarchical group, within which there are many different levels of groups. Through this way, the coupled relationships between the behaviors are hopefully captured in a finer granularity. The detailed definition for the similarity measure for coupling patterns is discussed in the following. Each CHMM represents the corresponding coupling pattern for behaviors in each particle group, our proposed similarity measure is based on the distance/similarity between two CHMMs. Inspired by [7], we put forward a novel similarity measure based on the Kullback-Leibler (KL) divergence [9, 6], which is a standard measure for the similarity between probability density functions. To be more specific, for two particle groups i and j, represented by λ_i and λ_j respectively, there are corresponding interval activities sets $\{\mathbf{b}_{\mathbf{IA}}^{\mathbf{n,i}}\}$ $(1 \le n \le N)$ and $\{\mathbf{b}_{\mathbf{IA}}^{\mathbf{n,j}}\}$ $(1 \le n \le N)$, where N is the number of the trading days. The likelihood of the behaviors $\mathbf{b}_{\mathbf{IA}}^{\mathbf{n,i}}$ under λ_j is denoted as ξ_{ij}^n. For all the coupled behaviors in the set $\{\mathbf{b}_{\mathbf{IA}}^{\mathbf{n,i}}\}$, we obtain a likelihood subspace $\xi_{ij} = \{\xi_{ij}^1, \xi_{ij}^2, \ldots, \xi_{ij}^N\}$, which are "intelligently" sampled points from the model space representing the fitness of the coupled behaviors set to the CHMM λ_j. Similarly, we obtain $\xi_{ii} = \{\xi_{ii}^1, \xi_{ii}^2, \ldots, \xi_{ii}^N\}$ to denote the fitness of the coupled behaviors set $\{\mathbf{b}_{\mathbf{IA}}^{\mathbf{n,i}}\}$ to the CHMM λ_i. If we normalize ξ_{ij} and ξ_{ii}, the corresponding probability density functions $f_{\xi_{ij}}$ and $f_{\xi_{ii}}$ can be obtained. Then, the distance/similarity between two set of coupled behaviors is converted to the similarity measure between probability density functions, for which the KL divergence is a suitable choice. Its formulation for the discrete case is as follows:

$$D_{KL}(f_{\xi_{ii}}|f_{\xi_{ij}}) = \sum_n f_{\xi_{ii}}(n) \log \frac{f_{\xi_{ii}}(n)}{f_{\xi_{ij}}(n)} \quad (4)$$

In the same way, $D_{KL}(f_{\xi_{jj}}|f_{\xi_{ji}})$ reflects the similarity between the CHMMs λ_i and λ_j from the angle of the coupled behaviors set $\{\mathbf{b}_{\mathbf{IA}}^{\mathbf{n,j}}\}$. Finally, the symmetric distance between the coupled behaviors of two particle groups of λ_i and λ_j is defined as:

$$D_{KL}(\lambda_i|\lambda_j) = \frac{1}{2}[D_{KL}(f_{\xi_{ii}}|f_{\xi_{ij}}) + D_{KL}(f_{\xi_{jj}}|f_{\xi_{ji}})] \quad (5)$$

By calculating the similarities between particle groups, hierarchical clustering [15] is used on the basis of the similarity matrix to reveal the coupling structure in a hierarchical way, which is expected to make a full-scale modeling and can reflect different levels of couplings between behaviors.

4.2 Quantitative Analysis: Hierarchical Modeling of Coupled Behaviors

After the qualitative analysis of hierarchically grouping the investors and their corresponding behaviors. For the coupled behaviors of each group in different levels, we can learn the corresponding CHMM (for further details, please refer to [4, 3]). Then these CHMMs are the quantitative models that capture the couplings between the behaviors and provide helpful information for further anomaly detection.

4.3 The Anomaly Detection Algorithm

After hierarchically grouping (HG) of all the investors and quantitatively modeling their coupled behaviors in multi-level groups, we are also able to detect the abnormal coupled behaviors. Algorithm 3 illustrates the process.

Algorithm 3 The Anomaly Detection Algorithm of HG-based CBA

Input: A Training set $\{\mathbf{b^i}\}$ $(1 \le i \le N)$,
A Testing set $\{\mathbf{b^k}\}$ $(1 \le k \le M)$,
An Initial Grouping $\{PG_l\}$,
A Threshold Tho.
Output: An anomaly set $\mathcal{A}$.

for all Particle group PG_l in the Training set **do**
  Construct its interval activity behavioral sequences $\{\mathbf{b_{IA}^{1,PG_l}}, \mathbf{b_{IA}^{2,PG_l}}, \cdots, \mathbf{b_{IA}^{N,PG_l}}\}$.
end for
Hierarchically cluster the Particle group $\{PG_l\}$ and generate a hierarchical grouping $\{G_{l'}\}$;
for all Groups $\{G_{l'}\}$ in the Training set **do**
  Train the corresponding CHMM $\lambda_{G_{l'}}$ for each group's behaviors $\{\mathbf{b_{IA}^{1,G_{l'}}}, \mathbf{b_{IA}^{2,G_{l'}}}, \cdots, \mathbf{b_{IA}^{N,G_{l'}}}\}$.
end for
for all Groups $\{G_{l'}\}$ in the Testing set **do**
  Construct its interval activity behavioral sequences $\{\mathbf{b_{IA}^{1,G_{l'}}}, \mathbf{b_{IA}^{2,G_{l'}}}, \cdots, \mathbf{b_{IA}^{M,G_{l'}}}\}$
  Calculate their likelihood $p(\mathbf{b_{IA}^{k,G_{l'}}}|\lambda_{G_{l'}})$ given the corresponding model.
end for
for all Trading day k in the testing set, **do**
  we choose $L_k = \arg\min_{l}\{p(\mathbf{b_{IA}^{k,G_{l'}}}|\lambda_{G_{l'}})\}$
  if $L_k < Tho$ **then**
    $\mathbf{b^k} \rightarrow \mathcal{A}$
  end if
end for

5. EXPERIMENTS

5.1 Experimental Data

Our algorithms are tested on a real data set from a major Asian stock exchange. The tick data covers 388 valid trading days from 1 June 2004 to 31 December 2005. It consists of 58333 traders, and 174416 buy orders, 178464 sell orders, and 109140 trades. The data is partitioned into two sets suggested by domain experts. The training data set is extracted from the transactions from 1 June 2004 to 31 December 2004 and those transactions associated with the identified alerts is filtered. Models are trained on such labeled normal data to capture the characteristics in so-called 'normal' coupled trading behaviors. The test set consists of the remaining transactional data and is made up of both normal and abnormal coupled trading behaviors. For evaluating the performance of the proposed approaches, true positive TP, true negative TN, false positive FP and false negative FN are counted in terms of treating the abnormal cases as the positive class. Then four generally accepted measures, accuracy $(\frac{TP+TN}{TP+FN+FP+TN})$, precision $(\frac{TP}{TP+FP})$, recall $(\frac{TP}{TP+FN})$, and specificity $(\frac{TN}{FP+TN})$ are adopted as the technical performance measures.

5.2 The Performance of the HC-based Framework

We tested the HC-based CBA framework using the RDN model (denoted as 'CBA-RDN') on the test data set and compared it to the CHMM-based CBA framework (denoted as 'CBA-CHMM')[2]. Figure 4 shows the technical performance. We vary the threshold Tho in Algorithm 2 for detecting different numbers of anomalies and compare the corresponding performance for both the algorithms. By doing this, we expect to provide a comprehensive comparison without considering the influence of the threshold. The horizontal axis (P-Num) stands for the number of detected group-based abnormal behaviors (i.e., the number of trading days with abnormal coupled behaviors), and the vertical axis represents the values of technical measures (accuracy, precision, recall or specificity). Figure 4 shows the four technical measures of the HC-based and CHMM-based CBA frameworks. Generally speaking, the former performs better than the latter in terms of all the metrics. For instance, the precision[3] of the CBA-RDN framework of $P - num = 45$ is 0.38 while that of the CBA-HMM framework is 0.28, which improves the precision of 35% higher than that of the CHMM-based framework. With respect to other measures, the CBA-RDN has better results as well, which proves that the HC-based CBA framework can characterize the coupled behaviors with more comprehensive information than the CHMM-based framework. This may lead to better anomaly detection performance to some extent.

5.3 The Performance of the HG-based Framework

For the HG-based framework, here we study seven variant strategies for detecting abnormal coupled behaviors.

- CBA-CHMM: The behaviors of all the investors are collected together to construct corresponding coupled

[2]The performance results are the averaged values of different time sliding windows [4].

[3]The precision looks very low, since we use the alerts from the market surveillance system as the benchmark, which is known with high overall false positive rate.

Models \ P-Num	45	46	47	48	49	50	51	52	53	54	55	56	57	58	59	60
CBA-RDN	0.88	0.88	0.88	0.87	0.87	0.87	0.86	0.86	0.86	0.85	0.85	0.85	0.84	0.84	0.84	0.83
CBA-CHMM	0.85	0.85	0.85	0.85	0.84	0.84	0.84	0.84	0.83	0.83	0.82	0.82	0.81	0.81	0.81	0.80

(a) Accuracy

Models \ P-Num	45	46	47	48	49	50	51	52	53	54	55	56	57	58	59	60
CBA-RDN	0.38	0.39	0.38	0.37	0.36	0.36	0.35	0.34	0.34	0.33	0.33	0.32	0.31	0.31	0.30	0.29
CBA-CHMM	0.28	0.28	0.28	0.28	0.27	0.26	0.26	0.26	0.26	0.25	0.24	0.24	0.23	0.23	0.23	0.22

(b) Precision

Models \ P-Num	45	46	47	48	49	50	51	52	53	54	55	56	57	58	59	60
CBA-RDN	0.92	0.91	0.91	0.90	0.90	0.90	0.89	0.89	0.88	0.88	0.88	0.87	0.87	0.86	0.86	0.85
CBA-CHMM	0.90	0.90	0.89	0.89	0.89	0.88	0.88	0.87	0.87	0.87	0.86	0.86	0.85	0.85	0.84	0.84

(c) Specificity

Models \ P-Num	45	46	47	48	49	50	51	52	53	54	55	56	57	58	59	60
CBA-RDN	0.52	0.55	0.56	0.56	0.56	0.57	0.58	0.58	0.58	0.58	0.59	0.59	0.59	0.60	0.60	0.60
CBA-CHMM	0.39	0.40	0.41	0.42	0.42	0.42	0.43	0.44	0.44	0.44	0.44	0.44	0.44	0.44	0.45	0.45

(d) Recall

Figure 4: Technical Performance of the Two Frameworks

behavior sequences and a CHMM is trained to represent the characteristics of the group-based coupled behaviors.

- CBA-PG, CBA-PG3: The investors are divided into different particle groups based on different predefined domain knowledge and then their behaviors are analyzed separately for each particle group. A set of CHMMs are trained for each particle group.
- CBA-PG2: The investors are randomly divided into different particle groups. The other processing is the same as that of CBA-PG and CBA-PG3.
- CBA-HG, CBA-HG3: On top of the CBA-PG and CBA-PG3 respectively, the proposed hierarchical clustering method is adopted to provide a comprehensive profile of the investors' behaviors. Consequently, the behaviors are analyzed in different scales and the corresponding CHMMs for each group is set up, which is expected for more accurate analysis of anomalies.
- CBA-HG2: On the basis of CBA-PG2, particle groups are randomly merged into a hierarchical grouping structure. The other parts of processing are the same as CBA-HG and CBA-HG3.

We tested the above seven strategies on the test dataset by setting various window sizes (*winsize*) and the results reported here are the averaged ones over different window sizes. Figure 5 shows their technical performance. The horizontal axis and the vertical axis have the same meanings in Figure 4. The performance of CBA-PG, CBA-PG2 and CBA-PG3 are worse than CBA-CHMM. This is because dividing investors into small particle groups only models the couplings within these groups and ignores the coupled relationships between particle groups. By contrast, while CBA-HG and CBA-HG3 perform better than other schemes in most cases, CBA-HG2 does not. A possible explanation is that the former two schemes integrate a hierarchical group structure based on reasonable similarity measures rather than a random merger. CBA-HG generally performs best out of the three strategies at general, which indicates suitable domain knowledge and a reasonable hierarchical structure is valuable for a more accurate grouping and

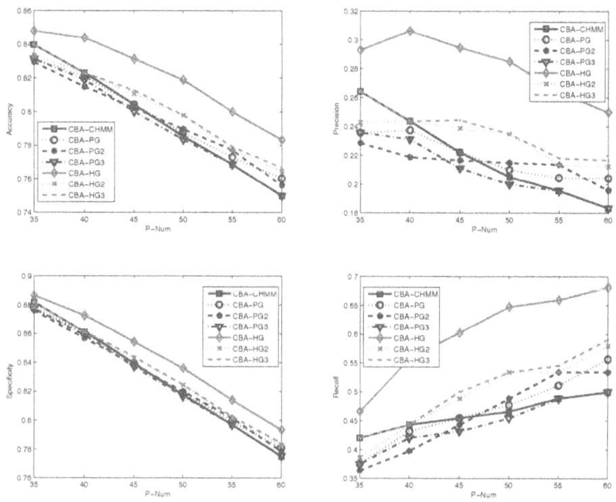

Figure 5: Comparison of the Seven Strategies

corresponding anomaly detection of the investors. Although the technical measures of CBA-HG is not much higher than those of other strategies when P-Num is small (smaller than 45), they are significantly higher as P-Num increases. For instance, as shown in Figure 5, when $P - Num = 40$, the precision of CBA-HG is 0.33, while that of CBA-PG is 0.24 and that of CBA-CHMM is 0.25. The precision of CBA-HG can be 32% higher than that of CBA-CHMM. It reveals that our proposed framework performs best and is most stable than other strategies.

5.4 Comparisons of the Three Frameworks

The above experiments show the performance of the two variant CBA frameworks respectively. To further compare their performance, Figure 6 shows the performance comparison of the two variant frameworks and the CHMM-based framework. As can be seen from the figure, the CBA-HG framework obtains the best performance in terms of all the technical measures. This is because the proper domain knowledge directs us to model proper and more comprehensive

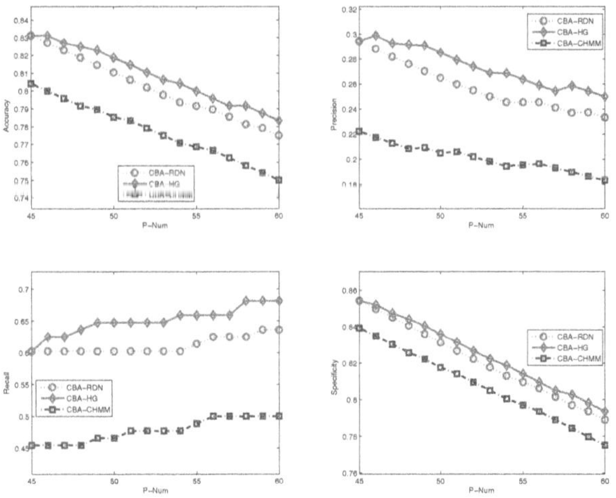

Figure 6: Comparison of the Three Frameworks

couplings between behaviors for anomaly detection. In addition, this proves integrating the proper domain knowledge for CBA could enhance its performance to some extent. The CBA-RDN performs better than the CBA-CHMM framework, which may benefit from the modeling of more comprehensive coupling relationships. When there is no prior domain knowledge, it is reasonable to assume hybrid couplings between the behaviors and give a comprehensive modeling. This method is still advantageous compared to the CBA-CHMM framework, which aggregates all investors' behaviors and may omit important coupled relationships. To sum up, the HC-based CBA considers hybrid couplings between behaviors for modeling is helpful when there is little knowledge about the coupling structures while HG-based CBA could provide better analysis of the coupled behaviors when the proper domain knowledge is set up for the underlying couplings.

6. CONCLUSIONS

This paper examined a challenging issue of detecting group-based market manipulations from the perspective of coupled behavior analysis. In order to analyze the rich couplings among behaviors and detect anomalies more accurately, we proposed a three-stage general CBA framework for abnormal behavior detection, which consists of *qualitative* analysis, *quantitative* analysis and anomaly detection stages. To cater for different situations of prior domain knowledge about the couplings, two variant implementation approaches have been proposed. The experimental results on a real-world data set in a major Asian stock market exhibited that the proposed approaches generally outperform the previous CHMM-based one by taking the miscellaneous alerts fired in the market surveillance system as a benchmark. In addition, we also found that integrating domain knowledge into abnormal coupled behavior detection can significantly improve the performance while detecting anomalies without additional domain knowledge is still possible. Future research could be on exploration of how to integrate more sophisticated domain knowledge for CBA and considering other application domains.

7. ACKNOWLEDGEMENT

This work is supported by the Australian Research Council (ARC) Discovery Grant (DP1096218), ARC Linkage Grant (LP100200774), the National 863 Program of China (2012AA011005), and the US NASA Research Award (NNX09AK86G).

8. REFERENCES

[1] H. Blau. A visual query language for relational knowledge discovery. Technical report, University of Massachusetts Amherst, 2001.

[2] M. Brand, N. Oliver, and A. Pentland. Coupled hidden markov models for complex action recognition. In *Proceedings of the IEEE Computer Society Conference on Computer Vision and Pattern Recognition*, pages 994–999, 1997.

[3] L. Cao, Y. Ou, and P. Yu. Coupled behavior analysis with applications. *IEEE Transactions on Knowledge and Data Engineering*, 2011.

[4] L. Cao, Y. Ou, P. Yu, and G. Wei. Detecting abnormal coupled sequences and sequence changes in group-based manipulative trading behaviors. In *Proceedings of the 16th ACM SIGKDD International Conference on Knowledge Discovery and Data Mining*, pages 85–94. ACM, 2010.

[5] D. Cohen. *JB Watson, the founder of behaviourism: a biography*. Routledge and Kegan Paul, 1979.

[6] J. Friedman, T. Hastie, and R. Tibshirani. *The elements of statistical learning*, volume 1. Springer Series in Statistics, 2001.

[7] D. Garcia-Garcia, E. Hernandez, and F. Diaz de Maria. A new distance measure for model-based sequence clustering. *IEEE Transactions on Pattern Analysis and Machine Intelligence*, 31(7):1325–1331, 2009.

[8] L. Getoor and B. Taskar. *Introduction to statistical relational learning*. The MIT Press, 2007.

[9] S. Kullback and R. Leibler. On information and sufficiency. *The Annals of Mathematical Statistics*, 22(1):79–86, 1951.

[10] H. Liu, J. Salerno, and M. Young. *Social computing, behavioral modeling, and prediction*. Springer-Verlag New York Inc, 2008.

[11] S. Mallat and Z. Zhang. Matching pursuits with time-frequency dictionaries. *Signal Processing, IEEE Transactions on*, 41(12):3397–3415, 1993.

[12] J. Neville. *Statistical models and analysis techniques for learning in relational data*. PhD thesis, 2006.

[13] B. Skinner. About behaviorism, alfred a, 1974.

[14] B. Taskar, P. Abbeel, and D. Koller. Discriminative probabilistic models for relational data. In *Proceedings of the Eighteenth Conference on Uncertainty in Artificial Intelligence (UAI02)*, pages 895–902, 2002.

[15] J. Ward. Hierarchical grouping to optimize an objective function. *Journal of the American statistical association*, 58(301):236–244, 1963.

HySAD: A Semi-Supervised Hybrid Shilling Attack Detector for Trustworthy Product Recommendation

Zhiang Wu[1], Junjie Wu[2*], Jie Cao[1], and Dacheng Tao[3]
[1]Jiangsu Provincial Key Laboratory of E-Business, Nanjing University of Finance and Economics, China
[2*](Corresponding Author) School of Economics and Management, Beihang University, China
[3]Centre for Quantum Computation & Intelligent Systems, University of Technology, Sydney
zawu@seu.edu.cn, wujj@buaa.edu.cn, caojie690929@163.com,
Dacheng.Tao@uts.edu.au

ABSTRACT

Shilling attackers apply biased rating profiles to recommender systems for manipulating online product recommendations. Although many studies have been devoted to shilling attack detection, few of them can handle the *hybrid* shilling attacks that usually happen in practice, and the studies for real-life applications are rarely seen. Moreover, little attention has yet been paid to modeling both labeled and unlabeled user profiles, although there are often a few labeled but numerous unlabeled users available in practice. This paper presents a Hybrid Shilling Attack Detector, or HySAD for short, to tackle these problems. In particular, HySAD introduces MC-Relief to select effective detection metrics, and Semi-supervised Naïve Bayes (SNB_λ) to precisely separate Random-Filler model attackers and Average-Filler model attackers from normal users. Thorough experiments on MovieLens and Netflix datasets demonstrate the effectiveness of HySAD in detecting hybrid shilling attacks, and its robustness for various obfuscated strategies. A real-life case study on product reviews of Amazon.cn is also provided, which further demonstrates that HySAD can effectively improve the accuracy of a collaborative-filtering based recommender system, and provide interesting opportunities for in-depth analysis of attacker behaviors. These, in turn, justify the value of HySAD for real-world applications.

Categories and Subject Descriptors

H.2.8 [**Database Management**]: Database Applications—*Data Mining*

General Terms

Algorithms, Experimentation

Keywords

Hybrid Shilling Attack, Semi-supervised Learning, Naïve Bayes, Recommendation Systems

1. INTRODUCTION

Recent years have witnessed the rapid growth of the Internet. More and more people now prefer online shopping over conventional shopping. The all-round infiltration of Web 2.0 these days further promotes this process. People enjoy new online shopping experiences by publishing, browsing, or sharing product reviews written by themselves or others. Indeed, research shows that people rely on the opinions of others when selecting something for the first time [1]. This selection behavior, together with the increasingly apparent problem of information overload, has motivated the development of recommender systems for automatic and personalized recommendation of books, movies, electronics, etc.

However, there is always a natural profit incentive to promote one's own products by leaving biased online comments and/or extreme ratings for the competition's products, which has spawned the so-called "shilling attacks". It appears that shilling attacks are successfully threatening recommender systems, and continuously generating huge volumes of spam or misleading review comments. Shilling attacks are therefore emerging as a considerable challenge to the sustainable development of online shopping.

In the literature, a great deal of research has been undertaken to detect shilling attacks from large-scale rating profiles. These studies mainly focus on the three subareas: the shilling attack generation models [21, 15], the shilling attack detection metrics [3, 6, 21, 22], and the shilling attack classification methods [6, 21, 13, 8, 10], which have greatly advanced the research onto a much higher level.

However, existing studies have some limitations. First, hybrid attacks consisting of multiple attack models are still a challenging problem in both academia and industry. Moreover, most existing studies used either supervised or unsupervised learning methods for attack detection, which do not agree with the fact that, in practice, we are often given only a few labeled but a majority of unlabeled user profiles. Finally, most existing studies are only validated by simulation results on artificially injected attacker profiles, rather than real-life applications. These drawbacks severely limit the use of the shilling attack detection methods in practice.

In light of this, we present Hybrid Shilling Attack Detector, or HySAD for short, to solve these problems. In general, HySAD has two distinct properties. First, HySAD is a hybrid-attack oriented system that collects many popular shilling attack detection metrics for the purpose of feature selection via a wrapper called MC-Relief. These metrics then become the informative features of the training data.

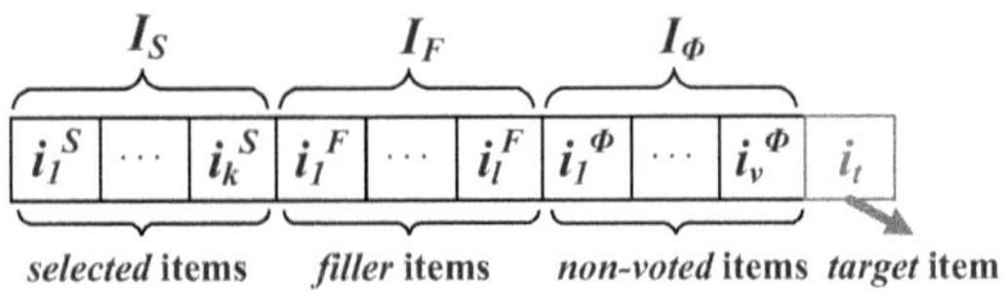

Figure 1: The illustration of a shilling profile.

Second, HySAD is a semi-supervised learning system that employs the Semi-supervised Naïve Bayes (SNB_λ) classifier for the categorization of both labeled and unlabeled profiles.

Extensive experiments on both the MovieLens and Netflix datasets demonstrate that, compared with some state-of-the-art methods proposed in the literature, HySAD is particularly effective for hybrid shilling attacks, even when attack variants generated by some obfuscated strategies are presented. A real-life application on product recommendation for Amazon.cn is also provided to demonstrate the effectiveness of HySAD. The results indicate that HySAD indeed improves the accuracy of a collaborative-filtering based recommender system, identifies some deeply hidden shilling attackers on Amazon.cn, and provides interesting opportunities for further study of attacker behaviors from various perspctives.

2. RELATED WORK

The word "shilling" was first termed in 2004 [9, 17]. Since then, several attack profile generation models have been proposed in the literature [21, 15], and a lot of research has been undertaken to employ supervised learning for shilling attack detection [3, 14]. For instance, a simple detector using the average similarity and the Rating Deviation from Mean Agreement (RDMA) metric was presented in [6]. A decision-tree based detector was also proposed in [21]. Many detection metrics were also presented to characterize the attacker profiles [6, 21, 3, 22]. An early unsupervised shilling attack detector is PCASelectUsers [13], which employs the principal component analysis on the original rating data. Hurley et al. presented the Neyman-Pearson statistical detector, with both supervised and unsupervised versions [8]. Recently, Lee et al. proposed a new detector using a clustering method and the Group RDMA (GRDMA) metric [10]. Other specific detectors include the segment-attack detector [4], the group-attack detector [19], and the time-series based detector [22]. Given the limited space, it is difficult to include all the related work in, and we hope the cited review [18] about robust collaborative recommendation can point to some of those missing references.

3. PRELIMINARIES AND THE SYSTEM OVERVIEW

Shilling attackers often have three intents: *push*, *nuke* and *vandalism* [21]. An attacker may insert ratings to make an item more likely (push) or less likely (nuke) to be recommended, or just make the entire recommender system malfunction (vandalism). As we only consider the intents that bring economic benefits to attackers, vandalism will not be considered in this study.

The rating records of a user on various products (items) construct the profile of that user. The profile of a shilling attacker (or a *shilling profile* for short) usually consists of the ratings on four types of items: target item, filler items, selected items, and non-voted items, as shown in Fig. 1. A target item often has the highest rating in a push attack, or the lowest rating in a nuke attack. Filler items can make a shilling profile look normal, yet have a profound impact on a recommender system. Selected items are often used to make friends with as many genuine users as possible. Finally, non-voted items form the remaining unrated items.

Table 1: Four shilling attack models (intent: push).

Type	Model	Ratings
RFM	random attack	$I_S=\emptyset$; Give random ratings to items in I_F; $r(i_t)=r_{\max}$.
	bandwagon attack (random)	I_S contains frequently-rated items, and $r(i^S)=r_{\max}$; Give random ratings to items in I_F; $r(i_t)=r_{\max}$.
AFM	average attack	$I_S=\emptyset$; The ratings to items in I_F are distributed around the mean of each item i^F; $r(i_t)=r_{\max}$.
	bandwagon attack (average)	I_S contains frequently-rated items, and $r(i^S)=r_{\max}$; The ratings to items in I_F are distributed around the mean of each item i^F; $r(i_t)=r_{\max}$.

Note: $r_{\max}$ ($r_{\min}$) - the highest (lowest) rating to an item.

Table 1 includes four generative models, i.e. random, average, bandwagon (random), and bandwagon (average), which are popular for generating shilling profiles by carefully rating these four types of items. Note that this is the case for the push intent, and the nuke-intent case can therefore be easily figured out. We can further categorize the four models into two types, i.e. Random-Filler models (RFM) and Average-Filler models (AFM). As a result, we have three types of user profiles in total: Normal users (N), RFM attackers (RF), and AFM attackers (AF).

Two obfuscated attack techniques, i.e. noise-injection and target-shifting, are often used for shilling attackers to avoid detection [21]. Recently, a simple, but effective strategy named Average-over-Popular (AoP) was also proposed to obfuscate the average attack [8]. The three techniques are listed below:

Noise-injection: Add a Gaussian distributed random number multiplied by α to each rating within a subset of filler items. This noise can be used to blur the profile characteristics that are associated with the above four attack types.

Target-shifting: For the push intent, this technique shifts the rating given to the target item from the maximum rating to a rating one step lower; or for the nuke attack, it increases the target rating to one step above the lowest rating. It can also be used with all the four types of attacks.

AoP: This technique chooses filler items with equal probability from the top $x\%$ of the most popular items, instead of the entire items. It is often used with the average attack.

3.1 Problem Definition

The combined use of the four attack models and the three obfuscated techniques leads to the *hybrid* shilling attacks, which inject various types of shilling profiles into a recommender system simultaneously. From a practical view, a hybrid shilling attack is very likely to be adopted by malicious users to make their attacks much more difficult to detect. Moreover, different groups of attackers may use different attack models for the same online system, which will, practically, result in hybrid attacks. However, most existing algorithms concentrate on detecting shilling profiles generated by a single model, and have not been evaluated by hybrid attacks. To narrow the gap, the first concern is:

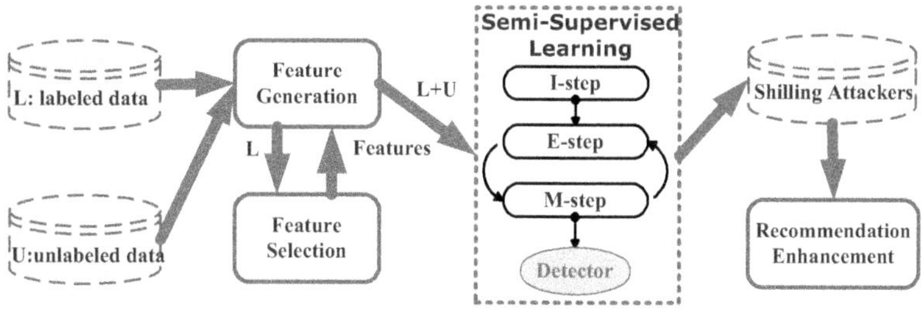

Figure 2: The procedure of HySAD.

T1: Design a detector to identify hybrid shilling attacks.

Another challenge in shilling attack detection is the lack of labeled users. It is known that, with the guidance of the label information, supervised learning generally has higher accuracy than unsupervised learning in data categorization [5]. However, given the huge volume of users in an online shopping system, such as Amazon.com, to manually label even ten percent of users is prohibitively expensive. Therefore, the real situation is, we are to be given a vast number of unlabeled users, together with a very small seed-set of labeled users, for the shilling attack detection. This directly leads to the second concern of this study:

T2: Design a detector that can use both labeled and unlabeled data.

T1 and T2 clearly define the problem we study in this paper. Specifically, a system named HySAD is proposed for hybrid shilling attack detection in the following subsection.

3.2 System Overview

Fig. 2 illustrates the diagram of the HySAD system. We provide a brief explanation as follows.

Firstly, we are given the user profile data, including a majority of unlabeled profiles U, and a small seed-set of labeled profiles L. To capture the essential information from different attacks, we collect as many as possible widely-adopted evaluation metrics in the literature, and then generate new features for all the users, as indicated by the "Feature Generation" box. These features will then be subjected to a feature-selection phase by using a wrapper method named MC-Relief on the labeled users, as indicated by the "Feature Selection" box. The training data is now ready for user profile classification.

A semi-supervised learning algorithm called Semi-supervised Naïve Bayes (SNB_λ) will then be launched for classification. That is, the labeled data will be firstly used to train a Naïve Bayes classifier, and predict the posterior probabilities of the unlabeled data; then the initial classifier will be improved by using an expectation-maximization-like iterative process, until certain stopping criterion is met. We finally obtain details of all the shilling attackers with higher probabilities for attacker classes. This valuable information will be further utilized to enhance the performance of a recommender system, as indicated by the "Recommendation Enhancement" box.

Discussion. Altogether we used ten metrics, i.e. Entropy, DegSim, LengthVar, RDMA, WDMA, WDA, MeanVar, FMTD, GFMV, and TMF, collected from the literature [3, 6, 21, 22] for feature generation. As a metric is often designed purposefully for one attack model, some may not be very suitable for hybrid attack detection, which is why a feature selection phase is required for HySAD. The reason for employing a semi-supervised learning in the classification modeling phase is also straightforward; that is, it will not only make use of the valuable label information, but also capture the proximity information between labeled and unlabeled data, and thus is more suitable for the shilling attack detection. The use of MC-Relief and SNB_λ is indeed optional, although these two algorithms do work surprisingly well in our study. Moreover, both models are very simple and explainable, which are the important merits for real-world applications. Some other classifiers, such as SVMs, may not have good interpretability, and thus are not considered for HySAD.

```
MC-Relief
Input:
    L: the set of labeled user profiles
    S: the sampling times
    m: the number of total features
    d: the number of features to select
    c: the number of classes
Output:
    F: the set of selected features
Variable:
    ω: the set of feature weights
Procedure:
1.  for l=1:m
2.      ω_l = 0;
3.  end for
4.  for j=1:S
5.      u=RandomSelect(L);
6.      u_p=SNN(u);
7.      (u_n^(1), ··· , u_n^(c−1))=DNN(u);
8.      for l=1:m
9.          Update(ω_l, u_p, u_n^(1), ··· , u_n^(c−1));
10.     end for
11. end for
12. F = {f_l | ω_l is among the top-d weights};
```

Figure 3: The MC-Relief algorithm.

4. FEATURE SELECTION

In this section, we present a simple heuristic MC-Relief to select the right metrics for the subsequent modeling task. MC-Relief is an extension from Relief [11], a feature selection algorithm for binary-class data. As MC-Relief is a wrapper method using the labeled data, we should first determine the number of classes we should use.

In the literature, user profiles are often categorized into two classes, i.e. normal users and attackers. However, from a hybrid attack perspective, setting only one attacker class may not be adequate. Indeed, the attacker using an average attack and the attacker using a random attack may have quite different feature values on metrics, such as WDMA and MeanVar, that use average ratings of items. The former attacker's ratings to filler items have a strong correlation with the average ratings, whereas the latter attacker's ratings tend to have a much weaker correlation with the average ratings. This implies that we should further divide the attackers into two subclass according to the attack models outlined in Section 3. This results in three types of users in total: normal users (N), AFM attackers (AF), and RFM attackers (RF). We will also demonstrate the benefits of setting three, rather than two classes in experiments.

We then describe the feature selection heuristic. MC-Relief is actually an extension of the Relief algorithm for multi-class problems. In general, MC-Relief aims to estimate the quality of features to distinguish the user profiles that are near to each other. Fig. 3 shows the pseudocodes, where ω_l denotes the weight of feature l, $l = 1, \cdots, m$, and the d features with top-d weights are finally selected. The weights will be updated S times during the selection process (Line 4). Each time MC-Relief randomly selects a profile u from L (Line 5), searches L for u's c nearest neighbors in c different classes (Lines 6 and 7), and then updates the weights sequentially. Note that the SNN function (Line 6) finds the nearest neighbor u_p in the same class of u, whereas the DNN function (Line 7) finds the nearest neighbors $\{u_n^{(1)}, \cdots, u_n^{c-1}\}$ in other classes. The proximity function used in SNN and DNN is the Pearson correlation coefficient. The Update function (Line 9) calls Eq. 1:

$$\omega_l \leftarrow \omega_l - \frac{|x_{u,l} - x_{u_p,l}|}{S} + \frac{\sum_{k=1}^{c-1} |x_{u,l} - x^{(k)}_{u_n,l}|}{S(c-1)} \quad (1)$$

to update the weights, where $x_{u,l}$ denotes the l-th feature value of u. To avoid the scale bias, we should normalize the feature values to [0,1] before calling MC-Relief.

5. CLASSIFICATION

Feature generation and selection provide training data that contains a very small portion of labeled data. We then propose a semi-supervised learning scheme named SNB$_\lambda$ for classification. In general, SNB$_\lambda$ is an EM-like algorithm that extends the Naïve Bayes classifier [20] to the situation where both labeled and unlabeled data are present.

Suppose we are given a dataset $\mathcal{D} = \{\mathbf{x}_i\}_{i=1}^n$ of n instances drawn independently from a mixture density of c components:

$$p(\mathbf{x}_i|\boldsymbol{\theta}) = \sum_{j=1}^{c} p(\mathbf{x}_i|C_j, \boldsymbol{\theta}_j)P(C_j), \quad (2)$$

where $\boldsymbol{\theta} = (\boldsymbol{\theta}_1, \cdots, \boldsymbol{\theta}_c)$ contains unknown parameter $\boldsymbol{\theta}_j$ that uniquely determines $p(\mathbf{x}_i|C_j)$, $P(C_j)$ is the prior probability of class C_j, $j = 1, \cdots, c$. Assume the class-conditional probability of each dimension of $\mathbf{x}_i$ is independent of other dimensions and satisfies a normal distribution, i.e., $p(x_{il}|C_j, \boldsymbol{\theta}_j) = \frac{1}{\sqrt{2\pi}\sigma_{jl}} \exp(\frac{(x_{il}-\mu_{jl})^2}{2\sigma_{jl}^2})$, $1 \le l \le d$.

As $\mathcal{D}$ consists of a few labeled but majority unlabeled instances, we let $\mathcal{D} = \mathcal{D}^U \bigcup \mathcal{D}^{L_1} \bigcup \cdots \bigcup \mathcal{D}^{L_c}$, where $\mathcal{D}^U$ contains unlabeled instances, and $\mathcal{D}^{L_j}$ contains instances from class C_j. A weight $\lambda \in [0, 1]$ is also introduced to lower the impact of unlabeled instances on the classifier modeling. Given the above settings, we launch the maximum-likelihood estimation to find the value $\hat{\boldsymbol{\theta}}$ that maximizes $p(\mathcal{D}|\boldsymbol{\theta})$ (A similar method named EM$_\lambda$ can be found in [16], but it uses a Bayesian estimation, and is designed purposefully for text classification on discrete attributes.).

Given instance independency and the weight λ, we have

$$p(\mathcal{D}|\boldsymbol{\theta}) = (\Pi_{\mathbf{x}_i \in \mathcal{D}^U} p(\mathbf{x}_i|\boldsymbol{\theta}))^\lambda \Pi_{j=1}^c (\Pi_{\mathbf{x}_i \in \mathcal{D}^{L_j}} p(\mathbf{x}_i|\boldsymbol{\theta})). \quad (3)$$

Taking the natural logarithm, we obtain the objective function as follows:

$$\max_{\boldsymbol{\theta}} \sum_{\mathbf{x}_i \in \mathcal{D}} \Lambda_i \ln p(\mathbf{x}_i|\boldsymbol{\theta}) \quad (4)$$
$$s.t. \sum_{j=1}^{c} P(C_j) = 1,$$

where

$$\Lambda_i = \begin{cases} \lambda, \text{ if } \mathbf{x}_i \in \mathcal{D}^U, \\ 1, \text{ otherwise.} \end{cases} \quad (5)$$

Let $\mathcal{L} = \ln p(\mathcal{D}|\boldsymbol{\theta}) - \rho(\sum_{j=1}^c P(C_j) - 1)$. Since $p(\mathbf{x}_i|\boldsymbol{\theta}) = \sum_{j=1}^c p(\mathbf{x}_i|C_j, \boldsymbol{\theta}_j)P(C_j)$, we have

$$\nabla_{\boldsymbol{\theta}_j} \mathcal{L} = \sum_{\mathbf{x}_i \in \mathcal{D}} \Lambda_i \frac{1}{p(\mathbf{x}_i|\boldsymbol{\theta})} \nabla_{\boldsymbol{\theta}_j} p(\mathbf{x}_i|C_j, \boldsymbol{\theta}_j)P(C_j). \quad (6)$$

Note that

$$P(C_j|\mathbf{x}_i, \boldsymbol{\theta}) = \frac{p(\mathbf{x}_i|C_j, \boldsymbol{\theta}_j)P(C_j)}{p(\mathbf{x}_i|\boldsymbol{\theta})}. \quad (7)$$

If we substitute $p(\mathbf{x}_i|\boldsymbol{\theta})$ in Eq. 6 by the one in Eq. 7, we have

$$\nabla_{\boldsymbol{\theta}_j} \mathcal{L} = \sum_{\mathbf{x}_i \in \mathcal{D}} \Lambda_i P(C_j|\mathbf{x}_i, \boldsymbol{\theta}) \nabla_{\boldsymbol{\theta}_j} \ln p(\mathbf{x}_i|C_j, \boldsymbol{\theta}_j). \quad (8)$$

Let $\nabla_{\boldsymbol{\theta}_j} \mathcal{L} = 0$. Since

$$p(\mathbf{x}_i|C_j, \boldsymbol{\theta}_j) = \Pi_{l=1}^d p(x_{il}|C_j, \boldsymbol{\theta}_j)$$
$$= \Pi_{l=1}^d \frac{1}{\sqrt{2\pi}\sigma_{jl}} \exp(\frac{(x_{il} - \mu_{jl})^2}{2\sigma_{jl}^2}), \quad (9)$$

we can easily have $\forall\ 1 \le j \le c$, $1 \le l \le d$,

$$\hat{\mu}_{jl} = \frac{\lambda \sum_{\mathbf{x}_i \in \mathcal{D}^U} P(C_j|\mathbf{x}_i, \hat{\boldsymbol{\theta}}) x_{il} + \sum_{\mathbf{x}_i \in \mathcal{D}^{L_j}} x_{il}}{\lambda \sum_{\mathbf{x}_i \in \mathcal{D}^U} P(C_j|\mathbf{x}_i, \hat{\boldsymbol{\theta}}) + |\mathcal{D}^{L_j}|}, \quad (10)$$

$$\hat{\sigma}_{jl}^2 = \frac{\lambda \sum_{\mathbf{x}_i \in \mathcal{D}^U} P(C_j|\mathbf{x}_i, \hat{\boldsymbol{\theta}})(x_{il} - \hat{\mu}_{jl})^2 + \sum_{\mathbf{x}_i \in \mathcal{D}^{L_j}} (x_{il} - \hat{\mu}_{jl})^2}{\lambda \sum_{\mathbf{x}_i \in \mathcal{D}^U} P(C_j|\mathbf{x}_i, \hat{\boldsymbol{\theta}}) + |\mathcal{D}^{L_j}|}. \quad (11)$$

Furthermore, let $\frac{\partial \mathcal{L}}{\partial P(C_j)} = 0$, we have $\forall\ 1 \le j \le c$

$$\hat{P}(C_j) = \frac{\lambda \sum_{\mathbf{x}_i \in \mathcal{D}^U} P(C_j|\mathbf{x}_i, \hat{\boldsymbol{\theta}}) + |\mathcal{D}^{L_j}|}{\lambda |\mathcal{D}^U| + \sum_{j=1}^c |\mathcal{D}^{L_j}|}. \quad (12)$$

Combining the above results produces expectation-maximization iterative process as follows:

- **Initial step**: $\forall\ j, l$, compute $\hat{\mu}_{jl}$, $\hat{\sigma}_{jl}^2$ and $\hat{P}(C_j)$ using Eqs. 10, 11 and 12, respectively, on labeled data. Then for $\mathbf{x}_i \in \mathcal{D}^U$, compute $p(\mathbf{x}_i|C_j, \hat{\boldsymbol{\theta}}_j)$ using Eq. 9. (This step is equivalent to building the Naïve Bayes classifier and using it to classify unlabeled data.)

- **E-step**: $\forall\ j$, compute $P(C_j|\mathbf{x}_i, \hat{\boldsymbol{\theta}})$ for all $\mathbf{x}_i \in \mathcal{D}^U$ using Eq. 7. For $\mathbf{x}_i \in \mathcal{D}^{L_j}$, let $P(C_j|\mathbf{x}_i, \hat{\boldsymbol{\theta}}) = 1$; and for $\mathbf{x}_i \in \mathcal{D}^{L_k}$, $k \ne j$, let $P(C_j|\mathbf{x}_i, \hat{\boldsymbol{\theta}}) = 0$.

Table 2: Experimental data sets.

Name	#User	#Movie	#Rating	Density
`MovieLens_u2.test`	943	1682	20000	1.26%
`Netflix_s1`	2000	2000	234467	5.86%

Table 3: The five selected features.

Data set	No.1	No.2	No.3	No.4	No.5
`MovieLens`	DegSim	TMF	Entropy	MeanVar	GFMV
`Netflix`	TMF	DegSim	Entropy	LengthVar	MeanVar

- **M-step:** $\forall\, j, l$, compute $\hat{\mu}_{jl}$, $\hat{\sigma}^2_{jl}$ and $\hat{P}(C_j)$ using Eqs. 10, 11 and 12, respectively. Then for $\mathbf{x}_i \in \mathcal{D}^U$, compute $p(\mathbf{x}_i|C_j, \hat{\boldsymbol{\theta}}_j)$ using Eq. 9.

The iterative process will be suspended if there is a very small change in the parameters of the objective-function in Eq. 4, so we have $P(C_j|\mathbf{x}_i, \hat{\boldsymbol{\theta}})$ for all $\mathbf{x}_i \in \mathcal{D}^U$ and all classes. Returning to the shilling-attack detection task, we have only three classes: N, AF, and RF. We let

$$\Omega_{AF}(\mathbf{x}_i) = \frac{P(AF|\mathbf{x}_i, \hat{\boldsymbol{\theta}})}{P(N|\mathbf{x}_i, \hat{\boldsymbol{\theta}})},\ \Omega_{RF}(\mathbf{x}_i) = \frac{P(RF|\mathbf{x}_i, \hat{\boldsymbol{\theta}})}{P(N|\mathbf{x}_i, \hat{\boldsymbol{\theta}})}, \quad (13)$$

and label $\forall\ \mathbf{x}_i \in \mathcal{D}^U$ as an attacker if $\Omega_{AF}(\mathbf{x}_i) > \eta$ or $\Omega_{RF}(\mathbf{x}_i) > \eta$, where η is an empirical threshold.

6. EXPERIMENTAL VALIDATION

In this section, we present experimental results on two well-known real-world datasets: `MovieLens` and `Netflix`. We demonstrate that three factors, i.e. the semi-supervised learning, the feature selection, and the three-class setting, are crucial for obtaining excellent performance from HySAD.

6.1 Experimental Setup

Datasets. Table 2 lists the information of the two datasets. `MovieLens` is a benchmark movie-evaluation dataset widely used in previous studies [9, 21, 13, 8, 6], and `u2.test` is one of its subsets. `Netflix` is also a well-known movie-evaluation dataset [2], from which a subset `s1` was obtained for our study. In detail, we first extracted 2000 movies whose sizes of rating files ranged from 170K to 1.44M; then we randomly extracted a sample of 2000 users who had rated no less than 50 of the selected movies. Note that these two datasets have quite different densities, and only the sub-sets were used since one of the comparative detectors, i.e. PCASelectUsers (PCA for short), which will be introduced below, does not work for large-scale data.

Tools. Four shilling attack detectors, i.e. HySAD, NB, C4.5, and PCA, were used in the experiments for the purpose of comparison. HySAD employs a semi-supervised learning scheme, NB (Naïve Bayes classifier) and C4.5 [20] employ supervised learning schemes, and PCA (PCASelectUsers) [13] employs an unsupervised learning scheme. Both HySAD and NB were coded in C++ and used on the data with generated features, with $\eta = 1$. However, PCA was coded in MATLAB to facilitate the principal-component computation, and used on the original rating data. C4.5 was the J48 version provided by WEKA with the default settings on the generated data. We selected C4.5 and PCA in this instance because they had been used for shilling attack detection and achieved good performance on `MovieLens` [21, 13].

Settings. We assumed the user profiles in the datasets were normal, and injected attacker profiles into them according to the four attack models and three obfuscated methods

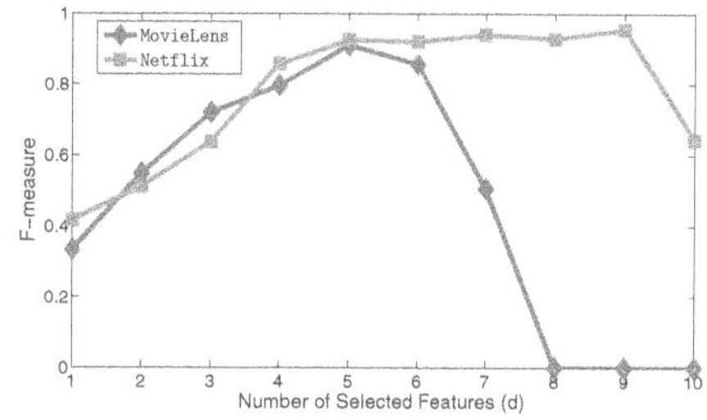

Figure 4: Impact of the number of selected features.

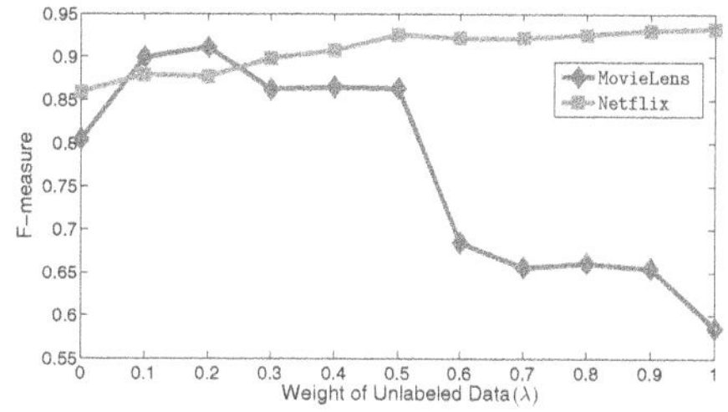

Figure 5: Impact of the weight of unlabeled data.

mentioned in Section 3. In detail, for `MovieLens` data, we sampled about 10% users (94 users) as labeled normal users, injected about 5% attackers (48 users) as labeled attackers, and thus formed the labeled data L with $|L| = 142$. To test the performance of detectors, 100 attackers were also injected into the remaining 849 users, and formed the unlabeled data U with $|U| = 949$. The `Netflix` was processed in a similar way, with 100 attackers and 200 normal users in L, and 200 attackers and 1800 normal users in U. For the hybrid attacks, attackers were divided evenly for different models, and the AFM and RFM attackers were labeled as AF and RF, respectively. Finally, note that the obfuscated methods were used for all the attackers in the unlabeled data, to verify whether detectors can adapt to attack variants.

Measures. We adopted the widely-used recall (R), precision (P), and F-measure (F) for the performance evaluation [20]. Specifically, we focused on the ability of detectors to recognize the hybrid attackers, where

$$P = \frac{TP}{TP + FP},\ R = \frac{TP}{TP + FN},\ F = \frac{2PR}{P + R}, \quad (14)$$

with TP being the number of truly identified attackers, TN the number of truly identified normal users, FP the number of wrongly identified attackers, and FN the number of missed attackers. In general, R and P highlight the completeness and accuracy of a detector, respectively, and F provides a global view.

6.2 Parameter Analysis for HySAD

Here, we investigate the impact of the two parameters, i.e. the number of selected features (d) and the weight for unlabeled data (λ), on the performance of HySAD. We set the filler size (the size of filler-item set) to 10% of the total item size, i.e. $|I^F| = 10\%|I|$. The injected hybrid attack, denoted as "hyb.", was the mixture of four types of attacks: random, average, bandwagon(random), and bandwagon(average). No obfuscated methods were used. Ten-fold cross-validation was employed to provide robust results.

Fig. 4 shows the performance of HySAD with different numbers of selected features, when the weight $\lambda = 0.5$. As can be seen, when $d = 5$, the maximum F-measure value is

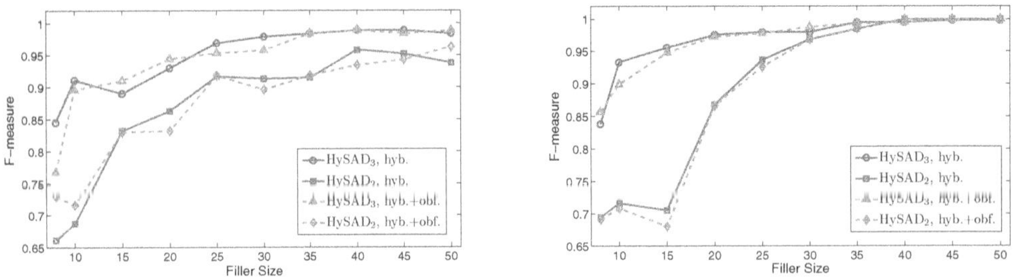

(a) MovieLens (b) Netflix

Figure 6: The effect of three-class modeling of HySAD.

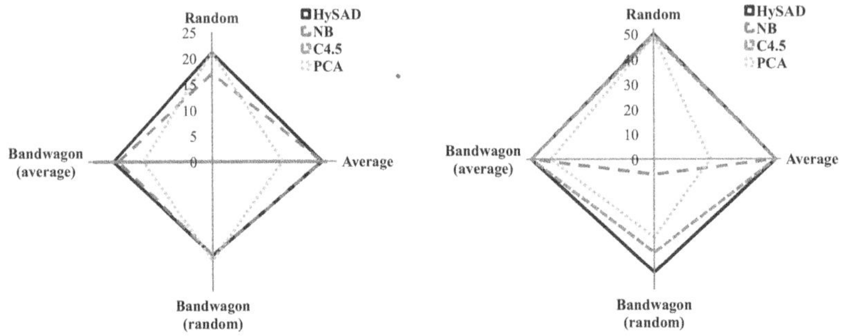

(a) MovieLens (b) Netflix

Figure 7: The performance of detectors against attacks of different types.

obtained for the MovieLens dataset. Moreover, although the Netflix dataset reaches the the maximum F-measure value when $d = 9$, $d = 5$ still provides a fairly good performance. As a result, we set $d = 5$ for HySAD in all the experiments. Table 3 also lists the selected five features on MovieLens and Netflix, respectively. As can be seen, the two sets of features are very similar to each other, except for GFMV and LengthVar. This implies that the feature selection algorithm MC-Relief is fairly robust. Fig. 5 shows the performance of HySAD given different weights of unlabeled data. Similarly to d, we find that $\lambda = 0.5$ is a relatively robust choice, becoming the default setting in our experiments.

6.3 The Necessity of MultiClass Modeling

In Section 4, we mentioned that we would like to label user profiles by one normal class (N) and two attacker classes (AF and RF). Here we demonstrate why taking only one attacker class is not suitable for HySAD. The hybrid attack "hyb.", defined in Section 6.2, was again injected into data. We also used two obfuscated methods, i.e. noise-injection ($\alpha = 0.2$) and target shifting, on all the attacker profiles in unlabeled data after the injection of "hyb.". We denote this more complicated attack as "hyb.+obf.". The filler size was changed from 8 to 50, to test the consistency of results.

Fig. 6 shows the results after employing HySAD on three-class data (denoted as HySAD_3) and binary-class data (denoted asHySAD_2), respectively. As can be seen, the impacts of the "hyb." and "hyb.+obf." attacks on HySAD are not significantly different. This implies that HySAD is robust for some variants of attacks. More importantly, HySAD_3 shows consistently higher F-measure values than HySAD_2, although the gap tends to be narrowed with the increase of the filler size. This indicates that it is better to divide attackers into AFM attackers and RFM attackers for the modeling of HySAD.

To explain the observation, let us look into the recall (R) and precision (P) values of HySAD_3 and HySAD_2. As can be seen from Table 4, HySAD_2 may have slightly higher recall values, e.g. on Netflix, but its precision values are typically much smaller than the values of HySAD_3. This implies that employing HySAD on binary data may help to find more attackers, but at the cost of wrongly classifying much more normal users as attackers, which largely degrades the overall performance. This clearly demonstrates that the random attack and the average attack indeed behave very differently, as discussed in Section 4.

6.4 The Comparison of Different Detectors

This section compares the performance of the four detectors: HySAD, NB, C4.5, and PCA, to demonstrate the effectiveness of semi-supervised learning for hybrid attack detection. Two hybrid attacks, i.e. "hyb." and "hyb.+obf.", were again injected. The filler size was changed from 8 to 30. Note that NB and C4.5 only uses the labeled data L for modeling, whereas PCA works on the original rating data. We assumed that PCA knew the number of injected attackers k, and returned the top-k users as attackers.

Table 4 lists the evaluation results of the four detectors, where the value larger than the one of HySAD is in italics. As can be seen, according to the F-measure, HySAD_3 performs the best among the four detectors in most of the cases, especially when the filler size is relatively small. As the filler size increases, both HySAD_3 and NB provide better prediction power, and the gap narrows. In contrast, PCA generally has the poorest performance for the two hybrid attacks, and the situation becomes even worse as the filler size increases. This implies that PCA may not be very suitable for hybrid attack detection. C4.5 is a bit unusual; that is, it is generally poorer than NB and better than PCA, but shows fluctuant results as the filler size increases.

We take a closer look at the recall and precision values of NB. As can be seen, NB often has a slightly higher preci-

Table 4: The performance of detectors against hybrid attacks.

Attack	Measure	Detector	MovieLens 8	MovieLens 15	MovieLens 20	MovieLens 25	Netflix 8	Netflix 15	Netflix 20	Netflix 25
			Filler size(%)							
Hyb.	R	$HySAD_3$	0.957	0.862	0.989	0.989	0.765	0.995	1	1
		$HySAD_2$	0.819	*0.872*	0.936	*1*	*1*	*1*	1	1
		NB	0.872	0.809	0.862	0.936	0.765	0.780	0.855	1
		C4.5	0.500	0.500	0.500	0.750	*0.820*	0.930	0.675	1
		PCA	0.798	0.723	0.564	0.170	0.755	0.725	0.725	0.700
	P	$HySAD_3$	0.756	0.920	0.877	0.949	0.927	0.917	0.952	0.962
		$HySAD_2$	0.554	0.796	0.800	0.847	0.532	0.545	0.766	0.881
		NB	0.683	0.894	*0.910*	0.946	*0.968*	*0.945*	*0.967*	*0.995*
		C4.5	*1*	0.691	*0.979*	0.949	0.854	*0.949*	*0.988*	*0.971*
		PCA	*0.798*	0.723	0.564	0.170	0.755	0.725	0.725	0.700
	F	$HySAD_3$	0.845	0.890	0.930	0.969	0.838	0.954	0.976	0.980
		$HySAD_2$	0.661	0.832	0.863	0.917	0.694	0.716	0.705	0.868
		NB	0.766	0.849	0.885	0.941	*0.855*	0.855	0.924	*0.998*
		C4.5	0.667	0.580	0.662	0.867	0.837	0.939	0.802	*0.985*
		PCA	0.798	0.723	0.564	0.170	0.755	0.725	0.725	0.700
Hyb.+Obf.	R	$HySAD_3$	0.670	0.968	0.979	0.979	0.795	1	1	1
		$HySAD_2$	*0.957*	0.777	0.894	0.957	*1*	1	1	1
		NB	*0.872*	0.734	0.862	0.915	0.760	0.750	0.805	1
		C4.5	0.479	0.500	0.500	0.766	*0.810*	0.880	0.675	1
		PCA	*0.777*	0.723	0.564	0.255	0.785	0.755	0.725	0.700
	P	$HySAD_3$	0.900	0.858	0.911	0.929	0.930	0.901	0.948	0.957
		$HySAD_2$	0.588	*0.890*	0.778	0.882	0.528	0.515	0.763	0.862
		NB	0.732	*0.908*	0.910	*0.945*	*0.968*	*0.949*	*0.970*	*0.990*
		C4.5	*1*	0.373	*0.916*	*0.935*	0.806	*0.941*	*0.988*	*0.971*
		PCA	0.777	0.723	0.564	0.255	0.785	0.755	0.720	0.695
	F	$HySAD_3$	0.768	0.910	0.944	0.953	0.857	0.948	0.973	0.978
		$HySAD_2$	0.729	0.830	0.832	0.918	0.691	0.680	0.866	0.926
		NB	*0.796*	0.812	0.885	0.930	0.852	0.838	0.880	*0.995*
		C4.5	0.648	0.427	0.662	0.842	0.808	0.909	0.802	*0.985*
		PCA	*0.777*	0.723	0.564	0.255	0.785	0.755	0.720	0.695

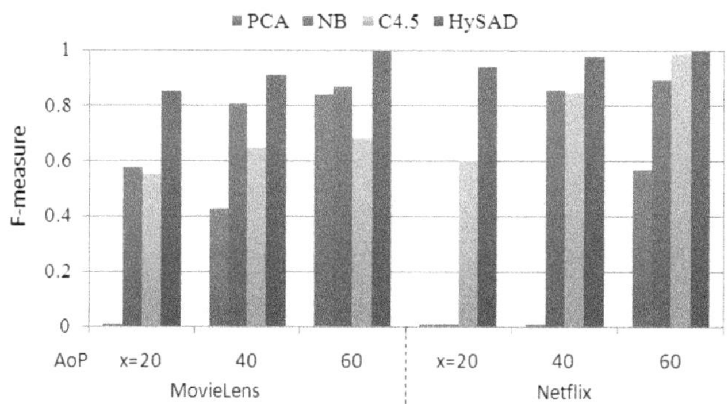

Figure 8: The performance of AoP attack detection.

sion value than $HySAD_3$, but its recall values are typically much smaller than the values of $HySAD_3$. This observation indicates that $HySAD_3$ indeed achieves a subtle balance between NB and $HySAD_2$, to detect as many hybrid attackers as possible, but avoids many false alarms in the meanwhile.

We also observe the comprehensiveness of the four detectors in detecting different types of attacks. Fig. 7 shows the numbers of recognized attackers generated by different attack models, where "hyb." was injected and filler size was set to 15. As can be seen, compared with $HySAD_3$, NB and C4.5 seem mediocre for the random attack, and PCA works poorly for the average attack. In contrast, $HySAD_3$ detects all types of attacks simultaneously, thereby demonstrating that it is particularly suitable for hybrid attack detection.

It was reported in [8] that, AoP attack is a simple and effective obfuscated strategy, which is hard to detect with an average attack. We therefore also tested the four detectors on the average attack with AoP, where the parameter $x = 20, 40, 60$, respectively. Note that to increase the difficulty, we adjusted the set of labeled users L to contain only 60 normal users and 30 attackers for both datasets. Empirical results suggested that $d = 5$ and $\lambda = 1$ for HySAD. Fig. 8 displays the comparative results. As can be seen, HySAD performs the best among the four detectors, and the performance is relatively robust with all the x values. In contrast, NB and PCA do not clearly detect AoP attacks, especially when x is small. To our surprise, C4.5 is second only to HySAD in AoP attack detection.

7. APPLICATION TO PRODUCT RECOMMENDATION: THE AMAZON.CN CASE

Amazon China (http://www.amazon.cn), founded in May 2000 and headquartered in Beijing, is the China operation of Amazon, the world's largest e-commerce company. Everyday, over 2.6 million products are browsed by tens of thousands of users on Amazon.cn, and a huge volume of product reviews are published online continuously. These reviews provide valuable information about products to consumers, but are probably fraudulently used by shilling attackers to promote special products. In this case study, we exploit HySAD for shilling attack detection on Amazon.cn.

7.1 Data Preprocessing

A review dataset from Amazon.cn was used in this situation, which contained 2347178 reviews from 49289 users on 504170 products. Each record contains the information with the following attributes: review_ID, User_ID, ASIN (the product identifier), review title, overall rating, created date, updated date, and is_verified_purchase (a boolean variable indicates whether the user indeed bought that item).

Considering the fact that target items tend to have many ratings, we first extracted the products which had been rated over 100 times. We then selected the users who had rated more than 15 extracted products. After that, we obtained a

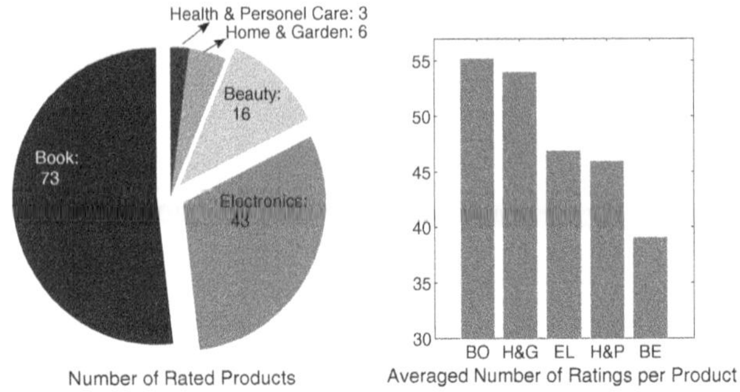

Figure 9: Product categories vulnerable to attacks.

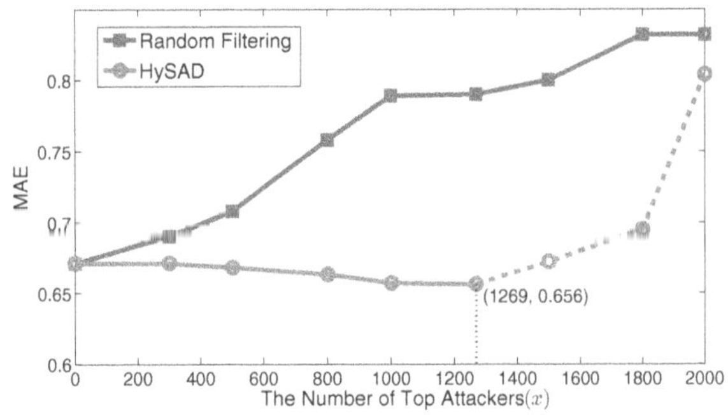

Figure 10: The enhancement of UCF by HySAD.

user subset D, which contained 130540 ratings of 3005 users on 2321 products. In general, D is expected to contain a much bigger proportion of attackers than the raw data.

7.2 Attacker Recognition

Two steps were employed for attacker recognition:

Step 1: Generating L**.** Let $L = \emptyset$, $d = 10$, $\lambda = 1$, and $\eta = 1$. We ran HySAD$_2$ on D to obtain the unsupervised classification results for two classes. The results were then sent to the experts at Amazon.cn for manual labeling, from whom we received 50 attackers and 100 normal users. We further divided the 50 attackers into 34 AFM attackers and 16 RFM attackers, according to their feature values, and finally obtained L of three classes.

Step 2: Running HySAD. We ran HySAD$_3$ on D using L, with $d = 5$, $\lambda = 1$, and $\eta = 1$, and got 1269 attackers and 1736 normal users. We then ranked the attackers in the decreasing order of $\max\{\Omega_{AF}, \Omega_{RF}\}$. The selected five features are TMF, WDA, $LengthVar$, $RDMA$ and $MeanVar$, which are quite different to the ones for the `MovieLens` and `Netflix` data sets.

We also investigated what types of products were more easily subjected to shilling attacks on Amazon.cn. To this end, we counted the ratings of attackers on the frequently rated products (≥ 30 ratings). As can be seen from Fig. 9, the five categories, Book (BO), Electronics (EL), Beauty (BE), Home & Garden (H&G), and Health & Personal Care (H&P), contain the products most rated by the attacks, although the average number of ratings per product indicates a different order of the five categories.

7.3 Recommendation Enhancement

Given the ranked 1269 attackers, we can now improve the accuracy of a recommender system. The User-based Collaborative Filtering (UCF) method [7] was used for product recommendation. It adopts the weighted Pearson correlation coefficient as the similarity measure (with a threshold 0.1), and sets the number of nearest neighbors to 20. The products with top-10 scores were recommended to users in the test set. The widely adopted measure Mean Absolute Error (MAE) [12], was used for recommendation evaluation. A smaller MAE indicates a higher recommendation quality.

Fig. 10 shows the recommendation quality of UCF after filtering out top-x attackers. As can be seen from the dotted line, the MAE value firstly decreases with the increase of x, until the maximum value 1269 is met. It then increases with $x \geq 1500$. This implies that the attackers detected by HySAD indeed degrade the performance of UCF, which in turn justifies the effectiveness of HySAD. For comparison, we also tested UCF after filtering out x users randomly (denoted as the *random filtering* scheme), and obtained the squared line in Fig. 10. Apparently, random filtering harms, rather than produces a good response for UCF.

7.4 Attacker Analysis

Here, we take a closer look at the attacker behaviors. We selected the top-20 attackers and analyzed them from three aspects: review behavior, purchase behavior, and Amazon.cn ranking. The review and purchase information in the original data and the ranking information on Amazon.cn were used for this study. It is interesting to note that the top-20 attackers can be further divided into three categories:

- **Pusher** (9 users). Pushers are the evident attackers, who use almost the same adwords as product reviews, purchase none of the reviewed products, and have no ranking from Amazon.cn. For instance, the attacker with ID 1095061968 rated many electronic products, but only left the following review: *Dirty cheap! Believe it or not! 40% discount for all products!*

- **Tricker** (7 users). Trickers are more cautious attackers. They often generate diverse reviews, and have Amazon.cn rankings as normal users, although the rankings may be low. However, the purchase behaviors betray them. They seldom buy rated products, although often claim that they did. Moreover, they only review products in the same category. The attacker "joe5138" is such an example, who gave five points to all the books in a certain financial series, but actually never bought any of them (information can be found at http://www.amazon.cn).

- **Lurker** (4 users). Lurkers act almost like normal users. They review diverse products, give differnt ratings and abundant reviews, buy some of the rated products, and may have a high Amazon.cn ranking. The only problem is, they often rate a lot of products in a very short period. From this aspect, a lurker may be a professional/parttime product reviewer of Amazon.cn, or a normal user who often seeks online discounts by publishing reviews. For instance, the user "Xiao'an" is lurker who reviewed two Motorola cell-phones, two Nokia cell-phones, one laptop, seven books, one sunscreen, and three bags for men and women in a very short period at September 11, 2008 (information can be found at http://www.amazon.cn).

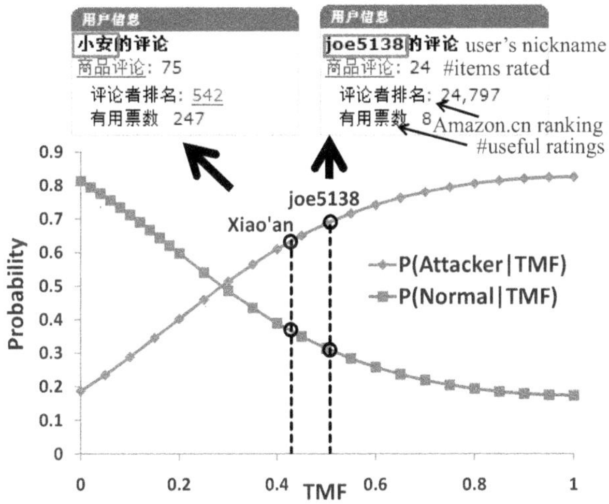

Figure 11: The TMF of two hidden attackers.

Fig. 11 shows one reason why HySAD considered "joe5138" and "Xiao'an" as attackers. As can be seen, judged by the Target Model Focus (TMF) metric, these two users deviate heavily from the normal users. This implies that both of them tend to give high ratings to items that are rated frequently and highly by some other users, i.e. the potential target items in shilling attacks. This, in turn, illustrates that HySAD has a good model interpretability, which is very important for real-world applications. Note that the two upper boxes in Fig. 11 are given by Amazon.cn.

8. CONCLUSIONS

This paper proposes a system called HySAD for hybrid shilling attack detection. In general, HySAD is a semi-supervised learning system that makes use of both unlabeled and labeled user profiles for multi-class modeling. Experimental results demonstrate that HySAD is particularly effective against hybrid attacks, even when presented with obfuscated strategies. A real-life case study on Amazon.cn also demonstrates the effectiveness of HySAD in improving the performance of a collaborative-filtering recommender system, and the ability of HySAD to help explore interesting attacker behaviors. These, in turn, justify the value of HySAD for real-world applications.

ACKNOWLEDGEMENTS

This research was partially supported by the National Natural Science Foundation of China (NSFC) (Nos. 61103229, 71072172), Industry Projects in the Jiangsu S&T Pillar Program (No. BE2011198), and Jiangsu Provincial Colleges and Universities Outstanding S&T Innovation Team Fund(No. 2001013). The second author was also supported in part by the National Natural Science Foundation of China (NSFC) (Nos. 70901002, 71171007, 70890080, 71028002).

9. REFERENCES

[1] S. Asch. Effects of group pressure upon the modification and distortion of judgments. In H. Guetzkow, editor, *Groups, Leadership, and Men: Research in Human Relations*, pages 17–190. Pittsburgh: Carnegie Press, 1951.

[2] J. Bennett and S. Lanning. The netflix prize. In *Proceedings of KDD Cup and Workshop*, San Jose, California, USA, 2007.

[3] R. Burke and B. M. et al. Classification features for attack detection in collaborative recommendation systems. In *KDD'06*, 2006.

[4] R. Burke, B. M. C. Williams, and R. Bhaumik. Segment-based injection attacks against collaborative filtering recommender systems. In *ICDM'05*, 2005.

[5] V. Castelli and T. Cover. On the exponential value of labeled samples. *Pattern Recognition Letters*, 16(1):105–111, 1995.

[6] P. Chirita, W. Nejdl, and C. Zamfir. Preventing shilling attacks in online recommender systems. In *WIDM'05*, pages 67–74, 2005.

[7] J. Herlocker, J. Konstan, L. Terveen, and J. Riedl. Evaluating collaborative filtering recommender systems. *TOIS*, 22(1):5–53, 2004.

[8] N. Hurley, Z. Cheng, and M. Zhang. Statistical attack detection. In *RecSys'09*, 2009.

[9] S. Lam and J. Riedl. Shilling recommender systems for fun and profit. In *WWW'04*, pages 393–402, 2004.

[10] J. Lee and D. Zhu. Shilling attack detection—a new approach for a trustworthy recommender system. *INFORMS Journal on Computing*.

[11] H. Liu, H. Motoda, and L. Yu. Feature selection with selective sampling. In *ICML'02*, 2002.

[12] Q. Liu, E. Chen, H. Xiong, H. Ding, and J. Chen. Enhancing collaborative filtering by user interest expansion via personalized ranking. *TSMCB*, 2011.

[13] B. Mehta and W. Nejdl. Unsupervised strategies for shilling detection and robust collaborative filtering. *User Modeling and User-Adapted Interaction*, 19(1-2):65–97, 2009.

[14] B. Mobasher, R. Burke, C. Williams, and R. Bhaumik. Analysis and detection of segment-focused attacks against collaborative recommendation. In *WebKDD Workshop*, 2006.

[15] B. Mobasher and R. B. et al. Toward trustworthy recommender systems: An analysis of attack models and algorithm robustness. *TOIT*, 7(4):1–40, 2007.

[16] K. Nigam, A. Mccallum, S. Thrun, and T. Mitchill. Text classification from labeled and unlabeled documents using em. *ML*, 39(2):103–134, 2000.

[17] M. O'Mahony, N. Hurley, N. Kushmerick, and G. Silvestre. Collaborative recommendation: A robustness analysis. *TOIT*, 4:344–377, 2004.

[18] F. Ricci, L. Rokach, B. Shapira, and P. Kantor. *Recommender Systems Handbook*. Spinger, 2011.

[19] X. Su, H.-J. Zeng, and Z. Chen. Finding group shilling in recommendation system. In *WWW'05*, 2005.

[20] P. Tan, M. Steinbach, and V. Kumar. *Introduction to Data Mining*. Addison-Wesley, 2005.

[21] C. Williams. Profile injection attack detection for securing collaborative recommender systems. Technical report, DePaul University, 2006.

[22] S. Zhang, A. Chakrabarti, J. Ford, and F. Makedon. Attack detection in time series for recommender systems. In *KDD'06*, 2006.

Following the Electrons: Methods for Power Management in Commercial Buildings

Gowtham Bellala, Manish Marwah, Martin Arlitt, Geoff Lyon, Cullen Bash
Hewlett Packard Laboratories
firstname.lastname@hp.com

ABSTRACT

Commercial buildings are significant consumers of electricity. The first step towards better energy management in commercial buildings is monitoring consumption. However, instrumenting every electrical panel in a large commercial building is expensive and wasteful. In this paper, we propose a greedy meter (sensor) placement algorithm based on maximization of information gained, subject to a cost constraint. The algorithm provides a near-optimal solution guarantee. Furthermore, to identify power saving opportunities, we use an unsupervised anomaly detection technique based on a low-dimensional embedding. Further, to better manage resources such as lighting and HVAC, we propose a semi-supervised approach combining hidden Markov models (HMM) and a standard classifier to model occupancy based on readily available port-level network statistics.

Categories and Subject Descriptors

H.4 [**Information Systems Applications**]: Miscellaneous

General Terms

Algorithms, Measurement, Performance

Keywords

Commercial buildings, power management, meter placement, anomaly detection, occupancy modeling

1. INTRODUCTION

In the United States alone, there are an estimated five million commercial buildings. In 2010, these buildings consumed about 1.3 trillion kWh of electricity, roughly one third of the electricity generated in the country. The energy costs for commercial buildings exceeds $100 billion annually. Due to recent economic turmoil, and increased awareness of environmental concerns (e.g., global climate change), many companies want to reduce power use in their buildings. Often, they turn to consulting firms for services like building energy efficiency analyses. The work described in this paper addresses shortcomings of existing analyses of this sort.

A first challenge for improving power use in a building is understanding how much power each appliance or device in the building uses. One option is to install power meters on all electrical panels, to collect usage data near the consumers, and get a (approximate) per-appliance breakdown of power use. The main disadvantage of this approach is the cost to buy and install the meters. For companies that own a lot of buildings (e.g., Walmart has more than 10,000 stores globally), this cost becomes prohibitively expensive. Thus, one research question we address is where to place a limited set of meters in a building, while minimizing the information loss. We propose an efficient greedy algorithm that provides a near-optimal solution.

A second challenge we investigate is how to systematically monitor building energy use and automatically detect problems that arise over time. A limitation of manual consulting services is that they can only identify issues that are occurring at the time the analysis is conducted, and typically only a limited number of panels are monitored, identified by an expert based on the likelihood of energy savings. Having a consultant repeat the study on a regular (e.g., daily) basis is not cost effective, so an automated technique is highly desired. We present results from applying our unsupervised anomaly (fault) detection and ranking methods for monitoring tens of meters over a six month period.

Lastly, consulting studies will typically recommend static solutions to reduce building energy use. For example, turn on all lights only during work hours (e.g., 8am to 6pm), and turn most off otherwise. While such techniques do help reduce power use in a building, further savings are possible. One approach is to only turn on lights (or HVAC systems) in areas where people are currently in, and to turn them off when the people leave. To facilitate such dynamic resource management, we developed a semi-supervised method for occupancy modeling.

Our group is instrumenting three large commercial buildings on the HP Labs campus in Palo Alto, CA. This instrumentation will provide extensive data on the campus power use, which will establish the "ground truth" against which we will evaluate our power management methods.

The paper makes the following contributions:

- It proposes a greedy algorithm for meter placement in a building's electrical infrastructure, to maximize mutual information while minimizing the cost of metering. Besides being computationally efficient, we also show that the proposed greedy algorithm guarantees a

KDD'12, August 12–16, 2012, Beijing, China.

Figure 1: The HP Labs Palo Alto Campus.

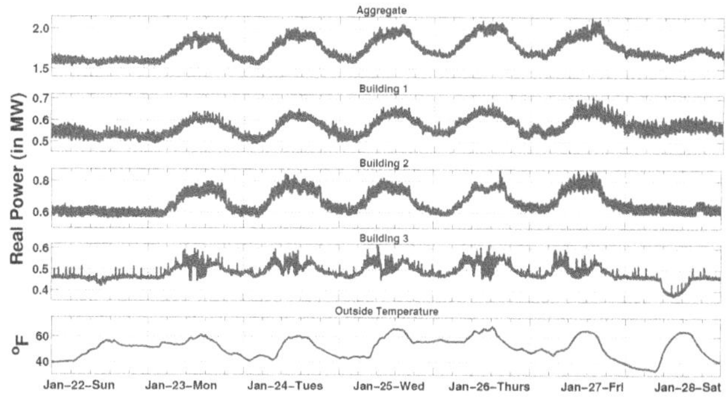

Figure 2: Campus power use and outside temperature.

near-optimal solution. In particular, we show that mutual information becomes submodular under a special graphical structure that arises in distribution networks such as power, water and gas.

- The meter placement results gauged by the ability of the selected meters to predict measurements of the unselected ones are better on average by about 15% over other methods considered.
- The results are demonstrated for six months of data from a large test bed (three buildings totaling 300,000 sq. ft.). The anomaly detection, and occupancy modeling techniques, described in more detail in [3], are validated over this data set.

The remainder of the paper is organized as follows. Section 2 provides an overview of the HP Labs campus, the power delivery and measurement infrastructure, and the campus power use characteristics. Section 3 describes our KDD methods. Section 4 evaluates our methods. Section 5 discusses related work. Section 6 summarizes our work and future directions.

2. CAMPUS OVERVIEW

The HP Labs campus contains six main buildings with a total footprint of 700,000 sq. ft. We are instrumenting three two-storey buildings (1, 2, 3), as highlighted in Figure 1. These three buildings have a 300,000 sq. ft. footprint and host about 500 occupants.

2.1 Power Distribution Topology

Buildings 1, 2 and 3 are powered by a single utility feed (3-phase 12.5kV). An emergency generator (3-phase 480V) maintains critical loads in the event of a utility failure. Automatic transfer switches (ATS) are used to revert from the utility to backup power. Each building has a main distribution panel (3-phase 480V) that branches to about 10 major sub-loads or sub-panels. A 135kW photo voltaic array on top of Building 3 offsets power demand during daylight hours.

2.2 Power Data Collection

To date, 33 power meters have been deployed on our campus. These include meters for building and top-level load distribution panels in Buildings 1-3. We are now instrumenting the second-tier distribution panels within each building, to obtain finer grained electrical data for our future work.

The installed electrical meters are commercial (3-phase) devices from Schneider Electric (`www.schneider-electric.com`). Data is retrieved from each meter every 10 seconds using the MODBUS over Ethernet protocol. The data includes metrics such as line voltage, real and apparent power, power factor, current and frequency. The data is stored in a PI-Server from OSIsoft (`www.osisoft.com`).

2.3 Campus Power Use Characteristics

As further motivation for the challenges addressed in this paper, we briefly examine some characteristics of the campus power use.[1] The top graph in Figure 2 shows the total power use for Buildings 1-3 over a one week period (from Jan. 22 through Jan. 28, 2012). The peak load is nearly 2 MW; understanding how to reduce this would translate directly to operational savings for the company. The base load is roughly 1.5 MW. An implication of this is very little insight on what is responsible for campus power consumption can be gleaned (e.g., via disaggregation techniques like [9] since none of the algorithms scale up to handle hundreds to thousands of loads present in commercial buildings, and further, none of the methods disaggregate base load) from the aggregate power. This means that more meters must be installed. Our meter placement algorithm addresses the issue of how many meters are needed and where they are needed, to minimize the cost while maximizing the information obtained.

The middle three graphs in Figure 2 show the total power demand for Buildings 1, 2 and 3, respectively. The bottom graph shows the outside temperature. Comparing this graph to the others reveals a correlation between outside temperature, occupancy (i.e., work hours) and power use. This motivates our investigation in Section 3.3 of occupancy modeling, to reduce the use of heating or cooling in areas of the building that people are not actively using.

3. METHODS

Figure 3 shows the overall framework of our approach. The meter placement algorithm forms the basis for instrumenting a building power infrastructure. For building power management, we propose an unsupervised anomaly detection and ranking method based on low dimensional embed-

[1] We expect these characteristics to exist with many other commercial buildings as well.

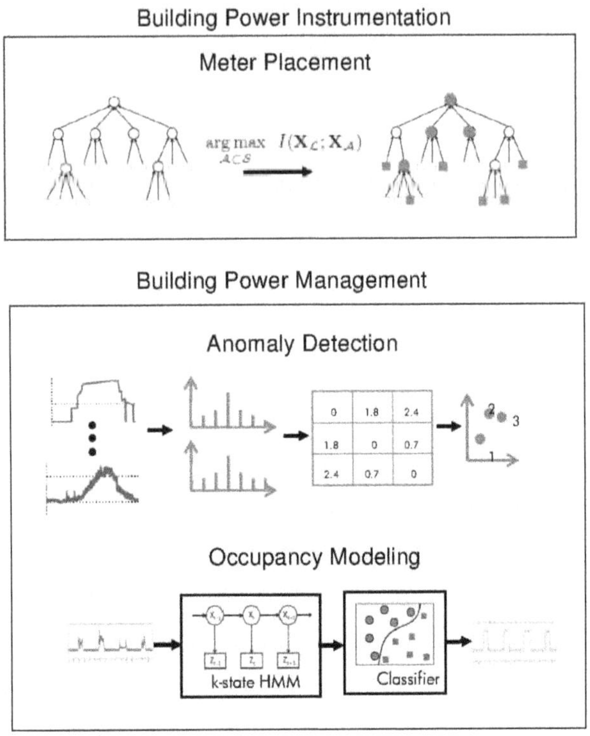

Figure 3: Overview of the methods used.

ding and k-nearest neighbors. For dynamic control of lighting and HVAC resources, we describe a semi-supervised approach that uses network port statistics to model occupancy.

3.1 Meter Placement

As noted in Section 2.3, the significant base load in the power demand of these buildings and the sheer number of devices in a large commercial building make known load disaggregation methods unreliable, thus requiring extensive metering of different electrical panels in each of these buildings for fine-grained power monitoring. However, one issue with this approach is that the total number of panels that could potentially be monitored can be very large, to the extent that meter deployment at all these locations is not economical (the cost of each power meter ranges between \$900 and \$3,000. This raises an interesting research question as to how and which panels should be selected for power meter deployment.

There are several criteria one could use to choose the panels for meter deployment. They include the total energy consumption of a panel, variability in the energy consumption, number of sub-panels/loads, predictability of panel power demand, or an information-theoretic measure. We choose mutual information, an information-theoretic measure that in a loose sense chooses panels that are highly unpredictable in terms of their power demands. As we show in Section 4.1, the panels selected using this criterion are superior to those selected using criterion such as the total energy consumption or variability in energy consumption.

Next, we demonstrate how this problem can be formulated as an optimization problem with the goal of choosing the set of panels with maximum information content.

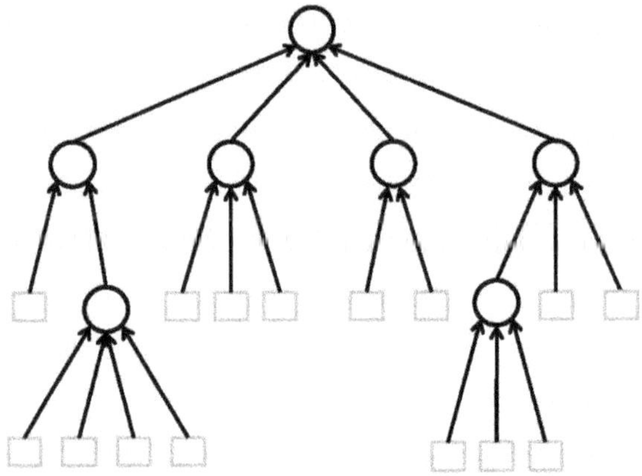

Figure 4: Example topology of building electrical panels where meters can be installed.

3.1.1 *Problem Formulation*

Before we formulate the problem, we need to introduce some notation. The panels at different locations on the site are related in a topological manner that can be represented by a tree, as shown in Figure 4. Each node in this tree denotes a panel, where the leaf nodes (denoted by squares) correspond to panels that directly feed either a single load (e.g., a chiller or a compressor) or a set of loads (e.g., lighting load). The remaining nodes in the tree topology (denoted by circles) correspond to panels that feed other panels given by their child nodes in the tree.

Let $\mathcal{S}$ denote the entire set of panels, i.e., all the nodes in a given tree, and let $\mathcal{L} \subset \mathcal{S}$ denote the set of leaf nodes. For any node $i \in \mathcal{S}$, let X_i be a random variable denoting the power consumption recorded at panel i. Then, for any set of nodes $\mathcal{A} \subset \mathcal{S}$, we denote by $\mathbf{X}_\mathcal{A}$ the random variables associated with the nodes in $\mathcal{A}$.

Given a constraint on the number of meters that can be afforded (k), we use mutual information as a criteria to choose the best panels for meter deployment, which can be formulated as an optimization problem shown below.

$$\arg\max_{\mathcal{A}\subset\mathcal{S}} \; I(\mathbf{X}_\mathcal{L};\mathbf{X}_\mathcal{A}) \quad \text{s.t.} \quad |\mathcal{A}| \le k, \tag{1}$$

where $I(\mathbf{X}_\mathcal{L};\mathbf{X}_\mathcal{A})$ denotes the amount of information conveyed by monitoring power consumption at panels in $\mathcal{A}$ about the power consumption at panels in $\mathcal{L}$. Note that when $k \ge |\mathcal{L}|$, i.e., in the scenario where one could afford to deploy meters at each of the leaf nodes that directly feed a bunch of loads, the mutual information is maximized by choosing $\mathcal{A}$ to be the set of all the panels in $\mathcal{L}$. On the other hand when $k < |\mathcal{L}|$, the above optimization problem attempts to find the best set of panels that provide maximum information about power consumption at each of these leaf nodes (the last layer of panels in the hierarchy).

3.1.2 *Proposed Solution*

Mutual Information is given by

$$I(\mathbf{X}_\mathcal{L};\mathbf{X}_\mathcal{A}) = H(\mathbf{X}_\mathcal{L}) - H(\mathbf{X}_\mathcal{L}|\mathbf{X}_\mathcal{A}),$$

which corresponds to the reduction in uncertainty about power consumption at panels in $\mathcal{L}$ given the power consumption information at panels in $\mathcal{A}$, where

$$H(\mathbf{X}_{\mathcal{L}}) = -\sum_{\mathbf{x}_{\mathcal{L}}} \Pr(\mathbf{X}_{\mathcal{L}} = \mathbf{x}_{\mathcal{L}}) \log_2 (\Pr(\mathbf{X}_{\mathcal{L}} = \mathbf{x}_{\mathcal{L}})), \quad \text{and}$$

$$H(\mathbf{X}_{\mathcal{L}}|\mathbf{X}_{\mathcal{A}}) = -\sum_{\mathbf{x}_{\mathcal{L}}, \mathbf{x}_{\mathcal{A}}} \Pr(\mathbf{X}_{\mathcal{L}} = \mathbf{x}_{\mathcal{L}}, \mathbf{X}_{\mathcal{A}} = \mathbf{x}_{\mathcal{A}}) \log_2 (\Pr(\mathbf{X}_{\mathcal{L}} = \mathbf{x}_{\mathcal{L}} | \mathbf{X}_{\mathcal{A}} = \mathbf{x}_{\mathcal{A}})).$$

Unfortunately, the optimization problem in (1) is NP-hard. Hence, we propose a greedy approach to optimize the given problem. The greedy algorithm chooses panels for meter deployment in a sequential manner, where given the set of panels that have already been chosen by the algorithm (denoted by $\mathcal{A}$), the next best panel is chosen to be the one that maximizes the gain in mutual information, i.e.,

$$j^* = \arg\max_{j \notin \mathcal{A}} I(\mathbf{X}_{\mathcal{L}}; \mathbf{X}_{\mathcal{A} \cup j}) - I(\mathbf{X}_{\mathcal{L}}; \mathbf{X}_{\mathcal{A}}).$$

The solution obtained using the above greedy algorithm is not necessarily an optimal solution for the optimization problem in (1). However, we show below that the obtained greedy solution is guaranteed to be near-optimal.

3.1.3 Near-optimality of greedy solution

To show that the solution obtained using the above greedy approach is near-optimal, we rely on the theory of submodularity introduced by Nemhauser *et al.* [21] and popularized by the work of Krause *et al.* [14, 13].

Krause *et al.* [14] study budgeted maximization problems of the form

$$\arg\max_{\mathcal{A} \subset \mathcal{S}} F(\mathcal{A}) \quad \text{s.t. } |\mathcal{A}| \leq k,$$

where $\mathcal{S} = \{1, \cdots, N\}$ is a set of elements and $F : \mathcal{A} \to \mathbb{R}$ is a function that maps the set of elements to the real line. A greedy solution to this problem is to select elements sequentially according to

$$j^* = \arg\max_{j \notin \mathcal{A}} F(\mathcal{A} \cup j) - F(\mathcal{A}).$$

Krause *et al.* [14] show that the solution obtained using this greedy approach is near-optimal in the following sense

$$F_{\text{greedy}} \geq \left(1 - \frac{1}{e}\right) F_{\text{opt}},$$

iff the objective function F is submodular, where submodularity is defined below.

DEFINITION 1. **(Submodularity)** *Let F be a function that maps from a set of elements $\mathcal{S}$ to the real line $\mathbb{R}$. Then, F is said to be submodular iff $\forall \mathcal{A} \subseteq \mathcal{B} \subseteq \mathcal{S}$ and for any $j \notin \mathcal{B}$,*

$$F(\mathcal{A} \cup j) - F(\mathcal{A}) \geq F(\mathcal{B} \cup j) - F(\mathcal{B}).$$

In our optimization problem, the objective function is mutual information, which unfortunately is not submodular, except for some known special cases [13, 16, 17]. However, as we will show below, in our problem setting, mutual information turns out to be submodular, thus guaranteeing near-optimality of the above greedy algorithm.

LEMMA 1. *Given the tree topology described in Section 3.1, let $\mathcal{S}$ denote the set of nodes in the tree and $\mathcal{L}$ the set of leaf nodes. Then, $\forall \mathcal{A} \subseteq \mathcal{B} \subseteq \mathcal{S}$, and for any $j \notin \mathcal{B}$,*

$$I(\mathbf{X}_{\mathcal{L}}; \mathbf{X}_{\mathcal{A} \cup j}) - I(\mathbf{X}_{\mathcal{L}}; \mathbf{X}_{\mathcal{A}}) \geq I(\mathbf{X}_{\mathcal{L}}; \mathbf{X}_{\mathcal{B} \cup j}) - I(\mathbf{X}_{\mathcal{L}}; \mathbf{X}_{\mathcal{B}}) \tag{2}$$

PROOF. From the definition of mutual information, we have

$$\begin{aligned} I(\mathbf{X}_{\mathcal{L}}; \mathbf{X}_{\mathcal{A} \cup j}) - I(\mathbf{X}_{\mathcal{L}}; \mathbf{X}_{\mathcal{A}}) &= H(\mathbf{X}_{\mathcal{L}}|\mathbf{X}_{\mathcal{A}}) - H(\mathbf{X}_{\mathcal{L}}|\mathbf{X}_{\mathcal{A} \cup j}) \\ &= H(X_j|\mathbf{X}_{\mathcal{A}}) - H(X_j|\mathbf{X}_{\mathcal{L}}, \mathbf{X}_{\mathcal{A}}), \end{aligned} \tag{3}$$

where the second equality follows from the first by expanding the entropy terms and by simple manipulation of the resulting terms. Note that the second term in (3) is equal to 0, i.e., $H(X_j|\mathbf{X}_{\mathcal{L}}, \mathbf{X}_{\mathcal{A}}) = 0$, as given the power consumption at all the leaf nodes, the power consumption at any panel upstream is completely deterministic.

Hence, the relation in (2) reduces to showing

$$H(X_j|\mathbf{X}_{\mathcal{A}}) \geq H(X_j|\mathbf{X}_{\mathcal{B}}),$$

which follows from the principle of "information never hurts" in information theory [5]. Thus, proving the submodularity of mutual information under the given tree topology. □

3.1.4 Use of Granger Causality

Another strategy to select meters would be by applying Granger causality, which considers the *direction* of flow of information unlike mutual information. Note that this could be remedied by the use of Transfer entropy, which is a version of mutual information that can detect the direction of information flow [24], however, transfer entropy is currently restricted to bivariate situations.

Granger Causality (or G-causality) test, which was initially introduced in the field of economics [8], is a statistical hypothesis test for determining whether one time series is useful in forecasting another. It is normally tested in the context of linear regression models. For example, let $X(t)$ and $Y(t)$ be two time series. Consider the following two auto-regressive models for predicting $X(t)$

$$X(t) = \sum_{j=1}^{p} a_j X(t-j) + e_1(t)$$

$$X(t) = \sum_{j=1}^{p} a_j X(t-j) + \sum_{j=1}^{p} b_j Y(t-j) + e_2(t),$$

where p is the maximum number of lagged observations included in the model, and $e_1(t), e_2(t)$ are the prediction errors (residuals) for the two regression models. If the variance in the prediction error is reduced by the inclusion of $Y(t)$ in the model, then Y is said to G-cause X. In other words, Y is said to G-cause X if the coefficients in $\{b_j\}_{j=1}^{p}$ are jointly significantly different from zero.

This test could potentially be used to reveal any hidden causal relationships between the loads (leaf nodes in the tree topology). Incorporating these relationships could further lead to a better choice of panels for meter deployment.

3.2 Anomaly Detection

Anomaly (or fault) detection is useful in detecting abnormal behavior in the power usage data collected from a building. Note that an anomaly indicates an irregular usage pattern and may not always correspond to a component failure or faulty operation. Since labeled data is difficult to obtain, we propose an unsupervised cluster-based algorithm that detects anomalous points via a low-dimensional embedding of the power data. This algorithm takes as input the power time series of a meter over a period of time, and outputs the probability of a particular day being anomalous. The probability scores can be used to rank the days in terms of anomalousness, providing a building administrator with a prioritized list of data points that require further inspection.

We refer to power data measured by a single meter over a 24 hour period (i.e., one day) as one observation or as a single power-time curve. As mentioned, we use an unsupervised approach where we cluster the power-time curves of each meter. The intuition behind this approach is that the data points that exhibit normal behavior will form tight clusters while anomalous points will lie outside these clusters.

To compare two power-time curves, we use the standard Euclidean distance measure, or the l_2 norm, between the frequency spectrum of the two power-time curves. While the frequency spectrum consists of two components - magnitude and phase, we restrict our attention to the magnitude of the frequency spectrum as it contains all the necessary information regarding the power consumption behavior.

Our algorithm consists of five steps. First, missing values in a power-time curve are imputed. Second, the frequency spectrum of the imputed power-time curve is computed. Third, the standard Euclidean distance measure is used to determine the dissimilarity between the power consumption profiles of any two days. Fourth, a low dimensional embedding of the power-curves. The fifth step uses this low dimensional embedding to compute the probability score of each observation being anomalous. We achieve this using a k-NN (nearest neighbor) density estimation algorithm. A more detailed explanation of our algorithm is provided in [3].

3.3 Occupancy Modeling

Occupancy modeling forms another important component for efficient power management in buildings. Many commercial buildings employ either a fixed time L-HVAC (lighting, heating ventilation and cooling) schedule or a fixed temperature set point schedule. This often leads to unnecessary conditioning of the building, especially when the actual occupancy is low. Hence, some recent work has suggested occupancy-based L-HVAC scheduling for efficient power management. However, most of this work assumes the availability of occupancy sensors, whose installation and maintenance may be prohibitive on a large campus.

Melfi et al. [20] propose an alternative method that uses existing network infrastructure to estimate occupancy. They studied the use of Dynamic Host Control Protocol (DHCP) logs and other explicit ways such as monitoring PC activity in estimating occupancy. We instead developed an implicit occupancy sensing procedure, where we use traffic statistics associated with layer 2 network ports in each cubicle to build occupancy models. Network switches typically maintain counters (for each physical layer 2 port) for the amount of in and out flowing traffic. We retrieve these statistics from the switches in the buildings every 30 minutes. The estimated occupancies at cube level are then used to estimate occupancy of a zone (e.g., multiple cubicles), which

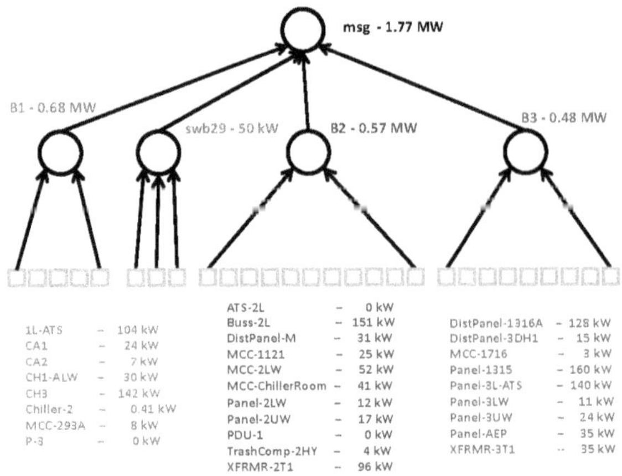

Figure 5: Tree topology of the 33 meters

can further be used for occupancy-based L-HVAC scheduling of that zone.

A primary challenge with using network data to estimate occupancy is the lack of labeled data. To address this, we consider two different approaches. The first is an unsupervised approach where we use hidden Markov model (HMM) [6] to estimate occupancy from network data. The second is a two-stage semi-supervised approach. Its first stage involves unsupervised learning using HMM, while the second trains a classifier using minimal labeled data. The two approaches are described in more detail in [3].

4. EXPERIMENTAL RESULTS

4.1 Meter Placement

To assess our meter placement method, we used the greedy algorithm described in Section 3.1 to select the most informative power meters among the 33 installed in our campus. The tree topology corresponding to these power meters is shown in Figure 5. The figure also shows their average power consumption values. For simplicity, we assumed in our experiments that the random variables corresponding to the power consumption at different panels are Gaussian.

Next, we greedily selected the meters in a sequential manner using the greedy algorithm described in Section 3.1 under three different criteria: mutual information, total power consumption and variability in power consumption. Table 1 shows a ranked list of the meters in the order in which they are selected using these three criterion. Figure 6 shows plots comparing the three ranked lists. The diagonal line (dotted red line) in these plots correspond to the scenario where the two ranked lists are exactly equal.

Given this ranked list and a budget ($t < 33$) on the number of panels that can be metered, the top t panels from the ranked list can be chosen to be metered. The power consumption measured at these metered panels can then be used to predict the power consumption at the remaining panels. We use this predictive ability as a measure of goodness of the selected meters. We compare the above three criteria based on the predictive ability of the selected panels. A random selection is included as a baseline. Figure 7(a) shows the average RMS (root mean squared) prediction error over all non-metered panels as a function of the number of panels metered (t). Similarly, Figure 7(b) shows the average normalized RMS prediction error, where the nor-

#	Total Power Consumption	Variability in Power Consumption	Mutual Information
1	msg	swb29-main	swb29-main
2	swb29-main	msg	msg
3	b1-main	b1-main	b2-Buss-2L
4	b2-main	b2-main	b1-main
5	b3-Panel-1315	b3-Panel-AEP	b1-CH1-ALW
6	b1-CH-3	b1-CH-3	b2-main
7	b3-Panel-3L-ATS	b2-DistPanel-M	b3-Panel-AEP
8	b3-DistPanel-1316A	b1-CH1-ALW	b1-CH-3
9	b1-1L-ATS	swb29-Chiller-2	b2-DistPanel-M
10	b2-XFRMR-2T1	b2-MCC-2LW	b2-MCC-2LW
11	b2-Buss-2L	b3-Panel-3UW	b1-CA-2
12	b2-MCC-2LW	b2-Panel-2UW	b3-Panel-1315

Table 1: Selection order of first 12 meters

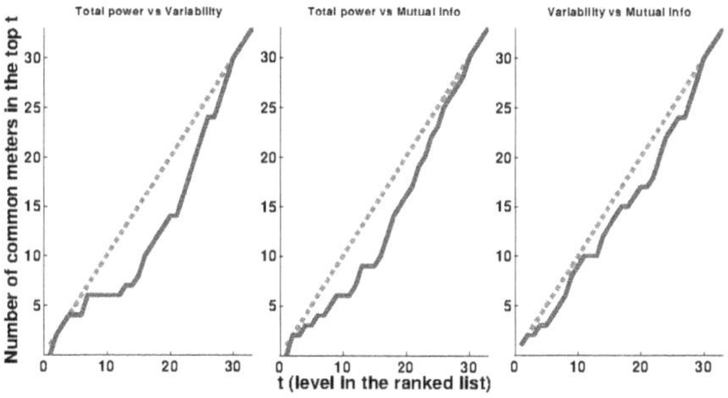

Figure 6: Comparison of ranked list similarity

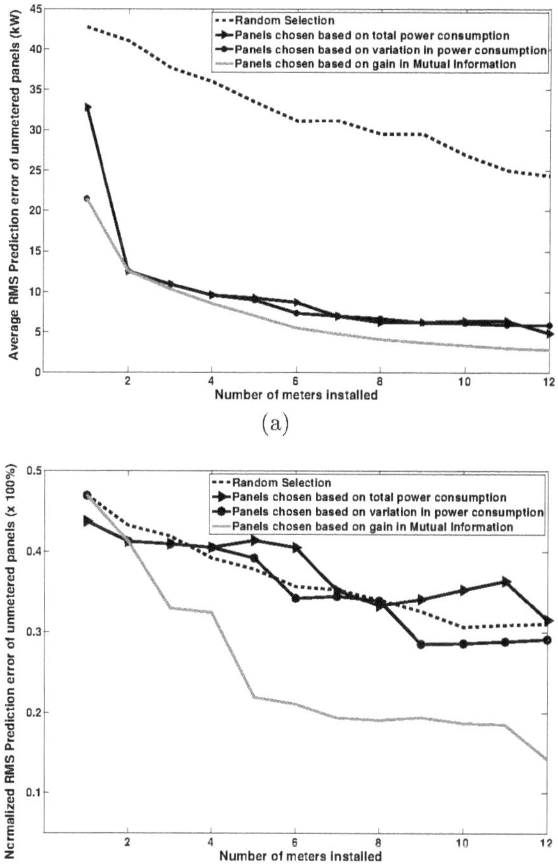

Figure 7: Comparison of the predictive ability of the panels selected for metering: (a) Average RMS prediction error (b) Average Normalized RMS prediction error

malization is based on the average power consumption of a meter. These two figures reveal that the proposed mutual information based meter deployment outperforms those based on the total power consumption and the variability in power consumption by an average of about 15%. The curve corresponding to the random selection is averaged over 100 different random orderings of the 33 meters.

Figure 8 shows the top 12 panels selected using mutual information. This solution can be verified intuitively. For example, panel b3-main is not selected as it is completely deterministic given the aggregate meter (msg) and the other three main meters (b1-main, swb29-main and b2-main). Similarly, most of the selected leaf node panels consist of loads that are less predictable given the others. For example,"b3-Panel-AEP" directly measures the power generated by the photo-voltaic array installed on building 3. This panel's output is less predictable and hence can be considered as a good choice for meter deployment.

4.1.1 Discussion and Extensions

One limitation of our current implementation is the Gaussian assumption on the distribution of the random variables. This is not a strictly valid assumption, as most panels have at least two distinct operating states, one with higher power consumption during business hours and the other with a baseload power consumption during non-business hours. Hence, a more accurate approach would be to model these random variables as a mixture of Gaussians. However, one limitation of using a Gaussian mixture model is that there is no closed form expression for entropy of a Gaussian mixture density, and hence one would need to approximate it.

4.1.2 Use of Granger Causality

As described in Section 3.1.4, we investigated applying

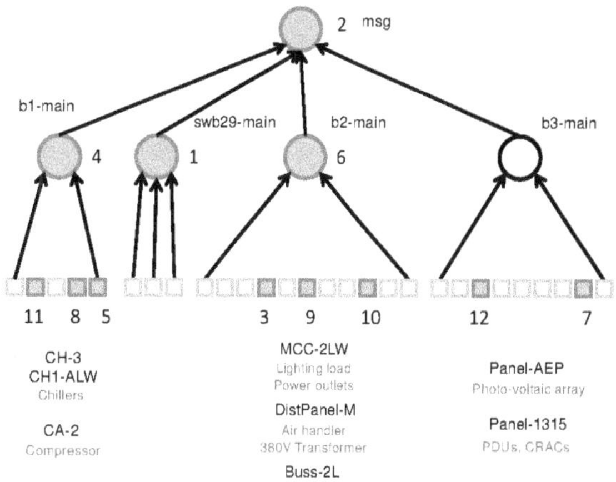

Figure 8: The panels selected by the greedy algorithm and mutual information criterion

Granger causality to a subset of meters. Figure 9 shows interesting causal relationships between 8 sub-panels in Building 1. The loads on these panels are as follows: panels b1-CA-1 and b1-CA-2 feed two different compressors, while the panels b1-CH-3, b1-CH1-ALW and swb29-Chiller-2 feed three different Chillers. The loads on the remaining 3 panels

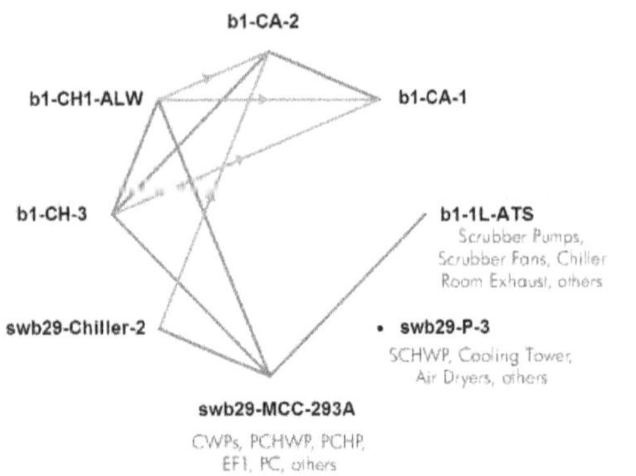

Figure 9: The causal relationship between different sub-panels in Building 1

Meter name	AUC
b1-main	0.87
b2-main	0.96
b3-main	0.99

(a)

	Category	# of Anomalies
1	High power usage	66
2	Low power usage	65
3	Irregular Shutdown	6
4	Irregular (time) usage	9
5	Oscillatory behavior	28
6	Abnormal drop/rise	29

(b)

Figure 10: Anomaly detection measurements: (a) AUC (b) Anomaly types and number.

are listed in the figure. The undirected edges demonstrate strong bi-directional causal relationships, while the directed edges demonstrate strong uni-directional causal relationship in the direction given by the arrow. Note from this figure that there is a strong causal relationship between the chillers and the compressors. For example, there is a strong causal relationship from chiller-2 to compressor-2, while chiller-3 seems to strongly G-cause compressor-1.

Furthermore, we used the G-causal test to rank the panels based on their predictive ability (results omitted for brevity). However, the mutual information based ranking performs better than the G-causal ranking with respect to the RMS prediction error on the non-metered panels. This could be due to the fact that the G-causal test is currently limited to linear regression models, whereas information theoretic measures are also sensitive to any non-linear relationships. Although extensions of the G-causal test to non-linear models exist, they are computationally less efficient and their statistical properties are not well studied [1].

4.2 Anomaly detection

We performed anomaly detection on six months of data from the 33 power meters. To validate our results, for three meters (b1-main, b2-main and b3-main) we obtained the ground truth by consulting with the building administrator, who looked at the entire time series data and marked days with potential anomalous regions. As described in Section 3.2, our algorithm assigns a probability score to each day, which can be used to obtain a ranked list of days in decreasing order of them being anomalous.

Given this ranked list, a building administrator could choose a threshold k and declare the top k points as anomalies for further inspection, and the remaining as normal, where k could vary from 0 to the maximum number of points in the input data (M). Each choice of k results in a certain number of false positives and false negatives. For example, when $k = 0$, i.e., when all the points are declared as normal, the false positive rate (FPR) is 0 while the false negative rate (FNR) is 1. On the other hand, when $k = M$, the associated FPR is 1 and FNR is 0. Varying this threshold k results in different values of FPR and FNR, leading to a receiver operating characteristic (ROC) curve. The area under the ROC curve (AUC) defines the quality of the obtained ranking. In the ideal case, where all the anomalous points are ranked at the top followed by normal points, the AUC takes the maximum value of 1. On the other hand, a random ranking achieves an AUC value of 0.5. We use AUC as a performance metric for our algorithm. Figure 10(a) shows the performance of our algorithm on 3 meters.

Further, we applied our algorithm on the remaining 30 meters, where we obtained a ranked list of anomalous days for each meter. We then manually characterized the top anomalies (for a conservative k value) by assigning them categories, as shown in Figure 10(b). Note that a particular anomaly could belong to multiple categories. Detecting these anomalies could potentially offer several benefits such as energy savings, detecting faulty equipment resulting in savings in maintenance costs, etc. Potential power savings in the high power usage and irregular time usage anomalies varied from around 50 to 2000 kWh per anomaly. In Figure 11, we demonstrate 4 of these 6 categories.

Figure 11(a) corresponds to the air handlers in a building, while Figure 11(b) corresponds to a chiller load. The low-dimensional embeddings obtained using MDS in both cases show clusters of normal behavior (June 30th and June 17th), and points (circled) that were detected as anomalous.

For the fan load, two anomalous points are seen (July 6th and July 7th) corresponding to high and irregular time usage (categories 1 and 4), where the air handlers were operating all through the night. Detecting and correcting these anomalies could have potentially saved 70 kWh over these two days. For the chiller load, three anomalous points corresponding to three consecutive days have been detected (July 5th and July 6th shown in the figure), where the chiller was abruptly shut down (categories 2 and 3) during business hours. If this was not caused due to a maintenance schedule, it could potentially correspond to a failed component.

4.3 Occupancy modeling

In this section, we demonstrate the superior performance of the proposed two-stage approach for occupancy estimation. In particular, we show that the use of k-state HMM as a pre-processing step in the two stage approach leads to a better classification accuracy over directly using the network switch port statistics in the classification algorithm. We compare the performance of the 2-stage approach with that of a 1-stage approach where the classifier is trained directly based on the network switch level port statistics.

To quantify the estimation accuracy of these algorithms, we collected ground truth data from 10 occupants over a pe-

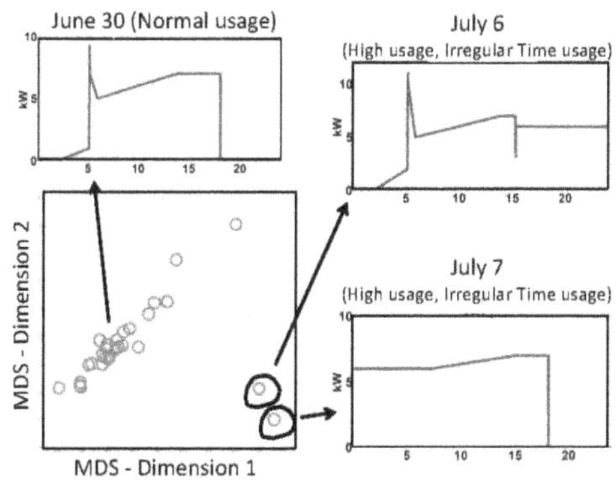

(a) Load corresponding to air handlers.

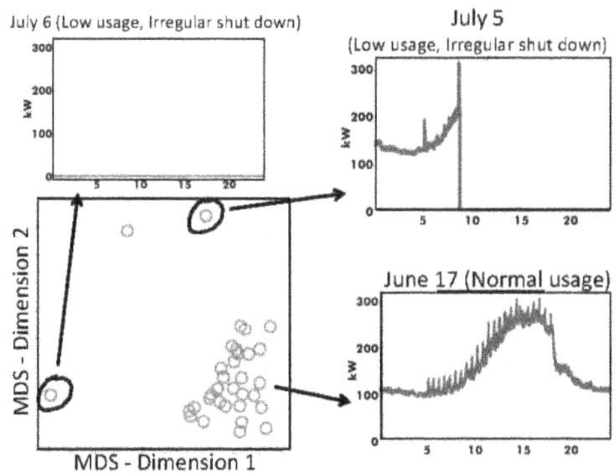

(b) Load corresponding to a chiller.

Figure 11: Examples of low dimensional embedding

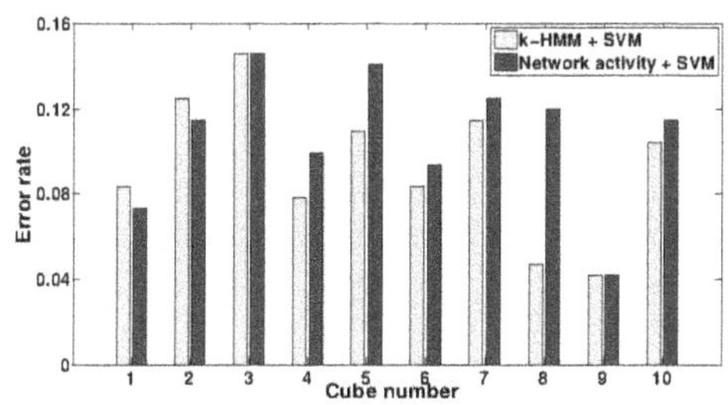

(a)

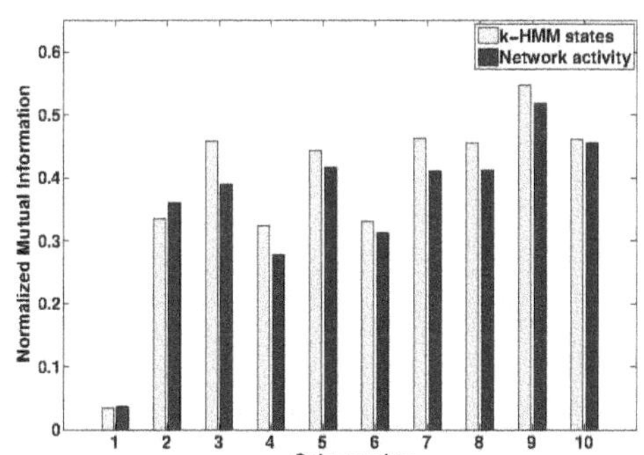

(b)

Figure 12: (a) Average error rates of models. (b) Feature quality.

riod of 16 weekdays. The occupants recorded their presence in their cube at a time resolution of 30 minutes, where an occupant marks their presence only if they are present for a majority of that 30 minute period. The in and out flowing network switch statistics are also collected every 30 minutes.

Figure 12 shows the experimental results. Figure 12(a) compares the average error rate between the two approaches, where the error rate is averaged over 16 different test cases. Figure 12(b) compares the quality of the two features (k-HMM output and network statistics) in terms of estimating the occupancy states. The feature quality is measured using normalized mutual information between the feature states and the true occupancy labels. The figures show that the k-HMM output has a better feature quality resulting in an improved classification accuracy.

The estimated occupancy states for each cube are then aggregated to estimate the occupancy of a zone. We further show that the estimated zone occupancy using the proposed 2-stage approach can be used to dynamically control the lighting in that zone, resulting in an energy savings of around 9.53%. More details on use of this approach to control lighting are provided in [3].

5. RELATED WORK

Commercial buildings consume a lot of energy [25], which motivates research to improve building energy efficiency. As discussed in Section 1, there are a variety of challenges to address. The problem of selecting optimal locations for meter placement can be framed as a budgeted optimization problem. This problem has been well studied in the literature in different contexts, such as in the case of sensor placement in a water distribution network [18] or observation selection in an autonomous robotic exploration [15]. Several different criteria have been proposed in the literature for selecting these optimal locations [15]. The most popular among them being mutual information [16, 17]. However, as we discussed earlier, this constrained optimization problem with mutual information as an objective function is known to be NP-hard, and hence requires use of greedy, near-optimal strategies to solve.

Examining data for anomalies is a known approach for identifying abnormal system behavior. Catterson et al. use this approach to monitor old power transformers [4]. Their goal is to pro-actively search for abnormal behavior that may indicate the transformer is about to fail. Li et al. [19] search for anomalies in building power consumption, where they employ simple statistical tests such as the Q-test to detect time points with abnormal power usage. On the other hand, Jakkula and Cook [11] demonstrate the superiority of a clustering based approach over such simple statistical tests in the context of identifying abnormal activities in household power consumption data. Our work on anomaly detection is built on observations in these studies.

Occupants of a building contribute to its energy footprint. Unfortunately, directly tracking the number of people in a building is often more difficult than one might think. To estimate the occupancy, we create models based on data retrieved from periodic scans of the computer network in the campus. This is a similar approach to that of Newsham and Birt [22]. Erickson *et al.* [7], Agarwal *et al.* [2], and Kim et al. [12] model occupancy through a variety of means. Rice et al. develop a model of building energy consumption, to offer insights on where energy is used [23]. Hay and Rice investigate how to assign power use to individuals, who may be able to adjust their behaviors to reduce the aggregate power consumption [10]. Our work is complementary.

6. CONCLUSIONS

Commercial buildings consume significant amounts of energy. Concerns over energy prices and global climate change are motivating building operators to reduce energy consumption. In this paper, we propose and evaluate three methods to aid in this effort. Our meter placement algorithm is both efficient and effective, guaranteeing a near optimal solution to information maximization by exploiting submodularity. In comparisons with other methods, the ability of the meter set selected using our algorithm to predict the measurements of the unselected meter set were found to be superior (by an average of about 15%). Our anomaly detection method is shown to identify numerous types of unexpected consumption patterns. Lastly, our occupancy modeling approach can be used to dynamically control lighting or HVAC resources, thereby reducing their energy consumption.

We plan to extend our work in several ways. We intend to leverage occupancy modeling results for enhancing anomaly detection. Further, we plan to automate the anomaly characterization task, and extend our algorithm to incorporate feedback from a building administrator. In addition, we are increasing instrumentation on our campus, to aid in validating our methods. Finally, further methods may be developed as we evolve our test bed into a demonstrator.

7. REFERENCES

[1] `http://www.scholarpedia.org/article/Granger_causality`.

[2] Y. Agarwal, B. Balaji, J. Lyles, M. Wei, and T. Weng. Occupancy-driven energy management for smart building automation. In *ACM Workshop on Embedded Sensing Systems for Energy-Efficiency in Buildings (BuildSys)*, Zurich, Switzerland, 2010.

[3] G. Bellala, M. Manish, M. Arlitt, G. Lyon, and C. Bash. Towards an understanding of campus-scale power consumption. In *ACM Workshop on Embedded Sensing Systems for Energy-Efficiency in Buildings (BuildSys)*, 2011.

[4] V. Catterson, S. McArthur, and G. Moss. Online conditional anomaly detection in multivariate data for transformer monitoring. *IEEE Transactions on Power Delivery*, 25(4):2556–2564, 2010.

[5] T. M. Cover and J. A. Thomas. *Elements of Information Theory.* Wiley Interscience, 1991.

[6] R. O. Duda, P. E. Hart, and D. G. Stork. *Pattern Classification.* Wiley, New York, 2. edition, 2001.

[7] V. Erickson, Y. Lin, A. Kamthe, and R. Brahme. Energy efficient building environment control strategies using real-time occupancy measurements. In *ACM Workshop on Embedded Sensing Systems for Energy-Efficiency in Buildings (BuildSys)*, Berkeley, CA, 2009.

[8] C. W. J. Granger. Investigating causal relations by econometric models and cross-spectral methods. *Econometrica*, 1969.

[9] G. Hart. Nonintrusive appliance load monitoring. *Proceedings of the IEEE*, 80(2):1870–1891, 1992.

[10] S. Hay and A. Rice. The case for apportionment. In *ACM Workshop on Embedded Sensing Systems for Energy-Efficiency in Buildings (BuildSys)*, Berkeley, CA, 2009.

[11] V. Jakkula and D. Cook. Outlier detection in smart environment structured power datasets. In *IEEE Intelligent Systems*, London, UK, 2010.

[12] Y. Kim, R. Balani, H. Zhao, and M. Srivastava. Granger causality analysis on ip traffic and circuit-level energy monitoring. In *ACM Workshop on Embedded Sensing Systems for Energy-Efficiency in Buildings (BuildSys)*, Zurich, Switzerland, 2010.

[13] A. Krause and C. Guestrin. Near-optimal nonmyopic value of information in graphical models. *Uncertainty in Artificial Intelligence (UAI)*, 2005.

[14] A. Krause and C. Guestrin. A note on the budgeted maximization of submodular functions. Technical report, CMU-CALD-05-103, 2005.

[15] A. Krause and C. Guestrin. Near-optimal observation selection using submodular functions. *National Conference on Artificial Intelligence (AAAI)*, 2007.

[16] A. Krause, C. Guestrin, A. Gupta, and J. Kleinberg. Near-optimal sensor placements: Maximizing information while minimizing communication cost. *International Symposium on Information Processing in Sensor Networks (IPSN)*, 2006.

[17] A. Krause, A. Singh, and C. Guestrin. Near-optimal sensor placements in gaussian processes: Theory, efficient algorithms and empirical studies. *Journal of Machine Learning Research*, 9:235–284, 2008.

[18] J. Leskovec, A. Krause, C. Guestrin, C. Faloutsos, J. VanBriesen, and N. Glance. Cost-effective outbreak detection in networks. *ACM SIGKDD International Conference on Knowledge Discovery and Data Mining (KDD)*, pages 420–429, 2007.

[19] X. Li, C. Bowers, and T. Schnier. Classification of energy consumption of a building with outlier detection. *IEEE Transactions on Industrial Electronics*, 57(11):3639–3644, 2010.

[20] R. Melfi, , B. Rosenblum, B. Nordman, and K. Christensen. Measuring building occupancy using existing network infrastructure. *International Green Computing Conference*, 2011.

[21] G. Nemhauser, L. Wolsey, and M. Fisher. An analysis of the approximations for maximizing submodular set functions. *Mathematical Programming*, 1978.

[22] G. Newsham and B. Birt. Building-level occupancy data to improve ARIMA-based electricity use forecasts. In *ACM Workshop on Embedded Sensing Systems for Energy-Efficiency in Buildings (BuildSys)*, Zurich, Switzerland, 2010.

[23] A. Rice, S. Hay, and D. Ryder-Cook. A limited-data model of building energy consumption. In *ACM Workshop on Embedded Sensing Systems for Energy-Efficiency in Buildings (BuildSys)*, Zurich, Switzerland, 2010.

[24] T. Schreiber. Measuring information transfer. *Physical Review Letters*, 85:461–464, 2000.

[25] United States Energy Information Administration. Annual energy review 2010. `http://www.eia.gov/aer`, 2011.

Industry Practice Expo Invited Talk

Ensembles and Model Delivery for Tax Compliance

Graham Williams
Australian Taxation Office
Australia
graham.williams@togaware.com

Abstract

Revenue authorities characteristically have large stores of historic audit data, with outcomes, ready for analysis. The Australian Taxation Office established one of the largest data mining teams in Australia in 2004 as a foundation to becoming a knowledge-based organization. Today, every tax return lodged in Australia is risk assessed by one or more models developed through data mining, generally based on historic data. We observe that any of the traditional modeling approaches, particularly including random forests, generally deliver similar models in terms of accuracy. We take advantage of combining different model types and modeling approaches for risk scoring, and in particular report on recent research that increases the diversity of trees that make up a random forest. We also review, in a practical context, how such models are evaluated and delivered.

Categories & Subject Descriptors: H.2.8 [Database Management]: Data Mining.

Author Keywords: Ensemble Models, Random Forests, Risk Scoring, Model Evaluation.

Bio

Dr. Graham Williams is Director of Data Mining at the Australian Taxation Office, and previously Principal Computer Scientist for Data Mining with CSIRO. He is a Senior International Expert and Visiting Professor of the Chinese Academy of Sciences at the Shenzhen Institutes of Advanced Technologies, and Adjunct Professor in Data Mining, Fraud Prevention, Security, at the University of Canberra and Australian National University. Graham is an active machine learning researcher and regularly teaches data mining courses. He is author of the freely available Rattle software for data mining and of the Rattle book published by Springer in 2011: Data Mining with Rattle and R: The Art of Excavating Knowledge from Data. Graham has been involved in data mining projects for clients from government and industry for over 25 years. His research developments include ensemble learning (1988) and hot spots discovery (1997). He is involved in numerous international artificial intelligence and data mining research activities and conferences and has edited a number of books and has authored many academic and industry papers. He is chair of the Pacific Asia Conference on Knowledge Discovery and Data Mining (PAKDD), and the Australasian Conference on Data Mining (AusDM). His passion is in ensuring data mining technology is readily accessible and available to all who wish, supporting innovation and the sharing of our knowledge widely.

KDD'12, August 12–16, 2012, Beijing, China.
ACM 978-1-4503-1462-6/12/08.

Industry Practice Expo Invited Talk

Leveraging Predictive Modeling to Reduce Signal Theft in a Multi-Service Organization Environment

Seymour Douglas
Deloitte Financial Advisory Services
USA
sedouglas@deloitte.com

Abstract

Signal theft can be defined as the interdiction, consumption or usage of carrier signal from a provider's network without payment or payment of an amount less than the level of service consumed. High levels of signal theft can potentially reflect open technical network issues, failure of electronic countermeasures or operational gaps that are estimated to cost the cable industry providers more than$5 billion annually. This session will discuss the business challenges associated with the quantification of signal theft-related losses, outline some of the countermeasures taken by MSOs, and then provide views on the development of predictive models to help identify the potential likelihood of signal theft in a given environment. We will examine the performance of certain machine learning algorithms as well as data challenges associated with both the architecture construction and analytical efforts, and conclude with a lessons-learned discussion and views on future approaches.

Categories & Subject Descriptors: H.2.8 [Database Management]: Data Mining.

Author Keywords: Telecommunications, Signal-theft, Data Analytics.

Bio

Seymour Douglas is a Director in the Data Analytics group of the Analytic & Forensic Technology Consulting ("AFT") practice within Deloitte Financial Advisory Services LLP ("Deloitte FAS") and has more than 20 years of experience in customer, predictive and data analytics. He specializes in designing and deploying high performance predictive modeling systems that can support fraud detection and monitoring, recommender systems, high frequency forecasting, data enrichment, text mining and revenue assurance. Seymour has led numerous projects using analytics and information technology to help identify improper payments and financial transactions. Prior to joining Deloitte, Seymour held responsibility for developing and deploying analytic solutions for fraud detection, customer valuation, analyzing telco billing data (CABS, CDR, switch data SS7, ISUP, Cabledata) for a communications firm. In addition, Seymour was part of the CRM Analytics practice of a consulting firm, focused on developing data driven analytics systems for the financial services industry. Seymour has consulted to the World Bank at Caribbean Development Bank focusing on developing and leveraging country risk models. He has also served on the faculty at Emory University where he taught undergraduate and graduate courses in microeconomics, international finance and economic development. Seymour received a Bachelor of Business Administration Degree in Math and Economics from the University of the West Indies, and holds a Ph.D. in Econometrics from Temple University.

KDD'12, August 12–16, 2012, Beijing, China.
ACM 978-1-4503-1462-6/12/08.

Capacitated Team Formation Problem on Social Networks

Samik Datta
Bell Labs, Bangalore
samik.datta@alcatel-lucent.com

Anirban Majumder
Bell Labs, Bangalore
anirban.majumder@alcatel-lucent.com

KVM Naidu*
Walmart Labs, Bangalore
naidukvm@walmartlabs.com

ABSTRACT

In a team formation problem, one is required to find a group of users that can match the requirements of a collaborative task. Example of such collaborative tasks abound, ranging from software product development to various participatory sensing tasks in knowledge creation. Due to the nature of the task, team members are often required to work on a co-operative basis. Previous studies [1, 2] have indicated that co-operation becomes effective in presence of social connections. Therefore, effective team selection requires the team members to be *socially close* as well as a division of the task among team members so that no user is overloaded by the assignment. In this work, we investigate how such teams can be formed on a social network.

Since our team formation problems are proven to be NP-hard, we design efficient approximate algorithms for finding near optimum teams with provable guarantees. As traditional data-sets from on-line social networks (e.g. Twitter, Facebook etc) typically do not contain instances of large scale collaboration, we have crawled millions of software repositories spanning a period of four years and hundreds of thousands of developers from GitHub, a popular open-source *social coding network*. We perform large scale experiments on this data-set to evaluate the accuracy and efficiency of our algorithms. Experimental results suggest that our algorithms achieve significant improvement in finding effective teams, as compared to naive strategies and scale well with the size of the data. Finally, we provide a validation of our techniques by comparing with existing software teams.

Categories and Subject Descriptors

H.2.8 [**Database Management**]: Database Applications—*Data mining*

*Work partially done while the author was at Bell Labs, Bangalore.

KDD'12, August 12–16, 2012, Beijing, China.

Keywords

social networks, team formation, capacity

1. INTRODUCTION

Social collaboration or team formation is gaining prominence in the web. There is a growing interest in the community to understand the process of social collaboration, namely, how people use social connections to form teams in challenging situations. To understand the sociological aspects of team formation, an on-line contest was recently organized by DARPA[1]. In this contest, ten balloons were raised into the air and the participants were asked to track their locations. Since no single person could track all of them, the point of the contest was to observe how people would use their social connections to form teams and collectively report the locations.

In today's web, large scale software systems are prominent embodiments of the team formation process. In a software project, collaboration among the developers is required at multiple stages of production. Therefore, it is important to ensure that the collaboration is effective, in order to attain the highest level of productivity. Previous studies [1, 2] suggest that presence of social connections are often good indicator of effective collaboration. In fact, in our experiments (see Section 4.2), we observed a strong positive correlation between activities of a project and social nature of the corresponding team. Moreover, due to proliferation of Web 2.0 phenomena, a growing number of Open Source Software sites (e.g. GitHub [3]) are becoming 'social' by imbibing social-networking features e.g. messaging, community formation, friendship links, for their users. It remains to study how one can facilitate the team formation process in this new generation of networks by designing specialized algorithms for team selection that are mindful of the social connections of the team members. Specifically, we ask the following question in this paper: *How to build an effective team of users that meets the requirement of a project and the selected team-members are socially close to each other ?*

However, team formation is not limited to the realm of software development only. Teams are fundamental to the concept of participatory sensing users contribute sensory information (through their mobile phones or other handheld devices) to constitute a body of knowledge, e.g. learning about the safety of biking tracks in a terrain [2] collecting

[1]http://news.cnet.com/8301-1023_3-10410403-93.html
[2]http://www.opencyclemap.org/

traffic patterns in a city [3] task need to collaborate among themselves in dividing the work. In this context, the social network represents their degree of co-operation and therefore, identifying the most effective community of users for a sensing task amounts to finding the 'best' team on their social network.

In summary, we believe that the problem of finding team of users on a social network (for a collaborative task), has far-reaching applications beyond the ones mentioned here and is an important problem to study. We consider the *social* team formation problem where the objective is to select a team of users from a social network and a division of the task so that the team members are socially 'close' to each other and no user is overloaded by the assignment. Below, we summarize our contributions.

1.1 Our Contributions

- Our key contribution is to account for capacity constraints in the team formation problem (on a social network). For a given task, our goal is to find a team of users from the social network who are 'socially effective' in terms of collaboration (see Section 2.3) and a division of the task among team members so that no user is overloaded by the assignment i.e. no user is assigned task beyond her capacity. To the best of our knowledge, ours is the first work to formulate the team formation problem in presence of a social network and capacity constraints on users (see Section 2.2), thereby showing that it gives rise to a novel problem previously unstudied in the literature.

  This is a major departure from existing works in Operations Research [4, 5] that primarily model team formation as a variant of the *bi-partite matching problem* [4] or other heuristics and therefore, completely ignores the social network information. The only known works consider the social network of users are by Lappas et al [6] and Anagnostopoulos et al [7]; however, their formulations do not account for capacity constraints on the users and therefore, are fundamentally different from ours (see Section 5 for a detailed comparison).

- As our team formation problems are proven to be NP-hard, we present efficient approximation algorithms to find nearly optimal teams with provable guarantees.

- We conduct a careful and detailed set of experiments to evaluate the performance of our algorithms. By crawling GitHub [3], a popular and the fastest growing open-source software site, we have collected large scale social networking graph and collaboration traces (hundred of thousands of users and nearly a million software repositories). Through experiments on this dataset, we have established that our algorithms achieve at much as 40% reduction in cost compared to other strategies.

  We present a validation of our algorithms by showing how our techniques can improve the collaboration cost (see Section 2.3) of existing software teams in GitHub. To the best of our knowledge, ours is the first attempt to collect and analyze large scale (in the order of hundreds of thousands of users and millions of software projects) collaboration traces from GitHub that enables us to derive some interesting insights about the nature of collaboration in this network (refer to Section 4.2).

- Further, to demonstrate the generality of our techniques, we present an additional set of experiments on the DBLP dataset. Experimental evidences suggest that our algorithms achieve at least 20% reduction in cost compared to other heuristics.

1.2 RoadMap

Our paper is organized as follows. In Section 2, we formulate the team formation problem on social networks, that we address in this paper. Section 3 presents the algorithms for team formation and analyze their properties and performance. We follow it up with detailed evaluation through experiments over real-world data-sets in Section 4. We survey the related works in this area in Section 5. Finally, we conclude in Section 6.

2. TEAM FORMATION PROBLEM

In this section, we introduce some notations and formally define our team formation problem on a social network.

2.1 Notation

We represent the social network as an undirected graph $G = (V, E, w)$ with vertices in V denoting the users and edges in E, the social connections between them. The edges are weighted by cost function $w : E \to \mathbb{R}^+$ indicating the cost of collaboration among neighboring users in the network. Therefore, for users u and v such that $(u, v) \in E$, if $w(u, v)$ is large, it indicates that they are unlikely to collaborate well with each other. The cost function w can be estimated by analyzing previous collaboration traces of the users [5].

Each user $v \in V$ is skilled with a set of *items*, where items are, for example, programming languages, operating systems etc that are needed for a software project. We denote the set of items for user v by I_v and the universe of all items in the network by $\mathbb{I}$ i.e. $\mathbb{I} = \cup_{v \in V} I_v$. For user v, let c_v denote her capacity i.e. the maximum number of items that can be assigned to v without overloading the user.

Finally, a task T is defined as a sub-set of items $\{i_1, i_2, \cdots i_k\} \subseteq \mathbb{I}$. A user u can be assigned an item i from the task only if she is skilled in it i.e. $i \in I_u$.

2.2 Feasibility Constraints

A team $U \subseteq V$ is said to be feasible for a given task T if it satisfies the following constraints:

- *Covering Constraints:* There is a valid assignment ψ of the items in T to users in U such that each item $i \in T$ is assigned to some user $\psi(i) \in U$ such that $i \in I_{\psi(i)}$.

- *Packing Constraints:* For each user $u \in U$, the total number of items assigned to u does not exceed her capacity i.e. $\sum_{i \in T : \psi(i) = u} 1 \leq c_u$.

[3] http://www.openstreetmap.org/

[4] http://en.wikipedia.org/wiki/Assignment_problem

[5] Refer to Section 4.3 on details of estimating edge costs from a given collaboration trace.

2.3 Social Collaboration Cost

By virtue of the cost function $w(\cdot)$, it is possible to calculate the collaboration cost between any pair of users u and v. If u and v are friends i.e. $(u,v) \in E$, then the cost is simply $w(u,v)$; otherwise, it is determined by the cost of the shortest path that connects u and v. However, it is not obvious how to extend this definition of collaboration cost for a team with more than two users.

We use the following measures of collaboration cost, borrowed from the work of Lappas et al [6]

- **Diameter Cost:** Given the social network $G = (V, E, w)$, the *diameter cost* of a team $U \subseteq V$ is defined to be the maximum cost between any pair of users in U.
- **Steiner Cost:** Given the social network $G = (V, E, w)$, the *steiner cost* of a team $U \subseteq V$ is defined to be the minimum cost of a tree that connects all the users in U. Stated more formally, steiner cost for a team U is the cost of a minimum cost steiner tree that connects all the users in U.
- **Bottleneck Edge** [6] **Cost:** Given the social network $G(V, E, w)$, and a team $U \subseteq V$, this cost function is defined as the minimum bottleneck cost of a steiner tree that spans U.

These cost models are intuitive and capture some desirable properties of a team. Observe that, while the diameter and bottleneck costs prohibit pair of users (for diameter) or neighboring users (for bottleneck cost) for whom there exists a large collaboration cost, steiner cost, on the other hand, is an aggregate measure and attempts to reduce the overall collaboration cost.

2.4 Problem Formulation

In a team formation problem, a user has a task in mind and is willing to collaborate with others from her social network to form a team, so that together, they accomplish the goal. Formally, it can be defined in the following way: *Given a social network $G(V, E, w)$, a user v who specifies a task T, find a group of other users $U \subseteq V$, so that the team $U \cup \{v\}$ is feasible for the task and minimizes the social collaboration cost (measured in diameter, steiner or the bottleneck cost).*

We refer to the team formation problem with diameter collaboration cost as MinDiamTeam; Similarly, the variants with steiner and bottleneck collaboration costs are referred to as MinAggrTeam and MinMaxTeam respectively.

In general, we assume that user v also specifies a maximum hop length h so that users who are more than h hops away from her, are not considered by the team selection process. Typical values of h are 1 (friend network), 2 (friend-of-friends network) and ∞ (unconstrained i.e. the entire network).

Observe that, as per our formulation, user v (who creates the task) is guaranteed to be a member of the team. We believe that this scenario is a representative of social collaboration esp. in a software development environment, where the user who creates the project also contributes to it. However, this assumption is not essential to our problem, since our algorithms, presented in Section 3, can be easily adapted for the case when v is not enforced to be part of the solution.

[6]The bottleneck cost of a tree is the weight of the maximum weighted edge.

Algorithm 1 The MinDiamSol algorithm for minimizing diameter cost

1. **Input** Social Network $G(V, E, w)$; User v; Task $T = \{i_1, i_2 \cdots, i_k\}$; maximum hop-length h.
2. **Output** Team $U \subseteq V$; allocation of T to U.
3. Pre-process the graph to exclude users who are more than h hops away from v.
4. Find the smallest radius r' such that MaxItems$(T_v(r')) = k$;
5. Let $Team_v$ be the team found;
6. **return** $Team_v$;

2.5 Hardness Result

Since the team formation problem considered in [6] is a specialization of our problem, namely, when all the user capacities are infinite, the hardness results established in their work directly carry over to our problem as well. We briefly summarize this result in the following lemma and refer to [6] for the proof. [7]

Lemma 1. MinDiamTeam *and* MinAggrTeam *problems are NP-hard.*

3. ALGORITHMS

Owing to the hardness result mentioned in Lemma 1, we can not hope to compute the optimum solutions for our team formation problems MinDiamTeam and MinAggrTeam. We first present approximate algorithms to compute nearly optimum teams (with provable guarantees) under these cost models and towards the end of the section present an exact algorithm for MinMaxTeam.

We first present an efficient procedure to identify feasible teams. Specifically, given a team of users U, we present techniques to determine whether U is feasible w.r.t. the task at hand. We describe it in the following lemma.

Lemma 2. MaxItems: *Given a task $T = \{i_1, i_2, \cdots, i_k\}$, and a team of users $U \subseteq V$, it can be computed in polynomial time, the maximum number of items that can be assigned to U so that no user in U is assigned items more than her capacity. (refer to Section 2.2). As a corollary, it can be decided whether U forms a feasible team for the task T.*

Proof. Given the task T and team U, we form a bipartite graph (L, R, E) as follows. For each item $i \in T$, we add a corresponding node l_i in L. Similarly, for each user $u \in U$, there is a corresponding node r_u in R. Add a directed edge (l_i, r_u) of capacity 1 between l_i and r_u if the item i can be assigned to u i.e. $i \in I_u$. Augment this network by adding source and sink nodes s and t. For each node $l_i \in L$, add a directed edge (s, l_i) of capacity 1. Similarly, for each $r_u \in R$, add a directed edge (r_u, t) of capacity c_u, i.e. the capacity of user u. We now seek to find the maximum flow between s and t.

Observe that if there is a feasible team, then each of the edges (s, l_i) will be saturated i.e. having 1 unit of flow through them. Therefore, the maximum flow is at least k. On the other hand, the maximum flow is bounded by the sum of the capacities of the edges (s, l_i), which is k.

[7]However, the MinMaxTeam problem is polynomially solvable (refer to Section 3).

Therefore, if the maximum flow of the network is k, we can conclude that there is a feasible team. Otherwise, it can be verified easily that the s-t max-flow gives us the maximum number of items that can be assigned to U. The allocation of the items to users in U can be decided by inspecting the set of edges (l_i, r_u) - if the edge (l_i, r_u) carries non-zero flow, then the item i is assigned to user u.

Time Complexity For a graph with n vertices and m edges, the best known algorithm for maximum flow has $O(mn \log m)$ time complexity. □

In the following discussion, we will use OPT to denote an optimum solution[8] and |OPT|, its cost. Algorithm MinDiamSol outlines the pseudo-code of our algorithm for the MinDiamTeam problem. Our idea is to guess the value of |OPT| and decide if there is a feasible team whose cost is well approximated by our guessed value. However, we can not hope to find the optimum solution by enumerating all possible values of |OPT|, since our problem is NP-Hard. Therefore, instead of minimizing the diameter cost of the team, we rather attempt to minimize the distance between the root user (i.e. v) and the team members.

Assume that r is our guess of the cost. We use the notation $T_v(r)$ to denote the set of users whose distance from v is at most r i.e. $T_v(r) = \{u | d(v,u) \leq r\}$, where $d(v,u)$ is the cost of the shortest path that connects v and u. Observe that $v \in T_v(r)$, for all values of r.

Our objective is to determine the minimum value of r so that the set of users $T_v(r)$ forms a feasible team for the given task.

Theorem 3.1. *Algorithm* MinDiamSol *obtains a 2-factor approximation algorithm for the* MinDiamTeam *problem.*

Proof. Let $\bar{r}$ be the minimum radius computed by Algorithm 3 and $r_m =$|OPT| be the cost of the optimum solution. We claim that $r_m \geq \bar{r}$. Otherwise, if $r_m < \bar{r}$, then $\text{OPT} \subseteq T_v(r_m)$ (since $v \in OPT$) implying that $T_v(r_m)$ contains a feasible team, which is a clearly a contradiction. Let p, q be any two users present in the solution computed by MinDiamSol. The distance between p and q can be bounded in the following way,

$$\begin{aligned} d(p,q) &\leq d(w,p) + d(w,q) \\ &\leq 2 \cdot \bar{r} \leq 2 \cdot r_m \end{aligned}$$

Here the first inequality follows by applying the triangle inequality for shortest path distances. Since the diameter of the team is being defined as the maximum shortest distance between pairs of users and the inequality holds for any such pair, the proof follows. □

Time Complexity The feasible team MinDiamSol can be found by performing a binary search on the diameter of the graph, that requires $O(\log n_h)$ invocations of Lemma 2 where n_h denotes the number of nodes that are within h hops of root user v. Therefore, the worst-case time complexity is $O(kn_h^2(\log n_h + \log k)\log n_h)$. However, in practice, the running time of this algorithm is much less than this worst-case analysis suggests [9].

[8]Observe that, as per our problem definition (Section 2.4) user v belongs to the team i.e. $v \in OPT$.

[9]refer to Section 4.4.3.

Our algorithm for MinAggrTeam problem is slightly more complicated than the diameter case. The MinAggrSol algorithm starts by transforming the social network into a simpler graph G' so that finding the team in G' is conceptually much easier than doing it in the original graph. Following that, the algorithm greedily picks nodes from G', based on a utility measure, until a feasible team is found. These steps of MinAggrSol are shown in Algorithm 2.

Algorithm 2 The MinAggrSol algorithm for minimizing steiner cost

1: **Input** Social Network $G(V, E, w)$; User v; Task $T = \{i_1, i_2, \cdots, i_k\}$; maximum hop length h.
2: **Output** Team $U \subseteq V$; allocation of T to U.
3: Pre-process the graph to exclude users who are more than h hops away from v.
4: $G'(V, E', \lambda) \leftarrow$ AugmentGraph(G).
5: $cover_v$:= $\{v\}$;
6: **while** $cover_v$ **not** feasible **do**
7: $\quad \bar{x} \leftarrow \underset{x \in \{V \setminus cover_v\}}{argmax} \left\{ \frac{\text{MaxItems}(cover_v \cup \{x\}) - \text{MaxItems}(cover_v)}{\lambda(v,x)} \right\}$;
8: $\quad cover_v \leftarrow cover_v \cup \{\bar{x}\}$
9: **end while**
10: $Team_v \leftarrow$ MinSteinerTree($cover_v$, G); /* *minimum cost steiner tree in G that connects all the users in* $cover_v$ */
11: **return** $Team_v$;

The procedure AugmentGraph (step 4 of MinAggrSol) creates a graph $G'(V, E', \lambda)$ in the following way - for each vertex $u \in V \setminus \{v\}$, it adds an edge $(v,u) \in E'$. The cost of the edge $(v,u) \in E'$ i.e. $\lambda(v,u)$ is defined as the cost of the shortest path between u and v in G. Conceptually, our construction produces a one level tree with user v being the root and all other users are at level 1. A feasible team in G' corresponds to a sub-tree of G' with user v as the root. We denote the optimum team in G' by OPT_λ.

Although G' is structurally much simpler than G, it turns out finding OPT_λ is still NP-hard, as it can be shown by a direct reduction from the set cover problem. We therefore resort to an approximation for it. To find an approximation to OPT_λ, we start with a partial team containing user v only. At each step, we greedily add a user from G' to the team only if it maximizes the *utility*. The utility of a node $u \in V \setminus \{v\}$ is defined as the ratio of the marginal benefit of adding u to the cover (in terms of the number of additional items it covers) to its cost $\lambda(v,u)$. We use the construction highlighted in Lemma 2 to derive the utility values. Once we find a feasible team, we construct a minimum cost steiner tree that connects all the users in the team and return it as a solution. Although computing minimum cost steiner tree is an NP-hard problem, there are well-known algorithms in the literature (c.f. [8]) that achieve factor of 2 approximation to it. The following lemma shows that the cost of the solution returned by MinAggrSol is not far from the cost of the optimum solution.

Theorem 3.2. *Algorithm* MinAggrSol *obtains an* $O(k \log k)$ *factor approximation to the* MinAggrTeam *problem, where* k *is the number of items required by the task.*

Our proof consists of two parts - as a first step, we find out how well OPT is approximated by OPT_λ. Following that, we prove bounds on the error we incur by approximating OPT_λ itself. We start with the following observation.

Algorithm 3 The MinMaxSol algorithm for minimizing bottleneck edge cost

1: **Input** Social Network $G(V, E, w)$; User v; Task $T = \{i_1, i_2 \cdots, i_k\}$; maximum hop-length h.
2: **Output** Team $U \subseteq V$; allocation of T to U.
3: Pre-process the graph to exclude users who are more than h hops away from v.
4: **for** $t = 0 \rightarrow maxweight(E)$ **do**
5: Remove all edge $e \in E$ such that $w(e) > t$; Let C be the component that contains v;
6: If MAXITEMS$(C) = k$, let $Team_t$ be the team found /* $Team_t \subseteq C$ */
7: **return** $Team_t$;
8: **end for**

LEMMA 3. *Cost of OPT_λ is at most $O(k)$ times the cost of OPT.*

PROOF. Consider any optimum solution OPT=$\{v, u_1, u_2, \cdots, u_{l-1}\}$ and let T_{OPT} be a minimum cost steiner tree in G that connects all users in OPT. Observe that in OPT, there can be at most k users who are assigned one or more items from the task i.e. $l \leq k$. In G', OPT is a 1-level tree with the vertex v at the root and all other vertices $\{u_1, u_2, \cdots, u_{l-1}\}$ being connected to v via an edge. Observe that OPT is also a feasible solution in G' whose cost is $\sum_j \lambda(v, u_j)$. Root the tree T_{OPT} at node v. It is easy to observe that the distance of $u_j \in OPT \setminus \{v\}$ from v is no more than |OPT|. Moreover, since $\lambda(v, u_j)$ corresponds to the shortest distance between v and u_j in G, we can write $\lambda(v, u_j) \leq |OPT|$. Therefore, the cost of OPT in G' can be bounded as $(k-1) \cdot |OPT|$. Finally, observe that OPT_λ is the minimum cost solution in G' and the inequality follows. □

In the next two lemmas, we derive the factor in approximating OPT_λ.

LEMMA 4. *The function* MAXITEMS*(S) over set of users $S \subseteq V$ is sub-modular*[10].

PROOF. See Appendix A for the proof. □

We use a known result on the sub-modular cover problem to complete the proof of Theorem 3.2. The **sub-modular cover problem** is defined as follows: Let $E = \{1, 2, \cdots, m\}$ be a ground set and C be a collection of sets defined over E i.e. $C \subseteq 2^E$. Let f be a sub-modular function defined as $f : 2^C \rightarrow \mathbb{Z}^+ \cup \{0\}$ such that $f(C) = m$, $f(\emptyset) = 0$ and f is monotone increasing i.e. for sets $C', C'' \in 2^C$ such that $C' \subseteq C''$, it implies $f(C'') \geq f(C')$. Each set $s \in C$ has a non-negative cost $w(s)$. A sub-collection $C' \subseteq C$ is said to form a feasible cover if $f(C') = f(C)$ and the cost of the cover is defined simply as the sum of the costs of the sets in it i.e. $\sum_{s \in C'} w(s)$. In the minimum cost sub-modular cover problem one is asked to find a feasible cover of minimum cost. Wolsey et al [9, 10] obtained the following result.

LEMMA 5. *[9, 10] The greedy algorithm that picks sets based on maximum utility, achieves an $O(\log k)$ factor approximation to the sub-modular set cover problem.*

[10]For a function $f : V \rightarrow \mathbb{Z}^+ \cup \{0\}$ to be sub-modular it means for all $S, T \subseteq V, f(S) + f(T) \geq f(S \cup T) + f(S \cap T)$

To put an analogy, the ground set E is the set of items in our requirement $T = \{i_1, i_2, \cdots, i_k\}$ and the collection of subsets C is the set of users who possesses a subset of items from T. Since the function MAXITEMS is sub-modular and satisfies all the requirements, we can conclude that through steps 8-11 of Algorithm 2) we compute an $O(\log k)$ approximate solution to OPT_λ. Combining this with Lemma 3, we obtain the result of Theorem 3.2.

Time Complexity Observe that in MinAggrSol, the size of $cover_v$ is at most k. Therefore, computing minimum cost team incurs a cost of $O(k^3 \log k + n_h k^2 + m)$ (steps 4 to 9). The steiner tree computation in step 10, can be performed in an additional $O(m + n \log n)$ time [11]. However, in practice, we find that MinAggrSol scales almost linearly with increasing size of the network (i.e. m and n) and number of items (i.e. k) [11].

Algorithm MinMaxSol outlines the pseudocode of our solution for the MINMAXTEAM problem. We first guess that the optimum team contains no edge with cost more than t and remove edges with higher cost. Following that, we identify the component of the graph that contains the root user v and determine whether it contains a feasible team. This is because any team that spans across multiple such components must use an edge of cost $> t$. Finally we search for the minimum value of t such that this component (containing the root v) consists of a feasible team. It can be verified easily that the solution returned by MinMaxSol is optimum.

Time Complexity The search for minimum value of t (in step 4) can be performed via binary search on the set of edges in the graph, that requires $O(\log m_h)$ invocations of Lemma 2; here m_h is the number of edges in the graph after the pre-processing step (i.e. step 3 in MinMaxSol). Hence the overall time complexity is $O(kn_h^2(\log n_h + \log k) \log m_h)$.

So far we have assumed that the root user has been specified and is required to be part of the solution. However, this restriction can be lifted in the following way - we repeat the algorithms over all choices of the root node and return the team that is of minimum cost. This operation preserves the approximation factors of the algorithm but increases the time complexity by a factor of n [12]. In practice, users are often paid for their participation and one would like to minimize the total cost (e.g. the sum of the collaboration and participation cost). We briefly mention that our team formation algorithms can be easily adapted to optimize over this new cost function and refer to the full version of the paper [12] for details.

4. EXPERIMENTS

We now report a detailed set of experiments carefully designed to evaluate the performance of our algorithms. Our first step is to describe the novel data-set on which our experiments are based.

4.1 Dataset

Traditional data-sets gathered from popular on-line social networks (e.g. Twitter, Facebook etc.) do not contain evidence of large scale collaboration and therefore, are not suitable for our experiments. We focus our attention on a popular social coding site, GitHub [3]. GitHub hosts a large number of software projects and provide social networking

[11]Please refer to Sections 4.4.2 and 4.4.3 for details.
[12]Refer to the full version of the paper [12] for proofs.

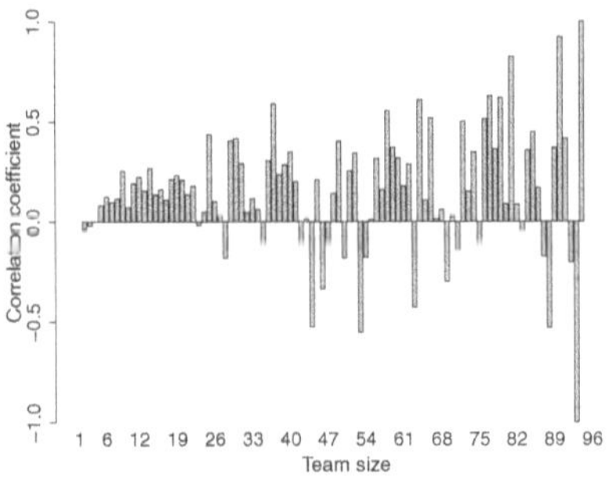

Figure 1: Correlation coefficients between number of commits of a project and number of social edges in the team for different team sizes.

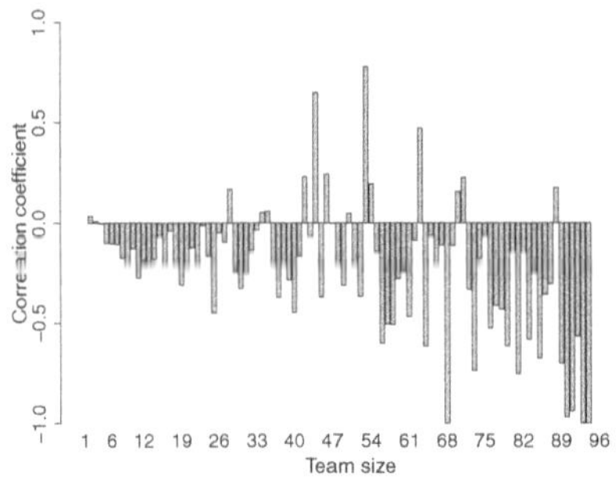

Figure 2: Correlation coefficients between number of commits of a project and number of connected components in the sub-graph induced by the team-members for different team sizes.

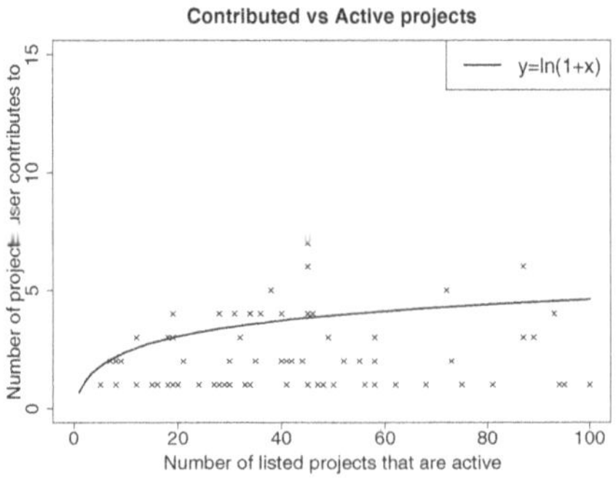

Figure 3: Number of projects actively contributed by a user vs. number of listed projects (for 2000 users).

features (e.g. messaging, activity streams, friendship links) for programmers working on these projects. Although there are other social coding sites (e.g. SourceForge, Google Codes etc.) we have selected GitHub for the following reasons - i) Unlike other sites, GitHub provides explicit social links through which users can connect with others, ii) GitHub APIs allowed us to extract richer quality of data and lastly, iii) it is the fastest-growing among others.

GitHub offers a novel social collaboration model in which a user can *fork* a copy of the software project owned by her friend. Contribution of the user in this forked copy can be merged with the original one, by communicating it to the owner. For our experiments, we have crawled publicly available information from GitHub consisting of 1,35,346 users and 9,05,000 software projects, during the month of August, 2011. Our data-set corresponds to 15% of the volume of GitHub and spans over a period of four years. For each project, we collected its composition in terms of programming languages, list of contributors, commit logs, and bug reports filed. Similarly, for each user, we collected the list of her followers and the list of the projects created and contributed by the user.

For our experiments, we crawled the following two datasets - data-set **D1** consists of 1,35,346 users and 9,05,000 software projects and several meta-data about the users and projects (e.g. commit logs, team composition etc.). This data-set is used for estimating parameters to our algorithms (refer to Section 4.3). Our second data-set **D2**, is used as test data points. This data-set consists of new set of 470 projects collected during the period September-December 2011 (i.e. following the crawl of D1) [13].

We also perform an additional set of experiments on a DBLP data-set to demonstrate the generality of our approach. The description of this dataset and the result of our experiments are presented in Section 4.5.

4.2 Evidence of Social Collaboration in GitHub

We analyzed the commit logs of 10k projects over a period of last three months (relative to the date of our crawl) and observed an interesting pattern between the activity of the project (measured in terms of number of commits) and 'social' nature of the corresponding team. For this experiment, we group the teams by their size (i.e. number of contributors)[14] and for each team size, report the correlation coefficient between the social nature of the team and number of commits of the project. We use two simple measures for evaluating 'social' nature of a team - a)number of social edges present in the team and b) number of connected components in the sub-graph induced by the team members.

Figure 1 and Figure 2 show the result of this experiment. We observe that teams with more edges (hence being more social) are more active in terms of number of commits in their projects. As a result, we see positive correlation coefficient across almost all different team sizes in Figure 1. Similarly, teams with larger number of connected components (hence less social) are less active and we observe negative correlation coefficient across almost all different teams sizes (Figure 2). These results suggest that in GitHub, social nature of a team has a strong correlation with the activity of the project.

4.3 Pre-processing

Below, we describe in detail how data set D1 is processed to generate the input parameters to our algorithms.

Social Network By virtue of the follower list, we construct a social network of the users included in our crawl. Since collaboration is symmetric in nature, we treat the edges as being undirected. For each pair of users u and v such that (u, v) is an edge, we assume their relationship strength to be proportional to the fraction of projects they have worked on together in the past. If N_u and N_v denote the set of projects in which u and v are listed as contributors, then their relationship strength is defined as $\sigma_{u,v} = \frac{|N_u \cap N_v|}{|N_u \cup N_v|}$. Finally, we use the following function to estimate the collaboration cost between u and v: $w(u, v) = 100 \cdot (1 - \sigma_{u,v})$. [15]. We experimentally verified that this cost function produces intuitive values for the edge weights such that the teams which are highly active (hence large number of commits), have small cost measured in diameter, steiner and bottleneck edge cost models.

[13]GitHub dataset can be obtained by mailing the authors.

[14]We believe that comparing number of commits of a smaller team with a larger one will be unfair. Therefore, we group teams by their size and compare among teams of same size.

[15]The constant 100 is arbitrary and is used to avoid rounding errors in our computation.

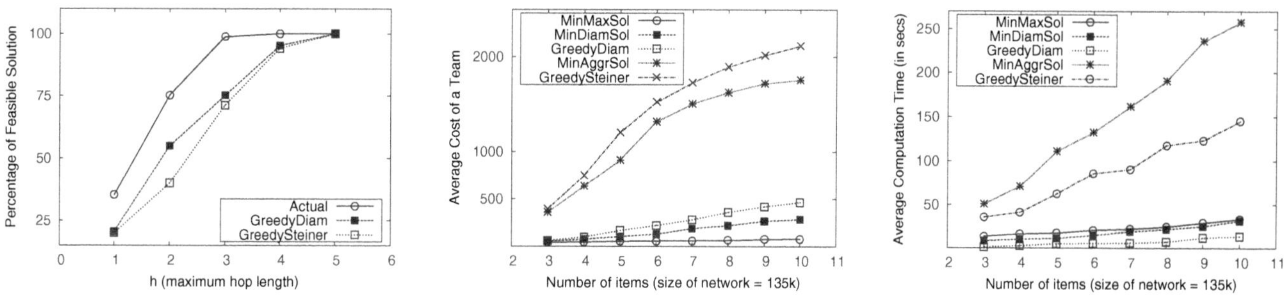

Figure 4: Experimental results for the GitHub dataset.

Items Items in data-set D1 correspond to programming languages required by the projects and there are 52 of them in our crawl. For each user, we construct her set of items as the collection of programming languages required by her projects.

Tasks In GitHub, tasks correspond to project requirements created by users. We use the projects in D2 and their requirements (in terms of programming languages) as tasks for our experiments. Observe that, D2 is not used for estimating other parameters since it might bias the experiment.

Further, we synthetically generate few more project requirements for our experiments. Unfortunately, a uniform random sampling of items is not guaranteed to generate realistic project requirements. Instead, we look at the co-occurrences of the items (bi-grams and n-grams in general) to generate synthetic requirements.

Capacity To get an understanding of capacities of users, we picked a set of ($\approx$ 2k) users who are believed to be active and looked at the commit logs for their listed projects over a period of one month. Among the listed projects[16], we declare a project to be active for that user, if she made at least one commit during that one month period. The result of this experiment is plotted in Figure 3. The plot reveals an interesting trend - the number of projects contributed by a user is often significantly less compared to the number of projects listed for the user. We strongly believe that this difference is due to the limited capacities of users. Finally, we compute the capacity of user u as $\ln(1 + N_u)$, where N_u is the number of projects contributed by u, as listed by GitHub.

4.4 Results

4.4.1 *Comparison with existing GitHub teams*

The first set of experiments is to highlight the fact that our techniques can significantly improve the social collaboration cost of existing projects in GitHub. In order to achieve that, we worked with projects in D2 and collected their composition in terms of the list of users who contribute to them and the set of programming languages, number of units of each language needed etc. For every project, we compute the solutions returned by algorithms MinDiamSol and MinAggrSol and compare their cost against the diameter and steiner cost of the actual team. For nearly 40% of the projects, we observed a reduction of cost in the range of 10% – 35%. In Figure 5, we plot the result for the MinAggrSol. The results for other algorithms are similar and not repeated here.

[16]All projects listed by GitHub are active i.e. they are being contributed to by some users in the network.

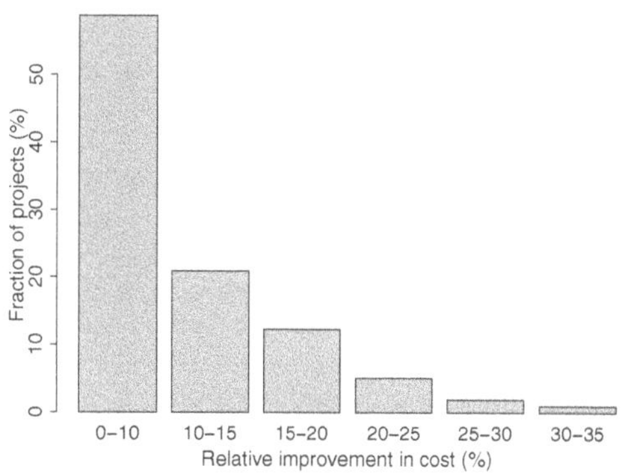

Figure 5: Improvement in collaboration cost as computed by MinAggrSol algorithm over existing teams in GitHub.

For approximately 5% of the projects, we observed that our algorithms obtained solution which has higher cost than the actual teams. We believe that this is due our imprecise modeling of the input parameters as the test data $D2$ was kept separate and not used for estimating cost, items and capacities of the users. For rest of the projects, our algorithm reported minor improvement ($< 5\%$) over the existing teams.

4.4.2 *Scalability*

For the purpose of this experiment, we generate subgraphs of the github network of varying sizes (between 10k and 135k). The subgraphs are created by randomly selecting a node and performing breadth-first search around it. We create synthetic requirements for a randomly selected root user, through the steps described in Section 4.3, and measure the time taken by our algorithms [17]. Finally, we report the average over 10 such measurements. In Figure 7, we plot the result of this experiment. It can be seen that, Algorithms MinMaxSol and MinDiamSol are highly efficient, taking approximately 30 secs on the 135k network. Algorithm MinAggrSol on the other hand scales almost linearly with increasing network size (nearly 6 min on the 135k subgraph).

4.4.3 *Comparison with Baseline*

Baseline Algorithms For baseline comparison, we implement an adapted version of the algorithms RarestFirst and

[17]For this experiment, we set h to ∞; i.e. the algorithms are run on the entire subgraph.

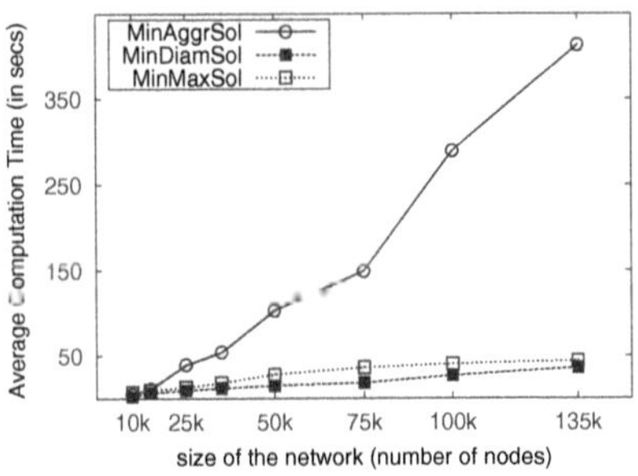

Figure 7: Computation time of different algorithms with varying network size (in github).

EnhancedSteiner, from the work of Lappas et al [6]. For a given task, these algorithms find a team of experts from a social network. However, they are not designed to handle capacity constraints on the users. We modify these algorithms as follows - first, we run the algorithm and inspect its solution. If the solution is feasible (c.f. Section 2.2), we declare it to be valid. Otherwise, for any user u whose capacity constraint is not met, we perform a reallocation of items. Among the items that are assigned to u, we order them based on their *rarity* - the minimum increase in cost to cover the item by other users who are not included in the current solution, and greedily assign the top b_u rarest items to u. After we have performed reallocation for all violating users, we contract the set of users into a single node of the graph and repeat the step, until a feasible solution is attained. We name these algorithms GreedyDiam and GreedySteiner respectively.

Results Our current set of experiments is designed to evaluate the performance of MinDiamSol and MinAggrSol with respect to the baseline heuristics. We first determine the minimum value of h, the maximum hop length, for which our input tasks have feasible solution. In Figure 4, we plot the result of this experiment (leftmost plot). As it can be seen, for a value of $h = 3$, our tasks (both real and synthetic) have feasible solutions. However, it turns out that both GreedyDiam and GreedySteiner fail to find feasible solutions for all of the tasks unless we increase h to 5. We therefore set h to 5 for the rest of the experiments.

Figure 4 summarizes the result of our experiment with real tasks. The experiments reveal that MinDiamSol achieves at least 25% reduction in cost as compared to GreedyDiam. The improvement is much more pronounced in the steiner cost version where our algorithm significantly outperforms the GreedySteiner heuristic by at least 40%. Our careful inspection of the steps of GreedySteiner reveals that by ignoring capacities of users in its decision making process, it actually ends up including a large number of steiner nodes in the solution and thereby, increasing the cost. The plot on running time (Figure 4) indicates that our algorithms scale linearly with the number of items in a task. [18]

4.5 Experiments on DBLP data

Our second data-set is obtained from DBLP [13] and consists of a snapshot of computer science publications taken on December 5th, 2011. Each publication is written by a set of authors. We follow the same pre-processing steps as described in Lappas et al [6] to generate input parameters for our algorithms. In addition, we determine capacity of an author u as the average number of publications co-authored by u in a year.

Unlike GitHub, DBLP dataset doesn't have an explicit notion of social graph. We generate the social network based on co-authorship: two authors are connected by an edge if they have co-authored at least two papers together. The collaboration cost of an edge (u, v) is estimated in the following way: If S_u (S_v) denotes the set of research articles co-authored by u (v resp.) then the cost of edge (u, v) is estimated as $100 \cdot (1 - \frac{|S_u \cap S_v|}{|S_u \cup S_v|})$. Once again, the constant 100 is arbitrary and is used to avoid any rounding error in computation. Following the pre-processing stage, the DBLP dataset contains 7332 authors, 19248 articles and 2763 distinct items.

4.5.1 *Results*

The result of our experiment is summarized in Figure 6. Since the DBLP network is slightly denser than GitHub, the baseline algorithms can find feasible teams within 4 hops of the root user. Therefore, for the purpose of this experiment, h is set to 4. We observe that MinDiamSol and MinAggrSol achieve $\approx 20\%$ improvement over the baseline heuristics. As mentioned earlier, our synthetic construction of the DBLP network is slightly denser than GitHub and contains users with large number of publications (hence large capacity). This fact has led to slight reduction of the gains reported by our algorithms as compared to GitHub experiments.

To conclude, through a fairly extensive set of experiments on real-world datasets, we have evaluated the performance of our team formation algorithms. Experimental results suggest that our algorithms outperform other naive strategies by a significant margin (20-40%) and scale well with hundreds of thousands of users.

5. RELATED WORK

Team formation is a well-studied problem in the Operations Research (OR) community [4, 5]In their setting, the goal is to find an allocation of tasks to different individuals so as to satisfy the project requirements. However, this body of work ignores the social relationship among people while deciding the best team and unfortunately, their techniques can not be applied to solve our problem.

Lappas et.al [6] considered the problem of finding team of experts on a social network. Given a requirement of skills, their goal is to find a team that minimizes the overall communication cost. Although they have a similar objective in mind, our problem is fundamentally very different from them. In [6], the authors don't deal with capacities on users. In effect, their problem can be thought of as *uncapacitated* version of our problem. As per our understanding, the notion of capacity changes the problem structure completely and their solutions can no longer be adapted to handle our requirement. Moreover, through detailed experiments (see Section 4), we have established that a natural extension of their algorithms perform very poorly compared to ours.

In [14], the authors studied a version of the team formation problem where the goal was to balance the load (*i.e.*the number of projects one is assigned to) of individuals. However, this version of the problem overlooks the social collaboration cost altogether. In a more recent study [7], the authors present algorithms which, in addition to load balance, also find teams with bounded social collaboration cost.

[18]We also performed experiments with synthetic tasks. The results are similar and not repeated here (see [12]).

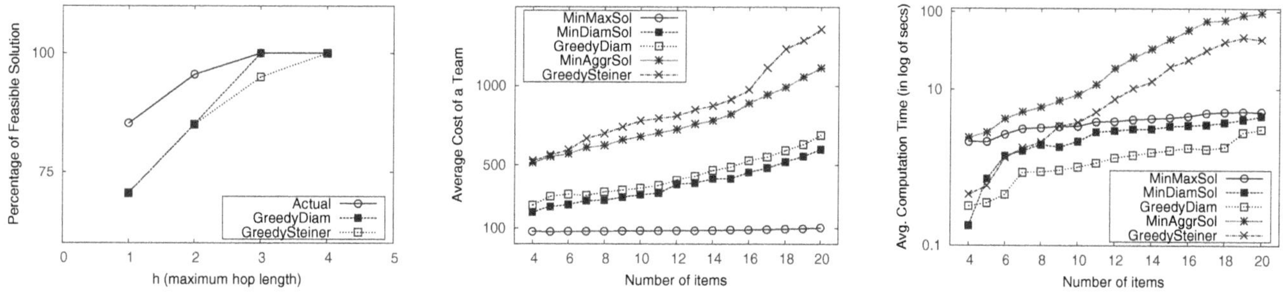

Figure 6: Experimental results for the DBLP dataset.

Their formulation is, however, different from ours - in addition to finding teams with bounded collaboration cost, they attempt to minimize the load on team members, whereas, we take the user capacities as constraint and attempt to minimize the social collaboration cost.

The specific techniques required to estimate the strength of relationship among individuals has been pursued in recent research works [15, 16]. However, these techniques can not be applied to estimate edge costs in our problem as they rely on peer interactions (e.g. e-mails exchanged etc.) which is not available for our data-sets. We believe that this direction of research is complimentary to our problem and beyond the scope and goal of this paper.

6. CONCLUSION

In this work, we presented a novel team-formation problem on social networks that attempts to find teams that are socially close as well as division of the task so that no user is overloaded by the assignment. We presented algorithms for this problem under different models of social collaboration and analyzed their performance thoroughly. Our experiments with real-life data-sets show that these techniques outperform the naive strategies by a significant margin.

7. REFERENCES

[1] D. McDonald, "Recommending collaboration with social networks: A comparative evaluation," in *CHI'03*, 2003.

[2] T. Wolf *et al.*, "Mining task-based social networks to explore collaboration in software teams," *Software, IEEE*, 2009.

[3] GitHub, "http://github.com."

[4] A. Baykasoglu *et al.*, "Project team selection using fuzzy optimization approach," *Cybern. Syst.*, 2007.

[5] H. Wi *et al.*, "A team formation model based on knowledge and collaboration," *Expert Syst. Appl.*, 2009.

[6] T. Lappas *et al.*, "Finding a team of experts in social networks," in *KDD '09*, 2009.

[7] A. Gionis *et al.*, "Online team formation in social networks," in *WWW '12*, 2012.

[8] V. V. Vazirani, *Approximation Algorithms*. Springer, 2004.

[9] L. Wolsey, "An analysis of the greedy algorithm for the submodular set covering problem," *Combinatorica*, vol. 2, pp. 385–393, 1982.

[10] G. Nemhauser and L. Wolsey, "Maximizing submodular set functions: Formulations and analysis of algorithms," in *Annals of Dis. Math*, 1981.

[11] K. Melhorn, "A faster approximation algorithm for steiner tree problem in graphs," *Inf Process. Lett.*, vol. 27, pp. 125–128, 1988.

[12] S. Datta, A. Majumder, and K. Naidu, "Capacitated Team Formation Problem on Social Networks," *arXiv:1205.3643v1*, May 2012.

[13] DBLP, "http://dblp.uni-trier.de."

[14] A. Anagnostopoulos *et al.*, "Power in unity: forming teams in large-scale community systems," in *CIKM '10*, 2010.

[15] R. Xiang *et al.*, "Modeling relationship strength in online social networks," in *WWW '10*, 2010.

[16] J. Leskovec *et al.*, "Predicting positive and negative links in online social networks," in *WWW '10*, 2010.

APPENDIX

A. PROOF OF LEMMA 4

PROOF. Observe that MAXITEMS is a monotone function i.e. for $S \subseteq T$, $\text{MAXITEMS}(S) \leq \text{MAXITEMS}(T)$. In order to prove sub-modularity, we need to establish the following result: for two arbitrary subsets A and B, $\text{MAXITEMS}(A) + \text{MAXITEMS}(B) \geq \text{MAXITEMS}(A \cup B) + \text{MAXITEMS}(A \cap B)$. As a first step, we prove it for sub-sets A and B such that $A \cap B = \emptyset$. For a given task T, consider the allocation of items by MAXITEMS on the set of users $A \cup B$. Let n_A and n_B denote the number of items assigned to sets A and B respectively. Since MAXITEMS(A) assigns the maximum possible items to A we can claim $n_A \leq \text{MAXITEMS}(A)$ and similarly, $n_B \leq \text{MAXITEMS}(B)$. The proof follows by observing that $\text{MAXITEMS}(A \cap B) = 0$ since A and B are disjoint.

For the general case, consider an allocation of the given task T to the set of users $A \cup B$ by $\text{MAXITEMS}(A \cup B)$. Let n_A, n_B and $n_{A \cap B}$ denote the number of items assigned to sets A, B and $A \cap B$ respectively. Therefore, $n_A + n_B - n_{A \cap B} = \text{MAXITEMS}(A \cup B)$. Applying a similar reasoning (as in the last paragraph) we get, $\text{MAXITEMS}(A) + \text{MAXITEMS}(B) \geq \text{MAXITEMS}(A \cup B) + n_{A \cap B}$. Now the only thing needs to be proved is whether there exists some solution of $\text{MAXITEMS}(A \cup B)$ such that $n_{A \cap B} = \text{MAXITEMS}(A \cap B)$. This can be achieved by constructing a minimum cost flow network in the following way: In the construction of Lemma 2, consider all edges of the form (l_i, r_u) where i is an item and $u \in A \cup B$. The edge is assigned a cost zero only if $u \in A \cap B$. For all other users, the cost is set to 1. For other set of edges, the cost is set to zero. Finally, we compute a minimum cost flow of value $\text{MAXITEMS}(A \cup B)$. It is easy to verify that this construction produces a re-allocation of $\text{MAXITEMS}(A \cup B)$ so that $n_{A \cap B} = \text{MAXITEMS}(A \cup B)$ and this completes our proof. □

Finding Trendsetters in Information Networks

Diego Saez-Trumper
Universitat Pompeu Fabra
Barcelona, Spain
diego.saez@upf.edu

Giovanni Comarela
UFMG
Belo Horizonte, Brazil
giovannicomarela@dcc.ufmg.br

Virgílio Almeida
UFMG
Belo Horizonte, Brazil
virgilio@dcc.ufmg.br

Ricardo Baeza-Yates
Yahoo! Research
Barcelona, Spain
rbaeza@acm.org

Fabrício Benevenuto
UFOP
Ouro Preto, Brazil
fabricio@dcc.ufmg.br

ABSTRACT

Influential people have an important role in the process of information diffusion. However, there are several ways to be influential, for example, to be the most popular or the first that adopts a new idea. In this paper we present a methodology to find trendsetters in information networks according to a specific topic of interest. Trendsetters are people that adopt and spread new ideas influencing other people before these ideas become popular. At the same time, not all early adopters are trendsetters because only few of them have the ability of propagating their ideas by their social contacts through word-of-mouth. Differently from other influence measures, a trendsetter is not necessarily popular or famous, but the one whose ideas spread over the graph successfully. Other metrics such as node in-degree or even standard Pagerank focus only in the static topology of the network. We propose a ranking strategy that focuses on the ability of some users to push new ideas that will be successful in the future. To that end, we combine temporal attributes of nodes and edges of the network with a Pagerank based algorithm to find the trendsetters for a given topic. To test our algorithm we conduct innovative experiments over a large Twitter dataset. We show that nodes with high in-degree tend to arrive late for new trends, while users in the top of our ranking tend to be early adopters that also influence their social contacts to adopt the new trend.

Categories and Subject Descriptors

H.3.3 [**Information Search and Retrieval**]: information filtering, retrieval models

General Terms

Algorithms, Design, Experimentation

Keywords

Information Networks, Influence, Social Networks

KDD'12, August 12–16, 2012, Beijing, China.

1. INTRODUCTION

The impressive growth of social networking services has made personal contacts and relationships more visible and quantifiable than ever before. Online information networks have been pointed out as places where users influence and are influenced by others, and have become ideal channels for spreading news or innovative ideas [11]. Online social networks have emerged as a popular medium where users discuss about everything, including noteworthy events, giving opinions and expressing sentiments concerning facts and ideas of daily life. Additionally, they pose opportunities for sharing information of local interest. For instance, local businesses actively reach out to their customers by announcing promotions and asking users to propagate them.

Online information networks data offers an opportunity to answer important questions related to information diffusion. Recently, the concept of *Follower Hubs* and *Innovative Hubs* has been borrowed from the economics literature, to describe how a new idea or product propagates over such networks [1]. Follower Hubs are nodes with high in-degree, hence they can deliver content to a larger audience than a normal user. However, previous research [21] shows that Follower Hubs usually have a high threshold for the adoption of new ideas. Here is where the Innovation Hubs are important. Innovation Hubs usually have lower in-degree than Follower Hubs, and also a lower threshold for the adoption of a new idea. Therefore, they have a key role in an information propagation process. In other words, the Followers Hubs are influencers, but the Innovation Hubs are trendsetters. Although these definitions are interesting, in traditional social experiments, it is not easy to identify the different and multiple roles of the participants without restricting the size of the study. Data collected from online information networks allow researchers to carry out detailed studies about dissemination of ideas and information with a large number of participants. Indeed, recent efforts quantified the level of influence of participants on online social networks [8] and proposed techniques to identify those who are likely to spread information to a large audience [16]. While marketing services actively search for potential influencers to promote various items, influencers actively search for innovative ideas and important innovators. In this paper, we address the problem of identifying trendsetters in information networks.

Trendsetters are people that adopt and spread new ideas (trends, fashions) before these ideas become popular. They are not necessarily well known news outlets, celebrities or politicians, but are the ones whose ideas spread widely and successfully through word-of-mouth. To be an innovator, a person needs to be one of the first people to pick up a new or nascent trend, which may be adopted by other members of a social or information network. On the other hand, not all the early adopters are trendsetters because only few of them have the ability of propagating their ideas to their social contacts through word-of-mouth.

To identify trendsetters there are two important aspects that we need to take into account. The first one is the area or topic of the innovator, as people have different levels of expertise on various subjects. For example, marketing services actively search for potential influential people in a specific domain or area to promote certain products or services. Influential people include "cool" teenagers, local leaders, and popular public figures. Thus, it is important to specify topics and themes that define the context where trendsetters will be identified.

Second, it is important to consider time information associated with the posting of innovative ideas. Traditional ranking algorithms on social networks, such as the standard Pagerank algorithm [22] do not consider time information concerned to ideas that become popular. Instead, they consider only aggregate usage statistics and a static network topology. For example, Figure 1 considers that for node X, $t_X = n$ represents that X adopted the trend h in time n. Thus, node G was the first one to adopt h, while node E was the last one to adopt the same trend. Note that, although node G is an innovator, it's information was passed to H but not to the rest of the network. Thus, node G cannot be considered a trendsetter. On the other hand, if we compute the standard Pagerank algorithm using this graph and ignore the time when trend h was adopted, node C would be considered the top ranked node although it has just incoming links from nodes A and E and simply spread it to a larger audience. However, if we pay attention to time, we will see that C adopted the trend before E, and therefore we cannot consider that C received information from E. We can also observe that nodes A and E have the same rank according to Pagerank, despite that A adopted the trend before E. In this example, the top trendsetter is node A because it was the first one to adopt this trend being followed - directly or indirectly - by many other participants of the network, such as nodes C, D, B, and F.

This paper presents a novel approach to identify trendsetters in information networks. Differently with previous work on ranking influential users in social and information networks, we introduce timing information on the social graph to be able to identify persons that spark the process of disseminating ideas that become popular in the network. We propose a robust way to model the dissemination of innovation, representing a topic as a collection of trends, that can be applied in several scenarios. We define a topic-sensitive weighted innovation graph that provides key information to understand who adopted a certain topic that triggered attention of others in the network. We then introduce a Pagerank inspired time-sensitive algorithm to find trendsetters. Next,

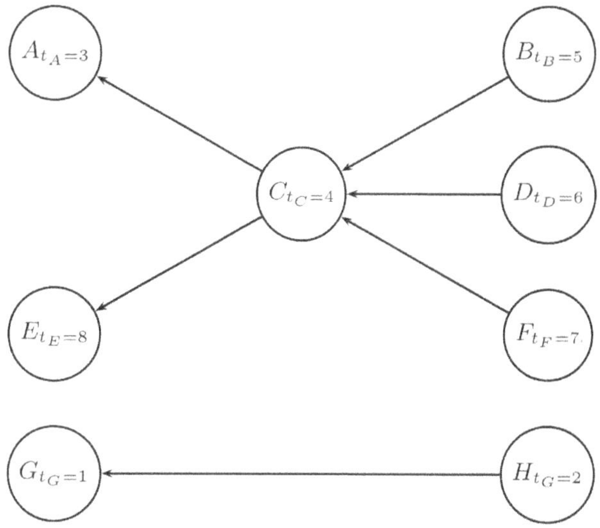

Figure 1: Illustrative example of timing importance: Without considering time information, nodes A and E are symmetric, regardless of whether A adopted the trend first. The edges represents social connections between nodes and the arrows goes opposite to the information flow.

we tested our algorithm using a robust dataset containing the complete snapshot of the Twitter network and containing all tweets from 2006 to the mid-2009. The result shows that the proposed algorithm is able to measure the direct and indirect influence adding also the early adoption as a key feature to be influential. This characteristic is useful to differentiate between trendsetters and other nodes that despite having a large in-degree, adopt the trends only after they became popular.

The rest of the paper is organized as follows. Section 2 reviews related work. Section 3 presents a formal definition of the trendsetters ranking. Section 4 describes the experimental evaluation and the results obtained. Finally, Section 5 concludes the paper summarizing its contributions and discussing future work.

2. RELATED WORK

The concept of influence has been studied by different disciplines. In the 1950s the social psychologist Solomon Asch published a well known study about the group's influence in individuals decisions [3]. Years later, in 1968, the marketing researcher Frank Bass proposed a model for the adoption of new technology on the market [7]. He considered that there are two types of new adopters: the innovators and the imitators. Bass models the relation between these two types with a differential equation. Other two important influence models based on individual thresholds were proposed at the end of 1970s by the economist Thomas Schelling [26] and by the sociologist Mark Granovetter [14]. Nowadays, the study of influence and information diffusion is a hot topic in the research community. Next, we review and summarize the different approaches related to our work.

Probabilistic Models: The relevance of viral marketing

has inspired studies looking for influential users that can maximize the information propagation in social networks. This problem has been faced by probabilistic models [10], and as a discrete optimization problem [16]. A complementary work in the same direction has been done by [9]. Most recently, a probabilistic approach to find topical authorities in microbloging sites has been proposed in [23]. In our case, we study users' ability of spreading an innovation as a ranking problem.

Group Influence: In [4] the authors shows that Livejournal users and also DBLP authors tends to join new groups when their *friends* joins too. In the same way, [24] has studied the adoption of *hashtags* in Twitter about different topics related with the number of *friends* that have used these tags previously. They show that users wait that their friends use some hashtag before them, and depending on how controversial is the topic, they wait for more friends to follow before they jump in. We have used the *hashtags* categorization done in this work as input for our analysis. However, those works focus in the direct influence of the group (friends or friend of friends) but does not take in account how the indirect influence spreads over the graph.

Early Adopters: The concept of Early Adopters was studied in [6], analyzing data from a popular on-line virtual world (Second Life), discovering that the trendsetters are usually users with few friends, i.e. nodes with low degree, and moreover, they are users that are not too evolved in the game (they play less hours than the average). These are key points for our work, because shows that users that can be considered outsiders in a trivial analysis gain importance when the time factor (to be an early adopter) is considered. We take the concept of early adopter, but we propose a way to differentiate those that create cascade behavior. That means that we are interested in influential early adopters.

Temporal Factor: The importance of the temporal factor in influence studies was remarked in [2]. Studying the different sources of correlation among users actions, the authors proposed three possible explanations to a group of users performing the same action: environmental factors, homophily and influence. An example of an environmental factor is the fact that a group of social media users living in the same city can post about the same event, because that event is taking place in their city. Homophily is similar, but corresponds to intrinsic characteristics of people. That means, that two users can post about the same topic because they have the same interests. The authors point out that we can only talk about social influence when exists a time causality associated to the actions among users. Another consideration about the time factor in information networks is described in [18], showing that considering only the topology is not enough to understand how the information spreads over an information network, because some edges could be *slower* than others and that in many cases the information can go faster through a multi-hop pathway that uses *faster* edges. Other important studies have been conducted taking in account the temporal factor to find the backbone of cascades produced on the Web [12], but they do not propose a ranking function neither model topics, and they only establish a temporal relation among nodes, looking to the most common path in cascades process, creating a influence pathway.

The work of [13] describes leaders as users that take actions that will be imitated by their friends later. They discover, among other things, that there are users that are tribe leaders, meaning that they are imitated in different actions by the same group of friends (the tribe). In this case to be the first is a signal of leadership. On the other hand, in [29] being the last is considered as a signal of expertise. This work studies the relation into a Java Forum among users making questions and giving answers for this programming language. These relations are model as a graph and ranking algorithms - such as PageRank [22] and HITS [17] - are used to find relevant users. Comparing their results with human evaluation they conclude that those algorithms allows to find expert users. HITS also was used to model influence and passivity in social media [25].

Memeshapes: In [28] the authors present the KSC-algorithm to cluster temporal series by their shape, applying it to *internet memes* and Twitter hashtags. They found different kinds of shapes and they explain them by the nature of the sources (such as bloggers, mainstream media, etc). This work is a fundamental input for our work, as we have used the algorithm proposed by them to cluster the trends in our dataset. However, the goal of our work is different as we are not interested in who is talking about a topic when it is popular, but just before it became popular. Differences about how we apply the KSC-algorithm are explained in Section 4.

Pagerank based algorithms: The idea to use Pagerank to evaluate user's influence in Social Media was also developed in [27]. Here, the authors used a topic-sensitive Pagerank extension [15] proposing a *TwitterRank* to evaluate Twitter users. In fact, this work is not focused on influence but in homophily, measuring the similarity among users, avoiding the temporal factor and considering the amount of information that each user posts (i.e. number of tweets) in a given topic to assign importance to each node for this topic. Something similar has been done in [20]. Other rankings on Twitter have been studied by [8], showing that the number of followers (node in-degree) is not necessarily an indicator of influence, naming this fact as: "The Million Follower Fallacy". In [19] they also ranked Twitter users, showing the differences between a node degree based ranking versus the results of Pagerank. However, all those works have been using the social graph without consider the temporal dynamics of communication.

Differences with our approach: Note that previous work has used different definitions of what is an influential user. Different from other works using a ranking based on the network topology, our approach also considers the early adoption as a key to be a trendsetter. To the best of our knowledge, this is the first paper that considers Pagerank and temporal factors to find influential people in information networks. Additionally, our algorithm presents a flexible way to model topics that is adaptable to different scenarios. Also, the influence as a function of time can be easily adjusted with a single parameter. Hence, we believe that our approach is innovative and complementary with existing approaches.

3. RANKING TRENDSETTERS

This section presents our algorithm to rank trendsetters in an information network according to some topic of interest. We start with basic definitions related to the concept of a *topic*, network graphs, and the interactions among nodes over time. We represent a network as a directed graph $G(N, E)$, where N is the set of nodes and E the set of edges. Each edge is an ordered pair (u, v), $u, v \in N$, representing a relation between u and v. Furthermore, we define $In_G(v) = \{w | (w, v) \in E\}$, $Out_G(v) = \{w | (v, w) \in E\}$, the incoming and outgoing neighbor sets respectively, and $|S|$ is the cardinality of a set S.

As we are interested in ranking nodes according to a specific topic, we look only at nodes that are related with the topic. The two next definitions formalize what a topic is and how to select the nodes.

Definition 1. We define a topic as a collection of trends related to a specific theme. We denote this collection by $\{h_1, \ldots, h_{n_k}\}$. Each one of the n_k trends could be a word, a phrase, a meme, a tag, an URL, or any other kind of label that can be associated with a node.

Definition 2. We denote $G_k(N_k, E_k)$ as the induced graph of $G(N, E)$ over the topic k. The set N_k is obtained by considering all nodes of N that used at least one trend of k and E_k represent all edges (u, v) such that, if $(u, v) \in E$ and $u, v \in N_k$ then $(u, v) \in E_k$.

As mentioned in the introduction, the timing information is the key to determine social influence. We include this information in the temporal attributes of nodes and edges of $G_k(N_k, E_k)$ in the following definition.

Definition 3. Let $t_i(v)$ be the time when node $v \in N_k$ adopts the trend $h_i \in k$ ($t_i(v) = 0$, if v does not adopt h_i). We define two vectors, $s_1(v)$ (for all $v \in N_k$) and $s_2(u, v)$ (for all $(u, v) \in E_k$), each one with n_k components given respectively by:

$$s_1(v)_i = \begin{cases} 1, & \text{if } t_i(v) > 0, \\ 0, & \text{otherwise} \end{cases} \quad (1)$$

and

$$s_2(u, v)_i = \begin{cases} e^{-\frac{\Delta}{\alpha}}, & \text{if } t_i(v) > 0 \text{ and } t_i(v) < t_i(u), \\ 0, & \text{otherwise} \end{cases} \quad (2)$$

for $i = 1, \ldots, n_k$, where $\Delta = t_i(u) - t_i(v)$ and $\alpha > 0$.

Vector $s_1(v)$ informs if node v adopted (or not) each trend of k, while $s_2(u, v)$ shows if u adopted these trends after v and weights the relation as a function of the period of time between $t_i(u)$ and $t_i(v)$. For a fixed α, if $\Delta \to 0^+$ then $e^{-\frac{\Delta}{\alpha}} \to 1$ and if $\Delta \to +\infty$ then $e^{-\frac{\Delta}{\alpha}} \to 0$. These limits mean that if the node u adopts a trend just after v then $s_1(v)_i$ is very close to $s_2(u, v)_i$, and, on the other hand, if u adopts the trend after a long time, we have that $s_1(v)_i$ and $s_2(u, v)_i$ are very different. The exponential time decay to compute influence has been proposed in previous work related to temporal factors in the web graph [5].

The α parameter allows to control the time window that will be considered to compute $s_2(u, v)$. This settable parameter is useful because it can be adapted to different scenarios. Depending on the nature of the problem, we want to consider that one node is strongly influencing another if the second one imitates the first one in few seconds, and in other cases we want to use a longer span of time. Moreover, for the same problem we could be interested in studying the influence of a short span of time, or a long term influence.

So, when many components of $s_1(v)$ and $s_2(u, v)$ are similar and different from 0, we assume that v has a strong influence over u according to a topic k. Based on the previous definitions we can now define influence:

Definition 4. Let $G_k(N_k, E_k)$ be an induced graph of a network $G(N, E)$ over a topic k with n_k trends. For each $(u, v) \in E_k$ we define the influence of v over u by:

$$I_k^*(u, v) = \left(\frac{s_1(v) \cdot s_2(u, v)}{||s_1(v)|| \times ||s_2(u, v)||} \right) \times \left(\frac{L(s_2(u, v))}{n_k} \right), \quad (3)$$

where the operator $\cdot$ refers to the scalar product, $||x||$ to the Euclidian norm of any vector x, and $L(s_2(u, v))$ to the number of components of $s_2(u, v)$ that are different from 0. If $||s_2(u, v)|| = 0$, we define $I^*(u, v) = 0$. It is important to notice that, by definition, $||s_1(v)|| \neq 0$ for all $v \in N_k$.

Equation 3 is the main outcome of our previous discussion. The first part is given by the cosine similarity between $s_1(v)$ and $s_2(u, v)$, which is close to 1 if u adopted the same trends than v in a reasonable lag of time, and close to 0, otherwise. The second term is the fraction of trends of k that u adopted after v. We use this to indicate that if u adopted more trends influenced by v than by other node z, then the influence of v over u is greater than the influence of z.

One important fact is that u can be influenced to adopt a trend of k by several nodes in $G_k(N_k, E_k)$. So, we normalize $I^*(u, v)$ as follows:

$$I_k(u, v) = \frac{I_k^*(u, v)}{\sum_{w \in Out_{G_k}(u)} I_k^*(u, w)}, \quad (4)$$

noticing that if the denominator of Equation 4 is zero, we define $I_k(u, v)$ as 0.

The next definition presents how we rank trendsetters according to a Pagerank-like algorithm.

Definition 5. The trendsetters (TS) rank of node v in a network $G_k(N_k, E_k)$, denoted by $TS_k(v)$, is given by:

$$TS_k(v) = d\, D_k(v) + (1 - d) \sum_{w \in In_{G_k}(v)} TS_k(w) I_k(w, v), \quad (5)$$

where $0 \leq d \leq 1$ is the damping factor and D_k is a probability distribution over all nodes of $G_k(N_k, E_k)$. In this paper we consider a uniform $D_k(v) = 1/|N_k|$ for all $v \in N_k$, but this distribution could be topic dependent.

Making an analogy with the random surfer model in the Pagerank algorithm presented in [22] on graph $G_k(N_k, E_k)$ we can analyze Equation 5 in the following way: consider that the surfer is in any node of $G_k(N_k, E_k)$, for example u. With probability $1-d$, the surfer leaves u and goes to other node in $Out_{G_k}(u)$, and with probability d, to any node in N_k. In the first case the node $v \in Out_{G_k}(u)$ will be visited with probability $I_k(u,v)$. So, the node that influences more u has a higher probability to be visited. In the second case, any $v \in N_k$ will be visited with probability $D_k(v)$, reflecting the independent adoption of that topic. Hence, in the steady state the surfer will spend more time in the most influential nodes of the network.

Let us now see an example in Twitter: The Iran election was an important topic during 2009. The main hashtag used to talk about this was #iranelection, and other related tags where #iran and #tehran. So using definition 1, the topic Iran Election could be represented by: $k_{\text{Iran Election}}$ = [#iranelection, #iran, #tehran]. Following the methodology proposed previously, we compute the graph for all the nodes that used at least one of the trends. Next, we compute the PageRank(PR), InDegree Rank(ID) and the TS rank for this graph. PR and ID selects @cnnbr (CNN Breaking News) as top user, while TS selects a user named @Lara, self-described as "Reporting from the Middle East for ABC News and Bloomberg Television." This user twitted with the two most popular hashtags in this topic, adopting them before than they became popular (see Figure 2). In other cases related with politics we have also find other activists or reporters "on site" being ranked on the top of TS, while PR and ID selects CNN for all of them.

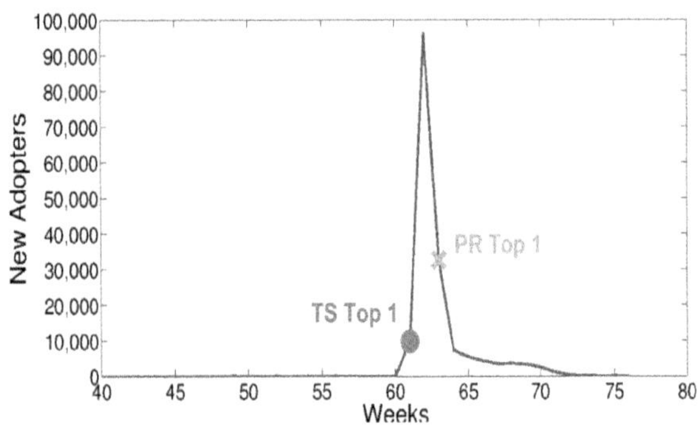

Figure 2: Iran Election Topic Timeline: comparison between top TS and top PR users.

Another interesting example is the idiom #musicmonday, which is one of the most popular in Twitter. Its name is very descriptive because it is used to share music on Mondays. Considering that we have almost the complete Twitter information from its beginning, we can know who invented this tag: *@rubenharris*. This fact should identify that user as influential in this trend. However, if we analyze this topic using PR, that user is ranked in the position 164,970 among 179,119 users. But using TS this user appears in the 4th position. Note that, as we explained before, to be an innovator - and thus an early adopter - a necessary but not sufficient characteristic is to be a trendsetter. TS considers that the most trendsetter for #musicmonday is user *@twtfm*, which is the corporate user of the site http://twt.fm, a company that offers a service to share and search music using Twitter. However this user was the 76th to adopt the trend. Now, note that PR and ID selects the same user as the top one: *@perezhilton*. He is a famous professional blogger, and he has been indicated as one of the users with more followers in Twitter [19]. However, if we check *@perezhilton*, he was the 18,718th user to adopt the trend, therefore we cannot consider he as an innovator. However, because he is prestigious, TS ranked it in the top-100. The example of #musicmonday is useful to understand that TS captures both characteristics that we consider important for a trendsetter: the early adoption and the capacity to spread the trend over the graph.

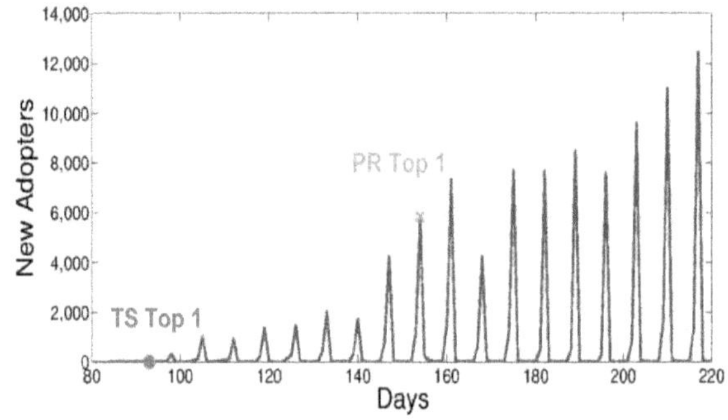

Figure 3: #musicmonday new adopters timeline: comparison between top TS and top PR users.

4. EXPERIMENTAL EVALUATION

In order to test the TS ranking we have conducted a set of experiments over a huge Twitter dataset. We consider the Twitter social graph, where the connections among users are directed. Using the notation described in the previous section the Twitter graph will be $G(N, E)$, where an edge $(u, v) \in E$ means that user u *follows* v. Trends are modeled using *hashtags*, so a topic k is a collection of hashtags, that is $k = [\#tag_1, \ldots, \#tag_{n_k}]$. Next, we create the induced graph G_k considering all the nodes that have posted at least a tweet with one hashtag of k. Over this graph we compute the TS ranking using a time window of one day ($\alpha = 86,400$ seconds) in Equation 2 and $d = 0.2$ in Equation 5, following the original PageRank value. We have tested other values and they do not change the results significantly.

Our hypothesis is that other measures of influence are not suitable to find trendsetters because they tend to favor nodes that do not propose new trends, but follow those that are already popular. To test this, we grouped the trends by different methodologies: first we group them by categories related with topics such as music, sports, movies, etc., next we grouped the new adopters curve shape. In each case we compare the TS ranking with In-Degree (ID) ranking - where nodes are sorted by incoming links; and the traditional Pagerank, PR. We also quantify the followers influenced by the top users of each ranking and we compute how similar are the rankings under study.

4.1 Dataset

We have used a dataset containing almost the total information in Twitter until August 2009. We have over 50 millions users, with all their social connections (*Followers* and *Followees*) and approximately 1.6 billions of Tweets. Note that differently from other works that use a big amount of tweets, we also have the complete social graph, so we do not need to use heuristics to infer it. A detailed description of this dataset can be found in [8].

To select the hashtag for the experiment, we use the classification made by Romero *et al.* [24], where each of the 500 most popular hashtags in their dataset was assigned to a category such as politics, music, or celebrities (see Table 1). From those 500 hashtags, only 370 are mentioned among the 2,000 most popular of our dataset, with #followfriday being the most popular with 3,051,316 mentions and #jemi the least mentioned, with only 1,810 occurrences. The 130 remaining hashtags do not appear or have a very low level of mentions. This is because each dataset was obtained on different dates.

To complete the topic modeling, we looked for other hashtags related with the main one. For the 370 hashtags we searched for others that had a co-occurrence of at least 5% with the main one. This means that each of the 370 topics is modeled by a vector containing the main hashtag and others related to it. For example, the topic modeled with more hasthtags was #realstate, having other 20 related hashtags. Over 74% of the topics were modeled with at least two hashtags. Note that these related hashtags creates the vectors that are described in Definition 2. The categories are used only to facilitate the analysis of the results.

4.2 Adoption before Peak: Categories

Our first approach to answer this question is to analyze the percent of users of each ranking adopting the trend before the peak of adoption. By peak of adoption we refer to the time when a trend had its bigger number of new adopters. To do that, first we obtained the peak of adoption from each of the 370 topics studied. We denote by P_k the peak of adoption of trend k. Next, we have to compare it with the time of adoption of the top-p users of each ranking, where $T(i)_{k_r}$ represents the time in which user i from ranking r adopted topic k. Therefore, if $P_k - T(i)_{k_r} < 0$, this means that user i adopted the trend before the peak. Finally, we grouped all the topics k by their category, and we computed the percentage of users adopting the trend after the peak for each ranking. The results presented have been calculated with $p = 100$, but values from 5 to 1000 do not present significant variations.

Figure 4 shows that in categories such as music, celebrity and idioms, most of the nodes in the top of ID and PR start talking about these topics after the peak, and only in sports and technology they obtain a good performance. In contrast, in 6 of the 9 categories, more than 50% of the TS top users adopted the trend before the peak. One motivation to develop the TS ranking was our intuition that nodes with high in-degree do not propose or push new trends but follow those that are already popular. The performance of ID in the previous experiment tends to confirm this intuition. In order to better understand how the in-degree is

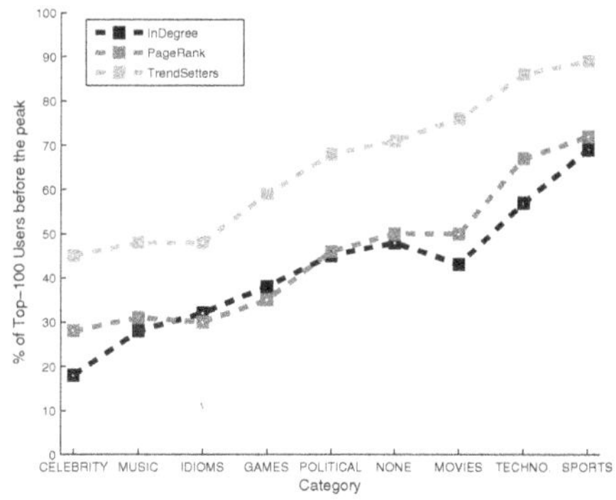

Figure 4: Percentage of top-100 users of each ranking that adopts the trend before the peak.

related with the adoption time, we repeated the previous experiment, but instead of computing only if $P_k - T(i)_{k_r}$ is > 0, we recorded this time span as well as the user i in-degree. Therefore, for each ranking in each trend we have a list of tuples representing the time span and the in-degree of the top-p nodes. Again we group the trends by their category, and at the end we computed the median of the time span and of the in-degree of each ranking for each category. In Figure 5 we plot the time span median in the horizontal axis and the in-degree median in the vertical axis for each ranking. It is clear that top users of TS adopt trends before the peak and they have a smaller in-degree than top users of the other rankings. These results confirm that nodes with high in-degree tend to be *slower* than other nodes.

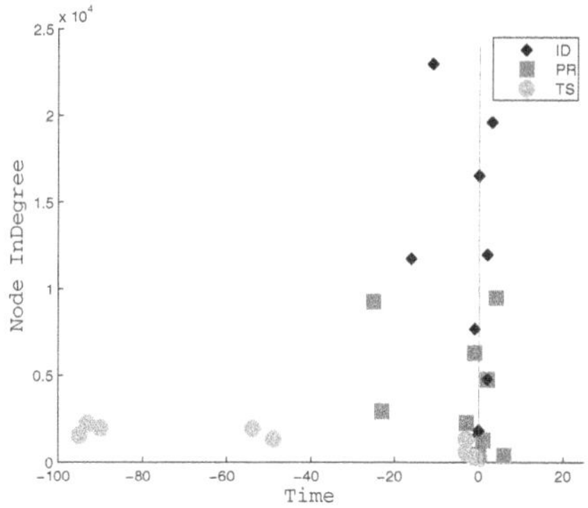

Figure 5: Relation among time span and in-degree for the top-100 users of each ranking in all the categories (peak is at time 0).

4.3 Adoption before Peak: Shapes

The categories by topic are very descriptive, but the nature of the TS ranking suggests that the quality is also related with the shape of the curve of adoption. For this reason we grouped the trends by their curve of new adopters. For this aim we have used the KSC-algorithm [28], that receives as input a set of time series, and gives as an output a classification by shape and the centroids of each cluster, providing a visual representation. Note that, unlike that paper, we are interested in the adoption of the trend, that is, the first

Table 1: Summary of categories. Note that some hashtags could belong to more than one Topic.

Category	#Topics	Example of Hashtags	#Tweets
Celebrity	16	#michaeljackson, #niley	1,036,101
Games	13	#mafiawars, #ps3 #	2,556,437
Idioms	35	#musicmonday,#followfriday	7,882,209
Movies	29	#heroes,#tv	1,769,945
Music	33	#lastfm, #musicmonday	2,705,522
None	153	#quotes, #sale	2,227,971
Political	39	#honduras, #Iranelection,	8,156,786
Sports	27	#soccer, #rugby	1,914,061
Technology	41	#twitter,#android	7,459,471
Total	370	-	41,442,741

time that the hashtag is mentioned by a user. Additionally, we are interested in all the popular trends, not only in those with a short duration. Hence, our time discretization is done by days, not hours.

To apply the KSC-algorithm we have created a time series to represent the curve of new adopters from each trend, considering that the time of adoption is the first mention of any of the hashtags in the topic (repeated or later mentions are not taken in account). We have created time series of 128 elements, where each element represents a day. Next, we align the peaks of all the time series at 2/3, that is position 86. This is different than the 1/3 peak centering used in [28]. Our reason to move the peak to the right is because we are more interested in what happens before the peak, rather than later. The last step, was to select the number of clusters K to use. We tried with values from 2 to 12, finding that with more than 4 clusters we found only small variations of the 4 main clusters. Figure 6 shows the shapes of the 4 clusters obtained. Next, we repeatead the calculations described in the previous subsection to find the time span and the median of time adoption of the top users of each ranking but now grouped by cluster. Finally, we plot these points over the curves.

Table 2: Number of topics in KSC Clusters.

#Cluster	1	2	3	4
#Topics	91	115	**128**	36

Table 2 show that most of the topics corresponds to clusters with a clear peak of adoption such as cluster 3. In figure 6 we can see that TS appears clearly before the peak in all the clusters. In contrast, the top users of ID and PR only appears before the peak in cluster 2, that is, in the cluster with the less pronounced peak. Specially interesting are the results for cluster 1, where TS appears over a little first peak before the largest one. This suggests that TS is detecting a topic that will be potentially interesting in the future.

4.4 Influenced Followers Ratio

Now we try to understand how many of the social contacts were influenced by the top users of each ranking, that is, how many of their total followers adopt the trends after them. To evaluate this, we create a simple indicator that we call *Influenced Followers* ratio for a topic k, $IF_k(v)$, defined as the fraction of followers of v that adopted at least one trend of the topic k after v.

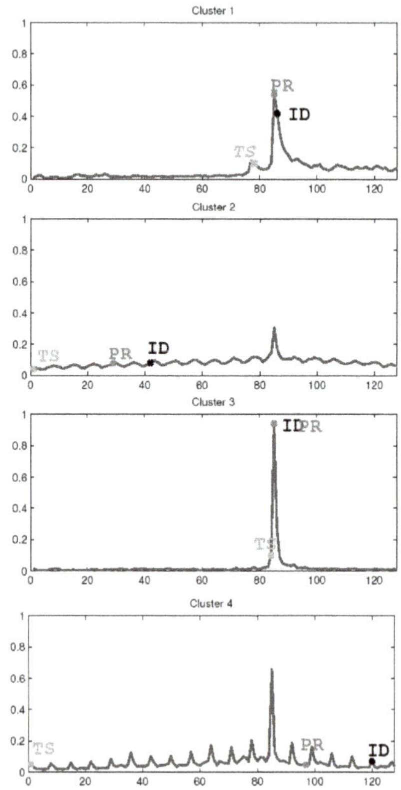

Figure 6: KSC clusters. Each ranking is represented with the median of time deviation with respect to the peak in each cluster.

Table 3 shows that TS top users have a bigger IF ratio than for PR and ID. It is interesting to note that in the category Political, the TS rankings obtain the best performance, and in all of them is always over 0.06. Note that in 7 of the 9 categories TS is one order of magnitude better than ID and almost doubles PR. This confirms that TS users influence more their social contacts than other rankings.

4.5 Ranking Similarities

Whereas one of the main features of TS ranking is to capture the early adoption behavior, makes sense to compare it with an Early Adoption EA ranking. That is, a ranking where

Table 3: **Influenced Followers (IF) ratio for top-100 users of each ranking.**

Category	(%)ID	(%)PR	(%)TS
Political	0.013	0.084	**0.174**
Celebrity	0.015	0.089	**0.148**
Music	0.013	0.096	**0.160**
Games	0.022	0.058	**0.115**
Sports	0.004	0.054	**0.098**
Idioms	0.001	0.034	**0.088**
None	0.011	0.001	**0.085**
Technology	0.006	0.054	**0.078**
Movies	0.006	0.043	**0.067**

the top one will be the first adopter and the next position will be assigned by the adoption time.

To compare rankings we use the Kendall Rank Correlation Coefficient τ. This coefficient gives an idea of the agreement between two rankings. It varies in the interval $[-1, 1]$, where 1 means total agreement and -1 means that one ranking is the reverse of the other.

For this experiment we use the trends with more mentions in each category and then we compute the average among trends for the four rankings: EA, TS, ID and PR.

Table 4 shows that PR and ID tend to be similar but completely different from EA. TS is not too similar with any of them but presents a nice balance among them. This results shows that TS has the ability to mix different characteristics of the other rankings. It also shows that not all the early adopters are trendsetters.

Table 4: Kendall τ comparison among rankings.

	EA	PR	ID
EA	-	-	-
PR	0.11	-	-
ID	0.09	0.74	-
TS	0.37	0.56	0.48

4.6 Ranking with Partial Information

Previous results show that TS give high scores to the early adopters. Considering this we can conjecture that probably it is not necessary to use the information about all users to find the top ones. To answer this question we conducted the following experiment: first we selected the topic with more users for each category to use it as representative of this category. Next, we ordered the users by adoption time and then we compute the ranking considering only the first 10% of them, then 20%, and so on in increments of 10%. Next, we compared it with the final ranking (i.e. with the 100% of users). For all the trends, we were able to find the top-one user, considering only the initial 10%. Moreover, we found 7 of the top 10 users, and more than 70 of the top-100 users if we consider the 20% of initial users. In contrast, PR could find the top-one with the 10% only in one case, requiring more than 50% of the users in the other cases. Moreover, PR required over 60% of users, to find at least 7 of the top-10 users.

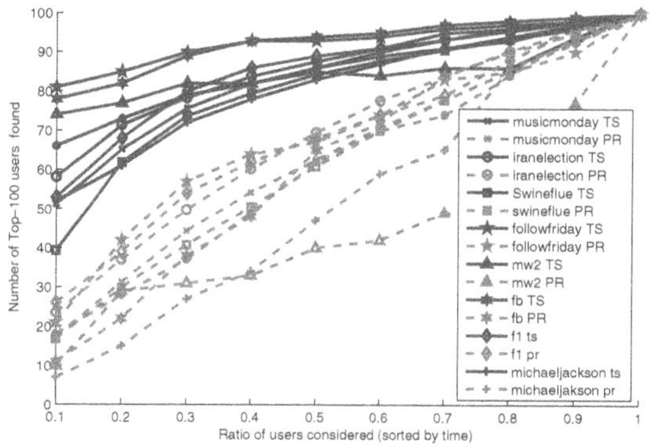

Figure 7: Number of top-100 users found using a only a fraction of total users sorted by time. A Comparison between PR and TS in three trends.

Figure 7 shows the total number of top-100 found considering different fractions of users. These results suggest that TS is able to find the most influential users faster than PR. This behavior can be explained considering that TS ranks on the top many early adopters, unlike PR that is more sensitive to the arrival of a node with high in-degree at anytime that they arrive. The time decay used makes TS less sensitive if those nodes arrive late.

5. CONCLUSIONS

We have proposed a robust algorithm to rank trendsetters, presenting the problem of the spread of an innovation as a ranking problem considering the temporal factor. We have also presented a sound and extensible way to model topics and influence allowing to run this algorithm in different contexts. Although we have conducted experiments only on Twitter, the problem formulation makes it possible to apply this algorithm to other information networks. We have also presented an innovative methodology to evaluate our algorithm, using different types of classifications such as categories and curve shapes.

One important finding is that users with high in-degree do not propose the ideas that became popular, as usually they adopt them when they are already popular. This confirms the importance of developing new techniques such as TS to find the users that create or early adopt these trends. This appear to be critical in topics related with celebrities, music, idioms and politics.

The results presented in Section 4.6 highlight two important advantages of TS over other algorithms. First, the possibility to find a big fraction of trendsetters requiring only the first 10% of trend adopters, something very useful in real-time scenarios. Second, the differences in the behavior along the time of TS against PR results could be explained because when nodes with a high in-degree adopt a trend late, the time decay function reduces their impact in the final rank.

In future work, using machine learning techniques we will compare the trendsetters with other users that appear to be similar but that do not achieve success, trying to identify the key characteristics of trendsetters. We will also test our algorithms in other data sets as they can be used in any social network. We also want to explore the impact of the parameters α and d as well as other functions to model the temporal behavior.

Acknowledgements

This work has been partially funded by the HIPERGRAPH project (TIN2009-14560-C03-01) from the Spanish Economy and Competitiveness Ministry, and partially funded by the Brazilian National Institute of Science and Technology for the Web (MCT/CNPq/INCT grant number 573871/2008-6).

6. REFERENCES

[1] P. Adams. *Grouped: How Small Groups of Friends Are the Key to Influence on the Social Web.* Voices That Matter. Pearson Education, 2011.

[2] A. Anagnostopoulos, R. Kumar, and M. Mahdian. Influence and correlation in social networks. In *Proc. of Int'l conf. on Knowledge discovery and data mining*, KDD'08, pages 7–15, NY, USA, 2008. ACM.

[3] S. E. Asch. Effects of group pressure upon the modification and distortion of judgments. In H. Guetzkow, editor, *Groups, Leadership, and Men*, pages 177–190. Carnegie Press, Pittsburgh, PA, 1951.

[4] L. Backstrom, D. Huttenlocher, J. Kleinberg, and X. Lan. Group formation in large social networks: membership, growth, and evolution. In *Proc.of Int'l conf. on Knowledge discovery and data mining*, KDD'06, pages 44–54, NY,USA, 2006. ACM.

[5] R. Baeza-Yates and E. Davis. Web page ranking using link attributes. In *Proc.of Int'l conf. World Wide Web*, WWW'04, pages 328–329, NY, USA, 2004. ACM.

[6] E. Bakshy, B. Karrer, and L. Adamic. Social influence and the diffusion of user-created content. In *Proc.of conf. on Electronic commerce*, EC '09, pages 325–334, NY, USA, 2009. ACM.

[7] F. Bass. A new product growth for model consumer durables. *Management Sciences*, 15(1):215–227, 1969.

[8] M. Cha, H. Haddadi, F. Benevenuto, and K. Gummadi. Measuring User Influence in Twitter: The Million Follower Fallacy. In *Proc.of the 4th Int'l AAAI conf. on Weblogs and Social Media (ICWSM)*, Washington DC, USA, 2010.

[9] W. Chen, Y. Wang, and S. Yang. Efficient influence maximization in social networks. In *Proc. Int'l conf. on Knowledge discovery and data mining*, KDD '09, pages 199–208, NY, USA, 2009. ACM.

[10] P. Domingos and M. Richardson. Mining the network value of customers. In *Proc.of Int'l conf. on Knowledge discovery and data mining*, KDD '01, pages 57–66, NY, USA, 2001. ACM.

[11] *A special report on social networking, The Economist*, Jan 2010. http://tinyurl.com/ylxtsek. Accessed 07/2011.

[12] M. Gomez-Rodriguez, J. Leskovec, and A. Krause. Inferring networks of diffusion and influence. *Networks*, Proceeding:1019–1028, 2010.

[13] A. Goyal, F. Bonchi, and L. Lakshmanan. Discovering leaders from community actions. In *Proc. of Int'l conf. on Information and knowledge management*, CIKM '08, pages 499–508, NY, USA, 2008. ACM.

[14] M. Granovetter. Threshold Models of Collective Behavior. *Amercan Journal of Sociology*, 15:1420 – 1443, 1978.

[15] T. Haveliwala. Topic-sensitive pagerank: A context-sensitive ranking algorithm for web search. *IEEE Transactions on Knowledge and Data Engineering*, 15:784–796, 2003.

[16] D. Kempe, J. Kleinberg, and E. Tardos. Maximizing the spread of influence through a social network. In *Proc.of Int'l conf. on Knowledge discovery and data mining*, KDD'03, pages 137–146, NY, USA, 2003. ACM.

[17] J. Kleinberg. Authoritative sources in a hyperlinked environment. *J. ACM*, 46:604–632, September 1999.

[18] G. Kossinets, J. Kleinberg, and D. Watts. The structure of information pathways in a social communication network. In *Proc. Int'l conf. on Knowledge discovery and data mining*, KDD '08, pages 435–443, NY, USA, 2008. ACM.

[19] H. Kwak, C. Lee, H. Park, and S. Moon. What is twitter, a social network or a news media? In *Proc.of Int'l conf. on World wide web*, WWW'10, pages 591–600, NY, USA, 2010. ACM.

[20] L. Liu, J. Tang, J. Han, M. Jiang, and S. Yang. Mining topic-level influence in heterogeneous networks. In *Proc.of Int'l conf. on Information and knowledge management*, CIKM '10, pages 199–208, NY, USA, 2010. ACM.

[21] G. Moore. *Crossing the Chasm.* HarperBusiness, revised edition, Sept. 2002.

[22] L. Page, S. Brin, R. Motwani, and T. Winograd. The pagerank citation ranking: Bringing order to the web. Technical Report 1999-66, Stanford InfoLab, November 1999.

[23] A. Pal and S. Counts. Identifying topical authorities in microblogs. In *ACM WSDM*, pages 45–54, 2011.

[24] D. Romero, B. Meeder, and J. Kleinberg. Differences in the mechanics of information diffusion across topics: idioms, political hashtags, and complex contagion on twitter. In *Proc. of Int'l conf. on World wide web*, WWW'11, pages 695–704, NY, USA, 2011. ACM.

[25] W. Romero, D.and Galuba, S. Asur, and B. Huberman. Influence and passivity in social media. In *ECML/PKDD (3)*, pages 18–33, 2011.

[26] T. Schelling. *Micromotives and Macrobehavior.* Norton, 1978.

[27] J. Weng, E. Lim, J. Jiang, and Q. He. Twitterrank: finding topic-sensitive influential twitterers. In *Proc.of Int'l conf. on Web search and data mining*, WSDM '10, pages 261–270, NY, USA, 2010. ACM.

[28] J. Yang and J. Leskovec. Patterns of temporal variation in online media. In *Proc.of Int'l conf. on Web search and data mining*, WSDM'11, pages 177–186, NY, USA, 2011. ACM.

[29] J. Zhang, M. Ackerman, and L. Adamic. Expertise networks in online communities: structure and algorithms. In *Proc.of the 16th Int'l conf. on World Wide Web*, WWW '07, pages 221–230, NY, USA, 2007. ACM.

Towards Social User Profiling: Unified and Discriminative Influence Model for Inferring Home Locations*

Rui Li[†], Shengjie Wang[†], Hongbo Deng[†], Rui Wang[†], Kevin Chen-Chuan Chang[†,*]
{ruili1, wang260, hbdeng, ruiwang3, kcchang}@illinois.edu
[†] Department of Computer Science, University of Illinois at Urbana-Champaign, Urbana, IL, USA
[*] Advanced Digital Sciences Center, Illinois at Singapore, Singapore

ABSTRACT

Users' locations are important to many applications such as targeted advertisement and news recommendation. In this paper, we focus on the problem of profiling users' home locations in the context of social network (Twitter). The problem is nontrivial, because signals, which may help to identify a user's location, are *scarce* and *noisy*. We propose a unified discriminative influence model, named as $\mathcal{UDI}$, to solve the problem. To overcome the challenge of scarce signals, $\mathcal{UDI}$ integrates signals observed from both social network (friends) and user-centric data (tweets) in a unified probabilistic framework. To overcome the challenge of noisy signals, $\mathcal{UDI}$ captures how likely a user connects to a signal with respect to 1) the distance between the user and the signal, and 2) the influence scope of the signal. Based on the model, we develop *local* and *global* location prediction methods. The experiments on a large scale data set show that our methods improve the state-of-the-art methods by 13%, and achieve the best performance.

Categories and Subject Descriptors

H.2.8 [**Data Management**]: Database Applications - Data Mining; H.4.0 [**Information Systems**]: General

General Terms

Algorithms

Keywords

Social Network, Influence Model, Location Profiling

1. INTRODUCTION

User profiling, which infers a user's essential attributes, such as gender, location and interests, has been a holy grail in enabling effective information services. For example, profiling a user's location (which we will focus) or topic interests enables search engines to provide personalized search results, news sites to recommend localized news, and advertisers to serve targeted ads. To profile a user, traditional approaches leverage limited user-centric data (*e.g.*, search log or purchase history).

The emergence of social network services raises both challenges and opportunities for effective user profiling. Recently, online social network services such as Facebook and Twitter become important platforms for users to connect with friends as well as share information. For example, Twitter, a social network for users to follow each other and publish tweets, now has 140 million active users and generates 340 million tweets daily. On one hand, those services need to "understand" their users better, because old tasks (*e.g.*, targeted ads) now become even more challenging (*e.g.*, serving ads without queries), and new tasks (*e.g.*, recommending "friends") arise in the context of social network. On the other hand, those services generate additional information to leverage, because not only user-centric data (*e.g.*, tweets) is available, but also information from others can be propagated through users' social connections.

In this paper, we are particularly interested in profiling "home locations" for Twitter users with both social network (the following network) and user-centric data (tweets). We define a user's *home location* as the place where most of his activities happen. First, a home location is a static geo *scope* (*e.g.*, Chicago) instead of a real-time geo *point* (*e.g.*, the Starbucks on 5th Ave.). Second, it is a user's "permanent" location instead of other locations that are "temporally" related to him (*e.g.*, the places where he is traveling). A user's home location, even when he is "out of town", captures his *major* and *static* geographic scope of interests, which is therefore a useful target for many location-based services as just mentioned.

On Twitter, a user's home location can not be obtained readily. Only a few people (16%) register city level locations (*e.g.*, Chicago, IL) in their profiles. Most of users leave general (*e.g.*, "IL"), nonsensical (*e.g.*, "my home") or even blank information. Although Twitter supports users to add GPS tags in their tweets, even fewer people (0.5%) use this feature due to privacy concerns. Thus, we aim to profile users' locations in the absence of GPS tags.

Intuitively, a user's following network and tweets provide valuable signals for profiling his home location, as he is likely to 1) follow users, who live close, and 2) tweet nearby locations. However, we face two challenges when utilizing the two types of signals.

- **Scarce Signals:** Based on our crawled data, we find that 1) a user has 126 social connections on average, but only 16% of them provide locations, and 2) there are only about 6 location related terms in every 100 messages. Each type of signals alone is not sufficient to profile all users' locations. It is possible that a user has few social connections and none of them provides a location. It is also possible that a user does not tweet but only consumes information from others.

*This material is based upon work partially supported by NSF Grant IIS 1018723 and the Advanced Digital Science Center of the University of Illinois at Urbana-Champaign. Any opinions, findings, and conclusions or recommendations expressed in this publication are those of the author(s) and do not necessarily reflect the views of the funding agencies.

KDD'12, August 12–16, 2012, Beijing, China.

- **Noisy Signals:** A user follows friends from or publishes tweets about different locations other than his home location. Some of them are far away. For example, a user in Chicago may follow Lady Gaga in New York or President Obama in Washington, and tweet about Houston Rocket's game or his vacation in Honolulu.

In this paper, we propose a unified discriminative "influence" model, named as $\mathcal{UDI}$, to tackle the above challenges.

Unified Signals With respect to the scarce signal challenge, $\mathcal{UDI}$ integrates the two types of signals in a unified probabilistic framework. To the best of our knowledge, it is the first that integrates social network and user-centric data for the location profiling task.

To integrate different types of signals (*e.g.*, locations of friends and from tweets), we first abstract them with a unified view. Specifically, we view them as a heterogenous graph, where a user connects to the two types of signals via "following" and "tweeting" edges. Then, we take a probabilistic generative approach to model them jointly. We assume every edge (*e.g.*, a tweeting edge) is "generated" according to the two end nodes' locations (*e.g.*, a user and a tweeted venue), and model the *joint conditional probability* of generating all the edges given the nodes' locations. We estimate the unknown locations as latent variables in the probability.

Discriminative Influence With respect to the noisy signal challenge, $\mathcal{UDI}$ models how likely an edge is "generated" from a head node (*e.g.*, a user) to a tail node (*e.g.*, a tweeted venue) with respect to 1) the distance between them, and 2) the influence scope of the tail node. It successfully captures "closeness" and "credibility" of each signal, and therefore is robust to noisy signals.

- **Influence at different distances:** $\mathcal{UDI}$ captures that 1) a node (*e.g.*, a user) has *influence probabilities* at different locations to attract a user there to build an edge (*e.g.*, a following edge), and 2) a node's influence probability at a location decreases as its distance to the node increases. Thus, $\mathcal{UDI}$ not only exploits our intuition that a user is likely to follow users from or tweet about nearby locations, but also tolerates noisy signals that he may follow friends from and tweet about locations far away. When predicting his location, our model can successfully identify that his location is close to the most dominating region among those of his friends and tweeted venues. *E.g.*, a user has three friends from New York, Chicago, and Champaign (a small town in Illinois) respectively, our model is able to find that he is in Illinois.
- **Influence Scope of each node:** $\mathcal{UDI}$ captures that each node has its own *influence scope*. Intuitively, an influential node (*e.g.*, Lady Gaga) with a "broad" influence scope is more likely than a regular node (*e.g.*, a real friend) to be followed or tweeted by a user far away, and therefore its location is more likely to be a noisy signal for predicting the user's location. Thus, our model overcomes noisy signals by discriminating the locations of influential nodes from the locations of regular nodes. When predicting a user's location, our model can automatically weigh a node (*e.g.*, a real friend) with a narrow influence scope more than a node (*e.g.*, Lady Gaga) with a broad scope.

To mathematically model all users' influence models, we choose a set of discriminative Gaussian distributions. For each node, a gaussian distribution has its center L and variance σ representing the node's location and its influence scope, respectively. A node's influence probability at a location L' is measured as the probability at the corresponding distance of L' from L in the distribution. The simplicity of a gaussian distribution enables us to learn its parameters for each node with scarce signals, and thus results in "rich" modeling– every node has its own unique influence model.

Based on $\mathcal{UDI}$, we develop two location prediction methods with the maximum likelihood (MLE) principle. Our *local prediction method* predicts a user's location by maximizing the probability of generating edges to his "local" signals, *i.e.*, locations of his friends and tweets. We further extend the local scheme to a *global prediction method*. Intuitively, a user's unlabeled friends are useful since their own labeled friends or tweets may indicate their locations explicitly, so as to enhance the prediction of the given user. Thus, we maximize the probability of generating edges to all the signals on the entire graph, and derive an iterative algorithm to make more accurate predictions. We also prove the convergence of the algorithm. In addition, we enhance our prediction methods by using human knowledge (*e.g.*, users only live in cities but not arbitrary geo points) as *constraints*. Those constraints help us to learn a more accurate model with scarce signals.

As a byproduct, $\mathcal{UDI}$ also identifies the influence scope of each node, which is new and different from the "influence score" studied by earlier work [5]. The influence scope measures the broadness in terms of physical distance of a node's influence over the geo space, while the influence score measures how good a node is in spreading information over a social network. A node (*e.g.*, the New York weather channel) can have a large influence score but a small influence scope. In this paper, we use the influence scope to discriminate the credibility of each node in predicting locations, but we see many interesting applications beyond this setting, such as differentiating global authorities (*e.g.*, Lady Gaga) and local authorities (*e.g.*, Texas Representative).

Finally, we conduct extensive experiments to evaluate our prediction methods and compare with the state-of-the-art methods [4, 7] based on a large-scale Twitter data set containing about 160K users and 50 million tweets. The experimental results show that our prediction methods significantly improve the best baseline method by 13%, and achieve accurate results. Particularly, our global method can place 66% users within 100 miles, and the average error distance for its top 60% predictions is less than 5 miles.

2. RELATED WORK

In this section, we discuss some related work, including user profiling and location prediction.

User Profiling Due to the importance of user profiling, many interesting studies have been done on this problem. Most of them focus on profiling users' "topic interests" to serve personalized search [13, 17], targeted advertisement [1, 12], and news recommendation [16]. They mainly explore user-centric data, including query logs [13], browsing behaviors [16] and other types of user generated data [12, 17]. Our work is different in two aspects. First, we aim to profile locations. Second, we explore not only user-centric data (*i.e.*, tweets) but also social network data.

As the rise of social network services, some seminal studies [18, 11] explore social network for user profiling. Yang et al. [18] propose a model to propagate interests of an item among users via their friendships. However, users' locations are different from their interests of an item, and can not be propagated directly. Mislove et al. [11] use friendships to infer Facebook users' attributes. They apply a clustering algorithm to find communities in the network and assign an identical attribute value to users in the same community. Although this method is supposed to work for different types of attributes, it fails in predicting locations, as users follow others living far away and communities are not directly formed based on users' locations. It does not leverage user-centric data as well.

Location Prediction As we focus on profiling users' locations, our work is related to identifying geographical scopes for various kinds of online entities, such as pages [2], queries [3], tags [14], and photos [8]. However, they predict locations for different types of entities with different resources. For example, Amitay et al. [2] explore a web page's content to predict its geo scope based on heuristic rules. Their method extracts location signals (*e.g.*, city names) from a page and uses a gazetteer to find the geo region that covers most of the signals as the region of the page. Our work is different, as we take a probabilistic approach to profile users' locations. Backstrom et al. [3] propose a probabilistic model to assign a geographic center and a rate of diffusion to a query based on the usage of the query. Our method is different from it, as we focus on utilizing social network and tweets in a unified and discriminative approach. Furthermore, our prediction methods are able to utilize additional human knowledge.

Our work is most related to [7, 4], as they also focus on the same user location prediction problem. Cheng et al. [7] estimate a user's location based on the content of his tweets. Specifically, they identify a set of location related words (*e.g.*, "chicago") and use them as features to classify the user to locations. Recently, Chandra et. al. [6] improve this model slightly by associating a user's original tweets to him, and his retweets to the initial user. However, they both treat local words and locations as discrete labels and overlook their explicit relations (*e.g.*, distances between them). Backstrom et al. [4] estimate a user's location based on his friends on Facebook. They first learn a function, which assigns the probability of being friends given the distance of two users, and then estimate a user's location based on MLE. However, their model assumes the probability of being friends given the same distance is the same for different users. This assumption usually does not hold, especially on Twitter. *E.g.*, a famous user is more likely to have a follower far away than a regular user does. Therefore, their model can not differentiate signals with different credibilities. $\mathcal{UDI}$ not only overcomes the disadvantages of the above methods, but also has the following advantages: 1) it models both content and social network, 2) it utilizes relationships from both labeled and unlabeled users, and 3) it supports integrating additional human knowledge.

3. PROBLEM FORMULATION

In this section, we first abstract different types of signals as a heterogeneous graph, and then formalize our problem from there.

Twitter is a social network, where users follow others and publish messages. Given a user, we identify two important types of signals: 1) *following relationships* between the user and other users, and 2) *tweets or messages* tweeted by the user. We note that following relationships are "directional", which means if a user u_i follows a user u_j, u_j does not necessarily follow back. Thus, we further divide a user's following relationships into *followers* who follow the user and *friends* who are followed by the user.

Both types of signals are useful for inferring a user's location. As Sec. 1 mentioned, a user is likely to 1) follow and be followed by users, who live close to him, and 2) mention some "venues" (*e.g.*, Chicago), which may indicate his location. We refer a *venue* as a signal for a place, which could be a city (*e.g.*, Chicago), a place (*e.g.*, Time Square), or an entity with a specific geo position (*e.g.*, Stanford University). If some of a user's followers or friends provide locations in their profiles, we can propagate their locations to him. If a user mentions some venues in his messages, we can use them to infer his location as well.

As shown in Fig. 1, we abstract different types of signals as a directed heterogeneous graph $G = (N, E)$, where N is a set of nodes n_i and E is a set of edges $e\langle n_i, n_j\rangle$ from a tail node n_i to a head node n_j. N contains two types of nodes, *user nodes* U representing all the users and *venue nodes* V representing all the venues tweeted by users. $N = U \cup V$. E contains two types

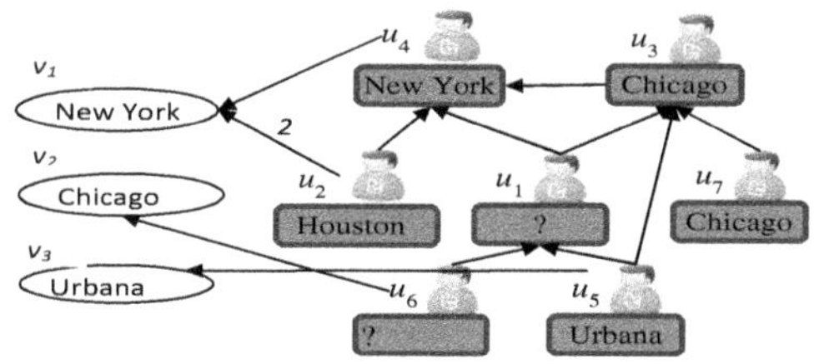

Figure 1: An Example of Twitter Graph.

of edges, each of which designates a specific type of relationships between nodes: 1) *following edges* F between user nodes, and 2) *tweeting edges* T between user nodes and venue nodes. $E = F \cup T$. A *following edge* $f\langle u_i, u_j\rangle$ is formed from a user u_i to another user u_j when u_i follows u_j, where u_i is a *follower* of u_j, and u_j is a *friend* of u_i. A *tweeting edge* $t\langle u_i, v_j\rangle$ is formed from a user u_i to a venue v_j, when u_i tweets v_j. As u_i can tweet v_j many times, we use w_{ij} to denote the frequency.

Generally, every node n_i in the graph is associated with a location, denoted as $\mathcal{L}_{n_i}$. We view $\mathcal{L}_{n_i}$ as a point (X, Y) on the geo space, where X denotes the latitude and Y denotes the longitude. Some user nodes' locations are missing. Our goal is to profile them. We call the users with known locations as *labeled users*, denoted as U^*, and the remaining users as *unlabeled users*, denoted as U^N. $U = U^* \cup U^N$. Formally, our problem can be stated as:

Location Profiling Problem Given a Twitter graph $G(U \cup V, T \cup F)$, $\mathcal{L}_{u_j}$ for $u_j \in U^*$, and $\mathcal{L}_{v_j}$ for $v_j \in V$, estimate a location $\hat{\mathcal{L}}_{u_i}$ for each user $u_i \in U^N$ so as to make $\hat{\mathcal{L}}_{u_i}$ close to u_i's true location $\mathcal{L}_{u_i}$.

As we motivated in Sec. 1, a user is related to inconsistent and noisy locations on the graph, so the problem is non-trivial. We propose a unified discriminative influence based probabilistic framework ($\mathcal{UDI}$) to solve it. Specifically, in Sec. 4, we describe our probabilistic model, which measures how likely an edge is generated between two nodes with respect to their locations. In Sec. 5, we present our prediction methods, which estimate a user's location by maximizing the probability of generating the observed edges.

Notation Before our discussion, we introduce some notations. Generally, we use $\mathcal{I}_e(n)$ and $\mathcal{O}_e(n)$ to denote incoming neighbor nodes of a node n through type e edges, and outgoing neighbors of n through type e edges respectively. Specifically,

- $\mathcal{I}_f(u_i) = \{u_j \in U | f\langle u_j, u_i\rangle \in F\}$ denotes the followers of u_i, and $\mathcal{I}^*_f(u_i) = \mathcal{I}_f(u_i) \cap U^*$ denotes the *labeled followers* of u_i
- $\mathcal{O}_f(u_i) = \{u_j \in U | f\langle u_i, u_j\rangle \in F\}$ denotes the friends of u_i, and $\mathcal{O}^*_f(u_i) = \mathcal{O}_f(u_i) \cap U^*$ denotes the *labeled friends* of u_i.
- $\mathcal{O}_t(u_i) = \{v_j \in V | t\langle u_i, v_j\rangle \in T\}$ denotes venues tweeted by u_i.
- $\mathcal{I}_t(v_i) = \{u_j \in U | t\langle u_j, v_i\rangle \in T\}$ denotes the users who tweet v_i. $\mathcal{I}^*_t(v_i) = \mathcal{I}_t(v_i) \cap U^*$ denotes the labeled users who tweet v_i.

4. INFLUENCE MODEL

In this section, we introduce a probabilistic model named as *influence model* to measure how likely a tail node n_j (*e.g.*, a user u_j) at a location $\mathcal{L}_{n_j}$ builds an edge $e\langle n_j, n_i\rangle$ (*e.g.*, a following edge) to a head node n_i (*e.g.*, a user u_i) at a location $\mathcal{L}_{n_i}$.

4.1 Motivation

To motivate our model, we investigate about 139,180 randomly crawled Twitter users and observe two key characteristics of the probability that there is $e\langle n_j, n_i\rangle$ from n_j to n_i.

First, the probability decreases as the distance from n_j to n_i increases. Specifically, Fig. 2(a) and 2(b) show the average numbers of followers of a user and the average numbers of users who tweet

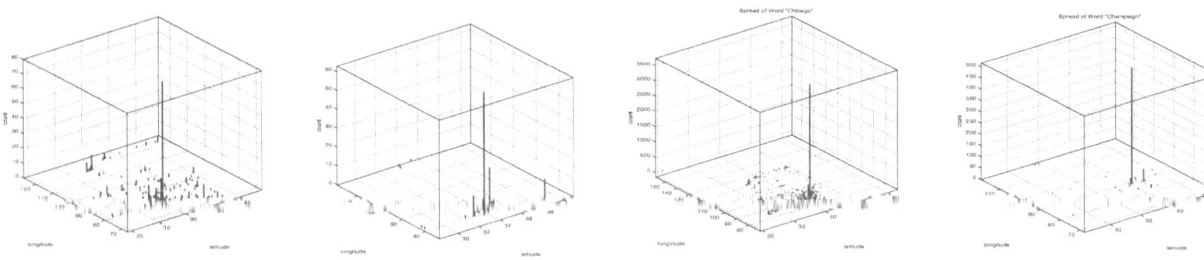

(a) Anonymous1's followers (b) Anonymous2's followers (c) Chicago's Users (d) Champaign's Users

Figure 3: Numbers of Relations over the Geo Space

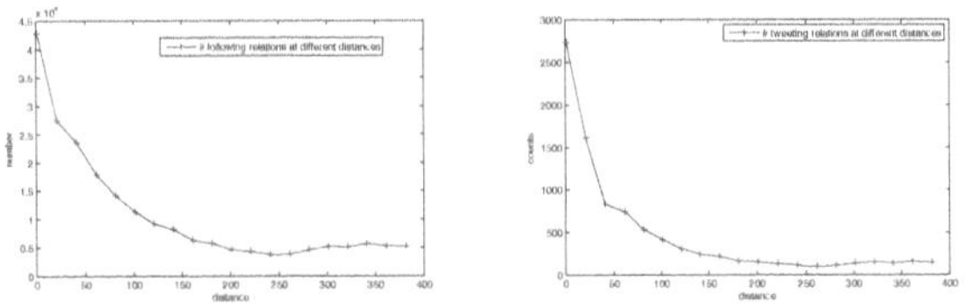

(a) Following Edges (b) Tweeting Edges

Figure 2: Numbers of Edges versus Distances

a venue at different distances. Fig. 2(a) illustrates that generally users have more followers living close than far away, which means that a user, as head node, is more likely to attract users living close to follow. The reason might be that a user's followers tend to know him in real life and are likely to live close to him. This property has also been observed from Facebook network [4] and other social networks [10]. Here we validate it on Twitter network. Similarly, Fig. 2(b) shows that a venue, as a head node, is more likely to attract users living close to tweet about it, because users are more likely to be interested in things happening around.

Second, at the same distance, different head nodes have different probabilities to attract tail nodes. Fig. 3(a) and 3(b) show the numbers of followers of two specific users on Twitter, Anonymous1 and Anonymous2, over the geographic space. Comparing Fig. 3(a) and 3(b), we can tell that Anonymous1, as an influential user, is more likely to attract users who live far away to build following edges than a regular user Anonymous2, because Anonymous1 has a broader influence scope than a regular user in real life. Fig. 3(c) and 3(d) show the numbers of users, who tweet two specific locations, Chicago and Champaign, at different locations. Similarly, we find that Chicago, as an influential city, is much more likely to be tweeted by users who live far away than Champaign, as cities such as Chicago or New York, are more influential than regular cities.

4.2 Model Formulation

Our influence model aims to capture the above characteristics. Conceptually, the *influence model* of a node n_i, denoted as θ_{n_i}, is a probability distribution over the geographic plane, which assigns an "influence probability" to any geo point in the plane. n_i's *influence probability* at a point L represents the probability that n_i influences another node n_j at L to build an edge $e\langle n_j, n_i\rangle$ to it. The higher n_i's influencing probability is, the more likely n_j is to build $e\langle n_j, n_i\rangle$ to n_i. Different nodes have different *influence scopes*. A node with a "broad" influence scope has a larger influence probability at a point far away than a node with a "narrow" influence scope does.

The influence model enables us to measure the probability of observing $e\langle n_j, n_i\rangle$ from n_j to n_i in a generative way. Specifically, we can assume $e\langle n_j, n_i\rangle$ is "generated" according to n_i's influence probability at $\mathcal{L}_{n_j}$, $P(e\langle n_j, n_i\rangle|\theta_{n_i}, \mathcal{L}_{n_j}) = P(\mathcal{L}_{n_j}|\theta_{n_i})$.

Probability Model Mathematically, we need a probability distribution to represent a node's influence model. We reason that an "ideal" distribution should satisfy the following requirements.

- *Expressiveness:* It should capture: 1) probabilities decrease as distances increase, and 2) each node has its own influence scope.
- *Simplicity:* Its parameters should be simple to estimate, as we only have a few observations for each node.

In this paper, we choose a gaussian distribution to capture a node's influence model. In terms of expressiveness, either the heavy tailed distribution [4, 3] or the gaussian distribution [15, 19], which has been widely used for modeling probabilities over the geo space, can be used in our case. In terms of simplicity, a heavy tailed distribution uses several parameters (*e.g.*, α and β in the form of $(\alpha + d)^{\beta}$ in [4]), while a simple gaussian uses only one parameter (*e.g.*, σ in the form of $N(0, \sigma)$). Thus, a heavy tailed distribution requires more observations than a gaussian for estimating parameters. *E.g.*, in [4], they use observations from all the users to estimate one heavy tailed distribution, and use it to model all the users. In our case, as we aim to estimate a unique gaussian distribution for each node with scarce observations related to the node, we choose a simple gaussian distribution for each node.

We must emphasize that our choice of the gaussian distribution neither conflicts with the heavy tailed distribution observed in [4], nor limits our model's prediction power. First, the heavy tailed distribution is observed based on the aggregation of all users, but we use a gaussian to model each individual. Second, our model uses millions of gaussian distributions, each of which is tailored to a user. It fits each individual better and is more flexible in general than one heavy tailed distribution. As our experiment in Sec. 6 will show, it profiles users' locations more accurately than the method [4] based on the heavy tailed distribution with the same amount of observations.

Specifically, we model a node n_i's influence model θ_{n_i} as a bivariate gaussian distribution, $N(\mathcal{L}_{n_i}, \Sigma_{u_i})$, centered at n_i's location $\mathcal{L}_{n_i} = (X_{n_i}, Y_{n_i})$ and with the covariance matrix Σ_{u_i} as its influence scope. While our model can generally take different variances along the X and Y dimensions as well as their covariances, we assume the influence scope of a node on the X and Y dimensions is the same, as it is easy to estimate with few observations and there isn't clear evidence for "non-symmetric" distributions on X and Y. Therefore, $\Sigma_{u_i} = \begin{pmatrix} \sigma_{n_i} & 0 \\ 0 & \sigma_{n_i} \end{pmatrix}$, and n_i's influence probability at a location L is measured as follows.

$$P(L|\theta_{n_i}) = \frac{1}{2\pi\sigma_{n_i}^2} e^{\frac{(X_{n_i} - X_L)^2}{-2\sigma_{n_i}^2} + \frac{(Y_{u_i} - Y_L)^2}{-2\sigma_{n_i}^2}} \quad (1)$$

To measure probabilities of generating following and tweeting edges, we instantiate two types of influence models.

User Influence Model is to measure $P(f\langle u_j, u_i\rangle|\theta_{u_i}, \mathcal{L}_{u_j})$, the conditional probability that a user u_i influences a user u_j at a location $\mathcal{L}_{u_j}$ to build a following edge $f\langle u_j, u_i\rangle$ to him given u_i's influence model θ_{u_i} and $\mathcal{L}_{u_j}$. We interpret it as follows.

$$P(f\langle u_j, u_i\rangle|\theta_{u_i}, \mathcal{L}_{u_j}) = \frac{1}{2\pi\sigma^2_{u_i}} e^{\frac{(X_{u_i}-X_{u_j})^2+(Y_{u_i}-Y_{u_j})^2}{-2\sigma^2_{u_i}}} \quad (2)$$

Venue Influence Model is to measure $P(t\langle u_j, v_i\rangle|\theta_{v_i}, \mathcal{L}_{u_j})$. Similarly, we interpret it as follows.

$$P(t\langle u_j, v_i\rangle|\theta_{v_i}, \mathcal{L}_{u_j}) = \frac{1}{2\pi\sigma^2_{v_i}} e^{\frac{(X_{v_i}-X_{u_j})^2+(Y_{v_i}-Y_{u_j})^2}{-2\sigma^2_{v_i}}} \quad (3)$$

Conditional Independence Assumption When modeling the probability of generating an edge, we take a *conditional independence assumption*. Specifically, we assume that *each edge (e.g., a tweeting edge) from a tail node (e.g., a user) to a head node (e.g., a venue) is conditionally independent given the head node's influence model and the tail node's location*. In other words, if the head node's influence model and the tail node's location are given, any additional observation (*e.g.*, other nodes or edges) will not affect the probability of generating the edge.

We are aware that, in reality, various factors affect the probability of generating an edge between two nodes. For example, if two nodes share common neighbors, the probability that there is an edge will increase. However, capturing any additional dependency requires additional parameters. The scarce observations and the complexity of estimation prevent us from modeling those comprehensive dependencies. To focus on the location factor only, we simplify our model with the above assumption. This assumption is widely applied in generative models (*e.g.*, Naive Bayes and topic modeling), which our model belongs to, for simplifying models and focusing on key factors. As our experiments will show, like other generative models, our model achieves promising results with the assumption. We further note that this assumption has also been used in other location prediction tasks [3, 4].

5. LOCATION PROFILING METHODS

In this section, we develop our location profiling methods based on the *Maximum Likelihood Estimation* (MLE) principle under the $\mathcal{UDI}$ framework. Specifically, we profile a user's location as the location that maximizes the joint probability of generating following and tweeting edges from and to his followers, friends and tweeted venues. We derive two prediction methods, a local one and a global one, which aim to balance efficiency and effectiveness.

5.1 Local Prediction Method

We first develop a *local prediction method*, which infers a user u_i's location via using locations observed from his "local" edges directly. A user's local edges are the edges which directly connect to him. However, some of them connect to nodes without locations (*e.g.*, an unlabeled friend), and they do not provide any location signal directly. In this setting, to simplify the problem and derive an efficient algorithm, we assume *we only observe the edges between the user and the label nodes*. Specifically, they are: 1) the following edges from his labeled followers, denoted as $f\langle U^*, u_i\rangle = \{f\langle u_j, u_i\rangle \in F | u_j \in U^*\}$, 2) the following edges to his labeled friends, denoted as $f\langle u_i, U^*\rangle = \{f\langle u_i, u_j\rangle \in F | u_j \in U^*\}$, and 3) the tweeting edges to the venues tweeted by him, denoted as $t\langle u_i, V\rangle = \{t\langle u_i, v_j\rangle \in T | v_j \in V\}$.

Based on our influence model, the probability of observing those edges depends on the following factors: 1) the probability of observing $f\langle U^*, u_i\rangle$ from u_i's labeled followers $\mathcal{I}^*_f(u_i)$ to u_i depends on u_i's influence model θ_{u_i} and the locations of $\mathcal{I}^*_f(u_i)$, denoted as $\mathcal{L}_{\mathcal{I}^*_f(u_i)}$, 2) the probability of observing $f\langle u_i, U^*\rangle$ from u_i to his labeled friends $\mathcal{O}^*_f(u_i)$ depends on u_i's location $\mathcal{L}_{u_i}$ and the influence models of $\mathcal{O}^*_f(u_i)$, denoted as $\theta_{\mathcal{O}^*_f(u_i)}$, and 3) the probability of observing $t\langle u_i, V\rangle$ from u_i to his tweeted venues $\mathcal{O}_t(u_i)$ depends on u_i's location $\mathcal{L}_{u_i}$ and the influence models of $\mathcal{O}_t(u_i)$, denoted as $\theta_{\mathcal{O}_t(u_i)}$.

Likelihood Function Given parameters $\theta_{u_i}, \mathcal{L}_{u_i}, \mathcal{L}_{\mathcal{I}^*_f(u_i)}, \theta_{\mathcal{O}^*_f(u_i)}$ and $\theta_{\mathcal{O}_t(u_i)}$, we write the joint conditional probability (the likelihood function) of observing $f\langle U^*, u_i\rangle$, $f\langle u_i, U^*\rangle$ and $t\langle u_i, V\rangle$ as Eq. (4). At step 1, we express the joint conditional probability as the product of $P(e\langle n_j, n_i\rangle|\theta_{n_i}, \mathcal{L}_{n_j})$ based on the conditional independence assumption. $t\langle u_i, v_j\rangle$ is multiplied w_{ij} times, as each $t\langle u_i, v_j\rangle$ appears w_{ij} times in $t\langle u_i, V\rangle$. At step 2, we represent $P(e\langle n_j, n_i\rangle|\theta_{n_i}, \mathcal{L}_{n_j})$ as n_i's influence probability at $\mathcal{L}_{n_j}$ based on our influence model.

$$\begin{aligned}
&P(f\langle U^*, u_i\rangle, f\langle u_i, U^*\rangle, t\langle u_i, V\rangle|\mathcal{L}_{u_i}, \theta_{u_i}, \mathcal{L}_{\mathcal{I}^*_f(u_i)}, \theta_{\mathcal{O}^*_f(u_i)}, \theta_{\mathcal{O}_t(u_i)}) \\
&=^1 \prod_{u_j\in\mathcal{I}^*_f(u_i)} P(f\langle u_j, u_i\rangle|\theta_{u_i}, \mathcal{L}_{u_j}) \times \prod_{u_j\in\mathcal{O}^*_f(u_i)} P(f\langle u_i, u_j\rangle|\theta_{u_j}, \mathcal{L}_{u_i}) \\
&\times \prod_{v_j\in\mathcal{O}_t(u_i)} P(t\langle u_i, v_j\rangle|\mathcal{L}_{u_i}, \theta_{v_j})^{w_{ij}} \\
&=^2 \prod_{u_j\in\mathcal{I}^*_f(u_i)} \frac{1}{2\pi\sigma^2_{u_i}} e^{\frac{(X_{u_i}-X_{u_j})^2+(Y_{u_i}-Y_{u_j})^2}{-2\sigma^2_{u_i}}} \\
&\times \prod_{u_j\in\mathcal{O}^*_f(u_i)} \frac{1}{2\pi\sigma^2_{u_j}} e^{\frac{(X_{u_i}-X_{u_j}+(Y_{u_i}-Y_{u_j})^2)^2}{-2\sigma^2_{u_j}}} \\
&\times \prod_{v_j\in\mathcal{O}_t(u_i)} (\frac{1}{2\pi\sigma^2_{v_j}} e^{\frac{(X_{u_i}-X_{v_j})^2+(Y_{u_i}-Y_{v_j})^2}{-2\sigma^2_{v_i}}})^{w_{ij}}
\end{aligned} \quad (4)$$

Based on MLE, we find parameters, u_i's location $\mathcal{L}_{u_i}$ and u_i's influence scope σ_{u_i}, by maximizing the above equation, and use the estimated $\mathcal{L}_{u_i}$ as u_i's location.

However, in Eq. (4), besides $\mathcal{L}_{u_i}$ and σ_{u_i}, which we aim to estimate, there are other unknown parameters. Particularly, for each labeled friend $u_j \in \mathcal{O}^*_f(u_i)$ and each tweeted venue $v_j \in \mathcal{O}_t(u_i)$, their influence scopes σ_{u_j} and σ_{v_j} are unknown, as we only observe their locations. In our local prediction setting, we assume each labeled node's influence scope can be accurately estimated with its labeled neighbors as well. Thus, we estimate them before predicting the user's location, and view them as the known parameters. Next, we discuss how to estimate them.

Influence Scope of a Friend To estimate σ_{u_j} in a labeled friend u_j's influence model θ_{u_j}, we can use u_j's following relationships from his labeled followers. Among u_j's edges, only u_j's following edges $f\langle U, u_j\rangle$ from his followers depend on θ_{u_j}. As those edges also depend on his followers' locations, we use u_j's following edges $f\langle U^*, u_j\rangle$ from his labeled followers $\mathcal{I}^*_f(u_j)$ as observations, and estimate θ_{u_j} by maximizing the joint conditional probability of observing $f\langle U^*, u_j\rangle$ given θ_{u_j} and $\mathcal{L}_{\mathcal{I}_f(u_j)}$. We write the probability as Eq. (5).

$$\begin{aligned}
P(f\langle U^*, u_j\rangle|\theta_{u_j}, \mathcal{L}_{\mathcal{I}^*_f(u_j)}) &= \prod_{u_k\in\mathcal{I}^*_f(u_j)} P(f\langle u_k, u_j\rangle|\theta_{u_j}, \mathcal{L}_{u_k}) \\
&= \prod_{u_k\in\mathcal{I}^*_f(u_j)} \frac{1}{2\pi\sigma^2_{u_j}} e^{\frac{(X_{u_j}-X_{u_k})^2+(Y_{u_j}-Y_{u_k})^2}{-2\sigma^2_{u_j}}}
\end{aligned} \quad (5)$$

In Eq. (5), σ_{u_j} is the only unknown variable, as u_j is a labeled user and u_k is his labeled follower. We directly estimate σ_{u_j} by maximizing Eq. (5). Technically, we get its closed-form solution by differentiating Eq. (5) with respect to σ_{u_j} and setting the result to zero. Eq. (6) shows the solution.

$$\sigma^2_{u_j} = \sum_{u_k \in \mathcal{I}^*_f(u_j)} \frac{(X_{u_j} - X_{u_k})^2 + (Y_{u_j} - Y_{u_k})^2}{2|\mathcal{I}^*_f(u_j)|} \tag{6}$$

Influence Scope of a Venue Similarly, to estimate a venue v_j's influence scope σ_{v_j}, we use the tweeting edges from v_j's labeled twitters, denoted as $t\langle U^*, v_j\rangle = \{t\langle u_i, v_j\rangle \in T | u_i \in U^*\}$. We derive σ_{v_j} by maximizing the conditional probability of generating $t\langle U^*, v_j\rangle$ given v_j's influence model θ_{v_j} and labeled twitter's locations $\mathcal{L}_{\mathcal{I}^*_t(v_j)}$. We write the condition probability as Eq. (7), and derive σ_{v_j} in Eq. (8).

$$P(t\langle U^*, v_j\rangle | \theta_{v_j}, \mathcal{L}_{\mathcal{I}^*_t(v_j)}) = \prod_{u_i \in \mathcal{I}^*_t(v_j)} P(t\langle u_i, v_j\rangle | \theta_{v_j}, \mathcal{L}_{u_i})^{w_{ij}} \tag{7}$$

$$\sigma^2_{v_j} = \sum_{u_i \in \mathcal{I}^*_t(v_j)} \frac{w_{ij}((X_{u_i} - X_{v_j})^2 + (Y_{u_i} - Y_{v_j})^2)}{2\sum_{u_i \in \mathcal{I}^*_t(v_j)} w_{ij}}. \tag{8}$$

Solution Now each tweeted venue v_j's σ_{v_j} and $\mathcal{L}_{v_j}$, each labeled friend u_j's $\mathcal{L}_{u_j}$ and σ_{u_j}, and each labeled follower u_j's $\mathcal{L}_{u_j}$ are known. $\mathcal{L}_{u_i}$ and σ_{u_i} are the unknown variables left. We estimate them by maximizing Eq. (4). We first differentiate Eq. (4) with regard to $\mathcal{L}_{u_i}$ and σ_{u_i}, and obtain Eq. (9) and Eq. (10), which show $\mathcal{L}_{u_i}$ and σ_{u_i} depend on each other. We substitute Eq. (10) for σ_{u_i} in Eq. (9), and obtain a polynomial function of $\mathcal{L}_{u_i}$. We apply the Newton–Raphson method to find its solution, and derive σ_{u_i} accordingly. We note that because X_{u_i} and Y_{u_i} are symmetric in Eq. (4), the solutions for X_{u_i} and Y_{u_i} are in the same form. Due to the space limit, we only give the solution for X_{u_i}.

$$X_{u_i} = \frac{\sum_{u_j \in \mathcal{I}^*_f(u_i)} \frac{X_{u_j}}{\sigma^2_{u_i}} + \sum_{u_j \in \mathcal{O}^*_f(u_i)} \frac{X_{u_j}}{\sigma^2_{u_j}} + \sum_{v_j \in \mathcal{O}_t(u_i)} \frac{w_{ij} X_{v_j}}{\sigma^2_{v_j}}}{\sum_{u_j \in \mathcal{I}^*_f(u_i)} \frac{1}{\sigma^2_{u_i}} + \sum_{u_j \in \mathcal{O}^*_f(u_i)} \frac{1}{\sigma^2_{u_j}} + \sum_{v_j \in \mathcal{O}_t(u_i)} \frac{w_{ij}}{\sigma^2_{v_j}}} \tag{9}$$

$$\sigma^2_{u_i} = \sum_{u_j \in \mathcal{I}^*_f(u_i)} \frac{(X_{u_j} - X_{u_i})^2 + (Y_{u_j} - Y_{u_i})^2}{2|\mathcal{I}^*_f(u_i)|} \tag{10}$$

The above solution also works for the cases that only a subset of resources (*e.g.*, tweets) is used, as we can simply view the unused resource as an empty set in our solution.

Interpretation The above solution can be interpreted meaningfully. As Eq. (10) shows, the influence scope of u_i will be large if u_i's followers are far away from him. Celebrities (*e.g.*, Lady Gaga) will get large influence scopes as their followers are distributed broadly. As Eq. (9) shows, when we estimate a user's location, each node contributes differently, where the weight of a node is inversely proportional to its influence scope. *E.g.*, if we profile a user's location using two friends of him, *e.g.*, Lady Gaga and a regular user, the prediction is close to the regular user, as Lady Gaga has a broad influence scope, and her location is likely to be a noisy signal.

Computation Complexity The algorithm computes a user's location in $O(K^2)$, where K is the average number of edges associated with a user and is less than a hundred. Specifically, it first computes influence scopes for K neighbors of the user, and each of them requires $O(K)$. Then, it uses $O(tK)$ to estimate the location with K edges, where t is the number of iterations in the Newton method. Theoretically, t is $O(d \log^2(d))$ for d digits precision, which is a small constant and can be ignored. In practice, we can precompute the influence scope for each labeled node, and the complexity is reduced to $O(K)$. The algorithm can be viewed as an online algorithm, which efficiently infers a user's location at real-time.

5.2 Global Prediction Method

We further develop a *global prediction method*, which infers a user's location via using all the edges in the graph, and profile users' locations more accurately than the local one.

To motivate our method, we argue that unlabeled users are valuable as we can propagate locations of their tweets, followers and friends to them. Let us revisit the example in Fig. 1. Although u_6 is unlabeled, we can tell u_6 is close to Chicago as he tweets Chicago. As a result, u_6 becomes an additional observation, which suggests that u_1 should be close to Chicago. However, unlabeled users can not be directly used, because we can not tell which unlabeled user we should predict first, say, u_1 or u_6, and how to propagate a user's predicted location to others.

We develop our global prediction method to model all the edges in the graph and utilize all the observed locations. Specifically, it models the joint conditional probability of observing all the following edges F and tweeting edges T in the graph given all the nodes' locations and influence models, and estimates all unlabeled users' locations together via maximizing the probability.

We write the probability as Eq. (11). Step 1 is based on the independence assumption, and step 2 is based on our influence model.

$$\begin{aligned} & P(F, T | \theta_U, \mathcal{L}_U, \theta_V, \mathcal{L}_V) \\ =^1 & \prod_{f\langle u_i, u_j\rangle \in F} P(f\langle u_i, u_j\rangle | \theta_{u_j}, \mathcal{L}_{u_i}) \prod_{t\langle u_i, v_j\rangle \in T} p(t\langle u_i, v_j\rangle | \theta_{v_j}, \mathcal{L}_{u_i})^{w_{ij}} \\ =^2 & \prod_{f\langle u_i, u_j\rangle \in F} \frac{1}{2\pi\sigma^2_{u_i}} e^{\frac{(X_{u_i} - X_{u_j})^2 + (Y_{u_i} - Y_{u_j})^2}{-2\sigma^2_{u_i}}} \\ \times & \prod_{t\langle u_i, v_j\rangle \in T} (\frac{1}{2\pi\sigma^2_{v_j}} e^{\frac{(X_{u_i} - X_{v_j})^2 + (Y_{u_i} - Y_{v_j})^2}{-2\sigma^2_{v_j}}} +)^{w_{ij}} \end{aligned} \tag{11}$$

In the above equation, for $u_i \in U^N$, both $\mathcal{L}_{u_i}$ and σ_{u_i} are unknown; for $u_i \in U^*$ and $v_j \in V$, σ_{u_i} and σ_{v_j} are unknown. We estimate their values by maximizing the probability. To derive them, we first differentiate Eq. (11) with regard to every unknown variable, and obtain the following equations.

$$X_{u_i} = \frac{\sum_{u_j \in \mathcal{I}_f(u_i)} \frac{X_{u_j}}{\sigma^2_{u_i}} + \sum_{u_j \in \mathcal{O}_f(u_i)} \frac{X_{u_j}}{\sigma^2_{u_j}} + \sum_{v_j \in \mathcal{O}_t(u_i)} \frac{w_{ij} X_{v_j}}{\sigma^2_{v_j}}}{\sum_{u_j \in \mathcal{I}_f(u_i)} 1/\sigma^2_{u_i} + \sum_{u_j \in \mathcal{O}_f(u_i)} 1/\sigma^2_{u_j} + \sum_{v_j \in \mathcal{O}_t(u_i)} w_{ij}/\sigma^2_{v_j}} \tag{12}$$

$$\sigma^2_{u_i} = \sum_{u_j \in \mathcal{I}_f(u_i)} \frac{(X_{u_j} - X_{u_i})^2 + (Y_{u_j} - Y_{u_i})^2}{2|\mathcal{I}_f(u_i)|} \tag{13}$$

$$\sigma^2_{v_j} = \sum_{u_i \in \mathcal{I}_t(v_j)} \frac{w_{ij}((X_{u_i} - X_{v_j})^2 + (Y_{u_i} - Y_{v_j})^2)}{2\sum_{u_i \in \mathcal{I}_t(v_j)} w_{ij}}. \tag{14}$$

In these equations, the unknown variables are dependent on each other. Their closed-form solutions are not easy to get. However, if we assume σ_{u_i} and σ_{v_j} for each $u_i \in U$ and each $v_j \in V$ are known, X_{u_i} only depends on $X_{u_j} \in U$ and $X_{v_j} \in V$. In this case, Eq. (12) tries to find X_{u_i} for each $u_i \in U^N$ such that $\sum_{f\langle u_i, u_j\rangle \in F} 1/\sigma^2_{u_j} (X_{u_i} - X_{u_j})^2 + \sum_{t\langle u_i, v_j\rangle \in T} w_{ij}/\sigma^2_{v_j} (X_{u_i} - X_{v_j})^2$ is minimized. An iterative algorithm, which updates each X_{u_i} based on other X_{u_j} iteratively, has been proposed to find X_{u_i} for this problem [20]. When X_{u_i} and Y_{u_i} are derived, σ_{u_i} and σ_{v_j} can be derived directly based on Eq. (13) and (14).

Therefore, we develop a two stage iterative algorithm based on the above intuition. The algorithm is shown in Algorithm 1. At step 1-2, it initializes all $u_i \in U^N$. At step 3-14, the algorithm does the iterative computation. There are two iterations. The outer iteration updates σ_{u_i} and σ_{v_j} according to $\mathcal{L}_{u_i}$ based on Eq. (13) and (14), while the inner iteration (from step 8 to 11) takes a set of fixed σ_{u_i} and σ_{v_j} as inputs and iteratively computes $\mathcal{L}_{u_i}$ based on Eq. (12). The newly obtained $\mathcal{L}_{u_i}$ is then used to update σ_{u_i} and σ_{v_j} again. The algorithm stops until the likelihood converges.

Algorithm 1: Global Prediction Algorithm
Input: $G, \mathcal{L}_{u_i} \forall u_i \in U^*$
Output: $\mathcal{L}_{u_i}, \forall u_i \in U^N$
// Initialization
1 **foreach** $u_i \in U^N$
2 $\quad X_{u_i} = Random$ and $Y_{u_i} = Random$
3 **repeat** //Outer Iteration
4 $\quad$ **foreach** $u_i \in U$
5 $\quad\quad$ update $\sigma^2_{u_i}$ based on Eq. (13)
6 $\quad$ **foreach** $v_j \in V$
7 $\quad\quad$ update $\sigma^2_{v_j}$ based on Eq. (14)
8 $\quad$ **repeat** // Inner Iteration
9 $\quad\quad$ **for** $u_i \in U^N$
10 $\quad\quad\quad$ update $X^{n+1}_{u_i}$ and $Y^{n+1}_{u_i}$ based on Eq. (12)
11 $\quad$ **until** converge
12 $\quad$ **foreach** $u_i \in U^N$
13 $\quad\quad X_{u_i} = X^{n+1}_{u_i}, Y_{u_i} = Y^{n+1}_{u_i}$
14 **until** converge

We can formally prove the convergence of the algorithm based on the following theorem.

Theorem *The global prediction algorithm converges.*

The proof of the theorem is derived based on the intuition of the algorithm stated above. In the inner iteration, the method can converge and yield $\mathcal{L}_{u_i}$ that maximizes the probability with fixed σ_{u_i} and σ_{v_j}, as shown in [20]. Second, the outer iteration directly computes σ_{u_i} and σ_{v_j} that maximize the probability given fixed $\mathcal{L}_{u_i}$ computed in the previous iteration, because Eq. (13) and (14) are the closed-form solutions for maximizing the probability when a set of $\mathcal{L}_{u_i}$ is given. In summary, each iterative step monotonically increases the probability and the probability has a maximum value, so the algorithm must converge.

The above algorithm, like many of other iterative algorithms (*e.g.*, EM), may converge to a local maximum. To avoid that, we can initialize the unknown variables with the values obtained from the local prediction method. The above iterative algorithm will always generate a better solution than the local one as each iteration improves the likelihood monotonically.

Complexity Analysis As each inner iteration requires $O(|E|)$ to update every user's location, the algorithm runs in $O(t|E|)$, where t is the number of iterations and $|E|$ is the number of edges of the graph. In our experiment, it converges after three outer iterations. As our algorithm uses all the edges in the graph, it can be viewed as an offline algorithm, which effectively profiles all users' locations.

5.3 Incorporating Constraints

To further improve our methods, we utilize human knowledge as constraints in our prediction methods. To motivate, let us revisit the example in Fig. 1. Most of u_1's followers and friends are in or close to Chicago (*e.g.*, u_5, u_3) except one (u_4) in New York. Our algorithms will estimate u_1's location to be near but not exactly Chicago. If we ask a human to predict u_1's location, he will definitely pick a city instead of an arbitrary geo point, and he is likely to choose one from Chicago, Urbana and New York, because he knows a user usually has some friends living in the same city.

We model such human knowledge as *constraints* in our prediction methods. A *constraint* specifies the set of candidate locations when we maximize a likelihood function. There are different choices of constraints, such as a candidate must be a city or within 30 miles of a city. Particularly, we apply the following assumption as the constraint in our implementation. We assume that a user's location must be the same as one of his friends, followers or tweeted venues. The assumption is generally valid. In our data, an incomplete crawl of Twitter, there are about 92% of users whose locations appear in their followers, friends or tweets. We note that this constraint may not be the best one. We use it to illustrate how our methods can incorporate constraints.

The constraint version of the local prediction method becomes maximizing Eq. (4) subject to $\{\mathcal{L}_{u_i} \in \mathcal{L}_{\mathcal{I}^*_f(u_i)} \cup \mathcal{L}_{\mathcal{O}^*_f(u_i)} \cup \mathcal{L}_{\mathcal{O}_t(u_i)}\}$. To solve it, we can rank each candidate location $\mathcal{L}_{u_i}$ according to Eq. (4), and use the top one as the prediction.

The constraint version of the global prediction method becomes maximizing Eq. (11) subject to $\{\mathcal{L}_{u_i} \in \mathcal{L}_{\mathcal{I}^*_f(u_i)} \cup \mathcal{L}_{\mathcal{O}^*_f(u_i)} \cup \mathcal{L}_{\mathcal{O}_t(u_i)}\}$ for any $u_i \in U^N$. If we rank all candidate solutions, which consist of all the combinations $\mathcal{L}_{u_i}$ for all $u_i \in U^N$, the complexity of the algorithm is $O(K^N)$, where K is the average number of candidate locations per user (it is usually larger than 2), and N is the number of unlabeled users (about millions). Instead, we propose an approximation algorithm based on the relax and round paradigm, which is widely used by approximation algorithms for optimization with constraints [9]. We first use the global algorithm to find $\mathcal{L}'_{u_i}$ for each u_i without any constraint, then find the closest location $\mathcal{L}_{u_i}$ that satisfies the constraint.

6. EXPERIMENTAL RESULTS

In this section, we conduct experiments on a large-scale data set and show the effectiveness of our methods from different aspects.

6.1 Experiment Setup

Data Set We constructed our data set by crawling Twitter. We randomly selected 100,000 users as seeds to crawl in May 2011. For each user, we crawled his profile, followers and friends. We obtained 3,980,061 users' profiles and their social network. Then, we extracted their registered locations from their profiles based on the rules described in [7]. Specifically, we extracted locations with city-level labels in the form of "cityName, stateName" and "cityName, stateAbbreviation," where we considered all cities listed in the Census 2000 U.S. Gazetteer. We found 630,187 users, who provided city level locations, and treated them as labeled users. Among them, we found 158,220 users, who had at least one labeled friend or follower. We further crawled their tweets and extracted venues from those tweets based on the same gazetteer. We crawled at most 600 tweets for each user. As we could not get some users' tweets due to their privacy settings or lack of tweets, only 139,180 users' tweets were crawled.

We used the 139,180 users with their following relationships and tweets, as our data set. There are 14.8 friends, 14.9 followers, and 29.0 venues per user. We took their registered locations as their home locations, and applied five fold validation, which means that we used 80% of users as labeled users and 20% of users as unlabeled users and reported our results based on the average of 5 runs.

We note that we directly take users' registered locations as their home locations and predict locations for only U.S. users, because we want to set up our experiments in the same way as the existing methods [7, 4]. We are aware that some registered locations are incorrect, but we believe they are rare, as leaving profiles empty is always an easy option. Thus, our results are reliable. Our method can predict locations for international users in the same way.

Methods To fully evaluate our methods, we not only compare them with two state-of-the-art methods in [4] and [7], but also evaluate our prediction methods with different settings. Specifically, our experiments evaluate the following methods.

- $Base_U$ is the method developed in [4], which predicts a user's location based on his social network. Twitter is a directional network, so we treat both followers and friends of a user as his undirected connections ("friends") in this method.
- $Base_C$ is the method developed in [7]. It assigns a location to a user based on a set of local words identified from his tweets.
- UDI$_U$ is our local prediction method, but only uses a user's friends and followers as signals.
- UDI$_C$ is our local prediction method, but only uses venues identified from a user's tweets as signals.
- UDI$_I$ is our local prediction method discussed in Sec. 5.1, which integrates different types of resources.
- UDI$_G$ is our global prediction method discussed in Sec. 5.2.

Measurement We use *average error distance in miles* (*AED*) and *accuracy within 100 miles* (*ACC*) proposed in [7] as measures. Specifically, let $Err(u_i)$ be the error distance between a user's home location and an estimated location. For a set of users U, $AED(U)$ is $\frac{\sum_{u_i \in U} Err(u_i)}{|U|}$, and $ACC(U)$ is $\frac{|\{u_i | u_i \in U \wedge Err(u_i) \leq 100\}|}{|U|}$.

However, as *AED* is easily affected by outliers in results, we report *AED* at different percentiles (60%, 80% and 100%) of users ranked by their error distances. *E.g.*, *AED@60%* is the average error distance of the top 60% of users ranked by their error distances.

We use T-test to conduct *significance tests* between our methods and baseline methods. If a method passes the significant test, we make it **boldface** in result tables.

6.2 Experiment Results

User-based Prediction We first compare *UDI*$_U$ with $Base_U$. Both of them profile a user's location based on his social network.

Tab. 1 shows the performance of each method. The results demonstrate that generally our method performs better than $Base_U$. When using the same amount of information, *UDI*$_U$ improves $Base_U$ by 4% in terms of *ACC*. Such an improvement soundly proves our assumption that different users have different influence scopes and we should model them discriminatively.

AED@60% tells that the average error distance of the top 60% of predictions of *UDI*$_U$ is 20 miles, which is fairly accurate. However, when comparing *AED@80%* and *AED@100%*, we find that *AED* dramatically increases from 159 to 525, because *AED* is easily affected by a small set of users, who are not accurately predicted. Therefore, we should not only focus on *AED@100%*.

To illustrate our results in detail, we plot an *accumulative accuracy at distances*(*AAD*) curve for each method in Fig. 4(a). A point (X, Y) in the curve means that Y percentages of users are accurate within X miles. From the figure, we can tell that *UDI*$_U$ has higher accuracy than $Base_U$ within different distances. *E.g.*, *UDI*$_U$ places about 47% of users within 25 miles, while $Base_U$ only places 44% of users within that range.

Content-based Prediction In this experiment, we compare *UDI*$_C$ with $Base_C$. Both of them profile a user's location with his tweets.

We show results and *AAD* curves of two methods in Tab. 1 and Fig. 4(b) respectively. From them, we can see that 1) *UDI*$_C$ significantly improves $Base_C$ by 10% in terms of *ACC*, 2) the improvement is consistent at any distance level, and 3) *UDI*$_C$ achieves very good results by making good use of content. The average error distance for the top 60% of its prediction is less than 10 miles. From

Table 1: Prediction Results

Model	$Base_U$	$Base_C$	UDI_U	UDI_C	UDI_I	UDI_G
ACC	52.4%	49.7%	**56.0%**	**60.0%**	64.4%	**65.9%**
AED@60%	33.7	21.8	**20.6**	**9.5**	**6.6**	**4.4**
AED@80%	200.0	161.5	**159.6**	**123.6**	**97.0**	**75.0**
AED@100%	616.9	542.5	**524.5**	**483.6**	**440.4**	**421.3**

Table 2: Discriminative vs. Non-discriminative

Model	ACC	$AED@60$	$AED@80$	$AED@100$
$Base_I$	58.5%	11.9	138.4	504.4
***UDI*$_I$**	**64.4%**	**6.6**	**97.0**	**440.4**

the results, we can safely conclude that our method is much better than $Base_C$ as our model captures the relation between a user' location and locations from his tweets in a meaningful way.

We clarify that $Base_C$ requires human labeling to train a model to select local words, which are the features for the classification model, and $Base_C$'s performance highly depends on the selected words. As labeling is a subjective task, by no means could we get the same set of local words in the original paper. We test performances of $Base_C$ with various local word sets, we get *ACC* ranging from 35.98% to 49.67%. We choose the highest one to report. Our method advances $Base_C$ in this aspect, as we do not require any labeling work, and only use location names in a gazetteer.

Integrated vs. Non-Integrated In this experiment, we evaluate whether our framework can take advantage of integrating more resources. Specifically, we compare *UDI*$_I$ with $Base_U$, $Base_C$, *UDI*$_C$ and *UDI*$_U$. Tab. 1 shows the performance of each method. As expected, *UDI*$_I$ gives a significant improvement (12%) over the best baseline method, and advances *UDI*$_C$ and *UDI*$_U$ by 4.4% and 8.4%. Fig. 4(c) shows that those improvements are consistent at any distance level. We can safely conclude that integrating different types of resources is useful for profiling locations. Meanwhile, we can find that *UDI*$_I$ is very accurate. It correctly places 57% of users within 25 miles. Its *AED* is only 6 miles for the top 60% of its predictions, and less than 100 miles for the top 80%.

Discriminative vs. Non-discriminative In this experiment, we demonstrate the power of discriminative modeling by comparing our methods based on a discriminative model with the methods based on a non-discriminative one. As the user-based prediction experiment has already shown that, when only using social network signals, a discriminative method (*UDI*$_U$) is better than a non-discriminative one ($Base_U$), we now compare the methods that use all the types of resources. We develop a new baseline method $Base_I$, which integrates different resources in a non-discriminative way. Specifically, we first learn one probabilistic distribution for following edges and one for tweeting edges based on [4], and then we apply the prediction method in [4]. Tab. 2 and Fig. 4(d) show the results. We can find that, although $Base_I$ uses the same amount of information as *UDI*$_I$, it is 6% lower than *UDI*$_I$ in accuracy, which suggests that we should model observations discriminatively.

Global vs. Local To investigate the usefulness of our global prediction method, we compare *UDI*$_G$ with *UDI*$_I$ and the two baselines.

We first evaluate the methods on the data set used in the previous experiments, which includes 20% unlabeled users and 80% labeled ones. The last column in Tab. 1 gives the results of *UDI*$_G$. We can see that, although *UDI*$_G$ improves *UDI*$_I$ slightly (1.5%) in terms of *ACC*, it reduces *AED@80%* a lot, and Fig. 4(e) shows that the improvement is consistent at any level. We believe that the improvement here is limited because there is already enough information from the labeled users and the iterative based method can not add much help. We expect that *UDI*$_G$ improves *UDI*$_I$ significantly in a more realistic scenario, where less users are labeled.

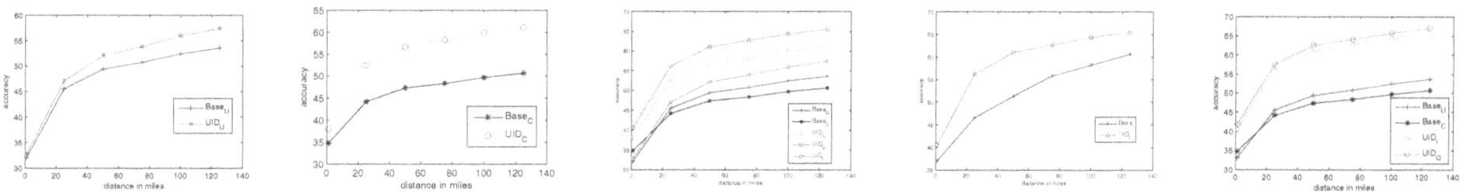

(a) User Results (b) Content Results (c) Integrated Results (d) Discriminative Results (e) Global Results

Figure 4: Accumulative Accuracy at Various Distance

Table 3: Local vs. Global with 80% Test Users

Model	$Base_U$	$Base_C$	UDI_I	UDI_G
ACC	34.0%	42.4%	**57.0%**	**66.0%**
AED@60	116.9	60.9	**11.7**	**4.3**
AED@80	347.7	259.3	**133.9**	**71.6**
AED@100	897.4	679.9	**514.1**	**415.3**

To test this conjecture, we evaluate those methods in another data set, where only 20% of users are labeled and 80% users are unlabeled. This scenario is more close to the real-world case, where only about 16% users have registered locations. Tab. 3 shows the results. We find that 1) UDI_G significantly outperforms the other three methods, as it can utilize information from even unlabeled users, 2) compared to the preceding experiment, UDI_G achieves nearly comparable results, but the other three methods perform much worse, as they make predictions with limited amount of information. We can conclude that UDI_G utilizes both labeled and unlabeled information and achieves better profiling.

We evaluate UDI_G for its convergence, and find it takes 3 outer iterations to converge. Due to space limit, the figure is omitted.

Table 4: Case Studies

Users	Follower No.	σ	Cities	σ
MythBusters Official	860688	1.127	Honolulu	0.970
Lady Gaga	18428360	0.633	San Francisco	0.582
National Geographic	162870	0.655	New York	0.551
NY Knicks	178297	0.172	Austin	0.11
Philadelphia 76ers	62210	0.161	Houston	0.12
timpawlenty	63896	0.239	Dallas	0.14

Case Studies for Influence Scope We give some concrete examples of influence scopes derived by our methods to illustrate their correctness and usefulness. Tab. 4 shows influence scopes of some Twitter users and venues. For easy understanding, we only choose verified users (celebrities). In Tab. 4, we can clearly distinguish local authorities (*e.g.*, "timpawlenty", a former governor of Minnesota), and national celebrities (*e.g.*, "Lady Gaga"). We note that we can not easily tell the difference between "national graphic" and "NY Knicks" just by the numbers of their followers. Similarly, our methods identify that Honolulu, a famous vacation destination, has a broad influence scope and is likely to be a noisy signal.

7. CONCLUSION

Profiling users' locations is an important problem. In this paper, we have made the following contributions to this problem. 1) We explore both social network and user-centric data for profiling users' locations. 2) We introduce a unified discriminative influence model ($\mathcal{UDI}$), which captures how likely a user follows a user or tweets a venue. 3) We develop two effective location prediction methods. The local method integrates locations observed from his friends, followers and tweets in a discriminative way and profiles users' locations efficiently. The global method extends the local one by using additional unlabeled users, and profiles users' locations more accurately. 4) We extend the two methods by modeling additional human knowledge as constraints. 5) We conduct comprehensive experiments on a large scale data set and demonstrate the effectiveness of our methods.

8. REFERENCES

[1] A. Ahmed, Y. Low, M. Aly, V. Josifovski, and A. J. Smola. Scalable distributed inference of dynamic user interests for behavioral targeting. In *KDD '11*, pages 114–122, 2011.

[2] E. Amitay, N. Har'El, R. Sivan, and A. Soffer. Web-a-where: geotagging web content. In *SIGIR '04*, pages 273–280, 2004.

[3] L. Backstrom, J. Kleinberg, R. Kumar, and J. Novak. Spatial variation in search engine queries. In *WWW '08*, pages 357–366, 2008.

[4] L. Backstrom, E. Sun, and C. Marlow. Find me if you can: improving geographical prediction with social and spatial proximity. In *WWW '10*, pages 61–70, 2010.

[5] E. Bakshy, J. M. Hofman, W. A. Mason, and D. J. Watts. Everyone's an influencer: quantifying influence on twitter. In *WSDM '11*, pages 65–74, 2011.

[6] S. Chandra, L. Khan, and F. Muhaya. Estimating twitter user location using social interactions–a content based approach. In *2011 ieee third international conference on social computing*, pages 838 –843, 2011.

[7] Z. Cheng, J. Caverlee, and K. Lee. You are where you tweet: a content-based approach to geo-locating twitter users. In *CIKM '10*, pages 759–768, 2010.

[8] D. J. Crandall, L. Backstrom, D. Huttenlocher, and J. Kleinberg. Mapping the world's photos. In *WWW '09*, pages 761–770, 2009.

[9] T. F. Gonzalez. *Handbook of Approximation Algorithms and Metaheuristics (Chapman & Hall/Crc Computer & Information Science Series)*. Chapman & Hall/CRC, 2007.

[10] D. Liben-Nowell, J. Novak, R. Kumar, P. Raghavan, and A. Tomkins. *Proceedings of the National Academy of Sciences of the United States of America*, (33), Aug 2005.

[11] A. Mislove, B. Viswanath, K. P. Gummadi, and P. Druschel. You are who you know: inferring user profiles in online social networks. In *WSDM '10*, pages 251–260, 2010.

[12] F. Provost, B. Dalessandro, R. Hook, X. Zhang, and A. Murray. Audience selection for on-line brand advertising: privacy-friendly social network targeting. In *KDD '09*, pages 707–716, 2009.

[13] F. Qiu and J. Cho. Automatic identification of user interest for personalized search. In *WWW '06*, pages 727–736, 2006.

[14] T. Rattenbury, N. Good, and M. Naaman. Towards automatic extraction of event and place semantics from flickr tags. In *SIGIR '07*, pages 103–110, 2007.

[15] S. Sizov. Geofolk: latent spatial semantics in web 2.0 social media. In *WSDM '10*, pages 281–290, 2010.

[16] R. W. White, P. Bailey, and L. Chen. Predicting user interests from contextual information. In *SIGIR '09*, pages 363–370, 2009.

[17] S. Xu, S. Bao, B. Fei, Z. Su, and Y. Yu. Exploring folksonomy for personalized search. In *SIGIR '08*, pages 155–162, 2008.

[18] S.-H. Yang, B. Long, A. Smola, N. Sadagopan, Z. Zheng, and H. Zha. Like like alike: joint friendship and interest propagation in social networks. In *WWW '11*, pages 537–546, 2011.

[19] Z. Yin, L. Cao, J. Han, C. Zhai, and T. Huang. Geographical topic discovery and comparison. In *WWW '11*, pages 247–256, 2011.

[20] Z. Yin, R. Li, Q. Mei, and J. Han. Exploring social tagging graph for web object classification. In *KDD '09*, pages 957–966, 2009.

Event-based Social Networks: Linking the Online and Offline Social Worlds

Xingjie Liu⋆, Qi He†, Yuanyuan Tian†, Wang-Chien Lee⋆, John McPherson†, Jiawei Han⋄
⋆ The Pennsylvania State University, † IBM Almaden Research Center,
⋄ University of Illinois at Urbana-Champaign
⋆ {xzl106, wlee}@cse.psu.edu, † {heq, ytian, jmcphers}@us.ibm.com,⋄ hanj@cs.uiuc.edu

ABSTRACT

Newly emerged event-based online social services, such as Meetup and Plancast, have experienced increased popularity and rapid growth. From these services, we observed a new type of social network – *event-based social network* (EBSN). An EBSN does not only contain online social interactions as in other conventional online social networks, but also includes valuable *offline* social interactions captured in offline activities. By analyzing real data collected from Meetup, we investigated EBSN properties and discovered many unique and interesting characteristics, such as heavy-tailed degree distributions and strong locality of social interactions.

We subsequently studied the heterogeneous nature (co-existence of both online and offline social interactions) of EBSNs on two challenging problems: community detection and information flow. We found that communities detected in EBSNs are more cohesive than those in other types of social networks (e.g. location-based social networks). In the context of information flow, we studied the event recommendation problem. By experimenting various information diffusion patterns, we found that a community-based diffusion model that takes into account of both online and offline interactions provides the best prediction power.

This paper is the first research to study EBSNs at scale and paves the way for future studies on this new type of social network. A sample dataset of this study can be downloaded from `http://www.largenetwork.org/ebsn`.

Categories and Subject Descriptors

H.3.4 [**Information Storage and Retrieval**]: Systems and Software - *Information networks*

General Terms

Algorithms, Experimentation.

Keywords

Event based Social Networks, Social Network Analysis, Social Event Recommendation, Online and Offline Social Behaviors, Heterogeneous Network

KDD'12, August 12–16, 2012, Beijing, China.

1. INTRODUCTION

Newly emerged event-based online social services, such as Meetup (`www.meetup.com`), Plancast (`www.plancast.com`), Yahoo! Upcoming (`upcoming.yahoo.com`) and Eventbrite (`www.eventbrite.com`) have provided convenient online platforms for people to create, distribute and organize social events. On these web services, people may propose social events, ranging from informal get-togethers (e.g. movie night and dining out) to formal activities (e.g. technical conferences and business meetings). In addition to supporting typical online social networking facilities (e.g. sharing comments and photos), these event-based services also promote face-to-face *offline* social interactions. To date, many of these services have attracted a huge number of users and have been experiencing rapid business growth. For example, Meetup has 9.5 million active users, creating 280,000 social events every month; Plancast has over 100,000 registered users and over 230,000 visits per month.

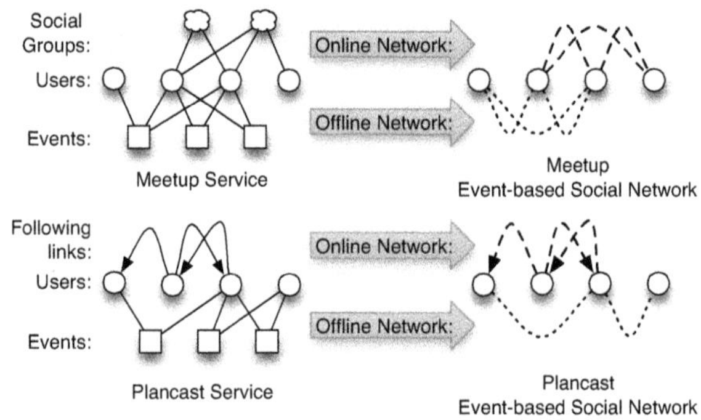

Figure 1: Event-based Social Network Examples

As these event-based services continue to expand, we identify a new type of social network – *event-based social network* (EBSN) – emerging from them. Like conventional online social networks, EBSNs provide an online virtual world where users exchange thoughts and share experiences. But what distinguishes EBSNs from conventional social networks is that EBSNs also capture the face-to-face social interactions in participating events in the offline physical world. Fig. 1 depicts two example EBSNs from Meetup and Plancast. In Meetup, users may share comments, photos and event plans with members in the same online social groups (e.g. "bay area photographers", "Nevada county walkers"). In Plancast, users may directly "follow" others' event calendars. Bi-directional co-memberships of online social groups in Meetup or uni-directional subscriptions in Plancast ultimately constitute an *online social network* represented as the dashed lines on the right side of Fig. 1. Meanwhile, in both cases, users' co-participations of the same events derive their offline social connections. These connections collectively form an *offline social network* denoted as dotted lines in Fig. 1. The online and offline social interactions jointly define an EBSN.

Recent location-based online social networking services, such as Foursquare (`foursquare.com`) and Gowalla (`gowalla.com`), represent another type of popular social network, called a location-based social network (LBSN). They are somewhat similar to EBSNs, as they capture online social interactions as well as offline location checkins. However, unlike the offline social events that incur a group of people with social interactions, location checkins from LBSNs mostly represent individual behaviors, i.e. a particular user was at a specific location at a specific time. Although in [5], adjacent checkins were treated as one kind of reason for social network tie creation. It is estimated that adjacent checkins have only a 24% chance to lead to a new social friendship in Gowalla. Therefore, in this paper, we only compare EBSNs against the online social networks in LBSNs.

To the best of our knowledge, this paper is the first work to identify an event-based social network as a co-existence of both online and offline social interactions, and comprehensively study its properties. Our study revealed the many aspects of EBSNs that are significantly different from conventional social networks. As to be shown in our analysis, social events present very regular temporal and spatial patterns. In addition, both online and offline social interactions in EBSNs are extremely local. For example, we found that 70.65% of Meetup online friends and 84.61% of Meetup offline friends live within 10 miles of each other. To our surprise, the degree distributions of the Meetup EBSN do not follow the usual power law distribution, but are more heavy-tailed than power law. Furthermore, we found that the online and offline social interactions in an EBSN are positively correlated, implying a synergistic relationship between the two parts.

Community structure detection is a very useful approach for analyzing social networks. However, to correctly detect communities in an EBSN, one has to consider both online and offline social interactions. In this paper, we employ an extended Fiedler method to incorporate this heterogeneity during the community detection process. Through experiments, we demonstrate the advantage of this method to other approaches. We also observed that the detected communities in the Meetup EBSN are more cohesive than those of the Gowalla LBSN.

To further investigate information flow over EBSNs, we also study the problem of event participation recommendation. Due to the short life time of an event, the event participation recommendation problem significantly differs from the usual recommendation problem for movies or places. Recommendation of an event is only valid after the event is created and before the event starts. This leads to a cold-start problem. In this paper, we design a number of diffusion patterns that capture the information flow over the heterogeneous EBSNs. Through experiments we demonstrate that the diffusion pattern that takes the community structures into account yields the best prediction power.

The rest of this paper is organized as follows. We describe the related work in Section 2 and formally define EBSNs in Section 3 . We examine the properties of EBSNs in Section 4 and further investigate the community structures in Section 5. In Section 6, we tackle the event participation prediction problem to study the information flow over EBSNs. Finally, we conclude the paper in Section 7.

2. RELATED WORK

Offline social interactions in the physical world have always been important in sociology [9]. One line of work is to study the origin of social relationships. In [12], Feld proposed a focus theory in which individuals organize their social interactions around foci, such as workplaces, families, etc; whereas [20, 16, 3] utilized affiliation to explain the construction of social connections. Chapter 4 of [11] provides a nice summary on these topics. Under the above theories, social events can be viewed as one type of focus or affiliation that creates the social interactions between participants.

Thanks to the popularity of event-based social network services, such as Meetup and Plancast, we are now able to get our hands on large scale social data with rich information on both online activities and offline social events. In [24], Sander and Seminar attended 40 social events in Meetup and concluded that participants in Meetup social events have social structures instead of just strangers meeting strangers.

Similar to event-based social networks, location-based social networks also contains "online" social interactions and "offline" checkin information. Although adjacent location checkins may indicate implicit social interactions and social ties [5], checkins are usually sporadic [21] and largely represent individual behaviors. The geographical features of users were also examined to infer social ties in [7, 26]. In comparison to these work, the "offline" information (social events) studied in this paper does not only contain location, but also time and people involved.

3. EVENT-BASED SOCIAL NETWORKS

In this section, motivated by popular event-based social services, we define event-based social networks and describe how to construct the networks from collected datasets.

3.1 Event-based social services

As various online social networking services become prevalent, a new type of event-based social service has emerged. These web services help users to create social event proposals, disseminate the proposals to related people, and keep track of all participants. To foster efficient communication and sharing, these event-based services also provide online social networking platforms to connect users with others with similar interests. Below, we describe two examples of such event-based social services: Meetup and Plancast.

Meetup is an online social event service that helps people publish and participate in social events. On Meetup, a social event is created by a user by specifying when, where and what the event is. Then, the created social event is made available to selected users or public, controlled by the event creators. Other users may express their intent to join the event by RSVP ("yes", "no" or "maybe") online. To facilitate online interactions, meetup.com also allows users to form social groups (e.g. "bay area single moms", "Nevada county walkers") to share comments, photos and event plans.

Similar to meetup.com, Plancast is another web service that helps users create and organize events online. Users also RSVP to express their intent to join social events. In

Meetup		Gowalla	
# Users	5,153,886	# Users	565,642
# Events	5,183,840	# Locations	2,838,143
# RSVPs	42,733,136	# Checkins	36,804,656
# Groups	97,587	# Social links	2,431,625
# Memberships	10,704,068		

Table 1: Dataset Statistics

contract to Meetup which adopts social groups to connect users online, Plancast allows users to "follow" others' social event calendars to establish online connections.

3.2 Event-based Social Networks Definition

Based on the event-based social services described above, we formulate a new type of social network, called an event-based social network (EBSN).

Like any social network, EBSNs capture social interactions among users. However, different from others, ESBNs incorporate two forms of social interactions: *online social interactions* and *offline social interactions.*

Online social interactions. In EBSNs, users can interact with each other online without the need of physical contact. For example, people can share thoughts and experiences with those in the same social group in Meetup. In Plancast, user comments and event plans are pushed to those who "follow" the user.

Offline social interactions. Social events play a major role in ESBNs. In a social event, people physically get together at a specific time and location, and do something together. Therefore, the social events in EBSNs represent the offline social interactions among event participants.

Definition: Formally, we define an EBSN as a heterogeneous network $G = \langle U, A^{\text{on}}, A^{\text{off}} \rangle$, where U represents the set of users (vertices) with $|U| = n$, A^{on} stands for the set of online social interactions (arcs), and A^{off} denotes the set of offline social interactions (arcs). The online social interactions of an EBSN form an online social network $G^{\text{on}} = \langle U, A^{\text{on}} \rangle$, and the offline interactions of an EBSN compose an offline social network $G^{\text{off}} = \langle U, A^{\text{off}} \rangle$. □

Note that the online social network or the offline social network of a EBSN can be either directed or undirected. For simplicity, we only focus on undirected online and offline networks in this paper.

The online social network [1, 18] or the offline social network [2, 22] alone is not new and has been studied extensively before. But the co-existence of both is what makes EBSNs special. As shown later in this paper, these two forms of social networks in EBSNs are intertwined but also have their own distinct characteristics at the same time.

3.3 Representative Datasets Description

To effectively study EBSNs and explore the unique properties against related LBSNs, we collected data from the popular event-based web services Meetup and the popular location-based social service Gowalla. In this section, we introduce the basic dataset statistics, as well as how EBSN and LBSN are established from these datasets.

Meetup EBSN. We crawled meetup.com from Oct 2011 to Jan 2012. The collected data statistics are shown in Table 1. With the Meetup dataset, the online EBSN is constructed by capturing the co-membership of online social groups: users u_i and u_j are connected in the online social network G^{on} if they are members of the same social group. Let g_r denote a group with $|g_r|$ members, then $(u_i, u_j) \in A^{\text{on}}$ if and only if $\exists g_r$ such that $u_i \in g_r$ and $u_j \in g_r$. We consider users of a smaller group more closely connected than those of a larger group. Therefore, we adopt a similar approach as in [19] to define the edge weights:

$$w_{i,j}^{\text{on}} = \sum_{\forall g_k, u_i \in g_k \wedge u_j \in g_k} \frac{1}{|g_k|}. \tag{1}$$

The offline social network of the EBSN, G^{off}, is constructed in a similar way based on the co-participation of social events: user u_i and u_j are connected if they co-participated in the same social event. If we use e_k to represent a social event with $|e_k|$ participants, and $u_i \in e_k$ to denote the fact that u_i participated e_k, then the weight of the offline social interaction between u_i and u_j is defined as

$$w_{i,j}^{\text{off}} = \sum_{\forall e_k, u_i \in e_k \wedge u_j \in e_k} \frac{1}{|e_k|}. \tag{2}$$

Gowalla LBSN. Gowalla is a popular online location-based social networking service that allows individual user to "checkin" their current locations (as well as comments/photos) and share with their friends. Gowalla requires users to explicitly specify their friends. Users need to mutually accept each other as friends to establish an online social link.

We crawled Gowalla from Sep 2011 to Nov 2011 and collected a subset of the users' online social networks and place checkins. The total numbers of users and locations are also summarized in Table 1. As discussed before, although this LBSN provides offline location checkins, these checkins cannot directly form an offline social network. Thus, the Gowalla LBSN only has an online social network in this study.

4. PROPERTIES OF EBSNS

In this section, we analyze the Meetup dataset to highlight the unique properties of EBSNs. As social events play a central role in EBSNs, we first study those properties specifically associated with social events. Then, we examine the network properties of EBSNs.

4.1 Social Events

Social events provide a platform for users to get-together physically. A social event is characterized by two major features: *event time* and *event location.* First, we observe

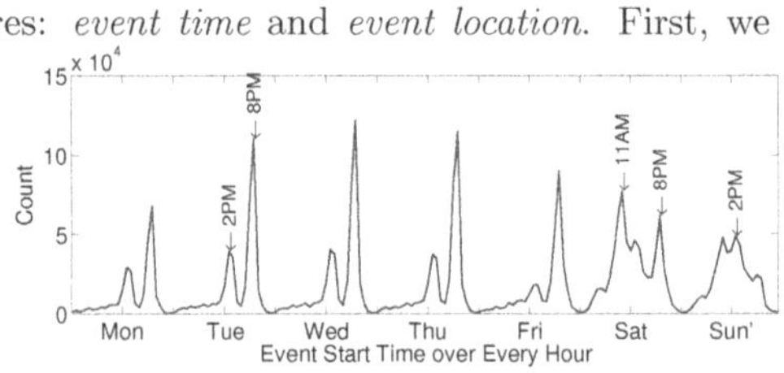

Figure 2: Social event time histogram over every hour of one week.

that social events exhibit regular temporal patterns. Fig. 2 depicts the social event time pattern on weekly scale. It is clear that in every weekday there is a small spike around 2pm in the afternoon, followed by a higher spike at 8pm in the evening. On weekends, events distribute relatively even throughout the day.

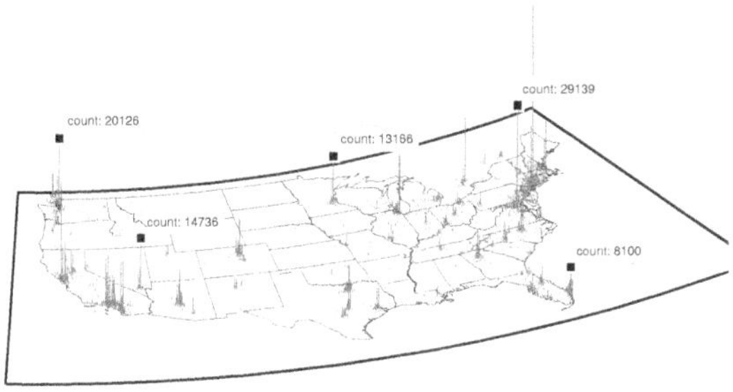

Figure 3: Social event geographical histogram. Each bar represents the number of social events in 100 square miles.

We also observe that social events are mainly located in urban areas. Fig. 3 depicts a US event geographical histogram with 100 square miles as a geographical unit.

4.2 Event and Group Participation

To understand the basic network properties of the Meetup EBSN, we need to first study the event participation and group membership in Meetup. As shown in Fig. 4(a), most of the events are small with just a few participants, but big events with a large number of participants (the heavy tail) do exist in a non-trivial quantity. Similarly, Fig. 4(b) shows that large groups do have significant presence. We examine how these two distributions fit the power law curve by Kolmogorov-Smirnov test [6]. This approach estimates the following 3 parameters:

- xmin: the best fitted cutoff value so that *only* values larger than $xmin$ fit a power-law distribution;
- $\hat{\alpha}$: the slope of the best fitted power-law distribution so that values larger than $xmin$ follow distribution $x^{-\hat{\alpha}}$;
- p-value: the statistical significance of the goodness of the power-law fitting, (p-value larger than 0.1 suggests a significant good fit).

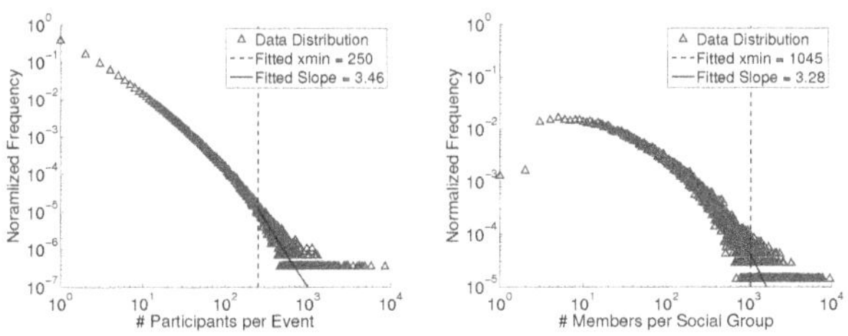

(a) # participants per event (b) # members per group

Figure 4: Histogram of the number of participants per event and number of members per group.

By estimating the above parameters, we find that only after xmin= 250 does the event size follow a power-law distribution with a high statistical significance (with p-value 0.357). Similarly, the number of members per group follows a power-law distribution non-significantly with $\hat{\alpha} = 3.28$ only after the number of events is greater than 1045 (with p-value 0.088). These two results suggest that although most events and social groups are in small scale, large events and large groups do show significant presence in the Meetup dataset.

4.3 Network Properties

Now we study the network properties of the Meetup ESBN by comparing it against the Gowalla LBSN. Table 2 lists some network properties of the Meetup EBSN online social network G^{on}, offline social network G^{off}, combined network G as well as the Gowalla LBSN social network. First, it can be clearly seen that the EBSN online social network is much denser than the EBSN offline social network, (larger strongly connected component SCC, higher clustering coefficient and lower average degree of separation). This is due to the fact that a user connects to more people online than in actual social events. Secondly, all three EBSN social networks (G^{on}, G^{off} and G) are much denser than the Gowalla LBSN, because Meetup users interact with each other by co-joining social groups or co-participating social events whereas Gowalla users have to mutually establish friendships to get connected.

	Meetup EBSN			Gowalla LBSN
	G^{on}	G^{off}	G	
Mean Degree	1,786.1	140.7	1,560.6	10.64
Median Degree	623	40	463	3
SCC. Ratio	0.999	0.993	0.997	0.987
Clustering Coef.	0.438	0.267	0.429	0.137
Degree Separation	3.00	4.25	3.07	4.47
Degree Fitted xmin	3,765	536	7,490	47
Degree Fitted $\hat{\alpha}$	2.49	2.53	2.50	2.53
Degree Fitting p-value	0.000	0.000	0.000	0.124

Table 2: Network statistics comparison between EBSN and LBSN.

To dig deeper into the network properties of EBSN, we first study the degree distributions in Fig. 5. Again, we apply the Kolmogorov-Smirnov statistic to examine whether these distributions fit the power law distribution. The estimated parameters are listed in the bottom of Table 2. While the Gowalla LBSN conforms to the power law distribution, all three of the EBSN forms are more heavy-tailed than power law. This heavy tail phenomenon in the Meetup EBSN is correlated with the significant presence of big events and big social groups found in Section 4.2.

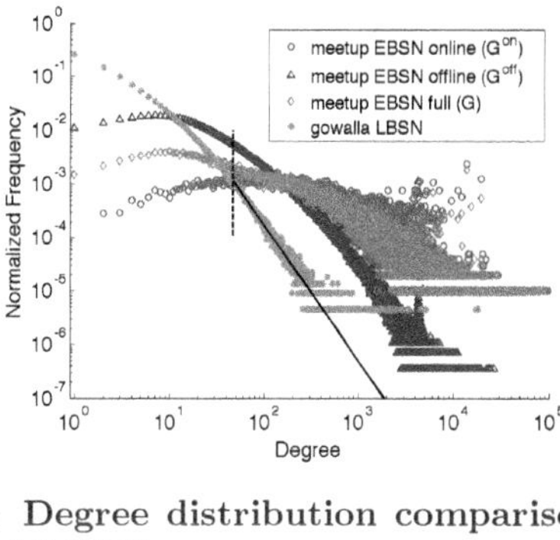

Figure 5: Degree distribution comparison between EBSN and LBSN.

Next, we analyze the correlation between each user's online interactions and offline interactions. By applying Pearson correlation, we observe positive correlation between online and offline degrees (0.368) as well as between online and offline cluster coefficients (0.393). This implies that the online social network and the offline social network work together synergistically in the Meetup EBSN – each have a positive effect on the other.

4.4 Locality of Social Interactions

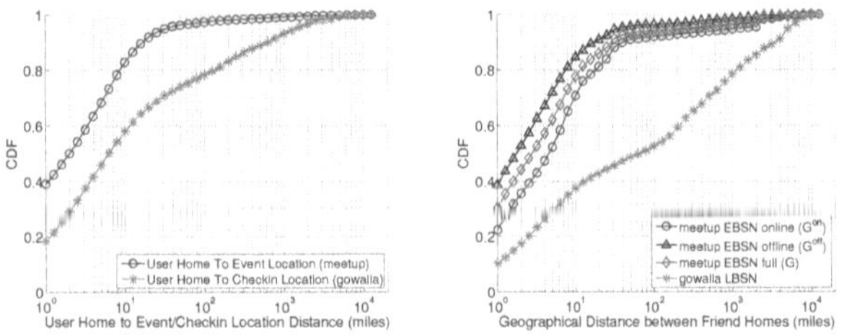

(a) locality of events (b) locality of friends

Figure 6: Localities of Meetup EBSN and Gowalla LBSN.

In the following, we further analyze on the geographic aspects of social interactions. In Fig. 6(a), we examine the distance of a Meetup event location and a Gowalla checkin location to the user's home location [4, 5]. As illustrated by this figure, although both events and checkins tend to be local to users' home locations, the possibility of an event participation in Meetup decreases more dramatically as the distance increases. As observed, 81.93% of events participated in by a user are within 10 miles of his/her home location. This indicates that people's social activities are much more location constrained than place checkins. This is because people's checkins are usually sporadic [21] and largely represent individual behaviors. Social events, which need all participants to meet at the same spot, must be located close to all the participants in most cases.

Next we compare the distances between friends' home locations in the Meetup EBSN against the Gowalla LBSN. As depicted in Fig. 6(b), friends in Meetup, no matter in online, offline, or the combined social networks, are much geographically closer to each other than in Gowalla LBSN. This is because both online and offline social networks in Meetup EBSN revolve around social events, which require participants to physically get together at the same location. In comparison, it is perfectly fine and usual for a Gowalla user to share a location checkin when he/she visits some new places. Not surprisingly, offline friends in Meetup EBSN tend to live closer to each other than the online friends. 84.61% of offline friends live within 10 miles to each other.

5. EBSNS COMMUNITY STRUCTURE

In this section, we investigate the community structures of EBSNs. Due to the heterogeneity of EBSNs, communities are defined by both online and offline interactions [1]. As a result, previous community detection algorithms on homogeneous networks do not directly apply to EBSNs. Thus, we employ an extended Fiedler method to detect communities in EBSNs and compare it against the previous approaches. We also use the Gowalla LBSN as a comparison to further study the unique features of the Meetup EBSN.

5.1 Clustering on Homogeneous Networks

For homogeneous social networks like the online or offline network of an EBSN, we use the popular Fiedler method offered by the Graclus tool [10] to partition networks. The partitioned clusters are treated as user communities. Let A define the adjacency matrix of a network. The popular Normalized Cut (NCut) [27] shown in Eq. 3 is applied as the graph partition objective function for each binary cut.

$$\min \frac{\mathbf{y}^T L \mathbf{y}}{\mathbf{y}^T D \mathbf{y}}, \quad \textit{subject to } \mathbf{y}^T D \mathbf{1} = 0, \mathbf{y} \neq 0. \tag{3}$$

In Eq. 3, D is the diagonal matrix in which each diagonal value is the sum of the corresponding row ($D_{ii} = \sum_j A_{ij}$), $L = D - A$ is the Laplacian matrix, $\mathbf{y}$ is the column vector with $y_i \in \{1, -b\}$ and b is some data-dependent constant. The column vector $\mathbf{y}$ represents the graph cutting results of the current binary cut, since all nodes with $\mathbf{y}_i = 1$ are clustered into one cluster and the other nodes with $\mathbf{y}_i = -b$ are clustered into another cluster. If $\mathbf{y}$ is relaxed to take on real values, Eq. 3 is equivalent to solving the generalized eigenvalue system $L\mathbf{y} = \lambda D\mathbf{y}$, where $\mathbf{y}$ is the Fiedler vector corresponding to the second smallest eigenvalue.

5.2 Clustering on Heterogeneous EBSNs

5.2.1 Baseline 1: Linear Combination

Given an EBSN G, we have two separate but correlated networks $G^{\text{on}} = \langle U, A^{\text{on}} \rangle$ and $G^{\text{off}} = \langle U, A^{\text{off}} \rangle$. Both G^{on} and G^{off} share the same user set U. As a result, the clustering process should consider the correlation between G^{on} and G^{off}. The simplest way to leverage both online and offline social interactions is to combine them linearly

$$A = \gamma * A^{\text{on}} + (1 - \gamma) * A^{\text{off}}. \tag{4}$$

Here A defines a linearly combined adjacency matrix with a weighting parameter γ to differentiate two types of interactions. We name this naive method as *LinearComb* and use it as a baseline for comparison. The major problem of *LinearComb* is that after the linear combination, the social interaction type information is missing in the new matrix A.

5.2.2 Baseline 2: Generalized SVD

As another baseline, we utilize Generalized Singular Vector Decomposition (GSVD) to incorporate online and offline social interactions in the clustering process by following Theorem 5.1.

THEOREM 5.1. *Given two EBSN social interaction matrices $A^{on} \in R^{n \times n}$ and $A^{off} \in R^{n \times n}$, there exists unitary matrics $\mu, \nu \in R^{n \times n}$, reversible matrix $Y \in R^{n \times n}$ and rectangular diagonal matrices Σ_1 and Σ_2 such that:*

$$A^{on} = \mu \Sigma_1 Y^T, \quad A^{off} = Y \Sigma_2 \nu^T.$$

The proof of Theorem 5.1 can be found in [14]. In Theorem 5.1, the singular vectors of matrix Y (from the second columns and onwards) collectively offer a consistent clustering on users by leveraging both online and offline social interactions. In this method, the singular vectors of the 2nd to m^{th} smallest singular values are used as $m - 1$ dimensional indicator vectors for users. Then, a classic K-means algorithm is conducted on this space to generate user communities. We name this method *GSVD*.

One shortcoming of *GSVD* is that as Y is not a unitary matrix, its values on different column vectors vary a lot in ranges. Therefore, the partitioning information embedded in Y cannot be simply differentiated by the symbol sign as the classic SVD does. In experiments, we also found that the performance of *GSVD* is rather sensitive to the choice

[1] Although a *group* or an *event* in Meetup somewhat captures the behaviors of a set of users either online or offline, it is the combination of online and offline interactions that defines a community in EBSNs.

Algorithm 1: HeteroClu

```
Input: EBSN G = ⟨U, A^on, A^off⟩, # clusters K
Output: User cluster set C
Initialize C = {C_1, C_2, ..., C_n}, where each C_i = {u_i};
Initialize normalized weights
    w̄_ij ← (Σ_{u_a∈C_i, u_b∈C_j} w_ab)/(|C_i| · |C_j|) for connected C_i, C_j;
while |C|>M do                          /* bottom-up cluster */
    Find the largest w̄_ij;
    Merge C_i and C_j, update related normalized weights;
while |C| < K do                        /* top-down partition */
    Binary cut all M clusters following the objective Eq. 5;
    if C_i is the cluster with the minimum cut cost then
        delete C_i from C;
        Add spitted parts of C_i into C;
return C
```

of similarity measures on the singular vectors of Y. After many comparions, we chose the *city block* similarity measure for *GSVD*.

5.2.3 Extended Fiedler Method

We now propose an algorithm that clusters online and offline interactions at the same time. This algorithm employs the following objective function based on normalized cut (Eq. 3):

$$\min \alpha \frac{\mathbf{y}^T(D^{\text{on}} - A^{\text{on}})\mathbf{y}}{\mathbf{y}^T D^{\text{on}} \mathbf{y}} + (1-\alpha) \frac{\mathbf{y}^T(D^{\text{off}} - A^{\text{off}})\mathbf{y}}{\mathbf{y}^T D^{\text{off}} \mathbf{y}}, \quad (5)$$
$$\textit{subject to } \mathbf{y}^T D^{\text{on}} \mathbf{1} = 0, \mathbf{y}^T D^{\text{off}} \mathbf{1} = 0, \mathbf{y} \neq 0.$$

The above objective function contains two parts, each part alone is a normalized cut objective function on individual online or offline social networks. But the linear combination of both defines a global optimization over the heterogeneous EBSN. Coupling factor α is used to weigh the importance of each network. Note that each part is a normalized value between 0 and 1. Therefore, the size of the individual online or offline network is not captured in Eq. 5. A naive way to assign the importance of the two parts is to set $\alpha = 0.5$. However, since online and offline networks have different network density, we set α as $\frac{sum(A^{\text{on}})}{sum(A^{\text{on}})+sum(A^{\text{off}})}$.

Similar objective functions to Eq. 5 have been used in the high-order co-clustering problem on multiple types of heterogeneous objects [13]. Solving the new objective function (Eq. 5) is non-trivial, as it represents a typical quadratic fractional programming problem. In [13], the similar function was first approximated to be a quadratically constrained quadratic programming problem by fixing two denominators of the function as constants. Then, the standard semi-definite programming is applied to compute $\mathbf{y}$ efficiently.

In this paper, we use a heuristic algorithm shown in Algorithm 1 to solve the clustering problem with the objective function defined in Eq. 5. This algorithm first employs a bottom-up clustering algorithm on the linear combination of online and offline social networks as defined in Eq. 4, to generate M ($M << K$) giant loose clusters in a bottom-up fashion. This step defines a local greedy merge procedure. Then it uses the top-down recursive binary cut procedure to cut large clusters to smaller ones until K clusters are achieved. This step defines a global recursive cut procedure.

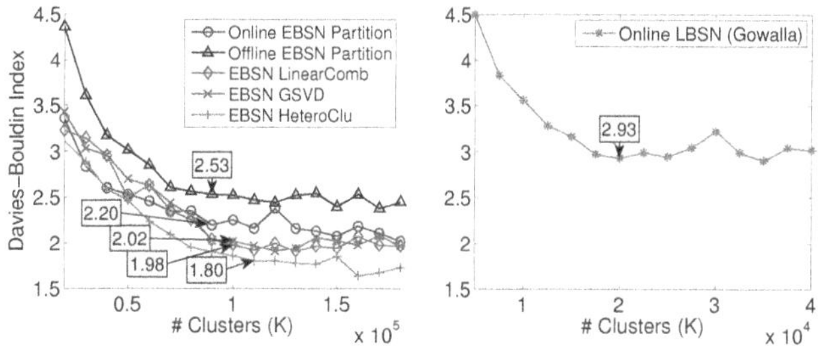

Figure 7: Community dectection performance. The score inside the grey rectangle is the DB index under the optimal K based on the "knee" method.

5.3 Community Structure Evaluation

5.3.1 Evaluation Settings

To measure the quality of user communities, we use the collected user tags as the external ground truth of latent community semantics. 78,158 unique user tags were collected from Meetup and treated as the Meetup tag space T with $|T| = m$. For each user u_i, we built a binary user-tag vector $\mathbf{u_i} = \{t_{i1}, t_{i2}, \ldots, t_{im}\}$ where $t_{ik} = 1$ if u_i selects the tag t_k; otherwise $t_{ik} = 0$. After normalization, the similarity between two users u_i and u_j is measured by the cosine similarity $\mathbf{u_i} \cdot \mathbf{u_j}$. There are no user tags available in Gowalla. Instead, we aggregated all location tags of a user's checkins to build the user-tag vector, in which t_{ik} is the number of checkins associated to tag t_k of user u_i. In total, 680 unique tags were collected in Gowalla.

The standard Davies-Bouldin (DB) index [8] was used to measure the cohesiveness of communities, which is given by

$$DB = \frac{1}{K} \sum_{k=1}^{K} \max_{k \neq j} \left(\frac{2 - \sigma_k - \sigma_j}{1 - \mathbf{c_k} \cdot \mathbf{c_j}} \right), \quad (6)$$

where K is the number of communities, $\mathbf{c_k} = 1/|C_k| \sum_{u_i \in C_k} \mathbf{u_i}$ is the centroid vector of cluster C_k after renormalization, and $\sigma_k = 1/|C_k| \sum_{u_i \in C_k} \mathbf{u_i} \cdot \mathbf{c_k}$ is the average similarity of users in cluster C_k to their centroid. A smaller DB index value indicates a more cohesive community.

5.3.2 Results

Determining the optimal K for a clustering has been an open problem for decades. For a fair comparison on various approaches and datasets, we used a simple yet popular method that identifies the "knee" [15] in the plot of DB index vs. K to determine the optimal K for each clustering first; and then compare the corresponding DB index under the optimal K. The DB index value corresponding to the "knee" can be seen as the best clustering performance that one method can achieve.

Fig. 7 compares the best DB index of each method based on the "knee" method. Note that since the DB index averages over all the worst separated clustering pairs, it is possible that the DB index has a value greater than 2.

As shown in Figure 7, the communities for the Meetup EBSN are more cohesive than those for Gowalla LBSN. One interesting finding is that users in online Meetup EBSN communities are more cohesive than users in offline Meetup EBSN communities (by 0.33), indicating that users tend to have more similar interests if they belong to same groups, compared to those who participated similar events. However, the combination of online and offline interactions does play an important role in the clustering process, as three methods *LinearCom*, *GSVD* and *HeteroClu* outperformed individual networks. The *LinearCom* is only slightly better than individual networks (by 0.18) but worse than *HeteroClu* (by 0.22), indicating that a simple linear combination cannot differentiate heterogeneous types of social interactions effectively. The *GSVD* has almost the same performance as *LinearCom*, suggesting that after relaxing the constraint on the unitary matrix of SVD decomposition, the generalized SVD lost some disambiguation power on clustering. Lastly, *HeteroClu* leads the pack in comparisons. It is the only method that achieved the best DB index (around 1.8) *sufficiently* under 2, indicating that its worst pairs of clusters were reasonably separated.

6. EBSNS INFORMATION FLOW

In this section, we study how information flows over this unique network structure. A good scenario that can be used to examine the information flow on EBSNs is the problem of recommending users to participate in social events *only* based on the topological structure of EBSNs. With this application, we can study how information flows from one user to the online/offline friends and how the information flow pathways latently drive the social event participation process.

Unlike classic movie/book recommendations, event participation recommendation is more challenging due to the short life time of social events. An event is non-existent until its creation time t_c. And after the start time t_s of an event, participation recommendation becomes meaningless. Due to the very limited history of an event from time t_c to t_s, event participation recommendation suffers from the cold-start problem heavily.

Now, let's formally define the event participation problem as follows: given an event e, at time t ($t_c < t < t_s$), the task is to predict users who will RSVP "yes" to event e between t and t_s. The EBSN built upon the collective data before t will serve as the network structure and all the users who responded "yes" to e between t_c and t are the positive training examples for the prediction, notated as set S [2].

6.1 Event-Centric Diffusion

Not to deviate from our goal of studying the information flow over the EBSNs' unique network structures, we only rely on the topological structure of EBSNs and the already responded users for event participation prediction.

6.1.1 Basic Event-Centric Diffusion

We design a simple yet efficient event-centric diffusion model for the problem. We define $f_i \geq 0$ as the initial score of node u_i, where only users in set S (the set of users already RSVPed "yes") have $f > 0$ and the rest of the users have $f = 0$. For simplicity, we initialize $f = 1/|S|$ for users in S. We use the column vector $\mathbf{v}^k = \{v_1^k, v_2^k, \ldots, v_n^k\}$ to represent the probabilities that users have been visited after the k-th diffusion step, and $v_i^0 = f_i$.

The basic event-centric diffusion, named *DIF*, can be expressed as $\mathbf{v}^{k+1} = \mathcal{D} \cdot \mathbf{v}^k$, where $\mathcal{D}$ defines the non-symmetric information transition matrix of a network for time t. Each

[2]For simplicity, the event creator is treated as the first user with RSVP "yes".

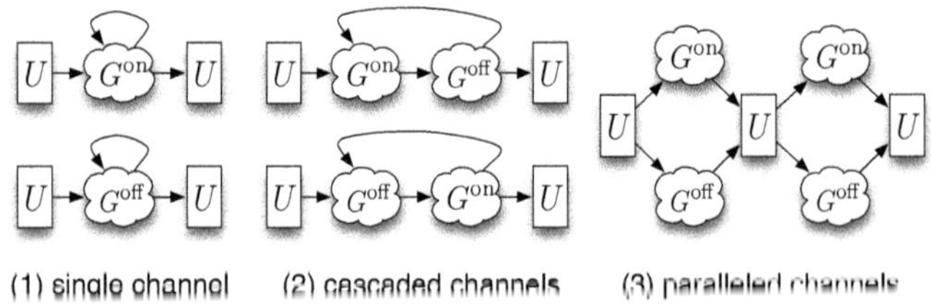

Figure 8: Typical EBSN information flow patterns.

element in $\mathcal{D}$ is defined as $d_{ij} = \frac{w_{ij}}{\sum_l w_{il}}$. If we run the model on the heterogeneous EBSN, we can use the linearly combined adjacency matrix (Eq. 4). d_{ij} is the empirical probability of information flow from user u_i to user u_j. Clearly, $d_{ij} \neq d_{ji}$. If u_i has a larger degree than u_j, the influence of u_i on u_j is less than that of u_j on u_i.

This basic diffusion model is event-centric because $\mathbf{v}^k$ represents personalized probabilities only corresponding to the current event e. A similar diffusion method has also been studied by [17] for link prediction. Because this diffusion process does not converge to the stationary distribution of information flow, a self-loop on every node is necessary; otherwise the information will be diverged far away quickly. The self-loop weight follows the same definitions of Eq. 1 and Eq. 2.

6.1.2 Diffusion over EBSNs

An EBSN contains both online and offline social interactions, but the basic diffusion model *DIF* does not take this heterogeneity into account. Accommodating different forms of social interactions, there exist at least three information flow patterns, as shown in Figure 8. The online and offline social networks G^{on} and G^{off} of an EBSN basically defines two kinds of channels for the flow of information. Figure 8(1) depicts the basic diffusion model *DIF* over a single channel exclusively, whereas Figure 8(2) define a cascade model, abbreviated as *DIF-cascade*, in which information interchangeably flows from one channel to the other. The simplest cascade diffusion model can be defined as $\mathbf{v}^{k+1} = \mathcal{D}_c \cdot \mathbf{v}^k$, where $\mathcal{D}_c$ is a cascaded transition matrix for time t, and $\mathcal{D}_c = \mathcal{D}^{\text{on}} \cdot \mathcal{D}^{\text{off}}$ or $\mathcal{D}^{\text{off}} \cdot \mathcal{D}^{\text{on}}$. Finally, in Figure 8(3), information flows over two channels concurrently. We call this model *DIF-parallel*. The simplest parallel diffusion model is $\mathbf{v}^{k+1} = \mathcal{D}_p \cdot \mathbf{v}^k$, where $\mathcal{D}_p$ defines a linearly combined transition matrix for time t, and $\mathcal{D}_p = \gamma\mathcal{D}^{\text{on}} + (1-\gamma)\mathcal{D}^{\text{off}}$. The parameter γ is used to measure the importance of each type of social interactions. It plays the same role of γ in Eq. 4. Thus, *DIF-parallel* is equivalent to *DIF* on the linearly combined adjacency matrix (Eq. 4). Undoubtedly, there are more complex information diffusion processes (i.e., a mixture of *DIF-cascade* and *DIF-parallel*). But we will leave them for future work.

6.1.3 Community-Based Diffusion

Information is often circulated more rapidly inside its own community, especially for those small-scale local communities. As a result, we design a community-based diffusion model in which information tends to, but is not restricted to, flow within the scope of its own community.

Specifically, in this model, $\mathbf{v}^{k+1} = \mathcal{D}_m \cdot \mathbf{v}^k$, where $\mathcal{D}_m$ defines the community-based information transition matrix. Each element of $\mathcal{D}_m$ is defined as

$$d'_{ij} = \begin{cases} \frac{(1-\beta)w_{ij}}{N} & \text{if } u_j \notin C(u_i), \\ \frac{\beta w_{ij}}{N} & \text{if } u_j \in C(u_i), \end{cases}$$

where $C(u_i)$ is the community of u_i, β is a parameter used to control weight of information flows inside its community versus outside, and N is the normalization factor so that $\sum_j d'ij = 1$. We name this model *DIF-com.*

Since *DIF-com* only adjusts the weights of edges on top of the basic *DIF* model (can be seen as a combination with *DIF*), it can be further combined with other complex diffusion models, including *DIF-cascade* and *DIF-parallel.* The names of the two combinations are *DIF-com-cascade* and *DIF-com-parallel*, respectively. Note that *DIF-com* on G based on the linearly combined adjacency matrix (Eq. 4) is equivalent to *DIF-com-parallel.*

6.2 Information Flow Evaluation

6.2.1 *Experimental Settings*

As discussed before, event participation recommendation suffer from a typical cold-start problem. When an event is created, except for the creator, it is unknown to all the other users. To simplify the problem, we treat the event creator as the first user who responded "yes" to the event. In evaluation, we can start the recommendation process immediately after the event creation, or wait for a while until there are a few responded users. We first focus on the latter case: given a testing event, we set the first k responded participants as the seed users, where k is randomly determined. The former case is a much harder problem and is examined at the end of the evaluation.

We split the Meetup data into two sequential parts (cut around Mar 2011). The first part of data (on or before Mar 2011, take up 80%) are used for training and the second part of data (after Mar 2012, take up 20%) are used for testing. Given a testing event, we recommend top 5, 10, 20, 50, 100, 200, 400, 800 users to it respectively. We choose to recommend a large number of users, because 1) in practice event organizers often broadly advertise their events to the public; and 2) we want to see the long-term trend of such a recommendation system. For the recommended top N users, we compute *recall* to evaluate the performance. *recall* is defined as the percentage of users who would respond "yes" to the testing event that are covered by the top N recommendations. Finally, we average the *recall* for all testing events under the same top N.

6.2.2 *Compare Event-Centric Diffusion Models with Classic Baselines*

There are two popular baselines found in the prior art that can be efficiently applied to such an event participation recommendation problem. One is Collaborative Filtering (CF) [25], and the other is the random walk model [23]. Note that due to the extremely short life time of events, most supervised recommendation (link prediction) methods suffer from severe sparsity of labeled data. As a result, they do not apply to the event participation recommendation problem.

For the baseline CF, the users who ever participated in similar groups or events in the Meetup training data are recommendation candidates. They are then ranked by their Jaccard similarities to the responded users. The Jaccard similarity between two users is simply based on their past group or event participation count vectors.

For the baseline random walk model, we applied the *random walk with restart* (RWR) model. In the RWR baseline, there is a certain chance (probability β) with which the information will flow back to the starting users at each step of information flow. By setting various β, we have various RWR baselines with names like RWR (0.3). When $\beta = 0$, RWR downgrades to the basic random walk model.

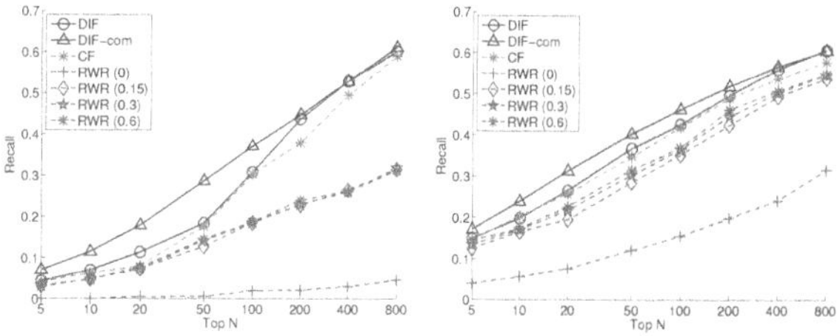

(a) Online EBSN (b) Offline EBSN

Figure 9: Prediction on individual EBSNs.

As both CF and RWR were initially designed for homogeneous networks, we compared them with the basic event-centric diffusion models on individual G^{on} and G^{off} in Fig. 9. From all diffusion models on G^{on} in Fig. 9(a) and G^{off} in Fig. 9(b), *DIF-com* outperforms *DIF* and *CF*, and RWR models perform the worst. By soft-restricting information flow in the same user communities, *DIF-com* can guarantee most closely related friends are recommended. The weighting strategies of *DIF* and *CF* differ only slightly, thus they yield similar prediction results. The poor performance of *RWR* indicates that identified network hubs are not relevant to the testing event. By raising return probabilities of RWR, the prediction performance does not improve much even with β as high as 0.6. In addition, by comparing Fig. 9(a) and Fig. 9(b), we find the offline EBSN has better prediction power when N is small but online EBSN gradually catches up and even surpasses the offline EBSN as N grows large. This is because offline social interactions are able to capture closely related friends who are very likely to participate in the same events, but the recommended users tend to be regulars to similar events. In comparison, online social interaction can introduce non-regulars to the events and increase the coverage of the recommendation.

6.2.3 *Compare Various Diffusion Patterns on EBSNs*

In the previous section, we showed that *DIF-com* has the best recommendation performance for individual online and offline social networks of an EBSN. As discussed in Section 6.1.3, *DIF-com* actually represents one kind of diffusion pattern on a whole EBSN (equivalent to *DIF-com-parallel* based on the linearly combined adjacency matrix (Eq. 4)). It is thus interesting to further compare various diffusion models we discussed in Section 6.1.2 on the whole EBSNs (with both online and offline social interactions). All diffusion models can be enhanced by communities since *DIF-com* has been shown to outperform the rest of the methods in the previous section. For a fair comparison, we use communities detected by Algorithm 1 for all methods. The detailed comparisons are given by Fig. 10. Fig. 10(a) compares three diffusion models over the heterogeneous EBSNs against individual online/offline networks. Only the paralleled diffusion model outperforms the online or offline only model. This means that the joint presence of online and offline social interactions can improve the prediction performance. The reason that cascade diffusions are worse is because values are diffused twice to those far away users. Similarly, In

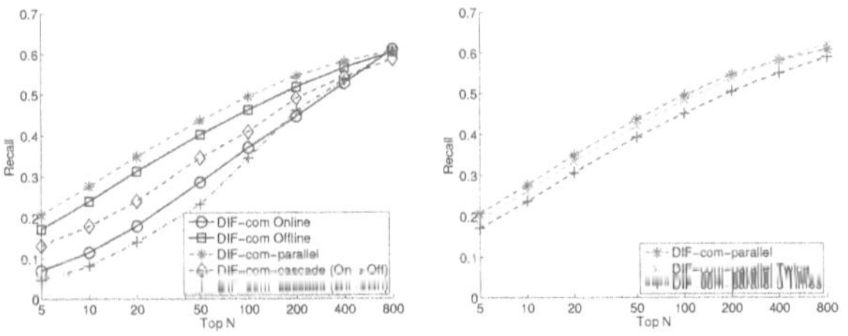

(a) EBSN diffusion patterns (b) EBSN recursive diffusion

Figure 10: Prediction on the heterogeneous EBSNs.

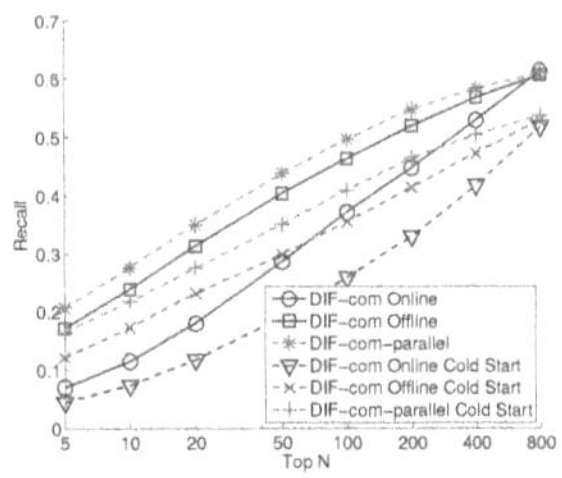

Figure 11: Comparison to cold-start scenarios.

Fig. 10(b), we see that repeating the parallel diffusion model also deteriorates the performance.

6.2.4 Examine the Effect of Cold-Start

In this section, we would like to examine how the cold-start phenomena hurts the recommendation performance. It is well-accepted that as the size of responded users decreases, the recommendation performance will get worse. We simply verify this well-known conjecture using Fig. 11. In Fig.11, the prediction performances for those cold start cases (the event creator is the only seed for an event) are slightly worse than random-start cases. However, the recalls achieved by diffusion from a single user are still fairly good, indicating that using diffusion to predict event participation on EBSNs is satisfactory even on the extreme cold start cases.

7. CONCLUSION

In this paper, we have identified and formally defined a new type of social network, EBSN. By using the Meetup dataset, we studied the unique features of EBSNs including basic network properties, community structures and information flow over EBSNs. Our research revealed many aspects of EBSNs that are significantly different from conventional social networks and LBSNs. We hope this paper paves the way for future studies on this interesting type of social networks.

Acknowledgements

We would like to thank Jon Kleinberg for helping us nail down the background of the problem, Bin Gao for his explanation on the related work [13] and Jiang Bian and Mao Ye for their valuable discussions.

8. REFERENCES

[1] Y. Ahn, S. Han, H. Kwak, S. Moon, and H. Jeong. Analysis of topological characteristics of huge online social networking services. In *WWW*, 2007.

[2] P. S. Bearman, J. Moody, and K. Stovel. Chains of Affection: The Structure of Adolescent Romantic and Sexual Networks. *American Journal of Sociology*, 2004.

[3] C. Borgs, J. Chayes, J. Ding, and B. Lucier. The hitchhiker's guide to affiliation networks: A game-theoretic approach. *arXiv:1008.1516v1*, 2010.

[4] Z. Cheng, J. Caverlee, K. Lee, and D. Sui. Exploring millions of footprints in location sharing services. In *ICWSM*, 2011.

[5] E. Cho, S. A. Myers, and J. Leskovec. Friendship and mobility: user movement in location-based social networks. In *KDD*, 2011.

[6] A. Clauset, C. Shalizi, and M. Newman. Power-law distributions in empirical data. *Arxiv preprint arxiv:0706.1062*, 2007.

[7] D. Crandall, L. Backstrom, D. Cosley, S. Suri, D. Huttenlocher, and J. Kleinberg. Inferring social ties from geographic coincidences. *PNAS*, 2010.

[8] D. Davies and D. Bouldin. A cluster separation measure. *Pattern Analysis and Machine Intelligence, IEEE Transactions on*, 1979.

[9] I. de Sola Pool Manfred. Contacts and influence. *Social networks*, 1979.

[10] I. Dhillon, Y. Guan, and B. Kulis. Kernel k-means: spectral clustering and normalized cuts. In *KDD*, 2004.

[11] D. Easley and J. Kleinberg. *Networks, Crowds, and Markets: Reasoning About a Highly Connected World.* Cambridge University Press, 2010.

[12] S. L. Feld. The focused organization of social ties. *American Journal of Sociology*, 1981.

[13] B. Gao, T.-Y. Liu, X. Zheng, Q.-S. Cheng, and W.-Y. Ma. Consistent bipartite graph co-partitioning for starstructured high-order heterogeneous data co-clustering. In *KDD*, 2005.

[14] G. Golub and C. Loan. *Matrix Computations.* Johns Hopkins Univ. Press, 1996.

[15] A. K. Jain and R. C. Dubes. *Algorithms for Clustering Data.* Prentice-Hall Prentice-Hall advanced reference series, 1988.

[16] S. Lattanzi and D. Sivakumar. Affiliation networks. In *STOC*, 2009.

[17] R. N. Lichtenwalter, J. T. Lussier, and N. V. Chawla. New perspectives and methods in link prediction. In *KDD*, 2010.

[18] A. Mislove, M. Marcon, K. Gummadi, P. Druschel, and B. Bhattacharjee. Measurement and analysis of online social networks. In *SIGCOMM*, 2007.

[19] M. Newman. Scientific collaboration networks. ii. shortest paths, weighted networks, and centrality". *Physical Review E*, 2001.

[20] M. E. J. Newman, D. J. Watts, and S. H. Strogatz. Random graph models of social networks. In *National Academy of Sciences*, 2002.

[21] A. Noulas, S. Scellato, C. Mascolo, and M. Pontil. An empirical study of geographic user activity patterns in foursquare. In *ICWSM*, 2011.

[22] J. F. Padgett and C. K. Ansell. Robust Action and the Rise of the Medici, 1400-1434. *The American Journal of Sociology*, 1993.

[23] L. Page, S. Brin, R. Motwani, and T. Winograd. The pagerank citation ranking: Bringing order to the web. 1999.

[24] T. Sander and S. Seminar. E-associations? using technology to connect citizens: The case of meetup.com. In *Annual Meeting of the American Political Science Association*, 2005.

[25] B. Sarwar, G. Karypis, J. Konstan, and J. Reidl. Item-based collaborative filtering recommendation algorithms. In *WWW*, 2001.

[26] S. Scellato, A. Noulas, and C. Mascolo. Exploiting place features in link prediction on location-based social networks. In *KDD*, 2011.

[27] J. Shi and J. Malik. Normalized cuts and image segmentation. *TPAMI*, 2000.

Differential Identifiability*

Jaewoo Lee
Dept. of Computer Science
Purdue University, West Lafayette, IN, USA
jaewoo@cs.purdue.edu

Chris Clifton
Dept. of Computer Science / CERIAS
Purdue University, West Lafayette, IN, USA
clifton@cs.purdue.edu

ABSTRACT

A key challenge in privacy-preserving data mining is ensuring that a data mining result does not inherently violate privacy. ϵ-Differential Privacy appears to provide a solution to this problem. However, there are no clear guidelines on how to set ϵ to satisfy a privacy policy. We give an alternate formulation, *Differential Identifiability*, parameterized by the probability of individual identification. This provides the strong privacy guarantees of differential privacy, while letting policy makers set parameters based on the established privacy concept of individual identifiability.

Categories and Subject Descriptors

K.4.1 [**Public Policy Issues**]: Privacy; H.2.8 [**Database Applications**]: Data mining

General Terms

Security

Keywords

Differential Privacy; Identifiability

1. INTRODUCTION

Privacy-preserving data mining has seen many advances, and today we can construct many data mining models without disclosing the input data [1,21]. One key challenge remains: does the produced model inherently violate privacy? *Differential Privacy* [7] provides a means to address this challenge. The basic idea is to add enough noise to the outcome (e.g., the model resulting from training) to hide the contribution of any single individual to that outcome.

This appears to address the challenge perfectly. From a data mining perspective, the first privacy issue is revealing information about an individual in the training data. Differential privacy essentially hides an individual by ensuring that the resulting model is nearly indistinguishable from the one without that individual – *for any individual.* Formally, given the query function f, $\forall S \subseteq Range(\mathcal{M})$ an ϵ-differentially private mechanism $\mathcal{M}$ satisfies:

$$\frac{Pr[\mathcal{M}_f(D_1) \in S]}{Pr[\mathcal{M}_f(D_2) \in S]} \leq e^{\epsilon} \quad (1)$$

where D_1 and D_2 are two databases differing by at most one element.[1] In data mining terms, $\mathcal{M}_f$ is the learning algorithm, f is the resulting model, and D_1 and D_2 are nearly identical training databases. Since the (randomized) learning algorithm guarantees that the results are indistinguishable for **any** two training sets that differ by one individual, we can claim that the resulting model does not disclose information about any single individual in the training set.

Unfortunately, indistinguishability only holds for $\epsilon = 0$, which makes the resulting model useless. The larger the value of ϵ, the less noise needed in the model, and the more a single individual can impact that model (thus risking disclosure of information about that individual). The problem is that ϵ limits how much one individual can affect the resulting model, not how much information is revealed about an individual. This does not match legal definitions of privacy, which require protection of *individually identifiable data* [8,11].

We instead propose a parameterization based on the probability that an individual contributes to the model. This corresponds to legal definitions, and we can use regulations such as the U.S. HIPAA safe harbor rule [11] to determine a probabilistic intent of the regulation. The HIPAA safe harbor rule requires removal of names, addresses, and identifying numbers. However, it does allow geographic units as small as 20,000 people, age in years (if less than 90), gender, and ethnicity. Given that less than 1.7% of the U.S. population is male and 85 or older[2], knowing the age, gender, and address of someone over 85 would allow us to limit them to one of 68 people (on average) in safe-harbor de-identified data. In practice, the privacy provided could be much worse; e.g., in a college town there may be few older people. How-

*Support for this work was provided by MURI award FA9550-08-1-0265 from the Air Force Office of Scientific Research.

KDD '12, August 12–16, 2012, Beijing, China
Copyright 2012 ACM 978-1-4503-1462-6 /12/08 ...$15.00.

[1]There are several formulations of the definition of differential privacy, such as a difference bound rather than the ratio given in Equation 1; we present the one from [7]. The differences between definitions is not critical to this paper.
[2]U.S. Census, 2010 data

ever, from this we can deduce that the goal of the privacy policy is met if we limit the estimate of the probability that an individual is in the data to approximately 1.5%.

The ϵ in ϵ-differential privacy does not correspond to such a probability; it has been shown that for a given value of ϵ, the probability of identification can vary depending on data values, or even on values of individuals not in the data set [13]. Nor does ϵ correspond to ability to infer private data values for an individual [4]. We give a definition ρ-*differential identifiability* that provides the same guarantees as differential privacy (proof against an arbitrarily strong adversary), but the parameter ρ bounds the probability estimate that an individual contributed to the resulting model.

Differential Identifiability is a subtle but important variation of differential privacy, and this paper shows that the general Laplacian noise addition mechanism for differential privacy can be adapted to provide differential identifiability. However, the mathematical formulation shows significant differences; there is no direct translation from ρ to ϵ; the relationship depends on additional information outside the scope of setting policy. The result is a method corresponding to real-world privacy policy (e.g., $\rho = .015$ provides privacy equivalent to what appears intended by the HIPAA safe harbor rules), with the strong formal guarantees of the adversary model used in differential privacy.

2. RELATED WORK

While many privacy definitions have been proposed, the common goal is to allow learning information about a group of individuals while protecting information of each individual in the group. Samarati and Sweeney proposed k-anonymity [19, 20]. k-anonymity ensures that the identifying information for at least k tuples is identical, ensuring that individuals cannot be uniquely re-identified.

While k-anonymity prevents linking a record to an individual, it may still disclose sensitive information. ℓ-diversity [14] shows that k-anonymous tables are vulnerable to homogeneity. Their definitions require that each equivalence class with identical identifying information have at least ℓ distinct values for each sensitive attribute.

While these and related approaches prevent the adversary from uniquely identifying an individual's record, they assume little prior knowledge available to the adversary. δ-presence [18] protects against determining if an individual is in a dataset even if the adversary has full knowledge of values of individuals. Generalization/suppression bounds the adversary's probability of inferring that an individual is in the database to the range $\delta = (\delta_{min}, \delta_{max})$.

A big advantage of the above methods is that the outcomes are guaranteed true, even though specificity may be lost through generalization/suppression. However, they assume the adversary's knowledge is limited. For example, in k-anonymity and ℓ-diversity, protection targets are not met if the adversary knows sensitive values of other individuals.

Differential privacy [7] avoids modeling prior knowledge of the adversary. To do this, it gives up the correctness guarantees of the above methods, instead providing a noisy result that hides the impact of any single individual on the result. The idea is that what is learned from a dataset with a particular individual can also be learned from a dataset without that individual. Therefore, it hides presence or absence of an individual in the database by making the response generated by two datasets (one with the individual and the other without the individual) indistinguishable. As stated previously, we follow in this model, but provide a parameterization based on the risk of identifying an individual.

Table 1: Notations

U	Universe
$D \subset U$	Database to be queried
$D' = D - i^*$	Subset of D missing one individual
$i \in U$	Data associated with an individual
$I(i)$	Identity of an individual corresponding to i

3. PRELIMINARIES

We now give background on differential privacy, the problem of re-identification, and introduce a possible worlds adversary and sensitivity model. We first introduce notation.

3.1 Notation

A database D can be modeled as a (multi)set. Each element x_i takes a fixed value from the universe U. Each entry in U corresponds to an individual whose privacy must be protected; $I(i)$ denotes the identity of the individual corresponding to database entry i. The set of individuals who contributed their data to D is denoted by $\mathcal{I}_D = \{I(i)|i \in D\}$. Let $D' \subset D$ denote a database having one less element than D (i.e., $|D'| = |D| - 1$). As with differential privacy, a query function f can be any function that extracts information from a database. Examples from differential privacy include aggregate queries (count, mean, sum, ...) used by a data mining algorithm [5, 15, 22], a data anonymizer [17], or a learning algorithm such as ID3 [10] or logistic regression model [3]. These notations are summarized in Table 1.

Another concept borrowed from differential privacy is sensitivity, which measures the maximum impact a single individual can have on the query result:

DEFINITION 1 (SENSITIVITY). *The sensitivity of a query function f for bounded differential privacy [6] is defined as*

$$\Delta f = \max_{x, x' \subset U} |f(x) - f(x')|$$

where x' can be obtained by replacing one element in x with another.

To attempt to dispel confusion, we note that there are different ways of defining sensitivity, based on the definition of neighboring databases D and D' differing by removal of an individual (*unbounded*) or replacement of an individual (*bounded*). Unless we explicitly state otherwise, we use bounded differential privacy in this paper. Further discussion of these differences can be found in [12].

3.2 Problem Statement

The goal of privacy-preserving data mining is to release the mining outcome without revealing identities of individuals in the database. Precisely, given $\rho \in [0, 1]$, the adversary's expectation that any individual corresponding to $i \in U$ *not previously known to be in* D is in D is at most ρ. This can be thought of as a game between a privacy mechanism and an adversary. The privacy mechanism $\mathcal{M}$ builds the model $f(D)$ and adds noise to produce the perturbed result (*response*) $R = \mathcal{M}_f(D)$. The adversary tries to identify individuals whose data is in D from the given response R. If

R enables the adversary to state any new individual belongs to D with confidence exceeding ρ, privacy is breached.

3.3 Adversary Model

This paper assumes the same strong adversary as differential privacy. The adversary's prior knowledge is represented as a triplet $\mathcal{L} = \langle U, D', \mathcal{I}_{D'} \rangle$. The adversary has complete knowledge on the universe; every value in U is known. The adversary knows every tuple in D except one. In other words, the adversary has D'. The adversary also has $\mathcal{I}_{D'}$, the identities of the individuals corresponding to those tuples. The only piece of information the adversary does not have is who the nth individual of $\mathcal{I}_D$ is. The adversary also knows the privacy mechanism $\mathcal{M}_f$, i.e., how the mechanism works and the noise distribution. This type of adversary is called an *informed adversary* [6].[3]

In our model, the goal of adversary is to determine the membership of the unknown individual in D with high confidence. To find out the identity of the missing individual, the adversary interacts with a randomized mechanism $\mathcal{M}$; issues a query and receives a noisy response $R = \mathcal{M}_f(D)$. The adversary uses the response and prior knowledge to reduce uncertainty about the missing individual.

To measure the adversary's confidence in making an inference, we use a possible worlds model. The adversary considers the set of all possible databases. Given the prior knowledge $\mathcal{L}$ and R, the adversary creates a set of all possible databases, called *possible worlds*, that may be the D that generated the perturbed answer R. Since the adversary only needs to determine the membership of one missing individual, each possible world is the union of D' and one data entry from U. Given the adversary's prior knowledge $\mathcal{L}$, the set of all possible worlds, denoted by Ψ, is

$$\Psi = \{D' \cup \{i\} | i \in U \wedge i \notin D'\}$$

Notice that exactly one of the worlds in Ψ is the true database that produced R. When the adversary knows k rows of D, the size of Ψ is $|\Psi| = \binom{|U|-k}{n-k}$. Let $\Psi_{\{i\}}$ and $\Psi^C_{\{i\}}$ denote the set of possible worlds that contains and doesn't contain a data entry i, respectively.

Before seeing the response R, we assume every possible world is equally likely to be D (we discuss relaxing this assumption at the end of Section 4.1.) Once the adversary receives R, for each possible world $\omega \in \Psi$, the adversary computes the probability that ω is the original database D that generated the perturbed response R:

$$Pr[\omega = D | \mathcal{M}_f(D) = R]$$

These probabilities give the adversary an updated belief on each possible world. Among all possible worlds, the one with the highest probability will be the adversary's "best guess". If the mechanism allows the adversary to make a correct guess on the missing data entry i with high confidence, the privacy of the individual corresponding to i is at risk. Therefore, the goal of our privacy mechanism is to bound the probability that the adversary identifies an individual's presence in the database.

[3] As with differential privacy, we assume the adversary does *not* know $U-D$, the individuals not in the dataset, as knowing $U-D$ and D' reveals D and there is no privacy left to protect. Assuming a large universe U, knowledge of a few individuals not in D has little impact, so the assumption that the adversary knows D' is a stronger practical assumption.

3.4 Sensitive Range

To determine the noise needed to hide the impact of any individual, differential identifiability (and differential privacy) use the *sensitivity* of the result to the contribution of any single individual. The greater the variation from the contribution of a single individual, the more noise must be added. Given the query function f, the contribution of an individual can be stated as the change in the range of f due to having that individual in its domain. The formal definition of individual contribution is:

DEFINITION 2 (CONTRIBUTION OF AN INDIVIDUAL). *The contribution of an individual corresponding to i to a query function f, $\mathcal{C}_f(i)$, is defined as:*

$$\mathcal{C}_f(i) = \max_{\omega_1, \omega_2} \|f(\omega_1) - f(\omega_2)\|$$

where $\omega_1 \in \Psi_{\{i\}}$ and $\omega_2 \in \Psi^C_{\{i\}}$.

To capture the largest contribution that can be made by any single individual in the universe, the *sensitive range* is defined as the range of a query function over the domain Ψ. This is the maximum distance over the range of f between two possible worlds, *for any set of possible worlds* (since we don't know which individual the adversary doesn't know.) The maximum contribution is the largest contribution that can be made by a single individual:

DEFINITION 3 (SENSITIVE RANGE $\mathcal{S}(f)$). *The sensitive range of a query function f is the range of f.*

$$\mathcal{S}(f) = \max_{\omega_1, \omega_2 \in \Psi} \|f(\omega_1) - f(\omega_2)\|$$

where Ψ is the set of possible worlds under the prior knowledge $\mathcal{L}$.

Note that $\mathcal{S}(f) = \max_i \mathcal{C}_f(i)$.

3.5 Disclosure Risk

Our goal is to hide identities of data contributors; we measure the adversary's computed probability that any given individual is in the database. This is called *identifiability risk*. In an interactive privacy mechanism, the information to be disclosed is the answer to an aggregate query that does not relate to a specific individual. However, even though published statistics are presented in aggregated form, it is still possible they leak some information about an individual. This is especially true when the database contains an individual whose contribution to the query answer is significantly larger (or smaller) than that of others.

To illustrate, we give an example where the mean $\mathcal{M}$ released by a differentially private mechanism enables the adversary to guess the missing element with high probability. Given $D = \{1, 2, 3, 10\}$ drawn from $U = \{1, 2, 3, 4, 5, 10\}$, the sensitivity of the query function f = mean is $\frac{9}{4}$. Assume the adversary already knows $\{1, 2, 3\} \subset D$. The possible worlds are $\omega_1 = \{1, 2, 3, 4\}$, $\omega_2 = \{1, 2, 3, 5\}$, and $\omega_3 = \{1, 2, 3, 10\}$. Assume that $\epsilon = 2$ and the response $R = 5.041$. The adversary computes the probability $Pr[\mathcal{M}_f(\omega_i){=}R], 1{\le}i{\le}3$ that R came from each distribution, and compares their ratio. $Pr[\mathcal{M}_f(\omega_3){=}5.041] = 0.1762$ is much larger than the other two, $Pr[\mathcal{M}_f(\omega_1){=}5.041] = 0.0464$ and $Pr[\mathcal{M}_f(\omega_2){=}5.041] = 0.0580$. The adversary concludes that the missing element is 10 with confidence $\frac{Pr[\mathcal{M}_f(\omega_3)=R]}{\sum_i Pr[\mathcal{M}_f(\omega_i)=R]} = \frac{0.1762}{0.1762+0.0464+0.0580} = 0.6278$. (For the same R and a smaller value of ϵ the confidence would be lower; see [13].)

4. DIFFERENTIAL IDENTIFIABILITY

Given the above, we can now provide a formal definition that satisfies the problem statement given in Section 3.2.

Definition 4 (ρ-differential identifiability). *Given a query function f, a randomized mechanism $\mathcal{M}$ is said to satisfy ρ-differential identifiability if for all databases D, $\forall D' = D - i^*$, and $\forall i \in U - D'$:*

$$Pr[I(i) \in \mathcal{I}_D | \mathcal{M}_f(D) = R, D'] \le \rho$$

A randomized mechanism $\mathcal{M}$ satisfying the above definition ensures that the identifiability risk of any individual in the universe is less than or equal to ρ. Basically, every possible world becomes indistinguishable within a factor of ρ. The parameter ρ in our work can be interpreted as the degree of indistinguishability between possible worlds, where the possible worlds differ by (any) one individual – providing an upper bound on the confidence that the individual is the difference between the worlds (and thus identifiable.) This differs from the ϵ in differential privacy, which measures the difference in the query result given different possible worlds, not the difference in the likelihood of those worlds.

4.1 Achieving Differential Identifiability

We now show how to calibrate noise to achieve ρ-differential identifiability, given the sensitive range of a query function. As with the mechanism for differential privacy introduced in [6], noise Y is added to every query response, $R = f(D) + Y$, where Y is an i.i.d. random variable drawn from a Laplace distribution.

Let $\Gamma(i)$ be the identifiability risk for the individual $I(i)$. $\Gamma(i)$ represents the degree to which an adversary believes $I(i)$ is in D given $\mathcal{M}_f(D) = R$. An upper bound on $\Gamma(i)$ can be obtained as follows:

$$\Gamma(i) = Pr[I(i) \in \mathcal{I}_D | \mathcal{M}_f(D){=}R, D'] \quad (2)$$

$$= Pr[D{=}D' \cup \{i\} | \mathcal{M}_f(D){=}R, D'] \quad (3)$$

$$= \frac{Pr[D{=}D' \cup \{i\}]}{Pr[\mathcal{M}_f(D){=}R]} \cdot Pr[\mathcal{M}_f(D){=}R | D{=}D' \cup \{i\}] \quad (4)$$

$$= \frac{Pr[D{=}D' \cup \{i\}] \cdot Pr[\mathcal{M}_f(D' \cup \{i\}){=}R]}{\sum_{\omega \in \Psi} Pr[\omega] \cdot Pr[\mathcal{M}_f(\omega){=}R]} \quad (5)$$

$$= \frac{e^{-\frac{|R-f(D)|}{\lambda}}}{e^{-\frac{|R-f(D)|}{\lambda}} + \sum_{\omega \in \Psi, \omega \neq D} e^{-\frac{|R-f(\omega)|}{\lambda}}} \quad (6)$$

$$= \frac{e^{-\frac{|R-f(D)|}{\lambda}}}{e^{-\frac{|R-f(D)|}{\lambda}} + e^{-\frac{|R-f(\omega_{j_1})|}{\lambda}} + \ldots + e^{-\frac{|R-f(\omega_{j_{m-1}})|}{\lambda}}} \quad (7)$$

Dividing numerator and denominator by $e^{-\frac{|R-f(D)|}{\lambda}}$ gives

$$\le \frac{1}{1 + e^{-\frac{|f(D)-f(\omega_{j_1})|}{\lambda}} + \ldots + e^{-\frac{|f(D)-f(\omega_{j_{m-1}})|}{\lambda}}} \quad (8)$$

Since $\forall k, 1 \le k \le m, |f(D) - f(\omega_{i_k})| \le \mathcal{S}(f)$, simple application of triangle inequality yields

$$\le \frac{1}{1+(m-1) \cdot e^{-\frac{\mathcal{S}(f)}{\lambda}}} \quad (9)$$

where $m = |\Psi| = |U| - |D'|$.

Since $(m-1) \cdot \exp(-\frac{\mathcal{S}(f)}{\lambda}) \le (m-1)$, it is trivial to see that the lower bound of Equation (9) is

$$\frac{1}{1+(m-1)} = \frac{1}{m} = \frac{1}{|\Psi|} = \frac{1}{|U| - |D'|}$$

This implies that it is impossible to protect the privacy of individuals in the database with the probability less than an adversary's probability of a correct random guess.

To find λ that ensures $\forall i, \Gamma(i) \le \rho$, it is sufficient to satisfy the following inequality

$$\frac{1}{1+(m-1) \cdot \exp\left(-\frac{\mathcal{S}(f)}{\lambda}\right)} \le \rho \quad (10)$$

$$1+(m-1) \cdot \exp\left(-\frac{\mathcal{S}(f)}{\lambda}\right) \ge \frac{1}{\rho} \quad (11)$$

$$\exp\left(-\frac{\mathcal{S}(f)}{\lambda}\right) \ge \frac{1-\rho}{(m-1)\rho} \quad (12)$$

Since $\rho \le 1$, taking the natural log of both sides yields

$$-\frac{\mathcal{S}(f)}{\lambda} \ge \ln \frac{1-\rho}{(m-1)\rho} \quad (13)$$

$$\frac{\mathcal{S}(f)}{\lambda} \le \ln \frac{(m-1)\rho}{1-\rho} \quad (14)$$

When $\frac{(m-1)\rho}{1-\rho} \le 1$, i.e.,$\rho \le \frac{1}{m}$, (14) can never be satisfied. For $\rho \ge \frac{1}{m}$,

$$\lambda \ge \frac{\mathcal{S}(f)}{\ln \frac{(m-1)\rho}{1-\rho}} \quad (15)$$

The above leads to (and serves as a proof of):

Theorem 1. *For an arbitrary adversary $\mathcal{A}$, if $\lambda = \frac{\mathcal{S}(f)}{\ln \frac{(m-1)\rho}{1-\rho}}$, $\mathcal{M}$ satisfies ρ-differential identifiability where $m = |\Psi|$.*

The construction given assumes that the prior probability of an individual being in D is the same for all individuals. In practice, some individuals may have a higher prior. This may make providing ρ-differential identifiability impossible: If the prior probability $Pr[D = D' \cup \{i\}] > \rho$, then the privacy goal is inherently violated and no privacy mechanism can restore it. For less severe cases, the value for m in Equation (15) can be replaced with $1/\max_\Psi(Pr[D = D' \cup \{i\}])$. This essentially says that the adversary's best guess is no better than the average calculated in Equation (5).

While this seems to require additional knowledge of the capabilities of an adversary, it actually shows that differential privacy does not provide guarantees on individual identifiability. Even if an adversary already has sufficient prior knowledge to identify an individual, differential privacy blindly produces the same (noisy) result as if the adversary had no such prior knowledge. The protection of differential privacy measures only the impact of an individual on the output, not the ability to identify an individual [13], or even the ability to infer data values for an individual [4].

Under the assumption that every possible world is equally likely and the number of possible worlds is known, there is a relationship between our definition and differential privacy. Any ϵ-differentially private mechanism satisfies $\frac{1}{1+(m-1)e^{-\epsilon}}$-differential identifiability. This is easy to see once we apply

Table 2: Possible worlds

Possible world	mean	median
$\omega_1 = \{1,2,3\}$	2	2
$\omega_2 = \{1,3,4\}$	$\frac{8}{3}$	3
$\omega_3 = \{1,3,5\}$	3	3
$\omega_4 = \{1,3,6\}$	$\frac{10}{3}$	3
$\omega_5 = \{1,3,7\}$	$\frac{11}{3}$	3
$\omega_6 = \{1,3,8\}$	4	3
$\omega_7 = \{1,3,9\}$	$\frac{13}{3}$	3
$\omega_8 = \{1,3,10\}$	$\frac{14}{3}$	3

the differential privacy guarantee ,$\forall j, Pr[\mathcal{M}_f(\omega_j) = R] \geq e^{-\epsilon} Pr[\mathcal{M}_f(D) = R]$, to Equation (6). Alternatively, $\epsilon \leq \ln \frac{(m-1)\rho}{1-\rho}$. This provides an upper bound on ϵ for the given ρ, not an optimal value. Note that even setting this upper bound for ϵ requires knowing the number of possible worlds m, making it difficult to develop a policy for a value of ϵ to prevent re-identification.

Since the upper bound on the identifiability risk is computed by approximating the distances between the original database and other possible worlds, $|f(D) - f(\omega_k)|$, with $\mathcal{S}(f)$, the calibrated noise could be greater than what is actually required. For example, assume $U = \{1, 2, \cdots, 10\}$, $D = \{1, 2, 3\}$, and the subset of D known to the adversary is $D' = \{1, 3\}$. Since the adversary already knows 1 and 3 belong to D and only needs to determine the membership of one missing element, the possible worlds generated by the adversary would be Table 2. Given the query function $f_{mean}(X)$ returning the mean of elements in X, the sensitive range is:

$$\mathcal{S}(f_{mean}) = \left|\frac{14}{3} - 2\right| = \frac{8}{3}$$

Assuming that the privacy goal is to ensure that the probability of identifying any individual in the database is no greater than $\frac{1}{3}$ (i.e., $\rho = \frac{1}{3}$),

$$\lambda = \frac{\frac{8}{3}}{\ln \frac{7 \cdot \frac{1}{3}}{1-\frac{1}{3}}} = \frac{\frac{8}{3}}{\ln \frac{7}{2}} = \frac{8}{3 \ln \frac{7}{2}}$$

Assume the response to the adversary $R = 2$. This is the worst case, as it maximizes the distance between the expectation that $\omega_1 = D$ and other possible worlds. Given $\lambda = \frac{8}{3 \ln \frac{7}{2}}$ and $R = 2$, the identifiability risk for $I(2)$ is

$$\Gamma(2) = \frac{\exp\left(-\frac{|R-f(\omega_1)|}{\lambda}\right)}{\sum_{k=1}^{8} \exp\left(-\frac{|R-f(\omega_k)|}{\lambda}\right)} = 0.2294 < \frac{1}{3}.$$

The actual identifiability risk is less than the threshold ρ, thus it is possible to choose noise from a tighter distribution while still satisfying the privacy constraint. Figure 1(a) shows the change of identifiability risk by varying ρ. However, the bound is tight for some function f. Consider the case where the query function is median. Notice that the median of every possible world is 3 except $\omega_1 = D$. In this case, the sensitive range is $\mathcal{S}(f_{median}) = |3 - 2| = 1$ and $|f(D) - f(\omega_k)| = \mathcal{S}(f)$ for $2 \leq k \leq 8$. Therefore, Equation (15) holds with equality. In other words, the amount of noise computed by the upper bound is the amount actually required. Figure 1(b) shows the tightness of the bound.

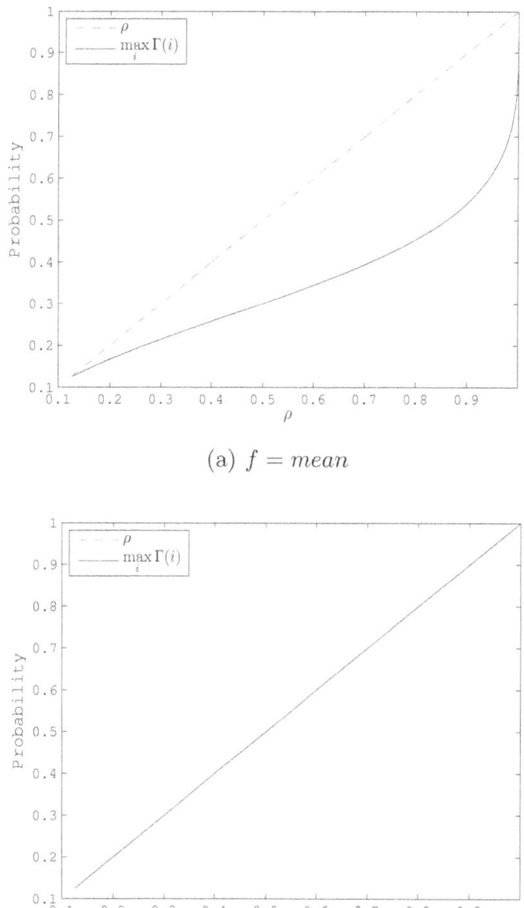

(a) $f = mean$

(b) $f = median$

Figure 1: Change of $\Gamma(i)$ by varying ρ

THEOREM 2. *The upper bound on the identifiability risk, $\Gamma(i)$, is tight, that is there exists a case where the bound holds with equality.*

PROOF. The conditions under which Equation (8) and (9) hold with equality are

1. $R \geq f(D) \geq f(\omega_i) \vee R \leq f(D) \leq f(\omega_i)$ and
2. $\forall \omega, \omega \neq D, |f(D) - f(\omega)| = \mathcal{S}(f)$

respectively. Consider the case where the size of database to publish is one less than that of universe (i.e., $|D| = |U| - 1$). In this case, there exists only two possible worlds, namely ω_1 and ω_2. Without loss of generality, assume $f(\omega_1) < f(\omega_2)$. If $\omega_1 = D$, $Pr[R \leq f(D)] = \frac{1}{2}$. If $\omega_2 = D$, $Pr[R \geq f(D)] = \frac{1}{2}$. Clearly there always exists an R that satisfies the first condition. According to the definition of sensitive range, $\mathcal{S}(f) = |f(\omega_1) - f(\omega_2)|$. Hence, the second condition is always satisfied. Therefore, for any function f, there exists a case that satisfies both conditions at the same time. □

5. EXAMPLE

We now look at practical applicability of differential identifiability. Due to space constraints, we only show the case

Table 3: Description of Adult database

Attribute	Max.	Min.
age(AG)	90	17
education-num(EN)	16	1
capital-gain(CG)	99999	0
capital-loss(CL)	4356	0
hours-per-week(HW)	99	1

where f is a simple aggregate query. This mechanism can be applied to more complex queries (such as a data mining model) in the same manner as the Laplace noise mechanism for differential privacy.

We use the Adult Database from the UCI Machine Learning Repository [9], comprised of 48,842 individuals from the 1994 U.S. Census, as our example database. This database contains 9 categorical and 5 numerical attributes. Only the numerical attributes (shown in Table 3) are used in this example. Since the example is census data, we assume the universe is all US residents. Assume we wish to release the ρ-differentially identifiable mean of hours-per-week. Let DB denote the example database, $D = \Pi_{hours-per-week}(DB)$ (Π is relational projection), and D' be the database obtained by removing an element from D. We assume that the maximum and minimum hours-per-week in the universe are 99 and 1, respectively. This is a reasonable assumption, since Census data typically uses top and bottom-coding to prevent rare values from being identifiable (clearly, [0, 168] could also be used as bounds.)

To determine the noise distribution, we must calculate $\mathcal{S}(f)$. Assume the adversary knows hours-per-week of every individual except one (i.e., the adversary has D'). The possible worlds the adversary would generate are $\omega_1 = D' \cup \{1\}, \omega_2 = D' \cup \{2\}, \cdots, \omega_{99} = D' \cup \{99\}$. Thus, the sensitive range $\mathcal{S}(f) = |f(\omega_{99}) - f(\omega_1)| = \frac{98}{48842} \approx 0.0020$. For $\rho = \frac{1}{10}$, this gives

$$\lambda = \frac{\mathcal{S}(f)}{\ln \frac{(m-1)\rho}{1-\rho}} = \frac{\frac{98}{48842}}{\ln \frac{98\times 0.1}{1-0.1}} = \frac{49}{24421 \cdot \ln \frac{98}{9}} \approx 8.4032 \times 10^{-4}$$

Table 4 shows the parameters and three responses for both mean and median of each of the three attributes for $\rho = 0.1$ and 0.001. (This is assuming the adversary sees only a single one of these responses, returning all would require sharing the "privacy budget" as with differential privacy.) Notice that when $\rho = 0.001$, the amount of noise required to enforce $\Gamma(i) \leq \rho$ for the attributes age, education-num and hours-per-week becomes infinite; the released statistics are essentially random noise and do not give any information about individuals in the database. This is because a random guess that D contains an individual with (say) 12 years of education is almost certainly correct.

To demonstrate the reliability of results from differential identifiability, Figure 2 shows the results of 1000 queries for mean as ρ is varied. This illustrates how often a querier would be seriously misled by the differentially identifiable result. The vertical axis gives the noise ratio:

$$\text{Noise ratio (NR)} = \frac{R - f(D)}{U_{range}}$$

where R is a response and $U_{range}(= U_{max} - U_{min})$ is the range of the domain. Note that the scale is $\times 10^{-3}$, so except for the rightmost trial on each plot, all the responses are close to the true answer. The band and cross near the middle represent the median and mean of responses, respectively. The boxplot is omitted when the magnitude of noise added to the response is typically greater than any possible value in the domain (i.e., $NR > 1$). From the figure, it is clear that the smaller the value of ρ (i.e., the higher the desired privacy), the more noise is required, responses become less useful. When the value of ρ is close to the probability of a random guess being correct, the mean and median of responses are not in range even with 1000 trials. Note that for everything except years of education, answers for $\rho = 1.5\%$ are highly likely to be close to the true answer.

Figure 3 shows the same information for differential privacy as the value of ϵ varies. (Only Capital-gain and Capital-loss are shown due to space constraints; the other figures are similar.) Note the similarity of the figures; it is clear that ϵ-differential privacy and ρ-differential identifiability are comparable in terms of privacy. However, setting ϵ to achieve this privacy is not an easy problem. While the plots appear similar, the scale of ϵ is very different across the two plots. Interpretation of the semantics of epsilon with respect to re-identification is very difficult.

The effect of database size on the noise needed is shown in Figure 4. For this experiment, two databases of different sizes (1000 and 10,000) are constructed by randomly sampling from the original dataset. The red (left) column of each pair shows the noise ratio for the database of size 1000; the right (blue) is for the database of size 10,000. (The ρ values for each pair are the same.) We see that, for $f = mean$, the noise needed shrinks with the size of the dataset. However, for $f = sum$, the noise is independent of dataset size. This is because the change in a sum based on one individual is the same regardless of the number of individuals, whereas for mean the impact shrinks with the number of individuals. Thus for mean it becomes harder to identify an individual from the released statistics as the database grows.

6. CONCLUSION

Differential identifiability (as with differential privacy) can often be satisfied with little impact on the resulting model. Data mining models should not be too dependent on a single individual; this would suggest that the model would not generalize well to unseen data. In addition to the general Laplace noise addition method of [7], several specialized techniques have already been developed for differentially private data mining [2,10,16,23]. We have shown that the general Laplace noise addition approach can be used to satisfy differential identifiability; we expect that analogous methods to other differentially private mechanisms can be developed to support differential identifiability as well.

7. REFERENCES

[1] C. C. Aggarwal and P. S. Yu, Eds., *Privacy-Preserving Data Mining: Models and Algorithms*, ser. Advances in Database Systems. Springer, 2008, vol. 34.

[2] R. Bhaskar, S. Laxman, A. Smith, and A. Thakurta, "Discovering frequent patterns in sensitive data," in *Proceedings of the 16th ACM SIGKDD international conference on Knowledge discovery and data mining (KDD'10)*. New York, NY, USA: ACM, 2010, pp. 503–512. http://doi.acm.org/10.1145/1835804.1835869

[3] K. Chaudhuri and C. Monteleoni, "Privacy-preserving logistic regression," in *Proceeding of the 22nd Annual*

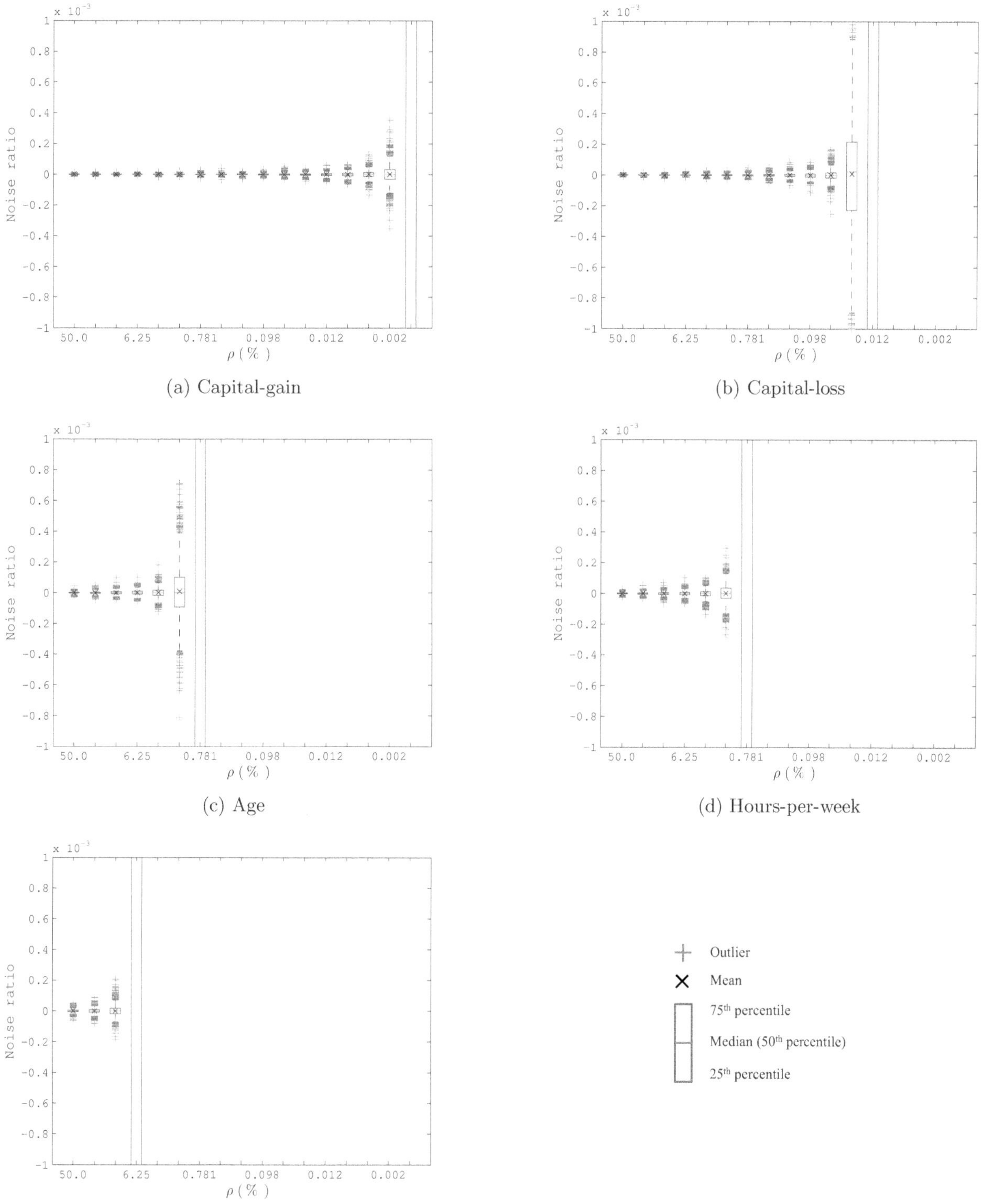

(a) Capital-gain

(b) Capital-loss

(c) Age

(d) Hours-per-week

(e) Education Number

(f) Legend

Figure 2: Noise Ratio

Table 4: Example of Three Query Responses for Mean and Standard Deviation

f	Attr.	$\mathcal{S}(f)$	$f(D)$	$\rho = 0.1$				$\rho = 0.001$			
				λ	R_1	R_2	R_3	λ	R_1	R_2	R_3
Mean	AG	0.0015	38.6435	0.0007	38.6431	38.6438	38.6438	∞	6410.178	36984.106	-20388.622
	EN	0.0003	10.0780	0.0006	10.0784	10.0776	10.0780	∞	276944.55	6481.767	-43022.968
	CG	2.0474	1079.067	0.2198	1079.027	1079.320	1079.308	0.4445	1080.4969	1078.2953	1079.1254
	CL	0.0892	87.5023	0.0144	87.5077	87.5179	87.5050	0.0606	87.4522	87.5130	87.4442
	HW	0.0020	40.4223	0.0008	40.4207	40.4204	40.4224	∞	3717.595	218292.256	32256.161
Std. Dev.	AG	0.0019	13.7105	0.0009	13.7114	13.7120	13.7093	∞	66620	-24260	37263.7
	EN	0.0251	2.5709	0.0491	2.5970	2.4357	2.5419	∞	-594100	445487	371312
	CG	26.8833	7452.019	2.8858	7454.0	7450.1	7452.1	5.8364	7458.7	7448.1	7457.8
	CL	0.4623	403.0045	0.0748	402.9782	403.0856	403.0185	0.3139	402.4125	402.3056	403.0245
	HW	0.0056	12.3914	0.0023	12.3937	12.3952	12.3882	∞	-115431	283352	245743

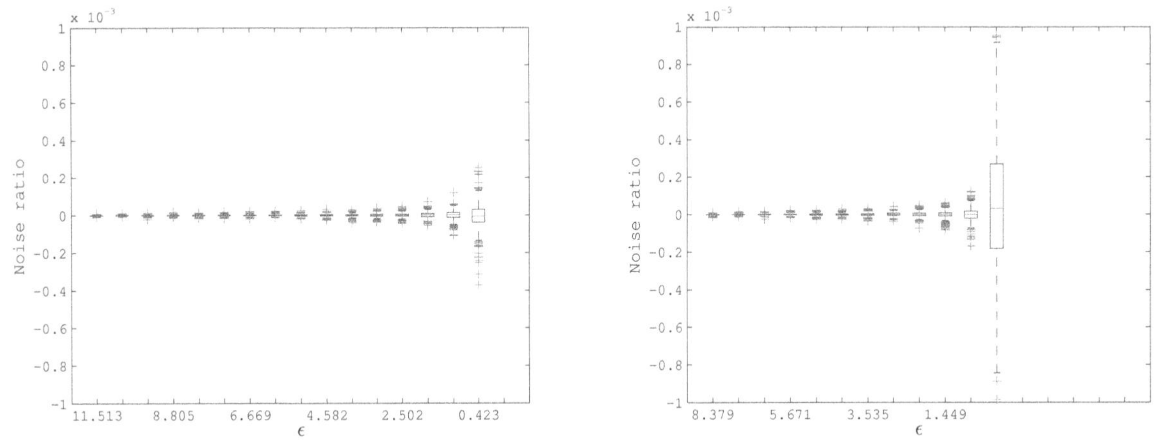

(a) Capital-gain (b) Capital-loss

Figure 3: Noise Ratio for Differential Privacy

Conference on Neural Information Processing Systems (NIPS), 2008, pp. 289–296.

[4] G. Cormode, "Personal privacy vs population privacy: learning to attack anonymization," in *Proceedings of the 17th ACM SIGKDD international conference on Knowledge discovery and data mining (KDD'11)*. New York, NY, USA: ACM, 2011, pp. 1253–1261. http://doi.acm.org/10.1145/2020408.2020598

[5] B. Ding, M. Winslett, J. Han, and Z. Li, "Differentially private data cubes: optimizing noise sources and consistency," in *Proceedings of the 2011 international conference on Management of data (SIGMOD'11)*. New York, NY, USA: ACM, 2011, pp. 217–228. http://doi.acm.org/10.1145/1989323.1989347

[6] C. Dwork, F. McSherry, K. Nissim, and A. Smith, "Calibrating noise to sensitivity in private data analysis," in *Proc. of the 3rd Theory of Cryptography Conference*. Springer, 2006, pp. 265–284.

[7] C. Dwork, "Differential privacy," in *33rd International Colloquium on Automata, Languages and Programming (ICALP 2006)*, Venice, Italy, Jul. 9-16 2006, pp. 1–12. http://dx.doi.org/10.1007/11787006_1

[8] "Directive 95/46/EC of the European Parliament and of the Council of 24 October 1995 on the protection of individuals with regard to the processing of personal data and on the free movement of such data," *Official Journal of the European Communities*, vol. No I., no. 281, pp. 31–50, Oct. 24 1995. http://ec.europa.eu/justice_home/fsj/privacy/law/index_en.htm

[9] A. Frank and A. Asuncion, "UCI machine learning repository," 2010. http://archive.ics.uci.edu/ml

[10] A. Friedman and A. Schuster, "Data mining with differential privacy," in *Proceedings of the 16th ACM SIGKDD international conference on Knowledge discovery and data mining (KDD'11)*. New York, NY, USA: ACM, 2010, pp. 493–502. http://doi.acm.org/10.1145/1835804.1835868

[11] "Standard for privacy of individually identifiable health information," *Federal Register*, vol. 67, no. 157, pp. 53 181–53 273, Aug. 14 2002. http://www.hhs.gov/ocr/privacy/hipaa/administrative/privacyrule/index.h%tml

[12] D. Kifer and A. Machanavajjhala, "No free lunch in data privacy," in *Proceedings of the 2011 Intl. Conf. on Management of data*. 2011, pp. 193–204.

[13] J. Lee and C. Clifton, "How much is enough? choosing ϵ for differential privacy," in *Information Security*, ser. Lecture Notes in Computer Science, X. Lai, J. Zhou, and H. Li, Eds. Springer Berlin / Heidelberg, 2011, vol. 7001, pp. 325–340.

[14] A. Machanavajjhala, D. Kifer, J. Gehrke, and M. Venkitasubramaniam, "l-diversity: Privacy beyond

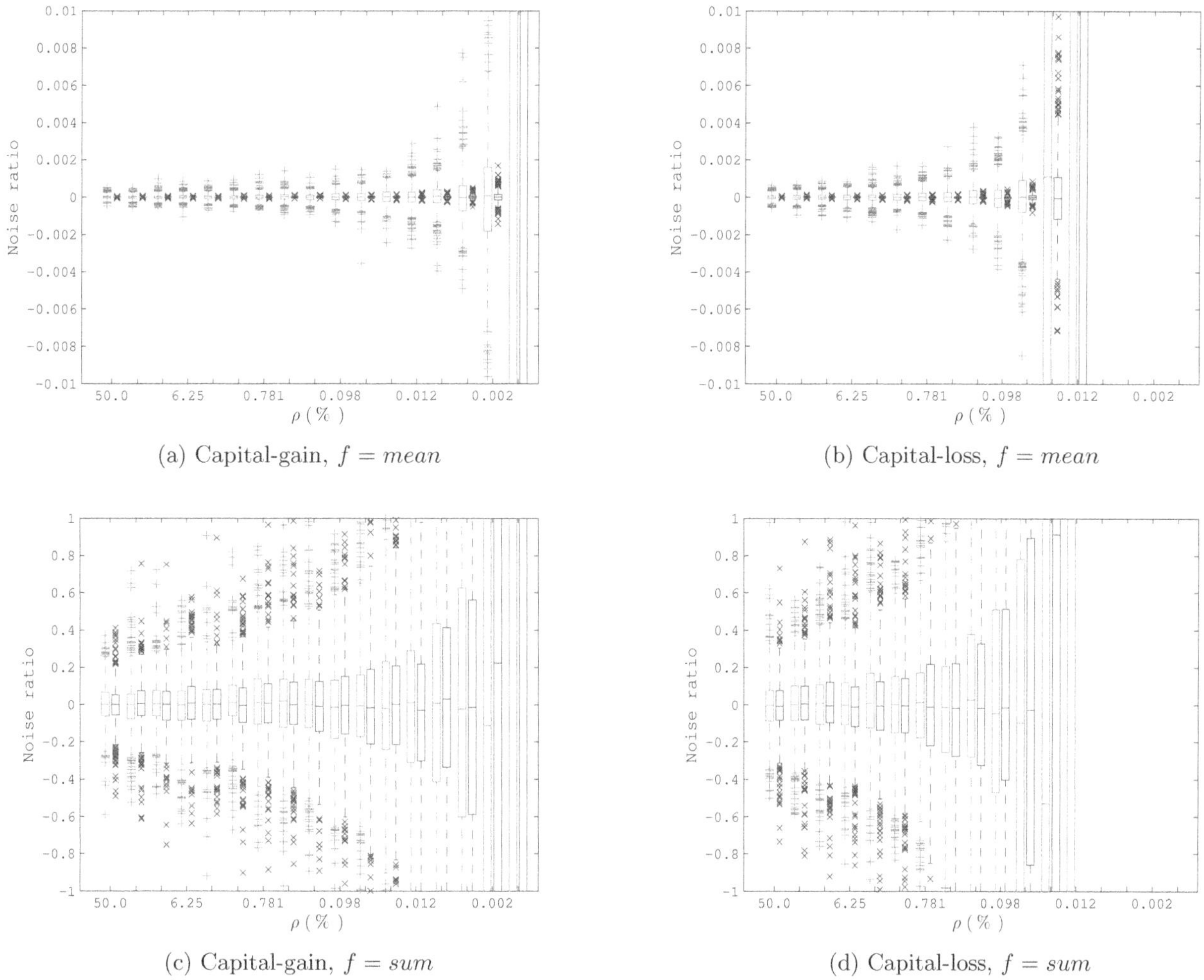

(a) Capital-gain, $f = mean$

(b) Capital-loss, $f = mean$

(c) Capital-gain, $f = sum$

(d) Capital-loss, $f = sum$

Figure 4: Noise Ratio with small (1000) and large (10,000) item databases

k-anonymity," *ACM Trans. on Knowledge Discovery from Data (TKDD)*, vol. 1, no. 1, pp. 3–es, 2007.

[15] F. McSherry, "Privacy integrated queries: an extensible platform for privacy-preserving data analysis," *Commun. ACM*, vol. 53, pp. 89–97, Sep. 2010. http://doi.acm.org/10.1145/1810891.1810916

[16] F. McSherry and I. Mironov, "Differentially-private recommender systems: Building privacy into the netflix prize contenders," in *Proceedings of the 15th ACM SIGKDD International Conference on Knowledge Discovery and Data Mining*, Paris, France, Jun. 28-Jul. 1 2009.

[17] N. Mohammed, R. Chen, B. C. Fung, and P. S. Yu, "Differentially private data release for data mining," in *Proceedings of the 17th ACM SIGKDD international conference on Knowledge discovery and data mining (KDD'11)*. ACM, 2011, pp. 493–501. http://doi.acm.org/10.1145/2020408.2020487

[18] M. E. Nergiz, M. Atzori, and C. Clifton, "Hiding the presence of individuals from shared databases," in *Proceedings of the 2007 ACM SIGMOD international conference on Management of data*. 2007, pp. 665–676. http://doi.acm.org/10.1145/1247480.1247554

[19] P. Samarati, "Protecting respondents' identities in microdata release," *IEEE Trans. on Knowl. and Data Eng.*, vol. 13, pp. 1010–1027, Nov. 2001. http://dx.doi.org/10.1109/69.971193

[20] L. Sweeney, "k-anonymity: a model for protecting privacy," *Int. J. Uncertain. Fuzziness Knowl.-Based Syst.*, vol. 10, pp. 557–570, Oct. 2002. http://dl.acm.org/citation.cfm?id=774544.774552

[21] J. Vaidya, C. Clifton, and M. Zhu, *Privacy Preserving Data Mining*, ser. Advances in Information Security. Springer, 2006, vol. 19. http://www.springer.com/computer/database+management+%26+information+retrieval/book/978-0-387-25886-7

[22] X. Xiao, G. Wang, and J. Gehrke, "Differential privacy via wavelet transforms," *IEEE Trans. on Knowledge and Data Engineering*, vol. 23, no. 8, pp. 1200–1214, Aug. 2011.

[23] N. Zhang, M. Li, and W. Lou, "Distributed data mining with differential privacy," in *2011 IEEE International Conference on Communications (ICC)*, Jun. 2011, pp. 1–5.

Anonymizing Set-Valued Data by Nonreciprocal Recoding*

Mingqiang Xue* Panagiotis Karras# Chedy Raïssi◇ Jaideep Vaidya# Kian-Lee Tan*

*National University of Singapore #Rutgers University ◇INRIA, Nancy Grand-Est, France

ABSTRACT

Today there is a strong interest in publishing set-valued data in a privacy-preserving manner. Such data associate individuals to sets of values (e.g., preferences, shopping items, symptoms, query logs). In addition, an individual can be associated with a sensitive label (e.g., marital status, religious or political conviction). Anonymizing such data implies ensuring that an adversary should not be able to (1) identify an individual's record, and (2) infer a sensitive label, if such exists. Existing research on this problem either perturbs the data, publishes them in disjoint groups disassociated from their sensitive labels, or generalizes their values by assuming the availability of a generalization hierarchy. In this paper, we propose a novel alternative. Our publication method also puts data in a generalized form, but does *not* require that published records form disjoint groups and does not assume a hierarchy either; instead, it employs *generalized bitmaps* and recasts data values in a *nonreciprocal* manner; formally, the bipartite graph from original to anonymized records does *not* have to be composed of disjoint complete subgraphs. We configure our schemes to provide popular privacy guarantees while resisting attacks proposed in recent research, and demonstrate experimentally that we gain a clear utility advantage over the previous state of the art.

Categories and Subject Descriptors

H.2.7 [**Database Management**]: Database Administration—*Security, integrity, and protection*; H.2.8 [**Database Management**]: Database applications—*Data mining*; K.4.1 [**Computers and Society**]: Public Policy Issues—*Privacy*

Keywords

privacy, anonymization, set-valued data, nonreciprocal recoding

1. INTRODUCTION

Assume a data vendor wants to publish a data set $\mathcal{D}$ of *set-valued* data, where a record $r_i \in \mathcal{D}$ consists of a set of items, $r_i = \{o_1, \ldots, o_n\}$, drawn from a universe $\mathcal{I}$. Moreover, each record r_i can potentially be associated with a *sensitive label* s_i, denoting a piece of information such as marital status, sexual orientation, political conviction, or income group. Several real-world data sharing problems can be formulated by this model, even when the data does not originally arise in a set-valued form; the set-valued data may describe data originally presented as a bipartite graph matching, e.g., users to preferences, or even relational database data, where each r_i contains a tuple's attribute values.

Publishing such data in their original form, even without identifiers, compromises privacy. Thus, there is a need to transform the data in a way that preserves information while alleviating privacy threats. There are two desiderata: First, a record r_i should not be clearly distinguishable from other records, leading to direct exposure of its subject's identity. Second, a sensitive label, when present, should not be easily associable to a certain individual.

ID	Jogging	Swimming	Tennis	Soccer	Religion
r_1	1	1	0	0	Christian
r_2	0	1	1	0	Christian
r_3	1	1	0	1	Muslim
r_4	0	1	1	1	Buddhist
r_5	1	1	1	0	Buddhist
r_6	1	0	1	1	Muslim

Table 1: Original set-valued data

Table 1 shows an example of set-valued data about the sport preferences and religious affiliation of certain individuals. For each record r_i, a value of 1 at position j indicates that item j is present in r_i, whereas a 0 indicates absence. Each record in Table 1 is uniquely identifiable by its bitmap. Thus, an adversary who is aware of the itemset this bitmap represents can infer an individual's presence in the data and sensitive label. For example, if Alex knows that Barbara likes *only* jogging and swimming, he can identify her record as r_1, and also infer that she is a Christian. We aim to publish the data in a form that prevents such disclosures.

Previous research has noted the importance of transforming set-valued data for privacy-preserving publication [8, 7, 9, 25, 23, 14, 2, 4], but employed transformation operations mostly unsuitable for the nature of the data at hand. Works such as [8, 7, 2] employ *random perturbation*, adding noise to the data. Yet random perturbation provides no information about the extent to which a particular record has been perturbed, and renders *outliers* vulnerable to an adversary with external knowledge [9]. On the other hand, *syntactic* data transformations, such as those in [9, 25, 23, 14, 4], recast the data so that they maintain a consistency to their original form, despite the obfuscation they undergo [17, 3]. Among them, [25] strives for a privacy objective by selectively *suppressing* some items (i.e., withholding them from publication); more refined *generalization* methods are employed in [23, 14, 4], based on the

*Work supported by Singapore's A*STAR grant 1021580037 and a Rutgers Business School Research Resources Committee grant.

assumption that a *generalization hierarchy* is applicable on the data items in $\mathcal{I}$. However, such hierarchies are not always available in practice; for example, in the case where the set-valued data represent query logs, their construction is, by itself, a non-trivial problem [14]. The experimental studies of [23, 14, 4] use ad hoc hierarchies, which are clearly arbitrary. Another suggestion [15] adds and suppresses query log objects so as to render users indistinguishable by a loose measure of user similarity. Last, [9] publishes exact (public) itemsets in groups, along with a separate summary table of (private) sensitive labels for each group. Unfortunately, this *transparent publication* method is vulnerable to attacks by adversaries with background knowledge of some sensitive associations: an adversary who sees the *exact* items in a record can carry out a chain of reasoning leading to an inference of a sensitive label, which would be hindered if these items were obfuscated by generalization [4]. Besides, the publication model of [9] does not provide protection against identity disclosure as generalization does [10].

ID	Jogging	Swimming	Tennis	Soccer	Religion
r_1	1	1	*	*	Christian
r_3	1	1	*	*	Muslim
r_5	1	1	*	*	Buddhist
r_2	*	*	1	*	Christian
r_4	*	*	1	*	Buddhist
r_6	*	*	1	*	Muslim

Table 2: Data anonymized by suppression

A conventional syntactic anonymization method may partition records in distinct groups, where all records in a group are interchangeable with each other. Table 2 shows an example along these lines, applied on the data of Table 1. The privacy objective is that, for each original record r_i, there should be (at least) *three* records that may be an obfuscated form of (or *match*) r_i's bitmap, and three different sensitive labels that may be associated to r_i. To achieve this objective, one can suppress some bit values, so that it is not disclosed whether the item in question is present or not, and form two distinct groups, with records in the same group having indistinguishable bitmaps and different sensitive labels. Yet even in this simple example, a significant number of suppressions is required to achieve the desired privacy, compromising the utility of the data.

However, it is *not* necessary that privacy be achieved via the formation of distinct groups, as above, while the obfuscation mechanism does *not* have to be suppression (or generalization along an arbitrary hierarchy) either. In this paper, we propose an alternative model. Our scheme ensures that each original record *matches* a group of generalized records, yet this effect is *not* brought about by creating groups of records recast so as to be identical to each other; instead, original records match anonymized ones in a *nonreciprocal* manner: when an original record s matches the anonymized form t' of another record t, then *it is not necessary* that t also matches s'. We recast each record's bitmap r_i by only altering some of its bits (i.e., adding or deleting items), and publish a *base bitmap* r'_i along with a *distance bitmap* d_i, and an *edit-distance threshold* t_i. In order to detect pairs of records of small Hamming distance, which can be easily recast so as to match each other, we employ the *Gray order* of bitmaps, enhanced by applying an approximation algorithm for the Traveling Salesman Problem (TSP).

Table 3 shows a way of publishing the data of Table 1 by our method that achieves the same privacy as the publication in Table 2, but much higher utility. For each original record r_i, the table shows its anonymized bitmap r'_i, a sensitive label, a distance bitmap d_i that indicates the positions where an error may occur in r'_i, and an edit-distance threshold t_i that indicates the maximum possible number of errors among the positions indicated in d_i.

For example, the distance bitmap for r'_5 is 0011, denoting that an

ID	Jogging	Swimming	Tennis	Soccer	Religion	d_i	t_i
r'_1	1	1	0	1	Christian	1 0 1 1	2 bits
r'_2	1	1	1	0	Christian	1 1 0 1	2 bits
r'_3	0	1	1	1	Muslim	1 0 1 1	2 bits
r'_4	0	1	1	1	Buddhist	1 1 0 1	2 bits
r'_5	1	1	0	0	Buddhist	0 0 1 1	1 bit
r'_6	1	1	1	0	Muslim	0 1 1 1	2 bits

Table 3: Data anonymized by our method

original record r represented by r'_5 *may* differ from it at the 3rd or 4th bit. The error threshold indicates that r may only differ from r'_5 by at most 1 bit, which reduces our options to *either* the 3rd bit, or the 4th, or none. Thus, three *possible worlds* [5] are defined, as r may be either 1100, or 1110, or 1101. In the first case, r is r_1, in the second case it is r_5, and in the third case it is r_3. We emphasize that *some* possible worlds might not correspond to any real record, yet *all* real records that have to match an anonymized one by our scheme are always found among the possible worlds.

Original	Matches	Anonymized	Matches
r_1	r'_1, r'_5, r'_6	r'_1	r_1, r_3, r_4
r_2	r'_2, r'_3, r'_4	r'_2	r_2, r_5, r_6
r_3	r'_1, r'_3, r'_5	r'_3	r_2, r_3, r_4
r_4	r'_1, r'_3, r'_4	r'_4	r_2, r_4, r_6
r_5	r'_2, r'_5, r'_6	r'_5	r_1, r_3, r_5
r_6	r'_2, r'_4, r'_6	r'_6	r_1, r_5, r_6

Table 4: Original/anonymized data correspondence

Table 4 shows the correspondence between original and anonymized records, i.e., the anonymized records in Table 3 that each original record in Table 1 is *compatible* with, and vice versa. As each anonymized record matches three original records, and *vice versa*, a privacy guarantee of 3-*anonymity* is achieved [20].

2. BACKGROUND AND RELATED WORK

Our work draws from two sources. The former involves the privacy-preserving sharing of set-valued data in general, while the latter is about the transformation by nonreciprocal recoding.

2.1 Anonymizing Set-valued Data

Research on preserving privacy in set-valued data has recently focused on transforming the data in a way that provides a generic privacy guarantee. The pioneering work in the field [11] transforms the data into a band matrix by permutating rows and columns in the original table, and forms anonymized groups on this matrix, offering the privacy guarantee that the probability of associating a record with a particular sensitive label does not exceed a threshold $\frac{1}{p}$. This method is augmented by two more approaches in [9]. The best performer in terms of both data utility and execution time is a scheme that interprets itemsets as Gray codes and sorts them by their Gray-code rank, so that consecutive records have low Hamming distance, facilitating group formation. Still, the publication model of [11, 9] publishes *exact* public items together with a summary of the frequencies of sensitive labels per group; this transparency renders it vulnerable to attacks by adversaries who are already aware of some associations and wish to infer others [4].

Another alternative [25] opts to selectively *suppress* some items, and ensures that an adversary can link an individual to (none, or) at least k records, with at most $h\%$ thereof sharing the same sensitive label; the h parameter is thus equivalent to $\frac{1}{p}$ in [11, 9]. However, in contrast to [11, 9], [25] assumes that an adversary's knowledge is limited to at most p items in a record. Besides, the suppression technique of [25] results in high information loss [4, 23].

More recently, [23, 14, 4] use hierarchy-based generalization to anonymize set-valued data, and provide privacy guarantees against an adversary's capacity to link an individual to a small number of records [23, 14], or to confidently infer any sensitive item among the items in a record themselves [4]. However, a generalization hierarchy is not always applicable and/or available, and its construction is by itself a non-trivial problem [14]. In their experimental studies, [23, 14, 4] construct synthetic hierarchies. Under such a synthetic hierarchy, [14] applies its proposal on the anonymization of query logs. On the other hand, [15] anonymizes query logs, without assuming a generalization hierarchy over query objects; users are rendered indistinguishable according to a loose similarity measure, by adding and suppressing query objects.

All methods discussed above use *syntactic* transformations. Another line of research uses *random perturbation* to anonymize data [6, 21, 8, 7, 19, 2]. However, perturbation techniques can expose the privacy of *outliers* in a way that syntactic methods do not [9]. The sketch-based method of [1] tries to avoid such drawbacks, providing a guarantee that renders records hardly distinguishable from their k nearest neighbors. However, as it may not always be possible to satisfy this privacy condition, [1] resorts to suppressing outliers. Besides, perturbation-based transformations provide no information on how much a given record has been perturbed; in other words, they render data in an *inaccurate* form, hence limit the purposes they can be useful for [17]. On the other hand, syntactic transformations hamper the data's *precision*, but not its *accuracy*.

2.2 Nonreciprocal Recoding

As discussed, a syntactic transformation recasts the data by a still accurate representation, albeit imprecise and coarse, with an explicit margin of error. Past research [25, 11, 9, 23, 14] applied syntactic transformations under the premise that, for any two records s, t, if s is recoded so as to match t, then t should also be recoded so as to match s. This premise alone leads to *reciprocal recoding*. Past research has also assumed that the published records need to form disjoint groups, so that (the public parts of) *all* records in the same group are recoded so as to mutually match each other.

Nevertheless, this *reciprocity* assumption is not required by a privacy condition; it is redundant. This redundancy was noted by [3], observing that "there is no privacy reason" therefor. Contemporaneously, [12] revisited this question in the context of microdata anonymization, and noted that dropping the reciprocity assumption allows for improved data utility; the model of global $(1, k)$-anonymity [12] guarantees, by nonreciprocal recoding, that an individual is associated with at least k recoded records, as the popular k-anonymity model conventionally does using reciprocal recoding. Later, [24] observed that the techniques of [12] do not ensure that each such association is equiprobable, and provided a nonreciprocal-recoding algorithm that guarantees k associations of probability $\frac{1}{k}$, using randomization.

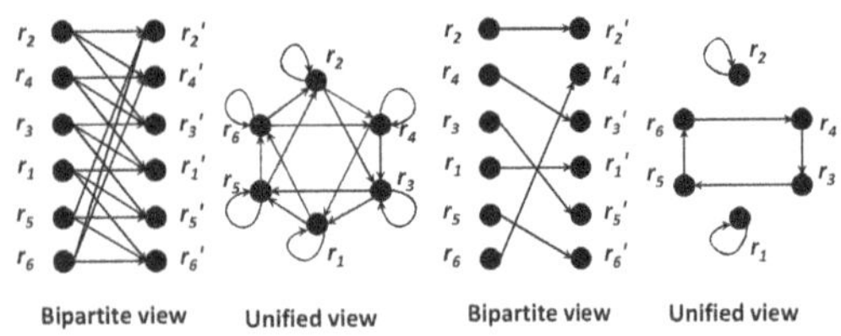

(a) Generalization graph (b) Sample assignment

Figure 1: Nonreciprocal recoding in graph view

We illustrate nonreciprocal recoding with two kinds of directed graphs. A *generalization graph* shows how the values of original records match those of anonymized records. A directed edge (r_i, r'_j) in a generalization graph indicates that the anonymized record r'_j should include original record r_i among its possible worlds. Figure 1(a) shows the generalization graph for the example in the previous section. We present two views of this graph: a *bipartite* view, as well as as a *unified* view where a single node represents both the original record r_i and the anonymized record r'_i. For instance the fact that r'_1 matches r_1, r_3, and r_4 is represented by the edges (r_1, r'_1), (r_3, r'_1) and (r_4, r'_1), respectively.

The privacy principle of k-anonymity [20] requires that each original record r_i have *at least k equally probable* matches among anonymized records R'. Under the conventional reciprocity assumption, this property is easily satisfied by forming groups of k records mutually matching each other within each group. However, when we drop the reciprocity assumption, we need to spell out the requirements for k-anonymity to be satisfied. It has been shown by [12, 24] that, to achieve k-anonymity by nonreciprocal recoding, it suffices to ensure that each original record r_i has exactly k matches in R' (i.e., k outgoing edges in the generalization graph), and each anonymized record r'_i also has exactly k matches in R (i.e., incoming edges); of course the same effect can be achieved with any $k' > k$, but then k'-anonymity is attained. In other words, it suffices to ensure that the data's generalization graph is *k-regular*. From such a graph we can generate k disjoint assignments [24]. The generalization graph in Figure 1(a) is 3-regular, hence ensures 3-anonymity. In order to create a k-regular generalization graph, [24] suggests the method of *ring generalization*: given k, a generalization graph is constructed as a ring, linking each of n records, r_i, to itself and its $k-1$ successors by a given cyclical order. The generalization graph in Figure 1(a) is a ring generalization graph for the order $\{r_2, r_4, r_3, r_1, r_5, r_6\}$.

On the other hand, an *assignment graph* shows a particular one-to-one correspondence between original and anonymized records (i.e., an assignment); it provides the assumed identities of anonymized records, and may be used as a guide when assigning non-generalized attributes (e.g., sensitive labels) to them. An assignment graph is a subset of the generalization graph. Figure 1(b) shows a possible assignment for our example in bipartite and unified view. To satisfy the equal probability requirement of k-anonymity, we should ensure that each edge in a generalization graph is equally likely to participate in a chosen assignment. This result can be achieved by selecting one of k disjoint assignments uniformly at random. Furthermore, in order to resist attacks based on knowledge of some anonymized tuples' identities and/or of the algorithm itself, the set of k disjoint assignments to choose from is generated by a randomization scheme [24]. Each assignment is generated by iteratively extracting cycles from the generalization graph (in unified view) via random walks, until all records are covered. We illustrate a simple example of this process in Figure 2.

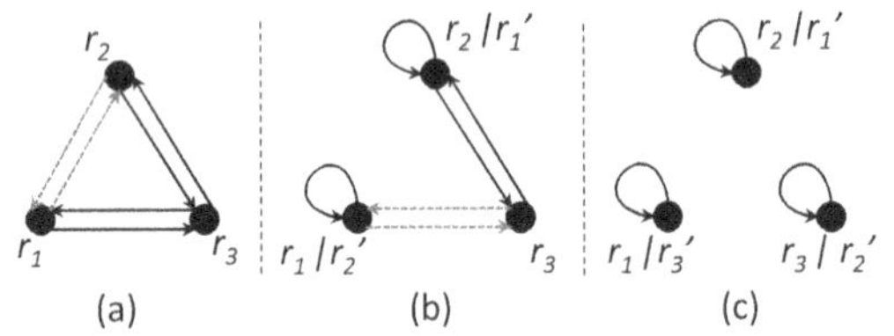

Figure 2: Iterative cycle extraction

Figure 2(a) depicts a 2-regular generalization graph for a data set of 3 records, and the first step of the process, which extracts the cycle $r_1 \rightarrow r_2 \rightarrow r_1$ by random walk. Then, the graph is updated to reflect the matching choices made so far. The node that originally stood for r_1 (and r'_1) now stands for r_1 and its match, r'_2, while the node that stood for r_2 (and r'_2) now stands for r_2 and r'_1; thus, the two chosen matches now appear as self-loops (Figure 2(b)). We can now proceed to extract another cycle, potentially destroying some of the previously selected matches (i.e., de-selecting the self-loops of those nodes as matches of our choice) in case the new cycle passes through the same nodes, yet without ever reducing the number of matched nodes; some matches may be replaced by others, but no previously matched node is left orphan. Such a new cycle, namely $r_3 \rightarrow r_1/r'_2 \rightarrow r_3$, is shown in Figure 2(b). This cycle replaces the match of r_1 to r'_3, while it matches r_3 to r'_2 instead. With these new matches our task is completed, as all records in the generalization graph have been covered. Figure 2(c) shows the chosen *assignment graph*, composed of self-loop singletons.

Unfortunately, the time complexity of the randomization-based scheme in [24] is $O(kn^2)$. Noting this complexity, [24] suggests that this scheme be applied *on top* of a partitioning scheme, so as to improve the utility within each partition. We aim to provide a general-purpose anonymization scheme by nonreciprocal recoding that can be applied on a full set-valued data set (or any data set amenable to bitmap representation) and achieve high data utility.

3. DEFINITIONS AND PRINCIPLES

We consider a set-valued dataset $\mathcal{D} = (R, S)$ of n records. $R = \{r_1, \ldots, r_n\}$, where r_i is the non-sensitive part of record i and $S = \{s_1, \ldots, s_n\}$ is a set of sensitive labels of records, with the sensitive label of record i denoted as s_i. Each r_i is represented as a bitmap of b bits, where b is the cardinality of the universe I a record draws items from. The value of the bit at position j, $r_{i,j}$, denotes the presence or absence of the jth item in I in/from r_i. We aim to obfuscate the non-sensitive parts of records, producing $R' = \{r'_1, \ldots, r'_n\}$, where r'_i is the anonymized version of r_i.

We say that an original record r_i and an obfuscated record r'_j *match* each other when r'_j is possibly an obfuscated from of r_i. We then define the privacy guarantees of k-anonymity [20] and ℓ-diversity [18] in the context of set-valued data as follows:

DEFINITION 1. *An* anonymized *set-valued data set* $\mathcal{D}' = (R', S)$ *satisfies* k-anonymity *with respect to the original data* $\mathcal{D} = (R, S)$ *iff each original record* $r_i \in \mathcal{D}$ *matches at least k published records in* $\mathcal{D}'$, *each having, from an adversary's perspective, equal probability (at most* $\frac{1}{k}$*) to be the* true match *of* r_i. $\mathcal{D}'$ *satisfies* ℓ-diversity *with respect to* $\mathcal{D}$ *iff each* $r_i \in \mathcal{D}$ *matches at least* ℓ *published records, each associated with a different sensitive label* $s \in S$ *and having equal probability (at most* $\frac{1}{\ell}$*) to be the* true match *of* r_i.

These guarantees ensure that an adversary knowing the non-sensitive part of all records, i.e. R, shall not be able to identify the *true match* of a record r_i (and its sensitive value) with probability higher than $\frac{1}{k}$ $(\frac{1}{\ell})$. The twin problems of k-anonymization and ℓ-diversification for set-valued data call for satisfying these guarantees with a low reduction of the utility of the original data:

PROBLEM 1. *Given a data set* $\mathcal{D} = (R, S)$, transform $\mathcal{D}$ *to an anonymized form* $\mathcal{D}'$ *that satisfies k-anonymity* (ℓ*-diversity), maintaining as much of the data utility as possible.*

We describe a collection of matches encompassing a complete set of original and anonymized records as an *assignment*.

DEFINITION 2. *Given a set-valued data set* $\mathcal{D} = (R, S)$ *and an anonymized version thereof,* $\mathcal{D}' = (R', S)$, *an* assignment α *from* $\mathcal{D}$ *to* $\mathcal{D}'$ *is an one-to-one mapping from* $\mathcal{D}$ *to* D', *denoted as* $\alpha = \{(r_{i_1}, r'_{j_1}), \ldots, (r_{i_n}, r'_{j_n})\}$, *such that each* $r_i \in \mathcal{D}$ *is mapped to exactly one* $r'_j \in D'$, *where* r_i matches r'_j. *In each pair* $(r_i, r'_j) \in \alpha$, *we say that* r_i *is the* preimage *of* r'_j *and* r'_j *is the* postimage *of* r_i. *Two assignments* α_p *and* α_q *are* disjoint *if* $\alpha_p \cap \alpha_q = \emptyset$.

In order to achieve k-anonymity, we need to ensure that there exist k disjoint assignments from original records in $\mathcal{D}$ to records in $\mathcal{D}'$. After we have constructed a set of k such desired assignments, we can determine the values of records in $\mathcal{D}'$ therefrom, such that each record $r'_i \in D'$ is indeed compatible to (i.e., matches) the records mapped to it. Last, we can select one of these k assignments as the one that defines the *true matches* between $\mathcal{D}$ and $\mathcal{D}'$ and publish any other attributes of our data accordingly. This reasoning extends to the case of ℓ-diversity, with the additional provision that the ℓ matches assigned to a record r in ℓ different assignments should have different sensitive labels from each other.

A set of m disjoint assignments defines m distinct matches in $\mathcal{D}'$ for each $r_i \in \mathcal{D}$ (i.e., one by each assignment), and *vice versa*, i.e., m distinct matches in $\mathcal{D}$ for each $r'_i \in \mathcal{D}'$. The net result can be represented by means of a *generalization graph* [24].

DEFINITION 3. *Given a set-valued data set* $\mathcal{D} = (R, S)$ *and its anonymized version* $\mathcal{D}' = (R', S)$, *a* generalization graph $G = (V, E)$ *is a directed graph in which each vertex* $v \in V$ *stands for an original/anonymized record* $r_i \in \mathcal{D}$ *and* $r'_i \in \mathcal{D}'$, *and an edge* $(v_i, v_j) \in E$ *is present iff* r_i *matches* r'_j.

Our definition corresponds to the *unified* view of such a graph (see Figure 1(a)). In a *bipartite* view, the vertex standing for an original record r_i is separate from that standing for its anonymized form r'_i. A set of m disjoint assignments defines a generalization graph in which each vertex has exactly m outgoing and m incoming edges, i.e., an m-regular generalization graph. As [24] has shown, the reverse is also true, that is, an m-regular generalization graph effectively defines m disjoint assignments.

In our publication model, we publish the anonymized data $\mathcal{D}' = (R', S)$, while for each anonymized record r'_i we also publish a distance bitmap d_i, which denotes with value 1 the bits where r'_i may differ from any of its matches, and a distance threshold t_i, which upper-bounds the number of different bits between r'_i and its matches, hence t_i does not exceed the number of 1 bits in d_i. Taken together, d_i and t_i compactly define a set of *possible worlds* [5], one of which corresponds to the true match of r'_i.

4. METHODOLOGY

Our overall methodology consists of the following five steps.

First, we order the data records by a cyclical order, the **Gray-TSP order**. The utility achieved by our anonymization scheme depends on the extent to which neighboring records in this order are close to each other by some distance metric, hence limit the afflicted information loss. In order to achieve such an outcome, we start out with the order defined by the Gray code of itemset bitmaps, also used by [9], and *enhance* it further via a local approximate solution to the Traveling Salesman Problem (TSP). For the same purpose [24] uses the order defined by a Hilbert curve in the space of attribute value domains; this approach is unsuitable for the high-dimensional space defined by set-valued data.

Second, we create an m-regular generalization graph, where m is k or ℓ. For k-anonymization, we build such a graph as a ring over the Gray-TSP order. On the other hand, in the case of ℓ-diversification, a ring generalization graph would not satisfy the privacy requirements. Therefore, we propose a **Greedy Assignment Extraction** algorithm, which extracts ℓ disjoint assignments from the dataset's complete graph under a constraint derived from the ℓ-diversity requirement, guided by the Gray-TSP order, and forms an ℓ-regular generalization graph from their union; the greedy character of this process aims to achieve low information loss.

Third, we extract m random disjoint assignments from the generalization graph, employing a *random walk*, as in [24] (see Section 2.2). Yet, in contrast to [24], we do not aim to create *cycles* via the walk, *backtracking* whenever we reach a dead-end. We propose a **Closed Walk** method instead: we allow the followed path to revisit vertices and continue, unobstructed by dead-ends. Thus, we gain a significant efficiency advantage that enables our algorithm to scale and run smoothly over a *full* data set. The random character of this process renders our scheme resistant to adversaries having knowledge of the algorithm [5] or of some anonymized tuples' identities[1] [24]. Besides, this same closed walk is employed for greedy assignment extraction (see above) as well.

Fourth, we pick up one of the extracted k (ℓ) assignments uniformly at random. This assignment defines the putative identity and (when such exists) sensitive label of each anonymized record r'_i. The non-deterministic nature of this step guarantees that each preimage of r'_i has the same probability to be chosen.

Fifth, for each anonymized record, we set its base bitmap r'_i, distance bitmap d_i, and distance threshold t_i, as a function of its m preimages. Let $\mathcal{P}(r'_i)$ be the set of m preimages of r'_i. For the sake of data utility, the values in r'_i should be similar to those of its preimages. To achieve this result, we employ a *bit voting* method: the pth bit of r'_i is set as the most common p^{th} bit value among its preimages (ties are resolved arbitrarily). For example, if $\mathcal{P}(r'_i) = \{1100, 1011, 0101\}$, then r'_i is set to be 1101; while r'_i is not identical to any of its preimages, each one of its bits has the most common value among those in $\mathcal{P}(r'_i)$. Thus, the value of r'_i minimizes the sum of Hamming distances among r'_i and its preimages. We emphasize that there is *no privacy loss* caused by this provision. The match of a record is chosen with equal probability among all the matches in the generalization graph. The bit voting method has no effect on this choice; it only reveals information on what *single items* are frequent in the data, which is the kind of information we wish to give. Next, the value of the pth bit of d_i is set to 0 iff the pth bit is the same among all preimages of r'_i; otherwise it is set to 1, denoting that at least one preimage differs from r'_i in that position. Last, the distance threshold t_i is measured as the maximum Hamming distance among r'_i and its preimages, $t_i = \max\{\mathcal{H}(r'_i, r_j) \forall r_j \in \mathcal{P}(r'_i)\}$. Eventually, d_i and t_i define a set of *possible worlds* that is a superset of $\mathcal{P}(r'_i)$.

We now elaborate on the elements of our approach.

4.1 The Gray-TSP Order

The *Gray code*, or *reflected binary code* [13], is a binary numeral system where two successive values differ in only one bit, i.e. their *Hamming distance* is 1. Table 5 depicts an example of Gray encoding for the decimals from 0 to 7.

Decimal	0	1	2	3	4	5	6	7
Binary	000	001	010	011	100	101	110	111
Gray	000	001	011	010	110	111	101	100

Table 5: An example of Gray coding

An itemset drawing items from a universe $\mathcal{I}$ of b items may take one of 2^b values. A *Gray order* defined over these values, expressed as bitmaps, provides a guide for *sorting* a dataset $\mathcal{D}$ of records drawing items from $\mathcal{I}$. Nevertheless, a typical real-world data set $\mathcal{D}$ contains much fewer records than the 2^b possible records (bitmaps) of size b. In effect, even after the records in $\mathcal{D}$ are sorted by the Gray order of their bitmaps, there will still be large gaps, i.e. large Hamming distances, between consecutive records.

To mitigate this drawback, we use the Gray order only as an initialization step, and then enhance it via a local application of an approximation algorithm for the Traveling Salesman Problem (TSP). In particular, we first sort $\mathcal{D}$ by its Gray order, to obtain a sorted version, $\sigma(\mathcal{D})$. Then we divide $\sigma(\mathcal{D})$ into segments. In each segment S_i, we fix the position of the first and last record, r_f and r_l, and treat each record $r_i \in S_i$ as a node v_i in a complete weighted graph $\mathcal{G}(V, E)$, where each edge $(v_i, v_j) \in E$ is weighted by the Hamming distance among the records corresponding to its incident nodes, $\mathcal{H}(r_i, r_j)$. We aim to locally reorder the internal records in S_i so as to reduce the total sum of Hamming distances among consecutive records. This problem amounts to solving the TSP on $\mathcal{G}$. As the TSP is NP-hard, we apply an efficient genetic algorithm therefor [22], with v_f as origin and v_l as destination.

We divide $\sigma(\mathcal{D})$ into segments so as to avoid applying the TSP algorithm on the full size of the data. We emphasize that our strategy does not aim to acquire the optimal TSP solution, but only to leverage a TSP algorithm in order to improve upon the Gray order. We fix the first and last record in each segment so as to facilitate the transitions among segments, preserving the Hamming distances provided by the Gray order at these breakpoints. Ideally, these breakpoints should be placed at positions where the Hamming distance between consecutive records in the Gray order is small. To achieve this effect, we design a dynamic programming (DP) algorithm that finds appropriate breakpoints. This DP algorithm receives as parameters the minimum and maximum segment size allowed, m and M respectively, and detects the *optimal* way of partitioning $\mathcal{D}$ into segments under these constraints, so that the sum of Hamming distances at breakpoints is minimized. Let $C(i)$ be the minimum sum of Hamming distances for partitioning the first i records in $\sigma(\mathcal{D})$. $C(i)$ is recursively computed as:

$$C(i) = \min_{j \in [i-M, i-m]} \{C(j) + \mathcal{H}(r_j, r_{j+1})\}, \quad C(0) = 0 \quad (1)$$

In Equation 1, the j variable goes through all the allowed positions for the last breakpoint in the examined prefix of $\sigma(\mathcal{D})$, and chooses the best among them. The overall solution is obtained by computing $C(n)$ in $O\big((M-m)n\big) = O(n)$. Eventually, after partitioning $\sigma(\mathcal{D})$ into segments and locally enhancing each of them by TSP, we arrive at a Gray-TSP order of $\mathcal{D}$, denoted as $\phi(R)$.

4.2 The Closed Walk

We now describe our Closed Walk algorithm for assignment extraction. We apply this algorithm in both our k-anonymization and ℓ-diversification algorithms. In the former, we use it only to extract k disjoint assignments from a k-regular ring generalization graph over the Gray-TSP order, using all its $n \times k$ edges and making walk choices in a *random* manner. In the latter, we use it first to extract ℓ assignments from the *complete* directed graph of the data so as to define our ℓ-regular generalization graph of $n \times \ell$ edges, making walk choices in a *greedy* manner and assisted by the Gray-TSP order (see Section 4.4); then, we reapply a *random* closed walk to extract ℓ disjoint assignments from this ℓ-regular graph, so as to render our scheme proof against sophisticated adversaries.

Our algorithm works in m rounds. Each round generates an assignment A_i, disjoint from previously generated ones, by iterative cycle extraction (see Section 2.2); it repetitively starts from a random node, takes a walk to build a cycle along edges that have not been traversed before (neither in previous rounds nor in the current one); when the walk is closed, the graph is updated so as to render all selected edges as self-loops; this process is repeated until all nodes are covered; the final set of selected edges represents the generated assignment; m rounds generate m disjoint assignments.

The algorithm in [24], which we call WMC, obeys the constraint that a node cannot be revisited by the same random walk. Thus, WMC encounters a *dead-end* in situations where there is no avail-

[1]Furthermore, our scheme impedes attacks that calculate the statistical likelihood of possible worlds, such as the deFinetti attack [16]; to launch such an attack, an adversary would have to calculate the likelihood of each possible assignment, and therefor find the number of possible assignments, a #P-complete problem.

able next hop to move to, as it has previously traversed all nodes adjacent to its current position; then it *backtracks* and attempts to correct a previous decision. Such backtracking may occupy most of its running time, manifesting its worst-case $O(kn^2)$ complexity.

In contrast, when our algorithm arrives at a position where all next hops have been visited by the current walk, it *revisits* one of them, say u, anyway; thereby, it creates a *deviant cycle* starting from and ending at u. This deviant cycle is henceforward ignored, and the walk proceeds until it closes by reaching the node it started from. In graph theory terms, while WMC strives to directly build a *cycle*, i.e., a closed walk that does not revisit any vertex, our algorithm takes a plain *closed walk* and simply ignores deviant cycles.

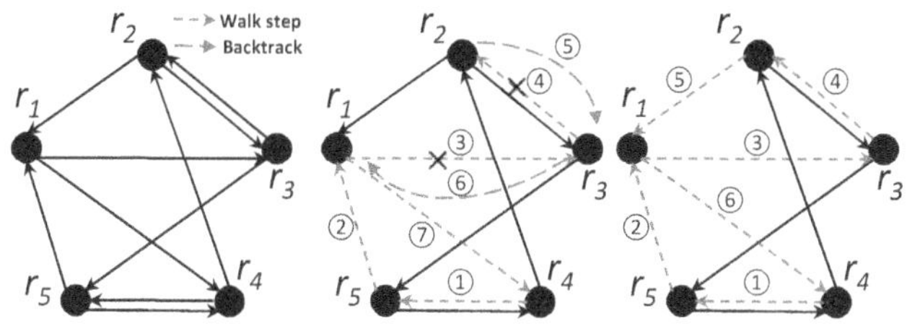

(a) Generalization graph (b) Backtracking (c) Closed-walking

Figure 3: Backtracking vs. Closed-walking

We illustrate the difference between backtracking and closed-walking by extracting a cycle from the 2-regular generalization graph in Figure 3(a). Let the first round start from r_4, and randomly pick its first 4 hops as in Figure 3(b). Then WMC encounters a *dead-end*, as r_1 and r_3, the two adjacent nodes of r_2, are already in the walk; thus, it *backtracks* to r_3 (Step 5). At r_3, there is still no other available next hop, as r_5 has been visited. In effect, WMC backtracks onto r_1 (Step 6), where it eventually selects a legitimate alternative next hop, r_4, and thus completes a cycle (Step 7). Altogether, it takes 7 steps to detect cycle $r_4 \rightarrow r_5 \rightarrow r_1 \rightarrow r_4$.

Figure 3(c) shows how our closed-walk algorithm resolves the same conflict. At Step 5, instead of backtracking, we revisit r_1, thereby creating *deviant cycle* $r_1 \rightarrow r_3 \rightarrow r_2 \rightarrow r_1$. Nodes r_3 and r_2, are duly removed from the cycle. In step 6, we move on to r_4 and close cycle $r_4 \rightarrow r_5 \rightarrow r_1 \rightarrow r_4$, constructed in only 6 steps. The step difference between backtracking and closed-walking can be arbitrarily large; for a deviant cycle of p edges, backtracking may have to perform p extra steps so as to annul the deviation; as we show in Section 5.3, such $O(p)$ differences, accumulated over many deviations, translate to a significant efficiency advantage.

Algorithm 1: Assignment extraction by Closed Walk

Data: The dataset $\phi(R)$ and $\phi(R')$ sorted in Gray-TSP order; The privacy level m; Current round r
Result: An assignment A_r

1 $A_r \leftarrow \{(u_i, u'_i)\}$ where $u_i \in \phi(R)$ and $u'_i \in \phi(R')$;
2 $L \leftarrow R$;
3 **while** $L \neq \emptyset$ **do**
4 $\quad visited \leftarrow$ new empty list;
5 $\quad$ Pick $u_i \in L$ at random;
6 $\quad u'_j \leftarrow$ Pick($u_i, \phi(R), \phi(R'), visited$);
7 $\quad$ add (u_i, u'_j) to $visited$;
8 $\quad$ **while** $u'_j \neq u'_i$ **do**
9 $\quad\quad u_x \leftarrow u$ s.t. (u, u'_j) in A_r;
10 $\quad\quad u'_y \leftarrow$ Pick($u_x, \phi(R), \phi(R'), visited$);
11 $\quad\quad$ add (u_x, u'_y) to $visited$; set the child of u'_j to be u'_y;
12 $\quad\quad u'_j \leftarrow u'_y$;
13 $\quad$ Update A_r with the matchings in the cycle;
14 $\quad$ Remove nodes matched with nodes in the cycle from L;
15 **return** A_r;

Algorithm 1 provides the pseudo-code for assignment extraction by closed walk. It first initializes an assignment A_r (Line 1), in which each u_i is matched with u'_i. This assignment does not need to be valid; some of the matches (edges) in it may have already been used by previous assignments. Our task is to *update* A_r with valid matchings. We set L as the list of unprocessed nodes, initially all nodes in the graph (Line 2). After a cycle is found, its nodes are removed from L, hence $|L|$ is monotonically decreasing. Then we enter a cycle-discovery loop, to be terminated when all nodes have been assigned to a cycle, i.e. when $L = \emptyset$ (Lines 3-14). For each cycle to be created, we initialize a *visited* data structure (Line 4), which keeps track of each visited node and its previously traversed next hops. This structure facilitates two objectives: (i) we prefer visiting previously unvisited nodes, so that we do not create deviant cycles; we only do so when no unvisited next hop node is available; (ii) when we do revisit a node v, we should not reselect a previously traversed next hop, lest we reiterate the same deviant cycle.

We initiate a cycle by picking up a node $u_i \in L$ at random (Line 5). Then we select a next hop, u'_j (Line 6); our method for picking up u'_j is either *random* or *greedy*; this point makes the difference between a *Random Walk*, used for extracting random assignments from a generalization graph with both our k-anonymization and ℓ-diversification schemes, and a *Greedy Walk*, used for extracting assignments from the complete graph to build an ℓ-regular generalization graph for ℓ-diversification. In both cases, we always choose a next hop not used in a previous assignment; the choice (either random or greedy) is preferably made among next hops not already visited in the current walk either; if such options are not available, then we choose among visited ones, creating a deviant cycle. We elaborate further on the *greedy* choice in the next section.

Once the next hop has been chosen, the pair (u_i, u'_j) is added to the $visited$ data structure (Line 7). Then a loop iterates until the cycle under construction is closed by reaching u'_i (Lines 8-12). At each iteration, we pick (Line 9) the current preimage u_x of the selected next hop u'_j in assignment A_r, choose a new next hop, u'_y, for u_x (Line 10), add the pair (u_x, u'_y) to the *visited* structure, and set u'_y as the child of u'_j, so as to retrieve the created cycle later (Line 11). The matching (u_x, u'_y) is *not* registered in the extracted assignment A_r at this point, as it may yet be updated by later steps of the same walk. We then assign u'_y to u'_j and proceed with the next hop (Line 12). When the internal **while** loop (Lines 8-12) terminates, a cycle has been discovered; then assignment A_r is *updated* with the matchings in that discovered cycle (Line 13). This update may annul some matchings created by a previous cycle. Yet the overall process is progressive, as *at least one new record* from L is added to the set of matched records with each cycle; previously matched records may re-orient their matches (i.e., their preimage and postimage), but they do not become unmatched. Last, the set of newly matched nodes is removed from L, hence cannot be selected as a starting point of a cycle again (Line 14). Once all nodes are removed from L, an assignment has been extracted.

While our algorithm's worst-case complexity is quadratic, it performs less redundant steps than WMC [24], and is therefore more efficient. This algorithm rests on the assumption that the walk can always be closed by returning to the starting node without reusing any edge. The following theorem justifies this assumption.

THEOREM 4.1. *In a directed graph G where each node u has the same number m_u of incoming and outgoing edges, if there is a path from node v to v', then there exists a path from v' to v that does not reuse any edge in the path from v to v'.*

PROOF. Consider the graph G' consisting of all nodes and edges in G *except* the edges along the path from v to v', and *with* an additional edge from v to v'. Each node in G' has the same number of incoming and outgoing edges, as we have deleted one incoming and one outgoing edge from each node along the path, and the added

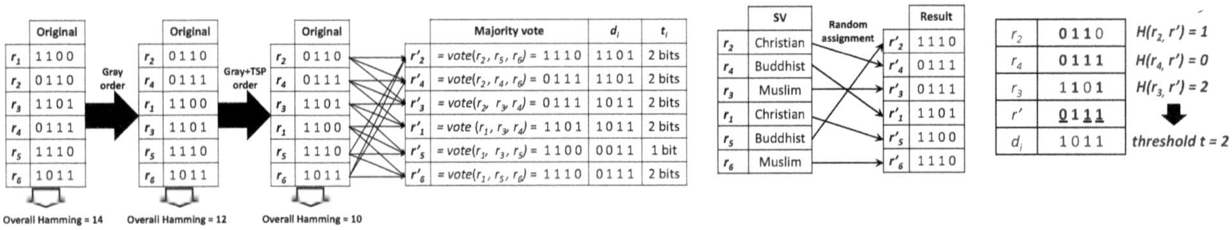

(a) Workflow (b) SV Assignment (c) Bit voting

Figure 4: Workflow and publication details in our methodology

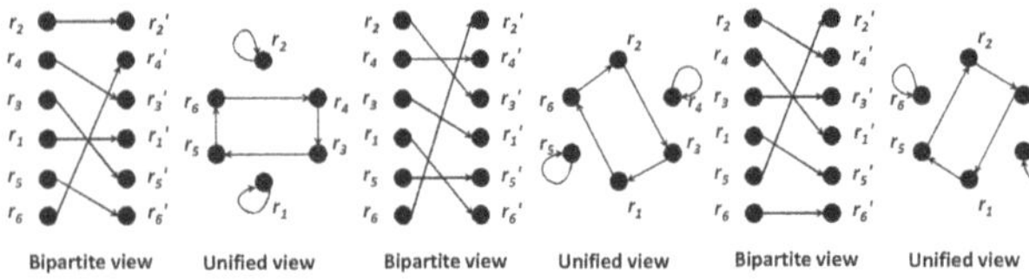

(a) Assignment 1 (b) Assignment 2 (c) Assignment 3

Figure 5: Extracted assignments in our example

edge from v to v' compensates for the edges these nodes have lost. If a path from v' to v exists in G', then it also exists in G, and, by the definition of G', does not reuse any edge in the path from v to v'. Thus, it suffices to prove that such a path exists in G'.

Assume there is no such path. Then consider W, the set of nodes in G' that can be reached from v'; v' is in W and has at least one outgoing edge (given that it has an incoming edge), hence W is non-empty. By definition, each outgoing edge from a node in W leads to a node in W, hence is an incoming edge to W. Since each node in G' has an equal number of incoming and outgoing edges, it follows that each edge incoming to W is also outgoing from W. By our assumption, v does not belong to W, hence the edge from v to v' is incoming to, but not outgoing from W. By reductio ad absurdum, it follows that there is a path from v' to v in G', hence in G, that does not reuse any edge in the path from v to v'. □

4.3 A Coherent Example

Figure 4 carries the example in the introduction forward by illustrating all elements of our methodology. The 3-regular ring generalization graph in Figure 1(a) is already defined on the Gray-TSP order over the dataset. Figure 4(a) shows how this order is created. The six records are first sorted by their Gray order, reducing the sum of their Hamming distances from 14 to 12. The application of the TSP algorithm further reduces this distance to 10. The Gray-TSP order $(r_2, r_4, r_1, r_3, r_5, r_6)$ is then used in the graph of Figure 1(a), whose edges are also shown in Figure 4(a). The values of anonymized records are defined by the *majority vote* of each record's preimages in the graph, as also shown in Figure 4(a). The details of voting are shown for record r'_3 as example, in Figure 4(c). Furthermore, Figure 5 depicts the three disjoint assignments we extract. Eventually, we randomly pick one of these; assume the one in Figure 4(c) is chosen. We use this assignment as a guide to assign presumed identities and any other attributes, such as sensitive labels, to our six records, as in Figure 4(b). The anonymized data we obtain are the same as those in Table 3. However, for the sake of simplicity, in that table we did not yet present the effect of assigning sensitive values according to a randomly selected assignment.

4.4 Greedy Assignment Extraction

The solution in our example applies our k-anonymization algorithm and satisfies 3-anonymity. By chance, it also happens to satisfy 3-diversity, as each original record matches three anonymized records of different sensitive values. However, in order to systematically address the ℓ-diversification problem, we need to ensure that the generalization graph we work with satisfies the ℓ-diversity requirement, i.e., matches each original record to ℓ anonymized postimages of different sensitive values. Such a generalization graph cannot be built by applying a simple rule over a given order. However, we can eschew the a priori construction of a generalization graph altogether. Instead, we start out by assuming a *complete generalization graph*, i.e. a graph where an edge exists from every preimage to every postimage, extract ℓ assignments therefrom, and build the generalization graph we eventually use as the union of these ℓ assignments. Assuming the full data set satisfies ℓ-diversity (is ℓ-eligible [18]), such ℓ assignments can be extracted, so that each record obtains ℓ-diverse matches. The burden falls upon our closed-walk algorithm to take sensitive values in consideration when *picking* next hops. We now outline our method for picking up next hops in a manner that satisfies the ℓ-diversity requirement, i.e., ensures that each postimage a record is matched to a sensitive value different from those it was previously matched to, while otherwise making greedy decisions for the benefit of utility. Algorithm 2 presents a pseudo-code for this greedyPick method, to be used in our closed-walk algorithm (Section 4.2).

Algorithm 2: greedyPick(u, $\phi(R)$, $\phi(R')$, $visited$)

1 $i \leftarrow$ the rank of u in $\phi(R)$;
2 $last \leftarrow$ false;
3 **for** $j \leftarrow 0$ *to* $\frac{n}{2}+1$ **do**
4 $\quad u'_1 \leftarrow$ record at rank $i+j \mod n$ in $\phi(R')$;
5 $\quad u'_2 \leftarrow$ record at rank $i-j \mod n$ in $\phi(R')$;
6 $\quad S_u \leftarrow$ sens. labels of records previously matched with u;
7 $\quad$ **for** $p \leftarrow 1$ *to* 2 **do**
8 $\quad\quad$ **if** $(u, u'_p) \in$ *any* $A_1 \ldots A_{r-1}$ *or* $visited$ **then**
9 $\quad\quad\quad u'_p \leftarrow null$;
10 $\quad\quad$ **if** $u'_p.s \in S_u$ **then**
11 $\quad\quad\quad u'_p \leftarrow null$;
12 $\quad$ **if** u'_1 *and* u'_2 *both are null* **then**
13 $\quad\quad$ continue loop;
14 $\quad u' \leftarrow u'_p \in \{u'_1, u'_2\}$ s.t. $H(u'_p, u)$ is minimum;
15 $\quad$ **if** $\nexists$ u_x, *s.t.* $(u_x, u') \in visited$ **then**
16 $\quad\quad u'' \leftarrow u'$; break loop;
17 $\quad$ **if** $last$ = *false* **then**
18 $\quad\quad u'' \leftarrow u'$; $last \leftarrow$ true;
19 **return** u'';

In a nutshell, given a preimage u and the TSP-Gray-sorted node lists $\phi(R)$ and $\phi(R')$, greedyPick aims to return an eligible postimage for u that is close to u by Hamming distance, while preferring unvisited nodes to visited ones. The rank of u in $\phi(R)$ is denoted as i (Line 1). We use a boolean, initialized as false (Line 2), which indicates whether an option of *last resort* has been reached, so that a deviant cycle may be created by picking up as next hop a node already visited in the current walk. While such an option is not preferred, it can be opted for if no other choice is available. For the sake of utility, we prefer to select a postimage that is close to u in the Gray-TSP order. We progressively search for such a postimage in Lines 3-20. In each iteration we consider the next two candidate records, u'_1 and u'_2, that are one position further away from u (in two directions along the Gray-TSP order) than previously considered ones (Lines 4-5), and try to match either u'_1 or u'_2 with u, while satisfying the following criteria: (i) u cannot be matched to a record it has been matched to in a previous assignment; (ii) in case u is being revisited (i.e., a deviant cycle is created), it cannot be matched again to a next-hop record it was already matched to in this walk, lest we reiterate the same deviant cycle indefinitely (see Section 4.2); (iii) for ℓ-diversity to be satisfied, u cannot be matched to a record having the same sensitive label as a match of u in a previous assignment. In case both u'_1 and u'_2 fail these criteria, the loop continues to the next iteration (Lines 6-13). Otherwise, we pick the one that has the lowest Hamming distance to u as u' (Line 14), while also ensuring that a node not previously visited in the current walk is preferred to an already visited one. If u' has *not* been previously visited, the loop terminates and u' is returned as u'' (Lines 15-16). Otherwise, if no option of last resort has been set before, u' is marked as the best such option (Lines 17-18). Thus, u' will be eventually returned, unless a more preferable option is found in a subsequent iteration.

We emphasize the greedy character of the process. As $\phi(R)$ is sorted by the Gray-TSP order, and we always pick up u' as close as possible to u, we expect their Hamming distance to be small; at the same time, we avoid u' with sensitive labels already picked up in previous assignments. To that end we maintain the set S_u of sensitive labels already assigned to u (Line 6). After u' is picked as a match for u, its label is also added to S_u. Eventually, our generalization graph is created as the union of ℓ disjoint assignments extracted by closed walk using our greedyPick method.

Dataset	# records n	Avg. size	Universe size $\|I\|$
Chess	3,196	37	75
Pumsb	49,046	75	7,117

Table 6: Dataset information

5. EXPERIMENTAL EVALUATION

We now evaluate our schemes experimentally. We use two real-life set-valued data: Pumbs and Chess, available at the UCI Machine Learning Repository.[2] Table 6 presents the data specifications. Pumsb contains transactions representing a sample of responses from the Los Angeles – Long Beach area census questionnaire. Such data sets are used in targeted marketing campaigns for identifying a population likely to respond to a particular promotion. Chess contains 37-attribute board-descriptions for chess endgames. The first 36 attributes describe the board, while the last attribute is the classification: "win" or "nowin". For the evaluation of our ℓ-diversification scheme, we have introduced sensitive labels in all data in a consistent manner. We obtain the empirical distribution of sensitive labels from the histogram of occupation values from the census data[3] of 1990, and assign to each record a randomly sampled sensitive label. The extracted census data has 3,030,728 records with 470 distinct occupation attribute values.

We evaluate our schemes in: (i) the information loss incurred by the anonymization process; (ii) the accuracy in answering aggregate queries over the data; and (iii) runtime efficiency and scalability. Our algorithms were implemented in Java and experiments ran on a 4 CPU, 2.4GHz Linux server with 8GB RAM.

5.1 Information Loss

We first assess the information loss caused by our techniques. We evaluate our k-anonymization scheme on the benefit brought about by the TSP-Gray sorting, in terms of reducing information loss. In the case of ℓ-diversification, we compare against CAHD (Correlation-aware Anonymization of High-dimensional Data), the most recommended anonymization scheme proposed in [9].

[2]Online at http://archive.ics.uci.edu/ml/datasets/
[3]Online at http://usa.ipums.org/usa/

CAHD partitions records in groups, assisted by a Gray order, so that the distribution of sensitive labels within groups satisfies a privacy requirement p, equivalent to ℓ-diversity for $p = \frac{1}{\ell}$. Eventually, the data is published by breaking the associations among individual records and their sensitive labels. In order to render CAHD comparable to our scheme, we apply our publication model on the data obtained from CAHD as well, i.e., we generalize the bitmaps of records within a group to their most representative bit values by our bit voting scheme. To measure the error inflicted by this model, we propose an Error Rate (ER) metric, defined as the average ratio of the number of bits flipped in the published base bitmap r'_i of an original record r_i to the number of bits valued 1 in r_i.

We measure ER for the anonymized Pumsb and Chess data. In all our experiments, we set the chunk-size range in Gray-TSP sorting to $[300, 350]$. To evaluate the benefit brought about by our sorting scheme, we prepare each data set in two different orders: one using the Gray order only and another using our Gray-TSP order, and apply ring-based nonreciprocal generalization on each. Figures 6(a,e) show our ER results as a function of the k parameter. Remarkably, lower ER values are achieved with the Gray-TSP order than with the plain Gray order; this result confirms that the TSP enhancement bears fruits in terms of containing information loss. We emphasize that the Gray-only technique is *also* using nonreciprocal recoding. Figures 6(b,f) show our results on ℓ-diversification, comparing our complete nonreciprocal method (NR) to CAHD, as a function of ℓ. The results show a clear utility advantage for NR, which is gained thanks to both nonreciprocal recoding and our TSP-based enhancement of the Gray order.

5.2 Answering Aggregation Queries

Next, we study the accuracy achieved with anonymized data over aggregation queries. We propose two types of queries, which count records based on whether a certain itemset is present in or absent from them. Given $In \subseteq I$ and $Ex \subseteq I$, these types are defined as:

Type I: Select COUNT(r) FROM R' WHERE $In \subseteq IS(r_i)$;

Type II: Select COUNT(r) FROM R' WHERE $Ex \cap IS(r_i) = \emptyset$;

A Type I (II) query counts records with certain items present (absent). We first specify the size of In and Ex based on the average number of records and the universe size in each dataset. In particular, the values of $(|In|, |Ex|)$ for Pumsb and Chess are $(1, 5)$ and $(3, 4)$, respectively. We randomly select $|In|$ items from I to form In, and $|Ex|$ items from I to form Ex. For each tested value of k, we run 500 random queries, and measure the query error (QE), defined as $QE = \frac{|C_o - C_a|}{n}$, where C_o (C_a) is the result obtained from the original (anonymized) data and n the size of the dataset. Figures 6(c,d,g,h) show the average QE results. Again, our TSP-based method permits lower query error than the variant using only a Gray-code order, while our nonreciprocal ℓ-diversification scheme clearly outperforms CAHD.

5.3 Runtime Results

We now evaluate the benefit brought about by our closed-walk algorithm for assignment extraction as compared to the backtracking algorithm in [24]. Figure 7(a) presents the time needed for assignment generation in k-anonymization by both algorithms on the Pumsb data, as a function of k. Our closed walk offers a clear efficiency benefit. We also examine scalability in data size. We obtain data sets of size $2\times$, $4\times$, $8\times$ and $16\times$ that of Chess by duplication and random perturbation. We ran both compared methods on these data, with k set to 16. Figure 7(b) shows our results on *logarithmic* axes. Our closed-walk method maintains an advantage of almost one order of magnitude with increasing data size. We also evaluate

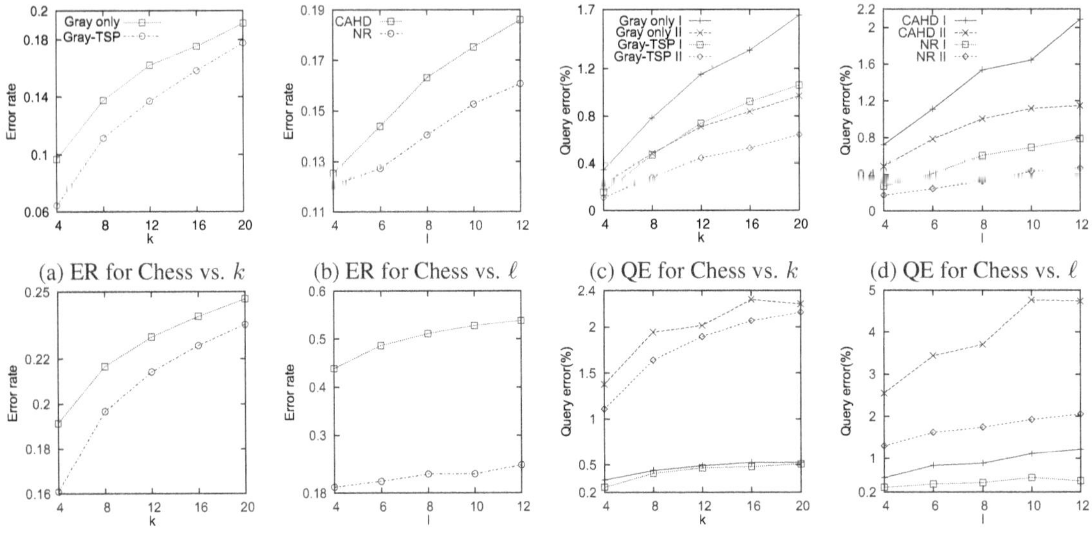

(a) ER for Chess vs. k (b) ER for Chess vs. ℓ (c) QE for Chess vs. k (d) QE for Chess vs. ℓ

(e) ER for Pumsb vs. k (f) ER for Pumsb vs. ℓ (g) QE for Pumsb vs. k (h) QE for Pumsb vs. ℓ

Figure 6: Bit Error Rate and Query Error in k-anonymization and ℓ-diversification

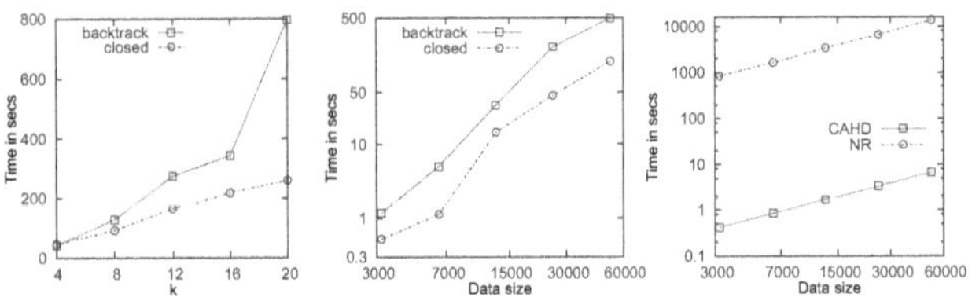

(a) Time with Pumsb (b) k-anonymization (c) ℓ-diversification

Figure 7: Runtime vs. k and size

the scalability of our ℓ-diversification technique vis-à-vis CAHD on the same data, setting ℓ to 6. Figure 7(c) shows our results. For our technique, the measured time includes the time for TSP-Gray sorting, greedy assignment generation for building the generalization graph, and random assignment generation for the sake of privacy (see Section 4). Expectedly, our method requires more time than CAHD, but presents a similarly scalable growth trend. Arguably, the extra time is a reasonable cost for the utility benefits it brings.

6. CONCLUSION

In this paper we revisited the problem of sharing set-valued data while conforming to k-anonymity-like and ℓ-diversity-like privacy guarantees. We proposed a novel *nonreciprocal* anonymization scheme for such data, whereby it is *not* required that original records match anonymized ones in groups. In the process, we brought the state of the art for nonreciprocal anonymization forward in terms of efficiency, applied it on whole data sets, and developed a special method for nonreciprocal ℓ-diversification. Our technique comes along with a novel way to devise a *cyclical order* over set-valued records, employing the Gray-code order and improving on it by applying a TSP algorithm. Our experimental study demonstrates that our schemes preserve data utility to a degree not achieved by previous methods; the extra runtime required compared to CAHD is an affordable price to pay for the benefits we gain. In the future, we plan to investigate how nonreciprocal anonymization techniques can be applied to other types of data, e.g. spatial data.

Acknowledgments

We thank Gabriel Ghinița who shared the CAHD code with us, and the anonymous reviewers for their constructive feedback.

7. REFERENCES

[1] C. C. Aggarwal and P. S. Yu. On privacy-preservation of text and sparse binary data with sketches. In *SDM*, 2007.

[2] S. Agrawal, J. R. Haritsa, and B. A. Prakash. FRAPP: A framework for high-accuracy privacy-preserving mining. *Data Min. Knowl. Discov.*, 18(1):101–139, 2009.

[3] J. Brickell and V. Shmatikov. The cost of privacy: destruction of data-mining utility in anonymized data publishing. In *KDD*, 2008.

[4] J. Cao, P. Karras, C. Raïssi, and K.-L. Tan. ρ-uncertainty: Inference-proof transaction anonymization. *PVLDB*, 3(1):1033–1044, 2010.

[5] G. Cormode, N. Li, T. Li, and D. Srivastava. Minimizing minimality and maximizing utility: Analyzing method-based attacks on anonymized data. *PVLDB*, 3(1):1045–1056, 2010.

[6] E. Dasseni, V. S. Verykios, A. K. Elmagarmid, and E. Bertino. Hiding association rules by using confidence and support. In *IHW*, 2001.

[7] A. Evfimievski, J. Gehrke, and R. Srikant. Limiting privacy breaches in privacy preserving data mining. In *PODS*, 2003.

[8] A. Evfimievski, R. Srikant, R. Agrawal, and J. Gehrke. Privacy preserving mining of association rules. In *KDD*, 2002.

[9] G. Ghinita, P. Kalnis, and Y. Tao. Anonymous publication of sensitive transactional data. *IEEE TKDE*, 23(2):161–174, 2011.

[10] G. Ghinita, P. Karras, P. Kalnis, and N. Mamoulis. A framework for efficient data anonymization under privacy and accuracy constraints. *ACM TODS*, 34(2):1–47, 2009.

[11] G. Ghinita, Y. Tao, and P. Kalnis. On the anonymization of sparse high-dimensional data. In *ICDE*, 2008.

[12] A. Gionis, A. Mazza, and T. Tassa. k-anonymization revisited. In *ICDE*, 2008.

[13] F. Gray. Pulse code communication. US Patent 2632058, 1953.

[14] Y. He and J. F. Naughton. Anonymization of set-valued data via top-down, local generalization. *PVLDB*, 2(1):934–945, 2009.

[15] Y. Hong, X. He, J. Vaidya, N. R. Adam, and V. Atluri. Effective anonymization of query logs. In *CIKM*, 2009.

[16] D. Kifer. Attacks on privacy and deFinetti's theorem. In *SIGMOD*, 2009.

[17] K. LeFevre, D. J. DeWitt, and R. Ramakrishnan. Workload-aware anonymization techniques for large-scale datasets. *ACM TODS*, 33(3):17:1–17:47, 2008.

[18] A. Machanavajjhala, D. Kifer, J. Gehrke, and M. Venkitasubramaniam. ℓ-diversity: Privacy beyond k-anonymity. *ACM TKDD*, 1(1):3, 2007.

[19] S. J. Rizvi and J. R. Haritsa. Maintaining data privacy in association rule mining. In *VLDB*, 2002.

[20] P. Samarati. Protecting respondents' identities in microdata release. *IEEE TKDE*, 13(6):1010–1027, 2001.

[21] Y. Saygin, V. S. Verykios, and C. Clifton. Using unknowns to prevent discovery of association rules. *SIGMOD Rec.*, 30(4):45–54, 2001.

[22] H. Sengoku and I. Yoshihara. A fast TSP solver using GA on JAVA. In *AROB*, 1998.

[23] M. Terrovitis, N. Mamoulis, and P. Kalnis. Local and global recoding methods for anonymizing set-valued data. *The VLDB Journal*, 20(1):83–106, 2011.

[24] W. K. Wong, N. Mamoulis, and D. W. L. Cheung. Non-homogeneous generalization in privacy preserving data publishing. In *SIGMOD*, 2010.

[25] Y. Xu, K. Wang, A. W.-C. Fu, and P. S. Yu. Anonymizing transaction databases for publication. In *KDD*, 2008.

Adversarial Support Vector Machine Learning

Yan Zhou   Murat Kantarcioglu   Bhavani Thuraisingham
Computer Science Department
University of Texas at Dallas
Richardson, TX 75080
yan.zhou2@utdallas.edu, muratk@utdallas.edu, bxt043000@utdallas.edu

Bowei Xi
Department of Statistics
Purdue University
West Lafayette, IN 47907
xbw@stat.purdue.edu

ABSTRACT

Many learning tasks such as spam filtering and credit card fraud detection face an active adversary that tries to avoid detection. For learning problems that deal with an active adversary, it is important to model the adversary's attack strategy and develop robust learning models to mitigate the attack. These are the two objectives of this paper. We consider two attack models: a *free-range* attack model that permits arbitrary data corruption and a *restrained* attack model that anticipates more realistic attacks that a reasonable adversary would devise under penalties. We then develop optimal SVM learning strategies against the two attack models. The learning algorithms minimize the hinge loss while assuming the adversary is modifying data to maximize the loss. Experiments are performed on both artificial and real data sets. We demonstrate that optimal solutions may be overly pessimistic when the actual attacks are much weaker than expected. More important, we demonstrate that it is possible to develop a much more resilient SVM learning model while making loose assumptions on the data corruption models. When derived under the *restrained* attack model, our optimal SVM learning strategy provides more robust overall performance under a wide range of attack parameters.

Categories and Subject Descriptors

I.5.1 [**Computing Methodologies**]: Pattern Recognition—*Models*; I.2.6 [**Computing Methodologies**]: Artificial Intelligence —*Learning*

General Terms

Theory, Algorithms

KDD'12, August 12–16, 2012, Beijing, China.

Keywords

adversarial learning, attack models, robust SVM

1. INTRODUCTION

Many learning tasks, such as intrusion detection and spam filtering, face adversarial attacks. Adversarial exploits create additional challenges to existing learning paradigms. Generalization of a learning model over future data cannot be achieved under the assumption that current and future data share identical properties, which is essential to the traditional approaches. In the presence of active adversaries, data used for training in a learning system is unlikely to represent future data the system would observe. The difference is not just simple random noise which most learning algorithms have already taken into consideration when they are designed. What typically flunk these learning algorithms are targeted attacks that aim to make the learning system dysfunctional by disguising malicious data that otherwise would be detected. Existing learning algorithms cannot be easily tailored to counter this kind of attack because there is a great deal of uncertainty in terms of how much the attacks would affect the structure of the sample space. Despite the sample size and distribution of malicious data given at training time, we would need to make an educated guess about how much the malicious data would change, as sophisticated attackers adapt quickly to evade detection. Attack models, that foretell how far an adversary would go in order to breach the system, need to be incorporated into learning algorithms to build a robust decision surface. In this paper, we present two attack models that cover a *wide range of attacks* tailored to match the adversary's motives. Each attack model makes a simple and realistic assumption on what is known to the adversary. Optimal SVM learning strategies are then derived against the attack models.

Some earlier work lays important theoretical foundations for problems in adversarial learning [15, 6, 20]. However, earlier work often makes strong assumptions such as unlimited computing resource and both sides having a complete knowledge of their opponents. Some proposes attack models that may not permit changes made to arbitrary sets of features [20]. In security applications, some existing research mainly explores practical means of defeating learning algorithms used in a given application domain [25, 19, 22].

Meanwhile, various learning strategies are proposed to fix application-specific weaknesses in learning algorithms [24, 21, 17], but only to find new doors open for future attacks [10, 22]. The main challenge remains as attackers continually exploit unknown weaknesses of a learning system. Regardless of how well designed a learning system appears to be, there are always "blind" spots it fails to detect, leading to escalating threats as the technical strengths on both sides develop. Threats are often divided into two groups, with one group aiming to smuggle malicious content past learning based detection mechanism, while the other trying to undermine the credibility of a learning system by raising both false positive and false negative rates [3]. The grey area in between is scarcely researched. In this work, we set ourselves free from handling application-specific attacks and addressing specific weaknesses of a learning algorithm. Our main contributions lie in the following three aspects:

- We develop a learning strategy that solves a general convex optimization problem where the strength of the constraints is tied to the strength of attacks.
- We derive optimal support vector machine learning models against an adversary whose attack strategy is defined under a general and reasonable assumption.
- We investigate how the performance of the resulting optimal solutions change with different parameter values in two different attack models. The empirical results suggest our proposed adversarial SVM learning algorithms are quite robust against various degrees of attacks.

The rest of the paper is organized as follows. Section 2 presents the related work in the area of adversarial learning. Section 3 formally defines the problem. Section 4 presents the attack models and Section 5 derives the adversarial SVM models. Section 6 presents experimental results on both artificial and real data sets. Section 7 concludes our work and presents future directions.

2. RELATED WORK

Kearns and Li [15] provide theoretical upper bounds on tolerable malicious error rates for learning in the presence of malicious errors. They assume the adversary has unbounded computational resource. In addition, they assume the adversary has the knowledge of the target concept, target distributions, and internal states of the learning algorithm. They demonstrate that error tolerance needs not come at the expense of efficiency or simplicity, and there are strong ties between learning with malicious errors and standard optimization problems.

Dalvi et al. [6] propose a game theoretic framework for learning problems where there is an optimal opponent. They define the problem as a game between two cost-sensitive opponents: a naive Bayes classifier and an adversary playing optimal strategies. They assume all parameters of both players are known to each other and the adversary knows the exact form of the classifier. Their adversary-aware algorithm makes predictions according to the class that maximizes the conditional utility. Finding optimal solutions remains to be computational intensive, which is typical in game theory.

Lowed and Meek [20] point out that assuming the adversary has perfect knowledge of the classifier is unrealistic. Instead they suggest the adversary can confirm the membership of an arbitrary instance by sending queries to the classifier. They also assume the adversary has available an adversarial cost function over the sample space that maps samples to cost values. This assumption essentially means the adversary needs to know the entire feature space to issue optimal attacks. They propose an adversarial classifier reverse engineering (ACRE) algorithm to learn vulnerabilities of given learning algorithms.

Adversarial learning problems are often modeled as games played between two opponents. Brückner and Scheffer model adversarial prediction problems as Stackelberg games [5]. To guarantee optimality, the model assumes adversaries behave rationally. However, it does not require a unique equilibrium. Kantarcioglu et al. [14] treat the problem as a sequential Stackelberg game. They assume the two players know each other's payoff function. They use simulated annealing and genetic algorithm to search for a Nash equilibrium. Later on such an equilibrium is used to choose optimal set of attributes that give good equilibrium performance. Improved models in which Nash strategies are played have also been proposed [4, 18].

Other game theoretic models play zero-sum minimax strategies. Globerson and Roweis [11] consider a problem where some features may be missing at testing time. This is related to adversarial learning in that the adversary may simply delete highly weighted features in malicious data to increase its chance to evade detection. They develop a game theoretic framework in which classifiers are constructed to be optimal in the worst case scenario. Their idea is to prevent assigning too much weight on any single feature. They use the support vector machine model which optimally minimizes the hinge loss when at most K features can be deleted. El Ghaoui et al [9] apply a minimax model to training data bounded by hyper-rectangles. Their model minimizes the worst-case loss over data in given intervals. Other robust learning algorithms for handling classification-time noise are also proposed [16, 23, 7, 8].

Our work differs from the existing ones in several respects. First of all, we do not make strong assumptions on what is known to either side of the players. Second, both wide-range attacks and targeted attacks are considered and incorporated into the SVM learning framework. Finally, the robustness of the minimax solutions against attacks over a wide range of parameters is investigated.

3. PROBLEM DEFINITION

Denote a sample set by $\{(x_i, y_i) \in (\mathcal{X}, \mathcal{Y})\}_{i=1}^n$, where x_i is the ith sample and $y_i \in \{-1, 1\}$ is its label, $\mathcal{X} \subseteq \mathbb{R}^d$ is a d-dimensional feature space, n is the total number of samples. We consider an adversarial learning problem where the adversary modifies malicious data to avoid detection and hence achieves his planned goals. The adversary has the freedom to move only the malicious data ($y_i = 1$) in any direction by adding a non-zero displacement vector δ_i to $x_i|_{y_i=1}$. For example, in spam-filtering the adversary may add good words to spam e-mail to defeat spam filters. On the other hand, adversary will not be able to modify legitimate e-mail.

We make no specific assumptions on the adversary's knowledge of the learning system. Instead, we simply assume there is a trade-off or cost of changing malicious data. For example, a practical strategy often employed by an adversary is to move the malicious data in the feature space as close as possible to where the innocuous data is frequently observed. However, the adversary can only alter a malicious data point so much that its malicious utility is not completely lost. If the adversary moves a data point too far away from its own class in the feature space, the adversary may have to sacrifice much of the malicious utility of the original data point. For example, in the problem of credit card fraud detection, an attacker may choose the "right" amount to spent with a stolen credit card to mimic a legitimate purchase. By doing so, the attacker will lose some potential profit.

4. ADVERSARIAL ATTACK MODELS

We present two attack models—*free-range* and *restrained*, each of which makes a simple and realistic assumption about how much is known to the adversary. The models differ in their implications for 1) the adversary's knowledge of the innocuous data, and 2) the loss of utility as a result of changing the malicious data. The *free-range* attack model assumes the adversary has the freedom to move data anywhere in the feature space. The *restrained* attack model is a more conservative attack model. The model is built under the intuition that the adversary would be reluctant to let a data point move far away from its original position in the feature space. The reason is that greater displacement often entails loss of malicious utility.

4.1 Free-Range Attack

The only knowledge the adversary needs is the valid range of each feature. Let $x^{max}_{.j}$ and $x^{min}_{.j}$ be the largest and the smallest values that the jth feature of a data point x_i—x_{ij}—can take. For all practical purposes, we assume both $x^{max}_{.j}$ and $x^{min}_{.j}$ are bounded. For example, for a Gaussian distribution, they can be set to the 0.01 and 0.99 quantiles. The resulting range would cover most of the data points and discard a few extreme values. An attack is then bounded in the following form:

$$C_f(x^{min}_{.j} - x_{ij}) \leq \delta_{ij} \leq C_f(x^{max}_{.j} - x_{ij}), \forall j \in [1, d],$$

where $C_f \in [0, 1]$ controls the aggressiveness of attacks. $C_f = 0$ means no attacks, while $C_f = 1$ corresponds to the most aggressive attacks involving the widest range of permitted data movement.

The great advantage of this attack model is that it is sufficiently general to cover all possible attack scenarios as far as data modification is concerned. When paired with a learning model, the combination would produce good performance against the most severe attacks. However, when there are mild attacks, the learning model becomes too "paranoid" and its performance suffers accordingly. Next, we present a more realistic model for attacks where significant data alteration is penalized.

4.2 Restrained Attack

Let x_i be a malicious data point the adversary aims to alter. Let x^t_i, a d-dimensional vector, be a potential target to which the adversary would like to push x_i. The adversary chooses x^t_i according to his estimate of the innocuous data distribution. Ideally, the adversary would optimize x^t_i for each x_i to minimize the cost of changing it and maximize the goal it can achieve. Optimally choosing x^t_i is desired, but often requires a great deal of knowledge about the feature space and sometimes the inner working of a learning algorithm [6, 20]. More realistically, the adversary can set x^t_i to be the estimated centroid of innocuous data, a data point sampled from the observed innocuous data, or an artificial data point generated from the estimated innocuous data distribution. Note that x^t_i could be a rough guess if the adversary has a very limited knowledge of the innocuous data, or a very accurate one if the adversary knows the exact make up of the training data.

In most cases, the adversary cannot change x_i to x^t_i as desired since x_i may lose too much of its malicious utility. Therefore, for each attribute j in the d-dimensional feature space, we assume the adversary adds δ_{ij} to x_{ij} where

$$|\delta_{ij}| \leq |x^t_{ij} - x_{ij}|, \ \forall\, j \in d.$$

Furthermore, we place an upper bound on the amount of displacement for attribute j as follows:

$$0 \leq (x^t_{ij} - x_{ij})\delta_{ij} \leq \left(1 - C_\delta \frac{|x^t_{ij} - x_{ij}|}{|x_{ij}| + |x^t_{ij}|}\right)(x^t_{ij} - x_{ij})^2,$$

where $C_\delta \in [0, 1]$ is a constant modeling the loss of malicious utility as a result of the movement δ_{ij}. This attack model specifies how much the adversary can push x_{ij} towards x^t_{ij} based on how far apart they are from each other. The term $1 - C_\delta \frac{|x^t_{ij} - x_{ij}|}{|x_{ij}| + |x^t_{ij}|}$ is the percentage of $x^t_{ij} - x_{ij}$ that δ_{ij} is allowed to be at most. When C_δ is fixed, the closer x_{ij} is to x^t_{ij}, the more x_{ij} is allowed to move towards x^t_{ij} percentage wise. The opposite is also true. The farther apart x_{ij} and x^t_{ij}, the smaller $|\delta_{ij}|$ will be. For example, when x_{ij} and x^t_{ij} reside on different sides of the origin, that is, one is positive and the other is negative, then no movement is permitted (that is, $\delta_{ij} = 0$) when $C_\delta = 1$. This model balances between the needs of disguising maliciousness of data and retaining its malicious utility in the mean time. $(x^t_{ij} - x_{ij})\delta_{ij} \geq 0$ ensures δ_{ij} moves in the same direction as $x^t_{ij} - x_{ij}$. C_δ is related to the loss of malicious utility after the data has been modified. C_δ sets how much malicious utility the adversary is willing to sacrifice for breaking through the decision boundary. A larger C_δ means smaller loss of malicious utility, while a smaller C_δ models greater loss of malicious utility. Hence a larger C_δ leads to less aggressive attacks while a smaller C_δ leads to more aggress attacks.

The attack model works great for well-separated data as shown in Figure 1(a). When data from both classes are near the separation boundary as shown in Figure 1(b), slightly changing attribute values would be sufficient to push the data across the boundary. In this case, even if C_δ is set to 1, the attack from the above model would still be too aggressive compared with what is needed. We could allow $C_\delta > 1$ to further reduce the aggressiveness of attacks, however, for simplicity and more straightforward control, we instead apply a discount factor C_ξ to $|x^t_{ij} - x_{ij}|$ directly to model the severeness of attacks:

$$0 \leq (x^t_{ij} - x_{ij})\delta_{ij} \leq C_\xi \left(1 - \frac{|x^t_{ij} - x_{ij}|}{|x_{ij}| + |x^t_{ij}|}\right)(x^t_{ij} - x_{ij})^2,$$

where $C_\xi \in [0, 1]$. A large C_ξ gives rise to a greater amount of data movement, and a small C_ξ sets a narrower limit on data movement. Combining these two cases, the *restrained-attack* model is given as follows:

$$0 \leq (x^t_{ij} - x_{ij})\delta_{ij} \leq C_\xi \left(1 - C_\delta \frac{|x^t_{ij} - x_{ij}|}{|x_{ij}| + |x^t_{ij}|}\right)(x^t_{ij} - x_{ij})^2.$$

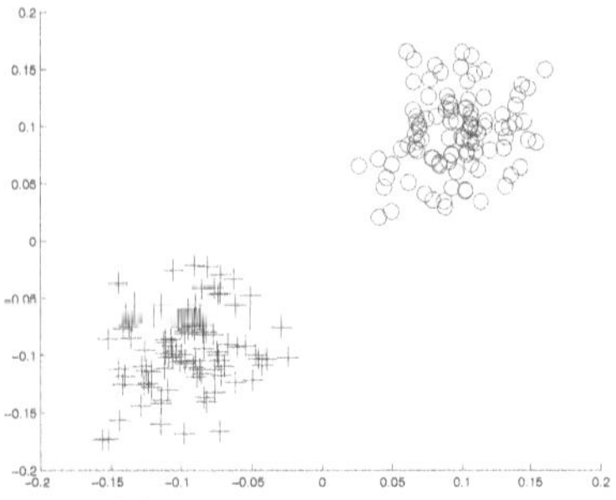

(a) Data well separated

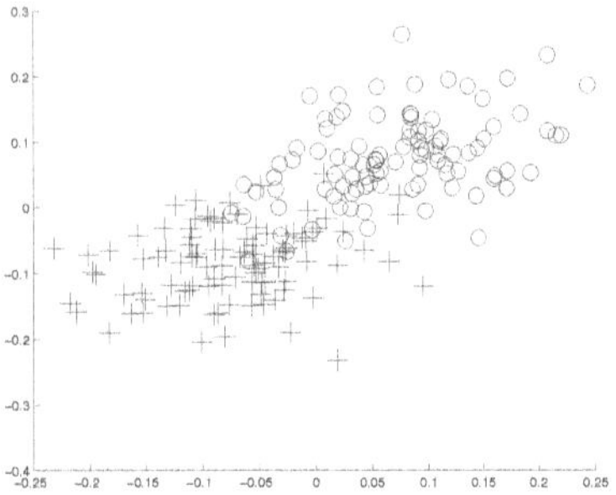

(b) Data cluttered near boundary

Figure 1: Data well separated and data cluttered near separating boundary.

5. ADVERSARIAL SVM LEARNING

We now present an adversarial support vector machine model (AD-SVM) against each of the two attack models discussed in the previous section. We assume the adversary cannot modify the innocuous data. Note that this assumption can be relaxed to model cases where the innocuous data may also be altered.

5.1 AD-SVM against Free-range Attack Model

We first consider the free-range attack model. The hinge loss model is given as follows:

$$\begin{array}{rcl} h(w,b,x_i) & = & \left\{ \begin{array}{ll} \max\limits_{\delta_i} \lfloor 1-(w\cdot(x_i+\delta_i)+b)\rfloor_+ & \text{if } y_i=1 \\ \lfloor 1+(w\cdot x_i+b)\rfloor_+ & \text{if } y_i=-1 \end{array} \right. \\ s.t. & & \\ & & \delta_i \preceq C_f(x^{max}-x_i) \\ & & \delta_i \succeq C_f(x^{min}-x_i) \end{array}$$

where δ_i is the displacement vector for x_i, $\preceq$ and $\succeq$ denote component-wise inequality.

Following the standard SVM risk formulation, we have

$$\begin{array}{ll} \underset{w,b}{\operatorname{argmin}} & \sum_{\{i|y_i=1\}} \max\limits_{\delta_i} \lfloor 1-(w\cdot(x_i+\delta_i)+b)\rfloor_+ \\ & +\sum_{\{i|y_i=-1\}} \lfloor 1+(w\cdot x_i+b)\rfloor_+ \\ & +\mu\|w\|^2 \end{array}$$

Combining cases for positive and negative instances, this is equivalent to:

$$\begin{array}{ll} \underset{w,b}{\operatorname{argmin}} & \sum\limits_i \max\limits_{\delta_i} \lfloor 1-y_i(w\cdot x_i+b)-\frac{1}{2}(1+y_i)w\cdot\delta_i\rfloor_+ \\ & +\mu\|w\|^2 \end{array}$$

Note that the worst case hinge loss of x_i is obtained when δ_i is chosen to minimize its contribution to the margin, that is,

$$\begin{array}{rcl} f_i & = & \min\limits_{\delta_i} \frac{1}{2}(1+y_i)w\cdot\delta_i \\ s.t. & & \delta_i \preceq C_f(x^{max}-x_i) \\ & & \delta_i \succeq C_f(x^{min}-x_i) \end{array}$$

This is a disjoint bilinear problem with resect to w and δ_i. Here, we are interested in discovering optimal assignment to δ_i with a given w. We can reduce the bilinear problem to the following asymmetric dual problem over $u_i \in \mathbb{R}^d$, $v_i \in \mathbb{R}^d$ where d is the dimension of the feature space:

$$\begin{array}{rcl} g_i & = & \max -\sum_j C_f\left(v_{ij}(x_j^{max}-x_{ij})-u_{ij}(x_j^{min}-x_{ij})\right) \\ \text{or} & & \\ g_i & = & \min \sum_j C_f\left(v_{ij}(x_j^{max}-x_{ij})-u_{ij}(x_j^{min}-x_{ij})\right) \\ s.t. & & (u_i-v_i)=\frac{1}{2}(1+y_i)w \\ & & u_i \succeq 0 \\ & & v_i \succeq 0 \end{array}$$

The SVM risk minimization problem can be rewritten as follows:

$$\begin{array}{ll} \underset{w,b,t_i,u_i,v_i}{\operatorname{argmin}} & \frac{1}{2}\|w\|^2 + C\sum_i \lfloor 1-y_i\cdot(w\cdot x_i+b)+t_i\rfloor_+ \\ s.t. & t_i \geq \sum_j C_f\left(v_{ij}(x_j^{max}-x_{ij})-u_{ij}(x_j^{min}-x_{ij})\right) \\ & u_i-v_i=\frac{1}{2}(1+y_i)w \\ & u_i \succeq 0 \\ & v_i \succeq 0 \end{array}$$

Adding a slack variable and linear constraints to remove the non-differentiality of the hinge loss, we can rewrite the problem as follows:

$$\begin{array}{ll} \underset{w,b,\xi_i,t_i,u_i,v_i}{\operatorname{argmin}} & \frac{1}{2}\|w\|^2 + C\sum_i \xi_i \\ s.t. & \xi_i \geq 0 \\ & \xi_i \geq 1-y_i\cdot(w\cdot x_i+b)+t_i \\ & t_i \geq \sum_j C_f\left(v_{ij}(x_j^{max}-x_{ij})-u_{ij}(x_j^{min}-x_{ij})\right) \\ & u_i-v_i=\frac{1}{2}(1+y_i)w \\ & u_i \succeq 0 \\ & v_i \succeq 0 \end{array}$$

5.2 AD-SVM against Restrained Attack Model

With the restrained attack model, we modify the hinge loss model and solve the problem following the same steps:

$$h(w,b,x_i) = \left\{ \begin{array}{ll} \max\limits_{\delta_i} \lfloor 1-(w\cdot(x_i+\delta_i)+b)\rfloor_+ & \text{if } y_i=1 \\ \lfloor 1+(w\cdot x_i+b)\rfloor_+ & \text{if } y_i=-1 \end{array} \right.$$

$$\begin{array}{l} s.t. \\ (x_i^t-x_i)\circ\delta_i \preceq C_\xi\left(1-C_\delta\frac{|x_i^t-x_i|}{|x_i|+|x_i^t|}\right)\circ(x_i^t-x_i)^{\circ 2} \\ (x_i^t-x_i)\circ\delta_i \succeq 0 \end{array}$$

where δ_i denotes the modification to x_i, $\preceq$ is component-wise inequality, and $\circ$ denotes component-wise operations.

The worst case hinge loss is obtained by solving the following minimization problem:

$$\begin{array}{rcl} f_i & = & \min\limits_{\delta_i} \frac{1}{2}(1+y_i)w\cdot\delta_i \\ s.t. & & (x_i^t-x_i)\circ\delta_i \preceq C_\xi\left(1-C_\delta\frac{|x_i^t-x_i|}{|x_i|+|x_i^t|}\right)\circ(x_i^t-x_i)^{\circ 2} \\ & & (x_i^t-x_i)\circ\delta_i \succeq 0 \end{array}$$

Let

$$e_{ij} = C_\xi\left(1-C_\delta\frac{|x_{ij}^t-x_{ij}|}{|x_{ij}|+|x_{ij}^t|}\right)(x_{ij}^t-x_{ij})^2.$$

We reduce the bilinear problem to the following asymmetric dual problem over $u_i \in \mathbb{R}^d$, $v_i \in \mathbb{R}^d$ where d is the dimension of the feature space:

$$\begin{array}{lll} g_i & = & \max - \sum_j e_{ij} u_{ij}, \text{ or} \\ g_i & = & \min \sum_j e_{ij} u_{ij} \\ s.t. & & (-u_i + v_i) \circ (x_i^t - x_i) = \frac{1}{2}(1 + y_i) w \\ & & u_i \succeq 0 \\ & & v_i \succeq 0 \end{array}$$

The SVM risk minimization problem can be rewritten as follows:

$$\begin{array}{ll} \underset{w,b,t_i,u_i,v_i}{\operatorname{argmin}} & \frac{1}{2}||w||^2 + C \sum_i \lfloor 1 - y_i \cdot (w \cdot x_i + b) + t_i \rfloor_+ \\ s.t. & t_i \geq \sum_j e_{ij} u_{ij} \\ & (-u_i + v_i) \circ (x_i^t - x_i) = \frac{1}{2}(1 + y_i) w \\ & u_i \succeq 0 \\ & v_i \succeq 0 \end{array}$$

After removing the non-differentiality of the hinge loss, we can rewrite the problem as follows:

$$\begin{array}{ll} \underset{w,b,\xi_i,t_i,u_i,v_i}{\operatorname{argmin}} & \frac{1}{2}||w||^2 + C \sum_i \xi_i \\ s.t. & \xi_i \geq 0 \\ & \xi_i \geq 1 - y_i \cdot (w \cdot x_i + b) + t_i \\ & t_i \geq \sum_j e_{ij} u_{ij} \\ & (-u_i + v_i) \circ (x_i^t - x_i) = \frac{1}{2}(1 + y_i) w \\ & u_i \succeq 0 \\ & v_i \succeq 0 \end{array}$$

6. EXPERIMENT

We test the AD-SVM models on both artificial and real data sets. In our experiments, we investigate the robustness of the AD-SVM models as we increase the severeness of the attacks. We let x_i^t be the centroid of the innocuous data in our AD-SVM model against restrained attacks. We also tried setting x_i^t to a random innocuous data point in the training or test set, and the results are similar. Due to space limitations, we do not report the results in the latter cases.

Attacks on the test data used in the experiments are simulated using the following model:

$$\delta_{ij} = f_{attack}(x_{ij}^- - x_{ij})$$

where x_i^- is an innocuous data point randomly chosen from the test set, and $f_{attack} > 0$ sets a limit for the adversary to move the test data toward the target innocuous data points. By controlling the value of f_{attack}, we can dictate the severity of attacks in the simulation. The actual attacks on the test data are intentionally designed not to match the attack models in AD-SVM so that the results are not biased. For each parameter C_f, C_δ and C_ξ in the attack models considered in AD-SVM, we tried different values as f_{attack} increases. This allows us to test the robustness of our AD-SVM model in all cases where there are no attacks and attacks that are much more severe than the model has anticipated. We compare our AD-SVM model to the standard SVM and one-class SVM models. We implemented our AD-SVM algorithms in CVX—a package for specifying and solving convex programs [12]. Experiments using SVM and one-class SVM are implemented using Weka [13].

6.1 Experiments on Artificial Dataset

We generate two artificial data sets from bivariate normal distributions with specified means and covariance matrices. Data in the first data set is well separated. The second data set consists of data more cluttered near the separating boundary. All results are averaged over 100 random runs.

6.1.1 *Data Points Well Separated*

Figure 2 illustrates the data distributions when different levels of distortion are applied to the malicious data by setting f_{attack} to 0 (original distribution), 0.3, 0.5, 0.7, and 1.0. As can be observed, as f_{attack} increases, the malicious data points are moved more aggressively towards innocuous data.

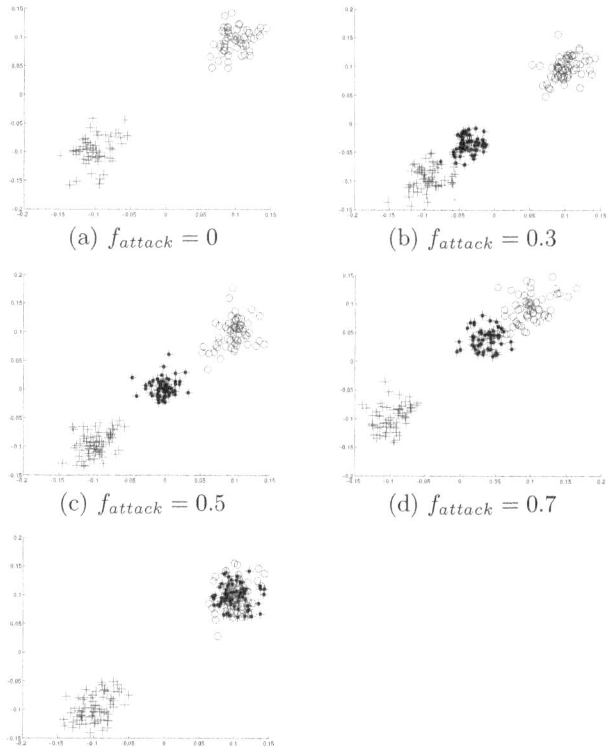

(a) $f_{attack} = 0$ (b) $f_{attack} = 0.3$ (c) $f_{attack} = 0.5$ (d) $f_{attack} = 0.7$ (e) $f_{attack} = 1.0$

Figure 2: Data distributions of the *first* data set after attacks. f_{attack} varies from 0 (no attack) to 1.0 (most aggressive). Plain "+" marks the original positive data points, "+" with a central black square marks positive data points after alteration, and "o" represents negative data.

Table 1 lists the predictive accuracy of our AD-SVM algorithm with the free-range attack model, the standard SVM algorithm, and the one-class SVM algorithm. AD-SVM clearly outperforms both SVM and one-class SVM when it assumes reasonable adversity ($C_f \in [0.1, 0.5]$). When there is mild attack or no attack at all, AD-SVM with more aggressive free-range assumptions ($C_f \in [0.5, 0.9]$) suffers great performance loss as we expect from such pessimistic model.

Compared to the free-range attack model, the restrained attack model works much more consistently across the entire spectrum of the learning and attack parameters. Here C_δ reflects the aggressiveness of attacks in our AD-SVM learning algorithm. Table 2 shows the classification results as C_δ decreases, from less aggressive ($C_\delta = 0.9$) to very aggressive ($C_\delta = 0.1$). Clearly, the most impressive results are lined up along the diagonal when the assumptions on the attacks

Table 1: **Accuracy of *free-range* AD-SVM, SVM, and one-class SVM under data distributions shown in Figure 2(a), 2(b), 2(c), 2(d), and 2(e). C_f *increases* as the learning model assumes more aggressive attacks.**

		$f_{attack} = 0$	$f_{attack} = 0.3$	$f_{attack} = 0.5$	$f_{attack} = 0.7$	$f_{attack} = 1.0$
AD-SVM	$C_f = 0.1$	1.000	**1.000**	**0.887**	**0.512**	0.500
	$C_f = 0.3$	1.000	**1.000**	**0.997**	**0.641**	0.500
	$C_f = 0.5$	0.996	0.996	**0.996**	**0.930**	0.500
	$C_f = 0.7$	0.882	0.886	**0.890**	**0.891**	0.500
	$C_f = 0.9$	0.500	0.500	0.500	0.500	0.500
SVM		1.000	0.999	0.751	0.502	0.500
One-class SVM		1.000	0.873	0.500	0.500	0.500

Table 2: **Accuracy of *restrained* AD-SVM, SVM, and one-class SVM under data distributions shown in Figure 2(a), 2(b), 2(c), 2(d), and 2(e). C_δ *decreases* as the learning model assumes more aggressive attacks.**

		$f_{attack} = 0$	$f_{attack} = 0.3$	$f_{attack} = 0.5$	$f_{attack} = 0.7$	$f_{attack} = 1.0$
AD-SVM ($C_\xi = 1$)	$C_\delta = 0.9$	1.000	**1.000**	**0.856**	**0.505**	0.500
	$C_\delta = 0.7$	1.000	**1.000**	**0.975**	**0.567**	0.500
	$C_\delta = 0.5$	1.000	**1.000**	**0.999**	**0.758**	0.500
	$C_\delta = 0.3$	0.994	0.994	**0.994**	**0.954**	0.500
	$C_\delta = 0.1$	0.878	0.876	**0.878**	**0.878**	0.500
SVM		1.000	0.998	0.748	0.501	0.500
One-class SVM		1.000	0.873	0.500	0.500	0.500

made in the learning model match the real attacks. The results of our AD-SVM in the rest of the experiments are mostly superior to both SVM and one-class SVM too. This relax the requirement of finding the best C_δ. Regardless of what C_δ value is chosen, our model delivers solid performance.

6.1.2 Data Cluttered Near Separating Boundary

Figure 3 illustrates the distributions of our second artificial data set under different levels of attacks. Malicious data points can be pushed across the boundary with little modification. We again consider both the free-range and the restrained attack models. Similar conclusions can be drawn: restrained AD-SVM is more robust than free-range AD-SVM; AD-SVMs in general cope much better with mild adversarial attacks than standard SVM and one-class SVM models.

Table 3 lists the predictive accuracy of our AD-SVM algorithm with the free-range attack model on the second data set. The results of the standard SVM algorithm and the one-class SVM algorithm are also listed. The free-range model is overly pessimistic in many cases, which overshadows its resilience against the most severe attacks. For the restrained attack model, since the two classes are not well separated originally, C_ξ is used (not combined with C_δ) to reflect the aggressiveness of attacks in AD-SVM. A larger C_ξ is more aggressive while a smaller C_ξ assumes mild attacks. Table 4 shows the classification results as C_ξ increases, from less aggressive ($C_\xi = 0.1$) to very aggressive ($C_\xi = 0.9$).

The restrained AD-SVM model still manages to improve the predictive accuracy compared to SVM and one-class SVM, although the improvement is much less impressive. This is understandable since the data set is generated to make it harder to differentiate between malicious and innocuous data, with or without attacks. The model suffers no performance loss when there are no attacks.

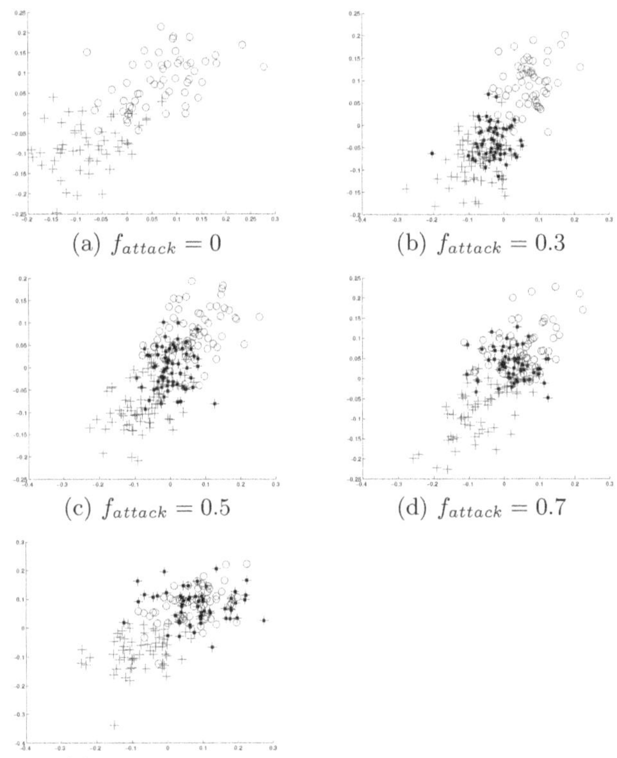

(a) $f_{attack} = 0$ (b) $f_{attack} = 0.3$ (c) $f_{attack} = 0.5$ (d) $f_{attack} = 0.7$ (e) $f_{attack} = 1.0$

Figure 3: Data distributions of the *second* data set after attacks. f_{attack} varies from 0 (none) to 1.0 (most aggressive). Plain "+" marks the original positive data points, "+" with a central black square is for positive data points after alteration, and "○" represents negative data.

Table 3: Accuracy of *free-range* AD-SVM, SVM, and one-class SVM under data distributions shown in Figure 3(a), 3(b), 3(c), 3(d), and 3(e). C_f *increases* as the learning model assumes more aggressive attacks.

		$f_{attack}=0$	$f_{attack}=0.3$	$f_{attack}=0.5$	$f_{attack}=0.7$	$f_{attack}=1.0$
AD-SVM	$C_f=0.1$	0.928	**0.884**	**0.771**	**0.609**	0.500
	$C_f=0.3$	0.859	0.848	**0.807**	**0.687**	0.500
	$C_f=0.5$	0.654	0.649	0.658	**0.638**	0.500
	$C_f=0.7$	0.500	0.500	0.500	0.500	0.500
	$C_f=0.9$	0.500	0.500	0.500	0.500	0.500
SVM		0.932	0.859	0.715	0.575	0.500
One-class SVM		0.936	0.758	0.611	0.527	0.500

Table 4: Accuracy of *restrained* AD-SVM, SVM, and one-class SVM under data distributions shown in Figure 3(a), 3(b), 3(c), 3(d), and 3(e). C_ξ *increases* as the learning model assumes more aggressive attacks.

		$f_{attack}=0$	$f_{attack}=0.3$	$f_{attack}=0.5$	$f_{attack}=0.7$	$f_{attack}=1.0$
AD-SVM ($C_\delta=1$)	$C_\xi=0.9$	0.932	**0.860**	**0.719**	**0.575**	0.500
	$C_\xi=0.7$	0.930	**0.858**	**0.717**	**0.576**	0.500
	$C_\xi=0.5$	**0.935**	**0.860**	**0.721**	**0.578**	0.500
	$C_\xi=0.3$	0.931	0.855	**0.718**	**0.577**	0.500
	$C_\xi=0.1$	0.933	**0.858**	**0.718**	**0.575**	0.500
SVM		0.930	0.856	0.714	0.574	0.500
One-class SVM		0.933	0.772	0.605	0.525	0.500

6.2 Experiments on Real Datasets

We also test our AD-SVM model on two real datasets: *spam base* taken from the UCI data repository [2], and *web spam* taken from the LibSVM website [1].

In the *spam base* data set, the spam concept includes advertisements, make money fast scams, chain letters, etc. The spam collection came from the postmaster and individuals who had filed spam. The non-spam e-mail collection came from filed work and personal e-mails [2]. The dataset consists of 4601 total number of instances, among which 39.4% is spam. There are 57 attributes and one class label. We divide the data sets into equal halves, with one half T_r for training and the other half T_s for test only. Learning models are built from 10% of random samples selected from T_r. The results are averaged over 10 random runs.

We took the second data set from the LibSVM website [1]. According to the website, the *web spam* data is the subset used in the Pascal Large Scale Learning Challenge. All positive examples were kept in the data set while the negative examples were created by randomly traversing the Internet starting at well known web-sites. They treat continuous n bytes as a word and use word count as the feature value and normalize each instance to unit length. We use their unigram data set in which the number of features is 254. The total number of instances is 350,000. We again divide the data set into equal halves for training and test. We use 2% of the samples in the training set to build the learning models and report the results averaged over 10 random runs.

Table 5 and Table 6 show the results on the *spam base* data set. AD-SVM, with both the free-range and the restrained attack models, achieved solid improvement on this data set. C_δ alone is used in the restrained learning model. Except for the most pessimistic cases, AD-SVM suffers no performance loss when there are no attacks. On the other hand, it achieved much more superior classification accuracy than SVM and one-class SVM when there are attacks.

Table 7 and Table 8 illustrate the results on the *web spam* data set. Unlike the *spam base* data set where data is well separated, *web spam* data is more like the second artificial data set. The AD-SVM model exhibits similar classification performance as on the second artificial data set. The free-range model is too pessimistic when there are no attacks, while the restrained model performs consistently better than SVM and one-class SVM and, more importantly, suffers no loss when there are no attacks. We use C_ξ alone in our learning model. Which parameter, C_ξ or C_δ, to use in the restrained attack model can be determined through cross validation on the initial data. Next subsection has a more detailed discussion on model parameters.

6.3 Setting C_f, C_ξ, and C_δ

The remaining question is how to set the parameters in the attack models. The AD-SVM algorithms proposed in this paper assume either a free-range attack model or a restrained attack model. In reality we might not know the exact attack model or the true utility function of the attackers. However, as Tables 1–8 demonstrate, although the actual attacks may not match what we have anticipated, our AD-SVM algorithm using the restrained attack model exhibits overall robust performance by setting C_δ or C_ξ values for more aggressive attacks. If we use the restrained attack model, choosing $C_\delta \leq 0.5$ ($C_\xi \geq 0.5$) consistently returns robust results against all f_{attack} values. If we use the free-range attack model in AD-SVM, we will have to set parameter values to avoid the very pessimistic results for mild attacks. Hence choosing $C_f \leq 0.3$ in general returns good classification results against all f_{attack} values.

As a general guideline, the baseline of C_f, C_δ or C_ξ has to be chosen to work well against attack parameters suggested by domain experts. This can be done through cross-validation for various attack scenarios. From there, we gradually increase C_f or C_ξ, or decrease in the case of C_δ. The best value of C_f, C_δ or C_ξ is reached right before perfor-

Table 5: Accuracy of AD-SVM, SVM, and one-class SVM on the *spambase* dataset as attacks intensify. The *free-range* attack is used in the learning model. C_f *increases* as attacks become more aggressive.

		$f_{attack} = 0$	$f_{attack} = 0.3$	$f_{attack} = 0.5$	$f_{attack} = 0.7$	$f_{attack} = 1.0$
AD-SVM	$C_f = 0.1$	**0.882**	**0.852**	**0.817**	**0.757**	**0.593**
	$C_f = 0.3$	0.880	**0.864**	**0.833**	**0.772**	**0.588**
	$C_f = 0.5$	0.870	**0.860**	**0.836**	**0.804**	**0.591**
	$C_f = 0.7$	0.859	**0.847**	**0.841**	**0.814**	**0.592**
	$C_f = 0.9$	0.824	**0.829**	**0.815**	**0.802**	**0.598**
SVM		0.881	0.809	0.742	0.680	0.586
One-Class SVM		0.695	0.686	0.667	0.653	0.572

Table 6: Accuracy of AD-SVM and SVM on *spambase* dataset as attacks intensify. The *restrained* attack model is used in the learning model. C_δ *decreases* as attacks become more aggressive.

		$f_{attack} = 0$	$f_{attack} = 0.3$	$f_{attack} = 0.5$	$f_{attack} = 0.7$	$f_{attack} = 1.0$
AD-SVM ($C_\xi = 1$)	$C_\delta = 0.9$	0.874	**0.821**	**0.766**	**0.720**	0.579
	$C_\delta = 0.7$	**0.888**	**0.860**	**0.821**	**0.776**	0.581
	$C_\delta = 0.5$	0.874	**0.860**	**0.849**	**0.804**	0.586
	$C_\delta = 0.3$	0.867	**0.855**	**0.845**	**0.809**	0.590
	$C_\delta = 0.1$	0.836	**0.840**	**0.839**	**0.815**	**0.597**
SVM		0.884	0.812	0.761	0.686	0.591
One-class SVM		0.695	0.687	0.676	0.653	0.574

Table 7: Accuracy of AD-SVM, SVM, and one-class SVM on *webspam* dataset as attacks intensify. The *free-range* attack model is used in the learning model. C_f *increases* as attacks become more aggressive.

		$f_{attack} = 0$	$f_{attack} = 0.3$	$f_{attack} = 0.5$	$f_{attack} = 0.7$	$f_{attack} = 1.0$
AD-SVM	$C_f = 0.1$	0.814	**0.790**	**0.727**	**0.591**	**0.463**
	$C_f = 0.3$	0.760	0.746	**0.732**	**0.643**	**0.436**
	$C_f = 0.5$	0.684	0.649	0.617	**0.658**	**0.572**
	$C_f = 0.7$	0.606	0.606	0.606	**0.606**	**0.606**
	$C_f = 0.9$	0.606	0.606	0.606	**0.606**	**0.606**
SVM		0.874	0.769	0.644	0.534	0.427
One-class SVM		0.685	0.438	0.405	0.399	0.399

Table 8: Accuracy of AD-SVM, SVM, and one-class SVM on *webspam* dataset as attacks intensify. The *restrained* attack model is used in the learning model. C_ξ *increases* as attacks become more aggressive.

		$f_{attack} = 0$	$f_{attack} = 0.3$	$f_{attack} = 0.5$	$f_{attack} = 0.7$	$f_{attack} = 1.0$
AD-SVM ($C_\delta = 1$)	$C_\xi = 0.1$	**0.873**	**0.822**	**0.699**	**0.552**	**0.435**
	$C_\xi = 0.3$	0.870	**0.837**	**0.748**	**0.597**	**0.444**
	$C_\xi = 0.5$	0.855	**0.833**	**0.772**	**0.641**	**0.454**
	$C_\xi = 0.7$	0.841	**0.820**	**0.773**	**0.663**	**0.467**
	$C_\xi = 0.9$	0.822	**0.803**	**0.749**	**0.671**	**0.478**
SVM		0.871	0.769	0.659	0.512	0.428
One-class SVM		0.684	0.436	0.406	0.399	0.400

mance deteriorates. Also note that it is sufficient to set only one of C_ξ and C_δ while fixing the other to 1. Furthermore, C_f, C_δ and C_ξ do not have to be a scalar parameter. In many applications, it is clear some attributes can be changed while others cannot. A C_f, C_δ/C_ξ parameter vector would help enforce these additional rules.

7. CONCLUSIONS AND FUTURE WORK

Adversarial attacks can lead to severe misrepresentation of real data distributions in the feature space. Learning algorithms lacking the flexibility of handling the structural change in the samples would not cope well with attacks that modify data to change the make up of the sample space. We present two attack models and an adversarial SVM learning model against each attack model. We demonstrate that our adversarial SVM model is much more resilient to adversarial attacks than standard SVM and one-class SVM models. We also show that optimal learning strategies derived to counter overly pessimistic attack models can produce unsatisfactory results when the real attacks are much weaker. On the other hand, learning models built on restrained attack models perform more consistently as attack parameters vary. One future direction for this work is to add cost-sensitive metrics into the learning models. Another direction is to extend the single learning model to an ensemble in which each base learner handles a different set of attacks.

8. ACKNOWLEDGEMENTS

This work was partially supported by Air Force Office of Scientific Research MURI Grant FA9550-08-1-0265, National Institutes of Health Grant 1R01LM009989, National Science Foundation (NSF) Grant Career-CNS-0845803, and NSF Grants CNS-0964350, CNS-1016343, CNS-1111529.

9. REFERENCES

[1] *LIBSVM Data: Classification, Regression, and Multi-label*, 2012.

[2] *UCI Machine Learning Repository*, 2012.

[3] M. Barreno, B. Nelson, R. Sears, A. D. Joseph, and J. D. Tygar. Can machine learning be secure? In *Proceedings of the 2006 ACM Symposium on Information, computer and communications security*, pages 16–25, New York, NY, USA, 2006. ACM.

[4] M. Bruckner and T. Scheffer. Nash equilibria of static prediction games. In *Advances in Neural Information Processing Systems*. MIT Press, 2009.

[5] M. Bruckner and T. Scheffer. Stackelberg games for adversarial prediction problems. In *Proceedings of the 17th ACM SIGKDD International Conference on Knowledge Discovery and Data Mining*. ACM, 2011.

[6] N. Dalvi, P. Domingos, Mausam, S. Sanghai, and D. Verma. Adversarial classification. In *Proceedings of the tenth ACM SIGKDD international conference on Knowledge discovery and data mining*, KDD '04, pages 99–108, New York, NY, USA, 2004. ACM.

[7] O. Dekel and O. Shamir. Learning to classify with missing and corrupted features. In *Proceedings of the International Conference on Machine Learning*, pages 216–223. ACM, 2008.

[8] O. Dekel, O. Shamir, and L. Xiao. Learning to classify with missing and corrupted features. *Machine Learning*, 81(2):149–178, 2010.

[9] L. El Ghaoui, G. R. G. Lanckriet, and G. Natsoulis. Robust classification with interval data. Technical Report UCB/CSD-03-1279, EECS Department, University of California, Berkeley, Oct 2003.

[10] P. Fogla and W. Lee. Evading network anomaly detection systems: formal reasoning and practical techniques. In *Proceedings of the 13th ACM conference on Computer and communications security*, CCS '06, pages 59–68, New York, NY, USA, 2006. ACM.

[11] A. Globerson and S. Roweis. Nightmare at test time: robust learning by feature deletion. In *Proceedings of the 23rd international conference on Machine learning*, ICML '06, pages 353–360. ACM, 2006.

[12] M. Grant and S. Boyd. CVX: Matlab software for disciplined convex programming, version 1.21. `http://cvxr.com/cvx/`, Apr. 2011.

[13] M. Hall, E. Frank, G. Holmes, B. Pfahringer, P. Reutemann, and I. H. Witten. The weka data mining software: an update. *SIGKDD Explor. Newsl.*, 11:10–18, November 2009.

[14] M. Kantarcioglu, B. Xi, and C. Clifton. Classifier evaluation and attribute selection against active adversaries. *Data Min. Knowl. Discov.*, 22:291–335, January 2011.

[15] M. Kearns and M. Li. Learning in the presence of malicious errors. *SIAM Journal on Computing*, 22:807–837, 1993.

[16] G. R. G. Lanckriet, L. E. Ghaoui, C. Bhattacharyya, and J. M. I. A robust minimax approach to classification. *Journal of Machine Learning Research*, 3:555–582, 2002.

[17] Z. Li, M. Sanghi, Y. Chen, M.-Y. Kao, and B. Chavez. Hamsa: Fast signature generation for zero-day polymorphic worms with provable attack resilience. In *Proceedings of the 2006 IEEE Symposium on Security and Privacy*. IEEE Computer Society, 2006.

[18] W. Liu and S. Chawla. Mining adversarial patterns via regularized loss minimization. *Mach. Learn.*, 81:69–83, October 2010.

[19] D. Lowd. Good word attacks on statistical spam filters. In *In Proceedings of the Second Conference on Email and Anti-Spam (CEAS)*, 2005.

[20] D. Lowd and C. Meek. Adversarial learning. In *Proceedings of the eleventh ACM SIGKDD international conference on Knowledge discovery in data mining*, KDD '05, pages 641–647, 2005.

[21] J. Newsome, B. Karp, and D. X. Song. Polygraph: Automatically generating signatures for polymorphic worms. In *2005 IEEE Symposium on Security and Privacy, 8-11 May 2005, Oakland, CA, USA*, pages 226–241. IEEE Computer Society, 2005.

[22] R. Perdisci, D. Dagon, W. Lee, P. Fogla, and M. Sharif. Misleadingworm signature generators using deliberate noise injection. In *Proceedings of the 2006 IEEE Symposium on Security and Privacy*, pages 17–31, 2006.

[23] C. H. Teo, A. Globerson, S. T. Roweis, and A. J. Smola. Convex learning with invariances. In *Advances in Neural Information Processing Systems*, 2007.

[24] K. Wang, J. J. Parekh, and S. J. Stolfo. Anagram: A content anomaly detector resistant to mimicry attack. In *Recent Advances in Intrusion Detection, 9th International Symposium*, pages 226–248, 2006.

[25] G. L. Wittel and S. F. Wu. On attacking statistical spam filters. In *Proceedings of the first Conference on Email and Anti-Spam (CEAS)*, 2004.

Web Image Prediction Using Multivariate Point Processes

Gunhee Kim
Computer Science Department
Carnegie Mellon University
Pittsburgh, 15213 PA
gunhee@cs.cmu.edu

Li Fei-Fei
Computer Science Department
Stanford University
Stanford, 94305 CA
feifeili@cs.stanford.edu

Eric P. Xing
Computer Science Department
Carnegie Mellon University
Pittsburgh, 15213 PA
epxing@cs.cmu.edu

ABSTRACT

In this paper, we investigate a problem of predicting *what images are likely to appear on the Web at a future time point*, given a query word and a database of historical image streams that potentiates learning of uploading patterns of previous user images and associated metadata. We address such a *Web image prediction* problem at both a collective group level and an individual user level. We develop a predictive framework based on the multivariate point process, which employs a stochastic parametric model to solve the relations between image occurrence and the covariates that influence it, in a flexible, scalable, and globally optimal way. Using Flickr datasets of more than ten million images of 40 topics, our empirical results show that the proposed algorithm is more successful in predicting unseen Web images than other candidate methods, including forecasting on semantic meanings only, a PageRank-based image retrieval, and a generative author-time topic model.

Categories and Subject Descriptors

H.3.3 [**Information Storage and Retrieval**]: Information Search and Retrieval—*Retrieval models*

Keywords

Web image prediction, multivariate point processes, penalized Poisson regression, personalization

1. INTRODUCTION

The prevalence of digital cameras and smartphones has led to an explosion of pictures being uploaded and shared online, across websites, platforms and social networks. This phenomenon poses great challenges and opportunities in multimedia data mining research. In this paper, we address an interesting problem along this line – predicting likely images to appear on the Web at a future time point and retrieving images similar to them from the database, after learning patterns of previous user images and associated metadata.

KDD'12, August 12–16, 2012, Beijing, China.

Fig.1 shows our problem statement with an example of a query *world+cup*. Suppose that we have the image database downloaded from Flickr for the *world+cup* up to 12/31/2008[1]. Can we then estimate what would be the most likely pictures that are taken in a future query time[2] 6/6/2009, and retrieve images similar to them from the database? As Fig.1.(c) has shown, the pictures actually taken at 6/6/2009 and shared on Flickr are not necessarily about the best possible world cup pictures (if the definition of *best* is even possible). Instead, they are the pictures that not only reflect the semantic meaning of the keyword, but also people's intends at that given moment of time. Furthermore, if a user cue is supplemented, the image prediction becomes highly personalized as shown in Fig.1.(d), given that individual users have their own preferences and photo-taking styles.

The problem in this paper is closely related to one active area of research in information retrieval: *exploring the temporal dynamics of user behaviors on Web queries* [5, 16, 18, 22]. The popularity of queries and their best search results change over time as people's interests evolve. For example, in [18], it is reported that more than 7% of queries are the ones that do not actually contain a year, but the user implicitly formulate with a specific year in mind (*e.g.* miss universe, Olympics). Moreover, many of them are connected to the events that have occurred with predictable periodicity. This line of research aims to improve search relevance by identifying what search terms are sensitive to time, what documents should be retrieved to the query time, and what webpages are likely to be clicked by a user at a particular time point. However, much of previous work has targeted at the search of documents such as blogs and news archives by analyzing the query log data; modeling and predicting temporal dynamics of Web user images has yet received little attention, even though photos are another popular modality to share the information on the Web.

Consequently, one important application of our image pre-

[1]Strictly speaking, we address a varient of *image re-ranking*; we assume that a text-based image search engine (*e.g.* Flickr search engine) provides a large-scale pool of unordered Web images for a given query word. Then, our goal is to re-rank those images to be fit for a query time. Image re-ranking following a text-based image search is the de facto pipeline for major image search engines such as Google and Bing [4].

[2]We are interested in future as a query time point rather than past or present because it is most interesting and challenging. For a query time in the past, we may trivially retrieve the images taken at that time from the database. However, if the query time is in future, we have to learn users' photo-taking patterns and extrapolate likely images to appear for the query time.

Figure 1: (a) Given an image sequence of *world+cup* up to 12/31/2008, can we guess what images are likely to appear at a future time point t_q=6/6/2009? (c) Collective image prediction. The *world+cup* usually refers to the soccer event, so a soccer scene can be a reasonable guess. However, the actual Web images are diverse because they reflect different users' experiences and preferences. (d) Personalized image prediction for a user u_6. A user's unique angle of seeing the topic can make the prediction more focused. The images are sampled from Flickr at each time.

diction is *time and user sensitive Web image re-ranking*. Suppose that a user submits a query *world+cup* into *Google and Bing image search*, which then invariably retrieve redundant photos of soccer in the first page. Although the term *world+cup* usually refers to the international soccer event, it is also commonly used in other international sports and competitions (*e.g.* ski, skate, bicycle, or horse riding, as shown in Fig.1.(a)). Therefore, if the *world+cup* is submitted in winter by a user who likes skiing, it is more desirable to include ski world cup photos in the retrieved result. Our image prediction framework can enable the re-ranking of the retrieved images, so that various views of the query word are shown, according to who searches, and when the search takes place. With the majority of Web photos now coming from hundreds of millions of general users with different experiences and preferences, the contents of images that are associated even with the same keyword can be highly variable according to owners and temporal information.

On the technical aspect, we develop an image prediction algorithm using a multivariate point process, which is a stochastic process that consists of a series of random events occurring at points in time and space [6]. In our method, an observed image stream is viewed as an instance of the multivariate point process. Although this well-established statistical model has been employed for analysis of neural spiking activities [27], and for event detection in video [21], no attempt has been made for image retrieval or re-ranking so far. Nonetheless, we adapt it to offer several key advantages for large-scale image prediction as follows: (i) *Flexibility*: The image occurrence on the Web is correlated with a wide range of factors or covariates (*e.g.* season, time, user preference, and other external events). A parametric model can be easily set up to relate the image occurrence probability with any number of factors that influence it (section 3.3). (ii) *Optimality*: The sparse globally-optimal MLE solution is computed to identify only a small number of key factors and their relative weights (section 3.2). (iii) *Scalability*: The learning and prediction are performed in a linear time with respect to all parameters, including time steps and the number of covariates (section 3.4). (iv) *Prediction accuracies*: Our experiments on more than ten millions of Flickr images have demonstrated compelling results on both collective and personalized image forecast over various 40 topic keywords. Indeed we show that our approach outperforms other methods including a PageRank-based image retrieval [15] and a generative author-time topic model [23] (section 4).

1.1 Relations to Previous work

The problem of image prediction using large-scale Web photo collections remains an under-addressed topic in the image retrieval literature. Our work is remotely related to following four lines of research, but is significantly different on the task, utility and methodology. Due to vast volume of literatures on these topics, we introduce only some selected papers that are most closely related to our work.

Web content dynamics: This research aims at large-scale analyses to describe how the Web content changes over time. Most previous work [1, 28] has dealt with the textual content on the Web such as news articles and scientific libraries. In the image domain, the most related work to ours may be [15] in that both involve studying topic evolution in large-scale Flickr photos. However, the main tasks of [15] were subtopic outbreak detection and classification of noisy web images. They did not address the image prediction, which is our main task here. Also, they did not explore any issues regarding personalization, as done in this work.

Similar image retrieval: The image prediction problem is also related to similar image retrieval, a well-studied topic in computer vision [8, 20, 26]. They are related in a way that in both cases, given a query, relevant images are returned from the database. Yet, there are a number of key differences. Traditional similar image retrieval tends to focus solely on the semantic meaning of the query word and feature-wise image similarity, whereas our image prediction additionally emphasizes the temporal trends and user histories associated with the images.

Image based collaborative filtering: The goal of this research is to mine the trends of people's interests from community photos such as Flickr. Examples include the social trends in politics and market [13], and spatio-temporal events [24]. However, most existing work has used images as the source of information to infer other phenomena rather than taking themselves as a subject to be forecasted.

Leveraging Web photos to infer missing information: The final related work is on inferring missing information by leveraging a large-scale Web image corpus. Some notable examples include scene completion [12], geo-location estimation of a photo sequence [14], 3-D models of landmarks [25], semantic image hierarchy [17], and people

Figure 2: A multivariate point process for a short image stream of the penguin. (a) Each image is assigned to a timestamp (t) and one of three visual clusters (v), which indicate {*ice hockey*, *animal penguin*, and *snowy mountain*}. (b) The image stream is modeled by a discrete-time trivariate point process according to visual clusters.

matching [11]. However, future image occurrence has not been explored as missing information to be inferred.

1.2 Summary of Contributions

Departing from the literatures reviewed above, the main contributions of our work can be summarized as follows:

(1) We develop a method for collective and personalized image prediction. To the best of our knowledge, there have been few attempts so far on such prediction tasks using large-scale Web photos. Our work can be used in several interesting data mining applications, such as time and user based image suggestion and re-ranking.

(2) We design our algorithm using multivariate point processes. We are not aware of any prior instances of multivariate point process in image re-ranking applications; here we adapt this well-founded statistical model to address a number of key challenges of Web image prediction, including flexibility, optimality, scalability, and prediction accuracies.

2. PROBLEM STATEMENT

We define the image prediction as a variant of the time and user sensitive image re-ranking problem. As an input, an image database consists of Flickr photos in $[0, T)$ that are downloaded by a topic keyword, together with their metadata including timestamps and user IDs. Then, given a future time point $t_q > T$ in the form of (M/D/Y), we retrieve L number of the most likely images from the database. Actual Web images to be predicted at any days are usually hundreds or more in volume and extremely diverse in content. Therefore, we first predict the trends of image clusters, and sample multiple L images as output accordingly, in order to cover various aspects of the topic.

We address both *collective* and *personalized* image prediction. The former refers to a generic prediction for arbitrary individuals using all collected information; and the latter concerns a customized forecast for a particular individual u_q to be specified at test time. The personalized prediction focuses on an individual user's history, whereas the collective prediction deals with societally aggregated trends.

Our problem involves learning a model of the image occurrences with related factors or covariates, and then building a forecast algorithm to sample the likely images based on the learned model. Multivariate point processes are a unified statistical framework to solve these problems, which will be discussed in detail in the next section.

In this paper, we exploit three information modalities based on which a prediction is made: image description, user description, and timestamps at which photos are taken. For clarity, we explain below the preprocessing steps of the first two modalities, and the third one is self-explanatory.

Image Description: All images are clustered into M different groups, which is called as *visual clusters* in this paper. We first extract two types of features for each image, spatial pyramids of dense HSV SIFT and HOG[3]. Then, we construct a visual dictionary of M clusters (*e.g.* $M = 500$) for each topic by applying K-means to randomly selected $100K$ features. Finally, each image is assigned to the nearest visual cluster in the feature space.

User Description: Measuring user propensity is important in collaborative filtering [7] because a user's future behavior is likely to be correlated with those of users who are similar to her. Intuitively, each user can be represented by a set of images that she has posted. We first compute an M-dimensional histogram for each user where each bin represents the count of images belonging to the corresponding visual cluster. Instead of directly using the user descriptor, we perform the pLSI-based user clustering proposed by Google News personalization [7]. In pLSI, the distribution of visual cluster v in a user u_i's images $p(v|u_i)$ is given by the following generative model:

$$p(v|u_i) = \sum_{z \in \mathcal{Z}} p(v|z)p(z|u_i). \tag{1}$$

The latent variable $z \in \mathcal{Z}$ is assumed to represent the cluster of user propensity. Thus, $p(z|u_i)$ is proportional to the fractional membership of user i to cluster z. We denote $p(z|u_i)$ by $\mathbf{u}_i$, which is used as the descriptor of a user u_i. The $\mathbf{u}_i$ is an L-1 normalized $|\mathcal{Z}|$-dimensional vector (*i.e.* $|\mathcal{Z}| = 50$).

For simplicity and better exposition of our point process framework, we use relatively simple image and user descriptors, and assume that the images in the same visual cluster are interchangeable. However, it is straightforward to enhance our method by replacing them with richer descriptors (*e.g.* soft assignment of visual clusters) or by adding other types of information (*e.g.* text tags).

3. POINT PROCESSES FOR WEB PHOTO STREAMS

3.1 Multivariate Point Processes

We employ a multivariate point process to model a stream of input images, as illustrated in Fig.2. Formally, a multivariate point process can be described by a counting process $\mathbf{N}(t) = (N^1(t), \cdots, N^M(t))^T$ where M is the number of visual clusters and $N^i(t)$ is the total number of observed images assigned to the i-th visual cluster in the interval $(0, t]$. Then, $N^i(t + \Delta) - N^i(t)$ represents the number of images in a small interval Δ. By letting $\Delta \to 0$, we obtain the *intensity function* $\lambda^i(t)$ (*i.e.* image occurrence rate) at t, which indicates the infinitesimal expected occurrence rate of the

[3]The codes for dense SIFT and HOG are available at http://www.vlfeat.org/ and http://www.robots.ox.ac.uk/~vgg/software/, respectively.

images of the i-th visual cluster at time t [6]:

$$\lambda^i(t) = \lim_{\Delta\to 0} \frac{P[N^i(t+\Delta)-N^i(t)=1]}{\Delta}, \; i \in \{1,\dots,M\}. \quad (2)$$

Data likelihood: Suppose that we partition the interval $(0,T]$ by a sufficiently large number K (*i.e.* $\Delta = T/K$) so that in each time bin Δ only one or zero image occurs. In other words, if we let $\Delta N_k^i = N_k^i - N_{k-1}^i$ be the number of images of the i-th visual cluster occurred between t_{k-1} and t_k, then ΔN_k^i can be zero or one. Here, t_k is the k-th interval ($t_k = k\Delta$). Now we can denote the sequence of images up to T by $N_{1:K}^i = (\Delta N_1^i, \cdots, \Delta N_K^i)$. This discretization induces that the log-likelihood function is represented by [27]

$$l(N_{1:K}^i|\boldsymbol{\theta}^i) = \sum_{k=1}^{K} \log(\lambda^i(t_k|\boldsymbol{\theta})\Delta)\Delta N_k^i - \sum_{k=1}^{K} \lambda^i(t_k|\boldsymbol{\theta})\Delta \quad (3)$$

where $\lambda^i(t_k|\boldsymbol{\theta})$ is the parametric form of the intensity function at k-th interval.

3.2 Regularized Generalized Linear Model

In order to relate the image occurrence with covariates, we model the intensity function as the exponential of a linear combination of functions f_j^i of the covariates x_k:

$$\log \lambda^i(t_k|\boldsymbol{\theta}^i) = \sum_{j=1}^{J} \theta_j^i f_j^i(x_1,\cdots,x_L), \; i \in \{1,\dots,M\} \quad (4)$$

where $\boldsymbol{\theta}^i = (\theta_1^i, \cdots, \theta_J^i)$ is a vector of model parameters and J is the number of covariate functions. It is shown in [27] that the likelihood of a point process in Eq.(3) along with λ^i of Eq.(4) is identical to the likelihood of a *generalized linear model* (GLM) under a Poisson probability model and a log link function, which is also known as the *Poisson regression.*

L1 regularized likelihood: It is reasonable to assume that although numerous factors affect image occurrences, each visual cluster depends on only a small subset of them. Hence, it is important to detect a small number of strong covariates by encouraging a sparse estimator of $\boldsymbol{\theta}^i$, and we maximize the likelihood with ℓ_1 penalty:

$$l_R(N_{1:K}^i|\boldsymbol{\theta}^i) = l(N_{1:K}^i|\boldsymbol{\theta}^i) - \mu \sum_{j=1}^{J} |\theta_j^i|. \quad (5)$$

We can efficiently solve the MLE solution to Eq.(5) (*i.e.* generalized linear models with ℓ_1 norm regularization) by using the cyclical coordinate descent in [10]. We use the regularized path to find the best regularization parameter μ; we perform a 10-fold cross validation procedure and choose μ that minimizes the mean cross-validated error.

Example: Here, we introduce a toy example to intuitively show how the proposed model predicts the image occurrence. For simplicity of the example, we assume that the intensity function is affected by only year and month covariates:

$$\log \lambda^i(t_k|\boldsymbol{\theta}^i) = \theta_0^i + \sum_{y=2003}^{2009} \theta_y^i I_y(t_k) + \sum_{m=1}^{12} \theta_m^i I_m(t_k) \quad (6)$$

where the parameter set comprises seven θ_y^i and twelve θ_m^i. $I_y(t_k)$ is an indicator function that is 1 if the year of t_k is y, and 0 otherwise (*e.g.* $I_y(t_k) = 1$ if $y = 2009$ and $t_k = 03/01/2009$). $I_m(t_k)$ is an indicator for the month.

Fig.3 shows the learned intensity functions $\lambda^i(t)$ of two visual clusters N^1 and N^2 with respect to years and months.

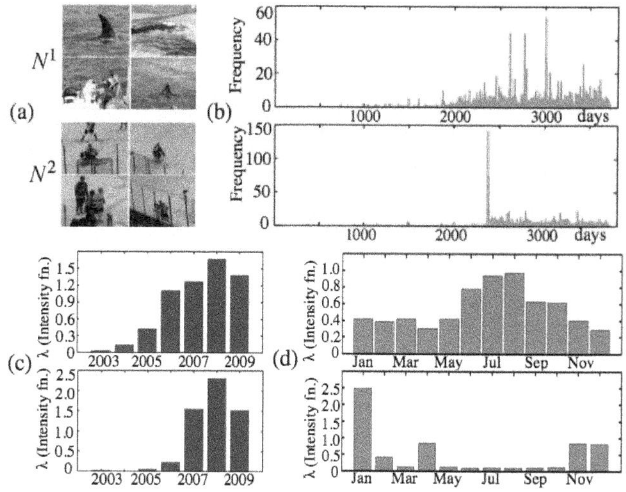

Figure 3: An example of the Poisson regression model for two visual clusters (N^1, N^2) of the *Shark*: {*dolphins in the sea, ice hockey team*}. (a) Four images sampled from N^1 and N^2. (b) Observed occurrence data. (c)-(d) The estimated intensity functions for years and months. In (d), N^1(top) and N^2(bottom) show different intensify functions peaked in summer and winter, respectively.

Fig.3.(b) presents the observed image sequences. For both N^1 and N^2, the intensity functions increase every year (See Fig.3.(c)). The rates decrease in 2009 because the *shark* dataset was gathered up to mid 2009. Interestingly, N^1 and N^2 show different monthly behaviors (See Fig.3.(d)). The N^1 for *dolphins in the sea* has a higher intensity value (*i.e.* more frequently occurred) in summer, whereas the N^2 for the *ice hockey team* peaks around January. This observation is reasonable because sea tours are popular in summer and the ice hockey season takes place during winter.

The learned intensity functions can be used for a simple image prediction. For example, if the month of query time t_q is January, then $\lambda^2(t_q)(\approx 2.5) > \lambda^1(t_q)(\approx 0.4)$, and we can sample the images from N^2 six times more than from N^1.

3.3 A Composite Model of Intensity Functions

Now we introduce the full model of the intensity function λ^i that can be used in image prediction. Note that any probable factors can be flexibly included into the model without any performance loss, because our objective function in Eq.(5) encourages a sparse solution in which the weights of irrelevant covariates are zeros.

We assume that the occurrence of each visual cluster is affected by three types of covariates: (i) its own history, (ii) behaviors of other visual clusters, and (iii) external covariates. It leads to the following composite intensity function:

$$\lambda^i(t_k|\boldsymbol{\theta}^i) = \lambda_h^i(t_k|\boldsymbol{\theta}_h^i)\lambda_e^i(t_k|\boldsymbol{\theta}_e^i)\lambda_x^i(t_k|\boldsymbol{\theta}_x^i), \; i \in \{1,...,M\} \quad (7)$$

where the λ_h^i, λ_e^i, and λ_x^i are called the components of intensity functions for history, correlation, and external covariates, respectively. They are described in Eq.(8)-(10) with an example of Fig.4. For brevity, we omit the superscript i in the following equations.

The first history component is modeled as a linear autore-

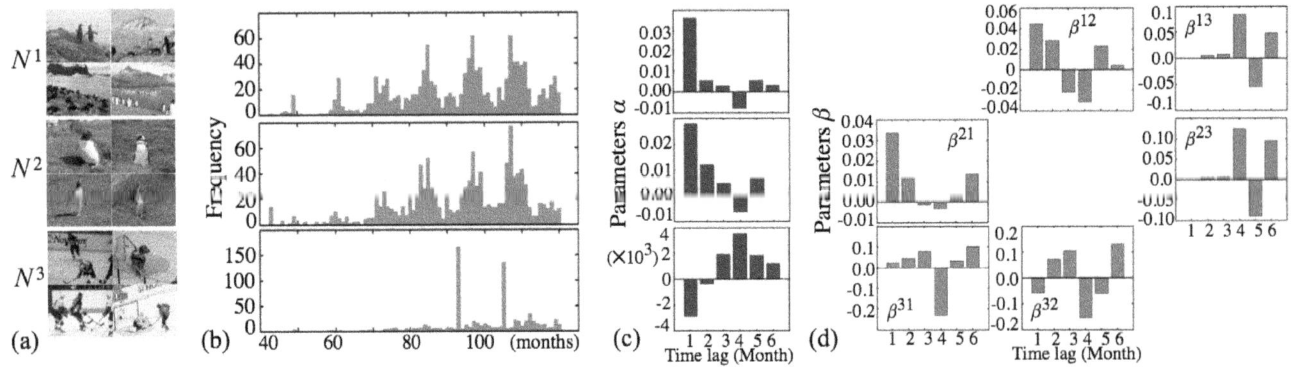

Figure 4: Examples of the *Penguin* topic for the learned parameters of history and correlation components. Visual clusters are {*penguins in landscape, penguins on grass, ice hockey team*}. (a) Four images sampled from each visual cluster. (b) Observed occurrence data. The N^1 and N^2 are strongly synchronized and periodically peaked in summer, whereas the N^3 has two high peaks in winter. (c)-(d) Learned parameters of history and correlation components, respectively.

gressive (AR) process of order P with $\boldsymbol{\theta}_h = \{\alpha_0, \cdots, \alpha_P\}$:

$$\log \lambda_h(t_k|\boldsymbol{\theta}_h) = \alpha_0 + \sum_{p=1}^{P} \alpha_p \Delta N\big(t_k - pd, t_k - (p-1)d\big). \quad (8)$$

$\Delta N(t_1, t_2)$ denotes the number of images during $[t_1, t_2)$, and d is the width of the time window (*e.g.* if $\Delta = 1$ day and $d = 7$, then $\Delta N(t_k - d, t_k)$ is the number of images occurred during previous one week from t_k). The history component reflects the dynamic behavior of a visual cluster. As shown in Fig.4.(c), the learned parameters of N^1 (top) and N^2 (middle) show the typical patterns for yearly periodic behaviors, whereas the parameters of N^3 (bottom) are biphasic, which indicates a bursty occurrence.

The second correlation component models the influence from the history of other visual clusters:

$$\log \lambda_e(t_k|\boldsymbol{\theta}_e) = \beta_0 + \sum_{\substack{c=1 \\ c \neq i}}^{M} \sum_{q=1}^{R} \beta_j^{ic} \Delta N^c\big(t_k - qd, t_k - (q-1)d\big) \quad (9)$$

where the parameter $\boldsymbol{\theta}_e$ consists of $(M-1) \times R + 1$ parameters of β in the full model. This correlation component is quite useful for the actual prediction in the Flickr dataset; we observe that there are strong correlations between visual clusters, and thus the existence or absence of a particular visual cluster gives a strong clue for others' prediction. The learned parameters β in Fig.4.(d) clearly present the correlations observed in Fig.4.(b). For example, the subfigures of β^{12} and β^{21} in Fig.4.(d) show that the occurrence of N^1 and N^2 are highly synchronized, whereas the subfigures of β^{13} and β^{23} illustrate the occurrence of N^3 precedes those of N^1 and N^2 by about four months. For fast computation, instead of using the full pairwise model, we learn the correlations of each N^i with top K most frequent visual clusters.

The extrinsic component incorporates any types of factors that are likely to influence the image occurrence. In this paper, we use months and user descriptors as covariates:

$$\log \lambda_x(t_k|\boldsymbol{\theta}_x) = \gamma_0 + \sum_{m=1}^{12} \gamma_m g(t_k - m) + \sum_{z=1}^{Z} \gamma_z \mathbf{u}_{t_k\text{-}d:t_k}(z). \quad (10)$$

We use $g(t_k - m) \propto \exp(-\alpha(t_k - m)^2)$ for month covariates. The idea is that if an image occurs in June, some contributions are also given on nearby months like May and July, assuming that images are smoothly changed as time goes. The user covariate is the average of user preferences of the images in $[t_k - d, t_k)$. The $\mathbf{u}_{t\text{-}d:t}(z)$ is the mean of z-th elements of user descriptors for the images in $[t_k - d, t_k)$.

In this paper, we introduce only three types of covariates for modeling of image occurrences, but one can freely add or remove covariate functions according to the characteristics of image topics unless they contradict the definition of Eq.(4). For example, other textual or social factors may be supplemented as covariates; or the AR model can be replaced by a more general linear temporal model such as ARMA (AutoRegressive Moving-Average).

3.4 Learning and Prediction

The learning corresponds to obtain MLE solution $\boldsymbol{\theta}^{i*}$ of Eq.(5) from the observe image sequences $N^i_{i:K}$ by solving

$$\max_{\boldsymbol{\theta}} \left(\sum_{k=1}^{K} \log \lambda^i(t_k|\boldsymbol{\theta}) \Delta N^i_k - \sum_{k=1}^{K} \lambda^i(t_k|\boldsymbol{\theta}) - \mu \sum_{j=1}^{J} |\theta^i_j| \right) \quad (11)$$

where $\lambda^i(t_k|\boldsymbol{\theta})$ has the form of Eq.(7). We use the cyclical coordinate descent in [10].

In the prediction step, given a query time t_q, we first obtain the set of $\lambda^i(t_q|\boldsymbol{\theta}^{i*})$ for $i = \{1, \ldots, M\}$, which indicates the occurrence rates of each visual cluster for t_q. It is computed by gathering covariate values at t_q, and plugging them with $\boldsymbol{\theta}^*$ into the Eq.(7). The final output is L number of most likely images for t_q, which is sampled according to $\lambda^i(t_q|\theta^*)$. The images of visual clusters with higher $\lambda^i(t_q|\theta^*)$ are more likely to be chosen for t_q. We use the thinning algorithm [19], which is a rejection sampling to simulate new samples from intensity functions.

Our parametric model is scalable. The learning time is $O(MTJ)$ where T is the number of time steps (*e.g.* discretized by day) and J is the number of covariates. Our code written in Matlab takes about 30 minutes to learn the model for the 810K of *soccer* images with $M = 200$, $T = 1,500$, and $J = 118$. The complexity of prediction time is $O(MJ)$. In the same experiment, it takes far less than one second.

3.5 Personalization

Given a query user u_q, the idea of personalization is to weight more the history of pictures taken by u_q or similar users to u_q during learning. For collective prediction, one

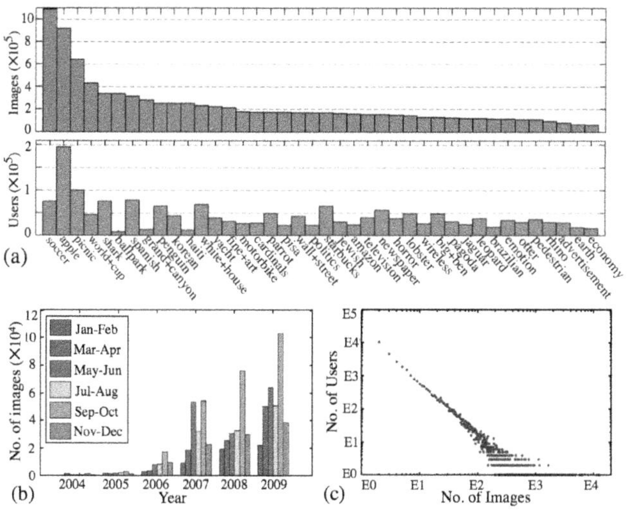

Figure 5: Flickr datasets. (a) The numbers of images and users for the 40 topics. (b) The seasonal distribution and (c) the log-log plot between the number of images and users for the *soccer* topic.

image occurrence is counted by equally one (*e.g.* the occurrence data in Fig.3.(b) simply count the number of images taken in each day). On the other hand, for personalized prediction, an image by u_q is weighted by a larger value so that the model fitting is more biased to the images of u_q. Likewise, the weight of an image occurrence can be assigned according to the similarity between its owner and u_q.

We implemented this idea by using the locally weighted learning framework [2], which is a form of lazy learning for a regression to adjust the weighting of data samples according to a query. More specifically, the weights of image data of any user u_x are assigned by $w_x = \sqrt{K(d(\mathbf{u}_q, \mathbf{u}_x))}$ where $\mathbf{u}_q$ is the user descriptor of a query user u_q, d is the distance function $d(\mathbf{u}_q, \mathbf{u}_x) = (\mathbf{u}_q - \mathbf{u}_x)^2$, and K is the Gaussian kernel function $K(d) = \exp(-d^2/\sigma)$.

In our lazy learning personalization, the training is deferred until a query user is assigned. For fast processing, if the number of users to be considered is very large, we can first perform user clustering (*e.g.* [7]), and learn the personalized prediction model offline for each group of users.

4. RESULTS

We evaluate the performance of our algorithm for collective and personalized image prediction using Flickr datasets. A simplified MATLAB demo code is available at our webpage `http://www.cs.cmu.edu/~gunhee`.

4.1 Evaluation Setting

Datasets: Our dataset consists of 10,284,945 images of 40 topics from Flickr. Some topics are re-used from the datasets of [15] and others are newly downloaded. Both datasets are collected by the same protocol, in which the topic name is used as a search word and all queried images are downloaded without any filtering. For the timestamp, the *date_taken* field is used. Fig.5 summarizes some statistics of our Flickr dataset. Fig.5.(a) shows the numbers of images and users of all 40 topics, which are roughly classified into {*nations*, *places*, *animals*, *objects*, *activities*, *abstract*, *hot topics*}. Fig.5.(b) shows a seasonal variation of the *soccer* dataset; the photo-taking peaks in autumn but falls in winter. Fig.5.(c) is a log-log plot between the numbers of images (x-axis) and users (y-axis). The number of images per user follows Zipf's law in almost all topics. That is, only a few users contribute the majority of images, and most users have only a small number of images.

Tasks: We first divide all image sets into training and test sets by time; training sets $\mathcal{I}_T$ consist of the images taken up to 12/31/2008 and test sets are the others. In the following experiments, $\mathcal{I}_T$ is used as both the database for retrieval and training data to learn the image occurrence patterns.

The collective image prediction is performed as follows; a topic name and a future time point t_q are given in a form of (M/D/Y) (*i.e.* t_q is a time point in 2009 or 2010). The images that are actually taken in $[t_q \pm 1$ days$]$ are the positive test set $\mathcal{I}_+$ to be estimated. The goal is to select L images $\mathcal{I}_e$ from $\mathcal{I}_T$ so that $\mathcal{I}_e$ and $\mathcal{I}_+$ are as similar as possible to each other. We set $L = 200$ in our experiments. In almost all test cases, the sizes of positive test sets are larger than L (*i.e.* $|\mathcal{I}_+| > L$).

The personalized image prediction is tested similarly only except that a query user u_q is additionally specified at test time. The goal of is to predict L likely images so that they are similar to the actual images taken by u_q at t_q, which are used as the positive test set $\mathcal{I}_+$.

For each topic, we randomly generate 20 t_q values and 20 (t_q, u_q) pairs as test cases of collective and personalized image forecast, respectively. A user is considered as u_q if she has a sufficiently large number of images in both training and test sets (*i.e.* at least 500 images in the training set and at least 100 images in the test set).

Baselines and Competitors: Since the Web image prediction is relatively novel, there are few existing methods to be compared. Hence, we come up with three alternatives for image prediction, and quantitatively compare them with our algorithm. Table 1 summarizes the baselines.

The (`SemIN`) [9] represents the prediction based on semantic meaning only. It is compared to show that the semantic meaning of a topic word is not enough to predict the user images on the Web. The (`RetPR`) [15] and (`TopAT`) [23][4] are the state-of-the-art methods for PageRank-based image retrieval and generative topic modeling, respectively.

In the personalized forecast, the locally weighted learning is also applied to all the other competitors except `SemIN`, which is a random sampling from the ImageNet dataset.

Evaluation Measures: We evaluated the performance of all algorithms by measuring the similarity between the estimated images $\mathcal{I}_e$ and actual images $\mathcal{I}_+$ at t_q. Due to lack of a perfect measure for image similarity, we calculate three popular metrics in image retrieval according to information levels: `L2`, `Tiny`, and average precision (`AP`), as shown in Table 2. `L2` is the most low-level metric by feature-wise comparison, and `AP` is the most high-level one based on classification ability. No single measure may be perfect, but one algorithm can be fairly said *better* if it constantly outperforms others in all three metrics. For `L2` and `Tiny`, we first find the one-to-one correspondences between estimated $\mathcal{I}_e$ and actual $\mathcal{I}_+$, and then calculate average distances. Since `L2` and `Tiny` are distance measures, a lower value means a better prediction, whereas in the `AP`, the higher is the better.

[4]We modified the toolbox at http://psiexp.ss.uci.edu/research/programs_data/toolbox.htm.

Method	Rationale	Description
Sampling from ImageNet (SemIN) [9]	Using semantic meaning only	ImageNet data are representative images of each topic cleaned by human annotation. We randomly sample L images as predicted images $\mathcal{I}_e$ for t_q.
PageRank-based prediction (RetPR) [15]	State-of-the-art retrieval algorithm	We first build a similarity graph between the images taken in the similar month to t_q from $\mathcal{I}_T$, and sample highly-ranked images by PageRank [3].
Author-Time Topic Model (TopAT) [20]	State-of-the-art generative topic modeling	We modify Author-Topic model [23] to jointly model image contents, users, and month data. We first estimate the subtopic distribution of each month, which means the popularity of visual clusters per month. We then sample the images according to the subtopic distributions of the month of t_q.

Table 1: Summary of the three baselines used for the quantitative comparison.

Metric	Description
L2	L2 distance between image descriptors (*i.e.* Spatial pyramids of denseSIFT and HOG features).
tiny	Inspired by [26], we first resize the images to 32×32 tiny color images, and compute the SSD (the sum of squared differences between pixels of images).
AP	Let $\mathcal{I}_+$ be actual images at t_q (*i.e.* positive test data) and $\mathcal{I}_-$ be negative data by randomly selecting the same number images outside of $[t_q \pm 3$ months$]$. Each algorithm ranks top L images out of $(\mathcal{I}_+ \cup \mathcal{I}_-)$, from which average precisions are computed.

Table 2: Description of three evaluation metrics. For L2 and Tiny, we first find the one-to-one correspondences between estimated $\mathcal{I}_e$ and actual $\mathcal{I}_+$, and then calculate average distances.

4.2 Results of Collective Image Prediction

Fig.6 summarizes the quantitative comparison between our method and three baselines. In each figure, the leftmost bar set is the average performance of 40 topics, and the results of 15 sampled topics follow. Our algorithm significantly outperformed all the competitors in most measures. In the average performance, the L2(tiny) measure of our method is smaller by 5.1(8.8)%, 17.1(6.5)%, and 34.2(15.5)% over the RetPR, TopAT, and SemIN, respectively. Our AP is also higher than the best of baselines by 8 %. Among the baselines, the RetPR was the best, and the SemIN was the worst.

Fig.7 shows several examples of collective prediction for the topics of *world+cup*, *cardinals*, *shark*, and the *penguin* in several months. Each figure is obtained as follows. We first find the one-to-one correspondences between the estimated $\mathcal{I}_e$ and the actual $\mathcal{I}_+$ by the L2 measure. Out of L matched pairs ($L = 200$), we only sample five matches and show the predicted images by our algorithm in the first row, and their matched actual images in the second row. The five examples may be too few compared to 200 matched pairs, but here we focus on qualitative analysis, since we already discuss the quantitative superiority of our algorithm in Fig.6.

The term *world+cup* is commonly used in different sports and competitions (*e.g.* soccer, ski, skating, cycling, horse riding, and even cocktail competitions), and the popular sports in the images are changed according to the query times. The topic *cardinal* is also used in different meanings, including a bird, a baseball team, and an American football team. The football images are frequent from fall to winter, whereas the baseball images are dominant from spring to fall. They agree with the scheduled seasons of corresponding sports. The bird images are also varied according to the query times. The popular backgrounds of bird images are snowy fields in winter and leafy trees in summer. The images about eggs and baby cardinals also appear in summer.

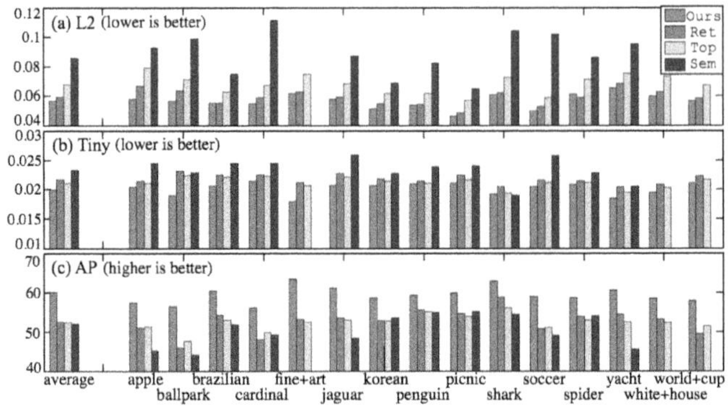

Figure 6: Quantitative comparison between our method and three baselines (RetPG[15], TopAT[23], SemIN[9]) for collective image prediction using three metrics in (a)-(c).

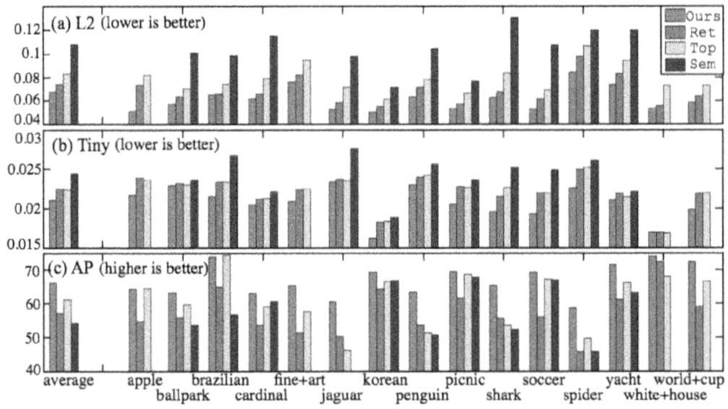

Figure 8: Quantitative comparison between our method and three baselines (RetPG[15], TopAT[23], SemIN[9]) for personalized image prediction using three metrics in (a)-(c).

Similar observations can be made as well in the *shark* and *penguin* topics, as shown in Fig.7.(g)-(l).

This observation concludes that indeed the Web image collections are extremely diverse, but some topics follow predictable patterns. Specifically, our predictive model works well for polysemous topics that show strong annual or periodic trends, and is promisingly applicable to time-sensitive image suggestion or re-ranking.

4.3 Results of Personalized Image Prediction

Fig.8 shows the quantitative results of personalized image prediction for the same 15 topics in Fig.6. In the average performance, our method is far better than all the baselines. The personalized prediction is more accurate than the collective forecast, because knowing the user at query time provides a strong clue to predict the images.

Figure 7: Examples of collective image prediction for the topics of *world+cup* ((a)-(c)), *cardinal* ((d)-(f)), *shark* ((g)-(i)), and *penguin* ((j)-(l)) in some selected months. In all sets, we first find one-to-one correspondences between the estimated images $\mathcal{I}_e$ and the actual images $\mathcal{I}_+$ by the L2 measure, and then sample five image pairs per month. The first row shows the estimated images by our method, and the second row depicts their matched actual images.

Fig.9 delivers a clear evidence for the importance of personalization in image prediction tasks. Even with the same keyword, users show various preferences. As shown in Fig.9.(a)-(c), the meanings of the term *fine+art* are differently recognized according to the users, such as paintings, classes, and photography. Other examples in Fig.9, including *Brazilian*, *apple*, and *picnic*, also show that this personal variation is quite common in online user photo sets, but it can be correctly treated once the user history is learned.

This observation presents that our method can be employed in the image search where a query word has a board range of concepts, which are varied much according to people's thoughts and interests. This personalized search has been actively studied in textual information retrieval, but our analysis reveals that images can convey more delicate information about user preferences that are hardly captured by text descriptions. For example, in the *fine+art* topic, following questions can be effectively addressed: What styles of paintings does the user like? How does the class presentation look like?

5. CONCLUSION

We studied the collective and personalized image prediction tasks, which can be applicable to a time and user sensitive Web image re-ranking using large-scale online images. The multivariate point process model was successfully tailored to achieve the flexibility, optimality, scalability, and prediction accuracy. As a promising direction of future work, it is interesting to incorporate other meta data surrounding Flickr photos such as comments or favs for better forecast.

6. ACKNOWLEDGMENTS

This work is supported by Google, ONR N000140910758, AFOSR FA9550010247, NSF IIS-0713379, and NSF DBI-0640543. L.F-F is supported by grant from NSF-IIS-1115313.

7. REFERENCES

[1] A. Ahmed, Q. Ho, C. H. Teo, J. Eisenstein, A. J. Smola, and E. P. Xing. Online Inference for the Infinite Topic-Cluster Model: Storylines from Streaming Text. In *AISTAT*, 2011.

[2] C. G. Atkeson, A. W. Moore, and S. Schaal. Locally Weighted Learning. *AI Review*, 11(1):11–73, 1997.

[3] S. Brin and L. Page. The Anatomy of a Large-scale Hypertextual Web Search Engine. In *WWW*, 1998.

[4] J. Cui, F. Wen, and X. Tang. Real Time Google and Live Image Search Re-ranking. In *MM*, 2008.

[5] W. Dakka, L. Gravano, and P. G. Ipeirotis. Answering General Time-Sensitive Queries. In *CIKM*, 2008.

[6] D. Daley and D. Vere-Jones. *An Introduction to the Theory of Point Processes*. Springer, 2003.

[7] A. S. Das, M. Datar, , A. Garg, and S. Rajaram. Google News Personalization: Scalable Online Collaborative Filtering. In *WWW*, 2007.

[8] J. Deng, A. C. Berg, and L. Fei-Fei. Hierarchical Semantic Indexing for Large Scale Image Retrieval. In *CVPR*, 2011.

[9] J. Deng, W. Dong, R. Socher, L.-J. Li, K. Li, and L. Fei-Fei. ImageNet: A Large-Scale Hierarchical Image Database. In *CVPR*, 2009.

Figure 9: Examples of personalized image prediction for the topics of *fine+art* ((a)-(c)), *Brazilian* ((d)-(f)), *apple* ((g)-(i)) and *picnic* ((j)-(l)) for some selected users. Similarly to Fig.7, in all sets, the first row shows the predicted images, and the second row is their matched actual images. The themes of images are largely varied across the users.

[10] J. Friedman, T. Hastie, and R. Tibshirani. Regularization Paths for Generalized Linear Models via Coordinate Descent. *J. Stat. Soft.*, 33:1–22, 2010.

[11] R. Garg, D. Ramanan, S. Seitz, and N. Snavely. Where's Waldo: Matching People in Images of Crowds. In *CVPR*, 2011.

[12] J. Hays and A. A. Efros. Scene Completion Using Millions of Photographs. *SIGGRAPH*, 26(3), 2007.

[13] X. Jin, A. Gallagher, L. Cao, J. Luo, and J. Han. The Wisdom of Social Multimedia: Using Flickr for Prediction and Forecast. In *ACM MM*, 2010.

[14] E. Kalogerakis, O. Vesselova, J. Hays, A. A. Efros, and A. Hertzmann. Image Sequence Geolocation with Human Travel Priors. In *ICCV*, 2009.

[15] G. Kim, E. P. Xing, and A. Torralba. Modeling and Analysis of Dynamic Behaviors of Web Image Collections. In *ECCV*, 2010.

[16] A. Kulkarni, J. Teevan, K. M. Svore, and S. T. Dumais. Understanding Temporal Query Dynamics. In *WSDM*, 2011.

[17] L.-J. Li, C. Wang, Y. Lim, D. Blei, and L. Fei-Fei. Building and Using a Semantivisual Image Hierarchy. In *CVPR*, 2010.

[18] D. Metzler, R. Jones, F. Peng, and R. Zhang. Understanding Temporal Query Dynamics. In *SIGIR*, 2009.

[19] Y. Ogata. On Lewis' Simulation Method for Point Processes. *IEEE Info. Theo.*, 27(1):23–31, 1981.

[20] J. Philbin, O. Chum, M. Isard, J. Sivic, and A. Zisserman. Lost in Quantization: Improving Particular Object Retrieval in Large Scale Image Databases. In *CVPR*, 2008.

[21] K. Prabhakar, S. Oh, P. Wang, G. Abowd, and J. M. Rehg. Temporal Causality and the Analysis of Interactions in Video. In *CVPR*, 2010.

[22] K. Radinsky, K. Svore, S. Dumais, J. Teevan, A. Bocharov, and E. Horvitz. Modeling and Predicting Behavioral Dynamics on the Web. In *WWW*, 2012.

[23] M. Rosen-Zvi, T. Griffiths, M. Steyvers, and P. Smyth. The Author-Topic Model for Authors and Documents. In *UAI*, 2004.

[24] V. K. Singh, M. Gao, and R. Jain. Social Pixels: Genesis and Evaluation. In *ACM MM*, 2010.

[25] N. Snavely, I. Simon, M. Goesele, R. Szeliski, and S. M. Seitz. Scene Reconstruction and Visualization From Community Photo Collections. *Proc. IEEE*, 98(8), 2010.

[26] A. Torralba and W. T. F. Rob Fergus. 80 Million Tiny Images: A Large Data Set for Nonparametric Object and Scene Recognition. *IEEE PAMI*, 30:1958–1970, 2008.

[27] W. Truccolo, U. T. Eden, M. R. Fellows, J. P. Donoghue, and E. N. Brown. A Point Process Framework for Relating Neural Spiking Activity to Spiking History, Neural Ensemble, and Extrinsic Covariate Effects. *J. Neurophysiol*, 93(2):1074–1089, 2005.

[28] X. Wang and A. McCallum. Topics Over Time: a Non-Markov Continuous-Time Model of Topical Trends. In *KDD*, 2006.

Transductive Multi-label Ensemble Classification for Protein Function Prediction

Guoxian Yu
School of Comp. Sci. & Tech.
South China Univ. of Tech.
Guangzhou, 510006, China
guoxian.yu@mail.scut.edu.cn

Carlotta Domeniconi
Dept. of Computer Science
George Mason University
Fairfax, 22030,VA
carlotta@cs.gmu.edu

Huzefa Rangwala
Dept. of Computer Science
George Mason University
Fairfax, 22030, VA
rangwala@cs.gmu.edu

Guoji Zhang
School of Sciences
South China Univ. of Tech.
Guangzhou, 510640, China
magjzh@scut.edu.cn

Zhiwen Yu
School of Comp. Sci. & Tech.
South China Univ. of Tech.
Guangzhou, 510006, China
zhwyu@scut.edu.cn

ABSTRACT

Advances in biotechnology have made available multitudes of heterogeneous proteomic and genomic data. Integrating these heterogeneous data sources, to automatically infer the function of proteins, is a fundamental challenge in computational biology. Several approaches represent each data source with a kernel (similarity) function. The resulting kernels are then integrated to determine a composite kernel, which is used for developing a function prediction model. Proteins are also found to have multiple roles and functions. As such, several approaches cast the protein function prediction problem within a multi-label learning framework. In our work we develop an approach that takes advantage of several unlabeled proteins, along with multiple data sources and multiple functions of proteins. We develop a graph-based *transductive multi-label classifier* (TMC) that is evaluated on a composite kernel, and also propose a method for data integration using the ensemble framework, called *transductive multi-label ensemble classifier* (TMEC). The TMEC approach trains a graph-based multi-label classifier for each individual kernel, and then combines the predictions of the individual models. Our contribution is the use of a bi-relational *directed* graph that captures relationships between pairs of proteins, between pairs of functions, and between proteins and functions. We evaluate the ability of TMC and TMEC to predict the functions of proteins by using two yeast datasets. We show that our approach performs better than recently proposed protein function prediction methods on composite and multiple kernels.

KDD'12, August 12–16, 2012, Beijing, China.

Categories and Subject Descriptors

I.5.2 [**Pattern Recognition**]: Design Methodology- Classifier Design and Evaluation; J.3 [**Life and Medical Sciences**]: Biology and Genetics

General Terms

Algorithms, Performance, Experimentation

Keywords

Multi-label Ensemble Classifier, Directed Bi-relation Graph, Protein Function Prediction

1. INTRODUCTION

Rapid advances in biotechnology have resulted in a variety of high throughput experimentally obtained genomic and proteomic datasets. Examples include protein-protein interaction networks, microarrays, genome sequences, protein structures, and genetic interaction networks, each of which provide a complementary view of the underlying mechanisms within a living cell. Manually annotating a protein, i.e. determining the "protein function", using the vast volumes of data available from heterogeneous sources is challenging and low throughput. As such, various computational methods have been developed for predicting protein functions by integrating the available biological data [17, 18].

Kernel based approaches [12, 14] have been very popular for developing several bioinformatics tools. The data is represented by means of a kernel function, $\mathcal{K}$, that computes pairwise similarities between proteins (or genes). Kernel functions capture the underlying biological complexity associated with the data. For each data source, a unique kernel function is defined, and each kernel function captures a different notion of similarity. For example, for protein sequences a string kernel [13] can be defined, and for protein-protein interaction (PPI) data a random walk kernel [23] function can be used. Both the sequence and PPI datasets are now defined by different kernel functions, each of which captures similarities between protein pairs within different feature spaces (or embeddings). Several methods [17, 24] have been developed to take advantage of the complementary embeddings induced by different data sources. Many approaches

[12, 15, 27] use a weighted combination (optimal or ad hoc) of multiple kernels derived from the different sources. This kind of approaches can be coined as *data integration*. In addition, supervised ensemble approaches [20, 21] have been developed to integrate the multiple data sources.

Several supervised [20] and semi-supervised [24, 27, 29] approaches have been introduced for predicting the function of proteins. Transductive or semi-supervised approaches are able to take advantage of the large number of available unannotated (unlabeled) proteins to improve the accuracy of function prediction algorithms. Further, proteins are generally involved in more than one biological process, and as such are annotated with multiple functions. Several approaches [9, 10, 19, 30] formulate the protein function prediction problem within a multi-label framework. By treating the dependencies between the different function classes, multi-label approaches achieve superior classification performance in comparison to single-labeled prediction methods.

In this paper we develop a protein function prediction method called *Transductive Multi-label Classifier* (TMC) that treats the relationship between proteins and functions as a directed bi-relation graph. To integrate the heterogeneous sources of protein data, we also develop an ensemble based classifier called *Transductive Multi-label Ensemble Classifier* (TMEC). We can summarize our key contributions as follows:

1. We analyze the use of an undirected bi-relation graph [28] within the label propagation framework, and discuss the advantage of a *directed* bi-relation graph instead.

2. We design a TMC on the directed bi-relation graph, and a weighted ensemble of TMCs (TMEC) trained on different graphs to take advantage of multiple complimentary data sources.

3. We compare *classifier integration* against *data integration*, and show the former is often more effective for protein function prediction.

We performed comprehensive experiments evaluating the performance of TMC and TMEC on two yeast protein function prediction benchmark sets. One of the datasets contains 5 kernels, whereas the other one contains 44 kernels. Our results show that the use of a directed bi-relation graph achieves higher accuracy than the undirected one. Our approaches outperform state-of-the-art protein function prediction approaches; namely, two transductive multi-label classification approaches [9, 30] and a transductive classifier [15].

The rest of the paper is organized as follows. In Section 2, we review related work on protein function prediction using multi-label learning and multiple data sources. In Section 3, we introduce the directed bi-relation graph and the corresponding training procedure. We also describe our ensemble approach to make use of multiple data sources. Section 4 details the experimental protocol, and Section 5 discusses the experimental results. In Section 6, we provide conclusions along with directions for future work.

2. PRIOR WORK

Numerous computational approaches have been developed for protein function prediction. They vary in terms of methodology, input data, and even problem definition. We refer the reader to a comprehensive review on this topic [18], and discuss here only the work most relevant to the scope of the paper.

2.1 Multi-label Learning in Protein Function Prediction

Traditional function prediction methods represent proteins in a feature space and train binary classification models, treating each functional class independently [20]. Given the fact that proteins are involved in multiple functions, and structured relationships are prevalent within protein function annotation databases (e.g., GO[1] is a directed acyclic graph), researchers have formulated the protein function prediction as a multi-label classification problem [26]. RankSVM [7] incorporates a ranking loss function within the minimization function. The work of Chen et. al. [4] improves the RankSVM approach by explicitly including label correlations within the objective function using a hypergraph of interrelated proteins. Specifically, a hypergraph is defined where proteins are connected to each other if they share the same function. Since, the protein function databases like Gene Ontology [5] and FunCat [22] represent proteins within a hierarchy (or a directed acyclic graph), several approaches incorporate the parent-children relationship within the algorithm. The work of Barutcuoglu et. al. [1], first trains independent binary SVM classification models for each of the GO function classes, and then integrates the prediction by incorporating GO's hierarchical structure within a Bayes formulation. Pandey et. al. [19] defined a pairwise similarity term between the different GO labels and incorporated it within a weighted multi-label kNN classifier.

Using protein-protein interaction data, several semi-supervised multi-label learning algorithms have been developed. MCSL [10] uses an objective function that is similar to the local and global consistency method [31]. The approach in [10] incorporates a pairwise function correlation term within the regularization penalty resulting in a Kronecker matrix. To address the computational complexity associated with storing a Kronecker matrix in memory, PfunBG [9] uses an *undirected* bi-relational graph [28] to represent the relationships between proteins and functions. The bi-relational graph captures three types of relationships: (i) protein-protein similarities, (ii) function-function similarities and (iii) protein-function associations. The GRF method [30] uses Jaccard coefficients to measure pairwise function-function similarities, which are incorporated within a manifold regularization framework [2]. All the methods described, MCSL, PfunBG and GRF, utilize pairwise label correlations within a semi-supervised learning framework, but are developed for protein function prediction using a single data source only.

2.2 Data Integration in Protein Function Prediction

Several protein function prediction approaches that capture the complementary information associated with multiple heterogeneous data sources have been developed [17]. Within the kernel optimization framework, Lanckriet et. al. [12] represent each data source as an individual kernel and determine the optimal weighted combination of kernels by solving a semi-definite problem (SDP). This optimization does not scale with large number of proteins, and the work of Tsuda et.

[1]http://www.geneontology.org/

al. [27] use a dual problem and gradient descent to determine the optimal combination of kernels. Shin et. al. [24] seek to determine weights using the EM algorithm [6], by iterating over reducing the prediction error and combining weights. Mostafavi et. al. [16] proposed a heuristic ridge-regression algorithm to combine multiple kernels. We refer the reader to a recent survey of multiple kernel learning methods [8].

The composite kernel determined as a linear combination of individual kernels obtained from the methods described above can be used within SVM-based or graph-based classifiers for protein function prediction. These methods determine the set of weights per function class, which results in increased time complexity. On the other hand, Mostafavi et. al. [15] proposed a method that simultaneously learns a set of weights for a group of correlated functions. This approach was called "Simultaneous Weighting (SW)". SW optimizes a set of weights for a group of functions, constructs a composite kernel for the functional groups, and then uses a graph-based semi-supervised classification scheme. Tsuda et. al. [27], Lewis [14] and Gönen et. al. [8] observe that a composite kernel combined with optimized weights has similar performance to a composite kernel combined with equal weights, i.e. without optimization.

In this paper we develop approaches that differ from traditional kernel integration methods [12, 15, 27]. Traditional methods first combine the kernels, and then annotate proteins using the composite kernels. In contrast, our approach first trains a transductive multi-label classifier (TMC) on each of the kernels representing a data source, and then integrates the predictions using an ensemble classification framework (TMEC). Our experimental evaluation demonstrates that, for the protein function prediction problem, TMEC outperforms methods that train classifiers on composite kernels. In addition, we observe that TMEC outperforms the TMC trained on an individual kernel. This result confirms that the ensemble approach is effective, and therefore the transductive multi-label classifiers trained on individual kernels are complementary to each other.

3. PROBLEM FORMULATION

We consider R different kinds of features that describe the same set of N proteins with C functions. Different kinds of features provide different representations for proteins (*e.g.* as vectors, trees, or networks). We assume that the first l proteins have known functions, and the remaining u proteins are not annotated ($l + u = N$). The R different sources of proteins are transformed into R kernels $[K_r]_{r=1}^{R} (K_r \in R^{N \times N})$, one kernel per source. Our objective is to first train a TMC on a directed bi-relation graph adapted from the kernel K_r, and then combine these TMCs into an ensemble classifier, thus giving TMEC. Finally, we use TMEC to annotate the u proteins. In this section, we first review the bi-relation graph and analyze its drawbacks when used for label propagation. Next, we propose a directed bi-relation graph and train TMC on this graph. We then define our TMEC on multiple kernels.

3.1 Transductive Multi-label Classification on a Directed Bi-relation Graph

Most graph-based multi-label learning methods explicitly incorporate a label correlation term into the general framework of graph-based semi-supervised learning to handle multi-labels [10, 30]. Unlike these methods, Wang *et al.* [28] design an undirected bi-relation graph for image classification and apply a random walk on it [25]. This graph includes both images and labels as nodes. For consistency, hereinafter, we use proteins instead of images and functions instead of labels. A bi-relation graph is composed of three kinds of edges: between proteins, between functions, and between proteins and functions. For the latter, if protein i has function c, an edge is set between them.

A random walk on a graph is often described by a transition probability matrix. For a random walk on a bi-relation graph, the transition probability matrix W is defined as:

$$W = \begin{bmatrix} \beta W_{PP} & (1-\beta)W_{PF} \\ (1-\beta)W_{FP} & \beta W_{FF} \end{bmatrix} \tag{1}$$

where W_{PP} and W_{FF} are the transition probability matrices of the intra-subgraphs of proteins and functions, respectively. W_{PF} and W_{FP} are the inter-subgraph transition probability matrices between proteins and functions, and β controls the relative importance of the intra- and the inter- subgraphs. W_{PP} and W_{FF} are computed as:

$$W_{PP} = D_{PP}^{-1} S_{PP} \quad W_{FF} = D_{FF}^{-1} S_{FF} \tag{2}$$

where $S_{PP} \in R^{N \times N}$ is the similarity matrix of proteins, and S_{FF} is the correlation matrix between functions. D_{PP} and D_{FF} are the diagonal matrices of the row sums of S_{PP} and S_{FF}, respectively. The correlation between functions can be defined in various ways [9, 19, 30]. Here we define the correlation between functions m and n using the cosine similarity as follows:

$$S_{FF}(m,n) = \frac{\mathbf{f}_m^T \mathbf{f}_n}{\|\mathbf{f}_m\| \|\mathbf{f}_n\|} \tag{3}$$

where $\mathbf{f}_m \in R^N (1 \leq m \leq C)$ is the m-th function vector on all proteins: if protein i has function m, then $\mathbf{f}_m(i) = 1$, otherwise $\mathbf{f}_m(i) = 0$. W_{PF} and W_{FP} are calculated as:

$$W_{PF} = D_{PF}^{-\frac{1}{2}} S_{PF} D_{FP}^{-\frac{1}{2}} \quad W_{FP} = D_{FP}^{-\frac{1}{2}} S_{FP} D_{PF}^{-\frac{1}{2}}, \tag{4}$$

where S_{PF} is the relation matrix between proteins and functions and S_{FP} is the transpose of S_{PF}. D_{PF} is the diagonal matrix of the column sums of S_{PF} and D_{FP} is the diagonal matrix of the row sums of S_{PF}. We observe that if protein i has function c then $S_{PF}(i,c) = 1$; otherwise $S_{PF}(i,c) = 0$.

Similarly to hypergraph-based multi-label learning [4], also in the bi-relation graph the c-th function node and the proteins annotated with this function are considered as a group:

$$G_c = v_c^F \cup \{v_i^P | S_{PF}(i,c) = 1\} \tag{5}$$

where v_c^F is the c-th function node and v_i^P is the i-th protein node of the bi-relation graph. In the bi-relation graph, instead of computing the node-to-node relevance between a function node and an unannotated protein node, the relevance between a protein and a group G_c is considered. For the c-th function, the distribution vector $\tilde{Y}_c$ is:

$$\tilde{Y}_c = \begin{bmatrix} \gamma \tilde{Y}_c^P \\ (1-\gamma)\tilde{Y}_c^F \end{bmatrix} \in R^{N+C} \tag{6}$$

where $\tilde{Y}_c^P(i) = \frac{1}{\sum_{i=1}^{N} S_{PF}(i,c)}$ if $S_{PF}(i,c) = 1$ and $\tilde{Y}_c^P(i) = 0$ otherwise; $\tilde{Y}_c^F(j) = 1$ if $j = c$, and $\tilde{Y}_c^F(j) = 0$ otherwise. γ controls the probability for the random walker to jump from a protein subgraph to a function subgraph.

Based on these preliminaries, an iterative objective function, also applied in our TMC, is defined on this bi-relation graph as follows:

$$F^{(t+1)}(j) = (1-\alpha)\sum_{i=1}^{N+C} F^{(t)}(i)W(i,j) + \alpha\tilde{Y}_j \quad (7)$$

where $F^{(t)}(j)$ is the predicted likelihood score vector of the j-th protein in the t-th iteration, α is a scalar value to balance the tradeoff between the initial function set and the predicted function set. From Eq. (7), we can see that the functions of a protein are predicted by the functions of its connected nodes. This makes Eq. (7) a direct protein function prediction method [23].

However, the application of Eq. (7) for protein function prediction has a major drawback. Suppose i is a protein vertex annotated with a function vertex j. The function j may be overwritten by the functions of the proteins connected to i, thus causing the loss of reliable information. As such, the functions of initially annotated proteins may be changed in the iterative label propagation. This phenomenon is similar to the one occurring in the local and global consistency method [31], and should be avoided.

A formal analysis of the above phenomenon is as follows. For simplification, the parameter β in Eq. (1) is not included in the following. Eq. (7) can be rewritten as follows:

$$\begin{aligned}\begin{bmatrix}F_P^{(t+1)}\\F_F^{(t+1)}\end{bmatrix} &= (1-\alpha)\begin{bmatrix}W_{PP} & W_{PF}\\W_{FP} & W_{FF}\end{bmatrix}\begin{bmatrix}F_P^{(t)}\\F_F^{(t)}\end{bmatrix} + \alpha\begin{bmatrix}\tilde{Y}_P\\\tilde{Y}_F\end{bmatrix}\\ &= (1-\alpha)\begin{bmatrix}W_{PP}F_P^{(t)} + W_{PF}F_F^{(t)}\\W_{FP}F_P^{(t)} + W_{FF}F_F^{(t)}\end{bmatrix} + \alpha\begin{bmatrix}\tilde{Y}_P\\\tilde{Y}_F\end{bmatrix}\end{aligned}$$

$$F_P^{(t+1)} = (1-\alpha)(W_{PP}F_P^{(t)} + W_{PF}F_F^{(t)}) + \alpha\tilde{Y}_P \quad (8)$$

$$F_F^{(t+1)} = (1-\alpha)(W_{FP}F_P^{(t)} + W_{FF}F_F^{(t)}) + \alpha\tilde{Y}_F \quad (9)$$

From Eqs. (8-9), we can see that W_{PF} propagates function information from function to protein nodes, and W_{FP} propagates function information from proteins to function nodes. In a bi-relation graph, we expect that information propagates from function to protein nodes, but not vice versa. Thus, we change the undirected bi-relation graph into a directed one. The resulting directed bi-relation graph is shown in Figure 1. In this graph, information can be propagated in the intra-subgraphs W_{PP} and W_{FF}, and in the inter-subgraph W_{PF}, but not in the inter-subgraph W_{FP}. Therefore, we define a new transition probability matrix W_d on the directed bi-relation graph as follows:

$$W_d = \begin{bmatrix}W_{PP} & W_{PF}\\ \mathbf{0} & W_{FF}\end{bmatrix} \quad (10)$$

where $\mathbf{0} \in R^{C\times N}$. In the case where proteins have incorrect annotations (i.e., noisy labels), it will be advantageous to use undirected relationships between proteins and functions.

Based on Eq. (7), setting $F^{(1)} = \tilde{Y}$, we have:

$$F^{(t+1)} = ((1-\alpha)W_d)^{(t)}\tilde{Y} + \alpha\sum_{k=1}^{t}((1-\alpha)W_d)^k\tilde{Y} \quad (11)$$

Since $0 < \alpha < 1$ and $0 \leq (1-\alpha)W_d < 1$, the first term in Eq. (11) is bound to 0, and the second term (excluding $\tilde{Y}$) is a geometric series with the following limit:

$$\lim_{t\to\infty}\sum_{k=1}^{t}((1-\alpha)W_d)^k = (I-(1-\alpha)W_d)^{-1} \quad (12)$$

where $I \in R^{(N+C)\times(N+C)}$ is the identity matrix. Thus the equilibrium solution F of Eq. (7) is:

$$F = \alpha(I-(1-\alpha)W_d)^{-1}\tilde{Y} \quad (13)$$

The predicted $F(j)$ is a real value vector with size C, where each entry reflects the likelihood that protein j has the corresponding function. Thus, we also refer to $F(j)$ as the predicted likelihood score vector of protein j. From Eq. (13), we can see that F is determined by W_d and a well-structured bi-relation graph can produce a competent F.

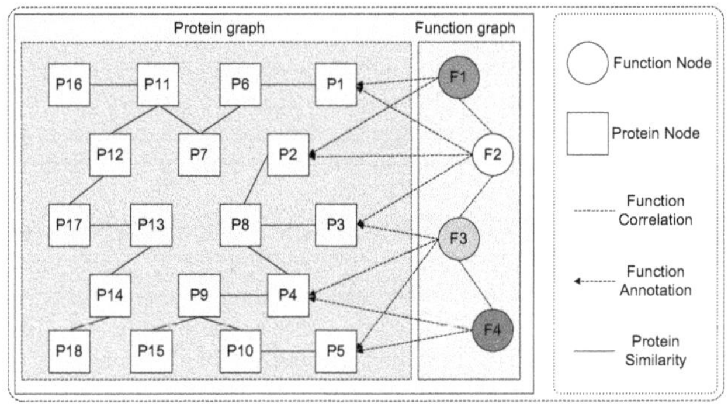

Figure 1: Directed bi-relation graph

3.2 Transductive Multi-label Ensemble Classification

TMC avoids the risk of overwriting the information given by function nodes. However, because of the noisy edges and isolated proteins present in a single bi-relation graph, it is still limited in providing a confident likelihood score vector $F(j)$ from a single data source. To avoid this limitation, we can leverage the various graphs (or kernels) associated with the same set of proteins (*e.g.*, PPI network, gene interaction network, and co-participation network in a protein complex) [17, 24]. These graphs are, to some extent, independent to one another, and also carry partially complementary information. Some researchers have advocated integrating such multiple kernels into a composite kernel [15, 16, 17]. The experimental results showed the annotator trained on the composite kernel has a superior likelihood score vector than the annotator trained on the single kernel. But the classifiers used on the composite kernel are binary and cannot make use of the correlation between the functions.

Here we predict protein functions using multiple kernels derived from multiple sources by performing *classifiers integration*. More specifically, we first transform each kernel into a directed bi-relation graph. We then train a TMC on each of the graphs. Finally, we combine these TMCs into a transductive multi-label ensemble classifier, TMEC. TMEC is described in **Algorithm 1**. In Eq. (14), we combine the F_r values using a weighted majority vote. The motivation is that different kernels have different qualities and have different levels of confidence on the predicted functions of a protein. For example, if kernel K_1 is more confident on annotating protein i with function m, and K_2 is more confident on annotating protein i with function n, then K_1 will have more influence on determining the m-th function of protein i, and K_2 will have more influence on determining the n-th function of protein i.

Algorithm 1 TMEC: Transductive Multi-label Ensemble Classification

Input:
$\{K_r\}_{r=1}^R$ from R data sources
$Y = [\mathbf{y}_1, \mathbf{y}_2, \ldots, \mathbf{y}_l]$
α, β, γ

Output:
Predicted likelihood score vectors $\{F(j)\}_{j=l+1}^N$

Specify $\widetilde{Y}$ using Eq.(6)
for $r = 1$ to R **do**
Set $W_{PP} = K_r$ and construct a directed bi-relation graph using Eqs.(2-4) and Eq.(10)
Get the rth annotator F_r using Eq.(13)
end for
Ensemble the R annotators $\{F_r\}_{r=1}^R$ as:

$$F(j) = \frac{1}{R}\sum_{r=1}^{R} F_r(j) \quad (14)$$

Due to the different structures across different kernels, the base classifiers F_r in Eq. (14) are diverse. In addition, because of the complementary information between different kernels, the predicted likelihood score vectors $F_r(j)$ are also complementary to each other. In contrast, the annotator trained on the composite graph cannot make use of these predicted likelihood score vectors. In ensemble learning, diversity between base classifiers is paramount to gain a consensus classifier with a good generalization ability [11]. For these reasons, TMEC can annotate proteins with higher confidence than the annotator trained on the composite kernel. Our experimental results in Section 5 confirm this advantage. An additional merit of TMEC is that it does not require to have all the data sources available beforehand, and each TMC can be trained individually or sequentially. In addition, new data sources can be appended into TMEC without repeating the entire training process.

4. EXPERIMENTAL SETUP

4.1 Dataset Description

We evaluate the performance of our algorithm on two previously defined protein function prediction benchmarks. Both these datasets provide heterogeneous protein information for the yeast (*Saccharomyces cerevisiae*) organism. The first dataset obtained from Tsuda *et. al.* [27] [2] consists of 3588 proteins, annotated with 13 highest-level functional classes from the MIPS Comprehensive Yeast Genome Data (MIPS CYGD)[3]. This dataset, called **yeast1** here, represents pairwise protein similarities as five different kernel functions. These kernels are obtained from the following sources: Pfam domain structure (K_1), co-participation within protein complexes (K_2), PPI network (K_3), genetic interaction network (K_4), and cell cycle and gene expression measurements (K_5). We refer the reader to the original paper [27] for more details.

The second dataset was obtained from the study by Mostafavi *et. al.* [15][4]. This dataset includes 3904 proteins annotated with 1188 protein functions, according to the biological process terms of the Gene Ontology [5]. The dataset provides 44 different kernel functions, most of which are protein-protein interactions obtained from different experiments [15]. As done in the previous study [15], we filtered the dataset to include only those GO functions that had at least 100 proteins and at most 300 proteins. This resulted in a dataset containing 1809 proteins annotated with 57 different functions. We refer to this dataset as **yeast2**.

4.2 Evaluation Metrics

We evaluate the protein function prediction problem as a multi-label classification problem. Given C different protein functions, our approach results in a predicted likelihood vector that assigns a protein j to a function c with probability $F(j, c)$. To convert the probabilistic assignment into a hard function assignment, we choose the top k most probable function assignments. For each protein, the k largest likelihood scores are chosen as relevant functions [3, 30].

We compute the Macro $F1$ score (MacroF1) across all the protein functions:

$$MacroF1 = \frac{1}{C}\sum_{c=1}^{C}\frac{2p_c r_c}{p_c + r_c}$$

where p_c and r_c are the precision and recall of the c-th function.

We also compute the Ranking loss. Ranking loss evaluates the average fraction of function label pairs that are not correctly ordered:

$$RankingLoss = \frac{1}{u}\sum_{i=l+1}^{N}\frac{1}{|\mathbf{y}_i||\bar{\mathbf{y}}_i|}|\{(y_1, y_2) \in \mathbf{y}_i \times \bar{\mathbf{y}}_i | F(i, y_1) \leq F(i, y_2)\}|$$

where $\mathbf{y}_i$ is the function set of protein i, and $\bar{\mathbf{y}}_i$ is the complementary set of $\mathbf{y}_i$. The performance is perfect when $RankingLoss = 0$, and the smaller the value, the better the performance. To keep consistency with $MacroF1$, we use $1 - RankingLoss$ instead of $RankingLoss$.

5. EXPERIMENT ANALYSIS

In this section, we evaluate our TMC and TMEC by comparing them against PfunBG [9], GRF [30] and SW [15]. PfunBG and GRF are recently proposed semi-supervised multi-label classifiers based on PPI networks for protein function prediction. SW is a recently introduced efficient protein function prediction method based on composite kernels. TMC and PfunBG have a similar objective function. The main difference between them is that TMC is trained on the *directed* bi-relation graph and PfunBG is trained on the *undirected* bi-relation graph. Here, we view function and protein nodes as equal, and set the parameters β and γ in the bi-relation graph equal to 0.5. Similarly to the local and global consistency method [31] and PfunBG [9], α in Eq. (7) is set to 0.01.

[2]http://www.cbrc.jp/ tsuda/code/eccb05.html
[3]http://mips.helmholtz-muenchen.de/genre/proj/yeast/
[4]http://morrislab.med.utoronto.ca/ sara/SW/

Yeast1 has 5482 annotations on 3588 proteins, thus on average each protein is annotated with 1.52 functions. Among the 3588 proteins, 3489 (97%) proteins have ≤3 functions, so we evaluate all the methods on yeast1 with $k \in \{1, 2, 3\}$. Yeast2 has 7874 functions on 1809 proteins, thus on average each protein has 4.35 functions. Among the 1809 proteins, 1333 proteins (73.69%) have ≤5 functions and 1656 proteins (91.54%) have ≤10 functions. Therefore, we evaluate all methods on yeast2 with k from 1 to 10.

As the authors reported in [14] and [27], the composite kernel combined with different weights has similar performance to the composite kernel combined with equal weights. Therefore, for simplicity, TMC, PfunBG and GRF are all trained on the composite kernel combined with equal weights. In addition, we take the recently proposed SW, which gives different weights to different kernels, as a baseline method. In Subsection 5.2, we investigate the performance of TMC on each single kernel. In the following experiments, unless otherwise specified, all the results are the average of 100 runs. In each run, 80% of the proteins are randomly selected for training, and the remaining 20% are used for testing.

5.1 Directed Bi-relation Graph vs. Undirected Bi-relation Graph

To investigate the difference between directed and undirected bi-relation graphs, we compare our TMC against PfunBG and GRF on the composite kernel, and TMEC against ensemble PfunBG (PfunBG-MK) and ensemble GRF (GRF-MK) on yeast1 and yeast2. The base classifiers of PfunBG-MK and GRF-MK on these 5 kernels are combined in the same way as TMEC in Eq. (14). Table 1 and Table 2 list the corresponding macro F1 scores and RankingLoss on the composite kernel and multiple kernels of yeast1. Table 3 reports the RankingLoss on the composite kernel of yeast2, and Table 4 records the RankingLoss on the multiple kernels of yeast2. Figure 2 plots macro F1 scores on the composite kernel and multiple kernels of yeast2. In these tables, results reported in boldface are significantly better, with significance level 95% in 100 runs using paired t-test. Standard deviations are also reported. The same t-test is also used to analyze the results in Figure 2. In these figures, the highest bar in each index indicates a significantly better result.

From these tables and figure, we can observe that, in most cases, TMC trained on the directed bi-relation graph is capable of achieving a higher performance than PfunBG trained on the undirected bi-relation graph. These results show the advantage of using a directed bi-relation graph. SW takes advantage of regression to seek the optimal combining weights, and binary classification to predict protein functions; it achieves a higher RankingLoss on yeast1, but it loses to PfunBG and TMC on the macro F1 score. As to yeast2, TMC significantly outperforms the other three methods on MacroF1 and RankingLoss. The ensemble classifiers are capable of achieving a better performance than the corresponding classifiers trained on the composite kernel. This result supports the use of multi-label ensemble classification for protein function prediction.

5.2 Multi Kernels vs. Single Kernel

In this section, we conduct additional experiments to investigate the difference between the TMC on the composite kernel, the TMC on a single kernel from one data source, and the TMEC on multiple kernels. Since the average number of functions of a protein is 1.52 in yeast1 and 4.35 in yeast2, we set $k = 2$ on yeast1 and $k = 5$ on yeast2. The results are plotted in Figures 3 and 4. The first two bars in each figure represent TMEC and TMC on the composite kernel; the remaining bars describe the results of TMC trained on a single kernel. The highest bar in each index indicates that the corresponding result is significantly better than the others bars for that index.

From Figures 3 and 4, we can observe that TMC trained on the composite kernel always outperforms TMC trained on a single kernel. This can be attributed to the complementary information across different kernels. TMEC performs better than TMC trained on the single kernel, and it outperforms TMC trained on the composite kernel (except in Figure 3(b)). The explanation is that TMEC not only takes advantage of the complementary information between different kernels, but also makes use of the structural difference among different kernels and the complementary likelihood score vectors. These results support the benefits of *classifier integration* over *data integration*.

5.3 Parameter Sensitivity Analysis

TMC and TMEC have three parameters: α, β and γ. α is a parameter common to label propagation methods and often is given a small value. In this section, we analyze the sensitivity of our methods with respect to β and γ. We vary β and γ between 0.1 and 0.9 with step size 0.1, and record the macro F1 score and Ranking loss. The experimental results are given in Figures 5 and 6.

From these figures, we can observe that TMEC is less sensitive than TMC to parameter selection. TMEC has wider ranges of effective parameter values than TMC. We also computed the maximum, minimum, average, and median values of MacroF1 and RankingLoss for the different values of β and γ. Due to space limit, we do not report them here. With respect to these four statistics, the values of MacroF1 and RankingLoss of TMEC are always better than that of TMC. This result again supports the advantage of *classifier integration* over *data integration*.

6. CONCLUSIONS

In this paper, we analyze the drawback of using undirected bi-relation graphs for protein function prediction. To avoid this limitation, we propose to use a directed bi-relation graph, and define a TMC on it. We further improve the performance by combining various TMCs trained on multiple data sources (TMEC). Different from traditional methods that make use of multiple data sources by data integration, TMEC takes advantage of multiple data sources by classifier integration. TMEC does not require to collect all the data sources beforehand. Our experimental results show that classifier integration is a valuable methodology to leverage multiple biological data sources.

The experimental results show that different kernels have different levels of quality. We will investigate a scheme that gives optimal weights to multi-label classifiers trained on different kernels, and then combine such classifiers using the weights for improved protein function prediction.

7. ACKNOWLEDGEMENT

This paper is partially supported by grants from NSF IIS 0905117, Natural Science Foundation of China (Project Nos.

Table 1: **MacroF1 and 1-RankingLoss on composite kernel of yeast1.**

Metric	MacroF1			1-RankingLoss
Method	$k = 1$	$k = 2$	$k = 3$	
SW	35.24 ± 1.25	45.08 ± 1.76	46.05 ± 1.08	$\mathbf{84.35 \pm 0.73}$
GRF	44.81 ± 1.50	49.53 ± 1.31	45.89 ± 1.36	80.79 ± 1.03
PfunBG	45.44 ± 1.52	49.85 ± 1.26	47.32 ± 1.54	80.76 ± 0.84
TMC	$\mathbf{47.66 \pm 1.45}$	$\mathbf{50.22 \pm 1.25}$	47.17 ± 1.03	80.18 ± 0.93

Table 2: MacroF1 and 1-RankingLoss on multiple kernels of yeast1.

Metric	MacroF1			1-RankingLoss
Method	$k = 1$	$k = 2$	$k = 3$	
GRF-MK	45.99 ± 1.59	50.65 ± 1.40	46.70 ± 1.30	80.93 ± 0.99
PfunBG-MK	47.79 ± 1.62	51.42 ± 1.27	47.40 ± 1.25	80.50 ± 0.87
TMEC	$\mathbf{49.75 \pm 1.60}$	$\mathbf{51.98 \pm 1.19}$	47.11 ± 1.01	80.79 ± 1.01

Table 3: 1-RankingLoss on composite kernel of yeast2.

Metric	1-RankingLoss			
Method	SW	GRF	PfunBG	TMC
	74.38 ± 1.42	71.66 ± 1.22	64.14 ± 0.89	$\mathbf{79.85 \pm 0.84}$

Table 4: 1-RankingLoss on multiple kernels of yeast2.

Metric	1-RankingLoss		
Method	GRF-MK	PfunBG-MK	TMEC
	72.97 ± 1.28	76.50 ± 1.28	$\mathbf{80.44 \pm 0.88}$

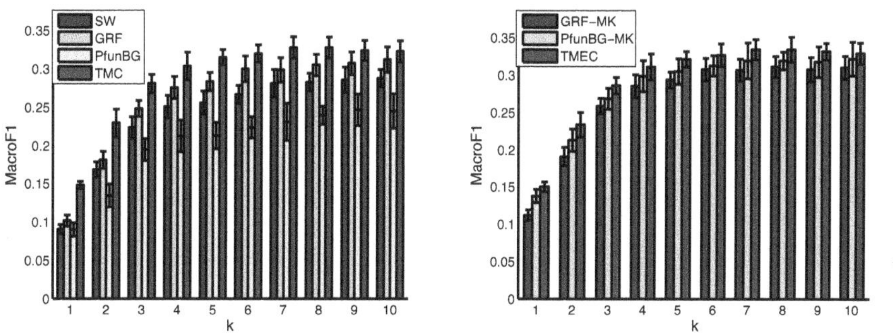

(a) composite kernel (b) multiple kernels

Figure 2: MacroF1 on the composite kernel and multiple kernels of yeast2.

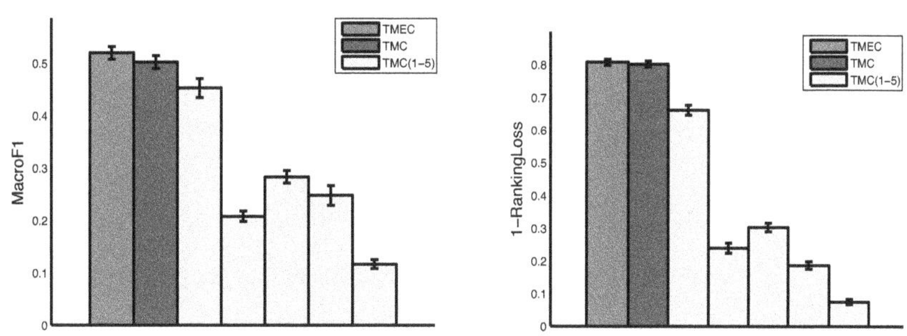

(a) MacroF1 (b) 1-RankingLoss

Figure 3: Difference between multiple kernels, composite kernel and single kernels of yeast1. TMC(1-5) denotes TMC on the single kernels of yeast1

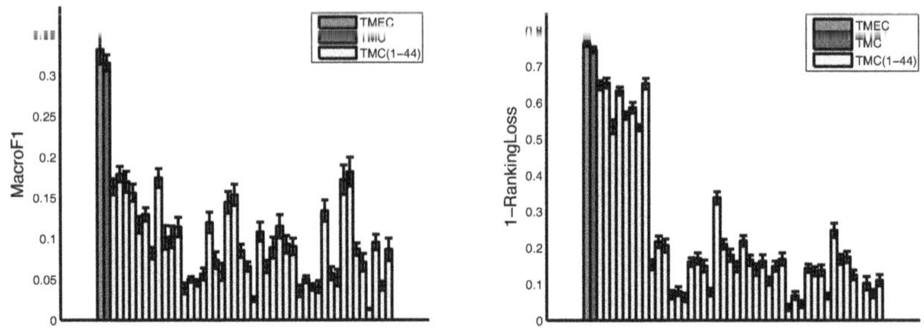

(a) MacroF1 (b) 1-RankingLoss

Figure 4: Difference between multiple kernels, composite kernel and single kernels of yeast2. TMC(1-44) denotes TMC on the single kernels of yeast2.

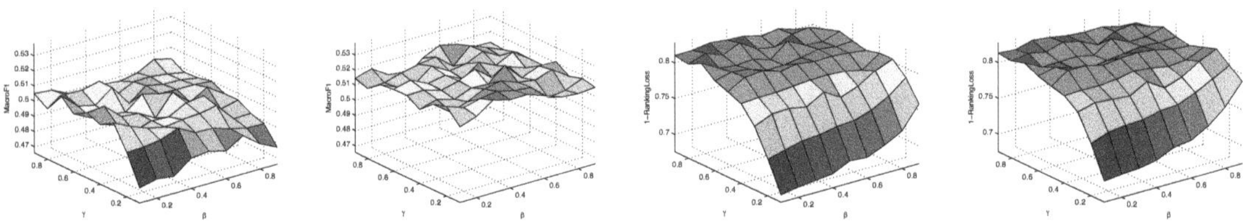

(a) TMC (MacroF1) (b) TMEC (MacroF1) (c) TMC (RankingLoss) (d) TMEC (RankingLoss)

Figure 5: MacroF1 and 1-RankingLoss on different β and γ (yeast1).

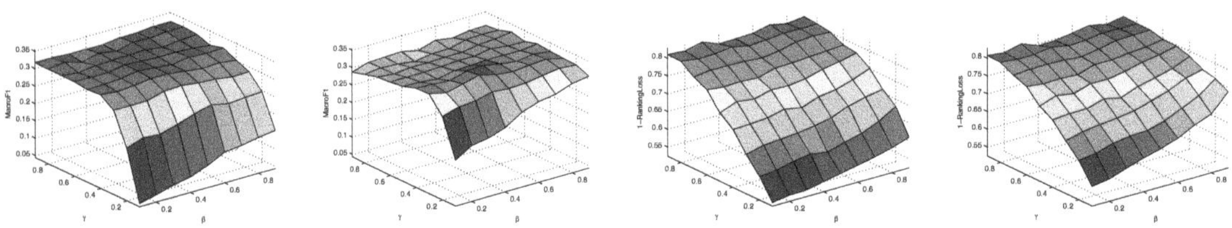

(a) TMC(MacroF1) (b) TMEC(MacroF1) (c) TMC(RankingLoss) (d) TMEC(RankingLoss)

Figure 6: MacroF1 and 1-RankingLoss on different β and γ (yeast2).

60973083, 61070090, 61003174 and 61170080), grants from the NSFC-Guangdong Joint Fund (Project No. U1035004 and U1135004) and China Scholarship Council (CSC).

8. REFERENCES

[1] Z. Barutcuoglu, R. Schapire, and O. Troyanskaya. Hierarchical multi-label prediction of gene function. *Bioinformatics*, 22(7):830–836, 2006.

[2] M. Belkin, P. Niyogi, and V. Sindhwani. Manifold regularization: a geometric framework for learning from labeled and unlabeled examples. *Journal of Machine Learning Research*, 7:2399–2434, 2006.

[3] P. Bogdanov and A. Singh. Molecular function prediction using neighborhood features. *IEEE/ACM Transactions on Computational Biology and Bioinformatics (TCBB)*, 7(2):208–217, 2010.

[4] G. Chen, J. Zhang, F. Wang, C. Zhang, and Y. Gao. Efficient multi-label classification with hypergraph regularization. In *Computer Vision and Pattern Recognition (CVPR), 2009 IEEE Conference on*, pages 1658–1665. IEEE, 2009.

[5] G. O. Consortium et al. Gene ontology: tool for the unification of biology. *Nature Genetics*, 25(1):25–29, 2000.

[6] A. Dempster, N. Laird, and D. Rubin. Maximum likelihood from incomplete data via the em algorithm. *Journal of the Royal Statistical Society. Series B (Methodological)*, pages 1–38, 1977.

[7] A. Elisseeff and J. Weston. A kernel method for multi-labelled classification. *Advances in Neural Information Processing Systems*, 14:681–687, 2001.

[8] M. Gönen and E. Alpaydin. Multiple kernel learning algorithms. *Journal of Machine Learning Research*, 12:2211–2268, 2011.

[9] J. Jiang. Learning protein functions from bi-relational graph of proteins and function annotations. *Algorithms in Bioinformatics*, pages 128–138, 2011.

[10] J. Jiang and L. McQuay. Predicting protein function by multi-label correlated semi-supervised learning. *Computational Biology and Bioinformatics, IEEE/ACM Transactions on*, (99):1–1, 2011.

[11] L. Kuncheva and C. Whitaker. Measures of diversity in classifier ensembles and their relationship with the ensemble accuracy. *Machine Learning*, 51(2):181–207, 2003.

[12] G. Lanckriet, T. De Bie, N. Cristianini, M. Jordan, and W. Noble. A statistical framework for genomic data fusion. *Bioinformatics*, 20(16):2626–2635, 2004.

[13] C. Leslie, E. Eskin, A. Cohen, J. Weston, and W. Noble. Mismatch string kernels for discriminative protein classification. *Bioinformatics*, 20(4):467, 2004.

[14] D. Lewis. *Combining kernels for classification.* PhD thesis, Columbia University, 2006.

[15] S. Mostafavi and Q. Morris. Fast integration of heterogeneous data sources for predicting gene function with limited annotation. *Bioinformatics*, 26(14):1759–1765, 2010.

[16] S. Mostafavi, D. Ray, D. Warde-Farley, C. Grouios, and Q. Morris. Genemania: a real-time multiple association network integration algorithm for predicting gene function. *Genome Biology*, 9(Suppl 1):S4, 2008.

[17] W. Noble and A. Ben-Hur. Integrating information for protein function prediction. *Bioinformatics-From Genomes to Therapies*, pages 1297–1314, 2007.

[18] G. Pandey, V. Kumar, and M. Steinbach. Computational approaches for protein function prediction. Technical Report TR 06-028, Department of Computer Science and Engineering, University of Minnesota, Twin Cities, 2006.

[19] G. Pandey, C. Myers, and V. Kumar. Incorporating functional inter-relationships into protein function prediction algorithms. *BMC Bioinformatics*, 10(1):142, 2009.

[20] P. Pavlidis, J. Weston, J. Cai, and W. Noble. Learning gene functional classifications from multiple data types. *Journal of Computational Biology*, 9(2):401–411, 2002.

[21] M. Re and G. Valentini. Ensemble based data fusion for gene function prediction. *Multiple Classifier Systems*, pages 448–457, 2009.

[22] A. Ruepp, A. Zollner, D. Maier, K. Albermann, J. Hani, M. Mokrejs, I. Tetko, U. Güldener, G. Mannhaupt, M. Münsterkötter, et al. The funcat, a functional annotation scheme for systematic classification of proteins from whole genomes. *Nucleic Acids Research*, 32(18):5539–5545, 2004.

[23] R. Sharan, I. Ulitsky, and R. Shamir. Network-based prediction of protein function. *Molecular Systems Biology*, 3(1), 2007.

[24] H. Shin, K. Tsuda, and B. Schölkopf. Protein functional class prediction with a combined graph. *Expert Systems with Applications*, 36(2):3284–3292, 2009.

[25] H. Tong, C. Faloutsos, and J. Pan. Random walk with restart: fast solutions and applications. *Knowledge and Information Systems*, 14(3):327–346, 2008.

[26] G. Tsoumakas, I. Katakis, and I. Vlahavas. Mining multi-label data. *Data Mining and Knowledge Discovery Handbook*, pages 667–685, 2010.

[27] K. Tsuda, H. Shin, and B. Schölkopf. Fast protein classification with multiple networks. *Bioinformatics*, 21(suppl 2):ii59, 2005.

[28] H. Wang, H. Huang, and C. Ding. Image annotation using bi-relational graph of images and semantic labels. In *Computer Vision and Pattern Recognition (CVPR), 2011 IEEE Conference on*, pages 793–800. IEEE, 2011.

[29] J. Weston, C. Leslie, E. Ie, D. Zhou, A. Elisseeff, and W. Noble. Semi-supervised protein classification using cluster kernels. *Bioinformatics*, 21(15):3241–3247, 2005.

[30] X. Zhang and D. Dai. A framework for incorporating functional inter-relationships into protein function prediction algorithms. *Computational Biology and Bioinformatics, IEEE/ACM Transactions on*, (99):1–1, 2011.

[31] D. Zhou, O. Bousquet, T. Lal, J. Weston, and B. Schölkopf. Learning with local and global consistency. *Advances in Neural Information Processing Systems*, 16:321–328, 2004.

Multi-Domain Active Learning for Text Classification

Lianghao Li[†] Xiaoming Jin[†] Sinno Jialin Pan[‡] Jian Tao Sun[§]
[†]School of Software, Tsinghua University, Beijing 100084, P.R. China
[‡]Institute for Infocomm Research, Singapore 138632
[§]Microsoft Research Asia, Beijing 100080, P.R. China
lianghaoli@yahoo.com, xmjin@tsinghua.edu.cn, jspan@i2r.a-star.edu.sg, jtsun@microsoft.com

ABSTRACT

Active learning has been proven to be effective in reducing labeling efforts for supervised learning. However, existing active learning work has mainly focused on training models for a single domain. In practical applications, it is common to simultaneously train classifiers for multiple domains. For example, some merchant web sites (like Amazon.com) may need a set of classifiers to predict the sentiment polarity of product reviews collected from various domains (e.g., electronics, books, shoes). Though different domains have their own unique features, they may share some common latent features. If we apply active learning on each domain separately, some data instances selected from different domains may contain duplicate knowledge due to the common features. Therefore, how to choose the data from multiple domains to label is crucial to further reducing the human labeling efforts in multi-domain learning. In this paper, we propose a novel *multi-domain active learning* framework to jointly select data instances from all domains with duplicate information considered. In our solution, a shared subspace is first learned to represent common latent features of different domains. By considering the common and the domain-specific features together, the model loss reduction induced by each data instance can be decomposed into a common part and a domain-specific part. In this way, the duplicate information across domains can be encoded into the common part of model loss reduction and taken into account when querying. We compare our method with the state-of-the-art active learning approaches on several text classification tasks: sentiment classification, newsgroup classification and email spam filtering. The experiment results show that our method reduces the human labeling efforts by 33.2%, 42.9% and 68.7% on the three tasks, respectively.

Categories and Subject Descriptors

I.2.6 [**Artificial Intelligence**]: Learning—*knowledge acquisition, concept learning*; I.5.2 [**Pattern Recognition**]: Design Methodology—*Classifier design and evaluation*

General Terms

Algorithms, Experimentation

Keywords

Active Learning, Transfer Learning, Text Classification

1. INTRODUCTION

Text classification has drawn much research attention in the literature. Typically, supervised classification algorithms require sufficient labeled data to train accurate classifiers, while the data labeling cost may be expensive. Active learning has been proven to be effective in reducing the human labeling efforts by actively choosing the most informative data to label. Existing active learning work has mainly focused on training models for a single domain. But in many applications, data of interest are from multiple domains and a group of classifiers need to be trained simultaneously for all the domains. For example, Amazon.com has organized user reviews of many products. A sentiment classifier [3] of each product class (domain) is highly desirable to automatically organize reviews according to user demands. Since different words can be used to express sentiment in different domains [17], training a single classifier for all domains would not generalize well across various domains. For instance, words like "blur", "fast", "sharp" are used to comment *electronics* products, while they do not carry opinion in *books* domain. Therefore, each domain should have its own sentiment classifier. Email spam filtering is another example [8]. Since users may have different backgrounds and interests, it is reasonable to customize spam filters for individual users.

Active learning for multi-domain text classification is a novel research problem. The algorithm of selecting data instances to label is not trivial. If we simply apply active learning on each domain separately, some data instances selected from different domains may contain duplicate information due to the inherent relationship among domains. For example, in sentiment classification, reviews containing common sentiment words like "wonderful", "perfect" may be selected to label by active learners of each domain, which may cause redundant labeling efforts. On the other hand, if we apply active learning for all domains together, the query strategy may be affected by the distribution gap between different domains. Therefore, how to measure the informativeness of data instances across domains is crucial. In this paper, we propose a novel global optimization based active learning framework for multi-domain text classification. The proposed query strategy aims to select unlabeled instances which can maximally reduce the model loss of all classifiers once labeled. In our solution, a shared subspace is first learned to represent common latent features of different domains. By splitting the feature space into a common part and a domain-specific part, the model loss reduction induced by each data candidate can be decomposed into the domain-specific loss reduction of the classifier on its corresponding domain, and the common loss reduction of the classifiers on all domains. By jointly querying instances, the common model loss of all classifiers can be reduced simultaneously, and the redundant labeling efforts can be saved.

It is worth noting that the problem setting of multi-domain classification is different from that of cross-domain classification. In cross-domain classification, data of interest are assumed to come from a source domain and a target domain. Sufficient labeled data are available in the source domain while no or few labeled data are available in the target domain. The goal is to train a classifier of the target domain by leveraging the labeled data of the source domain. In multi-domain classification, no domain is assumed to have sufficient labeled data. The goal is to simultaneously train classifiers for multiple domains by leveraging common knowledge among them. Active learning for multi-domain classification aims to jointly select data to label for training accurate classifiers on all domains.

The main contributions of our work include: 1) We studied an important practical problem for active learning in multiple domains. To the best of our knowledge, this is the first work which aims to actively build text classifiers for multiple domains simultaneously. 2) We proposed an efficient multi-domain active learning framework and showed its effectiveness on three real-world applications, i.e. sentiment classification, newsgroup classification and email spam filtering. The experiment results on the three tasks demonstrate that our proposed method can save more than 33% labeling efforts compared with the state-of-the-art active learning approaches, and save more than 50% labeling efforts compared with the random query methods.

The rest of this paper is organized as follows: we begin by reviewing the related works in the next section. After that, we describe the problem statement in Section 3, and present our solution in Section 4. The experiment results are discussed in Section 5. Finally, we conclude the paper and discuss some future work in Section 6.

2. RELATED WORK

The performance of supervised classification highly relies on labeled data. However, to collect sufficient training data is difficult and time-consuming. Active learning is an alternative learning framework which allows classification algorithms to choose the data they learn from. Existing active learning algorithms can be generally put into three categories: 1) uncertainty sampling [13, 25], which selects the data instances that are the most uncertainly predicted by the current classifier; 2) query by committee [22] selects the data instances about which the "committee" disagree most; and 3) expected error reduction [20], which aims to select the instance that can contribute the largest model loss reduction for the current classifier once labeled. Recently, Donmez and Carbonell proposed the proactive learning framework which relaxes some unrealistic assumptions of active learning in practical applications [7]. Beygelzimer *et al.* proposed an importance weighting method to avoid label-sampling bias in active learning [2]. In [15] and [5], the authors proposed the active learning methods for data with multiple views. In multi-view learning, every data instance is assumed to have several different descriptions, each of which can be used to learn concepts of interest.

Transfer learning is another technology to save the labeling efforts for supervised learning. Dredze *et al.* developed a multi-domain learning method based on parameter combination [8]. Xie *et al.* proposed the LatentMap algorithm to leverage the shared features for transfer learning [26]. Given an oracle and a lot of labeled data from a source domain, some researchers proposed to combine active learning and transfer learning to train an accurate classifier for a target domain [18, 23]. Shi *et al.* proposed to use the source domain classifier to answer the target domain queries as often as possible, and query the oracle only when necessary [23]. In [18], Rai *et al.* considered to use the source domain classifier as an initial classifier for the target domain. And the source domain data are further used to rule out the target domain queries which appear similar to the source domain data. Different from their works, we aim to build classifiers for multiple domains together, while they targeted at training the classifier of target domain by using the knowledge from the source domain.

Our work is also related to multi-task active learning, which has been studied to solve the problem where data instances are labeled in multiple ways for different tasks. Reichart *et al.* proposed a novel active learning method to label data instances with several linguistic annotations, such as named entities, syntactic parse trees, etc. [19]. Zhang tried to solve the multi-task active learning problem where outputs of different tasks are coupled by constraints [27]. Harpale *et al.* proposed an active learning method for multi-task adaptive filtering [11]. An adaptive filtering system monitors a set of documents to find and deliver the relevant items to a particular task. Its performance is boosted with the relevance feedback received on the delivered items. In [11], the items which lead to the maximal relevance feedback will be selected to deliver. Different from their works, we focus on a single task with multiple domains. In our problem, different domains share the same target concepts but have different data distributions. In addition, our work aims at proposing an active learning method for classification problems instead of adaptive filtering or natural language annotation. This makes the optimization goal of our proposed query strategy different from theirs.

3. PROBLEM DEFINITION

In this section, we introduce some definitions and the problem statement.

Definition 1. *(Domain) A domain consists of a set of data instances which are generated from the same data distribution $P(x)$, where $x \in \mathcal{X}$ and $\mathcal{X}$ is a feature space.*

For example, a set of user reviews for electronics products can be regarded as one domain, while reviews for different types of products, such as books, movies, can be regarded as *books* and *movies* domains, respectively. Data instances from one domain are assumed to be independent and identically distributed (*i.i.d.*). But data distributions across domains may be different. In this paper, the domain each data instance belongs to is assumed to be known. The multi-domain classification problem is defined as follows:

Definition 2. *(Multi-Domain Classification) Given a set of data instances collected from K different domains, where each domain has its own data distribution. Let $\mathcal{X}$ be a feature space[1] and $\mathcal{Y}$ be a pre-defined label set. The task is to train K classifiers $f^\ell : \mathcal{X} \to \mathcal{Y}$, $\ell = 1, 2, \ldots, K$, for all the domains.*

Based on the definitions above, we now define the problem we aim to address in this paper as follows:

Definition 3. *(Active Learning for Multi-Domain Classification) Let $\mathcal{P} = \{\mathcal{P}^1, \mathcal{P}^2, \ldots, \mathcal{P}^K\}$ be an unlabeled data pool which consists of data instances collected from K different domains. Here $\mathcal{P}^\ell = \{\mathbf{x}_1^\ell, \mathbf{x}_2^\ell, \ldots, \mathbf{x}_{N^\ell}^\ell\}$ includes N^ℓ data instances come from the ℓ'th domain. The task is to build K accurate classifiers $f^\ell : \mathcal{X} \to \mathcal{Y}$, $\ell = 1, 2, \ldots, K$, by selecting data instances to label as few as possible.*

Our active learning framework is based on pool-based sampling [13, 21]. In pool-based sampling, active learning is iteratively performed on an unlabeled data pool, which is usually assumed to be closed (i.e. stationary) [21]. Typically, in each iteration, the active learner scans the unlabeled data pool and chooses the most informative data candidates to label.

4. OUR SOLUTION

In this section, we describe our solution for multi-domain active learning. The main notations are listed in Table 1.

Table 1: Notations

Symbols	Description
K	total number of domains
$\mathbf{x}_i^\ell$	the i'th labeled data in the ℓ'th domain
y_i^ℓ	ground truth of $\mathbf{x}_i^\ell$
θ	learned shared subspace transformation matrix
$\mathbf{w}^\ell$	weight vector specific to the ℓ'th domain
$\mathbf{v}$	weight vector associated with the shared subspace
$f_\mathcal{D}^\ell$	predictive function of the ℓ'th domain
$L(\cdot)$	model loss of a classifier
λ^ℓ	domain weight specified by users
$\mathcal{L}_\mathcal{D}$	global model loss of all classifiers
$\mathcal{V}^\ell$	version space of the ℓ'th domain
$\mathcal{W}^\ell$	parameter space of the ℓ'th domain
$V_\mathcal{D}^\ell$	the size of $\mathcal{V}^\ell$

4.1 A General Optimization Framework

Recall that, in active learning for a single domain, an active learner attempts to select the most informative data instances to label in order to train an accurate classifier using as few labeling efforts as possible. In active learning for multiple domains, the goal is to choose the data instances which are not only informative for their corresponding domains but also for other domains such that all classifiers can benefit from the labeling.

Suppose that $L(f_\mathcal{D}^\ell)$ is the model loss of classifier $f_\mathcal{D}^\ell$, the global model loss of all classifiers is defined as:

$$\mathcal{L}_\mathcal{D} = \sum_{\ell=1}^{K} \lambda^\ell L(f_\mathcal{D}^\ell), \qquad (1)$$

[1]In this work, we assume all domains share the same vocabulary (i.e. feature space).

where $\{\lambda^\ell\}_{\ell=1}^K$ are user specified weights for different domains. The goal of our query strategy is to select an unlabeled instance $\mathbf{x}^*$ which can maximally reduce the global model loss once labeled. The optimization objective can be formulated as:

$$\begin{aligned} \mathbf{x}^* &= \arg\max_{\mathbf{x}^*} \mathcal{L}_\mathcal{D} - \mathcal{L}_{\mathcal{D}+(\mathbf{x}^*, y^*)} \\ &= \arg\max_{\mathbf{x}^*} \sum_{\ell=1}^{K} \lambda^\ell \cdot \left(L(f_\mathcal{D}^\ell) - L(f_{\mathcal{D}+(\mathbf{x}^*, y^*)}^\ell) \right), \end{aligned} \qquad (2)$$

where $\mathcal{D}+(\mathbf{x}^*, y^*)$ is the expanded training set after data instance $\mathbf{x}^*$ and its ground truth y^* are added. In some real-world applications, different domains may have different priorities. For example, users may require high classification performance or fast model convergency for some particular domains. In this case, one can assign larger weights for such domains. However, in many other scenarios, users may not have these requirements. Under such case, one can simply set the same weight for each domain. Without loss of generality, we set $\lambda^\ell = 1$ for all domains in this paper.

In practice, we do not know ground truth y^* of data instance $\mathbf{x}^*$ before querying. Therefore, we are not able to estimate the model loss in (2) directly. Instead, we use the expectation loss over all possible labels to approximate the true model loss. As a result, we can replace (2) by the following objective:

$$\mathbf{x}^* = \arg\max_{\mathbf{x}^*} \sum_{y \in \mathcal{Y}} \hat{P}(y|\mathbf{x}^*) \sum_{\ell=1}^{K} \left(L(f_\mathcal{D}^\ell) - L(f_{\mathcal{D}+(\mathbf{x}^*, y)}^\ell) \right), \qquad (3)$$

where $\hat{P}(y|\mathbf{x}^*)$ is the conditional probability of label y given data instance $\mathbf{x}^*$ estimated by the current classifier.

4.2 Multi-Domain Classification with SVM

Before describing our solution for multi-domain active learning, we first present an SVM-based multi-domain classification method which is used as the classification model in our optimization framework.

Support Vector Machines (SVMs) have been widely used for text classification [12, 25]. In this paper, we incorporate a shared subspace to represent common latent features into SVM for multi-domain classification. The predictive function $f_\mathcal{D}^\ell$ of the ℓ'th ($\ell \in \{1, ..., K\}$) domain is defined as:

$$f_\mathcal{D}^\ell(\mathbf{x}^\ell) = \mathbf{w}^\ell \cdot \Phi(\mathbf{x}^\ell) + \mathbf{v} \cdot \Phi(\theta \mathbf{x}^\ell), \qquad (4)$$

which consists of two parts: one is performed on the original feature space, and the other is derived for the shared subspace. Here $\mathcal{D}$ is a training set, Φ is a feature map, $\mathbf{w}^\ell$ and $\mathbf{v}$ are two weight vectors, θ is a learned transformation matrix to map the original feature space to the shared low-dimensional subspace. The shared parameters $\mathbf{v}$ and θ are leveraged to capture the common latent features across domains. Note that the idea of the formulation above is similar to that in multi-task learning [1, 9]. However, in this paper, we focus on proposing a novel *active learning* framework for multi-domain classification instead of a novel multi-domain classification method. In [1], Ando and Zhang proposed to learn the parameters $\{\mathbf{w}^\ell\}$'s, $\mathbf{v}$ and θ jointly by updating them iteratively. In each iteration, the singular value decomposition is required to update θ, which is not efficient, especially for active learning.

We propose to learn the parameters in two steps. In the first step, we apply Spectral Feature Alignment (SFA) [17], which is an unsupervised shared subspace learning method, to estimate θ. Note that besides SFA, many other effective approaches to shared subspace learning can be integrated into our framework, such as Structural Correspondence learning (SCL) [4], Maximum Mean Discrepancy Embedding (MMDE) [16], etc. In SFA, a set of domain independent features are firstly identified, and a bipartite graph is constructed to model the co-occurrence between the domain-independent features and the domain-specific features. Then a spectral clustering algorithm is adapted on the bipartite graph to co-align the two kinds of features into unified clusters. The space spanned by the unified clusters is then considered as the shared subspace across domains. In the second step, we estimate $\{\mathbf{w}^\ell\}$'s and $\mathbf{v}$ by solving the SVM optimization problem as follows[2]:

$$\min_{\{\mathbf{w}^\ell\}\text{'s},\mathbf{v}} \quad \frac{1}{2}\|\mathbf{v}\|^2 + \frac{1}{2}\sum_{\ell=1}^{K}\|\mathbf{w}^\ell\|^2, \tag{5}$$
$$s.t. \quad y_i^\ell(\mathbf{w}^\ell \cdot \Phi(\mathbf{x}_i^\ell) + \mathbf{v}\cdot\Phi(\theta\mathbf{x}_i^\ell)) \geq 1, \ \ \ell = 1, ..., K.$$

Note that for text classification, data instances are often linearly-separable due to the high dimensionality of its feature space. Therefore, in this paper, we present our framework in the linearly-separable manner and leave the nonseparable case to our future work. It can be shown that the optimization problem (5) can be directly linked to a standard SVM problem with a proper feature map [9] and solved by a standard SVM solver.

In our approach, the weight vector $\mathbf{v}$ is derived from the shared subspace, and learned from all training data across domains. Therefore, it can reflect the common discriminative information of all domains. The weight vectors $\{\mathbf{w}^\ell\}$'s are only affected by the training data in the corresponding domain, which implies that they should reflect the domain-specific discriminative information. By splitting the feature space into the two parts, we can measure both the common and the domain-specific model loss reduction induced by each data instance.

4.3 Multi-Domain Active Learning

In this section, we describe our solution for the proposed optimization framework (3) based on the multi-domain SVM. According to (1), the global model loss can be decomposed into the model loss of the classifier in each domain. So our problem becomes to measure the model loss reduction $\{L(f_\mathcal{D}^\ell) - L(f_{\mathcal{D}+(\mathbf{x}^*,y)}^\ell)\}_{\ell=1}^K$ of each classifier. As suggested by Tong and Koller [24], we can measure the model loss of each classifier by the size of version space. A version space $\mathcal{V}$ is a set of hypotheses that are consistent with the current training data instances [14]. For the ℓ'th domain, the version space $\mathcal{V}^\ell$ is defined as:

$$\mathcal{V}^\ell = \left\{\frac{\mathbf{u}^\ell}{\|\mathbf{u}^\ell\|} \,\middle|\, \mathbf{u}^\ell \in \mathcal{W}^\ell, \forall i\; y_i^\ell(\mathbf{w}^\ell\Phi(\mathbf{x}_i^\ell) + \mathbf{v}\Phi(\theta\mathbf{x}_i^\ell)) > 0\right\}, \tag{6}$$

where $\mathbf{u}^\ell = [\mathbf{w}^\ell, \mathbf{v}]$ and $\mathcal{W}^\ell$ is the parameter space. Since we can simply multiply a non-zero scale to a consistent hypothesis to get another one, we normalize the weight vectors to eliminate this freedom.

For SVM, we can use the margin of SVM as an indicator of the size of version space. Suppose we have a pool of unlabeled instances, we can evaluate each candidate by adding it into $\mathcal{D}$ and re-training an SVM based on (5) to estimate the new margin. We then select the data candidate which contributes the largest reduction of all version spaces to label. However, this process is very expensive in computation, especially when the candidate pool is large. To make it more practical, we apply a heuristic idea as proposed in [24](cf. page 34) to simplify the computation by mapping the size of new version space to the size of current version space. Denote $V_\mathcal{D}^\ell$ the size of current version space, the size of new version space (i.e. $V_{\mathcal{D}+(\mathbf{x}^*,y)}^\ell$) after adding $(\mathbf{x}^*, y)$ into the training set can be approximated as:

$$V_{\mathcal{D}+(\mathbf{x}^*,y)}^\ell \approx \frac{1 + yf_\mathcal{D}^\ell(\mathbf{x}^*)}{2}V_\mathcal{D}^\ell. \tag{7}$$

Based on the approximation above, the model loss reduction of each classifier in (3) can be rewritten as:

$$L(f_\mathcal{D}^\ell) - L(f_{\mathcal{D}+(\mathbf{x}^*,y)}^\ell) = V_\mathcal{D}^\ell - V_{\mathcal{D}+(\mathbf{x}^*,y)}^\ell \approx \frac{1 - yf_\mathcal{D}^\ell(\mathbf{x}^*)}{2}V_\mathcal{D}^\ell. \tag{8}$$

An intuitive explanation for the above estimation is that if data candidate $\mathbf{x}^*$ can be correctly predicted by the current model, that is $y = \text{sgn}(f_\mathcal{D}^\ell(\mathbf{x}^*))$, then the smaller the value of $\|f_\mathcal{D}^\ell(\mathbf{x}^*)\|$ is, the less confidence on $\mathbf{x}^*$ the current model has. As a result, data candidate $\mathbf{x}^*$ tend to be queried for labeling. On the other hand, if data candidate $\mathbf{x}^*$ cannot be correctly predicted, then the larger the value of $\|f_\mathcal{D}^\ell(\mathbf{x}^*)\|$ is, the more errors the current model makes. In this case, querying $\mathbf{x}^*$ can greatly improve the current model.

Recall that, given classifier $f_\mathcal{D}^\ell$ of the ℓ'th domain, if data candidate $\mathbf{x}^*$ is not from the ℓ'th domain, then $\mathbf{x}^*$ can only affect the version space of the ℓ'th domain via the shared subspace when queried. Correspondingly, classifier $f_\mathcal{D}^\ell$ can only make prediction on data candidate $\mathbf{x}^*$ through the common weight vector $\mathbf{v}$. So we propose to use the following predictive function $f_\mathcal{D}^\ell(\mathbf{x}^*)$ to calculate the model loss reduction in (8),

$$f_\mathcal{D}^\ell(\mathbf{x}^*) = \begin{cases} \mathbf{w}^\ell\cdot\Phi(\mathbf{x}^*) + \mathbf{v}\cdot\Phi(\theta\mathbf{x}^*) & \mathbf{x}^* \in \mathcal{P}^\ell, \\ \mathbf{v}\cdot\Phi(\theta\mathbf{x}^*) & \mathbf{x}^* \notin \mathcal{P}^\ell. \end{cases}$$

Therefore, the model loss reduction induced by each data candidate is decomposed into two parts: 1) the version space reduction of its corresponding domain in the whole feature space, and 2) the version space reduction of other domains in the shared subspace. In this way, the common model loss of all classifiers can be reduced together, and more labeling efforts can be saved. Since we learn all the classifiers jointly, there is no guarantee that the solutions of (5) can lead to the maximal margin solution for the classifier of each domain. However, because the low-dimensional subspace is shared by all domains, the hyperplane learned onto it should be consistent with the data instances from all domains. Therefore, the hyperplane of each domain learned by (5) is a good approximation of the hyperplane learned on the labeled data only from its corresponding domain.

By using the size of SVM margin as the indicator of $V_\mathcal{D}^\ell$, and substitute (8) into (3), our final query strategy for multi-domain active learning can be written as:

$$\mathbf{x}^* = \arg\max_{\mathbf{x}^*} \sum_{y=\pm1} \hat{P}(y|\mathbf{x}^*)\sum_{\ell=1}^{K}\frac{1 - yf_\mathcal{D}^\ell(\mathbf{x}^*)}{\|\mathbf{u}^\ell\|}. \tag{9}$$

[2]Here we introduce $\Phi_0(\mathbf{x}) = 1$ to replace the bias parameter of SVM.

Algorithm 1: Multi-Domain Active Learning

Input : (1) A pool $\mathcal{P}$ of unlabeled instances which are collected from K domains, (2) Number of initial training data in each domain M, (3) Number of iterations T, (4) Number of queried instances per iteration S

Output: K classifiers

Randomly label M data instances of each domain, and form the initial training set $\mathcal{D}$;

Learn the low-dimensional shared subspace using SFA;

for $t \leftarrow 1$ **to** T **do**

  Train K classifiers in the training set $\mathcal{D}$ using (5);

  foreach $\mathbf{x}_n^\ell \in \mathcal{P}$ **do**

    Estimate the global model loss reduction via (9);

  end

  Query the labels Y^* of S unlabeled instances U^* which have the largest global model loss reduction;

  Update the training set by $\mathcal{D} \leftarrow \mathcal{D} \cup (U^*, Y^*)$, and remove U^* from $\mathcal{P}$;

end

In order to calculate $\hat{P}(y|\mathbf{x}^*)$ in (9), we train a Logistic Regression classifier on all training data by maximizing the log-likelihood $J(\mathbf{w}^1, \cdots, \mathbf{w}^K, \mathbf{v}) = \sum_{\ell,i} \log \sigma(y_i^\ell(\mathbf{w}^\ell \mathbf{x}_i^\ell + \mathbf{v}\theta\mathbf{x}_i^\ell))$, and use it to estimate the probabilities. The complete process of our proposed method is summarized in Algorithm 1. The proposed method is very efficient because it only needs to learn one SVM per iteration, and in each iteration, it estimates the global model loss reduction induced by each candidate efficiently via (9).

For the classification problem having more than two categories, one simple and effective way is to use the one-vs-all technique. Suppose we have C classes, we can train C binary classifiers $\{f_\mathcal{D}^{\ell,c}\}_{c=1}^C$, where the classifier $f_\mathcal{D}^{\ell,c}$ is used to predict whether an instance belongs to the c'th class or not. Our multi-domain active learning method can be applied accordingly.

5. EXPERIMENTS

In this section, we conduct experiments on three real-world applications (i.e., sentiment classification, newsgroup classification and email spam filtering) to evaluate the effectiveness of our method.

5.1 Datasets

5.1.1 Multi-Domain Sentiment Dataset

The Multi-Domain Sentiment Dataset [3] has been widely used as a benchmark dataset for domain adaptation and sentiment analysis. It contains a collection of product reviews from Amazon.com. The reviews are about four product domains: *Book* (**B**), *DVD* (**D**), *Electronics* (**E**) and *Kitchen* (**K**). Each review has been annotated as positive or negative sentiment polarity according to users' rating scores. The summary of this dataset is described in Table 2.

From this dataset, we construct five multi-domain sentiment classification tasks: **B+D+E**, **B+D+K**, **B+E+K**, **D+E+K** and **B+D+E+K**, where each boldfaced letter corresponds with a domain. For example, **B+D+E** denotes sentiment classification in *Book*, *DVD* and *Electronics* domains.

Table 2: Summary of Multi-Domain Sentiment Dataset

Domain	# Reviews	# Pos	# Neg	# Features
Book	6,465	3,264	3,201	17,465
DVD	5,585	2,807	2,778	15,437
Electronics	7,677	3,853	3,824	13,687
Kitchen	7,945	3,954	3,991	12,439

5.1.2 20Newsgroups

The 20Newsgroups dataset[3] has been widely used for newsgroup classification and cross-domain text classification. As in the previous work [6], we generate four newsgroup domains from the dataset by utilizing its hierarchical structure. Table 3 shows the generated newsgroup domains. For example, domain NG-1 contains documents from four sub-categories, which are under four top-categories, respectively. The classification task is defined in the top-category level, where our goal is to classify documents into one of the four top-categories: *comp*, *rec*, *sci* and *talk*. This domain generation strategy can ensure the domains are different but related, because different domains consist of documents in different sub-categories, but are under the same top-categories.

Table 3: Four Domains Generated from 20Newsgroups

Domain	Newsgroups	
NG-1	comp.graphics sci.crypt	rec.autos talk.politics.guns
NG-2	comp.os.ms-windows.misc sci.electronics	rec.motorcycles talk.politics.mideast
NG-3	comp.sys.ibm.pc.hardware sci.med	rec.sport.baseball talk.politics.misc
NG-4	comp.sys.mac.hardware sci.space	rec.sport.hockey talk.religion.misc

By using the generated domains, we construct four multi-domain newsgroup classification tasks: **NG-123**, **NG-124**, **NG-134** and **NG-234**, where each digit denotes a domain. For example, **NG-123** denotes the multi-domain newsgroup classification in NG-1, NG-2 and NG-3 domains.

5.1.3 Email Spam Filtering Dataset

The email spam filtering dataset[4] released by ECML/PKDD 2006 discovery challenge contains 15 separate inboxes for users u00∼u14, where "u**" is a user id. For each inbox, there are 200 spam and 200 non-spam emails. In our experiments, each inbox is regarded as a domain and the learning task is to train a spam filter for each user to classify whether a new mail is a spam or not. From this dataset, we construct four multi-domain spam filtering tasks: **u00-u04**, **u05-u09**, **u10-u14** and **u00-u14**. For example, **u00-u04** denotes the email spam filtering in u00∼u04 domains.

5.2 Comparison Methods

In order to test the effectiveness of our method (which is referred to as MultiAL), we compare it with several active learning approaches. The first method is to perform a single-domain active learning for each domain independently. We call it SingleAL. The second method is to merge all domain data into a unified pool and perform active learning in the unified pool to train a single classifier for prediction. We call this approach UnifiedAL. In addition, once the shared subspace is identified, we can embed data instances from all domains into the shared subspace and generate a new

[3]http://people.csail.mit.edu/jrennie/20Newsgroups/
[4]http://www.ecmlpkdd2006.org/challenge.html

unified domain. We perform active learning in the new unified domain and train a single classifier for prediction. We call this method EmbedAL. We also test the Random query method which chooses unlabeled instances to label at random. In this paper, the SVM-based Simple-Margin active learning method proposed in [25] is adopted as the basic active learner for SingleAL, UnifiedAL and EmbedAL.

An alternative solution for multi-domain active learning is to apply existing active learning algorithms in each domain independently, and then apply existing transfer learning techniques to train more accurate classifiers by leveraging labeled data among domains. Here, we adopt the multi-domain SVM described in (5) as the classification method for SingleAL and Random to get another two comparison methods. We call them SingleAL+ and Random+, respectively.

5.3 Experiment Settings

For data preprocessing, we convert all words to lower cases and remove the stop words. Term frequency is used for feature weighting in all methods. Linear kernel is used as the feature map for SVM because of its good performance in text classification [12]. LIBLINEAR SVM [10] is used as the base classifier for all methods, and all parameters are set to their default values. In using SFA to learn the shared subspace for the multi-domain SVM, we adopt the same parameter setting adopted in the original paper [17]. Specifically, we set the number of domain-independent features to 500, and the dimensionality of shared subspace to 100.

The classification accuracy is adopted as the evaluation criteria. It is defined as:

$$\text{Accuracy} = \frac{\left|\{\mathbf{x}|\mathbf{x} \in \mathcal{D}^{\ell}_{tst} \cap c^{\ell}(\mathbf{x}) = y(\mathbf{x})\}\right|}{\left|\{\mathbf{x}|\mathbf{x} \in \mathcal{D}^{\ell}_{tst}\}\right|},$$

where $\mathcal{D}^{\ell}_{tst}$ denotes test data, $y(\mathbf{x})$ is the ground truth and $c^{\ell}(\mathbf{x})$ is the predicted label. For evaluating the overall classification performance on all domains, we adopt the domain average accuracy as the evaluation measure. All experiments are run on a machine with a 2.4GHz Intel Xeon processor and 16G RAM. The average results of 20 random runs are reported.

5.4 Results and Discussions

5.4.1 *Results on Sentiment and Newsgroups Datasets*

In this section, we conduct experiments on the multi-domain classification tasks constructed from Multi-Domain Sentiment Dataset and 20Newsgroups. In the experiment on each task, we first randomly select 100 labeled instances from each domain to form an initial training set, and use the remaining data instances to form an unlabeled pool. Active learning is iteratively performed several iterations until the learner achieves a sufficient accuracy. In each iteration, every active learner labels 30 data instances from unlabeled pool and move them to the training set. Once the labeled instances are incorporated, each active learner re-trains classifiers on the expanded training set and its performance is evaluated on the remaining unlabeled instances.

Figure 1 shows the overall performance of each method on sentiment classification task **B+D+K**. As can be seen, MultiAL consistently outperforms each comparison method when increasing number of new labeled instances are added. This result suggests that our method can take advantage of the multi-domain structure for querying, and effectively optimize all domain classifiers together. From the figure, we can also observe that the transfer learning baselines SingleAL+ and Random+ perform much better than the non-transfer baselines SingleAL and Random, respectively. The improvement is large especially when only a few data instances are queried to be labeled. However, as more new labeled instances are added, the performance of SingleAL+ and SingleAL becomes close, while MultiAL constantly outperforms both SingleAL+ and SingleAL. In addition, MultiAL increasingly outperforms EmbedAL when the number of queried data instances increases. It implies that the classifier trained in the shared subspace alone may not be able to generalize well across different domains. The overall performance on other sentiment classification tasks is presented in Figure 2. From the figures, we can observe the similar trends on all tasks.

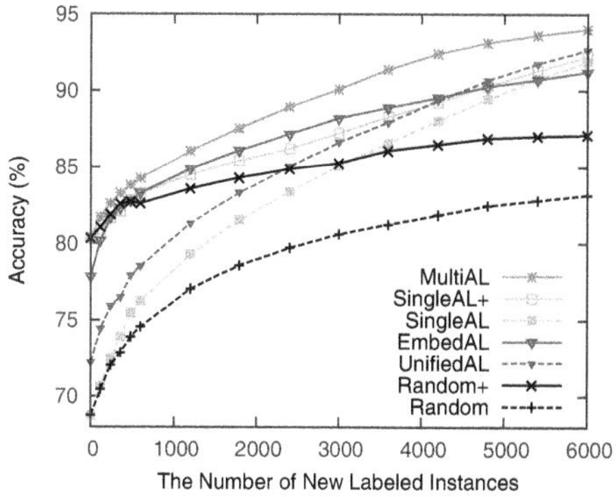

Figure 1: The sentiment classification results on **B+D+K**

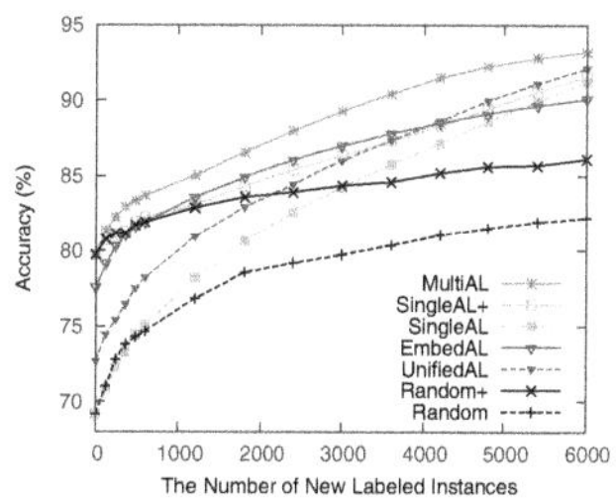

(a) Results on **B+D+E**

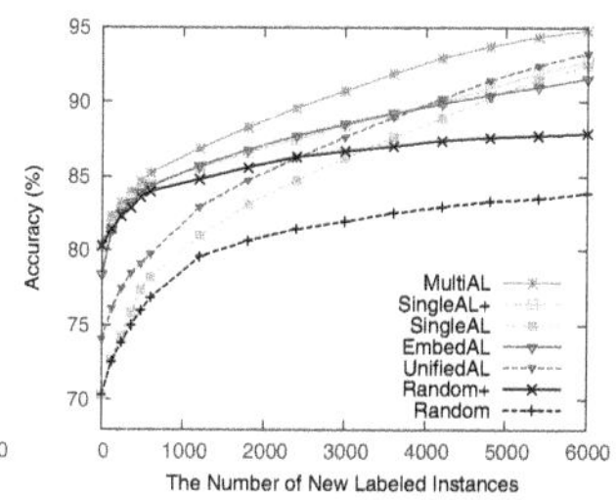

(b) Results on **B+E+K**

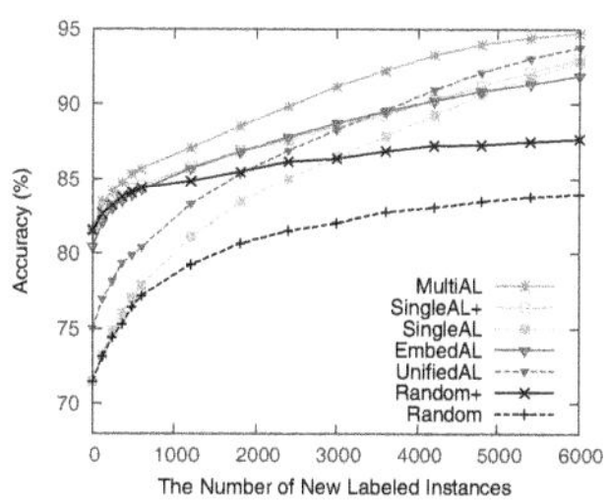

(c) Results on **D+E+K**

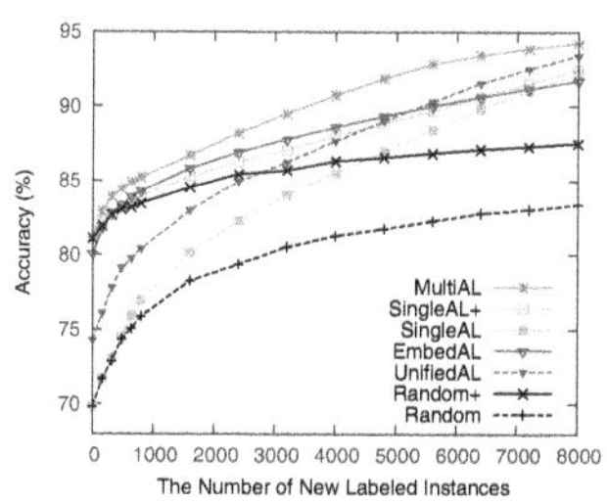

(d) Results on **B+D+E+K**

Figure 2: The sentiment classification results on the tasks constructed from Multi-Domain Sentiment Dataset

Table 4 summarizes the classification accuracy on each domain of task **B+D+K**. From the table, we can observe that MultiAL outperforms all comparison methods on each individual domain.

Furthermore, one more practical and interesting question is that how many human labeling efforts can be saved by using MultiAL? Table 5 shows how many new labeled instances

Table 4: The Classification Accuracy (%) on Task **B+D+K** after 4,000 New Labeled Instances Added

Domain	Random	Random+	UnifiedAL	EmbedAL	SingleAL	SingleAL+	MultiAL
Book	79.73±0.60	84.95±0.41	86.63±0.33	88.48±0.34	85.19±0.25	86.62±0.31	90.95±0.19
DVD	79.81±0.50	85.01±0.47	87.42±0.80	88.12±0.10	85.85±0.29	87.56±0.23	90.33±0.36
Kitchen	85.30±0.31	89.11±0.23	92.39±0.22	91.34±0.12	91.38±0.29	92.24±0.32	94.80±0.15
Average	81.62±0.26	86.36±0.32	88.81±0.33	89.31±0.10	87.47±0.12	88.81±0.14	92.03±0.14

Table 5: The Number of New Labeled Instances Needed for Each Learner to Achieve 90% Accuracy on Sentiment Classification

Task	Random	Random+	UnifiedAL	EmbedAL	SingleAL	SingleAL+	MultiAL
B+D+E	>6,000	>6,000	4,860	5,820	5,460	5,100	3,360
B+D+K	>6,000	>6,000	4,500	4,560	5,100	4,680	3,000
B+E+K	>6,000	>6,000	4,140	4,320	4,680	4,200	2,700
D+E+K	>6,000	>6,000	3,780	4,020	4,560	4,080	2,520
B+D+E+K	>8,000	>8,000	5,440	5,600	6,560	5,920	3,600
Average	>6,400	>6,400	4,544	4,864	5,272	4,796	3,036

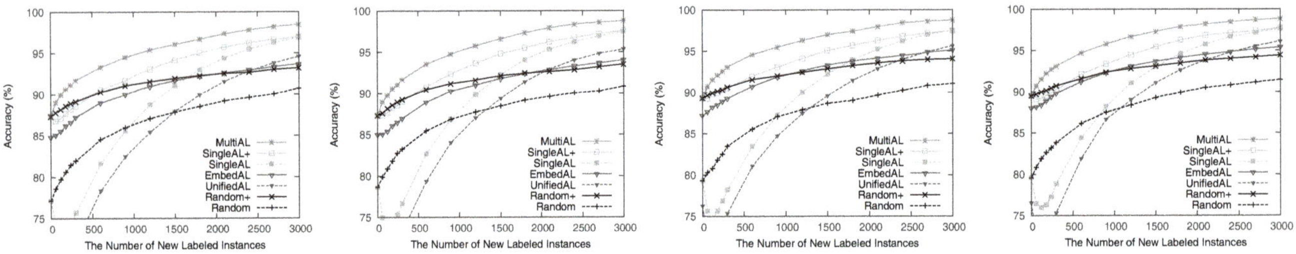

(a) Results on **NG-123** (b) Results on **NG-124** (c) Results on **NG-134** (d) Results on **NG-234**

Figure 3: The newsgroup classification results on the tasks constructed from 20Newsgroups

Table 6: The Number of New Labeled Instances Needed for Each Learner to Achieve 95% Accuracy on Newsgroup Classification

Task	Random	Random+	UnifiedAL	EmbedAL	SingleAL	SingleAL+	MultiAL
NG-123	>3,000	>3,000	>3,000	>3,000	2,280	1,800	1,080
NG-124	>3,000	>3,000	2,820	>3,000	2,040	1,620	1,020
NG-134	>3,000	>3,000	2,760	2,880	2,100	1,500	780
NG-234	>3,000	>3,000	2,520	2,580	1,920	1,380	720
Average	>3,000	>3,000	>2,775	>2,865	2,085	1,575	900

are needed for each active method to achieve a satisfactory classification accuracy (i.e., 90%). From Table 5, we can find that MultiAL saves at least 33.2% labeling efforts on average compared with all comparison methods. For example, on task **B+D+E+K**, MultiAL only needs to label 3,600 data instances to achieve 90% classification accuracy, while the best active learning baseline UnifiedAL requires 5,440 new labeled instances. The random query methods Random and Random+ cannot achieve the desired classification accuracy even if 8,000 new labeled instances are added. The result suggests that our method can effectively save the redundant labeling efforts by optimizing the classifiers of all domains together.

In the following, we report the experiment results on the newsgroup classification tasks. Figure 3 illustrates the overall performance on the four multi-domain newsgroup classification tasks. As can be seen from the figures, MultiAL consistently outperforms the comparison methods on all tasks. In addition, we can find that UnifiedAL always performs worse than SingleAL. An explanation is that when the domain gap is large, the query strategy would be affected by the inherent difference between domains. Table 6 shows the number of new labeled instances needed for each method to achieve 95% newsgroup classification accuracy. As presented in the table, MultiAL saves more than 42.9% labeling efforts compared with all comparison methods.

5.4.2 Results on Email Spam Filtering Dataset

In this section, we discuss our experiments on the email spam filtering dataset. The experiments are conducted in the inductive setting. For each task, we randomly select 10 emails of each user to form an initial training set, and select 100 emails of each user to form a test set. The remaining emails are used to form an unlabeled pool. Active learning is iteratively performed several iterations with 5 new labeled emails are added per iteration. Figures 4 shows the classification results on the test sets for the four spam filtering tasks. As illustrated in the figures, the accuracy curves of MultiAL grow very fast and achieve satisfactory performance after a few iterations. But other methods need much more querying iterations to obtain the comparable performance. Table 7 shows how many new labeled instances are needed for each method to achieve 95% classification accuracy on each task. From the table, we can observe that MultiAL saves more than 68.7% labeling efforts on average compared with all baseline methods.

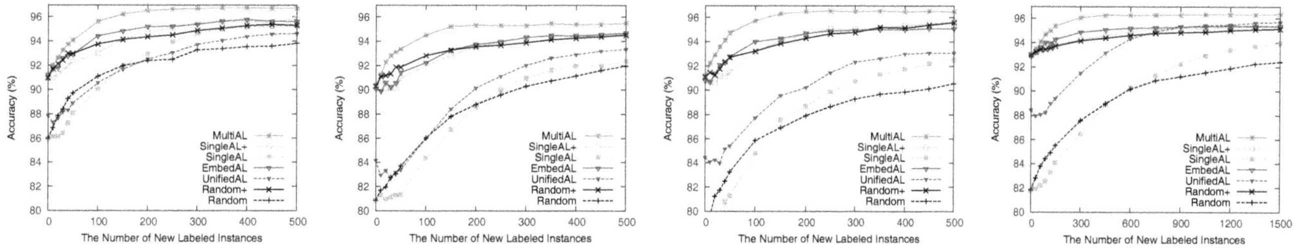

(a) Results on **u00-u04** (b) Results on **u05-u09** (c) Results on **u10-u14** (d) Results on **u00-u14**

Figure 4: The email spam filtering results on the tasks constructed from Email Spam Filtering Dataset

Table 7: The Number of New Labeled Instances Needed for Each Learner to Achieve 95% Accuracy on Email Spam Filtering

Task	Random	Random+	UnifiedAL	EmbedAL	SingleAL	SingleAL+	MultiAL
u00-u04	>500	310	>500	190	360	230	80
u05-u09	>500	>500	>500	>500	>500	>500	150
u10-u14	>500	340	>500	290	>500	250	70
u00-u14	>1,500	1,140	780	360	>1,500	720	120
Average	>750	>572	>570	>335	>715	>425	105

5.4.3 *Parameter Sensitivity Analysis*

There are two important parameters for active learning methods: 1) the size of initial training set, and 2) the number of queried instances per iteration. In addition, the dimensionality of the shared space is an important parameter of the multi-domain classification method in our proposed framework. In this section, we test the sensitivity of these parameters. When testing a specific parameter, we fix other parameters and vary the value of the parameter of our interest. For example, when testing the influence of initial training set size, we set the dimensionality of shared subspace to 100 for all tasks, and set the number of queried instances per iteration to 300 and 5 for the sentiment/newsgroup classification and the spam filtering tasks, respectively.

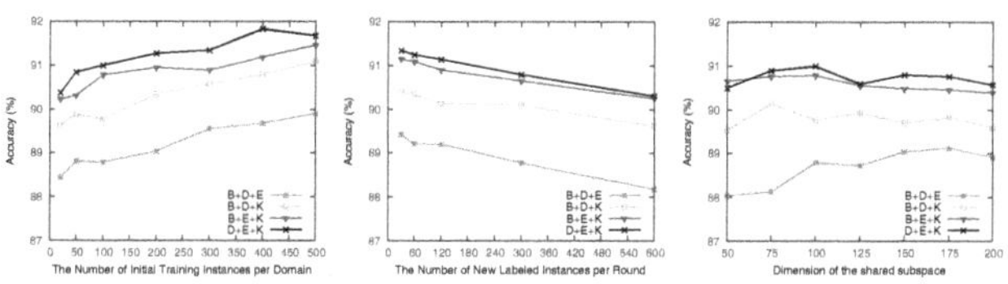

(a) Parameter sensitivity on the sentiment datasets

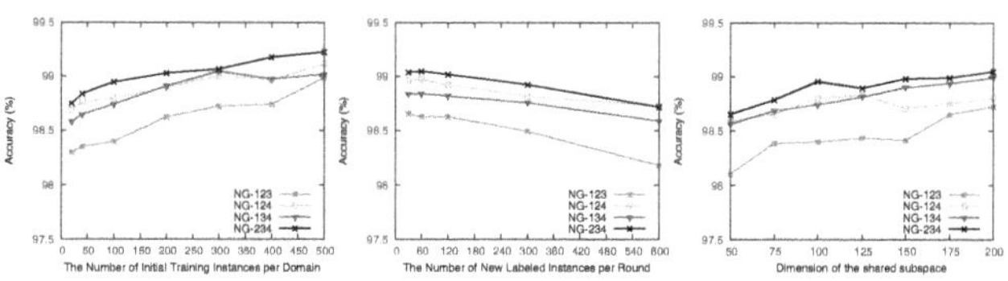

(b) Parameter sensitivity on the newsgroups datasets

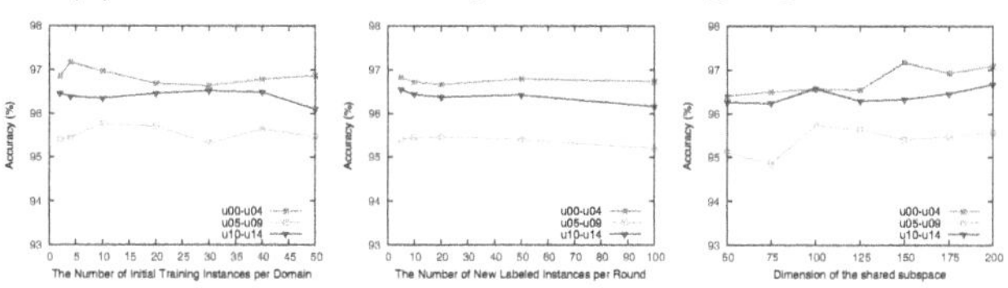

(c) Parameter sensitivity on the email spam datasets

Figure 5: Parameter sensitivity of: 1) numbers of initial training instances per domain, 2) numbers of new labeled instances per iteration, 3) dimensionality of shared subspaces

Figure 5 shows the parameter sensitivity of our method after 3000, 3000 and 500 new labeled data instances are added on the sentiment classification, the newsgroup classification and the spam filtering tasks, respectively. As presented in the figures, the performance of MultiAL is stable and consistent under different parameter settings. In general, the performance of MultiAL improves when more initial training data instances are available. And when the total number of queried instances are fixed, the performance of MultiAL drops when the number of queried instances per iteration increases. The reason may be that for each iteration, the more instances the active learner queries, the more duplicate information the active learner may get. Finally, we can also observe that MultiAL works well and stably when the dimensionality of the shared subspace ranges from 50 to 200.

5.4.4 *Scalability*

In this section, we investigate the scalability of the proposed method. In our experiment, we use the re-sampling strategy on both Multi-Domain Sentiment Dataset and 20Newsgroups to construct a set of data pools for experiments. In the experiment, we fix the number of iterations to 10, and fix the number of queried instances per iteration to 400. Figure 6 demonstrates the different running time when the size of unlabeled data pool varying from 20,000 to 1,000,000. From the figure, we can observe that the running time linearly increases under varying sizes of the unlabeled data pool. The result suggests that our proposed method is efficient and capable of dealing with large-scale applications.

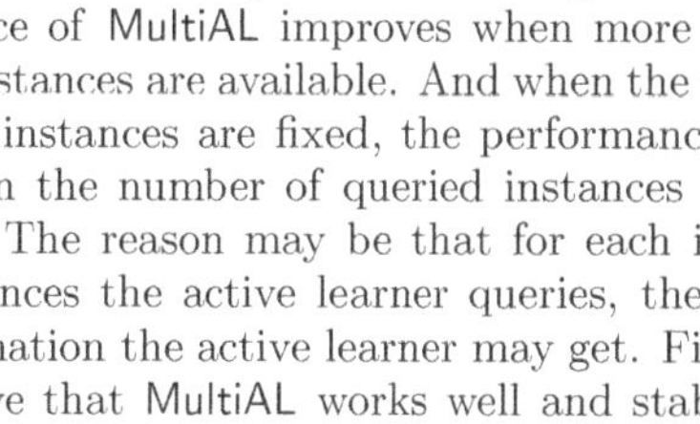

Figure 6: Running time under different size of data pool

6. CONCLUSIONS AND FUTURE WORK

In this work, we aim to solve a novel active learning problem for building classifiers of multiple domains simultaneously. Different from conventional active learning algorithms which focus on improving a single domain classifier, the proposed method aims to query the data instance which can not only improve the classifier of its corresponding domain but also improve the classifiers of other domains. The experiment results on three real-world applications show that our method respectively reduce the human labeling efforts by 33.2%, 42.9% and 68.7% on these applications. In addition, the proposed approach has been verified to be efficient and easily applied to large-scale applications. In the future, we plan to extend our work in the following directions: 1) In this work, we use a score function to rank unlabeled data instances for querying. However, this criteria can be biased by some data instances which contain rare patterns and are far away from existing labeled instances. It is not clear whether we can correct such label-sampling bias with importance weighting. 2) Given a large number of domains, some features may be shared by a subset of domains instead of all domains. It is interesting to jointly query instances under a hierarchical structure among domains. 3) With the increasing number of new labeled instances, it would be helpful to re-build the shared subspace after each iteration of active learning. 4) How to apply our active learning framework to other classification methods is also an interesting problem.

7. ACKNOWLEDGMENT

The work was supported by National Natural Science Foundation of China (60973103,90924003) and HGJ National Key Project (2010ZX01042-002-002).

References

[1] R. K. Ando and T. Zhang. A framework for learning predictive structures from multiple tasks and unlabeled data. *J. Mach. Learn. Res.*, 6:1817–1853, Dec. 2005.

[2] A. Beygelzimer, S. Dasgupta, and J. Langford. Importance weighted active learning. In *Proceedings of ICML*, pages 49–56, Montreal, Quebec, Canada, 2009. ACM.

[3] J. Blitzer, M. Dredze, and F. Pereira. Biographies, bollywood, boom-boxes and blenders: Domain adaptation for sentiment classification. In *Proceedings of ACL*, Prague, Czech Republic, 2007. ACL.

[4] J. Blitzer, R. McDonald, and F. Pereira. Domain adaptation with structural correspondence learning. In *Proceedings of EMNLP*, pages 120–128, Sydney, Australia, 2006. ACL.

[5] N. Cebron and M. R. Berthold. Active learning in parallel universes. In *Proceedings of CIKM*, pages 1621–1624, New York, NY, USA, 2010. ACM.

[6] W. Dai, Q. Yang, G.-R. Xue, and Y. Yu. Boosting for transfer learning. In *Proceedings of ICML*, pages 193–200, Corvalis, Oregon, USA, 2007. ACM.

[7] P. Donmez and J. G. Carbonell. Proactive learning: cost-sensitive active learning with multiple imperfect oracles. In *Proceeding of CIKM*, pages 619–628, Napa Valley, California, USA, 2008. ACM.

[8] M. Dredze, A. Kulesza, and K. Crammer. Multi-domain learning by confidence-weighted parameter combination. *Mach. Learn.*, 79(1-2):123–149, May 2010.

[9] T. Evgeniou and M. Pontil. Regularized multi–task learning. In *Proceedings of KDD*, pages 109–117, Seattle, WA, USA, 2004. ACM.

[10] R.-E. Fan, K.-W. Chang, C.-J. Hsieh, X.-R. Wang, and C.-J. Lin. LIBLINEAR: A library for large linear classification. *J. Mach. Learn. Res.*, 9:1871–1874, 2008.

[11] A. Harpale and Y. Yang. Active learning for multi-task adaptive filtering. In *Proceedings of ICML*, pages 431–438. Omnipress, 2010.

[12] T. Joachims. Text categorization with support vector machines: Learning with many relevant features. In *Proceedings of ECML*, pages 137–142, Berlin, Germany, 1998. Springer.

[13] D. D. Lewis and W. A. Gale. A sequential algorithm for training text classifiers. In *Proceedings of SIGIR*, pages 3–12, Dublin, Ireland, 1994. Springer-Verlag New York.

[14] T. M. Mitchell. Generalization as search. *Artif. Int.*, 18(2):203 – 226, 1982.

[15] I. Muslea, S. Minton, and C. A. Knoblock. Active learning with multiple views. *J. Artif. Int. Res.*, 27(1):203–233, Oct. 2006.

[16] S. J. Pan, J. T. Kwok, and Q. Yang. Transfer learning via dimensionality reduction. In *Proceedings of AAAI*, pages 677–682, Chicago, Illinois, USA, 2008. AAAI.

[17] S. J. Pan, X. Ni, J.-T. Sun, Q. Yang, and Z. Chen. Cross-domain sentiment classification via spectral feature alignment. In *Proceedings of WWW*, pages 751–760, Raleigh, North Carolina, USA, 2010. ACM.

[18] P. Rai, A. Saha, H. Daumé, III, and S. Venkatasubramanian. Domain adaptation meets active learning. In *Proceedings of the NAACL HLT 2010*, pages 27–32, Los Angeles, California, USA, 2010. ACL.

[19] R. Reichart, K. Tomanek, U. Hahn, and A. Rappoport. Multi-task active learning for linguistic annotations. In *Proceedings of ACL-08: HLT*, pages 861–869, Columbus, Ohio, USA, June 2008. ACL.

[20] N. Roy and A. McCallum. Toward optimal active learning through sampling estimation of error reduction. In *Proceedings of ICML*, pages 441–448, San Francisco, CA, USA, 2001. Morgan Kaufmann Publishers Inc.

[21] B. Settles. Active learning literature survey. Computer Sciences Technical Report 1648, University of Wisconsin–Madison, 2009.

[22] H. S. Seung, M. Opper, and H. Sompolinsky. Query by committee. In *Proceedings of COLT*, pages 287–294, Pittsburgh, Pennsylvania, USA, 1992. ACM.

[23] X. Shi, W. Fan, and J. Ren. Actively transfer domain knowledge. In *Proceedings of ECML/PKDD*, pages 342–357, Antwerp, Belgium, 2008. Springer-Verlag.

[24] S. Tong. *Active learning: theory and applications*. PhD thesis, 2001.

[25] S. Tong and D. Koller. Support vector machine active learning with applications to text classification. *J. Mach. Learn. Res.*, 2:45–66, Mar. 2002.

[26] S. Xie, W. Fan, J. Peng, O. Verscheure, and J. Ren. Latent space domain transfer between high dimensional overlapping distributions. In *Proceedings of WWW*, pages 91–100. ACM, 2009.

[27] Y. Zhang. Multi-task active learning with output constraints. In *Proceedings of AAAI*, Atlanta, Georgia, USA, 2010. AAAI.

Modeling Disease Progression via Fused Sparse Group Lasso

Jiayu Zhou[1,2], Jun Liu[1], Vaibhav A. Narayan[3], Jieping Ye[1,2]
[1]Center for Evolutionary Medicine and Informatics, The Biodesign Institute, ASU, Tempe, AZ
[2]Department of Computer Science and Engineering, ASU, Tempe, AZ
[3]Johnson & Johnson Pharmaceutical Research & Development, LLC, Titusville, NJ

ABSTRACT

Alzheimer's Disease (AD) is the most common neurodegenerative disorder associated with aging. Understanding how the disease progresses and identifying related pathological biomarkers for the progression is of primary importance in the clinical diagnosis and prognosis of Alzheimer's disease. In this paper, we develop novel multi-task learning techniques to predict the disease progression measured by cognitive scores and select biomarkers predictive of the progression. In multi-task learning, the prediction of cognitive scores at each time point is considered as a task, and multiple prediction tasks at different time points are performed simultaneously to capture the temporal smoothness of the prediction models across different time points. Specifically, we propose a novel convex fused sparse group Lasso (cFSGL) formulation that allows the simultaneous selection of a common set of biomarkers for multiple time points and specific sets of biomarkers for different time points using the sparse group Lasso penalty and in the meantime incorporates the temporal smoothness using the fused Lasso penalty. The proposed formulation is challenging to solve due to the use of several non-smooth penalties. One of the main technical contributions of this paper is to show that the proximal operator associated with the proposed formulation exhibits a certain decomposition property and can be computed efficiently; thus cFSGL can be solved efficiently using the accelerated gradient method. To further improve the model, we propose two non-convex formulations to reduce the shrinkage bias inherent in the convex formulation. We employ the difference of convex (DC) programming technique to solve the non-convex formulations. We have performed extensive experiments using data from the Alzheimer's Disease Neuroimaging Initiative (ADNI). Results demonstrate the effectiveness of the proposed progression models in comparison with existing methods for disease progression. We also perform longitudinal stability selection to identify and analyze the temporal patterns of biomarkers in disease progression.

KDD'12, August 12–16, 2012, Beijing, China.

Categories and Subject Descriptors

H.2.8 [**Database Management**]: Database Applications—*Data Mining*; J.3 [**Life and Medical Sciences**]: Health, Medical information systems

General Terms

Algorithms

Keywords

Alzheimer's Disease, regression, multi-task learning, fused Lasso, sparse group Lasso, cognitive score

1. INTRODUCTION

Alzheimer's disease (AD), accounting for 60-70% of age-related dementia, is a severe neurodegenerative disorder. AD is characterized by loss of memory and declination of cognitive function due to progressive impairment of neurons and their connections, leading directly to death [21]. In 2011 there are approximately 30 million individuals afflicted with dementia and the number is projected to be over 114 million by 2050 [36]. Currently there is no cure for Alzheimer's and efforts are underway to develop sensitive and consistent biomarkers for AD.

In order to better understand the disease, an important area that has recently received increasing attention is to understand how the disease progresses and identify related pathological biomarkers for the progression. Realizing its importance, NIH in 2003 funded the Alzheimer's Disease Neuroimaging Initiative (ADNI). The initiative is facilitating the scientific evaluation of neuroimaging data including magnetic resonance imaging (MRI), positron emission tomography (PET), other biomarkers, and clinical and neuropsychological assessments for predicting the onset and progression of MCI (Mild Cognitive Impairment) and AD. The identification of sensitive and specific markers of very early AD progression will facilitate the diagnosis of early AD and the development, assessment, and monitoring of new treatments. There are two types of progression models that have been commonly used in the literature: the regression model [10, 31] and the survival model [30, 34]. Many existing work consider a small number of input features, and the model building involves an iterative process in which each feature is evaluated individually by adding to the model and testing the performance of predicting the target representing the *disease status* [18, 35]. The disease status can be measured by a clinical score such as Mini Mental State Examination (MMSE) or Alzheimer's Disease Assessment Scale cognitive subscale (ADAS-Cog) [10, 31], or the volume of a certain brain region [16], or clinically defined categories [9, 26]. When high-dimensional data, such as neuroimages (i.e., MRI and/or PET) are used as input features, the methods of sequentially evaluating individual features are suboptimal. In such cases, dimension reduction techniques such as principle component analysis are commonly applied to project the data into a lower-dimensional space [10]. One disadvantage of using dimension reduction is that the models are no longer interpretable. A better alternative is to use feature selection in modeling the disease progression [31]. Most existing work focus on the prediction of target at a single time point (baseline [31], or one year [10]); however, a joint analysis of data from multiple time points is expected to improve the performance especially when the number of subjects is small and the number of input features is large.

To address the aforementioned challenges, multi-task learning techniques have recently been proposed to model the disease progression [39, 43]. The idea of multi-task learning is to utilize the intrinsic relationships among multiple related tasks in order to improve the generalization performance; it is most effective when the number of samples for each task is small. One of the key issues in multi-task learning is to identify how the tasks are related and build learning models to capture such task relatedness. One way of modeling multi-task relationship is to assume all tasks are related and task models are closed to each other [11], or tasks are clustered into groups [4, 20, 32, 41]. Alternatively, one can assume that the tasks share a common subspace [2, 7], or a common set of features [3, 29]. In [39], the prediction of different types of targets such as MMSE and ADAS-Cog is modeled as a multi-task learning problem and all models are constrained to share a common set of features. In [43], multi-task learning is used to model the longitudinal disease progression. Given the set of baseline features of a patient, the prediction of the patient's disease status at each time point can be considered as a regression task. Multiple prediction tasks at different time points are performed simultaneously to capture the temporal smoothness of the prediction models across different time points. However, similar to [39], the formulation in [43] constrains the models at all time points to select a common set of features, thus failing to capture the *temporal patterns* of the biomarkers in disease progression [6, 19]. It is thus desirable to develop formulations that allow the simultaneous selection of a common set of biomarkers for multiple time points and specific sets of biomarkers for different time points.

In this paper, we propose novel multi-task learning formulations for predicting the disease progression measured by the clinical scores (ADAS-Cog and MMSE). Specifically, we propose a convex fused sparse group Lasso (cFSGL) formulation that simultaneously selects a common set of biomarkers for all time points and selects a specific set of biomarkers at different time points using the sparse group Lasso penalty [14], and in the meantime incorporates the temporal smoothness using the fused Lasso penalty [33]. The proposed formulation is, however, challenging to solve due to the use of several non-smooth penalties including the sparse group Lasso and fused Lasso penalties. We show that the proximal operator associated with the optimization problem in cFSGL exhibits a certain decomposition property and can be solved efficiently. Therefore cFSGL can be efficiently solved using the accelerated gradient method [27, 28]. The convex sparsity-inducing penalties are known to introduce shrinkage bias [12]. To further improve the progression model and reduce the shrinkage bias in cFSGL, we propose two non-convex progression formulations. We employ the difference of convex (DC) programming technique to solve the non-convex formulations, which iteratively solves a sequence of convex relaxed optimization problems. We show that at each step the convex relaxed problems are equivalent to reweighted sparse learning problems [5].

We have performed extensive experiments to demonstrate the effectiveness of the proposed models using data from the Alzheimer's Disease Neuroimaging Initiative (ADNI). We have also performed longitudinal stability selection [43] using our proposed formulations to identify and analyze the temporal patterns of biomarkers in disease progression.

2. A CONVEX FORMULATION OF MODELING DISEASE PROGRESSION

In the longitudinal AD study, cognitive scores of selected patients are repeatedly measured at multiple time points. The prediction of cognitive scores at each time point can be considered as a regression problem, and the prediction of cognitive scores at multiple time points can be treated as a multi-task regression problem. By employing multi-task regression, the temporal information among different tasks can be incorporated into the model to improve the prediction performance.

Consider a multi-task regression problem of t tasks with n samples of d features. Let $\{\mathbf{x}_1, \cdots, \mathbf{x}_n\}$ be the input data at the baseline, and let $\{\mathbf{y}_1, \cdots, \mathbf{y}_n\}$ be the targets, where each $\mathbf{x}_i \in \mathbb{R}^d$ represents a sample (patient), and $y_i \in \mathbb{R}^t$ is the corresponding targets (clinical scores) at different time points. We collectively denote $X = [\mathbf{x}_1, \cdots, \mathbf{x}_n]^T \in \mathbb{R}^{n\times d}$ as the data matrix, $Y = [\mathbf{y}_1, \cdots, \mathbf{y}_n]^T \in \mathbb{R}^{n\times t}$ as the target matrix, and $W = [\mathbf{w}^1, \cdots, \mathbf{w}^t] \in \mathbb{R}^{d\times t}$ as the weight matrix. To consider the missing values from the target, we denote the loss function as:

$$L(W) = \|S \odot (XW - Y)\|_F^2, \tag{1}$$

where matrix $S \in \mathbb{R}^{n\times t}$ indicates missing target values: $S_{i,j} = 0$ if the target value of sample i is missing at the jth time point, and $S_{i,j} = 1$ otherwise. The component-wise operator $\odot$ is defined as follows: $Z = A \odot B$ denotes $Z_{i,j} = A_{i,j}B_{i,j}$, for all i, j. The multi-task regression solves the following optimization problem: $\min_W L(W) + \Omega(W)$, where $\Omega(W)$ is a regularization term that captures the task relatedness.

In the multi-task setting for modeling disease progression, each task is to predict a specific target (e.g., MMSE) for a set of subjects at different time points. It is thus reasonable to assume that the difference of the predictions between immediate time points is small, i.e., the temporal smoothness [43]. It is also well believed in the literature that a small subset of biomarkers are related to the disease progression, and biomarkers involved at different stages may be different [19]. To this end, we propose a novel multi-task learning formulation for modeling disease progression which allows simultaneous joint feature selection for multiple tasks and task-specific feature selection, and in the meantime incorporates the temporal smoothness. Mathematically, the proposed formulation solves the following convex optimization problem:

$$\min_W L(W) + \lambda_1 \|W\|_1 + \lambda_2 \left\|RW^T\right\|_1 + \lambda_3 \|W\|_{2,1}, \quad (2)$$

where $\|W\|_1$ is the Lasso penalty, the group Lasso penalty $\|W\|_{2,1}$ is given by $\sum_{i=1}^d \sqrt{\sum_{j=1}^t W_{ij}^2}$, $\left\|RW^T\right\|_1$ is the fused Lasso penalty, R is an $(t-1)\times t$ sparse matrix in which $R_{i,i}=1$ and $R_{i,i+1}=-1$, and λ_1, λ_2 and λ_3 are regularization parameters. The combination of Lasso and group Lasso penalties is also known as the sparse group Lasso penalty, which allows simultaneous joint feature selection for all tasks and selection of a specific set of features for each task. The fused Lasso penalty is employed to incorporate the temporal smoothness. We call the formulation in Eq. (2) "convex fused sparse group Lasso" (cFSGL). The cFSGL formulation involves three non-smooth terms, and is thus challenging to solve. We propose to solve the optimization problem by the accelerated gradient method (AGM) [27, 28]. One of the key steps in using AGM is the computation of the proximal operator associated with the composite of non-smooth penalties defined as follows:

$$\pi(V) = \arg\min_W \frac{1}{2}\|W - V\|_F^2 + \lambda_1\|W\|_1 + \lambda_2\|RW^T\|_1 + \lambda_3\|W\|_{2,1}. \quad (3)$$

It is clear that each row of W is decoupled in Eq. (3). Thus for obtaining the ith row $\mathbf{w}_i$, we only need to solve the following optimization problem:

$$\pi(\mathbf{v}_i) = \arg\min_{\mathbf{w}_i} \frac{1}{2}\|\mathbf{w}_i - \mathbf{v}_i\|_2^2 + \lambda_1\|\mathbf{w}_i\|_1 + \lambda_2\|R\mathbf{w}_i\|_1 + \lambda_3\|\mathbf{w}_i\|_2, \quad (4)$$

where $\mathbf{v}_i$ is the ith row of V. The proximal operator in Eq. (4) is challenging to compute due to the presence of three non-smooth terms. One of the key technical contributions of this paper is to show that the proximal operator exhibits a certain decomposition property, based on which we can efficiently compute the proximal operator in two stages, as summarized in the following theorem:

THEOREM 1. *Define*

$$\pi_{\rm FL}(\mathbf{v}) = \arg\min_{\mathbf{w}} \frac{1}{2}\|\mathbf{w} - \mathbf{v}\|_2^2 + \lambda_1\|\mathbf{w}\|_1 + \lambda_2\|R\mathbf{w}\|_1 \quad (5)$$

$$\pi_{\rm GL}(\mathbf{v}) = \arg\min_{\mathbf{w}} \frac{1}{2}\|\mathbf{w} - \mathbf{v}\|_2^2 + \lambda_3\|\mathbf{w}\|_2. \quad (6)$$

Then the following holds:

$$\pi(\mathbf{v}) = \pi_{\rm GL}(\pi_{\rm FL}(\mathbf{v})). \quad (7)$$

Proof: The necessary and sufficient optimality conditions for (4), (5), and (6) can be written as:

$$\mathbf{0} \in \pi(\mathbf{v}) - \mathbf{v} + \lambda_1 \mathrm{SGN}(\pi(\mathbf{v})) + \lambda_2 R^T \mathrm{SGN}(R\pi(\mathbf{v})) + \lambda_3 \partial g(\pi(\mathbf{v})), \quad (8)$$

$$\mathbf{0} \in \pi_{\rm FL}(\mathbf{v}) - \mathbf{v} + \lambda_1 \mathrm{SGN}(\pi_{\rm FL}(\mathbf{v})) + \lambda_2 R^T \mathrm{SGN}(R\pi_{\rm FL}(\mathbf{v})), \quad (9)$$

$$\mathbf{0} \in \pi_{\rm GL}(\pi_{\rm FL}(\mathbf{v})) - \pi_{\rm FL}(\mathbf{v}) + \lambda_3 \partial g(\pi_{\rm GL}(\pi_{\rm FL}(\mathbf{v}))), \quad (10)$$

where $\mathrm{SGN}(\mathbf{x})$ is a set defined in a componentwise manner as:

$$(\mathrm{SGN}(\mathbf{x}))_i = \begin{cases} [-1,1] & x_i = 0 \\ \{1\} & x_i > 0 \\ \{-1\} & x_i < 0, \end{cases} \quad (11)$$

and

$$\partial g(\mathbf{x}) = \begin{cases} \frac{\mathbf{x}}{\|\mathbf{x}\|_2} & \mathbf{x} \neq \mathbf{0} \\ \{\mathbf{y} : \|\mathbf{y}\|_2 \leq 1\} & \mathbf{x} = \mathbf{0}. \end{cases} \quad (12)$$

It follows from (10) and (12) that: 1) if $\|\pi_{\rm FL}(\mathbf{v})\|_2 \leq \lambda_3$, then $\pi_{\rm GL}(\pi_{\rm FL}(\mathbf{v})) = \mathbf{0}$; and 2) if $\|\pi_{\rm FL}(\mathbf{v})\|_2 > \lambda_3$, then $\pi_{\rm GL}(\pi_{\rm FL}(\mathbf{v})) = \frac{\|\pi_{\rm FL}(\mathbf{v})\|_2 - \lambda_3}{\|\pi_{\rm FL}(\mathbf{v})\|_2}\pi_{\rm FL}(\mathbf{v})$.

It is easy to observe that, 1) if the i-th entry of $\pi_{\rm FL}(\mathbf{v})$ is zero, so is the i-th entry of $\pi_{\rm GL}(\pi_{\rm FL}(\mathbf{v}))$; 2) if the i-th entry of $\pi_{\rm FL}(\mathbf{v})$ is positive (or negative), so is the i-th entry of $\pi_{\rm GL}(\pi_{\rm FL}(\mathbf{v}))$. Therefore, we have:

$$\mathrm{SGN}(\pi_{\rm FL}(\mathbf{v})) \subseteq \mathrm{SGN}(\pi_{\rm GL}(\pi_{\rm FL}(\mathbf{v}))). \quad (13)$$

Meanwhile, 1) if the i-th and the $(i+1)$-th entries of $\pi_{\rm FL}(\mathbf{v})$ are identical, so are those of $\pi_{\rm GL}(\pi_{\rm FL}(\mathbf{v}))$; 2) if the i-th entry is larger (or smaller) than the $(i+1)$-th entry in $\pi_{\rm FL}(\mathbf{v})$, so is in $\pi_{\rm GL}(\pi_{\rm FL}(\mathbf{v}))$. Therefore, we have:

$$\mathrm{SGN}(R\pi_{\rm FL}(\mathbf{v})) \subseteq \mathrm{SGN}(R\pi_{\rm GL}(\pi_{\rm FL}(\mathbf{v}))). \quad (14)$$

It follows from (9), (10), (13), and (14) that:

$$\mathbf{0} \in \pi_{\rm GL}(\pi_{\rm FL}(\mathbf{v})) - \mathbf{v} + \lambda_1 \mathrm{SGN}(\pi_{\rm GL}(\pi_{\rm FL}(\mathbf{v}))) + \lambda_2 R^T \mathrm{SGN}(R\pi_{\rm GL}(\pi_{\rm FL}(\mathbf{v}))) + \lambda_3 \partial g(\pi_{\rm GL}(\pi_{\rm FL}(\mathbf{v}))). \quad (15)$$

Since (4) has a unique solution, we can get (7) from (8) and (15). □

Note that the fused Lasso signal approximator [13] in Eq.(5) can be effectively solved using [24]. The complete algorithm for computing the proximal operator associated with cFSGL is given in Algorithm 1.

Algorithm 1 Proximal operator associated with the Convex Fused Sparse Group Lasso (cFSGL)

Input: $V \in \mathbb{R}^{d\times t}$, $R \in \mathbb{R}^{t-1\times t}$, λ_1, λ_2, λ_3
Output: $W \in \mathbb{R}^{d\times t}$
1: **for** i = 1 : d **do**
2: $\mathbf{u}_i = \arg\min_{\mathbf{w}} \frac{1}{2}\|\mathbf{w} - \mathbf{v}_i\|_2^2 + \lambda_1\|\mathbf{w}\|_1 + \lambda_2\|R\mathbf{w}\|_1$
3: $\mathbf{w}_i = \arg\min_{\mathbf{w}} \frac{1}{2}\|\mathbf{w} - \mathbf{u}_i\|_2^2 + \lambda_3\|\mathbf{w}\|_2$
4: **end for**

3. NON-CONVEX PROGRESSION MODELS

In cFSGL, we aim to select task-shared and task-specific features using the sparse group Lasso penalty. However, the decomposition property shown in Theorem 1 implies that a simple composition of the ℓ_1-norm penalty and $\ell_{2,1}$-norm penalty may be sub-optimal. Besides, the sparsity-inducing penalties are known to lead to biased estimates [12]. To this end, we propose the following non-convex multi-task regression formulation for modeling disease progression:

$$\min_W L(W) + \lambda \sum_{i=1}^d \sqrt{\|\mathbf{w}_i\|_1} + \gamma\|RW^T\|_1, \quad (16)$$

where the second term is the summation of the squared root of ℓ_1-norm of $\mathbf{w}_i$ ($\mathbf{w}_i$ is the ith row of W), and is called the composite $\ell_{(0.5,1)}$-norm regularization. Note that it is in fact not a valid norm due to its non-convexity. It is known that the $\ell_{0.5}$ penalty leads to a sparse solution, thus many of the rows of W will be zero, i.e., the features corresponding to the zero rows will be removed from all tasks. In addition, for the nonzero rows, due to the use of the ℓ_1 penalty for the rows, many features within these nonzero rows will be zero, resulting in task-specific features. Thus, the use of $\ell_{(0.5,1)}$ penalty leads to a tight coupling of between-task and within-task feature selection. In addition, the $\ell_{0.5}$ penalty is expected to reduce the estimation bias associated with the convex sparsity-inducing penalties.

We also consider an alternative non-convex formulation which includes the fused Lasso term of each row within the square root, resulting in a composite $\ell_{(0.5,1)}$-like penalty:

$$\min_W L(W) + \lambda \sum_{i=1}^{d} \sqrt{\|R\mathbf{w}_i^T\|_1 + \beta\|\mathbf{w}_i\|_1}. \quad (17)$$

A good merit of using non-convex penalties is that they are closer to the optimal ℓ_0-'norm' (minimizing which is NP-hard) and give better sparsity [15]. In addition, a practical advantage of the non-convex progression models presented in Eqs. (16) and (17) is that there are only 2 regularization parameters to be estimated, compared to 3 parameters in the convex formulation in Eq. (2). However, one disadvantage of the non-convex penalties is that the associated optimization problems are non-convex and global solutions are not guaranteed. A well-known method for solving non-convex problems is to approximate the non-convex formulation by a convex relaxation via the difference of convex (DC) programming techniques [17]. Next, we show how the non-convex problems can be solved using DC programming and then relate the relaxed formulations to reweighted convex formulations.

3.1 DC Programming

The formulations in Eq. (16) and Eq. (17) can be expressed in the following general form:

$$\min_W \ell(W) + \sqrt{h(W)}, \quad (18)$$

where $\ell(W)$ and $h(W)$ are convex. Since $x - \sqrt{x}$ is convex, we decompose the objective function in Eq. (18) into the following form:

$$\min_W \ell(W) + h(W) - (h(W) - \sqrt{h(W)}).$$

Denote the two functions as $f(W) = \ell(W) + h(W)$ and $g(h(W)) = h(W) - \sqrt{h(W)}$. We can express the formulation in Eq. (18) in the form of difference of two functions:

$$\min_W f(W) - g(h(W)).$$

Using the convex-concave procedure (CCCP) algorithm [38], we can linearize $g(h(W))$ using the 1st-order Taylor expansion at the current point W' as:

$$\begin{aligned} f(W) - g(h(W)) &= f(W) - g(h(W')) \\ &\quad - \langle \nabla g(h(W')), (h(W) - h(W')) \rangle, \quad (19) \end{aligned}$$

which is the convex upper bound of the non-convex problem. In every iteration of the CCCP algorithm, we minimize the upper bound:

$$W_{(k+1)} = \operatorname*{argmin}_W f(W) - \langle \nabla g(h(W_{(k)})), h(W) \rangle, \quad (20)$$

and the objective function is guaranteed to decrease. We obtain a local optimal W^* of Eq. (18) by iteratively solving Eq. (20). The CCCP algorithm has been applied successfully to solve many non-convex problems [8, 22, 37].

3.2 Reweighting Interpretation of Non-Convex Fused Sparse Group Lasso

We first consider the non-convex optimization problem in Eq. (16), whose convex relaxed form corresponding to Eq. (20) is given by:

$$\begin{aligned} W_{(k+1)} &= \operatorname*{argmin}_W L(W) \\ &\quad + \frac{\lambda}{2} \sum_{i=1}^{d} \mu_i \|\mathbf{w}_i\|_1 + \gamma \|RW^T\|_1, \quad (21) \end{aligned}$$

where $\mu_i = 1/\sqrt{\|\mathbf{w}_{i(k)}\|_1 + \epsilon}$ and ϵ is a small number included to avoid singularity. It is clear that the convex relaxed problem in each iteration is a fused Lasso problem with a reweighted ℓ_1-norm term. If we omit the fused term, the general $\ell_{(1,0.5)}$-regularized optimization problem is of the following form:

$$\min_W L(W) + \lambda \sum_{i=1}^{d} \sqrt{\|\mathbf{w}_i\|_1},$$

which, under DC programming, involves solving a series of reweighted Lasso [5, 23] problems:

$$W_{(k+1)} = \operatorname*{argmin}_W L(W) + \frac{\lambda}{2} \sum_{i=1}^{d} \mu_i \|\mathbf{w}_i\|_1.$$

It is known that the reweighted Lasso reduces the estimation bias of Lasso, thus leading to a better solution. Similarly, for the non-convex optimization problem in Eq. (17), we iteratively solve the following convex problem:

$$\begin{aligned} W_{(k+1)} &= \operatorname*{argmin}_W L(W) \\ &\quad + \frac{\lambda}{2} \sum_{i=1}^{d} \nu_i \|R\mathbf{w}_i^T\|_1 + \frac{\lambda\beta}{2} \sum_{i=1}^{d} \nu_i \|\mathbf{w}_i\|_1, \quad (22) \end{aligned}$$

where $\nu_i = 1/\sqrt{\|R\mathbf{w}_{i(k)}^T\|_1 + \beta\|\mathbf{w}_{i(k)}\|_1 + \epsilon}$. In this case, in each iteration, we solve a fused Lasso problem with a reweighted ℓ_1-term and a reweighted fused term.

The non-convex optimization problems may be sensitive to the starting point. In our algorithm in Eq. (21), for example, if all elements in row i of the model $\mathbf{w}_i$ are initialized to be close to 0, then in the next iteration μ_i will be set to a very large number. The large penalty forces the row to stay at 0 in later iterations. Therefore, in our convex relaxed algorithms in Eq. (21) and Eq. (22), we propose to use the solution of a problem similar to fused Lasso as the starting point. For example, the starting point we use in Eq. (21) is:

$$W_{(0)} = \operatorname*{argmin}_W L(W) + \lambda \sum_{i=1}^{d} \|\mathbf{w}_i\|_1 + \gamma \|RW^T\|_1. \quad (23)$$

This is equivalent to setting $\mu_i/2 = 1$. Similarly, in Eq. (22) we set $\nu_i/2 = 1$.

4. ANALYZE TEMPORAL PATTERNS OF BIOMARKERS USING LONGITUDINAL STABILITY SELECTION

We propose to employ longitudinal stability selection to quantify the importance of the features selected by the proposed formulations for disease progression. The idea of longitudinal stability selection is to apply stability selection [25] to multi-task learning models for longitudinal study. The stability score (between 0 and 1) of each feature is indicative of the importance of the specific feature for disease progression. In this paper, we propose to use longitudinal stability selection with cFSGL and nFSGL to analyze the temporal patterns of biomarkers. The temporal pattern of stability scores of the features selected at different time points can potentially reveal how disease progresses temporally and spatially.

The longitudinal stability selection algorithm with cFSGL and nFSGL is given as follows. Let F be the index set of features, and let $f \in F$ denote the index of a particular feature. Let Δ be the regularization parameter space and let the stability iteration number be denoted as γ. For cFSGL an element $\delta \in \Delta$ is a triple $\langle\lambda_1, \lambda_2, \lambda_3\rangle$, and for nFSGL is a tuple of the corresponding parameter pairs. Let $B_{(i)} = \{X_{(i)}, Y_{(i)}\}$ be a random subsample from input data $\{X, Y\}$ of size $\lfloor n/2 \rfloor$ without replacement. For a given $\delta \in \Delta$, let $\hat{W}^{(i)}$ be the optimal solution of cFSGL or nFSGL on $B_{(i)}$. The set of features selected by the model $\hat{W}^{(i)}$ of the task at time point p is denoted by:

$$U_p^\delta(B_{(i)}) = \{f : \hat{W}_{f,p}^{(i)} \neq 0\}.$$

We repeat this process for γ times and obtain the *selection probability* $\hat{\Pi}_{f,p}^\delta$ of each feature f at time point p:

$$\hat{\Pi}_{f,p}^\delta = \sum_{i=1}^{\gamma} I(f \in U_p^\delta(B_{(i)}))/\gamma,$$

where $I(.)$ is the indicator function defined as: $I(c) = 1$ if c is true and $I(c) = 0$ otherwise. Repeat the above procedure for all $\delta \in \Delta$, we obtain the *stability score* for each feature f at time point p:

$$\mathcal{S}_p(f) = \max_{\delta \in \Delta}(\hat{\Pi}_{f,p}^\delta).$$

The *stability vector* of a feature f at all t time points is given by: $\mathcal{S}(f) = [\mathcal{S}_1(f) \ldots \mathcal{S}_t(f)]$, which reveals the change of the importance of feature f at different time points. We define the stable features at time point p as:

$$\hat{U}_p = \{f : \mathcal{S}_p(f) \text{ ranks among top } \eta \text{ in } F\}$$

and choose $\eta = 20$ in our experiments. We are interested in the stable features at all time points, i.e., $f \in \hat{U} = \cup_{p=1}^t \hat{U}_p$. Note that $\mathcal{S}(f)$ is dependent on the progression model used.

We emphasize here that unlike the previous work which gives a list of features common for all time points [43], our proposed approaches yield a different list of features at different time points. Note that in the above stability selection we use temporal information via fused Lasso. Consequently the distribution of stability scores also has temporal smoothness property: for each feature the stability scores are smooth across different time points (as shown in experimental results in Section 6.3). If simply using Lasso in stability selection, then we obtain independent probability lists at each time point, and therefore such temporal smooth pattern cannot be captured.

5. RELATION TO PREVIOUS WORK

In our previous work [43], we proposed to use the temporal group Lasso (TGL) regularization to capture task relatedness, which involves the following optimization problem:

$$\min_W L(W) + \theta_1 \|W\|_F^2 + \theta_2 \left\|RW^T\right\|_F^2 + \theta_3 \|W\|_{2,1}, \quad (24)$$

where θ_1, θ_2 and θ_3 are regularization parameters. The TGL formulation in Eq. (24) contains three penalty terms. The first term penalize the ℓ_2-norm of the model to prevent overfitting; the second term enforces temporal smoothness using ℓ_2-norm, which is equivalent to a Laplacian term, and the last $\ell_{2,1}$-norm introduces joint feature selection. We argue that it is more natural to incorporate the within-task feature selection and temporal smoothness using a composite penalty as in our proposed cFSGL formulation in Eq. (2).

For example, the only sparsity-inducing term in TGL formulation in Eq. (24) is the $\ell_{2,1}$-norm regularized joint feature selection. Therefore an obvious disadvantage of this formulation is that it restricts all models from different time points to select a common set of features; however, different features may be involved at different time points. In addition, one key advantage of fused Lasso compared with the Laplacian-based smoothing used in [43] is that under the fused Lasso penalty the selected features across different time points are smooth, i.e., nearby time points tend to select similar features, while the Laplacian-based penalty focuses on the smoothing of the prediction models across different time points. Thus, the fused Lasso penalty better captures the temporal smoothness of the selected features, which is closer to the real-world disease progression mechanism.

In the TGL formulation, the temporal smoothness is enforced using a smooth Laplacian term, though fused Lasso in cFSGL indeed has better properties such as sparsity continuity. We have used this restrictive model in TGL, in order to avoid the computational difficulties introduced by the composite of non-smooth terms ($\ell_{2,1}$-norm and fused Lasso). We show in this paper that the proximal operator associated with the optimization problem in cFSGL exhibits a certain decomposition property and can be computed efficiently (Theorem 1); thus cFSGL can be solved efficiently using accelerated gradient method. Another contribution of this paper is that we extend our progression model using a composite of non-convex sparsity-inducing terms, and we further propose to employ the DC programming to solve the non-convex formulations.

6. EXPERIMENTS

In this section we evaluate the proposed progression models on the data sets from the Alzheimer's Disease Neuroimaging Initiative (ADNI)[1]. The source codes can be found in the Muli-tAsk Learning via StructurAl Regularization (MALSAR) package [42].

6.1 Experimental Setup

The ADNI project is a longitudinal study, where a variety of measurements are collected from selected subjects including Alzheimer's disease patients (AD), mild cognitive impairment patients (MCI) and normal controls (NL), repeatedly over a 6-month or 1-year interval. The measurements include MRI scans (M), PET scans (P), CSF measurements (C), and cognitive scores such as MMSE and ADAS-Cog. We denote all measurements other than the three types of

[1]www.loni.ucla.edu/ADNI

Table 1: The sample size and feature dimensionality of different data sets used in the experiments. M denotes baseline MMSE features and E denotes baseline META features.

Target	Source	M06	M12	M24	M36	M48	Dim.
MMSE	M	648	642	569	389	87	306
	M+E	648	642	569	389	87	371
ADAS	M	648	638	564	377	85	306
	M+E	648	642	569	389	87	371

Table 2: Features included in the META dataset. In META, we include baseline cognitive scores as features to predict the future cognitive scores. A detailed explanation of each cognitive score and lab test can be found at [1].

Type	Features
Demographic	age, years of education, gender
Genetic	ApoE-ε4 information
Baseline cognitive scores	MMSE, ADAS-Cog, ADAS-MOD, ADAS sub-scores, CDR, FAQ, GDS, Hachinski, Neuropsychological Battery, WMS-R Logical Memory
Lab tests	RCT1, RCT11, RCT12, RCT13, RCT14, RCT1407, RCT1408, RCT183, RCT19, RCT20, RCT29, RCT3, RCT392, RCT4, RCT5, RCT6, RCT8

biomarkers (M, P, C) as META (E). A detailed list of the META data is given in Table 2. The date when the patient performs the screening in the hospital for the first time is called *baseline*, and the time point for the follow-up visits is denoted by the duration starting from the baseline. For instance, we use the notation "M06" to denote the time point half year after the first visit. Currently ADNI has up to 48 months' follow-up data for some patients. However, many patients drop out from the study for many reasons (e.g. deceased). In our experiments, we predict future MMSE and ADAS-Cog scores using various measurements at the baseline. For each target we build a prediction model using a data set that only contains baseline MRI features (M), and another data set that contains both MRI and META features (M+E). In the current study, CSF and PET are not used due to the small sample size. The MRI features are extracted in the same way as in [43]. There are 5 types of MRI features used: white matter parcellation volume (Vol.WM.), cortical parcellation volume (Vol.C.), surface area (Surf. Area), cortical thickness average (CTA), cortical thickness standard deviation (CTStd). The sample size and dimensionality for each time point and feature combination is given in Table 1.

6.2 Prediction Performance

In the first experiment, we compare the proposed methods including Convex Fused Sparse Group Lasso (cFSGL) and the two Non-Convex Fused Group Lasso: nFSGL1 in Eq. (16) and nFSGL2 in Eq. (17) with ridge regression (Ridge) and Temporal Group Lasso (TGL) on the prediction of MMSE and ADAS-Cog using selected types of feature combinations, namely M and M+E. Note that Lasso is a special case of cFSGL when both λ_2 and λ_3 are set to 0. For each feature combination, we randomly split the data into training and testing sets using a ratio 9 : 1. The 5-fold cross validation is used to select model parameters. For the regression performance measures, we use Normalized Mean Squared Error (nMSE) as used in the multi-task learning literature [40, 3] and weighted correlation coefficient (R-value) as employed in the medical literature addressing AD progression problems [10, 31, 18]. We report the mean and standard deviation based on 20 iterations of experiments on different splits of data. To investigate the effects of the fused Lasso term, in cFSGL we fix the value of λ_2 in Eq.(2) to be $20, 50, 100$, and perform cross validation to select λ_1 and λ_3. The three configurations are labeled as cFSGL1, cFSGL2 and cFSGL3 respectively.

The experimental results using 90% training data on MRI and MRI+META are presented in Table 3 and Table 4. Overall our proposed approaches outperform Ridge and TGL, in terms of both nMSE and correlation coefficient. We have the following observations: 1) The fused Lasso term is effective. We witness significant improvement in cFSGL when changing the parameter value for the fused Lasso term. 2) The proposed cFSGL and nFSGL formulations witness significant improvement for later time points. This may be due to the data sparseness at later time points (see Table 1), as the proposed sparsity-inducing models are expected to achieve better generalization performance in this case. 3) The non-convex nFSGL formulations are better than cFSGL in many tasks. One practical strength of the non-convex nFSGL formulations is that they have fewer parameters to be estimated (only 2 parameters).

6.3 Temporal Patterns of Biomarkers

One of the strengthens of the proposed formulations is that they facilitate the identification of temporal patterns of biomarkers. In this experiment we study the temporal patterns of biomarkers using longitudinal stability selection with cFSGL and nFSGL. Note that because the sample size at the M48 time point is too small, we perform stability selection for M06, M12, M24, and M36 only.

The stability vectors of MRI stable features using cFSGL nFSGL1 and nFSGL2 formulations are given in Figure 1, Figure 2 and Figure 3 respectively. In the figures, we collectively list the stable features ($\eta = 20$) at the 4 time points. The total number of features may be less than 80 because one feature may be identified as a stable feature at multiple time points. In Figure 1(a), we observe that cortical thickness average of left middle temporal, cortical thickness average of left and right Entorhinal, and white matter volume of left Hippocampus are important biomarkers for all time points, which agrees with the previous findings [43]. Cortical volume of left Entorhinal provides significant information in later stages than in the first 6 months. Several biomarkers including white matter volume of left and right Amygdala, and surface area of right Bankssts provide useful information only in later time points. On the contrary, some biomarkers have a large stability score during the first 2 years after baseline screening, such as cortical thickness average of left inferior temporal, left inferior parietal, and cortical thickness standard deviation of left isthmus cingulate, right lingual, left inferior parietal, and cortical volume of right precentral, right isthmus cingulate, and left middle temporal cortex.

The stability vector of stable MRI features for MMSE are given in Figure 1(b). We obtain very different patterns from ADAS-Cog. We find that most biomarkers provide significant information for the first 2 years and very few of them

Table 3: Comparison of our proposed approaches (cFSGL and nFSGL) and existing approaches (Ridge and TGL) on longitudinal MMSE and ADAS-Cog prediction using MRI features (M) in terms of normalized mean squared error (nMSE), average correlation coefficient (R) and mean squared error (MSE) for each time point. 90 percent of data is used as training data.

	Ridge	TGL	cFSGL1	cFSGL2	cFSGL3	nFSGL1	nFSGL2
				Target: MMSE			
nMSE	0.548 ± 0.057	0.449 ± 0.045	0.428 ± 0.052	0.400 ± 0.053	$\mathbf{0.395 \pm 0.052}$	0.412 ± 0.054	0.408 ± 0.056
R	0.689 ± 0.030	0.755 ± 0.029	0.772 ± 0.030	0.790 ± 0.032	$\mathbf{0.796 \pm 0.031}$	0.788 ± 0.031	0.792 ± 0.031
M06 MSE	2.269 ± 0.207	$\mathbf{2.038 \pm 0.262}$	2.117 ± 0.209	2.069 ± 0.209	2.071 ± 0.213	2.149 ± 0.194	2.181 ± 0.201
M12 MSE	3.266 ± 0.556	2.923 ± 0.643	2.900 ± 0.629	2.803 ± 0.662	$\mathbf{2.762 \pm 0.669}$	2.835 ± 0.662	2.793 ± 0.659
M24 MSE	3.494 ± 0.599	3.363 ± 0.733	3.125 ± 0.612	3.016 ± 0.624	3.000 ± 0.642	3.031 ± 0.604	$\mathbf{2.979 \pm 0.546}$
M36 MSE	4.003 ± 0.853	3.768 ± 0.962	3.456 ± 0.766	3.302 ± 0.781	3.265 ± 0.803	3.263 ± 0.785	$\mathbf{3.211 \pm 0.786}$
M48 MSE	4.328 ± 1.310	3.631 ± 1.226	2.857 ± 0.892	$\mathbf{2.787 \pm 0.871}$	2.871 ± 0.884	2.780 ± 0.855	2.766 ± 0.826
				Target: ADAS-Cog			
nMSE	0.532 ± 0.095	0.464 ± 0.067	0.444 ± 0.059	0.404 ± 0.055	0.391 ± 0.059	0.386 ± 0.060	$\mathbf{0.381 \pm 0.057}$
R	0.705 ± 0.043	0.747 ± 0.033	0.765 ± 0.032	0.791 ± 0.026	0.803 ± 0.024	$\mathbf{0.809 \pm 0.023}$	$\mathbf{0.809 \pm 0.023}$
M06 MSE	5.213 ± 0.522	4.820 ± 0.489	4.779 ± 0.421	4.543 ± 0.374	4.451 ± 0.340	4.458 ± 0.354	$\mathbf{4.428 \pm 0.351}$
M12 MSE	6.079 ± 0.775	5.813 ± 0.697	5.605 ± 0.622	5.363 ± 0.595	5.230 ± 0.589	5.183 ± 0.597	$\mathbf{5.136 \pm 0.617}$
M24 MSE	7.409 ± 1.154	6.835 ± 1.052	6.893 ± 0.950	6.456 ± 0.974	6.249 ± 0.996	6.174 ± 0.943	$\mathbf{6.153 \pm 0.911}$
M36 MSE	7.143 ± 1.351	6.938 ± 1.363	6.475 ± 1.135	6.101 ± 1.071	5.928 ± 1.064	$\mathbf{5.819 \pm 0.945}$	5.879 ± 0.972
M48 MSE	6.644 ± 2.750	6.000 ± 2.738	5.767 ± 2.189	5.751 ± 2.081	5.980 ± 1.979	5.889 ± 1.848	$\mathbf{5.837 \pm 2.160}$

Table 4: Comparison of our proposed approaches (cFSGL and nFSGL) and existing approaches (Ridge and TGL) on longitudinal MMSE and ADAS-Cog prediction using MRI+META features (M+E) in terms of normalized mean squared error (nMSE), average correlation coefficient (R) and mean squared error (MSE) for each time point. 90 percent of data is used as training data.

	Ridge	TGL	cFSGL1	cFSGL2	cFSGL3	nFSGL1	nFSGL2
				Target: MMSE			
nMSE	0.404 ± 0.056	0.320 ± 0.044	0.310 ± 0.042	0.311 ± 0.042	0.312 ± 0.043	0.308 ± 0.046	$\mathbf{0.303 \pm 0.046}$
R	0.788 ± 0.032	0.839 ± 0.027	0.842 ± 0.026	0.841 ± 0.026	0.840 ± 0.026	0.839 ± 0.027	$\mathbf{0.843 \pm 0.027}$
M06 MSE	2.188 ± 0.194	1.943 ± 0.161	1.918 ± 0.155	1.912 ± 0.153	1.907 ± 0.149	1.935 ± 0.150	$\mathbf{1.906 \pm 0.149}$
M12 MSE	2.744 ± 0.638	2.366 ± 0.722	2.355 ± 0.716	2.356 ± 0.713	2.357 ± 0.711	2.374 ± 0.696	$\mathbf{2.326 \pm 0.707}$
M24 MSE	3.113 ± 0.560	2.821 ± 0.664	2.790 ± 0.653	2.823 ± 0.656	2.875 ± 0.675	2.766 ± 0.601	$\mathbf{2.730 \pm 0.604}$
M36 MSE	3.150 ± 0.517	2.933 ± 0.657	2.851 ± 0.635	2.878 ± 0.640	2.905 ± 0.646	$\mathbf{2.755 \pm 0.550}$	2.792 ± 0.523
M48 MSE	3.639 ± 0.959	3.544 ± 1.136	3.233 ± 1.070	3.098 ± 1.013	2.956 ± 0.924	$\mathbf{2.942 \pm 0.928}$	2.961 ± 0.969
				Target: ADAS-Cog			
nMSE	0.314 ± 0.036	0.278 ± 0.034	0.238 ± 0.033	$\mathbf{0.233 \pm 0.035}$	0.235 ± 0.035	0.238 ± 0.035	0.243 ± 0.035
R	0.840 ± 0.015	0.868 ± 0.016	0.882 ± 0.013	$\mathbf{0.886 \pm 0.014}$	$\mathbf{0.886 \pm 0.014}$	0.884 ± 0.015	0.880 ± 0.013
M06 MSE	3.972 ± 0.415	3.560 ± 0.469	3.566 ± 0.380	3.553 ± 0.375	3.617 ± 0.362	3.659 ± 0.356	$\mathbf{3.535 \pm 0.403}$
M12 MSE	4.365 ± 0.469	4.080 ± 0.598	3.742 ± 0.394	3.678 ± 0.389	$\mathbf{3.659 \pm 0.393}$	3.739 ± 0.367	3.742 ± 0.430
M24 MSE	6.028 ± 1.128	5.888 ± 1.641	5.226 ± 1.201	5.115 ± 1.277	5.122 ± 1.338	$\mathbf{5.111 \pm 1.222}$	5.257 ± 1.337
M36 MSE	5.824 ± 1.076	5.639 ± 1.339	4.871 ± 0.894	4.747 ± 0.957	$\mathbf{4.712 \pm 1.002}$	4.737 ± 0.917	5.055 ± 1.033
M48 MSE	6.192 ± 2.327	6.337 ± 2.487	5.133 ± 1.499	5.065 ± 1.446	5.103 ± 1.527	$\mathbf{4.968 \pm 1.339}$	5.404 ± 1.802

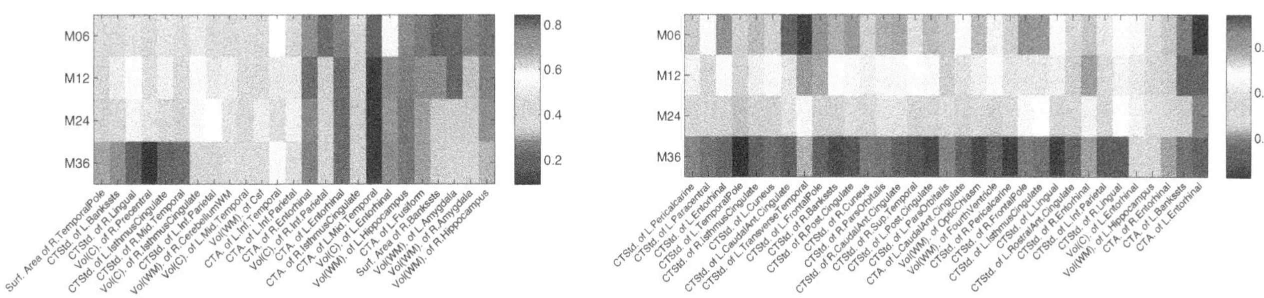

(a) Target: ADAS-Cog (25 stable features) (b) Target: MMSE (33 stable features)

Figure 1: The stability vector of stable MRI features using Convex Fused Sparse Group Lasso (cFSGL).

contain information about the progression in later stages. The lacking of predictable MRI biomarkers in later stages is a potential factor that contributes to the lower predictive performance of MMSE than that of ADAS-Cog in our study and other related studies [39]. These results suggest that ADAS-Cog may be a better cognitive measurement for lon-

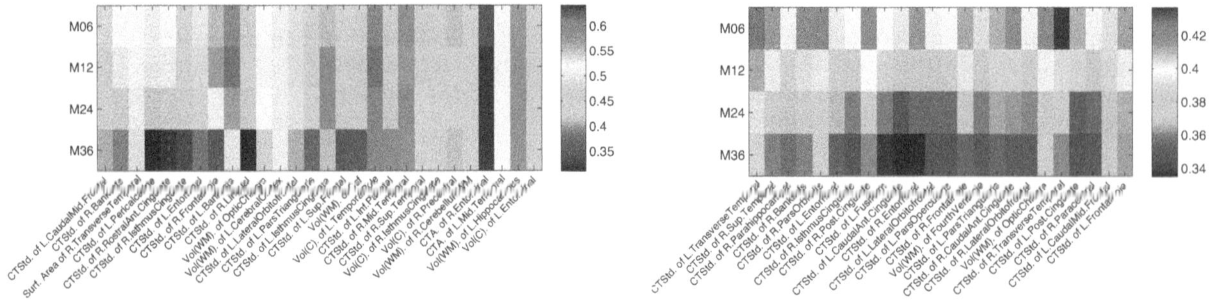

(a) Target: ADAS-Cog (28 stable features) (b) Target: MMSE (24 stable features)

Figure 2: The stability vector of stable MRI features using Non-Convex Fused Sparse Group Lasso (nFSGL1).

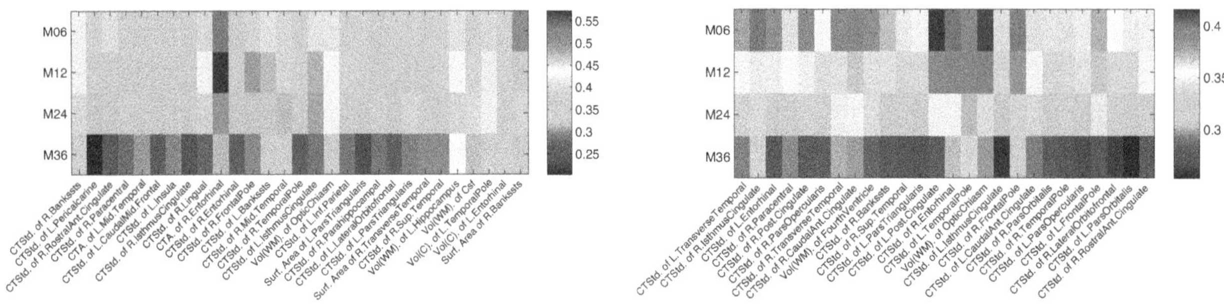

(a) Target: ADAS-Cog (29 stable features) (b) Target: MMSE (26 stable features)

Figure 3: The stability vector of stable MRI features using Non-Convex Fused Sparse Group Lasso (nFSGL2).

gitudinal study. The different temporal patterns of biomarkers for these two scores also suggest that restricting the two models for predicting these two scores to share a common set of features as in [39] may lead to sub-optimal performance.

We also perform stability selection of nFSGL1 and nFSGL2 using only MRI biomarkers. The results are given in Figure 2 and Figure 3. We observe that most biomarkers identified in cFSGL are also included in the top feature lists in nFSGL. This demonstrates the consistency between these two approaches. We also observe that the patterns of temporal selection stability differ from that of cFSGL in that fewer features have high probability. In nFSGL2 there is only one feature, namely cortical thickness average of right Entorhinal cortex, that has high probability at all time points, compared to 5 in cFSGL longitudinal stability selection. In nFSGL2 we observe that white matter volume of left Hippocampus also maintains a high stability vector. The higher temporal sparsity observed in nFSGL may be due to the non-convex $\ell_{(0.5,1)}$-norm penalty.

7. CONCLUSION

In this paper, we propose a convex fused sparse group Lasso (cFSGL) formulation for modeling disease progression. cFSGL allows the simultaneous selection of a common set of biomarkers for multiple time points and specific sets of biomarkers for different time points using the sparse group Lasso penalty and at the same time incorporates the temporal smoothness using the fused Lasso penalty. We show that the proximal operator associated with the optimization problem exhibits a certain decomposition property and thus can be solved effectively. To further improve the model, we propose two non-convex formulations, which are expected to reduce the shrinkage bias in the convex formulation. We employ the difference of convex (DC) programming technique to solve the non-convex formulations. The effectiveness of the proposed progression models is evaluated by extensive experimental studies on data sets from the Alzheimer's Disease Neuroimaging Initiative (ADNI) data sets. Results show that the proposed progression models are more effective than an existing multi-task learning formulation for disease progression. We also perform longitudinal stability selection to identify and analyze the temporal patterns of biomarkers for MMSE and ADAS-Cog respectively. The presented analysis can potentially provide novel insights into the AD progression.

Our proposed formulations for disease progression assume that the training data is complete, i.e., there are no missing values in the feature matrix X. We plan to extend our formulations to deal with missing data.

Acknowledgments

This work was supported in part by NIH R01 LM010730, NSF IIS-0812551, IIS-0953662, MCB-1026710, and CCF-1025177.

8. REFERENCES

[1] www.public.asu.edu/~jye02/FSGL.

[2] R. Ando and T. Zhang. A framework for learning predictive structures from multiple tasks and unlabeled data. *The Journal of Machine Learning Research*, 6:1817–1853, 2005.

[3] A. Argyriou, T. Evgeniou, and M. Pontil. Convex multi-task feature learning. *Machine Learning*, 73(3):243–272, 2008.

[4] B. Bakker and T. Heskes. Task clustering and gating for bayesian multitask learning. *The Journal of Machine Learning Research*, 4:83–99, 2003.

[5] E. Candes, M. Wakin, and S. Boyd. Enhancing sparsity by reweighted ℓ_1 minimization. *Journal of Fourier Analysis and Applications*, 14(5):877–905, 2008.

[6] A. Caroli, G. Frisoni, et al. The dynamics of alzheimer's disease biomarkers in the alzheimer's disease neuroimaging initiative cohort. *Neurobiology of aging*, 31(8):1263–1274, 2010.

[7] J. Chen, L. Tang, J. Liu, and J. Ye. A convex formulation for learning shared structures from multiple tasks. In *Proceedings of the 26th Annual International Conference on Machine Learning*, pages 137–144. ACM, 2009.

[8] R. Collobert, F. Sinz, J. Weston, and L. Bottou. Trading convexity for scalability. In *Proceedings of the 23rd international conference on Machine learning*, pages 201–208. ACM, 2006.

[9] R. Desikan, H. Cabral, F. Settecase, C. Hess, W. Dillon, C. Glastonbury, M. Weiner, N. Schmansky, D. Salat, B. Fischl, et al. Automated mri measures predict progression to alzheimer's disease. *Neurobiology of aging*, 31(8):1364–1374, 2010.

[10] S. Duchesne, A. Caroli, C. Geroldi, D. Collins, and G. Frisoni. Relating one-year cognitive change in mild cognitive impairment to baseline MRI features. *NeuroImage*, 47(4):1363–1370, 2009.

[11] T. Evgeniou, C. Micchelli, and M. Pontil. Learning multiple tasks with kernel methods. *Journal of Machine Learning Research*, 6(1):615, 2006.

[12] J. Fan and R. Li. Variable selection via nonconcave penalized likelihood and its oracle properties. *Journal of the American Statistical Association*, 96(456):1348–1360, 2001.

[13] J. Friedman, T. Hastie, H. Höfling, and R. Tibshirani. Pathwise coordinate optimization. *Annals of Applied Statistics*, 1(2):302–332, 2007.

[14] J. Friedman, T. Hastie, and R. Tibshirani. A note on the group lasso and a sparse group lasso. *Arxiv preprint arXiv:1001.0736*, 2010.

[15] G. Gasso, A. Rakotomamonjy, and S. Canu. Recovering sparse signals with a certain family of nonconvex penalties and dc programming. *Signal Processing, IEEE Transactions on*, 57(12):4686–4698, 2009.

[16] D. Holland, J. Brewer, D. Hagler, C. Fennema-Notestine, A. Dale, M. Weiner, L. Thal, R. Petersen, C. Jack, W. Jagust, et al. Subregional neuroanatomical change as a biomarker for alzheimer's disease. *Proceedings of the National Academy of Sciences*, 106(49):20954, 2009.

[17] R. Horst and N. Thoai. Dc programming: overview. *Journal of Optimization Theory and Applications*, 103(1):1–43, 1999.

[18] K. Ito et al. Disease progression model for cognitive deterioration from Alzheimer's Disease Neuroimaging Initiative database. *Alzheimer's and Dementia*, 6(1):39–53, 2010.

[19] C. Jack Jr, D. Knopman, W. Jagust, L. Shaw, P. Aisen, M. Weiner, R. Petersen, and J. Trojanowski. Hypothetical model of dynamic biomarkers of the alzheimer's pathological cascade. *The Lancet Neurology*, 9(1):119–128, 2010.

[20] L. Jacob, F. Bach, and J. Vert. Clustered multi-task learning: A convex formulation. *Advances in Neural Information Processing Systems*, 2008.

[21] Z. Khachaturian. Diagnosis of Alzheimer's disease. *Archives of Neurology*, 42(11):1097, 1985.

[22] A. Kumar and S. Zilberstein. Message-passing algorithms for quadratic programming formulations of MAP estimation. In *Proceedings of the Twenty-Seventh Conference on Uncertainty in Artificial Intelligence*, pages 428–435, Barcelona, Spain, 2011.

[23] Q. Ling, Z. Wen, and W. Yin. Decentralized jointly sparse signal recovery by reweighted ℓ_q minimization. submitted (2011).

[24] J. Liu, L. Yuan, and J. Ye. An efficient algorithm for a class of fused lasso problems. In *Proceedings of the 16th ACM SIGKDD international conference on Knowledge discovery and data mining*, KDD '10, pages 323–332. ACM, 2010.

[25] N. Meinshausen and P. Bühlmann. Stability selection. *Journal of the Royal Statistical Society: Series B (Statistical Methodology)*, 72(4):417–473, 2010.

[26] C. Misra, Y. Fan, and C. Davatzikos. Baseline and longitudinal patterns of brain atrophy in mci patients, and their use in prediction of short-term conversion to ad: results from adni. *Neuroimage*, 44(4):1415–1422, 2009.

[27] A. Nemirovski. Efficient methods in convex programming. 2005.

[28] Y. Nesterov. *Introductory lectures on convex optimization: A basic course.* Springer Netherlands, 2004.

[29] G. Obozinski, B. Taskar, and M. Jordan. Multi-task feature selection. *Statistics Department, UC Berkeley, Tech. Rep*, 2006.

[30] R. Pearson, R. Kingan, and A. Hochberg. Disease progression modeling from historical clinical databases. In *Proceedings of the eleventh ACM SIGKDD international conference on Knowledge discovery in data mining*, pages 788–793. ACM, 2005.

[31] C. Stonnington, C. Chu, S. Klöppel, C. Jack Jr, J. Ashburner, and R. Frackowiak. Predicting clinical scores from magnetic resonance scans in Alzheimer's disease. *NeuroImage*, 51(4):1405–1413, 2010.

[32] S. Thrun and J. O'Sullivan. Clustering learning tasks and the selective cross-task transfer of knowledge. *Learning to learn*, pages 181–209, 1998.

[33] R. Tibshirani, M. Saunders, S. Rosset, J. Zhu, and K. Knight. Sparsity and smoothness via the fused lasso. *Journal of the Royal Statistical Society: Series B (Statistical Methodology)*, 67(1):91–108, 2005.

[34] P. Vemuri et al. MRI and CSF biomarkers in normal, MCI, and AD subjects: predicting future clinical change. *Neurology*, 73(4):294, 2009.

[35] K. Walhovd et al. Combining MR imaging, positron-emission tomography, and CSF biomarkers in the diagnosis and prognosis of Alzheimer disease. *American Journal of Neuroradiology*, 31(2):347, 2010.

[36] A. Wimo, B. Winblad, H. Aguero-Torres, and E. von Strauss. The magnitude of dementia occurrence in the world. *Alzheimer Disease & Associated Disorders*, 17(2):63, 2003.

[37] C. Yu and T. Joachims. Learning structural svms with latent variables. In *Proceedings of the 26th Annual International Conference on Machine Learning*, pages 1169–1176. ACM, 2009.

[38] A. Yuille and A. Rangarajan. The concave-convex procedure (cccp). *Advances in Neural Information Processing Systems*, 2:1033–1040, 2002.

[39] D. Zhang and D. Shen. Multi-modal multi-task learning for joint prediction of multiple regression and classification variables in alzheimer's disease. *NeuroImage*, 2011.

[40] Y. Zhang and D.-Y. Yeung. Multi-task learning using generalized t process. 2010.

[41] J. Zhou, J. Chen, and J. Ye. Clustered multi-task learning: A convex formulation. *Advances in Neural Information Processing Systems*, 2011.

[42] J. Zhou, J. Chen, and J. Ye. *MALSAR: Multi-tAsk Learning via StructurAl Regularization.* Arizona State University, 2011. `www.public.asu.edu/~jye02/Software/MALSAR`

[43] J. Zhou, L. Yuan, J. Liu, and J. Ye. A multi-task learning formulation for predicting disease progression. In *Proceedings of the 17th ACM SIGKDD international conference on Knowledge discovery and data mining*, pages 814–822. ACM, 2011.

Open Domain Event Extraction from Twitter

Alan Ritter
University of Washington
Computer Sci. & Eng.
Seattle, WA
aritter@cs.washington.edu

Mausam
University of Washington
Computer Sci. & Eng.
Seattle, WA
mausam@cs.washington.edu

Oren Etzioni
University of Washington
Computer Sci. & Eng.
Seattle, WA
etzioni@cs.washington.edu

Sam Clark*
Decide, Inc.
Seattle, WA
sclark.uw@gmail.com

ABSTRACT

Tweets are the most up-to-date and inclusive stream of information and commentary on current events, but they are also fragmented and noisy, motivating the need for systems that can extract, aggregate and categorize important events. Previous work on extracting structured representations of events has focused largely on newswire text; Twitter's unique characteristics present new challenges and opportunities for open-domain event extraction. This paper describes TwiCal— the first open-domain event-extraction and categorization system for Twitter. We demonstrate that accurately extracting an open-domain calendar of significant events from Twitter is indeed feasible. In addition, we present a novel approach for discovering important event categories and classifying extracted events based on latent variable models. By leveraging large volumes of unlabeled data, our approach achieves a 14% increase in maximum F1 over a supervised baseline. A continuously updating demonstration of our system can be viewed at `http://statuscalendar.com`; Our NLP tools are available at `http://github.com/aritter/twitter_nlp`.

Categories and Subject Descriptors

I.2.7 [**Natural Language Processing**]: Language parsing and understanding; H.2.8 [**Database Management**]: Database applications—*data mining*

General Terms

Algorithms, Experimentation

1. INTRODUCTION

Social networking sites such as Facebook and Twitter present the most up-to-date information and buzz about current events. Yet the number of tweets posted daily has recently exceeded two-hundred million, many of which are either redundant [57], or of limited interest, leading to information overload.[1] Clearly, we can benefit from more structured representations of events that are *synthesized* from individual tweets.

Entity	Event Phrase	Date	Type
Steve Jobs	died	10/6/11	Death
iPhone	announcement	10/4/11	ProductLaunch
GOP	debate	9/7/11	PoliticalEvent
Amanda Knox	verdict	10/3/11	Trial

Table 1: Examples of events extracted by TwiCal.

Previous work in event extraction [21, 1, 54, 18, 43, 11, 7] has focused largely on news articles, as historically this genre of text has been the best source of information on current events. In the meantime, social networking sites such as Facebook and Twitter have become an important complementary source of such information. While status messages contain a wealth of useful information, they are very disorganized motivating the need for automatic extraction, aggregation and categorization. Although there has been much interest in tracking trends or memes in social media [26, 29], little work has addressed the challenges arising from extracting structured representations of events from short or informal texts.

Extracting useful structured representations of events from this disorganized corpus of noisy text is a challenging problem. On the other hand, individual tweets are short and self-contained and are therefore not composed of complex discourse structure as is the case for texts containing narratives. In this paper we demonstrate that **open-domain event extraction** from Twitter is indeed feasible, for example our highest-confidence extracted future events are 90% accurate as demonstrated in §8.

Twitter has several characteristics which present unique *challenges* and *opportunities* for the task of open-domain event extraction.

Challenges: Twitter users frequently mention mundane events in their daily lives (such as what they ate for lunch) which are only of interest to their immediate social network. In contrast, if an event is mentioned in newswire text, it

*This work was conducted at the University of Washington

[1] `http://blog.twitter.com/2011/06/200-million-tweets-per-day.html`

KDD'12, August 12–16, 2012, Beijing, China.

is safe to assume it is of general importance. Individual tweets are also very terse, often lacking sufficient context to categorize them into topics of interest (e.g. SPORTS, POLITICS, PRODUCTRELEASE etc...). Further because Twitter users can talk about whatever they choose, it is unclear in advance which set of event types are appropriate. Finally, tweets are written in an informal style causing NLP tools designed for edited texts to perform extremely poorly.

Opportunities: The short and self-contained nature of tweets means they have very simple discourse and pragmatic structure, issues which still challenge state-of-the-art NLP systems. For example in newswire, complex reasoning about relations between events (e.g. *before* and *after*) is often required to accurately relate events to temporal expressions [32, 8]. The volume of Tweets is also much larger than the volume of news articles, so redundancy of information can be exploited more easily.

To address Twitter's noisy style, we follow recent work on NLP in noisy text [46, 31, 19], annotating a corpus of Tweets with events, which is then used as training data for sequence-labeling models to identify event mentions in millions of messages.

Because of the terse, sometimes mundane, but highly redundant nature of tweets, we were motivated to focus on extracting an aggregate representation of events which provides additional context for tasks such as event categorization, and also filters out mundane events by exploiting redundancy of information. We propose identifying important events as those whose mentions are strongly associated with references to a unique date as opposed to dates which are evenly distributed across the calendar.

Twitter users discuss a wide variety of topics, making it unclear in advance what set of event types are appropriate for categorization. To address the diversity of events discussed on Twitter, we introduce a novel approach to discovering important event types and categorizing aggregate events within a new domain.

Supervised or semi-supervised approaches to event categorization would require first designing annotation guidelines (including selecting an appropriate set of types to annotate), then annotating a large corpus of events found in Twitter. This approach has several drawbacks, as it is apriori unclear what set of types should be annotated; a large amount of effort would be required to manually annotate a corpus of events while simultaneously refining annotation standards.

We propose an approach to open-domain event categorization based on latent variable models that uncovers an appropriate set of types which match the data. The automatically discovered types are subsequently inspected to filter out any which are incoherent and the rest are annotated with informative labels;[2] examples of types discovered using our approach are listed in figure 3. The resulting set of types are then applied to categorize hundreds of millions of extracted events without the use of any manually annotated examples. By leveraging large quantities of unlabeled data, our approach results in a 14% improvement in F_1 score over a supervised baseline which uses the same set of types.

[2]This annotation and filtering takes minimal effort. One of the authors spent roughly 30 minutes inspecting and annotating the automatically discovered event types.

	P	R	F_1	F_1 inc.
Stanford NER	0.62	0.35	0.44	-
T-SEG	0.73	0.61	0.67	52%

Table 2: By training on in-domain data, we obtain a 52% improvement in F_1 score over the Stanford Named Entity Recognizer at segmenting entities in Tweets [46].

2. SYSTEM OVERVIEW

TWICAL extracts a 4-tuple representation of events which includes a named entity, event phrase, calendar date, and event type (see Table 1). This representation was chosen to closely match the way important events are typically mentioned in Twitter.

An overview of the various components of our system for extracting events from Twitter is presented in Figure 1. Given a raw stream of tweets, our system extracts named entities in association with event phrases and unambiguous dates which are involved in significant events. First the tweets are POS tagged, then named entities and event phrases are extracted, temporal expressions resolved, and the extracted events are categorized into types. Finally we measure the strength of association between each named entity and date based on the number of tweets they co-occur in, in order to determine whether an event is significant.

NLP tools, such as named entity segmenters and part of speech taggers which were designed to process edited texts (e.g. news articles) perform very poorly when applied to Twitter text due to its noisy and unique style. To address these issues, we utilize a named entity tagger and part of speech tagger trained on in-domain Twitter data presented in previous work [46]. We also develop an event tagger trained on in-domain annotated data as described in §4.

3. NAMED ENTITY SEGMENTATION

NLP tools, such as named entity segmenters and part of speech taggers which were designed to process edited texts (e.g. news articles) perform very poorly when applied to Twitter text due to its noisy and unique style.

For instance, capitalization is a key feature for named entity extraction within news, but this feature is highly unreliable in tweets; words are often capitalized simply for emphasis, and named entities are often left all lowercase. In addition, tweets contain a higher proportion of out-of-vocabulary words, due to Twitter's 140 character limit and the creative spelling of its users.

To address these issues, we utilize a named entity tagger trained on in-domain Twitter data presented in previous work [46].[3]

Training on tweets vastly improves performance at segmenting Named Entities. For example, performance compared against the state-of-the-art news-trained Stanford Named Entity Recognizer [17] is presented in Table 2. Our system obtains a 52% increase in F_1 score over the Stanford Tagger at segmenting named entities.

4. EXTRACTING EVENT MENTIONS

In order to extract event mentions from Twitter's noisy text, we first annotate a corpus of tweets, which is then

[3]Available at `http://github.com/aritter/twitter_nlp`.

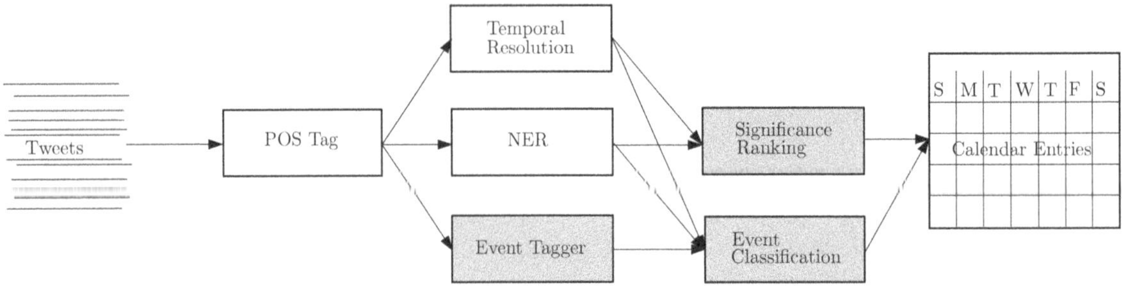

Figure 1: Processing pipeline for extracting events from Twitter. New components developed as part of this work are shaded in grey.

used to train sequence models to extract events. While we apply an established approach to sequence-labeling tasks in noisy text [46, 31, 19], this is the first work to extract event-referring phrases in Twitter.

Event phrases can consist of many different parts of speech as illustrated in the following examples:

- **Verbs:** Apple to *Announce* iPhone 5 on October 4th?! YES!
- **Nouns:** iPhone 5 *announcement* coming Oct 4th
- **Adjectives:** WOOOHOO *NEW* IPHONE TODAY! CAN'T WAIT!

These phrases provide important context, for example extracting the entity, **Steve Jobs** and the event phrase **died** in connection with October 5th, is much more informative than simply extracting **Steve Jobs**. In addition, event mentions are helpful in upstream tasks such as categorizing events into types, as described in §6.

In order to build a tagger for recognizing events, we annotated 1,000 tweets (19,484 tokens) with event phrases, following annotation guidelines similar to those developed for the EVENT tags in Timebank [43]. We treat the problem of recognizing event triggers as a sequence labeling task, using Conditional Random Fields for learning and inference [24]. Linear Chain CRFs model dependencies between the predicted labels of adjacent words, which is beneficial for extracting multi-word event phrases. We use contextual, dictionary, and orthographic features, and also include features based on our Twitter-tuned POS tagger [46], and dictionaries of event terms gathered from WordNet by Sauri et al. [50].

The precision and recall at segmenting event phrases are reported in Table 3. Our classifier, TWICAL-EVENT, obtains an F-score of 0.64. To demonstrate the need for in-domain training data, we compare against a baseline of training our system on the Timebank corpus.

	precision	recall	F1
TWICAL-EVENT	0.56	0.74	0.64
No POS	0.48	0.70	0.57
Timebank	0.24	0.11	0.15

Table 3: Precision and recall at event phrase extraction. All results are reported using 4-fold cross validation over the 1,000 manually annotated tweets (about 19K tokens). We compare against a system which doesn't make use of features generated based on our Twitter trained POS Tagger, in addition to a system trained on the Timebank corpus which uses the same set of features.

5. EXTRACTING AND RESOLVING TEMPORAL EXPRESSIONS

In addition to extracting events and related named entities, we also need to extract when they occur. In general there are many different ways users can refer to the same calendar date, for example "next Friday", "August 12th", "tomorrow" or "yesterday" could all refer to the same day, depending on when the tweet was written. To resolve temporal expressions we make use of TempEx [33], which takes as input a reference date, some text, and parts of speech (from our Twitter-trained POS tagger) and marks temporal expressions with unambiguous calendar references. Although this mostly rule-based system was designed for use on newswire text, we find its precision on Tweets (94% - estimated over as sample of 268 extractions) is sufficiently high to be useful for our purposes. TempEx's high precision on Tweets can be explained by the fact that some temporal expressions are relatively unambiguous. Although there appears to be room for improving the recall of temporal extraction on Twitter by handling noisy temporal expressions (for example see Ritter et. al. [46] for a list of over 50 spelling variations on the word "tomorrow"), we leave adapting temporal extraction to Twitter as potential future work.

6. CLASSIFICATION OF EVENT TYPES

To categorize the extracted events into types we propose an approach based on latent variable models which infers an appropriate set of event types to match our data, and also classifies events into types by leveraging large amounts of unlabeled data.

Supervised or semi-supervised classification of event categories is problematic for a number of reasons. First, it is *a priori* unclear which categories are appropriate for Twitter. Secondly, a large amount of manual effort is required to annotate tweets with event types. Third, the set of important categories (and entities) is likely to shift over time, or within a focused user demographic. Finally many important categories are relatively infrequent, so even a large annotated dataset may contain just a few examples of these categories, making classification difficult.

For these reasons we were motivated to investigate un-

Sports	7.45%		Conflict	0.69%
Party	3.66%		Prize	0.68%
TV	3.04%		Legal	0.67%
Politics	2.92%		Death	0.66%
Celebrity	2.38%		Sale	0.66%
Music	1.96%		VideoGameRelease	0.65%
Movie	1.92%		Graduation	0.63%
Food	1.87%		Racing	0.61%
Concert	1.53%		Fundraiser/Drive	0.60%
Performance	1.42%		Exhibit	0.60%
Fitness	1.11%		Celebration	0.60%
Interview	1.01%		Books	0.58%
ProductRelease	0.95%		Film	0.50%
Meeting	0.88%		Opening/Closing	0.49%
Fashion	0.87%		Wedding	0.46%
Finance	0.85%		Holiday	0.45%
School	0.85%		Medical	0.42%
AlbumRelease	0.78%		Wrestling	0.41%
Religion	0.71%		OTHER	53.45%

Figure 2: Complete list of automatically discovered event types with percentage of data covered. Interpretable types representing significant events cover roughly half of the data.

supervised approaches that will automatically induce event types which match the data. We adopt an approach based on latent variable models inspired by recent work on modeling selectional preferences [47, 39, 22, 52, 48], and unsupervised information extraction [4, 55, 7].

Each event indicator phrase in our data, e, is modeled as a mixture of types. For example the event phrase "cheered" might appear as part of either a POLITICALEVENT, or a SPORTSEVENT. Each type corresponds to a distribution over named entities n involved in specific instances of the type, in addition to a distribution over dates d on which events of the type occur. Including calendar dates in our model has the effect of encouraging (though not requiring) events which occur on the same date to be assigned the same type. This is helpful in guiding inference, because distinct references to the same event should also have the same type.

The generative story for our data is based on LinkLDA [15], and is presented as Algorithm 1. This approach has the advantage that information about an event phrase's type distribution is shared across it's mentions, while ambiguity is also naturally preserved. In addition, because the approach is based on generative a probabilistic model, it is straightforward to perform many different probabilistic queries about the data. This is useful for example when categorizing aggregate events.

For inference we use collapsed Gibbs Sampling [20] where each hidden variable, z_i, is sampled in turn, and parameters are integrated out. Example types are displayed in Figure 3. To estimate the distribution over types for a given event, a sample of the corresponding hidden variables is taken from the Gibbs markov chain after sufficient burn in. Prediction for new data is performed using a streaming approach to inference [56].

6.1 Evaluation

To evaluate the ability of our model to classify significant events, we gathered 65 million extracted events of the form

Label	Top 5 Event Phrases	Top 5 Entities
Sports	tailgate - scrimmage - tailgating - homecoming - regular season	espn - ncaa - tigers - eagles - varsity
Concert	concert - presale - performs - concerts - tickets	taylor swift - toronto - britney spears - rihanna - rock
Perform	matinee - musical - priscilla - seeing - wicked	shrek - les mis - lee evans - wicked - broadway
TV	new season - season finale - finished season - episodes - new episode	jersey shore - true blood - glee - dvr - hbo
Movie	watch love - dialogue theme - inception - hall pass - movie	netflix - black swan - insidious - tron - scott pilgrim
Sports	inning - innings - pitched - homered - homer	mlb - red sox - yankees - twins - dl
Politics	presidential debate - osama - presidential candidate - republican debate - debate performance	obama - president obama - gop - cnn - america
TV	network news broadcast - airing - primetime drama - channel - stream	nbc - espn - abc - fox - mtv
Product	unveils - unveiled - announces - launches - wraps off	apple - google - microsoft - uk - sony
Meeting	shows trading - hall - mtg - zoning - briefing	town hall - city hall - club - commerce - white house
Finance	stocks - tumbled - trading report - opened higher - tumbles	reuters - new york - u.s. - china - euro
School	maths - english test - exam - revise - physics	english - maths - german - bio - twitter
Album	in stores - album out - debut album - drops on - hits stores	itunes - ep - uk - amazon - cd
TV	voted off - idol - scotty - idol season - dividend-paying	lady gaga - american idol - america - beyonce - glee
Religion	sermon - preaching - preached - worship - preach	church - jesus - pastor - faith - god
Conflict	declared war - war - shelling - opened fire - wounded	libya - afghanistan - #syria - syria - nato
Politics	senate - legislation - repeal - budget - election	senate - house - congress - obama - gop
Prize	winners - lotto results - enter - winner - contest	ipad - award - facebook - good luck - winners
Legal	bail plea - murder trial - sentenced - plea - convicted	casey anthony - court - india - new delhi - supreme court
Movie	film festival - screening - starring - film - gosling	hollywood - nyc - la - los angeles - new york
Death	live forever - passed away - sad news - condolences - burried	michael jackson - afghanistan - john lennon - young - peace
Sale	add into - 50% off - up - shipping - save up	groupon - early bird - facebook - @etsy - etsy
Drive	donate - tornado relief - disaster relief - donated - raise money	japan - red cross - joplin - june - africa

Figure 3: Example event types discovered by our model. For each type t, we list the top 5 entities which have highest probability given t, and the 5 event phrases which assign highest probability to t.

Algorithm 1 Generative story for our data involving event types as hidden variables. Bayesian Inference techniques are applied to invert the generative process and infer an appropriate set of types to describe the observed events.

for each event type $t = 1 \ldots T$ **do**
  Generate β_t^n according to symmetric Dirichlet distribution $Dir(\eta_n)$.
  Generate β_t^d according to symmetric Dirichlet distribution $Dir(\eta_d)$.
end for
for each unique event phrase $e = 1 \ldots |E|$ **do**
  Generate θ_e according to Dirichlet distribution $Dir(\alpha)$.
  for each entity which co-occurs with e, $i = 1 \ldots N_e$ **do**
    Generate $z_{e,i}^n$ from Multinomial(θ_e).
    Generate the entity $n_{e,i}$ from Multinomial($\beta_{z_{e,i}^n}$).
  end for
  for each date which co-occurs with e, $i = 1 \ldots N_d$ **do**
    Generate $z_{e,i}^d$ from Multinomial(θ_e).
    Generate the date $d_{e,i}$ from Multinomial($\beta_{z_{d,i}^n}$).
  end for
end for

listed in Figure 1 (not including the type). We then ran Gibbs Sampling with 100 types for 1,000 iterations of burn-in, keeping the hidden variable assignments found in the last sample.[4]

One of the authors manually inspected the resulting types and assigned them labels such as SPORTS, POLITICS, MUSICRELEASE and so on, based on their distribution over entities, and the event words which assign highest probability to that type. Out of the 100 types, we found 52 to correspond to coherent event types which referred to significant events;[5] the other types were either incoherent, or covered types of events which are not of general interest, for example there was a cluster of phrases such as *applied*, *call*, *contact*, *job interview*, etc... which correspond to users discussing events related to searching for a job. Such event types which do not correspond to significant events of general interest were simply marked as *OTHER*. A complete list of labels used to annotate the automatically discovered event types along with the coverage of each type is listed in figure 2. Note that this assignment of labels to types only needs to be done once and produces a labeling for an arbitrarily large number of event instances. Additionally the same set of types can easily be used to classify new event instances using streaming inference techniques [56]. One interesting direction for future work is automatic labeling and coherence evaluation of automatically discovered event types analogous to recent work on topic models [38, 25].

In order to evaluate the ability of our model to classify aggregate events, we grouped together all (entity,date) pairs which occur 20 or more times the data, then annotated the 500 with highest association (see §7) using the event types discovered by our model.

To help demonstrate the benefits of leveraging large quantities of unlabeled data for event classification, we compare against a supervised Maximum Entropy baseline which makes use of the 500 annotated events using 10-fold cross validation. For features, we treat the set of event phrases that co-occur with each (entity, date) pair as a bag-of-words, and also include the associated entity. Because many event categories are infrequent, there are often few or no training examples for a category, leading to low performance.

	Precision	Recall	F_1
TWICAL-CLASSIFY	0.85	0.55	0.67
Supervised Baseline	0.61	0.57	0.59

Table 4: Precision and recall of event type categorization at the point of maximum F_1 score.

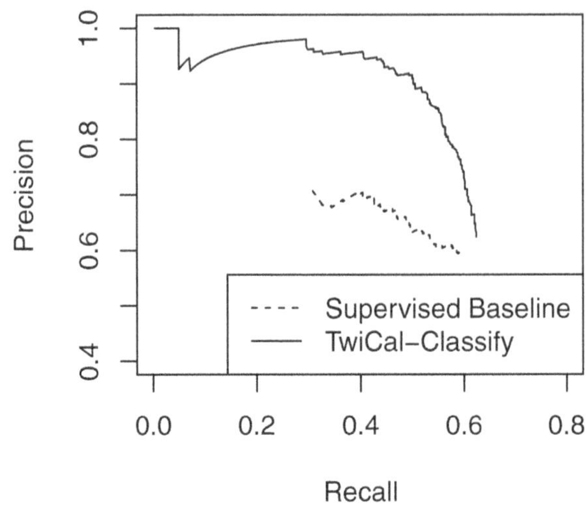

Figure 4: Precision and recall predicting event types.

Figure 4 compares the performance of our unsupervised approach to the supervised baseline, via a precision-recall curve obtained by varying the threshold on the probability of the most likely type. In addition table 4 compares precision and recall at the point of maximum F-score. Our unsupervised approach to event categorization achieves a 14% increase in maximum F_1 score over the supervised baseline.

Figure 5 plots the maximum F_1 score as the amount of training data used by the baseline is varied. It seems likely that with more data, performance will reach that of our approach which does not make use of any annotated events, however our approach both automatically discovers an appropriate set of event types and provides an initial classifier with minimal effort, making it useful as a first step in situations where annotated data is not immediately available.

7. RANKING EVENTS

Simply using frequency to determine which events are significant is insufficient, because many tweets refer to common events in user's daily lives. As an example, users often mention what they are eating for lunch, therefore entities such as *McDonalds* occur relatively frequently in association with references to most calendar days. Important events can be distinguished as those which have strong association with a unique date as opposed to being spread evenly across days on the calendar. To extract significant events of general interest from Twitter, we thus need some way to measure the strength of association between an entity and a date.

In order to measure the association strength between an

[4]To scale up to larger datasets, we performed inference in parallel on 40 cores using an approximation to the Gibbs Sampling procedure analogous to that presented by Newmann et. al. [37].

[5]After labeling some types were combined resulting in 37 distinct labels.

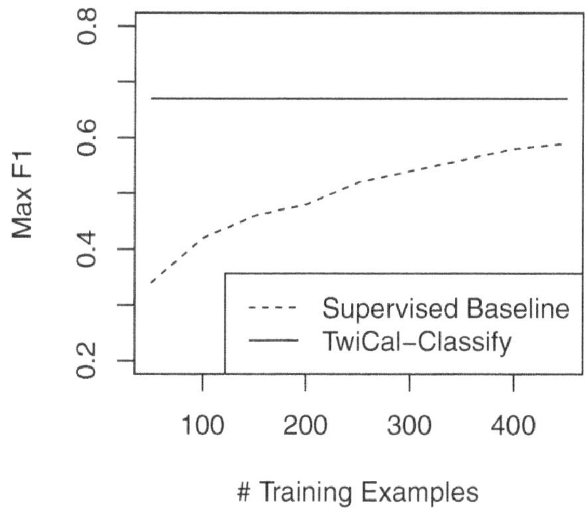

Figure 5: Maximum F_1 score of the supervised baseline as the amount of training data is varied.

entity and a specific date, we utilize the G^2 log likelihood ratio statistic. G^2 has been argued to be more appropriate for text analysis tasks than χ^2 [12]. Although Fisher's Exact test would produce more accurate p-values [34], given the amount of data with which we are working (sample size greater than 10^{11}), it proves difficult to compute Fisher's Exact Test Statistic, which results in floating point overflow even when using 64-bit operations. The G^2 test works sufficiently well in our setting, however, as computing association between entities and dates produces less sparse contingency tables than when working with pairs of entities (or words).

The G^2 test is based on the likelihood ratio between a model in which the entity is conditioned on the date, and a model of independence between entities and date references. For a given entity e and date d this statistic can be computed as follows:

$$G^2 = \sum_{x\in\{e,\neg e\},y\in\{d,\neg d\}} O_{x,y} \times \ln\left(\frac{O_{x,y}}{E_{x,y}}\right)$$

Where $O_{e,d}$ is the observed fraction of tweets containing both e and d, $O_{e,\neg d}$ is the observed fraction of tweets containing e, but not d, and so on. Similarly $E_{e,d}$ is the expected fraction of tweets containing both e and d assuming a model of independence.

8. EXPERIMENTS

To estimate the quality of the calendar entries generated using our approach we manually evaluated a sample of the top 100, 500 and 1,000 calendar entries occurring within a 2-week future window of November 3rd.

8.1 Data

For evaluation purposes, we gathered roughly the 100 million most recent tweets on November 3rd 2011 (collected using the Twitter Streaming API[6], and tracking a broad set of temporal keywords, including "today", "tomorrow", names of weekdays, months, etc.).

We extracted named entities in addition to event phrases, and temporal expressions from the text of each of the 100M tweets. We then added the extracted triples to the dataset used for inferring event types described in §6, and performed 50 iterations of Gibbs sampling for predicting event types on the new data, holding the hidden variables in the original data constant. This *streaming* approach to inference is similar to that presented by Yao et al. [56].

We then ranked the extracted events as described in §7, and randomly sampled 50 events from the top ranked 100, 500, and 1,000. We annotated the events with 4 separate criteria:

1. Is there a significant event involving the extracted entity which will take place on the extracted date?
2. Is the most frequently extracted event phrase informative?
3. Is the event's type correctly classified?
4. Are each of (1-3) correct? That is, does the event contain a correct entity, date, event phrase, and type?

Note that if (1) is marked as incorrect for a specific event, subsequent criteria are always marked incorrect.

8.2 Baseline

To demonstrate the importance of natural language processing and information extraction techniques in extracting informative events, we compare against a simple baseline which does not make use of the Ritter et. al. named entity recognizer or our event recognizer; instead, it considers all 1-4 grams in each tweet as candidate calendar entries, relying on the G^2 test to filter out phrases which have low association with each date.

8.3 Results

The results of the evaluation are displayed in table 5. The table shows the precision of the systems at different yield levels (number of aggregate events). These are obtained by varying the thresholds in the G^2 statistic. Note that the baseline is only comparable to the third column, i.e., the precision of (entity, date) pairs, since the baseline is not performing event identification and classification. Although in some cases ngrams do correspond to informative calendar entries, the precision of the ngram baseline is extremely low compared with our system.

In many cases the ngrams don't correspond to salient entities related to events; they often consist of single words which are difficult to interpret, for example "Breaking" which is part of the movie "Twilight: Breaking Dawn" released on November 18. Although the word "Breaking" has a strong association with November 18, by itself it is not very informative to present to a user.[7]

Our high-confidence calendar entries are surprisingly high quality. If we limit the data to the 100 highest ranked calendar entries over a two-week date range in the future, the precision of extracted (entity, date) pairs is quite good (90%) - an 80% increase over the ngram baseline. As expected precision drops as more calendar entries are displayed, but

[6]https://dev.twitter.com/docs/streaming-api

[7]In addition, we notice that the ngram baseline tends to produce many near-duplicate calendar entries, for example: "Twilight Breaking", "Breaking Dawn", and "Twilight Breaking Dawn". While each of these entries was annotated as correct, it would be problematic to show this many entries describing the same event to a user.

November 2011						
Mon Nov 7	Tue Nov 8	Wed Nov 9	Thu Nov 10	Fri Nov 11	Sat Nov 12	Sun Nov 13
Justin *meet* *Other*	Paris *love* *Other*	EAS *test* *Other*	Robert Pattinson *show* *Performance*	iPhone *debut* *Product Release*	Sydney *perform* *Other*	Playstation *answers* *Product Release*
Motorola Pro+ *kick* *Product Release*	iPhone *holding* *Product Release*	The Feds *cut off* *Other*	James Murdoch *give evidence* *Other*	Remembrance Day *open* *Performance*	Pullman Ballroom *promoted* *Other*	Samsung Galaxy Tab *launch* *Product Release*
Nook Color 2 *launch* *Product Release*	Election Day *vote* *Political Event*	Toca Rivera *promoted* *Performance*	RTL-TVI *post* *TV Event*	France *play* *Other*	Fox *fight* *Other*	Sony *answers* *Product Release*
Eid-ul-Azha *celebrated* *Performance*	Blue Slide Park *listening* *Music Release*	Alert System *test* *Other*	Gotti Live *work* *Other*	Veterans Day *closed* *Other*	Plaza *party* *Party*	Chibi Chibi Burger *other*
MW3 *midnight release* *Other*	Hedley *album* *Music Release*	Max Day *give* *Other*	Bambi Awards *perform* *Performance*	Skyrim *arrives* *Product Release*	Red Carpet *invited* *Party*	Jiexpo Kemayoran *promoted* *TV Event*

Figure 6: Example future calendar entries extracted by our system for the week of November 7th. Data was collected up to November 5th. For each day, we list the top 5 events including the entity, *event phrase*, and *event type*. While there are several errors, the majority of calendar entries are informative, for example: the Muslim holiday eid-ul-azha, the release of several videogames: Modern Warfare 3 (MW3) and Skyrim, in addition to the release of the new playstation 3D display on Nov 13th, and the new iPhone 4S in Hong Kong on Nov 11th.

	precision				
# calendar entries	ngram baseline	entity + date	event phrase	event type	entity + date + event + type
100	0.50	0.90	0.86	0.72	0.70
500	0.46	0.66	0.56	0.54	0.42
1,000	0.44	0.52	0.42	0.40	0.32

Table 5: Evaluation of precision at different recall levels (generated by varying the threshold of the G^2 statistic). We evaluate the top 100, 500 and 1,000 (entity, date) pairs. In addition we evaluate the precision of the most frequently extracted event phrase, and the predicted event type in association with these calendar entries. Also listed is the fraction of cases where all predictions ("entity + date + event + type") are correct. We also compare against the precision of a simple ngram baseline which does not make use of our NLP tools. Note that the ngram baseline is only comparable to the entity+date precision (column 3) since it does not include event phrases or types.

remains high enough to display to users (in a ranked list). In addition to being less likely to come from extraction errors, highly ranked entity/date pairs are more likely to relate to popular or important events, and are therefore of greater interest to users.

In addition we present a sample of extracted future events on a calendar in figure 6 in order to give an example of how they might be presented to a user. We present the top 5 entities associated with each date, in addition to the most frequently extracted event phrase, and highest probability event type.

8.4 Error Analysis

We found 2 main causes for why entity/date pairs were uninformative for display on a calendar, which occur in roughly equal proportion:

Segmentation Errors Some extracted "entities" or ngrams don't correspond to named entities or are generally uninformative because they are mis-segmented. Examples include "RSVP", "Breaking" and "Yikes".

Weak Association between Entity and Date In some cases, entities are properly segmented, but are uninformative because they are not strongly associated with a specific event on the associated date, or are involved in many different events which happen to occur on that day. Examples include locations such as "New York", and frequently mentioned entities, such as "Twitter".

9. RELATED WORK

While we are the first to study open domain event extraction within Twitter, there are two key related strands of research: extracting specific types of events from Twitter, and extracting open-domain events from news [43].

Recently there has been much interest in information extraction and event identification within Twitter. Benson et al. [5] use distant supervision to train a relation extractor which identifies artists and venues mentioned within tweets of users who list their location as New York City. Sakaki et al. [49] train a classifier to recognize tweets reporting earthquakes in Japan; they demonstrate their system is capable of recognizing almost all earthquakes reported by the Japan Meteorological Agency. Additionally there is recent work on detecting events or tracking topics [29] in Twitter which does not extract structured representations, but has the advantage that it is not limited to a narrow domain. Petrović et al. investigate a streaming approach to identifying Tweets which are the first to report a breaking news story using Locally Sensitive Hash Functions [40]. Becker et al. [3], Popescu et al. [42, 41] and Lin et al. [28] investigate discovering clusters of related words or tweets which correspond to events in progress. In contrast to previous work on Twitter event identification, our approach is independent of event type or domain and is thus more widely applicable. Additionally, our work focuses on extracting a calendar of events (including those occurring in the future), extracting event-referring expressions and categorizing events into types.

Also relevant is work on identifying events [23, 10, 6], and extracting timelines [30] from news articles.[8] Twitter status messages present both unique challenges and opportunities when compared with news articles. Twitter's noisy text presents serious challenges for NLP tools. On the other hand, it contains a higher proportion of references to present and future dates. Tweets do not require complex reasoning about relations between events in order to place them on a timeline as is typically necessary in long texts containing narratives [51]. Additionally, unlike News, Tweets often discus mundane events which are not of general interest, so it is crucial to exploit redundancy of information to assess whether an event is significant.

Previous work on open-domain information extraction [2, 53, 16] has mostly focused on extracting relations (as opposed to events) from web corpora and has also extracted relations based on verbs. In contrast, this work extracts events, using tools adapted to Twitter's noisy text, and extracts event phrases which are often adjectives or nouns, for example: *Super Bowl* **Party** *on Feb 5th.*

Finally we note that there has recently been increasing interest in applying NLP techniques to short informal messages such as those found on Twitter. For example, recent work has explored Part of Speech tagging [19], geographical variation in language found on Twitter [13, 14], modeling informal conversations [44, 45, 9], and also applying NLP techniques to help crisis workers with the flood of information following natural disasters [35, 27, 36].

10. CONCLUSIONS

We have presented a scalable and open-domain approach to extracting and categorizing events from status messages. We evaluated the quality of these events in a manual evaluation showing a clear improvement in performance over an ngram baseline

We proposed a novel approach to categorizing events in an open-domain text genre with unknown types. Our approach based on latent variable models first discovers event types which match the data, which are then used to classify aggregate events without any annotated examples. Because this approach is able to leverage large quantities of unlabeled data, it outperforms a supervised baseline by 14%.

A possible avenue for future work is extraction of even richer event representations, while maintaining domain independence. For example: grouping together related entities, classifying entities in relation to their roles in the event, thereby, extracting a frame-based representation of events.

A continuously updating demonstration of our system can be viewed at `http://statuscalendar.com`; Our NLP tools are available at `http://github.com/aritter/twitter_nlp`.

[8] `http://newstimeline.googlelabs.com/`

11. ACKNOWLEDGEMENTS

The authors would like to thank Luke Zettlemoyer and the anonymous reviewers for helpful feedback on a previous draft. This research was supported in part by NSF grant IIS-0803481 and ONR grant N00014-08-1-0431 and carried out at the University of Washington's Turing Center.

12. REFERENCES

[1] J. Allan, R. Papka, and V. Lavrenko. On-line new event detection and tracking. In *SIGIR*, 1998.

[2] M. Banko, M. J. Cafarella, S. Soderl, M. Broadhead, and O. Etzioni. Open information extraction from the web. In *In IJCAI*, 2007.

[3] H. Becker, M. Naaman, and L. Gravano. Beyond trending topics: Real-world event identification on twitter. In *ICWSM*, 2011.

[4] C. Bejan, M. Titsworth, A. Hickl, and S. Harabagiu. Nonparametric bayesian models for unsupervised event coreference resolution. In *NIPS*. 2009.

[5] E. Benson, A. Haghighi, and R. Barzilay. Event discovery in social media feeds. In *ACL*, 2011.

[6] S. Bethard and J. H. Martin. Identification of event mentions and their semantic class. In *EMNLP*, 2006.

[7] N. Chambers and D. Jurafsky. Template-based information extraction without the templates. In *Proceedings of ACL*, 2011.

[8] N. Chambers, S. Wang, and D. Jurafsky. Classifying temporal relations between events. In *ACL*, 2007.

[9] C. Danescu-Niculescu-Mizil, M. Gamon, and S. Dumais. Mark my words! Linguistic style accommodation in social media. In *Proceedings of WWW*, pages 745–754, 2011.

[10] A. Das Sarma, A. Jain, and C. Yu. Dynamic relationship and event discovery. In *WSDM*, 2011.

[11] G. Doddington, A. Mitchell, M. Przybocki, L. Ramshaw, S. Strassel, and R. Weischedel. The Automatic Content Extraction (ACE) Program–Tasks, Data, and Evaluation. *LREC*, 2004.

[12] T. Dunning. Accurate methods for the statistics of surprise and coincidence. *Comput. Linguist.*, 1993.

[13] J. Eisenstein, B. O'Connor, N. A. Smith, and E. P. Xing. A latent variable model for geographic lexical variation. In *EMNLP*, 2010.

[14] J. Eisenstein, N. A. Smith, and E. P. Xing. Discovering sociolinguistic associations with structured sparsity. In *ACL-HLT*, 2011.

[15] E. Erosheva, S. Fienberg, and J. Lafferty. Mixed-membership models of scientific publications. *PNAS*, 2004.

[16] A. Fader, S. Soderland, and O. Etzioni. Identifying relations for open information extraction. In *EMNLP*, 2011.

[17] J. R. Finkel, T. Grenager, and C. Manning. Incorporating non-local information into information extraction systems by gibbs sampling. In *ACL*, 2005.

[18] E. Gabrilovich, S. Dumais, and E. Horvitz. Newsjunkie: providing personalized newsfeeds via analysis of information novelty. In *WWW*, 2004.

[19] K. Gimpel, N. Schneider, B. O'Connor, D. Das, D. Mills, J. Eisenstein, M. Heilman, D. Yogatama, J. Flanigan, and N. A. Smith. Part-of-speech tagging

for twitter: Annotation, features, and experiments. In *ACL*, 2011.

[20] T. L. Griffiths and M. Steyvers. Finding scientific topics. *Proc Natl Acad Sci U S A*, 101 Suppl 1, 2004.

[21] R. Grishman and B. Sundheim. Message understanding conference - 6: A brief history. In *Proceedings of the International Conference on Computational Linguistics*, 1996.

[22] Z. Kozareva and E. Hovy. Learning arguments and supertypes of semantic relations using recursive patterns. In *ACL*, 2010.

[23] G. Kumaran and J. Allan. Text classification and named entities for new event detection. In *SIGIR*, 2004.

[24] J. D. Lafferty, A. McCallum, and F. C. N. Pereira. Conditional random fields: Probabilistic models for segmenting and labeling sequence data. In *ICML*, 2001.

[25] J. H. Lau, K. Grieser, D. Newman, and T. Baldwin. Automatic labelling of topic models. In *ACL*, 2011.

[26] J. Leskovec, L. Backstrom, and J. Kleinberg. Meme-tracking and the dynamics of the news cycle. In *KDD*, 2009.

[27] W. Lewis, R. Munro, and S. Vogel. Crisis mt: Developing a cookbook for mt in crisis situations. In *Proceedings of the Sixth Workshop on Statistical Machine Translation*, 2011.

[28] C. X. Lin, B. Zhao, Q. Mei, and J. Han. PET: a statistical model for popular events tracking in social communities. In *KDD*, 2010.

[29] J. Lin, R. Snow, and W. Morgan. Smoothing techniques for adaptive online language models: Topic tracking in tweet streams. In *KDD*, 2011.

[30] X. Ling and D. S. Weld. Temporal information extraction. In *AAAI*, 2010.

[31] X. Liu, S. Zhang, F. Wei, and M. Zhou. Recognizing named entities in tweets. In *ACL*, 2011.

[32] I. Mani, M. Verhagen, B. Wellner, C. M. Lee, and J. Pustejovsky. Machine learning of temporal relations. In *ACL*, 2006.

[33] I. Mani and G. Wilson. Robust temporal processing of news. In *ACL*, 2000.

[34] R. C. Moore. On log-likelihood-ratios and the significance of rare events. In *EMNLP*, 2004.

[35] R. Munro. Subword and spatiotemporal models for identifying actionable information in Haitian Kreyol. In *CoNLL*, 2011.

[36] G. Neubig, Y. Matsubayashi, M. Hagiwara, and K. Murakami. Safety information mining - what can NLP do in a disaster -. In *IJCNLP*, 2011.

[37] D. Newman, A. U. Asuncion, P. Smyth, and M. Welling. Distributed inference for latent dirichlet allocation. In *NIPS*, 2007.

[38] D. Newman, J. H. Lau, K. Grieser, and T. Baldwin. Automatic evaluation of topic coherence. In *HLT-NAACL*, 2010.

[39] D. Ó Séaghdha. Latent variable models of selectional preference. In *ACL*, ACL '10, 2010.

[40] S. Petrović, M. Osborne, and V. Lavrenko. Streaming first story detection with application to twitter. In *HLT-NAACL*, 2010.

[41] A.-M. Popescu and M. Pennacchiotti. Dancing with the stars, nba games, politics: An exploration of twitter users' response to events. In *ICWSM*, 2011.

[42] A.-M. Popescu, M. Pennacchiotti, and D. A. Paranjpe. Extracting events and event descriptions from twitter. In *WWW*, 2011.

[43] J. Pustejovsky, P. Hanks, R. Sauri, A. See, R. Gaizauskas, A. Setzer, D. Radev, B. Sundheim, D. Day, L. Ferro, and M. Lazo. The TIMEBANK corpus. In *Proceedings of Corpus Linguistics 2003*, 2003.

[44] A. Ritter, C. Cherry, and B. Dolan. Unsupervised modeling of twitter conversations. In *HLT-NAACL*, 2010.

[45] A. Ritter, C. Cherry, and W. B. Dolan. Data-driven response generation in social media. In *EMNLP*, 2011.

[46] A. Ritter, S. Clark, Mausam, and O. Etzioni. Named entity recognition in tweets: An experimental study. *EMNLP*, 2011.

[47] A. Ritter, Mausam, and O. Etzioni. A latent dirichlet allocation method for selectional preferences. In *ACL*, 2010.

[48] K. Roberts and S. M. Harabagiu. Unsupervised learning of selectional restrictions and detection of argument coercions. In *EMNLP*, 2011.

[49] T. Sakaki, M. Okazaki, and Y. Matsuo. Earthquake shakes twitter users: real-time event detection by social sensors. In *WWW*, 2010.

[50] R. Saurí, R. Knippen, M. Verhagen, and J. Pustejovsky. Evita: a robust event recognizer for qa systems. In *HLT-EMNLP*, 2005.

[51] F. Song and R. Cohen. Tense interpretation in the context of narrative. In *Proceedings of the ninth National conference on Artificial intelligence - Volume 1*, AAAI'91, 1991.

[52] B. Van Durme and D. Gildea. Topic models for corpus-centric knowledge generalization. In *Technical Report TR-946, Department of Computer Science, University of Rochester, Rochester*, 2009.

[53] D. S. Weld, R. Hoffmann, and F. Wu. Using wikipedia to bootstrap open information extraction. *SIGMOD Rec.*, 2009.

[54] Y. Yang, T. Pierce, and J. Carbonell. A study of retrospective and on-line event detection. In *Proceedings of the 21st annual international ACM SIGIR conference on Research and development in information retrieval*, SIGIR '98, 1998.

[55] L. Yao, A. Haghighi, S. Riedel, and A. McCallum. Structured relation discovery using generative models. In *EMNLP*, 2011.

[56] L. Yao, D. Mimno, and A. McCallum. Efficient methods for topic model inference on streaming document collections. In *KDD*, 2009.

[57] F. M. Zanzotto, M. Pennacchiotti, and K. Tsioutsiouliklis. Linguistic redundancy in twitter. In *EMNLP*, 2011.

Stratified K-means Clustering Over A Deep Web Data Source

Tantan Liu and Gagan Agrawal
Dept. of Computer Science and Engineering, The Ohio State University
Columbus, OH, US
liut@cse.ohio-state.edu, agrawal@cse.ohio-state.edu

ABSTRACT

This paper focuses on the problem of clustering data from a *hidden* or a deep web data source. A key characteristic of deep web data sources is that data can only be accessed through the limited *query interface* they support. Because the underlying data set cannot be accessed directly, data mining must be performed based on sampling of the datasets. The samples, in turn, can only be obtained by querying the deep web databases with specific inputs.

We have developed a new stratified clustering method addressing this problem for a deep web data source. Specifically, we have developed a stratified k-means clustering method. In our approach, the space of input attributes of a deep web data source is stratified for capturing the relationship between the input and the output attributes. The space of output attributes of a deep web data source is partitioned into sub-spaces. Three representative sampling methods are developed in this paper, with the goal of achieving a *good estimation* of the *statistics*, including proportions and centers, within the sub-spaces of the output attributes.

We have evaluated our methods using two synthetic and two real datasets. Our comparison shows significant gains in estimation accuracy from both the novel aspects of our work, i.e., the use of stratification(5%-55%), and our and representative sampling methods(up to 54%).

Categories and Subject Descriptors: H.2.8 [DATABASE MANAGEMENT]: Database Applications

General Terms: Algorithms.

Keywords: Deep web, clustering, sampling.

1. INTRODUCTION

In recent years, one mode of data dissemination has become extremely popular, which is the *deep web*. Deep web is the term coined to describe the contents that are stored in the databases and can be retrieved over the internet by querying through HTML forms, which are also called *query interfaces*.

The deep web has been a subject of much investigation[20, 8, 33, 17, 27, 26]. Most existing effort have focused on providing deep web querying systems[20, 8, 33]. However, given the volume of information contained in the deep web, it is desirable to obtain summary or key insights from one or more deep web data sources. Unfortunately, mining a deep web data source involves several unique challenges, which have not yet been adequately addressed.

KDD'12, August 12–16, 2012, Beijing, China.

Table 1: An Example of Back-end database for real-estate

ID	Year	Bedroom	Bathroom	Price($)	Square Feet
1	1980	3	1	90,000	1,100
2	1980	3	2	105,000	1,000
3	1980	4	2	140,000	1,250
4	1980	4	1	110,000	1,400
5	1990	3	1	150,000	1,500
6	1990	3	1	210,000	1,700
7	1990	4	2	225,000	1,850
8	1990	4	2	140,000	1,650
9	2000	3	1	210,000	2,000
10	2000	3	2	200,000	2,100
11	2000	4	1	215,000	2,200
12	2000	4	2	230,000	2,400
13	2008	3	1	250,000	2,400
14	2008	3	1	240,000	2,500
15	2008	4	2	280,000	2,500
16	2008	4	1	250,000	2,400

This paper specifically focuses on the problem of clustering data from a deep web data source. There are many examples where clustering data from a deep web data source can help obtain a useful summary of the entire data set. As one simple example, let us consider a county real-estate data source. Table 1 shows an example of the back-end database for a deep web data source of real-state. The database contains 16 properties described by 5 attributes, including *ID*, the *Year* of construction, the number of *Bedrooms*, the numbers of *Bathrooms*, *Price*, and the *Square Footage* of each property. Typically, such web-sites make records on all residential properties in the county available to any interested party. A person considering relocation to the county may wish to obtain a summary of the residences in the county, in terms of their value and square footage. Such a summary can be obtained through the clustering process, and can help a person know their options while looking to purchase a property.

Clustering in particular, and data mining in general, on the deep web is challenging because the databases cannot be accessed directly. Instead, the data can only be accessed through *query interface(s)*, which are based on *input attribute(s)*. A user query involves specifying value(s) for these attributes, and in response to such a query, dynamically generated HTML pages are returned as the output, comprising one or more *output attribute(s)*. Downloading the entire database is simply not practical. Thus, the only practical method for mining a deep web source is to sample the dataset. The samples, in turn, can only be obtained by querying the deep web databases with specific inputs. In Table 1, the query interface contains three input attributes, year of construction, number of bedrooms and number of bathrooms. The returned output html web-page(s) provide the information of two output attributes, which are the price and the square footage.

The clustering problem is clearly one of the most widely studied problems in the data mining community [18, 28, 25, 37, 16], but there is no existing work on clustering a hidden or a deep web data source. Sampling for efficient clustering has also been quite widely studied [19, 7, 21, 29, 15]. These sampling methods have the goal of reducing the computation and memory costs. None of these methods can be applied to the problem of clustering data from a deep web data source, since the entire dataset is not accessible, and the samples can only be obtained by querying the interface.

The overall goal while clustering over a deep web data source is to discover the underlying clusters of output attributes so that the estimated centers for clusters are close to the true centers of underlying clusters. However, estimating the centers of underlying clusters is itself a challenge. Furthermore, unlike sampling based methods developed for other types of data, computation or memory costs are not the dominant factor while mining the deep web. The key consideration, instead, is the *sampling cost*, which refers to the number of distinct queries that need to be issued in order to obtain the sample from the deep web. Thus, in developing sampling methods for clustering on a deep web data source, the two challenges are: 1) how to achieve a high estimation accuracy on mining results when the distribution of data is unknown, and 2) how to achieve a high estimation accuracy with a low sampling cost.

This paper presents and evaluates a k-means clustering method based on stratified sampling. First, we have developed a scheme for stratifying the space of input attributes of a deep web data source. In our method, the stratification is done through a tree that also models the relation between the input and output attributes. Second, for solving the challenge where the cluster identities of sampled data records are unavailable, the space of output attributes of a deep web data source is partitioned into sub-spaces based on a pilot sample. Third, we have developed sampling methods of obtaining a *representative sample*, considering the sub-spaces of output attributes of a deep web data source. *Statistics*, including *proportions* and *centers* of sub-spaces, are chosen for describing sub-spaces of output attributes. Corresponding to these statistics, three representative sampling methods are proposed so that a *good estimation* of sub-spaces of output attributes is achieved. Focusing on the *proportions* of sub-spaces of output attributes, an active learning based sampling method is developed. For *centers* of sub-spaces of output attributes, two sampling methods are developed, including an optimized sampling method and a method that uses active learning. These sampling methods are used in a stratified k-means clustering algorithm, which weighs different sampled points differently. Also, unlike the original k-means algorithm, our approach includes a method for deciding the parameter k in the k-means clustering, specific to the challenge of clustering a deep web data source.

We have evaluated our method using two synthetic and two real datasets. Our comparison shows significant gains in estimation accuracy from our novel representative sampling methods. Compared against simple random sampling, our representative sampling methods achieve 5%-55% improvement in accuracy of clustering. Compared with original k-means clustering, our stratified k-means clustering improves the accuracy of clustering by up to 54%.

2. BASIC IDEA IN OUR APPROACH

In this section, we introduce our method of partitioning the space of output attributes.

The key challenge in mining (or even querying) a deep web data source arises because the data in the back-end database is inaccessible. Typically, given an query composed of values of one or more of the input attributes, a deep web data source will return the number of data records satisfying the input query. Thus, in this paper, we assume the a deep web data source provides the *prior probability* of different queries, since it can be derived from the number of data records satisfying the input query on the entire database, which is provided by a large number of deep web data sources. Furthermore, using this information, the distribution, as well as clustering, on input attributes can be obtained. However, since the distribution of output attributes is unknown, discovering the clusters on output attributes is difficult. Still, as we will show later, the knowledge about prior probabilities of queries turns to be critical for output attribute clustering.

In traditional k-means clustering, the population to be clustered is partitioned into k clusters, where the distance between data objects

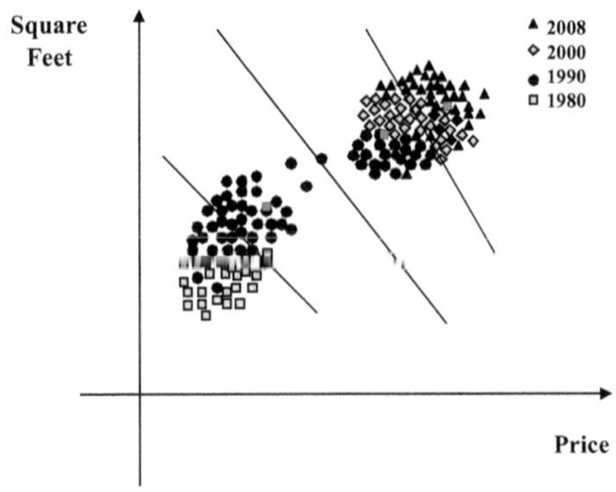

Figure 1: Partitioning the Space of Output Attributes of the Real-estate Data

within each cluster is minimized. For a deep web data source, where the data is not accessible directly, our goal has to be to estimate k centers for the k underlying clusters, so that the estimated k centers based on the sample are close to the k true centers.

Estimating the k centers for a data source would be trivial if the k partitions on the entire underlying population are available. This is because the k partitions for the underlying population can be used to divide the sampled data objects, and then the centers for k clusters can be estimated. However, the cluster labels or the k partitions on the entire hidden population are not available directly, which makes the task of estimating the k centers difficult. A possible solution for estimating the k partitions on the entire underlying population would be to use a *pilot sample*, which would be a small set of data records randomly drawn from the deep web. Clustering can first be performed on the pilot sample, yielding the k partitions as estimator for the true k partitions over the entire population.

Unfortunately, this method may not be effective when the pilot sample is small, as the differences between the estimated k partitions and the true k partitions may be large. Thus, in order to preserve the underlying true partitions, we target at generating partitions with cardinality that is a multiple of k. Formally, in our method, we generate $c \times k$ partitions over the space of output attributes, where $c \geq 1$ is an integer. The $c \times k$ partitions are generated by performing k-means clustering on a pilot sample and computing the corresponding $c \times k$ *sub-centers*. For a given data record, its distance with the $c \times k$ sub-centers is computed, and the data record is classified into the sub-space based on the sub-center with which it has the smallest distance.

To illustrate the idea described above, we revisit our running example. Figure 1 shows partitions on the output space of the real-estate data source which was presented earlier in Table 1. To explain our point, we assume that the dataset has many more data records (as compared to the 16 records shown in Table 1), but the same trends are maintained. The two axes of this figure correspond to the two output attributes, which are the price and the square footage. In this figure, in order to perform k-means clustering where $k = 2$, the space of output attributes is partitioned into four sub-spaces. Our sampling methods will aim at obtaining a representative sample considering these four sub-spaces.

3. STRATIFICATION OF THE INPUT SPACE

This section describes our approaches for stratification of the input space.

Unlike *simple random sampling*, which draws a sample from the population in entirety, stratified sampling picks separate samples from H groups, which are also called *strata* or *sub-populations* [10]. Stratified sampling helps improve performance when data varies considerably across *sub-populations*, whereas the variance within each *sub-population* is small. Thus, in our algorithm, stratification is performed so that data records contained in the same stratum are as similar as possible. On a deep web data source, where records can only be obtained by submitting queries, stratification clearly needs to be performed on the query space composed of input attributes in the query interface. The data in a deep web source can be considered to correspond to the entire query (input) space, whereas the *sub-populations* correspond to query (input) *sub-spaces*. More precisely, a sub-population comprises of data records that can be obtained by submitting queries from the corresponding query (input) sub-spaces.

Overall, in our method, the stratification is achieved by building a query (input) sub-space tree recursively, i.e, each node in the tree represents a query (input) sub-space. Associated with the node are a set of potential splitting input attributes, one of which needs to be chosen to further stratify the query (input) sub-space of the node. This is done in a greedy fashion, with the goal being to create strata in a way that the *radius* of the data objects within the strata is small. Therefore, at each step, for a leaf node of the tree, the input attribute that would maximally decrease the radius of the corresponding sub-population is selected. This greedy stratifying process stops when the radius associated with all leaf nodes is smaller than a pre-specified threshold.

In the example of real-estate data source shown earlier in Table 1, we can observe the following trend. The square footage and the price of the properties have increased with the year of construction, reflecting the trend that lower interest rates prompted demand for bigger (and more expensive) new properties. In comparison, there is no clear trend with respect to the other two input parameters, which are the number of bedrooms and bathrooms. Thus, by creating different strata using the attribute *year of construction*, we will obtain more *homogeneous* query (input) sub-spaces, i.e., the radius within each stratum will be lower.

Formally, for a deep web data source DP, let $IS = \{I_1, \ldots, I_p\}$ denote the set of input attributes and $OS = \{O_1, \ldots, O_q\}$ denote the set of output attributes. For a leaf node LN in the tree, let Q represent the corresponding input query, which is composed of SI, a subset of input attributes. The potential splitting input attributes for the node LN, which is represented by $PI = IS - SI$, is composed of input attributes that are not contained in the query Q. Under the query (input) space of node LN, the radius for the corresponding sub-population, R, is estimated by:

$$R = \sqrt{\frac{\sum_i (DR_i(OS) - C)^2}{N}} \qquad (1)$$

where, $DR_i(OS) = \{DR_i(O_1), \ldots, DR_i(O_q)\}$ corresponds to a data record DR_i of node LN's sub-population, and $DR_i(O_j), j = 1, \ldots, q$ denote values for output attributes in DR_i. $C = \frac{\sum_i DR_i(OS)}{N}$ denotes the center of the sub-population of the node LN, and N represents the size of the sub-population corresponding to the node LN. For a deep web data source where the data is not directly accessible, the radius R is estimated based on a sample.

For the potential splitting input attribute $P_i \in PI$ associated with the domain $DM_i = \{a_{i,1}, \ldots, a_{i,t}\}$, the decrease of radius is computed as:

$$\Delta R_i = R - \sum_{k=1}^{t} p(P_i = a_{i,k}|Q) \times R_{i,k}$$

where, $p(P_i = a_{i,k}|Q) = \frac{p(P_i = a_{i,k}, Q)}{p(Q)}$ represents the conditional probability that the input attribute P_i assigned by the value $a_{i,k}$ under the space of the input query Q. With the assumption that a deep web data source provides the prior probability of different values of each input attributes, such as $p(P_i = a_{i,k}, Q)$ and $p(Q)$, the conditional probability of $p(P_i = a_{i,k}|Q)$ can also be obtained.

Using the potential splitting input attribute P_i to stratify the query space of LN, there are t potential children generated, by assigning different values to the input attribute P_i. $R_{i,k}$ denotes the radius for the kth potential child node generated by splitting input attribute P_i, and the computation is similar to that of R. The potential splitting input attribute P_i with the largest decrease of radius ΔR_i is chosen to split the subspace of node LF.

In our stratified sampling process, the strata are the leaf nodes of the tree built on the query space of input attributes. The obtained strata are later related to the sub-spaces of the output space obtained from the pilot sample, and used for the representative sampling we will describe in the next section.

4. SAMPLING METHODS

In Section 2, we presented a method for solving the first challenge in performing clustering over a deep web data source. Specifically, we proposed to create a $c \times k$ partitions and generate $c \times k$ sub-spaces of the output attributes. In this section, we discuss how we address the second challenge, which is how to obtain a sample so that the estimated centers are close to the true centers.

Our solutions involve obtaining a representative sample from the data source based on the *statistics* of the sub-spaces of output attributes. In our method, *statistics*, which are either the *centers* or the *proportions*, are used to describe the $c \times k$ sub-spaces of the output attributes. The *centers* of each sub-space here are different from the *sub-centers* of each sub-space introduced in Section 2. The sub-centers are computed based on a pilot sample, which is then used for generating $c \times k$ partitions on the space of output attributes. Once the initial pilot sample has been drawn, these sub-centers are fixed during the sampling process. In comparison, the center of each sub-space is the mean vector of output attributes of all the underlying data records in that sub-space, which will be estimated during the sampling process. The statistics of sub-spaces can be estimated based on the sample we have obtained. Particularly, a sample is considered to be *representative* of the entire population if the estimated statistics of sub-spaces are close to the true values. However, for a deep web data sources where the data is not available directly, the true values of statistics are not available. Thus, in our problem, we target at obtaining a *good estimation* of the statistics of sub-spaces. Furthermore, as it is time consuming to obtain data from a deep web data source, we focus on developing *efficient* sampling methods. Considering the centers of sub-spaces, two sampling methods, which are the *optimized sampling method* and an *active learning* based sampling method, are proposed. Next, focusing on proportions of sub-spaces, another *active learning* based sampling method is proposed for greedily reducing the *risk* of incorrect estimation for proportions of sub-spaces.

4.1 Representative Sampling Based on Centers of Sub-Spaces

The overall goal of the clustering process is to estimate k centers that are close to the true k cluster centers. Thus, it is natural to choose the centers as the statistics for each sub-space. In this section, we describe two representative sampling methods which both focus on obtaining good estimation of centers of sub-spaces.

We initially develop a model of centers of sub-spaces. Then, we present our two sampling methods.

Statistic Model for the Centers of Sub-spaces: Let $sc_i = \{sc_{i,1}, \ldots, sc_{i,q}\}$, $i = 1, \ldots, c \times k$ denote the center of ith sub-space, where $sc_{i,m}$ corresponds to the mth output attribute. The center for the ith sub-space is computed as $sc_i = \frac{\sum_{r=1}^{N_i} Y_{i,r}}{N_i}$, where $Y_{i,r}$ denotes the vector of output attributes for a data record belonging to the ith sub-space, and N_i denotes the number of data records belonging to the ith sub-space in the data source. As we know, the output attributes of the deep web data source are not directly available, making $\sum_{r=1}^{N_i} Y_{i,r}$, the sum of vectors of output attributes of data records, and N_i, the size of the ith sub-space unavailable. However, the centers for the sub-spaces can be computed based on a sample drawn from the deep web.

In order to estimate the centers for sub-spaces, we define variables for the vectors of output attributes and classification for a data record with respects to each sub-space. Let the variable $y_i = \{y_i(O_1), \ldots, y_i(O_q)\}$ denote the vector of output attributes for a data record DR with respect to the ith sub-space. For a data object DR:

$$y_i = \begin{cases} \{DR(O_1), \ldots, DRO_q)\} & \text{if } DR \text{ belongs to } i\text{th sub-space} \\ \{0, \ldots, 0\} & \text{otherwise} \end{cases}$$

Let the variable x_i denote the classification of data records with respect to the ith sub-space. For a data object DR:

$$x_i = \begin{cases} 1 & \text{if } DR \text{ belongs to the } i\text{th sub-space} \\ 0 & \text{otherwise} \end{cases}$$

Then, with the definition of variables y_i, x_i, the center of the ith sub-space can be computed. Let $t_i = \{t_{i,1}, \ldots, t_{i,q}\}$, where $t_{i,m}$ corresponds to mth output attribute, and c_i denote the sum of y_i, x_i for all data records of the data source. The center of ith sub-space, $sc_i = \{sc_{i,1}, \ldots, sc_{i,q}\}$, where $sc_{i,m}$ corresponds to the mth output attribute, is computed as:

$$sc_{i,m} = \frac{t_{i,m}}{c_i}, i = 1, \ldots, c \times k, m = 1, \ldots, q$$

Since the data records are not available directly, t_i, and c_i are estimated based on a sample. In the stratified sampling where the data records are drawn from the deep web data source independently from each stratum, t_i and c_i are estimated based on each stratum. Given a sample $S = \{S_1, \ldots, S_H\}$ obtained from each stratum, t_i is estimated by $\widehat{t_i} = \{\widehat{t_{i,1}}, \ldots, \widehat{t_{i,q}}\}$:

$$\widehat{t_{i,m}} = \sum_{j=1}^{H} N_j \times \widehat{y_i^j}(O_m), i = 1, \ldots, c \times k, m = 1, \ldots, q$$

where N_j denotes the size of jth stratum, and is available from the deep web data source. $\widehat{y_i^j}(O_m)$ represents the estimated mean of $y_i(O_m)$ based on S_j, the sample drawn from the jth stratum. Similarly, c_i is estimated by:

$$\widehat{c_i} = \sum_{j=1}^{H} N_j \times \widehat{x_i}^j, i = 1, \ldots, c \times k \quad (2)$$

where $\widehat{x_i}^j$ represents the estimated mean of x_i based on S_j, the sample drawn from the jth stratum.

THEOREM 4.1. *$\widehat{t_{i,m}}$ and $\widehat{c_i}$ are unbiased estimators for $t_{i,m}$ and c_i [32]: $E(\widehat{t_{i,m}}) = t_{i,m}, m = 1, \ldots, q$, $E(\widehat{c_i}) = c_i$. The variance for $\widehat{t_{i,m}}$ and $\widehat{c_i}$ are:*

$$Var(\widehat{t_{i,m}}) = \sum_{j=1}^{H} N_j^2 \times \frac{S^2(y_i^j(O_m))}{n_j}, m = 1, \ldots, q$$

$$Var(\widehat{c_i}) = \sum_{j=1}^{H} N_j^2 \times \frac{S^2(x_i^j)}{n_j}$$

where $S^2(y_i^j(O_m))$ and $S^2(x_i^j)$ are the sample variance of the $y_i(O_m)$ and x_i in the j stratum and n_j represents the size of sample drawn from jth stratum.

Based on the unbiased estimators $\widehat{t_i}, \widehat{c_i}$ for t_i and c_i, we can obtain an estimator $\widehat{sc_i} = \{\widehat{sc_{i,1}}, \ldots, \widehat{sc_{i,q}}\}$ for the center for the ith subspace, sc_i:

$$\widehat{sc_{i,m}} = \frac{\widehat{t_{i,m}}}{\widehat{c_i}}, i = 1, \ldots, c \times k, m = 1, \ldots, q \quad (3)$$

THEOREM 4.2. *The estimator $\widehat{sc_i}$ is a biased estimator [32]:*

$$\begin{aligned} &Bias(\widehat{sc_{i,m}}) = E(\widehat{sc_{i,m}}) - sc_{i,m} \\ &\approx \frac{1}{c_i^2}(Var(\widehat{c_i}) \times \frac{t_{i,m}}{c_i} - Cov(\widehat{t_{i,m}}, \widehat{c_i})), m = 1, \ldots, q \end{aligned} \quad (4)$$

where $Cov(\widehat{t_{i,m}}, \widehat{c_i})$ is the covariance of estimator $\widehat{t_{i,m}}$ and $\widehat{c_i}$.

As we can see that the bias of estimator $\widehat{sc_{i,m}}$ depends on $Var(\widehat{c_i})$, which decreases with the sample size of each stratum (as shown in Theorem 4.1). Thus, when the sample size is large, the bias of estimator $\widehat{sc_{i,m}}$ is negligible.

Integrated Variance: To facilitate our presentation, we introduce the notion of *integrated variance*. For the ith sub-space in jth stratum, and corresponding to the mth output attribute: we define the integrated variance $Q_{i,m}^j$

$$\begin{aligned} &Q_{i,m}^j = \\ &\frac{1}{c_i^2} \times (S^2(x_i^j) \times \frac{\widehat{t_{i,m}^2}}{\widehat{c_i^2}} + S^2(y_i^j(O_m)) - 2Cov(y_i^j(O_m), x_i^j) \times \frac{\widehat{t_{i,m}}}{\widehat{c_i}}) \end{aligned}$$

where $S^2(x_i^j)$, $S^2(y_i^j(O_m))$ denote the sample variance of x_i and $y_i(O_m)$ based on the sample S_j, $Cov(y_i^j(O_m), x_i^j)$ represents the sample covariance of x_i and $y_i(O_m)$ based on sample S_j, and $\widehat{t_{i,m}}$ and $\widehat{c_i}$ are the unbiased estimators for $t_{i,m}$ and c_i introduced in Theorem 4.1.

LEMMA 4.3. *Given a sample $S = \{S_1, \ldots, S_H\}$, the variance of estimator $\widehat{sc_i}$ is:*

$$Var(\widehat{sc_{i,m}}) = \sum_{j=1}^{H} \frac{N_j^2}{n_j} \times Q_{i,m}^j, i = 1, \ldots, c \times k, m = 1, \ldots, q$$

where N_j and n_j denote the size of population and the size of sample for the jth stratum respectively.

PROOF. Please see [23]. □

Distance Function: Our goal of sampling method is to obtain a sample so that the distance between the estimated centers $\widehat{SC} = \{\widehat{sc_i}, i = 1, \ldots, c \times k\}$ and the true centers $SC = \{sc_i, i = 1, \ldots, c \times k\}$ of sub-spaces is small. To capture the distance between the centers SC and estimators $\widehat{SC}$, a distance function is defined as the summation of the expected distance between each center and the corresponding estimator:

$$Dist^2(SC, \widehat{SC}) = \sum_{i=1}^{c \times k} E(dist^2(sc_i, \widehat{sc_i}))$$

The Euclidean distance is utilized to evaluate the distance between sc_i and its estimator, $\widehat{sc_i}$: $dist(\widehat{sc_i}, sc_i) = \sqrt{\sum_m^q (sc_{i,m} - \widehat{sc_{i,m}})^2}$.

In order to obtain a representative sample from the deep web, we need to obtain a sample so that, $Dist^2(SC, \widehat{SC})$, the distance between estimated centers and the true centers of sub-spaces, is small.

LEMMA 4.4. *For centers $SC = \{sc_i, i = 1, \ldots, c \times k\}$ of sub-spaces and its estimator $\widehat{SC} = \{\widehat{sc_i}, i = 1, \ldots, c \times k\}$, the distance function is:*

$$\begin{aligned} &Dist^2(SC, \widehat{SC}) \\ &= \sum_{i=1}^{c \times k} \sum_{m=1}^{q} Var(\widehat{sc_{i,m}}) + \sum_{i=1}^{c \times k} \sum_{m=1}^{q} Bias^2(\widehat{sc_{i,m}}) \end{aligned}$$

PROOF. Please see [23]. □

As in Lemma 4.4, $Dist^2(SC, \widehat{SC})$ is composed of two terms, the variance denoted by $SumVar = \sum_{i=1}^{c \times k} \sum_m^q Var(\widehat{sc_{i,m}})$ and the bias, $Bias^2 = \sum_{i=1}^{c \times k} \sum_m^q Bias^2(\widehat{sc_{i,m}})$. When sample size is large, the bias is small compared to the variance of $Var(\widehat{sc_{i,m}})$ [32]. Then, our goal of obtaining a sample where $Dist^2(SC, \widehat{SC})$ is small reduces to the problem of obtaining a sample where $SumVar$ is small. Combining Lemma 4.3, we have:

$$SumVar = \sum_{j=1}^{H} \frac{N_j^2}{n_j} \times \sum_i^{c \times k} \sum_m^q Q_{i,m}^j \quad (5)$$

Since $\sum_i^{c \times k} \sum_m^q Q_{i,m}^j$ can be estimated based on a pilot sample, $SumVar$ depends on $n_j, j = 1, \ldots, c \times k$, the size of sample assigned to the jth stratum.

Now, we revisit our running example. Recall the data shown in Table 1, and assume that the input attribute *Year of Construction* is chosen to stratify the input space of the data source. To demonstrate our method, assume 2 strata are generated: $Year \leq 1990$ and $Year > 1990$. Let the set of output attribute be $OS = \{Price, SquareFeet\}$. A pilot sample of data records with ID 1, 4, 6, 8, 9, 10, 14, and 16, is drawn, and we assume $c = 1$ and $k = 2$. Further, assume that the space of output attributes is partitioned into $c \times k = 2$ sub-spaces by two sub-centers (115,000, 1,350) and (230,000, 2,100).

Table 3 shows the integrated variance, $Q_{i,m}^j$, for each stratum and sub-space computed based on the pilot sample that is shown in Table 2. Columns 2-3 show the value of $Q_{i,m}^j$ of output attributes for the first sub-space, whereas, columns 4-5 show the value of $Q_{i,m}^j$ for the output attributes for the second sub-space. Column 6 shows the summation of $Q_{i,m}^j$ for each stratum. We will later explain how these values are used by the two sampling methods we have developed.

Table 2: A pilot sample for Sub-spaces of Output Attributes

ID	Stratum	$y_1(\times 1000)$	x_1	$y_2(\times 1000)$	x_2
1	$Year \leq 1990$	(90,1.1))	1	(0,0)	0
4	$Year \leq 1990$	(110, 1.4)	1	(0,0)	0
6	$Year \leq 1990$	(0,0)	0	(210,1.7)	1
8	$Year \leq 1990$	(140,1.65)	1	(0,0)	0
9	$Year > 1990$	(0,0)	0	(210,2)	1
10	$Year > 1990$	(0,0)	0	(200,2.1)	1
14	$Year > 1990$	(0,0)	0	(240,2.5)	1
16	$Year > 1990$	(0,0)	0	(250,2.4)	1

Table 3: Integrated Variance of $Q^j_{i,m}$ in the Example

Stratum	$Q_{1,1}$	$Q_{1,2}$	$Q_{2,1}$	$Q_{2,1}$	$\sum_{i,m} Q_{i,m}$
$Year \leq 1990$	8.8E6	1.05E3	2.7E5	363	9.1E6
$Year > 1990$	0.0	0.0	4.2E6	425	4.2E6

Optimized Sampling Method: We use this method to decide n_j, the size of the sample drawn from jth stratum so that the variance of estimators $\widehat{SC}$ for centers of sub-spaces SC, $SumVar$, is minimized. As a result, the expected distance between estimated centers $\widehat{SC}$ and centers SC will be minimized. The total number of data records drawn from all the strata is fixed, which is denoted by $n = \sum_{j=1}^{H} n_j$. We formulate our goal as:

Minimize $SumVar(n_1, \ldots, n_H) = \sum_j^H \frac{N_j^2}{n_j} \times \sum_i^{c\times k} \sum_m^q Q^j_{i,m}$
subject to $\sum_j n_j = n$

LEMMA 4.5. *The solution for the objective to be minimized above is*

$$n_j = \frac{N_j \times \sqrt{\sum_{i=1}^{c\times k} \sum_{m=1}^{q} \times Q^j_{i,m}}}{\sum_{r=1}^{H} N_r \times \sum_{i=1}^{c\times k} \sum_{m=1}^{q} \times Q^r_{i,m}} \times n$$

PROOF. The problem can be solved by using *Lagrange multipliers*, a well know optimization method.

Our optimized sampling method can be viewed as a generalization of the Neymann method [10], a well-known sample allocation method for stratified sampling. Neymann allocation has been proposed in the context of of estimating results for an aggregation query, e.g. sum or mean, on a single statistical variable. It also works only on a population where each data object contains the variable. Our optimized sampling method is proposed for estimating the mean vector of multiple output attributes within each sub-space, where the size of data records belonging to each sub-space is not known for each stratum.

Returning to our example, recall the integrated variance $Q^j_{i,m}$ shown in Table 3. By using the optimized sampling method, with a sample size $n = 5$, we will have $n_1 = 3$ and $n_2 = 2$. This implies that three data records will be drawn from the first stratum, and two data records will be drawn from the second stratum. This is because the distribution of the output attributes in the first stratum is spread in a wider area, as compared to the second stratum. Thus, more data records are needed to represent the population of the first stratum.

Active Learning based Sampling Method: The second method we propose is the active learning based method. Active learning [14, 11, 36] has been proposed in the context of machine learning, for cases where gathering data is costly and/or time-consuming. Compared with *passive learning*, which selects training data randomly from the entire population, *active learning* selects certain types of data records, to help build a better model faster. The choice of data records is based on the data that has been seen so far. In other words, the information that has already been learned about the data influences the decision with respect to the data record to be chosen next by an active learner. While mining on the deep web, active learning is clearly desirable, as samples can only be obtained by issuing queries over a network, making sampling cost a very important consideration.

The optimized sampling method we have already presented aims at optimally minimizing the expected distance between $sc_i, i = 1, \ldots, c \times k$, the centers of sub-spaces and their estimators, in the *long run*. When the sample size is small, however, it might not have good performance. In comparison, our active learning based sampling method greedily reduces the distance between $sc_i, i = 1, \ldots, c \times k$, the centers of sub-spaces and their estimators. Similar to optimized sampling method, our active learning based sampling method aims at reducing $SumVar(n_1, \ldots, n_H)$, the variance for estimators in Formula 5, which is also defined as the risk function $Risk(n_1, \ldots, n_H)$. Data is sampled for reducing the risk function greedily. The stratum with largest reduction in the risk function value is selected and the associated query is submitted to the data source. For the estimators for $sc_i, i = 1, \ldots, c \times k$, centers of sub-spaces, the estimated decrease of risk function for choosing a data record from the jth stratum is computed as:

$$\Delta_j = N_j^2 (\textstyle\sum_i^{c\times k} \sum_m^q \times Q^j_{i,m}) \times (\frac{1}{n_j} - \frac{1}{n_j+1}) \tag{6}$$

Once a data record DR is drawn from the the jth stratum of the deep web, it is classified to one of the $c \times k$ sub-spaces based on the $c \times k$ sub-centers computed from the pilot sample. The parameters $Q^j_{i,m}, i = 1, \ldots, c \times k, m = 1, \ldots, q$ of the jth stratum are updated accordingly. The sample size of the jth stratum is also updated: $n'_j = n_j + 1$, while the sample size of other strata stay the same: $n'_r = n_r, r \neq j$.

Now, returning to our running example (Table 3), we have $N_1 = N_2 = 8$ and $n_1 = n_2 = 2$. Based on Formula 6, the decrease in the distance function value from choosing the first stratum is 9.7E7, whereas the decrease of the distance function value for choosing the second stratum is 4.4E7. Thus, we will submit a query for the first stratum. As we can see, our active learning based sampling method is also focusing on the stratum where the distribution of output attributes is spread in a wider area. However, the difference is that it performs such calculation greedily at each step, rather than determining the number of samples from each stratum separately.

4.2 Representative Sampling Based on the Proportion of Sub-spaces

In this subsection, we introduce our representative sampling method based on the proportions of sub-spaces. The proportion of a sub-space of output attributes is computed as the proportion of data records belonging to the sub-space in the entire population of the deep web data source.

Statistic Model for the Proportion of Sub-Spaces: For ith sub-space, the proportion, which is denoted as pr_i, is computed as $\frac{N_i}{N}$, where N_i denotes the number of data records belonging to the ith sub-space, and N denotes the size of the entire population of the deep web data source. The computation for pr_i is based on the entire population of the deep web. However, since the space of input attributes is stratified into H strata, the computation of the proportion of the ith sub-space, pr_i, is also based on the H strata. Let $pr_{i,j}, i = 1, \ldots, c \times k, j = 1, \ldots, H$ denote the proportions of the ith sub-space in the jth stratum. Then the proportion of the ith sub-space, $pr_i = \sum_{j=1}^{H} p_j \times pr_{i,j}$, where p_j is the probability of the jth stratum, which is available from the information provided by the deep web data source. Since the output attributes of the deep web data source are not directly available, $pr_{i,j}, i = 1, \ldots, c \times k, j = 1, \ldots, H$ are unknown, and can only be estimated based on a sample from the jth stratum, which is denoted by S_j.

The goal of our sampling method is to obtain a sample where the estimation for proportion of sub-space pr_i are good. In our previous work on frequent itemset mining on a deep web data source [22], we proposed an active learning based sampling method which aims at obtaining a sample where the estimation for the support of 1-itemset composed of output attributes are good. As we can see the goal of our sampling method based on the proportion of sub-spaces for clustering on a deep web are similar to the task of frequent itemset mining on a deep web. So, we can develop a similar active learning based sampling method.

In using active learning for our goal, a *risk function* is defined to evaluate the loss of estimated proportions for sub-spaces, and determine which queries are chosen to be submitted to the data source in the sampling process. Recall that we are focusing on $pr_{i,j}, i = 1, \ldots, c \times k, j = 1, \ldots, H$, the proportions of corresponding sub-spaces in each stratum. *Dirichilet distribution* [30] is used in our work. In the jth stratum, the proportions of sub-spaces $PR_j = \{pr_{i,j}, i = 1, \ldots, c \times k\} \sim Dirichlet(\alpha_{1,j}, \ldots, \alpha_{c\times k,j})$. The *risk function* is estimated based on the parameter of Dirichilet distribution for each stratum.

In the stratified sampling, after a data record is drawn from a stratum, the risk function $Risk(PR)$ will be reduced. In our active learning based sampling method, data is sampled from the deep web for reducing the risk function in a greedy way, step by step. At each step, the stratum with largest reduction in the risk function is selected. The associated query is submitted to the deep web data source for sampling a data record. Once a data record DR is drawn from the deep web, the parameters of Dirichilet distribution of $pr_{i,j}$ is modified, resulting the change in risk function, $Risk(PR)$, which determines the query to be submitted to the deep web in the next step.

Specifically, if a data record DR is drawn from the jth stratum of the deep web, it is classified to one of the $c \times k$ sub-spaces. The parameters for the Dirichilet distribution of $PR_j = \{pr_{i,j}, i = 1, \ldots, c \times k\} \sim Dirichlet(\alpha_{1,j}, \ldots, \alpha_{c\times k,j})$ are updated: $\alpha_{j,r} = \alpha_{j,r} + 1$ if the sampled data record is classified to the rth sub-space; $\alpha_{j,r} = \alpha_{j,r}$, otherwise.

4.3 Stratified K-means Clustering over a Deep Web Data Source

We now introduce our method for clustering the data, based on the samples drawn using one of three methods introduced above.

The key observation in our method is that since we are using stratified sampling, the sample obtained is not a simple random sample on the entire population. Thus, an original clustering method, like the k-means clustering algorithm, cannot be directly applied on the sample. Instead, we use a novel *stratified k-means clustering* method. The main idea in our algorithm is that each sampled data record is considered as a representative of the population of the stratum. Let the sample obtained be denoted by NS, and assume n_j data records are drawn randomly from jth stratum, where the size of the corresponding sub-population is N_j. Then, the n_j data records are used to represent the N_j data records, i.e., each data record in the sample represents $\frac{N_j}{n_j}$ data records in jth stratum. Correspondingly, in our clustering process, each data record in the sample is associated with weight of $\frac{N_j}{n_j}$.

Our algorithm works in the same way as the original k-means algorithm, with the following difference. At each iteration, the center of the ith cluster with the associate data objects is updated as:

$$c_i = \frac{\sum_r \omega_r \times DR_r(OS)}{\sum_r \omega_r} \quad (7)$$

where ω_r denotes the weight associated with data record DR_r in the ith cluster.

As in the original k-means clustering algorithm, the result of stratified k-means clustering depends on the initial k centers that are chosen randomly from the sample NS. To decrease the effect of bad initial k centers, we conduct the stratified k-means clustering on the sample multiple times with different random initial k centers. The result of stratified k-clustering with the smallest *distance within clusters* is chosen as the final clustering result for output. In our method, the distance within clusters of a clustering result for k centers $c_i, i = 1, \ldots, k$ is computed as:

$$WDist = \sum_{i=1}^{k} \sum_{r=1}^{|C_i|} \omega_r \times dist(DR_r(OS), c_i)$$

where C_i denotes the set of data objects belonging to the ith cluster in the sample.

Similar to traditional k-means clustering, *stratified* k-means clustering is performed iteratively on the sampled data. Initially, k centers are randomly chosen from the sampled data. At each iteration, sampled data objects are grouped into clusters with the smallest distance between the data objects and the corresponding centers. The k centers are updated based on the newly generated k clusters according to the Expression 7. The process stops if the distance between updated k centers and the current k centers is smaller than a user-defined threshold λ, or the number of iteration is larger than a user-defined threshold.

4.4 Automatically Choosing Number of Clusters

Initial experiments with our methods lead to the observation that our stratified k-means clustering method has a significantly lower average square distance if the number of clusters k equals to the number of natural clusters in the data. Moreover, more often than not, users are more interested in the natural clusters, rather than a specific number of cluster centers.

The problem of obtaining the number of natural clusters in datasets has been studied by several researchers [34, 2, 5]. We adapt the approach based on the stability of clusters [2]. Specifically, we take the following approach. For each particular number k, stratified k-means clustering is performed on the data with different initial centers that are randomly drawn from the data. The distance between each pair of clustering results is computed. Then, $p(\alpha)$, the proportion of the pair of clustering results with similarity larger than α is computed. The k corresponding to the largest value of $p_k(\alpha) - p_{k+1}(\alpha)$ is considered to be the number of natural clusters of the population.

5. EVALUATION STUDY

In this section, we evaluate our proposed methods. Particularly, we compare our three methods for representative sampling against two other methods, to evaluate the benefits from the use of stratified clustering and representative sampling.

Our evaluation has been performed using a combination of real and synthetic datasets.

Synthetic data set: This is a data set generated by *minitab* [1], a statistical software. This data set contains 4,000 data records with 6 categorical attributes, including 4 input attributes and 2 output attributes. There are 4 clusters on the 2 output attributes which are generated by a Gaussian distribution. The output attributes are created to be dependent on the input attributes.

Noisy Synthetic data set: This is a data set generated by adding *noise data points*, numbering 10% of the total data points, in the synthetic data set described above. The noise data points are uniformly distributed in the space of the output attributes.

Yahoo! data set: The Yahoo! data set, which consists of the data crawled from a subset of a real-world hidden database at http://autos.yahoo.com/. Particularly, we download the data on used cars located within 50 miles of a zipcode address. This yields 8,000 data records. The data consists of 4 categorical input attributes and 1 numerical output attribute. The input attributes contain the age, mileage, brand, and the number of windows of the cars. The output attribute contains the price of the cars.

US Census data set: This is a data set obtained from the 2008 US Census on the income of US households. This data set contains 40,000 data records with 13 categorical input attributes and 2 numerical output attributes. The input attributes contain the Metropolitan status of the household as well as the education, age, occupation, etc, of the husband and wife of each household. The output attributes are the income of husband and wife of the households.

The criteria used for evaluation of all methods is *Average Square Distance*. It is computed based on the distance between the estimated centers and true centers of the clusters. For k clusters $c_1, \ldots, c_k$ and the estimated centers $\bar{c}_1, \ldots, \bar{c}_k$, then the average distance is computed as $AsqDist = \frac{1}{k}\sum_{i=1}^{k} dist^2(c_i, \bar{c}_i)$, where $dist(m_i, \bar{m}_i)$ denotes the Euclidean distance between c_i and $\bar{c}_i$. Obviously, a smaller average distance value implies that the method is working more accurately.

[1]Please see http://http://www.minitab.com

In all results we report, sampling process is repeated 200 times, and the results we report are the average result for these 200 executions.

5.1 Evaluation of Representative Sampling and Stratified Clustering

In this subsection, we focus on evaluating the benefits from representative sampling and stratified clustering. For this purpose, we compare our methods that combine stratified clustering and representative sampling based on the partitioning over the space of output attributes. Specifically, our methods include active learning for proportions of sub-spaces, optimized sampling that focuses on centers of sub-spaces, and active learning based on centers of sub-spaces. These three methods are compared with two other methods, which are both based on simple random sampling. While both these methods randomly choose data records from the deep web data source, they differ in how clustering is performed. In the *first method*, clustering is directly conducted on the simple random sample, applying the original k-means clustering method. In the *second method*, stratified k-means clustering is conducted on the simple random sample using the tree described in the Section 3.

While reporting the results from our experiments, our active learning based sampling method that focuses on proportions of sub-spaces is referred to as `prop_act`, the optimized sampling method that focuses on centers of sub-spaces is referred to as `cent_opt`, and the active learning based method that again focuses on centers of sub-spaces is referred to as `cent_act`. Among the two baseline methods, the first method described above is referred to as `rand`, and the second method is referred to as `rand_st`,

Figure 2 shows the average square distance achieved during clustering for the four datasets. The sub-figure a) shows the result for the synthetic dataset, with number of clusters, k, set to 4, and the number of sub-spaces per cluster, c, set to 3. A pilot sample of size 200 is used. We can see that compared with $rand$, the average square distance achieved with algorithms $rand\_st$, $prop\_act$, $cent\_opt$, and $cent\_act$ is smaller, and the average decrease of average square distance over all sample sizes for $rand\_st$, $prop\_act$, $cent\_opt$, and $cent\_act$ are 31.8%, 35.6%, 41.0% and 39.2% respectively, which shows the efficiency of stratified k-means clustering over the original k-means clustering. This also shows that the distribution of input attributes is helpful for identifying the clusters of output attributes, and the stratification on the population improves the performance of clustering. Furthermore, compared with $rand\_st$, the average square distance with our sampling methods $prop\_act$, $cent\_opt$, and $cent\_act$ is smaller, and the average decrease of average square distance over all sample sizes for $prop\_act$, $cent\_opt$, and $cent\_act$ are 5.6%, 13.5%, and 10.8% respectively, which shows the benefit of sampling based on a partition over the space of output attributes. We can also observe that compared with $prop\_act$, $cent\_opt$ and $cent\_act$ have better performance in terms of the average square distance. This is because $cent\_opt$ and $cent\_act$ aim at reducing the expected distance between the estimated centers and the true centers of sub-spaces of output attributes. In addition, when the sample size is large, $cent\_opt$ has better performance than $cent\_act$, whereas, when the sample size is small, $cent\_act$ has better performance than $cent\_opt$. The reason is that $cent\_act$ greedily reduces the expected distance between the estimated centers and true centers of sub-spaces. But, at the same time, it is not an optimized sampling method on the long run, and thus, it does not have as good performance as $cent\_opt$ when the sample size is large.

Figure 2, sub-figure b), shows the result for noisy synthetic dataset. Again, we have $k = 4$ and $c = 3$, and a pilot sample of size 200. The results also follow a very similar trend. The stratification based methods, $prop\_act$, $cent\_opt$, $cent\_act$, and $rand\_st$ all have better accuracy than the original k-means clustering. Compared with $rand$, the average decrease of average square distance over all sample sizes for $rand\_st$, $prop\_act$, $cent\_opt$, and $cent\_act$ are 26.9%, 35.5%, 37.4% and 38.6% respectively. The representative sampling methods, $prop\_act$, $cent\_opt$, and $cent\_act$, further improves the accuracy over the simple random sampling $rand\_st$. Compared with $rand\_st$, the average decrease of average square distance over all sample sizes for $prop\_act$, $cent\_opt$, and $cent\_act$ are 11.8%, 14.4% and 16.1% respectively. Representative sampling methods that focus on a good estimation of the centers of sub-spaces, $cent\_opt$ and $cent\_act$, have better performance than $prop\_act$. Optimized sampling method $cent\_opt$ has better performance than the active learning based sampling method $cent\_act$ when the sample size is large.

Figure 2, sub-figure c) shows the results on the Yahoo! data set by setting $k = 4$ and $c = 2$, with a pilot sample of 300. The result follows a very similar trend to those in the sub-figure a). The stratified sampling methods have better performance than the original k-means clustering. Compared with $rand$, the average decrease of average square distance over all sample sizes for $rand\_st$, $prop\_act$, $cent\_opt$, and $cent\_act$ are 7.2%, 13.2%, 15.0% and 16.8% respectively. But the improvements in accuracy are relatively lower. This is likely because the relationship between the input attributes and the output attributes is not as strong for this dataset. Furthermore, representative sampling methods improves the accuracy over the simple random sampling. Compared with $rand\_st$, the average decrease of average square distance over all sample sizes for $prop\_act$, $cent\_opt$, and $cent\_act$ are 6.6%, 8.5%, 10.5% respectively. Finally. the sub-figure d) shows the results on the US census dataset by setting $k = 3$ and $c = 2$, with a pilot sample of 2000. We can also observe the same trend to those in the sub-figure a). Compared with $rand$, the average decrease of average square distance over all sample sizes for $rand\_st$, $prop\_act$, $cent\_opt$, and $cent\_act$ are -3.3%, 30.2%, 31.5% and 54.3% respectively. Compared with $rand\_st$, the average decrease of average square distance over all sample sizes for $prop\_act$, $cent\_opt$, and $cent\_act$ are 32.5%, 33.8%, 55.8% respectively.

5.2 Evaluation of Scalability of Representative Sampling and Stratified Clustering

In this subsection, we focus on evaluating the scalability of our methods by applying them on data sets with different sizes. For this purpose, three data sets with size 40,000, 400,000 and 4000,000 are generated by performing sampling with replacement on the synthetic data set. Then we apply our three representative sampling methods, which are denoted by $prop\_act$, $cent\_opt$ and $cent\_act$. For each data set with population of size N, an initial sample with size $0.05 \times N$ is obtained and a further sample of size $0.1 \times N$ is drawn based on the representative sampling methods. For each representative sampling method on each data set, the time for stratification on the query space of input attributes, computing the representative sampling and stratified clustering is computed and reported in Table 4. The sampling process is repeated 10 times, and the results are the average result for these 10 executions.

Table 4: Evaluation of Scalability of Representative Sampling and Stratified Clustering

Data Set Size	$prop\_act$	$cent\_opt$	$cent\_act$
40,000	76.1s	63.7s	72.7s
400,000	892.3s	666.1s	809.0s
4000,000	10872.7s	9316.2s	9528.1s

As we can see, for each method, when the size of data set is increased by 10 times, the execution time for each method is increased by around 12 times, i.e. the increase is quite close to linear. This shows the scalability of our methods.

5.3 Impact of Number of Clusters on Accuracy

In this subsection, we evaluate our sampling methods with respect to different choices of k, the number of clusters. Table 5 shows the experimental data for the three datasets: the synthetic dataset, the Yahoo! dataset and the US. census dataset. In this table, the first column identifies the dataset. The second column shows the choice of k, and the third column shows the average value of $p(\alpha)$, the proportion of the pairs of clustering results with similarity larger than $\alpha = 0.9$ (as described in Subsection 4.4). The fourth to sixth columns show the average square distance for the three representative sampling methods, i.e., $prop\_act$, $cent\_opt$, and $cent\_act$.

Rows 2-4 show the results for the synthetic dataset obtained by

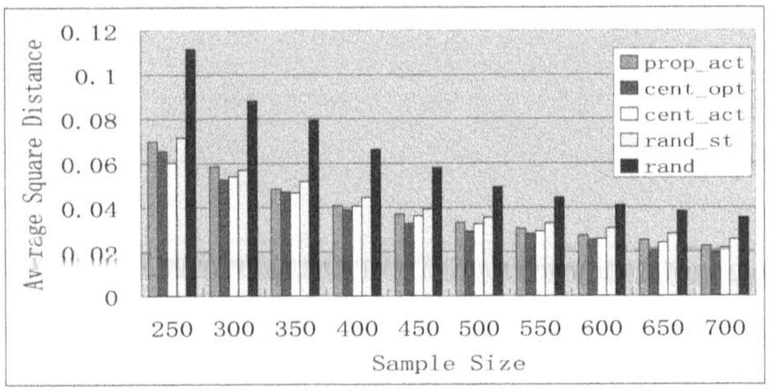

(a) Synthetic Data set

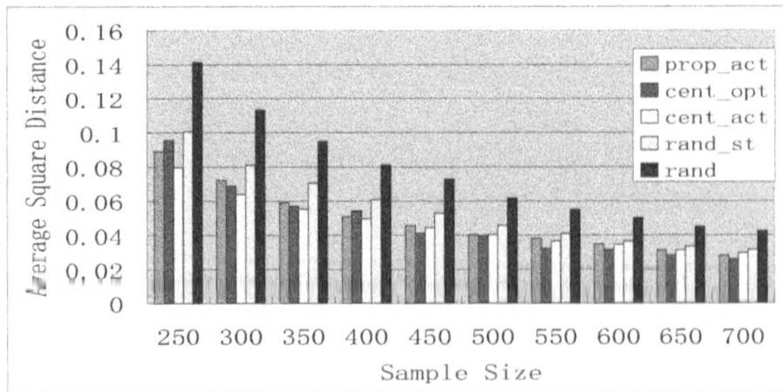

(b) Noisy Synthetic Data set

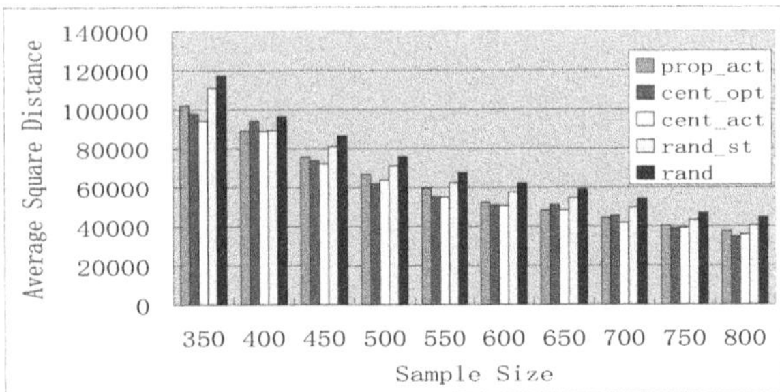

(c) Yahoo! Data set

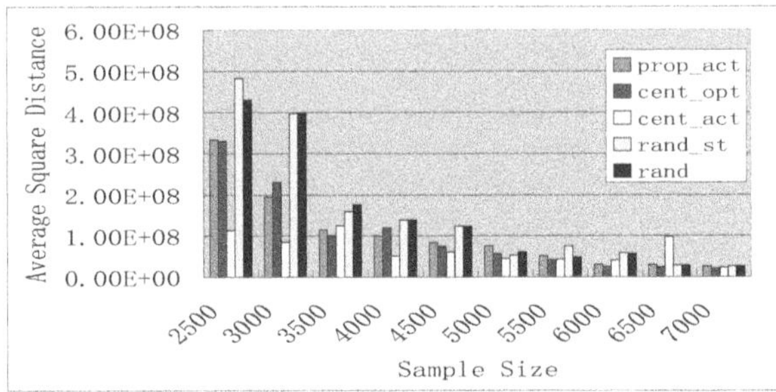

(d) US Census data set

Figure 2: Evaluation of Representative Sampling and Stratified Clustering (Average square Distance)

Table 5: Performance With Varying Number of Clusters

Dataset	k	$p(\alpha)$	*prop_act*	*cent_opt*	*cent_act*
synthetic	3	0.225	24.97	25.00	24.63
	4	0.620	0.033	0.029	0.032
	5	0.333	14.16	14.41	13.55
Yahoo!	2	0.990	52272.9	50734.3	50669.5
	3	0.559	170259.1	156108.9	128375.8
	4	0.454	150315.0	292893.9	171400.3
US Census	2	0.963	2.24E8	1.31E8	1.27E8
	3	0.90	7.50E7	5.68E7	4.50E7
	4	0.59	3.51E9	1.54E9	5.17E8

choosing $c = 3$, taking a sample size of 500 and a pilot sample size of 200. From the table we can see that $p(\alpha)$ has a large value at $k = 4$ and decreases sharply when we go from $k = 4$ to $k = 5$. Based on this observation, we can consider $k = 4$ to the number of *natural cluster* in the dataset. On the contrary, when $k = 3$ and 5, $p(\alpha)$ is small. Another observation we can make is that at $k = 4$, the average square distance is also small, whereas at $k = 3$ and $k = 5$, the average square distance is larger.

These observations show that our methods have good performance when k is chosen to be the number of natural clusters, which can be detected during the execution of the algorithm by considering the value of $p(\alpha)$. Thus, we not only detect the number of natural clusters, but can also reduce the inaccuracy in estimating their centers.

Rows 5-7 show the results for the Yahoo! dataset, obtained by by choosing $c = 2$, taking a sample size of 600 and a pilot sample size of 300. The results for the Yahoo! dataset are similar to the results for the synthetic dataset. The largest decrease in the value value $p(\alpha)$ in group from k to $k+1$ clusters occurs when $k = 2$. Correspondingly, the average square distance is also lowest at this point.

Similarly, rows 8-10 show the results for the US dataset, obtained by choosing $c = 2$, sample size of 5000 and a pilot sample size of 2000. The result are similar to those obtained for the other two datasets. The largest decrease of value of $p(\alpha)$ in going from k to $k + 1$ occurs where $k = 3$. Our sampling methods also achieve the best accuracy at $k = 3$, which also happens to be the number of natural clusters in the dataset.

5.4 Discussion

We can make several observations from the experimental results we have presented. By comparing *rand_st*, *prop_act*, *cent_opt*, and *cent_act* with *rand*, we can see that stratified k-means clustering has better performance than traditional k-means clustering. Compared with *rand*, the decrease in the average square distance for stratified sampling methods is up to 54%. Furthermore, compared with *rand_st*, the representative sampling methods, *prop_act*, *cent_opt*, and *cent_act* improve the accuracy of clustering, with the decrease in average square distance ranging from 5% to 55%.

In comparing the three representative sampling methods, we can see the following. As *cent_opt* and *cent_act* aim at obtaining a good estimation for centers of the sub-spaces, they have better performance than *prop_act*, which aims at obtaining good estimation for proportions of sub-spaces. But since there are more parameters to be estimated in *cent_opt* and *cent_act*, when c is large, *prop_act* has a better performance than *cent_opt* and *cent_act*. Furthermore, since *cent_act* greedily reduces the risk function, it has better performance when the sample size n is small. When the sample size n is large, *cent_opt*, the optimized method, has better accuracy.

6. RELATED WORK

We now compare our work with the existing work on sampling based methods for clustering, other data mining problems, and sampling work specifically targeting the deep web.

Sampling for Clustering: As we had listed in the Introduction, sampling for clustering has been studied by several researchers [19, 21, 29, 15, 4]. CLARA (Clustering LARge Applications) [19] uses sampling to find the potential medoids of the data. The entire dataset is assigned to potential medoids, and the best system of medoids is computed according to a particular objective function. Kollios *et al.* [21] investigate the use of biased sampling according to the density of the data set to speed up the operation of general data mining tasks, including clustering, on large multidimensional data sets. Meek *et al.* [29] examine the application of the learning-curve sampling method to the task of model-based clustering via the expectation-maximization (EM) algorithm. A fast and exact k-means clustering [15] is proposed to compute the same cluster centers as those reported by the original k-means algorithm. Shai *et al.* [4] present a theoretic analysis of sample-based clustering algorithms and prove that clustering methods, including k-means and k-median, converge to optimal clusterings with approximation bounds that depend on the sample sizes and accuracy parameters, but are independent of the generating data distribution and the dimensionality of the data. Our work is different from these sampling methods, since we consider the problem of clustering on a hidden deep web. Because the data records are hidden under limited query interfaces in these systems and the sampling cost is high, sampling involves very distinct challenges.

Sampling for Other Data Mining Problems: Sampling for frequent itemset mining has been studied by several researchers [35, 31, 9, 6]. Toivonen [35] developed a random sampling method to identify the association rules, which are then further verified on the entire database. Progressive sampling [31], which is based on equivalence classes, involves determining the required sample size for association rule mining. FAST [9], a two-phase sampling algorithm, has been proposed to select representative transactions, with the goal of reducing computation cost in association rule mining.

Sampling for outlier detection has also been studied [38, 1]. Wu *et al.* [38] have developed a sampling algorithm to efficiently detect distance-based outliers in domains where distance computation is very expensive. Abe *et al.* [1] present an approach to outlier detection based on classification. Their method invokes a selective sampling mechanism based on active learning to the reduced classification problem.

Hidden Web Sampling: There have been several recent research efforts [3, 12, 13, 24] on sampling from the deep web. Dasgupta *et al.*[12, 13] proposed HDSampler, a random walk scheme over the query space provided by the interface, to select a simple random sample from hidden database. Bar-Yossef *et al.*[3] proposed algorithms for sampling suggestions using the public suggestion interface. Our algorithm is different from their work, since our goal is sampling in the context of particular data mining tasks. We focus on achieving high accuracy for a specific task, instead of simple random sampling.

7. CONCLUSIONS

As a growing amount of useful information is available on the deep web, clustering such hidden data can provide useful summaries to various interested parties. This paper has presented a novel methodology for clustering data over a deep web data source. The input space of a deep web data source is initially stratified for both improving the effectiveness of sampling and utilizing the relationship between the input and the output attributes. The space of output attributes of a deep web data source is partitioned into sub-spaces, and three representative sampling methods are proposed. The goal of each of these three methods is achieving a *good estimation* of the *statistics*, which is either proportions or the centers, of sub-spaces of output attributes. Two of three approaches we have presented involve a novel application of active learning.

We have evaluated our method using two synthetic and two real datasets. Our comparison shows significant gains in estimation accuracy from both the novel aspects of our work, i.e., the use of stratified clustering and representative sampling.

8. REFERENCES

[1] Naoki Abe, Bianca Zadrozny, and John Langford. Outlier detection by active learning. In *Proceedings of the 12th ACM SIGKDD international conference on Knowledge discovery and data mining*, KDD '06, pages 504–509, New York, NY, USA, 2006. ACM.

[2] Isabelle Guyon Asa Ben-Hur, Andre Elisseeff. A stability based method for discovering structure in clustered data. In *Pacific Symposium on Biocomputing*, 2002.

[3] Ziv Bar-Yossef and Maxim Gurevich. Mining search engine query logs via suggestion sampling. *Proc. VLDB Endow.*, 1(1):54–65, 2008.

[4] Shai Ben-David. A framework for statistical clustering with constant time approximation algorithms for k-median and k-means clustering. *Mach. Learn.*, 66:243–257, March 2007.

[5] Shai Ben-David, Dávid Pál, and Hans Ulrich Simon. Stability of k-means clustering. In *Proceedings of the 20th annual conference on Learning theory*, COLT'07, pages 20–34, Berlin, Heidelberg, 2007. Springer-Verlag.

[6] Mario Boley and Henrik Grosskreutz. A randomized approach for approximating the number of frequent sets. In *ICDM '08: Proceedings of the 2008 Eighth IEEE International Conference on Data Mining*, pages 43–52, Washington, DC, USA, 2008. IEEE Computer Society.

[7] Paul S. Bradley and Usama M. Fayyad. Refining initial points for K-Means clustering. In *Proc. 15th International Conf. on Machine Learning*, pages 91–99. Morgan Kaufmann, San Francisco, CA, 1998.

[8] D. Braga, S. Ceri, F. Daniel, and D. Martinenghi. Optimization of Multi-domain Queries on the Web. *VLDB Endowment*, 1:562–673, 2008.

[9] Bin Chen, Peter Haas, and Peter Scheuermann. A new two-phase sampling based algorithm for discovering association rules. In *KDD '02: Proceedings of the eighth ACM SIGKDD international conference on Knowledge discovery and data mining*, pages 462–468, New York, NY, USA, 2002. ACM.

[10] W. Cochran. *Sampling Techniques*. Wiley and Sons, 1977.

[11] Ido Dagan and Sean P. Engelson. Committee-based sampling for training probabilistic classifiers. In *In Proceedings of the Twelfth International Conference on Machine Learning*, pages 150–157. Morgan Kaufmann, 1995.

[12] Arjun Dasgupta, Gautam Das, and Heikki Mannila. A random walk approach to sampling hidden databases. In *SIGMOD '07: Proceedings of the 2007 ACM SIGMOD international conference on Management of data*, pages 629–640, New York, NY, USA, 2007. ACM.

[13] Arjun Dasgupta, Nan Zhang, and Gautam Das. Leveraging count information in sampling hidden databases. In *ICDE '09: Proceedings of the 2009 IEEE International Conference on Data Engineering*, pages 329–340, Washington, DC, USA, 2009. IEEE Computer Society.

[14] Yoav Freund, H. Sebastian Seung, Eli Shamir, and Naftali Tishby. Selective sampling using the query by committee algorithm. In *Machine Learning*, pages 133–168, 1995.

[15] Anjan Goswami and Ruoming Jin. Fast and exact out-of-core k-means clustering. In *In ICDM*, pages 83–90. IEEE Computer Society, 2004.

[16] J. A. Hartigan and M. A. Wong. A K-means clustering algorithm. *Applied Statistics*, 28:100–108, 1979.

[17] H. He, W. Meng, C. Yu, and Z. Wu. Automatic integration of web search interfaces with wise_integrator. *The international Journal on Very Large Data Bases*, 12:256–273, 2004.

[18] Anil K. Jain and Richard C. Dubes. *Algorithms for clustering data*. Prentice-Hall, Inc., Upper Saddle River, NJ, USA, 1988.

[19] L. Kaufman and P.J. Rousseeuw. *Finding Groups in Data An Introduction to Cluster Analysis*. Wiley Interscience, New York, 1990.

[20] A. Kementsietsidis, F. Neven, D. Van de Craen, and S. Vansummeren. Scalable multi-query optimization for exploratory queries over federated scientific databases. *VLDB Endowment*, 1:16–27, 2008.

[21] George Kollios, Ieee Computer Society, Dimitrios Gunopulos, Nick Koudas, and Stefan Berchtold. Efficient biased sampling for approximate clustering and outlier detection in large datasets. *IEEE Transactions on Knowledge and Data Engineering*, 15:2003, 2003.

[22] Tantan Liu and Gagan Agrawal. Active learning based frequent itemset mining over the deep web. In *ICDE*, pages 219–230, 2011.

[23] Tantan Liu and Gagan Agrawal. Technical report: Stratified k-means clustering over a deep web data source, 2012. http://www.cse.ohio-state.edu/ liut/Paper.pdf.

[24] Tantan Liu, Fan Wang, and Gagan Agrawal. Stratified sampling for data mining on the deep web. In *ICDM*, pages 324–333, 2010.

[25] Stuart P. Lloyd. Least squares quantization in pcm. *IEEE Transactions on Information Theory*, 28(2):129–136, 1982.

[26] J. Madhavan, L. Afanasiev, L. Antova, and A. Halevy. Harnessing the deep web: Present and future. In *4th Biennial Conference on Innovative Data Systems Research (CIDR)*, 2009.

[27] J. Madhavan, D. Ko, L. Kot, V. Ganapathy, A. Rasmussen, and A. Halevy. Google's Deep Web Crawl. *VLDB Endowment*, 1:1241–1252, 2008.

[28] G.J. McLachlan and K.E. Basford. *Mixture Models: Inference and Applications to Clustering*. Marcel Dekker, New York, 1988.

[29] Christopher Meek, Bo Thiesson, David Heckerman, and Pack Kaelbling. The learning-curve sampling method applied to model-based clustering. *Journal of Machine Learning Research*, 2:397–418, 2001.

[30] Brian Peacock Merran Evans, N. A. J. Hastings. Wiley-interscience, 1993.

[31] Srinivasan Parthasarathy. Efficient progressive sampling for association rules. In *ICDM '02: Proceedings of the 2002 IEEE International Conference on Data Mining*, page 354, Washington, DC, USA, 2002. IEEE Computer Society.

[32] J.A. Rice. *Mathematical statistics and data analysis*. Duxbury Press, 2006.

[33] P. P. Talukdar, M. Jacob, M. S. Mehmood, K. Crammer, Z. G. Ives, F. Pereira, and S. Guha. Learning to create data-integrating queries. *VLDB Endowment*, 1:785–796, 2008.

[34] Robert Tibshirani, Guenther Walther, and Trevor Hastie. Estimating the number of clusters in a data set via the gap statistic. *Journal Of The Royal Statistical Society Series B*, 63(2):411–423, 2001.

[35] Hannu Toivonen. Sampling large databases for association rules. In *The VLDB Journal*, pages 134–145. Morgan Kaufmann, 1996.

[36] Simon Tong and Daphne Koller. Active learning for parameter estimation in bayesian networks. In *In NIPS*, pages 647–653, 2001.

[37] Jr. Ward. Hierarchical grouping to optimize an objective function. *Journal of the American Statistical Association*, 58:236–244, 1963.

[38] Mingxi Wu and Christopher Jermaine. C.: Outlier detection by sampling with accuracy guarantees. In *In: KDD (2006*, 2006.

Metro Maps of Science

Dafna Shahaf
Carnegie Mellon University
5000 Forbes Avenue
Pittsburgh, PA
dshahaf@cs.cmu.edu

Carlos Guestrin
Carnegie Mellon University
5000 Forbes Avenue
Pittsburgh, PA
guestrin@cs.cmu.edu

Eric Horvitz
Microsoft Research
One Microsoft Way
Redmond, WA
horvitz@microsoft.com

ABSTRACT

As the number of scientific publications soars, even the most enthusiastic reader can have trouble staying on top of the evolving literature. It is easy to focus on a narrow aspect of one's field and lose track of the big picture. Information overload is indeed a major challenge for scientists today, and is especially daunting for new investigators attempting to master a discipline and scientists who seek to cross disciplinary borders. In this paper, we propose metrics of influence, coverage, and connectivity for scientific literature. We use these metrics to create structured summaries of information, which we call *metro maps*. Most importantly, metro maps explicitly show the relations between papers in a way which captures developments in the field. Pilot user studies demonstrate that our method can help researchers acquire new knowledge efficiently: map users achieved better precision and recall scores and found more seminal papers while performing fewer searches.

Categories and Subject Descriptors

H.3.1 [**Information Storage and Retrieval**]: Content Analysis and Indexing; H.3.3 [**Information Storage and Retrieval**]: Information Search and Retrieval; H.5 [**Information Interfaces and Presentation**]

Keywords

Metro maps, Information, Summarization

1. INTRODUCTION

"Distringit librorum multitudo" (the abundance of books is a distraction), said Lucius Annaeus Seneca; he lived in the first century.

A lot has changed since the first century, but Lucius' problem has only become worse. The surge of the Web brought down the barriers of distribution, and the scientific community finds itself overwhelmed by the increasing numbers of publications; relevant data is often buried in an avalanche of publications, and locating it is difficult.

KDD'12, August 12–16, 2012, Beijing, China.

Search engines have been relied upon in recent years for accessing the scientific literature, and investments have even been made to create special academic search and retrieval tools. However, the search and browsing experience might be best characterized as providing keyhole views onto the literature: while search engines are highly effective in retrieving scientific publications, the task of fitting those publications into a coherent picture remains difficult.

In contrast, we are interested in methods that *explicitly* show the relationships among publications in a way that captures the main developments in the discipline. We believe that such methods can allow a user to explore a new, complex topic and discover hidden connections effectively. We consider as a sample motivation the creation of valuable literature exploration tools that could help people entering a new field, such as new graduate students or experts reaching beyond their traditional disciplinary borders.

Several tools already exist for summarizing and visualizing scientific literature (see [Borner, 2010] for a compendium). However, the output of these systems is often not suitable for a starting researcher. Some systems' level of granularity is too coarse: Boyack et al. [2009] provide a graph-summary of chemistry research, where each node corresponds to a cluster of disciplines ('Biology-Zoology-Ecology'). Bassecoulard and Zitt [1999] produce a hierarchical graph, where nodes correspond to clusters of journals.

We believe that in order to allow researchers to understand how a field is organized, a finer level of granularity is needed. For this reason, we chose *papers* as our unit of analysis. Most current tools that work at this level of granularity provide visualizations of citation (or co-citation) networks, where papers are nodes [Chen, 2004; Dunne et al., 2010]. Importantly, edges between papers are based on *local* computation: the edges are selected because they pass some threshold, or belong to a spanning tree. In such methods, there is no notion of coherent *lines of research*. We believe that the notion of story lines is essential, and facilitates users' knowledge acquisition and comprehension of the frontier and evolutionary history of ideas in a discipline.

Several systems have attempted to create story lines, especially in the news domain [Swan and Jensen, 2000; Yan et al., 2011; Allan et al., 2001]. However, this style of summarization only works for simple stories, which are linear in nature. In contrast, research fields display a very non-linear behaviour: lines of research branch like a tangle of spaghetti with side stories, dead ends, and intertwining narratives. In order to explore these stories, one needs a *map* as a guide through unfamiliar territory.

The metro map metaphor has been used before to display abstract knowledge. For example, Nesbitt's map shows interconnecting ideas running through his PhD thesis [Nesbitt, 2004]. However, these maps were all manually constructed. In this paper, we adapt the techniques of [Shahaf et al., 2012] (previously applied to news articles) to construct metro maps of scientific literature *automatically*. Our main contributions are as follows:

- Formalizing metrics characterizing good metro maps, taking advantage of the additional structure encoded in the scientific domain:
  - Characterizing the probability that ideas in two papers stem from a common source, then using this notion to define coherence of research lines.
  - Quantifying the impact of one paper on the corpus.
  - Proposing a notion of connectivity that captures how different lines of research can still interact with each other, despite not intersecting.
- Providing efficient methods with theoretical guarantees to compute these metrics and find a diverse set of high-impact, coherent research lines and their interactions.
- Integrating user preferences into our framework by providing an appropriate user-interaction model.
- Performing validation studies with users that highlight the promise of the methodology. Our method outperforms popular competitors.

2. OBJECTIVE

We first review the desired properties of a metro map, following the criteria outlined in [Shahaf et al., 2012]. We shall briefly present these criteria, motivate and formalize them. Later, we present a principled approach to constructing maps that optimizes tradeoffs among these criteria. Before we begin, we formally define metro maps.

Definition 2.1 (Metro Map [Shahaf et al., 2012]). A *metro map* $\mathcal{M}$ is a pair (G, Π), where $G = (V, E)$ is a directed graph and Π is a set of paths in G. We refer to paths as *metro lines*. Each $e \in E$ must belong to at least one line.

The vertices V correspond to scientific papers, and are denoted by $docs(\mathcal{M})$. The lines of Π correspond to aspects of the field. A key requirement is that each line is *coherent*: following the papers along a line should give the user a clear understanding of the evolution of a story.

Coherence is crucial for good maps, but is it sufficient as well? In order to put this matter to a test, we computed maximally coherent lines for the set of papers returned in response to the query 'support vector machines' (using methods detailed below). The results were discouraging. While the lines were indeed coherent, they were not *important*. Many of the lines revolved around narrow topics; many focused on a single research group, never expanding beyond it.

The example suggests that maximizing coherence does not guarantee good maps. Instead, the key challenge is balancing coherence and **coverage**: in addition to being coherent, lines should cover topics that are important to the user.

Finally, a map is more than just a set of lines; there is information in its *structure* as well. Publications offer a rich palette of interaction possibilities: assumption, affirmation, contrast, methodology, related work, and more. Therefore, our last property is **connectivity**. The map's **connectivity** should convey the underlying structure of the field, and how different lines of research interact with each other.

In Sections 3-5, we formalize **coherence**, **coverage** and **connectivity**. In Section 6, we explore tradeoffs among them and combine them into a single objective function to guide the construction of maps.

Chain A	Chain B
• Europe weights possibility of debt default in Greece	• Europe weights possibility of debt default in Greece
• Why Republicans don't fear a debt default	• Europe commits to action on Greek debt
• Italy; The Pope's leaning toward Republican ideas	• Europe union moves towards a bailout of Greece
• Italian-American groups protest 'Sopranos'	• Greece set to release austerity plan
• Greek workers protest austerity plan	• Greek workers protest austerity plan

3. COHERENCE

How should we measure coherence for a chain of papers? We rely on the notion of coherence developed in Connect-the-Dots (CTD) [Shahaf and Guestrin, 2010]. In the following, we briefly review this approach.

In order to define coherence, a natural first step is to measure similarity between each two consecutive papers along the chain. As a single bad transition can destroy the coherence of an entire chain, we measure the strength of the chain by the strength of its *weakest link*.

However, this simple approach can produce poor chains. Consider, for example, Chain A above. The transitions of Chain A are all reasonable when examined out of context. The first two articles are about debt default; the second and third mention Republicans. Despite these local connections, the overall effect is associative and incoherent.

Now, consider Chain B. This chain has the same endpoints, but it is significantly more coherent. Let us take a closer look at these two chains. Figure 1 shows word appearance along both chains. For example, the word 'Greece' appeared throughout Chain B. It is easy to spot the associative flow of Chain A in Figure 1. Words appear for short stretches; some words appear, then disappear and reappear. Contrast this with Chain B, where stretches are longer and transitions between documents are smoother. This observation motivates our definition of coherence.

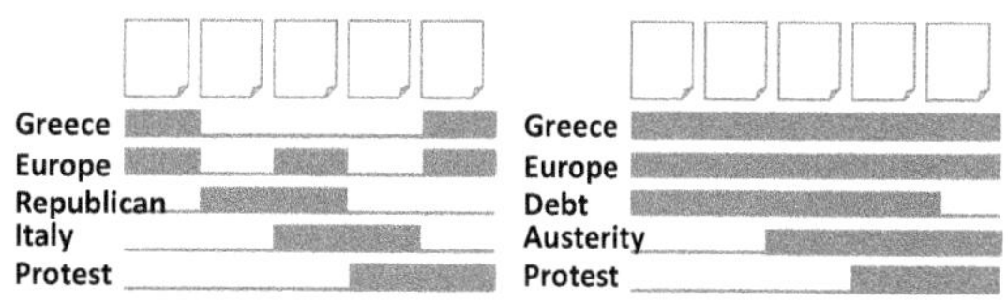

Figure 1: Word patterns in Chain A (left) and Chain B (right). Bars correspond to the appearance of a word in the articles depicted above them.

We represent documents as vectors of concepts (for the sake of presentation, assume concepts $\mathcal{C}$ are words). Given a chain of papers $(p_1, ..., p_n)$, we first score each transition $p_i \to p_{i+1}$ by the number of concepts both articles share:

$$Coherence(p_1, ..., p_n) = \min_{i=1...n-1} \sum_{c \in \mathcal{C}} \mathbb{1}(c \in p_i \cap p_{i+1})$$

However, word appearance is too noisy. Articles must use the exact same words; synonyms are treated as unrelated. Also, all words are treated equally: the word 'Greece' is as important as the word 'today'.

Therefore, we replaced the indicator function $\mathbb{1}(\cdot)$ with a notion of *influence* of concept c in a transition. Intuitively, $Influence(p_i, p_j \mid c)$ is high if (1) both documents are highly connected, and (2) c is important for the connectivity. Note that c does not have to appear in either of the documents.

After the introduction of influence, the objective becomes:

$$Coherence(p_1, ..., p_n) = \min_{i=1...n-1} \sum_c Influence(c \mid p_i, p_{i+1})$$

This objective guarantees good transitions, but associative chains like Chain A can still score well. However, these chains need to use many words in order to achieve high scores, as many of their transitions use a unique set of words. On the other hand, coherent chains (like Chain B) can often be characterized by a *small* set of words, which are important throughout many of the transitions.

Therefore, instead of summing $Influence(c \mid p_i, p_{i+1})$ over all concepts, the problem is transformed into an optimization problem, where the goal is to choose a small set of concepts (called 'active'), and score the chain based only on these concepts. Constraints on possible activations enforce a small number of words and smooth transitions, imitating the behaviour of Figure 1 (right). Formally,

$$Coherence(p_1, ..., p_n) = \max_{activations} \min_{i=1...n-1}$$

$$\sum_c Influence(c \mid p_i, p_{i+1}) \mathbb{1}(c \text{ active in } p_i, p_{i+1}) \quad (3.1)$$

Finally, the coherence of a map is defined as the minimal coherence across its lines Π.

3.1 Coherence for Scientific Papers

The coherence notion of [Shahaf and Guestrin, 2010] (Definition 3.1) was developed for the news domain, and relied exclusively on article *content*. It was designed to use very basic features, namely words. However, the simplicity of the representation can sometimes result in incoherent chains. To illustrate the problem, consider the following three papers:

p1: **Multiagent planning with factored MDPs / Guestrin et al** / *NIPS '01*

p2: **Timing and power issues in wireless sensor networks / Aakvaag et al** / *ICPP '05*

p3: **Social network analysis for routing in disconnected delay-tolerant manets / Daly et al** / *MobiHoc '07*

These papers share many words, such as 'network', 'probability' and 'cost', and thus can achieve a good coherence score. However, they clearly do not follow a coherent research line. The problem may be alleviated by higher-level features (e.g., distinguishing between different uses of 'network'); in this section, we choose instead to take advantage of the side information provided by the citation graph, and define a coherence notion more suited for scientific papers.

Upon close examination, our original coherence notion (Definition 3.1) is composed of two main ideas: computing the influence of concepts on transitions, and choosing a small set of active concepts that captures the story well. While the latter idea seems domain-independent, computing influence may benefit from the additional structure of the citation graph.

The citation graph explicitly captures the way papers influence each other: the content of a publication is often affected by cited work, the authors' prior work and novel insights. The influence notion proposed in BKS [El-Arini and Guestrin, 2011] captures exactly this behaviour. In BKS, the authors define a directed, acyclic graph G_c for every concept c in the corpus. Nodes represent papers that contain c and the edges represent citations and common authorship.

To capture the degree of influence, BKS defines a weight $\omega_{u,v}$ for each edge $u \to v$ in G_c, representing the probability of direct influence from paper u to paper v with respect to concept c. Some probability is assigned to 'novelty', the case that concept c in paper v was novel.

Given a concept-specific weight for each edge in G_c, BKS defines a probabilistic, concept-specific notion of influence between any two papers in the document collection:

Definition 3.1 (Direct Influence [El-Arini and Guestrin, 2011]). Let G_c^r be a random subgraph of G_c, where every edge $u \to v$ is included in G_c^r with probability $\omega_{u,v}$. The influence between papers p_i and p_j w.r.t. c is the probability there exists a directed path in G_c^r between p_i and p_j.

The BKS notion of influence has many attractive properties: it is simple, and it appears to capture the way ideas travel along the citation graph. However, using it for coherence severely limits the chains we can hope to identify. According to definition 3.1, the only pairs of papers that can have influence between them are ancestor-descendant pairs in G_c. Therefore, chains with high influence are likely to contain only papers that directly build on top of one another, especially papers by the same authors.

Consider papers $p2$ and $p3$ from above. Their notion of 'network' is similar, but there is no direct path from $p2$ to $p3$ in the corresponding graph. To mitigate this problem, we introduce a different notion of influence. Rather than requiring that p_i influence p_j, we are only interested in whether concept c in p_i and concept c in p_j refer to the same idea. To capture this property, we modify the notion of influence:

Definition 3.2 (Ancestral Influence). The influence between papers p_i and p_j with respect to concept c is the probability p_i and p_j have a common ancestor in G_c^r.

See Figure 2 for an illustration of the difference between direct influence (left) and ancestral influence (right). In order for p_i to have direct influence on p_j, there has to be a path from p_i to p_j. In order for p_i to have ancestral influence on p_j, it is sufficient that they have a common ancestor in the graph. The ancestor can also be p_i itself.

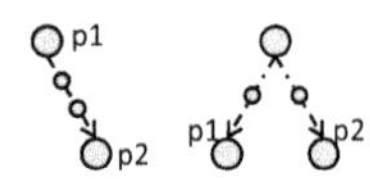

Figure 2: Direct (left) vs. ancestral influence (right).

As for $p2$ and $p3$: with no direct path among them, their direct influence is zero. However, as both cite Perkins' 1999 networks paper, their ancestral influence is non-zero.

4. COVERAGE

In addition to coherence, we need to ensure that the map has high coverage. Before defining coverage of a map, we need to understand which elements we wish to cover.

4.1 What to cover?

In [Shahaf et al., 2012], we only had the articles' content to rely upon, and thus the covered elements were *concepts*. We denoted the amount an article p covered a concept c by $cover_p(c)$, and looked for a set of articles that, when combined, achieved high coverage for many important concepts.

However, when we applied the same technique to scientific papers, we encountered a problem: papers with similar content may appear exchangeable w.r.t. their coverage, but they will not necessarily be equivalent in the user's eyes. For example, the user may notice that the papers aim at different communities, or that one paper is more seminal than the other. Consider the following two papers:

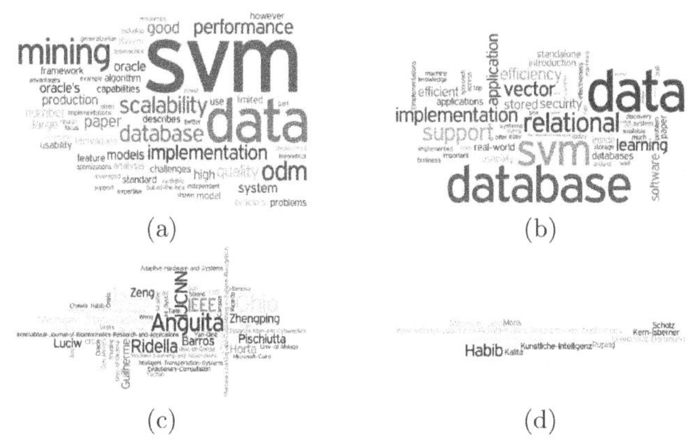

Figure 3: Tag clouds for $p1$ and $p2$. The size of a word is proportional to its frequency. (a-b) $p1$ and $p2$'s content, respectively. (c-d) Venues and authors of papers affected by $p1$ and $p2$, respectively. Note that (a) and (b) are very similar, but (c) and (d) are not.

p1: **SVM in Oracle database 10g: Removing the barriers to widespread adoption of support vector machines / Milenova et al**
VLDB '05 Proceedings of the 31st International Conference on Very Large Data Bases

p2: **Support Vector Machines in Relational Databases / Rüping**
SVM '02 Proceedings of the First International Workshop on Pattern Recognition with Support Vector Machines

The content of $p1$ and $p2$ is similar. Figures 3(a)-(b) display the papers as tag clouds: both papers share many of their important words ('data','database', 'svm', 'implementation'). Numerous other words have a closely related match ('performance'/ 'efficiency', 'Oracle'/ 'relational database').

One way to distinguish between the aforementioned papers is to examine their impact. Figures 3(c)-(d) show tag clouds of authors and venues for papers *citing* $p1$ and $p2$. Figure 3(c) has more words than 3(d), implying that $p1$ has affected more unique authors and venues than $p2$. Interestingly, despite the similar content of the papers, there is almost no intersection between the papers citing them; only a single paper cites both (Mona Habib from Microsoft Cairo).

Based on this intuition, we propose to use the papers themselves as elements of coverage. A paper p should cover itself and the papers it has had impact on. By this definition, a high-coverage set of papers consists of papers that, when combined, had impact on a large portion of the corpus.

The idea that a paper covers its descendants (and not its ancestors) may seem counterintuitive at first. After all, how can a paper cover future contributions? Nevertheless, we believe that examining a paper's ancestors merely helps understanding the context in which the paper was written, while its descendants truly reveal the gist of its contribution.

4.2 Coverage of a single paper

4.2.1 Desiderata

We would like papers to cover their descendants. Instead of a hard, binary notion of coverage, we prefer a softer notion, allowing us to express that descendants are covered to various degrees (depicted as a gradient in Figure 4a).

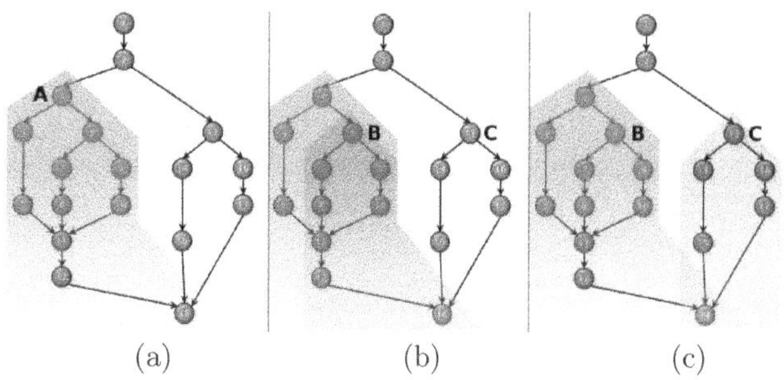

Figure 4: A simple citation graph. Edges traverse in the direction of impact, from cited to citing paper. (a) Coverage of document A. Gradient indicates different degrees of coverage. (b-c) The effect of adding papers B and C (respectively) to paper A. Since B's descendants are already covered to some extent by A, we prefer C.

Let us concentrate on the degree to which paper p covers its descendant q, $cover_p(q)$. In order to evaluate the impact that p had on q, we examine the way q is connected to p in the citation graph. Intuitively, if q can be reached from p by many paths, p had a high impact on q. Since impact is diluted with each step, shorter paths are more important than longer ones.

Before we devise a coverage formulation based on paths between p and q, we consider another point: impact is not necessarily transitive. Consider, for example, Figure 5. The figure outlines a (small) fraction of the descendants of Nicolo Cesa-Bianchi's paper, 'How to Use Expert Advice'. As before, edges indicate citation. A snippet from the citation text appears by each edge.

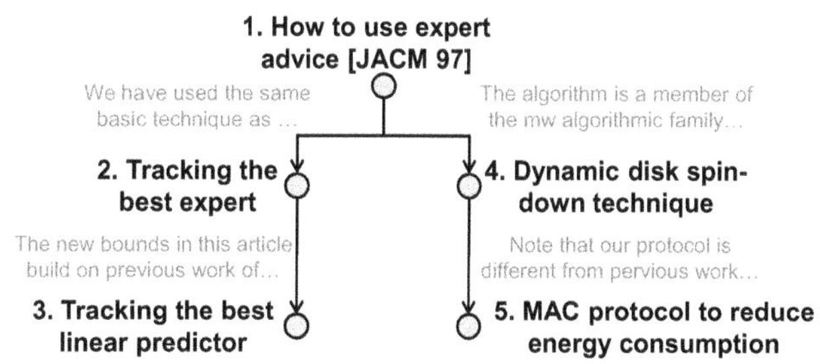

Figure 5: Two branches in the citation graph. The left branch is coherent; the right one is not.

The left branch of Figure 5 revolves around Online Learning Theory. The papers in this branch (#2 and #3) build on top of each other. Intuitively, the root paper had impact on both of them. In contrast, the right branch is more difficult to follow. Both descendants deal with extending the battery life of devices, but while paper #4 is a direct application of the root paper, paper #5 is not. In fact, when #5 cites #4, the citation reads 'Note that our protocol is different from previous work'. In other words, paper #5 is no longer relevant to the root node, and should not be covered by it.

The difference between the two branches can be captured by the coherence notion of Section 3: The left branch is much more coherent than the right one. Based on that intuition, we only want a paper to cover the descendants that can be reached by a *coherent* path. Unlike Section 3, we are only interested in direct-influence coherent chains (Definition 3.1), as they model the true impact of a paper.

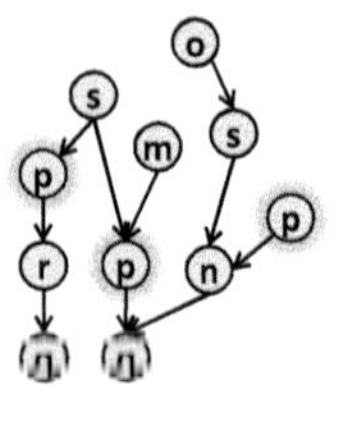

Figure 6: Coherence graph. Nodes represent papers (names appear inside). Paths represent coherent chains. Each paper may have multiple corresponding vertices: the highlighted vertices are all copies of paper p.

4.2.2 *Formulation*

In the previous section, we provided desiderata for $cover_p(q)$: coverage is high if there are many short and coherent paths between p and q. In order to formalize this idea, we employ the technique of random walks.

Let q be a paper. Consider a walk from q to its ancestors, taking only coherent paths into account. At each step, the walker either terminates (with probability α), or chooses an ancestor uniformly at random among the coherent paths that extend the current walk. If there are many short, coherent paths between p and q, there is a high probability that the walk reaches p before termination. We denote this probability by $cover_p(q)$.

Let us formalize this intuition now. Since we only consider coherent paths, it is more convenient to formulate coverage in terms of walks performed directly on a *coherence graph* G. A coherence graph is a graph representing all coherent chains in the domain (See Figure 6 for an example. In Section 7.1 we explain how to encode the graph compactly). Each vertex v of G corresponds to a single paper, which we denote $paper(v)$; each paper p may have multiple corresponding vertices in G, which we denote $copies(p)$. In Figure 6, $copies(p)$ are highlighted.

Let G be a coherence graph. For each paper q, we construct the graph G_q by reversing the direction of all edges in G and adding an additional vertex, v_q. v_q is the starting vertex of our walk. We connect v_q to each vertex of G which corresponds to paper q, $copies(q)$. This way, a walk from v_q will always proceed to a copy of q, and then to its ancestors in the coherence graph G. Since the graph is a DAG, the probability that a walk reaches vertex v is easy to compute. We first compute a topological ordering on G_q, and compute the probabilities in this order:

$$cover_v(q) = \begin{cases} P(v_q \to v), & v \in copies(q) \\ (1-\alpha) \cdot (\sum_{u:u \to v} P(u \to v) \cdot cover_u(q)), & \text{o/w} \end{cases}$$

where $P(u \to v)$ is the probability the walker chose to go from vertex u to vertex v. We want the walker to choose uniformly among the coherent paths that extend the current walk; in other words, we want to bias the walker towards ancestors that participate in many coherent paths. Therefore, we compute for each vertex v the number of coherent paths that end in v, $\#Path(v)$. For example, the number of paths that end in the vertex marked 'n' in Figure 6 is two (o,s,n and p,n). Since G_q is a DAG, computing the number of paths takes polynomial time. The probability that the walker chooses to go from vertex v to vertex u is proportional to $\#Path$:

$$P(u \to v) = \frac{\#Path(v)}{\sum_{w:u \to w} \#Path(w)}$$

We now have a coverage notion for vertices of $\mathbb{G}$. However, we are interested in a coverage notion for *papers*. In order to compute the coverage of paper p, we need to sum up the scores of all vertices in $copies(p)$:

$$cover_p(q) = \sum_{v \in copies(p)} cover_v(q)$$

This score corresponds to the probability of reaching p before termination. In particular, since p can never appear more than once along a path in G, this score always less than 1.

4.3 Map Coverage

Now that we have defined coverage of a single document, let us define coverage of a map. In order to encourage diversity, we view set coverage as a sampling procedure: each paper p_i in the map tries to cover document q with probability $cover_{p_i}(q)$. The coverage of q is the probability at least one of the documents succeeded.

$$cover_{\mathcal{M}}(q) = 1 - \prod_{p_i \in docs(\mathcal{M})} (1 - cover_{p_i}(q))$$

Thus, if the map already includes papers which cover q well, $cover_{\mathcal{M}}(q)$ is close to 1, and adding another paper which covers q well provides very little extra coverage of q. This encourages us to pick papers which cover new areas of the graph, promoting **diversity**.

Figures 4b and 4c illustrate this idea. Suppose we already have paper A in our map, and we need to choose between papers B and C, whose content is similar. Figures 4b and 4c show the effect of choosing B and C, respectively. Since B's descendants have already been covered by A, we would prefer to choose C. (Note that since our coverage is soft, choosing B will still provide gains in coverage.)

We now have a way to measure how well a map covers a single paper. Finally, we want to measure how well a map covers the entire *corpus*. Remember, our goal is to ensure that the map touches upon **important** aspects of the corpus. Therefore, we first assign weights λ_q to each paper q, signifying the importance of the paper. We model the amount $\mathcal{M}$ covers the corpus as the weighted sum of the amount it covers each paper:

$$Cover(\mathcal{M}) = \sum_q \lambda_q cover_{\mathcal{M}}(q)$$

The weights cause *Cover* to prefer maps which cover important papers. They offer a natural mechanism for personalization: With no prior knowledge about the user's preferences, we set all of the weights to 1. This is equivalent to asking for a map which covers as much of the corpus as possible. In Section 10 we discuss learning weights from user feedback, resulting in a personalized notion of coverage.

5. CONNECTIVITY

A map is more than just a set of lines; there is information in its *structure* as well. The map's **connectivity** should convey the underlying structure of the story, and how different aspects of the story interact with each other.

In [Shahaf et al., 2012] we simply define connectivity as the number of lines of Π that intersect:

$$Conn(M) = \sum_{i<j} \mathbb{1}(\pi_i \cap \pi_j \neq \emptyset)$$

Unfortunately, this simple objective does not suffice in the scientific domain. Consider the two chains in Figure 7: the top chain describes the progress of margin classifiers – from perceptrons, through linear SVMs, to kernel machines. The bottom chain describes the progress of face-recognition

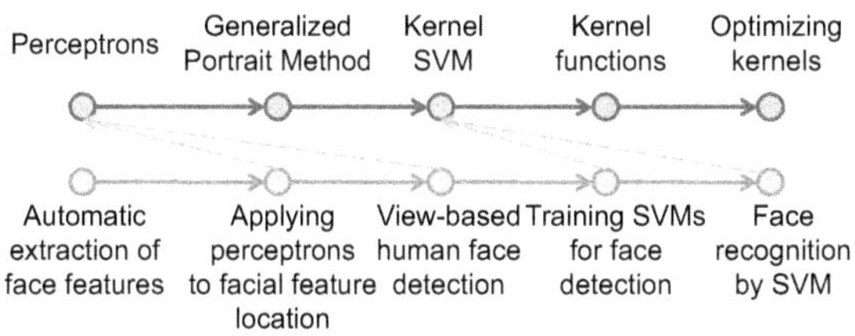

Figure 7: Two coherent chains (theory of SVMs, application of SVM to vision). The chains do not intersect, yet are related: the application chain uses tools from the theory chain. Dashed gray lines indicate impact.

challenge problems in vision: from facial feature location, through face detection, to face recognition. Both chains are clearly related; the vision papers use techniques from the theory chain. However, there is no way to find an article that would belong to both chains, unless we sacrifice coherence considerably. As a result, maps that optimize the aforementioned connectivity notion are often disconnected.

Finding papers that would belong to both chains may be difficult, but we can easily find theory papers that have had a big impact on vision papers. For example, some of the vision papers in Figure 7 directly cite papers from the theory chain. These citations are depicted as dashed lines.

Figure 7 motivates us to prefer a softer notion of intersection. Rather than requesting that the lines intersect, we also accept lines which are related to each other:

$$Conn(M) = \sum_{i<j} \mathbb{1}(\pi_i \cap \pi_j \neq \emptyset) \ + \gamma \cdot cover(\pi_i, \pi_j)$$

where $cover(\pi_i, \pi_j)$ is the maximal $cover_p(q)$ for $p \in \pi_i, q \in \pi_j$, or vice versa. We choose to use the maximum (instead of sum) in order to encourage connections between as many pairs of lines as possible. Scoring all the connections between π_i and π_j may lead to maps where only a few lines are very well-connected, and the rest are disconnected. The parameter γ is chosen empirically.

This softer notion of intersection is especially suited to scientific literature. Publications offer a rich palette of interaction possibilities, such as affirmation, criticism, contrast, methodology, and related work. Exposing the relationships between two lines of research can prove extremely valuable to researchers.

6. JOINT OBJECTIVE FUNCTION

Now that we have formally defined our three properties, we can combine them into one objective function. We need to consider tradeoffs among these properties: for example, maximizing coherence often results in repetitive, low-coverage chains. Maximizing connectivity encourages choosing similar chains, resulting in low coverage as well. Maximizing coverage leads to low connectivity, since there is no reason to re-use an article for more than one line.

The objective of [Shahaf et al., 2012] applies to the scientific domain as well. We include it here for completeness. For a full discussion, please refer to the paper.

Problem 6.1. Given a set of candidate documents $\mathcal{D}$, find a map $\mathcal{M} = (G, \Pi)$ over $\mathcal{D}$ which maximizes $Conn(\mathcal{M})$ s.t. $Coherence(\mathcal{M}) \geq \tau$ and $Cover(\mathcal{M}) \geq (1-\epsilon)\kappa$, where κ is the maximal coverage across maps with coherence $\geq \tau$ and ϵ is given.

There are several ways to restrict the size of $\mathcal{M}$; we chose to restrict $\mathcal{M}$ to K lines of length at most l. Alternatively, since some stories are more complex than others, one may prefer to add lines until coverage gains fall below a threshold.

7. ALGORITHM

In this section, we outline our approach for solving Problem 6.1. We adapt the algorithm of [Shahaf et al., 2012] to solve the problem. In the following we review the algorithm, highlighting the main differences.

We start by addressing the **coherence** constraint: In Section 7.1 we represent all coherent chains as a graph. In Section 7.2 we use this graph to find a set of K chains that maximize coverage; in Section 7.3, we increase connectivity without sacrificing coverage.

7.1 Representing all coherent chains

In order to pick good chains, we first wish to list all possible candidates. However, representing all chains whose coherence is at least τ is a non-trivial task. The number of possible chains may be exponential, and therefore it is infeasible to enumerate them all, let alone evaluate them.

The algorithm of [Shahaf et al., 2012] employs a divide-and-conquer approach to the problem, constructing long chains from shorter ones. This allows us to compactly encode many candidate chains in a graph structure which we call a *coherence graph*. $\mathbb{G}$ is a compact representation of the graph displayed in Figure 6. Vertices of $\mathbb{G}$ correspond to short coherent chains, and there is a directed edge between each pair of vertices which can be conjoined and maintain coherence. Importantly, this property is transitive: every path in $\mathbb{G}$, no matter how long, represents a coherent chain.

The only change in the algorithm lies in the computation of influence. Direct influence and ancestor influence are instances of the k-terminal reliability problem [Ball, 1986], which is $\#P$-complete, so we cannot hope for a polynomial-time solution. Instead, we apply approximations.

In BKS, the authors presented a deterministic, linear-time dynamic programming heuristic for calculating direct influence. This heuristic is based on the assumption that the paths between two nodes are independent of each other. Unfortunately, this assumption is too strong for ancestor influence. The paths between $p1, p2$, and possible ancestors are often dependent, and treating them as independent results in significant errors. Instead, we employ a simple Monte Carlo sampling method with theoretical guarantees (BKS also proposed a similar sampling approach).

In order to calculate m values with (ϵ, δ)-approximation guarantees (where ϵ and δ denote the upper bound of relative error and failure probability), we need $O(\frac{1}{\delta^2}\log(\frac{m}{\delta}))$ samples. m is the number of document-pairs with a common ancestor in the graph. In the worst case, m is quadratic in the number of papers (in practice, it is often much smaller). Therefore, the number of samples needed is logarithmic in the number of papers. Also note that influences can be pre-computed once and stored for future use.

7.2 Finding a high-coverage map

After representing all coherent chains as a graph $\mathbb{G}$, we wish to find a set of chains which maximize coverage, subject to map size constraints.

Problem 7.1. Given a coherence graph $\mathbb{G}$, find paths $\pi_1, ..., \pi_K$ in $\mathbb{G}$, $|docs(\pi_i)| \leq l$ that maximize $Cover(docs(\bigcup_i \pi_i))$.

We use the coverage-maximization algorithm of [Shahaf et al., 2012] to find a high-coverage map. The proof relies on formulating the problem in terms of *orienteering*. Orienteering problems are motivated by maximizing a function

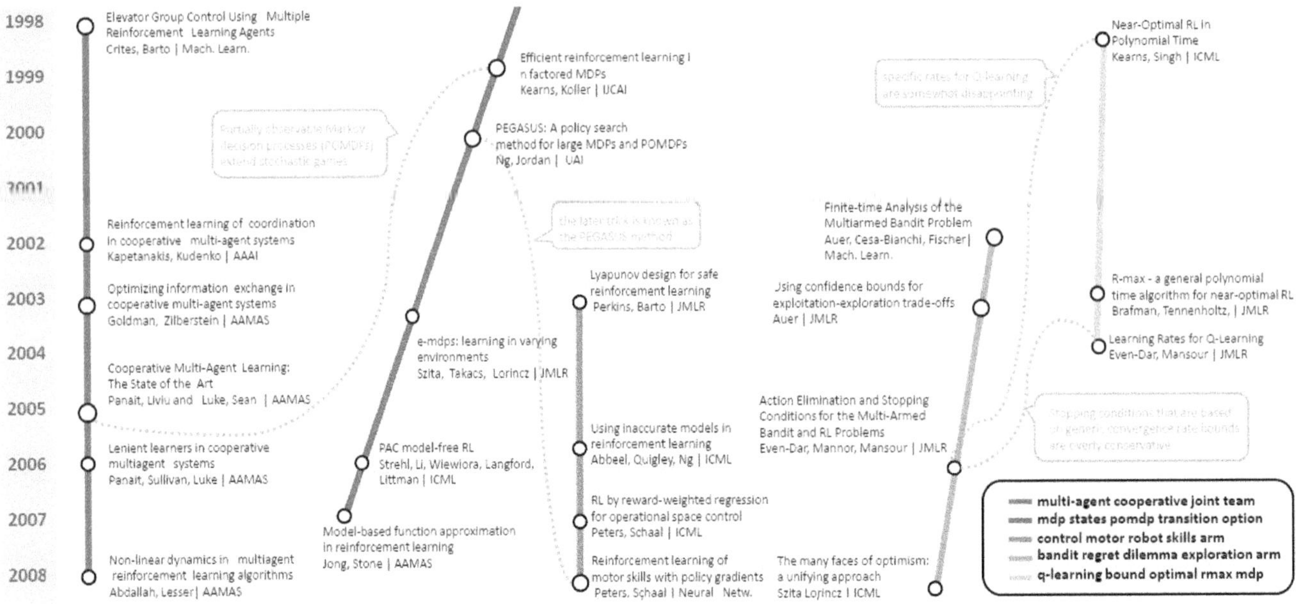

Figure 8: Part of the map computed for the query 'Reinforcement Learning'. The map depicts multiple lines of research (see legend at the bottom). Interactions between the lines are depicted as dashed gray lines, and relevant citation text appears near them.

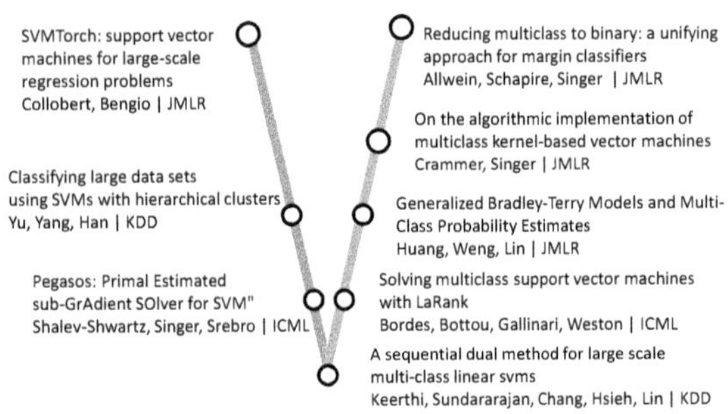

Figure 9: A segment of a map computed for the query SVM/ Support vector machine, showing the intersection of two lines: multi-class SVMs and large-scale SVM. In the interest of space, we condensed the timeline.

of nodes visited during a tour, subject to a budget on tour length. The [Shahaf et al., 2012] coverage notion is submodular, so we applied the Submodular orienteering algorithms of [Chekuri and Pal, 2005] to the problem.

In order to adapt the algorithm to the scientific domain, we changed only the way coverage is computed (see Section 4). Note that the new coverage notion is submodular. Figure 4 provides the intuition for that: adding a paper to a smaller set of papers helps more than adding it to a larger set (diminishing returns). Therefore, we can use the same submodular orienteering algorithm with the new coverage notion, and achieve the same guarantees.

7.3 Increasing connectivity

We now know how to find a high-coverage, coherent map. Our final step is to increase connectivity without sacrificing (more than an ϵ-fraction of) coverage.

In order to increase connectivity, we apply a local-search technique. It starts from map $\mathcal{M}_0$, and takes steps in the search space by applying local moves. Each local move replaces a single line in Π. At iteration i, we consider each path $p \in \Pi_{i-1}$. We hold the rest of the map fixed, and try to replace p by p' that increases connectivity (Section 5) and does not decrease coverage. At the end of the iteration, we pick the best move and apply it, resulting in $\mathcal{M}_i$. The full details of the algorithm are in [Shahaf et al., 2012].

8. EXAMPLE MAPS

Figure 8 shows a part of a map computed for the query 'Reinforcement Learning'. As can be seen, the map depicts multiple lines of research: MDPs, robotics and control, multi-agent cooperation, bounds and analysis, and exploration-exploitation tradeoffs. The map shows how the MDP line affects the multi-agent and robotics lines, and how the exploration-exploitation line interacts with the analysis line. Those relations are depicted as gray dashed paths. Note that the map does not capture all the interactions; for example, connections between MDPs and the analysis line are not captured.

As mentioned in Section 5, intersection is rare for broad queries. Figure 9 shows one such intersection between two lines in the SVM map. One line is about large-scale SVMs, the other is about multi-class SVMs. The lines intersect at Keerthi's paper about large scale multi-class linear SVMs.

9. USER STUDY

In our user study, we evaluated the effectiveness of metro maps in aiding users navigate, consume, and integrate different aspects of a specific, multi-faceted information need.

Evaluating metro maps in the scientific domain poses some significant challenges. Since the metro-map output is unique, we cannot conduct a double-blind comparison study, as subjects inevitably differentiate between the different systems. Therefore, we cannot have a within-subject study, but are instead forced to choose a between-subject design. This design, in itself, causes a new problem: since we need a different group of participants for each condition tested (metro-map or competitor), we cannot tailor the query to users.

Rather, we have to find a single domain such that all of our participants will (1) be able to read scientific publications in that domain and (2) not know the domain well in advance.

We recruited 30 participants from our university. All participants were graduate students with background in Machine Learning or related fields. The domain we chose was Reinforcement Learning. The machine learning background of the participants was enough to make them comfortable with the subject, but none of them had conducted research in the field or studied it extensively.

We asked participants to imagine themselves as first-year graduate students embarking on a research project in Reinforcement Learning. The participants were asked to conduct a quick literature survey. In particular, they were asked to update a survey paper from 1996: identify up to five research directions that should be included in the updated survey, and list a few relevant papers for each direction. We recorded participants' browsing histories, and took a snapshot of their progress every minute. We limited their time to 40 minutes to simulate a quick first pass on papers.

We used the ACM dataset to compute a map for the query 'Reinforcement learning'. The dataset contains more than 35,000 papers from ACM conferences and journals. As the number of papers is relatively small, scalability was not an issue. We extracted features as described in [El-Arini and Guestrin, 2011]. We had two conditions, GS and MP+GS: In GS, participants were allowed to use Google Scholar [1], a search engine that indexes scholarly literature. In the second condition (MP+GS), participants were given the pre-computed metro map, and asked to pretend that they stumbled upon it; they were not instructed how to use the map. In addition to the map, the participants could access Google Scholar.

We also included two simulated conditions in the study, MP and WK: In MP, we pretended our map was the user's output, and listed all of its papers. In WK, we used references from the Wikipedia article about reinforcement learning.

We decided to compare against Wikipedia and Google Scholar since they represent two of the most popular starting points for research queries today. Other systems we considered including in the comparative analysis were either unavailable for download, or very restricted in the span of the scientific domain represented.

Before grading, we discarded data from four participants. One did not understand the task, and wrote a (nice) essay about reinforcement learning. The others, despite visiting many web pages, listed less than 5 papers when time ran out.

We had an expert judge evaluate the results of the rest of the participants. We combined all of the papers that users had entered into one list. Each entry includes the paper's information and URL. In addition, we listed the labels that the users supplied for each paper. The judge did not know the method used to find the papers.

Our expert judge scored the papers on a 3-point scale: 0 – Irrelevant, 1 – 1: Relevant, 2 – Seminal. Each label was given a 0-1 score, based on whether it was a good match to the paper. The results are summarized below.

9.1 Results and Discussion

9.1.1 *Information collection patterns*

Avg:	Pages visited	Papers listed	Visited/Listed
GS	46	12.2	4.51
MP+GS	36.3	9.75	3.79

The table shows the average number of web pages visited throughout the session, the average number of papers listed by the user, and the average ratio of pages visited to papers listed. GS users visited more pages and listed more papers on average. However, when looking at the average ratio, only one out of 4.5 pages visited by GS users was added to their list, while MP+GS added one out of 3.8. In other words, the map users were more focused: they may have visited less pages, but they found these pages satisfactory.

9.1.2 *Precision*

Users' satisfaction level is important, but the real test is the expert's opinion. The next table shows the average normalized scores given by the judge: For each user, we calculate the average paper score and average label score. Then, we average over the users in each condition:

Avg:	Normalized Score	Normalized Label Score
GS	74.2%	71.6%
MP+GS	84.5%	80.2%

Both the paper and label scores of MP+GS users are higher than the scores of GS users (the median scores exhibit similar behaviour). In addition, the average number of seminal papers discovered by GS users was 1.2 , while MP+GS users have discovered on average 1.62 seminal papers.

The simulated Wikipedia user WK did not do well: out of 15 references, only four qualified for the study (papers published after 1996), and only two were deemed relevant. In Wikipedia's defense, the other references included seminal books, which could have been useful for our hypothetical first-year student.

Finally, let us examine the map (MP) user performance. Comparing the map directly to user output is challenging as the map contained 45 papers, many more than the average user. Out of these papers, seven were deemed seminal, and 21 were deemed relevant. Interestingly, many of the papers that were deemed irrelevant were used as bridges between relevant (or seminal) papers in the map.

The finding that many of the map users did not identify the seminal papers in the map is somewhat concerning. A possible explanation may be that the users were instructed to focus on at most five lines of research, while the seminal papers were spread among more lines. Note that despite this fact, the average normalized score of MP+GS users is still higher than the score for the map. In any case, this phenomenon highlights the need for more targeted research on locating and visualizing important nodes in the map.

9.1.3 *Recall*

In addition to measuring precision (the fraction of retrieved papers that are relevant), we also tested user's *recall* (the fraction of relevant papers retrieved). It is not enough for the users to find good papers; rather, it is also important that they do not overlook important research areas.

In order to measure recall, we have composed a list of the top-10 subareas of reinforcement learning by going over conference and workshop tracks and picking the most frequent topics. Each user had to list up to five research directions; for each user, we computed the fraction of these directions that appeared in our top-10 list. GS users received an average score of 46.4%, while MP+GS users outperformed them with an average score of 73.1%.

Finally, further analysis of the snapshots taken throughout the study provides anecdotal evidence of the utility of the map. Several MP+GS users started by composing a short

[1] http://scholar.google.com

list of research directions; throughout the session, these users have progressively added papers to each direction. GS users, in contrast, did not exhibit this 'big picture' behaviour.

9.2 User Comments

After the study, we asked the map users to tell us about their experience. Below are some of their comments:

Positive:	**Negative:**
"Helpful... gave me keywords to search for" / "I noticed directions I didn't know about... Haven't heard of predictive state representations before" / "Useful way to get a basic idea of what science is up to" / "That was a great starting point" / "Easy to identify research groups... in this context, this guy is good" / "Timeline is very useful"	"Takes a while to grasp" / "For a beginner, some papers are too specific... may be more useful after I read some more" / "Legend is confusing if you do not know the topic in advance" / "Didn't necessarily understand the logic behind edges... why don't you draw words on edges?" / "It is hard to get an idea from paper title alone"

Most importantly, many participants found the map useful in making sense of the field. Some of the participants had trouble interpreting elements of the map, or felt like the map was more suited for researchers with deeper background knowledge. We found that many of the negative comments could be addressed by improvements in the design of the user interface.

10. A NOTE ON PERSONALIZATION

When we defined our coverage notion (Secion 4), the weight of each paper was set to 1. In other words, the objective was to cover as much of the corpus as possible. However, some parts of the corpus may be more important to the user than others. In order to be useful, the model must be capable of representing the user's interests.

In this section, we rely on user feedback in order to learn their preferences and adjust the maps accordingly. We use the interaction algorithm of [Shahaf et al., 2012]. This algorithm lets the user provide *feature-based feedback*. Feature-based feedback is a very natural way for specifying preferences. We show the user a tag cloud describing the papers of the map. Clicking on a word lets the user adjust its importance. For example, importance of 0.9 implies that 90% of the documents in which the word appears are interesting to the user. The relative transparency of the model allows users to make sense of feature weights.

Feature-based feedback is especially useful in the research domain, as users can employ it to indicate which authors and venues they trust. In addition, since our coverage notion is biased against newer papers (new papers did not have enough time to make a big impact), the users can indicate their preferences for new, state-of-the-art papers.

When we increase the weight of the years 2005-2008 in the reinforcement learning map, the resulting map contains chains about more recent topics, such as hierarchical reinforcement learning. When biasing for AAMAS (a conference on autonomous agents and multiagent systems), the resulting map includes a new chain about robot soccer.

In the future, it may be interesting to formulate a notion of baseline personalization, where default weights are set based on authors' *reputations*: if an author has written many high-impact papers, his new paper is likely to be important. We may also explore other notions of personalized coverage, such as [El-Arini and Guestrin, 2011; Yue and Guestrin, 2011].

11. CONCLUSIONS AND FUTURE WORK

In this paper, we have devised a method for constructing metro maps of science. Given a query, our algorithm generates a metro map: a concise structured set of research lines which maximizes coverage of salient pieces of information. Most importantly, metro maps explicitly show the relations between the research lines.

We conducted promising pilot user studies, comparing our system to two systems that dominate today's research-related queries. The results indicate that our method can help users acquire knowledge efficiently.

In the future, we plan to experiment with richer forms of input, output, and interaction models. Promising directions include edge-annotation based on citation function, notions of coverage that combine structure and content, paper-based and line-based feedback mechanisms, and the integration of higher-level semantic features. We have also created a website that allows interactive visualization of metro maps, which we hope to launch soon. We believe that metro maps hold the potential to become effective tools to help researchers cope with information overload.

Acknowledgments: This work was partially supported by ONR PECASE N000141010672, ARO MURI W911NF0810242, ONR MURI N000141010934 and NSF Career IIS-0644225. Dafna Shahaf was supported in part by Microsoft Research Graduate Fellowship. An initial version of metro maps for science was created during an internship at Microsoft Research.

References

Allan, J., Gupta, R., and Khandelwal, V. (2001). Temporal summaries of new topics. In *SIGIR '01*.

Ball, M. O. (1986). Computational complexity of network reliability analysis: An overview. *IEEE Transactions on Reliability*, 35(3):230 -239.

Bassecoulard, E. and Zitt, M. (1999). Indicators in a research institute: A multi-level classification of scientific journals. *Scientometrics*, 44(3):323–345.

Borner, K. (2010). *Atlas of Science: Visualizing What We Know*. MIT Press.

Boyack, K., Börner, K., and Klavans, R. (2009). Mapping the structure and evolution of chemistry research. *Scientometrics*, 79:45–60.

Chekuri, C. and Pal, M. (2005). A recursive greedy algorithm for walks in directed graphs. In *FOCS '05*.

Chen, C. (2004). Searching for intellectual turning points: Progressive knowledge domain visualization. *PNAS*, 101(Suppl 1):5303–5310.

Dunne, C., Shneiderman, B., Dorr, B., and Klavans, J. (2010). iopener workbench: tools for rapid understanding of scientific literature. In *Proc. 27th Annual Human-Computer Interaction Lab Symposium*.

El-Arini, K. and Guestrin, C. (2011). Beyond keyword search: Discovering relevant scientific literature. In *KDD' 11*.

Nesbitt, K. (2004). Getting to more abstract places using the metro map metaphor. In *Information Visualisation '04*.

Shahaf, D. and Guestrin, C. (2010). Connecting the dots between news articles. In *KDD '10*.

Shahaf, D., Guestrin, C., and Horvitz, E. (2012). Trains of thought: Generating information maps. In *WWW '12*.

Swan, R. and Jensen, D. (2000). TimeMines: Constructing Timelines with Statistical Models of Word Usage. In *KDD' 00*.

Yan, R., Wan, X., Otterbacher, J., Kong, L., Li, X., and Zhang, Y. (2011). Evolutionary timeline summarization: a balanced optimization framework via iterative substitution. In *SIGIR' 11*.

Yue, Y. and Guestrin, C. (2011). Linear submodular bandits and their application to diversified retrieval. In *NIPS' 11*.

Active Sampling for Entity Matching

Kedar Bellare
Yahoo! Research
701 First Ave
Sunnyvale, CA 94089
kedar.bellare@gmail.com

Suresh Iyengar
Yahoo! Labs
EGL Business Park
Bangalore, India 560071
supartha@yahoo-inc.com

Aditya Parameswaran
Stanford University
353 Serra Mall
Stanford, CA 94305
adityagp@cs.stanford.edu

Vibhor Rastogi
Yahoo! Research
701 First Ave
Sunnyvale, CA 94089
vibhor.rastogi@gmail.com

ABSTRACT

In entity matching, a fundamental issue while training a classifier to label pairs of entities as either duplicates or non-duplicates is the one of selecting informative training examples. Although active learning presents an attractive solution to this problem, previous approaches minimize the misclassification rate (0-1 loss) of the classifier, which is an unsuitable metric for entity matching due to class imbalance (i.e., many more non-duplicate pairs than duplicate pairs). To address this, a recent paper [1] proposes to maximize recall of the classifier under the constraint that its precision should be greater than a specified threshold. However, the proposed technique requires the labels of all n input pairs in the worst-case.

Our main result is an active learning algorithm that approximately maximizes recall of the classifier while respecting a precision constraint with provably sub-linear label complexity (under certain distributional assumptions). Our algorithm uses as a black-box any active learning module that minimizes 0-1 loss. We show that label complexity of our algorithm is at most $\log n$ times the label complexity of the black-box, and also bound the difference in the recall of classifier learnt by our algorithm and the recall of the optimal classifier satisfying the precision constraint. We provide an empirical evaluation of our algorithm on several real-world matching data sets that demonstrates the effectiveness of our approach.

Categories and Subject Descriptors

H.2.8 [**Information Systems**]: Database Management—*Database Applications*[Data Mining]; H.3.3 [**Information Systems**]: Information Storage and Retrieval—*Information Search and Retrieval*[Clustering]

Keywords

entity matching, deduplication, active learning, imbalanced data

KDD'12, August 12–16, 2012, Beijing, China.

1. INTRODUCTION

Entity Matching (EM) is the problem of determining if two entities in a data set refer to the same real-world object. Entity matching is a complex and ubiquitous problem that appears in numerous application domains (including image processing, information extraction and integration, and natural language processing), often under different terminology (e.g., coreference resolution, record linkage, and deduplication [14]).

Machine learning approaches [31, 8, 6] for entity matching often learn a classifier over pairs of entities labeling them as duplicate or non-duplicate. The classifier is built over models such as SVM or logistic regression, using features like string similarity. The models are trained over labeled example pairs, which are usually costly to obtain. Active learning techniques [13, 19, 2, 16, 5, 4] are therefore used to carefully select the examples to label while learning a good classifier — one that minimizes the 0-1 loss. These algorithms provide label complexity guarantees, i.e., guarantees on the number of labeled examples required to learn the classifier.

In entity matching, the number of duplicate pairs is typically small, $o(m)$, for a dataset of m entities. On the other hand, the total number of pairs including non-duplicates can be $\Theta(m^2)$. While blocking techniques [30, 22] are used to reduce the number of pairs considered for entity matching from $\Theta(m^2)$ to a more manageable number, denoted n, the non-duplicates still vastly outnumber the duplicate pairs, often by a ratio of 100 to 1, as evident in many benchmark entity matching datasets. In such cases, minimizing 0-1 loss is insufficient: a classifier that labels all pairs as non-duplicates has a small 0-1 loss of less than 1%. Thus even this extremely poor classifier is considered good under 0-1 loss.

To address this, a recent paper [1] considers precision and recall[1] of the classifier as the objective functions. Precision in entity matching is the fraction of pairs labeled as duplicates that are true duplicates, and recall is the fraction of true duplicates labeled as duplicates. So the classifier that labels all pairs as non-duplicates, labels no true duplicates as duplicates, and has a recall of 0. Thus the classifier is correctly considered poor under the recall metric.

Arasu et al. [1] provide an active learning algorithm to maximize recall under a constraint that precision should be greater than a specified threshold. The algorithm makes a monotonicity assumption on the precision and recall of the classifier over its parameter space. The algorithm then

[1]That work actually considers an approximation of recall metric, but we ignore this distinction for now.

searches for the optimal classifier essentially through a binary search over classifiers in the high-dimensional parameter space. Due to this high-dimensional binary search, the algorithm has high label complexity (i.e., many labeled examples requested) and high computational complexity, and in the worst-case requires the labels of all n input pairs. Furthermore, the monotonicity assumption does not usually hold in practice, and while the algorithm still returns a feasible classifier satisfying the precision constraint, its recall is often poor.

In this paper, we propose an active learning algorithm for optimizing recall under the precision constraint, using as a black-box any active learning approach that minimizes 0-1 loss. We first use a Langrange multiplier to cast the precision constrained recall optimization problem into an unconstrained one with an objective that is a linear combination of precision and recall. For a fixed value of the Langrange multipier, the linear objective can be optimized using the given black-box. Then we search for the right value of the Langrange multiplier. For this we embed all classifiers in a two dimensional space, and perform a search along the convex hull [24] of the embedded classifiers.

A major challenge in our work is to ensure that the search over the embedded classifiers is efficient, and we show that via discretization techniques, we are able to achieve a rather low number of worst-case $O(\log^2 n)$ calls to the black-box. We also show that additional calls would not help: our output classifier is guaranteed to be the best one that can be found using any number of calls to the black-box. By comparison, [1] has exponential (in the number of dimensions) worst-case computational complexity.

While the classifier output by our algorithm need not be optimal in terms of its recall, we show that it is pareto-optimal (i.e., no other classifier dominates it in both recall and precision). We also provide additional guarantees on how close our output classifier is to the optimal by showing that they lie on the same edge of the convex hull of the embedded classifiers, and coincide in case the optimal is a vertex point.

Contributions and Outline:

- Our main result is an active learning algorithm that approximately maximizes recall of the classifier under the precision constraint using as a black-box any active learning approach that minimizes 0-1 loss. We show that label complexity of our algorithm is at most $O(\log^2 n)$ times the label complexity of the black-box. We also show that the classifier learnt by our algorithm is pareto-optimal, and close to the true optimal in terms of recall.
- We use the IWAL active learning algorithm [5] as the black-box for 0-1 loss minimization. IWAL has been shown to have a sublinear label complexity under certain low noise assumptions. Since our algorithm has a label complexity of at most $O(\log^2 n)$ times than that of IWAL, it also has sublinear label complexity under the same low noise assumptions. To our knowledge, this is the first active learning algorithm with sublinear label complexity for optimizing the precision-constrained recall objective.
- We provide an empirical evaluation of our algorithm on several real-world matching data sets and compare it with the technique in [1]. We show that our algorithm achieves better quality over these datasets while significantly reducing label and computational complexity.

We present background on active learning in Sec. 2, followed by our approach in Sec. 3. We then discuss experimental evaluation in Sec. 5 and conclude in Sec. 6.

2. BACKGROUND

In this section, we define the notation and setup the problem formally. We also briefly review the important active learning techniques.

2.1 Notation

Let E be the set of all entities for the matching task, and m be the size of E. We assume that the set of all candidate entity pairs to be matched from E has been generated (say by some blocking technique) and denote it as C. We denote $n = |C|$ be the number of candidate pairs. For a pair of entities (e_1, e_2), we assume that a d-dimensional feature vector $x = (x_1, x_2, \ldots, x_d)$ represents the similarity between entity e_1 and e_2, and let X be the set of all feature vectors corresponding to pairs in C. We say that the label of $x \in X$, denoted $y(x)$, is 1 if x corresponds to a duplicate pair, and -1 otherwise. In this paper, we consider linear classifiers defined as follows.

DEFINITION 2.1. *A linear classifier h is represented by a d-dimensional vector $w = (w_1, \ldots, w_d)$. h classifies a feature vector x as positive, i.e. $h(x) = 1$ if $w.x \geq 0$ and negative, i.e. $h(x) = -1$, otherwise.*

We let H be the set of all linear classifiers. For any classifier $h \in H$, we define number of false positives, false negatives, true positives as the following:

$$fp(h) = \sum_{x \in X} \mathbf{1}(h(x) = 1 \wedge y(x) = -1)$$

$$fn(h) = \sum_{x \in X} \mathbf{1}(h(x) = -1 \wedge y(x) = 1)$$

$$tp(h) = \sum_{x \in X} \mathbf{1}(h(x) = 1 \wedge y(x) = 1)$$

The precision and recall of a classifier are then defined as $\text{precison}(h) = \frac{tp(h)}{tp(h)+fp(h)}$ and $\text{recall}(h) = \frac{tp(h)}{tp(h)+fn(h)}$.

Problem. We wish to maximize recall under the precision constraint. Formally, this is stated as below.

PROBLEM 1 (RECALL). *Given $\tau \in [0, 1]$, find $h \in H$ to*

$$\textbf{maximize} \quad \textit{recall}(h)$$
$$\textbf{subject to} \quad \textit{precison}(h) \geq \tau$$

The RECALL problem is difficult to solve because recall(h) and precison(h) are complex functions of h.

2.2 Active Learning

Now we briefly review the main problems and techniques in active learning.

Problems. In active learning, the focus has primarily been to solve the problem of minimizing 0-1-loss. We call this problem as the 01-Loss problem. The goal of the problem[2] is to minimize the total number of false negatives and false positives. We state it below.

Problem 2 (01-Loss). *Find $h \in H$ to*

$$\textbf{minimize} \ \frac{fn(h) + fp(h)}{n}$$

A slight generalization of the problem considers a weighted loss function in which false negatives and false positives have different penalties. We denote the problem as 01-LossWeighted and define it below.

Problem 3 (01-LossWeighted). *Given $\alpha \in [0, 1]$, find $h \in H$ to*

$$\textbf{minimize} \ \frac{\alpha fn(h) + (1-\alpha) fp(h)}{n}$$

Techniques. One of the first active learning algorithms was given in [10]. The algorithm solves the 01-Loss problem for *separable* datasets – datasets for which a classifier exists having 0 empirical 0-1 loss. The paper showed that a good classifier can be learnt for separable datasets using only $O(\log n)$ labeled examples. The algorithm was based on the idea of selective sampling: each example point is queried with a probability, computed based on the point and previously labeled examples.

Since [10], several approaches have been proposed to handle non-separable datasets. Most recently, IWAL [5] proposed an efficient active learning algorithm having sublinear label complexity under some distributional assumptions. The algorithm is again based on selective sampling, and assigns a probability of querying an example based on the disagreement between two classifiers, each learnt on all previously labeled examples, but differing in the labels for the example of interest. The algorithm guarantees the following properties.

Theorem 2.2 (IWAL [5]). *IWAL approximately minimizes 01-loss using $O(error(h^*)n\theta + \sqrt{n}\log n\theta)$ labeled examples, where $error(h^*)$ is the 01-loss of the optimal classifier, and θ, the disagreement coefficient [16], is a parameter depending on the source distribution and the hypothesis class, but independent of the number of points n.*

Under certain distributional assumptions [5], θ is a small constant and $error(h^*) = o(1)$. Thus the label complexity is provably sublinear under those assumptions.

3. OUR LEARNING ALGORITHMS

In this section, we describe our approach to solve the Recall problem given a black-box to solve the 01-Loss problem. We use two algorithms: (i) ConvexHull algorithm that approximately solves Recall using a solution for the 01-LossWeighted problem, and (ii) RejectionSampling algorithm that reduces an instance of 01-LossWeighted problem into that of the 01-Loss problem. We describe each of the algorithms below. But we first begin by slightly generalizing the Recall problem.

[2]Learning literature considers a more difficult version of 01-Loss problem when the examples come from an unknown distribution, here we consider the simpler problem using the empirical distribution, for which the same techniques apply.

Problem Generalization: The Recall problem maximizes recall under the precision constraint. Maximizing recall(h) of a classifier h is equivalent to minimizing the fraction of false negatives, $fn(h)/n$. (Note that $tp(h) + fn(h)$ is a constant independent of h.) Instead of just minimizing this fraction, we consider here a more general problem that minimizes a linear combination of false negatives and false positives, $\frac{\alpha fn(h)+(1-\alpha)fp(h)}{n}$, under the precision constraint.

Further, the constraint on precision can be transformed into a simpler one. Denoting $\epsilon = (1-\tau)/\tau$, we can write.

$$\frac{tp(h)}{tp(h) + fp(h)} \geq \tau \equiv \epsilon \cdot tp(h) - fp(h) \geq 0$$

This gives us a generalized version of the Recall problem that we call as RecallWeighted.

Problem 4 (RecallWeighted). *Given $\alpha \in [0, 1]$ and $\epsilon \in [0, \infty)$, find $h \in H$ to*

$$\begin{array}{ll} \textbf{minimize} & \frac{\alpha fn(h)+(1-\alpha)fp(h)}{n} \\ \textbf{subject to} & \epsilon \cdot tp(h) - fp(h) \geq 0 \end{array}$$

Note that for $\alpha = 1$, the solution for RecallWeighted problem is same as that of Recall problem.

3.1 The ConvexHull Algorithm

Now we describe the ConvexHull algorithm that approximately solves the RecallWeighted problem by repeatedly solving the 01-LossWeighted problem. Note that the objective of both problems is the same, but RecallWeighted has an additional precision constraint. The ConvexHull algorithm essentially removes the constraint using a trick similar to Lagrange multipliers. We describe this below.

Embedding. We embed a classifier h as a point in two dimensional space with the first coordinate equal to negative of the objective and the second to the slack of the precision constraint, as shown below.

$$X(h) = \frac{-(\alpha fn(h) + (1-\alpha)fp(h))}{n} \quad (1)$$

$$Y(h) = \frac{\epsilon \cdot tp(h) - fp(h)}{n} \quad (2)$$

Thus, the RecallWeighted problem is equivalent to finding a classifier h that has the highest $X(h)$ under the constraint that $Y(h) \geq 0$. Note also that finding a classifier h that maximizes $X(h) + \lambda Y(h)$ for a given λ can be shown to be equivalent to the 01-LossWeighted problem (with appropriate α).

Let $P = \{(X(h), Y(h)) : h \in H\}$ be the set of all two-dimensional embeddings of all possible linear classifiers. While P need not be a convex set, we denote C to be the convex hull polytope of points in P and say a classifier h lies on C if $(X(h), Y(h))$ lies on an edge of C. Any classifier h lying on C is pareto-optimal: no other classifier h' exists that has both $-X(h')$ (i.e. objective) as well as $Y(h')$ (i.e. precision) better than h. We will show that ConvexHull algorithm returns classifiers on the convex hull. (Hence the name.)

Even though the set of all linear classifiers H is exponentially large in the number of dimensions, the size of P is bounded by $O(n^3)$, since many classifiers embed to the same point in P. To see this, note that embedded coordinates $X(h)$ and $Y(h)$ are functions of $fn(h)$, $fp(h)$, and $tp(h)$, each of which can vary from 0 to n.

Input: A set of n pairs X,
Black-box $B(\lambda)$ returning h with max $X(h) + \lambda Y(h)$
Output: Approximate solution for $RecallWeighted$
Compute sorted list Λ of all values λ, s.t. $-1/\lambda$ is a line slope in the embedded space.
Set $min = 0, max = |\Lambda|$.
while $min < max$ **do**
  Set $mid = (min + max)/2$
  Set λ to be $\Lambda[mid]$
  $h = B(\lambda)$
  if $Y(h) \geq 0$ set $max = mid$, else set $min = mid$
end while
return h

Algorithm 1: ConvexHull Algorithm

Since H is exponentially large, and P much smaller, we perform our search for optimal classifier in the embedded space. For the search, we define S the set of all possible slopes of lines joining any two points in P, and Λ a sorted array of all possible values λ where $-1/\lambda$ is a slope in S. The slopes in S have the form $\frac{Y(h')-Y(h)}{X(h')-X(h)}$, and it is easy to show that both S and Λ have at most $O(n^3)$ distinct values.

The ConvexHull Algorithm. For the algorithm, we assume a black-box B for the 01-LossWeighted problem that takes a λ and returns a h maximizing $X(h) + \lambda Y(h)$. The algorithm, shown in Algorithm 1, essentially does a binary search over values in Λ. Starting from the two extreme elements $\Lambda[min], \Lambda[max]$, the algorithm repeatedly picks their midpoint $\lambda = \Lambda[(max+min)/2]$, and then computes a classifier h maximizing $X(h) + \lambda Y(h)$ using the black-box B. Depending on whether $Y(h) \geq 0$ or not, the intervals are updated to ensure that we always have at least one extreme point that satisfies feasibility requirement $Y(h) \geq 0$. Finally the algorithm terminates with a feasible solution, i.e. a classifier h with $Y(h) \geq 0$. We can show following additional properties of the algorithm.

Theorem 3.1 (Complexity of ConvexHull). *The* ConvexHull *algorithm terminates with a feasible classifier (i.e. classifier satisfying the precision constraint) with label complexity at most* $3 \log n$ *times that of black-box B used in the algorithm.*

Proof. Since size of Λ is bounded by $O(n^3)$, the binary search procedure finishes in at most $3 \log n$ iterations. This immediately gives the required label and computational complexity bounds for the algorithm. The feasibility of the solution is guaranteed as a result of the binary search as long as one classifier h exists with $Y(h) \geq 0$, i.e satisfies the precision constraint. This is always true, for a linear classifier labeling all points as negative. □

On the optimality of the solution: In general, the solution returned by the ConvexHull algorithm need not be optimal. Recall the set C, the convex hull polytope of embedded points. Each classifier on C is pareto-optimal: i.e. no other classifier dominates it on both the value of objective and precision. The optimal classifer is guaranteed to lie on the convex hull, while the algorithm can return some other point on the same edge. Many times the two coincide, and the algorithm does return the optimal classifier. We state this result formally below.

Theorem 3.2. *The optimal solution lies on the convex hull C. The* ConvexHull *algorithm returns a classifier on the same edge of the convex hull. If the optimal is a vertex point of C, then the algorithm returns the optimal solution.*

Proof. First note that any pareto-optimal classifier lies on the convex hull. If not, then extending the line $Y = X$ from the point towards the convex hull results in a classifier dominating it in both objective value as well as precision. Since optimal is also pareto-optimal, it has to lie on the convex hull.

Next we show that the black-box $B(\lambda)$ also returns a h on the convex hull C. Assume the contrary, and suppose it returns a classifier h not on the convex hull. Then for h, there is a point on an edge AB of the convex hull that strictly dominates it in terms of both objective value and precision. Then one of the two vertices, either A or B, has as good or better $X + \lambda Y$ value, contradicting the assumption.

Furthermore, we show that $h = B(\lambda)$ lies on an edge AB, then its slope has to be $-1/\lambda$. This follows directly from linearity of the objective function $X + \lambda Y$. Thus our black box function gives us, for each λ, either a vertex of the convex hull, or a point on the line of the convex hull that has slope $-1/\lambda$. Let λ_0 be the smallest λ for which $h = B(\lambda)$ is feasible, i.e. $Y(h) \geq 0$. If $-1/\lambda_0$ is a slope whose value lies between slopes of two existing edges in the convex hull, then the binary search of the ConvexHull algorithm would give the vertex corresponding to λ_0. Furthermore, that vertex will be optimal. If $-1/\lambda_0$ is the slope of one of the edges (say AB) of the convex hull, then the binary search find λ_0 and $B(\lambda_0)$ will return a point on AB. Also the optimal will be on the same edge. □

On the efficiency of the algorithm: As stated, Algorithm 1 needs to explicitly construct the sorted list Λ that can have $O(n^3)$ elements. Thus the overall time complexity of the algorithm is $O(n^3) + 3 \log n \cdot T(B)$: $O(n^3)$ during construction of Λ and $3 \log n \cdot T(B)$ during active learning, where $T(B)$ is the time complexity of black-box B used in the algorithm.

Note that the $O(n^3)$ term might make the algorithm infeasible for large datasets. We now show how to eliminate the explicit construction of Λ, when α and ϵ are restricted to fractions of fixed bit length b (thus encompassing representation of floats in modern computer processors.) Our approach is to design a $\Lambda' \supseteq \Lambda$ whose constituent values are equally spaced apart (at a discretization factor γ). We may then simply do a binary search over the integral multiples of γ and avoid explicit enumeration of Λ'.

Since α and ϵ are fractions of bit length at most b, we can show using Equations 1 and 2 that numerators of $X(h)$ and $Y(h)$ are an integral multiple of $1/2^b$. Now, consider the smallest difference between two slopes in Λ. Let r/s and t/u be two slopes. We have: $r/s - t/u = (ru - ts)/su$. First, the smallest non-negative value of $ru - ts$ can be shown to be $1/(2^{2b}n^2)$. Second, the value of su is at most 1. Thus, the smallest difference between slopes is $1/(2^{2b}n^2)$. We use this value as our discretization factor γ. The largest value of $\lambda \in \Lambda$ is $O(n^3)$, and thus, the new size of Λ' is $O(n^3)/\gamma = O(n^5 2^{2b})$. Now, since Λ' contains all values from 0 to n^3 in multiples of $1/(2^{2b}n^2)$, we may perform binary search without explicitly enumerating the values in Λ'. Thus, the overall time complexity is $(5 \log n + 2b \log 2) \cdot T(B)$.

Input: A set of n points X,
A black-box B for 01-LOSS problem
Output: A solution for 01-LOSSWEIGHTED problem
Let $\bar{x} = (), \bar{y} = ()$ be empty sequences.
for each point x in X **do**
  If $B(\bar{x}, \bar{y}, x) =$ FALSE, continue to next point.
  Otherwise, query the point x. Let y be its label
  Toss a coin with success probability α if $y = 1$ and $1 - \alpha$ if $y = -1$
  If the coin returns failure, continue to next point
  Otherwise, add x and y to $\bar{x}$ and $\bar{y}$ respectively.
end for
return $B_h(\bar{x}, \bar{y})$

Algorithm 2: REJECTIONSAMPLING Algorithm

3.2 The REJECTIONSAMPLING Algorithm

In this section we describe the REJECTIONSAMPLING algorithm that reduces the 01-LOSSWEIGHTED problem into an instance of 01-LOSS problem. Recall that the difference in the two problems is that while the former minimizes any linear combination, $\frac{\alpha fn(h)+(1-\alpha)fp(h)}{n}$, of the false negatives and false positives, the latter only minimizes their sum. Both the problems are however unconstrained. Our algorithm is very similar to idea of rejection sampling used for transforming cost-sensitive binary classification into the standard setting [32, 23]. Our analysis is slightly different as we use empirical loss functions rather than distribution ones.

Black-box: We assume a black-box B for solving the 01-LOSS problem. We further assume that B reads all input points one by one, maintaining some internal state as it is reading the points, which it uses to determine whether or not to ask the label for the next point. We model this behavior as follows: B accepts as input a sequence of points $\bar{x} = x_1, \ldots, x_k$ along with their labels $\bar{y} = y_1, \ldots, y_k$, and a new point x, and returns *true* or *false* indicating whether or not to query the label for this point. Once all points have been considered, a function B_h accepts all the points $\bar{x}$ for which labels were asked, along with all their labels $\bar{y}$, and returns the classifier h minimizing 01-loss. Note that the label complexity of the black-box is exactly the size of sequence $\bar{x}$, since those are points that the black-box decided to query.

Since the 01-LOSSWEIGHTED problem has a penalty α for false negative and $1 - \alpha$ for false positive, one can use B for solving the 01-LOSSWEIGHTED problem if the distribution of false negatives and false positives is changed appropriately. This can be done simply by rejecting a positive point with probability $1 - \alpha$ and a negative point with probability α. However, given just a point we do not know its label, and thus cannot decide its rejection probability. To overcome this we query B to check whether or not query the point's label, and if it returns *true*, we use the label to set the rejection probability. This procedure works, but since we are rejecting even labeled points, the label complexity takes a hit.

The algorithm formally corresponding to the above intuition is defined in Algorithm 2. It begins with empty sequences $\bar{x}$, $\bar{y}$ for points and their labels. It then repeatedly picks a new point, and uses the black-box to determine whether or not to query the point's label. The black-box is provided all points $\bar{x}$ and their labels $\bar{y}$. If the black-box decides not to query the point, it is ignored and the algorithm moves to the next point. Otherwise, the points label is determined, and used to determine the rejection probability. If the point is rejected, then it is ignored even though its label has already been queried. Otherwise, the point is added to the sequence of labeled points $\bar{x}$. Finally, the black-box is fed all the labeled points in $\bar{x}$ and their labels, and the returned classifier is output.

Since REJECTIONSAMPLING algorithm is randomized, we can only show probability bounds on its optimality and label complexity. The following theorem shows that w.h.p the objective value of the returned classifier is within $O(1/\sqrt{n})$ away from the optimal. Additionally, it shows that label complexity is bounded in expectation. The same label complexity bound can be shown to hold w.h.p.

THEOREM 3.3. *Let h_{rs} be solution returned by the REJECTIONSAMPLING algorithm. Then with probability at least $1 - \delta$, the difference in the objective value of h_{rs} and the optimal is at most $O(\sqrt{\log \delta / n})$. Furthermore, the expected label complexity of the algorithm is at most $max(\frac{\alpha}{1-\alpha}, \frac{1-\alpha}{\alpha})$ times the label complexity of the black-box B for the 01-LOSS problem.*

PROOF. Denote $FN(h), FP(h)$ the set of false negatives and false positives for a classifier h. Since some false positives and false negatives are rejected in a random run of the REJECTIONSAMPLING algorithm, denote for a point x, $r(x)$ the random variable equal to 1 if x is selected in REJECTIONSAMPLING, and 0 if it is rejected.

The black-box B essentially minimizes the objective $Obj(h)$ equal to $\sum_{x:FN(h)} r(x)/n + \sum_{x':FP(h)} r(x')/n$. Also expectation $E(h)$ of $Obj(h)$ over the coin tosses of the algorithm is simply $\frac{\alpha fn(h)+(1-\alpha)fp(h)}{n}$, which is the right objective for the 01-LOSSWEIGHTED problem. Using Hoeffding, we can say that w.p. $1 - \delta$, $Obj(h)$ deviates from its expectation $E(h)$, by at most $O(\sqrt{\log \delta / n})$.

This shows that If h^* is an optimal classifier for the 01-LOSSWEIGHTED problem, w.p. $1 - \delta$, $|Obj(h^*) - E(Obj(h^*)|$ is bounded by $O(\sqrt{\log \delta / n})$. Similarly, w.p. $1 - \delta$, $|Obj(h_{rs}) - E(Obj(h_{rs})|$ is bounded by $O(\sqrt{\log \delta / n})$. Now we know that since the black-box returned h_{rs}, $Obj(h_{rs}) \leq Obj(h^*)$. Since h^* is optimal for the 01-LOSSWEIGHTED problem, and $E(h*)$ the objective for the same, we know $E(h*) \leq E(h_{rs})$. This shows that difference in $Obj(h_{rs})$ and $E(h*)$ is no more than $O(\sqrt{\log \delta / n})$. Hence proved.

The proof of expected label complexity follows directly from the expected number of labeled examples rejected by the REJECTIONSAMPLING algorithm. □

3.3 Overall Approach

Now we describe our overall approach. We do not introduce new techniques here, but explain and analyze how the various algorithms are run together. We begin by running the CONVEXHULL algorithm for solving the RECALL problem. During its run, CONVEXHULL might make calls to its black-box for solving the 01-LOSSWEIGHTED problem. Whenever a call is made, we invoke a run of the REJECTIONSAMPLING algorithm. When that in turn makes a call to its black-box for solving the 01-LOSS problem, we invoke a run of the IWAL algorithm [5]. We describe this process in detail below. We also compute the label complexity of the overall process.

Run of ConvexHull **algorithm:** We use ConvexHull algorithm to solve an instance of the RecallWeighted problem with $\alpha = 1 - 1/\log n$. Note that the objective that we are optimizing is then $\frac{(1-1/\log n)fn(h)+1/\log n fp(h)}{n}$, instead of $\frac{fn(n)}{n}$ that we need to do for solving the Recall problem. However, since $\alpha = 1 - 1/\log n$ is very close to 1, the two objectives can be shown to be at most $1/\log n$ away from each other. Thus an approximate solution for RecallWeighted for this α is a good approximate solution for the Recall problem. Here we solved RecallWeighted instead of Recall to ensure bounded labeled complexity when running the RejectionSampling algorithm, which we discuss next.

Run of RejectionSampling **algorithm:** During the above run of ConvexHull algorithm, whenever a call to the black-box for solving the 01-LossWeighted problem is made, we invoke the RejectionSampling algorithm. Note that the objective for the 01-LossWeighted problem is given by $X(h) + \lambda Y(h)$, which expands to

$$\frac{(1 - 1/\log n + \epsilon\lambda)fnh + (1/\log n + \lambda)fp(h)}{n}$$

Thus RejectionSampling algorithm solves an instance of 01-LossWeighted problem with

$$\alpha' = \frac{1 - 1/\log n + \epsilon\lambda}{1 + (1+\epsilon)\lambda}$$

This α' determines the rejection probabilities and the label complexity of the RejectionSampling algorithm. Finally, when the run is complete, we return the output classifier to the ConvexHull algorithm

Run of IWAL algorithm [5]: During the above run of RejectionSampling algorithm, whenever a call to the black-box for solving the 01-Loss problem is made, we invoke the IWAL algorithm, which is described in detail in [5]. We only use it as a black-box here, and return its output to the RejectionSampling algorithm.

Now we reason about the total number of examples that are queried in the above process.

Theorem 3.4 (Overall label complexity). *The label complexity of our overall approach is at most $O(\log^2 n)$ times that of the IWAL algorithm. Since IWAL algorithm has a label complexity of $O(error(h^*)n\theta + \sqrt{n \log n\theta})$, the overall label complexity is $O(2\log^2 n\left[error(h^*)n\theta + \sqrt{n\log n\theta}\right])$. Under certain distributional assumptions [5], this label complexity is sublinear.*

Proof. From theorem 3.1, the label complexity of ConvexHull is $2\log n$ times that of the black-box RejectionSampling used in the algorithm. Further, since

$$\alpha' = \frac{1 - 1/\log n + \epsilon\lambda}{1 + (1+\epsilon)\lambda} \text{ and } 1 - \alpha' = \frac{1/\log n + \lambda}{1 + (1+\epsilon)\lambda},$$

we can show that

$$max(1/\alpha', 1/(1-\alpha') \leq max(\log n, \frac{\epsilon}{1+\epsilon}, \frac{1}{1+\epsilon})$$

Since ϵ is a constant independent of n, $max(1/\alpha', 1/(1-\alpha'))$ is $O(\log n)$. Thus from Theorem 3.3, the label complexity of RejectionSampling is at most $O(\log n)$ times the label complexity of the black-box IWAL used. Finally, since the IWAL complexity is $O(error(h^*)n\theta + \sqrt{n \log n\theta})$ as shown in Theorem 2.2, we get the required result. □

4. RELATED WORK

The work related to us can be placed under three categories. We describe each of them in turn.

Entity Matching. Many techniques have been proposed for the entity matching problem [14, 21]. The ones most relevant to us are learning-based techniques that train a classifier over labeled pairs of examples. These include naive bayes [31], decision trees [8], SVMs [6]. All of these techniques are fully supervised, i.e., they do not try to reduce the label complexity by choosing the pairs whose labels to request. To reduce the number of labeled examples, [20] describes an algorithm that uses a heuristic string similarity function and then samples pairs having varied similarity scores. The algorithm cannot directly be applied for active learning as it is only for training data selection, but can in fact be used in conjunction with our active learning algorithm as a preprocessing step to select the pool of candidate pairs. Another training set construction method for deduplication is the described in [7]. The training examples selected by this approach are a mixture of examples with high textual similarity and randomly sampled examples. In contrast to this static approach, our active learning algorithm is more dynamic and systematically explores the example space while also providing guarantees on precision.

Active learning for entity matching. Several authors have previously studied the application of active learning to entity deduplication problems [9, 25, 26, 28]. However, these approaches do not provide any guarantees in terms of precision or recall, which is undesirable for datasets with highly imbalanced classes.

The previous work most similar to ours is [4], which also provides an active learning algorithm to maximize recall under a constraint that precision should be greater than a specified threshold. Their algorithm essentially performs a binary search in the high-dimensional parameter space by assuming monotonicity in precision with respect to parameters. In the worst-case the algorithm queries the labels of all the examples and its computational complexity is exponential in the number of parameters. Our approach, in contrast, provides guarantees on precision while being computationally and label efficient. In addition, it does not require a monotonicity assumption which may not hold in general and therefore can be applied to other imbalanced classification problems.

Active learning for general classification. Our method is also related to active learning for classification tasks. There is a large and growing body of work [27] on active learning for binary classification. A good summary of recent theoretical work in the area is provided in [13]. However, almost all related work on active learning for the general binary classification problem focuses on 0-1 loss minimization. We described two such related works in Section 2. In our work, we use IWAL [5] as a black-box active learner for 0-1 loss.

To our knowledge, [4] is the only active learning algorithm that minimizes general loss functions in addition to 0-1 loss. However, the algorithm cannot perform constrained optimization required for ensuring our precision constraint. Furthermore, no direct efficient implementation of algorithm is known for the class of linear classifiers. Previous approaches [2, 12, 16] also require maintaining a candidate set of hypotheses (called a version space), which is computationally infeasible. Recent agnostic active learning approaches, which our algorithm builds upon, achieve sub-linear label complexity [2, 4, 5, 16] when assumptions are made about low label noise in the data distribution. It is also known that under unbounded noise models, sub-linear label complexity is impossible [3, 17]. An exponential improvement in label complexity for unbounded noise was shown recently but it assumes that data has multiple views [29].

The majority of active learning research has focused on querying the most informative examples needed to learn the classifier. More recent papers have also considered querying representative examples [11], and querying examples that are both representative and informative [18].

5. EXPERIMENTS

In this section, we describe our experimental setup (Section 5.1) and present results comparing our approach against a previous state-of-the-art algorithm [1] on several real-world datasets (Section 5.2).

5.1 Setup

5.1.1 Data Sets

A brief description of the four real-world datasets used in our experiments is shown in Table 1. These include:

- Business: This is a dataset of local business listings used in the production system at Yahoo!. Each listing contain attributes like name, street, phone, etc. of the business. A set of labeled pairs is obtained as follows: we tokenize the name and street attributes into sets of k-grams. We then do blocking using a combination of prefix-filtering and min-hash to select pairs of entities that have a Jaccard overlap of more than 0.2 on the set of k-grams for either name or street attributes. Then using a heuristic matching function that gives a score to each pair, we select pairs having varied values for the scores, similar to the technique in [20]. Finally, the selected pairs are judged by human editors to generate a dataset of 3958 labeled pairs.
- Person: This is a record linkage dataset from the UCI machine learning repository [15]. It contains 574,913 pairs for which features have been computed and labels have been provided.
- DBLP-ACM [20]: This is a large bibliography record linkage task in which 494,437 matching records in dblp and acm have been manually labeled as either duplicates or non-duplicates.
- Scholar-DBLP [20]: This is a dataset of 589,326 pairs similar to dblp-acm. It however includes automatically extracted records from google scholar, which cause data quality problems and make matching harder.

The last three datasets are highly imbalanced.

5.1.2 Algorithms

We implement three algorithms for active learning.

- MONOTONE: This is our implementation of the algorithm described in [1]. The precision evaluations required for the algorithm is done over random samples of size 100. To ensure that the same examples be sampled for each precision evaluation whenever possible, a random permutation is chosen and fixed. Then each random sample is generated by selecting the first 100 applicable examples from this permutation.
- VW: This is an implementation of the IWAL algorithm [5] obtained from the open source Vowpal Wabbit [19]. The algorithm uses stochastic gradient descent to learn a linear classifier. The 01-loss is approximated as squared-loss for efficient implementation.
- CVHULL: This is an implementation of both CONVEXHULL and REJECTIONSAMPLING algorithms on top of IWAL as described in Sec. 3.3. Whenever CONVEXHULL calls its black-box, an implementation of REJECTIONSAMPLING is invoked. When REJECTIONSAMPLING calls for its black-box, VW is invoked. The VW algorithm reads examples one at a time, which we feed to the algorithm in a randomly chosen order kept fixed across its different invokation. The precision constraint check required in CONVEXHULL is implemented by a precision evaluation of over random samples of size 100, generated in the same manner as in MONOTONE.

Note that all of our datasets consist of labeled examples. The active learning algorithms are run on the datasets as follows: as the active learning algorithm reads the examples the labels are kept hidden. Whenever the algorithm requires a label for a specific example, its label is read from the dataset and given to the algorithm. This cuts out the need for a human involvement of labeling during our experiments.

5.2 Results

In Fig. 1, we report the F-1 achieved by MONOTONE and CVHULL on all datasets, as the threshold used for the precision constraint is varied. We do not report the F-1 for VW, since it returns classifier that often violates the precision constraint. The graphs show than CVHULL has consistently higher F-1 that MONOTONE over all datasets and precision thresholds. The difference in F-1 between the two algorithms is as big as 0.15 in some cases, but becomes smaller (around 0.05 on average) for highest precision threshold of 0.9. While this difference is still significant, it does indicate that the gains at high precision thresholds are limited, possibly owing to limited choices of classifiers satisfying the precision constraint.

In Fig. 2, we report the number of queries required by MONOTONE and CVHULL on all datasets, as the threshold used for the precision constraint is varied. We again do not report the number for VW, since it returns a classifier that often violates the precision constraint. The graphs show that CVHULL requires significantly lower number of queries than MONOTONE on all but 2 cases. The difference in number of examples is particularly stark for Person and Scholar-DBLP datasets, sometimes more than 3000 examples. A particularly attractive property of CVHULL is that it learns the classifier in around 500 points for all but one datasets and all threshold values.

In Fig. 3, we compare the computation time for the two algorithms MONOTONE and CVHULL as the number of dimensions is varied for the Person dataset. The figure clearly demonstrates that MONOTONE has an exponential complexity w.r.t number of dimensions, while CVHULL has an almost a constant dependence.

In Fig. 4, we show that that VW often fails to produce a

Dataset	Schema	Size	Ratio (+/-)	Blocking Function	Features
Business	name(N), street(S), city(C), zip(Z), phone(P)	3958	0.115	Jacc(N) $\geq$ 0.2, Jacc(S) $\geq$ 0.2, EQ(P)	5
Person	first-name(F), last-name(L), sex(S), birth-date(D), zip(Z)	574913	0.004	SoundEQ(F), SoundEQ(L), EQ(S), EQ(D)	9
DBLP-ACM	authors(A), title(T), venue(V), year(Y)	494437	0.005	Char3Jacc(T) $\geq$ 0.05	7
Scholar-DBLP	authors(A), title(T), venue(V), year(Y)	589326	0.009	Char3Jacc(T) $\geq$ 0.1	7

Table 1: Description of datasets used in our experiments. The blocking functions used to reduce the number of pairwise comparisons during matching are Jaccard similarity (Jacc), string equality (EQ), phonetic equality (SoundEQ) and trigram Jaccard similarity (Char3Jacc). The number of similarity features is shown in the last column.

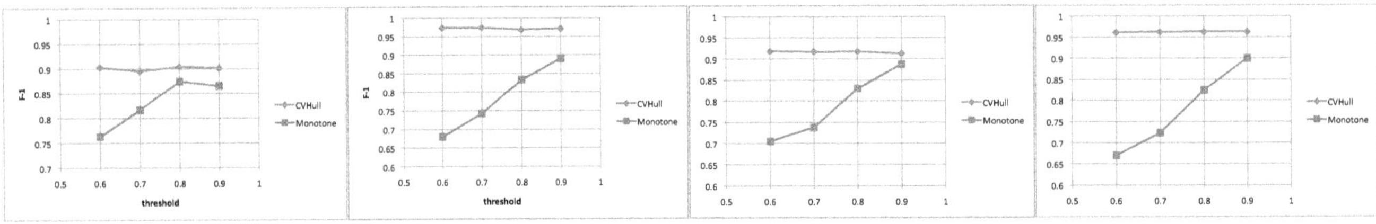

(a) Business (b) Person (c) Scholar-DBLP (d) DBLP-ACM

Figure 1: The effect of varying the precision threshold on the F-measure for different datasets.

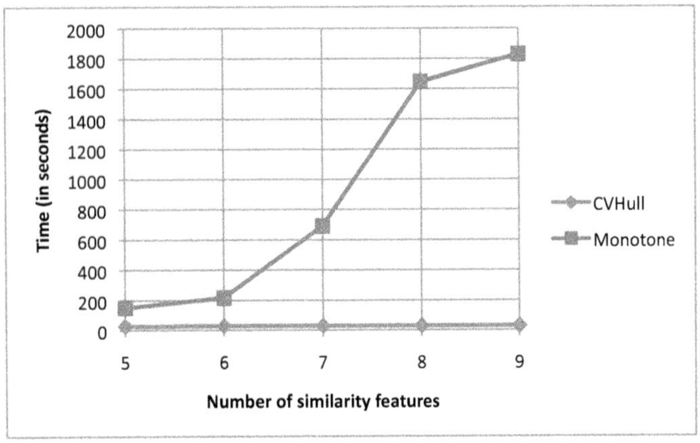

Figure 3: The computational complexity of the two algorithms as the dimension is varied.

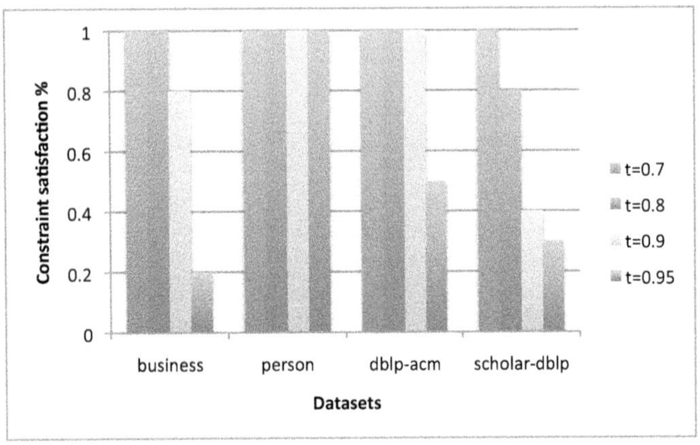

Figure 4: The constraint satisfaction percentage of VW active learning algorithm over 10 random runs for different datasets.

feasible classifier, i.e. one that satisfies the precision constraint. The graph plots the success rate, i.e. the fraction of times, over 10 random runs, the algorithm outputs a feasible classifier. Obviously as the precision threshold is increased, number of feasible classifiers decrease, and so does the success rate. This graph demonstrates the need for the CONVEXHULL and REJECTIONSAMPLING algorithms used in CVHULL on top of VW.

6. CONCLUSION

In this paper, we proposed an active learning algorithm for the entity matching problem. The algorithm tries to learn a classifier with maximum recall under a constraint that its precision should be greater than a given threshold. The algorithm uses any of the existing active learning technique for minimizing 01-loss as a black-box. We showed that the algorithm outputs a classifier having recall close to the optimal, and has good label and computation complexity. We also compared the algorithm against the state-of-the-art active learning algorithm for entity matching, and show that we outperform it in terms of metrics such as F1 of the trained classifier, number of labeled examples required, and computation time on several real-world datasets.

7. REFERENCES

[1] Arvind Arasu, Michaela Götz, and Raghav Kaushik. On active learning of record matching packages. In *SIGMOD Conference*, pages 783–794, 2010.

[2] Maria-Florina Balcan, Alina Beygelzimer, and John Langford. Agnostic active learning. *J. Comput. Syst. Sci.*, 75(1):78–89, 2009.

[3] Maria-Florina Balcan, Andrei Z. Broder, and Tong Zhang. Margin based active learning. In *COLT*, pages 35–50, 2007.

[4] Alina Beygelzimer, Sanjoy Dasgupta, and John Langford. Importance weighted active learning. In *ICML*, page 7, 2009.

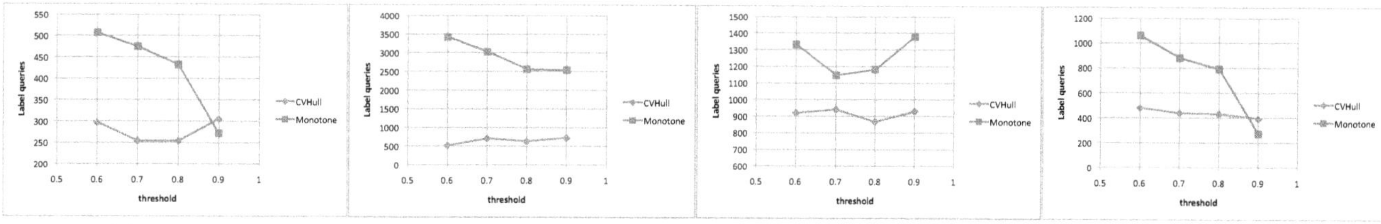

(a) Business (b) Person (c) Scholar-DBLP (d) DBLP-ACM

Figure 2: The effect of varying the precision threshold on the number of label queries for different datasets.

[5] Alina Beygelzimer, Daniel Hsu, John Langford, and Tong Zhang. Agnostic active learning without constraints. In *NIPS*, pages 199–207, 2010.

[6] Mikhail Bilenko and Raymond J. Mooney. Adaptive duplicate detection using learnable string similarity measures. In *Proceedings of the ninth ACM SIGKDD international conference on Knowledge discovery and data mining*, KDD '03, pages 39–48, New York, NY, USA, 2003. ACM.

[7] Mikhail Bilenko and Raymond J. Mooney. On evaluation and training-set construction for duplicate detection. In *Proceedings of the KDD-2003 Workshop on Data Cleaning, Record Linkage and Object Consolidation, Washington DC*, pages 7–12, 2003.

[8] Surajit Chaudhuri, Bee-Chung Chen, Venkatesh Ganti, and Raghav Kaushik. Example-driven design of efficient record matching queries. In *Proceedings of the 33rd international conference on Very large data bases*, VLDB '07, pages 327–338. VLDB Endowment, 2007.

[9] Peter Christen. Probabilistic data generation for deduplication and data linkage. In *IDEAL*, pages 109–116, 2005.

[10] David Cohn, Les Atlas, and Richard Ladner. Improving Generalization with Active Learning. *Mach. Learn.*, 15(2):201–221, May 1994.

[11] Sanjoy Dasgupta and Daniel Hsu. Hierarchical sampling for active learning. In *ICML*, pages 208–215, 2008.

[12] Sanjoy Dasgupta, Daniel Hsu, and Claire Monteleoni. A general agnostic active learning algorithm. In *NIPS*, 2007.

[13] Sanjoy Dasgupta and John Langford. Tutorial summary: Active learning. In *ICML*, page 178, 2009.

[14] Ahmed K. Elmagarmid, Panagiotis G. Ipeirotis, and Vassilios S. Verykios. Duplicate record detection: A survey. *IEEE Trans. on Knowl. and Data Eng.*, 19:1–16, January 2007.

[15] A. Frank and A. Asuncion. UCI machine learning repository, 2010.

[16] Steve Hanneke. A bound on the label complexity of agnostic active learning. In *ICML*, pages 353–360, 2007.

[17] Steve Hanneke. Adaptive rates of convergence in active learning. In *COLT*, 2009.

[18] Sheng-Jun Huang, Rong Jin, and Zhi-Hua Zhou. Active learning by querying informative and representative examples. In *NIPS*, pages 892–900, 2010.

[19] Nikos Karampatziakis and John Langford. Online importance weight aware updates. In *UAI*, pages 392–399, 2011.

[20] Hanna Köpcke and Erhard Rahm. Training selection for tuning entity matching. In *QDB/MUD*, pages 3–12, 2008.

[21] Hanna Köpcke and Erhard Rahm. Frameworks for entity matching: A comparison. *Data Knowl. Eng.*, 69:197–210, February 2010.

[22] Andrew McCallum, Kamal Nigam, and Lyle H. Ungar. Efficient clustering of high-dimensional data sets with application to reference matching. In *Proceedings of the sixth ACM SIGKDD international conference on Knowledge discovery and data mining*, KDD '00, pages 169–178, New York, NY, USA, 2000. ACM.

[23] Paul Mineiro. Cost-Sensitive Binary Classification and Active Learning, 2003.

[24] Franco P. Preparata and Michael I. Shamos. *Computational geometry: an introduction.* Springer-Verlag New York, Inc., New York, NY, USA, 1985.

[25] Steffen Rendle and Lars Schmidt-Thieme. Active learning of equivalence relations by minimizing the expected loss using constraint inference. In *ICDM*, pages 1001–1006, 2008.

[26] Sunita Sarawagi and Anuradha Bhamidipaty. Interactive deduplication using active learning. In *KDD*, pages 269–278, 2002.

[27] Burr Settles. Active learning literature survey. Computer Sciences Technical Report 1648, University of Wisconsin–Madison, 2009.

[28] Sheila Tejada, Craig A. Knoblock, and Steven Minton. Learning object identification rules for information integration. *Inf. Syst.*, 26:607–633, December 2001.

[29] Wei Wang and Zhi-Hua Zhou. Multi-view active learning in the non-realizable case. In *NIPS*, pages 2388–2396, 2010.

[30] Steven Euijong Whang, David Menestrina, Georgia Koutrika, Martin Theobald, and Hector Garcia-Molina. Entity resolution with iterative blocking. In *Proceedings of the 35th SIGMOD international conference on Management of data*, SIGMOD '09, pages 219–232, New York, NY, USA, 2009. ACM.

[31] William E. Winkler. The state of record linkage and current research problems. Technical report, Statistical Research Division, U.S. Census Bureau, 1999.

[32] Bianca Zadrozny, John Langford, and Naoki Abe. Cost-Sensitive Learning by Cost-Proportionate Example Weighting, 2012.

An Integrated Data Mining Approach to Real-time Clinical Monitoring and Deterioration Warning

Yi Mao*
Department of Computer Science and Engineering
Washington University in St. Louis, Saint Louis, USA
maoy@seas.wustl.edu

Wenlin Chen
Department of Computer Science and Engineering
Washington University in St. Louis, Saint Louis, USA
wenlinchen@wustl.edu

Yixin Chen
Department of Computer Science and Engineering
Washington University in St. Louis, Saint Louis, USA
chen@cse.wustl.edu

Chenyang Lu
Department of Computer Science and Engineering
Washington University in St. Louis, Saint Louis, USA
lu@cse.wustl.edu

Marin Kollef
Washington University School of Medicine
Washington University in St. Louis, Saint Louis, USA
mkollef@dom.wustl.edu

Thomas C. Bailey
Washington University School of Medicine
Washington University in St. Louis, Saint Louis, USA
tbailey@dom.wustl.edu

ABSTRACT

Clinical study found that early detection and intervention are essential for preventing clinical deterioration in patients, for patients both in intensive care units (ICU) as well as in general wards but under real-time data sensing (RDS). In this paper, we develop an integrated data mining approach to give early deterioration warnings for patients under real-time monitoring in ICU and RDS.

Existing work on mining real-time clinical data often focus on certain single vital sign and specific disease. In this paper, we consider an integrated data mining approach for general sudden deterioration warning. We synthesize a large feature set that includes first and second order time-series features, detrended fluctuation analysis (DFA), spectral analysis, approximative entropy, and cross-signal features. We then systematically apply and evaluate a series of established data mining methods, including forward feature selection, linear and nonlinear classification algorithms, and exploratory undersampling for class imbalance.

An extensive empirical study is conducted on real patient data collected between 2001 and 2008 from a variety of ICUs. Results show the benefit of each of the proposed techniques, and the final integrated approach significantly improves the prediction quality. The proposed clinical warning system is currently under integration with the electronic medical record system at Barnes-Jewish Hospital in preparation for a clinical trial. This work represents a promising step toward general early clinical warning which has the potential to significantly improve the quality of patient care in hospitals.

*Visiting doctoral candidate from Xidian University, China

KDD'12, August 12–16, 2012, Beijing, China.

Categories and Subject Descriptors

H.2.8 [**Database Management**]: Database Applications—*Data mining*; J.3 [**Computer Applications**]: Life and medical sciences

General Terms

Experimentation, Algorithms, Performance

Keywords

Real-time clinical monitoring, deterioration warning, time-series classification, feature selection

1. INTRODUCTION

Every year, 4-17% of patients undergo cardiopulmonary or respiratory arrest while in hospitals. Lots of these patients could have been saved if warning of serious clinical events could be provided early, before its occurrence rather than when it is happening. Early prediction based on real-time electronic monitoring data has become an apparent need in many clinical areas.

At Washington University, we have carried out a NIH-funded clinical trial of a real-time patient monitoring system in a step-down unit at Barnes-Jewish Hospital, one of the largest hospitals in the United States [9]. This clinical trial uses wireless sensing devices to collect real-time vital sign data for patients not only in ICU but also in general units. The goal of this pioneering study is to show the feasibility of using data mining algorithms to give early warning of sudden deterioration, ultimately leading to the prevention of death.

However, most prior studies focus on some specific disease prediction. For example, McQuatt et al. [2] introduced a decision tree method to analyze head injury. Loforte et al. [14] found statistical indexes for detecting sepsis by investigating the relationship between heart rate and respiration. Khosla et al. [6] applied multiple machine learning techniques for stroke prediction. There have been little study on general prediction and warning for serious clinical deterioration and death.

Data mining on clinical data has great potential to improve the treatment quality of hospitals and increase the survival rate of patients. Data-driven prediction technology strongly hinges on the data collection of patients' vital signs. In most hospitals, only intensive care units (ICUs) are equipped with real-time electronic medical sensors. In general hospital units, patients' vital signs are typically collected manually by a nurse, at a granularity of only a handful of readings per day, which confronts us with the challenged of sparseness and irregularity of data. However, most findings suggest that real-time monitoring data would be beneficial for a better treatment [10]. To handle this problem, our team has proposed a real-time data sensing (RDS) system, which enables patients' vital signs data in general hospital units to be collected via wireless sensors. Currently, RDS can provide constant monitoring of patients' heart rate and oxygen saturation rate. Through a pilot study at the Barnes-Jewish Hospital, the RDS system has been installed in its step-down unit. The success of RDS will dramatically enlarge the population that have real-time monitoring data. Hence, there is a critical need for a data mining system that can effectively utilize the multi-dimensional, real-time time-series data from ICU and RDS in order to prevent deterioration and mortality in hospitalized patients.

In this paper, we develop an integrated data mining approach to identify the signs of clinical deterioration and provide early warning for possible mortality. In particular, we build classification methods to monitor real-time signal of heart rate and oxygen saturation rate of patient and issue early warning alerts before clinical deterioration/death. This system enables at-risk patients to be timely checked and treated by healthcare professionals in order to prevent potential deterioration and death.

Studies have found that real-time clinical data has certain unique features, due to the underlying dynamics of biological systems [5]. Therefore, some dedicated algorithms based on nonlinear dynamics, such as detrended fluctuation analysis (DFA) and spectral analysis, have been proposed for clinical data. However, such prior work has two downsides. First, most of them consider only a single vital sign. For example, Penzel et al. [12] used DFA and spectral analysis for sleep apnea detection leveraging on the heart rates. Mining multiple time series is a more challenging problem. Second, time series data has rich information that previous work did not make full use of. For single time series, there are first-order and second-order features, as well as some sophisticated patterns, such as DFA, spectra and entropy. For multiple time series, features such as correlation and coherence can be used. Our approach not only leverages all these information but also performs feature selection to select the most relevant and discriminative features. For classification, researchers in the clinical community routinely use simple linear classifiers [5]. Our system incorporates more robust classifiers such as SVM with RBF kernels and logistic regression. Moreover, we use an exploratory undersampling method to address the challenge of class imbalance widely observed in clinical data.

In summary, this paper contains the following contributions:

1. We develop an integrated data mining approach to early deterioration warning based on real-time monitoring data. The approach is applicable to both ICU patients and patients in general hospital wards equipped with real-time sensing devices.
2. We bridge the gap between biomedical community and data mining community by incorporating popular features and methods from both areas.
3. We strengthen the early warning system by applying important data mining techniques such as feature selection, exploratory undersampling, and advanced classifiers to address the challenging multi-dimensional time-series classification problem.
4. We apply our integrated approach to a large collection of real patient data recorded from ICUs and show significant improvement over previous methods. The results also validate the effectiveness of the employed techniques.

The rest of this paper is organized as follows. Section 2 surveys the related work in detecting clinical deterioration. An overview on our early warning system is presented in Section 3. Section 4 describes our general approach and the evaluation criterion. Section 5 lists and describes all the features extracted from multiple vital sign time series. Section 6 and Section 7 describe the feature selection and prediction approach, respectively. Section 8 shows the experimental result of our real-time early warning system. Finally, we draw conclusions in Section 9.

2. RELATED WORK

Medical data mining is a key technique to extract useful clinical knowledge from medical records. A number of scoring systems exist that use medical knowledge for various medical conditions.

For example, Several Community-Acquired Pneumonia (SCAP) and Pneumonia Severity Index (PSI) were used to predict outcomes in patients with pneumonia [19]. Similarly, outcomes in patients with renal failures may be predicted using the Acute Physiology Score, Chronic Health Score, and APACHE score [18]. In [21], Zhou proposed a Multi-Task Learning Formulation for Predicting Alzheimer's Disease. The integration of heterogeneous data (neuroimages, demographic, and genetic measures) for AD prediction based on a kernel method was proposed in [20].

Detrended fluctuation analysis (DFA) and spectral analysis for heart rate variability were evaluated to classify sleep apnea and normal sleep [12]. RR (inter-beat) interval and spontaneous respiration were analyzed using approximated entropy(ApEn) and regularity index to distinguish sepsis [14]. Decision tree is introduced in predicting the outcome of head injury patients using both background (demographic) data and temporal (physiological) data [2]. Also, SVM and feature selection are employed to predict stroke [6].

However, most of these algorithms are designed for some specific diseases and to be used in some specialized hospital units. In contrast, the detection of clinical deterioration requires more general algorithms. For example, a team at the John Hopkins University developed the Modified Early Warning Score (MEWS) [7], which uses manually-collected systolic blood pressure, pulse rate, temperature, respiratory rate, age and BMI to predict clinical deterioration. Our team has also developed a learning algorithm to identify high-risk patients based on clinical data collected by nurses [9]. However, both of these works are applied to manually collected data which has only a handful of readings per day. Here, our goal is different. We are aiming at mining real-time vital signs read by electronic devices at ICU and wireless sensors in our project. Such data is very different from manually collected data, as they are regular and have high frequency (reading gaps being minutes instead of hours).

3. REAL-TIME MONITORING IN GENERAL HOSPITAL UNITS

Our work aims to prevent clinical deterioration in patients, for both patents in ICU as well as in general hospital units equipped with sensing devices, such as our RDS system.

In our RDS pilot study at the Barnes-Jewish Hospital, patients are provided with wireless sensor network (WSN) devices which collect and stream real-time vital sign data to the learning system. If deterioration is predicted, a warning is sent to nurses on the patient's floor over the hospital's paging system. The nurses may then intervene to prevent deterioration. Figure 1 shows a WSN-based wireless pulse oximeter device developed by our team, which is capable of collecting equipped patent's real-time heart rate and oxygen saturation rate and then route the data to a wired access point using an onboard radio based on the IEEE 802.15.4 radio standard. WSN network coverage is achieved by plugging additional TelosB nodes into electrical outlets in patients' rooms and in the hallway. These new nodes will autonomously locate other nearby nodes and participate in routing sensor data from patient nodes to a wired access point, where they are entered into our data mining system.

RDS enjoys robust system reliability and lifetime. It achieved high network reliability, with a median of 99.68% of packets successfully delivered to the base station. Network outages were infrequent and had a 95%-percentile time-to-recovery of 2.4 minutes. Patient nodes achieved a lifetime of up to 69 hours from a 9V battery power source.

The establishment of the RDS represents a important step toward early clinical warning that has the potential to significantly improve the quality and outcome of patient care in hospitals. RDS shows the feasibility that, real-time physiologic data will be available for not only patients at ICU, but also patients in the general hospital units with real-time monitoring. Due to the inevitable trend of popular uses of such sensing systems in hospitals, our data mining approach is meeting a critical challenge in the healthcare industry and has the potential of very broad usage.

4. OVERVIEW OF OUR APPROACH

In this section, we overview the proposed approach for early prediction of clinical deterioration/death based on real-time monitoring data from ICU and RDS. Specifically, in this work, we try to predict mortality (death) of hospitalized patients based on two vital signs that are most popular: heart rate and oxygen saturation rate. Our pulseox sensor can measure these two signs. The procedure consists of the following steps:

- Preprocess the data set by removing abnormal values.
- Extract features from the patient's collected real-time vital sign time series, including heart rate and oxygen saturation rate. The extracted features contains DFA, spectral analysis, first order and second order features, and multi-sign features. All features are normalized to the range of [0,1].
- Apply feature selection techniques to select the most relevant and discriminative features.
- Apply classification algorithms to train the model, and evaluate the prediction performance by cross validation. To deal with class imbalance widely observed in clinical data, we also use an exploratory undersampling method.

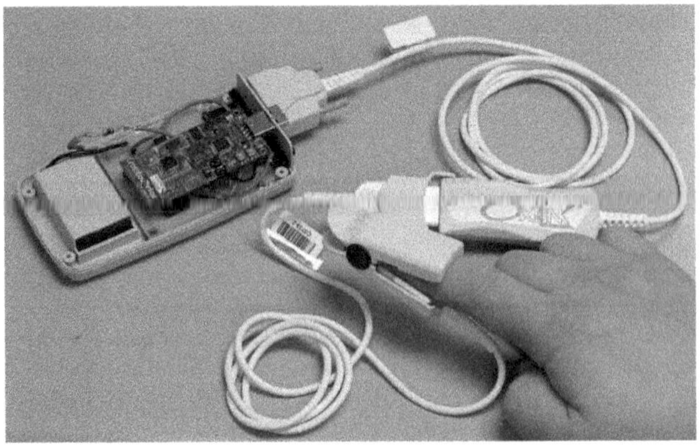

Figure 1: A wireless pulse-oximeter node developed at Washington University.

The evaluation of the prediction performance is based on the following criteria: AUC (Area Under receive operating characteristic Curve), PPV (Positive Predictive Value), NPV (Negative Predictive Value), sensitivity, and specificity. In clinical community, the PPV stands for the proportion of patients who actually suffer deterioration/death, among the candidate patients who are warned by our system. A high NPV means that patients who survived are rarely misclassified. PPV/NPV and sensitivity/specificity are trade-off pairs where typically lowering one makes the other higher. PPV and NPV are also sensitive to how imbalanced the dataset is. Hence, we adopt the AUC as our main metric since it is a comprehensive measurement combining sensitivity and specificity to deal with the imbalance dataset.

5. FEATURES

In this section, we describe all the features extracted from patients' vital sign time series - heart rate and oxygen saturation rate. There are in total 34 features from these two time series data, including features within single time series and features linking the two time series.

5.1 Detrended Fluctuation Analysis (DFA)

In stochastic processes, chaos theory and time series analysis, detrended fluctuation analysis (DFA) is a method for determining the statistical self-similarity of a signal [5]. Self-similarity is a key feature that is widely observed in natural systems, including human physiological signs. Mathematically, DFA is a scaling analysis method to reveal long-range power-law correlation exponents in noisy time series [5]. It

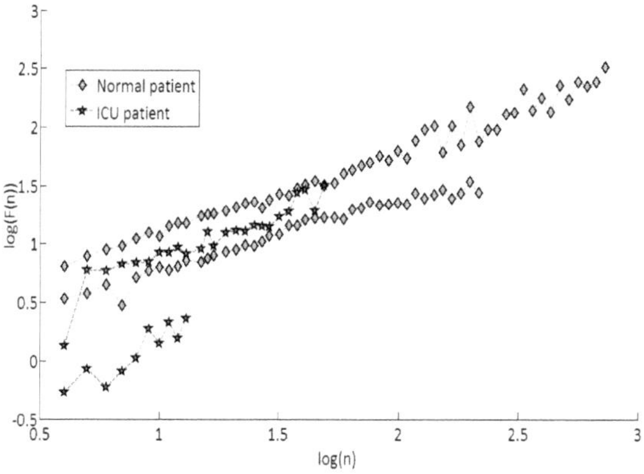

Figure 2: DFA analysis on the heart rates of two ICU and two non-ICU patients.

is most suitable for non-stationary time series with slowly varying trends, such as heart rate and oxygen saturation rate. The DFA of a time series is calculated as the average fitting error over all segments in different scales. Given a time series $\{x(i)\}$,$1 \leq i \leq N$, integration is performed to convert the original time series as follows:

$$y(j) = \sum_{i=1}^{j}[x(i) - \langle x\rangle], 1 \leq j \leq N$$

where

$$\langle x\rangle = \frac{1}{N}\sum_{i=1}^{N} x(i)$$

Next, the integrated time series $y(i)$ $(i = 1, 2, ...N)$ is divided into boxes of equal length n. A polynomial function y_n is fitted to each box of length n by minimizing the least square error. Then, we detrend the integrated time series y by subtracting y_n from each box. The root-mean-square fluctuation of the detrended time series is calculated by

$$F(n) = \sqrt{\frac{1}{N}\sum_{j=1}^{N}[y(j) - y_n(j)]^2}$$

Typically,$F(n)$ increases with n and follows the power law: $F(n) \sim n^{\alpha}$. Using a log-log plot, we can get a nearly linear curve as shown in Figure 2. The scaling exponent α characterizes the self-similarity level of original time series $x(t)$, which can be calculated using the slope of this curve.

As pointed out in [11], it is important to differentiate the short-range and long-range levels of self-similarity. Hence, we divide the curve into two pieces and fit a linear function to each piece of curve, which generates two slops - α_1 and α_2. α_1 represents the slope of curve $\log(F(n))$ vs. $\log(n)$ in the range $1 \leq n \leq \phi(N)$ while α_2 represents the slope of curve in the range $\phi(N) < n \leq N$. In this way, we can see that α_1 reflects the short-range self-similarity level and α_2 reflects the long-range self-similarity level. As different patients have time series of different length, we cannot apply the same curve-segmentation method as in [12]. Instead, we select the $\phi(N)$ by a ratio γ, where $\phi(N) = \gamma * N$. Regarding the selection of γ, we first sample two groups of died patients and survived patients, respectively. Next, for a fixed γ, we calculate the α_1 for each patient as well as the sum of all α_1 of each group. γ is selected to maximize the difference between sums of α_1 of the two groups.

5.2 Approximate entropy (ApEn)

Approximate entropy was introduced by Pincus to quantify the time series complexity closely related to entropy [13]. It is a measurement designed to quantify the degree of regularity versus unpredictability. It quantifies the unpredictability of fluctuations in a time series. A low value of the entropy indicates that the time series is deterministic while a high value means that the time series is unpredictable(randomness).

To compute the approximate entropy (ApEn) of a time series, we divide the time series into $N - m + 1$ sub-series, calculate the similarity between each other and then figure out the entropy. First, sub-series of vectors of length m, $v(n) = [x(n), x(n+1), ...x(n+m-1)]$, $n = 1, \cdots, N-m+1$, are derived from the original signal. The distance $D(i, j)$ between two vectors $v(i)$ and $v(j)$ is defined as the maximum difference in the scalar components of $v(i)$ and $v(j)$. Then $N^{m,r}(i)$, the number of vectors j such that the distance between the vectors $v(j)$ and the generic vector $v(i)$ is lower than r, is computed. The index r is a fixed parameter which sets the "tolerance" of the comparison. Then we consider $C^{m,r}(i)$, the probability to find a vector that differs from $v(i)$ by a distance less than r, as:

$$C^{m,r}(i) = N^{m,r}(i)/(N - m + 1) \quad (1)$$

and the logarithmic average over all the vectors of the $C^{m,r}(i)$ probability is calculated as follows:

$$F^{m,r} = \frac{\sum_{i=1}^{N-m+1}\ln(C^{m,r}(i)}{N - m + 1} \quad (2)$$

ApEn is given by:

$$ApEn^{m,r} = F^{m,r} - F^{m+1,r} \quad (3)$$

As recommended in [13], we use $m = 2$,$r = 20\%$ of the standard deviation of the time series in our analysis.

5.3 Spectral analysis

Spectral analysis is another major method for analyzing clinical time-series data [12]. For the calculation of the power spectra, the time series was resampled at 3.4 Hz using interpolation. The mean value, the standard deviation value was subtracted from the time series before applying the Fast Fourier Transformation (FFT). In case of having less than 2^N of records, zero-padding was used. The spectral analysis and the interpolation routine was implemented using Matlab 7.11.0. We calculated the component values for VLF (<=0.04HZ), LF (0.04-0.15HZ), HF (0.15-0.4HZ), and the ratio LF/HF for each time-series. Figure 3 shows an example spectral distribution of the heart rate of an ICU patient.

5.4 First order features

For first order features, we use some traditional statistical ones, such as mean (μ), standard deviation (σ), skewnes s(γ_1), and kurtosis (γ_2). In probability theory and statistics, skewness is a measure of the asymmetry of the probability distribution of a real-valued random variable. The skewness value can be positive or negative, or even undefined. Qualitatively, a negative skew indicates that the tail on the left side of the probability density function is longer than the

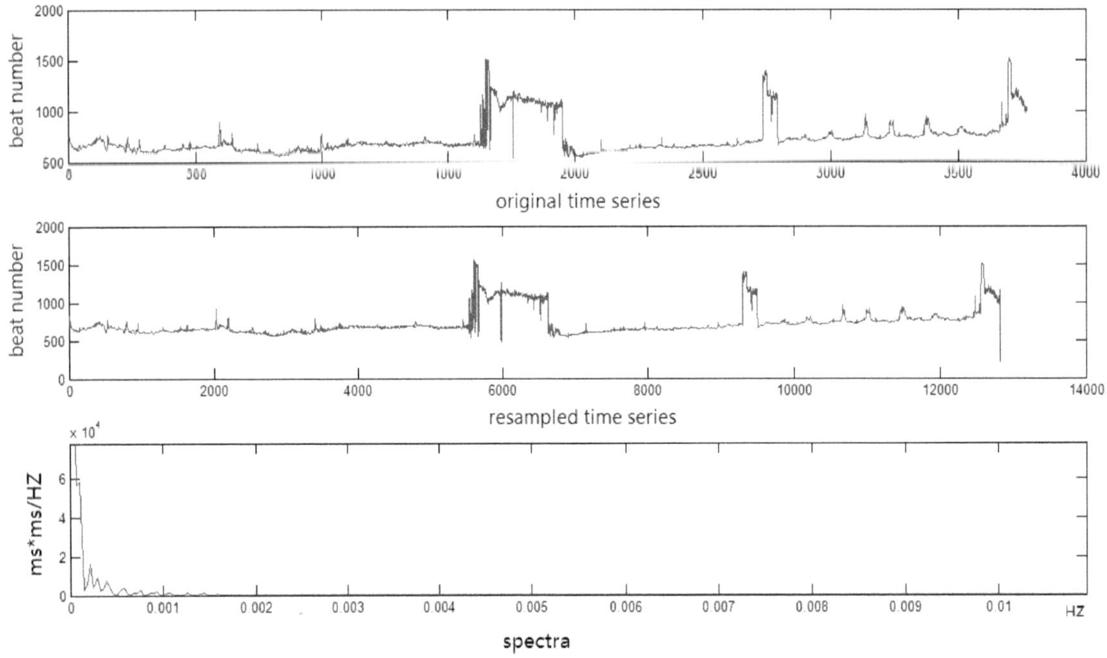

Figure 3: The calculation of the spectral features using FFT.

right side and the bulk of the values (possibly including the median) lie to the right of the mean. A positive skew indicates the opposite. A zero value indicates that the values are relatively evenly distributed on both sides of the mean, typically but not necessarily implying a symmetric distribution. Kurtosis is a measure of the "peakedness" of the probability distribution of a real-valued random variable. In a similar way to the concept of skewness, kurtosis is a descriptor of the shape of a probability distribution and, just as for skewness, there are different ways of quantifying it for a theoretical distribution and corresponding ways of estimating it from a sample from a population. The computation we used is as follows:

$$\mu = \frac{\sum_{i=1}^{N} x(i)}{N}$$

$$\sigma = \sqrt{\frac{\sum_{i=1}^{N}(x(i) - \mu)}{N}}$$

$$\gamma_1 = \frac{\sum_{i=1}^{N}(x(i) - \mu)^3}{n\sigma^3}$$

$$\gamma_2 = \frac{\sum_{i=1}^{N}(x(i) - \mu)^4}{n\sigma^4} - 3$$

5.5 Second order features

Here, we employ the description which related to co-occurrence features in one dimensional time series [1]. First, the data is quantized into Q levels. Second, a two dimensional matrix $c(i, j)$ is constructed ($1 \leq i, j \leq Q$). Point (i,j) in the matrix represents the number of times that a point in the sequence with level i is followed, at a distance d_1, by a point with level j. Figure 4 shows how this process works. Finally, five co-occurrence features, including energy (E), entropy

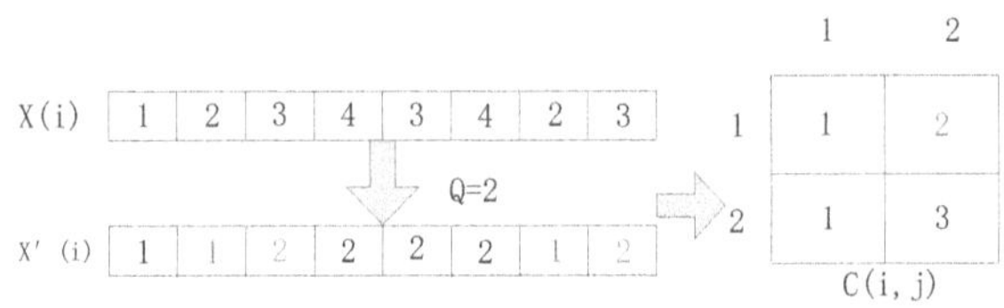

Figure 4: The process that transfers an one dimensional time series to two dimensional matrix.

(S), correlation (COR)(ρ_x, y), inertia (F), and local homogeneity (LH), are calculated using the following equations:

$$E = \sum_{i=1}^{Q}\sum_{j=1}^{Q} c(i,j)^2$$

$$S = \sum_{i=1}^{Q}\sum_{j=1}^{Q} c(i,j) * \log(c(i,j))$$

$$\rho_{x,y} = \frac{\sum_{i=1}^{Q}\sum_{j=1}^{Q}(i - \mu_x)(j - \mu_y)c(i,j)}{\sigma_x * \sigma_y}$$

where:

$$\mu_x = \frac{\sum_{i=1}^{Q} i \sum_{j=1}^{Q} c(i,j)}{Q}$$

$$\mu_y = \frac{\sum_{j=1}^{Q} j \sum_{i=1}^{Q} c(i,j)}{Q}$$

$$\sigma_x^2 = \frac{\sum_{i=1}^{Q}(i - \mu_x)^2 \sum_{j=1}^{Q} c(i,j)}{Q}$$

$$\sigma_x^2 = \frac{\sum_{j=1}^{Q}(j-\mu_y)^2 \sum_{i=1}^{Q} c(i,j)}{Q}$$

$$F = \sum_{i=1}^{Q}\sum_{j=1}^{Q}(i-j)^2 c(i,j)$$

$$LH = \sum_{i=1}^{Q}\sum_{j=1}^{Q}\frac{1}{1+(i-j)^2}c(i,j)$$

In our experiments, we set $Q = 10$.

5.6 Cross-sign features

We also consider features that link multiple vital signs together, including linear correlation and coherence.

5.6.1 *Linear Correlation*

Correlation indicates the strength and direction of a linear relationship between two random variables. In general, it refers to the departure of two variables from independence and equals:

$$\gamma_{1,2} = \frac{E[(X_1(t) - E(X_1(t)))(X_2(t) - E(X_2(t)))]}{Var[X_1(t)] \cdot Var[X_2(t)]}$$

5.6.2 *Coherence*

Coherence provides both amplitude and phase information about the frequencies held in common between the two time series and is defined by:

$$C_{1,2} = \frac{\phi_{X_1X_2}}{[\phi_{X_1X_1} \cdot \phi_{X_2X_2}]^{\frac{1}{2}}}$$

where $\phi_{x_1x_2}$ is the cross-spectral density, and $\phi_{x_1x_1}$ and $\phi_{x_2x_2}$ are autospectral densities. Coherence is a value between 0 and 1. If X_1 and X_2 correspondes to the single input and output of a constant parameter linear system, their coherence $C_{1,2}$ will always be equal to one. Otherwise, if X_1 and X_2 are completely unrelated, the coherence will be zero.

6. FEATURE SELECTION

Feature selection in supervised learning has been well studied, which aims to find the most relevant features and produce better classification performance than using all the features. In contrast to other dimensionality reduction techniques like those based on projection (e.g. principal component analysis) or compression (e.g. using information theory), feature selection techniques do not alter the original representation of the variables, but merely select a subset of them. Thus, besides reducing the utilization time and storage requirements, they preserve the original semantics of the variables, hence offering the advantage of interpretability to users [16].

While there are many classes of feature selection methods, here we adopt a forward feature selection algorithm which does not depend on a particular classifier. Forward feature selection is a simple search strategy to find useful features [4]. The basic idea is we starts with an empty feature subset and adds one variable each step until a predefined number of features is reached, or the approximation result does not improve any further.

We use two metrics for our forward selection, AUC and F-score. The AUC is the area under the ROC curve. F-score [3] is defined as:

$$F(i) \equiv \frac{(\overline{x_i}^{(+)} - \overline{x_i})^2 + (\overline{x_i}^{(-)} - \overline{x_i})^2}{\frac{1}{n_+-1}\sum_{k=1}^{n_+}(x_{k,i}^{(+)} - x_i^{(-)})^2 + \frac{1}{n_--1}\sum_{k=1}^{n_-}(x_{k,i}^{(-)} - x_i^{(-)})^2}$$

where $\overline{x_i}$, $\overline{x_i}^{(+)}$, $\overline{x_i}^{(-)}$ are the average of the ith feature of the whole, positive,and negative data sets, respectively; $x_{k,j}^{(+)}$ is the ith feature of the kth positive instance, and $x_{k,j}^{(-)}$ is the ith feature of the kth negative instance. The numerator indicates the discrimination between the positive and negative sets, and the denominator indicates the one within each of the two sets. The larger the F-score is, the more likely this feature is more discriminative.

7. CLASSIFICATION ALGORITHMS

In our approach, we apply Support Vector Machine (SVM) and logistic regression for prediction. In addition, to deal with the class imbalence of our dataset, we adopt the exploratory undersampling method.

7.1 Support vector machine

SVM is one of the most popular classification methods based on statistical learning theory. The key idea is to learn an optimal hyperplane that can separate the training data set with maximum margin [17]. Some previous work in DFA and spectral analysis use a linear separator [5, 11, 12] which corresponds to SVM with a liner kernel. Generally, by importing non-linear kernel, SVM has higher accuracy compared to other linear classifiers.

7.2 Logistic regression

Logistic regression is a model for predicting the probability of an event, which can also be used for binary classification. Logistic regression has the benefit of being able to output a numerical score to reflect the severity of the patient. Also, logistic regression allows us to control the sensitivity/specificity tradeoffs by adjusting the classification threshold.

7.3 Exploratory undersampling

Looking through the records, we have a skewed dataset. Among 772 records, there are 175 records that belongs to the positive (death) set. Undersampling [8] is a very popular method in dealing with the class-imbalance problem. The idea is to combine the minority class with only a subset of the majority class each time to generate a sampling set, and take the ensemble of multiple sampled models. We have tried undersampling on our data but obtained very modest improvements.

To improve the performance further, we used a recent method called exploratory undersampling [8], which makes better use of the majority class than simple undersampling. The idea is to iteratively remove those samples that can be correctly classified by a large margin to the class boundary by the existing model.

Specifically, we fix the number of the died patients, and then randomly choose the same amount of survived patients to build the training dataset at each iteration. The main difference to simple undersampling is that, each iteration, it removes 5% in both the majority class and the minority

Method	Features	AUC	Specificity	Sensitivity	PPV	NPV
linear SVM	DFA of heart rate (HR)	0.5759	0.9497	0.0755	0.2550	0.7781
Logistic Regression	DFA of HR	0.4742	0.9483	0.0729	0.3181	0.7555
kernel SVM	DFA of HR	0.5897	0.9497	0.1265	0.3643	0.7879
linear SVM	DFA of oxygen saturation rate (OS)	0.4473	0.9497	0.0346	0.1300	0.7705
Logistic Regression	DFA of OS	0.4902	0.9483	0.0313	0.1667	0.7473
kernel SVM	DFA of OS	0.5010	0.9497	0.0670	0.2150	0.7768
linear SVM	DFA of HR+OS	0.5757	0.9497	0.1416	0.3917	0.7694
Logistic Regression	DFA of HR+OS	0.5370	0.9483	0.0521	0.2500	0.7513
kernel SVM	DFA of HR+OS	**0.6332**	0.9497	**0.1428**	**0.4146**	**0.7911**

Table 1: The performance comparison of different classifiers using DFA in different time series and their combination.

class with the maximum classification margin. For logistic regression, we remove those died patients that are closest to 1 (the class label of death) and those survived patients that are closest to 0. For SVM, we remove those correctly classified patients with the maximum distance to the boundary.

8. EXPERIMENT RESULTS

In this section, we present the experimental result of the performance of our integrated learning algorithms. We first introduce the database of real-time vital signs used in our study. Then, we show and discuss the experimental results on the performance and advantages of various proposed techniques.

8.1 Database and experimental setup

Since our RDS system is still in a smaller scale clinical trial and does not yield enough data, we test our approach based on the MIMIC II (Multiparameter Intelligent Monitoring in Intensive Care) [15] database which contains comprehensive clinical data from tens of thousands of Intensive Care Unit (ICU) patients. Data were collected between 2001 and 2008 from a variety of ICUs (medical, surgical, coronary care, and neonatal). The database denotes the outcome of each patient while they are in ICU (died or survived). The database also includes thousands of records of continuous high-resolution physiologic waveforms and minute-by-minute numerical time series (trends) of physiologic measurements. Since our learning model is to be embedded into an early warning system that is based on heart rate and oxygen saturation rate collected by wireless sensors, we only extract the time series of heart rate and oxygen saturation rate of patients for training the model from MIMIC II. In addition, we only consider patients who died in hospital and who left hospital and was not reported dead at home, while excluding patients who left hospital but died at home. By doing this, we rule out the possibility of judging well-conditioned patients at hospital as soon-to-die cases because of their death at home. We are finally left with 772 patient records and realize that this extracted dataset suffers the class-imbalance problem, i.e. most patients in the dataset are from one class (no deterioration). To deal with this skewed dataset(597:175), later on we will adopt explorary undersampling and demonstrate its improvement on performance.

Our experiment is based on 10-fold cross validation. That is, we divide the data set into 10 smaller datasets with 9 training sets and 1 test set. Each subset is validated once as testing set. The results are the average of all the 10 validations. In addition to listing the AUC, we also give the sensitivity, specificity, PPV and NPV. For logistic regression, since we can vary its results by changing the threshold, we always set the threshold so that the specificity close to 0.95 by choosing a proper threshold when presenting sensitivity, PPV and NPV. For the implementation of nonlinear SVM, we use a RBF kernel.

8.2 Comparison of linear and nonlinear separation using DFA

Prior study [12] in clinical community only considers one single time series with linear separation. We evaluated a number combinations of classifiers and features listed in Table 1 to demonstrate that classifying multiple time series with nonlinear separation will improve the prediction performance for clinical data. For comparison, we employed different classifers with DFA features on heart rate only, oxygen saturation rate only, and both.

From Table 1, we could observe the following facts. First, on single time series, we discover that kernel SVM outperforms linear SVM, showing that clinical data with sparse features is better separated by a nonlinear classfier. Second, the combination of both time series greatly improve the performance of each classifier, which justifies our motivation of combining multiple time series.

8.3 Features combination

Previous methods only make use of limited features such as DFA [12]. In this section, we use a series of increasingly large feature set on two classifiers to see the performance of multiple features, as shown in Table 2. From the table, we can discover that as we add more features, the performance is improved. This is in contrast with Table 1, in which kernel SVM outperforms logistic regression when there are only a small number of features. It shows that all of the newly introduced features contribute to the improvement of performance. We can also observe that the logistic regression classifer outperforms SVM with RBF kernel in our dataset, which means that nonlinear SVM may suffer overfitting when the number of features becomes larger.

8.4 Features selection and exploratory undersampling

To avoid overfitting and improve the generalization ability, we perform the forward feature selection (FFS) technique based on SVM and logistic regression to select the most relevant features. We adopt two kinds of selection criteria: F-Score and AUC. Table 3 shows the performance compar-

Algorithms	Features	AUC
RBF Kernel SVM	DFA	0.6332
	DFA+Cross Feature	0.6565
	DFA+Cross Feature+ApEn	0.6753
	All Features	0.7090
Logistic Regression	DFA	0.5370
	DFA+Cross Feature	0.5731
	DFA+Cross Feature+ApEn	0.5974
	All Features	0.7402

Table 2: The performance comparison of different features.

ison of feature selection using SVM and logistic regression. We can observe that by using feature selection, both SVM and logistic regression get significant improvement on their performance. The selected features for SVM using F-score are standard deviation of Heart Rate, Inertia of Heart Rate, High Frequency of Oxygen Saturation, and Energy Oxygen Saturation. The selected features for SVM using AUC are standard deviation of Heart Rate, Approximate entropy of Heart Rate, Entropy of Oxygen Saturation, Local Homogeneity of Oxygen Saturation, and Inertia of Heart Rate. And, logistic regression outperforms SVM, which makes logistic regression our first choice for further experiments of our learning system. In addition, feature selection based on AUC outperforms the one based on F-Score, for both logistic regression and SVM. Finally, we can see that the number of features selected by logistic regression is larger than the one by SVM, which further demonstrates our conclusion that too many features tend to cause overfitting in SVM with RBF kernel.

Regarding the class-imbalance problem of our dataset, we apply an exploratory undersampling method whose result is shown in Table 4. We can see that, with all features used, logistic regression with exploratory undersampling trained on all features (AUC = 0.7767) outperforms the one without exploratory undersampling (AUC=0.7402). In addition, the combination of logistic regression, exploratory undersampling and forward feature selection with AUC further improves the performance (AUC = 0.8082), which forms the current learning model for our early warning system. Comparing the first row of Table 3 against the last row of Table 4, we can also see that exploratory undersampling also improves performance when feature selection is used on logistic regression.

8.5 Identifying leading risk factors

Other than just achieving better result on prediction performance, with our learning system, we also provide some insights on the leading risk factors for patient deterioration and mortality. Table 5 lists the first dozen of features by our feature selection method with AUC score. We can see that all kinds of proposed features are selected, including DFA, spectral analysis, first order, second order, ApEn and cross-sign features.

Table 6 provides the 10 most significant features of our final logistic regression model, ordered by the magnitude of their coefficients in the model. Note that all feature values are normalize to between 0 and 1, so the coefficient denotes the sensitivity of the model to a feature. With this table, we can identify some factors that are highly related to deterioration. For example, if the local homogenity of patent's heart rate (top ranked in Table 6) is low, then this patient is likely to suffer sudden clinical deterioration and death. The standard deviation of oxygen saturation rate is also a significant factor for clinical deterioration. It is confirmed by the clinical observation that high variation in a physiologic index strongly indicates the low stability of patients' health status.

Feature
standard deviation of heart rate
Apen of heart rate
Energy of oxygen saturation
LF of oxygen saturation in SPA
LF of heart rate in SPA
DFA of oxygen saturation
Mean of heart rate
HF of heart rate in SPA
Inertia of heart rate
Homogeneity of heart rate
Energy of heart rate
linear correlation of heart rate of oxygen saturation

Table 5: The first 12 selected features in logistic regression using forward feature selection with AUC.

Feature	Coefficient
local homogenity of heart rate	-14.50
standard deviation of oxygen saturation	10.20
entropy of oxygen saturation	10.17
low frequency of heart rate	8.62
local homogenity of oxygen saturation	7.77
LF/HF of oxygen saturation	4.53
inertia of heart rate	3.86
entropy of heart rate	2.97
low frequency of oxygen saturation	-2.89
mean of oxygen saturation	-2.86

Table 6: The 10 highest-weighted variables of our final logistical regression model (with exploratory undersampling and feature selection based on AUC).

9. CONCLUSION

Preventing clinical deterioration and death in hospital patients by mining electronic medical records is a promising and important trend in US hospitals. We have developed a predictive system that can provide early alert of deterioration for patients under real-time monitoring in ICUs and in general hospital units, as enabled by wireless sensing systems such as the RDS system we developed in Barnes-Jewish Hospital. Our approach integrated features from a diversity of fields including chaos theory (DFA), signal processing (spectral analysis and entropy), and machine learning (time-series features). We showed that the combined feature set gives significant performance improvement. We also showed that robust classifiers such as kernel SVM and logistic regression outperform previously used linear classifiers. Moreover, we showed that using established data mining methods, including feature selection and exploratory undersampling, can also improve the performance. With a AUC over 0.8 and sensitivity near 0.5 at 0.95 specificity, our final logistic regression model is approved by medical experts for a clinical trial at a major hospital.

Method	Number of Selected features	AUC	Specificity	Sensitivity	PPV	NPV
Logistic Regression (AUC)	23	**0.7844**	0.9483	0.5208	0.7692	0.8567
Logistic Regression (F-score)	26	0.7592	0.9483	0.5104	0.7656	0.8540
SVM (AUC)	5	0.7752	0.9654	0.4852	0.8041	0.8651
SVM (F-score)	4	0.7736	0.9497	0.4833	0.7163	0.8652

Table 3: The performance comparison of SVM and logistic regression combined with feature selection based on AUC score and F-score.

Method	AUC	Specificity	Sensitivity	PPV	NPV
Logistic Regression + all features	0.7402	0.9483	0.3646	0.7000	0.8185
Logistic Regression+all features+exploratory undersampling	0.7767	0.9500	0.4615	0.9000	0.6440
Logistic Regression+exploratory undersampling+feature selection	**0.8082**	0.9473	0.4865	0.9000	0.6546

Table 4: The performance of logistic regression using exploratory undersampling. Feature selection is based on the AUC.

10. REFERENCES

[1] R. J. Alcock and Y.Manolopoulos. Time-series similarity queries employing a fearture-based approach. pages 27–29, 1999.

[2] A.McQuatt, P.J.D.Andrews, D.Sleeman, V.Corruble, and P.A.Jones. The analysis of head injury data using decision tree techniques. *Artifical Intelligent in Medicine*, 1620:336–345, 1999.

[3] Y. Chen and C. Lin. Combining svms with various feature selection strategies. In *Taiwan University*, 2005.

[4] I. Guyon, S. Gunn, M. Nikravesh, and L. A.Zadeh, editors. *Feature Extraction: Foundations and Applications (Studies in Fuzziness and Soft Computing)*. 2006.

[5] K. Hu, P. Ch.Ivanov, Z. Chen, P. Carpena, and H. E. Stanley. Effect of trends on detrended fluctuation analysis. *Physical Review*, 2001.

[6] A. Khosla, Y. Cao, C. Lin, H. Chiu, J. Hu, and H. Lee. An integrated machine learning approach to stroke prediction. In *Prodeedings of the 16th ACM SIGKDD international conference on Knowledge discovery and data mining*, pages 183–192, 2010.

[7] J. Ko, J. H. Lim, Y. Chen, R. Musvaloiu-E, A. Terzis, G. M. Masson, T. Gao, W. Destler, and L. S. R. P. Dutton. Medisn: Medical emergency detection in sensor networks. In *Prodeedings of the 6th ACM coference on Embedded network sensor systems*, pages 361–362, 2010.

[8] X. Liu, J. Wu, and Z. Zhou. Exploratory under-sampling for class-imbalance learning. *Sixth IEEE International Conference on Data Mining*, 2006.

[9] Y. Mao, Y. Chen, G. Hackmann, M. Chen, C. Lu, M. Kollef, and T. Bailey. Early deterioration warning for hospitalized patients by mining clinical data. *International Journal of Knowledge Discovery in Bioinformatics*, 2(3):1–20, 2012.

[10] C. Otto. Telemedicine in the canadian high artic and other remote envirionments. 1999.

[11] C. Peng, S. Havlin, S. H. Eugene, and G. A. L. Quantification of scaling exponents and crossover phenomena in nonstationary heartbeat time series. *Chaos*, 5:82, 1995.

[12] T. Penzel, J. W.Kantelhardt, L. Grote, J.-H. Peter, and A. Bunde. Comparison of detrended fluctuation analysis and spectral analysis for heart rate variability in sleep and sleep apnea. *IEEE Transactions on Biomedical Engineering*, 50:10, 2003.

[13] S. Pincus. Approximate entropy as a measure of system complexity. volume 88, pages 2297–2301, 1991.

[14] R.Loforte, G.Carrault, L.Mainardi, and A.Beuche. Heart rate and respiration relationship as a diagnostic tool for late onset sepsis in sick preterm infants. *Computers in Cardiology*, 33:737–740, 2006.

[15] M. Saeed, M. Villarroel, A. T. Reisner, G. Clifford, L. W. Lehman, G. Moody, T. Heldt, T. H. Kyaw, B. Moody, and R. G. Mark. Multiparameter intelligent monitoring in intensive care ii: a public-access intensive care unit database. *Critical Care Medicine*, 39(5), 2011.

[16] Y. Saeys, I. Inza, and P. Larranaga. A review of feature selection techniques in bioinformatics. *Bioinformatics*, 23:2507–2517, 2007.

[17] W. Vladimir N. Vapnik. *Statistical Learning Theory*. 1998.

[18] W.A.Knaus, E.A.Draper, D.P.Wagner, and J.E.Zimmerman. Apache ii: a severity of disease classification system. *Critical Care Medicine*, 13(10):818–829, 1985.

[19] Yandiola, P. P. Espana, A. Capelastegui, J. Quintana, D. Rosa, G. Inmaculada, B. Amaia, Z. Rafael, M. Rosario, and T. Antonio. Prospective comparison of severity scores for predicting clinically relevant outcomes for patients hospitalized with community-acquired pneumonia. 135(6):1572–9, 2009.

[20] J. Ye, K. Chen, T. Wu, J. Li, Z. Zhao, R. Patel, M. Bae, R. Janardan, H. Liu, G. Alexander, and E. Reiman. Heterogeneous data fusion for alzheimer's disease study. pages 1025–1033, 2008.

[21] J. Zhou, Y. Lei, J. Liu, and J. Ye. A multi-task learning formulation for predicting disease progression. In *Proceedings of the 17th ACM SIGKDD international conference on Knowledge discovery and data mining*, pages 814–822, 2011.

Multi-Source Learning for Joint Analysis of Incomplete Multi-Modality Neuroimaging Data

Lei Yuan[1,2], Yalin Wang[1], Paul M. Thompson[3], Vaibhav A. Narayan[4], Jieping Ye[1,2]
[1]Center for Evolutionary Medicine and Informatics, The Biodesign Institute, ASU, Tempe, AZ
[2]Department of Computer Science and Engineering, ASU, Tempe, AZ
[3]Department of Neurology, UCLA, Los Angeles, CA
[4]Johnson & Johnson Pharmaceutical Research & Development, LLC, Titusville, NJ

ABSTRACT

Incomplete data present serious problems when integrating large-scale brain imaging data sets from different imaging modalities. In the Alzheimer's Disease Neuroimaging Initiative (ADNI), for example, over half of the subjects lack cerebrospinal fluid (CSF) measurements; an independent half of the subjects do not have fluorodeoxyglucose positron emission tomography (FDG-PET) scans; many lack proteomics measurements. Traditionally, subjects with missing measures are discarded, resulting in a severe loss of available information. We address this problem by proposing two novel learning methods where all the samples (with at least one available data source) can be used. In the first method, we divide our samples according to the availability of data sources, and we learn shared sets of features with state-of-the-art sparse learning methods. Our second method learns a base classifier for each data source independently, based on which we represent each source using a single column of prediction scores; we then estimate the missing prediction scores, which, combined with the existing prediction scores, are used to build a multi-source fusion model. To illustrate the proposed approaches, we classify patients from the ADNI study into groups with Alzheimer's disease (AD), mild cognitive impairment (MCI) and normal controls, based on the multi-modality data. At baseline, ADNI's 780 participants (172 AD, 397 MCI, 211 Normal), have at least one of four data types: magnetic resonance imaging (MRI), FDG-PET, CSF and proteomics. These data are used to test our algorithms. Comprehensive experiments show that our proposed methods yield stable and promising results.

Categories and Subject Descriptors

H.2.8 [**Database Management**]: Database Applications - Data Mining

General Terms

Algorithms

Keywords

Multi-source feature learning, multi-task learning, incomplete data

1. INTRODUCTION

Alzheimer's disease (AD) is a highly prevalent neurodegenerative disease, and is widely recognized as a major, escalating epidemic and a world-wide challenge to global health care systems [22]. AD is the the most common type of dementia, accounting for 60-80% of age-related dementia cases. The direct cost of care for AD patients by family members and healthcare professionals is more than $100 billion per year; this figure is expected to rise dramatically as the population ages over the next several decades [33]. In AD patients, neurons and their connections are progressively destroyed, leading to loss of cognitive function and ultimately death. The underlying pathology is thought to precede the onset of cognitive symptoms by many years [3, 19]. Efforts are underway to find early diagnostic markers to evaluate AD risk pre-symptomatically in a rapid and rigorous way. Such findings will help establish early interventions to prevent or at least postpone the onset of AD, or reduce the risk of developing the disease.

Neuroimaging is a powerful tool to measure disease progression and therapeutic efficacy in AD and mild cognitive impairment (MCI). Neuroimaging research offers great potential to discover features that can identify individuals early in the course of dementing illness; several candidate neuroimaging biomarkers have been examined in recent cross-sectional and longitudinal neuroimaging studies [9, 12]. Reduced fluorodeoxyglucose (FDG) PET measurements of the cerebral metabolic rate for glucose in brain regions preferentially affected by AD, structural MRI measures of brain shrinkage, and cerebrospinal fluid (CSF) measurements are among the best established biomarkers of AD progression and pathology [33]. Realizing the importance of combining neuroimaging and genetics, NIH in 2003 funded the Alzheimer's Disease Neuroimaging Initiative (ADNI [29, 20], PI: Michael W. Weiner). The initiative is facilitating the scientific evaluation of neuroimaging data including magnetic resonance imaging (MRI), positron emission tomography (PET), other biomarkers, and clinical and neuropsychological assessments for predicting the onset and progression of MCI and AD. By identifying more sensitive and specific markers of very early AD progression, these efforts should make it easier to diagnose AD earlier as well as develop, assess, and monitor new treatments.

Clinical and research studies commonly acquire complementary brain images, neuropsychological and genetic data for each participant for a more accurate and rigorous assessment of the disease status and likelihood of progression. Advances in image analysis make it possible to use one image modality to support the analysis of a complementary image modality [17, 6, 18, 23]. However, only a few systems, e.g., [40, 28, 11, 41, 38, 21, 39, 24, 43], applied data mining and machine learning techniques such as the multivariate linear model and partial least squares to characterize the

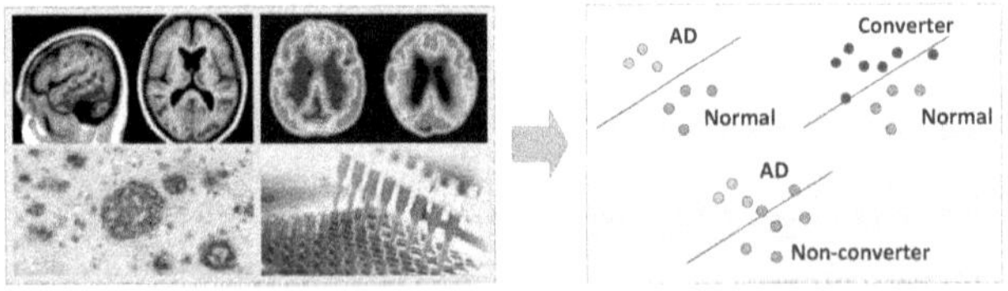

Figure 1: Illustration of integrating multiple heterogeneous data sources for disease status prediction tasks. More details on the different data sources and prediction tasks used in this study may be found in Section 3.

linkage between the patterns of information from the same individual's brain images and other biological measures. Instead, most researchers perform statistical analysis by analyzing different images separately. In general, these "unimodal" analysis could be improved by considering other sources of relevant information from multiple imaging modalities, e.g., PET and MRI, and non-imaging data sets from genomics and proteomics. It is a common belief that by integrating multiple heterogeneous sources (as illustrated in Figure 1), one may not only provide more accurate information on AD progression and pathology, but also better predict cognitive decline before the onset of illness, or at least in the earliest stages of disease.

One common problem that hampers the use of multi-modality imaging approach is the problem of *missing data*. Missing data present a special challenge when integrating large-scale biomedical data. Incomplete data is ubiquitous in real-world biomedical applications. In ADNI, over half of the subjects lack CSF measurements; an independent half of the subjects do not have FDG-PET; many lack proteomics measurements. Missing data may be due to the high cost of certain measures (e.g., PET scans), poor data quality, dropout of the patients from the study, etc. Some measures, such as CSF biomarkers, require more invasive procedures (such as lumbar puncture) which not all study participants are willing to consent to. Some subjects in a longitudinal study may miss at least one of the regular assessments, or their data quality may be insufficient for accurate analysis at some time points. The simplest approach removes all samples with missing values, but this throws away a vast amount of useful information and dramatically reduces the number of samples in the analysis. As a result, a subject with incomplete data cannot be studied for classification and prognosis. Moreover, with this approach, the resource and time devoted to those subjects with incomplete data are totally wasted. A number of previous works acknowledged the challenge of missing data and discussed general strategies [37, 14, 32]. An alternative and popular approach is to estimate missing entries based on the observed values. Many algorithms have been proposed for this [15, 34, 13, 35]. While these methods work well when missing data are rare, they are less effective when a significant amount of data is missing, e.g., when all PET features from half of the subjects are missing. Recently, trace norm minimization has been proposed for missing data estimation [4, 5]. This can be effective even when a large amount of data is missing. However, it does assume that the missing locations are random; it is less effective when a complete block of the data is missing, e.g., the complete block of all PET features from half of the subjects. Therefore, computational methods are needed to integrate heterogeneous data with a block-wise missing pattern ("block-wise missing" means a large chunk of data is missing for one or more data sources - an example is shown in Figure 2). Without such a method, it is quite challenging to build a highly accurate classifier to process any real multi-modality imaging data sets.

To achieve multi-modality integration while taking into account the block-wise missing nature of the data, we propose two novel learning frameworks. Our first system is based on a novel multi-task sparse learning framework, named incomplete multi-source feature learning (iMSF). Based on the availability of different feature sources, we divide the data set into several learning tasks, from each of which a unique classifier is learned. We then impose a structural sparse learning regularization onto these tasks, such that a common set of features is selected among these tasks. Therefore, we exploit the multi-task nature of the problem and the feature set is learned jointly among different tasks. In our second system, we tackle the difficulty of block-wise data completion by proposing a model score completion scheme (ScoreComp). Each data source is first treated independently, where a base classifier is learned such that the data source is converted into a single column consisting of model prediction scores. Thus, the missing data blocks become single missing values in the new representation of the data. Data imputation techniques are then applied and a new classifier is learned on the completed score matrix such that multiple sources are integrated together.

As an illustrative application, we study clinical group (diagnostic) classification problems in the ADNI baseline data set. Comprehensive experiments demonstrate the promising and stable performance of the proposed systems. 780 subjects in the ADNI baseline data set have their diagnosis (AD, MCI or Normal) available and have at least one type of features available (meaning an image or related clinical measure), including MRI, FDG-PET, CSF and proteomics. For the MCI subjects, we further make use of their 4-year follow up diagnosis to divide them into 2 sub-groups. We label those who had converted to AD by the time of a later visit as "converter" and those who stayed stable as "non-converter". We set out to use these data to solve clinical group classification problems (AD vs. Normal; AD vs. Non-converter and Converter vs. Normal). For our experiments, we obtained MRI, CSF and proteomics feature sets from the ADNI web site (`http://adni.loni.ucla.edu/`) and we processed FDG-PET data using the image analysis package, SPM (SPM8, `http://www.fil.ion.ucl.ac.uk/spm`) using the statistical region of interest (sROI) method. Besides our multi-source learning frameworks for incomplete data, we also include five other methods to estimate missing values: (1) the "Zero" method: a method that fills missing values with zeros; (2) EM: a missing value imputation method based on the expectation-maximization (EM) algorithm [34]; (3) SVD (singular value decomposition): a method for matrix completion using a low rank approximation to the full matrix; (4) KNN: a missing value imputation method based on the k-nearest neighbor principle [15]; and (5) SVT: a matrix completion method based on trace norm minimization [4, 5]. The experimental results show that our proposed methods are effective for incomplete multi-source data fusion.

The rest of the paper is organized as follows: in Section 2, we present two multi-source learning methods for a joint analysis of multi-modality data with a "block-wise" missing pattern; we have performed comprehensive experiments to evaluate the proposed methods and the results are reported in Section 3; finally, we conclude our paper in Section 4.

2. PROPOSED METHODS

In many applications, multiple data sources may suffer from a considerable amount of missing data. For example, in the ADNI data acquisition phase, many subjects lack a subset of measures, resulting in a scenario shown in Figure 2, where large chunks of missing data are marked by the white areas. A simple and popular

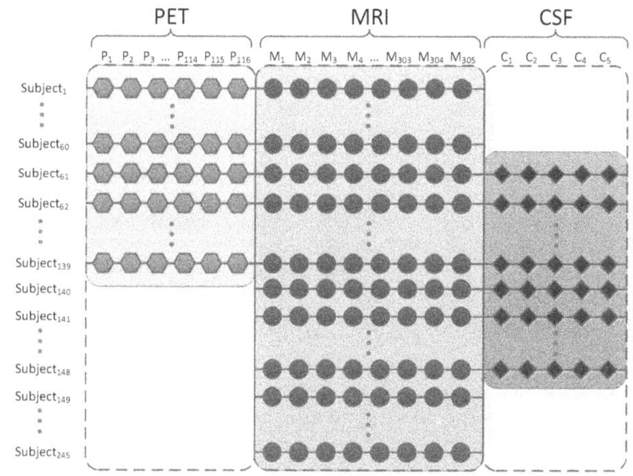

Figure 2: Illustration of the "block-wise" pattern of missing data for the ADNI data set. In this figure, we show AD and normal control subjects only. For simplicity, we focus on those subjects with complete MRI measures.

approach is to remove all the subjects with missing values, but this greatly reduces the number of samples and fails to fully use the information in the data set. In Figure 2, only 79 subjects (Subjects 61-139) out of a total of 245 subjects do not have missing values. Next, we present two methods for dealing with multi-source data with block-wise missing values.

2.1 Proposed Method I: Incomplete Multi-Source Feature Learning

In our feature learning framework described below, we fully use the multiple heterogeneous data with a block-wise missing pattern by exploiting the underlying structure in the multi-source data. Our proposed framework formulates the prediction problem as a multi-task learning problem [1, 2, 26, 44] by first decomposing the prediction problem into a set of tasks, one for each combination of data sources available, and then building the models for all tasks simultaneously.

For example, considering a data set with three sources (CSF, MRI, PET) and assuming all samples have MRI measures, we first partition the samples into multiple blocks (4 in this case), one for each combination of data sources available: (1) PET, MRI; (2) PET, MRI, CSF; (3) MRI, CSF; and (4) MRI. We then build four models, one for each block of data, resulting in four prediction tasks (Figure 3).

A simple approach to deal with the missing data is to build these four models separately, but that does not fully use the information in the multi-source data. Indeed, the sample size for each of these four tasks is even smaller, resulting in the *large dimension small sample size* problem. We address this by employing a joint feature learning formulation. We formulate our proposed framework as follows. Suppose the data set is divided into m tasks: $T^i = \{x_j^i, y_j^i\}, i = 1 \ldots m, j = 1 \ldots N_i$, where N_i is the number of subjects in the i-th task, and (x_j^i, y_j^i) is the j-th subject from the i-th task. For each task, we consider the following linear model:

$$f^i(x_j) = (\beta^i)^T x_j^i$$

where β^i is the weight vector, including the model parameters for the i-th task. Denote $\beta = \{\beta^1, \ldots, \beta^m\}$ as the collection of all model parameters. Assume that we have a total of S data sources, and the feature dimensionality of the s-th source is denoted as p_s. For notational convenience, we introduce an index function $I(s,k)$ as follows: $\beta_{I(s,k)}$ denotes all the model parameters corresponding to the k-th feature in the s-th data source. The proposed multi-task feature learning framework is:

$$\min_{\beta} \frac{1}{m} \sum_{i=1}^{m} \frac{1}{N_i} \sum_{j=1}^{N_i} L(x_j^i, y_j^i, \beta_i) + \lambda \sum_{s=1}^{S} \sum_{k=1}^{p_s} \left\| \beta_{I(s,k)} \right\|_2 \quad (1)$$

where $L(\cdot)$ is the loss function, and we adopt the logistic loss in our study. The second part of the formulation, which is essentially an $\ell_{2,1}$-norm regularization on the model parameters [42], leads to a solution with the desired sparsity, that is, all models involving a specific source are constrained to select a common set of features for this particular source. The proposed formulation is novel as it (1) formulates the incomplete multi-source fusion as a multi-task learning problem, and (2) extends existing multi-task feature learning formulations to accommodate missing feature values.

The regularization parameter λ in (1) controls the sparsity of the solution. Generally speaking, the larger λ is, the sparser the solution will be. However, in practice, the same λ value will induce different sparsity for different data sets. To select a proper range of parameters, we follow a similar approach as discussed by Liu et al. [27] to obtain a value λ_{max} for each specific problem such that if $\lambda \geq \lambda_{max}$, the optimal solution to (1) is $\mathbf{0}$. Therefore, we just need to set a *ratio* r such that $\lambda = r\lambda_{max}$, and r is selected in the region $(0, 1)$.

2.1.1 *Efficient Optimization*

The optimization problem proposed in Section 2.2 is the composition of a smooth term and a non-smooth term, which is challenging to solve. In this paper, we propose to solve it using the accelerated gradient descent (AGD) method [31, 30] as in [26] because of its fast convergence rate. Denote the empirical loss as:

$$\ell(\beta) = \frac{1}{m} \sum_{i=1}^{m} \frac{1}{N_i} \sum_{j=1}^{N_i} L(x_j^i, y_j^i, \beta_i),$$

and the non-smooth regularization as:

$$\phi_\lambda(\beta) = \lambda \sum_{s=1}^{S} \sum_{k=1}^{p_s} \left\| \beta_{I(s,k)} \right\|_2.$$

In AGD, we first approximate $\ell(\beta) + \phi_\lambda(\beta)$ by:

$$f_{L,\beta}(\theta) = \ell(\beta) + \langle \ell'(\beta), \theta - \beta \rangle + \theta_\lambda(\theta) + \frac{L}{2} \|\theta - \beta\|^2.$$

In the i-th step, a search point s_i is computed based on the past solutions of the previous steps by $s_i = \beta_i + \tau_i(\beta_i - \beta_{i-1})$. Then, the new solution β_{i+1} is obtained via the minimization of the model at the current search point, that is, $\beta_{i+1} = \arg\min_\theta f_{L,s_i}(\theta)$. This sub-problem is the key component to the optimization, and is often called the proximal operator [7]. A detailed discussion of how to solve this sub-problem efficiently is found in our previous work [26]. By doing so, we successfully bypass the difficulty of computing the sub-gradient of $\phi_\lambda(\cdot)$; algorithm details are summarized in Algorithm 1.

2.2 Proposed Method II: Model Score Completion

The iMSF framework proposed in Section 2.1 tackles the problem in a "row-wise" manner by dividing samples into different

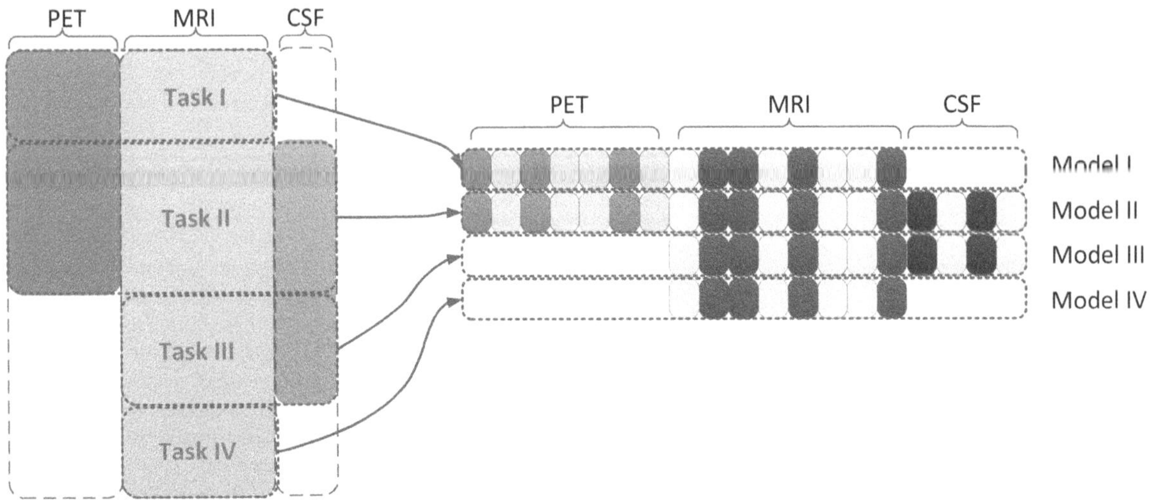

Figure 3: Illustration of the proposed multi-task feature learning framework for incomplete multi-source data fusion. In the proposed framework, we first partition the samples into multiple blocks (four blocks in this case), one for each combination of data sources available: (1) PET, MRI; (2) PET, MRI, CSF; (3) MRI, CSF; (4) MRI. We then build four models, one for each block of data, resulting in four prediction tasks. We use a joint feature learning framework that learns all models simultaneously. Specifically, all models involving a specific source are constrained to select a common set of features for that particular source.

Algorithm 1 Efficient Optimization for the Multi-Source Feature Learning Framework

Input: L_0, λ, β_0, n
Output: β_{n+1}
  Initialize $\beta_1 = \beta_0, \alpha_{-1} = 0, \alpha_0 = 1$, and $L = L_0$
  for $i = 1$ to n **do**
    Set $\tau_i = \frac{\alpha_{i-2}-1}{\alpha_{i-1}}$, $s_i = \beta_i + \tau_i(\beta_i - \beta_{i-1})$
    Find the smallest $L = L_{i-1}, 2L_{i-1}, \ldots$ such that $\ell(\beta_{i+1}) + \phi_\lambda(\beta_{i+1}) \leq f_{L,s_i}(\beta_{i+1})$ holds, where

$$\beta_{i+1} = \arg\min_\theta f_{L,s_i}(\theta)$$

    Set $L_i = L$ and $\alpha_{i+1} = \frac{1+\sqrt{1+4\alpha_i^2}}{2}$
  end for

groups. We next propose to tackle the problem in a "column-wise" manner. From Figure 2 we can observe another characteristic of this problem: if a certain data source is available for a particular sample (e.g., PET for subject 1), the complete set of features from this data source will be available. Intuitively, it is more challenging to estimate a complete block of missing values than a single value. This motivates us to design the model score completion scheme (ScoreComp). The overview of the ScoreComp is illustrated in Figure 4. Given an incomplete multi-source data set, we first train a base model on each individual data source using the available samples, and the base model is applied to produce prediction scores for the corresponding samples for this data source; thus each data source is represented by a single column of scores, and all data sources together are represented as a matrix of prediction scores with missing values. A missing value estimation method is then applied to obtain a complete set of model scores, which are treated as newly derived features to train our final classifier. That is, the prediction score from each data source is considered as a feature.

We formally describe our ScoreComp method as follows. Consider a labeled data set $\{\mathcal{D}_i, \mathcal{Y}_i\}, i = 1, \ldots, N$, with S incomplete

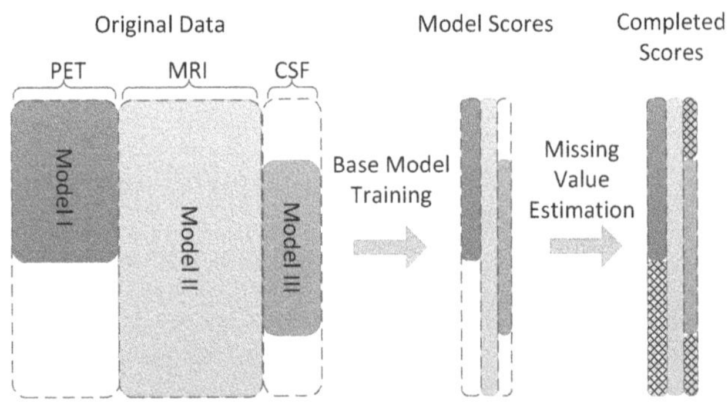

Figure 4: Illustration of the proposed model score completion scheme. We first train a base model on each individual data source using the available samples, and the base model is applied to produce prediction scores for this data source; thus each data source is represented by a single column of (incomplete) scores. A missing value estimation method is applied to obtain a complete set of model scores, which are treated as newly derived features to train our final classifier.

data sources. Let the set $sc(i) \subset \{1, \ldots, S\}$ denote the available data sources for the ith subject, such that $\mathcal{D}_i = \{X_i^s | s \in sc(i)\}$, where X_i^s is the feature vector of the ith subject from the sth source. The goal of the ScoreComp method is to derive a completed prediction score matrix $\tilde{A} \in \mathbb{R}^{N \times S}$ from the original data set. Details are given below:

Base Model Training Step. We first choose a classifier learning algorithm $\mathcal{L}$, based on which a prediction model is constructed for each data source:

$$\mathcal{M}_s = \mathcal{L}\left(\{(X_i^s, \mathcal{Y}_i) | s \in sc(i)\}\right), \quad s = 1, \ldots S.$$

Then, we use these models to construct an incomplete prediction score matrix $\hat{A} \in \mathbb{R}^{N \times S}$ given by:

$$\hat{A}_{i,s} = \begin{cases} \mathcal{M}_s(X_i^s) & \text{if } s \in sc(i) \\ \text{NaN} & \text{otherwise} \end{cases},$$

where $\mathcal{M}_s(X_i^s)$ is the prediction score of model $\mathcal{M}_s$ on feature vector X_i^s.

Missing Value Estimation Step. In this step, we choose a missing value estimation algorithm $\mathcal{E}$ such that $\tilde{A} = \mathcal{E}(\hat{A})$, where $\tilde{A}$ is the completed prediction score matrix. $\tilde{A}$ is then treated as the derived feature matrix for the original data set $\{\mathcal{D}_i, \mathcal{Y}_i\}$. The final model $\mathcal{M}$ is learned using $(\tilde{A}, \mathcal{Y})$ so that the data sources are integrated.

Prediction of Unlabeled Sample. Suppose we are given a set of unlabeled data $\{\mathcal{U}_j\}$, $j = 1, \ldots, M$, such that $\mathcal{U}_j = \{X_j^s | s \in sc(j)\}$. ScoreComp will first derive a completed feature matrix $\tilde{B} \in \mathbb{R}^{M \times S}$, which is then fed into $\mathcal{M}$ for prediction. To obtain $\tilde{B}$, we first use the models learned in the base model training step to construct an incomplete model score matrix $\hat{B} \in \mathbb{R}^{M \times S}$ given by:

$$\hat{B}_{j,s} = \begin{cases} \mathcal{M}_s(X_j^s) & \text{if } s \in sc(j) \\ \text{NaN} & \text{otherwise} \end{cases}.$$

Combining this with the previously obtained complete matrix $\tilde{A}$, we obtain:

$$C = \mathcal{E}\left(\begin{bmatrix} \tilde{A} \\ \hat{B} \end{bmatrix}\right), \quad C \in \mathbb{R}^{(N+M) \times S}.$$

Finally, by extracting the lower M rows of matrix C, we can obtain the derived feature matrix $\tilde{B}$ for the unlabeled data set.

Like the iMSF method, all available information is used in the integration process. Note that in ScoreComp, we still estimate missing values; but instead of estimating blocks of missing data, we only need to impute the prediction scores. Another advantage of this framework is its simplicity. No additional parameters are introduced, and one can choose any classification algorithms and/or missing value estimation method that suit the data set at hand. In this study, we chose the random forest classifier [25] as the base model learning algorithm $\mathcal{L}$, and our final model $\mathcal{M}$ was trained using ridge regression. We also tried various missing data estimation methods, and more details may be found in Section 3.

3. EXPERIMENTAL RESULTS

In this section, we report the results of our experiments to evaluate the effectiveness of our proposed methods. As noted earlier, we used all the subjects who had at least one feature type available among four different data sources including MRI, PET, CSF and proteomics, and challenge our method with the problem of distinguishing AD, MCI and NC subjects from each other. In our binary classification test scenarios, the relative performances of different methods are evaluated using several metrics including accuracy, sensitivity and specificity.

3.1 Subjects

Data used in this paper were obtained from the Alzheimer's Disease Neuroimaging Initiative (ADNI) database (`http://adni.loni.ucla.edu`). The ADNI was launched in 2003 by the National Institute on Aging (NIA), the National Institute of Biomedical Imaging and Bioengineering (NIBIB), the Food and Drug Administration (FDA), private pharmaceutical companies and non-profit organizations, as a $60 million, 5-year public-private partnership. The primary goal of ADNI has been to test whether serial magnetic resonance imaging (MRI), positron emission tomography (PET), other biological markers, and clinical and neuropsychological assessment can be combined to measure the progression of MCI and AD. Determination of sensitive and specific markers of very early AD progression is intended to aid researchers and clinicians to develop new treatments and monitor their effectiveness, as well as lessen the time and cost of clinical trials.

In terms of data collected at baseline, a total of 822 ADNI participants were recruited from 59 sites across the U.S. and Canada. These including 229 Normal (normal elderly controls), 405 with MCI, and 188 with AD, ranging in age from 55 to 90 years. Phenotype data included structural MRI scans acquired on 1.5T MRI scanners, and clinical and neuropsychological assessments. Additional data such as 3-Tesla MRI, FDG-PET, PIB-PET (a PET scanning method using the amyloid-sensitive ligand, Pittsburgh compound B), and fluid biomarkers are available for some subjects as well. In our experiments, we use pre-processed 1.5 Tesla (T) MRI imaging features. Besides these data, we were able to include other subjects who had at least one of three data types available: FDG-PET, CSF, and/or proteomics. As a result, baseline data from a total of 780 participants (172 AD, 397 MCI, 211 Normal) were used to test our algorithms.

The MRI image features in this study were based on the imaging data from the ADNI database processed by the UCSF team, who performed cortical reconstruction and volumetric segmentations with the FreeSurfer image analysis suite (`http://surfer.nmr.mgh.harvard.edu/`). The processed MRI features come from a total of 648 subjects (138 AD, 319 MCI and 191 Normal), and can be grouped into 5 categories: average cortical thickness, standard deviation in cortical thickness, the volumes of cortical parcellations, the volumes of specific white matter parcellations, and the total surface area of the cortex. There were 305 MRI features in total. We also downloaded FDG-PET images of 327 subjects (74 AD, 172 MCI, and 81 Normal) from the ADNI website. With SPM8 (`http://www.fil.ion.ucl.ac.uk/spm/`), we processed these FDG-PET images. We applied Automated Anatomical Labeling (AAL) [36] to extract each of the 116 anatomical volumes of interest (AVOI) and derived average image values from each AVOI, for every subject. Baseline CSF samples were acquired from 416 subjects (102 AD, 200 MCI and 114 Normal) by the ADNI Biomarker Core laboratory at the University of Pennsylvania Medical Center [36]. In our study, we use 5 measures obtained from the CSF, including levels of beta amyloid 1-42 ($A\beta_{1-42}$), tau protein (Tau), phosphorylated-tau protein 181 (pTau_{181p}) along with two CSF ratios (Tau/$A\beta_{1-42}$ and $\text{pTau}_{181p}/A\beta_{1-42}$). The proteomics data set (97 AD, 345 MCI, and 54 Normal) was produced by the Biomarkers Consortium Project "Use of Targeted Multiplex Proteomic Strategies to Identify Plasma-Based Biomarkers in Alzheimer's Disease"[1] (see URL in footnote). We use 147 measures from the proteomic data downloaded from the ADNI web site. As a result, for a subject with all four types of data available, a total of 573 measures were studied in our classification experiment. The number of samples from each category corresponding to each type of feature utilized in this study is summarized in Table 1.

3.2 Comparison of iMSF, ScoreComp and imputation methods

In our first set of experiments, we apply our proposed methods to the full multi-source data set including MRI, PET, proteomics and CSF for solving clinical group classification problems (AD vs. Normal; AD vs. Non-converter and Converter vs. Normal). 780

[1] `http://adni.loni.ucla.edu/wp-content/uploads/2010/11/BC_Plasma_Proteomics_Data_Primer.pdf`

Table 1: The number of available samples and features used in this study.

	MRI	PET	CSF	Proteomics
# of AD Subjects	138	74	102	97
# of MCI Subjects	319	172	200	345
# of Normal Subjects	191	81	114	54
# of Features	305	116	5	147

subjects were analyzed. Among them, each subject has at least one of the four data sources (MRI, FDG-PET, CSF and proteomics features) available. We first randomly select a portion (from 50% to 75%) of samples as the training set to learn the model, and then apply the model to predict the labels on the remaining data, used as a non-overlapping test set. We repeated this process 30 times; the average performance is reported.

For comparison purposes, we included the following missing value estimation methods:

Zero: this is the most intuitive way to impute missing values - we assign zero to any element that is missing. When the data set is first normalized to have zero mean and unit standard deviation, this is equivalent to mean value imputation.

KNN: missing value imputation using the k-nearest neighbor method [15]. The KNN method replaces the missing value in the data matrix with the corresponding value from the nearest column. That is to say, KNN will first identify the most similar feature to the current one with a missing value, and then use this feature as a guess for the missing one.

EM: this method imputes missing values using the expectation-maximization (EM) algorithm [34]. An iteration of the EM algorithm includes two steps. In the E step, we estimate the mean and covariance matrix from the data matrix (with missing values filled with guesses from previous M step, or initialized as zeros); then in the M step, the missing value of each data column is filled in with their conditional expectation values based on the available values and the estimated mean and the covariance. We then re-estimate the mean and the variance based on the new estimates, therefore entering the next EM iteration.

SVD: this is a standard method for matrix completion based on a low rank approximation. The SVD based estimation works in a similar way to the EM method above. We first provide some initial guesses (such as 0) to the missing data values, and then we apply singular value decomposition (SVD) to obtain a low-rank approximation of the filled-in matrix. Next, we update the missing values using their corresponding values in the low-rank estimation. Finally, we apply SVD to the updated matrix again and the process is repeated until convergence.

SVT: Recently, trace norm minimization has been proposed for missing data estimation [4, 5]. This can be effective even when a large amount of data is missing. Therefore, it will be interesting to see how this algorithm (singular value thresholding or SVT) performs in our particular setting. We acquire the SVT program online (`http://svt.stanford.edu`) and follow their suggestions for parameter setting.

The classification results are summarized in Table 2. For our proposed iMSF method, five ratios (0.001, 0.01, 0.1, 0.2 and 0.4) were used for the regularization parameter λ. We first run our iMSF method to learn a set of features for each different task, and then train a random forest classifier [25] on each learning task using the selected features. The best and average performance obtained using these five ratios are reported in Table 2, as "iMSF-Best" and "iMSF-Average" respectively. For the proposed ScoreComp scheme, we first use random forest to obtain the prediction score for the incomplete data set, and apply three different missing value estimation methods (Zero, EM and KNN) to obtain the completed score matrix. Then, ridge regression is applied to integrate the data sources together. The performance using three different missing value estimation methods is reported in Table 2 as "ScoreComp-Zero", "ScoreComp-EM" and "ScoreComp-KNN" respectively.

From Table 2, we can observe that for the AD vs. Normal problem, our ScoreComp performs best, with about 90% accuracy. The top 2 methods in terms of performance are "ScoreComp-EM" and "ScoreComp-KNN" in all training ratios, and they tend to produce comparable results. The AD vs. Normal problem is considered to be less challenging, and this might explain why its simplicity may give ScoreComp method an edge over iMSF.

In the more challenging settings where MCI subjects are involved, we obtain low sensitivity in the AD vs. Non-converter case and low specificity in the Converter vs. Normal case. In these settings, iMSF performs much better – it provides more balanced classification results on both the positive and negative classes. For example, in the Converter vs. Normal problem, using 75% of data for training, missing value estimation based methods only achieve about 70% specificity, but our proposed iMSF achieves an average of 89% among the five different parameters. Therefore, even though ScoreComp achieves a higher accuracy in the AD vs. Non-converter case, we still consider iMSF as the best method for these settings. This may be due to the fact that our iMSF algorithm took a more systematic approach in using multiple sources of information for classification. A detailed comparison with published results using the ADNI data set may be found in the Discussion section.

Among different variations of the ScoreComp method illustrated in Table 2, "ScoreComp-EM" and "ScoreComp-KNN" produce more stable results than "ScoreComp-Zero", where the missing scores are substituted with zeros. For example, in the AD vs. Non-converter case, all three variations yield comparable performance, while in the Converter vs. Normal case, "ScoreComp-Zero" yields much lower specificity. We can conclude that in the missing value estimation step of our ScoreComp method, an effective algorithm can indeed enhance the classification performance by using the model scores from other samples. Interestingly, the five other different missing value estimation methods (Zero, EM, KNN, SVD and SVT) perform comparably to each other. Thus, estimating the block-wise missing values directly does not give much edge over simply substituting missing elements with zeros. This further justifies the effectiveness of our ScoreComp method.

3.3 Comparison with single source classification

Though it is a common belief that by integrating multiple heterogeneous sources, one can predict AD progression more accurately, it is still interesting to see how much we improve classification performance by using multi-modality data. Therefore, we extract the 648 subjects that have MRI features available (with complete data), and perform leave-one-out classification on the same problems we discussed before. We then extract the classification results for the same 648 subjects from our proposed methods, so that the comparison can be made using the same sample pool. Results are summarized in Table 3.

As we see in Table 3, using multiple data sources greatly improves the performance in each case. This is because we not only learn from additional information from the current sample (when data sources other than MRI are available), but we also use the information from other samples that are thrown away in the unimodal case.

Table 2: Classification performance comparison of the proposed iMSF, ScoreComp and missing value estimation methods (Zero, EM, KNN, SVD and SVT) in terms of accuracy, sensitivity and specificity when the training percentage varies from 50% to 75%.

	AD vs. Normal			AD vs. Non-converter			Converter vs. Normal		
Training Size 50%	Accuracy	Sensitivity	Specificity	Accuracy	Sensitivity	Specificity	Accuracy	Sensitivity	Specificity
iMSF-Best	86.37%	85.64%	**87.65%**	78.05%	**57.34%**	89.91%	**91.20%**	94.11%	**89.59%**
iMSF-Average	83.00%	81.56%	84.80%	77.51%	55.97%	88.64%	90.34%	93.31%	84.18%
ScoreComp-Zero	87.31%	87.61%	87.35%	81.25%	53.26%	**95.68%**	83.15%	**99.32%**	48.12%
ScoreComp-EM	89.74%	94.13%	85.32%	81.05%	53.35%	95.31%	88.99%	98.73%	68.30%
ScoreComp-KNN	**90.13%**	**94.87%**	85.37%	**81.46%**	56.02%	94.58%	87.60%	98.89%	63.49%
Zero	85.38%	87.74%	83.23%	77.25%	44.10%	94.14%	89.48%	97.93%	71.36%
EM	87.20%	88.76%	85.75%	78.11%	47.25%	93.80%	89.40%	97.97%	70.95%
KNN	85.79%	88.10%	83.66%	75.15%	36.78%	94.59%	86.40%	97.88%	61.41%
SVD	83.89%	84.94%	82.96%	75.73%	43.00%	92.37%	87.57%	97.09%	67.07%
SVT	55.75%	61.31%	50.70%	81.15%	56.82%	93.48%	71.69%	87.81%	36.34%
Training Size 66.7%	Accuracy	Sensitivity	Specificity	Accuracy	Sensitivity	Specificity	Accuracy	Sensitivity	Specificity
iMSF-Best	88.77%	86.77%	**91.25%**	80.55%	**65.83%**	89.03%	**93.17%**	95.36%	**90.52%**
iMSF-Average	86.07%	83.23%	89.23%	80.12%	63.70%	88.16%	92.40%	94.72%	87.37%
ScoreComp-Zero	88.18%	86.48%	90.10%	**83.48%**	59.90%	**94.96%**	84.48%	**99.53%**	50.13%
ScoreComp-EM	**90.28%**	93.64%	86.61%	83.25%	60.85%	94.12%	90.82%	99.16%	72.07%
ScoreComp-KNN	90.19%	**94.48%**	85.51%	83.30%	62.25%	93.56%	89.56%	99.24%	67.66%
Zero	86.79%	88.80%	84.61%	80.87%	52.21%	94.56%	92.30%	98.84%	77.32%
EM	88.46%	88.40%	88.52%	80.90%	53.28%	93.96%	91.69%	98.76%	75.75%
KNN	87.20%	87.60%	86.75%	78.46%	44.24%	94.75%	89.07%	98.68%	66.84%
SVD	85.25%	85.19%	85.36%	78.52%	48.89%	92.51%	90.44%	98.13%	72.75%
SVT	57.14%	61.08%	53.39%	83.25%	60.71%	94.01%	75.30%	91.66%	38.03%
Training Size 75%	Accuracy	Sensitivity	Specificity	Accuracy	Sensitivity	Specificity	Accuracy	Sensitivity	Specificity
iMSF-Best	88.79%	87.16%	**90.92%**	81.33%	**66.02%**	89.06%	**93.19%**	95.94%	**90.58%**
iMSF-Average	85.81%	82.77%	89.38%	80.78%	65.20%	88.70%	92.98%	95.03%	88.87%
ScoreComp-Zero	88.53%	87.67%	89.75%	**84.51%**	61.48%	**96.00%**	84.96%	**99.60%**	52.74%
ScoreComp-EM	89.91%	92.97%	86.77%	83.80%	61.24%	94.95%	89.93%	99.30%	70.21%
ScoreComp-KNN	**90.35%**	**93.89%**	86.74%	84.35%	63.79%	94.60%	88.89%	99.11%	66.91%
Zero	86.49%	88.06%	85.13%	81.76%	55.54%	94.74%	91.48%	97.68%	78.49%
EM	88.96%	88.54%	89.54%	81.25%	55.72%	93.83%	90.74%	98.44%	74.38%
KNN	87.32%	88.20%	86.66%	77.73%	44.97%	93.66%	88.89%	98.43%	68.12%
SVD	85.93%	85.78%	86.23%	78.55%	50.13%	92.29%	89.19%	97.48%	70.92%
SVT	56.58%	59.38%	53.73%	81.92%	56.93%	94.17%	75.56%	90.23%	42.59%

Table 3: Classification performance comparison of using multi-modality data (iMSF and ScoreComp) and just using MRI data. The classification is performed on the same set of samples, so that a fair comparison can be made. Leave-one-out is used and the accuracy, sensitivity and specificity are reported.

	AD vs. Normal			AD vs. Non-converter			Converter vs. Normal		
	Accuracy	Sensitivity	Specificity	Accuracy	Sensitivity	Specificity	Accuracy	Sensitivity	Specificity
Baseline	86.45%	83.33%	89.36%	76.83%	50.60%	89.20%	85.80%	96.49%	60.42%
iMSF-Average	90.99%	90.28%	91.76%	77.84%	69.44%	83.84%	92.59%	94.34%	89.29%
ScoreComp-EM	90.82%	94.37%	87.02%	82.24%	63.89%	95.36%	90.66%	99.06%	71.43%

3.4 Comparison with methods that throw out missing data

An intrinsic advantage of our methods over throwing out missing data is that no sample will be wasted. The final learned model will benefit from all the samples, so long as at least one of the data sources is available. Also, unlike the one learned from a complete data set, our final model will be able to give a prediction for a newly arrived sample with any combination of the data sources. Still, it is interesting to investigate if this additional information can help improve the classification performance. Therefore, we extract the complete data set where each sample has all the four data sources (MRI, CSF, PET and proteomics) available. We then extract the classification results for the same 153 subjects from our methods (iMSF and ScoreComp), so that the comparison can be made using the same sample pool. Results are summarized in Table 4.

As we see in Table 4, using 153 subjects alone (about 20% of the 780 subjects we use) results in unsatisfactory performance. We can conclude that our method not only makes full use of the information available, but also greatly improves classification performance.

3.5 Effects of different λ ratios in the proposed iMSF

From Table 2, we can observe that in terms of classification performance, our iMSF method is not very sensitive to the parameter λ. Here we use a particular example to illustrate how the results vary when different λ ratios are chosen in our proposed iMSF method in Figure 5. We use the AD vs. Normal problem, and report leave-one-out results when we use different choices of λ ratio values (0.001, 0.01, 0.1, 0.2 and 0.4). As we can observe from the figure, as we increase λ, the number of features selected will gradually decrease, from about 25% of the features to 3%. This shows that by using a λ ratio instead of actual values, it is much easier to choose a range of parameters that lead to desired levels of sparsity. We can also observe that the best choice of λ lies in the middle of the region (in this example 0.2), but the performance is not very sensitive to the parameter.

4. DISCUSSION

This paper has two major contributions. First, we were able

Table 4: Classification comparison of using multi-modality data (iMSF and ScoreComp) and using the complete MRI + CSF + PET + Proteomics data. Classification is performed on the same set of samples, so that a fair comparison can be made. Leave-one-out is used and the accuracy, sensitivity and specificity are reported.

	AD vs. Normal			AD vs. Non-converter			Converter vs. Normal		
	Accuracy	Sensitivity	Specificity	Accuracy	Sensitivity	Specificity	Accuracy	Sensitivity	Specificity
Baseline	87.72%	100.00%	63.16%	76.19%	65.79%	84.78%	83.02%	97.06%	57.89%
iMSF-Average	95.79%	97.37%	92.63%	84.05%	79.47%	87.83%	88.68%	90.59%	85.26%
ScoreComp-EM	98.25%	97.37%	100.00%	83.33%	65.79%	97.83%	84.91%	97.06%	63.16%

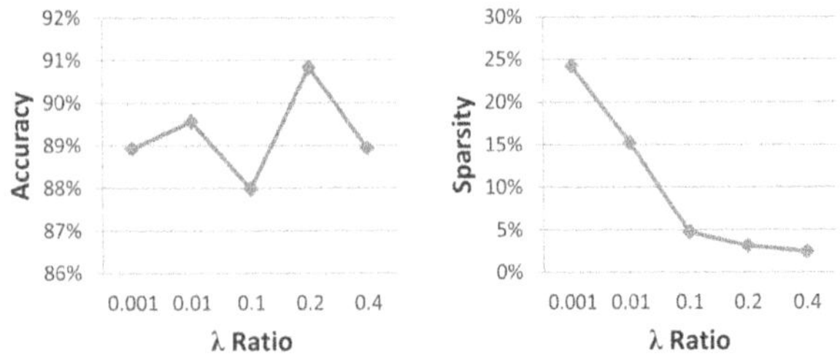

Figure 5: Illustration of the results obtained using different λ ratio values in our proposed iMSF method. We vary the λ ratio values from 0.001 to 0.4 (x-axis) and report the accuracy obtained (y-axis) in the left figure. In the right figure, we report the proportion of selected features (Sparsity, y-axis) when we increase λ ratio values from 0.001 to 0.4 (x-axis).

to use a large multi-modal data set for classification, even when large segments of the data were missing. Secondly, we propose two different multi-source learning schemes for block-wise incomplete data, and used them to construct automatic, robust classifiers. In our experiments, our systems greatly improved the classification accuracy on the ADNI data set. Our method (iMSF) has two major advantages: 1) All subjects, so long as at least one of the feature sources is available, can be used for feature learning, and all of them can contribute to the feature selection jointly; 2) the difficulty of guessing unknowns is bypassed, as the feature learning is only based on what data is available. To the best of our knowledge, in the ADNI data set, we are the first group who tried to utilize all the available information for classification by allowing the use of subjects with incomplete data. In our current pilot work, we assessed whether our multi-source learning models help to boost the statistical power in the whole data set. Except for some of the PET imaging measures (such as Pittsburgh compound B), we used all other measures that are publicly available at ADNI web site. We hope our work will increase interest in this important problem and that other groups might consider using this approach (not throwing out data) when performing future ADNI classification studies.

Pioneering work has been done on the automated diagnosis problem using the ADNI data set. López et al. (1995) applied principal component analysis to extract features from FDG-PET. In a data set of 211 subjects (53 AD, 114 MCI and 52 Normal), they achieved a best leave one out (LOO) accuracy 82% for classifying people into groups of AD vs. Normal and a best LOO accuracy of 81% on MCI vs. Normal. Cuingnet et al. [8] evaluated the performance of ten high dimensional classification methods using the ADNI MRI data. In their data set of 509 subjects, the best of the ten classifiers achieved 81%/95%, 65%/94% sensitivity/specificity for classification of AD vs. Normal, MCI vs. Normal, respectively. In our earlier work [21], we used support vector machines to combine several MRI measures, as well as PET and CSF biomarkers, etc. and we achieved a 90% LOO accuracy on AD vs. Normal and a 75% LOO accuracy on MCI vs. Normal classification. Notably, all of these studies were applied to a subset of the full available ADNI data used here. For example, in [21], 635 subjects were studied when only MRI-based measures were needed, but when both CSF and PET were also added to the set of predictors, the available sample size dropped dramatically to 166 subjects. Without a method to include subjects with missing data, it becomes quite difficult to train and test a classifier. The approach we outlined here still achieved comparable or better results than those in prior papers.

There are several possibilities for extending our current work. In this paper, we used numerical summary measures from MRI scans of 648 subjects, whose data were available at ADNI data set. In some of our earlier studies [16], we used tensor-based morphometry to study baseline and longitudinal MRI scans in ADNI, and these could be added to the feature set in the future. In addition, the second phase of the ADNI initiative is now collecting data from diffusion tensor imaging, arterial spin labeling, and resting state functional MRI. Although each of these features is likely to help with classification and for predicting decline, the 3 new imaging modalities will not all be performed on the same subjects - in fact, each of the ADNI subjects will be scanned using only one of the 3 additional modalities, because it was not feasible to prolong the scanning session to include all three in every subject. Such a situation lends itself to the data mining and machine learning approach developed here, as there will be considerable joint information available about the relationships between the new modalities and the traditional biomarkers, but not in the same subjects. Also, ensemble learning [10] can boost performance in general data mining and machine learning problems. By combining various models produced with different parameters, or even models from different methods, the ensemble method may produce even more stable and robust classifiers. In the future, we plan to enrich our model set and use ensemble method to tackle the incomplete data problem.

5. ACKNOWLEDGMENTS

This work was funded by the National Institute on Aging (AG016570 to PMT), the National Library of Medicine, the National Institute for Biomedical Imaging and Bioengineering, and the National Center for Research Resources (LM05639, EB01651, RR019771 to PMT), US National Science Foundation (NSF) (IIS-0812551, IIS-0953662, CCF-1025177 to JY), and National Library of Medicine (R01 LM010730 to JY).

6. REFERENCES

[1] R. Ando and T. Zhang. A framework for learning predictive structures from multiple tasks and unlabeled data. *The Journal of Machine Learning Research*, 6:1817–1853, 2005.

[2] A. Argyriou, T. Evgeniou, and M. Pontil. Convex multi-task feature learning. *Machine Learning*, 73(3):243–272, 2008.

[3] M. Braskie, A. Klunder, K. Hayashi, H. Protas, V. Kepe, K. Miller, S. Huang, J. Barrio, L. Ercoli, P. Siddarth, et al. Plaque and tangle imaging and cognition in normal aging and Alzheimer's disease. *Neurobiology of Aging*, 31(10):1669–1678, 2010.

[4] J. Cai, E. Candès, and Z. Shen. A singular value thresholding algorithm for matrix completion. *SIAM Journal of Optimization*, 20(4):1956–1982, 2010.

[5] E. Candes and T. Tao. The power of convex relaxation: Near-optimal matrix completion. *Information Theory, IEEE Transactions on*, 56(5):2053–2080, 2010.

[6] R. Casanova, R. Srikanth, A. Baer, P. Laurienti, J. Burdette, S. Hayasaka, L. Flowers, F. Wood, and J. Maldjian. Biological parametric mapping: a statistical toolbox for multimodality brain image analysis. *Neuroimage*, 34(1):137–143, 2007.

[7] P. Combettes and J. Pesquet. Proximal splitting methods in signal processing. *Fixed-Point Algorithms for Inverse Problems in Science and Engineering*, pages 185–212, 2011.

[8] R. Cuingnet, E. Gerardin, J. Tessieras, G. Auzias, S. Lehéricy, and M. Habert. Automatic classification of patients with Alzheimer's disease from structural MRI: A comparison of ten methods using the ADNI database. *Neuroimage*, 2010.

[9] D. Devanand, G. Pradhaban, X. Liu, A. Khandji, S. De Santi, S. Segal, H. Rusinek, G. Pelton, L. Honig, R. Mayeux, et al. Hippocampal and entorhinal atrophy in mild cognitive impairment. *Neurology*, 68(11):828–836, 2007.

[10] T. Dietterich. Ensemble methods in machine learning. *Multiple Classifier Systems*, pages 1–15, 2000.

[11] Y. Fan, S. Resnick, X. Wu, and C. Davatzikos. Structural and functional biomarkers of prodromal Alzheimer's disease: a high-dimensional pattern classification study. *Neuroimage*, 41(2):277–285, 2008.

[12] C. Fennema-Notestine, D. Hagler Jr, L. McEvoy, A. Fleisher, E. Wu, D. Karow, and A. Dale. Structural MRI biomarkers for preclinical and mild Alzheimer's disease. *Human Brain Mapping*, 30(10):3238–3253, 2009.

[13] S. Gao. A shared random effect parameter approach for longitudinal dementia data with non-ignorable missing data. *Statistics in Medicine*, 23(2):211–219, 2004.

[14] S. Hardy, H. Allore, and S. Studenski. Missing data: A special challenge in aging research. *Journal of the American Geriatrics Society*, 57(4):722–729, 2009.

[15] T. Hastie, R. Tibshirani, G. Sherlock, M. Eisen, P. Brown, and D. Botstein. Imputing missing data for gene expression arrays. *Technical Report*, 1999.

[16] X. Hua, B. Gutman, C. Boyle, P. Rajagopalan, A. Leow, I. Yanovsky, A. Kumar, A. Toga, C. Jack Jr, N. Schuff, et al. Accurate measurement of brain changes in longitudinal MRI scans using tensor-based morphometry. *Neuroimage*, 2011.

[17] V. Ibanez, P. Pietrini, G. Alexander, M. Furey, D. Teichberg, J. Rajapakse, S. Rapoport, M. Schapiro, and B. Horwitz. Regional glucose metabolic abnormalities are not the result of atrophy in Alzheimer's disease. *Neurology*, 50(6):1585–1593, 1998.

[18] C. Jack, V. Lowe, M. Senjem, S. Weigand, B. Kemp, M. Shiung, D. Knopman, B. Boeve, W. Klunk, C. Mathis, et al. [11C]-PiB and structural MRI provide complementary information in imaging of Alzheimer's disease and amnestic mild cognitive impairment. *Brain*, 131(3):665, 2008.

[19] C. Jack Jr, F. Barkhof, M. Bernstein, M. Cantillon, P. Cole, C. DeCarli, B. Dubois, S. Duchesne, N. Fox, G. Frisoni, et al. Steps to standardization and validation of hippocampal volumetry as a biomarker in clinical trials and diagnostic criterion for Alzheimer's disease. *Alzheimer's and Dementia*, 7(4):474–485, 2011.

[20] C. Jack Jr, M. Bernstein, N. Fox, P. Thompson, G. Alexander, D. Harvey, B. Borowski, P. Britson, J. L Whitwell, C. Ward, et al. The Alzheimer's disease neuroimaging initiative (ADNI): MRI methods. *Journal of Magnetic Resonance Imaging*, 27(4):685–691, 2008.

[21] O. Kohannim, X. Hua, D. Hibar, S. Lee, Y. Chou, A. Toga, C. Jack Jr, M. Weiner, P. Thompson, et al. Boosting power for clinical trials using classifiers based on multiple biomarkers. *Neurobiology of Aging*, 31(8):1429–1442, 2010.

[22] R. Kuljiš. Grand challenges in dementia 2010. *Frontiers in Neurology*, 1, 2010.

[23] S. Landau, D. Harvey, C. Madison, R. Koeppe, E. Reiman, N. Foster, M. Weiner, and W. Jagust. Associations between cognitive, functional, and FDG-PET measures of decline in AD and MCI. *Neurobiology of Aging*, 32(7):1207–1218, 2011.

[24] S. Lemm, B. Blankertz, T. Dickhaus, and K. Muller. Introduction to machine learning for brain imaging. *Neuroimage*, 2010.

[25] A. Liaw and M. Wiener. Classification and regression by randomforest. *R News*, 2(3):18–22, 2002.

[26] J. Liu, S. Ji, and J. Ye. Multi-task feature learning via efficient L2,1-Norm minimization. In *Proceedings of the Twenty-Fifth Conference on Uncertainty in Artificial Intelligence*, pages 339–348. AUAI Press, 2009.

[27] J. Liu, L. Yuan, and J. Ye. An efficient algorithm for a class of fused lasso problems. In *Proceedings of the 16th ACM SIGKDD international conference on Knowledge Discovery and Data Mining*, pages 323–332. ACM, 2010.

[28] E. Martinez-Montes, P. Valdés-Sosa, F. Miwakeichi, R. Goldman, and M. Cohen. Concurrent EEG/fMRI analysis by multiway partial least squares. *Neuroimage*, 22(3):1023–1034, 2004.

[29] S. Mueller, M. Weiner, L. Thal, R. Petersen, C. Jack, W. Jagust, J. Trojanowski, A. Toga, and L. Beckett. The Alzheimer's Disease Neuroimaging Initiative. *Neuroimaging Clinics of North America*, 15(4):869, 2005.

[30] Y. Nesterov. Gradient methods for minimizing composite objective function. *ReCALL*, 76(2007076), 2007.

[31] Y. Nesterov and I. Nesterov. *Introductory lectures on convex optimization: A basic course*, volume 87. Springer, 2004.

[32] R. Palmer and D. Royall. Missing data? Plan on it! *Journal of the American Geriatrics Society*, 58:S343–S348, 2010.

[33] E. Reiman, J. Langbaum, and P. Tariot. Alzheimer's prevention initiative: a proposal to evaluate presymptomatic treatments as quickly as possible. *Biomarkers*, 4(1):3–14, 2010.

[34] T. Schneider. Analysis of incomplete climate data: Estimation of mean values and covariance matrices and imputation of missing values. *Journal of Climate*, 14(5):853–871, 2001.

[35] J. Schott, J. Bartlett, J. Barnes, K. Leung, S. Ourselin, N. Fox, and ADNI. Reduced sample sizes for atrophy outcomes in Alzheimer's disease trials: baseline adjustment. *Neurobiology of Aging*, 31(8):1452, 2010.

[36] N. Tzourio-Mazoyer, B. Landeau, D. Papathanassiou, F. Crivello, O. Etard, N. Delcroix, B. Mazoyer, and M. Joliot. Automated anatomical labeling of activations in SPM using a macroscopic anatomical parcellation of the MNI MRI single-subject brain. *Neuroimage*, 15(1):273–289, 2002.

[37] P. Van Ness, T. Murphy, K. Araujo, M. Pisani, and H. Allore. The use of missingness screens in clinical epidemiologic research has implications for regression modeling. *Journal of clinical epidemiology*, 60(12):1239–1245, 2007.

[38] P. Vemuri, H. Wiste, S. Weigand, L. Shaw, J. Trojanowski, M. Weiner, D. Knopman, R. Petersen, C. J. Jack, and ADNI. MRI and CSF biomarkers in normal, MCI, and AD subjects: diagnostic discrimination and cognitive correlations. *Neurology*, 73(4):287–293, 2009.

[39] Y. Wang, Y. Fan, P. Bhatt, and C. Davatzikos. High-dimensional pattern regression using machine learning: From medical images to continuous clinical variables. *Neuroimage*, 50(4):1519–1535, 2010.

[40] K. Worsley, J. Poline, K. Friston, and A. Evans. Characterizing the response of PET and fMRI data using multivariate linear models. *Neuroimage*, 6(4):305–319, 1997.

[41] J. Ye, K. Chen, T. Wu, J. Li, Z. Zhao, R. Patel, M. Bae, R. Janardan, H. Liu, G. Alexander, et al. Heterogeneous data fusion for Alzheimer's disease study. In *Proceeding of the 14th ACM SIGKDD international conference on Knowledge Discovery and Data Mining*, pages 1025–1033. ACM, 2008.

[42] M. Yuan and Y. Lin. Model selection and estimation in regression with grouped variables. *Journal of the Royal Statistical Society: Series B (Statistical Methodology)*, 68(1):49–67, 2006.

[43] D. Zhang, Y. Wang, L. Zhou, H. Yuan, D. Shen, et al. Multimodal classification of Alzheimer's disease and mild cognitive impairment. *Neuroimage*, 2011.

[44] J. Zhou, J. Chen, and J. Ye. *MALSAR: Multi-tAsk Learning via StructurAl Regularization*. Arizona State University, 2011.

RainMon: An Integrated Approach to Mining Bursty Timeseries Monitoring Data

Ilari Shafer, Kai Ren, Vishnu Naresh Boddeti, Yoshihisa Abe, Gregory R. Ganger, Christos Faloutsos
Carnegie Mellon University

ABSTRACT

Metrics like disk activity and network traffic are widespread sources of diagnosis and monitoring information in datacenters and networks. However, as the scale of these systems increases, examining the raw data yields diminishing insight. We present RainMon, a novel end-to-end approach for mining timeseries monitoring data designed to handle its size and unique characteristics. Our system is able to (a) mine large, bursty, real-world monitoring data, (b) find significant trends and anomalies in the data, (c) compress the raw data effectively, and (d) estimate trends to make forecasts. Furthermore, RainMon integrates the full analysis process from data storage to the user interface to provide accessible long-term diagnosis. We apply RainMon to three real-world datasets from production systems and show its utility in discovering anomalous machines and time periods.

Categories and Subject Descriptors

K.6.2 [**Installation Management**]: Performance and usage measurement; H.2.8 [**Database Applications**]: Data mining

General Terms

Algorithms, Design, Management, Performance

Keywords

System Monitoring, PCA, Bursty Data

1. INTRODUCTION

Many modern computing clusters consist of dozens to thousands of machines that work together to perform a variety of tasks. The size and complexity of these systems has created a burden for administrators. Additionally, a move towards commodity hardware has produced more frequent failures that must be diagnosed and repaired [3]. These challenges have inspired considerable interest in monitoring tools catered towards system administrators, who are often also faced with monitoring external network links in addition to the datacenter itself.

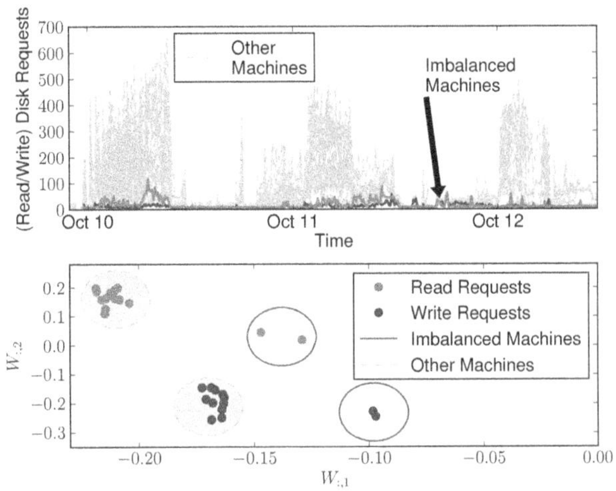

Figure 1: *Two anomalous machines discovered with RainMon.* The system can summarize bursty timeseries monitoring data (top plot) and allows easy discovery of groups of machines that share the same behavior: the four dots separated from the others in the bottom plot correspond to the imbalanced machines at top. Many tools used in current practice only offer the top view—without the helpful coloring. For details of the analysis, see Sec. 5.1.

Complicating matters further, analysis at the level of a single machine is often insufficient. To provide a concrete example that we analyze in this paper, applications like Hadoop [1] distribute work across multiple machines. Significant imbalances in monitoring observations between groups of machines are a problem worthy of human attention. A task of growing importance is understanding when problems like these occur, and determining which tasks, machines, or network links are responsible. Furthermore, administrators also would like to know about problems and potential capacity shortages as soon as possible [9], and predictions of future trends would be valuable.

To provide visibility into their behavior, systems emit a variety of timeseries streams — for example, CPU utilization, disk traffic, and network transfers. Such streams are widely used for datacenter monitoring through tools like Ganglia [24], Nagios [25], Zenoss [36], and Tivoli [13]. Typically, these tools provide summaries of performance through averages or roll-ups of streams across machines, or require administrators to look at machine status individually. Anomaly and outlier detection are often accomplished by thresholding individual metric values.

Unfortunately, the increased number of incoming monitoring streams due to the scale of modern systems makes diagnosis with these tools difficult. For example, simply overlaying monitoring data from many machines produces an unintelligible view (for example, at top in Fig. 1), yet similar views are common in the tools used in practice [24, 25, 36]. Another significant obstacle to human-intelligible monitoring is the burstiness of many of these streams: not only is the raw data visually noisy, it also poses difficulties for many timeseries analyses, such as modeling techniques that assume a smooth time evolution of data [17]. For example, alerts based on thresholds can produce false positives.

Despite the wide variety of anomaly detection and summarization approaches that have been proposed (we survey a few in Sec. 2), there exists a need for approaches that handle real-world data sources, focus on bursty data, and integrate the analysis process. To meet those goals, RainMon is an *end-to-end* system for mining anomalies and trends from bursty streams, compressing monitoring data, and forecasting trends. We have integrated RainMon with multiple real data streams produced by complex real systems to produce insight into datacenter behavior. It has isolated problems with machines and tasks like the ones shown in Fig. 1 in the Hadoop framework and unearthed network glitches. It can compress data more effectively than a non-integrated approach and can estimate future state. These applications are not disjoint, but rather the result of judicious combination of a few techniques from the literature into a knowledge discovery tool.

Contributions: We make three primary contributions. First, we describe a novel multi-stage analysis technique catered towards bursty timeseries monitoring streams from datacenters and networks. Second, we show its utility through a series of case studies on real-world monitoring streams. Third, we describe our end-to-end system that incorporates storage, modeling, and visualization.

2. RELATED WORK

A variety of data mining techniques have been applied to timeseries monitoring, many existing monitoring tools provide data infrastructure, and some consider effective visualization of the output [8]. Here we focus on RainMon's relation to the wide body of related work on stream anomaly detection and forecasting as applied to system monitoring. More background on the techniques we use is provided in Sec. 3; broader surveys of anomaly detection [7] and timeseries forecasting [6] are available.

Multiple data mining approaches have been proposed for summarizing relatively smooth portions of timeseries monitoring data. Patnaik et al. have developed an approach to cooling a datacenter based on finding frequent "motifs" [28]. The Intemon tool explores the use of dimensionality reduction to monitoring timeseries [12], and a case study considers applying the system to finding anomalies in environmental monitoring data. We use the same core algorithm (SPIRIT [27, 35]) as a technique for mining correlations and trends, and expand its applicability to cope with the bursty aspect of systems data. The symbolic SAX representation is also promising for anomaly detection and visualization [21].

Considerable work on automated detection of anomalies and bursts in timeseries data has resulted in a variety of techniques, such as wavelet decomposition [37], changepoint detection [10, 26], incremental nearest-neighbor computation [4], and others. PCA and ICA have been applied to monitoring data for a variety of features (e.g., by [16]). Other forms of matrix decomposition have also been applied to network monitoring data to find anomalies, though evaluations often focus on small or synthetic datasets [11]. Many other automated approaches (e.g., [5, 14]) complement this work: rather than defining what constitutes a violation of a trend, we focus on modeling and presenting the data.

Forecasting of timeseries monitoring data has often been examined independently of the mining techniques above. For example, ThermoCast [18] uses a specialized model for predicting timeseries temperature data in a datacenter. Some techniques like DynaMMo [19] and PLiF [20] learn linear dynamical systems for multiple time sequences for the purposes of both forecasting and summarization, and the latter is evaluated in part on network monitoring data (though for the purposes of clustering). Linear Gaussian models like the Kalman filter used here are surveyed in [31].

3. APPROACH

We address our three goals described in Sec. 1 in the following manner. First, in order to achieve efficient compression of monitoring data and facilitate the generation of its intelligible summaries, we decompose the raw data into spike data and streams that are amenable to these two objectives. Then, actual creation of summaries is performed using incremental PCA, which produces a lower-dimensional representation of the original data. Finally, we predict future system state by modeling the variables in the lower-dimensional representation. This process is illustrated in Fig. 2. Also, the core steps of the problem are formally defined as follows:

Problem Statement: Given N labeled timeseries streams, we have at each of T time ticks a vector of observations $y_t = [y_{t,1}, \ldots, y_{t,N}]$. Each reported value $y_{t,i} \in \mathbb{R}_{\geq 0}$. We seek to find $M < N$ streams $s_t = s_{t,1} \ldots s_{t,M}$ at each time tick that form a summary of the data, and other model parameters that can be displayed to indicate outliers and anomalies. Additionally, we seek to forecast s_{T+f} for some $f > 0$ — that is, predict future system trends.

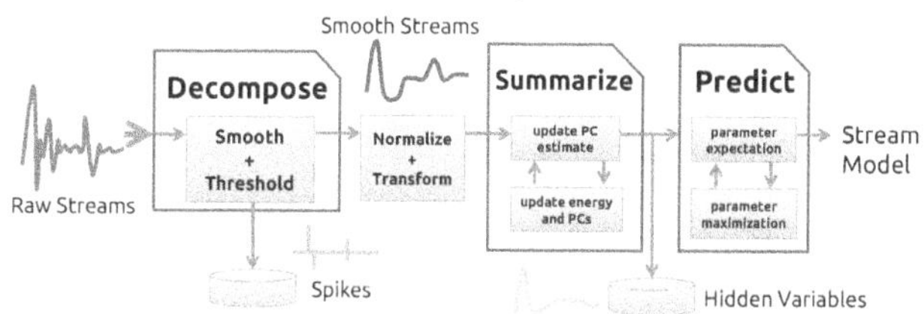

Figure 2: *Multi-stage RainMon data flow.* Raw streams are decomposed and then modeled.

In the following sections, we describe each step in detail. In each of these sections, we refer to the input of each stage as y_t and its output as x_t. Note that the decomposition and summarization stages of the analysis are *streaming* algorithms; that is, they can produce x_{t+1} given y_{t+1} and the model parameters estimated from $y_1 \ldots y_t$. This aspect is important in a monitoring setting, since data arrives in an incremental fashion as systems produce it; streaming analyses allow for efficiency through incremental updates.

3.1 Decomposition

One of the domain challenges of modeling datacenter timeseries is the burstiness of many system metrics, such as network and disk I/O [17]. Much of this burstiness is irrelevant for diagnosis, but significant bursts and long-term trends are useful features. This motivates us to borrow ideas from Cypress [30], a framework for decomposing datacenter timeseries data into smoothed trends, spiky bursts, and residual data. We show concretely how decomposition can be used to effectively compress relevant data in Sec. 5.5.

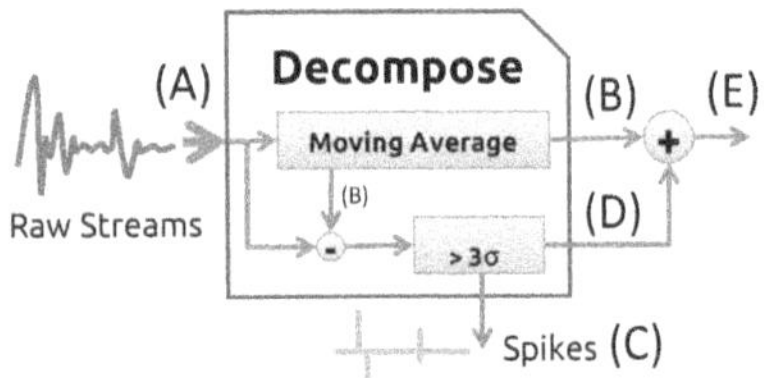

Figure 3: ***Stream decomposition:*** **data is low-pass filtered; spikes that are 3σ larger than the residuals are segregated and stored separately.**

In order to obtain a smoothed representation of the signal, the raw data (A in Fig. 3) is passed through a low-pass filter with cut off frequency $f_s/2m$ [29], where f_s is the sampling frequency of the timeseries and m is an application-specific parameter that is tunable based on the nature of the data streams. We use an exponential moving-average filter:

$$x_t = \alpha y_t + (1-\alpha)x_{t-1} \qquad \alpha = \frac{\Delta t}{m\Delta t/\pi + \Delta t}$$

where Δt is the interval between time ticks, and m can be experimentally determined by performing spectrum analysis on examples of the data streams [30]. Currently, we simply use $m = 60$ sec in the filtering of testing data.

The presence of significant spikes can be useful for time-based anomaly detection. In this kind of analysis, the most pronounced spikes in the signal are the most relevant. To detect these spikes, we apply a threshold to the "noise," which is the signal obtained by subtracting the band-limited signal (B) from the original signal (A). We choose 3σ as the threshold, where σ is the standard deviation of the "noise."

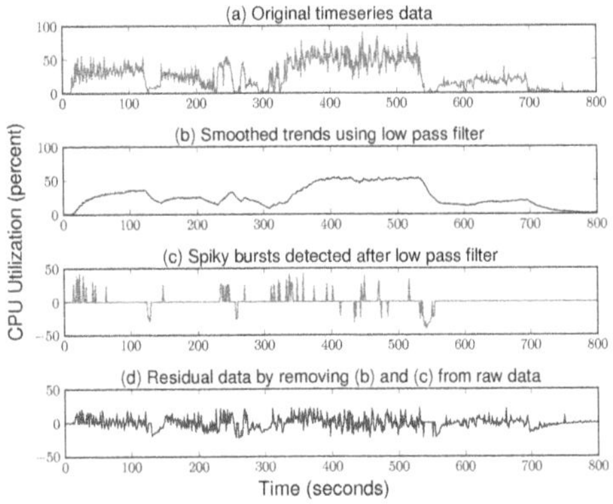

Figure 4: ***Sample of timeseries data decomposition.*** **Observe the burstiness of the CPU monitoring data.**

Fig. 4 illustrates a timeseries signal (CPU utilization) at each of the stages described above; the letters correspond to those in Fig. 3. We then pass the smoothed signal (E) with amplitude-constrained residuals to the next stage — summarization through dimensionality reduction.

3.2 Summarization

For the purposes of producing summaries that capture the overall behavior of the system, we use incremental PCA. We use the hidden variables it produces as timeseries summaries and its weight matrix to help identify anomalous streams. Additionally, the algorithm we use (SPIRIT [27]) adapts the number of hidden variables; addition or removal can signify a change in behavior.

The underlying model is that the N-dimensional data are well-modeled by $M \leq N$ hidden variables. As each new vector of observations y_t ((E) in Sec. 3.1) arrives, we update the model with the technique shown in Algorithm 1. We choose SPIRIT for two primary reasons. First, it is incremental, with complexity $O(MN)$. Second, in the datasets under examination, we expect linear correlations between streams in any case (e.g., the similar cluster resource utilization patterns in Sec. 5). The output x_t from this stage is used as the summary s_t.

Algorithm 1 SPIRIT update

Require: A number of principal components M_t, weight matrix W, new observation y_{t+1} of dimensionality N, energy vector d, energy thresholds f_E and F_E, previous energies E_x, E_y, $\lambda = 0.99$

Ensure: Updated W, d, M, reconstruction $\hat{y}_{t+1}$, hidden variables x_{t+1}

$r \leftarrow y_{t+1}$

for $i \leftarrow 1 \ldots M$ **do**

  $z = W_i^T \cdot r$ *(where W_i is the ith column of W)*

  $d_i \leftarrow \lambda d_i + z^2$

  $W_i \leftarrow W_i + \frac{z(r - zW_i)}{d_i}$

  $r \leftarrow r - zW_i$

end for

$W \leftarrow \text{orthonormalize}(W)$

$x_{t+1} \leftarrow W^T \cdot y_{t+1}$

$\hat{y}_{t+1} \leftarrow W \cdot x_{t+1}$

$E_x \leftarrow \lambda E_x + ||x_{t+1}||^2$

$E_y \leftarrow \lambda E_y + ||\hat{y}_{t+1}||^2$

if $E_x < f_E E_y$ **then**

  $M \leftarrow \max(0, M-1)$

else if $E_y > F_E E_x$ **then**

  $M \leftarrow \min(N, M+1)$

end if

PCA-based algorithms like SPIRIT function best when the magnitudes of the features are approximately equal. This is decidedly not true of monitoring data; metrics like network bytes written are on the order of 10^7, while CPU usage is delivered as a value between 0 and 100. For batch analysis, we simply normalize the data. For streaming analysis, we use domain knowledge of the data to associate a "maximum" value with each stream. This maximum is only accurate to an order of magnitude, but looking ahead in a stream to find the true maximum runs counter to the philosophy of incremental updates. We use a linear transform for data that is less bursty, and use a logarithmic transform for I/O-related metrics. For parameters R_{min} and R_{max}, which define the typical order-of-magnitude range of a value, the transform for a value v is:

$$\text{Linear:} \qquad f(v) = \frac{v - R_{min}}{R_{max} - R_{min}}$$

$$\text{Logarithmic:} \qquad f(v) = \frac{\ln(v+1)}{\ln(R_{max})}$$

3.3 Prediction

To forecast future system trends, we estimate future values of the streams output by the summarization stage. This problem amounts to multivariate timeseries forecasting, for which there is a wide body of work. We select a Kalman filter since it generalizes recursive linear regression. Other studies have compared forecasting models for datacenter event timeseries [33]. Alternative approaches like ARIMA [6] could be applied in this stage.

Given the response of SPIRIT (x_t in Sec. 3.2, denoted y_t here), we learn a state evolution model with hidden states x_t as follows:

$$x_{t+1} = Ax_t + w$$
$$y_t = Cx_t + v$$

where A is the state transition matrix, C captures the observation model, and $w \sim N(0, Q)$ and $v \sim N(0, R)$ are the state evolution and observation noise models, respectively. See Fig. 5 for a pictorial representation of the model evolution. The two main sub-problems associated with learning these models are *inference* and *parameter learning*. Inference deals with issues of estimating the unknown hidden variables given some observations and a given fixed model parameters. Parameter learning pertains to estimating the model parameters given only the observations.

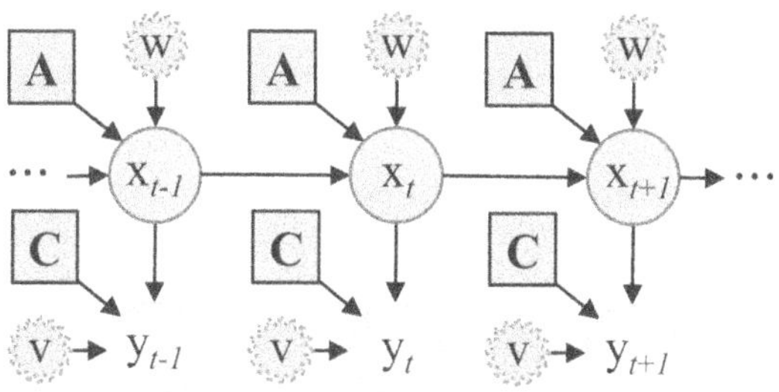

Figure 5: *Kalman filter model.* Hidden variables from dimensionality reduction (y) are further modeled with hidden states x.

With every observation y_t, we update the model parameters as detailed in Appendix A.1. Then, we smooth the predictions by iterating backwards (see Appendix A.2). With the forward predictions and smoothed reverse predictions, we use the standard Expectation-Maximization (EM) procedure both to learn the parameters and to predict the latent state variables (see Appendix A.3). That is, given the observations, we use the current model parameters to predict the latent state variables. Then given these latent state parameters and the observations, we determine the model parameters by maximum likelihood estimation.

4. IMPLEMENTATION

RainMon is an *end-to-end* system, accommodating the knowledge discovery process from storage through analysis to visualization. An overview of the system design is shown in Fig. 6. The tool can obtain data directly from existing monitoring systems using RRDtool [24, 32] and a database that stores terabyte-scale timeseries data [34]. Since both these data sources provide data in ranges, we run both streaming algorithms in batch fashion. The analysis process in RainMon is distributed; although we currently only run the analysis on a single machine, it can be partitioned and run in parallel. A web-based interface (shown in Fig. 7) accesses the analysis results and can display analysis results to multiple users simultaneously.

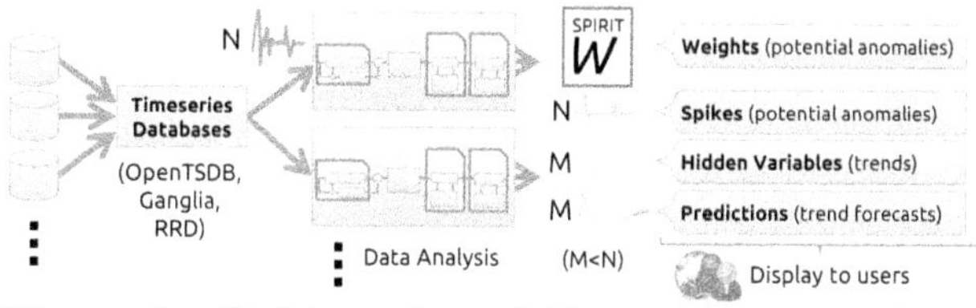

Figure 6: *End-to-end, scalable architecture.* RainMon can access multiple widely-deployed backing databases [24, 32], and is designed for scalability.

We have made RainMon open-source; additionally, we are releasing the CMU.net dataset, which we used as part of our evaluation, to the community. Both are available at `http://code.rainmon.com`.

5. APPLICATIONS

To assess the utility of RainMon, we demonstrate through a series of case studies how it was used to find problematic machines and time periods in real-world data. Note that the plots that follow were generated for clarity on paper, but all of the visualizations can be created in RainMon's interface. Using the techniques described in Sec. 3.1-3.3 and this tool, RainMon has been applied to three scenarios:

Hadoop Machine-level metrics from the OpenCloud Hadoop cluster at Carnegie Mellon University (CMU). Machines are numbered cloud1-cloud64.

CMU.net Time taken for a packet to make a round trip from CMU to other locations in the world, as measured by the ping program.

Abilene Network flows measured from the Abilene network backbone of Internet2 (courtesy [15])

Dataset	Nodes	Metrics	Size
Hadoop System Metrics	64	58	220GB
CMU.net Ping Times	6	18	17.1MB
Abilene Network Flows	121	1	5.7MB

Table 1: *Datasets used in case studies.*

In a cluster where all machines are shared across the same scheduler, such as many Hadoop clusters, a typical large job will span all machines in the cluster. Similar resource utilization patterns on all machines indicate that a job is performing normally, whereas a single machine or groups of machines that behave differently indicate anomalies or imbalance. We first consider the task of isolating a machine or small group with abnormal behavior.

For the analyses below, we do not provide summary statistics on the precision and recall of detection since determining whether a deviation is anomalous through root-cause diagnosis is a question in itself; further work is needed to establish complete ground truth and anomaly criteria for datasets like the Hadoop system metrics. Given a definition of an anomaly, a variety of outlier detection approaches can be applied (e.g., [5]). Here we present case studies for which further investigation has shown that anomalous behavior did indeed exist in the cluster or network.

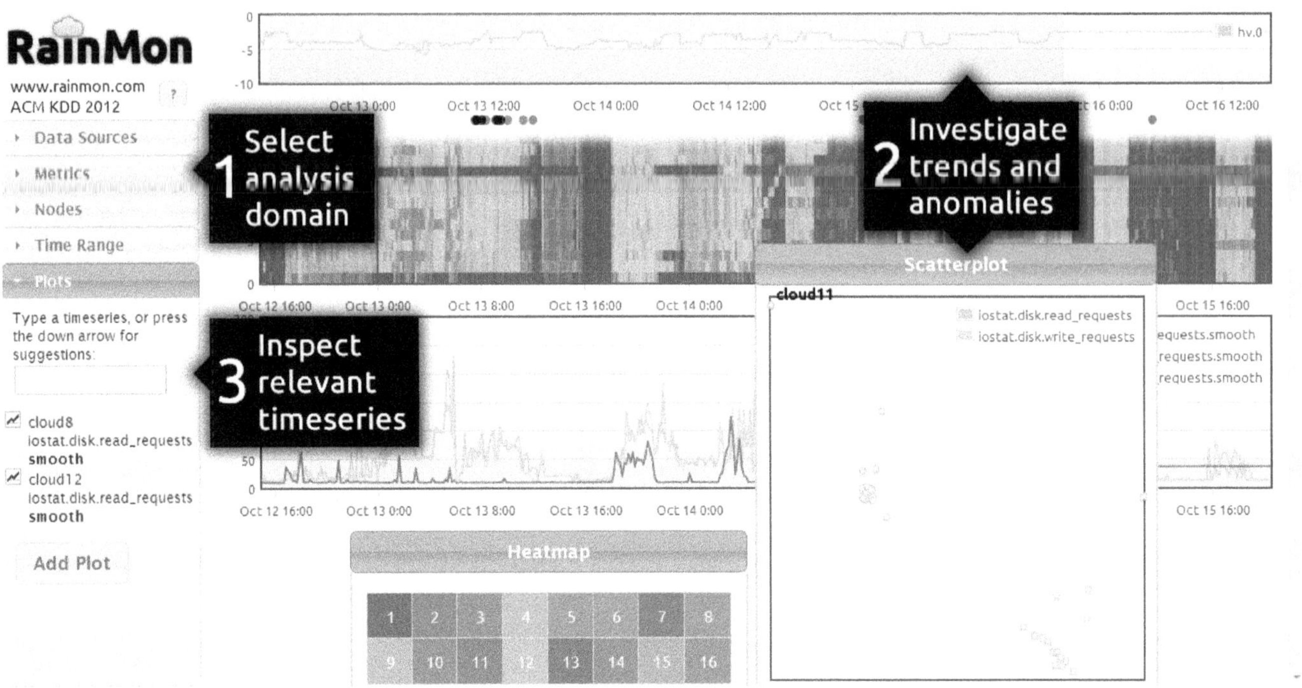

Figure 7: *RainMon interface.* Overlaid in black boxes is the workflow of the tool. At bottom are the scatterplot of $W_{:,2}$ vs $W_{:,1}$ and a machine "energy" heatmap. In the central pane are linked, zoomable, customizable timeseries plots. An interactive demonstration of the interface is available at `http://demo.rainmon.com`.

5.1 Outlier Machine Isolation

Caused by Machine: After selecting a region of data to analyze ((1) in Fig. 7), a useful visualization for quickly identifying machines that do not behave like others is a plot of the projection coefficients of the first two hidden variables to each smoothed data stream, i.e., $W_{:,2}$ vs $W_{:,1}$ of the PCA weight matrix W (from Algorithm 1, (2) in Fig. 7). If disk reads were closely correlated over time on all machines, and disk writes were also correlated, we would see two clusters on the plot — one for each metric. For example, in the case shown in Fig. 8, we see that this is the situation for almost all of the machines (points), but that the metrics for one machine (cloud11) were far from those for the others.

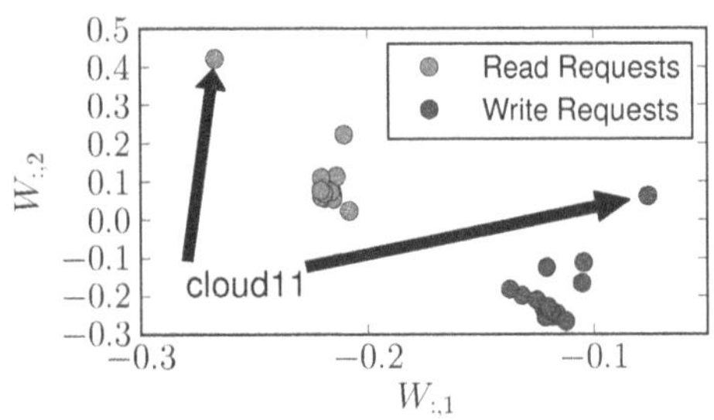

Figure 8: *Outlier node discovery.* RainMon's scatterplot of $W_{:,2}$ vs $W_{:,1}$ shows that the coefficients of cloud11 are separated from the other machines.

From this point, the tool provides the ability to easily construct overlaid timeseries plots of multiple metrics ((3) in Fig. 7). An examination of the disk read behavior of cloud11 compared with two other cluster members is shown in Fig. 9. Observe that during periods of heavy read activity on other machines it was idle (around Oct. 12), and that the collection process on the machine failed (the flat line from Oct. 13 onwards). Additionally, from the spike data we found that a burst of read activity on cloud11 occurred before a burst on most other nodes.

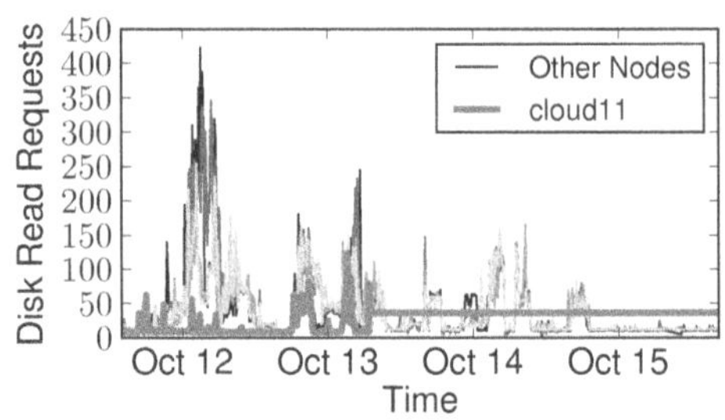

Figure 9: *Individual machine examination.* After identifying candidate outliers, RainMon allows users to build custom plots and overlay timeseries data.

Caused by Task: As another example of identifying outlier nodes in a representative cloud workload, we explicitly introduced load imbalance to a job running in the Hadoop cluster. The job is an email classification task running on a Hadoop-based machine learning framework [2]. Specifically, in the example input dataset, we generated a number of duplicated emails under a specific newsgroup topic, so that the total amount of input data is approximately an order of magnitude larger than that of the other topics. This caused the Mapper processes handling the topic to last longer and consume more resources than the others, because of the uneven input distribution.

Fig. 10 compares three different ways of visualizing CPU-related metrics of the Mahout workload in RainMon. The top graph shows raw user-level CPU usage of a set of machines that processed the task, and the middle graph shows spikes of this data extracted by decomposition. The bottom graph shows the first and second hidden variables computed from the set of CPU-related metrics including user-level CPU usage. The injected excessive input was processed by cloud9 and cloud28, increasing their resource usage. Even though the outliers are visible in the original data, they consist of multiple datapoints and require a threshold to distinguish from other behavior. In the extracted spike data, each single datapoint greater than zero can be treated as a potential anomaly, and general trends can be observed in the hidden variables hv0 and hv1. Note that spikes can also be negative, further emphasizing that domain knowledge is important to interpret the meaning. For example, a sudden workload increase may be witnessed by positive CPU spikes, whereas a brief network problem may manifest through negative network spikes.

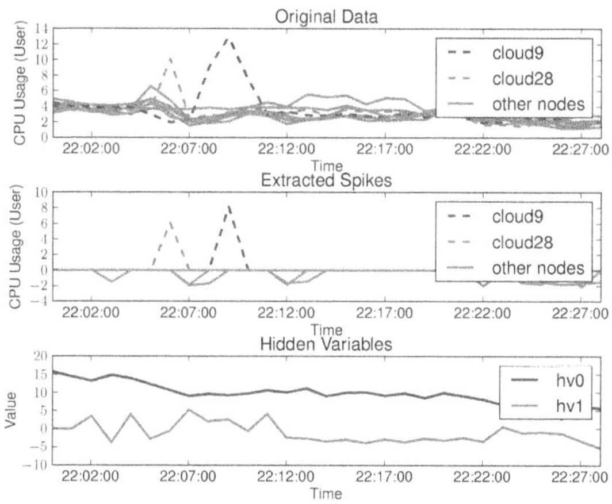

Figure 10: *Separation of trends and spikes.* Anomalous timeseries spikes caused by overburdened tasks and overall trends are distinguished by RainMon.

5.2 Machine Group Detection

It is not always the case that a single machine is an outlier. In many cases of uneven workload distribution across machines in a cluster, groups of machines may behave differently. For example, we identified a case with RainMon where all machines were *reading* data as expected, but there were two groups of *writers*—only about half the machines were writing heavily. Fig. 11, the plot of $W_{:,2}$ against $W_{:,1}$, illustrates the two groups of machines, which we have highlighted with gray rectangles. This was caused by a large Hadoop job whose tasks did not generate even output loads across machines. Some of those tasks generated more output data than other tasks, causing the machines running these tasks to experience higher disk write traffic. A programmer can fix this problem by partitioning the data more evenly across machines.

5.3 Detecting Correlated Routers

To demonstrate the applicability of RainMon to network monitoring, as well as within-datacenter monitoring, we analyze the packet flow count in the Abilene network [15]. Abilene is a nationwide high-speed data network for research and higher education. This public dataset was collected from 11 core routers with packet flow data between every

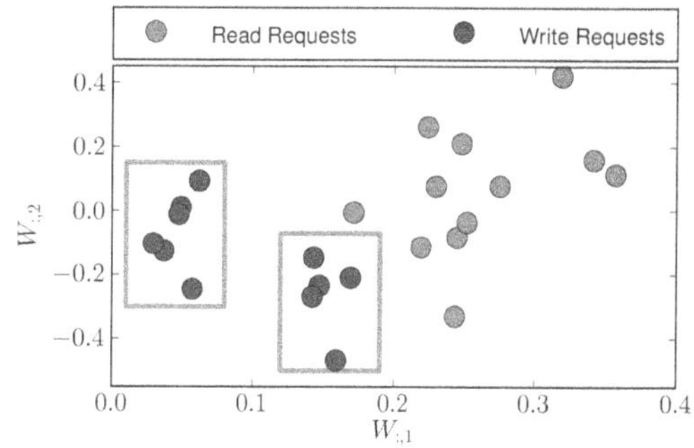

Figure 11: *Machine group discovery.* From the scatterplot, RainMon can also identify *groups* of machines with different behavior.

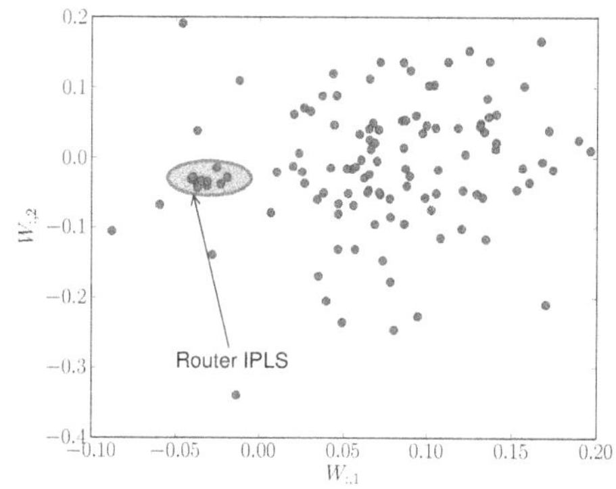

(a) Scatterplot of $W_{:,2}$ vs $W_{:,1}$

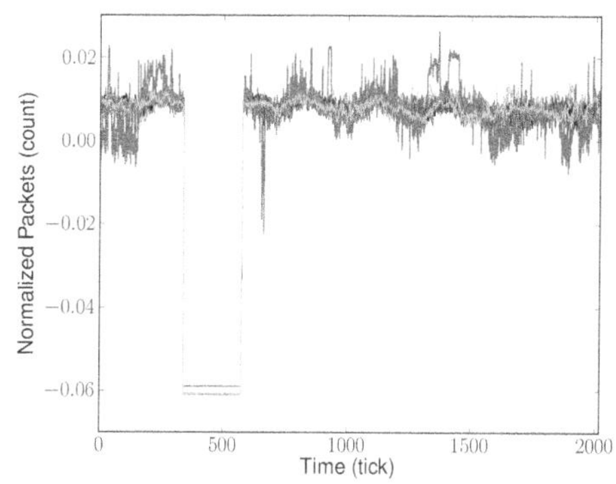

(b) Timeseries from the circled group in (a)

Figure 12: *Correlated anomaly identification.* RainMon's scatterplot illustrates a cluster of nodes and allows visualization of the anomalous streams. All streams shown in (b) correspond to a single router named "IPLS."

pair of nodes for a total of 121 packet flow streams. We analyzed a week's worth of data binned at 5 minute intervals for a total of 2016 time ticks. Visualizing this data via the scatterplot of $W_{:,2}$ vs $W_{:,1}$ reveals some tightly clustered streams (see Fig. 12(a)) that interestingly all correspond to packet flows from a single router named "IPLS." Examining in detail the corresponding data streams, this correlation between "IPLS" and other routers becomes quite evident (see Fig. 12(b)) in the abnormal behavior on its part around time tick 400.

5.4 Time Interval Anomaly Detection

In addition to finding anomalous machines, RainMon can be useful in detecting anomalous time intervals. The trends observed in hidden variables provide an overall picture of trends in smoothed data and anomalies across a multi-tick timescale. This can be helpful in finding unusual behavior in time from inspection of only a single trend.

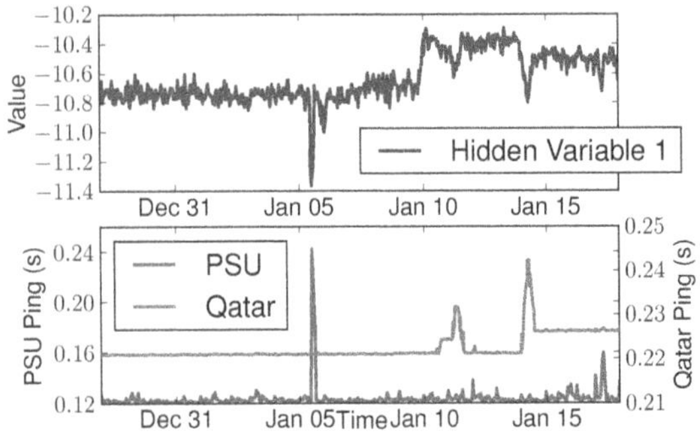

Figure 13: *Trend discovery.* Change in ping time behavior (Qatar) and sustained increase (PSU) found from the first hidden variable. Absolute values on the "Value" axis should not be interpreted.

When applying the tool to one year of data from the CMU.net dataset, we could rapidly identify changes in a single ping destination by examining the first hidden variable. Fig. 13 illustrates one of the cases: we observed a sudden point change in the trend that was retained after decomposition around Jan. 5, 2012, and an increase starting at approximately Jan. 10. From inspection of the weight coefficients of the first hidden variable, we isolated two unusual behaviors on two of the links. First, a point increase in ping time is clearly observable in the PSU timeseries. Second, the changes towards the end of the time window shown in the figure helped identify a change in the "normal" ping time to Qatar. This time was nearly constant at 0.221 sec before Jan. 10, and became 0.226 sec in the period after Jan. 15, a change difficult to localize from the traditional display currently used for the data. A network administrator confirmed that these sustained changes were legitimate and likely occur due to maintenance by a telecommunications provider.

5.5 Compression

To further show concretely how decomposition is effective, we show how RainMon can compress data, since the summary from dimensionality reduction can be projected back into the space of the original data. That is, by retaining hidden variables s_t and the weight matrix W, RainMon can store a lossy version of the timeseries data — but, by keeping spike data, it can also maintain potential anomalies with full fidelity. Since W is adapted over time in Algorithm 1, one would need to store this matrix at multiple points in time. Therefore, for this evaluation, we perform PCA over an interval of time, rather than use incremental PCA, and use a fixed number of hidden variables.

Fig. 14 shows the total compressed size of the data segment when stored with a combination of hidden variables and weight matrix (in red) and spike data (black). For comparison, we show two alternative compression approaches: using dimensionality reduction on the non-decomposed input (blue bars) and storing the original data (green line).

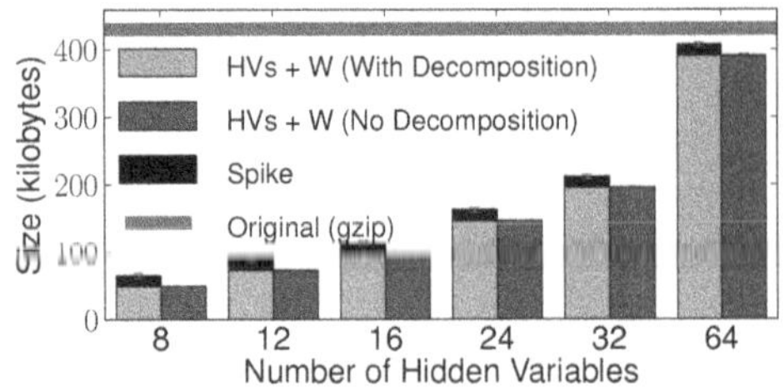

Figure 14: *Space savings:* storing hidden variables uses less space than the baseline lossless compression approach (green "Original" line).

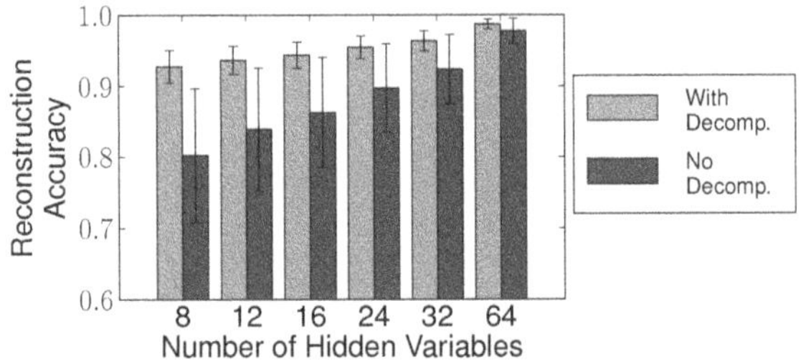

Figure 15: *Greater accuracy through decomposition:* Storing lossless spike data separately provides improved accuracy relative to no decomposition.

For fairness, we apply generic (**gzip**) compression to the data in all cases, which is a standard baseline approach to storing timeseries monitoring data [22]. For $M = 16$ hidden variables and eleven 56-hour intervals of 118 streams of disk access data from the Hadoop dataset, the reduced-dimensionality data and spikes together occupy 114 ± 5KB. This is 26.5% the size of the **gzip**-compressed original data (430 ± 80KB), and only requires 16KB (14%) of additional storage for the sparse, highly-compressible spike data.

Though spike data requires slightly more space, it yields better accuracy than using non-decomposed input. For the same data shown in Fig. 14, Fig. 15 shows the reconstruction accuracy of smoothed+spike data ("With Decomp.") and PCA as run on the original data ("No Decomp.")—the former has both higher mean accuracy and lower variance[1]. Additionally, since spikes are stored with full fidelity, anomaly detection and alerting algorithms that require precise values could operate without loss of correctness.

5.6 Prediction

We further consider how effectively the trends captured in hidden variables can be forecasted. If projected back into the original space, future machine utilization can be useful for synthetic workload generation and short-term capacity planning [9]. RainMon uses a Kalman filter as described in Sec. 3.3 to produce adaptive predictions. To provide an indirect comparison to other approaches, we instead force a fixed look-ahead and also run vector autoregression (VAR) [23] and trivial last-value prediction (Constant) for the same

[1]Reconstruction accuracy A is computed as the geometric mean of the coefficient of determination R^2 for each timeseries; we compare data where A is defined for both models:

$$A = \left(\prod_{i=1}^{N} 1 - \frac{\sum_{t=1}^{T} (y_{t,i} - \hat{y}_{t,i})^2}{\sum_{t=1}^{T} (y_{t,i} - \bar{y}_i)^2} \right)^{1/N}$$

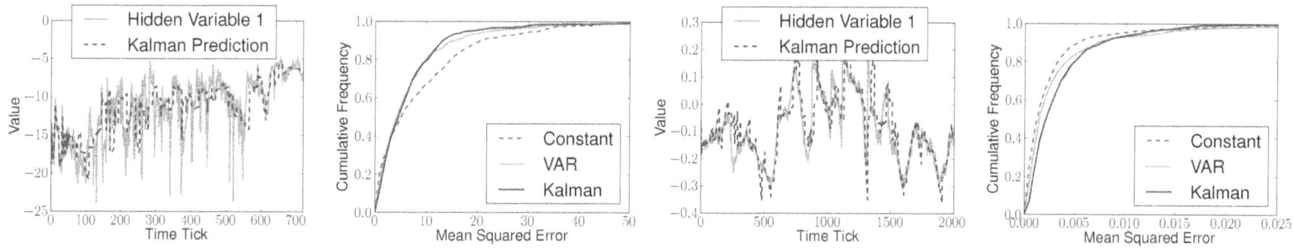

(a) Hadoop Prediction (b) Hadoop MSE (c) Abilene Prediction (d) Abilene MSE

Figure 16: *Kalman filter predictive performance.* A Kalman filter model was used to predict summarized hidden variables two hours into the future. Fig. (a) shows the prediction overlaid on the first hidden variable for a 5-day slice of memory and disk metrics on the Hadoop dataset; (b) shows a CDF of the mean squared error between the prediction and data as compared to vector autoregression and simple constant prediction. Figs. (c) and (d) show the same for the Abilene dataset.

look-ahead. As seen in Fig. 16, on a slice of Hadoop data, the Kalman filter slightly outperforms VAR, whereas both VAR and the Kalman filter have less predictive power than constant forecast for the Abilene data. Though further work is needed to fully characterize these datasets, this highlights the limitation of RainMon's model-based predictor on particularly self-similar or difficult data.

6. CONCLUSION AND DISCUSSION

Understanding usage and behavior in computing clusters is a significant and growing management problem. Integrating decomposition, dimensionality reduction, and prediction in an end-to-end system has given us enhanced ability to analyze monitoring data from real-world systems. RainMon has enabled exploration of cluster data at the granularity of the overall cluster and that of individual nodes, and allowed for diagnosis of anomalous machines and time periods.

Our experience with RainMon has helped to define its limitations, and we highlight three directions of ongoing work here. First, parameter selection is both involved and necessary given the diversity of datacenter streams, and as briefly glimpsed in Sec. 5.6 the ability to mine monitoring data varies across environments. Mining other datasets using similar techniques, or optimizing them for the ones we study, is an ongoing and future challenge.

Second, understanding how analysis results are interpreted is key to improving their presentation. Initial feedback from industry visitors and a few administrators has resulted in changes to RainMon's interface, but active deployment of RainMon on more systems and studies with administrators and cluster users are needed to enhance its utility.

Third, scaling these techniques to larger systems will require further towards performance tuning. Currently, the downsampling and slicing capabilities of our storage approach have enabled us to handle large datasets like the Hadoop streams. However, robustness at even greater scales remains to be demonstrated. Larger systems also complicate collection, aggregation, and fault-tolerance.

7. ACKNOWLEDGEMENTS

We greatly appreciate the CMU network operations team for enabling the use of RainMon on the CMU.net data and the assistance of OpenCloud administrators. Feedback from Lei Li, Raja Sambasivan, and the anonymous reviewers was very helpful in improving this paper. We thank the members and companies of the PDL Consortium (including Actifio, APC, EMC, Emulex, Facebook, Fusion-io, Google, Hewlett-Packard Labs, Hitachi, Intel, Microsoft Research, NEC Laboratories, NetApp, Oracle, Panasas, Riverbed, Samsung, Seagate, STEC, Symantec, VMware, and Western Digital) for their interest, insights, feedback, and support. This research was sponsored in part by Intel via the Intel Science and Technology Center for Cloud Computing (ISTC-CC). Ilari Shafer is supported in part by an NDSEG Fellowship, which is sponsored by the Department of Defense.

8. REFERENCES

[1] Apache Hadoop, `http://hadoop.apache.org/`.

[2] Apache Mahout: Scalable machine learning and data mining, `http://mahout.apache.org/`.

[3] L. Barroso and U. Hölzle. *The datacenter as a computer: An introduction to the design of warehouse-scale machines.* Morgan & Claypool Publishers, San Rafael, CA, 2009.

[4] K. Bhaduri, K. Das, and B. Matthews. Detecting abnormal machine characteristics in cloud infrastructures. In *Proc. ICDMW'11*, Vancouver, Canada.

[5] M. Breunig, H. Kriegel, R. Ng, and J. Sander. LOF: identifying density-based local outliers. In *Proc. SIGMOD'00*, Dallas, Texas. ACM.

[6] P. J. Brockwell and R. A. Davis. *Introduction to time series and forecasting.* Springer-Verlag, 2002.

[7] V. Chandola, A. Banerjee, and V. Kumar. Anomaly detection: A survey. *ACM Comput. Surv.*, 41(3):15:1–15:58, July 2009.

[8] D. Fisher, D. Maltz, A. Greenberg, X. Wang, H. Warncke, G. Robertson, and M. Czerwinski. Using visualization to support network and application management in a data center. In *Proc. INM'08*, Orlando, FL.

[9] D. Gmach, J. Rolia, L. Cherkasova, and A. Kemper. Workload analysis and demand prediction of enterprise data center applications. In *Proc. IISWC'07*, Boston, MA.

[10] V. Guralnik and J. Srivastava. Event detection from time series data. In *Proc. KDD'99*, San Diego, CA.

[11] S. Hirose, K. Yamanishi, T. Nakata, and R. Fujimaki. Network anomaly detection based on eigen equation compression. In *Proc. KDD'09*, Paris, France.

[12] E. Hoke, J. Sun, J. Strunk, G. Ganger, and C. Faloutsos. InteMon: continuous mining of sensor

data in large-scale self-infrastructures. *ACM SIGOPS Operating Systems Review*, 40(3):38–44, 2006.
[13] IBM Tivoli, `http://www.ibm.com/developerworks/tivoli/`.
[14] M. P. Kasick, J. Tan, R. Gandhi, and P. Narasimhan. Black-box problem diagnosis in parallel file systems. In *Proc. FAST'10*, San Jose, CA.
[15] A. Lakhina, M. Crovella, and C. Diot. Diagnosing network-wide traffic anomalies. In *Proc. SIGCOMM'04*, Portland, OR.
[16] Z. Lan, Z. Zheng, and Y. Li. Toward automated anomaly identification in large-scale systems. *IEEE Transactions on Parallel and Distributed Systems*, 21(2):174 –187, Feb. 2010.
[17] W. Leland, M. Taqqu, W. Willinger, and D. Wilson. On the self-similar nature of Ethernet traffic. In *Proc. SIGCOMM'93*, San Francisco, CA.
[18] L. Li, C. Liang, J. Liu, S. Nath, A. Terzis, and C. Faloutsos. ThermoCast: A cyber-physical forecasting model for data centers. In *Proc. KDD'11*, San Diego, CA.
[19] L. Li, J. McCann, N. Pollard, and C. Faloutsos. DynaMMo: Mining and summarization of coevolving sequences with missing values. In *Proc. KDD'09*, Paris, France.
[20] L. Li, B. A. Prakash, and C. Faloutsos. Parsimonious linear fingerprinting for time series. In *Proc. VLDB'10*, Singapore.
[21] J. Lin, E. Keogh, L. Wei, and S. Lonardi. Experiencing SAX: a novel symbolic representation of time series. *Data Min. Knowl. Discov.*, 15(2):107–144, Oct. 2007.
[22] C. Loboz, S. Smyl, and S. Nath. DataGarage: Warehousing massive performance data on commodity servers. In *Proc. VLDB'10*, Singapore.
[23] H. Lutkepohl. *New Introduction to Multiple Time Series Analysis*. Springer, 2007.
[24] M. L. Massie, B. N. Chun, and D. E. Culler. The ganglia distributed monitoring system: design, implementation, and experience. *Parallel Computing*, 30(7):817–840, July 2004.
[25] Nagios, `http://www.nagios.org`.
[26] H. Nguyen, Y. Tan, and X. Gu. PAL: Propagation-aware anomaly localization for cloud hosted distributed applications. In *Proc. SLAML'11*, Cascais, Portugal.
[27] S. Papadimitriou, J. Sun, and C. Faloutsos. Streaming pattern discovery in multiple time-series. In *Proc. VLDB'05*, Trondheim, Norway.
[28] D. Patnaik, M. Marwah, R. Sharma, and N. Ramakrishnan. Sustainable operation and management of data center chillers using temporal data mining. In *Proc. KDD'09*, Paris, France.
[29] J. G. Proakis and M. Salehi. *Fundamentals of Communication Systems*. Prentice Hall, 2004.
[30] G. Reeves, J. Liu, S. Nath, and F. Zhao. Cypress: Managing massive time series streams with multi-scale compressed trickles. In *Proc. VLDB'09*, Lyon, France.
[31] S. Roweis and Z. Ghahramani. A Unifying Review of Linear Gaussian Models. *Neural Computation*, 11(2):305–345, Feb. 1999.
[32] RRDtool, `http://www.mrtg.org/rrdtool/`.
[33] R. K. Sahoo, A. J. Oliner, I. Rish, M. Gupta, J. E. Moreira, S. Ma, R. Vilalta, and A. Sivasubramaniam. Critical event prediction for proactive management in large-scale computer clusters. In *Proc. KDD'03*, New York, NY.
[34] B. Sigoure. OpenTSDB: The distributed, scalable time series database. In *Proc. OSCON'11*, Portland, OR.
[35] J. Sun, S. Papadimitriou, and C. Faloutsos. Distributed pattern discovery in multiple streams. In *Proc. PAKDD'06*, Singapore.
[36] Zenoss, `http://www.zenoss.com/`.
[37] Y. Zhu and D. Shasha. Efficient elastic burst detection in data streams. In *Proc. KDD'03*, Washington, DC.

APPENDIX

A. KALMAN FILTER DETAILS

A.1 Prediction

Given the initial model parameters ($\mu_{t|t}$ and $P_{t|t}$) for the linear dynamical system and the current observation (y_t), we update the model parameters to compute $\mu_{t+1|t+1}$ and $P_{t+1|t+1}$ as follows:

$$\begin{aligned} V_t &= A P_{t|t} A^T + \Sigma_w \\ K_{t+1} &= V_t C^T (C V_t C^T + \Sigma_v)^{-1} \\ \hat{\mu}_{t+1|t+1} &= A \hat{\mu}_{t|t} + K_{t+1}(y_{t+1} - C A \hat{\mu}_{t|t}) \\ P_{t+1|t+1} &= V_t - V_t C^T (C V_t C^T + \Sigma_v)^{-1} C V_t \end{aligned}$$

A.2 Smoothing

Given the predictions $\hat{x}_{t|t}$ and $\hat{P}_{t|t}$ from above that were computed over the past T time samples, we compute the smoothed predictions using predictions from the future:

$$\begin{aligned} A_t^s &= P_{t|t} A^T (V_t)^{-1} \\ \hat{\mu}_t^s &= \hat{\mu}_{t|t} + A_t^s (x_{t+1}^s - A \hat{x}_{t|t}) \\ P_t^s &= P_{t|t} + A_t^s (P_{t+1}^s - V_t) A_t^{sT} \end{aligned}$$

where $\hat{\mu}_t^s$ and P_t^2 are the smoothed estimates of the model parameters computed by using the observations in the future. We start at $t = T$ and go backwards to $t = 1$. These are useful for parameter learning as described next.

A.3 Parameter Learning

Given the forward Kalman filter predictions and the smoothed reverse predictions we estimate all the model parameters as follows, where n refers to the EM iteration index:

$$\begin{aligned} E[x_t] &= \hat{\mu}_t^s \\ E[x_t x_{t-1}^T] &= P_t^s A_{t-1}^{sT} + \hat{\mu}_t^s \hat{\mu}_{t-1}^{sT} \\ E[x_t x_t^T] &= P_t^s + \hat{\mu}_t^s \hat{\mu}_t^{sT} \\ A^n &= (\textstyle\sum_{t=2}^T E[x_t x_{t-1}^T)(\sum_{t=1}^T E[x_t x_t^T])^{-1} \\ \Sigma_w^n &= \frac{\sum_{t=2}^T E[x_t x_t^T] + A^n E[x_{t-1} x_{t-1}^T] A^{nT}}{T-1} - \\ &\quad \frac{\sum_{t=2}^T E[x_t x_{t-1}] A^{nT} + A^n E[x_{t-1} x_t]}{T-1} \\ C^n &= (\textstyle\sum_{t=1}^T y_t E[x_t^T])(\sum_{t=1}^T E[x_t x_t^T])^{-1} \\ \Sigma_v^n &= \frac{\sum_{t=1}^T y_t y_t^T + C^n E[x_t x_t^T] C^{nT}}{T} - \\ &\quad \frac{y_t x_t^{sT} C^{nT} + C^n x_t^s y_t^T}{T} \\ \mu_0^n &= E[x_t] \\ \Sigma_0^n &= E[x_t x_t^T] - E[x_t] E[x_t]^T \end{aligned}$$

SympGraph: A Framework for Mining Clinical Notes through Symptom Relation Graphs

Parikshit Sondhi†, Jimeng Sun‡, Hanghang Tong‡, ChengXiang Zhai†
† Univ. of Illinois, Urbana, USA
‡IBM TJ Watson Research Center, USA
sondhi1@illinois.edu, jimeng@us.ibm.com, htong@us.ibm.com, czhai@illinois.edu

ABSTRACT

As an integral part of Electronic Health Records (EHRs), clinical notes pose special challenges for analyzing EHRs due to their unstructured nature. In this paper, we present a general mining framework SympGraph for modeling and analyzing symptom relationships in clinical notes.

A SympGraph has symptoms as nodes and co-occurrence relations between symptoms as edges, and can be constructed automatically through extracting symptoms over sequences of clinical notes for a large number of patients. We present an important clinical application of SympGraph: *symptom expansion*, which can expand a given set of symptoms to other related symptoms by analyzing the underlying SympGraph structure. We further propose a matrix update algorithm which provides a significant computational saving for dynamic updates to the graph. Comprehensive evaluation on 1 million longitudinal clinical notes over 13K patients shows that static symptom expansion can successfully expand a set of known symptoms to a disease with high agreement rate with physician input (average precision 0.46), a 31% improvement over baseline co-occurrence based methods. The experimental results also show that the expanded symptoms can serve as useful features for improving AUC measure for disease diagnosis prediction, thus confirming the potential clinical value of our work.

Categories and Subject Descriptors

H.3 [**INFORMATION STORAGE AND RETRIEVAL**]: Information Search and Retrieval

Keywords

symptom graphs, physician notes,random walk,patient records

1. INTRODUCTION

Electronic Health Records (EHRs) have become a standard practice in modern healthcare delivery. Beyond storing patient records, EHRs are an ever-growing data repository that enables clinical data mining applications, especially comparative effectiveness research. Heterogeneous sets of EHR data are available in both structured and unstructured formats. For example, diagnosis information such as International Classification of Diseases - ICD9 codes[1], medication information such as generic drug names, and lab results are commonly stored in structured formats. Such structured EHR data are readily usable for data mining applications. However, clinical notes, arguably the most important part of the patient records, are largely unstructured. Despite the standard practice based on which physicians write the notes, such as SOAP notes(sec 2.1), by and large the information in physician notes remains unstructured, making it a significant challenge to extract and understand clinical concepts both within and across patients. The following example illustrates some of the needs and specific challenges in mining clinical notes.

Clinical motivating example: Congestive Heart failure (CHF), affecting 1 in 5 US adults, is the single most costly health problem for Centers for Medicare & Medicaid Services (CMS). With an aging population, the individual and societal burden is expected to increase. CHF is a complex syndrome with multiple pathophysiological manifestations that frequently overlap with those of other diseases, making early diagnosis challenging. Thus it is usually diagnosed in primary care, often as a late stage disease. In order to increase the chance of early diagnosis of CHF, it is important to collect all directly and indirectly relevant symptoms from a patient, and have a good understanding of the criteria for diagnosis. Unfortunately, the only criteria currently available were published by the Framingham investigators in 1971 based on clinical data acquired in the 1950 and 60s [11]. Fortunately, clinical notes are excellent sources from which we can potentially extract relevant symptoms to diseases such as CHF.

Automatic identification of Framingham criteria can greatly enhance the understanding of their prevalence as well as incidence in a patient population over time. Clinicians are also interested in understanding in general how all signs and symptoms are related to each other in order to possibly expand Framingham criteria to a broader set of symptoms that serve as robust signals for early detection of CHF. The need for extracting clinical signs and symptoms from patient records and further analyzing them also exists for many other diseases.

In this paper, we study the following questions: How to *capture* the relations among different symptoms extracted from clinical notes? How to *expand* a set of known symptoms to other relevant symptoms? How to efficiently *update* such symptom expansion when the underlying symptom relations change? To the best of our knowledge, no previous work has systematically studied these questions.

To this end, we present a general mining framework SympGraph, that turns patient encounter notes into a symptom graph to system-

KDD'12, August 12–16, 2012, Beijing, China.

[1] *http://icd9cm.chrisendres.com/*

atically reveal all the symptoms and symptom relations buried in the notes. A SympGraph is a graph with extracted symptoms as vertices, and the associations of symptoms as edges. It provides a general representation of symptoms and their relations and helps support many different mining applications under a unified framework. As an example of the applications enabled by a symptom graph, we present an important clinical application: *symptom expansion* which expands a small initial set of known symptoms to a bigger set of relevant symptoms. We present two different algorithms for solving symptom expansion in different contexts. When the underlying symptom graph is static, we propose *static symptom expansion*, which adopts a random walk type of algorithm to rank related symptoms based on their relevance to the initial set. When the underlying symptom graph changes (e.g., due to addition of new symptom relations or updating existing ones), we propose *dynamic symptom expansion*, which is based on a novel matrix update method for low rank approximation of the symptom graph.

We evaluate the proposed SympGraph framework on a large-scale real world clinical database with 1 million clinical notes of over 13K patients over 7 years, and the experimental results are quite promising. We show that SympGraph can successfully expand a known set of CHF related symptoms with a high agreement rate compared to physician judgements (average precision 0.46), providing a 31% improvement over baseline methods that do not use SympGraph. We further demonstrate that the expanded symptoms can help achieve over 10% improvement of area under the curve (AUC) measure for predicting the onset of CHF. In terms of the scalability, we compare static and dynamic symptom expansion methods, where interesting workload trade-off is revealed. In general, dynamic symptom expansion is preferred when multiple initial symptom sets are present and underlying relation changes are small.

2. BACKGROUND

2.1 Clinical Notes

A clinical note contains unstructured details regarding a patient's encounter with a healthcare professional. The content of the note varies depending upon the type of encounter, and there are many different types of encounters. For example, a note for a *Pharmacy Visit*, contains information regarding medications and their side effects, while a *Physician Visit* contains complete details of patient symptoms, medications, social history etc. Other example types of encounters are *Laboratory Visit* and *Case Manager Visit*. Of all these, the most important and abundant are the *Physician Visit* notes. These are generally loosely organized into four SOAP sections: *Subjective*, *Objective*, *Assessment* and *Plan*. Each section contains a specific kind of information regarding the patient. A sample is shown in Figure 1.

Subjective: details of a patient's condition in her own words. Also other details such as social history, family history, current medications etc.

Objective: observable information such as findings from physical examination, test results, vital signs, age, height, weight etc.

Assessment: a list of potential diagnoses.

Plan: information on the subsequent steps of actions of the patient, such as a treatment plan.

2.2 Symptom Extraction

Clearly, in order to analyze and mine symptom-related knowledge from clinical notes, we first need to go through a Symptom Extraction step, in which we process each encounter to identify the symptom mentions present and filter out negated symptoms. In the proposed SympGraph framework, we would use the extracted symptoms and their statistical relations to constract a graph, which can then support various analysis tasks, especially symptom expansion, an application that we would study in detail in this paper.

Since improving the accuracy of symptom mention extraction is not our focus, we mostly rely on existing techniques and extend them systematically to extract symptom mentions. Specifically, we use the Apache Unstructured Information Management Architecture (UIMA) toolkit(http://uima.apache.org/) to construct a Natural Language Processing (NLP) pipeline for the task. The main idea behind a UIMA pipeline is to construct a series of annotators. Each annotator is a program that parses the document text and marks the start and end locations for a certain type of entity in the text. We adopt the UIMA toolkit as it allows us to efficiently create and interconnect such annotators. Figure 2 shows the architecture of our UIMA pipeline.

Word, Sentence Annotator At the lowest level we start with annotators, which identify the word, sentence and SOAP section boundaries in the text. These annotations, along with the original text are then supplied to the subsequent levels.

Symptom Annotator Symptom annotator annotates all symp-

Subjective:	**Objective:**
ANXIETY STATE NOS 300.00 DEPRESSIVE DISORDER NEC 311 ATRIAL FIBRILLATION 427.31 OLD MYOCARDIAL INFARCT 412 CONGESTIVE HEART FAILURE 428.0 Current outpatient prescriptions ** LOPRESSOR 50 MG PO TABS 1 tab two times a day 60 5	250.00 DM, CONTROLLED, TYPE II (primary encounter diagnosis) 428.0 CONGESTIVE HEART FAILURE 585.3 KIDNEY DZ, CHRONIC (GFR=30 59) STAGE III 412 OLD MYOCARDIAL INFARCT 715.09 GENERAL OSTEOARTHROSIS 427.31 ATRIAL FIBRILLATION
Assessment:	**Plan:**
BP 122/68 | Pulse 78 | Temp (Src) 98.1 (Oral) | Resp 22 | Wt 227 lbs Abdomen: abdomen soft, non–tender, obese and no masses or organomegaly Back: No CVA tenderness Extremities: No edema	Continue present medication(s): Referral(s) to: eye Injection(s) ordered: b12 Schedule labs: Labs on return.

Figure 1: A sample clinical note, highlighting the four sections

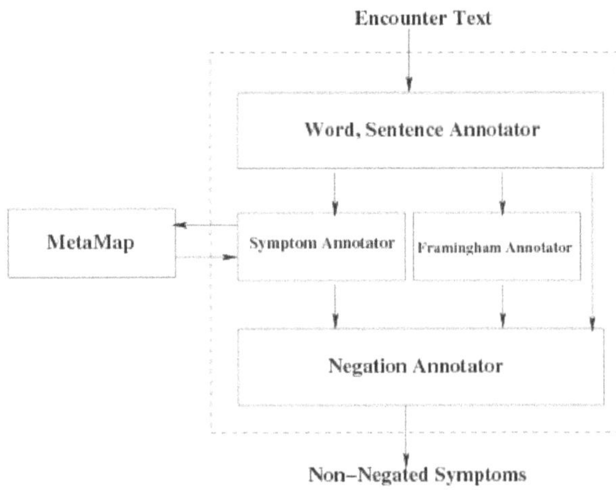

Figure 2: UIMA pipeline architecture for symptom extraction

tom mentions present in the text. Symptoms are identified using MetaMap (http://metamap.nlm.nih.gov/), a tool developed at the National Library of Medicine, for mapping raw English text to standardized medical concepts in the Unified Medical Language System (UMLS) metathesaurus(http://www.nlm.nih.gov/research/umls/). UMLS contains over a million medical and general English concepts, which are further organized under a hierarchy of 134 semantic types. Each concept is assigned one or more high level semantic types. For example "dsyn" type, contains all concepts belonging to the category of "Disease or Syndrome".

Since MetaMap returns all types of concepts present in the text, we filter out the returned concepts based on their semantic types. More specifically, we only keep concepts belonging to the following semantic types as symptom concepts:

{ *sosy, dsyn, neop, fngs, bact, virs, cgab, acab, lbtr, inpo, mobd, comd, anab* }

Framingham Annotator The general Symptom Annotator described above does not accurately identify all mentions of Framingham Symptoms for heart failure in the text. Since our experiments are focused on Congestive Heart Failure (CHF), we also built a separate annotator, which identifies Framingham Symptoms more accurately in the text using a dictionary of symptom mentions and simple heuristics. The symptom dictionary was built by manually analyzing clinical records. We used the Framingham Annotator to extract 15 out of 16 Framingham symptoms in total. One symptom - *Weight loss* $\geq$ *4.5 kg in 5 days in response to treatment*, needed deeper text analysis and was not extracted.

Negation Annotator Presence of a symptom in a clinical note does not necessarily imply an *Assertion* which is its presence in a patient. The negation annotator looks at the surrounding text of each symptom annotation and filters out symptom mentions found in negated contexts based on simple heuristics such as presence of negation related words like "denies", "without", and "no". In principle, negative symptom findings can also indicate interesting relationships. However for this work we will only focus on positive symptom occurrences.

3. SYMPGRAPH

From a medical application perspective, it is very important to study clinical signs and symptoms in clinical notes, especially their relations both within a patient and across patients. Recognizing mentions of symptoms in the clinical notes is only the first step; after recognizing all the mentions of potential symptoms, we also need to develop methods for further organization, abstraction, and analysis of the extracted symptoms. A major challenge here is how to support different applications in a general and efficient way. To this end, we propose a general symptom mining framework called SympGraph, which provides a general graph representation of symptoms and their relations extracted from the clinical notes. SympGraph can be regarded as an abstraction of clinical notes from the perspective of symptom analysis and mining in the sense that it contains essential and sufficient information about symptoms and their relations required by many different mining applications.

Below, we first present the overall process of building symptom graphs for clinical notes and then present the algorithms for constructing and aggregating them.

3.1 Overview

The construction of symptoms can be done in a multi-level fashion as shown in Figure 3. At the patient level, clinical notes of a patient can be modeled as event sequences. The events in this paper are mentions of the symptoms in the clinical notes during a specific time interval (e.g., a day). SympGraph summarizes the

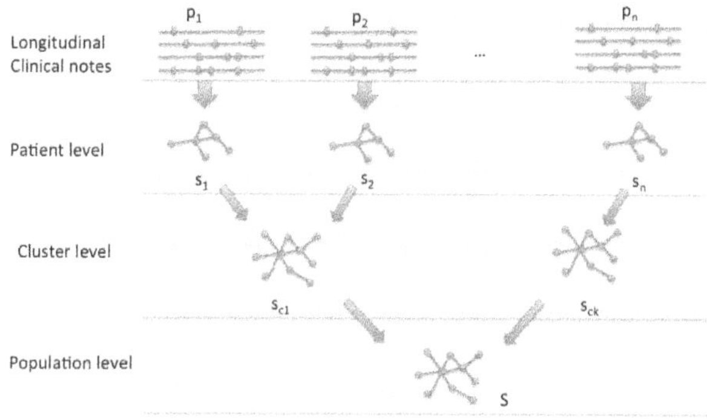

Figure 3: Overview of Multiple levels of SympGraphs

event sequences of a patient into a compact graph representation named patient (symptom) graph. A patient graph captures symptom co-occurrence relations for a given patient. The distance between patients can be defined based on the similarity of the underlying symptom graphs. We can aggregate individual patients' symptom graphs into a population-level symptom graph.

A symptom graph G is represented as $G = \{V, E, w\}$, where every node $v \in V$ represents a symptom, the edge $e = (v_1, v_2)$ represents the relationship between two symptoms v_1 and v_2, and weighting function $w : e \to \mathbb{R}^+$ maps the edge e to a positive value $w(e)$.

For a given patient p, such a symptom graph can be constructed, where nodes correspond to the symptoms extracted from p's clinical notes, and edges correspond to the relationship of symptoms exhibited in p's clinical notes.

3.2 Graph Construction

One simple way to construct the graph is to form edge (i, j) in G if symptoms i and j co-occurr in the same encounter note. Or formally, given a sequence of clinical encounters c_i of p over time $(1 \leq i \leq C_p)$, we can construct a symptom to encounter matrix $\mathbf{N}^p \in \mathbb{R}^{S \times C_p}$, where S is the total number of symptoms and C_p is the number of encounters for patient p, and the element in $\mathbf{N}^p$ is defined as

$$\mathbf{N}^p_{ij} = \begin{cases} 1 & \text{if symptom } i \text{ is in encounter note } j, \\ 0 & \text{otherwise.} \end{cases}$$

The i-th row vector $\mathbf{N}_{i:}$ of $\mathbf{N}$ corresponds to the patient p's encounters that contain symptom i. The j-th column vector $\mathbf{N}^p_{:j}$ corresponds to the symptoms extracted from the encounter note j. With the encounter matrix $\mathbf{N}^p$, the symptom co-occurrence matrix $\mathbf{G} \in \mathbb{R}^{S \times S}$ is

$$\mathbf{G} = \sum_p \mathbf{N}^p \cdot \mathbf{N}^{pT}. \quad (1)$$

The nonzero elements in $\mathbf{G}$ correspond to all the edges of the symptom graph G. Intuitively, the symptoms extracted from the same encounter note are connected to each other, and form a clique. All the cliques from different encounter notes of a patient can be summed together to form the symptom matrix $\mathbf{G}$. The weighting function $w(i, j)$ is exactly the element $\mathbf{G}_{ij}$.

Beyond this simple construction, we also extend the formulation to a location sensitive construction. The location sensitive idea arises out of the intuition that a physician will likely evaluate the presence of related symptoms in succession and they will likely appear closeby in the clinical notes. Thus if two symptoms are far away from each other in the encounter note, the edge weight between them should be small. If they are close, the weight should be large. In this paper, we use the inverse of the distance as the weight. Such formulation can still be captured by generalizing the multiplication operator as $\mathbf{u} \cdot \mathbf{v}^T = \sum_{1 \le i \le C_p} f(\mathbf{u}_i, \mathbf{v}_i)$ where $f(\mathbf{u}_i, \mathbf{v}_i) = 1/d$ and d is the location offset in words between symptom u and v in the encounter i.

Graph Normalization: In order to alleviate the problem where some symptoms are much more common than others, we further normalize a symptom matrix $\mathbf{G}$ constructed using a method described above through the following

$$\tilde{\mathbf{G}} = \mathbf{G}\mathbf{D}^{-1}$$

where $\mathbf{D}$ is a diagonal matrix with $\mathbf{D}_{ii} = \sum_j \mathbf{N}_{ij}$. The resulting matrix $\tilde{\mathbf{G}}$ will be Markovian, namely the column sums to 1. In this case, the popular symptoms will be penalized since the outgoing edges from them will be normalized. Note that the normalization does not preserve symmetric property of the original matrix $\mathbf{G}$. There are other normalization methods that can preserve the symmetric property such as the normalized Laplacian normalization $\tilde{\mathbf{G}} = \mathbf{D}^{-1/2}\mathbf{G}\mathbf{D}^{-1/2}$. In this paper, we pick the asymmetric normalization because we believe the relations are not always symmetric. For example, v is a common symptom with many neighbors including u, but u is only connected to v. In this case, the importance of u to v (i.e., $w(v, u)$) is small, but the importance of v to u (i.e., $w(u, v)$) is significant.

Aggregation: Finally, given a set of normalized symptom graphs $G_1, G_2, \ldots, G_K$, we can also easily combine them into an aggregated symptom graph G by averaging the symptom matrices:

$$\mathbf{G} = \frac{1}{K} \sum_i \mathbf{G}_i.$$

Since the symptom matrices $\mathbf{G}_i$ $(1 \le i \le K)$ are already normalized, the simple averaging will preserve the Markovian property. Aggregation provides a general and flexible way to analyze the data with different "resolutions"; this in combination with graph analysis algorithms naturally supports many different ways to analyze and exploit symptoms and their relations in a variety of applications.

4. STATIC SYMPTOM EXPANSION

Given a symptom graph, one important clinical application is to automatically explore and expand an existing set of symptoms. Such expansion is necessary to improve the diagnosis of diseases (one use case is described in Section 1 about extending Framingham criteria for CHF diagnosis). To facilitate the discussion, we define the following notations: Let ES be the set of the existing symptoms that one constructed (e.g., symptoms included in the Framingham criteria). Let vector $\mathbf{e} \in \mathbb{R}^S$ be the indicator vector of the existing symptom set, where

$$\mathbf{e}_i = \begin{cases} 1 & \text{if symptom } i \in ES, \\ 0 & \text{otherwise.} \end{cases}$$

Let $\mathbf{r} \in \mathbb{R}^S$ be the relevance score vector of all symptoms with respect to the existing set ES, which we hope to compute.

Intuitively, to perform symptom expansion, we would be interested in obtaining symptoms that co-occur frequently with the existing set of symptoms. Formally, such co-occurring symptoms can be captured through $\mathbf{r} = \mathbf{G}\mathbf{e}$, where highly ranked values in $\mathbf{r}$ correspond to the most commonly co-occurring symptoms with ES. Mathematically, this can be achieved by a one-step random walk from the existing set ES based on the symptom graph G.

In addition to the immediately co-occurring symptoms, we also perform the expansion recursively through random walk with restart [20]. Intuitively, random walk with restart (RWR) can be regarded as modeling a random particle that with probability $c (0 < c < 1)$ traverses randomly along edges of G, and probability $1 - c$ jumps back to one of the initial symptoms in ES. The recursion of random walk with restart is defined as

$$\mathbf{r} = c\mathbf{G}\mathbf{r} + (1 - c)\mathbf{e}. \quad (2)$$

The solution to the linear system eq-(2) is $\mathbf{r} = (1-c)(I - c\mathbf{G})^{-1}\mathbf{e}$. Many effective algorithms exist to solve eq-(2) when the underlying graph $\mathbf{G}$ is fixed. One simple and scalable method for solving this linear system is to use the power method to iteratively apply eq-2 with the initialization $\mathbf{r} = \mathbf{e}$ (referred to as 'Power-method'). Another effective way to solve eq-(2) is to use a low-rank approximation, followed by a matrix inversion of size $l \times l$ (where l is the rank of the low-rank approximation) to get all possible relevance scores. This solution [20], called NB_Lin, is summarized in Alg. 1 for completeness, where it is divided into two stages: NB_LIN_Pre() and NB_LIN_OQ(). In NB_LIN_Pre() (steps 1-3), a low-rank approximation is performed for the normalized adjacency matrix $\mathbf{A}$ and a matrix inversion $\mathbf{\Lambda}$ (referred to as 'core matrix') is computed. Next, in NB_LIN_OQ() (steps 4-5), only a small number of matrix-vector multiplications are computed to output the ranking vector. Therefore, NB_Lin is much more efficient for the query response, especially when we have multiple queries. (We can view the "seed symptoms" used for symptom expansion as a "query" and the task of symptom expansion as to "retrieve" additional related symptoms to the query.)

Algorithm 1 NB_Lin (repeated from [20] for completeness)

Input: The normalized adjacency matrix $\mathbf{G}$, the query vector $\mathbf{e}$ and c.

Output: The ranking vector for the source node $\mathbf{r}$.

1: **Pre-Compute Stage** (NB_LIN_Pre())
2: do low-rank approximation for $\mathbf{G} = \mathbf{U}\mathbf{V}$
3: pre-compute and store the core matrix $\mathbf{\Lambda} = (\mathbf{I} - c\mathbf{V}\mathbf{U})^{-1}$
4: **On-Line Query Stage** (NB_LIN_OQ())
5: output $\mathbf{r} = (1 - c)(\mathbf{e} + c\mathbf{U}\mathbf{\Lambda}\mathbf{V}\mathbf{e})$

In terms of applications, symptom expansion can be used at different levels of symptom graphs. At the patient level, users like physicians, nurses or even patients themselves can expand the existing set of symptoms from the current encounter to a more general set of symptoms based on the symptom graph built on the patient history. Those additional symptoms can be used as personalized query suggestions for diagnosis. One can also take the current symptoms from a patient p and perform symptom expansion based on the cluster symptom graph of p to immediately leverage patterns extracted from similar patients like p. Finally, at the population level, symptom expansion enables understanding of typical symptoms to a disease. "Typical symptoms" as described in medical books such as Framingham symptoms for CHF are just a small initial set of symptoms for diagnosing a disease such as CHF. Starting from an existing set of symptoms for a given disease, additional sets of symptoms can be obtained based on the population-level symptom graph using random walk with restart. The expansion set of symptoms can then be used as additional features for building predictive modeling for that disease, and also potentially enhance knowledge and understanding about the disease. We will present some initial clinical case studies in section 6 to show that the expansion set of symptoms discovered using our algorithm are indeed helpful for improving the prediction accuracy of the onset of CHF.

5. DYNAMIC SYMPTOM EXPANSION

In this section, we address the challenges in computing symptom expansion when the underlying symptom graph is changing. We first present our algorithm, and then analyze its accuracy as well as the efficiency.

5.1 Proposed Algorithm for Dynamic RWR

When the underlying symptom graph $\mathbf{G}$ changes over time, the results of symptom expansion would also have to be updated. In the case of very frequent changes, which can happen, e.g., due to additions of many new patient records daily, updating all the results can be computationally expensive. Specifically, let $\hat{\mathbf{G}}$ indicate the change of the symptom graph (i.e., $\hat{\mathbf{G}} + \mathbf{G}$ is the new normalized adjacency matrix). If we still want to apply NB_Lin to update the corresponding ranking vectors straight-forwardly, we need to re-compute the low-rank approximation as well as the core matrix. In other words, the computational cost in NB_Lin_Pre() now becomes part of the on-line query cost in the dynamic case, which might be too expensive.

Thus an interesting question is: how can we update the ranking vector efficiently? To address this issue, we propose an efficient algorithm to update the low rank approximation as well as the core matrix. Our key observation is as follows: for the application of symptom graph, $\hat{\mathbf{G}}$ itself can often be written or approximated by some low-rank approximation with a much lower rank size (say k, then $k << l$ where l is the rank of $\mathbf{G}$). In this case, we can easily update the low-rank approximation of the whole, new symptom matrix as well as the core matrix.

Algorithm 2 Update-RWR

Input: The previous low rank approximation $\mathbf{U}$ and $\mathbf{V}$, the previous core matrix $\mathbf{\Lambda}$, the change adjacency matrix $\hat{\mathbf{G}}$, the query vector $\mathbf{e}$ and c.

Output: The updated low rank approximation $\mathbf{U}$ and $\mathbf{V}$, the updated core matrix $\mathbf{\Lambda}$, and the updated ranking vector $\mathbf{r}$ for the query vector $\mathbf{e}$.

1: **Update U and V** (Update_LowRank())
2: Re-form or approximate $\hat{\mathbf{G}}$ as: $\hat{\mathbf{G}} = \mathbf{XY}$
3: Update: $\mathbf{U} \leftarrow [\mathbf{U}\ \mathbf{X}]$; $\mathbf{V} \leftarrow \begin{pmatrix}\mathbf{V}\\ \mathbf{Y}\end{pmatrix}$
4: **Update Core Matrix** (Update_Core())
5: Compute $\mathbf{L} = (\mathbf{I} - c\mathbf{YX} - c^2\mathbf{YU\Lambda VX})^{-1}$
6: Compute $\mathbf{P} = c\mathbf{\Lambda VX}$; and $\mathbf{Q} = c\mathbf{YU\Lambda}$
7: Update $\mathbf{\Lambda} \leftarrow \begin{pmatrix}\mathbf{\Lambda} + \mathbf{PLQ} & \mathbf{PL}\\ \mathbf{LQ} & \mathbf{L}\end{pmatrix}$
8: **Update Ranking Vector** (Update_Rank())
9: Update $\mathbf{r} = \mathrm{NB\_LIN\_OQ}(\mathbf{U}, \mathbf{V}, \mathbf{\Lambda}, c, \mathbf{e})$

5.2 Proofs and Analysis

The accuracy of the proposed Alg. 2 is summarized in Lemma 5.1.

LEMMA 5.1. **Effectiveness of Update-RWR.** *If* $\mathbf{G} = \mathbf{UV}$ *and* $\hat{\mathbf{G}} = \mathbf{XY}$, *Alg. 2 gives the correct ranking vector.*

PROOF. Let $\mathbf{A} = \mathbf{G} + \hat{\mathbf{G}}$, we have $\mathbf{A} = \hat{\mathbf{U}}\hat{\mathbf{V}}$, where $\hat{\mathbf{U}} = [\mathbf{U}\ \mathbf{X}]$; and $\mathbf{V} = \begin{pmatrix}\mathbf{V}\\ \mathbf{Y}\end{pmatrix}$.

Let $\hat{\mathbf{\Lambda}} = (\mathbf{I} - c\hat{\mathbf{V}}\hat{\mathbf{U}})^{-1}$. We have

$$\begin{aligned}\hat{\mathbf{\Lambda}} &= (\mathbf{I} - c\hat{\mathbf{V}}\hat{\mathbf{U}})^{-1}\\ &= \begin{pmatrix}\mathbf{I} - c\mathbf{VU} & -c\mathbf{VX}\\ -c\mathbf{YU} & \mathbf{I} - c\mathbf{YX}\end{pmatrix}^{-1}\end{aligned} \quad (3)$$

Applying the block matrix inverse lemma [3] to eq-(3), we can verify that the step 7 in Alg. 2 gives the exact $\hat{\mathbf{\Lambda}}$ matrix.

Then, for the updated ranking vector $\mathbf{r}$, we have

$$\begin{aligned}\mathbf{r} &= (1-c)(\mathbf{I} - c\mathbf{A})^{-1}\mathbf{e}\\ &= (1-c)(\mathbf{I} - c\hat{\mathbf{U}}\hat{\mathbf{V}})^{-1}\mathbf{e}\\ &= (1-c)(\mathbf{I} + c\hat{\mathbf{U}}\hat{\mathbf{\Lambda}}\hat{\mathbf{V}})\mathbf{e}\\ &= (1-c)(\mathbf{e} + c\hat{\mathbf{U}}\hat{\mathbf{\Lambda}}\hat{\mathbf{V}}\mathbf{e})\end{aligned} \quad (4)$$

Notice that the second to the last step is due to the Sherman-Morrison lemma [15]. This completes the proof. □

The efficiency of the proposed Alg. 2 is summarized in Lemma 5.2. It can be seen that it is much more efficient by (1) avoiding the re-computation of the low-rank approximation of the new normalized adjacency matrix, which takes $O(m)$ time; (2) avoiding directly updating the new core matrix, which takes $O(k+l)^3$.

LEMMA 5.2. **Efficiency of Update-RWR.** *Let* $\hat{m}$ *be the non-zero elements in* $\hat{\mathbf{G}}$, *the time complexity of Alg. 2 is* $O(\hat{m} + nkl)$, *where* k *and* l *are the rank of* $\mathbf{X}$ *and* $\mathbf{U}$, *respectively.*

PROOF. Step 2 takes $O(\hat{m})$ time to get the low-rank approximation of the matrix $\hat{\mathbf{G}}$. Step 3 takes $O(nk)$ time. Step 5 takes $O(nk^2 + nkl + k^3)$ time. Step 6 takes $O(nkl + l^2k)$ time. Step 7 takes $O(l^2k)$ time. Finally, step 9 takes $O(n(k+l) + (k+l)^2)$ time. Notice that $k \ll l \ll n$, therefore, the overall time complexity of Alg. 2 is $O(\hat{m} + nkl)$, which completes the proof. □

6. EXPERIMENTS AND RESULTS

The main motivation behind our experiments was to answer the following two questions: (1) **Symptom Expansion:** How useful are symptom graphs for the symptom expansion task? (2) **Dynamic Update:** How does the performance(efficiency/accuracy) of the proposed *Update-RWR* algorithm compare to the baseline *Power* method? The following subsections present a detailed description of our dataset, experiment design, evaluation metrics and the obtained results.

6.1 Dataset Description

Our dataset consists of 1 Million encounters of 13K patients. Among them, approximately 500K encounters (case subset) are cases (for 4.6K patients diagnosed with CHF), while the rest (control subset) are controls (8.4K patients without CHF). The case patients are defined by the operational criteria that include two or more mentions of CHF related diagnosis in outpatient visits and one or more mentions of CHF related diagnosis in the problem lists. Ten control patients are matched to each case patient on the age, gender and the clinic. Control patients do not have any CHF diagnosis by the diagnosis date of their corresponding case patient.

Each encounter is associated with a date, a patient ID and the type of visit. After processing the dataset with our UIMA pipeline, nearly 11.8K unique symptoms were extracted with an average of 12.7 positive symptoms and 5.7 negative symptoms per encounter.

6.2 Symptom Expansion Analysis

To evaluate the utility of a symptom graph for the symptom expansion task, we constructed six symptom graphs using the case subset (500K encounters) of the data. Four of them are constructed by using the four sections of the clinical notes (i.e., subjective, objective, assessment, and plan), respectively (all with location-sensitive weighting). The fifth was built by using text data in all the sections and location-sensitive weighting (LocSenseRWR). The sixth was also built by using all the sections, but with equal symptom weighing (EqRWR). That is, in the sixth graph, if two symptoms appeared together in a clinical note, their edge weight was increased by 1 instead of $1/d$, where d is the location offset in words. The first five allowed us to analyze the utility of different sections for the task. The last one allowed us to analyze the utility of location sensitive heuristic itself.

For evaluating each symptom graph, we started with the 15 Framingham symptoms as the initial vector and generated a ranked list of related symptoms using RWR. The accuracy of this ranked list was then evaluated in two ways - a) by comparing with expert judgements, b) by looking at the usefulness of the related symptoms for improving CHF prediction.

6.2.1 *Expert Judgment Evaluation*

Test Set Construction

The gold standard of related symptoms used for evaluating the ranked lists was generated via pooling [7], an approach used frequently in information retrieval evaluation. Each symptom graph provided a single ranked list of symptoms. These ranked lists along with an additional list obtained via a co-occurrence baseline which ranked related symptoms based on how frequently they co-occured with the Framingham symptoms in the clinical notes, were used for judgements. Top 50 symptoms from each ranked list, a total of 175 unique symptoms, were pooled together and judged by two medical experts. Finally, the 72 symptoms labeled as relevant by both experts were deemed as relevant and used for evaluation. The inter-annotation agreement was 81.8% (32 disagreements out of 175).

Evaluation Metrics

We used three standard information retrieval measures, i.e., Average Precision, Precision@10 and Recall@100, for quantitative evaluation, which are described below.

Average Precision intuitively captures the average of precision at every point when a new relevant symptom is retrieved. A higher AP implies that a greater number of relevant symptoms are being assigned higher ranks in the ranked list. Suppose for some ranking $r_i \in R$, there are k_i relevant symptoms. Further let $rank(j)$ be the rank of the jth relevant symptom and $P(rank(j))$ be the precision at the rank of the jth relevant symptom. Then

$$P(rank(j)) = \frac{\#\ Relevant\ Symptoms\ Till\ rank(j)}{\#\ Symptoms\ Till\ rank(j)} = \frac{j}{rank(j)}$$

Average precision of r_i is then given by: $AP(r_i) = \frac{\sum_{j=1}^{k_i} P(rank(j))}{k_i}$.

Precision@10 is defined as the percentage of relevant symptoms in the top 10 symptoms of the ranked list. $Recall@K$ is computed as the ratio of the number of relevant symptoms in the top K retrieved list to the total number of all relevant symptoms.

Comparison of SympGraph construction methods

Figure 4 shows the performance comparison of SympGraph with location sensitive heuristic (labeled LocSenseRWR) over two different baselines - symptom co-occurrence and SympGraph with equal weighing. All graphs were constructed over the case subset and symptom ranked lists were obtained by using the 15 framingham symptoms as the initial vector for RWR. The location sensitive method (LocSenseRWR) outperforms the baselines in all three metrics. With an average precision of 0.46, it improves over the two baselines by about 31%. In particular, seven out of top ten symptoms were found to be relevant and nearly 62% of known relevant symptoms were recovered in top 100. The results suggest that not

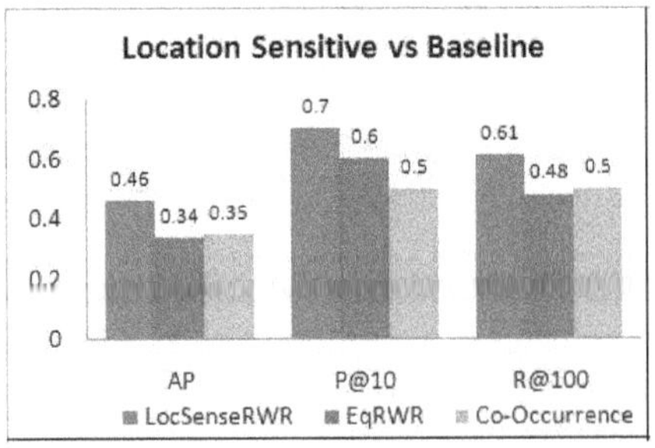

Figure 4: Comparison of location sensitive weighing with other baselines (31% improvement in AP over co-occurrence)

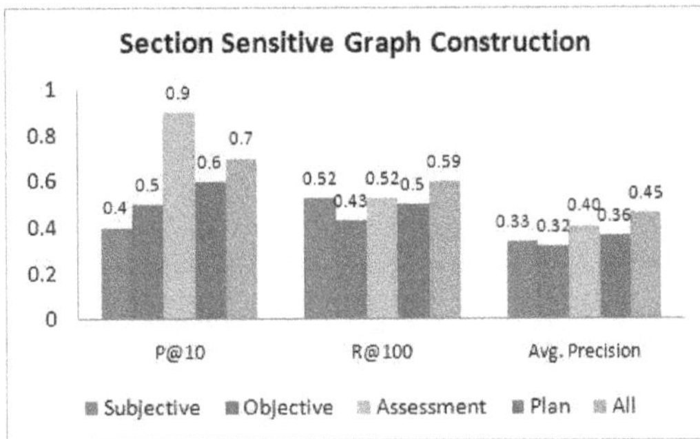

Figure 5: Location sensitive graphs over different sections

only are symptom graphs useful for the task, but the location sensitive heuristic indeed helps improve performance.

Figure 5 shows the performance comparison of SympGraphs constructed over different SOAP sections using the location sensitive heuristic. Performance varies significantly across sections.Graph based on Assessment section performed the best. This makes sense as the Assessment section primarily contains a concise summary of asserted symptoms and potential diagnoses. On the other hand, as one would expect, Subjective and Objective graphs did not do so well presumably since these sections are usually noisy with a lot of additional details. In practice, well formed section boundaries may not always be available. Therefore inspite of its slightly lower performance, we are still most interested in the graph built using the entire notes, and will continue to use it for subsequent experiments.

6.2.2 *CHF Prediction Evaluation*

In order to further evaluate the utility of related symptoms, we defined the CHF prediction task. The goal was to analyze a sequence of patient medical records and predict if a patient was likely to develop CHF in future, using only the list of related symptoms as features. For this task we used the entire dataset of 1M encounters.

For positive examples (i.e., case patients with CHF), we only used the data from clinical notes before a patient was diagnosed with CHF for constructing the feature vector. For negative examples (i.e., control patients without CHF), we used all available data. Each selected symptom became one feature, and its feature value was the number of occurrences of that symptom in the patient's records.

We compared the following methods for selecting features:

Framingham: Uses 15 Framingham symptoms + 35 randomly selected symptoms as features

Co-occurrence: Uses 15 Framingham symptoms + 35 additional symptoms that most commonly co-occurred with Framingham symptoms in the encounters.

	Fram.+Random	Fram+Co-Occ.	LocSenseRWR
AUC	0.590(14.24%)	0.649(3.85%)	**0.674**

Table 1: CHF prediction performance.Parenthesis show improvement achieved by LocSenseRWR over the method

Initial Fram. Symptoms	Top Related Symptoms
RCardiomegaly	Congestive Heart Failure
PNDyspnea	Chest Pain
DOExertion	Hypertensive Disease
Hepatomegaly	Coronary Arteriosclerosis
ICVPressure	Atherosclerosis
JVDistention	Obesity
Rales	Diabetes
PleuralEffusion	Hyperlipidemia
WeightLoss	Diabetes Mellitus (Non-insulin-Dependent)
APEdema	Benign hypertension (disorder)
AnkleEdema	Dyspnea
Tachycardia	
S3Gallop	
HJReflux	
NightCough	

Figure 6: Symptom expansion results

LocSenseRWR: Uses the top 50 ranked symptoms obtained from a symptom graph constructed with location sensitive heuristic.

Using the selected features, the model was trained on 90% patients and tested on the rest with 10 fold cross validation. Evaluation metric used was Area Under the ROC-Curve (AUC). The classification model was an SVM classifier with Gaussian kernel:

$$\mathbf{K}_{ij} = e^{-\frac{\|\mathbf{x}_i - \mathbf{x}_j\|^2}{2(a\bar{r}^2)}}, \tag{5}$$

where $\mathbf{x}_i$ and $\mathbf{x}_j$ are data samples and $\bar{r}$ is the average of pairwise distances among all the data samples. a is chosen from $[2^{-3}, 2^{-2}, 2^{-1}, 1, 2^1, 2^2, 2^3]$. The SVM trade off parameter C is chosen from $[0.01, 0.1, 1, 10, 100]$. We report the best results among all the combinations of a and C.

The results from CHF prediction task are shown in Table 1, which corroborate our observations from human judgement evaluation. The location sensitive graph (LocSenseRWR) outperforms the baselines, suggesting that the expanded symptoms are useful for the task. Figure 6 shows some of these top expanded symptoms. In particular, coronary arteriosclerosis, hypertension, diabetes etc. are all very related co-morbidity and risk factors to HF and have been confirmed by clinical experts.

6.3 Dynamic Update Analysis

In order to evaluate the efficiency of the proposed *Update-RWR* method we defined two real world update tasks: (1) **Symptom Extractor Update**: This task assumes that we have just updated our UIMA pipeline to extract a new symptoms from clinical notes. As a result the existing graph must be updated with a new symptom node and all its edges. (2) **Patient Update**: This task assumes that data for a new patient (a small patient subgraph) has joined and needs to be incorporated into an existing symptom graph.

Both tasks require incorporating a smaller subgraph (representing new information) into an existing symptom graph. We want to evaluate efficiency and effectiveness of Update-RWR algorithm compared to recomputation using the power method.

All dynamic update experiments were carried out on a 32-bit Windows Vista machine with 3Gb RAM and intel core-2 Duo 2.5 GHz processor. The initial symptom graph $\mathbf{G}$ consisted of $11.8K$ symptom nodes and 1.4 million edges. For both patient update and symptom update tasks, individual patient subgraphs usually contained less than 1000 edges, while for symptom update task, the symptom subgraphs contained up to 2500 edges.

6.3.1 Experimental Design

Accuracy Analysis: For accuracy evaluation, the top N ranked symptoms generated by the Update-RWR and the baseline methods (Power method) are compared by using the baseline symptoms as the gold standard. Evaluation metrics used are: Average Precision (AP), Precision at 50 ($P@50$), and Recall at N.

Intuitively precision at 50 tells us how many of the top-50 symptoms generated by Update-RWR, were found in the gold standard. Recall at N gives the percentage of gold standard symptoms that were recovered by Update-RWR. Finally AP takes a high value if both precision and recall are high.

Efficiency Analysis: Recall that both methods start with an initial normalized matrix $\mathbf{G}$ as their starting point. For the baseline, adding a new subgraph requires the modified graph matrix to be renormalized. For Update-RWR we need to calculate the $\mathbf{U}$,$\mathbf{V}$,and $\mathbf{\Lambda}$ once on the initial normalized matrix and update them whenever a new subgraph is added (refer to algorithms 1 and 2). As a result the speedup is evaluated by looking at three different times:

Initial one time matrix construction: In case of Update-RWR, this is the time for constructing the matrices $\mathbf{U}$,$\mathbf{V}$ and $\mathbf{\Lambda}$ on the large initial matrix as in algorithm 1. For the baseline this time is 0. This will happen only once.

Matrix update time: For the baseline, this is the time required to add the new subgraph matrix into the original symptom graph matrix and re-normalize the resulting graph. This is the time for computing the updated $\hat{\mathbf{U}}$, $\hat{\mathbf{V}}$ and $\hat{\mathbf{\Lambda}}$ as in algorithm 2. This will happen every time a new subgraph is added.

Online Query time: This is the time to perform random walk restart. In case of baseline, it is the time taken for applying the power method. For Update-RWR it is the time for performing the step $NB\_LIN\_OQ()$ in algorithm 1.

6.3.2 Results

Figure 7 presents the results for Symptom Update task for the symptom 'PNDyspnea'. Results for other symptoms were similar. The task was simulated by constructing a symptom graph without one of the Framingham symptom nodes and later updating it with all of missing symptom's edges. RWR was then run on the updated matrix using the new symptom as the initial vector. The accuracy was compared for top $N = 200$ symptoms (results for other values of N were similar). The low rank approximation parameter l for the initial normalized matrix $\mathbf{G}$ serves to control the trade-off between efficiency and accuracy of the method. The low rank approximation parameter k for the update matrix $\hat{\mathbf{G}}$ did not affect the results as much and was empirically set to 2. The low rank approximations were obtained using the signular value decomposition (SVD [3]) method. Increasing l results in improved average precision and recall@200, which both tend to 1 as l goes beyond 400. On the other hand even for small values eg. $l = 50$ the performance is still reasonably good. In particular, we observed a $P@50$ of 1 for all data points in Figure 7. This implies at all of the top 50 ranked symptoms by Update-RWR were found in the top 200 baseline symptoms. In addition, 89% symptoms were common in the two lists. Finally AP of 0.88 implies that most of the symptoms ranked high by Update-RWR were common to both lists.

In terms of efficiency, we observe that the speedup reduces as l increases. This is because a higher l implies a matrix multiplication between dense higher dimensional matrices. Assuming l as 50 we observe that while the difference in matrix update times is not that much, Update-RWR outperforms the baseline significantly in online query performance. We do not compare the performance of Update-RWR with the original NB_Lin in algorithm 1 as it

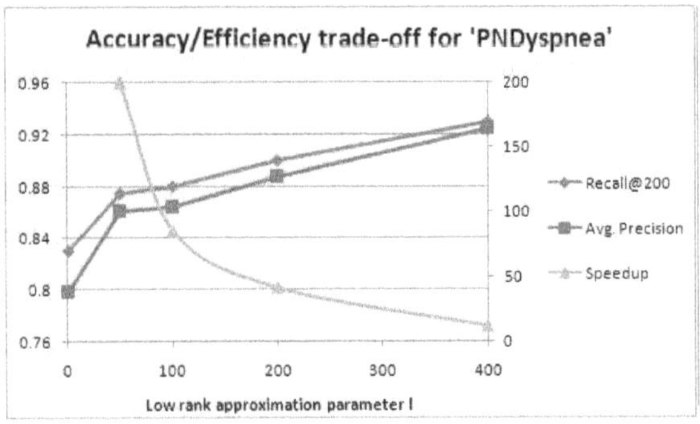

Figure 7: Symptom update results (speed up values are for online query performance)

Method	Initial Matrix Construction Time	Avg. Matrix Update Time	Avg. Online RWR Query Time
Update-RWR	5.28	3.067(+/-.046)	0.017(+/-.005)
Baseline(Power)	-	6.705(+/-.094)	1.336(+/-.028)
Times Speedup	-	2.186	78.59

Table 2: Time comparisons for patient update task. All values in secs. Averages are over 50 patient additions. Parenthesis provide standard deviations.

would require us to reconstruct the three $\mathbf{U},\mathbf{V},\mathbf{\Lambda}$ matrices on every update, and as a result the method would perform far worse than the other two, making the comparison not interesting.

Table 2 presents the different time metrics for Update-RWR and Power method for adding a new patient subgraph and running RWR. The time values are averaged over 50 different patient additions. The value of low rank approximation parameters l and k were fixed at 50 and 2, respectively. As expected, our proposed method is over 78 times faster than the baseline. This improves efficiency dramatically when multiple RWR queries need to be performed. Figure 8 illustrates this point.

Finally, Figure 9 compares the accuracy. Here we update $\mathbf{G}$ by repeatedly adding new patients using Update-RWR i.e. for adding x patients, Update-RWR gets applied x times consecutively. The accuracy of the updated matrix after say x patient additions, is evaluated by comparing against the ideal normalized matrix for those additions, i.e. the one we get after adding all x patient subgraphs to $\mathbf{G}$ and renormalizing. We observe that the accuracy continues to remain high inspite of over 400 consecutive new patient additions.

7. RELATED WORK

Information extraction from clinical records and medical text in general has been studied in the existing work (see, e.g., [4, 12, 23, 18, 16]). In most cases, standard information extraction techniques have been applied or adapted to the medical domain for recognizing various entities such as diseases [22] and treatments [2]. We however, go beyond symptom extraction to further construct symptom graphs and study how to leverage such graphs to convert raw symptom mentions into more useful knowledge.

Graph representations are frequently used to facilitate data mining. In most cases, a graph is naturally constructed based on observed data where the edges are directly available in an application. For example, Web graphs are often constructed with web pages as nodes and hyperlinks as edges [13, 8]. Also, information network

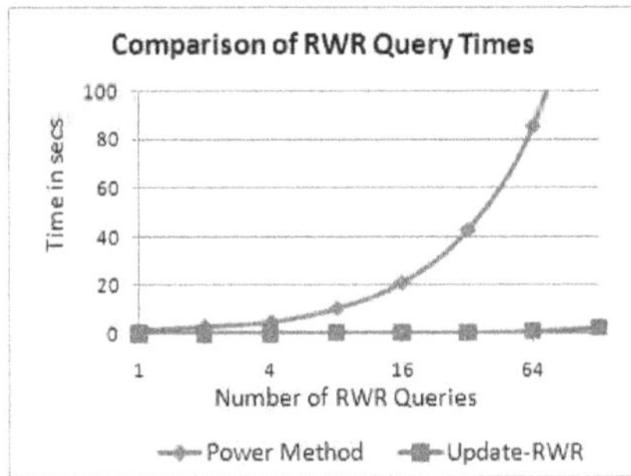

Figure 8: Online RWR query execution times. The scale on x-axis is logarithmic.

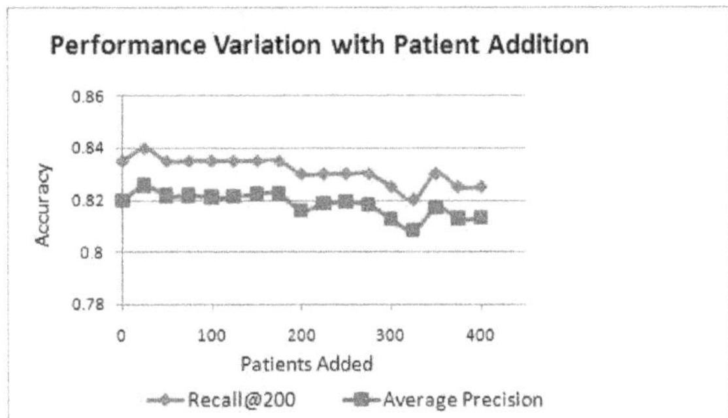

Figure 9: AP and Recall@200 for patient update task

mining has recently been studied (see e.g., [19]), especially bibliographical network and social networks. A main difference between the proposed SympGraph and these graphs lies in that both the nodes and edges in a SympGraph are *extracted* computationally from text data. An immediate consequence of this difference is that we need to address the issue of uncertainty in the edges of a SympGraph, which raises new challenges in designing graph mining algorithms.

Random Walk with Restart (RWR) [20] and related ideas have been applied to many problems such as Personalized PageRank [5] for Web search and image tagging [1]. Thanks to our graph viewpoint for the extracted symptoms, we are able to leverage this powerful tool to discover related patient symptoms. In terms of computation, most of the existing fast algorithms apply to the static graphs. In [21], the authors proposed an efficient on-line algorithm for *skewed bipartite* graphs, which does not apply to the symptom graph. Other remotely related works include dynamic PageRank [14, 17], Fast SimRank [10, 9], etc. Our work can be regarded as adding to this line of work a new application of RWR for finding related symptoms in graphs of patient symptoms.

Prediction of patient diseases based on patient records has been studied mostly by using the structured fields in the patient records (see e.g., [6]). Our work aims at tapping into the unstructured text data in clinical notes to extract symptom information, which can be used as extra features for prediction in a statistical prediction model, thus can be regarded as complementary with the study of prediction methods. Our experiment results show that the symptom features generated using the proposed SympGraph can be leveraged to improve the accuracy of prediction of CHF disease.

8. CONCLUSIONS

In this paper, we present SympGraph, a general mining framework for extracting and analyzing symptoms in longitudinal clinical notes. SympGraph constructs symptom graphs based on colocation relations among detected symptom mentions. Within the general formulation of symptom graphs, we present the important clinical mining application of symptom expansion. We also present an efficient dynamic update method to incorporate updates to the underlying symptom graphs.

Our evaluation on a large-scale real world clinical database with 1 million clinical notes of over 13K patients revealed an improvement of over 31% for the symptom expansion task and that the expanded symptoms were indeed useful for predicting the onset of Congestive Heart Failure. In terms of the scalability we show that the proposed dynamic symptom expansion approach is significantly faster than the baseline Power method when multiple online queries are involved.

It is worth noting that although we mainly explored the use of the proposed SympGraph for symptom expansion at the population level. SympGraph can easily support many other mining applications, particularly due to the possibility of constructing SympGraph in multiple resolutions. Indeed, we can construct SympGraphs corresponding to any meaningful ways of aggregating patient records (e.g., at the level of individual patients, patient groups, or aggregation over different time periods or geographic locations). Moreover, in addition to symptom expansion, SympGraph can also naturally support many other tasks such as patient stratification and clustering, comparative analysis of patient groups or mine temporal symptom patterns. Given the importance and promise of applying text mining to the health domain, we believe that the proposed SympGraph can serve as a general representation framework for developing sophisticated text mining systems in health domain.

9. ACKNOWLEDGEMENTS

This paper is based upon work supported in part by an IBM faculty award. Research was also partly sponsored by the Army Research Laboratory and was accomplished under Cooperative Agreement Number W911NF-09-2-0053.

10. REFERENCES

[1] T. Bailloeul, C. Zhu, and Y. Xu. Automatic image tagging as a random walk with priors on the canonical correlation subspace. In *MIR '08*, pages 75–82, New York, NY, USA, 2008. ACM.

[2] S. Doan and H. Xu. Recognizing medication related entities in hospital discharge summaries using support vector machine. In *COLING (Posters)*, pages 259–266, 2010.

[3] G.H. Golub and C.F.V. Loan. *Matrix Computation*. Johns Hopkins, 1996.

[4] H. Harkema, I. Roberts, R. Gaizauskas, and M. Hepple. Information extraction from clinical records. In *Proceedings of the 4th UK e-Science All Hands Meeting*, 2005. Nottingham, UK.

[5] T.H. Haveliwala. Topic-sensitive pagerank. In *WWW*, pages 517–526, 2002.

[6] B.E. Himes, Y. Dai, I.S. Kohane, S.T. Weiss, and M.F. Ramoni. Prediction of chronic obstructive pulmonary disease (copd) in asthma patients using electronic medical records. *JAMIA*, 16(3):371–379, 2009.

[7] K. Jones and C.J.V. Rijsbergen. Report on the need for and provision of an "ideal" information retrieval test collection. Technical Report British Library Research and Development Report 5266, Computer Laboratory, University of Cambridge, 1975.

[8] J.M. Kleinberg. Authoritative sources in a hyperlinked environment. *Journal of the ACM*, 46(5):604–632, 1999.

[9] C. Li, J. Han, G. He, X. Jin, Y. Sun, Y. Yu, and T. Wu. Fast computation of simrank for static and dynamic information networks. In *EDBT*, pages 465–476, 2010.

[10] D. Lizorkin, P. Velikhov, M.N. Grinev, and D. Turdakov. Accuracy estimate and optimization techniques for simrank computation. *PVLDB*, 1(1):422–433, 2008.

[11] P.A. McKee, W.P. Castelli, P.M. McNamara, and W.B. Kannel. The natural history of congestive heart failure: The framingham study. *N Engl J Med.*, 285:1441–1446, 1971.

[12] S. Meystre, G. Savova, K.K. Schuler, and J. Hurdle. Extracting information from textual documents in the electronic health record: A review of recent research. *IMIA Yearbook of Medical Informatics Methods Inf Med 2008*, 2008. 47 Suppl 1:128–44.

[13] L. Page, S. Brin, R. Motwani, and T. Winograd. The pagerank citation ranking: Bringing order to the web. Technical report, Stanford Digital Library Technologies Project, 1998.

[14] A. Pathak, S. Chakrabarti, and M.S. Gupta. Index design for dynamic personalized pagerank. In *ICDE*, pages 1489–1491, 2008.

[15] W.W. Piegorsch and G.E. Casella. Inverting a sum of matrices. In *SIAM Review*, volume 32, pages 470–470, 1990.

[16] A.R. Post and J.H. Harrison Jr. Protempa: A method for specifying and identifying temporal sequences in retrospective data for patient selection. *JAMIA*, 14(5):674–683, 2007.

[17] A.D. Sarma, S. Gollapudi, and R. Panigrahy. Estimating pagerank on graph streams. *J. ACM*, 58(3):13, 2011.

[18] G.K. Savova, J.J. Masanz, P.V. Ogren, J. Zheng, S. Sohn, K.K. Schuler, and C.G. Chute. Mayo clinical text analysis and knowledge extraction system (ctakes): architecture, component evaluation and applications. *JAMIA*, 17(5):507–513, 2010.

[19] Y. Sun, Y. Yu, and J. Han. Ranking-based clustering of heterogeneous information networks with star network schema. In John F. Elder IV, Françoise Fogelman-Soulié, Peter A. Flach, and Mohammed Javeed Zaki, editors, *KDD*, pages 797–806. ACM, 2009.

[20] H. Tong, C. Faloutsos, and J.Y. Pan. Random walk with restart: fast solutions and applications. *Knowl. Inf. Syst.*, 14:327–346, March 2008.

[21] H. Tong, S. Papadimitriou, P.S. Yu, and C. Faloutsos. Proximity tracking on time-evolving bipartite graphs. In *SDM*, pages 704–715, 2008.

[22] Y. Wang. Annotating and recognising named entities in clinical notes. In *ACL/AFNLP (Student Research Workshop)*, pages 18–26. The Association for Computer Linguistics, 2009.

[23] H.Xu, S.P. Stenner, S. Doan, K.B. Johnson, L.R. Waitman, and J.C. Denny. Medex: a medication information extraction system for clinical narratives. *Journal of American Medical Informatics Association*, 17(1):19–24, Jan-Feb 2010.

Industry Practice Expo Invited Talk

Experiences and Lessons in Developing Industry-Strength Machine Learning and Data Mining Software

Chih-Jen Lin
National Taiwan University and eBay Research Labs
cjlin@csie.ntu.edu.tw

Abstract

Traditionally academic machine learning and data mining researchers focus on proposing new algorithms. The task of implementing these methods is often left to companies that are developing software packages. However, the gap between the two sides has caused some problems. First, the practical deployment of new algorithms still involves some challenging issues that need to be studied by researchers. Second, without further investigation after publishing their papers, researchers have neither the opportunity to work with real problems nor see how their methods are used. We discuss the experiences in developing two machine learning packages LIBSVM and LIBLINEAR, that are widely used in both academia and industry. We demonstrate that the interaction with users leads us to identify some important research problems. For example, the decision to study and then support multi-class SVM was essential in the early stage of developing LIBSVM. The birth of LIBLINEAR was driven by the need to classify large-scale documents in Internet companies. For fast training of large-scale problems, we had to create new algorithms other than those used in LIBSVM for kernel SVM. We present some practical use of LIBLINEAR for Internet applications. Finally, we give lessons learned and future perspectives for developing industry-strength machine learning and data mining software.

Categories & Subject Descriptors: H.2.8 [Database Management]: Data Mining.

Author Keywords: Machine Learning, Document Classification, Software Development, Support Vector Machines.

Bio

Chih-Jen Lin is currently a distinguished professor at the Department of Computer Science, National Taiwan University and a visiting principal research scientist at eBay Research Labs. He obtained his B.S. degree from National Taiwan University in 1993 and Ph.D. degree from University of Michigan in 1998. His major research areas include machine learning, data mining, and numerical optimization. Dr. Lin is best known for his work on support vector machines (SVM) for data classification. His software LIBSVM is one of the most widely used and cited SVM packages. Several major companies use this software for classification and regression applications. More recently, his team developed the software LIBLINEAR for large-scale document classification. This package has quickly gained attention as Internet companies routinely use it for their applications. Dr. Lin has received many awards for his research work. A recent one is the ACM KDD 2010 best paper award. He is an IEEE fellow and an ACM distinguished scientist for his contribution to machine learning algorithms and software design. More information about him can be found at http://www.csie.ntu.edu.tw/~cjlin.

KDD'12, August 12–16, 2012, Beijing, China.
ACM 978-1-4503-1462-6/12/08.

Joint Optimization of Bid and Budget Allocation in Sponsored Search*

Weinan Zhang
Shanghai Jiao Tong University
Shanghai, 200240, P. R. China
wnzhang@apex.sjtu.edu.cn

Ying Zhang
Nankai University
Tianjin, 300071, P. R. China
zhangying@dbis.nankai.edu.cn

Bin Gao
Microsoft Research Asia
Beijing, 100080, P. R. China
bingao@microsoft.com

Yong Yu
Shanghai Jiao Tong University
Shanghai, 200240, P. R. China
yyu@apex.sjtu.edu.cn

Xiaojie Yuan
Nankai University
Tianjin, 300071, P. R. China
yuanxj@nankai.edu.cn

Tie-Yan Liu
Microsoft Research Asia
Beijing, 100080, P. R. China
tyliu@microsoft.com

ABSTRACT

This paper is concerned with the joint allocation of bid price and campaign budget in sponsored search. In this application, an advertiser can create a number of campaigns and set a budget for each of them. In a campaign, he/she can further create several ad groups with bid keywords and bid prices. Data analysis shows that many advertisers are dealing with a very large number of campaigns, bid keywords, and bid prices at the same time, which poses a great challenge to the optimality of their campaign management. As a result, the budgets of some campaigns might be too low to achieve the desired performance goals while those of some other campaigns might be wasted; the bid prices for some keywords may be too low to win competitive auctions while those of some other keywords may be unnecessarily high. In this paper, we propose a novel algorithm to automatically address this issue. In particular, we model the problem as a constrained optimization problem, which maximizes the expected advertiser revenue subject to the constraints of the total budget of the advertiser and the ranges of bid price change. By solving this optimization problem, we can obtain an optimal budget allocation plan as well as an optimal bid price setting. Our simulation results based on the sponsored search log of a commercial search engine have shown that by employing the proposed method, we can effectively improve the performances of the advertisers while at the same time we also see an increase in the revenue of the search engine. In addition, the results indicate that this method is robust to the second-order effects caused by the bid fluctuations from other advertisers.

*This work was performed when the first and the second authors were interns at Microsoft Research Asia.

KDD'12, August 12–16, 2012, Beijing, China.

Categories and Subject Descriptors

H.3.5 [**Information Systems**]: Information Storage and Retrieval - Online Information Services; J.0 [**Computer Applications**]: General

General Terms

Algorithms, Experimentation

Keywords

Budget allocation, Bid optimization, Sponsored search

1. INTRODUCTION

Sponsored search is a popular format of online advertising and is also the main revenue source for search engine companies. In sponsored search, a list of ads is displayed along with the organic search results in response to a given query. Sponsored search results are produced by a different mechanism from that of organic search, though they are displayed simultaneously and have similar appearance. Generally, the organic search results are mainly generated based on the relevance of each web page to the query, while the sponsored search results are generated based on an auction process [20, 2, 13].

An advertiser can create a number of campaigns under an account. In each campaign, he/she sets a campaign budget, builds several groups of ad copies (creatives), and bids on some keywords with their match types[1] for each ad group. Each keyword is an auction entry that is supposed to be triggered by some user queries. When a user submits a query, the search engine will first retrieve the most relevant ads as candidates according to a matching function between the bid keywords and the query. Then these candidate ads will participate in an auction, and some ads (e.g., with the largest expected revenue for the search engine) will win and be displayed on the search result page [13]. If an ad is clicked by the user, the corresponding advertiser will be charged by the search engine. Usually, the charged amount is determined by the generalized second price (GSP) [11] auction mechanism, which means that the advertiser's cost of a click depends on the bid price of the next ad in the ranking list of the auction. When a campaign runs out of budget, it will not be

[1]The match type might be exact match or broad match.

permitted to participate in any auctions until the budget is increased or the next budget period starts. For example, if the campaign budget is set at a monthly basis, the campaign will be re-involved in the auctions next month.

As can be seen above, besides creating ad groups and selecting bid keywords, an advertiser should also carefully consider two important problems as follows:

a) Bid Price Setting. Different keywords correspond to different opportunities (e.g., search volumes) and different degrees of competition. In many cases, the bids for some keywords are too low to win the auctions while the bids for some other keywords are unnecessarily high. Usually, the optimal bid price setting is very difficult for an individual advertiser to reach since he/she does not have the access to the related information (e.g., the bids of other advertisers) and his/her competitors are also adjusting their bid prices dynamically.

b) Campaign Budget Allocation. Similar to the case of keywords, different campaigns also have different opportunities and competition. As a result, under an account, some campaigns may run out of budget very quickly, some campaigns consume their budgets quite slowly, and the budgets for other campaigns may never be used at all. This will constrain the overall effectiveness for the advertiser to utilize his/her budget.

Both of the above issues are critical for advertisers, however, most advertisers have not been doing well in them according to our statistics (see Section 3). This is because many advertisers are managing hundreds of campaigns and tens of thousands of keywords, which makes it very difficult for them to manually tune the campaign budget allocation and keyword bid prices. There are some third-party tools to help the advertisers tune their bids; some advertisers even build tools themselves to manage the bids automatically. However, the market information they can get is still very limited, which restricts the effectiveness of the tools. In the research community, there have also been some attempts on preforming the task automatically (see Section 2). However, these works are still not sufficient to satisfy the practical requirements. For example, many works on keyword bid price optimization only consider the bid price when ranking the ads, but do not take relevance and position bias into consideration. For another example, although people have investigated keyword bid optimization, to the best of our knowledge, there is no work on campaign budget allocation yet in the literature.

In this paper, we propose a novel method to address the aforementioned issues. In particular, we propose jointly optimizing the campaign budget allocation and bid price setting. That is, for a given advertiser account with multiple campaigns and an account-level budget, we try to find the optimal allocation of the account-level budget into each campaign, and to set the optimal price[2,3] for each bid keyword in the campaign simultaneously. Here we focus on the joint optimization instead of optimizing campaign budget allocation and keyword bid setting separately due to the following reason. Suppose for some campaign, there are many high-utility keywords (in other words, these keywords contain a lot of opportunities of advertising). In order to achieve significant performance regarding these keywords, one has to put a lot of money on them. However, if we cannot increase the budget for this campaign, we will miss a lot of these opportunities.

We formulate the problem as a constrained optimization, which takes the campaign budgets and the keyword bid prices as variables and finds their optimal values by maximizing the advertiser revenue, with the constraint of the account-level budget. To efficiently solve the optimization problem, we employ the sequential quadratic programming method. Simulation results on the sponsored search log from a commercial search engine show that the proposed technology can effectively help advertisers improve their campaign performance under several metrics like click number, cost per click, and advertiser revenue. At the same time, we can also help the search engine obtain increased revenue. In addition, the proposed method is robust to the second-order effects caused by the advertisers' dynamical bid changes.

To sum up, the contributions of our work are listed as below. (i) We performed a comprehensive data study on the effectiveness of current campaign budget allocation and keyword bid price setting in sponsored search, and pointed out the importance and necessity of jointly optimizing them. (ii) We proposed a novel method for jointly optimizing bid and budget allocation. As far as we know, this is the first work on campaign budget allocation in the literature of sponsored search, and it is also the first work on consider keyword price setting and campaign budget allocation simultaneously.

2. RELATED WORK

As mentioned in the introduction, we focus on the joint optimization of campaign budget allocation and keyword bid price setting in this paper. That is, given an advertiser account with multiple campaigns and an account-level budget, we determine the optimal allocation of the account-level budget into each campaign, and set the optimal bid price for each bid keyword in the campaign. As far as we know, there is no work in the literature solving exactly the same problem. Instead, there is only some related work on keyword bid price optimization. We will briefly review such work in Section 2.1. Besides, there is some other work on budget allocation across different keywords [3], different search engines [8], or different online adverting markets [21], whose problem definitions are totally different with what we concern about in this paper.

2.1 Keyword Bid Price Setting

Chakrabarty *et al* [7] defined the weight and profit of each bid keyword, and proposed a knapsack based algorithm to find the optimal price setting that can maximize the advertiser revenue in sponsored search. The algorithm considered both single-slot and multi-slot auctions. Kitts *et al* [16] proposed a revenue optimization model based on the marketing factors that were related to ad slot positions, in order to solve the problem of keyword bid price setting. In [12, 17], a *budget optimization* problem was defined, in which the target is to find an optimal bid price setting to maximize the campaign performance under a given campaign budget.

[2]Note that not all clicks are created equal. An advertiser will give different bids for different keywords, for they have different value per click (VPC). In this work, we estimate the VPC of a keyword based on the idea proposed in [4, 20] and use the VPC as the upper bound of the bid price.

[3]Usually an advertiser observes the ad campaign performance and takes reactions to change the bid so as to approach the campaign goal. In this work, we find the optimal bid by maximizing the campaign goal directly, so the optimal bid is not a randomized value.

In particular, Feldman *et al* [12] defined the cost and click functions considering the position of an ad and the average click-through rate (CTR) on the position, and then developed a landscape algorithm to solve the optimization problem in approximation. Muthukrishnan *et al* [17] extended the above algorithm using a stochastic model, in which each keyword has a click distribution instead of an exactly known click number, in the context of single-slot auction.

In addition, the following works also discuss the problem of keyword bid price optimization, but in different scenarios from the above ones. Dar *et al* [10] studied how to improve the performance of broad match of bid keywords for a given query. They defined the weight and utility function of each bid keyword, and proposed a flow graph based algorithm to work out the optimal setting for keyword bid prices. Broder *et al* [6] pointed out that different matched queries for a bid keyword in broad match had different utilities according to their relevance to the bid keyword, and thus they should have different bid prices. They proposed a statistical approach to generate the corresponding bid prices. Borgs *et al* [5] studied the problem of keyword bid price setting given the budget on each keyword, and proposed an method to optimize the advertiser revenue across all keywords. More parts of the work are discussing the perturbation and convergence in their model.

3. DATA ANALYSIS ON SPONSORED SEARCH

In this section, we report our data analysis on sponsored search. We have used two kinds of data obtained from a mainstream search engine in our study: the auction log that records the detailed auction processes and the advertiser database that includes the bid keywords, bid prices, and the budget for each campaign. The data was collected in half a month, which contains over ten billion auctions and more than one hundred thousand advertiser accounts.

3.1 Campaign Budget

There can be several campaigns under the same advertiser account. In general, each campaign contains a set of ads (or ad groups) with the same campaign goal. Each campaign is assigned a budget, indicating the expected expense in a period of time (e.g., one month). In practice, due to the differences in the advertising settings and the market dynamics, it is quite common that some of the campaigns run out of budget while the other campaigns under the same account do not. We call this kind of accounts *partially-running-out-of-budget accounts* (or *p-accounts* for short). Here we give some statistics about the p-accounts in Table 1.

Table 1: Statistic of partially-running-out-budget accounts.

Number proportion	2.6%
Revenue proportion	31.6%
Potential revenue proportion	164.5%
Average campaign budget use ratio	45.1%
Total budget use ratio	11.5%
Average campaign number	15
Max campaign number	2,423
Average keyword number	10,735
Max keyword number	1,818,285

From Table 1 we have the following observations. (i) Although the number of the p-accounts is relatively small (2.6%), their contribution to the search engine revenue is considerably large (31.6%). It is clear that the individual contribution of each p-account is much larger than that of other accounts. (ii) The potential revenue of the p-accounts[4] is as much as 164.5% of the total revenue of sponsored search. This shows that improving p-accounts can result in a significant impact on the entire advertising system. (iii) The average campaign-level budget use ratio of the p-accounts is about 45.1%, and the total budget use ratio of the p-accounts is 11.5%. The potential of further increasing the budget use ratio for the p-accounts is higher than for the other accounts. This is because the p-accounts have at least one campaign (but not all campaigns) running out of budget, thus we can further improve their budget use ratio by simply reallocating the residual budget to that campaign(s). However, for other accounts this strategy will not help. (iv) For a p-account, the average campaign number is 15 and the maximum campaign number is 2,423. These large numbers suggest that it is difficult to manually adjust the campaign budget.

3.2 Bid Price

Bid price setting is also a non-trivial task. For a p-account, the average number of bid keywords is 10,735 and the maximum is 1,818,285. It is clearly infeasible to manually set keyword bid prices for the p-accounts. Instead, automatic keyword bid price setting is desired. The tools from the third-party usually cannot have adequate market information to aid the bid tuning. For example, we may need to consider the following information. (i) First, according to the commonly-used auction mechanisms in commercial search engines, higher bid prices will increase the probability of winning more auctions and obtaining higher ranking positions. Figure 1 shows the percentage of ads that will get at least one position up if we increase their corresponding keyword bid prices to a certain degree. In particular, 57.36% ads will get position up if their keyword bid prices are increased by 10%, and 78.84% ads will get position up if their keyword bid prices are increased by 40%. (ii) Second, higher ranking positions usually mean more attention and clicks [15], according to Figure 2, which shows the relative CTR[5] of the top ad slots in the commercial search engine. As a result, if an advertiser increases the bid price, the ad will have more opportunities to be clicked and the campaign goal of the advertiser will be better realized.

However, given the constraint of campaign budget, usually we cannot increase the bid prices for all the keywords. Instead, we have to balance between different keywords. Note that the utility of keywords are different from each other, and the return of lifting prices on some low-utility keywords might be very small. Therefore, we should consider the keyword utility when adjusting the keyword bid prices. For those keywords with low utility, the best choice may be to decrease their bid prices and instead put more money on the high utility keywords.

3.3 Joint Optimization

The data statistics reported in the previous section show that both campaign budget allocation and bid price setting are important to advertisers, but they are non-trivial to op-

[4]The potential revenue is calculated by summing up all the unused budgets of the p-accounts.

[5]The relative CTR is normalized by dividing the CTR on each position by the CTR on the first position.

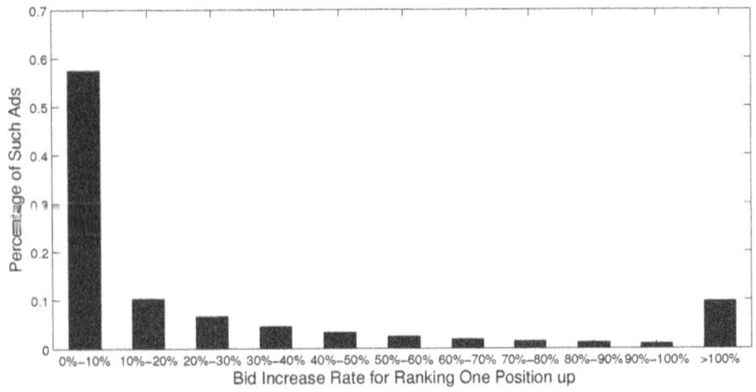

Figure 1: The proportion of ad volume ranking one position up with the increased bid price.

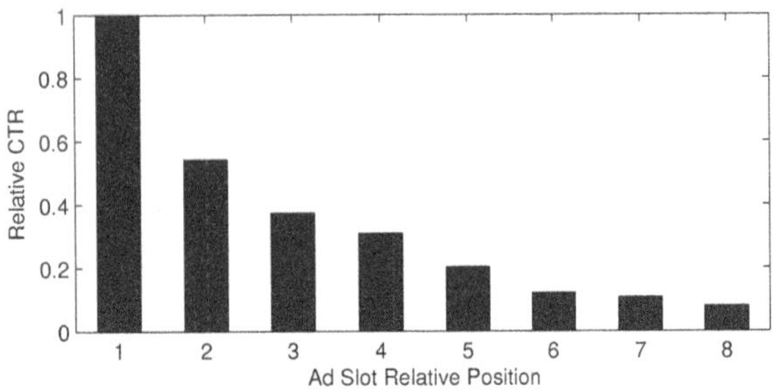

Figure 2: The relative CTR of each ad slot.

timize. If we want to jointly optimize them, the task may become even more difficult. However, we would like to point out that it is necessary to perform the joint optimization.

On one hand, if we only perform bid price optimization, each campaign will be optimized independently. For campaigns that have run out of budget, the help from bid price optimization will be limited because the potential capacity of these campaigns is constrained. For campaigns that have a lot of unused budget, bid price optimization can help achieve better performance, but it is hard to take full use of the budget due to the constraint of the value per click (VPC) of the bid keywords. On the other hand, if we only perform budget optimization, the unused budget will be reallocated to the campaigns that have already or tend to run out of budget, and thus their performance will be improved. However, the campaigns (no matter they run out of budget or not) will lose the opportunity to further improve their performance since their current bid price settings might not be optimal. Therefore, we had better consider both bid price optimization and campaign budget allocation simultaneously. In this way, the unused budget can be moved to the appropriate campaigns and can be effectively used on the best keyword candidates.

Note that in terms of optimizing the performances of advertisers, other efforts such as ad copy improvement, bid keyword selection, behavior and demography targeting, and landing page optimization are also important and effective. However, we will not discuss them as they are not in the scope of this paper.

4. JOINT OPTIMIZATION OF BID AND BUDGET ALLOCATION

In this section, we introduce the proposed method for joint optimization of bid price setting and campaign budget allocation. The key idea is to maximize the account-level advertiser revenue subject to the constraints of account-level budget. To better illustrate this idea, we first give some necessary notations including the definition of winning price interval, which serves as a basis of the following discussions. Then we adopt a probabilistic model to approximate the probability of winning a certain ad position given a bid price. After that, we define an optimization problem based on the probability model, and convert the problem to be a sequential quadratic programming problem. By solving the problem, we can get the optimal solution to campaign budget allocation and bid price setting.

4.1 Notations and Definitions

In the joint optimization of bid price setting and campaign budget allocation the input is an advertiser account $A = \{C_1, C_2, \ldots, C_m\}$, where m is the number of campaigns under account A and $C_i (i = 1, 2, \ldots, m)$ is the i-th campaign. For simplicity, we will not distinguish ad group and ad in the following discussions.[6] Accordingly, we can denote campaign C_i as $C_i = \{g_i^{(0)}, D_i, K_i\}$ $(i = 1, \ldots, m)$, where $g_i^{(0)}$ denotes the original periodical (e.g., monthly) budget set by the advertiser, D_i denotes the set of ads, and K_i denotes the set of bid keywords[7] in campaign C_i, respectively.

The ad set D_i can be written as $D_i = \{d_{i,1}, d_{i,2}, \ldots, d_{i,l_i}\}$, where l_i is the number of ads in campaign C_i and $d_{i,s}$ $(s = 1, 2, \ldots, l_i)$ denotes the s-th ad in the campaign. The bid keyword set K_i can be written as $K_i = \{(k_{i,1}, b_{i,1}^{(0)}, v_{i,1}), (k_{i,2}, b_{i,2}^{(0)}, v_{i,2}), \ldots, (k_{i,n_i}, b_{i,n_i}^{(0)}, v_{i,n_i})\}$ where n_i is the number of bid keywords[8] in campaign C_i, $k_{i,t}$ $(t = 1, 2, \ldots, n_i)$ denotes the t-th bid keyword, $b_{i,t}^{(0)}$ $(t = 1, 2, \ldots, n_i)$ denotes the original bid price for $k_{i,t}$, and $v_{i,t}$ $(t = 1, 2, \ldots, n_i)$ denotes the VPC that $k_{i,t}$ brings. We approximately estimate the VPC based on the idea proposed in [4, 20], and regard it as the upper bound of $b_{i,t}^{(0)}$ [2, 11]. In addition, we denote the minimum reserve price as ϵ_b, which serves as the lower bound of the valid bids.

In sponsored search, the advertiser can associate several keywords to his/her ad. When a query is issued, an auction might be triggered. If one of the associated keywords of an ad matches the query by the corresponding match functions to the match types of the keywords, the ad (together with the matched keyword) will be involved in the auction. Therefore, the candidates in the auction is actually a tuple as $\omega_{i,s,t} = (d_{i,s}, (k_{i,t}, b_{i,t}^{(0)}, v_{i,t}))$, where $s = 1, 2, \ldots, l_i$ and $t = 1, 2, \ldots, n_i$. We call the tuple *order item*. For ease of reference, for an order item ω, we also use $(\cdot)_w$ to denote the attribute associate with it, such as its keyword k_ω, bid price b_ω, and VPC v_ω.

We use Φ to denote the maximum number of ad slots in each search result page of the sponsored search system. Suppose the ads are ranked in the auction according to their rank scores, then we have the following definitions.

DEFINITION 1 (WINNING SCORE). *For an auction θ, its winning score at position ρ_ϕ (denoted by $\mu_{\phi,\theta}$, $\phi = 1, 2, \ldots, \Phi$)*

---

[6] In practice, the most relevant ad in an ad group will participate in the auction.

[7] A keyword may have different match types and different bid prices accordingly. For simplicity, we regard them as different keywords.

[8] The same keyword with different match types are regarded as different keywords in K_i.

is the least rank score that can make an order item get the ϕ-th ad slot ρ_ϕ in the auction. Let $\mu_{0,\theta} = +\infty$, then we have $\mu_{0,\theta} \geq \mu_{1,\theta} \geq \ldots \geq \mu_{\Phi,\theta}$.

DEFINITION 2 (WINNING SCORE INTERVAL). *For an auction θ, its winning score interval at position ρ_ϕ is $[\mu_{\phi,\theta}, \mu_{\phi-1,\theta})$ ($\phi = 1, 2, \ldots, \Phi$), which is the range of the rank score that can make an order item exactly get the ϕ-th ad slot ρ_ϕ in the auction.*

Mainstream search engines use the product of the bid price and the quality score as the rank score in their auctions [13]. Suppose the quality score of an order item ω in an auction θ is $r_{\omega,\theta}$, which can be calculated based on a group of features such as the query-ad similarity, semantic similarity, taxonomy, user query time, user query location and so on [14, 15, 19]. As indicated by the subscript, the quality score $r_{\omega,\theta}$ of an order item can be different in different auctions, due to some contextual information related to time, location, and user for the triggering query [14]. Usually such a quality score indicates the probability that an ad will be clicked after it is noticed by users. In this context, we have the following definitions of winning price and winning price interval.

DEFINITION 3 (WINNING PRICE). *Given an order item ω in an auction θ with its quality score $r_{\omega,\theta}$, its winning price at position ρ_ϕ (denoted by $\beta_{\omega,\phi,\theta}$, $\phi = 1, 2, \ldots, \Phi$) is $\frac{\mu_{\phi,\theta}}{r_{\omega,\theta}}$, which is the least bid price that can make ω get the ϕ-th ad slot ρ_ϕ in the auction. Let $\beta_{\omega,0,\theta} = +\infty$, and we have $\beta_{\omega,0,\theta} \geq \beta_{\omega,1,\theta} \geq \cdots \geq \beta_{\omega,\Phi,\theta}$.*

DEFINITION 4 (WINNING PRICE INTERVAL). *Given an order item ω in an auction θ with its quality score $r_{\omega,\theta}$, its winning price interval at position ρ_ϕ is $[\beta_{\omega,\phi,\theta}, \beta_{\omega,\phi-1,\theta})$ ($\phi = 1, 2, \ldots, \Phi$), which is the range of the bid price that can make ω exactly get the ϕ-th ad slot ρ_ϕ in the auction.*

4.2 Probabilistic Model for Ad Ranking

In order to compute the expected advertiser revenue, we need to get the probability for an order item ω with bid price b_ω to be ranked at position ρ_ϕ in the auctions.[9] More specifically, we define a probability distribution $P_\omega(b_\omega)$ as,

$$P_\omega(b_\omega) = (p_\omega(\rho_1|b_\omega), p_\omega(\rho_2|b_\omega), \ldots, p_\omega(\rho_\Phi|b_\omega), p_\omega(\rho_{\Phi+1}|b_\omega)),$$

where $p_\omega(\rho_\phi|b_\omega)$ ($\phi = 1, 2, \ldots, \Phi$) denotes the probability for ω to be ranked in slot ρ_ϕ when its bid price is b_ω, and $p_\omega(\rho_{\Phi+1}|b_\omega)$ denotes the probability for ω to lose the auction (i.e., to be ranked lower than ρ_Φ). It is clear that,

$$\sum_{\phi=1}^{\Phi+1} p_\omega(\rho_\phi|b_\omega) = 1.$$

To get the above probability distribution, we apply the Bayes theorem to each element of it.

$$p_\omega(\rho_\phi|b_\omega) = \frac{p_\omega(b_\omega|\rho_\phi)p_\omega(\rho_\phi)}{\sum_{j=1}^{\Phi+1} p_\omega(b_\omega|\rho_j)p_\omega(\rho_j)}$$

Here $p_\omega(\rho_\phi)$ is the probability of any ad being displayed at position ρ_ϕ in the auctions that ω participates in, which can be approximately obtained by simple counting in the historical auction log. $p_\omega(b_\omega|\rho_\phi)$ is the probability of observing b_ω in the winning price interval at position ρ_ϕ in the auction θ that ω participates in. A straightforward way is also to obtain this value by simple counting in the historical auction log. That is, for each auction θ of ω ($\theta = 1, 2, \ldots, \Theta_\omega$, where Θ_ω denotes the number of auctions ω participates in.), we calculate the winning price interval $[\beta_{\omega,\phi,\theta}, \beta_{\omega,\phi-1,\theta})$ for position ρ_ϕ from the auction log. If $b_\omega \in [\beta_{\omega,\phi,\theta}, \beta_{\omega,\phi-1,\theta})$, we say that there is an observation of price b_ω. However, the problem with this approach is that we need to go through the entire log for every possible value of b_ω, which will be too costly when we performing the optimization. Therefore we propose a new approach as described below that can be much more efficient without revisiting the entire auction logs during the optimization process.

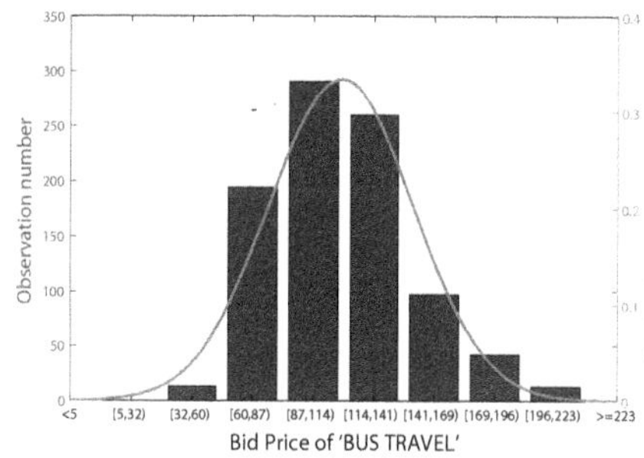

Figure 3: A case of Gaussian fitting for the bound of the winning price intervals.

For all auctions of ω, we can calculate their winning price intervals at position ρ_ϕ. As mentioned above, the lower bound and upper bound of the winning price interval are actually in fluctuation in different auctions. For simplicity, we use the following Gaussian distributions[10] to model the fluctuation of the bounds.

$$q_\omega^{(L)}(x|\rho_\phi) = \frac{1}{\sqrt{2\pi\sigma_{\omega,\phi}^2}} e^{-(x-\bar{\beta}_{\omega,\phi})^2/2\sigma_{\omega,\phi}^2}$$
$$q_\omega^{(U)}(y|\rho_\phi) = \frac{1}{\sqrt{2\pi\sigma_{\omega,\phi-1}^2}} e^{-(y-\bar{\beta}_{\omega,\phi-1})^2/2\sigma_{\omega,\phi-1}^2}$$

Here x and y are the random variables for the lower bound and upper bound of the winning price interval of ω at position ρ_ϕ, and the superscripts L and U stand for lower bound and upper bound respectively. In addition, $\bar{\beta}_{\omega,\phi}$ and $\sigma_{\omega,\phi}$ are the mean and standard deviation for the lower bounds of the winning price intervals at position ρ_ϕ for all auctions of ω. That is,

$$\bar{\beta}_{\omega,\phi} = \frac{1}{\Theta_\omega} \sum_{\theta=1}^{\Theta_\omega} \beta_{\omega,\phi,\theta}$$
$$\sigma_{\omega,\phi}^2 = \frac{1}{\Theta_\omega} \sum_{\theta=1}^{\Theta_\omega} (\beta_{\omega,\phi,\theta} - \frac{1}{\Theta_\omega} \sum_{\theta=1}^{\Theta_\omega} \beta_{\omega,\phi,\theta})^2$$

Similarly, $\bar{\beta}_{\omega,\phi-1}$ and $\sigma_{\omega,\phi-1}$ are the mean and standard deviation for the upper bounds of the winning price intervals at position ρ_ϕ for all auctions of ω.

[9]Note that we compute this probability at the order item level but not for each individual auction, mainly because of the concern of data sparseness.

[10]We have tested several possible distributions including Gaussian, Beta, and Gamma distributions, and found Gaussian is one of the best choices. Due to space limit, we will not show the parameter fitting for the distributions, but we can show an running example like Figure 3. As this is an approximation for the real data, we will ignore the negative values from the Gaussian distribution, just like what we usually do when we assume the heights of a group of people are sampled from a Gaussian distribution.

Thus $p_\omega(b_\omega|\rho_\phi)$ can be computed as below.

$$\begin{aligned} p_\omega(b_\omega|\rho_\phi) &= p_\omega(x \le b_\omega < y|\rho_\phi) \\ &= p_\omega(x \le b_\omega|\rho_\phi)p_\omega(b_\omega < y|\rho_\phi) \\ &= \int_{-\infty}^{b_\omega} q_\omega^{(L)}(x|\rho_\phi)dx \int_{b_\omega}^{\infty} q_\omega^{(U)}(y|\rho_\phi)dy \\ &= \emptyset(\frac{b_\omega - \bar{\beta}_{\omega,\phi}}{\sigma_{\omega,\phi}})(1 - \emptyset(\frac{b_\omega - \bar{\beta}_{\omega,\phi-1}}{\sigma_{\omega,\phi-1}})) \\ & \quad (\phi = 2, \ldots, \Phi) \end{aligned}$$

Here $\emptyset(\cdot)$ represents the cumulative distribution function of the standard normal distribution. In particular, for the first ad slot ρ_1, the upper bound y is infinity. Hence $p_\omega(b_\omega < y|\rho_1) \equiv 1$, and then,

$$p_\omega(b_\omega|\rho_1) = p_\omega(x \le b_\omega|\rho_1) = \emptyset(\frac{b_\omega - \bar{\beta}_{\omega,1}}{\sigma_{\omega,1}}).$$

Similarly, for $\rho_{\Phi+1}$, the lower bound x is zero. Hence $p_\omega(x \le b_\omega|\rho_{\Phi+1}) \equiv 1$, and then,

$$p_\omega(b_\omega|\rho_{\Phi+1}) = p_\omega(b_\omega < y|\rho_{\Phi+1}) = 1 - \emptyset(\frac{b_\omega - \bar{\beta}_{\omega,\Phi}}{\sigma_{\omega,\Phi}}).$$

Figure 4 uses an example to explain the calculation of the probability $p_\omega(b_\omega|\rho_\phi)$. Suppose the bid of an observation is 28 (cents), then the probability $p_\omega(b_\omega|\rho_\phi)$ equals to the product of the area of the left shadow (probability of lower bound < 28) and the area of the right shadow (probability of upper bound > 28).

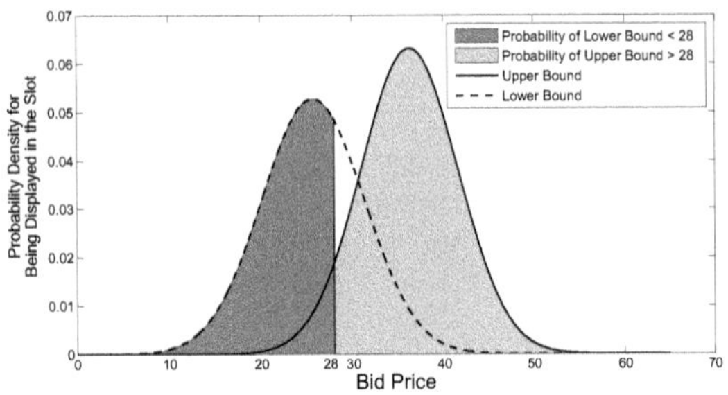

Figure 4: An example of the probability density distribution of the upper bound and lower bound of a winning price interval.

So far we have discussed our probabilistic model for ad ranking based on the ad auction log data. Compared with the conventional ranking models, the probabilistic model is smooth and easy to be directly optimized. Note that this model can be designed in other forms with different data formats in different scenarios.

4.3 Optimization Problem

Given the definition of the probabilistic model described in the previous subsection, we can define the expected advertiser revenue. To ease the illustration, we further introduce two notations as below. (i) τ_ϕ - the position bias at slot ρ_ϕ. As discussed in Section 3.2, the relative CTR (shown in Figure 2) indicates the probability of ads in the position ρ_ϕ being noticed. Further considering the definition of quality score $r_{\omega,\theta}$, the actual probability of an ad being clicked when ranked on the slot ρ_ϕ will be $\tau_\phi r_{\omega,\theta}$ [15]. (ii) $c_{\omega,\phi,\theta}$ - the cost for a click on ω in an auction θ where it is ranked on position ρ_ϕ. According to the GSP system, the cost can be calculated as $c_{\omega,\phi,\theta} = \frac{b_{\omega'} r_{\omega',\theta}}{r_{\omega,\theta}}$, where ω' is the order item that is ranked one slot lower than ω in the auction θ, and $b_{\omega'}$ is its bid price.

The objective of the optimization problem is to maximize the total revenue of the advertiser account, which reflects the final profit the advertiser can make from the sponsored search. The constraints are the bounds of the bid prices and the campaign budget.

For all the campaigns in an advertiser account, the total expected click number can be written as

$$\sum_{i=1}^m \sum_{\omega \in C_i} \sum_{\theta=1}^{\Theta_\omega} \sum_{\phi=1}^{\Phi} p_\omega(\rho_\phi|b_\omega)\tau_\phi r_{\omega,\theta}.$$

where the factor $\sum_{\phi=1}^{\Phi} p_\omega(\rho_\phi|b_\omega)\tau_\phi r_{\omega,\theta}$ is the probability of click on ω in one auction when the bid price is b_ω.

Considering the cost of click and the VPC of each bid keyword, we can get the expected advertiser revenue as follows,

$$\sum_{i=1}^m \sum_{\omega \in C_i} \sum_{\theta=1}^{\Theta_\omega} \sum_{\phi=1}^{\Phi} p_\omega(\rho_\phi|b_\omega)\tau_\phi r_{\omega,\theta}(v_\omega - c_{\omega,\phi,\theta}).$$

Given the above objective function, we can formulate the joint optimization as below, where g_i $(i = 1, 2, \ldots, m)$ and b_ω denote the variables of campaign budgets and keyword bid prices respectively. The minimum campaign budget is ϵ_g, for the advertiser might not like to entirely close a campaign by letting $g_i = 0$.

$$\begin{aligned} \max_{g_i, b_\omega} \quad & \sum_{i=1}^m \sum_{\omega \in C_i} \sum_{\theta=1}^{\Theta_\omega} \sum_{\phi=1}^{\Phi} p_\omega(\rho_\phi|b_\omega)\tau_\phi r_{\omega,\theta}(v_\omega - c_{\omega,\phi,\theta}) \\ s.t. \quad & \sum_i^m g_i = \sum_i^m g_i^{(0)} \\ & 0 \le \sum_{\omega \in C_i} \sum_{\theta=1}^{\Theta_\omega} \sum_{\phi=1}^{\Phi} p_\omega(\rho_\phi|b_\omega)\tau_\phi r_{\omega,\theta} c_{\omega,\phi,\theta} \le g_i \\ & (i = 1, 2, \ldots, m) \\ & \epsilon_g \le g_i \quad (i = 1, 2, \ldots, m) \\ & \epsilon_b \le b_\omega \le v_\omega \quad (\omega \in C_i, \; i = 1, 2, \ldots, m) \end{aligned}$$

4.4 Efficient Solution

The above optimization problem is a typical constrained optimization problem. It can be approximately solved by means of sequential quadratic programming (SQP) [9] in an efficient manner.

Suppose $\xi_1 = \{b_\omega\}$ $(\omega \in C_i, \; i = 1, 2, \ldots, m)$ denotes the vector of bid prices for all the order items in an advertiser account, and $\xi_2 = \{g_i\}$ $(i = 1, 2, \ldots, m)$ denotes the vector of campaign budgets. Then $\xi = (\xi_1^T, \xi_2^T)^T$ is the vector of all variables. We can rewrite the optimization problem as the following form.

$$\begin{aligned} \min_\xi \quad & f(\xi) \\ s.t. \quad & h_0(\xi) = 0 \\ & h_i(\xi) \ge 0 \quad (i = 1, 2, \ldots, 5) \end{aligned}$$

The functions $f(\xi)$ and $h_i(\xi)$ $(i = 0, 1, \ldots, 5)$ are written in the following forms,

$$\begin{aligned} f(\xi) &= -\sum_{i=1}^m \sum_{\omega \in C_i} \sum_{\theta=1}^{\Theta_\omega} \sum_{\phi=1}^{\Phi} p_\omega(\rho_\phi|b_\omega)\tau_\phi r_{\omega,\theta}(v_\omega - c_{\omega,\phi,\theta}) \\ h_0(\xi) &= \sum_i^m g_i - \sum_i^m g_i^{(0)} = 0 \\ h_1(\xi) &= \sum_{\omega \in C_i} \sum_{\theta=1}^{\Theta_\omega} \sum_{\phi=1}^{\Phi} p_\omega(\rho_\phi|b_\omega)\tau_\phi r_{\omega,\theta} c_{\omega,\phi,\theta} \ge 0 \\ h_2(\xi) &= g_i - \sum_{\omega \in C_i} \sum_{\theta=1}^{\Theta_\omega} \sum_{\phi=1}^{\Phi} p_\omega(\rho_\phi|b_\omega)\tau_\phi r_{\omega,\theta} c_{\omega,\phi,\theta} \ge 0 \\ & \quad (i = 1, 2, \ldots, m) \\ h_3(\xi) &= g_i - \epsilon_g \ge 0 \quad (i = 1, 2, \ldots, m) \\ h_4(\xi) &= b_\omega - \epsilon_b \ge 0 \quad (\omega \in C_i, \; i = 1, 2, \ldots, m) \\ h_5(\xi) &= v_\omega - b_\omega \ge 0 \quad (\omega \in C_i, \; i = 1, 2, \ldots, m) \end{aligned}$$

The above problem can be approximately solved by SQP. In SQP, a quadratic programming (QP) subproblem is solved in each iteration which is obtained by linearizing the constraints and approximating the following Lagrangian function $L(\xi, \eta)$ quadratically.

$$L(\xi, \eta) = f(\xi) - \sum_{i=0}^{5} \eta_i h_i(\xi)$$

Here $\eta = \{\eta_i\}$ is the Lagrangian multiplier. The optimization may start from any initial $\xi^{(0)}$. Suppose $\xi^{(j)}$ is the solution in the j-th iteration, $\eta^{(j)}$ is the corresponding Lagrangian multipliers, and $H^{(j)} = H(\xi^{(j)}, \eta^{(j)})$ is the Hessian of the Lagrangian function, then the following QP subproblem should be solved in the $(j+1)$-th iteration.

$$\begin{array}{ll} \min_z & \frac{1}{2} z^T H^{(j)} z + \nabla L(\xi, \eta)^T z \\ s.t. & \nabla h_0(\xi^{(j)})^T z + h_0(\xi^{(j)}) = 0 \\ & \nabla h_i(\xi^{(j)})^T z + h_i(\xi^{(j)}) \geq 0 \ (i = 1, \ldots, 5) \end{array}$$

Here ∇ denotes gradient calculus. If $z^{(j)}$ is the solution of the above QP subproblem and $w^{(j)}$ is the corresponding multiplier of this subproblem, then we use the following formulas to update the solution of the SQP problem.

$$\begin{array}{rcl} \xi^{(j+1)} & = & \xi^{(j)} + z^{(j)} \\ \eta^{(j+1)} & = & w^{(j)} \end{array}$$

The above iterations lead to a local approximation of the solution. The algorithm can be stabilized by line search. By solving this SQP problem, we can get the optimal campaign budgets as well as the optimal bid price for each order item.

5. EXPERIMENTAL EVALUATION

In this section, we first introduce our experimental settings, including the datasets, baseline algorithms, and evaluation measures. Then we report the experimental results on our proposed algorithm and make analysis and discussions.

5.1 Experimental Settings

5.1.1 Datasets

The data used in our experiments came from a mainstream commercial search engine. There are basically two types of data: auction log and advertiser database. The auction log was collected in a month of 2011, containing over one billion auction events. The log was partitioned into two parts, one for training and the other for testing. The training data was used as historical data to get the probability model for ad rank and the empirical values used in our algorithms. The test data was used for simulation [1] in order to evaluate the performance of each algorithm. The advertiser database is a snapshot in the same month, which contains about 150 thousand sponsored search accounts.

We sampled 400 p-accounts to study in our experiments. Accordingly, over 1.2 million related auction events were extracted from the auction log. We also got the bid price for each keyword and the budget for each campaign in these accounts from the advertiser database.

5.1.2 Baseline Algorithms

The proposed algorithm jointly optimizes the bid price and campaign budget. In order to understand the benefit of performing joint optimization, we will also investigate how it works if we only optimize bid price or campaign budget. This leads to two natural simplified methods for our algorithm. We also compare our algorithm with two state-of-the-art algorithms for bid price optimization. In addition, using the original bid prices and campaign budget is the pure baseline. Furthermore, we adopt a bidding strategy to mimic the second order effect by the bid fluctuations, and test the robustness of our proposed method. Therefore, as a whole, we have the following seven algorithms in our experiments.

Original Bid Price and Campaign Budget (ORI). This algorithm uses the original keyword bid prices and campaign budgets in the experiment. This is the pure baseline in the experiments.

Joint Optimization of Bid and Budget (JO). This is our proposed algorithm. Note that we approximately calculate the VPC according to the idea in [4], i.e., we ran a simulation on the auction log to get the incremental cost per click (ICPC) [4] for each keyword and use it as the estimated value for the VPC of the keyword.

Bid Price Only (BID). This algorithm uses our proposed algorithm, but only optimizes the keyword bid prices, without changing the campaign budgets. By comparing this method with JO, we can see the impact of joint optimization. This method can also be used to directly compare with other algorithms for bid optimization.

Campaign Budget Only (BGT). This algorithm uses our proposed algorithm, but only optimizes the campaign budget, without changing the keyword bid prices. By comparing this method with JO, we can also see the impact of joint optimization.

Knapsack Problem (KS). This algorithm is the multi-slot auction model proposed in [7], which adapts the problem of keyword bid price setting into a multi-choice knapsack problem. We set the t in the model as one day. That is, we will change the bid price daily according to remaining budget of each campaign.

Market Optimal Bid (MOB). This algorithm refers to the optimal bid model proposed in [16]. This model is an optimization framework that maximizes the advertiser revenue. Position is also considered in this model. The difference between this model and the BID model lies in that MOB captures the best position with fixed bid prices in each position to approach the observation instead of using a probability distribution for positions.

Joint Optimization with Advertiser Modeling (JO-AM). In the real online traffic, the advertisers would dynamically tune their bid prices in response to the changes of their campaign performances, and thus the changes of the bid prices will lead to the changes of the action outputs. Therefore, the optimal budget allocation and bid prices calculated from the historical log might not be so effective as expected in the real online experiment. We adopt a bidding strategy [18] by the advertisers to mimic the dynamic bid changes, and check whether the proposed JO method can still be robust with the possible bid changes by the advertisers.

Note that we do not compare with the algorithms in [12, 17], for their objective is to maximize the expected click number. The number of clicks can be a good measure for the campaign performance, but it may not be a good objective to optimize for the advertisers. They may care more about the quality of clicks or the value they desire from each click. In other words, the revenue might be more meaningful for the advertisers to optimize. We do not compare with the algorithms in [5, 6, 10] either, for they are in different scenarios with our setting.

5.1.3 *Evaluation Measures*

We used the following evaluation measures in our experiments.

Ad Impressions. After simulation on the test data, we can get the impressions for an advertiser account.

Expected Clicks. We use the adPredictor model [14] to calculate the probability of click, and transform the impressions to expected ad clicks.[11] More expected clicks mean better performance of an advertiser.

Advertiser Revenue. Since there is a cost and a VPC associated with each click, the advertiser revenue for each click can be calculated as the difference between the VPC and the cost. By summing up the advertiser revenue for all the clicks obtained by an advertiser account, we can get the overall advertiser revenue.

Search Engine Revenue. While the above measures mainly describe the performances of advertisers, this measure corresponds to the performance of the search engine. Note that the search engine revenue does not equal the expense of the target advertiser accounts. If the keyword auction is highly competitive and there is no empty ad slot, the impression of a new ad might not increase the expected search engine revenue since there is another ad losing the auction.

5.2 Experimental Results

We study the performances of the algorithms ORI, BID, BGT, KS, MOB, JO, and JO-AM which all take the advertiser revenue as the objective function. We report the performance of these algorithms with respect to ad impressions, expected clicks, advertiser revenue, and search engine revenue. Note that we normalized the values under each evaluation metric by dividing them by the maximum value in the corresponding results, to protect the business secrets of the search engine.

5.2.1 *Ad Impressions*

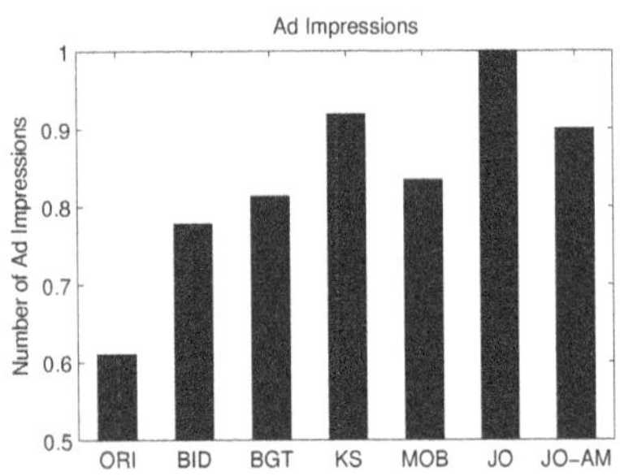

Figure 5: The average ad impressions among p-accounts.

The average ad impressions of each algorithm are shown in Figure 5. From the figure we have the following observations. (i) All the algorithms successfully achieve a lot more impressions as compared to ORI. This demonstrates that the p-accounts have large potential to improve their performance by tuning the bid prices or budget allocation. (ii) JO performs better than BID and BGT. Therefore, although BID and BGT can help improve the ad impressions, jointly optimizing both bid and budget will help achieve more. This shows the necessity of adopting our proposed method. (iii) The performance of JO-AM is hurt by the advertiser dynamics on bid changes. However, it is still comparable with the second highest performer KS. It shows the proposed method is robust against the second-order effects from the advertiser dynamics.

5.2.2 *Expected Clicks*

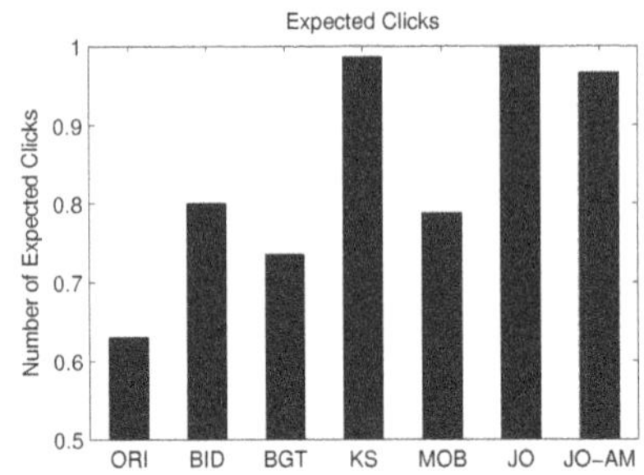

Figure 6: The average expected clicks among p-accounts.

Figure 6 depicts the number of expected clicks in the simulation period for the seven algorithms. From the figure we have the following observations. (i) BID, BGT, KS, MOB, JO and JO-AM all improve the click number as compared to ORI. This shows that using advertiser revenue as the optimization objective can also help improve the click number. (ii) BID performs better than MOB, indicating that our proposed ways of optimizing bid prices is more effective than some previous work. (iii) Further considering the budget allocation, JO performs the best. (iv) JO-AM is comparable with the second highest performer KS, again showing the robustness of the proposed method against the second-order effects.

5.2.3 *Advertiser Revenue*

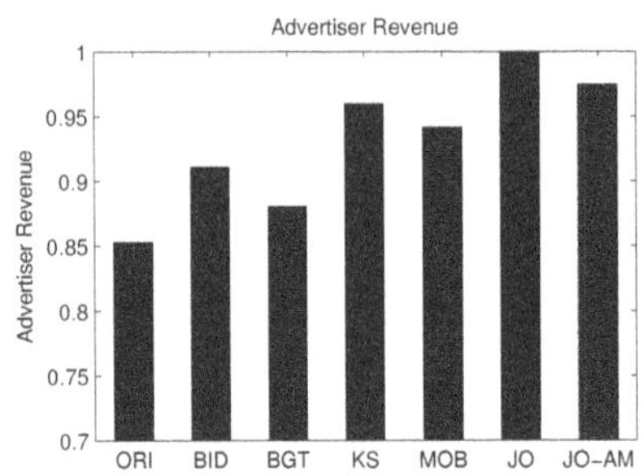

Figure 7: The average advertiser revenue among p-accounts.

In Figure 7, we evaluate the advertiser revenue, which is just the optimization objective of these algorithms. From the figure we have the following observations. (i) All the algorithms improve the advertiser revenue significantly. Though BID and BGT perform slightly worse than KS and MOB, by combining the advantages of BID and BGT, JO achieves better performance as compared to KS and MOB. It shows that the advertisers can benefit a lot from the joint optimization of bid price setting and budget allocation. (ii) JO-AM gets the second highest position in advertiser revenue. It even outperforms KS, showing that the proposed method is a good choice for the advertisers in practice when facing the bid dynamics.

[11] The adPredictor model performs quite well on our data and has a predict error of less than 10%.

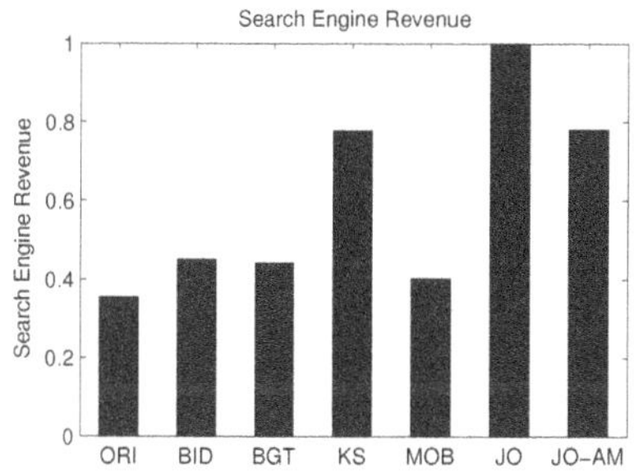

Figure 8: The average search engine revenue among p-accounts.

5.2.4 Search Engine Revenue

The performances in terms of search engine revenue are shown in Figure 8. From the figure, we can see that search engine can earn more money by using all the algorithms as compared to ORI. Among these algorithms, and JO still performs the best. Therefore, the joint optimization method can in return help the search engine improve the income.

To sum up all the aforementioned experimental results, we can get the following conclusions. (i) Bid price optimization (BID) can lead to high improvement on the ad impressions and expected clicks, and thus can largely increase both the advertiser revenue and the search engine revenue. (ii) Campaign budget optimization itself (BGT) seems not to perform as well as bid prices optimization (BID) in terms of the evaluation measures like expected clicks and advertiser revenue, however, it can ensure that only a very small number of advertisers will have worse performance than before after the optimization. (iii) By jointly optimizing both bid prices and budget allocation, JO perform the best among all the algorithms in all evaluation measures. This clearly demonstrates the effectiveness of our proposal for both the advertisers and the search engine.

6. CONCLUSION AND FUTURE WORK

In this paper, we studied the joint optimization of campaign budget allocation and bid price setting. For this purpose, we proposed a probability model for ad ranking, and proposed an integer optimization problem to maximize the expected advertiser revenue. We show that the problem can be approximately solved by means of alternately working on a binary integer optimization problem and another constraint optimization problem. Experimental results have shown that our proposed algorithm can increase the performance of advertisers in terms of several evaluation measures, as well as the search engine revenue.

For future work, we plan to further study like the following problems. For example, we will refine our model to perform the optimization for multiple accounts simultaneously. For this purpose, we need to consider the inter-competition between accounts, which will make the optimization problem much harder to solve. Furthermore, we want to apply the proposed method in online traffic to test its performance.

7. REFERENCES

[1] S. Acharya, P. Krishnamurthy, K. Deshp, T. W. Yan, and C. chao Chang. A simulation framework for evaluating designs for sponsored search markets. In *WWW 2007 Workshop on Sponsored Search Auctions.* ACM, 2007.

[2] G. Aggarwal, A. Goel, and R. Motwani. Truthful auctions for pricing search keywords. In *Proceedings of the 7th ACM conference on Electronic commerce*, 2006.

[3] N. Archak, V. Mirrokni, and M. Muthukrishnan. Budget optimization for online advertising campaigns with carryover effects. In *Sixth Ad Auctions Workshop.*, 2010.

[4] S. Atheya and D. Nekipelov. A structural model of sponsored search advertising auctions. Available at http://groups.haas.berkeley.edu/marketing/sics/pdf_2010/paper_athey.pdf.

[5] C. Borgs, J. Chayes, N. Immorlica, K. Jain, O. Etesami, and M. Mahdian. Dynamics of bid optimization in online advertisement auctions. In *Proceedings of the 16th international conference on World Wide Web*, WWW '07, pages 531–540, New York, NY, USA, 2007. ACM.

[6] A. Broder, E. Gabrilovich, V. Josifovski, G. Mavromatis, and A. Smola. Bid generation for advanced match in sponsored search. In *Proceedings of WSDM'11.*

[7] D. Chakrabarty, Y. Zhou, and R. Lukose. Budget constrained bidding in keyword auctions and online knapsack problems. In *Proceedings of the 16th World Wide Web Conference*, 2007.

[8] L. Chen and Y. Li. Allocating budget across portals in search engine advertising. In *Management Science and Engineering, 2009. ICMSE 2009. International Conference on*, pages 679 –685, 2009.

[9] R. W. Cottle, J.-S. Pang, and R. E. Stone. *The linear complementarity problem.* Academic Press, Inc., 1992.

[10] E. Dar, V. Mirrokni, S. Muthukrishnan, Y. Mansour, and U. Nadav. Bid optimization for broad match ad auctions. In *Proceedings of WWW'09*, 2009.

[11] B. Edelman, M. Ostrovsky, and M. Schwarz. Internet advertising and the generalized second-price auction: Selling billions of dollars worth of keywords. *The American Economic Review*, 97(1):242–259, 2007.

[12] J. Feldman, S. Muthukrishnan, M. Pĺcl, and C. Stein. Budget optimization in search-based advertising auctions. In *Proceedings of the 8th ACM conference on Electronic commerce*, 2007.

[13] J. Feng, H. Bhargava, and D. Pennock. Comparison of allocation rules for paid placement advertising in search engines. In *Proceedings of the 5th international conference on Electronic commerce*, pages 294–299. ACM ICEC, 2003.

[14] T. Graepel, J. Q. Candela, T. Borchert, and R. Herbrich. Web-scale bayesian click-through rate prediction for sponsored search advertising in microsoft's bing search engine. In *Proceedings of the 27th International Conference on Machine Learning.* ACM ICML, 2010.

[15] D. Hillard, S. Schroedl, and E. Manavoglu. Improving ad relevance in sponsored search. In *Proceedings of WSDM'10.*

[16] B. Kitts and B. Leblanc. Optimal bidding on keyword auctions. *Electronic Markets*, 14(3):186–201, 2004.

[17] S. Muthukrishnan, M. Pĺcl, and Z. Svitkina. Stochastic models for budget optimization in search-based advertising. In *Proceedings of WWW'07*, 2007.

[18] C. Nittala and Y. Narahari. Optimal equilibrium bidding strategies for budget constrained bidders in sponsored search auctions. In *Operational Research: An International Journal.* Springer, 2011.

[19] F. Radlinski, A. Broder, P. Ciccolo, E. Gabrilovich, V. Josifovski, and L. Riedel. Optimizing relevance and revenue in ad search: A query substitution approach. In *proceeding of SIGIR'08*, 2008.

[20] H. R. Varian. Position auctions. In *International Journal of Industrial Organization*, 2006.

[21] N. Virk. Is your search marketing budget allocation right? Available at http://www.internetseer.com/services/article.xtp?id=37080.

The Untold Story of the Clones: Content-agnostic Factors that Impact YouTube Video Popularity

Youmna Borghol
NICTA & UNSW
New South Wales, Australia

Sebastien Ardon
NICTA
Alexandria, NSW, Australia

Niklas Carlsson
Linköping University
Linköping, Sweden

Derek Eager
University of Saskatchewan
Saskatoon, SK, Canada

Anirban Mahanti
NICTA
Alexandria, NSW, Australia

ABSTRACT

Video dissemination through sites such as YouTube can have widespread impacts on opinions, thoughts, and cultures. Not all videos will reach the same popularity and have the same impact. Popularity differences arise not only because of differences in video content, but also because of other "content-agnostic" factors. The latter factors are of considerable interest but it has been difficult to accurately study them. For example, videos uploaded by users with large social networks may tend to be more popular because they tend to have more interesting content, not because social network size has a substantial direct impact on popularity.

In this paper, we develop and apply a methodology that is able to accurately assess, both qualitatively and quantitatively, the impacts of various content-agnostic factors on video popularity. When controlling for video content, we observe a strong linear "rich-get-richer" behavior, with the total number of previous views as the most important factor except for very young videos. The second most important factor is found to be video age. We analyze a number of phenomena that may contribute to rich-get-richer, including the first-mover advantage, and search bias towards popular videos. For young videos we find that factors other than the total number of previous views, such as uploader characteristics and number of keywords, become relatively more important. Our findings also confirm that inaccurate conclusions can be reached when not controlling for content.

Categories and Subject Descriptors

E.0 [**Data**]: General; C.4 [**Computer Systems Organization**]: Performance of Systems; H.3 [**Information Systems**]: Information Storage and Retrieval

Keywords

Popularity, Youtube, Rich-get-richer, Clones

KDD'12, August 12–16, 2012, Beijing, China.

1. INTRODUCTION

A vast amount of new video, audio, image, and text content is created each year, much of it disseminated via the Internet. What determines which items become popular and seen/heard/read by many people, and which do not? Although the content of the item (is it interesting, is it topical, is it high-quality, and so on) plays an important role, it has been widely recognized that other "content-agnostic" factors can also have a substantial impact on popularity.

For videos shared through a site such as YouTube, for example, content-agnostic factors impacting a video's current viewing rate include the video uploader's social network size, the total number of previous views to the video, the number of associated keywords, and the time that has elapsed since the video was uploaded (the video "age"). Such factors can directly impact the choices of potential viewers, as well as indirectly impact these choices through their influence on the service provider's search and featuring algorithms.

There has been considerable work on characterizing, modeling, and predicting the popularities of user-generated videos. User-generated video accesses at campus networks have been characterized [6,13]. Both static and temporal properties of view counts to a collection of user-generated videos have been studied [3,4,7,10]. Models have also been proposed for video popularity evolution [3,9,10]. Many of these models are based on the classical *rich-get-richer* phenomenon [2], which suggests that a video will attract new views at a rate proportional to the number of views already acquired.

Since both content-related and content-agnostic factors impact popularity, however, understanding how the various content-agnostic factors influence popularity has been challenging. For example, videos uploaded by users with large social networks may tend to become more popular because such users generally upload more interesting content, not because social network size has any direct impact on popularity. Prior studies have used datasets consisting of videos with widely-varying contents, and thus are unable to rigorously distinguish the impacts of content-agnostic factors on popularity, from the impacts arising from differing contents.

In this paper, we develop and apply a methodology that is able to accurately assess the impacts various content-agnostic factors have on video popularity. Our methodology is based on studying popularity differences among videos that have essentially the same content; i.e., can be considered as "clones" of each other. Popularity differences among clones can only be due to content-agnostic factors.

Using data we collected for sets of manually-identified

YouTube video clones, we apply multivariate linear regression and other statistical methods to systematically determine the content-agnostic factors that most influence a video's current popularity. In particular, by analyzing a large number of explicit measurable factors that are provided through the YouTube API, we find that the most significant content-agnostic factors are the total number of previous views and the video age. We also show that determining the relative importance of these factors without controlling for video content (i.e., ignoring clone set memberships) would result in inaccurate results; in particular, the relative importance of factors such as video age and the number of followers of the uploader would be significantly overestimated.

When controlling for video content, we find that "rich-get-richer" preferential selection based on the total number of previous views appears to provide a good model of video popularity evolution. Specifically, using regression analysis we show that current video popularity, among videos of similar "generation" (age within a multi-year window), follows a scale-free rich-get-richer model with power-law exponent of approximately one. We also show that carrying out this analysis without controlling for content would result in erroneously concluding that preferential selection is significantly weaker, not scale-free, with a power-law exponent smaller than one. We investigate a number of possible contributors to the observed rich-get-richer behavior, including the "first-mover" advantage and search bias towards popular videos.

The total number of previous views becomes less significant for very young (newly-uploaded) videos that have not yet accumulated many views. For such videos, we show that other factors such as uploader characteristics and the number of keywords become much more significant. Their significance is substantially underestimated, however, when not controlling for video content.

The remainder of this paper is organized as follows. Section 2 describes our data collection methodology and analysis approach. Section 3 presents an analysis for the relative impacts of the measured content-agnostic factors on current video popularity, while Section 4 shows the importance of controlling for video content in this analysis. Section 5 studies the applicability of rich-get-richer preferential selection models, and examines contributors to rich-get-richer behavior. Section 6 analyzes the content-agnostic factors impacting the popularity of newly-uploaded videos. Related work is discussed in Section 7. Section 8 concludes the paper.

2. METHODOLOGY

2.1 Data Collection

To analyze factors influencing video popularity, we start by identifying sets of identical or nearly identical videos on YouTube. By identical we mean the same video content and audio soundtrack. We allow subtitles, variations in encodings (quality), and small variations in video duration. In this paper, we refer to such a set of nearly identical videos as a *clone set* and videos in such a set as *clones*. Through extensive exploration, search, and viewing of YouTube videos, we manually identified 48 clone sets, each of which contain between 17 and 94 clones, with a median size of 29.5.[1] In total, we identified 1,761 videos. (Our initial dataset was somewhat larger, but we removed all videos whose duration deviated more than 15% from the median duration within their clone set.)

We developed a web-based collection system that allows us to easily enter clone video urls into a database. Each video entered is assigned a clone set id and a video id. Once in the database, the system then extracts video and uploader information using both the YouTube developer's API [11] and through HTML scraping. The system collects three types of information:

- **Video statistics:** These include statistics such as view count, uploader's followers count, number of comments, "likes" and "favourite" events and average rating. For each clone set, two snapshots were collected, spaced one week apart. For all videos in a clone set, the data collection was done within minutes. Table 1 describes all variables collected.
- **Historical view count:** When available, we extract historical video view counts from the YouTube HTML page. This information is referred to by YouTube as "insight data". We programmatically obtain this historical view count information by intercepting the URL request which the YouTube website uses to plot the view history graph. This URL contains 100 points with date/view count pairs.
- **Influential events:** The YouTube insight data also contains information on how users discover a video. It reveals the top 10 "most significant" sources of discovery, or where the video was linked from. Common sources of discovery include "discovered through YouTube search" and "embedded on Facebook". We also collect this list of referrers and, for each referrer, the first date of referral and the associated view count.

The dataset used in this work was collected between February 2010 and April 2011.

While the YouTube insight data provides valuable information regarding a video's popularity evolution, it has some limitations. First, this data is not available for all videos, as uploaders can choose to hide it from public view. We could retrieve the insight data for approximately 40% of the videos in our dataset. Second, the historical view count data includes only 100 points, irrespective of the video's age. To extract the view count at a specific point in time, we applied linear interpolation, which introduces an error dependent on video age. Finally, the referrer data only reveals 10 referrers, with the exact method used by YouTube to select which referrer to include in the list being unknown. This limits the number of views that can be mapped to a specific source, but also leaves some uncertainty in whether there are other more significant sources not accounted for. In our analysis we try to minimize the effect of these limitations.

2.2 Analysis Approach

In this section, we introduce our analysis approach. Since our dataset contains multiple sets of (near) identical content, we are able to apply a range of techniques, both on individual clone sets and on the overall collection of videos across all clone sets. When using the overall collection, we can then choose to take the content (clone set id) into consideration or not. This allows us to identify factors impacting video

[1]Our dataset is available at `http://www.ida.liu.se/~nikca/papers/kdd12.html`.

Variable	Description	Type	Scale	Category
Clone set ID	Unique clone set identifier	–	–	–
Capture time	Time at which this video data was captured	–	–	–
Upload time	Time at which the video was first published	–	–	–
Update time	Time at which the video was last updated	–	–	–
Categories count	Number of categories associated with this video	–	–	–
Next week views	Number of views between two weeks	Predicted	log	Video popularity
Rating average	Average rating (min and max ratings also measured)	Predictor	linear	Video popularity
Total comments	Number of comments	Predictor	log	Video popularity
Total dislikes	Number of 'dislike' events	Predictor	log	Video popularity
Total favourites	Number of time this video was 'favourited'	Predictor	log	Video popularity
Total likes	Number of 'like' events	Predictor	log	Video popularity
Total ratings	Number of ratings	Predictor	log	Video popularity
Total view count	Number of views	Predictor	log	Video popularity
Uploader age	Age of the uploader	Predictor	log	Uploader characteristics
Uploader contacts	Number of (YouTube) 'friends' of the uploader	Predictor	log	Uploader popularity
Uploader followers	Number of followers for the uploader	Predictor	log	Uploader popularity
Uploader video count	Number of videos uploaded by the uploader	Predictor	log	Uploader popularity
Uploader view count	Number of time any of the uploader's videos were viewed	Predictor	log	Uploader popularity
Video age	Age of the video	Predictor	log	Video characteristics
Video keywords	Number of keywords assigned to the video	Predictor	log	Video characteristics
Video quality	The best quality (frame size) available for this video (higher is better)	Predictor	linear	Video characteristics

Table 1: Variables collected and analyzed.

popularity, as well as evaluate the errors of other methods that do not take into account the impacts of differing video contents. Specifically, we focus on the following:

- **Individual clone set statistics**: These are calculated for each clone set. We present summaries of these as well as results for example clone sets.
- **Content-based statistics**: These are calculated across all videos using an extended model that takes into account each video's clone set identity.
- **Aggregate video statistics**: These are calculated across all videos, ignoring clone set identity. These statistics are used for comparison.

Our analysis focuses on the content-agnostic factors that most influence a video's popularity, as measured by the view count over a week. To evaluate the relative influence of different factors, we use three statistical tools. First, we characterize the relationships between variables using Principal Component Analysis (PCA). This technique allows us to identify groups of variables which are responsible for different parts of the variation. Second, we use correlation and collinearity analysis to identify interrelated variables, which can have a negative effect on regression results. For this purpose, we leverage a number of different statistical techniques, including pair-wise correlation matrices and auxiliary regression. Third, we use multi-linear regression with variable selection, to identify a subset of the variables that captures the majority of the variations, and eliminate variables that do not provide much information regarding popularity. Where appropriate, we apply standard hypothesis testing to assess the significance of our results.

Several techniques used in the following assume a linear relationship between variables and normally distributed errors. To validate these assumptions, we first performed a univariate linear regression to examine the relationship between the response variable (weekly view count) and each other variable. Second, we examine the residual plots and corresponding tests to check that the conditions for using linear regression are satisfied. Due to space limitations, we do not detail this preliminary analysis. We find that to ensure linearity with regards to the weekly view count, some variables require log transformation. In addition, some other variables clearly are weak predictors, with higher variation in their residuals. To avoid introducing subjective biases, we did not remove such variables. Instead, we allow the analysis to help us identify suitable candidates. This turned out to be important as some variables are weak predictors on their own, but complement other variables well. The resulting variables used in the remainder of this paper and any transformations used are summarized in Table 1.

2.3 Multi-linear Regression

In this section, we describe how we use multi-linear regression to determine which factors most influence video popularity. For this purpose, we define the response variable as the weekly view count (difference in view count between our two data collections), and the measured factors (also called predictors) as all the other variables. The use of linear regression is motivated by the observed linear relationships between the measured predictors and the response variable.

We perform three types of multi-linear analysis. We first use the standard multi-linear regression model

$$Y_i = \beta_0 + \sum_{p=1}^{P} X_{i,p}\beta_p + \epsilon_i,$$

where the response variable Y_i is modelled as a linear function of the independent variables ($X_{i,p}$), and the method of least squares is used to estimate the coefficients β_p for the P predictors. *Individual clone set statistics* are obtained by applying the above model on each clone set independently; this allows us to determine which factors are the best predictors for each clone set. We then apply this model on all videos together, regardless of the clone set identity, to obtain *aggregate clone set statistics*. This allows us to evaluate the error when not using our content-aware approach as discussed below.

In order to obtain *content-based statistics*, we design an extended model that incorporates a categorical variable for the clone set identity. This model is useful in understanding the influence of individual clone sets on the regression, and whether or not the classification makes a difference. Assuming that we have K clone sets (or categories), we introduce $K-1$ additional category variables, each capturing the relative difference against a reference clone set. The extended multi-linear model is then given as:

$$Y_i = \beta_0 + \sum_{p=1}^{P} X_{i,p}\beta_p + \sum_{k=2}^{K} Z_{i,k}\gamma_k + \epsilon_i,$$

where K is the number of clone sets; P is the number of predictors; and $Z_{i,k}$ is the category regressor, encoded as $Z_{i,k} = 1$ if clone i is from clone set k, and as 0 otherwise. Note that γ_k can be interpreted as the relative distance between the regression lines of clone sets 1 and k, or in other words, a measure of their relative popularity.

3. FACTOR STRENGTH

3.1 Preliminary Analysis

Before looking at which factors best capture the future popularity, we perform a preliminary analysis to discover any correlations between the factors themselves, and if there are groups of variables that provide redundant information and/or explain the same variation. First, we investigate the strength of the linear relationships among the variables using Pearson's correlation. Figure 1 shows the correlation matrix plot for an example clone set. The variables in the matrix plot are ordered based on their correlation with the response variable, and each entry shows the pairwise correlations between the corresponding two variables. The correlation's magnitude is represented by the ellipse symbol, and its sign is represented by colors (and slope), with red (with slope to the left) used for negative values and blue (with slope to the right) for positive values. We note that many of the variables have high pairwise correlation and very similar clustering of the pairwise correlation for most clone sets. In particular, two sets can be identified: (i) the set of variables related to the past video popularity (i.e., the total view count, favourite count, comment count, ratings count, likes and dislikes), and (ii) the set of variables related to the uploader characteristics (e.g., the number of uploader followers, contacts, videos, and views).

Second, we apply Principal Component Analysis (PCA) on each of the individual clone sets. We find the two aforementioned variable groups to correspond to the two primary principal components, particularly for younger clone sets. Figure 2 shows a PCA plot of the first two principal components for one such clone set. Referring to Table 1, these roughly correspond to *video popularity* and *uploader popularity* metrics, respectively. For many other clone sets, particularly clone sets with big variation in video age, other *video characteristics* (such as video age and video quality) forms a third important component.

Understanding and detecting collinearity is important, as interrelated variables could negatively affect the regression results. To find out whether predictor X_i is a linear combination of other predictors, we run auxiliary regressions to determine the coefficient of determination R_i^2 of how well the remaining explanatory variables $X_{j \neq i}$ explain X_i.

While the full results are omitted due to lack of space, the auxiliary regressions on all individual clone sets and on all videos aggregated across clone sets show that the R_i^2 values of the following regressor factors exceed the overall R^2 value of the model including all the explanatory variables: the total view count, the number of times a video was favourited, the number of comments, the number of ratings, the number of times the video was "liked" or "disliked", as well as the total number of views to all videos uploaded by the uploader, and the count of the uploader's followers. We note that these factors fall into the two previously identified groups of correlated variables. Overall, these results provide evidence of a serious collinearity and its sources.

3.2 Variable Selection within Clone Sets

To determine which predictors have the most impact on the popularity of a clone within a clone set, we applied multivariate regression analysis on individual clone sets.

To limit the impact of collinearity and additional noise on the regression models, we eliminate redundant variables

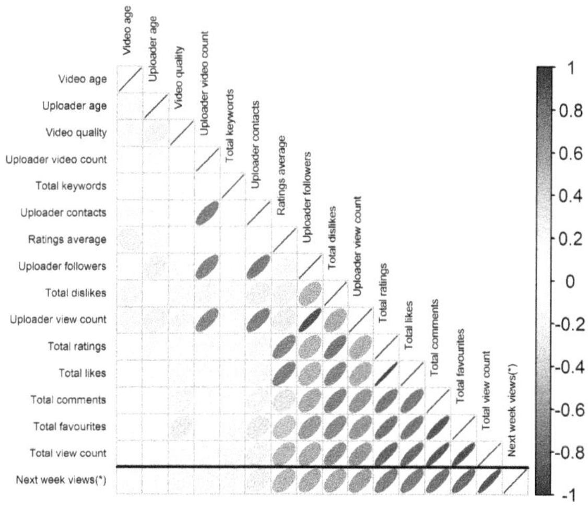

Figure 1: Correlation matrix for clone set 41.

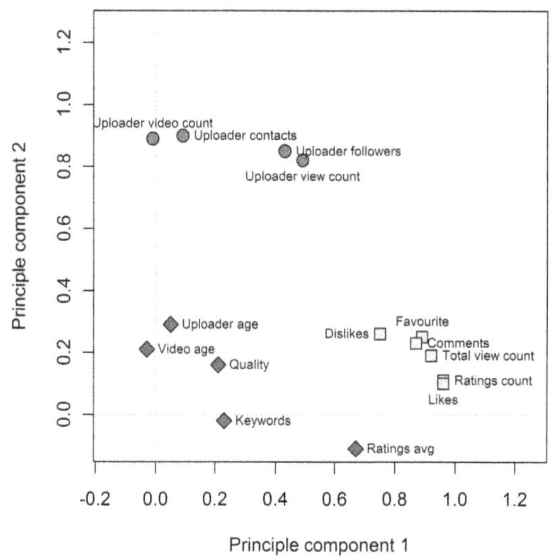

Figure 2: Principal components plot for clone set 41.

using the best subset search technique and Mallow's C_p as the selection criterion [1]. We have obtained qualitatively similar results using other commonly used regression methods and selection criteria. The results in Figure 3 show that the total view count is the most important explanatory variable. It is selected in 92% of the total set of "best models", and is determined to be highly significant. The video age is the second most important predictor, being very significant and being the second most common variable in the models. While the video age did not appear to be a good predictor on its own, as exemplified by the ordering in Figure 1 and low individual R^2 values (with a median of 0.081), its frequent inclusion indicates that it accounts for different variations than the total view count. This has also been observed in some of our PCA analyses. It is also interesting to note that other independent variables, such as variables related to the uploader characteristics, did not appear important in the original regression are now significant when selected in the final model, and are often significant for younger clone sets. One factor that seldomly is significant (even when included) is the video quality. In part, this may be a consequence

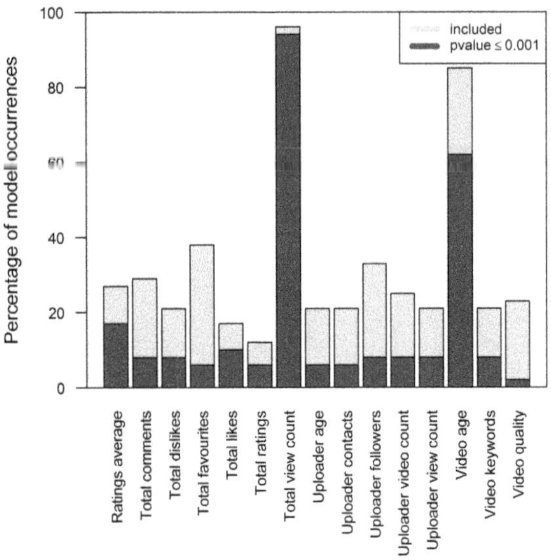

Figure 3: Percentage of occurrences in the set of "best models", using the best subset approach with Mallow's C_p. Dark color shows fraction of models in which the variable was selected while having a p-value smaller than 0.001 in the final model. In the remaining occurrences the variable was selected, but with a higher p-value.

of use of default encodings. However, although our analysis does not find a significant linear relationship, we believe that quality differences may be important in clone sets with wide variations in video age and associated wide variations in quality. The quality variations in such cases may play a role in making age our second most important predictor.

From Figure 3, we can see that the best subset approach with Mallow's C_p, on average, reduces the number of variables by about 60%. The multiple R^2 values for the chosen models are then only slightly smaller than the original R^2 value of the full model.

An interesting observation is that the most influential factors also are the only statistics available to the YouTube users, when searching for a video.

4. IMPACT OF CONTENT IDENTITY

The regression analysis presented in the preceding section was applied on individual clone sets. Using the model extension presented in Section 2.3, we perform regression analysis over the entire dataset while taking into account the content identity, and thus by extension study the impact of the video content on popularity dynamics. Evaluating the importance of the clone set categorical variable is important as it allows us to separate the impact of content-related and content-agnostic factors.

We perform the content-based regression analysis using the most important explanatory variables identified in Section 3.2. We use our default clone set ordering, where sets are numbered from 1 to 48, and choose one clone set as the baseline set.

Summary results are presented in Table 2, for the baseline clone set number 1. The coefficients of the category variables (γ_k) explain by how much the intercept of the selected clone set differs from the intercept of the baseline clone set. The significance of the categorization, i.e., the impact of video

	Estimate	Std. Error	t-value	p-value
Total view count (β_i)	1.100	0.013	87.83	0.000 * * *
Video age (β_i)	-1.008	0.039	-25.80	0.000 * * *
Clone set ($\min_k \gamma_k$)	-0.727	0.348	-2.08	0.037 *
Clone set ($\max_k \gamma_k$)	2.802	0.345	8.08	0.000 * * *

Table 2: Summary of extended regression analysis using categorical variables for clone set identification. With 95% confidence, the rejection rate of the hypothesis that the category variables (γ_k) are equal to zero is 94%.

	View count (1 variable)	+ age (2 var.)	+ followers (3 var.)	all (15 var.)
Individual (mean)	0.788	0.864	0.871	0.933
Individual (median)	0.803	0.873	0.875	0.940
Individual (41)	0.861	0.870	0.874	0.895
Content-based	0.792	0.850	0.852	0.855
Aggregate	0.707	0.808	0.808	0.821

Table 3: Summary of R^2 values for example models.

content, is then measured by the corresponding p-values. We also report range values $\min_k \gamma_k$ and $\max_k \gamma_k$, across the 47 non-baseline clone sets.

We find that 44 out of 47 category variables have p-value smaller than 0.05. When averaging over all possible baseline clone sets, we found approximately 60% of the category variables to be significant. This illustrates the importance of taking clone identity into consideration.

As a second step to evaluate the importance of video content, we compare the regression analysis results of the content-aware extended model and the regular individual clone set models with the aggregate model which ignores clone identity.

For each model type, we used four different models: three partial models and one full model. The first partial model includes only the view count variable, the second model includes both the view count and the video age, and the third model further adds the uploader followers.

Table 3 shows the coefficient of determination R^2 for each model when running the regression analysis on each clone set individually ("Individual"), across all clones and clone sets as an aggregate ("Aggregate"), and when we take the clone identity into account using category variables ("Content-based"). Comparing the last two rows, we note that the "Content-based" models consistently explain a larger portion of the variation, as evidenced by higher R^2 values. This is another indication that taking into account the clone identity is important in modelling video popularity.

Table 3 also reveals that the view count by itself explains the biggest percentage of the variance, especially when taking into account the clone identity. Adding the video age variable increases the R^2 values relatively significantly. Adding the uploader followers variable can result in an occasional incremental increase in the goodness of fit, while the other variables impact is even less important.

However, perhaps more importantly, this table also shows that if one tried to analyze the relative importance of age, followers, etc., without controlling for video content, one would conclude that factors such as age and followers are relatively more important (compared to view count) than they really are. This is illustrated by comparing the difference in values from left to right, for the aggregate and the content-based models. In one case, R^2 is improved by 0.114, and in the other by only 0.063.

The next section will take a closer look at the impact clone identity may have on predictive models, such as the rich-get-richer model.

	Slope estimate	Confidence intervals	
Metric	α (σ)	90%	95%
Individual	1.027 (0.091)	0.988-1.065	0.981-1.073
Content-based	1.003 (0.014)	0.98-1.027	0.976-1.031
Aggregate	0.932 (0.016)	0.906-0.958	0.901-0.963

Table 4: Rich-get-richer slope estimates.

	1st	2nd	3rd	4th	5th	later
Winner uploaded	27.1	12.5	8.3	6.3	6.3	39.6
Winner searched	66.7	8.3	0.0	8.3	8.3	8.3

Table 5: The percentage of times a video clone that obtained the highest total view count was the first, second, third, fourth, fifth (or later) among the videos in the clone set with respect to being uploaded or searched. (Clone sets with relevant statistics considered.)

5. RICH-GET-RICHER

Prior works have suggested that video popularity evolves according to rich-gets-richer preferential selection [2] or a variant thereof (e.g., [3, 9]), wherein the current viewing rate of a video is proportional to the total number of views the video has already acquired. In Section 5.1, we evaluate whether or not our data is consistent with a rich-get-richer model of popularity evolution. Section 5.2 considers a more restricted form of rich-get-richer behavior, the "first mover" advantage. Finally, Section 5.3 explores other phenomena that may result in rich-get-richer behavior, including search bias towards popular videos.

5.1 Models

We consider rich-get-richer models wherein the probability $\Pi(v_i)$ that a video i with v_i views will be selected for viewing follows a power law

$$\Pi(v_i) \propto v^{\alpha},$$

where α is the power exponent.

Perhaps most interesting is when $\alpha = 1$. This case corresponds to linear preferential selection, was considered by Barabasi and Albert [2], and can be shown to result in a scale-free distribution (in our context, of total view counts).

Basic rich-get-richer models as described above consider only the number of accumulated views as a determinant of the rate of acquiring additional views. With YouTube videos, however, user interest in particular subjects changes over time, causing a deviation from rich-get-richer behavior when one considers a collection of such videos with differing contents. An important question is whether a rich-get-richer model is applicable when one removes the impact of changing user interests, as we are able to do with our clone-based methodology.

To answer this question, we first identify within each clone set videos of similar "generation" (age within a multi-year window). We restrict attention to videos of similar generation to avoid our analysis being impacted by wide variations in video quality (or other generation-related effects). Specifically, for each clone set, we first find the video clone with the highest current popularity (i.e., the video that acquired the most additional views during our one week measurement window). We then consider only the videos in the clone set that were uploaded within two years of the upload time of this video.

We now take a closer look at the impact differences in video identity can have on the rich-get-richer phenomena. We examine how the rate at which videos attain new views depends on the total view count using univariate linear regression (using log-transformed data). All three analysis approaches, namely regression analysis on individual clone sets, on the aggregate, and the aggregate considering content identity, were applied. Table 4 summarizes our results.

The first column in Table 4 shows the coefficient estimates and standard deviation resulting from the univariate regression analysis. The second and third columns show the corresponding confidence intervals. For the individual clone sets, and the extended content-based model, α is typically equal or slightly higher than one. The selection rate is linearly dependent on the current total view count, suggesting that the popularity evolution is scale free, and strongly controlled by rich-get-richer behavior. For the aggregate model, α is less than one, indicating popularity evolution that could result in a much more even popularity distribution than that suggested by the pure (linear) rich-get-richer dynamics.

5.2 First Mover Advantage

Rich-get-richer behavior may result in part from a "first mover" advantage. The first video to include particular content may have already achieved significant dissemination by the time that clones appear, causing it to acquire new views at a higher rate (for example, via recommendations from previous viewers, featuring, or bias in search algorithms). Using our clone-based methodology, we now evaluate the advantage of being the first to upload particular content.

To track video popularity over time, we use YouTube's insight data collected through HTML scraping. As a first step, we consider the success of the first mover in each clone-set, where a success event for a particular video is defined as when that video accumulates the largest number of total views compared to all other videos within the clone set. We first consider how often the most successful video within a clone set is the first to either be uploaded or discovered through search. Table 5 shows the number of times the video clone that obtained the highest total view count was first, second, third, fourth, or fifth, among the videos in the clone set, to be uploaded or found through search. Overall, the winner was uploaded first among the videos in the clone set in 27.1% of the observed cases, and was among the first five in 60.4% of the cases. Similarly, the winner is the first to be found through search in 66.7% of the cases for which we have (insight data) statistics, and among the first five to be found through search in 92% of the cases. Clearly, there is a significant advantage to being first mover.

While these results suggest that the first mover typically is relatively successful, it is interesting to note that there are cases where other videos have been able to surpass the first mover in popularity. What is it that allows some other video to overtake the spot as the most popular clone? Section 6 takes a closer look at some influences that can cause such overtakings.

5.3 Video Discovery and Featuring

We now examine the roles that video discovery and featuring mechanisms may play in the observed rich-get-richer preferential selection behavior. Aspects such as featuring on YouTube, ranking of a video in YouTube search, and embedding of a video on external sites, are difficult to capture over time. Nonetheless, the "video referrers" part of the YouTube

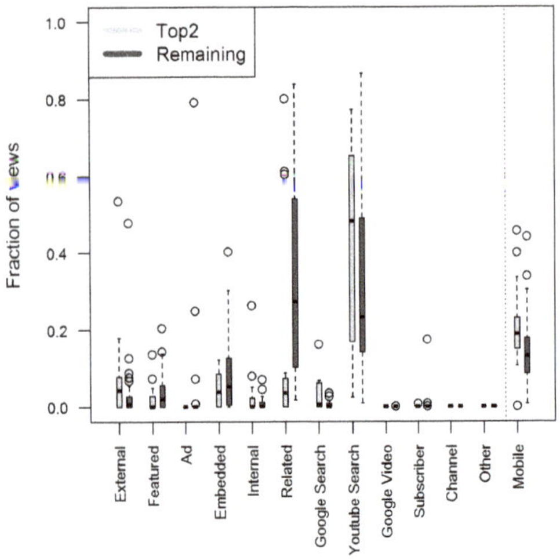

Figure 4: Boxplot of the average fraction of views (per clone-set) coming through different referrer categories.

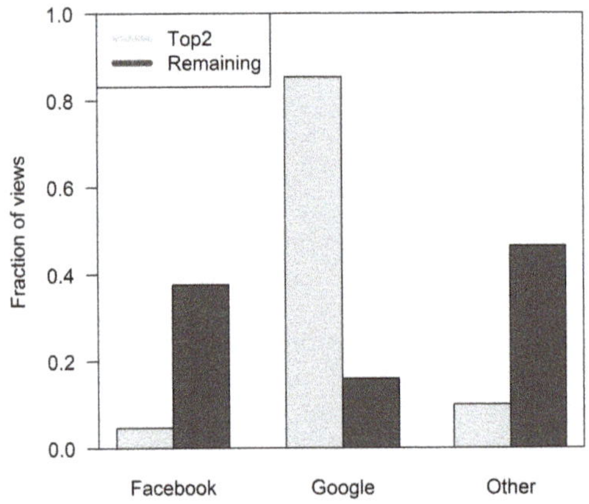

Figure 5: The fraction of views coming through external sources, for clones that are externally linked.

insight data provides (for some videos) additional information necessary for our analyses. The results presented here are based on analysis of clone sets that have multiple videos with insight data. We use YouTube's classification of registered referrers.

We first consider how the most popular videos within each clone set have obtained their views, compared to their less popular counterparts. Figure 4 compares the average fraction of views coming through different referrer types for the most popular clones, with that of the remaining clones.[2]

The results are somewhat counter-intuitive. Notice that the "Top 2" most popular videos are not necessarily the videos that are prominently featured or externally linked. Instead, the search discovery method alone accounts for most of the difference. For example, for the search referrer category, the median of the top clones is almost equal to the 90th quartile of the remaining videos. The less successful clones get most of their views through related (video) referrals.

Figure 5 shows the fraction of views coming through external referrers only (not including embeds). Note that Google is shown as an external source of traffic and it is driving most of the external views of the popular clones. Google is considered an external referrer because views may come from a number of Google non-search services such as Google News, Google Reader, and Google Group posts.

Overall, the highest fraction of clicks to a video is coming through the search referrers. As all videos can potentially be found through search, but not all videos are featured or embedded on external websites, we take a closer look at these referrers. Figures 6(a) and 6(b) show the corresponding boxplots of the fraction of views coming through different referrer types for only the clones that are featured and externally linked, respectively. The same conclusion applies to these data subsets. Search referrers are the most powerful in terms of the percentage of traffic they bring. Further, the biggest differences between successful and less successful videos can be seen in the fraction of views owing to search and mobile referrers.

Recall that we are considering multiple videos containing essentially the same content, and this allows us to remove biases introduced because of differences in content (e.g., popular content is more likely to be searched than non-popular content). Our results suggest that successful videos are much more prominently selected through searches. This could occur because of YouTube's internal search mechanism, the keywords associated with the videos, the keywords entered by the users, user biases when selecting among search results, or a combination thereof. For example, people may be more likely to pick the first search results than pick items lower down on the list, or to pick videos with higher view counts (visible to the user at the time of selection) [8].

As previously discussed, the first mover advantage can be important for the success of a video. In addition to being uploaded, it is important that the video is discovered and/or made available through different paths. Using correlation analysis, we have observed that there is often a significant positive correlation between the total view count and the order in which clones are first referred, featured, or accessed through mobile devices. While omitted, these results suggest that there also is a *first-discovery advantage*, where videos discovered earlier through internal search methods, featured earlier, or that are accessed through mobiles earlier, tend to be ranked higher.

6. FACTORS IMPACTING INITIAL POPULARITY

This section considers factors impacting the view count early in a video's life, which in turns impact the overall video popularity due to the rich-get-richer behavior, as shown in the previous section.

6.1 Uploader Characteristics

We analyzed the YouTube social network size of the uploaders observed in our dataset. In general, uploaders of top-ranked videos have large social networks. Furthermore, manual examination of the top uploaders confirmed that they are often commercial entities. Usually commercial uploaders are the "first-movers". In fact, even when they were not, it appears that their videos often manage to move ahead in popularity. Figure 7 shows an example clone set where

[2]We present the mobile referrers separately as it is not a source of discovery per se, but it nevertheless impacts discoverability, as more users are accessing videos exclusively through mobile devices.

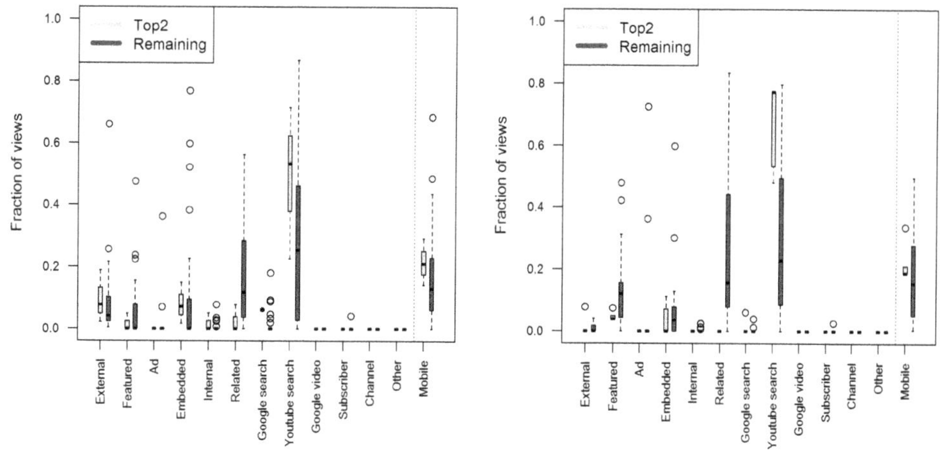

(a) Externally linked clones (b) Featured clones

Figure 6: Boxplot of the fraction of views of clones externally linked and featured, coming through different referrer categories.

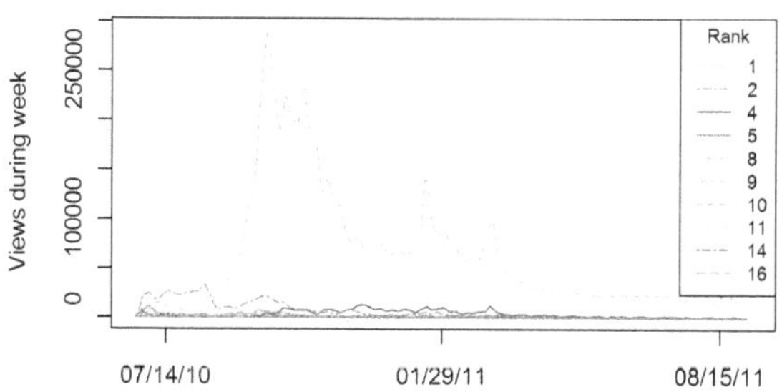

Figure 7: The weekly views for a number of example videos in clone set 14 (18 clones).

	Aggregate				Content-based			
Predictor / Age	1d	3d	7d	14d	1d	3d	7d	14d
View count	0.44	0.42	0.50	0.55	0.60	0.59	0.66	0.70
Video quality	0.08				0.35			
Number of keywords	0.04				0.36			
Uploader view count	0.41				0.64			
Uploader followers	0.40				0.58			
Uploader contacts	0.19				0.42			
Uploader video count	0.08				0.38			
Uploader age	0.02				0.35			

Table 6: Age effect on R^2 values when taking into account clone set identity (content-based) and when not (aggregate).

a commercial user (video with rank 1) catches up and surpasses a private uploader (video with rank 2) even though the former was not the first uploader. This is a typical example of the impact of uploader characteristics on the popularity.

6.2 Age-based Analysis

While the total view count can be an important factor when predicting a video's future popularity, it is less useful for young videos and not useful at all for a newly uploaded video which starts with a view count of zero. For such videos, other predictors such as the size of the uploader social network and the prior success of the uploader may be important, as seen in Section 6.1 and in our PCA analysis in Section 3. We now perform an age-based regression analysis to determine how the relative importance of the total view count changes with time, relative to these more static factors.

Table 6 shows the coefficient of determination R^2 between the predictors in the first two weeks since a video's upload and the total view count at the half-year point since upload. We calculate the total view count of videos at 1 day, 3 days, 1 week, 2 weeks, and half a year using the historical view statistics. Linear interpolation is needed to calculate the approximate total view count at specific time thresholds, as the data provides only 100 points, equally spaced through the video's lifetime. The file-related information and the uploader characteristics properties are assumed constant. The first four columns show results for the aggregate set of videos and the last four columns show results when clone set identity is accounted for.

These results show that the total view count quickly becomes the strongest predictor of the view count at the half-year point. The results also confirm that during the early stages of a video's lifetime, the uploader's social network is a more significant factor than the total view count. Indeed, already at upload, approximately 64% of the variation in views can be explained by the uploader view count alone, and it takes a week for the total view count to become a similar or better predictor than the uploader social network. The impact of the uploader characteristics are significant in the beginning, probably because an established social network is a source of initial views from subscribers.

Finally, we note that some factors have much more impact when the influence of the content is considered through the clone set identity factor. For instance, factors such as the number of keywords and the video quality, have a great impact in the early stages of a video's lifetime. The keyword metric, although appearing to be insignificant in the aggregate analysis, is an important factor when a video is first uploaded, explaining up to 36% of the variation in views. This may suggest that keywords in fact may be one of the main factors in helping find the video in the first place (when competing against videos with the same content). The more targeted keywords a video has, the greater the probability that it will be discovered after its upload.

7. RELATED WORK

To the best of our knowledge, no prior work has separated out the impacts of content-related and content-agnostic factors on video popularity. However, there has been considerable prior work concerning measurements, analyses of these measurements, and/or models, for various user-generated video properties including popularity.

Many prior works have analyzed different aspects of user-generated video metrics such as total views, total ratings, total comments, and uploader social network size (e.g., see [3, 4, 7]). For instance, Mitra et al. [7] compared four video sharing workloads and established the presence of "invariants" among their characteristics, such as heavy-tailed total view count distributions and positive correlation between total views and total ratings to a video.

Cha et al. [3] postulated that heavy-tailed view counts can be explained by combining a "rich-get-richer" model [2] with a limited fetch model. Szabo and Huberman [9] found that the total views received soon after a video is uploaded provides a strong indication of its total future view count; they leveraged this observation to develop a prediction model for video views. More recently, Borghol et al. [10] empirically demonstrated that individual video popularity is highly unstable and unpredictable, and proposed a model for how the popularity statistics of a collection of recently-uploaded videos evolve over time, instead of considering popularity evolution for individual videos.

YouTube's internal search and recommendation engines have been noted to be an important source of video views [5, 12]. For instance, Zhou et al. [12] observed strong correlation between the total view count of a video and the view count of its "related" videos. Similarly, Figueiredo et al. [5] noted that search and other internal mechanisms are the most important sources of views for Youtube videos. Our work is complementary to these as we have also sought to understand factors influencing video popularity, but unlike these prior works we are able to study the significance and impact of content-agnostic factors while controlling for differences in video content.

Cha et al. [3] noted the presence of YouTube video clones which they referred to as "aliases". They observe that aliases tends to "dilute" popularity, as the views for the same content are spread out over several videos. The authors did not use aliases to study how different factors influence content popularity, as we have done in our work.

8. CONCLUSIONS

Video sharing services provide a convenient platform for widespread dissemination of content. Every day, millions of videos are uploaded and there are billions of videos viewed for YouTube alone. Over time, some videos reach iconic status, while many others are simply forgotten.

Our first contribution is a methodology that is able to accurately assess the impact various content-agnostic factors have on popularity. We identify and collect a large dataset that consists of multiple near-identical copies (called clones) of a range of different content; we make this dataset available to the research community. We then develop a rigorous analysis framework, which allows us to control bias introduced when studying videos that do not have the same content.

Using our clone-based methodology, we provide several findings. First, we show that inaccurate conclusions may be drawn when not controlling for video content. Second, controlling for video content, we observe scale-free rich-get-richer behavior, with view count being the most important factor except for very young videos. Third, we find that while the total view count is the strongest predictor, other content-agnostic factors can help explain various other aspects of the popularity dynamics. For example, the uploader's social network can be a good predictor for newly uploaded videos. Finally, we present concrete evidence of the first-mover advantage where early uploaders have an edge over later uploaders of the same content.

While this paper considers video popularity, we note that the methodology presented and employed may be applicable to other domains and research questions. For example, a popular news story will result in many "clones" disseminated through different forums. The relative popularity of each such clone will depend on content-agnostic factors such as age, previous popularity, and publisher. Text-based content raises some interesting new methodological issues, as it may permit a more objective definition of "clone". Such studies are left for future work.

9. ACKNOWLEDGEMENTS

The authors are grateful to Shahriar Kaisar for his work on the data collection. This work was supported by National ICT Australia (NICTA), the Natural Sciences and Engineering Research Council (NSERC) of Canada, and CENIIT at Linköping University.

10. REFERENCES

[1] A. Allen. *Probability, Statistics, and Queuing Theory with Computer Science Applications.* Academic Press, 1990.

[2] A. Barabási and R. Albert. Emergence of Scaling in Random Networks. *Science*, 286:509–512, October 1999.

[3] M. Cha, H. Kwak, P. Rodriguez, Y. Ahn, and S. Moon. Analyzing the Video Popularity Characteristics of Large-Scale User Generated Content Systems. *ACM/IEEE Transactions on Networking*, 17(5):1357–1370, October 2009.

[4] X. Cheng, C. Dale, and J. Lui. Statistics and Social Network of YouTube Videos. In *Proc. International Workshop on Quality of Service (IWQoS)*, pages 229 – 238, Enskede, The Netherlands, June 2008.

[5] F. Figueiredo, F. Benevenuto, and J. M. Almeida. The Tube over Time: Characterizing Popularity Growth of YouTube Videos. In *Proc. ACM International Conference on Web Search and Data Mining (WSDM)*, pages 745–754, Hong Kong, China, February 2011.

[6] P. Gill, M. Arlitt, Z. Li, and A. Mahanti. YouTube Traffic Characterization: A View from the Edge. In *Proc. ACM Internet Measurement Conference (IMC)*, pages 15–28, San Deigo, CA, October 2007.

[7] S. Mitra, M. Agrawal, A. Yadav, N. Carlsson, D. Eager, and A. Mahanti. Characterizing Web-based Video Sharing Workloads. *ACM Transactions on the Web*, (2):8:1–8:27, May 2011.

[8] M. J. Salganik and D. Watts. Leading the Herd Astray: An Experimental Study of Self-fulfilling Prophecies in an Artificial Cultural Market. *Social Psychology Quarterly*, 71:338–355, December 2008.

[9] G. Szabo and B. A. Huberman. Predicting the Popularity of Online Content. *Commun. ACM*, 53(8):80–88, August 2010.

[10] Y. Borghol and S. Mitra and S. Ardon and N. Carlsson and D. Eager and A. Mahanti. Characterizing and Modelling Popularity of User-generated Videos. *Performance Evaluation*, 68(11):1037 – 1055, November 2011.

[11] YouTube. http://code.google.com/apis/youtube/overview.html.

[12] R. Zhou, S. Khemmarat, and L. Gao. The Impact of YouTube Recommendation System on Video Views. In *Proc. ACM Internet Measurement Conference (IMC)*, pages 404–410, Melbourne, Australia, November 2010.

[13] M. Zink, K. Suh, and J. Kurose. Watch Global, Cache Local: YouTube Network Traffic at a Campus Network - Measurements and Implications. In *Proc. SPIE Multimedia Computing and Networking (MMCN) Conference*, San Jose, CA, January 2008.

SHALE: An Efficient Algorithm for Allocation of Guaranteed Display Advertising

Vijay Bharadwaj
Netflix
bharadwaj.vijay@gmail.com

Peiji Chen
Yahoo! Labs
peiji@yahoo-inc.com

Wenjing Ma
Yahoo! Labs
wenjingm@yahoo-inc.com

Chandrashekhar Nagarajan
Yahoo! Labs
i.amchandra@yahoo.com

John Tomlin
opTomax Solutions
johntomlin@acm.org

Sergei Vassilvitskii
Google
sergei@cs.stanford.edu

Erik Vee
Facebook
erikvee@fb.com

Jian Yang
Yahoo! Labs
jianyang@yahoo-inc.com

ABSTRACT

Motivated by the problem of optimizing allocation in guaranteed display advertising, we develop an efficient, lightweight method of generating a compact *allocation plan* that can be used to guide ad server decisions. The plan itself uses just $O(1)$ state per guaranteed contract, is robust to noise, and allows us to serve (provably) nearly optimally. The optimization method we develop is scalable, with a small in-memory footprint, and working in linear time per iteration. It is also "stop-anytime," meaning that time-critical applications can stop early and still get a good serving solution. Thus, it is particularly useful for optimizing the large problems arising in the context of display advertising. We demonstrate the effectiveness of our algorithm using actual Yahoo! data.

Categories and Subject Descriptors

I.0 [**Computing Methodologies**]: General

General Terms

Algorithms, Experimentation

Keywords

Display Advertising, Online Advertising

1. INTRODUCTION

A key problem in display advertising is how to efficiently serve in some (nearly) optimal way. As internet publishers and advertisers become increasingly sophisticated, it is not enough to simply make serving choices "correctly" or "acceptably". Improving objective goals by just a few percent can often improve revenue by tens of millions of dollars for publishers, as well as improving advertiser or user experience. Serving needs to be done in such a way that we maximize the potential for users, advertisers, and publishers.

In this paper, we address serving display advertising in the guaranteed display marketplace, providing a lightweight optimization framework that allows real servers to allocate ads efficiently and with little overhead. Recall that in guaranteed display advertising, advertisers may target particular types of users visiting particular types of sites over a specified time period. Publishers guarantee to serve their ad some promised number of times to users matching the advertiser's criteria over the specified duration. We refer to this as a *contract*.

In [7], the authors show that given a forecast of future inventory, it is possible to create an optimal *allocation plan*, which consists of labeling each contract with just $O(1)$ additional information. Since it is so compact, this allocation plan can efficiently be communicated to ad servers. It requires no online state, which removes the need for maintaining immediately accessible impression counts. (An *impression* is generated whenever there is an opportunity to display an ad somewhere on a web page for a user.) Given the plan, each ad server can easily decide which ad to serve each impression, even when the impression is one that the forecast never predicted. The delivery produced by following the plan is nearly optimal. Note that simply using an optimizer to find an optimal allocation of contracts to impressions would not produce such a result, since the solution is too large and does not generalize to unpredicted outputs.

The method to generate the allocation plan outlined in [7] relies on the ability to solve large, non-linear optimization problems; it takes as input a bipartite graph representing the set of contracts and a sample of predicted user visits, which can have hundreds of millions of arcs or more. There are commercially available solvers that can be used to create allocation plans. However, they have several drawbacks. The most prominent of these is that such solvers aim towards finding good primal solutions, while the allocation plan generated is not directly tied to the quality of such solutions. (The allocation plan relies on the dual solution of the problem.) In particular, there is no guarantee of how close to optimal the allocation plan really is. Hence, although creating a good allocation plan is

KDD'12, August 12–16, 2012, Beijing, China.

time critical, stopping the optimizer early with sub-optimal values can have undesirable effects for serving.

For our particular problem, the graph we wish to optimize is extremely large and scalability becomes a real concern. For this reason, and given the other disadvantages of using complex third party software, we propose a new solution, called 'SHALE.' It addresses all of these concerns, having many desirable properties:

- It has the "stop anytime" property. That is, after completing any iteration, we can stop SHALE and produce a good answer.

- It is a multi-pass streaming algorithm. Each iteration of SHALE runs as a streaming algorithm, reading the arcs off disk one at a time. The total online memory is proportional to the number of contracts and samples used, and is independent of the number of edges in the graph. Because of this, it is possible to handle inputs that are prohibitively large for many commercial solvers without special modifications.

- It is guaranteed to converge to the true optimal solution if it runs for enough iterations. It is robust to sampling, so the input can be generated by sampling rather than using a full input.

- Each contract is annotated with just $O(1)$ information, which can be used to produce nearly optimal serving. Thus, the solution generated creates a practical allocation plan, useable in real serving systems.

The SHALE solver uses the idea of [7] as a starting point, but it provides an additional twist that allows the solver to stop after any number of iterations and still produce a good allocation plan. For this reason, SHALE is often five times faster than solving the full problem using a commercial solver.

1.1 Related Work

The allocation problem facing a display advertising publisher has been the subject of increased attention in the past few years. Often modeled as a special version of a stochastic optimization, several theoretical solutions have been developed [4, 6]. A similar formulation of the problem was done by Devanur and Hayes [2],who added an assumption that user arrivals are drawn independently and identically from some distribution, and then proceed to develop allocation plans based on the learned distribution. In contrast, Vee et al. [7] did not assume independence of arrivals, but require the knowledge of the user distributions to formulate the optimization problem.

Bridging the gap between theory and practice, Feldman et al. [3] demonstrated that primal-dual methods can be effective for solving the allocation problem. However, it is not clear how to scale their algorithm to instances on billions of nodes and tens of billions of edges. A different approach was given by Chen et al. [1] who used the *structure* of the allocation problem to develop control theory based methods to guide the online allocation and mitigate the impact of potential forecast errors.

Finally, a crucial piece of all of the above allocation problems is the underlying optimization function. Ghosh et al [5] define representative allocations, which minimize the average ℓ_2^2 distance between an allocation given to a specific advertiser, and the ideal one which allocates every eligible impression with equal probability. Feldman et al. [3] define a similar notion of *fair* allocations, which attempt to minimize an ℓ_1 distance between the achieved allocation and a similarly defined ideal.

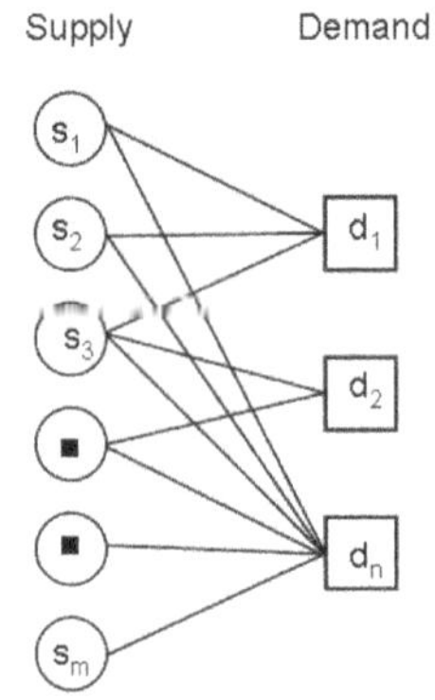

Figure 1: Example bipartite graph

2. PROBLEM STATEMENT

In this section, we begin by defining the notion of an optimal allocation of ads to users/impressions (Section 2.1). Our goal will then be to serve as close as possible to this optimal allocation. In Section 2.2, we describe the notion of generating an allocation plan, which will be used to produce nearly optimal serving.

2.1 Optimal Allocation

In guaranteed display advertising, we have a large number of forecast impressions together with a number of contracts. These contracts specify a *demand* as well as a target; we must deliver a number of impressions at least as large as the specified demand, and further, each impression must match the target specified by the contract. We model this as a bipartite graph. On one side are *supply nodes*, representing impressions. On the other side are *demand nodes*, representing contracts. We add an arc from a given supply node to a given demand node if and only if the impression that the supply node represents is *eligible* (i.e. matches the target profile) for the contract represented by the demand node. Further, demand nodes are labeled with a *demand*, which is precisely the amount of impressions guaranteed to the represented contract. In general, supply nodes will represent several impressions each, thus each supply node is labeled with a weight s_i, leading to a weighted graph (see [7] for more details). Figure 1 shows a simple example.

An optimal allocation must both be feasible and minimize some objective function. Here, our objective balances two goals: minimizing penalty, and maximizing *representativeness*. Each demand node/contract j has an associated penalty, p_j. Let u_j be the *under-delivery*, i.e. the number of impressions delivered less than d_j. Then our total penalty is $\sum_j p_j u_j$.

Representativeness is a measure of how close our allocation is to some target. For each impression i and contract j, we define a target, θ_{ij}. In this paper, we set $\theta_{ij} = d_j/S_j$, where $S_j = \sum_{i \in \Gamma(j)} s_i$, the total eligible supply for contract j. This has the effect of aiming for an equal mix of all possible matching impressions. (Here, $\Gamma(j)$ is the neighborhood of j, likewise, we denote the neighborhood of i by $\Gamma(i)$.) The non-representativeness for contract j is the weighted L_2 distance from the target θ_{ij} and the proposed allocation, x_{ij}. Specifically,

$$\frac{1}{2} \sum_{i \in \Gamma(j)} s_i \frac{V_j}{\theta_{ij}} (x_{ij} - \theta_{ij})^2,$$

where V_j is the relative priority of the contract j; a larger V_j means that representativeness is more important. Notice that we weight by s_i to account for the fact that some sample impressions have more weight than others. Representativeness is key for advertiser satisfaction. Simply giving an advertiser the least desirable type of users (say, three-year-olds with a history of not spending money) or attempting to serve out an entire contract in a few hours decreases long-term revenue by driving advertisers away. See [5] for more discussion on this idea.

Given these goals, we may write our optimal allocation in terms of a convex optimization problem:

$$\begin{aligned} \text{Minimize} \quad & \tfrac{1}{2}\textstyle\sum_{j,i\in\Gamma(j)} s_i \frac{V_j}{\theta_{ij}}(x_{ij}-\theta_{ij})^2 + \sum_j p_j u_j & & \\ \text{s.t.} \quad & \textstyle\sum_{i\in\Gamma(j)} s_i x_{ij} + u_j \ge d_j & \forall j \quad & (1) \\ & \textstyle\sum_{j\in\Gamma(i)} x_{ij} \le 1 & \forall i \quad & (2) \\ & x_{ij}, u_j \ge 0 & \forall i,j \quad & (3) \end{aligned}$$

Constraints 1 are called *demand constraints*. They guarantee that u_j precisely represents the total underdelivery to contract j. Constraints 2 are *supply constraints*, and they specify that we serve no more than one ad for each impression. Constraints 3 are simply *non-negativity constraints*.

The *optimal allocation* for the guaranteed display ad problem is the solution to the above problem, where the input bipartite graph represents the full set of contracts and the *full set of impressions!* Of course, generating the full set of impressions is impossible in practice. The work of [7] shows that using a sample of impressions still produces an approximately optimal fractional allocation. We interpret the fractions as the *probabilities* that a given impression should be allocated to a given contract. Since there are billions of impressions, this leads to serving that is nearly identical.

Although this paper focuses on the above problem, we note that our techniques can be extended to more general objectives. For example, in related work, [8] described a multi-objective model for the allocation of inventory to guaranteed delivery, which combined penalties and representativeness (as above) with revenue made on the non-guaranteed display (NGD) spot market and the potential revenue gained from supplying clicks to contracts. SHALE can easily be extended to handle these variants.

2.2 Compact Serving

In the previous subsection, we defined the notion of optimal allocation. However, serving such an allocation is itself a different problem. Following [7], we define the problem of online serving with forecasts as follows.

We are given as input a bipartite graph, as described in the previous subsection. (We assume this graph is an approximation of the future inventory, although it is not necessary for this definition.) We proceed in two phases.

- **Offline Phase**: Given the bipartite graph as input, we must annotate each demand node (corresponding to a contract) with $O(1)$ information. This information will guide the allocation during the online phase.

- **Online Phase**: During the online phase, impressions arrive one at a time. For each impression, we are given the set of eligible contracts, together with the annotation computed during the offline phase of each returned contract. Using only this information, we must decide which contract to serve to the impression.

The *online allocation* is the actual allocation of impressions to contracts given during the online phase. Our goal is to produce an online allocation that is as close to optimal as possible.

Remarkably, the work of [1] shows that there is an algorithm that solves the above problem nearly optimally. If the input bipartite graph exactly models the future impressions, then the online allocation produced is optimal. If the input bipartite graph is generated by sampling from the future, then the online allocation produced is provably approximately optimal.

However, the previous work simply assumed that an optimal solution can be found during the Offline Phase. Although this is true, it does not address many of the practical concerns that come with solving large-scale non-linear optimization problems. In the following sections, we describe our solution, which in addition to solving the problem of compact serving, is fast, simple, and robust.

3. ALGORITHMS

3.1 Plan creation using full solution

The proposal of [7] to create an allocation plan was to solve the problem of Section 2.1 using standard methods. From this, we can compute the *duals* of the problem. In particular, we may write the problem in terms of its Lagrangian (more formally, we use the KKT conditions). Every constraint then has a corresponding dual variable. (Intuitively, the harder a constraint is to satisfy, the larger its dual variable in the optimal solution.)

The allocation plan then consists of the demand duals of the problem, denoted α. So each contract j was labeled with the demand dual from the corresponding demand constraint, α_j. The supply duals, denoted β, and the non-negativity duals were simply thrown out.

A key insight of this earlier work is that we can reconstruct the optimal solution using only the α values. When impression i arrives, the value of β_i can be found online by solving the equation $\sum_{j\in\Gamma(i)} g_{ij}(\alpha_j - \beta_i) = 1$, resetting $\beta_i = 0$ if the solution is less than 0. Here, $g_{ij}(z) = \max\{0, \theta_{ij}(1 + z/V_j)\}$. We then set $x_{ij} = g_{ij}(\alpha_j - \beta_i)$ for each $j \in \Gamma(i)$. Somewhat surprisingly, this yields an optimal allocation. (And when the value of α is obtained by solving a sampled problem, it is approximately optimal.)

As mentioned in the introduction, although this solution has many nice properties, solving the optimization problem using standard methods is slower than desirable. Thus, we have a need for faster methods.

3.2 Greedy solution (HWM)

An alternate approach to solving the allocation problem is the *High Water Mark* (HWM) algorithm, based on a greedy heuristic. This method first orders all the contracts by their *allocation order*. Here, the allocation order puts contracts with smaller S_j (i.e. total eligible supply) before contracts with larger S_j. Then, the algorithm goes through each contract one after another, trying to allocate an equal fraction from all the eligible ad opportunities. This fraction is denoted ζ for each contract, and corresponds roughly to its demand dual. Contract j is given fraction ζ_j from each eligible impression, *unless* previous contracts have taken more than a $1-\zeta_j$ fraction already. In this case, contract j gets whatever fraction is left (possibly 0).

If there is very little contention (or contract j comes early in the allocation order), then $\zeta_j = d_j/S_j$. This will give exactly the right amount of inventory to contract j. However, if a lot of inventory has already been allocated when j is processed, its ζ_j value may be larger than this to accommodate the fact that it gets less than ζ_j for some impressions. Setting $\zeta = 1$ will give a contract all inventory that has not already been allocated. We do this in the case that there is not enough remaining inventory to satisfy the demand of j.

The pseudo-code is summarized as follows.

1. Order all demand nodes in decreasing contention order (d_j/S_j).
2. For each supply node i, initialize the available weight $\tilde{s_i} = s_i$.
3. For each demand node j, in allocation order:
   (a) Find ζ_j such that
   $$\sum_{i \in B_j} \min\{\tilde{s_i}, \zeta_j s_i\} = d_j,$$
   setting $\zeta_j = \infty$ if the above has no solution.
   (b) For each matching supply nodes $i \in B_j$
   Update $\tilde{s_i} = \tilde{s_i} - \min\{\tilde{s_i}, \zeta_j s_i\}$.

We note that the computation in Step 3a can be done in time linear in the size of $|B_j|$. Hence, the total runtime of the HWM algorithm is linear in the number of arcs in the graph.

3.3 SHALE

Obtaining a full solution using traditional methods is too slow (and more precise than needed), while the HWM heuristic, although very fast, sacrifices optimality. SHALE is a method that spans the two approaches. If it runs for enough iterations, it produces the true optimal solution. Running it for 0 iterations (plus an additional step at the end) produces the HWM allocation. So we can easily balance precision with running time. In our experience (see Section 4), just 10 or 20 iterations of SHALE yield remarkably good results; for serving, even using 5 iterations works quite well since forecast errors and other issues generally dwarf small variations in the solution. Further, SHALE is amenable to "warm-starts," using the previous allocation plan as a starting point. In this case, it is even better.

SHALE is based on the solution using optimal duals. The key innovation, however, is the ability to take *any* dual solution and convert it into a good primal solution. We do this by extending the simple heuristic HWM to incorporate dual values. Thus, the SHALE algorithm has two pieces. The first piece finds reasonable duals. This piece is an iterative algorithm. On each iteration, the dual solution will generally improve. (And repeated iterations converge to the true optimal.) The second piece converts the reasonable set of duals we found (more precisely, the α values, as described earlier) into a good primal solution.

The optimization for SHALE relies heavily on the machinery provided by the KKT conditions. Interested readers may find a more detailed discussion in the Appendix. Here, we note the following. If α^* and β^* are optimal dual values, then

1. The optimal primal solution is given by $x^*_{ij} = g_{ij}(\alpha^*_j - \beta^*_i)$, where $g_{ij}(z) = \max\{0, \theta_{ij}(1 + z/V_j)\}$.
2. For all j, $0 \leq \alpha^*_j \leq p_j$. Further, either $\alpha^*_j = p_j$ or $\sum_{i \in \Gamma(j)} s_i x^*_{ij} = d_j$.
3. For all i, $\beta_i \geq 0$. Further, either $\beta_i = 0$ or $\sum_{j \in \Gamma(i)} x^*_{ij} = 1$.

The pseudo-code for SHALE is shown below.

- **Initialize**. Set $\alpha_j = 0$ for all j.
- **Stage One**. Repeat until we run out of time:
  1. For each impression i, find β_i that satisfies
  $$\sum_{j \in \Gamma(i)} g_{ij}(\alpha_j - \beta_i) = 1$$
  If $\beta_i < 0$ or no solution exists, update $\beta_i = 0$.
  2. For each contract j, find α_j that satisfies
  $$\sum_{i \in \Gamma(j)} s_i g_{ij}(\alpha_j - \beta_i) = d_j$$
  If $\alpha_j > p_j$ or no solution exists, update $\alpha_j = p_j$.
- **Stage Two**.
  1. Initialize $\tilde{s}_i = 1$ for all i.
  2. For each impression i, find β_i that satisfies
  $$\sum_{j \in \Gamma(i)} g_{ij}(\alpha_j - \beta_i) = 1$$
  If $\beta_i < 0$ or no solution exists, update $\beta_i = 0$.
  3. For each contract j, in allocation order, do:
     (a) Find ζ_j that satisfies
     $$\sum_{i \in \Gamma(j)} \min\{\tilde{s}_i, s_i g_{ij}(\zeta_j - \beta_i)\} = d_j,$$
     setting $\zeta_j = \infty$ if there is no solution.
     (b) For each impression i eligible for j, update $\tilde{s}_i = \tilde{s}_i - \min\{\tilde{s}_i, s_i g_{ij}(\zeta_j - \beta_i)\}$.
- **Output** The α_j and ζ_j values for each j.

Our implementation of SHALE runs in linear time (in the number of arcs in the input graph) per iteration.

During Stage One, we iteratively improve the α values by assuming that the β values are correct and solving the equation for α. Recall that $x_{ij} = g_{ij}(\alpha_j - \beta_i)$. Thus, we are simply solving the equation $\sum_{i \in \Gamma(j)} s_i x_{ij} = d_j$ for α_j. In order to find better β values, we assume the α is correct and solve for β using $\sum_{j \in \Gamma(i)} x_{ij} = 1$. The following theorem shows that this simple iterative technique converges, and yields an ε approximation in polynomial steps.

More precisely, define $d_j(\alpha) = \sum_{i \in \Gamma(j)} s_i g_{ij}(\alpha_j - \beta_i)$, where β is determined as in Step 1 of Stage One of SHALE. (We think of this as the projected delivery for contract j using only Stage One of SHALE.) We say a given α solution produces an *ε-approximate delivery* if for all j, either $\alpha_j = p_j$ or $d_j(\alpha) \geq (1 - \varepsilon)d_j$. Note that an optimal α_j is at most p_j; the intuitive reason for this is that growing α_j any larger will cause the non-representativeness of the contract's delivery to be even more costly than the under-delivery penalty. Thus, an ε-approximate delivery means that every contract is projected to deliver within ε of the desired amount, or its α_j is "maxed-out."

We can now state our theorem. Its proof is in the appendix.

THEOREM 1. *Stage One of SHALE converges to the optimal solution of the guaranteed display allocation problem. Further, let $\varepsilon > 0$. Then within $\frac{1}{\varepsilon} n \max_j\{p_j/V_j\}$ iterations, the output α produces an ε-approximate delivery.*

Note that Stage One is effectively a form of coordinate descent. In general, it could be replaced with any standard optimization technique that allows us to recover a set of approximate dual values. However, the form we use is simple to understand, use, and debug. Further, it works very well in practice.

In Stage Two, we calculate ζ values in a way similar to HWM. We calculate β values based on the α values generated from Stage One. Using these, we calculate ζ values to give d_j allocation (if possible) to each contract. Notice that in Stage Two, we must be cognizant of the actual allocation. Thus, we maintain a remaining fraction left, $\tilde{s}_i$, that we cannot exceed. Thus, contracts allocated latest may not be able to get the full amount specified by g_{ij}, if the fraction taken from impression i is too great.

We note that in our actual implementation, we use a two-pass version of Stage Two. In the first pass, we bound ζ_j by α_j for each j. In the second pass, we find a second set of ζ values (with no upper bounds), utilizing any left-over inventory. This is somewhat "truer" to the allocation produced by SHALE in Stage One, and gives slightly better online allocation.

3.3.1 *Online Serving with SHALE*

Recall that SHALE produces two values for each contract j, namely α_j and ζ_j. Given impression i, the α values for eligible contracts are used to calculate the β_i value, which is used together with the ζ values to produce the allocation. The pseudo-code is below.

Input: Impression i and the set of eligible contracts.

1. Set $\tilde{s}_i = 1$ and find β_i such that
$$\sum_{j \in \Gamma(i)} g_{ij}(\alpha_j - \beta_i) = 1$$
If $\beta_i < 0$ or no solution exists, set $\beta_i = 0$.
2. For each matching contract j, in allocation order, compute $x_{ij} = \min\{\tilde{s}_i, g_{ij}(\zeta_i - \beta_i)\}$ and update $\tilde{s}_i \leftarrow \tilde{s}_i - x_{ij}$.
3. Select contract j with probability x_{ij}. (If $\sum_{j\Gamma(i)} x_{ij} < 1$, then there is some chance that no contract is selected.)

4. EXPERIMENTS

We have implemented both the HWM and SHALE algorithms described in Section 3 and benchmarked their performance against the full solution approach (known hereafter as XPRESS) on historical booked contract sets. First we describe these datasets and our chosen performance metrics and then present our evaluation results.

4.1 Experimental setup

In order to test the "real-world" performance of all three algorithms we considered 6 sets of real GD contracts booked and active in the recent past. In particular, we chose three periods of time as described in Table 1 and two ad positions LREC and SKY for each of these time periods.

Contracts Booked before	Contracts Active between
11/16/09	11/16/09 - 11/30/09
01/03/10	01/03/10 - 01/17/10
04/13/10	04/13/10 - 04/20/10

Table 1: Contract Time Periods

We considered US region contracts booked to the aforementioned positions and time periods and also excluded all frequency capped contracts and all contracts with time-of-day and other custom targets. Also, all remaining contracts that were active for longer than the specified date ranges were truncated and their demands were proportionally reduced. Next, we generated a bipartite graph for each contract set as in Figure 1; by sampling 50 eligible impressions for each contract in the set. This sampling procedure is described in detail in [7]. We then ran HWM, SHALE and XPRESS on each of the 6 graphs and evaluated the following metrics.

1. **Under-delivery Rate** : This represents the total under-delivered impressions as a proportion of the booked demand, i.e.,
$$U = \frac{\sum_j u_j}{\sum_j d_j} \tag{4}$$
2. **Penalty Cost** : This represents the penalty incurred by the publisher for failing to deliver the guaranteed number of impressions to booked GD contracts. Note that the true long-term penalty due to under-delivery is not known since we cannot easily forecast how an advertiser's future business with the publisher will change due to under-delivery on a booked contract. Here we define the total penalty cost to be
$$P = \sum_j p_j u_j \tag{5}$$
where u_j is the number of under-delivered impressions to contract j and p_j is the cost for each under-delivered impression. For our experiments, we set p_j to be $p_j = 0.005 + q_j$ where q_j is the revenue per delivered impression from contract j. Indeed, it is intuitive and reasonable to expect that contracts that are more valuable to the advertiser incur larger penalties for under-delivery. The offset (here $\$5CPM$) serves to ensure that our algorithms attempt to fully deliver even the contracts with low booking prices.
3. **L2 Distance** : This metric shows how much the generated allocation deviates from a desired allocation (for example a perfectly representative one). In particular, the L2 distance is the non-representativeness function $\frac{1}{2}\sum_{i \in \Gamma(j)} s_i \frac{V_j}{\theta_{ij}}(x_{ij} - \theta_{ij})^2$, the first term of the objective function in Section 2, corresponding to the weighted ℓ_2^2 distance between target and allocation.

4.2 Experiment 1

As we mentioned earlier, SHALE was designed to provide a trade-off between the speed of execution of HWM and the quality of solutions output by XPRESS. Accordingly in our first experiment we measured the performance of SHALE (run for 0, 5, 10, 20 and 50 iterations) as compared to XPRESS against our chosen metrics. Since SHALE at 0 iterations is the same as HWM, we label it as such. Figure 2 shows the penalty cost, under-delivery rate, L2

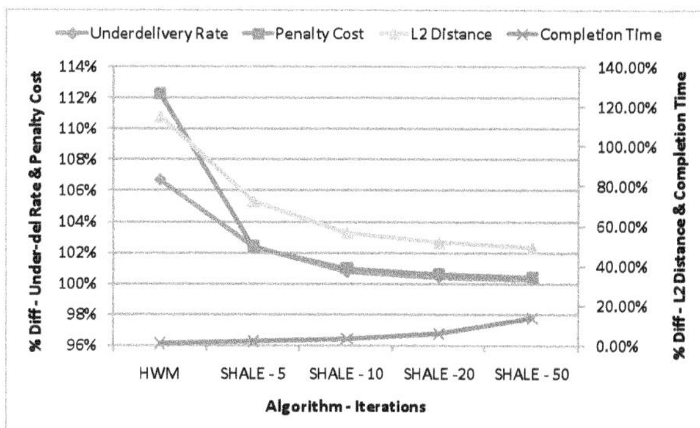

Figure 2: Performance Vs. Completion time

distance and completion for HWM and SHALE run for 5, 10, 20 and 50 iterations respectively as a percentage of the corresponding metric for XPRESS, averaged over our 6 chosen contract sets. Note that the y-axis labels for the under-delivery rate and penalty cost are on the left, while the labels for the L2 distance and completion time are on the right.

It is immediately clear that SHALE after only 10 iterations is within 2% of XPRESS with respect to penalty cost and under-delivery rate. Further, note that SHALE after 10 iterations is able to provide an allocation whose L2 distance is less than half that of XPRESS. (Recall smaller L2 distance means the solution is more representative, so SHALE is doing twice as well on this metric.) Remarkably, SHALE is able to generate a high quality solution while requiring less than 20% of the time taken by XPRESS.

4.3 Experiment 2

Next, we decided to fix the iteration count for SHALE at 20 and test its performance under varying supply levels. Specifically, for each of our 6 contract sets, we artificially reduced the supply weight on each of the supply nodes while keeping the graph structure fixed in order to simulate the increasing scarcity of supply. We define the average supply contention (ASC) metric to represent the scarcity of supply, as follows

$$\text{ASC} = \frac{\sum_i s_i \left(\sum_{j \in i} \frac{d_j}{S_j}\right)}{\sum_i s_i} \qquad (6)$$

where s_i represents the supply weight and d_j and S_j represent the demand and eligible supply for contract j. In Figure 3, we show the under-delivery rate, penalty cost and L2 distance for SHALE as a percentage of the corresponding metric for HWM for various levels of ASC. First we note that each of our metrics for SHALE is lower

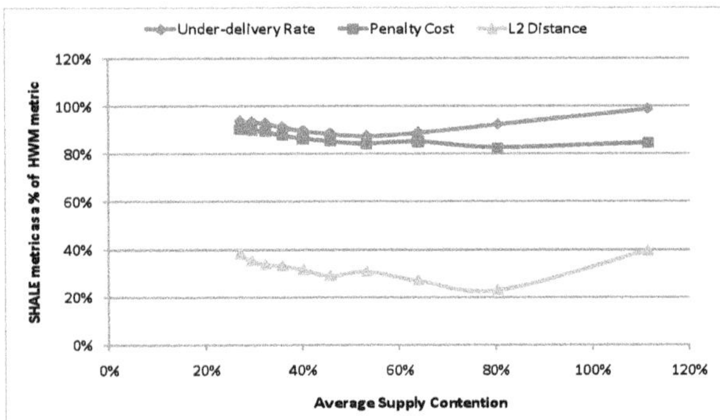

Figure 3: SHALE Vs. HWM

than the corresponding metric for HWM for all values of ASC. Indeed, the SHALE L2 distance is less than 50% of that for HWM. Also note that the SHALE penalty cost consistently improves compared to HWM as the ASC increases.

4.4 Experiment 3

Recall that the allocation plan produced by SHALE or HWM in production is expected to be used not on the input graph itself but on real impressions as they arrive. Thus, the graph on which the primal solution is reconstructed could potentially be very different from the sampled graph used for optimization. Whereas a "true" test of SHALE in production is out of the scope of this work, we did compare the robustness of SHALE (run for 20 iterations) and HWM by reconstructing the allocation plan generated be each algorithm on graphs different from those used for optimization. In particular, corresponding to each of our 6 contract sets, we first ran SHALE and HWM on corresponding 50 sample graphs to generate allocation plans. Then, for each contract set, we generated 6 different 200 sample graphs using 6 different random seeds. We also varied the ASC in the same fashion as in Experiment 2 in each of these 6 graphs. We then reconstructed primal solutions from the plans generated by HWM and SHALE on these graphs and evaluated our chosen metrics. Figure 4 shows the comparison of

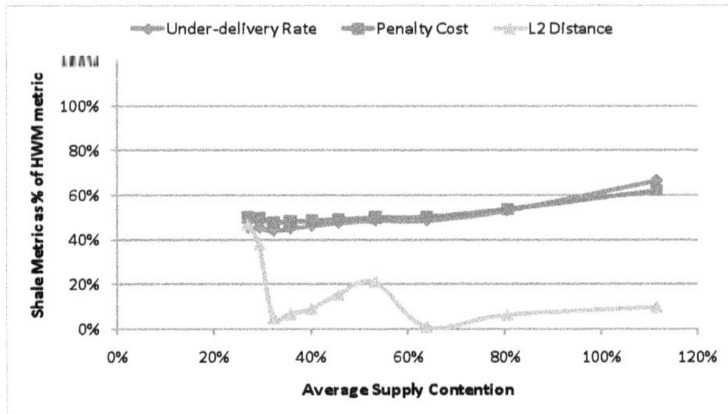

Figure 4: SHALE Vs. HWM reconstructed

under-delivery rate, penalty cost and L2 distance for SHALE as a percentage of the corresponding metric for HWM averaged over 36 graphs (6 different contract sets and 6 graphs for each contract set) for various values of ASC. Here, we can clearly see that SHALE performs significantly better than HWM on all three metrics. It turns out that the HWM allocation plan resulted in much higher under-delivery rates, penalty costs and L2 distances when reconstructed on the new 200 sample graphs as compared to the primal solution on the original 50 sample graph; whereas the SHALE allocation plan did not suffer such a degradation in the solution quality upon reconstruction on the 200 sample graphs. Finally, note that the L2 distance ratio, unlike penalty cost and under-delivery date is not monotonic in the ASC. We would like to point out that in fact, the L2 distance for SHALE was monotonically increasing in the ASC; whereas the L2 distance for HWM varied erratically. This caused the SHALE L2 distance as a percentage of the HWM L2 distance to be non-monotonic.

4.5 Experiment 4

The experiments above compare how SHALE performs with respect to the optimal algorithm under knowledge of supply landscape of the contracts. In this experiment we compare how these algorithms perform when the solution is used to serve real world sampled impressions from actual server logs. This experiment uses real contracts and real adserver logs (downsampled) for performing the complete offline simulation.

4.5.1 Setup

Here we take three new datasets which consists of real guaranteed delivery contracts from Yahoo! active during different one to two week periods in the past year. We run our optimization algorithms and serve real downsampled serving logs for two hours using the solution computed. Then after collecting the serving stats we reoptimize the contracts with updated goal and supply forecasts as the contract demands would have reduced after two hours of serving. This cycle continues where we optimize, serve adlogs and update stats every two hour for the entire test period of one two two weeks.

4.5.2 Algorithms compared

At the end of the simulation, we look at the contracts that start and end within the simulation period and compare how metrics of under delivery and penalty across HWM, SHALE and "Optimal" algorithms. HWM algorithm is essentially SHALE algorithm with 0 iterations. The SHALE algorithms are run with setting of 5, 10 and 20 iterations. Here the "Optimal" solution is obtained by running a coordinate gradient descent algorithm till the objective function convergence.

We performed serving using the reconstruction algorithm described in Section 3.3.1.

4.5.3 *Metrics*

The metrics include the underdelivery metric and penalty metrics as defined in Equation 4 and in Equation 5 For these set of experiments, we set p_j to be $p_j = 0.002 + 4 * q_j$ where q_j is the revenue per delivered impression from contract j.

We also compare another metric called pacing between these algorithms. This captures how representative contracts are with respect to time dimension while delivering these contracts. Pacing is defined as the percentage of contracts that are within 12% of the linear delivery goal atleast 80% of their active duration.

4.5.4 *Results*

Figures 5, 6 and 7 show that the under delivery and penalty cost for HWM (SHALE with 0 iterations) algorithm is the worst. Further as the number of SHALE iterations increase it gets very close to the "Optimal" algorithm. Note that even SHALE with 5 or 10 iterations performs as good or sometimes slightly better than the "Optimal" algorithm. This can be attributed to different reasons; one being the fact that there are forecasting errors intrinsic to using real serving logs. The other reason might be the fact that the objective function of "Optimal" algorithm is not just optimizing for these two metrics.

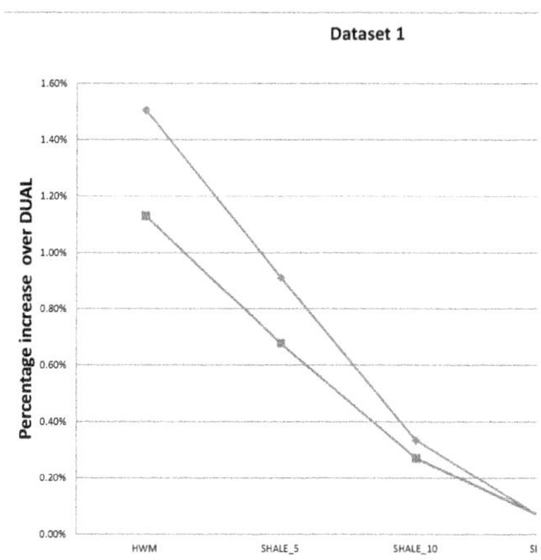

Figure 5: Dataset 1: Under Delivery and Penalty Cost Comparison

Figure 8 shows how these algorithm perform with respect to pacing. The pacing is pretty similar for all three datasets SHALE with 5, 10 and 20 iterations when compared with "Optimal" algorithm but HWM has better pacing than SHALE and "Optimal" for the other two datasets. The possible reasons here can be that SHALE and "Optimal" algorithm gives better under delivery and penalty cost compromising some pacing. Also note that time dimension is just one of the possible dimensions for the representativeness part f the objective function and SHALE and "Optimal" algorithm optimizes for all possible dimensions.

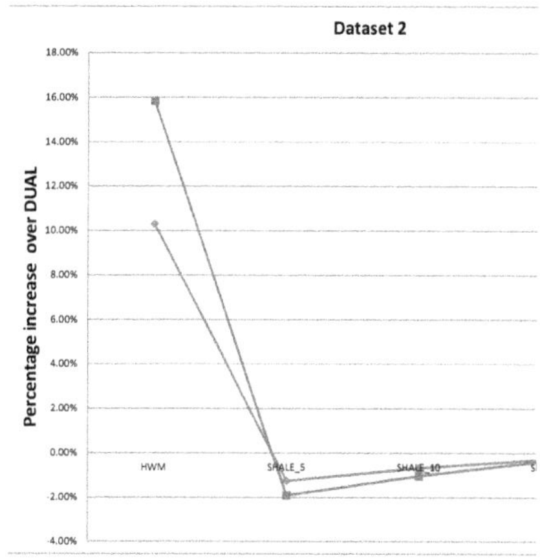

Figure 6: Dataset 2: Under Delivery and Penalty Cost Comparison

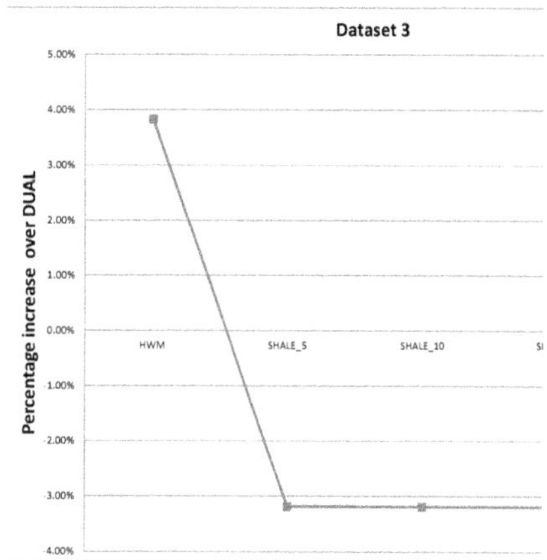

Figure 7: Dataset 3: Under Delivery and Penalty Cost Comparison

5. CONCLUSION

We described the SHALE algorithm, which is used to generate compact allocation plans leading to near-optimal serving. Our algorithm is scalable, efficient, and has the stop-anytime property, making it particularly useful in time-sensitive applications. Our experiments demonstrate that it is many times faster than using commercially available general purpose solvers, while still leading to near-optimal solutions. On the other side, it produces a much better and more robust solution than the simple HWM heuristic. Due to its stop-anytime property, it can be configured to give the desired tradeoff between running time and optimality of the solution. Furthermore, SHALE can handle "warm starts," using a previous allocation plan as a starting point for future iterations.

SHALE is easily modified to handle additional goals, such as maximizing revenue in the non-guaranteed market or click-through rate of advertisement. In fact, the technique appears to be amenable to other classes of problems involving many users with supply con-

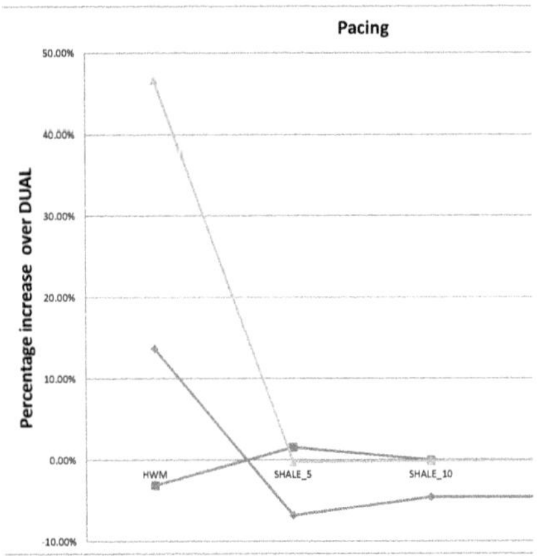

Figure 8: Pacing Comparisons on all three datasets

straints (e.g. each user is shown only one item). Thus, although SHALE is particularly well-suited to optimizing guaranteed display ad delivery, it is also an effective lightweight optimizer. It can handle huge, memory-intensive inputs, and the underlying techniques we use provide a useful method of mapping non-optimal dual solutions into nearly optimal primal results.

6. ADDITIONAL AUTHORS

7. REFERENCES

[1] Y. Chen, P. Berkhin, B. Anderson, and N. R. Devanur. Real-time bidding algorithms for performance-based display ad allocation. In C. Apté, J. Ghosh, and P. Smyth, editors, *KDD*, pages 1307–1315. ACM, 2011.

[2] N. R. Devenur and T. P. Hayes. The adwords problem: online keyword matching with budgeted bidders under random permutations. In J. Chuang, L. Fortnow, and P. Pu, editors, *ACM Conference on Electronic Commerce*, pages 71–78. ACM, 2009.

[3] J. Feldman, M. Henzinger, N. Korula, V. S. Mirrokni, and C. Stein. Online stochastic packing applied to display ad allocation. In M. de Berg and U. Meyer, editors, *ESA (1)*, volume 6346 of *Lecture Notes in Computer Science*, pages 182–194. Springer, 2010.

[4] J. Feldman, A. Mehta, V. S. Mirrokni, and S. Muthukrishnan. Online stochastic matching: Beating 1-1/e. In *FOCS*, pages 117–126. IEEE Computer Society, 2009.

[5] A. Ghosh, P. McAfee, K. Papineni, and S. Vassilvitskii. Bidding for representative allocations for display advertising. In S. Leonardi, editor, *WINE*, volume 5929 of *Lecture Notes in Computer Science*, pages 208–219. Springer, 2009.

[6] V. S. Mirrokni, S. O. Gharan, and M. Zadimoghaddam. Simultaneous approximations for adversarial and stochastic online budgeted allocation. In D. Randall, editor, *SODA*, pages 1690–1701. SIAM, 2012.

[7] E. Vee, S. Vassilvitskii, and J. Shanmugasundaram. Optimal online assignment with forecasts. In D. C. Parkes, C. Dellarocas, and M. Tennenholtz, editors, *ACM Conference on Electronic Commerce*, pages 109–118. ACM, 2010.

[8] J. Yang, E. Vee, S. Vassilvitskii, J. Tomlin, J. Shanmugasundaram, T. Anastasakos, and O. Kennedy. Inventory allocation for online graphical display advertising. *CoRR*, abs/1008.3551, 2010.

Appendix

Recall that our optimization problem is

$$\begin{aligned} \text{Minimize} \quad & \tfrac{1}{2}\textstyle\sum_{j,i\in\Gamma(j)} s_i \frac{V_j}{\theta_{ij}}(x_{ij}-\theta_{ij})^2 + \sum_j p_j u_j & & \\ \text{s.t.} \quad & \textstyle\sum_{i\in\Gamma(j)} s_i x_{ij} + u_j \geq d_j & \forall j \quad & (7) \\ & s_i \textstyle\sum_{j\in\Gamma(i)} x_{ij} \leq s_i & \forall i \quad & (8) \\ & x_{ij}, u_j \geq 0 & \forall i,j \quad & (9) \end{aligned}$$

Notice that we have multiplied the supply constraints by s_i to aid our mathematics later.

The KKT conditions generalize the somewhat more familiar Lagrangian. Let α_j denote the demand duals. Let β_i denote the supply duals. Let γ_{ij} denote the non-negativity duals for x_{ij}, and let ψ_j denote the non-negativity dual for u_j. For our problem, the KKT conditions tell us the optimal primal-dual solution must satisfy the following

Stationarity:

For all i, j, $s_i \frac{V_j}{\theta_{ij}}(x_{ij}-\theta_{ij}) - s_i\alpha_j + s_i\beta_i - \gamma_{ij}$

For all i, $p_j - \alpha_j - \psi_j = 0$

Complementary slackness:

For all j, either $\alpha_j = 0$ or $\sum_{i\in\Gamma(j)} s_i x_{ij} + u_j = d_j$.

For all i, either $\beta_i = 0$ or $\sum_{j\in\Gamma(i)} s_i x_{ij} = s_i$.

For all i, j, either $\gamma_{ij} = 0$ or $x_{ij} = 0$.

For all j, either $\psi_j = 0$ or $u_j = 0$.

The dual feasibity conditions also tell us that $\alpha_j \geq 0$, $\beta_i \geq 0$, $\gamma_{ij} \geq 0$, and $\psi_j \geq 0$ for all i, j. (While the primal feasibility conditions tell us that the constraints in the original problem must be satified.) Since our objective is convex, and primal-dual solution satisfying the KKT conditions is in fact optimal.

Notice that the stationarity conditions are effectively like taking the derivative of the Lagrangian. The first of these tells us that

$$x_{ij} = \theta_{ij}(1 + \frac{\alpha_j - \beta_i + \gamma_{ij}/s_i}{V_j})$$

The complementary slackness condition for the γ_{ij} tells us that $\gamma_{ij} = 0$ unless $x_{ij} = 0$. This has the effect that when the expression $\theta_{ij}(1 + \frac{\alpha_j - \beta_i}{V_j})$ is negative, γ_{ij} will increase just enough to make $x_{ij} = 0$. In particular, this implies

$$x_{ij} = \max\{0, \theta_{ij}(1 + \frac{\alpha_j - \beta_i}{V_j})\} = g_{ij}(\alpha_j - \beta_i)$$

The second stationarity condition shows $\alpha_j = p_j - \psi_j$. Since $\psi_j \geq 0$, this immediately shows that $\alpha_j \leq p_j$. Further, the complementary slackness condition for ψ_j implies that $\psi = 0$ unless $u_j = 0$. That is, either $\alpha_j = p_j$ or $\sum_{i\in\Gamma(j)} s_i x_{ij} \geq d_j$. By complementary slackness of α_j, we see in fact that equality must hold (i.e. $\sum_{i\in\Gamma(j)} s_i x_{ij} = d_j$) unless $\alpha_j = 0$. But when $\alpha_j = 0$, inspection reveals that $\sum_{i\in\Gamma(j)} s_i x_{ij} = \sum_{i\in\Gamma(j)} s_i g_{ij}(-\beta_i) \leq d_j$. Hence, even when $\alpha_j = 0$, equality must hold for an optimal α_j.

Finally, the complementary slackness condition on β_i implies either $\beta_i = 0$ or $\sum_{j \in \Gamma(i)} x_{ij} = 1$. Putting all of this together, we see that

1. The optimal primal solution is given by $x^*_{ij} = g_{ij}(\alpha^*_j - \beta^*_i)$, where $g_{ij}(z) = \max\{0, \theta_{ij}(1 + z/V_j)\}$.
2. For all j, $0 \le \alpha^*_j \le p_j$. Further, either $\alpha^*_j = p_j$ or $\sum_{i \in \Gamma(j)} s_i x^*_{ij} = d_j$.
3. For all i, $\beta_i \ge 0$. Further, either $\beta_i = 0$ or $\sum_{j \in \Gamma(i)} x^*_{ij} = 1$.

as we claimed in Section 3.

PROOF OF THEOREM 1. First, note that α_j is bounded above by p_j. We will show that α_j is non-decreasing on each iteration. Let α^t refer to the value of alpha computed during the t-th iteration, where $\alpha^0_j = 0$ for all j. We show by induction that $d_j(\alpha^t) \le d_j$ for all $t \ge 0$. The base case follows by definition, since $\beta_i \ge 0$ for all i: $d_j(\alpha^0) \le \sum_{i \in \Gamma(j)} s_i g_{ij}(0 - 0) = \sum_{i \in \Gamma(j)} s_i \theta_{ij} = d_j$.

So assume for some $t \ge 0$ that $d_j(\alpha^t) \le d_j$ for all j. Let β^t be the value computed in Step 1 of Stage One of SHALE, given α^t. We see that

$$
\begin{aligned}
d_j(\alpha^t) &= \sum_{i \in \Gamma(j)} s_i g_{ij}(\alpha^t_j - \beta^t_i) \\
&= \sum_{i \in \Gamma(j)} s_i \max\{0, \theta_{ij}(1 + \frac{\alpha^t_j - \beta^t_i}{V_j})\}
\end{aligned}
$$

Further, by the way in which α^{t+1} is calculated (in Stage One, Step 2), we have that α^{t+1}_j must either be p_j or satisfy the following:

$$
\begin{aligned}
d_j &= \sum_{i \in \Gamma(j)} s_i g_{ij}(\alpha^{t+1}_j - \beta^t_i) \\
&= \sum_{i \in \Gamma(j)} s_i \max\{0, \theta_{ij}(1 + \frac{\alpha^{t+1}_j - \beta^t_i}{V_j})\}
\end{aligned}
$$

Using the fact that for any numbers $a \ge b$ that $\max\{0, a\} - \max\{0, b\} \le a - b$ (which can be shown by an easy case analysis), we have

$$
\begin{aligned}
d_j - d_j(\alpha^t) &= \sum_{i \in \Gamma(j)} s_i \max\{0, \theta_{ij}(1 + \frac{\alpha^{t+1}_j - \beta^t_i}{V_j})\} \\
&\quad - \sum_{i \in \Gamma(j)} s_i \max\{0, \theta_{ij}(1 + \frac{\alpha^t_j - \beta^t_i}{V_j})\} \\
&\le \sum_{i \in \Gamma(j)} s_i \theta_{ij}(\alpha^{t+1}_j - \alpha^t_j)/V_j \\
&= d_j(\alpha^{t+1}_j - \alpha^t_j)/V_j
\end{aligned}
$$

That is, either $\alpha^{t+1}_j = p_j$ or

$$
\alpha^{t+1}_j = \alpha^t_j + V_j(1 - \frac{d_j(\alpha^t)}{d_j}) \tag{10}
$$

Since $d_j(\alpha^t) \le d_j$ by assumption, this shows that $\alpha^{t+1}_j \ge \alpha^t_j$ for each j. We must still prove that $d_j(\alpha^{t+1}) \le d_j$. To this end, note that the β^{t+1} generated in Step 1 for the given α^{t+1} must greater than or equal to β^t, since $\alpha^{t+1} \ge \alpha^t$. That is, $\beta^{t+1}_i \ge \beta^t_i$ for all i.

Thus,

$$
\begin{aligned}
d_j(\alpha^{t+1}) &= \sum_{i \in \Gamma(j)} s_i \max\{0, \theta_{ij}(1 + \frac{\alpha^{t+1}_j - \beta^{t+1}_i}{V_j})\} \\
&\le \sum_{i \in \Gamma(j)} s_i \max\{0, \theta_{ij}(1 + \frac{\alpha^{t+1}_j - \beta^t_i}{V_j})\} \\
&= d_j
\end{aligned}
$$

as we wanted.

In general, we can use the fact that $d_j(\alpha^t) \le d_j$ for all t, together with Equation 10, to see that the α_j values are non-decreasing at each iteration. From this (together with the fact that α_j is bounded by p_j), it immediately follows that the algorithm converges.

To see that the algorithm converges to the optimal solution, we note that the dual values generated by SHALE satisfy the KKT conditions at convergence: for all j, either $\alpha_j = p_j$ or $d_j(\alpha) = d_j$ (i.e. $p_j - \alpha_j - \psi_j = 0$ with either $\psi_j = 0$ or $u_j = 0$), with similar arguments holding for the other duals. Since the problem we study is convex, this shows that the primal solution generated must be the optimal.

As for our second claim, suppose that there is some j for which $\alpha^t_j \ne p_j$ but $d_j(\alpha^t_j) \le (1 - \varepsilon)d_j$. Then by Equation 10, we see

$$
\alpha^{t+1}_j = \alpha^t_j + V_j(1 - \frac{d_j(\alpha^t)}{d_j}) \ge \alpha^t_j + V_j\varepsilon
$$

That is, α^{t+1}_j increases (over α^t_j) by at least εV_j. Since α^t_j starts at 0, is bounded by p_j, and never decreases, we see that this can happen at most $p_j/(\varepsilon V_j)$ times for each j. In this worst case, this happens for every j, giving us the bound we claim.

□

Factoring Past Exposure in Display Advertising Targeting

Neha Gupta‡, Abhimanyu Das†, Sandeep Pandey†, Vijay K. Narayanan†

‡ University of Maryland, College Park, MD 20742, USA

† Yahoo! Labs, Santa Clara, CA 95054, USA

neha@cs.umd.edu | {abhidas | spandey | vnarayan}@yahoo-inc.com

ABSTRACT

Online advertising is increasingly becoming more performance oriented, where the decision to show an advertisement to a user is made based on the user's propensity to respond to the ad in a positive manner (e.g., purchasing a product, subscribing to an email list, etc). The user response depends on how well the ad campaign matches the user's interest, as well as the amount of the user's past exposure to the campaign – a factor shown to be impactful in controlled experimental studies. Past exposure builds brand-awareness and familiarity with the user, which in turn leads to a higher propensity of the user to buy/convert on the ad impression. In this paper we propose a model of the user response to an ad campaign as a function of both interest match and past exposure, where the interest match is estimated using historical search/browse activities of the user.

The goal of this paper is two-fold. First, we demonstrate the role played by the user interest and the past exposure in modeling user response by jointly estimating the parameters of these factors. We test this response model over hundreds of real ad campaigns. Second, we use the findings from this joint model to identify more relevant target users for ad campaigns. In particular, we show that on real advertising data this joint model identifies better target users compared to conventional targeting models.

Categories and Subject Descriptors

I.2.6 [**Artificial Intelligence**]: Learning; G.3 [**Mathematics of Computing**]: Probability and Statistics

General Terms

Algorithms, Experimentation

Keywords

Advertising, Targeting, User Modeling, Latent Factors

1. INTRODUCTION

Online advertising is growing at a rapid pace with more and more advertisers using the internet to reach out to their potential customers. This is not surprising given that users are spending an unprecedented amount of time performing online activities ranging from sending emails, searching and browsing, to dating and shopping. The advertisers (or intermediaries such as ad networks, online exchanges) use these past online activities of the users to identify those who are most likely to respond positively to their advertising campaigns. This is called behavioral targeting [15, 12, 7, 19], whereby models are built based on past user behavior to target likely potential customers. Behavioral targeting benefits both the parties involved: it allows advertisers to spend their money effectively, while it helps users by providing them more relevant ads.

Effective targeting requires deeper understanding of the factors influencing a user response to an ad. Broadly speaking, for a given advertising campaign this involves: (a) understanding user interests and identifying whether she is likely to be interested in the products/services offered by the advertiser (called "interest match"), and (b) making the user "aware" of the advertiser's product by repetitively exposing her to the ad so as to elicit a positive response (called "past exposure"). Previous work has shown how each of these factors can influence the likelihood of a user to pursue the ad. While the effect of the "interest match" factor is fairly natural and intuitive (e.g., the more relevant the ad campaign is to the user, the more likely she is to pursue it), the effect of past exposure is more complex. Controlled experiments have been done by economists and social scientists to identify the effect of past exposure [16, 13, 9]. While the results from these studies differ in some aspects, largely it has been shown that with increased past exposure the user is more likely to pursue the ad. Intuitively, "past exposure" to an ad might help in several ways such as increased brand-awareness and familiarity with the advertised product, or even an increased probability of the user to notice the ad. At the same time, some studies have also shown an "ad fatigue" effect where users might tire of an ad if it is displayed too often [1].

Our goal in this paper is to improve user targeting by accounting for the hidden interplay of the interest match and past exposure factors in a real world advertising environment. This is challenging for several reasons. First, when we receive a positive response from a user for an ad campaign, it is unclear how much of this is due to repeated past exposure of the ad, as opposed to the user interests matching with the campaign objectives. Most previous work has been limited to investigating these factors individually in a controlled experimental setting. Second, these past exposure and interest match factors themselves are complex and difficult to characterize precisely. For example, as discussed in [17], inferring user interests from their profiles requires dealing with millions of features and is challenging technically as well as computationally. Third, the contribution of these factors to a positive user response might be different for different advertising campaigns. For exam-

KDD'12, August 12–16, 2012, Beijing, China.

ple, past exposure might play a positive role for certain campaigns, be unrelated to user response for other campaigns, and might even lead to ad fatigue for a third set of campaigns. Lastly, in our study we define a positive user response in terms of "conversions", which represent desired user actions as specified by the advertiser in the form of purchases and product information request. While conversions are advertiser-defined and thus are clearly more tangible indicators of user interest compare to clicks, time spent or other implicit feedback, conversions are much rarer as well. Thus, we have to take necessary precautions while performing inference or learning from such sparse data.

We deal with the above mentioned issues by using mathematical models that jointly account for the two factors involved: past exposure and interest match. Our models use three sources of information for a given user and advertising campaign: (a) the number of previous ads that the user has seen from the campaign in consideration, (b) a rich user profile in terms of her past online activities that include, but are not limited to, search queries issued, pages browsed and the associated timestamps and (c) users who have responded well to the campaign in the past (called positive users). The number of previously viewed ads is used to model the past exposure factor, while the user profile is leveraged for gauging interest match with the advertiser. By jointly accounting and optimizing for past exposure and interest match with respect to the given positive and negative users, we are able to separate their influence [16, 13, 9]. Intuitively speaking, given a set of users with similar interest match but with different past exposure, the role of past exposure can be estimated and vice versa. However, doing so makes the model for characterizing interest match to depend on the given model for past exposure and vice versa, thus requiring a joint optimization.

Our work can have significant implications for display advertising and user targeting. We show how the two factors, past exposure and interest match, can be modeled jointly to perform more accurate prediction of potential converters. Current state of the art in targeting is largely focused on matching interested users with advertisers, but does not give deserved attention to past exposure. Through our experiments on hundreds of real advertising campaigns, we show how past exposure, along with interest match, can substantially improve the targeting performance. Also, understanding the effect of past exposure allows advertisers to allocate and spend their advertising budget more judiciously. For example, if their campaigns require large amount of past exposure, then it makes sense for them to find interested users and pursue them for a reasonable period before expecting a positive response. On the other hand, advertisers who only need small past exposure should shuffle through users quickly and avoid spending much resources on any particular user (since if the user is likely to convert, she would convert promptly for such advertisers). On our dataset we find, through our modeling approach, that different campaigns have sufficiently different needs in terms of past exposure and interest match.

Contributions. We make the following contributions in this paper:

- We study the effect of past exposure and interest match in terms of eliciting positive user response in a real world advertising environment. To the best of our knowledge, this is the first study that investigates the hidden interplay of the two factors in a non-controlled setting.
- We propose mathematical models that jointly account for both the factors. We give several variants to capture different kinds of advertising campaigns and user conversion models.
- Using several sources of data (involving user profiles and ad campaigns), we validate our models and surface the role played by past exposure for different campaigns.
- We use our models to show how past exposure, along with interest match, can help in significantly improving the targeting systems. From empirical analysis on 200 advertising campaigns, we show substantial improvement over the conventional targeting methods.

1.1 Related Work

Behavioral targeting systems for display advertising are rapidly increasing on the Internet. Utilizing historical online user information to target users with display ads has been shown to be highly effective, resulting in an increase in the performance of ad-campaigns [19]. Several optimization techniques have been suggested [15, 12, 7] which use different user features such as demographics, past views, past searches, pseudo social-networks, etc. to differentiate between converters and non-converters.

Different statistical models can be applied to capture the user behavior effectively. Regression models have been introduced in [3, 4, 10] in this domain. Bayesian factor-based models [2, 6] have also been proposed in literature. In [2] the authors used *ad factors* whose parameters are derived from different types of Markov models to generalize user behavior patterns for ad-campaigns. The goal of this study was on providing additional insight about the users to the advertisers. In [6] the authors use latent factor models similar to LDA for targeting [5], but do not consider the effect of past user exposure. Also, there is related work on user browsing models (UBM) which, for organic and sponsored search, separates the click-through rate into an "examination" probability and perceived relevance probability. However, these models apply for search results and do not consider any effect due to repeated exposure [18].

The effect of user exposure has been studied in [9, 13, 16] in a controlled setting, where it has been shown that multiple exposure to an advertisement can have varying effects on the purchasing decision of the users. In [16] the authors study the effect of temporal spacing between ads and show that at a purchase occasion, the probability of a product purchase increases if its past ads are spread apart rather than bunched together. In [13] the authors show that the purchase probability of a user varies as a function of banner advertising exposure. They also show that the number of websites and number of pages on which a user is exposed to advertisements can have an effect on the purchase probabilities.

2. TARGETING WITH PAST EXPOSURE AND INTEREST MATCH

Before we explain our modeling approach, we next describe the problem setup in detail.

2.1 Problem Formulation

The focus of our study is *performance based* display advertising campaigns, which are set up with conversions goals, where conversions are advertiser specified actions (e.g., email subscription, form fill, product purchase) that show positive user intent. For each campaign, the goal is to identify and target users who are most likely to convert, also known as *converters*. In the following section, we formulate this task mathematically.

We use the following sources of information for a given campaign:

- Past ad impressions x_i: the number of previous ads that user i, denoted by u_i, has seen from the campaign.

- User profile vector $\mathbf{f}_i$: representing the past online activities from user u_i. These activities include page visits and search queries, which are analyzed using established text processing techniques to construct a feature vector. More details are given in Section 4.1.

- Seed users $\mathcal{S}$: users who have been targeted for the campaign in the past along with their response values. In other words, for these seed users, we know whether they converted on the ad campaign or not.

We denote the user response using binary variable y_i. A y_i value of 1 represents a converter, and 0 represents a non-converter.

Let us denote the probability of user u_i converting by the time she has been served x_i ad impressions by $\mathrm{P}[y_i = 1|\mathbf{f}_i, x_i]$. Then the goal of ad targeting is to identify users with the largest values of $\mathrm{P}[y_i = 1|\mathbf{f}_i, x_i]$. There are several technical questions involved in doing so. For instance, it is worth investigating the gain achieved by accounting for the number of adviews x_i versus ignoring it (see Section 2.2). How does the user profile vector $\mathbf{f}_i$ interact with x_i? As described in Section 2.4, a naive solution is to treat x_i as another feature in the profile vector, but this leads to over-simplification and does not model the effect of x_i correctly. Note that, in our setting, the dimension of $\mathbf{f}_i$ is extremely large since it represents sparse user activities. Furthermore, the number of positive examples (i.e., y_i =1) in the given seed set $\mathcal{S}$ is typically small since conversions are rare events, making the problem harder.

Next we describe our proposed factor model for user targeting that accounts for both past exposure and interest match.

2.2 Proposed Factor Model (EFM)

We believe that the user conversion for a campaign comes from a two-stage process. In the first stage, the user is repeatedly exposed to the ad to get her attention. According to past work, this may lead to increased user *awareness* about the product/brand, making her more familiar with the ad offering and increasing her trust in the advertisement. Of course, an excess of repeated exposure to the ad can negatively affect the user sentiments about the advertiser. Once the user has become aware, denoted by the *awareness* random variable ϕ_i (defined precisely in Section 2.2.1), she moves to the second stage.

In the second stage, the user evaluates the offering and decides whether to pursue the ad or not. This decision is based on several other variables such as whether the user is interested in the offered product, whether the timing and price is appropriate,etc. We call this the *intrinsic conversion* probability and denote it by $\mathrm{P}[y_i = 1|\mathbf{f}_i, \phi_i = 1]$. Thus, our model factorizes the probability of user conversion into the product of two probabilities, the awareness probability ($\mathrm{P}[\phi_i = 1|x_i]$) and intrinsic conversion probability ($\mathrm{P}[y_i = 1|\mathbf{f}_i, \phi_i = 1]$). In other words,

$$\begin{aligned} \mathrm{P}[y_i = 1|\mathbf{f}_i, x_i] &= \mathrm{P}[\phi_i = 1|x_i] \cdot \mathrm{P}[y_i = 1|\mathbf{f}_i, \phi_i = 1] + \\ &\quad \mathrm{P}[\phi_i = 0|x_i] \cdot \mathrm{P}[y_i = 1|\mathbf{f}_i, \phi_i = 0] \\ &= \mathrm{P}[\phi_i = 1|x_i] \cdot \mathrm{P}[y_i = 1|\mathbf{f}_i, \phi_i = 1] \end{aligned}$$

where the last equation arises since the user cannot convert unless she is aware of the ad.

Note that our model decouples the effect of previous ad impressions x_i and profile vector $\mathbf{f}_i$, whereby x_i influences the awareness probability while the profile vector is used for modeling the intrinsic conversion probability. While we can envision the awareness probability to be a function of the profile vector as well (i.e., different users may build awareness in different manners) and the intrinsic probability to depend on the number of impressions, this could make the two stages fairly similar and mathematically unidentifiable. Hence, for the ease of model interpretation we keep the two stages decoupled as described above.

We refer to this model as the *Exposure-based Factor Model* for User Targeting (EFM). Next we describe the two factors in more detail.

2.2.1 *Modeling Awareness Probability*

For a given advertising campaign and a user, the awareness probability captures the likelihood with which the user is aware of the campaign and considers it for evaluation (i.e., moves to the second stage). We represent this as a function of the number of previous ad impressions x_i of the campaign that the user has been exposed to.

Below we describe two possible distributions that can be used to model the awareness probability.

1. *Geometric Process*: Let us assume that each time the user is shown the ad, she notices the ad with probability α. If each of these Bernoulli trials are independent, then the probability of the user becoming aware by noticing the ad on the ith impression is a geometric distribution. In other words, $\mathrm{P}[\phi_i = 1|x_i] = \sum_{j=1}^{x_i}(1-\alpha)^{j-1}\alpha = 1 - (1-\alpha)^{x_i}$. We denote this EFM model that uses this Geometric process for modeling awareness probability as EFMG.

2. *Poisson Process*: Here we model the number of times a user notices the ad as a Poisson process, with an average rate of $\lambda = \alpha \cdot x_i$ (where α is the probability of noticing an ad impression). Under the Poisson process, the probability of k events is $\frac{(\alpha \cdot x_i)^k e^{-\alpha \cdot x_i}}{k!}$. Hence, the probability of the user noticing the ad at least once and being aware of it is $\mathrm{P}[\phi_i = 1|x_i] = 1 - e^{-\alpha \cdot x_i}$.

   We denote this model by EFMP.

Both the above models are intuitive in nature and capture the fact that with increased exposure, the awareness probability increases (as found in previous studies). In other words, the more ads the user is exposed to, the higher is her awareness probability. While this is largely true, it is possible that with excess exposure the user gets annoyed and does not consider the ad for evaluation (i.e., the second stage). More specifically, the awareness may decrease due to negative sentiments.

We account for such negative sentiments by proposing a *Multinomial* distribution for awareness probability where $\mathrm{P}[\phi_i = 1|x_i] = \{\pi_1, \pi_2, \ldots\}$. Here π_x denotes the awareness probability after x number of previous ad impressions and is learned from the data during joint optimization (parameter estimation is described in Section 3). Hence, if there is excess exposure which leads to negative sentiments, π_x would start decreasing beyond a certain number of ad impressions (x).

2.2.2 *Modeling Intrinsic Conversion Probability*

As describe earlier, the intrinsic conversion probability for user u_i represents the likelihood with which the user converts on the ad when she evaluates it. The probability depends on many user attributes such as demographics, her interests (short-term and long-term), online shopping tendency. We model this using a logistic function of the features from the user profile vector:

$$\mathrm{P}[y_i = 1|\mathbf{f}_i, \phi_i = 1] = \frac{1}{1 + e^{-\mathbf{w}^T\mathbf{f}_i}}$$

In other words, *logit*($\mathrm{P}[y_i = 1|\mathbf{f}_i, \phi_i = 1]$) $= \mathbf{w}^T\mathbf{f}_i$ where $\mathbf{w} = \{w_1, w_2, \ldots, w_n\}$ denotes the unknown weight vector. The weight vector is campaign specific since it models the targeting constraints of a campaign and needs to be learned separately for each campaign.

Note that the choice of logistic regression for modeling intrinsic conversion probability is not central to our factor model and can be easily substituted by other approaches. Methods for identifying user interests is a research topic by itself and has been focus of many previous work on advertising and other applications such as news browsing, personalized search, etc (see related work). Many models such as Logistic regression, SVM, Naive-Bayes, Nearest-neighbor have been studied in this context and can potentially be used for our work.

2.3 Incorporating Delay Factor in the Model

In our factor model we described how the user converts on a campaign in a two step process — in the first step the user becomes aware of the ad and the advertiser, while in the second step she evaluates the ad and decides whether to convert on it or not. Another dimension that is worth investigating is the time delay between the first and the second step. For example, say the user is exposed to the ads from a cruise line and after a few exposures she becomes aware of it. Since she is not planning any vacation for the next few months, she decides to not react or evaluate the ad at the time. But when she finally gets to the vacation period, the awareness might have faded away. We make this more formal next.

Suppose the user has been targeted with a display advertisement for the campaign x_i times so far. Let the timestamp for the x-th adview for this user be $t_i(x)$, and suppose we know that the user has converted by time θ_i.[1] Let us denote the probability of this conversion event by $P[y_i = 1|\mathbf{f}_i, x_i, \theta_i]$. Our generative model for the conversion is as follows: first, the user becomes aware at the time of the x-th adview (where $1 \leq x \leq x_i$). After that she waits for a time interval t (where $0 \leq t \leq \theta_i$), before deciding whether to convert or not convert. In other words, the probability of conversion is the product of the following three terms - the probability of the user becoming aware at the x-th adview (denoted by $P[\phi_{i,x} = 1]$),[2] the probability of the user incurring a delay of time t in making her decision (denoted by $P[\Delta_i = t]$), and the intrinsic conversion probability of the user given that she has noticed the ad and is ready to make a decision (denoted by $P[y_i = 1|\mathbf{f}_i, \phi_i = 1]$). Thus, we have

$$P[y_i = 1|\mathbf{f}_i, x_i, \theta_i] = \sum_{x=1}^{x_i} \sum_{t=0}^{\theta_i - t_i(x)} (P[\phi_{i,x} = 1] \cdot P[\Delta_i = t] \cdot P[y_i = 1|\mathbf{f}_i, \phi_i = 1])$$

Assuming that the impressions are shown to users uniformly over time, we can approximate the time interval $\theta_i - t_i(x)$ in terms of the difference in the ad impression counts, that is, $\theta_i - t_i(x)$ is proportional to $x_i - x$. Hence,

$$\begin{aligned} P[y_i = 1|\mathbf{f}_i, x_i] &= \sum_{x=1}^{x_i} \sum_{t=0}^{x_i - x} (P[\phi_{i,x} = 1] \\ &\quad \cdot P[\Delta_i = t] \cdot P[y_i = 1|\mathbf{f}_i, \phi_i = 1]) \\ &= P[y_i = 1|\mathbf{f}_i, \phi_i = 1] \cdot \\ &\quad \sum_{x=1}^{x_i} \sum_{t=0}^{x_i - x} (P[\phi_{i,x} = 1] \cdot P[\Delta_i = t]) \end{aligned}$$

If it is the case that the user, after becoming aware, immediately decides whether to convert (without waiting for future ad impressions), i.e., $P[\Delta_i = 0] = 1$, then $P[y_i = 1|\mathbf{f}_i, x_i]$ simplifies to $P[y_i = 1|\mathbf{f}_i, \phi_i = 1] \cdot P[\phi_i = 1|x]$. Thus, we obtain the model described in Section 2.2 as a special case of this delay model.

More generally, if the probability $P[\Delta_i = t]$ decays obeys an exponentially decaying probability distribution, i.e., $P[\Delta_i = t] = \gamma e^{-\gamma t}$, where γ is the exponential parameter, then we get:

$$\begin{aligned} P[y_i = 1|\mathbf{f}_i, x_i] &= P[y_i = 1|\mathbf{f}_i, \phi_i = 1] \cdot \\ &\quad \sum_{x=1}^{x_i} \sum_{t=0}^{x_i - x} (P[\phi_{i,x} = 1] \cdot \gamma e^{-\gamma t}) \end{aligned}$$

We denote this model by EFMD.

2.4 Alternative Approaches for User Targeting

We start by describing the conventional targeting strategy which does not take exposure into account [3, 4]. In other words, this approach only accounts for the intrinsic conversion probability, $P[y_i = 1|\mathbf{f}_i, \phi_i = 1]$. The probability is typically modeled using a SVM or Logistic function of the user features including geographic, demographic, behavioral and/or social attributes (see Section 4.1 for more details about the type of features used). We refer to this baseline model by LR (for logistic regression). Note that this is a special case of our factor model from Section 2.2 where the bernoulli probability α is set to 1.

We propose another baseline method which takes exposure into account but in a rather simplistic manner. In particular, we can think of the past impression count x_i as another feature in the profile vector $\mathbf{f}_i$. Hence, instead of doing logistic regression over just the profile features as in LR, now we regress over both x_i and $\mathbf{f}_i$. We denote this by LR+ and study its performance in the experiment section. As we will see in the results section, while leveraging past exposure benefits LR+ over LR, it is substantially outperformed by our factor models.

3. PARAMETER ESTIMATION FOR FACTOR MODEL

We now present optimization methods for estimating the model parameters (α and $\mathbf{w}$) for our factor model. Note that the parameters α and $\mathbf{w}$ are specific to each campaign and are estimated separately.

We provide two different optimization approaches for this problem: an Alternate Maximization method and an Expectation Maximization method.

3.1 Alternate Maximization

For the ease of explanation, we consider the zero-delay factor model from Section 2.2. Also, let us assume $P[\phi_i = 1|x]$ to be a

[1]Note that the precise time of a user conversion is difficult to determine in practice since the conversion, unlike click, does not happen right after the ad impression; the user may evaluate the ad, like it and then buy the product few days later.

[2]Note that awareness probability $P[\phi_i = 1|x] = \sum_{k=1}^{x} P[\phi_{i,k} = 1]$. For the Geometric model described in Section 2.2.1, $P[\phi_{i,x} = 1] = (1-\alpha)^{x-1}\alpha$.

Geometric process with parameter α and $P[y_i = 1|\mathbf{f}_i, \phi_i = 1] = \frac{1}{1+e^{-\mathbf{w}^T\mathbf{f}_i}}$.

Given a set of users $U = \{u_i, \ldots, u_n\}$ along with corresponding labels $Y = \{y_i, \ldots, y_n\}$, feature vectors $F = \{\mathbf{f}_i, \ldots, \mathbf{f}_n\}$ and past ad impression counts $X = \{x_i, \ldots, x_n\}$, our goal is to find the unknown logistic parameters $\mathbf{w}$ and the Geometric Parameter α. Using $\Theta = \{\mathbf{w}, \alpha\}$ to represent the model parameters, $D = \{Y, F, X\}$ to represent the observed data, and using the expression for $P[y_i = 1|\mathbf{f}_i, \phi_i = 1]$ from Section 2.2, we can express the log-likelihood function for the data as:

$$\begin{aligned} L[\Theta; D] &= \sum_{i=1}^{n}(y_i \log(P[\phi_i = 1|x_i] \cdot P[y_i = 1|\mathbf{f}_i, \phi_i = 1]) + \\ &\quad (1-y_i)\log(1 - P[\phi_i = 1|x_i] \cdot P[y_i = 1|\mathbf{f}_i, \phi_i = 1]) \\ &= \sum_{i=1}^{n}(y_i \log((1-(1-\alpha)^{x_i}) \cdot \frac{1}{1+e^{-\mathbf{w}^T\mathbf{f}_i}}) + \\ &\quad (1-y_i)\log(1-(1-(1-\alpha)^{x_i}) \cdot \frac{1}{1+e^{-\mathbf{w}^T\mathbf{f}_i}})) \end{aligned}$$

To solve this maximum-likelihood optimization problem, we use an alternating maximization algorithm consisting of a sequence of iterations, each comprising of two steps: in the first step (α-step), we optimize for α while keeping $\mathbf{w}$ constant, and in the second step ($\mathbf{w}$-step), we optimize for $\mathbf{w}$ while keeping α constant.

- α-step: In this step, the value of $\mathbf{w}$ (and hence $\frac{1}{1+e^{-\mathbf{w}^T\mathbf{f}_i}}$) is kept constant. We denote these constant terms $\frac{1}{1+e^{-\mathbf{w}^T\mathbf{f}_i}}$ by c_i. The optimization step is therefore:

$$\begin{aligned} \underset{\alpha}{\operatorname{argmax}}\, g(\alpha) &= \sum_{i=1}^{n}(y_i \log((1-(1-\alpha)^{x_i}) \cdot c_i) + \\ &\quad (1-y_i)\log(1-(1-(1-\alpha)^{x_i}) \cdot c_i)). \end{aligned}$$

  While the above equation does not lead to a closed form solution, maximizing $g(\alpha)$ can be efficiently solved using grid search since it contains only one unknown $\alpha \in [0, 1]$.

- $\mathbf{w}$-step: In this step, we use the value of α obtained from the previous step. Hence, the $1-(1-\alpha)^{x_i}$ terms, which we denote by a_i, are kept constant. The optimization problem is then:

$$\begin{aligned} \underset{\mathbf{w}}{\operatorname{argmax}}\, f(\mathbf{w}) &= \sum_{i=1}^{n}(y_i \log(a_i \cdot \frac{1}{1+e^{-\mathbf{w}^T\mathbf{f}_i}}) + \\ &\quad (1-y_i)\log(1-(a_i \cdot \frac{1}{1+e^{-\mathbf{w}^T\mathbf{f}_i}}))). \end{aligned}$$

While the above function $f(\mathbf{w})$ is not concave, we can approximate it by another function that is concave:

$$\begin{aligned} f'(\mathbf{w}) &= \sum_{i=1}^{n}(y_i \log(a_i \cdot \frac{1}{1+e^{-\mathbf{w}^T\mathbf{f}_i}}) + \\ &\quad (1-y_i)\log(1-\frac{1}{1+e^{-\mathbf{w}^T\mathbf{f}_i}})^{a_i}). \end{aligned}$$

Essentially, we are approximating $(1 - P[\phi_i = 1|x_i] \cdot P[y_i = 1|\mathbf{f}_i, \phi_i = 1])$ by $(1 - P[y_i = 1|\mathbf{f}_i, \phi_i = 1])^{P[\phi_i=1|x_i]}$ which is known to be a good approximation if $P[y_i = 1|\mathbf{f}_i, \phi_i = 1]$ is small. Since this approximation is performed only in the case of those users for which $y_i = 0$, we expect $P[y_i = 1|\mathbf{f}_i, \phi_i = 1]$ to indeed be small for such users.

We can now solve the optimization problem $\operatorname{argmax}_{\mathbf{w}} f'(\mathbf{w})$ efficiently, since $f'(\mathbf{w})$ is a concave function of $\mathbf{w}$. Specifically, we performed L-BFGS gradient descent using the MALLET package [14].

LEMMA 3.1. *$f'(\mathbf{w})$ is a concave function of $\mathbf{w}$*

Proof. Let $l_i(w) = \frac{1}{1+e^{-\mathbf{w}^T\mathbf{f}_i}}$. Hence

$$\begin{aligned} f'(\mathbf{w}) &= \sum_{i=1}^{n}(y_i \log(a_i \cdot l_i(w)) + (1-y_i)\log(1-l_i(w))^{a_i}) \\ &= \sum_{i=1}^{n}(y_i \log(a_i \cdot l_i(w)) + (a_i - a_i y_i)\log(1-l_i(w))) \\ &= \sum_{i=1}^{n}(y_i(1-a_i)\log(l_i(w))) + \\ &\quad \sum_{i=1}^{n}(a_i(y_i \log l_i + (1-y_i)\log(1-l_i(w)))) \end{aligned}$$

The second term is the Logistic Regression log-likelihood function, which is concave. For the first term, it suffices to show that $-\log l_i(w)$ is convex.

Now $\frac{\partial(-\log l_i(w))}{\partial w_p} = -x_p(1-l_i(w))$. Therefore $\frac{\partial^2(-\log l_i(w))}{\partial w_p^2} = x_p^2 l_i(w)(1-l_i(w))$, and $\frac{\partial^2(-\log l_i(w))}{\partial w_p w_q} = x_p x_q l_i(w)(1-l_i(w))$.

Thus, the Hessian $\nabla(-\log l_i(w)) = l_i(w)(1-l_i(w))(\mathbf{x}\mathbf{x}^T)$ where $\mathbf{x} = [x_1, x_2, \ldots, x_n]^T$. This is clearly a positive-semidefinite matrix, and hence $-\log l_i(w)$ is convex.

Hence, $f'(\mathbf{w})$ is concave. ■

3.2 Expectation-Maximization

We can also perform model estimation using the Expectation Maximization framework. We use the same definitions for U, Y, F, Θ and X as before. In addition, for each user u_i we have an associated hidden (or latent) variable z_i that takes a value of 1 if the user is aware of the ad (with probability $P[\phi_i = 1|x_i]$), and 0 otherwise. We define $\mathbf{Z} = \{z_1, z_2, \ldots, z_n\}$. For ease of notation, we denote $P[y_i = 1|\mathbf{f}_i, \phi_i = 1]) = \frac{1}{1+e^{-\mathbf{w}^T\mathbf{f}_i}}$ by p_i, and $P[\phi_i = 1|x_i]$ by q_i.

Given the hidden variables $Z = \{z_i\}$ and data $D = \{Y, F, X\}$, we first compute the log-likelihood of the model $L[\Theta; D, Z]$. For each user, clearly $P[y_i = 1|z_i = 1] = q_i p_i$, $P[y_i = 0|z_i = 1] = q_i(1-p_i)$, $P[y_i = 1|z_i = 0] = 0$ and $P[y_i = 0|z_i = 0] = 1 - q_i$. Thus,

$$\begin{aligned} L[\Theta; D, Z] &= \sum_{i=1}^{n} y_i \log(z_i q_i p_i) + \\ &\quad (1-y_i)\log(z_i q_i(1-p_i) + (1-z_i)(1-q_i)) \\ &= \sum_{i=1}^{n} y_i \log(G_i) + (1-y_i)\log(H_i), \end{aligned}$$

where we use $G_i = z_i q_i p_i$ and $H_i = z_i q_i(1-p_i) + (1-z_i)(1-q_i)$.

Then, in the E-step we consider the expected value of the likelihood w.r.t. the conditional distribution of Z given the data and model parameters, i.e., $E_{Z/\Theta,D}[L[\Theta; D, Z]]$. Thus,

$$E_{Z/\Theta,D}[L[\Theta; D, Z]] = \sum_{\mathbf{Z}} \mathrm{P}[Z|\Theta, D] \cdot L[\Theta; D, Z]$$
$$= \sum_{\mathbf{Z}} \mathrm{P}[Z|\Theta, D] \cdot \sum_{i=1}^{n}(y_i \log(G_i) + (1 - y_i)\log(H_i))$$
$$= \sum_{i:y_i=1} \sum_{z_i} \mathrm{P}[z_i|\Theta, y_i = 1] \log(G_i)$$
$$+ \sum_{i:y_i=0} \sum_{z_i} \mathrm{P}[z_i|\Theta, y_i = 0] \log(H_i)$$
$$= \sum_{i:y_i=1} \log(q_i p_i) + \sum_{i:y_i=0} \mathrm{P}[z_i = 1|\Theta, y_i = 0] \log(q_i(1 - p_i))$$
$$+ \mathrm{P}[z_i = 0|\Theta, y_i = 0] \log(1 - q_i)$$

where, the last equality follows since $\mathrm{P}[z_i = 1|\Theta, y_i = 1] = 1$ and $\mathrm{P}[z_i = 0|\Theta, y_i = 1] = 0$. Also, we have

$$\mathrm{P}[z_i = 1|\Theta, y_i = 0] = \frac{q_i \cdot (1-p_i)}{q_i \cdot (1-p_i) + (1-q_i) \cdot 1} = \frac{q_i \cdot (1-p_i)}{1 - q_i \cdot p_i}.$$

Thus, we can further simplify:

$$\begin{aligned} E_{Z/\Theta,D}[L[\Theta; D, Z]] &= \sum_{i:y_i=1} \log(q_i p_i) \\ &+ \sum_{i:y_i=0} \frac{q_i \cdot (1-p_i)}{1 - q_i \cdot p_i} \log(q_i(1 - p_i)) \\ &+ \sum_{i:y_i=0} (1 - \frac{q_i \cdot (1-p_i)}{1 - q_i \cdot p_i}) \log(1 - q_i) \\ &= \sum_{i:y_i=1} \log(q_i p_i) + \sum_{i:y_i=0} \log(1 - q_i) \\ &+ \sum_{i:y_i=0} \frac{q_i \cdot (1-p_i)}{1 - q_i \cdot p_i} \cdot \log(q_i \frac{1 - p_i}{1 - q_i}) \end{aligned}$$

Thus we obtain the **E-step** expression:

$$\begin{aligned} E_{Z/\Theta,D}[L[\Theta; D, Z]] &= \sum_{i:y_i=1} \log(q_i p_i) + \sum_{i:y_i=0} \log(1 - q_i) \\ &+ \sum_{i:y_i=0} \frac{q_i \cdot (1-p_i)}{1 - q_i \cdot p_i} \cdot \log(q_i \frac{1 - p_i}{1 - q_i}) \end{aligned}$$

In the M-step, we aim to estimate the model parameters α and $\mathbf{w}$ that maximizes the above expression. Notice that p_i is a function of $\mathbf{w}$ and q_i is a function of α. Hence, in the M-step we can again use an alternating maximization algorithm consisting of a sequence of iterations, each comprising two steps: in the first step (α-step), we optimize for α while keeping $\mathbf{w}$ constant, and in the second step ($\mathbf{w}$-step), we optimize for $\mathbf{w}$, keeping α constant.

- α-step: In this step, the value of $\mathbf{w}$ (and hence p_i) is kept constant. Then the above expression can be efficiently maximized using grid search over the unknown parameter $\alpha \in [0, 1]$.
- $\mathbf{w}$-step: In this step, we use the value of α obtained from the previous step. Hence, the $q_i = 1 - (1 - \alpha)^{x_i}$ terms are kept constant. The optimization problem is then

$$\begin{aligned} \operatorname*{argmax}_{\mathbf{w}} \quad & \{ \sum_{i:y_i=1} \log(p_i) \\ & + \sum_{i:y_i=0} \frac{q_i \cdot (1-p_i)}{1 - q_i \cdot p_i} \cdot \log(q_i \frac{1 - p_i}{1 - q_i}) \} \end{aligned}$$

While the above function $f(\mathbf{w})$ is not concave, we use a gradient descent approach to reach a local maxima and obtain a reasonable estimate of the $\mathbf{w}$ parameter, by running the gradient descent solver using MALLET with multiple starting points [14].

4. EXPERIMENTS

In this section we describe the experimental setup and the data used to test our user targeting models proposed in Section 2.1.

4.1 Data Description

Our goal in these experiments is to build a conversion model for online display advertisement campaigns. Essentially, this amounts to training a discriminative classifier for identifying potential converters versus non-converters, using a training dataset comprising of previous converters and non-converters (similar to [3, 4]). We collect 4 weeks of advertisement data for a set of 200 campaigns from a historical time period. The campaigns were chosen in a non-uniform manner to ensure adequate representation of campaigns across the full range of conversion volumes, where the conversion volume of a campaign denotes the number of conversions obtained by the campaign over a fixed time period (more details below).[3] The data consists of the online activity of users (such as page views, search queries) over a period of 4 weeks, along with information about whether a user converted on a campaign or not, and how many times (within the 4 week period) that the user was exposed to the ads for that campaign.

The activities of the users are a sequence of events collected from server logs. The user's feature vector comprises both raw and categorized event counts for that user for the following types of events:

- Pages visited: Features include a unique identifier of the page and the category of the page derived using an existing hierarchical page categorizer into a category taxonomy.
- Search queries: Searches issued, clicks on search links, clicks on search advertising links. Features include the category of the query, the click information and the unigrams/bigrams in the query.

For each campaign, we therefore have a dataset of users (u_i) along with their user feature vectors ($\mathbf{f}_i$) , the number of times the user was targeted with the campaign ad (x_i), and whether the user converted or not (y_i).

Since the total dimension of the above feature space can be very high (of the order of millions), we use a Mutual-Information filter to select the top $30,000$ user features in each campaign for the subsequent modeling experiments. We further down-sample the total number of users (i.e., training and test instances) used by our models to around $100,000$ users per campaign.

4.2 Evaluation Methodology

For a thorough empirical analysis of our models, we run our experiments over the entire set of $\sim$ 200 display advertising campaigns described in subsection 4.1, using an efficient Map-Reduce implementation [8]. We bin each campaign into one of 6 buckets (based on the conversion volume in the campaign). Instead of showing performance over individual campaigns, to avoid cluttering we present the average performance of models for campaigns in each bucket. The buckets correspond to an increasing log-scale in the number of conversions, and span a few orders of magnitude in conversion volume. Figure 1 plots the histogram of the number of campaigns in each bucket.

[3] We note here that users that opt out of targeting are not profiled and are therefore not included in the experiments or in the actual campaigns.

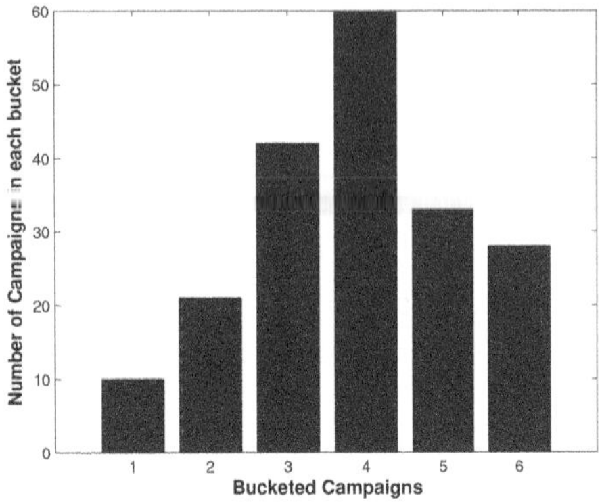

Figure 1: Number of campaigns in each conversion-volume bucket (the buckets correspond to an increasing log-scale in terms of the number of conversions).

In all our experiments, 66% of the data from each campaign is used for training the models, and the remaining 34% is used for testing, with 2-fold cross-validation. We train and evaluate the performance of the models independently for each campaign, and also estimate the average performance across all the 200 campaigns.

We use the area under the Receiver Operating Characteristic (ROC) curve to evaluate the ranked list of users produced by the different targeting models. The Area Under Curve (AUC) gives the probability that the targeting model assigns a higher score to a random positive example than a random negative example (i.e., probability of concordance) [11]. So, a purely random selection method will have an area under the curve of exactly 0.5. An algorithm that achieves AUC of 0.6 can distinguish a positive user from a negative user with 60% probability, and is thus 20% better than a random method.

An alternative metric could be to measure precision/recall at a certain rank in the list. Note that different campaigns may have different requirements in terms of precision and recall. For example, a small campaign whose reach is limited would prefer higher recall, while a large campaign that reaches out to many users might prefer higher precision. Consequently, selecting a rank at which to evaluate precision such that it would be suitable for all campaigns, is not possible. Hence, we use the AUC as a performance metric since it summarizes the prediction performance over all ranks in a single number.

4.3 Results

In this section, we show and discuss the AUC performance of the various models described in Section 2.1. This includes the baseline approaches such as logistic regression without and with the number of past impressions as a feature (denoted by LR and LR+ respectively). Our model variants include the geometric factor model (EFMG), the poisson factor model (EFMP) and the delayed factor model (EFMD) with alternate maximization being used for model inferencing. Lastly, EFMG_{EM} is the geometric model learned using the EM based inference method. We do not report the multinomial model from Section 2.1 since it did not perform well (primarily due to too many parameters being estimated). Table 1 provides a high-level overview of the average AUC performance of each of these methods over the full set of 200 campaigns. In the remainder of this section, we discuss the results of each of these methods separately, and also analyze their performance and model parameters for each stratified bucket of campaigns.

LR	LR+	EFMG	EFMP	EFMD	EFMG_{EM}
0.67	0.687	0.716	0.699	0.717	0.675

Table 1: Average AUC for the various models over the full set of 200 campaigns.

4.3.1 *Using Past Exposure as a feature*

We first obtain a baseline by using the Logistic Regression (LR) model (specified in Section 2.4), that uses $L1$-regularized logistic regression over the user feature vectors to model conversions for each campaign (ignoring information about past exposure of the user to the ad campaign in consideration). Figure 2 plots the AUC performance of this model for each stratified bucket of campaigns. The average AUC for LR over all the 200 campaigns is 0.67, and as seen from the figure, the AUC increases as the number of conversions available for training increases.

Next, we compare the performance of the LR+ model that additionally uses the number of past impressions (x_i) as another feature in the user feature vector $\mathbf{f}_i$, which is then modeled using logistic regression. As we see from Figure 1, using this simple method alone increases the AUC by 2.5% to 0.687. This demonstrates that past user exposure clearly has some discriminative signal for predicting user conversions, and suggests scope for exploiting this signal better by using a richer model.

4.3.2 *Factor Models for Past Exposure*

We now move on to experiments using our factor models for user exposure: EFMG (that uses a Geometric prior for $\text{P}[\phi_i = 1|x_i]$) and EFMP (that uses a Poisson prior for $\text{P}[\phi_i = 1|x_i]$). As seen in Table 1, EFMG yields an average AUC value of 0.716, and outperforms LR, LR+, and EFMP by around 7%, 4.2% and 2.5%, respectively. The fact that the EFMG factor model gives a substantial improvement over the LR+ and even the EFMP model, even though all of them use the past user campaign exposures, suggests that the Geometric model for modeling awareness might be a more accurate framework for accounting the effect of user exposure on conversion propensity.

While the EFMP model also improves over LR and LR+ by around 4.3% and 1.5% respectively, it does not perform as well as EFMG on average.

Figure 2 shows the average AUC performance for EFMG and EFMP for each campaign bucket. Interestingly, we see that the difference in performance among the models is more pronounced in campaigns with a smaller number of conversions (smaller bucket indices). In bucket 6 all the models perform nearly the same (except EFMP), while in bucket 1 EFMG has about a 20% higher AUC compared to the LR.

4.3.3 *Effect of Past Exposure on Different Campaigns*

Figure 3 shows the average value of the optimal Geometric parameter α (which represents the Bernoulli probability of noticing an ad) computed by the Alternate Maximization algorithm in the EFMG model, and the optimal Poisson parameter α in the EFMP model, in different buckets. Except for bucket 2 in the EFMP model, campaigns with a larger number of conversions (larger bucket indices) generally have higher α values. Recall from Section 2.2.1 that as α goes to 1, $\text{P}[\phi_i = 1|x_i]$ moves closer to 1 regardless of x_i. Hence, in such cases $\text{P}[y_i|\mathbf{f}_i, x_i]$ is relatively unaffected by the past impression count x_i, and all the user exposure models perform similarly in this situation (including the LR model that does not include user exposure).

We believe that the α parameter for each campaign is a measure

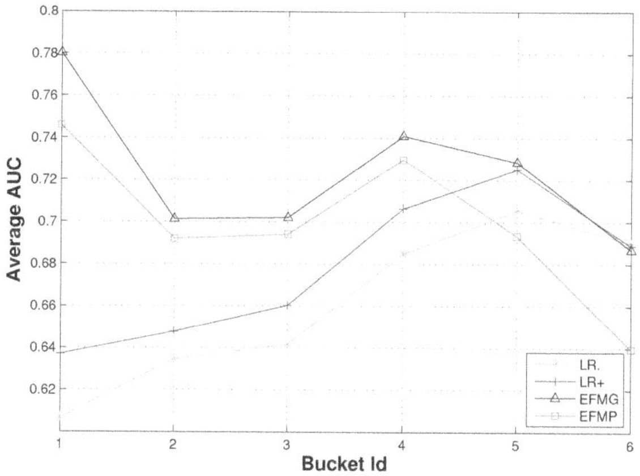

Figure 2: Average AUC of the campaigns in each conversion volume bucket for the LR, LR+, EFMG and EFMP models.

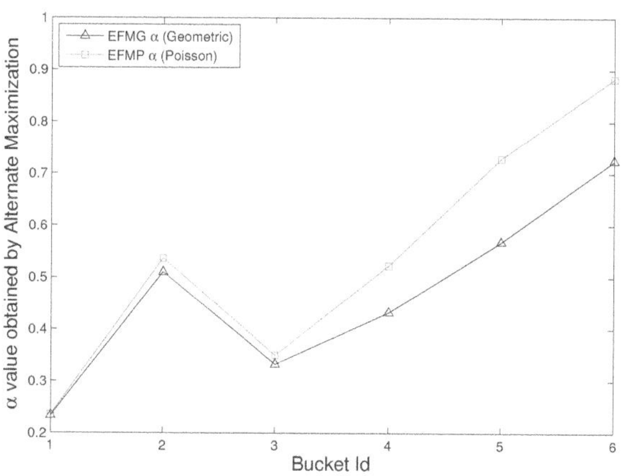

Figure 3: Average probability of noticing the ad (α parameter) for campaigns in each conversion volume bucket, for the EFMG (Geometric Distribution) model and EFMP (Poisson) models.

of the required past exposure and is unrelated to how well the campaign matches the user interest. The α parameter (noticeability) of the ad campaign depends on many hidden campaign characteristics such as brand awareness of the campaign, the product trustworthiness as well as other observable campaign characteristics such as the ad image attributes (e.g., size, color, text), the context where the ad is displayed, the location on the page where the ad is displayed (e.g. at the top of the page, above/below the fold). Modeling the ad noticeability as a function of these non-user attributes is a subject for future research.

4.3.4 Factor Model with Delay

We repeat the above experiment for the EFMD model, which incorporates an additional exponentially decaying delay factor with parameter γ in the conversion model. As described in Section 2.3, we build this delay model on top of the Geometric distribution with parameter α, and solve the resulting maximum likelihood estimation problem using alternate maximization. Table 1 shows that the performance of EFMD (AUC of 0.717) is almost identical to that of the EFM model (AUC of 0.716). Figure 4 also shows that the average AUC of the EFMD model and the EFM models are very similar over all campaign buckets. Figure 5 shows the delay parameter γ across all buckets, and this variation is non-monotonic. We believe that the delay period represents a phase when a user is considering whether to convert or not, and that our EFMD model without using any additional data source may not be rich enough to effectively model this consideration phase. Figure 5 shows the geometric parameter α (noticeability) for the EFMD model, and as with the case for EFMG and EFMP models, α increases with the number of conversions.

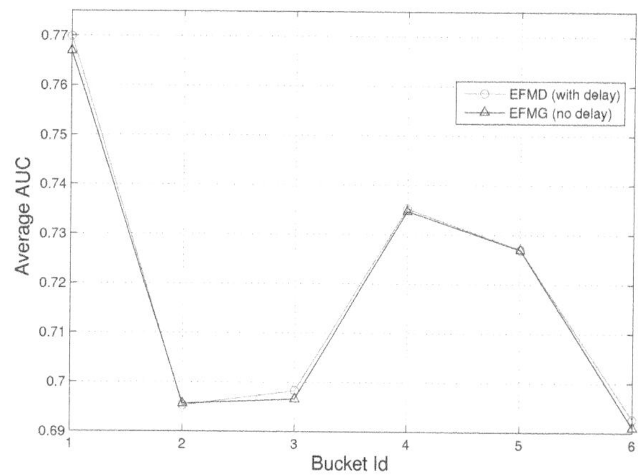

Figure 4: Average AUC of the campaigns in each conversion volume bucket for EFMG and EFMP models, with and without the additional delay factor (drawn from an exponential distribution) between the user noticing an ad and deciding whether or not to convert on it.

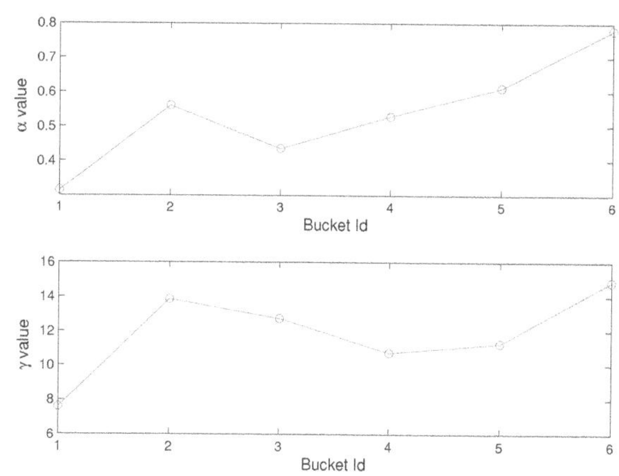

Figure 5: Top: Average probability of noticing the ad (α parameter) for campaigns in each conversion volume bucket, for the EFMD delay model. Bottom: Average value of the parameter (γ) in the exponential distribution of the delay between the user noticing an ad and making a conversion decision.

4.3.5 Effect of the Model Estimation Method

All the previous results for the factor models used Alternate Maximization (AM) for estimating the unknown model parameters. Next we explore whether the use of other optimization techniques such

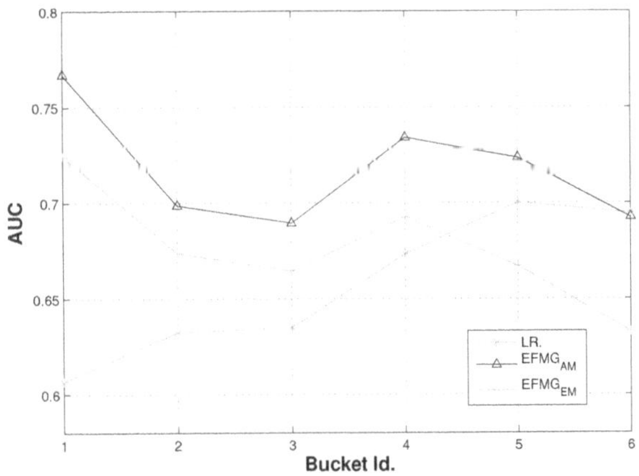

Figure 6: Average AUC of the campaigns in each conversion volume bucket for the EFMG models, with parameters estimated using Alternate Maximization ($\mathrm{EFMG_{AM}}$) and Expectation Maximization ($\mathrm{EFMG_{EM}}$), compared with the LR model

as Expectation Maximization (EM) affects the performance of the models. For this experiment we first learned the geometric factor model using the alternate maximization (denoted by EFMG) and then using the expectation maximization (denoted by $\mathrm{EFMG_{EM}}$).

Figure 6 compares the AUC performance of $\mathrm{EFMG_{EM}}$ and EFMG across all the buckets, on campaigns that converged successfully (a few models in $\mathrm{EFMG_{EM}}$ did not successfully converge). We observe that EFMG significantly outperforms $\mathrm{EFMG_{EM}}$ in all the buckets: the average AUC for $\mathrm{EFMG_{EM}}$ is 0.675 compared to 0.716 for EFMG. Further, in our experiments with $\mathrm{EFMG_{EM}}$, we observed that EM was much slower to converge than the AM approach and often encountered numerical stability issues with the M-step iterations. The reason for this poor performance with EM is likely due to the fact that we use a gradient-descent method for the M-step iterations even though the optimization objective is not convex.

5. DISCUSSION AND FUTURE WORK

In this paper we have presented an ad-exposure based factor model framework for capturing the joint effect of past ad exposure and user interest on conversion propensity for display ads. Our experimental results over a large set of 200 real-world online ad campaigns provide insights into the role that a user's past exposure to an ad campaign plays in predicting her response to the campaign. Our EFM models obtain more than a 4 to 7% gain in AUC over traditional targeting schemes that either do not consider past exposure at all, or use it naively as yet another user feature. This suggests that our models can indeed effectively factor out the separate components in terms of the interest-match component and the past-exposure component.

We can leverage this capability in two ways: first, this allows our models to target potential converters more accurately, as evident in the AUC performance. More interestingly, the α parameter that we obtain from the joint modeling of two factors in EFMG and EFMP, gives us a single metric for capturing the "effectiveness" of different ad campaigns. Advertisers can potentially use this information to determine aspects of their campaign strategy such as finding the right amount of past exposures needed by an ad to effectively target an interested user.

6. REFERENCES

[1] Zoë Abrams and Erik Vee. Personalized ad delivery when ads fatigue: an approximation algorithm. WINE'07, pages 535–540, Berlin, Heidelberg, 2007. Springer-Verlag.

[2] N. Archak, V. S Mirrokni, and S. Muthukrishnan. Mining advertiser-specific user behavior using adfactors. In *WWW*, pages 31–40, 2010.

[3] Abraham Bagherjeiran, Andrew O. Hatch, and Advait Ratnaparkhi. Ranking for the conversion funnel. In *SIGIR*, 2010.

[4] Abraham Bagherjeiran, Andrew O. Hatch, Advait Ratnaparkhi, and Rajesh Parekh. Large-scale customized models for advertisers. In *ICDMW*, 2010.

[5] David M. Blei, Andrew Y. Ng, and Michael I. Jordan. Latent dirichlet allocation. *The Journal of Machine Learning Research*, 3(4-5):993–1022, 2003.

[6] Ye Chen, Michael Kapralov, Dmitry Pavlov, and John F. Canny. Factor modeling for advertisement targeting. In *NIPS*, 2009.

[7] Ye Chen, Dmitry Pavlov, and John F. Canny. Large-scale behavioral targeting. In *KDD*, 2009.

[8] Jeffrey Dean and Sanjay Ghemawat. Mapreduce: simplified data processing on large clusters. *Commun. ACM*, 51:107–113, January 2008.

[9] Xiang Fang, Surendra Singh, and Rohini Alhuwalia. An examination of different explanations for the mere exposure effect. *Journal of consumer research*, 34(1):97–103, 2007.

[10] Thore Graepel, Joaquin Quinonero Candela, Thomas Borchert, and Ralf Herbrich. Web-scale bayesian click-through rate prediction for sponsored search advertising in bing search engine. In *ICML*, 2010.

[11] J. A. Hanley. *Receiver Operating Characteristic (ROC) Curves*. John Wiley & Sons, Ltd, 2005.

[12] Wei Li, Xuerui Wang, Ruofei Zhang, Ying Cui, Yun Jiang, and Zheng Chen. Exploitation and exploration in a performance based contextual advertising system. In *KDD*, 2010.

[13] Puneet Manchanda, Jean-Pierre Dube, Khim Yong Goh, and Pradeep K. Chintagunta. The effect of banner advertising on internet purchasing. *Journal of Marketing Research*, 43(1):98–108, 2006.

[14] Andrew Kachites McCallum. Mallet: A machine learning for language toolkit. http://www.cs.umass.edu/ mccallum/mallet, 2002.

[15] Foster Provost, Brian Dalessandro, Rod Hook, Xiaohan Zhang, and Alan Murray. Audience selection for on-line brand advertising: Privacy-friendly social network targeting. In *KDD*, 2009.

[16] Navdeep Sahni. Effect of temporal spacing between advertising exposures: Evidence from an online field experiment. To appear.

[17] Xiaoxiao Shi, Kevin L. Chang, Vijay K. Narayanan, Vanja Josifovski, and Alex Smola. A compression framework for user profile generation. In *SIGIR Workshop on Feature Generation and Selection for Information Retrieval*, 2010.

[18] Ramakrishnan Srikant, Sugato Basu, Ni Wang, and Daryl Pregibon. User browsing models: Relevance versus examination. In *KDD*, 2010.

[19] Jun Yan, Ning Liu, Gang Wang, Wen Zhang, Jianchang Mao, and Rong Jin. How much can behavioral targeting help online advertising? In *WWW*, 2009.

Online Allocation of Display Ads with Smooth Delivery

Anand Bhalgat*
University of Pennsylvania
bhalgat@seas.upenn.edu

Jon Feldman
Google Inc, New York
jonfeld@google.com

Vahab Mirrokni
Google Inc, New York
mirrokni@google.com

ABSTRACT

Display ads on the Internet are often sold in bundles of thousands or millions of impressions over a particular time period, typically weeks or months. Ad serving systems that assign ads to pages on behalf of publishers must satisfy these contracts, but at the same time try to maximize overall quality of placement. This is usually modeled in the literature as an *online allocation problem*, where contracts are represented by overall delivery constraints over a finite time horizon. However this model misses an important aspect of ad delivery: time homogeneity. Advertisers who buy these packages expect their ad to be shown *smoothly* throughout the purchased time period, in order to reach a wider audience, to have a sustained impact, and to support the ads they are running on other media (e.g., television). In this paper we formalize this problem using several nested packing constraints, and develop a tight $(1-1/e)$-competitive online algorithm for this problem. Our algorithms and analysis require novel techniques as they involve online computation of multiple dual variables per ad. We then show the effectiveness of our algorithms through exhaustive simulation studies on real data sets.

Categories and Subject Descriptors

F.2.2 [**Theory of Computation**]: Nonnumerical Algorithms and Problems; H.4.0 [**Information Systems**]: General

Keywords

Online Matching, Ad Allocation, Display Ads, Smooth Delivery

1. INTRODUCTION

Advertisers purchase bundles of thousands or even millions of display ad impressions from web publishers, and these bundles often represent just one piece of an overall seasonal marketing campaign. Think for example of a national clothing store: the summer campaign is carefully designed to reach as many customers as possible through similarly-themed ads on myriad different websites, TV stations and other media. It is essential that customers see a consistent message across media, and that throughout the time period customers are being exposed to ads.

Display ad serving systems that assign ads to pages on behalf of web publishers must satisfy the contracts with advertisers, respecting targeting criteria and delivery goals. Modulo this, publishers try to allocate ads intelligently to maximize overall quality (measured for example, by clicks). This has been modeled in the literature (e.g., [3, 7, 8]) as an online allocation problem, where quality is represented by edge weights, and contracts are enforced by overall delivery constraints: advertiser i may not receive more than $N(i)$ impressions. There is a $(1-1/e)$-approximate algorithm known for this problem using primal-dual techniques. While advertisers certainly appreciate getting high-quality placements, this treatment of the problem could lead to very undesirable allocations; nothing in the model prevents the publisher from showing a particular ad only on one day out of a month-long campaign, or only between 1:00 and 2:00am. *We note that, most current ad serving systems implement the smooth delivery constraint in some form to avoid such scenario, however their techniques do not achieve any bounded approximation guarantee in the adversarial case.*

Our Results and Techniques. In this paper we consider the problem of *time-homogenous* online ad assignment in a display ad serving system. We introduce *smooth delivery* constraints, where advertiser i may not receive more than $N(i,t)$ impressions before time t. The objective is to maximize the overall weight of assignment while respecting these constraints. (We give a more formal model in the next section.) We give a $(1-1/e)$-approximate algorithm using primal-dual techniques for the online ad assignment problem under arbitrary smooth delivery constraints in the *free disposal* model [7]. Building on the previous primal-dual algorithms that maintain one dual variable per advertiser, our algorithm and its analysis require new techniques for handling an entire vector of dual variables for each advertiser. Thankfully the online portion of the algorithm remains simple and can be implemented efficiently.

Our main technical contribution is how we handle the update of multiple, interacting dual variables simultaneously. In previous primal-dual algorithms, each incoming ad is assigned to the advertiser that minimizes an *adjusted* weight, equal to the edge weight minus the dual variable corresponding to that advertiser. The art is then to come up with a dual update rule that will maintain dual feasibility and a bounded gap between the primal and dual solutions. The natural extension to smoothness constraints subtracts off an entire *vector* of dual variables from the edge weight for each advertiser, and thus the design space for update rules is considerably larger, with complex interactions between the dual variables. To overcome this challenge, we derive careful accounting rules for the dual variables, where each variable corresponds to a set of impres-

*This work was done when the author was interning at Google Research, New York.

KDD'12, August 12–16, 2012, Beijing, China.

sions, and has a value equal to the exponential average of the set associated with it (or possibly the marginal value of that set over a later set). The heart of the algorithm lies in a *merge* operation where the impression sets assigned to two dual variables are joined, and we must prove a key technical lemma about a certain property of exponential average functions: for two sequences S_1 and S_2 with weighted exponential average δ_1 and δ_2, the weighted exponential average of their merged sequence is at most $\frac{\delta_1|S_1|+\delta_2|S_2|}{|S_1|+|S_2|}$.

Finally, we study the performance of our algorithms on real data for several web publishers against algorithms in [3, 7, 8], as well as some natural heuristics used in practice to ensure smooth delivery. Because *free disposal* is a stylized model largely necessitated by worst-case analysis, we look at overall metrics as well as smooth delivery metrics. Our algorithm matches [3,7,8] in the total weight of the assignment, it ensures substantially better delivery guarantees than both, and improves on the average quality of assignment (average CTR). It is contrary to perception that the delivery guarantees of our algorithm are substantially better than the heuristics used in practice for smooth delivery, as they are specifically tailored towards this objective. Thus, not only are our algorithms applicable to adversarial settings with traffic spikes, they also achieve superior performance on real-world data sets and metrics.

Related Work. Our work is closely related to online ad allocation problems, including the *Display Ads Allocation (DA)* problem [1, 6, 7, 11], and the *AdWords (AW)* problem [5, 8]. In both of these problems, the publisher must assign online impressions to an inventory of ads, optimizing efficiency or revenue of the allocation while respecting pre-specified contracts. In the AdWords(AW) problem [5, 8], advertiser i has a budget $B(i)$ on the total spend, and assigning impression j to advertiser i consumes $w(i, j)$ of his budget; whereas in the DisplayAds (DA) problem, advertiser i is associated with capacity $N(i)$, and assigning impression j to advertiser i consumes 1 unit from his capacity. In both problems, the objective is to maximize the total welfare. These problems have been studied in the stochastic as well as the adversarial arrival model. For the adversarial arrival model, a (1-1/e) approximation is known for both problems [5,7,8]. In the stochastic arrival model, a $(1-\varepsilon)$-approximation has been recently developed using primal-dual techniques [1,5,6,11]. Control-based adaptive algorithms have also been applied in the stochastic model; they achieve asymptotic optimality following an updating rule inspired by the primal-dual algorithms [10]. We note that none of the stochastic algorithms provide a guaranteed approximation in the adversarial model. As a real world application can experience unexpected traffic spikes, the desirable algorithms should be able to deal with unexpected traffic spikes while performing better for stochastic models [9].

We describe some of the other related work. Alaei *et al* [2] consider the problem of balanced allocation in the context of off-line ad allocation problem. Recently, Chen *et al* [4] gave a scheme that enables advertisers to alter their bids in real time.

We would like to mention that that none of these results consider *multiple budgets or capacity constraints* per advertiser. Our analysis requires a new set of techniques as we need to deal with computing multiple dual variables per ad in an online manner.

Organization We formally define the smooth delivery model for the Display Ads Allocation problem in Section 2. In Section 3, we describe our algorithm and prove the main result. Finally, we highlight important experimental observations in Section 4.

2. PRELIMINARIES

In this section, we formally define the Display Ads Allocation problem under *smooth delivery constraint*. There are n advertisers, $\mathbb{A}_1, \mathbb{A}_2, \dots, \mathbb{A}_n$. Impressions arrive one-by-one; when an impression arrives, it can be assigned to one of the advertisers. We denote the jth impression by $\mathbb{I}_j$ and the welfare of assigning $\mathbb{I}_j$ to $\mathbb{A}_i$ by $w(i, j)$. The total number of impressions is m.

The period of impressions' arrival is split into t intervals and an advertiser specifies the nature of impressions' delivery over these intervals. In particular, $\mathbb{A}_i$ does not wish to be assigned more than $N(i,k)$ impressions in first k intervals[1], for each $1 \le k \le t$. We refer to such capacity constraint as the *smooth delivery constraint.* The objective is to maximize the total welfare of the impressions assigned subject to the advertisers' capacity constraints.

We denote the number of impressions that arrive in first k intervals by $M(k)$, and the interval in which $\mathbb{I}_j$ arrives by $T(j)$. We assume $N(i,k+1) \ge N(i,k)$ for each k and $N(i,0) = 0$ for each i.

To enforce the capacity constraints, we apply the *free disposal* model [7], which says that capacity constraints are not strictly enforced during the run of the algorithm, rather they are used to determine the final value of the solution. In the smooth delivery setting, that means the following: Let S_i be the set of impressions assigned to advertiser i. Now let $S'_i \subseteq S_i$ be the maximum-weight subset such that S'_i has no more than $N(i,k)$ impressions from the first k intervals, for every k. Then, S'_i is used in the objective function to determine the value of the solution.

3. THE AD ALLOCATION ALGORITHM

In this section, we present a primal-dual based algorithm for the display ads problem with smooth delivery constraints. The LP for the offline matching problem is given below. The variable $x(i, j)$ is the fraction of $\mathbb{I}_j$ assigned to $\mathbb{A}_i$. The objective function is to maximize total welfare, the first set of constraints are the capacity constraints that guarantee the smooth-delivery of impressions, and the second set of constraints indicate that each impression is assigned to at most one advertiser.

$$\begin{array}{rll} \text{Maximize:} & \sum_j w(i,j)x(i,j) & \\ \text{Subject to:} & & \\ \text{For each } 1 \le i \le n, 1 \le k \le t: & \sum_{1\le j \le M(k)} x(i,j) & \le N(i,k) \\ \text{For each } 1 \le j \le m: & \sum_i x(i,j) & \le 1 \\ \text{For each } i,j: & x(i,j) & \ge 0 \end{array}$$

The following LP is its dual.

$$\begin{array}{rl} \text{Minimize:} & \sum_{i,k} \beta(i,k)N(i,k) + \sum_j z(j) \\ \text{Subject to:} & \\ \text{For each } 1 \le i \le n, 1 \le j \le m: & \sum_{T(j)\le l \le t} \beta(i,l) + z(j) \ge w(i,j) \\ \text{For each } 1 \le i \le n, 1 \le k \le t: & \beta(i,k) \ge 0 \\ \text{For each } j: & z(j) \ge 0 \end{array}$$

Algorithm.

We first illustrate the overall structure of dual variables. There are t beta variables corresponding to an advertiser, one for each of t capacity constraints. A beta variable $\beta(i,k)$ goes through three phases during the course of the algorithm: (a) inactive, (b) active, and (c) dead. It is *inactive* at the start of the algorithm, it becomes *active* when the first impression in the kth interval arrives and *may*

[1] In practice, the advertiser only specifies the value of total delivery and its expected delivery pattern. The display ad serving system computes the values of $N(i,k)$ for $1 \le k \le t$ based on this information. However, the algorithm and its approximation factor are independent of the way $N(i,k)$s are computed.

become dead in some later interval $k' > k$. The value of a beta variable is 0 when it is inactive or dead.

At any given state in the algorithm, for any i,k, let $F(i,k)$ be the largest integer k' such that $k' < k$ and $\beta(i,k')$ is active. If no such k' exists, then we define $F(i,k)$ to be 0. During the course of the algorithm, an active beta variable for an advertiser is associated with a (sub)set of impressions (already) assigned to him. If $\beta(i,k)$ is active when $\mathbb{I}_j$ arrives, then the set of impressions associated with it is the set of impressions assigned to $\mathbb{A}_i$ from the $(F(i,k)+1)^{th}$ interval up to the kth interval. We denote this set by $S(i,k)$. *Thus the sets associated with an advertiser's active beta variables form a partition over impressions assigned to him up to that stage.*

We propose three different ways by which the value of an active beta variable is determined; and they correspond to three algorithms that we design, namely (a) smooth-greedy (b) smooth-avg, (c) smooth-exp: we compute a candidate value $\delta(i,k)$ for an active beta variable $\beta(i,k)$ in these three different algorithms as follows.

1. *Smooth-Exp*: Let $w_1, w_2, ..., w_{|S(i,k)|}$ be the weights of impressions in $S(i,k)$ in a decreasing order. Then $\delta(i,k) = \frac{1}{\left(\left(1+\frac{1}{|S(i,k)|}\right)^{|S(i,k)|}-1\right)|S(i,k)|} \sum_{1\le j\le |S(i,k)|} \left(1+\frac{1}{|S(i,k)|}\right)^{j-1} w_j$
2. *Smooth-Greedy*: $\delta(i,k)$ is the smallest weight of an impression in $S(i,k)$.
3. *Smooth-Avg*: $\delta(i,k)$ is the average weight of impressions in $S(i,k)$.

We illustrate the smooth-avg algorithm in Section 3.1 and its analysis is given in Section 3.2. The smooth-greedy algorithm is exactly same as the smooth-avg algorithm (other than computing the value of an active beta variable) and we skip its analysis for lack of space. The smooth-exp algorithm uses the same basic framework as the smooth-avg algorithm with certain crucial differences; we illustrate the differences in the smooth-exp algorithm, and its analysis in Section 3.3.

Our results for smooth-greedy and smooth-avg hold even when t is as large as m, i.e. the advertiser can specify his capacity constraint from the beginning to the arrival of each impression. For the $(1-1/e)$-approximation, the smooth-exp algorithm makes certain assumptions (to be described later).

3.1 The Smooth-Avg Algorithm

We now illustrate the smooth-avg algorithm. At the start of the algorithm, (a) for each i,k, $\beta(i,k) = 0$, (b) the set $S(i,k)$ has $N(i,k) - N(i,k-1)$ elements and each element is 0, and (c) for each $j, 1 \le j \le m$, $z_j = 0$. Algorithm 1 illustrates one iteration of the algorithm: the incoming impression is $\mathbb{I}_j$ and the current interval is k. The algorithm either assigns the impression to one of the advertisers or leaves it unassigned.

Given an iteration of the algorithm, we use $\beta_{start}(i,l), \beta_{end}(i,l)$ to indicate the value of a beta variable at the start and the end of the iteration respectively, and $\beta(i,l)$ refers its current value. We define $F_{start}(i,k)$, $F_{end}(i,k)$, $\delta_{start}(i,k)$, $\delta_{end}(i,k)$, $S_{start}(i,k)$ and $S_{end}(i,k)$ similarly to indicate corresponding quantities at the start and the end of the iteration respectively, and $F(i,k)$, $\delta(i,k)$ and $S(i,k)$ refer to their current values. We define $\Delta(\beta(i,k))$ to be $\beta_{end}(i,k) - \beta_{start}(i,k)$.

Interpretation of the Algorithm.

We now provide a simple interpretation of the algorithm. We consider an instance with 2 intervals. Up to the end of the first interval, $\beta(i,1)$ is the average weight of impressions in $S(i,1)$, i.e. the set of $N(i,1)$ *top* impressions assigned to $\mathbb{A}_i$ in the first interval. In the second interval, there are two phases.

(1) In the first phase, $S(i,2)$ is the set of *top* $(N(i,2)-N(i,1))$ impressions assigned to $\mathbb{A}_i$ in the second interval. In this phase, the average weight of impressions in $S(i,2)$ is less than the average weight of impressions in $S(i,1)$. During this phase, $\beta(i,2)$ and $(\beta(i,1)+\beta(i,2))$ are the average weights of impressions in $S(i,2)$ and $S(i,1)$ respectively. Thus $\beta(i,1)$ stores the *marginal* over $\beta(i,2)$.

(2) When the average weight of impressions in $S(i,2)$ exceeds the average weight of impressions in $S(i,1)$ for the first time, then (a) the set $S(i,1)$ merges with $S(i,2)$ and $S(i,2)$ has size $N(i,2)$ after merge, (b) $\beta(i,1)$ is dead, and (c) $\beta(i,2)$ is the average weight of *top* $N(i,2)$ impressions assigned to $\mathbb{A}_i$ so far.

Figure 3.1 illustrates these phases of the algorithm.

Algorithm 1 One Iteration of Smooth-Avg Algorithm

Find advertiser $\mathbb{A}_i$ which maximizes $w(i,j) - \sum_{k\le l\le t}\beta(i,l)$.
if $\sum_{k\le l\le t}\beta(i,l) < w(i,j)$ **then**
  Assign $\mathbb{I}_j$ to $\mathbb{A}_i$.
  $z_j \Leftarrow b(i,j) - \sum_{k\le l\le t}\beta(i,l)$.
  Let w_{min} be the minimum weight element in the set $S(i,k)$.
  Then $S(i,k) \leftarrow S(i,k) \setminus \{w_{min}\} \cup \{w(i,j)\}$.
  Compute $\delta(i,k)$ for the set $S(i,k)$.
  $\beta(i,k) \Leftarrow \delta(i,k)$
  while $\beta(i,k) \ge \sum_{F(i,k)\le l\le t}\beta_{start}(i,l)$ **do**
    $\beta(i,F(i,k)) \Leftarrow 0$ and change its state to dead.
    $S(i,k) \Leftarrow S(i,k) \cup S(i,F(i,k))$.
    Compute $\delta(i,k)$ for the set $S(i,k)$.
    $\beta(i,k) \Leftarrow \delta(i,k)$
  end while
  $\beta(i,F(i,k)) \leftarrow \beta(i,F(i,k)) - \sum_{F(i,k)+1\le l\le k}(\beta_{end}(i,l) - \beta_{start}(i,l))$
end if

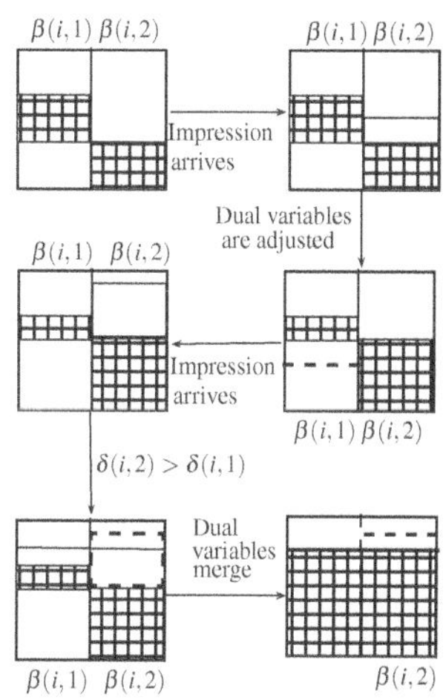

Figure 1: Smooth-Avg Algorithm. The left box represents the first interval and the right box represents the second. The height of the shaded area indicates the value of corresponding beta variable.

3.2 Analysis of the Smooth-Avg Algorithm

The goal of this section is to prove the following theorem:

THEOREM 3.1. *The approximation ratio of the smooth-avg algorithm is* $1/2$.

We first establish some important properties of beta variables. We call an iteration to be *merge-free* if no beta variables change their state to dead in the iteration. We note an important property of a merge free iteration.

FACT 1. *In a merge-free iteration of the algorithm, at most two beta variables change their value. Further more, if* $\mathbb{A}_i$ *is assigned the impression and the current interval is k, then*

$$\Delta(\beta(i,k)) = -\Delta(\beta(i,F(i,k)))$$

and remaining beta variables remain unchanged.

In the following lemma, we establish an important invariant maintained by the algorithm.

LEMMA 3.1. *For any* i,l*, when a beta variable* $\beta(i,l)$ *is active, then* $\delta(i,l) = \sum_{l \le p \le t} \beta(i,p)$.

PROOF. Given a beta variable $\beta(i,l)$, we first consider the lth interval of the algorithm. In the lth interval, $\beta(i,p) = 0$ for $p > l$ and the algorithm ensures that $\beta(i,l) = \delta(i,l)$. The set associated with $\beta(i,l)$ remains unchanged from the start of the $(l+1)^{th}$ iteration until $\beta(i,l)$ becomes dead. Hence it suffices to show that, while $\beta(i,l)$ is still active, $\sum_{l \le p \le t} \beta(i,p)$ does not change.

Consider the jth iteration of the algorithm, and let the corresponding interval be $k(> l)$. There are two cases based on the type of the iteration. If that iteration is merge-free, then as $\beta(i,l)$ is still active, $F(i,k) \ge l$, and by using Fact 1, we get $\sum_{l \le p \le t} \beta_{end}(i,p) = \sum_{l \le p \le t} \beta_{start}(i,p)$.

Now we consider the case when the jth iteration involves a merge operation. In this case, the algorithm ensures that

$$\Delta(\beta(i,F_{end}(i,k))) = -\left(\sum_{F_{end}(i,k)+1 \le l \le k} \Delta(\beta(i,l))\right)$$

This proves the lemma. □

We now prove the correctness of the smooth-avg algorithm by establishing two properties (a) the dual at the end of the algorithm is feasible, and (b) in every iteration, (the change in the dual)/(the change in the primal)≤ 2. The feasibility of the dual solution follows from the following lemma:

LEMMA 3.2. *The sum* $\sum_{l \le p \le t} \beta(i,p)$ *never decreases during the course of the algorithm for any* i,l.

PROOF. We prove the claim by induction on iterations of the algorithm. We consider j^{th} iteration of the algorithm and let k be the corresponding interval. If $\mathbb{I}_j$ is not assigned to any advertiser, then the claim follows by the induction assumption as no beta variable is changed. Now we consider the case when it is assigned to $\mathbb{A}_i$. We show that $\sum_{l \le p \le t} \beta(i,p)$ increases for $F_{end}(i,k) \le l \le k$ and remains unchanged otherwise. The latter follows as the algorithm ensures,

$$\Delta(\beta(i,F_{end}(i,k))) = -\left(\sum_{F_{end}(i,k)+1 \le l \le k} \Delta(\beta(i,l))\right)$$

Now we show that $\sum_{l \le p \le t} \beta(i,p)$ increases for $F_{end}(i,k) \le l \le k$. If the iteration is merge free and I_j is assigned to $\mathbb{A}_i$, then $\Delta(\beta(i,k)) > 0$, $\Delta(\beta(i,F_{start}(i,k))) = -\Delta(\beta(i,k))$, and remaining beta variables remain unchanged. Thus the claim holds in this case. Now we consider the case when the iteration is not merge free. Let $\{\beta(i,k_1), \beta(i,k_2), ..., \beta(i,k_d)\}$ (with $k_1 < k_2 < ... < k_d$) be the set of beta variables that die in this iteration. We note that $F_{start}(i,k_l) = k_{l-1}$ for $2 \le l \le d$, $F_{start}(i,k) = k_d$ and $F_{start}(i,k_1) = F_{end}(i,k)$.

Applying the precondition for merge operation on the last merge operation of the iteration, we get that the average weight of impressions in the set $(\cup_{1 \le p \le d} S_{start}(i,k_p)) \cup S(i,k) \cup \{w(i,j)\}/\{w_{min}\}$ is greater than $\delta_{start}(i,k_1)$ i.e. the average weight of impressions in $S_{start}(i,k_1)$. Thus $\beta_{end}(i,k)$, which is the average weight of impressions in $S_{end}(i,k) = (\cup_{1 \le p \le d} S_{start}(i,k_p)) \cup S(i,k) \cup \{w(i,j)\}/\{w_{min}\}$, is greater than $\delta_{start}(i,k_1) = \sum_{k_1 \le p \le k} \beta_{start}(i,p)$. Thus we get

$$\beta_{end}(i,k) > \sum_{k_1 \le p \le k} \beta_{start}(i,p) = \sum_{F_{end}(i,k)+1 \le p \le t} \beta_{start}(i,p)$$

as the other beta variables in the sum are 0. This completes the proof of the lemma. □

We are now ready to prove Theorem 3.1:

PROOF. (Theorem 3.1) We compute the change in the primal and dual in the jth iteration of the algorithm. If $\mathbb{I}_j$ remains unassigned, then the primal and the dual solutions do not change. When it is assigned to $\mathbb{A}_i$, the change in the primal is $w(i,j) - w_{min}$ and it suffices to show that the change in the dual is at most $2(w(i,j) - w_{min})$ to establish the theorem.

We first consider the case when the jth iteration is merge-free. In this case, by Lemma 3.1, we have $\Delta(\beta(i,k)) = -\Delta(\beta(i,F(i,k))) = \frac{w(i,j)-w_{min}}{N(i,k)-N(i,F(i,k))}$ and other dual variables remains unchanged. Thus the total change in the dual solution is

$$\begin{aligned} &= \Delta(\beta(i,F(i,k)))N(i,F(i,k)) + \Delta(\beta(i,k))N(i,k) + z_j \\ &= w(i,j) - w_{min} + z_j \end{aligned}$$

Moreover $z_j = w(i,j) - \beta(i,k) \le w(i,j) - w_{min}$. Thus the change in the dual is at most $2(w(i,j) - w_{min})$.

Now we consider the case when the jth iteration is not merge free. Let $S_{start}(i,k_1), S_{start}(i,k_2), ..., S_{start}(i,k_d)$ be the sets that merge with $S_{start}(i,k)$ in the current iteration, such that $k_1 < k_2 < ... < k_d$. As a result, the beta variables $\beta(i,k_1), \beta(i,k_2), ..., \beta(i,k_d)$ change their state to dead. For simplicity, we denote $F_{end}(i,k)$ at the end of the iteration by k_0.

The value of $\delta_{end}(i,k)$ is the average weight of impressions in $S_{end}(i,k) = (\cup_{1 \le p \le d} S_{start}(i,k_p)) \cup S_{start}(i,k) \cup \{w(i,j)\}/\{w_{min}\}$. Now we compute the average weight of impressions in $S_{end}(i,k)$. The average weight of impressions in $S_{start}(i,k_l)$ is $\delta_{start}(i,k_l)$ and $|S_{start}(i,k_l)| = N(i,k_l) - N(i,k_{l-1})$ for $1 \le l \le d$. By Lemma 3.1, for an active beta variable $\beta(i,l)$, $\delta_{start}(i,l) = \sum_{l \le p \le t} \beta_{start}(i,p)$. As $\beta(i,p) = 0$ for $p > k$, we get

$$\begin{aligned} &\beta_{end}(i,k)(N(i,k) - N(i,k_0)) \\ &= \delta_{start}(i,k)(N(i,k) - N(i,k_d)) \\ &+ \sum_{1 \le l \le d} \delta_{start}(i,k_d)(N(i,k_l) - N(i,k_{l-1})) + w(i,j) - w_{min} \\ &= \beta_{start}(i,k)(N(i,k) - N(i,k_0)) \\ &+ \sum_{1 \le l \le d} \beta_{start}(i,k_l)(N(i,k_l) - N(i,k_0)) + w(i,j) - w_{min} \qquad (1) \end{aligned}$$

Thus we get

$$\Delta(\beta(i,k)) = \frac{\sum_{1 \le l \le d} \beta_{start}(i,k_l)(N(i,k_l) - N(i,k_0)) + w(i,j) - w_{min}}{N(i,k) - N(i,k_0)}$$

The variable $\beta(i,k_0)$ is active at the end of iteration. Using Lemma 3.1, we get

$$\delta_{start}(i,k_0) = \delta_{end}(i,k_0) = \sum_{k_0 \le l \le t} \beta_{end}(i,l) = \beta_{end}(i,k_0) + \beta_{end}(i,k)$$

as other beta variables are 0. Thus we get,

$$\begin{aligned}\Delta(\beta(i,k_0)) &= -\sum_{k_0<l\le t}\Delta(\beta(i,l)) \\ &= -\Delta(\beta(i,k)) - \sum_{1\le p\le d}\beta_{start}(i,k_p) \qquad (2)\end{aligned}$$

The change in the dual is equal to

$$= \Delta(\beta(i,k))N(i,k) + \sum_{0\le l\le d}\Delta(\beta(i,k_l))N(i,k_l) + z_j$$

Using Equations 1 and 2, we get

$$= \sum_{1\le l\le d}\beta_{start}(i,k_l)\left(N(i,k_l)-N(i,k_0)\right)$$
$$- \sum_{1\le l\le d}\beta_{start}(i,k_l)\left(N(i,k_l)-N(i,k_0)\right) + w(i,j) - w_{min} + z_j$$
$$= w(i,j) - w_{min} + z_j \le 2(w(i,j)-w_{min})$$

This completes the proof of the theorem. □

3.3 Smooth-Exp Algorithm

In this section, we illustrate our result for the smooth-exp algorithm. The algorithm uses the same basic framework as the smooth-avg algorithm; we illustrate the differences between the two algorithms and its correctness proof in this section.

We first establish an important property of weighted exponential average functions in the following lemma, that will be crucial to the smooth-exp algorithm.

LEMMA 3.3. *Given two sequences S_1 and S_2, with weighted exponential averages δ_1 and δ_2 respectively, the weighted exponential average of their merged sequence $S_1 \cup S_2$ is at most $\frac{\delta_1|S_1|+\delta_2|S_2|}{|S_1|+|S_2|}$*

PROOF. Let $n_1 = |S_1|, n_2 = |S_2|$, and $n = n_1 + n_2$. Let $a_1, a_2, ..., a_{n_1}$ and $b_1, b_2, ..., b_{n_2}$, be elements in S_1, S_2 in an ascending order. Let $S = c_1, c_2, c_3, ..., c_n$ be their merged sequence. We shall construct an ordered sequence $S' = d_1, d_2, d_3, ..., d_n$ such that its weighted exponential average is no more than $\frac{\delta_1 n_1 + \delta_2 n_2}{n_1+n_2}$ and S' ensures following property:

PROPERTY 1. *For every $1 \le i \le n$, $\sum_{1\le j\le i} c_j \le \sum_{1\le j\le i} d_j$, and $\sum_{1\le j\le n} c_j = \sum_{1\le j\le n} d_j$.*

Let $\alpha(i,n_1) = \frac{(1+1/n_1)^{n_1-i}}{n_1((1+1/n_1)^{n_1}-1)}$, i.e the ith term in exponential weights for a sequence of size n_1. Similarly, we define $\alpha(i,n_2)$ and $\alpha(i,n)$. The weighted exponential averages of S and S' are $\sum_{1\le i\le n}\alpha(i,n)c_i$ and $\sum_{1\le i\le n}\alpha(i,n)d_i$ respectively. As S and S' are in an ascending order, using Property 1, we get,

$$\sum_{1\le i\le n}\alpha(i,n)c_i \le \sum_{1\le i\le n}\alpha(i,n)d_i$$

which proves the lemma. So it remains to establish the existence of sequence S'.

Let $\gamma = n_1/n$. For any sequence $Q = q_1, q_2, q_3, ..., q_{|Q|}$ and $0 \le r \le |Q|$, we define $\texttt{Prefix}(Q,r) = \sum_{1\le j\le\lfloor r\rfloor} q_j + (r - \lfloor r\rfloor) * q_{\lceil r\rceil}$. We construct S' as follows: for every $i, 1 \le i \le n$

$$d_i = \gamma R(1,i) + (1-\gamma)R(2,i)$$

where

$$R(1,i) = \texttt{Prefix}(S_1, i\gamma) - \texttt{Prefix}(S_1,(i-1)\gamma) \quad \text{and}$$
$$R(2,i) = \texttt{Prefix}(S_2, i(1-\gamma)) - \texttt{Prefix}(S_2,(i-1)(1-\gamma))$$

Now we check properties of S': (a) as S_1 and S_2 are sorted, S' is also sorted in an ascending order, and (b) as the sum of first i elements in S' is the sum of first $i \times n_1/n$ and $i \times n_2/n$ elements from S_1 and S_2 respectively, it easily follows that S' satisfies Property 1.

Now it remains to establish the bound on the exponential weighted average of S'. We first note that δ_1, i.e. the exponential average of S_1, can be written as

$$\sum_{1\le i\le n_1} a_i\alpha(i,n_1)$$
$$= a_1\left(\sum_{1\le i\le n_1}\alpha(i,n_1)\right) + \sum_{2\le i\le n_1}\left((a_i - a_{i-1})\left(\sum_{i\le j\le n_1}\alpha(j,n_1)\right)\right)$$

It suffices to show that the weighted exponential average of sequence $R_1 = R(1,1), R(1,2), ..., R(1,n)$ is upper bounded by δ_1. Then, by symmetry, the weighted exponential average of sequence $R_2 = R(2,1), R(2,2), ..., R(2,n)$ is upper bounded by δ_2, and by definition of S', we get the required upper bound on its weighed exponential average.

The weighted exponential average of R_1 can be written as

$$a_1\sum_{1\le i\le n}\alpha(1,i) + \sum_{2\le i\le n_1}(a_i - a_{i-1})\left(\sum_{\lceil\frac{i-1}{\gamma}\rceil+1\le j\le n}\alpha(j,n)\right)$$
$$+\sum_{2\le i\le n_1}(a_i - a_{i-1})\left(\left\lceil\frac{i-1}{\gamma}\right\rceil - \frac{i-1}{\gamma}\right)\alpha\left(\left\lceil\frac{i-1}{\gamma}\right\rceil, n\right)$$

Let $Z_1(i)$ and $Z(i)$ be multipliers of term $(a_i - a_{i-1})$ for sequences S_1 and R_1 respectively. As $\sum_{1\le i\le n}\alpha(1,i) = \sum_{1\le i\le n_1}\alpha(i,n_1) = 1$, and $\forall i \ge 2, (a_i - a_{i-1}) \ge 0$, it suffice to show that $Z_1(i) \ge Z(i)$ for each $2 \le i \le n_1$. Then we have

$$Z_1(i) = \frac{(1+1/n_1)^{(n_1-i+1)}-1}{(1+1/n_1)^{n_1}-1} \quad \text{and}$$
$$Z(i) = \frac{(1+1/n)^{(n_1-i+1)/\gamma}-1}{(1+1/n)^{n}-1}$$

We note an important property in the following lemma, it can be easily proven by differentiation.

LEMMA 3.4. *For any fixed $c, 0 \le c \le 1$, the function $\frac{(1+1/n)^{cn}-1}{(1+1/n)^{n}-1}$ is non-increasing in n.*

By choosing $c = (n_1 - i + 1)/n_1$, we get $Z_1(i) \ge Z(i)$. This completes the proof. □

Algorithm: The algorithm is similar to the smooth-avg algorithm with one exception: the difference occurs in merge operation due to different behavior shown by exponential average function compared to "average" function. For any two sequences S_1 and S_2 with exponential average δ_1 and δ_2, the merged sequence can have exponential average less than $\frac{\delta_1|S_1|+\delta_2|S_2|}{|S_1|+|S_2|}$ (Lemma 3.3). This creates issue in the feasibility of dual if we follow the same algorithm as smooth-avg. We handle the merge operation as follows: in the iteration where $\beta(i,k)$ merges with $\beta(i,F(i,k))$, $\mathbb{I}_j$ has been assigned to $\mathbb{A}_i$ before the merge operation. Let $S(i,k) = S_{start}(i,k) \cup w(i,j)\backslash w_{min}$, and $\delta(i,k)$ be its weighted exponential average. Let $\gamma = \max\{\beta_{start}(i,k), \delta(i,k)\}$. Then we assign the following value to $\beta(i,k)$ as result of the merge operation

$$\frac{\gamma|S_{start}(i,k)| + (\beta_{start}(i,k) + \beta_{start}(i,F(i,k)))|S_{start}(i,F(i,k))|}{|S_{start}(i,F(i,k))| + |S_{start}(i,k)|}$$

Similar to the smooth-avg algorithm, among the variables that are active at the end of the iteration, the value changes for only two of them: $\beta(i,k)$ and $\beta(i,F_{end}(i,k))$. Furthermore, $\beta(i,F_{end}(i,k))$ is changed such that, we have

$$\Delta(\beta(i,F_{end}(i,k))) = -\sum_{F_{end}(i,k)+1\le l\le t}\Delta(\beta(i,l))$$

Thus they continue to hold the marginal over the next active beta variable. Now we note important properties ensured by the algorithm.

FACT 2. *In the kth interval, (a) before any merge operation involving $\beta(i,k)$, the algorithm ensures $\beta(i,k) = \delta(i,k)$, (b) after a merge operation involving $\beta(i,k) \geq \delta(i,k)$, and (c) $\beta(i,k)$ never decreases.*

FACT 3. *For any i,l, when a variable $\beta(i,l)$ is active, then $\sum_{l \leq p \leq t} \beta(i,p) \geq \delta(i,l)$.*

FACT 4. *During the course of the algorithm, $\sum_{l \leq p \leq t} \beta(i,p)$ does not decrease for any i,l.*

It can be checked that these properties continue to hold for a merge-free iteration. Now we consider an iteration in which $\beta(i,k)$ merges with $\beta(i,F(i,k))$; we have: (a) the current interval is k^{th} interval and $\beta(i,>k) = 0$, (b) $\delta_{start}(i,k) \leq \beta_{start}(i,k)$, $\beta(i,>k) = 0$, and (c) $\delta_{start}(i,F(i,k)) \leq \beta_{start}(i,k) + \beta_{start}(i,F(i,k))$. By Lemma 3.3, the weighed exponential average of $S_{end}(i,k)$ after merging is upper bounded by

$$\frac{\gamma|S_{start}(i,k)| + \delta_{start}(i,F(i,k))|S_{start}(i,F(i,k))|}{|S_{start}(i,F(i,k))| + |S_{start}(i,k)|} \leq$$
$$\frac{\gamma|S_{start}(i,k)| + (\beta_{start}(i,k) + \beta_{start}(i,F(i,k)))|S_{start}(i,F(i,k))|}{|S_{start}(i,F(i,k))| + |S_{start}(i,k)|}$$

This ensures that $\delta_{end}(i,k) \leq \beta_{end}(i,k)$. Furthermore, it can be checked that the merge operation does not increase the value of the dual solution and the dual continues to remain feasible. When more than one merge operation take place in the same iteration for an advertiser, we treat it as a sequence of merge operations such that in step, one beta variable merges with $\beta(i,k)$, and each step is treated in the same way as discussed above. We now establish the performance ratio of the algorithm.

THEOREM 3.2. *If $(N(i,k) - N(i,k-1))$ is large for every i,k, then the performance ratio of the smooth-exp algorithm is $(1 - 1/e)$.*

PROOF. We compare the change in the primal and the dual solution in the jth iteration of the algorithm, let k be the corresponding interval. If $\mathbb{I}_j$ remains unassigned, then the primal and the dual solutions do not change. If $\mathbb{I}_j$ is assigned to $\mathbb{A}_i$, then the change in the primal is $w(i,j) - w_{min}$. If the jth iteration is merge free, then the change in the dual is $\Delta(\beta(i,k))N(i,k) - \Delta(\beta(i,k))N(i,F(i,k)) + z_j$. Furthermore, we have

$$\Delta(\beta(i,k)) \leq \delta_{end}(i,k) - \beta_{start}(i,k) \leq \delta_{end}(i,k) - \delta_{start}(i,k)$$
$$\leq \frac{w(i,j)}{(N(i,k) - N(i,F(i,k)))(e-1)} + \frac{\delta_{start}(i,k)}{N(i,k) - N(i,F(i,k))} - \frac{e \cdot w_{min}}{(e-1)(N(i,k) - N(i,F(i,k)))}$$

Thus the change in the dual is

$$= \Delta(\beta(i,k))N(i,k) - \Delta(\beta(i,k))N(i,F(i,k)) + z_j$$
$$\leq \frac{w(i,j)}{e-1} + \delta_{start}(i,k) - \frac{e \cdot w_{min}}{e-1} + w(i,j) - \sum_{k \leq l \leq t} \beta_{start}(i,l)$$

Using $\beta_{start}(i,p) = 0$ for $p > k$ and $\beta_{start}(i,k) \geq \delta_{start}(i,k)$, the change in the dual is bounded by

$$\leq \frac{w(i,j)}{e-1} + \beta_{start}(i,k) - \frac{e \cdot w_{min}}{e-1} + w(i,j) - \beta_{start}(i,k)$$
$$= \frac{(w(i,j) - w_{min})e}{e-1}$$

Thus the change in the dual is at most $e/(e-1)$ times the change in the primal. When the iteration involves a merge operation, we consider two stages involved in the iteration, (a) in the first stage, we add the impression to $S(i,k)$, $\beta(i,k)$ increases and $\beta(i,F(i,k))$ decreases and the change in this step is bounded by $(e/(e-1))(w(i,j) - w_{min})$, (b) as the value of $\beta(i,F(i,k))$ is now negative, $\beta(i,k)$ and $\beta(i,F(i,k))$ merge (potentially followed by a sequence of more merge operations), and using Lemma 3.3, there is no increase in the dual objective in this step. This completes the proof. □

Recall that, the algorithm in [7] requires each advertiser to have a large capacity to get a $(1 - 1/e)$ approximation. We now show that, even a stronger version of this assumption does not suffice to get a $(1 - 1/e)$-approximation in the smooth delivery setting, and the assumption made in Theorem 3.2 is indeed required. We defer its proof to the full version.

LEMMA 3.5. *For the Display Ads Allocation problem, no deterministic algorithm can do better than $1/2$, even when $N(i,k)$ is large for every i and large k.*

4. EXPERIMENTAL EVALUATION

We study the performance of our algorithm on display ads data for a set of 10 anonymous publishers working with Google (DoubleClick) display advertising system. The data set is collected over a period of one week for each publisher. The number of impressions in a data set range from 200 thousands to 3 millions.

Weight of an Advertiser-Impression Pair: We associate the CTR for an impression-advertiser pair with the advertiser's welfare from the assignment. Thus the objective of a display ad system is to assign impressions subject to the capacity constraints so that the (expected) number of clicks is maximized.

The Delivery Model and Penalty: We assume a linear delivery model for every advertiser, i.e. the capacity of $\mathbb{A}_i$ after arrival of j impressions is $N(i,j) = \frac{j}{m}N(i)$. We measure under-delivery and over-delivery of the assignment at 200 equally spaced milestones during the course of the algorithm.

As there is a penalty for under-delivery of impressions to a publisher, the algorithm should keep the under-delivery as small as possible. Even though there is no penalty for assigning impressions more than the capacity of the advertiser in the free-disposal model, *the impressions that are not assigned can be used for other properties in Google, hence it is imperative to keep even the over-delivery of impressions as small as possible.*

Algorithms Compared: We analyze the performance of smooth-avg, smooth-exp and smooth-greedy against the two reference algorithms:

Pd-Avg: We compare against a baseline online matching algorithm with free disposal [7] considering the overall capacity constraint but ignoring the smooth delivery constraints. In particular, we consider the pd-avg online matching algorithm developed by [7]. The algorithm is as follows: For advertiser $\mathbb{A}_i$, let $S(i)$ be the set of *top* $N(i)$ impressions assigned to $\mathbb{A}_i$; if there are less than $N(i)$ impressions assigned to $\mathbb{A}_i$, then we add elements with weight 0 so that $|S(i)| = N(i)$. The algorithm associates a dual variables $\beta(i)$ to $\mathbb{A}_i$, where the value of $\beta(i)$ is the average weight of impressions in $S(i)$. The algorithm assigns the impression to the advertiser which maximizes $w(i,j) - \beta(i)$. We expect this algorithm to achieve a better total welfare, but more overdelivery/underdelivery as it does not obey the tighter smooth delivery constraints.

A Heuristic: It is a natural baseline heuristic used in practice that adopts the pd-avg algorithm from [7] to ensure smooth delivery. It

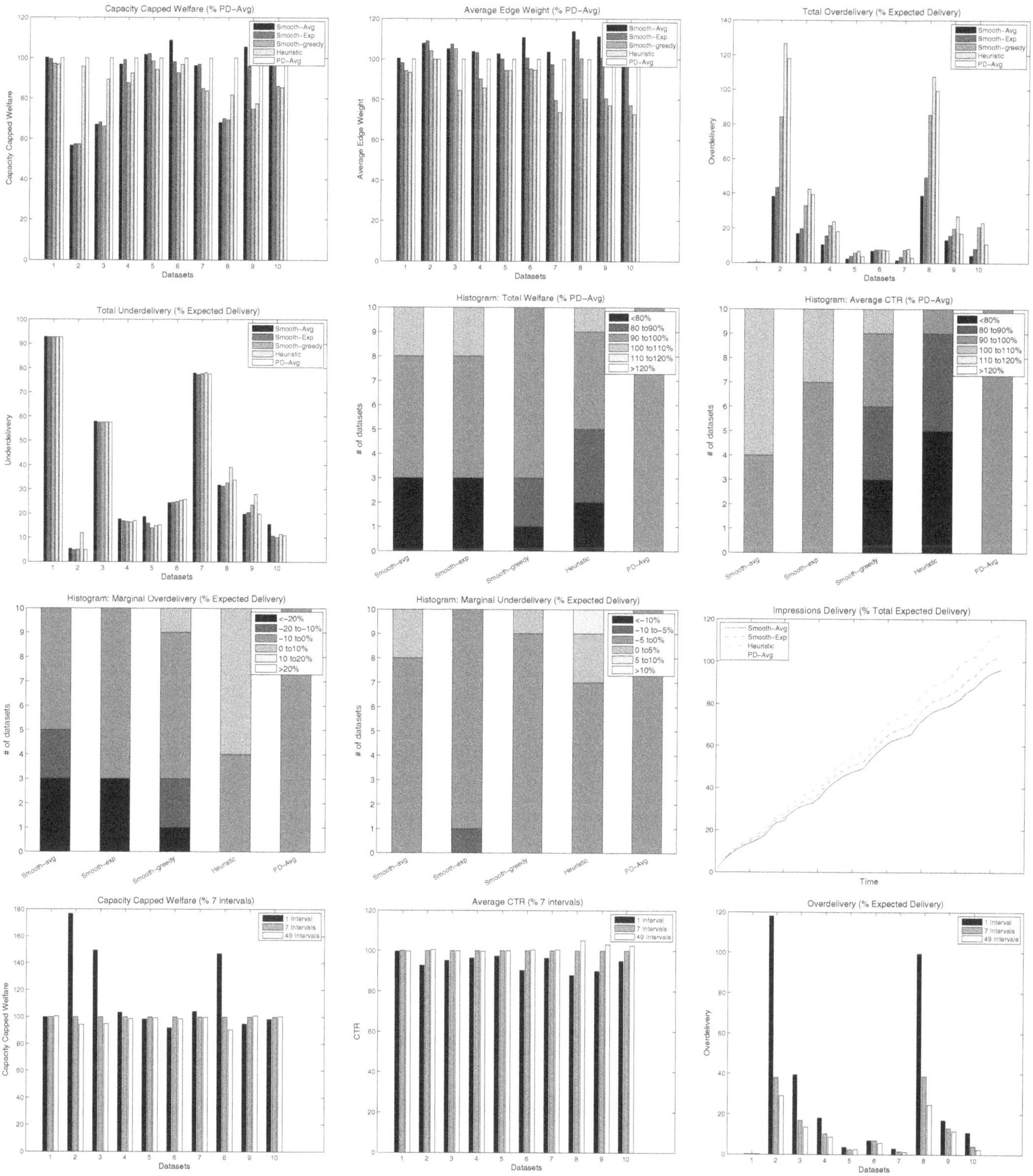

Figure 2: First four figures (all in the first row and the first in the second row) plot performance metrics of various smooth delivery algorithms for each data-set, the next four figures are histograms of data-sets based on various performance metrics for these algorithms, and the sixth figure shows time characteristics of impressions delivery for a sample data-set. The figures in the last row plot performance metrics for different number of intervals in each data-set for smooth-avg.

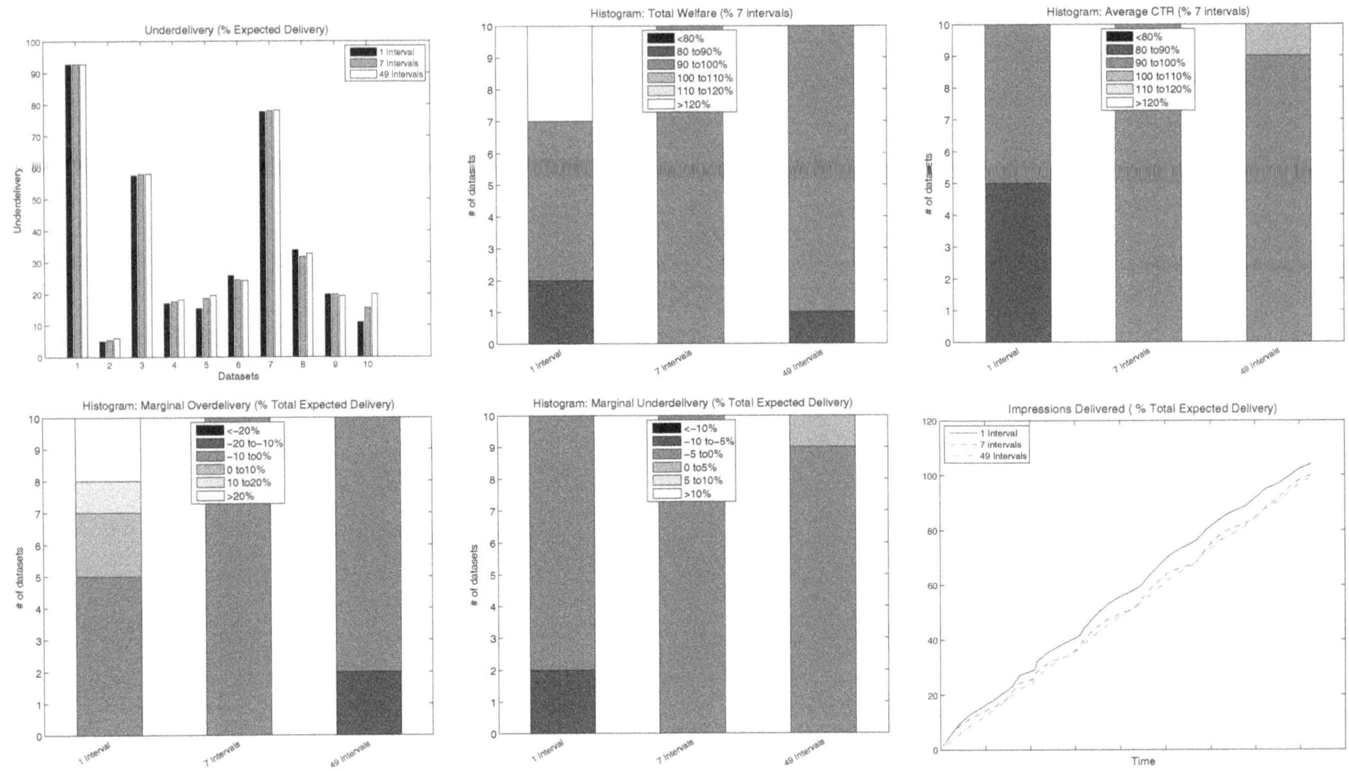

Figure 3: The first figure plots the value of under delivery for different number of intervals in each data-set for smooth avg, the next four figures are histograms of data-sets based on various performance metrics, and the last figure in the last row show time characteristics of impressions delivery for a sample data-set.

is very similar to the algorithm described above, the only difference is that in this heuristic, before arrival of $\mathbb{I}_j$, the capacity of $\mathbb{A}_i$ is considered to be $\frac{j}{m}N(i)$ (instead of $N(i)$). Therefore, in the algorithm above, $S(i)$ for heuristic algorithm is a set of $\frac{j}{m}N(i)$ edge weights corresponding to the *top* $\frac{j}{m}N(i)$ impressions assigned to $\mathbb{A}_i$. We expect this algorithm to have better delivery guarantee, and worse total weight of the assignment.

We use 7 intervals in the implementation of smooth algorithms, and we measure delivery guarantees at 200 equally spaced milestones.

Results and Metrics: The average statistics over 10 data sets can be found in the Table 1. It uses the following set of metrics for the comparison.

(1) *Total Welfare* is the total weight of the assignment regardless of the delivery constraint, relative to the pd-avg algorithm.
(2) *Capacity Capped Welfare* is the total weight of the assignment taking the smooth capacity constraint into consideration, relative to the pd-avg algorithm. This is the most relevant metric.
(3) *Average edge weight* in the assignment, relative to the pd-avg algorithm.
(4) *Under-delivery/over-delivery* at the end of the algorithm as a fraction of the expected delivery.
(5) *Accumulated under-delivery/over-delivery* summed over 200 milestones, as a fraction of the accumulated expected delivery.

These statistics for individual data-sets can be found in the Figure 2. We also plot histograms of data-set based on the performance metrics (Figure 2), they show the number of data-sets achieving a certain performance for the given metric relative to the pd-avg algorithm. The under-delivery/over-delivery histograms show the marginal under-delivery/over-delivery compared to the pd-avg algorithm, measured as a fraction of the total expected delivery. All other plots measure the performance metric as a fraction of the pd-avg algorithm.

Salient Observations.

Overall, smooth-exp and smooth-avg algorithms ensure significantly less over-delivery (by about 15% of the expected delivery) than the pd-avg algorithm and the heuristic, and have a matching under-delivery guarantee. Although they (smooth-exp and smooth-avg algorithms) achieve a marginally lower overall weight of the assignment, they ensure significantly larger *average edge weight in the assignment.*

Delivery Guarantees of Smooth Algrorithms: It is interesting to note that smooth-avg and smooth-exp have *less over-delivery* and *more average edge weight* in the assignment *for every data* set compared to the pd-avg and the heuristic algorithm. *This is contrary to expectations since the heuristic is specifically designed to ensure smooth delivery, at a cost of less overall weight of the assignment.* While smooth-exp has under-delivery less than the two reference algorithm on all datasets, smooth-avg performs better in 8 out of 10 datasets. Furthermore, smooth-avg has less over-delivery than smooth-exp for every data set.

We plot values of various performance metrics measured at 200 observation points for a sample data-set (Figure 2). The performance is measured relative to the pd-avg algorithm. In each plot, we can observe 7 concave regions, they correspond to the seven intervals. At the beginning of the interval, the *current* beta variable is

Table 1: Performance of various smooth algorithms averaged over 10 Data Sets

Metric	Smooth-Exp	Smooth-Avg	Smooth-Greedy	Heuristic	Pd-Avg
Total Welfare	94.22	95.69	95.69	93.35	100
Capacity Capped Welfare	90.28	89.25	81.51	89.45	100
Average Edge Weight	106.48	102.64	92.17	85.68	100
Over-delivery	11.51	15.13	28.14	36.54	26.30
Accumulated Over-delivery	13.24	16.72	28.58	37.35	31.68
Total Under-delivery	26.16	24.44	24.17	26.20	24.91
Accumulated Under-delivery	36.15	35.22	35.50	37.52	35.53

Table 2: Effect of Number of Intervals

Metric	1 Interval	7 Intervals	49 Intervals
Total Welfare	109.41	100	98.66
Average Edge Weight	94.04	100	101.19
Over-delivery	26.29	11.50	9.85
Accumulated Over-delivery	31.68	13.24	9.96
Total Under-delivery	24.91	26.15	26.84
Accumulated Over-delivery	35.52	36.16	36.87

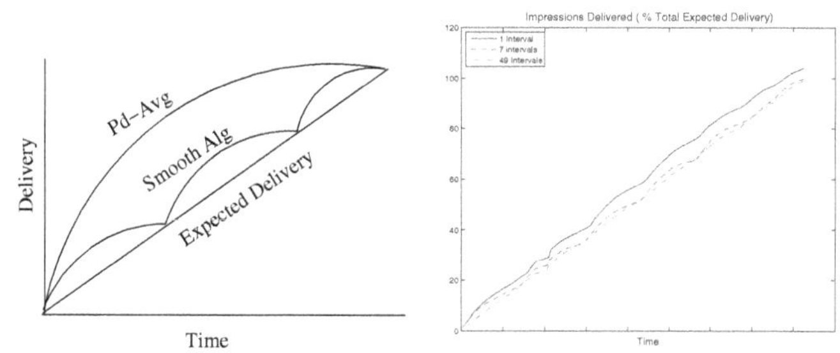

Figure 4: The figure on the left illustrates the reason for the less over-delivery of smooth-algorithms. The figure on the right is the delivery curve for a sample data-set over different values of intervals.

zero and hence impressions are assigned as a faster rate. As the *current* beta variable increases, the rate of assignment of impressions reduces.

Smooth-Avg vs Smooth-Exp Algorithm: Even though the smooth-exp algorithm has a better approximation guarantee, its implementation requires storing all impressions assigned to an advertiser so far and the update rules are computationally expensive as it involves computing the weighted exponential average of a set. In comparison, the smooth-avg algorithm only needs to maintain the value of beta variables and its update rules are simple. Furthermore, the performance of the smooth-avg algorithm is no worse than the smooth-exp algorithm on data. This makes the smooth-avg algorithm a better candidate for practical applications.

Number of Intervals and Smoothness: We analyze the effect of increasing the number of intervals. Towards this, we use three different values of intervals: 1, 7 and 49. We use smooth-avg algorithm and measure over-delivery and under-delivery at 200 uniformly spaced milestones. The average statistics can be found in the Table 2. These statistics for individual data-sets are given in the Figures 2 and 3. We also plot histograms of data-sets based on these performance parameters, and the values of various performance metrics measured at 200 observation points for a sample data-set (Figure 3). The performance is measured relative to the smooth-avg algorithm with 7 intervals.

We observe that the overall smoothness of the delivery increases as we increase the number of intervals. Though the average edge weight and the delivery guarantees improve with the increase in the number of intervals from 1 to 7, the corresponding gains by increasing the number of intervals to 49 are marginal and it leads to the drop the total weight of the assignment. We note that the over-delivery for every data-set reduces as we increase the number of intervals from 1 to 7 as well as from 7 to 49.

Reasons for Better Over-Delivery Guarantee of Smooth Algorithms.

In the pd-avg algorithm, the value of a beta variables increase from 0 to to its final value by the end of the algorithm and an impression is assigned only when its weight is more than the beta variable's value. If we assume an IID model of arrival, then as the value of a beta variable increases, the rate of delivery decreases as less impressions have weight more than the value of the beta variable. Thus the effective delivery curve is *concave*. With multiple intervals, the beta value is *reset to* 0 multiple times, thus the eventual delivery curve is made up of multiple small concave regions and its sum of distance form a linear expected delivery is less. (See Figure 1 for an illustration.)

5. REFERENCES

[1] S. Agrawal, Z. Wang, and Y. Ye. A dynamic near-optimal algorithm for online linear programming. Working paper posted at http://www.stanford.edu/ yyye/.

[2] S. Alaei, R. Kumar, A. Malekian, and E. Vee. Balanced allocation with succinct representation. In *KDD*, pages 523–532, 2010.

[3] N. Buchbinder, K. Jain, and J. Naor. Online Primal-Dual Algorithms for Maximizing Ad-Auctions Revenue. In *ESA*. Springer, 2007.

[4] Y. Chen, P. Berkhin, B. Anderson, and N. R. Devanur. Real-time bidding algorithms for performance-based display ad allocation. In *KDD*, pages 1307–1315, 2011.

[5] N. Devanur and T. Hayes. The adwords problem: Online keyword matching with budgeted bidders under random permutations. In *ACM EC*, 2009.

[6] J. Feldman, M. Henzinger, N. Korula, V. Mirrokni, and C. Stein. Online stochastic packing applied to display ad allocation. In *ESA*, 2010.

[7] J. Feldman, N. Korula, V. Mirrokni, S. Muthukrishnan, and M. Pal. Online ad assignment with free disposal. In *WINE*, 2009.

[8] A. Mehta, A. Saberi, U. Vazirani, and V. Vazirani. Adwords and generalized online matching. In *FOCS*, 2005.

[9] V. Mirrokni, S. O. Gharan, and M. ZadiMoghaddam. Simultaneous approximations for adversarial and stochastic online budgeted allocation problems. In *SODA*, 2012.

[10] B. Tan and R. Srikant. Online advertisement, optimization and stochastic networks. *CoRR*, abs/1009.0870, 2010.

[11] E. Vee, S. Vassilvitskii, and J. Shanmugasundaram. Optimal online assignment with forecasts. In *ACM EC*, 2010.

Streaming Graph Partitioning for Large Distributed Graphs

Isabelle Stanton
University of California Berkeley
Berkeley, CA
isabelle@eecs.berkeley.edu

Gabriel Kliot
Microsoft Research
Redmond, WA
gkliot@microsoft.com

ABSTRACT

Extracting knowledge by performing computations on graphs is becoming increasingly challenging as graphs grow in size. A standard approach distributes the graph over a cluster of nodes, but performing computations on a distributed graph is expensive if large amount of data have to be moved. Without partitioning the graph, communication quickly becomes a limiting factor in scaling the system up. Existing graph partitioning heuristics incur high computation and communication cost on large graphs, sometimes as high as the future computation itself. Observing that the graph has to be loaded into the cluster, we ask if the partitioning can be done at the same time with a lightweight streaming algorithm.

We propose natural, simple heuristics and compare their performance to hashing and METIS, a fast, offline heuristic. We show on a large collection of graph datasets that our heuristics are a significant improvement, with the best obtaining an average gain of 76%. The heuristics are scalable in the size of the graphs and the number of partitions. Using our streaming partitioning methods, we are able to speed up PageRank computations on Spark [32], a distributed computation system, by 18% to 39% for large social networks.

Categories and Subject Descriptors

G.2.2 [**Mathematics of Computing**]: Discrete Mathematics—*Graph Theory, Graph Algorithms*; D.2.8 [**Software Engineering**]: Metrics—*Complexity measures, Performance measures*

General Terms

Algorithms, Experimentation

Keywords

Graph Partitioning, Streaming Algorithms, Distributed Graphs, Experimental Evaluation

1. INTRODUCTION

Modern graph datasets are huge. The clearest example is the World Wide Web where crawls by large search engines currently consist of over one trillion links and are expected to exceed ten trillion within the year. Individual websites also contain enormous graph data. In Jan 2012, Facebook consisted of over 800 million active users, with hundreds of billions friend links [1]. There are over 900 million additional objects (communities, pages, events, etc.) that interact with the user nodes. In July 2009, Twitter had over 41.7 million users with over 1.47 billion social relations [21]. Since then, it has been estimated that Twitter has grown to over 200 million users. Examples of large graph datasets are not limited to the Internet and social networks - biological networks, like protein interaction networks, are of a similar size. Despite the size of these graphs, it is still necessary to perform computations over the data, such as calculating PageRank, broadcasting Twitter updates, identify protein associations, as well as many other applications.

The graphs consist of terabytes of compressed data when stored on disks and are all far too large for a single commodity type machine to efficiently perform computations. A standard solution is to split the data across a large cluster of commodity machines and use parallel, distributed algorithms for the computation. This approach introduces a host of systems engineering problems of which we focus only on the problem of data layout. For graph data, this is called *balanced graph partitioning*. The goal is to minimize the number of cross partition edges, while keeping the number of nodes (or edges) in every partition approximately even.

Good graph partitioning algorithms are very useful for many reasons. First, graphs that we encounter and care about in practice are not random. The edges display a great deal of locality, whether due to the vertices being geographically close in social networks, or related by topic or domain on the web. This locality gives us hope that good partitions, or at least partitions that are significantly better than random cuts, exist in real graphs. Next, inter-machine communication, even on the same local network, is substantially more expensive than inter-processor communication. Network latency is measured in microseconds while inter-process communication is measured in nanoseconds. This disparity substantially slows down processing when the network must be used. For large graphs, the data to be moved may border on gigabytes, causing network links to become saturated.

The primary problem with partitioning complicated graph data is that it is difficult to create a linear ordering of the data that maintains locality of the edges i.e. if it is possible to embed the vertices of a graph into a line such that none of the edges are 'too long', then a good balanced cut exists in the graph. Such an ordering may not even exist at all. There is a strong connection between graph partitioning and the eigenvectors and eigenvalues of the corresponding Laplacian matrix of the graph via the Cheeger bound. This connection has inspired many spectral solutions to the problem, including ARV [11] and the many works that followed.

However, spectral methods do not scale to big data. This is in part due to the running time and in part because current formulations require full graph information. When a graph does not physically fit on one machine, maintaining a coherent view of the entire state is impossible. This has led to local spectral partitioning methods, like EvoCut [9], but local methods still require access to large portions of the graph, rely on complex distributed coordination and large computation after the data has been loaded. Thus, we look for a new type of solution. A *graph loader* is a program that reads serial graph data from a disk onto a cluster. It must make a decision about the location of each node as it is loaded. The goal is to find a close to optimal balanced partitioning with as little computation as possible. This problem is also called *streaming graph partitioning*.

For some graphs, partitioning can be entirely bypassed by using meta data associated with the vertices, e.g. clustering web pages by URL produces a good partitioning for the web. In social networks, people tend to be friends with people who are geographically nearby. When such data is available, this produces an improved cut over a node ID hashing approach. Unfortunately, this data is not always be available, and even if it is, it is not always clear which features are useful for partitioning. Our goal in this work is to find a general streaming algorithm that relies only on the graph structure and works regardless of the meta data.

1.1 Applications

Our motivating example for studying this problem is a large distributed graph computation system. All distributed computation frameworks, like MapReduce, Hadoop, Orleans [15] and Spark [32] have methods for handling the distribution of data across the cluster. Unfortunately, for graphs, these methods are not tuned to minimize communication complexity, and saturating the network becomes a significant barrier to scaling the system up.

The interest in building distributed systems for graph computation has recently exploded, especially within the database community. Examples of these systems include Pregel [25], GraphLab [24], InfiniteGraph, HyperGraphDB, Ne04j, and Microsoft's Trinity [4] and Horton [3], to name but a few. Even for these graph specific systems, the graphs are laid out using a hash of the node ID to select a partition. If a good pseudorandom hash function is chosen, this is equivalent to using a random cut as graph partitioning and will result in approximately balanced partitions. However, computations on the graph run more slowly when a hash partitioning is used instead of a better partitioning, due to the high communication cost. Fortunately, these systems tend to support custom partitioning, so it is relatively easy to substitute a more sophisticated method, provided it scales to the size of the graph. As our experiments show, even using our simple streaming partitioning techniques can allow systems of this type to complete computations at least 20-40% faster.

1.2 Theoretical Difficulties - Lower Bound

Theoretically, a good streaming partitioning algorithm is impossible. It is easy to create graphs and orderings for any algorithm that will cause it to perform poorly. A simple example of this lower bound is a cycle. The optimal balanced 2-partition cuts only 2 edges. However, if the vertices are given in an order of 'all even nodes then all odd nodes', we won't observe any edges until the odd nodes arrive. Without any information, the best an algorithm could is to try and balance the number of vertices it has seen across the 2 partitions. This leads to an expected cut of $\frac{n}{4}$ edges. The worst algorithm might put all even nodes in one partition leading to all edges being cut!

We can partially bypass this problem by picking the input ordering. The three popular orderings considered in the literature are adversarial, random, and stochastic. The above cycle example is an adversarial order and demonstrates that the streaming graph partitioning problem may have arbitrarily bad solutions under that input model. Given that adversarial input is unrealistic in our setting - we have control over the data - we focus on input that results from either a random ordering, or the output of a graph search algorithm. The second option is a simplification of the ordering returned by a graph crawler.

THEOREM 1. *One-pass streaming balanced graph partitioning with an adversarial stream order can not be approximated within $o(n)$.*

THEOREM 2. *One-pass streaming balanced graph partitioning with a random stream order can not be approximated within $o(n)$.*

The full proofs are elided due to space. Theorem 1 can be proved with the above cycle discussion. Theorem 2 can be proved by analyzing the expected number of vertices in a random order that arrive with no edges (a third). Each of these vertices contributes an edge to the cut in expectation. This means, in expectation, a random cut will cut $O(n)$ edges, while an optimal partitioning cuts only 2.

We leave open the theoretical problem of analyzing the performance of our heuristics. While there are current approaches to analyzing streaming algorithms, our use of breadth-first and depth-first stream orders is novel and previous approaches can not be applied. Theorem 1 shows we should not hope to analyze any algorithm with an adversarial order, while a random ordering will always hide edges in sparse graphs until $O(\sqrt{n})$ vertices arrive, making competitive analysis difficult.

1.3 The Streaming Model

We consider a simple streaming graph model. We have a cluster of k machines, each with memory capacity C, such that the total capacity, kC, is large enough to hold the whole graph. The graph is $G = (V, E)$ where V is the vertices, and E the edges. The graph may be either directed or undirected. The vertices arrive in a stream with the set of edges where it is a member so for undirected graphs, each edge appears twice in the stream. We consider three orders: random, breadth-first search and depth-first search. As vertices arrive, a partitioner decides to place the vertex on one of the k machines. A vertex is never moved after it has been placed. In order to give the heuristics maximal flexibility, we allow the partitioning algorithm access to the entire subgraph defined by all vertices previously seen. This is a strong assumption, but the heuristics studied in this paper use only local (depth 1) information about this subgraph. We extend the model by allowing a buffer of size C so that the partitioning algorithm may decide to place any node in the buffer, rather than the one at the front of the stream.

Our model assumes serial input and a single loader. This is somewhat unrealistic for a real system where there may be many graph loaders working in parallel on independent portions of the stream. While we will not explore this option, the heuristics we investigate can be easily adapted to a parallel setting where each loads its portion of the graph independently from the others, sharing information only through a distributed lookup table of vertices to partition IDs.

1.4 Contributions

We provide a rigorous, empirical study of a set of natural heuristics for streaming balanced graph partitioning. To the best of our knowledge, this is a first attempt to study this problem. We evaluate these heuristics on a large collection of graph datasets, from various domains: the World Wide Web, social networks, finite-element meshes and synthetic datasets from some popular generative models - preferential-attachment [13], RMAT [23] and Watts-Strogatz [30]. We compare the results of our streaming heuristics to both the hash based partitioning, and METIS [19], a well-regarded, fast, offline partitioning heuristic.

Our results show that some of the heuristics are good and some are surprisingly bad. Our best performing heuristic is a weighted variant of the greedy algorithm. It has a significant improvement over the hashing approach without significantly increasing the computational overhead and obtains an average gain of 76% of the possible improvement in the number of edges cut. On some graphs, with some orderings, a variety of heuristics obtain results which are very close to the offline METIS result. By using the synthetic datasets, we are also able to show that our heuristics scale with the size of the graph and the number of partitions. We demonstrate the value of the best heuristic by using it to partition both the LiveJournal and the Twitter graph for PageRank computation using the Spark cluster system [32]. These are large crawls of real social networks, and we are able to improve the running time of the PageRank algorithm by 18% to 39% by changing the data layout alone. Our experimental results motivate us to recommend that this is an interesting problem worthy of future research and is a viable preprocessing step for graph computation systems.

Our streaming partitioning is not intended to substitute for a full information graph partitioning. Certain systems or applications that need as good a partitioning as possible will still want to repartition the graph after it has been fully loaded onto the cluster. These systems can still greatly benefit from our optimization as a distributed offline partitioning algorithm started from an already reasonably partitioned graph will require less communication and may need to move fewer vertices, causing it to run faster. Our streaming partitioning algorithms can be viewed as a preprocessing optimization step that cannot hurt in exchange for a very small additional computation cost for every loaded vertex.

2. RELATED WORK

Graph partitioning has a rich history. It encompasses many problems and has many proposed solutions, from the very simple to the very sophisticated. We cannot hope to cover the whole field and will only focus on the most relevant formulation - balanced k-partitioning. The goal is, given a graph G as input and a number k, to cut G into k balanced pieces while minimizing the number of edges cut. This problem is known to be NP-Hard, even if one relaxes the balanced constraint to 'approximately' balanced [10]. Andreev and Racke give an LP-based solution that obtains a $O(\log n)$ approximation [10]. Even *et al.* [16] provide another LP formulation based on spreading metrics that also obtains an $O(\log n)$ approximation. Both require full information about the graph. There are many heuristics that solve this problem with an unknown performance guarantee, like METIS [19], PMRSB [14], and Chaco [17]. In practice, these heuristics are quite effective, but many are intended for scientific computing purposes. One can recursively use any balanced 2-partitioning algorithm to approximate a balanced k-partitioning when k is a power of 2 [11].

While we are unaware of any previous work on the exact problem statement that we study - one pass balanced k partitioning - there has been much work on many related streaming problems, primarily graph sparsification in the semi-streaming model, cut projections in the streaming model as well as online algorithms in general, like online bipartite matching. This work includes both algorithms and lower bounds on space requirements.

The work on streaming graph problems where multiple passes on the stream are allowed includes estimating PageRank [29] and cut projections [28]. While PageRank has been used for local partitioning [8], the approach in [8] uses personalized PageRank vectors which does not easily generalize the approach in [29]. Additionally, cut projections do not maintain our balanced criterion.

Bahmani *et al.* [12] maintain an accurate estimate of the PageRank in one pass in the semi-streaming model, where the nodes are fixed but edges arrive in an adversarial order. In the semi-streaming model, further results are known with regards to finding minimum cuts, i.e. no balance requirement. Jin Ahn and Guha [6] give a one pass $\tilde{O}(n/\epsilon^2)$ space algorithm that sparsifies a graph such that each cut is approximated to within a $(1+\epsilon)$ factor. Kelner and Levin [20] produce a spectral sparsifier with $O(n \log n/\epsilon^2)$ edges in $\tilde{O}(m)$ time. While sparsifiers are related to partitioning, we do not have a prespecified computation task, so we cannot be sure that a sparsified graph will give accurate answers. Zelke [33] shows lower bounds of $o(n^2)$ space to find max and min cuts in one pass. Zelke [33] has shown that this cannot be computed in one pass with $o(n^2)$ space. By contrast, our methods require only access to a distributed lookup table and a buffer of size C.

3. HEURISTICS AND STREAM ORDERS

In this paper, we examine multiple heuristics and stream orders. We now formally define each one.

3.1 Heuristics

The notation P^t refers to the set of partitions at time t. Each individual partition is referred to by its index $P^t(i)$ so $\cup_{i=1}^{k} P^t(i)$ is equal to all of the vertices placed so far. Let v denote the vertex that arrives at time t in the stream, $\Gamma(v)$ refers to the set of vertices that v neighbors and $|S|$ refers to the number of elements in a set S. C is the capacity constraint on each partition. Each of the heuristics gives an algorithm for selecting the index ind of the partition where

v is assigned. The first seven heuristics do not use a buffer, while the last three do.

1. Balanced - Assign v to a partition of minimal size, breaking ties randomly:
$$ind = \arg\min_{i\in[k]}\{|P^t(i)|\}$$

2. Chunking - Divide the stream into chunks of size C and fill the partitions completely in order:
$$ind = \lceil t/C \rceil$$

3. Hashing - Given a hash function $H : V \to \{1 \cdots k\}$, assign v to $ind = H(v)$. We use:
$$H(v) = (v \mod k) + 1$$

4. (Weighted) Deterministic Greedy - Assign v to the partition where it has the most edges. Weight this by a penalty function based on the capacity of the partition, penalizing larger partitions. Break ties using Balanced.
$$ind = \arg\max_{i\in[k]}\{|P^t(i) \cap \Gamma(v)|w(t,i)\}$$
where $w(t,i)$ is a weighted penalty function:
$w(t,i) = 1$ for unweighted greedy
$w(t,i) = 1 - \frac{|P^t(i)|}{C}$ for linear weighted
$w(t,i) = 1-\exp\{|P^t(i)|-C\}$ for exponentially weighted

5. (Weighted) Randomized Greedy - Assign v according to the distribution defined by
$$Pr(i) = |P^t(i) \cap \Gamma(v)|w(t,i)/Z$$
where Z is the normalizing constant and $w(t,i)$ is the above 3 penalty functions.

6. (Weighted) Triangles - Assign v according to
$$\arg\max_{i\in[k]}\{\frac{|E(P^t(i)\cap\Gamma(v), P^t(i)\cap\Gamma(v))|}{\binom{|P^t(i)\cap\Gamma(v)|}{2}}w(t,i)\}$$
where $w(t,i)$ is the above 3 penalty functions and $E(S,T)$ is the set of edges between the nodes in S and T.

7. Balance Big - Given a way of differentiating high and low degree nodes, if v is high-degree, use Balanced. If it is low-degree, use Deterministic Greedy.

The following heuristics all use a buffer.

8. Prefer Big - Maintain a buffer of size C. Assign all high degree nodes with Balanced, and then stream in more nodes. If the buffer is entirely low degree nodes, then use Deterministic Greedy to clear the buffer.

9. Avoid Big - Maintain a buffer of size C and a threshold on large nodes. Greedily assign all small nodes in the buffer. When the buffer is entirely large nodes, use Deterministic Greedy to clear the buffer.

10. Greedy EvoCut - Use EvoCut [9] on the buffer to find small Nibbles with good conductance. Select a partition for each Nibble using Deterministic Greedy.

Each of these heuristics has a different motivation with some arguably more natural than others. Balanced and Chunking are simple ways of load balancing while ignoring the graph structure.

Hashing is currently used by many real systems [25]. The benefit of Hashing is that every vertex can be quickly found, from any machine in the cluster, without the need to maintain a distributed mapping table. If the IDs of the nodes are consecutive, the hash function $H(v) = (v \mod k) + 1$ makes Balanced and Hashing equivalent. More generally, a pseudorandom hash function should be used, making Hashing equivalent to a random cut.

The greedy approach is standard, although the weighted penalty is inspired by analysis of other online algorithms. The randomized versions of these algorithms were explored because adding randomness can often be shown to theoretically improve the worst-case performance.

The (Weighted) Triangles heuristic exploits work showing that social networks have high clustering coefficients by finding triangles completed triangles among the vertices neighbors in a partition and overweighting their importance.

Heuristics Balance Big, Prefer Big, and Avoid Big assume we have a way to differentiate high and low degree nodes. This assumption is based on the fact that many graphs have power law degree distributions. These three heuristics propose different treatments for the small number of high degree nodes and the large number of low degree nodes.

Balance Big uses the high degree nodes as seeds for the partitions to 'attract' the low degree nodes. The buffered version, Prefer Big, allows the algorithm more choice in finding these seeds. Avoid Big explores the idea that the high degree nodes form the expander portion of the graph, so perhaps the low degrees nodes can be partitioned after the high degree nodes have been removed.

The final heuristic, Greedy EvoCut, uses EvoCut [9], a local partitioning algorithm, on the buffer. This algorithm has very good theoretical guarantees with regards to the found cuts, and the amount of work spent to find them, but the guarantees do not apply to the way we use it.

Edge Balancing: While our experiments focus on partitions that are node balanced, in part because this is what our comparator algorithm METIS produces, there is nothing that prevents these heuristics from being used to produce edge-balanced partitions instead, i.e. each partition holds at most $C = (1+\epsilon)|E|/k$ edges. An edge-balanced partition may be preferable for power-law distributed graphs when the computation to be performed has complexity in terms of the number of edges and not the number of vertices. In fact, in our second set of experiments with the PageRank algorithm in Section 6 we used the edge-balanced versions of the algorithms instead, for the above reason.

3.2 Stream Orders

In a sense, the stream ordering is the key to having a heuristic perform well. A simple example is Chunking, where, if we had an optimal partitioning, and then created an ordering consisting of all nodes in partition 1, then all nodes in partition 2 and so on, Chunking would also return an optimal partition. For each heuristic, we can define optimal orderings, but, unfortunately, actually generating them reduces to solving balanced graph partitioning so we must settle for orderings that are easy to compute.

We consider the following three stream orderings:

- *Random* - This is a standard ordering in streaming literature and assumes that the vertices arrive in an order given by a random permutation of the vertices.
- *BFS* - This ordering is generated by selecting a starting node from each connected component of the graph uniformly at random and is the result of a breadth-first search that starts at the given node. If there are multiple connected components, the component ordering is done at random.
- *DFS* - This ordering is identical to the *BFS* ordering except that depth-first search is used.

Each of these stream orderings has a different justification. The random ordering is a standard assumption when theoretically analyzing streaming algorithms. While we generate these orderings by selecting a random permutation of the vertices, one could view this as a special case of a generic ordering that does not respect connectivity of the graph. The benefit of a random ordering is that it avoids adversarially bad orderings. The downside is that it does not preserve any locality in the edges so we expect it to do poorly for statistical reasons like the Birthday paradox. Via the Birthday paradox, we can argue that for sparse graphs, we expect to go through $O(\sqrt{n})$ of the vertices before we find a first edge.

Both BFS and DFS are natural ways of linearizing graphs and are highly simplified models of a web crawler. In practice, web crawlers are a combination of local search approaches - they follow links, but fully explore domains and sub-domains before moving on. This is breadth-first search between domains, and depth-first search within. The main benefit of both orderings is that they guarantee that the partitioner sees edges in the stream immediately. Additionally, they maintain some locality. Each has their drawbacks, but it should be noted that BFS is a subroutine that is often used in partitioning algorithms to find a good cut, particularly for rounding fractional solutions to LPs [16].

4. EVALUATION SETUP

We conducted extensive experimental evaluation to discover the performance and trends of stream partitioning heuristics on a variety of graphs. The questions we ask are: Which of these heuristics are reasonable? Can we recommend a best heuristic, restricted to graph type? Do these heuristics scale to larger graphs? Our intent is to use this style of solution for graphs that include trillions of edges, yet in our initial experiments our largest graph has 1.4 million edges. We address this last question by using synthetic datasets to show that the heuristics scale and in Section 6 use our heuristics on two larger social networks successfully.

4.1 Datasets

We used several sources to collect multiple datasets for our experiments. From the SNAP [22] archive, we used soc-Slashdot0811, wiki-Vote and web-NotreDame. From the Graph Partitioning Archive [5] we used : 3elt, 4elt, and vibrobox. We also used: Astrophysics collaborations (astro-ph) [27], C. Elegans Neural Network (celegans) [30], and the Marvel Comics social network [7]. We used two large social networks (LiveJournal [26] and Twitter [21]) to evaluate our heuristics in a real system in Section 6.

We created synthetic datasets using popular generative models, preferential attachment (BA) [13], Watts-Strogatz (WS) [30], the RMAT generator [23], and a power-law graph generator with clustering (PL) [18]. Three of the synthetic datasets, BA, WS, and PL were created with the NetworkX python package. For each model, we created a degree distribution with average degree $O(\log n)$ (average degree of 10 edges for 1,000 nodes, 13 for 10,000, and 25 for 50,000). This fully specifies the BA model. For WS and PL we used .1 as the rewiring probability. The RMAT datasets were created with the Python Web Graph Generator, a variant of the RMAT generator [2]. The RMAT or Kronecker parameters used by this implementation are [0.45,0.15;0.15,0.25].

The datasets were chosen to balance both size and variety. All are small enough so that we can find offline solutions with METIS so that our results are reproducable, while still big enough to capture the asymptotic behavior of these graph types. The collection captures a variety of real graphs, focusing on finite-element meshes (FEM) and power-law graphs. FEMs are used for scientific computing purposes to model simulations like the flow over a wing, while power-law (and other heavy-tailed) distributions capture nearly all 'natural' graphs, like the World Wide Web, social networks, and protein networks. In general, it is known that FEMs have good partitions because their edges are highly local, while natural graphs are more difficult to partition because they have high expansion and low diameter. The basic statistics about each graph, as well as its type and source are in Table 1.

Name	$\|V\|$	$\|E\|$	Type	Source
3elt	4720	13,722	FEM	[5]
4elt	15606	45,878	FEM	[5]
vibrobox	12,328	165,250	FEM	[5]
celegans	297	2,148	Protein	[30]
astro-ph	18,772	396,160	Citation	[27]
Slashdot0811	77,360	504,230	Social	[22]
wiki-Vote	7,115	99,291	Social	[22]
Marvel	6,486	427,018	Social	[7]
web-ND	325,729	1,497,134	Web	[22]
BA	1,000	9,900	Synth.	[13]
BA	10,000	129,831	Synth.	[13]
BA	50,000	1,249,375	Synth.	[13]
RMAT	1,000	9,175	Synth.	[23]
RMAT	10,000	129,015	Synth.	[23]
RMAT	50,000	1,231,907	Synth.	[23]
WS	1,000	5,000	Synth.	[30]
WS	10,000	120,000	Synth.	[30]
WS	50,000	3,400,000	Synth.	[30]
PL	1,000	9,878	Synth.	[18]
PL	10,000	129,763	Synth.	[18]
PL	50,000	1,249,044	Synth.	[18]
LiveJournal	$4.6*10^6$	$77.4*10^6$	Social	[26]
Twitter	$41.7*10^6$	$1.468*10^9$	Social	[21]

Table 1: Graph datasets summary

4.2 Methodology

We examined all the combinations of datasets, heuristics and steam orders and ran each experiment 5 times on each combination. The *Random* ordering is a random permutation of the vertices, while *BFS* and *DFS* were created by sampling a random vertex to be the root of the BFS or DFS algorithm. Each of the heuristics was run on the same ordering. We ran each experiment on 2, 4, 8, and 16 partitions and fixed the imbalance such that no partition held more than 5% more vertices than its share. The imbalance was chosen as a reasonable setting of this parameter in practice.

5. EVALUATION RESULTS

In all of the following figures, the y-axis has been scaled to zoom in on the data. The ordering of the heuristics in the figures is the one given in Table 2.

5.1 Upper and lower bounds

In order to evaluate the quality of our heuristics, we must establish good upper and lower bounds for the performance. A natural upper bound is the approach currently used in practice - hashing the node ID and mapping it to a partition. This approach completely ignores the edges so its expected performance is cutting a $\frac{k-1}{k}$ fraction of edges for k partitions. This bound is marked by the upper black line in our figures. We expect Balanced and Hashing to always perform at this level, as well as Chunking on a random order.

The lower bound can be picked in many more ways. Finding an optimal lower bound is NP-hard, so we focus on more realistic approaches. We compare against a practical and fast approach, the partition produced by METIS v4.0.3. While METIS has no theoretical guarantees, it is widely respected and produces good cuts in practice, and is thus a good offline comparison for our empirical work. This METIS value is marked as the lower black line in our figures. Note that METIS is given significantly more information than the streaming heuristics, so we would not expect them to produce partitioning of the same quality. Any heuristic between these two lines is an improvement.

5.2 Performance on three graph types

We have included figures of the results for three of the graphs, a synthetic graph, a social network graph and a FEM with the goal of covering all three major types of graphs.

Figure 1 depicts the performance on the PowerLaw Clustered graph [18] of size 1,000 with 4 partitions. This is one of our synthetic graphs where the model is intended to capture power law graphs observed in nature. The lower bound provided by METIS is 58.9% of the edges cut, while the upper bound for 4 partitions is 75%. The first heuristic, Avoid Big, is worse than a random cut. Linear Deterministic Greedy and Balance Big both perform very well for all 3 stream orderings. These each had a best average performance of 61.7% and 63.2% of the edges cut respectively, corresponding to 82% and 73% of the possible gain in performance. This gain was calculated as the fraction of edges cut by the random minus the fraction cut by the heuristic, divided by the fraction cut by a random cut minus the fraction cut by METIS ($\frac{\text{random}-\text{heuristic}}{\text{random}-\text{METIS}}$).

Figure 2 is our results for a social network, the Marvel Comics network [7], with 8 partitions. The Marvel network is synthetic, as it is the result of character interactions in books, but studies have shown it is similar to real social networks. The lower bound from METIS cuts only 32.2% of edges. The upper bound is 7/8 = 87.5% cut. The two heuristics at the upper bound level are Balanced and Hashing, with Chunking on the random order also performing poorly, as expected. Again, the best heuristic is Linear Deterministic Greedy, with 48%, 48.7% and 50.8% edges cut for the *BFS*, *DFS* and *Random* orderings respectively. This constitutes a gain of 71.3%, 70% and 66%.

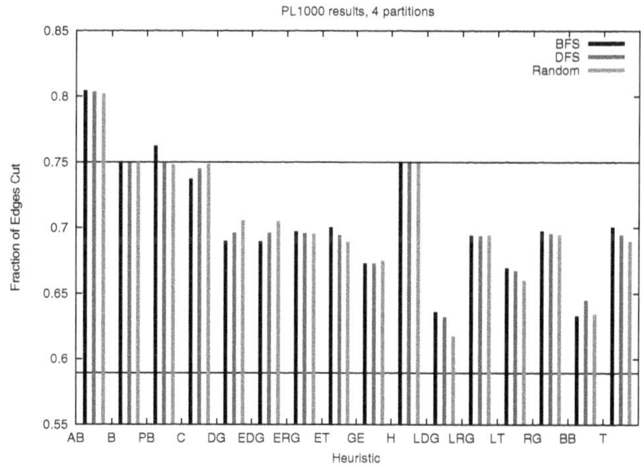

Figure 1: PL1000 results. The top line is the cost of a random cut and the bottom line is METIS. The best heuristic is Linear Deterministic Greedy. The figures are best viewed in color.

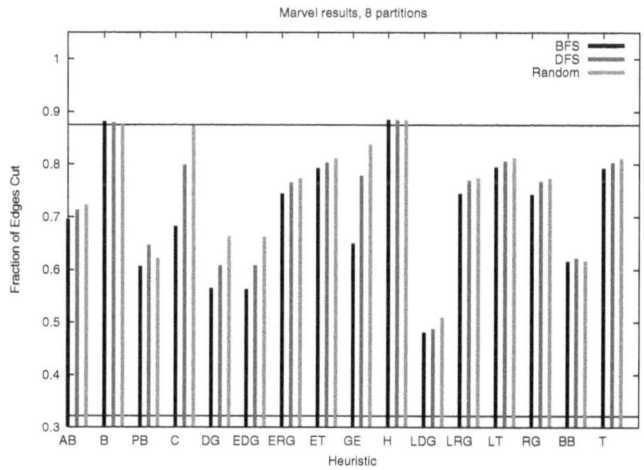

Figure 2: Marvel results. The top line is the cost of a random cut and the bottom line is METIS. The best heuristic is Linear Deterministic Greedy.

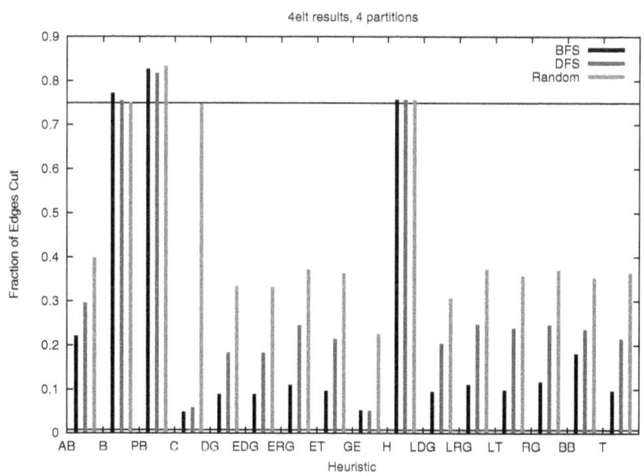

Figure 3: 4elt results. The top line is a random cut and the bottom line is METIS (0.7% edges cut).

Heuristic		*BFS*	*DFS*	*Random*
Avoid Big	AB	-27.3	-38.6	-46.4
Balanced	B	-1.5	-1.3	-0.2
Prefer Big	PB	-9.5	-18.6	-23.1
Chunking	C	37.6	35.7	0.7
Deterministic Greedy	DG	57.7	54.7	45.4
Exp. Det. Greedy	EDG	59.4	56.2	47.5
Exp. Rand. Greedy	ERG	45.6	45.6	38.8
Exp. Triangles	ET	50.7	49.3	41.6
Greedy EvoCut	GE	60.3	58.6	43.1
Hashing	H	-1.9	-2.1	-1.7
Linear Det. Greedy	LDG	76	73	75.3
Linear Rand. Greedy	LRG	46.4	44.9	39.1
Linear Triangles	LT	55.4	54.6	49.3
Randomized Greedy	RG	45.5	44.9	38.7
Balance Big	BB	67.8	68.5	63.3
Triangles	T	49.7	48.4	40.2

Table 2: The average gain of each heuristic over all of our datasets and partitions sizes.

Figure 3 contains the results for a FEM, 4elt [5], with 4 partitions. The change in graph structure gives us quite different results, not the least of which is that METIS now cuts only 0.7% of edges. The upper bound remains at 75%, providing a huge range for improvement. Surprisingly, Chunking performs extremely well here for the *BFS* and *DFS* orders, at 4.7% and 5.7% cut respectively. Translating into gain provides 94.7% and 93.3% of the optimal improvement. Chunking performs poorly on the *Random* order as expected. The other heuristic that performs well is Greedy EvoCut, obtaining 5.1% and 5% cuts for *BFS* and *DFS* respectively. Linear Deterministic Greedy obtains 9.4%, 20.3%, and 30.6% cuts for *BFS*, *DFS* and *Random* respectively. In fact, all of the heuristics beyond Balanced and Hashing are vast improvements. The *BFS* ordering is also a strict improvement for all approaches over the *DFS* and *Random* orderings.

5.3 Performance on all graphs: discussion

We present the gain in the performance of each heuristic in Table 2, averaged over all datasets from Table 1 (except for LiveJournal and Twitter) and all runs, for each ordering. The best heuristic is Linear Deterministic Greedy for all orderings, followed by Balance Big. Greedy EvoCut is also successful on the *BFS* and *DFS* orderings, but is computationally much more expensive than the other two approaches. Note that Balance Big is a combination of the Greedy and Balanced strategies, assigned based on node degree. There are universally bad heuristics, namely Prefer Big and Avoid Big. Both of these are significantly worse than Hashing.

We further restrict the results by type of graphs. As stated earlier, FEMs have good balanced edge cuts. For these types of graphs, no heuristic performed worse than the Hashing approach, and most did significantly better. For the *BFS* ordering, Linear Deterministic Greedy had an average 86.6% gain, with Deterministic Greedy closely behind at 84.2%. For the *DFS* ordering, the Greedy EvoCut approach performed best at 78.8%, with all 3 deterministic greedy approaches closely behind at 74.9% (exp), 74.8% (unweighted) and 75.8% (linear). Finally, as always, the *Random* ordering was the hardest, but Linear Deterministic Greedy was also the best with 63% improvement. No other method achieved more than 56%. The surprising result for FEMs is how well the Chunking heuristic performed: an 80% improvement for

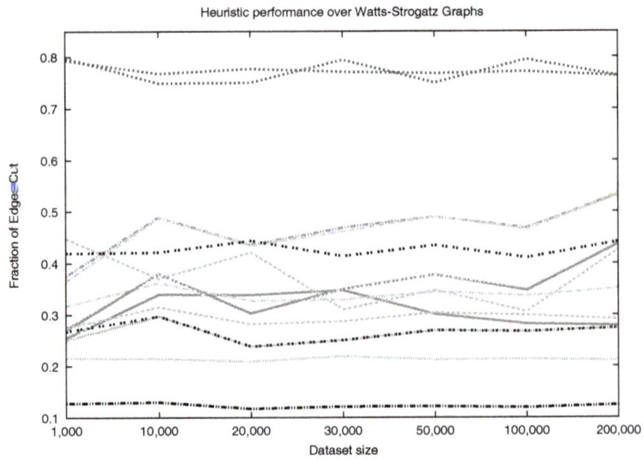

Figure 4: *BFS* with 4 partitions. Each line is a heuristics performance over 7 sizes of WS graph. The bottom line is METIS. The bottom purple line is Linear Deterministic Greedy. Best viewed in color.

BFS and 72% for DFS. This is a huge improvement for such a simple heuristic, although it is due to the topology of the networks and the fact that *BFS* is used in partitioning algorithms to find good cuts. When given a *Random* ordering, Chunking had only a 0.2% average improvement.

The social networks results were more varied. Here, the Prefer Big and Avoid Big both have large negative improvements, meaning both should never be used for power law degree networks with high expansion. For all three orderings, Linear Deterministic Greedy was clearly the superior approach with 71% improvement for *BFS*nd 70% for *DFS*. The second best performance was from both Exponential Deterministic Greedy and Deterministic Greedy at 60.5% for *BFS* and 52.9% for *DFS*. Finally, for a *Random* ordering, Linear Deterministic Greedy achieved a 64% improvement, with the other greedy approaches at only 42%.

Given that the Linear Deterministic Greedy algorithm performed so well, even compared with the other variants, one may ask why. At a high level, the penalty functions form a continuum. The unweighted version has a very strict cutoff - the penalty only applies when the partition is full and gives no indication that this restriction is approaching. The exponential penalty function has similar performance to the unweighted version because while the exponential function does not indicate that the partition is nearly full until it is very close to the limit. The linear weighting optimally balances the greedy choices with preferring less loaded partitions. Since $1 - x \approx e^{-x}$ when $0 < x < 1$, the linear weighting can be seen as a normalized exponential weighting. This normalization term allows the penalty to take effect much earlier in the process and smooths the information by preventing the size of the partition from affecting the prediction. As this is a continuum, this parameter could be further fine-tuned for different types of graphs. Additionally, the implementation of the unweighted greedy algorithm in this paper breaks ties lexicographically. Breaking ties by load is equivalent to an indicator penalty function and its performance is very close to the linear penalty function.

5.4 Scalability in the graph size

All of our datasets discussed so far are tiny when compared with graphs used in practice. While the above results are promising, it is important to understand whether the heuristics scale with the size of the graph. We used the synthetic datasets in order to control for the variance in different graphs. The key assumption is that using the same generative model with similar parameter settings will guarantee similar graph statistics while allowing the number of edges and nodes to vary. We began by looking at the results for the four generative models, BA, RMAT, WS, and PL. For each of these we had 3 data points: 1,000 vertices, 10,000 vertices, and 50,000 vertices. In order to get a better picture, we created additional graphs with 20,000, 30,000, 100,000 and 200,000 vertices. We will present only the results for the Watts-Strogatz graphs, but all other graphs exhibit quite similar results. Note that these results will scale to any size graph created by the same generative model because of the statistical properties of the generated graphs.

The labels in Figure 4 have been elided for clarity of the image. The bottom black line is METIS. This shows that our idea that the fraction of edges cut should scale with the size of the graph holds - it is approximately 12% for each graph. Next, there is clearly a best heuristic for this type of graph, the purple line. It corresponds to the Linear Deterministic Greedy heuristic. It has an average edge cut of 21% over all sizes of the graphs. Finally, all of the lines are approximately constant. The noise in the performance of each algorithm is due to the random nature of the orderings, and would decrease with further trials.

5.5 Scalability in the number of partitions

The other question is how the partitioning quality scales with the number of partitions. The fraction of edges cut must necessarily increase as we increase the number of partitions. Also, we are not trying to find an optimal number of partitions for the graph. As before, we only present data on one graph in Figure 5, the 50,000 node PowerLaw Clustered graph, but all graphs have similar characteristics. The heuristics performance closely tracks that of METIS.

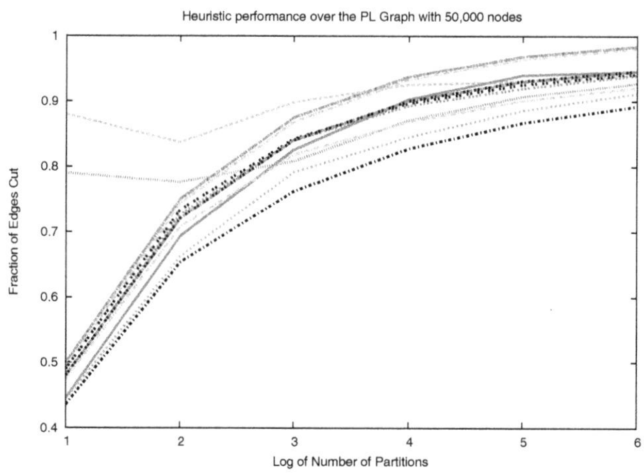

Figure 5: *BFS* with 2-64 partitions. Each line connects a heuristics performance over the 6 partition sizes. The bottom line is METIS. The bottom purple line is Linear Deterministic Greedy.

6. RESULTS ON A REAL SYSTEM

After evaluating the performance of the partitioning algorithms, we naturally ask whether the improvement in the partitioning makes any measurable difference for real computations. To evaluate our partitioning scheme in a cluster application, we used an implementation of PageRank in Spark [32], a cluster computing framework for iterative applications. Spark provides the ability to keep the working set of the application (the graph topology and PageRank values) in memory across iterations, so the algorithm is primarily limited by communication between nodes. Other recent frameworks for large-scale graph processing, like Pregel [25] and GraphLab [24], also keep data in memory and are expected to exhibit similar performance characteristics.

There are many graph algorithms implemented for the Spark system, but we chose PageRank for two reasons. One is the popularity of this specific algorithm, and the other is its generality. PageRank is a specialized matrix multiplication, and many graph algorithms can be expressed similarly. Additionally, Spark has two implementations of PageRank: a naïve version that sends a message on the network for each edge, and a more sophisticated combiner version that aggregates all messages between each partition [31].

We used Linear Deterministic Greedy, as it performed best in our previous experiments. We tried both a vertex balanced version and an edge-balanced version. However, our datasets are social networks and follow a power-law degree distribution. For PageRank, the quantity that should be balanced is the number of edges in each partition as this controls the amount of computation performed in sparse matrix multiplication and we want this to be equal for all partitions. The existence of very high degree nodes means that some partitions contain many more edges than others, resulting in unbalanced computation times between the different cluster machines. We therefore modified Linear Deterministic Greedy to use the number of edges in a partition for the weight penalty. We used two datasets, LiveJournal [26] with 4.6 million nodes and 77.4 million edges, and Twitter [21] with 41.7 million nodes and 1.468 billion edges. While neither are Internet scale, they are both realistic for medium sized web systems and large enough to show the effects of reduced communication on a distributed computation.

LiveJournal.

We used 100 partitions, with imbalance of 2% and the stream order provided by the authors of the dataset which is an unknown ordering. Linear Deterministic Greedy reduced the number of edges cut to 47,361,254 edges compared with 76,234,872 for Hashing. We ran 5 iterations of both versions of PageRank, and repeated this experiment 5 times. With the improved partitioning, naïve PageRank was 38.7% faster than the hashed partitioning version.The timing information, along with standard deviations, is summarized in Table 3. We used 10 "large" machines (7.5GB memory and 2 CPUS) on Amazon's EC2. The combiner version with our partitioning was 28.8% faster than the hashed version. This reduction in computation time is obtained entirely by laying out the data in a slightly smarter way.

Twitter.

We repeated the experiment for Twitter [21]. This graph is one of the largest publicly available datasets. Twitter was partitioned into 400 pieces with a maximum imbalance of 2%. Linear Deterministic Greedy cut 1.341 billion edges, while Hashing cut 1.464 billion. We used 50 "large" machines with 100 cores. The total computation time is much longer

	LJ Hash	LJ Streamed
Naïve PR Mean	296.2s	181.5s
Naïve PR STD	5.5 s	2.2 s
Combiner PR Mean	155.1 s	110.4 s
Combiner PR STD	1.5 s	0.8 s
	Twitter Hash	Twitter Streamed
Naïve PR Mean	1199.4 s	969.3 s
Naïve PR STD	81.2 s	16.9 s
Combiner PR Mean	599.4 s	486.8 s
Combiner PR STD	14.4 s	5.9 s

Table 3: Timing data (mean and standard deviation) for 5 iterations of PageRank computation on Spark for LiveJournal and Twitter graphs, Hashing vs. Linear Deterministic Greedy.

due to the increase in size. The naïve PageRank was 19.1% faster with our partitioning while the combiner version was 18.8% faster. For both graphs, there was additional time associated with loading the graph, about 200 seconds for Twitter and 80 seconds for LiveJournal, but this was not affected by the partitioning method.

These results show that with very little engineering effort, a simple preprocessing step that considers the graph edges can yield a large improvement in the running time. The best heuristic can be computed for each arriving node in time that is linear in the number of edges, given access to the distributed lookup table for the cluster and knowledge of the current loads of the machines. The improvement in running time is entirely due to the reduced network communication.

7. CONCLUSIONS AND FUTURE WORK

We have demonstrated that simple, one-pass streaming graph partitioning heuristics can dramatically improve the edge-cut in distributed graphs. Our best performing heuristic is the linear weighted variant of the greedy algorithm. This is a simple and effective preprocessing step for large graph computation systems, as the data must be loaded onto the cluster any way. One might need to perform a full graph partitioning once the graph has been fully loaded, however, as it will be re-partitioning an already partitioned graph, there will be less communication cost and it potentially may need to move fewer vertices, and will be faster. Using our approach as preprocessing step can only benefit any future computation while incurring only small cost.

There are several future directions for our work. First, there is the theoretical work. A framework should be developed for proving the performance of these heuristics. The main complications are the addition of the *BFS* and *DFS* stream orderings, and the fact that the offline optimal solution is NP-hard to compute. However, the best heuristic also performed well on the *Random* ordering, so it may be possible to prove a bound on its performance with additional assumptions like the graph is generated by a specific model.

The second direction is to address using parallel loaders. In reality, using a single machine to load terabytes of data will be far too slow. We expect the performance of running parallel loaders on independent portions of the graph stream to be similar to our experiments, requiring only access to the distributed lookup table.

8. REFERENCES

[1] http://facebook.com/press/info.php?statistics, Jan 2012.

[2] http://pywebgraph.sourceforge.net.

[3] http://research.microsoft.com/ldg, Jan 2012.

[4] http://research.microsoft.com/trinity, Jan 2012.

[5] http://staffweb.cms.gre.ac.uk/~wc06/partition.

[6] K. Jin Ahn and S. Guha. Graph sparsification in the semi-streaming model. *ICALP*, 2009.

[7] R. Alberich, J. Miro Julia, and F. Rossello. Marvel universe looks almost like a real social network. *arXiv*, 2002.

[8] R. Andersen, F. Chung, and K. Lang. Local graph partitioning using pagerank vectors. In *FOCS*, 2006.

[9] R. Andersen and Y. Peres. Finding sparse cuts locally using evolving sets. In *STOC*, pages 235–244, 2009.

[10] K. Andreev and H. Racke. Balanced graph partitions. *Theory of Computing Systems*, 39:929–939, 2006.

[11] S. Arora, S. Rao, and U. Vazirani. Expander flows, geo -metric embeddings and graph partitioning. *J.ACM*, 2009.

[12] B. Bahmani, A. Chowdhury, and A. Goel. Fast incremental and personalized pagerank. *PVLDB*, 4(3):173–184, 2010.

[13] A-L Barabasi and R Albert. Emergence of scaling in random networks. *Science*, 286(5439):509–512, 1999.

[14] S. Barnard. PMRSB: Parallel multilevel recursive spectral bisection. In *Supercomputing*, 1995.

[15] S. Bykov, A. Geller, G. Kliot, J. Larus, R. Pandya, and J. Thelin. Orleans: Cloud computing for everyone. In *ACM Symposium on Cloud Computing*, 2011.

[16] G. Even, J. Naor, S. Rao, and B. Schieber. Fast approximate graph partitioning algorithms. *SIAM J. Comput*, 28(6):2187–2214, 1999.

[17] B. Hendrickson and R. Leland. A multilevel algorithm for partitioning graphs. In *Supercomputing*, 1995.

[18] P. Holme and B. J. Kim. Growing scale-free networks with tunable clustering. Phys. Rev. E, 2002.

[19] G. Karypis and V. Kumar. Multilevel graph partitioning schemes. In *ICPP*, pages 113–122, 1995.

[20] J. Kelner and A. Levin. Spectral sparsification in the semi-streaming setting. *STACS*, pages 440–451, 2011.

[21] H. Kwak, C. Lee, H. Park, and S. Moon. What is Twitter, a social network or a news media? In *WWW*, 2010.

[22] J. Leskovec. http://snap.stanford.edu/snap, 2012.

[23] J. Leskovec, D. Chakrabarti, J. Kleinberg, C. Faloutsos, and Z. Ghahramani. Kronecker graphs: An approach to modeling networks. *JMLR*, 2010.

[24] Y. Low, J. Gonzalez, A. Kyrola, D. Bickson, C. Guestrin, and J. Hellerstein. GraphLab: A new framework for parallel machine learning. In *UAI*, 2010.

[25] G. Malewicz, M. Austern, A. Bik, J. Dehnert, I. Horn, N. Leiser, and G. Czajkowski. Pregel: a system for large-scale graph processing. PODC, 2009.

[26] A. Mislove, M. Marcon, K. Gummadi, P. Druschel, and B. Bhattacharjee. Measurement and analysis of online social networks. In *ACM/USENIX IMC*, 2007.

[27] M. E. J. Newman. The structure of scientific collaboration networks. *Natl Acad Sci*, 98:404–9, 2001.

[28] A. Das Sarma, S. Gollapudi, and R. Panigrahy. Sparse cut projections in graph streams. In *ESA*, pages 480–491, 2009.

[29] A. Das Sarma, S. Gollapudi, and R. Panigrahy. Estimating pagerank on graph streams. *J. ACM*, 58(3):13, 2011.

[30] D. J. Watts and S. H. Strogatz. Collective dynamics of 'small-world' networks. *Nature*, 393:440–442, 1998.

[31] M. Zaharia, M. Chowdhury, T. Das, A. Dave, J. Ma, M. McCauley, M.J. Franklin, S. Shenker, , and I. Stoica. Resilient distributed datasets: A fault-tolerant abstraction for in-memory cluster computing. *NSDI*, 2012.

[32] M. Zaharia, M. Chowdhury, M. J. Franklin, S. Shenker, and I. Stoica. Spark: Cluster Computing with Working Sets. In *HotCloud*, 2010.

[33] M. Zelke. Intractability of min- and max-cut in streaming graphs. *IPL*, 111(3):145 – 150, 2011.

RolX: Structural Role Extraction & Mining in Large Graphs

Keith Henderson and Brian Gallagher
Lawrence Livermore National Laboratory
{keith, bgallagher}@llnl.gov

Tina Eliassi-Rad
Rutgers University
tina@eliassi.org

Hanghang Tong
IBM Watson
htong@us.ibm.com

Sugato Basu
Google Research
sugato@google.com

Leman Akoglu, Danai Koutra, Christos Faloutsos, and Lei Li
Carnegie Mellon University
{lakoglu, danai, christos, leili}@cs.cmu.edu

ABSTRACT

Given a network, intuitively two nodes belong to the same role if they have similar structural behavior. Roles should be automatically determined from the data, and could be, for example, "clique-members," "periphery-nodes," etc. Roles enable numerous novel and useful network-mining tasks, such as sense-making, searching for similar nodes, and node classification. This paper addresses the question: Given a graph, how can we automatically discover *roles* for nodes? We propose *RolX* (*Role eXtraction*), a scalable (linear in the number of edges), unsupervised learning approach for automatically extracting structural roles from general network data. We demonstrate the effectiveness of *RolX* on several network-mining tasks: from exploratory data analysis to network transfer learning. Moreover, we compare network role discovery with network community discovery. We highlight fundamental differences between the two (e.g., roles generalize across disconnected networks, communities do not); and show that the two approaches are complimentary in nature.

Categories and Subject Descriptors

H.2.8 [**Database Applications**]: Data mining; E.1 [**Data Structures**]: Graphs and networks

General Terms

Algorithms, Design, Performance, Experimentation.

Keywords

Graph mining, structural role discovery, network classification, similarity search, sense-making

1. INTRODUCTION

Given a network, we want to automatically capture the structural behavior (or function) of nodes via *roles*. Examples of possible roles include: centers of stars, members of cliques, peripheral nodes, etc. To this end, we propose a novel approach, called *RolX* (*Role eXtraction*), which automatically and effectively summarizes the behavior of nodes in large graphs. More precisely, *RolX* achieves the following two objectives. First, with *no* prior knowledge of the kinds of roles that may exist, it automatically determines the underlying roles in a network. Second, it appropriately assigns a mixed-membership of these roles to each node in the network. *RolX* is important because its roles form a basis for a number of novel and interesting network data analysis tasks such as network transfer learning, measuring structural similarity, sense-making (i.e., understanding the underlying behavior in a network), and network visualization. For instance, given two IP communication graphs from enterprise networks, we can use the extracted roles in one graph to build a relational classifier that can be used for a classification task in the other graph, effectively performing across-network classification or transfer learning on graphs.

RolX is an unsupervised learning approach for automatically extracting structural roles from general network data sets. Through extensive experiments, we demonstrate that the derived roles are effective in exploratory data analysis tasks (such as sense-making and node-similarity) and in prediction tasks such as across-network transfer learning. In the latter setting, we use the ability of roles to generalize behavior across networks as a way to perform network learning without relying on homophily, or on the availability of class labels in the target graph.

In our framework, roles are derived from structural features. In the absence of any other information, the problem of extracting roles from a network dataset is ill-defined, since there can be an infinite number of structural features that can be derived from the data. Once we choose a set of such features, the problem of role extraction can be well-formulated. Given a set of structural features that are extracted for a dataset, we define the role extraction problem as (1) finding the basis vectors in this structural feature space (where the number of basis vectors is determined by model selection), and (2) determining how much each network node belongs to each role. The structural features that are used for role extraction are domain-dependent. For example, for social networks, we propose a set of structural features that agree with the domain knowledge of sociologists.

The contributions of our work are as follows:

- *Effectiveness*: *RolX* enables numerous graph mining tasks, including:
  - *Role Generalization/Transfer Learning*: The structural roles of *RolX* generalize across disjoint networks.
  - *Structural Similarity*: *RolX* provides a natural

KDD'12, August 12–16, 2012, Beijing, China.

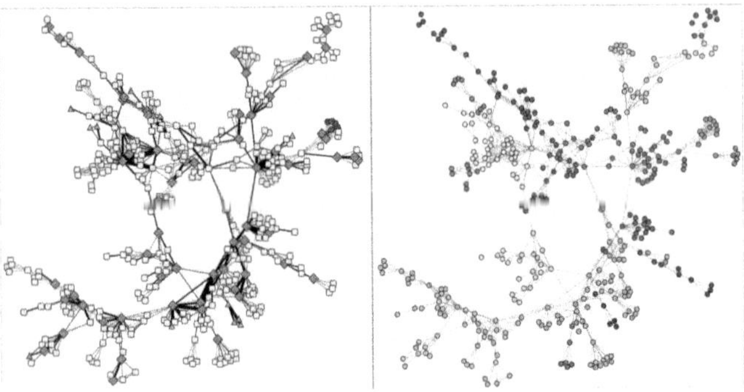

Figure 1: Role discovery and community discovery are complementary approaches to network analysis. Left: The 4 roles that *RolX* discovers on the largest connected component of the Network Science Co-authorship Graph: "bridge" nodes (as red diamonds), "main-stream" nodes (gray squares), etc - see text. Right: The 22 communities that Fast Modularity [6] finds on the same co-authorship graph. Roles capture node-level behaviors and generalize across networks whilst communities cannot.

way to determine similarity between nodes by comparing their role distributions.[1]

- *Sense-making*: The structural roles of *RolX* can be understood intuitively by summarizing their characteristics (*NodeSense*) and their neighbors (*NeighborSense*).

- *Automation*: *RolX* is carefully designed to be fully automatic, without requiring user-specified parameters.
- *Scalability*: The runtime complexity of *RolX* is linear on the number of edges.

We want to emphasize that *RolX* as a role discovery approach is fundamentally different from (and complementary to) community detection: the former groups nodes of similar *behavior*; the latter groups nodes that are well-connected to each other.

Figure 1 depicts the difference between role discovery and community discovery for the largest connected component of a weighted co-authorship network [25]. *RolX* automatically discovers 4 roles vs. the 22 communities that the popular *Fast Modularity* [6] community discovery algorithm finds. *RolX* is a mixed-membership approach, which assigns each node a distribution over the set of discovered, structural roles. The node colors for *RolX* correspond to the node's primary role, and for Fast Modularity correspond to the node's community. Our four discovered roles represent these behaviors: "bridge" nodes (red diamonds) representing central and prolific authors, "main-stream" nodes (gray squares) representing neighborhoods of bridge nodes, "pathy" nodes (green triangles) representing peripheral authors with high edge-weight, and "tight-knit" nodes (blue circles) representing authors with many coauthors and homophilic neighborhoods.

The rest of the paper is organized as follows: proposed method, experimental results for the mining tasks outlined above, related work, and conclusions.

[1] *RolX* is a mixed-membership approach, which assigns each node a distribution over the set of discovered roles.

2. PROPOSED METHOD

Given a network, the goal of *RolX* is to automatically discover a set of underlying (latent) roles, which summarize the structural behavior of nodes in the network. *RolX* consists of three components: feature extraction, feature grouping, and model selection.

2.1 Feature Extraction

In its first step, *RolX* describes each node as a feature vector. Examples of node features are the number of neighbors a node has, the number of triangles a node participates in, etc. *RolX* can use any set of features deemed important. Among the numerous choices for feature extraction from graphs, we choose the structural feature discovery algorithm described in [15] since it is scalable and has shown good performance for a number of tasks. For a given node v, it extracts local and egonet features based on counts (weighted and unweighted) of links adjacent to v and within and adjacent to the egonet of v. It also aggregates egonet-based features in a recursive fashion until no informative feature can be added. Examples of these recursive features include degree and number of within-egonet edges, as well as aggregates such as "average neighbor degree" and "maximum neighbor degree." Again, *RolX* is flexible in terms of a feature discovery algorithm, so *RolX*'s main results would hold for other structural feature extraction techniques as well.

2.2 Feature Grouping

After feature extraction, we have n vectors (one per node) of f numerical entries each. How should we create groups of nodes with similar structural behavior/features? How can we make it fully automatic, requiring *no* input from the user?

We propose to use soft clustering in the structural feature space (where each node has a mixed-membership across various discovered roles); and specifically, an automatic version of matrix factorization.

Given a node-feature matrix $V_{n\times f}$, the next step of the *RolX* algorithm is to generate a rank r approximation $GF \approx V$ where each row of $G_{n\times r}$ represents a node's membership in each role and each column of $F_{r\times f}$ specifies how membership in a specific role contributes to estimated feature values. There are many methods to generate such an approximation (e.g., SVD, spectral decomposition) and *RolX* is not tied to any particular approach. For this study, we chose Non-negative Matrix Factorization because it is computationally efficient and non-negative factors simplify the interpretation of roles and memberships.

Formally, we seek two non-negative low rank matrices G and F to satisfy: $\text{argmin}_{G,F}\|V-GF\|_{fro}$, s.t. $G \geq 0$, $F \geq 0$, where $\|\cdot\|_{fro}$ is the Frobenius norm. The non-negativity constraint generally leads to a sparse, part-based representation of the original data set, which is often semantically more meaningful than other factorization methods. While it is difficult to find the optimal factorization of a matrix because of the non-convexity of the objective function, several efficient approximation algorithms exist (e.g., multiplicative update [18] and projective gradient decent [20]). *RolX* uses multiplicative update because of its simplicity. It is worth pointing out that *RolX* can naturally incorporate other variants of matrix factorization such as imposing sparseness constraint on F and/or G by incorporating some regularization terms in the objective function [10]). *RolX* can also use a general Bregman divergence [8] to measure approximation

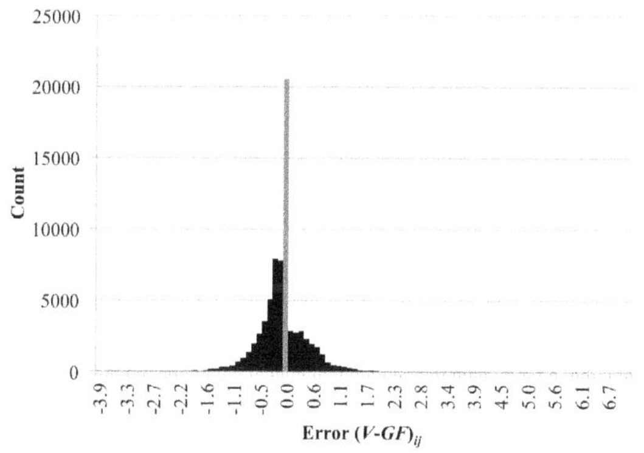

Figure 2: Errors do not appear to be normally distributed when approximating V in the Network Sciences Co-authorship graph. The spike at zero suggests that the Frobenius norm is not a good measure of model likelihood. *RolX* uses KL divergence to compute error description costs.

accuracy instead of using the Frobenius norm – this enables *RolX* to use other divergence functions (e.g., KL divergence) that can be more appropriate in some cases, as explained in Section 2.3.

One practical issue with feature grouping algorithms is that the model size (i.e., the number of roles) must be prespecified. In general, it is unrealistic to expect a practitioner to manually select an appropriate value for this parameter. Therefore, we explore several approaches for automatic model selection.

2.3 Automating the Method: Model Selection

Since roles summarize behavior, they can be used to compress the feature matrix V. We propose to use the Minimum Description Length criterion [27], to select the model size r that results in best compression. For a given model, we can compute the resulting description length in two parts: (1) the number of bits required to describe the model itself, and (2) the cost of describing the reconstruction errors in $V-GF$ (to achieve lossless compression). The selected model is the one that minimizes the description length $\mathcal{L}$, which is the sum of model description cost $\mathcal{M}$ and the coding cost (or equivalently, the cost of correcting the errors of our model) $\mathcal{E}$. That is, $\mathcal{L} = \mathcal{M} + \mathcal{E}$.

Assuming G and F are not sparse, the cost of describing the model using b bits per value is $\mathcal{M} = br(n + f)$.

How should we determine the representation cost of correcting errors in the reconstruction? That is, how do we compute the log-likelihood of a given model? Figure 2 suggests that the errors in $V-GF$ are not distributed normally, making the standard Frobenius norm a poor choice. Instead, we use KL divergence to compute the error description cost: $\mathcal{E} = \sum_{i,j}(V_{i,j} \log \frac{V_{i,j}}{(GF)_{i,j}} - V_{i,j} + (GF)_{i,j})$.

Because the model can contain high-precision floating point values, we combine Lloyd-Max quantization [22, 21] with Huffman codes [17] to increase compression. Note that with Huffman codes, the cost of encoding the model changes to $\bar{b}r(n + f)$, where $\bar{b}$ is the mean number of bits required per value. As a default, we choose $\log_2(n)$ quantization bins. However, the number of bins can be selected through param-

		Log2(# Quantization Bins)								
# Roles	1	2	3	4	5	6	7	8	9	10
1	37420	33855	31069	31347	31155	33015	34569	36579	39189	42098
2	35516	31433	27106	27572	27786	30492	33271	36562	40326	45127
3	32878	27769	23376	22149	24704	28723	32546	36486	41416	47242
4	37231	26295	23875	22198	25518	30485	34719	39282	44911	51674
5	46674	31456	25722	22245	25899	31398	35883	40947	46960	53941
6	46028	29327	27692	23849	29383	34753	39707	45016	51090	58691
7	40685	33922	29555	25561	30837	37667	42761	49399	56660	64456
8	42065	30322	28649	27526	34360	40804	47369	53842	61541	70812
9	39426	29422	29508	32557	38143	45765	52931	61155	69426	79495
10	45052	37736	31395	32844	41555	48523	56535	65402	74460	86220

Figure 3: Description length (in bits) is minimized when using 2^4 bins and 3 or 4 roles in the Network Science Co-authorship graph. Too many bins or roles increases the model description cost, while too few increases the cost of describing errors.

eter selection by choosing the number of bins and roles that minimizes description length. Figure 3 shows that for the Network Science Co-authorship graph, description lengths are minimized when we use $2^4 = 16$ quantization bins and 3 or 4 roles.

2.4 Computational Complexity

Let n be the number of nodes, m be number of edges, f = number of features, and r = number of roles.

LEMMA 1. *The running time complexity of* RolX *is linear on the number of edges, and specifically is $O(mf + nfr)$.*

PROOF. We give the complexity of each of the three steps of *RolX*.

Feature Extraction. This is $O(f(m + nf))$ [15].

Model Selection. The error computation takes $O(nrf)$ to multiply an $n \times r$ matrix by an $r \times f$ matrix. Quantization has a complexity of $O(nfilog(K))$, where K is the number of quantization bins and i is the number of iterations that we run the quantizer. Default for K is $log(n)$, so this becomes $O(nfilog(log(n)))$. Notice that the term of $O(log(log(n)))$ is a very small number. For example, for a graph with 1 billion nodes, this term is just about 3.1. So, the complexity for the quantization is roughly $O(nfi)$. There is also a term for the Huffman coding which is $O(nf + Klog(K))$. The $O(Klog(K))$ term is to build the tree that holds the codes. But this number is very small and therefore can be neglected.

Feature Grouping. We use the multiplicative update method for *RolX*, which has worst case complexity $O(nfr + nr^2 + fr^2) = O(nfr)$. □

2.5 Remarks

We experimented with several other options for clustering, model sizes criterion, and compression. For example, the information criterion proposed by Akaike (AIC) [1] can be used in place of compression. *RolX* can use as a drop-in replacement any other matrix factorization method, either in the usual form or the sparse counterpart (e.g., [10]).

Similarly, there are several representational choices for compressing floating points. We experimented with numerous of these choices, but we omit the details for brevity. Thus, unless otherwise stated *RolX* employs the feature extraction algorithm described in [15], non-negative matrix factorization for clustering, MDL for model selection, and KL divergence to measure likelihood.

	IP-A1	IP-A2	IP-A3	IP-A4	IP-B
# Nodes	81,450	57,415	154,103	206,704	181,267
(# labeled)	29,868	16,112	30,955	67,944	27,649
# Links	968,138	432,797	1,266,341	1,756,082	1,945,215
(# unique)	206,112	137822	358,851	465,869	397,925
% Web	32%	38%	38%	18%	42%
% DNS	36%	49%	39%	20%	42%
% P2P	32%	12%	20%	62%	16%

Table 1: Extracted real-world network trace data

		Test Graph			
		IP-A2	IP-A3	IP-A4	IP-B
Train Graph	IP-A1	✓	✓	✓	✓
	IP-A2		✓	✓	✓
	IP-A3			✓	✓
	IP-A4				✓
	IP-A1 to IP-A4				✓

Table 2: Across-network experiments performed on the network trace data

3. ROLE GENERALIZATION / TRANSFER LEARNING

In this section, we present experiments on role effectiveness for the across-network classification task (i.e., network transfer learning).

Data. We conduct experiments on two real-world data sets: IP communication networks and bluetooth proximity networks.

IP data: IP-A and IP-B are real network-trace data sets collected roughly one year apart on separate enterprise networks. The nodes are IP addresses and the links are communications between the IPs. The IP-A trace begins at midnight on day 1 and continues up to 12pm on day 5. The IP-B trace begins at midnight on day 1 and continues up to ≈5pm on day 6. For days 1-4 of the IP-A dataset (IP-A1 to IP-A4), we extract flows in the period from 12pm-1pm. We exclude day 5 because the trace ended at 12pm. For IP-B, we extract flows from 12pm-1pm for day 3 only. We then label all flows using a payload signature-based classification tool. Once network flows are labeled, we transfer labels to hosts by selecting the most frequent class-labels from among the host's flows. The payload classifier can distinguish between over 15 classes of traffic (e.g., Web, DNS, SMTP, P2P). However, since we found that 3 classes (namely, Web, DNS, and P2P) made up the dominant traffic type for over 90% of the labeled hosts, we remove all other labels and focus on the 3-class classification problem. Table 1 summarizes the data that we extracted. Notice the differences in the size and class distribution across these networks.

Reality Mining Device data: This dataset is constructed based on the data provided by the Reality Mining project [9]. That study was conducted in July 2004-June 2005 at the MIT Media Laboratory, with the participation of 94 human subjects using mobile phones pre-installed with several pieces of software, which recorded and sent to the research center various data including information about Bluetooth devices in proximity of approximately 5 meters. Subjects were tracked over 12 months and included students and faculty from the MIT Media Lab and the Sloan Business School. Within that period, about two million device scans were reported.

Classifiers. To test the predictive ability of the roles discovered by *RolX*, we use logistic regression with the *RolX* role memberships as features. In order to compare the predictive power of the *RolX* roles to the raw features that *RolX* uses as input, we also compare to a classifier that uses these raw features as input. The classifiers we compare are:

- *RolX*: a logistic regression model, which uses *RolX* role memberships as features
- *Feat*: a logForest model, which uses the same raw structural features as *RolX*, but does not decompose them into roles. The logForest is a bagged model, composed of a set of logistic regression classifiers, where each is given a subset of $\log(f) + 1$ of the f total features [13]. Note that for these raw features, logForest achieves vastly superior classification accuracy than logistic regression. Therefore, we omit logistic regression results for this classifier. See [15] for details.

The standard relational classifiers are not applicable for these transfer learning tasks since these methods rely on the availability of some known class labels in the test graph to seed the inference process. The test graphs here are completely unlabeled.

Methodology. For each experiment, the training graph has all known labels available. The test graph is *completely* unlabeled. Each classifier is evaluated on all known ground truth labels in the test graph. We use an identical set of roles for all data sets, which comes from running *RolX* on the IP-A1 data set. Table 2 summarizes the across-network experiments.

Results. We discuss predictive performance of roles next.

IP data: We ran *RolX* on a series of across-network transfer learning tasks (see Table 2). We train on one network where all known labels are available, and test on a separate network that is completely unlabeled. These tasks are difficult, given the (sometime extreme) differences in class distributions between data sets (see Table 1). The performance of the *Default* classifier is a good indicator of the difficulty of each task, since this model makes predictions based solely on the most frequent class from the training set. *Feat* uses the full set of 373 structural features extracted from IP-A1. *RolX* summarizes these features into 9 roles.

We see from Figure 4 that the roles produced by *RolX* effectively summarize the behavior of hosts in an IP network. In particular, *RolX* is able to generalize more effectively than *Feat* from network A to network B (*RolX* =85%, *Feat*=71% accuracy, p-value=0.01[2]). The results for transfer learning tasks across different days of network A are omitted since we cannot differentiate the performance of *RolX* and *Feat* (p-value=0.25).

Figures 5 and 6 demonstrate that the model selection criterion used by *RolX* is quite effective for our IP network classification task. *RolX* chooses a model size of 9 roles, which is right in the middle of the peak accuracy range shown in Figure 5. Figure 6a shows that the model selection criterion used by *RolX* is highly correlated with classification accuracy (Pearson correlation is -0.91). Figure 6b shows the default *RolX* model selection criterion decomposed into its constituent parts. *Model cost* is the cost associated with representing the model itself while *error cost* is the cost of

[2]The p-values are obtained from a one-tailed paired t-test.

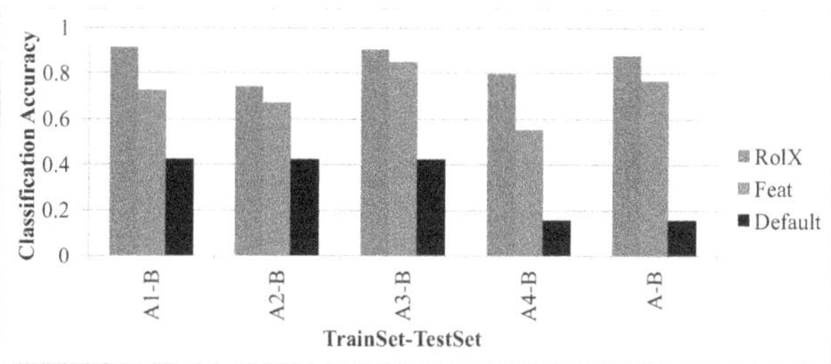

Figure 4: *RolX* provides better generalization performance between enterprise IP networks A and B (mean accuracy of *RolX* =85%, *Feat*=71%, p-value=0.01).

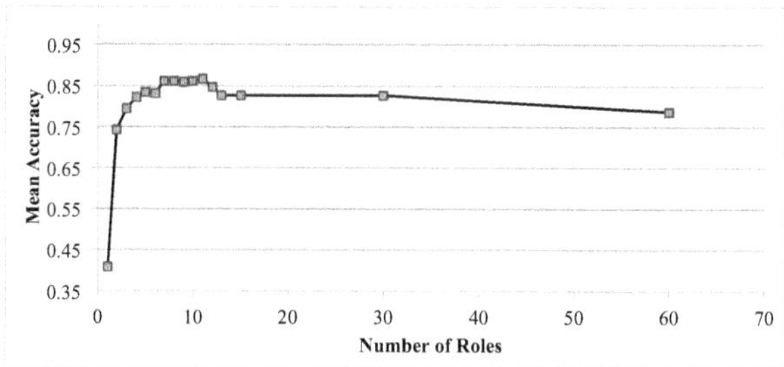

Figure 5: *RolX* chooses a high accuracy model size of 9 roles, in the middle of the peak accuracy range of 7-11 roles. The Y-axis depicts the mean classification accuracy using *RolX* (over all 4 test sets) by model size.

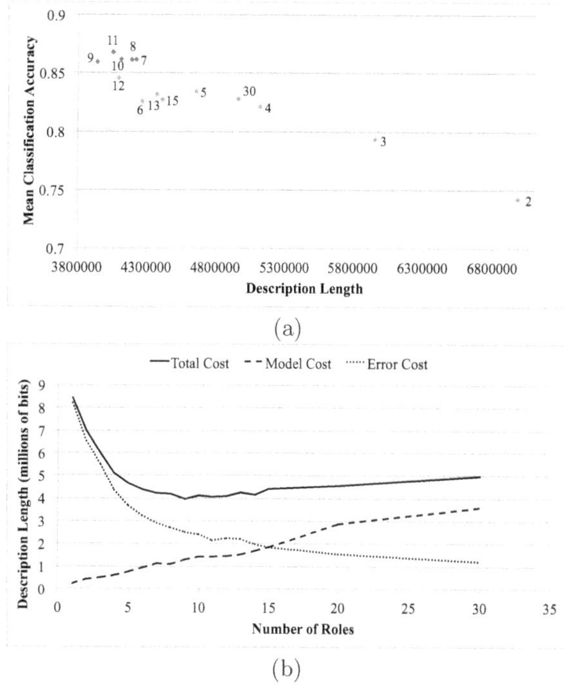

Figure 6: *RolX*'s model selection is effective: (a) Classification accuracy is highest when *RolX* selection criterion is minimized. Red markers indicate the peak performing model sizes of 7-11 roles (b) *RolX*'s model selection criterion balances model size and reconstruction accuracy.

representing the differences between the original feature values and the estimated feature values reconstructed using the model. As expected, we see a consistent increase in model cost and a consistent decrease in error cost as the number of roles increases.

Figure 7 shows that IP traffic classes are well-separated in the *RolX* "role space", with as few as 3 roles (extracted from the original 373 structural features). Note that we achieve even better separation with the automatically selected model size of 9 roles (see Figure 4), but we can only clearly visualize up to 3.

We omit for brevity the "sense-making" table for the 3-role IP experiment. It shows that Roles 1 and 2 are lower-volume IPs while Role 3 is high-volume servers or P2P nodes. Role 3 contains nodes of all three types (Web, DNS, P2P). This Role is overloaded since the model size of 3 is not as predictive as larger model sizes (see Figure 5).

Reality Mining Device data: We conducted two sets of transfer learning experiments on this data. The first set of experiments involves a binary classification task where we try to predict whether a given subject is a business school student or not. The second set is similar, where we try to predict whether a subject is a graduate student in the Media Lab or not. As train and test sets, we used each pair of consecutive months in our dataset. In Figure 8, we show the accuracy of *RolX*. The Baseline is a classifier that learns to always predict the majority class of the training set on the test set. The time labels denote the month for the train data, and the month following that is used as the test data. We also use all the data in 2004 and 2005 as train and test data, respectively. Notice that *RolX* outperforms the baseline classifier most of the time with an average of 83% and 76% accuracy for the two experiment sets, respectively. We notice that *RolX*'s accuracy drops when September and May data is used as training, possibly because these months correspond to the start and end of the school semesters; the behavior of the subjects would be generally different than usual in these months, thus providing not as much predictive information as the other months would.

4. STRUCTURAL SIMILARITY

Here we describe experiments in which *RolX* is used for its most basic task: grouping nodes based on their structural similarity.

Network Science Coauthorship Data. Our first data set is a weighted co-authorship graph with 1589 authors (from the network science community) and 2743 weighted edges [25]. Figure 9 shows (a) the role-colored graph (where each node is colored by the primary role that *RolX* finds) and (b) the role affinity heat map. *RolX* finds four roles. Based on further analysis of the network and its roles, we discovered that the roles correspond to the following: (Disclaimer: The relative position in the graph does not reflect the total magnitude of contributions of the individual researchers. It is just a snapshot of networks-science-related data, and specifically in 2006.)

- *blue circle*: *tightly knit*, nodes that participate in tightly-

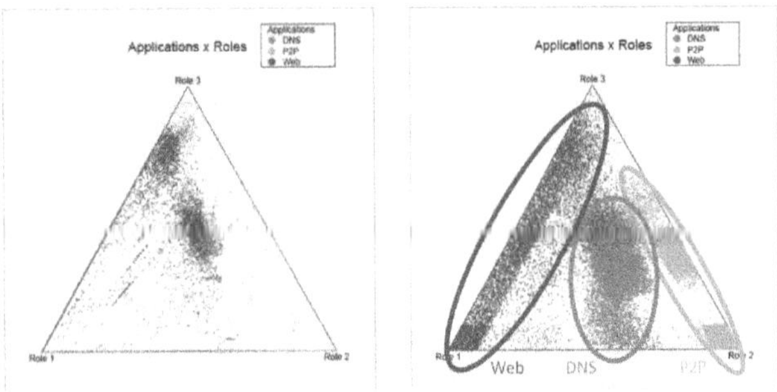

(a) (b)

Figure 7: IP traffic classes are well-separated in the *RolX* "role space" with as few as 3 roles. (a) Ternary plot showing the degree of membership of each DNS, P2P, and Web host in each of three roles. (b) Pseudo-density plot obtained by adding uniform noise to (a) to reveal overlapping points.

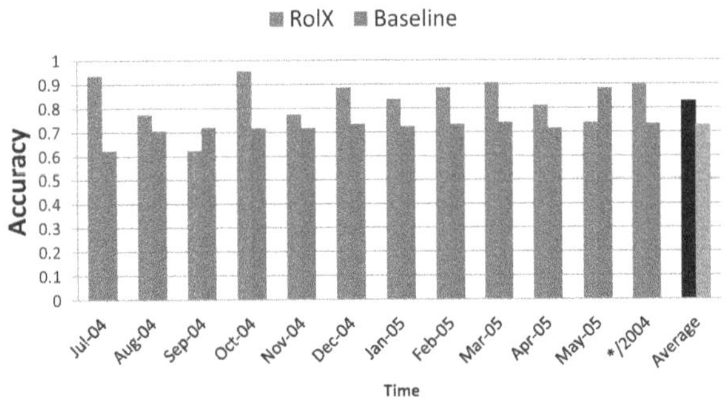

(a) Business Student vs. Rest

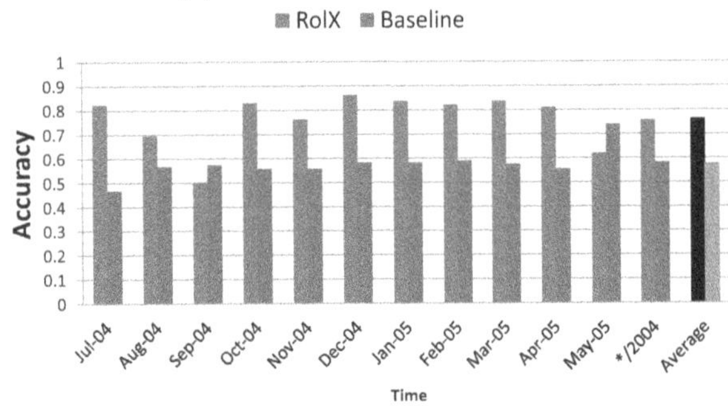

(b) Graduate Student vs. Rest

Figure 8: *RolX* (in blue) effectively generalizes behavior across time (higher is better). Figure shows results of across-network transfer learning on the Reality Mining Device dataset with *RolX*. Notice that *RolX* almost always performs well on the two different learning tasks with an average accuracy of 83% and 76%, respectively.

coupled groups. Examples are Andrei Broder and Christos Faloutsos.

- *red diamond*: *bridge* nodes, that connect groups of (typically, 'main-stream') nodes. Examples of bridges are Albert-Laszlo Barabasi and Mark Newman.

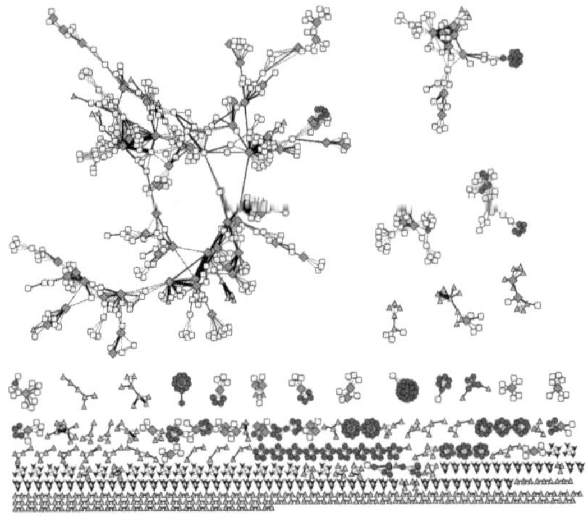

(a) Role-colored Visualization of the Network

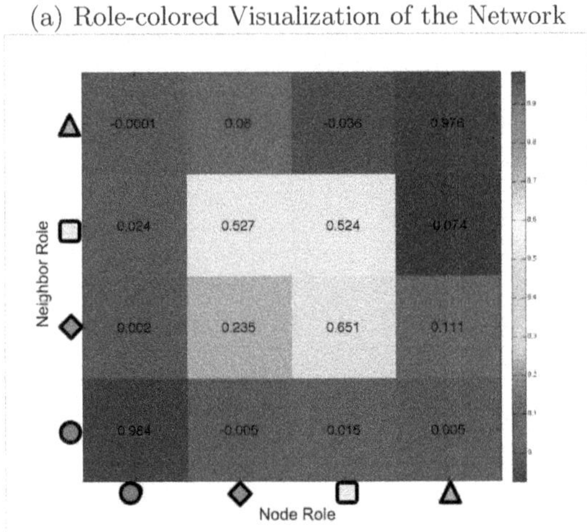

(b) Role Affinity Heat Map

Figure 9: *RolX* effectively discovers roles in the Network Science Co-authorship Graph. (a) Author network *RolX* discovered four roles, like the heterophilous bridges (*red diamond*), as well as the homophilous "pathy" nodes (*green triangle*) (b) Affinity matrix (red is high score, blue is low) - strong homophily for roles #1 and #4.

- *gray rectangle*: *main-stream*, the vast majority of nodes - neither on a clique, nor a chain. Examples are John Hopcroft and Jon Kleinberg.
- *green triangle*: *pathy*, nodes that belong to elongated clusters. For example, Lada Adamic and Bernardo Huberman.

RolX's roles allow us to find similar nodes by comparing their role distributions. Figure 10 depicts node similarity for three (target) authors for the Network Science Co-authorship Graph: Mark Newman, F. Robert, and J. Rinzel. The primary roles for these three authors are different. Mark Newman's primary role is a broker (a prolific author); F. Robert's primary role places him in a tight-knit group (an author with homophilous neighborhood), and J. Rinzel's primary role places him in the periphery (an author with homophilous but "pathy" neighborhood). In each node-similarity picture, the target author is colored in yellow. The more similar nodes are red and less similar nodes are blue. Due to the generality of roles, *RolX* is able to find similar nodes across the entire graph even though it has many disconnected components.

Political Books Co-purchase Data. We gave the 2000 Amazon Political Books Co-purchasing Network[3] to *RolX*. This graph has 105 nodes (representing books) and 441 edges (representing frequent co-purchasing of the books by the same buyers). *RolX* is able to effectively capture the purchasing behavior of customers by separating the "locally central" books from the "peripheral" books. Figure 11 depicts the "local central-ness" and "peripheral-ness" of the books.[4]

For the readers' convenience, we also present the human-provided labels for the nodes: conservative books (in circles), liberal books (in squares), and neutral books (in diamonds). Examples of highly central books are "Off With Their Heads" (conservative) and "Bushwhacked" (liberal). Highly peripheral books include "The Right Man" (conservative) and "Shrub" (liberal).

Node positions in Figure 11 are determined by a standard force-directed layout. Communities (conservative vs. liberal) are separated while nodes within a community are organized by role (central vs. peripheral) *RolX* can be used in conjunction with community discovery algorithms to find similar nodes in disparate communities or networks.

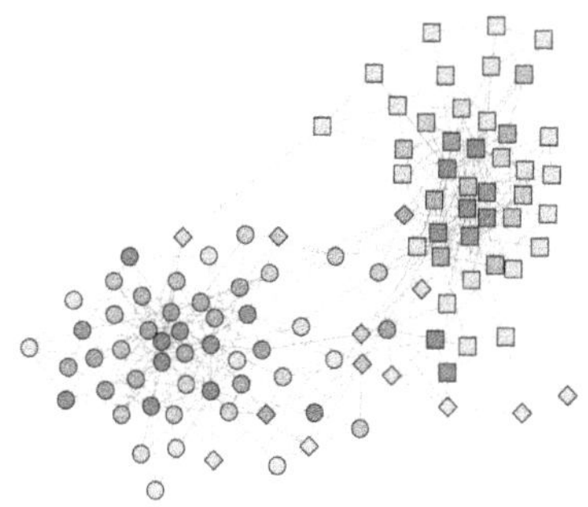

(a) Bright red nodes are locally central nodes.

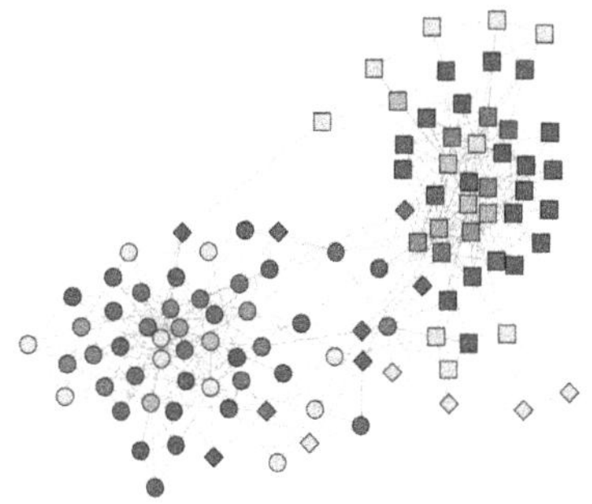

(b) Bright blue nodes are peripheral nodes.

Figure 11: *RolX* effectively discovers roles in the 2000 Amazon Political Books Co-purchasing Network – illustrating how *RolX*'s roles can be used to find similar nodes in disparate communities. *RolX* finds two roles: locally central nodes and peripheral nodes. The redness of a node corresponds to its percentage membership in Role 1 (its "local centralness"). Similarly, the blueness of a node corresponds to its percentage membership in Role 2 (its "peripheral-ness"). The node shapes corresponds to the human-provided labels of conservative (circle), liberal (square), and neutral (diamond).

5. SENSE-MAKING

To make "sense" of roles, we introduce two methods. One based on node measurements (*NodeSense*) and another based on neighbor measurements (*NeighborSense*).

NodeSense takes as input *RolX*'s node-by-role matrix, G, and a matrix of node measurements, M. For our experiments, we use the following node measurements: a node's degree, weighted degree, clustering coefficient, eccentricity (i.e., the longest geodesic from a node), PageRank, gatekeeper (i.e., whether a node is an articulation point for some pairs of nodes), local gatekeeper, pivot (i.e., a node with high betweenness), and structural hole (i.e., to what extent are a node's links redundant). *NodeSense* then computes a nonnegative matrix E such that $G \cdot E \approx M$. The matrix E represents the role contribution to node measurements. A default matrix E' is also computed by using $G' = ones(n, 1)$, where the n nodes belong to one role. Then, for each role r and for each measurement s, *NodeSense* computes $\frac{E(r,s)}{E'(r,s)}$. This ratio provides the role-contribution to node-measurements compared to the default contribution.

NeighborSense is similar to *NodeSense*–except instead of the matrix M, we use a neighbor matrix N, where the rows represent nodes and columns represent roles. $N(i, j)$ is the fraction of node i's neighborhood that is in role j. Then *NeighborSense* computes a nonnegative matrix Q such that $G \cdot Q \approx N$. The matrix Q represents the role affinities. A default matrix Q' is also computed using $G' = ones(n, 1)$, where the n nodes belong to one role. Then, for each pair of roles r_1 and r_2, *NeighborSense* computes $\frac{Q(r_1,r_2)}{Q'(r_1,r_2)}$. This ratio is the role-affinities compared to the default affinities.

Figure 12 depicts the results of *NodeSense* and *NeighborSense* on the Network Science Co-Authorship Graph. Recall that *RolX* found four roles on this graph. **Role 1** nodes (*blue circles* in Figure 9a) are authors with many coauthors and homophilic neighborhoods. They have high degree, high clustering coefficient, and high homophily. They are never gatekeepers (i.e. articulation points for some pairs of nodes) or pivotal nodes (i.e., with high betweenness). **Role 2** nodes (*red diamonds* in Figure 9a) represent authors who are central and prolific with high total weight. They have low clustering coefficient but high degree, high PageRank, and high affinity for Role 3 nodes (i.e., *gray rectangles*). Removal of Role 2 nodes severely interrupts graph connectivity because they are often gatekeepers and pivotal nodes. **Role 3** nodes (*gray squares* in Figure 9a) are peripheral authors. They have low degree and high eccentricity (i.e., nodes in the network periphery). They are almost never gatekeepers, but can be pivotal (i.e. they do not disconnect the graph, but they often increase geodesic lengths when removed). **Role 4** nodes (*green triangles* in Figure 9a) are isolated authors with high average edge weight and homophilic neighborhoods. Their links are not redundant (w.r.t. structural holes), but have low scores for most other measures (except homophily).

This sense-making analysis can be extremely useful for large networks, which cannot be easily visualized. By using

[3]Valdis Krebs, http://www.orgnet.com/.

[4]A third "super-peripheral" role is omitted for brevity. These nodes are gray in both (a) and (b).

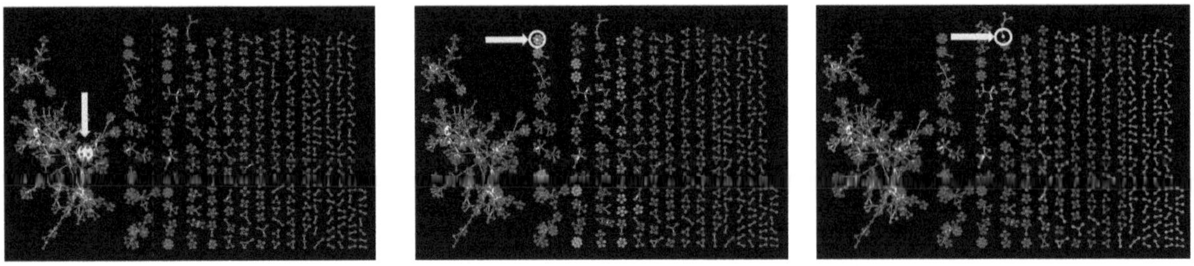

(a) Node similarity for Mark Newman (b) Node similarity for F. Robert (c) Node similarity for J. Rinzel

Figure 10: *RolX* produces meaningful node-similarity across (disconnected) components of a graph. For each chosen node (in yellow circle), we use 'red' for the nodes with high structural similarity, and blue for the rest. (a) For Mark Newman (who is a "broker"), the red nodes are fairly central nodes, bridging others. (b) For F. Robert (who is from a tight-knit and homophilous neighborhood): the reds are clique members (of disconnected cliques) (c) For J. Rinzel (who is from a "pathy" but homophilous neighborhood): red nodes form small chains.

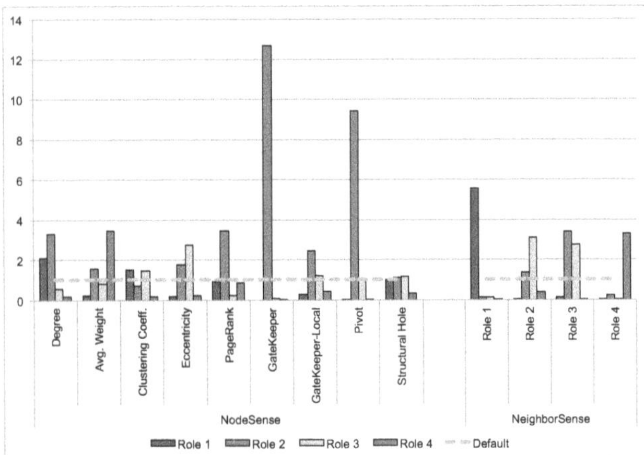

Figure 12: *NodeSense* and *NeighborSense* explain roles in the network science co-authorship graph. The *blue circle* authors (Role 1) are members of tight-knit communities and are role-homophilous. The *red diamond* authors (Role 2) are least homophilous. They are mostly brokers/bridges and are neighbors of *gray rectangles* (Role 3). The *gray rectangle* nodes (Role 3) are peripheral authors (i.e., have unusually high eccentricity). The *green triangle* nodes (Role 4) are isolated authors with disconnected coauthors.

role-homophily and topological measures, we can interpret roles regardless of network size.

6. RELATED WORK

Related research can be categorized into three parts: (1) graph features, (2) role discovery, and (3) transfer learning.

Graph Features. Features have been extracted from graphs for several data mining tasks. In [19], the authors propose extracting topological features for pairs of nodes for link prediction. In [14], the authors develop a multilevel framework to detect anomalies in time-varying graphs based on graph, sub-graph, and node level features. Their approach relies on extracting graph-level (global) features and tracking these metrics over time. In [2], the authors propose to detect abnormal nodes from weighted graphs based on features and patterns from egonets. There has also been work on using local and global structural features to improve the performance of network classifiers [12]. Some methods for feature extraction explicitly preserve the multi-cluster structure in the data [4]. Our work builds upon the approach of *recursive feature extraction* [15].

Role discovery. We propose using recursive graph features for role discovery of nodes. The task of role discovery has been studied in different types of graphs (e.g., social networks [23]). Different approaches have been used for role discovery, including Bayesian frameworks using MCMC sampling algorithm for learning multiple roles of data points [28], semi-supervised semantic role labeling [11], etc. These approaches do not scale up to handle large graphs.

There is another related body of work in role mining, a nice overview of which is given by Molloy et al. [24]. Role mining is somewhat different from the role discovery problem we discuss in this paper. It addresses the access permissions for different users in different roles in an access-controlled system. However, role mining algorithms use techniques similar to role discovery for inferring roles for nodes in a graph (e.g., hierarchical clustering).

In addition to using the inferred roles for exploratory graph mining (such as structural similarity and sense-making tasks), we use the inferred roles for improving classification. Previous approaches include using cluster structure for predicting class labels on graphs [16], and using cluster kernels for semi-supervised classification [30]. *RolX* is scalable.

RolX is different than generalized blockmodeling [26], which is commonly used in social network analysis. In particular, (1) *RolX* roles generalize across networks; (2) RolX is scalable; and (3) RolX incorporates local structure in addition to regular equivalence, and natively supports node attributes when they are available.

Transfer learning. Another aspect of our work is effective transfer learning in graphs. In the context of graph data, nonparametric models have been proposed for transfer learning for the task of collective link prediction [5]. The general framework of EigenTransfer constructs a graph to represent the source-target transfer learning task [7], while similarity matrix approximations of a hybrid graph have been explored for transfer learning [29]. Relevant supervision has also been transferred across domains to improve the performance of clustering algorithms [3]. In all existing work, the features are *given* as the input and the goal is to leverage the *given* features to boost performance in the target domain.

7. CONCLUSIONS

Our main contribution is the careful design and extensive experimental validation of *RolX*, a novel role discovery approach with the following properties:

- *Effectiveness*: *RolX* enables numerous mining tasks, including: *Role Generalization/Transfer Learning*, (§ 3), *Structural Similarity* (§ 4), and *Sense-making* (§ 5).
- *Automation*: *RolX* is fully automatic, requiring no user-specified parameters.
- *Scalability*: Runtime is linear on the number of edges.

8. ACKNOWLEDGEMENTS

This work was performed under the auspices of the U.S. Department of Energy by Lawrence Livermore National Laboratory under Contract No. DE-AC52-07NA27344, and supported in part by IARPA via AFRL Contract No. FA8650-10-C-7061 and in part by DAPRA under SMISC Program Agreement No. W911NF-12-C-0028 and ARL No. W911NF-09-2-0053. The U.S. Government is authorized to reproduce and distribute reprints for Government purposes notwithstanding any copyright annotation thereon. The views and conclusions contained in this document are those of the authors and should not be interpreted as representing the official policies, either expressed or implied, of IARPA, AFRL, DARPA, or the U.S. Government.

9. REFERENCES

[1] H. Akaike. Information theory and an extension of the maximum likelihood principle. In *Proc. of the 2nd Int'l Symp. on Information Theory*, pages 267–281, 1972.

[2] L. Akoglu, M. McGlohon, and C. Faloutsos. Oddball: Spotting anomalies in weighted graphs. In *PAKDD*, pages 410–421, 2010.

[3] I. Bhattacharya, S. Godbole, S. Joshi, and A. Verma. Cross-guided clustering: Transfer of relevant supervision across domains for improved clustering. In *ICDM*, pages 41–50, 2009.

[4] D. Cai, C. Zhang, and X. He. Unsupervised feature selection for multi-cluster data. In *KDD*, pages 333–342, 2010.

[5] B. Cao, N. Liu, and Q. Yang. Transfer learning for collective link prediction in multiple heterogenous domains. In *ICML*, pages 159–166, 2010.

[6] A. Clauset, M. Newman, and C. Moore. Finding community structure in very large networks. *Phys. Rev. E*, 70:066111, 2004.

[7] W. Dai, O. Jin, G.-R. Xue, Q. Yang, and Y. Yu. Eigentransfer: a unified framework for transfer learning. In *ICML*, pages 193–200, 2009.

[8] I. S. Dhillon and S. Sra. Generalized nonnegative matrix approximations with Bregman divergences. In *NIPS*, pages 283–290, 2005.

[9] N. Eagle, A. Pentland, and D. Lazer. Inferring social network structure using mobile phone data. *PNAS*, 106(36):15274–15278, 2009.

[10] J. Eggert and E. Korner. Sparse coding and NMF. In *IJCNN*, pages 2529–2533, 2004.

[11] H. Fürstenau and M. Lapata. Semi-supervised semantic role labeling. In *EACL*, pages 220–228, 2009.

[12] B. Gallagher and T. Eliassi-Rad. Leveraging label-independent features for classification in sparsely labeled networks: An empirical study. *Lecture Notes in Computer Science*, 5498:1–19, 2010.

[13] B. Gallagher, H. Tong, T. Eliassi-Rad, and C. Faloutsos. Using ghost edges for classification in sparsely labeled networks. In *KDD*, pages 256–264, 2008.

[14] K. Henderson, T. Eliassi-Rad, C. Faloutsos, L. Akoglu, L. Li, K. Maruhashi, B. A. Prakash, and H. Tong. Metric forensics: A multi-level approach for mining volatile graphs. In *KDD*, pages 163–172, 2010.

[15] K. Henderson, B. Gallagher, L. Li, L. Akoglu, T. Eliassi-Rad, H. Tong, and C. Faloutsos. It's who you know: Graph mining using recursive structural features. In *KDD*, pages 663–671, 2011.

[16] M. Herbster. Exploiting cluster-structure to predict the labeling of a graph. In *ALT*, pages 54–69, 2008.

[17] D. Huffman. A method for the construction of minimum-redundancy codes. In *Proc. of the IRE*, pages 1098–1101, 1952.

[18] D. D. Lee and H. S. Seung. Learning the parts of objects by non-negative matrix factorization. *Nature*, 401(6755):788–791, 1999.

[19] R. N. Lichtenwalter, J. T. Lussier, and N. V. Chawla. New perspectives and methods in link prediction. In *KDD*, pages 243–252, 2010.

[20] C.-J. Lin. Projected Gradient Methods for Nonnegative Matrix Factorization. *Neural Computation*, 19(10):2756–2779, 2007.

[21] S. P. Lloyd. Least squares quantization in PCM. *IEEE Trans. on Info. Theory*, IT-28(2):129–137, 1982.

[22] J. Max. Quantizing for minimum distortion. *IRE Trans. on Information Theory*, IT-6:7–12, 1960.

[23] A. Mccallum, X. Wang, and A. Corrada-Emmanuel. Topic and role discovery in social networks with experiments on enron and academic email. *JAIR*, 30(1):249–272, 2007.

[24] I. Molloy, N. Li, T. Li, Z. Mao, Q. Wang, and J. Lobo. Evaluating role mining algorithms. In *SACMAT*, pages 95–104, 2009.

[25] M. E. J. Newman. Finding community structure in networks using the eigenvectors of matrices. *Phys. Rev. E.*, 74:036104, 2006.

[26] A. F. Patrick Doreian, Vladimir Batagelj. *Generalized Blockmodeling*. Cambridge University Press, 2005.

[27] J. Rissanen. Modeling by shortest data description. *Automatica*, 14:465–471, 1978.

[28] M. Somaiya, C. Jermaine, and S. Ranka. Mixture models for learning low-dimensional roles in high-dimensional data. In *KDD*, pages 909–918, 2010.

[29] Z. Wang, Y. Song, and C. Zhang. Knowledge transfer on hybrid graph. In *IJCAI*, pages 1291–1296, 2009.

[30] J. Weston, C. Leslie, E. Ie, D. Zhou, A. Elisseeff, and W. S. Noble. Semi-supervised protein classification using cluster kernels. *Bioinformatics*, 21:3241–3247, 2005.

Fast Algorithms for Maximal Clique Enumeration with Limited Memory

James Cheng
Nanyang Technological University
Singapore
j.cheng@acm.org

Linhong Zhu
Institute for Infocomm Research
Singapore
lzhu@i2r.a-star.edu.sg

Yiping Ke
Institute of High Performance Computing
Singapore
keyp@ihpc.a-star.edu.sg

Shumo Chu
Nanyang Technological University
Singapore
shumo.chu@acm.org

ABSTRACT

Maximal clique enumeration (*MCE*) is a long-standing problem in graph theory and has numerous important applications. Though extensively studied, most existing algorithms become impractical when the input graph is too large and is disk-resident. We first propose an efficient partition-based algorithm for MCE that addresses the problem of processing large graphs with limited memory. We then further reduce the high cost of CPU computation of MCE by a careful nested partition based on a cost model. Finally, we parallelize our algorithm to further reduce the overall running time. We verified the efficiency of our algorithms by experiments in large real-world graphs.

Categories and Subject Descriptors

H.2.8 [**DATABASE MANAGEMENT**]: Database Applications—*Data mining*; G.2.2 [**DISCRETE MATHEMATICS**]: Graph Theory—*Graph algorithms*

General Terms

Algorithms, Experimentation, Performance

Keywords

Maximal clique enumeration, I/O efficient, parallel algorithm, massive networks, sparse graphs

1. INTRODUCTION

Maximal clique enumeration (**MCE**) [3, 9] is one of the fundamental problems in graph theory. It is closely related to many other important graph problems, such as maximal independent sets (or minimal vertex covers), graph coloring, maximal common induced subgraphs, maximal common edge subgraphs, etc. Besides graph theory, MCE has numerous other applications, such as social network analysis [20], hierarchy detection through email networks [16], study of structures in behavioral and cognitive networks [5], statistical analysis of financial networks [7], clustering in dynamic networks [28], the detection of emergent patterns in terrorist networks [6], etc. Moreover, MCE is also closely tied to various applications in computational biology [1], including the detection of protein-protein interaction complex and clustering protein sequences.

The problem of MCE is NP-hard theoretically but because of its significance in real applications, many practical algorithms [1, 3, 9, 10, 18, 19, 21, 23, 24, 25, 26, 28, 29, 30, 31] have been proposed. However, many of these algorithms have become impractical today due to the fast growing size of graphs in the real world. For example, the Web graph has over 1 trillion webpages (by Google in 2008); most social networks (e.g., Facebook, LinkedIn, Twitter, Google+) and communication networks (e.g., MSN, phone, SMS, and email networks) have up to billions of users; other networks such as transportation networks, citation networks, stock-market networks, etc., are also massively large.

The existing algorithms are *in-memory* algorithms, which require space that is asymptotically linear in the size of the input graph. However, the massive size of many graphs has outpaced the advance in the memory available on commodity hardware. MCE computation accesses vertices in a rather arbitrary manner and this results in random access. When memory is insufficient and the graph has to be resident on disk, random disk access incurs high I/O cost.

To process such large graphs, Cheng et al. proposed efficient algorithms [12, 13] which enumerate maximal cliques in local subgraphs that fit in main memory as to eliminate the high I/O cost due to random access. However, MCE intrinsically has a high CPU time complexity and thus reducing the I/O cost alone does not fully address the problem.

To address the intensity of MCE computation, several parallel algorithms [17, 27] have been proposed. However, they still require a copy of the entire input graph to be resident in memory at each computing node, which ends at the same predicament faced by the existing in-memory sequential MCE algorithms.

MapReduce has been popularly used to handle massive data. A MapReduce algorithm [33] was proposed recently for MCE. The MapReduce model, however, may not be efficient for enumeration tasks such as MCE and triangle listing [14, 15] in large graphs due to the huge amount of intermediate data produced in the shuffling phase between Mappers and Reducers.

In this paper, we propose new algorithms for MCE that achieve the following three objectives.

1. We reduce the I/O cost by a partition-based strategy, which avoids random access for MCE in large graphs that cannot fit in memory.

2. We reduce the cost of CPU computation by investigating a neglected (by existing work) but non-negligible cost in MCE; that is, most of the operations at each step of MCE require only constant time but some set intersections require linear time. We devise a cost model to reduce this cost which significantly speeds up the entire MCE process.

3. We further reduce the overall running time by parallelizing MCE based on our partitioning strategy. Instead of requiring to keep the entire input graph at each computing node as in the existing parallel algorithms [17, 27], our algorithm requires only limited memory at any computing node.

Extensive experiments on large real-world datasets verify the effectiveness of our algorithms in reducing both the I/O cost and CPU cost. The results show that our algorithms significantly outperform the state-of-the-art MCE algorithms [12, 13, 18, 19, 29], especially in the case when the input graph is too large to fit in main memory.

Paper organization. The remaining of the paper is organized as follows. Section 2 defines the problem and basic notations. Section 3 describes a conventional algorithm for MCE and points out its weaknesses. Section 4 discusses the details of our algorithms. Section 5 reports the experimental results. Section 6 discusses the related work and Section 7 concludes the paper.

2. NOTATIONS AND PROBLEM DEFINITION

Let $G = (V, E)$ be a simple undirected graph. We define the *size* of G, denoted by $|G|$, as $|G| = (|V| + |E|)$. Given a subset of vertices $S \subseteq V$, we define the *induced subgraph* of G by S as $G_S = (V_S, E_S)$, where $V_S = S$ and $E_S = \{(u, v) : u, v \in S, (u, v) \in E\}$. We define the set of *adjacent vertices* of a vertex v in G as $adj(v) = \{u : (u, v) \in E\}$, and the *degree* of v in G as $deg(v) = |adj(v)|$. Similarly, we define $adj(v, G_S) = \{u : (u, v) \in E_S\}$ and $deg(v, G_S) = |adj(v, G_S)|$.

We assume that all graphs are stored (whether in memory or on disk) in adjacency list representation, where vertices are assigned unique IDs and ordered according to their IDs.

A *clique* C in a graph G is a subset of vertices, where $C \subseteq V$, such that G_C is a complete subgraph of G. C is called a *maximal clique* in G if there exists no clique C' in G such that $C' \supset C$.

Problem definition. The problem of **MCE** is: *given a graph G, find the set of all maximal cliques in G.*

We focus on *sparse graphs*, for which $|E| \ll B \cdot |V|$, and B is the disk block size. Most large and many fast growing real-world networks are sparse. For processing these large sparse graphs, random disk access in the process of MCE is prohibitively expensive since data transferred from/to disk is in blocks, while the exact amount of data used in each step of MCE is much less than the amount of data transferred for each random access, since $deg(v) \ll B$ for most $v \in V$.

Algorithm 1 *IM-MCE*

Input: a graph $G = (V, E)$
Output: all maximal cliques in G

```
1. IM-MCE-Step(∅, V, ∅);
```

Procedure 2 *IM-MCE-Step*$(C, todo, done)$

```
1. if(todo = ∅ and done = ∅)
2.     output C as a maximal clique;
3. else
4.     choose a pivot vertex v_p from (todo ∪ done);
5.     doing := todo\adj(v_p);
6.     for each v ∈ doing do
7.         todo := todo\{v};
8.         IM-MCE-Step(C ∪ {v}, todo ∩ adj(v), done ∩ adj(v));
9.         done := done ∪ {v};
```

3. CONVENTIONAL MCE ALGORITHM

We first discuss the conventional algorithms for MCE and their shortcomings. Algorithm 1 and Procedure 2 sketch a general algorithm framework for MCE, which is adopted by most existing MCE algorithms [9, 23, 29]. The state-of-the-art parallel MCE algorithm [27] is also developed based on this framework. This framework is also used in later sections to explain our algorithms.

Algorithm 1 calls Procedure 2. In Procedure 2, we use the notations ***todo***, ***doing***, and ***done*** to represent the set of vertices *to be processed*, *being processed*, and *already processed*, respectively.

The algorithm starts from the set of all vertices in G, i.e., $todo = V$, and $done = \emptyset$, by calling Procedure 2. Procedure 2 recursively calls itself to grow a clique C in a depth-first manner until C becomes maximal; that is, when $todo = \emptyset$, i.e., there is no more vertex for C to grow with, and $done = \emptyset$, i.e., C has not been enumerated before (if $done \neq \emptyset$, then $\exists C' \supset C$ such that C' has been found as a maximal clique).

The depth-first MCE process essentially constructs a search tree, or more precisely a search forest joined by a (virtual) root. At each call of Procedure 2, we first pick a *pivot* vertex v_p, which is used to prune all the neighbors of v_p, because any maximal clique containing a vertex $u \in adj(v_p)$ can be enumerated from either v_p or another vertex $v \in adj(u)$, where $v \notin adj(v_p)$. Therefore, all the search subtrees rooted at each $u \in adj(v_p)$ can be pruned.

We then construct $doing$, which is the set of vertices being processed in the current call of Procedure 2. For each vertex $v \in doing$, we grow the current clique C by adding v to C. To further grow $(C \cup \{v\})$ to a bigger clique in the subsequent recursive call, we need to make sure that every vertex in $todo$ must be a neighbor of v. After the recursive call returns, we add v to $done$ to indicate that v has been processed in the current search subtree.

Shortcomings. Algorithm 1 requires $O(3^{|V|/3})$ time in the worst case, but has shown to be the optimal worst-case complexity [29]. In practice, the existing algorithms that adopt the framework of Algorithm 1 are reasonably fast for processing relatively small real-world graphs. However, these algorithms are in-memory algorithms and require $\Omega(|V| + |E|)$ memory space. If memory is not sufficient or the input graph is disk-resident, the process immediately becomes impractical. As we observe in Line 8 of Procedure 2, the MCE process requires accesses to the neighbor set of each vertex $v \in doing$, i.e., $adj(v)$, which may scatter in different locations in the graph resident on disk. Thus, random disk access leads to huge I/O cost and severely degrades the performance of the in-memory algorithm. In addition, some branches of the search tree constructed by Algorithm 1 can be potentially parallelized. Intuitively, the search subtrees rooted at each of the siblings of the search tree can be constructed in parallel with careful design. We address these issues in Section 4.

4. FASTER MCE ALGORITHMS

In this section, we address the shortcomings of the conventional algorithm for MCE. In particular, we have the following three main objectives: *(1) reducing the I/O cost, (2) reducing the CPU cost, and (3) further reducing the overall running time by parallelization.*

4.1 Reducing the I/O Cost

When the input graph cannot fit in main memory, reducing the I/O cost by avoiding random disk accesses becomes the key to the efficiency of MCE. The main idea of our algorithm is to repeatedly extract a subgraph that fits in memory and compute the maximal cliques locally from the subgraph. However, we should also preserve both the *global* correctness and completeness of the results computed from the *local* subgraphs.

We first define the subgraph to be extracted for MCE as follows.

Definition 1 (SEED VERTICES/SUBGRAPH). *Given a graph $G = (V, E)$, denote S to be a set of* ***seed vertices*** *selected from V, where $S \subseteq V$. The* ***seed subgraph*** *of G, denoted by $G_S = (V_S, E_S)$, is defined as the induced subgraph of G by S.*

Using the seed subgraph G_S alone is not sufficient to ensure the completeness of MCE since some seed vertices may form a clique with vertices not in G_S. To address this, we extend G_S as follows.

Definition 2 (EXTENDED VERTICES/SUBGRAPH). *Given a set of seed vertices S of a graph $G = (V, E)$, the set of* ***extended seed vertices****, or simply* ***extended vertices****, denoted by S^+, is defined as $S^+ = S \cup \{v : v \in adj(u), u \in S\}$. The* ***extended seed subgraph****, or simply* ***extended subgraph****, denoted by G_{S^+}, is defined as the induced subgraph of G by S^+.*

Note that the above definition of subgraph is different from the one used in [12, 13], where they do not include the edges among the vertices in $(S^+ \backslash S)$. This difference renders the design of the algorithm totally different, since the subgraphs in [12, 13] still need to access the input graph for MCE while ours do not. Compared with the algorithms in [12, 13], our algorithm is simpler, more efficient, and natural to be parallelized.

The following example illustrates the concepts.

Example 1. Consider the graph G shown in Figure 1. If we choose $S = \{0, 1, 2\}$ as the set of seed vertices, we obtain the seed subgraph G_S as shown in Figure 2 (left). It is easy to see that the seed subgraph alone cannot produce any maximal clique of G. So we extend the seed vertices to be $S^+ = \{0, 1, 2, 3, 4, 5, 7\}$ and obtain the extended subgraph G_{S^+}, as given in Figure 2 (right). The extended subgraph makes possible the local enumeration of global maximal cliques, i.e., $\{0, 1, 2, 3\}, \{1, 4, 5\}, \{2, 7\}$, since G_{S^+} captures fully the neighborhood information of seed vertices. □

With the above formulation of extended subgraph, we first prove that the maximal cliques computed locally in each extended subgraph are also globally maximal.

Let $\mathcal{M}(G)$ and $\mathcal{M}(G_{S^+})$ be the set of maximal cliques in G and G_{S^+}, respectively. Let $\mathcal{M}_S(G) = \{C : C \in \mathcal{M}(G), C \cap S \neq \emptyset\}$ and $\mathcal{M}_S(G_{S^+}) = \{C : C \in \mathcal{M}(G_{S^+}), C \cap S \neq \emptyset\}$ be the set of maximal cliques, respectively in G and G_{S^+}, that contain at least one vertex in S.

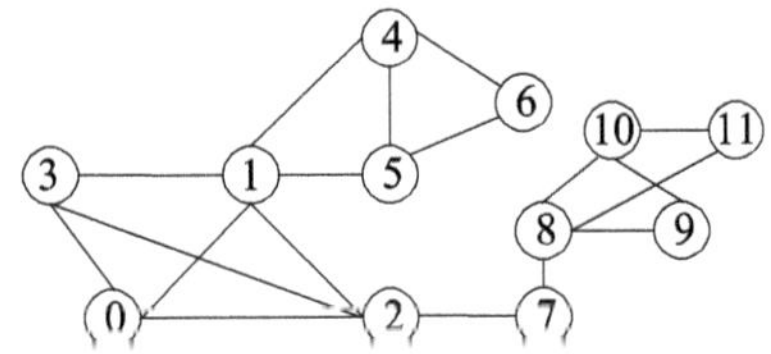

Figure 1: An Example of Input Graph, G

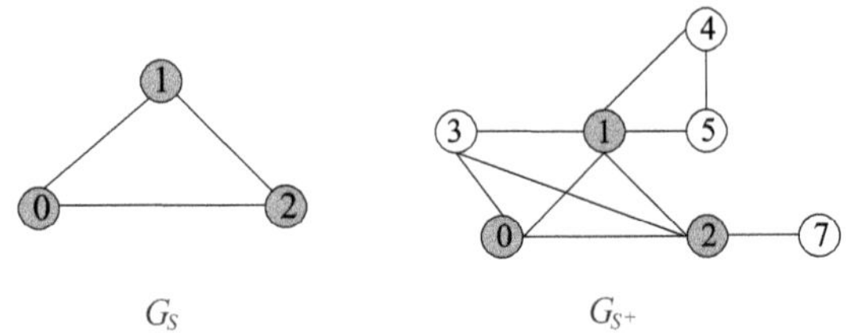

Figure 2: Seed Subgraph and Extended Subgraph

LEMMA 1. $\mathcal{M}_S(G_{S^+}) = \mathcal{M}_S(G)$.

PROOF. We first prove $\mathcal{M}_S(G_{S^+}) \subseteq \mathcal{M}_S(G)$. We begin by proving that $\forall C \in \mathcal{M}_S(G_{S^+})$, $C \in \mathcal{M}(G)$. Suppose $C \notin \mathcal{M}(G)$, then $\exists C' \in \mathcal{M}(G)$ such that $C' \supset C$. Then $\exists v \in C'$ and $v \notin S^+$ (otherwise $C' \in \mathcal{M}_S(G_{S^+})$ and hence $C \notin \mathcal{M}_S(G_{S^+})$). However, $v \notin S^+$ implies that $(v, u) \notin E$ for some vertex $u \in (C \cap S)$, which contradicts that C' is a clique. Thus, $C \in \mathcal{M}(G)$ and it follows that $C \in \mathcal{M}_S(G)$ since $C \cap S \neq \emptyset$.

We then prove $\mathcal{M}_S(G) \subseteq \mathcal{M}_S(G_{S^+})$. $\forall C \in \mathcal{M}_S(G)$, we have $C \in \mathcal{M}(G)$ and $C \cap S \neq \emptyset$. Let $u \in (C \cap S)$. Then $\forall v \in C \backslash \{u\}$, we have $(u, v) \in E$ and thus $v \in S^+$. Therefore, $C \in \mathcal{M}(G_{S^+})$ and it follows that $C \in \mathcal{M}_S(G_{S^+})$. □

Lemma 1 implies that all maximal cliques in G that contain at least one seed vertex in S can be computed from G_{S^+} alone. This leads to the design of an algorithm that repeatedly extracts a subgraph G_{S^+} that can fit in main memory, computes $\mathcal{M}_S(G_{S^+})$ from G_{S^+} in memory, and then continues to select another set of seed vertices from $(V \backslash S)$, until all vertices in V are processed. The following theorem guarantees the correctness and completeness of the set of maximal cliques so computed.

THEOREM 1. *Let $\mathcal{S} = \{S_1, \ldots, S_k\}$, where $\bigcup_{1 \leq i \leq k} S_i = V$ and $S_i \cap S_j = \emptyset$ for $i \neq j$. Let $\mathcal{M}_{\mathcal{S}} = \bigcup_{1 \leq i \leq k} \mathcal{M}_{S_i}(G_{S_i^+})$. Then, $\mathcal{M}_{\mathcal{S}} = \mathcal{M}(G)$.*

PROOF. First, $\forall S_i, \mathcal{M}_{S_i}(G_{S_i^+}) \subseteq \mathcal{M}(G)$ according to Lemma 1. Thus, $\mathcal{M}_{\mathcal{S}} \subseteq \mathcal{M}(G)$. Next, $\forall C \in \mathcal{M}(G)$, $\exists S_i$ such that $C \in \mathcal{M}_{S_i}(G_{S_i^+})$, where $C \cap S_i \neq \emptyset$ (note that the existence of S_i is because $\bigcup_{1 \leq i \leq k} S_i = V$). Thus, $\mathcal{M}(G) \subseteq \mathcal{M}_{\mathcal{S}}$. □

Theorem 1 immediately leads to the design of an efficient partition-based algorithm, as shown in Algorithm 3.

The algorithm sequentially scans the input graph G to select a set of seed vertices S, extracts G_{S^+} by another scan of G, computes $\mathcal{M}_S(G_{S^+})$ from G_{S^+}, and then continues to select another set of seed vertices until all vertices in V are processed as seed vertices.

The algorithm determines the size of G_{S^+} in Line 4, where a parameter ϕ_{deg} is used to estimate the size of G_{S^+}, and $0 < c < 1$

Algorithm 3 *Partition-Based MCE*

Input: a graph $G = (V, E)$

Output: all maximal cliques in G

```
1. S := ∅, S+ := ∅;
2. for each v ∈ V do
3.     S := (S ∪ {v}), S+ := (S+ ∪ {v} ∪ adj(v));
4.     if((φ_deg · |S+|) ≥ cM)
5.         scan G once to extract G_S+;
6.         apply in-memory MCE to G_S+;
7.         for each C ∈ M(G_S+) do
8.             if((C ∩ S) ≠ ∅ and (∄u ∈ C s.t. u ≺ S))
9.                 output C as a maximal clique;
10.        S := ∅, S+ := ∅;
```

is to ensure the estimated size is less than M[1], where M is the available memory size. Here, ϕ_{deg} can be the average or maximum vertex degree in G. If ϕ_{deg} is the average vertex degree, it is possible that $|G_{S^+}| > M$; however, this can be easily fixed by further splitting G_{S^+} into smaller extended subgraphs with smaller seed vertex sets. Since only some selection of S can lead to the case "$|G_{S^+}| > M$", in practice the total number of extended subgraphs to be extracted remains relatively stable. If ϕ_{deg} is the maximum vertex degree, we can guarantee that $|G_{S^+}| \leq M$. However, this may lead to under-utilization of the available memory. This is also true for splitting a large G_{S^+} into smaller extended subgraphs in the case of setting ϕ_{deg} as the average vertex degree. However, we shall show in Section 4.2 that fully utilizing the available memory may actually lead to an even higher cost in the in-memory computation of MCE.

After computing the set of local maximal cliques in G_{S^+}, i.e., $\mathcal{M}(G_{S^+})$, the algorithm outputs only those cliques containing at least one seed vertex to ensure the correctness according to Lemma 1. However, it is possible that a maximal clique C is enumerated in more than one G_{S^+}, if the vertices in C are in different sets of seed vertices, i.e., $\exists u, v \in C$ such that $u \in S_i$ and $v \in S_j$, where $u \neq v$ and $i \neq j$. To avoid duplicate output of a maximal clique, Line 8 sets another condition, ($\nexists u \in C$ s.t. $u \prec S$). Here, $u \prec S$ means that u is selected as a seed vertex (in an earlier iteration of Lines 5-10), before any vertex in S is selected (in the current iteration). Thus, Lines 7-9 do not output a maximal clique C if C contains a vertex that has already been selected as a seed vertex before S is selected as the seed vertex set.

Greater Pruning. The condition "($\nexists u \in C$ s.t. $u \prec S$)" also implies that we do not need to include into G_{S^+} any edge (u, w), $\forall u, w \in S^+$ and $u, w \prec S$. Furthermore, we can push the condition into the in-memory MCE process to achieve greater pruning as follows. Recall that the search tree (implicitly) constructed by Algorithm 1 is a prefix tree. During the MCE process, we can process the seed vertices in S before the vertices in $S^+ \backslash S$. Then we do not grow the current clique C by any vertex $v \prec S$ in Line 6 of Procedure 2. In this way, we avoid duplicate enumeration of maximal cliques as well as achieve greater pruning effect for MCE.

Complexity Analysis. The following theorem gives the complexity of Algorithm 3. We use the following standard I/O complexity notations [2] in the complexity analysis: M is the main memory size, B is the disk block size, $scan(N) = \Theta(N/B)$ I/Os, where $1 \ll B \leq M/2$ and N is the amount of data being read/written from/to disk.

THEOREM 2. *Algorithm 3 requires $O(k \cdot scan(|G|))$ I/Os, $O(kT)$ CPU time, and $O(M)$ memory space, where $k = min\{\frac{|V|(\phi_{deg})^2}{M}, |V|\}$, and T is the CPU time complexity of the in-memory algorithm for computing MCE in an extended subgraph G_{S^+} with $|G_{S^+}| \leq M$.*

PROOF. Algorithm 3 makes $(k + 1)$ scans of G, once in Line 1 and k times in Line 5, where k is the total number of extended subgraphs G_{S^+} extracted. From Line 5 we have $(\phi_{deg} \cdot |S^+|) \geq cM$, but we can easily move the last vertex in S to the next round of seed vertex selection to obtain $|G_{S^+}| \leq (\phi_{deg} \cdot |S^+|) = O(M)$. Thus, we have $((\phi_{deg})^2 \cdot |S|) = O(M)$ since $|S^+| \simeq (\phi_{deg} \cdot |S|)$. Since V is divided into k sets of seed vertices, we have $k = O(\frac{|V|}{|S|}) = O(\frac{|V|(\phi_{deg})^2}{M})$. In the worst case, each S contains only one vertex and thus $k \leq |V|$.

The selection of seed vertices and extraction of extended subgraphs require only linear time; thus, the CPU time is bounded by the number of times the in-memory algorithm is invoked to compute MCE on an extended subgraph G_{S^+}, where the maximum size of any G_{S^+} is M (we refer the readers to [29] for the details on the CPU time complexity analysis on the in-memory algorithm). The memory space requirement is $|G_{S^+}| = O(M)$. □

4.2 Reducing the CPU Cost

In processing large graphs that cannot fit in main memory, the bottleneck of the in-memory algorithms is the huge I/O cost due to random disk access. However, by processing these large graphs using Algorithm 3, the bottleneck may no longer be the I/O cost, but rather the cost of the in-memory computation of MCE in each extracted extended subgraph.

4.2.1 A Neglected but Non-Negligible Cost

The cost of in-memory MCE computation can be broken down into two main types: *the cost of constructing the search tree* and *the cost of set intersection.*

Conventional algorithms focus on reducing the cost of constructing the search tree by employing various pruning techniques to reduce the size of search tree. Although these pruning techniques are vital for efficient MCE, we have observed that we can further reduce the cost of CPU computation as follows.

Among all individual operations in the process of MCE, the most expensive one is the set intersection: two in Line 8 of Procedure 2 (and the set subtraction in Line 5 may also be considered as one). These set intersections can be significantly more costly to process than the other operations that require only constant time.

There are approximation algorithms for set intersection, but for MCE we require an exact answer. To compute $X \cap Y = Z$, if exact set intersection is required, then the cost of the intersection is at least $(|X| + |Y|)$. However, if $|Z|$ is significantly smaller than $|X|$ and $|Y|$, then the majority of the processing is "wasted" on processing *non-contributing* elements in X and Y, i.e., elements in $X \backslash Z$ and $Y \backslash Z$. Thus, the objective here is to reduce the number of non-contributing elements in X and Y.

Reducing the number of non-contributing elements in X and Y in Procedure 2 means removing non-contributing elements in *todo*, *done*, and in particular $adj(v)$ since $adj(v)$ is often significantly larger than *todo* and *done* (except in the first call of Procedure 2).

[1] We assume that if $|S| = 1$, then $|G_{S^+}| \leq M$. In the case of a high-degree vertex v, $|G_{S^+}|$ with $S = \{v\}$ can be large. For sparse real-world graphs, we may effectively reduce $|G_{S^+}|$ by sorting the vertex set V in ascending order of the vertex degree, since we actually do not need to include into G_{S^+} any edge (u, w) if u and w are ordered before v, for all $u, w \in S^+$ (as implied by Line 8 of Algorithm 3).

4.2.2 Cost Reduction of Set Intersection

To reduce the portion of the non-contributing elements in *todo*, *done*, and $adj(v)$, we transform the search space from G to G_{S^+}. In this way, the search space is immediately reduced from V to S^+ for *todo* and *done*, and from $adj(v, G)$ to $adj(v, G_{S^+})$. However, which S^+ and hence G_{S^+} should we select in order to minimize the cost?

To avoid expensive random disk access, G_{S^+} should have size smaller than M. For this purpose, Algorithm 3 naturally fulfills the requirement. However, Algorithm 3 attempts to fully utilize the available memory, i.e., $|G_{S^+}|$ is close to M. But the analysis in Section 4.2.1 suggests that a smaller G_{S^+} gives a smaller cost of set intersection.

Extracting a smaller G_{S^+} in Algorithm 3 can be easily done by setting a smaller c in Line 4 of Algorithm 3. However, doing so proportionally increases the number of scans of G in Line 5 and hence the overall I/O cost. The following lemma enables us to totally avoid any extra I/O in extracting smaller G_{S^+}.

LEMMA 2. *Given two sets of seed vertices, S_{big} and S_{small}, if $S_{small} \subseteq S_{big}$, then $G_{S^+_{small}}$ is a subgraph of $G_{S^+_{big}}$.*

PROOF. Since $S_{small} \subseteq S_{big}$, by Definition 2, $S^+_{small} \subseteq S^+_{big}$. Then we also have $E_{S^+_{small}} = \{(u, v) : u, v \in S^+_{small}, (u, v) \in E\} \subseteq E_{S^+_{big}} = \{(u, v) : u, v \in S^+_{big}, (u, v) \in E\}$. Thus, $G_{S^+_{small}}$ is a subgraph of $G_{S^+_{big}}$. □

Lemma 2 shows that it is possible to extract a smaller extended subgraph $G_{S^+_{small}}$ from another bigger extended subgraph $G_{S^+_{big}}$ (which is resident in memory) instead of from the original input graph G (which is resident on disk). However, we still need to determine how small this $G_{S^+_{small}}$ should be.

4.2.3 A Cost Model

We propose a cost model for choosing the right size for the extended subgraph. Suppose that we now have a set of extended subgraphs $\mathcal{G}_\beta$ resident in main memory for MCE computation. Each subgraph $G_{S^+_\beta}$ in $\mathcal{G}_\beta$ is roughly of the same size. Initially, $\mathcal{G}_\beta$ contains only one extended subgraph G_{S^+} extracted in Lines 4-5 of Algorithm 3. We determine (iteratively) whether extracting smaller extended subgraphs from $\mathcal{G}_\beta$ can achieve better efficiency for in-memory MCE computation.

For each $G_{S^+_\beta} \in \mathcal{G}_\beta$, we consider to split $G_{S^+_\beta}$ into a set of smaller extended subgraphs $\{G_{S^+_\alpha}\}$, each of them is roughly of the same size. Let $\mathcal{G}_\alpha$ be the set of all such smaller extended subgraphs extracted from $\mathcal{G}_\beta$.

First, having a smaller $adj(v, G_{S^+_\alpha})$, instead of $adj(v, G_{S^+_\beta})$, in the process of MCE leads to a lower cost of set intersection. The *gain* obtained by preferring $\mathcal{G}_\alpha$ over $\mathcal{G}_\beta$ can be estimated as follows.

$$
\begin{aligned}
Gain &= \sum_{G_{S^+_\beta} \in \mathcal{G}_\beta} |T_{S^+_\beta}| \cdot \overline{deg}(v, G_{S^+_\beta}) \\
&\quad - \sum_{G_{S^+_\alpha} \in \mathcal{G}_\alpha} |T_{S^+_\alpha}| \cdot \overline{deg}(v, G_{S^+_\alpha}) \\
&= \sum_{G_{S^+_\beta} \in \mathcal{G}_\beta} |T_{S^+_\beta}| \cdot (|E_{S^+_\beta}|/|S^+_\beta|) \\
&\quad - \sum_{G_{S^+_\alpha} \in \mathcal{G}_\alpha} |T_{S^+_\alpha}| \cdot (|E_{S^+_\alpha}|/|S^+_\alpha|), \qquad (1)
\end{aligned}
$$

where $|T_{S^+_\alpha}|$ is the number of nodes in the search tree $T_{S^+_\alpha}$ constructed by Algorithm 1 with $G_{S^+_\alpha}$ as the input, and $\overline{deg}(v, G_{S^+_\alpha})$ is the average degree of a vertex v in $G_{S^+_\alpha}$; and similarly for $|T_{S^+_\beta}|$ and $\overline{deg}(v, G_{S^+_\beta})$.

In Equation (1), the gain obtained from the reduction in the cost of set intersection with a smaller $adj(v, G_{S^+_\alpha})$ instead of $adj(v, G_{S^+_\beta})$ is reflected by the average degree $\overline{deg}(v, G_{S^+_\alpha})$ and $\overline{deg}(v, G_{S^+_\beta})$. And we multiply the average degree by the number of nodes in the search tree because at each node in the search tree, we need to perform the set intersection as shown in Line 8 of Procedure 2.

If choosing $\mathcal{G}_\alpha$ instead of $\mathcal{G}_\beta$ only results in a gain for MCE, then the optimal choice is by setting $S_\alpha = \{v\}$ for each single vertex $v \in V$. However, preferring $\mathcal{G}_\alpha$ over $\mathcal{G}_\beta$ may also result in some loss due to the extraction of a large number of smaller extended subgraphs and the construction of their search trees during the process of MCE.

First, if we further split $G_{S^+_\beta}$ into a set of smaller $G_{S^+_\alpha}$, we have extra extraction costs. Second, the size of the search tree constructed from $G_{S^+_\beta}$ is smaller than the total size of the search trees constructed from the set $\{G_{S^+_\alpha}\}$ extracted from $G_{S^+_\beta}$. The *loss* of preferring $\mathcal{G}_\alpha$ over $\mathcal{G}_\beta$ is given as follows.

$$
\begin{aligned}
Loss &= \Big(\sum_{G_{S^+_\beta} \in \mathcal{G}_\beta} \sum_{G_{S^+_\alpha} \subset G_{S^+_\beta}} (|G_{S^+_\alpha}| + |G_{S^+_\beta}|)\Big) \\
&\quad + \Big(\sum_{G_{S^+_\alpha} \in \mathcal{G}_\alpha} |T_{S^+_\alpha}| - \sum_{G_{S^+_\beta} \in \mathcal{G}_\beta} |T_{S^+_\beta}|\Big). \qquad (2)
\end{aligned}
$$

In Equation (2), the first half gives the cost of extracting all $G_{S^+_\alpha}$ from each $G_{S^+_\beta} \in \mathcal{G}_\beta$. Since we scan each $G_{S^+_\beta}$ at most once to extract each $G_{S^+_\alpha}$, we add $|G_{S^+_\beta}|$ to the total cost. The second half is the difference in the total size of the search trees constructed from all $G_{S^+_\alpha}$ and from all $G_{S^+_\beta}$.

Equation (1) and Equation (2) represent a tradeoff: we trade off *(1) the cost of set intersection* with *(2) the cost of subgraph extraction and that of search tree construction*; that is, using smaller extended subgraphs reduces (1) but increases (2), while using larger extended subgraphs results in the opposite. We quantify this tradeoff by the following cost model.

$$
TotalGain = Gain - Loss. \qquad (3)
$$

Finally, in Equation (1) and Equation (2), $|G_{S^+_\alpha}|$ and $|G_{S^+_\beta}|$ are known after we extract the subgraphs, while $|T_{S^+_\alpha}|$ and $|T_{S^+_\beta}|$ can be estimated by a variation of Knuth's method [22] for estimating the size of a backtracking tree of MCE proposed in [12].

4.2.4 An Improved Algorithm for MCE

With the results of the previous subsections, we propose an improved partition-based algorithm for MCE, as shown in Algorithm 4. We name this algorithm as **SeqMCE** (for **Seq**uential **MCE**), to distinguish from the parallel algorithm proposed in Section 4.3.

As shown in Algorithm 4 and Procedure 5, the extraction of ex-

Algorithm 4 *SeqMCE*

Input: a graph $G = (V, E)$
Output: all maximal cliques in G

Replace Lines 6-9 of Algorithm 3 by: *MCE-Step*(G_{S^+});

Procedure 5 *MCE-Step*$(H = (V_H, E_H))$

1. $\mathcal{G}_\alpha := \{H\}$;
2. $TotalGain := \infty$;
3. **while**$(TotalGain > 0)$
4. $\quad \mathcal{G}_\beta := \mathcal{G}_\alpha, \mathcal{G}_\alpha := \emptyset$;
5. $\quad$ **for each** $G_{S^+_\beta} \in \mathcal{G}_\beta$ **do**
6. $\quad\quad$ divide S_β into two equal halves: $S_{\alpha 1}$ and $S_{\alpha 2}$;
7. $\quad\quad$ extract $G_{S^+_{\alpha 1}}$ and $G_{S^+_{\alpha 2}}$ from $G_{S^+_\beta}$;
8. $\quad\quad \mathcal{G}_\alpha := \mathcal{G}_\alpha \cup \{G_{S^+_{\alpha 1}}, G_{S^+_{\alpha 2}}\}$;
9. $\quad$ compute $TotalGain$ from $\mathcal{G}_\alpha$ and $\mathcal{G}_\beta$;
10. $\mathcal{G}_\alpha := \mathcal{G}_\beta$;
11. **for each** $G_{S^+_\alpha} \in \mathcal{G}_\alpha$ **do**
12. $\quad$ apply in-memory MCE to $G_{S^+_\alpha}$;

tended subgraphs is processed at two levels, one aiming to minimize the I/O cost while the other aiming to reduce the CPU cost.

The first level is to extract bigger extended subgraphs, which is done in a similar way as in Algorithm 3 but by replacing Lines 6-9 with a call to Procedure 5. At this level, the size of each G_{S+} should be close to M to minimize the number of scans of G and hence the I/O cost.

Then, at the second level as shown in Procedure 5, we extract smaller extended subgraphs from each bigger extended subgraph H obtained at the first level. Whether or not to further extract smaller extended subgraphs is determined by the cost model given by Equation (3).

Computing the optimal $\mathcal{G}_\alpha$ to maximize $TotalGain$ is similar to finding the optimal graph partition from H, which is APX-hard [4]. Thus, this process alone would dominate the overall cost of MCE. However, if we do not select the seed vertices from H randomly but rather select them sequentially, the selection process can be made much more efficient.

Another challenge of applying Equation (3) is that Equation (3) consists of Equations (1) and (2), both of which require the entire sets of extended subgraphs, $\mathcal{G}_\alpha$ and $\mathcal{G}_\beta$, to be known. Even if we select the seed vertices sequentially, there are still exponentially many different permutations of $\mathcal{G}_\alpha$ and $\mathcal{G}_\beta$.

To avoid the costly intermediate process of subgraph extraction, we consider the search space as a binary tree, where the set of nodes at each level of the tree is a set of extended subgraphs. We construct the binary tree level-wise (Lines 1-10). The first level consists of only one extended subgraph, i.e., H itself. The two children of any internal node in the tree are constructed by dividing the set of seed vertices of the parent sequentially into two sets of seed vertices with equal size, and then extract the corresponding extended subgraphs from the parent (the correctness of the extraction is guaranteed by Lemma 2). Then at each level, we compute $TotalGain$. We stop constructing a new level of the binary tree when there is no longer a gain. Then (in Lines 10-12), we take the corresponding $\mathcal{G}_\alpha$ as the set of extended subgraphs, and process MCE in each $G_{S^+_\alpha} \in \mathcal{G}_\alpha$ as is done before in Algorithm 3.

The above scheme for subgraph extraction, though heuristic, is effective and efficient for the following important reasons: first, it fits seamlessly into the design of the partition-based algorithm; second, it supports effective parallelization; lastly, it avoids extra overhead in re-assigning the vertex order or relabeling the vertices,

Algorithm 6 *ParMCE*

Input: a graph $G = (V, E)$
Output: all maximal cliques in G

$S := \emptyset, S^+ := \emptyset$;
for each $v \in V$ **do**
$\quad S := (S \cup \{v\}), S^+ := (S^+ \cup \{v\} \cup adj(v))$;
$\quad$ **if**$((\phi_{deg} \cdot |S^+|) \geq cM)$
$\quad\quad$ scan G once to extract G_{S+};
$\quad\quad$ **while**(no idle computing node) **wait**;
$\quad\quad$ distribute the task *MCE-Job*(G_{S+})
$\quad\quad\quad$ to any idle computing node;
$\quad\quad S := \emptyset, S^+ := \emptyset$;

Procedure 7 *MCE-Job*$(H = (V_H, E_H))$

$\mathcal{G}_\alpha := \{H\}$;
$TotalGain := \infty$;
while$((TotalGain > 0)$ or
$\quad$ (# of idle computing nodes $> |\mathcal{G}_\beta|$))
$\quad \mathcal{G}_\beta := \mathcal{G}_\alpha, \mathcal{G}_\alpha := \emptyset$;
$\quad$ **for each** $G_{S^+_\beta} \in \mathcal{G}_\beta$ **do**
$\quad\quad$ divide S_β into two equal halves: $S_{\alpha 1}$ and $S_{\alpha 2}$;
$\quad\quad$ extract $G_{S^+_{\alpha 1}}$ and $G_{S^+_{\alpha 2}}$ from $G_{S^+_\beta}$;
$\quad\quad \mathcal{G}_\alpha := \mathcal{G}_\alpha \cup \{G_{S^+_{\alpha 1}}, G_{S^+_{\alpha 2}}\}$;
$\quad$ compute $TotalGain$ from $\mathcal{G}_\alpha$ and $\mathcal{G}_\beta$;
$\mathcal{G}_\alpha := \mathcal{G}_\beta$;
for each $G_{S^+_\alpha} \in \mathcal{G}_\alpha$ **do**
$\quad$ **while**(no idle computing node) **wait**;
$\quad$ distribute $G_{S^+_\alpha}$ to an idle computing node, X, and
$\quad$ compute in-memory MCE in $G_{S^+_\alpha}$, further parallelizing
$\quad$ the task among multiple cores or threads within X,
$\quad$ or any other idle computing node(s), if any;

which is necessary for the task of MCE when vertices are selected out of order into $G_{S^+_\alpha}$.

4.3 Parallel Maximal Clique Enumeration

Existing parallel algorithms for MCE [17, 27] are in-memory algorithms that require the entire graph to be resident in main memory of each computing node, and thus are not scalable as the graph size increases and main memory is not sufficient to hold the graph.

We adopt our partition-based MCE framework and propose a parallel algorithm for MCE that requires only limited memory at each computing node. We describe the algorithm, named as **ParMCE** (for **Par**allel **MCE**), in Algorithm 6 and Procedure 7.

Algorithm 6 uses one computing node as the *master node*. The master node reads the input graph G from disk, extracts extended subgraphs from G, and distributes them to the idle nodes, if any. To utilize parallelism (e.g., multi-cores, hyper threading, etc.) within the master node, we create two threads in the master node. One thread extracts extended subgraphs and pushes it into the *pool* of un-computed subgraphs, and the other one takes the subgraphs from the *pool* and sends them to any available idle nodes. In case that the total number of available computing nodes becomes too large so that the computation at the master node might become a bottleneck, our algorithm easily allows us to split the input graph and create multiple master nodes to serve the increasing number of computing nodes.

Procedure 7 then describes that when a computing node receives an extended subgraph H (distributed by Algorithm 6), it further extracts smaller extended subgraphs to improve the efficiency of MCE, as done in Procedure 5. If we have extra idle computing nodes, we may further divide extended subgraphs into smaller ones to maximize parallelization (note that the bottleneck is at the MCE computation rather than at the subgraph extraction, both of which are now performed in-memory). This task itself can also be easily parallelized, by simply distributing the extended subgraphs in $\mathcal{G}_\beta$ to new computing nodes and call Procedure 7. But since this process is not the bottleneck, it should be parallelized only when computing nodes are excessive.

After we obtain the set of extended subgraphs $\mathcal{G}_\alpha$, we distribute each small extended subgraph $G_{S_\alpha^+} \in \mathcal{G}_\alpha$ to an idle computing node, X. Then at X, we apply the in-memory algorithm to process MCE in $G_{S_\alpha^+}$. The fine-grained parallelization of MCE proposed in [27] can be further applied if X has multiple cores or threads, or if there are more idle computing nodes available.

5. EXPERIMENTAL EVALUATION

In this section, we evaluate the performance of our algorithms. We compared with the algorithm that has the optimal time complexity for MCE in memory proposed by Tomita et al. [29] (denoted by *TomitaTT*), a recent algorithm for MCE in d-degenerate graphs proposed by Eppstein et al. [18, 19] (denoted by *EppsteinLS*), and the I/O-efficient MCE algorithm by Cheng et al. [13] (denoted by *ChengKFYZ*).

For all the sequential programs, we ran the experiments on a machine with an Intel Xeon 2.67GHz CPU and 4GB RAM, running CentOS 5.4 (Linux). For the parallel program (using the MPI), we ran the experiments on a cluster, with each computing nodes having 2.93GHz CPU and 4GB RAM.

Datasets. We use the following four datasets: `blog`, `LJ`, `Web`, and `BTC`. The `blog` network is collected from the top-15 popular queries published by Technorati (technorati.com) every three hours from Nov 2006 to Mar 2008. For each query, the top-50 results are retrieved. In the `blog` network, vertices are blogs and edges indicate that two blogs appear in the search result of the same query. `LJ` is the free online community called *LiveJournal*, where vertices are members and edges represent friendship between members. The `LJ` dataset is available from snap.stanford.edu. The `Web` graph is obtained from the YAHOO webspam dataset (barcelona.research.yahoo.net/webspam), where vertices are webpages and edges are hyperlinks. The `BTC` dataset is a semantic graph converted from the *Billion Triple Challenge 2009 RDF* dataset (http://vmlion25.deri.ie), where each vertex represents an object such as a person, a document, and an event, and each edge represents the relationship between two vertices such as "as-author", "links-to", and "has-title". We list some details of the datasets (number of vertices and edges, physical storage size) in Table 1.

Table 1: Datasets (M = 1,000,000)

	`blog`	`LJ`	`Web`	`BTC`
$\|V\|$	1M	4.8M	52.9M	165M
$\|E\|$	6.5M	43M	274.8M	773M
Storage size	186MB	1310MB	5GB	14.5GB

Among the four datasets, `blog` and `LJ` are two relatively smaller graphs, while `Web` and `BTC` are two larger graphs. We use the smaller graphs to compare the performance of our algorithm with the in-memory algorithms, while we use the larger graphs to evaluate the performance of our algorithms when memory of a single machine is insufficient to hold the input graph.

5.1 Effectiveness of Cost Model

We first examine whether the reduction of set intersection cost by extracting smaller extended subgraphs, rather than extracting extended subgraphs that fill the available memory, can indeed improve the efficiency of MCE computation. We also assess the effectiveness of our cost model, given in Section 4.2.3, for choosing the right size for the extended subgraphs to be extracted. We test the settings on *SeqMCE*, i.e., Algorithm 4.

Figure 3 reports the running time of *SeqMCE* for `blog` and `Web`. We extract extended subgraphs of size from 0.001% to 10% of the available memory size at the second level of Algorithm 4, i.e., each $G_{S_\alpha^+} \in \mathcal{G}_\alpha$ in Lines 11-12 of Procedure 5 is of size xM, where $x \in \{0.001\%, 0.01\%, 0.1\%, 1\%, 10\%\}$ and M is the available memory size, which is set to 1 GB in this experiment. We also report the running time of *SeqMCE* that extracts extended subgraphs by our cost model, represented by "**CM**" on the x-axis. From Figure 3, the sizes of the extended subgraphs extracted by "**CM**" are around 2% for `blog` and 0.05% for `Web`.

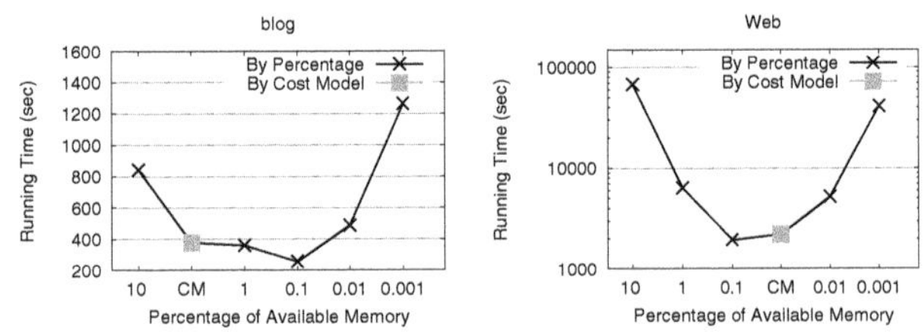

Figure 3: Running time (wall-clock time in seconds) of *SeqMCE* for MCE with varying sizes of extended subgraphs

The results show that for both graphs, the efficiency of MCE is first improved significantly when smaller extended subgraphs are used at the second level of the algorithm, but there is an optimal point after which further decreasing the size of the extended subgraphs reports a significantly deteriorated performance. The trend of the running time for different sizes of extended subgraphs can be explained by our analysis of the gain and loss, i.e., Equation (1) and Equation (2), in Section 4.2.3, which represent a tradeoff between *(1) the cost of set intersection* and *(2) the cost of subgraph extraction and search tree construction*. The same tradeoff can be also be clearly observed from the `LJ` and `BTC` graphs (details omitted due to lack of space).

Having shown the tradeoff, we show that the results obtained by the cost model is near the optimal point. Relatively speaking, the running time reported for the cost model for `blog` is further away from the optimal point than that for `Web`. This is because the `blog` graph is small and hence determining the right subgraph size by the cost model takes a considerable portion of the total time. When the input graph is large, the cost of computation involving the cost model becomes negligible compared to the cost of MCE.

In the subsequent experiments, the algorithm *SeqMCE* always extracts extended subgraphs by the cost model.

5.2 Performance of Sequential Algorithms

We now compare our algorithm *SeqMCE* with other state-of-the-art sequential algorithms for MCE.

Table 2 reports the running time of the four algorithms. For the smaller datasets, `blog` and `LJ`, *EppsteinLS* is the fastest. The *EppsteinLS* algorithm uses a d-degeneracy ordering[2] to limit the depth

[2]A graph is d-degenerate if it has a maximum k-core number of d [18].

Table 2: Running time (wall-clock time in seconds)

	blog	LJ	Web	BTC
TomitaTT [29]	11,876	150,122	–	–
EppsteinLS [19]	68	67	–	–
ChengKFYZ [13]	329	6,941	22,840	134,951
SeqMCE	378	175	2,209	28,410

Table 3: Peak memory consumption (in GB)

	blog	LJ	Web	BTC
TomitaTT [29]	0.2	0.9	–	–
EppsteinLS [19]	1.3	4.0	–	–
ChengKFYZ [13]	0.1	1.0	1.0	1.0
SeqMCE	0.1	1.0	1.0	1.0

of recursive calls in the *TomitaTT* algorithm to d, where d is not large for many real-world sparse graphs. Our algorithm *SeqMCE* can effectively reduce the cost of set intersection as well as limit the depth of recursive calls; however, it is a semi-streaming algorithm designed for processing large datasets, while *EppsteinLS* is an in-memory algorithm. Thus, *SeqMCE* needs to scan the input graph many times, which explains why it is slower than *EppsteinLS*. However, *EppsteinLS* uses significantly more memory than *SeqMCE* and ran out of memory for the larger graphs, Web and BTC. On the contrary, with the available memory set at only 1 GB, *SeqMCE* still processes MCE efficiently on both large graphs, and is up to an order of magnitude faster than the state-of-the-art I/O-efficient MCE algorithm, *ChengKFYZ*.

Compared with the in-memory algorithm *TomitaTT*, which also ran out of memory for Web and BTC, *SeqMCE* is up to two orders of magnitude faster for processing blog and LJ. Since the smaller datasets can be processed in memory, the main difference between *SeqMCE* and *TomitaTT* for in-memory processing is the new adoption of cost reduction on set intersection, we conclude that the performance improvement of *SeqMCE* over *TomitaTT* is mainly due to our proposal of cost reduction on set intersection. This result thus further demonstrates the effectiveness of the CPU cost reduction method proposed in Section 4.2.

5.3 Performance of Parallel Algorithm

We now evaluate the performance of the parallel algorithm (i.e., Algorithm 6), denoted by *ParMCE*. There are some recent algorithms for parallel MCE [17, 27, 33], but we were not able to obtain their code for comparison.

We report the running time of *ParMCE* in Figure 4. To show that our method is truly effective in handling graphs that cannot fit in memory, we set the available memory to only 64 MB for blog and LJ, and 256 MB for the two large graphs Web and BTC.

The figures show that when two machines are used, the running time is nearly halved for all the datasets. The efficiency continues to improve when more machines are used, although the speed-up becomes milder when more machines are used. With only eight machines, we can finish computing MCE in the largest dataset in about an hour.

6. RELATED WORK

Maximal clique enumeration has been studied extensively and comprehensive reviews can be found in [10] and [8] (the latter also discusses maximum clique finding). The first algorithms were the *backtracking* method [3, 9] that use $O(|V|^2)$ memory space. Then effective pruning strategy by selecting good *pivots* was employed

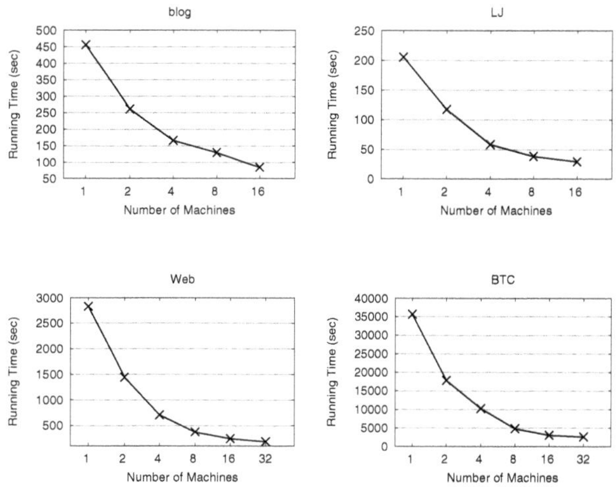

Figure 4: Running time (wall-clock time in seconds) of *ParMCE*

to further reduce the search space [10, 23, 29]. Algorithm for d-degenerate graphs was also proposed [18, 19], which achieves a time complexity of $O(d|V|3^{d/3})$ by utilizing a d-degeneracy ordering. However, all these studies did not focus on reducing the memory complexity and require $\Omega(|V| + |E|)$ memory space, which may not be practical for large disk-resident graphs.

Recently, several parallel algorithms were proposed for MCE. Most of these parallel algorithms [17, 27] still require the entire input graph to be resident in main memory of each computing node, and thus are not practical for processing large graphs that cannot fit in memory. A MapReduce algorithm [33] was also proposed for MCE. The MapReduce model, however, is slow in practice for enumeration tasks such as MCE and triangle listing in large graphs, mainly because of the huge amount of intermediate data produced in the shuffling phase between Mappers and Reducers.

Algorithm for output-sensitive MCE was also introduced which is based on reverse search [30]. The time delay was reduced to $O(d_{max}^4)$ for sparse graphs using matrix multiplication [25], where d_{max} is the maximum degree of a graph; but the algorithm requires $O(|V| \cdot |E|)$ preprocessing time. Other algorithms, such as computing a k-clique by joining two $(k-1)$-cliques [24], by making use of triangles [31], and enumerating maximal cliques of size larger than a threshold [26], were also studied. However, all these algorithms require memory space at least $\Omega(|V| + |E|)$.

Stix [28] proposed a streaming algorithm that updates the set of maximal cliques upon each edge insertion, but the update is expensive and it also requires to keep all maximal cliques in memory, which has been verified in [12].

Recently, Cheng et al. [12, 13] proposed an efficient algorithm that recursively extracts a core part of the input graph for local MCE computation. This idea is similar to the algorithm described in Section 4.1, but a fundamental difference in the formulation of the subgraphs to be extracted, i.e., their subgraphs still need to access the input graph for MCE while ours do not, making it nontrivial to parallelize their algorithm as what we do. We have also verified in Section 5 that our algorithm is significantly more efficient.

Other related works that also avoid random disk access by extracting small subgraphs include core/truss decomposition [11, 32], triangle listing [14, 15]. However, the subgraphs used in these works cannot guarantee the maximality of the cliques computed and their algorithm frameworks are also not suitable for the task of MCE.

7. CONCLUSIONS

We presented efficient algorithms to reduce both the I/O cost and CPU cost of MCE in massive networks. We verified the performance of our algorithms comparing with the state-of-the-art algorithms for MCE [12, 13, 18, 19, 29]. Our results first demonstrate that, by reducing the cost of set intersection in MCE, we are able to achieve significant speed-ups in both cases when the input graph can fit in main memory or cannot fit in main memory. Then, we also showed that our parallel algorithm for MCE significantly speeds up the MCE computation compared with the sequential algorithm.

8. ACKNOWLEDGMENTS

The authors would like to thank the reviewers of this paper for their constructive comments. This research is supported in part by the A*STAR Thematic Strategic Research Programme Grants (102 158 0034 and 112 172 0013).

9. REFERENCES

[1] F. N. Abu-Khzam, N. E. Baldwin, M. A. Langston, and N. F. Samatova. On the relative efficiency of maximal clique enumeration algorithms, with applications to high-throughput computational biology. In *International Conference on Research Trends in Science and Technology*, 2005.

[2] A. Aggarwal and S. Vitter, Jeffrey. The input/output complexity of sorting and related problems. *Commun. ACM*, 31(9):1116–1127, 1988.

[3] E. A. Akkoyunlu. The enumeration of maximal cliques of large graphs. *SIAM J. Comput.*, 2(1):1–6, 1973.

[4] K. Andreev and H. Racke. Balanced graph partitioning. In *SPAA*, pages 120–124, 2004.

[5] H. R. Bernard, P. D. Killworth, and L. Sailer. Informant accuracy in social network data iv: a comparison of clique-level structure in behavioral and cognitive network data. *Social Networks*, 2(3):191–218, 1979.

[6] N. M. Berry, T. H. Ko, T. Moy, J. Smrcka, J. Turnley, and B. Wu. Emergent clique formation in terrorist recruitment. In *The AAAI-04 Workshop on Agent Organizations: Theory and Practice*, 2004.

[7] V. Boginski, S. Butenko, and P. M. Pardalos. Statistical analysis of financial networks. *Computational Statistics & Data Analysis*, 48(2):431–443, 2005.

[8] I. M. Bomze, M. Budinich, P. M. Pardalos, and M. Pelillo. The maximum clique problem. In *Handbook of Combinatorial Optimization*, pages 1–74. Kluwer Academic Publishers, 1999.

[9] C. Bron and J. Kerbosch. Algorithm 457: finding all cliques of an undirected graph. *Commun. ACM*, 16(9):575–577, 1973.

[10] F. Cazals and C. Karande. A note on the problem of reporting maximal cliques. *Theor. Comput. Sci.*, 407(1-3):564–568, 2008.

[11] J. Cheng, Y. Ke, S. Chu, and M. T. Özsu. Efficient core decomposition in massive networks. In *ICDE*, pages 51–62, 2011.

[12] J. Cheng, Y. Ke, A. W.-C. Fu, J. X. Yu, and L. Zhu. Finding maximal cliques in massive networks by h*-graph. In *SIGMOD Conference*, pages 447–458, 2010.

[13] J. Cheng, Y. Ke, A. W.-C. Fu, J. X. Yu, and L. Zhu. Finding maximal cliques in massive networks. *ACM Trans. Database Syst.*, 36(4):21, 2011.

[14] S. Chu and J. Cheng. Triangle listing in massive networks. *To appear in ACM Transactions on Knowledge Discovery from Data, 2012.*

[15] S. Chu and J. Cheng. Triangle listing in massive networks and its applications. In *KDD*, pages 672–680, 2011.

[16] G. Creamer, R. Rowe, S. Hershkop, and S. J. Stolfo. Segmentation and automated social hierarchy detection through email network analysis. In *WebKDD/SNA-KDD*, pages 40–58, 2007.

[17] N. Du, B. Wu, L. Xu, B. Wang, and P. Xin. Parallel algorithm for enumerating maximal cliques in complex network. In *Mining Complex Data*, pages 207–221. 2009.

[18] D. Eppstein, M. Löffler, and D. Strash. Listing all maximal cliques in sparse graphs in near-optimal time. In *ISAAC (1)*, pages 403–414, 2010.

[19] D. Eppstein and D. Strash. Listing all maximal cliques in large sparse real-world graphs. In *SEA*, pages 364–375, 2011.

[20] K. Faust and S. Wasserman. Social network analysis: Methods and applications. *Cambridge University Press*, 1995.

[21] K. Gouda and M. J. Zaki. Efficiently mining maximal frequent itemsets. In *ICDM*, pages 163–170, 2001.

[22] D. E. Knuth. Estimating the efficiency of backtrack programs. *Mathematics of Computation*, 29(129):121–136, 1975.

[23] I. Koch. Enumerating all connected maximal common subgraphs in two graphs. *Theor. Comput. Sci.*, 250(1-2):1–30, 2001.

[24] F. Kose, W. Weckwerth, T. Linke, and O. Fiehn. Visualizing plant metabolomic correlation networks using clique-metabolite matrices. *Bioinformatics*, 17(12):1198–1208, 2001.

[25] K. Makino and T. Uno. New algorithms for enumerating all maximal cliques. In *SWAT*, pages 260–272, 2004.

[26] N. Modani and K. Dey. Large maximal cliques enumeration in sparse graphs. In *CIKM*, pages 1377–1378, 2008.

[27] M. C. Schmidt, N. F. Samatova, K. Thomas, and B.-H. Park. A scalable, parallel algorithm for maximal clique enumeration. *J. Parallel Distrib. Comput.*, 69(4):417–428, 2009.

[28] V. Stix. Finding all maximal cliques in dynamic graphs. *Computational Optimization and applications*, 27:173–186, 2004.

[29] E. Tomita, A. Tanaka, and H. Takahashi. The worst-case time complexity for generating all maximal cliques and computational experiments. *Theor. Comput. Sci.*, 363(1):28–42, 2006.

[30] S. Tsukiyama, M. Ide, H. Ariyoshi, and I. Shirakawa. A new algorithm for generating all the maximal independent sets. *SIAM J. Comput.*, 6(3):505–517, 1977.

[31] L. Wan, B. Wu, N. Du, Q. Ye, and P. Chen. A new algorithm for enumerating all maximal cliques in complex network. In *ADMA*, pages 606–617, 2006.

[32] J. Wang and J. Cheng. Truss decomposition in massive networks. *To appear in Proceedings of the Very Large Database Endowment, 2012.*

[33] B. Wu, S. Yang, H. Zhao, and B. Wang. A distributed algorithm to enumerate all maximal cliques in mapreduce. In *Proceedings of the Fourth International Conference on Frontier of Computer Science and Technology*, pages 45–51, 2009.

Summarization-based Mining Bipartite Graphs

Jing Feng[1], Xiao He[1], Bettina Konte[1], Christian Böhm[1], Claudia Plant[2]
[1]: University of Munich, [2]: Florida State University
{feng, he, konte, boehm}@dbs.ifi.lmu.de, cplant@fsu.edu

ABSTRACT

How to extract the truly relevant information from a large relational data set? The answer of this paper is a technique integrating graph summarization, graph clustering, link prediction and the discovery of the hidden structure on the basis of data compression. Our novel algorithm *SCMiner* (for Summarization-Compression Miner) reduces a large bipartite input graph to a highly compact representation which is very useful for different data mining tasks: 1) Clustering: The compact summary graph contains the truly relevant clusters of both types of nodes of a bipartite graph. 2) Link prediction: The compression scheme of *SCMiner* reveals suspicious edges which are probably erroneous as well as missing edges, i.e. pairs of nodes which should be connected by an edge. 3) Discovery of the hidden structure: Unlike traditional co-clustering methods, the result of *SCMiner* is not limited to row- and column-clusters. Besides the clusters, the summary graph also contains the essential relationships between both types of clusters and thus reveals the hidden structure of the data. Extensive experiments on synthetic and real data demonstrate that *SCMiner* outperforms state-of-the-art techniques for clustering and link prediction. Moreover, *SCMiner* discovers the hidden structure and reports it in an interpretable way to the user. Based on data compression, our technique does not rely on any input parameters which are difficult to estimate.

Categories and Subject Descriptors

H.2.8 [**Database applications**]: Data Mining

Keywords

bipartite graph, summarization, clustering, link prediction

1. MOTIVATION

Relational or graph-structured data are prevalent in nature, science and economics. Many aspects of real life can be well represented as a bipartite graph which has two types of vertices and edges representing the connections between them. Consider for example newsgroups where one type of vertices represents persons and the other type of vertices represent groups. An edge between a person and a group means that he or she is member of this group. Or consider the interaction between drugs and proteins: An edge between a particular substance and a protein means that the corresponding protein is responding to the drug. Such bipartite graphs are stored as large adjacency matrices often having millions of vertices and edges. Effective and efficient data mining methods are essential for answering high-level domain specific questions like: Which users are potentially interested to join a newsgroup? Or, which combination of substances is most effective against a certain disease?

Therefore, in recent years the research topic of mining bipartite graphs has attracted much attention, with a large volume of research papers, e.g. [1, 3, 5, 10, 11, 14] to mention a few. To extract knowledge from a large bipartite graph, existing techniques apply one of the following two basic strategies: (1) Clustering. These approaches reduce the complexity by partitioning the large input graph into smaller groups of similar vertices which can be inspected and interpreted by the user. In particular, approaches to co-clustering like [1, 3] cluster both types of vertices, i.e. the rows and the columns of the adjacency matrix simultaneously guided by the idea that the clustering of rows and columns can profit from another. The output of co-clustering is a set of row-clusters and a set of column clusters. (2) Summarization. These approaches reduce the complexity not by grouping but by a global abstraction. The output of summarization techniques like [14] is a bipartite graph which is much smaller than the original input graph. Ideally, it distills the major characteristics from the input data and is small enough to be accessible for the user. A third line of papers focuses on a different, however closely related topic: Link prediction. These approaches like [11] study the question whether there should be an edge between two currently disconnected vertices. Link prediction is closely related to summarization and clustering since a technique for link prediction must capture at least the local structure of the graph to provide reasonable predictions. Also clustering and summarization are closely related since during the process of abstraction, both approaches must identify the relevant major characteristics of the graph.

Contributions

In this paper, we therefore propose *SCMiner*, a technique integrating summarization, clustering and link prediction on bipartite graphs. The name *SCMiner* stands for Summarization-Compression Miner and the principle of data compression also known as the Minimum Description Length Principle (MDL) [16] is the basis of our technique. The basic idea is to transform the original graph into a very compact summary graph. During the process of transformation which is controlled by the MDL principle, our technique discovers the major clusters of both vertex types as well as the major connection patterns between those clusters. The result of *SCMiner* comprises a compressed graph, the row- and column-clusters and their link patterns. The major contributions of our approach can be summarized as follows:

- **Clustering plus hidden structure mining.** Like state-of-the-art co-clustering methods, *SCMiner* accurately identifies the row- and column clusters of bipartite graphs and even outperforms them on some data sets. As a key feature of our approach, the result does not only consist of two sets of clusters. *SCMiner* also reveals the relationships between the clusters which are essential for interpretation.
- **Accurate link prediction.** *SCMiner* accurately predicts missing or future links and removes noise edges.
- **Unsupervised graph mining all in one.** *SCMiner* integrates summarization, clustering and link prediction and thus comprehensively supports unsupervised graph mining.
- **Results validated by data compression.** Data compression is an intuitive optimization goal with many benefits: By natural balancing goodness of fit and model complexity, overfitting is avoided. The results are thus simple and interpretable. Moreover, supported by the MDL principle *SCMiner* does not rely on any difficult to estimate input parameters.

The remainder of this paper is organized as follows: In the following section, we give the model formulation. Section 3 presents the algorithm in detail. Section 4 contains an extensive experimental evaluation. Section 5 briefly surveys related work and Section 6 concludes the paper.

2. COMPRESSING A BIPARTITE GRAPH

In this section, we first present a simple example to introduce the terminology of graph summarization. Then an MDL based coding schema is derived to find the best summarization of a bipartite graph. At last, we propose a strategy to discover hidden relations between vertices of different type.

Notation and Example. Figure 1 depicts a simple example for graph summarization of a bipartite graph. $G = (V_1, V_2, E)$ is an unweighted bipartite graph where $V_1 = \{V_{11}, ..., V_{16}\}$ and $V_2 = \{V_{21}, ..., V_{26}\}$ denote two types of vertices and E denotes the edges between them. The summarization of graph G consists of two bipartite graphs, a summary graph G_S and an additional graph G_A. The summary graph $G_S = (S_1, S_2, E')$ is an aggregated graph and is composed of four super nodes $S_{11} = \{V_{11}, V_{12}, V_{13}\}$, $S_{12} = \{V_{14}, V_{15}, V_{16}\}$, $S_{21} = \{V_{21}, V_{22}, V_{23}\}$, $S_{22} = \{V_{24}, V_{25}, V_{26}\}$, and super edges E'. The super nodes themselves are composed of vertices exhibiting the exact same link pattern. They indicate the local cluster structure of each type of vertices, whereas the super edges represent the global relations between local clusters. The additional graph $G_A = (V_1, V_2, E'')$ contains normal nodes and correction edges which are required to reconstruct the bipartite graph G. The $+$ or $-$ symbols above the edges indicate whether it is required

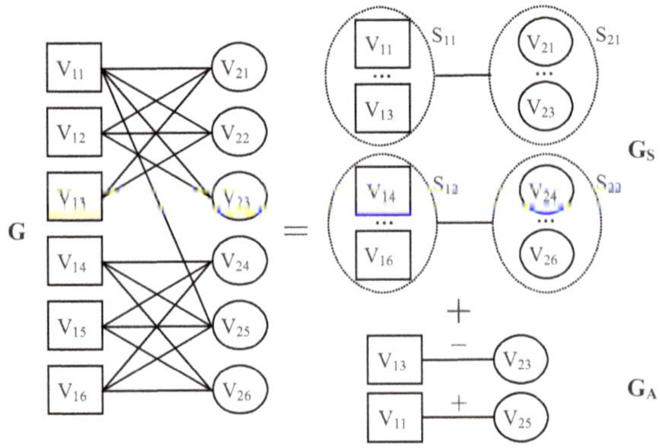

Figure 1: Summarization and Compression.

to add or remove them from G_S to recreate G. The correction edges describe the revealed hidden relations between different types of vertices.

2.1 Coding Scheme

A bipartite graph can be represented by thousands of summarizations, however, the challenge is to find out the one that best represents the data and reflects the hidden structure behind the surface data. The Minimum Description Length (MDL) principle is an intuitive choice for model selection [16]. It follows the assumption that the more we are able to compress the data, the more we have learned about its underlying patterns. Formally, the goodness of the model can be stated as shown in Eq.(1), where $L(M)$ denotes the cost for coding the model parameters and $L(D|M)$ represents the cost of describing the data D under the model M. As the model has to be coded with the data and too complex models result in high compression cost, MDL naturally avoids overfitting.

$$L(M, D) = L(D|M) + L(M). \quad (1)$$

Inspired by the MDL principle, we propose a coding schema to choose the best graph summarization. The most direct and simple way to represent a bipartite graph $G = (V_1, V_2, E)$ is to compress its adjacency matrix $A \in |V_1| \times |V_2|$, with $a_{ij} = 1$ if $(V_{1i}, V_{2j}) \in E$. The coding cost of the adjacency matrix A is lower bounded by its entropy which is provided by:

$$CC(G) = -|V_1| \cdot |V_2| \cdot H(A), \quad (2)$$

where $H(A) = -(p_n(A) \cdot \log_2 p_n(A) + p_r(A) \cdot \log_2 p_r(A))$, $p_n(A)$ and $p_r(A)$ are the probabilities of finding 1 and 0 entries in the adjacency matrix A of G, i.e. the probabilities to observe edges or not.

As mentioned above, the summarization of a bipartite graph G is composed of two bipartite graphs, the summary graph G_S and the additional graph G_A. Instead of transferring G from a sender to a receiver, we can transfer G_S, G_A and the group information of super nodes in G_S. In addition, there is no need to send the symbol information of edges in G_A, since this information can be obtained by comparing G_A and G_S. If the symbol of an edge in G_A is $+$, this edge is not present in G_S, and vice versa, if the symbol is $-$, G_S contains the edge. The following equation defines the coding cost of a summarization of the graph.

DEFINITION 1 (CODING COST OF A GRAPH.).

$$CC(G) = CC(G_S) + CC(G_A) + \sum_{i=1}^{K}\sum_{j=1}^{N_i} |S_{ij}| log_2 \frac{|V_i|}{|S_{ij}|}, \quad (3)$$

where $CC(G_S)$ and $CC(G_A)$ denote the coding cost of summary graph G_S and the additional graph G_A defined by Eq.(2). The third term is the cost of coding the group information, where K is the number of node types, N_i is the number of super nodes in type i, $|S_{ij}|$ is the number of members in super node S_{ij}, $|V_i|$ is the number of original nodes in type i.

$L(D|M) = CC(G_S)$ is the description of the data under the model M with coding cost $L(M) = CC(G_A) + CC(group)$. The optimization goal of our algorithm *SCMiner* is to find the best model or summarization that minimizes Eq.(3).

2.2 Hidden Relations Between Vertices

The data we record in real life applications does often only approximately represent the ground truth due to inconsistencies and measurement errors. For example, the same user often joins newsgroups under different nicknames and email addresses. Or a protein might show a strong response to a substance simply due to a measurement error. Thus real world graphs are often spoiled by erroneous connections on the one hand and are also missing important links on the other hand.

Take a close look at the graph G in Figure 1, obviously we have the feeling that edge (V_{13}, V_{23}) is probably missing, and edge (V_{11}, V_{25}) maybe presents an artifact of noise. Therefore, if we add edge (V_{13}, V_{23}) to G and remove edge (V_{11}, V_{25}) from G, we can form four super nodes, whose members exhibit the exact same connection patterns. These connections probably reflect the true relationships. Based on these observations, we propose the following strategy to discover the hidden relations between vertices.

Figure 2 describes our strategy for merging nodes, suppose all the nodes are super nodes. The nodes in Group 1 share a similar link pattern and could therefore be merged into a super node. Nodes in Group 2 and Group 3 are both hop two neighbors of node S_{2k}, specifically nodes in Group 2 are common neighbors of nodes in Group 1 and nodes in Group 3 are not. To form a new super node of nodes in Group 1 their link pattern should be exactly the same. However, the link pattern of node S_{1p} in Group 1 is similar to those of the other nodes, but not the same. Concretely, S_{1p} has an extra link with S_{2k} that the other nodes lack. As we can see from Figure 2, two methods can be adopted to make nodes in Group 1 exhibiting the same link pattern: we could either remove edge (S_{1p}, S_{2k}) or add edges $(S_{11}, S_{2k}), (S_{12}, S_{2k}), ..., (S_{1p-1}, S_{2k})$. The question is, how to distinguish whether edges should be removed or added? We can decide if we add or remove edges by calculating some cost function. We define the cost as the number of edges we add or delete, which is highly related to the MDL costs of Eq.(3), in order to make the link patterns of merging nodes equal. Specifically, as shown in Figure 2, there are p nodes in Group 1 $S_{11}, S_{12}, ..., S_{1p}$, among which S_{1p} exhibits a similar but not exact same link pattern as the other nodes. Therefore, the cost of removing edge (S_{1p}, S_{2k}) is 1 and the cost of adding edges $(S_{11}, S_{2k}), (S_{12}, S_{2k}), ..., (S_{1p-1}, S_{2k})$ is $p-1$. Obviously, the former method should be selected because of the lower cost. The pseudocode of modifying the edges of a merging group is shown in Algorithm 1. At first we combine neighbors and common neighbors of nodes in merging groups, then we need to modify the edges of those nodes which are neighbors but not common neighbors of the merging group to make the link pattern of all group members exactly the same. Suppose the merging group contains $S_{11}, S_{12}, ..., S_{1p}$ and S_{2k} is one of their neighbors but not a common neighbor. The cost of removing and adding edges can be calculated by Eq.(4) and Eq.(5). The cost of a super edge is calculated as $|S_{1i}| \cdot |S_{2k}|$, where $|.|$ is the number of normal nodes contained in a super node. However, in some cases the costs for removing might be the same as for adding edges. If so, we use the similarity proposed in the next section to decide which action to take. Naturally, if S_{2k} is more similar to the nodes of Group 2 compared to those of Group 3, we add edges for merging, while otherwise we

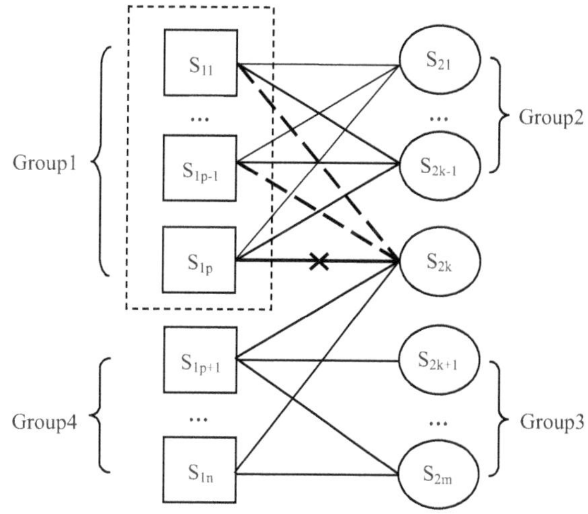

Group1: Nodes to be merged
Group2: Hop 2 neighbors of S_{2k} and common neighbor of Group1
Group3: Hop 2 neighbors of S_{2k} but not common neighbor of Group1
Group4: Neighbors of S_{2k}

—✕— : The edge to be deleted
- - - : The edge to be added

Figure 2: The strategy used for merging nodes

Algorithm 1 *ModifyEdge*

//Modify edges of *group* to make their link same
Input: Group nodes *group*, G_S, G_A
Output: G_S, G_A, *hop2Sim*

$alln$ = Neighbor($group$);
cn = CommonNeighbor($group$);
for Each node $S \in alln$ and $S \notin cn$ **do**
  Using Eq.(4) and Eq.(5) to add or remove edge;
  Add or remove edges in G_S;
  Add additional edges to G_A;
end for
Update *hop2Sim* for each $S \in alln$ and $S \notin cn$;
return G_S, G_A, *hop2Sim*;

---

remove edges.

$$Cost_{remove} = \sum_{i=1}^{p} \begin{cases} |S_{1i}| \cdot |S_{2k}| & \text{if } S_{1i} \text{ links to } S_{2k} \\ 0 & \text{otherwise.} \end{cases} \quad (4)$$

$$Cost_{add} = \sum_{i=1}^{p} \begin{cases} 0 & \text{if } S_{1i} \text{ links to } S_{2k} \\ |S_{1i}| \cdot |S_{2k}| & \text{otherwise.} \end{cases} \quad (5)$$

3. ALGORITHM SCMINER

In this section, we propose our algorithm *SCMiner* to find the best summarization of a bipartite graph. It can be proven that finding the global optimal summarization is NP-hard, therefore *SCMiner* follows a heuristic approach to search the local optima.

Basic Idea. The idea behind the algorithm *SCMiner* is that nodes with similar link patterns can be merged to groups, if the similarity between each pair of nodes in the group is bigger than some threshold th. By adding and removing edges as proposed in Section 2 we accomplish that all group nodes share the exact same link pattern and so can form a super node. *SCMiner* iteratively merges groups of nodes or super nodes whose similarities are bigger than th. The initial threshold is 1 and th is reduced stepwise by ϵ when no pair of nodes can be merged. In each iteration we calculate the new summarization coding cost. Then the MDL principle is used to choose the best summarization. The algorithm terminates when th reaches 0.

Finding Super Node Candidates. To find suitable candidate groups of nodes where merging might pay-off, we introduce the notion of hop two similarity. Suppose two super nodes S_{1i} and S_{1j} have n common neighbors $\{S_{21}...S_{2n}\}$ and m neighbors $\{S_{2(n+1)}...S_{2(n+m)}\}$ that are connected to only one of the two super nodes. Intuitively, if the two nodes have more common neighbors than neighbors only linking to one node, they are more similar in link pattern, then different. We can define their similarity as

DEFINITION 2 (HOP TWO SIMILARITY.).

$$sim(S_{1i}, S_{1j}) = \frac{\sum_{k=1}^{n} |S_{2k}|}{\sum_{k=1}^{n+m} |S_{2k}|} \quad (6)$$

where $|S_{2i}|$ is the number of normal nodes contained in super node S_{2i}. This similarity measure ranges from 0 to 1.

As described above, we only need to calculate the similarity between two nodes if they share at least one common neighbor and therefore are hop two neighbors of each other. In the following we call the similarity between a node and all its hop two neighbors its hop two similarity. **Algorithm.** Now we describe our algorithm *SCMiner*, the pseudocode is provided in algorithm 2. The input parameters of *SCMiner* are the bipartite graph $G = (V, E)$, where $V = (V_1, V_2)$ and E are the edges between V_1 and V_2, and stepsize ϵ for reducing th. The output of *SCMiner* is the summarization of G, including the summary graph $G_S = (S, E_S)$ composed of super nodes $S = (S_1, S_2)$ and the additional graph $G_A = (V, E')$ composed of single nodes $V = (V_1, V_2)$, which has the minimum coding cost regarding the proposed coding scheme. In the initialization phase, we first set the summary graph G_S to the input graph G, which means that all single nodes are treated as super nodes containing only one normal node, and set the additional graph G_A empty. Then we initialize the coding cost *mincc* using *Eq.*(3) with G_S and G_A. Afterwards we compute the similarities between each node and its hop two neighbors of same node type. In the searching phase, when $th > 0$, we do the following steps: First we search for groups of nodes that have at least one hop two neighbor with similarity larger than th and then we merge every group we found. When there is no more group of nodes that can be merged, we decrease the threshold th by ϵ. In the merging phase, we use the proposed method shown in algorithm 1 to modify the edges of the merging group that are present in G_S to get nodes with exact same link structure. Subsequently we add the corresponding additional edges to G_A and update the hop two similarity for affected nodes, which are neighbors of merging group nodes but not their common neighbors. During the merging phase, nodes with similar link patterns are merged, which decreases the data cost and increases the model cost, while the total cost is reduced in most cases. After each merging step, we calculate the coding cost using Eq.(3) with current G_S and G_A and the best summarization with minimum coding cost is stored in $bestG_S$ and $bestG_A$. Finally, we output $bestG_S$ and $bestG_A$ with coding cost.

Algorithm 2 *SCMiner*

```
Input: Bipartite graph G = (V, E), Reduce step ε
Output: Summary Graph G_S, Addition Graph G_A
//Initialization
G_S = G, G_A = (V, ∅);
Compute mincc using Eq.(3) with G_S and G_A;
bestG_S = G_S, bestG_A = G_A;
Compute hop2Sim for each S ∈ G_S using Eq.(6);
//Searching for best Summarization
while th > 0 do
  for each node S ∈ G_S do
    Get SN with S' ∈ SN and hop2Sim(S, S') > th;
  end for
  Combine SN and get non-overlapped groups allgroup;
  for each group ∈ allgroup do
    ModifyEdge(group, G_S, G_A);
    Merge nodes of G_S with same link pattern;
    Compute cc using Eq.(3) with G_S and G_A;
    Record bestG_S, bestG_A, and mincc if cc < mincc;
  end for
  if allgroup == ∅ then
    th = th − ε;
  else
    th = 1.0;
  end if
end while
return bestG_S, bestG_A;
```

Properties. We adjust the parameter ϵ using the MDL principle. Extensive experiments on synthetic and real data showed that a suitable range for ϵ is around 0.01 to 0.1. Therefore we try out every setting with a step size of 0.01 and let MDL select the best result. The runtime complexity for the computation of the similarity between each vertex v and its hop two neighbors is $O(N \cdot d_{av}^3)$, where N is the number of vertices and d_{av} is the average degree of each vertex. During each merging step in *SCMiner*, we only compute the similarities between some affected vertices and their two hop neighbors. Therefore the runtime complexity is roughly $O(d_{av}^4)$. The number of merging steps, affected by the re-

Table 1: Synthetic bipartite graphs

Data Set	S	T
BP1	$\begin{pmatrix} 0.8 & 0.2 \\ 0.1 & 0.9 \end{pmatrix}$	$\begin{pmatrix} 1 & 0 \\ 0 & 1 \end{pmatrix}$
BP2	$\begin{pmatrix} 0.9 & 0.8 & 0.1 \\ 0.1 & 0.9 & 0.8 \\ 0.1 & 0.2 & 0.9 \end{pmatrix}$	$\begin{pmatrix} 1 & 1 & 0 \\ 0 & 1 & 1 \\ 0 & 0 & 1 \end{pmatrix}$
BP3	$\begin{pmatrix} 0.8 & 0.7 & 0.2 & 0.8 \\ 0.9 & 0.3 & 0.8 & 0.2 \\ 0.3 & 0.8 & 0.2 & 0.7 \\ 0.9 & 0.8 & 0.7 & 0.2 \end{pmatrix}$	$\begin{pmatrix} 1 & 1 & 0 & 1 \\ 1 & 0 & 1 & 0 \\ 0 & 1 & 0 & 1 \\ 1 & 1 & 1 & 0 \end{pmatrix}$

duction stepsize ϵ, is N in average. So the whole runtime complexity is $O(N \cdot d_{av}^4)$.

4. EXPERIMENTS

This section provides empirical evidence to show the effectiveness of *SCMiner* on synthetic and real data. In particular, we evaluate *SCMiner* three aspects: First, we compare *SCMiner* with state-of-the-art co-clustering algorithms in terms of quality of the clusters detected on each type of nodes. Secondly, we evaluate the hidden structure, i.e. the relationships between both types of nodes found by *SCMiner*. Finally, we compare *SCMiner* with some state-of-the-art link prediction methods to evaluate the validity of hidden relationships discovered by *SCMiner*.

Data Sets. The generated synthetic bipartite graphs with different parameters are shown in Table 1. Both V_1 and V_2 contain the same number of clusters, and each cluster has 100 nodes. The matrix T shows the ground truth links between clusters of different type, where T_{pq} can take the values 1 or 0, which means the pth cluster of V_1 and the qth cluster of V_2 are fully connected or separated. The matrix S introduces link parameters to matrix T, where S_{pq} denotes the percentage of links generated between the pth cluster of V_1 and the qth cluster of V_2. In other words, if link parameters are introduced based on 0, noisy links are added to the ground truth graph. If link parameters are introduced based on 1, links are removed from the ground truth graph, where the percentage is 1 minus the link parameters.

Three real data sets are evaluated in our experiments. World cities[1] data consists of the distribution of offices from 46 global advanced producer service firms over 55 world cities. Global firms are defined as firms owning offices in at least 15 different cities. Service values for a firm in a city are given as 3,2,1 and 0. We binarize the data set such that positive service values become 1 and then generate the bipartite graph. The advanced producer service firms can be categorized into 4 clusters: accountancy firms, advertising firms, banking and finance firms and law firms.

MovieLens[2] data was collected through the MovieLens web site during the seven-month period from September 19th, 1997 to April 22nd, 1998 by the GroupLens Research Project at the University of Minnesota. It consists of 100,000 ratings (1-5) from 943 users on 1682 movies. We preprocess the data by removing movies which are rated by less than 30 users and users that rated less than 30 movies. Therefore, we got a bipartite graph of 361 users and 334 movies. Then we binarize the preprocessed data set such that 3-5 entries become 1 and others become 0.

[1]http://www.lboro.ac.uk/gawc/datasets/da6.html
[2]http://www.grouplens.org/node/12

Table 2: Clustering Performance on Synthetic data.

	BP1	BP2	BP3
SCMiner	**1**	**1**	**0.9949**
CA	0.6683	0.7897	0.8750
ITCC	**1**	**1**	0.8750
GS	0.2568	0.4069	0.5493

Jester[3] is a joke rating data set. The original data set contains over 1.7 million continuous ratings (-10.00 to +10.00, +10.00 best) of 150 jokes from 63974 users collected between April 2006 to May 2009. We remove 22 jokes which are never rated or rated by less than 0.01 of users, and randomly pick 1000 users who rate all the picked jokes. Then we binarize the data set such that 5-10 entries become 1 and others become 0. The ground truth is generated for evaluating link prediction, such that the non-negative entries become 1 and the negative entries become 0.

4.1 Clustering Quality

Firstly, we evaluate the quality of clusters detected by *SCMiner*. *SCMiner* can be used as a parameter-free bipartite graph partition method and therefore we choose the approaches Cross-association (*CA*) [1] and Information-theoretic Co-clustering (*ITCC*) [4] as comparison methods. In addition, we compare *SCMiner* to the graph summarization technique (*GS*) of [14]. The algorithms *SCMiner*, *CA* and *GS* are both parameter-free, *ITCC* requires the number of clusters in rows and columns. The algorithm *GS* does not output a clustering, however, the summarized nodes can also be regarded as clusters. We therefore create a cluster for each summarized node of the algorithm. For synthetic data we set the number of clusters of *ITCC* to the true number of the data set. We use the Normalized Mutual Information (NMI) [21] to measure the clustering performance. The value of NMI ranges between 0 and 1. The higher the value the better the clustering. We further report the Adjusted Mutual Information (AMI) and Adjusted Variation Information (AVI) scores proposed in [21].

Synthetic Data. Table 2 depicts the clustering performance comparison on synthetic data sets evaluated by NMI, which shows that *SCMiner* yields better results than *CA*, *ITCC* and *GS*. For BP1 and BP2 both *ITCC* and *SCMiner* give perfect results, however *ITCC* needs the true number of clusters as input parameter, whereas *SCMiner* determines the number of clusters automatically without user input. *CA* outputs worse NMI results, because it splits the clusters into some smaller ones. Worst NMI results yields *GS*, this is mainly because *GS* is designed for summarization but not for clustering. For space limitations, Table 2 reports only NMI but the other scores are similar.

For *SCMiner* we try out several ϵ and choose the best results with the minimum MDL. Figure 3 shows the clustering results for all synthetic data sets with different ϵ and one can see that the results are quite stable on a wide range of ϵ. We also test the relationship between NMI and MDL, for space limitation we only mark several MDL values for synthetic data BP3 in Figure 3. The coding costs are 127102 bits when $\epsilon = 0.01$ and $NMI = 0.89$, and it costs 123723 bits

[3]http://eigentaste.berkeley.edu/dataset/

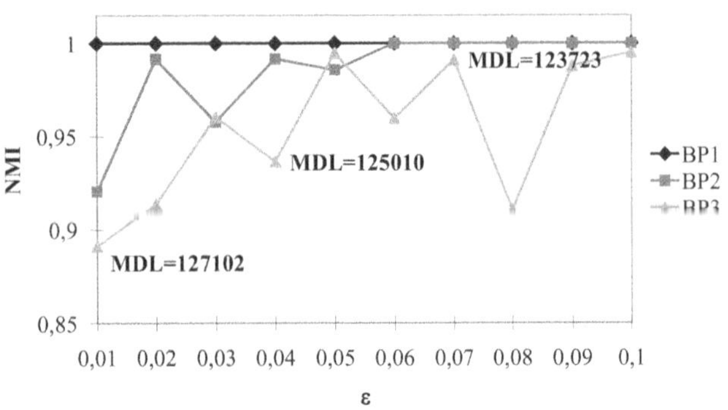

Figure 3: Results for Various ϵ.

when $\epsilon = 0.07$ and $NMI = 0.99$, which proofs that smaller MDL values lead to better NMI results.

World Cities Data. The World cities real data set contains cluster labels of global firms and thus we can use NMI to evaluate clustering quality of this type of nodes. We run *SCMiner*, *CA*, *ITCC* and *GS* on this data set. *SCMiner*, *CA* and *GS* are all parameter-free methods (the chosen ϵ of *SCMiner* for cities is 0.01). We set the true number of clusters of global firms and 4 as the number of clusters of world cities as input parameter for *ITCC*. The NMI results for global firms are depicted in Table 3 and the table shows that *SCMiner* clearly outperforms *CA*, *ITCC* and *GS* in all clustering quality scores. The evaluation of cities type clusters is much more difficult, since the cluster labels are not provided along with the data set. Looking in detail at the cluster contents, *SCMiner* finds 3 clusters and a separated city Washington, DC. The first cluster contains 13 cities, including Atlanta, Boston, Dallas, Munich, Montreal etc. and all these cities are strong in economics. In detail, all 5 accountancy firms have services in these cities, and there are 3 advertising, 5 banking and 2 law companies in average owning offices in these 13 cities. The second cluster contains 17 cities, including Toronto, Paris, London, New York, and Beijing. All these cities are metropolis in the world. Moreover most of these cities are capital of their country. In terms of service, all 5 accountancy firms have services in these cities, and there are 9 advertising, 11 banking and 7 law companies in average having offices in these 17 cities. The third cluster contains 24 cities, including Amsterdam, Barcelona, Seoul, Shanghai etc., which are all kind of financial cities. In terms of service, all 5 accountancy firms have services in these cities as well, and there are 7 advertising, 8 banking and 2 law companies in average having offices in these 24 cities. The cluster analysis shows that *SCMiner* outputs reasonable clusters regarding the cities type nodes. To sum up, the cities can be categorized into 3 types, capital metropolis, financial cities and economic cities. Capital metropolis are the economic, financial and politic center of a country, therefore all kinds of companies have offices in these cities. Financial cities offer a lot of banking and advertising company services, but lack law services, because they are not politically oriented. Some local manufactories are located in economic cities, whereas advertising, banking and law companies are not. Washington, DC is quite different compared to the other cities, since it is a politic, but not a financial city and therefore owns lots of law firms' offices but fewer advertising and banking firms' offices. Thus it is reasonable that this city is separated in its own cluster.

Table 3: Results on World Cities Data.

	NMI	AMI	AVI
SCMiner	**0.4345**	**0.3807**	**0.3824**
CA	0.3109	0.2447	0.2604
ITCC	0.2522	0.1845	0.1891
GS	0.2515	0.0467	0.0683

Movielens Data. MovieLens data set does not provide cluster labels, however, it provides movie categories and personal information of users that can be used to analyze the cluster contents. We separately perform *SCMiner*, *CA*, *ITCC* and *GS* on this data set, *SCMiner*, *CA* and *GS* are both parameter-free (the chosen ϵ of *SCMiner* for MovieLens is 0.05). *CA* outputs 9 user clusters and 8 movie clusters. In addition some isolated nodes and small clusters with less than 5 instances are found. *SCMiner* gives 10 user clusters and 15 movie clusters, whereas all the clusters found by *GS* are single nodes or just contain a few nodes (< 5). To be fair, we set the number of user and movie clusters to 10 and 15 for *ITCC*, which corresponds to the number of clusters found by *SCMiner*. In this data set, movies are classified into 19 genres, such as action, adventure, animation, etc, and a movie can be categorized into several genres at once. According to the basic concept of clustering that objects in the same cluster are similar, we define purity P to evaluate the movie clusters. By counting genres of movies, we can acquire the genre that dominates the cluster and let this genre be the cluster representative. The purity of a cluster is defined as the percentage of movies belonging to the most represented genre. We calculate the purity P for each movie cluster detected by *SCMiner*, *CA* and *ITCC*, and sort them by p value, which is shown in Figure 4. The figure shows that *SCMiner* outputs more pure movie clusters than the two comparison methods. In terms of user clusters, it is difficult to compare the results. Analyzing the content of user clusters detected by *SCMiner*, reveals that some clusters contain old users, some are composed of young users, some groups contain only males, while others own mainly women. This reflects that *SCMiner* outputs meaningful user clusters.

4.2 Hidden Structure

For bipartite graph data, we do only want to analyze the clusters in each type, but we also want to evaluate the relationship between clusters of different types. Besides our *SCMiner* algorithm, *CA* is the only comparison method providing information about these relationships (in the form of a re-arranged adjacency matrix) to users.

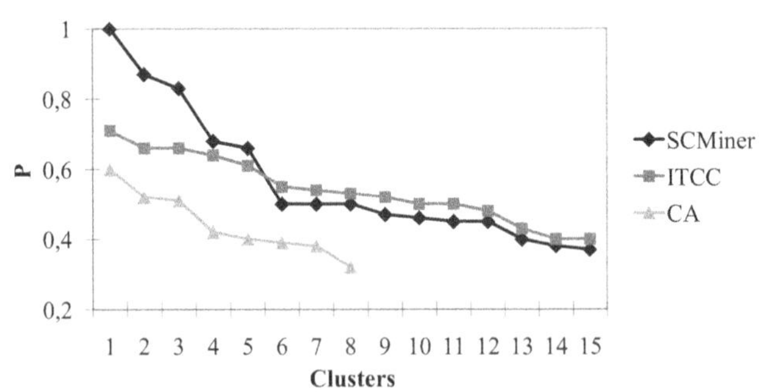

Figure 4: Cluster Purity on Movielens Data.

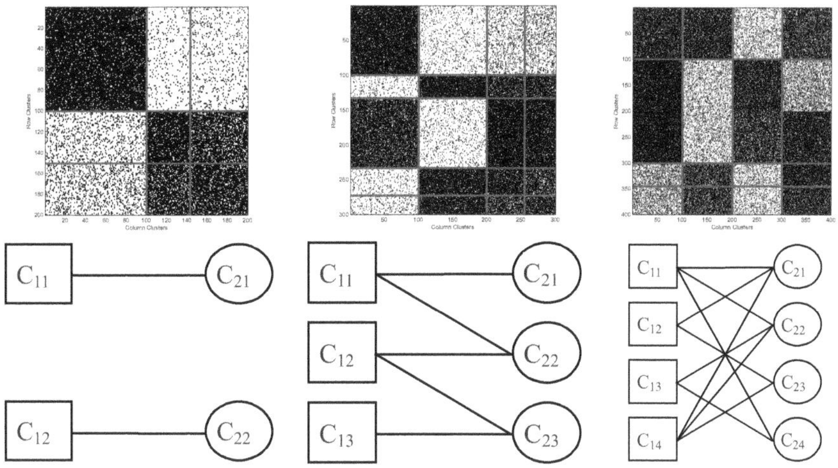

Figure 5: Hidden Structure Detected by *SCMiner* and *CA*. From Left to Right: Data Set BP1, BP2, BP3.

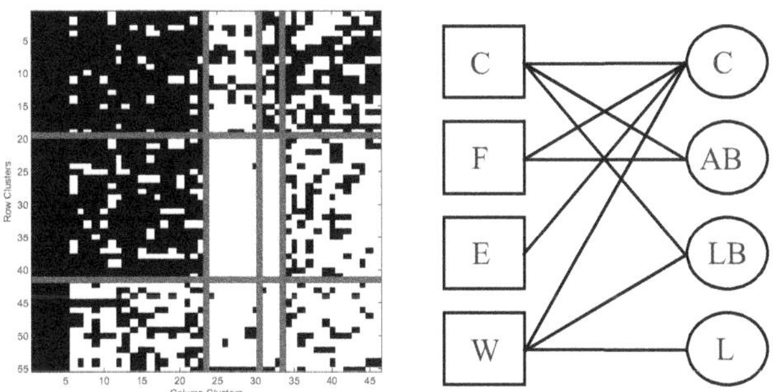

Figure 6: Hidden structure of cities detected by *CA* (left) and *SCMiner* (right). For *SCMiner* results, Square C represents a cluster consisting of capitals, Square F financial cities, Square E economic cities and Square W is the isolated city Washington, DC. On the other side, the cluster represented by Circle C mainly contains accountancy firms, Circle AB advertising and banking companies, Circle LB banking and law firms, and Circle L law firms.

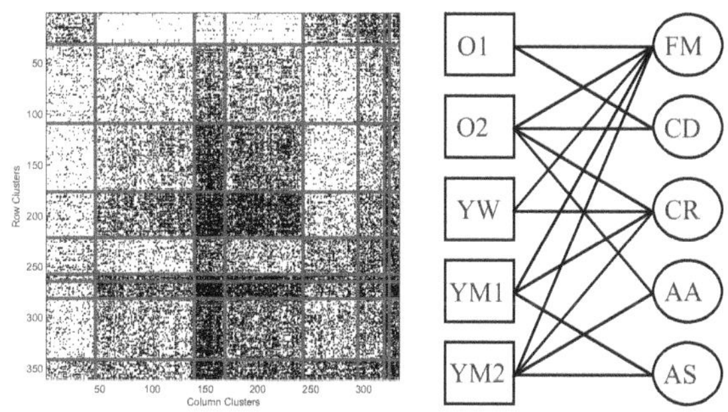

Figure 7: Hidden structure of MovieLens detected by*CA* (left) and *SCMiner* (right). For *SCMiner* results, Square $O1$ and $O2$ denote clusters containing old users, Square YW represents a cluster of young women, and Square $YM1$ and $YM2$ young man. On the other side, the cluster represented by Circle FM represents high scored movies, Circle CD comedy and drama, Circle CR action, romance and comedy. Circles AA and AS represent adventure, action, thriller movies and action, sci-fi, thriller movies, respectively.

Synthetic Data. Figure 5 depicts the hidden structure detected by *SCMiner* and *CA*, the top row shows the re-arranged adjacency matrix of data output by *CA*, the bottom row depicts the hidden structure found by *SCMiner*, where squares and circles denote the two different types of clusters. For BP1 and BP2 *SCMiner* gives perfect results and for BP3 just one node is categorized incorrectly, as cluster C_{12} contains 99 nodes and clusterC_{14} contains 101 nodes, but the whole structure is correct, whereas the cross association output by *CA* for BP3 is incorrect and it is really hard to tell the relationship between the second row and fourth column cluster. In summary, the visualization of cross-associations is only clear and interpretable for data having a relatively easy structure.

World Cities Data. Figure 6 depicts the hidden structure of World cities data set detected by *SCMiner* and *CA*. The left shows the re-arranged adjacency matrix of data output by *CA*. It is hard to identify the relationship between two types of nodes from the matrix itself. The right depicts the hidden structure found by *SCMiner*, the squares represent the cities clusters and circles denote clusters of companies. The figure shows that capital metropolis have connections to all kind of firms, financial cities do not have law companies services, most service in economic cities are from accountancy companies, and Washington, DC owns lots of law companies but fewer banking and advertising firms. From the figure, the major structure of the complex network becomes obvious at first glance. The result of *SCMiner* is a highly compact bipartite graph, a data representation which is easy to understand for the user. In contrast, the re-arranged adjacency matrix is still quite noisy and it is very difficult to infer the structure from this representation.

Movielens Data. Figure 7 depicts the hidden structure of MovieLens data set detected by *SCMiner* and *CA*, the left shows the re-arranged adjacency matrix of data output by *CA*, which is hard to understand, the right depicts the hidden structure found by *SCMiner* which is much easier to analyze. For clarity we only show the relation between the 5 biggest clusters in each type. Squares and circles represent the user and movies cluster. Cluster $O1$ and $O2$ contain user groups that are older than the average regarding the whole data set, and their male-to-female ratio is just about whole data set average. Square YW represents a user group with a much larger female ratio compared to the average, and the users are younger than the average as well. Square $YM1$ and $YM2$ denote clusters with groups of users containing almost all young man. On the other side, circle FM represents a cluster of famous movies, containing Schindler's List, Shawshank Redemption, and Seven etc. that all have high rating scores in IMDB, which shows that all groups of users like it. This fact is embodied in the revealed hidden structure, since this cluster has connections to all user groups. Circle CD is mainly consisting of movies from comedy and drama category, so it makes sense that older people like it. The movies in circle CR are mostly from action, romance and comedy genre, so young women and young men like it. Circle AA and AS represent adventure action thriller movies and action sci-fi thriller movies respectively, therefore young man like them. The above analysis shows that the hidden structure found by *SCMiner* is reasonable.

4.3 Link Prediction Accuracy

SCMiner outputs the summarization of the input graph that yields the minimum coding cost. The summarization itself consists of a summary graph and an additional graph, where the "-" edges in the additional graph denote missing links which should be added to the original graph, and "+" edges might be noisy links which should be removed from the original graph. Since it is hard to determine whether a "-" edge represents noise, we only use link prediction to evaluate whether a "+" edge is a missing link.

The link prediction problem has been studied on graphs by several approaches which can be divided into two categories, supervised, e.g. [11], [6] and unsupervised methods, e.g. [10]. Since *SCMiner* is unsupervised, we only compare our results to unsupervised approaches. There are two types of unsupervised methods: based on node neighbors and based on paths between nodes. However, some of these methods, like common neighbor, are not suitable for link prediction on bipartite graph data and therefore we choose two methods, *PA* preferential attachment [15] and *Katz* [8], that are suitable for bipartite graphs. We use precision and recall to evaluate the accuracy. *SCMiner* automatically outputs K predicted edges and for reasons of fairness we choose the top K predictions of the ranking list of *PA* and *Katz* to compare the precision and recall of the prediction results. We also compare our approach to *GS* Graph Summarization, since the algorithm changes the edges of the original graph as well. Table 4 shows the link prediction comparison on our synthetic data sets as well as on the real data set Jester. All the results are averaged over runs on 10 randomly generated or the selected data sets. *SCMiner* predicts the missing links of BP1 and BP2 completely and those of BP3 nearly completely correct and therefore yields better results on all synthetic data sets than all comparison methods. Moreover it outperforms the other approaches on the Jester data set. Interestingly, *GS* performs better on the synthetic data sets than on Jester. The reason might be that the Jester data set is sparser than the synthetic data sets, and therefore *GS* reaches a local minimum very fast, which results in fewer predicted edges.

5. RELATED WORK

During past decades, many algorithms were proposed for graph clustering, graph compression, graph summarization and link prediction. Due to space limitations, we only provide a very brief survey on some related research directions.

Co-clustering. Bi-clustering or co-clustering is a creative approach which simultaneously clusters rows and columns of a data matrix. It avoids the problems caused by sparseness and high-dimensionality that traditional one way clustering algorithms suffer from. There are some state-of-the-art co-clustering algorithms, such as Information- theoretic Co-clustering [4], Cross Association [1] etc. Specifically, Information theoretic co-clustering [4] simultaneously maps row elements to row clusters and column elements to column clusters, mutual information of each clustering state is calculated and compared to the initial state. Thus, the optimal co-clustering result is obtained when the mutual information loss is minimal. However, the drawback of the method is that the number of both row and column clusters must be predetermined. Cross Association [1] is a MDL-based parameter-free co-clustering method that processes a binary matrix and seeks clusters of rows and columns alternately. Then the matrix is divided into homogeneous rectangles which represent underlying structure of the data. However, compared with our algorithm, it only addresses the clustering problem. Moreover, Long et al. [13] proposed a framework for co-clustering named block value decomposition (BVD), which formulates co-clustering as an optimization problem of matrix decomposition. Similarly, in [12], Long et al. reconstruct a bipartite graph based on some hidden nodes and thus an optimal co-clustering result is obtained from the new bipartite graph which mostly approximates the origin graph. However, these two algorithms both need the number of clusters as input parameter. Besides, Dhillon [3] proposed a spectral algorithm for bipartite graph partition. Shan and Banerjee [17] proposed a Bayesian co-clustering model and considered co-clustering as a generative mixture modeling problem. George and Merugu proposed a co-clustering algorithm based on the collaborative filtering framework [5]. In terms of real life data sets, [2] applied co-clustering on gene expression data and [3] effectively processed documents and words data.

Graph Compression and Summarization. In real life, it is common that a graph consists of tens of thousands nodes and complex linkages. Graph compression and graph summarization [14, 20, 22] are effective ways to simplify the original large graph and to extract useful information. Many algorithms are based on Subdue [7], which is a classical graph compression system. It makes use of the MDL Principle to find a subgraph suitable for compression. Bayesian Model Merging (BMM) [18, 19] also is a kind of compression method which is based on Bayesian formula. The best compressed model can be achieved by maximizing the posterior probability. Navlakha et al. [14] represented a graph by a summary graph and a correction matrix, and summarization is implemented by greedy merging and randomized algorithms. MDL is used to find the local optimum. However, the algorithm is designed for compressing only and performs poorly in clustering or link prediction. In [20], according to group nodes based on their attributes and relationships, which are selected by the user, Tian et al. propose a graph summarization algorithm.

Link Prediction. Predicting whether two disconnected nodes will be connected in the future, based on available network information is known as the challenge of link prediction. Liben-Nowell and Kleinberg [10] summarize some

Table 4: Link Prediction Performances.

Algorithm	BP1		BP2		BP3		Jester	
	Precision	Recall	Precision	Recall	Precision	Recall	Precision	Recall
PA	0.084	0.084	0.436	0.436	0.442	0.443	0.406	0.369
Katz	0.984	0.984	0.943	0.943	0.547	0.548	0.406	0.369
GS	0.965	**1**	0.981	1	0.994	0.973	0.356	0.05
SCMiner	**1**	**1**	**1**	**1**	**0.997**	**1**	**0.431**	**0.389**

unsupervised link prediction approaches for social networks. For example, common neighbor, Jaccard's coefficient, preferential attachment [15], *Katz* [8] etc. Specifically, preferential attachment is based on the idea that two nodes with higher degree have higher probability to be connected. *Katz* [8] defines a score that sums up the number of all paths between two nodes where short paths are weighted stronger. By ranking these scores, the probability of whether two disconnected nodes will be linked in the future can be acquired. However, when dealing with bipartite graphs, Kunegis et al. [9] stated that scores based on common neighbor are not suitable, because two connected nodes do not have any common neighbors in a bipartite graph. But scores like preferential attachment and *Katz*, which are used in this paper as comparison methods are reasonable.

6. CONCLUSION

In this paper, we propose *SCMiner*, a technique which integrates graph summarization, bipartite graph clustering, link prediction and hidden structure mining. Based on the sound optimization goal of data compression, our algorithm finds a compact summary representation of a large graph. In addition, while compressing the graph *SCMiner* detects the truly relevant clusters of both node types and their hidden relationships. Thus, *SCMiner* is a framework comprehensively supporting the major tasks in unsupervised graph mining. Our experiments have demonstrated that *SCMiner* outperforms specialized state-of-the-art techniques for co-clustering and link prediction. In ongoing and future work we want to extend this idea to support multi-partite graphs as well as graphs with different edge types.

Acknowledgments

Jing Feng and Xiao He are supported by the China Scholarship Council (CSC). Claudia Plant is supported by the Alexander von Humboldt Foundation.

7. REFERENCES

[1] D. Chakrabarti, S. Papadimitriou, D. S. Modha, and C. Faloutsos. Fully automatic cross-associations. In *KDD*, pages 79–88, 2004.

[2] H. Cho, I. S. Dhillon, Y. Guan, and S. Sra. Minimum sum-squared residue co-clustering of gene expression data. In *SDM*, 2004.

[3] I. S. Dhillon. Co-clustering documents and words using bipartite spectral graph partitioning. In *KDD*, pages 269–274, 2001.

[4] I. S. Dhillon, S. Mallela, and D. S. Modha. Information-theoretic co-clustering. In *KDD*, pages 89–98, 2003.

[5] T. George and S. Merugu. A scalable collaborative filtering framework based on co-clustering. In *ICDM*, pages 625–628, 2005.

[6] M. A. Hasan, V. Chaoji, S. Salem, and M. Zaki. Link prediction using supervised learning. In *Proc. of SDM Workshop on Link Analysis*, 2006.

[7] L. B. Holder, D. J. Cook, and S. Djoko. Substucture discovery in the subdue system. In *KDD Workshop*, pages 169–180, 1994.

[8] L. Katz. A new status index derived from sociometric analysis. *PSYCHOMETRIKA*, 18(1):39–43, 1953.

[9] J. Kunegis, E. W. D. Luca, and S. Albayrak. The link prediction problem in bipartite networks. *CoRR*, abs/1006.5367, 2010.

[10] D. Liben-Nowell and J. M. Kleinberg. The link prediction problem for social networks. In *CIKM*, pages 556–559, 2003.

[11] R. Lichtenwalter, J. T. Lussier, and N. V. Chawla. New perspectives and methods in link prediction. In *KDD*, pages 243–252, 2010.

[12] B. Long, X. Wu, Z. M. Zhang, P. S. Yu, and P. S. Yu. Unsupervised learning on k-partite graphs. In *KDD*, pages 317–326, 2006.

[13] B. Long, Z. M. Zhang, P. S. Yu, and P. S. Yu. Co-clustering by block value decomposition. In *KDD*, pages 635–640, 2005.

[14] S. Navlakha, R. Rastogi, and N. Shrivastava. Graph summarization with bounded error. In *SIGMOD*, pages 419–432, 2008.

[15] M. E. J. Newman. Clustering and preferential attachment in growing networks. *PHYS.REV.E*, 64:025102, 2001.

[16] J. Rissanen. *Information and Complexity in Statistical Modeling*. Springer, 2007.

[17] H. Shan and A. Banerjee. Bayesian co-clustering. In *ICDM*, pages 530–539, 2008.

[18] A. Stolcke and S. M. Omohundro. Hidden markov model induction by bayesian model merging. In *NIPS*, pages 11–18, 1992.

[19] A. Stolcke and S. M. Omohundro. Inducing probabilistic grammars by bayesian model merging. In *ICGI*, pages 106–118, 1994.

[20] Y. Tian, R. A. Hankins, and J. M. Patel. Efficient aggregation for graph summarization. In *SIGMOD*, pages 567–580, 2008.

[21] N. X. Vinh, J. Epps, and J. Bailey. Information theoretic measures for clusterings comparison: is a correction for chance necessary? In *ICML*, pages 1073–1080, 2009.

[22] N. Zhang, Y. Tian, and J. M. Patel. Discovery-driven graph summarization. In *ICDE*, pages 880–891, 2010.

Mining Coherent Subgraphs in Multi-Layer Graphs with Edge Labels

Brigitte Boden, Stephan Günnemann, Holger Hoffmann, and Thomas Seidl
Data Management and Data Exploration Group
RWTH Aachen University, Germany
{boden, guennemann, h.hoffmann, seidl}@cs.rwth-aachen.de

ABSTRACT

Mining dense subgraphs such as cliques or quasi-cliques is an important graph mining problem and closely related to the notion of graph clustering. In various applications, graphs are enriched by additional information. For example, we can observe graphs representing different types of relations between the vertices. These multiple edge types can also be viewed as different "layers" of the same graph, which is denoted as a "multi-layer graph" in this work. Additionally, each edge might be annotated by a label characterizing the given relation in more detail. By exploiting all these different kinds of information, the detection of more interesting clusters in the graph can be supported.

In this work, we introduce the multi-layer coherent subgraph (MLCS) model, which defines clusters of vertices that are *densely connected* by edges with *similar labels* in a *subset* of the graph layers. We avoid redundancy in the result by selecting only the most interesting, non-redundant clusters for the output. Based on this model, we introduce the best-first search algorithm MiMAG. In thorough experiments we demonstrate the strengths of MiMAG in comparison with related approaches on synthetic as well as real-world datasets.

Categories and Subject Descriptors: H.2.8 Database management: Database applications [Data mining]

Keywords: dense subgraphs, graph clustering, networks

1. INTRODUCTION

Mining graph and network data has gained much attention in recent years. One important mining task is *graph clustering* that aims at grouping the vertices of a graph into so-called *clusters* such that many edges between vertices of the same cluster exist, i.e. the vertices are *densely connected*. This task is often also referred to as "dense subgraph mining" including the detection of cliques or quasi-cliques [12].

Besides the mere graph data, real-world data often contains additional information, which can be exploited by clustering approaches. Several approaches have been proposed considering additional information about the *vertices* of a graph (e.g. [19, 14, 7, 6]). In this work, however, we consider additional information about the *edges* of a graph.

For example, a graph can contain *different types of edges*, which represent different types of relations between vertices. Such different types can occur, for example, when we combine information from several information networks: e.g., combining a co-author network with a citation network. In the first graph, authors are connected if they have common papers; in the second graph, if a paper of one author cited a paper of the other author. Thus, we will get two edge types: "co-authorship" and "citation". Furthermore, each edge might also be associated with a label, e.g. the number of co-authored (or cited) papers. We denote such a graph with multiple edge types as a "multi-layer graph". It is defined as a set of graphs (called "layers") where each graph is based on the same set of vertices and represents the edges of one certain type. Accordingly, in each layer a different edge set is given. These layers can also be viewed as "dimensions" of the graph. (In the following, we use the terms "layers" and "dimensions" interchangeably.) An exemplary multi-layer graph is depicted in Fig. 1; several real-world examples are described in the experimental section.

For graphs with edge labels, we can distinguish between two possible interpretations of the labels: First, labels can be regarded as edge *weights* that denote the strength of the relation between the incident vertices. In this paper, however, we consider a second interpretation: the edge labels represent *characteristics* of the relations. For example, a co-author network might contain information about the collaboration between two authors, as the begin or end time of the collaboration, research topics, conferences/journals where the joint papers were published etc.

Overall, in this work, we aim at finding clusters of vertices that are *densely connected* by edges with *similar* labels in a *subset* of the graph layers. These clusters are denoted as (multi-layer) *coherent subgraphs*.

We want to highlight that the coherent subgraphs need not to appear across all layers, but we detect them in subsets of the layers. This is important as some of the edge types might not be relevant for finding interesting coherent subgraphs at all; other types might be relevant only for certain subgraphs. Thus, for each coherent subgraph we find an *individual* set of relevant layers. This principle is motivated by the field of *subspace clustering* [10] that aims at analyzing subsets of the dimensions in a vector space and that stems from the fact that in higher-dimensional vector data it is unlikely to find objects that are similar w.r.t. all

KDD'12, August 12–16, 2012, Beijing, China.

of their characteristics; each cluster is associated with an individual subspace projection. Exploiting these observations in our model, the detected coherent subgraphs are useful in several scenarios: We might find a dense cluster of authors who started their collaboration at a similar time and co-authored papers at the same conferences. The authors in another dense cluster might have cited each others' papers on similar research topics, but not have published joint papers. Similar, in a co-actor graph representing the joint work of actors (cf. Sec. 5), a cluster might be a group of actors who worked together on movies with similar success.

Additionally, we consider the fact that a vertex can naturally belong to more than one cluster, e.g. an author might of course participate in several working groups. Thus, we allow our clusters to overlap. However, similar to subspace clustering, allowing overlap can lead to a huge number of valid clusters that mostly represent redundant information [13, 7]. Thus, we propose a clustering model that allows clusters to overlap to a certain extend, but avoids redundancy in the resulting set of clusters. This final set of clusters ("clustering") should contain the *most interesting clusters* w.r.t. a quality function which can be specified by the user.

Finally, since determining the overall clustering according to our model is NP-hard (as also with most dense subgraph mining models on a single graph), we introduce the algorithm MiMAG using a best-first search [16] to find an approximate solution. Best-first search is an established search principle to explore a graph, which in our case is a search tree for enumerating subgraphs, in an informed fashion. Starting in an initial node (in our case: the root node of the search tree), best-first search algorithms iteratively expand the "most promising" node based on a given heuristic. In MiMAG, the most promising subgraphs are expanded to detect the most interesting clusters first. This concept is related to the well-known A* algorithm for finding minimum-cost paths in a graph [9].

The main contributions of this paper are the following:

1. We propose the new paradigm of clustering multi-layer graphs with edge labels.
2. We introduce the clustering model MLCS, which avoids redundancy in the result set.
3. We propose the best-first search algorithm MiMAG to approximate the MLCS clustering.

2. RELATED WORK

For mining graph data there exist various mining tasks [1]. Some of the most active areas are graph clustering, graph classification, and frequent subgraph mining. In this work, we concentrate on *clustering graph/network data.* An overview of the various existing models and techniques is given in [1] and [4]. The term "graph clustering" is somewhat ambiguous as it is (a) used for the clustering of graph databases, where a cluster represents a *set of graphs*, and (b) for clustering in one large graph, where the clusters represent *sets of vertices* from the graph. The latter is often also referred to as "dense subgraph mining", and is the meaning that is used in this paper. For the definition of dense subgraphs, several models exist. Two of the most widely-used models are cliques and γ-quasi-cliques [17].

The concept of subspace clustering was developed for the task of clustering vector data. Traditionally, clustering is done by using all dimensions of the feature space. However, full-space clustering does not scale to high-dimensional data since locally irrelevant dimensions may obfuscate the clustering structure [2, 10]. As a solution, *subspace clustering* methods detect an individual set of relevant dimensions for each cluster [10]. For subspace clustering, several models and algorithms have been proposed. E.g., cell-based subspace clustering methods obtain high-quality results and are efficiently computable [15].

Some clustering approaches have been proposed that consider graphs with labeled *vertices* (here, the vertex labels are vectors). These approaches can be seen as a combination of graph clustering with clustering approaches for vector data. However, they mostly rely on fullspace-clustering on the vertex attributes (e.g. [19]). Recently, the approaches [14, 7, 6] were introduced to deal with the combination of subspace clustering and dense subgraph mining. In these approaches, clusters are ensured to be densely connected and vertices in a cluster are similar in subsets of their attribute values. Although these cluster models are related to the model introduced in this paper, adapting these methods to handle *edge* labels does not lead to the desired results. Two approaches for such an adaption are discussed and evaluated in the experimental section.

Graphs with a *single* edge type and labels in terms of edge *weights* can be considered by some graph clustering approaches like minimum cut [1] and spectral clustering [19].

To the best of our knowledge, there are no previous approaches for clustering in *multi-layer graphs with edge labels.* Also in the survey by Fortunato [4] it is mentioned that such graphs have not been dealt with by any algorithm. Even though the authors of [11] mention the existence of different types of relations in a network (which they call "levels of relation"), they just summarize all the different relations between two vertices into a single edge weight.

A concept which is related to our approach is the detection of cross-graph quasi-cliques [17]. Given a database of graphs each having the same vertices, a cross-graph quasi-clique is defined as a set of vertices that forms a quasi-clique in *all* of the graphs. Only maximal sets having this property are output. The approaches [20] and [21] also work on a graph database and mine sets of vertices that form a clique [20] or quasi-clique [21] in at least a certain percentage of the graphs in the database (which is called the "support" of the (quasi-)clique). Both approaches aim at mining *closed* (quasi-)cliques, i.e. a (quasi-)clique O is not contained in the output if one of O's supersets also forms a (quasi-)clique having the same support. In [3], cross-graph cliques are detected in a dynamic graph represented as a 3-dimensional boolean cube. To adapt these approaches to our problem setting, the graphs in the graph database could be seen as the different layers of our input graph. However, edge labels are not considered by these approaches. Furthermore, the existing methods do not avoid redundancy in the result set apart from simply excluding *subsets* of (quasi-)cliques. Thus their output can often contain a large set of highly overlapping vertex sets. In our experimental section, we compare our approach to an adaption of the closed quasi-clique mining algorithm Cocain [21].

3. MODEL

In this section, we introduce the MLCS ("Multi-layer coherent subgraph") model for the clustering of graphs with different types of edges. We start by providing a formal definition of the input graph. For ease of presentation, we represent the input graph as a *set* of graphs (called "multi-layer graph") each having the same vertex set V; each graph contains the edges of one type with their corresponding labels. Formally, the layer graph is defined as:

DEFINITION 1 (MULTI-LAYER GRAPH). *A multi-layer graph $\mathcal{G}$ for a set of dimensions $Dim = \{1, \ldots, d\}$ is a set $\mathcal{G} = \{G_i \mid i \in Dim\}$ of graphs*

$$G_i = (V, E_i, l_i), E_i \subseteq V \times V, l_i : E_i \to \mathbb{R}$$

where each graph layer $G_i, i \in Dim$ is an undirected graph without self-loops and with an edge labeling function l_i.

We can easily handle graphs with different vertex sets V_i by simply considering the union $V = \bigcup V_i$. The remainder of this section is structured as follows: In Section 3.1, we introduce our definition for a single cluster. We define our redundancy model and selection criteria for the final clustering in Section 3.2. In Section 3.3 we introduce the cluster quality function that is used in our experiments.

3.1 Cluster model

As discussed in the introduction, an MLCS cluster is a set of vertices which are connected with a *high density* by edges with *similar labels* in a *subspace of the multi-layer graph* (i.e. in a subset of the graph layers).

Cluster property for a single graph layer. First, we consider a single graph layer G_i. For the density of a subgraph, we use the established *quasi-clique* model [17, 21, 12]. The quasi-clique model defines dense subgraphs based on their intra-cluster connectivity. Formally,

DEFINITION 2 (γ-QUASI-CLIQUE). *A vertex set $O \subseteq V$ in a graph $G = (V, E)$ is a γ-quasi-clique for $\gamma \in [0, 1]$ if*

$$\forall v \in O : deg_G^O(v) \geq \lceil \gamma \cdot (|O| - 1) \rceil$$

where $deg_G^O(v) = |\{u \in O \mid (u, v) \in E\}|$. The density of a quasi-clique O in graph layer G_i is defined by

$$\gamma_{G_i}(O) = \frac{\min_{v \in O}\{deg_{G_i}^O(v)\}}{|O| - 1}$$

For our cluster model, we consider a vertex set as dense if it is a 0.5-quasi-clique, i.e. its quasi-clique density is at least 0.5. As shown in [21], for $\gamma \geq 0.5$ the vertices in a γ-quasi-clique are connected "tightly and relatively evenly". This also ensures that the subgraph is connected in the graph [21]. For the similarity of the edge labels, we use a cell-based cluster model [15]. To be considered similar, the labels of the edges in a cluster may vary at most by a threshold w. Formally, we define a cluster in a graph layer G_i as follows:

DEFINITION 3 (ONE-DIMENSIONAL MLCS CLUSTER). *A vertex set $O \subseteq V$ is a one-dimensional MLCS cluster in a graph layer $G_i = (V, E_i, l_i)$ (w.r.t. threshold w and distance function dist) if it forms a 0.5-quasi-clique in the graph G_i and*

$$\forall x, y \in E_i(O) : dist(l_i(x), l_i(y)) \leq w$$

where the edge set $E_i(O)$ is defined as $E_i(O) = \{(u, v) \in E_i \mid u, v \in O\}$

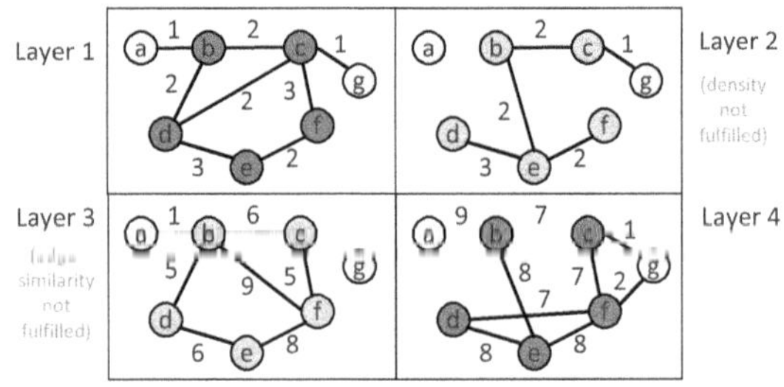

Figure 1: Exemplary MLCS cluster in layer 1 & 4

Please note that the threshold w is only needed if the edge labels are continuous valued. If we have categorical labels or the layer graphs are unlabeled, we can simply set $w = 0$. Additionally, since two nodes connected by a single edge trivially fulfill the definition, we only consider subgraphs with at least 3 vertices as clusters.

Cluster property in subspaces of the multi-layer graph. Next, we consider clusters located in subspaces of the layer graph. Naturally, the vertex set of a multi-dimensional cluster should fulfill the one-dimensional cluster property for all of the dimensions in the subspace. This idea leads to some important observations: If an edge (u, v) exists in one graph layer, it does not automatically exist in another layer. Thus, when we consider the *same vertex set* in different graph layers, the corresponding *edge sets can differ* from each other. Thus, in our model, we ensure the density of the subgraph for each layer individually. Formally,

DEFINITION 4 (MLCS CLUSTER). *An MLCS cluster $C = (O, S)$ in a multi-layer graph $\mathcal{G} = \{G_i \mid i \in Dim\}$ consists of a vertex set $O \subseteq V$ and a non-empty set of relevant layers $S \subseteq Dim$ such that $\forall i \in Dim : i \in S \Leftrightarrow O$ is an MLCS cluster in the graph layer G_i.*

The density of the cluster $C = (O, S)$ is defined as

$$\gamma_S(O) = \tfrac{1}{|S|} \textstyle\sum_{i \in S} \gamma_{G_i}(O)$$

Since the edge sets per layer may differ, also the cluster's density in each layer may vary. Thus, we define the density of the cluster as the average density over all layers in the subspace. Note that in the case of unlabeled layer graphs, our cluster model resembles the definition of cross-graph quasi-cliques [17] or closed quasi-cliques [21].

In Fig. 1, the vertex set $O = \{b, c, d, e, f\}$ forms an MLCS cluster for $w = 1$ in the layers 1 and 4. In layer 2, O is not a quasi-clique and in layer 3, the edge labels of $E_3(O)$ are not similar, thus O does not form a cluster in these layers.

3.2 Clustering model

In the previous section we introduced the properties that a vertex set has to fulfill to form an MLCS cluster. As motivated in the introduction, the clusters are allowed to overlap. However, just outputting all valid clusters can lead to a large amount of valid clusters that are possibly very similar to each other and thus contain redundant information. An example (for simplicity without edge labels) is shown in Fig. 2, where the clusters C_2 and C_3 highly overlap in layer 1. Thus, the final clustering result should be a non-redundant set of the "most interesting" clusters. This result set is called the *MLCS clustering*.

As the "interestingness" of a cluster can be highly application dependent, it is defined by a quality function $Q(C)$,

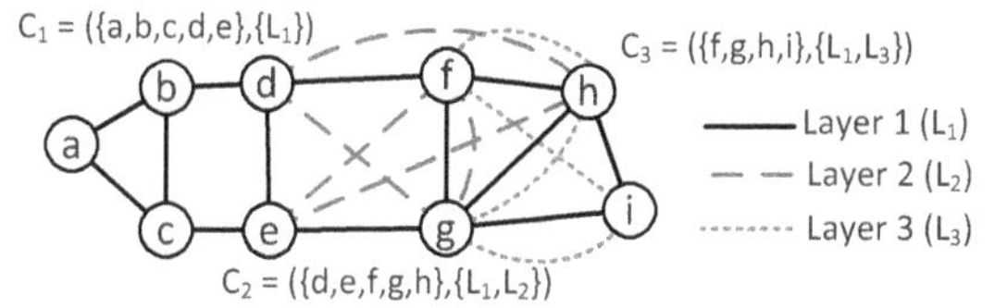

Figure 2: Overlapping clusters with given qualities $Q(C_1) = 2.5$, $Q(C_2) = 5$ and $Q(C_3) = 5.3$

which can be specified by the user. The default quality function that was used in our experiments is introduced in Section 3.3.

For the avoidance of redundancy, we first introduce a redundancy relation. We define a cluster C to be redundant w.r.t. a cluster C' if a significant fraction of C's edges is also covered by C' (thus, they represent similar information) and the quality of C' is not smaller than that of C. Formally,

DEFINITION 5 (REDUNDANCY RELATION). *A cluster $C = (O, S)$ is redundant w.r.t. a cluster $C' = (O', S')$ (short: $C \prec_{red} C'$) if*

$$C \neq C' \wedge Q(C) \leq Q(C') \wedge \frac{1}{|S|} \sum_{i \in S \cap S'} \frac{|E_i(O) \cap E_i(O')|}{|E_i(O)|} \geq r$$

for the redundancy parameter $r \in (0, 1]$.

In our experiments, $r = 0.25$ proved to be a good choice, thus this is used as the default redundancy parameter. In Fig. 2, the cluster C_2 is redundant w.r.t. the cluster C_3. In contrast, C_1 is not redundant w.r.t. C_2. Although it's quality is lower, the edge overlap between the clusters is below the threshold. Please note that two clusters with equal quality might be pairwise redundant w.r.t. each other.

Based on this redundancy relation we now select the maximum-quality clustering *Result* from the set $\mathcal{A}$ of all valid clusters. This clustering should not contain clusters that are redundant w.r.t. each other and at the same time it should maximize the sum of the qualities of the selected clusters:

DEFINITION 6 (MLCS CLUSTERING). *Given a multi-layer graph $\mathcal{G}$ and the set $\mathcal{A}$ of all valid MLCS clusters, the maximum-quality clustering $Result \subseteq \mathcal{A}$ fulfills:*

- *Redundancy-freeness: $\neg \exists C, C' \in Result : C \prec_{red} C'$*
- *Maximum quality sum: $\neg \exists Result' \subseteq \mathcal{A}$: $Result'$ is redundancy-free and $\sum_{C \in Result'} Q(C) > \sum_{C \in Result} Q(C)$.*

In Fig. 2, the clustering solution would be $\{C_1, C_3\}$.

Complexity results. We briefly describe the main result of our complexity analysis:

THEOREM 1. *Given a layer graph $\mathcal{G}$ over the vertices V, determining the MLCS clustering is NP-hard w.r.t. $|V|$.*

PROOF. We prove this theorem by a polynomial reduction of the NP-hard k-clique problem ("Is there a clique with at least k vertices"?) to the determination of an *MLCS* clustering. Given a graph $G = (V, E)$ and an integer k, we can solve the k-clique problem as follows: Take $\mathcal{G} = \{G_1 = (V, E, l_1)\}$ with $l_1(e) = 0 \; \forall e \in E$ as the input of the *MLCS* clustering. As quality function for a cluster $C = (O, S)$ we choose $Q(C) = \begin{cases} |O| & |O| \geq k \wedge \gamma_{G_1}(O) = 1 \\ -1 & else \end{cases}$. Since the MLCS clustering has maximum quality sum it contains only the cliques ($\gamma_{G_1}(O) = 1$) of the graph G with at least k vertices. The answer to the k-clique problem is 'no', if the MLCS clustering is empty, and 'yes', else. This proof can even be extended to show the #P-hardness of MLCS. □

3.3 Instantiation of our model

In this section we introduce a default cluster quality function for MLCS clusters. In most settings, clusters containing many vertices are considered more interesting than smaller ones. Therefore, approaches for mining quasi-cliques mostly aim at finding maximal quasi-cliques w.r.t. the number of vertices. However, just maximizing the number of vertices in a cluster can lead to the detection of low-dimensional clusters with low density. Thus, our quality function realizes a trade-off between the contradicting objective functions size, dimensionality and density. Furthermore, we are not interested in clusters that are too small (here: less than 8 vertices) or that are only one-dimensional. Thus, the quality of a cluster $C = (O, S)$ in our instantiation is defined as

$$Q(C) = \begin{cases} |O| \cdot |S| \cdot \gamma_S(O) & |O| \geq 8 \wedge |S| \geq 2 \\ -1 & else \end{cases}$$

Clusters that are not considered interesting are assigned a quality of -1 and will thus never be included in an MLCS clustering, as they would lower the overall quality sum of the clustering. As distance function for the edge labels we use the Manhattan distance. In all experiments in Section 5, these instantiations are used. Though, our model and the algorithm can easily be used with other instantiations, which might be more applicable for some applications.

4. ALGORITHM

In this section we give an overview of the MiMAG (**Mi**ning **M**ulti-layered, **A**ttributed **G**raphs) algorithm. Due to Theorem 1, we cannot expect to find an efficient algorithm computing an exact MLCS clustering. Thus, MiMAG computes an approximate solution: Instead of determining a redundancy-free clustering with *maximum* quality, we compute a *maximal*, redundancy-free clustering with *high quality*. That is, we determine a clustering to which no further cluster C with $Q(C) > 0$ can be added without violating the redundancy-freeness property.

MiMAG is partly based on the Quick algorithm [12] for finding quasi-cliques. In this algorithm, vertex sets $O \subseteq V$ are enumerated by a depth-first traversal in the *set enumeration tree* [18].[1] Each set visited by the depth-first traversal is tested for the quasi-clique property. An exemplary tree for a graph with three vertices is shown in Fig. 3 (top left). Each node O is associated with a candidate set $cand_O$, which contains all vertices that are ordered behind the vertices in O in a given order $\prec$. A child node O'' extends its parent node O by adding one of the vertices from $cand_O$. Basically, the set enumeration tree contains all possible vertex sets $O \subseteq V$. However, the search space can be reduced: If O's candidate set contains a vertex v that can never be part of a quasi-clique $O' \supset O$, we can delete v from the candidate set. For example, in Fig. 3 (top left) if the vertex v_2 is deleted from the candidate set of O, the subtree rooted at

[1]To avoid confusion, we use the term "vertex" for a vertex in the original graph and the term "node" for the nodes of the set enumeration tree, which represent *sets* of vertices.

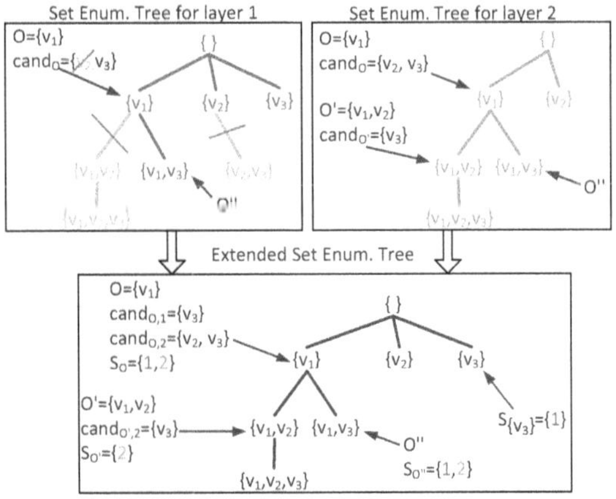

Figure 3: Synchronizing set enumeration trees

$\{v_1, v_2\}$ is pruned from the tree. Techniques how to detect such vertices were introduced in [12].

Synchronized Tree Traversal. A naive approach to determine the MLCS clustering would be: (1) use the quick algorithm on each of the graph layers individually to find all one-dimensional MLCS clusters[2], (2) compose the resulting patterns to multidimensional clusters, and (3) remove redundant clusters. This naive, *sequential* approach, however, is not suitable for the detection of the MLCS clustering: too many (intermediate) patterns are generated which anyway would not be included in the final result due to their redundancy. Thus, we interweave all steps.

We first combine the steps (1)+(2) by proposing a "synchronized traversal" of *all* set enumeration trees *simultaneously*, i.e. all instances of the tree perform the *same* order of traversal. Trees in which a node O was pruned temporarily pause their traversal. Another view on this synchronized traversal is that we use an *extended set enumeration tree* (cf. Fig. 3, bottom). In this tree, each node O has a set of *active dimensions* S_O (which represent the set of dimensions in which the node O has not been pruned from the set enum. tree) and candidate sets $cand_{O,i}$ for each dimension $i \in S_O$. For each set O we visit during the traversal, we check if O forms an MLCS cluster in a subset of its active dimensions. Please do not confuse the active dimensions S_O of a node O and the subspace S of the potential cluster $C = (O, S)$; it holds $S \subseteq S_O$ but the sets are not necessarily equal. We show in Sec. 4.1/4.2 how the set of active dimensions can be used to prune the tree.

Informed Best-First Traversal. We now combine the steps (1)-(3): Instead of first generating all clusters, we let the final (redundancy-free) clustering grow incrementally. Since we want to maximize the quality of the overall clustering, we aim at generating the clusters in decreasing order of their quality and adding the non-redundant clusters with highest quality to the result first. In this case, it is crucial to use a good traversal strategy for the extended set enum. tree.[3] Therefore, we propose an informed best-first traversal: For each node O, we compute a quality estimation that provides an *upper bound* for the maximal quality of any cluster that can be found in the subtree rooted at O. We start the traversal at the root node and in each search step we expand the node O having the highest estimated quality (i.e. MiMAG descends one step into the subtree rooted at O).

[2]Please note that for each layer we get a different set enum. tree (cf. Fig. 3, top) as different subtrees might be pruned.

[3]If one is interested in generating *all* patterns, an arbitrary traversal strategy can be used. We, however, want to determine only a *subset* of the patterns (the non-redundant, high quality ones).

Algorithm 1 MiMAG: Best-first search for MLCS clusters

Require: ML-Graph $\mathcal{G} = \{G_i \mid i \in Dim\}$ with $G_i = (V, E_i, l_i)$
Ensure: Redundancy-free, maximal clustering *Result*
1: $Result := \emptyset$
2: $queue := \{(\emptyset, Dim, \{cand_{\emptyset,i} = V \mid i \in Dim\})\}$
3: **while** $queue \neq \emptyset$ **do**
4: $\quad Obj := queue.\text{pop}()$
5: $\quad$ **if** Obj is cluster $C = (O, S)$ **then**
6: $\quad\quad$ **if** $\neg\exists C' \in Result : C \prec_{red} C'$ **then** $Result.\text{add}(C)$
7: $\quad$ **else** $\quad \triangleright$ Obj is $ST = (O, S_O, \{cand_{O,i} \mid i \in S_O\})$
8: $\quad\quad neighbors := \bigcup_{i \in S_O} \{v \in cand_{O,i} \mid \exists x \in O : (x, v) \in E_i\}$
9: $\quad\quad u := \arg\max_{v \in neighbors} \{\sum_{i \in S_O} deg^O_{G_i}(v)\}$
10: $\quad\quad$ EXPAND$(O, u, S_O, \{cand_{O,i} \mid i \in S_O\})$
11: **return** Result
12: **procedure** EXPAND$(O, u, S_O, \{cand_{O,i} \mid i \in S_O\})$
13: $\quad O_{next} := O \cup \{u\}$, $S_{O_{next}} := \{i \in S_O \mid u \in cand_{O,i}\}$
14: $\quad$ **for all** $i \in S_{O_{next}}$ **do** $cand_{O_{next},i} := cand_{O,i} \setminus \{u\}$
15: $\quad$ Prune $S_{O_{next}}$ and $cand_{O_{next},i}$ $(\forall i \in S_{O_{next}})$
16: $\quad ST_{next} = (O_{next}, S_{O_{next}}, \{cand_{O_{next},i} \mid i \in S_{O_{next}}\})$
17: $\quad$ **if** $Q_{est}(ST_{next}) \geq 0$ **then** $queue.\text{insert}(ST_{next})$
18: $\quad$ **for all** $i \in S_O$ **do** $cand_{O,i} := cand_{O,i} \setminus \{u\}$
19: $\quad$ Prune S_O and $cand_{O,i}$ $(\forall i \in S_O)$
20: $\quad ST_{remain} = (O, S_O, \{cand_{O,i} \mid i \in S_O\})$
21: $\quad$ **if** $Q_{est}(ST_{remain}) \geq 0$ **then** $queue.\text{insert}(ST_{remain})$
22: $\quad$ **if** $\exists$ cluster $C = (O_{next}, S)$, $S \subseteq S_{O_{next}}$ **then**
23: $\quad\quad$ **if** $\neg\exists C' \in Result : C \prec_{red} C'$ **then** $queue.\text{insert}(C)$

One important aspect has to be considered: Even if a cluster C is found at the currently expanded node, it can not be added to the result directly. Since the quality estimation *upper bounds* the quality of the *subtree*, C itself might have a lower quality. Thus, there might exist other subtrees (and potential clusters) with higher (estimated) qualities. Therefore, MiMAG maintains a priority queue which contains the set of subtrees that are still to process (similar to the list *OPEN* in best-first search) as well as the set of already detected clusters that could not be added to the result so far. This queue is sorted by the (estimated) quality values of the subtrees and clusters. If the first element of the queue is a cluster, no better clusters exist; in this case (and if the cluster is non-redundant to previously selected clusters), we can finally add it to the result set.

In the queue, a subtree (short: ST) is represented by a 3-tuple $ST = (O, S_O, \{cand_{O,i} \mid i \in S_O\})$ where O is the vertex set in the root node of ST, S_O is the set of active dimensions for O and $cand_{O,i}$ are the candidate sets. $Q_{est}(ST)$ denotes the upper bound for the quality of clusters of this subtree. We discuss these upper bounds in Sec. 4.1.

Overall Processing Scheme. The processing of MiMAG is shown in Algorithm 1. Given the input multi-layer graph $\mathcal{G}$, MiMAG computes a redundancy-free, maximal clustering *Result*. Initially, the set *Result* is empty (line 1); it will be iteratively filled during the processing. At the beginning, the queue contains one element which represents the root node of the extended set enum. tree (line 2). As long as the queue contains elements, the object with the highest (estimated) quality is taken from the queue. If the object is a cluster, no cluster with higher quality can be found anymore, thus we add it to the result set if it is not redundant w.r.t. an

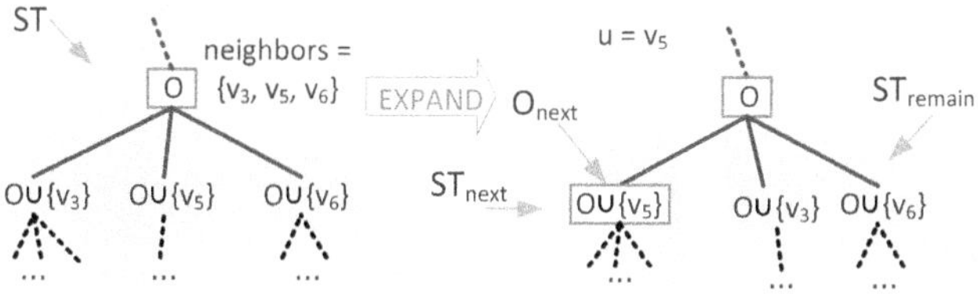

Figure 4: Expansion of a node O

already selected cluster (line 6). If the object is a subtree, we expand the represented set O by one neighboring vertex u that is contained in the candidate sets; we use the vertex having the highest degree w.r.t. O since it most probably leads to dense subgraphs.

The node expansion is illustrated in Fig. 4, where $u = v_5$. MiMAG calls the $EXPAND$ procedure for the subtree rooted at O. In this procedure, at first the sets O_{next}, $S_{O_{next}}$ and the candidate sets $cand_{O_{next},i}$ are determined. $S_{O_{next}}$ can only contain dimensions i for which vertex u was contained in the candidate set $cand_{O,i}$ (line 13). The candidate sets are reduced using pruning techniques (cf. Section 4.2). These sets represent the new subtree ST_{next} rooted at O_{next}, and it is added to the queue if the estimated quality is non-negative (lines 16,17). Similar steps are done for the remaining subtree ST_{remain} rooted at O (lines 20,21), which contains the sets $O' \supset O$ with $u \notin O'$ (cf. Fig. 4). Note that we get a new quality estimate, since u is removed from the candidate sets $cand_{O,i}$. Finally, if O_{next} is a valid (non-redundant) cluster it is also added to the queue.

4.1 Quality Bounds for Subtrees

In the following, we present upper bounds for the quality of subtrees (all proofs are available on our website[4]). Even by allowing arbitrary quality functions, we can derive some generally applicable bounds. First, we exploit the fact that in some cases the subtree does not contain any interesting cluster at all; the quality can be upper bounded by -1.

The first case uses the active dimensions: If no active dimensions are left in the node O, we know that there cannot exist any valid cluster in the subtree rooted at O. This result holds since a cluster's subspace is a subset of the active dimensions and the active dimensions fulfill the anti-monotonicity property[5]: If a dimension i is not active for the set O, then there cannot exist a superset $O' \supset O$ such that i is active for O'.

In the second case, we exploit our redundancy model to determine the bound: If all clusters C contained in subtree ST (i.e. clusters $C = (X, S_X)$ with $S_X \subseteq S_O$ and $O \subset X \subseteq O \cup \bigcup_{i \in S_O} cand_{O,i}$) would be redundant w.r.t. a cluster $C' \in Result$ we cannot add them to the final clustering. Thus, even if their quality is larger than 0, we can safely estimate the subtree's quality with -1. To check the redundancy w.r.t. a cluster $C' = (O', S') \in Result$, we have to check the properties from Def. 5. The properties $C \neq C'$ and $Q(C) \leq Q(C')$ are trivially fulfilled for every possible C due to the ordering of the queue; just the edge overlap property ($\frac{1}{|S_X|} \sum_{i \in S_X \cap S'} \frac{|E_i(X) \cap E_i(O')|}{|E_i(X)|} \geq r$) has to be checked. Therefore, we determine a lower bound ovl_{min} for the edge overlap such that $ovl_{min} \leq \frac{1}{|S_X|} \sum_{i \in S_X \cap S'} \frac{|E_i(X) \cap E_i(O')|}{|E_i(X)|}$ for all possible clusters C from the subtree . Then, if $ovl_{min} \geq r$ we get $Q_{est}(ST) = -1$. For every subtree ST and every cluster $C' = (O', S') \in Result$ with $S' \supseteq S_O$ we get:

$$ovl_{min} = \min_{i \in S_O} \frac{|E_i(O \cap O')| + \max\{\frac{1}{4} \cdot (|O|^2 + |O|) - |E_i(O \cap O')| - k, 0\}}{|E_i(O \cap O')| + k + \max\{\frac{1}{4} \cdot (|O|^2 + |O|) - |E_i(O \cap O')| - k, 0\}}$$
$$\text{with } k = |E_i(O \cup cand_{O,i}) \setminus E_i((O \cup cand_{O,i}) \cap O')|$$

For example, in the case $O' \supseteq O \cup \bigcup_{i \in S_O} cand_{O,i}$ we get $ovl_{min} = 1$ and thus $Q_{est}(ST) = -1$.

Upper bounding cluster properties. Useful properties to incorporate in quality functions are the density and cardinality of clusters. Thus, we develop upper bounds for these cluster properties that can be used for specific instantiations of the quality function. Given a subtree $ST = (O, S_O, \{cand_{O,i} \mid i \in S_O\})$, for each one-dimensional MLCS cluster X in dimension $i \in S_O$ with $O \subset X \subseteq O \cup cand_{O,i}$ the following bounds apply:

- $\gamma(X) \leq \min\{\frac{min\_deg_i}{|O|}, 1\} =: \gamma_i^{max}$ with $min\_deg_{G_i} = \min_{v \in O}\{deg^{O \cup cand_{O,i}}(v)\}$
- $|X| \leq \min(\left\lfloor \frac{min\_deg_i}{0.5} \right\rfloor + 1, |O \cup cand_{O,i}|) =: n_i^{max}$
- $|E_i(X)| \leq |E_i(O)| + (n_i^{max} - |O|) \cdot \max_{v \in cand_O} \{deg_{G_i}^{O \cup cand_{O,i}}(v)\}$

Furthermore, we have for each multi-dimensional MLCS cluster (X, S_X): $|S_X| \leq |S_O|$ due to the anti-monotonicity of the active dimensions.

Specific instantiation. We can use the above bounds for our default instantiation of the quality function: the quality of the subtree ST is upper bounded by

$$Q_{est}(ST) = \max_{k \in \{1,\dots,|S_O|\}} \{max_k(n_i^{max}) \cdot \sum_{m=1}^{k} max_m(\gamma_i^{max})\}$$

where $max_x(y_i)$ denotes the x-th highest value of all $\{y_i \mid i \in S_O\}$. Furthermore, if we have $\max_{i \in S_O}(n_i^{max}) < 8$ or $|S_O| < 2$, the subtree can not contain any cluster with positive quality; in this case, the estimation is $Q_{est}(ST) = -1$.

4.2 Pruning Techniques

MiMAG exploits the introduced quality bounds twofold: first, to realize the best-first traversal using a priority queue; and second, to prune the search space if the estimate is negative (lines 17, 21). To further enhance the efficiency, MiMAG exploits pruning techniques for the set of active dimensions and the candidate sets (lines 15, 19).

One example is the *pruning by edge similarity*: Due to Def. 3, a one-dim. MLCS cluster (O, S) must only contain edges with similar labels. Thus, if the set $E_i(O)$ contains *any* two edges with label distance greater than w, O (and also all supersets $O' \supset O$) cannot be a valid cluster. We use this property to prune the candidate sets $cand_{O,i}$ as follows: If for a vertex $v \in cand_{O,i}$ it holds that $E' = E_i(O) \cup \{(v, o) \in E_i \mid o \in O\}$ does not fulfill the similarity property, we can remove v from $cand_{O,i}$ as no set $O' \supseteq O \cup \{v\}$ could form an MLCS cluster in dimension i.

Deleting a vertex from a candidate set can change properties (e.g. the degree) of other vertices from the set, thus we prune the sets iteratively until no more vertices can be deleted. If after the pruning we have $cand_{O,i} = \emptyset$ for a dimension i, i becomes inactive and can thus be removed from

[4]http://dme.rwth-aachen.de/mlcs

[5]Note: This property does not hold for the cluster model itself (neither for the set of vertices nor for the relevant dimensions).

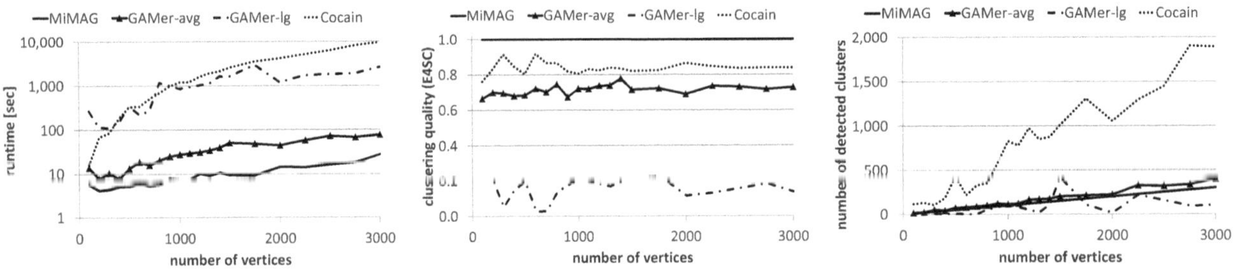

(a) Runtime vs. graph size (b) Clustering quality vs. graph size (c) #Detected clusters vs. graph size

Figure 5: Experimental evaluation on synthetic datasets (1)

S_O. More pruning techniques are left out here due to space limitations. Besides the pruning techniques developed especially for the MLCS model, MiMAG also uses the pruning techniques from the Quick algorithm [12].

5. EXPERIMENTAL EVALUATION

We evaluate the clustering quality and runtime of MiMAG experimentally on synthetic and real-world datasets. All experiments were conducted on Opteron 2.3 GHz CPU's using Java6 64bit. For the synthetic data, the clustering quality is determined by comparing the clustering results to the ground truth using the E4SC measure, which was developed for the evaluation of subspace clustering results [5]. For the real-world datasets, there is no ground truth available, which hinders an evaluation of the clustering quality. Thus, for those datasets we provide some key characteristics of the clustering results as well as exemplary clusters to illustrate the results of MiMAG. If not specified otherwise, the redundancy parameter r is set to $r = 0.25$ for all experiments.

Baseline approaches. We compare MiMAG with 3 baseline approaches: The closed quasi-clique mining algorithm Cocain [21] (cf. Section 2) is used on our input graph by considering each of the graph layers as a graph in a graph database. To best match our cluster model, the minimum support parameter of Cocain is set to $min\_sup = \frac{1}{|Dim|}$ and the minimum quasi-clique density to $\gamma_{min} = 0.5$.

Furthermore, we present two different ideas to adapt the GAMer algorithm [7], developed for clustering graphs with vertex labels, to our problem. Both ideas transform the multi-layer graph covering Dim layers to a graph with Dim-dimensional attribute vectors at the vertices. The resulting graph can then be clustered by GAMer. In the first idea (GAMer-avg), the transformed graph is obtained as follows: the vertices of the original graph are kept; the edges are determined by the union of the edge sets from all graph layers (i.e. $E = \bigcup E_i$; the edge labels are deleted). The i-th entry of a vertex v's attribute vector is the average label value of v's incident edges from layer i. In the second idea (GAMer-lg) we use the well-known concept of the *line graph* [8]. Each vertex of a line graph represents an edge of the original graph and vice versa. In our case, a line graph vertex $v^{lg} = (v_1, v_2)$ represents *all* the edges (v_1, v_2) from the different layers. The i-th entry of v^{lg}'s attribute vector corresponds to the label value $l_i(v_1, v_2)$, if $(v_1, v_2) \in E_i$ and $\perp$, else (where $\perp$ is considered not similar to any value).

5.1 Evaluation on synthetic graphs

For the evaluation of MiMAG, we generated various synthetic multi-layer graphs with edge labels containing overlapping MLCS clusters as well as "noise" vertices and "noise" edges that do not belong to any cluster. The generated edge labels lie in the range $[0, 1]$. In our experiments, the parameter w for MiMAG (and also the corresponding parameter for GAMer) is set to $w = 0.1$.

Results for varying graph sizes. First, we analyze the behavior of the approaches for varying graph sizes. The generated graphs consist of 10 layers, the number of generated ("hidden") clusters increases linearly from 10 to 300. Each cluster contains 10 vertices and 3 relevant layers, with quasi-clique densities of 0.6. 10% of the vertices in the graph are noise vertices and in each layer we have 60 noise edges.

Although the runtimes of all approaches (cf. Fig. 5(a)) increase with increasing graph sizes, MiMAG constantly shows the lowest runtimes. Considering the clustering quality (cf. Fig. 5(b)), MiMAG reaches perfect or nearly perfect E4SC values on all datasets. The number of detected clusters (Fig. 5(c)) matches the number of hidden clusters. Cocain also achieves quite good quality values (ca. 0.8 to 0.9), as the closed quasi-clique model is closely related to our MLCS model. However, Cocain outputs a huge amount of quasi-cliques (e.g. nearly 2000 instead of the hidden 300 clusters) because it does not avoid redundancy in the result. This also explains the high runtimes of Cocain. For GAMer-avg, the number of detected clusters approximately matches the number of hidden clusters. However, the clustering quality is significantly lower as MiMAG's as the averaged label values distort the cluster structure. For GAMer-lg the number of found clusters varies very much and the clustering quality is low. This is caused by an important problem with the line graph approach: from the density of a subgraph in the line graph, it is not possible to draw conclusions about the density of the corresponding original subgraph, which hinders the detection of dense subgraphs in the original graph.

Results for varying dimensionality. Next, we analyze the behavior of the different approaches for varying dimensionalities (i.e. varying numbers of graph layers) of the input graph. The number of graph layers varies between 5 and 50. The generated multi-layer graphs each contain 30 clusters, each having 10 vertices and 3 relevant layers, with quasi-clique densities of 0.6. Again, we have 10% noise vertices and 60 noise edges per layer.

Comparing the runtimes and clustering qualities of the approaches (Fig. 6(a) and Fig. 6(b)), we observe that MiMAG again achieves the lowest runtime and highest quality. For most approaches, the runtime and the clustering quality remain relatively stable for increasing dimensionality. Just for GAMer-avg the runtime significantly increases, while the E4SC values dramatically drop. This is caused by the graph

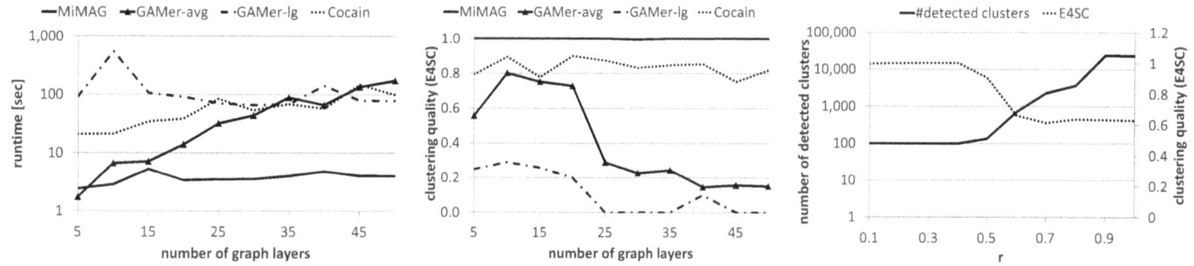

(a) Runtime vs. dimensionality (b) Clustering quality vs. dim. (c) #Detected clusters vs. parameter r

Figure 6: Experimental evaluation on synthetic datasets (2)

transformation: As the edges of the transformed graph are the union of the edge sets from all graph layers, by combining an increasing number of graph layers the transformed graph gets very dense, such for high dimensionalities GAMer-avg detects many clusters that do not exist in the original graph.

Results for varying redundancy parameter. In Fig. 6(c), we analyze how the redundancy parameter r of our clustering model affects the results of MiMAG, using a graph with 10 layers and 100 hidden clusters; the cluster size varies between 10 and 15. We observe that for $r < 0.5$, the correct number of clusters is found with a high clustering quality. For $r \geq 0.5$, the number of found clusters increases dramatically and the clustering quality drops. For high values for r, less clusters are considered redundant w.r.t. other clusters, which leads to a clustering that contains many low-quality clusters that would be considered redundant for lower r values. Thus, we propose using $r = 0.25$ as a reasonable default setting for r.

5.2 Evaluation on real-world data

Besides synthetic graphs, we also evaluate our approach on three real-world datasets: The first one is a multi-layer graph with edge labels extracted from the IMDB movie Database[6]. In this graph, the vertices represent actors; the labeled edges represent information about movies in which the actors worked together. The four layers of the graph are: 1. "First year of collaboration", 2. "Last year of collaboration", 3. "Rental fees" (the average earnings of all joint movies between two actors), 4. "Sold tickets" (the average number of sold tickets of all joint movies between two actors). All label values were normalized to the range $[0, 1]$, and we used $w = 0.03$ for this experiment. In this special case, the same edge sets exist in all layers; though, the edge labels differ. Overall, the IMDB graph contains 300 vertices (the most prolific actors) and 18368 edges. An exemplary cluster from MiMAG's clustering result is shown in Fig. 7. Please note that the cluster does not form a clique (its quasi-clique density is 0.625), thus not all actors worked together in the same movie. Actually, all actors connected by an edge worked together (among other movies) in the movie "Con Air" or "The Rock" (or both).

[6]http://imdb.com

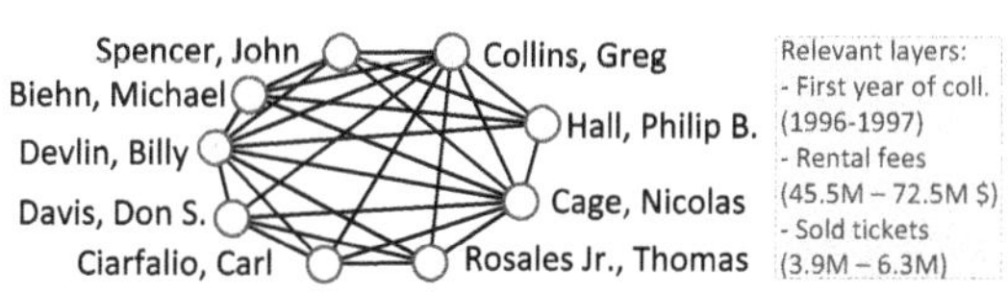

Figure 7: Exemplary cluster from IMDB

In our next experiment, we evaluate the potential of our approach to handle also multi-layer graphs without edge labels. The second dataset was constructed from an extract of the Arxiv publication database[7]. Here, each vertex represents a publication. From the abstracts of the publications, we extracted the 300 most common keywords. Each layer of the graph represents a certain keyword, and an edge of layer i represents a citation between two publications with the common topic i. Overall, the Arxiv graph contains 13396 vertices and 673800 edges. For example, the largest cluster found by MiMAG consists of 19 papers from the field of string theory. The 7 relevant layers of this cluster correspond to the keywords given in Fig 8:

symmetry	model	supersymmetric	intersect
brane	super	metric	

Figure 8: Keywords for a cluster from Arxiv

Our third real-world dataset is a co-author graph extracted from the DBLP database[8]. In this graph, the vertices represent authors and the layers represent the 50 conferences in computer science having the most publications. Two authors are connected by an edge in layer i if they co-authored at least two papers that were published at the corresponding conference. Overall, the DBLP graph contains 17291 vertices and 22896 edges. As we expect co-author groups to be rather small, for this experiment we adapted our quality function to consider clusters with at least 4 vertices as interesting. Fig. 7 shows three exemplary clusters detected by MiMAG and their corresponding conferences. Please note that each of the clusters has different relevant layers. While two of the clusters form cliques in both of their layers, in the top right cluster the edge sets of the layers differ.

Clustering results on real-world datasets. In Table 1, we summarize key characteristics of the clustering results of the different approaches on the real-world datasets. Experiments that did not finish within 2 days were aborted. For each approach and dataset we provide the runtime as well as the average number of vertices, density and number of layers of the found clusters. Note that for the adaptions of GAMer, the density and subspace are determined on the corresponding *transformed* graphs (whose densities are generally higher than in the original graph); the clusters do *not* correspond to MLCS clusters in the *original* multi-layer graphs.

[7]http://www.cs.cornell.edu/projects/kddcup/datasets.html
[8]http://dblp.uni-trier.de

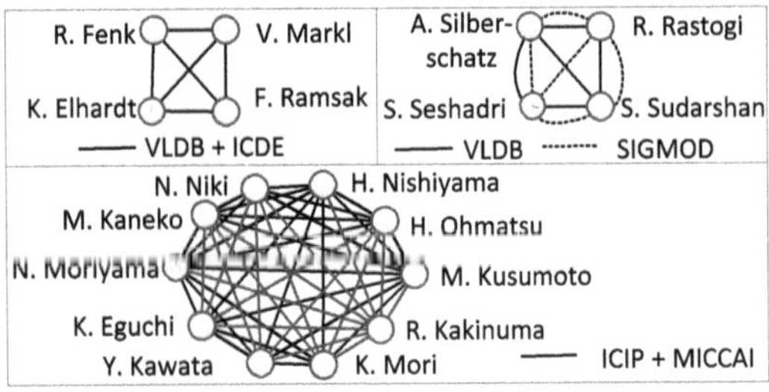

Figure 9: Exemplary clusters from DBLP

Cocain did not finish on any of the datasets within 2 days; GAMer-lg finished only on the DBLP graph, however with a much higher runtime than the other approaches due to the size of the constructed line graph. MiMAG and GAMer-avg have similar runtimes for all datasets. On the IMDB graph, MiMAG detects clusters with a significantly higher average density and dimensionality than GAMer-avg. On Arxiv, the density of GAMer-avg's clusters is slightly higher, which is caused by the fact that GAMer-avg unions the edge sets from all 300 layers and thus obtains a very dense graph. On DBLP, the clusters detected by MiMAG again show the highest average density, while having similar average size and dimensionality to the other approaches.

	IMDB		Arxiv		DBLP		
	MiMAG	*G.-avg*	*MiMAG*	*G.-avg*	*MiMAG*	*G.-avg*	*G.-lg*
runtime [sec]	22	26	623	661	6	9	2390
$avg(\|O\|)$	9.42	9.17	13.6	15.0	4.28	4.48	6.29
$avg(\gamma_S)$	0.94	0.64*	0.62	0.65*	0.87	0.40*	0.81*
$avg(\|S\|)$	2.58	2.00	9.00	9.00	2.05	2.17	2.01

Table 1: Key characteristics of the clustering results (* density in the transformed graph)

6. CONCLUSION

We proposed the new paradigm of clustering multi-layer graphs with edge labels. Besides the mere graph data, additional information about the edges is considered for finding coherent subgraphs. We introduced the clustering model MLCS, which defines clusters of vertices that are *densely connected* by edges with *similar edge labels* in a *subset* of the graph layers. Redundancy in the result set is avoided by selecting only the most interesting clusters. Based on this model, we introduced the efficient best-first search algorithm MiMAG. The performance and clustering quality of MiMAG were demonstrated in our experimental analysis.

Acknowledgments. This work has been supported by the B-IT Research School of the Bonn-Aachen International Center for Information Technology and the UMIC Research Centre, RWTH Aachen University, Germany.

7. REFERENCES

[1] C. Aggarwal and H. Wang. *Managing and Mining Graph Data.* Springer, New York, 2010.

[2] K. S. Beyer, J. Goldstein, R. Ramakrishnan, and U. Shaft. When is "nearest neighbor" meaningful? In *ICDT*, pages 217–235, 1999.

[3] L. Cerf, T. B. N. Nguyen, and J.-F. Boulicaut. Discovering relevant cross-graph cliques in dynamic networks. In *ISMIS*, pages 513–522, 2009.

[4] S. Fortunato. Community detection in graphs. *Physics Reports*, 486(3-5):75–174, 2010.

[5] S. Günnemann, I. Färber, E. Müller, I. Assent, and T. Seidl. External evaluation measures for subspace clustering. In *CIKM*, pages 1363–1372, 2011.

[6] S. Günnemann, B. Boden, and T. Seidl. DB-CSC: A density-based approach for subspace clustering in graphs with feature vectors. In *ECML/PKDD (1)*, pages 565–580, 2011.

[7] S. Günnemann, I. Färber, B. Boden, and T. Seidl. Subspace clustering meets dense subgraph mining: A synthesis of two paradigms. In *ICDM*, pages 845–850, 2010.

[8] F. Harary and R. Norman. Some properties of line digraphs. *Rendiconti del Circolo Matematico di Palermo*, 9(2):161–168, 1960.

[9] P. Hart, N. Nilsson, and B. Raphael. A formal basis for the heuristic determination of minimum cost paths. *Systems Science and Cybernetics*, 4(2):100 –107, 1968.

[10] H.-P. Kriegel, P. Kröger, and A. Zimek. Clustering high-dimensional data: A survey on subspace clustering, pattern-based clustering, and correlation clustering. *TKDD*, 3(1):1–58, 2009.

[11] M. Li, Y. Fan, J. Chen, L. Gao, Z. Di, and J. Wu. Weighted networks of scientific communication: the measurement and topological role of weight. *Physica A: Statistical Mechanics and its Applications*, 350(2):643–656, 2005.

[12] G. Liu and L. Wong. Effective pruning techniques for mining quasi-cliques. In *ECML/PKDD (2)*, pages 33–49, 2008.

[13] E. Müller, I. Assent, S. Günnemann, R. Krieger, and T. Seidl. Relevant subspace clustering: Mining the most interesting non-redundant concepts in high dimensional data. In *ICDM*, pages 377–386, 2009.

[14] F. Moser, R. Colak, A. Rafiey, and M. Ester. Mining cohesive patterns from graphs with feature vectors. In *SDM*, pages 593–604, 2009.

[15] E. Müller, S. Günnemann, I. Assent, and T. Seidl. Evaluating clustering in subspace projections of high dimensional data. In *VLDB*, pages 1270–1281, 2009.

[16] J. Pearl. *Heuristics: Intelligent Search Strategies for Computer Problem Solving.* Addison Wesley, 1984.

[17] J. Pei, D. Jiang, and A. Zhang. On mining cross-graph quasi-cliques. In *SIGKDD*, pages 228–238, 2005.

[18] R. Rymon. Search through systematic set enumeration. In *KR*, pages 539–550, 1992.

[19] M. Shiga, I. Takigawa, and H. Mamitsuka. A spectral clustering approach to optimally combining numerical vectors with a modular network. In *SIGKDD*, pages 647–656, 2007.

[20] J. Wang, Z. Zeng, and L. Zhou. Clan: An algorithm for mining closed cliques from large dense graph databases. In *ICDE*, page 73, 2006.

[21] Z. Zeng, J. Wang, L. Zhou, and G. Karypis. Coherent closed quasi-clique discovery from large dense graph databases. In *SIGKDD*, pages 797–802, 2006.

Circle-based Recommendation in Online Social Networks

Xiwang Yang
ECE Department
Polytechnic Institute of NYU
Brooklyn, New York
xyang01@students.poly.edu

Harald Steck*
Bell Labs
Alcatel-Lucent
Murray Hill, New Jersey
hsteck@gmail.com

Yong Liu
ECE Department
Polytechnic Institute of NYU
Brooklyn, New York
yongliu@poly.edu

ABSTRACT

Online social network information promises to increase recommendation accuracy beyond the capabilities of purely rating/feedback-driven recommender systems (RS). As to better serve users' activities across different domains, many online social networks now support a new feature of "Friends Circles", which refines the domain-oblivious "Friends" concept. RS should also benefit from domain-specific "Trust Circles". Intuitively, a user may trust different subsets of friends regarding different domains. Unfortunately, in most existing multi-category rating datasets, a user's social connections from all categories are mixed together. This paper presents an effort to develop circle-based RS. We focus on inferring category-specific social trust circles from available rating data combined with social network data. We outline several variants of weighting friends within circles based on their inferred expertise levels. Through experiments on publicly available data, we demonstrate that the proposed circle-based recommendation models can better utilize user's social trust information, resulting in increased recommendation accuracy.

Categories and Subject Descriptors

H.2.8 [**Database Management**]: Database Applications–Data Mining

General Terms

Algorithms

Keywords

collaborative filtering, friends circles, online social networks, recommender systems

1. INTRODUCTION

Recommender Systems (RS) deal with information overload by suggesting to users the items that are potentially of their interests. Traditional collaborative filtering approaches predict users' interests by mining user rating history data [1], [2], [4], [6], [16], [23] and [24]. The increasingly popular online social networks provide additional information to enhance pure rating-based RSes. Several social-trust based RSes have recently been proposed to improve recommendation accuracy, to just name a few, [9], [10], [11], [12], [13], [15], [17], [18], and [19]. The common rationale behind all of them is that a user's taste is *similar to* and/or *influenced by* her trusted friends in social networks. Meanwhile, another obvious fact is that users' social life, being online or offline, is intrinsically *multifaceted*. To better serve a user's activities across different domains, many online social networks now support a new feature of "Friends Circles", which refines the *domain-oblivious* "Friends" concept. Google+ is the first to introduce "Circles", the function that let users assign classmates, family members, colleagues and others to different groups. Facebook, which has long had Friend lists, also launched its "Groups" feature to assign users to groups for finer granular information sharing: a user can share different information with different groups. In Twitter, users can organize people who they follow (followees) into "lists". When a user clicks to view a list, she will see a stream of Tweets from all her followees in that list.

RSes should also benefit from domain-specific "Trust Circles". Intuitively, a user trusts different subsets of friends in different domains. For example, in the context of multi-category recommendation, a user u may trust user v in Cars category while not trust v in Kids' TV Show category. Therefore, u should care less about v's ratings in Kids' TV Show category than in Cars category. Ideally, if we know users' trust circles in different categories, to predict ratings in one category, we probably should only use trust circles specific to that category. We call it *circle-based recommendation*. Unfortunately, in most existing multi-category rating datasets, a user's social connections from all categories are mixed together. So if we use all social trust information for rating prediction in a specific category, we misuse social trust information from other categories, which compromises the rating prediction accuracy. Apart from that, even if the circles were explicitly known, e.g. Circles in Google+ or Facebook, they may not correspond to particular item categories that a recommender system may be concerned with. Therefore, *inferred* circles concerning each item-category may be of value by themselves, besides the explicitly known circles.

This paper presents an effort to develop circle-based RS. We focus on inferring category-specific social trust circles from available rating data combined with social network data

*Now at Netflix Inc. Work was done while at Bell Labs.

KDD'12, August 12–16, 2012, Beijing, China.

data where social trust links across all categories are mixed together. We propose a set of algorithms to infer category-specific circles of friends and to infer the trust value on each link based on user rating activities in each category. To infer the trust value of a link in a circle, we first estimate a user's *expertise level* in a category based on the rating activities of *herself as well as all users trusting her.* We then assign to users trust values proportional to their expertise levels. The reconstructed trust circles are used to develop a low-rank matrix factorization type of RS. Through experiments on publicly available data, we demonstrate that the proposed circle-based RSes can better utilize user's social trust information and achieve more accurate recommendation than the traditional matrix factorization approaches that do not use any social trust information, and the existing social-trust based RSes that use mixed social trust information across all categories.

The rest of the paper is organized as follows. Section 2 presents the related work. In Section 3, we first introduce the concept of trust circle, then propose three variants of assigning weights to users within each circle. Finally, we present circle-based training models, based on either ratings from one category or ratings from all categories. Experimental results are presented in Section 4. The paper is concluded in Section 5.

2. RELATED WORK

In this paper, we focus on low-rank matrix factorization models, as they were found to be one of the most accurate single models for collaborative filtering [5,7,8,20,21]. In the following, we briefly review the ones relevant to this paper.

2.1 Matrix Factorization (MF)

While there are various sophisticated approaches (e.g. [5, 7, 8, 20, 21]), we here briefly review the basic low-rank matrix factorization (MF) approach, which will be extended towards social network information in the remainder of this paper. The matrix of predicted ratings $\hat{R} \in \mathbb{R}^{u_0 \times i_0}$, where u_0 denotes the number of users, and i_0 the number of items, is modeled as:

$$\hat{R} = r_m + QP^\top, \tag{1}$$

with matrices $P \in \mathbb{R}^{i_0 \times d}$ and $Q \in \mathbb{R}^{u_0 \times d}$, where d is the rank (or dimension of the latent space), with $d \ll i_0, u_0$, and $r_m \in \mathbb{R}$ is a (global) offset value.

This model is trained on the observed rating data by minimizing the square error (with the usual Frobenius/L2-norm regularization) (see also [5, 20]):

$$\frac{1}{2} \sum_{(u,i)\text{obs.}} \left(R_{u,i} - \hat{R}_{u,i}\right)^2 + \frac{\lambda}{2}\left(||P||_F^2 + ||Q||_F^2\right), \tag{2}$$

where $\hat{R}_{u,i}$ denotes the ratings predicted by the model in Eq. (1); and $R_{u,i}$ are the actual rating values in the training data for item i from user u. This objective function can be minimized efficiently using gradient descent method [13].

Once the low-rank matrices P and Q have been learned, rating values can be predicted according to Eq. (1) for any user-item pair (u, i).

2.2 MF and Social Networks

The usage of social network data has been found to improve the prediction accuracy of rating values, and various models for integrating these two data sources have been proposed, like Social Recommendation (SoRec) [11], Social Trust Ensemble (STE) [9], Recommender Systems with Social Regularization [12], Adaptive social similarities for recommender systems [14], among which the SocialMF model [13] was found to achieve a particularly low RMSE value, and is hence used as a baseline model in our experimental comparison study.

2.2.1 *SocialMF Model*

The SocialMF model was proposed in [13], and was found to outperform SoRec and STE with respect to RMSE. The social network information is represented by a matrix $S \in \mathbb{R}^{u_0 \times u_0}$, where u_0 is the number of users. The directed and weighted social relationship of user u with user v (e.g. user u trusts/knows/follows user v) is represented by a positive value $S_{u,v} \in (0, 1]$. An absent or unobserved social relationship is reflected by $S_{u,v} = s_m$, where typically $s_m = 0$. Each of the rows of the social network matrix S is normalized to 1, resulting in the new matrix S^* with $S^*_{u,v} \propto S_{u,v}$, and $\sum_v S^*_{u,v} = 1$ for each user u.

The idea underlying SocialMF is that neighbors in the social network may have similar interests. This similarity is enforced by the second term in the objective function in equation (3), which says that user profile Q_u should be similar to the (weighted) average of his/her friends' profiles Q_v (measured in terms of the square error):

$$\begin{aligned} &\frac{1}{2} \sum_{(u,i)obs.} \left(R_{u,i} - \hat{R}_{u,i}\right)^2 \\ + &\frac{\beta}{2} \sum_{\text{all } u} \left((Q_u - \sum_v S^*_{u,v} Q_v)(Q_u - \sum_v S^*_{u,v} Q_v)^\top \right) \\ + &\frac{\lambda}{2}\left(||P||_F^2 + ||Q||_F^2\right), \end{aligned} \tag{3}$$

where the ratings $\hat{R}_{u,i}$ predicted by this model are obtained according to Eq. (1). Note that we omitted the logistic function from the original publication [13], as we found its effect rather negligible in our experiments. The trade-off between the feedback data (ratings) and the social network information is determined by a weight $\beta \geq 0$. Obviously, the social network information is ignored if $\beta = 0$, and increasing β shifts the trade-off more and more towards the social network information.

Eq. (3) can be optimized by the gradient descent approach (see the update equations (13) and (14) in [13]).

Once the model is trained, the soft constraint that neighbors should have similar user profiles is captured in the user latent feature matrix Q. The rating value for any user concerning any item can be predicted according to Eq. (1).

3. CIRCLE-BASED RECOMMENDATION MODELS

Our proposed Circle-based Recommendation (CircleCon) models may be viewed as an extension of the SocialMF model [13] to social networks with *inferred circles* of friends.

3.1 Trust Circle Inference

We infer the circles of friends from rating (or other feedback) data concerning items *that can be divided into different categories (or genres etc.).* The basic idea is that a user may trust each friend only concerning certain item categories but not regarding others. For instance, the circle of friends concerning cars may differ significantly from the circle regarding kids' TV shows.

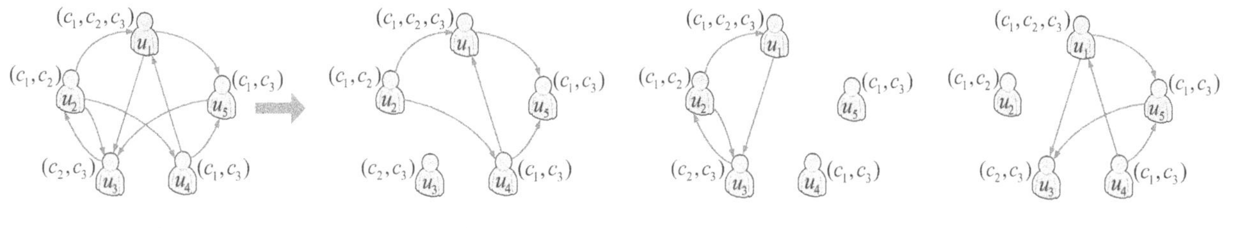

Figure 1: Illustration of inferred circles, each user is labeled with the categories in which she has ratings. a): the original social network; b), c) and d): inferred circles for categories c_1, c_2 and c_3 respectively.

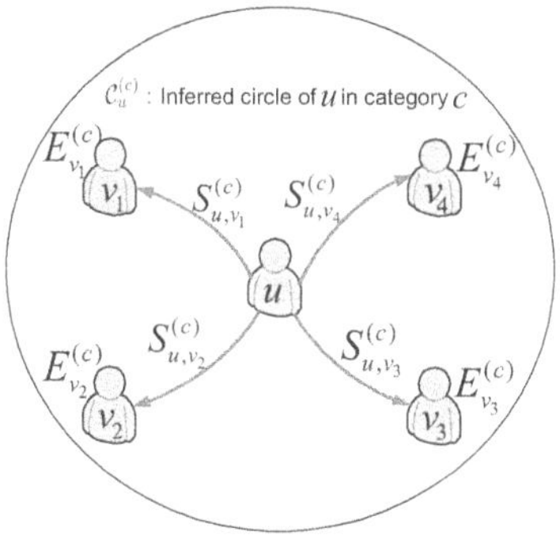

Figure 2: Illustration of expertise-based trust-assignment in category c.

To this end, we divide the social network S of all trust relationships into several sub-networks $S^{(c)}$, each of which concerning a single category c of items.

Definition (Inferred Circle): *Regarding each category* c*, a user* v *is in the* inferred circle *of user* u*, i.e., in the set* $\mathcal{C}_u^{(c)}$*, if and only if the following two conditions hold:*

- $S_{u,v} > 0$ *in the (original) social network, and*
- $N_u^{(c)} > 0$ *and* $N_v^{(c)} > 0$ *in the rating data,*

where $N_u^{(c)}$ *denotes the number of ratings that user* u *has assigned to items in category* c*. Otherwise, user* v *is not in the circle of* u *concerning category* c*, i.e.,* $v \notin \mathcal{C}_u^{(c)}$.

This is illustrated for a toy example in Figure 1.

3.2 Trust Value Assignment

The trust values between friends in the same inferred circle (based on item category c) are captured in a social network matrix $S^{(c)}$, such that $S_{u,v}^{(c)} = 0$ if $v \notin \mathcal{C}_u^{(c)}$, $S_{u,v}^{(c)} > 0$ if $v \in \mathcal{C}_u^{(c)}$. In the following, we consider three variants of defining the positive values $S_{u,v}^{(c)} > 0$ when user v is in the inferred circle of user u regarding category c. They are then experimentally evaluated in Section 4.

3.2.1 CircleCon1: Equal Trust

We start with the simplest variant of defining trust values $S_{u,v}^{(c)} > 0$ within inferred circles regarding item category c: each user v in the inferred circle of user u gets assigned the same trust value, i.e., $S_{u,v}^{(c)*} = \text{const}$ if $v \in \mathcal{C}_u^{(c)}$. The constant is determined by the normalization constraint $\sum_{v\in\mathcal{C}_u^c} S_{u,v}^{(c)*} = 1$. In other words, $S_{u,v}^{(c)*} = 1/|\mathcal{C}_u^{(c)}|, \forall v \in \mathcal{C}_u^{(c)}$.

3.2.2 CircleCon2: Expertise-based Trust

In this section, we outline two variants of assigning *different* trust values to friends within a trust circle. The goal is to assign a higher trust value or weight to the friends that are experts in the circle / category. As an approximation to their level of expertise, we use the numbers of ratings they assigned to items in the category. The idea is that an expert in a category may have rated more items in that category than users who are not experts in that category.

We formalize this as follows. We consider directed trust relationships; undirected/mutual trust relationships (e.g., friendship) can be viewed as a special case of directed trust. If user u trusts user v in category c, we say u follows v in category c, i.e., u is the follower of v, and v is a followee of u. All of user u's followees in category c form the trust circle $\mathcal{C}_u^{(c)}$ of u in c. We also denote u's followers in category c as $\mathcal{F}_u^{(c)}$. Finally, a user u's expertise level in category c is denoted as $E_u^{(c)}$. This is illustrated in Figure 2.

We assign trust values to u's followees in circle $\mathcal{C}_u^{(c)}$to be proportional to their expertise levels in category c. Based on this idea, we consider two variants in the following:

- **Variant a:** In this case, user $v's$ expertise level in category c is equal to the number of ratings that v assigned in category c, i.e., $E_v^{(c)} = N_v^{(c)}$. Thus,

$$S_{u,v}^{(c)} = \begin{cases} N_v^{(c)} & \text{if } v \in \mathcal{C}_u^c \\ 0 & \text{otherwise.} \end{cases}$$

We then normalize each row of $S^{(c)}$ matrix as follows

$$S_{u,v}^{(c)*} = \frac{S_{u,v}^{(c)}}{\sum_{v\in\mathcal{C}_u^{(c)}} S_{u,v}^{(c)}}, \tag{4}$$

which ensures that, for each user u, the weights across all users v in each circle are normalized to unity:

$$\sum_{v\in\mathcal{C}_u^{(c)}} S_{u,v}^{(c)*} = 1.$$

- **Variant b:** In this case, the expertise level of user v in category c is the product of two components: the first component is the number of ratings that v assigned in category c, the second component is some voting value in category c from all her followers in $\mathcal{F}_v^{(c)}$. The intuition is that if most of v's followers have lots of ratings in category c, and they all trust v, it is a good indication that v is an expert in category c.

We denote the voting value from followers of v in category c by $\phi_v^{(c)}$. For each follower $w \in \mathcal{F}_v^{(c)}$, we compute the distribution of her ratings in each individual category. We denote $\mathcal{D}_w$ as a distribution vector over all the categories,

$$\mathcal{D}_w = \left(\frac{N_w(1)}{N_w}, \frac{N_w(2)}{N_w}, ..., \frac{N_w(m)}{N_w}\right), \tag{5}$$

where m is the number of categories, and $N_w(c)$ with $c = 1, ..., m$ is the number of ratings assigned by user w in category c; N_w is the total number of ratings assigned by user w, $N_w = \sum_c N_w(c)$. Thus, $\mathcal{D}_w$ records the proportions of ratings user w assigned in all categories. It reflects the interest distribution of w cross all categories.

The second component, namely the voting value from all followers is defined as $\phi_v^{(c)} = \sum_{w \in \mathcal{F}_v^{(c)}} \mathcal{D}_w(c)$.

Combining both components, we have the following expression for v's expertise level:

$$E_v^{(c)} = N_v^{(c)} \cdot \sum_{w \in \mathcal{F}_v^{(c)}} \mathcal{D}_w(c)$$

which results in the trust values

$$S_{u,v}^{(c)} = \begin{cases} N_v^{(c)} \cdot \sum_{w \in \mathcal{F}_v^{(c)}} \mathcal{D}_w(c) & \text{if } v \in \mathcal{C}_u^{(c)} \\ 0 & \text{otherwise.} \end{cases}$$

As in each of the above cases, also here we finally normalize each row of the $S^{(c)}$ matrix (across v):

$$S_{u,v}^{(c)*} = S_{u,v}^{(c)} / \sum_{v \in \mathcal{C}_u^{(c)}} S_{u,v}^{(c)}.$$

3.2.3 CircleCon3: Trust Splitting

The previous circle inference and trust value assignment essentially assume that if u issues a trust statement towards v, and u and v simultaneously have ratings in a category c, then u trusts v in c. The trust value assignment is done in each circle separately. In practice, user u might issue a trust statement towards v just because of v's ratings in a subset of categories in which they simultaneously have ratings. The trust value of u towards v in category c should reflect the likelihood that u issues the trust statement towards v due to v's ratings in c. One simple heuristic is to make the likelihood proportional to the number of v's ratings in category c. In other words, given that u trusts v, if v has more ratings in category c_1 than in c_2, it is more likely that u trusts v because of v's ratings in c_1 than v's ratings in c_2. Now if u and v simultaneously have ratings in multiple categories, the trust value of u towards v should be *split* cross those commonly rated categories.

Essentially, we now normalize trust values across c,

$$S_{u,v}^{(c)} = \begin{cases} \frac{N_v^{(c)}}{\sum_{c: v \in \mathcal{C}_u^{(c)}} N_v^{(c)}} & \text{if } v \in \mathcal{C}_u^{(c)} \\ 0 & \text{otherwise.} \end{cases}$$

To illustrate this *trust splitting*, let us look at Figure 1: user u_2 trusts user u_1 and both of them have ratings in category c_1 and c_2. Assume the number of ratings u_1 issued in category c_1 and c_2 are 9 and 1 respectively. The trust value in original social network is $S_{u_2,u_1} = 1$. Now after *trust splitting*, we get $S_{u_2,u_1}^{(c_1)} = 0.9$ and $S_{u_2,u_1}^{(c_2)} = 0.1$.

Like before, we then also normalize each row of $S^{(c)}$ matrix (across v), as to make the trust values independent of the activity levels of the users in each circle:

$$S_{u,v}^{(c)*} = S_{u,v}^{(c)} / \sum_{v \in \mathcal{C}_u^{(c)}} S_{u,v}^{(c)}.$$

We note that the normalizations across c and then v may also be viewed as the first step of an iterative procedure called *iterative proportional fitting* [25]. In short, when this procedure is iterated until convergence, it results in an exact *joint* normalization regarding both c and v: $\sum_c \sum_v S_{u,v}^{(c)} = const$, where $\sum_c S_{u,v}^{(c)} = 1$ for each v, and $\sum_v S_{u,v}^{(c)} = const$ for each c. While the iterative procedure yields exact normalization, it is computationally expensive. For the latter reason, the reported results in our experiment section are obtained after only one iteration.

3.3 Model Training

3.3.1 Training with ratings from each category

Using the (normalized) trust network $S^{(c)*}$, as defined above, we train a separate matrix factorization model for each category c. For each kind of inferred circles of friends, we obtain a separate user profile $Q^{(c)}$ and item profile $P^{(c)}$ for each c. Similar to the SocialMF model [13], but with the crucial difference of using inferred social circles of friends, we use the following training objective function

$$\begin{aligned} &\mathcal{L}^{(c)}(R^{(c)}, Q^{(c)}, P^{(c)}, S^{(c)*}) = \\ &\frac{1}{2} \sum_{(u,i)\text{obs.}} \left(R_{u,i}^{(c)} - \hat{R}_{u,i}^{(c)} \right)^2 \\ &+ \frac{\beta}{2} \sum_{\text{all } u} \left((Q_u^{(c)} - \sum_v S_{u,v}^{(c)*} Q_v^{(c)})(Q_u^{(c)} - \sum_v S_{u,v}^{(c)*} Q_v^{(c)})^\top \right) \\ &+ \frac{\lambda}{2} \left(||P^{(c)}||_F^2 + ||Q^{(c)}||_F^2 \right), \end{aligned} \tag{6}$$

where we only use ratings $R_{u,i}^{(c)}$ in category c; $\hat{R}_{u,i}^{(c)}$ is the predicted rating of item i in category c,

$$\hat{R}_{u,i}^{(c)} = r_m^{(c)} + Q_u^{(c)} P_i^{(c)\top}, \tag{7}$$

where we define the global bias term $r_m^{(c)}$ as the average value of observed training rating in category c (see also Table 4). The summation in Eq. (6) extends over all observed user-item pairs (u, i) where item i belongs to category c. Note that this model only captures user and item profiles in category c, i.e., $Q^{(c)}$ and $P^{(c)}$. $P^{(c)} \in \mathbb{R}^{i_0^{(c)} \times d}$, where $i_0^{(c)}$ is the number of items in category c and $Q^{(c)} \in \mathbb{R}^{u_0 \times d}$. Eq. (6) can be minimized by the gradient decent approach, analogous to [13]:

$$\begin{aligned} &\frac{\partial \mathcal{L}^{(c)}}{\partial Q_u^{(c)}} = \\ &\sum_{i:cat(i)=c} I_{u,i}^{R^{(c)}} \left(r_m^{(c)} + Q_u^{(c)} P_i^{(c)T} - R_{u,i}^{(c)} \right) P_i^{(c)} + \lambda Q_u^{(c)} \\ &+ \beta \left(Q_u^{(c)} - \sum_{v \in \mathcal{C}_u^{(c)}} S_{u,v}^{(c)*} Q_v^{(c)} \right) \\ &- \beta \sum_{v: u \in \mathcal{C}_v^{(c)}} S_{v,u}^{(c)*} \left(Q_v^{(c)} - \sum_{w \in \mathcal{C}_v^{(c)}} S_{v,w}^{(c)*} Q_w^{(c)} \right), \end{aligned} \tag{8}$$

where $cat(i)$ is the category of item i.

Table 1: Epinions Data: Top-10 Category Statistics.

Category	User Count	Item Count	Rating Count	Sparsity	Trust Fraction	Original Degree	Degree in Circle
Videos & DVDs	17,312	10,065	94,261	0.999459	44.64%	18.1	13.1
Books	11,296	21,662	47,889	0.999804	36.09%	23.4	16.3
Music	10,188	14,905	43,079	0.999716	21.48%	19.6	10.7
Video Games	9,124	2,389	29,661	0.998639	13.32%	18.2	7.4
Toys	6,373	3,344	26,789	0.998743	21.49%	30.3	17.2
Online Stores& Services	8,074	973	22,661	0.997115	28.55%	29.6	18.0
Software	8,290	1,624	19,400	0.998559	22.05%	25.9	13.5
Destinations	7,438	1475	19,395	0.998232	23.12%	27.6	15.8
Cars	10,847	3,108	17,604	0.999478	19.35%	18.3	9.1
Kids' TV Shows	4,784	259	11,203	0.990958	10.85%	29.0	11.6

$$\frac{\partial \mathcal{L}^{(c)}}{\partial P_i^{(c)}} = \sum_{all\ u} I_{u,i}^{R^{(c)}} \left(r_m^{(c)} + Q_u^{(c)} P_i^{(c)T} - R_{u,i}^{(c)} \right) Q_u^{(c)} + \lambda P_i^{(c)}, \tag{9}$$

where $I_{u,i}^{R^{(c)}}$ is the indicator function that is equal to 1 if u has rated i in category c, and equal to 0 otherwise. The initial values of $Q^{(c)}$ and $P^{(c)}$ are sampled from the normal distribution with zero mean. In each iteration, $Q^{(c)}$ and $P^{(c)}$ are updated based on the latent variables from the previous iteration.

Once $Q^{(c)}$ and $P^{(c)}$ are learned for each category c, this model can be used to predict ratings for user-item pairs (u, i) according to Eq. (7), where the category c of item i determines the matrices $Q_u^{(c)}$ and $P_i^{(c)}$ to be used.

3.3.2 Training with ratings for all categories

As an alternative training objective function, we also considered using *all* ratings in the data, instead of only the ratings in category c. The only difference to Eq. (6) is that the first line is replaced by

$$\frac{1}{2} \sum_{(u,i)\text{obs.}} \left(R_{u,i} - \hat{R}_{u,i} \right)^2, \tag{10}$$

where the summation extends over all observed user-item pairs (u, i) from all categories. As before, we train a separate model for each category c, i.e., $Q^{(c)}$ and $P^{(c)}$, with $P^{(c)} \in \mathbb{R}^{i_0 \times d}$, and $Q^{(c)} \in \mathbb{R}^{u_0 \times d}$.

4. EXPERIMENTS

In this section, we evaluate our different variants of Circle-based recommendation and compare them to the existing approaches using the Epinions dataset[1].

4.1 Dataset

Epinions is a consumer opinion website where users can review items (such as cars, movies, books, software,...) and also assign them numeric ratings in the range of 1 (min) to 5 (max). Users can also express their *trust* to other users, such as reviewers whose reviews and ratings they have consistently found to be valuable. Each user has a list of trusted users. A user issues a trust statement to another user by adding the user to her trust list. In the Epinions dataset, the trust values between users are binary: if user B is in user A's trust list, then user A's trust value towards B is 1, otherwise it is 0.

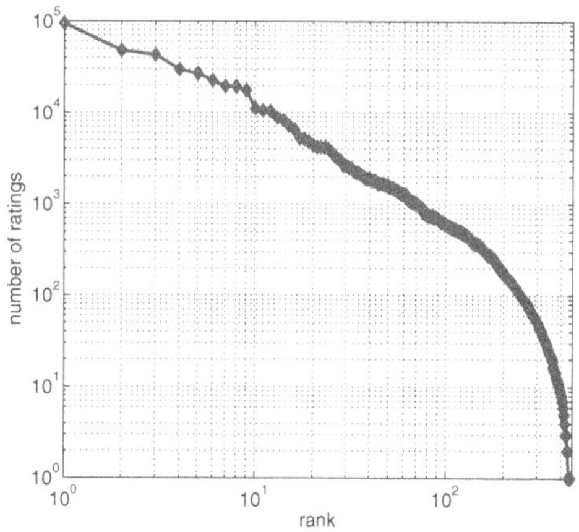

Figure 7: Distribution of Number of Ratings across Categories.

We use the version of the Epinions dataset[2] published by the authors of [3]. It consists of ratings from 71,002 users who rated a total of 104,356 different items from 451 categories. The total number of ratings is 571,235. The distribution of the ratings cross all categories is plotted in Figure 7. A large number of ratings fall into a small number of large categories. The distribution of users and items in the top-10 categories is presented in Table 1.

The total number of issued trust statements is 508,960. We apply the circle inference algorithms presented in Section 3.1 to the Epinions dataset. The fraction of trust links with $S_{u,v}^{(c)} > 0$ for each category c, out of all trust links in the entire original social network is shown in Table 1 column *Trust Fraction*. We can see that the inferred social network of each category is much smaller than the original one. For users who have ratings in each category, we also compare

[1]http://www.epinions.com/

[2]http://alchemy.cs.washington.edu/data/epinions/

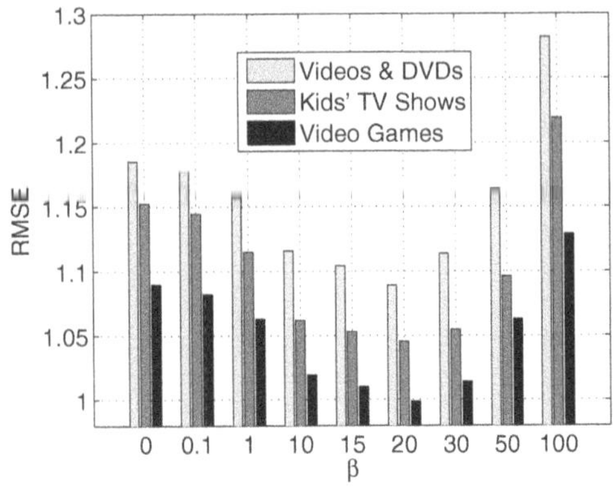

Figure 3: Impact of social information weight β on the RMSE performance using all category ratings in CircleCon3.

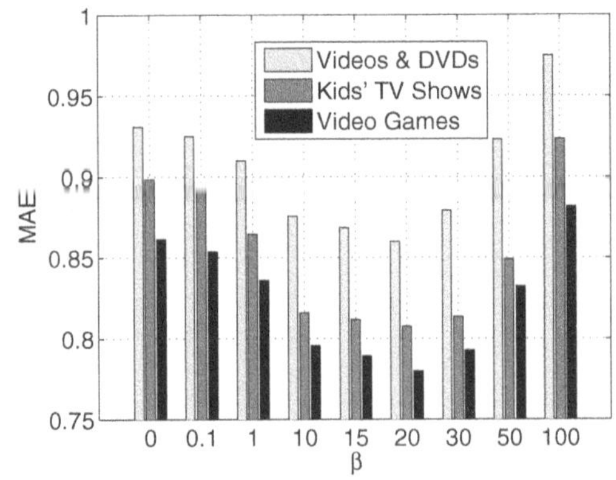

Figure 4: Impact of social information weight β on the MAE performance using all category ratings in CircleCon3.

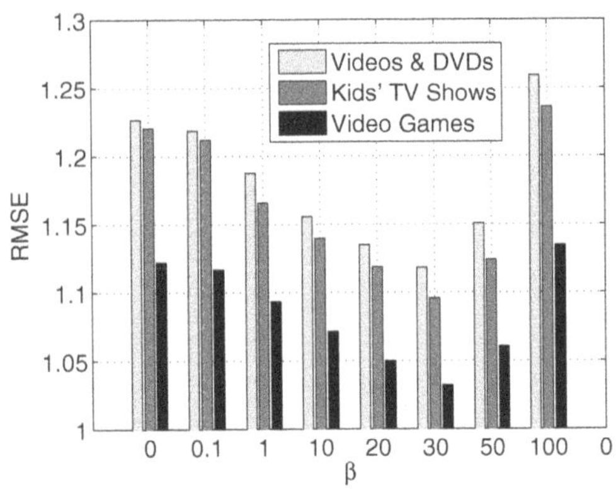

Figure 5: Impact of social information weight β on the RMSE performance using one category ratings in CircleCon3.

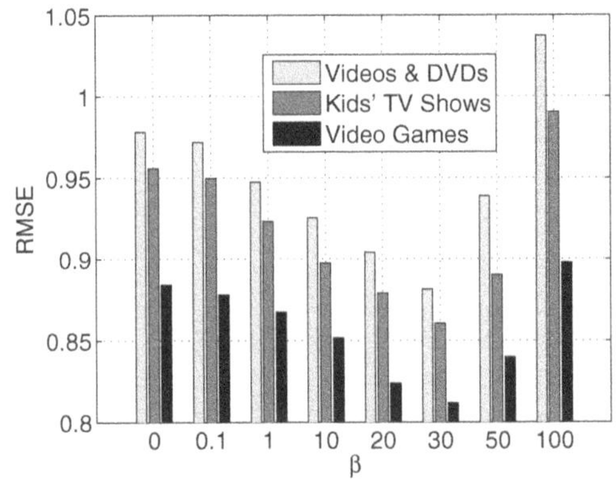

Figure 6: Impact of social information weight β on the MAE performance using one category ratings in CircleCon3.

their followee numbers in the original social network with those in the inferred circles for that category. The average number of followees in the original social network is shown in Table 1 column *Original Degree*. The average number of followees in the inferred circles is shown in Table 1 column *Degree in Circle*. A pair of users connected by a trust link in the original social network are not always in the same inferred circle. For instance, recommendations in the Videos & DVDs category are based on about 72% of a user's friends on average, and in the Kids' TV Shows category only about 40% of friends are relevant on average.

4.2 Performance Measures

We perform 5-fold cross validation in our experiments. In each fold, we use 80% of data as the training set and the remaining 20% as the test set. The evaluation metrics we use in our experiments are Root Mean Square Error (RMSE) and Mean Absolute Error (MAE), as these are the most popular accuracy measures in the literature of recommender systems. RMSE is defined as

$$RMSE = \sqrt{\frac{\sum_{(u,i)\in\mathcal{R}_{test}}(R_{u,i} - \hat{R}_{u,i})^2}{|\mathcal{R}_{test}|}}, \quad (11)$$

where $\mathcal{R}_{test}$ is the set of all user-item pairs (u, i) in the test set. MAE is defined as

$$MAE = \frac{\sum_{(u,i)\in\mathcal{R}_{test}}|R_{u,i} - \hat{R}_{u,i}|}{|\mathcal{R}_{test}|}. \quad (12)$$

4.3 Evaluation

As to demonstrate the effectiveness of the proposed circle reconstruction approaches, we compare the recommendation results of the following approaches:

- **BaseMF**: This method is the baseline matrix factorization approach proposed in [5] and [22], which does not take into account the social network.
- **SocialMF**: This method is proposed in [13]. It improves the recommendation accuracy of BaseMF by taking into social trust between users. It always uses all social links available in the dataset.
- **CircleCon1**: For recommendation in one category c, a social link will be used if and only if the pair of users connected by the link both have ratings in category c. The social trust values are calculated as outlined in Section 3.2.1.
- **∼CircleCon1**: This is the complementary case of CircleCon1. It uses all social links except for the links used by CircleCon1. The trust value assignment is same as **CircleCon1**.

Table 2: *RMSE* comparisons for the ten largest categories using all ratings (dimensionality $d = 10$). The percentage numbers in each cell are the relative improvements of CircleCon3 over the various baseline models. The standard deviations of the results are about 0.005.

Category	BaseMF	SocialMF	~CircleCon1	CircleCon1	CircleCon2a	CircleCon2b	CircleCon3
Videos & DVDs	1.186 8.15%	1.130 3.65%	1.147 5.04%	1.098	1.109	**1.091**	**1.089**
Books	1.054 5.88%	1.023 3.09%	1.031 3.76%	1.002	1.000	**0.991**	**0.992**
Music	1.038 6.22%	0.990 1.75%	1.002 2.92%	0.979	0.982	**0.973**	**0.973**
Video Games	1.090 8.36%	1.036 3.63%	1.057 5.50%	1.005	**0.999**	**1.000**	**0.999**
Toys	1.084 9.18%	1.025 3.94%	1.031 4.56%	0.990	0.995	**0.988**	**0.984**
Online Stores & Services	1.329 11.05%	1.236 4.31%	1.257 5.95%	1.189	**1.182**	1.190	**1.182**
Software	1.153 7.54%	1.093 2.50%	1.107 3.76%	1.072	1.075	**1.061**	**1.066**
Destinations	1.032 7.49%	0.984 3.03%	0.993 3.85%	0.961	**0.959**	0.963	**0.955**
Cars	1.123 4.66%	1.085 1.35%	1.094 2.12%	1.076	1.080	**1.073**	**1.070**
Kids' TV Shows	1.153 9.28%	1.083 3.48%	1.095 4.50%	1.052	1.051	**1.042**	**1.046**

Table 3: *MAE* comparison for the ten largest categories using all ratings (dimensionality = 10). The percentage numbers in each cell are the relative improvements of CircleCon3 over the various baseline models. The standard deviations of the results are about 0.005.

Category	BaseMF	SocialMF	~CircleCon1	CircleCon1	CircleCon2a	CircleCon2b	CircleCon3
Videos & DVDs	0.931 7.66%	0.890 3.44%	0.901 4.54%	**0.863**	0.874	**0.862**	**0.860**
Books	0.862 7.36%	0.834 4.23%	0.842 5.16%	0.812	0.809	**0.797**	**0.799**
Music	0.849 7.14%	0.806 2.27%	0.811 2.80%	0.794	0.798	**0.788**	**0.788**
Video Games	0.861 9.49%	0.809 3.67%	0.824 5.35%	0.786	**0.781**	**0.781**	**0.780**
Toys	0.859 10.31%	0.808 4.69%	0.814 5.38%	0.777	0.782	**0.773**	**0.770**
Online Stores & Services	1.050 9.78%	0.994 4.77%	1.008 6.03%	0.955	**0.947**	0.953	**0.947**
Software	0.910 8.23%	0.858 2.64%	0.869 3.93%	0.841	0.842	**0.831**	**0.835**
Destinations	0.838 9.40%	0.795 4.44%	0.802 5.37%	0.766	0.766	0.769	**0.759**
Cars	0.867 4.86%	0.834 1.08%	0.841 1.90%	0.832	**0.828**	**0.829**	**0.825**
Kids' TV Shows	0.899 10.13%	0.846 4.49%	0.852 5.23%	0.813	0.812	**0.802**	0.808

- **CircleCon2**: It uses the same subset of social links used by **CircleCon1**. But the social trust values are calculated according to the two expertise-based normalization algorithms presented in Section 3.2.2, resulting into two variations: **CircleCon2a** and **CircleCon2b**.
- **CircleCon3**: It uses the same subset of social links used by **CircleCon1**. But the social trust values are calculated according to the trust-splitting algorithm presented in Section 3.2.3.

In all our experiments, we set the dimensionality for low-

Table 4: Performance comparison when training on *ratings of the given category only.* The standard deviations of the results are about 0.005.

Category	avg. rating	BaseMF		SocialMF		CircleCon3	
		RMSE	MAE	RMSE	MAE	RMSE	MAE
Videos & DVDs	3.77	1.227 8.84%	0.978 9.89%	1.160 3.59%	0.921 4.28%	**1.118**	**0.882**
Books	4.30	1.065 5.79%	0.869 5.90%	1.029 2.47%	0.841 2.80%	**1.003**	**0.818**
Music	4.30	1.055 7.25%	0.855 6.72%	0.999 2.06%	0.812 1.69%	**0.979**	**0.798**
Video Games	4.06	1.122 8.04%	0.884 8.20%	1.074 3.92%	0.844 3.85%	**1.032**	**0.812**
Toys	4.14	1.137 11.12%	0.887 9.89%	1.063 4.90%	0.832 3.90%	**1.011**	**0.799**
Online Stores & Services	3.52	1.446 15.28%	1.172 15.99%	1.277 4.07%	1.034 4.75%	**1.225**	**0.985**
Software	4.06	1.202 8.49%	0.955 9.11%	1.157 4.95%	0.916 5.18%	**1.099**	**0.868**
Destinations	4.38	1.049 7.01%	0.851 7.81%	0.992 1.62%	0.804 2.44%	**0.975**	**0.785**
Cars	4.17	1.140 5.33%	0.871 4.94%	1.099 1.82%	0.845 2.06%	**1.079**	**0.828**
Kids' TV Shows	4.14	1.221 10.23%	0.956 9.98%	1.154 5.04%	0.904 4.84%	**1.096**	**0.860**

rank matrix factorization to be $d = 10$ and the regularization constant to be $\lambda = 0.1$.

4.3.1 Training with ratings from all categories

In this section, we consider the variant of using all ratings for training the various models, as outlined in Section 3.3.2. The other variant, which uses only the ratings of a single category at a time, will be evaluated in the next section.

In detail, regarding **BaseMF**, we use all ratings from all categories as input to train for the latent features of all items and all users; for **SocialMF**, we use all category ratings and all trust links as input to train for the latent features of all items and all users. For all the circle-based methods, we conduct separate trainings for individual categories, as discussed in Section 3.3.2.

When trained with all ratings, for **SocialMF**, the optimal social information weight is $\beta = 15$. For **CircleCon1**, **CircleCon2** and **CircleCon3**, the optimal social information weights are all around $\beta = 20$. We plot the RMSE and MAE of **CircleCon3** as a function of β in Figures 3 and 4, respectively. The trends for **CircleCon1** and **CircleCon2** are similar. This is because after we filtered out the trust links which do not belong to the current category, the similarity between a follower and followee connected by a surviving trust link should be higher. In ~CircleCon1, we set $\beta = 15$.

The performance of the five methods are compared in Tables 2 and 3 regarding RMSE and MAE, respectively. The standard deviations of the results are about 0.005. Values that are within the standard deviation of the best result are highlighted in bold. We can see from the tables that **CircleCon1** is better than **SocialMF**, and **~CircleCon1** is worse than **SocialMF**, in terms of both RMSE and MAE. This demonstrates from two sides the benefit of reconstructing trust circles for individual categories. Over all categories, **CircleCon3** has the best performance, but **CircleCon2b** is slightly (but not significantly) better than **CircleCon3** in the categories of Books, Software and Kids' TV Shows.

4.3.2 Training with per-category ratings.

As outlined in Section 3.3.1, another training alternative is to use only the ratings pertaining to the category that the model is trained for. In detail, for **BaseMF**, we only use ratings in the current category as input. For **SocialMF**, we use ratings in the current category and all trust links as input. For circle-based RSes, as discussed in 3.3.1, we use ratings in the current category and weighted trust links obtained from circle construction methods. Among the different variants, we only presents results for **CircleCon3** in this section, as we found it to be the best approach in the previous section.

When trained with per-category ratings, for **SocialMF** the optimal social information weight is $\beta = 15$. As illustrated in Figures 5 and 6, for **CircleCon3**, the optimal social information weight is $\beta = 30$. Similar to the case of training with all ratings, this is again because the latent features between friends in circles established for each category should be more similar to each other. The detailed results of per-category training are shown in Table 4.

We can see from Table 4, **CircleCon3** is better than **SocialMF** in terms of RMSE and MAE.

4.4 Observations

Comparing the performance of **BaseMF** in Table 2 and Table 4 (also Table 3 and Table 4), we can see that more rating information enables BaseMF to learn user's interest more accurately. The same conclusion holds when comparing the performance of **SocialMF** in Table 2 and Table 4 (also Table 3 and Table 4). Comparing **CircleCon3** in Table 2 and Table 4 (also Table 3 and Table 4), we can see that all category ratings combined with per-category Circle trust relationships provides the best prediction accuracy in all the compared cases. This is because all category ratings provide us more information to learn user's interests, and circles reconstructed for individual categories alleviate the ambiguity resulting from the mixed trust statements issued cross different categories.

Thus, we find that the proposed variant **CircleCon3** with all category ratings achieves the lowest RMSE and MAE values overall.

5. CONCLUSIONS

In this paper, we presented a novel approach to improving recommendation accuracy by introducing the concept of "inferred circles of friends". The idea is to determine the best subset of a user's friends, i.e., an inferred circle, for making recommendations in an item category of interest. As these inferred circles are tailored towards the various item categories, they may differ from explicit circles of friends that have recently become popular in online social networks. We proposed methods for inferring category-specific circles, and to assign weights to the friends within each circle. In our experiments on publicly available data, we showed significant improvements over existing approaches that use mixed social network information.

6. ACKNOWLEDGMENTS

The authors would like to thank Debasis Mitra and Shiv Panwar for initiating this collaboration. H.S. would also like to thank Tin Kam Ho for her encouragement and support of this work.

7. REFERENCES

[1] G. Adomavicius and A. Tuzhilin. Toward the next generation of recommender systems: A survey of the state-of-the-art and possible extensions. *IEEE Transactions on Knowledge and Data Engineering*, 17:734–49, 2005.

[2] R. Bell, Y. Koren, and C. Volinsky. Modeling relationships at multiple scales to improve accuracy of large recommender systems. In Proc. of KDD '07, pages 95-104, San Jose, California, USA, 2007.

[3] M. Richardson and P. Domingos. Mining Knowledge-Sharing Sites for Viral Marketing, In Proc. of KDD, 2002.

[4] M. Jahrer, A. Toscher, and R. Legenstein. Combining predictions for accurate recommender systems. In Proc. of KDD '10.

[5] S. Funk. Netflix update: Try this at home, 2006. `http://sifter.org/ simon/journal/20061211.html`.

[6] Y. Zhang, B. Cao, and D. Y. Yeung. Multi-domain collaborative filtering. In Proceedings of the 26th Conference on Uncertainty in Artificial Intelligence (UAI), Catalina Island, California, USA, 2010.

[7] R. Keshavan, A. Montanari, and S. Oh. Matrix completion from noisy entries. *Journal of Machine Learning Research*, 11:2057–78, 2010.

[8] Y. Koren. Factorization meets the neighborhood: a multifaceted collaborative filtering model. In Proc. KDD, 2008.

[9] H. Ma, I. King, and M. R. Lyu. Learning to recommend with social trust ensemble. In *ACM conference on Research and development in information retrieval (SIGIR)*, 2009.

[10] X. Yang, Y. Guo and Y. Liu. "Bayesian-inference based recommendation in online social networks". The 30th Annual IEEE International Conference on Computer Communications (INFOCOM 2011).

[11] H. Ma, H. Yang, M. R. Lyu, and I. King. Sorec: Social recommendation using probabilistic matrix factorization. In *International Conference on Information and Knowledge Management (CIKM)*, 2008.

[12] H. Ma, D. Zhou, C. Liu, M. R. Lyu, and I. King. Recommender Systems with Social Regularization. In *ACM International Conference on Web Search and Data Mining (WSDM)*, 2011.

[13] M. Jamali and M. Ester. A matrix factorization technique with trust propagation for recommendation in social networks. In *Proceedings of the fourth ACM conference on Recommender systems(RecSys)*, 2010.

[14] L. Yu, R. Pan, and Z Li. Adaptive social similarities for recommender systems. In *Proceedings of the fifth ACM conference on Recommender systems(RecSys)*, 2011.

[15] P. Bedi, H. Kaur, and S. Marwaha. Trust based recommender system for semantic web. In Proc. of IJCAI '07, pages 2677-2682, 2007.

[16] Y. Koren. Collaborative filtering with temporal dynamics. In Proc. of KDD '09, pages 447-456, Paris, France, 2009.

[17] F. Liu and H. J. Lee. Use of social network information to enhance collaborative filtering performance. Expert Syst. Appl., 37(7):4772-4778, 2010.

[18] P. Massa and P. Avesani. Trust-aware recommender systems. In Proc. of RecSys '07, pages 17-24, Minneapolis, MN, USA, 2007.

[19] J. O 'Donovan and B. Smyth. Trust in recommender systems. In Proc. of IUI '05, pages 167-174, San Diego, California, USA, 2005.

[20] A. Paterek. Improving regularized singular value decomposition for collaborative filtering. In *KDDCup*, 2007.

[21] R. Salakhutdinov, A. Mnih, and G. Hinton. Restricted Boltzmann machines for collaborative filtering. In *International Conference on Machine Learning (ICML)*, 2007.

[22] R. Salakhutdinov and A. Mnih Probabilistic matrix factorization. In NIPS 2008, volume 20.

[23] J. Wang, A. P. de Vries, and M. J. T. Reinders. Unifying user-based and item-based collaborative filtering approaches by similarity fusion. In Proc. of SIGIR '06, Seattle, Washington, USA, 2006.

[24] G -R Xue, C Lin, Q Yang, W Xi, H -J Zeng, Y Yu,and Z Chen. Scalable collaborative filtering using cluster-based smoothing. In Proc. of SIGIR '05, pages 114-121, Salvador, Brazil, 2005.

[25] W. Deming and F. Stephan, On least square adjustment of sampled frequency tables when the expected marginal totals are known, *Ann. Math. Statist.*, 6, pp. 427-44, 1940.

Incorporating Heterogeneous Information for Personalized Tag Recommendation in Social Tagging Systems

Wei Feng
Tsinghua University
Beijing, China
feng-w10@mails.tsinghua.edu.cn

Jianyong Wang
Tsinghua University
Beijing, China
jianyong@tsinghua.edu.cn

ABSTRACT

A social tagging system provides users an effective way to collaboratively annotate and organize items with their own tags. A social tagging system contains heterogeneous information like users' tagging behaviors, social networks, tag semantics and item profiles. All the heterogeneous information helps alleviate the cold start problem due to data sparsity. In this paper, we model a social tagging system as a multi-type graph. To learn the weights of different types of nodes and edges, we propose an optimization framework, called OptRank. OptRank can be characterized as follows:(1) Edges and nodes are represented by features. Different types of edges and nodes have different set of features. (2) OptRank learns the best feature weights by maximizing the average AUC (Area Under the ROC Curve) of the tag recommender. We conducted experiments on two publicly available datasets, i.e., Delicious and Last.fm. Experimental results show that: (1) OptRank outperforms the existing graph based methods when only <user, tag, item> relation is available. (2) OptRank successfully improves the results by incorporating social network, tag semantics and item profiles.

Categories and Subject Descriptors

H.3.3 [**Information Storage and Retrieval**]: Information Search and Retrieval—*Information Filtering, Retrieval Models, Selection Process*

General Terms

Algorithms

Keywords

Recommender System, Social Tagging System

1. INTRODUCTION

In social tagging systems, users can annotate and organize items with their own tags for future search and sharing. For example, users can annotate and share Web pages in Delicious[1]. Besides Delicious, there are many other social tagging system like Last.fm[2] and YouTube[3] in entertainment domain and CiteULike[4] in the research domain.

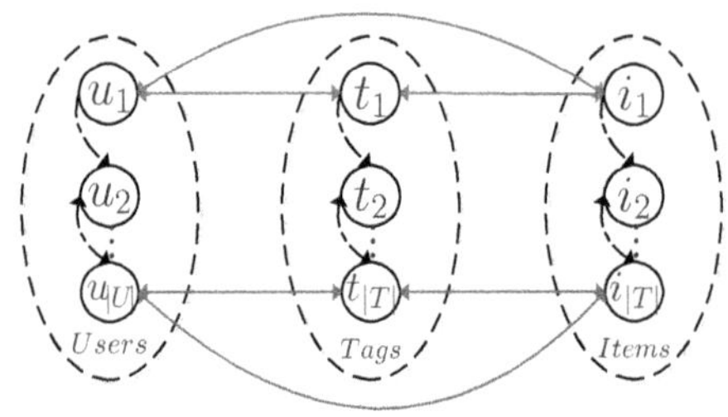

Figure 1: Social Tagging System

Personalized tag recommendation is the key part of a social tagging system. When a user wants to annotate an item, the user may have his/her own vocabulary to organize items. Personalized tag recommendation tries to find the tags that can precisely describe the item with the user's vocabulary.

A social tagging system, as shown in Figure 1, contains heterogeneous information and can be modeled as a graph:

- Users(U), tags(T) and items(I) co-exist in the graph.
- Inter-relation. Edges between users, tags and items can be derived from annotation behaviors <user, tag, item>. Suppose we have $u \in U$ and $t \in T$, the weight of <u, t> is the times of tag t being used by user u. The same rule applies to <u, i> and <i, t> ($i \in I$).
- Intra-relation. (1) Social network among users.(2) Tag semantic network based on semantic relatedness. (3) Item network based on content similarities.

While the inter-relation has been well studied in previous work [4, 5, 12, 13, 16, 17], few work tries to incorporate all the intra-relation into a unified model. Incorporating the intra-relation may solve the cold start problem due to data sparsity. Users in a social network may influence each other by sharing some annotated items. Semantically related tags may co-occur to describe an item. Items that have similar contents may be annotated with the same tag.

When a user u wants to annotate an item i, the recommended tags should meet two requirements: (1) Highly relevant to user u because users have their own way to organize items. (2) Highly relevant to item i because tags should precisely describe the item. To rank the tags, we can perform

KDD'12, August 12–16, 2012, Beijing, China.

[1]http://delicious.com
[2]http://www.last.fm
[3]http://www.youtube.com
[4]http://www.citeulike.org

a random walk with restart at user u and item i to assign each tag a visiting probability, which is used as the ranking score. Only tags that are both relevant to u and i can get high scores. However, two problems arise when the random walk is performed on the multi-type graph:

- Different types of edges have different meanings and thus are measured in different metrics. For example, the edge weights of a social network may be binary and they have completely different meanings from other types of edges, such as the edges formed by tagging behaviors <*user*, *tag*, *item*>. To perform a random walk, they need to be measured under the same metric.
- The random walker can either restart from the user u or the item i. The probabilities of restart at u and at i should be estimated.

To solve the above two problems, we propose an optimization framework called OptRank. OptRank can be characterized as follows:

- Edges are represented by features. Different types of edges have different set of features. For example, <u_1, u_2> ($u_1, u_2 \in U$) in a social network is represented by the feature set {*the number of common tags, the number of common items*}. The edge <t, u> ($u \in U, t \in T$) is represented by the feature {*the times of t being used by u*}. Each feature has a feature weight. The edge weight is decided by both the features and the feature weights.
- User u and item i for recommendation are represented by a constant feature but their feature weights are learned separately.
- OptRank learns the feature weights by maximizing the average AUC (Area under the ROC Curve) of the tag recommender.

Although graph based methods have been studied in the field of personalized tag recommendation by many researchers [4, 5, 17], most of them belong to the unsupervised approach, in which the edge weights and restart probabilities of u and i are empirically assigned. Inspired by the recent development of semi-supervised learning [3] and graph-based learning [1], we are able to turn the existing unsupervised graph-based methods into supervised methods. More specifically, we extend the supervised random walk proposed in [1] for link prediction into the setting of personalized tag recommendation. This paper has two major differences from [1] : (1) The graph in our setting contains different types of edges, each of them has their own set of features and the corresponding feature weights are learned separately. (2) Since we have two nodes for restart, we further introduce node features.

To summarize, our contributions are as follows:

- To solve the cold start problem due to data sparsity, we are among the first to explore the three new relations: social network, tag semantic relatedness and item content similarities.
- We propose a graph model and extend the random walk with restart to the multi-type graph to handle different types of relations uniformly.
- We propose an optimization framework to learn the best edge weights and node weights by maximizing the average AUC of the tag recommender.

The remainder of this paper is organized as follows. The problem we addressed is formulated in Section 2. Graph model and random walk with restart are introduced in Section 3. Our optimization framework OptRank is introduced in Section3. Experimental study is described in Section 5. Related work is introduced in Section 6. We conclude the paper and discuss the future work in Section 7.

2. PROBLEM STATEMENT AND BASIC FRAMEWORK

Personalized Tag Recommendation. Given a user u and an item i, personalized tag recommendation tries to find tags to describe or classify the item i precisely according to u's vocabulary. Inter-relations and intra-relations among users, items and tags are considered, which makes the graph as a multi-type graph (as shown in Figure 1).

Highly ranked tags should be relevant to both u and i. To achieve this goal, a random walk with restart is performed on the multi-type graph with restart at user u and item i. Only tags that are both near to u and item i can get a high visiting probability. Formally, the random walk with restart is performed according to the following equation:

$$\begin{pmatrix} \mathbf{p}_U \\ \mathbf{p}_T \\ \mathbf{p}_I \end{pmatrix}^{(t+1)} = (1-\alpha)\overline{\mathbf{A}} \begin{pmatrix} \mathbf{p}_U \\ \mathbf{p}_T \\ \mathbf{p}_I \end{pmatrix}^{(t)} + \alpha \begin{pmatrix} \overline{\mathbf{q}}_U \\ \mathbf{0} \\ \overline{\mathbf{q}}_I \end{pmatrix} \quad (1)$$

where

- α is the restart probability. (1 - α) means that the random walker has the probability of (1-α) to perform a random jump based on his current state.
- $\mathbf{p}^T = (\mathbf{p}_U^T, \mathbf{p}_T^T, \mathbf{p}_I^T)$ is a vector of visiting probabilities of all nodes. $\mathbf{p}_T$ contains the ranking scores for each tag.
- $\overline{\mathbf{A}}$ is the transition matrix that stores graph structure information. $\overline{\mathbf{A}}$ is obtained by normalizing each column of the adjacency matrix $\mathbf{A}$ to sum to 1.
- $\overline{\mathbf{q}}^T = (\overline{\mathbf{q}}_U^T, \mathbf{0}^T, \overline{\mathbf{q}}_I^T)$ is the preference vector that contains the restart probabilities of each node. $\overline{\mathbf{q}}$ is obtained by normalizing the node weight vector $\mathbf{q}$ to sum to 1.

The transition matrix $\overline{\mathbf{A}}$ and the preference vector $\overline{\mathbf{q}}$ will be introduced in detail in Section 3.

Optimization Framework To get a good ranking by following Equation 1, the transition matrix $\overline{\mathbf{A}}$ and the preference vector $\overline{\mathbf{q}}$ need to be carefully assigned. Thus we develop an optimization framework called OptRank.

Given a user u and an item i for personalized tag recommendation, suppose u has finally annotated i with tags $(t_1, t_2, ...t_k)$, these tags are defined to be positive tags, denoted by PT. The rest tags are defined to be negative tags, denoted by NT. In other words, the whole tag set T is divided into two parts, i.e. $T = PT \cup NT$.

A good ranking function defined by Equation 1 should rank all the positive tags higher than the negative tags. For a randomly picked positive tag t_1 and a negative tag t_2, a good ranking function has a high probability of ranking t_1 higher than t_2. This is the idea of AUC (Area Under the ROC Curve) metric. Formally, AUC is defined by the following equation:

$$AUC = \frac{\sum_{i\in PT}\sum_{j\in NT}\mathbb{I}(\mathbf{p}_T(i) - \mathbf{p}_T(j))}{|PT||NT|} \quad (2)$$

where $\mathbb{I}(x)$ is 1 when $x > 0$. Otherwise $\mathbb{I}(x)$ is 0.

Our goal is to find the best transition matrix $\overline{\mathbf{A}}$ and the preference vector $\overline{\mathbf{q}}$ to maximize the AUC. To achieve this, edges are represented by features $\mathbf{X}$ and nodes u and i are represented by features $\mathbf{Y}$. To better illustrate the idea, we can assume the adjacency matrix $\mathbf{A}$ only contains edges of the same type. $\mathbf{A}$ with different types of edges will be introduced in Section 3.1.

- Each edge $<v, u>$ ($u,v \in U \cup T \cup I$) is represented by a feature vector $\mathbf{X}(u,v)$. Let $\boldsymbol{\theta}$ represent the vector of feature weights, the edge weight $\mathbf{A}(u,v)$ is computed by $\mathbf{A}(u,v) = f_{edge}(\boldsymbol{\theta}^T\mathbf{X}(u,v))$, where f_{edge}:$\mathbf{R} \rightarrow \mathbf{R}^+$.
- User u and item i are respectively represented by feature vector[5] $\mathbf{Y}_U = (1)$ and $\mathbf{Y}_I = (1)$. Let $\boldsymbol{\xi}$ denote the feature weights. The node weights $\mathbf{q}_U(u)$ and $\mathbf{q}_I(i)$ are computed by $\mathbf{q}_U(u)$=$f_{node}(\boldsymbol{\xi}_U^T\mathbf{Y}_U)$ and $\mathbf{q}_I(i)$=$f_{node}(\boldsymbol{\xi}_I^T\mathbf{Y}_I)$, where f_{node}:$\mathbf{R} \rightarrow \mathbf{R}^+$. Other entries of $\mathbf{q}_U$ and $\mathbf{q}_I$ are all 0.

According to the above representation, the transition matrix $\overline{\mathbf{A}}$ and the adjacency matrix $\mathbf{A}$ can be rewritten to $\overline{\mathbf{A}}(\boldsymbol{\theta})$ and $\mathbf{A}(\boldsymbol{\theta})$. $\overline{\mathbf{q}}$ and $\mathbf{q}$ can be rewritten to $\overline{\mathbf{q}}(\boldsymbol{\xi})$ and $\mathbf{q}(\boldsymbol{\xi})$. This means they are respectively decided by parameters $\boldsymbol{\theta}$ and $\boldsymbol{\xi}$. Since the random walk is defined by $\overline{\mathbf{A}}(\boldsymbol{\theta})$ and $\overline{\mathbf{q}}(\boldsymbol{\xi})$ according to Equation 1, we know that $\mathbf{p}$ can be rewritten to $\mathbf{p}(\boldsymbol{\theta},\boldsymbol{\xi})$, which means the final ranking scores are parameterized by $\boldsymbol{\theta}$ and $\boldsymbol{\xi}$. However, to make the following formulae more clear, we will not rewrite the above notations with parameters $\boldsymbol{\theta}$ and $\boldsymbol{\xi}$.

With edges and nodes parameterized by $\boldsymbol{\theta}$ and $\boldsymbol{\xi}$, we give a formal description of our optimization framework. Given a user u and an item i for tag recommendation and the positive tag set, the optimization problem is

$$\max_{\boldsymbol{\theta},\boldsymbol{\xi}} AUC(\boldsymbol{\theta},\boldsymbol{\xi}) = \frac{\sum_{i \in PT}\sum_{j \in NT}\mathbb{I}(\mathbf{p}_T(i) - \mathbf{p}_T(j))}{|PT||NT|}$$

However, the above equation only considers a single training instance. When m instances $\{< u_k, i_k, PT_k >\}_{k=1}^m$ are considered, the cost function $J(\boldsymbol{\theta},\boldsymbol{\xi})$ is defined as the average AUC:

$$\max_{\boldsymbol{\theta},\boldsymbol{\xi}} J(\boldsymbol{\theta},\boldsymbol{\xi}) = \frac{1}{m}\sum_{k=1}^{m}\frac{\sum_{i \in PT_k}\sum_{j \in NT_k}\mathbb{I}(\mathbf{p}_T(i) - \mathbf{p}_T(j))}{|PT_k||NT_k|} \tag{3}$$

where $NT_k = T - PT_k$.

The optimization framework OptRank and its solution will be introduced in Section 4.

3. GRAPH MODEL

Before introducing the optimization problem, we first introduce more details about Equation 1. Section 3.1 introduces the transition matrix. Section 3.2 describes the preference vector. Section 3.3 introduces more intuitions and details of the random walk with restart.

3.1 Transition Matrix

Transition matrix stores the graph structure information. Before defining the transition matrix, we first introduce how to construct a graph from a social tagging system. The graph shown in Figure 1 is constructed with three steps: (1) Users, tags and items are mapped as the nodes. (2) All the binary relations, i.e., social network, tag semantic relatedness and item content similarities are mapped to edges. (3) For ternary relation $<user, tag, item>$ where three nodes are involved, binary relations can be derived by projections on each dimension. For example, suppose we have $<u,t,i>$ ($u \in U$, $t \in T$, $i \in I$), $<i,t>$ can be derived by projecting on the user dimention. $<i,t>$ is described by the feature which is the times of i annotated with t.

Now we define the adjacency matrix. Let G denote the whole graph as shown in Figure 1 and $\mathbf{A}$ denote its adjacency matrix. Let G_{MN} ($M,N \in \{U,T,I\}$) denote the each sub-graph made up by relation $<m,n>$ ($m \in M, n \in N$) and $\mathbf{A}_{MN}$ denote its adjacency matrix. We have G=$\bigcup_{M,N\in\{U,T,I\}} G_{MN}$ and $\mathbf{A}$ is composed of sub-matrices $\mathbf{A}_{MN}$:

$$\mathbf{A} = \begin{bmatrix} \mathbf{A}_{UU} & \mathbf{A}_{UT} & \mathbf{A}_{UI} \\ \mathbf{A}_{TU} & \mathbf{A}_{TT} & \mathbf{A}_{TI} \\ \mathbf{A}_{IU} & \mathbf{A}_{IT} & \mathbf{A}_{II} \end{bmatrix} \tag{4}$$

Recall that edges are represented by features. In Section 2, the edge feature set is denoted by $\mathbf{X}$ and the feature weights is denoted by $\boldsymbol{\theta}$. Since different types of edges have different features and feature weights. We have $\mathbf{X}$=$\{\mathbf{X}_{MN} \mid M,N \in \{U,T,I\}\}$ and $\boldsymbol{\theta}$=$\{\boldsymbol{\theta}_{MN} | M,N \in \{U,T,I\}\}$. Given an edge $<m,n> \in \{M,N\}$, $\mathbf{A}_{MN}(m,n)$ is defined by

$$\mathbf{A}_{MN}(m,n) = f_{edge}(\boldsymbol{\theta}_{MN}^T\mathbf{X}_{MN}(m,n)) \tag{5}$$

Note that $\mathbf{X}_{MN}(m,n)$ is a vector and $\mathbf{X}_{MN}$ is an array of three dimensions. In this paper, f_{edge} : $\mathbf{R} \rightarrow \mathbf{R}^+$ is the sigmoid function:

$$f_{edge}(x) = \frac{1}{1+e^{-x}} \tag{6}$$

Transition matrix $\overline{\mathbf{A}}$ is obtained by normalizing each column of $\mathbf{A}$:

$$\overline{\mathbf{A}} = \begin{pmatrix} \mathbf{A}_{UU}\mathbf{D}_U^{-1} & \mathbf{A}_{UT}\mathbf{D}_T^{-1} & \mathbf{A}_{UI}\mathbf{D}_I^{-1} \\ \mathbf{A}_{TU}\mathbf{D}_U^{-1} & \mathbf{A}_{TT}\mathbf{D}_T^{-1} & \mathbf{A}_{TI}\mathbf{D}_I^{-1} \\ \mathbf{A}_{IU}\mathbf{D}_U^{-1} & \mathbf{A}_{IT}\mathbf{D}_T^{-1} & \mathbf{A}_{II}\mathbf{D}_I^{-1} \end{pmatrix} \tag{7}$$

where $\mathbf{D}_U$, $\mathbf{D}_T$ and $\mathbf{D}_I$ are diagonal matrices. The i-th entry in the diagonal of $\mathbf{D}_U$ is the out-degree of the i-th user. For $u \in U$, we have

$$\mathbf{D}_U^{-1}(u,u) = \frac{1}{\sum_{M\in\{U,T,I\}}\sum_{k=1}^{|M|}\mathbf{A}_{MU}(k,u)} \tag{8}$$

$\mathbf{D}_T$ and $\mathbf{D}_I$ are defined in the same way. Following this definition, each column of A will be normalized to sum to 1.

3.2 Preference Vector

Given a user u and an item i for tag recommendation, the preference vector $\overline{\mathbf{q}}^T = (\overline{\mathbf{q}}_U^T, \mathbf{0}^T, \overline{\mathbf{q}}_I^T)$ specifies the restart probability at u and i. As introduced in Section 2, User u and item i are respectively represented by feature vector $\mathbf{Y}_U = (1)$ and $\mathbf{Y}_I = (1)$. Let $\boldsymbol{\xi} = \{\boldsymbol{\xi}_U, \boldsymbol{\xi}_I\}$ denote the feature weights. Node weight $\mathbf{q}_M(m)$ ($M \in \{U,I\}, m \in \{u,i\}$) is computed by

$$\mathbf{q}_M(m) = f_{node}(\boldsymbol{\xi}_M^T\mathbf{Y}_M) \tag{9}$$

The other entries of $\mathbf{q}_U$ and $\mathbf{q}_I$ are all set to 0. f_{node} : $\mathbf{R} \rightarrow \mathbf{R}^+$ is the sigmoid function in this paper:

$$f_{node}(x) = \frac{1}{1+e^{-x}} \tag{10}$$

[5]Nodes are allowed to have more than one feature, so $\mathbf{Y}_U$ and $\mathbf{Y}_I$ are still in bold to represent vectors.

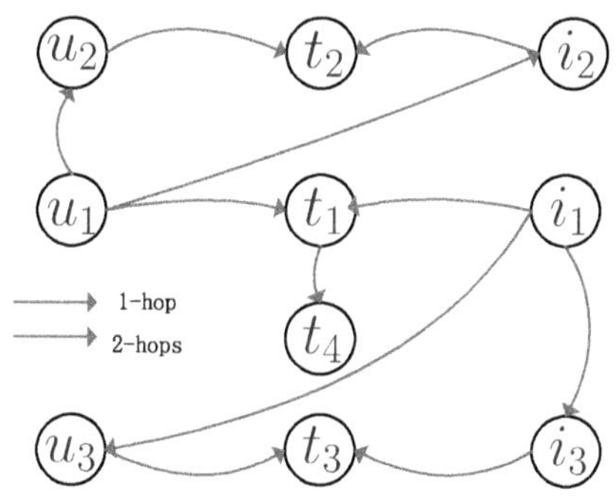

Figure 2: The random walker restart at u_1 and i_1 in no more than 2-hops

The preference vector $\overline{\mathbf{q}}^T = (\overline{\mathbf{q}}_U^T, \mathbf{0}^T, \overline{\mathbf{q}}_I^T)$ is obtained by normalizing $\mathbf{q}^T = (\mathbf{q}_U^T, \mathbf{0}, \mathbf{q}_I^T)$ to sum to 1:

$$\overline{\mathbf{q}} = \begin{pmatrix} \mathbf{q}_U D_q^{-1} \\ \mathbf{0} \\ \mathbf{q}_I D_q^{-1} \end{pmatrix} \tag{11}$$

where D_q is the summation of each entry in $\mathbf{q}_U$ and $\mathbf{q}_I$. Formally, D_q^{-1} is defined as the following equation:

$$D_q^{-1} = \frac{1}{\sum_{M \in \{U,I\}} \sum_{k=1}^{|M|} \mathbf{q}_M(k)} \tag{12}$$

Equation 11 ensures that $\overline{\mathbf{q}}$ sums to 1.

3.3 Random Walk With Restart

In this section, we introduce more intuitions of the random walk with restart for personalized tag recommendation.

As we introduced in Section 2, the random walker can frequently restart at u and i to rank the tags. We illustrate this idea with an example shown in Figure 2. In Figure 2, we want to recommend tags for user u_1 to annotate i_1, so the random walker restarts frequently from u_1 and i_1. The edges indicate how the random walker jumps from node to node. u_1 has the history that she/he has annotated i_2 before. i_1 has the history that it has been annotated by u_3. Besides annotation relation, u_2 is a friend of u_1, i_3 has similar contents with i_1, and t_4 has high semantic relatedness with t_1. Now we discuss how the random walker behaves in no more than two hops from u_1 and i_1:

- When the random walker is only allowed to jump one hop from user u_1 and item i_1, the recommended tags either have been used by user u_1 or have been annotated on item i_1 by other users. As we can see from Figure 2, t_1 is such a tag. When u_1 has annotated many items and i_1 has been annotated by many users, the random walker will find the best common tags in both sets of u_1's tags and i_1's tags.

- When the random walker is allowed to jump within two hops, the recommended tags come from different sources: (1) Items annotated by u_1. For example, i_2 has been annotated by u_1 and i_2 has a tag t_2. t_2 may reflect the interests of u_1. (2) Users that have annotated item i_1. Since u_3 has annotated i_1, the tags annotated by u_3 may reflect the content of i_1. (3) Friends of u_1. u_2 is a friend of u_1 and his/her tags may also be adopted by u_1. (4) Similar items. Since i_3 and i_1 have similar content, the tags of i_3 may also be the tags of i_1. (5)Semantically related tags. t_4 and t_1 are semantically related, which means that they may co-occur in the annotation. When data is sparse, i.e., u_1 and i_1 are both inactive, more information can be taken into account by jumping more than two-hops away.

Now we introduce another intuition behind the random walk. With the transition matrix $\overline{\mathbf{A}}$ defined by Equation 7, we can rewrite Equation 1 as follows:

$$\mathbf{p}_U = (1-\alpha)(\overline{\mathbf{A}}_{UU}\mathbf{p}_U + \overline{\mathbf{A}}_{UT}\mathbf{p}_T + \overline{\mathbf{A}}_{UI}\mathbf{p}_I) + \alpha\overline{\mathbf{q}}_U \tag{13}$$

$$\mathbf{p}_T = (1-\alpha)(\overline{\mathbf{A}}_{TU}\mathbf{p}_U + \overline{\mathbf{A}}_{TT}\mathbf{p}_T + \overline{\mathbf{A}}_{TI}\mathbf{p}_I) \tag{14}$$

$$\mathbf{p}_I = (1-\alpha)(\overline{\mathbf{A}}_{IU}\mathbf{p}_U + \overline{\mathbf{A}}_{IT}\mathbf{p}_T + \overline{\mathbf{A}}_{II}\mathbf{p}_I) + \alpha\overline{\mathbf{q}}_I \tag{15}$$

where $\overline{\mathbf{A}}_{MN}=\mathbf{A}_{MN}\mathbf{D}_N^{-1}(M, N \in \{U,T,I\})$. $\overline{\mathbf{A}}_{MN}\mathbf{p}_N$ $(M, N \in \{U,T,I\})$ means that $\mathbf{p}_N$ is spread to its neighbor nodes through the transition matrix $\overline{\mathbf{A}}_{MN}$.

First we discuss the extreme case that α equals to 0. Taking $\mathbf{p}_T$ as an example, $\mathbf{p}_T$ receives scores from $\mathbf{p}_U$ through $\overline{\mathbf{A}}_{TU}$, $\mathbf{p}_T$ through $\overline{\mathbf{A}}_{TT}$ and $\mathbf{p}_I$ through $\overline{\mathbf{A}}_{TI}$. For $t \in T$, $\mathbf{p}_T(t)$ will have a high score if t has highly ranked user neighbors, tag neighbors and item neighbors. The same rule applies to $\mathbf{p}_U$ and $\mathbf{p}_I$. In other words, users, tags and items reinforce each other iteratively until a stable state is reached. However, there is no personalized information considered. Given a user u and an item i for tag recommendation, when α is greater than 0, the random walker will restart at u and i. Besides reinforcement rule, $\mathbf{p}_U$, $\mathbf{p}_T$ and $\mathbf{p}_I$ are also influenced by the distance from u and i. Nodes that are near to u and i will get a higher ranking.

4. OPTIMIZATION BASED FRAMEWORK

In this section, we focus on how to find the best feature weights to achieve an optimal random walk with restart. Section 4.1 describes the objective function for optimization. Section 4.2 introduces how to solve the optimization problem. Section 4.3 introduces the derivatives of the random walk with respect to the feature weights, which belongs to the details in solving the optimization problem.

4.1 Objective Function

As we introduced in Section 2, we want to maximize the average AUC of the tag recommender according to Equation 3. To convert this problem into a minimization problem, we can rewrite Equation 2 to an equivalent form:

$$AUC = 1 - \frac{\sum_{i \in PT}\sum_{j \in NT}\mathbb{I}(\mathbf{p}_T(j) - \mathbf{p}_T(i))}{|PT||NT|} \tag{16}$$

This equation tells us that to maximize AUC is equivalent to minimize $\sum_{i \in PT}\sum_{j \in NT}\mathbb{I}(\mathbf{p}_T(j) - \mathbf{p}_T(i))/|PT||NT|$. We propose an equivalent minimization problem of Equation 3:

$$\min_{\boldsymbol{\theta},\boldsymbol{\xi}} J(\boldsymbol{\theta},\boldsymbol{\xi}) = \frac{1}{m}\sum_{k=1}^{m}\frac{\sum_{i \in PT_k}\sum_{j \in NT_k}\mathbb{I}(\mathbf{p}_T(j) - \mathbf{p}_T(i))}{|PT_k||NT_k|} \tag{17}$$

Since $J(\boldsymbol{\theta},\boldsymbol{\xi})$ is not differentiable, we can use the sigmoid function with parameter β as a differentiable approximation:

$$S(x;\beta) = \frac{1}{1+e^{-\beta x}} \tag{18}$$

The bigger the β is, the smaller the approximate error is. However, when β is big, the steep gradient will cause a numerical problem. β is empirically assigned. Now we have a new objective function:

$$\min_{\boldsymbol{\theta},\boldsymbol{\xi}} J(\boldsymbol{\theta},\boldsymbol{\xi}) = \frac{1}{m}\sum_{k=1}^{m}\frac{\sum_{i\in PT_k}\sum_{j\in NT_k} S(\mathbf{p}_T(j)-\mathbf{p}_T(i))}{|PT_k||NT_k|} \tag{19}$$

4.2 Solving the Optimization Problem

We use gradient descent to solve the optimization problem. The basic idea of gradient descent is to find the direction (gradient) that the objective function drops down and make a small step towards the direction to update $\boldsymbol{\theta}$ and $\boldsymbol{\xi}$. However, the cost function defined in Equation 19 requires to sum up all the training instances to perform one update, which is too costly. So we update $\boldsymbol{\theta}$ and $\boldsymbol{\xi}$ based on each training instance, which is called stochastic gradient descent. The algorithm is shown in Algorithm 1.

Algorithm 1: Stochastic Gradient Descent

Input: m training instances
lr: learning rate
Output: optimal $\boldsymbol{\theta}$ and $\boldsymbol{\xi}$

1 t=0;
2 initialize $\boldsymbol{\theta}^{(0)}$ and $\boldsymbol{\xi}^{(0)}$;
3 **while** *$J(\boldsymbol{\theta},\boldsymbol{\xi})$ has not converged* **do**
4   Randomly shuffle the m training instances;
    foreach *training instance k* **do**
5         $\boldsymbol{\theta}^{(t+1)} = \boldsymbol{\theta}^{(t)} - lr\ \frac{\partial J_k(\boldsymbol{\theta}^{(t)},\boldsymbol{\xi}^{(t)})}{\partial \boldsymbol{\theta}}$
6         $\boldsymbol{\xi}^{(t+1)} = \boldsymbol{\xi}^{(t)} - lr\ \frac{\partial J_k(\boldsymbol{\theta}^{(t)},\boldsymbol{\xi}^{(t)})}{\partial \boldsymbol{\xi}}$
7   t = t + 1;

where $J_k(\boldsymbol{\theta},\boldsymbol{\xi})$ is the cost based on the k-th instance:

$$J_k(\boldsymbol{\theta},\boldsymbol{\xi}) = \frac{\sum_{i\in PT_k}\sum_{j\in NT_k} S(\mathbf{p}_T(j)-(\mathbf{p}_T(i))}{|PT_k||NT_k|} \tag{20}$$

Learning rate lr decides the step size towards the dropping direction. The random shuffle at Line 4 is required by stochastic descent for convergence. The updating rules for $\boldsymbol{\theta}$ and $\boldsymbol{\xi}$ are shown in Lines 5 and 6. We will discuss how to compute $\partial J_k(\boldsymbol{\theta},\boldsymbol{\xi})/\partial\boldsymbol{\theta}$ and $\partial J_k(\boldsymbol{\theta},\boldsymbol{\xi})/\partial\boldsymbol{\xi}$ in detail in the following.

$$\frac{\partial J_k(\boldsymbol{\theta},\boldsymbol{\xi})}{\partial\boldsymbol{\theta}} = \frac{\sum_{i\in PT_k\wedge j\in NT_k}\frac{\partial S(\delta_{ji})}{\partial\delta_{ji}}\left(\frac{\partial\mathbf{p}_T(j)}{\partial\boldsymbol{\theta}}-\frac{\partial\mathbf{p}_T(i)}{\partial\boldsymbol{\theta}}\right)}{|PT_k||NT_k|} \tag{21}$$

$$\frac{\partial J_k(\boldsymbol{\theta},\boldsymbol{\xi})}{\partial\boldsymbol{\xi}} = \frac{\sum_{i\in PT_k\wedge j\in NT_k}\frac{\partial S(\delta_{ji})}{\partial\delta_{ji}}\left(\frac{\partial\mathbf{p}_T(j)}{\partial\boldsymbol{\xi}}-\frac{\partial\mathbf{p}_T(i)}{\partial\boldsymbol{\xi}}\right)}{|PT_k||NT_k|} \tag{22}$$

where $\delta_{ji} = \mathbf{p}_T(j)-\mathbf{p}_T(i)$. $\partial S(\delta_{ji})/\partial\delta_{ji}$ is easy to compute. According to Equation 18, we can derive that $\partial S(\delta_{ji})/\partial\delta_{ji}$ $= \beta S(\delta_{ji})(1-S(\delta_{ji}))$. The remaining question is how to compute $\partial\mathbf{p}_T(j)/\partial\boldsymbol{\theta}$ and $\partial\mathbf{p}_T(i)/\partial\boldsymbol{\xi}$, which will be discussed in the next section.

4.3 Derivatives of the Random Walk

In this section, we will discuss how to compute the derivatives of the random walk. Suppose $\mathbf{p}^T = (\mathbf{p}_U^T,\mathbf{p}_T^T,\mathbf{p}_I^T)^T$, we want to compute $\partial\mathbf{p}/\partial\boldsymbol{\theta}$ and $\partial\mathbf{p}/\partial\boldsymbol{\xi}$. The basic idea is that we can derive a similar iterative way to compute derivatives from the definition of random walk.

Derivatives with respect to $\boldsymbol{\theta}$. Since $\partial\mathbf{p}/\partial\boldsymbol{\theta}$ is composed of $\partial\mathbf{p}/\partial\boldsymbol{\theta}_{MN}$ $(M,N\in\{U,T,I\})$, without loss of generality, we introduce how to compute $\partial\mathbf{p}/\partial\boldsymbol{\theta}_{UU}$. Taking the derivatives with respect to $\boldsymbol{\theta}_{UU}$ on both sides of the Equations 13, 14, 15, we can get

$$\frac{\partial\mathbf{p}_U}{\partial\boldsymbol{\theta}_{UU}} = (1-\alpha)\sum_{N\in\{U,T,I\}}\left(\overline{\mathbf{A}}_{UN}\frac{\partial\mathbf{p}_N}{\partial\boldsymbol{\theta}_{UU}}+\frac{\partial\overline{\mathbf{A}}_{UN}}{\partial\boldsymbol{\theta}_{UU}}\mathbf{p}_N\right) \tag{23}$$

$$\frac{\partial\mathbf{p}_T}{\partial\boldsymbol{\theta}_{UU}} = (1-\alpha)\sum_{N\in\{U,T,I\}}\left(\overline{\mathbf{A}}_{TN}\frac{\partial\mathbf{p}_N}{\partial\boldsymbol{\theta}_{UU}}+\frac{\partial\overline{\mathbf{A}}_{TN}}{\partial\boldsymbol{\theta}_{UU}}\mathbf{p}_N\right) \tag{24}$$

$$\frac{\partial\mathbf{p}_I}{\partial\boldsymbol{\theta}_{UU}} = (1-\alpha)\sum_{N\in\{U,T,I\}}\left(\overline{\mathbf{A}}_{IN}\frac{\partial\mathbf{p}_N}{\partial\boldsymbol{\theta}_{UU}}+\frac{\partial\overline{\mathbf{A}}_{IN}}{\partial\boldsymbol{\theta}_{UU}}\mathbf{p}_N\right) \tag{25}$$

Following the same rule, we can compute the derivatives with respect to any $\boldsymbol{\theta}_{MN}$ $(M,N\in\{U,T,I\})$, which all lead to the same form with the above three equations. To better illustrate the connections between computing $\mathbf{p}$ and computing $\partial\mathbf{p}/\partial\boldsymbol{\theta}_{MN}$, we can rewrite the above three equations with $\boldsymbol{\theta}_{UU}$ replaced by $\boldsymbol{\theta}_{MN}$ in the matrix form:

$$\begin{pmatrix}\frac{\partial\mathbf{p}_U}{\partial\boldsymbol{\theta}_{MN}}\\ \frac{\partial\mathbf{p}_T}{\partial\boldsymbol{\theta}_{MN}}\\ \frac{\partial\mathbf{p}_I}{\partial\boldsymbol{\theta}_{MN}}\end{pmatrix} = (1-\alpha)\overline{\mathbf{A}}\begin{pmatrix}\frac{\partial\mathbf{p}_U}{\partial\boldsymbol{\theta}_{MN}}\\ \frac{\partial\mathbf{p}_T}{\partial\boldsymbol{\theta}_{MN}}\\ \frac{\partial\mathbf{p}_I}{\partial\boldsymbol{\theta}_{MN}}\end{pmatrix} + (1-\alpha)\frac{\partial\overline{\mathbf{A}}}{\partial\boldsymbol{\theta}_{MN}}\begin{pmatrix}\mathbf{p}_U\\ \mathbf{p}_T\\ \mathbf{p}_I\end{pmatrix} \tag{26}$$

where $\overline{\mathbf{A}}$ is the transition matrix defined in the original random walk. Comparing the above equation with Equation 1 for computing $\mathbf{p}$, we can find two differences: (1) $\mathbf{p}$ is replaced by $\partial\mathbf{p}/\partial\boldsymbol{\theta}_{MN}$. (2) The last term on the right side is totally changed. However, only the first term $(1-\alpha)\overline{\mathbf{A}}\partial\mathbf{p}/\partial\boldsymbol{\theta}_{MN}$ decides whether Equation 26 will converge to a stable state. More details about the convergence are discussed in the appendix.

The last detail is how to compute $\partial\overline{\mathbf{A}}/\partial\boldsymbol{\theta}_{MN}$. Without loss of generality, we discuss how to compute $\partial\overline{\mathbf{A}}/\partial\boldsymbol{\theta}_{UU}$. Recall that $\overline{\mathbf{A}}$ is composed of sub-matrices $\{\overline{\mathbf{A}}_{MN}|M,N\in\{U,T,I\}\}$ and not all $\overline{\mathbf{A}}_{MN}$ are related with $\partial\boldsymbol{\theta}_{UU}$. According to Equation 7, only $\overline{\mathbf{A}}_{UU}$, $\overline{\mathbf{A}}_{TU}$ and $\overline{\mathbf{A}}_{IU}$ can be influenced by $\boldsymbol{\theta}_{UU}$. So we only need to compute $\partial\overline{\mathbf{A}}_{UU}/\partial\boldsymbol{\theta}_{UU}$, $\partial\overline{\mathbf{A}}_{TU}/\partial\boldsymbol{\theta}_{UU}$, $\partial\overline{\mathbf{A}}_{IU}/\partial\boldsymbol{\theta}_{UU}$. Take $\partial\overline{\mathbf{A}}_{UU}/\partial\boldsymbol{\theta}_{UU}$ for example, we can get

$$\frac{\partial\overline{\mathbf{A}}_{UU}}{\partial\boldsymbol{\theta}_{UU}} = \frac{\partial\mathbf{A}_{UU}}{\partial\boldsymbol{\theta}_{UU}}\mathbf{D}_U^{-1}+\mathbf{A}_{UU}\frac{\partial\mathbf{D}_U^{-1}}{\boldsymbol{\theta}_{UU}} \tag{27}$$

Each entry of $\mathbf{A}_{UU}$ is defined according to Equation 5. For $u_1,u_2\in U$, we have

$$\frac{\partial\mathbf{A}_{UU}(u_1,u_2)}{\partial\boldsymbol{\theta}_{UU}} = \frac{\partial f_{edge}(\boldsymbol{\theta}_{UU}^T\mathbf{X}_{UU}(u_1,u_2))}{\partial\boldsymbol{\theta}_{UU}} \tag{28}$$

Each entry in the diagonal of $\mathbf{D}_U^{-1}$ is the out-degree of a user. According to Equation 8, for $u\in U$, the derivative is

$$\frac{\partial\mathbf{D}_U^{-1}(u,u)}{\partial\boldsymbol{\theta}_{UU}} = -\frac{\sum_{k=1}^{|U|}\frac{\partial\mathbf{A}_{UU}(k,u)}{\partial\boldsymbol{\theta}_{UU}}}{(\sum_{M\in\{U,T,I\}}\sum_{k=1}^{|M|}\mathbf{A}_{MU}(k,u))^2} \tag{29}$$

So far we have explained how to compute $\partial\overline{\mathbf{A}}_{UU}/\partial\boldsymbol{\theta}_{UU}$. The same process can be used for computing $\partial\overline{\mathbf{A}}_{TU}/\partial\boldsymbol{\theta}_{UU}$ and $\partial\overline{\mathbf{A}}_{IU}/\partial\boldsymbol{\theta}_{UU}$.

Derivatives with respect to $\boldsymbol{\xi}$. Computing $\partial\mathbf{p}/\partial\boldsymbol{\xi}$ is analogous to computing $\partial\mathbf{p}/\partial\boldsymbol{\theta}$. Since $\partial\mathbf{p}/\partial\boldsymbol{\xi}$ is composed of $\partial\mathbf{p}/\partial\boldsymbol{\xi}_M$ $(M\in\{U,I\})$, without loss of generality, we first focus on how to compute $\partial \mathbf{p}/\partial \boldsymbol{\xi}_U$. Taking the partial derivatives with respect to $\boldsymbol{\xi}_U$ on both sides of Equations 13, 14 and 15, we can get

$$\frac{\partial \mathbf{p}_U}{\partial \boldsymbol{\xi}_U} = (1-\alpha) \sum_{N\in\{U,T,I\}} \overline{\mathbf{A}}_{UN} \frac{\partial \mathbf{p}_N}{\partial \boldsymbol{\xi}_U} + \alpha \frac{\partial \overline{\mathbf{q}}_U}{\partial \boldsymbol{\xi}_U} \tag{30}$$

$$\frac{\partial \mathbf{p}_T}{\partial \boldsymbol{\xi}_U} = (1-\alpha) \sum_{N\in\{U,T,I\}} \overline{\mathbf{A}}_{TN} \frac{\partial \mathbf{p}_N}{\partial \boldsymbol{\xi}_U} + \alpha \frac{\partial \overline{\mathbf{q}}_T}{\partial \boldsymbol{\xi}_U} \tag{31}$$

$$\frac{\partial \mathbf{p}_I}{\partial \boldsymbol{\xi}_U} = (1-\alpha) \sum_{N\in\{U,T,I\}} \overline{\mathbf{A}}_{IN} \frac{\partial \mathbf{p}_N}{\partial \boldsymbol{\xi}_U} + \alpha \frac{\partial \overline{\mathbf{q}}_I}{\partial \boldsymbol{\xi}_U} \tag{32}$$

Following the same rule, $\partial \mathbf{p}/\partial \boldsymbol{\xi}_I$ can also be obtained. Replacing $\boldsymbol{\xi}_I$ with $\boldsymbol{\xi}_M$ ($M \in \{U, I\}$), we can rewrite the above three equations to a single equation in the matrix form:

$$\begin{pmatrix} \frac{\partial \mathbf{p}_U}{\partial \boldsymbol{\xi}_M} \\ \frac{\partial \mathbf{p}_T}{\partial \boldsymbol{\xi}_M} \\ \frac{\partial \mathbf{p}_I}{\partial \boldsymbol{\xi}_M} \end{pmatrix} = (1-\alpha)\overline{\mathbf{A}} \begin{pmatrix} \frac{\partial \mathbf{p}_U}{\partial \boldsymbol{\xi}_M} \\ \frac{\partial \mathbf{p}_T}{\partial \boldsymbol{\xi}_M} \\ \frac{\partial \mathbf{p}_I}{\partial \boldsymbol{\xi}_M} \end{pmatrix} + \alpha \begin{pmatrix} \frac{\partial \overline{\mathbf{q}}_U}{\partial \boldsymbol{\xi}_M} \\ \frac{\partial \overline{\mathbf{q}}_T}{\partial \boldsymbol{\xi}_M} \\ \frac{\partial \overline{\mathbf{q}}_I}{\partial \boldsymbol{\xi}_M} \end{pmatrix} \tag{33}$$

From the above equation, we can see that computing $\partial \mathbf{p}/\partial \boldsymbol{\xi}_M$ also has the same form with Equation 1. More details on the convergence will be discussed in the appendix.

The last detail is how to compute $\partial \overline{\mathbf{q}}/\partial \boldsymbol{\xi}_M$ ($M \in \{U, I\}$). Without loss of generality, suppose M is U, according to Equation 11, we have

$$\frac{\partial \overline{\mathbf{q}}}{\partial \boldsymbol{\xi}_U} = \begin{pmatrix} \frac{\partial \mathbf{q}_U}{\partial \boldsymbol{\xi}_U} D_q^{-1} + \mathbf{q}_U \frac{\partial D_q^{-1}}{\partial \boldsymbol{\xi}_U} \\ \mathbf{0} \\ \mathbf{q}_I \frac{\partial D_q^{-1}}{\partial \boldsymbol{\xi}_U} \end{pmatrix} \tag{34}$$

Each entry of $\mathbf{q}_U$ is defined according to Equation 9. For $u \in U$, we have

$$\frac{\partial \mathbf{q}(u)}{\partial \boldsymbol{\xi}_U} = \frac{\partial f_{node}(\boldsymbol{\xi}_U^T \mathbf{Y}_U)}{\partial \boldsymbol{\xi}_U} \tag{35}$$

When f_{node} is the sigmoid function, we know that $df_{node}(x) / dx = [f_{node}(x)][1 - f_{node}(x)]$. D_q^{-1} is defined according to Equation 12 and the derivative is

$$\frac{\partial D_q^{-1}}{\partial \boldsymbol{\xi}_U} = -\frac{\sum_{k=1}^{|M|} \frac{\partial \mathbf{q}_U(k)}{\partial \boldsymbol{\xi}_U}}{(\sum_{M\in\{U,I\}} \sum_{k=1}^{|M|} \mathbf{q}_M(k))^2} \tag{36}$$

So far we have described how to compute $\partial \overline{\mathbf{q}}/\partial \boldsymbol{\xi}_U$. The same process can be performed to compute $\partial \overline{\mathbf{q}}/\partial \boldsymbol{\xi}_I$

To sum up, we have introduced how to compute $\partial \mathbf{p}/\partial \boldsymbol{\theta}$ and $\partial \mathbf{p}/\partial \boldsymbol{\xi}$, which can be summarized by Algorithm 2.

5. EXPERIMENTAL STUDY

5.1 Datasets

We test OptRank on two publicly available datasets[6]: Delicious and Last.fm, which are published by [2] as benchmarks. Delicious contains 437593 posts involving 1867 users, 40678 tags, 69223 items, 15328 user relations, 197438 tag relations and 151971 item relations. All types of intra-relations we studied are included in Delicious. Posts are represented by <*user*, *tag*, *item*>. Last.fm contains 24164 posts involving 1892 users, 9749 tags, 12523 items and 25434 user relations. Last.fm is a smaller dataset and only user relations are available. We introduce each type of relation and its features as follows.

[6]http://www.grouplens.org/node/462

Algorithm 2: Derivatives of the random walk

Input: Transition matrix $\overline{\mathbf{A}}$ and preference vector $\overline{\mathbf{q}}$
Output: $\frac{\partial \mathbf{p}}{\partial \boldsymbol{\theta}}$ and $\frac{\partial \mathbf{p}}{\partial \boldsymbol{\xi}}$

t=0;
Initialize $\mathbf{p}^{(t)}$
while *p has not converged* **do**
  $\mathbf{p}^{(t+1)} = (1 - \alpha)\overline{\mathbf{A}}\mathbf{p}^{(t)} + \alpha\, \overline{\mathbf{q}}$
  t = t + 1;
t=0;
Initialize $\frac{\partial \mathbf{p}}{\partial \boldsymbol{\theta}}^{(0)}$;
while $\frac{\partial p}{\partial \boldsymbol{\theta}}$ *has not converged* **do**
  Computing $\frac{\partial \mathbf{p}}{\partial \boldsymbol{\theta}}^{(t+1)}$ according to Equation 26
  t = t + 1;
t=0;
Initialize $\frac{\partial \mathbf{p}}{\partial \boldsymbol{\xi}}^{(0)}$;
while $\frac{\partial p}{\partial \boldsymbol{\xi}}$ *has not converged* **do**
  Computing $\frac{\partial \mathbf{p}}{\partial \boldsymbol{\xi}}^{(t+1)}$ according to Equation 33
  t = t + 1;

Inter-relation. For edge <*m*,*n*> ($m \in M \wedge n \in N \wedge M, N \in \{U,T,I\} \wedge M \neq N$), the feature vector $\boldsymbol{X}_{MN}(m,n)$ = (*the times of m co-occurred with n in the posts*). For example, suppose we have <*u*, *t*> ($u \in U \wedge t \in T$), $\boldsymbol{X}_{UT}(u,t)$ = (*the times of u co-occurred with t in the posts*), which means the times of t used by u. In our experiments, we use the same feature set to denote <*m*,*n*> and <*n*,*m*>. This means that $\mathbf{A}_{MN}$ and $\mathbf{A}_{NM}$ are both decided by $\boldsymbol{\xi}_{MN}$ and $\boldsymbol{\theta}_{MN}$.

User Relation. User relations are formed by the social network. Each relation is bi-direction and binary weighted. To find the strength of a user relation, we check their items and tags in common. More formally, user u can be represented by an item vector $\mathbf{A}_{IU}(\cdot, u)$ and a tag vector $\mathbf{A}_{TU}(\cdot, u)$. Each entry of $\mathbf{A}_{IU}$ and $\mathbf{A}_{TU}$ is re-weighted by TF-IDF. Users and items can be viewed as documents and words in the information retrieval. Let $\widetilde{\mathbf{A}}_{MN}$ ($M, N \in \{U,T,I\}$) denote the $\mathbf{A}_{MN}$ re-weighted by TF-IDF. For edge <u_1, u_2> ($u_1, u_2 \in U$), the feature vector $\mathbf{X}_{UU}(u_1, u_2)$ = [cos($\widetilde{\mathbf{A}}_{TU}(\cdot, u_1)$, $\widetilde{\mathbf{A}}_{TU}(\cdot, u_2)$), cos($\widetilde{\mathbf{A}}_{IU}(\cdot, u_1)$, $\widetilde{\mathbf{A}}_{IU}(\cdot, u_2)$)]

Tag Relation. Tag semantic relatedness is computed with the help of Wikipedia[7]. To be more specific, 47% tags are article titles in Wikipedia. Articles link to each other by anchor texts. Semantic relatedness of tag pairs can be inferred from the the number of links between article pairs. We use WikipediaMiner [10], which is an off-the-shelf tool, to calculate semantic relatedness. Only tag pairs that have semantic relatedness larger than 0.25 are retained. To refine the edge weights, tags are also represented by user vectors and item vectors. We perform the same TF-IDF weighting technique to $\mathbf{A}_{UT}$ and $\mathbf{A}_{IT}$. Let $\widetilde{\mathbf{A}}_{UT}$ and $\widetilde{\mathbf{A}}_{IT}$ denote the TF-IDF weighted matrix. For edge (t_1, t_2) ($t_1, t_2 \in T$), edge

[7]http://www.wikipedia.org

feature $\mathbf{X}_{TT}(t_1, t_2)$ = [semantic relatedness, $\cos(\widetilde{\mathbf{A}}_{UT}(\cdot, t_1), \widetilde{\mathbf{A}}_{UT}(\cdot, t_2))$, $\cos(\widetilde{\mathbf{A}}_{IT}(\cdot, t_1), \widetilde{\mathbf{A}}_{IT}(\cdot, t_2))$].

Item Relation. We calculate item similarities based on Web page titles in Delicious. A title is a vector of words with TF-IDF weighting on each entry. Besides content similarities, we refine edge weight with TF-IDF weighted $\widetilde{\mathbf{A}}_{UI}$ and $\widetilde{\mathbf{A}}_{TI}$. For <$i_1, i_2$> ($i_1, i_2 \in I$), $\mathbf{X}_{II}(i_1, i_2)$ = [$\cos(title_1, title_2)$, $\cos(\widetilde{\mathbf{A}}_{UI}(\cdot, i_1), \widetilde{\mathbf{A}}_{UI}(\cdot, i_2))$, $\cos(\widetilde{\mathbf{A}}_{TI}(\cdot, i_1), \widetilde{\mathbf{A}}_{TI}(\cdot, i_2))$]

Like logistic regression, we add a constant feature 1 to each feature set $\mathbf{X}_{MN}$ and all the features are normalized to have mean 0 and standard deviation 1.

5.2 Baselines

Since OptRank is an extension of existing graph-based methods, we want to prove two points: (1) OptRank outperforms existing graph-based methods when only <*user*, *tag*, *item*> is available. (2) OptRank further improves the performance by incorporating social networks, tag semantic relatedness, item content similarities. we choose two graph based methods as our baselines.

Random Walk with Restart. Random Walk with Restart, called RWR for short, is the unsupervised version of OptRank. RWR performs on the graph defined by <*user*, *tag*, *item*>. The weight of the edge <*m*,*n*> ($m \in M \wedge n \in N \wedge M, N \in \{U, T, I\} \wedge M \neq N$) is the times of m cooccurred with n in the posts. Given a user u and an item i for tag recommendation, when the random walker decides to restart, it has the probability of 0.5 to restart at u and 0.5 to restart at i. RWR has been adopted in [6] to incorporate social networks, but the different types of edges are normalized empirically and are hard to reproduce.

FolkRank. FolkRank is a state-of-the-art graph-based algorithm. The graph is defined in the same way with RWR. FolkRank can be summarized as three steps: (1) Calculate a global PageRank score p_{global} for each node. (2) Calculate a personalized PageRank score p_{pref} with special preference to u and i for each node. (3) Calculate FolkRank score as the wins and loses between the personalized PageRank p_{pref} and the global PageRank p_{global}, i.e., $score = p_{pref} - p_{global}$. In our experiments, we set the damping factor to 0.7, which achieves the best performance for FolkRank. In our experiments, FolkRank is denoted by 'FR'.

We are aware that there are many methods based on tensor factorization[12, 13, 15]. However, tensor factorization needs to learn a low rank approximation vector for each user, item and tag. In OptRank, a user can even not exist in the training set but can still get recommendation if she/he has neighbors in the test set. OptRank only needs about 3000 training instances to reach its best performance. However, tensor factorization would fail with such a small training set, which is unfair. For this reason, we did not choose these methods as baselines.

5.3 Evaluation Methodology

Performance Measurements. We use average precision, precision-recall curve and average AUC (Area under the ROC Curve) to measure the performance. We are aware that the optimal of AUC is not necessarily the optimal of average precision/recall. To trade-off between best AUC and best precision, we choose the model that has both high AUC and precision in the cross validation set. Then the model is evaluated on the test set.

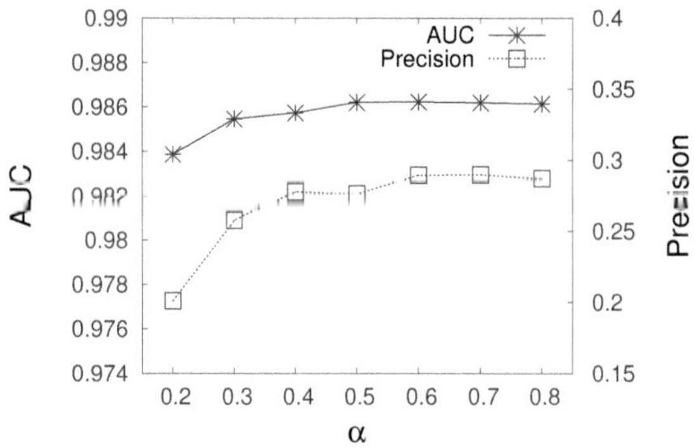

Figure 3: The effect of α

Training/Cross Validation/Test Set. Posts are aggregated into records <u, i, PT> ($u \in U$, $i \in I$). For each dataset, we randomly picked 5000, 3000, and 3000 records as the training set, cross validation set, and test set.

5.4 Parameters

β and learning rate. β in Equation 18 controls the error of approximating $\mathbb{I}(x)$. The bigger β is, the smaller the approximate error is. However, when β gets too big, the derivative at $x = 0$ will also get too steep and will cause a numeric problem. When β gets too small, minimizing $J(\boldsymbol{\theta}, \boldsymbol{\xi})$ would fail to maximize AUC. From Equations 21 and 22, we can know that the summation of the derivatives is divided by $|PT_k||NT_k|$. Since large dataset has big $|PT_k||NT_k|$, we can use a big β. In our experiments, β is 10^9 in Delicious and 10^6 in Last.fm. Learning rate lr is strongly related to β. When lr gets too big, stochastic gradient descent would fail to converge. lr is set to 10 in both datasets.

Restart Probability α. α controls how frequently the random walker chooses to restart. We evaluate how AUC and precision change by differing α from 0.2 to 0.8 in Delicious. The results are shown in Figure 3. OptRank was run on the inter-relation formed by <*user*, *tag*, *item*>. When precision and AUC are both considered, $\alpha \in$[0.6, 0.8] seems to be a good choice. Finally, we set α to 0.7.

5.5 Experimental Results

Results on Delicious. Results on Delicious are shown in Table 1 and Figure 4. FR denote FolkRank. OptRank_Edge, OptRank_Node and OptRank_EN denote OptRank with only edge features enabled, only node features enabled , and both features enabled, respectively. Firstly, we compare the algorithms that are only performed on inter-relations formed by <*user*, *tag*, *item*>. Since RWR always performs better than FR, we only compare OptRank with RWR in the following. When only edge features are enabled, OptRank_Edge has comparable performance with RWR. This indicates that the original transition matrix of RWR and FR is nearly optimal. When only node features are enabled, OptRank_Node learns the best weights for u and i, which improves the top-1 precision by 3.3% compared with RWR. This indicates the original node weight is not optimal. When edge features and node features are both enabled, OptRank_EN futher improves the top-1 precision by 2.4% based on OptRank_Node. From Figure 4 we can know that the OptRank_EN outperforms RWR at top-5 but the advantage disappears at top-10. However, since a user usually annotates an item with less than 5 tags, top-5 performance is considered more important than top-10 performance. In terms of AUC, FolkRank

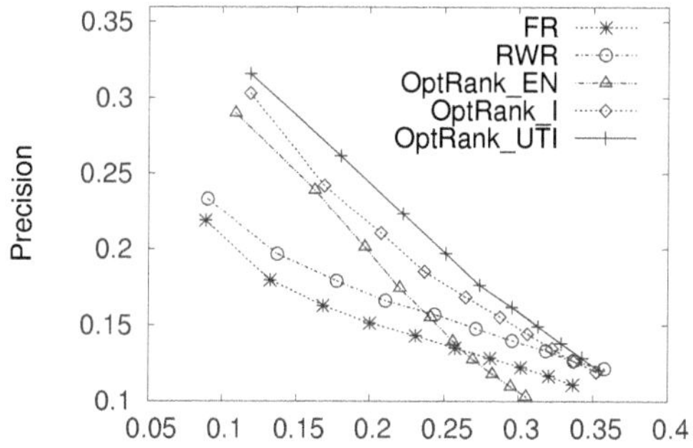

Figure 4: Precision-Recall Curve on Delicious

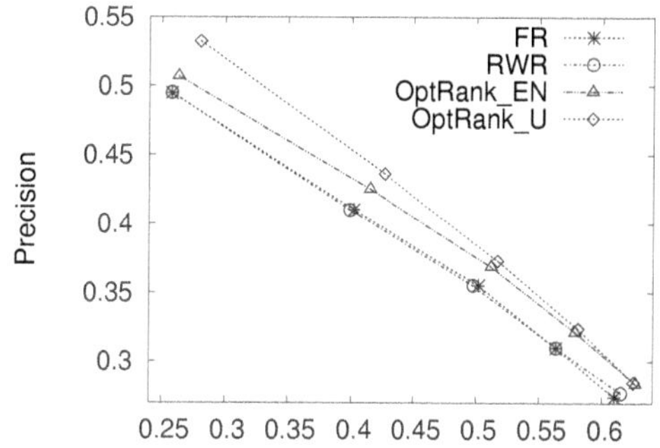

Figure 5: Precision-Recall Curve on Last.fm

Table 1: Precision and AUC on Delicious

Algorithm	P@1	P@2	P@3	AUC
FR	0.219	0.180	0.163	0.6851
RWR	0.233	0.197	0.179	0.9812
OptRank_Edge	0.234	0.194	0.171	0.9851
OptRank_Node	0.266	0.204	0.179	0.9833
OptRank_EN	0.290	0.239	0.201	0.9862
OptRank_U	0.297	0.247	0.215	0.9862
OptRank_T	0.302	0.245	0.213	0.9862
OptRank_I	0.303	0.242	0.210	0.9863
OptRank_UTI	**0.316**	**0.262**	**0.223**	**0.9869**

Table 2: Precision and AUC on Last.fm

Algorithm	P@1	P@2	P@3	AUC
FR	0.495	0.410	0.355	0.9509
RWR	0.495	0.410	0.355	0.9969
OptRank_EN	0.507	0.425	0.369	0.9973
OptRank_U	**0.532**	**0.436**	**0.373**	**0.9975**

has relatively poor performance, worse than the precision. In contrast, RWR has a much better average AUC. This is probably because FolkRank is an empirically designed algorithm and relies too much on the global information. We can see that a high precision does not indicate a high AUC.

Now we discuss how OptRank performs when extra user relations, tag relations and item relations exist. When each type of relation is considered separately, OptRank_U, OptRank_T and OptRank_I improve the top-1 precision by around 1% based on OptRank_EN, which is not very significant compared with previous improvement. However, as we can see from Figure 4, the top-10 performance of OptRank_I is significantly improved compared with OptRank_EN. Since OptRank_U, OptRank_T and OptRank_I are comparable, only OptRank_I is shown in Figure 4. When all the relations are combined, we can see that OptRank_UTI achieves the best performance at all top-k performance. In terms of AUC, OptRank_UTI also achieves the best performance.

Results on Last.fm. The results are shown in Figure 5 and Table 2. The results are significantly better than the results on Delicious. This can be explained in terms of data sparsity. When only inter-relations are considered, a post can be viewed as an entry in the three-dimension array spanned by users, tags and items. $1.05 \times 10^{(-7)}$ and $0.83 \times 10^{(-7)}$ of the entries in Last.fm and Delicious are known, respectively. Thus Last.fm is less sparse and more predictable than Delicious. In Last.fm, all algorithms have comparable performance at top-10. So we mainly focus on the top-5 performance in this experiment and this is reasonable since users usually annotate an item within 5 tags. From Figure 5 we can know that FolkRank and RWR have comparable performances in term of precision, which is different from the results on Delicious. When node features and edge features are both considered, OptRank_EN improves P@1, P@2 and P@3 by 1.2%, 1.5%, 1.5% respectively compared with FR and RWR. Although Last.fm is less sparse than Delicious, when the social network is combined, OptRank_U successfully improves the top-1 precision by 3.7% compared with the two baselines. In terms of AUC, empirically designed FR still falls behind other methods. OptRank_U achieves the highest AUC.

To sum up, we have two conclusions from the experiments: (1) When only <*user*, *tag*, *item*> is available, OptRank outperforms RWR and FolkRank. (2) OptRank successfully combined extra relations to improve the performance. Now we discuss some details about the training process. Since Delicious is bigger and takes more time, the training size and running time are reported according to Delicious.

Over-fitting Issues. Over-fitting does not seem to be a problem in our model since we only have 18 parameters when all the relations are combined[8]. OptRank_UTI achieves nearly the same top-1 precision in the cross validation set and test set.

Training Size. The training size is really small compared with tensor factorization. OptRank_EN achieves its best performance when 600 training instances are passed. OptRank_UTI achieves its best performance when 1200 training instances are passed.

Running Time. The experiments were conducted on a single PC with a 2-core 3.2GHz CPU and 2G main memory. We implemented the algorithm in Matlab with full vectorization. When all the relations are combined, each training instance takes nearly 3.5 seconds. Prediction takes around 0.1 seconds per instance and most of the time is spent on computing the gradients. Training with 5000 instances would take 4.8 hours at most. However, all the algorithms in our experiments achieve their best performance within 2000 training instances.

6. RELATED WORK

There are mainly three approaches for personalized recommendation in social tagging systems: (1) Graph-based approach [4, 5, 17]. (2) Tensor decomposition [12, 13, 15]. The annotation relation is modeled as a cube with many

[8]Each inter relation has 2 parameters, user relation has 3 parameters, tag relation and item relation has 4 parameters, respectively.

unknown entries. After performing tensor decomposition, we can predict the unknown entries by low-rank approximations. (3) User/Item based collaborative filtering [8, 11, 18]. The original user-item matrix is extended by including tag information so that we can apply user/item based collaborative filtering methods.

Besides annotation behaviors, user space, tag space and item space have also been explored. [9] has studied trust networks and proposed a factor analysis approach based on probabilistic matrix factorization. [6] incorporates social network for item recommendation, but fails to improve the performance significantly. [14] links social tags from Flickr into WordNet. [7] introduces item taxonomies into recommender systems.

This paper is mainly inspired by two recent work on graph-based learning [1] and semi-supervised learning [3]. [1] proposes supervised random walks to learn the edge weights for link prediction in homogenous graph. This paper extends [1] with multi-type edges and nodes. [3] has proposed similar idea to learn edge weights and node weights with an inductive learning framework in homogenous graph. Since a recommender should have the ability to predict for future events, our framework is different from [3] in that ours belongs to transductive learning.

7. CONCLUSION AND FUTURE WORK

In this paper, we propose an optimization-based graph method for personalized tag recommendation. To alleviate data sparsity, different sources of information are incorporated into the optimization framework. There are some problems unsolved for future work: (1) Reducing the graph size. Since the random walker frequently restarts at u and i, nodes that are far away from u and i may be cut without influencing the final ranking. (2) Comparing with tensor factorization methods under a suitable experiment setting. (3) More features can be explored to further improve the results, such as the temporal factors.

8. ACKNOWLEDGMENTS

This work was supported in part by National Basic Research Program of China (973 Program) under Grant No. 2011CB302206, and National Natural Science Foundation of China under Grant No. 60833003.

9. REFERENCES

[1] L. Backstrom and J. Leskovec. Supervised random walks: predicting and recommending links in social networks. In *WSDM*, pages 635–644, 2011.

[2] I. Cantador, P. Brusilovsky, and T. Kuflik. Workshop hetrec 2011. RecSys 2011. ACM, 2011.

[3] B. Gao, T.-Y. Liu, W. Wei, T. Wang, and H. Li. Semi-supervised ranking on very large graphs with rich metadata. In *KDD*, pages 96–104, 2011.

[4] Z. Guan, J. Bu, Q. Mei, C. Chen, and C. Wang. Personalized tag recommendation using graph-based ranking on multi-type interrelated objects. In *SIGIR*, pages 540–547, 2009.

[5] R. Jäschke, L. B. Marinho, A. Hotho, L. Schmidt-Thieme, and G. Stumme. Tag recommendations in folksonomies. In *PKDD*, pages 506–514, 2007.

[6] I. Konstas, V. Stathopoulos, and J. M. Jose. On social networks and collaborative recommendation. In *SIGIR*, pages 195–202, 2009.

[7] H. Liang, Y. Xu, Y. Li, and R. Nayak. Personalized recommender system based on item taxonomy and folksonomy. CIKM '10, pages 1641–1644, 2010.

[8] H. Liang, Y. Xu, Y. Li, R. Nayak, and X. Tao. Connecting users and items with weighted tags for personalized item recommendations. HT '10, pages 51–60. ACM, 2010.

[9] H. Ma, T. C. Zhou, M. R. Lyu, and I. King. Improving recommender systems by incorporating social contextual information. *ACM Trans. Inf. Syst.*, 29:9:1–9:23, Apr. 2011.

[10] D. Milne. *An Open-Source Toolkit for Mining Wikipedia*, volume 2889. 2009.

[11] J. Peng, D. D. Zeng, H. Zhao, and F.-y. Wang. Collaborative filtering in social tagging systems based on joint item-tag recommendations. CIKM '10, pages 809–818. ACM, 2010.

[12] S. Rendle, L. B. Marinho, A. Nanopoulos, and L. Schmidt-Thieme. Learning optimal ranking with tensor factorization for tag recommendation. In *KDD*, pages 727–736, 2009.

[13] S. Rendle and L. Schmidt-Thieme. Pairwise interaction tensor factorization for personalized tag recommendation. In *WSDM*, pages 81–90, 2010.

[14] B. Sigurbjörnsson and R. van Zwol. Flickr tag recommendation based on collective knowledge. WWW '08, pages 327–336. ACM, 2008.

[15] P. Symeonidis, A. Nanopoulos, and Y. Manolopoulos. Tag recommendations based on tensor dimensionality reduction. In *RecSys*, pages 43–50, 2008.

[16] P. Symeonidis, A. Nanopoulos, and Y. Manolopoulos. A unified framework for providing recommendations in social tagging systems based on ternary semantic analysis. *TKDE*, 22(2):179–192, 2010.

[17] H. Yildirim and M. S. Krishnamoorthy. A random walk method for alleviating the sparsity problem in collaborative filtering. In *RecSys*, pages 131–138, 2008.

[18] Y. Zhen, W.-J. Li, and D.-Y. Yeung. Tagicofi: tag informed collaborative filtering. RecSys '09, pages 69–76. ACM, 2009.

APPENDIX

We prove the convergence of Equations 26 and 33. Both the equations can be rewritten to a more general form:

$$\mathbf{p}^{(t+1)} = \lambda\overline{\mathbf{A}}\mathbf{p}^{(t)} + \mu\mathbf{q}$$

where $0 \leq \lambda, \mu \leq 1$, $\overline{\mathbf{A}}$ is a transition matrix with each column summing to 1 and $\mathbf{q}$ can be any vector with the same dimension of $\mathbf{p}$. Suppose $\mathbf{p}^{(0)} = \boldsymbol{\pi}$, we have $\mathbf{p}^{(1)} = \lambda\overline{\mathbf{A}}\boldsymbol{\pi} + \mu\mathbf{q}$, $\mathbf{p}^{(2)} = (\lambda\overline{\mathbf{A}})^2\boldsymbol{\pi} + \lambda\overline{\mathbf{A}}\mu\mathbf{q} + \mu\mathbf{q}$, ..., $\mathbf{p}^{(n)} = (\lambda\overline{\mathbf{A}})^n\boldsymbol{\pi} + \sum_{k=0}^{n-1}(\lambda\overline{\mathbf{A}})^k\mu\mathbf{q}$. Since $0 \leq \lambda, \mu \leq 1$ and the eigenvalues of the transition matrix $\overline{\mathbf{A}}$ are in [-1, 1], we have $\lim_{n\to\infty}(\lambda\overline{\mathbf{A}})^n = \mathbf{0}$ and $\lim_{n\to\infty}\sum_{k=0}^{n-1}(\lambda\overline{\mathbf{A}})^k = (\mathbf{I} - \lambda\overline{\mathbf{A}})^{-1}$. So $\mathbf{p}^{(n)}$ finally converges to $\mathbf{p}^* = (\mathbf{I} - \lambda\overline{\mathbf{A}})^{-1}\mu\mathbf{q}$.

Cross-domain Collaboration Recommendation

Jie Tang[†], Sen Wu[†], Jimeng Sun[‡], and Hang Su[†]
[†]Department of Computer Science and Technology, Tsinghua University
[‡]IBM TJ Watson Research Center, USA
jietang@tsinghua.edu.cn, ronaldosen@gmail.com, jimeng@us.ibm.com, suhang@sse.buaa.edu.cn

ABSTRACT

Interdisciplinary collaborations have generated huge impact to society. However, it is often hard for researchers to establish such cross-domain collaborations. What are the patterns of cross-domain collaborations? How do those collaborations form? Can we predict this type of collaborations?

Cross-domain collaborations exhibit very different patterns compared to traditional collaborations in the same domain: 1) **sparse connection:** cross-domain collaborations are rare; 2) **complementary expertise:** cross-domain collaborators often have different expertise and interest; 3) **topic skewness:** cross-domain collaboration topics are focused on a subset of topics. All these patterns violate fundamental assumptions of traditional recommendation systems.

In this paper, we analyze the cross-domain collaboration data from research publications and confirm the above patterns. We propose the Cross-domain Topic Learning (CTL) model to address these challenges. For handling sparse connections, CTL consolidates the existing cross-domain collaborations through topic layers instead of at author layers, which alleviates the sparseness issue. For handling complementary expertise, CTL models topic distributions from source and target domains separately, as well as the correlation across domains. For handling topic skewness, CTL only models relevant topics to the cross-domain collaboration.

We compare CTL with several baseline approaches on large publication datasets from different domains. CTL outperforms baselines significantly on multiple recommendation metrics. Beyond accurate recommendation performance, CTL is also insensitive to parameter tuning as confirmed in the sensitivity analysis.

Categories and Subject Descriptors

H.3.3 [**Information Search and Retrieval**]: Text Mining; J.4 [**Social Behavioral Sciences**]: Miscellaneous

General Terms

Algorithms, Experimentation

Keywords

Collaboration recommendation, Social network, Social influence

KDD'12, August 12–16, 2012, Beijing, China.

1. INTRODUCTION

Social network analysis focuses on modeling interactions between people. Researchers have studied various issues in social networks, such as network properties [6, 11] and generation processes [18], link predictions [19, 20, 21, 32] and recommendations [2, 7, 17]. Despite all the existing research in social networks, little has been done on analyzing collaborations across two different domains.

Interdisciplinary collaborations have generated huge impact to society. For example, collaborations between biology and computer science revolutionized the field of bioinformatics. Because of these cross-domain collaborations, originally extremely expensive tasks such DNA sequencing have become scalable and affordable to a much broader population. Now medicine and data mining are working together in the field of medical informatics, which is a big growth area that is expected to have huge impact on medicine [24]. Indeed, cross-domain collaboration has become increasingly important. Figure 1 shows the increasing trend of cross-domain collaborations over the past fifteen years across different domains in a publication database (Cf. § 4 for details). In most of the cases, there exists a clear increasing trend of the cross-domain collaborations.

However, it is often hard for researchers to establish such cross-domain collaborations. What are the patterns of cross-domain collaborations? How do those collaborations form? Can we predict this type of collaborations? Cross-domain collaborations often exhibit very different challenges compared to traditional collaborations in the same domain:

First, **sparse connection**, cross-domain collaborations are rare compared to traditional collaborations within a domain, partly because it is difficult for an outsider to find the right collaborator in the field that one does not know. This also makes it challenging to directly use a supervised learning approach due to the lack of training samples.

Second, **complementary expertise**, cross-domain collaborators often have different expertise and interest; For example, data mining researchers can easily identify who they want to work with in the data mining field, because the topics are known to them. However, for a cardiologist who wants to apply data mining techniques to predict heart failures, it will be difficult for her to find the right collaborators in data mining. Because these two fields (cardiology and data mining) are completely different with different terminology and problems. It is very difficult for one from cardiology to identify the right topics in data mining to look for collaborators.

Third, **topic skewness**, not all topics are relevant for cross-domain collaborations. In fact, in our study, only less than 9% of all possible topics pairs across domains have collaborations. Therefore, for the task of cross-domain collaboration recommendation,

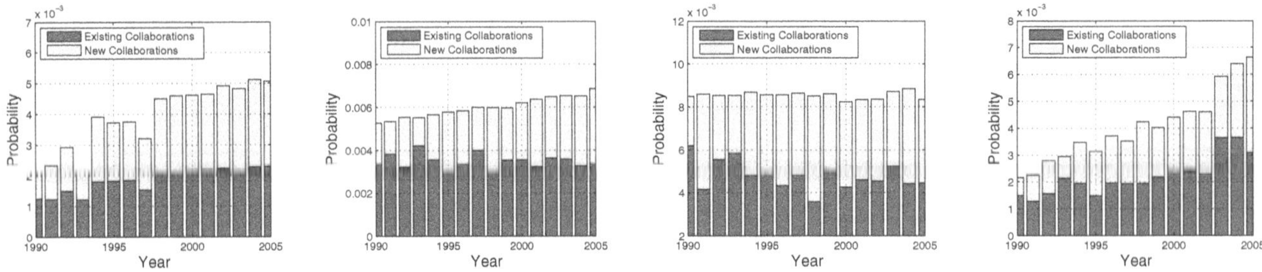

(a) DM - TH (b) DM - MI (c) DM - VIS (d) MI - DB

Figure 1: The comparison of existing collaboration and new collaboration trends over years. DM - Data Mining domain; MI - Medical Informatics domain; TH - Theory domain; VIS - Visualization domain; DB - Database domain. The trends of cross-domain collaborations in all but one case are growing (The exception between DM and VIS remain roughly constant over time). Newly formed cross-domain collaborations are significantly in all cases.

we should focus on better modeling those topics with high probability of having cross-domain collaborations.

Despite of the above challenges, once such cross-domain collaboration is successfully formed, its impact is usually tremendous. In our study, cross-domain collaborations constitute a small portion of all possible collaborations as shown in Figure 1. The trends of cross-domain collaboration in many cases are growing. Newly formed cross-domain collaborations are significant in all cases, which confirmed the potential need for cross-domain collaborations.

Based on these observations, we propose the Cross-domain Topic Learning (CTL) method that addresses all three challenges including sparse connection, complementary expertise and topic skewness. CTL is a generative topic model that differentiates relevant topics to cross-domain collaboration from other topics.

We compare CTL with several baseline approaches on large publication data sets of different domains. CTL outperforms others significantly on recommendation metrics. Beyond accurate recommendation performance, CTL is also insensitive to parameter tuning as confirmed in the sensitivity analysis. Finally, we integrate CTL into a large-scale web application for recommending cross-domain research collaborators, which further demonstrates the scalability of CTL in handling real-time queries.

The rest of this paper is organized as follows: Section 2 formulates the cross-domain recommendation problem formally; Section 3 presents our proposed methods on cross-domain recommendation; Section 4 describes the experiments; Section 5 presents the related work; then we conclude in Section 6.

2. PROBLEM DEFINITION

We present required definitions and formulate the problem of cross-domain collaboration recommendation. Without loss of generality, we assume there are two domains, the source domain and the target domain. Our goal is to recommend potential collaborators in the target domain for a specific user from the source domain.

Definition 1. **Source/Target domain.** The source (or target) domain can be represented as a social network $G = (V, E, X)$, where V is a set of $|V| = N$ users and $E \subseteq V \times V$ is a set of undirected (collaborative) relationships between users, X is an $N \times d$ attribute matrix in which every row corresponds to a vector of attribute values of a user. We use x_j to denote the jth attribute.

We use superscript ^{S} and ^{T} to differentiate the source domain and the target. If there is no ambiguity, we will omit ^{S} for the source domain and use superscript $'$ for the target, for brevity. Suppose each user v_i is associated with d attributes. For example, in the research collaboration network, each user is associated with a set of publication papers or a set of words appearing in those papers. Given this, we have the following definition:

Definition 2. **Domain-specific topic models.** A topic model θ_i of a user v_i is a multinomial distribution of attributes $\{P(x_j|\theta_i)\}_j$. Then a domain is considered as a mixture of multiple user-specific topic models. The assumption behind is that attributes associated with the user are sampled following a distribution corresponding to each topic, i.e., $P(x|\theta_i)$.

Such a definition is usually used in the LDA/PLSI style topic models [4, 15]. According to the above definition, attributes with the highest probability associated with each topic would suggest the semantics represented by the topic. For example, a "Data Mining" topic discovered from the publication data can be represented by keywords "clustering", "learning", "classification", etc.

The input of our problem consists of a source domain G^S and a target domain G^T, each associated with topic models. Please note that the source domain and the target domain can be overlapping, i.e., $V^S \cap V^T \neq \varnothing$. Given this, we can precisely define the following problem:

Problem 1. **Cross-domain collaboration recommendation.** Given (1) a source domain G^S and a target domain G^T, (2) topic models θ and θ' associated with users in the two domains respectively, the goal is to rank and recommend potential collaborators in the target domain for a specific user v_q from the source domain.

The fundamental challenge of this problem is how to capture the collaboration patterns across different domains. Within the same domain, homophily is often considered as the driven force for the formation of collaborative relationships, which suggests that people with the similar interest (topic model θ) tend to collaborate with each other. However, in the cross-domain setting, the problem is very different. Technically, it is challenging to extract and discriminate topics in the two domains. In particular, given a specific user and her topic distribution from the source domain, on *which topics* and with *whom* should she collaborate in the target domains?

3. CROSS-DOMAIN TOPIC LEARNING

We begin by considering some baseline solutions and then propose our cross-domain topic learning approach. A simple approach to the problem is to construct a collaboration graph connecting users between source and target domains and then use a random walk with restart algorithm [28] to rank collaborators in the target

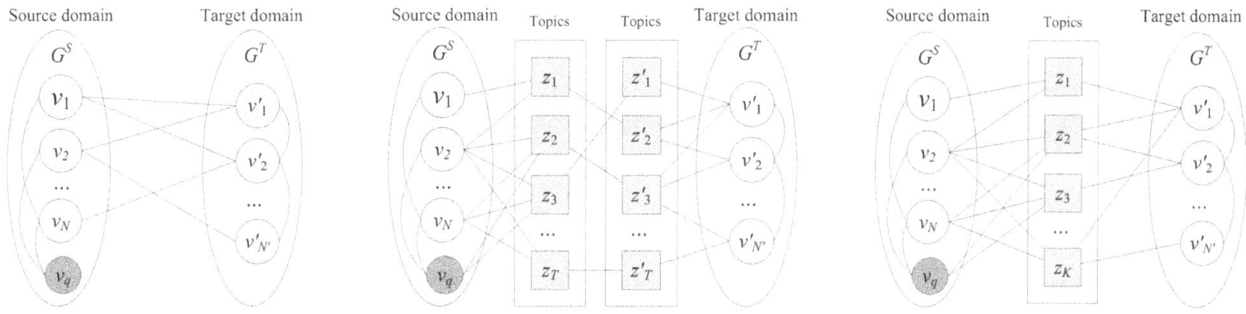

(a) Author matching (b) Topic matching (c) CTL

Figure 2: Graphical representation of the three recommendation models: author matching, topic matching, and CTL.

domain. We call this method *Author Matching*. The details of the algorithm are described in Section 3.1.

The problem with Author Matching is the sparse connections between authors across two domains. To alleviate this problem, the second model is to consolidate the correlation between the underlying topics. Suppose each domain has T different topics and each user has a distribution over the topics. We can augment the collaboration graph with two topic layers (as shown in Figure 2(b)). The links between the two topic layers indicate the alignment between topics, which implicitly represents the complementary expertise between users. Based on this representation, a random walk with restart algorithm can be again applied to the graph to rank (both topic and user) nodes in the target domain. We call this method *Topic Matching*, and details are described in Section 3.2.

Topic matching improves the cross domain connections through a subset of topic pairs from source domain to target domain. However, not all topic pairs are relevant for collaboration (topic skewness). Therefore, blindly computing all topics from source and target domains are not necessary for collaboration recommendation and often lead to sub optimal results. One challenge here is how to differentiate relevant "collaboration" topics from other topics. We further design a Cross-domain Topic Learning (CTL) algorithm to address this challenge in Section 3.3.

3.1 Author Matching

Based on the historic cross-domain collaborations, we create a collaboration graph, as shown in Figure 2(a). The problem is to rank relevant nodes in the target domain G^T for a given query node v_q in the source domain G^S. Measuring the relatedness of two nodes in the graph can be achieved using the Random Walks with Restarts (RWR) theory [22, 28]. Starting from node v_q, a RWR is performed by following a link to another node according to the weight of the link at each step.[1] Also, in every step, there is a probability τ to return the node v_q. The relatedness score of node v_i wrt node v_q is defined as the stationary probability r_i that the random walk will finally arrive node v_i, i.e.,

$$\mathbf{r}^{(t+1)} = (1-\tau)\mathbf{S} \cdot \mathbf{r}^{(t)} + \tau \mathbf{q} \tag{1}$$

where $\mathbf{r}^{(t)}$ is a vector with each element r_i^t denoting the probability that the random walk at step t arrives at node v_i; $\mathbf{q}$ is a vector of zero with the element corresponding to the starting node v_q set to 1, i.e., $q_{v_q} = 1$; $\mathbf{S}$ defines the transition probability of the random walk, with element S_{ij} denoting the random walking probability from node v_i to node v_j.

3.2 Topic Matching

The author matching method only considers the network structure information, but ignores the content (topic) information. How do people collaborate across different domains? And what are the hottest topics on which people from different domains tend to collaborate?

Recently, probabilistic topic models have been successfully applied to multiple text mining tasks to extract topics from text [4, 15, 27]. We employ an Author-Conference-Topic (ACT) model [31], which utilizes the topic distribution to represent the interdependencies among authors, papers, and publication venues.[2] The model simulates the process when people collaborate on a work, e.g., writing a scientific paper, using a series of probabilistic steps. In essence, for each object it estimates a mixture of topic distributions which represent the probability of the object associated with every topic. Such as for each author v, we have a set of probabilities $\{P(z_i|v)\}_i$ or $\{\theta_{vz_i}\}_i$, respectively denoting how likely author v is interested in topic z_i. Similarly, we have $\{P(x_j|z)\}_j$ or $\{\phi_{zx_j}\}_j$, the probability of attribute x_j (e.g., a keyword) given topic z. We use Gibbs sampling to learn the probabilities. The interested reader can refer to [31] for more details.

Combining topic model into random walk. We now discuss how to combine the topic model into the random walk framework. First, we apply the ACT model to the source and the target domains respectively and obtain two sets of topic distributions. Then we estimate the alignment between topics of these two domains. We calculate the alignment according to the historic cross-domain collaborations. Specifically, the strength of the alignment between topic z_i from the source domain and topic z'_j from the target domain is estimated by:

$$S_{z_i z'_j} = \frac{1}{\kappa} \sum_{(v,v') \in E^{ST}} [P(z_i|v) + P(z'_j|v')] \tag{2}$$

where κ is a normalization factor; $(v, v') \in E^{ST}$ indicates a cross-domain collaboration between v and v'.

We augment the graph generated in the author matching method with topic nodes $\{z\}$ and $\{z'\}$ extracted from the two domains. Figure 2(b) shows the graphical structure, which suggests that a random walk can be performed from a user v to a topic z and from

[1]In the author matching method, we use a uniform weight, i.e., weights of links of a node v to its neighbors are defined as $\frac{1}{NB(v)}$, where $NB(v)$ is the number of neighbors of node v. In §3.2, we will introduce how to define the weight based on topic model.

[2]The ACT model can be considered as an extension of LDA [4], but considers the collaborative relationships between users and the difference of various objects (e.g., author, paper, and conference/journal).

Input: a source domain G^S and a target domain G^T
Output: estimated parameters θ,θ',ϕ, ϑ, and λ

Initialize an ACT model in G^S by learning from documents written by authors only from G^S;
Similarly, initialize an ACT model for target domain G^T;
foreach *collaborated document d* **do**
  foreach *word* $x_{di} \in d$ **do**
    Toss a coin s_{di} according to $bernoulli(s_{di}) \sim beta(\gamma_t, \gamma)$, where $beta(.)$ is a Beta distribution, and γ_t and γ are two parameters;
    if $s_{di} = 0$ **then**
      Randomly select a pair (v, v') from d's authors, where v is an author from G^S and v' from G^T;
      Draw a topic $z_{di} \sim multi(\vartheta_{vv'})$ from the topic mixture $\vartheta_{vv'}$ specific to (v, v');
    end
    if $s_{di} = 1$ **then**
      Randomly select a user v;
      Draw a topic $z_{di} \sim multi(\theta_v)$ from the topic model of user v;
    end
  end
  Draw a word $x_{di} \sim multi(\phi_{z_{di}})$ from z_{di}-specific word distribution;
end

Algorithm 1: Probabilistic generative process in CTL.

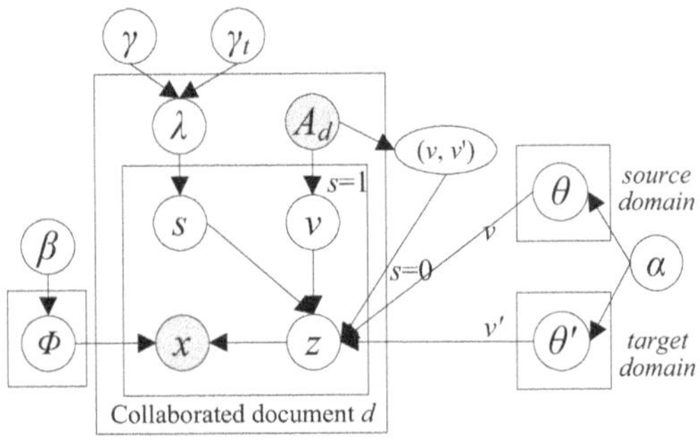

Figure 3: Graphical representation of CTL model.

a topic z of the source domain to a topic z' of the target domain (and vice versa). The link weight between user node v and topic node z is defined as the probability $P(z|v)$ obtained from the ACT model. Then the relatedness of the query node to a target topic z' is defined by a similar formula as that in Eq. 1 and analogously we can define the relatedness between the query node and user nodes in the target domain.

3.3 Cross-domain Topic Learning (CTL)

The topic matching method does not discriminate the "collaboration" topics from those topics existing in only one domain. As a result, the "irrelevant" topics (irrelevant to collaboration) may hurt the collaboration recommendation performance. We develop a new topic modeling approach called Cross-domain Topic Learning (CTL) to model topics of the source domain and the target domain simultaneously.

Model description. The basic idea here is to use two correlated generative processes to model the source and the target domains together. The first process is to model documents written by authors from single domain (either source or target). The second process is to model collaborated documents. For each word in a collaborated document, we use a Bernoulli distribution to determine whether it is generated from a "collaboration" topic or a topic-specific to one domain only. Figure 3 shows the graphical structure of the CTL model. (For simplicity, we omit the modeling part for single domain and focus on the modeling of the collaborated documents.) CTL models each cross-domain collaborated document using topic models of authors from the source domain and the target domain.

Table 1: Notations in the CTL model.

SYMBOL	DESCRIPTION
T	number of topics
d	a collaborated document
A_d	a set of authors of document d
x_{di}	the ith attribute (word) in document d
z_{di}	the topic assigned to attribute x_{di}
s_{di}	if x_{di} is a word from a single domain or a cross domain
θ_v	multinomial distribution over topics specific to author v
$\vartheta_{vv'}$	multinomial distribution over topics specific to author pair (v,v')
ϕ_z	multinomial distribution over words specific to topic z
α, β	Dirichlet priors to multinomial distributions θ, θ' and ϕ
λ	parameter for sampling the binary variable s
γ, γ_t	Beta parameters to generate λ

Let us briefly introduce notations. A_d is a set of authors of document d; v is an author and (v, v') is an author pair randomly sampled to be responsible for word x; s is a binary variable indicating whether the current word inherits the topic from a single domain ($s = 1$) or by a cross-domain collaboration $s = 0$; θ and θ' are topic models from the source domain and the target domain, respectively; $\vartheta_{vv'}$ is a collaboration topic model specific to author pair (v, v'); α is the Dirichlet hyperparameter; λ is a parameter for sampling the binary variable s; γ and γ_t are Beta parameters to generate λ. Table 1 summarizes the notations used in the CTL model.

Formally, the generative process is described in Algorithm 1: first, documents of the two domains G^S and G^T are partitioned into three clusters: documents written by authors only from the source domain, documents written by authors only from the target domain, and documents collaborated by authors from both domains. Then CTL respectively extracts topics of authors from the first two document clusters (without cross-domain collaborations) according to the distribution$p(\theta_v|\alpha)$ and $p(\theta'_{v'}|\alpha)$, where α is the Dirichlet prior. For simplicity, we use the same prior α for both source and target domains.

Second, CTL models the cross domain collaboration documents. For each word x_{di} in document d, a coin s is tossed according to $p(s|d) \sim beta(\gamma_t, \gamma)$, where $beta(.)$ is a Beta distribution. When $s = 1$, a single user v (or v') is chosen according to a uniform distribution, then the word x_{di} is sampled from a selected topic z_{di} specific to the user v, according to θ_v (therefore, this is not a cross-domain collaboration). When $s = 0$, a pair of cross-domain collaborators (v, v') are selected, and a new multinomial distribution $\vartheta_{vv'}$ is constructed by combining θ_v and $\theta_{v'}$ (therefore, cross-domain collaboration is formed). More specifically, we first expand the source and target topic spaces to be of the same dimension. For example, if source domain has 10 topics and target domain 5 topics, the expanded topic space will have 15 topics (10 from source domain and 5 from target domain). The expanded source topic distribution $\tilde{\theta}_v = < \theta_v, 0, \ldots, 0 >$, where we set 0 on the target topics. Similarly, we define the expanded target topic distribution to be $\tilde{\theta}'_{v'} = < 0, \ldots, 0, \theta'_v >$. The new distribution $\vartheta_{vv'}$ is then defined as $\tilde{\theta}_v + \tilde{\theta}_{v'}$, a simple mixture of the two expanded multinomials of θ_v and $\theta_{v'}$ [5]. Finally the word x_{di} is sampled from a collaboration topic z_{di} according to the new distribution $\vartheta_{vv'}$.

Figure 4 illustrates an example of CTL learning. Before CTL learning, each author only has topic distribution in either source or

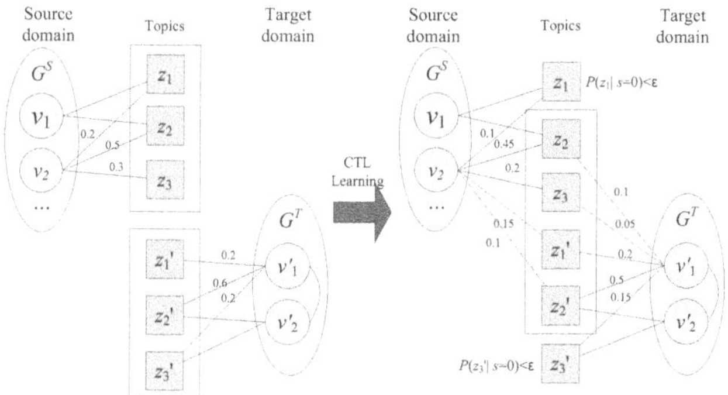

Figure 4: Intuitive explanation of the CTL learning. ϵ **is a parameter to select collaboration topics.**

target domain (zero probability on topics from the other domain). Then, CTL smoothes topics distributions across the two domains. Users from the source domain will also have a probability over topics extracted from the target domain, and vice versa. After training the CTL model, we also obtain a set of "collaboration topics" between the two domains, i.e., topics with the highest posterior probabilities $P(z|s=0,\cdot)$ (or $P(z|s=0,\cdot) > \epsilon$) in the collaborated documents. (Here, $\cdot$ indicates all the other parameters we should consider when calculating the probability.) For example in right hand side of Figure 4, the box indicates those collaboration topics.

Model inference. We use Gibbs sampling to estimate unknown parameters $\{\theta, \theta', \vartheta, \phi, \lambda\}$ in the CTL model. In particular, we evaluate (a) the posterior distribution on z' (or z) for each word in the document written by authors only from a single domain and then use the results to infer θ' (or θ); (b) the posterior distribution on s, and then use the sampling results of z and z' according to s to update ϑ, θ and θ'. Finally, λ and ϕ can be inferred from the obtained topic models. More specifically, we begin with the joint probability of all documents in the two domains, and then using the chain rule, we obtain the posterior probability of sampling the topic for each word. For (a) we use the same sampling algorithm as that for the LDA model (or the ACT model) (cf. [13] or [31]), i.e. with the posterior probability:

$$P(z_{di}|\mathbf{z}_{-di}, \mathbf{x}, \cdot) = \frac{n_{vz_{di}}^{-di} + \alpha}{\sum_z (n_{vz}^{-di} + \alpha)} \times \frac{m_{z_{di}x_{di}}^{-di} + \beta}{\sum_x (m_{z_{di}x}^{-di} + \beta)} \quad (3)$$

where n_{vz} is the number of times that topic z has been sampled from the multinomial distribution specific to a randomly selected author v; m_{zx} is the number of times that word x has been generated by topic z; the number n^{-di} with the superscript $-di$ denotes a quantity, excluding the current instance. We use a similar process for both domains.

For parameter estimation in (b), we consider a two-step Gibbs sampling. We first sample the coin s according to the posterior probability: (Detailed derivation is given in Appendix.)

$$\begin{aligned} P(s_{di}=0|\mathbf{s}_{-di}, \mathbf{z}, \cdot) = & \frac{n_{ds_0}^{-di} + \gamma_t}{n_{ds_0}^{-di} + n_{ds_1}^{-di} + \gamma_t + \gamma} \\ & \times \frac{n_{vv'z_{di}}^{-di} + (n_{vz_{di}} + n_{v'z_{di}}) + \alpha}{\sum_z (n_{vv'z}^{-di} + (n_{vz_{di}} + n_{v'z_{di}}) + \alpha)} \end{aligned} \quad (4)$$

where n_{ds_0} is the number of times that $s=0$ has been sampled in document d; (v, v') is the selected user pair to be responsible for x_{di}; $n_{vv'z}$ is the number of times that topic z has been sampled from user pair (v, v'). $P(s_{di}=1|\cdot)$ can be analogously defined as the above equation. The only difference is to replace the sum of the two terms $(n_{vz_{di}} + n_{v'z_{di}})$ with the number by a selected single user v (or v').

The posterior probability of topic z is defined as:

$$\begin{aligned} P(z_{di}|s_{di}=0, \mathbf{x}, \mathbf{z}_{-di}, \cdot) = & \frac{m_{z_{di}x_{di}}^{-di} + m_{z_{di}x_{di}} + m'_{z_{di}x_{di}} + \beta}{\sum_x (m_{z_{di}x}^{-di} + m_{z_{di}x} + m'_{z_{di}x} + \beta)} \\ & \times \frac{n_{vv'z_{di}}^{-di} + (n_{vz_{di}} + n_{v'z_{di}}) + \alpha}{\sum_z (n_{vv'z}^{-di} + (n_{vz} + n_{v'z}) + \alpha)} \end{aligned} \quad (5)$$

where m_{zx}^{-di} is the number of times that word x has been generated by topic z in the collaborated documents; m_{zx} and m'_{zx} respectively represents the number of times that word x has been generated by topic z in the source domain and that in the target domain.

During the parameter estimation, the algorithm keeps track of a $V \times T$ (user by topic) count matrix for both domains, a $D \times 2$ (collaborated document by coin), a $2 \times T$ (coin by topic) count matrices, and a $AP \times T$ (user pair by topic) count matrix (AP is the number of user pairs). Given these matrices, we can estimate the probabilities of θ, θ', ϑ, ϕ, and λ.

Cross-domain recommendation via random walk. We combine the learned "collaboration" topics by CTL into the collaboration graph (Cf. Figure 2(c)). In principle, there could be a link between any user node and topic node (the difference is the link weight). To control the density of the constructed network, we define a parameter ϵ and add links between users and topics only when $P(z|s=0,\cdot) > \epsilon$. A smaller ϵ results in a more dense network. Random walk with restart is then performed on the topic augmented graph to calculate the relatedness between users from the target domain and the query user node in an analogous way as done in Eq. 1. Finally we rank users in the target domain according to the estimated relatedness scores and recommend users with the highest relatedness. One advantage of the CTL model is that it is able to recommend "related" collaboration topics based on the relatedness scores between the query node and the topic nodes. In topic matching, we could also consider recommending topics based on the relatedness scores; however, the recommended topics might be irrelevant to collaboration. In CTL, the recommended topics directly reflect existing collaborations across the two domains.

The CTL model can be also generalized to multiple domains. The basic idea is to use a multinomial distribution to replace the Bernoulli distribution. The multinomial represents collaboration topics among multiple domains, between two specific domains, or those in single domain. Based on the learned topics, we can construct a topic-centered network (similar to Figure 2(c)). Then the random walk with restart can be performed on the network to estimate the relatedness scores of users from different domains.

4. EXPERIMENTAL RESULTS

In this section, we evaluate the proposed methods on large publication datasets of different domains. All data sets and codes are publicly available[3].

4.1 Experimental Setup

Data sets. The data set is extracted from Arnetminer.org [31], an academic search system, which contains 1,436,990 authors and

[3]http://arnetminer.org/collaboration

1,932,442 publications. The data we used in our experiments spans from 1990 to 2005. We consider the following five sub-domains:

- **Data Mining:** We use papers of the following data mining conferences: KDD, SDM, ICDM, WSDM and PKDD as ground truth, which result in a network with 6,282 authors and 22,862 co-author relationships.
- **Medical Informatics:** We include the following journals: Journal of the American Medical Informatics Association, Journal of Biomedical Informatics, Artificial Intelligence in Medicine, IEEE Trans. Med. Imaging and IEEE Transactions on Information and Technology in Biomedicine, from which we obtain a network of 9,150 authors and 31,851 co-author relationships.
- **Theory:** We include the following conferences, i.e., STOC, FOCS and SODA, from which we get 5,449 authors and 27,712 co-author relationships.
- **Visualization:** We include the following conferences and journals, CVPR, ICCV, VAST, TVCG, IEEE Visualization and Information Visualization. The obtained coauthor network is comprised of 5,268 authors and 19,261 co-author relationships.
- **Database:** We include the following conferences, i.e., SIGMOD, VLDB and ICDE. From those conferences, we extract 7,590 authors and 37,592 co-author relationships.

Based on the above five sub domains, we create four cross-domain test cases: *Data Mining* to *Theory*, *Medical Informatics* to *Database*, *Medical Informatics* to *Data Mining*, and *Visualization* to *Data Mining*.

Comparison methods. We compare the following methods for collaboration recommendation:

Content Similarity (Content): It calculates similarity between authors based on papers published by them. Specifically, we construct feature vector $\mathbf{w}_q$ and $\mathbf{w}_{v'}$ of words used in papers published by query author q and target author v', respectively. Those feature vectors are normalized by TFIDF [1]. The similarity score is the Cosine similarity between $\mathbf{w}_q$ and $\mathbf{w}_{v'}$

$$Sim(v_q, v') = \frac{\mathbf{w}_q \cdot \mathbf{w}_{v'}}{\|\mathbf{w}_q\|\|\mathbf{w}_{v'}\|} \quad (6)$$

Collaborative Filtering (CF): It leverages the existing collaborations to make the recommendation. The basic idea is that if a query author q has the same or similar collaborators as a person x within the same domain, q is then likely to have the same cross-domain collaborators as x. We employ a memory-based collaborative filtering algorithm [8], in which recommendations are made for a query user q using the following formula:

$$CF\_score(q, v') = \sum_{x \in V^S} I(x, v') r(q, x) \quad (7)$$

where $r(q, x)$ is the similarity between authors in the source domain, e.g., Cosine similarity based on collaboration connections; the indicator variable $I(x, v')$ is 1 if the author x has a cross-domain collaboration with v' and 0 otherwise.

Hybrid: It considers a linear combination of the scores obtained by the Content and the CF methods, specifically,

$$Hybrid(v_q, v') = \mu CF\_score(v_q, v') + (1-\mu) Sim(v_q, v') \quad (8)$$

where μ is a balance parameter. We empirically set it as 0.5.

Katz: It is the best link predictor in [20]. It sums over all possible paths between the query user and a candidate user, and then use the summation score to rank all candidates.

Author Matching: (Cf. §3.1) It makes recommendation by performing the random walk with restart on the collaboration graph.

Topic Matching: (Cf. §3.2) It makes recommendation by combining the extracted topics into random walking algorithm.

CTL: (Cf. §3.3) It is the proposed method, which considers topic skewness and extracts relevant topics to cross-domain collaboration. The relevant topics are then integrated into the random walk framework for recommendation.[4]

Evaluation metrics. To quantitatively evaluate the proposed methods, in each test case, we use historic collaboration data (data before 2001) for training and the last four years (2001-2005) for validation. In evaluation, we consider those candidates who already have cross-domain collaborations and then our task is to predict if they will maintain the collaborations or expand new cross-domain collaborations. If the system recommends a cross-domain collaboration and later the collaboration has been built, then we say the system made a correct recommendation; otherwise we say the system made a wrong recommendation. Based on this, we evaluate the recommendation performance in terms of P@10 (Precision for the top 10 recommended results), P@20, R@100 (Recall for the top 100 results), MAP (Mean Average Precision), and Average Reciprocal Hit-Rank (ARHR) [9].

All codes are implemented in C++, and all the experiments are conducted on an x64 server with E7520 1.87GHz Intel Xeon CPU and 128G RAM. The operation system is Microsoft Windows Sever 2008 R2 Enterprise. For training the ACT and the CTL models, it takes about 12 hours and 15 hours respectively on the entire data set (1,436,990 authors and 1,932,442 publications). Recognizing the computation complexity of LDA style models, we are currently looking into developing more efficient computation mechanism to speed up the process.

4.2 Recommendation Performance Analysis

Table 2 lists the performance of cross-domain collaboration recommendation by the comparison methods on the four different test cases. The proposed CTL method clearly outperforms the baseline methods (+2.2-30% in terms of MAP). Content only considers the content information, which leads to a bad performance. The two methods (Hybrid and Topic Matching), combining the content and the network information, improve the recommendation performance compared to the simple baselines such as Content, CF and Author Matching. Moreover, Topic Matching considers the topic information extracted from the two domains, and thus performs better than the Hybrid method adopting a simple combination. CTL differentiates "collaboration topics" from those irrelevant topics and obtains significant improvement over both Hybrid and Topic Matching.

Cross-domain topics analysis. How many topics are enough for the cross-domain recommendation? We perform an analysis by varying the number of cross-domain topics in the proposed CTL method. Figure 5(a) shows its MAP performance with the num-

[4] As for the hyperparameters α, α_t, and β, following LDA [4], we empirically take fixed values (i.e., $\alpha = \alpha_q = 50/T$, and $\beta = 0.01$). γ and γ_t are defined to represent our preference for cross-domain collaborations (i.e., $\gamma_q = 3.0$ and $\gamma = 0.1$). We did try different settings and found that the estimated topic models are not very sensitive to the hyperparameters.

Table 2: **Recommendation performance by different methods on the four cross-domain test cases (%). Content– Content Similarity; CF– Collaborative Filtering; Author– Author Matching; Topic– Topic Matching.**

Cross domain	ALG	P@10	P@20	MAP	R@100	ARHR -10	ARHR -20
Data Mining (S) to Theory (T)	Content	10.3	10.2	10.9	31.4	4.9	2.1
	CF	15.6	13.3	23.1	26.2	4.9	2.8
	Hybrid	17.4	19.1	20.0	29.5	5.0	2.4
	Author	27.2	22.3	25.7	32.4	10.1	6.4
	Topic	28.0	26.0	32.4	33.5	13.4	7.1
	Katz	30.4	29.8	31.6	27.4	11.2	5.9
	CTL	**37.7**	**36.4**	**40.6**	**35.6**	**14.3**	**7.5**
Medical Info. (S) to Database (T)	Content	10.1	10.9	12.5	45.9	3.6	2.1
	CF	18.3	20.2	21.4	47.6	5.3	3.9
	Hybrid	25.0	26.5	28.4	59.1	6.4	4.2
	Author	26.2	29.6	32.2	54.8	10.5	**5.4**
	Topic	29.4	26.3	34.7	59.3	**11.5**	5.2
	Katz	27.5	28.3	30.7	57.2	10.5	5.0
	CTL	**32.5**	**30.0**	**36.9**	**59.8**	11.4	**5.4**
Medical Info. (S) to Data Mining (T)	Content	5.8	5.7	9.5	19.8	1.9	0.9
	CF	13.7	17.8	18.9	34.3	2.7	1.3
	Hybrid	18.0	19.0	19.8	36.7	3.4	1.3
	Author	20.1	23.8	29.3	**64.4**	5.3	2.1
	Topic	26.0	**25.0**	33.9	48.1	10.7	5.6
	Katz	21.2	23.8	32.4	48.1	10.2	4.8
	CTL	**30.0**	24.0	**35.6**	49.6	**12.2**	**6.0**
Visual. (S) to Data Mining (T)	Content	9.6	11.8	13.2	18.9	3.1	1.8
	CF	14.0	20.8	26.4	29.4	6.9	4.3
	Hybrid	16.0	20.0	27.6	30.1	6.3	4.4
	Author	22.0	25.2	27.7	31.1	11.9	6.7
	Topic	26.3	25.0	32.3	31.4	13.2	8.8
	Katz	23.0	25.1	29.3	30.2	10.4	5.4
	CTL	**28.3**	**26.0**	**32.8**	**36.3**	**14.0**	**9.1**

ber of cross-domain topics varied. We see, when the number is small (< 80), increasing the number often obtains a performance improvement. The trend becomes stable when the number is up to 150. This demonstrates the stability of the CTL method with respect to the number of topics.

Hyperparameter analysis. We use α as the example to analyze how hyperparameter influences the performance of the CTL method. Figure 5(b) shows the performance of CTL with the parameter α varied (all the other hyperparameters fixed and the number of topics is set as $T = 120$). We see although the performance changes when varying the value of α, the largest difference is less than 0.03 This confirms CTL method is not sensitive to the particular choice of α.

Restart parameter analysis. We study how the parameter τ influences the process of random walk with restart. Figure 5(c) plots the performance of the CTL method on the four test cases with the parameter τ varied. In general, the recommendation performance is not sensitive to the restart parameter τ. By a careful investigation, we find that a small τ makes the random walk diffuse too quickly thus can hurt the precision, while a large τ limits the diffusion process and thus can result in a lower recall.

Convergence analysis. We further investigate the convergence of the random walk with restart algorithm. Figure 5(d) shows the convergence analysis of different models on the test case of Visualization-Data Mining. We see all the three models converge within 10 iterations and CTL achieved even faster convergence

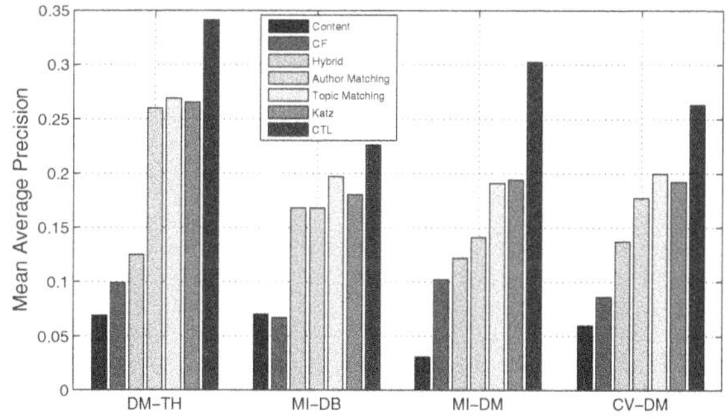

Figure 6: Performance on new collaboration prediction of all algorithms.

(within 5 iterations). This fast convergence on CTL model enable real time query support that is crucial in the deployed system we will discuss next.

New Collaboration Prediction The collaboration network is dynamic in nature, with collaborative relationships created over time. In general, there are two types of collaborative behaviors, maintaining existing collaborations and building new collaborations. Can we predict who will create a new collaboration in the future? This is a more difficult task. We conduct an experiment to evaluate the performance of the proposed method for new collaboration prediction. In particular, we still use the publication data before 2001 for training and the data between 2001-2005 for test, and in the evaluation, we only consider new collaborations in the test data. Figure 6 shows the performance of new collaboration prediction by the six comparison algorithms. On average, the performance of all algorithms drops a bit, but all algorithms have similar behaviors as that in Table 2. In particular, it is exciting to see that CTL can still maintain about 0.3 in terms of MAP which is significantly higher than the baseline methods.

4.3 Prototype System

We have developed and deployed a web application for cross-domain recommendation based on the proposed CTL method[5]. The system trained a CTL model offline using all the publication data (about 1,932,442 publication papers) in Arnetminer.org. When a user wants to find cross-domain collaborators, he first inputs his profile (including organization and research interest) or use an existing author profile via the Arnetminer system, which includes more than 1 million researcher profiles. Then the user inputs the target domain (by keywords) in which he wants to find collaborations. The system performs the random walk with restart algorithm (Cf. §3.3) online against the CTL model to rank potential topics/collaborators in the target domain.

5. RELATED WORK

Collaboration recommendation plays an important role in many fields and has attracted a lot of research interest. Chen et al. [7] have developed a system called CollabSeer for discovering potential collaborators for a given author based on the structure of the coauthor network and the user's research interests. This is the most relevant paper to our work. However, it does not consider the cross-domain problem. Konstas et al. [17] investigated how social relationships can help recommendation. They developed a

[5]http://arnetminer.org/collaborator

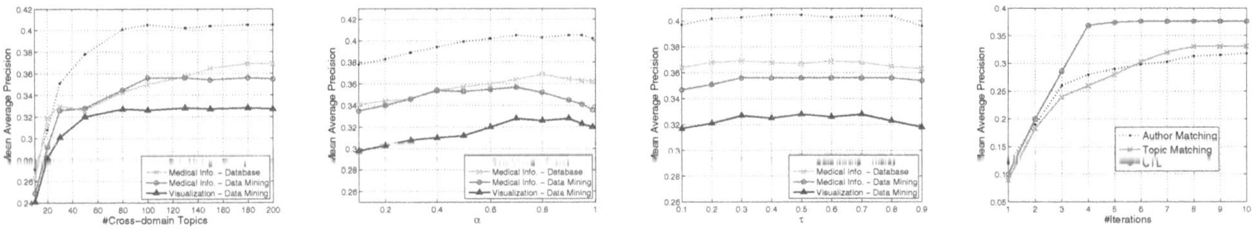

(a) number of topics T (b) Hyperparameter α (c) RWR parameter τ (d) Convergence analysis

Figure 5: Parameter analysis. (a) Performance of cross-domain topic learning model by varying the number of topics T; (b) Performance of cross-domain topic learning (CTL) is stable when varying α parameter; (c) Performance of CTL is stable when varying the restart parameter τ in the random walk process on the four test cases; (d) Convergence analysis of different models on the test case of Visualization-Data Mining.

track recommendation system by considering both social annotation and friendship inherent in the social graph established among users, items and tags. Kautz et al. [16] introduced a system called ReferralWeb which attempts to combine social networks for collaborative filtering. There are a large body of research on collaborative filtering. For example [2] introduced a system called Fab by combining content-based filtering and collaborative filtering. Shi et al. [26] proposed a large scale machine learning system for recommending heterogeneous content in social networks and Sculley et al. [25] presented a method to rank which combines regression and ranking. Yuan et al. [35] aimed to fuse heterogeneous social relationships for recommendation using factorization and regularization technologies. Wang and Blei [34] developed an algorithm to recommend scientific articles to users of an online community by combining traditional collaborative filtering and probabilistic topic modeling. However, most existing works only consider the recommendation problem within one single domain, but do not consider the cross-domain recommendation problem. In addition, we propose a novel cross-domain topic learning method, which supports recommending collaboration topics as well.

Our work is also related to expert finding [3, 30, 36] and expertise matching [23, 33]. Mimno et al. [23] and Tang et al. [33] studied the problem of paper-reviewer recommendation, a subtask of expert finding. The proposed algorithms can be leveraged for collaboration recommendations. However, expert finding and expertise matching are in nature different from the problem of collaboration recommendation. The idea of differentiating irrelevant topics has been also studied in previous work such as the query-oriented topic model (qLDA) proposed in [29], which tries to identify relevant topics to queries in multi-document summarization.

6. CONCLUSION

In this paper, we study the problem of cross-domain collaboration recommendation. We precisely define the problem and present three models for ranking and recommending potential collaborators. A cross-domain topic modeling approach has been proposed to learn and differentiate collaboration topics from other topics. Experimental results in a coauthor network demonstrate the effectiveness and efficiency of the proposed approach.

As for the future work, it is intriguing to connect cross-domain collaborative relationships with social theories. For example, how cross-domain relationships correlate with strong/weak ties [12] and how such correlation can help spread knowledge from one domain to another domain. It would be also interesting to apply the proposed method to other networks, e.g., software development.

Acknowledgements. The work is supported by the Natural Science Foundation of China (No. 61073073, No. 61170061) and Chinese National Key Foundation Research (No. 60933013, No.61035004), 973 Program (No. 2011CB302302), a special fund for Fast Sharing of Science Paper in Net Era by CSTD, and Tsinghua-Tencent innovation funding.

7. REFERENCES

[1] R. Baeza-Yates and B. Ribeiro-Neto. *Modern Information Retrieval*. ACM Press, 1999.

[2] M. Balabanović and Y. Shoham. Fab: content-based, collaborative recommendation. *Commun. ACM*, 40:66–72, March 1997.

[3] K. Balog, L. Azzopardi, and M. de Rijke. Formal models for expert finding in enterprise corpora. In *SIGIR'06*, pages 43–55, 2006.

[4] D. M. Blei, A. Y. Ng, and M. I. Jordan. Latent dirichlet allocation. *JMLR*, 3:993–1022, 2003.

[5] W. Buntine and A. Jakulin. Applying discrete pca in data analysis. In *UAI'04*, pages 59–66, 2004.

[6] D. Chakrabarti and C. Faloutsos. Graph mining: Laws, generators, and algorithms. *ACM Comput. Surv.*, 38(1):2, 2006.

[7] H.-H. Chen, L. Gou, X. Zhang, and C. L. Giles. Collabseer: a search engine for collaboration discovery. In *JCDL'11*, pages 231–240, 2011.

[8] A. Das, M. Datar, A. Garg, and S. Rajaram. Google news personalization: Scalable online collaborative filtering. In *WWW'07*, 2007.

[9] M. Deshpande and G. Karypis. Item-based top-n recommendation algorithms. *ACM Trans. Inf. Syst.*, 22(1):143–177, Jan. 2004.

[10] A. Doucet, N. de Freitas, K. Murphy, and S. Russell. Rao-blackwellised particle filtering for dynamic bayesian networks. In *UAI'00*, pages 176–183, 2000.

[11] M. Faloutsos, P. Faloutsos, and C. Faloutsos. On power-law relationships of the internet topology. In *SIGCOMM'99*, pages 251–262, 1999.

[12] M. Granovetter. The strength of weak ties. *American Journal of Sociology*, 78(6):1360–1380, 1973.

[13] T. L. Griffiths and M. Steyvers. Finding scientific topics. In *PNAS'04*, pages 5228–5235, 2004.

[14] G. Heinrich. Parameter estimation for text analysis. Technical report, University of Leipzig, Germany, 2004.

[15] T. Hofmann. Probabilistic latent semantic indexing. In *SIGIR'99*, pages 50–57, 1999.

[16] H. Kautz, B. Selman, and M. Shah. Referral web: Combining social networks and collaborative filtering. *Communications of the ACM*, 40(3):63–65, 1997.

[17] I. Konstas, V. Stathopoulos, and J. M. Jose. On social networks and collaborative recommendation. In *SIGIR'09*, pages 195–202, 2009.

[18] J. Leskovec and C. Faloutsos. Sampling from large graphs. In *KDD'06*, pages 631–636, 2006.

[19] J. Leskovec, D. Huttenlocher, and J. Kleinberg. Predicting positive and negative links in online social networks. In *WWW'10*, pages 641–650, 2010.

[20] D. Liben-Nowell and J. M. Kleinberg. The link-prediction problem for social networks. *JASIST*, 58(7):1019–1031, 2007.

[21] R. Lichtenwalter, J. T. Lussier, and N. V. Chawla. New perspectives and methods in link prediction. In *KDD'10*, pages 243–252, 2010.

[22] L. Lovasz. Random walks on graphs: A survey. *Combinatorics*, 2(1):1?6, 1993.

[23] D. Mimno and A. McCallum. Expertise modeling for matching papers with reviewers. In *KDD'07*, pages 500–509, 2007.

[24] J. Quackenbush. Microarray analysis and tumor classification. *New England Journal of Medicine*, 354:2463–2472, June 2006.

[25] D. Sculley. Combined regression and ranking. In *KDD'10*, pages 979–988, 2010.

[26] Y. Shi, D. Ye, A. Goder, and S. Narayanan. A large scale machine learning system for recommending heterogeneous content in social networks. In *SIGIR'11*, pages 1337–1338, 2011.

[27] M. Steyvers, P. Smyth, and T. Griffiths. Probabilistic author-topic models for information discovery. In *KDD'04*, pages 306–315, 2004.

[28] J. Sun, H. Qu, D. Chakrabarti, and C. Faloutsos. Neighborhood formation and anomaly detection in bipartite graphs. In *ICDM'05*, pages 418–425, 2005.

[29] J. Tang, L. Yao, and D. Chen. Multi-topic based query-oriented summarization. In *SDM'09*, pages 1147–1158, 2009.

[30] J. Tang, J. Zhang, R. Jin, Z. Yang, K. Cai, L. Zhang, and Z. Su. Topic level expertise search over heterogeneous networks. *Machine Learning Journal*, 82(2):211–237, 2011.

[31] J. Tang, J. Zhang, L. Yao, J. Li, L. Zhang, and Z. Su. Arnetminer: Extraction and mining of academic social networks. In *KDD'08*, pages 990–998, 2008.

[32] L. Tang and H. Liu. Relational learning via latent social dimensions. In *KDD'09*, pages 817–826, 2009.

[33] W. Tang, J. Tang, T. Lei, C. Tan, B. Gao, and T. Li. On optimization of expertise matching with various constraints. *Neurocomputing*, 76(1):71–83, 2012.

[34] C. Wang and D. M. Blei. Collaborative topic modeling for recommending scientific articles. In *KDD'11*, pages 448–456, 2011.

[35] Q. Yuan, L. Chen, and S. Zhao. Factorization vs. regularization: fusing heterogeneous social relationships in top-n recommendation. In *RecSys'11*, pages 245–252, 2011.

[36] J. Zhang, J. Tang, and J. Li. Expert finding in a social network. In *DASFAA'07*, pages 1066–1069, 2007.

8. APPENDIX

According to the generative process, we could integrate out the multinomial (Bernoulli) distributions $\theta, \theta', \vartheta, \lambda, \phi$, because the model only uses conjugate priors [10]. We use Eq. 4 as the example to explain its derivation. First we write the joint probability:

$$\begin{aligned} & P(\mathbf{x}, \mathbf{x}', \mathbf{z}, \mathbf{z}', \mathbf{s}, \mathbf{v}, \mathbf{v}' | \alpha, \gamma, \gamma_t, \beta, \mathbf{A}) \\ & \propto \int P(\mathbf{s}|\lambda) P(\lambda|\gamma, \gamma_t) d\lambda \int P(\mathbf{v}|\mathbf{A}) P(\mathbf{z}|\mathbf{v}, \mathbf{s}, \theta) P(\theta|\alpha) d\theta \\ & \int P(\mathbf{v}'|\mathbf{A}') P(\mathbf{z}'|\mathbf{v}', \mathbf{s}, \theta') P(\theta'|\alpha) d\theta' \int P(\mathbf{x}|\mathbf{z}, \phi) P(\phi|\beta) d\phi \\ & \int P((\mathbf{v}, \mathbf{v}')|\mathbf{A}) P(\mathbf{z}|(\mathbf{v}, \mathbf{v}'), \mathbf{s}, \vartheta) P(\vartheta|\alpha) d\vartheta \end{aligned} \tag{9}$$

The conditional of s_i is obtained by dividing the joint distribution of all variables by the joint with all variables but s_i (denoted by $\mathbf{s}_{-i}$) and canceling factors that do not depend on $\mathbf{s}_{-i}$.

$$\begin{aligned} p(s_i = 0 | \mathbf{s}_{-i}, \mathbf{z}, .) &= \frac{P(\mathbf{x}, \mathbf{x}', \mathbf{z}, \mathbf{z}', \mathbf{s}, \mathbf{v}, \mathbf{v}' | \alpha, \gamma, \gamma_t, \beta, \mathbf{A})}{P(\mathbf{x}, \mathbf{x}', \mathbf{z}, \mathbf{z}', \mathbf{s}_{-i}, \mathbf{v}, \mathbf{v}' | \alpha, \gamma, \gamma_t, \beta, \mathbf{A})} \\ &= \frac{\int P(\mathbf{s}|\lambda) P(\lambda|\gamma, \gamma_t) d\lambda}{\int P(\mathbf{s}_{-i}|\lambda) P(\lambda|\gamma, \gamma_t) d\lambda} \\ &\cdot \frac{\int P((\mathbf{v}, \mathbf{v}')|\mathbf{A}) P(\mathbf{z}|(\mathbf{v}, \mathbf{v}'), \mathbf{s}, \vartheta) P(\vartheta|\alpha) d\vartheta}{\int P((\mathbf{v}, \mathbf{v}')|\mathbf{A}) P(\mathbf{z}|(\mathbf{v}, \mathbf{v}'), \mathbf{s}_{-i}, \vartheta) P(\vartheta|\alpha) d\vartheta} \end{aligned} \tag{10}$$

We now derive the first fraction of Eq. 10. As we assume that s_i is generated from a Bernoulli distribution λ whose Beta parameters are γ, γ_t, then we can get $p(\mathbf{s}|\lambda) = \prod_d \lambda_d^{n_{ds_0}} \cdot (1 - \lambda_d)^{n_{ds_1}}$, where n_{ds_0} is the number of times that $s = 0$ has been sampled in document d and n_{ds_1} represents the number of times that $s =$ 1 has been sampled in d. Because Beta is the conjugate prior of Bernoulli, we could solve the Bernoulli-Beta integral using Gibbs sampling. Specifically,

$$\begin{aligned} & \int P(\mathbf{s}|\lambda) P(\lambda|\gamma, \gamma_t) d\lambda \\ &= \prod_d \frac{1}{B(\gamma_t, \gamma)} \int_0^1 \lambda_d^{n_{ds_0} + \gamma_t - 1} (1 - \lambda_d)^{n_{ds_1} + \gamma - 1} d\lambda_d \\ &= \prod_d \frac{B(n_{ds_0} + \gamma_t, n_{ds_1} + \gamma)}{B(\gamma_t, \gamma)} \\ &= \prod_d \frac{\Gamma(n_{ds_0} + \gamma_t)\Gamma(n_{ds_1} + \gamma)\Gamma(\gamma_t + \gamma)}{\Gamma(n_{ds_0} + n_{ds_1} + \gamma_t + \gamma)} \end{aligned} \tag{11}$$

To yield the first fraction of Eq. 10, we apply the above equation twice and obtain the following equation:

$$\begin{aligned} \frac{\int P(\mathbf{s}|\lambda) P(\lambda|\gamma, \gamma_t) d\lambda}{\int P(\mathbf{s}_{-i}|\lambda) P(\lambda|\gamma, \gamma_t) d\lambda} &= \frac{\prod_d \frac{\Gamma(n_{ds_0} + \gamma_t)\Gamma(n_{ds_1} + \gamma)\Gamma(\gamma_t + \gamma)}{\Gamma(n_{ds_0} + n_{ds_1} + \gamma_t + \gamma)}}{\prod_d \frac{\Gamma(n_{ds_0}^{-di} + \gamma_t)\Gamma(n_{ds_1}^{-di} + \gamma)\Gamma(\gamma_t + \gamma)}{\Gamma(n_{ds_0}^{-di} + n_{ds_1}^{-di} + \gamma_t + \gamma)}} \\ &= \frac{n_{ds_0}^{-di} + \gamma_t}{n_{ds_0}^{-di} + n_{ds_1}^{-di} + \gamma_t + \gamma} \end{aligned} \tag{12}$$

Here, we use the identity $\Gamma(x + 1) = x\Gamma(x)$; the superscript $-di$ denotes a quantity, excluding the current instance. The second fraction of Eq. 10 can be derived analogously. Specifically, as $P((\mathbf{v}, \mathbf{v}')|\mathbf{A})$ is a uniform distribution, $P(\mathbf{z}|(\mathbf{v}, \mathbf{v}', \mathbf{s}, \vartheta)$ and $P(\vartheta|\alpha)$ are conjugate pair of Multinomial-Dirichlet, we can obtain [14]:

$$\begin{aligned} & \int P((\mathbf{v}, \mathbf{v}')|\mathbf{A}) P(\mathbf{z}|(\mathbf{v}, \mathbf{v}'), \mathbf{s}, \vartheta) P(\vartheta|\alpha) d\vartheta \\ &= \prod_d \frac{1}{\sigma(A_d)} \cdot \frac{1}{\Delta(\alpha)} \int \prod_z \vartheta_{vv'z}^{n_{vz} + n_{v'z} + n_{vv'z} + \alpha - 1} d\vartheta_{vv'} \\ &= \prod_d \frac{1}{\sigma(A_d)} \frac{\Delta(\vec{n_d} + \alpha)}{\Delta(\alpha)}, \\ & \text{with } \vec{n_d} = \{n_{vz} + n_{v'z} + n_{vv'z}\}_{z=1}^{T} \end{aligned} \tag{13}$$

where $\sigma(A_d)$ is the total number of cross-domain user pairs generated from authors of document d (for a specific document, the number will be a constant); $\Delta(\alpha) = \frac{\Gamma(\alpha)^T}{\Gamma(T\alpha)}$; $n_{vv'z}$ denotes the number of times that topic z has been sampled by user pair (v, v'); n_{vz} and $n_{v'z}$ are two numbers obtained when combining the two distributions θ_v and $\theta_{v'}$; please note that though we write it as the sum of the two numbers, in practice, when sampling a specific topic, we will only consider one of them. This is because, for example, if a topic z is from the source domain, the number $n_{v'z}$ will be 0. Accordingly, the second fraction of Eq. 10 can be written as:

$$\begin{aligned} & \frac{\int P((\mathbf{v}, \mathbf{v}')|\mathbf{A}) P(\mathbf{z}|(\mathbf{v}, \mathbf{v}'), \mathbf{s}, \vartheta) P(\vartheta|\alpha) d\vartheta}{\int P((\mathbf{v}, \mathbf{v}')|\mathbf{A}) P(\mathbf{z}|(\mathbf{v}, \mathbf{v}'), \mathbf{s}_{-i}, \vartheta) P(\vartheta|\alpha) d\vartheta} \\ &= \frac{\prod_d \frac{1}{\sigma(A_d)} \frac{\Delta(\vec{n_d} + \alpha)}{\Delta(\alpha)}}{\prod_d \frac{1}{\sigma(A_d)} \frac{\Delta(\vec{n}_{d,\neg i} + \alpha)}{\Delta(\alpha)}} \\ &= \frac{\frac{\Gamma(n_{vv'z} + n_{vz} + n_{v'z} + \alpha)}{\Gamma(\sum_{z'}(n_{vv'z'} + n_{vz'} + n_{v'z'} + \alpha))}}{\frac{\Gamma(n_{vv'z} + n_{vz} + n_{v'z} + \alpha - 1)}{\Gamma([\sum_{z'}(n_{vv'z'}^{-di} + n_{vz'} + n_{v'z'} + \alpha)] - 1)}} \\ &= \frac{n_{vv'z_{di}}^{-di} + (n_{vz_{di}} + n_{v'z_{di}}) + \alpha}{\sum_z (n_{vv'z}^{-di} + (n_{vz_{di}} + n_{v'z_{di}}) + \alpha)} \end{aligned} \tag{14}$$

Finally, by combining Eqs. 12 and 14, we obtain Eq. 4.

RecMax: Exploiting Recommender Systems for Fun and Profit

Amit Goyal
University of British Columbia
Vancouver, BC, Canada
goyal@cs.ubc.ca

Laks V. S. Lakshmanan
University of British Columbia
Vancouver, BC, Canada
laks@cs.ubc.ca

ABSTRACT

In recent times, collaborative filtering based Recommender Systems (RS) have become extremely popular. While research in recommender systems has mostly focused on improving the accuracy of recommendations, in this paper, we look at the "flip" side of a RS. That is, instead of improving existing recommender algorithms, we ask whether we can use an existing operational RS to launch a targeted marketing campaign. To this end, we propose a novel problem called RECMAX that aims to select a set of "seed" users for a marketing campaign for a new product, such that if they endorse the product by providing relatively high ratings, the number of other users to whom the product is recommended by the underlying RS algorithm is maximum. We motivate RECMAX with real world applications. We show that seeding can make a substantial difference, if done carefully. We prove that RECMAX is not only NP-hard to solve optimally, it is NP-hard to even approximate within any reasonable factor. Given this hardness, we explore several natural heuristics on 3 real world datasets – Movielens, Yahoo! Music and Jester Joke and report our findings. We show that even though RECMAX is hard to approximate, simple natural heuristics may provide impressive gains, for targeted marketing using RS.

Categories and Subject Descriptors H.2.8 [Database Management]: Database Applications - *Data Mining*
General Terms: Algorithms, Theory, Experimentation.
Keywords: Recommender Systems, Collaborative Filtering, Targeted Marketing, Seed Set Selection, Maximization.

1. INTRODUCTION

There are many applications like online shopping where the opinions of other users who bought and rated a product are important for a user trying to decide which product to buy. Recommender systems (RS) have emerged as a complementary paradigm for search in order to fulfill users' information needs in such applications, by providing mass personalization [14]. Much of their popularity was spurred by the early success of collaborative filtering techniques [9], which exploit the existing ratings in a system to estimate the expected rating a user might give a product. Today, RS form the backbone of the business of many companies like Amazon and Netflix.

RS research has mostly focused on improving the accuracy with which the algorithm predicts the likely rating a user will provide an item she has not experienced before. The predicted ratings are then used for recommending items to users, e.g., by picking the top-ℓ items with highest predicted rating for the active user. In this paper, we take a look at the "flip" side of a RS. That is, instead of improving existing recommender algorithms, we ask whether we can use an *existing* operational RS to launch a targeted marketing campaign. More concretely, you have a product you want to sell in an online market place powered by RS technology. Suppose you give free samples of your product to a select number of users, called the *seed* users. Based on its quality, the seed users rate the product, preferably with high ratings. E.g., Amazon's Vine program employs a similar scheme. The question is, under the condition that the seed users endorse the product with high ratings, can this lead to the product being recommended by the system to a large number of other users? If so, this represents a huge opportunity for the client companies launching the campaign as it helps effectively advertise their product via the RS. It is a business opportunity for the host company as well since it can offer seeding as a service, whereby it selects effective seeds on behalf of the clients. It is beneficial to the seed users as they get free or discounted samples of a new product. Finally, it is helpful to the rest of the users as they receive recommendations of new products earlier than they otherwise would, a well recognized problem in RS [11].

In this paper, we will show the answer to the above question is "yes" and that the manner in which seeds are selected can make a difference. We focus on the case where the seed users who are targeted like the new product and endorse it with relatively high ratings. As example applications, Warner Brothers can target a select number of Netflix users in order to give free samples of their new movie release. A publisher can target customers of Amazon in a similar way. Motivated by these applications, we study the following problem, called RECMAX: Given a collaborative RS, a number k and a new product ρ, find k users (called *seed set*) to whom ρ should be marketed such that if these users rate the new product with relatively high ratings, the number of users to whom the product is recommended by the system is maximum.

Many ventures like *Increase YouTube Views*[1] and *Mile-*

KDD'12, August 12–16, 2012, Beijing, China.

[1] www.increaseyoutubeviews.com

Stone Internet Marketing[2] have emerged that offer services to increase/improve the ratings and reviews of their clients. Amazon's Vine program operates an interesting ecosystem, whereby reviewers (users) ranked highly by other users based on their past reviews are invited to review new items. These reviewers in turn are offered pre-release versions of products for the purpose of their review. We are not aware of any research works that investigate the mechanism used by the above ventures or by Amazon.

RECMAX has an interesting application for the cold-start items problem [11, 2], for the manufacturer of the item: for a newly introduced item, there may be few ratings provided by users. As a RS based on collaborative filtering relies on existing ratings, the new item will not be recommended to users until it gets enough ratings. Using RECMAX, when a new item is introduced, the item manufacturer has the opportunity to market it to the seed users and have the system recommend it to other users. Further comparison with works dealing with the cold-start problem appears in §2. There has been substantial work on detecting spam in RS and making them robust against spam. Mobasher [12] describes an attack called shilling attack whereby user profiles are injected into the system and reviewers are made to write positive reviews. The goal of RECMAX is *not* to spam a RS. Rather, it is to leverage a normal working RS for purposes of marketing. In particular, the ratings provided by the seed users to the new product are not influenced or interfered with in any way. They are free to rate it as they see fit. We focus on the case where the seed users like the new product and provide a relatively high rating.

The single most important challenge in studying the RECMAX problem is the wide diversity of RS algorithms (see [14], and [1] for comprehensive surveys) that are used in real applications. While User-based [9] and Item-based [15] collaborative filtering methods making use of neighborhood are extensively used, recently model-based approaches such as Matrix Factorization [16] have attracted a lot of attention. All these methods have many variants thus making the problem very difficult to formulate and study. In this work, we focus on User-based and Item-based methods since they are used in many real systems and are representative.

Targeted marketing in RS by selecting seed users has been recognized before [5, 13, 2, 3]. All of them use the notion of influence that a user has might exert in a RS, and based on their definition of influence, they select the seed users. The definition of influence and hence the goal is different in each of these works (as elaborated in §2). While the motivation and overall strategy are similar, that is, to select a set of seed users for marketing, RECMAX focuses on selecting seed users for maximizing the number of (other) users to whom a new item will be recommended by the RS, directly based on a recommender algorithm, as opposed to using an auxiliary notion of influence and resorting to social influence maximization. One of our main contributions is a thorough theoretical analysis of the complexity of RECMAX. As we shall show, RECMAX is not only a hard problem, it's even NP-hard to approximate within any reasonable factor. Given this, we explore various natural heuristics for solving RECMAX. We undertake a detailed analysis of three diverse real data sets, evaluate several natural heuristics for seed selection on those data sets and report our findings. One of the key contributions is showing that RECMAX is a real practical problem where selecting good seeds can yield a big payoff. To our knowledge, *we are the first to study the problem of identifying seed users to market a product to, in order to trigger a large number of recommendations of the product to other users from an existing RS.* We make the following contributions.

- We propose a novel problem RECMAX. It aims to find a set of seed users to whom a new product should be initially marketed such that if they endorse the product, the number of users to whom the product is recommended is maximum. We offer early empirical evidence that seeding does help in boosting the number of recommendations (§4).
- We perform a thorough theoretical analysis of RECMAX. We show that RECMAX is not only NP-hard to solve optimally, it is NP-hard to approximate within a factor of $1/(|V|^{1-\epsilon})$ for any fixed $\epsilon > 0$, both in User-based and Item-based methods (§5), under the settings we study. We also present intuitions behind where the intrinsic hardness of RECMAX comes from.
- Given the hardness, we explore several natural heuristics on 3 real datasets (§6). Some of the key observations we make are: a) If enough budget is allowed, seeding can make a substantial difference in the number of recommendations a new product can get; b) The gains that can be achieved saturates after some point, in both methods, suggesting that the seeding does not help after a certain budget; c) The overall gains that can be achieved in User-based systems are much higher than can be achieved in Item-based systems, though saturation is attained much quicker in Item-based systems; d) Choice of the seed set is critical.

Related work is reviewed in §2 while in §3, we provide a brief background and define RECMAX formally. Finally, we summarize the paper and discuss future research in §7.

2. RELATED WORK

Recommender Systems: The majority of works in RS (see [14] and [1] for detailed surveys) focus on improving the quality of the algorithms w.r.t. prediction accuracy. RS in general can be content-based or based on collaborative filtering. The most popular methodology in RS is based on collaborative filtering, which seeks to predict the expected rating that a user may provide to an item which she hasn't experienced before. Collaborative filtering methods are further classified into memory(or neighborhood)-based (e.g., see Chapter 4 of [14]) or model-based (e.g., matrix factorization [14], Chapter 5). This wide variety in RS makes RECMAX a very challenging problem to define and study. In this paper, we study both User-based and Item-based neighborhood methods, when the predicted ratings are estimated through weighted average.

A by-product of RECMAX is a solution to the cold-start problem [11], for item manufacturers. Various approaches have been proposed to solve the cold start problem including hybrid methods which in addition to existing ratings, utilize the item content data [11]. A recent work by Anand and Griffiths [2] employs an interesting incentive based approach which, given a collection of new items, calls for offering a list of new items for every user in the system. A user gets a fixed payment for every new item she rates. The

[2]`www.milestoneinternet.com/products/social-media/hotel-internet-marketing-reviews.aspx`

payment is determined using the influence of a user in the RS. The authors provide general guidelines on what factors the influence should depend on without explicitly defining it. They infer a social graph and apply existing social influence maximizing heuristics like Degree Discount [4]. As such this is a "proxy" to the original problem motivated by them. Moreover, degree discount is proposed for the independent cascade model where attempts of influence on a user by her neighbors are assumed to be independent, an assumption that, strictly speaking, doesn't hold in their framework. As the authors themselves acknowledge, their framework is vulnerable to fake ratings as the ratings provided by the seed users may be compromised by the free payments they get in return. The key differences from this work are as follows: a) Solving the cold start problem is not our main goal, although it is an interesting by-product; b) We look to pick seed users in a way that maximizes the number of users to whom the item is recommended directly using the underlying algorithms the RS use (e.g., User-based or Item-Based), instead of relying on social influence maximization; c) As mentioned earlier, ratings provided by seed users are not dictated or interfered with in anyway, avoiding fake ratings.

Another related line of work is spam in RS and its detection [12]. As mentioned earlier, the goal of RECMAX is not to spam the RS or to encourage fake ratings for the sake of item promotion. Instead, our goal is to leverage RS for ethical marketing. If seed users do not endorse a new item by providing high ratings, that item would simply not be recommended to other users. In a way, the seed users also play a role of initial customer feedback in our framework.

Influence Maximization: Our study is related in spirit to the problem of influence maximization in social networks as well as to the related problems of adoption and revenue maximization [5, 10, 7, 3]. In fact, the notion of influence from a data mining perspective was first studied in the context of RS [5]. Later Kempe et al. [10] formalized the problem as a discrete optimization problem. To the best of our knowledge, till date, there have been 4 papers which measure users' influence for marketing in RS by selecting seed users [5, 13, 2, 3]. Domingos et al. [5] define influence as the expected lift in profit and aim to maximize it. Anand and Griffiths [2] on the other hand, calculate influence empirically by exploiting social influence maximization heuristics. We provided a detailed account of the differences with our work above. Rashid et al. [13] focus on measuring influence scores of users in a RS and define it as a function of user's ability to change the predicted ratings of other users by δ where δ is the difference between consecutive rating valies (e.g., in a standard 1-5 rating scale, $\delta = 1$). Their main goal is to calculate influence scores of users, not to select a seed set. Bhagat et al. [3] on the other hand, develop a model for product adoption and use it to select seed users to maximize a new product adoption, from an influence maximization perspective.

Several factors set RECMAX apart from influence maximization. A fundamental distinction is that in RECMAX, the goal is to maximize the number of users to whom the system will *recommend* the item. By contrast, in influence maximization, the goal is to maximize the number of users who are influenced by the seed users and *adopt* the item. Second, no explicit social network is assumed as input for RECMAX, whereas for influence/adoption/revenue maximization, the basic backbone is a social network with influence weights. While in principle, one can induce a social network from a RS as [2] does, the resulting problem formulated on the social network is at best a proxy for the original problem of recommendation maximization. Third, unlike in influence maximization, there is no underlying propagation model (such as indepndent cascade or linear threshold – see [10]) in RECMAX.

3. BACKGROUND AND PROBLEM STUDIED

Recommender systems serve the top-ℓ items with the highest predicted ratings for a user as recommendations to that user, where ℓ is the desired length of the recommendation list. While User-based [9] and Item-based [15] are among the most popular collaborative filtering methods, recently hybrid approaches have been proposed [17]. Even more recently, Matrix factorization based methods [16] have gained significant attention. For excellent surveys, see Chapters 4 and 5 of [14]. In this paper, we study RECMAX on User-based and Item-based methods. With $\hat{R}(v,i)$, we denote the expected rating that user v gives an item i. Among User-based methods, perhaps the most popular approach to estimate $\hat{R}(v,i)$ is to use the weighted average:

$$\hat{R}(v,i) = \frac{\sum_{u \in N_i(v)} w(u,v) \cdot R(u,i)}{\sum_{u \in N_i(v)} abs(w(u,v))} \tag{1}$$

where $R(u,i)$ is the rating given to item i by user u, $abs(\cdot)$ is the absolute value function and $N_i(v)$ is the set of nearest neighbors of v, based on the similarity scores $w(\cdot,v)$, who have rated i. The similarity scores are calculated using cosine similarity or Pearson correlation or one of their variations (see [14], Ch. 4). In this paper, we employ the Pearson correlation as the similarity measure for User-based methods. Let $I(u)$ denote the set of items rated by user u and let $\mathcal{I} = I(u) \cap I(v)$. Then the similarity $w(u,v)$ using Pearson correlation is computed as

$$\frac{\sum_{i \in \mathcal{I}} (R(u,i) - \bar{R}_u) \cdot (R(v,i) - \bar{R}_v)}{\sqrt{\sum_{i \in \mathcal{I}} (R(u,i) - \bar{R}_u)^2} \cdot \sqrt{\sum_{i \in \mathcal{I}} (R(v,i) - \bar{R}_v)^2}} \tag{2}$$

where $\bar{R}_u$ is the average of u's ratings over various items.

Item-based methods on the other hand, use the similarities among items to estimate the predicted ratings. For instance, using the weighted average,

$$\hat{R}(v,j) = \frac{\sum_{i \in N_v(j)} w(i,j) \cdot R(v,i)}{\sum_{i \in N_v(j)} abs(w(i,j))} \tag{3}$$

where $N_v(j)$ is the set of nearest neighbors of (i.e., the most similar items to) j that are rated by v. Again, the similarities can be computed based on cosine, Pearson, their variants or other methods (see [14], Ch. 4). In this paper, we focus on adjusted cosine similarity, which is shown to be the most accurate similarity measure for Item-based methods [15]. Let $V(i)$ denote that set of users who rate item i, and let $U = V(i) \cap V(j)$. Then the adjusted cosine similarity between items i and j is

$$\frac{\sum_{u \in U} (R(u,i) - \bar{R}_u) \cdot (R(u,j) - \bar{R}_u)}{\sqrt{\sum_{u \in U} (R(u,i) - \bar{R}_u)^2} \cdot \sqrt{\sum_{u \in U} (R(u,j) - \bar{R}_u)^2}} \tag{4}$$

In both User-based and Item-based methods, the number of nearest neighbors considered is often restricted to a limited number d, usually between 20 and 50. This has been found to improve not only scalability, but even accuracy [14, 9].

Problem Studied. In addition to the log of past ratings, we assume we know the algorithm used by the RS. In this paper, we focus on both User-based and Item-based methods. For User-based, we employ Pearson correlation similarity measure, while for Item-based, we utilize adjusted cosine similarity measure, both defined above.

With ρ, we denote the new item to be marketed. The number of items that can be recommended to a user v is limited and as a result various items are in competition to enter the recommendation lists of users. Clearly, for ρ to appear in the recommendation list of user v, the expected rating $\hat{R}(v, \rho)$ must be more than the *rating threshold* of user v, which is the predicted rating of v for the last item in its recommendation list. We use θ_v to refer to the rating threshold of user v. We do not necessarily assume that the new item ρ has no prior ratings.

Let V be the set of users in the system. The problem we study in this paper is to select a set $S \subseteq V$ of k users (called *seed set*) such that by convincing them to provide relatively high ratings to the new item ρ, the number of users to whom it is recommended is maximized. We leave the definition of "relatively high rating" open for now and argue that if the new item is not a good item causing the seed users to provide relatively low ratings, then in any case, it should *not* receive many recommendations. The goal of this work is not to promote bad items. In our experiments, we derive a rating $R(u, \rho)$ for a seed user u by taking an average of the top-20% highest ratings provided by u.

We use $H(S)$ to denote the set of users to whom the item is recommended by virtue of the seed set S. Clearly, $H(S) \subseteq V \setminus S$ as the users in S have already adopted the item and there is no value to recommending the item to them. Intuitively, users in the seed set S should have high "influence" where the influence flows indirectly via the recommendations. We define $f(S) := |H(S)|$, the *hit score* of seed set S as:

$$f(S) = \sum_{v \in V-S} I(\hat{R}(v, \rho) > \theta_v) \quad (5)$$

where $I(\cdot)$ is an indicator function which is 1 if $\hat{R}(v, \rho) > \theta_v$ and 0 otherwise. Formally, the problem is defined as follows.

PROBLEM 1 (RECMAX). Given a recommender system and rating thresholds θ_v for each user v in the system, and a number k, find a set S of k users s.t. $f(S)$ is maximized.

4. DOES SEEDING HELP?

Before we study the RECMAX problem of how to select an optimal seed set, we address several natural questions: Does seeding help? What are the gains that may be achieved? How does hit score vary with respect to the seed set size?

To answer these questions, in this section, we show the results from preliminary experiments, using the popular Movielens data set. More detailed experiments are discussed in §6. Predicted ratings are computed according to weighted average, both for User-based and Item-based methods (see Eq. 1 and 3). The similarity measure we use is Pearson correlation for User-based (Eq., 2) and adjusted cosine for Item-based (Eq. 4). See §6 for explicit experiment settings.

Next, we run a RANDOM heuristic to select the seed set and calculate the hit score achieved, both in User-based and Item-based methods. We assume that a seed user $u \in S$ provides a relatively high rating to the new item. In our experimental evaluation, we set this rating as the average of the top-20% highest ratings provided by user u. Given a budget k, a seed set of size k is randomly selected and the hit score is computed. We repeat this process 100 times and take the average. Note that it is important to repeat the process several times as in some cases, the seed set picked by RANDOM may be really good with a large hit score, while in other cases, very poor with a low hit score. Fig. 1 shows the results. As can be seen, the hit score achieved is remarkable, under both methods, with a much higher hit score under User-based. For example, a budget of 500 can get a hit score of 5091 on User-based and a budget of 20 can achieve a hit score of 636 on Item-based.

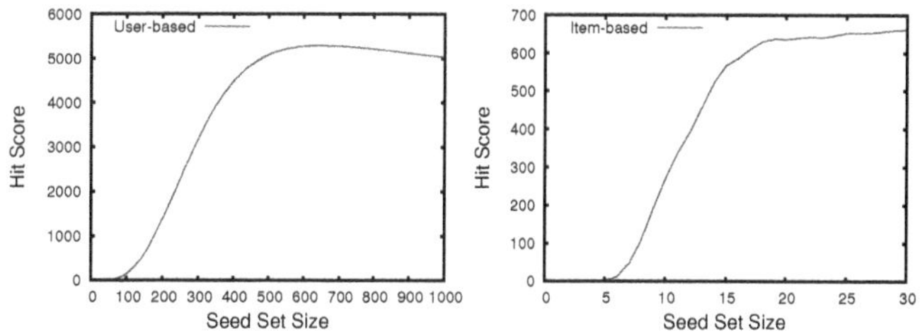

Figure 1: Hit Rate achieved by random seed set on Movielens dataset on User-based (left) and Item-based (right). The plots show that even when the seed sets are selected randomly, seeding does help and exhibits impressive gains in hit score.

This immediately suggests that *seeding does help and establishes the case for* RECMAX. Another interesting observation is that the hit score curve resembles the classic sigmoid curve, implying that if sufficient budget is allowed, then the gains achieved can be substantial. Moreover, if we continue to increase the budget, the hit score plateaus, and sometimes, it may even start decreasing (unlike sigmoid). These interesting observations inspire us to perform a deeper analysis of RECMAX– both theoretical and empirical – and we do so in the next sections.

5. COMPLEXITY OF RECMAX

In this section, we study the complexity of RECMAX. Unfortunately, it turns out to be intractable: in fact, it is hard to approximate within any reasonable factor, unless P=NP. Due to the wide variations in RS methods, it is tedious to study the complexity for everyone of them. Instead we present formal proofs for cases where the underlying methods are either User-based or Item-based, with Pearson and adjusted cosine as similarity functions respectively. We believe these are representative cases and our results give an indication that RECMAX may indeed be a very hard problem for known RS algorithms in general.

We also provide important insights as to why RECMAX is so hard. First, it is easy to show that the function $f(S)$ defining the hit score of a seed set is in general non-monotone and non-submodular. Intuitively, $f(\cdot)$ is based on predicted ratings computed using weighted average, which is neither monotone nor submodular. Indeed, the plot in Fig. 1 (left) shows an example where $f(\cdot)$ is not monotone and both (left) and (right) plots show it is not submodular in general. To help us prove the hardness results, we introduce a helper problem that we call *Maximum Encirclement Problem* (MEP). We show that MEP is as hard to approximate as the classical *Maximum Independent Set Problem* (MIS). Recall that in an undirected graph $G = (V, E)$, a set $S \subseteq V$ is an independent set iff no two nodes in S are adjacent. MIS cannot be approximated within a factor of $1/(|V|^{1-\epsilon})$ for any fixed $\epsilon > 0$, unless P=NP [8]. We show that RECMAX is as hard to approximate as MEP and our result follows.

Given an undirected graph $G = (V, E)$ and a set $S \subseteq V$, we say a node $v \in V \setminus S$ is *encircled* by S, provided v has at least one neighbor and all its neighbors are in S.

PROBLEM 2 (MEP). Given an undirected graph $G = (V, E)$ and an integer k, find a set $S \subseteq V$ such that $|S| \leq k$ and S encircles the maximum number of nodes.

For the sake of simplicity, we assume there are no isolated (i.e., zero degree) nodes in the graph. As an insight, notice that MEP is very close to the minimum vertex cover problem (MVC) which asks if there is a set $S \subseteq V$ of size $\leq k$, given $k \leq |V|$, such that every edge of the graph is incident on at least one node in S. Notice, S is a vertex cover iff for any node $v \in V \setminus S$, all its neighbors are in S, i.e., iff v is encircled by S (assuming there are no isolated nodes). Thus, MVC is equivalent to asking if there is a set of nodes $S \subseteq V$ of size k such that it encircles rest of the nodes in the graph. From this, it follows that MEP is NP-hard, which is not very surprising. What is interesting is that while MVC enjoys 2-approximation, MEP is not approximable, as we show next.

LEMMA 1. *The Maximum Encirclement Problem (*MEP*) cannot be approximated within a factor of $\frac{1}{|V|^{1-\epsilon}}$ for any fixed $\epsilon > 0$, unless P=NP.*

PROOF. Consider an instance of MIS, consisting of a graph $G = (V, E)$. Create an instance of MEP by keeping the graph same. Clearly, a set $S \subseteq V$ is an independent set of G if and only if the set $V \setminus S$ encircles each node in S. In particular, S is an optimal solution to MIS iff $V \setminus S$ is an optimal solution to MEP where the budget is set to $|V| - |S|$. Assume there is a β-approximation algorithm for MEP. For $k = 1, ..., |V|$, run the approximation algorithm on the MEP instance with the budget set to k. Let $\hat{S}$ be a set of nodes output by this algorithm for some value of $\hat{k}$: $|\hat{S}| \leq \hat{k}$ and the number of encircled nodes is the maximum among all values of k. Clearly, the number of nodes encircled by $\hat{S}$ is $\geq \beta \cdot (|V| - \hat{k})$, since for some budget, there must exist a set that encircles every node outside the set. Let T be the set of nodes encircled by $\hat{S}$. Clearly, T is an independent set of size $\geq \beta \cdot (|V| - \hat{k})$ which thus is a β-approximate solution to MIS. Therefore, MEP is as hard to approximate as MIS. □

Now, we are ready to prove hardness results for RECMAX.

THEOREM 1. *Under User-based Collaborative Filtering that uses Eq. 1 and 2 to compute predicted ratings,* RECMAX *is NP-hard. Moreover, it cannot be approximated within a factor of $\frac{1}{|V|^{1-\epsilon}}$ for any $\epsilon > 0$, unless P=NP.*

PROOF. We prove the theorem by reducing MEP to RECMAX. From an instance $\mathcal{I}$ of MEP consisting of graph $G = (V, E)$, create an instance $\mathcal{J}$ of RECMAX as follows. For each node $u \in V$, create a user u in instance $\mathcal{J}$. For each edge $(u, v) \in E$, create an item i_{uv} such that users u and v rate the item i_{uv} with rating 2. Add $|V|$ dummy items to the instance $\mathcal{J}$ such that each user rates exactly one of these dummy items, with rating 1. Let d be the maximum number of nearest neighbors that are being considered by the RS, then also add d dummy users (call this set of dummy users X) in instance $\mathcal{J}$ such that each of these dummy users $x \in X$ rates all $|V|$ dummy items with rating 2. Hence, in our construction, we have $|V| + d$ users, $|E| + |V|$ items and $2 \cdot |E| + (d+1) \cdot |V|$ ratings. Let every seed user provide the same rating to the new item, say 2. Next, let each dummy user provide rating 1 to the new item ρ. We will decide the rating threshold θ_v later.

Let $S \subseteq V$ be any seed set. Then, we claim that a node $v \in V \setminus S$ is encircled by S (in instance $\mathcal{I}$) iff the new item is recommended to v, that is, $v \in H(S)$ (in instance $\mathcal{J}$). We prove this claim below. From this claim, it is easy to see that a set S of size k encircles η nodes in instance $\mathcal{I}$ if and only if $|H(S)| = \eta$ in instance $\mathcal{J}$. Therefore, RECMAX is as hard to approximate as MEP, following the same logic used in the proof of Lemma 1, and this proves the theorem.

Consider a user $v \notin S$. According to Eq. 2, the similarity between v and a user $u \in S$ is 1. Likewise, the similarity among v and a dummy user $x \in X$ is -1 With $deg(v)$, we denote the degree of user v in instance $\mathcal{I}$. If $l \leq deg(v)$ (non-dummy) neighbors of v rate the new item ρ, then, according to Eq. 1,

$$\hat{R}(v, \rho) = \frac{\sum_{u \in N_\rho(v)} w(u, v) \cdot R(u, i)}{\sum_{u \in N_\rho(v)} abs(w(u, v))}$$

$$= \frac{l \cdot 1 \cdot 2 + (d - l) \cdot (-1) \cdot 1}{abs(l \cdot 1) + abs((d - l) \cdot (-1))} = \frac{3 \cdot l - d}{d}$$

Set the rating threshold $\theta_v = (3 \cdot deg(v) - d)/d - \delta$ where δ is a small number to ensure that $\hat{R}(v, \rho)$ is $(3 \cdot deg(v) - d)/d$ iff the new item is recommended to v. This rating threshold can be achieved iff all neighbors of v rate the new item. As a result, an item is recommended to a user v iff all of its neighbors are in S. that is, iff v is encircled by S. This was to be shown. □

THEOREM 2. *Under Item-based Collaborative Filtering that uses Eq. 3 and 4 to compute predicted ratings,* RECMAX *is NP-hard. Moreover, it cannot be approximated within a factor of $\frac{1}{|V|^{1-\epsilon}}$ for any fixed $\epsilon > 0$, unless P=NP.*

PROOF. As above, we prove the claim by reducing MEP to RECMAX under the Item-based method that uses weighted average along with adjusted cosine similarity (see Eq. 3 and 4). Consider an instance $\mathcal{I}$ of MEP consisting of an undirected graph $G = (V, E)$. Create an instance $\mathcal{J}$ of RECMAX as follows. Each node $v \in V$ corresponds to a user. Create $|E|$ items in instance $\mathcal{J}$, one for each edge in instance $\mathcal{I}$. An item i_{uv} corresponding to edge $(u, v) \in E$ is rated by users u and v with rating 2. Add a special item j such that each user rates it with rating 1. Thus, in instance $\mathcal{J}$, we have $|V|$ users, $|E| + 1$ items and $2 \cdot |E| + |V|$ ratings. We will decide the values of rating thresholds later.

Let $S \subseteq V$ be any seed set. Like above, we claim that a node $v \in V \setminus S$ will be in $H(S)$ (in instance $\mathcal{J}$) iff v is encircled by S (in instance $\mathcal{I}$). The proof then follows from the same logic used in the proof of Theorem 1.

We now show the above claim. Say, each seed user provides a rating 2 to the new item. Then, for a user $u \in S$, $\bar{R}_u = (2 \cdot deg(u) + 1 + 2)/(deg(u) + 2)$, as it provides rating 2 to all the items that correspond to the edges in $\mathcal{I}$ and 1 to the special item j, in addition to rating 2 to the new item ρ. Considering the adjusted cosine similarity function among items (see Eq. 4), for any item i that corresponds to an edge in instance $\mathcal{I}$, the deviation term is $2 - (2 \cdot deg(u) + 3)/(deg(u) + 2) = 1/(deg(u) + 2)$. Let us call this x_u. The similarity of i with ρ would then be

$$w(i,\rho) = \frac{\sum_{u \in U} x_u \cdot x_u}{\sqrt{\sum_{u \in U} x_u^2} \cdot \sqrt{\sum_{u \in U} x_u^2}} = 1$$

where $U = V(i) \cap V(\rho) = V(i) \cap S$. Similarly, for the special item j, the deviation term is $y_u = 1 - (2 \cdot deg(u) + 3)/(deg(u) + 2) < 0$. It implies that the similarity between j and ρ is strictly less than 0. Let it be z. Thus, from Eq. 3, the expected rating of a user v on item ρ is

$$\hat{R}(v,\rho) = \frac{\sum_{i \in I(v) \cap I(S)} w(i,\rho) \cdot R(v,i)}{\sum_{i \in I(v) \cap I(S)} abs(w(i,\rho))} \quad (6)$$

where $I(S) = \bigcup_{u \in S} I(u)$ is the set of items rated by any seed user in S. Note that if an item i is not rated by any user in S, then it cannot be among the neighbors of new item ρ because ρ is rated only by users in S. That's why we iterate over all items $i \in I(v) \cap I(S)$ in Eq. 6. Moreover, $|I(v)| = 1 + deg(v)$. Clearly, the special item j is in $I(S)$, as all users rate j. Next, any item $i \neq j$, if added to $I(S)$, cannot decrease $\hat{R}(v,\rho)$ as all such items are rated with rating 2. Hence, the maximum possible predicted rating that v could give the new item ρ is realized when all the items rated by v are in $I(S)$, i.e., $I(v) \subseteq I(S)$. Following Eq. 6, this maximum rating is

$$R_{max}(v) = \frac{2 \cdot deg(v) - z}{deg(v) + z}$$

Thus, we can set θ_v as $R_{max}(v) - \delta$ where δ is an extremely small number which ensures that the item ρ is recommended to v if and only if the predicted rating $\hat{R}(v,\rho) = R_{max}$. It means that the user $v \in H(S)$ if and only if $I(v) \subseteq I(S)$. However, an item $i_{uv} \in I(v) \setminus \{j\}$ can be in $I(S)$ if and only if the neighbor u of v is in S (because only u and v have rated the item i_{uv}). Thus, $I(v) \subseteq I(S)$ iff all neighbors of v are in S, i.e., iff S encircles v. This was to be shown. □

It should be noted that a slight modification in the reduction shown above shows that the RECMAX under Item-based method (that uses weighted average) is as hard as MEP even when the similarity function is cosine or Pearson. We omit the details for brevity.

Discussion. By now, it is clear that the RECMAX problem cannot be approximated within any reasonable factor, for the specific settings we focus on in this paper. Many real RS are based on the User-based and Item-based methods considered in our settings of RECMAX and thus our results apply to RECMAX over those systems. What can we say about RS that are based on the hybrid of content-based and collaborative filtering, on matrix factorization etc.? Given the complexities of systems based on such methods, it is very likely that RECMAX continues to be hard (to approximate) on these systems. The main reason behind this hardness of RECMAX is its similarity with MEP: in order to push an item to the recommendation list of a user, several other users may need to rate the item. This has a flavor similar to the user being "encircled" by other users. Since the hit score function is neither monotone nor submodular, as noted in the beginning of the section, it is not clear a priori which heuristics will work well for RECMAX. So, the question arises: What can we do with RECMAX? Does it still have a case? As we show in §4, the answer is yes. Even if the problem is too hard to approximate, it still makes a good sense for targeted marketing, as the gains (in terms of hit score) achieved are impressive, even with the RANDOM heuristic. Clearly, we cannot develop an algorithm with theoretical guarantees, but we can try several heuristics and see what works best and under what conditions – which is what we do in the next section.

6. EXPERIMENTS

Algorithms. Given that RECMAX cannot be approximated within any reasonable factor, in this section we explore several natural heuristics, and then gauge their performance on 3 real datasets – Movielens, Yahoo! Music and Jester– and analyze the results. Let k be the budget on seed set size. We explore the following heuristics in our evaluation.

RANDOM: Seed set is selected randomly. The process is repeated 100 times and the average hit score of different choices is taken. We take this as a baseline.

MOST-ACTIVE: Choose the top-k users with most number of ratings. The intuition here is that the users who are most active "control" most of the ratings in the system, and thus can be seen as a good target for marketing.

MOST-POSITIVE: Choose the top-k users with most positive average ratings as seeds. It is another natural way for targeted marketing, as many manufacturers may want to avoid bad ratings/opinions about their product. Thus, targeting positive users is a "safe" marketing choice.

MOST-CRITICAL: Choose the top-k users with most critical average ratings. This is another extreme, where it may be argued that if the most critical users endorse a product, the chances of success (i.e., large hit score) are high.

MOST-CENTRAL: For each user, we compute its similarity with every other user. Then, we compute its aggregate similarity score $agg(u) = \sum_{v \in V} sim(u,v)$. Next, we select top-$k$ users with highest aggregate similarity scores as the seed set. In case of User-based, we compute the similarity according to the Pearson correlation, which is what is used in estimating predicted ratings.

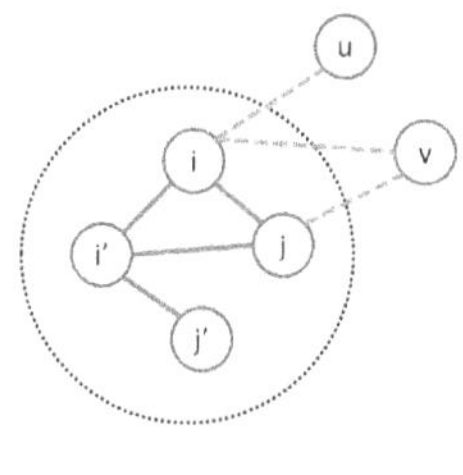

Figure 2: Example.

For Item-based, the recommendations are generated using similarities among items, and not users. Hence, it is not clear how to compute similarities among users in case of Item-based. For instance, consider the example shown in Fig. 2. It has 4 items i, j, i', j', and we know the weights on the red edges: they are computed according to Eq. 4. No two users are directly connected in Fig. 2. Hence, to compute the similarity between users u and v, we take the weighted average of ratings provided by the users u and v on every pair of items they rate, as follows.

$$sim(u,v) = \frac{\sum_{i \in I(u), j \in I(v)} w(i,j) \cdot sim(R(u,i), R(v,j))}{\sum_{i \in I(u), j \in I(v)} w(i,j)}$$

where $sim(R(u,i), R(v,j))$ is the similarity between the ratings provided by user u on item i and user v on item j. If users u and v rate a common item i, i.e., $i = j$, then, $w(i,j) = w(i,i) = 1$. Intuitively, if the ratings are nearly equal, $w(R(u,i), R(v,j))$ should be close to 1 and if the ratings are very different, the similarity score should be close

	Movielens	Yahoo	Jester
#Users	6040	10K	25K
#Items	3706	5069	100
#Ratings	1M	1M	1.8M
Mean	3.58	51.9	10.88
Std. Dev.	1.12	39.9	5.23

(a) Dataset statistics

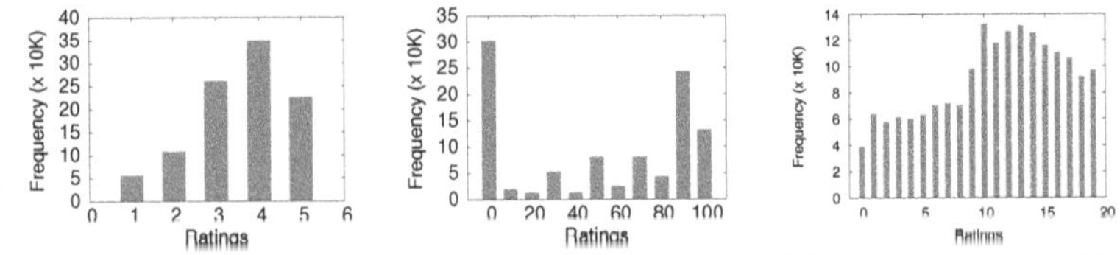

(b) Movielens Ratings Distribution (c) Yahoo! Music Ratings Distribution (d) Jester Ratings Distribution

Figure 3: (a) Summary of datasets; (b)-(d) Distributions of ratings.

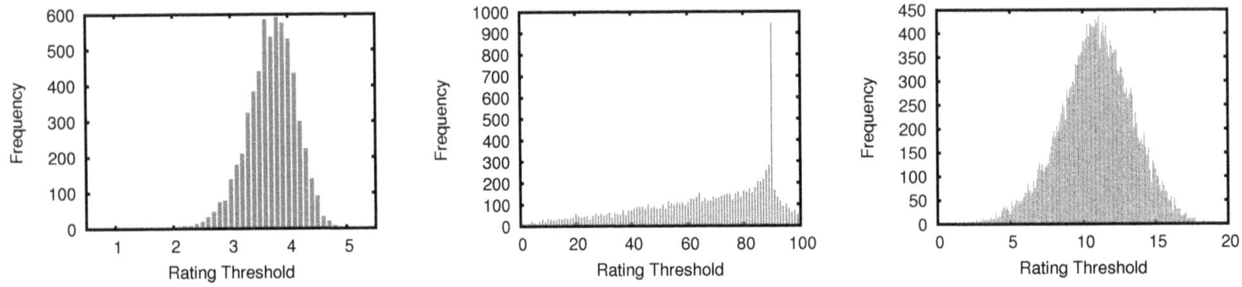

(a) Movielens users' ratings thresholds (b) Yahoo! users' ratings thresholds (c) Jester users' ratings thresholds

Figure 4: Distributions of users's rating thresholds.

to 0. One way to define it is

$$sim(R(u,i), R(v,j)) = 1 - \frac{abs(R(u,i) - R(v,j))}{(R_{max} - R_{min})}$$

where R_{max} and R_{min} are the maximum and minimum ratings in the system and $abs(\cdot)$ is the absolute value function.

Datasets. We run experiments on three real world datasets, whose statistics are given in Fig. 3(a). The first dataset is Movielens. It consists of 1M ratings given by 6040 users distributed over 3706 movies. The ratings are on a scale of 1-5. Fig. 3(b) shows the distribution of ratings which follows the normal distribution with mean 3.58 and standard deviation 1.12. Next, we use Yahoo! Music[3] data set, provided as part of the Yahoo! Research Alliance Webscope program. It represents a sample of Yahoo! users' ratings of musical artists, gathered over a thirty-day period sometime prior to March 2004. The raw data contains 11.5M ratings over 98K artists given by 1.9M users. The ratings are integers ranging from 0 to 100, except 255 (a special rating meaning "never play again"). From this data set, we randomly sampled 10K users who assigned 20 or more ratings. From the sample, we discarded all the artists who received less than 20 ratings. This pre-processing resulted in 1M ratings over 5069 artists. We ignored the special rating 255 in the pre-processing and kept only explicit ratings. The rating distribution of the resulting data set is presented in Fig. 3(c). Notice that unlike in Movielens, there is a large number of ratings with value 0 in Yahoo!. Finally, we use the Jester Joke collaborative filtering data set released by Ken Goldberg from UC Berkeley[4][6]. It has 100 jokes rated by 25K users. There are a total of 1.8M ratings, on a continuous scale of -10 to 10. Since we use the weighted average to compute expected ratings (according to Eq. 1 and 3) which is meant for positive ratings, we shift the ratings from the $[-10, 10]$ scale to $[0, 20]$, by adding 10 to each rating. The ratings distribution is presented in Fig. 3(d). Again, unlike the movie ratings in Movielens, there is a significant number of negative ratings in Jester. In our experiments, we derive a rating $R(u, \rho)$ for a seed user u by taking an average of the top-20% of the highest ratings provided by u. Finally, while computing $\hat{R}(v, \rho)$, we ignore the small changes in similarity values among users (in case of User-based) and existing items (in case of Item-based) that happen because of ratings provided by seed users to the new item ρ. We evaluate our heuristics for RECMAX on both User-based and Item-based collaborative filtering methods.

User-Based collaborative filtering. We first report our findings in User-based systems. Predicted ratings are computed using weighted average along with Pearson correlation (see Eq. 1 and 2). For $\hat{R}(v,i)$ to be non-zero, we require that at least 5 of v's nearest neighbors must rate the item i, i.e., $|N_i(v)| \geq 5$. Similarly, for the similarity between users u and v to be non-zero, we require them to rate at least 5 items in common, i.e., $|I(u) \cap I(v)| \geq 5$. Finally, we consider at most 25 nearest neighbors of v while computing $\hat{R}(v,i)$. These settings are used and recommended by previous works (E.g., see [14, 9]). On Movielens and Yahoo!, we set the length of the recommendation list ℓ as 15, as popular recommendation music/movies systems like Yahoo! Music, Movielens, Youtube usually show 15-20 recommendations on a single page. On Jester, ℓ is set to 1 because only one joke is recommended at a time on the Jester website. Based on these settings, we compute the rating thresholds θ_v of every user v. The distributions of the rating thresholds for the three data sets are shown in Fig. 4.

Fig. 5 compares the various heuristics, described above, on all 3 datasets. The plots reveal many interesting points. (i) On all 3 datasets, we see that MOST-ACTIVE and MOST-CRITICAL perform poorly, and MOST-POSITIVE and MOST-CENTRAL perform relatively better. Thus, simply choosing users who provide lots of ratings or users who are very critical does not seem to help. Surprisingly, even RANDOM exhibits a relatively good performance. For instance, on Yahoo! (Fig. 5(b)), with a budget of 500, RANDOM is able to achieve a hit score of 3719. With the same budget, MOST-CENTRAL and MOST-POSITIVE achieve 4628 and 5073, that is, a 24.4% and a 36.4% improvement over RANDOM, respectively. By contrast, MOST-ACTIVE and MOST-CRITICAL

[3]www.music.yahoo.com

[4]eigentaste.berkeley.edu/user

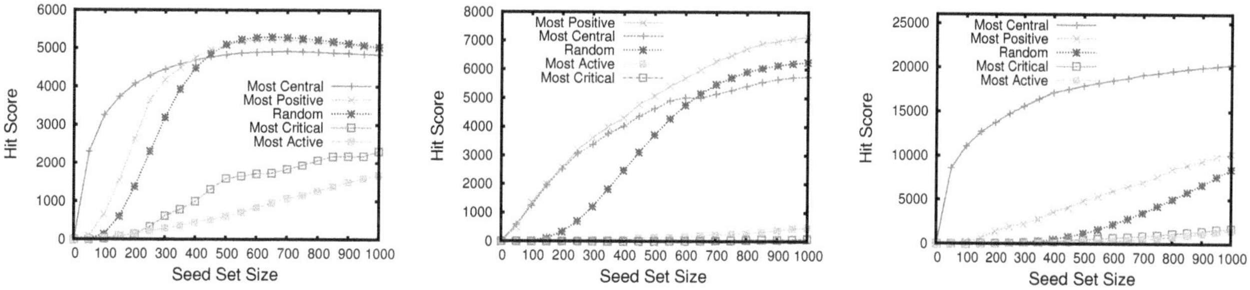

(a) Movielens (b) Yahoo! (c) Jester

Figure 5: Hit Score achieved with various algorithms on different datasets on User-based RS.

achieve poor hit scores of only 132 and 2 respectively. This clearly establishes that *the choice of seed sets is critical and can make a substantial difference.* Except on Yahoo! where MOST-POSITIVE wins, MOST-CENTRAL is found to be the best. MOST-CENTRAL picks seeds who have the greatest affinity to other users in the aggregate and in the context of User-based collaborative filtering, this does make sense. (ii) In general, the hit score achieved is impressive. For instance, with a budget of only 300, MOST-CENTRAL attains a hit score of 4444, 3377 and 15.6K on Movielens, Yahoo! and Jester respectively. It shows even the simple heuristic strategies for seed selection make RECMAX relevant and useful for targeted marketing, despite the problem being inapproximable within any reasonable factor. (iii) Depending on the data set and the seed set selected, we may encounter a "tipping point", a point at which a slight increase in budget can make a significant difference in the hit score achieved. For example, on Movielens, using MOST-POSITIVE, the hit score with a budget of 50 is only 288, i.e., the average hit score per seed is 5.76. On the other hand, the overall hit score shoots up to 3656 with a the budget of 250, i.e., the average hit score for the last 200 seeds is 16.84. The rate of growth in hit score slows down as the budget is increased beyond a point. E.g., when the budget is extended futher by 200 to 450, the hit score increases to 4962, that is, the average hit score for the last 200 seeds drops to 6.53. When we continue to expand the budget, the hit score plateaus and in some cases it may even decrease. For instance, on Movielens with MOST-POSITIVE, if we increase the budget from 700 to 1000, the hit score falls from 5215 to 5008.

Item-Based collaborative filtering. We now report our findings in Item-based collaborative filtering. Again, to compute the expected rating $\hat{R}(v, i)$, we use the weighted average with similarities among items computed using adjusted cosine (see Eq. 3 and 4). As earlier, we require for $\hat{R}(v, j) > 0$, that there be at least 5 similar items to j that are rated by v, that is, $|N_v(j)| \geq 5$. Similarly, the similarity among items i and j can be more than 0 only if they are rated by at least 5 common users, i.e., $|V(i) \cap V(j)| \geq 5$. Finally, we consider at most 25 most similar items to j to compute $\hat{R}(v, j)$. We keep the length of the recommendation list ℓ the same as before, that is, 15, 15 and 1 for Movielens, Yahoo! and Jester respectively. Based on these settings, the rating thresholds of all users are computed. We found their distributions to be very similar to those for User-based (see Fig. 4) and so suppress their plots for brevity.

In Fig. 6, we show the hit score achieved by the various heuristics. Note that the MOST-CENTRAL heuristic is fundamentally different in Item-based. Out of curiosity, we also include in our comparison the MOST-CENTRAL heuristic of User-based method. For clarity, we refer to the latter as UB-MOST-CENTRAL in Fig. 6. Again, many interesting observations are made. (i) On all 3 datasets, the overall hit score that is achieved in Item-based is much lower than in User-based. Moreover, on all the datasets, the hit score plateaus much faster in Item-based than in User-based. For example, on Movielens with MOST-CENTRAL heuristics, the hit score saturates at 1238 at the budget of 200 in case of Item-based. In User-based, on the other hand, the hit score saturates at 4825 at the budget of 500 (see Fig. 5(a)). As a result, much less seeding is required to achieve the maximum possible hit score in Item-based. (ii) Except in Jester, MOST-CENTRAL beats every other algorithm. For instance, on Movielens, with a budget of 200, while MOST-CENTRAL gets the hit score of 1238, RANDOM achieves just 712. MOST-ACTIVE, MOST-CRITICAL and MOST-POSITIVE attain the scores 692, 587 and 481 respectively. (iii) Another interesting observation is that while MOST-POSITIVE performs quite well in User-based, it performs poorly in Item-based. This shows strategies that work well in User-based need not work well in Item-based. However, interestingly enough, the intuition underlying MOST-CENTRAL seems to be borne out well by the results for both User-based and Item-based.

Next, we undertake a comparison of User-based with Item-based. Fig. 7 presents a zoomed-in comparison of hit scores achieved in User-based and Item-based methods, with the heuristic MOST-CENTRAL. Except in Movielens, the initial rise of hit score is much steeper in Item-based than in User-based. And as the budget increases, hit score in User-based continues to increase well beyond the peak value of Item-based and it plateaus at a much higher budget than Item-based. Finally, we look at the intersection of seed sets obtained from MOST-CENTRAL heuristic in both cases. Out of 1000 seeds, the number of common seeds are 103, 219 and 62 on Movielens, Yahoo! and Jester, respectively, suggesting that the seed sets are different in both methods.

In summary, the hit scores behave very differently in User-based and Item-based methods. While the overall hit scores that are achieved in User-based are much higher, the saturation in hit scores is achieved much faster in case of Item-based. In both, respective versions of MOST-CENTRAL are found to be most effective, although other heuristics behave differently. For instance, MOST-POSITIVE performs quite well in User-based, while its performance in Item-based is poor. These observations suggest that different approaches are required to select good seed sets on different systems, and no single rule of thumb works well for all systems.

7. CONCLUSIONS AND FUTURE WORK

The main goal of this paper is to propose and study a

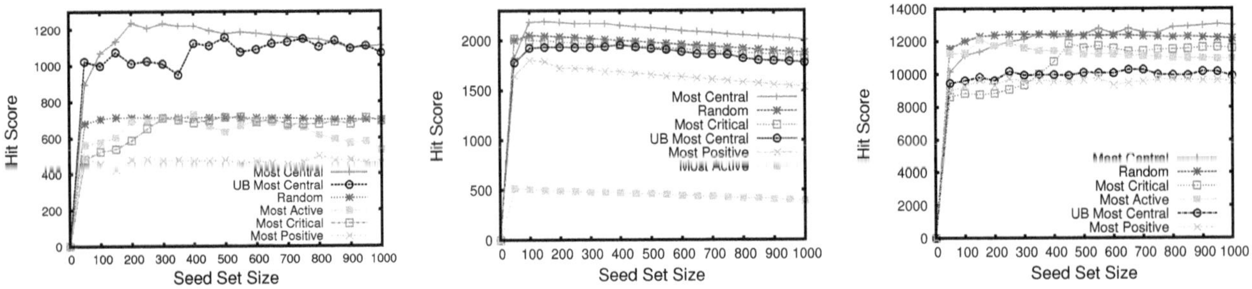

(a) Movielens (b) Yahoo! (c) Jester

Figure 6: Hit Score achieved with various algorithms on different datasets on Item-based RS.

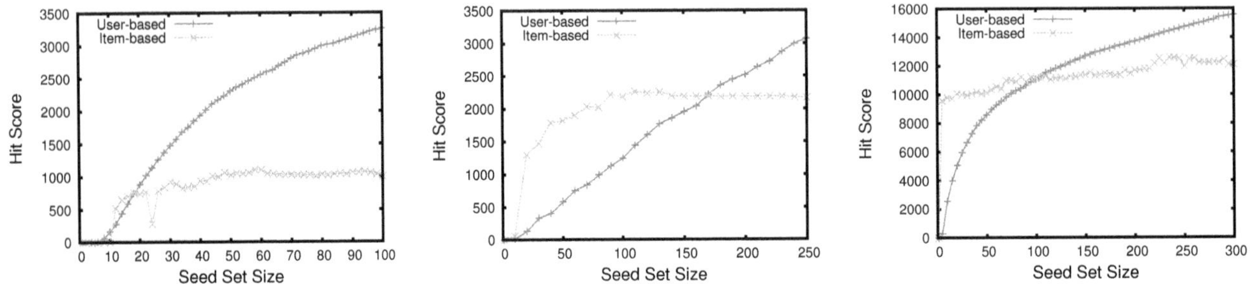

(a) Movielens (b) Yahoo! (c) Jester

Figure 7: Comparison of User-based and Item-based RS with the algorithm Most-Central.

novel problem that we call RECMAX. It aims to develop a technology to select seed users in a collborative filtering based RS such that if they endorse a new product with relatively high ratings, the new product is recommended to a large number of users, solely because of the underlying mechanics of the RS. We motivate the problem with real world applications. We focus on the two widely used methods – User-based and Item-based. We perform a thorough theoretical analysis and show that RECMAX is not only NP-hard to solve optimally, it is NP-hard to approximate within any reasonable factor. Given that, we explore various natural heuristics and show that, even though the problem is inapproximable, simple heuristics like MOST-CENTRAL can fetch impressive gains. This makes RECMAX an interesting problem for targeted marketing in RS.

This work opens up a wide array of challenges. First, developing more effective heuristics is important, interesting and challenging, given that the hit score function is neither monotone nor submodular. We also need to calibrate the proposed and new heuristics on a wide array of real data sets. Second, as we saw in our empirical evaluation, the hit score function behaves distinctly on User-based and Item-based systems. It would be interesting to see how it behaves when mixed approaches are employed. Third, studying RECMAX on more recent RS methodologies, for example, Matrix factorization [16] – both theoretically and empirically, would be exciting. Finally, the vision behind RECMAX is marketing based on an operational recommender *system*, which is not just a simple RS algorithm but has a much greater complexity. Formulating and solving RECMAX and launching it on an operational RS is a fascinating challenge with great potential.

Acknowledgments. We thank Suresh Venkatasubramanian and Nick Harvey for helpful discussions. We acknowledge Yun Lou's involvement in the initial phase of the project. We appreciate anonymous reviewer's feedback that helped us in improving the presentation of the paper.

8. REFERENCES

[1] G. Adomavicius and A. Tuzhilin. Toward the next generation of recommender systems: A survey of the state-of-the-art and possible extensions. *IEEE Trans. on Knowl. and Data Eng.*, 17, 2005.

[2] S. S. Anand and N. Griffiths. A market-based approach to address the new item problem. In *RecSys*, 2011.

[3] S. Bhagat, A. Goyal, and L. V. S. Lakshmanan. Maximizing product adoption in social networks. In *WSDM*, 2012.

[4] W. Chen, Y. Wang, and S. Yang. Efficient influence maximization in social networks. In *KDD*, 2009.

[5] P. Domingos and M. Richardson. Mining the network value of customers. In *KDD*, 2001.

[6] K. Y. Goldberg et al. Eigentaste: A constant time collaborative filtering algorithm. *Inf. Retr.*, 4(2), 2001.

[7] J. D. Hartline et al. Optimal marketing strategies over social networks. In *WWW*, 2008.

[8] J. Hastad. Clique is hard to approximate within $n^{1-\epsilon}$. In *FOCS*, 1996.

[9] J. L. Herlocker et al. An algorithmic framework for performing collaborative filtering. In *SIGIR*, 1999.

[10] D. Kempe, J. M. Kleinberg, and É. Tardos. Maximizing the spread of influence through a social network. In *KDD*, 2003.

[11] X. N. Lam et al. Addressing cold-start problem in recommendation systems. In *ICUIMC*, 2008.

[12] B. Mobasher et al. Toward trustworthy recommender systems: An analysis of attack models and algorithm robustness. *ACM Trans. Internet Techn.*, 7(4), 2007.

[13] A. Rashid, G. Karypis, and J. Riedl. Influence in ratings-based recommender systems: An algorithm-independent approach. In *SDM*, 2005.

[14] F. Ricci, L. Rokach, B. Shapira, and P. B. Kantor, editors. *Recommender Systems Handbook*. Springer, 2011.

[15] B. Sarwar, G. Karypis, J. Konstan, and J. Reidl. Item-based collaborative filtering recommendation algorithms. In *WWW*, 2001.

[16] G. Takács et al. Matrix factorization and neighbor based algorithms for the netflix prize problem. In *RecSys*, 2008.

[17] J. Wang, A. P. de Vries, and M. J. T. Reinders. Unifying user-based and item-based collaborative filtering approaches by similarity fusion. In *SIGIR*, 2006.

Learning Personal+Social Latent Factor Model for Social Recommendation

Yelong Shen
Department of Computer Science
Kent State University
yshen@cs.kent.edu

Ruoming Jin
Department of Computer Science
Kent State University
jin@cs.kent.edu

ABSTRACT

Social recommendation, which aims to systematically leverage the social relationships between users as well as their past behaviors for automatic recommendation, attract much attention recently. The belief is that users linked with each other in social networks tend to share *certain* common interests or have similar tastes (*homophily principle*); such similarity is expected to help improve the recommendation accuracy and quality. There have been a few studies on social recommendations; however, they almost completely ignored the heterogeneity and diversity of the social relationship.

In this paper, we develop a joint personal and social latent factor (PSLF) model for social recommendation. Specifically, it combines the state-of-the-art collaborative filtering and the social network modeling approaches for social recommendation. Especially, the PSLF extracts the social factor vectors for each user based on the state-of-the-art mixture membership stochastic blockmodel, which can explicitly express the varieties of the social relationship. To optimize the PSLF model, we develop a scalable expectation-maximization (EM) algorithm for fast expectation computation. We compare our approach with the latest social recommendation approaches on two real datasets, Flixter and Douban. With similar training cost, our approach has shown a significant improvement in terms of prediction accuracy criteria over the existing approaches.

Categories and Subject Descriptors

H.3.3 [**Information Search and Retrieval**]: :Information Filtering; J.4 [**Computer Applications**]: :Social and Behavioral Sciences

Keywords

Social Recommender Systems, Personal + social Factor

1. INTRODUCTION

Recommendation systems are playing increasingly important role for Etailers and service providers: providing each individual with the "best" options matching with their tastes and needs. By doing so, companies can foster customers' satisfaction and loyalty, and even boost the sale and attract more potential customers. In the meantime, users may view recommendation itself as an indispensable service as it can help them save time and effort in discovering what they like or need. In the past, recommendation systems mainly focus on utilizing users' historical behaviors, such as their preferences on the purchased products/services (often represented in terms a user-item rating matrix R, illustrated in Figure 1(a)) for collaborative filtering [1, 10].

Thanks to the booming online social networking websites, users are explicitly linked and often (un)knowingly recommend products/services to friends. Numerous websites [16] directly utilize the social networks to enable users to share opinions and recommends stuffs, such as books, movies, and/or musics, etc. to one another. More recently, there have been lots of interest in *social recommendation*, which aims to systematically leverage the social relationships between users (Figure 1(b)) as well as their past behaviors for automatic recommendation. The belief here is that users linked with each other in social networks tend to share *certain* common interests or have similar tastes (*homophily principle* [12]), which can help increase the recommendation accuracy. However, how to discover and utilize the common denominators hidden in the complex and massive social network is not a trivial problem.

There have been a few recent attempts at social recommendations [5, 11, 18], which are all based on the assumption that any pair of friends in the social network shall have similar interests. The recent studies [11, 18] incorporate such a network-based similarity property between users into the state-of-the-art matrix factorization recommendation approaches [10]. The matrix factorization approaches map both users and products to a common latent factor space $\mathbb{R}^k$ (each dimension encodes a latent factor). In movie recommendation, for instance, one latent factor (dimension) may represent the degree of actions and/or violence and another one may encode the movie cost. Each user u_i is characterized by a latent factor vector $U_i \in \mathbb{R}^k$, which represents her or his personal interests/tastes; and each item v_j is also represented by a vector $V_j \in \mathbb{R}^k$, describing its key features and compositions. Given this, the inner product $(U_i^T V_j)$ of these two latent factor vectors (U_i and V_j) is used to predict the likely rating of user u_i on item v_j. The higher is the value $(U_i^T V_j)$, the more likely is a match (between user u_i and item v_j). Mao *et al.* [11] propose a social-network based regulation on top of the latent factor model, which targets to constrain the difference between the latent vectors of user u_i's friends and user u_i, i.e., $||U_i - U_f||$ shall be small where u_f is u_i's friend. Yang *et al.* [18] take one step further and they require the inner product $(U_i^T U_f)$ between two users u_i and u_f can directly help to recover whether u_i and u_j is linked in the social network. Basically, the higher is the

KDD'12, August 12–16, 2012, Beijing, China.

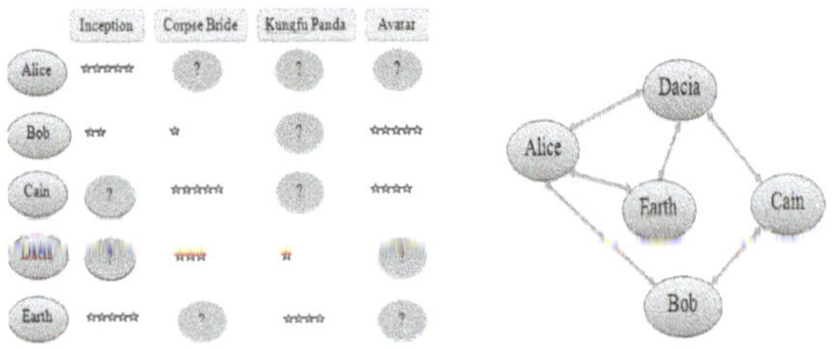

(a) User-Item Rating Matrix $\mathcal{R}$ (b) User-Social Network $\mathcal{G}$

Figure 1: Social Recommendation Data Sources

value $U_i^T U_f$, the more similar they are and the more likely they are friends. Both approaches have shown reasonable improvement over the state-of-art recommendation approaches which do not utilize the social factors.

However, the basic underlying assumption about social relationships used in the existing social recommendation approaches is too strict to be realistic: they almost completely ignored the heterogeneity and diversity of the social relationship. Users in an online social network, such as Facebook, are linked or become "friends" because of different reasons, including family, friends, classmates, or even business relationships, among many others. For different types of interactions, the common denominators (shared interests or preferences) might be quite different. From a user-centered viewpoint, each user u_i may be characterized by a set of social tags (factors), such as "car dealer", "skiing enthusiast", "food-lover", etc.; one of his neighbors u_f in the social network might only share the common attribute "car dealer", and another one u'_f with may be his ski-buddies who teaches in the nearby college. Thus, an interest on an adventure movie, may be propagated between u_i and his "skiing enthusiast" friend, but may not necessarily be shared with his "car dealer" colleague. On the other hand, two users at different states with many similar interests may not know one another and never become friends.

Thus, the (dis)similarity measure of the latent factors, such as the difference $||U_i - U_f||$ or the inner product $U_i^T U_f$ may not be an appropriate factor to determine the likelihood of existing social relationship. In the meantime, however, the social factors of an individual do directly affect her or his preferences towards an item. Given this, the key challenge is how to discover those latent social factors of individual user and how to effectively utilize them to boost the recommendation accuracy.

1.1 Our Contribution

In this paper, we propose a joint personal and social latent factor (PSLF) model for social recommendation, which utilize both users' past behaviors and the social relationships. Similar to the matrix factorization approaches, each user u_i (and each item v_j) is represented by a personal (item) latent factor vector, U_i (V_j) in a unified user-item factor space $\mathbb{R}^k$. However, instead of using the social relationship to constraint those personal factors, the new model explicitly represent each user u_i with an additional social factor vector Π_i in another space $\mathbb{S}^d$, which can also be linearly transformed and mapped to the user-item factor space $\mathbb{R}^k$, denoted as $M^T \Pi_i$, where M is the linear transformation matrix. Given this, the model utilizes the joint predictions from both personal and social latent factors, $U_i V_j + \Pi_i^T M V_j$, for the likely rating from u_i on item v_j. Clearly, the major challenge here is how to discover the right social latent factors which can complement and also reinforce the personal latent factors, which have been extensively studied [10].

In this work, we extract the social factor vectors for each user based on the mixture membership stochastic blockmodel [2], which can simultaneously factorize the social network and infer the latent social structure. Specifically, in this blockmodel, the network is assumed to base on a number of social factors (attributes), and these social factors may interact with one another in certain probability (represented as a social interaction/connection matrix B). Furthermore, each user u_i is represented as a mixture (social factor vector Π_i) of social factors; and $\Pi_i^T B \Pi_j$ represents the likelihood whether user u_i and u_f are linked.

Even though both personal latent factor model and mixture membership blockmodel for social factors have been studied independently before, to the best of our knowledge, this is the first study which bridges them. Here, we combine the latent factor model and mixture membership blockmodel in a unified probabilistic model for social recommendation; and we study how to optimize the joint model and scale it on large social networks. Especially, we note that in the joint personal and social modeling, the social latent factors should not only reflect the underlying social structures, but also directly contribute to improvise the accuracy of the ratings. In other words, users' past behaviors are also served as the feedback for factorizing the social network.

To sum, we make the following contributions in this work. We first propose a novel joint personal and social latent factor model which can effectively utilize both users' past behaviors and the social network. Our approach combines the collaborative filtering and the social network modeling approaches for social recommendation. We develop a fast expectation-maximization (EM) algorithm to optimize the joint factor model. We compare our approach with the latest social recommendation approaches on two real datasets, Flixster and Douban. In the experiments, our approach has shown a significant improvement in terms of prediction accuracy criteria over the existing approaches.

Paper Organization: In Section 2, we formally describe the social recommendation problem and discuss the basic latent factor modeling and its adoption for the problem. In Section 3, we present the joint personal and social latent factor (PSLF) modeling. In Section 4, we introduce the fast EM based parameter inference algorithm for the PSLF model. In Section 5, we report the detailed experiments results. Finally, we provide a short review of the related work in Section 6 and conclude the paper in Section 7.

2. PROBLEM DEFINITION AND LATENT FACTOR MODELING

The social recommendation problem considers two major data sources: 1) the user-item rating matrix $\mathcal{R}$ (recording users' past behaviors), where R_{ij} indicates the user u_i's preference to item v_j; 2) the social network $\mathcal{G} = (V, E)$, where $(i, f) \in E$ indicate users u_i and u_f are linked. Here, we consider the social relationship is mutual and thus G is an undirected graph. Figure 1(a) illustrates the rating matrix $\mathcal{R}$ and Figure 1(b) shows the social network $\mathcal{R}$. Given this, the social recommendation problem can be defined as learning a model which can effectively predict the missing values in the user-item rating matrix $\mathcal{R}$ by employing both $\mathcal{R}$ and $\mathcal{G}$.

In the following, we will introduce the basics of latent factor modeling for collaborative filtering (Subsection 2.1). Then, in Subsection 2.2, we will given an overview on the latest studies [11, 18] which incorporates the social networks with the latent factor modeling for social recommendation.

2.1 Latent Factor Modeling

The latent factor modeling approach maps both users and items to a common latent factor space $\mathbb{R}^k$ (each dimension encodes a latent factor). Each user u_i is characterized by a latent factor vector $U_i \in \mathbb{R}^k$, which represents her or his personal interests/tastes; and each item v_j also represented by a vector $V_j \in \mathbb{R}^k$, describing its key features and compositions. Given this, the inner product ($U_i^T V_j$) of these two latent factor vectors (U_i and V_j) is used to predict R_{ij}, the rating of user u_i on item v_j.

Now, we follow the probabilistic matrix factorization (PMF) notation to formally describe the latent factor modeling approach. The rating R_{ij} is modeled using the normal distribution $\mathcal{N}(x|\mu, \sigma^2)$ with mean μ and variance σ^2:

$$R_{ij} \sim p(R_{ij}|U_i^T V_j, \sigma^2) = \mathcal{N}(R_{ij}|U_i^T V_j, \sigma^2) \quad (1)$$

Furthermore, the user (item) latent factor vectors are also modeled using the normal distribution with zero mean:

$$U_i \sim p(U_i|\sigma_u^2) = \mathcal{N}(U_i|0, \sigma_u^2 \mathbf{I}) \quad (2)$$

$$V_j \sim p(V_j|\sigma_v^2) = \mathcal{N}(V_j|0, \sigma_v^2 \mathbf{I}) \quad (3)$$

Parameters $U = (U_i)$,$V = (V_j)$ are estimated through maximizing the *log-posterior* over user rating behaviors ($\mathcal{R}$):

$$\ln p(U, V|\mathcal{R}, \sigma^2, \sigma_u^2, \sigma_v^2) = \ln p(\mathcal{R}|U, V, \sigma^2) + \ln p(U|\sigma_u^2) + \ln p(V|\sigma_v^2) + C, \quad (4)$$

where C is a parameter-independent constant. Specifically,

$$p(\mathcal{R}|U, V, \sigma^2) = \prod_{i,j} \mathcal{N}(R_{ij}|U_i^T V_j, \sigma^2)^{I_{ij}}$$

$$p(U|\sigma_u^2) = \prod_i \mathcal{N}(U_i|0, \sigma_u^2 \mathbf{I}),\ p(V|\sigma_v^2) = \prod_j \mathcal{N}(V_j|0, \sigma_v^2 \mathbf{I}) \quad (5)$$

where I_{ij} is the indicator: $I_{ij} = 1$ if user u_i rates item v_j, and $I_{ij} = 0$, otherwise. Maximizing the log-posterior with respect to U and V is equivalent to minimize the sum-of-squared-errors objective function with quadratic regulation terms:

$$\min_{U,V} \sum_{i,j} I_{ij}(R_{ij} - U_i^T V_j)^2 + \lambda_U \sum_i ||U_i||^2 + \lambda_V \sum_j ||V_j||^2 \quad (6)$$

where $\lambda_U = \sigma^2/\sigma_U^2$ and $\lambda_V = \sigma^2/\sigma_V^2$. Usually, an iterative method, such as gradient descent method, can be employed to find the local optimum of U and V.

Recently, Koren in [9] make a major improvement over the existing latent factor model by taking the similarity between items (users) into consideration. The neighborhood-based latent factor model naturally combines the neighborhood model with the latent factor model, yielding better performances over pure neighborhood and pure latent factor models. Specially, the basic neighborhood based latent factor model utilizes the sum: $U_i^T V_j + (B_{ij} + |R(i)|^{-1/2} \sum_{j' \in R(i)} (R_{ij'} - B_{ij'}) W_{jj'})$ to predict R_{ij}, where $R(i)$ is the set of items user u_i rated, B_{ij} is the baseline estimator of R_{ij} [1], and ($W_{jj'}$) are the user-independent parameters for describing the similarity between item j and j'. In [9], both the baseline estimator and similarity parameters ($W_{jj'}$) can be computed to minimize the estimation accuracy, and different variants such as using $R^k(j; i)$, which is the set of top k similar items user i has rated, to replace $R(i)$ are also discussed.

2.2 Social Recommendation Models

As we mentioned before, there have been a few studies [11, 18] on social recommendations recently. They all based on the assumption that any pair of friends in the social network shall have similar interests and try to incorporate such a network-based similarity property between users into the latent factor modeling. Mao *et al.* [11] introduces the *social regulation*, i.e., using the social relationship explicitly regulate the latent factor model. Specifically, the individual-based regulation (the best approach in [11]) is modeled as follows:

$$\min_{U,V} \sum_{i,j} I_{ij}(R_{ij} - U_i^T V_j)^2 + \lambda_U \sum_i ||U_i||^2 + \lambda_V \sum_j ||V_j||^2 + \lambda_E \sum_{(i,f) \in E} Sim(i, f)||U_i - U_f||^2, \quad (7)$$

where the last one is the social regulation term: it targets to minimize the difference between the latent vectors of user u_i and her or his friend u_f. $Sim(i, f)$ is the similarity between users u_i and u_f and can be defined in terms of either Vector Space Similarity (VSS) or Person Correction Coefficient (PCC) [11].

In [18], Yang *et al.* proposes the *Friendship-Interest Propagation* (FIP) model, which utilizes the latent space vectors not only for predicting the rating ($U_i^T V_j$), but also for link prediction. Basically, the inner product ($U_i^T U_f$) between two users u_i and u_f can directly help to recover whether u_i and u_j is linked in the social network. Note that Yang *et al.* [18] study slightly different contexts where both users and items have additional features (contents) and the rating is only binary (item recommendation). To facilitate the discussion, we adopt their approach to the typical social recommendation. Thus, the basic FIP model can be described as follows:

$$\min_{U,V} \sum_{i,j} I_{ij}(R_{ij} - U_i^T V_j)^2 + \lambda_E \sum_{(i,f) \in E} \mathcal{L}(1, U_i^T U_f) + \lambda_U \sum_i ||U_i||^2 + \lambda_V \sum_j ||V_j||^2, \quad (8)$$

where the second term is the error induced by using the user's latent factor similarity to predict their social relationship. The function $\mathcal{L}(x, y)$ is a loss function for measuring the difference between a binary variable x and a continuous variable y [18]. For instance, the logistic regression $log(x, y) = \log[1 + exp(-xy)]$ can be applied here.

As we argued earlier, even though linked users often share *certain* common denominators (interests, tastes, etc.), (*homophily principle*), this is not equivalent to say that they shall be "similar". In fact, the similarity on certain interests and tastes between two friends can often be outweighed by their difference on most other aspects. Clearly, the existing approaches have largely ignored the heterogeneity and diversity of the social relationship. Using the (dis)similarity measure of the latent factors, such as the difference $||U_i - U_f||$ or the inner product $U_i^T U_f$, to regulate or predict social relationship is clearly not fully reflect or exploit the underlying dimensionality of social networks. In this work, we utilize the social network modeling to help discover the latent social factors S_i of an individual user and combine it with the (personal) latent factors (U_i) to solve the social recommendation problems.

3. PERSONAL+SOCIAL LATENT FACTOR MODEL

In the section, we present a joint personal and social latent factor (PSLF) model, which utilize both users' past behaviors and the social relationships for social recommendation. For the personal latent factor, it is similar to the matrix factorization approaches, where each user u_i is represented by a personal latent factor vector, U_i in a unified user-item factor space $\mathbb{R}^k$. For

[1] $B_{ij} = \mu + B_i + B_j$, where μ is the overall average rating and B_i and B_j are the observed deviations of user u_i and item v_j, respectively.

the social latent factor, it is based on the state-of-the-art mixture membership stochastic blockmodel [2], which can simultaneously factorize the social network and infer the latent social structure. The social factor vector of each user u_i is represented in terms of his or her mixture membership Π_i in the social network. Given this, the model utilizes the joint predictions from both personal and social latent factors, $U_i V_j + \Pi_i^T M V_j$, for the likely rating from u_i on item v_j.

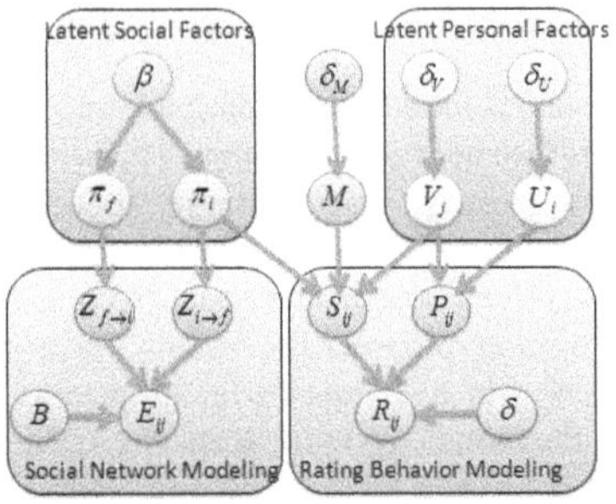

Figure 2: Social-interest Factor model for recommendation

Figure 2 shows the graphical model of PSLF. The generative process of PSLF model is as follows:

1. For each user u_i,
   - **(1.a)** Draw a personal latent factor vector $U_i \in \mathbb{R}^k \sim p(U_i|\sigma_u^2) = \mathcal{N}(U_i|0, \sigma_u^2 \mathbf{I})$.
   - **(1.b)** Draw a social latent factor vector (mixture membership) $\Pi_i \in \mathbb{S}^d \sim p(\Pi_i|\beta) = Dirichlet(\beta)$.
2. For each item v_j, draw an item latent vector $V_j \in \mathcal{R}^k \sim p(V_j|\sigma_v^2) = \mathcal{N}(V_j|0, \sigma_v^2 \mathbf{I})$.
3. For each pair of users (u_i, u_f),
   - **(3.a)** Draw membership indicator $z_{i\to f} \sim p(z_{i\to f}|\Pi_i) = Multi(z_{i\to f}|\Pi_i)$.
   - **(3.b)** Draw membership indicator $z_{f\to i} \sim p(z_{f\to i}|\Pi_f) = Multi(z_{f\to i}|\Pi_f)$.
   - **(3.c)** Sample the value of their social relationship, $E_{if} \sim p(E_{if}|z_{i\to f}^T B z_{f\to i}) = Bernoulli(z_{i\to f}^T B z_{f\to i})$.
4. For each user-item pair (u_i, v_j), draw the response $R_{ij} \sim p(R_{ij}|P_{ij} + S_{ij}, \sigma^2) = \mathcal{N}(R_{ij}|U_i^T V_j + \Pi_i^T M V_j, \sigma^2)$. Here P_{ij} and S_{ij} can be considered as the predictions drawing from the personal latent factors $(U_i^T V_j)$ and social latent factors $(\Pi_i^T M V_j)$, respectively. Furthermore, each cell M_{ij} in the matrix M is also considered to be generated from a normal distribution: $M_{ij} \sim p(M_{ij}|0, \sigma_M^2) = \mathcal{N}(M_{ij}|0, \sigma_M^2)$.
5. For the item pair similarity measure $\mathcal{S} = V^T L^T L V$, draw its value $\mathcal{S} \sim p(\mathcal{S}|0, \sigma_s^2) = N(\mathcal{S}|0, \sigma_s^2)$. Here, L is the Laplace matrix defined as $L = D - W$, where matrix W is the pearson coefficient matrix, and D is the diagonal matrix with $D_{jj} = \sum_{j' \in \Omega_j} W_{jj'}$. Also, Ω_i is the neighborhoods of item v_i that the two items are neighbors indicates that they at least rated by one common user.

We make the following notes of the joint personal and social latent factor (PSLF) model:

1) The generative steps (Steps 1.b and 3) forms the core of the mixture membership stochastic blockmodeling as described in [2]. Recall that in the typical block modeling, each user is considered to be associated with only one group and a block structure can represent at high level how likely one group may interact with another group. The stochastic blockmodel assumes there is an underlying block structure (describe in the matrix $B_{d\times d}$), and each user may belong to several groups (latent social factors), which are specified by Π_i. Thus, the social factor vector Π_i can help characterize each user's unique underlying social interests and preferences.

2) Because the social latent factor vector Π_i is located in the different space $\mathbb{S}^d$ as the unified user-item latent space $\mathbb{R}^k$, an additional matrix M (Step 4) is utilized to linearly transform and map each social vector Π_i to the user-item space $M^T \Pi_i$. The new vector $M^T \Pi_i$ can be viewed as the social latent factor in the user-item space $\mathbb{R}^k$ which complements the personal latent vector U_i. We note that the generative representation of matrix M is for penalizing the model complexity.

3) The last step (Step 5) is to incorporate the neighborhood item similarity constraint into the latent factor model, which was initially proposed by Koren in [9]. However, since our approach is based on generative modeling, for the simplicity (and uniformity) of technical treatment, we utilize the neighborhood preserving regulation $(V^T L^T L V)$ used in matrix factorization [6] and consider it as a response being generated through a normal distribution. We note that also for simplicity, Figure 2 does not explicitly reflect this constraint.

Now, let $\Theta = (U, V, \Pi, M, B)$ be the model parameter set in the PSLF model; let $\Phi = (\sigma, \beta, \sigma_s, \sigma_u, \sigma_v, \sigma_M)$ be the hyper-parameters. Given this, the posterior probability given the user-item rating matrix $\mathcal{R}$ and the social work $\mathcal{G}$ $(p(\Theta, \Phi|\mathcal{R}, \mathcal{G}))$ is proportional to:

$$\propto \prod_{(u_i,v_j)} p(R_{ij}|U_i^T V_j + \pi_i^T M V_j, \sigma^2)^{I_{ij}} \prod_{i,j} p(M_{ij}|\sigma_M^2)$$
$$\prod_{(u_i,u_f)} \int_{z_{i\to f}} \int_{z_{f\to i}} p(z_{i\to f}|\Pi_i) p(z_{f\to i}|\Pi_j) p(E_{if}|z_{i\to f}^T B z_{f\to i})$$
$$\prod_{u_i} p(\Pi_i|\beta) \prod_{u_i} p(U_i|\sigma_u^2) \prod_{v_i} p(V_i|\sigma_v^2) \prod_{v_i,v_j} p(V_i^T L^T L V_j|\sigma_s^2) \quad (9)$$

Thus, the social recommendation problem needs to find the optimal model parameters Θ which can maximize the posterior probability given the user-item rating matrix $\mathcal{R}$ and the social work $\mathcal{G}$:

$$\max_{\Theta} \ln p(\Theta, \Phi|\mathcal{R}, \mathcal{G}) \quad (10)$$

In the next section, we will discuss how to efficiently infer the model parameters Θ.

4. PARAMETERS INFERENCE ON PSLF MODEL

In this section, we present an efficient algorithm for parameter inference , which aims to maximize the posteriori distribution (MAP) of the PSLF model.

Since there are hidden variables Z (in the integral form) being included in the PSLF model, naturally the expectation-maximization (EM) method can be utilized: computing Z first in the E-step given parameters Θ, and then update model parameters in the M-step. In general, the M-step can be solved by the gradient based optimization to update model parameters Θ when the hidden variables Z is explicit estimated; for the E-step, the hidden parameters Z can be estimated by Gibbs sampling (or variational bayesian method), such as:

$$p(z_{i\to f} = m, z_{f\to i} = n | E_{if}, \Pi_i, \Pi_f, B) \propto \pi_{im} * \pi_{fn} * Bernoulli(E_{if}, B_{mn}) \quad (11)$$

However, both Gibbs sampling and variational bayesian method [2] can lead to $O(N^2K^2)$ [2] time complexity in each E-step, which can be too computationally expensive for large networks. To address this problem, in this work, we propose a novel approximate mean-field approximation method for E-step. The new method can reduce the time complexity of E-step to $O(EK^2)$ [3]. In the following two subsections, we elaborate M-step and scalable E-step for model parameter inference.

4.1 Parameters Inference : M-step

The posterior distribution over social latent factors Π_i for user u_i can be written as

$$p(\Pi_i | R, E, \Theta / \Pi, Z; \Phi) \propto L_{[\Pi_i]} = Dir(\Pi_i; Z_{i,\bullet} + \beta) * \prod_{v_j \in R_{ij}} p(R_{ij}; U_i^T V_j + \Pi_i^T M V_j, \sigma), \quad (12)$$

where the dimension of latent social factors denotes K, and let $Z_{(i,\bullet)}$ be a K dimensional vector, i.e., $Z_{i,\bullet} = (Z_{i,1}, Z_{i,2}, ..Z_{i,K})^T$. Here each element $Z_{i,k}$ indicates the count of the k_{th} social attribute (factor) sampled by user u_i, $Z_{(i,k)} = \sum_{u_j} I(z_{i\to j} = k)$, I is the indicator function. The posterior distribution over Π_i is the joint probability of modeling social networks and user rating behaviors.

Since the normal distribution and Dirichlet distribution are non-conjugate, we update Π using the gradient-based approach to maximize posterior distribution over Π.

Update Π:

$$\frac{\partial L_{[\Pi_i]}}{\partial \Pi_i} = (Z_{(i,\bullet)} + \beta - 1) \circ (\frac{1}{\Pi_i}) + \sum_{v_j \in R_{ij}} \frac{1}{\sigma} * (R_{ij} - U_i^T V_j - \Pi_i^T M V_j) M V_j \quad (13)$$

where $\circ$ is the pairwise product operator. Since Π_i is specified as the Dirichlet distribution, which places linear constraints on Π_i (Eqn 14). Thus, the active set method can be utilized to project gradient into feasible region [3]. Here we omit the details due to space limitation.

$$\sum_{k=1}^{K} \Pi_{i,k} = 1 \qquad 0 \le \Pi_{i,k} \le 1 \quad (14)$$

Similarly, by isolating U, V and M terms in posterior distribution of model, the parameters can be updated by moving in the direction of the gradient, yielding:

Update U, V, M: ($e_{ij} = R_{ij} - U_i^T V_j - \Pi_i^T M V_j$)

$$U_i = U_i - \lambda\sigma_u U_i + \lambda\sigma \sum_{v_j} e_{ij} V_j) \quad (15)$$

$$V_j = V_j - \lambda\sigma_v V_j + \lambda\sigma \sum_{u_i} e_{ij}(U_i + \Pi_i M) + \lambda\sigma_s \sum_{j' \in \Omega_j} L^T L V_{j'} \quad (16)$$

$$M = M - \lambda\sigma_M M + \lambda\sigma \sum_{(u_i, v_j)} e_{ij}(\Pi_i V_j^T) \quad (17)$$

[2] N is the user number in social networks, K is the dimension of latent social factors

[3] E is the number of connections in social networks

4.2 Parameters Inference : Scalable E-step

In the earlier discussion, we point out that the classical statistical methods, such as Gibbs sampling and variational inference, can be too costly to estimate Z ($O(N^2K^2)$ time complexity). Here, we introduced an scale EM method to reduce the time complexity to $O(EK^2)$. The basic idea is to utilize an clustering based social network modeling method. Let $C = (C_1, C_2, ...C_T)$ be a set of clusters for Π, each Π_i has an mixture membership to the clusters C, $\sum_{t=1}^{T} p(C_t|\Pi_i) = 1$. Figure 3 illustrates the clustering based approximation. Given this, the distribution over $z_{i\to f}$ and $z_{f\to i}$ can be rewritten in Eqn. 18.

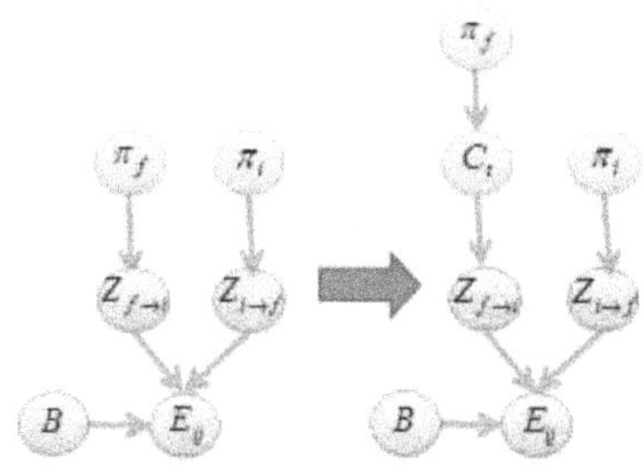

Figure 3: clustering social factors to approximate social network modeling

$$p(z_{i\to f} = m, z_{f\to i} = n | E_{if}, \Pi_i, \Pi_f, B, C) \propto \sum_{t=1}^{T} \Pi_{im} C_{tn} Bernoulli(E_{if}; B_{mn}) p(C_t|\Pi_f) \quad (18)$$

Furthermore, a key observation is as follows: *Based on Eqn 13, it is not necessary to infer hidden variables Z for any pair of users, i.e.* $z_{(i\to f)}, z_{(f\to i)}$. *Instead, only the count of social attributes (factors), i.e.* $Z_{i,\bullet} = (Z_{i,1}, Z_{i,2}, ..Z_{i,K})^T$ *is needed for further parameters updating process.* Given this, let us introduce $Z^+_{i,m,n}$ and $Z^-_{i,m,n}$:

$Z^+_{i,m,n}$: the count of m_{th} and n_{th} social attributes (factors) sampled by user u_i with her/his connected users. According to Eqn. 18, the expectation of $Z^+_{i,m,n}$ can be rewritten as:

$$E(Z^+_{i,m,n}) = \sum_{u_f|E_{if}=1} \sum_{t=1}^{T} \frac{\Pi_{im} C_{tn} B_{mn}}{\sum_{m',n'} \Pi_{im'} C_{tn'} B_{m'n'}} p(C_t|\Pi_f) = \sum_{t=1}^{T} \frac{\Pi_{im} C_{tn} B_{mn}}{\sum_{m',n'} \Pi_{im'} C_{tn'} B_{m'n'}} \sum_{u_f|E_{if}=1} p(C_t|\Pi_f) \quad (19)$$

$Z^-_{i,m,n}$: the count of m_{th} and n_{th} social attributes (factors) sampled by user u_i with her/his non-connected users.

$$E(Z^-_{i,m,n}) = \sum_{u_f|E_{if}=0} \sum_{t=1}^{T} p^-(C_{tn}, \Pi_{im}, B_{mn}) p(C_t|\Pi_f) = \sum_{t=1}^{T} p^-(C_{tn}, \Pi_{im}, B_{mn})(T(C_t) - p(C_t|\Pi_i) - \sum_{u_f|E_{if}=1} p(C_t|\Pi_f)) \quad (20)$$

$$p^-(C_{tn}, \Pi_{im}, B_{mn}) = \frac{\Pi_{im} C_{tn}(1 - B_{mn})}{\sum_{m',n'} \Pi_{im'} C_{tn'}(1 - B_{m'n'})} \quad (21)$$

where $T(C_t) = \sum_{u_i} p(C_t|\Pi_i)$

Given this, the expectation of $Z_{i,m}$ can be calculated based on $Z^{+}_{i,m,n}$ and $Z^{-}_{i,m,n}$:

$$E(Z_{i,m}) = \sum_{n=1}^{K} E(Z^{+}_{i,m,n}) + E(Z^{-}_{i,m,n}) \tag{22}$$

Note that in this approach, the time complexity for estimating $Z_{i,\bullet}$ is $O(TEK^2)$ (at each E-step), where T is the number of the clusters.

Update B : In addition, we can utilize this method to infer B in the M-step:

$$B(m,n) = \frac{\sum_{u_i} E(Z^{+}_{i,m,n})}{\sum_{u_i}(1-\rho)(E(Z^{+}_{i,m,n}) + E(Z^{-}_{i,m,n}))} \tag{23}$$

where ρ is the sparsity parameter to capture non-interaction of the social network [2]. And ρ can be estimated by:

$$\rho = \frac{\sum_{u_i}\sum_{m,n} E(Z^{-}_{i,m,n})}{\sum_{u_i}\sum_{m,n}(E(Z^{+}_{i,m,n}) + E(Z^{-}_{i,m,n}))} \tag{24}$$

4.3 Overall EM Algorithm

Algorithm 1 EM-PSFL-Inference($\mathcal{R}$, $\mathcal{G}$, Φ)

Parameter: $\mathcal{R}$:user-item rating matrix; $\mathcal{G}$: user social network; Φ: model hyperparameters;

```
1: Random Initialize parameters Θ = (U, V, Π, M, B).
2: repeat
3:   Scalable E-Step:
4:     Online K-Means Clustering on Θ.
5:     Estimate E(Z+_{i,k,l}), E(Z-_{i,k,l}) and E(Z_{i,k}) using Eqn. 19, 20
       and 22
6:   M-Step:
7:     Update parameters U, V, M using Eqn. 15, 16 and 17
8:     Update Π according Eqn. 13 and 14.
9:     Update B using Eqn. 23
10: until Repeat the E-M steps until Θ convergence.
```

The parameters inference method for PSFL is outlined in Algorithm 1. The time complexity for the E-step and M-step are $O(TEK^2)$ and $O(RKN)$ [4], respectively. In the Algorithm 1, we use the online K-Means clustering algorithm to obtain C, which leads to $O(KTN)$ time complexity. In practice, the number of clusters T has a relative small affect to our proposed PSFL model (we use 300 in this work). For the hyper-parameters Φ in PSFL model, they are determined by cross-validation. We will further elaborate it in the experiment section.

5. EXPERIMENTS

In this section, we use the real world user rating data and their corresponding social network to empirically validate the effectiveness of the proposed joint personal and social latent factor (PSLF) model for social recommendation. We compare it with the existing social recommendation methods and the state-of-the-art collaborative filtering approaches without considering the social relationships. Specifically, the following five recommendation models are compared:

SIM item-oriented neighborhood model(SIM) is the classical collaborative filtering method based on item similarity. SIM predicts the rating score of the item according to the user historical ratings on the similar items. We implement the SIM as described in [15].

[4] N is the dimension of latent interest factors

MMMF maximum-margin matrix factorization model(MMMF) places a latent factor vector on each user and item. In the training step, user-item latent factors are computed by user-rating matrix decomposition. For prediction, rating scores is calculated as the inner product between user latent factors and item latent factors. We implement MMMF as described in [14]. In addition, we also incorporate the item-neighborhood information based on [9]. In MMMF, there are three hyper-parameters, regularization terms σ_u,σ_v on factors U and V respectively and σ_s item similarity constraint terms. The three hyper-parameters are determined by cross-validation and the results reported in all experimental results are based on the parameter configurations which produce the best results.

FIP Friend-Interest Propagation(FIP) model [18] utilizes the latent factors of users not only for predicting the ratings, but also for link prediction. The inner product between two user latent factors can directly help whether they are linked in social network. Note that the original FIP model mainly targets for the item recommendation (rating is only binary). For comparison purpose, we extend their approach to the rating prediction, as in Eqn. 8. Four hyper-parameters in the model, λ_s, λ_u, λ_v (the first three are the same as the MMMF model), and λ_E are all determined by cross-validation.

SR-LFM Social regularization based latent factor model (SR-LFM) [11] utilizes the social relationships explicitly to regulate the latent facts of users. Specifically, the individual-based regulation is modeled as in Eqn 7. For comparison purpose, we also add neighborhood item similarity constraint to the SR-LFM model. There are four parameters, λ_s,λ_u, λ_v (the first three are the same as the MMMF model), and λ_E, are determined by cross-validation.

PSLF Joint Personal and Social latent Factor model(PSLF) proposed in the paper, utilizes both users' past behaviors and social relationships for social recommendation. In the PSLF model, there are six hyper-parameters: λ_s,λ_u and λ_v are the same as MMMF model; β is a prior Dirichlet parameter (assigned as a fixed value *i.e.* 1.0); and σ_M and σ. All these parameters except β are determined by cross-validation.

In the experimental study, we use the two popular metrics, Mean Absolute Error (MAE) and Root Mean Square Error (RMSE) to measure the prediction quality of our proposed PSLF model in comparison with other collaborative filtering and social recommendation methods.

MAE is defined as:

$$MAE = \frac{1}{T}\sum_{(u_i,v_j)} |R_{ij} - R'_{ij}| \tag{25}$$

RMSE is defined as:

$$RMSE = \sqrt{\frac{1}{T}\sum_{(u_i,v_j)} (R_{ij} - R'_{ij})^2} \tag{26}$$

where R_{ij} denotes the rating score user u_i gave to movie v_j, R'_{ij} denotes the predicted rating score user u_i gave to movie v_j, and T denotes the number of tested ratings. The smaller MAE or RMSE value means a better performance.

5.1 Experimental Datasets

Flixster Dataset. Flixster is a social networking service in which users can rate movies [5]. Users can add other users to their friend list and create a social network. The social relations

[5]The flixster dataset is public, and it can be download from http://www.sfu.ca/ sja25/datasets/

Table 1: General Statistic of Flixster and DouBan

Statistics	Flixster	DouBan
Users	786,936	129,490
Social Relations	7,058,819	1,692,950
Ratings	8,196,077	8,415,420
Items	48,794	58,541

Table 2: Paired t-Test(2-tail) results

dataset	t-Test	MMMF	FIP	SR-LFM
Douban	PSLF(MAE)	$3.38e-8$	$3.16e-7$	$2.42e-4$
	PSLF(RMSE)	$5.73e-9$	$2.22e-6$	$6.52e-7$
flixster	PSLF(MAE)	$7.47e-4$	$1.06e-3$	$3.09e-4$
	PSLF(RMSE)	$1.22e-4$	$1.08e-4$	$1.12e-3$

in Flixster are undirected. It also contains ratings expressed by users in the period from November 2005 to November 2009.

Possible rating values in Flixster dataset are 10 discrete numbers in the range $[0.5, 5]$ with step size 0.5. There are totally $786,936$ users, and $48,794$ movies in this dataset. The overall number of social relations and rating historical records are $7,058,819$ and $8,196,077$, respectively.

Douban Dataset. Douban is a Chinese social website providing user rating, review and recommendation services for movie, books and music [6]. It provides Facebook-like social networking services that users can make friends with each other through the email communication. Douban dataset is crawled and shared with us by Ma Hao [11]. In the dataset, users can assign 5 integer ratings (1 to 5) to movies, books and musics. There are overall $129,490$ unique users and $58,541$ unique items. The number of social relations and rating records are $1,692,950$ and $8,415,420$ respectively. The basic statistics of the Flixster and Douban dataset are shown in Table 5.1.

5.2 Experiment Results

In this subsection, we report the performance of different (social) recommendation approaches. The users' rating dataset is randomly divided into 2 folds. In the experiments, we use 70 percent of the rating data for training and the other 30 percent for testing. The random selection was carried out 5 times independently, and we report the average results. Note that except SIM, the other four models MMMF, FIP, SR-LFM and PSLF need select the dimension of the latent (personal) factors which is denoted by N. Thus, we show the performance of MMMF, FIP SR-LFM and PSLF models with different N, which are (4, 6, 8, 10, 20) respectively. For PSLF model, additional social factor dimension K is set to be $K = 50$. Later, we will further analyze the performance of PSLF when K varies.

Rating Prediction Varying N (Number of Latent Factors): First, we evaluate the five different methods by varying the number of latent factors N. Both MAE and RMSE metrics are used to measure the prediction quality. As shown in Figure 4, the proposed PSLF model consistently outperforms the other four methods. The performance of SIM is generally the worst among all these methods in both Douban and flixster dataset. This is as expected because it does not utilize any latent factors (a straight line in these figures). The MMMF is better than SIM as it utilizes the latent factors and item neighborhood information. We observe the three recommendation approaches FIP, SR-LFM, and our PSLF are all consistently better than MMMF and SIM. This provides a strong evidence that the social recommendation indeed is useful and can be used to improve the recommendation accuracy. In these social recommendation approaches, SR-LFM is slightly better than FIP in Douban dataset, and comparable with FIP in flixster dataset; and our PSLF are always better than both of them.

[6]http://www.douban.com

Table 3: Performance Comparison with MAE and RMSE on flixster dataset

Model	MAE	RMSE
SIM	0.1594	0.1963
MMMF	$0.1429 \pm (0.0010)$	$0.1886 \pm (0.0007)$
FIP	$0.1400 \pm (0.0006)$	$0.1863 \pm (0.0009)$
SR-LFM	$0.1389 \pm (0.0018)$	$0.1864 \pm (0.0017)$
PSLF	$\mathbf{0.1339 \pm (0.0007)}$	$\mathbf{0.1831 \pm (0.0013)}$

Table 4: Performance Comparison with MAE and RMSE on douban dataset

Model	MAE	RMSE
SIM	0.1443	0.1828
MMMF	$0.1427 \pm (0.0011)$	$0.1785 \pm (0.0010)$
FIP	$0.1397 \pm (0.0005)$	$0.1726 \pm (0.0010)$
SR-LFM	$0.1367 \pm (0.0008)$	$0.1718 \pm (0.0012)$
PSLF	$\mathbf{0.1326 \pm (0.0018)}$	$\mathbf{0.1694 \pm (0.0013)}$

From the Figure 4, we observe that a convergence effect of N: when we increase the latent factor dimension N to be around 10, there seem to be little improvement for any large N. This suggests that a small number of latent factors (such as 10) is enough for all the models, including MMMF, FIP, SR-LFM, and PSLF.

Detailed Performance Analysis for $N = 10$ In Table 5.2 and 5.2, we provide a detailed comparison of these five approaches (for the four latent factor based approaches, the number of latent factor N is set to be 10.) We observe in terms of MAE in flixster dataset, PSLF model can improve the performance as high as 3.60% in contrast to SR-LFM model, 4.36% and 6.30% in contrast to FIP and MMMF models, respectively. In terms of RMSE in flixster dataset, PSLF model improves the performance as high as 1.39%, 1.71% and 2.91% in contrast to SR-LFM,FIP, and MMMF, respectively. In Douban dataset, PSLF model improves the performance as high as 2.99%, 5.06%, 7.07% in terms of MAE, and 1.39%, 1.85%, 2.91% in terms of RMSE in contrast to the other three latent factor based approaches, such as SR-LFM, FIP, and MMMF, respectively.

Finally, to validate the statistical significance of our experiments, we perform the paired t-test (2-tail) over the MAE and RMSE of the experiential result. As shown in Table 5.1, all the t-test results are less than 0.01, which means the improvements of PSLF over other methods are statistically significant.

Parameter Sensitivity Analysis: Here, we analyze the performance of PSLF model when varying the dimension of social factors K. In the experiments, we compare the performance on MAE with different social factor dimensions, which are (20, 50, 80). As shown in the Figure 5, we observe that the performance with $K = 50$ and the performance with $K = 80$ are comparable; they are both slighter better than $K = 20$. We note that in most of the cases, the performance with $K = 50$ is even slightly better than the performance with $K = 80$. This indicates a large number of social factors (beyond 50) may not help much for performance improvement.

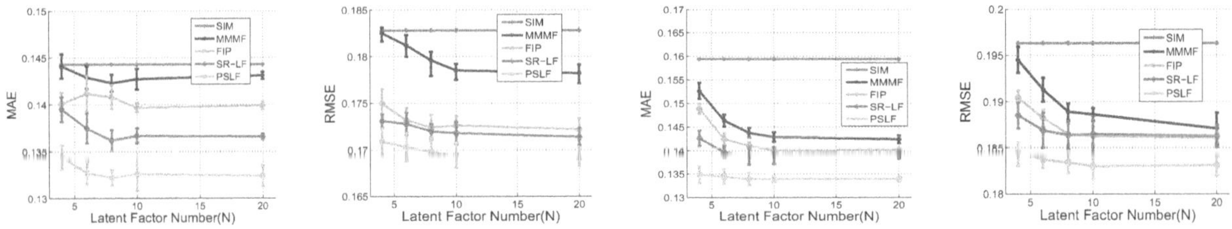

(a) MAE (Douban) (b) RMSE (Douban) (c) MAE (flixster) (d) RMSE (flixster)

Figure 4: Performance Comparisons with MAE and RMSE on flixster and Douban

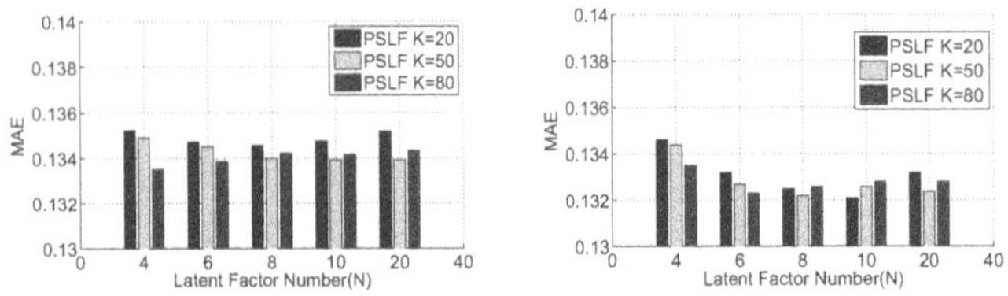

(a) flixster (b) douban

Figure 5: Sensitivity Analysis on K and N

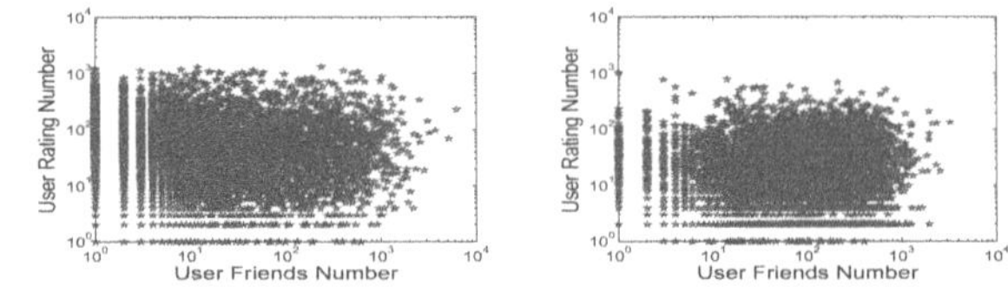

(a) flixster (b) Douban

Figure 6: Correlation between user's rating behaviors and social activities

Table 5: Comparison of Pearson coefficient with different sampling strategies

Sampling Method	flixster	Douban
Randomly Sample	0.0504 ± 0.0025	0.2554 ± 0.0027
Social-aware Sample	0.0561 ± 0.0026	0.2654 ± 0.0016

5.3 Statistical Data Analysis for Social Recommendation

In this subsection, we perform a detailed statistical analysis to help analyze some underlying assumptions which form the basis of the existing social recommendation methods. Such an analysis also provides an insights into their recommendation performance. First, we analyze the correlations between users' rating behaviors and their social activities. As in the Figure 6, the correlation coefficient between users' rating number and their friends number is relative small, i.e 0.045 in flixster dataset. This indicates that users who have a large number of friends may rate only a small number of items. In other words, the behaviors of user's rating and making friends in social network seem to be independent. This also provides a statistical evidence for the proposed PSLF model as it treats the personal and social latent factors as being independent. Note that both FIP and SR-LFM models all try to use the same latent factors to represent both users' rating behaviors and their social relationships.

Secondly, we further analyze whether friends share similar opinions (with similar rating to the same items). To achieve this, we utilize two sampling strategies: the first one is to randomly sample 100,000 user pairs, from the overall 786, 936 users in flixster and 129, 490 users in Douban; the second sampling approach is to randomly sample 100,000 user pairs, who are directly linked in the sample, from 7,058,819 social relations in flixster and 1,692,950 social relations in Douban. Then, for each sample set, we compute the interest coefficient [7] between any two user in each sample. The higher interest coefficient is, the more similar interests users have.

In the Table 5.3, we report the comparison with average interest coefficient on the two sampling approaches. In flixster dataset, the average interest coefficient is 0.0524 based on random sampling method (random pair), and 0.0561 based on second sampling method (random friends) with nearly 7 percent improvement. In Douban dataset, the average interest coefficients are 0.2554 and 0.2654 based on random sampling method and friends sampling method, respectively. There is 4 percent improvement for social-aware sampling method. Therefore, simply assuming users have similar interest with their friends in social networks may still be helpful when incorporating into recommender system, though the improvement maybe limited.

Finally, we compare the distribution of Pearson correlation coefficient(PCC) between the two sample sets generate by the two sampling approaches. First, PCC is sorted in ascending and descending order respectively. For each order, we get Top N percentage of samples, and calculate the average PCC. In Figure 5.3, we show the comparison with Top(N) average PCC in ascending order on random sampling set and friend sampling set. From the Figure 5.3, we can observe that the friend sampling method's PCC curve is above random sampling method's in both flixster and douban dataset. This indicates that friends in social network have less probability to have opposite interests. In Figure 5.3, we report the comparison with Top(N) average PCC in descending order between the two sampling approaches. Here, we found that the friend sampling method's PCC curve is below random sampling method's. It indicates that there are many users who have similar interests may not be friends with each other in social network. This again suggests that using the (personal) latent factor to measure the likelihood of being friends is not accurate.

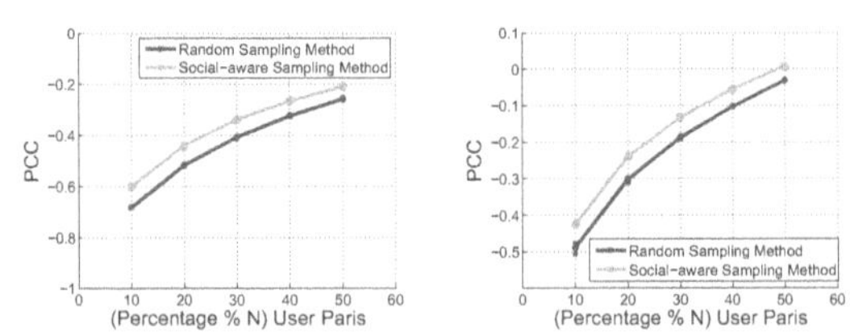

(a) flixster (b) Douban

Figure 7: Comparison with Top(N) PCC in descending order

6. RELATED WORK

Recently studies show users' trust relationship can be employed to enhance traditional recommender systems[13]. A few trust-aware recommendation methods have been proposed [7][4]. How-

[7]PCC between the two users, ranges between [-1, 1]. We only report the PCC between two users with no less than 5 common rated items

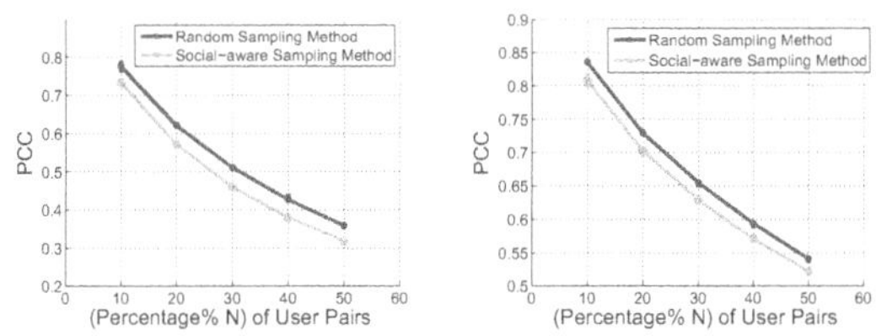

(a) flixster (b) Douban

Figure 8: Comparison with Top(N) PCC in ascending order

ever, trust-based recommendation approaches are different from social recommendation in many aspects. Typically, on the website, when a user A likes a review by another user B, user A probably will add user B to his/her trust list [11]. This process of trust generation is a unilateral action that does not require user A to confirm the relationship. However, the social relationship refers to the cooperative and mutual relationships that surround us, such as classmates, colleagues, or relatives, etc. In addition, trust-based recommender systems are based on the assumption that users have similar tastes with other users they trust. This hypothesis may not always be true in social recommendation systems since the tastes among the user and her/his connected users may vary significantly. A more detailed analysis on the difference between the trust-based recommendation approach and the social recommendation approach can be found in [11].

There have been a few attempts on social recommendations lately [5, 11, 18], which are all based on the assumption that any pair of friends in the social network shall have similar interests. The recent studies [11, 18] incorporate such a network-based similarity property between users into the state-of-the-art matrix factorization recommendation approaches [10]. However, they almost completely ignored the heterogeneity and diversity of the social relationship.

Social attribute (factor) extraction was first proposed by Holland et al. [8] and Harrison et al.[17]. They are also referred to as the blockmodel, which can be used to describe the role or position of actors in the social network. In [8] and [17], users in social network have only one factor(position) being extracted, and the interaction of the positions is captured in the latent social structures. Recently, more complicated blockmodel, mixed-membership blockmodel [2], proposed to relax the assumption of single position bloackmodel, allow users to have a more natural, mixed-membership of social attributes. However, the exiting parameter inference method has scalability bottleneck, which requires $O(n^2)$ time complexity in each iteration, where n is the user number of social networks. In this work, we develop a scale EM approach with time complexity $O(E)$ in each iteration, where E is the number of edges in the social network.

7. CONCLUSION

In this paper, we develop a joint personal and social latent factor (PSLF) model which combines the collaborative filtering and social network modeling approaches for social recommendation. Our approach has shown to have better prediction accuracy over the existing social network approaches. In the future work, we plan to study the following aspects of social recommendations: 1) can we scale the social recommendation used the map-reduce (Hadoop) computation framework to handle tens or hundreds of millions of users? 2) how to deal with privacy issue? Can social commendation be done with minimal (or coarse) network information?

8. ACKNOWLEDGMENTS

The authors appreciate the anonymous reviewers for their extensive and informative comments to help improve the paper. We also thank Dr Hao Ma for sharing Douban Dataset. Yelong Shen and Ruoming Jin's work in this paper is partially supported by National Science Foundation under CAREER Award IIS-0953950.

9. REFERENCES

[1] Gediminas Adomavicius and Alexander Tuzhilin. Toward the next generation of recommender systems: A survey of the state-of-the-art and possible extensions. *IEEE Trans. on Knowl. and Data Eng.*, 17:734–749, June 2005.

[2] Edoardo M. Airoldi, David M. Blei, Stephen E. Fienberg, and Eirc P. Xing. Mixed membership stochastic blockmodels. In *JMLR' 08. The Journal of Machine Learning Research*, pages 1981–2014. ACM, 2008.

[3] Paul H. Calamai and Jorge J. More:9A. Projected gradient methods for linearly constrained problems. *Math. Program.*, 39:93–116, October 1987.

[4] J.O' Donovan and B. Smyth. Trust in recommender systems. In *IUI '05. Proceedings of the 10th international conference on Intelligent User Interfaces*, pages 167–174. ACM, 2005.

[5] H. J. Lee F. Liu. Use of social network information to enhace collaborative filtering performance. In *ESA' 10. Expert Systems with Applications*, pages 4772–4778. Elsevier Ltd, 2010.

[6] Quanquan Gu and Jie Zhou. neighborhood preserving nonnegative matrix factorization. In *BMVC*, pages 1–11, 2009.

[7] Michael R. Lyu Hao Ma, Irwin King. Learning to recommend with social trust ensemble. In *SIGIR '09. Proceedings of the 32th International Conference on information retrieval*, pages 203–210. ACM, 2009.

[8] P W Holland, K B Laskey, and S Leinhardt. Stochastic blockmodels: First steps. *Social Networks*, 5(2):109–137, 1983.

[9] Yehuda Koren. Factorization meets the neighborhood: a multifaceted collaborative filtering model. In *KDD' 08. Proceedings of the 14th ACM SIGKDD international conference on Knowledge discovery and data mining*. ACM, 2008.

[10] Yehuda Koren, Robert Bell, and Chris Volinsky. Matrix factorization techniques for recommender systems. *Computer*, 42:30–37, August 2009.

[11] Hao Ma, Dengyong Zhou, Chao Liu, Michael R. Lyu, and Irwin King. Recommender systems with social regularization. In *WSDM '11. Proceedings of the fourth ACM international conference on Web search and data mining*, pages 287–196. ACM, 2011.

[12] Miller McPherson, Lynn S. Lovin, and James M. Cook. Birds of a feather: Homophily in social networks. *Annual Review of Sociology*, 27(1):415–444, 2001.

[13] Sudeep Marwaha Punam Bedi, Harmeet Kaur. Trust based recommender system for semantic web. In *IJCAI '07. Proceedings of the 2007 International Joint Conference on Artificial Intelligence*, pages 2677–2682. ACM, 2007.

[14] Jason D. M. Rennie and Nathan Srebro. Fast maximum margin matrix factorization for collaborative prediction. In *ICML '05. Proceedings of the 22th International Conference on Machine Learning*, pages 713–719. ACM, 2005.

[15] Badrul Sarwar, George Karypis, Joseph Konstan, and John Reidl. Item-based collaborative filtering recommendation algorithms. In *Proceedings of the 10th international conference on World Wide Web*, WWW '01, pages 285–295, New York, NY, USA, 2001. ACM.

[16] `http://en.wikipedia.org/wiki/List_of_social_networking_websites`.

[17] Harrison C. White, Scott A. Boorman, and Ronald L. Breiger. Social structure from multiple networks. i. blockmodels of roles and positions. *American Journal of Sociology*, 81(4):730–780, 1976.

[18] Shuang Hong Yang, Alex Smola H. Bo Long, Narayanan Sadagopan, Zhaohui Zheng, and Hongyuan Zha. Like like alike - joint friendship and interest propagation in social networks. In *WWW' 11. Proceedings of the 20th international conference on World Wide Web*. ACM, 2011.

Two Approaches To Understanding When Constraints Help Clustering

Ian Davidson
Computer Science
University of California - Davis
davidson@cs.ucdavis.edu

ABSTRACT

Most algorithm work in data mining focuses on designing algorithms to address a discovery problem. Here we focus our attention on designing algorithms to determine the ease or difficulty of a problem instance. The area of clustering under constraints has recently received much attention in the data mining community. We can view the constraints as restricting (either directly or indirectly) the search space of a clustering algorithm to just **feasible** clusterings. However, to our knowledge no work explores methods to count the feasible clusterings or other measures of difficulty nor the importance of these measures. We present two approaches to efficiently characterize the difficulty of satisfying must-link (ML) and cannot-link (CL) constraints: calculating the fractional chromatic polynomial of the constraint graph using Linear Programming (LP) and approximately counting the number of feasible clusterings using Markov Chain Monte Carlo (MCMC) samplers. We show that these measures are correlated to the classical performance measures of constrained clustering algorithms. From these insights and our algorithms we construct new methods of generating and pruning constraints and empirically demonstrate their usefulness.

Categories and Subject Descriptors

H.2.8 [**Database Management**]: Database Applications-Data Mining

Keywords

Clustering, constraints, semi-supervised learning

1. INTRODUCTION AND MOTIVATION

The last decade has seen extensive work on incorporating instance-level constraints into a variety of clustering and metric learning methods [2]. The two typical instance level constraints are must-link (ML) where two points must be in the same cluster and cannot-link (CL) where the points must be in different clusters. The use of constraints *restricts* the clustering algorithm to explore only those clusterings consistent with users expectations (as given by the constraints). All possible clusterings are then effectively divided into those that are **feasible** (i.e. satisfy all constraints) and those that are **infeasible**. Some algorithms such as COP-k-means algorithm [13] only search the set of feasible clustering while others attempt to satisfy all or most constraints while other still learn a distance function to be used for clustering so that ML (CL) constrained points are close together (far apart).

Pragmatically these constraints can be generated from small amounts of labeled data by generating CL constraints between points with different labels and ML constraints between points with the same label. Alternatively they can be used to enforce geometric properties on the clusters [13]. While most previous work showed that as the size of constraint set becomes larger, the accuracy **on average** of the clustering algorithms increased, a negative result [5] showed that many constraint sets produced a **decrease** in accuracy compared to using no constraints. A valid question is then what differentiates those constraint sets that help constrained clustering versus those that do not. Our work provides several insights:

- We show that the number of feasible clusterings (NFC) and fractional chromatic number (FCN) of the constraints represented as a graph varies greatly for constraint sets of the same size generated using the exact same mechanism.
- The NFC and FCN are highly correlated to the clustering algorithms performance. The former is a measure of the size of the search space, the later the difficulty of generating a legal clustering and transitioning from one state to another.
- Existing constrained clustering algorithms work best when the NFC is large and FCN is small (see Figures 3 and 4).
- The above insights and computational methods can be used to generate new constraint generating and pruning mechanisms to maximize algorithm performance (see section 6 and Figures 5, 6 and 7).

2. BACKGROUND

Given a set X of n points to cluster, the number of possible *unique* clusterings into k groups is given by a Stirling number of the second kind written as $S(n,k)$. However, most clustering algorithms allow both $\{[a,b],[c,d]\}$ and $\{[c,d],[a,b]\}$

KDD'12, August 12–16, 2012, Beijing, China.

to be two different and distinct clusterings since though a, b are together in both clusterings, they are assigned to different cluster numbers. Therefore, the size of the search space of non-hierarchical clustering algorithms is $NF_{\emptyset} = k!S(n,k)$ clusterings where $S(n,k) = \frac{1}{k!}\sum_{i=0}^{k}(-1)^i\binom{k}{i}(k-i)^n$. NF is our ongoing notation meaning the **N**umber of **F**easible clusterings under the constraint set given by the subscript which is in this case, the empty set. *For the remainder of this paper when we refer to the number of feasible clusterings, we shall effectively refer to the number of feasible clustering of **constrained** points.* We can easily determine the number of feasible clusterings of all points from the number of feasible clusterings of just constrained points.

Constraint Graphs. Here we show how to convert constraints into a graphical form. To understand the easiness and difficulty of clustering with constraints consider the following problem of clustering under the set of constraints: *C={ML(a,b), ML(a,c), ML(d,e), ML(f,g), ML(h,i), ML(j,k), CL(a,e), CL(i,j), CL(d,k), CL(e,l)}*. We can represent the problem of finding a single feasible clustering in graphical form as shown in Figure 1 where must-linked points are represented by the same node and cannot-linked points have an edge between them. These nodes and edges form the constraint-graph and to find a feasible clustering is then to assign each node a value between 1 through k so that no two nodes with a common edge have the same value. This is equivalent to the graph coloring problem and forms the basis of the **NP**-Complete results of clustering with constraints [6]. These results indicate that finding a *single* feasible clustering is intractable and it is not surprising that **counting** the number of clusterings/colorings is also intractable [11]. It is important to note that in constraint graphs, after performing a transitive closure over all ML constraints, each connected component can be represented as **one** node in Figure 1.

Chromatic Numbers. The chromatic number of a graph is the minimum number of colors required to color the vertices and its calculation is **NP**-Complete [11]. However the recent notion of fractional graph coloring, allows each vertex to be assigned multiple colors but still requires that a legal coloring has no two nodes connected by an edge sharing a common color. A graph has a legal b-fold coloring if color sets of size no more than b are assigned to each vertex and adjacent vertices have non-overlapping sets. Similarly, an a:b-coloring produces a b-fold coloring when a colors are available. Finally, the b-fold fractional chromatic number is the least value of a such that an a:b-coloring exists. We shall see that the fractional coloring problem is a relaxation of regular coloring and the fractional chromatic number can be calculated by a linear programming relaxation of an integer programming problem.

3. APPROACH 1: AN MCMC SAMPLER TO COUNT THE NUMBER OF FEASIBLE CLUSTERINGS

Though MCMC samplers have been used extensively in statistics, data mining and machine learning [9] the use of these algorithms **for counting** is novel having being relatively recently proposed in computer science theory [10]. Counting problems are a special application of samplers since the equilibrium distribution of the chain needs to be uniform which has the benefit of allowing strong performance bounds

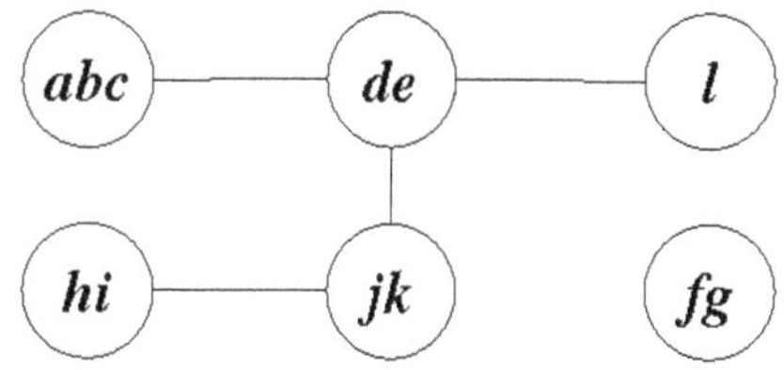

Figure 1: Constraint Graphs. A graphical representation of the feasibility problem for *ML(a,b), ML(a,c), ML(d,e), ML(f,g), ML(h,i), ML(j,k), CL(a,e), CL(i,j), CL(d,k), CL(e,l)*

to be created. In particular, provably efficient *rapidly mixing* samplers [10] are possible and there is no need to rely on typical statistical experimental approaches to test for convergence such as variance estimation or estimating the spectral radius. However, not all counting problems have an easily implementable uniform sampler as we shall see the counting of constrained clusterings does. Gomes et' al [7] note the difficulty in creating uniform samplers for SAT counting problems and that samplers not converging to a uniform equilibrium distribution can significantly over or under estimates counts.

The MCMC sampler we shall create at its core is a rejection sampler but unlike typical applications we shall use **many rejection samplers**, and many chains for each sampler and couple their results together. Our approach will be explained in four parts which are outlined in the following four subsections.

- Firstly, we shall create a **sufficient condition** when creating a feasible clustering is easy and use this to initialize our sampler. This sufficient condition ensures a completed connected state space.

- Next, we shall describe how to create **the rejection sampler** to determine the ratio $\frac{NF_{C-i}}{NF_{C-(i+1)}}$ which is the number of feasible clusterings for the entire constraint set less i specific CL constraints to the number of feasible clusterings for the same constraint set less **just one more CL constraint**. Note that the ratio will always be less then one since the denominator problem is a *relaxed* version of the numerator problem and the removal of a constraint can only increase the number of feasible clusterings. Note that ML constraints are not considered in our discussion because as mentioned earlier, they are merged into single nodes in the constraint graph (see Figure 1).

- Thirdly, we use a coupling (multiplying) approach to count the number of clusterings by multiplying the ratios of the rejection samplers together. It should be noted for clarity that we create many samplers and N_{chains} chains for each sampler and run each chain for N_{draws} draws after which it will reach equilibrium.

- Finally, we discuss how to determine values for N_{draws} (see equation 4) and N_{chains} (see equation 5) which can bound the error of our calculations.

We create a rejection sampler for all values of $i = 0 \ldots |C_{\neq}| - 1$ where $C_{\neq}$ is the number of CL constraints. For the coupling approach to work deleting a constraint corresponds to deleting all equivalent constraints and effectively deletes an edge in the constraint graph. Consider two connected components formed by ML constraints: $\{a,b,c\}$ and $\{d,f,g\}$ and two CL constraints are $CL(a,d)$ and $CL(b,f)$ then the deletion of $CL(a,d)$ still leaves an edge between the two connected components in the constraint graph so $CL(b,f)$ would also need to be deleted to remove the edge. To simplify our notation, the constraint set C will contain only unique constraints, that is each CL constraint corresponds to only one unique edge in the constraint graph.

3.1 A Sufficient Condition

Consider the set of constraints in Figure 1. If the sufficient condition $k > \Delta$ holds where k is the number of clusters and Δ is the the most number of CL constraints on a single instance (i.e. the maximum degree of our constraint graph), then regardless of what order the instances are assigned to clusters, we can always produce a feasible clustering. **This is important since it guarantees a completely connected state space since in effect there is always one "free" cluster to move any point to.** This result is from the well known result, called Brooks's Theorem, in graph theory [11]. In our example (Figure 1) if $k = 4$ we can just proceed and assign the instances in any order and we will always find a feasible clustering. This sufficient condition does create a limitation when this sampler can be used but as discussed earlier typically a small number of constraints are used, hence Δ will be small so this should not be a limitation.

3.2 The MCMC Sampler

The sampler estimates the ratio of the number of feasible clusterings for a constraint set to the number of feasible clusterings for the same constraint set less one constraint. It takes in the original set of ML and CL constraints and removes one CL constraint (edge from the constraint graph). It then performs a random walk over the set of feasible clusterings for the **smaller** constraint set to reach equilibrium with the last state drawn being $\mathcal{X}$. The previously removed constraint is added back and if $\mathcal{X}$ satisfies this original larger constraint set then we add 1 to a success count otherwise we reject the sampled state. The proportion of successes gives us an estimate of the ratio. Figure 2 shows our algorithm, in a later section we shall show how to derive bounds for N_{draws} and N_{chains}. Note, this approach only works because the feasible clusterings of the larger constraint set is a proper subset of the feasible clusterings of the reduced constraint set. It can be viewed as a rejection sampler by noting that we are sampling from a larger set of constrained clusterings (given the smaller number of constraints) and then rejecting if a clustering does not also satisfy the additional constraint.

In our context the state space of the random walk is the space of all feasible clusterings and since each is equally important to us (we are just counting) the equilibrium distribution is the uniform distribution. An individual chain is essentially defined by step 8 in Figure 2 which chooses an instance at random and then assigns it to a new cluster. Clearly this satisfies the detailed balance requirement and will produce a finite, irreducible, aperiodic and hence ergodic chain.

Algorithm MCMC-Rejection Sampler

Input:
X: the set of points to cluster, k: number of clusters
$C_{\neq}$: the set of cannot-link constraints
$C_{=}$: the set of must-link constraints
N_{draws} and N_{chains}: as calculated from equations 4 and 5 respectively
Output: $\frac{NF_C}{(NF_{C-1})}$: The number of feasible clusterings ratio for a constraint set and the same set less one constraint.

1. $G(V,E)$=*GenerateConstraintGraph*$(X, C_{\neq}, C_{=}, k)$ (See section 2.)
2. Let Δ be the maximum degree of $G(V,E)$. If $k \leq \Delta$ exit k *not large enough.*
3. Create $C'_{\neq} = C_{\neq} - c(i,j)$ /*A single CL constraint is removed*/
4. $G'(V,E')$=*GenerateConstraintGraph*$(X, C'_{\neq}, C_{=}, k)$ (See section 2.)
5. $\mathcal{X}$=*GenerateInitialClustering*(X, G', k)
6. **for** c = 1 to N_{chains}
7. $Success_c = 0$
8. **for** d = 1 to N_{draws}
   (a) Let q be a random integer $\in [1,k]$
   (b) From $\mathcal{X}$ take a randomly chosen v and assign to a new cluster q to derive $\mathcal{X}_{Candidate}$
   (c) If Feasible($\mathcal{X}_{Candidate}$,$G'(V,E')$) then $\mathcal{X} = \mathcal{X}_{Candidate}$

   end
9. If Feasible($\mathcal{X}$,$G(V,E)$) then $Success_c = 1$ /*Note the random walk is on G' and we now test feasibility against G*/
10. **end**
11. **return** $\sum_i Success_i / N_{chains}$

Figure 2: A MCMC Rejection Sampler. The number of draws from each chain (N_{draws}) and the number of chains (N_{chains}) are specified in section 3.4.

3.3 Coupling Arrangement to Estimate Number of Feasible Clusterings

The above subsection describes how to create a single chain to calculate the ratio $\frac{NF_C}{NF_{C-1}}$, we now show how to use a series of such chains to calculate the total number of feasible clusterings NF_C. Our approach begins by creating a rejection sampler to calculate the ratio of feasible clusterings using all constraints to feasible clusterings for all constraints less one particular constraint. This is multiplied by the ratio of all feasible clusterings for the reduced constraint set to feasible clusterings for the same constraint set less one additional specific constraint and so on. We can then couple/multiply the results of the rejection samplers to achieve the final number of feasible clusterings by:

$$NF_C = \frac{NF_C}{NF_{C-1}} \times \frac{NF_{C-1}}{NF_{C-2}} \times \dots \frac{NF_{C-(|C|-1)}}{NF_\emptyset} NF_\emptyset \quad (1)$$

Where NF_{C-i} is the number of feasible clusterings using the constraint set C less i specific CL constraints. The key to understanding why equation 1 is computable is to note that $NF_\emptyset = k!S(n,k)$ where n is the number of nodes in the constraint graph (i.e. CL constrained nodes) and that $S(n,k)$ can be calculated as described earlier in Section 2.

3.4 How Many Chains and How Long To Run Each Chain

Perhaps where MCMC algorithms for counting differ most than previous uses of samplers in learning is the existence of strong results for bounding the number of steps until convergence. This is possible since the sampler's equilibrium distribution is the uniform distribution. We use the measure of variation distance in equation 2 between the current distribution and the equilibrium distribution over the state space, Ω, starting from an **initial state** x to get an upper-bound on the convergence time (t) shown in equation 3.

$$\delta_x(t) = \frac{1}{2}\Sigma_{y\in\Omega}|P_x^t(y) - \pi(y)| \quad (2)$$

$$\tau_x(\epsilon) = min\{t : \delta_x(t') \leq \epsilon \ \forall t' \geq t\} \quad (3)$$

We use a result from [4] that the time for the chain to reach equilibrium is upper-bounded as shown in equation 4.

$$N_{draws} = \tau_x(\epsilon) \geq qlog(q\epsilon^{-1}) \quad (4)$$

Where q is the number of constrained instances (a large connected component counts as one point) and ϵ a measure of our choice. However, knowing how many draws to reach equilibrium is only half of our requirements. We must also know how many samples to draw after equilibrium is reached to bound the accuracy of our count. As is typical in the counting MCMC literature, we obtain our estimates from **multiple** Markov chains rather than sampling multiple times from the same chain. Skipping over much lengthy but standard math and substituting and rearranging a Chebyshev inequality we derive a bound shown in equation 5.

$$N_{chains} \geq \frac{1}{(\delta \times (\epsilon)^2)^{ln(ln(|C|))}} \quad (5)$$

where δ is our chance of failure.

This allows us to set the key parameters in our algorithm (Figure 2) to be a function of the error ($0 < \epsilon < 1$) of our estimate and chance of the bound failing ($0 < \delta < 0.5$). It is possible to show that this approach can be extended to a fully polynomial-time randomized approximation scheme and hence is capable of rapid mixing.

4. APPROACH 2: DETERMINING CLUSTER ASSIGNMENT DIFFICULTY USING FRACTIONAL CHROMATIC NUMBERS

Figure 1 shows the relationship between graph coloring and constrained clustering. With traditional graph coloring, each node is assigned exactly one color and the chromatic number of a graph is the minimum number of colors to color it. The chromatic number of a graph can then be determined by the following integer program. As before let the vertices of G (the constraint graph) be numbered from 1 to n and the maximal independent sets of vertices of G numbered from 1 to m. Recall an independent set is a subset of all vertices where no two vertices share an edge and hence in our context all vertices in an independent set can be assigned to the same cluster. Let A be a $n \times m$ matrix with $a_{i,j} = 1$ if the ith vertex is in the jth independent set, and 0 otherwise. Then the integer programming problem is:

$$\begin{aligned} &minimize \ \mathbf{x}.\mathbf{1} \\ subject\ to: \ &A\mathbf{x} \geq \mathbf{1}, \mathbf{x} \geq \mathbf{0} \end{aligned} \quad (6)$$

The indicator vector $\mathbf{x}$ represents which independent sets are required and the objective function just counts the number required. The first constraint requires each vertex to be part of at least one independent set (cluster) and the second to prevent the trivial solution. We can then view fractional graph coloring as a relaxation of this problem where $\mathbf{x} \in [0,1]$ and hence a vertex can be assigned fractionally to different independent sets (therefore having multiple colors) and we can easily see this can be solved as a linear programming problem. As we shall see the number of fractional colors associated with an instance is a measure of how **easy** it is to assign this point and the b-fold chromatic number a measure of how difficult the entire constraint set is to satisfy.

5. EXPERIMENTAL INSIGHTS

We use four core algorithms in our experiments. They are chosen because they are some of the seminal work in the field and hence are widely used with stable freely available implementations. Furthermore, they cover a wide range of different ways of using constraints. The **CKM** algorithm is the original COP-k-means algorithm [13] that attempts to satisfy **all** constraints. The **PKM** algorithm of Basu and collaborators [1] allows constraints to be violated but tries to minimize this number. The related **MKM** algorithm is a metric learning algorithm that was shown to perform comparable or better than the seminal work in the field [15]. After the metric space is learnt, we apply regular unconstrained k-means. Finally the **MPKM** algorithm combines metric learning and constraint satisfaction by modeling the constraints as enforcing a prior using a hidden Markov random field. Similarly, we choose our four data sets due to their variety in size, attribute type and most importantly number of extrinsic classes. We always set k to equal the number of extrinsic labels (unless otherwise specified) and generate constraint randomly by selecting pairs of instances at random and comparing them: if the labels agree then a

Table 1: **Fraction of 1000 randomly created 25-constraint sets that caused a drop in accuracy (measured by the Rand index), compared to an unconstrained run with the same centroid initialization.**

Data	Algorithm			
	CKM	PKM	MKM	MPKM
Glass	31%	7%	16%	3%
Ionosphere	26%	68%	3%	80%
Iris	27%	23%	31%	41%
Wine	35%	38%	82%	69%

must-link is generated otherwise a cannot-link is generated. We use the following data sets with number of extrinsic labels (k), instances (n) and dimensions (m) in parentheses, Iris($k = 3$, $n = 150$, $m = 4$), Wine($k = 3$, $n = 178$, $m = 13$), Ionsphere($k = 2$, $n = 351$, $m = 34$) and Glass($k = 6$, $n = 214$, $m = 10$).

In this section we investigate several questions with our proposed work but no doubt there are other important questions. We begin by exploring a counter-intuitive result published earlier [5] that showed that constraints can **hurt** performance of algorithms. In that work, they showed that even though on average (over many constraint sets of the same size) the accuracy of a variety of algorithms (as measured by the Rand index between the ground truth partition defined by the labels and the partition/clustering found by the algorithms) increased with the amount of constraints given to the algorithm, there were a significant number of individual constraint sets where performance was degraded (but not enough to bring down the average significantly). This leads to our first experimental question.

Q1: For those constraint sets where performance is ***worse*** *than not using any constraints, was there a significant difference in the number of feasible clusterings compared to constraint sets that helped clustering performance.*

We verified earlier results [5] and see in Table 1 that the fraction of these 1000 trials that caused **a decrease in clustering accuracy** (compared to using no constraints) is significant. Since each trial involved the same initialization mechanism for both unconstrained and constraint experiments, performance differences are due to the use of constraints.

A valid question is then: *Do the constraint sets where the algorithms perform poorly, correspond to those with fewer feasible clusterings?* To answer this question we split the 1000 constraint sets for each algorithm into those where the the constraint set produced no change or a decrease in accuracy (hurt) and those that produced an increase in accuracy compared to not using constraints (help). We then used our sampler to approximately count how many feasible clustering (on average) each sub-population contained. Results in a comparative bar chart are in Figure 3 and show that constraint sets that hurt clustering accuracy have a smaller number of feasible clusterings on average than those that helped.

Q2: Is the b*-fold Chromatic Number A Useful Measure of Constraint Difficulty?*

In these experiments, we attempt to see how the Rand index varies depending on the minimum b-fold chromatic number. For each of our data sets we generate 100 constraint sets of size 25. For each constraint set, we solved our linear program to determine the fractional chromatic number. We plot this as a scatter plot with the x-axis being the inverse of fractional chromatic number (the larger the easier the graph is to color) and the y-axis the Rand index. The scatter plot for each data set is shown in Figure 4 and shows a strong positive correlation between the x and y axes.

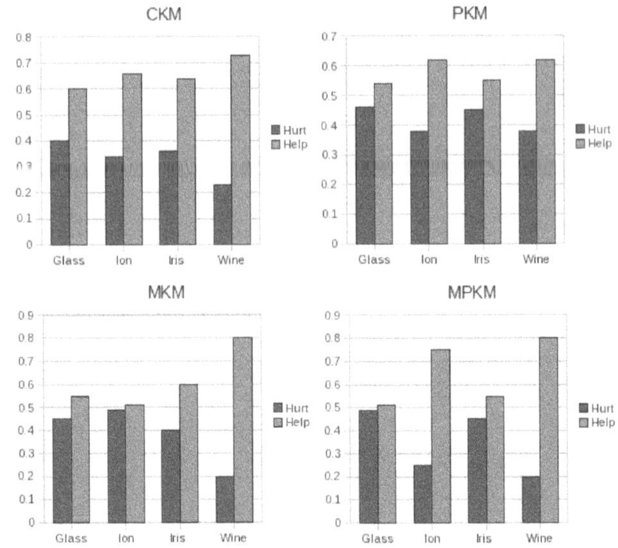

Figure 3: The average ratio of the number of feasible clusterings to total clusterings for two subpopulations: constraint sets that help performance and those that hurt performance.

6. SEVERAL USES OF OUR WORK

Our two approaches allow us to estimate how difficult a constraint set is to satisfy which has many potential applications. In this section we outline several uses of our algorithms. The first is useful when the user has the possibility to generate many different constraint sets easily and allows them to generate the most useful set of constraints (see Figure 5). The second is useful when the user is given just a single constraint set and can remove constraints to improve the algorithm performance (see Figure 6).

6.1 Use 1: Constraint Generating Methods

Our experimental insights regarding the ability of the algorithm to recover the set partition the constraints were generated from can be summarized as follows. Constraint sets that allow a too large **infeasible** set of clusterings cause the CKM, PKM, MKM and MPKM algorithms to perform poorly with respect to the Rand index (see Figure 3). However, as others have shown the more constraints given to the algorithm the better. **Therefore, our aim is to generate as many constraints as possible without overly restricting the algorithm.**

To achieve this we create a **balanced** sampling approach for CL constraints as follows. Before we generate the ith CL constraint involving instance j, all other instances must have $i-1$ CL constraints on them. In this way we make the degree of nodes across the constraint graph uniform. ML constraint generation does not change. We then compare this approach of generating constraints to the typical ap-

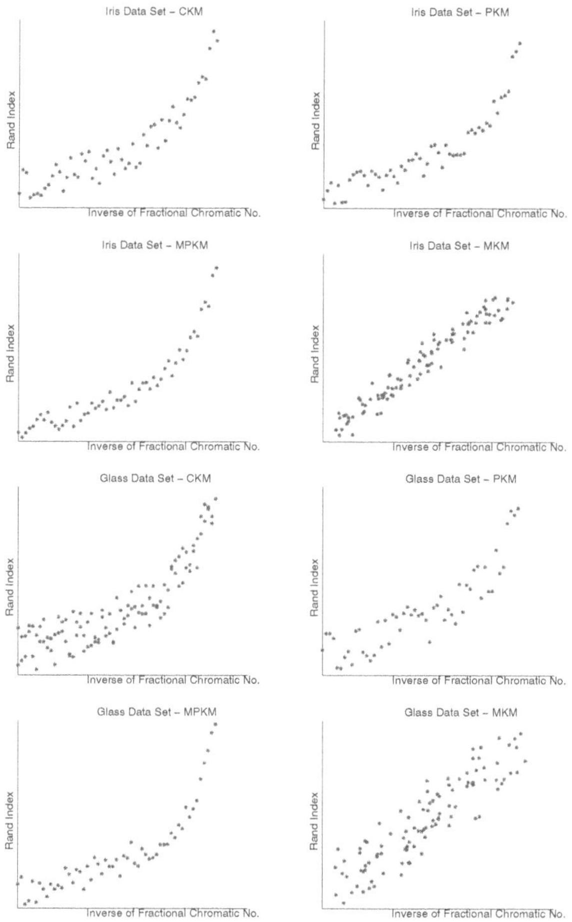

Figure 4: The fractional chromatic number inverse(x-axis) (the larger the easier the problem) versus the Rand index (y-axis) for one hundred constraint sets for a variety of algorithms. Similar relationships hold for other data sets.

proach of randomly selecting points on which to generate constraints. We ensure generating equal number of ML and CL constraints for both styles of constraint generation.

We plot the average Rand index (over 100 constraint sets) for increasing amounts of constraints for a variety of algorithms and data sets for the two methods. We found that on average the new approach of generating constraints outperformed the traditional approach by a statistically significant amount at the 99% confidence interval using a student t-test after just twenty constraints. Results are shown in Figure 5. We see that initially the random approach of generating constraints performs similar to our own since for small number of constraints it is unlikely that any balancing is needed. However, when constraint sets became larger our balanced sampling approach produces significantly better results. We tested our work on two differing styles of constrained clustering algorithm: **CKM** which attempts to satisfy all constraints and **MPKM** which both learns a distance metric and satisfies as many constraints as possible.

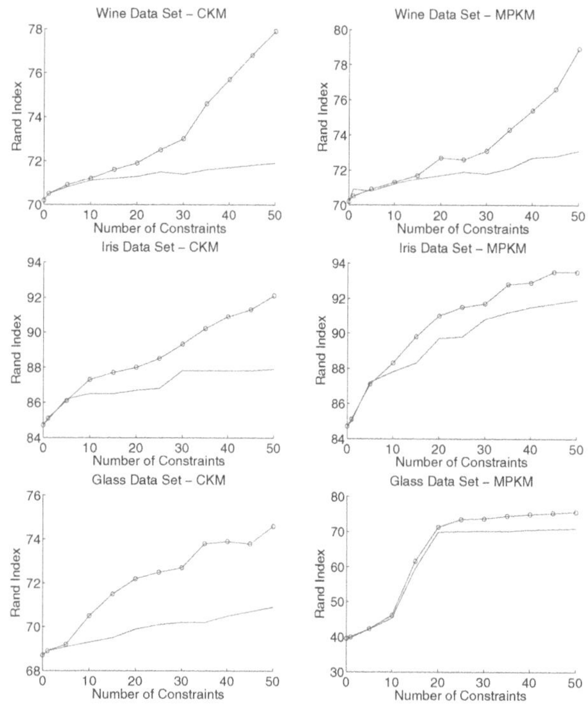

Figure 5: The Rand index versus the number of constraints. The solid line (—) is for constraints generated by random selection while the other line (-o-) is our balanced generation approach. The Rand index is averaged over 100 constraint sets.

6.2 Use 2: Pruning Constraint Sets

An output of the linear program solution of equation 6 is effectively a measure of how flexible (or conversely how difficult) a point is to assign. If the solution indicates that point i belongs to many independent sets and point j only one, then it is more difficult to assign the latter than the former since there are fewer options. To the graph of the constrained points (recall edges indicate cannot link constraints) we add their k furthest neighbors and corresponding edges (indicating unlikely points to be grouped with). We then solve equation 6 to get a better estimate of the difficulty of assigning each of the constrained points. In our experiments we use the five furthest neighbors.

A natural method of pruning constraint sets is then to remove the points that are part of the least number of independent sets and corresponding constraints they are part of. This set of points are those though potentially useful, are difficult for algorithms to handle since there is little freedom in assigning them to clusters. This is particularly important since most constrained clustering algorithms are iterative and repetitively attempt to assign a point to a cluster and incrementally build up the clustering. Our experimental results in Figure 6 show the Rand index increases as the constraints are pruned. A valid question for future work is when to stop pruning which we side-step by generating many constraints and only pruning a few.

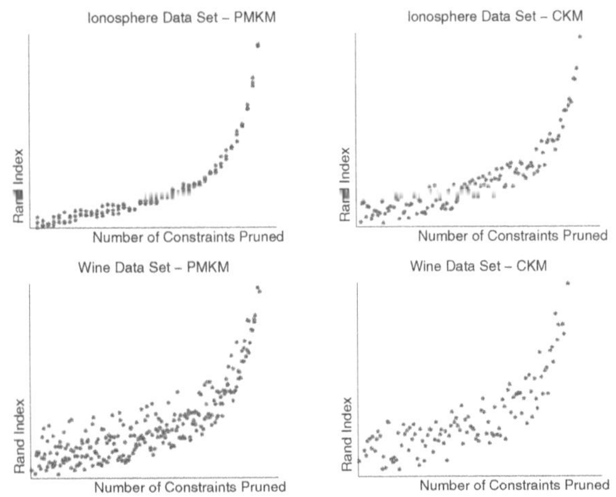

Figure 6: Typical results of the Rand index versus the number of constraints pruned (from 1 through 10) from a constraint set of size 100. The results over 100 experiments are shown.

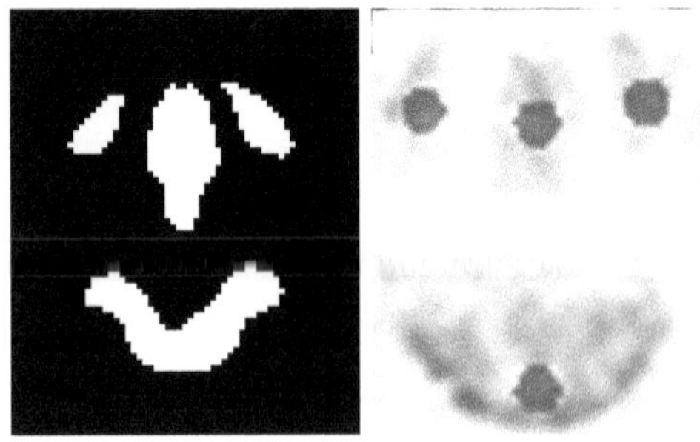

Figure 7: The idealized default mode network (left) from which many constraints can be generated. The resultant network found (right) with constraints actually used (i.e. not pruned) shown in darker color.

6.3 Use 3 - Simplest Geometric Constraints

Functional Magnetic Resonance Imaging (fMRI) is extensively used for capturing brain activity as it processes information in real time. A key science question is clustering the voxels/pixels in the images (represented as time sequences) into two groups (correlated or networked versus other or background). Constraints can help guide clustering algorithms since they can be used to represent geometric properties [13][6] such as maximum diameter and maximum separation. Consider the default mode network (DMN) shown in Figure 7 (left). Each of the four regions can be represented as a large number of must-link constraints and we can require that the surrounding areas not merge into the regions using cannot-link constraints. However, this will generate a huge number of constraints that can easily over-constrain the algorithms. In all our experiments with this data using all generated constraints the CKM algorithm which attempts to satisfy all constraints did not converge (being over-constrained) and the metric learning algorithms (such as MKM) returned poor results.

We apply our constraint pruning approach described in the previous sub-section to leave just 10% of all possible constraints and the resultant clustering (and subset of constraints produced) are shown in Figure 7 (right). We see two clusters (light blue: DMN, white: background) are discovered and a reasonable subset set of constraints are produced (shown in dark blue).

7. CONCLUSION AND FUTURE WORK

In this work we proposed two answers to the problem:" Which constraint sets help constrained clustering algorithms ?". We posed the novel question: "Can the number of feasible clusterings that satisfy all constraints be counted?" Though this problem is intractable in general, we showed that under a reasonable sufficient condition a simple rapidly mixing MCMC sampler can approximately count the number of feasible clusterings. There are many uses of this particular sampler for analysis and we focused on the open question: "Why do some constraint sets adversely effect clustering performance to the point that it would have been better **not** to have used constraints?" We showed that those constraint sets that hurt performance had far less feasible clusterings than those that helped performance. We then proposed a method of creating larger constraint sets without over-constraining the algorithms and showed it was superior than the traditional approach (see Figure 3).

We also showed that the difficultly in fractionally coloring the constraint graph was reflective of how useful the constraint set was to the clustering algorithm's performance with respect to accuracy (see Figure 4). To do this we created a LP that determine the minimum b-fold chromatic number. A side benefit of the LP solution is that it tells us how many independent sets a constrained point belonged to. The fewer the number the less available clusters the algorithm has to place them in without violating constraints. We showed that removing/pruning constraints on difficult to assign points produced improved performance on the algorithms we studied and that for real world fMRI data the approach is a reasonable way of pruning the many thousands of constraints that can be generated from geometric properties to enforce on the clustering (see Figure 7).

We can therefore conclude that all constraint sets are not generated equally, some more restrict the possible clusterings and understanding which do is important for algorithm designers and practitioners alike. We hope that this work will make some progress towards this and other important questions.

8. ACKNOWLEDGMENTS

The authors gratefully acknowledge support of this research from the NSF (IIS-0801528) and ONR (N000140910712).

9. REFERENCES

[1] S. Basu, M. Bilenko, R.J. Mooney, A probabilistic framework for semi-supervised clustering, ACM KDD, 2004.

[2] *Constrained Clustering: Advances in Algorithms, Theory, and Applications* Editors: Sugato Basu, Ian Davidson, Kiri L. Wagstaff CRC Press

[3] A. Bar-Hillel, T. Hertz, N. Shental, D. Weinshall, Learning a Mahalanobis metric from equivalence constraints. *JMLR* **6** (2005)

[4] R.Bubley and M. Dyer., Path coupling: A technique for proving rapid mixing in Markov chains, Proceedings of 38th FOCS, 1997.

[5] I. Davidson, K. Wagstaff, S. Basu, Measuring Constraint-Set Utility for Partitional Clustering Algorithms, Proceedings of ECML/PKDD 2006.

[6] I. Davidson and S. S. Ravi, "The Complexity of Non-Hierarchical Clustering with Constraints", *Journal of Knowledge Discovery and Data Mining* (DMKD), Volume 14, Number 1, Pages 25-61. 2007.

[7] C. Gomes, A. Sabharwal, and B. Selman, From Sampling to Model Counting, IJCAI, Hyderabad, India, Jan 2007.

[8] L. Goodman, The Variance of the Product of K Random Variables, JASA V 57, No 297 p 54-60, 1962.

[9] R. Neal, Probabilistic Inference Using Markov Chain Monte Carlo Methods, Technical Report CRG-TR-93-1, Department of Computer Science, University of Toronto.

[10] M. Jerrum, A. Sinclair, "The MCMC method: an approach to approximate counting and integration", In *Approximations for NP-hard Problems*, 1996.

[11] D. B. West, *Introduction to Graph Theory*, 2nd Edition, Prentice Hall, Inc., 2001.

[12] K. Wagstaff & C. Cardie. Clustering with Instance-Level Constraints, ICML 2000.

[13] K. Wagstaff, C. Cardie, S. Rogers & S. Schroedl, "Constrained k-means Clustering with Background Knowledge", ICML, 2001.

[14] K. Wagstaff, *Intelligent Clustering with Instance-Level Constraints*, Ph.D. Dissertation, Cornell University, 2002.

[15] E. Xing, A. Ng, M. Jordan, and S. Russell. Distance metric learning, with application to clustering with side-information. NIPS 15, 2003.

Chromatic Correlation Clustering

Francesco Bonchi Aristides Gionis Francesco Gullo Antti Ukkonen
Yahoo! Research – Barcelona, Spain
{bonchi,gionis,gullo,aukkonen}@yahoo-inc.com

ABSTRACT

We study a novel clustering problem in which the pairwise relations between objects are *categorical*. This problem can be viewed as clustering the vertices of a graph whose edges are of different types (*colors*). We introduce an objective function that aims at partitioning the graph such that the edges within each cluster have, as much as possible, the same color. We show that the problem is **NP**-hard and propose a randomized algorithm with approximation guarantee proportional to the maximum degree of the input graph. The algorithm iteratively picks a random edge as pivot, builds a cluster around it, and removes the cluster from the graph. Although being fast, easy-to-implement, and parameter free, this algorithm tends to produce a relatively large number of clusters. To overcome this issue we introduce a variant algorithm, which modifies how the pivot is chosen and and how the cluster is built around the pivot. Finally, to address the case where a fixed number of output clusters is required, we devise a third algorithm that directly optimizes the objective function via a strategy based on the *alternating minimization* paradigm.

We test our algorithms on synthetic and real data from the domains of protein-interaction networks, social media, and bibliometrics. Experimental evidence show that our algorithms outperform a baseline algorithm both in the task of reconstructing a ground-truth clustering and in terms of objective function value.

Categories and Subject Descriptors: H.2.8 [**Database Management**]: Database Applications - *Data Mining*
Keywords: Clustering, Edge-labeled graphs.

1. INTRODUCTION

Clustering is one of the most well-studied problems in data mining. The goal of clustering is to partition a set of objects in different clusters, so that objects in the same cluster are more similar to each other than to objects in other clusters. A common trait underlying most clustering paradigms is the existence of a function $\text{sim}(x, y)$ representing the similarity between pairs of objects x and y. The similarity function is either provided explicitly as input, or it can be computed implicitly from the representation of the objects.

KDD'12, August 12–16, 2012, Beijing, China.

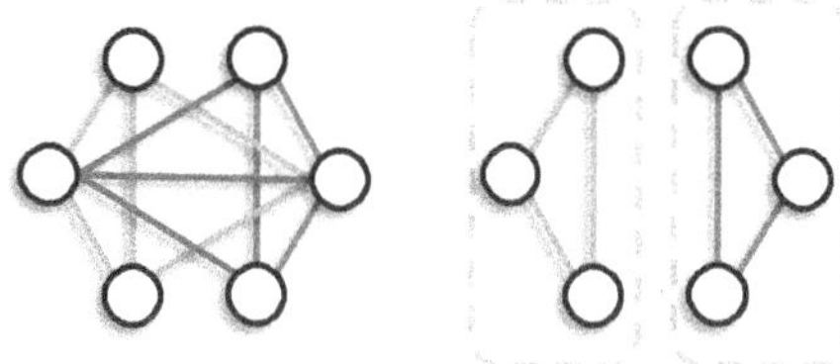

(a) (b)

Figure 1: An example of chromatic clustering: (a) input graph, (b) the optimal solution for chromatic-correlation-clustering (Problem 2).

In this paper, we consider a different clustering setting where the relationship among objects is represented by a relation type, such as a label $\ell(x, y)$ from a finite set of possible labels L. In other words, the *range* of the similarity function $\text{sim}(x, y)$ can be viewed as being *categorical*, instead of *numerical*. Moreover, we model the case where two objects x and y do not have any relation with a special label $l_0 \notin L$. Our framework has a natural graph interpretation: the input can be viewed as an edge-labeled graph $G = (V, E, L, \ell)$, where the set of vertices V is the set of objects to be clustered, the set of edges $E \subseteq V \times V$ is implicitly defined as $E = \{(x, y) \in V \times V \mid \ell(x, y) \neq l_0\}$, and each edge has a *label* in L or, as we like to think about it, a *color*.

The key objective in our framework is to find a partition of the vertices of the graph such that the edges in each cluster have, as much as possible, the same color (an example is shown in Figure 1). Intuitively, a `red` edge (x, y) provides positive evidence that the vertices x and y should be clustered in such a way that the edges in the subgraph induced by that cluster are mostly `red`. Furthermore, in the case that most edges of a cluster are `red`, it is reasonable to label the whole cluster with the `red` color. Note that a clustering algorithm for this problem should also deal with inconsistent evidence, as a `red` edge (x, y) provides evidence for the vertex x to participate in a cluster with `red` edges, while a `green` edge (x, z) provides contradicting evidence for the vertex x to participate in a cluster with `green` edges. Aggregating such inconsistent information is resolved by optimizing a properly-defined objective function.

Applications. The study of edge-labeled graphs is motivated by many real-world applications and is receiving increasing attention in the data-mining literature [8, 10, 16]. As an example, biologists study protein-protein interaction networks, where vertices represent proteins and edges represent interactions occurring when two or more proteins bind together to carry out their biological function. Those interactions can be of different types, e.g., physical association, direct interaction, co-localization, etc. In these networks, for instance, a cluster containing mainly edges labeled as co-localization, might represent a *protein complex*, i.e., a group of proteins that interact with each other at the same time and place, forming a single multi-molecular machine [11].

As a further example, social networks are commonly represented as graphs, where the vertices represent individuals and the edges capture relationships among these individuals. Again, these relationships can be of various types, e.g., colleagues, neighbors, schoolmates, football-mates.

In bibliographic data, co-authorship networks represent collaborations among authors: in this case the topic of the collaboration can be seen as an edge label, and a cluster of vertices represents a topic-coherent community of researchers. In our experiments in Section 5 we show how our framework can be applied in all the above domains.

Contributions. In this paper we address the problem of clustering data with categorical similarity, achieving the following contributions:

- We define CHROMATIC-CORRELATION-CLUSTERING, a novel clustering problem for objects with categorical similarity, by revisiting the well-studied *correlation clustering* framework [3]. We show that our problem is a generalization of the traditional CORRELATION-CLUSTERING problem, implying that it is **NP**-hard.
- We introduce a randomized algorithm, named Chromatic Balls, that provides approximation guarantee proportional to the maximum degree of the graph.
- Though of theoretical interest, Chromatic Balls has some limits when it comes to practice. Trying to overcome these limits, we introduce two alternative algorithms: a more practical *lazy* version of Chromatic Balls, and an algorithm that directly optimizes the proposed objective function via an iterative process based on the *alternating minimization* paradigm.
- We empirically assess our algorithms both on synthetic and real datasets. Experiments on synthetic data show that our algorithms outperform a baseline algorithm in the task of reconstructing a ground-truth clustering. Experiments on real-world data confirm that CHROMATIC-CORRELATION-CLUSTERING provides meaningful clusters.

The rest of the paper is organized as follows. In the next section we recall the traditional correlation clustering problem and introduce our new formulation. In Section 3 we introduce the Chromatic Balls algorithm and we prove its approximation guarantees. In Section 4 we present the two more practical algorithms, namely Lazy Chromatic Balls and Alternating Minimization. In Section 5 we report our experimental analysis. In Section 6 we discuss related work.

2. PROBLEM DEFINITION

Given a set of objects V, a clustering problem asks to partition the set V into clusters of similar objects. Assuming that cluster identifiers are represented by natural numbers, a clustering $\mathcal{C}$ can be seen as a function $\mathcal{C} : V \to \mathbb{N}$. Typically, the goal is to find a clustering $\mathcal{C}$ that optimizes an objective function that measures the quality of the clustering Numerous formulations and objective functions have been considered in the literature. One of these, considered both in the area of theoretical computer science and data mining, is that at the basis of the CORRELATION-CLUSTERING problem [3].

Problem 1 (CORRELATION-CLUSTERING)
Given a set of objects V and a pairwise similarity function $\mathrm{sim} : V \times V \to [0, 1]$, find a clustering $\mathcal{C} : V \to \mathbb{N}$ that minimizes the cost

$$\mathrm{cost}(\mathcal{C}) = \sum_{\substack{(x,y) \in V \times V \\ \mathcal{C}(x) = \mathcal{C}(y)}} (1 - \mathrm{sim}(x, y)) + \sum_{\substack{(x,y) \in V \times V \\ \mathcal{C}(x) \neq \mathcal{C}(y)}} \mathrm{sim}(x, y). \quad (1)$$

The intuition underlying the above problem is that the cost of assigning two objects x and y to the same cluster should be equal to the dissimilarity $1 - \mathrm{sim}(x, y)$, while the cost of assigning the objects in different clusters should correspond to their similarity $\mathrm{sim}(x, y)$. A common case is when the similarity is binary, that is, $\mathrm{sim} : V \times V \to \{0, 1\}$. In this case, Equation (1) reduces to counting the number of pairs of objects that have similarity 0 and are put in the same cluster plus the number of pairs of objects that have similarity 1 and belong to different clusters. Or equivalently, in a graph-based terminology, the objective function counts the number of "positive" edges that are cut plus the number of "negative" (i.e., non-existing) edges that are not cut.

In CHROMATIC-CORRELATION-CLUSTERING, which we formally define below, we still have negative edges (i.e., l_0-edges), but the positive edges may have different colors, representing different kinds of relations among the objects.

Problem 2 (CHROMATIC-CORRELATION-CLUSTERING)
Given a set V of objects, a set L of labels, a special label l_0, and a pairwise labeling function $\ell : V \times V \to L \cup \{l_0\}$, find a clustering $\mathcal{C} : V \to \mathbb{N}$ and a cluster labeling function $c\ell : \mathcal{C}[V] \to L$ so to minimize the cost

$$\mathrm{cost}(\mathcal{C}, c\ell) = \sum_{\substack{(x,y) \in V \times V, \\ \mathcal{C}(x) = \mathcal{C}(y)}} (1 - \mathrm{I}[\ell(x, y) = c\ell(\mathcal{C}(x))]) + \sum_{\substack{(x,y) \in V \times V, \\ \mathcal{C}(x) \neq \mathcal{C}(y)}} \mathrm{I}[\ell(x, y) \neq l_0]. \quad (2)$$

Equation (2) is composed by two terms, representing intra- and inter-cluster costs, respectively. In particular, according to the intra-cluster cost term, any pair of objects (x, y) assigned to the same cluster should pay a cost if and only if their relation type $\ell(x, y)$ is other than the predominant relation type of the cluster indicated by the function $c\ell$. For the inter-cluster cost, the objective function does not penalize a pair of objects (x, y) only if they do not have any relation, i.e., $\ell(x, y) = l_0$. If $\ell(x, y) \neq l_0$, the objective function incurs a cost, regardless of the label $\ell(x, y)$.

Example 1 *For the problem instance in Figure 1(a), the solution in Figure 1(b) has a cost of 5: there is no intra-cluster cost, because the two clusters are cliques and their edges are monochromatic, while we have an inter-cluster cost of 5 as equal to the number of edges that are cut.*

It is trivial to observe that, when $|L| = 1$, the CHROMATIC-CORRELATION-CLUSTERING problem corresponds to the binary version of CORRELATION-CLUSTERING. Thus, our problem is a generalization of the standard problem. Since CORRELATION-CLUSTERING is **NP**-hard, we can easily conclude that CHROMATIC-CORRELATION-CLUSTERING is **NP**-hard too.

The previous observation motivates us to consider whether applying standard CORRELATION-CLUSTERING algorithms, just ignoring the different colors, is a good solution to the problem. As we show in the following example, such an approach does not guarantee to produce good solutions.

Example 2 *For the problem instance in Figure 1(a), the optimal solution for the standard* CORRELATION-CLUSTERING *which does not consider the different colors, would be composed by a single cluster containing all the six vertices, as, according to Equation (1), this solution has a (minimum) cost of 4 corresponding to the number of missing edges within the cluster. Conversely, this solution has a non-optimal cost 12 when evaluated according to the* CHROMATIC-CORRELATION-CLUSTERING *formulation, i.e., according to Equation (2). Instead, the optimum in this case would correspond to the cost 5 solution depicted in Figure 1(b).*

Although the example shows that for the chromatic version of the problem we cannot directly apply algorithms developed for the CORRELATION-CLUSTERING problem, we can use such algorithms at least as a starting point, as shown in the next section.

3. THE Chromatic Balls ALGORITHM

We present next a randomized approximation algorithm for the CHROMATIC-CORRELATION-CLUSTERING problem. This algorithm, called Chromatic Balls, is motivated by the Balls algorithm [1], which is an approximation algorithm for standard CORRELATION-CLUSTERING.

For completeness, we briefly review the Balls algorithm. The algorithm works in iterations. Initially all objects are considered *uncovered*. In each iteration the algorithm produces a cluster, and the objects participating in the cluster are considered *covered*. In particular, the algorithm picks as pivot a random object currently uncovered, and forms a cluster consisting of the pivot itself along with all currently uncovered objects that are connected to the pivot.

The outline of our Chromatic Balls is summarized in Algorithm 1. The main difference with the Balls algorithm is that the edge labels are taken into account in order to build clusters around the pivots. To this end, the pivot chosen at each iteration of Chromatic Balls is an edge, thus a pair of objects, rather than a single object. The Chromatic Balls algorithm employs a set V' to keep all the objects that have not been assigned to any cluster yet; hence, initially, $V' = V$. At each iteration, a random edge (u, v) such that both objects u and v are currently in the set V' is selected as pivot (line 3). Given the pivot (u, v), a cluster C is formed around it. Beyond the objects u and v, the cluster C additionally contains all other objects $x \in V'$ for which the *triangle* (u, v, x) is monochromatic, that is, $\ell(u, x) = \ell(v, x) = \ell(u, v)$ (lines 4 and 5). Since the label $\ell(u, v)$ forms the basis for creating the cluster C, the cluster is labeled with this label (line 6). All objects added in C are removed from V' (line 7), and the algorithm terminates when V' does not contain any pair of objects that share an edge, i.e., that is labeled with a label other than l_0 (line 2). All objects remaining in the set V', if any, are eventually made singleton clusters (lines 8-11).

Computational complexity. The complexity of the Chromatic Balls algorithm is determined by two steps: (*i*) picking the pivots (line 3), and (*ii*) building the clusters (line 4). Choosing the pivots requires $\mathcal{O}(m \log n)$ time, where $n = |V|$ and $m = |E|$, as selecting random edges can be implemented by building a priority queue of edges with random priorities, and subsequently removing edges; each edge is removed once from the priority queue, whether it is selected as pivot or not. Building a single cluster C, instead, requires to access all neighbors of the pivot edge (u, v). As the current cluster is removed from the set of uncovered objects at the end of each iteration, the neighbors of any pivot are not considered again in the remainder of the algorithm. Thus, the step of selecting the objects to be included into the current clusters requires visiting each edge at most once; therefore, the process takes $\mathcal{O}(m)$ time. In conclusion, we can state that the computational complexity of the Chromatic Balls algorithm is $\mathcal{O}(m \log n)$.

Algorithm 1 Chromatic Balls

Input: Edge-labeled graph $G = (V, E, L, \ell)$
Output: Clustering $\mathcal{C} : V \to \mathbb{N}$; cluster labeling function $c\ell : \mathcal{C}[V] \to L$

1: $V' \leftarrow V$; $i \leftarrow 1$
2: **while** there exist $u, v \in V'$ such that $(u, v) \in E$ **do**
3:   randomly pick $u, v \in V'$ such that $(u, v) \in E$
4:   $C \leftarrow \{u, v\} \cup \{x \in V' \mid \ell(u, x) = \ell(v, x) = \ell(u, v)\}$
5:   **for all** $x \in C$ **do** $\mathcal{C}(x) \leftarrow i$
6:   $c\ell(i) = \ell(u, v)$
7:   $V' \leftarrow V' \setminus C$; $i \leftarrow i + 1$
8: **for all** $x \in V'$ **do**
9:   $\mathcal{C}(x) \leftarrow i$
10:   $c\ell(i) \leftarrow$ a random label from L
11:   $i \leftarrow i + 1$

3.1 Theoretical analysis

We analyze next the quality of the solutions obtained by Chromatic Balls. Our main result, given in Theorem 1, shows that the approximation guarantee of the algorithm depends on the number of *bad triplets* incident to a pair of objects in the input dataset. The notion of bad triplet is defined below; however, here we note that this result gives a constant-factor guarantee for bounded-degree graphs.

Even though the Chromatic Balls algorithm is similar to the Balls algorithm, which can be shown to provide a constant-factor approximation guarantee for general graphs too, the theoretical analysis of Chromatic Balls is much more complicated and requires several additional and nontrivial arguments. Due to the limited space of this paper, we report next only an outline of our analysis. Further details, including complete proofs, can be found in an extended technical report.[1]

We begin our analysis by defining special types of triplets and quadruples among the vertices of the graph.

Definition 1 (SC-triplet) *We say that* $\{x, y, z\}$ *is a* same-color triplet *(SC-triplet) if the induced triangle is monochromatic, i.e.,* $\ell(x, y) = \ell(x, z) = \ell(y, z) \neq l_0$.

Definition 2 (B-triplet) *We say that* $\{x, y, z\}$ *is a* bad triplet *(B-triplet) if the induced triangle is non-monochromatic and it has at most one pair labeled with* l_0.

Definition 3 (B-quadruple) *A* Bad-quadruple *is a set* $\{x, y, z, w\} \subseteq V$ *that contains at least one SC-triplet and at least one B-triplet.*

Note that, according to the cost function of our problem as defined in Equation (2), there is no way to partition a B-triplet without paying any cost. Next we define the notions of *hitting* and *d-hitting*.

Definition 4 (hitting) *Consider a pair of objects* (x, y) *and a triplet* t*, which can be either SC-triplet or B-triplet. We say that* t hits (x, y) *if* $x \in t$ *and* $y \in t$*. Additionally, if*

[1] `http://francescobonchi.com/CCC.pdf`

q is a B-quadruple, we say that q hits (x, y) *if* $x \in q$, $y \in q$, *and there exists* $z \in q$ *such that* $\{x, y, z\}$ *is a B-triplet.*

Definition 5 (*d*-hitting) *Given any pair of objects* (x, y) *and any B-quadruple* $q = \{x, y, z, w\}$, *we say that* q deeply hits *(*d-hits*)* (x, y) *if* q *hits* (x, y) *and either* $\{x, z, w\}$ *or* $\{y, z, w\}$ *is an SC-triplet.*

In reference to the above notions, we hereinafter denote by $\mathcal{S}$, $\mathcal{T}$, and $\mathcal{Q}$ the sets of all SC-triplets, B-triplets, and B-quadruples for an instance of our problem. Moreover, given a pair $(x, y) \in V \times V$ we define the following sets: $\mathcal{T}_{xy} \subseteq \mathcal{T}$ denotes the set of all B-triplets in $\mathcal{T}$ that hit (x, y); $\mathcal{Q}_{xy} \subseteq \mathcal{Q}$ denotes the set of all B-quadruples in $\mathcal{Q}$ that hit (x, y); $\mathcal{Q}^d_{xy} \subseteq \mathcal{Q}_{xy} \subseteq \mathcal{Q}$ denotes the set of all B-quadruples in $\mathcal{Q}$ that d-hit (x, y).

Let us now consider some events that may arise during the execution of the Chromatic Balls algorithm. Given an object $x \in V$, $P^{(i)}_x$ denotes the event "*x is chosen as pivot in the i-th iteration.*" Given a set $\{x_1, \ldots, x_n\} \subseteq V$, with $n \geq 2$, $A^{(i)}_{x_1 \cdots x_n}$ denotes the event "*all objects $x_1, \ldots, x_n$ enter the i-th iteration of the algorithm, while two of them are chosen as pivot in the same iteration.*"

Additionally, the events $T^{(i)}_{z|xy}$ and $Q^{(i)}_{zw|xy}$ are defined in reference to a pair (x, y). Given a B-triplet $\{x, y, z\} \in \mathcal{T}_{xy}$, $T^{(i)}_{z|xy}$ denotes the event "*$A^{(i)}_{xyz}$ occurs while x and y are not chosen both as pivots in the i-th iteration.*" Given a B-quadruple $\{x, y, z, w\} \in \mathcal{Q}^d_{xy}$, $Q^{(i)}_{zw|xy}$ denotes the event "*$A^{(i)}_{xyzw}$ occurs while neither x nor y are chosen as pivots in i-th iteration.*"

For the events $A^{(i)}_{x_1 \cdots x_n}$, $T^{(i)}_{z|xy}$, and $Q^{(i)}_{zw|xy}$, defined above, we also consider their counterparts that assert that the events occur at *some* iteration i. For instance, $A_{x_1 \cdots x_n}$ denotes the event "*$A^{(i)}_{x_1 \cdots x_n}$ happens at some iteration i,*" while $T_{z|xy}$ and $Q_{zw|xy}$ are defined analogously. Formally:

$$A_{x_1 \cdots x_n} \Leftrightarrow \bigvee_i A^{(i)}_{x_1 \cdots x_n}, \tag{3}$$

$$T_{z|xy} \Leftrightarrow \bigvee_i T^{(i)}_{z|xy} \Leftrightarrow \bigvee_i \left(A^{(i)}_{xyz} \wedge \neg \left(P^{(i)}_x \wedge P^{(i)}_y \right) \right), \tag{4}$$

$$Q_{zw|xy} \Leftrightarrow \bigvee_i Q^{(i)}_{zw|xy} \Leftrightarrow \bigvee_i \left(A^{(i)}_{xyzw} \wedge \neg P^{(i)}_x \wedge \neg P^{(i)}_y \right). \tag{5}$$

As reported in the next two lemmas, the probabilities of the events $T_{z|xy}$ and $Q_{zw|xy}$ can be expressed in terms of the probabilities of the events A_{xyz} and A_{xyzw}.

Lemma 1 *Given a pair $(x, y) \in V \times V$ and a B-triplet $\{x, y, z\} \in \mathcal{T}_{xy}$, it holds that $\frac{1}{2} \Pr[A_{xyz}] \leq \Pr[T_{z|xy}] \leq \Pr[A_{xyz}]$.*

Lemma 2 *Given a pair $(x, y) \in V \times V$ and a B-quadruple $\{x, y, z, w\} \in \mathcal{Q}^d_{xy}$, it holds that $\frac{1}{6} \Pr[A_{xyzw}] \leq \Pr[Q_{zw|xy}] \leq \frac{1}{4} \Pr[A_{xyzw}]$.*

Analyzing carefully the probabilities of events $T_{z|xy}$ and $Q_{zw|xy}$ is crucial for deriving the desired approximation factor, as shown next.

We consider an instance $G = (V, E, L, \ell)$ of our problem and rewrite the cost function in Equation (2) as sum of the costs paid by any single pair (x, y). To this end, in order to simplify the notation, we hereinafter write the cost by omitting $\mathcal{C}$ and $c\ell$ while keeping G only:

$$c(G) = \sum_{(x,y) \in V \times V} c_{xy}(G), \tag{6}$$

where $c_{xy}(G)$ denotes the aforementioned contribution of the pair (x, y) to the total cost. Moreover, let $\mathrm{E}[c(G)]$ denote the expected cost of Chromatic Balls over the random choices made by the algorithm. By the linearity of expectation, the expected cost $\mathrm{E}[c(G)]$ can be expressed as

$$\mathrm{E}[c(G)] = \sum_{(x,y) \in V \times V} \mathrm{E}\left[c_{xy}(G)\right]. \tag{7}$$

Finally, let $c^*(G)$ be the cost of the optimal solution on G.

To derive an approximation factor $r(G)$ on the performance of the Chromatic Balls algorithm, we look for an upper bound $Ub(G)$ on the expected cost $\mathrm{E}[c(G)]$ of the algorithm, and a lower bound $Lb(G)$ on the cost $c^*(G)$ of the optimal solution, so that

$$\frac{\mathrm{E}[c(G)]}{c^*(G)} \leq \frac{Ub(G)}{Lb(G)} = r(G). \tag{8}$$

We next show how to derive such upper and lower bounds.

Deriving the upper bound $Ub(G)$. For a pair (x, y) we define the collection of events $\Omega_{xy} = \{T_{z|xy} \mid \{x, y, z\} \in \mathcal{T}_{xy}\} \cup \{Q_{zw|xy} \mid \{x, y, z, w\} \in \mathcal{Q}^d_{xy}\}$. As the following two lemmas show, if pair (x, y) contributes to the cost paid by the algorithm, then exactly one of the events in Ω_{xy} occurs.

Lemma 3 *If $c_{xy}(\mathcal{C}, c\ell, G) > 0$ then at least one of the events in Ω_{xy} occurs.*

Lemma 4 *The events within the collection Ω_{xy} are disjoint.*

Combining Lemmas 3 and 4 with the expressions of the probabilities of the events $T_{z|xy}$ (Lemma 1) and $Q_{zw|xy}$ (Lemma 2) we can derive an upper bound on the expected contribution $\mathrm{E}[c_{xy}(G)]$ of a pair (x, y) to the total cost.

Lemma 5 *For a pair $(x, y) \in V \times V$ the following bound holds.*

$$\mathrm{E}[c_{xy}(G)] \leq \sum_{\{x,y,z\} \in \mathcal{T}_{xy}} \Pr[A_{xyz}] + \sum_{\{x,y,z,w\} \in \mathcal{Q}^d_{xy}} \frac{1}{4} \Pr[A_{xyzw}].$$

The bound in Lemma 5 together with Equation (7) can be used to give the desired (upper) bound on the overall expected cost $\mathrm{E}[c(G)]$.

Lemma 6 *The expected cost $\mathrm{E}[c(G)]$ of the Chromatic Balls algorithm can be bounded as follows*

$$\mathrm{E}[c(G)] \leq Ub(G) = \sum_{\{x,y,z\} \in \mathcal{T}} \left(3 \Pr[A_{xyz}] + \frac{3}{4} X_{xyz} + \frac{1}{2} Y_{xyz} \right),$$

where:

$$X_{xyz} = \sum_{w \in W_{xyz}} \frac{\Pr[A_{xyzw}]}{\tau_{xyzw}}, \quad Y_{xyz} = Y^{xy}_{xyz} + Y^{xz}_{xyz} + Y^{yz}_{xyz},$$

$$Y^{xy}_{xyz} = \sum_{w \in W^{xy}_{xyz}} \frac{\Pr[A_{xyzw}]}{\tau_{xyzw}}, \quad Y^{xz}_{xyz} = \sum_{w \in W^{xz}_{xyz}} \frac{\Pr[A_{xyzw}]}{\tau_{xyzw}},$$

$$\text{and } Y^{yz}_{xyz} = \sum_{w \in W^{yz}_{xyz}} \frac{\Pr[A_{xyzw}]}{\tau_{xyzw}}.$$

Finally, τ_{xyzw} denotes the number of B-triplets contained in any B-quadruple $\{x, y, z, w\}$.

Deriving the lower bound $Lb(G)$**.** Recalling that a B-triplet incurs a non-zero cost in any solution, a lower bound on the cost of the optimal solution $c^*(G)$ can be obtained by counting the number of disjoint B-triplets in the input. Considering the set $\mathcal{T}$ of B-triplets we can restate the following result of Ailon et al. [1] that provides a lower bound on the optimal by "fractionally assigning" all pairs of objects in $V \times V$ to the triplets in $\mathcal{T}$.

Lemma 7 (Ailon et al. [1]) *Let* $\{\alpha_{xyz} \mid \{x, y, z\} \in \mathcal{T}\}$ *be any assignment of nonnegative weights to the B-triplets in* $\mathcal{T}$ *satisfying* $\sum_{\{x,y,z\}\in\mathcal{T}_{x'y'}} \alpha_{xyz} \leq 1$ *for all* $(x', y') \in V \times V$*. It holds that* $c^*(G) \geq \sum_{\{x,y,z\}\in\mathcal{T}} \alpha_{xyz}$*.*

We can then obtain a lower bound on the optimal solution by finding a suitable set of weights α_{xyz} that satisfies the conditions of the previous lemma. We derive such a set of weights in the following further lemma.

Lemma 8 *For any pair* $(x, y) \in V \times V$ *the following condition holds.*

$$\sum_{\{x,y,z\}\in\mathcal{T}_{xy}} \frac{1}{1+|\mathcal{T}_{xy}|}\left(\frac{1}{2}\ \Pr\left[A_{xyz}\right] + \frac{1}{6}X_{xyz} + \frac{1}{6}Y_{xyz}\right) \leq 1.$$

Thus, combining Lemmas 7 and 8, we can obtain the desired lower bound $Lb(G)$ as follows.

Lemma 9 *The cost* $c^*(G)$ *of the optimal solution on any input instance* G *is lower bounded as follows*

$$c^*(G) \ \geq\ Lb(G) \ =$$

$$= \sum_{\{x,y,z\}\in\mathcal{T}} \frac{1}{1+t_{max}}\left(\frac{1}{2}\Pr\left[A_{xyz}\right] + \frac{1}{6}X_{xyz} + \frac{1}{6}Y_{xyz}\right),$$

where $t_{max} = \max_{(x,y)\in V\times V} |\mathcal{T}_{xy}|$ *is the maximum number of B-triplets that hit a pair of objects.*

The approximation ratio $r(G)$**.** The upper and lower bounds obtained in Lemmas 6 and 9 are at the basis if the final form of the approximation ratio of Chromatic Balls.

Theorem 1 *The approximation ratio of the Chromatic Balls algorithm on any input instance* G *is*

$$r(G) = \frac{\mathrm{E}[c(G)]}{c^*(G)} \leq 6\ (1 + t_{max}),$$

where $t_{max} = \max_{(x,y)\in V\times V} |\mathcal{T}_{xy}|$ *is the maximum number of B-triplets that hit a pair of objects.*

Theorem 1 shows that the approximation factor of the Chromatic Balls algorithm is bounded by the maximum number t_{max} of B-triplets that hit a pair of objects. The result is meaningful as it quantifies the quality of the performance of the algorithm as a property of the input graph. For example, as the following corollary shows, the algorithm provides a constant-factor approximation for bounded-degree graphs.

Corollary 1 *The approximation ratio of the Chromatic Balls algorithm on any input instance* G *is*

$$r(G) \leq 6\,(2D_{max} - 1)\,,$$

where $D_{max} = \max_{x\in V} |\{y \mid y \in V \wedge \ell(x, y) \neq l_0\}|$ *is the maximum degree in the problem instance.*

4. OTHER ALGORITHMS

In this section we present two additional algorithms for the CHROMATIC-CORRELATION-CLUSTERING problem. The first one is a variant of the Chromatic Balls algorithm that attempts to overcome some weaknesses of Chromatic Balls by employing two heuristics, one for pivot selection and one for cluster selection. The second one is an alternating minimization method that is designed to optimize directly the objective function.

4.1 Lazy Chromatic Balls

The algorithm we present next is motivated by the following example, in which we discuss what may go wrong during the execution of the Chromatic Balls algorithm.

Example 3 *Consider the graph in Figure 2: it has a fairly evident* **green** *cluster formed by vertices* {U,V,R,X,Y,W,Z}*.*

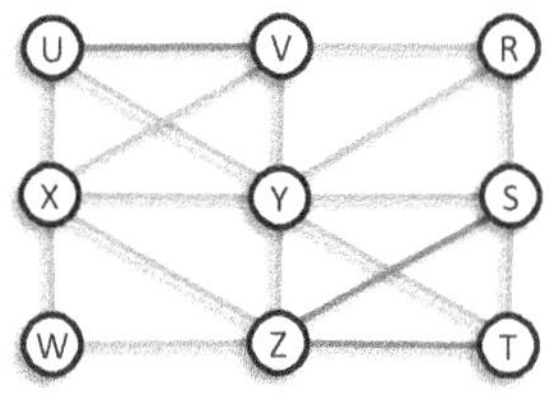

Figure 2: An example of an edge-labeled graph.

However, as all the edges have the same probability of being selected as pivots, Chromatic Balls might miss this **green** *cluster, depending on which edge is selected first. For instance, suppose that the first pivot chosen is (Y,S). Chromatic Balls forms the* **red** *cluster {Y,S,T} and removes it from the graph. Removing vertex Y makes the edge (X,Y) missing, which would have been a good pivot to build a* **green** *cluster. At this point, even if the second selected pivot edge is a* **green** *one, say (X,Z), Chromatic Balls would form only a small* **green** *cluster {X,W,Z}.*

Motivated by the previous example we introduce the Lazy Chromatic Balls heuristic, which tries to minimize the risk of bad choices. Given a vertex $x \in V$, and a label $l \in L$, let $d(x, l)$ be the number of edges incident to x having label l. Also, we denote by $\Delta(x) = \max_{l\in L} d(x, l)$, and $\lambda(x) = \arg\max_{l\in L} d(x, l)$. Lazy Chromatic Balls differs from Chromatic Balls in two ways:

Pivot random selection. At each iteration Lazy Chromatic Balls selects a pivot edge in two steps. First, a vertex u is picked up with probability directly proportional to $\Delta(u)$. Then, a second vertex v is selected among the neighbors of u with probability proportional to $d(v, \lambda(u))$.

Ball formation. Given the pivot (u, v), Chromatic Balls forms a cluster by adding all vertices x such that $\langle u, v, x\rangle$ is a monochromatic triangle. Lazy Chromatic Balls instead, iteratively adds vertices x in the cluster as long as they form a triangle $\langle X, Z, w\rangle$ of color $\ell(u, v)$, where X is either u or v, and Z can be any other vertex already belonging to the current cluster.

Example 4 *Consider again the example in Figure 2. Vertices X and Y have the maximum number of edges of one color: they both have 5* **green** *edges. Hence, one of them is chosen as first pivot vertex* u *by Lazy Chromatic Balls with higher probability than the remaining vertices. Suppose that*

Algorithm 2 Alternating Minimization (AM)

Input: Edge-labeled graph $G = (V, E, L, \ell)$; number K of output clusters

Output: Clustering $\mathcal{C} : V \rightarrow \mathbb{N}$; cluster labeling function $c\ell : \mathcal{C}[V] \rightarrow L$

initialize $\mathbf{A} = [\mathbf{a}_1, \ldots, \mathbf{a}_N]$ and $\mathbf{C} = [\mathbf{c}_1, \ldots, \mathbf{c}_K]$ at random
repeat
  for all $x \in V$ compute optimal $\mathbf{a}_x$ according to Proposition 1
  for all $k \in [1..K]$ compute optimal $\mathbf{c}_k$ according to Proposition 2
until neither $\mathbf{A}$ nor $\mathbf{C}$ changed

X is picked up, i.e., $u = X$. Given this choice, the second pivot v is chosen among the neighbors of X with probability proportional to $d(v, \lambda(u))$, i.e., the higher the number of green edges of the neighbor, the higher the probability for it to be chosen. In this case, hence, Lazy Chromatic Balls would likely choose Y as a second pivot vertex v, thus making (X,Y) the selected pivot edge. Afterwards, Lazy Chromatic Balls adds to the being formed cluster the vertices {U,V,Z} because each of them forms a green triangle with the pivot edge. Then, R enters the cluster too, because it forms a green triangle with Y and V, which is already in the cluster. Similarly, W enters the cluster thanks to Z.

Computational complexity. Like Chromatic Balls, the running time of the Lazy Chromatic Balls algorithm is determined by picking the pivots and building the various clusters. Picking the first pivot u can be implemented with a priority queue with priorities $\Delta \times rnd$, where rnd is a random number. This requires computing Δ for all objects, which takes $\mathcal{O}(nh + m)$ (where $h = |L|$). Managing the priority queue itself requires instead $\mathcal{O}(n \log n)$, as each object is put into/removed from the queue only once during the execution of the algorithm. Given u, the second pivot v is selected by probing all (non-chosen) neighbors of u. This takes $\mathcal{O}(m)$ time, as for each pivot u, its neighbors are accessed only once throughout the execution of the algorithm. Finally, building the current cluster takes $\mathcal{O}(m)$ time, as it requires a visit of the graph, where each edge is accessed $\mathcal{O}(1)$ times. In conclusion, the computational complexity of Lazy Chromatic Balls is $\mathcal{O}(n(\log n + h) + m)$, which, for small h, is better than the complexity of Chromatic Balls.

4.2 An alternating-minimization approach

A nice feature of the previous algorithms is that they are parameter-free: they produce clusterings by using information that is local to the pivot edges, without forcing the number of output clusters in any way. However, in some cases, it could be desired having an output clustering composed by a pre-specified number K of clusters. To this purpose, we present here an algorithm based on the *alternating minimization* paradigm [7], that receives in input the number K of output clusters and attempts to minimize Equation (2) directly. The pseudocode of the proposed algorithm, called Alternating Minimization, is given in Algorithm 2.

In a nutshell, AM tries to produce a solution by alternating between two optimization steps. In the first step the algorithm finds the best cluster assignment for every $x \in V$ given the assignments of every other $y \in V$ and the current cluster labels. In the second step, it finds the best label for every cluster given the current assignment of objects to clusters. Below we show that both steps can be solved optimally. As a consequence the value of Equation (2) is guaranteed to decrease in every step, until convergence. Finding the global minimum is obviously hard, but the algorithm is guaranteed to converge to a local optimum.

Definitions. For presentation sake, we adopt matrix notation. We denote matrices by uppercase boldface romans and vectors by lowercase boldface romans. We write $\mathbf{X}_{ij}$ for the (i, j) coordinate of matrix $\mathbf{X}$, and $\mathbf{x}(i)$ for the i-th coordinate of vector $\mathbf{x}$.

The parameter space of Problem 2 consists of a *cluster assignment* for every object $x \in V$, given by the binary matrix $\mathbf{A}$, and a *label assignment* for every cluster $k \in \{1, \ldots, K\}$, given by the binary matrix $\mathbf{C}$. We have $\mathbf{A}_{kx} = 1$ when object x is assigned to cluster k, and $\mathbf{A}_{kx} = 0$ otherwise. Similarly, we set $\mathbf{C}_{lk} = 1$ when label l is assigned to cluster k, and $\mathbf{C}_{lk} = 0$ otherwise. Since every object must belong to one and only one cluster, and every cluster must have one and only one label assigned, both $\mathbf{A}$ and $\mathbf{C}$ are constrained to consist of all zeros with a single 1 on every column. Denote by $\mathbf{a}_x$ the column of $\mathbf{A}$ that corresponds to object x.

The input is represented by a set of binary matrices, with a matrix $\mathbf{Z}_x$ for every $x \in V$. These matrices encode the labeling function ℓ as follows. Let $\mathbf{z}_{xy}$ denote the column of $\mathbf{Z}_x$ that corresponds to the object $y \in V$. We have $\mathbf{z}_{xy}(l) = 1$ if and only if $\ell(x, y) = l$, otherwise $\mathbf{z}_{xy}(l) = 0$. Every $\mathbf{Z}_x$ consists thus of zeros, with exactly one 1 on every column. Finally, denote by $\mathbf{b}$ a special binary vector where $\mathbf{b}(l) = 1$ when $l = l_0$ and $\mathbf{b}(l) = 0$ otherwise. We have then $\mathbf{z}_{xy}^{\mathrm{T}}\mathbf{b} = 1$ if and only if $\ell(x, y) = l_0$.

The above formulation of the problem assumes that the input is represented by many large matrices. Note however that this representation is only conceptual. In the actual implementation we do not have to materialize these matrices and we can represent the input with the minimal amount of space required, as shown next. The benefit of our formulation is that it allows to write our objective function and our optimization process using linear-algebra operations, and argue about the optimality of the local optimization steps.

Optimal cluster assignment. Denote by N_{xk}^{-} the number of objects $y \in V$ in cluster k that have $\ell(x, y) = l_0$. Since $\ell(x, y) = l_0 \Leftrightarrow \mathbf{z}_{xy}\mathbf{b} = 1$, we have $N_{xk}^{-} = (\mathbf{A}\mathbf{Z}_x\mathbf{b})(k)$. Similarly, let N_{xk}^{+} denote the number of objects $y \in V$ in cluster k that have $\ell(x, y) = c\ell(k)$. Since $y \in k$, we have $\ell(x, y) = c\ell(k) \Leftrightarrow \mathbf{z}_{xy}\mathbf{C}\mathbf{a}_y = 1$ and can write $N_{xk}^{+} = (\mathbf{A}\mathbf{w}_x)(k)$, where $\mathbf{w}_x = [\mathbf{z}_{x1}^{\mathrm{T}}\mathbf{C}\mathbf{a}_1 \ldots \mathbf{z}_{xn}^{\mathrm{T}}\mathbf{C}\mathbf{a}_n]$.

Proposition 1 *The optimal cluster assignment for $x \in V$ given $\mathbf{A}$ and $\mathbf{C}$ is $k^* = \arg\min_k N_{xk}^{-} - N_{xk}^{+}$.*

PROOF. We can rewrite Equation (2) as follows:

$$\begin{aligned} &\textstyle\sum_{x,y} \mathbf{a}_x^{\mathrm{T}}\mathbf{a}_y(1 - \mathbf{z}_{xy}^{\mathrm{T}}\mathbf{C}\mathbf{a}_y) + (1 - \mathbf{a}_x^{\mathrm{T}}\mathbf{a}_y)(1 - \mathbf{z}_{xy}^{\mathrm{T}}\mathbf{b}) = \\ &= \textstyle\sum_x \mathbf{a}_x^{\mathrm{T}}\mathbf{A}(\mathbb{1} - \mathbf{w}_x) + (\mathbb{1}^{\mathrm{T}} - \mathbf{a}_x^{\mathrm{T}}\mathbf{A})(\mathbb{1} - \mathbf{Z}_x^{\mathrm{T}}\mathbf{b}), \end{aligned} \quad (9)$$

where $\mathbf{w}_x$ is defined as above, and $\mathbb{1}$ denotes the $|V|$-dimensional vector of all 1s. Terms that correspond to a fixed $x \in V$ further simplify to

$$\mathbf{a}_x^{\mathrm{T}}\mathbf{A}^{\mathrm{T}}\mathbf{Z}_x\mathbf{b} - \mathbf{a}_x^{\mathrm{T}}\mathbf{A}\mathbf{w}_x + d_x,$$

where the constant $d_x = \mathbb{1}^{\mathrm{T}}\mathbb{1} - \mathbb{1}^{\mathrm{T}}\mathbf{Z}_x^{\mathrm{T}}\mathbf{b}$ is the "degree" of object x, the number of objects $y \in V$ where $\ell(x, y) \neq l_0$.

Since we must assign exactly one cluster for x, the above expression is minimized simply by assigning x to the cluster k that minimizes $(\mathbf{A}\mathbf{Z}_x^{\mathrm{T}}\mathbf{b})(k) - (\mathbf{A}\mathbf{w}_x)(k) = N_{xk}^{-} - N_{xk}^{+}$.

The result is quite intuitive. The best cluster for x is the one having the least "push" in terms of l_0 connections, and the most "pull" given by connections having the appropriate label. However, evaluating N_{xk}^{-} in practice is very slow, as it involves checking all l_0 connections of x. Ideally the update rule should only require access to edges having some label other than l_0. This is easy to achieve, however.

Let N_{xk}^{0} denote the remaining objects in cluster k, that is, those with $\ell(x, y) \neq c\ell(k) \neq l_0$. Also, let S_k denote the size of cluster k. Clearly we have $S_k = N_{xk}^{+} + N_{xk}^{0} + N_{xk}^{-}$ for every $x \in V$. Using this we obtain $N_{xk}^{-} - N_{xk}^{+} = S_k - 2N_{xk}^{+} - N_{xk}^{0}$, which is much faster to evaluate.

Optimal label assignment. The update rule for the cluster label is intuitive as well. Denote by E_k the number of ordered (x, y) pairs so that both x and y belong to cluster k, and $\ell(x, y) = c\ell(k)$.

Proposition 2 *The optimal label assignment for cluster k given $\mathbf{A}$ is $l^* = \arg\min_l S_k^2 - E_k$.*

PROOF. We can partition the cost in Equation (9) as a sum over clusters. That is, for a fixed cluster k we sum only over those x and y that belong both to k. Also, the second term in Equation (9) does not depend on $\mathbf{C}$ and can therefore be omitted. This leaves us with the sum

$$\sum_{x \in k, y \in k} (1 - \mathbf{z}_{xy}^{\mathrm{T}} \mathbf{C} \mathbf{a}_y),$$

where we can replace $\mathbf{C}\mathbf{a}_y$ with the binary vector $\mathbf{c}_k$ that indicates the label assigned to cluster k. Clearly we have $\sum_{x \in k, y \in k} 1 = S_k^2$, and it is easy to see that $\sum_{x \in k, y \in k} \mathbf{z}_{xy}\mathbf{c}_k$ counts all (x, y) pairs having the same label that is currently assigned to k, which is by definition equal to E_k.

This means that the optimal label for cluster k is simply the label shared by the majority of the pairs in k.

Computational complexity. The running time of Alternating Minimization depends on the (optimal) cluster and label assignment steps. Cluster assignment requires two sub-steps: evaluating $S_k - 2N_{xk}^{+} - N_{xk}^{0}$ for each vertex and cluster, which can be performed in $\mathcal{O}(m)$ by a simple visit of the input graph, and looking at all clusters to choose the best one for each vertex, which clearly takes $\mathcal{O}(Kn)$. Label assignment requires to compute the number of intra-cluster edge labels for each cluster k and label l. This takes $\mathcal{O}(m)$, as it can be performed, again, by visiting the input graph. Then, the assignment of labels to clusters by evaluating $S_k^2 - E_k$ can be performed in $\mathcal{O}(Kh)$. In conclusion, as usually $h = |L| \ll n$, the computational complexity of Alternating Minimization is $\mathcal{O}(s(Kn + m))$, where s is the number of iterations to convergence.

5. EXPERIMENTAL EVALUATION

In this section, we report our empirical assessments. We experiment with all three proposed algorithms, Chromatic Balls, Lazy Chromatic Balls, and Alternating Minimization, to which we refer by CB, LCB, and AM, respectively. We also evaluate the performance of the baseline described in the Introduction, namely the "standard" Balls algorithm [1] that ignores colors. We refer to this baseline as B. All measurements reported are averaged over 50 runs.

Algorithm 3 Synthetic data generator

```
Input: number of vertices n, number of clusters K, number
    of labels h, probability p of intra-cluster edges, proba-
    bility q of inter-cluster edges, probability w that an edge
    inside a cluster has a color different from the cluster
Output: edge labeled graph G = (V, E, L, ℓ)
V ← [1, n],  E ← ∅,  L ← {l_1, ..., l_h}
assign each vertex x ∈ V to a randomly selected cluster
assign to each cluster a randomly selected label from L
for all pairs (x, y) ∈ V × V do
   pick 3 random numbers r_1, r_2, r_3 ranging within [0, 1]
   if C(x) = C(y) then
      if r_1 < p then
         if r_2 < w then
            E ← E ∪ (x, y)
            ℓ(x, y) ← a random label from L \ {cℓ(C(x))}
         else
            E ← E ∪ (x, y)
            ℓ(x, y) ← cℓ(C(x));
   else if r_3 < q then
      E ← E ∪ (x, y)
      ℓ(x, y) ← a random label from L
```

5.1 Experiments on synthetic data

We evaluate our algorithms on synthetic datasets generated by the process outlined in Algorithm 3. In a nutshell, the generator initially assigns vertices and labels to clusters uniformly at random, and then adds noise according to the probability parameters p, q, and w. Given the assignment of vertices to clusters, intra-cluster edges are sampled with probability p, and they are given the correct label (the label of the cluster they are assigned to) with probability $1 - w$, while, inter-cluster edges are sampled with probability q.

The initial assignment of objects and labels to clusters can be interpreted as a ground truth underlying the corresponding synthetic dataset. We compare the resulting clusterings with the ground-truth clustering using the well-known F-measure external cluster-validity criterion. Given a ground-truth clustering $\hat{\mathcal{C}}$ and a clustering solution $\mathcal{C}$ having $\hat{K}$ and K clusters, respectively, F-measure is defined in terms of *precision* and *recall* as follows:

$$F(\mathcal{C}, \widetilde{\mathcal{C}}) = \frac{1}{n} \sum_{\hat{k}=1}^{\hat{K}} S_{\hat{k}} \max_{k \in [1..K]} F_{\hat{k}k},$$

where $F_{\hat{k}k} = (2P_{\hat{k}k}R_{\hat{k}k})/(P_{\hat{k}k} + R_{\hat{k}k})$ such that $P_{\hat{k}k} = S_{\hat{k} \cap k}/S_k$ and $R_{\hat{k}k} = S_{\hat{k} \cap k}/S_{\hat{k}}$, while $S_{\hat{k} \cap k}$ denotes the number of common objects between the $\hat{k}$-th cluster of $\widetilde{\mathcal{C}}$ and the k-th cluster of $\mathcal{C}$, and $S_{\hat{k}}$ and $S_{\hat{k}}$ are the sizes of clusters $\hat{k}$ and k, respectively. It easy to see that $F \in [0, 1]$.

We generate datasets with a fixed number of objects ($n = 1000$), and we vary (i) the noise level (controlled by playing with p, q, and w); (ii) the number of labels h; and (iii) the number of clusters K in the ground truth. Even though we perform tests by varying all parameters p, q, and w, due to space limitations we only report results obtained for varying q and keeping p and w equal to 0.5.

For the number of clusters required as input for the AM algorithm, we consider two options: the average number of clusters produced by the CB algorithm, and the number of clusters in the ground truth. We refer to these two settings by AM and AM*, respectively. In Figure 3 we report the performance of our algorithms in terms of F-measure, as well as solution cost (Equation (2)).

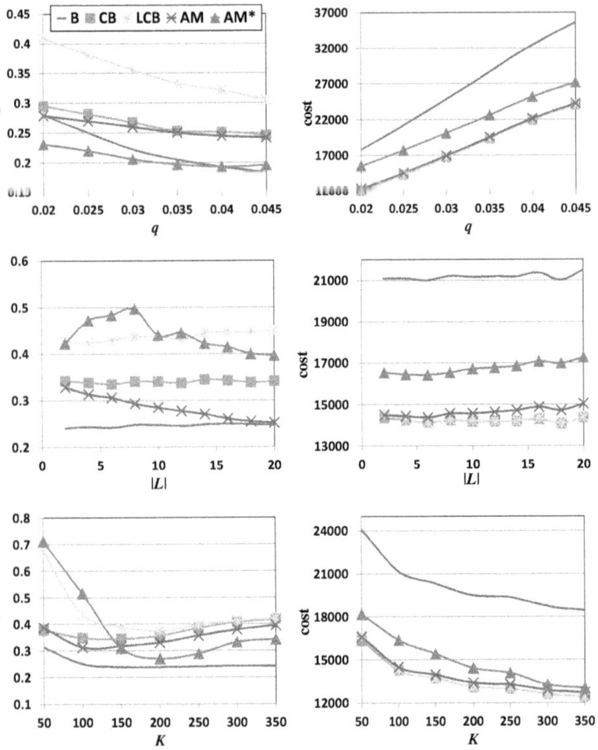

Figure 3: Accuracy on synthetic datasets in terms of F-measure (left) and solution cost (right), by varying level of noise (1st row), number of labels (2nd row), and number of ground-truth clusters (3rd row).

All trends observed by varying the parameters q, h, and K are intuitive. Indeed, for all methods, the performance decreases as the noise level q increases (Figure 3, 1st row). On the other hand, all methods give better solutions, in terms of cost, as the number of ground truth clusters K increases (Figure 3, 3rd row right). The reason is that since CB and LCB tend to produce a large number of clusters, by setting a larger K the difference tends to disappear.

All proposed methods generally achieve both F-measure and solution cost results evidently better than the baseline. Particularly, in terms of solution cost, CB, LCB, and AM perform very close to each other and generally better than AM*. In terms of F-measure, instead, LCB is recognized as the best method in most cases.

5.2 Experiments on real data

We experiment with three real datasets (Table 1).

String. A protein-protein interaction (PPI) network obtained from `string-db.org`, i.e., a database of known protein interactions for a large number of organisms. The dataset is an undirected graph where vertices represent proteins and edges represent protein interactions. Edges are labeled with 4 types of interactions. The PPI datasets are usually very sparse, therefore, we keep only the 30-core of the entire network, i.e., we recursively remove the vertices with degree less than 30 until a fix-point has been reached.

Youtube. This dataset represents a network of associations in the `youtube` site. The vertices of the network represent users, videos, and channels. Entities in the network have five different types of associations: *contact*, *co-contact*, *co-subscription*, *co-subscribed*, and *favorite*; these are the edge labels considered by our algorithms. For edges with multiple labels we picked one label at random from the available ones. The dataset has been compiled by Tang et al. [14] and it is available at `http://www.public.asu.edu/~ltang9/`.

Table 1: Characteristics of real data. n: number of vertices; m: number of edges; d: average degree; $|L|$: number of labels; c: clustering coefficient.

dataset	n	m	d	$\|L\|$	c
String	18 152	401 582	44.25	4	0.731
Youtube	15 088	19 923 067	2 640.92	5	0.495
DBLP	312 416	2 110 470	13.51	100	0.204

DBLP. We obtain a recent snapshot of the DBLP co-authorship network (`http://dblp.uni-trier.de/xml/`). For each co-authorship edge, we consider the bag of words obtained by merging the titles of all papers coauthored by the two authors. Words are stemmed and stop-words are removed. We then apply *Latent Dirichlet Allocation* (LDA) [5] to automatically identify 100 topics on each edge. After LDA topic-modeling, for each edge, we assign its most prominent topic discovered as edge label.

Results. Table 2 summarizes the results obtained on real data. Like in synthetic data, all proposed algorithms clearly outperform the baseline B. CB is the best method on Youtube and DBLP, achieving up to 27.74% of improvement with respect to the baseline in terms of solution cost. Instead, CB is slightly outperformed by LCB and AM on String, while LCB outperforms AM on String and DBLP.

As far as the runtime, we observe that the baseline is faster than the proposed methods, as expected. This is mainly due to a smaller complexity in choosing vertex pivots compared to choosing edge pivots. However, all proposed methods remain very efficient, as they take a few seconds (CB and LCB) or minutes (AM) on large and dense graphs like Youtube and DBLP. All runtimes comply with the computational complexity analysis reported previously. Indeed, AM is the slowest method, mostly due to the typically high number of iterations needed to convergence, while LCB is faster than CB, especially on dense datasets like Youtube.

Finally, Figure 4 shows an example cluster from the DBLP co-authorship network recognized by the LCB algorithm, containing 23 authors (vertices). Among the 71 intra-cluster edges, 58 have the same label, i.e., `Topic 18`, whose most representative (stemmed) keywords are: **`queri, effici, spatial, tempor, search, index, similar, data, dimension, aggreg`**. Other topics (edge colors) that appears are "sensor networks", "frequent pattern mining", "algorithms on graphs and trees", "support vector machines", "classifiers and Bayesian learning".

6. RELATED WORK

Edge-labeled graphs and multidimensional networks. Graphs in which edges are labeled with a type of relation occurring among the connected vertices are receiving increasingly attention. To the best of our knowledge no previous work has investigated the problem of clustering in such graphs. The problems studied so far on this kind of graphs are mainly on label-constrained reachability queries [8, 10, 12, 16], whose main goal is to answer whether a vertex u can reach vertex v trough a path whose edge labels belong to a given set. Clustering has been studied, instead, in so called *multidimensional networks*, i.e., networks defined as a col-

Table 2: Results on real datasets: average cost, runtime (s), and average number of output clusters

dataset	cost				runtime (s)				#clusters			
	B	CB	LCB	AM	B	CB	LCB	AM	B	CB	LCB	AM
String	163 305	160 060	155 881	156 976	0.5	1.4	1.3	21.0	1 086	1 451	784	1 451
Youtube	23 550 213	18 956 000	22 644 858	19 670 899	22.4	117.8	40.5	1 038.9	568	1 078	672	1 078
DBLP	2 260 065	1 633 149	1 678 714	2 018 952	4.3	10.2	5.5	2 116.1	66 276	123 197	99 948	123 197

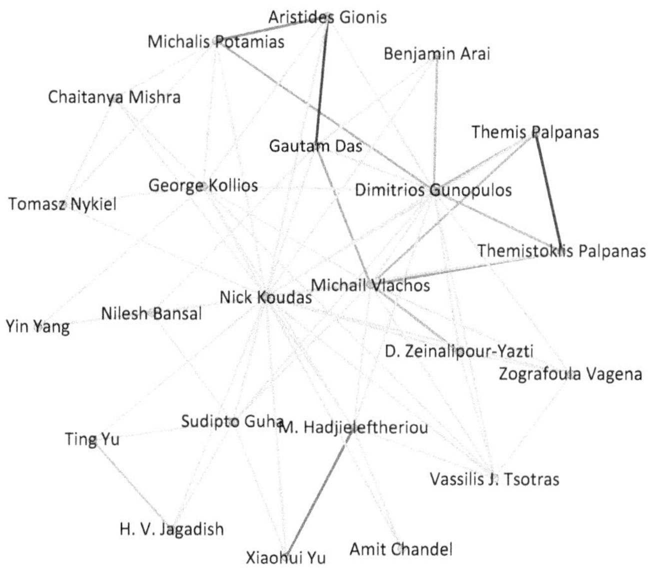

Figure 4: An example cluster from DBLP.

lection of multiple networks over the same set of actors. In our jargon these are simply graphs where each edge can have more than one color [4, 13, 15]. Although the input of that problem might seem close to ours, the objective is semantically far away. In clustering multidimensional networks, the objective is to find a partitioning of vertices which is meaningful and relevant in *all dimensions at the same time*. Taking again the colors metaphor, in that setting is a clustering is considered as good if it makes sense in the `green` network *and* as well as the `red` network, and so on. In our work, we are rather interested in finding groups of objects that induce color-coherent clusters while looking at all the colors together.

Correlation Clustering. The problem of CORRELATION-CLUSTERING was first defined by Bansal et al. [3] in its binary version. Ailon et al. [1] proposed the Balls algorithm that achieves expected approximation factor 5 if the weights obey the probability condition. If the weights X_{ij} obey also the triangle inequality, then the algorithm achieves expected approximation factor 2. Giotis and Guruswami [9] consider correlation clustering when the number of clusters is given, while Ailon and Liberty [2] study a variant of correlation clustering where the goal is to minimize the number of disagreements between the produced clustering and a given ground truth clustering. We recently extended correlation clustering to allow overlaps, i.e., objects belonging to more than one cluster [6].

7. CONCLUSIONS

In this paper, we introduce a variant of the correlation-clustering problem, in which the pairwise relations between objects are categorical. The problem has interesting applications, such as clustering social networks where individuals are connected with different types of relations, or clustering protein networks, where proteins are associated with different types of interactions. We propose three algorithms that we evaluate on synthetic and real datasets.

Our problem is a novel clustering formulation well-suited for mining multi-labeled and heterogeneous datasets that are becoming increasingly common. We believe that there are many interesting extensions and fruitful future research directions. For example, we would like to extend the problem formulation in order to capture overlapping clusters as well as multiple-labeled edges.

Acknowledgements. This research was partially supported by the Torres Quevedo Program of the Spanish Ministry of Science and Innovation, co-funded by the European Social Fund, and by the Spanish Centre for the Development of Industrial Technology under the CENIT program, project CEN-20101037, "Social Media" (`http://www.cenitsocialmedia.es/`).

8. REFERENCES

[1] N. Ailon, M. Charikar, and A. Newman. Aggregating inconsistent information: Ranking and clustering. *JACM*, 55:23:1–23:27, 2008.

[2] N. Ailon and E. Liberty. Correlation clustering revisited: The "true" cost of error minimization problems. In *ICALP*, 2009.

[3] N. Bansal, A. Blum, and S. Chawla. Correlation clustering. *Machine Learning*, 56(1–3), 2004.

[4] M. Berlingerio, M. Coscia, and F. Giannotti. Finding and Characterizing Communities in Multidimensional Networks. In *ASONAM*, pages 490–494, 2011.

[5] D. M. Blei, A. Y. Ng, and M. I. Jordan. Latent dirichlet allocation. *JMLR*, 3:993–1022, 2003.

[6] F. Bonchi, A. Gionis, and A. Ukkonen. Overlapping correlation clustering. In *ICDM*, pages 51–60, 2011.

[7] I. Csiszar and G. Tusnady. Information geometry and alternating minimization procedures. *Statistics and Decisions*, 1984.

[8] W. Fan, J. Li, S. Ma, N. Tang, and Y. Wu. Adding Regular Expressions to Graph Reachability and Pattern Queries. In *ICDE*, pages 39–50, 2011.

[9] I. Giotis and V. Guruswami. Correlation clustering with a fixed number of clusters. In *SODA*, 2006.

[10] R. J. H. Hong, H. Wang, N. Ruan, and Y. Xiang. Computing Label-Constraint Reachability in Graph Databases. In *SIGMOD*, pages 123–134, 2010.

[11] C. Lin et al. Clustering methods in protein-protein interaction networks. In *Knowledge Discovery in Bioinformatics: Techniques, Methods and Application.*

[12] M. Rice and V. J. Tsotras. Graph indexing of road networks for shortest path queries with label restrictions. *PVLDB*, 4:69–80, 2010.

[13] M. Rocklin and A. Pinar. On Clustering on Graphs with Multiple Edge Types. In *WAW*, pages 38–49, 2011.

[14] L. Tang, X. Wang, and H. Liu. Uncovering groups via heterogeneous interaction analysis. In *ICDM '09: Proceedings of IEEE International Conference on Data Mining*, pages 503–512, 2009.

[15] L. Tang, X. Wang, and H. Liu. Community detection via heterogeneous interaction analysis. *Data Mining and Knowledge Discovery*, pages 1–33, 2011.

[16] K. Xu, L. Zou, J. X. Yu, L. Chen, Y. Xiao, and D. Zhao. Answering Label-Constraint Reachability in Large Graphs. In *CIKM*, pages 1595–1600, 2011.

Locally-Scaled Spectral Clustering using Empty Region Graphs

Carlos D. Correa
Center for Advanced Scientific Computing
Lawrence Livermore National Laboratory
correac@llnl.gov

Peter Lindstrom
Center for Advanced Scientific Computing
Lawrence Livermore National Laboratory
pl@llnl.gov

ABSTRACT

This paper introduces a new method for estimating the local neighborhood and scale of data points to improve the robustness of spectral clustering algorithms. We employ a subset of empty region graphs – the β-skeleton – and non-linear diffusion to define a locally-adapted affinity matrix, which, as we demonstrate, provides higher quality clustering than conventional approaches based on k nearest neighbors or global scale parameters. Moreover, we show that the clustering quality is far less sensitive to the choice of β and other algorithm parameters, and to transformations such as geometric distortion and random perturbation. We summarize the results of an empirical study that applies our method to a number of 2D synthetic data sets, consisting of clusters of arbitrary shape and scale, and to real multi-dimensional classification examples from benchmarks, including image segmentation.

Categories and Subject Descriptors

I.5.3 [**Clustering**]: Algorithms; H.2.8 [**Database applications**]: Data mining

Keywords

Spectral Clustering, Proximity Graphs

1. INTRODUCTION

Clustering is at the core of modern data mining tools. Common techniques, such as those based on K-means or explicit density models, are being replaced by *spectral methods* for clustering, where points are clustered based on a spectral analysis of a matrix of pairwise similarities or affinities, instead of relying on a particular cluster model.

Spectral clustering has been applied successfully in a number of fields, including image segmentation, text mining, and data analysis in general. However, there remain a number of open questions: (1) How to define the neighborhood around data points to estimate a "good" affinity matrix, (2) how to adapt the algorithm to account for variations in local scale or density of the data, and (3) how to automatically select the number of clusters. This paper concerns the former two questions.

KDD'12, August 12–16, 2012, Beijing, China.
Copyright 2012 ACM 978-1-4503-1462-6 /12/08. ...$10.00.

The most common approaches to date rely on simple neighborhood definitions, such as k-nearest neighbor (kNN) graphs or ε-graphs, both which involve parameters that govern the graph density. However, clustering results may change dramatically for different values of k or ε. In particular, when the neighborhood graph is too sparse, clusters break up into individual components that cannot be aggregated by spectral clustering, while the spectral method can be unreliable for identifying clusters in an overconnected, dense graph. Alternatively, one can simply connect all points in a fully connected graph and rely on a single scale parameter σ to define the affinity between pairs of points in a weighted graph, which can be thought of as a fuzzy instance of ε-graphs. In either case, the optimal choice of these parameters varies with the dimensionality and across data sets, and more importantly often *within* a data set, as the resulting selection of neighbors or affinities does not adapt to the local density or distribution of points.

In this paper, we exploit *empty region graphs* (ERGs) to construct neighborhoods without requiring a particular choice of the neighborhood extents. In contrast to kNN graphs, which prescribe the number of neighbors without regard to their relative locations, empty region graphs account for the spatial distribution of points to define neighborhoods of varying extent and cardinality, and do in general not suffer from missing or redundant connections. We show that these graphs generally improve the accuracy of spectral clustering algorithms. We also introduce a diffusion-based mechanism that estimates the density based on the average neighborhood size around a point to define affinities. We show that this local scaling algorithm, when combined with empty region neighborhoods, results in a better classification that is robust to noise and geometric transformations of the data points.

We present results on a number of synthetic benchmark data sets, as well as real multi-dimensional classification problems, including image segmentation.

2. RELATED WORK

Spectral Clustering. Spectral clustering is becoming a successful alternative to techniques based on K-means [21] or density models [10], and dates back to Donath and Hoffman [8] and Fiedler [11]. Recently, spectral clustering has found a niche in image segmentation [28], text mining [7] and as a data mining tool in general [26, 17]. Since then, there has been a trend in improving spectral clustering through a detailed analysis of the underlying graph structure [22], the scale and density parameters [34, 1], and the stability [15] and consistency [33] of the algorithm. Most related to our work are the techniques that attempt to estimate the local scale or density to improve spectral clustering of data with varying densities, shapes and levels of noise. Among the first to address this problem for data mining were Zelnik-Manor and Perona [34], who improve the general algorithm by Ng et al. [26] with local scaling. This approach, although effective even in high dimensions, was shown to be suboptimal for noisy data sets, or for data with clusters of different densities [25]. To alleviate this problem, Nadler and Galun [25] introduce a coherence measure of a set of points belonging to the same cluster. Although not exclusive of spectral methods, the authors show that it alleviates some of the intrinsic limitations of spectral clustering. To deal with noise, Li et al. [19] propose a warping model that maps the data into a new space more suitable for clustering and more resilient to noise. Other methods are able to cluster data consisting of regions of arbitrary shapes, such as density based clustering [27], and, in a similar spirit to Zelnik-Manor and Perona's method, locally scaled density based clustering [1].

In this paper, we address the problem of locally-scaled and noise robust spectral clustering. We take a different approach and identify the problem as early as the selection of the neighborhood graph. Maier et al. suggest that the construction of the graph has a measurable effect on the results of spectral clustering [22]. Inspired by this paper, we turned to alternative neighborhood graphs, namely *empty region graphs* [3], in an effort to obtain better neighborhoods.

Empty Region Graphs. Neighborhood or proximity graphs create a geometric structure that connects two points if they are close in some sense. These graphs have been well studied and include the relative neighborhood graph [16], the Gabriel graph [14], β-skeletons [18], σ-local graphs [2] and Delaunay triangulations [12]. A subset of these, called the empty region graphs, define a neighborhood graph where two points are connected if a geometric region parameterized by those points does not contain any other point [3]. These graphs have been well studied in terms of their geometric properties [6, 3], and have been applied in geographic analysis, pattern recognition and machine learning. Proximity graphs have been applied to clustering as well. Urquhart et al. [32] use the Gabriel graph and the Relative Neighbor graph to improve hierarchical clustering, noting that these graphs result in natural clusters that can be separated depending on the local graph density [32]. Carreira and Zemel apply an ensemble of minimum spanning trees to form neighborhood graphs that are more resilient to noise and varying densities [4]. Choo et al. propose an agglomerate method for hierarchical clustering that merges candidate clusters that belong to the same connected component in the Gabriel graph [5].

In this paper, we propose the use of the one-parameter β-skeleton empty region graph to construct locally-scaled affinity matrices that improve the accuracy of spectral clustering. We show that this approach is more effective when combined with a diffusion step that enhances the block structure of the affinity matrix and, thus, the separability of clusters.

3. BACKGROUND

Our approach combines neighborhoods defined by empty region graphs with density estimation techniques and spectral clustering.

3.1 Spectral Clustering

Spectral clustering refers to a general algorithm where data are clustered into groups based on spectral analysis of a matrix of pairwise affinities or similarities between data points. The intuition is that, based on a similarity graph between points, a good clustering should partition the graph such that points in the same group are similar and points in different groups are dissimilar to each other. The spectral properties of the graph Laplacian helps us partition the graph in that manner, based on one of the properties of the graph Laplacian, which states the graph Laplacian has eigenvalue 0 with multiplicity equal to the number of connected components of the affinity matrix.

A general algorithm for spectral clustering can be implemented as follows [26]: Given a set of n points $S = \{s_1, s_2, \ldots, s_n\}$ in $\mathbb{R}^d$ to be partitioned into K clusters,

- Construct a neighborhood graph (S, E) (e.g. based on k nearest neighbors) over the point set S.
- Define the affinity matrix $A \in \mathbb{R}^{n\times n}$, where
$$A_{ij} = \begin{cases} \exp\left(\frac{-d(s_i,s_j)^2}{\sigma^2}\right) & ij \in E \\ 0 & \text{otherwise} \end{cases} \tag{1}$$
d is a distance function, commonly Euclidean, and σ is a scale parameter.
- Define D as the diagonal matrix $D_{ii} = \sum_{j=1}^{n} A_{ij}$.
- Define the normalized Laplacian matrix $L = I - D^{-1/2}AD^{-1/2}$.
- Find the K eigenvectors corresponding to the smallest eigenvalues of L, and form the matrix $X \in \mathbb{R}^{n\times K}$ with these eigenvectors as columns.
- Form the matrix Y by normalizing the rows of X, so that $Y_{ij} = X_{ij}/\sqrt{\sum_j X_{ij}^2}$.
- Treat each row of Y as a point in $\mathbb{R}^K$ and cluster via K-means [21].
- Each point s_i is assigned to a given cluster c if the corresponding row i in Y is assigned to cluster c.

Clearly, the accuracy of the clustering depends, among other factors, on the graph density k and the scale parameter σ. Fig. 1 shows how $k = 3$ and $k = 7$ nearest neighbor graphs with a fixed scale parameter are used to cluster groups of 2D points, two of which define small dense clusters, while the third forms a sparse background. When k is small (Fig. 1(a)), important connections are missing within the background cluster, which is separated into two components. Increasing k helps connect the background cluster (Fig. 1(b)), but adds many redundant edges between clusters that diffuse them and cause the algorithm to misclassify background points. Varying k and σ together may improve the results, though when the point density varies significantly, it may be that no combination of k and σ yields the correct clustering.

To deal with disparate densities, Zelnik-Manor and Perona define a more general affinity that incorporates local scaling [34]. Instead of a single scale parameter, they define the affinity between two points as:

$$A_{ij} = \exp\left(\frac{-d(s_i,s_j)^2}{\sigma_i\sigma_j}\right) \tag{2}$$

where σ_i and σ_j are the local scale parameters estimated for points s_i and s_j, respectively. In the original paper, this parameter is defined as $\sigma_i = d(s_i, s_J^{(i)})$, where $s_J^{(i)}$ is the Jth neighbor of s_i. In practice, it was found that a single setting, $J = 7$, gave acceptable results.

Although local scaling tends to improve the clustering, we found that the quality of the results using this approach still depends on finding the right combination of k and J, and that these choices are dependent on the dimensionality of the domain. Furthermore, as we will discuss in Section 5, a single value of J may not correctly cluster data in the presence of noise or under nonlinear geometric transformations.

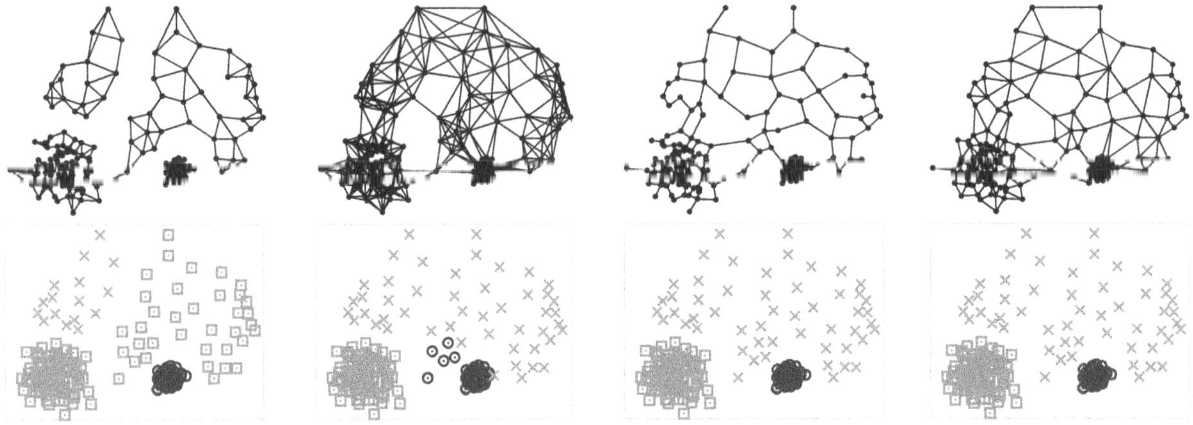

(a) 3NN (b) 7NN (c) 2-Skeleton (d) 1-Skeleton

Figure 1: Proximity graphs and clusters for kNN and the β-skeleton. The sparsity of 3NN disconnects the "background" cluster, while 7NN adds many spurious connections between clusters, leading to poor separation. By constrast, at only 2.5 edges per point, the 2-skeleton generates the correct clustering via a more judicious choice of edges, as does the 1-skeleton using 3.9 edges per point.

3.2 Empty Region Graphs

In addition to graphs based solely on absolute or relative distances between points, a number of alternative proximity graphs have been proposed, such as the relative neighbor graph (RNG) and the Gabriel graph (GG), as surveyed by Jaromczyk et al. [16]. A family of these, known collectively as the *empty region graphs*, are more representative of the neighborhood of a point and less redundant than kNN, and are more efficient to compute than simplicial tessellations such as the Delaunay triangulation, particularly in high dimensions.

Definition 1. A graph $G(S,R) = (S,E)$ is an empty region graph if for every edge $(p,q) \in E$, a canonical region $R(p,q) \subseteq \mathbb{R}^d$ does not contain any other point in S:

$$pq \in E \iff R(p,q) \cap S = \varnothing \quad (3)$$

where R defines the neighborhood and is called the *empty region.*

Some common ERGs are:

Nearest Neighbor Graph (NNG). This is the directed graph that results from the empty region $R(p,q)$ formed by the open d-ball centered on p with radius $d(p,q)$.

$$pq \in E \iff \forall r \in S,\ d(p,r) \geq d(p,q) \quad (4)$$

Relative Neighborhood Graph (RNG). This graph is defined by a lune-shaped region consisting of the intersection of two d-balls of radius $d(p,q)$, one centered on p and the other centered on q, i.e.,

$$pq \in E \iff \forall r \in S,\ \max\{d(p,r),d(q,r)\} \geq d(p,q) \quad (5)$$

Gabriel Graph (GG). This is the graph defined by a d-ball centered at $\frac{1}{2}(p+q)$ with diameter $d(p,q)$, i.e.,

$$pq \in E \iff \forall r \in S,\ \sqrt{d(p,r)^2 + d(q,r)^2} \geq d(p,q) \quad (6)$$

β-Skeleton. The so-called lune-based β-skeleton is a one-parameter generalization of the RNG and GG, defined as follows:

- For $0 < \beta < 1$, the empty region is the intersection of all d-balls with diameter $d(p,q)/\beta$ that have p and q on the boundary.

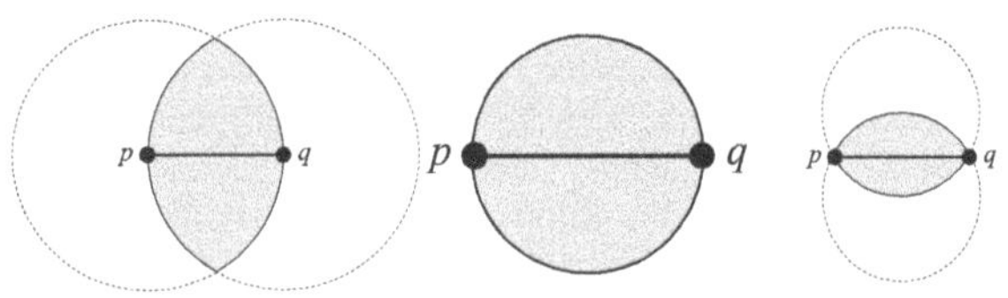

(a) $1 < \beta \leq 2$ (b) $\beta = 1$ (c) $0 < \beta < 1$

Figure 2: Empty regions parameterized by β.

- For $\beta \geq 1$, the empty region is the intersection of two d-balls with diameter $\beta d(p,q)$ centered at $(1-\frac{\beta}{2})p + \frac{\beta}{2}q$ and $\frac{\beta}{2}p + (1-\frac{\beta}{2})q$.

It follows that $\beta = 2$ gives the RNG, while $\beta = 1$ is the GG. Fig. 2 depicts the geometric regions associated with different values of β. Finally, we note that geometric inclusion of one region within another also implies a partial order of the resulting neighborhood graphs (in terms of their edges), so that:

$$RNG \subseteq GG \subseteq (\beta \leq 1)\text{-skeleton} \quad (7)$$

This observation is key, since it allows us to explore neighborhood graphs of varying density using a single parameter, β, without the problems associated with kNN or ε-graphs. Section 5 provides empirical results that suggest that the clustering is far more stable for different values of β than they are for variations in k and σ.

4. APPROACH

We now motivate the use of empty region graphs for representing the neighborhood around a point, and consequently, for shaping the affinity matrix, and describe a general method for its application in spectral clustering.

4.1 Constructing the Neighborhood Graph

As a first step, we construct the β-skeleton of the data points for a given value $\beta \in (0,2]$. As described above, β-skeletons parameterize the neighborhood graph of a collection of points in a different

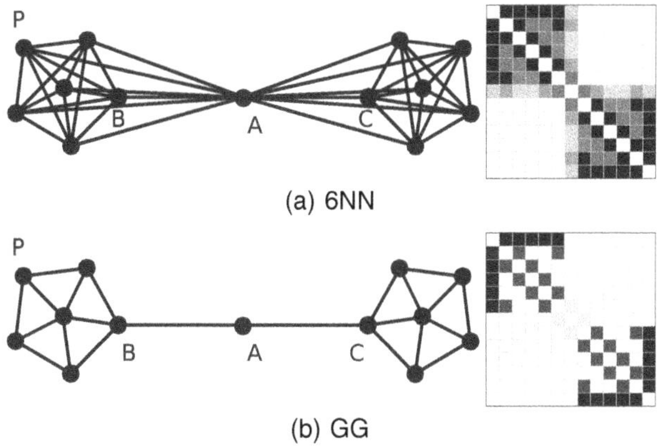

Figure 3: Two proximity graphs and their corresponding affinity matrices (a) 6NN, (b) 1-Skeleton, or Gabriel graph (GG). The bridging node between clusters destroys the block structure of the affinity matrix. While this is pronounced for the 6NN, it only affects two nodes (B and C) for the GG.

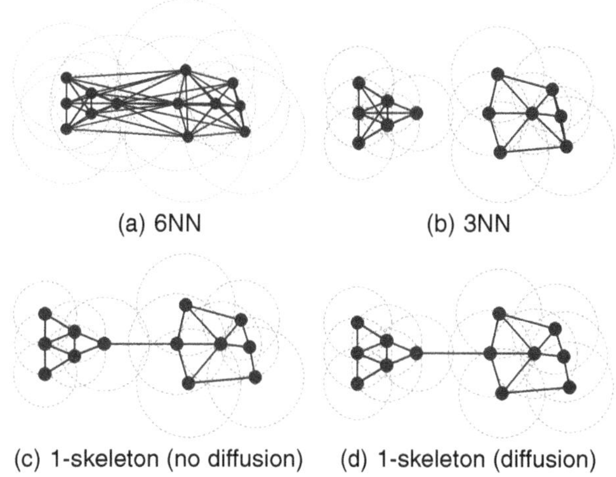

Figure 4: Average distance to neighbors as a measure of local scale. (a) Poor scale estimate due to an overconnected graph. (b) Better scale estimate using a sparser graph. (c) GG further improves the local scale, except for cluster boundary nodes. (d) Diffusion corrects the scale of boundary nodes.

way than kNN does. In this paper we show that those graphs lead to better clustering than kNN graphs.

Graphs such as the k-nearest neighbor graph are susceptible to short circuiting nearby clusters when extra points lie between the clusters. As shown in Fig. 3(a), separating the two clusters is difficult due to the connecting node. In fact, the corresponding affinity matrix is formed by two blocks that overlap, and a large number of off-diagonal elements.

A β-skeleton alleviates this problem, as illustrated in Fig. 3(b). In this case, the connecting node (which may be due to noise or the presence of a smaller cluster) is joined to each cluster via a single edge. In the resulting affinity matrix, there are three blocks, but the off-diagonal elements are confined to the vicinity of point A.

4.2 Local Scaling

Now we show that β-skeletons provide better estimates than kNN of the local scale of a point. This local value defines the scale parameter for the computation of the affinity matrix. Using local scaling allows a pair of points within a high-density cluster to be assigned the same affinity as a pair of points in a low-density cluster when their separation in relation to the local scale is the same.

A natural measure of the local scale around a point include functions of the distance to its neighbors, such as the mean or the median distance. These measures can be brittle in kNN graphs, as suggested by Zelnik and Perona [34], and as studied by Maier et al. [22]. Picking the distance to an arbitrary nearest neighbor may prove more effective, but is sensitive to density changes and noise.

Here, we provide an initial estimate of the local scale using the mean or the median distance to a point's neighbors in an empty region graph. These measures make sense for these graphs since they approximate locally the spatial extents associated with each point. To illustrate this, consider the points in Fig. 4(a), connected in a 6NN graph. The dashed circle associated with each point has a radius equal to the average distance of the point to its neighbors, and can be understood as a representation of the local scale. Naturally, over-connecting the points results in artificially large local scales. The larger the local scale, the higher the affinity is of a point with a neighbor enclosed in its respective dashed circle. In Fig. 4(a), there is a high affinity between the points near the boundary of both clusters. The 3NN graph, in contrast, produces smaller local scales and clearly separates the two clusters (Fig. 4(b)). However, finding the appropriate k parameter for a kNN graph proves difficult. In contrast, the mean distance to the neighbors in the 1-Skeleton is a good estimator of the local scales required to cluster the points accurately, as shown in Fig. 4(c). Note that the local scales for each cluster is roughly the same as in the 3NN, except for the extremes of the edge connecting the two clusters, where the local scale is larger than expected, and one runs the risk of clustering them together.

This behavior, the estimation of larger scales for nodes connected via intercluster edges, is the result of using a β-skeleton, which is *well connected*. One might consider the use of the median distance to exclude outliers and solve the problem, but this technique may fail when the neighborhood graph is sparse A more fundamental problem are small "cliques" of a few close points that are embedded in a larger cluster. Their median neighbor distance may be far smaller than the scale suggested by the surrounding density, resulting in artificially small local scales and poor affinity with the rest of the cluster. To avoid this, one must analyze the local scale by looking not only at the immediate neighbors of a point, but at a possibly larger set.

To address this, we introduce a propagation mechanism based on non-linear diffusion, which improves the estimate of the local scale of a point by querying the scale of its neighbors, similar to reachability in density based clustering [27].

4.3 Diffusion-based Scale Refinement

To deal with the local scale of boundary points, one must ensure that a boundary point has a local scale so that points outside the cluster exhibit less affinity than those within the same cluster. In turn, those neighbors in the same cluster should exhibit affinity with their neighbors, and so on. Thus, the local scale of a point is affected by points that may not be immediate neighbors.

To determine the local scale, we use non-linear diffusion, such that the local density of a point (inverse of the local scale) is iteratively blended with the local densities of its neighboring points. Because shorter edges are likely to correspond to points in the same cluster, we use inverse distance weighted kernels, such as Gaussian or inverse polynomials.

The method works as follows: we start from an estimate of the local scale σ_i^0 of a point s_i as the mean or median distance to its neighbors in the neighborhood graph. We iteratively refine the local scale for some iterations $t \in \{1,\dots,T\}$,

$$\sigma_i^{(t)} = \left(\sum_{j \subset N(s_i) \cup \{s_i\}} \hat{w}_{ij}^{(t-1)} \frac{1}{\sigma_j^{(t-1)}} \right)^{-1} \quad (8)$$

where $N(s_i)$ is the neighborhood of point s_i (using a β-skeleton), and the weights are normalized kernels, defined as the product of two Gaussians $G(d,\rho) = \exp(-d^2/\rho)$,

$$\hat{w}_{ij}^{(t)} = w_{ij}^{(t)} / \sum_k w_{ik}^{(t)} \quad (9)$$

$$w_{ij}^{(t)} = G(d(s_i,s_j),\rho_D) \times G(|\sigma_i^{(t)} - \sigma_j^{(t)}|,\rho_C) \quad (10)$$

The first kernel blends the scales of nearby points, and ensures that intracluster scales are made more uniform than intercluster scales. The parameter ρ_D, called *diffusivity*, controls the speed at which diffusion propagates the local scales in terms of the distance between points. Diffusivity alone, however, makes the scales converge to a uniform value for the entire graph. We then introduce an additional kernel that penalizes the weight when the difference in scale is high, similar to bilateral filtering in image denoising [30]. The parameter ρ_C, or *conductivity*, controls how fast the diffusion propagates along scale discontinuities.

Note that we diffuse the local density instead of the local scales, similar to equivalent kernel density estimators [9], where the reciprocal of the local scale approximates the density of a point. We found this approach more accurate than blending the local scales.

4.3.1 *Parameter Selection*

Our approach, although designed to eliminate the selection of a global parameter k for the number of neighbors or σ for the global scale, requires the selection of different parameters, namely β, which controls the density of the neighborhood graph, and the diffusion parameters, T, ρ_D and ρ_C. Unlike the exploration of k and σ, we have found that parameterizing the graph density via β allows for more resilience to changes in point density, e.g. by limiting the number of intercluster edges. On the other hand, the diffusion parameters are inter-dependent. A large ρ_D may result in convergence to the same solution as a small ρ_D with only a fraction of the number of iterations T. Moreover, these diffusion parameters are similar to those used in kernel density estimation and diffusion in general, and have been well studied [20].

To illustrate the sensitivity of our algorithm to these parameters, we conducted an experiment to find the pair of parameters that yields the best clustering of the data set depicted in Fig. 5(a). We compared five scenarios: (1) Global scaling [26], defined in terms of number of neighbors k and global scale σ, (2) local scaling [34], in terms of number of neighbors k and local scale neighbor J, (3) our local scaling using graphs of different density via the parameter β, (4) our diffusion approach for a fixed $\beta = 1$ and $\rho_C = 1$, in terms of diffusivity ρ_D and number of iterations T, and (5) our non-linear diffusion approach, in terms of the diffusivity and conductivity parameters, while keeping a constant number of iterations $T = 10$. Fig. 5 shows the results for this experiment, depicted as surfaces of the normalized mutual information (NMI)—higher is better—for a discretization of their respective parameters. Global scaling is, not surprisingly, the most sensitive approach, and the optimal clustering is only achieved within a narrow interval of values. Local scaling in this case exhibits optimality for a fixed interval of the local scale. However, overshooting this interval produces drastically sub-optimal results. In contrast, exploring the graph density using β instead of k exhibits little sensitivity for $\beta > 0.7$. The same can be said about the diffusion parameters. Typically, we set ρ_D

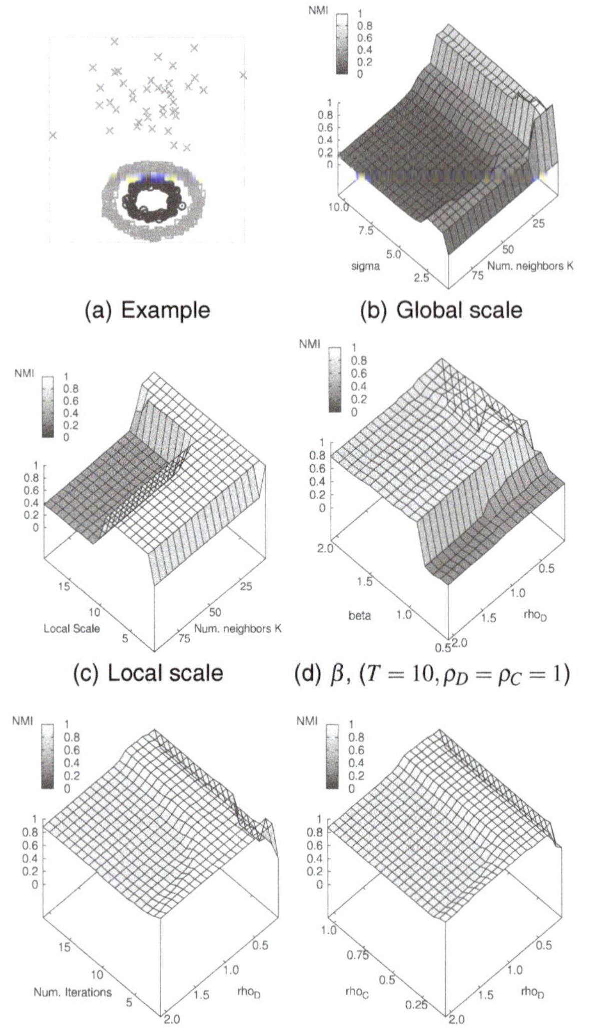

(a) Example (b) Global scale

(c) Local scale (d) β, $(T = 10, \rho_D = \rho_C = 1)$

(e) Diffusion,$(\rho_C = 1, \beta = 1)$ (f) Conductivity $(T = 10, \beta = 1)$

Figure 5: Sensitivity of clustering to various sets of parameters.

and ρ_C to 1. We believe bandwidth selection algorithms for kernel density estimation can be used towards improving these initial estimates [9].

4.4 Constructing the Affinity Matrix

Finally, once we determine the local scale associated with each point, we construct the affinity matrix as

$$A_{ij} = \begin{cases} \exp\left(\frac{-d(s_i,s_j)^2}{\sigma_i^{(T)}\sigma_j^{(T)}}\right) & (i,j) \in G(S,R(\beta)) \\ 0 & \text{otherwise} \end{cases} \quad (11)$$

where $R(\beta)$ is an empty region template, parameterized by β. Algorithm 1 summarizes the full algorithm.

4.5 Complexity and Time Analysis

We now describe the computational cost of the key steps in our algorithm.

Construction of ERG. Constructing an ERG can be expensive. A brute-force implementation requires $O(n^3)$ time, which is prohibitively expensive for most practical applications. How-

Algorithm 1: New algorithm for spectral clustering using empty region graphs.

```
input  : Data points S = {s_1, ..., s_n}, number of clusters K,
         number of iterations T, diffusion parameters ρ_D, ρ_C
output: Classification C
G ← ERG(S)                                    Construct ERG
for i ← 1 to n do
    N_i ← NEIGHBORS(G, s_i)
    σ_i^(0) ← LOCALSCALE(s_i, N_i)            Estimate initial local scale
for t ← 1 to T do
    for i ← 1 to n do
        N_i ← NEIGHBORS(G, s_i)
        Σ_i ← {σ_i^(t−1)}
        for j ∈ N_i do
            Σ_i ← Σ_i ∪ {σ_j^(t−1)}
        σ_i^(t) ← DIFFUSE(Σ_i, ρ_D, ρ_C)      Update local scale
A ← AFFINITY({s_i}, {σ_i})                    Compute affinity matrix
C ← SPECTRALCLUSTER(A)                        Cluster using Laplacian of A [26]
```

ever, there are known algorithms that compute the RNG and GG in $O(n^2)$ time [31, 24].

We further reduce the computation cost of obtaining an ERG by restricting the neighbor search to the k_{max} nearest neighbors of a point, where k_{max} is usually a constant factor larger than the k value selected for k nearest neighbor graphs, but $k_{max} \ll n$. The overall complexity of computing such a kNN graph is

$$O(n^2 \log k_{max}),$$

and the additional cost of computing an ERG becomes

$$O(nk_{max}^2) \text{ time.}$$

Diffusion. The diffusion process involves a sequential walk on the neighborhood graph and requires $O(|E|T)$ time, where T is the number of iterations and $|E| \leq nk_{max}$ is the number of edges in the graph.

Solution of Eigenvector Problem. In general, computing the eigenvectors of the Laplacian matrix takes $O(n^3)$ time, but, as described by Song et al. [29], sparse eigensolvers, such as the variants of Lanczos/Arnoldi factorization (e.g., ARPACK), have a cost of

$$O(m^3) + (O(nm) + O(nk_{max}) + O(m-K)) \times (\text{\# restarted Arnoldi})$$

where $m > K$ is the Arnoldi length used to compute the first K eigenvectors of the affinity matrix.

Clustering the spectrum. Finally, using K-means to cluster the eigenvectors has a cost of $O(nK) \times$ (# K-means iterations).

Overall, as suggested by Song et al. [29], as the data size grows larger, the cost of the clustering becomes dependent on the construction of the affinity matrix. Nonetheless, the additional cost of computing an ERG instead of a kNN is relatively small. According to our results, this marginal increase is well worth the benefits of using the β-skeleton instead of k-nearest neighbors.

5. RESULTS

We have validated our algorithm with a number of low dimensional synthetic data sets and a few (higher-dimensional) real classification problems. To compare the quality of these datasets, we measure the normalized mutual information (NMI) between the clustering X and the ground truth classification Y:

$$NMI(X;Y) = \frac{2I(X;Y)}{H(X)+H(Y)} \tag{12}$$

where $I(X;Y)$ is the mutual information between X and Y and $H(X)$ and $H(Y)$ are their entropies, respectively.

5.1 Sensitivity to Transformations

To illustrate the benefits of using the β-skeleton, we analyzed the results of our algorithm compared to traditional approaches using k-Nearest Neighbors (kNN) when applied to transformations of a synthetic data set. We compare three types of transformations: geometric distortion (shear transformation), decimation (where we remove $0.05Dn$ points, for a decimation factor $D \in \{1, \ldots, 10\}$, and noise (where we perturb the data with Gaussian noise of increasing standard deviation). Fig. 6(a) compares the result of clustering a 2D data set consisting of three concentric rings under these three transformations. Fig. 6(b) shows quality surfaces for the different transformations and different values of the main parameters for our method (β and T) vs. the number of neighbors J used to define the local scale in kNN-based methods (as a reference, Zelnik and Perona's method uses $J = 7$). The quality of the clustering increases as the color of the surface approaches yellow. Notice how the optimal value for kNN methods (bottom) varies depending on the degree of distortion, decimation or noise. For our method, the quality converges as we increase the number of iterations and is less sensitive to the transformation itself.

A similar analysis was performed for other data sets, as shown in Fig. 7. Here, we show the mean, minimum and maximum quality for different values of β using our approach (blue), and for different values of k (global scale—green) and J (local scale—red) for kNN methods. In general, we observed a higher quality for empty region graphs and a lower variance when compared to globally-scaled clustering. Particularly for the first two rows, our approach is also better than locally-scaled clustering based on kNN. Note an important exception, the fourth row, consisting of small clusters surrounded by a random noisy background. β-skeletons do not cluster data as well on this data set, and in other similar cases. Locally-scaled kNN based methods are able to segment these because a small number of neighbors is able to keep them disconnected, while ERGs are always well-connected.

5.2 UCI Benchmarks

We validated our approach on multi-dimensional data sets from synthetic generators and the UCI Machine Learning repository [13]. The results are summarized in Table 1. We compare our approach using the β-skeleton (the parameter β chosen and number of iterations are reported next to each, for $\rho_D = 0.1$ and $\rho_C = 1$) with conventional clustering using kNN and (1) global scaling, (2) local scaling [34], and (3) DBSCAN, a density-based approach [27]. In all these cases, we report the best results obtained after exhaustively exploring their key parameters (k and σ for global-kNN and DBSCAN, k for local-kNN and β and T for ours). As seen in the table, it was possible to find a suitable neighborhood graph using the β parameter that produces better results than exhaustive search of the parameters of other conventional algorithms. Although the density of the graph increases with the number of dimensions, the exploration of the β parameter allows us to get the necessary density to cluster the higher-dimensional data sets. Similar to the results in Fig. 7, we also observed that quality is less sensitive to β than to values of K.

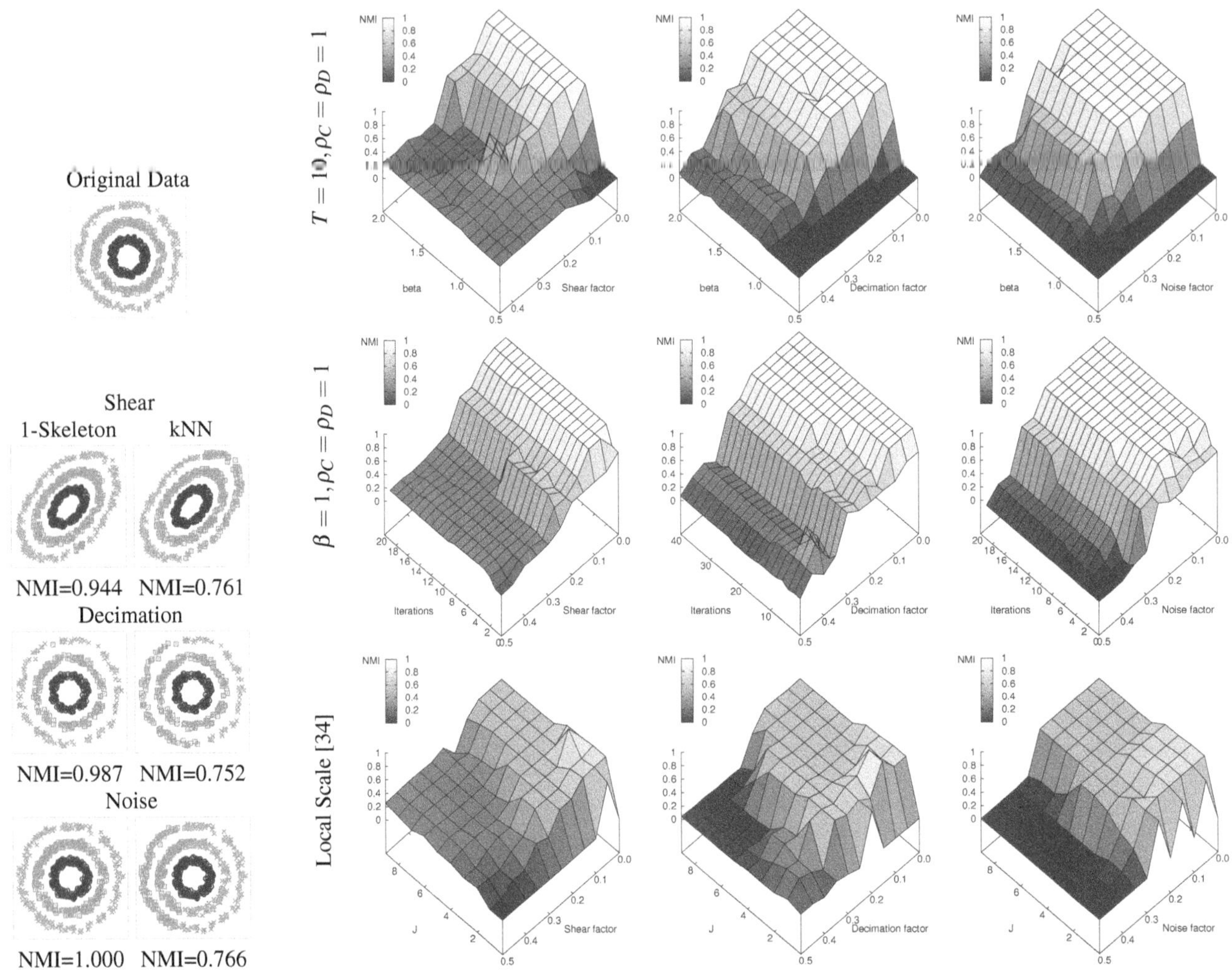

(a) Example data set

(b) Clustering quality as a function of transformation severity and algorithm parameter

Figure 6: (a) Results of clustering data undergoing transformations (geometric distortion, decimation and noise). (b) Clustering quality in terms of the transformation severity and algorithm parameter. From top to bottom: β and T in our algorithm, and the local scale given by J in [34].

5.3 Image Segmentation

Finally, we applied our method to image segmentation, where each pixel is defines a five dimensional point of its pixel coordinates x and y, and the color intensities in the $L^*u^*v^*$ color space. In all these results, the number of clusters is picked manually. Fig. 8 shows three examples from the Berkeley Segmentation Dataset and Benchmark [23]. Note how ERG based methods produce visually better clusters, while methods such as local scaling result in over-segmentation. Notably, Fig. 8(c) demonstrates the importance of good neighborhood graphs for local scaling. Attempting to separate this image into two segments proves difficult with a global scale using kNN, and users must resort to over-segmentation (4 clusters instead of 2). In our case (leftmost panels), the Gabriel graph is able to segment the airplane using both 2 and 4 clusters.

6. SUMMARY AND CONCLUSION

A fundamental problem in clustering is defining a neighborhood graph that defines how similar two data points are. This paper introduces a more natural parameterization of the neighborhood density based on the β-skeleton. We showed that using β to define the affinity between points provides higher quality than the prevalent approach of picking k nearest neighbors or finding a global scale parameter. We have also shown that our clustering results are far less sensitive to the choice of β and the diffusion parameters (diffusivity and conductivity), and to data transformations such as perturbations and geometric distortion.

Our diffusion-based local scaling approach proves effective for clustering irregular data sets and estimating the correct local scale at each point, despite the fact that the empty region graphs we explore (supersets of the relative neighbor graph), are well-connected. We must point out that we introduce additional parameters to tune the diffusion mechanism, but these are well known in other domains where diffusion is applied, and there are methods for choosing them. From a practical standpoint, one can define heuristics to explore the parameter space efficiently. As a rule of thumb, one defines the diffusivity parameter as the smallest scale one wants to preserve in the data set, if that information is known, for example,

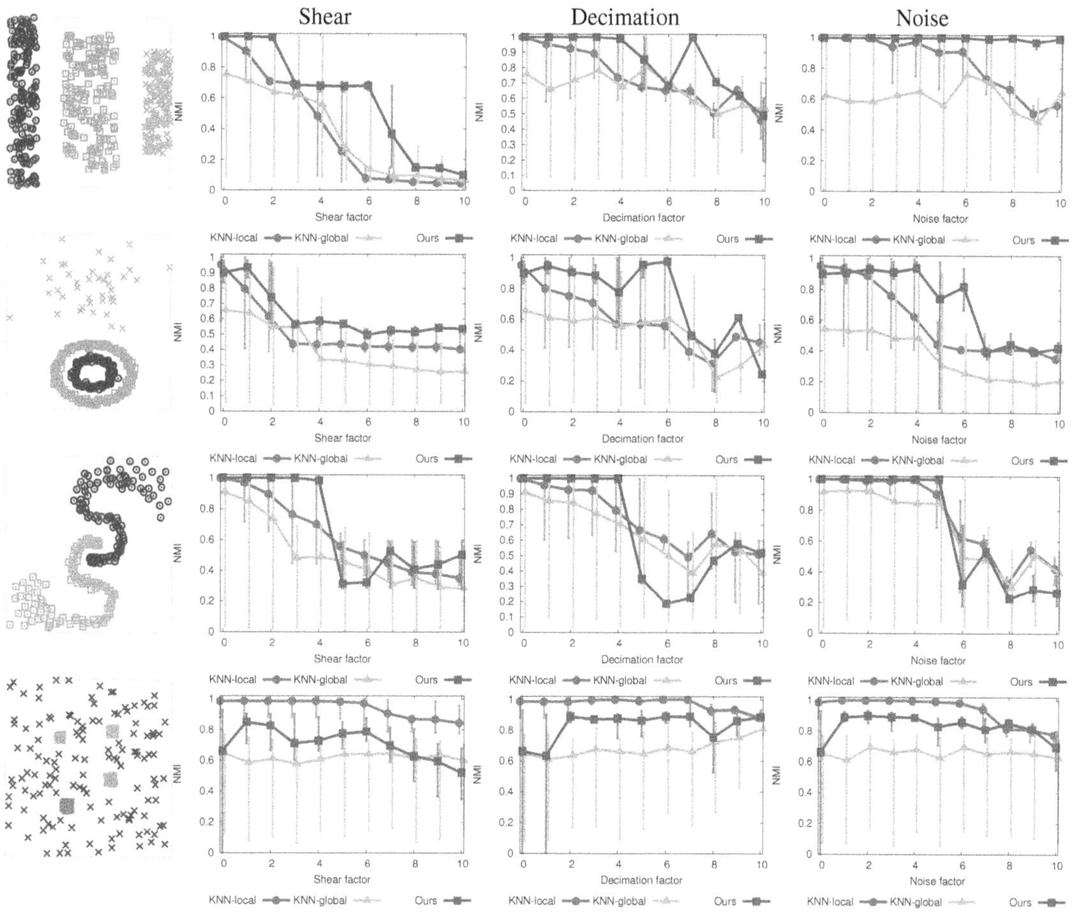

Figure 7: Average clustering quality (NMI – higher is better) of various 2D data sets as a function of transformation severity for our algorithm (blue), globally- (green) and locally-scaled (red) clustering based on kNN. Each curve shows the mean, maximum and minimum NMI while varying $\beta \in [0.8, 2.0]$ (blue), $k \in [2, 20]$ (green) or local scale $J \in [1, 20]$ (red). The β-skeleton provides higher quality than global scaling, and far less variance. Compared to local scaling, our algorithm performed better except in the last row.

when interested in the presence (or absence) of data features of a given size (e.g., in medical image segmentation).

In our experiments, we often apply the 1-Skeleton as an initial candidate for generating the affinity matrix. Over-segmentation may be an indication that the graph is too sparse and one might explore other graphs with $\beta < 1$. Conversely, when one suspects that the result is under-segmented, one may explore sparse graphs, with $1 < \beta \leq 2$. Our approach can be extended in a number of ways to retrieve the number of clusters automatically, as suggested by approaches like [34, 1]. We believe our approach, proving to be resilient to noise and other types of data perturbations, is a step forward towards robust spectral clustering, and may have broader applications where a neighborhood graph is required.

Acknowledgements

Prepared by LLNL under Contract DE-AC52-07NA27344. LLNL-CONF-513768.

7. REFERENCES

[1] E. Biçici and D. Yuret. Locally scaled density based clustering. In *Proc. 8th int. conf. on Adaptive and Natural Computing Algorithms, Part I*, ICANNGA '07, pages 739–748, 2007.

[2] P. Bose, S. Collette, S. Langerman, A. Maheshwari, P. Morin, and M. Smid. Sigma-local graphs. *J. of Discrete Algorithms*, 8:15–23, 2010.

[3] J. Cardinal, S. Collette, and S. Langerman. Empty region graphs. *Comput. Geom. Theory Appl.*, 42:183–195, 2009.

[4] M. A. Carreira-Perpiñán and R. S. Zemel. Proximity graphs for clustering and manifold learning. In *Advances in Neural Information Processing Systems*, pages 225–232. MIT Press, 2005.

[5] J. Choo, R. Jiamthapthaksin, C.-S. Chen, O. U. Celepcikay, C. Giusti, and C. F. Eick. Mosaic: A proximity graph approach for agglomerative clustering. In *DaWaK*, volume 4654 of *Lecture Notes in Computer Science*, pages 231–240. Springer, 2007.

[6] R. J. Cimikowski. Properties of some euclidean proximity graphs. *Pattern Recogn. Lett.*, 13:417–423, 1992.

[7] I. S. Dhillon. Co-clustering documents and words using bipartite spectral graph partitioning. In *Proc. of ACM SIGKDD int. conf. on Knowledge discovery and data mining*, pages 269–274, 2001.

[8] W. Donath and A. Hoffman. Lower bounds for partitioning of graphs. *IBM J. Res. Dev.*, 17:420–425, 1973.

[9] V. A. Epanechnikov. Non-parametric estimation of a multivariate probability density. *Theory of Probability and Its Applications*, 14, 1969.

[10] M. Ester, H. peter Kriegel, J. Sander, and X. Xu. A density-based algorithm for discovering clusters in large spatial databases with noise. In *Knowledge Discovery and Data Mining*, pages 226–231, 1996.

[11] M. Fiedler. Algebraic connectivity of graphs. *Czechoslovak Mathematical Journal*, 1973.

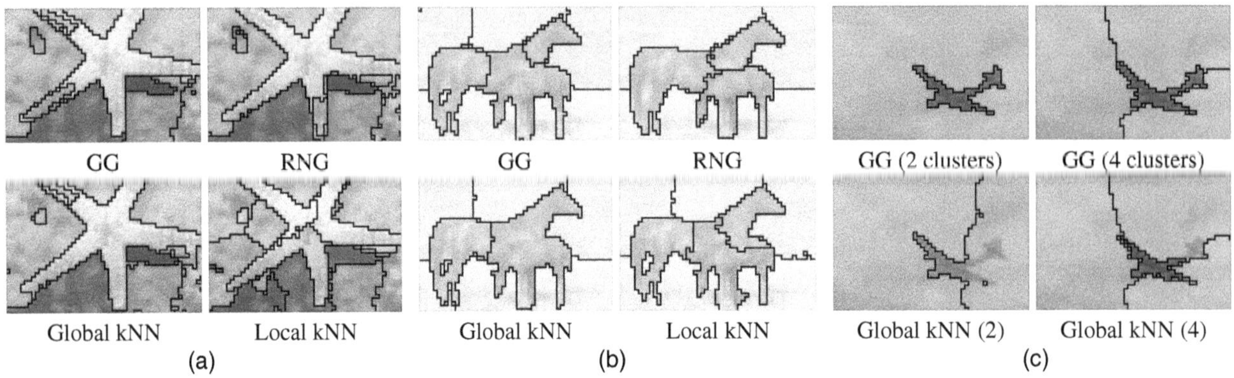

Figure 8: Image Segmentation in $L^*u^*v^*$. ERG based methods are able to adapt to local densities and produce better segmentations. In (c), finding the appropriate k and σ proves difficult for background-foreground segmentation and the user resorts to over-segmentation. In contrast, our approach produces good clusters even for over- segmented cases.

Table 1: Summary of experiments on multi-dimensional data.

Data set	Dimensions	Num. Clusters	Ours (β, T)	Global (kNN)	Local (kNN)	DBSCAN
Gaussians	3	3	**0.982** (1.0, 1)	0.822	**0.982** (J=7)	**0.982**
Noisy Rings	3	2	**1.000** (2.0, 5)	0.983	0.910	0.957
Ellipsoids	3	3	**0.975** (1.0, 20)	0.958	0.960	0.670
Iris	4	3	**0.843** (1.5, 2)	0.833	0.790	0.731
Ellipsoids5D	5	5	**0.816** (1.5, 70)	0.728	0.746	0.537
Auto-mpg	5	5	**0.713** (1.9, 2)	0.648	0.635	0.471
E.coli	7	8	**0.675** (1.0, 42)	0.671	0.620	0.437
Breast	9	2	**0.782** (1.7,8)	0.741	0.735	0.695
Glass	9	6	**0.466** (0.99,8)	0.355	0.366	0.459
Wine	13	3	**0.947** (1.9, 46)	0.938	0.866	0.527

[12] S. Fortune. Voronoi diagrams and delaunay triangulations. In J. E. Goodman and J. O'Rourke, editors, *Handbook of discrete and computational geometry*, pages 377–388. 1997.

[13] A. Frank and A. Asuncion. UCI machine learning repository, 2010.

[14] R. K. Gabriel and R. R. Sokal. A new statistical approach to geographic variation analysis. *Systematic Zoology*, 18(3):259–278, 1969.

[15] L. Huang, D. Yan, M. I. Jordan, and N. Taft. Spectral clustering with perturbed data. In *Neural Information Processing Systems*, pages 705–712, 2008.

[16] J. Jaromczyk and G. Toussaint. Relative neighborhood graphs and their relatives. *Proc. of the IEEE*, 80(9):1502 –1517, 1992.

[17] R. Kannan, S. Vempala, and A. Vetta. On clusterings: Good, bad and spectral. *J. The ACM*, 51:497–515, 2004.

[18] D. Kirkpatrick and J. Radke. A framework for computational morphology. *CG*, 85:217–248, 1985.

[19] Z. Li, J. Liu, S. Chen, and X. Tang. Noise robust spectral clustering. In *IEEE int. conf. on Computer Vision, 2007*, pages 1 –8, 2007.

[20] T. Lindeberg. *Scale-Space Theory in Computer Vision*. Kluwer Academic Publishers, 1994.

[21] J. B. MacQueen. Some methods for classification and analysis of multivariate observations. In L. M. L. Cam and J. Neyman, editors, *Proc. of the 5th Berkeley Symp. on Mathematical Statistics and Probability*, volume 1, pages 281–297, 1967.

[22] M. Maier, U. von Luxburg, and M. Hein. How the result of graph clustering methods depends on the construction of the graph. *CoRR*, abs/1102.2075, 2011. informal publication.

[23] D. Martin, C. Fowlkes, D. Tal, and J. Malik. A database of human segmented natural images and its application to evaluating segmentation algorithms and measuring ecological statistics. In *Proc. 8th Int'l Conf. Computer Vision*, volume 2, pages 416–423, July 2001.

[24] D. L. Millman and V. Verma. A slow algorithm for computing the gabriel graph with double precision. In *Proc. of the 23nd Canadian Conf. on Computational Geometry*, pages 485–487, 2011.

[25] B. Nadler and M. Galun. Fundamental limitations of spectral clustering. In *Neural Information Processing Systems*, pages 1017–1024, 2006.

[26] A. Y. Ng, M. I. Jordan, and Y. Weiss. On spectral clustering: Analysis and an algorithm. In *Advances in Neural Information Processing Systems*, pages 849–856. MIT Press, 2001.

[27] J. Sander, M. Ester, H.-P. Kriegel, and X. Xu. Density-based clustering in spatial databases: The algorithm gdbscan and its applications. *Data Min. Knowl. Discov.*, 2:169–194, 1998.

[28] J. Shi and J. Malik. Normalized cuts and image segmentation. *IEEE Transactions on Pattern Analysis and Machine Intelligence*, 22(8):888 – 905, 2000.

[29] Y. Song, W.-Y. Chen, H. Bai, C.-J. Lin, and E. Y. Chang. Parallel spectral clustering. In *ECML PKDD '08*, pages 374–389, 2008.

[30] C. Tomasi and R. Manduchi. Bilateral filtering for gray and color images. In *Proc. of the Sixth int. conf. on Computer Vision*, ICCV '98, pages 839–, 1998.

[31] G. T. Toussaint. The relative neighbourhood graph of a finite planar set. *Pattern Recognition*, 12:261–268, 1980.

[32] R. Urquhart. Graph theoretical clustering based on limited neighbourhood sets. *Pattern Recognition*, 15(3):173 – 187, 1982.

[33] U. von Luxburg, M. Belkin, and O. Bousquet. Consistency of spectral clustering. *Annals of Statistics*, 36:555–586, 2008.

[34] L. Zelnik-Manor and P. Perona. Self-tuning spectral clustering. In *NIPS*, 2004.

Active Spectral Clustering via Iterative Uncertainty Reduction

Fabian L. Wauthier
Computer Science Division
UC Berkeley
Berkeley, CA-94720
flw@cs.berkeley.edu

Nebojsa Jojic
Microsoft Research
Redmond, WA-98052
jojic@microsoft.com

Michael I. Jordan
Computer Science Division
UC Berkeley
Berkeley, CA-94720
jordan@cs.berkeley.edu

ABSTRACT

Spectral clustering is a widely used method for organizing data that only relies on pairwise similarity measurements. This makes its application to non-vectorial data straightforward in principle, as long as all pairwise similarities are available. However, in recent years, numerous examples have emerged in which the cost of assessing similarities is substantial or prohibitive. We propose an active learning algorithm for spectral clustering that incrementally measures only those similarities that are most likely to remove uncertainty in an intermediate clustering solution. In many applications, similarities are not only costly to compute, but also noisy. We extend our algorithm to maintain running estimates of the true similarities, as well as estimates of their accuracy. Using this information, the algorithm updates only those estimates which are relatively inaccurate and whose update would most likely remove clustering uncertainty. We compare our methods on several datasets, including a realistic example where similarities are expensive and noisy. The results show a significant improvement in performance compared to the alternatives.

Categories and Subject Descriptors

H.3.3 [**Information Search and Retrieval**]: Information Search and Retrieval; I.5.3 [**Pattern Recognition**]: Clustering

General Terms

Algorithms

Keywords

Spectral Clustering, Active Learning

1. INTRODUCTION

Clustering is a fundamental problem involving summarizing, indexing and classifying various types of data. As data sets become larger and more complex, algorithms that depend on pairwise similarities—rather than fixed length feature vector representations—are growing increasingly popular. An important example is spectral clustering, which partitions data through a spectral analysis of the Laplacian matrix induced by the similarity graph.

Although methods based on pairwise similarities are growing in popularity, a practical difficulty is that pairwise similarities can be expensive to acquire, be it due to computational requirements, need for human input, or lack of observability. In protein clustering, for example, a computationally expensive alignment process may be necessary before two proteins can be compared. Other examples in computational biology require a combinatorial search for each pairwise similarity, even when the datapoint can be represented in a compact form (a protein sequence is usually less than 1000 letters long). A counterpart to these computational issues is that often the only practical way to obtain similarities is to query human annotators. Here, measurements are not only expensive, but frequently also noisy. In this paper we consider the task of organizing a stream of snapshots taken by a wearable camera at a rate of about one photo per 20 seconds [12]. Clustering these snapshots is beyond the capabilities of existing computer vision algorithms, so human guidance is necessary to either cluster the images, or learn improved models to do the clustering for us. As the human subject (e.g., an Alzheimer's patient), wears the camera during an open-ended observation period, it is not clear a priori what the clusters should be. A way to tackle this problem is to ask human annotators to rate how similar any two photos are and then to cluster using this data. (For example, photos may be deemed similar if they were taken in similar locations.) This is one of many examples where crowdsourcing, albeit expensive, can be used to collect pairwise similarity measurements. As a final example, in some situations the objects that are being compared can disappear over time, making retrospective comparisons difficult. Consider viral strains, which, if not preserved in a laboratory, may disappear, leaving behind only indirect assessments with other viruses. While similarities among preserved viruses can be acquired at a relatively high cost in the lab (e.g., crossreactivity of the immune responses), similarities involving the extinct strain are not available at any cost. In addition to this time barrier, geographic, legal and policy barriers can also make certain pairwise similarities inaccessible. All these examples illustrate that similarities may be noisy and arbitrarily expensive to compute, to the extreme where certain similarities are completely unavailable.

KDD'12, August 12–16, 2012, Beijing, China.
Copyright 2012 ACM 978-1-4503-1462-6 /12/08 ...$15.00.

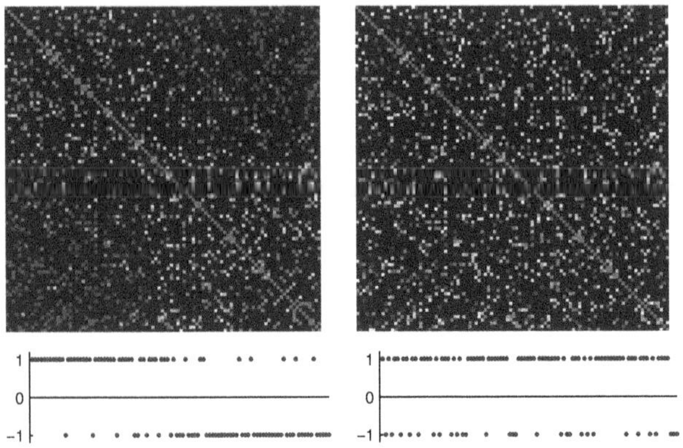

Figure 1: Two incomplete similarity matrices. The left was constructed from median image similarities, measured using Amazon Mechanical Turk (see Section 6.3). We permuted the rows and columns so that any clusters would become visible as diagonal blocks. Then we set 82% of the similarities to 0 (black regions). The right matrix was constructed similarly, but starting from similarities sampled uniformly in $[0, 1]$. The left matrix still shows clustering structure, which is also visible in the sign vector of the second Laplacian eigenvector, plotted below (see Sections 3 and 4 for details). The right matrix had almost no structure to start with, so no structure is visible in the corresponding eigenvector.

The potentially significant cost of obtaining pairwise similarities motivates the search for tradeoffs between desired clustering quality and the required amount of data. In this paper, we study this question in the setting of the spectral clustering of n objects when we do not have access to all pairwise measurements initially, but we can iteratively query the similarities from an external black-box procedure (which may impose restrictions on which of the subset of all $n(n-1)/2$ similarities can be queried). In this active learning formulation the goal is to find a good approximation to the true clustering based on as few similarity evaluations as possible, thus reducing the overall cost (i.e. compute cycles, human tasks performed, laboratory material and other data collection expenses).

A recent contribution in this direction has been made by Shamir and Tishby [18]. Their approach was designed for querying arbitrary similarity matrices, including those where no clustering structure is apparent. This paper significantly improves on their method by exploiting the fact that most realistic pairwise similarity matrices, even if incomplete, do exhibit clustering structure. Consider Figure 1, where on the left we show an incomplete matrix that we might realistically encounter and on the right a matrix constructed from random similarities. Shamir and Tishby assume no structure in the matrix (such as in the matrix on the right) and query measurements that maximally change the overall clustering solution. In contrast, we tailor our active learning algorithm to work well with *realistic* matrices (such as the one on the left) where information about the true clustering emerges quickly and can be leveraged to guide an improved query selection strategy.

An aspect of spectral clustering that is commonly ignored is that similarity measurements are generally noisy. Active spectral clustering methods have so far not taken these uncertainties into account. We extend our algorithm in this direction to allow repeat measurements of noisy similarities, and use these to compute running estimates of the true similarities, as well as estimates of their accuracy. Using this information, we extend our algorithm to measure that similarity which is relatively inaccurate and whose update would most likely remove clustering uncertainty.

The paper is organized as follows. In Section 2 we review related research. Section 3 presents some background on spectral clustering. Next, we describe our active learning algorithm in Section 4. In Section 5 we extend the algorithm to take measurement noise into account. We present experiments on synthetic and real datasets in Section 6 and conclude with final remarks in Section 7.

2. RELATED RESEARCH

Spectral Clustering.

Spectral clustering was popularized in the machine learning community by Shi and Malik [20] and shortly afterwards revisited by Ng, Jordan and Weiss [14]. Since then, it has permeated the literature and become a firm part of the practitioner's toolbox. Over the years, numerous connections to other research fields have been made, a comprehensive review of which can be found in [24]. However, very little work in the spectral clustering literature has explicitly investigated situations when only a subset of all similarities is known, possibly contaminated by noise.

Matrix Completion.

One simple approach to adapting spectral clustering to the case of missing similarities is to exploit the burgeoning literature on matrix completion methods. A particularly straightforward approach is to impute a constant value (e.g., zero) for the missing similarities. Such approaches are often used in practice, and some of its properties have been analyzed theoretically [18].

More sophisticated methods can be deployed under the assumption that entire rows or columns of the similarity matrix can be measured. The driving assumption behind these methods is that the true matrix is of low rank, so that a small subset of elements approximately captures the global matrix structure. Among these approaches, the Nyström method [6, 26] is perhaps the most well known. Other algorithms that use row/column sampling include for instance [4, 5, 9]. Applications of some of these methods to spectral clustering are given in [7, 17]. In less controlled situations, we do not have access to entire rows/columns of measurements, but only an arbitrary subset; in this setting it is still possible to exploit a low-rank assumption for matrix completion [1, 22]. There is debate about the value of these methods in the spectral clustering setting; in particular, Shamir and Tishby [18] argued that the low rank assumptions can be unrealistic in many spectral clustering applications and demonstrated that the Nyström method often performs poorly. Additionally, most of the row/column sampling methods require that the sampling distribution depends on the entire similarity matrix [4, 5, 6, 9]. Because this matrix is unknown, these methods are of limited applicapability in our setting. Finally, we highlight that with the exception of Huang et al. [11], relatively little work has been done on analyzing the influence of incomplete or perturbed similarity matrices on the spectral clustering solution.

Active Learning.

Until recently, the study of active learning for spectral clustering was restricted to settings where the entire similarity matrix is known (perhaps approximately) and an external oracle can be repeatedly queried for additional *linkage constraints* between objects (of the form *must-link* or *cannot-link*). When the similarity matrix only approximately captures the desired clustering, adding such constraints iteratively can help resolve ambiguous boundary cases. Relevant examples include [2, 13, 25, 27]. We note in particular the work of Xu et al. [27], in which the constraints are absorbed by modifying the similarity matrix in a way that is akin to measuring similarities of higher quality. The focus in active learning for spectral clustering has only recently shifted to scenarios in which explicit costs are imposed on the measurement of similarities. This focus is exemplified by Shamir and Tishby [18], who propose and analyze an active learning method based on matrix perturbation theory [21].

3. SPECTRAL CLUSTERING

We begin by presenting our notation and summarizing the key ideas of spectral clustering. For further details and various interpretations of spectral clustering we refer the reader to von Luxburg [24]. Given n objects, denote by W the $n \times n$ symmetric matrix of pairwise similarities among these objects. Typically, $0 \leq w_{ij} \leq 1, i, j = 1, \ldots, n$ and $w_{ii} = 1, i = 1, \ldots, n$. Let $D = \mathrm{diag}(W\mathbf{1})$ be the diagonal matrix of row sums of W. The *unnormalized Laplacian matrix* is then given by

$$L = D - W. \tag{1}$$

Spectral clustering partitions the n objects into two groups by thresholding the second eigenvector v_2 of L. Specifically, if we let the partition be encoded by variables $c_i \in \{-1, +1\}, i = 1, \ldots, n$, then

$$c_i = 2\,[v_2(i) > 0] - 1. \tag{2}$$

Here, we use the notation $v_2(i)$ to indicate the ith component of the vector v_2. Because the partitioning is trivial to compute from the second eigenvector, we will occasionally refer to the eigenvector itself as the spectral clustering solution, rather than the partitioning.

Spectral clustering only sees the data as filtered through the matrix W. Thus it is possible to adapt the spectral approach to the clustering of non-vectorial data such as graphs, sequences and sets; it suffices that similarity scores can be computed for these objects. This is generally accomplished via a kernel function, and computationally efficient kernels are available for certain kinds of structured objects [10, 19]. Unfortunately, however, kernel formulations are often too rigid to be adapted to specific needs, and often lack interpretability. As we move to more complex datasets, the notion of similarity a practitioner is interested in may not be captured by a kernel. Indeed, as highlighted in the Introduction, in many practical examples the similarities cannot be evaluated by a computer at all, but must be provided by an experiment or human annotator.

4. ACTIVE LEARNING

In this section we propose an active learning strategy that attempts to alleviate the above issues. Our work is based on a matrix perturbation argument for an intermediate estimate of the Laplacian matrix. Given incomplete measurements, we estimate the true Laplacian matrix as

$$\hat{L} = \hat{D} - \hat{W}, \tag{3}$$

where $\hat{W}$ is the matrix of all pairwise measurements with zero imputed for unknown entries, and $\hat{D} = \mathrm{diag}(\hat{W}\mathbf{1})$. The motivation for imputation with zero can be seen by rewriting the spectral clustering problem. The second eigenvector of the Laplacian $\hat{L}$ can be found as

$$\hat{v}_2 = \mathrm{argmin}_v v^\top \hat{L} v = \mathrm{argmin}_v \sum_{ij} \hat{w}_{ij}(v(i) - v(j))^2 \tag{4}$$

$$\text{s.t.} \quad v^\top v = 1 \tag{5}$$

$$v^\top \mathbf{1} = 0. \tag{6}$$

Thus, similarities act as weights on soft constraints between eigenvector components. By imputing zero for missing similarities we merely ignore those constraints which are not supported by a measurement.

For any set of similarities $\hat{W}$, the second eigenvector $\hat{v}_2$ gives the best guess for an embedding of the objects on the line. The embedding is such that two groups of similar objects are embedded away from zero, on the negative or positive orthant, respectively. Any objects that are approximately equally similar to all remaining objects are embedded near zero. This is intuitive, for these are the objects that cannot clearly be assigned to either of the two groups. Indeed, since a mean can be found by minimizing a mean squared error, we see from Eq. (4) that an object i with approximately constant similarities $\hat{w}_{ij}$ to remaining objects j should be embedded near the average of their embedding locations $\hat{v}_2(j)$. On the other hand, if the data actually clusters well and is reasonably balanced, then we expect the second eigenvector v_2 of the true Laplacian L to have elements with magnitude on the order of $1/\sqrt{n}$, since $v_2^\top v_2 = 1$. In this way, the elements of most realistic embeddings v_2 should be expected to be bounded away from zero. Spectral clustering based on incomplete data $\hat{W}$ partitions the objects by looking at the signs of the embedding $\hat{v}_2$ (Eq. (2), with threshold at zero). Consequently, objects which are embedded near zero are the objects about whose cluster label we should be most "uncertain" about.

In many practical cases, a relatively small amount of data suffices so that $\hat{v}_2$ already indicates a useful clustering. The left sign vector shown in Figure 1 demonstrates this on a real dataset. We use such partial information as a guide towards measurements that more quickly reveal the true nature of the clustering. In this approach, our earlier intuition about the magnitude of $\hat{v}_2$ components plays a crucial role. More specifically, our active learning strategy uses matrix perturbation theory to reveal that entry of $\hat{W}$ for which a constant perturbation would change the *minimum magnitude element* of $\hat{v}_2$ the most. The rationale is that by focussing on small magnitude components, we more quickly move them away from the cluster boundary (i.e. 0), and thus reduce uncertainty in the partial clustering. In effect, we try to choose measurements that help us push the embedding clusters further apart. If the data actually clusters well, this should quickly guide us to the clean clustering we expect to find.

Algorithm 1: IU-RED

$S = \{(i,j) : i,j \in \{1,\dots,n\}, i < j\}$
$\hat{W} = I$
for $t = 1,\dots,n(n-1)/2$
  $\hat{L} = \text{diag}(\hat{W}\mathbf{1}) - \hat{W} = \sum_{p=1}^{n} \hat{\lambda}_p \hat{v}_p \hat{v}_p^\top$
  $k_{min} = \text{argmin}_k |\hat{v}_2(k)|$ (1)
  $(i^*, j^*) = \text{argmax}_{(i,j)\in S} \left| \frac{d\hat{v}_2(k_{min})}{d\hat{w}_{ij}} \right|$ (2)
  $= \text{argmax}_{(i,j)\in S} \left| \sum_{p>2}^{n} \frac{\hat{v}_2^\top [\partial \hat{L}/\partial \hat{w}_{ij}] \hat{v}_p}{\hat{\lambda}_2 - \hat{\lambda}_p} \hat{v}_p(k_{min}) \right|$ (3)
  $S = S \setminus \{(i^*, j^*)\}$
  $\hat{w}_{i^*j^*} = w_{i^*j^*}, \hat{w}_{j^*i^*} = w_{j^*i^*}$
return Second eigenvector of $\hat{L} = \text{diag}(\hat{W}\mathbf{1}) - \hat{W}$

Algorithm 2: S&T [18]

$S = \{(i,j) : i,j \in \{1,\dots,n\}, i < j\}$
$\hat{W} = I$
for $t = 1,\dots,n(n-1)/2$
  $\hat{L} = \text{diag}(\hat{W}\mathbf{1}) - \hat{W} = \sum_{p=1}^{n} \hat{\lambda}_p \hat{v}_p \hat{v}_p^\top$ (1)
  $(i^*, j^*) = \text{argmax}_{(i,j)\in S} \left\| \frac{d\hat{v}_2}{d\hat{w}_{ij}} \right\|_2^2$ (2)
  $= \text{argmax}_{(i,j)\in S} \left\| \sum_{p>2}^{n} \frac{\hat{v}_2^\top [\partial \hat{L}/\partial \hat{w}_{ij}] \hat{v}_p}{\hat{\lambda}_2 - \hat{\lambda}_p} \hat{v}_p \right\|_2^2$ (3)
  $S = S \setminus \{(i^*, j^*)\}$
  $\hat{w}_{i^*j^*} = w_{i^*j^*}, \hat{w}_{j^*i^*} = w_{j^*i^*}$
return Second eigenvector of $\hat{L} = \text{diag}(\hat{W}\mathbf{1}) - \hat{W}$

Suppose we have the Laplacian eigenvector decomposition $\hat{L} = \sum_{p=1}^{n} \hat{\lambda}_p \hat{v}_p \hat{v}_p^\top$ and that $\hat{\lambda}_1 \leq \hat{\lambda}_2 \ldots \leq \hat{\lambda}_n$. For spectral clustering, $\hat{\lambda}_1 = 0$ and $v_1 = \mathbf{1}/\sqrt{n}$. Matrix perturbation theory (e.g. Stewart and Sun [21], Chapter V, Section 2.3) gives the first order change of the second eigenvector as

$$\frac{d\hat{v}_2}{d\hat{w}_{ij}} = \sum_{p>2}^{n} \frac{\hat{v}_2^\top \left[\partial \hat{L}/\partial \hat{w}_{ij}\right] \hat{v}_p}{\hat{\lambda}_2 - \hat{\lambda}_p} \hat{v}_p, \quad (7)$$

provided $\hat{\lambda}_2$ has multiplicity 1. Note that $\partial \hat{L}/\partial \hat{w}_{ij} = (e_i - e_j)(e_i - e_j)^\top$, where e_i is the indicator vector of i. If $k_{min} = \text{argmin}_k |\hat{v}_2(k)|$, the change to the smallest magnitude element of $\hat{v}_2$ is $d\hat{v}_2(k_{min})/d\hat{w}_{ij}$. Our proposed active learning algorithm, IU-RED, is given in Algorithm 1.

A recent algorithm due to Shamir and Tishby [18] has a similar structure. The main steps are shown in Algorithm 2, which we refer to as S&T throughout.[1] The algorithm chooses measurements that maximize the *global* change to $\hat{v}_2$ by maximizing the norm on line 2. The reasoning is the following: As more measurements are acquired, the estimate $\hat{v}_2$ will necessarily converge to the true eigenvector v_2, regardless of the query ordering, since only a finite number of measurements can be made. Since constant perturbations to elements of $\hat{W}$ can have varying effects on $\hat{v}_2$, we should choose to update that element where the effect is largest.

If the similarity matrices were random, we would not expect to see partial clusterings emerge in $\hat{v}_2$, even with fairly large amounts of data. Figure 1 has highlighted this. In this unstructured setting, Shamir and Tishby's method may well be the best we can do, for it targets the global change in the clustering solution. Our algorithm exploits that practical similarity matrices are highly structured even when severely subsampled and uses this partial information as a guide for query selection. Our experiments emphasize that the empirical improvements of our method are significant, even though the algorithmic differences may at first appear minor.

[1] The full algorithm requires a "budget" parameter b which specifies the maximum number of measurements that can be requested from an oracle. For this paper, we set $b = n(n-1)/2$. Another version of their algorithm interleaves active selection with random selection, which we consider in our experiments.

5. MEASUREMENT NOISE

In many settings, only noisy similarities can be measured. In the Section 6, for example, we consider a crowdsourcing application where similarities are manually assigned by human labelers. A significant factor there is that even cooperative workers may disagree on similarity scores. Noisy similarities can be a fundamental problem, yet their impact on spectral clustering has not been thoroughly understood. Huang et al. [11] are among the few to investigate the effects of perturbations when all similarities are known. To our knowledge, active spectral clustering with costly and noisy measurements has not been considered.

The simplest way to deal with noise is to take the mean or median of multiple repeated measurements. However, given m repeated measurements of normally distributed similarities, both the mean and median have a standard deviation that is only a factor of $O(1/\sqrt{m})$ smaller than that of a single measurement. Thus, to halve the standard deviation we need about four times as many measurements. Thus, measuring every similarity multiple times is a fairly expensive way to reduce the effects of noise. It is especially wasteful since it is likely that only similarities of objects close to the cluster boundaries need to be known accurately to resolve the decision boundary. This section gives an active learning algorithm that asks for repeat measurements only when the measurement can significantly change the current solution and when our uncertainty in the true similarity is large.

We have extended IU-RED to maintain a "running median" estimate for each similarity. At any time, the true similarity is estimated as the median of any repeat measurements. Additionally, we maintain for each similarity estimate $\hat{w}_{ij}$ an estimate of its standard deviation, $\hat{\sigma}_{ij}$. When no measurements were made, we let the standard deviation be that of a uniform on [0, 1]; i.e., $\hat{\sigma}_{ij} = \sqrt{1/12} \approx 0.2887$. After a single measurement we set $\hat{\sigma}_{ij} = s$, an estimate of the population standard deviation, and we let $\hat{\sigma}_{ij} = s/\sqrt{m}$ for m repeat measurements.[2] IU-RED was then modified to choose that measurement (possibly a repeat) where the product $\hat{\sigma}_{ij}|d\hat{v}_2(k_{min})/d\hat{w}_{ij}|$ is maximal. This amounts to

[2] Several variations of this theme could be considered. Given enough samples, frequentist confidence intervals of the median could be estimated using the bootstrap. Alternatively, given prior information one could use Bayesian techniques to estimate posterior means and variances.

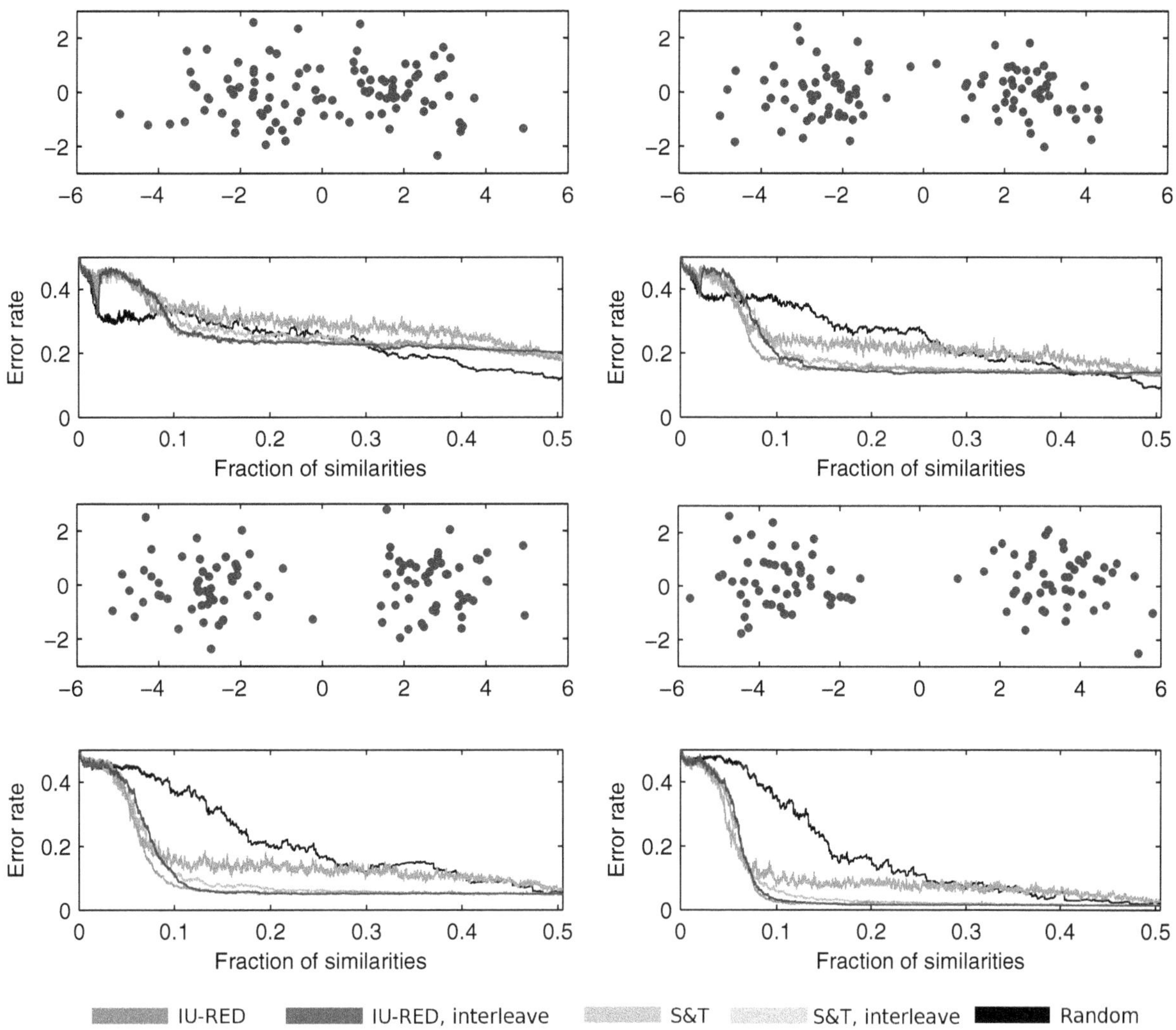

Figure 2: Results on synthetic datasets. For each dataset we sampled a total of 200 points from two Gaussians of increasing separation. Methods are evaluated on the average misclustering error rate, relative to a spectral clustering solution with complete data. Our proposed methods are "IU-RED" and "IU-RED, interleave".

choosing that measurement where our current estimate is uncertain *and* where the uncertainty matters. The S&T algorithm can be similarly modified and is considered in that form during our experiments.

6. RESULTS

We begin this section by evaluating the basic IU-RED algorithm of Section 4 on synthetic and real datasets. Subsection 6.3 then considers the extension to noisy measurements.

Our methods include IU-RED and a version of IU-RED where active selection is interleaved with random selection. We compared against three alternatives: S&T, S&T with interleaved random selection, and random selection only. The last three methods have been previously evaluated in Shamir and Tishby [18] using a similar evaluation methodology and on similar datasets as we consider here. In particular, we consider binary classification, which can be extended to more than two clusters by recursive splitting or by expanding the reasoning outlined here to more eigenvectors. Shamir and Tishby also evaluated an algorithm based on the Nyström method [7], but often found performance to be poor if the low rank assumption was not met. We evaluate all methods on the misclustering error, relative to a spectral clustering solution with complete dat and give average results over 20 runs.

6.1 Synthetic Datasets

We first present results on a simple clustering task in which the data is drawn from mixtures of Gaussians with two components. The data and results are shown in Figure 2. For each dataset we sampled a total of 200 points from two Gaussians of increasing separation. We normalized the data to lie in the unit hypercube and used a standard radial basis function kernel to compute similarities. As expected, random selection usually performs worst, except when the cluster separation is minimal. Compared to our two algorithms, S&T does poorly even on easy problems. As reported in [18], interleaving with random selection significantly boosts performance. IU-RED outperforms both

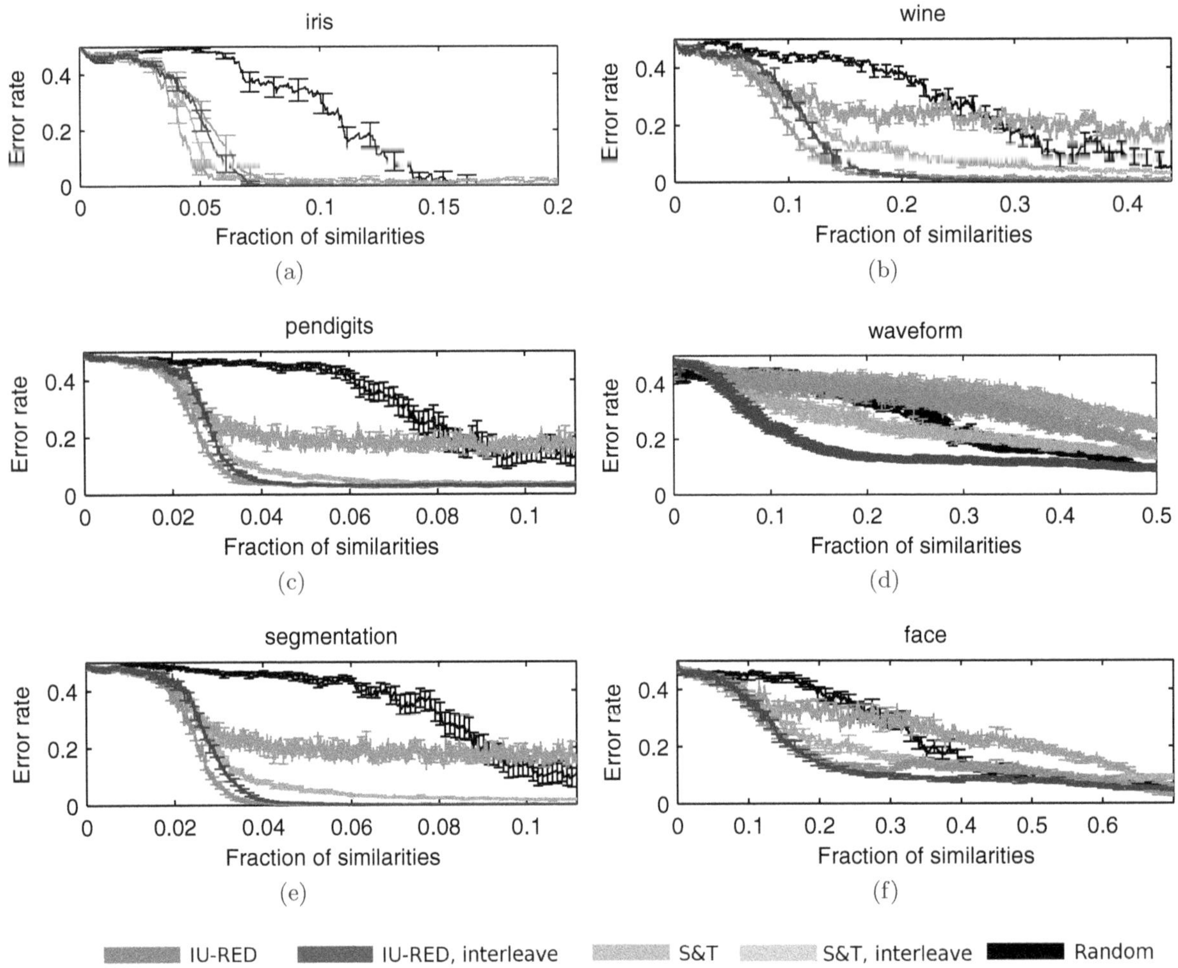

Figure 3: Results on several real datasets. Methods are evaluated on the average misclustering error rate, relative to a spectral clustering solution with complete data. Our proposed methods are "IU-RED" and "IU-RED, interleave". Note that the scaling of the x-axis changes between plots.

versions of S&T early on, but ties with them towards the end. Interestingly, while interleaving IU-RED appears to eventually stabilize the error rates, it slightly hurts performance early on.

6.2 Real Datasets

We have also evaluated our algorithm on a variety of real datasets. Five of the sets in this subsection are from the UCI repository [8] (iris, wine, pendigits, waveform, segmentation). An additional dataset concerning the similarity of faces is available from the University of Washington [15]. We followed [11, 18] and normalized the data to lie in the unit hypercube and used the Gaussian kernel to compute similarities.[3] Figures 3(a)–(e) show the results on the UCI datasets. Figure 3(f) shows results on the face dataset. Note that the scaling of the x-axis changes between plots. The difference between methods is amplified on these datasets. Except for the iris dataset in Figure 3(a), S&T performs relatively poorly, and is eventually outperformed by random selection. On three of five UCI datasets IU-RED outperforms all other methods early on. Interleaving usually increases the error initially, but eventually leads to a more stable algorithm with marginally lower error. The exception is the waveform dataset in Figure 3(d) where interleaving helps significantly. Lastly, on the face dataset IU-RED also outperforms S&T early on, with slight gains for interleaving.

We conducted a further experiment to assess whether the superior performance of IU-RED over S&T can be seen after a single active learning step, or only emerges after many such steps. In this experiment, we sampled a subset of similarities of approximately constant size uniformly at random and measured the decrease in error rate over one active selection step. These results were averaged over 30000 restarts. The first five rows of Table 1 show results for UCI data, the sixth row for the face data, and the last row for similarity matrices with off-diagonal entries uniform in [0, 1]. On four out of five UCI datasets and on the face dataset, IU-RED decreases the error more than S&T. The one dataset where we perform

[3]Although the UCI datasets were previously analyzed in [18], the results are not directly comparable, since their evaluations used different kernel parameters. Also, since each of these datasets contains more than two classes, it is possible that we chose two different classes for evaluating the spectral clustering.

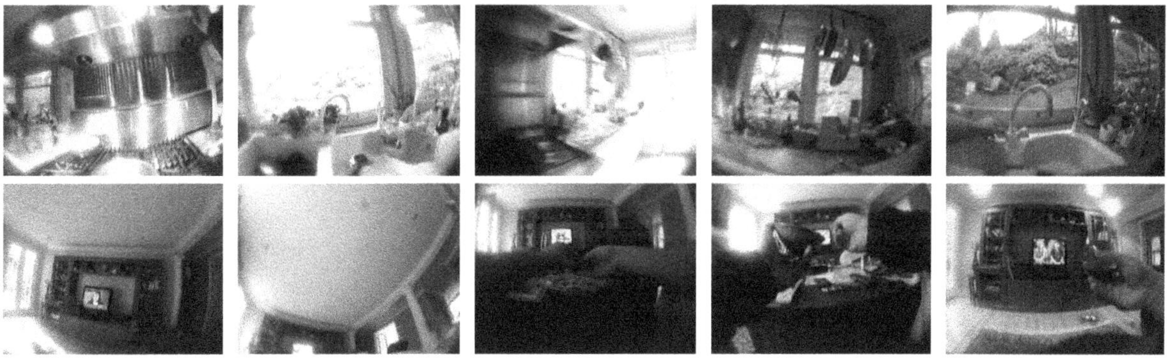

Figure 4: Spectral clustering of photos with complete data. The top row shows example views of the kitchen, and the bottom row example views of the living room. Humans can easily determine that photos in each row were probably taken in the same room, but a computer algorithm would have difficulty solving this task.

worse is the waveform dataset, which Figure 3(d) shows to be challenging for all methods. Overall, our method performs much better than S&T on structured similarity matrices. On random matrices both algorithms perform poorly, but now S&T performs better than IU-RED.

6.3 Wearable Camera Dataset

Our next experiment focuses on the realistic example outlined in the Introduction where similarities are hard to compute and noisy. The data of interest is a photo stream, acquired by a wearable camera at a rate of about one photo per 20 seconds. Clustering the data by the location at which an image was taken may be useful in a variety of applications, ranging from health (e.g., in diagnosis and life quality improvement for Alzheimer's patients) to summarization of personal memories. Because the data is collected in an entirely unconstrained way, analyzing it is beyond the capabilities of current unsupervised algorithms. The top row of Figure 4, for example, shows five images taken in the same kitchen. Clustering clearly requires some human input; at the very least a preliminary annotation that could be used to train supervised computer vision algorithms. It is impractical to ask annotators to simply label images by their location, since salient locations and their number only become evident as the stream progresses and may change from week to week, and from subject to subject. Also, locations may be interconnected, and multiple locations might be visible from the same viewpoint. In our data, for example, an open kitchen connects to the living room so that large parts of the space can be perceived to belong to both rooms. It is much more natural (and cost effective) to collect similarities between images and to infer a clustering from that data.

We took this approach in order to cluster 100 images taken from the photo stream described above [12]. Of these, about 50 were taken in an open kitchen, and 50 were taken in the adjacent living room. Some example images are shown in Figure 4. We asked workers on Amazon Mechanical Turk to rate, on a scale from 1 to 10, how likely it was that a given pair of images was taken in the same room, with 10 indicating certainty. The user ratings were divided by 10 and then used as similarities. Humans are adept at matching rooms by a loose jumble of visible objects, making this task fairly realistic. Indeed, the two rows of Figure 4 show representative examples from a partition that was found by spectral clustering using the complete median similarity matrix, with the median running over three repeat measurements. A subsampled version of the median similarity matrix was shown in Figure 1 on the left. To collect one similarity for each pair of photos costs a total of US\$74, so the three repeats required for the median cost a total of US\$222.

We first evaluated our algorithms on the median similarity matrix using the same methods as before. The results are shown in Figure 5(a). The legend is the same as in Figure 2. Note that the x-axis is scaled to extend beyond 1.0, to account for the three repeat measurements necessary to compute one median similarity. A fraction of f indicates that a total of $fn(n-1)/2$ pairwise measurements were made. As before, our method outperforms a number of competitors early on. The results can be also interpreted in terms of the amount of money that must be expended to achieve a clustering result of fixed quality. Each image comparison cost us US\$0.045 on Amazon Mechanical Turk. Table 2 shows the resulting approximate cost in US\$ for each algorithm in order to achieve an error rate of 0.05. IU-RED is at least 4 times cheaper than S&T, which costs more than 30% of the complete-labelling cost. This difference can easily render larger image clustering tasks than ours impractical.

We also evaluated how IU-RED and S&T compare over only one active choice. The result is shown in the row of Table 1 labeled "photos." As before, our active learning framework outperforms that of Shamir and Tishby.

Next, we consider the extension of IU-RED to deal with noisy similarities, as outlined in Section 5. Figure 6 illustrates the type of noise encountered in this labelling task. We allow up to three repeat measurements of similarities that are known with high uncertainty and which can potentially change the current solution. The results are shown in Figure 5(b). For comparison, Figure 5(c) shows results when no repeat measurements are allowed and the standard deviation is not estimated. The latter is the extreme counterpart to measuring every similarity three times. All error rates are relative to a spectral clustering computed from the complete median similarity matrix, averaged over 20 runs. As before, we scaled the x-axes to show the *effective* fraction of pairwise measurements that was made. For the no-repeats framework in Figure 5(c) this fraction cannot be larger than 1.0. Another important consequence of this measuring framework is that all algorithms should yield approximately the same

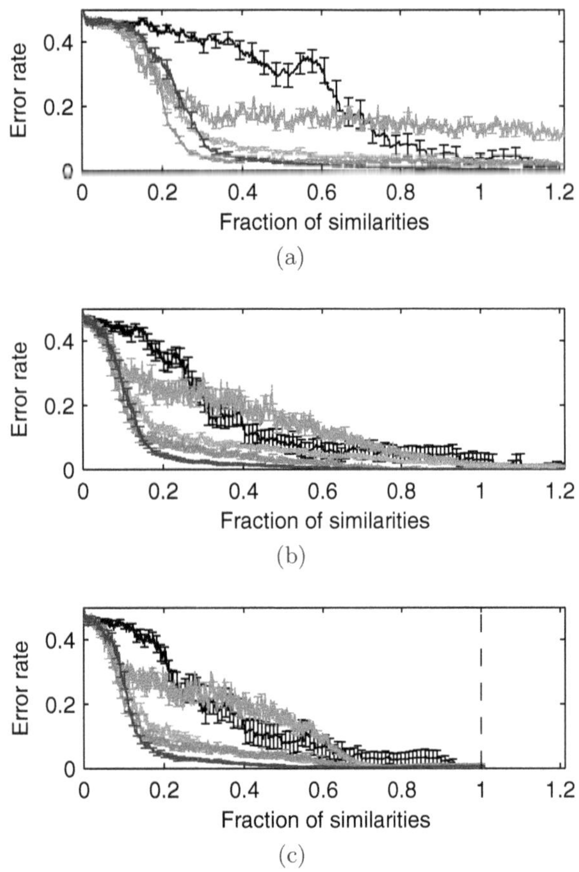

Figure 5: Results on the "photos" dataset. Figure (a) shows results when true similarities are estimated as the median of three measurements. Figure (b) shows results when the algorithm is allowed choose which repeat measurements to make. Up to three repeats are allowed. Figure (c) shows results when similarities are estimated by a single noisy measurement. The legend is the same as in Figure 3.

average error rate at a fraction of 1.0, since at that point every algorithm has observed one complete set of (noisy) similarities. The differences between algorithms are thus only appreciated in the first half of the Figure 5(c).

Both versions of IU-RED continue to beat the remaining algorithms in either of the two new settings. However, random interleaving now helps slightly, where it was detrimental before. With the exception of S&T, most methods improve early on compared to Figure 5(a). On the one hand this is intuitive, since as long as the similarities are not extremely noisy, three measurements do not convey three times as much information as one. One the other hand, it suggests that moderately noisy measurements can still be quite informative. Even so, we emphasize again that all algorithms should perform identically at a fraction of 1.0 in Figure 5(c). Maintaining running estimates and their accuracies is therefore preferable as it does not force performance to equalize once a fixed measurement quantum has been reached. Indeed, both IU-RED and IU-RED with random interleaving perform marginally better in Figure 5(b) than Figure 5(c) once a fraction of 1.0 measurements is reached.

Dataset	IU-RED	S&T
iris	0.0078 ± 0.0002	0.0016 ± 0.0001
wine	0.0103 ± 0.0003	-0.0010 ± 0.0003
pendigits	0.0067 ± 0.0002	-0.0007 ± 0.0002
waveform	-0.0018 ± 0.0002	0.0008 ± 0.0001
segmentation	0.0104 ± 0.0002	0.0002 ± 0.0002
face	0.0009 ± 0.0001	0.0001 ± 0.0001
photos	0.0126 ± 0.0003	-0.0021 ± 0.0002
uniform	-0.0057 ± 0.0009	-0.0037 ± 0.0007

Table 1: Average decrease in error rate across one selection step. IU-RED generally decreases the error more than S&T.

Random	S&T	S&T, inter.	IU-RED	IU-RED, inter.
\$53	> \$70	\$32	\$17	\$21

Table 2: Approximate labelling costs in US\$ to achieve a 0.05 error rate on the photos dataset.

Figure 6: Worker disagreement for two image comparisons on Amazon Mechanical Turk. For the left two photos, workers agreed they were certainly taken in the same room; for the right two, one worker asserted they were definitely not.

7. CONCLUSION

In this paper we have presented and evaluated an active learning algorithm for spectral clustering. Our main insight is that similarity matrices are not random, but usually exhibit clear clustering structure. Even when observing only a small fraction of the data, this structure becomes evident. Furthermore, assuming that the data clusters well, the final v_2 will usually have elements well away from zero. Motivated by these observations, our algorithm uses the current estimate $\hat{v}_2$ to choose measurements that will be most useful in removing elements close to zero, i.e., to push the two clusters in $\hat{v}_2$ apart. We have applied this algorithm to a range of datasets and showed that it generally outperforms a related algorithm by Shamir and Tishby.

The effects of costly and noisy similarities have so far been ignored in the active learning setting. We propose an extension of our algorithm that maintains running estimates of the true similarities as well as their accuracies. By taking these accuracies into account during query selection, we can potentially avoid unnecessary repeat measurements and speed up the learning process in noisy settings.

Rahimi and Recht [16] previously showed that a version of spectral clustering related to normalized cuts [20] clusters data by finding a hyperplane that cuts the data in a lifted space. The signed distances of points to the hyperplane are given by rescaled elements of an Laplacian eigenvector, and the partitioning can be done by taking the sign of the distances. If we have that $W\mathbf{1} = c\mathbf{1}$, for some $c > 0$, then their result implies that our version of spectral clustering also finds such a hyperplane, and that the signed distances are proportional to the second eigenvector v_2. Our active learning approach can then be interpreted as choosing measurements that can maximally perturb the margin between a hyperplane and the lifted datapoints. Rahimi and Recht's observation has recently been used to derive an active learning rule for the spectral graph transducer [2]. Here W is completely known, but for each object an additional binary class label can be queried. The rule chooses to label that point next which is currently closest to a hyperplane. Similar heuristics have also been employed in a number of other classifiers and clustering frameworks [3, 13, 23, 27]. In all these methods, however, the pairwise similarities are assumed to be known initially (either implicitly or explicitly) but additional labels or constraints can be queried. In contrast, our setting allows for incomplete similarities which we can (perhaps only noisily) measure at high cost.

8. REFERENCES

[1] D. Achlioptas and F. McSherry. Fast Computation of Low-Rank Matrix Approximations. *Journal of the ACM*, 54, 2007.

[2] Z. Bodó, Z. Minier, and L. Csató. Active Learning with Clustering. *Journal of Machine Learning Research*, 16:127–139, 2011.

[3] C. Campbell, N. Cristianini, and A. Smola. Query Learning with Large Margin Classifiers. In *Proceedings of the International Conference on Machine Learning (ICML)*, pages 111–118. Morgan Kaufmann, 2000.

[4] P. Drineas and R. Kannan. Pass-Efficient Algorithms for Approximating Large Matrices. In *Proceedings of the Annual Symposium on Discrete Algorithms*, pages 223–232, 2003.

[5] P. Drineas, R. Kannan, and M. W. Mahoney. Fast Monte Carlo Algorithms for Matrices II: Computing a Low-Rank Approximation to a Matrix. *SIAM Journal on Computing*, 36:158–183, 2006.

[6] P. Drineas and M. W. Mahoney. On the Nyström Method for Approximating a Gram Matrix for Improved Kernel-Based Learning. *Journal of Machine Learning Research*, 6:2153–2175, 2005.

[7] C. Fowlkes, S. Belongie, F. Chung, and J. Malik. Spectral Grouping using the Nyström Method. *IEEE Transactions on Pattern Analysis and Machine Intelligence*, 26, 2004.

[8] A. Frank and A. Asuncion. UCI Machine Learning Repository, 2010.

[9] A. Frieze, R. Kannan, and S. Vempala. Fast Monte-Carlo Algorithms for Finding Low-Rank Approximations. *Journal of the ACM*, 51:1025–1041, 2004.

[10] T. Gärtner. A Survey of Kernels for Structured Data. *SIGKDD Explorations*, 2003.

[11] L. Huang, D. Yan, M. I. Jordan, and N. Taft. Spectral Clustering with Perturbed Data. In *Advances in Neural Information Processing Systems 21 (NIPS)*, pages 705–712, 2009.

[12] N. Jojic, A. Perina, and V. Murino. Structural Epitome: A Way to Summarize One's Visual Experience. In *Advances in Neural Information Processing Systems 23 (NIPS)*, pages 1027–1035. 2011.

[13] P. K. Mallapragada, R. Jin, and A. K. Jain. Active Query Selection for Semi-Supervised Clustering. In *ICPR*, pages 1–4. IEEE, 2008.

[14] A. Y. Ng, M. I. Jordan, and Y. Weiss. On Spectral Clustering: Analysis and an Algorithm. In *Advances in Neural Information Processing Systems 14 (NIPS)*, pages 849–856. MIT Press, 2002.

[15] University of Washington Information Design Lab. [idl.ee.washington.edu/SimilarityLearning/Applications/Datasets/]. Face Similarity Data, 2012.

[16] A. Rahimi and B. Recht. Clustering with Normalized Cuts is Clustering with a Hyperplane. In *Statistical Learning in Computer Vision*, 2004.

[17] T. Sakai and A. Imiya. Fast Spectral Clustering with Random Projection and Sampling. In *Proceedings of the International Conference on Machine Learning and Data Mining in Pattern Recognition*, pages 372–384, Berlin, Heidelberg, 2009. Springer-Verlag.

[18] O. Shamir and N. Tishby. Spectral Clustering on a Budget. *Proceedings of the Infernational Conference on Artificial Intelligence and Statistics (AISTATS)*, 2011.

[19] J. Shawe-Taylor and N. Cristianini. *Kernel Methods for Pattern Analysis*. Cambridge University Press, New York, NY, USA, 2004.

[20] J. Shi and J. Malik. Normalized Cuts and Image Segmentation. *IEEE Transactions on Pattern Analysis and Machine Intelligence*, 22(8):888–905, 2000.

[21] G. W. Stewart and J. Sun. *Matrix Perturbation Theory*. Computer Science and Scientific Computing. Academic Press, 1990.

[22] G. Takács, I. Pilászy, B. Németh, and D. Tikk. Investigation of Various Matrix Factorization Methods for Large Recommender Systems. In *Proceedings of the 2nd KDD Workshop on Large-Scale Recommender Systems and the Netflix Prize Competition*, pages 6:1–6:8, New York, NY, USA, 2008. ACM.

[23] S. Tong and D. Koller. Support Vector Machine Active Learning with Applications to Text Classification. *Journal of Machine Learning Research*, 2:45–66, 2002.

[24] U. von Luxburg. A Tutorial on Spectral Clustering. *Statistics and Computing*, 17:395–416, 2007.

[25] X. Wang and I. Davidson. Active Spectral Clustering. In *IEEE International Conference on Data Mining*, pages 561–568, 2010.

[26] C. K. I. Williams and M. Seeger. Using the Nyström Method to Speed Up Kernel Machines. In *Advances in Neural Information Processing Systems 13 (NIPS)*, pages 682–688. MIT Press, 2001.

[27] Q. Xu, M. desJardins, and K. L. Wagstaff. Active Constrained Clustering by Examining Spectral Eigenvectors. In *Proceedings of the International Conference on Discovery Science*, pages 294–307, 2005.

Integrating Meta-Path Selection with User-Guided Object Clustering in Heterogeneous Information Networks*

Yizhou Sun† Brandon Norick† Jiawei Han† Xifeng Yan‡ Philip S. Yu§ Xiao Yu†
† University of Illinois at Urbana-Champaign, Urbana, IL
‡ University of California at Santa Barbara, Santa Barbara, CA
§ University of Illinois at Chicago, Chicago, IL
†{sun22, bnorick, hanj,xiaoyu1}@illinois.edu ‡xyan@cs.ucsb.edu §psyu@cs.uic.edu

ABSTRACT

Real-world, multiple-typed objects are often interconnected, forming heterogeneous information networks. A major challenge for link-based clustering in such networks is its potential to generate many different results, carrying rather diverse semantic meanings. In order to generate desired clustering, we propose to use *meta-path*, a path that connects object types via a sequence of relations, to control clustering with distinct semantics. Nevertheless, it is easier for a user to provide a few examples ("seeds") than a weighted combination of sophisticated meta-paths to specify her clustering preference. Thus, we propose to integrate *meta-path selection* with *user-guided clustering* to cluster objects in networks, where a user first provides a small set of object seeds for each cluster as guidance. Then the system learns the weights for each meta-path that are consistent with the clustering result implied by the guidance, and generates clusters under the learned weights of meta-paths. A probabilistic approach is proposed to solve the problem, and an effective and efficient iterative algorithm, *PathSelClus*, is proposed to learn the model, where the clustering quality and the meta-path weights are mutually enhancing each other. Our experiments with several clustering tasks in two real networks demonstrate the power of the algorithm in comparison with the baselines.

Categories and Subject Descriptors

H.2.8 [**Database Management**]: Database Applications—*Data mining*

Keywords

Heterogeneous information networks, meta-path selection, user guided clustering

*The work was supported in part by the U.S. Army Research Laboratory under Cooperative Agreement No. W911NF-09-2-0053 (NS-CTA), NSF IIS-1017362, MIAS, a DHS-IDS Center for Multimodal Information Access and Synthesis at UIUC, and U.S. Air Force Office of Scientific Research MURI award FA9550-08-1-0265. The views and conclusions contained in this paper are those of the authors and should not be interpreted as representing any funding agencies.

KDD'12, August 12–16, 2012, Beijing, China.

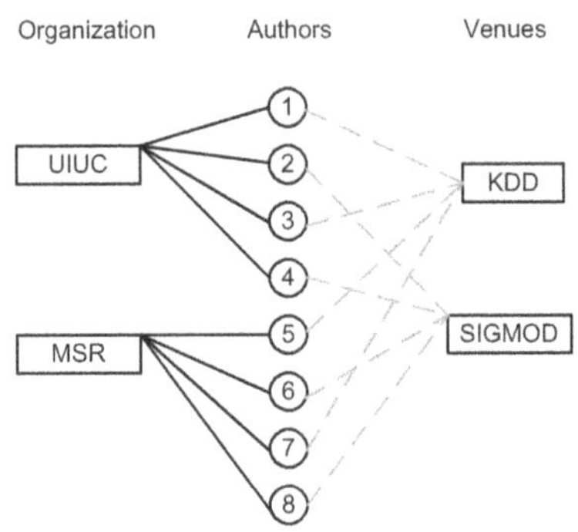

Figure 1: A toy heterogeneous information network containing organizations, authors and venues.

1. INTRODUCTION

With the advent of massive social and information networks, link-based clustering of objects in networks becomes increasingly important since it may help discover hidden knowledge in large networks. Link-based clustering groups objects based on their links instead of attribute values. This is especially useful when attributes of objects cannot be fully obtained. Most existing link-based clustering algorithms are on homogeneous networks where links carry the same semantic meaning and only differ in their strengths (*i.e.*, weights). However, most real-world networks are heterogeneous, where objects are of multiple types and are linked via different types of relations or sequences of relations, forming a set of *meta-paths* [21]. These meta-paths imply diverse semantics, and thus clustering on different meta-paths will generate rather different results, as shown below.

Example 1.1. (Meta-path-based clustering) A toy heterogeneous information network is shown in Figure 1, which contains three types of objects: organization (O), author (A) and venue (V), and two types of links: solid line represents the affiliation relation between author and organization, whereas the dashed one the publication relation between author and venue. Authors are then connected (indirectly) via different meta-paths. For example, $A - O - A$ is a meta-path denoting a relation between authors via organizations (*i.e.*, colleagues), whereas $A - V - A$ denotes a relation between authors via venues (*i.e.*, publishing in the same venues). A question then raises: *which type of connections should we use to cluster the authors?*

Obviously, there is no unique answer to this question: Different meta-paths lead to different author connection graphs, which may lead to different clustering results. In Figure 2(a), authors are connected via organizations and form two clusters: $\{1, 2, 3, 4\}$ and

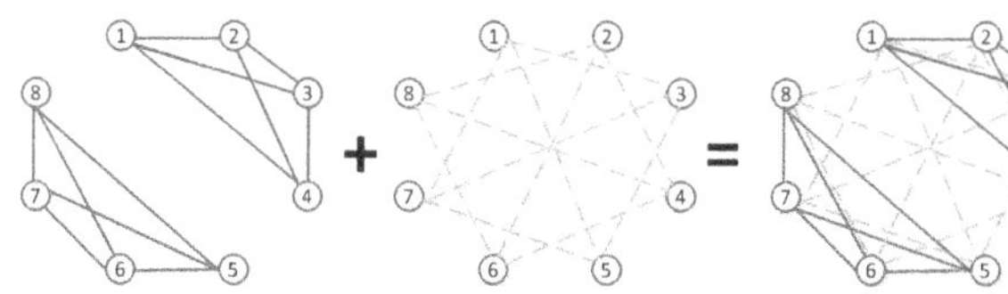

Figure 2: Author connection graphs under different meta-paths.

$\{5, 6, 7, 8\}$; in Figure 2(b), authors are connected via venues and form two different clusters: $\{1, 3, 5, 7\}$ and $\{2, 4, 6, 8\}$; whereas in Figure 2(c), a connection graph combining both meta-paths generate 4 clusters: $\{1, 3\}, \{2, 4\}, \{5, 7\}$ and $\{6, 8\}$. ∎

This toy example shows that all the three clusterings look reasonable but they carry diverse semantics. It should be a user's responsibility to choose her desired meta-path(s). However, it is often difficult to ask her to explicitly specify one or a weighted combination of meta-paths. Instead, it is easier for her to give some guidance in other forms, such as giving one or a couple of examples for each cluster. For example, it may not be hard to give a few known conferences in each cluster (*i.e.*, field) if one wants to cluster them into K research areas (for a user-desired K), or ask a user to name a few restaurants if one wants to cluster them into different categories in a business review website (*e.g.*, Yelp).

On the other hand, since we are dealing with heterogeneous networks, the previous work on user-guided clustering or semi-supervised learning approaches on (homogeneous) graphs [11, 30, 31] cannot apply. We need to explore meta-paths that represent heterogeneous connections across objects, leading to rich semantic meanings, hence diverse clustering results. With user guidance, a system will be able to learn the most appropriate meta-paths or their weighted combinations. The learned meta-paths will in turn provide an insightful view to help understand the underneath mechanism for the formation of a specific type of clustering. For example, which meta-path is more important to determine a restaurant's category?—the meta-path connecting them via customers, or the one connecting them via text in reviews, or the kNN relation determined by their locations?

In this paper, we integrate the meta-path selection with the user-guided clustering for better clustering a user-specified type of objects, *i.e.*, the *target objects*, in a heterogeneous information network, where the user guidance is given as a small set of seeds in each cluster. For example, to cluster authors into 2 clusters in Example 1.1, a user may seed $\{1\}$ and $\{5\}$ for two clusters, which implies a selection of meta-path $A - O - A$; or seed $\{1\}, \{2\}, \{5\}$, and $\{6\}$ for four clusters, which implies a combination of both meta-paths $A - O - A$ and $A - V - A$ with about equal weights. Our goal is to (1) determine the weight of each meta-path for a particular clustering task, which should be consistent with the clustering results implied by the limited user guidance, and (2) output the clustering result according to the user guidance and under the learned weights for each meta-path.

We propose a probabilistic model that models the hidden clusters for target objects, the user guidance, and the quality weights for different meta-paths in a unified framework. An effective and efficient iterative algorithm *PathSelClus* is developed to learn the model, where the clustering quality and the meta-paths quality mutually enhance each other. The experiments with different tasks on two real networks show our algorithm outperforms the baselines. Our contributions are summarized as follows:

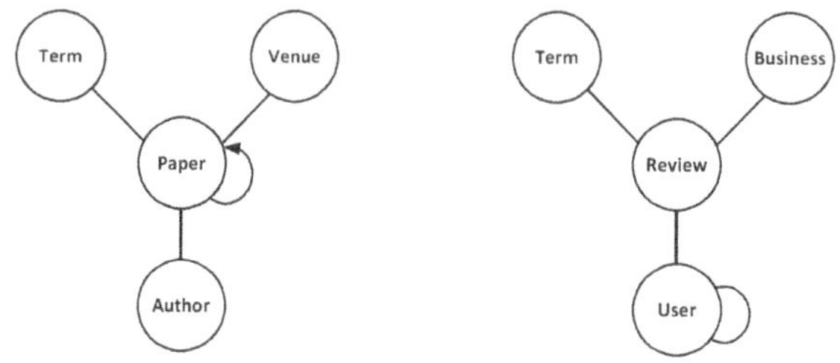

Figure 3: Examples of heterogeneous information networks.

1. We propose to integrate meta-path selection with user-guided clustering for arbitrary heterogeneous networks, and study a specific form of guidance: seeding some objects in each cluster;
2. A probabilistic model is proposed to put hidden clusters, user guidance, and the quality of meta-paths into one unified framework, and an iterative algorithm is developed where the clustering result and weights for each meta-path are learned alternatively and mutually enhance each other; and
3. Experiments on real heterogeneous information networks have shown the effectiveness and efficiency of our algorithm over baselines, and the learned weights of meta-paths provide knowledge for better understanding of the cluster formation.

2. PRELIMINARIES

In this section, we introduce preliminary concepts in heterogeneous information networks and define the problem of integrating meta-path selection with user-guided object clustering.

2.1 Heterogeneous Information Network

A heterogeneous information network [22] is an information network with multiple types of objects and/or multiple types of links. Here we introduce two heterogeneous information networks that are used in the experiment section in this paper, which are the D-BLP network and the Yelp network.

Example 2.1. (The DBLP bibliographic network[1]) DBLP is a typical heterogeneous information network (see schema in Figure 3(a)), which contains 4 types of objects, namely paper(P), author (A), term (T), and venue (V) including conferences and journals. Links exist between authors and papers by the relation of "write" and "written by", between papers and terms by "mention" and "mentioned by", and between venues and papers by "publish" and "published by". "Citation" relation between papers can be added further using other data source, such as Google scholar.

Example 2.2. (The Yelp network[2]) Yelp is a website where users can write reviews for businesses. The Yelp network (see schema in Figure 3(b)) used in this paper contains 4 types of objects, namely business (B), user (U), term (T), and review (R). Links exist between users and reviews by the relation of "write" and "written by", between reviews and terms by "mention" and " mentioned by", between businesses and reviews by "commented by" and "comment", and between users by "friendship" (not included in our dataset).

Following the work [21], we use the concept of **meta-path** to describe the possible relations that can be derived from a heterogeneous network between two types of objects in a meta level. Meta-path is defined by a sequence of relations in the network schema,

[1] http://www.informatik.uni-trier.de/~ley/db/
[2] http://www.yelp.com/

and can be described by a sequence of object types when there is no ambiguity. For example, $A - P - A$ is a meta-path denoting the co-authorship between authors, and $A - P - V$ is a meta-path denoting the publication relation between the author and the venue type. Note that, a single relation defined in the network schema can be viewed as a special case of meta-path, *e.g.*, the citation relation $P \to P$.

2.2 The Meta-Path Selection Problem

Link-based clustering is to cluster objects based on their connections to other objects in the network. In a heterogeneous information network, we need to specify more information for a meaningful clustering.

First, we need to specify the type of objects we want to cluster, which is called the **target type**. Second, we need to specify which type of connection, *i.e.*, meta-path, to use for the clustering task, where we call the object type that the target type is connecting to via the meta-path as the **feature type**. For example, when clustering authors based on the venues they have published papers in, the target type is the author type, the meta-path to use is $A - P - V$, and the feature type is the venue type.

In a heterogeneous information network, target objects could link to many types of feature objects by multiple meta-paths. For example, authors could connect to other authors by meta-path $A - P - A$, or connect to terms by meta-path $A - P - T$. The meta-path selection problem is then to determine which meta-paths or their weighted combination to use for a specific clustering task.

2.3 User-Guided Clustering

User guidance is critical for clustering objects in the network. In this study, we consider the guidance in the form of object seeds in each cluster given by users. For example, to cluster authors based on their (hidden) research areas, one can first provide several representative authors in each area. On one hand, these seeds are used as guidance for clustering all the target objects in the network. On the other hand, they provide information for selecting the most relevant meta-paths for the specific clustering task. Note that in practice, a user may not be able to provide seeds for *every* cluster, but only for *some* clusters they are most familiar with, which should be handled by the algorithm too.

2.4 The Problem Definition

In all, given a heterogeneous information network G, a user needs to specify the following as inputs for a clustering task:

1. The target type for clustering, type T.
2. The number of clusters, K, and the object seeds for each cluster, say $\mathcal{L}_1, \ldots, \mathcal{L}_K$, where $\mathcal{L}_k$ denotes the object seeds for cluster k, which could be an empty set. These seeds will be used as the hints to learn the purpose/preference of the clustering task.
3. A set of M meta-paths starting from type T, denoted as $\mathcal{P}_1, \mathcal{P}_2, \ldots, \mathcal{P}_M$, which might be helpful for the clustering task. These meta-paths can be determined either according to users' expert knowledge, or by traversing the network schema starting from type T with a length constraint.

For each meta-path $\mathcal{P}_m$, we calculate the adjacency matrix W_m, which we call *relation matrix*, between the target type T and the feature type F_m, by multiplying adjacency matrices for each relation along the meta-path. For example, the relation matrix W for meta-path $A-P-V$, denoting the number of papers published by an author in a venue, is calculated by $W = W_{AP} \times W_{PV}$, where W_{AP} and W_{PV} are the adjacency matrices for relation $A - P$ and $P - V$ respectively.

The output of the algorithm includes two parts: (1) to determine the weight $\alpha_m \geq 0$ of each meta-path $\mathcal{P}_m$ for a particular clustering task, which should be consistent with the clustering result implied by the limited user guidance, and (2) to output the clustering result according to the user guidance and under the learned weights for each meta-path, that is, to associate each target object t_i in T with a K-dimensional soft clustering probability vector, $\boldsymbol{\theta}_i = (\theta_{i1}, \ldots, \theta_{iK})$, where θ_{ik} is the probability of t_i belonging to cluster k, *i.e.*, $\theta_{ik} \geq 0$ and $\sum_{k=1}^{K} \theta_{ik} = 1$.

3. THE PROBABILISTIC MODEL

In this section, we propose a probabilistic approach to model the problem into a unified framework.

A good clustering result is determined by several factors: first, the clustering result should be consistent with the link structure; second, the clustering result should be consistent with the user guidance; third, the importance of each meta-path is implied by the user-guided clustering, which should be modeled and learned to further enhance the clustering quality. In the following, we first introduce the modeling for the three aspects respectively, and then propose a unified model that takes consideration of all of them.

3.1 Modeling the Relationship Generation

To model the consistency between a clustering result and a relation matrix, we propose a clustering-based generative model for relationship generation.

For a meta-path $\mathcal{P}_m$, let its corresponding relation matrix between the target type T and the feature type F_m be W_m. For each target object t_i, we model its relationships as generated from a mixture of multinomial distributions, where the probability of $t_i \in T$ connecting to $f_{j,m} \in F_m$ is conditionally independent on t_i given the hidden cluster label of the relationship is known. Let $\pi_{ij,m} = P(j|i,m)$ be the generative probability of the relationship starting from t_i and ending at $f_{j,m}$, where $\sum_j \pi_{ij,m} = 1$, then

$$\pi_{ij,m} = P(j|i,m) = \sum_k P(k|i)P(j|k,m) = \sum_k \theta_{ik}\beta_{kj,m} \quad (1)$$

where $\theta_{ik} = P(k|i)$ denotes the probability of t_i belonging to cluster k and $\beta_{kj,m} = P(j|k,m)$ denotes the probability of $f_{j,m}$ appearing in cluster k. In other words, let $\boldsymbol{\pi}_{i,m} = (\pi_{i1,m}, \ldots, \pi_{i|F_m|,m})$ be the generative probability vector for target object t_i, then each $\boldsymbol{\pi}_{i,m}$ can be factorized as a weighted summation of ranking distributions of feature objects in each cluster. The factorization idea is similar to that of PLSA [10], PHITS [7], and RankClus [22], but is built on meta-path-encoded relationships rather than immediate links. This extension will capture more and richer link-based features for clustering target objects in heterogeneous networks.

By assuming each target object t_i is independent with each other and each relationship generated by t_i is independent with each other, the probability of observing all the relationships between all the target objects and feature objects is the production of the probability of all the relationships following meta-path $\mathcal{P}_m$:

$$P(W_m|\Pi_m, \Theta, B_m) = \prod_i P(\mathbf{w}_{i,m}|\boldsymbol{\pi}_{i,m}, \Theta, B_m) = \prod_i \prod_j (\pi_{ij,m})^{w_{ij,m}} \quad (2)$$

where $\Pi_m = \Theta B_m$ is the probability matrix with cells as $\pi_{ij,m}$'s, Θ is the parameter matrix for θ_{ik}'s, B_m is the parameter matrix for $\beta_{kj,m}$'s. and $w_{ij,m}$ is the weight of the relationship between t_i and $f_{j,m}$. Note that, each meta-path $\mathcal{P}_m$ corresponds to a different generative probability matrix Π_m to model the relationship generation. The factorization of these probability matrices share the same soft clustering probabilities Θ, but different ranking distributions B_m in different meta-paths.

3.2 Modeling the Guidance from Users

Further, we take the user guidance in the form of object seeds for some clusters as the prior knowledge for the clustering result Θ, by modeling the prior as a Dirichlet distribution rather than treating them as hard labeled ones.

For each target object t_i, its clustering probability vector $\boldsymbol{\theta}_i$ is assumed to be a multinomial distribution, which is generated from some Dirichlet distribution. If t_i is labeled as a seed in cluster k^*, $\boldsymbol{\theta}_i$ is then modeled as being sampled from a Dirichlet distribution with parameter vector $\lambda \mathbf{e}_{k^*} + \mathbf{1}$, where $\mathbf{e}_{k^*}$ is a K-dimensional basis vector, with the k^*th element as 1 and 0 elsewhere. If t_i is not a seed, $\boldsymbol{\theta}_i$ is then assumed as being sampled from a uniform distribution, which can also be viewed as a Dirichlet distribution with parameter vector of $\mathbf{1}$. The density of $\boldsymbol{\theta}_i$ given such priors is:

$$P(\boldsymbol{\theta}_i|\lambda) \propto \begin{cases} \prod_k \theta_{ik}^{\mathbf{1}_{\{t_i \in \mathcal{L}_k\}}\lambda} = \theta_{ik^*}^{\lambda}, & \text{if } t_i \text{ is labeled and } t_i \in \mathcal{L}_{k^*}, \\ 1, & \text{if } t_i \text{ is not labeled.} \end{cases} \quad (3)$$

where $\mathbf{1}_{\{t_i \in \mathcal{L}_k\}}$ is an indicator function, which is 1 if $t_i \in \mathcal{L}_k$ holds, otherwise 0.

The hyper-parameter λ is a nonnegative value, which controls the strength of users' confidence over the object seeds in each cluster. From Eq. (3), we can find that:

- when $\lambda = 0$, the prior for $\boldsymbol{\theta}_i$ of a labeled target object becomes a uniform distribution, which means no guidance information will be used in the clustering process.
- when $\lambda \to \infty$, the prior for $\boldsymbol{\theta}_i$ of a labeled target object converges to a point mass, *i.e.*, $P(\boldsymbol{\theta}_i = \mathbf{e}_{k^*}) \to 1$ or $\boldsymbol{\theta}_i \to \mathbf{e}_{k^*}$, which means we will assign k^* as the hard cluster label for t_i.

In general, a larger λ indicates a higher probability of that $\boldsymbol{\theta}_i$ is around the point mass $\mathbf{e}_{k^*}$, and thus a higher confidence for the user guidance.

3.3 Modeling the Quality Weights for Meta-Path Selection

Different meta-paths may lead to different clustering results, therefore it is desirable to learn the quality for each meta-path for the specific clustering task. We propose to learn the quality weight for each meta-path by evaluating the consistency between its relation matrix and the user-guided clustering result.

In deciding the clustering result for target objects, a meta-path may be of low quality for the following reasons:

1. The relation matrix derived by the meta-path does not contain an inherent cluster structure. For example, target objects are connecting to the feature objects randomly.
2. The relation matrix derived by the meta-path itself has a good inherent cluster structure, however, it is not consistent with the user guidance. For example, in our motivating example, if the user gives a guidance as: $K = 2, \mathcal{L}_1 = \{1\}, \mathcal{L}_2 = \{2\}$, then the meta-path $A - O - A$ should have a lower impact in the clustering process for authors.

The general idea of measuring the quality of each meta-path is to see whether the relation matrix W_m is consistent with the detected hidden clusters Θ and thus the generative probability matrix Π_m, which is a function of Θ, *i.e.*, $\Pi_m = \Theta B_m$.

In order to quantify the weight for such quality, we model the weight α_m for meta-path $\mathcal{P}_m$ as the *relative weight* for each relationship between target objects and feature objects following $\mathcal{P}_m$. In other words, we treat our observations of the relation matrix as $\alpha_m W_m$ rather than original W_m. A larger α_m indicates a higher quality and a higher confidence of the observed relationships, and thus each relationship should count more.

Then, we assume the multinomial distribution $\boldsymbol{\pi}_{i,m}$ has a prior of Dirichlet distribution with parameter vector $\boldsymbol{\phi}_i$. In this paper, we consider a discrete uniform prior, which is a special case of Dirichlet distribution with parameters as an all-one vector, *i.e.*, $\boldsymbol{\phi}_{i,m} = \mathbf{1}$. The value of α_m is determined by the consistency between the observed relation matrix W_m and the generative probability matrix Π_m. The goal is to find the α_m^* that maximizes the posterior probability of $\boldsymbol{\pi}_{i,m}$ for all the target objects t_i, given the observation of relationships $\mathbf{w}_{i,m}$ with relative weight α_m:

$$\alpha_m^* = \arg\max_{\alpha_m} \prod_i P(\boldsymbol{\pi}_{i,m}|\alpha_m \mathbf{w}_{i,m}, \boldsymbol{\theta}_i, B_m) \quad (4)$$

The posterior of $\boldsymbol{\pi}_{i,m} = \boldsymbol{\theta}_i B_m$ is another Dirichlet distribution with the updated parameter vector as $\alpha_m \mathbf{w}_{i,m} + \mathbf{1}$, according to the multinomial-Dirichlet conjugate:

$$\boldsymbol{\pi}_{i,m}|\alpha_m \mathbf{w}_{i,m}, \boldsymbol{\theta}_i, B_m \sim Dir(\alpha_m w_{ij,m}+1, \ldots, \alpha_m w_{i|F_m|,m}+1) \quad (5)$$

which has the following density function:

$$P(\boldsymbol{\pi}_{i,m}|\alpha_m \mathbf{w}_{i,m}, \boldsymbol{\theta}_i, B_m) = \frac{\Gamma(\alpha_m n_{i,m} + |F_m|)}{\prod_j \Gamma(\alpha_m w_{ij,m} + 1)} \prod_j (\pi_{ij,m})^{\alpha_m w_{ij,m}} \quad (6)$$

where $n_{i,m} = \sum_j w_{ij,m}$, the total number of path instances from t_i following meta-path $\mathcal{P}_m$.

By modeling α_m in such a way, the meaning of α_m is quite clear:

- $\alpha_m w_{ij,m} + 1$ is the parameter of jth dimension for the new Dirichlet distribution.
- The larger α_m, the more likely it will generate a $\boldsymbol{\pi}_{i,m}$ with a distribution as the observed relationship distribution, *i.e.*, $\boldsymbol{\pi}_{i,m} \to \mathbf{w_{i,m}}/n_{i,m}$ when $\alpha_m \to \infty$, where $n_{i,m}$ is the total number of path instances from t_i following meta-path $\mathcal{P}_m$.
- The smaller α_m, the more likely it will generate a $\boldsymbol{\pi}_i$ with a uniform distribution (which means randomly), *i.e.*, $\boldsymbol{\pi}_{i,m} \to (1/|F_m|, \ldots, 1/|F_m|)$ when $\alpha_m \to 0$, where $|F_m|$ is the total size of feature objects in meta-path $\mathcal{P}_m$.

Note that, we do not consider negative α_m's in this model, which means relationships with a negative impact in the clustering process are not considered, and the extreme case of $\alpha_m = 0$ means the relationships in a meta-path are totally irrelevant for the clustering process.

3.4 The Unified Model

By putting all the three factors together, we have the joint probability of observing the relation matrices with relative weights α_m's, and the parameter matrices Π_m's and Θ:

$$\begin{aligned} &P(\{\alpha_m W_m\}_{m=1}^M, \Pi_{1:M}, \Theta | B_{1:M}, \Phi_{1:M}, \lambda) \\ &= \prod_i (\prod_m P(\alpha_m W_m | \Pi_m, \boldsymbol{\theta}_i, B_m) P(\Pi_m | \Phi_m)) P(\boldsymbol{\theta}_i|\lambda) \end{aligned} \quad (7)$$

where Φ_m is the Dirichlet prior parameter matrix for Π_m, and an all-one matrix in our case. We want to find the maximum a posteriori probability (MAP) estimate for Π_m's and Θ, which maximizes the logarithm of posterior probability of $\{\Pi_m\}_{m=1}^M$, given the observations of relation matrices with relative weights $\{\alpha_m W_m\}_{m=1}^M$ and Θ, plus a regularization term over $\boldsymbol{\theta}_i$ for each target object denoting the logarithm of prior density of $\boldsymbol{\theta}_i$:

$$J = \sum_i (\sum_m \log P(\boldsymbol{\pi}_{i,m}|\alpha_m \mathbf{w}_{i,m}, \boldsymbol{\theta}_i, B_m) + \sum_k \mathbf{1}_{\{t_i \in \mathcal{L}_k\}} \lambda \log \theta_{ik}) \quad (8)$$

By substituting the posterior probability formula in Eq. (6) and the factorization form for all $\boldsymbol{\pi}_{i,m}$, we get the final objective function:

$$J = \sum_i \Big(\sum_m \big(\sum_j \alpha_m w_{ij,m} \log \sum_k \theta_{ik} \beta_{kj,m} + \log \Gamma(\alpha_m n_{i,m} + |F_m|) - \sum_j \log \Gamma(\alpha_m w_{ij,m} + 1) \big) + \sum_k \mathbf{1}_{\{t_i \in \mathcal{L}_k\}} \lambda \log \theta_{ik} \Big) \quad (9)$$

4. THE LEARNING ALGORITHM

In this section, we introduce the learning algorithm, *PathSelClus*, for the model (Eq. (9)) proposed in Section 3. It is a two-step iterative algorithm, where the clustering result Θ and the weights for each meta-path $\boldsymbol{\alpha}$ mutually enhance each other. In the first step, we fix the weight vector $\boldsymbol{\alpha}$, and learn the best clustering results Θ under this weight. In the second step, we fix the clustering matrix Θ and learn the best weight vector $\boldsymbol{\alpha}$.

4.1 Optimize Θ Given α

When $\boldsymbol{\alpha}$ is fixed, the terms only involving $\boldsymbol{\alpha}$ can be discarded in the objective function Eq. (9), which is then reduced to:

$$J_1 = \sum_m \alpha_m \sum_i \sum_j w_{ij,m} \log \sum_k \theta_{ik} \beta_{kj,m} + \sum_i \sum_k \mathbf{1}_{\{t_i \in \mathcal{L}_k\}} \lambda \log \theta_{ik} \quad (10)$$

The new objective function can be viewed as a weighted summation of the log-likelihood for each relation matrix under each meta-path, where the weight α_m indicates the quality of each meta-path, plus a regularization term over Θ representing the user guidance. Θ and the augmented parameter B_m's can be learned using the standard EM algorithm, as follows.

E-step: In each relation matrix, we use $z_{ij,m}$ to denote the cluster label for each relationship between a target object t_i and a feature object $f_{j,m}$. According to the generative process described in Section 3.1, $P(z_{ij,m} = k) = \theta_{ik}$, and $f_{j,m}$ is picked with probability $\beta_{kj,m}$. The conditional probability of the hidden cluster label given the old Θ^{t-1} and B_m^{t-1} values is:

$$p(z_{ij,m} = k | \Theta^{t-1}, B_m^{t-1}) \propto \theta_{ik}^{t-1} \beta_{kj,m}^{t-1} \quad (11)$$

M-step: We have the updating formulas for Θ^t and B_m^t as:

$$\theta_{ik}^t \propto \sum_m \alpha_m \sum_j w_{ij,m} p(z_{ij,m} = k | \Theta^{t-1}, B_m^{t-1}) + \mathbf{1}_{\{t_i \in \mathcal{L}_k\}} \lambda \quad (12)$$

$$\beta_{kj,m}^t \propto \sum_i \sum_j w_{ij,m} p(z_{ij,m} = k | \Theta^{t-1}, B_m^{t-1}) \quad (13)$$

From Eq. (12), we can see that the clustering membership vector $\boldsymbol{\theta}_i$ for t_i is determined by the cluster labels of all its relationships to feature objects, in all the relation matrices. Besides, if t_i is labeled as a seed object in some cluster k^*, $\boldsymbol{\theta}_i$ is also determined by the label. The strength of impacts from these factors is determined by the weight of each meta-path α_m, and the strength of the cluster labels λ, where α_m's are learned automatically by our algorithm, and λ is given by users.

4.2 Optimize α Given Θ

Once given a clustering result Θ and the augmented parameter B_m's, we can calculate the generative probability matrix Π_m for each meta-path $\mathcal{P}_m$ by: $\Pi_m = \Theta B_m$. By discarding the irrelevant terms, the objective function of Eq. (9) can be reduced to:

$$J_2 = \sum_i \Big(\sum_m \big(\sum_j \alpha_m w_{ij,m} \log \pi_{ij,m} + \log \Gamma(\alpha_m n_{i,m} + |F_m|) - \sum_j \log \Gamma(\alpha_m w_{ij,m} + 1) \big) \Big) \quad (14)$$

It is easy to check that J_2 is a concave function, which means there is a unique $\boldsymbol{\alpha}$ that maximizes J_2. We use gradient descent approach to solve the problem, which is an iterative algorithm with the updating formula as: $\alpha_m^t = \alpha_m^{t-1} + \eta_m^t \frac{\partial J_2}{\partial \alpha_m}\Big|_{\alpha_m = \alpha_m^{t-1}}$, where the partial derivative of α_m can be derived as:

$$\frac{\partial J_2}{\partial \alpha_m} = \sum_i \sum_j w_{ij,m} \log \pi_{ij,m} + \sum_i \psi(\alpha_m n_{im} + |F_m|) n_{i,m} - \sum_i \sum_j \psi(\alpha_m w_{ij,m} + 1) w_{ij,m}$$

where $\psi(x)$ is the digamma function, the first derivative of $\log \Gamma(x)$. The step size η_m^t is usually set as a small enough number, to guarantee the increase of J_2. In this paper, we follow the trick used in non-negative matrix factorization (NMF) [12], and set $\eta_m^t = \frac{\alpha_m^{t-1}}{-\sum_i \sum_j w_{ij,m} \log \pi_{ij,m}}$. By using the above step size, we can get updating formula for α_m as:

$$\alpha_m^t = \alpha_m^{t-1} \frac{\sum_i (\psi(\alpha_m^{t-1} n_{im} + |F_m|) n_{i,m} - \sum_j \psi(\alpha_m^{t-1} w_{ij,m} + 1) w_{ij,m}}{-\sum_i \sum_j w_{ij,m} \log \pi_{ij,m}} \quad (15)$$

which guarantees to be a *non-negative* value. Also, by looking at the denominator of the formula, we can see that a larger log-likelihood of observing relationships $w_{ij,m}$ under model probability $\pi_{ij,m}$, which means a smaller denominator as log-likelihood is negative, generally leads to a larger α_m. This is also consistent with the human intuition.

4.3 The PathSelClus Algorithm

The *PathSelClus* algorithm is then summarized in Algorithm 1. Overall, it is an iterative algorithm that optimizes Θ and $\boldsymbol{\alpha}$ alternatively. The optimization of Θ contains an inner loop of EM-algorithm, and the optimization of $\boldsymbol{\alpha}$ contains another inner loop of gradient descent algorithm. We discuss some details of the algorithm implementation in the following.

The Weight Setting of Relation Matrices. Given a heterogeneous information network G, we calculate the relation matrix W_m for each given meta-path $\mathcal{P}_m$ by multiplying adjacency matrices along the meta-path. It can be shown that, scaling W_m by a factor of $1/c_m$ leads to a scaling of the learned relative weight α_m by a factor of c_m. Therefore, the performance of the clustering result will not be affected by the scaling of the relation matrix, which is a good property of our algorithm.

Initialization Issues. For the initial value of $\boldsymbol{\alpha}$, we set it as an all-one vector, which assumes all the meta-paths are equally important. For the initial value of Θ in the clustering step given $\boldsymbol{\alpha}$, if t_i is not labeled, we assign a random clustering vector to $\boldsymbol{\theta}_i$; while if t_i is labeled as a seed for a cluster k^*, we assign $\boldsymbol{\theta}_i = \mathbf{e}_k^*$.

Time Complexity Analysis. The *PathSelClus* algorithm is very efficient, as it is proportional to the number of relationships that are used in the clustering process, which is about linear to the number of target objects for short meta-paths in *sparse* networks. Formally, for the inner EM algorithm that optimizes Θ, the time complexity is $O(t_1(K \sum_m |E_m| + K|T| + K \sum_m |F_m|)) =$

Input: Network: G, Meta-path: $\{\mathcal{P}\}_{m=1}^{M}$, Number of cluster: K, Object seeds: $\{\mathcal{L}_1, \ldots, \mathcal{L}_K\}$, User belief: λ;
Output: The clustering result Θ; the weight vector for meta-paths $\boldsymbol{\alpha}$;
Normalize the weight of each relation matrix W_m into $\frac{W_m}{\sum_{ij} W_{ij,m}}$;
$\boldsymbol{\alpha} = \mathbf{1}$;
repeat
  Initialize Θ^0 and B^0;
  repeat
    1. E-step: update $p(z_{ij,m} = k|\Theta^{t-1}, B_m^{t-1})$ by Eq. (11);
    2. M-step: update Θ^t and B_m^t by Eqs. (12) and (13);
  until *reaches cluster change threshold*;
  $\Theta = \Theta^t$;
  $\boldsymbol{\alpha}^0 = \boldsymbol{\alpha}$;
  repeat
    1. update $\boldsymbol{\alpha}^t$ by Eq. (15) ;
  until *reaches inner $\boldsymbol{\alpha}$ difference threshold*;
  $\boldsymbol{\alpha} = \boldsymbol{\alpha}^t$;
until *reaches $\boldsymbol{\alpha}$ difference threshold*;
Output Θ and $\boldsymbol{\alpha}$;

Algorithm 1: The *PathSelClus* Algorithm.

$O(t_1(K\sum_m |E_m|))$, where $|E_m|$ is the number of non-empty relationships in relation matrix W_m, $|T|$ and $|F_m|$ are the numbers of target objects and feature objects in meta-path $\mathcal{P}_m$, which are typically smaller than $|E_m|$, and t_1 is the number of iterations. For the inner gradient descent algorithm, the time complexity is $O(t_2(\sum_m |E_m|))$, where t_2 is the number of iterations. The total time complexity for the whole algorithm is then $O(t(t_1(K\sum_m |E_m|)+t_2(\sum_m |E_m|)))$, where t is the number of outer iterations, which usually is a small number.

5. EXPERIMENTS

In this section, we will compare *PathSelClus* with several baselines, and show the effectiveness and efficiency of our algorithm.

5.1 Datasets

In this paper, we use two real information networks for performance test, the DBLP network and the Yelp network. For each network, we design multiple clustering tasks provided with different user guidance, which are introduced in the following.

1. The DBLP Network. For the DBLP network introduced in Example 2.1, we design three clustering tasks in the following.

- DBLP-T1: Cluster conferences in the "four-area dataset" [23], which contains 20 major conferences and all the related papers, authors and terms in DM, DB, IR, and ML fields, according to the *research areas* of the conferences. The candidate meta-paths include: $V-P-A-P-V$ and $V-P-T-P-V$.
- DBLP-T2: Cluster top-2000 authors (by their number of publications) in the "four-area dataset", according to their *research areas*. The candidate meta-paths include: $A-P-A$, $A-P-A-P-A$, $A-P-V-P-A$, and $A-P-T-P-A$.
- DBLP-T3: Cluster 165 authors who have been ever advised by Christos Faloutsos, Michael I. Jordan, Jiawei Han, and Dan Roth (including these professors), according to their *research groups*. The candidate meta-paths are the same as in DBLP-T2.

2. The Yelp Network. For the Yelp network introduced in Example 2.2, we are provided by Yelp a sub-network[3], which include 6900 businesses, 152327 reviews, and 65888 users. Hierarchical categories are provided for each business as well, such as "Restaurants", "Shopping" and so on. For Yelp network, we design three clustering tasks in the following.

- Yelp-T1: We select 4 relatively big categories ("Health and Medical", "Food", "Shopping", and "Beauty and Spas"), and cluster 2224 businesses with more than one reviews according to two meta-paths: $B-R-U-R-B$ and $B-R-T-R-B$.
- Yelp-T2: We select 6 relatively big sub-categories under the first-level category "Restaurant" ("Sandwiches", "Thai", "American (New)", "Mexican", "Italian", and "Chinese"), and cluster 554 businesses with more than one reviews according to the same two meta-paths.
- Yelp-T3: We select 6 relatively big sub-categories under the first-level category "Shopping" ("Eyewear & Opticians", "Books, Mags, Music and Video", "Sporting Goods", "Fashion", "Drugstores", and "Home & Garden"), and cluster 484 businesses with more than one reviews according to the same two meta-paths.

5.2 Effectiveness Study

First, we study the effectiveness of our algorithm under different tasks, and compare it with several baselines.

5.2.1 *Baselines*

Three baselines are used in this paper. Since none of them has considered the meta-path selection problem, we will use all the meta-paths as features and prepare them to fit the input of each of these algorithms. The first one is user-guided information theoretic-based k-means clustering (ITC), which is an adaption of seeded k-means algorithm proposed in [4], by replacing Euclidean distance to KL-divergence as used in information theoretic-based clustering algorithms [8, 2]. ITC is a hard clustering algorithm. For the input, we concatenate all the relation matrices side-by-side into one single relation matrix, and thus we get a very high dimensional feature vector for each target object.

The second baseline is the label propagation (LP) algorithm proposed in [31], which utilizes link structure to propagate labels to the rest of the network. For the input, we add all the relation matrices together to get one single relation matrix. As LP is designed for homogeneous networks, we confine our meta-paths to ones that start and end both in the target type. LP is a soft clustering algorithm.

The third baseline is the cluster ensemble algorithm proposed in [18], which can combine soft clustering results into a consensus, which we call ensemble_soft. Different from the previous two baselines that directly combine meta-paths at the input level, cluster ensemble combines the clustering results for different meta-paths at the output level. Besides, we also use majority voting as another baseline (ensemble_voting), which first maps each clustering result for each target object into a hard cluster label and then pick the cluster label that is the majority over different meta-paths. As we can use either ITC or LP as the clustering algorithm for each ensemble method, we then get four ensemble baselines in total: ITC_soft, ITC_voting, LP_soft, and LP_voting.

5.2.2 *Evaluation Methods*

Two evaluation methods are used to test the clustering result compared with the ground truth, where the soft clustering is mapped into hard cluster labels.

The first measure is *accuracy*, which is used when seeds are available for every cluster and is calculated as the percentage of target objects going to the correct cluster. Note that, in order to measure whether the seeds are indeed attracting objects to the right

[3]http://www.yelp.com/academic_dataset

Table 1: Clustering Accuracy for DBLP Tasks

(a) DBLP-T1

#S	Measure	PathSelClus	LP	ITC	LP_voting	LP_soft	ITC_voting	ITC_soft
1	Accuracy	**0.9950**	0.6500	0.6900	0.6500	0.6650	0.6450	0.5100
	NMI	**0.9906**	0.6181	0.6986	0.6181	0.5801	0.5903	0.5316
2	Accuracy	**1**	0.7500	0.8450	0.7500	0.8200	0.8950	0.8700
	NMI	**1**	0.6734	0.7752	0.6734	0.7492	0.8321	0.7942

(b) DBLP-T2

#S	Measure	PathSelClus	LP	ITC	LP_voting	LP_soft	ITC_voting	ITC_soft
1	Accuracy	**0.7951**	0.2122	0.3284	0.2109	0.3529	0.2513	0.2548
	NMI	**0.6770**	0.0312	0.1277	0.0267	0.0301	0.4317	0.4398
5	Accuracy	**0.8815**	0.2487	0.3223	0.5117	0.3685	0.3311	0.3495
	NMI	**0.6868**	0.0991	0.1102	0.4402	0.0760	0.3092	0.4316
10	Accuracy	**0.8863**	0.5586	0.3694	0.4297	0.3880	0.4891	0.2969
	NMI	**0.6947**	0.4025	0.1261	0.1788	0.1148	0.4045	0.4204

(c) DBLP-T3

#S	Measure	PathSelClus	LP	ITC	LP_voting	LP_soft	ITC_voting	ITC_soft
1	Accuracy	0.8067	**0.9273**	0.5376	0.7091	0.5424	0.4770	0.2358
	NMI	0.6050	**0.7966**	0.5120	0.5870	0.7182	0.3008	0.3416
2	Accuracy	0.9036	**0.9394**	0.5285	0.7333	0.3267	0.5176	0.4085
	NMI	0.7485	**0.8283**	0.5056	0.5986	0.8087	0.3898	0.3464
4	Accuracy	0.9248	**0.9576**	0.7624	0.7636	0.9255	0.6370	0.5485
	NMI	0.7933	0.8841	0.6280	0.6179	**0.9057**	0.4437	0.4634

Table 2: Clustering Accuracy for Yelp Tasks

(a) Yelp-T1

%S	Measure	PathSelClus	LP	ITC	LP_voting	LP_soft	ITC_voting	ITC_soft
1%	Accuracy	**0.5384**	0.3381	0.2619	0.1632	0.1632	0.2564	0.2769
	NMI	**0.5826**	0.0393	0.0042	0.0399	0.0399	0.1907	0.2435
2%	Accuracy	**0.5487**	0.3444	0.2798	0.1713	0.1713	0.3581	0.3790
	NMI	**0.5800**	0.0557	0.0062	0.0567	0.0567	0.2281	0.2734
5%	Accuracy	**0.5989**	0.3732	0.3136	0.1965	0.1965	0.5215	0.5250
	NMI	**0.5796**	0.1004	0.0098	0.0962	0.0962	0.2583	0.2878

(b) Yelp-T2

%S	Measure	PathSelClus	LP	ITC	LP_voting	LP_soft	ITC_voting	ITC_soft
1%	Accuracy	**0.7435**	0.1137	0.1758	0.2112	0.2112	0.2430	0.2022
	NMI	**0.6517**	0.0323	0.0178	0.0578	0.0578	0.2308	0.2490
2%	Accuracy	**0.8004**	0.1264	0.1910	0.2202	0.2202	0.2762	0.2792
	NMI	**0.6803**	0.0487	0.0150	0.0801	0.0801	0.2099	0.2907
5%	Accuracy	**0.8125**	0.2653	0.2200	0.2437	0.2437	0.3049	0.3240
	NMI	**0.6894**	0.1111	0.0220	0.1212	0.1212	0.2252	0.2692

(c) Yelp-T3

%S	Measure	PathSelClus	LP	ITC	LP_voting	LP_soft	ITC_voting	ITC_soft
1%	Accuracy	**0.4736**	0.2789	0.1893	0.0682	0.0682	0.2593	0.1775
	NMI	**0.4304**	0.0568	0.0155	0.0626	0.0626	0.1738	0.2065
2%	Accuracy	**0.4597**	0.4008	0.1948	0.0764	0.0764	0.2318	0.2033
	NMI	**0.4359**	0.0910	0.0172	0.0755	0.0755	0.1835	0.1822
5%	Accuracy	0.4393	**0.5351**	0.2233	0.1033	0.1033	0.3337	0.3083
	NMI	**0.4415**	0.1761	0.0194	0.1133	0.1133	0.1793	0.2285

cluster, we do not map the outcome cluster labels to the given class labels. The second measure is *normalized mutual information (N-MI)*, which does not require the mapping relation between ground truth labels and the cluster labels obtained by the clustering algorithm. The normalized mutual information of two partitions X and Y is calculated as: $NMI(X,Y) = \frac{I(X;Y)}{\sqrt{H(X)H(Y)}}$, where X and Y are vectors containing cluster labels for all the target objects. Both measures are in the range of 0 to 1, and a higher value indicates a better clustering result in terms of the ground truth.

5.2.3 Full Cluster Seeds

We first test the clustering accuracy when cluster seeds are given for every cluster. In this case, all the three baselines can be used and compared. Performances under different numbers of seeds in each cluster are tested. Each result is the average of 10 runs.

The accuracy for all the 6 tasks for two networks are summarized in Table 1 and Table 2 respectively. From the results we can see that, *PathSelClus* performs the best in most of the tasks. Even for the task such as DBLP-T3 where other methods give the best clustering result, *PathSelClus* still gives clustering results among the top. This means, *PathSelClus* can give consistently good results across different tasks in different networks. Also, by looking at the clustering accuracy trend along with the number of seeds used in each cluster, we can see that, more seeds generally leads to better clustering results.

5.2.4 Partial Cluster Seeds

We then test the clustering accuracy when cluster seeds are only available for some of the clusters. We perform this study on DBLP-T3 using *PathSelClus*, which includes 4 clusters, and the results are shown in Fig. 4. We can see that even if user guidance is only given to some clusters, those seeds can still be used to improve the clustering accuracy. In general, the fewer number of clusters with seeds, the worse the clustering accuracy, which is consistent with the human intuition. Note that, label propagation-based methods like LP cannot deal with partial cluster labels. However, in reality it is quite common that users are only familiar with some of the clusters and are only able to give good seeds in those clusters. That is another advantage of *PathSelClus*.

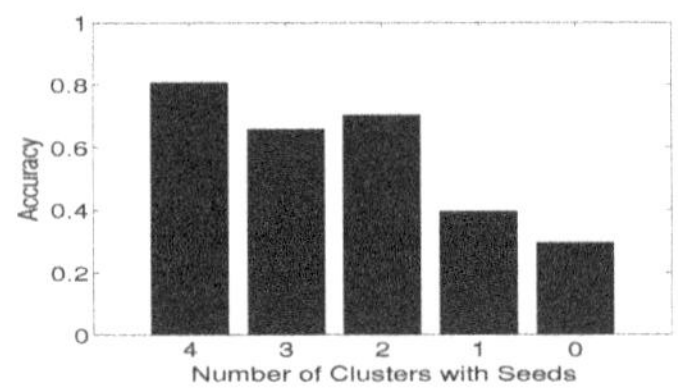

Figure 4: Clustering accuracy under partial guidance: DBLP-T3 with #seeds = 1.

5.3 Efficiency Study

Now, we study the scalability of our algorithm using synthetic datasets, due to that we can manipulate the size of network flexibly. In Fig. 5(a), we keep the size of target objects and the total number of relationships they issued as fixed, and vary the size of feature objects. We can see that the average running time for one iteration of the inner EM algorithm is about linear to the size of the feature objects; and the average running time for one iteration of the inner gradient descent algorithm is almost constant, as it is only linear to the number of relationships in the network. In Fig. 5(b), we keep the size of feature objects as fixed, and vary the number of target objects. We keep the average relationships for each target object as constant. From the result we can see that the average running time for one iteration of both the inner EM algorithm and the gradient descent algorithm is linear to the size of target objects, since the number of relationships is also increasing linearly with the size of target objects. From the efficiency test, we can see that *PathSelClus* is very scalable and can be applied to large-scale networks.

5.4 Parameter Study

In this section, we study the impact of the only parameter in the algorithm, λ, to the performance of our algorithm. We select DBLP-T1 and Yelp-T2 as the test tasks. From the results in Fig. 6, we can see that the clustering results is in general not sensitive to the value of λ, as long as it is a positive value. In practice, we set it as 100 for our experiments. Notice that in Fig. 6, we do not show

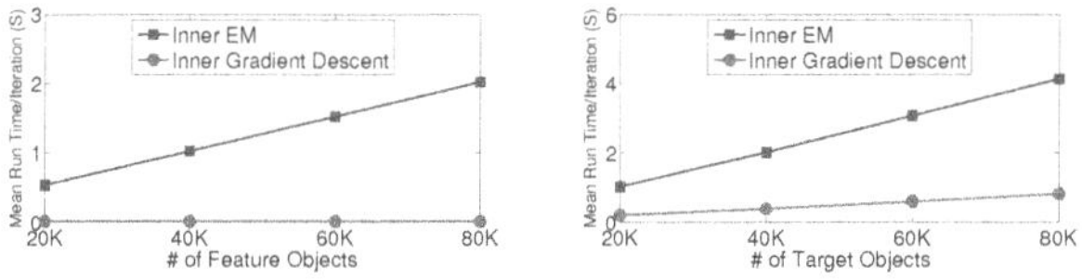

(a) Varying Feature Object Size (b) Varying Target Object Size

Figure 5: Scalability test on synthetic networks.

the accuracy value when $\lambda = 0$, as when there is no guidance from users, the accuracy cannot be correctly defined.

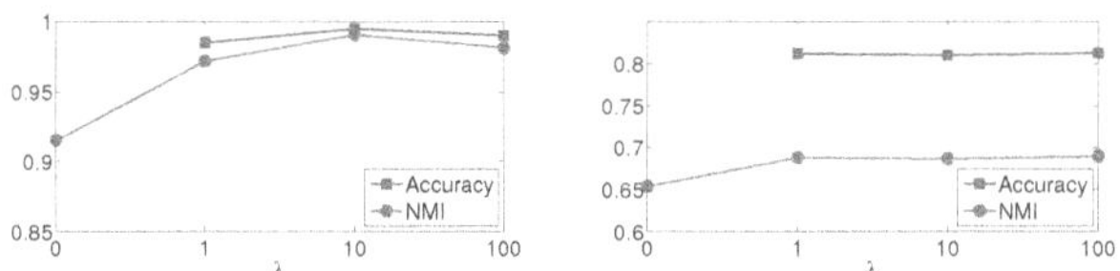

(a) DBLP-T1: #seeds = 1 (b) Yelp-T2: %seeds = 5%

Figure 6: Parameter study of λ.

5.5 Case Study on Meta-Path Weights

One of the major contributions of *PathSelClus* is that it can select the right meta-paths for a user-guided clustering task. We now show the learned weights of meta-paths for some of the tasks.

In DBLP-T1 task, the total weight α_m for meta-path $V - P - A - P - V$ is 1576, and the average weight per relationship (a concrete path instance following the meta-path) is 0.0017. The total weight for meta-path $V - P - T - P - V$ is 17001, while the average weight per relationship is 0.0003. This means that generally the relationships between two conferences that are connected by an author are more trustable than the ones that are connected by a term, which is consistent with human intuition since many terms can be used in different research areas and authors are typically more focused on confined research topics. However, as there are much more relationships following $V - P - T - P - V$ than following $V - P - A - P - V$, the former overall provide more information for clustering.

In the Yelp network, similar to DBLP-T1 task, in terms of the average weight for each relationship, meta-path $B - R - U - R - B$ is with higher weight than $B - R - T - U - B$; while in terms of total weight, meta-path $B - R - T - U - B$ is with higher weight. An interesting phenomenon is that, for Yelp-T2 task, which tries to cluster restaurants into different categories, the average weight for relationships following $B - R - U - R - B$ is 0.1716, much lower than the value (0.5864) for Yelp-T3 task, which tries to cluster shopping businesses into finer categories. This simply says that most users actually will try all different kinds of food, therefore they will not be served as a good connection between restaurants as they are in other categories.

6. DISCUSSION

In this section, we briefly discuss some interesting issues.

1. The Strength of Meta-Path Selection. Different meta-paths in heterogeneous networks could be viewed as different sources of information for defining link-based similarity between objects. There are several ways to handle different meta-paths: (1) to combine them at relation matrix level, such as in baselines ITC and LP; (2) to combine the clustering results at the output level, such as in ensemble baselines; (3) to learn and improve the quality weights for each meta-path iteratively, such as in *PathSelClus*. Only the third approach is able to select different meta-paths according to different clustering tasks, while the other two can only output an "average" clustering result using all the information. It turns out that, in most cases, the third approach is more flexible to combine information from different sources, and its advantage has been shown in the experiment section.

2. Meta-Paths vs. Path Instances. In this paper, we only consider the different semantics encoded by different meta-paths. In practice, different concrete paths (path instances) between two objects may also differ from each other, e.g., two objects may be linked via a "bridge" or via a "hub", indicating different meanings. The difference between the two concepts, *i.e.*, meta-path and path instance, is similar to the difference between *a source of features* and *a concrete feature* in a vector space. Due to limited scope, this paper only discusses the selection of meta-paths. It is possible to select path instance at the object level, and the concrete method is left for future research.

7. RELATED WORK

Recently, there are many clustering algorithms proposed for networks, such as spectral clustering-based methods [19, 15], link-based probabilistic models [7, 1], modularity function-based algorithms [17, 16], and density-based algorithms [26, 25] on homogenous networks; and ranking-based algorithms [22, 23], non-negative matrix factorization [12, 24], spectral clustering-based methods [13], and probabilistic approaches [14] on heterogeneous networks. However, while all these clustering methods use the information given in the networks, none considers that different users may have different purposes for clustering, nor do they ask users to help select different information for link-based clustering. In this paper, we show that different types of relationships encoded by meta-paths have different semantic meanings in determining the similarity between target objects, and the selection of these meta-paths should be done with user guidance in order to derive user-desired clustering results.

There are several lines of research on how to add user guidance to derive good clustering results, consistent with users' demand in vector space or networked data.

Clustering with constraints. In [4, 5, 11], clustering algorithms that consider constraints either in the form of seeds in each cluster or pairwise constraints as *must-link* or *cannot-link* are proposed. A probabilistic model with an HMRF (hidden Markov random field) as a hidden layer that models the must-link and cannot-link between objects is proposed to solve the problem [5]. This approach can also be extended to graph data with the use of kernels instead of vector-based features [11]. However, these methods assume there is one trustable information source to either define the feature of each object or define the network structure between objects. The goal is to output the clustering result that is consistent with both the similarity defined by the data as well as the user guidance. In this paper, we dig further and study which type of information source encoded with meta-paths is more trustable in a heterogeneous network.

Semi-supervised learning on graphs. In [30, 31], algorithms that propagate labels for a small portion of objects into the rest of the network are proposed, which are based on harmonic functions defined between objects using the network structure. Again, this kind of methods totally trust the given network and determine the best labels of the rest of the nodes according to the cost function defined on the network.

Semi-supervised metric learning. In [6, 3], algorithms that learn the best distance metric functions according to the constrains for the clustering task are proposed. This line of problem is closer to the meta-path selection problem, but still differs significantly. First, they study features of objects in vector space instead of network; second, the metric functions should be given in an explicit format, which is very difficult to determine in a network scenario. In this paper, we are not finding an explicit metric function that determines the similarity between any two target objects, instead, we model and learn the quality weight for each meta-path in the clustering process, which can be viewed as an implicit way to determine the similarity between two target objects.

User-guided clustering in relational data. CrossClus [28] deals with another type of guidance from users: the attribute set of the target object type. The algorithm extracts a set of highly relevant attributes in multiple relations connected via linkages defined in the database schema, and then use the whole attribute set as the feature set to apply traditional vector space-based clustering algorithm. CrossClus works for relational data with complete attributes, but not for purely link-based clustering.

Cluster ensemble [20, 18] is a method that combines clustering results of different methods or different datasets to a single consensus. Most of these cluster ensemble methods try to find a mean partition given different partitions of target objects. However, in reality these clusterings may conflict with each other, representing different purposes of clustering tasks, and a consensus does not necessarily lead to a clustering desired by users. In this study, we do not combine clustering results at the output level, but use intermediate clustering results as feedback to adjust the weight of each meta-path, and thus the clustering results and the quality weight for each meta-path can mutually enhance each other.

Our work also differs from traditional feature selection [9] and recently emerged semi-supervised feature selection [29, 27], which focus on vector space features, and do not have an immediate extension of solutions to our problem. For our meta-path selection problem, each meta-path provides *a source* of features instead of *a concrete* feature, and we have shown that simple combinations of features from different sources may lead to no good solution.

8. CONCLUSIONS

Link-based clustering for objects in heterogeneous information networks is an important task with many applications. Different from traditional clustering tasks where similarity functions between objects are given and with no ambiguity, objects in heterogeneous networks can be connected via different relationships, encoded by different meta-paths. In this paper, we integrate the meta-path selection problem with the user-guided clustering problem in heterogeneous networks. An algorithm *PathSelClus* that can utilize very limited guidance from users in the form of seeds in some of the clusters and automatically learn the best weights for each meta-path in the clustering process, is proposed. The experiments on different tasks on real datasets have demonstrated that our algorithm can output the most stable and accurate clustering results compared with the baselines. Also, the learned weights for each meta-path are very insightful to explain the hidden similarity between target objects under a particular clustering task.

9. REFERENCES

[1] E. M. Airoldi, D. M. Blei, S. E. Fienberg, and E. P. Xing. Mixed membership stochastic blockmodels. *J. Mach. Learn. Res.*, 9:1981–2014, June 2008.

[2] A. Banerjee, S. Merugu, I. S. Dhillon, and J. Ghosh. Clustering with bregman divergences. *J. Mach. Learn. Res.*, 6:1705–1749, December 2005.

[3] A. Bar-Hillel, T. Hertz, N. Shental, and D. Weinshall. Learning a mahalanobis metric from equivalence constraints. *JMLR*, 6, 2005.

[4] S. Basu, A. Banerjee, and R. Mooney. Semi-supervised clustering by seeding. In *ICML '02*, 2002.

[5] S. Basu, M. Bilenko, and R. J. Mooney. A probabilistic framework for semi-supervised clustering. KDD '04, pages 59–68, 2004.

[6] M. Bilenko, S. Basu, and R. J. Mooney. Integrating constraints and metric learning in semi-supervised clustering. In *ICML '04*, 2004.

[7] D. Cohn and H. Chang. Learning to probabilistically identify authoritative documents. In *ICML '00*, pages 167–174, 2000.

[8] I. S. Dhillon, S. Mallela, and R. Kumar. A divisive information-theoretic feature clustering algorithm for text classification. *JMLR*, 3:1265–1287, 2003.

[9] I. Guyon and A. Elisseeff. An introduction to variable and feature selection. *J. Mach. Learn. Res.*, 3:1157–1182, Mar. 2003.

[10] T. Hofmann. Probabilistic latent semantic indexing. SIGIR '99, pages 50–57, 1999.

[11] B. Kulis, S. Basu, I. Dhillon, and R. Mooney. Semi-supervised graph clustering: a kernel approach. ICML '05, pages 457–464, 2005.

[12] D. D. Lee and H. S. Seung. Algorithms for non-negative matrix factorization. In *NIPS '00*, pages 556–562, 2000.

[13] B. Long, Z. (mark Zhang, X. Wu, and P. S. Yu. Spectral clustering for multi-type relational data. In *ICML '06*, pages 585–592, 2006.

[14] B. Long, Z. M. Zhang, and P. S. Yu. A probabilistic framework for relational clustering. In *KDD '07*, pages 470–479, 2007.

[15] U. Luxburg. A tutorial on spectral clustering. *Statistics and Computing*, 17:395–416, December 2007.

[16] M. E. J. Newman. Fast algorithm for detecting community structure in networks. *Physical Review E (Statistical, Nonlinear, and Soft Matter Physics)*, 69(6), 2004.

[17] M. E. J. Newman and M. Girvan. Finding and evaluating community structure in networks. *Physical Review E (Statistical, Nonlinear, and Soft Matter Physics)*, 69(2), 2004.

[18] K. Punera and J. Ghosh. Consensus-based ensembles of soft clusterings. *Appl. Artif. Intell.*, 22:780–810, August 2008.

[19] J. Shi and J. Malik. Normalized cuts and image segmentation. *IEEE Transactions on Pattern Analysis and Machine Intelligence*, 22:888–905, 1997.

[20] A. Strehl, J. Ghosh, and C. Cardie. Cluster ensembles - a knowledge reuse framework for combining multiple partitions. *Journal of Machine Learning Research*, 3:583–617, 2002.

[21] Y. Sun, J. Han, X. Yan, P. S. Yu, and T. Wu. Pathsim: Meta path-based top-k similarity search in heterogeneous information networks. In *VLDB '11*, 2011.

[22] Y. Sun, J. Han, P. Zhao, Z. Yin, H. Cheng, and T. Wu. Rankclus: integrating clustering with ranking for heterogeneous information network analysis. In *EDBT '09*, pages 565–576, 2009.

[23] Y. Sun, Y. Yu, and J. Han. Ranking-based clustering of heterogeneous information networks with star network schema. In *KDD '09*, pages 797–806, 2009.

[24] F. Wang, T. Li, X. Wang, S. Zhu, and C. Ding. Community discovery using nonnegative matrix factorization. *Data Mining and Knowledge Discovery*, 20, 2010.

[25] N. Wang, S. Parthasarathy, K.-L. Tan, and A. K. H. Tung. Csv: visualizing and mining cohesive subgraphs. In *SIGMOD '08*, pages 445–458, 2008.

[26] X. Xu, N. Yuruk, Z. Feng, and T. A. J. Schweiger. Scan: a structural clustering algorithm for networks. In *KDD '07*, pages 824–833, 2007.

[27] Z. Xu, I. King, M. R.-T. Lyu, and R. Jin. Discriminative semi-supervised feature selection via manifold regularization. *Trans. Neur. Netw.*, 21:1033–1047, July 2010.

[28] X. Yin, J. Han, and P. S. Yu. Crossclus: user-guided multirelational clustering. *Data Mining and Knowledge Discovery*, 2007.

[29] Z. Zhao and H. Liu. Semi-supervised feature selection via spectral analysis. In *ICDM '07*, 2007.

[30] X. Zhu and Z. Ghahramani. Learning from labeled and unlabeled data with label propagation. Technical Report CMU-CALD-02-107, Carnegie Mellon University, 2002.

[31] X. Zhu, Z. Ghahramani, and J. D. Lafferty. Semi-Supervised learning using gaussian fields and harmonic functions. In *ICML '03*, pages 912–919, 2003.

Design Principles of Massive, Robust Prediction Systems

Troy Raeder,
Ori Stitelman
M6D Research
37 E. 18th Street
New York, NY 10003
troy,ori@m6d.com

Brian Dalessandro,
Claudia Perlich
M6D Research
37 E. 18th Street
New York, NY 10003
briand,claudia@m6d.com

Foster Provost
New York University
& M6D Research
44 W. 4th Street
New York, NY 10012
fprovost@stern.nyu.edu

ABSTRACT

Most data mining research is concerned with building high-quality classification models in isolation. In massive production systems, however, the ability to monitor and maintain performance over time while growing in size and scope is equally important. Many external factors may degrade classification performance including changes in data distribution, noise or bias in the source data, and the evolution of the system itself. A well-functioning system must gracefully handle all of these. This paper lays out a set of design principles for large-scale autonomous data mining systems and then demonstrates our application of these principles within the m6d automated ad targeting system. We demonstrate a comprehensive set of quality control processes that allow us monitor and maintain thousands of distinct classification models automatically, and to add new models, take on new data, and correct poorly-performing models without manual intervention or system disruption.

Categories and Subject Descriptors

I.5.4 [**Computing Methodologies**]: Pattern Recognition—*Applications*

General Terms

Reliability, Measurement

Keywords

Quality control, data mining systems, data monitoring

1. INTRODUCTION

Online display advertising, (broadly speaking, the showing of banner ads on web sites) is a large and growing industry, with consumer brands expected to pour almost US$30 billion into the medium in 2012 and over $34 billion in 2013. [20] The problem of *targeted display advertising* involves determining where, when, and to whom to show a particular display ad on the Internet.

KDD'12, August 12–16, 2012, Beijing, China.

Display targeting decomposes broadly into two broad categories: *Retargeting*, in which advertisers target users that they have interacted with before (such as users who have visited their website), and *Prospecting* in which advertisers target users with whom they have no prior interaction in order to improve the penetration of their brand.

At m6d, we operate a large-scale, machine-learning based display advertising system which delivers tens of millions of display ad impressions for hundreds of different advertisers every day. We deal primarily in prospecting, meaning that we must identify, for each brand, a set of previously-unseen Internet users who will respond to the brand's advertising. Broadly speaking, this means that we classify hundreds of millions of Internet browsers as either "good" or "bad" prospects for each of our client brands. Delivering strong classification performance in this environment poses a number of challenges. For example:

- We operate *thousands* of simultaneous classification models, since we train separate models for each brand with which we work, and a model may contain millions of features. Additionally, we need to be able to *add new models* automatically as we take on more business. The result is a dynamic, constantly-changing model base that is too large for human oversight.
- We need to perform well over a broad range of classification tasks. The problems on which we train our models vary wildly in terms of class skew (anywhere from 1 in 100 to 1 in 100,000 examples are positive-class) and the amount of available data. As a result, there is no single "best" classification model for each problem in our system.
- We need to *maintain* our thousands of models in the face of changing internal and external system conditions. That is, they need to run 24 hours a day in a rapidly-changing environment in truly *autonomous* fashion.

In our experience, meeting all of these demands requires more than just a good classification model. It requires an end-to-end data mining system with that has been designed with maintenance and quality control in mind. Based on our experience, we have devised a set of design principles to help guide the design of large-scale autonomous data mining systems like ours. The remainder of the paper presents these principles, the architecture of our system and a number of the quality-control processes that we have developed in fulfillment of the principles. Taken together, these processes help us scale and maintain the system by allowing us to add new models, take on new data, detect harmful changes in the environment, and correct underperforming models all with minimal or no human intervention.

2. DESIGN PRINCIPLES FOR AUTONOMOUS DATA MINING SYSTEMS

In developing principles for autonomous system design, we are concerned primarily with systems that maintain a large and potentially dynamic set of independent models and operate in near real-time. Examples would include systems for electronic stock trading [17], fraud detection [6], churn prediction [18], and online display advertising [8, 4].

As a result of their size and the diversity of their problem space, these systems need to function largely autonomously even in the face of changing data and populations. Specifically, a massive robust production system should:

Yield fail-safe predictions: The system must run well for every stakeholder or user, maintaining acceptable worst-case performance. Worst-case performance here has two different components: all models must perform well under normal operating conditions, and they must *continue* to perform well under reasonable deviations in the operating conditions. That is, small changes in data distribution should not destroy model performance.

In an ad-targeting system, it is better to provide solid performance on every campaign than excellent performance for apparel ads and poor performance for fast-food ads. A fraud detection system needs to be able to deal with ordinary activity fluctuations, such as those due to weekends and holidays without issuing a bunch of false alarms.

Scale and easily extend: The system should be designed for growth and be able to scale as the application requires.

Exactly what it means to grow depends on the application, but at the very least the system should be able to add new users and models gracefully. In many cases the system must also be able to incorporate new data.

Minimize human intervention: The system must be able to hold all of the above properties without excessive human intervention.

In other words, the processes that ensure fail-safe predictions, scalability, and extensibility should be as automatic as possible. Ideally, the system would be self-correcting but where that is not possible, it should be self-diagnosing. This way, when human intervention is required because of extraordinary changes in the operating environment, the intervention is minimal. For example, the system might automatically look for significant changes in data distribution or performance and issue alerts when they occur.

3. THE M6D TARGETING ENGINE

At m6d, we run an automated online display ad targeting platform. Our customers are consumer brands; they pay us to identify Internet browsers well-suited to their product and target them with display ads. In order to provide the highest quality of targeting to our customers, our system is *browser specific*, *dynamic*, and *brand specific*.

Browser-specificity means that we target individual browsers rather than static buckets of browsers, which allows for very fine-grained targeting. It is worth noting that when we speak of *browsers*, both here and throughout the paper, we are referring to an individual browser cookie. If an individual web user deletes his or her cookies or uses a different computer, the user becomes a completely different browser for the purposes of our system. We use the words "browser" and "cookie" interchangeably throughout the paper, and they always refer to the same thing.

Brand-specificity means that we build a separate classification model, using separate data, for each client,[1] and "dynamic" here means that we regularly re-evaluate and re-score browsers. A browser who is a good target today may be a bad target next week.

In order to achieve browser-level targeting, we collect browser-level data. Specifically, we target browsers based on the existence, recency, and frequency of their visits to various sites around the web. For each campaign we run, we place pixels on the customer's website. These pixels call back to `m6d.com` and allow us to create or modify cookies for any user who visits the customer site[2]. Additionally, we have pixels on non-brand sites around the web, as well as data from some third-party providers, which together present a snapshot of the browser's general web activity. It is worth noting that we only store anonymized identifiers, rather than actual URLs, at every point in our system.

Our primary classification model [4] computes a brand-affinity score based on the user's browsing activity. If many of the URLs in a browser's cookie correlate positively with conversion, the browser gets a high score, and if the user's browsing history correlates negatively with conversion, he or she gets a very low score. The targetable audience for a given campaign is some number of the highest-scoring browsers, depending on the campaign's budget. What exactly counts as a "conversion" is different for different campaigns, but usually it requires a purchase from the customer web site.

3.1 System

The above-described classification procedure runs as part of a large-scale, end-to-end data mining system. Our system responds to billions of ad-targeting opportunities each day and maintains well over 1,000 classification models while operating hundreds of different advertising campaigns. We interact with hundreds of millions of browsers per day, each of which is scored for every campaign that we run.

A diagrammatic overview of our targeting system appears in Figure 1. Our raw input data comes from two major external sources: *mapping* pixels and *action* pixels. Action pixels are placed on individual customer web sites, and we use them both to define positive browsers and to track the conversion rates associated with their campaigns. Mapping pixels are placed on content-generating sites (e.g. blogs) throughout the web, and they provide the visit history data that forms the core of our classification models. A more detailed discussion of action and mapping pixels and their role in our system appears in [4]. We discuss two quality controls on this data in Section 3.2.

These data form the basis of our low-level classification model: a linear model over the sites that a browser has visited. Specifically, mapping data define the **features** for our low-level model and action data define the **class**. The output of the low-level model, as well as some other features

[1] This is both a performance issue and a client privacy issue: data collected for one client should not not inadvertently help its competitors.

[2] This assumes, of course, that the user accepts cookies. We make no attempt to track users who have disabled cookies or opted out of our tracking.

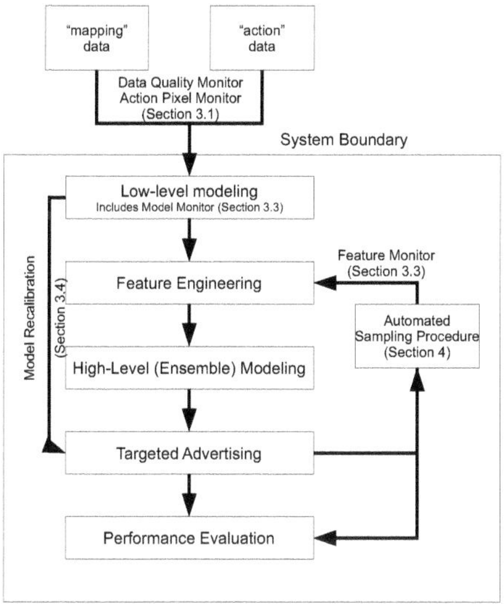

Figure 1: Our targeting system

computed from the user's cookie, form the basis of a "high-level" linear ensemble model. Both the low-level model and the ensemble model are available for user targeting. We discuss quality controls on the structure of the models themselves in Section 3.3. Once models are deployed, we evaluate their performance on a sample set that is carefully designed to represent the targetable population. The construction of the sample set and its appropriateness for model evaluation are discussed in Section 4.

It is worth briefly mentioning the *metrics* we use for evaluation, since we will need to quantify performance later in the paper. The most important feature of our classification model is its ability to rank. If the model ranks perfectly, then the optimal campaign-management strategy is to target as many browsers from the top of the list as the campaign's budget allows. Since most of our campaigns target only a small fraction of the browser population, metrics, (like ROC area) that evaluate ranking over the *entire* space of model scores can be misleading [9]. As a result, we measure performance using a more focused metric: *lift* at 5% of the population. Lift measures how many more converters (positive-class browsers) appear in the top 5% of model scores than would be expected from a random classifier.

We also track the *conversion rate* within the targeted browser population. The conversion rate for a campaign is the proportion of the targeted population (i.e. the browsers we have shown an ad) who convert within a short time of seeing the ad. Conversion rates depend on many factors other than raw classification performance, but since conversion rate is important to our customers, it serves as a measure of overall *system* performance.

In the absence of quality control, drastic changes in these performance metrics are often the only way to detect problems. The processes outlined in the rest of the paper allow us to notice changes before they affect performance.

3.2 Monitoring External System Interfaces

Our targeting system processes and incorporates a large portion of its data from sources that are either partly or entirely beyond our control. The pixels that we place on client websites and throughout the web, as well as the data we incorporate from external partners, are all critical to the functioning of our system. Changes in our client and partner systems, as well as incorporation of new partners, can lead to system disruptions if problems are not detected early on.

To this end, we have developed two separate processes aimed at monitoring this data stream. The first of these simply monitors the rate of activity on each of our action pixels. Visits to action pixels are critical elements of our model training because they form the "positive" browser population for a particular campaign. However, since this visibility depends on web servers outside of our control, the data stream could be disrupted at any time. Monitoring these streams allows us to detect disruptions before they affect system performance (ensuring *fail-safe predictions*) and reduces the human effort needed to investigate problems (*minimal intervention*).

Figure 2 shows performance statistics for a campaign that was flagged by our action pixel monitor system. Figure 2(a) plots the conversion rate among targeted browsers for one of our campaigns over time. This is a commonly-tracked business performance metric. Notice that it drops precipitously around the middle of the graph and remains low throughout.

Figure 2(b) plots conversion rate against our model's rank-order performance and Figure 2(c) plots conversion rate against action pixel activity for the same campaign and time window. Taking the two plots together, we see that both conversion rates and action pixel activity drop at exactly the same time, but that model rank-order performance (measured by lift) is not affected. The monitoring system was able to detect that external data, and not model performance, caused the drop in measured conversion rate.

In a smaller system, this type of anomaly could be detected fairly easily by human observers. As the system scales to handle more and more models, the *cause* of poor performance (or apparently poor performance) for any single model becomes increasingly difficult to identify. The installation of automated monitors such as these is an effective way to scale the system rapidly while controlling the amount of human effort actually required.

Monitoring external data sources.

A second monitoring process tracks the quality of mapping pixel (low-level feature) data from our external data providers. As we mentioned above, we incorporate browser-activity data from many different external sources. These data improve our visibility into browser activity on the web and provide most of the data that informs our models.

Monitoring our incoming data stream at the data-source level has two goals. First, we need to ensure that each source continues to provide quality data. Second, we need to understand the *risk* that would be posed to our system by losing a data source.

We incorporate data from dozens of external sources of varying sizes. The most relevant statistics we track are:

- *Reach*: the proportion of our browser population on which the source provides data. Since our data collection process seeks in part to increase the size of our targetable audience, we track both the proportion of the population that the source reaches in isolation and the proportion of the population reached the source's data removed.

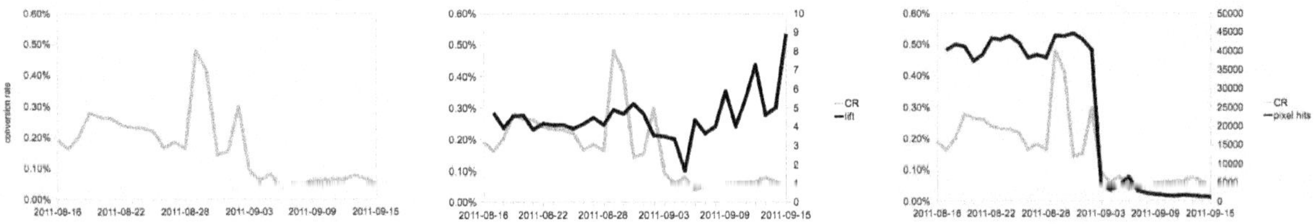

(a) Anomalous Conversion Rate (b) Model Performance vs. Conversion Rate (c) Pixel Activity vs. Conversion Rate

Figure 2: Anomaly detected with action pixel monitoring.

	reach	Prop Good	avg loss	worst loss	reach without
1	0.21	0.20	0.9964	0.9657	0.9999
2	0.22	0.00	0.9927	0.9649	0.9984
3	0.24	**0.45**	0.9928	0.9409	0.9998
4	0.26	0.05	0.9944	0.9642	0.9994
5	0.32	0.30	0.9951	0.9653	0.9996
6	0.37	0.40	**1.000**	0.9806	0.9997
7	0.89	0.80	0.9166	0.6659	0.9764
8	0.90	0.75	0.9109	0.5904	0.9862
9	0.89	0.70	0.9896	0.8445	0.9842

Table 1: Example data source quality report.

- *Performance*: In order to assess the quality of the data provided by an individual source, we estimate the performance of our model using only data from that source. Similarly, to understand the risk of losing a source, we estimate our model's performance with data from that source removed.

In combination, these reports show us both the extent to which a particular source's data is *predictive*, and the extent to which it is *redundant*. Following these reports over time assures us that each of the sources we use is continuing to add value, even when all others are considered.

Table 1 shows some typical results. Each metric that we compute is an aggregate over several campaigns. We present both average-case and worst-case analyses because we need to be mindful of any change that could potentially devastate one of our campaigns.

We present an evaluation of several of our sources on a diverse set of 20 campaigns. Data sources are anonymized for privacy reasons and numbered in order of reach. The other four columns are:

1. The proportion of campaigns on which the source's data provides a lift above a minimum performance threshold. This is useful for spotting sources that are especially predictive for a few campaigns.
2. The average performance loss after removing the data source, measured by lift at 1% (1.000 indicates no loss, 0.900 would be a 10% loss).
3. The worst-case loss over all campaigns after removing a data source. In larger studies, we sometimes report 5th or 10th percentile loss. Either way, this metric is designed to ensure that there will be no crises if we were to lose a source.
4. The proportion of our browser population that we still reach when removing the source.

Most of the columns correlate relatively strongly with reach, which is to be expected. The more data that comes from a particular source, the more browsers it will reach, the more it will contribute to performance, and the more it will hurt to lose. Of particular interest to us are sources that deviate from the general trend, as these sources are discernably better or worse than their comparably-sized counterparts. In the table above, for example, source 3 contributes significantly to many more campaigns than others of similar size and source 6 has the lowest average loss in the table.

Our application of data source tracking is in many ways more relative than absolute. If a particular data provider costs more than its comparably-performing peers, the report provides a quantitative basis for renegotiation or termination. If we notice a source's performance consistently degrading, we may try to engage the data provider and work toward a technical solution.

Our data quality reporting improves both *extensibility* and *scale*, and *stability* in our system. The ability to add new data seamlessly is a major growth driver for the reach of our targeting. Tracking the report's contents over time helps ensure that we are properly insulated against the loss of a data provider and gives us the knowledge and freedom to cut data providers, if necessary, if they become too expensive. As a result, we can easily take on new providers on a provisional basis and evaluate their impact on our ability to scale.

3.3 Monitoring Data Distributions

Once the raw input data that is discussed in the prior sections has been transformed into labeled feature vectors, it is available to train our models. At this point, we monitor both the input data and the output models for significant changes that may indicate systematic problems.

Model Monitor.

The quality-control process for our low-level models consists of a series of tests on model coefficients. As we mentioned above, each feature in our low-level classification model is a distinct (anonymized) URL and the model learns a single coefficient for each feature.

Each time one of these models is re-trained, it must pass two different quality checks before entering the production system. The first is simply a paired t-test of the model coefficients. The paired T-test tests the null hypothesis that the *mean difference* between the paired observations is zero. In our particular case, it tests whether the average change in model coefficients between two successive model builds is statistically indistinguishable from zero.

In an ideal world, where our model coefficients are unbiased estimators of some true quantity, the null hypothesis is exactly what one would expect: changes in model coefficients will amount to measurement error and the mean difference should be zero. Thus, the t-test serves as a safeguard against significant and unexpected bias in the model coefficients.

Second, we compute the rank correlation between sets of model coefficients in successive builds. A drastic change in the rank-ordering of the model coefficients indicates a higher-than-expected *variance* in our coefficient estimates.

A failure in either of the tests simply indicates that the model has changed appreciably and flags it for human examination. At this point, the system compiles a test failure report including the relevant statistics (t-score and rank correlation) as well as performance estimates for each (old and new) model on a recent hold-out sample. If the examiner approves the new model (usually because its performance is similar or improves) then the model passes into production. Otherwise, the most recent passed model remains until the source of the change is thoroughly investigated.

It would certainly be possible to skip the t-test and the rank test altogether and automatically pass any model whose performance stays "roughly the same" or improves by some measure, but there are advantages to our approach. The t-test and rank test are much faster than computing model performance. The latter requires scoring a sample of browsers and then ranking them while the former needs only mathematical operations on coefficients. As such, it is much more efficient to compute performance only for those models that fail the test.

Table 2 shows some results from one of our automated modeling runs. The thresholds for anomaly-flagging were a T-statistic greater than 2 in absolute value or a rank correlation less than 0.7. Boldfaced models showed significant improvement in model performance and so were allowed to pass. The ability to identify potentially problematic models cheaply, (both in terms of human and computer effort) is a big part of our ability to maintain thousands of effective models at once.

Feature Monitor.

A second similar process tracks the distributions and rank-ordering ability of each of the features in our high-level model as well as the model scores themselves. Specifically, we track *feature values*, *conversion rates*, and *lift* at various points on the distribution. This tracking allows us to see changes in both the distributions of features and their relative importance to model performance over time. Since the outputs or scores of our low-level models are also features of our high-level model, those outputs get tracked as a part of this process as well.

The ability to track changes in data distribution has many well-documented benefits. If one can identify situations where the input data have changed "significantly" in some sense, it becomes easier to determine when to re-train models or develop new ones. Our primary use of distribution monitoring, however, is to learn about the behavior of our system.

For example, Figure 3 plots the 98th percentile low-level model score for one of our campaigns over time. Since the top 2% of our audience is approximately what we target for the average campaign, this represents the approximate bottom of our targetable range. The black vertical lines (on 11-14 and 1-11) mark dates when the low-level model was retrained. Notice that the distribution changes dramatically a couple days after model retraining and then stabilizes a short time after. In our experience, stabilization takes about three to seven days, indicating that we should refresh our classification thresholds about a week after any retraining.

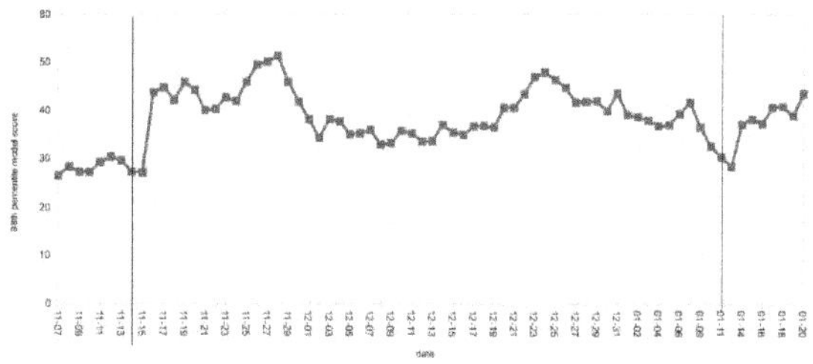

Figure 3: 98th percentile of a model score distribution over time. Black lines represent times of model retraining.

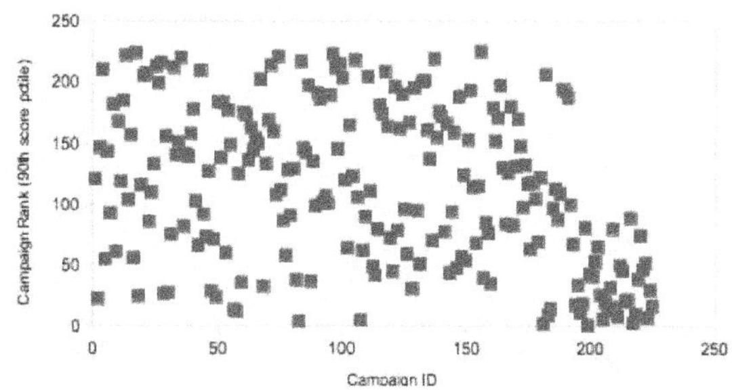

Figure 4: An emerging relationship between ID and model score can indicate a system change.

Figure 4 presents another interesting result. It shows the 90th percentile low-level model score (calculated across a sample of about one million targetable browsers) plotted against the internal ID number for the campaign associated with the model. The campaign ID is a meaningless primary key in our database, but since it is auto-incrementing, it is monotonic in the age of the campaign. That is, newer campaigns have higher IDs.

For the vast majority of campaigns, (up to about 200) there is absolutely no correlation between campaign ID and model score, exactly as we would expect. Conversely, campaigns with IDs greater than 200 appear to cluster and give very high model scores.

The phenomenon turned out to be a bug in the model-builder that affected any very-new campaigns that were also using very-new data. We fixed it very quickly after it was discovered. This result brings up an interesting point about the role of identifiers in maintaining data mining systems. We stressed earlier that automated systems need to remain stable, behaving relatively consistently in the face of "ordinary" changes in the operating environment. Figure 4 is a very clear violation of the stability principle. Our input data changed slightly (we were simply bringing on more data than we had in the past), but the behavior of the system changed substantially. The emergence of correlation between identifiers and system outputs strongly suggests that something fundamental in the system has changed.

3.4 Correcting underperforming models

Up to this point, we have discussed quality controls that take place prior to model construction. One might think of

(a) T-test

ID	T Statistic	Old lift	New lift
2829	2.7595	4.7579	2.1362
3132	5.0807	1.0830	**1.4904**
3579	2.1367	6.7901	4.7616
3934	2.4460	1.3513	**2.0831**
659	4.4058	8.7298	3.4879

(b) Rank correlation

ID	Rank Corr	Old lift	New lift
2679	0.6581	0.7860	0.7718
274	0.6726	1.9479	0.9114
2829	0.6293	4.7579	2.1362
3132	0.6925	1.0830	**1.4904**
3577	0.5651	10.7136	5.4022

Table 2: Sample model monitoring results.

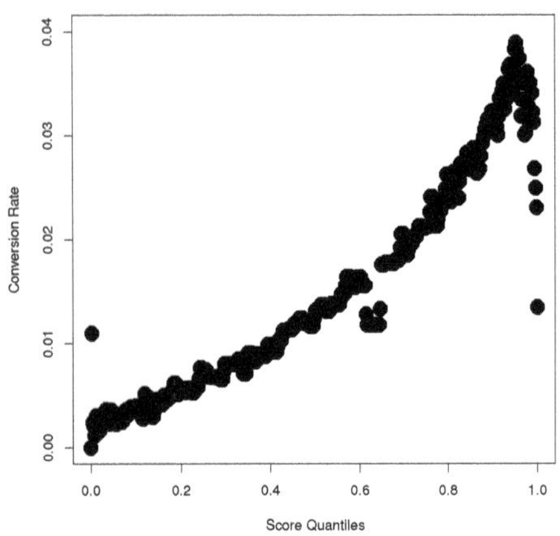

Figure 5: Binned estimates of actual conversion rate vs. quantile of score for a recalibration candidate in our system. The model mostly rank-orders well, but the highest-scoring browsers perform relatively poorly.

these controls as guarding against the pollution of innocent models by bad data or broken processes. The final quality control in our pipeline, however, goes beyond this: actually correcting for some degree of error in the models.

Both our low-level and ensemble classification models are ultimately linear functions of their constituent features. This decision has a lot of practical advantages. In addition to relatively strong performance, the storage requirements for the models are very low (just tables of coefficients) and scoring large groups of browsers is very efficient, requiring a single database join.

The downside to this approach is that, occasionally, the relationship between the conversion rate and model features is decidedly non-linear. In this case, our classification models will rank-order sub-optimally, with the highest-scoring browsers converting at less-than-optimal rates while lower-scoring browsers perform better. Similar behavior has been observed elsewhere, including the 2008 KDD Cup [14].

Since it is critical for us to perform well on every campaign (*fail-safe predictions*), we need to fix sub-optimal performance whenever we can. However, since we lack the computational resources to perform expensive searches over complicated hypothesis spaces to find the best model, we develop a novel re-calibration procedure that allows us to adjust the rank-order of suboptimal models when necessary without affecting any of the other models in the pipeline.

To see why such a procedure is necessary, simply observe Figure 5, which shows conversion probability, estimated in equal-frequency bins, against score quantiles from one of our low-level models. The top few quantiles of classifier score convert at a lower rate than the preceding quantiles despite the fact that the majority of the classifier scores rank order nicely. In this case the quantile-based conversion rates in Figure 1 could now be used to recalibrate the algorithm by re-ranking the browsers by estimated conversion rate. For most of our models, however, conversion rates are much smaller than 1% - 4%, and often smaller than 1 in 1,000. In this case, the bucketed quantiles will not provide good estimates of conversion rates. For this reason we use a generalized additive model (GAM) [10] with smoothing splines.

Figure 6(a) shows conversion rate as a function of score, for the campaign in Figure 5, as predicted by a GAM.[3] We recalibrate the scores by using the probabilities predicted by the GAM as the scores rather than the scores from the initial classifier. In this example those individuals in the top 1% as scored by the smoothing algorithm (the scores between the dotted lines on the plot) converted at a rate of about 4.0% while the top 1% of people scored by the initial algorithm (those scores to the right of the solid vertical line) converted at a rate of 2.6%. Thus, by using the re-calibrated scores we end up with a group of people that convert at a 50% higher rate than by using the initial algorithm alone. Figure 6(b) shows a campaign where the recalibrating algorithm does little to change the ranking of the browsers since those ranked in the top 1% by the GAM (between the dotted lines) have a large amount of overlap with the top 1% according to the initial algorithm (to the right of the solid vertical line). The difference in the conversion rate in this case is negligible (.159% vs .157%). In many other cases the score itself is monotonic in conversion rate and as a result the recalibration does not affect the ranking at all.

The use of GAM for re-calibration has a significant advantage over other recalibration approaches in the literature, such as Logistic [15] or isotonic [13, 5] regression in that its fit is potentially non-monotonic, allowing it to smooth over and reorder poor-performing regions. However the use of GAM is not magical. In practice, any smoothing method which can predict probabilities from a continuous feature will do.

In summary, we created a two stage classification algorithm with the following stages:

1. Fit an initial classification model on the training data.
2. Recalibrate the initial estimator using a smoothing algorithm, such as GAM, and use the predicted probability as the new score.

In situations where the relationship between the scores and

[3]Estimates were generated using the mgcv library in R.

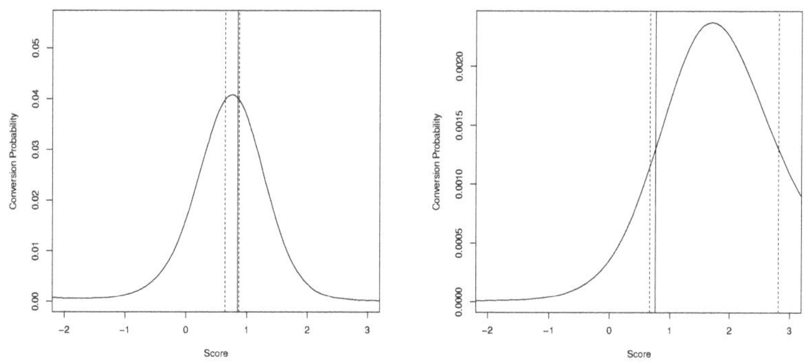

(a) (b)

Figure 6: GAM-predicted conversion rate vs. model score. Dashed lines enclose the top 1% of the population according to the GAM, while the black line marks the 99th percentile model score.

the conversion probabilities are monotonic this method does not change the ordering, but it will reorder those classifiers where the relationship is non-monotonic. By running this algorithm in production after the initial classifier is fit we can recalibrate its scores automatically and provide higher-quality models for the affected campaigns.

The ability to do this automatically and on demand has significant practical benefits for our system. It improves our ability to scale the system (we can take on more campaigns without changing models), maintains the *stability* of the system, since we can re-calibrate scores when things change, and helps make model predictions more fail-safe by allowing us to re-order model scores.

4. CONSTRUCTING REPRESENTATIVE BROWSER SAMPLES

Several different pieces of our system rely on having a "representative" sample of our reachable browser population. The construction of such a sample is complicated by a couple of factors. First, any sample of Internet browsers is naturally prone to activity bias [1]. Care must be taken to ensure that active browsers are not overrepresented in the sample. The second complicating factor is cookie decay. Since we respect a browser's right to delete his or her cookies (i.e. do not fingerprint or reconstruct cookies), a browser gets a new identifier in our system every time it clears its cookies. In the worst case (where it rejects cookies entirely), a browser may get a new identifier for every interaction. As a result, a large majority of browser identifiers are assigned to cookies that we see exactly once.

Broadly speaking, there are two different methods for correcting these types of bias: modeling and sampling. The Heckman correction [11] and its variants, for example produce unbiased estimates of the quantity of interest (in this case conversion rate) by explicitly modeling the selection process and including an estimate of the *selection probability* in the final classification model. Prior work [2, 19] has shown that this approach is effective in classification settings, but the size of our data and the number of factors influencing selection make the construction of an effective model difficult.

The second option is to sample more intelligently. The ultimate goal of any procedure we implement is to produce a representative sample of *targetable browsers*: browsers to which, broadly speaking, we could conceivably serve an ad. The set of such browsers changes over time, of course, as users get new computers or clear their cookies, but a very simple proxy for the targetable population is the set of browsers that *actually saw an ad* on a given day.

This approach is attractive on several levels. The set of browsers that saw an ad is certainly a subset of the targetable browser population. If any targetable browser is just as likely to see an ad as any other targetable browser, it is a perfectly representative sample of the population.

Unfortunately, this is not the case. Some browsers in our system qualify for dozens of campaigns, and these browsers are much more likely to see an ad than browsers who qualify for only a few campaigns. Additionally, this kind of impression-based sampling is heavily influenced by external factors. Whether a qualified browser actually sees an ad depends, among other things, on the amount of competition for the browser and how many ads we have already shown that day.

Our sampling algorithm accounts for these difficulties in the following manner. Each day, our system selects a random sample of browsers that meet the following criteria:

1. The browser is qualified for at least two of our campaigns. This guarantees that the cookie has survived long enough and accumulated enough information to be targetable.
2. We interacted with the browser on the day in question. This guarantees that the cookie is still active.

We find that this sampling methodology produces training and evaluation samples that generally outperform impression-based sampling. A fairly straightforward explanation appears in Figure 7, which shows distributions of a few high-level model features over both impression and qualification samples. It is easy to see that the qualification sampling gives access to a wider range of feature values, providing a more inclusive sample than impression-based sampling. In particular, the qualification sampling tends to get more representation from lower-valued regions of the feature space, which tend to contain less active browsers.

Performance estimates on this sample of browsers correlate surprisingly well with the "real" performance on which

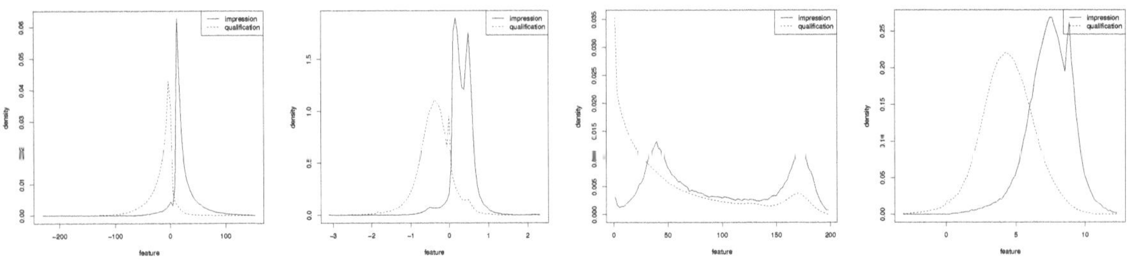

Figure 7: Distributions induced by different sampling schemes. Impression-based sampling tends to exclude less active browsers (i.e. those with lower feature values).

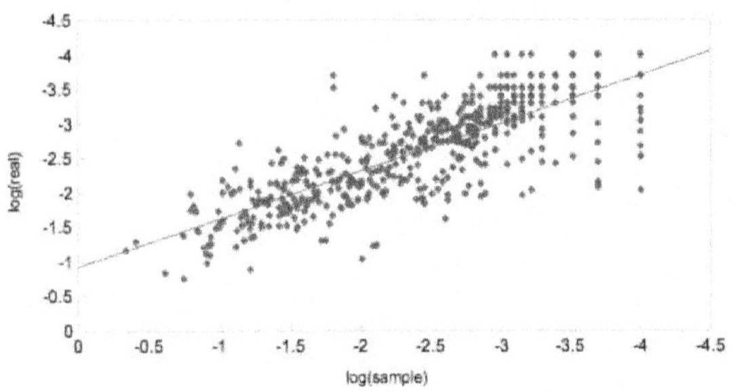

Figure 8: Correlation of sample performance estimates and real performance.

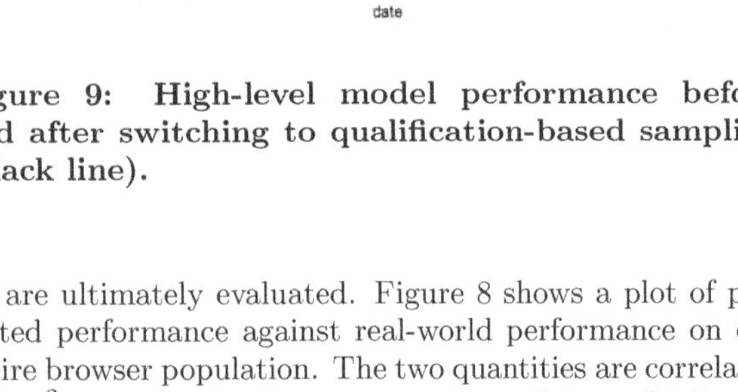

Figure 9: High-level model performance before and after switching to qualification-based sampling (black line).

we are ultimately evaluated. Figure 8 shows a plot of predicted performance against real-world performance on our entire browser population. The two quantities are correlated with $r^2 = 0.75$ and a Spearman rank coefficient of 0.8.

Further validation is available in Figure 9, which shows shows a plot of our median high-level model performance over time. On the date marked by the black line, we began training our high-level models on a qualification-based rather than an impression-based sample. The cutover was gradual, but after fully implementing this sampling procedure for training, the performance of the high-level model increased more than 50% from 1.88x (lift over untargeted-browser performance) to sustained performance above 3.0x going forward.

A consistent, automated, representative sampling procedure is, in our opinion, a critical component in a large-scale data mining system. Having a readily available automated sample ensures not only that the evaluation of new methods is consistent and correct and contributed to the development of most of the other quality-control systems described here.

5. RELATED WORK

We are not aware of any papers that discuss quality control in deployed systems as large as ours. Sculley et al [16] present a system for detecting malicious ads that works in a semi-automated fashion (consistent with "minimal intervention") and trains thousands of models (consistent with "scale"). The authors say that automated monitoring and recalibration tools are important aspects of their system, but they do not give any implementation details.

Ghani and Kumar [7] discuss an interactive quality-control improvement to a health-insurance-auditing application. They augment an existing classifier (which predicts overpayments in health insurance claims) with a "more-like-this" feature to reduce the time human auditors spend auditing claims.

Moreno-Torres et al [12] report on a situation where data generated for the same classification task from two different research labs were incompatible. In other words, the classifier trained on one lab's data was completely useless for the other lab even though the features and label were theoretically the same. They develop a genetic-programming-based feature-engineering algorithm that solves the problem in their case.

The problem of change detection has attracted considerable attention, although most of it in a research setting. The most relevant of these deal with change detection in production systems. Curry et al [3] develop a change-detection system for identifying anomalies in credit card payment records and Fawcett and Provost [6] describe a system for fraud detection from cellular phone records. Both of these systems serve to automatically detect adverse system changes with minimal human intervention. In both of these cases, however, change detection is a problem in and of itself, rather than a quality control within a production system.

6. PRACTICAL GUIDANCE

So far we have given a very general set of principles along with a very specific description of our own production system. The purpose of this final section is to offer a few practical suggestions for someone trying to implement our principles from scratch. The following simple suggestions, based on our experience, should help practitioners trying to get a new system off the ground.

- **Closely monitor data feeds** from any external source, including the Internet. Unless you control the data-generating process *completely*, it will eventually change.
- **Monitor interfaces** between critical internal systems. In a large evolving system, even intentional changes may have unintended consequences. It is best to detect these as quickly as possible.
- **Work, then scale, then excel**: It is easier to improve a system that provides adequate performance at scale than to scale a system that was not designed to grow. For example, simple models are fast to train, fast to score, and can be enhanced on a case-by-case basis as necessary.
- **Build a sandbox**: A consistent, automatically-generated data sample saves time when experimenting with new ideas, but also helps diagnose problems with the existing system. Data that is pulled the exact same way for two months makes identifying changes much easier.
- **Bound your error**: The simplest realization of the *fail-safe predictions* principle simply is to ensure that even dreadful model predictions cause limited damage to your system. We do this ourselves in a number of ways, for example by limiting the number of ad impressions any one browser can see.

7. CONCLUSION

Operating an end-to-end data mining system at scale requires more than just clever feature engineering or brilliant algorithmic design. The consistent need to grow and change the system while maintaining or improving performance means that *quality control* becomes increasingly important as the system matures.

In an effort to energize and focus the discussion of quality control in the data mining community, we have proposed three desirable criteria for a self-sufficient data mining system. Next, we present the quality-control processes that we have developed for our online display-ad targeting system in accordance with the principles outlined above. Many of these controls developed because of our need to maintain thousands of classification models simultaneously, but they should be useful in any system where the number of distinct components makes direct human oversight impractical.

We have automated monitoring of all of our external data, which allows us to scale and extend the system without increasing the quality-control burden on human operators. We monitor and flag significant changes in our model coefficients, which helps ensure that our system is *stable*: that is, that it continues to operate well in a changing environment. We have developed an algorithm, based on generalized additive models, which re-calibrates the output of a classification model and improves its rank-ordering performance. This naturally keeps performance "fail-safe", but also helps the system *scale*, as we can add new customers and be confident that our models will continue to perform well.

8. REFERENCES

[1] D. Chan, R. Ge, O. Gershony, T. Hesterberg, and D. Lambert. Evaluating online ad campaigns in a pipeline: causal models at scale. In *Proceedings of KDD*, pages 7–16. ACM, 2010.

[2] N. Chawla and G. Karakoulas. Learning from labeled and unlabeled data: An empirical study across techniques and domains. *Journal of Artificial Intelligence Research*, 23(1):331–366, 2005.

[3] C. Curry, R. Grossman, D. Locke, S. Vejcik, and J. Bugajski. Detecting changes in large data sets of payment card data: a case study. In *Proceedings of KDD*, pages 1018–1022. ACM, 2007.

[4] F. Provost et al. Audience selection for on-line brand advertising: privacy-friendly social network targeting.

[5] T. Fawcett and A. Niculescu-Mizil. PAV and the ROC convex hull. *Machine Learning*, 68(1):97–106, 2007.

[6] T. Fawcett and F. Provost. Adaptive fraud detection. *Data mining and knowledge discovery*, 1(3):291–316, 1997.

[7] R. Ghani and M. Kumar. Interactive learning for efficiently detecting errors in insurance claims. In *Proceedings of KDD*, pages 325–333. ACM, 2011.

[8] A. Goldfarb and C. Tucker. Online display advertising: Targeting and obtrusiveness. *Marketing Science*, 2010.

[9] D. Hand. Measuring classifier performance: a coherent alternative to the area under the roc curve. *Machine learning*, 77(1):103–123, 2009.

[10] T. Hastie and R. Tibshirani. *Generalized additive models*. Chapman & Hall/CRC, 1990.

[11] J. Heckman. Sample selection bias as a specification error. *Econometrica*, pages 153–161, 1979.

[12] J. Moreno-Torres, X. Llorà, D. Goldberg, and R. Bhargava. Repairing fractures between data using genetic programming-based feature extraction: A case study in cancer diagnosis. *Information Sciences*, 2010.

[13] A. Niculescu-Mizil and R. Caruana. Predicting good probabilities with supervised learning. In *Proceedings of ICML*, pages 625–632. ACM, 2005.

[14] C. Perlich, P. Melville, Y. Liu, G. Świrszcz, R. Lawrence, and S. Rosset. Breast cancer identification: Kdd cup winner's report. *ACM SIGKDD Explorations Newsletter*, 10(2):39–42, 2008.

[15] J. Platt. Sequential minimal optimization: A fast algorithm for training support vector machines. *Advances in Kernel Methods: Support Vector Learning*, 208(MSR-TR-98-14):1–21, 1998.

[16] D. Sculley, M. Otey, M. Pohl, B. Spitznagel, J. Hainsworth, and Y. Zhou. Detecting adversarial advertisements in the wild. In *Proceedings of KDD*, pages 274–282. ACM, 2011.

[17] H. Stoll. Electronic trading in stock markets. *J. Economic Perspectives*, 20(1):153–174, 2006.

[18] C. Wei, I. Chiu, et al. Turning telecommunications call details to churn prediction: a data mining approach. *Expert systems with applications*, 23(2):103–112, 2002.

[19] B. Zadrozny. Learning and evaluating classifiers under sample selection bias. In *Proceedings of ICML*, page 114. ACM, 2004.

[20] ZenithOptimedia. Global ad expenditure to return to pre-recession peak level this year. `http://www.zenithoptimedia.com/files/media/image/news/PressReleasefiles/2011/July/AdspendforecastsJuly2011.pdf`, 2011.

PatentMiner: Topic-driven Patent Analysis and Mining

Jie Tang†, Bo Wang†, Yang Yang†, Po Hu†, Yanting Zhao†, Xinyu Yan†, Bo Gao†, Minlie Huang†, Peng Xu♮, Weichang Li♮, and Adam K. Usadi♮
†Department of Computer Science and Technology, Tsinghua University, China
♮ExxonMobil Research and Engineering Company, New Jersey, USA
jietang@tsinghua.edu.cn

ABSTRACT

Patenting is one of the most important ways to protect company's core business concepts and proprietary technologies. Analyzing large volume of patent data can uncover the potential competitive or collaborative relations among companies in certain areas, which can provide valuable information to develop strategies for intellectual property (IP), R&D, and marketing. In this paper, we present a novel topic-driven patent analysis and mining system. Instead of merely searching over patent content, we focus on studying the heterogeneous patent network derived from the patent database, which is represented by several types of objects (companies, inventors, and technical content) jointly evolving over time. We design and implement a general topic-driven framework for analyzing and mining the heterogeneous patent network. Specifically, we propose a dynamic probabilistic model to characterize the topical evolution of these objects within the patent network. Based on this modeling framework, we derive several patent analytics tools that can be directly used for IP and R&D strategy planning, including a heterogeneous network co-ranking method, a topic-level competitor evolution analysis algorithm, and a method to summarize the search results. We evaluate the proposed methods on a real-world patent database. The experimental results show that the proposed techniques clearly outperform the corresponding baseline methods.

Categories and Subject Descriptors

H.3.3 [**Information Search and Retrieval**]: Text Mining; H.2.8 [**Database Management**]: Database Applications

General Terms

Algorithms, Experimentation

Keywords

Patent analysis, Competitor analysis, Company ranking, Social network

KDD'12, August 12–16, 2012, Beijing, China.
Copyright 2012 ACM 978-1-4503-1462-6/12/08... $15.00.

1. INTRODUCTION

Patenting becomes one of the most important ways to protect company's core business concepts and proprietary technologies. Before a company entering the market of a new field, a comprehensive patent landscape overview is always necessary, lest be faced with a flurry of third-party licensing opportunities or even lawsuits. Nowadays, the collection and retrieval of patent publications is a critical component of a company's intellectual property strategy. Within many companies (or organizations), patent analysts have the responsibility to determine how patent information is best made available and how it is best used within their organizations in a strategic manner. From the technical perspective, patent, as one of the few real indicators of future product releases, carries out the technical details of research of different companies long before the product reaches the marketplace. Keeping being aware of novel technology development and competitors' technological advancement also becomes more and more important for a company to make the decision on marketing and R&D strategies.

However, patent analysts in the 21st century now face many challenges. They must search over the huge volume of patents to find relevant patents, to recognize potential competitors (or collaborators), and to identify inventors with significant impact. Despite a great deal of theoretical development in information retrieval and data mining techniques, advanced search tools for patent professionals are still in their infancy. Most existing patent analysis systems such as Google Patent[1], WikiPatent[2], FreePatentsOnline[3] only focus on the search function. A few other systems such as Patents[4], PatentLens[5], and PriorArtSearch[6] provide more advanced analysis and mining capabilities. For example, the Patents system uses iBoogie to cluster the retrieved patents. It also provides a forum for people to discuss different patenting related problems. PatentLens provides a function called Patent Landscapes, which lists a number of "White Papers" discussing technologies relevant to life scientists. However, the Technology Landscapes require extensive searching and analytical work by people skilled in both science and intellectual property, thus infeasible to scale up to various topics.

[1] `http://www.google.com/patents`
[2] `http://www.wikipatents.com/`
[3] `http://www.freepatentsonline.com/`
[4] `http://www.patents.com/`
[5] `http://www.patentlens.net/`
[6] `http://www.priorartsearch.com/`

This paper reports the development of PatentMiner[7], a novel topic-driven patent analysis and mining system. PatentMiner is designed for an in-depth analysis of patent activity at the topic-level. The main unique characteristics of the PatentMiner system that distinguish it from traditional patent search systems are as follows: (1) topic-driven modeling; (2) heterogeneous network co-ranking; (3) intelligent competitive analysis; and (4) patent summarization.

1. Topic-driven modeling. The fundamental problem in most existing systems is that all patents are simply modeled based on keywords. In this work, we present a probabilistic model to simultaneously model the topical aspects of different objects in the heterogeneous patent network.
2. Heterogeneous network co-ranking. When a company plans to enter a new market or brainstorm novel ideas, several typical questions are: what are the most active companies in this area? what are the most relevant patents? and who are the most prolific inventors? We propose a heterogeneous co-ranking algorithm to address these questions.
3. Competitive analysis. It would be very helpful for a company to make right business strategies by identifying who are its competitors and what is the trend of a competitor's technology development. We define four measures to identify competitors, topic-level competitors, and competitors' evolutionary pattern based on the topic modeling results.
4. Patent summarization. It is always expensive to digest the large number of patents returned by a search engine. We present a maximum coverage method to automatically generate a summary for the results of patent search.

We conducted empirical evaluations of the proposed methods. Experimental results show that our methods clearly outperform the baseline methods for addressing the above issues. Our technical contributions in this paper include: (1) a proposal of a probabilistic topic modeling approach, (2) a proposal of a heterogeneous co-ranking method for search over the patent network, (3) a proposal of a topic-level competitive evolution analysis approach, and (4) a proposal of a maximum coverage model for patent summarization.

2. OVERVIEW

Figure 1 shows the architecture of the system. The system consists of five major components:

1. *Patent Network Extraction*: The patent data contains huge amount of information. From the patent data, we derive a heterogeneous information network consisting of different types of objects such as companies, inventors, and patents.
2. *Patent Network Storage*: It provides storage and indexing for the extracted patent networking data. Specifically, for storage it employs MySQL; for indexing, it employs the inverted file indexing method [20].

[7] `http://pminer.org`

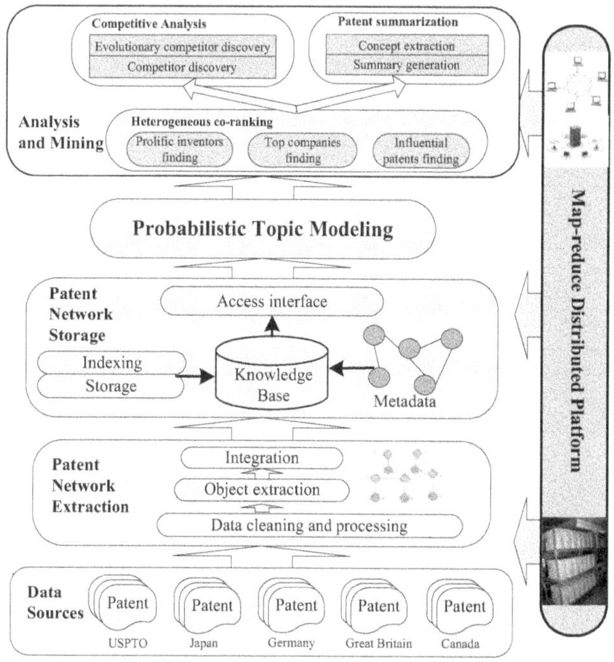

Figure 1: Architecture of PatentMiner.

3. *Probabilistic Topic Modeling*: It utilizes a generative probabilistic model to simultaneously model the different types of objects. After modeling, each object is associated with a topic distribution. The topic modeling is the basis for the analysis and mining component.
4. *Analysis and Mining*: This is the most important component in the PatentMiner system, and our major technical contribution also lies in this component. In summary, it provides three functions: heterogeneous co-ranking, competitive evolution analysis, and patent summarization.
5. *Distributed Platform*: The back-end system is built on the Map-reduce distributed platform [6], a programming platform for distributed processing of large data sets. For some analysis and mining tasks (such as topic model and competitive analysis), we implement the distributed version of the proposed algorithms.

At present, we maintain an English patent database extracted from USPTO.gov, which consists of nearly 4,000,000 patents, 2,000,000 inventors, and 400,000 companies. The system is very flexible and can be easily extended to multiple different sources.

Preliminaries Assume that a patent d contains a vector $\mathbf{w}_d$ of N_d words, in which each word w_{di} is chosen from a vocabulary of size V, and the patent d is developed by a group of inventors $\mathbf{a}_d$ and is owned by company c_d, then a collection of M patents can be represented as $\mathbf{D} = \{(\mathbf{a}_1, c_1, \mathbf{w}_1), \ldots, (\mathbf{a}_M, c_M, \mathbf{w}_M)\}$. Given a collection of patents $\mathbf{D}$, we extract the inventor and company information from each patent, and derive a heterogeneous patent network.

DEFINITION 1. **Heterogenous Patent Network.** *The heterogeneous patent network can be represented as a graph centered by the patent* $G = (V_d \cup V_a \cup V_c, E_{da} \cup E_{dc} \cup E_{dd'} \cup$

Table 1: Notations.

Symbol	Description
M	Number of patents
W	Number of unique words in patents
K	Number of topics
A	Number of inventors
C	Number of companies
N_d	Number of words in patent d
d, c, a	A patent, a company, and an inventor respectively
w_{di}	The i-th word in patent d
x_{di}	The chosen inventor to be responsible for word w_{di}
z_{di}	The topic assigned to the i-th word in patent d
θ_a	Multinomial on topics specific to inventor a
ϕ_z	Multinomial on words specific to topic z
ψ_c	Multinomial on topics specific to company c
α, β, μ	Dirichlet priors to the multinomials θ, ϕ, and ψ

E_{ac}), where V_d includes all patents, V_a includes all inventors, V_c includes all companies, and the edge $(v_d, v_a) \in E_{da}$ (or briefly e_{da}) suggests that there is a relationship between patent v_d and inventor v_a. Similarly we can define the other relationships e_{dc}, $e_{dd'}$, and e_{ac}.

The heterogeneous patent network is comprised of three different types of objects: inventors, companies, and patents. Each object may be associated with different topics. For example, a patent may talk about "web search" and "data mining". The goal of topic modeling over the patent network is to discover the latent topics associated with each object. Each topic z is defined as a mixture of words and their probabilities belonging to the topic, i.e., $\{(w_1, P(w_1|z)), \cdots, (w_{N1}, P(w_{N1}|z))\}$. The definition can be extended to other information sources. For example, we can extend the topic definition by companies, i.e., $\{(c_1, P(c_1|z)), \cdots, (c_{N1}, P(c_{N1}|z))\}$. After topic modeling, each object would be associated with a topic distribution, e.g., an inventor a is associated with $\{P(z|a)\}_z$. By further considering the time information, a patent network can be segmented into a network sequence $GS = (G^1, G^2, \cdots, G^T)$ according to the time-stamp associated with each object. Each sub network G^t in the sequence is comprised of objects in the time window t, e.g., patents published at time t. In this work, the time-stamp is defined as the published year of each patent. Table 1 lists the major notations.

3. MODELING PATENT NETWORK

Several topic models have been proposed and successfully applied to text mining tasks [1, 4, 9, 13, 18]. However, these models can only model patent contents and are not able to incorporate the company and inventor information, which contains valuable information for topic modeling. Moreover, they cannot model the time information. In this section, we will first present an Inventor-Company-Topic model which leverages interdependencies between different objects to learn the topic model, and then describe an extension of the model by combining time information.

3.1 Inventor-Company-Topic (ICT) Model

We present an Inventor-Company-Topic (ICT) model, which incorporates companies, inventors, and patents into a unified probabilistic model. The basic idea is to describe patent writing in a generative process. The generative process can be described as follows: when preparing a patent d, each inventor $x \in \mathbf{a}_d$ would suggest what topics to be included in patent according to his expertise (the associated topic distribution $P(z|\theta_x)$ or θ_{xz}); then the word w_{di} is sampled from a suggested topic z_{di} by the inventor according to $P(w_{di}|z_{di})$ or $\phi_{z_{di}w_{di}}$. In the generative process, all the suggested topics specific to the patent d are relevant to the own company c_d. Aggregating topics of all patents owned by company c_d could constitute a topic distribution of the company $P(z|\psi_c)$ or ψ_{cz}. Formally, we use a uniform distribution to associate each patent with its inventors, use a multinomial distribution (with a prior α) to associate each inventor with the topics, and use a similar multinomial distribution (with a prior β) to associate each topic with words. The company-topic distribution is represented as a mixture of topic distribution extracted from each patent (again can be considered as a multinomial distribution with a different prior μ). Finally, given a collection of patents $\mathbf{D}$, we could write its generative log-likelihood as:

$$\mathcal{L}(\mathbf{D}) = P(\mathbf{x}, \mathbf{z}, \mathbf{w}, \mathbf{c}|\Theta, \Phi, \Psi, \mathbf{a}) = \prod_{d=1}^{M}\prod_{i=1}^{N_d}\frac{1}{A_d} \times \prod_{z=1}^{K}\left(\prod_{x=1}^{A}\theta_{xz}^{m_{xz}}\prod_{j=1}^{W}\phi_{zw_j}^{n_{zw_j}}\prod_{c=1}^{C}\psi_{zc}^{n_{zc}}\right) \quad (1)$$

where m_{xz} is the number of times that topic z was associated with inventor x, n_{zw_j} is the number of times that word w_j is generated by topic z, n_{zc} is the number of times that company c is generated by topic z, N_d is the number of words in patent d, and A_d is the number of inventors for patent d.

Learning the ICT model is to estimate the unknown parameters in the ICT model. There are two sets of unknown parameters: (1) the distribution θ of A inventor-topics, the distribution ϕ of K topic-words, and the distribution ψ of K topic-companies; and (2) the corresponding topic z_{di} and inventor x_{di} for each word w_{di}. It is usually intractable to do exact inference in such a probabilistic model. A variety of algorithms have been proposed to conduct approximate inference, for example variational EM methods [1] and Gibbs sampling [7]. We chose Gibbs sampling for its ease of implementation. Specifically, we calculate the posterior distribution on z and then sample the topic for each word. Based on the sampling results, we could infer the distribution θ, ϕ, and ψ. For the hyperparameters α, β, and μ, for simplicity, we take fixed values (i.e., $\alpha = 50/K$, $\beta = 0.01$, and $\mu = 0.01$.

3.2 Dynamic ICT Model

Though the ICT model incorporates companies, inventors, and patents together, it still cannot capture the temporal information. We therefore propose a dynamic extension of the ICT model. The general idea is that topic distribution of an object (e.g., company) in adjacent time-stamps (e.g., two continuous years) should be similar. At each time-stamp, an ICT model is built, i.e., each object is associated with a topic distribution which will be used as a prior for the object in the next time-stamp. The prior has a smoothing effect to make the discovered topic models between adjacent time-stamps similar to each other. The new model is referred to as Dynamic Inventor-Company-Topic (DICT). To summarize, there are three smoothing requirements for the dynamic modeling:

- Inventor-topic smoothing. The topic distribution of

an inventor should be smooth over time, aka $\Omega_1 = \sum_z(\theta^t_{az} - \theta^{t-1}_{az})^2$ should be small, where θ^t_{az} indicates the probability of topic z given inventor a at time t.

- Company-topic smoothing. The topic distribution of a company should be smooth over time, aka $\Omega_2 = \sum_z(\psi^t_{cz} - \psi^{t-1}_{cz})^2$ should be small.

- Topic smoothing. The topic distribution itself should be smooth over time, aka $\Omega_3 = \sum_z(P(z)^t - P(z)^{t-1})^2$ should be small.

Now, the problem is how to combine the three smoothing hypothesis into the ICT model. One strategy is to use a regularization framework to describe the three smoothing factors as three regularization terms, and plug into the original log-likelihood function, thus we obtain a new objective function:

$$\mathcal{O}(\mathbf{D}) = -\mathcal{L}(\mathbf{D}) + \gamma_1\Omega_1 + \gamma_2\Omega_2 + \gamma_3\Omega_3 \quad (2)$$

where γ_1, γ_2, and γ_3 are three parameters to balance the importances of different smoothing factors.

It is intractable to solve the new objective function. In existing literatures, there are a few attempts to deal with the constrained regularization framework using approximation algorithms such as [24] and [11]. However, these methods cannot guarantee a convergence. In this paper, we consider an alternative method to solve the problem. Instead of plugging the regularization terms into the log-likelihood function, we use the learned topic model of previous time-stamp as the prior for the topic model of the current time-stamp. Specifically, we use the Gaussian distribution as the prior distribution, e.g. $\alpha_t|\alpha_{t-1} \sim \mathcal{N}(\alpha_{t-1}, \delta^2 I)$. In principle, we can also consider other prior distributions, such as Dirichlet distribution or Gamma distribution. We tested a few distributions and found that the Gaussian distribution has the best performance. With a prior distribution, we can incorporate the smoothing effect directly into the probabilistic generative process (as summarized in Algorithm 1).

To learn the Dynamic ICT model, we can still use the Gibbs sampling algorithm for parameter estimation of the DICT model. In an analogous way, we first estimate the posterior probability of sampling the topic z^t_{di} for each word w^t_{di} with time-stamp t, and then use the sampling results to infer θ^t, ϕ^t, and ψ^t. Specifically, with the learned topic model at time t, we can estimate the probability of a topic given an inventor θ^t_{xz}, the probability of a word given a topic ϕ^t_{zv}, and the probability of a company given a topic ψ^t_{zc} respectively by (Derivation is omitted for brevity.):

$$\theta^t_{xz} = \frac{m^t_{xz} + \alpha^t_z + \tau(m^{t-1}_{xz} + \alpha^{t-1}_z)}{\sum_{z'}(m^t_{x,z'} + \alpha^t_{z'}) + \tau\sum_{z'}(m^{t-1}_{xz'} + \alpha^{t-1}_{z'})} \quad (3)$$

$$\phi^t_{zw} = \frac{n^t_{zw} + \beta^t_w + \tau(n^{t-1}_{zw} + \beta^{t-1}_w)}{\sum_{w'}(n^t_{zw'} + \beta^t_{w'}) + \tau\sum_{w'}(n^{t-1}_{zw'} + \beta^{t-1}_{w'})} \quad (4)$$

$$\psi^t_{zc} = \frac{n^t_{zc} + \mu^t_c + \tau(n^{t-1}_{zc} + \mu^{t-1}_c)}{\sum_{c'}(n^t_{zc'} + \mu^t_{c'}) + \tau\sum_{c'}(n^{t-1}_{zc'} + \mu^{t-1}_{c'})} \quad (5)$$

where τ is a parameter to control the influence of the topic model of the previous time on the topic model of to the current time.

```
Initialize α^0 = 50/K, β^0 = 0.01, and μ^0 = 0.01;
foreach time-stamp t do
    Draw α^t|α^{t-1} ~ N(α^{t-1}, δ^2 I);
    Draw β^t|β^{t-1} ~ N(β^{t-1}, σ^2 I);
    Draw μ^t|μ^{t-1} ~ N(μ^{t-1}, ε^2 I);
    For each topic z^t, draw φ^t_z and ψ^t_z respectively from
    Dirichlet prior β^t and μ^t;
    foreach word w_di in patent d do
        Draw an inventor x_di from a_d uniformly;
        Draw a topic z^t_di from a multinomial distribution
        θ^t_{x_di} specific to inventor x_di, where θ^t is generated
        from the Dirichlet prior α^t;
        Draw a word w^t_di from multinomial φ^t_{z_di};
        Draw a company stamp c^t_di from multinomial ψ^t_{z_di};
    end
end
```

Algorithm 1: Probabilistic generative process in DICT.

4. HETEROGENEOUS CO-RANKING

The unique requirements of searching over the heterogeneous patent network give rises to several challenging issues and make them different from general search engines. First, the information seeking practice [8] is not only about patents, but also about other information sources, such as companies and inventors. In this spirit, a good patent search engine should provide supports not only for patents, but also for these information sources. Second, search over the patent network typically requires much higher retrieval accuracy. Given a query, such as "data mining", a user does not mean to find patents merely containing these two words. Her/his intention is to find patents on the data mining topic. Finally, these two issues are often intertwined.

Formally, given a heterogeneous patent network $G = (V, E)$, and a query $q = \{w_1, \cdots, w_n\}$, our objective is to leverage the power of both *textual content* (patent content) and the *network information* (relationships between different types of objects) in the patent network to obtain accurate ranking results for companies, inventors, and patents.

To deal with the ranking problem over the patent network, a straightforward method is to first represent each object with a bag of words, and then calculate the relevance score of each object with a given query q by using methods such as language model [22] or vector space model [20]. We use language model as the example to explain how to calculate the relevance score. Language model is one of the state-of-the-art approaches for information retrieval. It interprets the relevance between a document and a query word as a generative probability:

$$P_{LM}(w|d) = \frac{N_d}{N_d + \lambda} \cdot \frac{tf(w,d)}{N_d} + (1 - \frac{N_d}{N_d + \lambda}) \cdot \frac{tf(w,\mathbf{D})}{N_\mathbf{D}} \quad (6)$$

where N_d is the number of words in document (patent) d, $tf(w, d)$ is the word frequency (i.e., occurring number) of word w in d, $N_\mathbf{D}$ is the number of words in the entire collection, and $tf(w, \mathbf{D})$ is the word frequency of word w in the collection $\mathbf{D}$. λ is the Dirichlet smoothing factor and is commonly set according to the average document length in the collection [22]. Further, the probability of the document model d generating a query q can be defined as $P(q|d) = \Pi_{w\in q}P(w|d)$. For companies and inventors, we first combine all patents associated with each object and create a virtual document, and then use a similar formula to calculate the relevance score of company $P(q|c)$ and inventor $P(q|a)$.

However, such a method is only based on keyword matching and cannot leverage the topic modeling information. To take advantage of the topic modeling results, we define another relevance score:

$$P_{ICT}(w|d,\theta,\phi) = \sum_{z=1}^{K}\sum_{x=1}^{A_d} P(w|z)P(z|x)P(x|d) \quad (7)$$

where $P(w|z) = \phi_{zw}$, $P(z|x) = \theta_{xz}$, and $P(x|d) = \frac{1}{A_d}$. By combining the two relevance scores, we have:

$$P(w|d) = P_{LM}(w|d) \times P_{ICT}(w|d) \quad (8)$$

In practice, the learned topics by the topic model is usually general to a given query while the language model is specific to keywords in the query. Combining the two relevance scores achieves a balance between generality and specificity, thus could improve the ranking performance. However, this method still does not consider the network information. We therefore propose a heterogeneous co-ranking method to address this issue.

The basic idea of the heterogenous co-ranking method is to propagate the relevance score between the linked objects in the network. The intuition behind the method is as follows: (a) a patent applied by inventors with higher expertise degrees on a topic (query) is more likely to have a higher quality (or impact); (b) a company who owns many high quality patents on a topic is more likely to be ranked higher; (c) an inventor who applies many patents with high impacts should be ranked higher. Similar strategies have been also considered in [23, 14] for academic search. Based on this intuition, we propose a two-stage method. In the first stage, we use Eq. 8 to calculate the relevance score of each object to the given query q and select the top-ranked objects as candidates. In the second stage, we use the candidates to construct a heterogeneous subgraph and perform a score propagation on the subgraph. Finally, we use the new score to re-rank each type of objects. In the propagation, we calculate the new score by (here we use company as the example):

$$r^k[c] = (1-\xi_1-\xi_2)r^{k-1}[c] + \frac{\xi_1}{|V_a^c|}\sum_{d\in V_a^c} r^{k-1}[a] + \frac{\xi_2}{|V_d^c|}\sum_{d\in V_d^c} r^{k-1}[d]$$

where $r^k[c]$ is the ranking score of company c after the k-step propagation; the score is initialized by Eq. 8; V_a^c denotes a set of inventors related to company c and V_d^c denotes a set of patents owned by company c; ξ_1 and ξ_2 are two parameters to control the propagation. The number of propagation steps reflects how we trust the network information. Setting $k = 0$ indicates that we only use the content information, thus the method degrades to Eq. 8; while setting $k = \infty$ indicates that we only trust the network information, thus the algorithm obtains a result similar to that of PageRank [12] on the heterogenous network.

5. COMPETITIVE ANALYSIS

This component aims to quantitatively characterize the competitive relations between companies. Based on the modeling results of the DICT model, we define four measures to quantify the competitive relations.

Global competitor discovery If two companies compete in their major areas, we call these two companies global competitors of each other. For example, ExxonMobil and Shell Oil are two global competitors: they are two energy companies, competing in "oil exploration", "oil refinery", and "chemical". Given a company c, we define the following measures to rank its global competitors.

- Word-based similarity (WBS). It represents each company by a vector of words, and ranks the competitors based on (Cosine) similarity between company c and each candidate.
- Topic-based divergence (TBD). It represents each company using the topic distribution $\{P(z|c)\}_z$ (or ψ_c), and ranks the competitors by the KL-divergence between company c and each candidate c', i.e.,

$$KL(\psi_c||\psi_{c'}) = \sum_{i=1}^{K}\psi_{cz_i}\log\frac{\psi_{cz_i}}{\psi_{c'z_i}}.$$

- Probability-based correlation (PBC). It defines a correlation score to rank the candidate companies. For a company c and a candidate competitor c', the score is defined as:

$$S(c,c') = \sum_{i=1}^{K} p(z_i|c)p(z_i|c') + \eta(\ln(M_c) - \ln(M_{c'}))^2$$

where M_c is the number of patents by company c; η is balance parameter; $P(z_i|c)$ can be obtained using Bayes rule based on ψ_{z_ic}. The second term is used to avoid noise.

Topic-level competitor discovery Two companies may only compete in one or a few specific areas. For example, Apple and Amazon may not be global competitors, but they compete fiercely on "Tablet PC". Given a company c, we aim to find its competitors on a specific topic z. The simplest way is to utilize the topic distribution associated with each company. For two companies c and c', if $|P(c|z) - P(c'|z)| \leq \tau$, then we say that c and c' are competitors on topic z. The method is referred to as distribution-based competitor finding (DBC). However, this method ignores the correlation between topics. For example, companies who compete on "data mining" may also compete on "web search", as the two topics have a strong correlation with each other. To incorporate the topic correlation, we define a hybrid measure (HBC) as follows:

$$S(c,c',z) = (\psi_{zc} - \psi_{z'c})^2 + \eta\sum_{z'\neq z}\rho_{zz'}(\psi_{z'c} - \psi_{z'c'})^2$$

where $\rho_{zz'}$ is the correlation between topic z and topic z', could be calculated as the negative Kullback-Leibler divergence [22]: $\rho_{zz'} = -KL(\phi_z||\phi'_z)$.

Evolutionary competitor discovery Companies may change their IP and marketing strategies, thus the competitive relations between them would change over time as well. Based on the dynamic ICT model, we define the competitive degree between two companies c and c' at time t as:

$$S(c,c',t) = \sum_{t'=1}^{t}\pi_{tt'}\sum_{i=1}^{K} p(c|z_i,t')p(c'|z_i,t') + \eta(\ln(M_c^t) - \ln(M_{c'}^t))^2$$

where $P(z_i|c)$ can be obtained using Bayes rule based on $\psi^t_{z_i c}$. We use the parameter $\pi_{tt'}$ (defined as $e^{-|t-t'|}$) to model the historic information in the above equation, which means if two companies are competitors in a recent past time, it is also likely that they are competitors in the current time.

We can further extend the evolutionary competitor discovery to the topic level. The basic idea is to replace the inner summation in the above equation with the specific topic.

6. PATENT SUMMARIZATION

When a user performs a search in the patent mining system, a large number of objects (patents, companies, and inventors) may be returned. It is always expensive for the user to digest the large volume information. It is desirable that the system can automatically generate a concise and informative summary for the returned objects, so that the user can quickly grasp a global picture before 'click-and-view' each object. A high-quality summary should satisfy the following requirements: (1) cover the most important information in the returned objects, (2) be relevant to the query as well, and (3) minimize the redundancy in the generated summary.

To solve the patent summarization problem, we propose a maximum coverage method. The idea is to choose a set of representative sentences as the summary from the returned objects for a query. The method consists of three major steps. First, when the user issues a query, it retrieves relevant patents for the query. Second, it extracts concepts from each sentence in the patents. All the extracted concepts form the knowledge space for the query and each sentence is also represented by the extracted concepts. Finally, it employs integer linear programming to find a set of sentences whose concepts maximally cover the knowledge space.

Concept extraction In our maximum coverage method, concept is the basic unit to represent the knowledge. A concept can be a word, a phrase, a named entity (e.g., Person or Location), or even a parsed syntax subtree of a sentence. Each concept has an importance score to the query. The schemes of concept scoring vary from simple term frequency to sophisticated machine learning methods. In our method, candidate concepts are selected using bigrams and are weighted using $TF * IDF$. Specifically, all patents are preprocessed by (1) sentence splitting, (2) part-of-speech tagging, (3) stemming and phrase chunking. Then we collect all extracted noun phrases (obtained by phrase chunking) from the patents and further split them into bigrams as candidate concepts. The next step is to score each candidate concept. In particular, we segment each patent into five fields: Title, Abstract, Claim, Background, and Other. Each field has a weight to reflect its importance (we empirically set the field-weights as 2, 1.5, 1.5, 1.0 and 0.5 respectively). Then, the importance score of each candidate concept is defined as the sum of weighted frequencies, i.e., filed-weight×concept-frequency-in-the-field. Finally, we choose the top 50 candidate concepts with the highest scores to form the knowledge space of the given query.

Summary generation An ideal summary should cover as many important and diverse concepts as possible. The problem can be formulated as a 0-1 knapsack problem. Formally, it aims to maximize the total importance score of concepts that form the knowledge space. In addition, we need to consider several constraints. The first one is the summary length: a user would not want to read a long summary. Thus, we define a maximal number of words in the extracted summary, i.e., $MaxLength$. Another constraint is to maintain the logical consistency between variables. For example, if the summary contains an important concept, then it at least includes one sentence which contains this concept. By combining the objective and the constraints together, we define the following constrained optimization problem:

$$\begin{aligned} & \sum_i IS_i * C_i \\ \text{s.t.} \quad & \sum_j L_j * S_j \leq MaxLength \\ & S_j * Occ_{i,j} \leq C_i \;\forall i, j; \quad \sum_j S_j * Occ_{i,j} \geq C_i \;\forall i \end{aligned} \tag{9}$$

where C_i is an indicator to represent whether the i-th concept is included in the summary ($C_i = 1$) or not ($C_i = 0$), and IS_i is the importance score of the i-th concept. In the first constraint, L_j is the number of words in the j-th sentence, and S_i is an indicator of whether the j-th sentence is included in the summary. In the second and the third constraints, $Occ_{i,j}$ is an indicator of whether the i-th concept occurs in the j-th sentence.

We solve the above optimization problem using integer linear programming (ILP). Specifically, we employ an open source software, LP-Solve (http://lpsolve.sourceforge.net/). The obtained result is an optimal solution that maximizes the objective function. Finally, we construct the summary by selecting sentences with $S_j = 1$.

7. EXPERIMENTAL RESULTS

We evaluated the proposed methods in the context of the PatentMiner system[7], consisting of 3,880,211 patents, 2,134,211 inventors, and 421,032 companies. We conducted three experiments to evaluate the proposed methods: heterogeneous co-ranking, competitor analysis, and patent summarization.

7.1 Results on Heterogeneous Co-Ranking

Data Sets, Evaluation Measures, and Baselines To qualitatively evaluate the proposed methods and compare with existing methods, we collected a list of 50 popular queries (e.g., "data mining", "web search"). For each query, we independently request five annotators (two undergraduates, two PhD students, and one faculty) to provide human judgement on the top (20) returned objects (companies, patents, and inventors) by the system. The judgement is about relevant (Like) or irrelevant (DisLike). If there are more than two annotators saying that an object is irrelevant, we remove the object from the returned list. As it is really difficult to judge the expertise for inventors even for human, we only perform the evaluation for companies and patents. We conducted the evaluation in terms of P@N (Precision for top N results), mean average precision (MAP), and normalized discounted cumulative gain (NDCG) [2, 5].

We used language model (LM) as the baseline method. For language model, we used Eq. 6 to calculate the relevance between a query term and a patent and similar equations for an inventor/company, where an inventor is represented by

Table 2: Average ranking performance for the patents and companies. N@1 and N@5 indicate NDCG for the top 1 or 5 results. HCR-1 indicates our proposed HCR method with one step propagation.

Object	Method	P@1	P@5	MAP	N@1	N@5
Patent	LM	.7001	.6900	.6991	.7021	.6833
	HCR-1	.7592	.7102	.7359	.7592	.7310
	HCR-2	.7598	.7201	.7361	.7600	.7300
	HCR-5	.7600	.7298	.7400	.7678	.7367
Company	LM	.6931	.6790	.6654	.6888	.6532
	HCR-1	.7167	.6833	.7058	.7167	.6934
	HCR-2	.7189	.6900	.7100	.7200	.7000
	HCR-5	.7201	.6999	.7210	.7201	.7031

his/her published patents and a company is represented by its held patents. Our heterogeneous co-ranking method is referred to as HCR. We tried different settings for the propagation. For example, HCR-2 indicates the heterogeneous co-ranking method with 2-step propagation. We preprocessed each patent by (a) removing stopwords and numbers; (b) removing words that appear less than three times in the corpus; and (c) downcasing the obtained words. Moreover, we performed company name disambiguation (e.g., IBM versus IBM Corp.) based on a company name dictionary.

Results and Analysis Table 2 shows the ranking performances for patents and companies. We see that the proposed HCR method (with all settings) clearly outperforms the baseline method using language model. In terms of MAP, the improvement of HCR-5 over language model is 5.3% for patent ranking and 5.01% for company ranking. Our method benefits from the topic modeling results which consider the companies, patents, and inventors in a unified model while the language model can only use the content information. In addition, the propagation process in our HCR methods further leverages the network information.

We studied how the number of propagation step influences the ranking performance. Figure 2 shows the ranking performance in terms of MAP with varied propagation step. Increasing the propagation step from 1 to 5 results in improved performance. This is because that our methods integrated more network information with more propagation steps. However, continuing to increase the propagation step make the network information an dominate factor for the final ranking results, thus hurts the relevance performance.

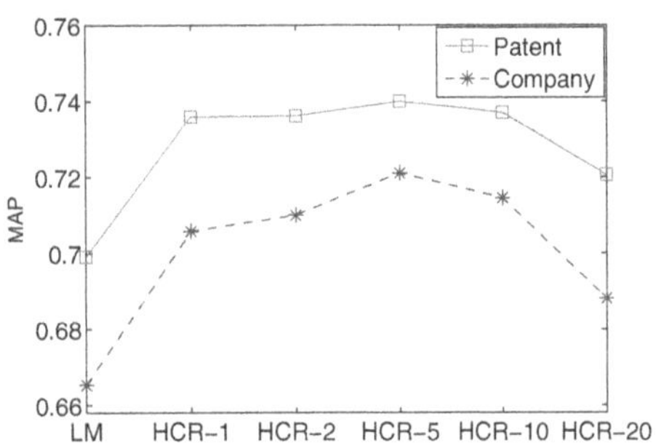

Figure 2: Ranking performance with varied propagation step.

7.2 Results on Competitive Analysis

Data Sets, Evaluation Measures, and Baselines It is difficult to obtain the ground truth for evaluating our method's performance on competitor analysis. For a relatively fair comparison, we have obtained the competitor information from Yahoo! Finance[8], which hosts information of all companies listed on NASDAQ, Dow Jones, S&P, etc. For each company, it gives a list of competitors based on their business performance (such as revenue and employees). It also provides the topic information for the competitors, such as Microsoft and Oracle compete on "Software". In summary, we obtained 543 companies and their global competitor information, and 326 companies and their competitors on 18 different topics.

We used P@N, MAP, and NDCG to evaluate our method (referred to as TopCom), and to compare with two baseline methods. The first one (referred to as WBS) is to represent each company as a bag of words (by the vector space model [20]), and for a given company, its competitors are ranked according to the Cosine similarity of the company with each candidate. This method can identify the global but not topic-level competitors. The second baseline method is for topic-level competitors analysis. We used Latent Dirichlet Allocation (LDA) [1] to generate the topic-word distribution and then combine the language model (LM) for competitor discovery. Specifically, we used all the patent titles to learn the LDA model, and used language model to find the relevant patents for a given query. Finally we obtained the competitive companies by summing all the scores of their corresponding patents. Hereafter we will use "LM+LDA" to denote this method. In addition, we compared our methods with different scoring measures (Cf. Section 5):

- **TopCom+TBD**: It ranks the competitors by KL-divergence of topic distribution between each candidate and the given company.
- **TopCom+PBC**: It ranks the competitors by the probability-based correlation between each candidate and the given company.
- **TopCom+DBC**: It ranks the competitors by the difference of its distribution in a specific topic between each candidate and the given company.
- **TopCom+HBC**: It ranks the competitors by the hybrid-based score between each candidate and the given company.

Results and Analysis Table 3 shows the performance of different methods on global and topic-level competitor analysis. We see that our method (TopCom) outperforms the baseline methods. For the global competitor analysis, our method with the probability-based correlation (PBC) scoring measure achieves the best performance in terms of P@1, P@5, N@1, and N@5. For the topic-level competitor analysis, the best performance is obtained by our method with the hybrid-based (HBC) scoring measure, which indicates that a scoring measure leveraging both topic and patent content information can achieve a better performance than using only one of the information. The advantage of our method lies in that in the proposed DICT model, we simultaneously model the topic distribution of companies, inventors, and patents;

[8]`http://finance.yahoo.com/`

Table 3: Performance of competitor analysis. N@1 and N@5 indicate NDCG for the top 1 or 5 returned competitors.

	Methods	P@1	P@5	MAP	N@1	N@5
Global	WBS	.2009	.1087	.2904	.2009	.2841
	TopCom+TBD	.1731	.0846	**.3078**	.1731	.2871
	TopCom+PBC	**.2098**	**.1161**	.2920	**.2098**	**.3085**
Topic	LM+LDA	.1536	.1221	.2643	.1536	.2524
	TopCom+DBC	.1369	.1270	.2388	.1469	.2446
	TopCom+HBC	**.1620**	**.1366**	**.2781**	**.1620**	**.2874**

Table 4: Examples for topic-level competitor evolution.

Cisco (Network Device)		**AT&T Corp.** (Communication)		
1996-2000	2006-2010	1996-2000	2001-2005	2006-2010
IBM	3Com	Lucent	Lucent	Lucent
Microsoft	Juniper	IBM	NEC	NEC
Lucent	Broadcom	NEC	Motorola	IBM
AT&T Corp.	Nortel	Verizon	IBM	Bell
Intel	Intel	Microsoft	Broadcom	Fujitsu
Sun	Canon	Samsung	Intel	Samsung
3Com	IBM	Motorola	Microsoft	Motorola
DEC	Fujitsu	Ericsson	Cisco	Verizon
HP	Sony	Alcatel	Samsung	AOL

while the two baseline methods only model the content information (WBS) or only model the topic distribution of patents (LM+LDA).

Case Study Table 4 shows example results of the topic-level competitor evolution analysis by our TopCom+PBC method. From the example, we have observed some interesting patterns. On topic "Network Devices", Cisco's early (1996-2000) competitors include IBM, Microsoft, Lucence, etc., but now it turns out to be 3Com, Juniper, and Broadcom, etc. Juniper seems to be a rising star in the "Network Device" field; while a few other companies (such as AT&T and Lucent) have passed their bloom on "Network Device" since 2001. Instead, AT&T and Lucent have become more focused in the "Communication" field.

7.3 Results on Patent Summarization

Data Sets, Evaluation Metrics, and Baselines The patent summarization method was first tested on benchmark data sets TAC 2008 and 2009 [9] before being applied to patent data. TAC 2008 and 2009 datasets respectively contain 48 and 44 topics (queries). The document collection for each topic is given. The task is, similar to our problem, to generate a 100-word summary from the document collection for each topic (query). Four human-written summaries are used as gold standard for each topic.

We compared our approach with two baseline methods that reported the state-of-the-art performance on this task. The baselines are: Maximal Marginal Relevance (MMR) [3] and Diversity Penalty (DP) [21]. We use ROUGE-1 and ROUGE-2, two commonly used evaluation metrics in document summarization, as the evaluation measures.

Results and Analysis Table 5 lists the results of different summarization methods on the TAC datasets. Our approach clearly outperforms the baseline systems on both datasets. The relative improvements over the baselines are about 6% and 10% in terms of ROUGE-1 and ROUGE-2. We also compared our generated results with the human-written results. The last column in Table 5 is the average results of the four human-written summaries for all topics. Therefore, these scores in the last column can be considered as the upper bound of the summarization task. As shown in Table 5, the average score of our approach (0.371/0.372 by ROUGE-1) reaches 86.63% of that of gold standard (0.414/0.444), 86.01% in terms of ROUGE-2, which further confirms the effectiveness of the proposed approach.

[9] `http://www.nist.gov/tac/`

Table 5: Summarization performance on the TAC datasets. ILP is our approach.

Data	Metrics	Methods			Gold
		DP	MMR	ILP	Standard
TAC2008	ROUGE-1	0.349	0.348	**0.371**	0.414
	ROUGE-2	0.097	0.096	**0.103**	0.116
TAC2009	ROUGE-1	0.334	0.343	**0.372**	0.444
	ROUGE-2	0.091	0.096	**0.105**	0.126

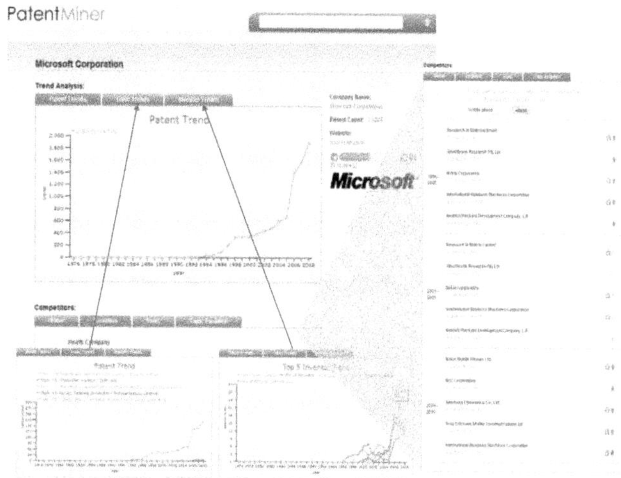

Figure 3: Demonstration system of PatentMiner.

7.4 Online System

We have developed a patent analysis and mining system: PatentMiner, and implemented the proposed methods in the system. Figure 3 shows the screenshot of the system. The top-left of is the profile page for "Microsoft Corporation". There are three plots respectively showing the patent application trend, topic trend, and major inventor trend. The right side is the results of competitor evolution analysis on topic "mobile phone".

8. RELATED WORK

There are a few systems for patent search and analysis such as Google Patent, WikiPatent, FreePatentsOnline, Patents, PatentLens, and PriorArtSearch. However, most of these systems focus on search and provide limited macro-level analytic functions. Few systems provide the user with insights into the micro-level analysis of the patent network. No existing system studies the problem of dynamic topic modeling and the topic-level competitor analysis. Tseng et al. [19] introduce a series of text mining techniques for patent analysis, including text segmentation and summary extraction. However, they merely employ existing text mining techniques for patent analysis.

Arnetminer [18] is a "sister" system of PatentMiner. It uses a combination approach to build profiles for academic researchers [16] and provides topic-level expertise search over academic social networks [17]. Compared with these prior works, the PatentMiner system distinguishes itself in the following aspects: dynamic topic driven modeling, heterogeneous network co-ranking, competitive analysis, and patent summarization, where we propose new approaches to overcome the drawbacks that exist in the traditional methods.

Considerable work has been conducted for extracting topics from text. For example, Hofmann [9] proposes the probabilistic latent semantic indexing (pLSI) and applies it to information retrieval. Blei et al. [1] propose Latent Dirichlet Allocation (LDA) by introducing a conjugate Dirichlet prior for all documents. Several extensions of the LDA model have been proposed, for example, the Author model [10], the Author-Topic model [13], and the Author-Conference-Topic model [18]. The major difference of our ICT and DICT models from existing models is that we simultaneously model dynamic topics of different objects in the patent network.

9. CONCLUSION

We introduce the architecture, algorithms, and main features of the PatentMiner system. We design and implement a general topic-driven framework for analyzing and mining the heterogeneous patent network. Specifically, we first propose a dynamic probabilistic model to model the topical evolution of different objects in the heterogeneous network. We then present a heterogeneous co-ranking approach to rank the multiple objects. We further propose an approach for topic-level competitor analysis. To help users digest the search result, we introduce a method to summarize the patent search results. We evaluate the proposed methods on a real-world patent database and the experimental results validate the effectiveness of our methods.

There are many directions of this work. It would be interesting to further study influence between companies [15]: how a company's technology innovation influences another company's marketing/R&D strategy? Another challenge is how to integrate domain knowledge into the mining process.

Acknolwedgements The work is supported by a research fund from ExxonMobil Corporation. Jie Tang has been supported in part by the Natural Science Foundation of China (No. 61073073, No. 61170061), Chinese National Key Foundation Research (No. 60933013, No. 61035004).

10. REFERENCES

[1] D. M. Blei, A. Y. Ng, and M. I. Jordan. Latent dirichlet allocation. *JMLR*, 3:993–1022, 2003.

[2] C. Buckley and E. M. Voorhees. Retrieval evaluation with incomplete information. In *SIGIR'2004*, pages 25–32, 2004.

[3] J. Carbonell and J. Goldstein. The use of mmr, diversity-based reranking for reordering documents and producing summaries. In *SIGIR'98*, pages 335–336, 1998.

[4] D. Cohn and H. Chang. Learning to probabilistically identify authoritative documents. In *ICML'00*, pages 167–174, 2000.

[5] N. Craswell, A. P. de Vries, and I. Soboroff. Overview of the trec-2005 enterprise track. In *TREC 2005 Conference Notebook*, pages 199–205, 2005.

[6] J. Dean and S. Ghemawat. Mapreduce: Simplified data processing on large clusters. In *OSDI'04*, pages 10–10, 2004.

[7] T. L. Griffiths and M. Steyvers. Finding scientific topics. In *PNAS'04*, pages 5228–5235, 2004.

[8] M. Hertzum and A. M. Pejtersen. The information-seeking practices of engineers: Searching for documents as well as for people. *Information Processing & Management*, 36(5):761–778, 2000.

[9] T. Hofmann. Probabilistic latent semantic indexing. In *SIGIR'99*, pages 50–57, 1999.

[10] A. McCallum. Multi-label text classification with a mixture model trained by em. In *Proceedings of AAAI'99 Workshop on Text Learning*, 1999.

[11] Q. Mei, X. Ling, M. Wondra, H. Su, and C. Zhai. Topic sentiment mixture: modeling facets and opinions in weblogs. In *WWW'07*, pages 171–180, 2007.

[12] L. Page, S. Brin, R. Motwani, and T. Winograd. The pagerank citation ranking: Bringing order to the web. Technical Report SIDL-WP-1999-0120, Stanford University, 1999.

[13] M. Steyvers, P. Smyth, and T. Griffiths. Probabilistic author-topic models for information discovery. In *KDD'04*, pages 306–315, 2004.

[14] J. Tang, R. Jin, and J. Zhang. A topic modeling approach and its integration into the random walk framework for academic search. In *ICDM'08*, pages 1055–1060, 2008.

[15] J. Tang, J. Sun, C. Wang, and Z. Yang. Social influence analysis in large-scale networks. In *KDD'09*, pages 807–816, 2009.

[16] J. Tang, L. Yao, D. Zhang, and J. Zhang. A combination approach to web user profiling. *ACM TKDD*, 5(1):1–44, 2010.

[17] J. Tang, J. Zhang, R. Jin, Z. Yang, K. Cai, L. Zhang, and Z. Su. Topic level expertise search over heterogeneous networks. *Machine Learning Journal*, 82(2):211–237, 2011.

[18] J. Tang, J. Zhang, L. Yao, J. Li, L. Zhang, and Z. Su. Arnetminer: Extraction and mining of academic social networks. In *KDD'08*, pages 990–998, 2008.

[19] Y.-H. Tseng, C.-J. Lin, and Y.-I. Lin. Text mining techniques for patent analysis. *Inf. Process. Manage.*, 43:1216–1247, September 2007.

[20] C. van Rijsbergen. *Information Retrieval.* But-terworths, London, 1979.

[21] X. Wan, J. Yang, and J. Xiao. Towards an iterative reinforcement approach for simultaneous document summarization and keyword extraction. In *ACL'07*, pages 552–559, 2007.

[22] C. Zhai and J. Lafferty. A study of smoothing methods for language models applied to ad hoc information retrieval. In *SIGIR'01*, pages 334–342, 2001.

[23] J. Zhang, J. Tang, and J. Li. Expert finding in a social network. In *DASFAA'07*, pages 1066–1069, 2007.

[24] X. Zhu and J. Lafferty. Harmonic mixtures: Combining mixture models and graph-based methods for inductive and scalable semi-supervised learning. In *ICML'05*, pages 1052–1059, 2005.

Storytelling in Entity Networks to Support Intelligence Analysts

M. Shahriar Hossain[1], Patrick Butler[1], Arnold P. Boedihardjo[2], Naren Ramakrishnan[1]
[1]Virginia Tech, Blacksburg, VA 24061
[2]U. S. Army Corps of Engineers, Alexandria , VA 22315
{msh, pabutler}@cs.vt.edu, arnold.p.boedihardjo@usace.army.mil, naren@cs.vt.edu

ABSTRACT

Intelligence analysts grapple with many challenges, chief among them is the need for software support in storytelling, i.e., automatically 'connecting the dots' between disparate entities (e.g., people, organizations) in an effort to form hypotheses and suggest non-obvious relationships. We present a system to automatically construct stories in entity networks that can help form directed chains of relationships, with support for co-referencing, evidence marshaling, and imposing syntactic constraints on the story generation process. A novel optimization technique based on concept lattice mining enables us to rapidly construct stories on massive datasets. Using several public domain datasets, we illustrate how our approach overcomes many limitations of current systems and enables the analyst to efficiently narrow down to hypotheses of interest and reason about alternative explanations.

Categories and Subject Descriptors

H.2.8 [**Database management**]: Database applications—*Data mining*; H.3.3 [**Information storage and retrieval**]: Information search and retrieval—*Search process, Retrieval models*

Keywords

Storytelling, connecting the dots, redescriptions, intelligence analysis

1 Introduction

Intelligence analysts today are faced with many challenges, chief among them being the need to fuse disparate streams of data, and rapidly arrive at analytical decisions and quantitative predictions for use by policy makers. Although there are available catalogs of problem solving strategies suitable for intelligence analysis (e.g., see [1, 2]) and several visual analytic tools (e.g. [3–8]), our understanding of underlying user needs is constantly evolving.

After a thorough user study, Kang and Stasko [9] suggested several design implications for systems supporting intelligence analysis. Along with several suggestions related to information management, two of the suggested design requirements are: (1) help analysts create a convincing production by supporting insight provenance and sanity checks, and (2) help analysts continuously build a conceptual model. In our work, we design an algorithmic framework to help intelligence analysts make connections by providing evidence and explanations to build a mental model.

Here, we focus on the task of storytelling [10], i.e., connecting the dots between disparate entities in an attempt to discover relationships between hitherto different concepts and suggest hypotheses. For example, what is the connection between Osama Bin Laden and Igor Kolokov? What other entities relate them and what documents provide evidence for the underlying connections?

1.1 Limitations of Current Tools

Current tools in this space—e.g., Entity Workspace [5], Jigsaw [8], NetLens [11], and Sentinel Visualizer [4]. Entity Workspace—use entity recognizers to infer a graph of relationships between entities (see Fig. 1). (There are other tools that we do not survey here, e.g., Palantir [7], but their characteristics are similar.) Entity Workspace focuses more on information representation goals and does not provide graph exploration or summarization capabilities, whereas Jigsaw, NetLens, and Sentinel Visualizer provide exploration techniques with different emphases. In Jigsaw and NetLens, the user can traverse from entities to documents (in which the entities appear), and vice versa. Sentinel Visualizer supports exploration of the entity network and can hide document level details by using concepts of degree centrality, betweenness centrality, and closeness. In all cases, however, manual exploration becomes difficult as networks get dense with increasing numbers of entities. More broadly, significant shortcomings of the above tools are:

A. *Lack of support for "evidence marshaling"*: The tools described above employ entity network models where the edges represent only boolean associations between entities, i.e., presence/absence in the same document(s). They require that the documents be manually read by analysts to marshal evidence.
B. *Lack of support for explanation:* Extracted and inferred relationships between entities should be explained by surrounding evidence. With the above tools, the user is relegated the task of explaining the visualized relationships. Because multiple explanations can exist for a relationship, the analyst is further burdened with the manual task of sorting through these explanations.
C. *Directed search:* Current tools do not support automated directed search to discover relationships between user-specified entities. Manual exploration often results in failed searches that loop back to the origin instead of leading towards a destination entity.
D. *Syntactic constraints:* Analysts bring in significant domain knowledge that manifest as syntactic constraints on path finding. In current systems, users must manually apply constraints at each step of the exploration which significantly prolongs the discovery process.
E. *Lack of support for entity disambiguation:* A person named "Igor Kolokov" might be referenced in different ways across

KDD'12, August 12–16, 2012, Beijing, China.

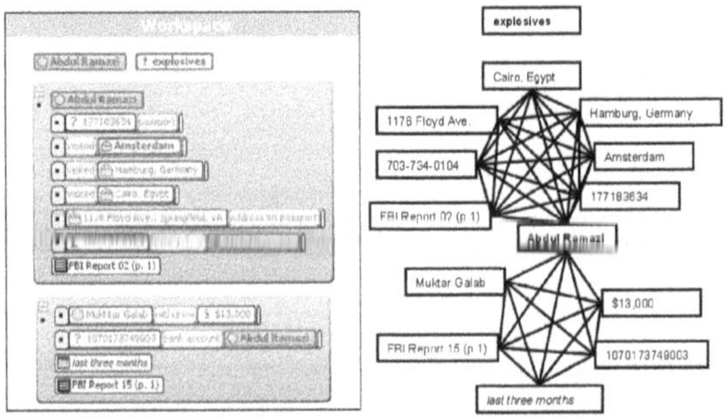

(a) Entity Workspace [5].

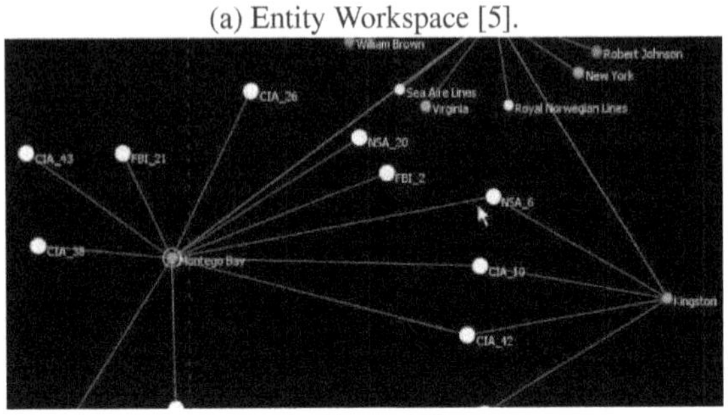

(b) Jigsaw [8].

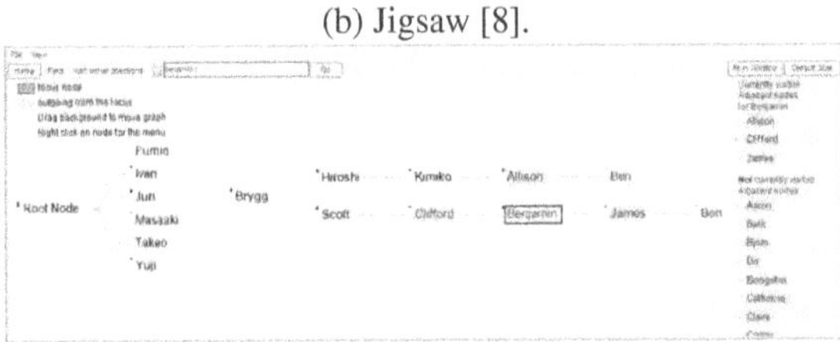

(c) NetLens [11].

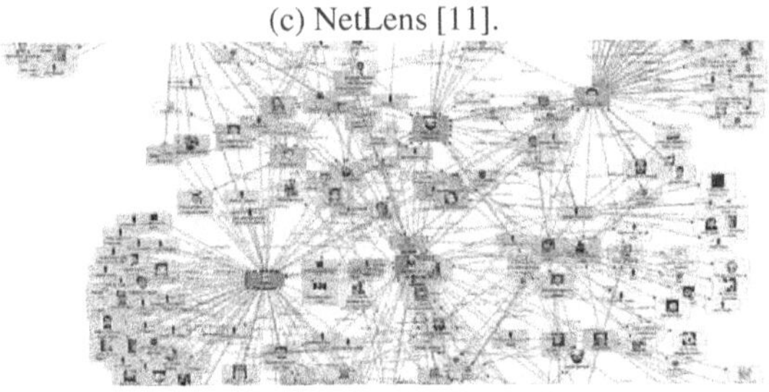

(d) Sentinel Visualizer [4].

Figure 1: State-of-the-art visual analytic tools for intelligence analysis.

a document (e.g., "Igor Kolokov" can be variously extracted as "Igor Kolokov", "Kolokov", and "Igor"). In current visual analytics tools for intelligence analysis, entity disambiguation is a manual process left to the user. Further, current entity recognition tools will be unable to extract an entity from a sentence if the sentence contains pronominal references (e.g., "that guy" instead of "Kolokov").

F. *The curse of large datasets and massive networks:* All the above tools require that a pre-generated or fully materialized network of all relationships be computed prior to exploration. As a result, exploration of large networks becomes computationally taxing and practically infeasible with even few tens of thousands of entities.

1.2 Contributions

The above shortcomings motivate our story generation methodology. A collection of documents is mined and indexed to provide efficient access to nearest-neighbor queries, and a storytelling algorithm is used to direct searches toward desired destination entities. Various pre- and post- processing techniques are utilized to discover stories and explain them. Our contributions are:

1. *Cliques:* We introduce a new network model that employs cliques to define weighted edges between entities (different from the boolean edge models of existing systems). Cliques are used as evidence to support a particular connection between two entities and serve as the primary building block of storytelling. This component addresses issue (A).
2. *Explanation Chain (Clique Chain):* To provide effective explanations, we propose a relationship model between two entities (a story) as a path traversed from one entity to another through a series of cliques. Thus the story between two entities is explained as a chain of cliques where evidence is marshalled by the entities' surrounding neighbors within their respective cliques. This component addresses issue (B).
3. *Efficient Automated Search for Storytelling:* We propose a formulation of heuristic search for finding explanations/clique chains between two entities. The search algorithm can efficiently provide multiple explanations for the identical start and end entities based on two user-defined parameters. This component address issue (C).
4. *Syntactic Storytelling:* User can provide syntactic constraints to the proposed search algorithm to obtain relevant stories and improve processing time. This contribution addresses issue (D).
5. *Coreferencing:* We use coreferencing to disambiguate pronominal references as well as references to the same person. This component addresses issue (E).
6. *Induced Similarity Networks:* Our algorithms operate directly on the vector space model without materializing the network to obtain significant computational efficiency. We demonstrate our ability to scale to large datasets and to rapidly generate/verify multiple hypotheses. This component addresses issue (F).

2 Related Projects

Intelligence analysis: Research work into software tools for intelligence analysis can be grouped into model-guided systems [12–14], multi-agent systems [15], graph-based analytic tools [16–19], and collaborative systems [5,20,21]. Our work falls in the category of graph-based analytic tools. We support exploration of the entity-entity graph (without materializing it) to help intelligence analysts to marshal evidence, explain connections, and form hypotheses.

Visual analytic tools: A different way to classify software tools is in terms of the activity they support, i.e., information foraging vs. sensemaking [22]. Some of the tools in the former category are *IN-SPIRE* [6], and *NetLens* [11]; they leave the reasoning processes to the analyst. Other tools, such as *Analyst's Notebook* [3], *Sentinel Visualizer* [4], *Entity Workspace* [5], *Jigsaw* [8], and *Palantir* [7] focus more on the the sensemaking process, and while many of them ostensibly support information foraging, some of these tools are primarily for late stage sensemaking and presentation.

Connecting the dots: The "connecting the dots" problem is not new and has appeared before in a variety of contexts: entity networks [23], image collections [24], cellular networks [25], social networks [26], and document collections [10,27,28]. While some of these works can be adapted toward our problem context, the notion of a story in intelligence analysis often deals with relating entities sequentially such that neighboring entities share commonality, whereas the above projects typically require a stronger connecting thread through all entities, not just neighboring entities. Swanson refers to the notion of neighboring commonality as complementary but disjoint (CBD) structures [29], whereby two arguments may exist separately that when considered together lead to new insights, but the objects exhibiting these two arguments are unaware of each other.

This paper builds upon our prior work in [10,30] in many important ways. First, we build stories through entity networks extracted

(a) Clique size, k=2 and distance threshold, θ=0.99: Laboratory technician Jose Escalante is connected to Omar Hanif, a key player of a possible terrorist attack and an Al-Queda operative. The connection is explained by a story with three junction nodes: Carlos Morales, Ali Sufaat, and Seashore Hotel.

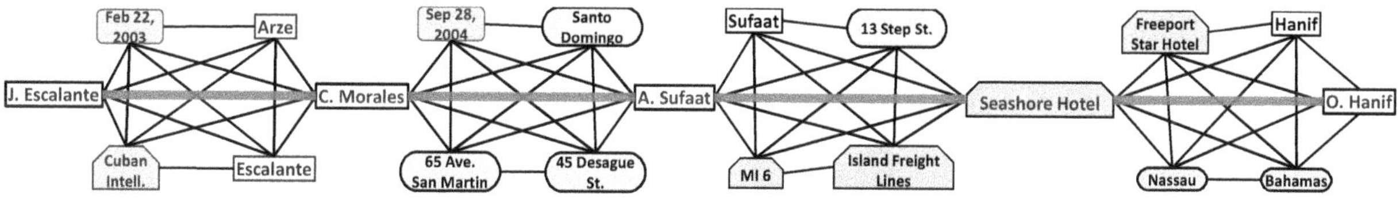

(b) Clique size, k=6 and distance threshold, θ=0.99: A larger clique size requirement adds more evidence to the story and better explains the connection.

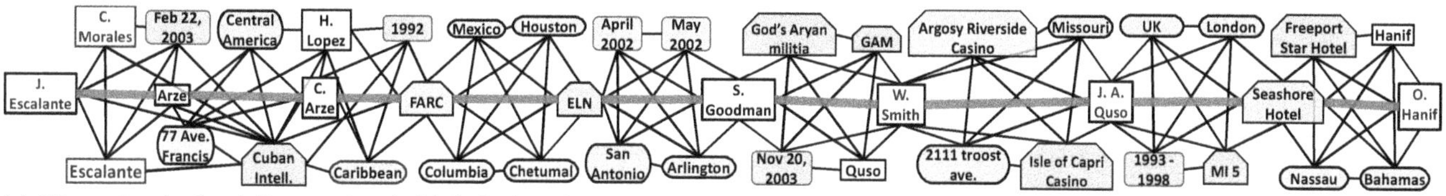

(c) Clique size, k=6 and distance threshold, θ=0.93. A longer clique-chain with $k = 6$ provides another detailed explanation of the connection between Jose Escalante and Omar Hanif.

Figure 2: Different explanations for the connection between two entities: Jose Escalante and Omar Hanif.

from documents whereas these prior projects build stories through documents directly. This emphasis on entity networks is closer to how intelligence analysts reason about connections. Second, the present paper significantly generalizes the work in [10] by incorporating the notion of cliques in stories, thus supporting evidence marshalling and explanation generation. Third, we present a novel optimization technique for large databases based on concept lattice mining to support faster story construction.

3 Problem Setting

A story between entities e_1 and e_t is a sequence of intermediate entities $e_2, e_3, ..., e_{t-1}$ such that every neighboring pair of entities satisfies some user defined criteria. We model entities and the documents they occur in using a traditional vector space model. The problem of finding a story then can be modeled as a path search problem in the induced entity-entity graph $\mathcal{E}$, but direct materialization of $\mathcal{E}$ with hundreds of thousands of entities and billions of edges is infeasible. What is needed is support for directed exploration of the graph toward desired entities.

Given a start and end entity, our algorithm induces the network on the fly from the vector space model and finds a path. We allow the analyst to influence the story construction using two distinct criteria: clique size and distance thresholds. Given a story connecting a start and an end entity (see Fig. 2(a)), analysts can perform one of two tasks: they can either aim to strengthen the individual connections resulting in a longer path (see Fig. 2(b)), or they can organize evidence around the given connection (see Fig. 2(c)). We use the notions of distance threshold and clique size to mimic these behaviors. The distance threshold refers to the maximum acceptable distance between two neighboring entities in a story. Lower distance thresholds impose stricter requirements and lead to longer paths. The clique size refers to the minimum size of the clique that every pair of neighboring entities must participate in. Greater clique sizes provide more evidence and tend to provide longer stories.

We use the term *edge* to refer to the basic unit of a direct link between two entities. A k-clique has k entities and is composed of $k(k-1)/2$ edges where every edge satisfies the distance threshold θ. A *clique chain* is composed of a number of consecutive cliques connecting as start and end entity. Clique chains of Fig. 2(a, b, and c) are respectively composed of 2-, 6-, and 6-cliques. Applied distance thresholds to these three clique chains are 0.99, 0.99, and 0.93. Each clique chain provides alternative explanations for the relationship between the same pair of entities. We use the term *story* to refer to a relation between two entities via the junction entities of the corresponding clique chain. The stories are highlighted by thick lines in the clique chains of Fig. 2.

We use the *Soergel distance* between two entities e_1 and e_2 to measure the strength between them:

$$\mathbb{D}(e_1, e_2) = \frac{\sum\limits_{f \in \mathcal{F}} |V(e_1, f) - V(e_2, f)|}{\sum\limits_{f \in \mathcal{F}} \max(V(e_1, f), V(e_2, f))}$$

where $V(e, f)$ indicates the weight of feature f for entity e. Here, the features are the different documents in which the entity appears. Let $e(f)$ be the set of entities associated with feature f, and $f(e)$ be the set of features associated with entity e. Soergel distance is a true distance measure: it is exactly 0.0 when the entities e_1 and e_2 have exactly the same features is symmetric, and obeys the triangle inequality. For entities in a document collection, the weight $V(e, f)$ can be defined as

$$V(e, f) = \frac{(1 + \log(n_{e,f}))\left(\log \frac{|\mathcal{E}|}{|e(f)|}\right)}{\sum_{j=1}^{|f(e)|}\left((1 + \log(n_{e,j}))\left(\log \frac{|\mathcal{E}|}{|e(j)|}\right)\right)^2}$$

where $n_{e,f}$ is the frequency of entity e in document f, $|e(f)|$ is the number of entities in document f, $|e(j)|$ is the number of entities in document j, and $|\mathcal{E}|$ is the total number of entities. Note that this is a variant of tf-idf modeling with cosine normalization in the entity-document space.

4 Approach

Figure 3 summarizes our storytelling framework. The framework takes a document corpus as input, applies algorithmic approaches to handle the research issues in story generation, and outputs stories at the end of the pipeline. We describe the entire process in detail in this section.

Our overall methodology is based on using a concept lattice framework to structure the search for stories. A concept lattice [31] structures the membership of entities in documents into sets of overlaps and relationships between these sets. Recall that the two parameters influencing the quality of the path—distance threshold and clique

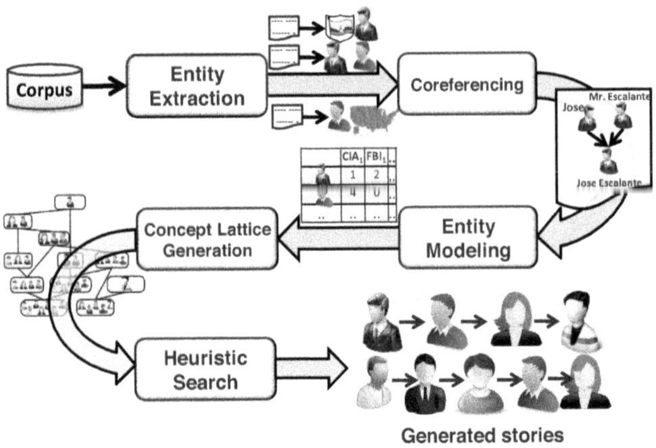

Figure 3: Storytelling pipeline.

size—impose a duality. The distance threshold is posed over feature sets whereas the clique size is over entities. We use the clique size to prune the concept lattice during construction (by incorporating it as a support constraint) and the distance threshold to select candidates for dynamic construction of paths. There are three key computational stages: (i) construction of the concept lattice, (ii) generating promising candidates for path following, and (iii) evaluating candidates for potential to lead to destination. Of these, the first stage can be viewed as a startup cost that can be amortized over storytelling tasks.

We adopt the CHARM-L [31] algorithm of Zaki for constructing concept lattices. The second and third stages are organized as part of an A* search algorithm that begins with the starting entity, uses the concept lattice to identify candidates satisfying the distance threshold and clique size requirements, and evaluates them heuristically for their promise in leading to the end entity. In practice, we will place a limit on the branching factor (b) of the search, thus sacrificing completeness for efficiency. We showcase these steps in detail below, including the construction of admissible heuristics.

4.1 Concept Lattice Construction

We employ the notion of a concept lattice [31] to capture similarities between entities. Each concept/closed set is a pair: (entity set, document set). Concepts capture a maximal co-occurrence between entity sets and document sets, i.e., it is not possible to add more entities to a concept without losing some documents, and vice versa. We order the entity list for each concept by the number of documents. Note that we can find an approximate set of nearest neighbors for an entity e from the entity list of the concept containing e and the longest document set. The concept lattice is a data structure that models conceptual clusters of entities and feature overlaps and is used here as a quick lookup of potential neighbors that will satisfy the distance threshold and clique constraints.

4.2 Successor Generation

Successor generation is the task of, given an entity, using the distance threshold and clique size requirements, to identify a set of possible successors for path following. Note that this does not use the end entity in its computation. We study three techniques for successor generation:

1. Cover Tree Nearest Neighbor,
2. Nearest Neighbors Approximation (NNA), and
3. k-Clique Near Neighbor (kCNN).

Among these three techniques, NNA and kCNN approaches are our contributions and the cover tree approach is used for comparison purpose only.

4.2.1 *Cover Tree Nearest Neighbor*

The cover tree [32] is a data structure for fast nearest neighbor operations in a space of entities organized alongside any distance

Algorithm 1 NNA(e)

Input: An entity $e \in \mathcal{E}$
  $fringe \leftarrow \top(e)$ order by feature set size
  $prospects \leftarrow \emptyset$
  while $fringe \neq \emptyset$ **do**
    $r \leftarrow$ dequeue from $fringe$
    while $prospects \neq \emptyset$ **do**
      $e' \leftarrow$ head $prospects$
      if $J(e,e') > \frac{|\text{Items}(e)|}{|\text{Items}(r)|}$ **then**
        yield e'
        dequeue $prospects$
      else
        break
    for all $r' \in$ ChildrenOf r **do**
      add r' to $fringe$ order by feature set size
      for all e' in $e(r')$ **do**
        add e' to $prospects$ order by $J(e,e')$

metric (here, we use the Soergel distance [33]). The space complexity is $O(\|\mathcal{E}\|)$, i.e., linear in the entity size of the database. A nearest neighbor query requires logarithmic time in the entity space $O\left(c^{12}\log\left(n\right)\right)$ where c is the expansion constant associated with the feature set dimension of the dataset (see [32] for details).

4.2.2 *Nearest Neighbors Approximation (NNA)*

The second mechanism we use for successor generation is to approximate the nearest neighbors of an entity using the concept lattice. We use the Jaccard coefficient between two entities as an indicator to inversely (and approximately) track the Soergel distance between the entities. In order to efficiently calculate an entity's nearest neighbors, however, we cannot simply calculate the Jaccard coefficient between it and every other entity. We harness the concept lattice to avoid wasteful comparisons.

A formal description of our NNA algorithm is shown in Algorithm 1. The set $\top(e)$ is the set of all redescriptions [31] which form the upper edge in the concept lattice where e appears. $J(e,e')$ of Algorithm 1 refers to *Jaccard coefficient* between two entities is defined as

$$J(e,e') = \frac{|f(e) \cap f(e')|}{|f(e) \cup f(e')|}$$

which is a measure of how similar two entities are based upon how many features they share in proportion to their overall size. NNA returns better approximate redescriptions of an entity first. This is still, however, an approximation since it uses the Jacccard coefficient rather than the Soergel distance.

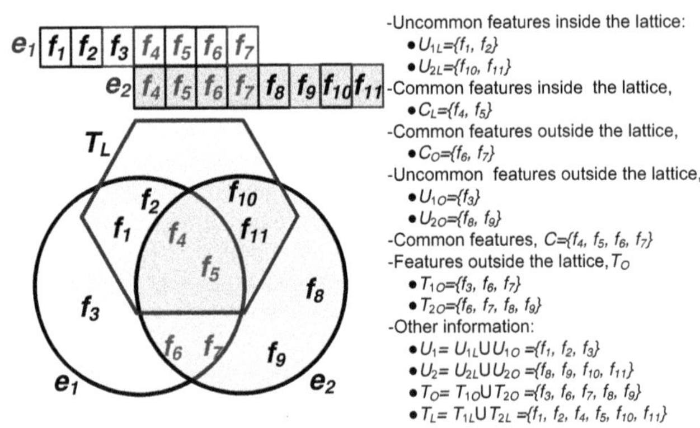

Figure 4: Distribution of common and uncommon features of entities e_1 and e_2 inside and outside the concept lattice. (The hexagon indicates the concept lattice).

$$\mathbb{D}_{\text{mixed}}(e_1, e_2) = \frac{|U_{1L}| \times \text{minw}(e_1) + |U_{2L}| \times \text{minw}(e_2) + \sum_{f \in C_L} |V(e_1, f) - V(e_2, f)|}{|U_{1L}| \times \text{minw}(e_1) + |U_{2L}| \times \text{minw}(e_2) + \sum_{f \in C_L} \max(V(e_1, f), V(e_2, f)) + |T_O| \times \max(\text{maxw}(e_1), \text{maxw}(e_2))}$$

Figure 5: The mixed mode Soergel distance equation.

4.2.3 *k-Clique Near Neighbor (kCNN)*

The basic idea of the kCNN approach is, in addition to finding a good set of successor nodes for a given entity e, to be able to have sufficient number of them so that, combinatorially, they contribute a desired number of cliques. With a clique size constraint of k, it is not sufficient to merely pick the top k neighbors of the given entity, since the successor generation function expects multiple clique candidates. Given that this function expects b clique candidates, minimum number m of candidate entities to identify can be cast as the solution to the inequalities:

$$\binom{m-1}{k} < b \text{ and } \binom{m}{k} \geq b$$

The entity list of each concept of the lattice is ordered in the number of features and this aids in picking the top m candidate entities for the given entity e. We pick up these m candidate entities for o from the entity list of the concept containing the longest feature set and redescription set containing e. Note that, in practice, the entity list of each concept is much larger than m and as a result kCNN does not need to traverse the lattice to obtain promising candidates. kCNN thus forms combinations of size k from these m entities to obtain a total of b k-cliques. Since m is calculated using the two inequalities, the total number of such combinations is equal to or slightly greater than b (but never less than b). Each clique is given an average distance score calculated from the distances of the entities of the clique and the current entity e. This aids kCNN in returning a priority queue of exactly b candidate k-cliques.

4.3 Evaluating Candidates

We now have a set of candidates that are close to the current entity and must determine which of these has potential to lead to the destination. We present two operational modes to rank candidates: (i) the normal mode and (ii) the mixed mode.

4.3.1 *Normal Mode*

The normal mode is suitable for the general case where we have all the entities and features resident in the database. The primary criteria of optimality for the A* search procedure is the cumulative Soergel distance of the path. We use the straight line Soergel distance for the heuristic. This can never overestimate the cost of a path from any entity e to the goal (and is hence admissible), because the Soergel distance maintains the triangle inequality.

4.3.2 *Mixed Mode*

The mixed mode distance measure is effective for large datasets where only important information is stored while other information is removed from the system after recording some of their aggregated information to save on space and cost. With the mixed mode approach, for simplicity, we assume that all the information about items outside the concept lattice are absent but some of their aggregated information like number of features truncated are provided. Figure 4 shows the distribution of common and uncommon features of entities e_1 and e_2 inside and outside a concept lattice.

Figure 5 shows our formula for the mixed mode approach. Consider the set of features T_O that do not appear in the lattice due to the support threshold of the concept lattice, *minsup*. Some features of T_O can be common to both entities e_1 and e_2. $|U_{1O}|$ and $|U_{2O}|$ are the numbers of uncommon features in entities e_1 and e_2, which are thus outside the frequent concept lattice. Length $|T_O|$ is a known variable due to the recorded aggregated information, but $|U_{1O}|$ and $|U_{2O}|$ are unknown. This is why $|U_{1O}|$ and $|U_{2O}|$ do not appear in $\mathbb{D}_{\text{mixed}}(e_1, e_2)$. For $\mathbb{D}_{\text{mixed}}(e_1, e_2)$, we consider that all the features of T_O (i.e., features outside the lattice) are common in both entities e_1 and e_2 and all these features have the same weight which is $\max(\text{maxw}(e_1), \text{maxw}(e_2))$.

To be able to use $\mathbb{D}_{\text{mixed}}(e_1, e_2)$ as a heuristic, it should be mentioned that $\mathbb{D}_{\text{mixed}}(e_1, e_2)$ must never overestimate the original Soergel distance $\mathbb{D}(e_1, e_2)$. The proof is omitted due to space constraints.

4.4 Implementation Details

The aim of the algorithms we have described so far is to support intelligence analysts in marshaling thoughts and evidence in order to generate hypotheses and then to generate defensible and persuasive arguments on hypotheses that are most favored by the evidence. Note that significant domain knowledge is still required to analyze a dataset to find a set of good stories. This raises some implementation issues regarding pre- and post processing, starting points, and exploration constraints. This subsection describes these implementation issues.

4.4.1 *Entity Extraction*

We used a number of named-entity recognition (NER) APIs to extract entities from a document collection. We used multiple NER APIs because we observed that some named entities are better extracted by one tool but missed by another. The NER APIs we used are LingPipe [34], OpenNLP [35], and Stanford NER [36]. We combined the entities extracted by these three named-entity recognizers and modeled the entities in the vector space model (entities are objects and documents are features).

4.4.2 *Syntactic Storytelling*

The kCNN approach already uses two constraints: clique size and distance threshold. It is possible to include a syntactic constraint to the successor generation process (Figure 6). For example, we can restrict the exploration in such a way that the junction nodes can be of certain types of entities, e.g., people or organizations. Other entity types such as places, dates, money amount, phone number, etc. are better used as surrounding evidence, and hence can be part of a clique but not as a junction point.

Figure 6(a) shows that the connection between "Osama Bin Laden" and "Igor Kolokov" has a place "Cairo" as a junction node. One way to interpret this connection is that Laden and Kolokov visited Cairo. This interpretation becomes unimportant if the dates of their travel to Cairo are far apart. On the other hand, Figure 6(b) shows that Laden and Kolokov are connected via "Saeed Hasham". This new junction node warrants further investigation about "Saeed Hasham". In the Atlantic Storm dataset discussed later, Saeed Hasham is a direct recruitee of Osama Bin Laden and Igor Kolokov is recruited by Saeed Hasham. There is no direct connection between Laden and Kolokov. Therefore, a syntactic constraint applied on the successor generation module can provide better connections. In the experimental results section we provide performance and quality comparison between two strategies: with and without person/organization as junction nodes (Section 5.4).

4.4.3 *Coreferencing*

Coreference is the art of determining when two entity mentions in a text refer to the same entity. We use LingPipe's heuristic coref-

(a) A city as an intermediate node

(b) A person as an intermediate node

Figure 6: Using syntactic constraints on story generation.

Text: A Russian named Igor Kolokov was arrested in Cairo on 29 January, 2003 and charged with assault on an Egyptian police officer who had attempted to arrest him for being drunk in public. Kolokov sells medical supplies throughout the Middle East and represents a company in Moscow called Medikat.

Coreferred text: A Russian named Igor Kolokov was arrested in Cairo on 29 January, 2003 and charged with assault on an Egyptian police officer who had attempted to arrest Igor Kolokov for being drunk in public. Igor Kolokov sells medical supplies throughout the Middle East and represents a company in Moscow called Medikat.

Figure 7: Example of coreferencing.

erence package [34] to resolve pronominal references to entities. LingPipe's coreference package is based on a greedy algorithm called CogNIAC [37] that visits each entity mentioned in a document in order, and for each mention either links it to a previous linked chain of mentions, or begins a new chain consisting only of the current mention. The resolution of a mention is guided by matchers and anti-matchers that score candidate antecedent mention chains based on properties such as the closest matching alias (using a complex comparison allowing for missing tokens), known alias associations, discourse proximity (how far away the last mention in a chain is and how many are intervening), and entity type. Figure 7 shows a simple example where "Kolokov" and some pronouns are replaced by "Igor Kolokov" using this approach.

4.4.4 *How does the Analyst Know where to Start?*

The question of how to find a starting point is very subjective and depends on the analyst's objectives. Some systems choose use graph-theoretic metrics such as betweenness centrality to identify key players in an entity network. We found significant benefits in classifying documents and using entities extracted from specific classes as candidate starting points. We use the AlchemyAPI [38] to assign each document to its most likely topic category (news, sports, business, law and crime, etc.). The analyst's further perusal of documents in each category helps narrow down the number of documents that might contain potential start and end entities. In section 5.6.2, we describe how we can reduce the start set of documents to solve a particular task with the VAST 2011 dataset.

4.4.5 *Modeling Issues*

So far, we have discussed our framework in the entity space. That is, the network we consider has entities as nodes and each entity is modeled as a vector of documents. Storytelling provides different explanations of a relationship between two entities as form of clique chains where each node of the clique chains is an entity. It is possible to reverse this model and traverse in the document space so that we can obtain clique chains of entities. In this reverse case, documents are modeled as vectors of entities and we can find explanation clique chains for a pair of documents instead of a pair of entities. This reverse modeling is sometimes useful where the investigation is less evidence based and the task is to find a small plot from a large volume of documents. In section 5.6.2, we explain how when we used documents as objects and entities as features, we can identify an imminent threat to a hypothetical city.

5 Experimental Results

Due to confidentiality reasons, our group is unable to disclose many intelligence analysis datasets that we have applied our algorithm on. For this paper, we demonstrate results on many public domain datasets, including i) the Atlantic Storm dataset developed in the Joint Military Intelligence College [39], ii) two datasets from the annual VAST challenge contests in 2010 and 2011, and iii) a dataset of politicians that we harvested from Wikipedia text. These datasets range from having 779 to 230,627 entities.

5.1 Evaluation measures

We use both quantitative and qualitative measures for our evaluation. To compare the performance of different successor generation strategies, we assess the number of nodes explored against the

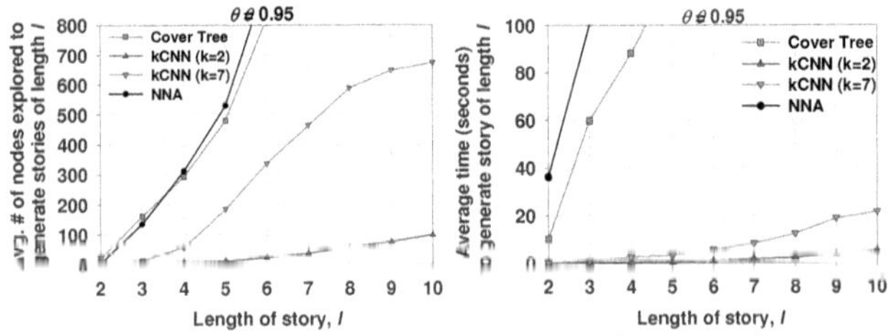

Figure 8: Comparison of successor generation approaches.

length of the story, and whether this growth is linear or exponential. For a numerical measure of story quality, we assess the pairwise Soergel distances between entities in a story (both consecutive and non-consecutive ones) and distill these distances into a dispersion coefficient. The dispersion coefficient assesses the overlap of the features of the entities of a story (not the graph structure of the clique chain) and, thus, evaluates the story, not the clique chain. An ideal story is one that meets the Soergel distance threshold only between consecutive pairs whereas a non-ideal story "oversatisfies" the distance threshold and meets it even between non-consecutive pairs. If n entities of a story are $e_0, e_1, \ldots, e_{n-1}$, then we quantify dispersion coefficient as:

$$\vartheta = 1 - \frac{1}{n-2} \sum_{i=0}^{n-3} \sum_{j=i+2}^{n-1} \text{disp}\,(e_i, e_j)$$

where
$$\text{disp}\,(e_i, e_j) = \begin{cases} \frac{1}{n+i-j}, & \text{if } \mathbb{D}\,(e_i, e_j) > \theta \\ 0, & \text{otherwise} \end{cases}$$

Thus, the dispersion coefficient is 1 for an ideal story and 0 in the worst case when every pair of entities of the story satisfies the distance threshold. Finally, we describe below the analysts interpretations and conclusions from the discovered stories. All the results presented in this paper were obtained using a regular desktop computer with Intel Core2 Quad CPU Q9450 @ 2.66GHz and 8 GB physical memory.

5.2 Evaluating Successor Generation Strategies

The goal of this experiment is to assess the number of nodes explored by the A* search and the time taken as a function of the discovered path length, and as a function of different successor generation strategies. For this purpose, we used the VAST11 dataset and aimed to generate 10,000 stories between randomly selected entity pairs, with a distance threshold of 0.95. Figure 8 depicts the results of the successful searches. As Figure 8 (left) shows, the cover tree and NNA approaches require much more number of node exploration than kCNN with k=2 and 7. The runtime trends shown in Figure 8(right) also mirror the number of nodes explored in Figure 8(left). This result is not surprising, as the cover tree algorithm does not factor into the clique constraint, thus preventing it from taking advantage of the search space reduction that this constraint provides. NNA does take advantage of this constraint, however, and it generates a strict ordering on the Jaccard's coefficient over the cliques, whereas kCNN simply generates some b candidate cliques. In practice, the kCNN relaxation results in the discovery of candidate cliques more rapidly than the NNA algorithm, while still remaining accurate. In both cases a post processing step is necessary to determine if a given candidate does in fact meet the search threshold. Through the remainder of this paper, we thus use the kCNN algorithm as it provides the best performance of the three algorithms.

5.3 Interplay between Clique and Distance Thresholds

We use the VAST11 dataset to study the effects of varying distance and clique size thresholds. As expected, the number of possible sto-

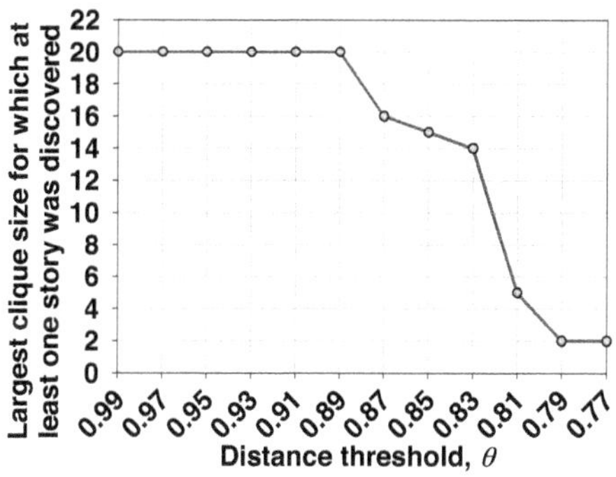

Figure 9: VAST 2011 Text Dataset (Entities are objects and documents are features): Relation between clique chain and distance threshold.

ries decreases monotonically with stricter distance and clique size requirements. Figure 9 shows the relationship between the largest available clique size as distance thresholds become progressively stricter.

5.4 Comparison between Syntactic and non-syntactic Storytelling

To explore this phenomena, we apply apply our algorithms on a dataset of politicians harvested from Wikipedia.org (contains 230,627 entities and 49,612 documents). We allow only person/organization type of entities as junction points of a clique chain in syntactic storytelling. On the other hand, non-syntactic storytelling can use any type of entities as junction nodes. To evaluate the performance of these two approaches, we generated 10,000 random pairs of politicians and invoked syntactic and non-syntactic storytelling with a range of distance threshold and clique size. Figure 10 compares the results of syntactic and non-syntactic storytelling with those start and end entity pairs for which at least one story was found by both the approaches. Figure 10 (left) shows that the average dispersion is better (i.e., higher) for syntactic storytelling with any distance threshold. This plot also depicts an increase in average dispersion with stricter (lower) distance thresholds for both syntactic and non-syntactic approaches.

Figure 10(middle) compares syntactic and non-syntactic versions of storytelling in terms of average clique size as a function of distance threshold. It shows that the average clique size is smaller with the syntactic approach at any distance threshold. This indicates that the extra syntactic constraint applied to the successor generator reduces the size of the neighborhood. As a result, the explanations (with cliques) are generally smaller than the non-syntactic version.

Figure 10(right) shows the distributions of the costs of the paths of the discovered stories for both syntactic and non-syntactic strategies. It shows that the syntactic approach discovers costlier paths than the non-syntactic approach. The extra syntactic restrictions at the junction nodes result in costlier and hence rare stories that the non-syntactic approach might not discover. Around 60% of the discovered stories for the non-syntactic approach have cost between 4.0 to 8.0 where only 36.5% of the stories with the syntactic approach fall into this range. Note that both the approaches yield a right skewed distribution, but the syntactic approach has a longer right skew than the non-syntactic approach indicating generation of costlier stories.

5.5 Comparison between Storytelling and an uninformed Search

We used the VAST 2011 dataset to compare storytelling against an uninformed search. Figure 11 (a) shows that the use of Soergel distance heuristic improves the average branching factor over the vanilla BFS (h=0). Overall improvement of average branching factor is more than 50%. Figure 11(b) shows that the use of the straight line Soergel distance for the heuristic exhibits lower runtime than exploration by the A* procedure over BFS (h=0), for a range of different clique sizes. The average time saved is more than 60%, even with the smallest clique size k=2. The heuristic tends to save additional time as larger clique size requirements are imposed.

Figure 11 (c) and (d) respectively depict the average effective branching factor and average time to generate stories as functions of clique size, for different approaches. Despite the use of the truncated dataset, Figure 11 (c) and (d) show that the mixed mode gains due to the heuristic over the BFS have a similar trend to the normal mode of Figure 11 (a) and (b). Therefore, the mixed mode analysis offers a practical mechanism to provide the best possible gains from lossy datasets without time consuming remodeling of the vector space (e.g., [10] uses a costly remodeling for post processing).

5.6 Use Case Studies

In this subsection we describe some of the illustrative results we obtained using some benchmark intelligence analysis datasets.

5.6.1 Atlantic Storm Dataset

The Atlantic Storm dataset was developed in the Joint Military Intelligence College as part of an evidence-based case study. We extracted 779 entities from the Atlantic Storm text dataset. An illustrative example of some stories are already shown in Figure 2 which provides multiple explanations of the relationship between two persons, Jose Escalante and Omar Hanif, who play an important role in transferring biological agents from Europe to the Caribbean.

After analyzing some stories, the user obtains a mental model of the attack. An illustrative mental model is shown in Figure 12. It depicts that the conspiracy starts from Osama Bin Laden in Afghanistan. Two of his close contacts are Saeed Hasham and Fahd al Badawi. Once these two contacts are discovered it becomes easy to find stories involving Igor Kolokov, Pyotr Safrygin, and Boris Bugarov. All these three people are former employees of Russian State Research Center of Virology and Biotechnology (Vector). Among them Boris Bugarov is known to be a bioweapon scientist. Another person named Abdellah Atmani, who works for Holland Orange Ship Lines, helps in smuggling the biological agents to the Caribbean from Morocco. After discovering the plot up to this point, a story involving four key entities (Escalante, Arze, Morales, and Sufaat) reveals that the biological agents will be transferred to the USA from the Bahamas. Omar Hanif and Adnan Hijaji are two key players who recruited Al Qaeda field agents to tansport the biological agents to the USA by several cruise ships.

5.6.2 VAST 2011 Dataset

The VAST11 dataset contains 4,447 documents. The task is to find any imminent threat to the imaginary city named "Vastopolis". We extracted a total of 55,109 entities from 4,447 documents. To find a starting set to work with, we first classify each of the documents using AlchemyAPI (Section 4.4.4). We reduced the set of 4,474 documents down to 122 by selecting the articles that were classified as "law and crime" or were considered "unclassifiable". This narrows down the potential number of terminal entities (start and end) to a few hundred from 55,109 entities. (Note that once given a start and end point, our storytelling algorithm still uses the entire collection.)

Since the number of entities is too large for an analyst to work with and the possible imminent threat is hidden in the news articles, we modeled the documents as vectors of entities (as described in Section 4.4.5). In the actual solution plot there are only around ten entities and thirteen documents involved. There are other stories that can be discovered from this dataset but they do not pose any imminent threats to Vastopolis.

An example story from the dataset is: [03435.txt → 00783.txt → 02566.txt → 01785.txt → 03212.txt]. The start document contains an entity named "Paramurderers of Chaos" which is the name of a terror group and the end document contains a report regard-

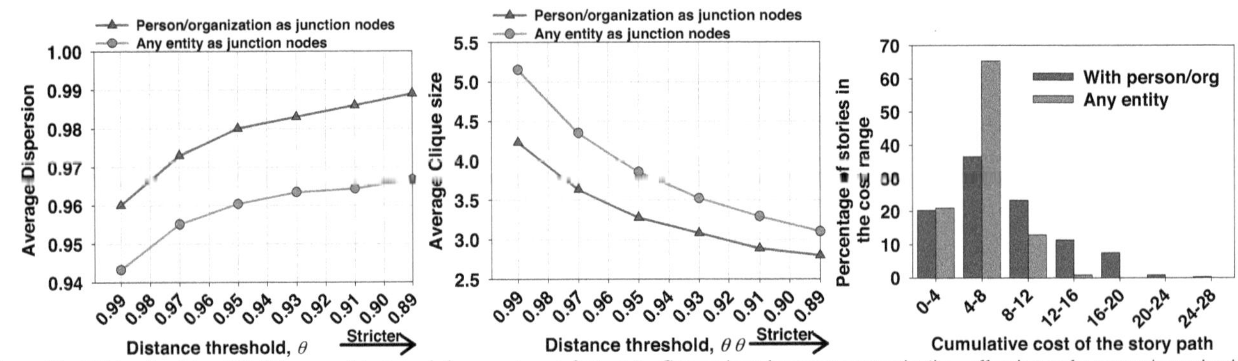

Figure 10: Wikipedia dataset(Entities are objects and documents are features). Comparison between syntactic (i.e., allowing only person/organization as junction nodes) and non-syntactic (e.g., allowing any type of entity as) approaches of storytelling: *(left)* Average dispersion as a function of distance threshold, *(middle)* Average clique size as a function of distance threshold, and *(right)* Cumulative cost distribution of the discovered stories.

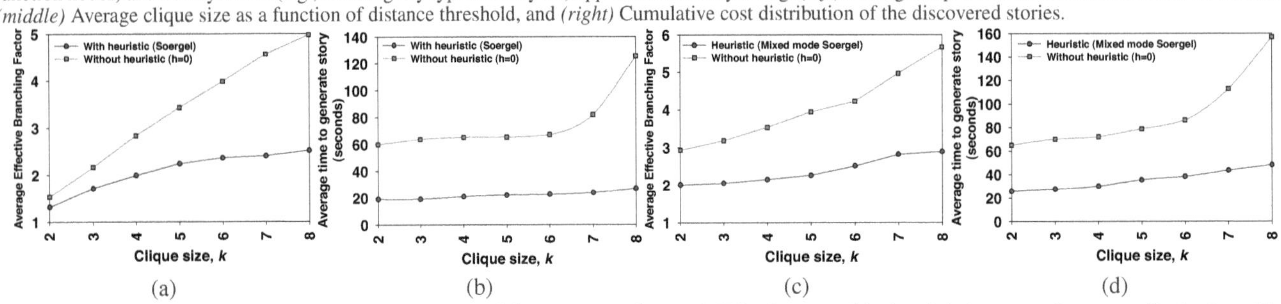

Figure 11: VAST 2011 Text Dataset (Entities are objects and documents are features). Effectiveness of the heuristic in terms of average effective branching factor and average runtime. (a) and (b) show a comparison between our storytelling and an uninformed search. (c) and (d) also depict similar plots but in the mixed operational mode.

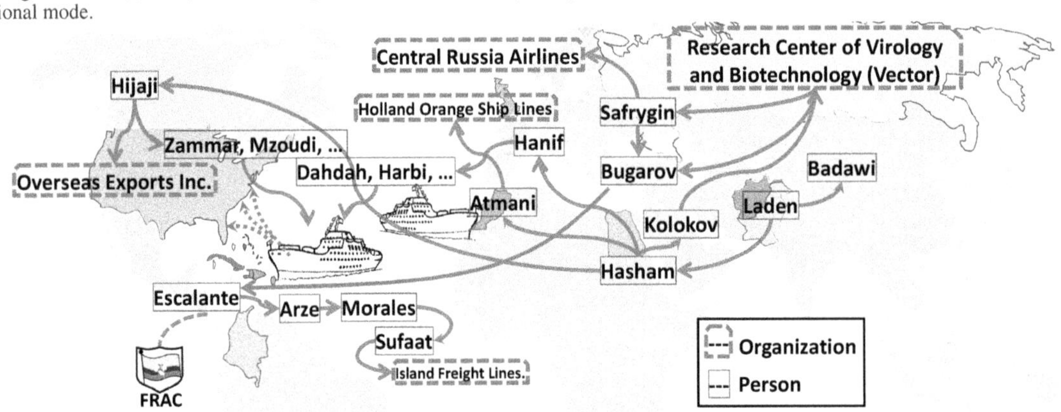

Figure 12: A sketch of the solution of the Atlantic Storm dataset.

ing a talk of professor (Edward Patino), another important entity in this plot. The algorithm selects documents 00783.txt, 02566.txt and 01785.txt as junction documents. The first two junction documents (00783.txt, 02566.txt) are related to computer viruses, worm threats, and security flaws in the Vast University. The next document (01785.txt) is related to a Robbery at Vast University (equipments of Professor Edward Patino were stolen). 01785.txt is one of the key documents in the solution which is properly picked by our algorithm. Note that document 00783.txt is considered a "false lead" in the solution planted by the VAST 2011 contest organizers. This study demonstrates that out algorithm was able to identify several key elements hidden inside a large corpora of news articles as well as a few false leads related to the actual plot. Several stories combined together and explanations provided by the cliques lead an analyst to the mental model of the whole plot.

5.6.3 VAST 2010 Dataset

Unlike the VAST 2011 dataset, VAST 2010 dataset is composed of transcribed phone calls, email messages, and reports from fields agents. The task is to investigate arms dealing. We extracted a total of 621 entities from this dataset, of which 102 are person entities. After reading a few documents, the user becomes interested in two people: Igor Sviatoslavich and Viktor Bout. The user first uses syntactic storytelling so that the junction points are people or organizations, but syntactic storytelling reported that there is no story between the given entities. A broader search reveals the result shown in Figure 13, where the junction nodes are locations. Both the two intermediate cliques of the chain are validated in the solution provided by the VAST 2010 Contest organizers. This story is part of an arms deal in the Iran region of the entire plot (called Iran network). Some places used to transport arms from North Korea to Iran were Colombo (Sri Lanka), Pyongyang, and Don Mueang. The story successfully reveals these locations. The story also reveals another person "Soltanzadeh" who is part of the Iran arms dealing network.

6 Discussion

We have presented a novel approach to storytelling between entities in large document collections, with applications to intelligence analysis. Our algorithms are both efficient at handling large datasets and effective at teasing out complicated plots from textual corpora. In the future, we aim to explore ways to automatically incorporate user feedback about presented stories, so as to dynami-

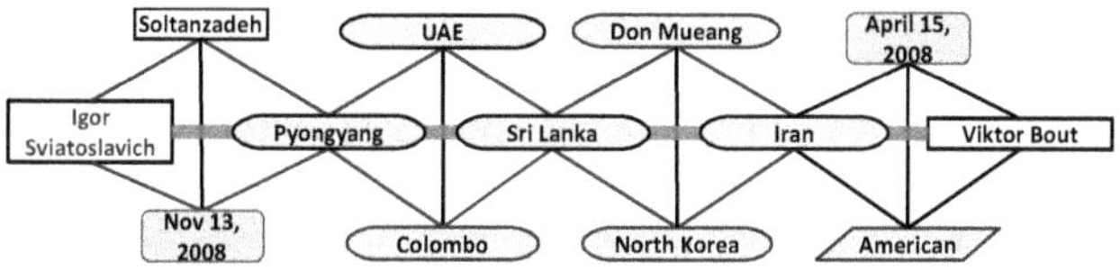

Figure 13: An example clique chain connecting Igor Sviatoslavich with Viktor Bout. Both of them are involved in arms dealing in the Iran network.

cally adjust the weightings of documents and/or the similarity functions. This will enable analysts to preferentially explore certain types of stories featuring preferred entity types or subplots. We will also explore incorporating additional sources of data, besides text documents, e.g., social media. Finally, we plan to continue our dialog with intelligence analysts to further develop compelling software tools for analytics.

7 Acknowledgements

This work is supported in part by the Institute for Critical Technology and Applied Science, Virginia Tech, and the US National Science Foundation through grant CCF-0937133.

8 References

[1] R. J. Heuer, *Psychology of Intelligence Analysis*. Center for the Study of Intelligence, CIA, 1999. [Online]. Available: https://www.cia.gov/library/

[2] R. Clark, *Intelligence Analysis: a Target-centric Approach*. CQ Press, 2003.

[3] i2group, "The Analyst's Notebook," Last accessed: May 26, 2011, http://www.i2group.com/us.

[4] FMS Advanced Systems Group, FMS Inc., "Sentinel Visualizer," Last accessed: May 26, 2011, http://www.fmsasg.com/.

[5] E. Bier, E. Ishak, and E. Chi, "Entity Workspace: An Evidence File That Aids Memory, Inference, and Reading," in *ISI '06*, 2006, pp. 466–472.

[6] PNNL, "Pacific Northwest National Laboratory, INSPIRE visual document analysis," Last accessed: May 26, 2011, http://in-spire.pnl.gov.

[7] H. Khurana, J. Basney, M. Bakht, M. Freemon, V. Welch, and R. Butler, "Palantir: a Framework for Collaborative Incident Response and Investigation," in *IDtrust*, 2009.

[8] Information Interfaces Research Lab., Georgia Tech, "Jigsaw: Visual Analytics for Exploring and Understanding Document Collections," Last accessed: February 9, 2012, http://www.cc.gatech.edu/gvu/ii/jigsaw/.

[9] Y. Kang and J. Stasko, "Characterizing the Intelligence Analysis Process: Informing Visual Analytics Design through a Longitudinal Field Study," in *VAST*, 2011.

[10] D. Kumar, N. Ramakrishnan, R. Helm, and M. Potts, "Algorithms for Storytelling," *TKDE*, vol. 20, no. 6, pp. 736–751, 2008.

[11] H. Kang, C. Plaisant, B. Lee, and B. B. Bederson, "NetLens: Iterative Exploration of Content-actor Network Data," *Info. Vis.*, vol. 6, no. 1, pp. 18–31, 2007.

[12] R. Alonso and H. Li, "Model-guided Information Discovery for Intelligence Analysis," in *CIKM '05*, 2005, pp. 269–270.

[13] A. Koltuksuz and S. Tekir, "Intelligence Analysis Modeling," in *ICHIT '06*, 2006.

[14] K. Chopra and C. Haimson, "Information fusion for intelligence analysis," in *HICSS '05*, 2005, p. 111a.

[15] E. Lindahl, S. O'Hara, and Q. Zhu, "A Multi-agent System of Evidential Reasoning for Intelligence Analyses," in *AAMAS '07*, 2007, pp. 279:1–279:6.

[16] J. Gersh, B. Lewis, J. Montemayor, C. Piatko, and R. Turner, "Supporting Insight-based Information Exploration in Intelligence Analysis," *Commun. ACM*, vol. 49, April 2006.

[17] T. Coffman, S. Greenblatt, and S. Marcus, "Graph-based Technologies for Intelligence Analysis," *Commun. ACM*, vol. 47, pp. 45–47, March 2004.

[18] P. Crossno, B. Wylie, A. Wilson, J. Greenfield, E. Stanton, T. Shead, L. Ice, K. Moreland, J. Baumes, and B. Geveci, "Intelligence Analysis Using Titan," in *IEEE Symposium on Visual Analytics Science and Technology*, 2007, pp. 241–242.

[19] G. Chin, O. A. Kuchar, P. D. Whitney, M. Powers, and K. E. Johnson, "Graph-based comparisons of scenarios in intelligence analysis," in *SMC '04*, vol. 4, 2004.

[20] E. Bier, S. Card, and J. Bodnar, "Principles and Tools for Collaborative Entity-Based Intelligence Analysis," *TVCG*, vol. 16, no. 2, pp. 178–191, 2010.

[21] M. Chau, J. J. Xu, and H. Chen, "Extracting Meaningful Entities from Police Narrative Reports," in *Annual National Conference on Digital Government Research*, 2002, pp. 1–5.

[22] P. Pirolli and S. Card, "The Sensemaking Process and Leverage Points for Analyst Technology as Identified through Cognitive Task Analysis," in *ICIA '05*, 2005.

[23] L. Fang, A. D. Sarma, C. Yu, and P. Bohannon, "Rex: explaining relationships between entity pairs," *Proc. VLDB Endow.*, vol. 5, no. 3, pp. 241–252, 2011.

[24] K. Heath, N. Gelfand, M. Ovsjanikov, M. Aanjaneya, and L. Guibas, "Image Webs: Computing and Exploiting Connectivity in Image Collections," in *CVPR*, 2010.

[25] J.-P. Brassard and J. Gecsei, "Path Building in Cellular Partitioning Networks," in *ISCA '80*, 1980, pp. 44–50.

[26] C. Faloutsos, K. S. McCurley, and A. Tomkins, "Fast Discovery of Connection Subgraphs," in *KDD '04*, 2004.

[27] M. S. Hossain, J. Gresock, Y. Edmonds, R. Helm, M. Potts, and N. Ramakrishnan, "Connecting the Dots between PubMed Abstracts," *PLoS ONE*, vol. 7, no. 1, p. e29509, 2012.

[28] D. Shahaf and C. Guestrin, "Connecting the Dots between News Articles," in *KDD '10*, 2010, pp. 623–632.

[29] D. R. Swanson, "Complementary Structures in Disjoint Science Literatures," in *SIGIR '91*, 1991, pp. 280–289.

[30] M. S. Hossain, C. Andrews, N. Ramakrishnan, and C. North, "Helping Intelligence Analysts Make Connections," in *AAAI '11 Workshop on Scalable Integration of Analytics and Visualization*, 2011.

[31] M. J. Zaki and N. Ramakrishnan, "Reasoning About Sets Using Redescription Mining," in *KDD '05*, 2005.

[32] A. Beygelzimer, S. Kakade, and J. Langford, "Cover Trees for Nearest Neighbor," in *ICML '06*, 2006, pp. 97–104.

[33] A. Leach and V. Gillet, *Introduction to Chemoinformatics*. Springer, 2007.

[34] Alias-i., "LingPipe 4.1.0," Last accessed: Jan 31, 2012, http://alias-i.com/lingpipe, 2008.

[35] Apache Software Foundation, "OpenNLP," Last accessed: Jan 31, 2012, http://incubator.apache.org/opennlp.

[36] Stanford Natural Language Processing Group, "Stanford NER: http://nlp.stanford.edu/software/CRF-NER.shtml," Last accessed: Jan 31, 2012.

[37] B. Baldwin, "CogNIAC: High Precision Coreference with Limited Knowledge and Linguistic Resources," in *ACL/EACL'97*, Spain, July 1997, pp. 38–45.

[38] AlchemyAPI., "AlchemyAPI: http://www.alchemyapi.com/api/categ/."

[39] F. J. Hughes, "Discovery, Proof, Choice: The Art and Science of the Process of Intelligence Analysis, Case Study 6, 'All Fall Down', Unpublished report," 2005.

A Framework for Robust Discovery of Entity Synonyms

Kaushik Chakrabarti, Surajit Chaudhuri, Tao Cheng, Dong Xin*
Microsoft Research
One Microsoft Way
Redmond, WA 98052
{kaushik, surajitc, taocheng}@microsoft.com, dongxin@google.com

ABSTRACT

Entity synonyms are critical for many applications like information retrieval and named entity recognition in documents. The current trend is to automatically discover entity synonyms using statistical techniques on web data. Prior techniques suffer from several limitations like click log sparsity and inability to distinguish between entities of different concept classes. In this paper, we propose a general framework for robustly discovering entity synonym with two novel similarity functions that overcome the limitations of prior techniques. We develop efficient and scalable techniques leveraging the MapReduce framework to discover synonyms at large scale. To handle long entity names with extraneous tokens, we propose techniques to effectively map long entity names to short queries in query log. Our experiments on real data from different entity domains demonstrate the superior quality of our synonyms as well as the efficiency of our algorithms. The entity synonyms produced by our system is in production in Bing Shopping and Video search, with experiments showing the significance it brings in improving search experience.

Categories and Subject Descriptors

H.2.8 [**DATABASE MANAGEMENT**]: Database applications—*Data mining*; H.3.3 [**INFORMATION STORAGE AND RETRIEVAL**]: Information Search and Retrieval

Keywords

entity synonym, robust synonym discovery, pseudo document similarity, query context similarity

1. INTRODUCTION

People often use several alternate strings to refer to the same named entity. For example, the product "Canon EOS 400d Digital Camera" is also referred to as "canon rebel xti" and "canon kiss k", the movie "Harry Potter and the Half Blood Prince" is also referred to as "harry potter 6" or simply "half blood prince", "Washington State Department of Licensing" is also referred to as "wa dol" and "wa dmv". We refer to these alternate strings as *entity synonyms*. Knowing the synonyms for the entities of interest is critical in effective search over entities.

At Microsoft, two concrete examples of searching over entities are Bing Shopping search and Video search (the two target applications of this work). In shopping search, the engine will fail to return the product entity named "Canon EOS 400d Digital Camera" for query "canon rebel xti" if the product description does not mention "rebel xti" and it does not know they are synonyms. Similarly in video search, a user asking for "harry potter 6" will not be able to find the "Harry Potter and the Half Blood Prince" video if the engine does not know they are synonymous. Typically, such vertical search applications support search over a catalog of entities (e.g., product entities, video entities). This work aims at discovering the synonyms for entities based on entity names (e.g., product names, video titles) offline and enriching the catalogs with the discovered synonyms. Synonym-enriched catalog can help boost recall and improve precision, and therefore help improve users' search experience. We will concretely study the positive effect of synonyms in improving these two search verticals in Section 7.

Entity synonyms are also very useful in many other applications. Applications like Voice of the Customer (VoC) and Social Media Analytics need to recognize mentions of named entities (e.g., products, organizations, people) in text documents (e.g., web pages, blogs, forum posts, tweets). Typically, these applications maintain a *reference table of entities* and require identification of mentions of *only* these entities in the documents [1, 3, 6]. For example, in VoC, an enterprise is typically interested in mining customer sentiment of its own and its competitors' products, so it needs to identify *only* those products in web documents. Exact matching and even approximate matching techniques, based on string similarity functions (e.g., Jaccard similarity), will miss many mentions. For example, "canon rebel xti" has very low string similarity with "Canon EOS 400d Digital Camera".

Review of State-of-the-art: To address the above needs, several similarity functions to automatically discover synonyms for entities have been proposed:

Click Similarity: Cheng et. al. identifies synonyms of entities using query click logs of a web search engine [6, 7]. They first identify webpage urls that are "good representatives" of the entity; for example, the urls clicked by users when the reference entity string is issued as query can be considered as good representatives. They then identify queries that have clicked at least one of the urls: these are "candidate synonyms strings" of the entity (henceforth, simply referred to as candidate synonyms). Finally, they identify the candidates that are strongly and exclusively related to the entity by inspecting click patterns on those representative urls; this is captured using two similarity functions which we refer to as *click similarity*

*Work done while author at MSR. Author's current address: Google.

KDD'12, August 12–16, 2012, Beijing, China.

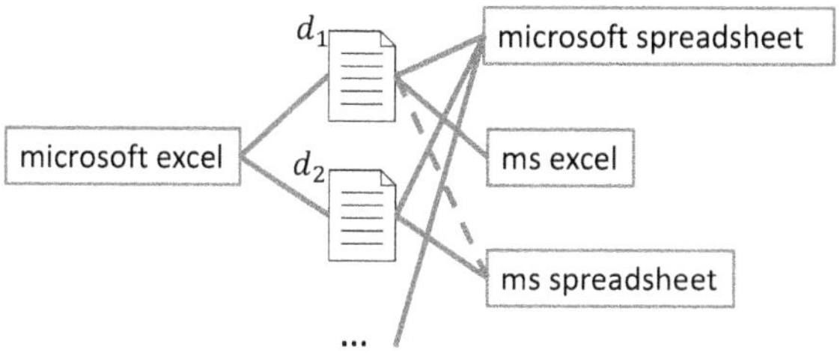

Figure 1: Motivating Example

(*ClickSim* in short).

Document Similarity: Turney proposes to identify synonyms based on coocurrence in web documents [18]. If the set of documents where the entity reference string occurs is strongly correlated with the set where a candidate synonym string occurs, it is adjudged a synonym of the entity. This is captured using a similarity measure which we refer to as *document similarity* (*DocSim* in short).

Distributional Similarity: The distribution hypothesis is that similar terms appear in similar contexts [11]. Although this has not been applied to entities, it has been used to compute semantically related terms (based on similarity of the contexts of their mentions in documents) [17] (*DistSim* in short).

Limitations of State-of-the-art: The above similarity measures suffer from several limitations:

• *Click Log Sparsity*: Often, many true synonyms of an entity are tail queries, i.e, they are asked by very few users and thus there are few clicked documents; this is often referred to as the *click log sparsity* problem. They often have few or no clicked documents in common with the representative documents for the entity. ClickSim will miss these synonyms.

We illustrate this using a real example from our experiments as shown in Figure 1. "microsoft excel" is the reference entity string, and "microsoft spreadsheet", "ms excel" and "ms spreadsheet" are three candidate synonyms. A solid edge between a query and a document represent a click on the document for that query. d_1 and d_2 are the representative documents for "microsoft excel". "ms spreadsheet" is a tail query and has only one clicked document in common (d_2) with the representative documents for "microsoft excel". Assuming the threshold is 2, "ms spreadsheet", in spite of being a true synonym, will not be adjudged a synonym.[1] ClickSim often misses such tail queries which results in *poor recall.* Note that this can be mitigated by lowering the threshold but this leads to drop in precision.

• *Inability to distinguish entities of different classes*: Consider the entity "microsoft excel" and the candidate synonym "ms excel tutorial". They might share many clicks with each other, hence it might be adjudged a synonym by ClickSim. Similarity, they might cooccur in many documents, hence it might be adjudged a synonym by DocSim as well. They are indeed very related but they do not belong to the same concept class; one is a tutorial whereas the other is a software product. To be a synonym, the entities must not only be highly related but also belong to the same concept class; the above techniques do not attempt to enforce the latter constraint. This leads to drop in precision.

Our Contributions: Our main contributions are summarized as follows:

• *General framework*: We first propose a set of *simple and natural properties* that entity synonyms should satisfy. We develop a novel synonym discovery framework that takes the individual similarity values as input and combines them and produces synonyms that satisfy the above properties. Our synonym framework differs from a standard classification model with the similarity values as features as the former enforces the synonym properties while the latter does not (Section 2).

• *Novel similarity measures*: We propose two novel similarity measures, *Pseudo Document Similarity* (*PseudoDocSim* in short) and *Query Context Similarity* (*QCSim* in short), to identify synonyms that overcome the limitations of ClickSim and DocSim. One of the main technical challenges to overcome the click log sparsity is whether we can derive additional "edges" between documents and queries in the click graph. We address this challenge using the following insight: even if a (tail) query q does not click on a document d, we can infer whether d is related to q by observing other queries that clicked on d. For example, in Figure 1, "ms spreadsheet" did not click on d_1 but "microsoft spreadsheet" and "ms excel" did. There is enough evidence that d_1 is related to "ms spreadsheet", so we add a new edge between "ms spreadsheet" and d_1 (shown by the dotted edge in Figure 1). In the above example, even with threshold 2, we will judge "ms spreadsheet" as a synonym. We propose the PseudoDocSim function that leverages the new edges to achieve higher recall than ClickSim without drop in precision (Section 4).

• *Efficient and scalable algorithms*: Often, we need to generate synonyms for millions of entities. To compute PseudoDocSim, we need to check the set containment of the tokens in each candidate synonym string and the "pseudo document" (bag of words constructed by concatenating the queries that clicked on it) of each representative document of the entity. This "all pairs" containment checking per entity is computationally challenging. We address this challenge using the following insight: for each entity, there is a high degree of overlap of tokens *both* among the pseudo documents as well as among the candidate synonyms. For example, in Figure 1, the tokens 'ms' and 'spreadsheet' are common among the candidates. We develop novel algorithms to exploit this overlap and avoid repeated work. Furthermore, we propose a MapReduce-based architecture for scalable discovery of synonyms and show how our algorithms can be incorporated into it (Section 5).

• *Handling long entity names with extraneous tokens*: Often times, entity catalogs contain long entity names which have many extraneous tokens. This makes it difficult in matching against query log, where queries are typically short. We propose search API based technique coupled with click information for finding more succinct strings of the entity to further improve the robustness of the framework (Section 6).

• *Experimental results*: We conduct extensive experiments using two real-life entity sets with different characteristics (location entities and software products). Our experiments show that (i) PseudoDocSim significantly outperform ClickSim and DocSim in terms of both precision and recall; (ii) our framework further improves the quality by enforcing the properties; (iii) our algorithms that share computation significantly outperform the baseline (by upto 6x); (iv) we demonstrate the usefulness of synonyms in improving search experience in real product settings (Section 7).

In this paper, we focus on entities with unambiguous reference strings and unambiguous candidate synonyms strings. Extending the framework to handle ambiguous reference strings and ambiguous candidate strings is an item of future work.

2. DEFINITIONS AND FRAMEWORK

In this section, we first define the synonym discovery problem and suggest a set of properties to define the synonym relation conceptually. Then, we present the notion of synonym similarity function and describe the general framework for discovering synonyms.

[1]For simplicity, we are thresholding based on the intersection count in this example. In practice, click ratios are used. The above limitation applies in that case as well.

2.1 Synonym Relation and Properties

For a given entity e, let r_e denote the entity reference string for the entity e. Let S_e be the set of candidate synonym strings of entity e[2]. Let $s_e \in S_e$ be a candidate synonym string of entity e. We first try to define the synonym relation on entity reference string r_e and candidate synonym strings S_e. We use the notation $r_e \equiv_{syn} s_e$ to denote that s_e is a synonym of r_e. In this work, we focus on unambiguous entity reference strings and synonym strings. An entity reference string r_e or a synonym string s_e is considered unambiguous if it uniquely identifies entity e. The synonym discovery problem is defined as follows in terms of input and output:

DEFINITION 1. ***(Synonym Discovery Problem)*** *Given a reference entity string r_e of entity e and a set of candidate synonym strings S_e, identify all candidate synonym strings $s_e \in S_e$ such that $r_e \equiv_{syn} s_e$*

What desired properties should r_e and s_e have in order for $r_e \equiv_{syn} s_e$ to hold true? As motivated in Section 1, we believe the following properties should be true for judging $r_e \equiv_{syn} s_e$:

PROPERTY 1. ***(Reflexivity)*** $r_e \equiv_{syn} r_e$, $s_e \equiv_{syn} s_e$

This property states that a string (either entity reference string, or candidate synonym string) is always a synonym of itself. *The meaning of this property is that the strings in the synonym relation are unambiguous, which is the scope of this study.* If a string could refer to multiple different entities, then reflexivity does not hold.

PROPERTY 2. ***(Symmetry)*** *if $r_e \equiv_{syn} s_e$, then $s_e \equiv_{syn} r_e$.*

This property states that if s_e is synonym to r_e as the entity reference string, then r_e is also synonym to s_e as the entity reference string. One key property of synonym relation is that it has to be *two-way*, which can be inferred from the symmetry property. One way checking of synonym from s_e to r_e often leads to poor precision; this was also observed in [2]. We will specifically show how this property leads to the design of our synonym discovery framework, which ensures high precision.

PROPERTY 3. ***(Similarity)*** *$r_e \equiv_{syn} s_e$, iff r_e and s_e are strongly related and both belong to the same concept class.*

This property requires two important aspects. First, entity reference string r_e and candidate synonym string s_e needs to be highly related with each other in order to be synonymous. Further, r_e and s_e should both belong to the same concept class. This is used to overcome the current approaches' limitation: inability to distinguish entities of different classes. It is important to notice that these two aspects need to be judiciously *combined* when synonym checking is performed.

These natural synonym properties allow us to more systematically study the limitation of current techniques, in that they do not fully satisfy these properties.

2.2 Synonym Similarity Function

The challenge is to instantiate the (r_e, s_e) pairs that satisfy the similarity property. We need evidence to check the similarity property; specifically, we need evidence of whether they are strongly related and whether they belong to the same concept class. We resort to synonym similarity functions for this purpose.

[2]We use previously proposed techniques to generate the set of candidate synonym strings S_e of any entity e. Specifically, any query that shares at least one common clicked document with the reference entity string is a candidate synonym string [6].

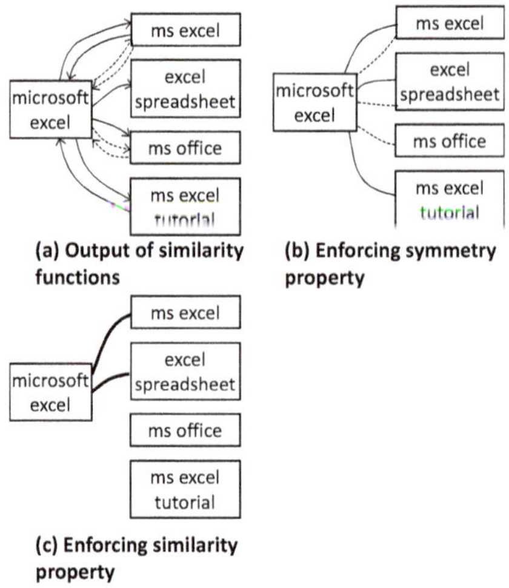

Figure 2: Synonym Discovery Steps

These functions serve as the starting point in populating the entire synonym relation between r_e and S_e. Figure 2 illustrates the 3 steps needed to discover synonyms, with Figure 2(a) focusing on instantiating relationship values based on two similarity functions (say $\mathcal{F}_1$ and $\mathcal{F}_2$). In the figure, solid thin edges represent relationship strength output from $\mathcal{F}_1$ and dashed edges represent relationship strength output from $\mathcal{F}_2$; thick edges refer to synonym relationship $\equiv_{syn}$.

As observed in prior works, the strings s_e and r_e alone are not enough for determining synonym relationship because string similarity between s_e and r_e is often not adequate [4, 3]. *As a result, we need to resort to auxiliary evidence for s_e and r_e.* Let $aux(s)$ denote the auxiliary evidence associated with a string s. One example auxiliary evidence $aux(s)$ associated with a string s can be the set of documents clicked by users for the web search query s or the set of documents in which s is mentioned.

Let a and b denote two strings.

DEFINITION 2. ***(Synonym Similarity Function)*** *A synonym similarity function $\mathcal{F}(a \to b)$ ($\mathcal{F}$ in short) takes input string a and its auxiliary evidence $aux(a)$ as well as input string b and its auxiliary evidence $aux(b)$, and computes the strength of relationship of a to b, formally:*
$\mathcal{F} : \{a, aux(a)\} \times \{b, aux(b)\} \to \mathcal{R} \in [0, 1]$

Note that the function needs access to auxiliary evidence (e.g, web documents or click logs). We omit those inputs from the notation $\mathcal{F}(a \to b)$ for simplicity. Intuitively, b has strong relationship to a if the auxiliary evidence $aux(b)$ of b that supports b is related to a is significant compared with the auxiliary evidence $aux(a)$ that does not support it. Note that this function does not need to be symmetric.

2.3 Synonym Discovery Framework

Given the available synonym similarity functions, a general framework is needed for discovering entity synonyms to make sure that the synonym relation properties are satisfied. Figure 3 shows the synonym relation discovery framework. We need to judiciously combine multiple synonym functions to satisfy the similarity property. In general, the framework can take a wide variety of *synonym similarity functions* $\mathcal{F}_1, \ldots, \mathcal{F}_n$ that can be used for checking synonym relationship. As a result, many existing useful similarity functions can be incorporated in this framework. Note that the similarity functions do not need to satisfy symmetry.

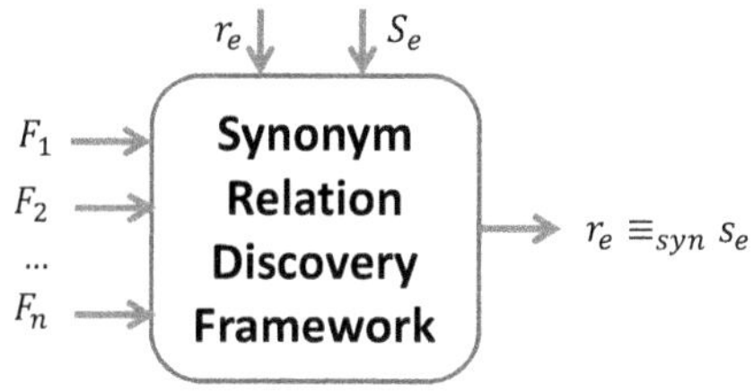

Figure 3: Synonym Discovery Framework

The framework can either be threshold based, or classifier based, which all perform checking based on the values output by synonym functions. This paper mainly focuses on a threshold based framework.

Synonym functions are not necessarily symmetric in that $\mathcal{F}(a \rightarrow b)$ may have different value from $\mathcal{F}(b \rightarrow a)$. We now discuss how our framework ensures symmetry. To ensure the symmetry property of synonym, the framework must perform *two-way checking* for asymmetric functions. In a threshold based framework (with threshold θ), we must make sure that the following condition is met to ensure symmetry:

$$\mathcal{F}(s_e \rightarrow r_e) \geq \theta \wedge \mathcal{F}(r_e \rightarrow s_e) \geq \theta \quad (1)$$

The above two-way checking states that s_e is a synonym of e if (i) s_e has strong relationship to r_e and (ii) r_e has strong relationship to s_e. As shown in Figure 2(b), by enforcing symmetry we can filter out candidates which only satisfy similarity one way (e.g., "ms office").

This two-way checking in Eq. 1 is essential for synonyms, i.e., the relationship has to be strong from both directions. As observed in [2, 6], this enables us to distinguish true synonyms from other semantically related terms (e.g., other "nyms" like hypernym and hyponyms). In general, the measure of strength is *directional* and both direction needs to be checked explicitly (e.g., in PseudoDocSim proposed in Section 4). In some cases, it might be possible to obtain a single similarity function that captures both $\mathcal{F}(s_e \rightarrow r_e)$ and $\mathcal{F}(r_e \rightarrow s_e)$. For example, when the similarity is based on set intersection, the Jaccard Similarity can capture both (e.g., QCSim). Another example is PMI when the similarity is based on correlation. In such cases, one check is sufficient.

The similarity property states that the two aspects of synonym, relatedness and same class relationship, need to be checked in *combination*. This requires that, among the *synonym similarity functions* $\mathcal{F}_1, \ldots, \mathcal{F}_n$ in the framework, there must exist at least one function for checking relatedness, and at least one function for making sure of the same class relationship.

As shown in Figure 2(c), by enforcing similarity property by judicious combination of various similarity functions, we can filter out candidates with only one aspect of the similarity property (e.g., "ms excel tutorial").

Being able to accommodate various similarity functions is an advantage of our framework, as compared to single similarity function based approaches. This enables us to support the two key aspects of the similarity property, and therefore achieve higher precision.

3. BASELINE SIMILARITY FUNCTIONS

In this section, we study two previously proposed approaches, based on two existing similarity functions, ClickSim and DocSim, for finding synonyms and discuss why they are inadequate.

3.1 Click Similarity

In ClickSim, proposed in [6], the documents clicked for the web search query s is the auxiliary evidence $aux(s)$ associated with s. We first consider the strength $\mathcal{F}_{csim}(s_e \rightarrow r_e)$ of the relationship of s_e to r_e. The supporting evidence is the number of documents $|aux(s_e) \cap aux(r_e)|$ clicked for web search query r_e that are also clicked for s_e. The non-supporting evidence is the number of documents $|aux(r_e)| - |aux(s_e) \cap aux(r_e)|$ clicked for r_e but not clicked for s_e. The *strength* of the relationship of s_e to r_e is the significance of the former compared with the latter and formalized as follows:

$\mathcal{F}_{csim}(s_e \rightarrow r_e) = \frac{|aux(s_e) \cap aux(r_e)|}{|aux(r_e)|}$

Reversely, checking the relationship the other way around indicates the *exclusiveness* from s_e to r_e

$\mathcal{F}_{csim}(r_e \rightarrow s_e) = \frac{|aux(r_e) \cap aux(s_e)|}{|aux(s_e)|}$

ClickSim adjudges s_e to be a synonym of e iff

$\mathcal{F}_{csim}(s_e \rightarrow r_e) \geq \theta \wedge \mathcal{F}_{cs}(r_e \rightarrow s_e) \geq \theta$

As we can see, the formalization in Eq.1 accommodates ClickSim by capturing both strength and exclusiveness. Note that this approach already ensures the symmetry property. However, it does not meet the similarity property, in that it does make sure that candidate string is of the same class of the reference entity string.

3.2 Document Similarity

In the original document similarity proposed in [18], the documents which s occurs in is the auxiliary evidence $aux(s)$ associated with s. Turney just considered one-way checks; he only considered the strength $\mathcal{F}_{dsim}(r_e \rightarrow s_e)$ of the relationship of r_e to s_e. The supporting evidence is the number of documents $|aux(r_e) \cap aux(s_e)|$ that both s_e and r_e occurs in; the non-supporting evidence is the number of documents $|aux(s_e)| - |aux(r_e) \cap aux(s_e)|$ that s_e occurs in but not r_e. As in ClickSim, the strength of the relationship of r_e to s_e is formalized as follows:

$\mathcal{F}_{dsim}(r_e \rightarrow s_e) = \log_2 \frac{|aux(r_e) \cap aux(s_e)|}{|aux(s_e)|}$

s_e is adjudged a synonym of iff $\mathcal{F}_{ds}(r_e \rightarrow s_e) > \theta$. Note that this function is not symmetric. It does not meet the similarity property either, by failing to check same class relationship.

4. NOVEL SIMILARITY FUNCTIONS

As discussed in Section 3, both ClickSim and DocSim do not satisfy the synonym properties. Further, ClickSim often misses valid synonyms due to the sparsity of the click logs and DocSim suffers from noise in document content. In this section, we propose two novel similarity functions, namely *Pseudo Document Similarity* and *Query Context Similarity* to ensure the synonym properties and overcome the limitations.

4.1 Pseudo Document Similarity

We propose pseudo document similarity (PseudoDocSim in short) to address the sparsity problem. The main insight is that a document d can be concisely and accurately captured by the set of queries which clicked on it. *As a result, although a tail query q may not click on a document d, we can infer whether q is related to d through the other queries that clicked on d.* Recall the example in Figure 1, "ms spreadsheet" did not click on d_1 but "microsoft spreadsheet" and "ms excel" did. Since its tokens are "covered" by the tokens of the latter two queries, we can infer d_1 is related to "ms spreadsheet". PseudoDocSim leverages this additional inferred evidence to overcome the sparsity problem of ClickSim.

To check whether a candidate synonym string is covered by queries clicked on a document, we construct the *pseudo document* for each document. The *pseudo document* of a document d (referred to as pseudodoc in short) is the set of all tokens from all the queries that clicked on document d.

DEFINITION 3. ***(Pseudo Document)*** *Given a query click log L, the pseudo document of document d $PseuDoc(d)$ is defined as:* $PseuDoc(d) = \{w | w \in q, s.t.\ q \text{ clicked on } d \text{ in log } L\}$

We typically use a query click log collected over a long period of time to construct comprehensive pseudo documents. For robustness, a minimal support (e.g., 5 clicks) is needed for a query, document pair to be included in the query click log.

The auxiliary information $aux(s)$ of string s is the set of documents clicked by query s. Formally, $aux(s) = \{d | s \text{ clicked on } d\}$

Consider a document $d \in aux(r_e)$. If d's pseudodoc contains all the tokens in s_e, it is evidence supporting r_e is related to s_e; otherwise, it is non-supporting evidence. The strength of the relationship of s_e to r_e, $F_{pdsim}(s_e \rightarrow r_e)$, is the fraction of documents in $aux(r_e)$ whose pseudo document contains all the tokens in s_e.

$$\mathcal{F}_{pdsim}(s_e \rightarrow r_e) = \frac{|\{d | s_e \in PseuDoc(d), d \in aux(r_e)\}|}{|aux(r_e)|} \quad (2)$$

Given Eq. 1, since PseudoDocSim is not symmetric in nature, we can enforce the two way checking by checking $\mathcal{F}_{pdsim}(r_e \rightarrow s_e)$ in addition to $\mathcal{F}_{pdsim}(s_e \rightarrow r_e)$, as follows:

$$\mathcal{F}_{pdsim}(r_e \rightarrow s_e) = \frac{|\{d | r_e \in PseuDoc(d), d \in aux(s_e)\}|}{|aux(s_e)|} \quad (3)$$

We refer to $F_{pdsim}(s_e \rightarrow r_e)$ and $F_{pdsim}(r_e \rightarrow s_e)$ as C-to-E (candidate-to-entity) and E-to-C (entity-to-candidate) similarities respectively. Similar enforcement can be applied to DocSim to ensure symmetry as well.

We now show that this two way checking of PseudoDocSim leads to higher recall than ClickSim as proved below.

LEMMA 1. ***(Improved Recall)*** *For the same threshold, pseudo document similarity has higher recall compared with click similarity.*

Proof: Consider a document $d_{common} \in (aux(s_e) \cap aux(r_e))$. Since s_e clicked on d_{common}, s_e is contained in d_{common}'s pseudo document, i.e., $s_e \subseteq PseudoDoc(d_{common})$. Hence, $d_{common} \in |\{d | s_e \in PseuDoc(d), d \in aux(r_e)\}|$
$\Rightarrow (aux(s_e) \cap aux(r_e)) \subseteq |\{d | s_e \in PseuDoc(d), d \in aux(r_e)\}|$
$\Rightarrow \frac{|(aux(s_e) \cap aux(r_e))|}{|aux(r_e)|} \leq \frac{|\{d | s_e \in PseuDoc(d), d \in aux(r_e)\}|}{|\{d | d \in aux(r_e)\}|}$
$\Rightarrow F_{csim}(s_e \rightarrow r_e) \leq F_{pdsim}(s_e \rightarrow r_e)$.
This implies $F_{csim}(s_e \rightarrow r_e) \geq \theta \Rightarrow F_{pdsim}(s_e \rightarrow r_e) \geq \theta$. Exactly in the same way, we can show that $F_{csim}(r_e \rightarrow s_e) \geq \theta \Rightarrow F_{pdsim}(r_e \rightarrow s_e) \geq \theta$ Hence, $F_{csim}(s_e \rightarrow r_e) \geq \theta \wedge F_{csim}(r_e \rightarrow s_e) \geq \theta \Rightarrow F_{pdsim}(s_e \rightarrow r_e) \geq \theta \wedge F_{pdsim}(r_e \rightarrow s_e) \geq \theta$ ■

There are two main benefits of using pseudo document similarity. *First*, it harvests strictly more supporting evidence than ClickSim. if $d \in aux(r_e)$ is supporting evidence of s_e in ClickSim (i.e., r_e clicked on d), it is also supporting evidence in pseudodoc. Even if d is not supporting evidence in ClickSim, it can serve as supporting evidence in PseudoDocSim based on additional inferred information.

Second, in contrast to DocSim, pseudo document allows us to focus on the essential parts of a document, rather than the complete content. Consider the example in Figure 1. Although document d_1 has many other words in its content, its pseudo document only contains words "microsoft", "spreadsheet", "ms" and "excel": a very succinct yet high quality representation of the document. Mining over pseudo documents yields higher precision, as compared to the document similarity approach. Furthermore, since pseudo documents are much shorter than real documents, it is much more efficient to compute as well.

4.2 Query Context Similarity

We propose query context similarity (QCSim in short) to make sure that candidate synonym string is of the same class of the entity. Since query strings are considered as candidate synonym strings, ClickSim often includes candidate synonym strings of other concept classes as synonyms. For example, "ms excel tutorial" could be adjudged as synonym for "microsoft excel" because they are strongly related to each other based on our auxiliary evidence. The technical challenge is to filter out candidate synonym strings that are of different concept classes.

Our main insight here is that the words that appear in the context of entity names in web search queries can help us distinguish between entities of different classes. These words describes the various facets of the concept class, and as a result tend to be similar for entities from the same class and different for entities from different classes. Contexts of a string are the additional words (consisting of $1, 2, 3$ words) occur immediately on its left and right in web search queries; we require the number of occurrences to be above a threshold to eliminate noise. For example, "microsoft excel" and its true synonyms like "microsoft spreadsheet", "ms excel" and "ms spreadsheet" have contexts like "download", "help", and "training" while "ms excel tutorial" have (very different) contexts like "book", "ppt" and "guide". We compute QCSim between r_e and s_e by taking the set similarity of their contexts. We use Jaccard Similarity in this paper; any other measure of set similarity (e.g., Cosine, Dice coefficient, etc.) can be used.

The auxiliary information $aux(s)$ of a string is the set of contexts in web search queries. In this case, we use a single similarity function to capture both $\mathcal{F}(s_e \rightarrow r_e)$ and $\mathcal{F}(r_e \rightarrow s_e)$:

$$\mathcal{F}_{qcsim}(s_e \rightarrow r_e) = \mathcal{F}_{qcsim}(r_e \rightarrow s_e) = \frac{|aux(s_e) \cap aux(r_e)|}{|aux(s_e) \cup aux(r_e)|} \quad (4)$$

Here, the two way checking is automatically satisfied.

Note that QCSim is very similar to distributional similarity using contexts [11, 14, 17]. However, most prior work uses contexts in documents; to the best of knowledge, this is the first time distributional similarity has been applied to contexts in web search queries.

4.3 Combining the Two Similarity Measures

Formally, the synonym discovery process in our framework can be stated as follows:

DEFINITION 4. ***(Synonym Discovery Process)*** *Given a reference entity string r_e of entity e and a set of candidate synonym strings S_e, identify all $s_e \in S_e$ such that*
(i) $\mathcal{F}_{pdsim}(s_e \rightarrow r_e) \geq \theta_1 \wedge \mathcal{F}_{pdsim}(r_e \rightarrow s_e) \geq \theta_1$ *and*
(ii) $\mathcal{F}_{qcsim}(s_e \rightarrow r_e)(= \mathcal{F}_{qcsim}(r_e \rightarrow s_e)) \geq \theta_2$

We follow the above approach in this paper. In practice, such hard thresholds on each similarity measure are difficult to determine and may be too restricting; a more practical approach is to use the similarity values as features and use a classifier to determine whether r_e and s_e are synonyms.

5. EFFICIENT AND SCALABLE ALGORITHM

Often, we need to generate synonyms for millions of entities, and therefore efficiency and scalability become critical. We first present the basic system architecture. Further, we observe that there is a high degree of overlap in computation; we develop algorithms that share computation and avoid repeated work. Finally we show how we can leverage the MapReduce framework to generate synonyms at such large scale.

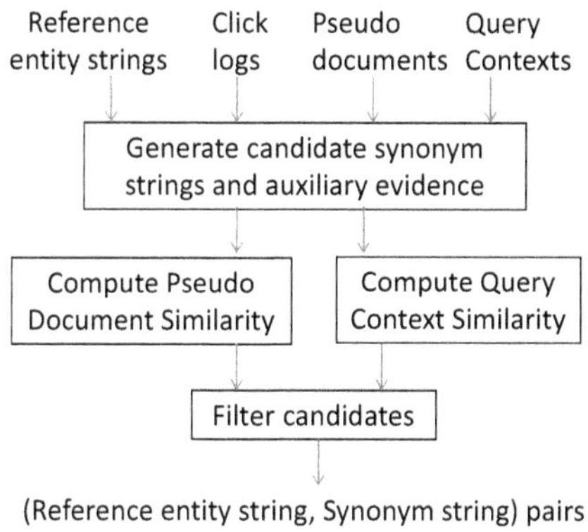

Figure 4: System Architecture

5.1 System Architecture

The architecture of our system is shown in Figure 4. We assume the pseudo documents for all documents (that have non-zero clicks in the click log) are computed in advance; this is a one-time job that can be reused for any reference entity set.[3] We also assume that the contexts of all query strings in the query log (in longer queries) are also computed in advance. Our architecture has 4 steps:

1) **Generation of Candidates and Auxiliary Evidence**: Given the reference entity strings and the click logs, this step generates (i) the candidate synonym strings of each entity and (ii) the auxiliary evidence for each reference entity string and each candidate synonym string.

2) **Pseudo Document Similarity Computation**: Given the (entity, candidate) pairs and the pseudodocs for both the reference entity strings and the candidates, this step computes the E-to-C similarity as well as C-to-E similarity based on Equations 2 and 3.

3) **Context Similarity Computation**: Given the (entity, candidate) pairs and the query contexts, this step computes the context similarity for each pair based on Equation 4.

4) **Filtering**: Given the (entity, candidate) pairs and their E-to-C similarities, C-to-E similarities and context similarities, this step filters out the non-synonyms and outputs the final (entity, synonym) pairs.

The most expensive computation component in the architecture is the PseudoDocSim computation, and as a result becomes the bottleneck of the framework. We focus on this step in the rest of the section.

5.2 PseudoDocSim Computation

We consider computing the C-to-E similarities; E-to-C similarities are computed in exactly the same way. There are two main decisions: how to save the computation cost of calculating PseudoDocSim (efficiency) and how to partition the task into subtasks (scalability).

5.2.1 *Efficient Computation*

We present three algorithms to calculate PseudoDocSim: a baseline algorithm for containment checking that does not exploit any overlap of tokens, an algorithm, called DocIndex, that exploits overlap on the document side but not on the candidate side and finally, an algorithm, called DualIndex, that exploits overlap on both document and candidate sides.

The task performed by the algorithms can be formally defined as follows.

DEFINITION 5. ***(PseudoDocSim Computation Task)*** *Given the reference entity string r_e, its pseudo documents $D(r_e)$ and its candidate synonym strings S_e, compute E-to-C similarities between the reference entity string r_e and each candidate $s_e \in S_e$.*

Baseline Algorithm: The naive algorithm is, for each candidate s_e and each pseudo document d_e, to check the containment of tokens in s_e in d_e. We tokenize the each pseudo document only once and insert the tokens of each pseudo document in a separate hash table to allow containment checking.

Cost analysis: Let $|T(s)|$ denote the number of tokens in the string s. The number of hash table lookups for candidate s_e is $|T(s_e)| \times |D(r_e)|$. The overall number of hash table lookups is $\sigma_{s_e \in S_e} |T(s_e)| \times |D(r_e)|$. The total cost is $C_h \times \sum_{s_e \in S_e} |T(s_e)| \times |D(r_e)|$ where C_h is the average cost of a hash lookup.

The naive algorithm is expensive as it performs too many hash lookups. For example, if an entity has 1000 candidates and 1000 representative documents and a candidate has an average of 5 tokens, the number of lookups is $5 * 1000 * 1000 = 5$ million. We observe that there is a high degree of overlap of tokens both among the pseudo documents in $D(r_e)$ and the candidates in S_e; it is possible to reduce the cost by exploiting this overlap.

Inverted Index on Pseudo Documents: We propose to build an inverted index on the pseudo documents. For each candidate s_e, we obtain the pseudo documents containing the tokens in s_e using the inverted index, i.e., by intersecting the posting lists corresponding to the tokens in s_e. We assume that the inverted index fits in memory; this is realistic since it is built on pseudo documents (which are short) of a single entity.

Cost analysis: We assume that the cost of accessing the inverted index and intersecting the posting lists for each candidate s_e is proportional to the number of tokens $|T(s_e)|$ in s_e, i.e., it is $C_l \times |T(s_e)|$ where C_l is the average access/intersection cost per token. The overall cost is $C_l \times \sum_{s_e \in S_e} |T(s_e)|$.

The above algorithm, referred to as *DocIndex*, is an improvement over the naive algorithm as it exploits the overlap of tokens among the pseudo documents. A token is looked up just one for each candidate compared with $|D(r_e)|$ times in the naive case. We observe that it is possible to further improve cost by exploiting overlap of tokens among candidates as well.

Inverted Index on both Pseudo Documents and Candidates: In addition to the inverted index on the pseudo documents, we propose to build an inverted index on the candidates. Subsequently, the algorithm iterates over each distinct token in the set S_e of candidates and constructs the Candidate-Document matrix (CD matrix) as follows. We first assign an index $ind(s_e)$ between 1 and $|S_e|$ to each candidate and an index $ind(d_e)$ between 1 and $|D_e|$ to each representative document. The (i, j)th cell $CD[i, j]$ in the CD matrix contains the number of tokens of the candidate with index i contained in the pseudo document with index j. We assume that the two inverted indexes and the CD matrix fits in memory.

Initially, all cells in the CD matrix are set to 0. For each distinct token t in S_e, we lookup the inverted indexes on pseudo documents and candidates. For each document d and each candidate s containing t, we increment $CD[ind(d), ind(s)]$ by 1. The CD matrix computation is completed when we have iterated over all distinct tokens in S_e.

After the CD matrix has been computed, we compute the E-to-C similarity between r_e and a candidate s_e as follows. We count the

[3]The pseudo documents need to be recomputed when the information in the click logs have changed significantly. Since we are using click logs collected over multiple years (say, 2 or 3 years), we anticipate this to happen once every several months (say, once in six months). Hence, we do not consider the cost of constructing pseudo documents as part of the synonym generation task.

Algorithm 1 DUALINDEX

Input: $S(e)$, $D(e)$
Output: E-to-C similarities
$\forall i, j$ CDMatrix[i,j] $\leftarrow 0$

```
1: if |S(e)| ≤ |D(e) then
2:     for t ∈ DisTok(S(e)) do
3:         S_t ← Index of candidates containing t
4:         D_t ← Index on pseudo documents containing t
5:         for i ∈ S_t do
6:             for j ∈ D_t do
7:                 CDMatrix[i,j] ← CDMatrix[i,j] + 1
8: else
9:     for t ∈ DisTok(D(e)) do
10:        // Same as lines 2 -5
11: for s ∈ S(e) do
12:    E − to − C − Sim(e, s) ← |d|d∈D(e)∧CD[ind(s),ind(d)]=|s|| / |D(e)|
13: return E − to − C − Sim(e, s)
```

number of documents $d_e \in D_e$ which contains all the tokens of s_e, i.e. for which $C[ind(s_e), ind(d_e)] = |T(s_e)|$. Dividing that count by the number of pseudo documents yields the E-to-C similarity.

Cost analysis: We assume the cost of accessing the two inverted indexes is proportional to the number of tokens it is accessed for. We assume the cost of updating the matrix is very efficient because it is direct access. Let $DisTok(S_e)$ denote the set of distinct tokens in the set S_e of candidates and $DisTok(D_e)$ denote the set of distinct tokens in the set D_e of candidates. The overall cost is therefore $C_a \times min(|DisTok(S_e)|, |DisTok(D_e)|)$ where C_a is the average access cost per token.

The above algorithm, referred to as *DualIndex*, further improves the cost over DocIndex by exploiting the overlap among candidates as well. A token t is looked up just once in DualIndex as opposed to $|C(t)|$ times where $|C(t)|$ is the number of candidates that contains that token.

5.2.2 *Partitioning the Task*

To scale the computation of PseudoDocSim, we leverage the MapReduce framework to partition the computation across various distributed nodes, which is achieved by specifying the appropriate key to the Map step. We propose to partition the computation into subtasks by entity. Each subtask computes the E-to-C similarities between a reference entity string and all its candidate synonym strings. Formally, the Map and Reduce steps are (the key is r_e):
Map: $\langle r_e, s_e, d_e\rangle \rightarrow \langle r_e, \langle s_e\rangle, \langle d_e\rangle\rangle$
Reduce: $\langle r_e, \langle s_e\rangle, \langle d_e\rangle\rangle \rightarrow \langle r_e, \langle s_e, \mathcal{F}_{pdsim}(r_e \rightarrow s_e)\rangle\rangle$

The Map step groups the set of candidate synonym string into $\langle s_e\rangle$, and the set of pseudo documents for r_e into $\langle d_e\rangle$. The reduce step performs the PseudoDocSim computation of all candidates with respect to r_e and output the $\mathcal{F}_{pdsim}(r_e \rightarrow s_e)$ value for each candidate string s_e.

Adapting the other steps in the system architecture to the MapReduce framework is straightforward. We skip the details to save space.

6. HANDLING LONG ENTITY NAMES

Often times, entity catalogs contain long entity names which have many extraneous tokens. Matching such long entity names directly against query log often yields very few or no queries, which makes subsequence synonym mining difficult or even impossible. To make the framework robust, can we identify the key tokens in a long entity name, and discard extraneous tokens, so that we can better match the entity with queries in query log?

It is common to have very long entity names which contain peripheral information about the entity. For instance, camera names in a camera catalog often includes spec information (e.g., megapixel, zoom, etc.). One such example is "Canon EOS 350D - digital camera, 8MP, 3x Optical Zoom". To deal with such cases, we propose to leverage search engine API to find proper subset of tokens (subset synonyms) that can still uniquely identify the entity.

Specifically, given such an entity reference string r_e, we first use search engine API to retrieve a set of documents by using the entity reference string as the query, and treat these documents as the auxiliary information $aux(r_e)$ for r_e. A query which clicked on at least one of the documents in this set, whose tokens is a subset of those in r_e, is regarded as a candidate s_e. Then we can perform click similarity analysis based on strength of relationship and exclusiveness, as described in Section 3.1, to find the subset synonyms. For instance, we may find that "Canon EOS 350D" is a qualifying subset synonym of "Canon EOS 350D - digital camera, 8MP, 3x Optical Zoom" using this analysis. It is worth noticing that here we are restricting to subsets only, which makes click similarity analysis more accurate. Further, pseudo document similarity does not work here since extraneous tokens such as "8MP, 3x Optical Zoom" often do not appear in pseudo documents.

Once we found such subset synonym of the entity, we can use it as the reference string of the entity and perform synonym discovery.

7. EXPERIMENTAL EVALUATION

In this section, we report our experiment results. We first describe the setting of our experiments. Then we report the quality results to validate the effectiveness of our framework. We further report efficiency and scalability results. Finally, we discuss the impact of the generated synonyms in improving search.

7.1 Experimental Setting

Our synonym discovery framework mainly leverages query log. Specifically, we leverage the query click log from "Bing" from 2009 to 2010. Note that due to proprietary and privacy concerns we cannot share all the details of the query click log.

To empirically evaluate the framework, we conduct experiments on two real life datasets, as summarized below:

- **Local Business Names (Local)**: 937 local business names sampled from "Bing" local catalog, e.g., *la police credit union*;
- **Software Names (Software)**: 10 software names, e.g., *microsoft excel*.

These two datasets, from two very different domains, are of very different characteristics. The local business names dataset, by its nature, tend to have niche entities. As a result, they do not have extensive appearance in query click log. Meanwhile, the entities from the software names datasets tend to be more popular. There are often a large number of click data available for such entities. The discovered synonyms are judged by human experts as to whether they are true synonyms or not.

We implemented our synonym discovery framework on top of COSMOS, a distributed MapReduce framework based on Dryad [12].

7.2 Quality Results

To give an intuitive feeling of the output, a few example entities with entity synonyms discovered by our framework are listed in Table 1.

Next, we systematically study the performance of our framework, and compare it to the state-of-the-art. Specifically, we report the results on the following 4 settings:
(I) ClickSim: click similarity (Section 3)

Domain	Entity	Synonyms
Local	la police credit union	lapfcu, los angeles police fcu, ...
Local	bemidji state university	bemidji state u, bemidji state univ, ...
Software	microsoft excel	ms excel, spreadsheet excel, microsoft office excel, ...
Software	microsoft sql server	ms sql server, sqlserver, mssql, ...

Table 1: Example Entity Synonyms Discovered

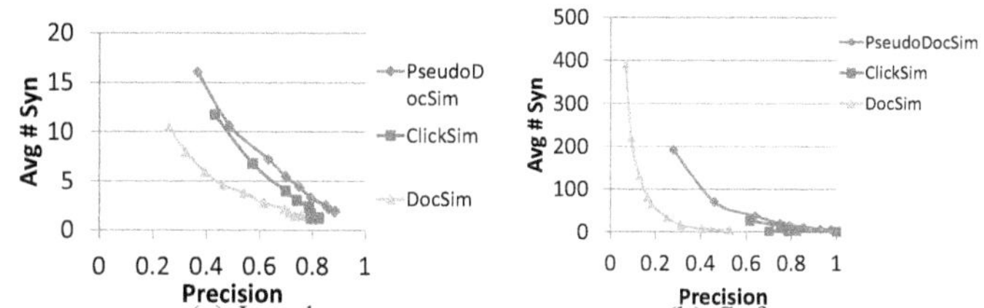

(a) Local (b) Software

Figure 5: Quality Results (Threshold)

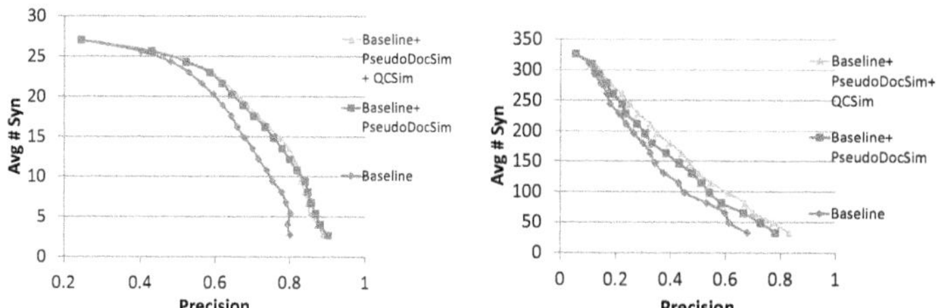

(a) Local (b) Software

Figure 6: Classification Results

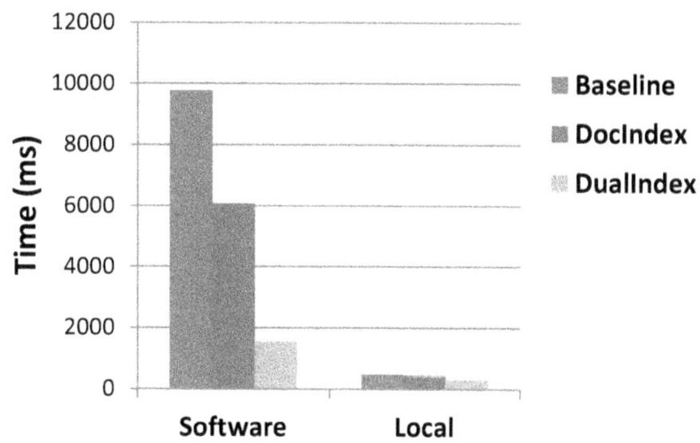

Figure 7: Efficiency Results

(II) DocSim: document similarity (Section 3)
(III) PseudoDocSim: pseudo document similarity (Section 4)
(IV) PseudoDocSim+QCSim: pseudo document similarity with context similarity (Section 4)

We use two main measures for effectiveness evaluation:
•Precision: number of true synonyms divided by the total number of synonyms output;
•AvgNumOfSynonym: Average Number of Synonyms Per Entity.[4]

We first examine the performance of PseudoDocSim when compared against ClickSim and DocSim. We vary the threshold value from 0 to 1.0 to examine the precision and recall tradeoff. Figure 5(a) and (b) report the results on Local and Software datasets respectively. As we can see, PseudoDocSim consistently outperforms ClickSim by outputting more number of synonyms per entity, while still maintaining high accuracy. This validates our design in that PseudoDocSim overcomes the sparsity problem of ClickSim to output more synonyms. Interestingly, it also significantly outperforms DocSim in both precision and recall. The improvement in precision is expected, since DocSim suffers from the noise from document content. The improvement in recall is due to the fact that search engines' ability to direct a query to a document (by query alternation, spell checking or partial match) although the query does not appear exactly in the document. Since PseudoDocSim leverages query log, it could harvest such rich signals. Comparing the results across the two domains, we also find that the software domain tend to have much higher number of synonyms generated per entity. This is due to the diverse characteristics of the two domains as discussed. The results show that we can generate ~12 synonyms per entity at ~85% precision for software entities, and ~4 synonyms per entity at ~80% precision for local entities.

We also study how the various similarity features contribute to the output result in using a classifier. We first examine the classification results over baseline (using only ClickSim and DocSim), then we study how the results change when we add in PseudoDocSim and QCSim as features. Figure 6(a) and (b) show the precision and recall tradeoff over the two domains, by using a standard boosted tree based classifier. As we can see, adding PseudoDocSim feature significantly improves the performance over baseline, and adding QCSim further improves the quality. The effect of QCSim is relatively minor for the Local dataset. This is due to the fact that many entities in this dataset are tail entities, and therefore having very limited query context information available.

[4]it is almost impossible to know the universal set of synonyms for each entity, and therefore hard to report the traditional recall numbers. As an alternative, we report the average number of synonyms generated per entity.

7.3 Efficiency Results

Now we report the processing efficiency results on the two real datasets. We report the total processing time with respect to the three schemes discussed in Section 5, referred to as *Baseline*, *DocIndex* and *DualIndex* respectively.

Figure 7 shows the overall processing time to calculate the PseudoDocSim score (the main computation of the framework) for the two datasets. As we can see, *DocIndex* consistently outperforms *Naive*, and *DualIndex* significantly improves over *DocIndex*. This is because *DualIndex* is able to fully exploit the overlap between candidates and pseudo documents, whereas *DocIndex* only leverage the overlap between pseudo documents and *Baseline* does not leverage any overlap. *DualIndex* is shown to offer more than 6x speedup over *Baseline* in the Software dataset, since entities in this dataset tends to have many more pseudo documents as well as candidates, as compared to the entities in the Local dataset. As a result, there is more overlap opportunities to exploit in the Software dataset, where *DualIndex* shines.

7.4 Impact on Improving Search

To see the impact of synonyms on search, we perform judgement on search results in two settings: setting (a) search over the original catalog versus setting (b) search over synonym augmented catalog. All other aspects of the two setting are identical.

Specially, expert judges first perform relevance judgement under setting (a) over a query set. The same judges then perform relevance judgement under setting (b) using the same query set. The classical normalized discounted cumulative gain (nDCG) is used to judge the quality of retrieved results.

Study was performed in two Bing products, Bing Shopping and Bing Video. 2000 queries were sampled from their perspective query logs, and used for relevance evaluation. For each query, the top 4 returned results are evaluated.

To get a concrete feeling, the table below shows a few examples, where we see the original entity name, the discovered synonym and the specific query the synonym helped in improving nDCG. As we can see, without the synonym, it would be hard to directly match the query with the entity name.

Entity Name	Synonym	Query
pbs kids play!	pbs kids org games	pbs kids.org
mitsubishi wd-73c9 73" rear projection TV	mitsubishi wd73c9	wd73c9

Overall, we see that the synonyms bring +0.1 nDCG (on 0-100 scale) in Bing Shopping search. Notice, we obtain this gain in the actual production setting of Bing Shopping, which is a highly optimized engine with many existing features. More interestingly, we zoomed into the set of difficult queries (94 queries with 0 nDCG in setting (a)). We see an nDCG improvement of +0.8 over these queries, a significant boost. For Bing Video search, we witness +0.2 nDCG improvement overall with the help of synonyms.

As we can see, the discovered entity synonyms have clearly helped in both search scenarios, resulting in higher nDCG numbers and therefore better search experience.

8. RELATED WORK

Researchers have proposed several approaches to automatically discovering synonyms using web data [6, 7, 18, 2, 11, 17, 3, 5]. They include click similarity [6, 7], document similarity [18, 2] and distributional similarity [11, 17]. As we discussed in Section 1, none of the above approaches satisfies all the properties and suffers from other limitations like click log sparsity, inability to distinguish between entities of different concept classes and difficulty to scale. Techniques to generate a particular class of synonyms, ones that are substrings of the given entity names, have been proposed recently [3, 5]. Our focus is to generate *all* classes of synonyms.

There exists a rich body of work on identifying similar queries; this can be used for query suggestions, query alteration, document ranking and ad matching [13, 8, 15]. Many techniques have been proposed to compute query similarities. For example, Craswell and Szummer compute it by using random walks on the click graph [8], Jones et. al. do so based on typical substitutions web searchers make in their queries [13] while Mei et. al. use hitting time on the query click graph [15] (e.g., using random walk on the click graph). They are not applicable to synonym discovery as they compute all similar queries, not just synonyms.

Approximate string matching techniques (when applied between reference string and candidate string) can be used to detect some classes of synonyms [16]. This can discover synonyms due to different different normalization (e.g., "canon eos-400d" vs. "Canon EOS 400d") or mispellings (e.g., "cannon eos 400d" vs. "Canon EOS 400d"), but not other types of variations like acronyms, semantic variations or subset/supersets.

Our work is related to the works on entity resolution (also known as entity conflation, reference reconciliation or record matching) which try to resolve difference references to the same real world entity [9]. They typically rely on a rich set of attributes to be present to produce high quality results. Such information is not available in a web setting, hence those techniques cannot be directly applied.

Our work is also related to the traditional word synonym discovery problem from text in NLP [10, 19]. The synonyms we focused on this this work are entity synonyms. Unlike words, it is non-trivial to identify entities of any domain from text. Furthermore, many legitimate entity synonyms do not necessary appear as one phrase in text. Another difference is that this work mainly leverages query log for mining synonyms. The mining space is much more succinct than that of text, and therefore is more practical for mining entity synonyms at large scale.

9. CONCLUSION

In this paper, we proposed a general framework for discovering entity synonyms. We study novel similarity functions that overcome the limitations of previously proposed functions. We developed efficient and scalable algorithms to generate such synonyms, and robust techniques to handle long entity names. Our experiments demonstrate superior quality of our synonyms and efficiency of our algorithms, as well as its impact in improving search.

10. REFERENCES

[1] S. Agrawal, K. Chakrabarti, S. Chaudhuri, and V. Ganti. Scalable ad-hoc entity extraction from text collections. *Proc. VLDB Endow.*, 2008.

[2] M. Baroni and S. Bisi. Using cooccurrence statistics and the web to discover synonyms in technical language. In *In Proceedings of LREC 2004*, pages 1725–1728, 2004.

[3] S. Chaudhuri, V. Ganti, and D. Xin. Exploiting web search to generate synonyms for entities. In *WWW Conference*, 2009.

[4] S. Chaudhuri, V. Ganti, and D. Xin. Mining document collections to facilitate accurate approximate entity matching. *PVLDB*, 2009.

[5] S. Chaudhuri, V. Ganti, and D. Xin. Mining document collections to facilitate accurate approximate entity matching. *PVLDB*, 2(1), 2009.

[6] T. Cheng, H. Lauw, and S. Paparizos. Fuzzy matching of web queries to structured data. In *ICDE*, 2010.

[7] T. Cheng, H. W. Lauw, and S. Paparizos. Entity synonyms for structured web search. *TKDE*, 2011.

[8] N. Craswell and M. Szummer. Random walks on the click graph. In *SIGIR*, 2007.

[9] X. Dong, A. Halevy, and J. Madhavan. Reference reconciliation in complex information spaces. In *SIGMOD*, 2005.

[10] G. W. Furnas, S. C. Deerwester, S. T. Dumais, T. K. Landauer, R. A. Harshman, L. A. Streeter, and K. E. Lochbaum. Information retrieval using a singular value decomposition model of latent semantic structure. In *SIGIR*, 1988.

[11] Z. Harris. Distributional structure. *Word*, 10(23), 1954.

[12] M. Isard, M. Budiu, Y. Yu, A. Birrell, and D. Fetterly. Dryad: distributed data-parallel programs from sequential building blocks. In *EuroSys*, 2007.

[13] R. Jones, B. Rey, O. Madani, and W. Greiner. Generating query substitutions. In *WWW*, 2006.

[14] C. D. Manning and H. Schütze. *Foundations of statistical natural language processing*. MIT Press, 1999.

[15] Q. Mei, D. Zhou, and K. Church. Query suggestion using hitting time. In *CIKM*, 2008.

[16] G. Navarro. A guided tour to approximate string matching. *ACM Comput. Surv.*, 2001.

[17] P. Pantel, E. Crestan, A. Borkovsky, A.-M. Popescu, and V. Vyas. Web-scale distributional similarity and entity set expansion. In *EMNLP*, 2009.

[18] P. D. Turney. Mining the web for synonyms: Pmi-ir versus lsa on toefl. *CoRR*, cs.LG/0212033, 2002.

[19] T. Wang and G. Hirst. Near-synonym lexical choice in latent semantic space. In *COLING*, 2010.

SmartDispatch: Enabling Efficient Ticket Dispatch in an IT Service Environment

Shivali Agarwal
IBM Research
Bengaluru, India
shivaaga@in.ibm.com

Renuka Sindhgatta
IBM Research
Bengaluru, India
renuka.sr@in.ibm.com

Bikram Sengupta
IBM Research
Bengaluru, India
bsengupt@in.ibm.com

ABSTRACT

In an IT service delivery environment, the speedy dispatch of a ticket to the correct resolution group is the crucial first step in the problem resolution process. The size and complexity of such environments make the dispatch decision challenging, and incorrect routing by a human dispatcher can lead to significant delays that degrade customer satisfaction, and also have adverse financial implications for both the customer and the IT vendor. In this paper, we present SmartDispatch, a learning-based tool that seeks to automate the process of ticket dispatch while maintaining high accuracy levels. SmartDispatch comes with two classification approaches - the well-known SVM method, and a discriminative term-based approach that we designed to address some of the issues in SVM classification that were empirically observed. Using a combination of these approaches, SmartDispatch is able to automate the dispatch of a ticket to the correct resolution group for a large share of the tickets, while for the rest, it is able to suggest a short list of 3-5 groups that contain the correct resolution group with a high probability. Empirical evaluation of SmartDispatch on data from 3 large service engagement projects in IBM demonstrate the efficacy and practical utility of the approach.

Categories and Subject Descriptors

H.4.0 [**Information Systems Applications**]: General; I.5.4 [**Pattern Recognition**]: Applications—*Text Processing*; I.5.2 [**Pattern Recognition**]: Design Methodology—*Feature Evaluation and Selection*

General Terms

Design, Experimentation

Keywords

Ticket resolution group, SVM classification, Discriminative term weighting, Automated and advisory mode dispatch

KDD'12, August 12–16, 2012, Beijing, China.

1. INTRODUCTION

Information technology (IT) is now a major enabler for most businesses. The size, diversity and complexity of such systems have increased manifold over the years, prompting organizations to outsource the maintenance of their IT systems to specialized service providers (IT vendors). These vendors employ skilled practitioners and organize them into teams with the responsibility of maintaining different parts of the IT system. For example, a team may be responsible for a specific process area of a large packaged application, a set of custom applications that leverage a common technology, or the like. For systems in production use, customers submit service requests to the vendor in the form of *tickets*, that represent a specific IT problem or need experienced by the end users (e.g. a failed transaction, user authentication expiry, data formatting issues etc.), and are generally small, atomic tasks that can be handled by a single practitioner within a short duration (e.g. a few minutes to a few days). The tickets are usually assigned to a practitioner in a two-step process. First, incoming tickets are received by a dispatcher, who reviews the problem description text (entered by the customer or end user) to try and understand which service team (henceforth called resolution group) is responsible for addressing the ticket, and then dispatches it to that group of practitioners. Next, within the group, the assignment of the ticket to a specific practitioner may be done by the group lead, or a practitioner may volunteer for the same, and this is usually based on criteria such as complexity of the ticket and expertise of the practitioner, the practitioner's availability and current workload etc. In this paper, we focus on the first step of the assignment process - namely the dispatching of a ticket to an appropriate resolution group based on the problem text description. Using text-based classification techniques applied on large-scale real-life data from IBM's services engagements, we study the extent to which this process may be automated and how practical tool support may be provided to aid the dispatcher when complete automation is not feasible.

The dispatch of a ticket - as soon as it arrives - to the correct group of practitioners, is a critical step in the speedy resolution of a ticket. If the dispatcher misinterprets the problem and routes the ticket to an incorrect group, then significant time may be wasted before the group reviews the problem, determines it is not in their area of responsibility, and transfers it back to the dispatcher, to begin the process anew. This calls for timely and intelligent handling of tickets by the dispatcher. However, a number of factors make the dispatcher's job challenging. First, s/he needs to have a reasonably broad knowledge of the entire IT portfolio being managed, along with the roles and responsibilities of the individual groups. Second, s/he needs to be able to quickly parse the ticket text describing the problem and map it to the right group, which is often not straightforward given the heterogeneous and informal nature of the problem description reported by human users. While a senior practitioner with a good overview of the customer's IT system may be able to discharge these responsibilities well, such practitioners are usually preoccupied with helping their colleagues resolve the more complex tickets and the routine dispatch task (that is also labor intensive when the ticket volume is high) is often assigned to one of the less experienced practitioners. High attrition in service delivery teams may further compound the problem, as a dispatcher who had developed a certain amount of expertise over a period of time, may leave the organization, and a new practitioner filling in will take time to develop into the role. Incorrect dispatch decisions that result in such situations can significantly increase the total turnaround time for ticket resolution. For example, we observed in a study of an actual production support system that the average turnaround time for a ticket jumps by as much as 100% as the number of transfers increase from 2 to 4. When such delays occur, the customer's business may be severely impacted, customer satisfaction degrades, and the vendor may also need to compensate the customer by paying a penalty in case of a breach in Service Level Agreement (SLA). Inefficiencies in dispatch may thus have serious business consequences that an IT vendor can ill-afford.

1.1 Smart Dispatch

The practical challenges associated with manual ticket dispatch motivated us to investigate how, and to what extent, we can automate the process of resolution group selection based on ticket text description. This has led to the development of a tool called SmartDispatch, which we describe and evaluate in this paper. Our goal is to have a performance baseline that is comparable to that of an expert human dispatcher, so the error rate (incorrect routings) should be low (within 10% of tickets). As our subjects of study, we selected large 3 production systems maintained by IBM (from 3 different domains and customers), where 2 of the systems had 25 resolution groups each, while the largest one had 79 resolution groups. The total number of tickets across these 3 data sets was more than 82,000.

To train the SmartDispatch tool in taking intelligent routing decisions, we decided to use a supervised learning approach, with 60% of tickets in each set being used to train a classification engine, while the remaining 40% of tickets was used to test the accuracy of classification. We applied text processing on the ticket text to transform it into a weighted vector of terms, and then used the well-known Support Vector Machine (SVM) method to build the classification engine. Our experiments revealed that the accuracy of SmartDispatch with a full-automated approach ranged from 69% to 81% in the three systems, thereby implying an incorrect dispatch of 19% to 31% of the tickets. Given the business consequences of incorrect routing as noted above, we concluded that blanket automation may not be a practical solution to the dispatch problem, as it may lead to unacceptably high error rates.

Next, we sought to determine the percentage of tickets we could automatically dispatch with a low error rate, by considering the confidence probabilities of classification as returned by the engine. The idea here is that if a reasonably high percentage of tickets can be correctly and automatically dispatched this way through the SmartDispatch system, it would significantly reduce the burden on an expert human dispatcher who can process the remaining tickets. As a threshold, we considered a confidence probability of 90% i.e. as long as the probability of a ticket belonging to a particular group was perceived to be >=90% by the classification engine, we would route the ticket to that group. We obtained mixed results using this approach. On the positive side, we found that when the confidence probability was >=90%, the error rate of SmartDispatch was only around 4%-6%. Unfortunately, we also found that while the percentage of tickets where the engine displayed such a high classification confidence was reasonably high for two data sets (55% to 62%) it was quite low (25%) for the other data set. We concluded that this was unlikely to be a useful generic approach when dispatching real-life service tickets, since the need for human involvement and judgement may continue to be very high.

Given this, our next goal was to see if we can devise a classification approach that is able to consistently classify a significant percentage of tickets (at least >50%) with high confidence probability, and with low error rate. The reason why we felt this may still be feasible was that on closer review of ticket text and analysis of how SVM was handling the terms in the text, we observed that discriminative terms - words or phrases that seemed to characterize one or a small subset of resolution groups - appeared to be not particularly well-leveraged by SVM, even when we experimented with the weights assigned to these terms. This motivated us to design a classification approach - the *discriminative term approach* (DTA) - that assigns weights to terms using a function called inverse group frequency, which is inspired by the notion of inverse document frequency (idf) used by search engines to score and rank a document's relevance given a user query. In this approach, we assumed the classification engine to display a high confidence probability in a resolution group if it gave it a higher score than any other group, and in such cases, the ticket is automatically dispatched to that group. Using this new approach, we obtained strong results - across the 3 groups, the percentage of tickets that could be automatically dispatched ranged from 59% to as high as 72%, with a 100% precision rate in all cases.

The final question to consider was how SmartDispatch could best handle tickets that did not have the necessary clarity for automatic dispatch to a specific group. Here again, the confidence scores returned by classification engines came in handy. We decided to adopt a dual mode dispatch strategy wherein SmartDispatch, when unable to automatically dispatch a ticket to a group, switches to an advisory mode and forwards the ticket to a human dispatcher, with suggestions on the top N groups the ticket may likely belong to (the groups having the top N confidence scores). Alternatively, if we still desire a fully automated system, SmartDispatch could offer the tickets through a limited broadcast to the top N groups, with the expectation that the correct group will identify the ticket as its own and take ownership. Here, interestingly, the results derived from SVM-based classification outperformed those derived from our discriminative term approach. In fact, very effective dispatch performance could be achieved by leveraging the complementary strengths of the two approaches - using the discriminative term approach for fully automated dispatch of a large percentage of tickets to the correct resolution group, and using SVM to advise on potential group(s) in case the decision was not unambiguous, with a combined error rate of well within 10%. Overall, our experience with SmartDispatch suggests that a combination of learning techniques, along with a dual mode dispatch strategy, can provide a satisfactory, near-automated solution to the problem of fast, accurate dispatch of service tickets to resolution groups.

The rest of the paper is structured as follows: Section 2 describes the SmartDispatch tool design, architecture and the learning methods used in the tool; Section 3 presents evaluations results; related work is discussed in Section 4, while Section 5 concludes the paper.

2. SmartDispatch TOOL DESIGN

The basic principle underlying the *SmartDispatch* tool is to build a prediction model for ticket dispatch using supervised learning on historical ticket data, and then use the model to guide subsequent dispatch decisions. Past ticket data is persisted in repositories, usually within the ticketing system itself. Two key fields recorded for each ticket are Description, which is a text field that describes the problem/need that needs to be addressed, and the Resolution Group, which is the team in which the practitioner who resolved the ticket belongs. While a ticket has many other fields as well (e.g. severity, open/close timestamps, practitioner name etc.) the (Description, Resolution Group) attributes are what we use to build a prediction model for dispatch based on ticket text. The prototypical text classification problem can be posed as done in [2]: "Given a set of labelled text documents $L = \{\langle x_i, c_i\rangle\}_{i=1}^{|L|}$ where $c_i \in C = \{1, 2, ..., |C|\}$ denotes the category of document x_i and $|C|$ and $|L|$ are the total number of predefined categories and labelled documents; learn a classifier that assigns a category label from 1 to $|C|$ to each document in the fresh set $U = \langle x_i\rangle_{i=1}^{|U|}$". This is a supervised learning approach, wherein it is assumed that the joint probability distribution of documents and categories is identical in sets U and L (although this may not be guaranteed in practice). Figure 1 depicts the architecture of SmartDispatch, and we outline the different components below.

2.1 Text processing

Text processing is necessary to generate a numeric form of description that can be consumed by classification methods like Support Vector Machine (SVM). The ticket description text is transformed into a vector space model. This includes extracting nouns and verbs as terms from the ticket description and reducing the terms to their morphological root. Stanford POS Tagger [11] is used to identify the nouns and verbs in the ticket description. Porter's stemming [7] is further used on the terms. Once the terms are extracted, any appropriate term weighting scheme can be applied on ticket description to obtain a vector representation. The text processing component of our tool is generic enough to handle data from different kinds of maintenance projects. The results presented in Section 3 have been arrived at by using this generic scheme of stop words and stemming. While account-specific dictionaries may help process ticket text more intelligently, such dictionaries may not always be available or up-to-date, hence the generic nature of text processing in SmartDispatch ensures wide applicability of the tool.

2.2 Generating Supervised Learning Model

There exists a number of supervised learning techniques that may be used to learn a classification model that uses ticket text description to predict resolution group. The SmartDispatch tool comes with the well-known classification technique of Support Vector Machine, and also employs another learning technique based on discriminative terms that has been developed in house. Both of these approaches are described in detail below with appropriate insights and motivation.

2.2.1 *Standard Classifier Approach*

We have chosen Support Vector Machine (SVM) as the standard classification engine in SmartDispatch based on existing literature [1] that puts it above the rest of the techniques for unstructured text. The choice was made after verifying this result with the sample data that we had. The tf*idf term weighting scheme was applied on each ticket description to obtain a vector representation for SVM. The SVM approach was found to be more robust than other techniques such as decision trees, Bayesian network, K-means etc. as it performed reasonably well for all data samples, and produced the best results in most cases. We also found the notion of confidence intervals reliable in case of SVMs and such intervals are the basis for designing the advisor module of our tool. The standard classifier approach will be used interchangeably with SVM based approach in the remaining paper. We have used the SVM implementation in SPSS [10], an industry standard statistical analysis package, within SmartDispatch.

However, one of the issues with the SVM approach that we observed was the tendency of biased prediction in favor of groups having large volume of tickets. For example, if groups A and B have significantly higher number of tickets as compared to the rest of the groups (which also have sufficient number of tickets to learn the model), then the mis-classified tickets of the rest of the groups were often found to labelled as A or B. We tried using different forms of term weight functions but with little improvement. Upon case based inspection of mis-classified tickets, we figured out that SVM was not able to effectively exploit the discriminatory terms present in those tickets in many cases. This led to the design of a new approach based on discriminative terms described below. Such an approach was envisioned to complement the SVM approach.

2.2.2 *Discriminative Term Approach*

While trying to use ticket descriptions for group prediction by exploiting the discriminative content that they possess, we developed a learning approach based on discriminative terms or keywords. The motivation for this approach stems from the fact that a resolution group typically has a set of discriminative terms related to the IT sub-system they manage, which are likely to appear in the tickets that come to them for resolution. If we identify the terms that correspond to each group by mining the descriptions associated with that group, then we can assign appropriate weights to all the terms in the entire data set to signify their extent of uniqueness with respect to groups. Using this as a model, the terms in a new ticket can be analyzed to arrive at a

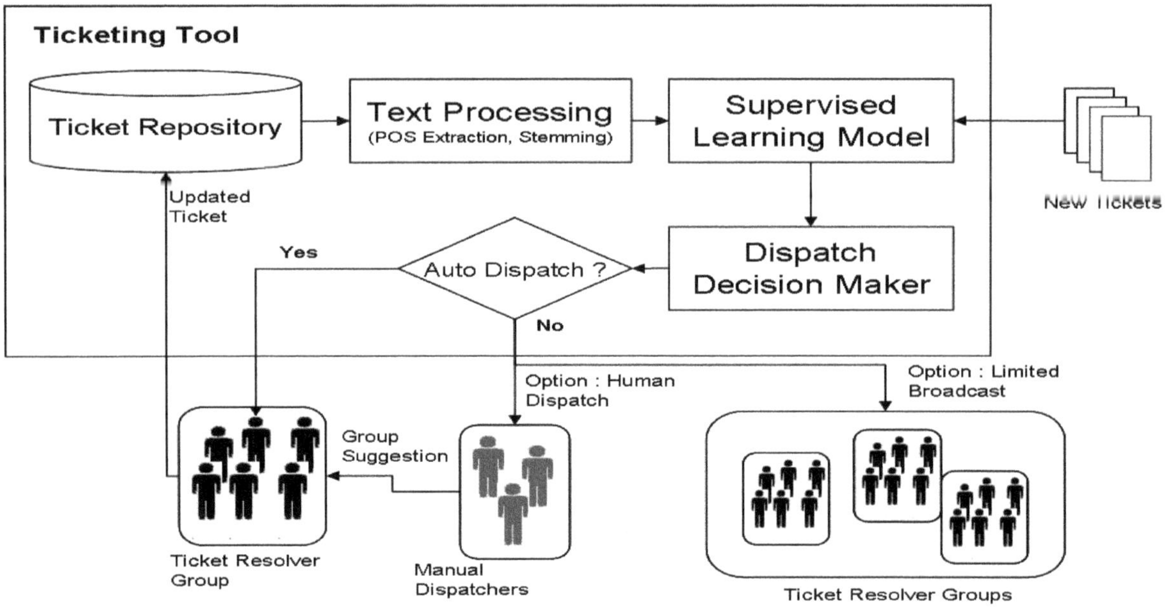

Figure 1: SmartDispatch Architecture Diagram

group closeness score, thus predicting the group to which the ticket should be dispatched. For example, a term like "error" that say, occurs in 8 out of 10 groups, is not discriminative as compared to a term like "password" that may occur in only 2 out of 10 groups. Any ticket that consists of the term "password" will have high closeness score with respect to those groups.

The steps involved in this approach consist of discriminative term weighting, term selection and association, and classifier function definition. We outline these below.

Discriminative term weighting: We have defined a weight function called *inverse group frequency (igf)*. This function abstracts away the role of number of documents (tickets) involved in arriving at the weight for a term and uses only the group cardinality. This ensures that the function performs equally well on small as well as large training datasets as long as the distribution of the sample is the same as the actual data. The formal definition is given below.

Let $\mathcal{T}$ be the set of terms in the dataset. Let w_t denote the discriminative weight of the term $t \in \mathcal{T}$. Let N denote all the groups in the data and let N_t denote the groups that have occurrence of t in them. The discriminative weight is given by the formula:

$$w_t = N/N_t$$

The value of w_t is what we refer to as *igf* of the term as it is analogous in concept to idf. Higher the value of igf for a term, higher is the discriminative nature of the term. The value of igf is computed for all the terms in the document space. If needed, a threshold can be used to restrict the number of terms in the space by allowing only those terms whose frequency of occurrence is above the threshold.

Term selection and association: Each resolution group needs to be associated with a set of terms that best describe it. To do this, we first find all the terms associated with a group through text processing of the ticket descriptions of all tickets belonging to this group. Next, we perform term selection for each group by discarding all terms that have igf value below a certain predefined threshold value. The threshold value can be easily arrived at by setting some lenient value upfront and then refining it over a period of time. Each group is thereby associated with a set of terms that meet the threshold criteria. Formally, we use $\mathcal{G}$ to denote the set of groups and T_g to denote the terms that have been selected for the group $g \in \mathcal{G}$.

Classifier function: This is the step that pools all information about groups and their terms and uses it for prediction. The igf value of each term belonging to a group gives us an idea of how discriminating that term is for the group. This information is pooled to obtain closeness score of a ticket with respect to each group. For each ticket, the terms in the ticket are used to compute a closeness score using a well defined linear function given below, with respect to each group. The group(s) with the highest score is(are) the group(s) that the ticket is predicted to belong .

More formally, let x denote a ticket description consisting of a set of terms T_x, and let $Val_x(g)$ denote the score of ticket x with respect to group $g \in \mathcal{G}$ computed using the linear discriminant function as below:

$$Val_x(g) = \sum_{t \in T_g \cap T_x} w_t$$

The use of discriminant function reduces the $|\mathcal{T}|$ dimensional space to $N = |\mathcal{G}|$ dimensional feature space, and $Val_x(g), \forall g \in \mathcal{G}$ defines the N-dimensional feature space. The classifier function for the ticket description x can be simply written as follows:

$$\hat{g}(x) = arg\ max_{g \in \mathcal{G}} Val_x(g)$$

such that $\hat{g}(x)$ denotes the group that is obtained by solving the straightforward optimization problem posed above using iterative technique. Note that there can be multiple groups with the same score. So, it is possible that for certain tickets, there is no total order on the group ranks based on score.

This approach works best if descriptions have discriminative nature for distinct groups. The prediction model is very simple in this case and once the discriminative terms enter the system, the model stabilizes very fast.

2.3 Dispatch Decision Maker

An incoming ticket for which a dispatch decision has to be made is first classified (mapped to resolution group(s)) using one of the supervised learning techniques described above. If there is sufficient confidence in the classification result, then the Dispatch Decision Maker will dispatch the ticket to that group. For SVM-based classification, we exercise this *Auto Dispatch Policy* if a ticket is classified to a group by SVM with a confidence probability of 0.9 or above. We chose this threshold based on the observation that the error rate of prediction by SVM is very low when the confidence probability is 0.9 or above, as we discuss in more detail during the evaluation of SmartDispatch in the next section. For the discriminatory term approach, where multiple groups may hold the top position based on having the same score through the discriminant function, we exercise the auto dispatch policy if and only if there is a clear winner i.e. there is only a single group at the top position.

There will be cases, however, when none of the classification approaches return a clear winner. In such situations, SmartDispatch resorts to an *Advisory Dispatch Policy*. Here, the tool selects a small subset of groups that may be expected to contain the correct resolution group with reasonably high confidence. If an expert human dispatcher is available, the tool forwards the ticket to him/her with an advisory that contains the identities of these selected groups. The expectation here is that the expert dispatcher will be able to take a well-judged dispatch decision, and if the advisory of the tool contains the correct group, it would have done its job well. If an expert dispatcher is not available, and/or if full automation is desired, then SmartDispatch may forward the ticket to each of the selected groups through a limited broadcast, with the assumption that the correct group (if present in the selected list) will take ownership of the ticket and resolve it, while others will ignore the ticket. If the correct group is not included in the shortlist compiled by SmartDispatcher, we consider it as an error in its prediction (thus we slightly relax the notion of correct prediction in advisory mode by allowing a small number of other groups to appear in the shortlist, along with the correct resolution group). In case of SVM-based classification, we exercise the advisory dispatch policy for predictions with confidence probability less than 0.9, and generate a small ranked list of between 1 and 5 groups, in decreasing order of confidence probabilities. For the discriminatory term based approach, when there are multiple groups having the highest score, then all the groups that have the same highest score are suggested as possible groups in the advisory mode.

2.4 Feedback Mechanism

The new tickets that have been dispatched by the system may have their resolution group updated in case of an incorrect dispatch. Other details (e.g. closure timestamps, resolving practitioner etc.) would also get updated, and upon closure, the final ticket details are persisted with in the ticket repository. The learning model should be generated at frequent intervals in order to leverage the new data available, and improve the prediction capabilities.

3. EVALUATION OF THE TOOL

We have evaluated the SmartDispatch tool on three ticket data sets, derived from three different ongoing services engagements involving IBM. To preserve client confidentiality, these data sets will henceforth be denoted by Dataset A, Dataset B and Dataset C. In order to test the wide applicability of the tool, the datasets were derived from three different domains: Media and Entertainment (A), Automotive (B) and Consumer Goods (C). The number of tickets in each data set, the number of resolution groups, and the duration of the dataset (derived from the timestamps of the constituent tickets) are shown in Figure 2. As can be seen, each data set covers a reasonably wide time window (with a minimum of two months) and has a significantly large number of tickets. Dataset C, of course, is by far the largest, although spanning over the shortest duration, since it comes from an account with very high ticket inflow. To build and test the prediction models, each data set was split into a training set and a testing set using a 60:40 ratio.

	Dataset A	Dataset B	Dataset C
Number of Tickets	15415	7062	59905
Number of Resolution Groups	25	25	79
Duration for the dataset (months)	12	8	2

Figure 2: Dataset Overview

We will now discuss the evaluation results. The results will be presented in the sequence in which the tool was incrementally developed as outlined in the Introduction. We will thus begin with SVM as the sole classification engine used for automated dispatch of *all* tickets (Section 3.1); next, we will consider automated dispatch of tickets having high prediction confidence, and incorporate the discriminative term approach to see if the volume of such tickets may be increased (Section 3.2); we will then evaluate the tool in the advisory dispatch mode for tickets that could not be automatically dispatched to a single group (Section 3.3); finally, we will consider a heterogeneous dispatch strategy leveraging DTA for automatic dispatch, and SVM for the advisory or limited broadcast mode (Section 3.4).

3.1 Fully automated approach using SVM

The very first set of experiments were carried out to evaluate the performance of fully automated dispatch of all tickets based on supervised learning using SVM. The results of running SVM model on test data are shown in table 1. As can be seen, the percentage of misrouted tickets is quite high in

Table 1: Full Auto-dispatch with SVM

Dataset	SVM precision (%)	% Misrouted
A	81%	19%
B	69%	31%
C	73%	27%

the 3 data sets, particularly for Dataset B and Dataset C. The error rates are considerably higher than our target performance baseline of $\leq 10\%$ (as mentioned in Section 1.1), and this suggested to us that full automation may not be practical. This led us to consider dispatch based on confidence scores, as we discuss next.

3.2 Auto-dispatch based on confidence scores

The ticket classification results from SVM contain confidence probabilities associated with each resolution group. We wanted to test if we could improve prediction accuracy of automated dispatch by only selecting tickets where there was a high confidence probability in a specific group, and if so, whether we could dispatch a significantly large share of tickets this way, so as to reduce the burden on a human dispatcher. Our experiments with SVM suggested that as the confidence probability increased, error rates went down significantly. This is depicted for all three data sets in Figures 3, 4 and 5. The left chart in the figures depict the percentage of tickets that fall in the confidence intervals of 0-0.1, 0.1-0.2,..., 0.9-1.0 where each bar depicts an interval. The chart on the right side shows the split of percentage of correct and incorrect predictions for each of these confidence intervals. For example, Figure 3 for dataset A shows that about 55% tickets occur in the range of 0.9 and above, out of which 4% are incorrect and rest are all correct predictions. This implies that 55% tickets can be dispatched automatically with 96% precision.

The results of auto dispatch policy for confidence level of 0.9 and above using SVM are shown in Table 2, columns two and three. We see that the error rates are low for all three data sets, ranging from only 4% to 6%. However, the percentage of tickets that can be routed this way with high confidence probability is not consistently high, and is, in fact, as low as 25% for Dataset B. This suggested to us that confidence-based routing using SVM, using thresholds that lead to low error rates, carries the risk of passing on a significant share of tickets to a human dispatcher for manual routing. As mentioned in Section 2.2.1, we also observed that SVM was often unable to effectively exploit discriminatory terms in ticket text, and we hypothesized that if we were able to devise a classification approach that leverages discriminatory terms well, then it may also be able to classify a higher number of tickets with sufficient confidence. This led us to design and incorporate the Discriminative Term Approach (DTA) within SmartDispatch.

Table 2: Auto-dispatch mode based on confidence probability

Dataset	%tickets SVM	SVM precision	%tickets DTA	DTA precision
A	55%	96%	70%	100%
B	25%	94%	72%	100%
C	62%	96%	59%	100%

The results for DTA are presented in Table 2. The tickets for which only one group obtained the highest score were the ones eligible for auto-dispatch and these percentage values are shown in column four of Table 2 for the three data sets. It is noteworthy that the accuracy of auto-dispatch was 100% for all datasets. The percentage of tickets that could be auto-dispatched range from a low of 59% to a high of 72%. The results are significantly better than SVM for Dataset A and Dataset B, and only marginally worse for Dataset C (though still better in terms of error rates). The threshold value for igf was set to 1 for all datasets. This is the most liberal setting and thus, the results are obtained for the most generic case. The evaluation indicates that DTA is a very good choice for auto dispatch of tickets. The relatively bad performance on Dataset C was due to large number of tickets having terms with low igf values. We believe that this problem can possibly be resolved by introducing a notion of discriminating phrase (consisting of a sequence of terms) in the learning method, which we plan to do in future.

Next, we consider the handling of tickets which are ineligible for auto-dispatch. The advisory mode designed to tackle this set is evaluated next.

3.3 Advisory mode evaluation

Table 3 presents evaluation results when the tool operates in advisory mode for SVM approach. These are obtained on the tickets that did not meet the criterion of auto-dispatch. The entry 'Top 3' in this table shows the percentage of times the correct group occurred in top 3 predicted groups ranked on confidence probability values. Similarly, 'Top 5' indicates the percentage of tickets that did not figure in top 3 but were fourth or fifth. The other columns are analogously defined. Thus, for Dataset A in the table, the correct resolution group occurred in top 3 of the ranked predicted groups 86.8% of the time (this was split as - 58.2% at rank one, 28.6% at ranks two or three), and occurred in top 5 (86.8 + 5.63)% or 92.43% of the time. This mode performs very well for Dataset B as well, although for Dataset C (which has 79 resolution groups), the results are less satisfactory in absolute terms, with the correct group occurring in the top 5 in 81% cases. Overall, it can be concluded that the SVM approach is reasonably reliable for advisory mode. Note that a correct value can be predicted at rank one by SVM, although with a low absolute confidence score.

As far as the advisory mode for DTA is concerned, all the tickets for which the top score is awarded to two or more groups are dispatched in advisory mode. Table 4 presents the results of this approach in advisory mode. Here again, only those tickets which were not eligible for auto-dispatch are the ones which are considered in advisory mode. The label 'Top 3' denotes the percentage of tickets out of this set for which there were 2 or 3 groups having highest score. Similarly, 'Top 5' denotes the set for which 4 or 5 groups have the top score. The rest of the labels are analogous to this. It can be seen that the precision falls at a very fast rate. For example, for dataset C, the correct resolution group appears in the top 3 in only 31.7% cases, thereby limiting the usefulness of the advisory mode in the DTA approach.

3.4 Combining SVM and DTA approaches

The results in the preceding sections suggest that the SVM and DTA approaches have complementary strengths. When it comes to the percentage of tickets that can be automatically dispatched to the correct group with high confidence (low error rates), DTA outperforms SVM in general, on the strength of being able to distinguish such groups better using discriminative terms, with a perfect precision record. On the other hand, for tickets where such a distinction cannot

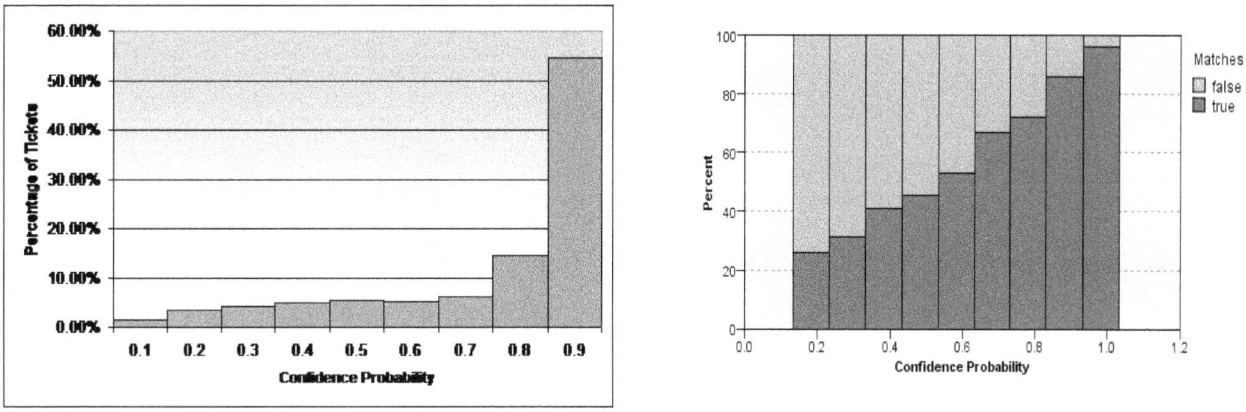

Figure 3: Distribution of confidence probabilities for Dataset A and corresponding true vs. false predictions

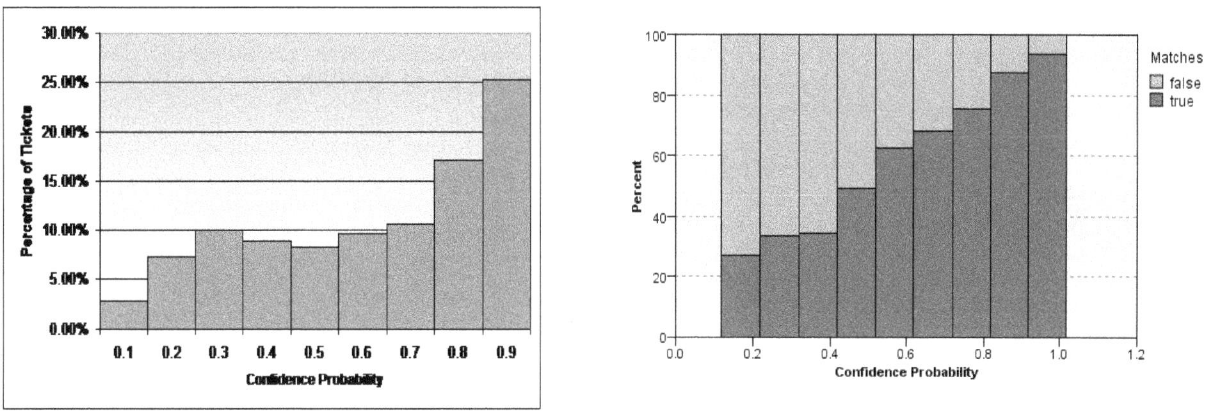

Figure 4: Distribution of confidence probabilities for Dataset B and corresponding true vs. false predictions

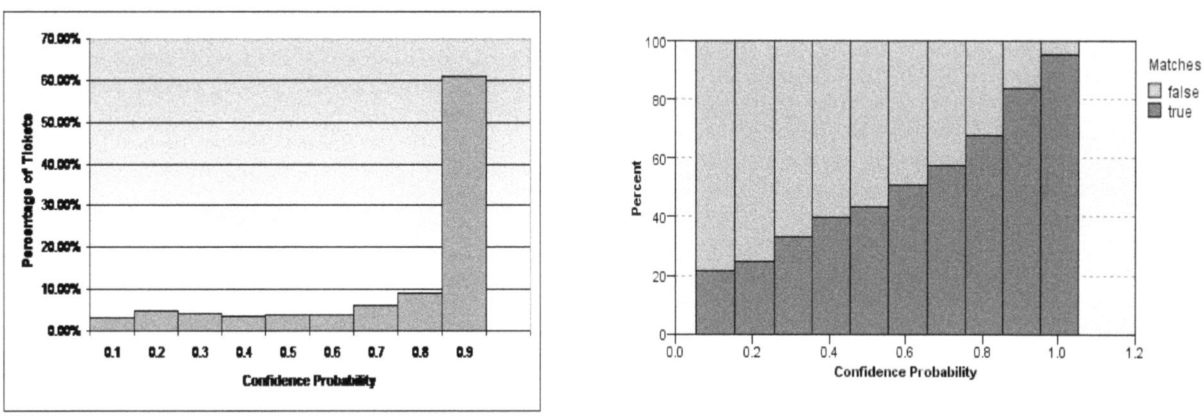

Figure 5: Distribution of confidence probabilities for Dataset C and corresponding true vs. false predictions

Table 3: Performance of SVM approach in advisory mode on the respective ticket set that it found ineligible for auto-dispatch

Dataset	Top 3	Top 5	Top 10	Top 15	Top 20	Top 25	>30
A	86.8%	5.63%	4.76%	1.5%	1.09%	0.25%	0%
B	88%	5.26%	3.98%	1.72%	0.74%	0.3%	0%
C	76.4%	4.68%	6.45%	3.6%	2.36%	1.48%	5.03%

Table 4: Performance of DTA in advisory mode on the respective ticket set that it found ineligible for auto-dispatch

Dataset	Top 3	Top 5	Top 10	Top 15	Top 20	Top 25	>30
A	50%	26%	20%	2%	2%	0%	0%
B	39.2%	21.4%	25%	3.6%	3.6%	7.2%	0%
C	31.7%	12.2%	17.1%	9.7%	7.4%	9.7%	12.2%

be made unambiguously, and the dispatch has to switch to an advisory mode, SVM's performance is clearly much more robust. This motivated us to experiment with a heterogeneous approach, tapping into the respective strengths of both the techniques within a single dispatch decision: that is, for a new ticket, we use DTA for auto-dispatch when a single resolution group receives the highest score, otherwise, we handle it using SVM's advisory dispatch mode.

The results for this combined approach are presented in Table 5. The percentage of tickets that that are automatically dispatched through DTA are shown in column two, and are derived from similar results presented earlier in Table 2. For each data set, the remaining tickets are dispatched in advisory (or limited broadcast) mode using SVM. Even when the advise (or broadcast) is limited to a single group (with the highest confidence probability), the error rate is very low, varying between 4% to 9%, and this comes down further to 2% to 6% when the top 3 resolution groups (by confidence score) returned by SVM are used. When compared to Table 1, we see that the percentage of misrouted tickets have substantially come down and this shows the effectiveness of the dual mode heterogeneous SmartDispatch approach over blanket automation using a single learning technique like SVM.

The complementary capabilities of SVM and DTA thus make them a good package to have in the dispatch tool. While they can be used together in the manner outlined above, we can also run both the techniques on historical data from an engagement and compare the precision values on test data. The technique which is able to automate higher percentage of ticket dispatch with low error rates may be chosen. This will provide more flexibility to handle the differing nature of ticket descriptions in different engagements; for example, while it would make more sense to adopt the DTA approach to decide on auto-dispatch for data sets A and B, the SVM based approach may also be adopted in case of Dataset C (where the overall performance across the two approaches is almost at par).

Besides the superior dispatch performance that results from this combination, the DTA option also provides scalability in learning since it can build a model very fast even when given a huge training set. At the same time, it can also handle learning with limited training data under the identical distribution assumption between training and actual data; this makes it very useful in cases where a new resolution group is added, but the ticket volume is not yet high enough to have a SVM-based model.

4. RELATED WORK

Several researchers have studied different aspects of the problem of routing tickets to practitioners [8], [9], [6]. The work in [9] approaches the problem by mining resolution sequence data and does not access ticket description at all, thus being completely different from our approach. Its objective is to come up with ticket transfer recommendations given the initial assignment information. The work in [8] mines historical ticket data and develops a probabilistic model of an enterprise social network that represents the functional relationships among various expert groups in ticket routing. Based on this network, the system then provides routing recommendations to new tickets. This work also focuses on ticket transfers between groups (given an initial assignment) like [9] without looking at the ticket text content. The work in [6] is different and approaches the problem from a queue perspective. This is more related to the issue of service times and becomes particularly relevant when the ticket that has been dispatched to a group needs to be assigned to an agent.

There are some papers which apply text classification techniques to handle tickets. [4] is close to our work and the objective is to automatically classify tickets based on description to route them to the right group. However, the work was applied on a small ticket set with only 8 groups. The accuracy of 84% in best case is something that was also not acceptable for the kind of reliable automation that we sought in our tool. The work in [3] attempts to classify the incoming change requests into one of the fine grained activities in a catalog by leveraging aggregated information associated with the change, like past failure reasons or best implementation practices. They use information retrieval and machine learning techniques in order to match change tickets to the activity that is most suitable for it. They suggest the top 5 activity group to the user as output and do not automate the process of assignment. Similar to our work, [2] shows the limitation of SVM-like techniques in terms of scalability and proposes a notion of discriminative keyword approach. However, we differ substantially in the defini-

Table 5: Combined SVM and DTA evaluation

Dataset	% Automated (DTA)	%Top 1 Advisory (SVM)	% Top 1 Advisory misrouted	%Top 3 Advisory (SVM)	% Top 3 Advisory misrouted
A	70%	26%	4%	28%	2%
B	72%	21%	7%	22%	6%
C	59%	32%	9%	37%	6%

tion of our discriminative term weighting function and our ability to handle a higher dimensional feature space, as also in the application domain, with [2] being more focused on commonly used text classification data sets like personalized spam filtering and movie reviews, rather than service tickets.

There has also been a large body of work on comparative analysis of various machine learning algorithms like SVM, decision trees etc. We used the conclusions in the work in [1] to use SVM as the algorithm for our analysis of ticket descriptions. We did carry out a preliminary analysis of comparing the precision and recall values of SVM, Bayesnet and C&RT and found SVM to be more robust and precise. We also referred to [5] to help decide what may be considered as a quality score for descriptions.

5. CONCLUSIONS

Ticket dispatch plays an important role in determining the turnaround time of a ticket because a misrouting can introduce significant delays. We have proposed a tool called SmartDispatch for efficient dispatch of tickets in an IT service environment, using supervised learning techniques to review ticket descriptions and predict the most appropriate resolution group. The tool uses a combination of the standard classification algorithm SVM and a new discriminative term based heuristic for carrying out the dispatch, and offers automated as well as advisory dispatch capabilities. Empirical evaluation of the tool on large ticket data sets from real-life services engagements at IBM demonstrate the efficacy of the approach. As a part of future work, we plan to incorporate the notion of discriminative phrases to handle descriptions that do not have discriminative terms but a combination of terms, that is a phrase, is unique to the group.

6. REFERENCES

[1] Shantanu Godbole and Shourya Roy. Text classification, business intelligence, and interactivity: automating c-sat analysis for services industry. In *Proceedings of the 14th ACM SIGKDD international conference on Knowledge discovery and data mining*, KDD '08, pages 911–919, New York, NY, USA, 2008. ACM.

[2] K.N. Junejo and A. Karim. A robust discriminative term weighting based linear discriminant method for text classification. In *Proceedings of the Eighth IEEE International Conference on Data Mining, 2008.*, ICDM '08, pages 323 – 332. IEEE, 2008.

[3] Cristina Kadar, Dorothea Wiesmann, Jose Iria, Dirk Husemann, and Mario Lucic. Automatic classification of change requests for improved it service quality. In *Proceedings of the 2011 Annual SRII Global Conference*, SRII '11, pages 430–439, Washington, DC, USA, 2011. IEEE Computer Society.

[4] G. di Lucca. An approach to classify software maintenance requests. In *Proceedings of the International Conference on Software Maintenance (ICSM'02)*, pages 93–, Washington, DC, USA, 2002. IEEE Computer Society.

[5] Debapriyo Majumdar, Rose Catherine, Shajith Ikbal, and Karthik Visweswariah. Privacy protected knowledge management in services with emphasis on quality data. In *Proceedings of the 20th ACM international conference on Information and knowledge management*, CIKM '11, pages 1889–1894, New York, NY, USA, 2011. ACM.

[6] Hoda Parvin, Abhijit Bose, and Mark P. Van Oyen. Priority-based routing with strict deadlines and server flexibility under uncertainty. In *Winter Simulation Conference*, WSC '09, pages 3181–3188. Winter Simulation Conference, 2009.

[7] M. F. Porter. Readings in information retrieval. chapter An algorithm for suffix stripping, pages 313–316. Morgan Kaufmann Publishers Inc., San Francisco, CA, USA, 1997.

[8] Qihong Shao, Yi Chen, Shu Tao, et al. Easyticket: a ticket routing recommendation engine for enterprise problem resolution. *Proc. VLDB Endow.*, 1:1436–1439, August 2008.

[9] Qihong Shao, Yi Chen, Shu Tao, Xifeng Yan, and Nikos Anerousis. Efficient ticket routing by resolution sequence mining. In *Proceedings of the 14th ACM SIGKDD international conference on Knowledge discovery and data mining*, KDD '08, pages 605–613, New York, NY, USA, 2008. ACM.

[10] IBM SPSS. In *http://spss.co.in/*.

[11] Kristina Toutanova, Dan Klein, Christopher D. Manning, and Yoram Singer. Feature-rich part-of-speech tagging with a cyclic dependency network. In *Proceedings of the 2003 Conference of the North American Chapter of the Association for Computational Linguistics on Human Language Technology - Volume 1*, NAACL '03, pages 173–180, Stroudsburg, PA, USA, 2003. Association for Computational Linguistics.

Social Media Data Analysis for Revealing Collective Behaviors

Aoying Zhou, Weinign Qian, Haixin Ma
Software Engineering Institute, Eastern Normal University
3663 Zhongshan Road (N.), Shanghai 200062, China
ayzhou@sei.ecnu.edu.cn

Abstract

Along with the development of Web 2.0 applications, social media services has attracted many users and become their hands-on toolkits for recording life, sharing ideas, and social networking. Though social media services are essentially web or mobile applications and services, they combine user-generated content and social networks together, so that information can be created, transmitted, transformed, and consumed in the cyberspace. Thus, social media somehow could be regarded as a kind of sensor to the real life of its users. In general, the data from social media is of low quality. Pieces of information in social media are usually short, with informal presentation, and in some specific context that is highly related to the physical world. Therefore, it is challenging to extract semantics from social media data. However, we argue that given sufficient social media data, users' collective behaviors could be sensed, studied, and even predicted in a certain circumstance. Our study is conducted on data from two services, i.e. Twitter, and Sina Weibo, the most popular microblogging services all over the world and in China, respectively. Collective behaviors are actions of a large amount of various people, which are neither conforming nor deviant. Various collective behaviors are studied in the context of social media. Our studies show that there are various information flow patterns in social media, some of which are similar to traditional media such as newspapers, while others are embedded deep in the social network structure. The evolution of hotspots is highly affected by external stimulation, the social network structure, and individual user's activities. Furthermore, social media tends to be immune to some repeated similar external stimulations. Last but not the least, there is considerable difference in users' behavior between Twitter and Sina Weibo.

Categories & Subject Descriptors: H. Information Systems: H.2 DATABASE MANAGEMENT: H.2.8 Database applications: Subjects: Data mining

Author Keywords: Data Analysis, Social Media, Collective Behavior,

Bio

Aoying Zhou, Professor and deputy dean of School of Software Engineering at East China Normal University (ECNU), where he directs the Institute of Massive Computing. He got his master and bachelor degree in Computer Science from Sichuan University, Chengdu, in 1988 and 1985 respectively, and he won his Ph.D. degree from Fudan University in 1993. Before joining ECNU in 2008, Aoying worked for Fudan University in the Computer Science Department from 1993 to 2007, where he was the department chair from 1999 to 2002. He worked as a visiting scholar in the Berkeley Scholar Program at UC Berkeley in 2005. He is the winner of the National Science Fund for Distinguished Young Scholars supported by NSFC and the professorship appointment under Cheung Kong Scholars Program. He is the vice-director of ACM SIGMOD China and Database Technology Committee of China Computer Federation. He is serving as a member of the editorial boards of prestigious journals, such as VLDB Journal, WWW Journal. His research interests include Web data management, data management for data-intensive computing, management of uncertain data, data mining and data streams, distributed storage and P2P computing.

KDD'12, August 12-16, 2012, Beijing, China.
ACM 978-1-4503-1462-6 /12/08.

Information Processing in Social Networks

Ming-Syan Chen
National Taiwan University
Taiwan
mschen@cc.ee.ntu.edu.tw

Abstract

In the current social network, a user may have hundreds of friends and find it very time consuming to categorize and tag every friend manually. When a user is going to initiate an activity by issuing a corresponding query, he/she needs to consider the relationship among candidate attendees to find a group of mutually close friends. Meanwhile, he/she also needs to consider the schedule of candidate attendees to find an activity period available for all attendees. It would certainly be desirable if the efficiency of such process is improved. In this talk, information processing in social networks will first be reviewed in three phrases, namely (i) from content to social relationship, (ii) mining on social relationship, and (iii) from social relationship to content organization. In addition, we shall present an effective procedure which helps a user to organize an event with proper attendees with minimum total social distance and commonly available time. Moreover, it is noted that the information retrieved from the social networks is also able to facilitate those user-dependent and human-centric services. In light of this, we shall explore the quality of recommendation through incorporating the notion of social filtering and collaborative filtering. Finally, it is recognized that the cloud computing has offered many new capabilities of storing and processing huge amounts of heterogeneous data in social networks. In view of this, we shall also examine how this paradigm shift will affect the information processing in social networks.

Categories & Subject Descriptors: H.2.8 Database applications: Subjects: Data mining

Author Keywords: Social Network; Recommendation Systems

Bio

Ming-Syan Chen received the M.S. and Ph.D. degrees in Computer, Information and Control Engineering from The University of Michigan, Ann Arbor, MI, USA, in 1985 and 1988, respectively. He is now a Distinguished Research Fellow and the Director of Research Center of Information Technology Innovation (CITI) in the Academia Sinica, Taiwan, and is also a Distinguished Professor in the EE Department, National Taiwan University. He was a research staff member at IBM Thomas J. Watson Research Center, Yorktown Heights, NY, USA from 1988 to 1996, the Director of Graduate Institute of Comm. Eng. at NTU from 2003 to 2006, and also the President/CEO of Institute for Information Industry (III), from 2007 to 2008. His research interests include databases, data mining, and multimedia networking. Dr. Chen is a recipient of the Academic Award of the Ministry of Education, Taiwan, the NSC (National Science Council) Distinguished Research Award, Pan Wen Yuan Distinguished Research Award, Teco Award, Honorary Medal of Information, K.-T. Li Research Breakthrough Award, and IBM Outstanding Innovation Award. Dr. Chen is a Fellow of ACM and a Fellow of IEEE.

KDD'12, August 12-16, 2012, Beijing, China.
ACM 978-1-4503-1462-6 /12/08.

Understanding Users' Satisfaction for Search Engine Evaluation

Gordon Sun
Tencent Technology
China
gordon.gzsun@gmail.com

Abstract

To fulfill users' search needs, the search engine must have good performance, easy-to-use functionalities, and good search result quality. Search quality evaluation becomes challenging when users' satisfaction may not be able to judge by a single search and even within a single search judgments from various sources are not consistent. In this talk, I will discuss how user's satisfaction is decomposed into different components in general, and how we measure them with various means - human judgment, automatic computation with query log, and outsourcing, and their pros and cons with operational implications. For an outlook, I will postulate potential evaluation approaches for a better user's satisfaction.

Categories & Subject Descriptors: H. Information Systems: H.2 DATABASE MANAGEMENT: H.2.8 Database applications: Subjects: Data mining

Author Keywords: Search Engine Performance

Bio

Gordon Sun has been working on algorithmic search technology since 1998 when he joined Inktomi (the leading US search engine company during 1990s) as the senior scientist and architect. He also worked for two search engine companies, WiseNut and LookSmart as the director of R&D during 2001 to 2003 before he joined Yahoo early 2004 where he was leading the Global Search Relevance team as the director of research until 2009. Gordon graduated from University of Science and Technology of China and went to the US through the CUSPEA program (sponsored by Nobel Price Winner Prof. T.D. Lee) in 1981 and received his Ph.D. in theoretical physics from University of Iowa, 1984. He worked as the Research faculty in University of Maryland for 9 years before he moved to Silicon Valley, 1993, and worked in Communication Intelligence Inc, a leading hand-writing recognition provider, as the Chief Scientist. He has broad work experiences, knowledge and publications in neural networks, pattern recognition, machine learning, data mining, information retrieval, speech recognition, hand-writing recognition and non-linear dynamics.

KDD'12, August 12-16, 2012, Beijing, China.
ACM 978-1-4503-1462-6 /12/08.

Similarity Search in Real World Networks

Cuiping Li
Renmin University
China
cuiping_li@263.net

Abstract

Recently there has been a lot of interest in graph-based analysis. One of the most important aspects of graph-based analysis is to measure similarity between nodes and to do similarity search in a graph. For example, in social networks such as Facebook, system may want to recommend potential friends to a particular user based on connections between users. In custom-product networks such as eBay, one may wish to recommend products to others based on purchases history. In this talk, I will introduce some methods on vertex similarities computations and their applications on similarity search in real world networks.

Categories & Subject Descriptors: H. Information Systems: H.2 DATABASE MANAGEMENT: H.2.8 Database applications: Subjects: Data mining

Author Keywords: Graph Mining; Similarity Query; Social Network

Bio

Dr. Cuiping Li is currently a Professor of the Information School, Renmin University of China. Her current research interests include profit-based data mining, large scale information network analysis, and data warehousing. She has published over 30 research papers in major international conferences and journals including SIGMOD, VLDB, and KDD.

KDD'12, August 12-16, 2012, Beijing, China.
ACM 978-1-4503-1462-6 /12/08.

Large-Scale Learning of Word Relatedness with Constraints

Guy Halawi[§], Gideon Dror[†], Evgeniy Gabrilovich[‡], Yehuda Koren[†],
[§]Tel Aviv University, Tel Aviv, Israel; [†]Yahoo! Research, Haifa, Israel; [‡]Yahoo! Research, Santa Clara, CA, USA
ghalawi@gmail.com,{gideondr|gabr|yehuda}@yahoo-inc.com

ABSTRACT

Prior work on computing semantic relatedness of words focused on representing their meaning *in isolation*, effectively disregarding inter-word affinities. We propose a large-scale data mining approach to *learning* word-word relatedness, where known *pairs* of related words impose *constraints* on the learning process. Our method, called CLEAR, is shown to significantly outperform previously published approaches. The proposed method is based on first principles, and is generic enough to exploit diverse types of text corpora, while having the flexibility to impose constraints on the derived word similarities. We also make publicly available a new labeled dataset for evaluating word relatedness algorithms, which we believe to be the largest such dataset to date.

Categories and Subject Descriptors

H.2.8 [**Database Applications**]: Data Mining

General Terms

Algorithms, Experimentation

Keywords

Semantic similarity, word relatedness

1. INTRODUCTION

Computing semantic relatedness of words is an enabling technology for many natural language applications [5]. In document clustering, assessment of word relatedness can be used for formulating a better distance metric. In word sense disambiguation, the correct sense in which a word appears in a given text can be determined by computing the relatedness of the different candidate senses to the context. Consider also correction of typing errors or speech recognition errors, where a word is mistakenly replaced by another valid (i.e., not misspelled) word. Estimating word relatedness in context can help us determine the user most likely meant "Web site" rather than "Web sight".[1]

KDD'12, August 12–16, 2012, Beijing, China.

Conventional approaches to modeling semantic relatedness represent the meaning of individual words in a multidimensional space, and then compute the distance between the resultant word vectors. However, prior works focused on representation that is completely agnostic of the task of assessing relatedness, whereas the meanings of words is determined *in isolation*. Research in human judgment of similarity shows that it crucially depends on the context and frame of reference [25]. Quoting Tversky's example [25], "when subjects are asked to assess the similarity between the USA and the USSR, they usually assume that the relevant context is the set of countries and that the relevant frame of reference includes all political, geographical, and cultural features". Such context is completely lost when each word is considered in isolation from others.

Here we propose to *learn* a suitable word representation—in a latent factor space—with the particular task (of computing word relatedness) in mind. Specifically, we learn to represent word meanings by having observed word co-occurrences within sentences, as well as numerous *pairs of words* with different degrees of relatedness. This is done by incorporating word pairs of known relatedness as *constraints* on the learning process. We call our method CLEAR, which stands for Constrained LEArning of Relatedness.

Computing semantic relatedness using the newly learned representation yields statistically significant improvements on a range of datasets. Importantly, explicit modeling of word relatedness allows us to learn a signal that is *complementary* to that learned from large-scale world knowledge repositories, which were used in the previous state of the art method (TSA) [17]. Indeed, combining CLEAR with TSA yields significantly better results than either method alone. On the WS-353 dataset [10], which is the standard reference in the field, the combination improves the correlation with human judgments from $r = 0.8$ to 0.85.

The contributions of this paper are threefold. First, we introduce CLEAR, a novel approach to learning a word relatedness metric through a latent space embedding of the words, which directly incorporates the relatedness of training pairs of words used as constraints. Second, the results of using CLEAR for computing semantic relatedness are superior to the previous state of the art on three different datasets. Finally, we make publicly available a new dataset of 771 word pairs with human relatedness judgments, which was acquired as part of this research. To the best of our knowledge, this is the largest such dataset to date.

[1]Albeit one can argue that the last example can also be resolved by simple co-occurrence statistics (e.g., bi-grams), this would only be true for adjacent words. On the other hand, computing word relatedness to the rest of the text can easily handle long-term dependencies, which are very common in natural language (e.g., "Many people liked my *site* [or *sight* ?], which I have recently uploaded to the Web").

2. RELATED WORK

Prior work on semantic relatedness of words pursued two main directions, using purely statistical techniques or using repositories of human knowledge.

Early work on word relatedness formulated the notion of distributional similarity [6, 15], judging the relatedness of words by the similarity of contexts in which they occur. Later, Latent Semantic Analysis (LSA) [7] was proposed, which also leverages word co-occurrence information from a large unlabeled corpus of text. LSA is essentially a dimensionality reduction technique that identifies a number of most prominent dimensions in the data, which are assumed to correspond to "latent concepts". This is done by applying Singular Value Decomposition to the words-by-documents co-occurrence matrix. Latent Dirichlet Allocation (LDA) [3] can also be used for computing word relatedness by representing words as vectors of probabilities over each topic. Sun et al. [23] used LDA in a related application of text segmentation, using a Fisher kernel.

Lexical databases such as the WordNet electronic dictionary [8] or Roget's Thesaurus [19] encode relations between words such as synonymy, hypernymy, and meronymy. Quite a few metrics have been defined that compute word relatedness using various properties of the underlying graph structure of these resources (see [5] for an extensive survey). An obvious drawback of these approaches is that creation of lexical resources requires lexicographic expertise as well as considerable time and effort, and consequently such resources cover only a small fraction of the language lexicon. Specifically, such resources contain few proper names, neologisms, slang, and domain-specific technical terms. Indeed, Zesch et al. [29] showed that using a collaboratively constructed dictionary (Wiktionary) is superior to both WordNet and GermaNet (a German version of WordNet, [14]).

Dictionaries and thesauri mainly contain information about individual words but little world knowledge in general. Explicit Semantic Analysis (ESA) [11] was proposed to incorporate substantially large amounts of human knowledge — such as the entire Open Directory or Wikipedia — into word relatedness computation. Zesch and Gurevych [28] showed that it is possible to devise measures of relatedness using lexical resources that are competitive with those based on collaboratively constructed resources such as Wikipedia. Later, Temporal Semantic Analysis (TSA) [17] was proposed, which further improved the performance of ESA by extending it with a temporal dimension. This way, the computation of word relatedness was augmented with patterns of word occurrence over time (e.g., in an archive of a 100 years worth of New York Times articles).

Our approach effectively bridges the above two directions in a principled way. Similarly to purely statistical approaches, it learns word relatedness from word occurrence statistics in large text corpora. However, it *constrains* the learning process using word pairs that are *known* to be related, thus incorporating human knowledge. In Section 6 we compare CLEAR to the best performing statistical and knowledge-based approaches, and show that it outperforms all of them.

In this work, we used word pairs from WordNet, but in general they can come from a variety sources. For example, we can use lists of entities from Wikipedia (thus implicitly assuming the entities in the list are related) or Freebase, or lists automatically mined from the World Wide Web [13]. Domain-specific pairs of related words can be naturally incorporated in CLEAR.

In the present study we focused on computing semantic relatedness of individual words. However, in many cases a need arises to quantify semantic relatedness of longer fragments of text, for instance, in applications such as information retrieval or text clustering. The conventional approach to comparing fragments of text in information retrieval represents them as vectors of words, using the vector space model [20]. A major limitation of this model is that it assumes words to be independent, which is an oversimplification of the richness of natural language. Generalized vector space model [26] no longer makes this assumption, and explicitly manipulates a matrix G of term dependencies. Under this model, the similarity of a pair of documents, a and b, is computed as $sim_{GVSM}(a,b) = \mathbf{a}^T \cdot G \cdot \mathbf{b}$. Our method for estimating word relatedness can be immediately used for computing the matrix G, hence the generalized vector space model provides a principled way for incorporating CLEAR to refine existing text similarity models.

It should be noted that in this paper we deal with "semantic relatedness" rather than "semantic similarity" or "semantic distance", which are also often used in the literature. In their extensive survey of relatedness measures, Budanitsky and Hirst [5] argued that the notion of relatedness is more general than that of similarity, as the former subsumes many different kinds of specific relations, including meronymy, antonymy, functional association, and others. They further maintained that computational linguistics applications often require measures of relatedness rather than the more narrowly defined measures of similarity. For example, word sense disambiguation can use any *related* words from the context, and not merely *similar* words.

3. MODELING RELATEDNESS OF WORDS

We learn relatedness between words by embedding them in a low-dimensional space (e.g., a 100-D space), which strives to capture their semantic relations. Positions of words in the latent space reflect their meaning within sentences. This embedding is constructed while modeling the probability of observing a word given its adjacent context (e.g., the rest of its host sentence).

Before delving into the details of the method, we provide some necessary notational conventions. We observe words arranged within sequences. Each sequence annotates a pivot word. The sequence can be a short sentence containing the pivot word, or when the pivot word is placed within a long sentence, we limit the sequence to the words close to the pivot word (e.g., up to 5 words away). In order to distinguish words from sequences, we index words by i, j and sequences by s.

Therefore, from the text corpus we extract sequences of at most $2K + 1$ consecutive words, which do not exceed single sentence boundaries. A typical value of K would be in the range 2–8. Each sequence characterizes its middle pivot word denoted by i_s. The pivot word is removed from the sequence, that is $i_s \notin s$. Note that the extracted sequences can overlap because multiple pivot words are extracted from the same sentence. The sequences are arranged within a train set $\mathcal{S}$. After the sequences are identified, the word order within each sequence is no longer important, and we treat a sequence as a set of words.

A key component underlying our model is a mapping of words, and indirectly also of sequences, into a joint low dimensional space (of dimension ℓ), which we refer to as the latent factor representation, as follows:

- Each word i is mapped into a vector $q_i \in \mathbb{R}^\ell$.
- Each sequence s is mapped into a vector $p_s \in \mathbb{R}^\ell$, defined by $p_s = \frac{1}{|s|}\sum_{i \in s} q_i$.

In addition, we introduce biases for words, such that the bias of word i is denoted by b_i. These biases reflect the varying frequencies of words, independent of the surrounding sequence.

We denote by r_{si} the affinity of word i to sequence s, defined as

$$r_{si} = b_i + q_i^T p_s \quad (1)$$

Common words will generally have high bias values, reflecting their tendency to frequently co-occur with many other words (i.e., similar to many words in a distributional sense). However, words that are "strongly explained" by their context get bias values much lower than what is "merited" by their frequency. One such example is the word "versa", which almost always appears in the phrase "vice versa", hence its learned bias value is very low (actually negative, -1.25). On the other hand, the word "vice" can occur with many other words (e.g., "vice president"), hence its bias is much higher (+1.89).

Both the latent factor representation and the biases are parameters that we need to learn. Henceforth, we denote the model parameters by Θ.

The latent space representation strives to capture the semantics of the words, such that affinities in the latent space reflect semantic relations. Typically, we use a latent space dimensionality of $\ell = 100-200$, which gives a good trade off between time and accuracy. We report the results of experimenting with other possible numbers of dimensions in Section 6.2.

The likelihood of observing word i within sequence s is modeled by the multinomial distribution

$$P(i|s;\Theta) = \frac{\exp(r_{si})}{\sum_j \exp(r_{sj})} \quad (2)$$

We seek model parameters (Θ) in a way that maximizes the log-likelihood of the training set

$$L(\mathcal{S};\Theta) \stackrel{\text{def}}{=} \sum_{s\in\mathcal{S}} \log P(i_s|s;\Theta) \quad (3)$$

This modeling follows *multinomial logistic regression* [12], albeit with latent factors that make the function non-convex.

In the following, we often omit Θ from the probability definition, using the notation $P(i|s)$.

3.1 Optimization process

Learning proceeds by stochastic gradient ascent [4, 22]. Given a training sequence s we update each parameter $\theta \in \Theta$ by

$$\Delta\theta = \eta \frac{\partial \log P(i_s|s)}{\partial\theta} = \eta \left(\frac{\partial r_{si_s}}{\partial\theta} - \sum_j P(j|s) \frac{\partial r_{sj}}{\partial\theta} \right) \quad (4)$$

where η is the learning rate.

However, such a training scheme would be too slow to be practical, as each update rule requires summing over all words. Thus, we resort to sampling the weighted sum in (4), based on the importance sampling idea proposed by Bengio and Senécal [2].

With importance sampling we draw words according to a *proposal distribution*. In our case we assign each word a probability proportional to its empirical frequency in the train set, and denote this proposal distribution by $P(i|\mathcal{S})$. Consequently, words are sampled with replacement from $P(i|\mathcal{S})$ into a list $\mathcal{J}$. Thus, the expensive-to-compute $P(i|s)$ probabilities are approximated with the weighting scheme

$$w(i|s) = \frac{\exp(r_{si})/P(i|\mathcal{S})}{\sum_{j\in\mathcal{J}} \exp(r_{sj})/P(j|\mathcal{S})} \quad (5)$$

Consequently, the approximated gradient ascent step given a training sequence s will be

$$\Delta\theta = \eta \left(\frac{\partial r_{si_s}}{\partial\theta} - \sum_{j\in\mathcal{J}} w(j|s) \frac{\partial r_{sj}}{\partial\theta} \right) \quad (6)$$

As mentioned in [2], it is desirable that the size of set $\mathcal{J}$ grows as the training process proceeds, because at later training phases more delicate parameter adjustments are needed. We employ a simple rule for controlling the sample size ($|\mathcal{J}|$) based on the fitness of current estimate. Given a training sequence s, we keep sampling words into $\mathcal{J}$ until the following condition is satisfied:

$$\sum_{j\in\mathcal{J}} P(j|s) > P(i_s|s) \Leftrightarrow \sum_{j\in\mathcal{J}} \exp(r_{sj}) > \exp(r_{si_s}) \quad (7)$$

The adaptive sampling automatically lets the sample size grow when parameters are nearing final values and the correct word is getting a relatively high probability. We impose a minimal size of 50 on the sample size. For efficiency we also limit the maximal sample size to 1500.

We now provide a few finer details on the stochastic gradient ascent algorithm. We cycle through random permutations of the training examples (pivot words) in order to achieve convergence. In our implementation we ran the process for 5 sweeps over the training data, though not much improvement was observed beyond 3 sweeps. Weight decay was not found to be helpful. When training on the t-th example, we set the learning rate to $\eta_t = \frac{\eta_0}{t+\tau}$. This learning rate schedule satisfies the Robbins-Monro conditions [18], $\sum \eta_t = \infty$ and $\sum \eta_t^2 < \infty$. Specifically, in our implementation we set $\eta_0 = 10^6$ and $\tau = 10^7$. All model parameters were randomly initialized by drawing each from $\mathcal{N}(0, 0.01)$.

3.2 Incorporating similarity constraints

Frequently we have external knowledge relating pairs of words. For example, WordNet [8] can supply us with numerous pairs of related words, including synonyms, hypernyms/hyponyms, and meronyms/holonyms. Other sources of such information can be domain-specific, expert-driven, or Web-based (see Section 2 for additional examples). We incorporate this knowledge into our approach through pairwise regularization terms. It should be emphasized that it is this step that allows CLEAR to incorporate world knowledge. This way, we no longer represent words in isolation, but rather induce a representation where related words are located close to one another.

Specifically, let us denote by $\mathcal{P}$ the set of word pairs known to be related. We encourage closeness between such pairs by enhancing our optimization goal (3) to be

$$L(\mathcal{S};\Theta) \stackrel{\text{def}}{=} \sum_{s\in\mathcal{S}} \log P(i_s|s,\Theta) - \lambda \sum_{(i_1,i_2)\in\mathcal{P}} \|q_{i_1} - q_{i_2}\|^2 \quad (8)$$

We used the value 0.01 for the constant λ, which controls the extent of pulling known related words towards each other. We report the results of experimenting with other possible values of this parameter in Section 6.2.

Note that we only use the fact that particular word pairs are related, but do not use the actual degree of their relatedness. In practice, automatic acquisition of related word pairs is fairly easy from electronic dictionaries, thesauri, or world knowledge repositories such as Wikipedia. Consider, for example, the list of mathematical functions in Wikipedia (`http://en.wikipedia.org/wiki/List_of_mathematical_functions`). Pairing all the entries in this list can easily create many pairs of related concepts, yet requiring each such pair to be accompanied with a human judgment of relatedness would adversely affect large-scale data acquisition.

In our future work, we plan to experiment with annotating constraints with automatic assessment of relatedness.

Prior work on semantic relatedness represented individual words in isolation, effectively disregarding known affinities among the words in the language. Thus, we view the easiness of incorporating such information as a core component of our method, which augments statistical processing with human world knowledge in a principled way.

3.3 Deriving word relatedness

The latent factors yield a compact representation of the words that allows their direct comparison. Given two words i and j, we estimate their relatedness by comparing their respective factor vectors q_i and q_j. In this work, the word-word relatedness is defined by the cosine function:

$$\text{rel}_{ij} = \frac{q_i^T q_j}{\|q_i\| \|q_j\|} \quad (9)$$

4. DATA CREATION AND PROCESSING

In this section we discuss the data sources used in this work, including the corpora used for model training, word relatedness constraints, and test datasets. The next section motivates the choice of evaluation metric and the baselines we used. Then, we report the experimental results in Section 6.

4.1 Text corpora

As explained in Section 3, our method learns word relatedness from text corpora. In this work, we used three text corpora from very different domains. With the intent of modeling the word relatedness judgments of a layman, we refrained from using more formal sources such as Reuters' RCV1 or Wikipedia[2], but focused on corpora that reflect informal language use:

- **Yahoo! Answers**: This dataset is available through the Yahoo! Webscope program[3]. The dataset contains questions and answers posted to the Yahoo! Answers service prior to October 2007. The corpus contains a wide spectrum of questions, such as factual, advice seeking, and social, on topics ranging from Arts & Entertainment to Sports, Travel, Health, or Politics. We used the first half of the corpus comprising of 2,215,396 questions. For the purpose of this work, the concatenation of all the text related to a single question, namely, the question title, body, and the best answer, was considered as a single document.
- **UKWaC** [1] is a corpus built by crawling of the .uk Web domain. It contains more than a billion words, and is considered one of the largest Web resources for British English. It is part-of-speech tagged and lemmatized. We used the first file of the UKWaC corpus distribution version 1.0, which contains 110,165 documents.
- **Subtitles**: We extracted English subtitles for 9,950 random movies and television series from the OpenSubtitle API[4].

4.2 Processing

Each corpus was separately processed using the following preprocessing steps:

1. Parsing, tokenization and stopword removal.

2. Lemmatization of tokens, which amounts to reducing each token to its morphological stem. For example, this step identifies as equivalent different tense forms of the same verb (e.g., 'climbed' and 'climb'), including irregular verbs (e.g., 'go' and 'went'). For this task we used the LemmaGen tool[5].

3. Removal of rare tokens: tokens occurring fewer than 30 times were removed from the dictionary as well as from the text. For the Subtitles dataset, which is considerably smaller, we reduced the dictionary size by simply taking the 40,000 most frequent tokens.

4. The corpus was split into sentences, and sentences with fewer than 4 tokens were discarded. We used the SharpNLP Project[6] for sentence boundary detection.

Table 1 details the characteristics of the processed datasets. Additionally, to give the reader a glimpse into the different corpora we used, Figure 1 pictorially depicts the most frequent tokens in each corpus using word clouds.

Corpus	# Sentences	Dictionary size	#Tokens
Y! Answers	4,778,784	41,102	41,170,886
UKWaC	3,499,361	42,717	34,382,199
Subtitles	695,482	40,000	4,927,282

Table 1: Number of sentences, dictionary size and total number of word tokens comprising the final corpora

4.3 WordNet synonyms as similarity constraints

As explained in Section 3.2, our method can be constrained with a collection of word pairs, which are known to be related. In Section 2 we discussed a variety of suitable resources that can provide lists of related word pairs. In this work, we used the WordNet electronic dictionary [8], and the constraints were based on the synonymy relation.

The basic unit of information in WordNet is a synset, which is a set of synonyms that share the same word sense. For each word in our datasets, we queried WordNet for synonyms. The most common synset was picked if the word was ambiguous. Overall, 10,148 tokens were found to be related through the synonymy relations. These provided a total of 21,929 synonym pairs, which were used by method as relatedness constraints.

4.4 Evaluation datasets

The standard practice of evaluating word relatedness models is to compute the correlation between their predictions and human judgments [5]. In this study, we used three evaluation datasets.

The WordSimilarity-353 (WS-353) is the standard reference dataset in the field, which contains 353 word pairs. Each word pair was judged by 13–16 human annotators. This dataset, which was so far the largest publicly available collection of this kind, was extensively used for word relatedness evaluation [29, 11, 28, 27, 17].

In addition, we used the dataset constructed by Radinsky et al. [17], comprising of 287 word pairs. In this dataset, word relatedness was evaluated by Amazon's Mechanical Turk workers, with an average of 23 worker ratings for each word pair. We call this dataset MTURK-287.

To enhance the statistical strength of our findings, we also constructed a third, larger dataset, which we make publicly available at `http://www2.mta.ac.il/~gideon/datasets/`. We discuss the process of its construction in the next section.

4.5 Constructing a new evaluation dataset

Word pairs were constructed to get a comprehensive sampling of both related and unrelated words, and we specifically aimed at

[2]Recent research shows that Wikipedia—despite being collaboratively authored by numerous contributors around the world—can hardly be viewed as easily readable text [24].

[3]`http://webscope.sandbox.yahoo.com/`

[4]`http://trac.opensubtitles.org/projects/opensubtitles`

[5]http://lemmatise.ijs.si/

[6]`http://sharpnlp.codeplex.com/`

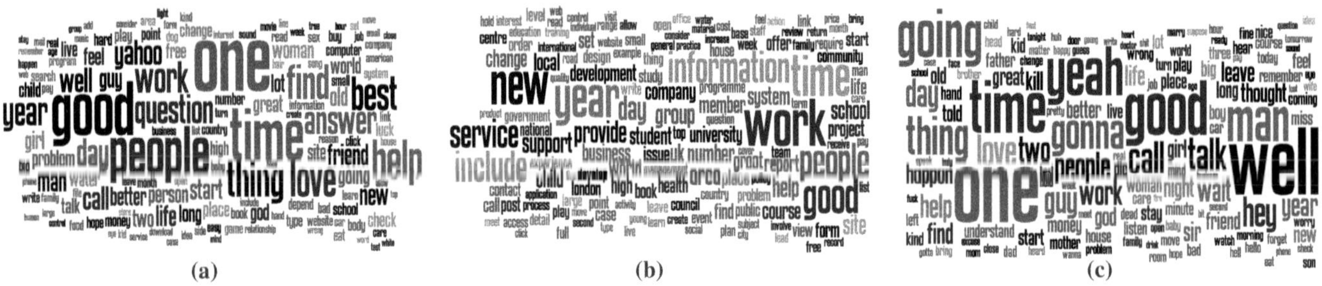

Figure 1: Word clouds depicting most frequent tokens in (a) Yahoo! Answers dataset; (b) UKWaC dataset; (c) Subtitles dataset. Displayed token size is proportional to token frequency. Pictures produced by `wordle.net`.

various types of relatedness. To this end we considered WordNet [8] as a graph linking nouns. For two nouns i and j, the following relations (graph edges) are possible:

- i and j are synonyms (synonymy relation).
- i is a part of j (meronymy relation), for example 'leg' and 'table'.
- i is a type of j (holonymy relation), for example 'table' and 'furniture'.

Construction of word pairs.

From this graph we uniformly sampled noun pairs with (undirected) graph distances between 1 and 4. In order to ensure quality of collected human evaluations, we eliminated rare words. To this end, we used the Yahoo! Web search engine to count the number of search results when a word is used as a query. We discarded all pairs containing a word with fewer than 40 million search results.

Human estimation of word relatedness.

Word relatedness was evaluated by Amazon's Mechanical Turk workers, with an average of 20 ratings for each word pair, where each judgment task consisted of a batch of 50 word pairs. Ratings were collected on a 1–5 scale, where 5 stands for "highly related" and 1 stands for "not related". In order to discard poor-quality work, each batch contained 10 trap word pairs with known extreme relatedness values (WordNet synonyms or extremely unrelated words as indicated by WS-353), serving as binary indicators. A batch that failed on more than one of the binary indicators was discarded. This guarantees an over 98% probability for detecting random workers (e.g., bots). The relatedness value of each word-pair was taken as the mean score given by the workers. This dataset has 771 word-pairs, and is accordingly named MTURK-771.

Figure 2 depicts the word-relatedness scores, sorted by their mean value. The error bars represent a one standard deviation confidence interval of each value. The horizontal axis represents the rank of each word-pair when sorted by relatedness in ascending order, such that the least related word-pair is ranked 1 and the most related word-pair is ranked 771. Importantly, our dataset includes the full range of word relatedness, with a clear signal, demonstrated by the relatively small error bars. In particular we observe that word-pairs which are with extremal value of relatedness have significantly lower variance in human judgements, as evident from the shorter error bars on both extremes of the relatedness range.

Consistency assessment.

To verify the agreement between raters, following Snow et al. [21], we randomly split the raters into two groups, each including 10 Mechanical Turk workers. We then averaged the numeric judgements for each word pair among the raters in each of the two sets, thus

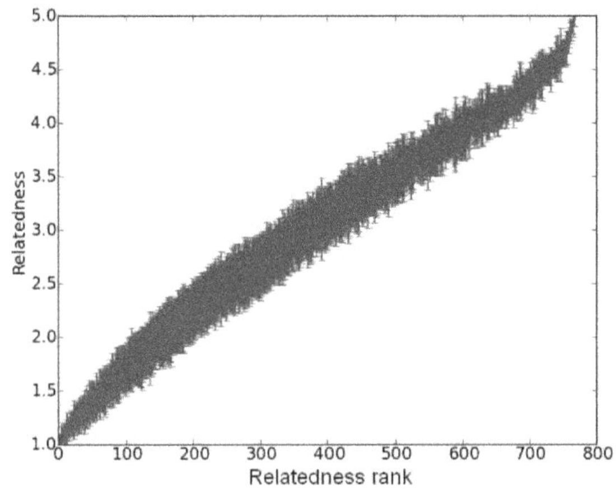

Figure 2: Word-pair relatedness (with error bars), sorted by value

yielding a (771 element long) vector of average judgments for each set. Finally, we computed the correlation between the vectors of the two sets. We repeated this process 1000 times, and over these 1000 random splits the mean correlation between the two sets of raters was 0.8957, with extremely small variance, attesting to the quality of the collected data.

5. EVALUATION SETUP

We now discuss the evaluation metric we employed, as well as the procedure for assessing the significance of the results observed.

Following prior literature [11, 17], we compute Spearman's rank-order correlation coefficient between the algorithm's predictions and the average human judgments on a list of word pairs. Being non-parametric, Spearman's correlation coefficient is considered to be much more robust than Pearson's linear correlation. We report Spearman's correlation separately for each test dataset, because the datasets have been collected by different methods.

5.1 Significance testing

We now discuss our methodology for testing the significance of the obtained results. Given two algorithms for computing word relatedness, let r_1 and r_2 be the values of their (Spearman rank) correlation with human judgments, obtained on a set of n word pairs. Let z_i be their Fisher transformed values [9]:

$$z_i = \sqrt{\frac{n-3}{1.06}}\frac{1}{2}\ln\frac{1+r_i}{1-r_i} \tag{10}$$

The z_i scores approximately follow a standard normal distribution, and therefore it is straightforward to determine whether the difference $z_1 - z_2$ is significantly different from zero. Specifically, to show the superiority of CLEAR we use a one-sided t-test.

5.2 Baseline methods

In what follows, we compare CLEAR to the two methods that showed best reported results to date, namely, ESA [11] and TSA [17] (see Section 2). We also compare CLEAR to two additional strong baselines, namely, distributional similarity and LDA, which share certain aspects with CLEAR. These two baselines are described below.

Distributional similarity (DS).

The notion of distributional similarity of words was formulated by Lee [15] and Dagan et al. [6].

Let n be the number of unique words in the dataset. For each word we maintain an n-dimensional vector, which reflects the frequency with which it co-occurs with every other word in the dataset. We consider two words to co-occur if they are collocated within the same sentence, no more than K tokens apart. We used $K = 3$, which yielded the best results. Word frequency was normalized by dividing it by the overall word count (standard IDF normalization was also tried, but yielded inferior results). Formally, let n_{ij} be the number of co-occurrences of words i and j, and let n_j be the overall frequency of word j. Then, word i is represented via $v_i \in \mathbb{R}^n$, where $v_{ij} = n_{ij}/n_j$. Finally, the distributional similarity (DS) between words i and j is defined by $\cos(i, j)$.

Distributional similarity shares with CLEAR the principle of defining the word semantics using the words that frequently co-occur with it. However, unlike CLEAR, it is not based on an optimization process, and does not use a latent factor representation for compactly capturing the words semantics.

Latent Dirichlet allocation (LDA).

LDA [3] is a generative model that explains word occurrences in documents through latent topics underlying the document and the word distributions. We used the open source LDA implementation called Mallet [16]. We report results using 200 topics (best performing setting). For each word i, we compute its probability distribution over topics, denoted by p_i. Semantic relatedness between words i and j is then computed as the Jensen-Shannon divergence between their respective probability distributions.

CLEAR shares resemblance with LDA in terms of modeling the words through latent factor vectors. However, CLEAR differs in modeling short word sequences, or sentences, whereas LDA requires longer documents for good performance. Furthermore, CLEAR incorporates external-supplied similarity relations, which are given as constraints.

5.3 New evaluation scenario: finding word synonyms

We also used a new evaluation scenario, where we employed CLEAR to identify word synonyms (which are obviously related in meaning), and used WordNet to validate our predictions. When doing so, we did not use WordNet synonyms as learning constraints (cf. Section 4.3). Note that WordNet synonyms comprise a larger dataset than any of the three word relatedness datasets (cf. Sections 4.4 and 4.5); however, this particular dataset lacks negative or weak positive examples.

6. EXPERIMENTAL RESULTS

We trained CLEAR on the three text corpora described in Section 4.1, and a combination thereof. The method was implemented in C#, and was run on a machine with Intel Dual Core E840 3GHz processor and 2GB RAM. Typical training time for 5 sweeps over the Yahoo! Answers corpus was 5 hours. To give the reader a flavor of the results, we show in Table 2 examples of related words found by our method.

In what follows, we first report the performance of our method on the three datasets described in Sections 4.4 and 4.5, and then on the task of identifying word synonyms described in Section 5.3.

6.1 Quantifying word relatedness with CLEAR

We compare the performance of CLEAR with that of prior methods (discussed in Sections 2 and 5.2). The choices of parameter values used for the experiments in this subsection, as well as the results of experimentation with other possible parameter settings, are discussed in Section 6.2.

Several variants of CLEAR are reported, which differ by the training corpus. First, we trained CLEAR separately on Y!Answers, UKWaC, and Subtitles. As can be seen in Table 3, models trained on Y!Answers deliver the best performance on all datasets, followed closely by UKWaC-trained models. Training on Subtitles yields significantly poorer results, which might be explained by the significantly smaller size of this corpus.

Clearly, there is no need to limit the training to only one of the corpora. Therefore, we also present the results obtained with the two more informative training corpora (Yahoo! Answers and UKWaC) combined, as well as the results due to the combination of all three corpora. When combining these corpora, we let the training process run on each, and then employ the average of the cosine similarities computed on each corpus separately. As we can see in Table 3, the performance of CLEAR is obviously improving when it learns from diverse corpora. Interestingly, even the smaller Subtitles corpus, which delivered poorer results on its own, adds a non-negligible value when integrated with the others. This probably reflects on its unique nature of representing spoken, rather than written, language.

In the remainder of this subsection (6.1), we report CLEAR results with training on all the three training corpora.

Method	WS-353	MTURK-287	MTURK-771
CLEAR on Y!Answers	0.771	0.697	0.690
CLEAR on UKWaC	0.748	0.653	0.673
CLEAR on Subtitles	0.635	0.636	0.610
CLEAR on Y!Answers+ UKWaC	0.795	0.712	0.716
CLEAR on Y!Answers+ UKWaC+Subtitles	**0.810**	**0.737**	**0.727**

Table 3: Performance of CLEAR on different training corpora and their combinations.

Table 4 compares CLEAR with previously published methods. The results of prior methods (ESA [11] and TSA [17]) were achieved using their original code through their respective authors. As we can readily see, CLEAR outperforms these state of the art methods with a notable margin, especially on the two MTURK test sets. In almost all the cases, the difference between CLEAR and each of the other methods is statistically significant. Table 4 shows the statistical significance of the difference between the performance of each method and that of CLEAR; we use the symbols § and † to represent significance levels of $\alpha = 0.0001$ and $\alpha = 0.01$, respectively.

coke	mile	religion	sheep	university	webcam
pepsi (0.813)	mi (0.826)	relgion (0.779)	ox (0.648)	suny (0.809)	cam (0.636)
cola (0.567)	kilometer (0.690)	abrahamic (0.771)	ewe (0.620)	nyu (0.806)	logitech (0.581)
sprite (0.491)	nautical (0.607)	spirituality (0.717)	goat (0.614)	devry (0.804)	messenge (0.519)
coca (0.477)	kilometre (0.589)	religon (0.715)	herd (0.612)	polytechnic (0.801)	messenger (0.484)
pepsico (0.471)	furlong (0.563)	secularism (0.674)	cattle (0.596)	univeristy (0.795)	camera (0.474)

Table 2: Word relatedness examples: top-5 lists of most related for six sample words, obtained by running our method on the Yahoo! Answers corpus; cosine similarity values are reported in parentheses. (Spelling errors are in original data.)

We remark that unlike ESA and TSA, CLEAR follows more general principles, as it does not require elaborate knowledge resource or text corpora spanning long periods of time. In fact, CLEAR can be trained on virtually any text corpus. Hence, we would expect the CLEAR advantage to grow even further when it is trained on more diverse corpora.

We further analyze the performance of CLEAR by comparing it to two other methods, which isolate two of its founding principles. First, we compare it to distributional similarity (DS), which models words based on their contextual neighborhood. The best results for this method were obtained when trained on the three corpora combined. Second, we compare CLEAR to LDA, which demonstrates the importance of mapping words to a latent factor space, thus capturing their semantic relations. Again, combining the three training text corpora improved LDA accuracy. We observe that both DS and LDA cannot match the performance of CLEAR. Yet, LDA delivers results much stronger than DS, indicating the greater importance of latent factor modeling.

Method	WS-353	MTURK-287	MTURK-771
CLEAR	**0.810**	**0.737**	**0.727**
TSA	0.8	0.61§	0.606§
ESA	0.75§	0.607§	0.603§
LDA	0.736§	0.677†	0.619§
DS	0.61§	0.625§	0.578§

Table 4: Comparing the performance of CLEAR with competing methods. The symbols § and † represent statistically significant differences (vs. CLEAR) at the levels of 0.0001 and 0.01, respectively.

We also evaluated whether other methods can add value on top of CLEAR. To this end, we formed linear combinations of CLEAR values with those produced by other methods. The linear combination coefficients were learned by linear regression on the human judgments. When evaluating on each one of the datasets, we used the other two datasets for training the regressor.

The results are reported in Table 5. We can see that the accuracy is further improved by combining CLEAR with other methods, implying that CLEAR learns signals that are complementary to the other methods. We also tried to combine the previous methods, without involving CLEAR (the bottom two rows of Table 5). We found that the linear combination of ESA and TSA could not improve performance. This is possible because linear regression is suboptimal when optimizing Spearman's correlation. We also tried a simple average, but it did not improve the performance either. Even though some smarter combinations of the two methods may be successful, we suspect that the signals captured by these two methods are not sufficiently different to justify their combination. Indeed, TSA extends the ESA model with temporal analysis, therefore, the results of the two methods are correlated. As for DS and LDA, their linear combination does improve the performance; this is not surprising given their very different nature. However, their combination is still inferior to the standalone CLEAR.

Method	WS-353	MTURK-287	MTURK-771
CLEAR + ESA	0.826	0.746	0.732
CLEAR + TSA	**0.850**	**0.751**	**0.742**
CLEAR + DS	0.809	0.738	0.729
CLEAR + LDA	0.818	0.749	0.731
ESA+TSA	0.772	0.601	0.604
DS + LDA	0.757	0.694	0.638

Table 5: Performance of pairs of methods combined

To further compare CLEAR with TSA, we examined the ranking of word pairs by their relatedness according to each algorithm. To this end, for each dataset we ranked all the words by their relatedness according to CLEAR, TSA, and humans. We denote the resultant rankings as $\mathcal{R}_{CLEAR}$, $\mathcal{R}_{TSA}$, and $\mathcal{R}_{human}$, respectively. We found $\mathcal{R}_{CLEAR}$ to be consistently closer to $\mathcal{R}_{human}$ than $\mathcal{R}_{TSA}$.

Indeed, on WS-353, the average improvement in rank from $\mathcal{R}_{TSA}$ to $\mathcal{R}_{CLEAR}$ was 5.8 positions (median 3.5). For MTURK-287, the average improvement was 10.2 positions (median 3). Finally, for MTURK-771, the average improvement was 29.8 positions (median 19).

6.2 Parameter setting study

We now explore the dependency of CLEAR performance on the following parameters:

(a) The parameter K controls the context size, i.e., the maximum distance between the pivot word and other words in its context (Section 3).

(b) The parameter λ controls the extent of using the similarity constraints (Section 3.2).

(c) The parameter ℓ represents the dimensionality of the latent factor space (Section 3).

The results reported here were obtained by training on the Yahoo! Answers corpus (the results using the other two training corpora exhibited very similar patterns).

Table 6 analyzes the effect of different context sizes. We see a mild variation of performance as K changes, with the best results around $K = 6$. Hence we set $K = 6$ throughout the other experiments. We also observe that the results on the WS-353 test set are consistently higher than those on the two MTURK datasets, which remains true through all our evaluations.

Table 7 studies the effect of the similarity constraints (see Section 3.2). For the WS-353 and MTURK-771 datasets, optimal performances is obtained when similarity constraints are taken with the weight of $\lambda = 0.01$; however, further emphasis of these constraints with $\lambda = 0.1$ becomes counter-productive. As for the smaller MTURK-287 test set, even $\lambda = 0.01$ was too large with a negative impact on performance. Therefore, we set $\lambda = 0.01$ for all our reported results.

Finally, we report in Table 8 the effect of the dimensionality of

Context size	WS-353	MTURK-287	MTURK-771
$K = 2$	0.744	0.664	0.682
$K = 4$	0.756	0.670	**0.700**
$K = 6$	**0.767**	**0.687**	0.695
$K = 7$	0.761	0.686	0.688
$K = 8$	0.747	0.678	0.686

Table 6: Impact of context size: CLEAR performance for various values of K (measured by Spearman correlation; higher is better). Here $\lambda = 0.01$ and $\ell = 100$.

λ	WS-353	MTURK-287	MTURK-771
0	0.744	**0.692**	0.674
0.01	**0.767**	0.687	**0.695**
0.1	0.742	0.684	0.666

Table 7: Impact of similarity constraints: CLEAR performance for various values of λ. Here $K = 6$ and $\ell = 100$.

the latent factor space. We see steady accuracy gains until reaching $\ell = 100 - 150$, demonstrating the added expressive power of the increased dimensionality. However, as dimensionality further increases towards 500, the sparser latent space does not translate into a measurably better performance. Therefore, we set $\ell = 150$ for the remainder of the experiments.

Latent dim.	WS-353	MTURK-287	MTURK-771
$\ell = 20$	0.681	0.662	0.610
$\ell = 50$	0.722	0.675	0.670
$\ell = 100$	0.767	0.687	0.695
$\ell = 150$	**0.771**	**0.697**	0.690
$\ell = 200$	0.759	0.668	0.680
$\ell = 500$	0.758	0.665	**0.700**

Table 8: Impact of dimensionality: CLEAR performance for various values of ℓ. Here $\lambda = 0.01$ and $K = 6$.

6.3 Identifying word synonyms

Test sets based on human judgments are expensive to collect and hence small in size. Therefore, we also evaluated the performance of CLEAR on an additional task, namely, identifying word synonyms. We used WordNet as a gold-standard repository of synonyms. In this experiment, we used a version of our algorithm trained without similarity constraints (i.e., we set $\lambda = 0$), so that no explicit knowledge on the synonyms leaks into the training phase (cf. Section 4.3).

First, we computed similarities between 21,929 WordNet synonym pairs, henceforth called *SynPairs*. Second, for each word in *SynPairs*, we formed 100 test instances by pairing it with 100 random words; we refer to this collection as *RndPairs*. Naturally, one would expect the similarities computed on *SynPairs* (i.e., between true synonyms) to be significantly higher than those computed on *RndPairs* (i.e., random pairs of words). We repeated the same experiment with LDA. As explained in Section 5.2, we used the Jensen-Shannon distance for comparing the LDA word vectors, which gave there better results than cosine similarity.

Figure 3 shows the performance of CLEAR and LDA on identifying word synonyms. For both methods, the results visibly indicate that the distribution of pairwise similarity values for synonyms (*SynPairs*) is very different from that for random word pairs (*RndPairs*). We used the Jensen-Shannon divergence to compute the distance between the two distributions. For CLEAR, the JS divergence between the two distributions is 0.275, whereas for LDA it is 0.178. This implies better discriminative power of CLEAR compared to LDA.

Note also that LDA topic vectors tend to be sparse (sparseness factor of 97.87%), so both *SynPairs* and *RndPairs* distributions are peaking near 1, indicating no overlap between the topic vectors of the respective words. In fact, we observed that the sparseness of LDA topic vectors, which is helpful for unsupervised exploratory analysis, harms its predictive abilities. As many topics are correlated, a sparse representation of words over topics masks important signals. At CLEAR, the sparseness factor is virtually zero, thus reducing the issues raised by correlative factors.

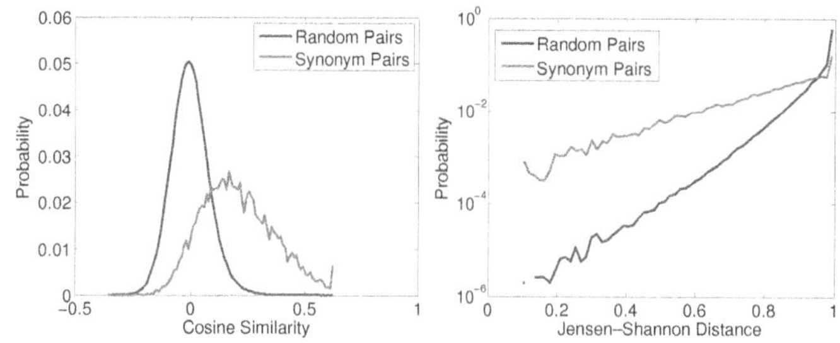

CLEAR **LDA**

Figure 3: The distributions of pairwise similarities (or, distances) for both WordNet synonyms and for random pairs.

6.4 The effect of the consistency of human judgments

Interestingly, we found a dependency between the accuracy of CLEAR and the consistency of human judgments. For the MTURK-771 dataset, we ranked all word pairs by the CLEAR relatedness and by the human-judged relatedness. Then, for each word pair we calculated the difference in its ranks according to CLEAR and according to humans, denoted as $\mathcal{D}$. We also calculated the variance between human raters for each word pair, denoted by $\mathcal{V}$.

We found $\mathcal{D}$ and $\mathcal{V}$ to be significantly correlated, with Pearson's coefficient $r = 0.18$. In other words, when raters tend to disagree about a particular word pair, we find CLEAR to systematically err more about the relatedness of these words. This result is highly significant statistically and cannot be explained by chance, with p-value $p = 1.96 \cdot 10^{-7}$.

7. CONCLUDING REMARKS

This paper introduced CLEAR, a method for estimating relatedness between natural language words. Prior works represented the meaning of words in isolation, even though cognitive research proves humans represent word meanings in context. CLEAR circumvents this limitation by learning word semantics from actual contexts in which the word occurs. CLEAR can be trained on any text corpus, without limiting the nature of the analyzed text, and hence can learn from virtually all kinds of textual corpora. Indeed, we have shown that training the method on texts from very different domains and styles improves its accuracy.

The main principle behind CLEAR is learning to embed words in a low-dimensional latent space, thus explaining the composition of short word sequences. Furthermore, CLEAR can leverage existing knowledge on word relatedness, which is directly encoded using similarity constraints.

We believe that the following ingredients contribute to the success of CLEAR:

• Modeling informal language, such as that used in the Yahoo! Answers and the movie subtitles corpora, was found beneficial to modeling human judgments of word relatedness.

• An ability to anchor the model with existing lists of related words boosts the accuracy of the method.

• Analysis of short contexts, rather than full documents or paragraphs, assists in better identification of related words.

• Embedding the words in a latent semantic space is helpful for identifying related words, and also for treating rare words correctly based on models learned for their more frequent relatives.

• A model learned through global optimization captures large scale signals, and thus shows higher robustness against local artifacts.

In a comprehensive set of empirical tests, CLEAR was shown to outperform prior works, as it achieves the best known results on a host of highly competitive benchmarks. We also showed that the signal learned by CLEAR is complementary to that learned by other state of the art methods. Indeed, combining CLEAR with TSA yields even better results. Interestingly, we found a notable correlation between the agreement of human raters and the performance of CLEAR—the method shines on word pairs that are unambiguous for humans, while tends to err more on word pairs that are also difficult for humans to agree on.

In the future work, we plan to augment our method by incorporating new types of constraints. For instance, in addition to synonyms, we can use other word relations such as hypernyms, hyponyms, meronyms, and holonyms, to name but a few. These relations imply different degrees of word relatedness, and quantifying the degree of relatedness in each constraint can further refine our method.

As an additional contribution of this research, we collected a new human-judged dataset for evaluating word relatedness algorithms. We believe this dataset, called MTURK-771, is the largest such test collection to date. We make it publicly available at `http://www2.mta.ac.il/~gideon/datasets/`.

Acknowledgments

We thank Kira Radinsky for running experiments on the TSA method. We also thank Greg Druck, Bo Pang, and Sujith Ravi for pointers to relevant literature.

8. REFERENCES

[1] M. Baroni, S. Bernardini, A. Ferraresi, and E. Zanchetta. The WaCky wide web: a collection of very large linguistically processed web-crawled corpora. *Language Resources and Evaluation*, 2009.

[2] Y. Bengio and J.-S. Senécal. Quick training of probabilistic neural nets by sampling. In *Proc. 9th International Workshop on Artificial Intelligence and Statistics (AISTATS'03)*, 2003.

[3] D. M. Blei, A. Y. Ng, and M. I. Jordan. Latent dirichlet allocation. *Journal of Machine Learning Research*, 3:993–1022, 2003.

[4] L. Bottou. Stochastic learning. In *Advanced Lectures on Machine Learning*, LNAI 3176, pages 146–168. Springer Verlag, 2004.

[5] A. Budanitsky and G. Hirst. Evaluating wordnet-based measures of lexical semantic relatedness. *Computational Linguistics*, 32(1):13–47, 2006.

[6] I. Dagan, L. Lee, and F. C. N. Pereira. Similarity-based models of word cooccurrence probabilities. *Machine Learning*, 34(1–3):43–69, 1999.

[7] S. Deerwester, S. Dumais, G. Furnas, T. Landauer, and R. Harshman. Indexing by latent semantic analysis. *JASIS*, 41(6):391–407, 1990.

[8] C. Fellbaum, editor. *WordNet: An Electronic Lexical Database*. MIT Press, Cambridge, MA, 1998.

[9] E. Fieller, H. Hartley, and E. Pearson. Tests for rank correlation coefficients. *Biometrika*, 44:470–Ű481, 1957.

[10] L. Finkelstein, E. Gabrilovich, Y. Matias, E. Rivlin, Z. Solan, G. Wolfman, and E. Ruppin. Placing search in context: The concept revisited. *ACM TOIS*, 20(1):116–131, January 2002.

[11] E. Gabrilovich and S. Markovitch. Wikipedia-based semantic interpretation for natural language processing. *Journal of Artificial Intelligence Research*, 34:443–498, 2009.

[12] T. Hastie, R. Tibshirani, and J. Friedman. *The Elements of Statistical Learning*. Springer Series in Statistics. Springer New York Inc., New York, NY, USA, 2009.

[13] R. Hoffmann, C. Zhang, and D. S. Weld. Learning 5000 relational extractors. In *ACL*, pages 286–295, 2010.

[14] C. Kunze. Computerlinguistik und sprachtechnologie. In *Lexikalisch-semantische Wortnetze*, pages 423–431. Spektrum Akademischer Verlag, 2004.

[15] L. Lee. Measures of distributional similarity. In *Proceedings of the 37th Annual Meeting of the ACL*, pages 25–32, 1999.

[16] A. K. McCallum. Mallet: A machine learning for language toolkit. http://mallet.cs.umass.edu, 2002.

[17] K. Radinsky, E. Agichtein, E. Gabrilovich, and S. Markovitch. A word at a time: Computing word relatedness using temporal semantic analysis. In *WWW*, 2011.

[18] H. Robbins and S. Monro. A stochastic approximation method. *Annals of Math. Statistics*, 22:400–407, 1951.

[19] P. Roget. *Roget's Thesaurus of English Words and Phrases*. Longman Group Ltd., 1852.

[20] G. Salton, editor. *The SMART Retrieval System: Experiments in Automatic Document Processing*. Prentice Hall, 1971.

[21] R. Snow, B. O'Connor, D. Jurafsky, and A. Y. Ng. Cheap and fast — but is it good? Evaluating non-expert annotations for natural language tasks. In *EMNLP*, 2008.

[22] J. C. Spall. *Introduction to Stochastic Search and Optimization*. John Wiley & Sons, Inc., 2003.

[23] Q. Sun, R. Li, D. Luo, and X. Wu. Text segmentation with LDA-based fisher kernel. In *ACL-HLT Short Papers*, pages 269–272, 2008.

[24] C. Tan, E. Gabrilovich, and B. Pang. To each his own: Personalized content selection based on text comprehensibility. In *WSDM*, 2012.

[25] A. Tversky. Features of similarity. *Psychological Review*, 84(4):327–352, 1977.

[26] S. K. M. Wong, W. Ziarko, and P. C. N. Wong. Generalized vector spaces model in information retrieval. In *SIGIR*, 1985.

[27] E. Yeh, D. Ramage, C. D. Manning, E. Agirre, and A. Soroa. Wikiwalk: Random walks on wikipedia for semantic relatedness. In *2009 TextGraphs-4 Workshop*, 2009.

[28] T. Zesch and I. Gurevych. Wisdom of crowds versus wisdom of linguists? measuring the semantic relatedness of words. *Natural Language Engineering*, 16(1):25–59, 2010.

[29] T. Zesch, C. Mueller, and I. Gurevych. Using Wiktionary for computing semantic relatedness. In *AAAI*, pages 861–866, 2008.

Latent Association Analysis of Document Pairs

Gengxin Miao[†], Ziyu Guan[†], Louise Moser[†], Xifeng Yan[†], Shu Tao[♯], Nikos Anerousis[♯], Jimeng Sun[♯]
[†]University of California, Santa Barbara
[♯]IBM T. J. Watson Research Center
[†]{miao, moser}@ece.ucsb.edu, {ziyuguan, xyan}@cs.ucsb.edu
[♯]{shutao,nikos, jimeng}@us.ibm.com

Abstract

This paper presents Latent Association Analysis (LAA), a generative model that analyzes the topics within two document sets simultaneously, as well as the correlations between the two topic structures, by considering the semantic associations among document pairs. LAA defines a correlation factor that represents the connection between two documents, and considers the topic proportion of paired documents based on this factor. Words in the documents are assumed to be randomly generated by particular topic assignments and topic-to-word probability distributions. The paper also presents a new ranking algorithm, based on LAA, that can be used to retrieve target documents that are potentially associated with a given source document. The ranking algorithm uses the latent factor in LAA to rank target documents by the strength of their semantic associations with the source document. We evaluate the LAA algorithm with real datasets, specifically, the IT-Change and the IT-Solution document sets from the IBM IT service environment and the Symptom-Treatment document sets from Google Health. Experimental results demonstrate that the LAA algorithm significantly outperforms existing algorithms.

Source Code
`http://www.uweb.ucsb.edu/~miao/resources.html`

Categories and Subject Descriptors

I.7.0 [**Computing Methodologies**]: Document and Text Processing

Keywords

Topic Model, Variational Inference, Ranking Algorithm

1. INTRODUCTION

The numerous and diverse documents generated in business and society present both challenges and opportunities for data mining research. Among the common, yet relatively unexplored, types of documents are the documents that occur in pairs. Examples of such document pairs include questions and answers, changes to IT systems and consequent problems, disease symptoms and diagnoses, *etc.* Such document pairs can be used to build valuable knowledge bases that help improve decisions in business and society.

Change (Source)	Problem (Target)
Set the schedule of weekly CARS backup: 3am on Sundays.	The backup is running for a long time, which is impacting the start of daytime BMP processing.
Replication of new data is loaded for all customer centers.	Server outage: User can ping the server but failed to access the database.
Back up authentication server.	User reported can access E-Pricer without inputting password.

Table 1: Example Change Problem Document Pairs.

Table 1 shows example document pairs from the IBM IT Change document sets that contain changes to IT systems (source documents) and the resulting problems (target documents). Given such document pairs, we seek to address two fundamental problems:

1. What is the underlying principle that makes the connection between a pair of documents? (*Modeling*)
2. Given a source document, how do we use this principle to rank the target documents based on how strongly they are related to the source document? (*Ranking*)

The solutions to the *Modeling* and *Ranking* problems can help us understand the semantic connection (*i.e.*, *latent association*) between paired documents and can provide tremendous value in real-world applications. For instance, in the IT service industry, changes are frequently made to an operational IT environment, and the service consultants need to evaluate the potential problems caused by a proposed change, so that they can make plans accordingly.

Both the modeling and the ranking problems present great challenges that cannot be readily addressed using existing approaches. For instance, topic models, such as CTM [4], LDA [5] and PLSI [12], are designed to model only single document sets. However, we need not only to model individual documents correctly, but also to capture the connection between the documents accurately. Furthermore, the existence of one-to-many or many-to-one mappings in a bipartite graph suggests possibly different interpretations of the topics of a document. For example, a question might refer to different topics if the answers emphasize different aspects of the question. What we need is a model that puts a document in the context of a document pair and allows its topic proportion to be interpreted differently in different contexts. Existing topic models do not support flexible topic proportions in the same document. The ranking problem is also non-trivial. Given a source document, the number of potentially related target documents can be huge. The model needs to be able to identify an appropriate target document from a large number of candidates accurately.

In this paper, we present our novel Latent Association Analysis (LAA), which models the topic structures and their correlations together. In the LAA model, each document pair is considered as a randomly drawn correlation factor that initiates the connection between the two documents. The topic proportions of the two documents are drawn conditionally depending on the correlation factor. Each word in the documents is assumed to be generated based on a topic assignment and the topic-to-word probability distribution.

For LAA, we adopt concepts from two well-known models, namely, Correlated Topic Model (CTM) [4] and Canonical Correlation Analysis (CCA) [2]. We then develop a novel ranking algorithm to retrieve target documents based on their latent associations with the given source document. We evaluate the ranking algorithm using the IT-Change and the IT-Solution document sets from the IBM IT service environment and the Symptom-Treatment document sets from Google Health. Experimental results show that the LAA algorithm significantly outperforms existing algorithms, which confirms that LAA successfully captures the semantic-level connections among document pairs.

To the best of our knowledge, this work is the first such work to model paired document sets within a unified framework. Our contributions are two-fold. First, we show that exploring document-level correlations is more effective at capturing semantic topic associations in document pairs, compared to using word-level or topic-level correlations. LAA considers a document pair as a whole and, thus, can deliver better association semantics than existing approaches. Second, the ranking algorithm based on LAA performs exceptionally well for target document retrieval. Through diverse experiments, we show that this ranking algorithm has broad applications in document analysis and retrieval.

2. PROBLEM FORMULATION

The problem we address involves a source document set $\mathcal{D}_s$ and a target document set $\mathcal{D}_t$. Each source document $d_s \in \mathcal{D}_s$ is paired with at least one target document $d_t \in \mathcal{D}_t$, and vice versa. The pairing between source and target document sets can be represented by a bipartite graph $\mathcal{G}$, with its two sets of vertices being the source document set and the target document set, and its set of edges corresponding to the source and target document pairs. Specifically,

- $\mathcal{G} = \{\mathcal{D}_s \bigcup \mathcal{D}_t, \mathcal{E}\}$ is a bipartite graph with its vertices defined by a set $\mathcal{D}_s$ of source documents, a set $\mathcal{D}_t$ of target documents, and a set $\mathcal{E}$ of edges between documents in $\mathcal{D}_s$ and documents in $\mathcal{D}_t$.
- Each edge $e_i = (d_{is}, d_{it})$ represents a document pair, where $d_{is} \in \mathcal{D}_s$, $d_{it} \in \mathcal{D}_t$ and $e_i \in \mathcal{E}$.
- The vocabulary set of $\mathcal{D}_s$ is $\mathcal{W}_s = \{w_{s1}, ..., w_{sN_s}\}$, and the vocabulary set of $\mathcal{D}_t$ is $\mathcal{W}_t = \{w_{t1}, ..., w_{tN_t}\}$.

In the example in Table 1, there is a one-to-one mapping between the source and target documents. However, one-to-many or many-to-one mappings are not uncommon in other paired document sets. In this study, we consider the other mappings as special cases of one-to-one mappings and convert them to multiple one-to-one document pairs.

Given the above formulation, we aim to solve two problems: (1) *Modeling*: Model the associations between the source documents in $\mathcal{D}_s$ and the target documents in $\mathcal{D}_t$; (2) *Ranking*: For a new source document d_s, rank and retrieve the target document d_t, that is most likely to be associated with d_s, from a repository of target documents.

3. LATENT ASSOCIATION ANALYSIS

The objective of our modeling problem is different from that of existing work [4, 5, 12]. Our focus is to model the association between a pair of documents. The task is also different from traditional information retrieval tasks: (1) Our query involves a document, which is much noisier than a keyword query in traditional information retrieval tasks; (2) The source (query) document and the target documents to be retrieved arise from two separate document sets, for which we do not assume any vocabulary overlap. Therefore, similarity-based relevance scores do not apply to this problem. Conceptually, the association between the source and target documents can be considered at three different levels of granularity, yielding three possible solutions:

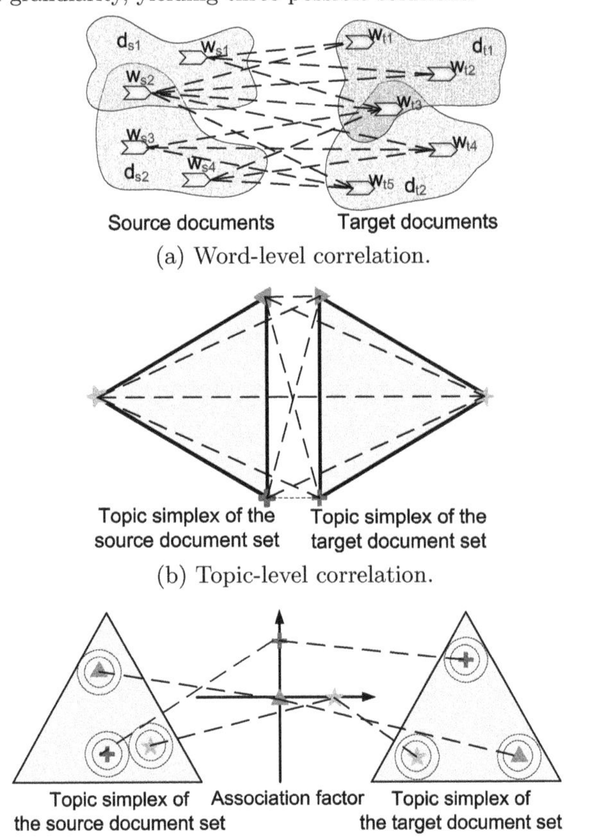

(a) Word-level correlation.

(b) Topic-level correlation.

(c) Document-level correlation.

Figure 1: Analyzing the Associations at Different Levels of Granularity.

Word-level correlation (Fig. 1(a)): Given individual words in the source documents, we can directly model whether and how they are correlated with the words in the target documents using a training dataset. Unfortunately, synonyms and polysemy in free text make the correlation at the word level noisy.

Topic-level correlation (Fig. 1(b)): Topics are more stable than words. Topic-level correlation can be analyzed in two ways: 1) learn two topic structures from the two document sets separately and then discover the mapping between the two topic spaces; 2) assume that the two document sets share the same topic space and analyze the common topics. A problem with the first approach is that topics learned separately might not reflect the associations in document pairs. A problem with the second approach is that the common topic space won't be able to capture the different semantic associations between pairs of documents.

Document-level correlation (Fig. 1(c)): Instead of generating topics separately, we can learn the topics for the source and target documents simultaneously. We define a correlation factor for a document pair. The topic proportions of the two documents are drawn based on this correlation factor. In this approach, the topic distribution of each (source or target) document is studied in the context of a document pair. This approach allows flexible topic assignment if the same source document is paired with different target documents, and vice versa. Thus, the same source document can have different topic assignments in different contexts. Hence, this approach handles the one-to-many or many-to-one mappings between two document sets smoothly, because mappings involving many documents are broken down into multiple document pairs that can be considered separately.

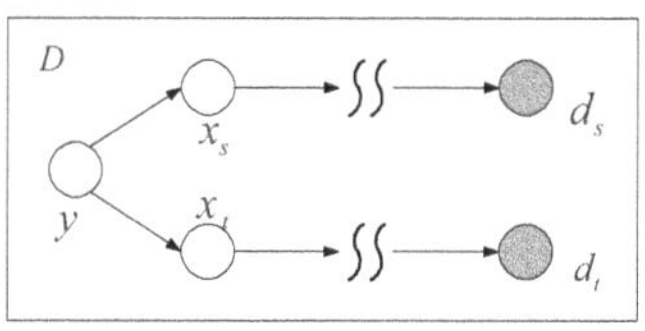

Figure 2: Basic LAA Framework.

The Latent Association Analysis (LAA) framework takes the document-level correlation approach. As shown in Fig. 2, the LAA framework consists of two components, the correlation factor y between two latent variables x_s and x_t, and the document-generation processes for d_s and d_t. We can instantiate LAA with different correlation models and topic models. Moreover, the models for generating source and target documents can differ. After learning based on training document pairs, LAA can be directly applied to solve our ranking problem: for a given query d_s, we can rank pairs (d_s, d_t) based on not only the topics of d_s and d_t, but also the correlation factor between them.

4. MODELING DOCUMENT PAIRS

In this section, we consider an instantiation of the LAA framework with the Canonical Correlation Analysis (CCA) [2] and the Correlated Topic Model (CTM) [4], and derive a variational method [3] to estimate the parameters for the model.

4.1 Canonical Correlation Analysis

Canonical Correlation Analysis [15] works on two sets of random variables and their covariance matrix. Two linear transformations are found for the two sets of random variables such that the two sets of projected variables have maximum correlation with each other. Bach *et al.* [2] gave a probabilistic interpretation of CCA and considered CCA as a model-based method that could be integrated with other probabilistic methods.

In CCA, the observed random variables $x_1 \in \mathbb{R}^{m_1}$ and $x_2 \in \mathbb{R}^{m_2}$ depend on a latent correlation factor $y \in \mathbb{R}^d$. The generative process can be described as follows.

- For a pair of variables, draw the correlation factor $y \sim \mathcal{N}(\mathbf{0}, \mathbf{I_d})$ where $\min\{m_1, m_2\} \geq d \geq 1$.

- For each set of random variables, draw
$x_1|y \sim \mathcal{N}(T_1 y + \mu_1, \Psi_1)$, $T_1 \in \mathbb{R}^{m_1 \times d}$, $\Psi_1 \succeq 0$
$x_2|y \sim \mathcal{N}(T_2 y + \mu_2, \Psi_2)$, $T_2 \in \mathbb{R}^{m_2 \times d}$, $\Psi_2 \succeq 0$.

In LAA, we can use CCA to capture the semantic association between the source document and the target document. The two random variables x_s and x_t are lower-dimensional representations of the source and target documents, respectively. The correlation factor y represents why these two documents are associated on a semantic level.

4.2 LAA

Whereas CCA can capture the semantic association in a document pair, other existing topic models can capture the topics of the two documents. These existing topic models include CTM [4], LDA [5], PLSI [12], *etc.* If PLSI is used, the random variables x_s and x_t are the topic proportions of the documents d_s and d_t. If LDA is used, the random variables x_s and x_t are the Dirichlet priors of the topic proportions in d_s and d_t. In both cases, the topics are assumed to be independent of each other; and the correlation between different topics cannot be properly modeled. If CTM is used, the topic proportion documents are assumed to have a multivariate Gaussian prior distribution, which is a natural fit with the Gaussian variables x_s and x_t in CCA. The correlation between different topics can be explicitly captured by the covariance matrix of the Gaussian distribution. In this paper, we choose CTM to instantiate LAA.

The instantiated LAA model is depicted in Fig. 3. The LAA model comprises the model parameters in the set $M = \{\Psi_s, T_s, \mu_s, \Psi_t, T_t, \mu_t, \beta_s, \beta_t\}$. For source and target documents d_s and d_t of lengths l_s and l_t, the words $w_{s,1:l_s}$ and $w_{t,1:l_t}$ in the source and target documents are the observable variables. The latent variables (*i.e.*, variables that are neither directly observable nor explicitly specified in the learned model) form the parameter set $V_l = \{y, x_s, x_t, z_{s,1:l_s}, z_{t,1:l_t}\}$.

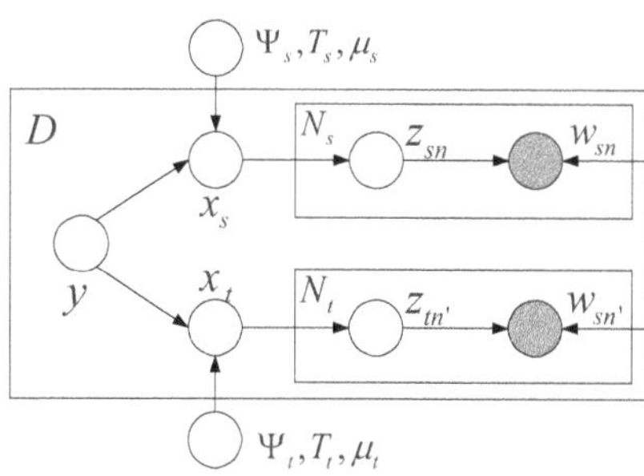

Figure 3: Instantiated LAA Model.

The generative process can be described as follows:

1. For each edge in the bipartite graph $\mathcal{G}$ (*i.e.*, a document pair), draw an L-dimensional Gaussian correlation factor: $y \in \mathcal{N}(0, I_L)$. The dimension L $<$ min $\{K_s, K_t\}$, where K_s is the number of topics in the source document set $\mathcal{D}_s$ and K_t is the number of topics in the target document set $\mathcal{D}_t$.

2. For each document pair connected by an edge, draw topic proportions as follows:
   For the source document, draw
   $x_s|y \sim \mathcal{N}(T_s y + \mu_s, \Psi_s)$; $T_s \in \mathbb{R}^{K_s \times L}$, $\Psi_s \succeq 0$.
   For the target document, draw
   $x_t|y \sim \mathcal{N}(T_t y + \mu_t, \Psi_t)$; $T_t \in \mathbb{R}^{K_t \times L}$, $\Psi_t \succeq 0$.

3. For each word in the source document, choose:
   (a) a topic $z_{sn}|x_s \sim \text{Mult}(\theta_s)$, where
   $\theta_{si} = \exp(x_{si})/\sum_j \exp(x_{sj})$ for $i \in \{1, 2, ...K_s\}$.
   (b) a word $w_{sn}|z_{sn}, \beta_s \sim \text{Mult}(\beta_{sz_{sn}})$.
   The topics and words in the target document are chosen in a similar manner.

Although the topic modeling portion of LAA stems from the idea of CTM, LAA is more complicated than the existing topic models: It is built on a set of document pairs, instead of a single document set as in existing topic models. As a result, the latent topic structures in the source and the target document sets, as well as their correlation, need to be analyzed simultaneously. LAA considers each edge in the bipartite graph as a correlation factor that initiates the connection between two documents. The generation process of the topic proportions depends on the correlation factor. That is, first, LAA decides what makes the connection between the source documents and the target documents at the document level. Then, LAA models the pair consisting of the source document and the target document as a co-occurrence interpreted by the correlation factor, instead of assuming a causal relationship between the two documents, which is difficult to validate.

It is worth noting that the topic proportion of a document is context-dependent. The same piece of text, in the eyes of different observers with different emphases, can belong to different topics. In LAA, each source or target document is put in the context of a pair, allowing the topic proportion of each document to be mutually enhanced and to be context-dependent. Doing so provides the flexibility of not deciding the topic of a document until we learn what is emphasized in the other document paired with it.

4.3 Variational Inference and Parameter Estimation

Given the LAA model described above, we solve the following problems: (1) Model fitting: Given a set of document pairs, how do we find model parameters that best fit the data? (2) Inference: For a new document pair, how do we decide the correlation factor y, the topic proportions x_s, x_t, and the topic assignments z for each word? The true posterior distributions are computationally intractable, when the hidden variables are not independent of each other, given an observed document pair. Similar to CTM, our LAA model employs a variational method to solve these problems.

4.3.1 Variational Inference

Consider a pair (d_s, d_t) of documents, represented as sets $\{w_{sn}\}$ and $\{w_{tn'}\}$ of words, where w_{sn} is the nth word in

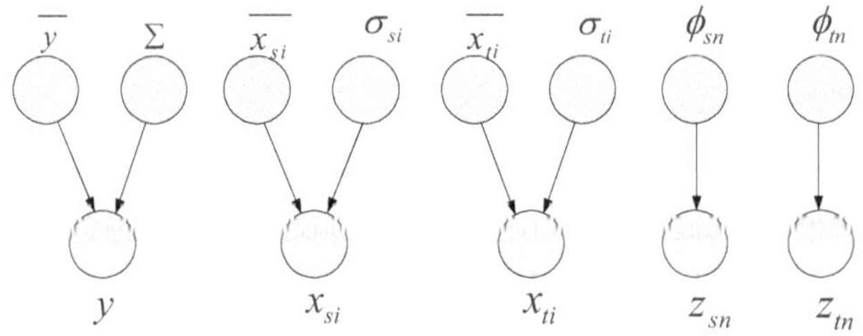

Figure 4: Variational Distribution.

d_s and $w_{tn'}$ is the n'th word in d_t, Eq. (1) gives the probability that the document pair arises from an LAA model represented by a parameter set M.

$$P(d_s, d_t|M) = \int_y \int_{x_s} \int_{x_t} P(y)P(x_s|y, M)P(x_t|y, M) \times \prod_{k'=1}^{K_t} \prod_{n'=1}^{l_t} (P(z_{tn'} = k'|x_t)P(w_{tn'}|z_{tn'}, \beta_t))d(x_t) \times \prod_{k=1}^{K_s} \prod_{n=1}^{l_s} (P(z_{sn} = k|x_s)P(w_{sn}|z_{sn}, \beta_s))d(x_s)d(y) \quad (1)$$

Ideally, the latent variables in the set V_l should be chosen to maximize the probability $P(d_s, d_t|M)$ to best fit the pair of documents. Unfortunately, it is computationally intractable to determine the true posterior distribution over V_l, because the latent variables are coupled together. Thus, we introduce a variational distribution $Q(V_l)$, in which the latent variables are independent of each other, to approximate the true posterior distribution $P(V_l|d_s, d_t)$. The graphical representation of Q is shown in Fig. 4. According to the variational distribution, $Q(y) \sim \mathcal{N}(\bar{y}, \Sigma)$, $Q(x_{si}) \sim \mathcal{N}(\bar{x}_{si}, \sigma_{si}^2)$, $Q(x_{ti}) \sim \mathcal{N}(\bar{x}_{ti}, \sigma_{ti}^2)$, $Q(z_{sn}) \sim \text{Mult}(\phi_{sn})$ and $Q(z_{tn}) \sim \text{Mult}(\phi_{tn})$. Note that each component in the topic proportions x_s and x_t is drawn independently. The variational parameters introduced in the variational distribution are fit such that the KL-divergence between $Q(V_l)$ and $P(V_l|d_s, d_t)$ is minimized.

Using the variational distribution and Jensen's inequality, we take the logarithm of the probability in Eq. (1) and rewrite the objective function in Eq. (2). Instead of maximizing the log likelihood directly, which is intractable, we maximize the lower bound of the log likelihood to obtain an approximation of the optimal value of the latent variables.

$$\log(P(d_s, d_t|M)) \geq E_Q \log(P(d_s, d_t|M)) + H(Q) = \lfloor \mathcal{L} \rfloor \quad (2)$$

The above maximization problem is a convex optimization problem and, thus, the optimal values of the variational parameters occur when the derivatives are zero. According to the decomposition of the marginal probability in Eq. (1), we expand the lower bound of the log likelihood as follows:

$$\lfloor \mathcal{L} \rfloor = \sum_n E_Q \log P(w_{sn}|z_{tn}, \beta_s) + \sum_{n'} E_Q \log P(w_{tn'}|z_{tn'}, \beta_t) + \sum_n E_Q \log P(z_{sn}|x_s) + \sum_{n'} E_Q \log P(z_{tn'}|x_t) + E_Q \log P(x_s|y, \Psi_s, T_s, \mu_s) + E_Q \log P(x_t|y, \Psi_t, T_t, \mu_t) + E_Q \log P(y) + H(Q(V_l)) \quad (3)$$

Each term on the right-hand side is a function over the variational parameters as shown in Eqs. (4) - (8):

$$\sum_n E_Q \log(P(w_{an}|z_{an},\beta_a)) = \sum_{n=1}^{l_a}\sum_{k=1}^{K_a} \phi_{ank}\log(\beta_{ank}) \quad (4)$$

Here, a represents the source document s or the target document t in a pair. Because a document pair is symmetric, we use the same set of equations with different subscripts.

According to LAA, the topic assignment z is drawn based on the Gaussian prior x, $P(z_n = k|x) = \frac{\exp(x_k)}{\sum_j \exp(x_j)}$. Let $\iota = \sum_j \exp(x_j)$. If we take the first-order Taylor expansion with respect to ι at point ζ to approximate $\log P(z_n = k|x)$, we have $\log P(z_n = k|x) = x_k - \log(\zeta) - \frac{1}{\zeta}(\sum_j \exp(x_j) - \zeta) + \mathcal{O}((\iota-\zeta)^2)$. Thus,

$$\sum_n E_Q \log(P(z_{an}|x_a)) \geq \sum_{n=1}^{l_a}\sum_{k=1}^{K_a} \phi_{ank}\bar{x}_{ak} - l_a\log(\zeta_a) - \frac{l_a}{\zeta_a}\sum_{k=1}^{K_a}\exp(\bar{x}_{ak} + \frac{\sigma_{ak}^2}{2}) + l_a \quad (5)$$

where ζ is an additional variational parameter.

$$E_Q\log(P(x_a)) = \frac{1}{2}\log(|\Psi_a^{-1}|) - \frac{1}{2}\mathrm{tr}(\mathrm{diag}(\sigma_a^2)\Psi_a^{-1}) - \frac{1}{2}\mathrm{tr}((T_a\bar{y} + \mu_a - \bar{x}_a)(\bar{y}^T T_a^T + \mu_a^T - \bar{x}_a^T)\Psi_a^{-1}) - \frac{1}{2}\mathrm{tr}(T_a\Sigma T_a^T\Psi_a^{-1}) + \mathrm{const} \quad (6)$$

$$E_Q\log(P(y)) = -\frac{1}{2}\log(2\pi) - \frac{1}{2}\mathrm{tr}(\Sigma) - \frac{1}{2}\bar{y}^T\bar{y} \quad (7)$$

$$H(Q) = -\sum_{a=s,t}\sum_{n=1}^{l_a}\sum_{k=1}^{K_a}\phi_{ank}\log(\phi_{ank}) + \frac{1}{2}\log(\det(\Sigma)) + \sum_{a=s,t}\sum_{k=1}^{K_a}\log(\sigma_{ak}) + \mathrm{const} \quad (8)$$

We substitute Eqs. (4)-(8) into Eq. (3), and then maximize the lower bound of the log likelihood by taking the partial derivatives with respect to each of the variational parameters and setting them to zero.

For the variational parameters ζ, ϕ, Σ and y, the optimal values that maximize the objective function are achieved by:

$$\zeta_a = \sum_k \exp(\bar{x}_{ak} + \frac{\sigma_{ak}^2}{2}) \quad (9)$$

$$\phi_{ank} \propto \beta_{akv}\exp(\bar{x}_{ak}) \text{ s.t. } w_{an}^v = 1 \quad (10)$$

$$\Sigma = \sum_{a=s,t} T_a^T\Psi_a^{-1}T_a + I_L \quad (11)$$

$$\bar{y} = \Sigma\sum_{a=s,t} T_a^T\Psi_a^{-1}(\bar{x}_a - \mu_a) \quad (12)$$

For the variational parameters $\bar{x}$ and σ, there are no analytical solutions. The optimal values of these variables are the solutions to Eqs. (13) and (14), which are solved iteratively using Newton's method.

$$\sum_n \phi_{an} - \frac{l_a}{\zeta_a}\exp(\bar{x}_a + \frac{\sigma_a^2}{2}) - \Psi_a^{-1}(T_a\bar{y} + \mu_a - \bar{x}_a) = 0 \quad (13)$$

$$\frac{l_a}{\zeta_a}\exp(\bar{x}_a + \frac{\sigma_a^2}{2}) + \mathrm{diag}(\Psi_a^{-1}) - \frac{1}{\sigma_a^2} = 0 \quad (14)$$

For each edge in the bipartite graph, we calculate the variational parameters using Eqs. (9) - (14) iteratively until the log likelihood lower bound in Eq. (3) no longer increases. The resulting variational parameter values are an approximation of the optimal values of the latent variables. Specifically, $y^* = \bar{y}$, $x_{ak}^* = \bar{x}_{ak}$, $z_{an}^* = \arg_k\max(\phi_{ank})$, where $a \in \{s,t\}$, $k \in \{1,2,...,K_a\}$, $n \in \{1,2,...l_a\}$.

4.3.2 *Parameter Estimation*

We estimate the model parameters using the variational expectation-maximization algorithm. In the E-Step, we update the variational parameters for each edge in the bipartite graph. In the M-Step, we update the model parameters, so that the sum of the log likelihood lower bound on each edge is maximized.

The process used in the M-Step is similar to that of variational inference. The goal here is to maximize the aggregated log likelihood of all the edges in the bipartite graph, rather than maximizing the log likelihood of a single edge. We sum the lower bounds of the log likelihood in Eq. (2) for each edge and take the partial derivative over the set M of model parameters. We then calculate the optimal values of the model parameters by setting the derivatives to zero.

$$\beta_{akv} \propto \sum_{e\in\mathcal{E}}\sum_n \phi_{adnk}1(w_{ean}^v = 1) \quad (15)$$
$$\text{s.t. } \textstyle\sum_v \beta_{akv} = 1$$

$$T_a = (\sum_{e\in\mathcal{E}}(\bar{x}_{ea}\bar{y}_e^T - \mu_a\bar{y}_e^T))(\sum_{e\in\mathcal{E}}(\bar{y}_e\bar{y}_e^T + \Sigma_e))^{-1} \quad (16)$$

$$\mu_a = \frac{1}{|\mathcal{E}|}(\sum_{e\in\mathcal{E}}\bar{x}_{ea} - T_a\sum_{e\in\mathcal{E}}\bar{y}_e) \quad (17)$$

$$\Psi_a = \frac{1}{|\mathcal{E}|}\sum_{e\in\mathcal{E}}(\mathrm{diag}(\sigma_{ea}^2) + T_a\Sigma_e T_a^T + (T_a\bar{y}_e + \mu_a - \bar{x}_{ea})(T_a\bar{y}_e + \mu_a - \bar{x}_{ea})^T) \quad (18)$$

The E-Step and the M-Step are performed iteratively until the model parameters converge, indicating that the model parameters fit the training dataset.

5. RANKING DOCUMENT PAIRS

Given an LAA model M learned from a training dataset, for a new source document d_s, we aim to rank the target documents in a test dataset according to their potential associations with the source document. In this section, we introduce three different approaches to this problem. In Section 6, we evaluate these three approaches, together with the PTM method proposed by Zhang *et al.* [25].

5.1 Two-Step Approach

First, we discuss the Two-Step approach that mines the topics in the target and source document sets independently and then determines the correlation between their topic structures. This method is used as the baseline for comparison with LAA.

The training process consists of two steps: (1) Find the topics in the source and target document sets; (2) Find the correlation between the source and target topic structures. In the first step, CTM is independently applied to the two document sets $\mathcal{D}_s$ and $\mathcal{D}_t$. The topic proportion priors x_s and x_t are obtained for $\mathcal{D}_s$ and $\mathcal{D}_t$, respectively, using the variational inference method presented in [4]. For each document pair (d_s, d_t), their corresponding topic proportion priors (x_s, x_t) form a pair. In the second step, these topic proportion priors (which follow Gaussian distributions) are fed into CCA. The CCA parameters T_1, T_2, μ_1, μ_2, Ψ_1, Ψ_2 are fit to the topic proportion pairs (x_s, x_t).

In the document retrieval task, given a new source document d_s, our goal is to rank the target documents in a test set. The candidates d_t are ranked based on the probability $P(d_t|d_s)$ that a target document d_t can be observed in a document pair containing the source document d_s.

We assume that the topic proportion priors x are a lower dimensional representation of the document d. Thus, $P(d_t|d_s) \propto P(x_t|x_s)$. In CCA, given x_1, the latent correlation factor y follows a normal distribution: $y|x_1 \sim \mathcal{N}(M_1^T U_{1d}^T(x_1 - \mu_1), I - M_1 M_1^T)$ [2], and given y, x_2 follows a normal distribution: $x_2|y \sim \mathcal{N}(T_2 y + \mu_2, \Psi_2)$. Thus, given the topic proportion prior x_s of a source document d_s, its corresponding document d_t has a topic proportion prior x_t that follows a normal distribution:

$$x_t|x_s \sim \mathcal{N}(T_1 M^T(x_s - \mu_1) + \mu_2, \Psi_2 + T_1(I - MM^T)T_1^T) \quad (19)$$

where $M = (P_l)^{1/2}$ and P_l is the diagonal matrix of the top l canonical correlations.

Given a source document d_s and a candidate target document d_t, their topic proportion priors x_s and x_t can be inferred using CTM. Thus, the target documents can be ranked using $P(x_t|x_s)$, calculated from Eq. (19).

5.2 LAA Direct Approach

The LAA model presented in Section 4 allows us to predict, for a new source document d_s, which target document d_t is more likely to be associated with d_s. A direct way of ranking target documents is to evaluate how likely a hypothetical document pair (d_s, d_t) arises from the underlying LAA model. The lower bound $\log(P(d_s, d_t|M))$ can be estimated by Eq. (3) using the variational inference method discussed in Section 4.3.1. Thus, we can use the function $R(d_s, d_t) = \lfloor \log(P(d_s, d_t|M)) \rfloor$ to rank the target documents. Because both the source and the target documents are considered to be a bag of interchangeable words in the LAA model, the generation probability of a long document is less than the generation probability of a short document. Note that, in this prediction method, the rank of a document pair is inversely proportional to the document length. To avoid unfairly penalizing long documents, we normalize all of the documents to unit length.

5.3 LAA Latent Approach

Although the above LAA direct approach is intuitive, it has some drawbacks. In ranking document pairs, the most important factor should be the semantic association between the source and target documents, whereas the exact wording of a document in expressing its semantic meaning should not be overemphasized. However, when evaluating a document pair using the probability that the document pair arises from the LAA model, the LAA direct approach considers all the words in the source and target documents to be equally important. As a consequence, if a target document contains rare words, it will have a low rank. The reason is that, even if the rare words in the target document might associate perfectly with the source document semantically, the probability of generating such words is still very small, which brings down the rank of the target document. Moreover, in our ranking method, the value of the correlation factor should not matter, as long as it interprets the semantic association in a document pair. The LAA direct approach cannot accommodate this feature either.

To address the aforementioned problems, we developed the LAA latent approach based on the semantic association between source and target documents. In this approach, only the topic association information is used to rank the document pairs. For any given source document d_s and candidate target document d_t, first we use variational inference to calculate the most probable correlation factor $y^* = \bar{y}$, and topic proportion $x_s^* = \bar{x}_s$ and $x_t^* = \bar{x}_t$, according to the variational distribution. Then, we evaluate how likely there exists an association between the two documents based on the topic proportion, and use the following ranking function to rank the target documents.

$$R(d_s, d_t) = P(x_s^*, x_t^*|y^*) = P(x_s^*|y^*)P(x_t^*|y^*) \quad (20)$$

In Eq. (20), $P(x_s|y^*) \sim \mathcal{N}(T_s y^* + \mu_s, \Psi_s)$, and $P(x_t|y^*) \sim \mathcal{N}(T_t y^* + \mu_t, \Psi_t)$.

6. EXPERIMENTS

We trained the LAA model based on real-world datasets and evaluated its performance for the document retrieval task. Two IT service datasets from IBM, the IT-Change and IT-Solution datasets, and a relatively smaller publicly available dataset from Google Health [1], the Symptom-Treatment dataset, were used to evaluate the effectiveness of the LAA ranking algorithm.

6.1 Datasets

The IT-Change dataset was obtained in the context of IT change management at IBM. In this dataset, each document pair consists of a change document, which describes the planned change, and a problem document, which describes the problem resulting from this change. Both the change and problem documents are written in free text, and the associations between them are established by a human expert. Given a historical IT-Change dataset, we built the LAA model and used it to retrieve the potential problem documents (from a set of problems reported) caused by a change request. The original dataset contains 24,317 pairs of documents. We randomly sampled 20,000 document pairs for training and used the rest to evaluate the performance of our ranking algorithm.

The IT-Solution dataset was obtained in the context of IT problem management at IBM. In this dataset, each document pair consists of a problem document and its corresponding solution document identified by a human expert. LAA is used to predict possible solutions for new problems. This dataset contains 19,696 pairs of documents. We ran-

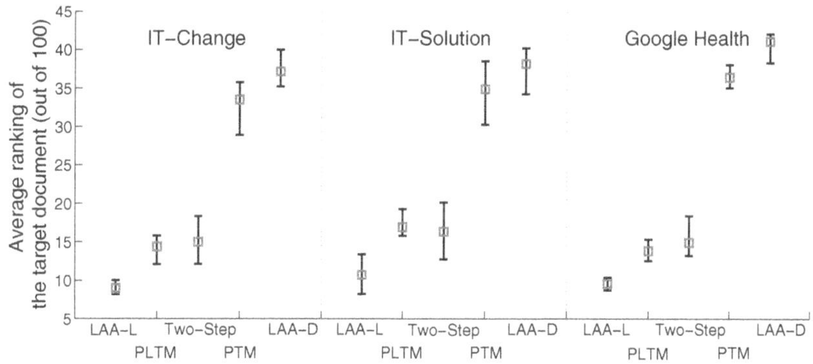

Figure 5: A Comparison of Retrieval Performance of the Different Methods Using Three Datasets.

domly selected 15,000 document pairs for training and the rest for testing.

The Google Health Symptom-Treatment dataset contains pairs of disease symptoms and treatments. This dataset is relatively small and contains 1,287 document pairs. We used 1,187 document pairs for training purposes and tested the model on the remaining 100 document pairs.

6.2 Accuracy Analysis

We compare our two LAA-based approaches, *i.e.*, LAA Direct (LAA-D) and LAA Latent (LAA-L), against the Two-Step method and the PTM method [25], as well as the Polylingual topic model (PLTM) [17], in terms of their accuracy in retrieving target documents for a given source document. For a given source document, PTM predicts a word distribution of its potential target document and compares it with the word distributions of the candidate documents. The word distribution of PTM has two components: one from the model, and the other from the similarity between the source and target documents. In LAA, we do not assume any overlap between the vocabularies of the source and target documents, which is a key advantage compared to PTM. For comparison purposes, we used only the model component in PTM as shown in Eq. (21) and adopted the KL-divergence distance [14] to evaluate the candidate target documents, as presented in [25].

$$P_{PTM}(w_t|d_s) = \sum_{i=1}^{K_s} P(w_t|\theta_i)P(\theta_i|d_s) \qquad (21)$$

Besides these methods, we also considered a two-way classification approach. We used the real source and target document pairs as positive samples, and randomly generated source and target document pairs as negative samples. Based on these labeled samples, we trained a classifier using SVM to predict future source and target document pairs. However, this approach does not work due to lack of good quality negative samples.

From each of the two datasets, we randomly selected a batch of 100 document pairs with one-to-one mappings between the source and target documents. Given a source document randomly selected within these 100 document pairs, we then ranked the 100 target documents based on the four different approaches. We used the average rank of the correct target document (the one actually paired with the selected source document) to measure the accuracy. We repeated this process for five batches (*i.e.*, 500 queries in total) for each datasets.

To train the LAA model, we varied the number of topics from 10 to 50, and chose the best performing models for the three datasets. For the IT-Change and IT-Solution datasets, we chose 20 topics for both the source and target document sets to train the three models. For the Google Health dataset, we chose 30 topics, where the model performed best. The dimensionality of the correlation factor was set to 10 for both the LAA models and the Two-Step method.

Fig. 5 compares the performance of these five approaches on the three datasets. The y-axis shows the average rank of the correct target document from the 100 target document candidates. For the IT-Change and IT-Solution datasets, each bar in the figure shows the performance range of one method over the five batches of test cases. The average over the five batches is marked in red on each bar. Because the Google Health dataset does not contain as many document pairs as the other two datasets, we investigated the accuracy of the model on only one batch of 100 test document pairs.

For all three datasets, LAA-L outperforms all other approaches, and the Two-Step method and PLTM perform closer to LAA-L. The key difference between LAA-L and the Two-Step method is that the topic structures of the source and target documents in the Two-Step method are learned independently without considering correlations between them. As a result, the performance of the Two-Step method is not as good as that of LAA-L.

PLTM, on the other hand, assumes a pair of linked documents that are identical in topic. A topic model is learned for all of the document pairs. For testing how likely a new source document and a new target document are associated, PLTM predicts their topic proportions independently and compares their similarities. PLTM is most effective when modeling the same set of articles written in different languages. In LAA, we don't assume that the topic proportions of a source document and the linked target document are the same. Hence, LAA is more general and can be applied to document sets that have arbitrary semantic associations, such as questions and answers, symptoms and diagnoses, *etc.*

LAA-D suffers from the problems discussed in Section 5.2 and does not perform well in our document retrieval task. Due to the noisy nature of word-level correlation (as noted in Section 3), the PTM method does not show good performance either. We also experimented with a modified version of PTM that compares the topic distributions, rather than the word distributions, between the source and target documents. The performance of this modified method is similar to that of the Two-Step method, but significantly worse than that of LAA-L.

6.3 Robustness Analysis

To show the robustness of the LAA-L model in capturing the semantic associations in document pairs, we trained the model with different numbers of topics and compared the results of the document retrieval task in an experimental setting similar to that in Section 6.2.

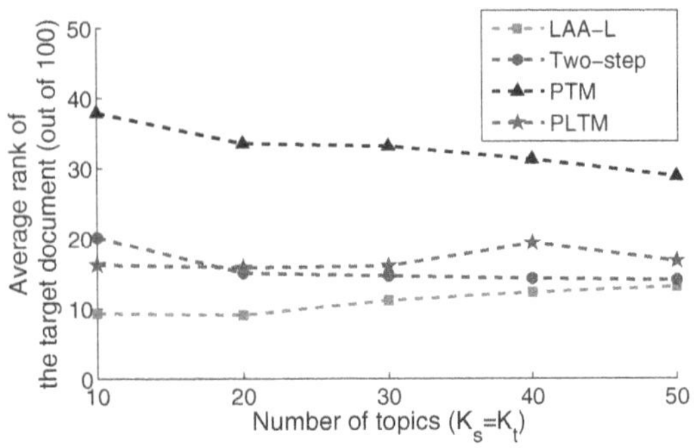

Figure 6: A Comparison of Ranks for the Different Methods Using Different Numbers of Topics.

Fig. 6 shows the experimental results for the IT-Change dataset. Limited by the space, we do not show the results for the IT-Solution and Google Health datasets, but the results are quite similar. We chose the same number of topics for the source and the target document sets, and the dimension of the correlation factor $L = \frac{1}{2}K_s = \frac{1}{2}K_t$. With different numbers of topics, the performance of the LAA-L approach remains stable, and is better than that of the other approaches.

6.4 Correlation Factor Analysis

The LAA framework assumes a correlation factor. The topic portion priors of a pair of documents are drawn centered around a point in their corresponding topic simplex. Because each point in the topic simplex implies a mixture of the topics and each topic is represented by a probability distribution of words, the point in the topic simplex can also be mapped to a distribution over words. Here, we show examples of correlation factors and the corresponding top-ranked words in the source and target documents. First, we choose a sample correlation factor, which can be mapped to the topic distributions in both the source and target document sets. The topic distribution can be further mapped to a word distribution using a linear combination of the topics. Then, we show the top-ranked word list. In these examples, the dimension of the correlation factor is set to 10. The number of topics in both the source and target document sets are set to 20. Note that the topic numbers in the source and target documents do not have to be the same.

As demonstrated in Fig. 7, the LAA model successfully captures the semantic-level connections between the source and target documents. Cases 1 and 2 were extracted from the IT-Change dataset, whereas cases 3 and 4 were from the IT-Solution dataset. For Cases 1 through 4, the top-ranked words indicate that the correlations between the source and target documents are around *Database, Network, Business,* and *Scheduling*, respectively[1].

[1]The labels for the correlation factors were added by the authors.

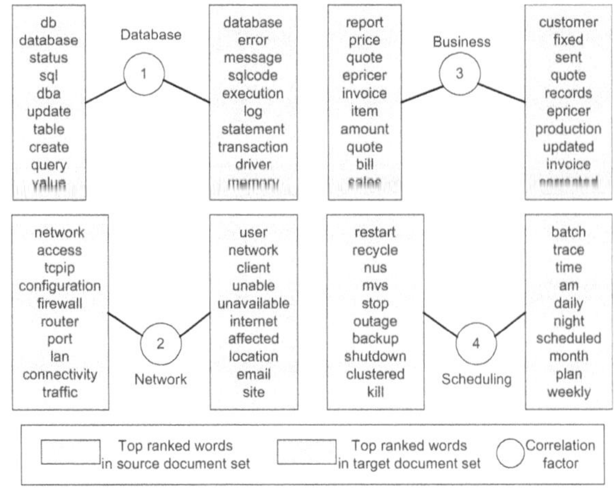

Figure 7: Sample Top Ranked Words Linked to the Same Correlation Factor.

7. RELATED WORK

Topic models have been extensively studied and have become a powerful tool for exploring the semantic content of large-scale document corpora. Most topic models deal with a single document corpus. LSI [8] uses SVD to approximate a high-dimensional document-to-word co-occurrence matrix using lower-dimensional document-to-topic and topic-to-word co-occurrence matrices. PLSI [12] introduces a probabilistic explanation of LSI. Neither LSI nor PLSI is naturally generalizable to new documents. To overcome this limitation, Blei *et al.* [5] proposed LDA, in which the topic proportions of documents are randomly drawn from a Dirichlet distribution. The Dirichlet prior is used to guide the generation of topic proportions for new documents. The CTM method [4] introduces a covariance matrix over the topic proportions and allows topics to be correlated with each other. IFTM [19] combines CTM with PCA [20] to allow exploration of a very large number of topics.

Besides the textual information in a document corpus, a number of topic models consider structural information. Steyvers *et al.* [21] use the authorship graph between authors and articles to explore author-to-topic relationships. Nallapati *et al.* [18] consider the citation graph for a document set to perform link predictions. Zhou *et al.* [28] study Web pages and tag graphs to explore user interests. Mei *et al.* [16] propose topic models with network regularization. Unlike those models, LAA focuses on document-to-document associations, and explores topics of two document sets simultaneously. Thus, LAA is better suited for ranking document pairs.

Researchers have studied topic structures of cross-lingual corpora. Zhao *et al.* [26, 27] explore probabilistic word alignments across languages using aligned bilingual document pairs, *i.e.*, the same set of articles written in two different languages. Mimno *et al.* [17] study the shared topic structure of an aligned document corpora over possibly many languages. Jagaralamudi *et al.* [13], assuming that a dictionary exists between words in two languages, analyze a single topic structure over bilingual unaligned document sets. MuTo [6] also utilizes word matchings in a dictionary to analyze the topics as distributions over the word pairs. Haghighi *et al.* [11] also applied the CCA model to learn bilingual translation lexicons.

8. CONCLUSION

This paper has presented one of the first attempts to tackle the problem of analyzing the topic structures of two document sets linked by a bipartite graph. The Latent Association Analysis (LAA) model draws the topic proportion priors of a pair of documents based on a correlation factor. Unlike other topic models, the goal of LAA is not only to provide a semantic-level explanation of the topics of the document pairs, but also to retrieve the associated target document, when a new source document is given. Using LAA, we introduced a document-level ranking method that can help to retrieve target documents associated with a source document. Experiments on real datasets confirm the effectiveness of our method for extracting semantic concepts of associated document pairs, and establish that LAA outperforms state-of-the-art algorithms in ranking document pairs. LAA can be extended to more complex association structures over multiple document sets. For other applications, the symmetric structure of the source and target documents can be replaced by an asymmetric structure, if that is more appropriate.

9. ACKNOWLEDGMENTS

The first author, Gengxin Miao, was supported by an IBM Ph.D. Fellowship. This research was also supported by the U.S. National Science Foundation under grant IIS-0954125 and by the Army Research Laboratory under cooperative agreement W911NF-09-2-0053 (NS-CTA). The views and conclusions contained herein are those of the authors and should not be interpreted as representing the official policies, either expressed or implied, of the Army Research Laboratory or the U.S. Government. The U.S. Government is authorized to reproduce and distribute reprints for Government purposes notwithstanding any copyright notice herein.

10. REFERENCES

[1] Google health: https://health.google.com.

[2] F. R. Bach and M. I. Jordan. A probabilistic interpretation of canonical correlation analysis. Technical report, Statistics Dept., UC Berkeley, 2006.

[3] C. M. Bishop. *Pattern Recognition and Machine Learning*. Springer, 2nd ed., October 2007.

[4] D. M. Blei and J. D. Lafferty. Correlated topic models. In *NIPS*, 2006.

[5] D. M. Blei, A. Y. Ng, and M. I. Jordan. Latent Dirichlet allocation. *JMLR*, 3:993–1022, 2003.

[6] J. Boyd-Graber and D. M. Blei. Multilingual topic models for unaligned text. In *UAI*, pages 75–82, 2009.

[7] H. T. Dang, D. Kelly, and J. J. Lin. Overview of the trec 2007 question answering track. In *TREC*, 2007.

[8] S. Deerwester, S. T. Dumais, G. W. Furnas, T. K. Landauer, and R. Harshman. Indexing by latent semantic analysis. *J. American Society for Information Science*, 41(6):391–407, 1990.

[9] P. Forner, A. Penas, E. Agirre, I. Alegria, C. Forascu, N. Moreau, P. Osenova, P. Prokopidis, P. Rocha, B. Sacaleanu, R. Sutcliffe, and E. Tjong Kim Sang. Overview of the clef 2008 multilingual question answering track. In *Evaluating Systems for Multilingual and Multimodal Information Access*, LNCS 5706, pages 262–295. 2009.

[10] J. Gao, K. Toutanova, and W. tau Yih. Clickthrough-based latent semantic models for Web search. In *SIGIR*, pages 675–684, 2011.

[11] A. Haghighi, P. Liang, T. Berg-Kirkpatrick, and D. Klein. Learning bilingual lexicons from monolingual corpora. In *ACL*, pages 771–779, 2008.

[12] T. Hofmann. Probabilistic latent semantic indexing. In *SIGIR*, pages 50–57, 1999.

[13] J. Jagaralamudi and H. Daumé. Extracting multilingual topics from unaligned corpora. In *ECIR*, 2010.

[14] J. Lafferty and C. Zhai. Document language models, query models, and risk minimization for information retrieval. In *SIGIR*, pages 111–119, 2001.

[15] K. V. Mardia, J. T. Kent, and J. M. Bibby. *Multivariate Analysis*. Academic Press, 1979.

[16] Q. Mei, D. Cai, D. Zhang, and C. Zhai. Topic modeling with network regularization. In *WWW*, pages 101–110, 2008.

[17] D. Mimno, H. M. Wallach, J. Naradowsky, D. A. Smith, and A. Mccallum. Polylingual topic models. In *EMNLP*, pages 880–889, Singapore, 2009.

[18] R. M. Nallapati, A. Ahmed, E. P. Xing, and W. W. Cohen. Joint latent topic models for text and citations. In *SIGKDD*, pages 542–550, 2008.

[19] D. P. Putthividhya, H. T. Attias, and S. Nagarajan. Independent factor topic models. In *ICML*, pages 833–840, 2009.

[20] J. Shlens. A tutorial on principal component analysis. In *Systems Neurobiology Laboratory, Salk Institute for Biological Studies*, 2005.

[21] M. Steyvers, P. Smyth, M. Rosen-Zvi, and T. Griffiths. Probabilistic author-topic models for information discovery. In *SIGKDD*, pages 306–315, 2004.

[22] T. Strohman, W. B. Croft, and D. Jensen. Recommending citations for academic papers. In *SIGIR*, pages 705–706, 2007.

[23] B. Taskar, M. F. Wong, P. Abbeel, and D. Koller. Link prediction in relational data. In *NIPS*, 2003.

[24] X. Xue, J. Jeon, and W. B. Croft. Retrieval models for question and answer archives. In *SIGIR*, pages 475–482, 2008.

[25] D. Zhang, J. Sun, C. Zhai, A. Bose, and N. Anerousis. PTM: Probabilistic topic mapping model for mining parallel document collections. In *CIKM*, pages 1653–1656, 2010.

[26] B. Zhao and E. P. Xing. Bitam: Bilingual topic admixture models for word alignment. In *COLING/ACL*, pages 969–976, 2006.

[27] B. Zhao and E. P. Xing. HM-BiTAM: Bilingual topic exploration, word alignment, and translation. In *NIPS*, 2007.

[28] D. Zhou, J. Bian, S. Zheng, H. Zha, and C. L. Giles. Exploring social annotations for information retrieval. In *WWW*, pages 715–724, 2008.

LIEGE: Link Entities in Web Lists with Knowledge Base

Wei Shen[1], Jianyong Wang[1], Ping Luo[2], Min Wang[2]
[1]Department of Computer Science and Technology, Tsinghua University, Beijing, China
[2]HP Labs China, Beijing, China
[1]chen-wei09@mails.tsinghua.edu.cn, jianyong@tsinghua.edu.cn
[2]{ping.luo, min.wang6}@hp.com

ABSTRACT

A critical step in bridging the knowledge base with the huge corpus of semi-structured Web list data is to link the entity mentions that appear in the Web lists with the corresponding real world entities in the knowledge base, which we call list linking task. This task can facilitate many different tasks such as knowledge base population, entity search and table annotation. However, the list linking task is challenging because a Web list has almost no textual context, and the only input for this task is a list of entity mentions extracted from the Web pages. In this paper, we propose LIEGE, the first general framework to Link the entIties in wEb lists with the knowledGe basE to the best of our knowledge. Our assumption is that entities mentioned in a Web list can be any collection of entities that have the same conceptual type that people have in mind. To annotate the list items in a Web list with entities that they likely mention, we leverage the prior probability of an entity being mentioned and the global coherence between the types of entities in the Web list. The interdependence between different entity assignments in a Web list makes the optimization of this list linking problem NP-hard. Accordingly, we propose a practical solution based on the iterative substitution to jointly optimize the identification of the mapping entities for the Web list items. We extensively evaluated the performance of our proposed framework over both manually annotated real Web lists extracted from the Web pages and two public data sets, and the experimental results show that our framework significantly outperforms the baseline method in terms of accuracy.

Categories and Subject Descriptors

H.3.3 [**Information Systems**]: Information Storage and Retrieval—*Information Search and Retrieval*

General Terms

Algorithms, Experimentation

Keywords

List linking, Knowledge base, Similarity metric, Iterative substitution

1. INTRODUCTION

A large number of Web pages contain data structured in the form of lists. A Web list on some Web page may enumerate a list of famous American basketball players, a list of best-selling albums in the United States or a list of films directed by James Cameron. In addition, table which is another major source of structured data on the Web can be regarded as a set of lists/columns. Therefore, lists are considered as a general data structure to express entity references. Items in Web lists often refer to entities, however, as being free text form, the list items are potentially ambiguous: the same textual name may refer to several different real world entities. For instance, the entity mention of "Michael Jordan" can refer to the famous basketball player, the computer science professor who is one of the keynote speakers in KDD'12, or some other persons.

Recently, the success of Wikipedia and the development of information extraction techniques have facilitated the automated construction of large scale machine-readable knowledge base about the world's entities, their semantic classes and their mutual relationships. Such kind of notable endeavors include DBpedia [2], KnowItAll [9], YAGO [21, 20] and KOG [23, 24]. Bridging these knowledge bases with the semi-structured Web lists is beneficial for the exploitation of this huge corpus of structured data on the Web. Additionally, the list linking task enables powerful join and union operations that can integrate information across different lists, tables and pages.

The list linking task is of practical importance and can be used in various applications. For instance, 75% of the tables on the Web typically have a column that is the subject of the table, and the subject column contains the set of entities the table is about [22]. Linking this subject column with the knowledge base is significantly helpful for the task of table annotation [16] and recovering the semantics of tables [22]. As another example, linking the Web lists or table columns with a knowledge base can enrich the existing knowledge base and impulse the trend to advance the traditional keyword-based search to the semantic entity-based search.

In recent years, considerable progresses have been made in linking entities in free text with a knowledge base [3, 6, 7, 13, 15, 19]. When linking entities in free text, the textual context is considered as the key evidence for disambiguation. The essential step in these previous approaches is to define a similarity measure between the text around the entity mention and the document associated with the entity. While in our setting, lists never have any header text information and textual context. The only input for the list linking task is a list of entity mentions extracted from the Web pages, such as the Web list on the left of Figure 1. On the other hand, most of the methods addressing the problem of linking entities in free text exploit the observation that entities mentioned from a single document are likely to be semantically related [6, 15, 19]. However, the entities in a Web list can be any set of entities that have the same conceptual type, and they are semantically similar, rather than semantically related. Accordingly, this observation for linking entities in free text clearly cannot be applied to the Web list data. From these two dimensions mentioned above, it can be seen that the list linking task is challenging and different from the task of linking entities in free text. Moreover, we are interested in linking these Web list items in a fully automatic manner, and avoid tedious tuning or parameter settings.

Given a knowledge base about the world's entities, their semantic classes and their mutual relationships, for each Web list in the list corpus, our goal is to link each list item in the Web list with the real world mapping entity existing in the knowledge base. In this paper, we propose LIEGE, a general framework to annotate the list items in the Web lists with entities based on the assumption that entities in a list can be any set of entities that have the same conceptual type. Specifically, we propose to measure the *linking quality* of the candidate mapping entities in a straightforward and comprehensive way. Intuitively, a candidate mapping entity is "good" for some list item if it has two key properties: (1) the prior probability of the entity being mentioned is high; (2) the type of the candidate mapping entity is coherent with the types of the other mapping entities in the same list, in the sense that they represent a list of entities having the same conceptual type. If the type of an entity is coherent with the type of another entity, we say these two entities are semantically similar. To calculate the semantic similarity between entities, we leverage two categories of information: (1) type hierarchy based similarity; (2) distributional context similarity. To combine these signals to give the *linking quality* for each candidate mapping entity, we use the max-margin technique to automatically learn the proper weights for different features. The interdependence between different entity assignments in a Web list makes the inference of this problem NP-hard. Thus, we develop a practical and effective solution based on the iterative substitution to jointly optimize the entity assignments for each Web list.

Contributions. The main contributions of this paper are summarized as follows.

- We propose LIEGE, the first framework that can effectively link list items in the Web lists with the mapping entities in the knowledge base to the best of our knowledge.
- We propose to use the max-margin technique to automatically learn the proper weights for different features to calculate the *link quality* for each candidate mapping entity, which allows LIEGE to run without tedious parameter tuning.
- We propose a practical and effective algorithm, called *iterative substitution algorithm*, to jointly optimize the identification of the mapping entities for the list items of each Web list.
- To verify the effectiveness of our framework, we evaluated our proposed framework LIEGE over both manually annotated real Web list data set and two public data sets, and the experimental results show that our framework significantly outperforms the baseline method in terms of accuracy.

The remainder of this paper is organized as follows. Section 2 introduces some preliminaries and notations. We present the framework of LIEGE in Section 3. Section 4 presents our experimental results and Section 5 discusses the related work. Finally, we conclude this paper in Section 6.

2. PRELIMINARIES AND NOTATIONS

In this section, we begin by describing the knowledge base and the task of list linking. Next, we introduce the generation of candidate mapping entities for each list item.

Knowledge base. The knowledge base consists of a type hierarchy and entities that are instances of types. The set of types is denoted by T, and each $t \in T$ is a type, such as the type *American singers*. Types are connected by the subtype relation $t_1 \subset t_2$, which means t_1 is a subtype of t_2. For example, *American singers* is a subtype of *Singers*. We use $t_1 \subset^* t_2$ to denote that t_2 is an ancestor node of t_1 in the type hierarchy. The set of entities existing in the knowledge base is denoted by E, and each $e \in E$ is an entity, such as the entity *Michael Jackson*. We say entity e is an instance of one type t, denoted by $e \in t$. For instance, the entity *Michael Jackson* is an instance of the type *American singers*. We also use $e \in^* t$ to denote that type t is an ancestor node of entity e in the hierarchy, thus, we can say, *Michael Jackson* $\in^*$ *Singers*. Let $T(e) = \{t|e \in t\}$ be the set of types of which entity e is the instance. Likewise, let $E(t) = \{e|e \in^* t\}$ be the set of entities having type t as an ancestor node in the hierarchy. In this paper, the knowledge base we adopt is YAGO [21, 20], an open-domain ontology combining Wikipedia and WordNet [10] with high coverage and quality. In YAGO, they use unique canonical strings from Wikipedia as the entity names. Currently, YAGO contains about 250,000 types and over one million entities.

List linking. The input of our framework LIEGE is a collection of Web lists, and let L be a Web list with $|L|$ items. We use $1 \leq i \leq |L|$ to index the list item in L, and the list item with index i is denoted by l_i. Each list item $l_i \in L$ is a token sequence of an entity mention that is potentially linked with an entity in the knowledge base (see Figure 1 for an example). For this list L, it is noted that we do not have a name for it (i.e., the type of entities this list L enumerates). And there are no textual context and header text about this list L. Here, we formally state the list linking task as follows. Given the set of entities E in the knowledge base and the Web list L, the goal is to identify the mapping entity list M, with the same size as L, such that each $m_i \in M$ is the mapping entity for the corresponding list item $l_i \in L$. In this paper, we assume that the knowledge base contains all the mapping entities for all the list items, i.e., $M \subset E$.

Candidate mapping entity. For each $l_i \in L$, the mapping entity m_i should be the entity that may be referred by

Table 1: A part of the dictionary D

K (Mention form)	$K.value$ (Mapping entity)
IBM	*IBM*
HP	*Hewlett-Packard*
Michael Jordan	*Michael Jordan* *Michael I. Jordan* *Michael Jordan (mycologist)* *Michael Jordan (footballer)* ...
Bill Hewlett	*William Reddington Hewlett*

the token sequence of l_i. Therefore, we firstly identify all the entities that may be referred by l_i, and denote this set of entities as the candidate mapping entity set R_i for the list item l_i. Let $R = \{R_i | l_i \in L\}$ be the set of candidate mapping entity sets for all the list items in the Web list L.

To identify R_i for each $l_i \in L$, we need to build a dictionary D that contains vast amount of information about various mention forms of the named entities, like name variations, abbreviations, confusable names, spelling variations, nicknames, etc. The structure of the Wikipedia provides a set of useful features for the creation of such a dictionary D. In addition, Wikipedia has high coverage of named entities [25], which is profitable for constructing the dictionary D as well. The dictionary D is a <key, value> mapping, where the column of the key K is a list of mention forms and the column of the mapping value $K.value$ is the set of named entities which are referred by the key K. We construct the dictionary D by leveraging the following four structures of Wikipedia:

Entity page: Each entity page in Wikipedia describes a single entity, and generally, the title of each entity page is the most common name for that entity, e.g., the page title "IBM" for that giant American company headquartered in Armonk. Thus, we add the title of the entity page to the key K, and add the entity described in this page to $K.value$.

Redirect page: A redirect page exists for each alternative name which can be used to refer to an existing entity in Wikipedia. For example, the redirect page titled "HP" contains a pointer to the entity page titled "Hewlett-Packard". Henceforth, we add the title of the redirect page to the key K, and add the pointed entity to $K.value$.

Disambiguation page: When multiple entities in Wikipedia could be given the same name, a disambiguation page is created to separate them and contains a list of references to those entities. For instance, the disambiguation page for the name "Michael Jordan" lists eight associated entities having the same name of "Michael Jordan", including the famous NBA player and the Berkeley professor. For each disambiguation page, the title of this page is added to the key K, and the entities listed in this page are added to $K.value$.

Hyperlink in Wikipedia article: The article in Wikipedia often contains some hyperlinks each of which links to the page of the corresponding entity mentioned in this article. For example, in the entity page titled "Hewlett-Packard", there is a hyperlink pointing to the entity *William Reddington Hewlett* whose anchor text is "Bill Hewlett". Then we add the anchor text of the hyperlink to the key K, and add the pointed entity to $K.value$.

Using the four structures of Wikipedia described above, we construct the dictionary D. A part of the dictionary D is shown in Table 1. For each list item $l_i \in L$, we look up the dictionary D and search for l_i in the column of the key K. If a hit is found, i.e., $l_i \in K$, we add the set of the entities $l_i.value$ to the candidate mapping entity set R_i. We denote the size of R_i as $|R_i|$, and use $1 \le j \le |R_i|$ to index the candidate entity in R_i. The candidate mapping entity with index j in R_i is denoted by $r_{i,j}$.

In most cases, the size of the candidate mapping entity set is larger than one. Figure 1 shows an example. The Web list in Figure 1 enumerates 6 best-selling single-volume books on the left. For each list item, we show its candidate mapping entity set generated from the dictionary D on the right of the figure, and the real mapping entity is underlined. It is noted that in Figure 1 each candidate entity has the name which is the unique canonical string for that entity in Wikipedia, and the size of the candidate mapping entity set for most of the list items (5 out of 6) is larger than 1.

3. LIST LINKING

In this section, we introduce how to pick the proper entity from R_i as the mapping entity m_i for the list item l_i, when $|R_i| > 1$. We firstly illustrate how to define the *linking quality* metric for each candidate mapping entity in Section 3.1. Next, we show how to learn the proper weights for different features to calculate the *link quality* for each candidate mapping entity in Section 3.2. Finally, we present an effective algorithm, called *iterative substitution algorithm*, to jointly optimize the identification of the mapping entities for the list items of each Web list in Section 3.3.

3.1 Linking quality metric

Since each list item can refer to several candidate entities, it is nontrivial to select the mapping entity of the list item from the candidate mapping entity set. In this section, we propose an intuitive and comprehensive metric to measure the *linking quality* of the candidate mapping entity.

Prior probability: The first observation we have is that, each candidate mapping entity $r_{i,j} \in R_i$ having the same mention form l_i has different popularity, and some entities are very obscure and rare for the given mention form l_i. For the example in Figure 1, for the list item "A Tale of Two Cities", the candidate entity *A Tale of Two Cities (musical)*, the stage musical by Jill Santoriello, is much rarer than the candidate entity *A Tale of Two Cities*, the novel by Charles Dickens, and in most cases when people mention "A Tale of Two Cities", they mean the novel rather than the stage musical whose name is also "A Tale of Two Cities". We formalize this observation via taking advantage of the count information from Wikipedia, and define the *prior probability* $P_{pr}(r_{i,j})$ for each candidate mapping entity $r_{i,j} \in R_i$ with respect to the list item l_i as the proportion of the links with the mention form l_i as the anchor text which point to the candidate mapping entity $r_{i,j}$:

$$P_{pr}(r_{i,j}) = \frac{count(r_{i,j})}{\sum_{u=1}^{|R_i|} count(r_{i,u})} \quad (1)$$

where $count(r_{i,j})$ is the number of links which point to entity $r_{i,j}$ and have the mention form l_i as the anchor text.

For the example in Figure 1, with respect to the list item "A Tale of Two Cities", the *prior probability* of the entity *A Tale of Two Cities*, the novel, is 0.6528, while the *prior probability* of the entity *A Tale of Two Cities (musical)*, the

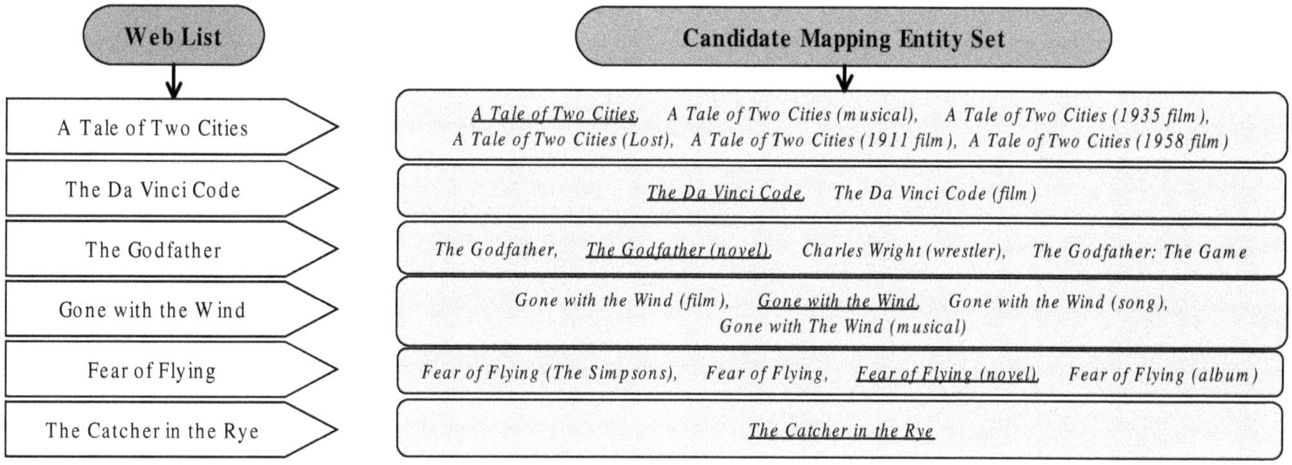

Figure 1: The candidate mapping entities for an example Web list

stage musical, is 0.1319. And the *prior probabilities* of all other candidate entities for the list item "A Tale of Two Cities", e.g., *A Tale of Two Cities (1935 film)*, *A Tale of Two Cities (Lost)*, are much smaller than that for the entity *A Tale of Two Cities*. Moreover, in Figure 1, the candidate mapping entities for each list item are ranked by their *prior probabilities* shown on the right of the figure in decreasing order. It can be seen that the notion of *prior probability* suitably expresses the popularity of the candidate mapping entity being mentioned given a mention form.

Coherence: A Web list usually enumerates some entities which have the same conceptual type. As an example, the Web list in Figure 1 enumerates some best-selling single-volume books. We observe that the definition of *prior probability* does not capture the contextual meaning the Web list represents. For the example in Figure 1, for the list item "The Godfather", the entity *The Godfather*, an American epic crime film, which has the highest *prior probability*, is not the corresponding mapping entity for this list item in this Web list. The same situation occurs for the list items "Gone with the Wind" and "Fear of Flying" in Figure 1. Accordingly, to choose the mapping entity for a list item, we should select the candidate entity whose type is coherent with the types of the other mapping entities in the same Web list. In other words, the mapping entity for some list item should be semantically similar to the other mapping entities in the same Web list. Therefore, we have the intuition that the more semantically similar the candidate mapping entity is to the other mapping entities in the same Web list, the more likely the candidate entity is the correct mapping entity for the list item. To capture this intuition, we formally define the notion of *coherence* $Coh(r_{i,j})$ for each candidate mapping entity $r_{i,j} \in R_i$ as:

$$Coh(r_{i,j}) = \frac{1}{|L|-1} \sum_{u=1, u \neq i}^{|L|} Sim(r_{i,j}, m_u) \tag{2}$$

where m_u is the mapping entity for the list item $l_u \in L$, and $Sim(e_1, e_2)$ is the function that measures the semantic similarity between entities e_1 and e_2, $e_1, e_2 \in E$.

To calculate the semantic similarity between entities, we leverage two categories of information in this paper: (1) type hierarchy based similarity; (2) distributional context similarity.

Type hierarchy based similarity: To measure the semantic similarity between entities based on type hierarchy, we have the assumption that two entities are semantically similar if they are in close places in the type hierarchy. Given two entities $e_1, e_2 \in E$, $T(e_1) = \{t|e_1 \in t\}$ is the set of types of which entity e_1 is the instance in the knowledge base, likewise, $T(e_2) = \{t|e_2 \in t\}$. To measure the semantic similarity $Sim_{hr}(e_1, e_2)$ between e_1 and e_2 based on type hierarchy, we firstly define how to calculate the semantic similarity between the sets of types $T(e_1)$ and $T(e_2)$. Since the sizes of $T(e_1)$ and $T(e_2)$, and the elements in $T(e_1)$ and $T(e_2)$ are likely to be different, we start by defining the correspondence between the elements of types from one set to another set. For each type $t_1 \in T(e_1)$, we assign a target type $\varepsilon(t_1)$ in another set $T(e_2)$ as follows: $\varepsilon(t_1) = \arg\max_{t_2 \in T(e_2)} Sim_{hr}(t_1, t_2)$, where $Sim_{hr}(t_1, t_2)$ is the semantic similarity between two types t_1 and t_2 based on type hierarchy, and $\varepsilon(t_1)$ is the type in $T(e_2)$ which maximizes the semantic similarity between these two types.

To compute $Sim_{hr}(t_1, t_2)$, we adopt the approach introduced in [17] which is an information-theoretic method. Assuming $t \in T$ is a type in the knowledge base, the amount of information contained in the statement "$x \in t$" is $-log(P(t))$, where $P(t)$ is the probability that a randomly selected entity e belongs to $E(t)$, which is the set of entities having the type t as an ancestor node in the hierarchy. We also assume that t_0 is the lowest common ancestor node for type nodes t_1 and t_2 in the hierarchy. The following is the definition of the semantic similarity between types t_1 and t_2 based on type hierarchy:

$$Sim_{hr}(t_1, t_2) = \frac{2 \times log(P(t_0))}{log(P(t_1)) + log(P(t_2))} \tag{3}$$

Next, we can calculate the semantic similarity from one set of types $T(e_1)$ to another set of types $T(e_2)$:

$$Sim_{hr}(T(e_1) \rightarrow T(e_2)) = \frac{\sum_{t_1 \in T(e_1)} Sim_{hr}(t_1, \varepsilon(t_1))}{|T(e_1)|} \tag{4}$$

Similarly, we can calculate the semantic similarity from $T(e_2)$ to $T(e_1)$, i.e., $Sim_{hr}(T(e_2) \rightarrow T(e_1))$, in the similar way to that in Formula 4. Based on the definitions mentioned above, we can define the semantic similarity between entities e_1 and e_2 based on type hierarchy as the average of the semantic similarity from $T(e_1)$ to $T(e_2)$ and that from $T(e_2)$ to $T(e_1)$:

$$Sim_{hr}(e_1, e_2) = \frac{Sim_{hr}(T(e_1) \to T(e_2)) + Sim_{hr}(T(e_2) \to T(e_1))}{2} \tag{5}$$

For the example in Figure 1, the semantic similarity between entities *A Tale of Two Cities* and *The Da Vinci Code*, a mystery-detective novel, based on the type hierarchy is 0.9527, while the semantic similarity between *A Tale of Two Cities (musical)* and *The Da Vinci Code* is much smaller, i.e., 0.3637.

Distributional context similarity: To measure the semantic similarity between entities based on the contexts where they appear in the external document corpus (e.g. the Wikipedia article corpus), we have the assumption that entities that occur in similar contexts are semantically similar, which is the extension of the distributional hypothesis [14]. We define the document context η_e for each entity $e \in E$ as the set of windows of words (removing all punctuation symbols) before and after each occurrence of the entity e in the external document corpus. Assume that an entity e of length $|e|$ words appears in a document at position p. The size-k document context η_e of entity e should contain these two windows of words, i.e., $w_{p-k}, \ldots, w_{p-1}$ and $w_{p+|e|}, \ldots, w_{p+|e|+k-1}$, around the occurrence of e. For instance, the entity *A Tale of Two Cities* occurs in a document containing such a sentence, "Simplified versions of *A Tale of Two Cities*, a novel by Charles Dickens, have been published ...". When the size k is set to 4, we should add the windows "Simplified versions of" and "a novel by Charles" to the document context of the entity *A Tale of Two Cities.* To compute the n-gram vector V_e for each entity $e \in E$, we firstly add all n-grams in the size-k document context η_e of entity e together with their frequencies, and then discard the top W most frequent n-grams which appear in this vector V_e. In the experiments, we set $k = 4$, $W = 50$. In order to measure the distributional context similarity between entities e_1 and e_2, we calculate the cosine similarity of the two n-gram vectors V_{e_1} and V_{e_2} for entities e_1 and e_2 respectively as follows:

$$Sim_{ds}(e_1, e_2) = \frac{\sum_{i=1}^{g} a_i * b_i}{\sqrt{\sum_{i=1}^{g} a_i^2} * \sqrt{\sum_{i=1}^{g} b_i^2}} \tag{6}$$

where g is the number of distinct n-grams in the union of the n-gram vectors for entities e_1 and e_2, each $a_i(b_i)$ is the frequency of the corresponding n-gram which appears in the vector $V_{e_1}(V_{e_2})$, and $V_{e_1} = \langle a_1, a_2, \ldots, a_g \rangle$, $V_{e_2} = \langle b_1, b_2, \ldots, b_g \rangle$.

For the example in Figure 1, the distributional context similarity between entities *A Tale of Two Cities* and *The Da Vinci Code* is 0.0934, while the distributional context similarity between *A Tale of Two Cities (musical)* and *The Da Vinci Code* is much smaller, i.e., 0.0137.

In this paper, we only leverage these two categories of information to calculate the semantic similarity between entities, the function Sim in Formula 2 could be either one of these two semantic similarity metrics, i.e., Sim_{hr} and Sim_{ds}, or their weighted sum. In addition, we emphasize that our framework is general and extensible enough that any other semantic similarity methods can be easily plugged in to be used.

Linking quality: Based on the observation that both *prior probability* and *coherence* contribute to the *linking quality* of candidate mapping entity, we define the *linking quality* $LQ(r_{i,j})$ for each candidate mapping entity $r_{i,j} \in R_i$ as the weighted sum of *prior probability* and *coherence* as follows:

$$LQ(r_{i,j}) = \alpha * P_{pr}(r_{i,j}) + (1 - \alpha) * Coh(r_{i,j}) \tag{7}$$

where α is a weight factor that balances the importance between *prior probability* and *coherence.*

With the definition of *linking quality* for each candidate mapping entity, we also define the *linking quality* for the mapping entity list M as the sum of the *linking qualities* of the mapping entities for all the list items with respect to the Web list L:

$$LQ(M) = \alpha * \sum_{s=1}^{|L|} P_{pr}(m_s) + (1 - \alpha) * \sum_{s=1}^{|L|} Coh(m_s) \tag{8}$$

where $m_s \in M$ and $Coh(m_s)$ can be calculated in the way introduced in Formula 2. Thus, we have

$$LQ(M) = \alpha * \sum_{s=1}^{|L|} P_{pr}(m_s) + \frac{1-\alpha}{|L|-1} * \sum_{s=1}^{|L|} \sum_{u=1, u \neq s}^{|L|} Sim(m_s, m_u) \tag{9}$$

Now, we formally state the list linking task as follows:

List linking: *Given the set of entities E in the knowledge base, the Web list L and the definition of linking quality in Formula 9, the goal is to identify the mapping entity list $M \subset E$, with size $|L|$, such that the objective function $LQ(M)$ is maximized.*

However, the inference problem of identifying the mapping entity list $M \subset E$, with size $|L|$, which maximizes the objective function $LQ(M)$ is NP-hard. The hardness can be shown using a reduction from the maximal clique problem[11]. Details of proof are omitted to save space.

3.2 Weight learner

To measure the *linking quality* $LQ(r_{i,j})$ for each candidate mapping entity $r_{i,j} \in R_i$, we use the definitions introduced in Formulae 7 and 2. Thus, we have

$$LQ(r_{i,j}) = \alpha * P_{pr}(r_{i,j}) + \frac{1-\alpha}{|L|-1} * \sum_{u=1, u \neq i}^{|L|} Sim(r_{i,j}, m_u) \tag{10}$$

where the function Sim could be the weighted sum of the two semantic similarity metrics, i.e., Sim_{hr} and Sim_{ds}, introduced in Formulae 5 and 6 respectively. Thus,

$$LQ(r_{i,j}) = \alpha * P_{pr}(r_{i,j}) + \beta * \frac{1}{|L|-1} \sum_{u=1, u \neq i}^{|L|} Sim_{hr}(r_{i,j}, m_u) + \gamma * \frac{1}{|L|-1} \sum_{u=1, u \neq i}^{|L|} Sim_{ds}(r_{i,j}, m_u) \tag{11}$$

where $\alpha + \beta + \gamma = 1$, and α, β and γ are weight factors that give different weights for different feature values in the calculation of the *linking quality* $LQ(r_{i,j})$. Here, we denote $\overrightarrow{w}$ as the weight vector, and $\overrightarrow{w} = \langle \alpha, \beta, \gamma \rangle$. In this section, we introduce how to learn the weight vector $\overrightarrow{w}$ based on the training data set.

To learn $\overrightarrow{w}$, we use a max-margin technique based on the training data set. Given the ground truth mapping entity $m_i \in M$ for each list item $l_i \in L$, we assume that the *linking quality* of the mapping entity $LQ(m_i)$ is larger than the *linking quality* of any other candidate entity $LQ(r_{i,j})$ with a margin, where $r_{i,j} \in R_i$ and $r_{i,j} \neq m_i$. This gives us the usual SVM linear constraints for all list items:

$$\forall l_i, \forall r_{i,j} \neq m_i \in R_i : LQ(m_i) - LQ(r_{i,j}) \geq \xi_{l_i} \quad (12)$$

and we maximize the objective $C_{l_i} \sum_{l_i} \xi_{l_i}$ where C_{l_i} is a constant with respect to ξ_{l_i}, to learn the weight vector $\overrightarrow{w} = \langle \alpha, \beta, \gamma \rangle$ such that $\alpha + \beta + \gamma = 1$.

If the assumption is violated by some list item l_i, that is to say, $LQ(m_i)$ is smaller than $LQ(r_{i,j})$ for all $r_{i,j} \neq m_i \in R_i$, we have $\xi_{l_i} < 0$. Therefore, for the list item l_i which violates the assumption, i.e., $\xi_{l_i} < 0$, we give some penalty to it and set $C_{l_i} = \theta$, where θ is a constant that is larger than 1, called penalty parameter; Otherwise, for the list item l_i, $\xi_{l_i} \geq 0$, we set $C_{l_i} = 1$. θ is the only parameter we have to set in our framework, and in the experiments, we show that the choice of θ does not affect the results of our framework greatly. Accordingly, our framework can run without tedious parameter tuning.

3.3 Iterative substitution algorithm

As the inference problem of identifying the mapping entity list $M \subset E$, with size $|L|$, which maximizes the objective function $LQ(M)$ is NP-hard, we propose an effective algorithm, called *iterative substitution algorithm*, to jointly optimize the identification of the mapping entity list M for each Web list L in this section.

The *iterative substitution algorithm* starts with a good guess of the mapping entity list from the candidate mapping entity sets, and then iteratively refines the mapping entity list to improve the *linking quality* as defined in Formula 9, until the algorithm converges and a local maximum of the *linking quality* of the mapping entity list is reached. To improve the *linking quality* of the mapping entity list in each iteration, the algorithm replaces the mapping entity of the previous iteration with the candidate mapping entity which maximizes the improvement of the overall *linking quality* of the mapping entity list. The details of the *iterative substitution algorithm* are described in Algorithm 1.

The *iterative substitution algorithm* depicted in Algorithm 1 takes the Web list L and the candidate mapping entity sets R as input, and outputs the mapping entity list M for the Web list L. We firstly calculate the *prior probability* $P_{pr}(r_{i,j})$ for each candidate entity $r_{i,j}$ in the candidate entity set R_i of each list item l_i, as defined in Formula 1, and pick the candidate entity which has the maximum *prior probability* as the initial estimate of the mapping entity $m_i^{(0)}$ for the list item l_i (line 1-line 3). Let $M^{(0)}$ be the initial mapping entity list for the Web list L (line 4). In the subsequent iterations in the while loop, we iteratively identify the new mapping entity list $M^{(iter)}$ based on the mapping entity list of previous iteration $M^{(iter-1)}$, and gradually improve the *linking quality* of the mapping entity list until the algorithm converges and a local maximum is reached (line 6-line 20). Specifically, in each iteration $iter$, for each candidate mapping entity $r_{i,j} \neq m_i^{(iter-1)} \in R_i$ of each list item $l_i \in L$, where $m_i^{(iter-1)}$ is the estimate of the mapping entity for l_i of previous iteration, we compute the new mapping entity

Algorithm 1 *Iterative Substitution Algorithm*

Input: Web list L, candidate mapping entity sets R.
Output: mapping entity list M.

1: **for** each $l_i \in L$ **do**
2: $\quad m_i^{(0)} = \arg\max_{r_{i,j}} P_{pr}(r_{i,j}),\ r_{i,j} \in R_i$
3: **end for**
4: $M^{(0)} = \{m_i^{(0)} | l_i \in L\}$
5: $iter = 1$
6: **while** true **do**
7: $\quad$ **for** each $l_i \in L$ **do**
8: $\quad\quad$ **for** each $r_{i,j} \neq m_i^{(iter-1)} \in R_i$ **do**
9: $\quad\quad\quad M_{r_{i,j}}^{(iter)} = (M^{(iter-1)} - \{m_i^{(iter-1)}\}) \bigcup \{r_{i,j}\}$
10: $\quad\quad\quad IncreLQ_{r_{i,j}} = LQ(M_{r_{i,j}}^{(iter)}) - LQ(M^{(iter-1)})$
11: $\quad\quad$ **end for**
12: $\quad$ **end for**
13: $\quad r_{i,j}^{max} = \arg\max_{r_{i,j}} IncreLQ_{r_{i,j}}, \quad r_{i,j} \in R_i, R_i \in R$
14: $\quad$ **if** $IncreLQ_{r_{i,j}^{max}} > 0$ **then**
15: $\quad\quad M^{(iter)} = (M^{(iter-1)} - \{m_i^{(iter-1)}\}) \bigcup \{r_{i,j}^{max}\}$
16: $\quad\quad iter++$
17: $\quad$ **else**
18: $\quad\quad$ break
19: $\quad$ **end if**
20: **end while**
21: $M = M^{(iter-1)}$

list $M_{r_{i,j}}^{(iter)}$ assuming that we substitute $r_{i,j}$ for $m_i^{(iter-1)}$ to choose $r_{i,j}$ as the mapping entity for l_i in iteration $iter$ (line 9), and then calculate the improvement of the *linking quality* of the mapping entity list $IncreLQ_{r_{i,j}}$ if this substitution is operated (line 10). Let $r_{i,j}^{max}$ be the candidate entity which achieves the maximum improvement of the *linking quality* of the mapping entity list (line 13). If $IncreLQ_{r_{i,j}^{max}} > 0$, we substitute $r_{i,j}^{max}$ for $m_i^{(iter-1)}$ to generate the mapping entity list $M^{(iter)}$ of iteration $iter$, and continue the iteration(line 14-line 16). Otherwise, if $IncreLQ_{r_{i,j}^{max}} \leq 0$, the algorithm has converged and reached a local maximum, thus, we stop the algorithm (line 18) and return $M^{(iter-1)}$ as the result of the mapping entity list M for L (line 21).

We state that the computation of the mapping entity list M in Algorithm 1 is guaranteed to **converge**, and the *iterative substitution algorithm* depicted in Algorithm 1 is bound to terminate. Here, we give out the proof of the convergence of the *iterative substitution algorithm*. We note that the *linking quality* of the mapping entity list $LQ(M^{(iter)})$ of each iteration $iter$ is greater than the *linking quality* of the mapping entity list $LQ(M^{(iter-1)})$ of the previous iteration $(iter - 1)$. Thus, we can say that the *linking quality* $LQ(M^{(iter)})$ is monotonically increasing with the number of iteration $iter$. Moreover, since $M \subset E$, the number of different mapping entity lists is finite. The linking quality $LQ(M)$ has an upper bound. Accordingly, we know that the *iterative substitution algorithm* is bound to stop and the computation of M in Algorithm 1 converges. Though we do not know the upper bound on the number of iterations Algorithm 1 may run until it terminates, in our experiments, we observe that it converges quickly and typically takes only a few iterations.

Table 2: Summary of the data sets

	# tables	# lists	# list items
Wiki_Manual	36	66	1691
Web_Manual	371	550	9239
Web_Lists	N/A	50	2520

Table 3: Experimental results over Wiki_Manual

Approach	# correctly linked	Accuracy
TableAnno	1419	0.8392
$\text{LIEGE}_{\beta=0,\gamma=0}$	1461	0.8640
$\text{LIEGE}_{\beta=0}$	1519	0.8983
$\text{LIEGE}_{\gamma=0}$	1498	0.8850
LIEGE_{full}	**1536**	**0.9083**

Table 4: Experimental results over Web_Manual

Approach	# correctly linked	Accuracy
TableAnno	7518	0.8137
$\text{LIEGE}_{\beta=0,\gamma=0}$	7925	0.8578
$\text{LIEGE}_{\beta=0}$	8219	0.8896
$\text{LIEGE}_{\gamma=0}$	8097	0.8764
LIEGE_{full}	**8249**	**0.8928**

4. EXPERIMENTS

To evaluate the effectiveness of LIEGE, we present a thorough experimental study in this section. We firstly describe the experimental setting in Section 4.1 and then show the experimental results in Section 4.2.

4.1 Experimental setting

To the best of our knowledge, there is no publicly available data set for the list linking task. However, we found that the table annotation task introduced in [16] has a subtask, whose goal is to annotate the table cells in Web tables with the mapping entities in the knowledge base. Though this subtask is not the same as our list linking task, we could regard each column of each table in the data sets as a Web list, and used the ground truth annotation in [16] to evaluate the performance of our framework. Specifically, we used two Web table data sets, i.e., Wiki_Manual and Web_Manual, introduced in [16]. The Wiki_Manual data set contains 36 (non-Infobox) tables selected from Wikipedia article text, and the Web_Manual data set consists of 371 Web tables similar to the Web tables in Wiki_Manual. The main difference between Wiki_Manual and Web_Manual is that the cells in the latter are more noisy. In both of these two data sets, the table cells whose mapping entities do not exist in the knowledge base have been dropped from the labeling task [16]. A summary of the data sets used in this paper is shown in Table 2. From the summary in Table 2, we can see that the average number of annotated columns for each table is less than 2 in both Wiki_Manual and Web_Manual data sets.

In addition, to verify the effectiveness of our framework over the real Web list data set, we collected 50 Web lists from the Web and manually annotated the list items with the mapping entities in the knowledge base, which we refer as the Web_Lists data set. The Web lists in our Web_Lists data set enumerate various kinds of entities, such as a list of American basketball coaches, a list of best-selling single-volume books and a list of best films winning the Empire Award. In our experiments, we evaluate the performance of LIEGE using only the list items whose mapping entities exist in the knowledge base. The summary of this data set is also shown in Table 2.

In the following experiments, we used YAGO(1)[1] of version 2008-w40-2 as the knowledge base, which is the same version as that used in [16]. We downloaded the May 2011 version of Wikipedia to construct the dictionary D introduced in Section 2. Then we used the dictionary D to generate the candidate mapping entity set R_i for each list item $l_i \in L$. If the size of the candidate mapping entity set $|R_i|$ of some list item l_i equals 0, we considered that the textual form of this list item has some noise. We processed this kind of list items by some methods, such as eliminating appositives (either within parentheses or following a comma), removing the sequence number at the beginning of the textual form, eliminating the redundant white spaces in the textual form and correcting the spelling errors using the query spelling correction supplied by Google. Then we generated the candidate mapping entity sets for these list items using the dictionary D again. To generate the document context for each entity to calculate the distributional context similarity, we employed these downloaded 3.5 million Wikipedia pages as the external document corpus, where each entity in the Wikitext has been converted to its canonical representation. To learn the weight vector introduced in Section 3.2, we set $\theta = 100$. In the next section, we will show that the results of our framework LIEGE is insensitive to the parameter θ and the choice of θ does not affect the results greatly. To evaluate the results of our framework, we calculated the *accuracy* as the number of correctly linked list items divided by the total number of all list items.

[1]http://www.mpi-inf.mpg.de/yago-naga/yago/

4.2 Experimental results

We compared our framework LIEGE with the algorithm proposed in [16], which we refer as *TableAnno*, over the Wiki_Manual and Web_Manual data sets. To give a fair comparison, we used the Wiki_Manual data set to learn the weight vector $\overrightarrow{w}$ and testing was done over the Wiki_Manual and Web_Manual data sets, which is the same way as that proposed in [16]. The experimental results of the baseline method *TableAnno* performing collective inference in the full model over the Wiki_Manual and Web_Manual data sets introduced in [16] are shown in Tables 3 and 4, respectively. The experimental results of our framework LIEGE over the Wiki_Manual and Web_Manual data sets are also presented in Tables 3 and 4 respectively. In these two tables, besides the accuracy, we also show the number of correctly linked list items. For our framework LIEGE, we do not only show the performance of LIEGE leveraging all the features introduced in this paper, which we refer as LIEGE_{full}, but also present the performance of LIEGE leveraging a subset of the features. When we calculated the *linking quality* using the Formula 11, if we set $\beta = 0$ and $\gamma = 0$, it means we only leveraged the feature of *prior probability* to address the list linking task, which we refer as $\text{LIEGE}_{\beta=0,\gamma=0}$. If we only set $\beta = 0$, it means that we leveraged the features of *prior probability* and distributional context similarity, which we refer as $\text{LIEGE}_{\beta=0}$. Likewise, if we only set $\gamma = 0$, it means that we leveraged the features of *prior probability* and type hierarchy based similarity, which we refer as $\text{LIEGE}_{\gamma=0}$. From

Table 5: Experimental results over Web_Lists

Approach	# correctly linked	Accuracy
$\text{LIEGE}_{\beta=0,\gamma=0}$	1969	0.7813
$\text{LIEGE}_{\beta=0}$	2329	0.9242
$\text{LIEGE}_{\gamma=0}$	2265	0.8988
LIEGE_{full}	**2352**	**0.9333**

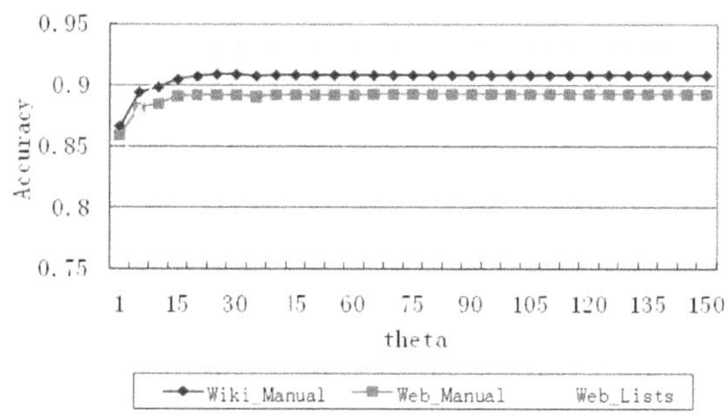

Figure 2: Sensitivity analysis to θ

the experimental results shown in Tables 3 and 4, we obtain the same conclusion that our framework leveraging different subsets of features achieves significantly higher accuracy than the baseline method *TableAnno*, which performs collective inference using entities, types and relationships. It can be also seen from the results in Tables 3 and 4 that every feature has a positive impact on the performance of our framework, and with the combination of all features LIEGE can obtain the best results.

The baseline method *TableAnno* is proposed to deal with the table annotation task [16], while for the Web list data set, *TableAnno* cannot perform collective inference using entities, types and relationships. Moreover, the approach $\text{LIEGE}_{\beta=0,\gamma=0}$, only leveraging the feature of *prior probability*, significantly outperforms the approach *TableAnno* over both Wiki_Manual and Web_Manual data sets. Thus, we did not compare our framework LIEGE with the *TableAnno* method over the Web_Lists data set. To learn the weight vector $\vec{w}$ on the Web_Lists data set, we used 2-fold cross validation. We show the experimental results of LIEGE leveraging different subsets of features over the Web_Lists data set in Table 5. From the results in Table 5, it can be seen that the list linking task over the Web_Lists data set is more challenging compared with that over the Wiki_Manual and Web_Manual data sets, as the accuracy achieved by the approach $\text{LIEGE}_{\beta=0,\gamma=0}$ over the Web_Lists data set (78.13%) is much smaller than those over the Wiki_Manual (86.40%) and Web_Manual (85.78%) data sets. However, the approach LIEGE_{full} leveraging all the features obtains very high accuracy over the Web_Lists data set, which demonstrates the effectiveness of our framework LIEGE over the Web list data set.

To better understand the performance characteristics of our proposed LIEGE framework, we conducted sensitivity analysis to understand the influence of the parameter θ to the results of LIEGE. Here, we used our framework leveraging all the features LIEGE_{full} as the example. Figure 2 depicts the performance of LIEGE_{full} with varied parameter θ over these three data sets, i.e., Wiki_Manual, Web_Manual and Web_Lists, respectively. Recall that the parameter θ is called the penalty parameter in Section 3.2, which gives some penalty to the list item which violates the assumption. From the trends plotted in Figure 2, it can be seen that when θ is set to be larger than 40, the accuracies achieved by LIEGE_{full} are stable with varied θ and remain the best over these three data sets, which demonstrates that the results of our framework are insensitive to the parameter θ, and the choice of θ does not affect the results greatly. Thus, we set $\theta = 100$ in all experiments introduced above. While we only report the performance of LIEGE_{full} over these three data sets, similar trends are observed for the approaches $\text{LIEGE}_{\beta=0}$ and $\text{LIEGE}_{\gamma=0}$ over all these three data sets.

5. RELATED WORK AND DISCUSSION

As more and more knowledge bases like DBpedia [2], KnowItAll [9], YAGO [21, 20] and KOG [23, 24] are available publicly, considerable progresses have been made in linking entities in free text with a knowledge base [3, 6, 7, 13, 15, 19]. Entity linking is the task to link a textual entity mention in the unstructured free text, with the corresponding real world entity in an existing knowledge base. Bunescu and Pasca [3] firstly tackled this problem by exploiting a set of useful features derived from Wikipedia for entity detection and disambiguation. They leveraged the bag of words model to measure the cosine similarity between the context of the mention and the text of the Wikipedia article, and selected the entity whose Wikipedia article is most similar to the context where the mention appears as the mapping entity for this mention. Cucerzan [6] proposed a solution which is the first system to recognize the global document-level topical coherence of the entities. The system addresses the entity linking problem through a process of maximizing the agreement between the context of the entity mention and the contextual information extracted from the Wikipedia, as well as the agreement among the categories associated with the candidate entities. The learning based solution in [7] focuses on the classification framework to resolve entity linking. It develops a comprehensive feature set based on the entity mention, the contextual document and the knowledge base entry, and then uses a SVM ranker to score each candidate entity. Han and Sun [13] proposed a generative probabilistic model for the entity linking task. This model incorporates multiple types of heterogenous entity knowledge, i.e., popularity knowledge, name knowledge and context knowledge. Our previous work [19] proposed LINDEN to deal with the entity linking task. LINDEN is a novel framework to link named entities in text with a knowledge base unifying Wikipedia and WordNet, by leveraging the rich semantic knowledge embedded in the Wikipedia and the taxonomy of the knowledge base. In all these work, the essential step is to define a similarity measure between the text around the entity mention and the document associated with the entity. While in our list linking task, lists never have any header text information and textual context. The only input for the list linking task is a list of entity mentions extracted from the Web pages. Therefore, these methods cannot be applied to our list linking task.

Kulkarni *et al.* [15] proposed a general collective disambiguation approach based on the observation that coherent documents refer to entities from one or a few related topics or domains, and entities mentioned from a single document are likely to be semantically related. In that paper, they gave precise formulations for the trade-off between local compatibility between mention and entity and measures of global coherence between entities. However, this observation cannot be applied to the Web list data, since the entity mentions in a Web list can be any set of entities that have the same conceptual type, that is to say, they are semantically similar, rather than semantically related. Accordingly, it can be seen that the list linking task is challenging and greatly different from the traditional entity linking task.

Another thread of research related to our work is managing structured data on the Web [1, 4, 5, 18, 8, 12, 22, 16]. These solutions were proposed to find, extract and integrate structured data on the Web. The work most related to our list linking task is the model proposed in [16] to address the problem of table annotation. In that paper, the table annotation task is defined as three subtasks: annotating each column of the table with one or more types, annotating pairs of columns with a binary relation in the knowledge base and mapping table cells with entities that they likely mention in the knowledge base. They proposed a new probabilistic graphical model for simultaneously associating entities for cells, types for columns and binary relations for column pairs. Specifically, they modeled the table annotation problem as a joint distribution over variables, and the goal is to find optimal values to the variables that maximize the joint probability. However, for the subtask of annotating table cells with entities, they did not consider the prior probability of entities being mentioned and the semantic similarity between each pair of entities in the same column or list, which have been shown to be significantly important and effective in our experiments for the list linking task.

6. CONCLUSION

In this paper, we have studied the problem of list linking. We propose LIEGE, the first framework that can effectively link list items in the Web lists with a knowledge base to the best of our knowledge. LIEGE is based on the observation that the type of the mapping entity should be coherent with the types of the other mapping entities in the same Web list. To evaluate the effectiveness of LIEGE, a thorough experimental study was conducted, and the experimental results demonstrate that our framework significantly outperforms the baseline method in terms of accuracy. Moreover, LIEGE can run in a fully automatic manner without tedious parameter tuning.

7. ACKNOWLEDGMENTS

This work was supported in part by National Natural Science Foundation of China under Grant No. 60833003, National Basic Research Program of China (973 Program) under Grant No. 2011CB302206, and an HP Labs Innovation Research Program award.

8. REFERENCES

[1] A. Arasu and H. Garcia-Molina. Extracting structured data from web pages. In *Proceedings of the 2003 ACM SIGMOD international conference on Management of data*, pages 337–348, 2003.

[2] S. Auer, C. Bizer, G. Kobilarov, J. Lehmann, and Z. Ives. Dbpedia: A nucleus for a web of open data. In *Proceedings of ISWC*, pages 11–15, 2007.

[3] R. Bunescu and M. Pasca. Using Encyclopedic Knowledge for Named Entity Disambiguation. In *Proceedings of EACL*, pages 9–16, 2006.

[4] M. J. Cafarella, A. Halevy, D. Z. Wang, E. Wu, and Y. Zhang. Webtables: exploring the power of tables on the web. *Proc. VLDB Endow.*, 1:538–549, August 2008.

[5] M. J. Cafarella, A. Halevy, Y. Zhang, D. Z. Wang, and E. Wu. Webtables: exploring the power of tables on the web. In *Proceedings of WebDB*, 2008.

[6] S. Cucerzan. Large-Scale Named Entity Disambiguation Based on Wikipedia Data. In *Proceedings of EMNLP-CoNLL*, pages 708–716, 2007.

[7] M. Dredze, P. McNamee, D. Rao, A. Gerber, and T. Finin. Entity disambiguation for knowledge base population. In *Proceedings of COLING*, pages 277–285, 2010.

[8] H. Elmeleegy, J. Madhavan, and A. Halevy. Harvesting relational tables from lists on the web. *Proc. VLDB Endow.*, 2:1078–1089, August 2009.

[9] O. Etzioni, M. Cafarella, D. Downey, S. Kok, A.-M. Popescu, T. Shaked, S. Soderland, D. S. Weld, and A. Yates. Web-scale information extraction in knowitall: (preliminary results). In *Proceedings of WWW*, pages 100–110, 2004.

[10] C. Fellbaum, editor. *WordNet: An Electronic Lexical Database.* MIT Press, Cambridge, MA, 1998.

[11] M. R. Garey and D. S. Johnson. *Computers and Intractability; A Guide to the Theory of NP-Completeness.* W. H. Freeman & Co., New York, NY, USA, 1990.

[12] R. Gupta and S. Sarawagi. Answering table augmentation queries from unstructured lists on the web. *Proc. VLDB Endow.*, 2:289–300, August 2009.

[13] X. Han and L. Sun. A generative entity-mention model for linking entities with knowledge base. In *Proceedings of ACL*, pages 945–954, 2011.

[14] Z. Harris. Distributional structure. *Word*, 10(23):146–162, 1954.

[15] S. Kulkarni, A. Singh, G. Ramakrishnan, and S. Chakrabarti. Collective annotation of wikipedia entities in web text. In *Proceedings of SIGKDD*, pages 457–466, 2009.

[16] G. Limaye, S. Sarawagi, and S. Chakrabarti. Annotating and searching web tables using entities, types and relationships. *Proc. VLDB Endow.*, 3:1338–1347, September 2010.

[17] D. Lin. An information-theoretic definition of similarity. In *Proceedings of ICML*, pages 296–304, 1998.

[18] J. Madhavan, D. Ko, L. Kot, V. Ganapathy, A. Rasmussen, and A. Halevy. Google's deep web crawl. *Proc. VLDB Endow.*, 1:1241–1252, August 2008.

[19] W. Shen, J. Wang, P. Luo, and M. Wang. Linden: linking named entities with knowledge base via semantic knowledge. In *Proceedings of WWW*, pages 449–458, 2012.

[20] F. Suchanek, G. Kasneci, and G. Weikum. Yago: A Large Ontology from Wikipedia and WordNet. *Journal of Web Semantics*, 6(3):203–217, 2008.

[21] F. M. Suchanek, G. Kasneci, and G. Weikum. Yago: A core of semantic knowledge unifying wordnet and wikipedia. In *Proceedings of WWW*, pages 697–706, 2007.

[22] P. Venetis, A. Halevy, J. Madhavan, M. Paşca, W. Shen, F. Wu, G. Miao, and C. Wu. Recovering semantics of tables on the web. *Proc. VLDB Endow.*, 4:528–538, June 2011.

[23] F. Wu and D. S. Weld. Autonomously semantifying wikipedia. In *Proceedings of CIKM*, pages 41–50, 2007.

[24] F. Wu and D. S. Weld. Automatically refining the wikipedia infobox ontology. In *Proceedings of WWW*, pages 635–644, 2008.

[25] T. Zesch, I. Gurevych, and M. Mühlhäuser. Analyzing and Accessing Wikipedia as a Lexical Semantic Resource. In *Biannual Conference of the Society for Computational Linguistics and Language Technology*, 2007.

Automatic Taxonomy Construction from Keywords

Xueqing Liu[§‡], Yangqiu Song[§], Shixia Liu[§], Haixun Wang[§]
[§]Microsoft Research Asia, Beijing, China; [‡]Tsinghua University
{v-xueqli,yangqiu.song,shliu,haixunw}@microsoft.com

ABSTRACT

Taxonomies, especially the ones in specific domains, are becoming indispensable to a growing number of applications. State-of-the-art approaches assume there exists a text corpus to accurately characterize the domain of interest, and that a taxonomy can be derived from the text corpus using information extraction techniques. In reality, neither assumption is valid, especially for highly focused or fast-changing domains. In this paper, we study a challenging problem: Deriving a taxonomy from a set of keyword phrases. A solution can benefit many real life applications because i) keywords give users the flexibility and ease to characterize a specific domain; and ii) in many applications, such as online advertisements, the domain of interest is already represented by a set of keywords. However, it is impossible to create a taxonomy out of a keyword set itself. We argue that additional knowledge and contexts are needed. To this end, we first use a general purpose knowledgebase and keyword search to supply the required knowledge and context. Then we develop a Bayesian approach to build a hierarchical taxonomy for a given set of keywords. We reduce the complexity of previous hierarchical clustering approaches from $O(n^2 \log n)$ to $O(n \log n)$, so that we can derive a domain specific taxonomy from one million keyword phrases in less than an hour. Finally, we conduct comprehensive large scale experiments to show the effectiveness and efficiency of our approach. A real life example of building an insurance-related query taxonomy illustrates the usefulness of our approach for specific domains.

Categories and Subject Descriptors

I.2.6 [**Artificial Intelligence**]: Learning; G.3 [**Probability and Statistics**]: *Nonparametric statistics*; H.2.8 [**Database Management**]: Database applications—*Data mining*

General Terms

Algorithms; Experimentation

Keywords

Knowledgebase, Taxonomy Building, Hierarchical Clustering, Bayesian Rose Tree, Query Understanding

KDD'12, August 12–16, 2012, Beijing, China.

1. INTRODUCTION

Taxonomy plays an important role in many applications. For example, in web search, organizing domain-specific queries into a hierarchy can help better understand the queries and improve search results [23] or help with query refinement [17]. In online advertising, taxonomies about specific domains (e.g., insurance, which is the most profitable domain in online ads) are used to decide the relatedness between a given query and bidding keywords.

Recently, much work has been devoted to taxonomy induction, particularly with respect to automatically creating a domain-specific ontology or taxonomy [14, 15, 16]. The value of automatic taxonomy constructing is obvious: Manual taxonomy construction is a laborious process, and the resulting taxonomy is often highly subjective, compared with taxonomies built by data-driven approaches. Furthermore, automatic approaches have the potential to enable humans or even machines to understand a highly focused and potentially fast changing domain.

Most state-of-the-art approaches for domain-specific taxonomy induction work as follows: First, it selects a text corpus as its input. The assumption is that the text corpus accurately represents the domain. Second, it uses some information extraction methods to extract ontological relationships from the text corpus, and uses the relationships to build a taxonomy. For instance, to derive a medical or biological taxonomy, a commonly used corpus is the entire body of biomedical literature from MEDLINE, life science journals, and online books (e.g., those on PubMed).

Although these text-corpus based approaches have achieved some success, they have several disadvantages. For example, for a highly focused domain, it is very difficult to find a text corpus that accurately characterizes that domain. Intuitively, it is easier to find a text corpus (e.g., the entire set of ACM publications) for big topics such as "computer science," but it is much more difficult to find one for a specific topic such as "big data for business intelligence," as articles about such topics are likely to be dispersed in many different fields and forums. Furthermore, we are often interested in new domains or fast changing domains, which makes it even more difficult to find a characterizing text corpus.

Furthermore, even if we can find a corpus that accurately characterizes the domain, we may still have a problem of data sparsity. Intuitively, the more highly focused the domain, the smaller the text corpus that is available for that domain. The problem is exacerbated by our limited power in understanding natural language text for identifying ontological relationships. To build a taxonomy from a text corpus, we usually bootstrap from a limited set of heuristic patterns. However, high quality patterns typically have very low recalls. For instance, it is well known that Hearst patterns [8] (i.e., "such as" patterns) have a high level of accuracy, but it is unrealistic to assume that the text corpus expresses every ontological relationship in "such as" or its derived patterns, especially when the text corpus is not large enough.

Instead of building taxonomies from a text corpus, we can also consider extracting a domain-specific taxonomy from a big, general purpose taxonomy such as the Open Directory Project (ODP)[1] or Wikipedia[2]. However, a general purpose knowledgebase usually has low coverage on a highly focused domain, and it may also produce ambiguous interpretations for highly specialized terms in the domain.

In this paper, we consider the challenge of inducing a taxonomy from a set of keyword phrases instead of from a text corpus. The problem is important because a set of keywords gives us the flexibility and ease to accurately characterize a domain, even if the domain is fast changing. Furthermore, in many cases, such a set of keywords is often readily available. For instance, search engine companies are interested in creating taxonomies for specific advertising domains. Each domain is described by a set of related ad keywords (bid phrases).

The problem of inducing a taxonomy from a set of keywords has one major challenge. Although by using a set of keywords we can more accurately characterize a highly focused, even fast-changing domain, the set of keywords itself does not contain explicit relationships from which a taxonomy can be constructed. One way to overcome this problem is to enrich the set of keyword phrases by aggregating the search results for each keyword phrase (i.e., throwing each keyword phrase into a search engine, and collecting its top k search result) into a text corpus. Then it treats the text corpus as a bag of words and constructs a taxonomy directly out of the bag of words using some hierarchical clustering approach [5, 18]. The problem with this approach is that the corpus represents the context of the keyword phrases, rather than the conceptual relationships that exist among the keyword phrases. For instance, the search results for the query "auto insurance" contain a very limited number of articles on how "auto insurance" is defined or characterized. The majority of articles either introduce a certain type of car insurance or talk about car insurance in passing. From such articles, we can extract context words such as "Florida," "Fords," or "accident." The resulting context can be arbitrary and not insurance related.

To tackle this challenge, we propose a novel, "knowledge+context" approach for taxonomy induction. We argue that, in order to create a taxonomy out of a set of keywords, we need knowledge and contexts beyond the set of keywords itself. For example, given two phrases "vehicle insurance" and "car insurance," humans know immediately that "car insurance" is a sub-concept of "vehicle insurance," because humans have the knowledge that a car is a vehicle. Without this knowledge, the machine can hardly derive this relationship unless the extended corpus from the keywords (e.g., using keyword search) happens to describe this relationship in a syntactic pattern that the machine can recognize (e.g., "vehicles such as cars"). But the context is also important. It is unlikely that the knowledgebase (especially a general purpose one) knows about every subsuming relationship in the specific domain. For example, it has no idea that x is a sub-concept of y. However, through the context, we may find that x is highly related to z, and in the knowledgebase z is a sub-concept of y. Thus, using knowledge and contexts, we can establish the relationship between x and y.

Incorporating both knowledge and contexts in taxonomy building is not easy. To this end, we formalize our approach as hierarchical clustering over features generated from a general knowledgebase and search context. More specifically, we first deduce a set of concepts for each keyword phrase using a general purpose knowledgebase [19] and then obtain its context information from a search engine. After enriching the keyword set using knowledge and contexts, we make use of Bayesian-based hierarchical clustering to automatically induce a new taxonomy. Our paper presents three technical contributions: First, we illustrate how to derive the concepts and context from each keyword. Second, we present the way to formulate the taxonomy building to a hierarchical clustering problem based on their concepts and context. And finally, we scale up the method to millions of keywords.

The rest of the paper is organized as follows. In Section 2, we introduce the background of hierarchical clustering and Bayesian rose trees. We then present algorithms, analyze their complexity, and discuss some implementation issues in Section 3. Section 4 describes experiments that demonstrate the effectiveness and efficiency of our approach. In Section 5, we conclude our work and present several future works.

[1] http://www.dmoz.org/

[2] http://www.wikipedia.org/

2. MULTI-BRANCH CLUSTERING

Hierarchical clustering is a widely used clustering method [9]. The advantage of hierarchical clustering is that it generates a tree structure (a dendrogram) which is easy to interpret. Two strategies are used for hierarchical clustering, agglomerative and divisive, where the agglomerative approach builds a tree from bottom up by combining the two most similar clusters at each step, and the divisive approach builds a tree from top down by splitting the current cluster into two clusters at each step.

Traditional hierarchical clustering algorithms construct binary trees. However, binary branches may not be the best model to describe a set of data's intrinsic structure in many applications. Fig. 1 gives an example. The goal here is to create a taxonomy from a set of insurance-related keyword phrases. It assumes we have a good similarity measure that enables us to group related keywords in an optimal way. Still, the outcome might be sub-optimal or unnatural. In the figure, "indiana cheap car insurance," "kentucky cheap car insurance," and "missouri cheap car insurance" are on different levels, but apparently they belong to the same cluster. This disadvantage is introduced by the model not the similarity measure, which means that no matter how accurately we understand the data, the result will still be sub-optimal.

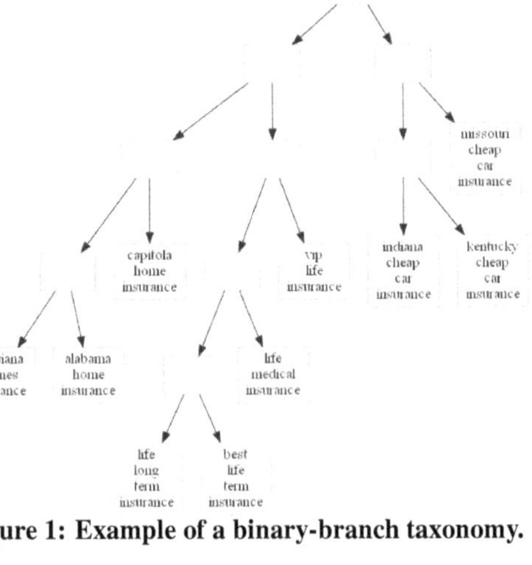

Figure 1: Example of a binary-branch taxonomy.

To remedy this, multi-branch trees are developed. Compared with binary trees, they have a simpler structure and better interpretability. An example of multi-branch clustering is shown in

Fig. 2, where nodes such as "indiana cheap car insurance," "kentucky cheap car insurance," and "missouri cheap car insurance" are grouped under the same parent node.

Currently, there are several multi-branch hierarchy clustering approaches [1, 3, 10]. The methods proposed by Adams et al [1] and Knowles et al [10] are based on the Dirichlet diffusion tree, which use an MCMC process to infer the model. Blundel et al [3] adopts a simple, deterministic, agglomerative approach called BRT (Bayesian Rose Tree). In this work, we adopt BRT as a basic algorithm for taxonomy induction. The major steps of BRT are shown in Algorithm 1.

Algorithm 1 is a greedy agglomerative approach. In the beginning, each data point is regarded as a tree on its own: $T_i = \{\mathbf{x}_i\}$ where $\mathbf{x}_i$ is the feature vector of ith data. For each step, the algorithm selects two trees T_i and T_j and merges them into a new tree T_m. Unlike binary hierarchical clustering, BRT uses three possible merging operations [3]:

- **Join:** $T_m = \{T_i, T_j\}$, that is, T_m has two child nodes.
- **Absorb:** $T_m = \{\text{children}(T_i) \cup T_j\}$, that is, T_m has $|T_i| + 1$ child nodes.
- **Collapse:** $T_m = \{\text{children}(T_i) \cup \text{children}(T_j)\}$, that is, T_m has $|T_i| + |T_j|$ child nodes.

Specifically, in each step, Algorithm 1 greedily finds two trees T_i and T_j to maximize the ratio of probability:

$$\frac{p(\mathcal{D}_m|T_m)}{p(\mathcal{D}_i|T_i)p(\mathcal{D}_j|T_j)} \tag{1}$$

where $p(\mathcal{D}_m|T_m)$ is the likelihood of data $\mathcal{D}_m$ given the tree T_m, $\mathcal{D}_m$ is all the leaf data of T_m, and $\mathcal{D}_m = \mathcal{D}_i \cup \mathcal{D}_j$. The probability $p(\mathcal{D}_m|T_m)$ is recursively defined on the children of T_m:

$$p(\mathcal{D}_m|T_m) = \pi_{T_m} f(\mathcal{D}_m) + (1 - \pi_{T_m}) \prod_{T_i \in \text{Children}(T_m)} p(\mathcal{D}_i|T_i) \tag{2}$$

where $f(\mathcal{D}_m)$ is the marginal probability of the data $\mathcal{D}_m$ and π_{T_m} is the "mixing proportion." Intuitively, π_{T_m} is the prior probability that all the data in T_m is kept in one cluster instead of partitioned into sub-trees. In BRT [3], π_{T_m} is defined as:

$$\pi_{T_m} = 1 - (1 - \gamma)^{n_{T_m} - 1} \tag{3}$$

where n_{T_m} is the number of children of T_m, and $0 \le \gamma \le 1$ is the hyperparameter to control the model. A larger γ leads to coarser partitions and a smaller γ leads to finer partitions.

The major cost of this bottom-up hierarchy construction approach is dominated by the following two steps:

(1) looking for pairs of clusters to merge;

(2) calculating the likelihood associated with the merged cluster (Eq. (1)).

Assume in the current round there are c clusters. The two steps above take $O(c^2)$ time. At the start of the algorithm, we have $c = n$, the number of data points. For all the clusters merging into one cluster, if we first compute the likelihood by Eq. (1), and sort them before we search for merging pairs, it will take $O(n^2 \cdot C_V + n^2 \log n)$ time complexity, where C_V is the maximum number of non-zero elements in all the initial vectors $\mathbf{x}_i$'s. For high-dimensional text data, the document will have hundreds of words on average. Therefore, C_V cannot be ignored when we analyze the overall complexity compared to $\log n$. This is not applicable for any large-scale data set. Moreover, this approach will have $O(n^2)$ memory cost. For

Algorithm 1 Bayesian Rose Tree (BRT).

Input: A set of documents $\mathcal{D}$.
$T_i \leftarrow \mathbf{x}_i$ for $i = 1, 2, \cdots, n$
$c \leftarrow n$
while $c > 1$ **do**
  1. Select T_i and T_j and merge them into T_m which maximizes

$$L(T_m) = \frac{p(\mathcal{D}_m|T_m)}{p(\mathcal{D}_i|T_i)p(\mathcal{D}_j|T_j)}, \tag{4}$$

  where the merge operation is join, absorb, or collapse.
  2. Replace T_i and T_j with T_m in the tree.
  3. $c \leftarrow c - 1$
end while

$100,000$ data points, this will take $3 \times 8 \times 10^{10} = 240G$ bytes memory to contain all the pairs' likelihood, if we use 8 bytes to store double-precision value and have three types of merging likelihoods ("join," "absorb," and "collapse").

3. KEYWORD TAXONOMY BUILDING

In this section, we introduce our approach for building a domain specific taxonomy from a set of keyword phrases augmented with knowledge and contexts. First, we obtain knowledge and contexts related to the keywords. In our approach, we obtain knowledge (concepts that correspond to each keyword phrase) using a technique called short text conceptualization [19] and a general purpose knowledgebase called Probase [11, 24], and we obtain contexts by submitting the queries to a commercial search engine to retrieve all snippet words. Second, we build the taxonomy using a multiple branch hierarchical clustering approach. In this section, we initially introduce how to leverage concepts and contexts, and then we present the methods that speed up the taxonomy building for a large set of keywords.

3.1 Knowledge and Context

We use information obtained from a general-purpose knowledgebase and a search engine to augment the given set of keyword phrases.

The knowledgebase we use is Probase [11, 24], which has been demonstrated useful for Web search [21, 22]. The core of Probase consists of a large set of *isa* relationships, which are extracted from a text corpus of 1.68 billion web pages. For example, "... Spanish artists such as Pablo Picasso ..." is considered a piece of evidence for the claim that "Pablo Picasso" is an instance of the concept *Spanish artist*. Probase also contains other information. For example, for each concept, it contains a set of attributes that describe the concept. One unique feature of Probase is the broadness of its coverage. Probase contains millions of concepts, from well-known ones such as "country" and "artists" to small but concrete ones such as "wedding dress designers" and "renewable energy techniques." The richness of Probase enables us to identify and understand millions of concepts people use in their daily communication.

The knowledgebase facilitates us in deriving concepts from keyword phrases and we can then use the concepts to enrich the keyword phrase. For instance, given "microsoft and apple," we derive concepts such as *IT companies*, *big companies*, etc., and given "apple and pear," we derive concepts such as *fruit* or *tree*. However, these are still not enough for understanding the keyword phrase. We need to enhance the knowledgebase in two aspects.

- In order to model text for inferencing, we need to make the knowledge in Probase probabilistic. To this end, we introduce a set of probabilistic measures. For example, *P(instance*

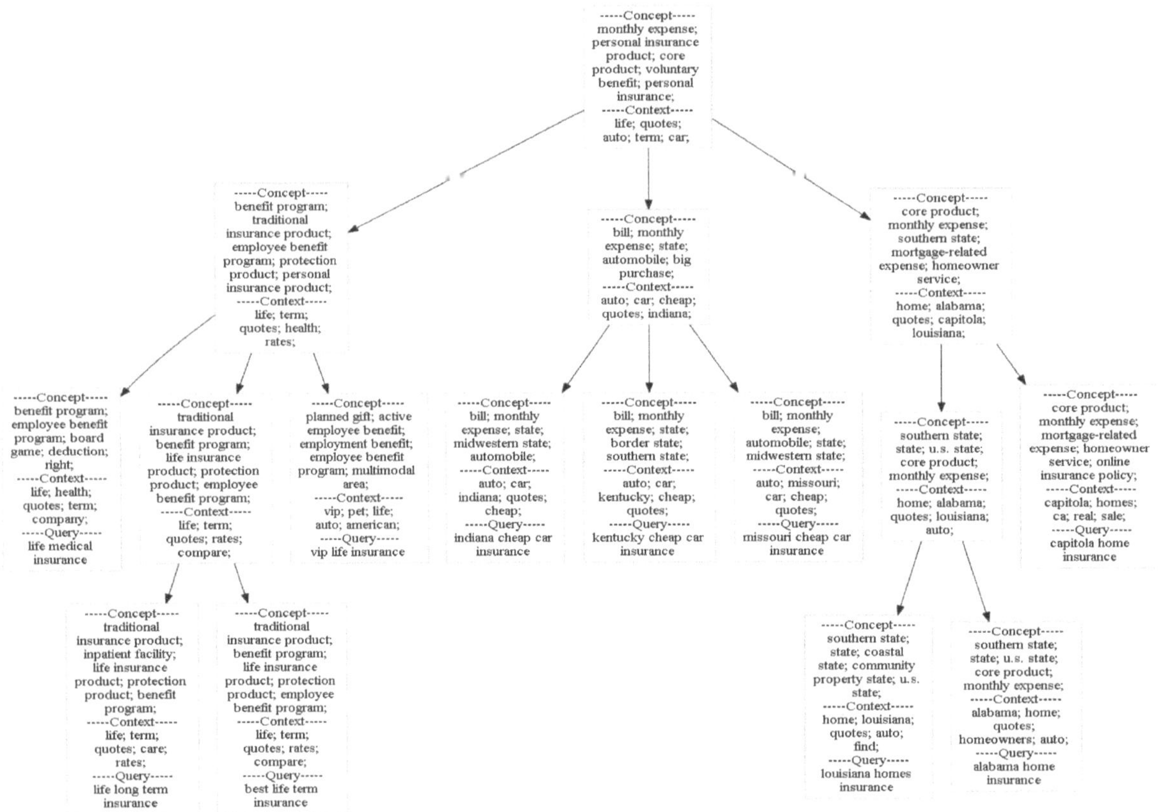

Figure 2: Example of Multi-branch Query Taxonomy.

$|concept)$ tells us how typical the *instance* in the given *concept* is. Intuitively, knowing that both "robin" and "penguin" are birds is not enough. We need to know "robin" is a much more typical bird than "penguin," that is, when people talk about birds, it is more likely that they are thinking about a robin than a penguin. Such information is essential for understanding the intent behind a piece of short text. Besides $P(instance|concept)$ we also obtain $P(concept|instance)$, $P(concept|attribute)$, and $P(attribute|concept)$. These values are calculated during the information extraction process, for example:

$$P(instance|concept) = \frac{n(instance, concept)}{n(concept)} \quad (5)$$

where $n(instance, concept)$ denotes the number of times that the*instance* and *concept* co-occur in the same sentence in a given corpus, and $n(concept)$ is the frequency of the *concept*.

- A keyword phrase may be syntactically and semantically complicated and require sophisticated chunking and parsing to identify meaningful terms. As shown in Fig. 3, we conceptualize "indiana cheap car insurance" by first recognizing the terms "indiana," "cheap car," and "car insurance" that appear in Probase, and then we derive concepts such as *state*, *car insurance*, *bill*, etc. Furthermore, each concept is associated with a probability score that indicates the strength of the concept. A detailed description of the conceptualization techniques can be found in [19].

Although Probase contains millions of concepts, we cannot expect it to cover everything. To remedy this, we collect the "context" of a keyword phrase, and use the context to supplement the concepts related to the phrase. To obtain the context, we submit the keyword phrase to a search engine, and collect the top ten snippets in the search results. The context is represented as a bag of words. The quality of the context is much lower than that of the concepts obtained from Probase, in the sense that for a given word in the bag-of-words context, we do not know its semantic relationship with the keyword. But still, they can be useful especially when the concepts we obtained are insufficient. As an example, consider two keyword phrases, "www.monster.com" and "monster.com." Probase knows that "monster.com" is a job site, but it knows nothing about "www.monster.com." Thus, conceptualization will report that the two phrases have zero similarity. Through the search engine, we find that "www.monster.com" is associated with phrases such as *web site, online job site, job board*, etc. Thus, by adding the context information, the query containing "www.monster.com" will have greater similarity to the query containing "monster.com."

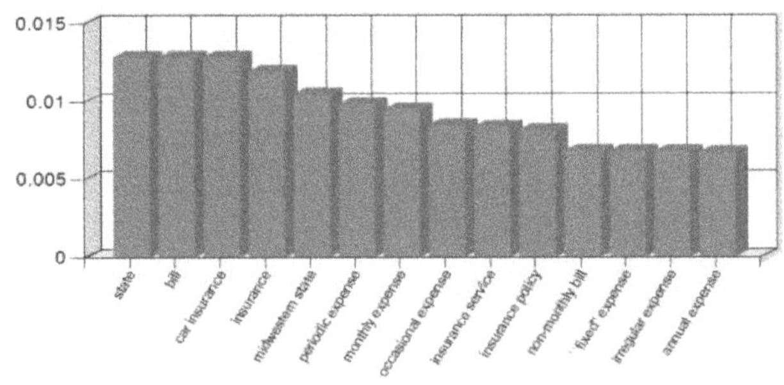

Figure 3: Conceptualization of "indiana cheap car insurance".

3.2 Text Modeling

To cluster the data into a hierarchy, we first need to model the data. This corresponds to calculating $f(\mathcal{D})$ in Eq.(2), the marginal distribution of data $\mathcal{D}$ (Section 2). The original BRT approach [3] assumes that the data can be modeled by a set of binary features that follow the Bernoulli distribution. In other words, features are not weighted. In our approach, we use features that consist of concepts and contexts to represent the data. Since even a short piece of text may contain multiple topics or concepts, it is important to rank them by their significance. Thus, unlike BRT, we incorporate weights into the marginal distribution $f(\mathcal{D})$.

Given a set of keyword phrases $\{keyword_1, \cdots, keyword_n\}$, we derive a list of $(term, weight)$ pairs for each keyword, where the *term* is either a concept produced by the knowledgebase, or a context word generated by search, and the *weight* is derived as follows:

$$weight_j = \lambda \cdot freq(term_j) + (1 - \lambda) \cdot \sum_i^n C_i \cdot P(term_j|keyword_i)$$

where λ is a parameter that controls how much we value the context compared to concepts; $freq(term_j)$ is the frequency of a term j in the context derived from search results; $P(term_j|keyword_i)$ is the probability of the term as a concept given keyword phrase $keyword_i$, and is provided by the knowledgebase (as in Eq (5)); C_i is the frequency of $keyword_i$ in the knowledgebase, and $C_i \cdot P(term_j|keyword_i)$ is used as the frequency of the term as a concept. We then set the feature vector $\mathbf{x}_i$ with the term frequencies $weight_j$'s for $keyword_i$.

In the hierarchical clustering algorithm, once two keywords or keyword clusters are grouped together, the grouped keyword cluster can contain multiple topics. For example, initially we have four keywords "China," "India," "Germany," and "France." Although these four keywords share some common concepts such as *country* and *nation*, we can still distinguish them based on the concepts with smaller weights. First, "China" and "India" will be grouped together since they share many concepts like *Asian country* and *emerging market*. "Germany" and "France" will also be grouped together because they share concepts like *European country* and *Western nation*. After that, these two clusters will be grouped together. The final cluster actually contains multiple topics, i.e. both *Asian country* and *European country*. Therefore, we need a distribution to better capture this characteristic.

To this end, we use the DCM distribution [13] to represent the marginal distribution $f(\mathcal{D})$. DCM is derived based on multinomial and Dirichlet conjugate distributions. Multinomial distribution can naturally characterize the co-occurrence counts of terms, while the prior distribution, i.e., Dirichlet distribution, can be regarded as smoothing over counts. The generative process of a document underlying this modeling is that we first sample a multinomial distribution from Dirichlet distribution, and then sample a document based on the multinomial distribution. Multinomial distribution can be regarded as a document-specific sub-topic distribution, which makes certain words appear more likely in a particular document [13]. DCM integrates out the intermediate multinomial distribution, and thus it represents either more general topics or multiple topics. In hierarchical clustering, we incrementally merge clusters. Therefore, DCM is more appropriate for evaluating whether two clusters (with multiple topics) should be merged.

Specifically, the likelihood of multinomial distribution $p(\mathbf{x}|\boldsymbol{\theta})$ is defined by:

$$p(\mathbf{x}|\boldsymbol{\theta}) = \frac{m!}{\prod_j^V x^{(j)}!} \prod_{j=1}^V p(x^{(j)}|\boldsymbol{\theta}) = \frac{m!}{\prod_j^V x^{(j)}!} \prod_{j=1}^V [\theta^{(j)}]^{x^{(j)}}, \quad (6)$$

Algorithm 2 Nearest-neighbor-based BRT.

Input: A set of documents $\mathcal{D}$.
Initialization 1: Set $T_i = \mathbf{x}_i$ for $i = 1, 2, \cdots, n$; number of clusters $c = n$.
Initialization 2: Find the nearest neighbors $\mathcal{N}(T_i)$ for each cluster, and compute all the likelihood scores.
while $c > 1$ **do**
1. Find T_i and T_j in all neighborhood sets $\{\mathcal{N}_k(T_i)\}$, whose merge maximizes Eq. (1), where $m \in$ {join, absorb, collapse}.
2. $T_m \leftarrow$ the result of merge on T_i and T_j
3. Delete T_i and T_j.
4. Find the nearest neighbors set $\mathcal{N}(T_m)$ for the new cluster.
5. $c \leftarrow c - 1$

end while

where V is the vocabulary size, $x^{(j)}$ is the frequency of term $v^{(j)}$, $m = \sum_j^V x^{(j)}$, and $\boldsymbol{\theta} = (\theta^{(1)}, \theta^{(2)}, \ldots, \theta^{(V)})^T \in \mathcal{R}^V$ are the parameters of multinomial distribution.

The Dirichlet distribution prior is:

$$p(\boldsymbol{\theta}|\boldsymbol{\alpha}) = \frac{\Gamma(\sum_{j=1}^V \alpha^{(j)})}{\prod_{j=1}^V \Gamma(\alpha^{(j)})} \prod_{j=1}^V [\theta^{(j)}]^{\alpha^{(j)}-1} = \frac{1}{\Delta(\boldsymbol{\alpha})} \prod_{j=1}^V [\theta^{(j)}]^{\alpha^{(j)}-1}, \quad (7)$$

where $\boldsymbol{\alpha} = (\alpha^{(1)}, \alpha^{(2)}, \ldots, \alpha^{(V)})^T \in \mathcal{R}^V$, and the Gamma function[3] has the property $\Gamma(x + 1) = x\Gamma(x)$. The "Dirichlet delta function" $\Delta(\boldsymbol{\alpha}) = \frac{\Gamma(\sum_{j=1}^V \alpha^{(j)})}{\prod_{j=1}^V \Gamma(\alpha^{(j)})}$ is introduced for convenience.

Then the marginal distribution $f(\mathcal{D})$ is given by:

$$f_{DCM}(\mathcal{D}) = \int_{\boldsymbol{\theta}} \prod_i^n p(\mathbf{x}_i|\boldsymbol{\theta}) p(\boldsymbol{\theta}|\boldsymbol{\alpha}) d\boldsymbol{\theta} = \prod_i^n \frac{m!}{\prod_j^V x_i^{(j)}!} \cdot \frac{\Delta(\boldsymbol{\alpha} + \sum_i \mathbf{x}_i)}{\Delta(\boldsymbol{\alpha})}. \quad (8)$$

Using this marginal distribution $f_{DCM}(\mathcal{D})$, we can seamlessly integrate the weights into the term feature vector. Next we will introduce how to construct the tree more efficiently.

3.3 Efficient Taxonomy Construction

As we show in Section 2, BRT has time complexity $O(n^2 \cdot C_V + n^2 \log n)$, and space complexity $O(n^2)$, which is not applicable to large-scale problems. The most time consuming process in agglomerative clustering lies in searching all candidate cluster pairs to find the best pairs to merge. If we can reduce the search space for BRT by pruning the pairs of keyword clusters that are most unlikely to be merged, then we can reduce the cost of searching agglomerative clustering. We propose to "cache" a set of nearest neighbors for each data point. Then the search complexity only depends on the number of the nearest neighbors. However, searching for nearest neighbors still incurs a cost of $O(n)$ for each data point. The time complexity of finding k nearest neighbors can be reduced to $O(\log n)$ using techniques such as KD-trees [2] and Metric trees [20]. However, these techniques are not suitable for high-dimensional data, since they partition the data space dimension by dimension. Approximation methods such as LSH (Locality-Sensitive Hashing) [7] can be used when the number of dimensions is large. Particularly, Spilltree [12] relaxes the non-overlapping constraints of Metric trees and incorporates the technique used in LSH, and thus combines the benefits of both methods.

In this section, we focus on adapting two major types of nearest neighbor approaches for efficient taxonomy construction: k-nearest-neighbor (kNN) and ϵ-ball-nearest-neighbor (ϵNN) [4]. kNN finds k nearest neighbors for each data and is not concerned the density of the data. ϵNN uses a spherical ball to bind all the nearest

[3]For integer variables, Gamma function is $\Gamma(x) = (x - 1)!$. For real numbers, it is $\Gamma(x) = \int_0^\infty t^{x-1} e^{-t} dt$.

neighbors within the ball. In our taxonomy construction approach, we significantly reduce the time complexity by using methods such as Spilltree [12] and PPJoin+ [25].

3.3.1 kNN-*Approximation*

We introduce two kNN-based approximation approaches based on BRT. A flowchart for using the nearest neighbors to approximate the construction procedure of BRT is shown in Algorithm 2.

kNN-BRT: Using the kNN approach, we first find the k nearest neighbors for each data point, and then we check the possibility of merging within the neighborhood set. We denote $\mathcal{N}_k(\mathbf{x})$ as the k nearest neighbor set of data $\mathbf{x}$. To find k nearest neighbors of a data, we keep a minheap with size k to maintain the data with largest similarities scores. When new data comes and the similarity score is larger than the top value (the smallest one in the minheap), we replace the top index with the new data. Compared to BRT, the space cost is significantly reduced from $O(n^2)$ to $O(nk)$. The time complexity is also reduced to $O(n^2 \cdot C_V + n^2 \log k)$.

Spilltree-BRT: Using the k nearest neighbors to construct BRT is still time consuming. We then use the Spilltree algorithm [12] to further reduce the time complexity.

Spilltree is a generalization of metric trees [20]. Metric trees partition the data space into binary trees, and retrieve the nearest neighbors by DFS (depth first search). Metric trees will be less efficient when the number of dimensionality is large (e.g., larger than 30 [12]). The Spilltree algorithm offers two major modifications:

1. Introduce random projection before partitioning the data space.

2. Introduce the overlapping/non-overlapping regions between nodes when partitioning each sub-tree. While searching for the nearest neighbors in the sub-trees with overlapping partitions, Spilltree searches one branch only.

According to the Johnson-Lindenstrauss Lemma [6], embedding a data set of dimension n to an $O(\log n)$ dimensional space has little distortions for pairwise distances. As a result, brute-force search in the projected space provides a $(1+\varepsilon)$-NN [12] in the original space. Thus, by projecting the data onto a much lower dimensional space, high precision can be guaranteed while the time cost is significantly reduced, especially when the original data has millions of dimensions.

Moreover, original metric trees perform a DFS to find the nearest neighbors. By introducing the overlapping nodes, Spilltree adopts a combined strategy of a defeatist search and DFS. The defeatist search may fail for non-overlapping nodes if a query and its nearest neighbors belong to different branches. However, it is guaranteed to be successful for the overlapping nodes when the shortest distance in the overlapping regions is larger than or equal to the distance between the query and its nearest neighbor. By setting an appropriate tolerance parameter τ, the accuracies of both overlapping and non-overlapping nodes are ensured [12]. Overall, the time complexity of search for Spilltree is $O(\log n)$ [12].

The random projection to d-dimensional space has the time complexity of $O(nd \cdot C_V)$. Building a Spilltree costs $O(nd \log n)$. To use Spilltree to search the k nearest neighbors, we also keep a minheap to maintain k data points when traversing the Spilltree. This step will cost $O(nd \log n \log k)$ time for all the data. In summary, using Spilltree to build BRT costs $O(nd \cdot C_V + nd \log n \log k)$. Compared to the kNN-BRT algorithm, using Spilltree will cost additional $O(Vd + nd)$ memory to store the random projection matrix and the Spilltree.

Table 1: Comparison of computational complexity and memory requirements of different algorithms. (C_V **is the number of non-zero elements in the vector x and** $L = \sum_j x^{(j)}$)

Algorithm	Time complexity	Memory requirement
BRT	$O(n^2 \cdot C_V + n^2 \log n)$	$O(n^2)$
kNN-BRT	$O(n^2 \cdot C_V + n^2 \log k)$	$O(nk)$
Spilltree-BRT	$O(nd \cdot C_V + nd \log n \log k)$	$O(nk + Vd + nd)$
PPJoin-BRT	$O(n^2[(1-\epsilon^2)L + \log L])$	$O(nf(\epsilon) + nL)$

3.3.2 ϵNN-*Approximation*

In ϵNN-approximation, for each data point, we keep its nearest neighbors whose similarity with the data point is larger than a predefined threshold ϵ. This reduces the time complexity to $O(n^2 \cdot C_V)$. The storage of ϵNN depends on the number of the neighbors that satisfy the ϵ threshold. However, we might need to re-run the ϵNN algorithm in order to ensure we can find candidates to be merged, since when the threshold ϵ is too large, ϵNN will not return any nearest neighbors.

PPJoin-BRT: To support ϵNN-approximation, we need to find ϵ neighbors of a data point efficiently. We adopt the PPJoin+ [25] approach for this purpose. PPJoin+ uses two types of filtering, prefix filtering and suffix filtering, to filter out the data points that do not satisfy certain constraints. In prefix filtering, it has been proven that the cosine similarity is larger than a threshold ϵ if and only if the number of overlapped terms between the two sets is larger than $\epsilon' = \lceil \epsilon \sqrt{L_i \cdot L_j} \rceil$, where $L_i = \sum_k x_i^{(k)}$ is the length of the document $\mathbf{x}_i$. Therefore, we can quickly filter out pairs of documents as if their overlap is larger than ϵ'. The time complexity of this step is reduced to $(1-\epsilon^2)\sum_j x^{(j)}, \epsilon < 1$ [25]. In suffix filtering, it first derives an upper bound of hamming distance H_{max} corresponding to the pre-defined threshold ϵ. Then we filter out the data if the lower bound of the hamming distance between two documents $H_{min}(\mathbf{x}_i, \mathbf{x}_j)$ is larger than the upper bound H_{max}. We also implemented an algorithm based on the binary search for the lower bound of the hamming distance. The overall time complexity of PPJoin+ is $O(n^2[(1-\epsilon^2)L + \log L])$, where L is the average length of documents. PPJoin-BRT takes $O(nf(\epsilon))$ memory to store the likelihood values of the nearest neighbors. Moreover, it needs an inverted index to facilitate prefix filtering, and the memory cost is $O(nL)$.

A comparison of all the algorithms is shown in Table 1. We can see that Spilltree-BRT has the least time complexity; however, it requires more memory.

4. EXPERIMENTS

To demonstrate the effectiveness and scalability of the proposed taxonomy building algorithms, we test the original BRT and the nearest-neighbor-based methods on three different data sets. The nearest-neighbor-based methods include kNN-BRT, Spilltree-BRT, and PPJoin-BRT. In this section, we introduce the evaluation results in detail.

4.1 Performance of Clustering

In this experiment, we use the 20-newsgroups data to evaluate the correctness of the algorithms. This data set forms a hierarchy with two levels. The first level has six clusters, and the second level contains 20 clusters. We randomly sample 2,000 documents to compare the clusters generated by different hierarchical clustering algorithms. We set all the parameters to be the same for Bayesian rose trees. In addition, k in kNN-BRT and Spilltree-BRT is set to 10. The dimension of random projection used in Spilltree-BRT is

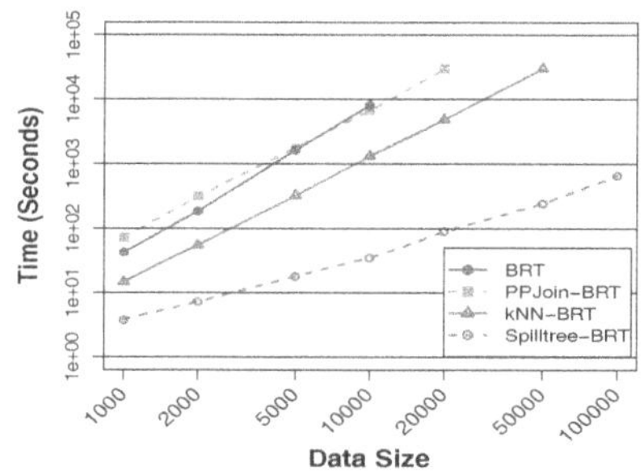

(a) End-to-end time for query data.

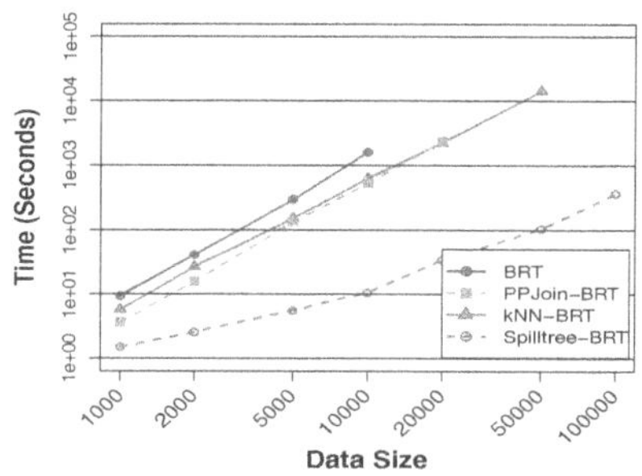

(b) Preprocessing time for query data.

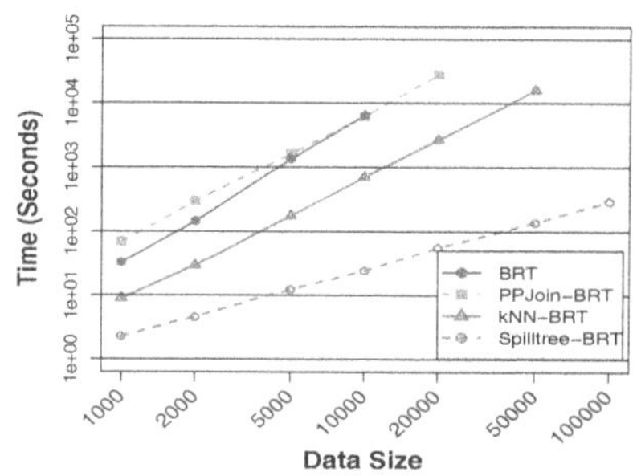

(c) Building time for query data.

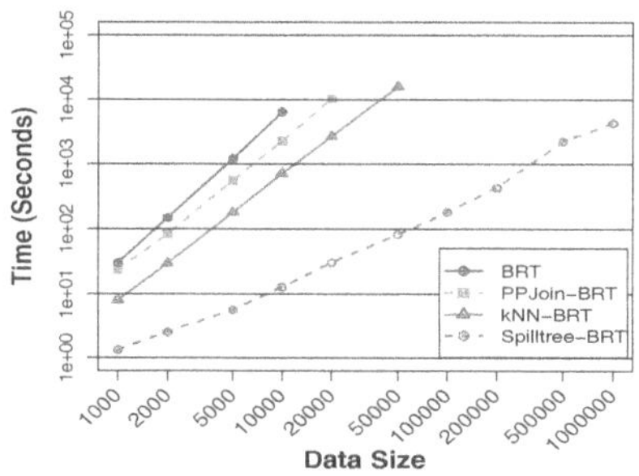

(d) End-to-end time for news data.

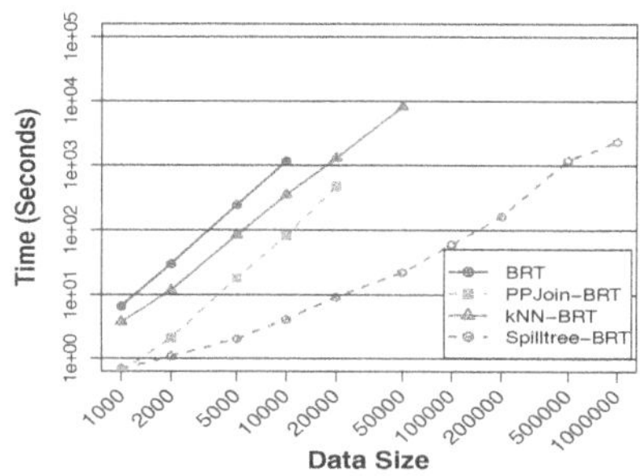

(e) Preprocessing time for news data.

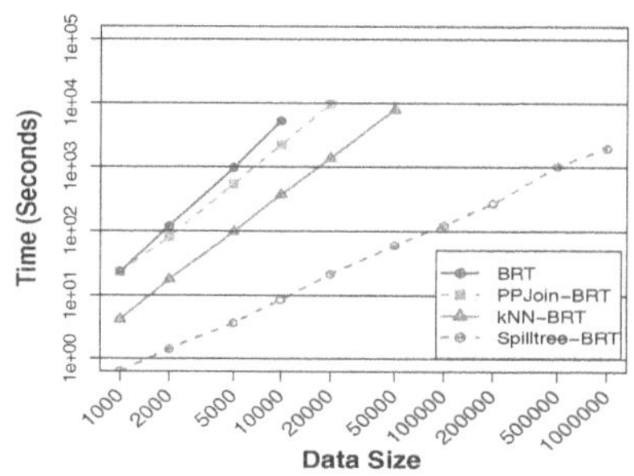

(f) Building time for news data.

Figure 4: Time cost comparison of different algorithms.

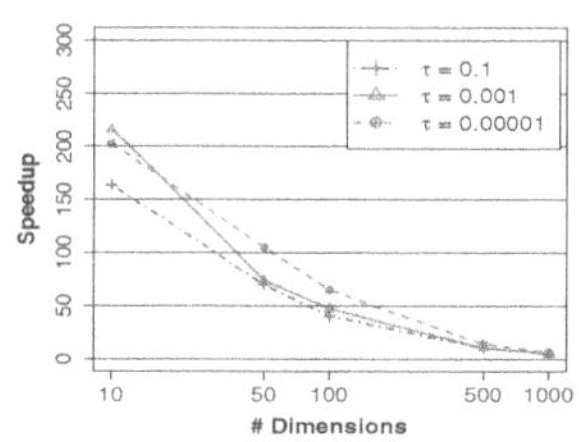

(a) Speedup over BRT with different parameters in Spilltree for query data.

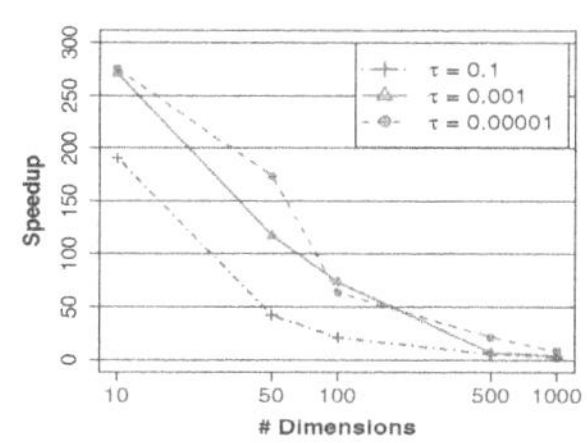

(b) Speedup over BRT with different parameters in Spilltree for news data.

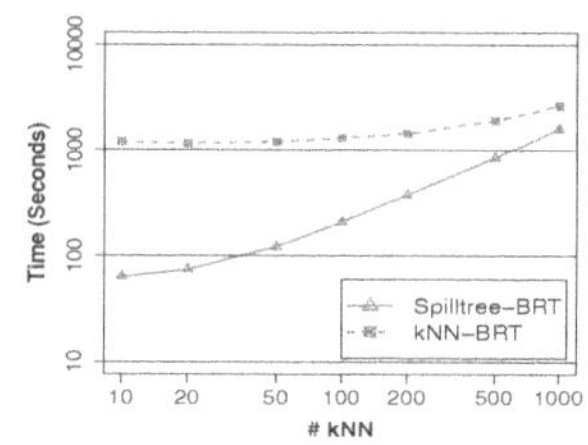

(c) Time cost comparison of k nearest neighbors for query data.

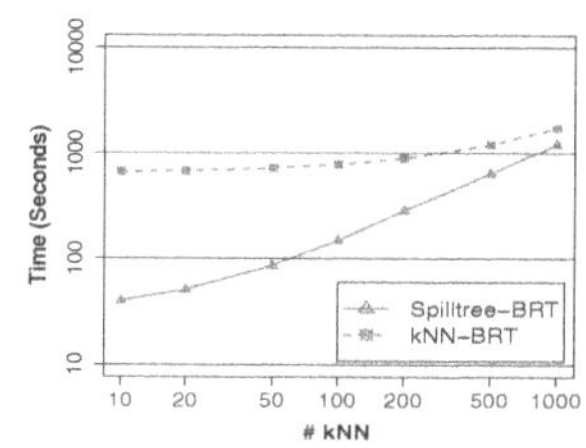

(d) Time cost comparison of k nearest neighbors for news data.

Figure 5: Comparison of the impact of different parameters and settings for *k*NN based methods (10,000 data samples).

set to 10. The overlapping parameter τ used in Spilltree [12] is set to 0.001.

We first compare the likelihood of different algorithms. As shown in Table 2, the nearest-neighbor-based methods are comparable with the original BRT. Particularly, the likelihood of kNN-BRT is better than the original BRT. The reason is that searching the candidate pairs from the nearest neighbors can significantly reduce the noise of the data. Thereby it leads to a better local optima. This phenomenon has also been observed in [4].

Then we leverage the NMI metric to compare the clusters of different levels in the generated trees with the human annotated ones (Table 3). All the results are based on ten trials of different executions. It can be seen that all the nearest-neighbor-based methods have similar performance with the original BRT. The kNN-BRT algorithm performs best with levels one and two, while the original BRT performs best with the third level. This observation is consistent with the likelihood results.

4.2 Scalability of Taxonomy Building

In this section, we investigate the scalability of the algorithms based on two data sets. The first one is a query data set consisting of 114,076 queries, where the concept and context information are extracted using the methods introduced in Section 3.1. The vocabulary size is 912,792 and the average number of words in the documents is 935. We also evaluate the algorithms on a larger news data set. It contains one million news articles. The vocabulary size is 252,174 and the average number of words is 242. All the experiments are conducted on a 64-bit server with 2.5GHz CPU and 32G of memory. The memory cost for the news data set is around 10G.

We first conduct the experiments to examine the "end-to-end" time cost of different algorithms. We set $k = 10$ for kNN-BRT and Spilltree-BRT. The dimension of random projection used in Spilltree-BRT is set 10. The overlapping parameter τ used in Spilltree is set to 0.001. As shown in Figs. 4(a) and 4(d), the Spilltree-BRT al-

Table 2: Comparison of likelihood for 20-newsgroups data.

Methods	Likelihood
BRT	$-1.441 \times 10^6 \pm 1.637 \times 10^5$
kNN-BRT	$\mathbf{-1.392 \times 10^6 \pm 1.053 \times 10^5}$
Spilltree-BRT	$-1.473 \times 10^6 \pm 1.837 \times 10^5$
PPJoin-BRT	$-1.484 \times 10^6 \pm 1.348 \times 10^5$

Table 3: Comparison of different algorithm with NMI scores.

Rose Tree Level	Level 1		Level 2		Level 3	
20-newsgroups cluster	6 Categories	20 Categories	6 Categories	20 Categories	6 Categories	20 Categories
BRT	0.055±0.006	0.075±0.008	0.202±0.010	0.295±0.016	**0.313±0.012**	**0.476±0.019**
*k*NN-BRT	**0.123±0.019**	**0.144±0.020**	**0.237±0.020**	**0.324±0.021**	0.311±0.014	0.454±0.020
Spilltree-BRT	0.076±0.004	0.101±0.007	0.189±0.007	0.273±0.114	0.279±0.007	0.423±0.011
PPJoin-BRT	0.080±0.010	0.113±0.012	0.190±0.033	0.269±0.002	0.238±0.038	0.389±0.003

gorithm is the fastest. *k*NN-BRT also performs faster than BRT and PPJoin-BRT. PPJoin-BRT is not as fast as expected because the process of finding the nearest neighbors must be re-run if there is no candidate cluster pair to merge. Particularly, for the query data set, PPJoin-BRT is even worse than the original BRT algorithm. This is due to the fact that PPJoin is significantly affected by the average length of documents. The average length of documents in query data is about four times that of the news data. For the news data set, PPJoin-BRT performs better than BRT.

To further analyze the performance of each algorithm in detail, we divide the execution into two parts: preprocessing and build. The detailed time costs for different algorithms are shown in Figs. 4(b), 4(c), 4(e), and 4(f). For BRT, during the preprocessing, we compute the likelihood values between data samples and then sort them. For the nearest neighbor based methods, the preprocessing mainly focuses on finding the nearest neighbors and computing the likelihood values. The building part of each algorithm gradually merges clusters. For different algorithms, merging clusters differs from searching for the candidate pair sets of different sizes. Moreover, after a new cluster is generated, different number of likelihood values will be computed, as illustrated in Algorithms 1 and 2. It can be concluded from the results that the time costs of *k*NN-BRT and Spilltree-BRT in these two parts is consistently lower than BRT. Specifically, the preprocessing of PPJoin-BRT is faster than *k*NN-BRT. However, for build is much slower. This again demonstrates our explanation that PPJoin-BRT will re-run the process of finding the nearest neighbors.

Since Spilltree-BRT is the fastest algorithm, we also investigate how different Spilltree parameters affect the time cost. The following experiments are conducted with 10,000 data samples. The comparison results between the nearest-neighbor-based methods and the original BRT are shown in Figs. 5(a) and 5(b). In the figures, different curves represent the time costs of the Spilltree algorithms with different overlapping tolerance parameters τ. This parameter controls how many data points we allow to be overlapped by different tree nodes in a Spilltree. As shown in the figures, the larger overlapping parameter results in slower algorithm execution, since it makes the algorithm backtrack more times back to the parent nodes [12]. Moreover, in each curve, we also show how the projected dimensions affect the time cost. Generally, fewer dimensions lead to faster algorithm execution. Spilltree-BRT can be 200–300 times faster than BRT when we project the data onto a ten-dimensional space. Finally, we evaluate how the number of the nearest neighbors affects the time cost. The results are shown in Figs. 5(c) and 5(d). We present the time costs of both *k*NN-BRT and Spilltree-BRT algorithms. It is shown that Spilltree-BRT performs better when the number of the nearest neighbors is small. This is also because it backtracks fewer times to the parent nodes when fewer neighbors are needed.

4.3 Top *K*NN Search

To investigate the quality of the proposed taxonomy building method, we also apply it to the top *K*NN search problem. This problem is defined as: given a query in the form of short text, we retrieve similar queries based on the concept and context features

Table 4: Comparison of the accuracy of top *K* search. (d is the dimension of random projection, and k is the number of the nearest neighbors.)

Algorithm	Top 5	Top 10
Spilltree (d = 10)	0.290±0.364	0.321±0.350
Spilltree (d = 50)	0.632±0.317	0.640±0.295
Spilltree (d = 100)	0.754±0.298	0.731±0.280
Spilltree (d = 500)	0.904±0.149	0.880±0.172
BRT	0.922±0.193	0.921±0.187
*k*NN-BRT (k = 1)	0.929±0.197	0.929±0.209
*k*NN-BRT (k = 5)	0.923±0.206	0.936±0.159
*k*NN-BRT (k = 20)	0.928±0.160	0.961±0.124
PPJoin-BRT	0.868±0.247	0.852±0.271
Spilltree-BRT (d = 10, k = 1)	0.512±0.468	0.496±0.463
Spilltree-BRT (d = 50, k = 1)	0.818±0.335	0.796±0.338
Spilltree-BRT (d = 100, k = 1)	0.852±0.300	0.843±0.297
Spilltree-BRT (d = 500, k = 1)	0.907±0.217	0.909±0.204
Spilltree-BRT (d = 10, k = 5)	0.600±0.451	0.587±0.437
Spilltree-BRT (d = 50, k = 5)	0.815±0.339	0.799±0.344
Spilltree-BRT (d = 100, k = 5)	0.844±0.292	0.824±0.299
Spilltree-BRT (d = 500, k = 5)	0.856±0.289	0.852±0.287
Spilltree-BRT (d = 10, k = 20)	0.777±0.365	0.777±0.340
Spilltree-BRT (d = 50, k = 20)	0.885±0.257	0.909±0.221
Spilltree-BRT (d = 100, k = 20)	0.891±0.242	0.902±0.227
Spilltree-BRT (d = 500, k = 20)	0.901±0.221	0.911±0.208

from an already built tree. We use K here to distinguish the notation of k used for *k*NN-based construction of taxonomy. In this experiment, we investigate whether Spilltree, *k*NN-BRT, and Spilltree-BRT can bring benefits to this problem.

We first select 1,000 queries to build the taxonomy trees by leveraging the Spilltree algorithm and different algorithms of BRTs. The experiments of Spilltree are conducted by doing a grid search for tolerance parameter $\tau = \{0.2, 0.3, 0.4\}$. The experiments of all BRT-related algorithms are conducted by doing a grid search for parameters $\alpha = \{5, 10, 15\}$ (Eq. (7)) and $\gamma = \{0.1, 0.5, 0.9\}$ (Eq. (3)). We choose the best results to be shown in this experiment. Then we randomly select 100 queries to search the *K*NN of each query. The ground truth is generated based on the cosine similarity. We evaluate the precision of the top K search problems for different algorithms, which is the proportion of the overlapped top K keywords retrieved by the generated trees and the brute-force search using the cosine similarity metric. The results are shown in Table 4. From the analysis of the results, we draw the following conclusions: First, the dimension of random projection significantly affects the accuracy of Spilltree. In general, the more random projection features we use, the better the accuracy is. The search accuracy can be improved from 30% to more than 90%. Second, the number of the nearest neighbors used to accelerate the building procedure does not affect the accuracy very much. For *k*NN-BRT, the accuracy does not show a significant change when changing the number of k. Third, Spilltree-BRT can further improve the accuracy of Spilltree. With the same projection dimensionality d, Spilltree-BRT results are significantly better than Spilltree. Increasing d or k can both improve the accuracy. This is because larger d results in a better searching accuracy of the nearest neighbors, while larger k leads

Table 5: Comparison of the time (in 10^{-6} seconds) of top K search. (d is the dimension of random projection.)

Algorithm	Top 5	Top 10
Spilltree ($d = 10$)	2.29±5.53	1.86±5.06
Spilltree ($d = 50$)	657.02±158.82	693.02±115.78
Spilltree ($d = 100$)	1,103.84±253.28	1,159.44±147.72
Spilltree ($d = 500$)	3,867.02±777.99	4,443.81±633.41
Spilltree-BRT ($d = 10, k = 1$)	34.38±109.55	35.94± 110.17
Spilltree-BRT ($d = 10, k = 5$)	48.44±84.71	40.63±78.50
Spilltree-BRT ($d = 10, k = 20$)	148.44±977.40	371.88±1,407.09
Spilltree-BRT ($d = 50, k = 1$)	143.75± 978.46	251.56± 1,464.60
Spilltree-BRT ($d = 50, k = 5$)	34.38± 64.73	43.75± 73.55
Spilltree-BRT ($d = 50, k = 20$)	50.00± 85.24	50.00± 98.53
Spilltree-BRT ($d = 100,k = 1$)	1,724.99±6,136.47	2,195.30 ± 6,855.77
Spilltree-BRT($d = 100,k = 5$)	1,782.82±8,498.16	1,814.07 ± 8,687.89
Spilltree-BRT($d = 100,k = 20$)	1,496.89±4,237.15	1,482.82 ± 4,233.09
Spilltree-BRT($d = 500,k = 1$)	2,425.03 ± 5,085.73	2,621.91 ± 5,237.34
Spilltree-BRT($d = 500,k = 5$)	2,135.97±5,025.30	2,223.47± 5,030.34
Spilltree-BRT($d = 500,k = 20$)	2,121.89±4,420.28	2,112.51 ± 4,458.08

to more candidate cluster pairs which increase the opportunity for finding the right clusters to merge.

We also test the searching time for Spilltree and Spilltree-BRT. 110K data is used to build the trees and 200 queries are randomly selected to test the retrieving time. As shown in Table 5, Spilltree performs faster with lower dimension of random projection. However, the accuracy is not good enough (see Table 4). With higher dimensions, the time cost of Spilltree increases very quickly. The major reasons are: (1) It cost more time to compare the similarity between two points for higher dimensionality; (2) Given the same parameter configuration, Spilltree will search more points in high dimensional space. We also perform a grid search for Spilltree-BRT. It can be seen that all results are achieved in acceptable time. The search time of Spilltree-BRT depends on the structure of the tree. Thus, changing d and k only affects the building time of Spilltree-BRT and does not monotonically affect the searching time.

5. CONCLUSION AND FUTURE WORK

In this paper, we present an approach that can automatically derive a domain-dependent taxonomy from a set of keyword phrases by leveraging both a general knowledgebase and keyword search. We first deduce concepts with the technique of conceptualization and extract context information from a search engine, and then induce the new taxonomy using a Bayesian rose tree. We provide three nearest-neighborhood-based methods to speed up the original Bayesian rose tree algorithm. Particularly, the Spilltree-based algorithm reduces the time and memory cost significantly. We also conducted a set of experiments to demonstrate the effectiveness and efficiency of the proposed algorithms.

We regard the work presented as initial, as there are improvements to be made as well as many directions to pursue. First, we will investigate how to use a set of random projections to exponentially reduce the errors of k nearest neighbor searches in the Spilltree algorithm. Second, we would like to use other locality sensitive hashing methods or latent semantic sensitive dimensionality reduction methods to improve the search accuracy in Spilltree. Third, we would like to apply our taxonomy building method to real-world applications (e.g., advertisement or personalized search) to demonstrate its effectiveness and usefulness.

Acknowledgements

We would like to thank Charles Blundell and Yee Whye Teh for their help on the implementation of the Bayesian rose tree, and thanks to Ting Liu for help on the implementation of Spilltree.

6. REFERENCES

[1] R. P. Adams, Z. Ghahramani, and M. I. Jordan. Tree-structured stick breaking for hierarchical data. In *NIPS*, 2010.

[2] J. L. Bentley. Multidimensional binary search trees used for associative searching. *Communications of the ACM*, 18(9):509–517, 1975.

[3] C. Blundell, Y. W. Teh, and K. A. Heller. Bayesian rose trees. In *UAI*, 2010.

[4] W.-Y. Chen, Y. Song, H. Bai, C.-J. Lin, and E. Y. Chang. Parallel spectral clustering in distributed systems. *IEEE Trans. Pattern Anal. Mach. Intell.*, 33(3):568–586, 2011.

[5] S.-L. Chuang and L.-F. Chien. Towards automatic generation of query taxonomy: A hierarchical query clustering approach. In *ICDM*, pages 75–82, 2002.

[6] S. Dasgupta and A. Gupta. An elementary proof of the Lohnson-Lindenstrauss lemma. Technical report, MIT, 1999. ICSI Technical Report TR-99-006.

[7] A. Gionis, P. Indyk, and R. Motwani. Similarity search in high dimensions via hashing. In *VLDB*, pages 518–529, 1999.

[8] M. A. Hearst. Automatic acquisition of hyponyms from large text corpora. In *COLING*, pages 539–545, 1992.

[9] A. K. Jain, M. N. Murty, and P. J. Flynn. Data clustering: a review. *ACM Comput. Surv.*, 31:264–323, September 1999.

[10] D. A. Knowles and Z. Ghahramani. Pitman-Yor diffusion trees. In *UAI*, 2010.

[11] T. Lee, Z. Wang, H. Wang, and S. Hwang. Web scale taxonomy cleansing. *PVLDB*, 4(12):1295–1306, 2011.

[12] T. Liu, A. W. Moore, A. Gray, and K. Yang. An investigation of practical approximate nearest neighbor algorithms. In *NIPS*, pages 825–832, 2005.

[13] R. E. Madsen, D. Kauchak, and C. Elkan. Modeling word burstiness using the Dirichlet distribution. In *ICML*, pages 545–552, 2005.

[14] I. Mani, K. Samuel, K. Concepcion, and D. Vogel. Automatcally inducing ontologies from corpora. In *Workshop on Computational Terminology*, 2004.

[15] R. Navigli, P. Velardi, and S. Faralli. A graph-based algorithm for inducing lexical taxonomies from scratch. In *IJCAI*, pages 1872–1877, 2011.

[16] H. Poon and P. Domingos. Unsupervised ontology induction from text. In *ACL*, pages 296–305, 2010.

[17] E. Sadikov, J. Madhavan, L. Wang, and A. Y. Halevy. Clustering query refinements by user intent. In *WWW*, pages 841–850, 2010.

[18] D. Shen, M. Qin, W. Chen, Q. Yang, and Z. Chen. Mining web query hierarchies from clickthrough data. In *AAAI*, pages 341–346, 2007.

[19] Y. Song, H. Wang, Z. Wang, H. Li, and W. Chen. Short text conceptualization using a probabilistic knowledgebase. In *IJCAI*, pages 2330–2336, 2011.

[20] J. K. Uhlmann. Satisfying general proximity/similarity queries with metric trees. *Information Processing Letters*, 40(4):175–179, 1991.

[21] J. Wang, H. Wang, Z. Wang, and K. Q. Zhu. Understanding tables on the web. In *ER*, 2012.

[22] Y. Wang, H. Li, H. Wang, and K. Q. Zhu. Toward topic search on the web. In *ER*, 2012.

[23] R. W. White, P. N. Bennett, and S. T. Dumais. Predicting short-term interests using activity-based search context. In *CIKM*, pages 1009–1018, 2010.

[24] W. Wu, H. Li, H. Wang, and K. Q. Zhu. Probase: A probabilistic taxonomy for text understanding. In *SIGMOD*, 2012.

[25] C. Xiao, W. Wang, X. Lin, J. X. Yu, and G. Wang. Efficient similarity joins for near-duplicate detection. *ACM Trans. Database Syst.*, 36(3):15, 2011.

An Enhanced Relevance Criterion For More Concise Supervised Pattern Discovery

Henrik Großkreutz
Fraunhofer IAIS
Schloss Birlinghoven
53754 St. Augustin, Germany
henrik.grosskreutz@iais.fraunhofer.de

Daniel Paurat
Computer Science
University of Bonn
53117 Bonn, Germany
daniel.paurat@uni-bonn.de

Stefan Rüping
Fraunhofer IAIS
Schloss Birlinghoven
53754 St. Augustin, Germany
stefan.rueping@iais.fraunhofer.de

ABSTRACT

Supervised local pattern discovery aims to find subsets of a database with a high statistical unusualness in the distribution of a target attribute. Local pattern discovery is often used to generate a human-understandable representation of the most interesting dependencies in a data set. Hence, the more crisp and concise the output is, the better. Unfortunately, standard algorithm often produce very large and redundant outputs.

In this paper, we introduce Δ-relevance, a definition of a more strict criterion of relevance. It will allow us to significantly reduce the output space, while being able to guarantee that every local pattern has a Δ-relevant representative which is almost as good in a clearly defined sense. We show empirically that Δ-relevance leads to a considerable reduction of the amount of returned patterns. We also demonstrate that in a top-k setting, the removal of not Δ-relevant patterns improves the quality of the result set.

Categories and Subject Descriptors

H.2.8 [**H.2.8 Database Applications**]: Data mining

General Terms

Theory,Algorithms

Keywords

Local Patterns, Subgroup Discovery, Theory of Relevance

1. INTRODUCTION

Supervised local pattern discovery is the task of finding patterns that describe subsets of a database with a high statistical unusualness in the distribution of a target attribute. Different approaches for supervised local pattern discovery have been proposed, which differ in the way in which the statistical unusualness is defined. Among these approaches are subgroup discovery [10] contrast set mining [2] and correlated itemset mining [20], all of which are also sometimes subsumed under the name supervised descriptive rule discovery [12]. Hence, in this paper we use the words *pattern* and *subgroup* interchangeably. Moreover, we will focus one the special case of a **binary** class label.

In many (if not most) applications of supervised pattern discovery, the practical usefulness of the approach depends on the ability to produce a concise, non-redundant output. Unfortunately, in particular in situations with some amount of noise, standard local pattern algorithms are often found to return a high number of very similar, correlated patterns.

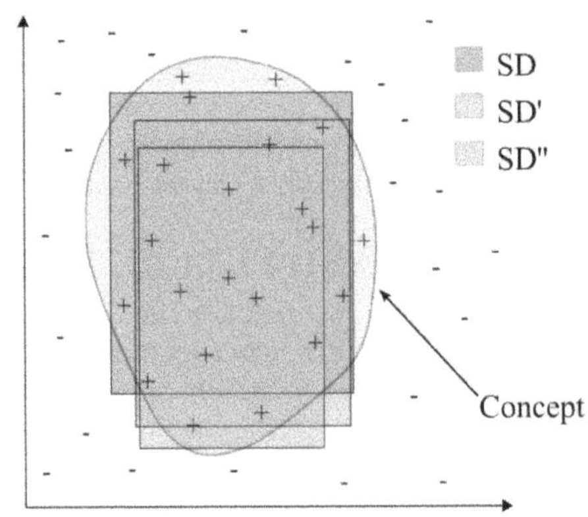

Figure 1: Highly correlated set of subgroups. If a small loss of precision is tolerable, each single subgroup already describes the target concept well.

The basic problem is depicted in Figure 1. Here, we have aligned (or projected) the instances in a two-dimensional space, and the green area highlights a subset with a high share of target-class instances ("+"). The figure also shows three subgroups, visualized by rectangular boxes. While it is clear that all subgroups are correct, non-identical descriptions of parts of the target concept, they are highly correlated. Hence, when one is willing to sacrifice a small amount of precision in favor of simplicity, one single subgroup suffices to describe the target concept reasonably well.

1.1 Goals and Contributions

Different techniques have been used to reduce the output space of supervised pattern discovery. One particularly interesting approach is the **theory of relevance** [7]. The

KDD'12, August 12–16, 2012, Beijing, China.

idea is to check whether a subgroup sd is better suited as a predictor of the label than another subgroup sd_{irr}, which holds true if all correct prediction from sd_{irr} can be made by sd as well, and all errors from sd are made by sd_{irr} as well. If so, then sd_{irr} is irrelevant and can be ignored. A pattern is then defined to be relevant if it is not **dominated** by another pattern in the above sense.

While the theory of relevance provides a nice theoretical approach to the suppression of useless patterns, and has shown to be of great use in practical applications [14], it is based on a stringent definition of dominance. Even if a pattern misclassifies hundreds or thousands of positives correctly matched by another pattern, but is better on a single negative, then the former pattern will not be considered as dominated by the latter pattern.

In this paper, we aim at an extended definition of relevance that allows for a controlled amount of lenience. To this end, we propose a **relaxed** criterion of dominance, which allows a dominating subgroup to predict a small number of examples worse than its dominated counterpart. Thereupon, we define a **more strict criterion of relevance**: Due to the relaxed criterion of dominance, more patterns may dominate a given pattern, such that it is harder for a pattern not to be dominated, i.e. to be relevant.

The resulting definition of Δ-relevance will allow us to significantly reduce the output space. At the same time, it will provide the guarantee that every local pattern sd's has a Δ-relevant representative which is almost as good, in the sense that if the dominated pattern has precision p (i.e. a share of positives p), then the Δ-relevant representative will (i) support all of sd's positives and (ii) will have at least precision $(1-\Delta)\cdot p$. That is, the loss in precision is limited by the factor Δ.

As the main contribution of our paper we see

- Definition 2 of the new, relaxed domination criterion ("Δ-domination"), and, building upon it, the Definition 4 of the new relevance criterion ("Δ-relevance");
- Propositions 2 and 5, showing that limiting the output of pattern discovery to only Δ-relevant patterns leads only to a limited loss of information compared to the full set of patterns;
- Corollary 6, showing that each dataset has a unique covering of Δ-relevant patterns;
- Algorithm 1 to compute this covering.

To demonstrate the usefulness of Δ-relevance we show experimentally that it results in a significant reduction of the number of resulting patterns. Moreover, to show that Δ-relevance keeps the "important" pattern and only removes patterns of little use, we will also apply it to top-k subgroup discovery [10]. The basic idea, depicted in Figure 2, is that removing subgroups which are not Δ-relevant from the top-k patterns allows other patterns, which cover different and thus more interesting aspects of pattern space, to make into the output.

Every Δ-relevant pattern is closed on the positives, meaning that the Δ-relevant patterns is a subset of the well-known closed patterns [6, 3]. Compared to heuristic approaches for redundancy avoidance, like weighted covering [13] or beam selection strategies [22], Δ-relevance is a principled approach that provides formal guarantees on the quality of the result.

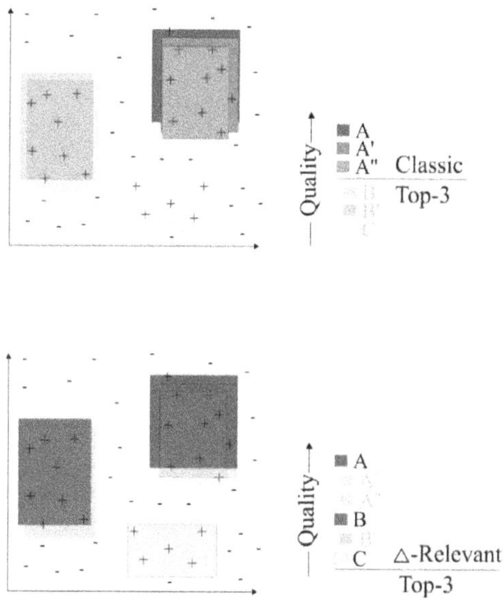

Figure 2: Top subfigure shows the classical top-3 subgroups, which are highly correlated; The bottom subfigure shows that choosing a representative for the sets of highly correlated subgroups allows other, non-redundant subgroup descriptions to enter the top-3 result list

Moreover, although (like the other approaches) it introduces a new parameter, this parameter has a clear interpretation (the loss in precision tolerated for the representatives). Finally, compared to Δ-closed itemsets [4], in spite of the similar name it has different characteristics: in our approach there is a guarantee that for every dominated pattern has a Δ-dominant representative, which is not guaranteed for Δ-closed itemsets.

The remainder of this paper is structured as follows: the next section formally introduces the notions of closure operators, domination and relevance. Section 3 describes our theoretical contribution, the definition of Δ-relevance, which is a more strict criterion of relevance. This is applied to the problem of subgroup discovery in Section 4. Experiments in Section 5 demonstrate that Δ-relevance leads to a considerable reduction of the size of the set of subgroups and that the combination with top-k approaches improves the quality of the outcome. Section 6 concludes.

2. PRELIMINARIES

We will now briefly review the (classical) definition of relevance and summarize some important results from that area.

2.1 Databases and Subgroup Descriptions

A **database** DB is a collection of data **records**, i.e. $DB = d_1, \ldots, d_m$. We assume every record d_i to be described by a set of n binary **features** $(f_1(d_i), \ldots, f_n(d_i)) \in \{0,1\}^n$. Moreover, we assume that all records have a binary **label**. Formally, the label is a special feature $class(d)$ with range $\{+,-\}$. A **subgroup description** sd is a subset of the feature set, i.e. $sd \subseteq \{f_1, \ldots, f_n\}$. In the following, we will sometimes simply write **subgroup** to refer to a subgroup description. A data record d satisfies sd if $f(d) = 1$ for all

$f \in sd$. Finally, $DB[sd]$ to denote the set of records $d \in DB$ of a database DB satisfying a subgroup description sd.

2.2 Domination and Relevance

The theory of relevance [15, 14] is aimed at eliminating irrelevant patterns. A subgroup sd_{irr} is considered as irrelevant if it is **dominated** (or **covered**) by another subgroup sd in the following sense:

DEFINITION 1. *The subgroup sd_{irr} is* ***dominated*** *by the subgroup sd in database DB iff.*

- $TP(DB, sd_{irr}) \subseteq TP(DB, sd)$ *and*
- $FP(DB, sd) \subseteq FP(DB, sd_{irr})$.

Here, TP denotes the **true positives**, which are defined as $TP(DB, sd) = \{c \in DB[sd] \mid class(c) = +\}$. Similarly, FP denotes the **false positives**, i.e. $FP(DB, sd) = \{c \in DB[sd] \mid class(c) = -\}$. Note that it is possible that two subgroups dominate each other, however only in the case that they have identical support. In this case, their closure can be used as their common unique representative.

The above notion allows to distinguish between **irrelevant** and **relevant** subgroups, the former being those dominated by a different subgroup. The idea of the theory of relevance is to restrict consideration to the relevant subgroups, because for each of the other subgroups there is a dominating relevant subgroup which is more valuable.

2.3 Closure Operators and their Connection to Relevance

As shown by Garriga et al. [7], the notion of relevance can be restated in terms of the following mapping between subgroup descriptions:

$$\Gamma^+(X) := \{f \mid \forall d \in TP(DB, X) : f[d] = 1\}. \quad (1)$$

Γ^+ is a **closure operator**, i.e. a function defined on the powerset of features $\mathcal{P}(\{f_1, \dots, f_n\})$ such that for all $X, Y \in \mathcal{P}(\{f_1, \dots, f_n\})$, (i) $X \subseteq \Gamma(X)$ (extensivity), (ii) $X \subseteq Y \Rightarrow \Gamma(X) \subseteq \Gamma(Y)$ (monotonicity), and (iii) $\Gamma(X) = \Gamma(\Gamma(X))$ (idempotence) holds.

The fixpoints of Γ^+, i.e. the subgroup descriptions sd such that $sd = \Gamma^+(sd)$, are called the **closed-on-the-positives**. The main result in [7] is that

PROPOSITION 1. *The space of relevant patterns consists of all patterns sd_{rel} satisfying the following:*

- *sd_{rel} is closed on the positives, and*
- *there is no generalization $sd \subsetneq sd_{rel}$ closed on the positives such that $|FP(sd)| = |FP(sd_{rel})|$.*

The connection between relevancy and closure operators is particularly interesting because closure operators have extensively been studied in the area of closed pattern mining (cf. [21]). However, unlike here in closed pattern mining the closure operator is defined solely on the **support**, without accounting for labels (i.e., $\Gamma_{sup}(X) = \{f \mid \forall d \in DB[X] : f[d] = 1\}$). The fixpoints of this closure operator are simply called **closed** patterns.

3. A MORE STRICT DEFINITION OF RELEVANCE

We will now present our relaxed dominance criterion which leads to a stricter definition of relevance. But before we do so, let us give a short example why such a criterion is necessary. Let sd_1 be a pattern which covers 1000 positive examples and 1 negative example. Let sd_2 be specialization of sd_1 that covers exactly the same examples, with the exception of one positive and the negative one. Obviously, neither of the subgroups dominates each other, because although the true positives of sd_2 are contained in the true positives of sd_1, the one false positive of sd_1 is missing in sd_2 (intuitively speaking, sd_1 is better than sd_2 on the positives, but worse on the negatives). However, in practice it is questionable whether such a small difference will have any significant impact.

Motivated by this example, we will introduce a definition of dominance that allows a percentage Δ of missing false positives in the dominated pattern. I.e. the dominated pattern may be better than the dominating one on the negatives, but only slightly so. Thus, in the above example sd_2 would be dominated by sd_1 (for an appropriate Δ).

It is obvious that larger datasets can be constructed according to the scheme of our example. In larger datasets the effect can be that the top-k subgroups all characterize very similar subgroups, while other, different and thus more interesting subgroups are pushed out of the result. To overcome this problem, we will now propose a relaxed definition of relevance.

3.1 A Generalized Definition of Dominance

The first step in defining a relaxed notion of relevance is to modify the definition of dominance. To this end, we introduce the notion of Δ-domination, where Δ is a real-valued parameter between 0 and 1. The larger the value of Δ, the lower the requirements for a subgroup to be dominated, and thus the more subgroups are (potentially) dominated.

DEFINITION 2. *(**Δ-dominance**) Let Δ be some value, $0 \leq \Delta < 1$. The subgroup sd_{irr} is Δ-dominated by the subgroup sd in database DB iff.*

- $TP(DB, sd_{irr}) \subseteq TP(DB, sd)$ *and*
- $|FP(DB, sd) \setminus FP(DB, sd_{irr})| \leq \frac{\Delta}{1-\Delta} |DB[sd_{irr}]|$

Intuitively, this definition says that sd_{irr} is Δ-dominated if it supports less positives than the dominating pattern, and although it may support less negatives than the dominating pattern, the number of negatives in this difference set is relatively small compared with the overall size of the subgroup sd_{irr}.

Note that also alternative definitions of the second constraint would be possible, e.g. using a constant bound on the number of additional false positives. The main advantage of the relative definition is that it allows us to quantify the relation between the share of positives in the dominated subgroup and in the dominating subgroups:

PROPOSITION 2. *If a subgroup sd_{irr} is Δ-dominated by a subgroup sd_{rel}, then the share of positives in sd_{rel} is no lower than $(1 - \Delta)$ times the share of positives in sd_{irr}. Formally,*

$$\frac{|TP(DB, sd_{rel})|}{|DB[sd_{rel}]|} \geq (1 - \Delta)\frac{|TP(DB, sd_{irr})|}{|DB[sd_{irr}]|}.$$

PROOF. We have that

$$|TP(DB, sd_{rel})| \,/\, |DB[sd_{rel}]| =$$
$$|TP(DB, sd_{rel})| \,/ (|TP(DB, sd_{rel})| + |FP(DB, sd_{rel})|) \geq$$
$$|TP(DB, sd_{rel})| \,/ (|TP(DB, sd_{rel})| +$$
$$|FP(DB, sd_{irr})| + |FP(DB, sd_{rel}) \setminus FP(DB, sd_{irr})|)$$

From the first condition of relevance, we can conclude that the above must be

$$\geq \frac{|TP(DB, sd_{irr})|}{|DB[sd_{irr})| + |FP(DB, sd_{rel}) \setminus FP(DB, sd_{irr})|}$$

Moreover, from the second condition we have

$$|FP(DB, sd_{rel}) \setminus FP(DB, sd_{irr})| \leq \frac{\Delta}{1-\Delta} |DB[sd_{irr}])|$$

which together from the earlier inequality implies the proposition. □

With this proposition, Δ becomes a parameter with a clearly defined semantic, namely the control of the trade-off of compression versus allowed loss of precision $p(sd) = \frac{|TP(DB, sd_{rel})|}{|DB[sd_{rel}]|}$. Hence, a user can easily choose an adequate value of Δ that is consistent with his practical application requirements. Note that the question of how much loss of precision is still considered as tolerable is an external decision, hence it is necessary to include a user-controllable parameter for this step.

3.2 Properties of the Generalized Dominance

In this part, we will prove some important properties of the generalized definition of dominance that will be of importance later. As already mention, a higher value of Δ has the effect that potentially more subgroups are dominated. In fact, the following implication holds:

LEMMA 3. *If a subgroup sd Δ-dominates another subgroup sd_{irr}, then the subgroup sd Δ'-dominates sd_{irr} for all $\Delta' > \Delta$.*

PROOF. This follows from the fact that the function $f(\Delta) = \frac{\Delta}{1-\Delta}$ is monotonically increasing for $\Delta < 1$. □

In particular, every subgroup dominated according to the classical definition of dominance is Δ-dominated for arbitrary Δ, as 0-dominance is equivalent to classical dominance. The definition of Δ-dominance implies additional properties, which are similar to those of the classical definition:

LEMMA 4. *The following holds:*

1. *Every subgroup sd_{notCl} not closed on the positives is dominated by some subgroup sd which is closed on the positives (and, hence, also Δ-dominated);*

2. *Let sd_1, sd_2 be different subgroups closed on the positives. If sd_1 is Δ-dominated by sd_2, then sd_2 is a generalization of sd_1;*

3. *Every subgroup that is closed on the positives and that is Δ-dominated by some subgroup is also Δ-dominated by a closed-on-the-positive.*

PROOF. Item 1: Let sd_{notCl} be some subgroup not closed on the positives. Then sd_{notCl} is dominated by $sd_{closed} = \Gamma^+(sd_{notCl})$. This can be verified by checking the conditions of the definition of domination: 1. both subgroups support the same set of positives (by definition), hence the first condition is satisfied. 2. sd_{closed} supports a subset of the examples supported by sd_{notCl}, hence the second condition is satisfied.

Item 2: By condition 1 of the definition of relevance, the TP supported by sd_1 are all supported by sd_2. Hence, the closure on the positives of sd_1 contains the subgroup description of sd_2. As sd_1 is closed on the positives, sd_1 must be a specialization of sd_2.

Item 3: Assume that sd_{irr} is dominated by some pattern sd_{notCl} not closed on the positives. Then, it must also be dominated by $sd_{closed} = \Gamma^+(sd_{notCl})$: first, sd_{closed} and sd_{notCl} support the same positives. Second, by Definition 2 we have $|FP(DB, sd_{notCl}) \setminus FP(DB, sd_{irr})| \leq \Delta/(1-\Delta)\,|DB[sd_{irr}]|$. Moreover, the false positives of sd_{notCl} are a subset of the false positives of sd_{closed}, which implies $|FP(DB, sd_{rel}) \setminus FP(DB, sd_{irr})| \leq \Delta/(1-\Delta)\,|DB[sd_{irr}]|$ and completes the proof. □

Finally, we will present an example to illustrate the definition and to show that dominance does **not** have one particular property, namely transitivity. Please consider the example dataset is given in Table 1. It includes three features, A, B and C, and the support of each of these features is a subset of the support of the previous features.

Id	Label	A	B	C
1	+	✓	✓	✓
2	-	✓	✓	-
3	+	✓	✓	-
4	-	✓	-	-
5	+	✓	-	-
6	-	-	-	-

Table 1: Example

The space of subgroup descriptions of this example is visualized in Figure 3, together with the records that support the different subgroups (positive records are rendered with a gray filling). The subgroup C (which is equivalent to ABC) supports only one record, which is positive; the subgroup B (resp. AB) supports three records, two of which are positive; and finally A supports 5 records, three of which are positive.

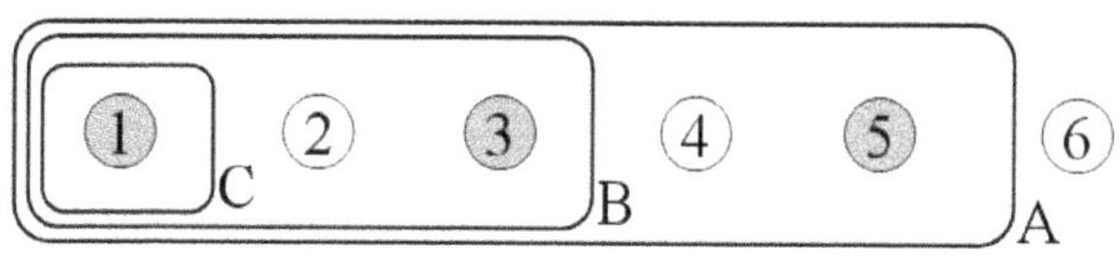

Figure 3: The dominance relation is not transitive

For $\Delta = 0$, Δ-domination does not differ from the classical definition of domination, so none of the above subgroup descriptions is dominated. For $\Delta = 0.5$, A Δ-dominates AB: the true positives of AB (examples 1 and 3) are also true positives of A, there exists 1 false positive of A that is no false positive of AB (example 4), AB covers a total of 3 examples (1,2, and 3), and $1 \leq 0.5 \cdot 3$. Similarly, it is easy to verify that AB 0.5-dominates ABC. However, A does **not** 0.5-dominate ABC, because $1 > 0.5 \cdot 1$: the Δ-dominance relation is **not transitive**!

3.3 A Generalized Definition of Relevance

Now that we have defined Δ-dominance, we turn to the definition of Δ-relevance. It might seem at first that Δ-relevance can be defined in complete analogy to classical relevance (where a subgroup is relevant if it is not dominated by any other subgroup). This, however, is problematic due to the different characteristics of Δ-dominance, namely to the missing transitivity.

If we would define patterns to be Δ-relevant if they are not being dominated by any other pattern, then there would be irrelevant patterns (wrt. such a definition) that are not dominated by relevant pattern. The effect would be that (unlike it classical relevance) patterns could be suppressed although the result does not contain a dominating pattern.

To avoid such undesirable situations, we base our definition of Δ-relevance on the notion of a covering of Δ-dominating subgroups:

DEFINITION 3. *Given a dataset DB, a set of subgroups S is called a* ***covering*** *of Δ-relevant subgroups for DB iff.*

- *For every subgroup s in DB, there is a subgroup $s' \in S$ that Δ-dominates s.*
- *There are no two subgroups $s_1, s_2 \in S$ such that s_1 Δ-dominates s_2.*
- *Every subgroup in S is closed on the positives.*

The first condition ensures that S is a covering, that is, **every subgroup has a Δ-relevant representative**. The second requires it to be **minimal**. The third condition says that we want the covering to consist only of subgroups **closed on the positives**, because as usual we want to use these as representatives.

The practical significance of this definition is that in combination with Proposition 2 we can now guarantee that if one is willing to tolerate a loss of precision of at most Δ, it suffices to look only at the subgroups in such a covering. Part 1 of the definition guarantees that for all other subgroups we can find a subgroup in the covering which is almost as good.

While this definition seems to leave a high degree of freedom, in fact it defines precisely one single set of patterns. These can be constructed iteratively, based on the specialization graph defined on the patterns closed-on-the-positives. This graph $G = (V, E)$ has, as vertex set V, the set of closed-on-the-positives, and its edge set consists of all (p, p') such that p' is a specialization of p (not necessarily a direct specialization). Based on this graph, the covering of Δ-relevant subgroups can be constructed as described in Algorithm 1.

We will now prove that these construction rules are correct, and yield a uniquely determine set of patterns:

PROPOSITION 5. *The algorithm calculates a set Cov such that (i) Cov is a covering; and (ii) any covering must include all patterns in Cov.*

PROOF. We first show inductively that all nodes in *Cov* **must** be part of the covering.

Algorithm 1 Covering of Δ-relevant Subgroups

```
1: let G = the specialization graph for the patterns
2: let Cov:= {c ∈ G|c has no predecessor in G}
3: while the vertex set of G is not empty do
4:     G := the graph obtained from G by removing all Δ-
       dominated specializations of nodes in Cov (and the
       corresponding edges).
5:     let Cov:= Cov∪{c ∈ G|c has no predecessor in G}
6: return Cov
```

(Base case:) The set of vertexes selected in Line 2 have to be part of the covering, because (i) they are closed on the positives, and (ii) there isn't any closed-on-the-positive generalization of them. Thus, according to Lemma 4 they are not Δ-dominated by any other pattern and hence they must be part of the covering.

(Inductive step:) All nodes removed in 4 cannot be part of any covering. This follows directly from the second part of Definition 3 together with the fact that the covering already includes a pattern that Δ-dominates them.

Moreover, all nodes added to the covering in Line 5 must be part of the covering. This follows from Lemma 4 and the facts that (i) the covering does not yet include a pattern which Δ-dominates them, and (ii) there isn't any Δ-dominating pattern which could alternatively be added to the covering, because for all generalizations we already know that they either cannot be part of the covering or are not Δ-dominating.

This completes the first part of the proof. It remains to show that the algorithms terminates, and that when it ends *Cov* contains a covering.

The fact that the algorithm ends follows from the facts that the (initial) vertex set is finite, and that in every loop the graph is replaced by a graph with strictly less vertexes (because G has no cycles).

Finally, *Cov* must be a covering because for every vertex resp. pattern, either it is in the covering or there is a dominating pattern in *Cov*. This directly follows from the construction of the algorithm for patterns that are closed on the positives. For all other patterns sd_{notCl}, either their closure in the positives, $sd_{closed} = \Gamma^+(sd_{notCl})$ is a member of *Cov*; then, they are obviously dominated. Else, their closure sd_{closed} is dominated by some member sd_{rel} of *Cov*. By statement 2 of Lemma 4, sd_{rel} is a generalization of sd_{closed}. Hence, the true positives of sd_{rel} are a superset of the true positives of sd_{closed}, resp. sd_{notCl} and the first condition of Definition 2 is satisfied. It remains to show that the second condition also holds.

sd_{rel} dominates sd_{closed}, hence by Definition 2 we have $|FP(DB, sd_{rel}) \setminus FP(DB, sd_{closed})| \leq \Delta/(1-\Delta)\,|DB[sd_{closed}]|$.

Moreover, the false positives of sd_{notCl} are a superset of the false positives of sd_{closed}, and the support set of sd_{notCl} is a superset of the support set of sd_{closed}. This implies $|FP(DB, sd_{rel}) \setminus FP(DB, sd_{notCl})| \leq \Delta/(1-\Delta)\,|DB[sd_{notCl}]|$.

□

COROLLARY 6. *Definition 3 defines a unique set of patterns.*

PROOF. This follows from the above proposition and the fact that a covering has to be minimal – i.e. from the second item in the definition. □

Based on Corollary 6, we finally define Δ-relevance as follows:

DEFINITION 4. *A subgroup is called a Δ-relevant for a dataset DB iff. it is a member of DB's unique covering of Δ-relevant patterns.*

3.4 Caveat

It is interesting to notice that a property like Lemma 3 (dealing with Δ-dominance) does not hold for Δ-relevance: it is possible that a subgroup becomes Δ-irrelevant for one value of Δ, but that for another $\Delta' > \Delta$, becomes Δ'-relevant again. This can lead to the situation that a covering for one value of Δ is actually **smaller** than that for a higher value Δ'. For example, consider the data set in Table 2. For $\Delta = 0.5$, the subgroup AB dominates the subgroups ABC and ABD, but is not dominated by A. Hence, the relevant subgroups for $\Delta = 0.5$ are A and AB. For $\Delta = 0.56$, A dominates AB, but does dominate neither ABC nor ABD, so there exists three relevant subgroups, A, ABC, and ABD. Again, this has to do with the missing transitivity of dominance: AB does still dominate ABC and ABD, but as AB is suppressed from the result set, this does not exclude its two specializations. Figure 4 show the graph with the dominance dependencies between these subgroups together with the minimal Δ for which the dominance holds.

Id	Label	A	B	C	D
1	+	✓	✓	✓	-
2	+	✓	✓	-	✓
3	+	✓	✓	-	-
4	+	✓	-	-	-
5	-	✓	-	-	-
6	-	✓	-	-	-
7	-	✓	✓	-	-
8	-	✓	-	-	-
9	-	✓	-	-	-
10	-	✓	-	-	-

Table 2: The size of the Δ-relevant pattern set is not monotonous in Δ

In the experiments, however, we will demonstrate that this problem usually does not occur in practice.

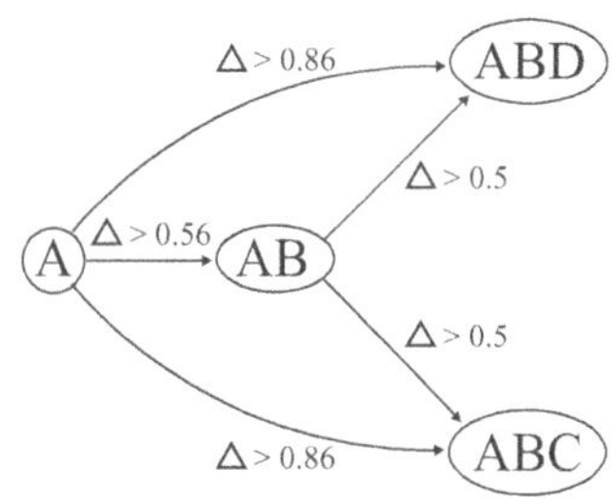

Figure 4: The dominance graph of Example 2.

4. EXTENSION: COMBINATION WITH TOP-K APPROACHES

Our algorithm from Section 3.3 computes the unique covering of Δ-relevant patterns for a database. While the covering of Δ-relevant patterns can be much smaller than the whole set of (relevant) patterns, depending on the database this set can still be unacceptably large. As already mentioned in the introduction, one standard approach to deal with this issue is to rank the pattern according to some quality function and keep only the top$-k$ patterns. In this section, we will describe how our new concept of Δ-relevance can be combined with top$-k$ approaches – more precisely, how it can be used to devise an improved subgroup discovery algorithm.

4.1 Classical Top$-k$ Subgroup Discovery

The interestingness of a subgroup description sd in the context of a database DB is measured by a **quality function** q that assigns a real-valued quality $q(sd, DB)$ to sd. In this paper, we only consider the following family of quality functions:

$$|DB[sd]|^a \cdot \left(\frac{|TP(DB, sd)|}{|DB[sd]|} - \frac{|TP(DB, \emptyset)|}{|DB|}\right) \qquad (2)$$

Here, a is a constant such that $0 \leq a \leq 1$. The family of quality functions characterized by Equation 2 includes some of the most popular quality functions: for $a = 1$, it is order equivalent to the Piatetsky-Shapiro quality function [10] and the weighted relative accuracy WRACC [16], while for $a = 0.5$ it corresponds to the binomial test quality function [10]. Based on the definition of a quality function, classical **top-k subgroup discovery** [10] is then concerned with finding the k highest-quality subgroups.

4.2 Top-k Δ-Relevant Subgroup Discovery

Using our generalization notion of relevance, we extend the task of subgroup discovery as follows:

TASK 1. ***Top-k Δ-Relevant Subgroup Discovery*** *Given a database DB, a quality function q, an integer $k > 0$ and a real value Δ, $0 \leq \Delta < 1$, find a set of subgroup descriptions G of size k, such that*

- *all subgroup descriptions in G are Δ-relevant, and*
- *all Δ-relevant subgroup descriptions not in R have a quality no higher than $\min_{sd \in R} q(DB, sd)$.*

4.3 Efficient Computation

Δ-relevant Subgroup Discovery can be performed following the algorithm from Section 3.3, where for every discovered pattern its quality is calculated. In a subsequent step, all but the top-k subgroups are then discarded.

However, it is not necessary to compute the graph G beforehand, as this can be done dynamically during the execution of the algorithm. The basic trick is that Property 2 of Lemma 4 allows to search through the space of closed patterns in a general-to-specific order. If one is only interested in the top-k patterns, then large parts of the specialization graph (used in the construction in Sec. 3.3) can be pruned using so-called optimistic estimators [24, 19, 9]. Essentially, all vertexes corresponding to subgroups with optimistic estimate below a minimum threshold can be ignored. Even if such a threshold is not specified beforehand, the threshold can dynamically be determined using the quality of the best k relevant subgroups so far considered. The overall algorithm is quite similar to the one in [8], and the computation is thus roughly as expensive as classical relevant pattern mining. The details are omitted for space reasons, computational aspects not being the focus of our investigation. We remark, however, that each experiment presented in Section 5 could be computed within less than 5 minutes on a Core-2 Duo PC, with most experiments completing in a few seconds.

5. RESULTS

In this section, we consider the effect of our new definition of relevance on several benchmark datasets. More precisely, we will analyze the following two questions:

1. To what extent does the new definition reduce the number of patterns?
2. Does the use of our stronger relevance criterion improve the quality of the top-k (filtered) patterns?

To answer these questions, we applied our algorithm on 8 datasets from the UCI repository [1], listed in Table 3 along with some of their properties.

Dataset	target class	# rec.	# feat.
credit-g	bad	1000	58
lymph	mal_lymph	148	50
mushroom	poisonous	8124	117
nursery	recommend	12960	27
sick	sick	3772	66
soybean	brown-spot	638	133
tic-tac-toe	positive	958	27
vote	republican	435	48

Table 3: Datasets

5.1 Reduction of the Number of Patterns

In this section, we aim to show that Δ-relevance significantly reduces the number of patterns that are found in a database. In [3] it has already been shown that closed subgroups very much reduce the number of patterns in comparison to all possible patterns, while in [7] it has been shown that going from closed pattern to relevant patterns again very much reduces the amount of patterns found. Hence, it suffices to show that going from relevant patterns, i.e. Δ-relevant patterns for $\Delta = 0$, to Δ-relevant patterns for $\Delta > 0$ reduces the number of patterns.

Figure 5 shows how the number of Δ-relevant patterns reduces depending on Δ. It can be seen that for all datasets, the number of patterns reduces with increasing Δ.

5.2 Quality of the Patterns

Despite the reduction of the output space, the number of Δ-relevant patterns found can still be too large to handle. Therefore, a combination with a top-k approach is advisable. The benefit that comes with the usage of Δ-relevant patterns is that the top-k Δ-relevant patterns are less redundant and more "interesting" than classical top−k patterns.

In the following, we will first illustrate the impact of our approach on the redundancy of the top subgroups using the visualization introduced in [22]. Thereafter, we will describe the effect of our approach using a set of performance figures. While optimizing accuracy is not the primary goal of subgroup discovery [16], it is a common approach to evaluate predictive accuracy in the absence of a better option to capture the "interestingness" of the patterns.

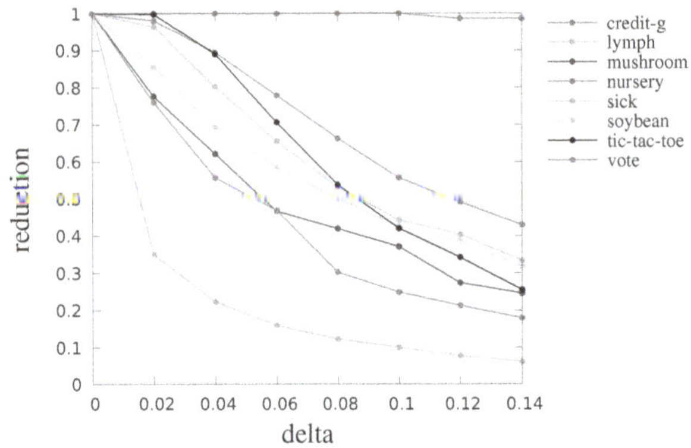

Figure 5: Number of Δ-relevant rules found (percentage, y-axis) depending on Δ (x-axis).

5.2.1 Redundancy

To illustrate how our approach affects redundancy, we use the visualization proposed by [22]. Here, the coverage of a set of subgroups, i.e. the set of records satisfied by the individual subgroups, is visualized as a rectangular plot of black and white pixels. The plot has one row of pixels for every subgroup. Similarly, there is one column for every record. The pixel at location (x, y) is plotted in black if the x-th subgroup includes record y; else, the pixel is plotted in white. If a set of subgroups is highly redundant, then the plot will reveal noticeable vertical patterns: the reason is that the coverage of the subgroups, and hence the rows visualizing them, will be very similar.

Figure 6 shows an individual plot for the top-k subgroups found using different approaches. On top, we show the plot for the top−20 classic subgroups; next, we show the plot for the top-20 closed subgroups; thereafter, we show the plot for the top-20 relevant subgroups; and finally, we show the plot for the top−20 Δ-relevant subgroups ($\Delta = 0.1$). It is obvious that the first three plots exhibit vertical patterns, meaning that there is a high degree of redundancy. In the last plot – visualizing the Δ-relevant subgroups – no such pattern is appearant, meaning that the Δ-relevant subgroups are much more diverse.

5.2.2 Predictive Accuracy

We use the following experimental setup: we convert a set of patterns in a predictive model in the following way: for any pattern sd we compute the class probability $p(sd) = \frac{|TP(DB,sd)|}{|DB[sd]|}$. To any example x that is covered by sd, we assign $p(sd)$ as the predicted class probability. In case x is covered by more than one pattern, we assign to it the maximum p of all covering patterns. If x is not covered by any pattern, we assign to it the default probability. This allows to compute the Area under the Curve (AUC) of a set of patterns, which is a measure of how good the set of patterns reproduces the underlying class distribution.

Figure 7 shows the AUC of the Top 10 Δ-relevant patterns for different values of Δ and the Piatetsky-Shapiro quality function. It can be seen that the AUC tends to increase for $\Delta > 0$ (for 5 datasets, there is a clear improvement; one

Figure 6: Redudancy of the top-k subgroups using classic, closed and relevant subgroups respectively Δ-relevant subgroups. The obvious regularity in the visualization of the subgroups for the existing approaches shows that these come up with highly redundant subgroups. For the Δ-relevant subgroups, no vertical pattern is apparent, meaning that they are much less redundant.

dataset ("nursery") is completely unaffected; and finally, for two datasets ("lymph" and "vote"), the plot shows that the AUC decreases after reaching a maximum for a value of Δ around 0.05). The results are similar for the binomial quality function in Figure 8: again, the AUC tends to increase when Δ-relevant patterns are considered instead of classical relevant patterns.

6. CONCLUSION

In this paper, we have presented Δ-relevance as an enhancement of the theory of relevance. It was shown that Δ-relevance can be defined in terms of a unique covering of a database. Δ-relevance allows to significantly reduce the output of local pattern detection tasks, while being able to guarantee that for every pattern that is excluded from the result, there is a pattern included in the result which is almost as good in a clearly defined sense.

In addition, algorithmic solutions for finding all and the top-k Δ-relevant patterns have been introduced. As Δ-relevance is built upon a weaker criterion of domination than classical relevance, there exists fewer Δ-relevant patterns than strictly relevant ones. We have shown empirically that this can very much reduce the amount of pattern that are found, while there is no negative effect on the usefulness of the patterns (in terms of the AUC when using the patterns as a predictive model).

Compared to other approaches targeting redundancy avoidance (e.g. [11, 5, 18, 23]), our approach considers labeled data and provides particular guarantees about the resulting set of patterns, as precised by Proposition 2. The paper [17] introduces an extension of classical relevance to subgroups similar to ours. However, it only defines what is called delta-dominance in this paper; it does not uniquely define delta-relevance of a single subgroup in the sense of Definition 4. Furthermore, the algorithm is not based on patterns that are closed on the positive. It is this asymmetric treatment of the positive labelled data that allows us to drastically reduce the size of the search space for our algorithm.

Acknowledgments

This publication has been produced in the context of the EU Collaborative Project "DICODE - Mastering Data-Intensive Collaboration and Decision Making" which is co-funded by the European Commission under the contract FP7-ICT--257184.

Part of this work was supported by the German Science Foundation (DFG) under 'GA 1615/1-1' and by the European Commission under 'ICT-FP7-LIFT-255951'.

7. REFERENCES

[1] Arthur Asuncion and David J. Newman. UCI machine learning repository, 2007.

[2] Stephen D. Bay and Michael J. Pazzani. Detecting group differences: Mining contrast sets. *Data Mining and Knowledge Discovery*, 5:213–246, July 2001.

[3] Mario Boley and Henrik Grosskreutz. Non-redundant subgroup discovery using a closure system. In *ECML/PKDD*, 2009.

[4] Mario Boley, Tamás Horváth, and Stefan Wrobel. Efficient discovery of interesting patterns based on strong closedness. In *SDM*, pages 1002–1013. SIAM, 2009.

[5] Björn Bringmann and Albrecht Zimmermann. The chosen few: On identifying valuable patterns. In *ICDM*, pages 63–72. IEEE Computer Society, 2007.

[6] Toon Calders, Christophe Rigotti, and Jean-Francois Boulicaut. A survey on condensed representations for frequent sets. In *Constraint Based Mining and Inductive Databases*, pages 64–80. Springer, 2005.

[7] Gemma C. Garriga, Petra Kralj, and Nada Lavrač. Closed sets for labeled data. *Journal of Machine Learning Research*, 9:559–580, 2008.

[8] Henrik Grosskreutz and Daniel Paurat. Fast and memory–efficient discovery of the top–k relevant subgroups in a reduced candidate space. In *ECML/PKDD*, 2011.

[9] Henrik Grosskreutz, Stefan Rüping, and Stefan Wrobel. Tight optimistic estimates for fast subgroup discovery. In *ECML/PKDD*, pages 440–456, 2008.

[10] Willi Klösgen. Explora: A multipattern and multistrategy discovery assistant. In *Advances in Knowledge Discovery and Data Mining*, pages 249–271. MIT Press, 1996.

[11] Arno J. Knobbe and Eric K. Y. Ho. Pattern teams. In Johannes Fürnkranz, Tobias Scheffer, and Myra Spiliopoulou, editors, *PKDD*, volume 4213 of *Lecture Notes in Computer Science*, pages 577–584. Springer, 2006.

[12] Petra Kralj Novak, Nada Lavrač, and Geoffrey I. Webb. Supervised descriptive rule discovery: A unifying survey of contrast set, emerging pattern and subgroup mining. *Journal of Machine Learning Research*, 10:377–403, 2009.

[13] Nada Lavrac, Peter A. Flach, Branko Kavsek, and Ljupco Todorovski. Adapting classification rule induction to subgroup discovery. In *ICDM*, pages 266–273, 2002.

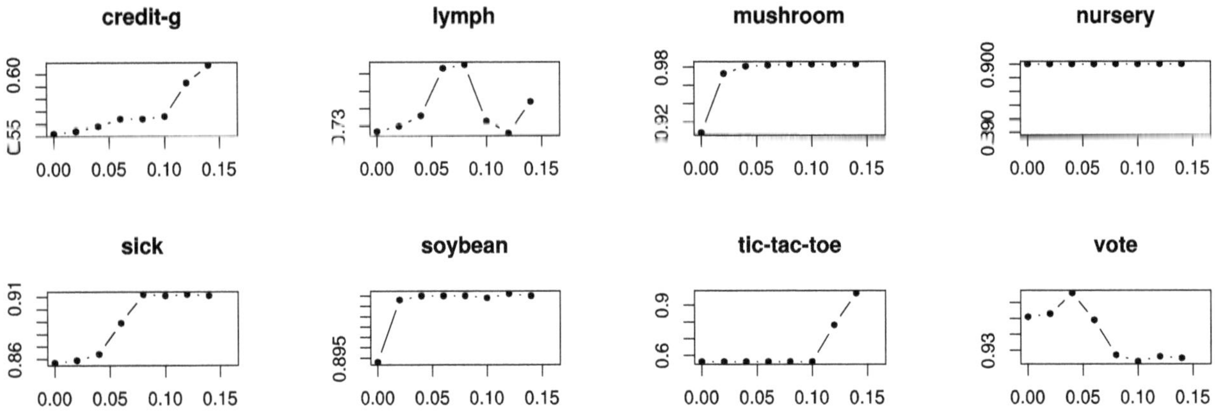

Figure 7: AUC of the top−10 Δ-relevant rule set (y-axis) depending on Δ (x-axis) (Piatetsky-Shapiro quality)

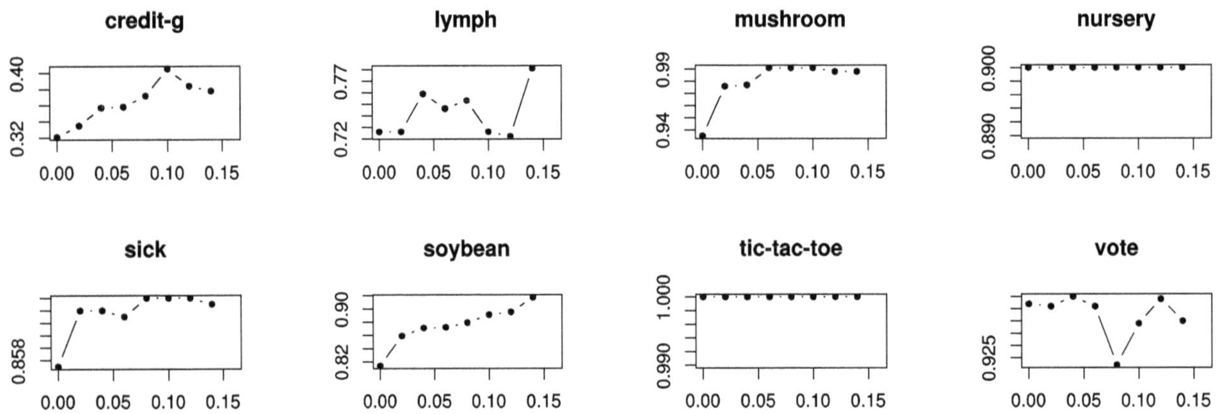

Figure 8: AUC of the top 10 Δ-relevant rule set (y-axis) depending on Δ (x-axis) (bin-test quality)

[14] Nada Lavrac and Dragan Gamberger. Relevancy in constraint-based subgroup discovery. In *Constraint-Based Mining and Inductive Databases*, 2005.

[15] Nada Lavrac, Dragan Gamberger, and Viktor Jovanoski. A study of relevance for learning in deductive databases. *Journal of Logic Programming*, 40(2-3):215–249, 1999.

[16] Nada Lavrac, Branko Kavsek, Peter Flach, and Ljupco Todorovski. Subgroup discovery with CN2-SD. *Journal of Machine Learning Research*, 5(Feb):153–188, 2004.

[17] Florian Lemmerich and Martin Atzmueller. Incorporating Exceptions: Efficient Mining of epsilon-Relevant Subgroup Patterns. In *Proc. LeGo-09: From Local Patterns to Global Models, Workshop at ECMLPKDD-2009*, 2009. accepted.

[18] Michael Mampaey, Nikolaj Tatti, and Jilles Vreeken. Tell me what i need to know: succinctly summarizing data with itemsets. In Chid Apté, Joydeep Ghosh, and Padhraic Smyth, editors, *KDD*, pages 573–581. ACM, 2011.

[19] Shinichi Morishita and Jun Sese. Traversing itemset lattice with statistical metric pruning. In *PODS*, 2000.

[20] Siegfried Nijssen, Tias Guns, and Luc De Raedt. Correlated itemset mining in roc space: a constraint programming approach. In *KDD*, pages 647–656, 2009.

[21] Nicolas Pasquier, Yves Bastide, Rafik Taouil, and Lotfi Lakhal. Efficient mining of association rules using closed itemset lattices. *Information Systems*, 24(1):25 – 46, 1999.

[22] Matthijs van Leeuwen and Arno J. Knobbe. Non-redundant subgroup discovery in large and complex data. In *ECML/PKDD*, pages 459–474, 2011.

[23] Geoffrey I. Webb. Self-sufficient itemsets: An approach to screening potentially interesting associations between items. *TKDD*, 4(1), 2010.

[24] Stefan Wrobel. An algorithm for multi-relational discovery of subgroups. In *PKDD*. Springer, 1997.

Efficient Frequent Item Counting in Multi-Core Hardware

Pratanu Roy Jens Teubner Gustavo Alonso
Systems Group, Dept. of Computer Science, ETH Zurich, Switzerland
{firstname.lastname}@inf.ethz.ch

ABSTRACT

The increasing number of cores and the rich instruction sets of modern hardware are opening up new opportunities for optimizing many traditional data mining tasks. In this paper we demonstrate how to speed up the performance of the computation of frequent items by almost one order of magnitude over the best published results by matching the algorithm to the underlying hardware architecture.

We start with the observation that frequent item counting, like other data mining tasks, assumes certain amount of skew in the data. We exploit this skew to design a new algorithm that uses a pre-filtering stage that can be implemented in a highly efficient manner through SIMD instructions. Using pipelining, we then combine this pre-filtering stage with a conventional frequent item algorithm (*Space-Saving*) that will process the remainder of the data. The resulting operator can be parallelized with a small number of cores, leading to a parallel implementation that does not suffer any of the overheads of existing parallel solutions when querying the results and offers significantly higher throughput.

Categories and Subject Descriptors

H.2.4 [**Database Management**]: Data Mining

Keywords

frequent items, parallelism, data flow

1. INTRODUCTION

Concerned by the looming data deluge, users are looking more than ever at the properties of their core data mining algorithms. Algorithms that adapt well to the characteristics of modern hardware—such as parallelism or advanced instruction sets (*e.g.*, SIMD)—can benefit from technology advances, which ultimately is the only way to escape a drowning in data [7, 17].

Unfortunately, key characteristics of data mining algorithms are often at odds with classical approaches to parallelism. For instance, *skew in the input data* often lies at the heart of the mining problem, but will lead to strong *load imbalances* in typical data partitioning schemes.

In this work we show how input skew can be turned into an advantage instead. Intuitively, we dynamically create an optimized code path for those input items that are frequent in the data set. An *input filter* routes each input item to its respective code path, making the common case fast without a noticeable slow-down of the remaining cases.

To illustrate the idea, we focus on the *frequent item counting problem*: given a data set, count the number of times each item appears in the set. In practice, this problem has to be answered with limited memory and with a single pass over the input data. Frequent item counting is used as a preliminary processing step to many data mining algorithms and it is a well-studied problem in the literature [5, 14]. Available sequential solutions are very efficient. For instance, *Space-Saving* can process close to 20 million items per second [15].

Besides being simple to describe and illustrate, the frequent item problem is interesting because it was shown to be difficult to parallelize by conventional means [6] and it is a good example of a data mining algorithm that is most meaningful when the input data is heavily skewed (otherwise all items has similar counts and none has a higher frequency than others). To date, there is no parallel implementation of frequent item counting that reaches the performance of the best sequential implementation of the algorithm.

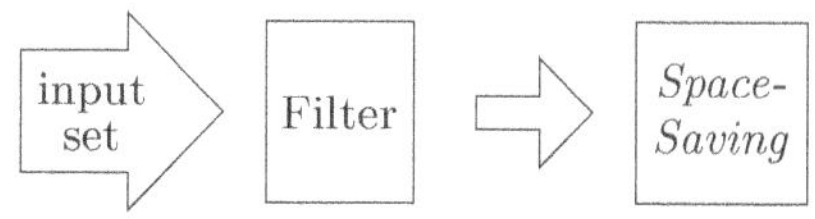

Figure 1: Input filtering for the frequent item problem. A filter absorbs much of the input data set and forwards only the remaining items to state-of-the-art *Space-Saving* instance.

Figure 1 sketches how we speed up frequent item counting through input filtering. A "Filter" stage at the front absorbs the most common cases with an optimized code path and routes only the remaining items to a conventional *Space-Saving* instance. Notice that, to speed up frequent item counting, we do not need to modify *Space-Saving* itself, but encapsulate all hardware awareness in the input filter. This makes our work complimentary to any optimizations that might be proposed for *Space-Saving* in the future.

As we show in the paper, input filtering can easily be parallelized using a small number of cores. Our actual im-

KDD'12, August 12–16, 2012, Beijing, China.

```
1 foreach stream item x ∈ S do
2     find bin b_x with b_x.item = x ;
3     if such a bin was found then
4         b_x.count ← b_x.count + 1 ;
5     else
6         b_min ← bin with minimum count value ;
7         b_min.count ← b_min.count + 1 ;
8         b_min.item ← x ;
```

Figure 2: Algorithm *Space-Saving*. A fixed number of bins monitors the most frequent items in the stream S [15].

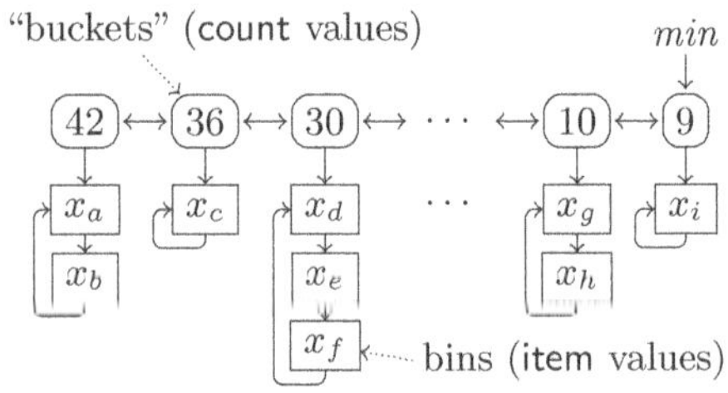

Figure 3: *Stream-Summary* data structure [15]. Bins with the same count value are grouped under one "bucket." Buckets form a double-linked list.

Zipf	data throughput	cycles/item
1.0	13.7×10^6 items/sec	135 cy/item
2.0	22.8×10^6 items/sec	82 cy/item
3.0	26.7×10^6 items/sec	70 cy/item

Table 1: Runtime characteristics of *Space-Saving*. Intel Nehalem-EX, 1.87 GHz; $k = 1{,}000$.

plementation reaches throughput rates (up to 200 million tuples per second) that are almost an order of magnitude faster than the best published results today. Moreover, we can sustain that throughput also in the presence of concurrent queries while the counting is in progress. Concurrent queries were shown to be a key performance blocker in earlier work [6].

2. COUNTING FREQUENT ITEMS

Several data mining techniques (such as top-k algorithms or a-priori [1]) start their data analysis by looking at the most frequently occurring items in the input data set. More formally, the *frequent item problem* is defined as

Given a data set S of size N and a threshold ϕ, return all items x that have a frequency f_x of at least ϕN in S.

To solve the problem accurately, the occurrences of *all* items have to be counted in memory, which requires an unrealistic $\Omega(N)$ space [5]. Fortunately, all common uses of frequent item counting can tolerate a small error ε in the counting result, allowing the result to include some additional items for which $(\phi - \varepsilon)N < f_x \leq \phi N$.

This *ε-approximate frequent item problem* can be solved very efficiently and with little space. ε-approximate solutions have been studied extensively (most recently by a survey article of Cormode and Hadjieleftheriou [5]), with the *Space-Saving* algorithm of Metwally *et al.* [15] (or variants thereof) generally seen as the most efficient solution.

2.1 State of the Art: *Space-Saving*

The basic idea behind *Space-Saving* is to limit space consumption by counting ("monitoring" in [15]) only the occurrences of those items that are actually frequent. The algorithm allocates a configurable number k of $\langle \mathsf{item}, \mathsf{count} \rangle$ pairs in main memory (we call them *bins*) that are supposed to monitor the most frequent items in S. Input items are then processed as listed in Figure 2. If an input item x is among those currently monitored, the corresponding count value is incremented. Otherwise, the bin with the lowest count value, b_{min} is replaced by the pair $\langle x, b_{\mathsf{min}}.\mathsf{count} + 1 \rangle$. In the latter case, item x receives the benefit of doubt: it could have occurred as often as b_{min}.count times before. *Space-Saving* never under-estimates frequencies and, hence, records b_{min}.count as the frequency estimate for x.

The number of bins k reserved for monitoring is a configuration parameter that can be used to trade accuracy for space. As rule of thumb, $\lceil 1/\varepsilon \rceil$ counters are required to find frequent items with an accuracy of ε. For details we refer to [5, 15].

Implementation-wise, *Space-Saving* is typically based on two data structures. A *linked-list* variant (termed *Stream-Summary* in [15]; cf. Figure 3) keeps all bins ordered by their count values to make line 6 in Algorithm *Space-Saving* fast. Lookups by item value (line 2) are performed using a *hash table*. Both data structures allow updates with (approximated) constant-time complexity. That is, the time spent per input item is independent of the bin count parameter k.

2.2 *Space-Saving* Characteristics

Space-Saving is primarily characterized by its extremely tight loop within which it accesses a very compact data structure. The iterations of the loop execute remarkably fast (cf. Table 1): several ten million input items are processed per second, leaving less than a hundred CPU cycles for each loop iteration on current hardware. These CPU cycles per item counts are similar to those reported for the most efficient implementations of join operators [3, 10].

The primary reason for this is the cache efficiency of *Space-Saving*. For typical problem sizes, all data structures conveniently fit into modern CPU caches. Skewed input data—the typical case for frequent item computation—further increases data locality. In spite of its random access behavior, *Space-Saving* thus processes its data almost entirely within the L1 cache on typical computing hardware.

The individual iterations of *Space-Saving* update the item and count fields. The resulting *data dependency* makes it difficult to apply local optimizations, such as *loop unrolling*, *vectorization*, or fine-grained *data parallelism*. Without such optimizations, implementations leave much of the strength of modern computing hardware entirely unused.

2.3 It is Hard to Parallelize *Space-Saving*

The prevalence of multi-core hardware has spurred interest in parallel variants of *Space-Saving* [4, 6]. But it turns out the problem is hard to parallelize, even though the single-core solution is well understood and very efficient.

2.3.1 Data Partitioning

Intuitively, *Space-Saving* can be parallelized by running multiple independent executions of the original algorithm, each of which gets one share of the input data stream. Depending on the application scenario, input data may already be provided as a set of disjoint streams (as in [6]) or additional logic performs, *e.g.*, round-robin partitioning:

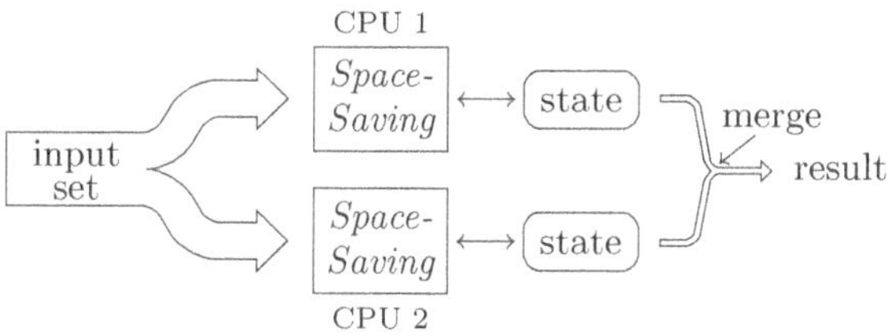

The overall counting result is then obtained by *merging* the data structures of the independent *Space-Saving* instances.

Result merging is a highly expensive operation that has to be performed each time an on-line query arrives. Das *et al.* [6] have shown that even in the presence of low query rates the overall execution time increases almost linearly with the number of parallel instances. Even for "hierarchical merging," which they showed to be the best strategy, merging is responsible for 65–98 % of the overall execution time.

Unfortunately, result merging cannot be avoided in partitioning-based schemes. Input sets to frequent item counting are usually heavily skewed (Manerikar and Palpanas report Zipfian skew in real-world data with at least $z \gtrsim 1.5$ [14]). Any value-based input partitioning (*e.g.*, by a hash on item values) will lead to strong load imbalances, leaving the setup bottlenecked in one of the *Space-Saving* instances.

Cafaro and Tempesta [4] have implemented the data partitioning strategy sketched above, using an MPI-based system. But their study ignores result merging and on-line querying and thus works around a key challenge in parallelizing the frequent item problem.

2.3.2 Shared Data Structures

Result merging *could* be avoided if all processors access the same *"shared"* data structure:

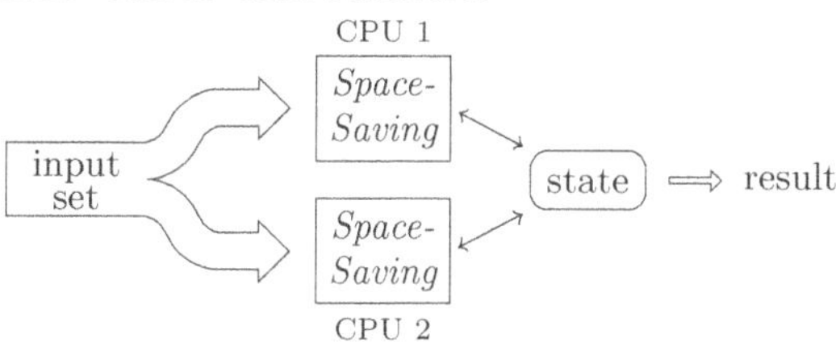

Queries would then get a consistent view on the counting state simply by reading out the shared data structure. This convenience, however, would come at a significant price. The shared state has to be protected with *locks* during every access. As mentioned before, the amount of time spent by *Space-Saving* on each input item is very small. Any additional lock maintenance code will immediately result in a noticeable performance degradation.

Cost of Cache Coherency. Given the very high cache locality of *Space-Saving*, participating processors will *not* actually share the "shared state" physically. Rather, the state ends up distributed over the respective L1 caches, depending on which piece was last accessed by which processor.

To mimic a shared memory, the system's *cache coherency protocol* will actively ship cache lines between cores whenever a requested data item cannot be found in a local cache.

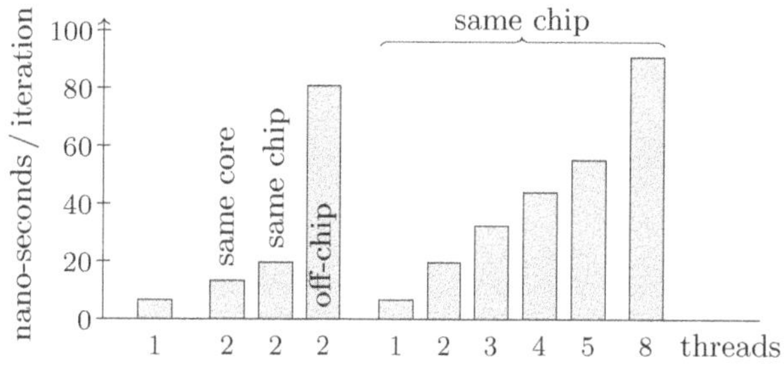

Figure 4: Cache coherency cost, depending on physical thread placement and degree of parallelism.

The cost of this can be significant: Molka *et al.* [16] measured a latency of 83 cycles for a single core-to-core cache line shipment in the Intel Nehalem architecture, which is similar to the processing time for a single item in *Space-Saving* (Table 1). The cost is intrinsic to shared data access and independent of any application-level locking strategy.[1]

A Micro-Benchmark for Cache Coherency Cost. To judge the impact that cache coherency cost can have on frequent item processing, we performed a micro-benchmark where a number of threads accesses a shared memory array. Each thread performs random counter increments in this array, following a Zipfian access pattern much like *Space-Saving* (no locking involved). On truly shared memory, thread performance should not depend on the number of threads in the system. The test platform was a 1.87 GHz Intel Nehalem EX (eight physical cores per CPU).

In the base case, exclusive data access by a single thread, each counter increment takes around 6.6 ns to complete. As Figure 4 shows, co-running threads significantly increase this access time to 20 ns (one co-runner) or even 84 ns (seven co-runners). In practice, cache coherency costs will offset any gain that parallel processing over shared data structures might bring. As mentioned before, the cost *cannot* be avoided by tuning the application's locking protocol (as proposed by [6]).

In summary, neither partitioning nor sharing can adequately leverage the capabilities of current hardware. In fact, the current trends toward de-centralization and lack of cache coherence protocols really work against using shared data structures.

3. INPUT FILTERING

The intuition behind input pre-filtering is simple: a *filter* is placed in front of an instance of *Space-Saving*, as shown in Figure 1. Out of a high-volume data stream, the filter takes out those input items that are particularly frequent and routes them through an optimized "shortcut" code path. If enough input items follow the shortcut, optimizing the filtering stage will lead to an improved overall throughput.

3.1 Algorithm

More formally, in Algorithm *Filter* we *partition* the in-memory bin set of *Space-Saving* into two groups X and Y. X consists of the *heavy hitters* for which we define a shortcut implementation. Only if an input item is not monitored

[1]In fact, locks are a shared data structure and thus will even exacerbate the problem.

1 **foreach** stream item $x \in S$ **do**
2   look-up bin b_x in X with b_x.item $= x$;
3   **if** such a bin was found **then**   */* shortcut */*
4   b_x.count $\leftarrow b_x$.count $+ 1$;
5   **else**   */* forward to Space-Saving */*
6   update Y according to *Space-Saving* ;
7   decrement consistency_limit ;
8   increment n' ;
9   **if** consistency_limit $= 0$ **then**
10       $b_{X\,\mathsf{min}} \leftarrow$ bin in X with min. count value ;
11   **if** $b_{X\,\mathsf{min}}$.count $\leq \frac{n'}{|Y|}$ **then**
        // actual violation of consistency limit
12         $b_{Y\,\mathsf{max}} \leftarrow$ bin in Y with max. count value ;
13   remove $b_{X\,\mathsf{min}}$ from X and add it to Y ;
14   remove $b_{Y\,\mathsf{max}}$ from Y and add it to X ;
15         $n' \leftarrow n' + b_{X\,\mathsf{min}}$.count $- b_{Y\,\mathsf{max}}$.count ;
16         $b_{X\,\mathsf{min}} \leftarrow$ bin in X with min. count value ;
17   consistency_limit $\leftarrow b_{X\,\mathsf{min}}$.count $- \left\lfloor \frac{n'}{|Y|} \right\rfloor$;

Figure 5: Algorithm *Filter*.

within X, we forward it to a *Space-Saving* instance that maintains the set Y. To achieve overall consistency with *Space-Saving* semantics, *Filter* must ensure the following invariant: *the item with the overall minimum count* b_{min} *must be monitored by the bin set* Y. This is further explained later in this section.

Filtering becomes efficient whenever the size of X is small, yet catches a relevant share of the input data stream. These assumptions are reasonable since any meaningful input to the frequent item problem will be skewed. For data that follows a Zipf distribution ($z \gtrsim 1$), we find that $|X|$ values between 4 and 16 are enough to achieve effective filtering (we study the impact of this parameter in the experimental evaluation).

Figure 5 shows Algorithm *Filter* in pseudo code. Each input item is first compared to the bins in set X. If the item can be found there, the respective bin count is updated. Otherwise, bin set Y is updated according to the *Space-Saving* algorithm (line 6). In practice, bin sets X and Y are kept in separate data structures and accessed independently.

Consistency with *Space-Saving*. A partitioned execution over X and Y is consistent with the semantics of *Space-Saving* only if the processed item is either a heavy hitter (*i.e.*, it can be found in X) or if b_{min}, the bin with the minimum count value, is part of the bin set Y (*i.e.*, $b_{\mathsf{min}} \notin X$). Otherwise, the forwarded item might overwrite a bin whose count value is not minimal. At the same time, we want to avoid checking $b_{\mathsf{min}} \notin X$ too often, because X is part of the shortcut code path and not optimized for count-based searches.

Avoiding Expensive b_{min} Lookups. count-based searches on X can be mostly avoided if we *(a)* regularly push high-count bins into X and low-count bins into Y and *(b)* conservatively *estimate* whether b_{min} could possibly be found within X. This is what lines 7–17 do in Algorithm *Filter*. In this code, consistency_limit tells how many items can still safely be forwarded to the *Space-Saving* part without violating the consistency constraint $b_{\mathsf{min}} \in Y$. This safety margin is decremented for every input item that is forwarded to *Space-Saving* (line 7).

Once the safety margin hits zero (line 9), consistency_limit is re-estimated based on $b_{X\,\mathsf{min}}$.count (the minimum count value in X) and n', the total number of items forwarded to *Space-Saving* (lines 10/16 and 17). If $b_{\mathsf{min}} \in Y$ can no longer be guaranteed from statistics alone, lines 11–16 push one high-count bin from Y to X and one low-count bin from X to Y (as motivated before).

The setting of consistency_limit can be motivated as follows. Let us assume we have forwarded n' items to *Space-Saving*. Let $|Y|$ denote the size of Y. Then, the following guarantee on the bin with minimum count in Y holds:

$$b_{Y\,\mathsf{min}}.\mathsf{count} \leq \left\lfloor \frac{n'}{|Y|} \right\rfloor . \qquad (1)$$

That is, the largest minimum count that is possible in Y can not be larger than this value (Lemma 3.3 in [15] identifies a similar bound for b_{min}.count in *Space-Saving*).

Observe that the value of $\lfloor n'/|Y| \rfloor$ changes only every $|Y|$ forwarded items. A well-engineered implementation[2] of *Filter* thus needs to perform consistency maintenance at most once every $|Y|$ forwarded items.

3.2 Hardware-Conscious Filtering

The complexity of the filtering stage (lines 2–4 in Figure 5) lies in the lookup of items x in the bin set X. A hash table was suggested for this task in *Space-Saving*, since it offers (approximate) $|X|$-independent lookup time. This asymptotic value becomes irrelevant, however, for the small bin counts $|X|$ we are considering here.

Thus, we can gain speed by implementing the lookup in line 2 as a *sequential scan* over X. Such a scan fits the pipelined execution model of modern processors, avoids random access and pointer chasing as it happens for a hash-based lookup.

Vectorized Search. Sequential scans can efficiently be implemented with *vectorized instructions*. By using the SIMD instruction sets of modern processors, four to eight[3] bin contents can be inspected in a single CPU cycle. As our evaluation in Section 6 shows, the use of SIMD dramatically improves the filtering throughput, particularly for real-world skew values.

The SIMD code that we use in our implementation is illustrated in Figure 6 for $|X| = 8$ and a SIMD width of 128 bits (*i.e.*, four items per SIMD register). The contents of X are held in four SIMD registers, two of which hold the eight item values (`itms.vec[0]` and `itms.vec[1]`) and two of which maintain the associated count values (`cnts.vec[0]` and `cnts.vec[1]`).

To prepare the vectorized search, the input item `x` is replicated into the four slots of the SIMD register `vec_x` (line 2). Comparison with the two item vectors (lines 4–5) yields vectors `cmp1` and `cmp2` that contain a '-1' where the item was found and '0' elsewhere. This means that count vectors can be updated by *subtracting* `cmp1` and `cmp2`, as done in lines 7 and 8. Finally, the comparison results are combined into a

[2]The value of $b_{X\,\mathsf{min}}$.count can be cached and used as a lower bound before actually executing lines 10–16.

[3]The AVX instruction set of Intel's *Sandy Bridge* architecture offers a SIMD width of 256 bits. In previous processor generations, this number was 128.

```
// load the input item into vector register
const __m128i vec_x = _mm_set1_epi32(x);

// compare it to the bin contents
__m128i cmp1 = _mm_cmpeq_epi32(itms.vec[0],vec_x);
__m128i cmp2 = _mm_cmpeq_epi32(itms.vec[1],vec_x);

// update the count values
cnts.vec[0] = _mm_sub_epi32(cnts.vec[0],cmp1);
cnts.vec[1] = _mm_sub_epi32(cnts.vec[1],cmp2);

// compute the overall result of the comparisons
cmp1 = _mm_or_si128(cmp2, cmp1);

// bring the result into the scalar part
bool found = _mm_movemask_ps((__m128) cmp1);
```

Figure 6: Vectorized filtering using x86 intrinsics.

single Boolean value (using a SIMD `or` and a `movemask` operation) to decide whether or not the item should be passed on to *Space-Saving*.

Observe that this code compares and updates bin contents eagerly. While this may lead to redundant instruction executions without effect (*e.g.*, we will often subtract '0' from the count registers), the absence of *branches* makes the code particularly efficient on actual hardware. We will evaluate the effectiveness of vectorization in Section 6.

3.3 *Filter* Characteristics

To understand the runtime characteristics of *Filter*, its per-item cost can be broken up into three terms:

$$\textit{lookup cost in } X \quad (2)$$
$$+ \sigma \times \textit{cost of Space-Saving on } Y \quad (3)$$
$$+ \sigma' \times \textit{cost of consistency maintenance} \ , \quad (4)$$

where σ and σ' are the probabilities that the code branches in lines 6–17 and lines 10–16 are entered for the input item (respectively).

Terms (2) and (4) are overhead that is not present in the plain *Space-Saving* algorithm. In return, the cost of *Space-Saving* is reduced by the factor σ. Vectorized execution will make the lookup cost in X very small. The code in Figure 6, *e.g.*, requires only seven assembly instructions to perform the filtering work.

Entry into the consistency maintenance code path might result in a noticeable cost, since it involves accesses to X and Y that are not supported by any data structure (*e.g.*, line 13 in Algorithm *Filter* is essentially an insertion step in a sorted list). But the factor σ' is very small in practice. To illustrate, if all bins in Y contain the same count value (which is the worst case that defines the bound in (1)), $|Y|$ items can be forwarded to *Space-Saving* before the minimum count value increases. In practice, we find that $\sigma' \ll \sigma \times {}^1/_{|Y|}$.

This indicates that the filter selectivity σ is the dominant factor in determining the benefit from filtering.

For Zipf-distributed data, σ can be described in closed form. The probability of finding an item x among the k most frequent elements of a Zipf distribution is

$$P(k, z, |A|) = \sum_{i=1}^{k} \frac{1}{i^z} \times \frac{1}{\sum_{j=1}^{|A|} \frac{1}{j^z}} \ . \quad (5)$$

That is, we sum up the first k probabilities of a Zipf distribution and normalize using the sum of all item probabilities.

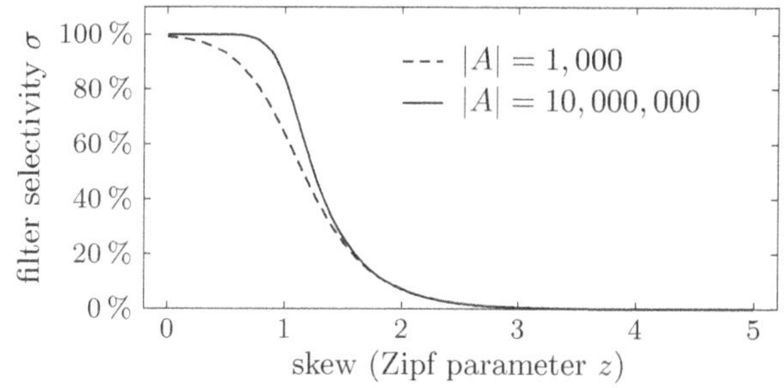

Figure 7: Filter selectivity ($|X| = 8$), depending on Zipf parameter z and alphabet size $|A|$.

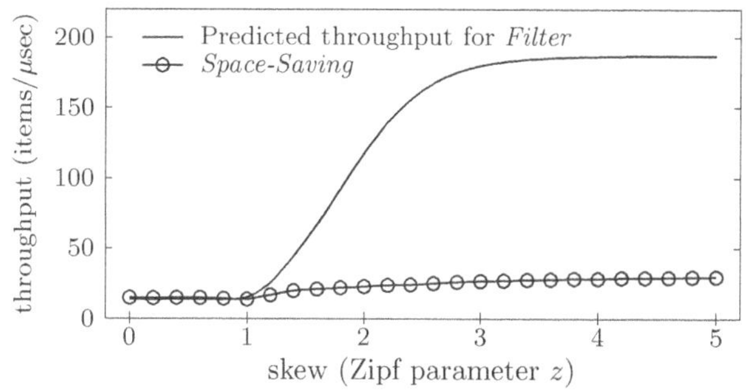

Figure 8: Predicted throughput for *Filter* assuming $k = 1000$, $|X| = 8$, *lookup cost in* $X = 10$ cycles, and an alphabet size $|A| = 5000000$.

The probability that an item passes the filter is thus

$$\sigma(|X|, z, |A|) = 1 - P(|X|, z, |A|) \ .$$

Assuming a filter stage with eight bins ($|X| = 8$, as reflected also in Figure 6), the resulting filter selectivity is illustrated in Figure 7. As can be seen in the figure, the effectiveness of filtering increases sharply as soon as the input data skew exceeds a Zipf parameter of around 1. For instance, for a skew of $z = 1$ and an alphabet size $|A| = 1000$, filtering already avoids more than 35 % of the *Space-Saving* work. Since real-world data sets exhibit Zipf values much larger than 1 ([14] provides a detailed study), we can expect a very high effectiveness of filtering.

3.4 Overall Cost

We are now ready to model the overall cost of an execution of *Filter*. Figure 6 lists the actual SIMD code that implements the lookup in X. With a loop body added, this code will require around 10 cycles to execute for each input item. Since we know σ and the cost of *Space-Saving* (from experiments, cf. Table 1), we can compute cost terms (2) and (3) and predict the throughput of *Filter* depending on data skew.

Such a prediction is illustrated in Figure 8. In this figure, we complemented experimental results for *Space-Saving* with a prediction on the throughput of *Filter*. For real-world skews (starting from around 1.5), we can expect several factors of throughput improvement. Filtering causes a slight cost increase for very low skew values ($z \lesssim 0.5$). We will verify and evaluate both characteristics in Section 6.

```
1  foreach stream item x ∈ S do
2      look-up bin b_x in X with b_x.item = x ;
3      if such a bin was found then
4          b_x.count ← b_x.count + 1 ;
5      else
6          send x to processor P_1 ;
7          decrement consistency_limit ;
8          increment n' ;
9          if consistency_limit = 0 then
10             b_Xmin ← bin in X with min. count value ;
11             if b_Xmin.count ≤ n'/|Y| then
                   // actual violation of consistency limit
12                 send b_Xmin to processor P_1 ;
13                 receive b_Ymax from processor P_1 ;
14                 n' = n' + b_Xmin.count − b_Ymax.count ;
15                 b_Xmin.item ← b_Ymax.item ;
16                 b_Xmin.count ← b_Ymax.count ;
17                 b_Xmin ← bin in X with min. count value ;
18             consistency_limit = b_Xmin.count − n'/|Y| ;
```

Figure 9: Algorithm *Parallel-Filter* for Processor P_0.

The above model does not include the cost of consistency maintenance (cost term (4)). In practice, it will have only marginal impact. This is because the operation is necessary at most once every $|Y|$ forwarded items, *i.e.*, with a probability of at most $\sigma \times {}^{1}/_{|Y|}$. If, say, we choose Y to contain 1,000 bins, this means that a consistency maintenance run would have to be at least a thousand times more expensive than *Space-Saving* to have noticeable impact.

4. PARALLELIZATION OF FILTER

The key benefit of Algorithm *Filter* comes from reducing the amount of data reaching the *Space-Saving* routine. On modern multi-core machines, this effect can be amplified by dividing the filtering and *Space-Saving* work over two or more processor cores. The structure of *Filter* describes a *data flow system* (cf. Figure 1), which can be mapped to *pipeline parallelism* on multi-core hardware.

4.1 *Parallel-Filter*

Intuitively, the task of input filtering is associated with one (possibly also more; see below) CPU core P_0, while a different core P_1 runs the *Space-Saving* part. The two cores interact through *asynchronous message channels* installed between the threads on P_0 and P_1.

The algorithm *Parallel-Filter* is illustrated in Figure 9 and 10. Essentially, all interaction with the bin set Y (*i.e.*, the *Space-Saving* part) is replaced by explicit *messaging instructions*, as shown in lines 6, 12, and 13.

The other end of these messages is a modified *Space-Saving* instance that runs on P_1. We listed its pseudo code in Figure 10. Input to this code are the messages received from P_0. The message is then dispatched either to run a regular *Space-Saving* update or perform bin pushing as discussed earlier in Section 3.1.

The most apparent advantage of *Parallel-Filter* is that operations on X and Y can now be executed in parallel. In particular, cost terms (2) and (3) in Section 3.3 now arise

```
foreach msg received from processor P_0 do
    if msg = bin b_Xmin then
        b_Ymax ← bin with max. count value ;
        send b_Ymax back to processor P_0 ;
        add b_Xmin to the bin set Y;
    else if msg = stream item x then
        run regular Space-Saving ;
```

Figure 10: Alg. *Parallel-Filter* for Processor P_1.

on separate cores, such that only the larger term determines the overall runtime.

This is particularly valuable if both of the terms are non-negligible. That is, a pipeline parallel execution could offer performance advantages especially for mid-range skew values $1 \lesssim z \lesssim 2$, where both algorithm parts take a considerable share of the input data (cf. Figure 7). This skew range matches what can be found in many real-world use cases.

***Parallel-Filter* and Modern Hardware.** Partitioning *Filter* over independent CPU cores also leads to routines with an extremely small code and data footprint. Most importantly, the filter task is simple enough to keep all bin contents within the (SIMD) registers of P_0. Such locality is an important ingredient to achieve high cycles-per-instruction (CPI) values on modern hardware.

Message Passing. Observe in Figure 9 that the bulk of the messages between P_0 and P_1 is sent fully asynchronously. Asynchronous message passing of this type is known to be a good fit for current hardware. In fact, hardware makers are developing new hardware architectures entirely based on message passing [9] and the operating systems community is working on full OS re-designs built around message passing primitives [2]. In our implementation, we adopt the message passing protocol of [2].

More Than Two Cores. Intuitively, the idea of *Parallel-Filter* can be extended in a pipelined mode, where multiple cores are running the filtering (cf. Figure 1). The performance advantage of such an approach will heavily depend on the data distribution, since each core has to take out enough share of the data to improve the overall throughput.

5. QUERIES

The key challenge in frequent item counting is to achieve high throughput, yet retain the ability to support *on-line queries* (*e.g.*, top-n queries), while the algorithm processes input. As analyzed in detail by Das *et al.* [6] and motivated briefly by us in Section 2.3, the cost of *result merging* may easily ruin any throughput advantages gained from parallelism or work distribution. For instance, Das *et al.* account more than 90 % of all CPU resources to query processing and result merging even for low query rates.

This problem does not arise in *Filter*, because all algorithm state is already partitioned by item values. All it takes to answer a top-n query is to return the bins in X and as many of the (count-sorted) bins from Y as needed to answer the query.

The advantages of *Filter* in the presence of on-line queries become even more pronounced when *Filter* is run in a parallel setting (cf. Section 4). The query can now be forwarded

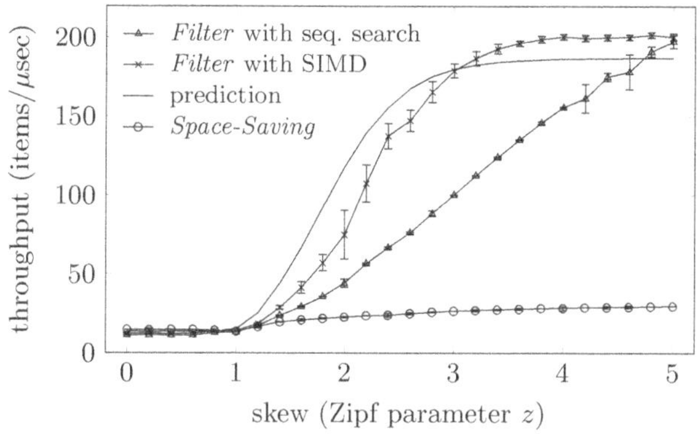

Figure 11: *Filter* performance, $k = 1000$, $|X| = 8$.

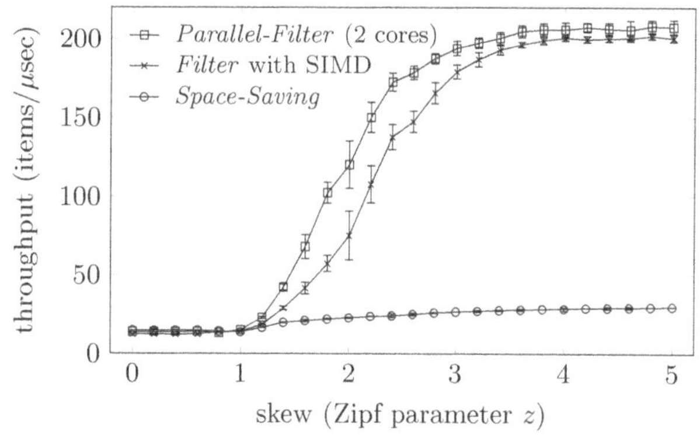

Figure 12: *Filter* vs. *Parallel-Filter* without querying, $k = 1000$, $|X| = 8$.

within the processing pipeline much like input items. Unlike in classical parallelization schemes, there is no need to suspend parallel processing because of an on-line query.

6. EVALUATION

6.1 Experimental Setup

To evaluate the potential of input filtering, we implemented the above algorithms using C (compiled with gcc version 4.5.2) on an Intel Nehalem CPU with a clock speed of 1.87 GHz (Intel model number L7555) and running Ubuntu 11.04. To ensure deterministic performance, we disabled the system's *hyper threading* and *turbo boost* features (which could lead to further throughput improvements in practice).

For evaluating the results, we generated synthetic data that follows a Zipf distribution. We ran the experiments on a skew range of 0.0 to 5.0. All the generated data sets contained 50 million items with an alphabet size of 5 million.

To keep the comparison meaningful, we did not implement the *Space-Saving* with linked list ourselves, instead we used the implementation from [5], which is publicly available. We recompiled that code using gcc and got similar results as presented in [5]. Therefore, we treat those results as the baseline for comparison of the performance.

6.2 Different Implementations of *Filter*

We implemented two variants of the *Filter* algorithm. One that uses a naïve sequential search and one based on the SIMD code shown in Figure 6. The performance of these two implementations along with the throughput of *Space-Saving* are shown in Figure 11. The figure shows the skew vs. throughput (items/μ-second) of the implementations for $k = 1000$, $|X| = 8$. We got similar graphs for $k = 100$ and 10000.

The results shown in the figure are consistent with the analytic assessment in Section 3.4 (repeated as a solid line in Figure 11). For very low skew (up to $z \lesssim 0.8$), *Filter* runs slightly slower than the baseline *Space-Saving* (up to $\approx 28\,\%$ loss for the sequential implementation, 2–17 % for the SIMD code). In this low-skew range, the overhead of filtering and consistency maintenance cannot be compensated by a reduced workload on *Space-Saving*.

As soon as the skew goes higher than 0.8, *Filter* becomes much faster than *Space-Saving*, whereby the SIMD implementation quite closely follows our analytical model. For very high skew we even see better throughput as predicted, which indicates that we over-estimated the cycle count needed per item in the SIMD code.

For mid-range skew values ($1.5 \lesssim z \lesssim 2.5$), the measured throughput stays behind our model. This is mainly because our model ignored a statistical effect. When filtering takes away the $|X|$ most frequent items from the input stream, the remaining data set is actually *not* Zipf-distributed any more. Rather, the skew perceived by *Space-Saving* is appreciably smaller than the one seen at the input. This leads to the under-estimation of the *Space-Saving* cost in our model seen in Figure 11.

The implementation based on sequential search clearly does not follow our cost model. This is because we assumed the eager execution model of our SIMD code, which leads to data-independent runtimes (we had assumed 10 cycles/item). This assumption does not hold for a non-hardware-optimized search that aborts the sequential search lazily. Yet, note that also this naïve implementation shows significant throughput advantages over an off-the-shelf *Space-Saving* implementation.

6.3 *Filter* vs. *Parallel-Filter*

In this section, we explore how *Filter* and *Parallel-Filter* perform with respect to each other. We analyze the performance both in the presence and in the absence of queries. We used the SIMD implementations for comparing performance.

6.3.1 *Without Querying*

In *Parallel-Filter*, the *Filter* and *Space-Saving* processing overlap. For very low skew values, this reduces the overhead of filtering. Since item lookups in X are now performed on a separate core, only consistency maintenance and a small communication overhead add to the cost of the baseline *Space-Saving*. More specifically, *Parallel-Filter* runs only 5 % slower than *Space-Saving* (cf. Figure 12).

As discussed already in Section 4, parallel execution becomes most effective if the contributions of terms (2) and (3) in our cost model are of comparable size, which is the case for mid-range skew values. Our throughput results in Figure 12 confirm this expectation. Skew ranges above 1.0 are most relevant in practice, and we see an improvement of *Parallel-Filter* over *Filter* of up to 80 % in this range (and a factor of up to six compared to plain *Space-Saving*).

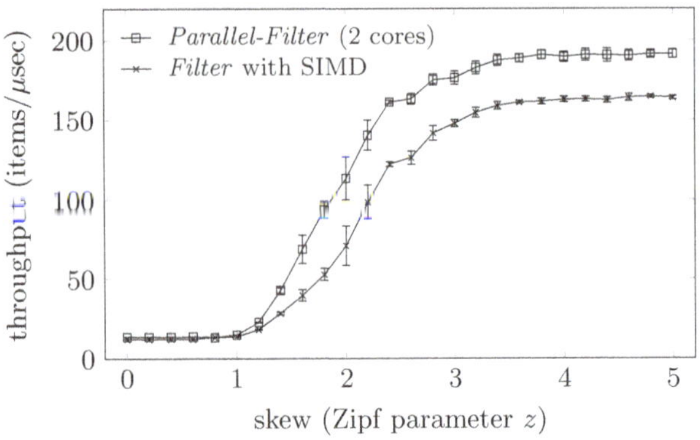

Figure 13: *Filter* vs. *Parallel-Filter* with querying, $k = 1000$, $|X| = 8$, query rate: 2000 queries/second.

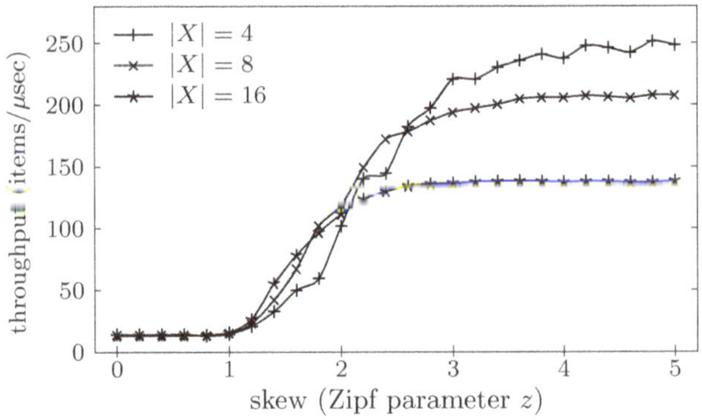

Figure 14: Impact of increasing sizes of X on *Parallel Filter* (2 cores), $k = 1000$.

For very high skew values, the advantage of parallel execution becomes less pronounced. In this range, the *Space-Saving* part of *Filter* is called very infrequently. Parallel execution of filtering and *Space-Saving* thus yields little benefit over the single-threaded case. Likewise, in additional experiments we found that parallelism beyond two cores will not significantly increase overall throughput any further.

6.3.2 *With Querying*

A key benefit that we expect from *Filter* is a better robustness against concurrent queries. To verify that property, we re-ran the experiments of Figure 12, but issued queries while the input was processed. To illustrate high robustness, we deliberately chose a very high query rate of 2,000 queries per second.

As shown in Figure 13, even such high query rates cause only little performance impact compared to the numbers we saw for input processing without queries (Figure 12). Most realistic workloads will use lower query rates, which means that on-line queries will cause negligible overhead in practice. This is in sharp contrast to the merging overhead reported by Das *et al.* [6], where on-line queries would immediately reduce input processing rates by several factors.

Also observe in Figure 13 how parallel processing is even more robust to on-line queries than our single-threaded implementation. This is because queries propagate from one CPU core to another. And while, *e.g.*, the last core in the pipeline collects bin contents from its *Stream-Summary* data structure, all other cores can already proceed with input processing.

6.4 Impact of the size of X

To see the impact of different sizes of X, we analyzed the performance of *Parallel-Filter* with $|X| = 4$, 8, and 16 (Figure 14). As expected, for a very low skew, they perform similarly because the added overhead by 4, 8 or 16 bins is too small in comparison to the *Space-Saving* cost. But for a very high skew, the performance will drop due to the increase in constant-time look up cost of X. As shown in the figure, the performance with 4 bins supersedes that with 8 and 16 bins, and reaches up to 250 million items per second. On the contrary, for a skew range of 1.0 to 1.6, $|X| = 16$ bins perform best, since it reduces the number of items that get forwarded to *Space-Saving*. Overall, $|X| = 8$ is an intermediate value that offers good performance balance for all skew ranges.

7. RELATED WORK

To leverage the advances in hardware technology, it has become unavoidable to re-design software systems such that they match the strengths of the underlying hardware. As Kim *et al.* [10] have shown, the changing hardware characteristics may even shift the balance between algorithmic approaches. More specifically, they conclude that sort-based join methods will soon overtake hash-based alternatives because sorting can better exploit modern instruction sets, most notably SIMD extensions.

The use of SIMD extensions proved effective also in our work, but only after we designed an algorithmic structure that would permit the use of SIMD. The necessity of careful algorithm designs to enable SIMD, but also the benefits that can be gained, were shown previously for a number of database tasks, including in-memory decompression [23] and sorted set intersection [18]. As in our case, the performance advantages obtained far exceed what would be expected from a classical cost analysis alone.

A number of research groups have re-designed database algorithms to better match the characteristics of caches and main-memory subsystems in modern hardware. Shatdal *et al.* [19] proposed adaptations to database join algorithms as early as 1994. Later their results were extended to match the cache characteristics of modern hardware, most notably in the MonetDB project [13]. More recently, Zukowski *et al.* [25] showed how lightweight data compression can better utilize real-world memory subsystems.

Probably most related to the frequent item counting problem is a recent paper by Ye *et al.* [24] that studies the performance of aggregation algorithms on modern hardware. Technically, the full aggregate of a data set contains all information needed to determine the most frequent item. But large memory requirements and necessary post-processing render the approach impractical for frequent item counting. Aside from that, Ye *et al.* achieve comparable throughput for the alphabet sizes we considered here, but require 8-way parallelism and much stronger CPUs to do so.

The resulting algorithm structure of our work resembles a *data flow system*, and there are numerous examples of how data flow-oriented designs can be mapped very efficiently to a given piece of hardware. In fact, most hardware designers first analyze the data flow of any given problem before they try to solve it.

A seminal work in stressing the importance of data flow-driven designs were the *systolic arrays* of Kung *et al.* [11, 12]. In the database world, one of the most notable studies has been done by Teeuw and Blanken [20]. Many of these results carry over to modern multi-core environments in the form of *pipeline parallelism*, as was emphasized recently, *e.g.*, by Giacomoni *et al.* [8].

Data flow-oriented processing proved effective also in some of our own recent work. In [21], we showed how it helps to parallelize the processing of *sliding-window joins* in many-core systems; similarly, we used a data flow-based design to solve the frequent item problem in (FPGA) hardware [22].

8. CONCLUSIONS

We have demonstrated the effectiveness of *pre-filtering* on modern hardware when applied to the *frequent item problem*. Filtering opens the door to using vectorized instructions on modern processor architectures. Depending on the input data skew, our proposed algorithm *Filter* improves performance over *Space-Saving* (the existing state of the art) by one order of magnitude.

We also show that *Filter* can easily be parallelized and thus make use of additional computing resources in multi-core systems. The proposed *Parallel-Filter* algorithm improves the performance of *Filter* significantly on the data with medium skew—the most common case in real-world applications. Both algorithms, *Filter* and *Parallel-Filter*, sustain their throughput properties even under high query load, since they avoid the merging overhead of earlier parallel frequent item solutions.

The improvements due to filtering are orthogonal to possible advances in the back-end algorithm (*Space-Saving* in our case). In fact, since filtering turns data skew into a throughput advantage, it could also complement other algorithms where skew often causes major performance problems.

Acknowledgements

This work was supported by the European Commission (FP7, Marie Curie Actions; project *Geocrowd*), by the Swiss National Science Foundation (*Ambizione* grant; project *Avalanche*), and by the Enterprise Computing Center (ECC) of ETH Zurich.

9. REFERENCES

[1] R. Agrawal and R. Srikant. Fast algorithms for mining association rules in large databases. In *Proc. VLDB*, 1994.

[2] A. Baumann, P. Barham, P.-E. Dagand, T. Harris, R. Isaacs, S. Peter, T. Roscoe, A. Schüpbach, and A. Singhania. The Multikernel: A new OS architecture for scalable multicore systems. In *Proc. ACM SOSP*, Big Sky, MT, USA, 2009.

[3] S. Blanas, Y. Li, and J. M. Patel. Design and evaluation of main memory hash join algorithms for multi-core cpus. In *Proc. ACM SIGMOD*, 2011.

[4] M. Cafaro and P. Tempesta. Finding frequent items in parallel. *Concurrency and Computation: Practice and Experience*, 2011. (online preprint).

[5] G. Cormode and M. Hadjieleftheriou. Finding frequent items in data streams. *Proc. VLDB Endowment (PVLDB)*, 1(2), 2008.

[6] S. Das, S. Antony, D. Agrawal, and A. E. Abbadi. Thread cooperation in multicore architectures for frequency counting over multiple data streams. *Proc. VLDB Endowment (PVLDB)*, 2(1), 2009.

[7] P. Dubey. Teraflops for the masses: Killer apps of tomorrow. In *Workshop on Edge Computing Using New Commodity Architectures*, 2006.

[8] J. Giacomoni, T. Moseley, and M. Vachharajani. FastForward for efficient pipeline parallelism: A cache-optimized concurrent lock-free queue. In *Proc. ACM SIGPLAN*, Salt Lake City, UT, USA, 2008.

[9] J. Howard, S. Dighe, Y. Hoskote, S. Vangal, D. Finan, G. Ruhl, D. Jenkins, H. Wilson, N. Borkar, G. Schrom, F. Pailet, S. Jain, T. Jacob, S. Yada, S. Marella, P. Salihundam, V. Erraguntla, M. Konow, M. Riepen, G. Droege, J. Lindemann, M. Gries, T. Apel, K. Henriss, T. Lund-Larsen, S. Steibl, S. Borkar, V. De, R. V. D. Wijngaart, and T. Mattson. A 48-core IA-32 message-passing processor with DVFS in 45nm CMOS. In *2010 IEEE Int'l Solid-State Circuits Conf.*, San Francisco, CA, USA, 2010.

[10] C. Kim, E. Sedlar, J. Chhugani, T. Kaldewey, A. D. Nguyen, A. D. Blas, V. W. Lee, N. Satish, and P. Dubey. Sort vs. hash revisited: Fast join implementation on modern multi-core CPUs. *Proc. VLDB Endowment (PVLDB)*, 2(2), 2009.

[11] H. T. Kung and C. E. Leiserson. Systolic arrays (for VLSI). In *Sparse Matrix Proceedings*, Knoxville, TN, USA, 1978.

[12] H. T. Kung and P. L. Lohman. Systolic (VLSI) arrays for relational database operations. In *Proc. ACM SIGMOD*, Santa Monica, CA, USA, 1980.

[13] S. Manegold, P. A. Boncz, and M. L. Kersten. Optimizing main-memory join on modern hardware. *IEEE TKDE*, 14(4), 2002.

[14] N. Manerikar and T. Palpanas. Frequent items in streaming data: An experimental evaluation of the state-of-the-art. *Data & Knowl. Eng.*, 68(4), 2009.

[15] A. Metwally, D. Agrawal, and A. E. Abbadi. An integrated efficient solution for computing frequent and top-*k* elements in data streams. *ACM TODS*, 31(3), 2006.

[16] D. Molka, D. Hackenberg, R. Schöne, and M. S. Müller. Memory performance and cache coherency effects on an Intel Nehalem multiprocessor system. In *Proc. PACT*, 2009.

[17] X. Qiu, G. Fox, H. Yuan, S.-H. Bae, G. Chrysanthakopoulos, and H. Nielsen. Parallel data mining on multicore clusters. In *Proc. GCC*, Bloomington, IN, USA, 2008.

[18] B. Schlegel, T. Willhalm, and W. Lehner. Fast sorted-set intersection using SIMD instructions. In *ADMS Workshop*, Seattle, WA, USA, 2011.

[19] A. Shatdal, C. Kant, and J. F. Naughton. Cache conscious algorithms for relational query processing. In *Proc. VLDB*, 1994.

[20] W. B. Teeuw and H. M. Blanken. Control versus data flow in parallel database machines. *IEEE TPDS*, 4(11), 1993.

[21] J. Teubner and R. Mueller. How soccer players would do stream joins. In *Proc. ACM SIGMOD*, Athens, Greece, 2011.

[22] J. Teubner, R. Mueller, and G. Alonso. FPGA acceleration for the frequent item problem. In *Proc. ICDE*, Long Beach, CA, USA, 2010.

[23] T. Willhalm, N. Popvici, Y. Boshmaf, H. Plattner, A. Zeier, and J. Schaffner. SIMD-scan: Ultra fast in-memory table scan using on-chip vector processing units. *Proc. VLDB Endowment (PVLDB)*, 2(2), 2009.

[24] Y. Ye, K. A. Ross, and N. Vesdapunt. Scalable aggregation on multicore processors. In *DaMoN Workshop*, 2011.

[25] M. Zukowski, S. Héman, N. Nes, and P. Boncz. Super-scalar RAM-CPU cache compression. In *Proc. ICDE*, Atlanta, GA, USA, 2006.

On Nested Palindromes in Clickstream Data

Michel Speiser[†‡]
msp@zurich.ibm.com

Gianluca Antonini[†]
gan@zurich.ibm.com

Abderrahim Labbi[†]
abl@zurich.ibm.com

Juliana Sutanto[‡]
jsutanto@ethz.ch

[†]Dept. of Mathematical & Computational Sciences
IBM Research - Zurich
Säumerstrasse 4
8803 Rüschlikon, Switzerland

[‡]Dept. of Management, Technology, and Economics
ETH Zürich
Weinbergstrasse 56/58
8092 Zürich, Switzerland

ABSTRACT

In this paper we discuss an interesting and useful property of clickstream data. Often a visit includes repeated views of the same page. We show that in three real datasets, sampled from the websites of technology and consulting groups and a news broadcaster, page repetitions occur for the majority as a very specific structure, namely in the form of nested palindromes. This can be explained by the widespread use of features which are available in any web browser: the "refresh" and "back" buttons. Among the types of patterns which can be mined from sequence data, many either stumble if symbol repetitions are involved, or else fail to capture interesting aspects related to symbol repetitions. In an attempt to remedy this, we characterize the palindromic structures, and discuss possible ways of making use of them. One way is to pre-process the sequence data by explicitly inserting these structures, in order to obtain a richer output from conventional mining algorithms. Another application we discuss is to use the information directly, in order to analyze certain aspects of the website under study. We also provide the simple linear-time algorithm which we developed to identify and extract the structures from our data.

Categories and Subject Descriptors

H.2.8 [**Database Management**]: Database Applications—*Data Mining*; E.m [**Data**]: Miscellaneous

General Terms

Algorithms, Measurement

Keywords

palindrome, web usage mining, backtrack, refresh

1. INTRODUCTION

The motivation of this research was to discover patterns in clickstream data. In this Section, we first give an insight into what clickstream data are, and how they can be obtained. We then briefly discuss some of the relevant patterns which were studied in data mining literature, and describe their difficulties in dealing with the specific structural property of palindromicity.

In Section 2 we describe why nested palindromes can be anticipated with normal web-browsing behavior, and provide a simple algorithm which extracts these structures in linear time (proof of correctness is provided in the appendix). In Section 3 we briefly describe the clickstream datasets studied, and show how the methods can be used for finer analysis. Finally, conclusions are given in Section 4.

1.1 Mining Clickstream Data

A clickstream, or visit, is defined as a sequence of URLs visited from a single device (and presumably by a single individual) within a single session. The notion of visit is necessarily arbitrary, since it corresponds to some form of contiguity in time; the scale of this contiguity is then a required parameter. In standard practice, if two consecutive web server log entries belonging to the same user are separated by a time lapse greater than 30 minutes, they are considered to belong to two distinct visits. A visits database can be obtained by transforming web server logs through a process called sessionization (see e.g. [5, 15]). Nowadays many tools exist to feed such databases in an ongoing manner, by incorporating active elements in the pages of the website, which is usually referred to as page tagging.

Since a visit can be seen as a sequence of pages, we can apply a host of data-mining techniques designed for sequence data, namely frequent pattern mining. For an overview see e.g. [13, 24]. In line with the usual vocabulary, given a pattern and a collection of sequences, we say that a sequence *supports* a pattern if the pattern occurs in the sequence. We call the number of sequences in the collection which support the pattern the *support* of the pattern. Furthermore, we say that a pattern is *frequent* if its support is at least min_sup (a user-defined threshold), and a pattern is *closed* if it has no superpattern of equal support.

Two basic patterns which can be mined from a database of sequences are "frequent subsets" and "association rules" [1, 18], both of which capture sets of symbols which frequently co-occur in the database. Classic *Apriori* type algorithms readily provide these [1]. Another well-studied pattern is the "sequential pattern" [2, 23, 20] which, in its simplest form, is a frequent (not necessarily contiguous) subsequence of maximal length. Among others, an efficient algorithm called *PrefixSpan* was proposed to extract such patterns [20].

The partial order pattern (partially ordered set, also called poset) was also studied [17, 4, 21]. It occurs in a sequence if all symbols of the poset are present, and they occur in an order which is compatible with the partial order defined by the poset. More general graph patterns can also be mined. For instance, one can extract from a set of graphs all frequent common subgraphs [8].

Each of these pattern types runs into some problems in capturing aspects of clickstream data which we hold to be important. The frequent subset discards ordering information, which we deem to be essential for the purpose at hand, since our objective is to study traffic flow, which intuitively includes the notion of direction. The sequential pattern is thus a closer fit, but it has a drawback in that it treats a symbol repetition in a rather neutral manner – essentially as just another symbol. The strength drawn from disregarding the contiguity of symbols can turn into a weakness for clickstreams, as we shall see. Symbol repetitions are downright problematic for partial orders, and indeed one of the hypotheses of the *Frecpo* [21] algorithm is that the sequences in the database are repetition-free. A similar problem affects the subgraph pattern; in the general case, for sequences containing symbol repetitions (which translate to cycles in graph representations), chronological precedence is ambiguous. Thus, it seems that none of these patterns is ideally suited to describe data in which repetitions carry a particular importance, as in our clickstream data which will be described in Section 2.1. We will now argue why this is to be expected, and what shape these repetitions take on.

2. NESTED PALINDROMES IN CLICKSTREAM DATA

Loosely speaking, a palindrome is a word which is the same whether it is read from left to right or from right to left, such as *level* or *redder*. It is a sequence with a central symmetry. Palindromes have been the subject of countless human expressions and inquiries since ancient Greece, attracting artistic and mathematical curiosity. Palindromes are investigated in biology; DNA segments often contain palindromic structures which are thought to have certain functional implications, like self-repair. Properties of palindromicity have also been investigated in proteins [11]. As far as computer science is concerned, palindromes are a classic example of an important language type in the Chomsky hierarchy [6]. The set of all palindromes on a given alphabet of symbols is context-free but not regular – no finite state machine can accept the language; at least a pushdown automaton is required.

We argue that palindromes are relevant to web usage mining, and we make this case both by arguing in terms of expected outcome of standard behavior, as well as by showing the patterns observed in real datasets. Imagine the following browsing experience. Catherine knows that the company Pumpkin Umbrellas will launch its new product line today, and lands on the website by typing the URL `pumpkin-umbrellas.com` into her browser. When the page is displayed, an announcement about membership with Pumpkin Umbrellas catches her eye, but she clicks on the "press releases" link instead, to find that the information she was expecting has not been published yet. She gets out of her chair to get a cup of coffee, comes back ten minutes later and hits the "refresh" button on her browser. Now the news item is displayed; she clicks on the link to see the press release. When she is done reading it, she hits the "back" button twice, and clicks on the membership promotion link she had seen earlier. However, membership looks too complicated, so she grows disinterested and walks away from her computer.

Stripping away the narrative, we are left with the sequence of pages through which the user navigated: Main, Press Releases, Press Releases, Product Launch, Press Releases, Main, Membership. We can encode this as the symbol sequence $ABBCBAD$, and visualize it as the graph in Figure 1; each node represents a symbol, and the arcs are labelled in chronological order of the symbols' appearance in the sequence. A page refresh always translates into a reflexive arc (e.g. $B \to B$), and a backtrack always translates into a pair of opposite arcs (e.g. $\{A \to B\ ,\ B \to A\}$).

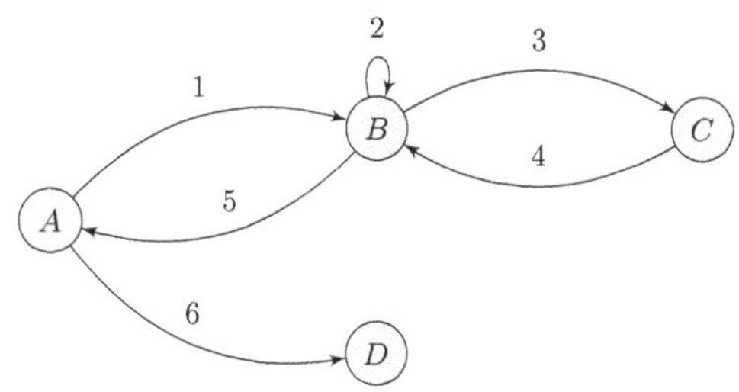

Figure 1: Graph of the sequence $ABBCBAD$.

Looking at the sequence $ABBCBAD$, we notice that there are three repetitions in this sequence; the symbol B is repeated twice and the symbol A is repeated once. We also see two contiguous subsequences which are palindromes, BB and BCB, corresponding to the page refresh and to the first backtrack, respectively. They overlap on their outermost symbol B. Next, we make the less obvious observation that $ABBCBA$ is "almost" a palindrome – it would be a palindrome if BB were replaced by a single B. Finally, notice that if we take the sequence $ABBCBAD$ and iteratively replace the first-ending palindrome by its outermost symbol, the resulting sequence AD does not contain any repetitions (see Table 1 for the steps). In other words, the repetitions in this sequence are all *accounted for* by short palindromes. These intuitions form the basis of our approach.

sequence	1st palindrome "compressed"
$A\mathbf{BB}CBAD$	$A\mathbf{B}CBAD$
$A\mathbf{BCB}AD$	$A\mathbf{B}AD$
$\mathbf{ABA}D$	$\mathbf{A}D$
AD	AD

Table 1: Successively replacing the first-ending palindrome transforms the sequence $ABBCBAD$ into the sequence AD, which contains no repetitions.

Many efficient (linear time) algorithms exist to extract different kinds of palindromes from sequences, e.g. maximal palindromes, palindromes with gaps, etc (see e.g. [14, 12]). However, we are not aware of an algorithm which performs the process we describe above. It is captured formally in the algorithm *extract-pals*, listed as Algorithm 1. For a proof of correctness, please see the appendix. The algorithm transforms the graph in a straightforward way. It iteratively

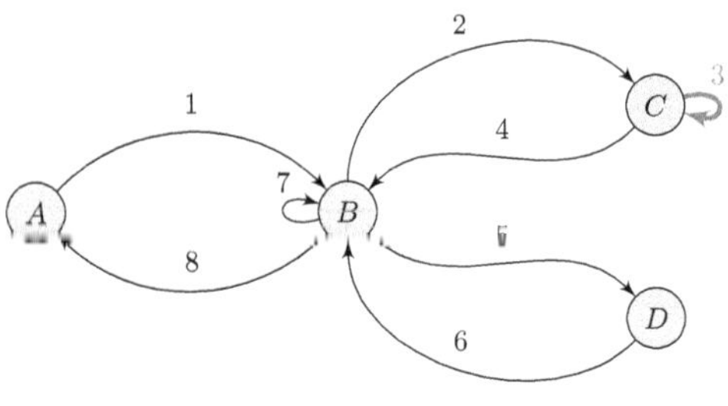

(a) $ABCCBDBBA$

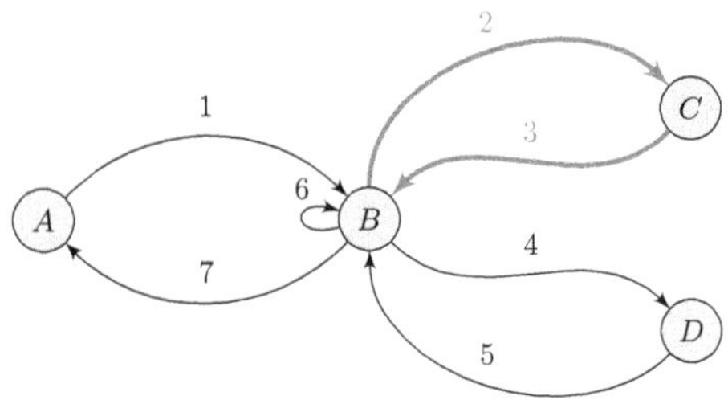

(b) $ABCBDBBA$

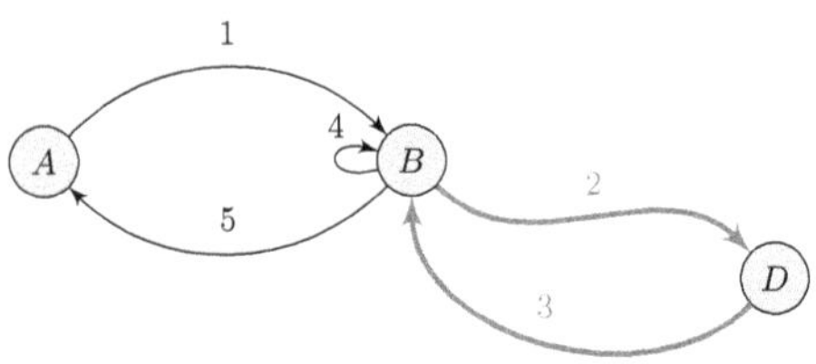

(c) $ABDBBA$

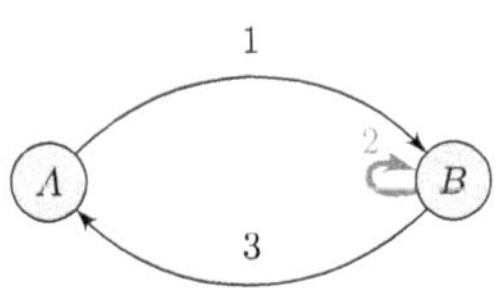

(d) $ABBA$

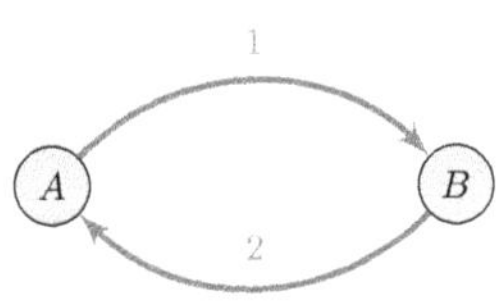

(e) ABA

(f) A

Figure 2: Successive removals of the first-ending palindrome in $ABCCBDBBA$ reduce the sequence to a single symbol.

Input: A sequence s
Output: The list (refreshes, backtracks, leftover)
R = empty set
B = empty set
T = empty stack
for $i = 1$ *to* $length(s)$ **do**
  if *the top of* T *equals* $s[i]$ **then**
    $R = R \cup \{s[i]\}$ `#refresh`
  else if *the symbol under the top of* T *equals* $s[i]$ **then**
    $B = B \cup \{(T.top, s[i])\}$ `#backtrack`
    $T.pop()$
  else
    $T.push(s[i])$ `#no palindrome`
  end
end
return (R, B, T)

Algorithm 1: extract-pals

i	T	R	B
1	A	$\emptyset$	$\emptyset$
2	AB	$\emptyset$	$\emptyset$
3	ABC	$\emptyset$	$\emptyset$
4	ABC	$\{C\}$	$\emptyset$
5	AB	$\{C\}$	$\{(C, B)\}$
6	ABD	$\{C\}$	$\{(C, B)\}$
7	AB	$\{C\}$	$\{(C, B), (D, B)\}$
8	AB	$\{C, B\}$	$\{(C, B), (D, B)\}$
9	A	$\{C, B\}$	$\{(C, B), (D, B), (B, A)\}$

Table 2: Steps of *extract-pals* for $ABCCBDBBA$.

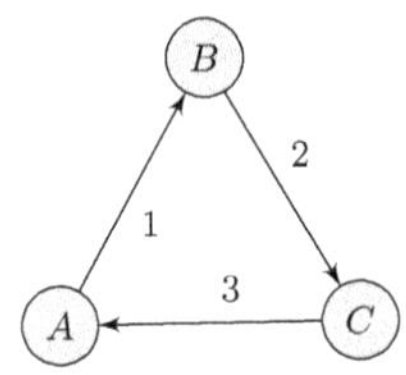

Figure 3: Graph of the sequence $ABCA$.

removes the first (and earliest in a chronological sense) of the following:

- a reflexive arc
- a pair of opposite arcs with consecutive label numbers

The complexity of the algorithm is linear in the sum of the lengths of the sequences in the database. The process is illustrated for the more complex sequence $ABCCBDBBA$; the successive steps are shown in Table 2 and represented graphically in Figure 2. Notice that here again, all repetitions are accounted for by palindromes.

This need of course not be the case for every sequence, for instance the sequence $ABCA$, shown in Figure 3, contains a repetition but no palindromes. If a sequence contains at least one repetition which is not accounted for by palindromes, we will call it *unaccounted*. Otherwise we will say that the sequence is *accounted*. In the next section, we will show that in our datasets, unaccounted sequences are a minority.

2.1 Evidence of Nested Palindromes

We now turn to real data, to show that palindromes are indeed a characteristic feature of clickstreams. We analyze three different datasets, the two first of which we will call *Blue* and *Orange* for anonymity purposes. The datasets are collections of visits to the websites of two distinct groups of a large technology and consulting company, from the year 2011, collected by a page tagging solution. The third dataset is a database of visits to `msnbc.com` on September 28, 1999, gathered from an IIS log, which we obtained from the UCI Machine Learning Repository [10]. It differs from the first two datasets in that the level of granularity is coarser; while Blue and Orange consist of sequences of URLs, a visit in the MSNBC dataset is given as a sequence of news categories. For example, if a user read an article about French politics, another on the tour de France, an opinion piece about doping in cycling, a second tour de France article, and finally the weather forecast, the corresponding visit was recorded as "frontpage, sports, opinion, sports, weather". In this study, we simply treat the categories as pages[1].

The sample sizes are $3.1 \cdot 10^5$, $3.2 \cdot 10^5$ and $9.9 \cdot 10^5$ visits, over about $1.8 \cdot 10^3$ pages, $8.8 \cdot 10^3$ pages, and seventeen categories, respectively (see Table 3 for a summary). Most visits are made up of very few pageviews, but a small percentage range into a length of several hundreds. Our goal is to study human behavior, and most likely very long visits were made by crawlers or similar programs. For this reason, and also to make the presentation of results easier, we remove from the databases all visits with length above 20 pageviews, since they correspond to a low proportion of 0.16%, 0.53% and 2.8% of the visits, respectively. The visit length distributions are shown as log-log plots in Figure 4. The first two datasets look quite regular in this respect, and visually they seem to be approximately Zipf distributed, although goodness-of-fit tests such as the Kolmogorov-Smirnoff test (cf. [7]) fail quite unequivocally. The MSNBC visits are a bit less regular in their length distribution, however clearly all datasets share the characteristic that visit lengths are rather heavy-tailed.

Applying our extraction algorithm, we obtain for each sequence the set of refreshes and the set of backtracks it contains, as well as the "leftover" sequence – the sequence that remains after all palindromes have been compressed. Notice that a sequence is unaccounted if and only if the leftover sequence contains at least one repetition. We find that the proportion of unaccounted sequences is as low as 0.86%, 1.6% and 5.4%, respectively. Of course, to be fair, it should be said that the shortest sequence which *can* be unaccounted[2] has length 4 (such as the one in Figure 3). However, even if we consider only the sequences which both contain repetitions and are of length ≥ 4, the proportion of unaccounted sequences remains low; the values are then 14%, 18% and 8.3%.

In order to get a more complete picture of this characteristic in our datasets, in Figure 5 we categorize visits by the number of refreshes and backtracks they contain. The blobs are sized according to the number of visits in the category, and the black spokes indicate the proportion of accounted sequences in each category – a vertical spoke means that the proportion is 1, while a horizontal spoke means that the proportion is 0. As can be seen, the proportion is large in most categories. For instance, in the Blue dataset, among the visits containing 3 page refreshes and 4 backtracks (i.e. 7 repetitions explained by palindromes) virtually none contain a repetition of another form. On the whole, in our data, it seems that palindromes account for the lion's share of repetitions all around.

Taking a slightly different approach, if we look at counts of non-palindromic *repetitions* (as opposed to counts of *visits containing non-palindromic repetitions*), we find that out of all repetitions, those explained by palindromes make up 95%, 92% and 96% of the respective datasets. The "palindromicity" throughout our data is thus confirmed from quite a few different angles. The strength of the presence of this property, and the independence of the datasets, together suggest that the same structure may be found in other clickstream databases as well.

3. APPLICATIONS

Being confident in the strong presence of palindromes in our datasets, we can now turn to discussing possible ways of making use of it. We identify at least two simple applications of the presented material. Firstly, it can be used in a pre-processing step to ensure richer output of existing algorithms. Secondly, we sketch how one can make a direct use of the extracted features in order to analyze navigational properties of a website.

3.1 Pre-processing for Sequence Mining

Recall the sequence $ABBCBAD$ studied above, which contains one refresh and two backtracks. This sequence is easily transformed to $AB\mathbf{X}BC\mathbf{Y}B\mathbf{Z}AD$, where we have inserted the new symbols X, Y and Z to specifically mark the places where the behaviors of interest occur; for instance, Y stands for "backtrack from C to B". The set of sequential patterns obtained from such a transformed dataset will be strictly richer than the set obtained from the original dataset; no information is lost, however the extra information can be put to good use. For instance, imagine the pattern $ABCYB$ is found to be frequent. Obviously, if we had run the algorithm on the original sequences, the pattern $ABCB$ would have been reported as frequent. However, $ABCYB$ contains more information, because it tells us that a backtrack from C to B occurs, whereas $ABCB$ could correspond to backtracks as well as sequences like $ABCDEB$. Thus, rather than reporting $ABCB$ we can report e.g. $A\widehat{BCB}$.

The same concept holds for the partial order pattern. In order to quantify the "enrichment" of the result set, we run the Frecpo algorithm on the three pre-processed datasets, setting the support thresholds so as to obtain a few hundred frequent patterns, and observe how many of them contain at least one of the added symbols. The proportions are quite high: 193/418 (46%), 313/339 (92%) and 317/437 (73%). This means that in our data, refreshes and backtracks are not only frequent as a general feature, but furthermore, spe-

[1]It should be noted that in this dataset, the number of actual refreshes will be over-estimated, since any intra-category transition will look like a refresh. Likewise, the backtracks will be both under-estimated (for the same reason) and over-estimated because "Skiing, Banking crisis, Basketball", will turn into "sports, finance, sports" and be interpreted as a backtrack. It should also be noted that this log-based dataset is likely more susceptible to caching effects.

[2]A sequence which contains no repetitions is trivially accounted.

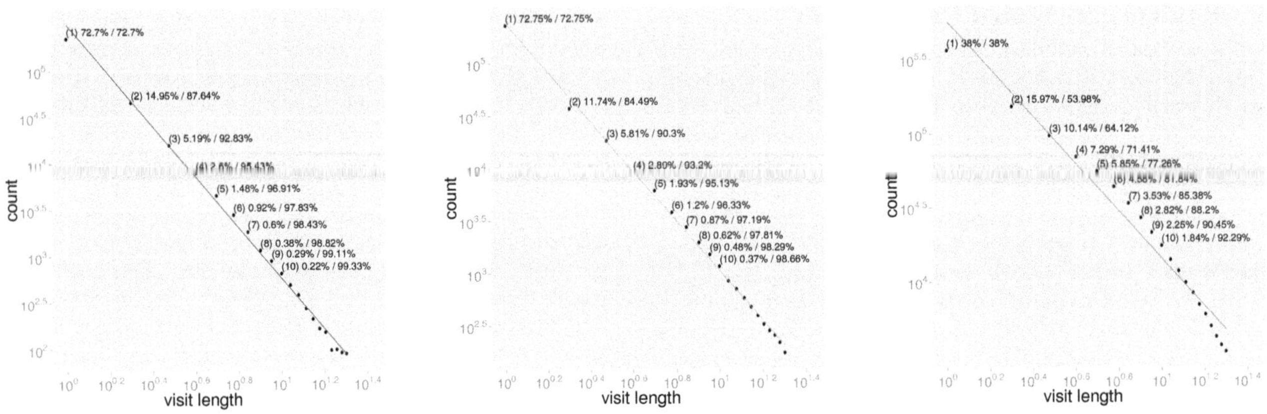

(a) Blue dataset (b) Orange dataset (c) MSNBC dataset

Figure 4: Distribution of visit lengths, in number of pageviews. The values next to points are the length (in parentheses), the proportion of sequences of that length, and the cumulative proportion.

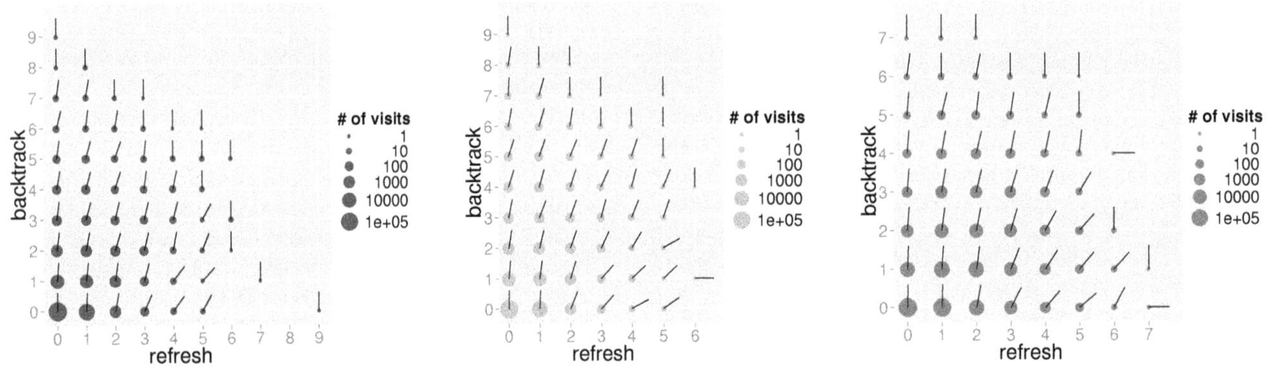

(a) Blue dataset (b) Orange dataset (c) MSNBC dataset

Figure 5: Visits are categorized by the number of refreshes and backtracks they contain. The blob sizes represent the number of visits in the category. The black spokes show the *proportion of accounted sequences* in the category (vertical means 100%, horizontal means 0).

statistic	Blue	Orange	MSNBC
sample size	$3.1 \cdot 10^5$	$3.2 \cdot 10^5$	$9.9 \cdot 10^5$
distinct items	1822	8822	17
visits over length 20 (removed)	0.16%	0.53%	2.8%
unaccounted visits among all visits	0.86%	1.6%	5.4%
unaccounted visits among visits of length ≥ 4 containing repetitions	14%	18%	8.3%
proportion of palindromic repetitions	95%	92%	96%
frequent closed partial orders containing added symbols	193/418 (46%)	313/339 (92%)	317/437 (73%)

Table 3: Summary view of the dataset statistics.

cific instances are also frequent, and part of larger frequent browsing patterns. For an example of how to graphically incorporate the additional information in a partial order pattern, see Figure 6.

One caveat which should be mentioned about our procedure of enriching sequences is that it may result in aggravating the redundancy in the result set, which is a much-reported problem in frequent pattern mining. Fortunately a lot of excellent research is being done to manage this redundancy (see e.g. [3, 16]).

3.2 Direct Interpretation for Web Analytics

Surely the tendencies of a page to be refreshed, or backtracked from, or backtracked to, are features of direct interest for anyone who aims to understand the dynamics of a website. In order to achieve these insights, we extract the palindromic patterns previously discussed. Here we opt for finding the *support* of the palindromes, rather than the occurrence count. This means that if a given backtrack (B, A) occurs $n \geq 1$ times during a single visit, we count 1 rather than n. This approach is popular in data mining, and from

(a) Original data

(b) Pre-processed data

Figure 6: Comparison of partial order patterns without and with pre-processing. From the original data (a), an example of pattern obtained is read as "A before D and A before B and B before C". With pre-processed data (b), a pattern can additionally express information like "refresh of D and backtrack from B to A".

a statistical robustness viewpoint a good choice. Indeed, the breakdown point[3] of the occurrence count is $1/N$ (where N is the number of sequences) since a single "bad" sequence with a large number of occurrences can perturb the statistic by an arbitrary amount. By contrast, the support statistic has no breakdown point, because it is always contained in the interval $[0, N]$; any observation can only perturb the statistic by $1/N$.

We provide an adaptation of Algorithm 1 to extract the support of all refreshes and backtracks from a visits database. It is called *sup-pals* and listed as Algorithm 2. Notice that unlike in the case of frequent pattern algorithms, no threshold parameter is required as input. The support $sup_{re}(x)$ equals the number of visits in which at least one refresh of x occurs, while supports $sup_{bf}(x)$ and $sup_{bt}(x)$ equal the number of visits containing at least one backtrack from and to x, respectively. Using these supports, we can now derive some quite informative metrics about web pages.

One straight-forward such metric is the *refresh rate* $REF(x)$ of page x, defined as

$$REF(x) = \frac{sup_{re}(x)}{sup(x)} \quad (1)$$

which is contained between 0 and 1. Depending on the intended function of a page x within a website, different values of $REF(x)$ may be desirable. For example, if an active newsfeed page has a high refresh rate, this can be taken as a good sign, since the implication is that many of the visitors are eager for more news items. If however a static page has a high refresh rate, it may indicate that the page often displays poorly in users' browsers for some reason, and should be checked by a webmaster for possible malfunction. It also bears mentioning that some pages reload automatically *by design*, which then needs to be kept in mind when analyzing the results. We further define the *cul-de-sac rate* $CDS(x)$ of page x as

$$CDS(x) = \frac{sup_{bf}(x)}{sup(x)} \quad (2)$$

which is also contained between 0 and 1. This metric reflects the tendency of the page's visitors to return to an earlier page. Here again, different values may be desirable depending on the context. A help page, for instance, will hopefully have a high CDS, indicating that visitors returned to the website, presumably because they found the help they needed on the help page. Conversely, if an "index" page designed to act as a hub has a high CDS, the page may need a redesign. Similarly, let us define the *pivot rate* $PIV(x)$ of a page as

$$PIV(x) = \frac{sup_{bt}(x)}{sup(x)} \quad (3)$$

which again falls into the interval $[0, 1]$. This metric indicates the tendency of visitors to return to the page, possibly in order to proceed elsewhere. An "index" page should probably have a relatively high PIV, whereas if a page in the checkout/ordering workflow of an online retailer has high PIV, it is probably indicative of a malfunction or of a problem in the web design. If for some page x, both $CDS(x)$ and $PIV(x)$ are high, i.e. visitors backtrack both from and to that page a lot, it could be indicative of some kind of "corridor" which visitors need to follow in order to get from A to B. Perhaps a direct link would be more convenient; it is also worthwhile to investigate whether x should be merged with

```
Input: A sequence database S
Output: The supports sup_re, sup_bf and sup_bt.
foreach sequence s ∈ S do
    R = empty set
    B = empty set
    T = empty stack
    for i = 1 to length(s) do
        if T.top equals s[i] then
            R = R ∪ {s[i]} #refresh
        else if T.undertop equals s[i] then
            B = B ∪ {(T.top, s[i])} #backtrack
            T.pop()
        else
            T.push(s[i]) #no palindrome
        end
    end
    foreach symbol x in R do
        add 1 to sup_re(x)
    end
    foreach pair (x, y) in B do
        add 1 to sup_bf(x)
        add 1 to sup_bt(y)
    end
end
return (sup_re, sup_bf, sup_bt)
```
Algorithm 2: *sup-pals*

[3]The breakdown point of a statistic is defined as the large-sample proportion of contaminated observations needed to change the value of a statistic by an arbitrarily large amount [9]. For a survey of the field of robust statistics see [19].

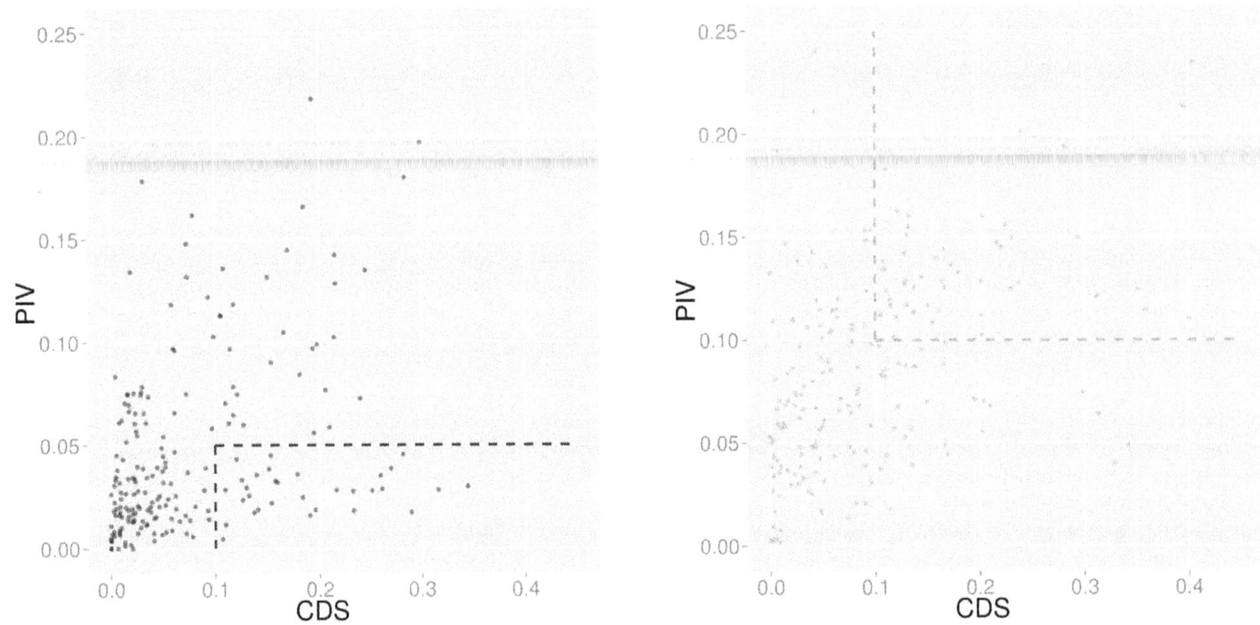

(a) Blue dataset (b) Orange dataset

Figure 7: Each point stands for a top-200 page in the website. There seem to be many low-PIV, high-CDS pages in the top Blue pages, while there are many high-PIV, high-CDS pages in the Orange pages.

a page people frequently backtrack to (from x), in order to spare visitors a click.

While it may be difficult to decide which absolute values are desirable, one can turn to a comparative analysis; are there outliers? Do the pages look like they are in their proper place in the distribution? Note that if additionally to the page sequences, we also had access to the time at which each click was made, we could incorporate this information to allow for a more precise interpretation – if a page refresh occurs after several minutes spent on the page, it is arguably a better sign than if it occurs shortly after the preceding view of the page.

Combined outlier analysis can also be of interest for diagnostics purposes. For instance, a plot of PIV vs CDS in Figure 7 simultaneously shows both tendencies of backtracking *from* and *to* a page. Here we plot only the top 200 pages (in terms of support) of the sites Blue and Orange. We can notice that in the Blue dataset, there are quite many low-PIV, high-CDS pages – 31 points in the delimited region, versus 9 in the same region in the Orange dataset. On the other hand, there are quite many high-PIV, high-CDS pages in the Orange dataset – 50 pages in the region vs 15 in the same region in the Blue dataset. Accordingly, the owner of the Blue website may wish to examine all those "dead ends", while the owner of the Orange website might want to investigate why it has so many "corridors".

4. CONCLUSIONS

We have illustrated that nested palindromes are strongly present in clickstream data; we first argued that standard browsing behavior generates clickstreams containing such structures. A simple stack-based algorithm was derived to extract such patterns (in linear time), and used to confirm the presence of palindromicity in three independent datasets of real data. We showed how sequence data can be preprocessed by insert new symbols which explicitly mark the phenomena in question, and illustrated ways in which the resulting patterns become richer. Furthermore, we showed examples of metrics which can be derived from the results, and how those can be interpreted. Such information is helpful to people in charge of designing and/or analyzing the usage of the website. In particular, it can be used to detect whether a page is failing in its intended function.

4.1 Limitations and Future Work

Our considerations in this work are limited to "first-order" palindromes, for instance for the sequence $ABCBA$ we produce backtracks (C, B) and (B, A). In some applications it may be of interest to know that there was an uninterrupted return from C to A, which would require extracting (C, B, A) or something similar.

In future work, we intend to use the discovered features to produce more accurate generative models which could improve the results of approaches such as we described e.g. in [22]. We are also in the process of developing website optimizations utilizing these results, and of validating the practical use of the findings with the websites' stakeholders.

Our approach was studied with web navigation in mind, but could in principle be useful in analyzing data arising from other processes with a similar structure. In particular, studies of navigation of all kinds could benefit, for instance, if the dataset consists in descriptions of daily itineraries, such as sequences of stations/stops in a public transportation network, or of areas in a roads network traversed by car.

5. REFERENCES

[1] R. Agrawal and R. Srikant. Fast algorithms for mining association rules. In *VLDB*, pages 487–499, 1994.

[2] R. Agrawal and R. Srikant. Mining sequential patterns. *Data Engineering, International Conference on*, 0:3, 1995.

[3] T. Calders and B. Goethals. Mining all non-derivable frequent itemsets. In *Proceedings of the 6th European Conference on Principles of Data Mining and Knowledge Discovery*, PKDD '02, pages 74–85, London, UK, UK, 2002. Springer-Verlag.

[4] G. Casas-Garriga. Summarizing sequential data with closed partial orders. In *Proceedings of the Fifth SIAM International Conference on Data Mining*, pages 380–390, 2005.

[5] S. Chakrabarti. *Mining the Web: Discovering Knowledge from Hypertext Data*. Morgan-Kauffman, 2002.

[6] N. Chomsky. Three models for the description of language. *Information Theory, IRE Transactions on*, 2(3):113 –124, september 1956.

[7] A. Clauset, C. R. Shalizi, and M. E. J. Newman. Power-law distributions in empirical data. *SIAM Reviews*, June 2007.

[8] D. J. Cook and L. B. Holder. *Mining Graph Data*. John Wiley & Sons Inc., 2007.

[9] A. Davison. *Statistical Models*. Cambridge University Press, The Pitt Building, Trumpington Street, Cambridge, UK, 2003.

[10] A. Frank and A. Asuncion. UCI machine learning repository, 2010.

[11] M. Giel-Pietraszuk, M. Hoffmann, S. Dolecka, J. Rychlewski, and J. Barciszewski. Palindromes in proteins. *Journal of Protein Chemistry*, 22:109–113, 2003. 10.1023/A:1023454111924.

[12] D. Gusfield. *Algorithms on strings, trees, and sequences: computer science and computational biology*. Cambridge University Press, New York, NY, USA, 1997.

[13] J. Han, H. Cheng, D. Xin, and X. Yan. Frequent pattern mining: Current status and future directions. *Data Mining and Knowledge Discovery*, 14(1), 2007.

[14] R. Kolpakov and G. Kucherov. Searching for gapped palindromes. In P. Ferragina and G. Landau, editors, *Combinatorial Pattern Matching*, volume 5029 of *Lecture Notes in Computer Science*, pages 18–30. Springer Berlin / Heidelberg, 2008.

[15] B. Liu. *Web Data Mining: Exploring Hyperlinks, Contents, and Usage Data (Data-Centric Systems and Applications)*. Springer-Verlag New York, Inc., Secaucus, NJ, USA, 2006.

[16] M. Mampaey, N. Tatti, and J. Vreeken. Tell me what i need to know: succinctly summarizing data with itemsets. In *KDD*, pages 573–581, 2011.

[17] H. Mannila and C. Meek. Global partial orders from sequential data. In *KDD '00: Proceedings of the sixth ACM SIGKDD International Conference on Knowledge Discovery and Data Mining*, pages 161–168. ACM, 2000.

[18] H. Mannila, H. Toivonen, and I. Verkamo. Efficient algorithms for discovering association rules. pages 181–192. AAAI Press, 1994.

[19] S. Morgenthaler. A survey of robust statistics. *Statistical Methods & Applications*, 16:171–172, 2007.

[20] J. Pei, J. Han, B. Mortazavi-Asl, J. Wang, H. Pinto, Q. Chen, U. Dayal, and M.-C. Hsu. Mining sequential patterns by pattern-growth: The prefixspan approach. *IEEE Transactions on Knowledge and Data Engineering*, 16(11):2004, 2004.

[21] J. Pei, H. Wang, J. Liu, K. Wang, J. Wang, and P. S. Yu. Discovering frequent closed partial orders from strings. *IEEE Transactions on Knowledge and Data Engineering*, 18:1467–1481, November 2006.

[22] M. Speiser, G. Antonini, and A. Labbi. Ranking web-based partial orders by significance using a markov reference model. In *IEEE 11th International Conference on Data Mining (ICDM)*, 2011.

[23] X. Yan, J. Han, and R. Afshar. Clospan: Mining closed sequential patterns in large datasets. In *In SDM*, pages 166–177, 2003.

[24] M. Zaki, N. Parimi, N. De, F. Gao, B. Phoophakdee, J. Urban, V. Chaoji, M. Hasan, and S. Salem. Towards generic pattern mining. In B. Ganter and R. Godin, editors, *Formal Concept Analysis*, volume 3403 of *Lecture Notes in Computer Science*, pages 1–20. Springer Berlin / Heidelberg, 2005.

APPENDIX

A. MINING PALINDROMIC STRUCTURES

If s is a sequence, then given integers $i \leq j$ we denote by $s[i:j]$ the contiguous subsequence of s from position i to position j. A subsequence $s[i:i]$ of length 1 can also be written as $s[i]$, and $s[i:j]$ with $i > j$ is interpreted as the empty sequence. We denote by $\rho(s)$ the reversed sequence (the symbols in reverse order), and we say that s is a *palindrome* if it has length > 1 and $s = \rho(s)$. If $s_1, s_2..., s_n$ are n sequences, we denote by $s_1 s_2 ... s_n$ the sequence obtained by their concatenation. Now, for a sequence s, let

$$\omega = min\{j : \exists \alpha < j : s[\alpha : j] = \rho(s[\alpha : j])\} \tag{4}$$

If such an ω exists, then α is unique, that is, $s[\alpha : \omega]$ is the unique first-ending palindrome of s. Indeed, suppose that α is not unique, i.e. that the statement holds for two different values $\alpha_1 < \alpha_2$. Since we have $s[\alpha_1 : \omega] = \rho(s[\alpha_1 : \omega])$ and $s[\alpha_2 : \omega] = \rho(s[\alpha_2 : \omega])$ it follows that $s[\alpha_1 : \alpha_1 + \omega - \alpha_2] = \rho(s[\alpha_1 : \alpha_1 + \omega - \alpha_2])$, i.e. there is a palindrome ending at $\alpha_1 + \omega - \alpha_2 < \omega$, which contradicts the definition of ω. This means that we can unambiguously define the function CFP as follows. If α and ω of equation (4) exist,

$$CFP(s) = s[1 : \alpha]s[\omega + 1 : \ell] \tag{5}$$

otherwise,

$$CFP(s) = s. \tag{6}$$

In words, CFP, which stands for Compress First Palindrome, is a function which takes as input a sequence s, and returns a sequence identical to s, except that the first-ending palindrome in s (if it exists) is replaced by its outermost symbol – we say that the palindrome is *compressed*. Table 2 shows a few examples of CFP preimages and images.

Notice that we know the lengths of palindromes compressed by CFP: if a sequence s contains a palindrome, the first-ending palindrome is of length 2 or 3. Indeed, suppose that s has a first-ending palindrome of length $\ell > 3$. Let α be the starting index of the palindrome, and $\omega = \alpha + \ell - 1$ its end index. Since $s[\alpha : \omega]$ is a palindrome, then so is $s[\alpha + 1 : \omega - 1]$, which has a length $\ell - 2 > 1$. But then, there is a palindrome ending at $\omega - 1$, i.e. before ω, which contradicts the hypothesis. As a consequence, $CFP(s)$ either leaves the sequence s unchanged, or compresses a palindrome of length 2 or 3. This is fortunate, because in terms of browsing behavior, CFP compresses either a page refresh (palindrome of length 2) or a backtrack (palindrome of length 3), which are precisely the features of interest to us. Denote by $CFP^{\infty}(s)$ the fixed point of CFP reached by successive applications of CFP to s, i.e.

$$CFP^{\infty}(s) = CFP \circ CFP \circ ... \circ CFP(s). \quad (7)$$

This fixed point exists for any sequence s of finite, positive length; the image is either identical to the preimage or shorter than the preimage, and any sequence of length 1 is obviously a fixed point, so a fixed point is reached in a finite number of iterations. As an example, for the sequence $s = ABCCBDBBA$, Table 2 tells us that $CFP^{\infty}(s) = A$. We now turn our attention to exploiting this structural property in order to mine features of interest. As a first step, an algorithm which computes CFP^{∞} is listed as Algorithm 3. The algorithm's complexity is linear in the length of the sequence.

Input: A sequence s
Output: The sequence $CFP^{\infty}(s)$
T = empty stack
for $i = 1$ *to length*(s) **do**
  if *the top of* T *equals* $s[i]$ **then**
    // Type #2: palindrome of length 2
    // do nothing
  else if *the symbol under the top of* T *equals* $s[i]$ **then**
    // Type #3: palindrome of length 3
    T.*pop*()
  else
    // Type #1: no palindrome ("trivial type")
    T.*push*$(s[i])$
  end
end
return T

Algorithm 3: rm-pals

THEOREM 1. *Given a sequence s, the algorithm rm-pals computes $CFP^{\infty}(s)$.*

We will prove a few intermediate steps first. During the execution of *rm-pals(s)*, we call the pair $(T, s[i : length(s)])$ observed immediately after i is modified the *state at* i. We say that a loop iteration is called *trivial* if it is of type #1; otherwise, it is called *non-trivial.*

LEMMA 1. *The execution* rm-pals(s) *contains only type #1 iterations until iteration ω, where ω is the end index of the first-ending palindrome of s.*

PROOF. Observe that while no non-trivial iteration has occurred, $T = s[1 : i - 1]$. Now, suppose a non-trivial iteration first occurs before ω, and consider the state for s before this iteration; we have that either $T.top = s[i]$ or

i	T	$s[i : length(s)]$	Type
1		$ABCCBDBBA$	#1
2	A	$BCCBDBBA$	#1
3	AB	$CCBDBBA$	#1
4	$AB\boldsymbol{C}$	$\boldsymbol{C}BDBBA$	#2
5	$A\boldsymbol{B}C$	$\boldsymbol{B}DBBA$	#3
6	AB	$DBBA$	#1
7	$A\boldsymbol{B}D$	$\boldsymbol{B}BA$	#3
8	$A\boldsymbol{B}$	$\boldsymbol{B}A$	#2
9	$\boldsymbol{A}B$	$\boldsymbol{A}$	#3

Table 4: Sequence of *rm-pals* states for the sequence $ABCCBDBBA$.

$T.undertop = s[i]$. In the first case $s[i - 1] = s[i]$, that is $s[i - 1 : i] = \rho(s[i - 1 : i])$, and in the second case $s[i - 2] = s[i]$, that is $s[i - 2 : i] = \rho(s[i - 2 : i])$. In either case, s contains a palindrome ending before ω, which contradicts the hypothesis. □

COROLLARY 1. *For an input s which contains no palindromes, rm-pals(s) terminates using only trivial loop iterations, and hence the algorithm returns s.*

LEMMA 2. *If sequence s has a first-ending palindrome of length ℓ, the first non-trivial loop iteration of* rm-pals(s) *is of type #ℓ.*

PROOF. Observe that while only type #1 iterations have occurred, $T = s[1 : i - 1]$. Hence if the first-ending palindrome $s[\alpha : \omega]$ is of length 2, at iteration ω we have

$$T.top = s[\alpha] = s[\omega] = s[i] \quad (8)$$

which results in type #2. Conversely, if $s[\alpha : \omega]$ is of length 3, this becomes

$$T.undertop = s[\alpha] = s[\omega] = s[i] \quad (9)$$

which results in type #3. □

LEMMA 3. *For an input sequence s with first-ending palindrome $s[\alpha : \omega]$, the state after the first non-trivial iteration is $(s[1 : \alpha], s[\omega + 1 : length(s)])$.*

PROOF. The first non-trivial loop iteration occurs at ω. If the first-ending palindrome has length 2, we have a type #2 iteration and the stack remains unchanged from the last iteration, i.e. $T = s[1 : \omega - 1]$. If the palindrome has length 3, we have a type #3 iteration and the top element is popped from the stack, yielding $T = s[1 : \omega - 2]$. In both events, the resulting stack is $T = s[1 : \alpha]$, and the remaining sequence is $s[\omega + 1 : length(s)]$. □

LEMMA 4. *For a sequence s with first-ending palindrome $s[\alpha : \omega]$, the execution rm-pals(CPF(s)) reaches the state $(s[1 : \alpha], s[\omega + 1 : length(s)])$ using only trivial loops.*

PROOF. First, notice that $CFP(s)[1 : \alpha] = s[1 : \alpha]$. Since the right-hand side can not contain a palindrome, all loop iterations until α are of type #1. Finally, recall that $CFP(s) = s[1 : \alpha]s[\omega + 1 : length(s)]$. □

Theorem 1, which states that the algorithm is correct, easily follows from Corollary 1 and Lemmas 3 and 4.

Mining Discriminative Components With Low-Rank And Sparsity Constraints for Face Recognition

Qiang Zhang, Baoxin Li
Computer Science and Engineering
Arizona State University
Tempe, AZ, 85281
qzhang53, baoxin.li@asu.edu

ABSTRACT

This paper introduces a novel image decomposition approach for an ensemble of correlated images, using low-rank and sparsity constraints. Each image is decomposed as a combination of three components: one common component, one condition component, which is assumed to be a low-rank matrix, and a sparse residual. For a set of face images of N subjects, the decomposition finds N common components, one for each subject, K low-rank components, each capturing a different global condition of the set (e.g., different illumination conditions), and a sparse residual for each input image. Through this decomposition, the proposed approach recovers a clean face image (the common component) for each subject and discovers the conditions (the condition components and the sparse residuals) of the images in the set. The set of $N+K$ images containing only the common and the low-rank components form a compact and discriminative representation for the original images. We design a classifier using only these $N+K$ images. Experiments on commonly-used face data sets demonstrate the effectiveness of the approach for face recognition through comparing with the leading state-of-the-art in the literature. The experiments further show good accuracy in classifying the condition of an input image, suggesting that the components from the proposed decomposition indeed capture physically meaningful features of the input.

Categories and Subject Descriptors

H.4 [**Information Systems Applications**]: Miscellaneous

General Terms

Feature extraction and preprocessing

Keywords

Subspace learning, Low-rank matrix, Sparse matrix, Face Recognition, Component Decomposition

1. INTRODUCTION

Face recognition has been an active research field for a few decades, and its challenges and importance continue to attract efforts from many researchers, resulting in many new approaches in recent years. The most recent literature may be divided into roughly two groups, where methods in the first group try to model the physical processes of image formation under different conditions (e.g., illumination, expression, pose etc.). For example, the approach of [10] models the face image under varying illumination conditions to be a linear combination of images of the same subject captured at 9 specially designed illumination conditions; the SRC algorithm of [19] further assumes that face images with illumination and expression conditions can be represented as a sparse linear combination of the training instances (i.e., the dictionary atoms). On the other hand, the second group of approaches utilizes mathematical/statistical tools to capture the latent relations among face images for classification. E.g., the SUN approach [7] uses the statistics of the human fixation of the images to recognize the face images, Volterrafaces [9] finds a latent space for face recognition, where the ratio of intra-class distance over inter-class distance is minimized. One major advantage of the techniques in the first class comes from their being generative in nature, which allows these methods to accomplish tasks like face relighting or novel pose generation in addition to recognition. The second group of methods in a sense ignores the physical property of the faces images and treats them as ordinary 2D signals.

Although the methods in the first group have the above nice property, a baseline implementation usually requires dictionaries with training images as atoms and thus may face the scalability issue in real-world applications with a huge number of subjects. Hence efforts have also been devoted to reducing the size of the dictionary while attempting to retain the level of performance of the original dictionary. Examples include those that generate more compact dictionaries through some learning procedure (e.g., [13]) and those that attempt to extract subject-specific features that are effectively used as dictionary atoms (e.g., [15]). Our approach belongs to the second group. Since the expressive power of the original dictionary-based techniques comes from largely the number of training images for each subject, a compact dictionary may suffer from degraded performance unless the reduced dictionary properly captures the conditions of the original data that are critical for a recognition task. For example, the method of [15], while shown to be effective for expression-invariant recognition, is difficulty to generalize to handle global conditions such as illumination change, which often introduce to the data non-sparse conditions that cannot be captured by the sparsity model proposed therein.

Recognizing that non-sparse conditions such as illumination change and large occlusion are critical for face recognition, and that for a typical application we may assume only a finite number of such conditions (e.g., a relatively small number of illumination conditions or other conditions), in this paper, we propose a model for representing a set of face images by decomposing them into three components: a common component shared by images of the same subject, a low-rank component capturing non-sparse global changes, and a sparse residual component. Such a decomposition is partially inspired by the observation that the reconstruction of the image with the top few singular values and the corresponding singular vectors often capture the global information of the image, which can be represented by a low-rank matrix. To this end, a generic algorithm is proposed, with theoretic analysis on the convergence and parameter selection. The learned common and low-rank components form a compact and discriminative representation of the original set of images. A classifier is then built based on comparison of subspaces spanned by these components and by a novel image to be classified. This is very compact compared with the number of atoms in an over-determined dictionary such as that in [19]. Further, by explicitly modeling non-sparse conditions, the proposed approach is able to handle both illumination changes and large occlusions, which would fail methods like [15].

To demonstrate the effectiveness of the proposed method, we first design synthetic experiments with known ground truth to verify its key capability in recovering the underlying common, low-rank and sparse components. Then we report results on three commonly-used data sets of real face images: the Extended YaleB dataset [4], the CMU PIE dataset [17] and the AR dataset [14].The experiments show that, the proposed approach obtained better performance than the SRC algorithm [19], which utilizes a much larger dictionary, and the SUN approach [7]. The proposed approach also achieves comparable result to Volterrafaces, which is the current state-of-the-art in the literature for a few commonly-used data sets. In addition, the proposed approach can explicitly model the most important feature of the subject and the conditions in the dataset. Experiments also show that the proposed method is robust to situations where a non-trivial percentage of the training images is unavailable. Further, the capability of the proposed approach for classifying the type of condition that an input image is subject to is also demonstrated by extensive experiments. This suggests that the proposed decomposition is able to obtain physically meaningful and thus potentially discriminative components.

We introduce the proposed method in Section 2, including the proposed model, the learning algorithm and the classification method. The experiments are reported and analyzed in Section 3. We conclude in Section 4 with a summary of the work and brief discussion on future work.

In the presentation, we use upper case bold font for matrices, e.g., $\mathbf{X}$, lower case bold font for vectors, e.g., $\mathbf{x}$ and normal font for scalars, e.g., x. $\{\mathbf{X}_{i,j}\}_{i=1,j=1}^{N,M}$ denotes a set of $N \times M$ matrices, with $\mathbf{X}_{i,j}$ as its $(i,j)_{th}$ member. We assume that N is the number of the subjects, and M the number of images per subject[1]. Thus $\mathbf{X}_{i,j}$ refers to j_{th} image of the i_{th} subject. When there is no confusion, we also use $\mathbb{X}$ to denote the set $\{\mathbf{X}_{i,j}\}_{i,j=1}^{N,M}$.

[1]For simplicity, we assume that each subject has the same number of images, which can always be achieved by using some blank images, a situation the proposed method can handle.

2. PROPOSED METHOD

In this section, we first present the general formulation of the proposed model in Section 2.1, and then present our algorithm for obtaining the desired decomposition in Section 2.2 and analysis of its convergence in Sec. 2.3. With these, a face recognition algorithm is then designed in Section 2.4.

2.1 Decomposing a Face Image Set

In many applications of image and signal processing, we often consider a set of correlated signals as an ensemble. For efficient representation, a signal in the ensemble can often be viewed as a combination of a common component, which is shared among all the signals in the ensemble, and an innovation component, which is unique to this signal. Many benefits can be drawn from this decomposition of the ensemble, such as obtaining better compression rate and being able to extract more relevant features. In face recognition, all the face images, especially the subset corresponding to a subject, may be naturally viewed as forming such an ensemble of correlated signals. In a sense, a sparse-coding approach like SRC *implicitly* figures out the correlation of the images in the ensemble via the sparse coefficients under the dictionary of the training images.

In this work, we aim at developing a new representation of this ensemble so that the face recognition task can be better supported. In particular, considering the common challenges such as illumination conditions and large occlusions, we want to have a representation that can *explicitly* model such conditions. To this end, we propose the following decomposition of face images $\mathbf{X}_{i,j}$ in the ensemble $\mathbb{X}$ as:

$$\mathbf{X}_{i,j} = \mathbf{C}_i + \mathbf{A}_j + \mathbf{E}_{i,j},\ \forall \mathbf{X}_{i,j} \in \mathbb{X} \tag{1}$$

where $\mathbf{C}_i$ is the common part for Subject i, $\mathbf{A}_j$ is a low-rank matrix, and $\mathbf{E}_{i,j}$ is a sparse residual.

One essential difference between the proposed method and Robust PCA (RPCA [18]), is that RPCA assumes the signals are linearly dependent, with some sparsely corrupted entries in the signals. As a result, they build a big matrix with each signal as a vector. The big matrix would naturally be low-rank (because of the assumed inter-image correlation), in addition to having a sparse set of entries. On the other hand, the proposed decomposition is partially inspired by the observation that the reconstruction of the image with first few singular values and the corresponding singular vectors often capture the global information of the image [12], e.g., illumination conditions, structured patterns, which can be represented by a low-rank matrix. Here the low-rank constraint arises from certain physical conditions (rather than due to inter-image correlation), and it is imposed on each individual image. Accordingly, we represent images by matrices rather than vectors, unlike other methods like [19, 18]. With this, we can expect that:

$\mathbf{C}_i$ is a matrix representing the common information of images for Subject i, i.e., the common components;

$\mathbf{A}_j$ is a low-rank matrix capturing the global information of the image $\mathbf{X}_{i,j}$, e.g., illumination conditions (Fig. 3), structured patterns (Fig. 1); and

$\mathbf{E}_{i,j}$ is a sparse matrix pertaining to image-specific details such as expression conditions or noise with sparse support in the images.

In this modeling, we have assumed M different low-rank matrices, which are responsible for M different global conditions such as illumination conditions or large occlusions, and they are shared among the images of different subjects. However, images of each subject do not necessarily contain all the M conditions, as we will show in Sec. 2.2.

We can also obtain a variant of the above model by considering the Retinex theory, in which image $\mathbf{I}$ can be represented as:

$$\mathbf{I}(p,q) = \mathbf{R}(p,q) \cdot \mathbf{L}(p,q) \quad (2)$$

where $\mathbf{R}(x,y)$ is the reflectance at location (x,y), which depends on the surface property, $\mathbf{L}(x,y)$ is the illumination, and $\cdot$ is element-wise product. Converting this into the logarithm domain, we have

$$log(\mathbf{I}) = log(\mathbf{R}) + log(\mathbf{L}) \quad (3)$$

The above equation indicates that we can represent the intensity of the face image as follows:

$$log(\mathbf{X}_{i,j}) = \mathbf{C}_i + \mathbf{A}_j + \mathbf{E}_{i,j},\ \forall \mathbf{X}_{i,j} \in \mathbb{X} \quad (4)$$

where $\mathbf{C}_i = log(\mathbf{R})$ captures the common property of the images for Subject i, $\mathbf{A}_j = log(\mathbf{L})$ captures the lighting conditions, and $\mathbf{E}_{i,j}$ captures the residual. This is a variant of the model in Eqn. 1, and is especially suitable for illumination-dominated datasets such as the extended YaleB dataset and the CMU-PIE dataset.

With the above decomposition, the entire dataset containing $N \times M$ images can be compactly represented by N common components and K low-rank components. If we extract the common component $\mathbf{C}_i$ for face images of Subject i under different conditions, we expect that this common component $\mathbf{C}_i$ represents the most significant feature of that subject. The set of all the learned low-rank components $\mathbb{A} = \{\mathbf{A}_j\}_{j=1}^{M}$ represents all possible global conditions of the images in the set. Hence we may use $\mathbb{A}$ and $\mathbf{C}_i$ to span the subspace of the face images for Subject i, where, in the ideal case, any face images of this subject should lie in, barring a sparse residual. This suggests that we can utilize the subspaces for face recognition by identifying which subspace a test image is more likely to lie in, which is detailed in Sec. 2.4.

2.2 An Algorithm for the Decomposition

Based on Eqn. 1, we formulate the decomposition task as the following constrained optimization problem, with an objective function derived from the requirement of decomposing a set of images into some common components, some low-rank matrices and the sparse residuals:

$$\begin{aligned}\mathbb{C},\mathbb{A},\mathbb{E} &= \operatorname*{argmin}_{\mathbb{C},\mathbb{A},\mathbb{E}} \sum_{i,j} \|\mathbf{A}_j\|_* + \lambda_{i,j}\|\mathbf{E}_{i,j}\|_1 \\ s.t.\quad & \mathbf{X}_{i,j} = \mathbf{C}_i + \mathbf{A}_j + \mathbf{E}_{i,j},\ \forall \mathbf{X}_{i,j} \in \mathbb{X} \quad (5)\end{aligned}$$

where $\|\mathbf{A}_j\|_* = \sum_i \sigma_i(\mathbf{A}_j)$ is the nuclear norm, $\|\mathbf{E}_{i,j}\|_1 = \sum_{p,q} |\mathbf{E}_{i,j}(p,q)|$ is the ℓ_1 norm and $\mathbb{E} = \{\mathbf{E}_{i,j}\}_{i,j=1}^{N,M}$. Note that, unlike [18] where a set of images are stacked as vectors of a low-rank matrix, we do not convert the image to a vector in the decomposition stage.

To absorb the constraints into the objective function, we can reformulate Eqn. 5 with augmented Lagrange multiplier as:

$$\begin{aligned}\mathbb{C},\mathbb{A},\mathbb{E} &= \operatorname*{argmin}_{\mathbb{C},\mathbb{A},\mathbb{E}} \sum_{i,j} \|\mathbf{A}_j\|_* + \lambda_{i,j}\|\mathbf{E}_{i,j}\|_1 \\ &+ \frac{\mu_{i,j}}{2}\|\mathbf{X}_{i,j} - \mathbf{C}_i - \mathbf{A}_j - \mathbf{E}_{i,j}\|_F^2 \\ &+ < \mathbf{Y}_{i,j}, \mathbf{X}_{i,j} - \mathbf{C}_i - \mathbf{A}_j - \mathbf{E}_{i,j} > \quad (6)\end{aligned}$$

where $\mathbf{Y}_{i,j}$ is the Lagrange multiplier, $\lambda_{i,j}$ and $\mu_{i,j}$ are scalars controlling the weight of sparsity and reconstruction error accordingly. When μ is sufficiently large, Eqn. 6 is equivalent to Eqn. 5. It is worth pointing out that, while for clarity we have written only the expression for Subject i, the optimization is actually done for the entire set of images, since the low-rank components are deemed as been shared by all images.

To solve the problem of Eqn. 6, a block coordinate descent algorithm may be designed, with each iterative step solving a convex optimization problem [3][18] for one of the unknowns. To this end, we first describe the following three sub-solutions that are needed in each iteration of such an algorithm, which correspond to solving only one of the unknowns (blocks) while fixing others.

Sub-solution 1: For finding an optimal $E_{i,j}$ in the t-th iteration, where the problem can be written as

$$\begin{aligned}\mathbf{E}_{i,j} &= \operatorname*{argmin}_{\mathbf{E}_{i,j}} \lambda_{i,j}\|\mathbf{E}_{i,j}\|_1 \quad (7) \\ &+ \frac{\mu_{i,j}}{2}\|\mathbf{X}_{i,j}^E - \mathbf{E}_{i,j}\|_F^2 + < \mathbf{Y}_{i,j}, \mathbf{X}_{i,j}^E - \mathbf{E}_{i,j} >\end{aligned}$$

with $\mathbf{X}_{i,j}^E = \mathbf{X}_{i,j} - \mathbf{C}_i - \mathbf{A}_j$. So we do the following update [6]:

$$\mathbf{E}_{i,j} = S_{\frac{\lambda}{\mu_{i,j}}}(\mathbf{X}_{i,j}^E + \frac{1}{\mu_{i,j}}\mathbf{Y}_{i,j}) \quad (8)$$

where $S_\tau(\mathbf{X}) = sign(\mathbf{X}) \cdot max(0, |\mathbf{X}| - \tau)$.

Sub-solution 2: For finding an optimal $\mathbf{A}_k$ in the t-th iteration, where the problem can be written as

$$\begin{aligned}\mathbf{A}_j &= \operatorname*{argmin}_{\mathbf{A}_j} \sum_i \|\mathbf{A}_j\|_* \quad (9) \\ &+ \frac{\mu_{i,j}}{2}\|\mathbf{X}_{i,j}^A - \mathbf{A}_j\|_F^2 + < \mathbf{Y}_{i,j}, \mathbf{X}_{i,j}^A - \mathbf{A}_j >\end{aligned}$$

We use the singular value thresholding algorithm [2, 5]:

$$\begin{aligned}\mathbf{U}\Sigma\mathbf{V}^T &\leftarrow \frac{\sum_i \mu_{i,j}\mathbf{X}_{i,j}^A + \mathbf{Y}_{i,j}}{\sum_i \mu_{i,j}} \\ \mathbf{A}_j &= \mathbf{U}S_\tau(\Sigma)\mathbf{V}^T\end{aligned}$$

with $\mathbf{X}_{i,j}^A = \mathbf{X}_{i,j} - \mathbf{C}_i - \mathbf{E}_{i,j}$ and $\tau = \frac{N}{\sum_i \mu_{i,j}}$.

Sub-solution 3: The solution to the problem of finding optimal $\mathbf{C}_i$

$$\operatorname*{argmin}_{\mathbf{C}_i} \frac{\mu_{i,j}}{2} \sum_j \|\mathbf{X}_{i,j}^C - \mathbf{C}_i\|_F^2 + < \mathbf{Y}_{i,j}, \mathbf{X}_{i,j}^C - \mathbf{C}_i > \quad (10)$$

where $\mathbf{X}_{i,j}^C = \mathbf{X}_{i,j} - \mathbf{A}_j - \mathbf{E}_{i,j}$, can be obtained directly (by taking derivatives of the objective function and setting to zero) as

$$\mathbf{C}_i = \frac{\sum_j \mathbf{Y}_{i,j} + \mu_{i,j}\mathbf{X}^C_{i,j}}{\sum_j \mu_{i,j}} \quad (11)$$

As alluded earlier, the images of any given subject may not range over all possible M conditions. This may be equivalently viewed as a problem of some images are missing for the subject. We now show how this can be addressed in a principled way. Assume that Ω is the set of (i, j) where $\mathbf{X}_{i,j}$ is available and $\bar{\Omega}$ is the complement of Ω. To deal with those missing entries, we only need to set $\mathbf{Y}_{i,j}$, $\mu_{i,j}$ and $\mathbf{X}_{i,j}$ to 0 for $(i,j) \in \bar{\Omega}$ in the initialization stage. In each iteration, we do not update $\mathbf{E}_{i,j}$ for $(i,j) \in \bar{\Omega}$. The proposed decomposition algorithm will automatically infer the missing images.

With the above preparation, we now propose the following Algorithm 1 to solve Eqn. 6:

Algorithm 1: Learning the Decomposition

Input: $\mathbb{X}$, Ω, N, M, ρ, λ and τ;
Output: $\{\mathbf{C}_i\}_{i=1}^N$, $\{\mathbf{A}_j\}_{j=1}^K$ and $\{\mathbf{E}_{i,j}\}_{i,j=1}^{N,M}$;
% Initialization
$t = 0$, $\mathbf{C}_i^0 = \mathbf{A}_j^0 = \mathbf{E}_{i,j}^0 = 0$;
$\mathbf{Y}_{i,j}^0 = \frac{\mathbf{X}_{i,j}}{\|\mathbf{X}_{i,j}\|_F}$, $\mu_{i,j}^0 = \frac{\tau}{\|\mathbf{X}_{i,j}\|_F}$ for $(i,j) \in \Omega$;
$\mathbf{Y}_{i,j}^0 = 0$, $\mu_{i,j}^0 = 0$ for $(i,j) \notin \Omega$;
while not converged do
  Solve $\mathbf{E}_{i,j}$ for $(i,j) \in \Omega$ by Sub-solution 1:
  Solve $\mathbf{A}_j$ for $j = 1, 2, ..., M$ with Sub-solution 2;
  Solve $\mathbf{C}_i$ for $i = 1, 2, ..., N$ using Sub-solution 3;
  %Update $\mathbf{Y}_{i,j}$ and $\mu_{i,j}$ for $(i,j) \in \Omega$:
  $\mathbf{Y}_{i,j}^{t+1} = \mathbf{Y}_{i,j}^t + \mu_{i,j}^t(\mathbf{X}_{i,j} - \mathbf{C}_i^{t+1} - \mathbf{A}_j^{t+1} - \mathbf{E}_{i,j}^{t+1})$;
  $\mu_{i,j}^{t+1} = \mu_{i,j}^t \rho$;
  $t = t + 1$;
end

---

where for convergence, we check $\frac{\sum_{i,j}\|\mathbf{X}_{i,j} - \mathbf{C}_i - \mathbf{A}_j - \mathbf{E}_{i,j}\|_F^2}{\sum_{i,j}\|\mathbf{X}_{i,j}\|_F^2}$ and if it is small enough (e.g., 10^{-6}), we terminate the algorithm. λ, τ and ρ are three parameters specified in input, which are discussed in Sec. 3.1.

2.3 Convergence of the Algorithm

The convergence property of an iterative optimization procedure like the algorithm proposed above is critical to its usefulness. The Algorithm 1 has similar convergence property as the methods described in [11], which are also augmented Lagrange multiplier based approaches. We can draw the following theorem:

Theorem 1 If $\sum_{t=1}^{\infty} \mu_{i,j}^{t+1}(\mu_{i,j}^t)^{-2} < \infty$ and $\lim_{t\to\infty} \mu_{i,j}^t(\mathbf{E}_{i,j}^{t+1} - \mathbf{E}_{i,j}^t) = 0\ \forall i,j$, then Algorithm 1 will converge to the optimal solution for the problem of Eqn. 5.

The proof of Theorem 1 is included in the appendix.

2.4 Face Recognition Using the Decomposition

With the components in Eqn. 1 estimated from the previous algorithm, we now discuss how to classify a test image. Recognizing that the sparse residual captures only image-specific details that have not been absorbed by the common or the global condition, we discard the sparse residuals from the decomposition (training) stage and keep only the common and the low-rank components.

Ideally a face image from Subject i should lie in a subspace spanned by its common component $\mathbf{C}_i$ and the low-rank components $\mathbb{A}$. Therefore, we propose the following classification scheme based on comparing the distance between subspaces spanned by the training components and those spanned by replacing the training common by the test image $\mathbf{y}$. We first build the subspace $\mathbf{S}_i$ for subject i, which contains all the linear combinations of the images of Subject i under all conditions, i.e.,

$$\mathbf{S}_i = \{\mathbf{x}|\mathbf{x} = \sum_k w_k \times (\mathbf{c}_i + \mathbf{a}_j)\forall \mathbf{w} \in \mathbb{R}^M\} \quad (12)$$

where $\mathbf{c}_i$ and $\mathbf{a}_j$ is the vectorized form of $\mathbf{C}_i$ and $\mathbf{A}_j$ respectively. Subspace $\mathbf{S}_i$ can be sufficiently represented by a set of "basis", i.e., $\{\mathbf{c}_i + \mathbf{a}_j\}_{j=1}^M$. Accordingly, we can build the subspace $\mathbf{S}_y$ for the test image y as the follows:

$$\mathbf{S}_y = \{\mathbf{x}|\mathbf{x} = \sum_k w_k \times (\mathbf{y} + \mathbf{a}_j)\forall \mathbf{w} \in \mathbb{R}^M\} \quad (13)$$

Then we use the principal angles [8] between these subspace to measure their similarities. In this paper, the principal angles measure the cosine distance between the subspaces, which is calculated as $s(\mathbf{S}_i, \mathbf{S}_y) = \sum_k cos^2(\theta_k)$, where θ_k is the k_{th} principal angle between $\mathbf{S}_i$ and $\mathbf{S}_y$. The assign i as the label of $\mathbf{f}$, for which $s(\mathbf{S}_i, \mathbf{S}_y)$ is maximal.

3. EXPERIMENTAL RESULTS

Experiments have been done to evaluate the proposed model and algorithms. In this section, we report several sets of results from such experiments. First, simulations (Sec. 3.1) are employed to demonstrate the convergence and parameter selection of the proposed decomposition algorithm. Then, we show the decomposition of the images from extended YaleB dataset and also how the learned components can be used to reconstruct new images in Sec. 3.2. Finally, we demonstrate the application of the proposed method and algorithms in classification tasks, including face recognition (Sec. 3.3) and identifying the conditions of the images (Sec. 3.4). The performance of the proposed method in face recognition task is compared with that of SRC [19], Volterrafaces [9] and SUN [7] on 2 commonly used datasets, i.e., extended YaleB [10] and CMU-PIE [17].

3.1 Simulation-based Experiments

In this subsection, we use synthetic data to demonstrate the convergence of the algorithm and selection of the parameters. The common components and condition components used in this experiment are shown in Fig. 1 (b,c), where the condition components are from [16] and both components are rescaled to range [0, 1]. The sparse components are sampled from a uniform distribution in the range of [0, 1]. We use those components to generate 25 images, which are used in this experiment, as Eqn. 1.

Algorithm 1 in Sec. 2.2 requires three parameters, ρ controls the convergence speed; λ controls the sparsity of the sparse residuals; and τ is a scalar. In [11], they suggest $\rho = 1.5$, $\tau = 1.25$ and $\lambda = \frac{1}{\sqrt{m}}$ for Robust PCA, where m is the width of $\mathbf{X}_{i,j}$. We have also found that $\lambda = \frac{1}{\sqrt{m}}$ is optimal from the experiments, thus we adopt this selection in our paper. From the experiment, we found that $\tau \in [0.125, 2]$ and $\rho = 1.25$ would be an optimal choice. Fig. 1 shows an example of the recovered common components

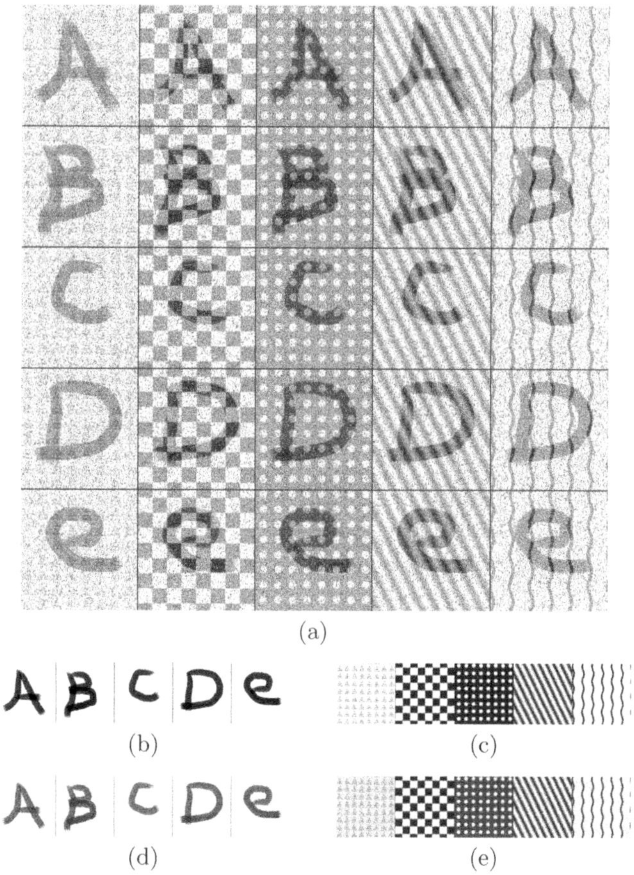

Figure 1: (a) shows the 25 images generated in the experiment, where the sparse part has 20% support of each image. (b,c) shows the ground truth of the common components and condition components accordingly. We also show the common components (d) and condition components (e) decomposed from (b) when $\rho = 1.25$ and $\tau = 2$.

(d) and condition components (e) when the sparse part has 20% support of the image.[2]

To demonstrate the robustness of the algorithm, when only part of data is available, we randomly remove 10 images from the 25 images (Fig. 2(a)) and run the algorithm with the same set of parameters. The results are shown in Fig. 2, where (b) is the recovered common components and (c) is the recovered condition components. These results suggest that the algorithm is still able to produce reasonable results even with 40% of the images missing.

3.2 Decomposing a Set of Images

In this subsection, we first demonstrate the decomposition of the set of images from Extended YaleB dataset[4]. All the 2432 images from 38 subjects under 64 illumination conditions were used. The common components and the condition components are illustrated in in Fig. 3. Comparing these with the original data, it is evident that the recovered commons are largely clean pictures of the subjects, while the condition components align well with the given illumination conditions. This experiment shows the capability of the proposed method with the Retinex model to discover the illumination conditions and the subject commons from a set of real images.

Next, we randomly pick 32 illumination conditions out of the decomposed 64 conditions and the common components of Subject 1 to form a subspace as described in Eqn. 14. Then we use the proposed method to identify whether an new image is in this subspace, by reconstructing this image as the linear combination of the "basis" of this subspace, i.e., $\mathbf{c}_1 + \mathbf{a}_j$. Fig. 4 shows an example, where the new image is also picked from Subject 1; and Fig. 5 shows another example, where the new image is picked from Subject 2. These examples suggest that the learned components can be used for identifying which subject an new image belongs to. Similarly, the learned components can also be used for identifying which conditions the new image is associated with. These two scenarios are further evaluated in the following two subsections, with real face images.

3.3 Recognizing the Face Images

In this subsection, we demonstrate the performance of the proposed method in face recognition task, with the comparison to SRC, Volterraface and SUN on the extended YaleB dataset and CMU PIE dataset. As these two datasets are dominated by illumination conditions, we use the Retinex model for the proposed method, i.e., the image is converted

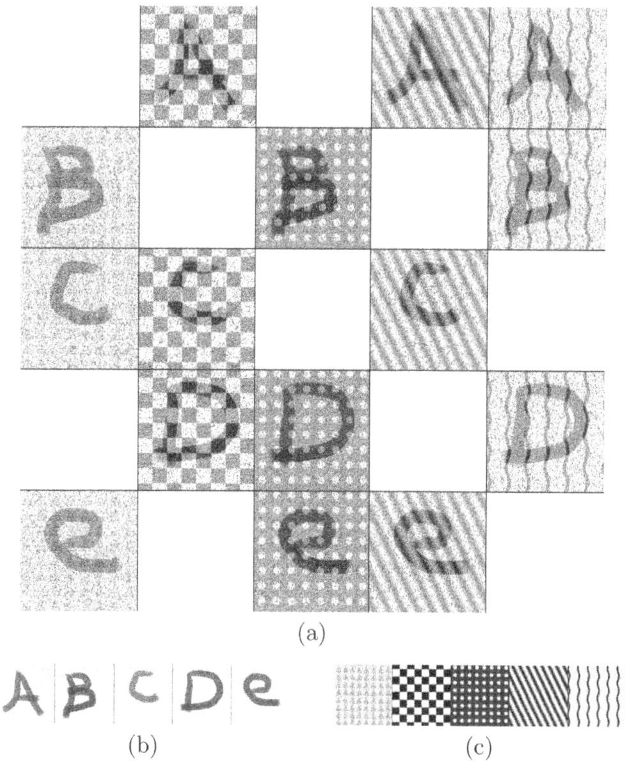

Figure 2: (a) the input data with 10 image manually removed, (b,c) is the common components and condition components decomposed from (a) accordingly.

[2] The recovered parts are subject to a linear shift and scaling. We identify the parameters for this linear shift and scaling then map them back with those parameters.

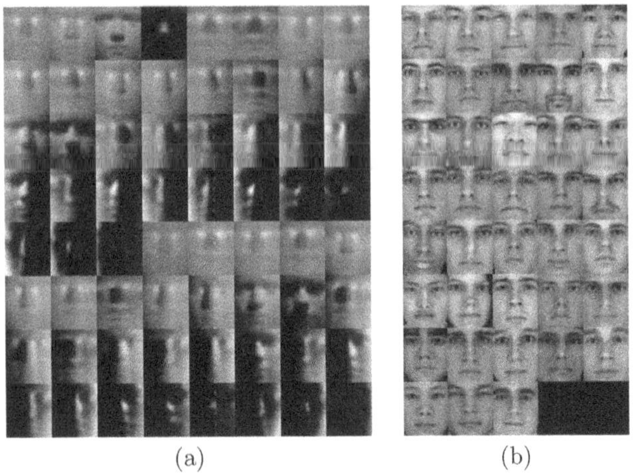

Figure 3: The decomposition of the extended YaleB dataset. We use all the 2432 images which contain 38 subjects (b) and 64 illumination conditions (a).

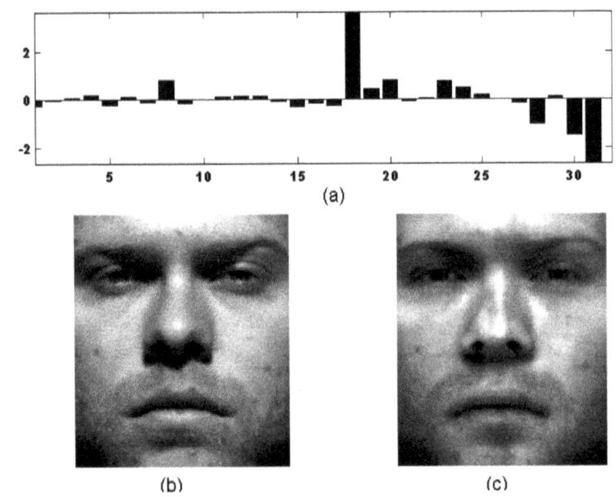

Figure 4: (a) the coefficient for the linear combination, (b) the input image, which is not observed in the images for training the 32 illumination conditions, and (c) the reconstructed image.

to logarithm. In the SRC method, we build the dictionary by containing all the training images as its columns. Since there is no code publicly available for SRC, we build our own implementation. For ℓ_1 optimization used by SRC, we used Orthonormal Matching Pursuit (OMP)[1] as the solver. We set the number of non-zero elements in the sparse coefficient (refer as K later) to be twice the number of conditions in the training data. In addition, each image is normalized to have zero mean and unit l_2 norm for SRC. For Volterrafaces and SUN, we use the author's original implementation and the provided parameters. For all the results, we present the both mean and standard deviation of the accuracies of 3 rounds of experiments.

To examine the robustness of the approaches with respect to the amount of training data, we use the following scheme. In the experiment, we only pick "#train per subject" images for each subject as the training instances, according to the randomly generated sample matrix, where some of the ele-

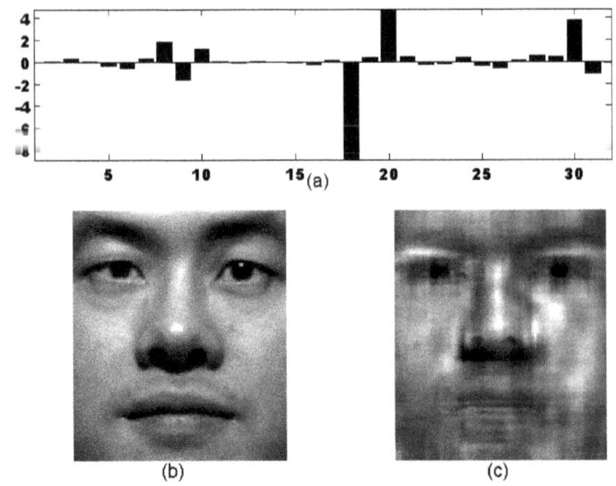

Figure 5: (a) the coefficient for the linear combination, (b) the input image and (c) the reconstructed image.

ments are set to 0 and the corresponding images won't be used for training.

The Extended YaleB dataset [4] contains $N = 38$ subjects with 64 images for each subject, which correspond to 64 illumination conditions in the dataset. The images are resized to 48×42. The results on the extended YaleB dataset are summarized in Tab. 1. From this table, we find that the proposed approach and Volterrafaces achieve the best results; and SUN get obviously the lowest accuracy. The performance of SRC degrade dramatically as the size of dictionary (i.e., number of training instances) reduced.

The CMU PIE dataset [17] contains $N = 68$ subjects with varying poses, illuminations and expressions etc.. For all the images, we manually crop the face region, according to the eye position, then resize them to 50×35. The results are summarized in Tab. 2. In Experiment 1, all 4 methods get similar results; in Experiment 2, the proposed method and Volterrafaces get the best result; and in Experiment 3, the proposed approach gets the best result. In addition, the proposed method is more robust to the missing of training images. The performance of SRC degrades obviously as the size of dictionary reduced.

To illustrate the speed performance of the proposed approach, we compared the time required to classify one image in our approach and the SRC approach. This time was about 0.84 seconds in our method, and about 1.59 seconds in SRC. The time for the decomposition (i.e., Algorithm 1) is less than 5 minutes. The most time consuming part for the proposed approach is the singular value decomposition (SVD), which is used in computing the principle angle, so an efficient implementation of SVD can make the proposed algorithm even faster.

3.4 Identifying the Conditions

Finally, we use an experiment to show how the proposed method can be applied to to identifying the conditions the testing images are associated with. The AR dataset [14] contains $N = 100$ subjects and 26 images for each subjects. The dataset contains 2 sessions, which are taken at different times. Each session contains 13 conditions: 4 for expressions, 3 for illuminations, 3 for sun glasses and 3 for scarves.

(a) Experiment 1

#train per subject	32	24	16	8
Proposed	99.78±0.24%	99.54±0.04%	99.18±0.14%	**95.15±1.03%**
SRC	96.48±0.44%	95.29±0.52%	91.90±0.94%	78.65±1.81%
Volterrafaces	**99.95±0.06%**	**99.80±0.26%**	**99.48±0.49%**	90.22±11.84%
SUN	89.61±1.85%	87.64±2.80%	76.91±3.71%	60.17±2.09%

(b) Experiment 2

#train per subject	16	12	8	4
Proposed	**99.56±0.00%**	**99.33±0.23%**	**98.32±0.03%**	80.03±2.17%
SRC	89.14±0.00%	87.88±0.44%	81.02±0.13%	58.54±1.26%
Volterrafaces	99.25±0.34%	99.17±0.39%	96.27±4.03%	**91.03±2.43%**
SUN	79.22±0.00%	76.75±0.00%	68.86±0.00%	51.60±0.00%

Table 1: The results on extended YaleB dataset. Experiment 1: we randomly pick $M = 32$ illumination conditions for training and the remaining for testing, i.e., we will obtain $N = 38$ common components and $M = 32$ conditions by the proposed method. Experiment 2: we manually pick $M = 16$ illumination conditions for training and the remaining for testing.

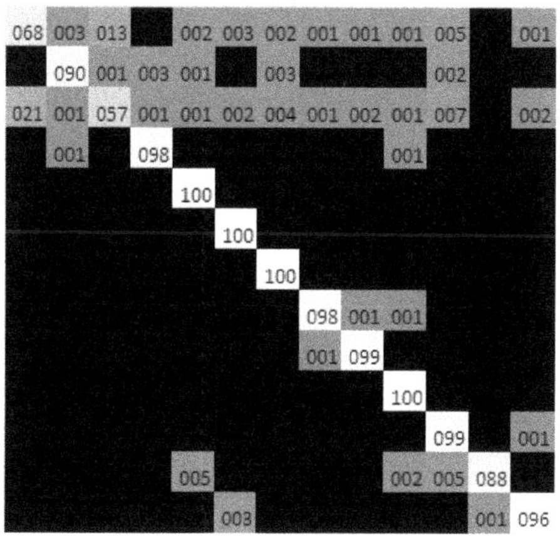

Figure 6: The confusion matrix (in percentage) of condition recognition result from the proposed method, where both axes are the condition index. The axis is index of the conditions.

In our experiments, we use one session for training and the other session for testing. The images are converted to gray scale and resized to 55×40. To recognized the associated condition, we slightly changes the formulation of the subspace:

$$\mathbf{S}_i = \{\mathbf{x} | \mathbf{x} = \sum_j w_j \times (\mathbf{a}_i + \mathbf{c}_j) \forall \mathbf{w} \in \mathbb{R}^N\} \quad (14)$$

$$\mathbf{S}_y = \{\mathbf{x} | \mathbf{x} = \sum_j w_j \times (\mathbf{y} + \mathbf{c}_j) \forall \mathbf{w} \in \mathbb{R}^N\} \quad (15)$$

where $\mathbf{S}_i$ is the subspace for condition i and $\mathbf{S}_y$ the subspace for the test image. The other settings were the same as those of previous face recognition experiments.

The proposed method achieves an accuracy of 91.77% in recognizing the conditions, with the confusion matrix given in Fig. 6, where we achieved over 96% accuracy for all but conditions 1, 2, 3 (3 expressions) and 12. This experiment again demonstrates the effectiveness of the proposed method in capturing the physical conditions in the form of low-rank components.

4. CONCLUSIONS AND FUTURE WORK

In this paper, we proposed a novel decomposition of a set of face images of multiple subjects, each with multiple images. The decomposition finds a common image and a low-rank image for each of the subjects in the set. All the low-rank images form a set that is used to capture all possible global conditions existing in the set of images. This facilitates explicit modeling of typical challenges in face recognition, such as illumination conditions and large occlusion. Based on the decomposition, a face classifier was designed, using the decomposed components for subspace reconstruction and comparison. The classification performance shows that the proposed approach can achieve state-of-the-art performance. Experiments also showed that the proposed method is robust with missing training images, which can be an important factor to consider in a practical system. We also demonstrated with experiments that the decomposition indeed captures physically meaningful conditions, with both synthetic data and real data.

There are a few possible directions for further development of the work. In particular, the current algorithm assumes that the low-rank conditions of the training images are known and given for each of them. In practice, if the data do not have such image-level label (but still with a finite set of low-rank conditions), it is possible to expand the current algorithm by incorporating another step that attempts to estimate a mapping matrix for assigning a condition label to each image, during the optimization iteration. For example, we may define a mapping matrix Φ with $\Phi_{i,j} = k$ defining that training image $\mathbf{X}_{i,j}$ is associated with condition $\mathbf{A}_k$. Eqn. 1 suggests a constraint that we may use to solve for Φ: the optimal mapping matrix should result in the most sparsity for $\mathbf{E}_{i,j}$ or the lowest rank for $\mathbf{A}_k$, given the same reconstruction error. If we use the first criterion, the problem of finding Φ can be formulated as $\Phi = \underset{\Phi}{\operatorname{argmin}} \sum_{i,j} \|\mathbf{X}_{i,j} - \mathbf{C}_i - \mathbf{A}_{\Phi_{i,j}}\|_1$.

5. ACKNOWLEDGMENT

The work was supported in part by a grant (Grant No. 0845469) from the National Science Foundation. Any opinions, findings, and conclusions or recommendations expressed

(a) Experiment 1

#train per subject	20	15	10	5
Proposed	**100±0.00%**	**100±0.00%**	99.65±0.37%	97.49±0.21%
SRC	99.88±0.07%	99.88±0.07%	99.73±0.14%	**97.73±0.54%**
Volterrafaces	**100±0.00%**	**100±0.00%**	**100±0.00%**	95.83±4.16%
SUN	**100%**	99.84±0.11%	99.45±0.43%	95.75±0.49%

(b) Experiment 2

#train per subject	12	9	6	3
Proposed	**100±0.00%**	99.960.08%	99.17±0.15%	**94.70±0.20%**
SRC	99.91±0.16%	98.89±1.74%	96.90±3.73%	87.18±1.78%
Volterrafaces	**100±0.00%**	**100±0.00%**	**99.54±0.31%**	94.30±4.72%
SUN	**100±0.00%**	99.84±0.05%	98.53±0.29%	88.75±4.72%

(c) Experiment 3

#train per subject	40	30	20	10
Proposed	**99.98±0.03%**	**99.92±0.06%**	**99.24±0.06%**	**90.95±0.70%**
SRC	**99.98±0.03%**	99.45±0.03%	96.79±0.28%	86.98±0.16%
Volterrafaces	99.60±0.22%	98.37±0.47%	97.63±0.28%	89.72±1.45%
SUN	99.93±0.05%	99.38±0.14%	97.89±0.30%	88.29±0.02%

Table 2: The result on CMU-PIE dataset. Experiment 1: we pick the images with frontal pose (C27), which include 43 illumination conditions for each subject. We randomly pick $M = 20$ conditions for training and the remaining for testing. Experiment 2: we again only pick the image with frontal pose, but we randomly pick $M = 12$ conditions for training and the remaining for testing. Experiment 3: we use all the images from 5 near frontal poses (C05, C07, C09, C27, C29), which includes 153 conditions for each subject. We randomly pick $M = 40$ conditions for training and the remaining for testing..

in this material are those of the authors and do not necessarily reflect the views of the National Science Foundation.

6. REFERENCES

[1] M. Aharon, M. Elad, and A. Bruckstein. K-SVD: Design of dictionaries for sparse representation. *Proceedings of SPARS*, 5, 2005.

[2] J. F. Cai, E. J. Candes, and Z. Shen. A singular value thresholding algorithm for matrix completion. *preprint*, 2008.

[3] E. Candes and Y. Plan. Matrix completion with noise. *Proceedings of the IEEE*, 2009.

[4] A. Georghiades, P. Belhumeur, and D. Kriegman. From few to many: Illumination cone models for face recognition under variable lighting and pose. *IEEE Transactions on Pattern Analysis and Machine Intelligence*, 23(6):643–660, 2001.

[5] D. Goldfarb and S. Ma. Convergence of fixed-point continuation algorithms for matrix rank minimization. *Foundations of Computational Mathematics*, pages 1–28, 2011.

[6] E. T. Hale, W. Yin, and Y. Zhang. Fixed-point continuation for ℓ_1-minimization: Methodology and convergence. *SIAM Journal on Optimization*, 19(3):1107–1130, 2008.

[7] C. Kanan and G. Cottrell. Robust classification of objects, faces, and flowers using natural image statistics. In *Computer Vision and Pattern Recognition (CVPR), 2010 IEEE Conference on*, pages 2472 –2479, june 2010.

[8] A. Knyazev and M. Argentati. Principal angles between subspaces in an A-based scalar product: algorithms and perturbation estimates. *SIAM Journal on Scientific Computing*, 23(6):2008–2040, 2002.

[9] R. Kumar, A. Banerjee, and B. Vemuri. Volterrafaces: Discriminant analysis using volterra kernels. In *Computer Vision and Pattern Recognition, 2009. CVPR 2009. IEEE Conference on*, pages 150 –155, june 2009.

[10] K. Lee, J. Ho, and D. Kriegman. Acquiring linear subspaces for face recognition under variable lighting. *IEEE Transactions on Pattern Analysis and Machine Intelligence*, pages 684–698, 2005.

[11] Z. Lin, M. Chen, L. Wu, and Y. Ma. The augmented lagrange multiplier method for exact recovery of corrupted low-rank matrices. *Arxiv preprint arXiv:1009.5055*, 2010.

[12] J. Liu, S. Chen, and X. Tan. Fractional order singular value decomposition representation for face recognition. *Pattern Recogn.*, 41:378–395, January 2008.

[13] J. Mairal, F. Bach, J. Ponce, G. Sapiro, and A. Zisserman. Discriminative learned dictionaries for local image analysis. In *Computer Vision and Pattern Recognition, 2008. CVPR 2008. IEEE Conference on*, pages 1–8. IEEE, 2008.

[14] A. Martinez and R. Benavente. The AR face database. Technical report, CVC Technical report, 1998.

[15] P. Nagesh and B. Li. A compressive sensing approach for expression-invariant face recognition. In *Computer Vision and Pattern Recognition, 2009. CVPR 2009. IEEE Conference on*, pages 1518 –1525, 2009.

[16] J. Portilla and E. Simoncelli. A parametric texture model based on joint statistics of complex wavelet coefficients. *International Journal of Computer Vision*, 40(1):49–70, 2000.

[17] T. Sim, S. Baker, and M. Bsat. The CMU pose, illumination, and expression (PIE) database. In

Proceedings of the 5th International Conference on Automatic Face and Gesture Recognition, 2002.

[18] J. Wright, A. Ganesh, S. Rao, Y. Peng, and Y. Ma. Robust Principal Component Analysis: Exact Recovery of Corrupted Low-Rank Matrices via Convex Optimization. In *Advances in Neural Information Processing Systems 22.*

[19] J. Wright, A. Yang, A. Ganesh, S. Sastry, and Y. Ma. Robust face recognition via sparse representation. *Pattern Analysis and Machine Intelligence, IEEE Transactions on*, 31(2):210–227, 2008.

APPENDIX

A. PROOF OF THEOREM 1

Proposition 1 The sequences of $\tilde{Y}^{t+1}_{i,j}$, $\sum_i \hat{Y}^{t+1}_{i,j}$, $\sum_j \mathbf{Y}^{t+1}_{i,j}$ and $\dot{Y}^{t+1}_{i,j}$ are all bounded $\forall i,j$, where

$$\begin{aligned}
\mathbf{Y}^{t+1}_{i,j} &= \mu^t_{i,j}(\mathbf{X}_{i,j} - \mathbf{C}^{t+1}_i - \mathbf{A}^{t+1}_j - \mathbf{E}^{t+1}_{i,j}) + \mathbf{Y}^t_{i,j}\\
\hat{Y}^{t+1}_{i,j} &= \mu^t_{i,j}(\mathbf{X}_{i,j} - \mathbf{C}^t_i - \mathbf{A}^{t+1}_j - \mathbf{E}^{t+1}_{i,j} + \mathbf{Y}^t_{i,j}\\
\tilde{Y}^{t+1}_{i,j} &= \mu^t_{i,j}(\mathbf{X}_{i,j} - \mathbf{C}^t_i - \mathbf{A}^t_j - \mathbf{E}^{t+1}_{i,j}) + \mathbf{Y}^t_{i,j}\\
\dot{Y}^{t+1}_{i,j} &= \mu^t_{i,j}(\mathbf{X}_{i,j} - \dot{C}^{t+1}_i - \dot{A}^{t+1}_j - \dot{E}^{t+1}_{i,j}) + \dot{Y}^t_{i,j}
\end{aligned}$$

and $(\dot{C}^{t+1}, \dot{A}^{t+1}, \dot{E}^{t+1})$ is the optimal solution to the problem $\min_{\mathbb{C},\mathbb{A},\mathbb{E}} L(\mathbb{C},\mathbb{A},\mathbb{E},\dot{Y}^t,\mu^t)$ with $\dot{Y}^t = \{\dot{Y}^t_{i,j}\}^{N,M}_{i,j=1}$.

Proof Let's write the Lagrange function in 6 as:

$$\begin{aligned}
& L(\{\mathbf{C}^t_i\}_i, \{\mathbf{A}^t_j\}_j, \{\mathbf{E}^t_{i,j}\}_{i,j}, \{\mathbf{Y}^t_{i,j}\}_{i,j}, \{\mu^t\}_{i,j})\\
=& \sum_{i,j} \|\mathbf{A}^t_j\|_* + \lambda_{i,j}\|\mathbf{E}^t_{i,j}\|_1\\
+& \frac{\mu^t_{i,j}}{2}\|\mathbf{X}_{i,j} - \mathbf{C}^t_i - \mathbf{A}^t_j - \mathbf{E}^t_{i,j}\|^2_F\\
+& < \mathbf{Y}^t_{i,j}, \mathbf{X}_{i,j} - \mathbf{C}^t_i - \mathbf{A}^t_j - \mathbf{E}^t_{i,j} >
\end{aligned}$$

For simplicity, we will use $L(\mathbb{C}^t, \mathbb{A}^t, \mathbb{E}^{t+1}, \mathbb{Y}^t, \mu^t)$ instead of $L(\{\mathbf{C}^t_i\}_i, \{\mathbf{A}^t_j\}_j, \{\mathbf{E}^{t+1}_{i,j}\}_{i,j}, \{\mathbf{Y}^t_{i,j}\}_{i,j}, \{\mu^t\}_{i,j})$. The subgradient of $L(\mathbb{C}^t, \mathbb{A}^t, \mathbb{E}, \mathbb{Y}^t, \mu_t)$ over $\mathbf{E}_{i,j}$ is

$$\lambda_{i,j}\partial\|\mathbf{E}_{i,j}\|_1 - \mu^t_{i,j}(\mathbf{X}_{i,j} - \mathbf{C}^t_i - \mathbf{A}^t_j - \mathbf{E}_{i,j}) - \mathbf{Y}^t_{i,j}$$

As $\mathbf{E}^{t+1}_{i,j}$ is optimal for the problem $\operatorname{argmin}_{\mathbf{E}_{i,j}} L(\mathbb{C}^t, \mathbb{A}^t, \mathbb{E}, \mathbb{Y}^t, \mu_t)$

$$0 \in \lambda_{i,j}\partial\|\mathbf{E}^t_{i,j}\|_1 - \tilde{Y}^{t+1}_{i,j}$$

i.e., $\tilde{Y}^{t+1}_{i,j} \in \lambda_{i,j}\|\mathbf{E}^{t+1}_{i,j}\|_1$; and according to the Theorem 3 of [11], $\tilde{Y}^{t+1}_{i,j}$ is bounded $\forall i,j$. Similarly, we can also show that $\sum_i \hat{Y}^{t+1}_{i,j}$, $\sum_j \mathbf{Y}^{t+1}_{i,j}$ and $\dot{Y}^{t+1}_{i,j}$ are bounded $\forall i,j$.

Proposition 2 The sequences of $(\mathbb{C}^{t+1}, \mathbb{A}^{t+1}, \mathbb{E}^{t+1})$ is bounded.

Proof For Algorithm 1, we can find that:

$$\begin{aligned}
L(\mathbb{C}^{t+1}, \mathbb{A}^{t+1}, \mathbb{E}^{t+1}, \mathbb{Y}^t, \mu^t) &\le L(\mathbb{C}^t, \mathbb{A}^{t+1}, \mathbb{E}^{t+1}, \mathbb{Y}^t, \mu^t)\\
\le L(\mathbb{C}^t, \mathbb{A}^t, \mathbb{E}^{t+1}, \mathbb{Y}^t, \mu^t) &\le L(\mathbb{C}^t, \mathbb{A}^t, \mathbb{E}^t, \mathbb{Y}^t, \mu^t)\\
= L(\mathbb{C}^t, \mathbb{A}^t, \mathbb{E}^t, \mathbb{Y}^{t-1}, \mu^{t-1}) &+ \sum_{i,j} \frac{\mu^{t-1}_{i,j} + \mu^t_{i,j}}{(\mu^t_{i,j})^2}\|\mathbf{Y}^t_{i,j} - \mathbf{Y}^{t-1}_{i,j}\|^2_F
\end{aligned}$$

By boundedness of assumption that $\sum^{\infty}_{t=1} \mu^{t+1}_{i,j}(\mu^t_{i,j})^{-2} < \infty$ and $\sum_j \mathbf{Y}^t_{i,j}$ $\forall i,j$, we have $L(\mathbb{C}^{t+1}, \mathbb{A}^{t+1}, \mathbb{E}^{t+1}, \mathbb{Y}^t, \mu^t)$ is upper bounded. Thus $\sum_{i,j}\|\mathbf{A}^t_j\|_* + \lambda_{i,j}\|\mathbf{E}^t_{i,j}\|_1$ is bounded.

Proposition 3 The accumulation point $(\dot{C}^*, \dot{A}^*, \dot{E}^*)$ for sequences $(\dot{C}^{t+1}, \dot{A}^{t+1}, \dot{E}^{t+1})$ is optimal for the problem in Eqn. 5.

Proof For $(\dot{C}^{t+1}, \dot{A}^{t+1}, \dot{E}^{t+1})$, we have the following:

$$\begin{aligned}
& L(\dot{C}^{t+1}, \dot{A}^{t+1}, \dot{E}^{t+1}, \dot{Y}^t, \mu^t) = \min_{\mathbb{C},\mathbb{A},\mathbb{E}} L(\mathbb{C}, \mathbb{A}, \mathbb{E}, \dot{Y}^t, \mu^t)\\
\le& \min_{\mathbf{C}_i+\mathbf{A}_j+\mathbf{E}_{i,j}=\mathbf{X}_{i,j},\forall(i,j)} L(\mathbb{C}, \mathbb{A}, \mathbb{E}, \dot{Y}^t, \mu^t)\\
\le& \min_{\mathbf{C}_i+\mathbf{A}_j+\mathbf{E}_{i,j}=\mathbf{X}_{i,j},\forall(i,j)} \sum_{i,j}\|\mathbf{A}_j\|_* + \lambda_{i,j}\|\mathbf{E}_{i,j}\|_1\\
=& f^*
\end{aligned}$$

We also have:

$$\begin{aligned}
& \sum_{i,j}\|\dot{A}^{t+1}_j\|_* + \lambda_{i,j}\|\dot{E}^{t+1}_{i,j}\|_1\\
=& L(\dot{C}^{t+1}, \dot{A}^{t+1}, \dot{E}^{t+1}, \dot{Y}^t, \mu^t) - \sum_{i,j}\frac{\|\dot{Y}^t_{i,j} - \dot{Y}^{t-1}_{i,j}\|^2_F}{2\mu^t_{i,j}}\\
\le& f^* - \sum_{i,j}\frac{\|\dot{Y}^t_{i,j} - \dot{Y}^{t-1}_{i,j}\|^2_F}{2\mu^t_{i,j}} = f^* + O(\sum_{i,j}(\mu^t_{i,j})^{-1})
\end{aligned}$$

where we use the knowledge that $\dot{Y}^{t+1}_{i,j}$ is bounded $\forall i,j$. Take $t \to \infty$, we have $\sum_{i,j}\|\dot{A}^*_j\|_* + \lambda_{i,j}\|\dot{E}^*_{i,j}\|_1 = f^*$. Using $(\dot{Y}^t_{i,j} - \dot{Y}^{t-1}_{i,j}) = \mu^{t-1}_{i,j}(\dot{X}_{i,j} - \dot{C}^{t-1}_i - \dot{A}^{t-1}_j - \dot{E}^{t-1}_{i,j})$ and boundedness of $\dot{Y}^{t+1}_{i,j}$ $\forall i,j$, we also have $\mathbf{X}_{i,j} - \dot{C}^*_i - \dot{A}^*_j - \dot{E}^*_{i,j} = 0$ $\forall i,j$. Thus $(\dot{C}^*, \dot{A}^*, \dot{E}^*)$ is the optimal solution for Eqn. 5.

By $\mathbf{X}_{i,j} - \mathbf{C}^{t+1}_i - \mathbf{A}^{t+1}_j - \mathbf{E}^{t+1}_{i,j} = \mu^t_{i,j}(\mathbf{Y}^{t+1}_{i,j} - \mathbf{Y}^t_{i,j})$ and boundedness of $\mathbf{Y}^t_{i,j}$, we have $\lim_{t\to\infty} \mathbf{C}^{t+1}_i + \mathbf{A}^{t+1}_j + \mathbf{E}^{t+1}_{i,j} = \mathbf{X}_{i,j}$ $\forall i,j$, i.e., $(\mathbb{C}^{t+1}, \mathbb{A}^{t+1}, \mathbb{E}^{t+1})$ approaches to a feasible solution. In addition, we have

$$\|\sum_i \mathbf{A}^{t+1}_j - \mathbf{A}^t_j\|_F = \|\sum_i (\mu^t_{i,j})^{-1}(\hat{Y}^{t+1}_{i,j} - \tilde{Y}^{t+1}_{i,j})\|_F$$

With the assumption $\sum^{\infty}_{t=1}(\mu^t_{i,j})^{-1} < \infty$, boundedness of $\sum_i \hat{Y}^{t+1}_{i,j}$ and $\tilde{Y}^t_{i,j}$, $\mathbf{A}^{t+1}_j$ has a limit $\mathbf{A}^*_j$. Similarly:

$$\|\sum_j \mathbf{A}^{t+1}_j - \mathbf{A}^t_j + \mathbf{C}^{t+1}_i - \mathbf{C}^t_i\|_F = \|\sum_j (\mu^t_{i,j})^{-1}(\mathbf{Y}^{t+1}_{i,j} - \tilde{Y}^{t+1}_{i,j})\|_F$$

Thus $\lim_{t\to\infty}\sum_j \mathbf{A}^{t+1}_j - \mathbf{A}^t_j + \mathbf{C}^{t+1}_i - \mathbf{C}^t_i = 0$. Since $\mathbf{A}^{t+1}_j$ has limit $\mathbf{A}^*_j$, then $\mathbf{C}^{t+1}_i$ has limit $\mathbf{C}^*_i$, then $\mathbf{E}^{t+1}_{i,j}$ has limit $\mathbf{X}_{i,j} - \mathbf{A}^*_j - \mathbf{C}^*_i$. So $(\mathbb{C}^*, \mathbb{A}^*, \mathbb{E}^*)$ is a feasible solution.

Considering the subgradients and the optimality of $\mathbf{E}^{t+1}_{i,j}$ and $\mathbf{A}^{t+1}_j$, we have $\tilde{Y}^{t+1}_{i,j} \in \partial\|\mathbf{E}^{t+1}_{i,j}\|_1$ and $\sum_i \hat{Y}^{t+1}_{i,j} \in \partial\|\mathbf{A}^{t+1}_j\|_*$. According to the property of subgradients:

$$\begin{aligned}
& (\sum_{i,j}\|\mathbf{A}^{t+1}_j\|_* + \lambda_{i,j}\|\mathbf{E}^{t+1}_{i,j}\|_1) - (\sum_{i,j}\|\dot{A}^{t+1}_j\|_* + \lambda_{i,j}\|\dot{E}^{t+1}_{i,j}\|_1)\\
\le& \sum_{i,j} - < \hat{Y}^{t+1}_{i,j}, \dot{A}^{t+1}_j - \mathbf{A}^{t+1}_j > - < \tilde{Y}^{t+1}_{i,j}, \dot{E}^{t+1}_{i,j} - \mathbf{E}^{t+1}_{i,j} >\\
=& \sum_{i,j} -\mu^t_{i,j} < \mathbf{E}^{t+1}_{i,j} - \mathbf{E}^t_{i,j}, \dot{A}^{t+1}_j - \mathbf{A}^{t+1}_j >\\
-& \frac{< \tilde{Y}^{t+1}_{i,j}, \dot{Y}^{t+1}_{i,j} - \dot{Y}^t_{i,j} >}{\mu^t_{i,j}} - \frac{< \tilde{Y}^{t+1}_{i,j}, \dot{Y}^{t+1}_{i,j} - \dot{Y}^t_{i,j} >}{\mu^t_{i,j}}
\end{aligned}$$

By Proposition 1 and 2 that $\mathbf{Y}^{t+1}_{i,j}$, $\dot{Y}^{t+1}_{i,j}$ are bounded; by Proposition 3 that $\sum_{i,j}\|\dot{A}^*_j\|_* + \lambda_{i,j}\|\dot{E}^*_{i,j}\|_1 = f^*$; and by assumption $\lim_{t\to\infty}\mu^t_{i,j}(\mathbf{E}^{t+1}_{i,j} - \mathbf{E}^t_{i,j}) = 0$, we have $\sum_{i,j}\|\mathbf{A}^*_j\|_* + \lambda_{i,j}\|\mathbf{E}^*_{i,j}\|_1 = f^*$. That is $(\mathbb{C}^*, \mathbb{A}^*, \mathbb{E}^*)$ is optimal for the problem in Eqn. 5. This completes the proof of Theorem 1.

Fast Algorithms for Comprehensive N-point Correlation Estimates

William B. March
Georgia Institute of Technology
266 Ferst Dr.
Atlanta, GA, USA
march@gatech.edu

Andrew J. Connolly
University of Washington
3910 15th Ave. NE Seattle, WA, USA
ajc@astro.washington.edu

Alexander G. Gray
Georgia Institute of Technology
266 Ferst Dr.
Atlanta, GA, USA
agray@cc.gatech.edu

ABSTRACT

The n-point correlation functions (npcf) are powerful spatial statistics capable of fully characterizing any set of multidimensional points. These functions are critical in key data analyses in astronomy and materials science, among other fields, for example to test whether two point sets come from the same distribution and to validate physical models and theories. For example, the npcf has been used to study the phenomenon of dark energy, considered one of the major breakthroughs in recent scientific discoveries. Unfortunately, directly estimating the continuous npcf at a single value requires $O(N^n)$ time for N points, and n may be 2, 3, 4 or even higher, depending on the sensitivity required. In order to draw useful conclusions about real scientific problems, we must repeat this expensive computation both for many different scales in order to derive a smooth estimate and over many different subsamples of our data in order to bound the variance.

We present the first comprehensive approach to the entire n-point correlation function estimation problem, including fast algorithms for the computation at multiple scales and for many subsamples. We extend the current state-of-the-art tree-based approach with these two algorithms. We show an order-of-magnitude speedup over the current best approach with each of our new algorithms and show that they can be used together to obtain over 500x speedups over the state-of-the-art in order to enable much larger datasets and more accurate scientific analyses than were possible previously.

Categories and Subject Descriptors

J.2 [**Physical Sciences and Engineering**]: Astronomy; G.4 [**Mathematical Software**]: Algorithm design and analysis

Keywords

N-point Correlation Functions, Jackknife Resampling

1. INTRODUCTION

In this paper, we discuss a hierarchy of powerful statistics: the *n-point correlation functions*, which constitute a widely-used approach for detailed characterizations of multivariate point sets. These functions, which are analogous to the moments of a univariate distribution, can completely describe any point process and are widely applicable.

Applications in astronomy. The n-point statistics have long constituted the state-of-the-art approach in many scientific areas, in particular for detailed characterization of the patterns in spatial data. They are a fundamental tool in astronomy for characterizing the large scale structure of the universe [20], fluctuations in the cosmic microwave background [28], the formation of clusters of galaxies [32], and the characterization of the galaxy-mass bias [17]. They can be used to compare observations to theoretical models through perturbation theory [1, 6]. A high-profile example of this was a study showing large-scale evidence for dark energy [8] – this study was written up as the Top Scientific Breakthrough of 2003 in *Science* [26]. In this study, due to the massive potential implications to fundamental physics of the outcome, the accuracy of the n-point statistics used and the hypothesis test based on them were a considerable focus of the scientific scrutiny of the results – underscoring both the centrality of n-point correlations as a tool to some of the most significant modern scientific problems, as well as the importance of their accurate estimation.

Materials science and medical imaging. The materials science community also makes extensive use of the n-point correlation functions. They are used to form three-dimensional models of microstructure [13] and to characterize that microstructure and relate it to macroscopic properties such as the diffusion coefficient, fluid permeability, and elastic modulus[31, 30]. The n-point correlations have also been used to create feature sets for medical image segmentation and classification [22, 19, 2].

Generality of npcf. In addition to these existing applications, the n-point correlations are completely general. Thus, they are a powerful tool for any multivariate or spatial data analysis problem. Ripley [23] showed that any point process consisting of multidimensional data can be completely determined by the distribution of counts in cells. The distribution of counts in cells can in turn be shown to be completely determined by the set of n-point correlation functions [20]. While ordinary statistical moments are defined in terms of the expectation of increasing powers of X, the n-point functions are determined by the cross-correlations of counts in increasing numbers of nearby regions. Thus, we have a sequence of increasingly complex statistics, analogous to the moments of ordinary distributions, with which to characterize any point process and which can be estimated from finite data. With this simple, rigorous characterization of our data and models, we can answer the key questions posed above in one statistical framework.

Computational challenge. Unfortunately, directly estimating the n-point correlation functions is extremely computationally expensive. As we will show below, estimating the npcf potentially requires enumerating all n-tuples of data points. Since this scales as $O(N^n)$ for N data points, this is prohibitively expensive for even modest-sized data sets and low-orders of correlation. Higher-order correlations are often necessary to fully understand and characterize data [32]. Furthermore, the npcf is a continuous quantity. In order to understand its behavior at all the scales of interest for a given problem, we must repeat this difficult computation many times. We also need to estimate the variance of our estimated npcf. This in general requires a resampling method in order to make the most use of our data. We must therefore repeat the $O(N^n)$ computation not only for many scales, but for many different subsamples of the data.

In the past, these computational difficulties have restricted the use of the n-point correlations, despite their power and generality. The largest 3-point correlation estimation thus far for the distribution of galaxies used only approximately 10^5 galaxies [16]. Higher-order correlations have been even more restricted by computational considerations.

Large data. Additionally, data sets are growing rapidly, and spatial data are no exception. The National Biodiversity Institute of Costa Rica has collected over 3 million observations of tropical species along with geographical data [11]. In astronomy, the Sloan Digital Sky Survey [25] spent eight years imagining the northern sky and collected tens of terabytes of data. The Large Synoptic Survey Telescope [14], scheduled to come online later this decade, will collect as much as 20 terabytes *per night* for ten years. These massive datasets will render n-point correlation estimation even more difficult without efficient algorithms.

Our contributions. These computational considerations have restricted the widespread use of the npcf in the past. We introduce two new algorithms, building on the previous state-of-the-art algorithm [9, 18], to address this entire computational challenge. We present the first algorithms to efficiently overcome two important computational bottlenecks.

- We **estimate the npcf at many scales simultaneously**, thus allowing smoother and more accurate estimates.
- We **efficiently handle jackknife resampling** by sharing work across different parts of the computation, allowing more effective variance estimation and more accurate results.

For each of these problems, we present new algorithms capable of sharing work between different parts of the computation. We prove a theorem which allows us to eliminate a critical redundancy in the computation over multiple scales. We also cast the computation over multiple subsamples in a novel way, allowing a much more efficient algorithm. Each of these new ideas allows an order-of-magnitude speedup over the existing state of the art. These algorithms are therefore able to render n-point correlation function estimation tractable for many large datasets for the first time by allowing N to increase and allow more sensitive and accurate scientific results for the first time by allowing multiple scales and resampling regions. Our work is the first to deal directly with the full computational task.

Overview. In Section 2, we define the n-point correlation functions and describe their estimators in detail. This leads to the $O(J \cdot M \cdot N^n)$ computational challenge mentioned above. We then introduce our two new algorithms for the entire npcf estimation problem in Section 3. We show experimental results in Section 4. Finally, we conclude in Section 5 by highlighting future work and extensions of our method.

1.1 Related Work

Due to the computational difficulty associated with estimating the full npcf, many alternatives to the full npcf have been developed, including those based on nearest-neighbor distances, quadrats, Dirichlet cells, and Ripley's K function (and related functions) (See [24] and [3] for an overview and further references). Counts-in-cells [29] and Fourier space methods are commonly used for astronomical data. However, these methods are generally less powerful than the full npcf. For instance, the counts-in-cells method cannot be corrected for errors due to the edges of the sample window. Fourier transform-based methods suffer from ringing effects and suboptimal variance. See [27] for more details.

Since we deal exclusively with estimating the exact npcf, we only compare against other methods for this task. The existing state-of-the-art methods for exact npcf estimation use multiple space-partitioning trees to overcome the $O(N^n)$ scaling of the n-point point estimator. This approach was first introduced in [9, 18]. It has been parallelized using the Ntropy framework [7]. We present the serial version here and leave the description of our ongoing work on parallelizing our approach to future work.

2. N-POINT CORRELATION FUNCTIONS

We now define the n-point correlation functions. We provide a high-level description; for a more thorough defintion, see [20, 27]. Once we have given a simple description of the npcf, we turn to the main problem of this paper: the computational task of estimating the npcf from real data. We give several common estimators for the npcf, and highlight the underlying counting problem in each. We also discuss the full computational task involved in a useful estimate of the npcf for real scientific problems.

Problem setting. Our data are drawn from a *point process*. The data consist of a set of points D in a subset of $\mathbb{R}^d$. Note that we are not assuming that the locations of individual points are independent, just that our data set is a fair sample from the underlying ensemble. We assume that distant parts of our sample window are uncorrelated, so that by averaging over them, we can approximate averages over multiple samples from the point process.

Following standard practice in astronomy, we assume that the process is homogeneous and isotropic. Note that the n-point correlations can be defined both for more general point processes and for continuous random fields. The estimators for these cases are similar to the ones described below and can be improved by similar algorithmic techniques.

Defining the npcf. We now turn to an informal, intuitive description of the hierarchy of n-point correlations. Since we have assumed that properties of the point process are translation and rotation invariant, the expected number of points in a given volume is proportional to a global density ρ. If we consider a small volume element dV, then the probability of finding a point in dV is given by:

$$dP = \rho dV \quad (1)$$

with dV suitably normalized. If the density ρ completely characterizes the process, we refer to it as a Poisson process.

Two-point correlation. The assumption of homogeneity and isotropy does not require the process to lack structure. The positions of points may still be correlated. The joint probability of finding objects in volume elements dV_1 and dV_2 separated by a distance r is given by:

$$dP_{12} = \rho^2 dV_1 dV_2 (1 + \xi(r)) \quad (2)$$

where the dV_i are again normalized. The two-point correlation $\xi(r)$ captures the increased or decreased probability of points occurring at a separation r. Note that the 2-point correlation is characterized by a single scale r and is a continuously varying function of this distance.

Three-point correlation. Higher-order correlations describe the probabilities of more than two points in a given configuration. We first consider three small volume elements, which form a triangle (See Fig. 1(b)). The joint probability of simultaneously finding points in volume elements dV_1, dV_2, and dV_3, separated by distances r_{12}, r_{13}, and r_{23}, is given by:

$$dP_{123} = \rho^3 dV_1 dV_2 dV_3 \left[1 + \xi(r_{12}) + \xi(r_{23}) + \xi(r_{13}) + \zeta(r_{12}, r_{23}, r_{13})\right] \quad (3)$$

The quantity in square brackets is sometimes called the *complete (or full) 3-point correlation function* and ζ is the *reduced 3-point correlation function.* We will often refer to ζ as simply the 3-point correlation function, since it will be the quantity of computational interest to us. Note that unlike the 2-point correlation, the 3-point correlation depends both on distance and configuration. The function varies continuously both as we increase the lengths of the sides of the triangle and as we vary its shape, for example by fixing two legs of the triangle and varying the angle between them.

Higher-order correlations. Higher-order correlation functions (such as the 4-point correlation in Fig. 1(c)) are defined in the same fashion. The probability of finding n-points in a given configuration can be written as a summation over the n-point correlation functions. For example, in addition to the reduced 4-point correlation function η, the complete 4-point correlation depends on the six 2-point terms (one for each pairwise distance), four 3-point terms (one for each triple of distances), and three products of two 2-point functions. The reduced four-point correlation is a function of all six pairwise distances. In general, we will denote the n-point correlation function as $\xi^{(n)}(\cdot)$, where the argument is understood to be $\binom{n}{2}$ pairwise distances. We refer to this set of pairwise distances as a *configuration*, or in the computational context, as a *matcher* (see below).

2.1 Estimating the NPCF

We have shown that the n-point correlation function is a fundamental spatial statistic and have sketched the definitions of the n-point correlation functions in terms of the underlying point process. We now turn to the central task of this paper: the problem of estimating the n-point correlation from real data. We describe several commonly used estimators and identify their common computational task.

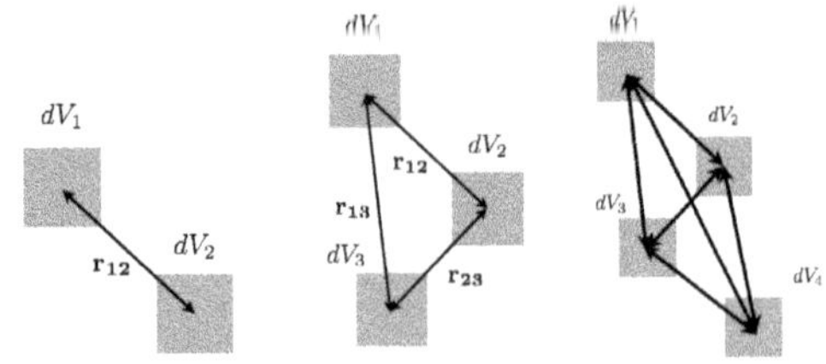

(a) 2-point (b) 3-point (c) 4-point

Figure 1: Visual interpretation of the n-point correlation functions.

We begin by considering the task of computing an estimate $\widehat{\xi}^{(n)}(\mathbf{r})$ for a given configuration. For simplicity, we consider the 2-point function first. Recall that $\xi(r)$ captures the increased (or decreased) probability of finding a pair of points at a distance r over finding the pair in a Poisson distributed set. This observation suggests a simple Monte Carlo estimator for $\xi(r)$. We generate a random set of points R from a Poisson distribution with the same (sample) density as our data and filling the same volume. We then compare the frequency with which points appear at a distance close to r in our data versus in the random set.

Simple estimator. Let DD(r) denote the number of pairs of points (x_i, x_j) in our data, normalized by the total number of possible pairs, whose pairwise distance $d(x_i, x_j)$ is close to r (in a way to be made precise below). Let RR(r) be the number of points whose pairwise distances are in the same interval (again normalized) from the random sample (DD stands for data-data, RR for random-random). Then, a simple estimator for the two-point correlation is [20, 27]:

$$\hat{\xi}(r) = \frac{\mathrm{DD}(r)}{\mathrm{RR}(r)} - 1 \quad (4)$$

This estimator captures the intuitive behavior we expect. If pairs of points at a distance near r are more common in our data than in a completely random (Poisson) distribution, we are likely to obtain a positive estimate for ξ.

This simple estimator suffers from suboptimal variance and sensitivity to noise. The Landy-Szalay estimator [12]

$$\hat{\xi}(r) = \frac{DD(r) - 2DR(r) + RR(r)}{RR(r)} \quad (5)$$

overcomes these difficulties. Here the notation $DR(r)$ denotes the number of pairs (x_i, y_j) at a distance near r where x_i is from the data and y_j is from the Poisson sample (DR – data-random pairs). Other widely used estimators use the same underlying quantities – pairs of points satisfying a given distance constraint [12, 10].

Three-point estimator. The 3-point correlation function depends on the pairwise distances between three points, rather than a single distance as before. We will therefore need to specify three distance constraints, and estimate the function for that configuration. The Landy-Szalay estimator for the 2-point function can be generalized to any value of n, and retains its improved bias and variance [29]. We again generate points from a Poisson distribution, and the estimator is also a function of quantities of the form $D^{(n)}$, or $D^{(i)}R^{(n-i)}$. These refer to the number of unique triples of points, all three from the data or two from the data and one from the Poisson set, with the property that their three pairwise distances lie close to the distances in the matcher.

All estimators count tuples of points. Any n-point correlation can be estimated using a sum of counts of n-tuples of points of the form $D^{(i)}R^{(n-i)}(\mathbf{r})$, where i ranges from zero to n. The argument is a vector of distances of length $\binom{n}{2}$, one for each pairwise distance needed to specify the configuration. We count unique tuples of points whose pairwise distances are close to the distances in the matcher in some ordering.

2.2 The Computational Task

Note that all the estimators described above depend on the same fundamental quantities: the number of tuples of points from the data/Poisson set that satisfy some set of distance constraints. Thus, our task is to compute this number given the data and a suitably large Poisson set. Enumerating all n-tuples requires $O(N^n)$ work for N data points. Therefore, we must seek a more efficient approach. We first give some terminology for our algorithm description below. We then present the entire computational task.

Matchers. We specify an n-tuple with $\binom{n}{2}$ constraints, one for each pairwise distance in the tuple. We mentioned above that we count tuples of points whose pairwise distances are "close" to the distance constraints. Each of the $\binom{n}{2}$ pairwise distance constraints consists of a lower and upper bound: $r_{ij}^{(l)}$ and $r_{ij}^{(u)}$. In the context of our algorithms, we refer to this collection of distance constraints $\mathbf{r}$ as a *matcher*. We refer to the entries of the matcher as $r_{ij}^{(l)}$ and $r_{ij}^{(u)}$, where the indices i and j refer to the volume elements introduced above (Fig. 1). We sometimes refer to an entry as simply r_{ij}, with the upper and lower bounds being understood.

Satisfying matchers. Given an n-tuple of points and a matcher $\mathbf{r}$, we say that the tuple *satisfies* the matcher if there exists a permutation of the points such that each pairwise distance does not violate the corresponding distance constraint in the matcher. More formally:

Definition 1. Given an n-tuple of points $(p_1, \ldots, p_n)$ and a matcher $\mathbf{r}$, we say that the tuple **satisfies** the matcher if there exists (at least one) permutation σ of $[1, \ldots, n]$ such that

$$r_{\sigma(i)\sigma(j)}^{(l)} < \|p_i - p_j\| < r_{\sigma(i)\sigma(j)}^{(u)} \quad (6)$$

for all indices $i, j \in [1, \ldots n]$ such that $i < j$.

The computational task. We can now formally define our basic computational task:

Definition 2. **Computational Task 1: Compute the counts of tuples $D^{(i)}R^{(j)}(\mathbf{r})$.** Given a data set D, random set R, and matcher $\mathbf{r}$, and $0 \leq i \leq n$, compute the number of unique n-tuples of points with i points from D and $n-i$ points from R, such that the tuple satisfies the matcher.

Computing these quantities directly requires enumerating all unique n-tuples of points, which takes $O(N^n)$ work and is prohibitively slow for even two-point correlations.

Multiple matchers. The estimators above give us a value $\widehat{\xi}^{(n)}(\mathbf{r})$ at a single configuration. However, the n-point correlations are continuous quantities. In order to fully characterize them, we must compute estimates for a wide range of configurations. In order to do this, we must repeat the computation in Defn. 2 for many matchers, both of different scales and configurations.

Definition 3. **Computational Task 2: Multiple matchers.** Given a data set D, random set R, and a collection of M matchers $\{\mathbf{r}_m\}$, compute $D^{(i)}R^{(j)}(\mathbf{r}_m)$ for each $1 \leq m \leq M$.

This task requires us to repeat Task 1 M times, where M controls the smoothness of our overall estimate of the npcf and our quantitative picture of its overall behavior. Thus, it is generally necessary for M to be large.

Resampling. Simply computing point estimates of any statistic is generally insufficient for most scientific applications. We also need to bound the variance of our estimator and compute error bars. In general, we must make the largest possible use of the available data, rather than withholding much of it for variance estimation. Thus, a resampling method is necessary.

Jackknife resampling is a widely used variance estimation method and is popular with astronomical data [15]. It is also used to study large scale structure by identifying variations in the npcf across different parts of the sample window [16]. We divide the data set into subregions. We eliminate each region from the data in turn, then compute our estimate of the npcf. We repeat this for each subset, and use the resulting estimates to bound the variance. This leads to our third and final computational task.

Definition 4. **Computational Task 3: Jackknife resampling.** We are given a data set D, random set R, a set of M matchers $\mathbf{r}_m$, and a partitioning of D into J subsets D_k. For each $1 \leq k \leq J$, construct the set $D_{(-k)} = D/D_k$. Then, compute $D_{(-k)}^{(i)}R^{(j)}(\mathbf{r})$.

This task requires us to repeat Task 1 J times on sets of size $D - D/J$. Note that J controls the quality of our variance estimation, with larger values necessary for a better estimate.

The complete computational task. We can now identify the complete computational task for n-point correlation estimation. Given our data and random sets, a collection of M matchers, and a partitioning of the data into J subregions, we must perform Task 3. This in turn requires us to perform Task 2 J times. Each iteration of Task 2 requires M computations of Task 1. Therefore, the entire computation requires $O(J \cdot M \cdot N^n)$ time if done in a brute-force fashion. In the next section, we describe our algorithmic approach to simultaneously computing all three parts of the computation, thus allowing significant savings in time.

3. ALGORITHMS

We have identified the full computational task of n-point correlation estimation. We now turn to our new algorithm. We begin by addressing previous work on efficiently computing the counts $D^{(i)}R^{(j)}(\mathbf{r})$ described above (Computational Task 1.) We first describe the multi-tree algorithm for computing these counts. We then give our new algorithm for directly solving computations with multiple matchers (Computational Task 2) and our method for efficiently computing counts for resampling regions (Computational Task 3).

3.1 Basic Algorithm

We build on previous, tree-based algorithms for the n-point correlation estimation problem [9, 18]. The key idea is to employ multiple kd-trees to improve on the $O(N^n)$ scaling of the brute-force approach.

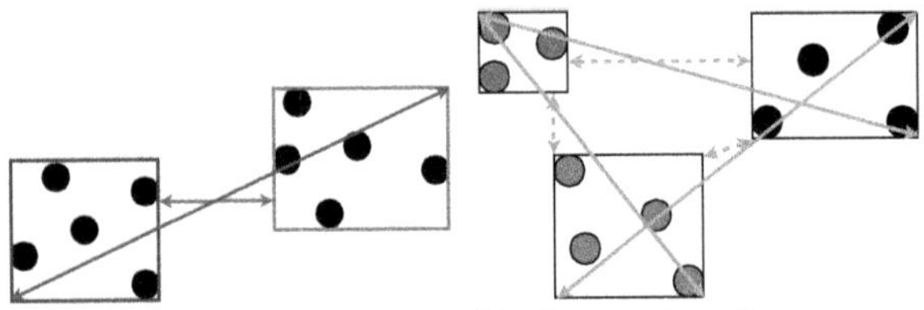

(a) Comparing two nodes. (b) Comparing three nodes.

Figure 2: Computing node-node bounds for pruning.

kd-trees. The kd-tree [21, 5] is a binary space partitioning tree which maintains a bounding box for all the points in each node. The root consists of the entire set. Children are formed recursively by splitting the parent's bounding box along the midpoint of its largest dimension and partitioning the points on either side. We can build a kd-tree on both the data and random sets as a pre-processing step. This requires only $O(N \log N)$ work and $O(N)$ space.

We employ the bounding boxes to speed up the naive computation by using them to identify opportunities for *pruning*. By computing the minimum and maximum distances between a pair of kd-tree nodes (Fig. 2), we can identify cases where it is impossible for any pair of points in the nodes to satisfy the matcher.

Dual-tree algorithm. For simplicity, we begin by considering the two-point correlation estimation (Alg. 1). Recall that the task is to count the number of unique pairs of points that satisfy a given matcher. We consider two tree nodes at a time, one from each set to be correlated. We compute the upper and lower bounds on distances between points in these nodes using the bounding boxes. We can then compare this to the matcher's lower and upper bounds. If the distance bounds prove that all pairs of points are either too far or too close to possibly satisfy the matcher, then we do not need to perform any more work on the nodes. We can thus *prune* all child nodes, and save $O(|T_1| \cdot |T_2|)$ work. If we cannot prune, then we split one (or both) nodes, and recursively consider the two (or four) resoling pairs of nodes. If our recursion reaches leaf nodes, we compare all pairs of points exhaustively.

We begin by calling the algorithm on the root nodes of the tree. If we wish to perform a DR count, we call the algorithm on the root of each tree. Note also that we only want to count unique pairs of points. Therefore, we can prune if T_2 comes before T_1 in an in-order tree traversal. This ensures that we see each pair of points at most once.

Multi-tree algorithm. We can extend this algorithm to the general n case. Instead of considering pairs of tree nodes, we compare an n-tuple of nodes in each step of the algorithm. This *multi-tree* algorithm uses the same basic idea – use bounding information between pairs of tree nodes to identify sets of nodes whose points cannot satisfy the matcher. We need only make two extensions to Alg. 1. First, we must do more work to determine if a particular

Algorithm 1 DualTree2pt (Tree node T_1, Tree node T_2, matcher **r**)

```
if T1 and T2 are leaves then
  for all points p1 ∈ T1, p2 ∈ T2 do
    if r12^(l) < ||p1 − p2|| < r12^(u) then
      result += 1
    end if
  end for
else if dmin(T1, T2) > r12^(u) or dmax(T1, T2) < r12^(l) then
  Prune
else
  DualTree2pt(T1.left, T2.left)
  DualTree2pt(T1.left, T2.right)
  DualTree2pt(T1.right, T2.left)
  DualTree2pt(T1.right, T2.right)
end if
```

Algorithm 2 MultiTreeNpt (Tree node $T_1, \ldots,$ Tree node T_n, matcher **r**)

```
if all nodes Ti are leaves then
  for all points p1 ∈ T1, ..., points pn ∈ Tn do
    if TestPointTuple(p1, ..., pn, r) then
      result += 1
    end if
  end for
else if not TestNodeTuple(T1, ..., Tn, r) then
  Prune
else
  Let Ti be the largest node
  MultiTreeNpt(T1, ..., Ti.left, ..., Tn, r)
  MultiTreeNpt(T1, ..., Ti.right, ..., Tn, r)
end if
```

tuple of points satisfies the matcher. We accomplish this in Alg. 3 by iterating over all permutations of the indices. Each permutation of indices corresponds to an assignment of pairwise distances to entries in the matcher. We can quickly check if this assignment is valid, and we only count tuples that have at least one valid assignment. The second extension is a similar one for checking if a tuple of nodes can be pruned (Alg. 4). We again iterate through all permutations and check if the distance bounds obtained from the bounding boxes fall within the upper and lower bounds of the matcher entry. As before, for an $D^{(i)}R^{(j)}$ count, we call the algorithm on i copies of the data tree root and j copies of the random tree root.

3.2 Multi-Matcher Algorithm

The algorithms presented above all focus on computing individual counts of points – *i.e.* Computational Task 1, from Sec. 2.2. This approach improves the overall dependence on the number of data points – N – and the order of the correlation – n. However, this does nothing for the other two parts of the overall computational complexity. We now turn to our novel algorithm to count tuples for many matchers simultaneously, thus addressing Computational Task 2.

Intuitively, computing counts for multiple matchers will repeat many calculations. For simplicity, consider the two-point correlation case illustrated in Fig. 3(a). We must count the number of pairs that satisfy two matchers, r_1 and r_2 (assume that the upper and lower bounds for each are very

Algorithm 3 TestPointTuple (points $p_1, \ldots, p_n$, matcher $\mathbf{r}$)

mark all permutations σ of $[1, \ldots, n]$ as valid
for all indices $i, j \in [1, n], i < j$ **do**
  $d_{ij} = \|p_i - p_j\|$
  for all permutations σ **do**
    if $r^{(l)}_{\sigma(i)\sigma(j)} > d_{ij}$ or $r^{(u)}_{\sigma(i)\sigma(j)} < d_{ij}$ **then**
      mark σ as invalid
    end if
  end for
end for
if At least one permutation σ is marked valid **then**
  return true
else
  return false
end if

Algorithm 4 TestNodeTuple (Tree node $T_1, \ldots,$ Tree node T_n, matcher $\mathbf{r}$)

mark all permutations σ of $[1, \ldots, n]$ as valid
for all indices $i \in [1, n-1]$ and indices $j > i$ **do**
  $d^{\max}_{ij} = d^{\max}(T_i, T_j)$; $d^{\min}_{ij} = d^{\min}(T_i, T_j)$
  for all permutations σ **do**
    if $r^{(l)}_{\sigma(i)\sigma(j)} > d^{\max}_{ij}$ or $r^{(u)}_{\sigma(i)\sigma(j)} < d^{\min}_{ij}$ **then**
      mark σ as invalid
    end if
  end for
end for
if At least one permutation σ is marked valid **then**
  return true
else
  return false
end if

close to the distances shown for simplicity). If we first perform the computation for r_1 using the dual-tree algorithm (Alg. 1), at some point we will consider the pair of nodes in the figure. We compute the lower bound distance from their bounding boxes and see that we can prune. After this algorithm has finished, we again use Alg. 1, this time with matcher r_2. We may again encounter the same pair of nodes, which requires us to compute the same distance bounds and make the same pruning decision. If we can consider the two matchers simultaneously, we can make the pruning decision for both and save the unnecessary work. We can also save work in the base case. We need only compute the distance between each pair of points once (if we have not been able to prune the pair completely). We can then immediately identify which matcher(s), if any, it satisfies.

Two-point case. In the two-point case, this improvement is straightforward, and has already been shown in [9]. We must only modify Alg. 3 and Alg. 4 to consider a collection of matchers. If the matchers are regularly spaced, then we can identify which (if any) the node or point pair may satisfy in constant time. For arbitrary matchers, we can sort them and find possible matching pairs in logarithmic time.

General case. The general n-point case requires more caution. The presence of permutations in Alg. 4 makes the straightforward approach mentioned above more difficult. Each pair of nodes in each permutation will possibly satisfy

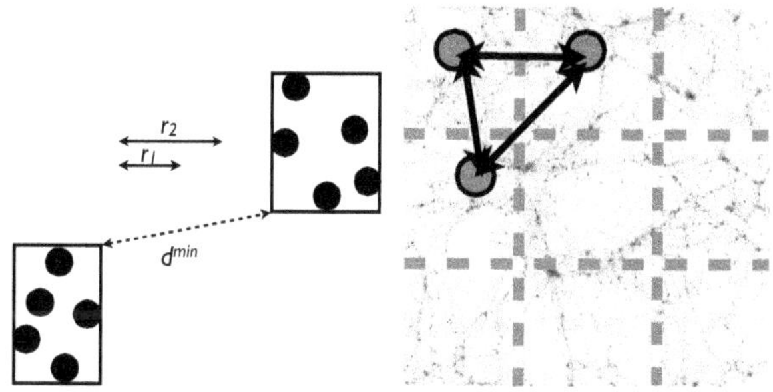

(a) Pruning for multiple matchers. (b) Resampling regions.

Figure 3: Our two new algorithmic ideas.

different matchers. It becomes prohibitively expensive to determine which, if any, matchers may be satisfied.

Instead, we can avoid searching all permutations entirely. We make use of the following observation, proven below: if the distance bounds violate a matcher in a particular order, they will violate it in all possible permutations.

THEOREM 3.1. *Given a matcher* $\mathbf{r}$, *let* $\{u_i : 1 \le i \le \binom{n}{2}\}$ *be the set of upper bounds* $r^{(u)}_{ij}$, *in the matcher, sorted in ascending order. Let* $\{d^l_i : 1 \le i \le \binom{n}{2}\}$ *be the set of lower-bound distances* d^{min}_{ij} *obtained from the bounding boxes of* n *tree nodes, also sorted in ascending order. Then, if* $d^l_i > u_i$ *for any* i, *no* n*-tuple of points from the nodes can satisfy the matcher.*

PROOF. Any permutation σ of the bounding boxes assigns each lower-bound distance d^l_i to some upper bound distance in the matcher $u_{\sigma(i)}$. In order for this permutation to work, we need that $d^l_i < u_{\sigma(i)}$ for all i. Let i' be the index such that $d^l_{i'} > u_{i'}$ in the condition of the theorem. Then, any permutation must map i' to an index j. If $j < i'$, then $d^l_{i'} > u_j = u_{\sigma(i')}$. If $j > i'$, then $\sigma(j) < i'$. Therefore, $d^l_j > u_{\sigma(j)}$. Therefore, no permutation can satisfy the matcher. □

We can easily arrive at a similar conclusion regarding upper bounds.

Multi-matcher pruning. Using these observations, we can improve the pruning rule in Alg. 4. With each n-tuple of nodes, we store the upper and lower bound distances, sorted in ascending order. We can compare these with the sorted distances in the matcher, using the observations above. If any lower bound distance is greater than a corresponding maximum matcher distance, we prune. When we recurse, we compute the $n-1$ new upper and lower bounds on node distances and update the sorted lists.

The total running time for pruning checks is therefore reduced from something proportional to $n!$ to a single loop of size $\binom{n}{2}$ along with comparable overhead from updating the sorted lists of bounds. Unfortunately, for common values of n (2 and 3), this is not a significant advantage. However, this approach makes a much greater difference in the multi-matcher version of the algorithm.

Specifying multiple matchers. We specify a set of matchers $\mathbf{r}_m$ by giving a minimum and maximum range, $r^{\min}_{ij}, r^{\max}_{ij}$ for each of its $\binom{n}{2}$ dimensions along with a num-

Algorithm 5 MultiTestNodeTuple (Tree node $T_1, \ldots,$ Tree node T_n, matcher minima $r_i^{\min}$, matcher maxima $r_i^{\max}$)

```
Compute node-node bounds l_i and u_i and sort
for i = 1 : (n choose 2) do
  if l_i > r_i^max or u_i < r_i^min then
    return false
  end if
end for
return true
```

Algorithm 6 EfficientResampling (Data sets $D_i : 1 \leq i \leq J$, matcher $\mathbf{r}$)

```
Construct a tree T_i on each D_i
for all unique n tuples of indices (i_1, ..., i_n) do
  result = MultiTreeNpt(T_{i_1}, ..., T_{i_n}, r)
  for all j ∉ {i_i, ..., i_n} do
    results[j] += result
  end for
end for
```

ber of equally-sized bins b_{ij} for each dimension. Each possible choice of bins, one from each dimension, then forms a single matcher. The total set of matchers consists of $\prod b_{ij}$ matchers, where the product runs over all dimensions of the matcher.

We can then provide a multi-matcher version of Alg. 4. We sort the minimum and maximum matcher ranges in ascending order. We can then compare these against the bounds from the nodes' bounding boxes.

We extend Alg. 3 by marking a permutation invalid if the point-point distance is greater than the maximum matcher distance or less than the minimum. If the distance falls in between, we can identify which bin contains it in constant time. We store a vector of possible bins for each permutation, and if a permutation has a valid bin for each dimension, we can increment our count for that dimension. Note that we still only count each tuple at most once.

Alternative matcher specifications. Our specification of multiple matchers may seem somewhat restrictive. On the one hand, our framework allows for a wide range of possible configurations by allowing each dimension to be specified separately. However, we have assumed that no bins overlap and that the thickness of each bin is fixed. Neither of these restrictions are fundamental to our method. We are currently developing an extension which will allow overlapping bins and varying thicknesses, such as commonly occurs in three point computations. This modification requires only limited extensions to the pruning rule and base case.

3.3 Efficient Resampling Algorithm

We now turn to our second new algorithm – a method to efficiently compute counts for resampling regions (Computational Task 3). Recall from Sec. 2.2 that we are given a partitioning of the data set into subsets D_i. We then construct i data sets $D_{(-i)} = \{i \in D | i \notin D_i\}$. We now compute counts which satisfy the matcher for each set $D^{(-i)}$. Assuming that the subregions each contain roughly the same number of points, we see that for J subregions and an n-point estimation algorithm which requires $T(N)$ time for N data points, we require $O(JT(N - N/J))$ time for each matcher. Instead, we can rearrange this computation to share work between different subcomputations.

Redundant work. The intuition for our new approach is shown in Fig. 3(b). Assume we are computing a count of the form $DDD(\mathbf{r})$ and that the three points shown in the figure satisfy the matcher. For all but the three regions in which the tuple's points lie, we will need to do the work to find and count the tuple since it factors into the total DDD count for all the $D_{(-i)}$. Therefore, we will perform all the work needed to find this tuple $J - 3$ times.

New algorithmic strategy. We can avoid this extra work by working with the subsets D_i directly. For instance, if we compute the count $D_i D_i D_i(\mathbf{r})$, this result will appear in the counts for all $D_{(-j)} D_{(-k)} D_{(-l)}(\mathbf{r})$. We can then compute this count once and add its intermediate result into the $J - 1$ final results. In general, we consider n distinct sets D_i, compute the number of tuples from them that satisfy the matcher, and add that intermediate count into the result for each $D_{(-j)}$ that does not appear in the computation. We show this approach in Alg. 6. We maintain an array of results of length J, where the jth entry corresponds to the count $D_{(-j)} \cdots D_{(-j)}(\mathbf{r})$. This method can be easily extended to include random sets by including the random set as one of the D_i in the input to Alg. 6.

For J resampling regions, each containing roughly N/J points, this algorithm requires $O(\binom{J}{n} \cdot T(N/J))$ time, where $T(N)$ is the time required for a single n-point correlation computation on N points. The naive version loops over all resampling regions, so it requires $O(J \cdot T(N))$ time. While the combinatorial dependence on n may seem to be a disadvantage, it is easily made up for by the reduced problem size for each n-point computation. As we will show in our experimental results, this method provides a considerable speedup.

We have presented two new algorithms which, along with the previous multi-tree algorithm [9, 18], address the entire computational problem of estimating n-point correlations. Our two algorithms can be used in conjunction for maximum speedups. We simply provide the set of matchers described in Sec. 3.2 to the efficient resampling algorithm (Alg. 6). We now turn to some empirical results for our new algorithms.

4. EXPERIMENTAL RESULTS

Algorithms. We have presented two new algorithms for n-point correlation estimation. We show results with our new *efficient resampling* algorithm (Alg. 6) and with a naive resampling ($O(J \cdot T(N))$) approach, which simply loops over resampling regions. We also show results with our *multi-matcher* method and a naive-matcher $O(M \cdot T(N))$ algorithm which simply loops over matchers and calls Alg. 2. We therefore present results for each new method alone, and in combination. We also show results for the original multi-tree algorithm [18], which we call the single-matcher, naive-resampling algorithm. We have also estimated runtimes for the brute-force $O(J \cdot M \cdot N^n)$ algorithm.

In our charts and tables, we use the following labels for these algorithms:

- *single-naive* – the original multi-tree algorithm [9] inside loops over resampling regions and matchers.
- *single-efficient* – the original multi-tree algorithm [9] inside a loop over matchers but using our improved resampling algorithm (Alg. 6).

- *multi-naive* – our improved multi-matcher algorithm inside a loop over resampling regions.
- *multi-efficient* – our multi-matcher algorithm used together with the efficient resampling method.

Algorithm	Time (s)	Speedup (brute-force)	Speedup (over [9])
multi-efficient	328.6	$\mathbf{1.4 \times 10^6}$	**105**
multi-naive	10229	4.6×10^3	3.36
single-efficient	1365.5	3.4×10^5	25.2
single-naive	34397	1.4×10^3	–

Table 1: Mock catalog experimental results for 2-point correlations, 10^6 points. 30 resampling regions, 20 matchers.

Algorithm	Time (s)	Speedup
multi-efficient	10057	$\mathbf{2.2 \times 10^5}$
multi-naive	96620	2.3×10^4
naive-efficient	21935	9.9×10^4

Table 2: Mock catalog experimental results for 3-point correlations, 10^6 points. 12 resampling regions, 18 matchers. Speedups are over the brute-force algorithm. The naive-naive algorithm was omitted because of time constraints.

Implementation details. We implemented our algorithms in C++. We used the *kd*-tree implementation in the MLPACK scalable machine learning library [4]. All experiments were performed in serial on a 6 core, AMD Phenom 3.3 GHz machine.

Datasets. We provide experimental results on uniform (Poisson data) in three dimensions and a mock galaxy catalog generated from N-body simulations. Both these sets are representative of the data used in actual n-point correlation estimation. Galaxy catalogs reproduce the correlation statistics of observed data. Computations involving Poisson distributed sets, such as those in the estimators in Section 2.1, represent a significant fraction of the total computational overhead.

Results. In Fig. 4, we show runtimes for all four algorithms on uniform data of different sizes. The numbers of matchers and resampling subsets are shown with each figure. Note that for all three figures, each of our new methods provides a large speedup, shown in Table 3. We see that in our experiments, each of our new algorithms provides roughly an order-of-magnitude speedup. These effects stack when used together, so we see speedups of well over 100.

The efficient resampling algorithm provides a greater advantage than the multi-matcher method in our experiments. However, this effect is less pronounced in our 4-point experiments (Fig. 4(c)). These experiments used more matchers than the others, suggesting that the savings due to the multi-matcher algorithm will increase with more matchers.

5. CONCLUSION & FUTURE WORK

We have described the first fast algorithms for the entire n-point correlation function estimation problem. Both of these new algorithms build on the current state-of-the-art tree-based approach by identifying computational bottlenecks in the entire npcf estimation problem. One of our

n	Algorithm	Speedup (brute-force)	Speedup (over [9])
2	multi-efficient	$\mathbf{1.08 \times 10^6}$	**77.4**
	multi-naive	4.95×10^4	3.6
	single-efficient	3.7×10^5	26.6
3	multi-efficient	$\mathbf{5.9 \times 10^4}$	**228.6**
	multi-naive	2.03×10^3	7.87
	single-efficient	8.47×10^3	32.8
4	multi-efficient	$\mathbf{2.3 \times 10^6}$	**583**
	multi-naive	5.28×10^3	21.3
	single-efficient	1.2×10^4	2.72

Table 3: Speedups over the brute-force algorithm and current state-of-the-art. Timings are from the largest values of N in Fig. 4.

methods computes the counts necessary for estimating the correlations at multiple scales in a single pass. The other efficiently incorporates the jackknife resampling step required to estimate the variance. We have shown that each of these methods can provide an order-of-magnitude speedup over the current best algorithms and that they can be used in conjunction for speedups up to 500 or greater.

We are currently developing two extensions of this approach. First, we are implementing another, more general multi-matcher algorithm which will be capable of handling overlapping bins. Second, we are working on a parallel implementation of our approach for the largest data sets.

6. REFERENCES

[1] J. Bardeen et al. The statistics of peaks of gaussian random fields. *The Astrophysical Journal*, 304:15–61, 1986.

[2] L. Cooper et al. Two-point correlation as a feature for histology images. In *Computer Vision and Pattern Recognition Workshops*, volume 13, pages 79–86, 2010.

[3] N. Cressie. *Statistics for Spatial Data.* John Wiley & Sons, 1991.

[4] R. R. Curtin et al. MLPACK: A Scalable C++ Machine Learning Library. In *BigLearning: Algorithms, Systems, and Tools for Learning at Scale*, 2011.

[5] J. H. Friedman et al. An Algorithm for Finding Best Matches in Logarithmic Expected Time. *ACM Trans. Math. Softw.*, 3:209–226, 1977.

[6] J. Fry. The galaxy correlation hierarchy in perturbation theory. *The Astrophysical Journal*, 279:499–510, 1984.

[7] J. Gardner et al. A framework for analyzing massive astrophysical datasets on a distributed grid. In *Astronomical Society of the Pacific Conference Series*, volume 376, page 69, 2007.

[8] T. Giannantonio et al. High redshift detection of the integrated Sachs-Wolfe effect. *Physical Review D*, 74(6):063520, 2006.

[9] A. G. Gray and A. W. Moore. 'N-Body' problems in statistical learning. In *Neural Information Processing Systems*, volume 4, pages 521–527, 2000.

[10] A. Hamilton. Toward better ways to measure the galaxy correlation function. *The Astrophysical Journal*, 417:19, 1993.

[11] INBio. *The National Biodiversity Institute of Costa Rica.* http://www.inbio.ac.cr/en.

[12] S. Landy and A. Szalay. Bias and variance of angular correlation functions. *The Astrophysical Journal*, 412:64–71, 1993.

[13] D. Li et al. 3D reconstruction of carbon nanotube composite microstructure using correlation functions. *Journal of Computational and Theoretical Nanoscience*, 7:1462–1468, 2010.

[14] LSST. *The Large Synoptic Survey Telescope.* www.lsst.org.

[15] R. Lupton et al. The SDSS imaging pipelines. In *Astronomical Data Analysis Software and Systems X*, volume 238, page 269, 2001.

[16] C. McBride. *Our Non-Gaussian Universe: Higher Order Correlation Functions in the Sloan Digital Sky Survey.* PhD thesis, University of Pittsburgh, 2010.

[17] C. McBride et al. Three-point correlation functions of SDSS galaxies: constraining galaxy-mass bias. *The Astrophysical Journal*, 739:85, 2011.

[18] A. Moore et al. Fast algorithms and efficient statistics: N-point correlation functions. *Mining the Sky*, pages 71–82, 2001.

[19] K. Mosaliganti et al. Tensor classification of n-point correlation function features for histology tissue segmentation. *Medical Image Analysis*, 13:156–166, 2009.

[20] P. Peebles. *The Large-Scale Structure of the Universe.* Princeton University Press, 1980.

[21] F. P. Preparata and M. I. Shamos. *Computational Geometry: An Introduction.* Springer, 1985.

[22] R. Ridgway et al. Image segmentation with tensor-based classification of n-point correlation functions. In *MICCAI Workshop on Medical Image Analysis with Applications in Biology*, 2006.

[23] B. Ripley. Locally finite random sets: Foundations for point process theory. *The Annals of Probability*, 4:983–994, 1976.

[24] B. Ripley. *Spatial statistics.* Wiley-Blackwell, 2004.

[25] SDSS. *The Sloan Digital Sky Survey.* www.sdss.org.

[26] C. Seife. Breakthrough of the year: Illuminating the dark universe. *Science*, 302(5653):2017–2172, December 19 2003.

[27] I. Szapudi. Introduction to higher order spatial statistics in cosmology. *Data Analysis in Cosmology*, pages 457–492, 2009.

[28] I. Szapudi et al. Fast cosmic microwave background analyses via correlation functions. *The Astrophysical Journal Letters*, 548:L115, 2001.

[29] I. Szapudi and A. Szalay. A new class of estimators for the N-point correlations. *The Astrophysical Journal Letters*, 494:L41, 1998.

[30] S. Torquato. *Random Heterogeneous Materials.* Springer, 2002.

[31] S. Torquato and G. Stell. Microstructure of two-phase random media. I. The n-point probability functions. *The Journal of Chemical Physics*, 77:2071, 1982.

[32] S. White. The hierarchy of correlation functions and its relation to other measures of galaxy clustering. *Monthly Notices of the Royal Astronomical Society*, 186:145–154, 1979.

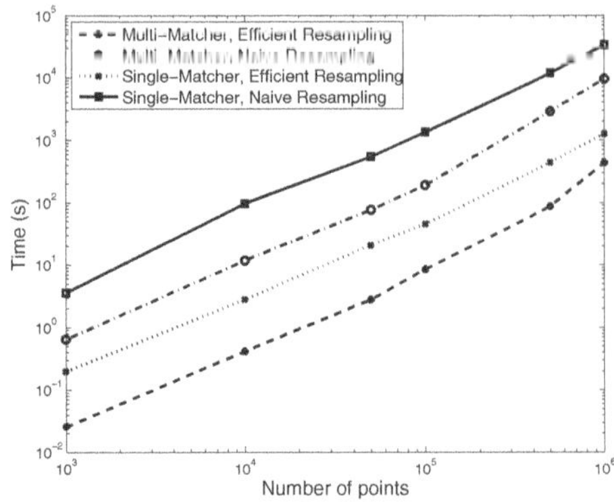

(a) Two-point correlation estimation on uniformly distributed data with 20 matchers and 30 resampling regions.

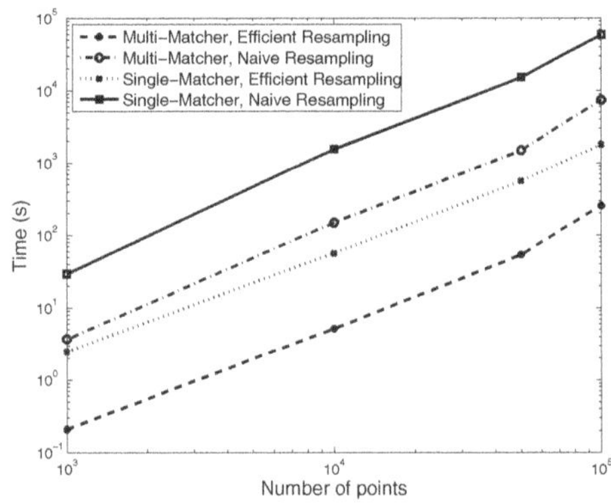

(b) Three-point correlation estimation on uniformly distributed data with 50 matchers and 30 resampling regions.

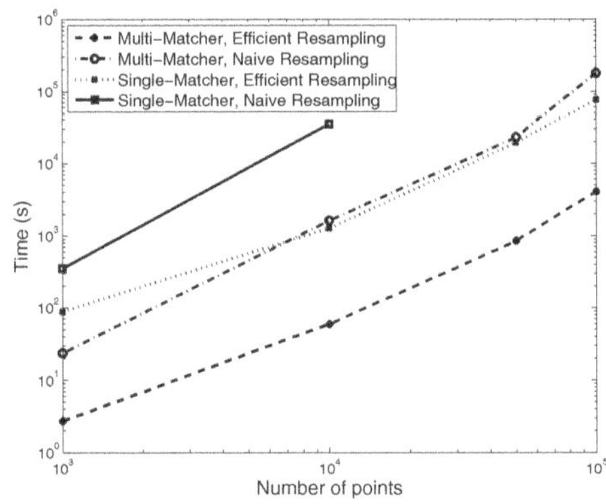

(c) Four-point correlation estimation on uniformly distributed data with 216 matchers and 30 resampling regions.

Figure 4: n-point correlation estimation computation times on log-log scale. All timings are in seconds.

On "One of the Few" Objects

You Wu† Pankaj K. Agarwal† Chengkai Li‡ Jun Yang† Cong Yu§
†Duke University, ‡University of Texas at Arlington, §Google Research

ABSTRACT

Objects with multiple numeric attributes can be compared within any "subspace" (subset of attributes). In applications such as computational journalism, users are interested in claims of the form: *Karl Malone is one of the only two players in NBA history with at least 25,000 points, 12,000 rebounds, and 5,000 assists in one's career.* One challenge in identifying such "one-of-the-k" claims ($k = 2$ above) is ensuring their "interestingness." A small k is not a good indicator for interestingness, as one can often make such claims for many objects by increasing the dimensionality of the subspace considered. We propose a uniqueness-based interestingness measure for one-of-the-few claims that is intuitive for non-technical users, and we design algorithms for finding all interesting claims (across all subspaces) from a dataset. Sometimes, users are interested primarily in the objects appearing in these claims. Building on our notion of interesting claims, we propose a scheme for ranking objects and an algorithm for computing the top-ranked objects. Using real-world datasets, we evaluate the efficiency of our algorithms as well as the advantage of our object-ranking scheme over popular methods such as Kemeny optimal rank aggregation and weighted-sum ranking.

Categories and Subject Descriptors

H.2.8 [**Database Management**]: Database Applications—*data mining*; H.2.4 [**Database Management**]: Systems—*query processing*; K.4.0 [**Computers and Society**]: General

Keywords

Computational journalism, fact checking, skyband, ranking

1 Introduction

Raw data in various domains are becoming more widely accessible, e.g., play-by-play game logs for sports, databases of campaign finance and voting records for politics, etc. An increasing number of news stories are driven by information extracted from data. Computational journalism [5, 6] is a nascent field about using computing to help improve effectiveness and reduce cost for journalism, which serves a vital role in our society. One important goal in computational journalism is *(semi-)automatic lead identification* from data, i.e., finding interesting information nuggets from raw data that lead to further investigation and/or news stories around them. In this paper, we take a first step toward this goal by considering a popular form of claims exemplified by the following:

- *There is no player in NBA history with more points, more rebounds, and more assists than Oscar Robertson in one's career.*
- *Rick Perry is one of the only three candidates in the 2012 US federal election cycle to have received at least $600k from "lawyers & lobbyists" (an interest group that is usually pro-Democrat) and $400k from "energy & natural resources" (usually pro-Republican).*

These two claims share a common structure: both are about an object being one of the few that "stand out" when compared according to a set of numeric attributes. More precisely, given a set of objects $\mathcal{O}$, each with a set $\mathcal{A}$ of numeric attributes, we consider *one-of-the-few* claims of the following form:

> ***Object** o **is dominated by fewer than** k **objects in a non-empty subset** $\mathcal{B} \subseteq \mathcal{A}$ **of attributes.***

Here, we say o' dominates o in $\mathcal{B}$ if o' is no worse than o for all attributes in $\mathcal{B}$, and o' is strictly better than o for at least one attribute in $\mathcal{B}$. Journalists are interested in two tasks: 1) finding all "interesting" one-of-the-few claims from a given dataset; 2) ranking objects based on what one-of-the-few claims can be made about them. The first task allows journalists to identify claims that can be used in stories or serve as leads for further investigation. The second task provides an object-centric view that allows journalists to prioritize their investigation of particular objects (especially when there are many interesting one-of-the-few claims).

Task 1: Finding Claims Our goal is to find interesting one-of-the-few claims in all "subspaces" (i.e., subsets of attributes). One-of-the-few claims are closely related to the concept of *k-skyband* for multi-dimensional data [15]. Intuitively, the k-skyband of a set $\mathcal{O}$ of objects in subspace $\mathcal{B}$ is the subset of objects each dominated by fewer than k other objects in $\mathcal{B}$. (The better-known notion of *skyline* is a special case of k-skyband where $k = 1$.) From the k-skyband in $\mathcal{B}$, a one-of-the-few claim can be generated for each object in the skyband straightforwardly. While various algorithms exist for computing a k-skyband given k and $\mathcal{B}$, they do not address the key challenge of ensuring "interestingness" of the claims they find in a way that is easy for users to control and interpret. Although the parameter k can be tuned, it is a poor indicator of interestingness, as illustrated by the following example.

Example 1. *Consider the set of nearly* 4000 *players in NBA history, with stats such as career total* points, rebounds, *and* assists. *Being one of the top* 50 *leading scorers—i.e., in the* 50*-skyband for the single-attribute subspace* {points}*—is quite an impressive*

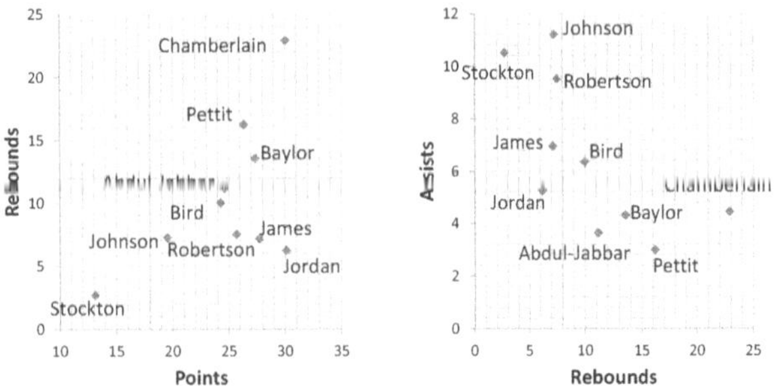

(a) Positive: *points* vs. *rebounds* (b) Negative: *rebounds* vs. *assists*

Figure 1: Correlation in NBA player stats.

feat. However, if we expand the subspace to {points, rebounds}, 142 *players now fit the bill—i.e., each is dominated by fewer than* 50 *others in* {points, rebounds}. *If we further include* assists *in the subspace,* 324 *(almost* 9% *of all) players will be in the* 50*-skyband.*

Example 1 clearly illustrates why we cannot use a universal k to ensure interestingness of one-of-the-few claims for different subspaces: the size of the skyband tends to increase rapidly as dimensionality goes up. For example, the expected number of 1-skyband (skyline) objects is $O(\ln^{|\mathcal{B}|-1}|\mathcal{O}|/(|\mathcal{B}|-1)!)$, if object ranks by individual attributes are uniformly and independently distributed [1], e.g., when objects are uniformly distributed in a box. With a fixed k, too many claims may be in high-dimensional subspaces, making them uninteresting. Clearly, k must be adjusted as $|\mathcal{B}|$ changes. Furthermore, the appropriate setting for k is not simply as a function of dimensionality, because data characteristics—e.g., correlation among attributes—also matter, as illustrated below.

Example 2. *We plot a subset of NBA players, with attributes* points, rebounds, *and* assists *per game, as points in subspaces* {points, rebounds} *(Figure 1a) and* {rebounds, assists} *(Figure 1b). It is easy to see that the skybands in Figure 1a tend to be smaller than those in Figure 1b, because of the positive correlation between* points *and* rebounds *and the negative correlation between* rebounds *and* assists. *For example, the* 3*-skyband in* {points, rebounds} *contains* 5 *players (Jordan, Chamberlain, James, Baylor, and Pettit), which translate into* 5 *one-of-the-*3 *claims; on the other hand, the* 3*-skyband in* {rebounds, assists} *contains* 9 *players (all except Jordan). Hence, no single choice of k is appropriate for these two subspaces of the same dimensionality.*

Example 2 above clearly illustrates that we cannot hope to define interestingness, which is data-dependent, by a function of k and $|\mathcal{B}|$ alone. Asking the user to pick the right k manually for each and every subspace is also infeasible. Our quest is to find an effective way of ensuring claim interestingness such that: 1) users are not required to tune lots of parameters; 2) the results are easy to understand and explain in layman's terms. Both properties are critical for computational journalism, where journalists are often non-technical and the results need to be explained to the general public in stories. Furthermore, given the interestingness measure, we need to address the challenge of finding interesting one-of-the-few claims in all subspaces efficiently.

Task 2: Ranking Objects Even with an appropriate definition of "interestingness," many objects may be the subject of at least one interesting one-of-the-few claim in some subspace. The task of ranking objects allows users to prioritize their effort in investigating objects. From our experience analyzing real data and preliminary user studies, different data domains and user preferences call for some degree of customization in ranking, as illustrated below.

Example 3. *Both John Stockton and Larry Bird are inductees into the Naismith Memorial Basketball Hall of Fame, but they have different playing styles. Stockton has the second highest assists per game in NBA history, but is not very impressive in points or rebounds. Bird ranks 17th in points, 60th rebounds, and 44th in assists. Stockton and Bird exemplify what we call "specialized" and "well-rounded" objects, respectively. How to rank specialized objects relative to well-rounded ones often depends on the context, or may simply be a matter of personal opinion.*

A popular method for ranking objects based on multiple input rankings is *Kemeny optimal rank aggregation* [7], or *Kemeny* for short. It produces a "consensus" ranking that minimizes the number of pairwise disagreements (in the relative ordering of two objects). When aggregating object rankings under individual attributes, Kemeny tends to downgrade objects that rank extremely high in few attributes but considerably low in other attributes. For Example 3 above, Bird, who is well-rounded, would be ranked as the 9th by Kemeny, while Stockton, who is specialized, would be as low as the 139th, which may not be acceptable to some.

While Kemeny leaves no option for customization, another popular method, *weighted-sum ranking*, exposes too many knobs. With weighted-sum, a user specifies a preference vector, whose components represent weights assigned to attributes; objects are ranked according to their projection onto this vector (i.e., weighted combination of their attribute values). For a d-dimensional dataset, the user needs to specify d weights; even if we learn these weights automatically, training examples must be provided. Such requirements may overwhelm journalists with little time or technical expertise. Our goal is to devise a ranking scheme with as few knobs as possible, which allows customization without overwhelming users.

Main Contributions First, we propose a simple but effective definition for the interestingness of a claim based on its "uniqueness." For a one-of-the-few claim (with a particular k in a particular subspace $\mathcal{B}$) to be interesting, we require that this claim (with the same k and $\mathcal{B}$) cannot be made for more than τ objects. Unlike k, τ is a user-defined threshold that applies universally to all subspaces, significantly reducing the burden on the user to define interestingness. For each subspace, our definition automatically adapts k in a data-dependent way, and naturally excludes those high-dimensional subspaces where no claims are unique enough. Furthermore, τ is easy to understand for non-technical users.

Based on this definition, we introduce the problem of finding all interesting one-of-the-few claims across all non-empty subspaces, given the uniqueness threshold τ. The fact that our k is data-dependent and not fixed raises unique challenges not addressed by previous work on computing skylines and skybands. We devise efficient algorithms that avoid redundant computation. In particular, we are able to improve the worst-case complexity of finding all interesting claims in a subspace from $O(|\mathcal{O}|^2)$ to $O(\tau|\mathcal{O}|)$, which is attractive because τ in practice is small for claims to be unique.

Building on the definition of interestingness, we propose a novel scheme for scoring and ranking objects based on the aggregated interestingness of claims involving them. One key insight distinguishing our scheme from others is that we in effect aggregate ranks across all non-empty subspaces as opposed to just individual attributes. Our scheme supports tuning by a single parameter α, which captures user preference between specialized and well-rounded objects, and overcomes the inflexibility of Kemeny without resorting to an overwhelming number of knobs like weighted-sum. Extending the algorithms for finding all interesting claims, we show how to compute top-ranked objects efficiently given α. We experimentally demonstrate, on real datasets, that our scheme is able to produce rankings comparable to Kemeny and weighted-sum while offering more effective customization.

2 Finding One-of-the-Few Claims

Preliminaries Consider a set $\mathcal{O}$ of n objects, each with d numeric attributes $\mathcal{A} = \{A_1, A_2, \ldots, A_d\}$. A *subspace* is (more precisely, spanned by) a subset of the attributes. The set of all subspaces of $\mathcal{A}$ forms a lattice under containment relation. We say that subspace $\mathcal{B}_1$ is an *ancestor* (*descendant*) of subspace $\mathcal{B}_2$ if $\mathcal{B}_1 \subseteq \mathcal{B}_2$ (resp. $\mathcal{B}_1 \supseteq \mathcal{B}_2$). We say $\mathcal{B}_1$ is a *parent* (*child*) of $\mathcal{B}_2$ if $\mathcal{B}_1 \subset \mathcal{B}_2$ (resp. $\mathcal{B}_1 \supset \mathcal{B}_2$) and their cardinalities differ by one.

We say o_1 *dominates* o_2 in subspace $\mathcal{B}$, denoted $o_1 \succ_{\mathcal{B}} o_2$, if i) $\forall A \in \mathcal{B}, o_1.A \geq o_2.A$, and ii) $\exists A \in \mathcal{B}, o_1.A > o_2.A$. Clearly, dominance is transitive: if $o_1 \succ_{\mathcal{B}} o_2$ and $o_2 \succ_{\mathcal{B}} o_3$, then $o_1 \succ_{\mathcal{B}} o_3$.

Definition 1 (Dominating Subset, k-Skyband, Skyline, Tier).

- *The* dominating subset *of $o \in \mathcal{O}$ in subspace $\mathcal{B} \subseteq \mathcal{A}$, denoted $\mathfrak{D}_{\mathcal{B}}(\mathcal{O}, o)$, is the subset of objects that dominate o in $\mathcal{B}$; i.e., $\mathfrak{D}_{\mathcal{B}}(\mathcal{O}, o) = \{o' \in \mathcal{O} \mid o' \succ_{\mathcal{B}} o\}$. Let $\delta_{\mathcal{B}}(\mathcal{O}, o) = |\mathfrak{D}_{\mathcal{B}}(\mathcal{O}, o)|$ denote the size of the dominating subset.*
- *The* k-skyband *($k \geq 1$) of $\mathcal{O}$ in subspace $\mathcal{B}$, denoted $\mathfrak{S}^k_{\mathcal{B}}(\mathcal{O})$, is the subset of objects in $\mathcal{O}$ where each is dominated by fewer than k objects in $\mathcal{O}$; i.e., $\mathfrak{S}^k_{\mathcal{B}}(\mathcal{O}) = \{o \in \mathcal{O} \mid \delta_{\mathcal{B}}(\mathcal{O}, o) < k\}$.*
- *The* skyline *of $\mathcal{O}$ in subspace $\mathcal{B}$ is $\mathfrak{S}^1_{\mathcal{B}}(\mathcal{O})$, i.e., the 1-skyband.*
- *The* i-th tier *($i \geq 1$) of $\mathcal{O}$ in subspace $\mathcal{B}$ is the subset of objects in $\mathcal{O}$ where each is dominated by exactly $i-1$ objects in $\mathcal{O}$; i.e., $\{o \in \mathcal{O} \mid \delta_{\mathcal{B}}(\mathcal{O}, o) = i - 1\}$.*

Clearly, by definition, the k-skyband $\mathfrak{S}^k_{\mathcal{B}}(\mathcal{O})$ is the disjoint union of all i-th tiers with $i \leq k$, and the difference between the k-skyband and the $(k-1)$-skyband is the k-th tier.[1]

To illustrate, consider the set $\mathcal{O}$ of 10 NBA players and subspace $\mathcal{B} = \{rebounds, assists\}$ shown in Figure 1b. $\mathfrak{D}_{\mathcal{B}}(\mathcal{O}, \text{Stockton}) = \{\text{Johnson}\}$, so $\delta_{\mathcal{B}}(\mathcal{O}, \text{Stockton}) = 1$. $\mathfrak{S}^1_{\mathcal{B}}(\mathcal{O}) = \{$Johnson, Robertson, Bird, Chamberlain$\}$ is the skyline (or 1-skyband), which is also the 1-st tier. $\mathfrak{S}^2_{\mathcal{B}}(\mathcal{O}) = \mathfrak{S}^1_{\mathcal{B}}(\mathcal{O}) \cup \{$Stockton, Baylor, Pettit$\}$ is the 2-skyband, where Stockton, Baylor, and Pettit are in the 2nd tier and each dominated by exactly one object in $\mathcal{O}$. $\mathfrak{S}^3_{\mathcal{B}}(\mathcal{O})$, the 3-skyband, additionally includes the 3rd tier $\{$James, Abdul-Jabbar$\}$, leaving only Jordan out, as mentioned in Example 2.

Problem Statement As motivated in Section 1, while each object in the k-skyband translates into a one-of-the-few claim, we measure the interestingness of this claim by the number of objects for which similar claims can be made, i.e., the size of the k-skyband. Instead of struggling with setting k, which depends on the subspace and object distribution, a user should be able to specify a single threshold τ that caps the number of similar claims. Therefore, we introduce the concept of *top-τ skyband* below. While the concept is closely related to k-skyband, a crucial difference is that a top-τ skyband is defined by its size, while a k-skyband, defined by its number of tiers, can be arbitrarily large.

Definition 2 (Top-τ Skyband). *Given $\tau \geq 1$, the* top-τ skyband *of a set of objects $\mathcal{O}$ in subspace $\mathcal{B}$, denoted $\Phi^\tau_{\mathcal{B}}(\mathcal{O})$ (or Φ^τ if context is clear), is the $\hat{k}$-skyband where $\hat{k} = \max\{k \mid \tau \geq |\mathfrak{S}^k_{\mathcal{B}}(\mathcal{O})|\}$.*

In other words, the top-τ skyband is the largest skyband whose size does not exceed τ.

The fact that an object o belongs to the top-τ skyband with the k-th tier as its last non-empty tier—or alternatively, the k-skyband with size no more than τ—translates into the following statement:

Object o is dominated by fewer than k objects in $\mathcal{B}$, and this claim cannot be made for more than τ objects.

Intuitively, τ measures the uniqueness of the claim made by the first part of the above statement. For example, in Figure 1a, suppose we set $\tau = 3$. $\Phi^\tau = \{$Chamberlain, Jordan$\}$ is the 1-skyband. The 2-skyband would be too big, because it also contains Pettit, Baylor, and James, and has size $5 > \tau$. Note that the 3rd tier is empty—no player is dominated by exactly two others in this example—so the 3-skyband (recall Example 2) is the same as the 2-skyband.

The problem of finding all interesting one-of-the-few claims can now be formulated as follows:

Definition 3 (Finding Top-τ Skybands in All Subspaces). *Given the set $\mathcal{O}$ of objects and a user-specified threshold τ, find $\Phi^\tau_{\mathcal{B}}(\mathcal{O})$ for every non-empty subspace $\mathcal{B} \subseteq \mathcal{A}$.*

For each subspace, the membership of an object in Φ^τ corresponds to a one-of-the-few claim that cannot be made for more than τ objects. This definition leads naturally to some desired features. In a single-attribute subspace, Φ^τ contains essentially the top τ objects ranked by this attribute. As the subspace dimensionality goes up, the number of tiers in Φ^τ decreases in an automatic, data-dependent manner until these tiers contain no more than τ objects. Thus, with this problem formulation, users need not manually pick the number of tiers in the skyband for each subspace. To illustrate, consider again Example 2. Suppose the user sets $\tau = 8$. For subspace $\{points, rebounds\}$ (Figure 1a), Φ^τ would be the 5-skyband. In contrast, for $\{rebounds, assists\}$ (Figure 1b), Φ^τ would be the 2-skyband. Finally, in high-dimensional subspaces where so many objects are on the skyline that no claims are interesting, our problem formulation correctly leads to an empty Φ^τ.

Overview of Solutions The rest of this section discusses how to find all interesting one-of-the-few claims. At a high level, we 1) traverse the lattice of subspaces in some manner, and 2) compute Φ^τ for each subspace we visit. Techniques for improving efficiency exist both across subspaces and within each subspace. For finding Φ^τ in a given subspace $\mathcal{B}$, we propose two algorithms in Sections 2.1 and 2.2. We then show in Section 2.3 how to explore the lattice of subspaces using these algorithms as subroutines.

Note that computing Φ^τ for a single-attribute subspace $\{A\}$ simply involves finding the top τ objects sorted by A; algorithms in Sections 2.1 and 2.2 are needed only when $|\mathcal{B}| > 1$.

Also note that it is possible to devise solutions by adapting existing techniques from literature. We present one such solution here, which we call *Baseline*. For lattice traversal, Baseline adopts the strategy of *bottom-up skyline (BUS)* of Pei et al. [17], who study the problem of computing the skyline in every subspace. BUS can be extended to compute k-skyband if k is given. In each subspace, Baseline starts with $k = 1$, and computes the k-skyband and increments k, iteratively, until the k-skyband contains at least τ objects. Obviously, this iterative process of finding the right k leads to a lot of redundant computation. Our new algorithms avoid such redundant computation, and we experimentally validate their advantages over Baseline in Section 4.

2.1 Progressive Top-τ Skyband Algorithm

As it turns out, all objects of $\mathcal{O}$ in the $(k+1)$-th tier must lie on the skyline of the set of remaining objects after those in the k-skyband are taken out. This simple but useful observation has probably been made in other contexts too; we state it as a lemma here for completeness (see [23] for proof):

Lemma 1. $\mathfrak{S}^{k+1}_{\mathcal{B}}(\mathcal{O}) \setminus \mathfrak{S}^k_{\mathcal{B}}(\mathcal{O}) \subseteq \mathfrak{S}^1_{\mathcal{B}}(\mathcal{O} \setminus \mathfrak{S}^k_{\mathcal{B}}(\mathcal{O}))$.

[1] Note that tiers differ from the well-known concept of *maximal layers*, where the next maximal layer is defined as the skyline of the set of objects that are not in previous layers.

Algorithm 1: Progressive$(\mathcal{O}, \mathcal{B}, \tau)$

Data: object set $\mathcal{O}$, subspace $\mathcal{B}$, and size threshold τ
Result: $\Phi^{\tau}_{\mathcal{B}}(\mathcal{O})$
1 $\Phi \leftarrow \varnothing; k \leftarrow 0;$
2 **while true do**
3 $\quad S \leftarrow \mathfrak{S}^{1}_{\mathcal{B}}(\mathcal{O} \setminus \Phi);$
4 $\quad k' \leftarrow \min\{\delta_{\mathcal{B}}(\Phi, o) + 1 \mid o \in S\};$
5 $\quad \Delta\Phi \leftarrow \{o \in S \mid \delta_{\mathcal{B}}(\Phi, o) + 1 = k'\};$
6 $\quad$ **if** $|\Phi \cup \Delta\Phi| > \tau$ **then break**;
7 $\quad \Phi \leftarrow \Phi \cup \Delta\Phi; k \leftarrow k';$
8 **return** Φ;

Lemma 1 suggests the following strategy, which we call *Progressive* (Algorithm 1), for computing the top-τ skyband for a given subspace. Given τ, Progressive computes the answer Φ tier by tier, starting from the first. By Lemma 1, to obtain the next non-empty tier, we first compute (Line 3) the skyline S for the set of remaining objects (those outside the current Φ). Objects in the next non-empty tier ($\Delta\Phi$ on Line 5) are those in S whose dominating subsets in $\mathcal{O}$ are the smallest in size. We add this tier to Φ as long as their set union has no more than τ objects. It is easy to see that at the end of each iteration, the invariant that $\Phi = \mathfrak{S}^{k}_{\mathcal{B}}(\mathcal{O})$ holds. Progressive terminates if the addition of the next non-empty tier causes the size of Φ to exceed τ.

Note that in Lines 4 and 5 we compute the size of the dominating subset for $o \in S$ in Φ instead of $\mathcal{O}$. This optimization is correct because, being on the skyline of $\mathcal{O} \setminus \Phi$, o is not dominated by any object in $\mathcal{O} \setminus \Phi$, so $\delta_{\mathcal{B}}(\Phi, o) = \delta_{\mathcal{B}}(\mathcal{O}, o)$.

Further Optimizations For clarity of presentation, Algorithm 1 leaves out some details, which we describe below. Suppose that in the previous iteration, the skyline computed was $\bar{S}$, and $\Delta\bar{\Phi} \subseteq \bar{S}$ was added to the answer set. For the current iteration, it is easy to see that $\bar{S} \setminus \Delta\bar{\Phi} \subseteq S$; i.e., all remaining objects in $\bar{S}$ will appear again in the skyline S to be computed. This observation leads to two optimizations. **1)** We can speed up successive skyline computations on Line 3 across iterations. Specifically, we adapt the *SUBSKY* algorithm of Tao et al. [19] (in general any skyline algorithm can be used). The original SUBSKY uses an index whose size is linear in $|\mathcal{O}|$ to help compute the skyline of $\mathcal{O}$ in any subspace. During execution, SUBSKY always maintains the skyline for the subset of objects that it has examined. In our adaption of SUBSKY, we remove from (a copy of) the SUBSKY index any object added to Φ, and we "seed" each invocation of SUBSKY with $\bar{S} \setminus \Delta\bar{\Phi}$ instead of starting it with an empty skyline. **2)** We can reduce the number of dominance tests involved in determining $\delta_{\mathcal{B}}(\Phi, o)$ for $o \in S$ on Lines 4 and 5. For any $o \in \bar{S} \setminus \Delta\bar{\Phi} \subseteq S$, we have already computed $\delta_{\mathcal{B}}(\mathcal{O}, o)$ in the previous iteration, so there is no need to recompute it.

Complexity Following convention [19], we measure the performance of our algorithms by the number of dominance tests. Progressive performs two types of such tests: 1) those involved in computing the skyline of the remaining objects, and 2) those involved in computing the sizes of the dominating subsets in $\mathcal{O}$ for objects on that skyline. The number of type-1 tests depends on the skyline algorithm; Tao et al. [19] describes various techniques to reduce it for SUBSKY. However, in the worst case, $|\Phi|$ is almost τ in the final iteration, while $|S|$ can be roughly $|\mathcal{O}| - \tau$ (i.e., the next non-empty tier contains nearly all remaining objects). In this case, the total number of dominance tests would be $\Theta(|\mathcal{O}|^2)$.

2.2 One-Pass Top-τ Skyband Algorithm

Progressive has poor worst-case complexity: it computes the entire next tier in order to decide whether to add that tier to the answer, but that tier can be larger than τ. In this section, we show how to tame the complexity with another algorithm *OnePass*. This algorithm works by considering objects one by one in a particular order. Each object is either added to the answer set Φ or dropped. Once Φ has more than τ objects, the last tier is peeled off. The processing order is chosen in a "safe" way, as defined below, which allows OnePass to cap $|\Phi|$ at τ at all times, thereby bounding the number of dominance tests to $\tau|\mathcal{O}|$, in contrast to $O(|\mathcal{O}|^2)$ by Progressive.

Algorithm 2: OnePass$(\mathcal{O}, \mathcal{B}, \tau)$

Data: object set $\mathcal{O}$, subspace $\mathcal{B}$, and size threshold τ
Result: $\Phi^{\tau}_{\mathcal{B}}(\mathcal{O})$
1 $\Phi \leftarrow \varnothing; k \leftarrow \tau;$
2 **foreach** $o \in \mathcal{O}$ *in safe order (Definition 4)* **do**
3 $\quad c[o] \leftarrow 0;$ *// count the number of objects in Φ dominating o*
4 $\quad$ **foreach** $o' \in \Phi$ **do** *// heuristically in ascending order of $c[o']$*
5 $\quad\quad$ **if** $o' \succ_{\mathcal{B}} o$ **then** $c[o] \leftarrow c[o] + 1;$
6 $\quad\quad$ **if** $c[o] \geq k$ **then break**; *// no need to count further*
7 $\quad$ **if** $c[o] < k$ **then**
8 $\quad\quad \Phi \leftarrow \Phi \cup \{o\};$
9 $\quad\quad$ **if** $|\Phi| > \tau$ **then** *// Φ is too big; remove the last tier*
10 $\quad\quad\quad k \leftarrow \max\{c[o'] \mid o' \in \Phi\};$
11 $\quad\quad\quad \Phi \leftarrow \Phi \setminus \{o' \in \Phi \mid c[o'] = k\};$
12 $\quad\quad\quad$ **if** $k = 0$ **then break**;
13 **return** Φ;

Definition 4 (Safe Order [2]). *An order for a set $\mathcal{O}$ of objects is* safe *(for OnePass) if o' precedes o whenever $o' \succ_{\mathcal{B}} o$.*

Algorithm 2 describes OnePass. The details of implementing the safe order will be given later in this section. Here, we first explain the algorithm and establish its correctness, the crux of which is captured by the lemma below (see [23] for proof).

Lemma 2. *The following invariants are true at the end of each iteration of OnePass's main loop, where $\mathcal{O}^{\star}$ denotes the set of all objects processed so far.*

(I-1) For all $o' \in \Phi$, $c[o'] = \delta_{\mathcal{B}}(\mathcal{O}, o')$.

(I-2) $\Phi = \mathfrak{S}^{k}_{\mathcal{B}}(\mathcal{O}^{\star})$.

(I-3) $|\mathfrak{S}^{k+1}_{\mathcal{B}}(\mathcal{O})| > \tau$ (if $|\mathcal{O}| > \tau$).

Consider the next object o in the safe order. OnePass first checks whether o is dominated by at least k objects in Φ (Lines 3–6). If yes, o is ignored because it would be in the $(k+1)$-th or later tier (by (I-1)) and therefore cannot be in $\Phi^{\tau}_{\mathcal{B}}(\mathcal{O})$ (by (I-3)). We stop counting as soon as $c[o]$ reaches k. Heuristically, we check o against "better" objects in Φ (i.e., those with smaller dominating sets) first, in hope of reaching k sooner with fewer dominance tests.

If $c[o] < k$, OnePass adds o to Φ (Lines 8) and remember the count $c[o]$. If doing so makes $|\Phi|$ exceed τ we remove the last tier from Φ and update k accordingly (Lines 9–11), to preserve (I-2) and (I-3). If k drops to 0 (Line 12), that means even the skyline has size bigger than τ (by (I-3)), so we can terminate (and return $\varnothing$) without processing the remaining objects. After all objects in $\mathcal{O}$ are processed, Φ is the top-τ skyband of $\mathcal{O}$ in $\mathcal{B}$, by (I-2) and (I-3).

Producing a Safe Order The simplest approach for OnePass to produce a safe processing order is to sort $\mathcal{O}$ by $\mathcal{B}$ (lexicographically, with an arbitrary ordering among the attributes), which takes $O(|\mathcal{O}| \log |\mathcal{O}|)$ time. To avoid the cost of a full sort, we precompute, for each of the d attributes in $\mathcal{A}$, a version of $\mathcal{O}$ sorted by that attribute. Given a subspace $\mathcal{B}$, OnePass picks the attribute $A \in \mathcal{B}$ with the largest domain (a heuristic also adopted in [2, 17]), and

[2] Note that a safe order is equivalent to a topological order.

use the version of $\mathcal{O}$ sorted by A. During processing, if OnePass finds that a group of objects tie in A, OnePass further sorts this group by the full $\mathcal{B}$. As a further optimization, before sorting this group, OnePass first performs Lines 3–6 on each object o in the group, and removes those with $c[o] \geq k$; the filtered group is then sorted and further processed. In the worst case, OnePass still needs to pay $O(|\mathcal{O}| \log |\mathcal{O}|)$ for sorting. In practice, however, we have found our heuristics effective in eliminating sorting, because most ties tend to occur later in processing; by that time, most objects will be eliminated by Lines 3–6. Furthermore, the cost of filtering is low because τ and k are typically small.

Complexity Because OnePass caps $|\Phi|$ at τ at all times, the number of dominance tests is bounded by $\tau|\mathcal{O}|$. As explained above, sorting adds $O(|\mathcal{O}| \log |\mathcal{O}|)$ in the worst case, though in practice the extra cost is rarely incurred. Furthermore, in high-dimensional subspaces, k decreases rapidly as OnePass examines more objects. It is likely that an object will be discarded after a few dominance tests. OnePass also detects the case when the size of the skyline would exceed τ, and is able to terminate without examining the whole $\mathcal{O}$. Thus, OnePass is expected to run faster in practice than the bound suggests, particularly for high-dimensional subspaces.

2.3 Lattice Traversal

Finding all interesting one-of-the-few claims requires computing Φ^τ in every non-empty subspace. We now describe, on a high level, how to accomplish this task using either Progressive or OnePass as the building block; details can be found in [23].

For Progressive, computation in every subspace starts with finding the skyline. For this part, we directly apply the techniques of Pei et al. [17], who study the problem of computing the skyline in every subspace. Their techniques traverse the lattice of subspaces in either bottom-up or top-down order, and try to share computation across subspaces. For a given subspace $\mathcal{B}$, once we have computed the skyline using these techniques, we proceed with Progressive to compute the rest of Φ^τ as discussed in Section 2.1.

For OnePass, we traverse the lattice of subspaces top-down, i.e., going from low- to high-dimensional subspaces. We use the top-down technique from Pei et al. [17] to help compute the skyline in a subspace using those found in its parent subspaces. Moreover, we use the Φ^τ in parent subspaces to fine-tune the safe processing order in the current subspace.

Furthermore, during a top-down lattice traversal, we use two tests to prune uninteresting high-dimensional subspaces from the search. 1) If the "distinct-count" of skyline objects in $\mathcal{B}$ (i.e., the number of distinct projections onto $\mathcal{B}$) is greater than τ, Φ^τ must be empty for all descendant subspaces. 2) Given $\mathcal{B}$, if the union of skyline objects from parent subspaces already contains more than τ objects, $\Phi^\tau_\mathcal{B}(\mathcal{O})$ must be empty.

3 Ranking Objects

This section presents our solution for ranking the set $\mathcal{O}$ of objects with attributes $\mathcal{A}$, based on what one-of-the-few claims can be made about them across subspaces, and how interesting these claims are. Section 3.1 proposes a novel scoring scheme that captures varying user preferences with a single parameter, while Section 3.2 describes how the algorithms in Section 2 can be leveraged to compute top-ranked objects.

3.1 Scoring Objects

A common approach for ranking a set $\mathcal{O}$ of objects (e.g., political candidates) is to combine multiple ranked lists of them (e.g., by voters). Traditionally, the scores for objects in a single list are assigned according to a *positional scoring vector (or function)* [25], v, which maps a rank i ($1 \leq i \leq |\mathcal{O}|$) to a numeric score $v(i)$, such that $v(i) \geq v(i+1)$. Some examples include *Borda*, where $v(i) = |\mathcal{O}| - i$, and *Plurality*, where $v(1) = 1$ and $v(i) = 0$ for $i > 1$. Then, the overall object ranking is done according to the aggregate score of each object, usually defined as the sum of its scores across all ranked lists.

A straightforward approach would be to have one ranked list of $\mathcal{O}$ by each attribute in $\mathcal{A}$, and sum up an object's scores across these lists. However, this approach has serious drawbacks, particularly in handling data with correlation. Suppose o_1 is ranked high for two correlated attributes (e.g., contributions from finance and real estate sectors, or minutes played and points scored), while o_2 is ranked equally high in two anti-correlated attributes (e.g., contributions from oil companies and environmental groups, or rebounds and assists). Since it is harder to rank high for two anti-correlated attributes, we should score o_2 higher than o_1 overall. However, the approach of summing scores over individual attributes will assign the same score to o_1 and o_2 (assuming all other factors are equal).

All-Subspace Positional Scoring with Ties (APST) To resolve the issue above, we propose *All-Subspace Positional Scoring with Ties*. The key novelty is to aggregate object scores not just across individual attributes, but instead over all non-empty subspaces. The dominance relationship in a multi-dimensional subspace $\mathcal{B}$ likely does not induce a totally ranked list; hence, we draw insight from Section 2 to score objects using the partial order in a way that reflects the uniqueness of one-of-the-few claims in $\mathcal{B}$. The result is a scoring scheme that naturally adapts to data distributions.

Definition 5 (All-Subspace Positional Scoring with Ties (APST)). *For each non-empty subspace $\mathcal{B} \subseteq \mathcal{A}$, sort $\mathcal{O}$ in non-descending order of $\delta_\mathcal{B}(\mathcal{O}, o)$, the size of the dominating subset for each $o \in \mathcal{O}$; ties are broken arbitrarily. Denote this ranking by $\pi_\mathcal{B}$, where $\pi_\mathcal{B}(o) \in [1, |\mathcal{O}|]$ is the rank of o in this ranking. Let $[\pi^\vdash_\mathcal{B}(o), \pi^\dashv_\mathcal{B}(o)]$ denote the range of ranks occupied by objects that tie with o in $\delta_\mathcal{B}(\mathcal{O}, o)$; i.e., $\pi^\vdash_\mathcal{B}(o) = \min\{\pi_\mathcal{B}(o') \mid \delta_\mathcal{B}(\mathcal{O}, o') = \delta_\mathcal{B}(\mathcal{O}, o)\}$ and $\pi^\dashv_\mathcal{B}(o) = \max\{\pi_\mathcal{B}(o') \mid \delta_\mathcal{B}(\mathcal{O}, o') = \delta_\mathcal{B}(\mathcal{O}, o)\}$. Given a positional scoring function v where $v(1) > v(2) > \cdots > v(|\mathcal{O}|)$, the* (APST) score of object *o in $\mathcal{B}$, denoted $\gamma_\mathcal{B}(o)$, is given by:*

$$\gamma_\mathcal{B}(o) = \frac{1}{\pi^\dashv_\mathcal{B}(o) - \pi^\vdash_\mathcal{B}(o) + 1} \cdot \sum_{i \in [\pi^\vdash_\mathcal{B}(o), \pi^\dashv_\mathcal{B}(o)]} v(i).$$

Overall, the APST *score of o, denoted $\Gamma(o)$, is the total of o's score over all non-empty subspaces: $\Gamma(o) = \sum_{\mathcal{B} \subseteq \mathcal{A}, \mathcal{B} \neq \varnothing} \gamma_\mathcal{B}(o)$.*

Intuitively, for each subspace $\mathcal{B}$, APST sorts objects by tiers, and each tier occupies a range of ranks. The total score assigned by v to such a range of ranks is distributed equally among objects in the corresponding tier, as we consider them ties in $\mathcal{B}$. The larger the tier, the less "unique" each object, and the smaller the share each object will receive. A number of desirable properties follow directly from the definition. For example, APST favors tiers that are smaller in size or occupy earlier ranges of ranks; see [23] for a more formal discussion.

Furthermore, aggregating scores over combinations of attributes make APST naturally adaptive to correlations in data. Consider again the example earlier in this section, where o_1 is ranked high for two correlated attributes $\{A_1, B_1\}$ and o_2 is ranked equally high in two anti-correlated attributes $\{A_2, B_2\}$. Since it is rare to rank high for anti-correlated attributes, few objects will be in o_2's tier or an earlier tier in $\{A_2, B_2\}$; therefore, APST will score o_2 high in $\{A_2, B_2\}$. On the other hand, for o_1, since A_1 and B_2 are correlated, there will likely be more objects dominating o_1 in $\{A_1, B_1\}$ than those dominating o_2 in $\{A_2, B_2\}$. Thus, all other factors being equal, APST will score o_2 higher than o_1 overall.

Adjustable Discounted APST (APST-α) What remains to be discussed is the choice of the positional scoring function v. To make our scoring scheme easy to use, we have so far consciously avoided introducing any tuning parameters. However, as motivated in Example 3, we would like some degree of customization for ranking "specialized" objects relative to "well-rounded" ones. Recall that a specialized object is exceptional in few attributes (such as Stockton in assists), while a well-rounded object is exceptional in none, but reasonably good in many, so as to be exceptional when all those attributes are combined (such as Bird). To capture user's wide ranging preferences for one or the other, we design our positional scoring function with a single tunable parameter to achieve that flexibility while retaining APST's desirable properties.

Definition 6 (Adjustable Discounted APST (APST-α))**.** *Let* α *be a real number in* $(0, 1)$*. The* adjustable discounted APST (APST-α) score *of an object* $o \in \mathcal{O}$ *is* o*'s APST score with positional scoring function* $v_\alpha(i) = \alpha^{i-1}$.

Intuitively, the discounting factor, α, controls how much more higher ranked objects weigh against lower ranked objects, thereby affecting how specialized and well-rounded objects score relatively overall. In a higher-dimensional subspace $\mathcal{B}$, tiers tend to be larger. Hence, an object that is dominated by few others in $\mathcal{B}$ (but by more objects in subsets of $\mathcal{B}$) tend to score lower in $\mathcal{B}$, compared with an object with the same number of dominating objects in a lower-dimensional subspace $\mathcal{B}'$. With a smaller α, the score gap is wider, so overall, it is more difficult for well-rounded objects to surpass specialized ones, whose scores come mostly from contributions by low-dimensional subspaces. In Section 4, we will see how effective α is as a tuning knob on real data—compared with weighted-sum (discussed in Section 1), APST-α has only 1 knob instead of d, but produces comparable rankings as highly tuned weighted-sum.

Comparison with Kemeny Optimal Rank Aggregation In addition to flexible approaches where users are allowed to specify their preferences, studies in social choice theory have also investigated an alternative where some notion of "optimality" is defined for the resulting ranks. A popular representative of this approach is *Kemeny (optimal rank aggregation)*. As discussed in Section 1, given a set of rankings for $\mathcal{O}$, a Kemeny optimal rank aggregation is a ranking that minimizes the total number of pairwise disagreements between this ranking and the input rankings.

One natural way to use Kemeny is to apply it to the d rankings according to the individual attributes in $\mathcal{A}$. This approach, which we call *Kemeny-d*, has several issues. First, finding a Kemeny optimal aggregation is NP-hard in $|\mathcal{O}|$ [7]. We would prefer an approach that is computationally more tractable. Indeed, ranking objects using APST-α has complexity polynomial in $|\mathcal{O}|$.

Second, by definition, Kemeny-d is strongly biased against specialized objects, which rank high in few attributes but low in many, because ranking them high overall will incur many disagreements. As discussed in Section 1 following Example 3, based on points, rebounds, and assists per game, Kemeny-d would rank John Stockton low, even though he is a Hall-of-Famer who has the second highest assists per game in NBA history. In contrast, with a small α, APST-α would rank it high, because it likely lies on a small skyband for roughly half of the $2^d - 1$ non-empty subspaces—namely those containing the attribute in which the object specializes.

Third, Kemeny-d sometimes fails to suggest a rank for a worthy object p. More precisely, there may be many consensus rankings that are all optimal in the Kemeny sense, where p is ranked differently, sometimes below objects that can be considered obviously inferior to p. For an illustrative example, as well as how APST-α avoids this issue, see [23].

Fourth, Kemeny-d does not allow for customization—if it fails to recognize a worthy object there is little that a user can do. On the other hand, the discounting factor α in APST-α provides a single, effective knob that allows users to choose their preference between specialized and well-rounded objects. Indeed, we have seen from above how the choice of α helps overcome the issues faced by Kemeny. More detailed results on real data are shown in Section 4.

Finally, instead of Kemeny-d, it is conceivable to use Kemeny to aggregate all $2^d - 1$ rankings according to all non-empty subsets of attributes in $\mathcal{A}$.[3] We are not aware of any previous work exploring this approach. While this approach could potentially alleviate the second and third issues above, it still suffers from the first (high computational complexity) and last (lack of any customization). This approach would require the same amount of effort as APST-α just to prepare the $2^d - 1$ input rankings in all subspaces; then, its rank aggregation is more expensive and not tunable.

3.2 Finding Top κ Objects

Computing the exact APST-α scores of all objects in subspace entails computing $\delta_{\mathcal{B}}(\mathcal{O}, o)$ for all $o \in \mathcal{O}$ and non-empty $\mathcal{B} \subseteq \mathcal{A}$, which takes $O(2^d|\mathcal{O}|^2)$ time using a naive algorithm. However, for the purpose of identifying objects most worthy of further investigation, we care only about the top-ranked objects. This observation leads to the following problem definition:

Definition 7 (Finding Top κ Objects)**.** *Given a set* $\mathcal{O}$ *of objects, a discounting factor* $\alpha \in (0, 1)$*, and* $\kappa \geq 1$*, find the top* κ *objects in* $\mathcal{O}$ *ranked by APST-*α *scores.*

We show how to extend the algorithms in Section 2 to efficiently compute approximate answers to the above question. We provide only high-level insights here; see [23] for a full discussion with more technical details. The key observation is that, in each subspace, we need to compute only enough number of tiers in order to not miss any top objects overall, because score contributions from memberships in subsequent tiers are so small that they have little influence over whether an object can be in the top κ overall.

Given an error tolerance $\epsilon > 0$, we can compute a list of objects, where each object o gets an approximate score $\tilde{\Gamma}(o) \in (\Gamma(o) - \epsilon, \Gamma(o)]$. Roughly speaking, we divide the error tolerance ϵ among the subspaces to be considered. Within a subspace $\mathcal{B}$ with share $\epsilon_{\mathcal{B}}$ of error tolerance, we use Progressive or OnePass to "grow" the skyband up to some top-τ skyband such that any object outside it will receive a score below $\epsilon_{\mathcal{B}}$ in $\mathcal{B}$. We add the objects in this skyband to the output list (or update their scores if they are already in it). With some care, we can ensure that OnePass retains its advantage over Progressive; i.e., it avoids computing the entire "next" tier, which could include all remaining objects. The idea is that we only need to see enough number of objects in this tier before knowing that all its objects must score below $\epsilon_{\mathcal{B}}$, because APST scores get "diluted" by larger tiers. When we are done with $\mathcal{B}$, we can derive a tighter bound (hopefully much less than $\epsilon_{\mathcal{B}}$) for errors in $\mathcal{B}$, and use it to update the error tolerance for remaining subspaces.

The user does not need to choose ϵ manually. A reasonable default is $\alpha^{\kappa-1}$, the value of the positional scoring function at rank κ. With this setting, we can guarantee that any object not in the output list cannot be among the top κ overall. The output list may contain more than κ objects, and ϵ can be used to determine which part of this ranking is guaranteed to be accurate. As future work, we are developing an "online" version of the algorithm where ϵ is incrementally tightened when given additional time or until the top κ objects can be accurately separated from the rest.

[3] More precisely, such rankings are partial orders induced by skyband tiers in their respective subspaces; Kemeny readily generalizes to partial orders.

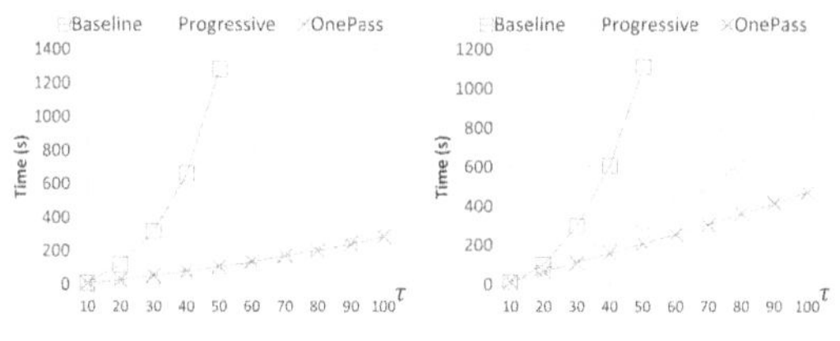

(a) NBA1 (b) NBA3

Figure 2: Running time on NBA1, NBA3 (varying τ).

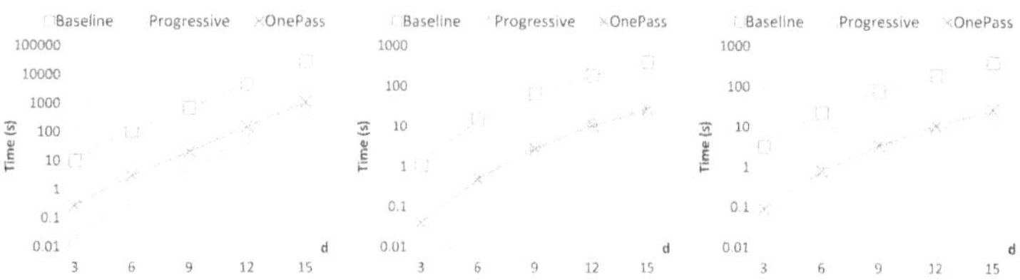

(a) CORR (b) ANTICORR (c) IND

Figure 3: Running time on synthetic data (varying d).

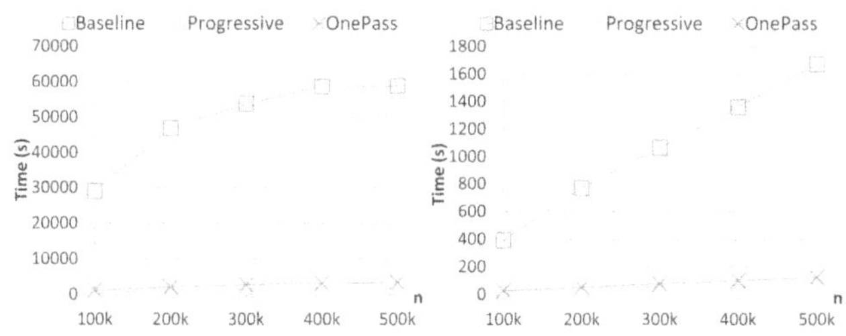

(a) CORR (b) IND

Figure 4: Running time on synthetic data (varying n).

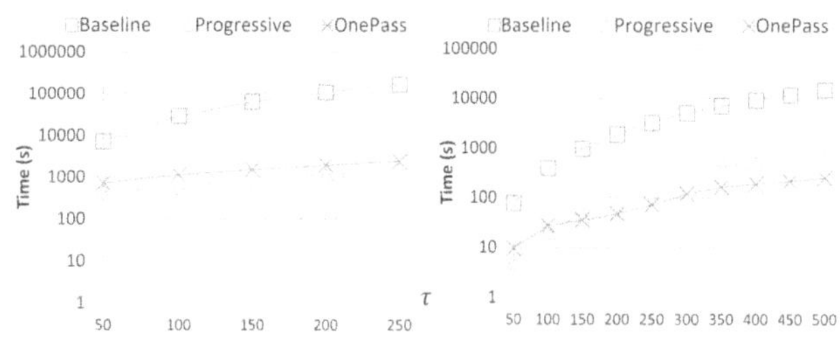

(a) CORR (b) IND

Figure 5: Running time on synthetic data (varying τ).

4 Experiments

All algorithms were implemented in C++ and tested on a machine with Intel Core i7-2600 3.4GHz processor and 7.8GB memory.

We use three datasets on NBA players.[4] **NBA1** contains the *career total* statistics for $n \approx$ 4K players. There are $d = 15$ performance attributes, including the total *number of games played*, *points*, *rebounds*, etc., over the players' whole careers. **NBA2** contains the *career average* statistics for the same set of $n \approx$ 4K players. It has the same set of attributes as NBA1 except *number of games played* (hence $d = 14$), and the attribute values for a player are derived by dividing the corresponding values in NBA1 by the number of games played by the player. **NBA3** contains the game-by-game statistics for each player. There are a total of $n \approx$ 400K records with $d = 14$ performance attributes.

We also use synthetic datasets to test algorithm performance—correlated (**CORR**), anti-correlated (**ANTICORR**), and independent (**IND**), with varying size and dimensionality. CORR and ANTICORR are generated by first sampling data points randomly from a multivariate Gaussian distribution; then, we stretch all points in the direction of $(1, 1, \ldots, 1)$ to produce CORR, and we shrink them in the direction of $(1, 1, \ldots, 1)$ to yield ANTICORR. This way, the attributes are pairwise correlated or anti-correlated.

Additional results are in [23], including those on the National Research Council survey of 127 computer science programs.

4.1 Efficiency of Top-τ Skyband Algorithms

Given a dataset, a particular τ value, and an algorithm, we use the algorithm to find the top-τ skyband for each and every subspace. The total elapsed time for the $2^d - 1$ nonempty subspaces measures the algorithm's efficiency. We compare Baseline (Section 2), Progressive (Algorithm 1), and OnePass (Algorithm 2).

4.1.1 Efficiency on Real Datasets

Figure 2 shows the execution time of Baseline, Progressive, and OnePass, under varying $\tau = 10, 20, \ldots, 100$, on both NBA1 ($n =$ 4K) and NBA3 ($n =$ 400K). On both the small and large datasets, our algorithms significantly outperform the baseline approach.

On the small NBA1 dataset (Figure 2(a)), OnePass is less efficient for small τ and starts to outperform Progressive as τ increases. The reason is that the dimensionalities of subspaces in which top-τ skyband is empty but cannot be pruned (by techniques in Section 2.3) increase with τ. Computing the skylines for these subspaces gets more expensive as SUBSKY becomes less efficient. Results on NBA2 are similar to NBA1 and hence omitted.

On the large NBA3 dataset (Figure 2(b)), we also see that the running time of Progressive grows faster than OnePass as τ increases, for the same reason above. Moreover, attributes in NBA3 have smaller correlations than in NBA1, which induce larger skylines, making Progressive even less efficient. Hence, OnePass starts to outperform Progressive when τ is small.

On both datasets, we observe the running time of OnePass to be roughly linear in τ, confirming the analysis in Section 2.2.

4.1.2 Efficiency on Synthetic Datasets

Varying d, Fixed $n =$ 100K and $\tau = 100$: Figure 3 shows that both Progressive and OnePass are faster than Baseline by orders of magnitude (vertical axis has logarithmic scale). Progressive runs faster than OnePass on correlated data (a). Their performances are comparable on anti-correlated (b) and independent data (c). We observe that the running times on CORR are much longer than those on ANTICORR and IND for all algorithms. The reason is that top-τ skybands in CORR may be non-empty even in high dimensional subspaces, while for ANTICORR and IND, they tend to be empty and can be quickly detected and pruned as discussed in Section 2.3. When the dimensionality is high, due to the way ANTICORR is generated for ensuring pairwise anti-correlation among all attributes, ANTICORR becomes similar to IND; hence, we omit the results on ANTICORR in the following discussion.

Varying n, Fixed $d = 15$ and $\tau = 100$: From Figure 4, we observe again that Progressive and OnePass outperform Baseline by orders of magnitude, and Progressive slightly outperforms OnePass. Their running times increase roughly linearly by n.

Varying τ, Fixed $n =$ 100K and $d = 15$: Figure 5 shows that Progressive and OnePass significantly outperform Baseline on both CORR and IND. For all three algorithms, their running times grow nearly exponentially in τ (vertical axis has logarithmic scale). Progressive is slightly faster than OnePass on CORR. On IND, OnePass is slower than Progressive under small τ but becomes faster as τ increases.

[4] `http://www.databasebasketball.com/`

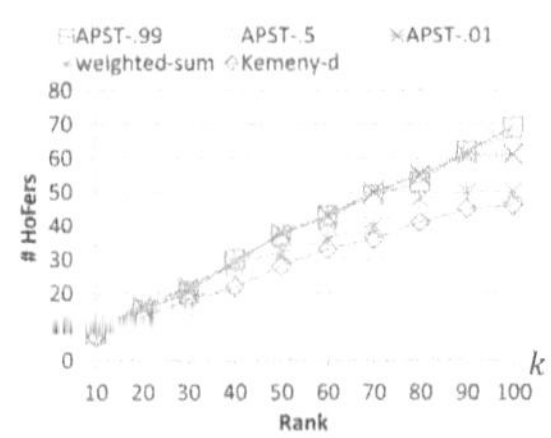

Figure 6: Comparison of rankings by number of HoFers in top-k.

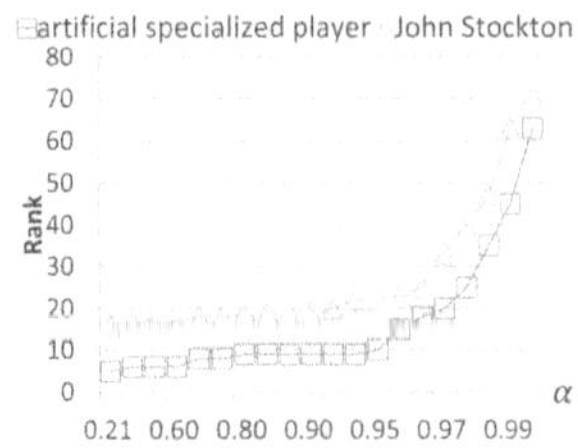

Figure 7: Ranks of an artificial player vs. Stockton as α varies.

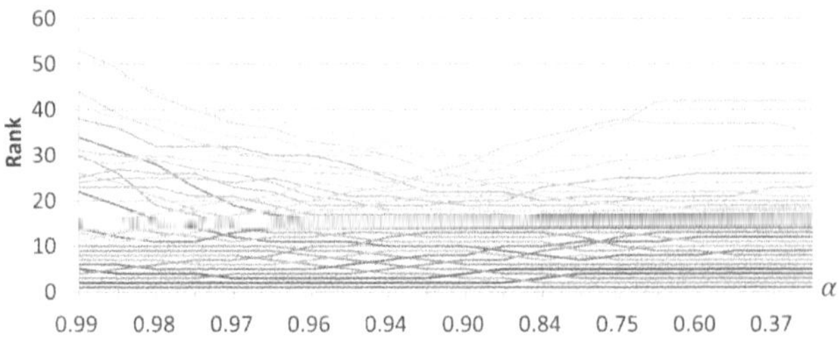

Figure 8: Effect of α on the APST-α ranking of NBA players.

Overall, these experiments further confirm the significant performance advantage of Progressive and OnePass over Baseline.

4.2 Quality of Ranking by APST-α

We evaluate the quality of the rankings by APST-α, Kemeny-d, and weighted-sum for the NBA2 dataset (career average statistics). For each ranking, we measure its quality by the number of Hall of Fame inductees (HoFers for short) found among the top-k players according the the ranking, under various k values.

We use 7 out of the 14 attributes in NBA2 for ranking because the dataset did not record statistics such as *steals*, *blocks*, and *minutes* for games played before 1971. Including these attributes would unfairly underrate the players from the early days. We do not use NBA1 (career total performance) because it would also underrate earlier players, as they did not play as many games as recent ones.

APST-α vs. Weighted-Sum We vary α in APST-α to produce different rankings. For weighted-sum, the weights on the attributes are determined as follows. We first find a linear classifier to separate HoFers from non-HoFers that minimizes the number of inaccurately classified players. We then use the unit vector perpendicular to the linear classifier as the weight vector in weighted-sum.

Figure 6 compares weighted-sum, APST-.99, APST-.5, and APST-.01, by the numbers of HoFers found among the top k players in their rankings, respectively (ignore the curve for Kemeny-d for now). We can see that APST-α contains visibly more HoFers in top-k under most combinations of α and k considered. Note that the performance of all ranking methods are negatively affected by active players who would be good candidate HoFers in the future, but will not be eligible until 5 years after retirement.[5] For example, at $k = 80$, the top k players identified by weighted-sum include 48 HoFers. Among the remaining 32, 23 are not yet eligible; 9 are eligible but not HoFers.

APST-α vs. Kemeny-d For Kemeny-d, solving for the optimal ranking proved computationally challenging on this real dataset, reinforcing our discussion in Section 3.1. We model the optimization as an integer program (IP) and solve it with CPLEX.[6] Recall that there are about 4K players. On our reasonably powerful machine, CPLEX caused memory overflow with close to 300 players, and it failed to find solutions with more than 200 players because of precision issues. Thus, we improvise by first identifying 200 players, who are the set union of the 7 top-40 lists for the 7 attributes used for ranking. Then, we run Kemeny-d on these 200 players only.

In Figure 6, we can see that in most cases APST-α rankings contain noticeably more HoFers in top-k than Kemeny-d. The scale limitation Kemeny-d is to blame: there are 91 HoFers in the 4K players in NBA2, but only 59 of them are among those 200 considered by Kemeny-d. In contrast, APST-α and weighted-sum have been computed over all 4K players. For comparison disregarding Kemeny's scale limitation, we have also used APST-α to rank the same subset of 200 players; in that case APST-α and Kemeny-d showed comparable performance (see [23] for results).

4.3 Effect of α in APST-α

To understand how the parameter α in APST-α helps in promoting specialized vs. well-rounded objects, we inject an artificial player into NBA2. Again, we use 7 attributes, as explained in Section 4.2. This artificial player has the highest *points* but the lowest values for all other attributes. Figure 7 shows how this player's rank changes in the APST-α ranking when α varies. As α decreases from 1, the artificial player quickly gets ranked high among real players. Its rank converges as α approaches 0, but never becomes the first because it cannot surpass real players who have the highest values on some other attributes. We have observed similar behaviors when the artificial player specializes in other attributes. This result agrees with the discussion in Section 3 that a smaller α favors specialized objects over well-rounded ones. An example of a specialized player is John Stockton, a HoFer, who is second only to Magic Johnson in assists per game, but is not ranked high in any other attributes considered. His ranks under various α values are also plotted in Figure 7, which show a similar trend to that for the artificial player.

In Figure 8, we focus on the top 30 players bound by APST-.9 in NBA2, under the three attributes: *points*, *rebounds*, and *assists*. The figure shows how their ranking positions change by α (horizontal axis has logarithmic scale). At the bottom of the figure, the top 9 players always remain in the top 13, because of their exceptional performance in multiple attributes. The ranks of the remaining players respond well to changes in α. We can categorize these players into two types: I) specialized players, who are exceptional on very few attributes; II) well-rounded players, who are not exceptional on any single attribute, but are reasonably good on multiple attributes. In Figure 8, the curves of Type-I players go down as α decreases, because small α favors them more against other players in at least half of the subspaces, i.e., those containing the attribute on which they specialize. On the contrary, the curves of Type-II players go up as α decreases. They get rewarded in higher-dimensional subspaces for not being dominated by many players in such subspaces, while they can be easily dominated by others on individual dimensions.

For a concrete example, consider the lowest-ranked players at largest and smallest α, respectively. The lowest ranked curve (53rd) at the largest α (on the leftmost) corresponds to Nate Thurmond, a HoFer, ranked 277th in *points*, 6th in *rebounds*, and 579th in *assists*. As a representative Type-I player, when α decreases, his overall rank becomes higher, ending eventually at 18th. In contrast, the lowest ranked player (42nd) at the smallest α, Charles Barkley (another HoFer), ranked 33rd, 23rd, and 223rd respectively in *points*, *rebounds*, and *assists*. As a representative Type-II player, when α decreases, his rank goes all the way down from 11th. A tunable α thus allows a user to specify personal preference between Thurmond and Barkley effectively.

[5] For weighted-sum, we excluded these players when training the weight vector, but included them in ranking as with other methods.

[6] `http://www.ibm.com/software/integration/optimization/cplex-optimizer/`

5 Related Work

Our work is closely related to skyline computation for multidimensional data, which can be roughly grouped into two classes. The first class [3, 4, 8] includes Block Nested Loop (BNL), Divide and Conquer (D&C) and their variants, and do not require precomputed indices. The second class [18, 11, 15] adopts B^+-tree or R-tree indices to prune unnecessary computation. Skyline computation for multiple (or all) subspaces are first studied by Pei et al. [17] (BUS and TDS algorithms) and by Tao et al. [19] (SUBSKY algorithm). The former are extensions of BNL and D&C algorithms that traverse the subspace lattice without using indices, while the latter follows the index-based approaches. Extending skyline to k-skyband was first studied in [15].

While our notion of top-τ skyband is the first to provide a universal parameter suitable for selecting the right set of objects regardless of the subspaces being considered, there are previous works proposing various advanced selection criteria when the size of the skyline is too large. For example, BBS [15] and PBT [24] focus on selecting points that dominate the most other points, and Lin et al. [13] focus on selecting a fixed sized set of points that collectively dominate the most other points. More recently, Lu et al. [14] propose the notion of layered skylines, where each layer is defined as the skyline after objects in previous layers are removed. Compared with these works, we believe our notion of top-τ skyband is more appealing in terms of usability, because it has a simple interpretation and a single parameter works across all subspaces.

Linear ranking of objects for the purpose of answering top-k queries has been studied extensively, including approaches using skyline and skybands [21, 22]. These studies focus on performance improvements and do not consider providing better control of the semantics of the ranking functions. Kemeny ranking [7], on the other hand, was proposed in social choice theory and offer good semantics. As discussed in Section 3.1, however, it does not provide a flexible knob, such as our α parameter, for adjusting the ranking based on the users' preference towards different types of interesting objects. Moreover, computing Kemeny is NP-hard.

Several lines of work on data mining, to various extents, share our focus on finding interesting claims that can be translated to simple, intuitive English statements. Local pattern discovery [26, 20] and subgroup discovery [12, 10] aim to find semantically describable subsets of data whose properties deviate strongly from the overall distribution. However, our subsets of interest, based on dominance, do not fit in their frameworks. Redescription mining [16] seeks to describe a given subset of data using a sequence of set operations. In contrast, we mine the subset in the first place, and our desired description of the subset involves dominance and counting instead. [9] finds "prominent streaks" (consecutive high/low values in a data sequence) and captures the significance of such streaks by skyline dominance test on streak length and value.

6 Conclusion

The tasks of finding one-of-the-few claims from data and ranking objects by such claims are important to the nascent field of computational journalism. We have introduced a simple and intuitive problem formulation for finding all interesting claims, using a single uniqueness threshold τ that automatically adapts to data characteristics and applies to all subspaces. We have proposed a novel scheme for ranking objects, overcoming the inflexibility of Kemeny without resorting to a large number of knobs like weighted-sum. We have devised efficient algorithms for both tasks, using techniques such as pruning and approximation to tame complexity. We believe that our attention to usability will appeal to journalists and citizens alike.

Acknowledgments Y.W., P.K.A., and J.Y. are supported by NSF grants CNS-05-40347 and IIS-07-13498. P.K.A. is additionally supported by NSF grants CCF-06-35000, CCF-09-40671, CCF-10-12254, by ARO grants W911NF-07-1-0376 and W911NF-08-1-0452, and by an ARL award W9132V-11-C-0003. J.Y. is additionally supported by NSF grant IIS-09-16027. C.L. is supported by NSF Grants IIS-10-18865 and CCF-11-17369. Both J.Y. and C.L. are also supported by HP Labs Innovation Research Awards.

References

[1] J. Bentley, H. Kung, M. Schkolnick, and C. Thompson. On the average number of maxima in a set of vectors and applications. *JACM*, 25(4):536–543, 1978.

[2] K. Beyer and R. Ramakrishnan. Bottom-up computation of sparse and iceberg cube. *ACM SIGMOD Record*, 28(2):359–370, 1999.

[3] S. Börzsönyi, D. Kossmann, and K. Stocker. The skyline operator. In *ICDE*, 2001.

[4] J. Chomicki, P. Godfrey, J. Gryz, and D. Liang. Skyline with presorting. In *ICDE*, 2003.

[5] S. Cohen, J. T. Hamilton, and F. Turner. Computational journalism. *Communications of the ACM*, 54(10):66–71, 2011.

[6] S. Cohen, C. Li, J. Yang, and C. Yu. Computational journalism: A call to arms to database researchers. In *CIDR*, 2011.

[7] C. Dwork, R. Kumar, M. Naor, and D. Sivakumar. Rank aggregation methods for the web. In *WWW*, 2001.

[8] P. Godfrey, R. Shipley, and J. Gryz. Maximal vector computation in large data sets. In *VLDB*, 2005.

[9] X. Jiang, C. Li, P. Luo, M. Wang, and Y. Yu. Prominent streak discovery in sequence data. In *KDD*, pages 1280–1288, 2011.

[10] B. Kavšek, N. Lavrač, and V. Jovanoski. Apriori-sd: Adapting association rule learning to subgroup discovery. *Advances in Intelligent Data Analysis V*, pages 230–241, 2003.

[11] D. Kossmann, F. Ramsak, and S. Rost. Shooting stars in the sky: An online algorithm for skyline queries. In *VLDB*, 2002.

[12] N. Lavrač, F. Železný, and P. Flach. Rsd: Relational subgroup discovery through first-order feature construction. *Inductive Logic Programming*, pages 149–165, 2003.

[13] X. Lin, Y. Yuan, Q. Zhang, and Y. Zhang. Selecting stars: The k most representative skyline operator. In *ICDE*, 2007.

[14] H. Lu, C. Jensen, and Z. Zhang. Skyline ordering: A flexible framework for efficient resolution of size constraints on skyline queries. Technical report, Aalborg University, 2010.

[15] D. Papadias, Y. Tao, G. Fu, and B. Seeger. Progressive skyline computation in database systems. *TODS*, 30(1):41–82, 2005.

[16] L. Parida and N. Ramakrishnan. Redescription mining: Structure theory and algorithms. *AAAI*, 20(2):837, 2005.

[17] J. Pei, Y. Yuan, X. Lin, W. Jin, M. Ester, Q. Liu, W. Wang, Y. Tao, J. Yu, and Q. Zhang. Towards multidimensional subspace skyline analysis. *TODS*, 31(4):1335–1381, 2006.

[18] K. Tan, P. Eng, B. Ooi, et al. Efficient progressive skyline computation. In *VLDB*, 2001.

[19] Y. Tao, X. Xiao, and J. Pei. Subsky: Efficient computation of skylines in subspaces. In *ICDE*, 2006.

[20] Y. Tian, G. Weiss, D. Hsu, and Q. Ma. A combinatorial fusion method for feature mining. In *KDD*, volume 7, 2007.

[21] P. Tsaparas, T. Palpanas, Y. Kotidis, N. Koudas, and D. Srivastava. Ranked join indices. In *ICDE*, 2003.

[22] A. Vlachou, C. Doulkeridis, K. Nørvåg, and M. Vazirgiannis. Skyline-based peer-to-peer top-k query processing. In *ICDE*, 2008.

[23] Y. Wu, P. K. Agarwal, C. Li, J. Yang, and C. Yu. On "one of the few" objects. Technical report, Duke University, Feb. 2012. `http://www.cs.duke.edu/dbgroup/papers/2012-WuEtAl-oneoffew.pdf`.

[24] M. Yiu and N. Mamoulis. Efficient processing of top-k dominating queries on multi-dimensional data. In *VLDB*, 2007.

[25] H. Young. Social choice scoring functions. *SIAM Journal on Applied Mathematics*, pages 824–838, 1975.

[26] S. Zhang and M. Zaki. Mining multiple data sources: local pattern analysis. *KDD*, 12(2):121–125, 2006.

BC-PDM: Data Mining, Social Network Analysis and Text Mining System Based on Cloud Computing

Le Yu
Beijing University of Posts and Telecommunications
Beijing 100876, China
yuleyule1987@gamil.com

Jian Zheng
Beijing University of Posts and Telecommunications
Beijing 100876, China
zhengjian8972@gmail.com

Bin Wu, Bai Wang
Beijing University of Posts and Telecommunications
Beijing 100876, China
wubin,wangbai@bupt.edu.cn

Chongwei Shen
Beijing University of Posts and Telecommunications
Beijing 100876, China
wsscwqx135@sina.com

Long Qian
Beijing University of Posts and Telecommunications
Beijing 100876, China
qianlonglarry@qq.com

Renbo Zhang
Beijing University of Posts and Telecommunications
Beijing 100876, China
zhrbocool@gmail.com

ABSTRACT

Telecom BI(Business Intelligence) system consists of a set of application programs and technologies for gathering, storing, analyzing and providing access to data, which contribute to manage business information and make decision precisely. However, traditional analysis algorithms meet new challenges as the continued exponential growth in both the volume and the complexity of telecom data. With the Cloud Computing development, some parallel data analysis systems have been emerging. However, existing systems rarely have comprehensive function, either providing data analysis service or providing social network analysis. We need a comprehensive tool to store and analysis large scale data efficiently. In response to the challenge, the SaaS (Software-as-a-Service) BI system, *BC-PDM* (Big Cloud-Parallel Data Mining), are proposed. *BC-PDM* supports parallel ETL process, statistical analysis, data mining, text mining and social network analysis which are based on Hadoop. This demo introduces three tasks: business recommendation, customer community detection and user preference classification by employing a real telecom data set. Experimental results show that *BC-PDM* is very efficient and effective for intelligence data analysis.

Categories and Subject Descriptors

H.2.8 [**Database Management**]: Database application-Data Mining

General Terms

Algorithms, Design, Experimentation

Keywords

Parallel data mining, Hadoop, SNA, Text mining

1. INTRODUCTION

Telecom BI(Business Intelligence) system consists of a set of application programs and technologies for gathering, storing, analyzing and providing access to data, which contribute to manage business information and make decision precisely. The telecommunication operator generates huge count of information and data. The study focus on mining potential significant information from massive mobile communication data efficiently. Current application mode has the following problems:

- Data storage and access: A middle level branch of CMCC(China Mobile Communication Corporation) will be 12-16 TB in a year[1], and there are many other data including network data, customer data and so on. Traditional data storage uses commercial database or data warehouse system, such as Oracle. When facing with large scale dataset, these storage solutions are unable to ensure high scalability and availability.

- Data analysis and process: SAS Enterprise Miner and SPSS Clementine are traditional BI systems. However, these tools are low scalability and high cost. With the Cloud Computing development, some parallel data analysis systems have been emerging[2]. Mahout [3] is a collection of scalable machine learning algorithms based on Hadoop, but it lacks an user-friendly interface and its learning cycle is long. Radoop[4] integrates HDFS, Hive and Mahout functionalities in the RapidMiner environment. PEGASUS[5] and Giraph[1] utilize the parallel computing framework to implement graph mining. However, these projects have single function and they cannot be used as BI system. Even it lacks the basic function of BI system, ETL.

In response to these challenges, the *BC-PDM* is proposed which is based on Hadoop. *BC-PDM* provides access to

[1]http://incubator.apache.org/giraph/

large telecom data and business solutions for telecom operators. The system is an important project of Big-Cloud(BC) which is proposed by CMRI(China Mobile Research Institute). It combines ETL, data mining (DM), social network analysis (SNA), statistical analysis (SA) and text mining (TM) with MapReduce. This demo has the following contributions:

- *BC-PDM* provides cloud-based data warehouse. Large-scale datasets are stored in HDFS and HBase.
- Computing model for meeting the capability of data intensive computing and nearly linear speedup of ETL, DM, SNA , SA and TM algorithms based on MapReduce and BSP (Bulk synchronous parallel)[6]. According to the characteristics of the algorithms, they are implemented in different computing model. *BC-PDM* also provides brilliant visualization for the presentation of results.
- Novel methods are proposed to assist operator marketing in real-world application for telecom industry. Moreover, *BC-PDM* has established Business Application Templates (BATs), such as statistical template, business recommended model, customer churning, community detection, etc.

This demo focuses on three tasks: business recommendation, customer community detection and user preference classification.

This demo introduces the following points. Section 2 shows the architecture and the core algorithms of *BC-PDM*. Section 3 experiments the performance and scalability of *BC-PDM* using large-scale datasets. Section 4 presents how the system solves the business tasks in telecommunication using novel data mining, social network analysis and text mining techniques.

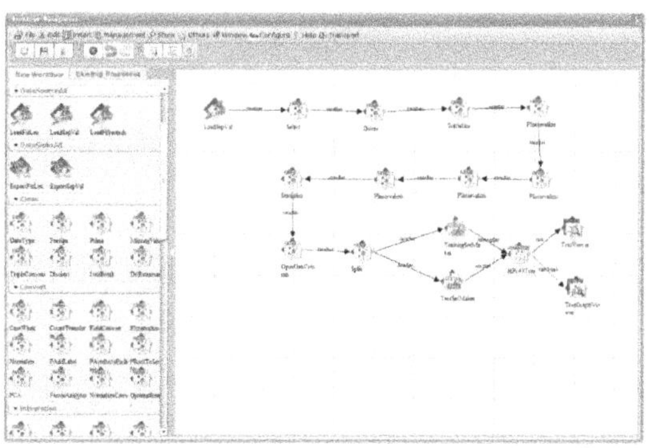

Figure 1: User Interface of *BC-PDM*.

2. SYSTEM OVERVIEW

The overview architecture of *BC-PDM* is presented in Fig.2. The system consists of three main layers. The function and feature of each layer is described as followed:

- *Cloud Computing Layer* provides storage and computational support. This layer uses HDFS, HBase and Hive as distributed file system.
- *Core Algorithms Layer* is the key of *BC-PDM* which includs ETL, DM, SA, SNA and TM algorithms.

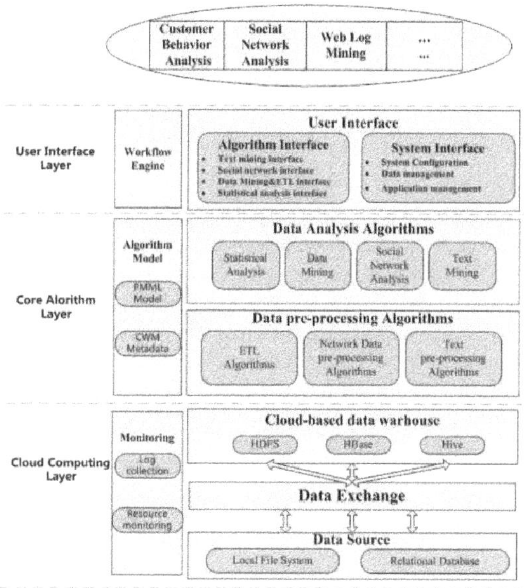

Figure 2: The Architecture of *BC-PDM*.

- *User Interface Layer* provides a Flex-based user interface. The functions of data storage and analysis are published as web service

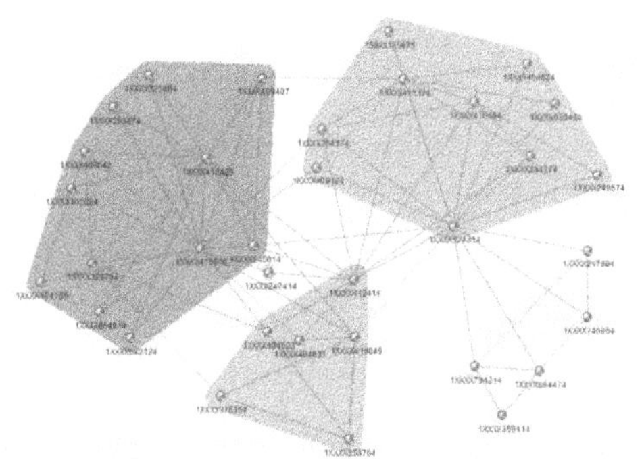

Figure 3: The community structure in a small mobile communication network.

Fig.3 shows the community structure of mobile communication network. Social network analysis provides many basic graph metrics including: degree, cluster coefficient, PageRank, network density, shortest distance and network diameter. Community detection and Community evolution analysis are also comprised in *BC-PDM*. The SNA has the following features:

- *Parallel Computing Framework: BC-PDM* employs MapReduce and BSP to implement the CPM (Clique percolation method)[7] which is an overlapping community detection method. The experiment indicates that BSP is more suitable for iterative graph algorithms than MapReduce.
- *High Applicability:* When analyzing small-scale data, serial computing could achieve good performance because the initiate time of Hadoop cannot neglect. *BC-PDM* offers serial algorithms in SNA as an alterna-

tive choice to guarantee the high practical applicability. System can select the most appropriate computing model for users according to the data size. Experiments have found the suitable inflexion point of the data size.

- *Message Passing Mechanism:* In order to improve the parallelism efficiency of graph algorithm and enable SNA to be flexible enough to express graph algorithms, *BC-PDM* build a multi-source message passing mechanism in *BC-PDM*. The message's state is modified to control the execution process of algorithm makes full use of every parallel computational job and avoid great amount of iteration.

- *Balanced Data Distribution: BC-PDM* proposes a novel high efficient parallel multi-level stepwise partitioning algorithm to reduce the communication and speed up the system.

Text mining refers to the process of deriving high-quality information from text. Text mining usually involves the process of structuring the input text, deriving patterns within the structured data, and finally evaluation and interpretation of the output. Typical text mining tasks include text categorization, text clustering, entity extraction, production of granular taxonomies, sentiment analysis, document summarization and entity relation modeling. *BC-PDM* provides text preprocessing algorithms, Bayes and Center Vector classification algorithms. Meanwhile, it also provides clustering algorithms such as Partitioning Methods and Canopy.

BC-PDM implements many clustering, classification and association rule algorithms. Moreover, *BC-PDM* creates and compares a set of different models based on the specified options. Then it ranks the best candidates according to the according to users' criteria. So users can choose the best approach for a given analysis. The data mining model are stored as PMML (Predictive Model Markup Language) and users can use PMML to migrate data mining model.

Parallel ETL can extract, transform and load variety kinds of data. The large-scale data are stored in HBase and HDFS. Corresponding metadata are kept at metadata repository. Technology metadata of each ETL component are conducted in accordance with the CWM (Common Warehouse Metamodel).

3. PERFORMANCE

The Chinese Software Testing Center (CSTC) has tested the *BC-PDM* in function, reliability, usability, efficiency, maintainability and portability. The evaluation has been performed on the 10 nodes Hadoop clusters, and each node consists of 4 Intel Xeon E5504 CPU, 8 GB main memory and 1024 GB hard drive. The evaluation data set is 403G.

Fig.4 shows the performance of typical algorithms. The average response time of 100 concurrent users accessing systems is 3.32 seconds. This experiment compares the performance of Groupby and MissValue component in different scale datasets. MissValue component is used to process the numerical incomplete problems. The result shows that the execution time presents linear speedup. Also,the social network algorithms have excellent performance. PageRank algorithm needs 17 minutes and 2 seconds to process 200,000 nodes and 800,000 edges, while Community Detection algorithm needs 1 hour 10 minutes and 17 seconds.

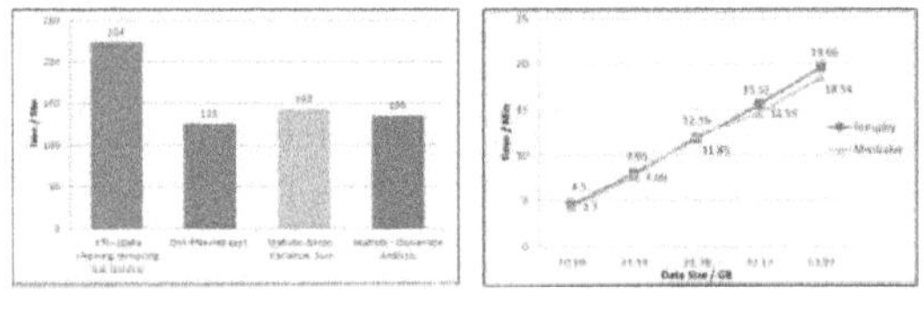

Figure 4: The performance of the DM and ETL algorithms.

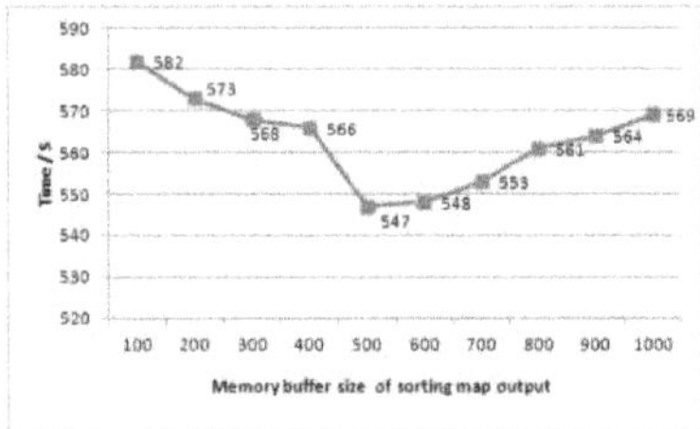

Figure 5: The effect of parameters.

Hadoop has many configuration parameters. Adjust parameters can take different effect. *BC-PDM* focuses on how to set the optimum parameters to improve system performance.The experiment results as follows (Cluster with 8 nodes, data sets 8GB):

- Memory buffer size: The left part of Fig.5 shows the execution time varying with memory buffer size. With the increase of memory buffer size, the execution time increases first and then decreases.

- Maximum of merge streams: The maximum of merge streams is the maximum number of streams to merge at once when sorting files. Fig.6 shows the execution time varying with maximum of merge streams. The execution time decreases with the increase of the maximum of merge streams and tend to certain stable value.

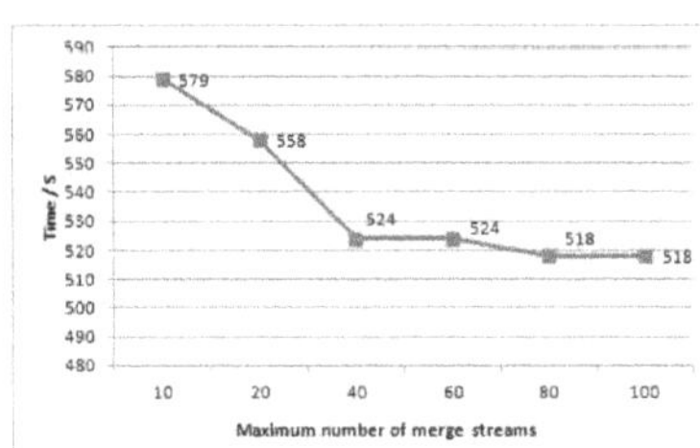

Figure 6: The effect of parameters.

4. APPLICATION SCENARIOS

BC-PDM analyzes user influence, user behavior, user preferences, network quality and the possibility of customer churn, such as telecommunications business or Internet search department.

4.1 Business recommendation

With rapidly growing of telecommunication users, users' consumption behaviors present some specific patterns. Discovering these patterns is conducive to business promotion.

Traditional analysis algorithms meet new challenges. *BC-PDM* uses the CDR (Calling Detail Records) and user information to establish the recommended model. First, *BC-PDM* selects long-distance calls, local calls, short message service and other fields from the CDRs as features. *BC-PDM* divides users into six categories using cluster algorithm. *BC-PDM* uses uses' category as the classification attribute and users' basic information to build the recommendation model. The experimental results show that the accuracy reaches 89.03%. *BC-PDM* provides business recommendation to 100 million users in 2 hours using the above model.

4.2 User preference classification

Reading on mobile phone is becoming part of everyday life. *BC-PDM* gets the hobby of user from the log which records the surfing of a specific user during a period of time based on the idea of the action of user. Browsing log records consists of much information such as IP address, Timestamp, encoding, page title, URL, etc. Through analyzing users' accessing page contents, *BC-PDM* can find users' preferences. Then, user preferences classification is converted into web page classification problems.

First, *BC-PDM* collects tens of thousands of pages as the original corpus for training classification model. The well-trained text categorization model has more than 30 categories and 73 sub-categories. Second, system uses the RMBoost classification algorithm which is proposed by *BC-PDM* and the accuracy rate can reach 90%. RMBoost is a centroid-based algorithm by calculating the centroids of different categories. The core of RMBoost algorithm is the centroid adjusting strategy. Centroid is the identifier of every category. RMBoost pushes the loose centroids farther while brings the compact centroid closer.

Meanwhile, it requires several iterations to make sure that the relative margin is greater than a given margin. Finally, the type of pages which users access for the most times and have the longest on-line time is the users' preference.

4.3 Overlapping customer community detection

A large account of complex systems can be modeled using complex networks. Mobile social networks consist of mobile users who communicate with one another using mobile phones. The structure of customer communication network provides us a way to understand customers' relationships. Mobile communication network is comparatively more common than other communications in everyday lives. Community structure is an important feature of mobile community detection. Generally, a community is a sub-graph whose nodes are densely connected within it but sparsely connected with the rest of the network. *BC-PDM* can also detect hierarchical community from mobile communication network.

This system employs CPM algorithm to detect hierarchical community. By combining with parallel computing framework, system has realized the parallel edition of CPM. Fig.7 shows the community structure in telecommunication network.

5. CONCLUSION AND FEATURE WORK

This demo introduces *BC-PDM* based on cloud computing. It has the ability to analyze the huge scale telecom data with data mining, social network analysis, text mining and statistical analysis and the high performance with linear speedup ratio. The *BC-PDM* shows its effectiveness on real world mobile communication data.

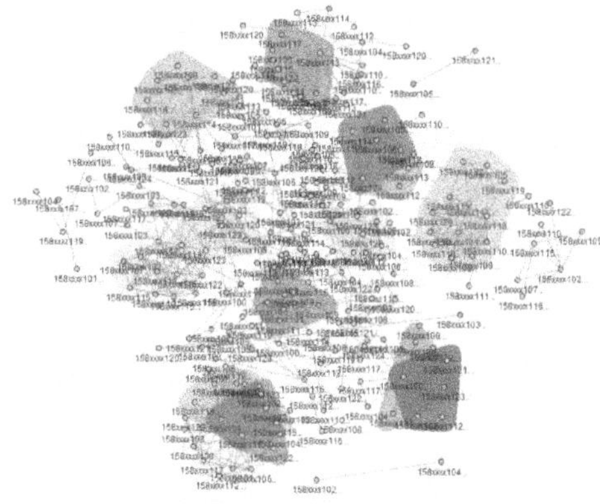

Figure 7: The result of community detection.

6. ACKNOWLEDGMENT

We would like to thank Dr. Deng Chao from China Mobile Research Institute for providing strong support on the project. This work is supported by the National Natural Science Foundation of China (Grant No.60905025, 90924029, 61074128). And the authors would like to acknowledge the anonymous reviewers.

7. REFERENCES

[1] M. Xu, D. Gao, C. Deng, Z. Luo, and S. Sun. Cloud computing boosts business intelligence of telecommunication industry. *Cloud Computing of Lecture Notes in Computer Science.*

[2] A. Ghoting, P. Kambadur, E. Pednault, and R. Kannan. Nimble: a toolkit for the implementation of parallel data mining and machine learning algorithms on mapreduce. In *Proceedings of the 17th ACM SIGKDD international conference on Knowledge discovery and data mining*, pages 334–342. ACM, 2011.

[3] S. Owen, R. Anil, T. Dunning, and E. Friedman. *Mahout in action.* Manning Publications Co., 2011.

[4] Z. Prekopcsk, G. Makrai, T. Henk, and C. Gspr-Papanek. Radoop: Analyzing big data with rapidminer and hadoop. In *Proceedings of the 2nd RapidMiner Community Meeting and Conference (RCOMM 2011)*, 2011.

[5] U. Kang, C. Tsourakakis, and C. Faloutsos. Pegasus: A peta-scale graph mining system implementation and observations. In *Data Mining, 2009. ICDM'09. Ninth IEEE International Conference on*, pages 229–238. IEEE, 2009.

[6] L. Valiant. A bridging model for parallel computation. *Communications of the ACM*, 33(8):103–111, 1990.

[7] G. Palla, I. Derényi, I. Farkas, and T. Vicsek. Uncovering the overlapping community structure of complex networks in nature and society. *Nature*, 435(7043):814–818, 2005.

Query-Driven Discovery of Semantically Similar Substructures in Heterogeneous Networks

Xiao Yu, Yizhou Sun, Peixiang Zhao, Jiawei Han
Department of Computer Science, University of Illinois at Urbana-Champaign
{xiaoyu1, sun22, pzhao4, hanj}@illinois.edu

ABSTRACT

Heterogeneous information networks that contain multiple types of objects and links are ubiquitous in the real world, such as bibliographic networks, cyber-physical networks, and social media networks. Although researchers have studied various data mining tasks in information networks, interactive query-based network exploration techniques have not been addressed systematically, which, in fact, are highly desirable for exploring large-scale information networks.

In this demo, we introduce and demonstrate our recent research project on query-driven discovery of semantically similar substructures in heterogeneous networks. Given a subgraph query, our system searches a given large information network and finds efficiently a list of subgraphs that are structurally identical and semantically similar. Since data mining methods are used to obtain semantically similar entities (nodes), we use *discovery* as a term to describe this process. In order to achieve high efficiency and scalability, we design and implement a filter-and-verification search framework, which can first generate promising subgraph candidates using off-line indices built by data mining results, and then verify candidates with a recursive pruning matching process. The proposed system demonstrates the effectiveness of our query-driven semantic similarity search framework and the efficiency of the proposed methodology on multiple real-world heterogeneous information networks.

Categories and Subject Descriptors

H.2.8 [**Database Management**]: Database applications—*Data Mining*; H.3.4 [**Information Storage and Retrieval**]: Systems and Software—*Information Networks*

General Terms

Experimentation, Algorithms

Keywords

Data Mining, Graph Query, Information Network

1. INTRODUCTION

Due to the rapid emergence of social networks and information networks extracted from various on-line databases, such as bibliographic databases, movie databases, and social media databases, heterogeneous information network analysis and mining begin to play an essential role in many large-scale systems. Problems including ranking, clustering [6], classification [1], entity similarity search [5] and relationship prediction [4] in information networks have been intensively studied and drawn research interests from a wide range of application domains. However, techniques which allow users to interactively explore large scale networks using query examples have not been studied yet.

Efficient subgraph isomorphism methods [7] [10] have been proposed in homogeneous information networks, with which users can locate identical subgraphs in a graph with a subgraph query. However, due to the rich information possessed in heterogeneous information networks, a user often wants to search for substructures with similar semantic meanings rather than identical subgraphs. Most of the time, it is easy for a user to use an example to describe a substructure, in order to find a list of semantically similar subgraphs. For example, a funding agency is looking for collaborations in academic institutes on graph analysis projects. They do not know many proficient researchers but they know that Christos Faloutsos and Jure Leskovec collaborate on graph analysis. Aiming to find more experts who collaborate on similar topics, a subgraph query can be written to represent a search criterion (Figure 1, left up corner). Desired results would be subgraphs that have identical structure and semantically similar entities so that more experts can be found. To our best knowledge, no existing search engine can answer such queries.

In this demo, we study and demonstrate our newly designed "Semantically Similar SubStructure" discovery system, namely the S^4 system, which takes a subgraph query as input, and retrieve from an information network a list of subgraphs that satisfy the query criteria as mentioned above. Our system, with off-line data mining results as indices, utilizes semi-structure information encoded in information networks and answers semantic similarity based substructure queries efficiently.

In the rest of the paper, we briefly introduce the framework of the new search technique, and demonstrate the power of S^4 system with real-world heterogeneous information networks. For instance, if we input the above query using our interactive web-based interface into the S^4 system, we can get a list of subgraphs as the retrieval results, part of which are presented in Figure 1. By examining the results, one could learn other graph analysis experts who have collaboration relationships, such as Christos Faloutsos and Jon Kleinberg worked on entity connection problems, and Philip Yu and Jimeng Sun are collaborators on large-scale graph

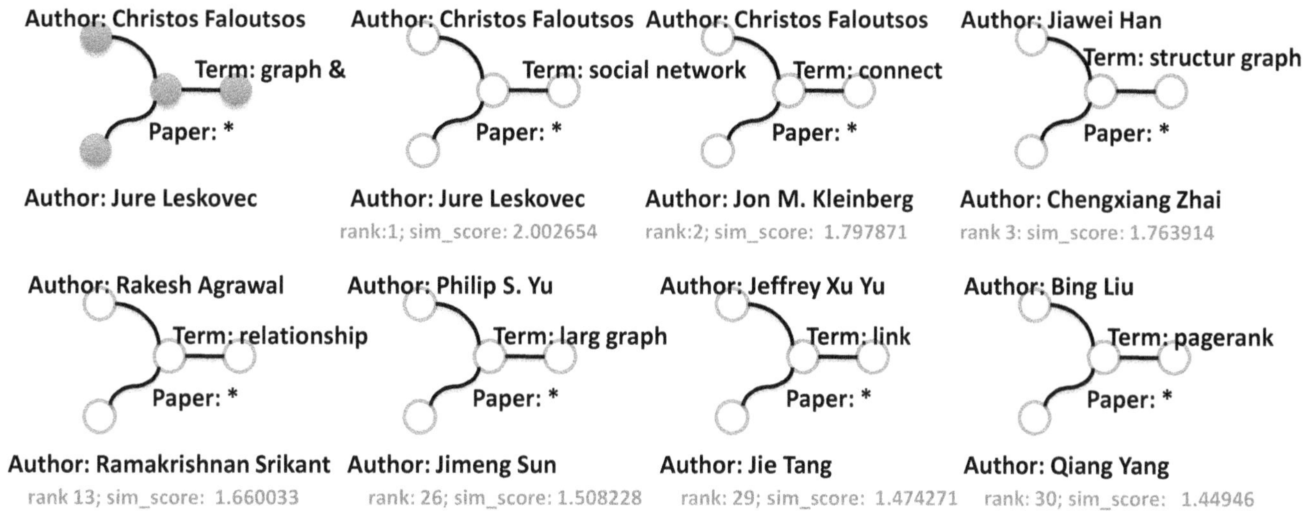

Figure 1: Example of entity similarity based subgraph search, where the subgraph with solid nodes is the query, and the subgraphs with hollow nodes are some retrieval results; similarity score (sim_score) and ranking ($rank$) in the entire retrieval results of each subgraph is also presented. Constraint notations including $*$ and $\&$ can be found in Section

analysis, and so on. Results from S^4 provide valuable information and help users explore the contents of the information network.

2. PROBLEM DESCRIPTION

We briefly introduce background concepts related to heterogeneous information networks and define semantically similar substructure discovery problem in this section.

As defined in [6], a heterogeneous information network is a directed graph, which contains multiple types of entities and / or multiple types of links. An information network is usually denoted as $G = (V, E)$, where V is the set of nodes (entities) and E is the set of edges (links between entities). If $|typeof(v \in V)| > 1$ and / or also $|typeof(e \in E)| > 1$, the network is a *heterogeneous information network*; otherwise it is a *homogeneous information network*.

Similar to relational databases, heterogeneous information networks usually follow a schema, in which rules of how entities and links coexist are defined. An example of heterogeneous information network and the corresponding network schema can be found as follows.

EXAMPLE 1. *DBLP[1] (Digital Bibliography & Library Project) is a computer science bibliographic dataset, which can be described as a heterogeneous information network. It contains four different types of entities (papers, venues, authors and terms). Links exist between papers and authors, papers and venues, papers and terms as well as within paper entities, representing citation relations. The schema of DBLP can be found in Figure 2.*

The semantically similar substructure discovery problem we study and present in this demo is defined in the scope of heterogeneous information networks, although it can also be applied on homogeneous networks. The problem can be defined as follows. Given a subgraph Q with concrete entities and valid links as query, *i.e.*, the query follows network schema, and a heterogeneous information network G, the system will return a Top-K list of subgraphs of G, each of which has identical same structure of of Q, but has

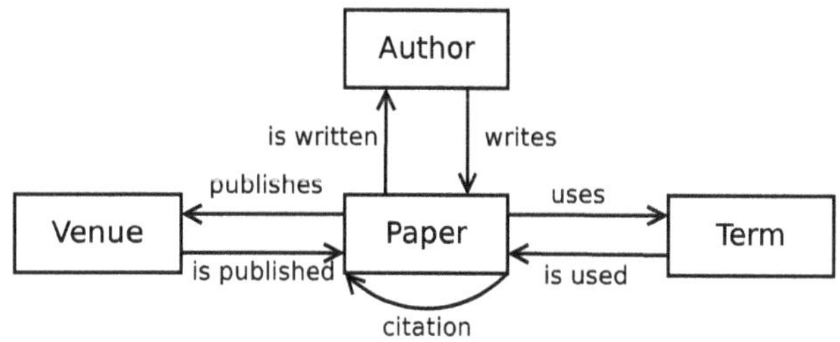

Figure 2: DBLP network schema

different yet semantically similar entities. As shown in Figure 1, retrieval results can help users access and explore Web-scale information networks with the issuing of the aforementioned structure similarity queries.

3. FRAMEWORK AND METHODS

As shown in Figure 3, the architecture of the S^4 system can be divided into two parts, which are *off-line analysis and indexing* and *on-line query answering*. Data mining and analysis over heterogeneous information network, including clustering, entity similarity measurement *etc*, are performed during the off-line stage. Two types of indices are built with the output of off-line mining and analysis. Similarity index utilizes the results of entity similarity calculation and indexes popular entities (entities with high rank or appear often in queries) with their semantically similar siblings. Structure index summarizes the output of structure index selectivity analysis and indexes frequent subgraph structures with a certain space budget.

During the on-line stage, given a subgraph query through a web-based interactive interface, the S^4 system will first verify the subgraph against network schema, and then pass the query down to index matching module. With the help of two indices built off-line, index matching module calculates possible query matching graph locations and entity combinations, denoted as subgraph candidates. If necessary, a revised subgraph isomorphism examination will be

[1] http://www.informatik.uni-trier.de/~ley/db/

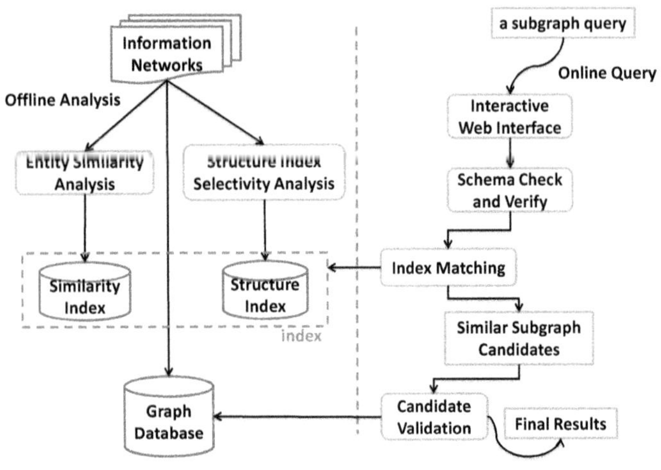

Figure 3: System Framework, where purple elements indicate off-line data flow, orange elements represent on-line data flow, and the green elements are system modules

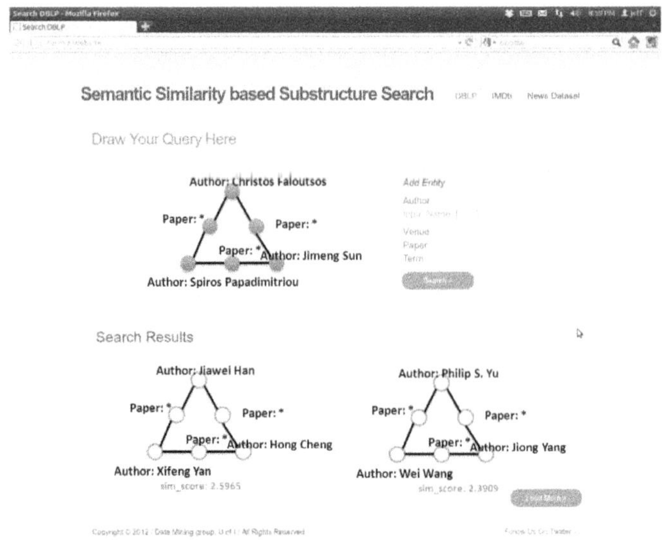

Figure 4: System Snapshot

applied to each subgraph candidate, and further verify the search criteria. More details of the important modules in the system are presented as follows.

3.1 Entity Similarity Analysis

Entity similarity calculation, as one of the most fundamental problems in heterogeneous information networks, has been studied from different aspects with various techniques [4] [3] [9]. Entity similarity analysis results can be used in link prediction, recommendation, and entity query systems. Previous studies [5] [8] also suggest similarity calculation along different *meta-paths* can be used to interpret different semantic meanings.

The similarity analysis module in this system measures entity similarity with different meta-path-based measurements, and stores results of popular entities as similarity index. Given an entity from the query subgraph, a set of ranked lists of entities of the same type which are semantically similar can be retrieved efficiently if indexed. The on-line index matching module will further investigate the semantic meaning of the query, select corresponding similar entities and pass the intermediate results to the following search module.

3.2 Structure Index Selectivity Analysis

Similarity index is an entity level semantic index, which can retrieve lists of similar entities with different semantic meanings, and find semantically similar entity combinations of the given query in the network efficiently. The other part of the search criteria is identical structure matching of the given subgraph query, which is a similar problem to subgraph isomorphism [7]. Subgraph isomorphism, which is a computational task in which two graphs G and H are given as input, and one must determine whether G contains a subgraph that is isomorphic to H, is NP-hard. Many recent studies [2] [11] [10] on subgraph query in graph or network propose different techniques to ease the subgraph isomorphism curse. Researchers discovered that with correct structure index over the large scale network, one can reduce the number of isomorphism checking significantly; hence reduce the overall query time.

However, structure index takes time and space to be built, and one can not index all possible subgraph structures off-line. A decision of which substructures should be indexed has to be made based on the availability of resource, selectivity of structures as well as frequency of substructures in information networks. The S^4 system takes different factors as well as the network schema into consideration when building structure index. Given a subgraph query, with proper structure index, the on-line index matching module retrieves and sorts graph locations which possibly possess the same substructure as the query. The candidate validation module verifies partial results generated from both similarity index and structure index and calculates final retrieval results.

3.3 Candidate Validation

With the assistance of similarity index and structure index, the S^4 system can calculate promising network locations and entity combinations efficiently, which are denoted as subgraph candidate. These candidates have high probability to match the structure of the subgraph identically, and have semantically similar entities as the subgraph query.

Candidate validation module is the last step of the on-line process. This module examines candidate in batch using a recursive strategy, picks up candidates which meet the criteria of the query subgraph and outputs them as the final retrieval results. The candidate validation process is similar to the subgraph isomorphism examination so the process can be very slow when the structure of subgraph query is large or complex.

To make the S^4 system response fast with most of the queries, two principles have been followed in system design. The first principle is to reduce the number of candidate validation as much as possible, which requires that in order to generate Top-K results, the number of query candidates has to be small and comparable to K. The second principle is to reduce the size of subgraph structure we need to verify as much as possible. To achieve the first principle, we need to improve the quality (selectivity) of the two indices during off-line data mining stage. To achieve the second principle, we need to analyze the subgraph query on-line, and calculate the best examine order for the recursive validation process. What's more, if similarity index and structure index can provide enough evidence for part of substructure, the system should be able to identify such scenarios and shrink the original subgraph query along with all candidates to an even smaller size, so that each validation will take less time. The S^4 system incorporates with both principles in the

```
N 1 author Christos Faloutsos
N 2 author Jure Leskovec
N 3 paper *
N 4 term graph &
E 1 3
E 2 3
E 3 4
```

Figure 5: Subgraph Definition Language Example

candidate validation module and improves the overall performance significantly.

3.4 Implementation Details

The S^4 system is designed to be scalable, efficient and user friendly. What's more, the system works well with limited resource, e.g., hard drive and memory. When the hard drive is limited, the system will create smaller indices, aiming to make the most common cases faster, and search unindexed entities or structures dynamically.

Similarity index is stored in relational database, and structure index is stored in a nonsql graph database, neo4j [2]. Both back-ends and front-ends modules are written in Python with networkx [3]. The web based interactive interface is implemented using Django [4] and jquery.

4. DEMONSTRATION

We demonstrate the power of the semantically similar substructure discovery system (the S^4 system) on multiple real life heterogeneous information datasets including DBLP and IMDb, and we are working on incorporating more newly generated datasets into the system as well.

A snapshot of the web based interactive interface can be found in Figure 4. From this simple interface, users can draw the subgraph query structure with a mouse or a stylus and a touch screen, and they can input the entity type and more information through the panel on the right. Alternatively, we provide a simple subgraph definition language input interface (which is not shown in the snapshot) for users who do not like drawing. The definition language is equivalent expressive as the drawing input method. An example of the definition language of the subgraph query in Figure 1 can be found in Figure 5.

In subgraph definition language, every line, which starts with either N as node or E as edge, defines a node or an edge in the query. For node definition, a node id within the query has to be specified, and the attributes of the node should be listed next in the same line. If the users do not know the attributes or do not need the actual node content for similarity matching, they can simply use $*$ to indicate this node is a dummy node, which only contribute to the structure of the query. Edges are defined using couples of node ids. By appending ^ at the end of an edge definition, it means this edge is directed, otherwise it's undirected. Similar to $*$ and ^, the S^4 system supports two more node constraints, which are $\&$ as shown in the example, which means this entity has to be substituted in the retrieval results, and also $\$$ which means this entity can not be changed in the retrieval results.

After query input, users need to click on the query button and the system will return a list of results, each of which has the identical structure, and shares similar semantic meanings of the query subgraph.

[2]NoSql open source graph database neo4j: http://neo4j.org/

[3]Python graph library: http://networkx.lanl.gov/

[4]Python web framework: https://www.djangoproject.com/

5. FURTHER DISCUSSION

We study and demonstrate the power of query driven discovery of semantically similar substructure, which is one of the several possible ways of exploring large-scale information networks with subgraph examples. Given a subgraph query, our system searches in an information network for identical structure match and semantically similar entity match. There can be alternative search standards, such has identical entity match but flexible structure match. This type of system can be useful when users need to query additional relationships among given entities. Also, one may prefer a more flexible search standard: given a subgraph query, return those with similar structure and similar entities. These alternative standards can be interesting and need further studies.

The prototype of S^4 system we implemented can be applied to many different scenarios, including new recommendation systems for B2C or movie rental services, multidimensional vertical similarity search engines for lawyers and journalists, expert community exploration on specific areas for scientific researchers, and even multidimensional candidates search for company recruiting.

6. ACKNOWLEDGMENTS

The work was supported in part by the U.S. Army Research Laboratory under Cooperative Agreement Number W911NF-09-2-0053 (NS-CTA), NSF IIS-09-05215, and U.S. Air Force Office of Scientific Research MURI award FA9550-08-1-0265.

7. REFERENCES

[1] M. Ji, J. Han, and M. Danilevsky. Ranking-based classification of heterogeneous information networks. In *Proceedings of SIGKDD*. ACM, 2011.

[2] A. Khan, N. Li, X. Yan, Z. Guan, S. Chakraborty, and S. Tao. Neighborhood based fast graph search in large networks. In *SIGMOD Conference*, 2011.

[3] N. Lao and W. W. Cohen. Fast query execution for retrieval models based on path-constrained random walks. In *Proceedings of SIGKDD*, 2010.

[4] Y. Sun, R. Barber, M. Gupta, C. Aggarwal, and J. Han. Co-Author Relationship Prediction in Heterogeneous Bibliographic Networks. In *ASONAM Conference*, 2011.

[5] Y. Sun, J. Han, X. Yan, S. P. Yu, and T. Wu. PathSim: Meta Path-Based Top-K Similarity Search in Heterogeneous Information Networks. In *VLDB*. ACM, 2011.

[6] Y. Sun, Y. Yu, and J. Han. Ranking-based clustering of heterogeneous information networks with star network schema. In *Proceedings of SIGKDD*. ACM, 2009.

[7] J. Ullmann. An algorithm for subgraph isomorphism. *Journal of the ACM (JACM)*, 1976.

[8] X. Yu, Q. Gu, M. Zhou, and J. Han. Citation prediction in heterogeneous bibliographic networks. In *Proccedings of the 2012 SIAM Conference on Data Mining (SDM 2012)*, 2012.

[9] X. Yu, A. Pan, L. Tang, Z. Li, and J. Han. Geo-friends recommendation in gps-based cyber-physical social network. In *ASONAM Conference*, 2011.

[10] P. Zhao and J. Han. On graph query optimization in large networks. *Proceedings of the VLDB Endowment*, 2010.

[11] P. Zhao, J. Yu, and P. Yu. Graph indexing: tree+ delta<= graph. In *Proceedings of the 33rd international conference on Very large data bases*. VLDB Endowment, 2007.

DAGger: Clustering Correlated Uncertain Data
(to predict asset failure in energy networks)

Dan Olteanu
Dept. of Computer Science, University of Oxford
Oxford OX1 3QD, United Kingdom
Dan.Olteanu@cs.ox.ac.uk

Sebastiaan J. van Schaik
Oxford e-Research Centre
Oxford OX1 3QG, United Kingdom
Sebastiaan.vanSchaik@oerc.ox.ac.uk

ABSTRACT

DAGger is a clustering algorithm for uncertain data. In contrast to prior work, DAGger can work on arbitrarily correlated data and can compute both exact and approximate clusterings with error guarantees.

We demonstrate DAGger using a real-world scenario in which partial discharge data from UK Power Networks is clustered to predict asset failure in the energy network.

Categories and Subject Descriptors

H.2.8 [**Database Management**]: Database Applications—*Data mining*

Keywords

Clustering, classification, uncertain data, probabilistic data, correlations, partial discharge, dagger.

1. CLUSTERING UNCERTAIN DATA

Recent years have witnessed a surge in the amount of digitally-born data. In many scenarios, this data is inherently uncertain or probabilistic, such as in automatic data extraction, image and voice detection (*e.g.*, processing handwriting, controlling mobile phones by voice), location detection, sensor networks, and measurement data [13]. Uncertain data calls for new processing approaches where uncertainty is explicitly accounted for, and it has led to a solid body of work on building probabilistic databases, such as MystiQ, Trio, and MayBMS. Albeit at a smaller scale, there is effort to adapt well-known data mining tasks to uncertain data, e.g., in discovery of frequent patterns and association rules [14], clustering [5], and classification [10]. However, to the best of our knowledge, prior work only considers limited probabilistic data models based on a simplifying independence assumption and circumvents the hardness of probability computation by the use of expected values and Monte-Carlo sampling. Expected values can lead to unintuitive results, for instance when data values and their probabilities follow skewed and non-aligned distributions. In case of correlated input events, the independence assumption can lead to results that are arbitrarily off from the ground truth.

In this paper we demonstrate DAGger, a novel approach to clustering correlated uncertain data. At its core, DAGger is a variant of the well-known k-medoids clustering algorithm adapted to accommodate uncertainty throughout the clustering process and probability computation.

DAGger has the following key features:

- The clustering outcome has a simple and intuitive meaning given by the possible worlds semantics: conceptually, it is equivalent to clustering in each possible world represented by the input data. This is in line with virtually all work in probabilistic databases [13] and thus allows for an easy integration of query processing and mining tasks.
- It supports arbitrarily correlated input data through a symbolic representation of probabilistic events. Complex events generated during the clustering process are expressible within the same representation formalism.
- At any stage in the clustering process, DAGger computes clustering events stating the membership of an object to a cluster and whether an object is a cluster medoid. The probability of such events can be computed exactly or approximately with absolute or relative error guarantees using a novel compilation technique of independent interest. This technique first represents the events of all objects and clusters at all iterations in a directed acyclic graph (DAG) where common factors are represented only once; each node in this graph thus represents an event. It then bulk-compiles all events into one decision diagram to the degree required to compute their probabilities.
- In addition to the events that are intrinsic to the clustering process, DAGger supports queries over the clustering output, e.g., to compute the probability that two given objects belong to the same cluster.

The purpose of the demonstration is to show how DAGger can be effectively used to cluster and classify sensor readings of a phenomenon in energy distribution networks, called *partial discharge*. This is used to predict asset failure in energy distribution networks. We will use real (anonymised) data from UK Power Networks consisting of known readings representing asset failures and new unclassified readings. These readings are naturally uncertain due to limited sensor sensitivity, hardware failure, and unreliable transmission channels [1, 3, 4]. By using DAGger, we can improve the quality

	(metadata) date/time	class	(uncertain) PD	load	(events) $\phi[o_i]$
...					
o_5	20/12 16:00	OK	5	140	$x_4 \wedge x_5 \wedge x_6$
o_6	20/12 17:00	OK	6	140	$x_5 \wedge x_6 \wedge x_7$
o_7	20/12 18:00	OK	9	150	$x_6 \wedge x_7 \wedge x_8$
o_8	20/12 19:00	OK	50	160	$x_7 \wedge x_8 \wedge x_9$
...					
o_{15}	10/01 03:00	warn	22	25	$x_{14} \wedge x_{15} \wedge x_{16}$
o_{16}	10/01 04:00	warn	20	25	$x_{15} \wedge x_{16} \wedge x_{17}$
o_{17}	10/01 05:00	warn	24	40	$x_{16} \wedge x_{17} \wedge x_{18}$
o_{18}	10/01 06:00	warn	25	50	$x_{17} \wedge x_{18} \wedge x_{19}$
...					
o_{25}	01/07 19:00	??	16	100	$x_{24} \wedge x_{25} \wedge x_{26}$
o_{26}	01/07 20:00	??	30	80	$x_{25} \wedge x_{26} \wedge x_{27}$

Table 1: Simplified data set. The labelled sensor readings are prior to a fault on January 11, 2011. The last two readings can be classified by clustering them with labelled data.

of the clustering for the set of new sensor readings and are able to distinguish spurious readings from readings that indicate an imminent failure of an asset (*e.g.*, a cable). The audience of this demonstration can explore the clustering outcome visually, as well as a ranked list of critical assets.

In the rest of this paper, we explain our demonstration scenario, show how DAGger clusters uncertain sensor readings, and detail on how the audience of our demonstration can interact with the system.

2. DEMONSTRATION SCENARIO: CLUSTERING PARTIAL DISCHARGE DATA

We demonstrate the clustering capability of DAGger in an application that predicts asset failure in energy networks.

2.1 Partial discharge

Partial discharge (PD) is an electrical discharge that does not fully bridge the insulation between two conducting electrodes. It has been identified as one of the major causes of long-term degradation and eventual failure of cables.

In order to minimise the customer minutes lost, energy distribution network operators (DNOs) are currently deploying sensors to monitor partial discharge activity in the distribution network, to be able to act preemptively [8, 9]. Unfortunately, monitoring partial discharge is not a straightforward task: the phenomenon is hard to detect, sensors often report spurious measurements and are prone to failure (as are the transmission channels).

The HiPerDNO project [15] aims to show the benefits of the introduction of cutting edge computational tools and techniques to improve electricity distribution network operations in partnership with UK Power Networks and other European DNOs.

2.2 Uncertain readings of PD and load

The data used to demonstrate our system is historical data on partial discharge activities in distribution networks, as well as records of network load and asset failure. It is gathered from two different types of sensors: (1) partial discharge sensors installed on switchgear and cables in substations of the distribution network, and (2) network load sensors in substations. By aggregating the number of partial discharge occurrences over the duration of an hour and subsequently pairing this value with the average network load during that hour, a data set like the one depicted in Table 1 is obtained. DAGger can deal with data with an arbitrary number of dimensions. For this demonstration each data point has the attributes load and partial discharge as described above. A single asset typically yields up to 24 data points per day.

DAGger interprets this data probabilistically. The rightmost column of Table 1 contains probabilistic events, i.e., arbitrary propositional formulas over independent Boolean random variables, that quantify the correlation and probability of readings. This probabilistic data formalism, whereby records are associated with probabilistic events, is called *probabilistic conditional tables*, or pc-tables for short, and is common in probabilistic databases [13].

We associate each sensor reading with a probabilistic event. The probability of that reading being true is thus given by the probability of the event. Each load and partial discharge reading has a probability of being accurate, which is inferred from sensor specification and measurement intervals in historical data. In the events used in DAGger, this is captured by independent Boolean random variables $x_0, \ldots x_{m-1}$.

Inference of probabilities and correlations can be done using many techniques, *e.g.* using inference in Bayesian networks or Markov Logic Networks [11, 6] and possibly based on the hardware specifications of the sensor manufacturer. In this specific application of DAGger, we construct a Markov chain in which each data point o_t at time t only depends on the data point o_{t-1} at time $t-1$. The conditional probabilities are then converted into events that can be processed by DAGger. As expected, consecutive sensor readings are strongly correlated [12]. In the example in Table 1, we used a sliding window of size three that yields events represented by conjunctions of three literals.

The possible worlds represented by our sample data are obtained by total assignments of the event variables. For instance, the worlds in which reading o_8 is correct are defined by assignments where x_7, x_8, and x_9 are *true*. Hence, the probability of o_8 being correct is given by the product of probabilities of these Boolean random variables being *true*. The readings o_5 and o_6 are positively correlated, since they both depend on x_5 and x_6. The readings o_8 and o_{15} are independent, since their events are independent.

2.3 Predicting asset failure

In order to predict asset failure, we perform the following procedure using DAGger:

1. Construct a clustering using both historical data (labelled readings), and the unclassified sensor readings.
2. For each unclassified reading, query the clustering for the probability that the reading is in the same cluster as one (or more) of the readings from the warn-labelled set. Depending on the type of labelled readings in the same cluster with the new readings, an expert user can also understand the type of failure.

After DAGger has constructed a probabilistic clustering, we can query it for the event that reading o_{25} is clustered into the same cluster as at least one reading from the set $R_{\texttt{warn}}$ with readings labelled warn. This query is constructed using clustering events (for clusters $C_1, \ldots, C_k$):

$$\phi[o_{25} \text{ is } \texttt{warn}] = \bigvee_{1 \le j \le k} \left(\phi\left[o_{25} \in C_j\right] \wedge \left(\bigvee_{o_w \in R_{\texttt{warn}}} \phi\left[o_w \in C_j\right] \right) \right)$$

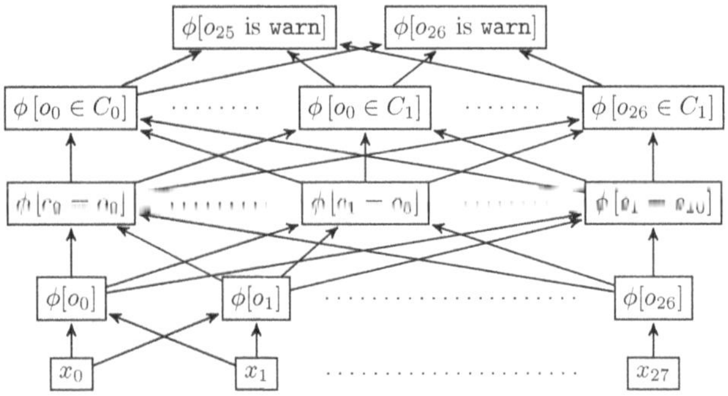

Figure 1: Partial DAG with five layers encoding clustering events for clusters C_0 (OK) and C_1 (warn) in our example.

In this expression, $\phi[o_i \in C_j]$ denotes the event that reading o_i belongs to cluster C_j. DAGger can cluster the data set from Table 1 and perform exact classification of o_{25} within seconds. The system can thus inform the user whether new readings indicate that a fault is imminent.

3. UNDER DAGGER'S HOOD

At the core of DAGger lies the well-known k-medoids clustering algorithm [2, 7], an unsupervised data mining technique that partitions a set of data points into k groups of similar points. It repeatedly assigns data points to clusters and re-elects cluster medoids, until convergence is reached.

In DAGger, the assignment of data points to clusters and selection of cluster medoids are probabilistic events. Therefore, a data point belongs to a cluster or is a cluster medoid with a certain probability. Conceptually, DAGger's outcome is equivalent to applying the standard k-medoids algorithm in each possible world. However, DAGger cannot afford to enumerate the exponentially many possible worlds and perform a clustering in each of them. Instead, its computation is more symbolic as it traces the clustering events and uses them to compute probabilities of possible clusterings to any approximation degree. This symbolic computation can be orders of magnitude faster than the more extensional approach based on explicit enumeration of the possible worlds.

In this section, we give some details on how DAGger works.

Constructing events. The events $\phi[o_i]$ associated with input readings are the building blocks for events that are subsequently created by DAGger to express medoid selection and cluster assignment. At each clustering step, such events depend solely on events from the previous step. All events can be represented in a layered structure, where each layer corresponds to a clustering step and where we factor out common expressions. This layered factorisation, which is a directed acyclic graph (DAG), is key to the compact representation of the events, as it exploits the combinatorial nature of clustering computation. For instance, the event $\phi[o_i \in C_j]$ that reading o_i belongs to cluster C_j is expressed as a conjunction of the event $\phi[o_i]$ and of events for all cases in which a reading o_l is the medoid of cluster C_j and the distance from o_i to o_l is the smallest among all distances from o_i to the other readings. Figure 1 partially depicts such a DAG. Clustering events are expressed using conditional expressions that involve propositional formulas and distances, since the selection of new cluster medoids depends on input events and distances between data points. They are expressed in the algebraic structure of the semimodule defined by the tensor product $\mathbb{B}[\mathbf{X}] \otimes \mathbb{R}$ of the Boolean semiring $\mathbb{B}[\mathbf{X}]$ freely generated by the set $\mathbf{X}$ of input random variables and the SUM monoid of real numbers $\mathbb{R}$. For instance, the following expression represents the total distance-sum of a reading o_i to the readings $o_0, \ldots, o_{n-1}$ in cluster C_j:

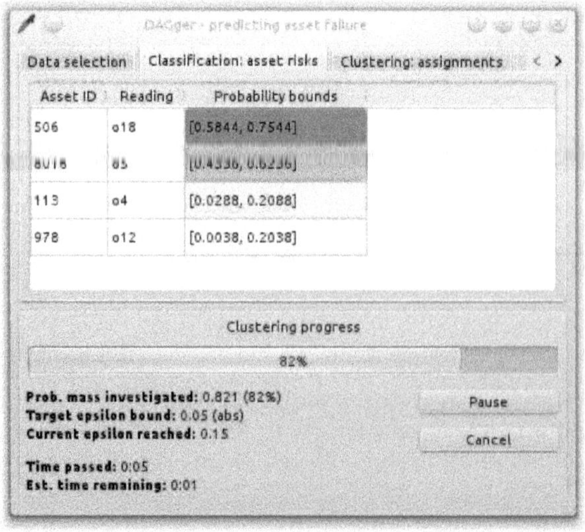

Figure 2: Screenshot of the system interface, showing an ordered list of assets of which sensor readings were classified as 'warning' with a high probability.

$$\Delta(C_j, o_i) = \sum_{0 \le a < n, a \neq i} (\phi[o_a \in C_j] \otimes d(o_i, o_a))$$

This expression represents a discrete probability distribution function over all possible distance-sums of o_i to readings in cluster C_j in a compact way. Indeed, for each possible truth assignment of random variables, this expression can yield a different distance-sum with a different probability. Such distance-sums are used inside inequalities to construct the events that describe medoid selection: the data point with the smallest distance-sum to the other points in the cluster is chosen as the new cluster medoid.

$$\phi[c_j = o_i] = \phi[o_i \in C_j] \wedge \bigwedge_{0 \le a < n, a \neq i} (\Delta(C_j, o_i) \le \Delta(C_j, o_a))$$

In the absence of the semimodule $\mathbb{B}[\mathbf{X}] \otimes \mathbb{R}$, these inequalities would only be expressible as propositional events of size exponential in the number of objects (or readings).

Once the clustering events are constructed, classification queries such as the one described in Section 2.3 are added to the DAG. The DAG in Figure 1 includes classification queries for objects o_{25} and o_{26} from Table 1 in the top layer.

Probability computation. DAGger uses a novel bulk compilation strategy to efficiently compute the probability of the events represented in a layered DAG structure. The core idea of this compilation technique is Shannon expansion: given a Boolean random variable x, the probability $P(\Phi)$ of an event Φ is the weighted sum of probabilities of the events $\Phi|_x$ and $\Phi|_{\neg x}$ obtained by setting x to *true* and respectively to *false* in Φ, i.e., $P(\Phi) = P(x) \cdot P(\Phi|_x) + P(\neg x) \cdot P(\Phi|_{\neg x})$.

The challenges faced by DAGger are to extend Shannon expansion (1) to work well on sets of events represented in a DAG structure and on semimodule expressions, and (2) to incrementally compute approximations to any degree.

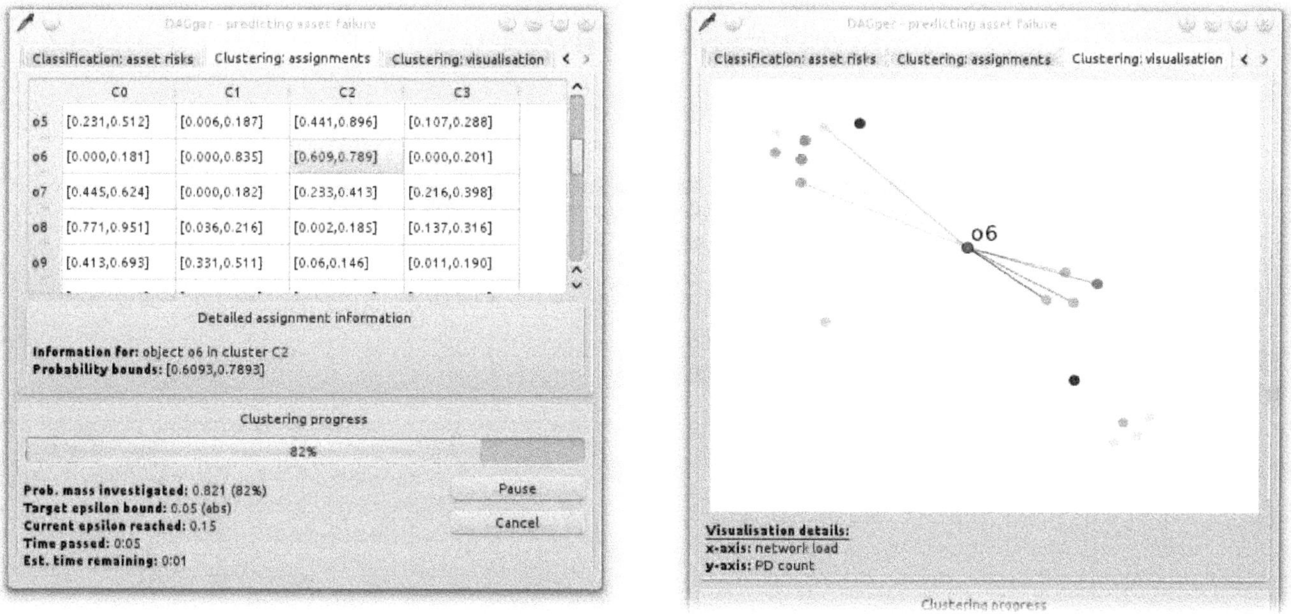

(a) Probabilistic assignment of data points to clusters (b) Visualisation of probabilistic clustering

Figure 3: Screenshots of the system interface, showing two different views of the clustering result.

4. DRIVING DAGGER

`DAGger` has a graphical user interface to present the clustering outcome, as well as the incremental probability computation of the clustering events. Screenshots of this interface are given in Figures 2 and 3.

On the first tab, the user can make a selection of the input data (both labelled and unlabelled data) which is to be analysed by `DAGger`. After the data analysis has started, the user can monitor the progress and examine the results.

On the tab "Classification: asset risks" (Figure 2), the system displays the results of the classification of the unlabelled data points. It lists the assets that were classified into the `warn` category in decreasing order of probability.

The tab "Clustering: assignments" (Figure 3a) shows the probabilistic assignment of data points to clusters.

The tab "Clustering: visualisation" (Figure 3b) presents the user with a visual representation of the uncertain clustering. By selecting a sensor reading (in this case: o_6), the interface will show the user the probability that the data point will be clustered into the same cluster as the closest neighbouring data points: the darker the line that connects o_6 to another data point, the higher the probability that the two data points end up in the same cluster.

Throughout the interface of the system, the user will see the exact lower and upper bounds of the probabilities, whilst the probabilities are being established. Unless `DAGger` is configured to compute approximate probabilities, the system will present the user with the exact probabilities once the lower and upper bounds have converged.

Acknowledgements

The authors would like to thank Peter Lang, Matthieu Michel, and Koen Tavernier (UK Power Networks, IPEC) for providing us with the data. This work is supported by EC FP7 HiPerDNO project under grant 248235 and EPSRC ADEPT project under grant EP/I000194/1.

5. REFERENCES

[1] C. C. Aggarwal. *Managing and Mining Uncertain Data*, volume 35 of *Advances in Database Systems*. Kluwer, 2009.

[2] C. M. Bishop. *Pattern Recognition and Machine Learning*. Springer-Verlag, 2006.

[3] R. Cheng and S. Prabhakar. Managing uncertainty in sensor database. *SIGMOD Rec.*, 32:41–46, 12 2003.

[4] A. Deshpande, C. Guestrin, S. Madden, J. Hellerstein, and W. Hong. Model-driven data acquisition in sensor networks. In *VLDB*, 2004.

[5] F. Gullo, G. Ponti, and A. Tagarelli. Clustering uncertain data via k-medoids. In *SUM*, 2008.

[6] A. Jha and D. Suciu. Probabilistic databases with markoviews. In *VLDB*, 2012.

[7] J. B. MacQueen. Some methods for classification and analysis of multivariate observations. In *Berkeley Symp. on Mathematical Statistics and Probability*, 1967.

[8] M. Michel. Innovative asset management and targeted investments using on-line partial discharge monitoring and mapping techniques. In *CED*, 2007.

[9] M. Michel and C. Eastham. Improving the management of MV underground cable circuits using automated on-line cable partial discharge mapping. In *CEED*, 2011.

[10] B. Qin, Y. Xia, R. Sathyesh, S. Prabhakar, and Y. Tu. urule: A rule-based classification system for uncertain data. In *ICDM Workshops*, 2010.

[11] M. Richardson and P. Domingos. Markov logic networks. *Machine learning*, 62(1):107–136, 2006.

[12] S. Sathe, H. Jeung, and K. Aberer. Creating probabilistic databases from imprecise time-series data. In *ICDE*, 2011.

[13] D. Suciu, D. Olteanu, C. Ré, and C. Koch. *Probabilistic Databases*. Morgan & Claypool Publishers, 2011.

[14] L. Sun, R. Cheng, D. W. Cheung, and J. Cheng. Mining uncertain data with probabilistic guarantees. In *KDD*, 2010.

[15] G. Taylor, D. Wallom, S. Grenard, A. Yunta Huete, and C. J. Axon. Recent developments towards novel high performance computing and communications solutions for smart distribution network operation. In *ISGT*, 2011.

UFIMT: An Uncertain Frequent Itemset Mining Toolbox

Yongxin Tong † Lei Chen † Philip S. Yu §
†Hong Kong University of Science & Technology, Hong Kong, China
§University of Illinois at Chicago, USA
†{yxtong, leichen}@cse.ust.hk, §psyu@cs.uic.edu

ABSTRACT

In recent years, mining frequent itemsets over uncertain data has attracted much attention in the data mining community. Unlike the corresponding problem in deterministic data, the frequent itemset under uncertain data has two different definitions: the expected support-based frequent itemset and the probabilistic frequent itemset. Most existing works only focus on one of the definitions and no comprehensive study is conducted to compare the two different definitions. Moreover, due to lacking the uniform implementation platform, existing solutions for the same definition even generate inconsistent results. In this demo, we present a demonstration called as *UFIMT* (Uncertain Frequent Itemset Mining Toolbox) which not only discovers frequent itemsets over uncertain data but also compares the performance of different algorithms and demonstrates the relationship between different definitions. In this demo, we firstly present important techniques and implementation skills of the mining problem, secondly, we show the system architecture of *UFIMT*, thirdly, we report an empirical analysis on extensive both real and synthetic benchmark data sets, which are used to compare different algorithms and to show the close relationship between two different frequent itemset definitions, and finally we discuss some existing challenges and new findings.

Categories and Subject Descriptors

H.2.8 [**Database Applications**]: Data Mining

General Terms

Algorithms, Experimentation

Keywords

Frequent Itemset Mining, Uncertain Database, UFIMT

1. INTRODUCTION

With the emerging of many new applications, such as sensor network monitoring, protein-protein interaction (PPI) network analysis, etc., uncertain data mining has become a new challenge in data mining communities. Due to the fundamental status of frequent itemset mining in the data mining field, mining frequent itemsets over uncertain databases has also attracted much attention [1, 2, 3, 4, 5, 6, 8, 9] recently. For instance, with the popularization of wireless sensor networks, wireless sensor network systems collect huge amount of data. However, due to the inherent uncertainty of sensors, the collected data is often inaccurate. For the probability-included uncertain data, how can we discover frequent patterns (itemsets) so that the users can find the hidden rules in data? The inherent probability property of data is ignored if we simply employ the traditional method of frequent itemset mining in deterministic data to uncertain data. Hence, it is necessary to develop specialized algorithms for mining frequent itemsets over uncertain databases.

Unlike the research of frequent itemset mining in deterministic data, the corresponding problem in uncertain data presents different semantic explanations and problem definitions. In deterministic data, frequent itemset has a unique definition, that is, an itemset is frequent if and only if its support (frequency) is no less than a specified minimum support, *min_sup*. However, the definition of a frequent itemset over uncertain data has two different semantic explanations: expected support-based frequent itemset [4] and probabilistic frequent itemset [2], both of which consider the support of an itemset as a discrete random variable. However, the two definitions employ different semantic explanations for the random variable. The former defines the expectation of the support of an itemset as the measurement, denoted as the expected support of this itemset. Thus, an itemset is frequent if and only if its expected support is no less than a specified minimum expected support threshold, *min_esup*. The latter uses the probability that an itemset appears at least the specified minimum support (*min_sup*) times as the measurement, denoted as the frequent probability of an itemset, therefore, an itemset is frequent if and only if its frequent probability is larger than a given probabilistic threshold. Therefore, most prior works study the above two definitions independently [2, 6].

In this work, through experimental verification and theoretical analysis, we find that the two definitions have a rather close connection. Generally speaking, this finding is reasonable since both definitions consider the support of an itemset as a random variable following a Poisson Binomial distribution, the expected support of an itemset equals to the expectation of the random variable. As a result, calculating the frequent probability of an itemset is equivalent to calculating the cumulative distribution function of this random variable. In addition, the existing mathematical theory shows that a Poisson distribution or a Normal distribution can approximate a Poisson Binomial distribution under high

KDD'12, August 12–16, 2012, Beijing, China.

confidence [3, 7, 9]. Thus, an interesting result is that the frequent probability of an itemset can be directly computed as long as we know the expected and variance of the support of the itemset when the uncertain database is enough large [7]. So, the efficiency of mining probabilistic frequent itemsets can be greatly improved by employing many efficient expected support-based frequent itemset mining algorithms. In this demo, based on our system, *UFIMT*, we verify this conclusion through extensive experimental comparisons.

Besides ignoring the hidden relationship between two above definitions, existing research on the same definition also shows contradictory conclusions. For example, in the research of mining expected support-based frequent itemsets, [5] shows that UFP-growth algorithm always outperforms UApriori algorithm with respect to the running time. However, [1] reports that UFP-growth algorithm is always slower than UApriori algorithm. These inconsistent conclusions make later researchers confused about which result is correct.

In addition, different experimental results also originate from the discrepancy among many implementation skills, blurring what the contributions of algorithms are. Therefore, a uniform baseline implementation is necessary, which is one of our important motivations to develop *UFIMT*.

Except verifying the relationship between two above definitions, clarifying inconsistent conclusions in current related researches, and providing uniform baseline implementations, we also study another variant problem, mining probabilistic frequent closed itemsets over uncertain data recently [8], which aims to compress the size of all frequent itemsets in order to help user better understand the result set. Therefore, the prototype system, UFIMT, provides solutions of some related problems of frequent itemset mining over uncertain data as well. For example, UFIMT can discover the probabilistic frequent closed itemsets.

Thus, in this demo, we try to achieve the following goals:

- Present a novel prototype system, *UFIMT*, for mining frequent itemsets over uncertain databases. The prototype system seamlessly integrates the uncertain data preprocessing module, the algorithm library of mining frequent itemsets over uncertain data, and the comparison and analysis of algorithms.
- Clarify the relationship of the two definitions of frequent itemsets over uncertain data. In fact, the two definitions can be integrated together due to the mathematical correlation between them. Based on this relationship, instead of paying expensive computation cost to mine probabilistic frequent itemsets, we can directly use the solutions for mining expected support-based itemsets when the size of data is large enough.
- Provide uniform baseline implementations for nine existing representative algorithms for mining frequent itemsets and mining frequent closed itemsets under uncertain databases. These implementations adopt common basic operations and offer a base for comparing with the future work in this area.
- Propose an objective and sufficient experimental evaluation platform. Meanwhile, we test the performances of the existing representative algorithms over extensive benchmarks and verify the contradictory conclusions in the existing research.

The rest of the demo is organized as follows. In Section 2, we introduce the technical specification of our prototype system, *UFIMT* (Uncertain Frequent Itemset Mining Toolbox). A system demonstration plan is proposed in Section 3. We conclude in Section 4.

2. TECHNICAL SPECIFICATION

In this section, we firstly introduce basic definitions about mining frequent itemsets over uncertain databases. Then, existing representative algorithms under the above two definitions are briefly reviewed. Finally, the system architecture of *UFIMT* is described and illustrated.

2.1 Frequent Itemsets over Uncertain Data

In this subsection, we generally introduce several basic definitions about mining frequent itemsets over uncertain databases.

Let $I = \{i_1, i_2, \ldots, i_n\}$ be a set of distinct items. We name a non-empty subset, X, of I as an itemset. For brevity, we use $X = x_1 x_2 \ldots x_n$ to denote itemset $X = \{x_1, x_2, \ldots, x_n\}$. X is a $l-itemset$ if it has l items. Given an uncertain transaction database UDB, each transaction is denoted as a tuple $< tid, Y >$ where tid is the transaction identifier, and $Y = \{y_1(p_1), y_2(p_2), \ldots, y_m(p_m)\}$. Y contains m units. Each unit has an item y_i and a probability, p_i, denoting the possibility of item y_i appearing in the tid tuple. The number of transactions containing X in UDB is a random variable following the Poisson Binomial distribution, denoted as $sup(X)$. Given an UDB, the expected support-based frequent itemset and the probabilistic frequent itemset are defined as follows.

Definition 1. (Expected Support) Given an uncertain transaction database UDB which includes N transactions, and an itemset X, the expected support of X is shows as follows:

$$esup(X) = \sum_{i=1}^{N} p_i(X)$$

Definition 2. (Expected-Support-based Frequent Itemset) Given an uncertain transaction database UDB which includes N transactions, and a minimum expected support ratio, min_esup, an itemset X is an expected support-based frequent itemset if and only if $esup(X) \geq N \times min\_esup$

Definition 3. (Frequent Probability) Given an uncertain transaction database UDB which includes N transactions, a minimum support ratio min_sup, and an itemset X, X's frequent probability, denoted as $Pr(X)$, is shown as follows:

$$Pr(X) = Pr\{sup(X) \geq N \times min\_sup\}$$

Definition 4. (Probabilistic Frequent Itemset) Given an uncertain transaction database UDB which includes N transactions, a minimum support ratio min_sup, and a probabilistic frequent threshold pft, an itemset X is a probabilistic frequent itemset if X's frequent probability is larger than the probabilistic frequent threshold, namely,

$$Pr(X) = Pr\{sup(X) \geq N \times min\_sup\} > pft$$

2.2 Uncertain Frequent Itemset Mining

In this subsection, we briefly review eight existing representative algorithms of mining frequent itemsets over uncertain data. These algorithms are also seamlessly integrated into our prototype system, *UFIMT*. We categorize the eight representative algorithms into three groups: expected support-based frequent itemset mining algorithms, exact probabilistic frequent itemset mining algorithms, and approximate probabilistic frequent itemset mining algorithms.

Expected support-based frequent itemset mining algorithms. These algorithms aim to find all expected support-based frequent itemsets. The complexity of computing the expected support of an itemset is $O(N)$, where N is the number of transactions.

In this categorization, *UFIMT* contains three representative algorithms: UApriori [4], UFP-growth [5], and UH-Mine [1]. UApriori is the first expected support-based frequent itemset mining algorithm which extends the well-known Apriori algorithm to the uncertain environment and employs the generate-and-test framework to find all expected support-based frequent itemsets. In our system, we also modify the Trie-Tree-based Apriori framework to speed up our algorithm. UFP-growth algorithm extends the well-known FP-growth algorithm. Similar to the traditional FP-growth algorithm, UFP-growth algorithm also firstly builds an index tree, called UFP-tree to store all information of the uncertain database. Then, based on the UFP-tree, the algorithm recursively builds conditional subtrees and finds expected support-based frequent itemsets. UH-Mine is also based on the divide-and-conquer framework. The algorithm is extended from the H-Mine algorithm which is a classical algorithm in deterministic frequent itemset mining. Similar to H-Mine, UH-Mine first builds the special data structure, UH-Struct, and then recursively discovers the expected support-based frequent itemsets based on the DFS strategy.

Exact probabilistic frequent itemset mining algorithms. These algorithms discover all probabilistic frequent itemsets and report exact frequent probability for each itemset. Due to computing the exact frequent probability instead of the simple expectation, these algorithms need to spend at least $O(NlogN)$ computation cost for each itemset. Moreover, in order to avoid redundant processing, the Chernoff bound-based pruning is the main factor that affects the running time of the algorithms in this.

In this categorization, *UFIMT* contains two algorithms: DP (Dynamic Programming-based Apriori algorithm) [2] and DC (Divide-and-Conquer-based Apriori Algorithm) [6]. Both of them are based on the Apriori framework. The main difference between the two algorithms is the method for calculating the frequent probability of each itemset. The time complexity of the DP algorithm calculating the frequent probability is $O(N^2 \times min\_sup)$, however, that of DC algorithm is $O(NlogN)$.

Approximate probabilistic frequent itemset mining algorithms. These algorithms can obtain the approximate frequent probability with high quality by only acquiring the first moment (expectation) and the second moment (variance). Due to the sound properties of the Poisson Binomial distribution, the time complexities of calculating the expectation and the variance of each itemset are $O(N)$ (The first type of algorithms have the same time complexity). Therefore, these algorithms are much faster than the exact probabilistic frequent itemset mining algorithms but obtain the similar probability information when the uncertain databases are large enough. To sum up, the third type of algorithms actually build a bridge between two different definitions of frequent itemsets over uncertain databases.

In this categorization, *UFIMT* contains three algorithms: PDUApriori (Poisson Distribution-based UApriori) [9], NDUApriori (Normal Distribution-based UApriori) [3], and NDUH-Mine (Normal Distribution-based UH-Mine) [7]. Because the support of an itemset follows a Poisson Binomial distribution that can be approximated by a Poisson distribution, based on cumulative distribution function (CDF) of the Poisson distribution, PDUApriori solves the corresponding expected support λ of the given pft and calls UApriori to find all approximate probabilistic frequent itemsets. Moreover, according to the *Lyapunov Central Limit Theory*, NDUApriori algorithm uses the cumulative distribution function of a standard Normal distribution to approximately calculate the frequent probability.

Although the above two algorithms can obtain good approximation, it is impractical to apply them on very large sparse uncertain databases due to their Apriori framework. Therefore, we propose a novel algorithm, NDUH-Mine which integrates the framework of UH-Mine and the Normal distribution approximation in order to achieve a win-win partnership in sparse uncertain databases. In the other words, we calculate the variance of each itemset when we obtain the expected support of each itemset. Through extensive experiments over *UFIMT*, we can observe that NDUH-Mine has a better performance than PDUApriori and NDUApriori on very large sparse uncertain databases, which confirms the goal of our design.

Therefore, the Normal distribution-based approximation algorithms build a bridge between the definition of expected support-based frequent itemset mining and definition of the probabilistic frequent itemset mining. In particular, existing efficient expected support-based mining algorithms can be directly reused in the problem of mining probabilistic frequent itemsets and retain their intrinsic properties. In addition, more experimental comparisons and analysis about above algorithms can be found in [7].

2.3 System Architecture of UFIMT

In this subsection, we focus on our system architecture of *UFIMT*. Figure 1(a) shows the software system architecture of *UFIMT*. It consists of the following modules.

Data Preprocessing Module: it provides the normalized uncertain data. In our prototype system, uncertain data originates from two kinds of data sources. The first kind of data comes from a real sensor monitoring network. Because different kinds of sensors generate different formal data, our system needs normalizes different kinds of uncertain data into the unique data format. Moreover, the second kind of data is generated from some classical deterministic benchmarks, e.g. mushroom, connect, etc. In our data preprocessing module, it contains an uncertain data generator which assigns probabilities to deterministic data following a Normal distribution or a Zipf distribution.

Uncertain Mining Engine and Algorithm Library: *UFIMT* includes an uncertain mining engine which can compare the performance of mining algorithms and analyze the mining results according to users' requirements. In addition, an algorithm library is an important module in *UFIMT* as well. The algorithm library is consisted of the eight representative uncertain frequent itemset mining algorithms above and the novel variant algorithm developed by us, mining probabilistic frequent closed itemsets [8], respectively. All algorithms are based on the same basic functions, so that the comparable results are fair.

Comparable Analysis and User Visualization: Different from the traditional frequent pattern mining tools, *UFIMT* not only shows the result of single mining algorith-

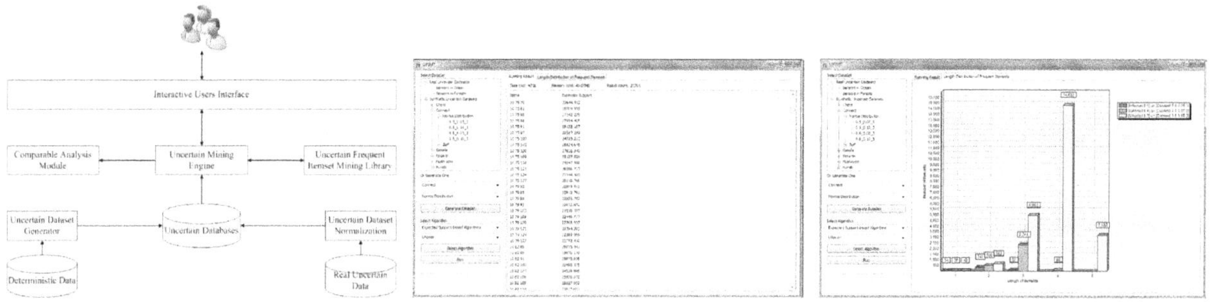

(a) System Architecture of *UFIMT* (b) Displaying A Running result in *UFIMT* (c) Length distribution of frequent itemsets

Figure 1: System Architecture and Screenshots of *UFIMT*

m, but also supports the performance comparison of different algorithms. For the visualization of the result of the single algorithm, *UFIMT* can show the running time, the memory usage, all frequent itemsets and their probability information. Moreover, *UFIMT* also uses the histograms to show all kinds of distributions of frequent itemsets. In particular, *UFIMT* can also demonstrate the effect of mining frequent closed itemsets. On the other hand, to visualize the comparison of multi-algorithms, *UFIMT* uses the visual methods to report the differences among the performances of the algorithms. Two screenshots of *UFIMT* are shown in Figure 1(b) and Figure 1(c), respectively. Figure 1(b) shows a running result of UApriori algorithm. Figure 1(c) reports the length distribution of all frequent itemsets under different minimum expected supports.

3. DEMONSTRATION PLAN

In the design and implementations of our prototype, *U-FIMT*, we mainly provide a practical platform of mining frequent itemsets over uncertain databases. In addition, *U-FIMT* seamlessly integrates eight existing representative algorithms of mining frequent itemsets over uncertain data [7] and a few novel variant solutions, such mining probabilistic frequent closed itemsets over uncertain databases [8].

We will introduce our prototype system thoroughly in our demo. In particular, we will focus on the following aspects.

Firstly, we will show the overview of *UFIMT*, including the motivations and the problems handled by this prototype system. We will briefly introduce the difference between frequent itemset mining over deterministic data and uncertain data to the audience. In particular, two different definitions of frequent itemsets over uncertain data will be explained, and several challenges about this topic will be reviewed, such as the contradictory conclusions in current researches.

Secondly, we will report the system architecture and the technical details in *UFIMT*, including the implementation details. We will discuss implementation details of all mining algorithms. In particular, we will show the audience how *UFIMT* implements the common basic functions in an efficient and effective way.

Thirdly, we will demonstrate our prototype system over both real and synthetic uncertain databases which includes on two real uncertain databases and six synthetic uncertain databases. We will show our visualization of *UFIMT* through the live presentation as well.

Finally, we will show our prototype system and invite audiences to use *UFIMT*. Audiences are encouraged to use the system on all kinds of datasets in order to further understand how to find frequent itemsets over uncertain databases.

4. CONCLUSIONS

In this demo, we present a novel prototype system, *U-FIMT*, which provides a practical platform for mining frequent itemsets over uncertain databases. Since there are two definitions of frequent itemsets over uncertain data, most existing researches are categorized into two directions. However, through our explorations, *UFIMT* firstly clarifies that there is a close relationship between the two different definitions. Secondly, *UFIMT* provides baseline implementations of eight existing representative algorithms and tests their performances. Finally, through extensive experiments, *U-FIMT* verifies several existing inconsistent conclusions and finds some new rules on this topic.

5. ACKNOWLEDGMENTS

This work is supported in part by the Hong Kong RGC GRF Project No.611411, National Grand Fundamental Research 973 Program of China under Grant 2012-CB316200, HP IRP Project 2011, Microsoft Research Asia Grant, M-RA11EG05, US NSF grants DBI-0960443, CNS-1115234, and IIS-0914934, and Google Mobile 2014 Program.

6. REFERENCES

[1] C. Aggarwal, Y. Li, J. Wang, and J. Wang. Frequent pattern mining with uncertain data. In *KDD'09*.

[2] T. Bernecker, H.-P. Kriegel, M. Renz, F. Verhein, and A. Züfle. Probabilistic frequent itemset mining in uncertain databases. In *KDD'09*.

[3] T. Calders, C. Garboni, and B. Goethals. Approximation of frequentness probability of itemsets in uncertain data. In *ICDM'10*.

[4] C. K. Chui, B. Kao, and E. Hung. Mining frequent itemsets from uncertain data. In *PAKDD'07*.

[5] C. K.-S. Leung, M. A. F. Mateo, and D. A. Brajczuk. A tree-based approach for frequent pattern mining from uncertain data. In *PAKDD'08*.

[6] L. Sun, R. Cheng, D. W. Cheung, and J. Cheng. Mining uncertain data with probabilistic guarantees. In *KDD'10*.

[7] Y. Tong, L. Chen, Y. Cheng, and P. S. Yu. Mining frequent itemsets over uncertain databases. In *VLDB'12*.

[8] Y. Tong, L. Chen, and B. Ding. Discovering threshold-based frequent closed itemsets over probabilistic data. In *ICDE'12*.

[9] L. Wang, R. Cheng, S. D. Lee, and D. W.-L. Cheung. Accelerating probabilistic frequent itemset mining: a model-based approach. In *CIKM'10*.

Visual Exploration of Collaboration Networks based on Graph Degeneracy

Christos Giatsidis
LIX, École Polytechnique
Palaiseau Cedex, France
xristosakamad@gmail.com

Klaus Berberich
LIX, École Polytechnique
Palaiseau Cedex, France
klaus@berberi.ch

Dimitrios M. Thilikos
Department of Mathematics,
National & Kapodistrian
University of Athens
Athens, Greece
sedthilk@math.uoa.gr

Michalis Vazirgiannis
Department of Informatics,
Athens University of
Economics and Business
Athens, Greece
mvazirg@aueb.gr

ABSTRACT

We demonstrate a system that supports the visual exploration of collaboration networks. The system leverages the notion of fractional cores introduced in earlier work to rank vertices in a collaboration network and filter vertices' neighborhoods. Fractional cores build on the idea of graph degeneracy as captured by the notion of k-cores in graph theory and extend it to undirected edge-weighted graphs. In a co-authorship network, for instance, the fractional core index of an author intuitively reflects the degree of collaboration with equally or higher-ranked authors. Our system has been deployed on a real-world co-authorship network derived from DBLP, demonstrating that the idea of fractional cores can be applied even to large-scale networks. The system provides an easy-to-use interface to query for the fractional core index of an author, to see who the closest equally or higher-ranked co-authors are, and explore the entire co-authorship network in an incremental manner.

Categories and Subject Descriptors

H.3.3 [**Information Search & Retrieval**]

General Terms

Algorithms, Experimentation.

Keywords

Collaboration networks, graph degeneracy, fractional cores.

KDD'12, August 12–16, 2012, Beijing, China.

1. INTRODUCTION

Our focus in this work is on providing tools to visually explore collaboration networks. Such networks arise in different contexts including science, entertainment and society. Co-authorship networks, as a concrete example from science, encode researchers' collaborations on joint publications. Given the large scale of such networks (e.g., the co-authorship network derived from DBLP that we use for our demo consists of more than 0.8M vertices and 4.4M edges), tools to explore them must provide a clutter-free view on vertices and their neighborhoods. This mandates meaningful ways to rank and filter vertices.

To these ends, we build on the idea of *graph degeneracy* that is tightly connected with the concept of k-cores. In a nutshell, the k-core of an undirected graph is its largest subgraph in which every vertex has a degree of at least k. The concept of k-cores is fundamental in graph theory and has been investigated since the 1960's [4,8,10]. The existence of k-cores of large size in sufficiently dense graphs, for instance, has been theoretically studied by [2,9,11] for random graphs generated by the Erdős-Rényi model [5].

In earlier work [6], we proposed the notion of fractional cores as an extension of the k-core concept to undirected edge-weighted graphs. This extension takes into account not only the number but also the strength of connections that a vertex in the graph has. When looking at a co-authorship network (e.g., the one derived from DBLP as our showcase application), we thus take into account both the number of collaborations that authors have as well as their contribution to each of them. Our demonstrated system leverages the notion of fractional cores to rank and filter vertices in the network. It is available at the following URL:

`http://www.graphdegeneracy.org/fcores/dblp/`

We stress that the visualization of the hop-1 coauthoring community we propose conveys much more meaning and information than the simple co-author graphs presented in other approaches such as the *Co-author Graph* at `http://academic.research.microsoft.com/` or the respective in Arnet Miner at `http://arnetminer.org/`). More specifically, in our case the visualization depicts the neighbors of authors in the DBLP co-authorship network that are *inside* the highest index core they belong to. This implies that the appearing co-authors is the subset of all coauthors that also belong to the current or better k-core. Thus these authors are those that are at least as collaborative as the one we are concerned. Therefore this graph is the best co-authorship community of the author bearing as well weights on the edges. These edges indicate the amount of the co-authorship effort shared among the authors at the ends of the edge.

Organization. The rest of this paper unfolds as follows: In Section 2, we describe the concept of fractional cores and explain how it can be used to rank and filter vertices in collaboration networks. Section 3 describes the architecture of our system. Our demo is outlined in Section 4. Finally, Section 5 lays out other potential application scenarios.

2. FRACTIONAL K-CORE RANKING

We now describe the notion of fractional cores and explain how it can be used to rank and filter vertices in a collaboration network.

Collaboration Networks are formally represented as follows: Consider a bipartite graph

$$G = (A, P, E)$$

where A is the set of authors, P is the set of papers, and E is a set of edges. Each edge $\{x, y\}$ (where $x \in A$ and $y \in P$) expresses the fact that x is one of the authors of paper y. We also assume that all papers are written by at least two authors. This is a safe assumption, given that single-author papers can be ignored for our application. Given G, we construct an edge-weighted graph $(H_G, \mathbf{w})$ whose vertex set is A and where an edge connects two authors if and only if they appear as co-authors in at least one paper. We call $(H_G, \mathbf{w})$ the *co-authorship graph* of G. The mere existence of some edge H_G does not convey how intensively the two authors have collaborated in the past. Therefore, we set up a weighing function $\mathbf{w}$ that assigns a weight $w(e)$ on each edge $e = \{x, x'\}$ of H_G according to the following scheme:

$$\mathbf{w}(e) = \sum_{y \in N_G(x) \cap N_G(x')} \frac{1}{|N_G(y)|}$$

where $N_G(x)$ is the set of neighbors in G of the vertex x, i.e., the set of papers that were authored by x. Notice that in the above formula, we implicitly assume that all authors of a paper have put equal effort in its preparation. Given that we have assigned a weight to each of the edges of G, we can extend the notion of the degree of a vertex x by defining:

$$\mathbf{deg}_{G,\mathbf{w}}(x) = \sum_{e \in E(x)} \mathbf{w}(e). \qquad (1)$$

Fractional k-Cores. Let $\mathbb{Q}^+$ be the set of all positive rational numbers. Given a $k \in \mathbb{Q}$, we define the *fractional k-core* of $(H_G, \mathbf{w})$ as the maximum size subgraph of H such that for each of its vertices, the sum of the weights of its incident edges is no smaller than k. It is easy to prove that this graph is unique. For this reason it can be computed easily by discarding from H_G vertices of fractional degree less than k until no such vertices exist anymore. We refer to this procedure as the *Trim* procedure. For more details and pseudo-code of this procedure, the reader is referred to [6]. The procedure runs in $O(n+m)$ time where n is the number of vertices and m is the number of edges in H_G [1].

Ranking. To determine a ranking of vertices in the graph (i.e., authors in our case), we consider the infinite sequence $\mathcal{G} = G_0, G_1, \ldots,$ recursively defined as follows: $G_0 = G, h_0 = 0$, and for $i > 0$, $G_i = Trim(G_{i-1}, h_{i-1})$ where $h_i = \delta(G_i, \mathbf{w}_{G_i})$ refers to the minimum weighted degree according to (1) in the graph G_i. Then, the *fractional core sequence* of an edge-weighted graph $(G, \mathbf{w})$ is the prefix of $\mathcal{G}$ that contains all the non-empty graphs of $\mathcal{G}$. Notice that this sequence divides the original graph into "levels of cohesion". That is, as we increase h_i the corresponding G_i contains fewer vertices – corresponding to those authors who have collaborated more often and/or more intensively. We define the *fractional core index* of a vertex x to be the maximum h_i for which x belongs to the fractional h_i-core G_i.

3. SYSTEM ARCHITECTURE

Figure 1 depicts the overall architecture of our system, which is the subject of this section. For our demonstration, we use a co-authorship network derived from the DBLP bibliographic dataset[1]

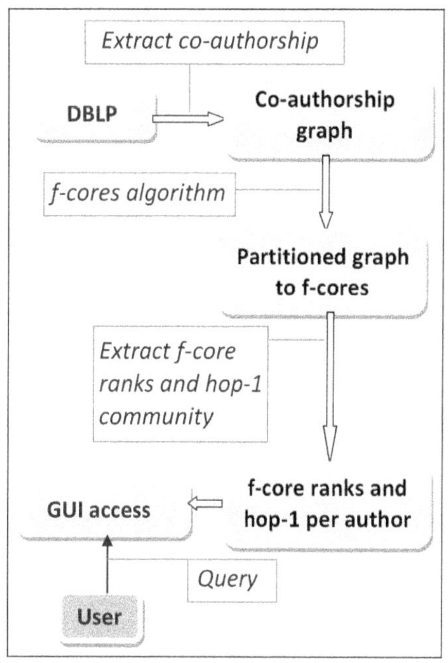

Figure 1: System Architecture

Going from top to bottom in Figure 1, we first convert the bibliographic dataset into an undirected edge-weighted co-authorship graph as described in Section 2. If two authors have co-authored a paper, this graph contains an undirected edge with a weight according to (1).

Next, as a one-time pre-computation, we iteratively compute the fractional core sequence of this graph. That is, we repeatedly invoke the *Trim* procedure, removing more and more vertices from the graph and thus implicitly partition it. When we remove a vertex from the graph, we keep track

[1]Freely available at `http://dblp.uni-trier.de`.

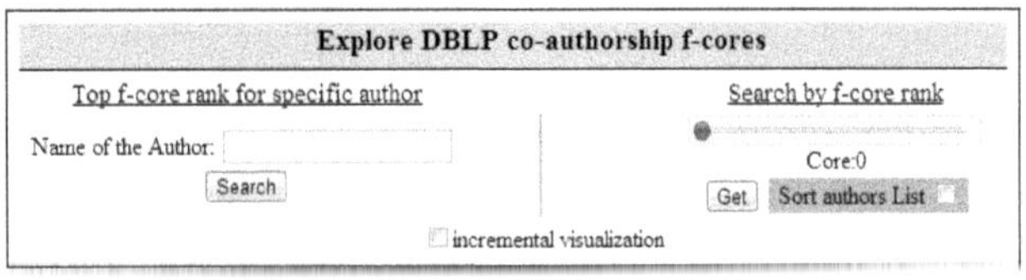

Figure 2: Main input interface

of its fractional core index and its hop-1 neighborhood consisting of immediate neighbors in the remaining graph. This information is stored in a relational database, so that it can be retrieved efficiently by our system at runtime. Note that, despite of the large scale of the DBLP co-authorship network, we were able to run the entire computation on a commodity notebook equipped with a 2-core CPU and 2 GB of main memory – an indication that fractional cores are computationally lightweight and can be applied to large-scale collaboration networks.

Users interact with our system through a web-based GUI that was implemented building on the Dracula Graph javascrpit library and can be accessed at the aforementioned URL. Its functionality, described in more detail in the following Section 4, includes showing rankings of authors by their fractional core index but also an interactive visualization of an author's neighborhood, displaying only those co-authors with an equal or higher fractional core index to provide a clutter-free view on the collaboration network.

4. DEMONSTRATION

The main user interface of our system is shown in Figure 2, offering users two options to interact. On the right, a slider allows users to select a threshold on the fractional core index and browse through qualifying authors. On the left, an input box allows users to search for a specific author by name – both exact match and fuzzy match are supported here. Either way, once an author has been selected, the system shows the fractional core index of the author together with a visualization of the surrounding hop-1 neighborhood, i.e., the author's closest co-authors who have at least an equally high fractional core index. Figure 3 shows an example hop-1 neighborhood (in this case for Michalis Vazirgiannis). From the visualization, users can see author's fractional core index (here 10.6) and his "tightest" collaborators each linked with a weighted edge indicating the "strength" of their partnership.

On this initial star-like graph the user can explore the surrounding authors by clicking on the "Find" function that appears when the mouse hovers over the author's vertex. If the "incremental visualization" option is not activated the result of the "Find" function is a fresh star-like graph centered around the newly selected author. Otherwise, if the option is activated, the user gets to explore the intersection of the two authors' (the original and the newly selected one) strongest collaborators. This "incremental" visualization can continue for multiple steps to reveal an increasingly broader and possibly highly interconnected community around an author. Figure 5 demonstrates this functionality building on our earlier example. Here, the star-like graph from Figure 3 was expanded by selecting Timos K. Sellis from the surrounding hop-1 neighborhood of collaborators. Interestingly, as can be observed from the figure, there is an overlap between the "tightest" collaborators of the two authors,

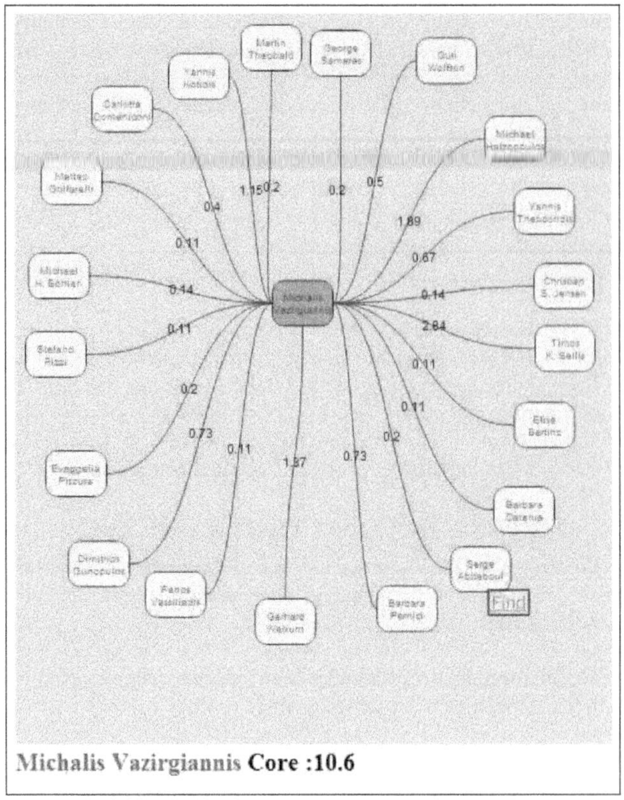

Figure 3: Output for the query "Vazirgiannis"

revealing a much richer view on the community that they belong to.

When the user selects a threshold for the fractional core index with the slider shown in Figure 2, using the "incremental" function more than one author can be selected and the user can see how different communities form within the same fractional core from the interconnection of the authors within that core. Figure 4 shows a small example based on authors from the 19.6-core – it is interesting to see the selected authors belong to two disconnected communities.

We will encourage conference attendants to interact with the system and use it to explore the(ir) DBLP co-authorship network. Until then, our system can be tried out online at the URL mentioned above. A screencast of the above test cases on our demo can be found at

`http://www.youtube.com/watch?v=XnzZqvzdOyo`

5. APPLICATION SCENARIOS

What are other application scenarios where a visual exploration of collaboration networks, as provided by our system, can provide useful insights?

Bibliographic data and measures derived therefrom (e.g., the H-Index [7] and G-Index [3]) nowadays play a big role in *academic hiring*. Measures like the aforementioned one have focused on citations and sought to capture a candidate's scientific impact. As networking skills and the ability to work in teams become more important, even in academia, our system provides the means to inspect a candidate in these regards. By relying on the notion of fractional cores, our system automatically zooms in on the connections to peers

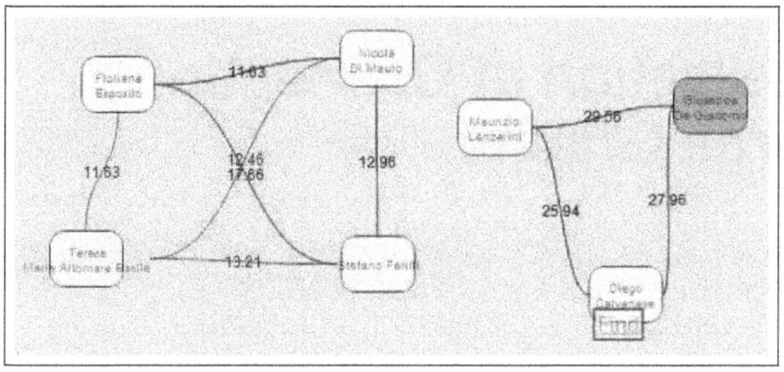

Figure 4: Example of browsing the 19.6-core with the "incremental" function activated

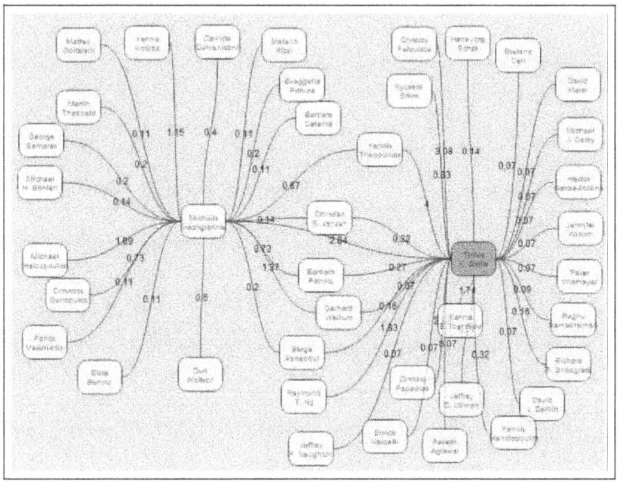

Figure 5: Example of browsing the hop-1 neighborhood with the "incremental" function activated

and more senior scientists and, as a consequence, provides a clutter-free view on the candidate's collaborations. Thus, collaborations that are ephemeral or with less prolific individuals (e.g., students who left academia after graduating) are automatically filtered out thanks to the use of fractional cores. We foresee similar applications for *human resources* and *team building* in industry, where collaboration networks can be derived from other datasets, e.g., patents (based on the listed inventor names), e-mails (based on recipient lists) or records about who worked together on which projects in the past. We believe that a visual exploration of collaboration networks can also turn out insightful for other collaboration networks, for example, those of actors who played in the same movie (e.g., derived from a movie database such as IMDB[2]) or politicians who co-signed a petition or participated in other joint activities.

The ideas behind our system are not limited to collaboration networks but can be applied to any dataset from which undirected weighted graphs can be derived in a sensible manner. This includes various facets of social networks with ties that signify, for instance, joint interests (based on group memberships) or reciprocal activities. Also in other contexts, the ability to visually explore large-scale datasets becomes more important in face of the ongoing data deluge. Some of the now available data has natural interpretations as graphs, for example, RDF datasets like those connected in the linked data cloud[3]. We expect that a visual exploration of such datasets can greatly profit from the use of fractional cores that, as in the applications above, help to get a clutter-free view on the data that focuses on essential highly-connected data items. Deploying our system on such datasets and evaluating its usefulness here is part of our ongoing work.

6. ACKNOWLEDGMENTS

All the authors of this paper are generously supported by the DIGITEO Chair grant LEVETONE in France

7. REFERENCES

[1] V. Batagelj and M. Zaversnik. An $o(m)$ algorithm for cores decomposition of networks. *CoRR*, cs.DS/0310049, 2003.

[2] B. Bollobás. The evolution of sparse graphs. In *Graph theory and combinatorics (Cambridge, 1983)*, pages 35–57. Academic Press, London, 1984.

[3] L. Egghe. Theory and practise of the g-index. *Scientometrics*, 69(1):131–152, 2006.

[4] P. Erdős. On the structure of linear graphs. *Israel J. Math.*, 1:156–160, 1963.

[5] P. Erdős and A. Rényi. On the evolution of random graphs. *Magyar Tud. Akad. Mat. Kutató Int. Közl.*, 5:17–61, 1960.

[6] C. Giatsidis, D. M. Thilikos, and M. Vazirgiannis. Evaluating cooperation in communities with the k-core structure. In *ASONAM*, pages 87–93, 2011.

[7] J. Hirsch. An index to quantify an individual's scientific research output. *Proceedings of the National Academy of Sciences of the United states of America*, 102(46):16569, 2005.

[8] D. W. Matula. A min–max theorem for graphs with application to graph coloring. *SIAM Reviews*, 10:481–482, 1968.

[9] B. Pittel, J. Spencer, and N. Wormald. Sudden emergence of a giant k-core in a random graph. *J. Combin. Theory Ser. B*, 67(1):111–151, 1996.

[10] G. Szekeres and H. S. Wilf. An inequality for the chromatic number of a graph. *J. Combinatorial Theory*, 4:1–3, 1968.

[11] T. Łuczak. Size and connectivity of the k-core of a random graph. *Discrete Mathematics*, pages 61–68, 1991.

[2] `http://www.imdb.com`

[3] `http://linkeddata.org`

TOURVIZ: Interactive Visualization of Connection Pathways in Large Graphs

Duen Horng (Polo) Chau
Carnegie Mellon University
dchau@cs.cmu.edu

Leman Akoglu
Carnegie Mellon University
lakoglu@cs.cmu.edu

Jilles Vreeken
University of Antwerp
jilles.vreeken@ua.ac.be

Hanghang Tong
IBM T.J. Watson Research
htong@us.ibm.com

Christos Faloutsos
Carnegie Mellon University
christos@cs.cmu.edu

ABSTRACT

We present TOURVIZ, a system that helps its users to interactively visualize and make sense in large network datasets. In particular, it takes as input a set of nodes the user specifies as of interest and presents the user with a visualization of connection subgraphs around these input nodes. Each connection subgraph contains good pathways that highlight succinct connections among a 'close-by' group of input nodes. TOURVIZ combines visualization with rich user interaction to engage and help the user to further understand the relations among the nodes of interest, by exploring their neighborhood on demand as well as modifying the set of interest nodes.

We demonstrate TOURVIZ's usage and benefits using the DBLP graph, consisting of authors and their co-authorship relations, while our system is designed generally to work with any kind of graph data. We will invite the audience to experiment with our system and comment on its usability, usefulness, and how our system can help with their research and improve the understanding of data in other domains.

Categories and Subject Descriptors

H.3.3 [**Information Storage and Retrieval**]; H.5.2 [**Information Interfaces and Presentation**]

General Terms

Algorithms, Design, Human Factors

Keywords

Sensemaking, Large networks, Connection subgraphs

1. INTRODUCTION

Finding associations among a set of objects is an important problem in many domains ranging from biology (gene/protein interactions), security (criminal/terrorist interactions), immunology (patient interactions), and so on. Often, these objects are connected with certain type of relations within a large network. In such a network setting, the task of finding associations among objects can be thought of finding succinct connection pathways among these objects. While these connection pathways reveal how the set of objects associate with one another in the network, the additional nodes (connectors) revealed on these pathways provide useful information about other nodes that might be of interest in understanding these associations.

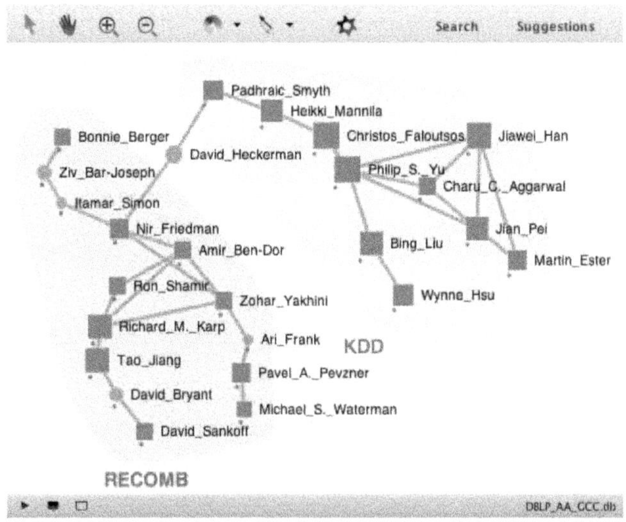

Figure 1: Screenshot of TOURVIZ showing a user exploring the connection subgraphs among a set of authors of interest (square nodes) in KDD and RECOMB (computational biology). Edges are co-authorship relations.

The above setting finds numerous applications in diverse domains. For example, given a gene interaction network, an experiment may reveal for particular conditions a number of genes to be up- (or down-) regulated, and a biologist might be interested in finding associations between these genes. This would give him/her a good summary of possible pathways the genes may be involved in. Another example relates to security; given a set of suspicious people detected by an anomaly detection algorithm, an analyst could use our system to group them to reveal associations; by finding how as well as through whom else they are connected in the network. Moreover, given an event affecting a set of people connected via a network, e.g. people in a geographical region affected by a certain disease, an immunolog can use our system to figure out the pathways through which the disease spread among these people, potentially discovering other affected people on the connection pathways. More applications can be given, however, the main point

KDD'12, August 12–16, 2012, Beijing, China.

is that the system we shortly introduce is quite general and can be used in various settings independent of a specific domain.

We developed TOURVIZ (Figure1), an interactive visualization system, for a domain analyst to explore and understand the associations among a set of objects (i.e. nodes) in a network. The analyst selects a set of nodes that s/he is interested in within the network and specifies them as 'marked'. Next, within TOURVIZ an efficient algorithm finds succinct connection subgraphs among the marked nodes. Intuitively, 'close-by' (highly associated nodes) in the network can be connected by simple paths, while 'far away' (not-so-highly associated) nodes are hard to link together. Therefore, the algorithm returns possibly multiple connection subgraphs for multiple groups of 'close-by' nodes. TOURVIZ offers visualization features to show the analyst these groups and their associated connection subgraphs found by our algorithm. Our system also embodies interaction features for the analyst to update the nodes of interest on demand.

We summarize our main contributions as follows:

- We build a new system called TOURVIZ to provide users with the understanding of how a set of nodes in a network are associated, through visualizing good connections and connectors among them. TOURVIZ integrates novel algorithms we developed [1] for finding succinct connection pathways among groups of highly associated nodes.
- TOURVIZ integrates our novel algorithm into an interactive environment that allows users to easily specify nodes of interest, reveal connections among them through visualization, and iteratively refine their specifications to improve their understanding.

2. DEMONSTRATING TOURVIZ

We will demonstrate TOURVIZ's usage, user interaction and algorithm through scenarios on understanding connections among researchers in various computer science fields in the DBLP[1] coauthorship graph, which contains about 329K authors (nodes) and 1094K coauthorship relations (edges).

Scenario. Here, we illustrate one example scenario, where our user uses TOURVIZ to explore and understand the connections between several researchers in KDD (data mining, machine learning) and RECOMB (computational biology). This scenario will touch upon major features of TOURVIZ.

Our user begins by searching for authors that he is familiar with, using TOURVIZ's search feature (Figure 2). Authors whose names contains the search text show up as a list. They can be sorted alphabetically, or by various metrics that TOURVIZ has pre-computed for the graph (the first time the graph is loaded), e.g., PageRank score, degree, etc. Once a match is found, our user drags the name into the visualization, which turns into a circle, its size proportional to its coauthor count (i.e., node degree).

Our user proceeds to drag in more authors he is familiar with, in the domains of KDD and RECOMB. Although the user is familiar with these researchers' work, s/he does not recall how they have been collaborating. In particular, s/he is interested in using TOURVIZ to figure out the researchers who have been working at the intersection of these two domains.

To help keep track of the two groups of researchers, our user groups them into KDD and RECOMB using TOURVIZ's *grouping* feature (Figure 3). Each group is assigned a color, and its nodes enclosed by a convex hull.

These are all the nodes that our user wants to create a connection subgraph for (Figure 3). To mark these nodes as inputs, our user

[1] http://dblp.uni-trier.de/

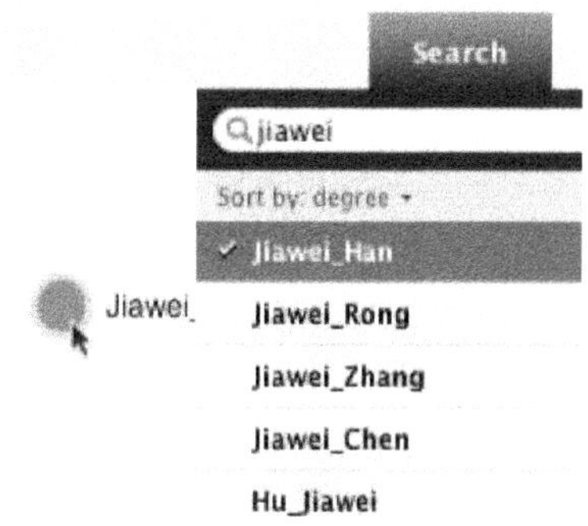

Figure 2: User searching for "jiawei". Matching authors shown in a list, sorted by the authors' coauthor counts (i.e., node *degrees* in the graph. Dragging the name of "Jiawei Han" into the visualization turns it into a circle; the name becomes the node label. Node size is scaled by degree. The yellow halo around the node indicates it is a match.

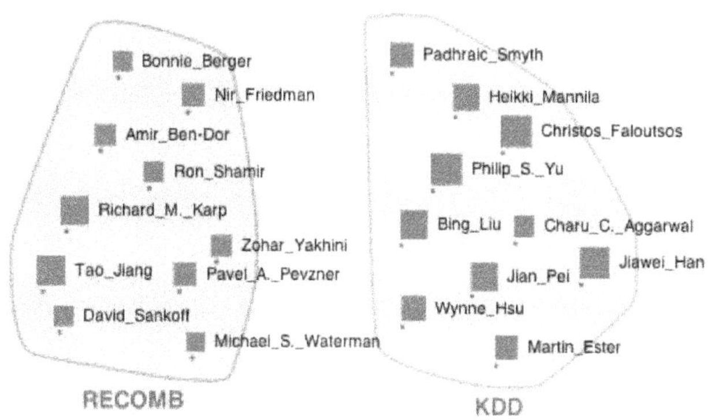

Figure 3: Our user has dragged multiple authors into the visualization, and grouped them into KDD and RECOMB using TOURVIZ's *grouping* feature. Each group is enclosed by a convex hull. Group names are provided by the user. Blue square nodes are the *marked* input nodes to TOURVIZ.

changes their shapes into squares (node colors do not matter). Next, they are given as input to TOURVIZ's algorithm that finds the best subgraph. We will explain how the algorithm works in more detail in Section 3. Simply put, it finds a simple subgraph spanning all the input nodes that also has as few edges and as few additional intermediary nodes as possible.

Figure 4 shows the result of the algorithm —a tree whose edges are shown as thick orange lines, connecting the *marked* nodes with a few *intermediary* nodes (orange circles). Thin edges are other relations among all the nodes being displayed, but not part of the tree. Most interesting to our user is the discovery of David Heckerman; a prolific researcher who have been publishing with authors who frequent KDD and RECOMB. Additional discoveries include the intermediary nodes, that is the authors such as Ziv Bar-Joseph and Ari Frank, who are good connectors among the authors that our user is interested in observing the relations.

Here, since the whole tree has few nodes, our user can rearrange the nodes manually to create a visually pleasing layout. Optionally, he can also use TOURVIZ's built-in force-directed *layout* feature to automatically layout the nodes, which often helps reduce node and edge overlap.

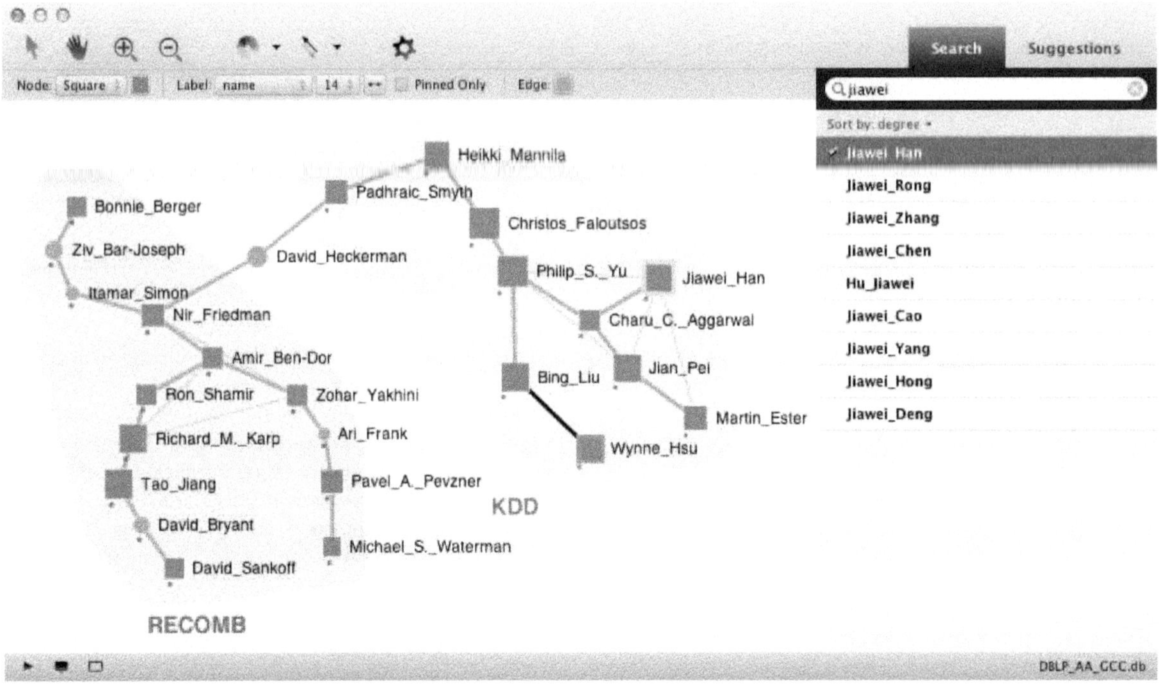

Figure 4: Screenshot of TOURVIZ showing our user exploring the connection subgraph among a set of authors of interest (blue, square nodes) in KDD and RECOMB (computational biology). Node shape is set using the first drop-down menu on the left; these nodes serve as input to the algorithm that finds the best tree (thick, orange edges) that connects them; other edges are shown as thin lines. Edges are co-authorship relations. Node size is scaled by the node's degree. TOURVIZ comes with useful visualization features: pan and zoom tool on the first row, color tools for nodes and edges, node label tool for specifying font size and node attribute to show (node "name" is chosen here). Our user can search for authors using the *Search Panel* on the right.

Our user can interactively add or remove nodes (marked or unmarked), and refresh the visualization with an updated connection subgraph by invoking the algorithm. Nodes that were previously in the visualization will maintain their positions, to help our user preserve his mental model about the connections.

Engaging Our Audience. We will invite our audience to try out TOURVIZ with their own set of authors, and collect their feedback on TOURVIZ's usability and usefulness. Since we created TOURVIZ to be a general tool, we will be particularly interested in discussing with our audience how TOURVIZ may help them with research and data visualization in their domains.

3. TECHNICAL DETAILS

In this section, we first provide details about how the algorithm in our system works, and then give information about implementation and integration with the visualization component.

3.1 Method Details

Idea of encoding. Our method addresses the problem of succinctly describing a given set of marked nodes in a graph. We formulate this problem using an encoding scheme, which involves a sender and a receiver. In this scheme both the sender and the receiver know the graph structure $G = (V, E)$, while only the sender knows the set of marked nodes. The goal of the sender, then, is to transmit to the receiver the information of which nodes are marked, using *as few bits as possible*.

Intuitively, the sender could use fewer bits to encode 'close-by' marked nodes; by following a (short) path from one to another. For each such path, the sender encodes the starting node using $\log |V|$ bits. The following nodes on the path are described by encoding the particular neighbor of the previous node i to go to the next node $i+1$, which requires $\log d_i < \log |V|$ bits since the degree of each node in the graph is bounded by $|V| - 1$. A *simple* connection subgraph for a group of 'close-by' nodes is the union of such paths.

Notice that the simplest subgraph is in fact a *tree* since it requires fewer bits to directly refer to a node that is already encoded, compared to following a path to it. In addition, low degree nodes are preferred over hub-like node on the paths, since it takes fewer bits to encode where to go next for such nodes. Intuitively, hub-like nodes are avoided in connecting the marked nodes since practically they connect everything in the graph and thus do not constitute interesting candidates as connectors. All in all, we find one simple tree for every group of 'close-by' marked nodes. Two groups are separated if no path of cost less than $\log |V|$ bits exists inbetween.

Steiner tree problem. Simplicity of a connection tree is determined by the number of nodes the sender visits in this encoding, how many unmarked nodes s/he visits, and in particular how easily per visited node s/he can identify which edge to follow next. We show that the problem of finding the simplest tree with the minimum encoding is NP-hard, with a reduction from the Directed Steiner tree problem: Given a directed weighted graph $G = (V, E)$ and a subset of (marked) nodes M, find the minimum cost arborescence that spans all (marked) nodes in M. The cost of the tree is the sum of the weights (encoding costs) of its edges. The tree may include (unmarked) nodes that are not in M, which are referred to as Steiner nodes.

Fast heuristic methods. As the directed Steiner tree problem is NP-hard, we develop four fast heuristic approximation algorithms for large graphs. (1) The first and simplest method only considers the connected components induced on the marked nodes. (2)

The second method first builds the transitive closure graph of the marked nodes in which each pair of marked nodes are connected by an edge of weight equal to the minimum cost path inbetween them (no edge if the path length is greater than $\log |V|$). Next, it runs a minimum arborescence algorithm on this small graph of M nodes. Finally each edge in the returned tree(s) is expanded to include the original nodes on the path represented by that edge. (3) The third method builds the minimum depth-1 tree(s) in which the root marked node is connected to each other marked node with the shortest path length. (4) Finally, the fourth method builds on the depth-1 tree(s) to build larger depth trees, by finding intermediate nodes that decrease the total cost. Our method returns the best tree among found by various heuristics that has the minimum cost.

3.2 System Details

The visualization component of TOURVIZ system is written in Java 1.7. built on top of the open-source JUNG network visualization library [8] and with design based on the APOLO [2] system. TOURVIZ stores the graph in a SQLite[2] embedded database, for its cross-platform portability. The graph database's schema was designed independently from the TOURVIZ system, so that different graphs that follow the schema can be readily used. TOURVIZ takes advantage of built-in features from SQLite, such as its full-text search capability to quickly locate nodes whose attribute values match users' search text (Figure 2).

When the user interactively specifies the set of marked nodes for which the connection subgraphs are to be found, the IDs of these nodes are written to a temporary file. This file as well as the directory for the network data are input to our algorithm which is implemented in Matlab 7.10. The algorithm then outputs the best connection tree(s) as well as small subgraphs around the seed nodes (candidate graph). TOURVIZ shows the candidate graph and highlights (in bold) the edges that correspond to the best tree edges.

4. RELATED WORK

TOURVIZ builds on a large body of research aimed at understanding and supporting how people can gain insights through network visualization [7]. It provides several features to help people specify the nodes of interest in a network and visualize connection subgraphs in context of local neighborhoods around these nodes that are not too overwhelming [2].

Much work has been done on finding connection subgraphs, introduced by [4], and extended by [9] and [11]. Related work include expanding communities around a given set of seed nodes [10, 12] such that the modularity or conductance of the subgraph containing the seed nodes is optimized. [13] finds the most 'centered' node that has strong connections (good paths) to most or all of the seed nodes. [6] finds the subgraph up to a certain size which retains most of the proximity between seed nodes. Proximity and connection subgraphs are also exploited for visualization and summarization [3, 5].

Few tools have integrated connection subgraphs algorithms to interactively help people make sense of associations among nodes in a graph, and they often only support some of the sensemaking features offered by TOURVIZ, e.g., showing (multiple) connection subgraphs only among highly associated *groups* of nodes, rather than a single large subgraph including all nodes at once.

5. CONCLUSIONS

We presented TOURVIZ, an interactive system to help people understand connections between sets of nodes in large graphs. Our system integrates 1) novel algorithms that find the best subgraphs for succinctly connecting these nodes; and 2) visualization and interaction features that help people interactively and visually explore such subgraphs.

We demonstrated TOURVIZ's usage and benefits using a DBLP co-authorship graph, which consists of 329K authors (nodes) and 1094K co-authorship relations (edges). We invite our audience to try TOURVIZ, comment on its usability and usefulness, and discuss how TOURVIZ may help with their work as well as data analytics in other domains.

[2]www.sqlite.org

6. ACKNOWLEDGEMENT

Research was sponsored by the National Science Foundation under Grant No. IIS1017415 and the Army Research Laboratory under Cooperative Agreement No. W911NF-09-2-0053. It is continuing through participation in the Anomaly Detection at Multiple Scales (ADAMS) program sponsored by the U.S. Defense Advanced Research Projects Agency (DARPA) under Agreements No. W911NF-11-C-0200 and W911NF-11-C-0088. The views and conclusions contained in this document are those of the authors and should not be interpreted as representing the official policies, either expressed or implied, of the Army Research Laboratory, of the National Science Foundation, of the U.S. Government, or any other funding parties. The U.S. Government is authorized to reproduce and distribute reprints for Government purposes notwithstanding any copyright notation here on. This work is also partially supported by an IBM Faculty Award.

Jilles Vreeken is supported by a Post-Doctoral Fellowship of the Research Foundation – Flanders (FWO).

7. REFERENCES

[1] L. Akoglu, J. Vreeken, H. Tong, D. H. Chau, and C. Faloutsos. Islands and bridges: Making sense of marked nodes in large graphs. Technical Report CMU-CS-12-124, Carnegie Mellon University, 2012.

[2] D. Chau, A. Kittur, J. I. Hong, and C. Faloutsos. Apolo: Making Sense of Large Network Data by Combining Rich User Interaction and Machine Learning. In *CHI*, 2011.

[3] D. H. Chau, C. Faloutsos, H. Tong, J. I. Hong, B. Gallagher, and T. Eliassi-Rad. Graphite: A visual query system for large graphs. In *ICDM Workshops*, pages 963–966, 2008.

[4] C. Faloutsos, K. S. McCurley, and A. Tomkins. Fast discovery of connection subgraphs. In *KDD*, 2004.

[5] J. F. R. Jr., H. Tong, A. J. M. Traina, C. Faloutsos, and J. Leskovec. Gmine: A system for scalable, interactive graph visualization and mining. In *VLDB*, pages 1195–1198, 2006.

[6] Y. Koren, S. C. North, and C. Volinsky. Measuring and extracting proximity in networks. In *KDD*, 2006.

[7] B. Kules. From keyword search to exploration: How result visualization aids discovery on the web.

[8] J. O'Madadhain, D. Fisher, P. Smyth, S. White, and Y. Boey. Analysis and visualization of network data using JUNG. *Journal of Statistical Software*, 10:1–35, 2005.

[9] C. Ramakrishnan, W. H. Milnor, M. Perry, and A. P. Sheth. Discovering informative connection subgraphs in multi-relational graphs. 7(2):56–63, 2005.

[10] J. Riedy, D. A. Bader, K. Jiang, P. Pande, , and R. Sharma. Detecting communities from given seeds in social networks. *Technical Report GT-CSE-11-01*, 2011.

[11] P. Sevon and L. Eronen. Subgraph queries by context-free grammars. *J. Integrative Bioinformatics*, 5(2), 2008.

[12] D. A. Spielman and S.-H. Teng. A local clustering algorithm for massive graphs and its application to nearly-linear time graph partitioning. *CoRR*, abs/0809.3232, 2008.

[13] H. Tong and C. Faloutsos. Center-piece subgraphs: problem definition and fast solutions. In *KDD*, pages 404–413, 2006.

D-INDEX: a Web Environment for Analyzing Dependences among Scientific Collaborators

Claudio Schifanella
Università di Torino
Torino, Italy
schi@di.unito.it

Luigi Di Caro
Università di Torino
Torino, Italy
dicaro@di.unito.it

Mario Cataldi
École Centrale Paris
Paris, France
mario.cataldi@ecp.fr

Marie-Aude Aufaure
École Centrale Paris
Paris, France
marie-aude.aufaure@ecp.fr

ABSTRACT

In this work, we demonstrate a web application, available at *http://d-index.di.unito.it*, that permits to analyze the scientific profiles of all the researchers indexed by DBLP[1] by focusing on the collaborations that contributed to define their curricula. The presented application allows the user to analyze the profile of a researcher, her dependence degrees on all the co-authors (along her entire scientific publication history) and to make comparisons among them in terms of dependence patterns. In particular, it is possible to estimate and visualize how much a researcher has benefited from collaboration with another researcher as well as the communities in which she has been involved. Moreover, the application permits to compare, in a single chart, each researcher with all the scientists indexed in DBLP by focusing on their dependences with respect to many other parameters like the total number of papers, the number of collaborations and the length of the scientific careers.

Categories and Subject Descriptors

H.3.5 [**Information Systems Applications**]: On-line Information Services; H.4 [**Information Systems Applications**]: Miscellaneous

General Terms

Experimentation

Keywords

Scientometrics, DBLP, Collaboration Graph

[1]www.informatik.uni-trier.de/~ley/db/

1. INTRODUCTION

The evaluation of the work of a researcher and its impact on the later literature has been widely studied because of its real and relevant applications, like recruitment, funding allocation, and so forth. With the growing of new on-line digital platforms, like DBLP, Google Scholar, Microsoft Academic Search, CiteSeer, etc., it is becoming easier than ever to explore and experiment ways of evaluating research products thanks to their aggregated information, like co-authorships, number of citations and related data. Despite this, even considering these web services, an author's publication and/or citation record gives only a partial account of the author's scientific profile. Indeed, in an evaluation process some co-authored works can unconditionally favor researchers who collaborated with those experts who were able to lead high-quality research projects. On the other hand, those who produced such relevant research products could not be distinguished (within their pure publication list) from their co-authors because of the typical assumption of a proportional collaboration among them.

Given these considerations, while many works evaluate the quantity and/or the quality of the research, (one among all, the *h*-index [2] and its different variations, a distinct part of the problem involves the study of co-authorship dependences, in terms of scientific influence among the authors. The evaluation of such collaboration networks is anyway a challenging task that, to the best of our knowledge, received few interests so far. Some tools like DBLPVis, ArnetMiner or Microsoft Academic Search permit to visualize the academic career of a researcher through her co-authorship relations; however, they only show the relationships among authors based on the number of co-authored papers and are not suitable for such a challenging task.

In this paper we demonstrate a way to estimate this *dependence degree* among co-authors and present a set of graphical tools, integrated in the web environment *http://d-index.di.unito.it*, for permitting analyses, comparisons and evaluations of researchers' dependences.

2. BACKGROUND: D-INDEX

In this paper we make use of a novel measure of dependence between two co-authors, presented in [1], called *d*-index, which is calculated based on the *co-authorship network* that represents the common environment they have

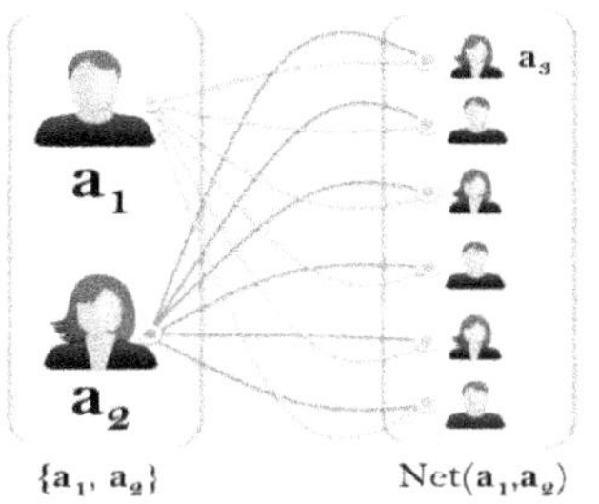

Figure 1: *Bipartite dependence Graph*: two authors a_1 and a_2 and the set of co-authors that they have in common (Net_{a_1,a_2}).

been working in. This is modeled through a *Bipartite Dependence Graph*, or *BDG*, which aim is to represent two authors in their scientific environment, defined as the set of co-authors they have in common. More in detail, given two authors a_i and a_j, we define their $BDG_{a_i,a_j} = \{V_{a_i,a_j}, E_{a_i,a_j}, w\}$, where

- $V_{a_i,a_j} = \{a_i, a_j\} \cup Net_{a_i,a_j}$, where Net_{a_i,a_j} is the set of researchers that co-authored at least one paper with both a_i and a_j;
- E_{a_i,a_j} contains the undirected edges representing collaborations between two authors (i.e., if $e_{a_x,a_y} \in E_{a_i,a_j}$ there is at least one paper co-authored by both a_x and a_y, with $a_x \in \{a_i, a_j\} \wedge a_y \in Net_{a_i,a_j}$);
- w is the weighting function.

The weight w of each edge within the *BDG* represents the *relative dependence* of a collaboration between two authors with respect to a co-author. In other words, each weight represents how much the collaboration between a pair of authors is dependent on the collaboration with a common co-author. Considering the example shown in Figure 1, given the authors a_1 and a_2 and one of their co-authors, a_3, the weight of the edge connecting a_1 and a_3 in BDG_{a_1,a_2} represents the dependence of the collaboration between a_1 and a_3 on the scientific assistance of a_2. This information quantifies how much the collaboration between a_1 and a_3 depends on the contribution of a_2. More formally, given two authors a_i and a_j and one of their common co-authors a_k, we define the relative dependence $w^{a_j}_{a_i,a_k}$ of the collaboration between a_i and a_k on a_j as

$$w^{a_j}_{a_i,a_k} = 1 - \frac{p_{a_i,a_j,a_k} + p_{a_i,a_k,\neg a_j}}{p_{a_i,a_j,a_k} + p_{a_i,a_k,\neg a_j} + p_{a_j,a_k,\neg a_i}}, \quad (1)$$

where

- p_{a_i,a_j,a_k} is the productivity of the collaboration among a_i, a_j, and a_k calculated as the number of papers that a_i, a_j and a_k co-authored together;
- $p_{a_i,a_k,\neg a_j}$ is the productivity of the collaboration between a_i and a_k without the contribution of a_j (i.e., calculated as the number of papers a_i and a_k co-authored without the assistance of a_j);
- $p_{a_j,a_k,\neg a_i}$ is the productivity of the collaboration between a_j and a_k without the contribution of a_i (i.e., calculated as the number of paper a_j and a_k co-authored without the assistance of a_i).

This relative dependence $w^{a_j}_{a_i,a_k}$ ranges from *0* to *1*; in particular, $w^{a_j}_{a_i,a_k} \approx 0$ indicates that the dependence of the scientific collaboration between a_i and a_k relatively to a_j is negligible, while a $w^{a_j}_{a_i,a_k} \approx 1$ highlights the contrary.

At this point, given two authors a_i and a_j, and their research network Net_{a_i,a_j}, it is possible to compute the dependence degree, *d*-index, of a_i on a_j by calculating the average dependence of all the scientific collaborations of a_i on the contribution of a_j. Thus, we calculate the dependence index, *d*-index, of a_i on a_j, as

$$d^{a_j}_{a_i} = \frac{p_{a_i,a_j}}{p_{a_i}} \times \frac{\sum_{a_k \in Net_{a_i,a_j}} w^{a_j}_{a_i,a_k}}{|Net_{a_i,a_j}|}, \quad (2)$$

where p_{a_i,a_j} is the productivity of a_i and a_j together (as before, calculated as the number of papers they co-authored together) and p_{a_i} is the total productivity of a_i.

It is important to notice that, while the first term permits to numerically quantify the impact of this scientific collaboration over the entire bibliographic record of a_i, the second term calculates the average of the relative dependences of the scientific collaborations of a_i on a_j. The formula lies in the range $[0,1]$ as well. The higher the value of the *d*-index, the higher the scientific dependence of a_i on the collaboration with a_j. Please notice that $d^{a_j}_{a_i} \neq d^{a_i}_{a_j}$; in fact, even if their scientific network is the same ($Net_{a_i,a_j} = Net_{a_j,a_i}$), their relative dependences on the co-authors can significantly differ, since they are based on their personal collaborations.

Now, given an author a_i and her list of *d*-index values related to her co-authors, we can also calculate her overall *dependence coefficient* as her dependence degree on the set of co-authors on whom she resulted more dependent. In a sense, we aim to quantify how much a researcher has been able to work without the scientists on whom she results more dependent. Thus, given an author a_i and the set of her co-authors on whom she resulted more dependent K_{a_i} (calculated applying an adaptive cut-off to the ordered list of d-index values), we calculate the dependence coefficient of a researcher a_i as her dependence degree on K_{a_i}. In particular, we first define the scientific network of a_i and K_{a_i} as $Net_{a_i,K_{a_i}} = Net_{a_i,a_1} \cup Net_{a_i,a_2} \cup \cdots \cup Net_{a_i,a_p}$, (where $K_{a_i} = \{a_1, a_2, \cdots a_p\}$). Then, for each co-author $a_k \in Net_{a_i,K_{a_i}}$, we calculate the relative dependence of the collaboration between a_i and a_k on the authors in K_{a_i} as

$$w^{K_{a_i}}_{a_i,a_k} = 1 - \frac{p_{a_i,K_{a_i},a_k} + p_{a_i,a_k,\neg K_{a_i}}}{p_{a_i,K_{a_i},a_k} + p_{a_i,a_k,\neg K_{a_i}} + p_{K_{a_i},a_k,\neg a_i}}, \quad (3)$$

where

- p_{a_i,K_{a_i},a_k} is the number of paper co-authored by a_i, a_k, and at least one author in K_{a_i};
- $p_{a_i,a_k,\neg K_{a_i}}$ is the number of paper co-authored by a_i and a_k without the contribution of K_{a_i} (i.e., excluding the research outputs in which is also involved at least one author in K_{a_i});
- $p_{K_{a_i},a_k,\neg a_i}$ is the number of paper co-authored by a least one author in K_{a_i} and a_k without the contribution of a_i (i.e., excluding the papers in which is also involved a_i);

At this step, we use all these relative dependences to calculate the dependence coefficient of a_i as

$$c_{a_i} = d^{K_{a_i}}_{a_i} = \frac{p_{a_i,K_{a_i}}}{p_{a_i}} \times \frac{\sum_{a_k \in Net_{a_i,K_{a_i}}} w^{K_{a_i}}_{a_i,a_k}}{|Net_{a_i,K_{a_i}}|}, \quad (4)$$

where $p_{a_i,K_{a_i}}$ is the productivity of a_i in collaboration with K_{a_i} (i.e., the number of research output co-authored by a_i and at least one author in K_{a_i}).

3. VISUALIZATION TOOLS

The web-based application, presented in Section 4, includes several tools for visualizing information about all the researchers indexed by the DBLP service. In this section we present them in detail.

3.1 Your and Others dependences

The first way to analyze the scientific dependences of a researcher is to plot the d-index values, in ascending order, related to her co-authors, as a curve within a Cartesian coordinate system (Figure 2(b)). This visualization scheme gives a first insight into an author's career by showing in a single chart the ordered dependences with respect to all her co-authors.

This curve can be also leveraged as an instrument for comparisons among different authors with respect to shared co-authors. However, considering that the co-authors of two researchers are most of the time different, in order to permit this comparison, we also present another chart where we map onto the x-axis a set of meta-authors where each one of them represents one co-author of each considered researcher.

More formally, given two authors a_i and a_j and their set of co-authors, $Net_{a_i} = \{a_{i,1}, a_{i,2} \cdots a_{i,n}\}$ and $Net_{a_j} = \{a_{j,1}, a_{j,2} \cdots a_{j,m}\}$ (where $a_{j,t}$ is the t-th co-author of a_j ordered by the d-index values, and n is not necessarily equals to m), we map onto the x-axis a set of meta-authors $Net_{meta} = \{a_{k,1}, a_{k,2} \cdots a_{k,r}\}$ where each author $a_{k,h} \in Net_{meta}$ represents one co-author of each researcher (i.e., $a_{k,h}$ represents $a_{i,n-r+h}$ and $a_{j,m-r+h}$ respectively) and $r = m$ if $m \leq n$, otherwise $r = n$.

This way, we permit to compare scientists based on their highest dependence values instead of their shared co-authors (that, obviously, not necessarily exist). In a sense, we compare researchers based on their absolute dependence values without taking into account on whom they are dependent. An example is shown in Figure 2(c).

3.2 You and your Collaborators

While the previous visualization scheme provides a simple way to analyze the dependences of a researcher, it does not permit to evaluate the reciprocal ones. In fact, given two scientists, it could be difficult to establish who of them is more dependent on the other by only analyzing their curves. For this reason, considering an author a_i, we introduce her *Mutual dependence Curve*, that plots all her co-authors onto the x-axis and, for each co-author a_k, it shows their *mutual dependence* calculated as $d_{a_i}^{a_k} - d_{a_k}^{a_i}$ onto the y-axis. The co-authors are ordered based on these values.

Using this simple tool, it is possible to distinguish the collaborators who depend on the considered researcher (those plotted under the x-axis) from those that more likely lead the scientific collaborations with the considered researcher (those plotted above the x-axis).

3.3 You and your Communities

Since researchers tend to work in communities, we provide a tool for analyzing scientific dependences among authors with respect to the communities they form. As the mutual dependence curve does, our tool called *Collaboration Map* shows the mutual dependences onto the y-axis. Regarding the x-axis, we aim to plot the co-authors based on the *local communities* they form with respect to the considered researcher. In particular, starting from an author a_i, we compute her square collaboration matrix C_i where both rows and columns represent her co-authors, and $C_i[j][k]$ is the number of papers of a_i co-authored by both a_j and a_k (the diagonal $C_i[j][j]$ simply reports the number of outcomes that a_i produced in collaboration with a_j). From this, we compute a dissimilarity matrix of co-authors D_i, where $D_i[j][k] = 1 - cos(C_i[j], C_i[k])$, where the function cos measures the cosine similarity between two vectors, $C_i[j]$ and $C_i[k]$, representing, respectively, the j-th and k-th rows of the collaboration matrix of the author a_i. We then apply the well-known X-Means clustering approach (which is able to automatically determine the optimal number of clusters), to the dissimilarity matrix in order to find clusters of co-authors who collaborated prolifically among them with respect to considered author (the communities are then visualized within the chart with different colors).

At this point, we need to map this information into a one-dimensional ordering (the x-axis). For this, without loss of generality, we use multi-dimensional scaling (MDS) proposed in [3] to embed the co-authors onto a 1-dimensional order. This chart allows us to graphically group the co-authors based on their scientific relations (i.e, the closer the authors onto the x-axis, the more productive is their collaboration with respect to the considered researcher), to identify the local communities in which the author is involved, and to estimate the roles the co-authors play within the local communities with respect to the considered researcher (for each co-author, the lower her y-value, the more scientifically dependent on the considered researcher). An example is shown in Figure 2(e).

3.4 You among All

Finally we provide a set of tools for comparing, from different points of view, the considered author with the all the scientists indexed in DBLP (1,097,418 researchers). In particular, we analyze, in three different charts, the relation between the dependence coefficient of an author (Section 2) and three parameters: the total number of her published papers, the total number of her co-authors and the length of her scientific career (expressed in years, from her first publication to her last one). Within these charts, all the researchers within DBLP are mapped with blue points, whereas the considered researcher is highlighted in red. This way, it is possible to compare each researcher with the entire community by focusing on different parameters, and according to the dependence coefficients. Moreover, within these charts, it is possible to map multiple authors and compare them with respect to the entire community.

4. DEMO SCENARIO

In this section we present a web environment, available at *http://d-index.di.unito.it*, for evaluation of scientific dependences among researchers. The considered data set contains information about the 1,097,418 authors and the 1,924,030 papers indexed by the DBLP bibliographic database[2]. Within this web platform it is possible to perform the following operations:

- visualization of the scientific profile of each researcher, including the information about her research papers and her collaborations over time;
- graphical analyses of scientific dependences with respect to the co-authors;

[2]Information updated on March 2012.

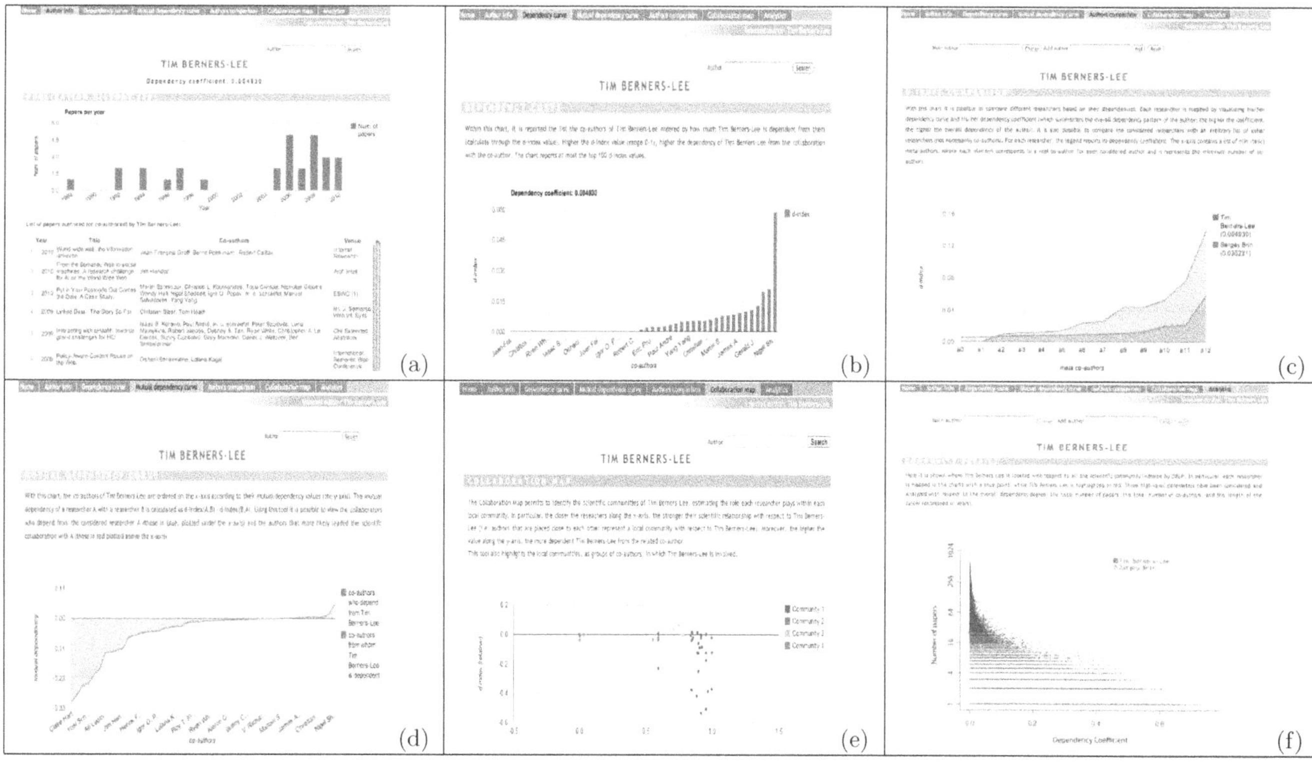

Figure 2: Different visualizations of the career of Dr. Tim Berners-Lee taken from *http://d-index.di.unito.it*; our web environment permits to visualize the information about the author (a), his dependence curve (here visualized as a histogram) (b), a comparison with other scientists (in this example only Dr. Sergey Brin)(c), his mutual dependences with respect to his co-authors (d), his local communities (e) and the relations between his dependence coefficient and his total number of papers compared with the whole scientific community (and, in this example, also focused on the comparison with Dr. Brin) (f).

- graphical comparisons among authors based on their dependence curves and coefficients;
- graphical analyses of the mutual dependences of the each researcher relatively to her co-authors;
- graphical analyses of the local communities in which the author is involved, estimating the dependence of each member on the considered researcher;
- comparisons with the entire community, focusing on the dependence coefficient, with respect to the total number of papers, total number of co-authors and length of career.

Figure 2 shows a set of screenshots taken from the presented web application. Within this system a user can search for authors and analyze their scientific profiles, according to the proposed measures. In particular, the system permits to query the database by typing an author's name and disambiguate, if it is necessary, the authors' list that match the query. The user can therefore analyze the scientific profile of the selected author (Figure 2(a)) by studying her scientific career (visualized as a histogram of papers per year), the complete list of scientific outcomes (through the standard information as the title, the name of the conference/journal, the year of the publication, etc.), the entire list of co-authors over the entire career, and much more.

Then, as shown in Figure 2(b), it is possible to analyze her dependence curve that visualizes her scientific dependences (plotted as explained in Section 3.1). The curve permits to graphically order her co-authors with respect to their *d*-index value. The user can visualize this in two different ways (curve or histogram).

Using the dependence curve, it is also possible to compare the considered researcher with different authors; an example is shown in Figure 2(c). Then, the user can analyze her scientific relationships with her co-authors by visualizing her Mutual Dependences Curve (Figure 2(d)), graphically separating the authors who depend on the considered researcher (in blue) from those he is dependent on (in red). Moreover, by visualizing the Collaboration Map (Figure 2(e)), it is possible to get an alternative view of her dependences by also taking into account her communities (intended as groups of co-authors). In this way it is possible to analyze the research groups in which the author has been involved and, for each of them, the relative dependence of each researcher belonging to it on the considered author. Finally, the application permits to compare the researcher with the entire community by focusing on the dependence coefficient with respect to different parameters (number of papers, number of co-authors and length of the career). Within these charts, it is possible to plot multiple authors (Figure 2(f)).

5. REFERENCES

[1] L. Di Caro, M. Cataldi, and C. Schifanella. The d-index: Discovering dependences among scientific collaborators from their bibliographic data records. *Scientometrics*, pages 1–25. 10.1007/s11192-012-0762-1.

[2] J. Hirsch. An index to quantify an individual's scientific research output. *Proceedings of the National Academy of Sciences of the United States of America*, 2005.

[3] W. S. Torgerson. *Theory and methods of scaling.* R.E. Krieger Pub. Co, 1958.

Information Propagation Game: a Tool to Acquire Human Playing Data for Multi-Player Influence Maximization on Social Networks

Hung-Hsuan Chen
Computer Science and Engineering
Pennsylvania State University
State College, PA, USA
hhchen@psu.edu

Yan-Bin Ciou
Computer Science and Information Engineering
National Taiwan University
Taipei, Taiwan
b97902012@ntu.edu.tw

Shou-De Lin
Computer Science and Information Engineering
National Taiwan University
Taipei, Taiwan
sdlin@csie.ntu.edu.tw

ABSTRACT
With the popularity of online social network services, influence maximization on social networks has drawn much attention in recent years. Most of these studies approximate a greedy based sub-optimal solution by proving the submodular nature of the utility function. Instead of using the analytical techniques, we are interested in solving the diffusion competition and influence maximization problem by a data-driven approach. We propose Information Propagation Game (IPG), a framework that can collect a large number of seed picking strategies for analysis. Through the IPG framework, human players are not only having fun but also helping contributing the seed picking strategies. Preliminary experiment suggests that centrality based heuristics are too simple for seed selection in a multiple player environment.

Categories and Subject Descriptors
G.2.2 [**Discrete Mathematics**]: Graph Theory—*Graph algorithms*; E.1 [**Data Structures**]: Graphs and networks; H.4 [**Information Systems Applications**]: Miscellaneous

General Terms
Design, Experimentation, Measurement

Keywords
Diffusion Network, Influence Maximization, Information Propagation, Game, Independent Cascade, Linear Threshold

KDD'12, August 12–16, 2012, Beijing, China.

1. INTRODUCTION
Studies have shown that people's decisions on whether to adopt an innovation or product are not purely based on the objective factors of the object, but also the colleagues' or friends' opinions [6, 10]. Therefore, to promote an item, it is essential to identify the key *influencers* to advertise to, with the hope that these influencers can disseminate the message to a larger group of individuals. Given a network, discovering the k most influential nodes that can eventually propagate certain information to the most nodes is defined as the *influence maximization* problem. Researchers have shown that influence maximization is NP-hardness [8]. Several selection strategies, such as greedy based approach and the centrality based heuristics, were posed to effectively select the initial nodes, called seeds, for influence maximization [8, 5, 9].

In real life, however, it is very likely that more than one mutually exclusive products compete with each other for the market share. For example, two competitive companies usually release similar products within a short range. Due to the exclusiveness natural of their products, each of the company would like to look for the influential personnels on social networks to maximize their benefit in advertisement. This kind of problems, in general called *diffusion competition problem*, have been studied by a number of researchers.

The previous works studied the seed picking strategy of diffusion competition and influence maximization by proposing some intuitive selection strategies [2, 3, 4]. While multiple participants are involved in competing for the seed nodes, the selection policy can become very complicated because every move of a participant is affected not only by its previous moves, but also the previous selections by other camps. Under such circumstance, the strategies designed for single-player influence maximization such as a centrality-based strategy might be too naïve to be effective. Here we argue that when multiple participants were involved, the seed-selection competition can be modeled as a multiple-player game, where each player has some budget to influence some seed nodes for propagation each turn. Thus, it is not hard to imagine that human players can derive better strategies with the accumulation of experiences on playing this game, just like that a novice promotion manager can gradually learn how to outwit their opponents and eventually become master in such advertisement campaign. Similarly, the increasing amount of historical playing record would allow an intelligent program to learn how to play such a game through machine learning (in particular reinforcement learning) models. To effectively collect a large number of seed picking strategies for advanced learning not only by human but also by machines, we design Information Propagation Game (IPG), a chess-like gaming engine in which the chessboard is a set of nodes and edges, and players compete with each other with the goal to maximize the influenced nodes. While the users are playing the game for fun, they are helping collecting data about sophisticated seed picking strategy for learning.

A demonstration page of IPG is available at `http://www.csie.ntu.edu.tw/~hhchen1/ipg/`.

2. IPG RULES

Before diving to the detail, we define some terms used in the paper. Each person involves in IPG is called a *player*. Each player takes turn to perform a legal action, called a *move*. The IPG performs information diffusion in a discrete step, named as a *round*. When the diffusion completes, the *utility* of a player is defined as the number of nodes activated by this player.

Although IPG is designed as a platform for multiple players, it also provides a single player mode. We introduce the rules for both scenarios in this section.

2.1 Rules of a Single Player Game

Given a social network and a known diffusion strategy such as Independent Cascade (IC) or Linear Threshold (LT) model, the player is asked to select k seeds to maximize the influence. Next, the IPG displays the diffusion process and returns the number of eventually activated nodes. To make the game more interesting, the IPG also shows the current best records given this network topology and diffusion strategy. This setup challenges the players to break the current record. The data collected can be used to analyze the influence maximization problem and facilitate the policy learning from machines.

2.2 Rules of a Multiple Player Game

In multi-player IPG game, each player is asked to choose same amount of seeds for propagation. The IPG performs diffusion until no more activations are possible. The side that occupies the most seeds after propagation wins the game. Unlike the single-player influence maximization problem, here several players may compete for activating an inactive node. Since most of the state-of-the-art diffusion models are designed for the non-competition scenario, we design two diffusion models for multi-player diffusion competition: Competitive Independent Cascade (CIC) model and Competitive Linear Threshold (CLT) model, which are natural extensions of the famous IC model and LT model, to deal with the competition scenario.

In IC model, each active node belong to only one person and has a single chance to activate each of its neighbors. In CIC model, each active node has to belong to one player (i.e. considered as activated by that player). Similar to IC model, in CIC when all active neighbors fail to activate a node, this node would remain inactive. If multiple nodes belonging to multiple players have successfully activated the same node, then the chance that this node is activated by a player will be proportional to the number of neighbor nodes belonging to this player that successfully activated this node. For example, if there are two players each has 2 and 3 nodes that successfully activated a target node, then there are $2/5$ and $3/5$ respectively chance this target node belongs to the first and second player.

For LT model, an inactive node is activated if the summation of the influential power of its active neighbors exceeds the threshold. In a diffusion competing scenario, if an inactive node can be activated by more than one player, the chances of the would-be-activated node belonging to a certain player is proportional to the accumulated influential power of that player. For example, if the threshold of an inactive node is $1/4$ and there are three players attempt to influence the node with the summation influential power be $1/5$, $1/3$, and $1/2$ respectively, the inactive node will choose the second player with probability $(1/3)/((1/3)+(1/2)) = 2/5$ and the third player with probability $(1/2)/((1/3)+(1/2)) = 3/5$. The first player cannot activate the node because its influential power does not exceed the threshold.

2.3 Extension Rules for Multiple Player Game

Assuming that each player can only select the seed nodes at the beginning might not be the case in many real world scenarios. In marketing, companies usually have advertising budgets allocated every month or every season; thus they are able to affect their customers in multiple rounds. In the case of epidemic disease prevention, the disease control center usually is aware of only a portion of the patients in the beginning. As the controlling process goes on, the center usually prevents the spread of infection in one area, and in the meanwhile can discover more patients in other areas. This can be viewed as one player (the disease) selects the nodes for propagation and the other player (the disease control center) adjust the inoculation strategy to minimize the spread in multiple rounds.

Motivated by this, the extension rules allow the players to select the seeds for multiple rounds. For example, one possible variation is each player can select k' nodes every round. Another possible variation is to provide each player k selection quota initially, and the players can decide when to use them during the play.

3. DESIGN NOVELTIES

The IPG is implemented using Java Universal Network Framework (JUNG)[1]. As shown in Figure 1, the system is highly modular so that the important components can be updated or enriched with little effort. We introduce the design novelties of IPG in this section.

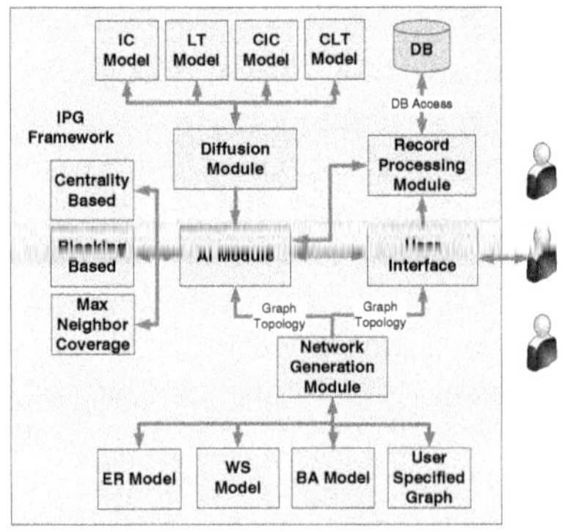

Figure 1: The system components

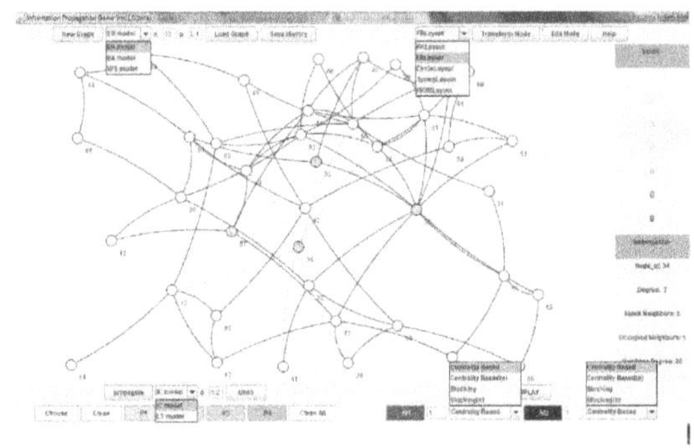

Figure 2: The snapshots of the IPG framework

3.1 AI Strategy

The player can choose to play with an AI agent in the multi-player game. The current AI strategies are based on three heuristics: the centrality based strategy, the blocking strategy, and the maximum neighbor coverage strategy.

Centrality measures are usually used to quantify the importance of a node within a network. The centrality based AI first chooses one centrality measure from the available options. It then selects the k inactive nodes with the highest centrality as the seeds. Currently, three important centrality measures are calculated: degree centrality, betweenness centrality, and closeness centrality. Other centrality measures, such as Katz centrality and Eigenvector centrality, can be easily integrated into the framework.

While the first player seems to have predominance by selecting the most influential nodes, an effective responding strategy of the second player could even up such advantage. Here, we propose two responding AI strategies: the blocking strategy and the maximum neighbor coverage strategy. The blocking AI examines the inactive neighbors of the seeds selected by the competitors, and among them chooses the ones with higher centrality values. By blocking the diffusion path that are potentially influential, the second player could hopefully decrease the first player's influence. The other responding strategy, maximum neighbor coverage, selects the nodes whose neighbors are largely overlapped with the neighbors of the first player's selected seeds. Maximum neighbor coverage AI aggressively competes the nodes with the first player in the beginning to prevent the first player gaining obvious initial advantage.

3.2 Network Topology Selection

Different seed picking strategies may gain different level of effectiveness on different types of network structures.

The IPG system allows the generation of different types of networks which facilitates further study about the relationship between network structure and the seed picking strategy. The current IPG framework can produce graphs of the following types: Erdős-Rényi (ER) network [7], Watts-Strogatz (WS) network [11], and Barabási-Albert (BA) network [1]. Furthermore, IPG also allows users to load an existing social network from file.

3.3 Interface Novelty

Users may find the IPG framework provides a novel interface that facilitates seed selection by human. We introduce several of the characteristics here.

Players can view the nodes' information, including the centrality values, the number of occupied and non-occupied neighbors, and the summation of neighbors' degree. These information can be useful clues for the players to decide which nodes to pick.

IPG allows the players to undo their decisions if they figure out a better move. Since we are interested in collecting effective strategies, we hope the users to play as well as they can.

In addition, the total number of occupied and unoccupied nodes are displayed in real time, as shown in Figure 2. This feature is especially helpful when applying

[1] `http://jung.sourceforge.net/`

the extension rules in which the players can select the seeds for multiple rounds. They can decide to use the remaining seed picking quota at a more proper moment.

3.4 AI to AI competition

While the human to human and human to AI competition allow us to collect valuable playing records with complicated seed picking strategies, AI to AI competitions enables us to accumulate a large number of playing records with little effort. IPG framework allows users to select the AI strategy from the available strategy list. Through the large number of automatic playing records, an reinforcement learning agent might be able to discover possible response strategy given different types of network topologies, diffusion models, and the competitor's seed picking strategies.

4. EXPERIMENTS AND DISCUSSION

Table 1: Comparison of the second player's strategy (BA network with 1000 nodes, CIC diffusion model with activation rate 0.1, the first player tend to pick high degree nodes, U_i: the number of activated nodes of player i)

	Deg.	B2n.	Cls.	Blk-Deg.
U_1	267 (0%)	261 (−2%)	272 (+2%)	259 (−3%)
U_2	152 (0%)	158 (+5%)	163 (+8%)	174 (+15%)

Table 2: Comparison of the second player's strategy (BA network with 1000 nodes, CLT diffusion model with threshold 0.6, influence value 0.3, the first player tend to pick high degree nodes, U_i: the number of activated nodes of player i)

	Deg.	B2n.	Cls.	Blk-Deg.
U_1	886 (0%)	876 (−1%)	860 (−3%)	876 (−1%)
U_2	114 (0%)	120 (+5%)	140 (+23%)	124 (+8%)

For a two player game, we investigate the second player's strategy when the first player tends to select the high degree nodes under BA network through IPG. By varying the second player's strategy be degree centrality (Deg.), betweenness centrality (B2n.), closeness centrality (Cls.), and the degree-based blocking strategy (Blk-Deg.), i.e., the second player selects high degree nodes from the inactive neighbors of the first player's seeds, the utility U_i (number of final influenced nodes) of player i, given the diffusion model be CIC and CLT, are shown in Table 1 and Table 2 respectively. Under CIC diffusion model, the second player's utility improves 15% by applying degree based blocking strategy instead of degree centrality. The result suggests that centrality heuristics are too simple when the competitors exist. Although the improvement under CLT model is not as obvious as the CIC model, degree based blocking strategy still shows the advantage over degree centrality and betweenness centrality strategies.

A questionnaire survey is conducted to the pilot player who played dozens of games in IPG. The report shows that the first player apparently has some advantages given small graphs. However, the second player can apply a more aggressive seed picking strategy, such as the maximum neighbor coverage strategy introduced in Section 3.1, to make up the disadvantage. The experiences shared by the real player also support our claim of simply selecting the high centrality nodes is too naïve in a competing scenario.

For future work, we will study the records retrieved by IPG systematically. In particular we plan to apply reinforcement learning, which uses the reward feedback, i.e., the utility in IPG, to learn a good policy for players in different positions. We are also interested in applying game theory studies to diffusion competition problem. Another interesting research topic is the relationship between rate of spread of diffusion and other player's next move.

5. ACKNOWLEDGMENTS

This work was also supported by National Science Council, National Taiwan University and Intel Corporation under Grants NSC 100-2911-I-002-001, and 101R7501.

6. REFERENCES

[1] A. Barabási and R. Albert. Emergence of scaling in random networks. *Science*, 286(5439):509–512, 1999.

[2] S. Bharathi, D. Kempe, and M. Salek. Competitive influence maximization in social networks. *Internet and Network Economics*, pages 306–311, 2007.

[3] C. Budak, D. Agrawal, and A. El Abbadi. Limiting the spread of misinformation in social networks. In *Proceedings of the 20th international conference on World wide web*, pages 665–674. ACM, 2011.

[4] T. Carnes, C. Nagarajan, S. Wild, and A. Van Zuylen. Maximizing influence in a competitive social network: a follower's perspective. In *Proceedings of the ninth international conference on electronic commerce*, pages 351–360. ACM, 2007.

[5] W. Chen, Y. Wang, and S. Yang. Efficient influence maximization in social networks. In *Proceedings of the 15th ACM SIGKDD international conference on knowledge discovery and data mining*, pages 199–208. ACM, 2009.

[6] J. Coleman, E. Katz, and H. Mentzel. Medical innovation: Diffusion of a medical drug among doctors. *Indianapolis: Bobbs-Merrill*, 1966.

[7] P. ERDdS and A. R&WI. On random graphs i. *Publ. Math. Debrecen*, 6:290–297, 1959.

[8] D. Kempe, J. Kleinberg, and É. Tardos. Maximizing the spread of influence through a social network. In *Proceedings of the ninth ACM SIGKDD international conference on knowledge discovery and data mining*, pages 137–146. ACM, 2003.

[9] J. Leskovec, A. Krause, C. Guestrin, C. Faloutsos, J. VanBriesen, and N. Glance. Cost-effective outbreak detection in networks. In *Proceedings of the 13th ACM SIGKDD international conference on Knowledge discovery and data mining*, pages 420–429. ACM, 2007.

[10] B. Ryan and N. Gross. The diffusion of hybrid seed corn in two iowa communities. *Rural sociology*, 8(1):15–24, 1943.

[11] D. Watts and S. Strogatz. Collective dynamics of small-worldnetworks. *Nature*, 393(6684):440–442, 1998.

MoodLens: An Emoticon-Based Sentiment Analysis System for Chinese Tweets

Jichang Zhao*, Li Dong*, Junjie Wu†, and Ke Xu*‡
*State Key Lab of Software Development Environment, Beihang University
†Beijing Key Laboratory of Emergency Support Simulation Technologies for City Operations, School of Economics and Management, Beihang University
‡Corresponding author
zhaojichang@nlsde.buaa.edu.cn, donglixp@gmail.com, wujj@buaa.edu.cn, kexu@nlsde.buaa.edu.cn

ABSTRACT

Recent years have witnessed the explosive growth of online social media. Weibo, a Twitter-like online social network in China, has attracted more than 300 million users in less than three years, with more than 1000 tweets generated in every second. These tweets not only convey the factual information, but also reflect the emotional states of the authors, which are very important for understanding user behaviors. However, a tweet in Weibo is extremely short and the words it contains evolve extraordinarily fast. Moreover, the Chinese corpus of sentiments is still very small, which prevents the conventional keyword-based methods from being used. In light of this, we build a system called *MoodLens*, which to our best knowledge is the first system for sentiment analysis of Chinese tweets in Weibo. In *MoodLens*, 95 emoticons are mapped into four categories of sentiments, i.e. *angry*, *disgusting*, *joyful*, and *sad*, which serve as the class labels of tweets. We then collect over 3.5 million labeled tweets as the corpus and train a fast Naïve Bayes classifier, with an empirical precision of 64.3%. *MoodLens* also implements an incremental learning method to tackle the problem of the sentiment shift and the generation of new words. Using *MoodLens* for real-time tweets obtained from Weibo, several interesting temporal and spatial patterns are observed. Also, sentiment variations are well-captured by *MoodLens* to effectively detect abnormal events in China. Finally, by using the highly efficient Naïve Bayes classifier, *MoodLens* is capable of online real-time sentiment monitoring. The demo of *MoodLens* can be found at *http://goo.gl/8DQ65*.

Categories and Subject Descriptors

H.2.8 [**Database Management**]: Database Applications—*Data Mining*; H.3.3 [**Information Search and Retrieval**]: [Text Mining]; J.4 [**Social and Behavioral Sciences**]: [Miscellaneous]

General Terms

Measurement, Experimentation

Keywords

Sentiment Analysis; Chinese Short Text; Online Social Media; Weibo

1. INTRODUCTION

The development of online social networks has attracted enormous Internet users in this decade. They are becoming the mainstream online social media for information sharing. Twitter (www.twitter.com), a microblog site launched in 2006, has over 300 million registered users, with over 140 million microblog posts, known as *tweets*, being published every day. In China, Weibo (www.weibo.com), a Twitter-like service launched in 2009, has accumulated more than 300 millions users in less than three years. Every second, more than 1000 Chinese tweets are posted in Weibo.

Each user in the network can be viewed as a social sensor, which publishes and propagates the information through the tweets. Therefore, the huge amount of tweets convey complicated signals of the authors and the real-world events, in which the sentiment is an essential part. In [3], the authors argued that the events in the social, political and cultural fields did have a significant effect on the users' mood, which could be detected by their tweets. It was also claimed in [2] that the stock market even could be predicted by the sentiment analysis of the Twitter users.

Disclosing the emotions in tweets therefore plays a key role in understanding the user behaviors in social media. However, both Twitter and Weibo only allow users to post messages up to 140 characters, which makes the tweets extremely short, and the sentiment analysis therefore becomes a very challenging task. In particular, few works have been done to reveal how to perform sentiment analysis for Chinese tweets in Weibo.

In light of this, we propose a system called *MoodLens* to perform the sentiment analysis for Chinese Weibo. The main contributions lie in the following aspects: (a) *Moodlens* employs an emoticon-based method for sentiment classification, which helps to tackle the longstanding sparsity problem of short texts; (b) *MoodLens* can detect four types of sentiments: *angry*, *disgusting*, *joyful*, and *sad*, which goes beyond the traditional binary sentiment (positive vs. negative) analysis studies, and is crucial for unveiling the abundant sentiments contained in tweets; (c) *MoodLens* implements an incremental learning scheme to deal with the problems of the sentiment shift of words and the generation of new words; (d) *MoodLens* is capable of real-time tweet processing and classification, and therefore can serve as a real-time abnormal event monitoring system. The demo of *MoodLens* is now available at *http://goo.gl/8DQ65*.

2. EMOTICON-BASED METHOD

We have noticed that the graphical emoticons are popular in Weibo. In recent work [1], it has been found that the graphical emoticons can convey strong sentiment. They help the users to express their mood when post the tweet. Hence, we could treat these emoticons as sentiment labels of the tweets. In fact, it is a kind of crowdsourcing, i.e., the users label the tweet with emoticons to express their emotion themselves. Because of this, categorizing the emoticons into different sentiments would make the tweets divided into different emotion classes. Among over 1000 emoticons, we manually select 95 ones as the sentiment labels(denoted as E) and divide them into four different sentiment categories, including *angry*, *disgusting*, *joyful* and *sadness*. As show in Figure 1, there are 9 emoticons in *angry*, 14 emoticons in *disgusting*, 50 emoticons in *joyful* and 22 emoticons in *sad*, respectively.

Sentiment	#Emoticons	Typical emoticons
Angry	*9*	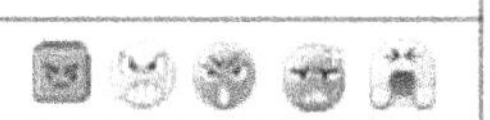
Disgusting	*14*	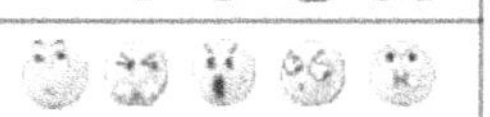
Joyful	*50*	
Sad	*22*	

Figure 1: Sentiment categories and the typical emoticons in each class.

From Dec. 2010 to Feb. 2011, *MoodLens* has collected more than 70 million tweets from Weibo. We extract over 3.5 million tweets that contains emoticons in E as the labeled tweets set, denoted as T. It indicates that in Weibo, there is nearly 5% of the tweets labeled by the sentiment emoticons. Finally we obtain 569,229 *angry* tweets, 290,444 *disgusting* tweets, 2,218,779 *joyful* tweets and 607,715 *sad* tweets. These tweets could be used to as a initial sentiment corpus for Weibo. For each tweet t in T, *MoodLens* converts it into a sequence of words $\{w_i\}$, where w_i is a word and i is its position in t.

In *MoodLens*, we employ the simple method of Naïve Bayes (NB) to build the classifier, which consumes little training time and predicts the category fast. From the labeled tweets, we could obtain the word w_i's prior probability of belonging to the sentiment category c_j is $P(w_i \parallel c_j) = \frac{n^{c_j}(w_i)+1}{\sum_q (n^{c_j}(w_q)+1)}$, where $j = 1, 2, 3$ *or* 4, $n^{c_j}(w_i)$ is the times that w_i appears in all the tweets in the category c_j and *Laplace smoothing* is used to avoid the problem of zero probability. Then we could establish the Naïve Bayes classifier as follows, for a unlabeled tweet t with word sequence $\{w_i\}$, its category could be obtained as $c^*(t) = arg \max_j P(c_j)\Pi_i P(w_i \parallel c_j)$, where $P(c_j)$ is the prior probability of c_j.

In order to validate the performance of the classifier, the set of labeled tweets is divided into two sets randomly, including training set, denoted as T_{train} and testing set, denoted as T_{test}. The fraction of T_{train}, i.e., the fraction of the training data, is denoted as $f_t = \frac{|T_{train}|}{|T|}$. In T_{train}, the set of tweets labeled as c_j is denoted as $T^{c_j}_{train}$, similarly, the tweets in T_{test} of c_j is denoted as $T^{c_j}_{test}$. In the testing set, the correctly predicted tweets of c_j is denoted as P^{c_j}. From these definitions, we mainly employ three metrics in this paper to describe the effectiveness of the classifier, which are listed as follows. **Precision** is defined as $p = \frac{\sum_{j=1}^{4} |P^{c_j}|}{|T_{test}|}$. **Recall** is defined as $r = \frac{1}{4}\sum_{j=1}^{4} \frac{|P^{c_j}|}{|T^{c_j}_{test}|}$. **F-measure** is defined as $f = 2pr/(p + r)$.

In this demo, we use a standard bag of words as the feature, set $f_t = 0.9$, $P(c_j) = 0.25$ and get a Naïve Bayes classifier, its precision is 64.3%, recall is 53.3% and F-measure is 58.3%.

We also present a simple incremental learning approach to complement the original Naïve Bayes classifier. Here, we could assume the tweets in Weibo is a stream, in which there is a fraction of tweets (denoted u) are sentimentally labeled, then these labeled tweets could be used to update the prior probability of words. To verify the effectiveness of the method, the following experiment is performed. we randomly shuffle T and divide it into 50 pieces of same size. Then we use the first piece as the training set and obtain an initial classifier. For the other 49 pieces, we treat them as the tweet stream, which means they enter into the classifier one by one, and in each of them, there is a fraction(u) of tweets are randomly selected as labeled tweets and could be used to update the classifier. As shown in Figure 2, as the index of pieces, denoted as s, grows, the p, r and f of the classifier indeed grows. Particularly, higher u means a larger fraction of labeled tweets are used to update the classifier, and then the more updates produce more improvements.

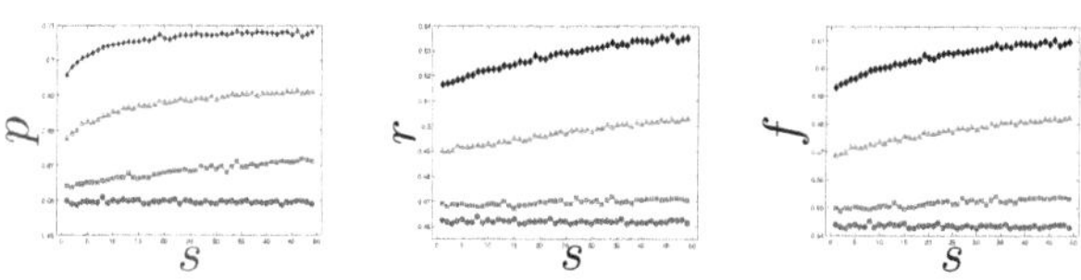

(a) Precision (b) Recall (c) F-measure

Figure 2: Experiments of incremental learning, $u = 0, 0.01, 0.05, 0.1$ from bottom to top, respectively.

In summary, *MoodLens* employs Naïve Bayes classifier with incremental learning to predict the detailed sentiment of the tweets. For other solutions, like Liblinear [4], which consumes much more training time while gain less than 5% improvement of precision. Moreover, it is also hard to incorporate incremental learning approaches into it.

3. APPLICATIONS

Data Collection Weibo has published its APIs since 2010 and through these APIs, it is easy to obtain the public tweets and some basic demographic attributes of the users. We build a Weibo application named *"Are you happy?!"* and

Weibo grant us the opportunity to access its APIs with the application-level. For the limitation of requesting the API, it is necessary to select some probes from Weibo and then collect data from them. From a large-scale user-pool we collected before 2011, which contains more than 2.2 million users, *MoodLens* randomly selects 6,800 active users, 200 users for each province or region in China. Here the "active users" means these users should be true users but not spam. A simple filtering rule is used to filter them out, which is that *MoodLens* only chooses the user with more than 200 but less than 3,000 followers and has published less than 3,000 tweets.

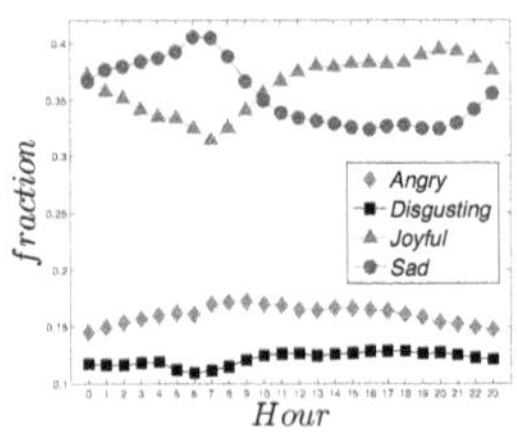

(a) Hourly pattern.

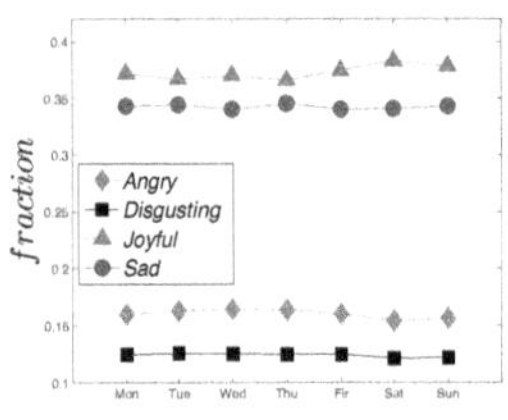

(b) Weekly pattern.

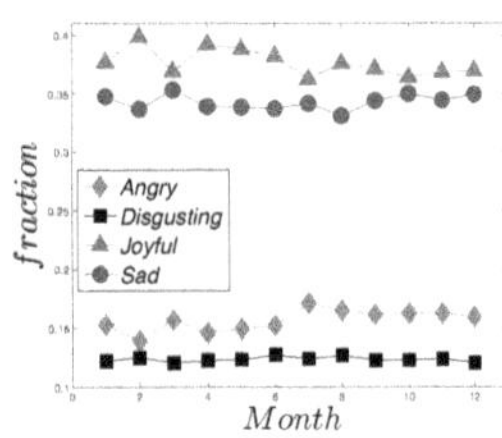

(c) Monthly pattern.

Figure 3: Temporal sentiment patterns.

Sentiment Patterns The hourly pattern of the sentiment is showed in Figure 3(a). It could be found that the time from 6:00 AM to 8:00 AM is the saddest moment, which is different from the recent study from Twitter [5]. In their data set, they found people are likely to be positive at early morning. While for Weibo, this period is also the angriest moment for most of the users during a day. Surprised by this difference, we carefully investigate the tweets published in Weibo from 6:00AM to 8:00AM and extract the commonly used words. And the results show that the "sad" mood is generally caused by the followed reasons. First, some people hate to get up early, but they have to. Second, some users do not want to work at this time. Third, some ones might have nightmare in the last night and have bad sleep. After 10:00 AM, users of Weibo seems to become more and more joyful gradually and the fraction of *joyful* tweets reaches the peak at 20:00 PM. The weekly pattern of the sentiment is showed in Figure 3(b). As can be seen, people seems to become happier since Friday, the *joyful* reaches peak at Saturday and then the mood of joy goes down as Sunday begins. As shown in Figure 3(c) is the monthly pattern of the sentiment. There are several outliers. For instance, in March of 2011, it shows the users of Weibo are sad and angry, it might be caused by the earthquake in Japan and the rumor that the iodized salt in China is also nuclear polluted. Another one is in July, the fraction of *angry* reaches the peak, it is mainly related with the accident of the bullet train. We also find the days of extreme sentiment in 2011. Namely, Jan. 1 is the most joyful day, Mar. 11 is the saddest day, Jul. 13 is the most disgusting day and Jul. 24 is the angriest day (refer to [6] for the link). *MoodLens* also draws the distribution graph of everyday sentiment for each region of China and show how the sentiment evolves day by day dynamically (refer to [7] for the link).

Abnormal Event Detection Intuitively, abnormal events in the real world would definitely affect the people's emotion, and then the mental change would be reflected by the tweets people publish. The basic idea of the detection method is first to find the turning point in the variation of the sentiment and then to extract information of event from the tweets. *MoodLens* defines a sequence of fraction for the sentiment c_j as $\{S_t^{c_j}\}$, where t is the observing time, its unit is likely to be a day or an hour. Assuming we observe the variation of the sentiment from $t = t_1$ to $t = t_2$, then the averaged fraction tweets in c_j could be defined as

$$\langle S_{t_1 \to t_2}^{c_j} \rangle = \frac{1}{t_2 - t_1} \sum_{t=t_1}^{t_2} S_t^{c_j}, \tag{1}$$

where$\Delta t = t_2 - t_1$ is the time window of observation. Hence, *MoodLens* could get the sequence of relative variation for c_j as

$$V_t^{c_j} = \frac{S_t^{c_j} - \langle S_{t_1 \to t_2}^{c_j} \rangle}{\langle S_{t_1 \to t_2}^{c_j} \rangle}. \tag{2}$$

Then *MoodLens* defines the sequence of sentiment variation as $\{\sum_{j=1}^{4} |V_t^{c_j}|\}$. This sequence could be sorted in descending order and the $top - k$ t is selected as the outlier time points, denoted as $\{t_1, t_2, .., t_k\}$. For each t_i, *MoodLens* could extract the tweets posted at that time and perform the information extraction for the event. Here *MoodLens* employs the simplest way, the top 5 bi-gram terms of high frequency would be extracted to depict the event happened. We perform this method on the data set of 2011 and find it could detect almost all the abnormal events happened during the whole year. As shown in Figure 4, we mark the $top - 10$ events detected from A to J. In these detected events, A,D and E correspond to the event of bullet train crash. C and B correspond to the fact that Japan was hit by a magnitude 9.0 earthquake, while J corresponds to the news that people in China rushed to purchase the salt because of rumors. It should be noted that for J, the fraction of *angry* is larger than C and B. F corresponds to New Years' Eve of 2011. G and I correspond to Spring Festival of 2011. H corresponds to the death of Steven Jobs. It is also interesting that different from C, B, J, A, D and E, for H, although the fraction of *sad* is high but the fraction of *angry* is low. It indicates that detailed negative sentiments are useful for analyzing the essence of the abnormal event.

Real-time Sentiment Monitoring The NB classifier with incremental learning is speedy enough for the real-time sentiment analysis of the tweets in Weibo. Through the API provided by Weibo, *MoodLens* could obtain the most recent 400 public tweets every minute and these tweets could be analyzed in less than one second. In order to guarantee the statistical significance, we set the cycle of collecting tweets as 30 minutes, which means *MoodLens* would download nearly 12,000 tweets in one monitoring cycle. Then these tweets would be categorized into different sentiment classes in less than 1 minute. As shown in Figure 5, we present a sample cycle from the real-time monitoring, which starts from 19:30

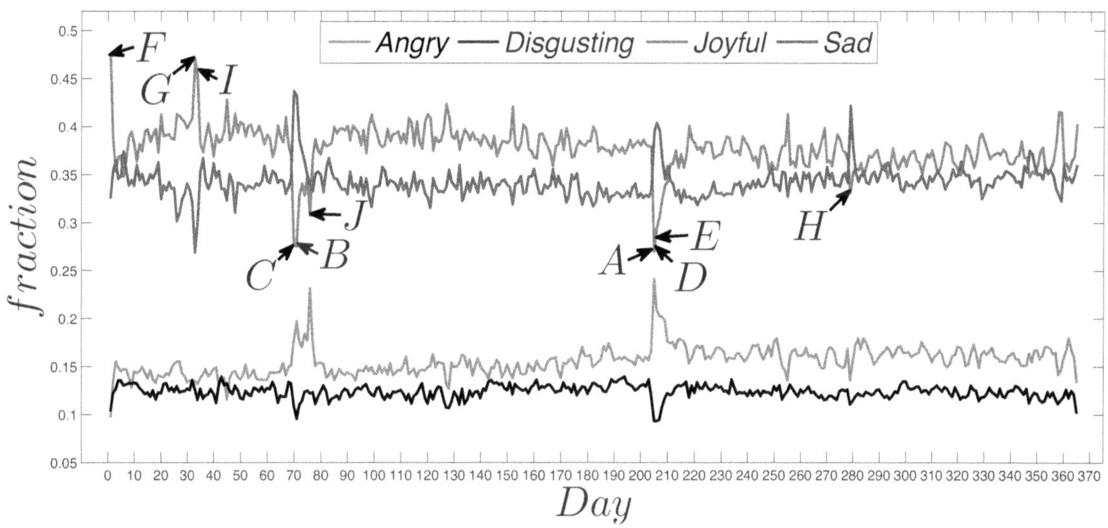

Figure 4: Abnormal event detection of 2011. We also provide an interactive version on the following link: http://gana.nlsde.buaa.edu.cn/hourly_happy/timeline_2011.html.

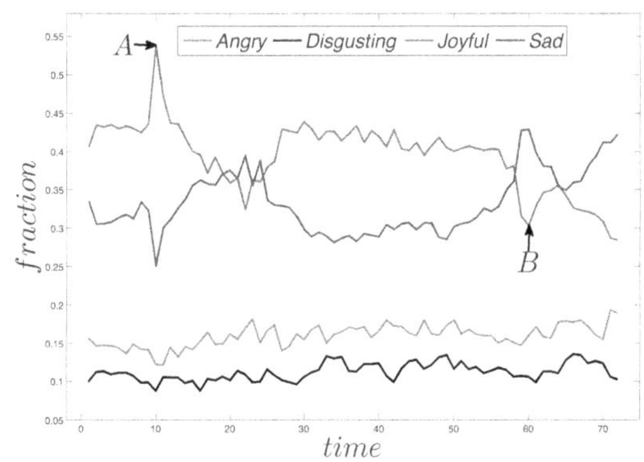

Figure 5: A sample from real-time monitoring. The online application could be accessed through the following link: gana.nlsde.buaa.edu.cn/hourly_happy/line_36h.html.

PM of Dec. 24, 2011 and ends to 7:00 AM of Dec. 26, 2011, the delay between two points is 30 minutes and 72 points are drew in all. As can be seen, the real-time event could be indeed monitored. For instance, regarding to the time marked by A, which is at 0:00 PM of Dec. 24, the sentiment of *joyful* reaches peak because everyone is celebrating the coming of the Christmas Day. While with respect to B, at the time of 1:00 AM of Dec. 26, the fraction of *sad* tweets rises suddenly, the bi-gram terms reveal that it is caused by the earthquake happened in Chengdu at that time.

4. CONCLUSION

MoodLens is an online sentiment analysis system for Chinese tweets in Weibo. It employs the emoticons for the generation of sentiment labels for tweets, and builds an incremental learning Naïve Bayes classifier for the categorization of four types of sentiments: *angry*, *disgusting*, *joyful*, and *sad*. *MoodLens* is now available online for temporal and spatial sentiment pattern discovery, abnormal events detection and illustration, and online real-time monitoring of sentiment fluctuations.

5. ACKNOWLEDGEMENTS

This works was supported by the fund of the State Key Laboratory of Software Development Environment (SKLSDE-2011ZX-02) and the Research Fund for the Doctoral Program of Higher Education of China (Grant No. 20111102110019). The third author was supported in part by the National Natural Science Foundation of China (NSFC) under Grants 71171007, 70901002, and 90924020.

6. REFERENCES

[1] Sho Aoki and Osamu Uchida. A method for automatically generating the emotional vectors of emoticons using weblog articles. ACACOS'11, pages 132–136, Stevens Point, Wisconsin, USA, 2011.

[2] Johan Bollen, Huina Mao, and Xiaojun Zeng. Twitter mood predicts the stock market. *Journal of Computational Science*, 2(1):1–8, 2011.

[3] Johan Bollen, Alberto Pepe, and Huina Mao. Modeling public mood and emotion: Twitter sentiment and socio-economic phenomena. 5th ICWSM, 2011.

[4] Rong-En Fan, Kai-Wei Chang, Cho-Jui Hsieh, Xiang-Rui Wang, and Chih-Jen Lin. Liblinear: A library for large linear classification. *J. Mach. Learn. Res.*, 9:1871–1874, June 2008.

[5] Scott A. Golder and Michael W. Macy. Diurnal and seasonal mood vary with work, sleep, and daylength across diverse cultures. *Science*, 333(6051):1878–1881, September 2011.

[6] http://gana.nlsde.buaa.edu.cn/hourly_happy/line_cycle.html.

[7] http://gana.nlsde.buaa.edu.cn/hourly_happy/map_pie.html.

Intelligent Advertising Framework for Digital Signage

Phil Tian
Intel Corporation
Raycom InfoTech Park A
2 Kexueyuan South Rd
Beijing 100190 PRC
+8610 82171645
phil.tian@intel.com

Addicam V Sanjay
Intel Corporation
5000 W. Chandler Blvd
Chandler, AZ 85226
USA
+1 480 552 0275
addicam.v.sanjay@intel.com

Kunapareddy Chiranjeevi
Intel Corporation
Thoobarahalli Village
Bangalore South Taluk
Bangalore 560037, India
+91 80 2513 2521
kunapareddy.chiranjeevi@intel.com

Shahzad Malik
Intel Corporation
15 Allstate Parkway
6th Floor, Markham
ON, Canada, L3R 5B4
+1 416 846 7209
shahzad.malik@intel.com

ABSTRACT

How to realize targeted advertising in digital signage is an interesting question. This paper proposed an Intelligent Advertising Framework (IAF), which pioneers the integration of Anonymous Viewer Analytics (AVA) and Data Mining technologies to achieve Targeted and interactive Advertising. IAF correlates AVA viewership information with point-of-sale (POS) data, and establishes a link between the response time to an ad by a certain demographic group and the effect on the sale of the advertised product. With the advertising models learned based on this correlation, IAF can provide advertisers and retailers with intelligence to show the right ads to right audience in right location at right time. Preliminary results indicate that IAF will greatly improve the effect and utility of advertising and maximize the Return on Investment (ROI) of advertisers and retailers. The demo shows Intel's leadership regarding intelligent advertising in the Digital Signage industry.

Categories and Subject Descriptors

H.2.8 [**Database Management**]: Database Applications---*data mining*; I.4.8 [**Image Processing and Computer Vision**]: Scene Analysis---*object recognition, tracking*; I.5.4 [**Pattern Recognition**]: Applications---*computer vision.*

General Terms

Algorithms, Measurement, Design, Experimentation

Keywords

Intelligent Advertising Framework, Digital Signage, Targeted Advertising, Anonymous Viewer Analytics, Data Mining

1. INTRODUCTION

Digital signage (DS) [1] [2] is the term that is often used to describe the use of LCD, LED, plasma, or projected displays to show news, ads, local announcements, and other multimedia content in public venues such as restaurants or malls. In recent years, the digital signage industry has experienced tremendous growth, and it is now only second to the Internet in terms of annual advertising revenue growth [3].

One of the main challenges in the digital signage industry has been providing signage operators with some clear ROI data. Fortunately, some recent technologies such as AVA are now available on the market to help digital signage operators to measure marketing ROI by capturing audience data such as total number of viewers, average attention span, and even the gender and age of viewers as they pass by a screen. More advanced data correlations are also possible, such as matching anonymous viewership data with point-of-sale data. AVA plus data correlation provides advertisers a more effective and accurate way to measure the effectiveness of their ads than traditional sampling and extrapolation method.

Besides measuring ad effectiveness, a more important problem that advertisers are concerned with is how to improve ROI, not just understand ROI. A typical approach is using the concept of targeted advertising. Although targeted advertising has been adopted in many industries [4] [5], such as banking, insurance, telecom marketing, social networks, it is still a new concept for digital signage industry. Quividi [6] and Tru-Media [7] are two popular companies that provide audience measurement solutions. Although their solutions also provide some targeted advertising capabilities, the advertising models are created manually rather than learned from historical viewership data automatically. Immersive Labs developed a prototype that realizes targeted advertising by mining the historical data [8]. But it hasn't yet publicized any details on the used data mining algorithms and targeting accuracy.

This paper proposed an Intelligent Advertising Framework (IAF), which integrates AVA and Data Mining technologies to achieve Targeted and interactive Advertising in digital signage. It uses AVA to capture human faces and recognize demographic information of the audiences, then correlate this information with ads playing list, point-of-sale (POS) data as well as other context information, such as time, location, weather etc., and use data mining algorithms to learn advertising models based on the correlation. Using these models, IAF is able to intelligently select and play the most appropriate ads to the audience in real time.

2. IAF ARCHITECTURE

Figure 1 demonstrates an end to end reference architecture of IAF. AIM Suite Analytics Server, Data Mining Engine, Data Mining Module (DMM) and Content Management System (CMS) run in the Cloud. AIM Suite and Digital Player run on the Client, i.e. the digital signs. IAF shows a wonderful integration of cloud based data mining and client based real time content triggering. The data mining happens in the cloud to take use of the computing resource as much as possible. And the content

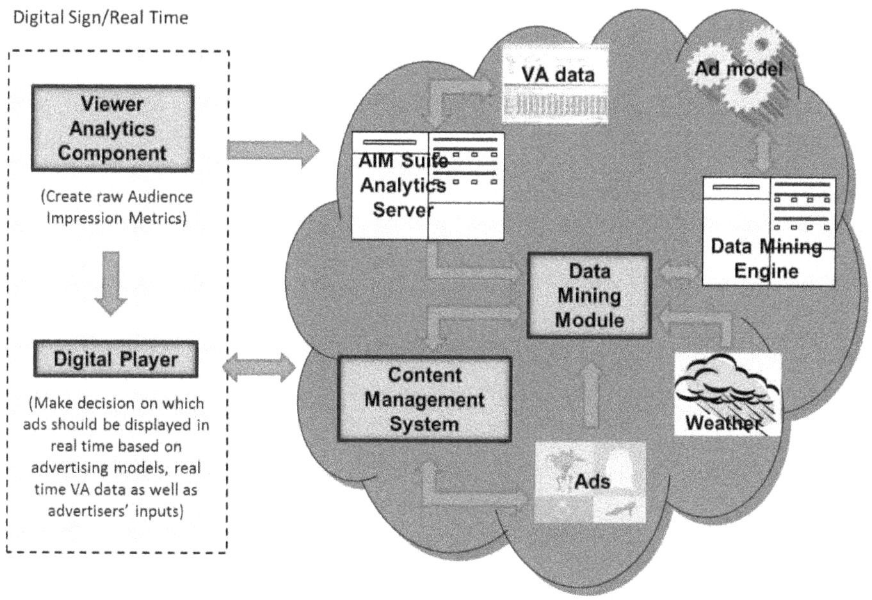

Figure 1. The IAF architecture.

selection and triggering happens in real time in the client independent of cloud end.

AIM Suite is an AVA component, which passively analyzes the video feed of the audience captured by an embedded camera in real-time, creates and sends viewership information to Analytic Server. After cleansed (removing noises and outliers) on Analytic Server, the viewership information is saved into the data repository in the Cloud. Analytic Server also works as a middleware to provide AVA data access and analytical reports to outside or other components. Data Mining Engine provides data mining algorithms and mechanism for learning and querying advertising models. DMM realizes the capabilities of data connection, predictive modeling, model query as well as rule extraction, and automate the processes so as to make these capabilities accessible from other components or applications through web services. CMS consumes advertising models learned by DMM, and take other advertising information as inputs to create customized advertising lists. It also realizes the configuration and management of digital signs, actual ads, advertisers etc. Digital Player takes use of real-time viewership information, advertising models, customized list from CMS and advertisers' inputs etc. to make the final decision in real-time on what ads should be displayed on the digital signs. It also performs the display of the actual ads, creates ad playlist, and sends the playlist to data repository in the cloud.

3. TARGETED ADVERTISING METHDOLOGY

Targeted advertising is a type of advertising whereby advertisements are placed so as to reach consumers based on various traits such as demographics, purchase history, or observed behavior [9]. On one hand, targeted advertising helps to identify potential customers, create a real-time relationship with these customers, improves their experience, and provides them cross-sell services to boost incremental revenue. On the other hand, it helps to reduce waste and improve advertisers' ROI by just placing advertisement to the potential purchasers rather than the whole population.

Targeted advertising in digital signage requires the digital signs have the capability to dynamically select and play advertisements according to the traits of the audiences in front of them, rather than select and play in a predefined or random order. Future audience belonging to the same demographic as previous audience will be targeted based on the viewing behavior of the previous audience.

3.1 Audience Targeting Methods

Here we use data mining algorithms to discover the patterns on viewing behaviors of the audience. The basic idea is to show the audience certain ads that have in the past been viewed for a reasonable amount of time by the audience belonging to the same demographics.

For the purpose of capturing the patterns contained in new coming data, two different ways are used to retrain the advertising models, regular retraining and on demand retraining. Regular retraining is triggered regularly, such as weekly or monthly. On-demand retraining is triggered when the performance of the models is lower than a predefined threshold or a retaining request is received from users or operators. Besides, to fully take use of the advantages of different data mining algorithms, Decision Tree, Association Rule and Naïve Bayes are used to train advertising models in parallel. The best advertising model or multiple advertising models will be used for ad selection.

We use the below three methods to target the audience. Many technical details on how to realize these methods are available in [10].

3.1.1 Seeing Based Targeting

Seeing based targeting means targeting the audience once the digital sign "sees" the audience. For example, 3 young females and 1 senior male are seen passing by the digital sign, then the advertising models are queried with this input and the most appropriate ad is selected to play. This is the most accurate targeting method give the demographic information of the audience has been captured and used.

3.1.2 Prediction Based Targeting

Prediction based targeting first predicts the passers coming in the future period of time and then targets them. For example, it is predicted that 3 young females and 1 senior male will pass by the digital sign within next 20 seconds, then the most appropriate ad is to be selected per the advertising models and prepared to play. This is quite useful in the below scenario. In some cases, if the time cost of the whole targeting process is longer than the audience's dwelling time, that means when the digital player gets the selected ad prepared and displayed on the screen, the audience has looked away and never look back, the seeing based targeting doesn't work.

3.1.3 Context Based Targeting

Context based targeting targets the ads just depending on the context, such as targeting date/time, device location, weather info etc. For example, in clear Wednesday morning between 9 AM and 11AM during November and December, an ad for senior males will be selected to play on digital sign A per the advertising models. This is useful when passer type prediction is not reliable or no passer patterns can be discovered from the training data.

3.2 Targeted Advertising Process

The process of targeted advertising can be broken down into four phases: creating viewer events, learning advertising models, creating playlists, and playing playlists.

3.2.1 Create Viewer Events

AIM Suite is responsible for creation of viewer events. It takes the video feeds from a camera as its input, and detects the human faces in each image frame, then recognizes the demographics (gender, age bracket) of the faces, and finally creates the viewer events [11].

It should be emphasized that AIM Suite is privacy friendly [12]. It only detects the presence of a mathematical human face as well as its demographic features, but it does not identify who the face belongs to. Moreover, only viewing events are recorded, which are completely anonymous. And no images or video footage are stored, so there is no way to link back to any specific individual from the viewing events. The audience's privacy is well protected.

3.2.2 Learn Advertising Models

DMM in IAF correlates the viewer events with player events (about what ads were played at what time and in what location) and other context information, and discovers interesting viewer patterns or advertising models from the correlated data. like when, where, under what weather and to what extent what group of audience is interested in what type of ads. DMM consists of following subcomponents.

Data Connector: Connects and gets access to the training data repository. The data is made of original AVA data, playlist data, weather data and ad data.

Data Preprocessor: Realizes necessary data preprocessing actions, like deriving new attributes from original attributes for modeling purpose.

Model Constructor: Defines data mining models with specified algorithm, training data scope and training parameters

Model Learner: Learn advertising models according to the model definition, also test the learned models against the testing data in terms of accuracy.

Query Engine: Both prediction result and model content (such as rules) can be queried against an advertising model. This enables extraction and deployment elsewhere of the model content to achieve better efficiency for real time applications.

3.2.3 Create Default Playlist

After the advertising models are generated, they get transferred to the CMS. CMS then extracts the Ad Categories from the models and creates Ad Category list. The ad information (such as actual ad location) corresponding to the Ad Categories are then fetched from the ad information table. Based on Ad category list, CMS creates initial ad lists, which are modified in Advertiser Input Scheduler based on the advertisers' inputs. Each Advertiser is assigned certain priority, which rearranges the initial ad lists in Advertiser Input Scheduler.

3.2.4 Finalize and Play the Playlist

Finally the shuffered ad lists get transferred to the Digital player. It generates the default playlist by extracting the path from the ad list and then getting the ads from the Ad Repository. The digital player operates in either online or offline mode. In online mode, Digital Player selects an ad based on the probability distribution calculated using advertising models. In the offline mode, Digital Player selects an ad from default playlist based on the scheduling time. It switches between these two modes depending on the confidence level of the advertising models. That means when the confidence beyond some predefined threshold, digital player works in online mode; otherwise, it works in offline mode.

4. INITIAL EXPERIMENTAL RESULTS

An IAF prototype was developed and on this basis an internal pilot was performed within Intel. We use both real internal GPTW (Great Place To Work) events and fake ads as playing content on digital sign. The experiment data was collected from 5 digital signs deployed globally. We use 70% collection data for training and the remaining 30% for testing. Three algorithms, Decision Tree (DT), Association Rule (AR) and Naïve Bayes (NB) in Microsoft SQL Server Analysis Service (SSAS) were used in the experiments.

Table 1. Initial experimental results on targeting accuracy.

	DT	AR	NB
Seeing based targeting model	71.72%	68.34%	64.26%
Context based targeting model	67.98%	67.66%	64.05%

The experimental results are as shown in Table 1, where each cell indicates the targeting accuracy of each model learned by different algorithms. Here the difference between Seeing Based Targeting model and Context Based Targeting model is that the former uses demographic info (gender and age bracket) as inputs and the latter doesn't. From Table1, we can see that Decision Tree algorithm can achieve the highest targeting accuracy for both types of models (71.72% and 67.98% respectively). Moreover, Seeing Based Targeting model can achieve higher targeting accuracy than Context Based Targeting model with Decision Tree algorithm.

This verifies that demographic info does help to improve the audience targeting accuracy. Finally, we found in Decision Tree model, playing ad is the most differentiable factor for targeting results, which indicates that different ads have very different attraction to the audiences. An interesting example is that the audiences show very different behaviors with respect to a focal evaluation ad when compared with other ads.

Since the training data was collected within Intel campuses, and most of the Intel employees are male young adults and male adults, it is not a good coverage of all the different audience groups (child, young adults, adults and senior). Furthermore, most of the playing content is quite generic, not gender and age specific, which results in different audience groups have similar interests in the same playing content. We believe the targeting accuracy of IAF can be significantly improved up to around 90% if it is deployed in public locations like restaurants, Disney, shopping mall and has gender and age differentiable content playing on the digital signs.

5. DEMONSTRATION

An IAF demo was developed to show the concept of targeted advertising in digital signage. Figure 2 shows a screenshot of IAF demo interface. The top right window shows the captured human face in a green circle. To its bottom shows the recognized demographics of the captured audience and corresponding number, here means one Male Young Adult (M.Y.A) is captured. To its left, shows a list of default ads, a list of recommended ads for the current audience and a list of relevant ads to the current playing ad. To its top, is the current playing advertisement.

Figure 2. A screenshot of IAF demo interface.

The demo plays default ads in predefined order (or random order) when no audience is noticed. Once an audience watches the played ads, the demo will notice, capture, and track his/her face, and recognize gender and age bracket in real time. Then the demo will play the ads that the audience would be most interested in along with a recommended ad list based on predictive modeling. In addition to watching the played ad, the audience can select and play any of the recommended ads. When the audience selects other ads, a new list relevant to the selected ad will be provided to the audience for selection while the selected ad plays. The viewer event by the audience will be recorded and input to the predictive modeling. The predictive modeling correlates the features of the audience with the content of ads, discovers strong associations between them and creates the recommended ad list.

6. CONCLUSION

This paper proposed an Intelligent Advertising Framework, which integrates AVA and data mining to realize targeted advertising. By analyzing AVA viewership data collected from previous audience in front of a display, some viewing patterns can be discovered with data mining technology. These viewing patterns or advertising models can be deployed to the digital signs and then used to choose specific ads from the inventory of available content to intelligently target future audiences.

An IAF demo was developed, shown at several internal events and industrial events and got wide recognition and great traction from the industry. The demo shows the latest advance of AVA technology and a novel usage of targeted advertising in digital signage industry. The demo also provides KDD community an excellent showcase of how to adopt intelligent technologies, AVA and data mining to bring customers real business values. An internal pilot of IAF was performed within Intel. The initial experimental results based on the collected data are very positive and validate the IAF solution.

7. REFERENCES

[1] Digital Signage. http://en.wikipedia.org/wiki/Digital_signage.

[2] Schaeffler, J. 2008. *Digital Signage: Software, Networks, Advertising, and Displays: A Primer for Understanding the business*. Focal press, Burlington, MA USA, 2008

[3] Müller, J., Wilmsmann, D., Exeler, J. et al 2009. Display Blindness: The Effect of Expectations on Attention towards Digital Signage, *Lecture Notes in Computer Science*, Volume 5538 (2009), 1-8.

[4] Galeotti, J. L. Moraga-Gonzalez 2004. *A Model of Strategic Targeted Advertising.* CESIFO Working Paper NO. 1196. May 2004

[5] Payne, T., David, E., Jennings, N. R. and Sharifi, M. 2006. Auction mechanisms for efficient advertisement selection on public displays. In *Proceedings of European Conference on Artificial Intelligence*, pages 285–289, 2006.

[6] Tru-Media. http://tru-media.com/.

[7] Quividi. http://www.quividi.com/.

[8] At Immersive Labs, Ads Watch Who Looks At Them. http://www.huffingtonpost.com/2011/04/25/immersive-labs_n_853555.html.

[9] Targeted Advertising. http://en.wikipedia.org/wiki/Targeted_advertising.

[10] Tian, P., Sanjay, A. V. Malik, S. et al. 2012. Realizing Targeted Advertising in Digital Signage with AVA and Data Mining. In *Proceedings of International MultiConference on Engineers and Computer Scientists 2012*, Mar. 14-16, 2012, Hong Kong.

[11] Intel AIM Suite. http://intel.cognovision.com/.

[12] Slawsky, R. *Audience Measurement with Anonymous Video Analytics*, http://global.networldalliance.com/downloads/white_papers/NEC_WP_AVA%20Measurement_To%20Launch.pdf

AssocExplorer: An Association Rule Visualization System for Exploratory Data Analysis

Guimei Liu
School of Computing
National University of Singapore
liugm@comp.nus.edu.sg

Andre Suchitra
School of Computing
National University of Singapore
suchitra@comp.nus.edu.sg

Haojun Zhang
School of Computing
National University of Singapore
zhanghao@comp.nus.edu.sg

Mengling Feng
Data Mining Department
Institute for Infocomm Research, Singapore
mfeng@i2r.a-star.edu.sg

See-Kiong Ng
Data Mining Department
Institute for Infocomm Research, Singapore
skng@i2r.a-star.edu.sg

Limsoon Wong
School of Computing
National University of Singapore
wongls@comp.nus.edu.sg

ABSTRACT

We present a system called AssocExplorer to support exploratory data analysis via association rule visualization and exploration. AssocExplorer is designed by following the visual information-seeking mantra: overview first, zoom and filter, then details on demand. It effectively uses coloring to deliver information so that users can easily detect things that are interesting to them. If users find a rule interesting, they can explore related rules for further analysis, which allows users to find interesting phenomenon that are difficult to detect when rules are examined separately. Our system also allows users to compare rules and inspect rules with similar item composition but different statistics so that the key factors that contribute to the difference can be isolated.

Categories and Subject Descriptors

H.2.8 [**DATABASE MANAGEMENT**]: Database Applications—*Data Mining*

Keywords

exploratory data analysis, rule visualization, rule exploration

1. INTRODUCTION

The main objective of exploratory data analysis is to summarize the main characteristics of datasets, often with visualization, to help users understand the data and to suggest hypotheses to test. Association rule mining is an important problem in the data mining area [1]. An association rule can be viewed as a summarization of a subset of the underlying dataset. Understanding association rules can help users understand the underlying dataset. Furthermore, the relationship and interaction among rules often reveal valuable information of the underlying data. Hence it is desirable to use association rules for exploratory data analysis.

Association rule mining often produces a large number of rules. Rules need to be organized and presented properly for easy comprehension. Here we present a system called AssocExplorer to support exploratory data analysis via association rule visualization and exploration. The main features of our system can be summarized as follows:

- We follow the visual information-seeking mantra [3] to design our system: we use a scatter plot to provide a global view of all rules; we allow users to filter rules based on various criteria; details of rules are displayed on demand.
- We use coloring to deliver information effectively. In particular, we color length-1 rules, and the whole collection of rules can be colored based on a selected attribute. This helps users find important attributes easily. Users can then start their analysis from there.
- If users find a rule interesting, they can explore related rules to have a deeper understanding of the rule. Bringing related rules together allows users to compare similar rules and find interesting phenomenon that are difficult to detect when rules are examined separately.
- Rules with similar item composition but very different statistics may represent inexpensive actions that we can take to make a big change. Our system allow users to inspect such rules under various contexts to isolate the key factors that contribute to the difference.
- We use proper structures to store and index rules and the original dataset, which ensures that our system can respond users' requests promptly.

In the rest of this paper, we first briefly describe the association rule mining problem and then present the AssocExplorer system.

KDD'12, August 12–16, 2012, Beijing, China.

2. ASSOCIATION RULE MINING

Association rule mining has been applied on both transactional datasets and attribute-valued datasets. In our system, we focus on attribute-valued datasets since they are prevalent in real-world applications.

Let $D = \{t_1, t_2, \cdots, t_n\}$ be a dataset containing a set of records. Each record is described by a set of attributes $\mathcal{A} = \{A_1, A_2, \cdots, A_m\}$. Attributes in $\mathcal{A}$ are either categorical or continuous. We use $t[A]$ to denote the value of attribute A in record t. Let A be a categorical attribute and v be a value taken by A. We call attribute-value pair $A = v$ an *item*. Let t be a record. If $t[A] = v$, then we say t *contains* item $A = v$. We use letter i to denote items.

DEFINITION 1 (PATTERN). *A pattern is a set of items* $\{i_1, i_2, \cdots, i_k\}$*, and* k *is called the length of the pattern.*

We use letter X to denote patterns. If a record t contains all the items in X, then we say t *contains* X, denoted as $X \subseteq t$. We use $T(X)$ to denote the set of records containing X, that is, $T(X) = \{t | t \in D \wedge X \subseteq t\}$. The *support* of a pattern X in a dataset D is defined as the number of records in D containing X, that is, $supp(X) = |T(X)|$.

In real applications, users are often interested in finding the association between patterns and a target attribute. For example, in business analysis, companies are often interested in finding patterns that may be associated with customer spending; in medical domain, knowing which group of people are more likely to contract a disease and their associated patterns can help the prevention and the diagnosis of the disease. Therefore, we focus on studying the association between patterns and a pre-specified target attribute in our system. The target attribute is supplied by users based on their interest. It can be either categorical or continuous. Below we mainly focus on the case where the target attribute is categorical.

To simplify the problem, we assume that users specify one target attribute for one analysis task. Let A_{tgt} be the target attribute specified by users and it is categorical. We ask users to choose a value of A_{tgt} that is the most interesting to them, and we call this value *target value*, denoted as v_{tgt}. Given a pattern X, we formulate the corresponding association rule as $R : X \Rightarrow v_{tgt}$. As in traditional association rule mining, we define the support of R as $supp(X \bigcup \{A_{tgt} = v_{tgt}\})$, denoted as $supp(R)$, and the confidence of R as $supp(R)/supp(X)$, denoted as $conf(R)$. The support of X is called the *coverage* of R.

In our system, we use p-value as an additional interestingness measure. The p-value of a rule R, denoted as $p\text{-}value(R)$, measures the statistically significance of R. It is the probability of observing R or a rule more extreme than R given the two sides of R are independent. The lower the p-value, the less likely the rule occurs by random chance, thus the more statistically significant the rule is.

We use the algorithm described in [2] to mine patterns and store them in a structure called CFP-tree. The CFP-tree structure is specially designed for storing and querying patterns [2]. Sub-pattern search, super-pattern search, immediate sub-pattern/super-pattern search and exact match can be efficiently processed on a CFP-tree. These operations are frequently used in rule filtering, rule exploration and comparative analysis. The efficiency of CFP-tree in supporting various queries ensures that our system has a reasonable response time.

3. THE ASSOCEXPLORER SYSTEM

In this section, we use dataset *adult* downloaded from UCI machine learning repository [1] to illustrate our system. Dataset *adult* contains the demographical information of 32,561 adults. There is a class attribute on this dataset, and it indicates whether the annual income of a person exceeds 50K. The class attribute takes two values: "*>50K*" and "*<=50K*". We pick the class attribute as the target attribute, and "*>50K*" as the target value.

3.1 Global view

We use a scatter plot to provide a global view of all the rules. The X-axis is coverage of rules and the Y-axis is confidence. Rules are mapped to points in the two-dimensional space. From the scatter plot, users can easily locate rules with high confidence and/or support. Figure 1 shows a snapshot of the AssocExplorer system. The lower-left panel displays the set of rules discovered from the *adult* dataset with minimum support threshold of 5%, minimum confidence threshold of 10% and maximum p-value of 0.05. The horizontal red line at 24.1% corresponds to the relative frequency of the target value "*>50K*" in the whole dataset.

Coloring length-1 rules. Length-1 rules are often of particular interest since they are simple and easy to comprehend. We highlight length-1 rules in the scatter plot using different colors as shown in Figure 1. Rules containing more than one item are colored in gray. Users can easily identify attributes and items that have strong association with the target value. Figure 1 shows that attributes *age*, *education*, *marital-status*, *occupation*, and *sex* are important for a person's income, while attribute *race* and *workclass* are not that important. The *native-country* attribute has no impact on income as most of the people in the dataset are Americans.

Coloring rules based on an attribute. Another coloring scheme is to color rules based on a selected attribute. Let A be an attribute selected by users. Rules that do not contain items of A are colored in gray. Rules that contain items of A are colored based on the items of A. This coloring scheme help users understand the impact of the items of A on the whole set of rules. For example, users can have a rough idea on the frequency of the items of A in the whole set of rules. It is also easy to know whether attribute A or its items dominate other attributes/items. Figure 2 shows the rules colored based on attribute *education*. Most rules containing "*education=Bachelors*" have higher confidence than rules containing "*education= Some-college*" or "*education=HS-grad*". It means that people with a bachelor degree are more likely to earn more than 50K per year than people with a lower degree. We observe that one rule containing "*education=Bachelors*" has very low confidence. It lies at the lower-left corner of the plot. By taking a closer look, we find the rule contains "*marital-status=never-married*". It implies item "*marital-status=never-married*" is more dominant than item "*education=Bachelors*".

3.2 Zooming and filtering

The number of rules generated from a dataset can be very large. Points in the scatter plot may get over-crowded. Users can utilize zooming and filtering to focus on rules that are interesting to them. Using the zooming function, users can

[1] `http://archive.ics.uci.edu/ml/datasets`

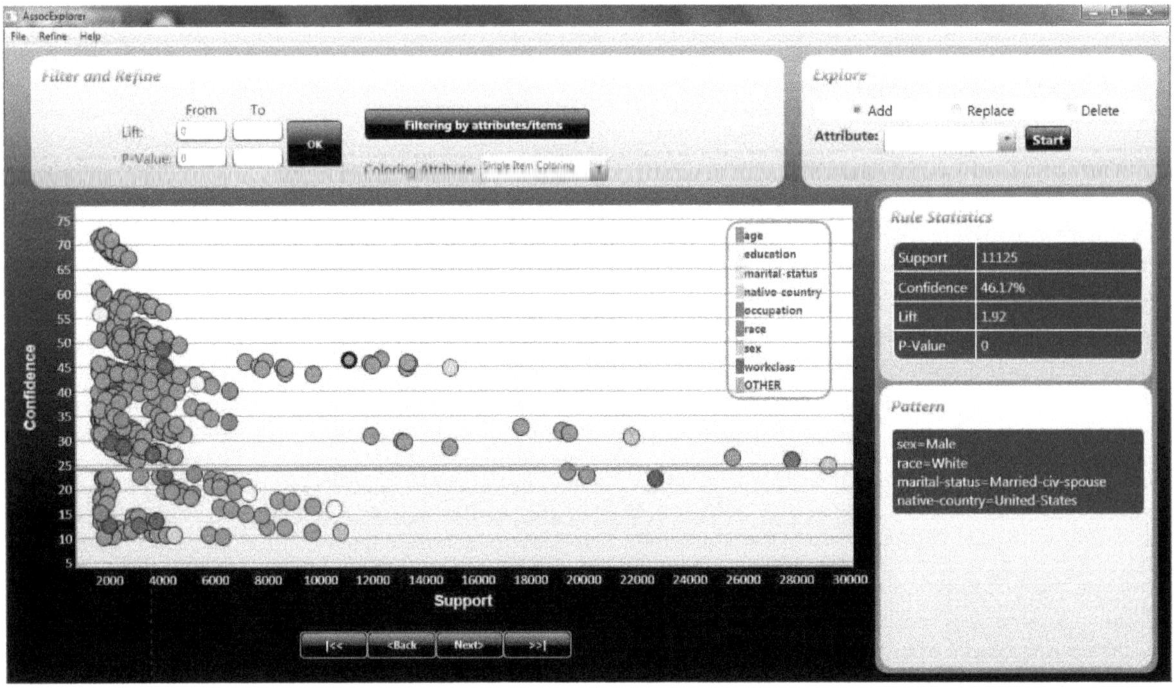

Figure 1: Overview of the AssocExplorer system

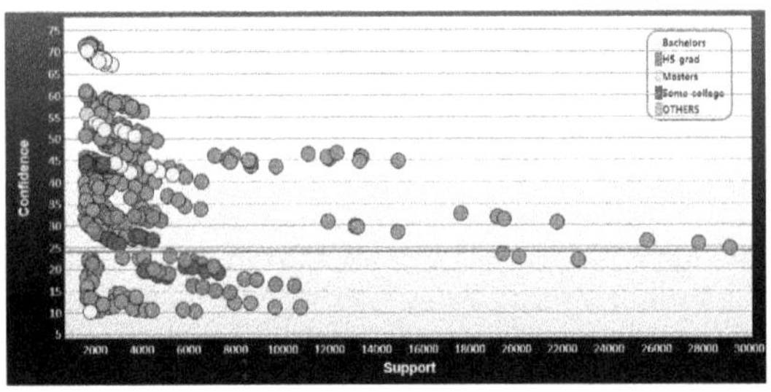

Figure 2: Coloring rules based on *education*

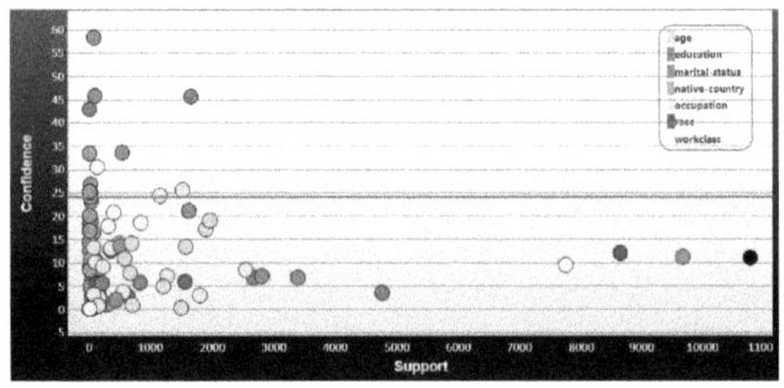

Figure 3: Adding one attribute to {sex=female}

focus on a particular region of the scatter plot. It is equivalent to filtering by support and confidence.

The filtering functions are located at the upper-left panel of Figure 1. Users can do filtering based on p-value by specifying a range for the p-value. Rules which fall out of the specified range are removed from the scatter plot.

Users can also narrow down the set of rules to be examined by specifying constraints on attributes and items. Attributes are put into three categories: attributes that must appear in rules (the "include" category), attributes that cannot appear in rules (the "exclude" category) and attributes that may or may not appear in rules (the "optional" category). Similarly, items are put into the three categories in accordance with the status of attributes. Initially, all the attributes and items are set to be optional. When users change the status of attributes and items, the consistency between attributes and items is automatically enforced by our system.

3.3 Details on demand

The detailed information of a rule is displayed at the lower-right panel when the rule is clicked. The clicked rule is highlighted in a bold black circle.

3.4 Exploring rules

When one rule is deemed to be interesting, it is often helpful to look at rules that are similar to it. We provide several operations to explore rules starting from a selected rule R: adding one more item to R, removing one item from R and replacing one item in R. Users can specify an attribute to be added, removed or replaced. If no attribute is specified, then any item whose attribute is outside R can be added, and any item inside R can be removed or be replaced by items from the same attribute. The resultant rules are still displayed in a scatter plot.

For the adding operation, the resultant rules are colored based on the added attributes. Rules that contain the same added attribute have the same color. Figure 3 shows the set of rules generated by adding one more attribute to rule $\{sex{=}female\}$. The original rule is colored in black, and it lies below the red line, which means that females are less likely to earn more than 50K than males. If we divide females into different age groups, we find that all the groups still lie below the red line. The situation is almost the same for attribute *occupation*. A few rules that are generated by

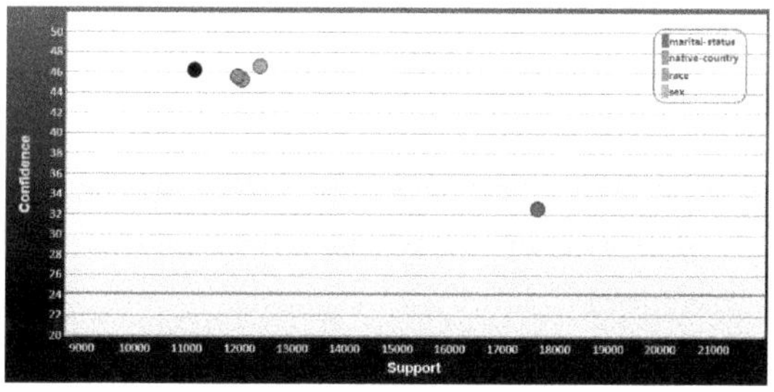

Figure 4: Remove one attribute from {*sex=Male, race=white, marital-status=Married-civ-spouse, native-country=United-State*}

adding items of attribute *education* or *marital-status* have high confidence. It implies that females can have higher income by getting a higher degree or changing marital status.

Figure 4 shows the rules generated by removing one item from {*sex=Male, race=white, marital-status=Married-civ-spouse, native-country=United-State*}. The original rule is colored in black. If item "*marital-status=Married-civ-spouse*" is removed, the confidence of the rule (the blue point) decreases a lot. It suggests that this item is key to the confidence of the original rule. On the contrary, removing any of the other three items does not change the confidence of the rule much. It implies that the other three items do not have much impact on the association between the original pattern and the target value.

3.5 Comparative analysis

When we replace one item in R and the confidence of the resultant rule R' is quite different from that of R, we get a situation where a small change in items causes a big change in confidence. It is often worthwhile to further examine such situations as they may suggest inexpensive actions that we can take to change things toward a desired direction. Such knowledge is called actionable knowledge [4].

Rules R and R' differ on only one attribute. Let X_c be the set of common items of R and R', A_{diff} be the attribute on which R and R' differ, and v and v' be two values of A_{diff} that appear in R and R' respectively. Pattern X_c constitutes the context where the impact of A_{diff} on the target value v_{tgt} is studied. We call A_{diff} a *comparing attribute*, and its two values, v and v', *comparing items*.

To have a comprehensive understanding of the impact of A_{diff} on A_{tgt}, we provide operations to examine the impact of A_{diff} on A_{tgt} in other contexts: (1) on the whole dataset, that is, X_c is empty; (2) add one item to X_c; (3) remove one item from X_c; and (4) X_c contains one single item, and this item can be any item except for items of A_{diff}.

Figure 5 shows the comparison between *occupation= Admin-clerical* and *occupation = Craft-repair* in the context of {*race =White*}. The bar plot on the left shows that when *race =White*, craft repairers are more likely to earn more than 50K per year than administrative clerks. The two comparing items exhibit similar difference in confidence on the whole dataset. The right panel of Figure 5 displays how the difference changes when we add one more attribute to the context. The top two bar plots show that when items of attributes *age* and *education* are added to the context respectively, the difference between the two comparing items does not change much. The bottom bar plot shows that for both males and

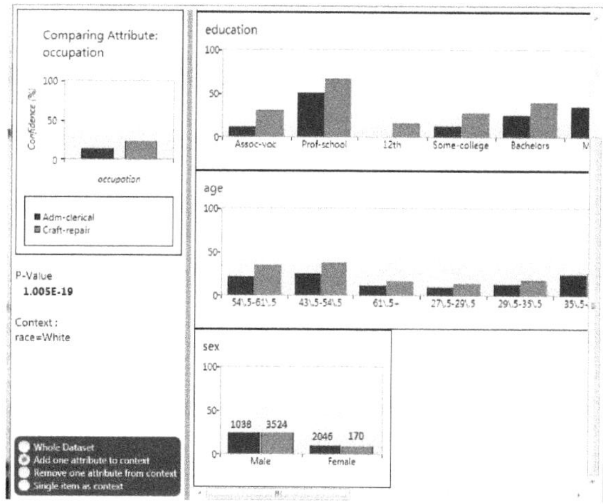

Figure 5: Comparing {*race=White, occupation=Admin-clerical*} with {*race=White, occupation=Craft-repair*}. The numbers on top of the bars are the support of the corresponding patterns.

females, craft-repairer are slightly less likely to earn more than 50K than administrative clerks. This contradicts the original finding shown in the left panel. We have a Simpson's paradox. By taking a closer look, we find that attribute *sex* is a confounding factor here. It has association with both attribute *occupation* and the target value: men generally earn more than women and many more men work as craft repairers than women. We use pie charts to visualize the interactions between comparing items and the added attribute, which are accessible from the right-click menu.

3.6 Managing history

In a data mining task, users often do not have a clear idea on what they are looking for at the beginning. They may need to iteratively examine rules from different points of view to find things that are interesting to them. To help users go back to results produced by previous operations, we store previous results in a sequence and we call it the history sequence. Users can move backward and forward along the history sequence. In Figure 1, the history bar is located under the scatter plot.

4. ACKNOWLEDGMENT

This work is supported in part by Singapore Agency for Science, Technology and Research grant SERC 102 101 0030.

5. REFERENCES

[1] R. Agrawal, T. Imielinski, and A. N. Swami. Mining association rules between sets of items in large databases. In *SIGMOD*, pages 207–216, 1993.

[2] G. Liu, H. Lu, and J. X. Yu. Cfp-tree: A compact disk-based structure for storing and querying frequent itemsets. *Information Systems*, 32(2):295–319, 2007.

[3] B. Shneiderman. The eyes have it: A task by data type taxonomy for information visualizations. In *IEEE Symposium on Visual Languages*, pages 336–343, 1996.

[4] Q. Yang, J. Yin, C. X. Ling, and R. Pan. Extracting actionable knowledge from decision trees. *TKDE*, 19(1):43–56, 2007.

GeoSearch: Georeferenced Video Retrieval System *

Youngwoo Kim, Jinha Kim, Hwanjo Yu†
Department of Computer Science and Engineering
Pohang University of Science and Technology(POSTECH)
Pohang, South Korea
{ywkim10, goldbar, hwanjoyu}@postech.ac.kr

ABSTRACT

Conventional video search systems, to find relevant videos, rely on textual data such as video titles, annotations, and text around the video. Nowadays, video recording devices such as cameras, smartphones and car blackboxes are equipped with GPS sensors and able to capture videos with spatiotemporal information such as time, location and camera direction. We call such videos *georeferenced videos*. This paper presents a georeferenced video retrieval system, GeoSearch, which efficiently retrieves videos containing a certain point or range in the map. To enable a fast search of georeferenced videos, GeoSearch adopts a novel data structure MB*T*R (Minimum Bounding *Tilted* Rectangle) in the leaf nodes of R-Tree. New algorithms are developed to build MB*T*Rs from georeferenced videos and to efficiently process point and range queries on MB*T*Rs. We demonstrate our system on real georeferenced videos, and show that, compared to previous methods, GeoSearch substantially reduces the index size and also improves the search speed for georeferenced video data. Our online demo is available at "http://dm.hwanjoyu.org/geosearch".

Categories and Subject Descriptors

H.2.4 [**Database Management**]: Systems—*Query processing*; H.2.4 [**Database Management**]: Systems—*Multimedia databases*; H.2.8 [**Database Management**]: Database Applications—*Spatial databases and GIS*

General Terms

Algorithms, Performance

Keywords

Georeferencing, Video search, Spatial Indexing

*This work was partially supported by the Brain Korea 21 Project in 2012 and Mid-career Researcher Program through NRF grant funded by the MEST (No. KRF-2011-0016029). This work was also supported by IT Consilience Creative Program of MKE and NIPA (C1515-1121-0003).

†corresponding author

KDD'12, August 12–16, 2012, Beijing, China.

1. INTRODUCTION

With the rapid popularization of video recording devices, not only the media made by professionals but also made by ordinary users called UCC (User-Created Contents) are taking a large portion in the web. Since identifying related video requires understanding of video contents, which is a very heavy and complex process, current video search systems mostly rely on textual data such as video titles, annotations, and text around the video.

Nowadays, video capturing devices such as cameras, smartphones and car blackboxes are equipped with GPS sensors and able to capture videos with spatiotemporal information such as time, location and camera direction. We call such videos *georeferenced videos*. For some applications, such spatiotemporal information plays key roles in querying georeferenced videos. For example, some people may want to find videos of specific event that occurred at specific time and location, e.g., videos of a traffic accident captured by car blackboxes, videos of a goal scene in a soccer play captured by users, or videos of a concert with celebrities captured by users.

This paper presents GeoSearch, a georeferenced video retrieval system, which efficiently retrieves videos containing a certain point or range in the map. GeoSearch adopts a novel data structure MB*T*R (Minimum Bounding *Tilted* Rectangle) in the leaf nodes of R-Tree, in order to enable a fast search of georeferenced videos. While traditional MBR (Minimum Bounding Rectangle) is popularly used to describe an area in spatial indexes such as R-Tree, MBR is not suitable for describing the areas of moving scenes where its location and direction are continously changing. MB*T*R is designed to describe an area (or scenes) of moving location and direction. New algorithms are developed to build MB*T*Rs from georeferenced videos and to efficiently process point and range queries on MB*T*Rs. We demonstrate our system on real georeferenced videos, and show that, compared to previous methods, by adopting MB*T*R in the R-Tree, GeoSearch substantially reduces the index size and also improves the search speed for georeferenced video data.

Our demo is available at "http://dm.hwanjoyu.org/geosearch". Due to space limitation, this paper focuses on a high-level overview of techniques and demonstration. Technical details are described in our technical report [10].

1.1 Related Work

Georeferenced Multimedia Search: There are several approaches to the use of location information in image search. Toyama et al [21] used metadata in image search and developed a database for it. They enabled spatial image search by recording images with longitudinal and latitudinal coordinates and timestamps. Several commercial websites, such as Flickr and Woophy [1], also provide georeferenced image search. They focus on showing static images of the locations in a map and support simple query such as nearest neighbor query. Google Street View [2] provides streams of street view images of their own. We can reference these images by camera's location and viewing direction.

Trajectory indexing methods were developed in order to efficiently store and search moving objects [16, 8]. Our indexing method for supporting moving *scenes* can be considered an extension of trajectory indexing which takes into consideration camera directions as well as the location of the cameras.

Research associated with "trajectory-based video indexing" [7, 17] and "spatial indexing for video" [20] have been published in the computer vision community. However, the problem they address is different from ours; their goal is to index the relative location of objects in the video, not the viewable scenes. They also use video content retrieval methods such as object segmentation and motion tracking to detect objects, while we use metadata to search georeferenced videos.

A viewable scene model for enabling georeferenced video search has been recently proposed by Ay et al. [3, 5]. Based on the viewable scene model, they developed methods for supporting point and range queries using MBR-based filtering. (We compare this method as a baseline method in our experiments in Section 3.) Our method builds an index GeoTree based on their viewable scene model.

They also developed a *relevance* video search method based on the viewable scene model, and proposed metrics to measure the relevance of video to the given range query [3]. The metrics compute the relevance scores based on the size of the overlapping area. Since computing the exact size of the overlapping area is computationally expensive, they approximate it using grids and histograms. However, their approach requires vast storage to keep all the videos stored in grids, and also the accuracy is compromised due to the running of the query on the gridded data instead of the original data. Moreover, the overlapping area-based relevance may not reflect the true relevance implied in the user's query; user's relevance may be more related to parts that are overlapped and the distance to the overlapping area. Inducing a good relevance function is itself a non-trivial research problem.

Ay et al. also proposed a method for generating synthetic metadata for georeferenced video search [4]. Since it is often difficult to obtain a large set of georeferenced video data, this method can be used for evaluating new methods for georeferenced video search.

Spatial Indexing: There are numerous works on spatial indexing and query processing in the database community. Many of the indexing structures are based on R-Tree [9, 13, 19]. Several works focus on querying location trajectories of moving objects [14, 18]. Also, several effective indexing structures such as STR-Tree and TB-tree were proposed [15]. These works mostly focus on dealing with temporal dimension and complex queries, rather than dealing with complex spatial data such as viewable scenes.

Spatiotemporal trajectory compressions for saving data storage and enabling fast query processing are also being researched [12, 8]. Their methods focus on the data of points or location trajectories that are not directly applicable to viewable scenes. There are also works that focus on indexing range data or region data that consider static rectangular objects [6, 11].

No effective indexing structure has yet been proposed that supports exact queries on camera viewable scenes of moving locations and directions.

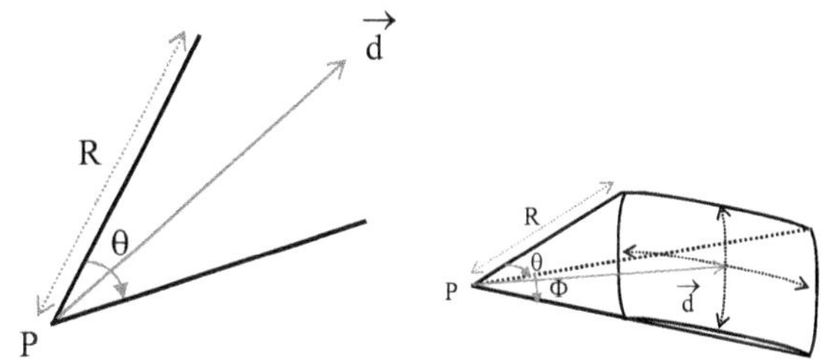

(a) FOVscene in 2D (b) FOVscene in 3D

Figure 1: Examples of FOVscene in 2D and 3D spaces

2. GEOTREE: SPATIAL INDEXING FOR GEO-REFERENCED VIDEO SEARCH

Preliminary: Viewable Scene Model: The viewable scene changes, as the camera moves or rotates. The area captured by the camera is referred to as the Field-Of-View scene (FOVscene) [5]. As illustrated in Figure 1(a), in a 2D space, four parameters are required to express a single FOVscene: (1) location of the camera P, (2) direction of the camera $\vec{d}$, (3) viewable angle of the camera θ, and (4) visible distance R. Camera location P is represented as a (latitude, longitude) pair that can be obtained using a GPS sensor. Camera direction $\vec{d}$ can be obtained using a compass sensor. Camera viewable angle θ and visible distance R can be obtained from the camera lens' property and zoom level. As assumed in [5, 3], we also fixed θ and R by assuming the use of static camera lens. (Some video recording devices such as smartphones and car blackboxes use static camera lenses.)

The camera view or the viewable scene information at a particular moment is entirely expressed by an FOVscene. An FOVscene corresponds to a frame in the video. A georeferenced video can be represented by a sequence of FOVscenes. We use the term FOVstream to denote a sequence of FOVscenes. As done in [5, 3], we restrict FOVscene to a 2D space, however it can be extended to a 3D space in a straightforward manner. Altitude and pitch should be considered in the 3D model (Figure 1(b)). but they do not alter the nature of the FOVscene model.

Index Construction and Query Processing: To enable an efficient indexing of georeferenced video search, videos must be recorded with the metadata of $(P, \vec{d}, \theta, R)$ for each FOVscene. Video recording devices such as car blackboxes and smartphones are nowadays equipped with sensors that have the ability to record metadata with videos. We construct a spatial index called GeoTree using the metadata. When a point or range query is submitted by users, it is processed on the GeoTree by finding the FOVstreams that overlap the query area.

GeoTree adopts a novel structure called Minimum Bounding *Tilted* Rectangle (MB*T*R). GeoTree uses MB*T*R instead of MBR (Minimum Bounding Rectangle) to represent an area of moving scenes in the index. GeoTree is a kind of R-tree using MBR in the nonleaf nodes and MB*T*R in the leaf nodes. Figure 2 depicts examples of MBR and MB*T*R representing areas of moving scenes. MB*T*R is more suitable for representing an area of moving scenes; as video recording devices such as car blackboxes are often moving piece-wise linearly, MB*T*R produces less false positive areas. For example, when a query, i.e., the red circle in the figure, is submitted, the MBR in Figure 2(a) includes the query area, thereby incurring a large area of false scanning of videos while the MB*T*R in Figure 2(b) efficiently prunes the videos.

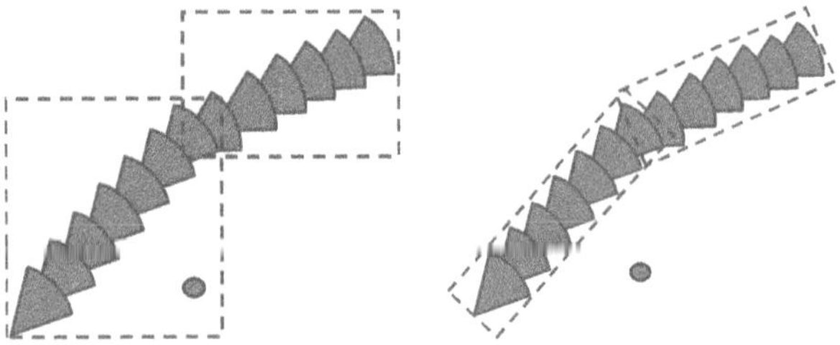

(a) MBR-based filtering (b) MBTR-based filtering

Figure 2: Examples of MBR (Minimum Bounding Rectangle) and MBTR (Minimum Bounding *Tilted* Rectangle). Red circle is the querying area. Blue circular sector is a viewable scene

	MBR-Filtering	R-Tree	GeoTree
Range Query (ms)	297,800	6,039.4	4,554.2
Point Query (ms)	68,297	1,302.0	1,264.5
Memory Use (MB)	16.6	27.3	2.83

Table 1: Comparison of Query Processing Time

Building MBTRs requires modeling moving scenes piece-wise linearly such that each MBTR covers as large an area as possible while producing as small a number of false positive areas as possible. Therefore, we first identify *markup* FOVscene*s* from moving scenes, while considering the changing patterns of P and $\vec{d}$. Markup FOVscenes are those at the edge of an MBTR, such that the FOVscenes between markup FOVscenes are moving linearly in terms of P and constant in terms of $\vec{d}$, and thus any FOVscenes can be estimated from the markup FOVscenes. Once a set of markup FOVscenes are found, MBTRs from pairs of adjacent markup FOVscenes are constructed.

A point or range query is processed in a similar fashion to R-Tree in the nonleaf nodes, as the nonleaf nodes of GeoTree are also described by MBRs. Once a query reaches a leaf node in the GeoTree, it is processed in two steps – (1) MBTR filtering and (2) MBTR lookup. MBTR filtering ascertains if the query can overlap the MBTR. If MBTR filtering returns *false*, this means that there is no FOVscene in the MBTR that overlaps the query. However, if MBTR filtering returns *true*, MBTR lookup is called to compute and return an expected subsequence of FOVscenes that overlap the query. Since an MBTR typically contains numerous FOVscenes, it would be inefficient to scan all the FOVscenes in the MBTR to find the overlapping FOVscenes. We directly compute, using the MBTR structure, a sequence of FOVscenes that is expected to contain the query point.

3. EXPERIMENTS

We compare the performance of GeoTree to R-Tree and MBR-Filter, i.e., the MBR-based filtering proposed in [3]. We evaluate the performance of processing point queries and range queries in terms of query processing time and also memory usage. Our experiments were done using a machine with the following specifications: dualcore CPU (2.4GHz) and 4GB of Memory.

DataSet: Experiments were performed on real FOVstream data sets. We captured real scenes using an Android mobile phone equipped with a GPS receiver and a 3D compass. We ignored altitude and pitch angles from the 3D compass, as we are only interested in 2D. Thirty FOVscenes were captured every second. Latitudinal and longitudinal data were converted into meter metrics in the 2D plane. No zoom level change was simulated, thus viewable angle θ and visible distance R were kept constant and thus fixed to $\theta = 55\,^{\circ}$ and $R = 50m$.

FOVscenes ranged in the area of 3.3km long in the north-south and 3.8km long in east-west. Test data corresponded to 11 streams with a total duration of 180 minutes. The number of FOVscenes was 325,313 in total. This number of streams corresponded to approximately 4.4GB of typical video data. The sum of all trajectories' length was approximately 68km. For the leaf nodes of GeoTree with less than 5 FOVscenes, we simply used simple one-by-one search and did not perform MBTR filtering and lookup, because, when an MBTR contains just a few FOVscenes, scanning FOVscenes one-by-one runs faster due to some overhead of MBTR filtering and lookup.

Result Summary: Table 1 summarizes the results of the query processing time for each method. For the range query test, we randomly generated 10,000 queries and measured the accumulated processing time for the queries. For the point query test, we randomly generated 100,000 queries and also measured the accumulated processing time for the queries. The processing times are averaged by 30 runs. For GeoTree, we first tuned the error threshold parameters on the dataset, and fixed the parameter values for all runs, these were. $\epsilon_P = 1m$ and $\epsilon_\theta = 10^{\circ}$

MBR-Filter was one hundred times slower than the other tree-based searches. We omitted the naive sequential search results because it was even much slower than MBR-Filter. GeoTree gave a consistently faster query processing time than R-Tree. Although the query processing times of R-Tree and GeoTree were not substantially different, their memory usages were an order of magnitude different. As Figure 3 shows, the performance difference became more significant, as data size increased.

4. DEMONSTRATION PLAN

We plan to demonstrate our system on a real map of the campus of POSTECH[1]. We captured various places of the campus and uploaded the videos to YouTube. We then built an online website, "http://dm.hwanjoyu.org/geosearch/", which can search corresponding video frames using point or range queries. In our online search website, a user submits a point or range query by mouse clicks on the map, and our system returns corresponding video frames using Tubechop[2]. Figure 4(a) illustrates an example of a range query in our website. Figure 4(b) shows the result in text and links to video views. Once the user clicks a link, our system plays corresponding video frames as shown in Figure 4(c).

5. REFERENCES

[1] Woophy. http://www.woophy.com.

[2] D. Anguelov, C. Dulong, D. Filip, C. Frueh, S. Lafon, R. Lyon, A. Ogale, L. Vincent, and J. Weaver. Google street view: Capturing the world at street level. *Computer*, 43:32–38, June 2010.

[3] S. Arslan Ay, R. Zimmermann, and S. Kim. Relevance ranking in georeferenced video search. *Multimedia Systems*, 16:105–125, 2010. 10.1007/s00530-009-0177-x.

[4] S. A. Ay, S. H. Kim, and R. Zimmermann. Generating synthetic meta-data for georeferenced video management. In *Proceedings of the 18th SIGSPATIAL International Conference on Advances in Geographic Information Systems*, GIS '10, pages 280–289, New York, NY, USA, 2010. ACM.

[5] S. A. Ay, R. Zimmermann, and S. H. Kim. Viewable scene modeling for geospatial video search. In *Proceedings of the 16th ACM*

[1] http://www.postech.ac.kr

[2] www.tubechop.com: a site that shows a segment of YouTube videos

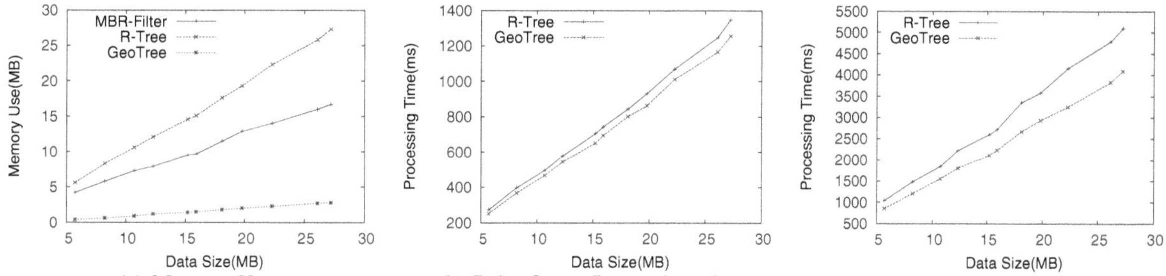

(a) Memory Use (b) Point Query Processing Time (c) Range Query Processing Time

Figure 3: Result of Varying Data Sizes

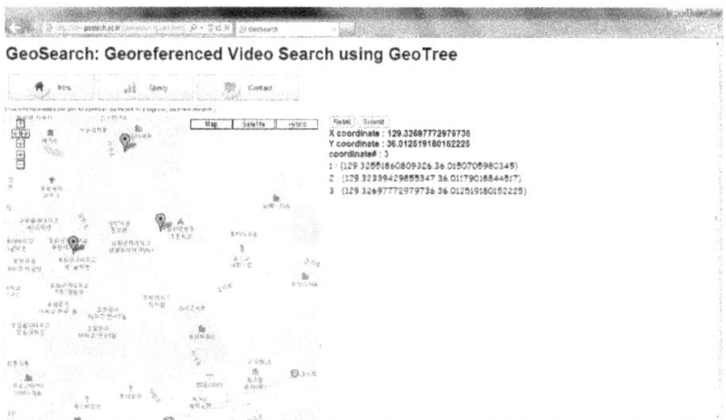

(a) Point Query

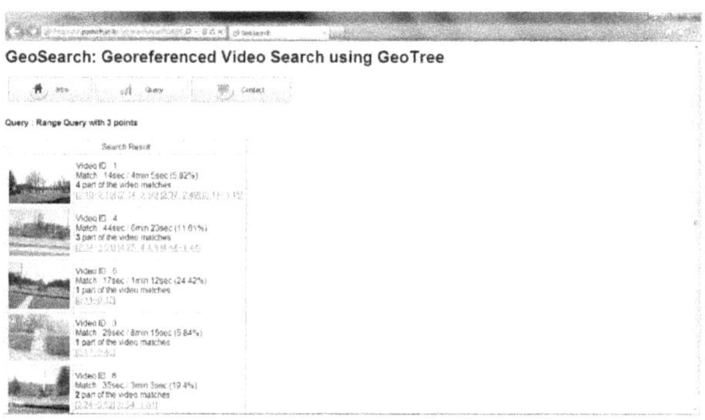

(b) Query Result

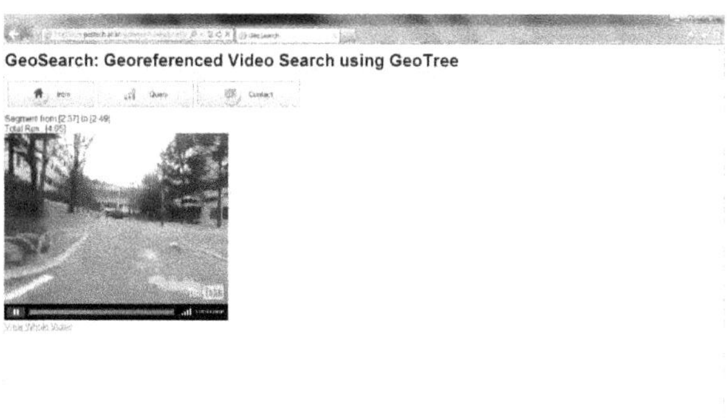

(c) Video view on YouTube

Figure 4: Demonstration Site

international conference on Multimedia, MM '08, pages 309–318, New York, NY, USA, 2008. ACM.

[6] M. Chaabouni and S. M. Chung. The point-range tree: a data structure for indexing intervals. In *Proceedings of the 1993 ACM conference on Computer science*, CSC '93, pages 453–460, New York, NY, USA, 1993. ACM.

[7] S. Dagtas, W. Al-Khatib, A. Ghafoor, and R. Kashyap. Models for motion-based video indexing and retrieval. *Image Processing, IEEE Transactions on*, 9(1):88 –101, jan 2000.

[8] E. Frentzos and Y. Theodoridis. On the effect of trajectory compression in spatiotemporal querying. In *Proc. of East European Conf. Advances in Databases and Information Systems*. Springer Berlin / Heidelberg, 2007.

[9] A. Guttman. R-trees: A dynamic index structure for spatial searching. In *INTERNATIONAL CONFERENCE ON MANAGEMENT OF DATA*, pages 47–57. ACM, 1984.

[10] Y. Kim and H. Yu. Geotree: Using spatial information for georeferenced video search. Technical report, POSTECH-CSE-2012-03, http://dm.postech.ac.kr/techreport/TechReport-POSTECH-CSE-2012-03-GeoTree.pdf, 2012.

[11] H.-P. Kriegel, M. PÃűtke, and T. Seidl. Interval sequences: An object-relational approach to manage spatial data. In C. Jensen, M. Schneider, B. Seeger, and V. Tsotras, editors, *Advances in Spatial and Temporal Databases*, volume 2121 of *Lecture Notes in Computer Science*, pages 481–501. Springer Berlin / Heidelberg, 2001.

[12] N. Meratnia and R. de By. Spatiotemporal compression techniques for moving point objects. In *Proc. of Int. Conf. on Extending Database Technology (EDBT 2004)*, 2004.

[13] M. F. Mokbel, T. M. Ghanem, and W. G. Aref. Spatio-temporal access methods. *IEEE Data Engineering Bulletin*, 26:40–49, 2003.

[14] D. Pfoser. Indexing the trajectories of moving objects. *IEEE Data Engineering Bulletin*, 25:3–9, 2002.

[15] D. Pfoser, C. S. Jensen, and Y. Theodoridis. Novel approaches to the indexing of moving object trajectories. pages 395–406, 2000.

[16] M. Potamias, K. Patroumpas, and T. Sellis. Sampling trajectory streams with spatiotemporal criteria. In *Scientific and Statistical Database Management, 2006. 18th International Conference on*, pages 275 –284, 0-0 2006.

[17] E. Sahouria and A. Zakhor. A trajectory based video indexing system for street surveillance. In *IEEE Int. Conf. on Image Processing*, pages 24–28, 1999.

[18] S. Saltenis, C. S. Jensen, S. T. Leutenegger, and M. A. Lopez. Indexing the positions of continuously moving objects, 2000.

[19] H. Samet. Spatial data structures. Addison-Wesley, 1995.

[20] K. Shearer, S. Venkatesh, and D. Kieronska. Spatial indexing for video databases. *Journal of Visual Communication and Image Representation*, 7(4):325 – 335, 1996.

[21] K. Toyama, R. Logan, and A. Roseway. Geographic location tags on digital images. In *Proceedings of the eleventh ACM international conference on Multimedia*, MULTIMEDIA '03, pages 156–166, New York, NY, USA, 2003. ACM.

Siren: An Interactive Tool for Mining and Visualizing Geospatial Redescriptions

[Demo]

Esther Galbrun
Helsinki Institute for Information Technology
Department of Computer Science
University of Helsinki, Finland
galbrun@cs.helsinki.fi

Pauli Miettinen
Max Planck Institute for Informatics
Saarbrücken, Germany
pmiettin@mpi-inf.mpg.de

ABSTRACT

We present SIREN, an interactive tool for mining and visualizing geospatial redescriptions. Redescription mining is a powerful data analysis tool that aims at finding alternative descriptions of the same entities. For example, in biology, an important task is to identify the bioclimatic constraints that allow some species to survive, that is, to describe geographical regions in terms of both the fauna that inhabits them and their bioclimatic conditions.

Using SIREN, users can explore geospatial data of their interest by visualizing the redescriptions on a map, interactively edit, extend and filter them[1].

To demonstrate the use of the tool, we focus on climatic niche-finding over Europe, as an example task. Yet, SIREN is by no means limited to a particular dataset or application.

Categories and Subject Descriptors

H.2.8 [**Information Systems**]: Database Applications—*Data Mining*

General Terms

Algorithms, Design

Keywords

Redescription Mining, Interactive Data Mining

1. INTRODUCTION

Finding multiple ways to characterize the same entities is a problem that appears in many areas of science. In medical sciences, one might want to find a subset of patients sharing similar symptoms and similar genes. Describing geographical regions in terms of both their bioclimatic conditions and the fauna that inhabits them is another example — and a task of great importance for biologists. A simple example of a redescription in this setting could state that areas where Moose live are areas where February's maximum temperature is between −10 and 0 degrees Celsius and July's maximum temperature between 12 and 25 degrees Celsius. This is the redescription shown in the front panel of Figure 1.

However, finding such alternative descriptions of the data generally requires to manually fix the query on one side before looking for the best matching query on the other side, using some type of classification. This typically prevents queries involving more than one variable to be tested. *Redescription Mining* aims at solving this tedious task by automatically identifying the best redescriptions.

More formally, we consider data that contains entities with two sets of characterizing variables, e.g. the fauna and the bioclimatic conditions. We refer to the two sets of variables as left and right hand side data, and the queries over them, respectively, as left and right hand side queries. The task consists in finding a pair of queries, one query for both sets of variables, such that both queries describe (almost) the same set of entities. Section 4 presents requisite background information about that problem.

The results of redescription mining, the redescriptions, can be approached from two points of view. On one hand, by considering the variables and conditions appearing in the queries, which provide valuable information in themselves; On the other hand, by studying the support set of the redescriptions, i.e. the subset of entities where both queries of a redescription hold. When the data is geospatial, that is, the entities are connected to geographical locations, the latter approach becomes even more important. A meaningful geospatial redescription should define coherent areas using expressive queries. The goal of SIREN is to facilitate the analysis of redescriptions using both of the approaches simultaneously.

Mining data is generally an iterative process, the results obtained at one step giving rise to hypotheses which will be tested at a further step, and redescription mining is no exception. Providing means to the user to easily interact with the mining process greatly improves the analysis. When dealing with geospatial data, visualizing the results on a map is crucial in order to interpret them. To answer these

[1]More details about SIREN's features, additional screenshots and a demonstration video are available online at `http://www.cs.helsinki.fi/u/galbrun/redescriptors/siren/`.

KDD'12, August 12–16, 2012, Beijing, China.

Figure 1: The Siren interactive mining and visualization tool. The panel in the background contains a list of redescriptions while the foreground panel displays the map of a selected redescription. In this example, left hand side queries are over fauna while right hand side queries are over monthly bioclimatic conditions, that is, temperatures and precipitation.

needs, we present SIREN, an interactive tool for mining and visualizing geospatial redescriptions.

Alternatively, experimenting with SIREN provides an efficient way for unfamiliar users to learn about redescription mining. The underlying concepts can be easily understood while visualizing the redescriptions and interacting with the system. Hence, it can also be used for educational purposes.

2. EXAMPLE APPLICATIONS

Our main example for demonstrating SIREN is an application to *bioclimatic niche-finding.*

Indeed, an important problem in biology, niche-finding, is a particular instance of redescription mining. The bioclimatic constraints that must be met for a certain species to survive constitute that species' bioclimatic envelope, or niche [3]. Finding such envelopes can help, e.g. to predict the results of global warming [9]. A number of methods, involving regression, neural networks, and genetic algorithms (see [11]) have been developed over the past ten year to model the bioclimatic envelope, BIOMOD [12] being a good example of a modelling tool used in this domain. But to the best of our knowledge, none of these methods allows automatically finding both the set of species and their envelope.

We give an example of the application of SIREN on this task using data that describes spatial areas of Europe, squares of side roughly 50 kilometers. The left hand side data contains information about the mammals living in these areas, while the right hand side consists of bioclimatic variables. The data comes from two publicly available datasets: European mammal atlas [6] and Worldclim climate data [4].

Nonetheless, SIREN is a flexible tool that can be used with different datasets from various application domains. For instance, it could help in sociological studies, with the exploration of statistical and political data. On the web page, we outline a usage scenario based on census statistics and electoral campaign funding of U.S. continental counties, as an alternative example.

3. USE-CASE SCENARIO

We exemplify the usage of SIREN by going through a generic work-flow of mining geospatial redescriptions, detailing typical steps in the process. A screenshot of the system, displaying a list of redescriptions with one particular redescription plotted on a map is shown in Figure 1.

Initial redescription mining.

A natural starting point for the analysis of any given data is to use a redescription mining algorithm to find an initial set of redescriptions. This can be done withing SIREN by running the extension mechanism on an empty redescription.

Extending a redescription.

Sometimes the user wants to focus only on one of the queries, on some particular variable of interest or on a part of an existing redescription. SIREN allows the user to auto-

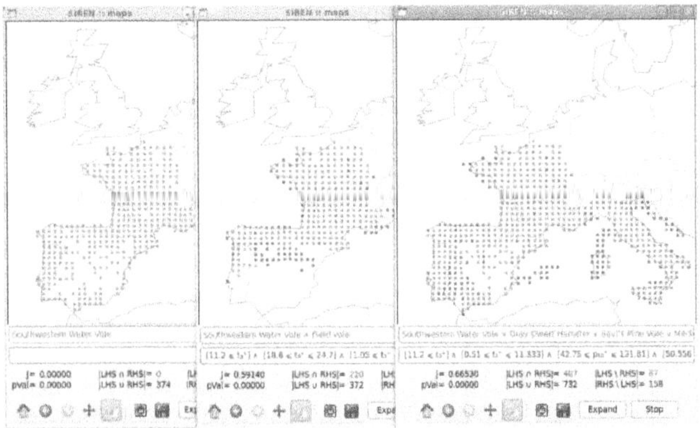

Figure 2: Several map panels. Comparing intermediate extensions automatically generated for a chosen starting variable. Red, blue and purple represents areas where only the left hand side query holds, only the right hand side query holds and where both queries hold, respectively.

matically extend a given redescription, i.e. let the algorithm add new literals to the queries to make the redescription as accurate as possible.

The extension mechanism of SIREN is based on the beam search implemented in the REREMI algorithm [1]. In this case, the intermediate redescriptions explored during the search are returned at each step, allowing to study more specific alternative extensions to a redescription that were discarded from the beam because they were not among the best extensions at some point of the search.

In the climatic niche-finding task, for instance, we might select a species, say, the Southwestern Water Vole and look for best extensions starting from that single variable. Returned extensions can be visualized side by side and compared as shown in Figure 2. Here, the best found extension has accuracy 0.665 (per Jaccard coefficient):

Southwestern Water Vole ∨ Gray Dwarf Hamster
∨ Savi's Pine Vole ∨ Mediterranean Monk Seal

$$[11.2 \leq t_3^+] \wedge [0.51 \leq t_1^= \leq 11.333]$$
$$\wedge [42.75 \leq p_{10}^= \leq 131.81] \wedge [50.556 \leq p_{11}^= \leq 176.75],$$

This redescription indicates that areas where any of the four species lives correspond to areas where the maximum temperature in March is above 11.2 degrees Celsius, the average temperature in January between 0.51 and 11.333 degrees Celsius and the average precipitations in October and November range from 42.75 to 131.81 millimeters and from 50.556 to 176.75 millimeters, respectively.

Editing a redescription.

It is typical that the user wants to edit some of the obtained redescriptions. For example, some results might be overly complex, or have exceedingly precise boundaries for numerical variables. The user can easily select a redescription to modify, open it in a map panel and edit it. Boundaries can be altered, literals added or removed. SIREN updates the map and important statistics (accuracy, p-value, etc.) of the redescription, allowing the user to see the effects of the modifications immediately and verify, e.g. whether the new redescription would still be acceptably accurate.

Continuing with our example above, we might want to reduce the precision of the climatic constraints to integers. We could edit the query as follows:

$$[11 \leq t_3^+] \wedge [0 \leq t_1^= \leq 12]$$
$$\wedge [42 \leq p_{10}^= \leq 132] \wedge [50 \leq p_{11}^= \leq 177],$$

and obtain a redescription of slightly decreased accuracy.

Using subsets of variables.

SIREN allows the user to specify variables to temporarily avoid when extending or mining redescriptions.

For example, when two variables are highly correlated, several redescriptions might contain them both. The user, however, might want to consider redescriptions with only one of these variables, not both. SIREN makes that simple: the user only has to select a redescription, remove the unwanted variable from the redescription and unselect it from the list of variables, then extend the redescription again.

Alternatively, in our running example, we might want to force the algorithm to search alternative redescriptions that do not involve any precipitation. For that purpose, we simply unselect all such variables before running the extension anew. We will obtain the best extensions containing only temperatures in the bioclimatic query, such as the following redescription of accuracy 0.653:

Southwestern Water Vole ∨ Cape Hare
∨ Savi's Pine Vole ∨ Mediterranean Monk Seal

$$([11.2 \leq t_3^+] \wedge [20.1 \leq t_7^+ \leq 32.9]$$
$$\wedge [0.51 \leq t_1^= \leq 11.333]) \vee [34.0 \leq t_8^+].$$

Note that this redescription was not returned previously since the beam search focused on better ones involving precipitation variables.

Filtering redundant redescriptions.

It is common to see a set of redescriptions that cover approximately the same area even if they have (somewhat) different sets of variables. Indeed, redescriptions belong to the family of local patterns, with each individual pattern independently describing a subset of the data. Mining local patterns typically returns redundant results that require filtering. In such cases, it is important to be able to recognize and remove redundant redescriptions, i.e. redescriptions that do not convey significant new information, lest the user be overwhelmed with the number of found redescriptions. Again, SIREN allows automatic filtering of redundant redescriptions. The user can select a redescription and ask SIREN either to filter out all redescriptions that are redundant with respect to the selected one, or to go through the whole list of redescriptions filtering out all redescriptions that are redundant with respect to some earlier-encountered (i.e. better) redescription. Naturally, the decisions made by SIREN can be reverted whenever the user wishes to.

For instance, the results returned during the extension mentioned previously may contain many redundant redescriptions found at different steps. We can easily sort them, e.g. by accuracy, select one of interest and filter all the following results redundant with respect to it.

Outputting the results.

Finally, SIREN facilitates the distribution of the results: redescriptions can be exported in easy-to-read format and the maps associated to redescriptions can be readily converted to publication-ready graphics.

4. REDESCRIPTION MINING

Redescription mining aims at simultaneously finding multiple descriptions of a subset of entities which is not previously specified. This is in contrast with other methods like Emerging Patterns Mining (EPM), Contrast Set Mining (CSM) and Subgroup Discovery (SD) (see [7] for a unifying survey) or general classification methods, where target subsets of entities are specified via labels. Currently, redescription mining is a purely descriptive approach, its predictive power remains to be explored. Since its introduction in [10] various algorithms have been proposed for Boolean redescription mining, based on approaches including decision trees [10, 5], co-clusters [8], and frequent itemsets [2].

At the core of SIREN is the REREMI redescription mining algorithm. This greedy algorithm uses an efficient on-the-fly discretization technique to extend redescription mining to categorical and numerical variables. Below, we give an outline of the concepts and algorithms involved. Full details can be found in the original publication [1].

We consider Boolean, categorical, and numerical variables, partitioned into two sets. Boolean variables can be interpreted as a truth value assignment in a natural way. For categorical and real-valued variables, truth value assignments are induced by relations $[v = c]$ and $[a \leq v \leq b]$, respectively, where c is some category and $[a, b]$ an interval. These truth assignments and their negations constitute *literals* which can be combined using the Boolean operators $\wedge$ (and) and $\vee$ (or) to form *queries*. Then, a redescription is simply a pair of queries over variables from the two sets. The support of a query is the subset of entities for which the query holds true. The *accuracy* of a redescription is measured by the *Jaccard coefficient* of the supports of its two queries; p-values indicating how likely it is to observe such an overlap for independent queries can be used to reject uninteresting redescriptions.

We use a strategy similar to beam-search to explore the solution space. The basic idea is to construct queries bottom-up, starting from singleton redescriptions (i.e. both queries contain only one literal) and progressively extending them by appending operators and literals. After evaluating all possible one-step extensions, we select the best candidates and extend them in turn. This process stops when no new redescription can be generated.

5. IMPLEMENTATION DETAILS

SIREN and REREMI are implemented in Python. The interface is built with the `wxPython` Open Source GUI toolkit, ensuring cross-platform compatibility. The `matplotlib` library enables to generate high quality figures, seamlessly integrated in the interface. SIREN allows for simple editing of the redescriptions thanks to flexible parsing of different representations. It can handle any data provided in a compatible format.

The formulation of redescription mining presented here assumes that the describing variables are partitioned into two sets apriori, and looks for a pairs of queries over these two sets, respectively. However, this can be naturally adapted to settings with a single set of describing variables. One might then search for pairs of queries, with the constraint that the two subsets of variables appearing in the queries of any redescription be disjoint or enable the user to interactively determine the split between the variables.

6. CONCLUSIONS

We present SIREN, a tool for mining geospatial redescriptions. It enables users to interactively mine, edit and extend redescriptions. It also features visualization of the redescriptions on a map, a key toward interpreting the results of geospatial data mining.

We will give chance to the public to experiment with SIREN and together consider how this tool could be used to explore their own geospatial data and help answer their data analysis need.

7. REFERENCES

[1] E. Galbrun and P. Miettinen. From Black and White to Full Colour: Extending Redescription Mining Outside the Boolean World. In *SDM*, pages 546–557, 2011.

[2] A. Gallo, P. Miettinen, and H. Mannila. Finding subgroups having several descriptions: Algorithms for redescription mining. In *SDM*, pages 334–345, 2008.

[3] J. Grinnell. The niche-relationships of the California Thrasher. *The Auk*, 34(4):427–433, 1917.

[4] R. J. Hijmans, S. Cameron, L. Parra, P. Jones, and A. Jarvis. Very high resolution interpolated climate surfaces for global land areas. *Int. J. Climatol.*, 25:1965–1978, 2005. `www.worldclim.org`.

[5] D. Kumar. *Redescription mining: Algorithms and applications in bioinformatics*. PhD thesis, Department of Computer Science, Virginia Tech, 2007.

[6] A. J. Mitchell-Jones, G. Amori, W. Bogdanowicz, B. Krystufek, P. Reijnders, F. Spitzenberger, M. Stubbe, J. Thissen, V. Vohralik, and J. Zima. *The atlas of European mammals*. Academic Press, London, 1999. `www.european-mammals.org`.

[7] P. K. Novak, N. Lavrac, and G. I. Webb. Supervised descriptive rule discovery: A unifying survey of contrast set, emerging pattern and subgroup mining. *J. Mach. Learn. Res.*, 10:377–403, 2009.

[8] L. Parida and N. Ramakrishnan. Redescription mining: Structure theory and algorithms. In *AAAI*, pages 837–844, 2005.

[9] R. G. Pearson and T. P. Dawson. Predicting the impacts of climate change on the distribution of species: Are bioclimate envelope models useful? *Global Ecol. Biogeogr.*, 12:361–371, 2003.

[10] N. Ramakrishnan, D. Kumar, B. Mishra, M. Potts, and R. F. Helm. Turning CARTwheels: An alternating algorithm for mining redescriptions. In *KDD*, pages 266–275, 2004.

[11] J. Soberón and A. T. Peterson. Interpretation of models of fundamental ecological niches and species' distributional areas. *Biodiv. Inform.*, 2(0), 2005.

[12] W. Thuiller, B. Lafourcade, R. Engler, and M. B. Araújo. Biomod – a platform for ensemble forecasting of species distributions. *Ecography*, 32(3):369–373, 2009.

Navigating Information Facets on Twitter (NIF-T)

Shamanth Kumar†, Fred Morstatter†, Grant Marshall†, Huan Liu†, Ullas Nambiar‡
† School of Computing, Informatics, and Decision Systems Engineering, Arizona State University
‡ IBM India Research Lab, New Delhi, India
{skumar34,fmorstat,gamarsha,hliu}@asu.edu,ubnambiar@in.ibm.com

ABSTRACT

Recent years have seen an exponential increase in the number of users of social media sites. As the number of users of these sites continues to grow at an extraordinary rate, the amount of data produced follows in magnitude. With this deluge of social media data, the need for comprehensive tools to analyze user interactions is ever increasing. In this paper, we present a novel tool, Navigating Information Facets on Twitter (NIF-T), which helps users to explore data generated on social media sites. Using the three dimensions or facets: time, location, and topic as an example of the many possible facets, we enable the users to explore large social media datasets. With the help of a large corpus of tweets collected from the Occupy Wall Street movement on the Twitter platform we show how our system can be used to identify important aspects of the event along these facets.

Categories and Subject Descriptors

H.3.3 [**Information Storage and Retrieval**]: Information Search and Retrieval—*Information filtering, Search process*

General Terms

Design, Experimentation

Keywords

Faceted Search, Social Media, and Visual Analytics

1. INTRODUCTION

Many social networking sites have hundreds of millions of active users who publish content on a regular basis. Twitter, for example, claims a daily tweet-publishing rate of 250 million[1]. Given this, we are now over-encumbered with data. The deluge of data has brought forth many new problems for data scientists, including the problem of search and navigation of information in the space of social media. NIF-T, our proposed system, is a web-based system that leverages faceted navigation to solve this problem using Twitter as a representative example of social media. A *facet* of the data extracts and organizes the information in the data along a specific dimension. Information on Twitter is known as tweets, which can consist of text of at most 140 characters. In the past year, Twitter has been used as a communication medium in several crises. Twitter has also been prominently used during the Arab Spring uprising in several countries in the Middle East. In September of 2011, the Occupy Wall Street movement was started with a presence on Twitter through the hashtag #occupywallstreet. To a user exploring social and political events, NIF-T extracts and presents the following facets which are generalizable enough to be used on most social media sites.

Influenced by Ranganathan's classic PMEST model for identifying information facets [8], we focus our effort on organization of tweets into 3 orthogonal facets or dimensions: time facet, geo facet, and topic facet. The system and the approach can be very easily expanded to include other dimensions based on existing domain knowledge, such as user demographics, resources shared within tweets, tweeters' social networks, etc.

Events are **temporal** by nature and span a limited amount of time. Using time as a facet of the data, significant temporal bursts of content are automatically extracted and proposed to the user for further investigation. **Location** is becoming increasingly popular in social media, with several popular social media sites now supporting location-based updates. Tweet location as a facet enables users of our system to detect prominent regions associated with an event. The **topics** of the tweets are indicative of the theme of their content. One prominent choice for topics is the hashtags used in the tweet. However, when discussing the navigation of event-related tweets, we need to look beyond hashtags to identify finer points of discussion in these tweets. Topics are effective in summarization of the data and can significantly aid user analysis.

[1] http://tinyurl.com/3ngck5x

KDD'12, August 12–16, 2012, Beijing, China.

2. DATASET

To show the effectiveness of our system we identify and collect a dataset that pertains to the Occupy Wall Street movement, which received much media attention and publicity last year. The movement was well-advertised before it officially began on Sept 17, 2011. The movement started as a protest against the growing social and economic disparity in US. Although the movement began in New York,

Table 1: Hashtags used to crawl tweets related to the Occupy Wall Street movement on Twitter

Event Name	Hashtags
Occupy Wall Street	#occupywallstreet, #ows, #occupyboston, #p2, #occupywallst, #occupy, #tcot, #occupyphoenix, #15o, #occupytogether, #teaparty, #99percent, #nypd, #takewallstreet, #occupydc,#occupychicago, #occupyla, #usdor, #occupyboston, #occupyoakland, #occupysf, #solidarity, #anonymous, #citizenradio, #gop, #sep17

it eventually spread across the country, and to many other countries around the world.

Advertisements distributed preceding this movement explicitly promoted use of the Twitter hashtag #occupywallstreet. Other hashtags such as #ows, #occupy and its variants for individual cities and countries were later used by people to discuss local impact of the movement. There are several reasons for selecting this particular event:
- The OWS movement was well advertised on social media platforms. The event explicitly used Twitter, to promote their ideas.
- Even though the event began as U.S.-centric, it quickly spread to several other countries and was closely followed by many. "Occupy London" is one such example. The penetration of both mobile technology[2] and Twitter[3] in the United States also makes this a suitable event to explore.

The dataset used in this paper was crawled using a list of hashtags and keywords related to the OWS movement. Tracking of the movement was started on September 14, 2011 with the advertised hashtag, #occupywallstreet, and later more specific local variants of the hashtags were added as the movement gained momentum. A full list of the parameters used to crawl the dataset is presented in Table 1. The dataset consists of 9,357,141 tweets generated by 908,269 users collected between Sept 14, 2011 to Dec 27, 2011. 85,752 of these tweets were geotagged; that is, their location information was made available. As an alternative, a user may provide some textual location information as part of his Twitter profile. If provided, this textual location is extracted from a Twitter user's profile and translated into geographic coordinates using a combination of the Nominatim service provided by OpenStreetMaps[4] and the GeoNames[5] dataset consisting of more than 10 million named locations. The coordinates are then stored as part of tweet metadata.

The dataset will be shared upon request according to Twitter data sharing guidelines.

3. OVERVIEW OF NIF-T

Our system is web-based, and uses a client-server architecture. The view consists of our faceted search interface, the contribution of this work. The faceted search interface consists of three components used to help the user navigate the facets. Our view is written in HTML5, CSS, and Javascript. Our server-side component, which hosts the dataset and performs operations such as retrieving data and returning basic views of the data was written in PHP, and uses MySQL as the data store. It is hosted on an Apache server. On starting the system, a user is immediately presented with the three facets computed from the entire dataset. Figure 2 provides an overview of the system from the OWS dataset from Nov 15.

[2]http://tinyurl.com/56vmkd
[3]http://tinyurl.com/5sjks7v
[4]http://wiki.openstreetmap.org/wiki/Nominatim
[5]http://www.geonames.org/

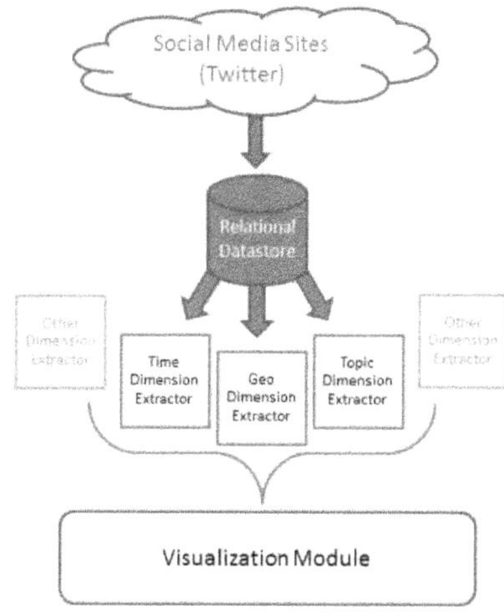

Figure 1: System Workflow

NIF-T organizes the information into three distinct facets:

3.1 Geo Facet

The Geo Facet is presented to the user in the form of a map. In Figure 2 we see the geo facet in the center of the map. Tweets that match the parameters set forth by the other two facets are displayed in the form of dots on the map. The map component is rendered using the Leaflet library[6] for JavaScript. Leaflet comes with the ability to draw map layers along with the ability to render map markers, zoom, and pan across the map. One strength of Leaflet is that it draws only the portion of the map that the user is currently viewing, with all other portions rendered "on demand" when the user pans to that region. To accommodate this, Leaflet takes the map images and cuts them into a series of smaller images, called tiles. CloudMade[7] serves these tiles. Effectively displaying a large number of tweets on the map was one of the major challenges. A reasonable query could easily return in excess of 100,000 tweets. A collection of this size would cause lag on the user interface, rendering the map almost unusable. To get around this issue, we decided not to render each individual tweet as a map marker, and instead to render the tweet locations as a series of tiles drawn by an HTML5 Canvas[8] element. The result is a series of tiles drawn in a manner exactly the same as the map tiles described earlier, providing the user with a seamless experience that takes a much lighter toll on the browser.

3.2 Topic Facet

Topics extracted from the tweets can help a user to understand their context and guide a user in further analysis. This facet is visualized in the form of a word cloud. The

[6]http://leaflet.cloudmade.com
[7]http://cloudmade.com/
[8]http://dev.w3.org/html5/2dcontext/

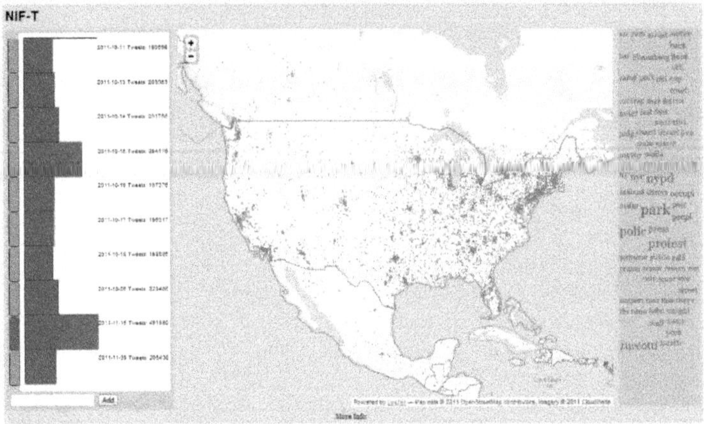

Figure 2: NIF-T system

word cloud is generated from tweets by ranking the words on their TF scores. Computation of IDF is replaced by removal of Twitter entities like URLs, usernames, hashtags, and an extensive list of stopwords as this is less expensive. Additionally, the words were stemmed using Porter Stemmer. An example of the topic visualization can be seen in Figure 2. The relevance of each word in the word cloud is highlighted by its font size which is proportional to its frequency of occurrence in the underlying tweets.

3.3 Time Facet

The Time facet is displayed following the concept of control charts. In a control chart, the observations are plotted along with a statistic such as the mean. The interestingness of an observation is determined based on upper and lower control limits, typically 3 standard deviations away from the mean. In addition, warning limits can also be set, such that a new observation that crosses the warning limit would trigger an alert. In our system, the observations are the daily recorded traffic of the tweet in the dataset, and we set the warning limit to 1 standard deviation, such that all observations above 1 standard deviation are presented to the user as interesting observations in the form of a histogram. This histogram can be viewed in the left panel of Figure 2. Relevant details accompany the visualization for faster understanding.

4. USING NIF-T FOR INSIGHTS

In this section, we present two specific insights gained from using our NIF-T on the OWS dataset. But, first we discuss how a user of the system can interact with the various facets in our system.

Geo Facet: A user can zoom or pan to different regions, the other two facets are updated automatically to show tweets characteristics of tweets from the region in the user's view. **Topic Facet:** A user can select one or more of these topics by clicking the tags to effect a change in the geospatial visualization and view the corresponding relevant checkpoints in the time facet as well. **Time Facet:** A user can select one or more of the time presented in this facet by clicking the accompanying buttons. The time facet is interactive like the other facets and user selections cause the information in the other facets to be filtered accordingly.

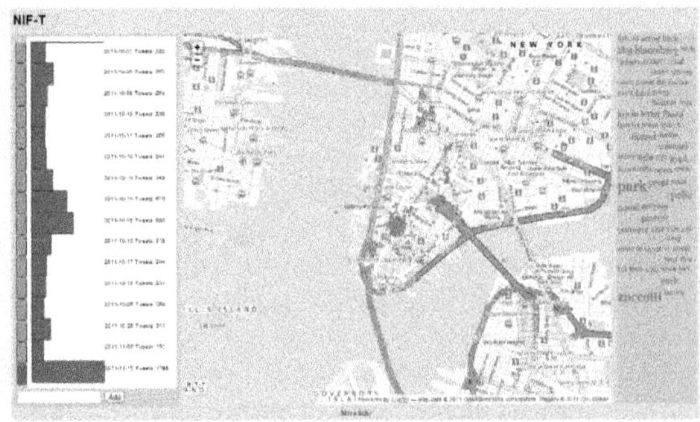

Figure 3: Geographical distribution of tweets from Nov 15, 2011

User interaction with any one facet causes the other two facets to react, updating their views to help the user navigate within the confines of the new selection. For example, panning and zooming the map to create a geographic sub-selection will cause the topic to update, showing the most relevant keywords from within the view and cause the temporal histogram to update showing the days within the specified region containing the most tweets.

From the time facet in Figure 2 we can clearly see that we capture many of the significant dates highlighted in the OWS event timeline on Wikipedia[9]. One of the largest peaks observed through the system occurs on Nov 15 with more than 490k tweets published that day. A closer look at New York shows a dense cluster of tweets around the Zuccotti park area as observed in Figure 3. On Nov 15, Zuccotti park was cleared by NYPD after almost 8 weeks of camping by the protestors. The density of tweets in the region increased considerably after this incident. The topics from this day, such as "zuccotti", "park", and "polic" also clearly indicate the general theme of the tweets.

In another example, we looked at the tweets from Western Europe, particularly the UK, where Twitter is also popular to verify if the large spike in tweets observed in the U.S. had also stirred the interest of people in this part of the world. A screenshot of the system for this region is presented in

[9]http://tinyurl.com/7g5q5st

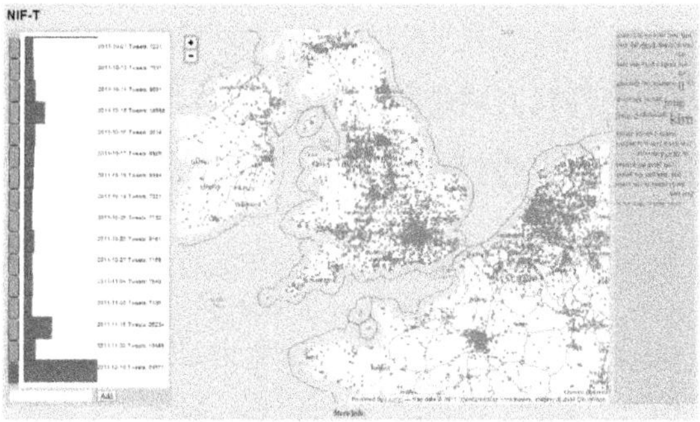

Figure 4: Geographical distribution of tweets from the UK

Figure 4. The topic in this case focuses on Kim Jong Il (referring to his death) and the most important date for this region was Nov 19 when the number of tweets was far greater than any other day. The absence of the impact of Zuccotti park incident on this region is interesting and points to the locality of such events even though the regions are connected by a common movement.

Given a sample of the Twitter stream our system would be helpful to anyone who wishes to investigate the underlying events that possibly generated the stream and help in investigating and understanding them.

5. RELATED WORK

We will discuss the related work to our research from two different areas: multi-faceted browsing, and Twitter analysis in the context of global events.

Faceted search as a means to investigate large corpora of data has been studied extensively. Facet Lens [4] exploits metadata to display relationships between the various facets of the data. It also aims to discover trends in the data and present them to the user in a clear and direct manner. Seeking to implement faceted search by automatically presenting facets to the user, [1] presents facets to users which best match their interests. In this work, the system acquires from the user the facets that are demanded most at each interaction, helping the user to quickly find the records of a structured database which are most useful. In the only example we found of the merging of faceted search with social media, [7] uses faceted search as a way to assist in searching through records labeled through folksonomy. By combining user-generated tags with more structured category definitions from the Classification Research Group, this approach allows users to search through articles using both structured and unstructured facets. In an approach that focuses on topics, [9] creates a system which dynamically creates facets from topics in the corpus that is being searched. Using PLSA to derive topics, the system gives each user an individual experience where they can choose topics that suit their interests. Discussions of the merits of faceted search through its ability to reduce effort in finding sought-after records are conducted in [2].

Twitter analysis in crisis scenarios is an active area of research. TwitterMonitor [5] is a system which constantly monitors a stream of tweets, looking for "bursts" in keywords or hashtags. When an influx occurs, the system then stores all of the tweets containing the keywords behind the burst. In a similar vein, TweetTracker [3] is a system to track events in real time. In this approach, the user is allowed to specify their own parameters for each individual event. The system then uses the Twitter Streaming API[10] to collect a sample of the tweets containing those keywords/hashtags. [6] investigates the propagation of rumors and facts in the aftermath of the Chilean earthquake.

6. SUMMARY

The idea of faceted browsing in library sciences is quite old. When combined with the many forms of information present in social media it can be a powerful tool to analyze large social media datasets. NIF-T focuses on visualizing unstructured social media stream through faceted browsing. This necessitates identification of meaningful and easily understandable facets to map this content. NIF-T uses the PMEST Classification Scheme from Library Sciences to derive these meaningful facets. In this work, we have implemented a system over a large real world social media data(specifically Twitter OWS data) and shown the effeciency and utility of faceted browsing.

7. ACKNOWLEDGMENTS

This work was sponsored, in part, by NSF grant #0812551 and ONR grant N000141010091.

8. REFERENCES

[1] Senjuti Basu Roy, Haidong Wang, Gautam Das, Ullas Nambiar, and Mukesh Mohania. Minimum-effort driven dynamic faceted search in structured databases. CIKM '08, pages 13–22, New York, NY, USA, 2008. ACM.

[2] C. He, X. Cheng, J. Guo, and H. Shen. Multi-select faceted navigation based on minimum description length principle. IJCAI'11, 2011.

[3] S. Kumar, G. Barbier, M.A. Abbasi, and H. Liu. Tweettracker: An analysis tool for humanitarian and disaster relief. ICWSM, 2011.

[4] B. Lee, G. Smith, G.G. Robertson, M. Czerwinski, and D.S. Tan. Facetlens: exposing trends and relationships to support sensemaking within faceted datasets. CHI'09, pages 1293–1302. ACM, 2009.

[5] Michael Mathioudakis and Nick Koudas. Twittermonitor: trend detection over the twitter stream. SIGMOD '10, pages 1155–1158, New York, NY, USA, 2010. ACM.

[6] Marcelo Mendoza, Barbara Poblete, and Carlos Castillo. Twitter under crisis: can we trust what we rt? SOMA '10, pages 71–79, New York, NY, USA, 2010. ACM.

[7] E. Quintarelli, A. Resmini, and L. Rosati. Information architecture: Facetag: Integrating bottom-up and top-down classification in a social tagging system. *Bulletin of the American Society for Information Science and Technology*, 33(5):10–15, 2007.

[8] S.R. Ranganathan. *Elements of library classification*, volume 8. Asia Pub. House, 1962.

[9] Raymond Chi-Wing Wong, Jian Pei, Ada Wai-Chee Fu, and Ke Wang. Mining favorable facets. KDD '07, pages 804–813, New York, NY, USA, 2007. ACM.

[10]https://dev.twitter.com/docs/streaming-api

HeteRecom: A Semantic-based Recommendation System in Heterogeneous Networks

Chuan Shi
Beijing University of Posts and Telecommunications
Beijing, China
shichuan@bupt.edu.cn

Chong Zhou
Beijing University of Posts and Telecommunications
Beijing, China
zhouchong90@gmail.com

Xiangnan Kong
University of Illinois at Chicago
IL, USA
xkong4@uic.edu

Philip S. Yu
University of Illinois at Chicago, IL, USA
King Abdulaziz University
Jeddah, Saudi Arabia
psyu@cs.uic.edu

Gang Liu
Beijing University of Posts and Telecommunications
Beijing, China
liugangofbupt@gmail.com

Bai Wang
Beijing University of Posts and Telecommunications
Beijing, China
wangbai@bupt.edu.cn

ABSTRACT

Making accurate recommendations for users has become an important function of e-commerce system with the rapid growth of WWW. Conventional recommendation systems usually recommend similar objects, which are of the same type with the query object without exploring the semantics of different similarity measures. In this paper, we organize objects in the recommendation system as a heterogeneous network. Through employing a path-based relevance measure to evaluate the relatedness between any-typed objects and capture the subtle semantic containing in each path, we implement a prototype system (called *HeteRecom*) for semantic-based recommendation. *HeteRecom* has the following unique properties: (1) It provides the semantic-based recommendation function according to the path specified by users. (2) It recommends the similar objects of the same type as well as related objects of different types. We demonstrate the effectiveness of our system with a real-world movie data set.

Categories and Subject Descriptors

H.2.8 [**Database Management**]: Database applications-Data Mining

General Terms

Algorithms, Design, Experimentation

Keywords

heterogeneous information network, recommendation, similarity, semantic search

1. INTRODUCTION

With the rapid growth of WWW, we are being surrounded by a large amount of information on the web. Recommendation is an effective way to reduce the cost for finding information. It has been widely used in many e-commerce applications, such as Amazon, eBay, and Taobao.

Many recommendation methods have been proposed, which can be roughly classified into two categories: content-based filtering (CB) and collaborative filtering (CF). CB analyzes correlations between the content of the items and the user's preferences [1]. CF analyzes the similarity between users or items [2]. These methods have been applied to recommendation systems and achieved great success. However, these recommendation systems have the following disadvantages.

- Conventional recommendation systems usually recommend similar products to users without exploring the semantics of different similarity measures. However, the similar products are often different based on similarity semantics. For example, in the movie recommendation, the similar movies based on the same actors are different from those based on the same directors. Conventional systems usually give a recommendation without considering the subtle implications of similarity semantics. The proposed system is more appealing to provide a semantic recommendation function, which will give more accurate recommendation when users know their intents.
- Conventional systems only recommend same-typed objects. However, a system may be more useful if it simultaneously recommends more related objects under different semantics. For example, when users select movies, the system not only recommends the similar movies, but also suggests some related actors and directors (note that they are not limited to the actors and directors of this movie). The user may find an interesting actor and then search the movies of the actor. The relevance recommendation will provide richer information and enhance user experience.

Nowadays, social networks consisting of different types of information become popular. Particularly, the advent of

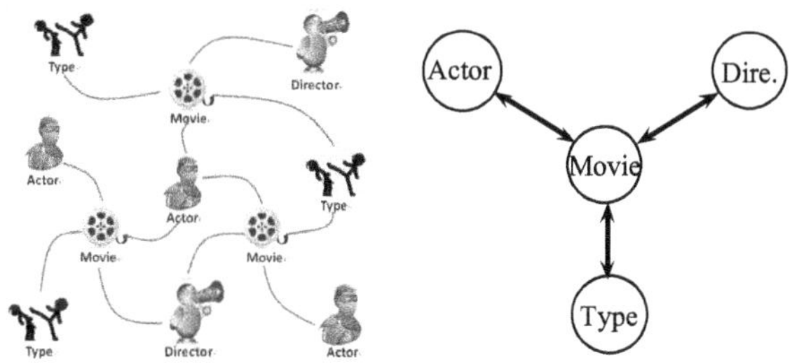

(a) Heterogeneous network of movie data (b) Network schema

Figure 1: An example of heterogeneous information network and its schema.

the Heterogeneous Information Networks (HIN) [3] provides a new perspective to design the recommendation system. HINs are the logical networks involving multiple-typed objects and multiple-typed links denoting different relations. It is clear that HINs are ubiquitous and form a critical component of modern information infrastructure [3]. Although the bipartite network [5] has been applied to organize components of recommendation system, HIN is a more general model which contains more comprehensive relations among objects and much richer semantic information. Fig. 1(a) shows an HIN example on the movie recommendation data. The network includes the richer objects (e.g., movie, actor, director) and their relations. The network structure can be represented with the star schema as shown in Fig. 1(b). HIN has an unique property [6, 7]: the different paths connecting two objects have different meanings. For example, in Fig. 1(b), movies can be connected via "Movie-Actor-Movie" (MAM) path, "Movie-Type-Movie" (MTM) path, and so on. It is clear that the semantics underneath these paths are different. The MAM path means that movies have the same actors, while the MTM path means that movies have the same types. Here the meta path connecting two-typed objects is defined as relevance path [6]. Obviously, the distinct semantics under different relevance paths will lead to different relatedness and recommendation.

Focusing on non-personalized recommendation, this paper demonstrates a semantic recommendation system, called *HeteRecom*. Different from conventional recommendation systems, it is based on HIN. Generally, *HeteRecom* has the following unique features. (1) Semantic recommendation. The system can recommend objects of the designated type based on the relevance path specified by users. (2) Relevance recommendation. Besides the same-typed objects recommendation, the system can recommend other related objects.

The implementation of *HeteRecom* faces the following challenges. (1) Relevance measure of heterogeneous objects. In order to recommend the different-typed objects, the system needs to measure the relatedness of different-typed objects. (2) The weight learning method. It is a key issue for an integrated recommendation to automatically determine the weights of different relevance paths. (3) Efficient computing strategies. In order to provide online service, the recommendation system needs to efficiently compute the relevance measure. In order to solve these challenges, the *HeteRecom* system first applies a path-based relevance measure, which can not only effectively measure the relatedness of any-typed objects but also subtly capture the semantics containing in the relevance path. Besides, a heuristic weight learning method can automatically determine the weights of different paths. Moreover, many computing strategies are designed to handle huge graph data. This paper demonstrates the effectiveness of *HeteRecom* on the real movie data through providing online semantic and relevance recommendation services.

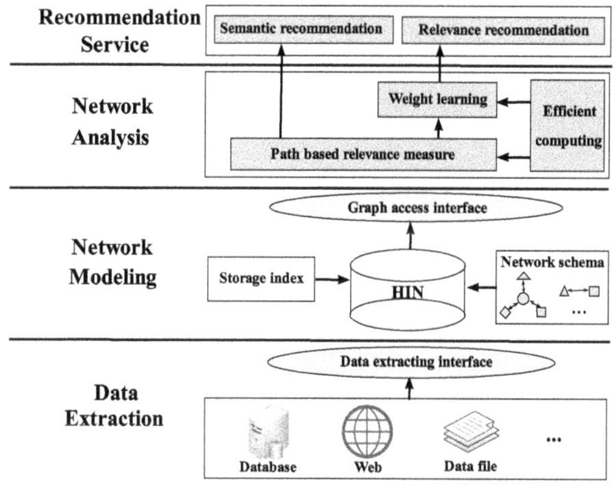

Figure 2: The architecture of *HeteRecom* system.

2. OVERVIEW OF SYSTEM

Fig. 2 shows the architecture of *HeteRecom*, which mainly consists of four components:

- Data extraction: it extracts data from different data source (e.g., database and web) to construct the network.
- Network modeling: it constructs the HIN with a given network schema. According to the structure of data, users can specify the network schema (e.g., bipartite, star or arbitrary schema) to construct the HIN database. The database provides the store and index functions of the node table and edge table of the HIN.
- Network analysis: it analyzes the HIN and provides the recommendation services. It first computes and stores the relevance matrix of object pairs by the path-based relevance measure. Based on the relevance matrix and efficient computing strategies, the system can provide the online semantic recommendation service. Through the weight learning method, it can combine the relevance information from different semantic paths and provide online relevance recommendation service.
- Recommendation service: it provides the succinct and friendly interface of recommendation services.

3. IMPLEMENTATION OF SYSTEM

It is challenging in many ways to implement these components. First, it is difficult to measure the relatedness of any-typed objects in a HIN. Second, It is not easy to combine those recommendation information on different semantic paths. Third, there are many challenges in the computation and storage of huge relevance matrix. In the following section, we will present the solutions to these challenges.

3.1 A Path-based Relevance Measure

This paper applied the *HeteSim* [6], a path-based relevance measure, to do semantic recommendation. The basic idea behind *HeteSim* is that similar objects are related to similar objects. The *HeteSim* is defined as follows.

DEFINITION 1. ***HeteSim** [6]: Given a relevance path $\mathcal{P} = R_1 \circ R_2 \circ \cdots \circ R_l$, HeteSim between two objects s and t ($s \in R_1.S$ and $t \in R_l.T$) is:*

$$HeteSim(s,t|R_1 \circ R_2 \circ \cdots \circ R_l) = \frac{1}{|O(s|R_1)||I(t|R_l)|} \sum_{i=1}^{|O(s|R_1)|} \sum_{j=1}^{|I(t|R_l)|} HeteSim(O_i(s|R_1), I_j(t|R_l)|R_2 \circ \cdots \circ R_{l-1}) \quad (1)$$

where $O(s|R_1)$ is the out-neighbors of s based on relation R_1, $I(t|R_l)$ is the in-neighbors of t based on relation R_l, and $R.S$ ($R.T$) represents the source (target) object of relation R, respectively.

Essentially, $HeteSim(s,t|\mathcal{P})$ is a pair-wise random walk based measure, which evaluates how likely s and t will meet at the same node when s follows along the path and t goes against the path. The path implies the semantic information and *HeteSim* evaluates the relatedness of any-typed object pairs according to the given path. The *HeteSim* measure has shown its potential in object profiling, experts finding, and relevance search. The detailed information can be seen in [6].

Since relevance paths embody different semantics, users can specify the path according to their intents. The semantic recommendation calculates the relevance matrix with *HeteSim* and recommends the top k objects.

3.2 Weight Learning Method

There are many relevance paths connecting the query object and related objects, so the relevance recommendation should comprehensively consider the relevance measures based on all relevance paths. It can be depicted as follows.

$$Sim(A,B) = \sum_{i=1}^{N} w_i * HeteSim(A,B|\mathcal{P}_i) \quad (2)$$

where N is the number of relevance paths, $\mathcal{P}_i$ is a relevance path connecting the object types A and B, w_i is the weight of path $\mathcal{P}_i$. Although there can be infinite relevance paths connecting two objects, we only need to consider those short paths, since the long paths are usually less important [7].

The next question is how to determine the weight w_i. The supervised learning [4] can be used to estimate these parameters. However, it is impractical for an online system: (1) It is time-consuming, even impractical, to learn these parameters on an online system. (2) It is very labor intensive and subjective work to label those learning instances. Here we propose a heuristic weight learning method.

The importance (I) of a path $\mathcal{P} = R_1 \circ R_2 \circ \cdots \circ R_l$ is determined by its strength (S) and length (l). Obviously, the path strength is decided by the strength of relations constructing the path, which can be defined as follows.

$$S(\mathcal{P}) = \prod_{i=1}^{l} S(R_i) \quad (3)$$

The strength of a relation $A \xrightarrow{R} B$ is related to the degree of A and B based on R. Intuitively, if the mutual connective links between A and B are smaller, they are more important to each other, so their relation strength is stronger. For example, the relation strength between movie and director (MD) is stronger than that between movie and type (MT). So we can define the relation strength as follows.

$$S(R) = (O(A|R)I(B|R))^{-\alpha} (\alpha \in [0,1]) \quad (4)$$

where $O(A|R)$ is the average out-degree of type A and $I(B|R)$ is the average in-degree of type B based on relation R.

The importance (I) of the path $\mathcal{P}$ is positively correlative to the path strength (S) and negatively correlative to the path length (l). Here we define it as follows.

$$I(\mathcal{P}) = f(S,l) = e^{S-l} \quad (5)$$

For multiple paths ($\mathcal{P}_1, \mathcal{P}_2, \cdots, \mathcal{P}_N$), the weight ($w_i$) of path $\mathcal{P}_i$ is

$$w_i = \frac{I_i}{\sum_{i=1}^{N} I_i} \quad (6)$$

In *HeteRecom*, we consider all relevance paths whose length is smaller than a threshold *Len*. The relevance recommendation combines the relevance measure results of all these paths with the weight learning method and makes an integrated recommendation.

3.3 Efficient Computing Strategies

As an online recommendation system, *HeteRecom* needs to do a real-time recommendation for user's query. However, a HIN is usually huge and the computation of *HeteSim* is time-consuming. So the system employed many efficient computing strategies. Three basic strategies are depicted as follows.

Off-line computation. The primary strategy is to compute relevance matrix off-line and make recommendations online. For frequently-used relevance paths, the relevance matrix $HeteSim(A,B|\mathcal{P})$ can be calculated ahead of time. The online recommendation on $HeteSim(a,B|\mathcal{P})$ will be very fast, since it only needs to locate the position in the matrix.

Fast matrix multiplications. The most time-consuming component in the system is the matrix multiplications in *HeteSim*. There are many frequent patterns in relevance paths. Since the matrix multiplications satisfy the associative law, we can precede to compute the product of frequent patterns iteratively. Moreover, those frequent patterns only need to be computed once. For example, we only need to compute the frequent pattern AMA once for the symmetric path $AMAMA$. Since the short pattern is more frequent, we only find the most frequent relation pair in each iteration.

Matrix sparsification. The relevance matrix often becomes denser along the matrix multiplications [4]. The dense matrix may cause two difficulties. (1) It is time and space expensive to do matrix multiplications. (2) It costs a lot of time and huge memory to load and search these dense relevance matrix. As a consequence, we need to sparsify the reachable probability matrix along the matrix multiplications without much loss of accuracy. The basic idea is to truncate those less important nodes whose relevance value is smaller than a threshold ε. The static threshold [4] is not suitable, since it may truncate some important nodes

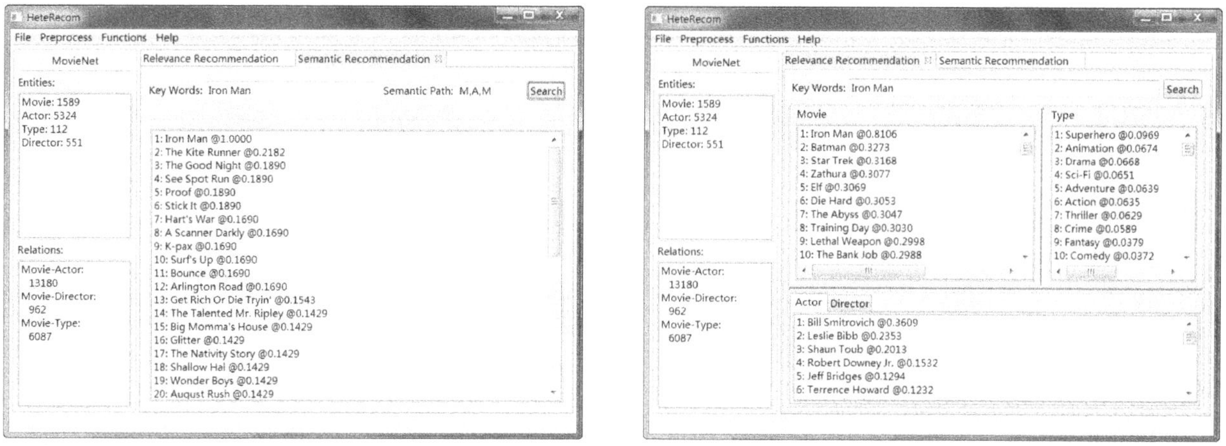

(a) Semantic recommendation based on *MAM* path (b) Relevance recommendation

Figure 3: The *HeteRecom* prototype system.

with small relevance values and keep those unimportant nodes with large relevance values. Since we usually pay close attention to the top k recommendation, we set the threshold ε as the top k relevance value of the matrix. The k is dynamically adjusted as follows.

$$k = \begin{cases} L & \text{if } L \leq W \\ \lfloor (L-W)^{\beta} \rfloor + W(\beta \in [0,1]) & \text{others} \end{cases}$$

where L is the vector length. W is the threshold which determines the size of non-zero elements. The larger W or β may lead to the denser matrix with less loss. In order to quickly determine the top k relevance value, it is approximately computed with the sample data from the raw matrix.

4. DEMONSTRATION

We showcase the *HeteRecom* prototype system using IMDB movie data as the example application. The IMDB movie data was downloaded from The Internet Movie Database [1]. The IMDB movie data collects 1591 movies before 2010. The related objects include actors, directors and types, which are organized as a star schema shown in Fig. 1(b).

Fig. 3 demonstrates the interface of the *HeteRecom* system, which is developed with Java. The left part of interface shows the basic information of the data set. The right part shows the recommendation results. In the semantic recommendation, users specify the key words and semantic path, the recommendation results will be exhibited in the panel. Fig. 3(a) shows the movies with the same actors of "Iron Man" by specified the "MAM" path. The *HeteRecom* can make many recommendations that conventional systems cannot do. For example, recommending the movies that have the same style with the movies of "Arnold Schwarzenegger" can be done by the path *AMTM*. In the relevance recommendation, the system can simultaneously recommend different-typed objects. Fig. 3(b) shows the recommendation results of the movie "Iron Man", which includes the similar movies and related actors, directors and types. We can make many interesting recommendations on *HeteRecom*. For example, if we want to know the information about the action movie, we can search "action". The system will recommend related action movies, actors and directors.

[1] www.imdb.com/

Note that this is an ongoing project. We will provide web service on internet and a more friendly interface will be implemented with visualization techniques. Moreover, *HeteRecom* is a general tool to do recommendation on HIN. Other recommendation tasks can be easily loaded into this system through extracting the HIN from the raw data. In addition, user preference can also be integrated into the *HeteRecom* system.

5. CONCLUSION

This paper studied the recommendation problem from the heterogeneous network angle and designed a novel recommendation system: *HeteRecom*. The *HeteRecom* system has two unique properties: semantic recommendation and relevance recommendation. The *HeteRecom* demonstrates its effectiveness on the real-world movie data set.

Acknowledgments.

It is supported by the National Natural Science Foundation of China (No. 60905025, 61074128, 61035003). It is also supported by the Fundamental Research Funds for the Central Universities.

6. REFERENCES

[1] M. Balabanovic and Y. Shoham. Content-based collaborative recommendation. *Commun. ACM*, 40(3):66–72, 1997.

[2] J. Breese, D. Heckerman, and C. Kadie. Empirical analysis of predictive algorithms for collaborative filtering. In *UAI*, pages 43–52, 1998.

[3] J. Han. Mining heterogeneous information networks by exploring the power of links. In *DS*, pages 13–30, 2009.

[4] N. Lao and W. Cohen. Fast query execution for retrieval models based on path constrained random walks. In *KDD*, pages 881–888, 2010.

[5] M. Shang, L. Lu, Y. Zhang, and T. Zhou. Empirical analysis of web-based user-object bipartite networks. In *EPL 90 (0120) 48006*, 2010.

[6] C. Shi, X. Kong, P. S. Yu, and S. Xie. Relevance search in heterogeneous networks. In *EDBT*, 2012.

[7] Y. Sun, J. Han, X. Yan, P. Yu, and T. Wu. Pathsim: Meta path-based top-k similarity search in heterogeneous information networks. In *VLDB*, pages 992–1003, 2011.

VOXSUP: A Social Engagement Framework

Yusheng Xie[1], Daniel Honbo[1], Kunpeng Zhang[2], Yu Cheng[2], Ankit Agrawal[2], Alok Choudhary[1]

[1]Voxsup Inc.
{yves,dan,alok}@voxsupinc.com

[2]Northwestern University
{kzh980,ych133,ankitag}@eecs.northwestern.edu

ABSTRACT

Social media websites are currently central hubs on the Internet. Major online social media platforms are not only places for individual users to socialize but are increasingly more important as channels for companies to advertise, public figures to engage, etc. In order to optimize such advertising and engaging efforts, there is an emerging challenge for knowledge discovery on today's Internet. The goal of knowledge discovery is to understand the entire online social landscape instead of merely summarizing the statistics. To answer this challenge, we have created VOXSUP as a unified social engagement framework. Unlike most existing tools, VOXSUP not only aggregates and filters social data from the Internet, but also provides what we call Voxsupian Knowledge Discovery (VKD). VKD consists of an almost human-level understanding of social conversations at any level of granularity from a single comment sentiment to multi-lingual inter-platform user demographics. Here we describe the technologies that are crucial to VKD, and subsequently go beyond experimental verification and present case studies from our live VOXSUP system.

Categories and Subject Descriptors

H.3.3 [**Information Storage And Retrieval**]: Information Search and Retrieval – *Information filtering, Selection process*

General Terms

Algorithms, Experimentation.

Keywords

Opinion mining, Topic model, Social ranking.

1. INTRODUCTION

Online social media websites are currently among the most popular Internet applications. Hundreds of millions of Internet users go to websites like Facebook and Twitter several times a day. Naturally, the massive use of public social media has become valuable for scientific research due to the large amount of human-generated contents. Social media can be used as datasets and attract a lot of academic interests ranging from large-scale complex network modeling to individual behavioral targeting [1]. Previous works dealing with social media data return impressive results in many well-defined problems. For example, sentence-level sentiment analysis done by [2] is used in real applications. Such research efforts help us to realize how valuable social media contents can be from many different viewpoints. However, since every major social networking service (e.g. Facebook, Twitter, LinkedIn, etc.) avidly supports Google-style advertising, just solving isolated problems is definitely not the only way researchers can interact with social media. Driven by commercial marketing interests, the addition of knowledge discovery to social media analysis will greatly increase product-marketing performance. The increase of performance does not emerge from a list of individual solutions like sentiment analysis; it has to come from a unified framework. Social media analysis needs such a framework.

VOXSUP is our answer to this need. VOXSUP exceeds the performance of most existing tools because it not only aggregates and filters social data from the Internet, but also performs what we call Voxsupian Knowledge Discovery (VKD). VKD provides an almost human-level understanding of social conversations at any level of granularity from a single comment sentiment to multi-lingual inter-platform user demographics. In the following sections, we describe the technologies that are crucial to VKD.

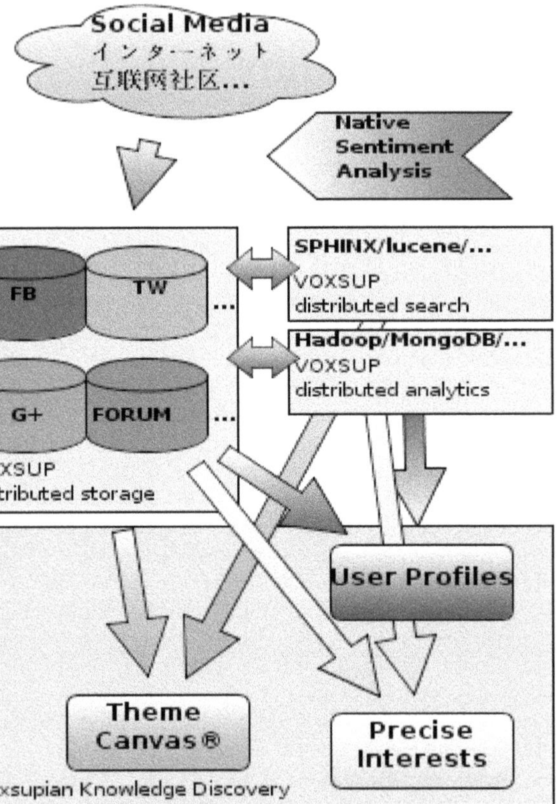

Figure 1. Overview of VOXSUP architecture.

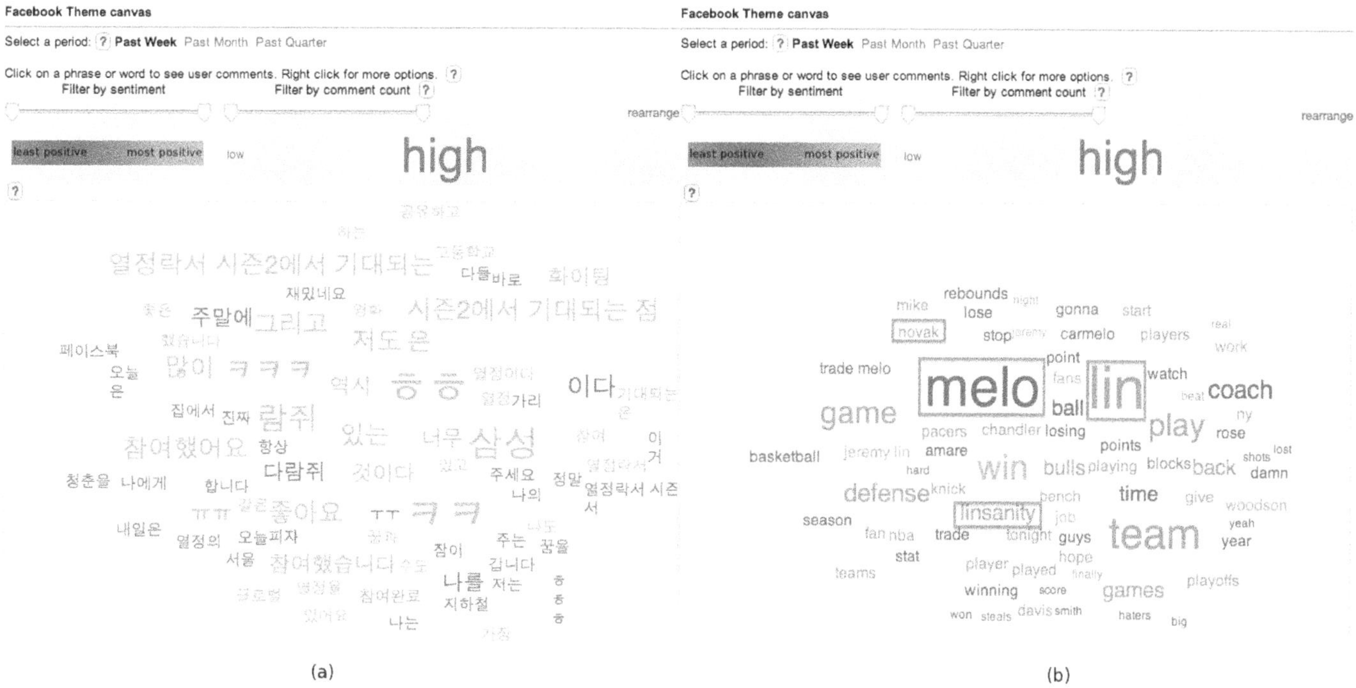

Figure 2. Theme Canvas® screenshots: (a) Samsung results showing multi-language capability. (b) New York Knicks results showing the quality by discovering frequently talked about Jeremy Lin, *Linsanity*, etc. Note that the results are fully tunable by changing the time period, sentiment, frequency filters and other parameters.

2. SYSTEM DESCRIPTION

VOXSUP architecture is shown in Figure 1. In short, VOXSUP monitors multi-lingual social media content, performs sentiment analysis on this content, pushes it to scalable infrastructure, and finally extracts the human-level knowledge from this content.

2.1 Media Monitored

VOXSUP monitors multiple channels of social media in more than 7 languages, these channels include over 10,000 of the most popular Facebook public walls, over 3,000 Twitter handles, over 800 YouTube Channels, over 2,000 fo the most popular Google+ public pages, over 1,500 LinkedIn company profiles, over 500 product categories with customer reviews from Amazon.com and over 300 active blog sites and online forums. For most of these sources, we have all its data to date since 2009 or its inception. In VOXSUP, we try to keep as much information as possible without violating any regulations. For example, for each Facebook wall, we keep all public comments, "likes", and public user profiles. Despite VOXSUP's enormous capacity, we can still keep our data synchronized with the providing media in soft real time.

2.2 Sentiment Analysis

For sentiment analysis, we use our state-of-the-art Sentiment Elicitation System (SES). Complete details can be found in [2].

Algorithm 1: CSR Compositional rule.

Input: *arg1*: sentimental word; *arg2*: sentimental word;
Output: *sentiment*: sentiment for the composition;

```
If arg1 is negative
    If arg2 is not neutral {return S(arg2)}
    Else {return -1}
    End if
Else if arg1 is positive and arg2 is not neutral {return S(arg2)}
Else if S(arg1) == S(arg2) {return 2*S(arg1)}
Else if (arg1 is positive and arg2 is neutral) or
      (arg2 is positive and arg1 is neutral) {return S(arg1)+S(arg2)}
Else {return 0}
End if
```

Compositional Semantic Rule (CSR) estimates the sentiment from a grammatical point of view. The algorithm looks for 12 specific patterns in the text, two of which we give as examples in Table 1 and our Compose function is described in Algorithm 1. Currently, we only apply this method to the English language.

Table 1. Two examples of CSR rules

Rules	Example
S([adj] to [verb])=Compose(adj,verb)	*Unlikely* to *harm* the Earth
S([noun] be [adj])=Compose(noun,adj)	*Damage* is *minimal*

Numeric Sentiment Identification (NSI) estimates the sentiment in a numeric scale, which provides a convenient feature in the later learning stage. The idea is to use a training set with labeled sentiment to assign a numeric score to each of the words in the training sentences; then assign a score to any new sentences based on the scores on words. We assign a score to each word by

$$\text{Score}(w) = \frac{\sum_{i \in P} (n_{r_i}/N) r_i f_{r_i}}{\sum_{r_i} (n_{r_i}/N) f_{r_i}}, \quad (1)$$

where P represents the set of appearances of word w, r_i represents the associated label in each appearance of w, N is the number of entities in our training data set, and f_{r_i} is the number of entities with label r_i. After obtaining a score for each word, the score for sentence is calculated by a weighted linear combination. Note that in our original work [2] we distinguish between adjectives and adverbs, but the basic idea is the same.

Bag-of-word and Rule-based (BR) is specially designed for social media type of text where people type a lot of nonstandard phrases like Internet sarcasm, emoticons (e.g. :)), acronyms (e.g. "lol" for "laughing out loud"), etc.

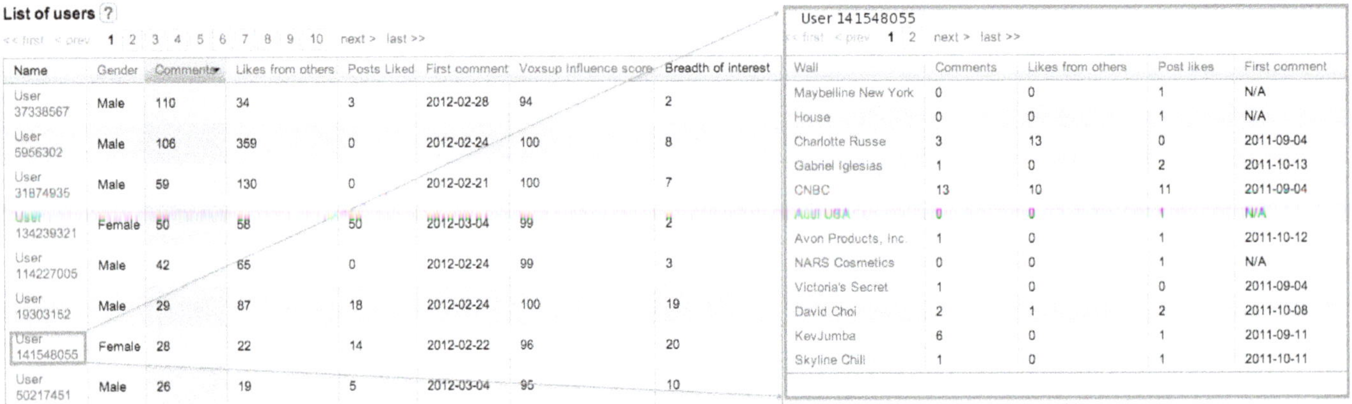

List of users ?

<< first < prev 1 2 3 4 5 6 7 8 9 10 next > last >>

Name	Gender	Comments	Likes from others	Posts Liked	First comment	Voxsup Influence score	Breadth of interest
User 37338567	Male	110	34	3	2012-02-28	94	2
User 5956302	Male	106	359	0	2012-02-24	100	8
User 31874935	Male	59	130	0	2012-02-21	100	7
User 134239321	Female	50	58	50	2012-03-04	99	2
User 114227005	Male	42	65	0	2012-02-24	99	3
User 19303152	Male	29	87	18	2012-02-24	100	19
User 141548055	Female	28	22	14	2012-02-22	96	20
User 50217451	Male	26	19	5	2012-03-04	95	10

(a)

User 141548055

<< first < prev 1 2 next > last >>

Wall	Comments	Likes from others	Post likes	First comment
Maybelline New York	0	0	1	N/A
House	0	0	1	N/A
Charlotte Russe	3	13	0	2011-09-04
Gabriel Iglesias	1	0	2	2011-10-13
CNBC	13	10	11	2011-09-04
Audi USA	0	0	1	N/A
Avon Products, Inc.	1	0	1	2011-10-12
NARS Cosmetics	0	0	1	N/A
Victoria's Secret	1	0	0	2011-09-04
David Choi	2	1	2	2011-10-08
KevJumba	6	0	1	2011-09-11
Skyline Chili	1	0	1	2011-10-11

(b)

Figure 3. User profile screenshots: (a) Partial list of the social users associated with the scenario *New York Knicks*. (b) More details about this particular user showing her activities on other subjects and interests. Note that all the statistics shown are contingent upon parameters (e.g. time window) chosen.

The final sentiment is obtained by combining the three results through a random forest model.

2.3 Distributed Solution for Big Data

VOXSUP is designed to be a cutting edge data mining system that is (almost) always available, highly durable, and easily scalable. Different from many data mining projects, which first receive a massive, static dataset and then perform mining tasks on it, VOXSUP contains a cluster of several transactional databases and high-dimensional data warehouses. Each social channel VOXSUP monitors, e.g. Facebook, has an individual transactional database that has to handle soft real time updates as the source channel updates. While enabling this feature for just the 10,000 walls Facebook is not trivial, VOXSUP does it for almost all major social media. What is more challenging is how to make sense of this massive amount of data from so many different yet correlated sources. The individual transactional database for each source in VOXSUP scales easily because such databases are independent of one another. However, this independency vanishes when we build the data warehouse. For example, an end-user may be interested in knowing what the hot topic talked about by certain group of social users is; he/she wants to know this for the entire social landscape. Traditional independent analytics on individual platforms will be, at best, biased estimates. VOXSUP can discover knowledge in real time from cross-platform heterogeneous information and therefore give end-users timely and unbiased insights.

To support demanding data mining tasks like the above example, we enable free text search on all of the text in our system through multiple scalable indexing / searching solutions.

2.4 Voxsupian Knowledge Discovery

VKD provides comprehensive, unbiased, actionable insights of the entire social topology through its 3 major components: Theme Canvas® discovery, user profile discovery, and precise interests discovery.

Theme Canvas® discovers the most talked about keywords and phrases for any given social channel in any given time interval. Different from traditional "word cloud" applications, Theme Canvas® encodes general social opinions associated with each term in gradients of two colors, and represents the scope or influence of each topic / term by its font size on canvas; clicking on any of the phrase takes the end-user to all of the original sentences/paragraphs that mentions the chosen phrase. We find the sentiment of each word (phrase) S_w on the canvas by latent topic models [3]:

$$S_w \propto \sum_{\substack{z \in \text{all} \\ \text{topics}}} \sum_{\substack{d \in \text{all} \\ \text{documents}}} S_d \cdot p(w|d,z), \tag{2}$$

where S_d is the sentiment for each document (e.g. comment, tweet) determined by SES. In addition, Theme Canvas® incorporates streaming data and returns results in real time. We achieve this by methods from item counting in streaming data [4]. Figure 2 visualizes this application.

User profile discovery in VKD analyzes each social user's public interests network. A Voxsupian user profile is the summary of this social user's presence and activities on different public pages across all platforms over a period of time. Like many available social profiling tools such as Klout, our user profile ranks the most influential users. But unlike most other social user profiling tools, the Voxsupian user profile distinguishes scenarios. For example, the online accounts for politicians and rock stars are influential and popular; but without distinguishing scenarios, their popularity does not translate into any useful information for, for example, a local business owner who wants to maximize viral reach by micro-targeting local residents who are influential for her brand and business. VOXSUP generates a customized user profile for each scenario. In the mathematical analogy, if a traditional user profile is represented as a vector of homogenous objects: $U = [o_1, o_2, \ldots, o_n]$, a Voxsupian user profile is essentially a tensor: $\tilde{U} = [T^{(o_1)}, T^{(o_1)}, \ldots, T^{(o_n)}]$. Tensors are confusing to many people, so we summarize all this information in each Voxsupian user profile into a single scenario-dependent measure, the Voxsup Influence Score, as an indicator of user's scenario-dependent influence power. To calculate this score, we map $\tilde{U}$, a Voxsupian user profile, to a score vector $SC \in \Re^n$. For each scenario $i \in \{1,\ldots,n\}$ in $\tilde{U}$, let $A_i = \{a_1^i, \ldots, a_m^i\}$ be his/her set of activities, $S_i = \{s_1^i, \ldots, s_m^i\}, s \in \Re$ be the corresponding set of sentiment representations, and $P_i = \{p_1^i, \ldots, p_m^i\}, p \in \Re^+$ be the corresponding set of popularity measures. Then we define the Voxsup Influence Score in an analogous fashion to that of the H-index [6]. For each scenario $i \in \{1,\ldots,n\}$, we define $SC[i] = \tilde{s}\tilde{p}$ where

$$\tilde{s} = \sup_{|s_j^i|} \left\{ |s_j^i| < \left| \left\{ s_k^i \in S_i : |s_k^i| \geq |s_j^i| \right\} \right| \right\}, \tag{3}$$

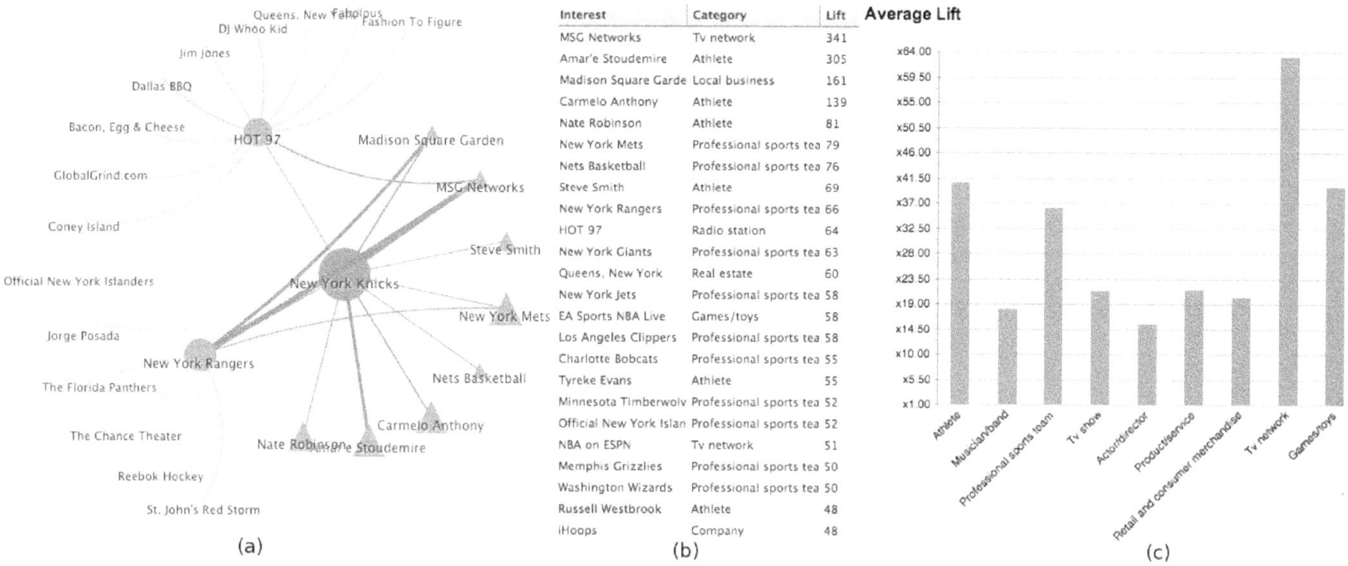

Interest	Category	Lift
MSG Networks	Tv network	341
Amar'e Stoudemire	Athlete	305
Madison Square Garde	Local business	161
Carmelo Anthony	Athlete	139
Nate Robinson	Athlete	81
New York Mets	Professional sports tea	79
Nets Basketball	Professional sports tea	76
Steve Smith	Athlete	69
New York Rangers	Professional sports tea	66
HOT 97	Radio station	64
New York Giants	Professional sports tea	63
Queens, New York	Real estate	60
New York Jets	Professional sports tea	58
EA Sports NBA Live	Games/toys	58
Los Angeles Clippers	Professional sports tea	58
Charlotte Bobcats	Professional sports tea	55
Tyreke Evans	Athlete	55
Minnesota Timberwolv	Professional sports tea	52
Official New York Islan	Professional sports tea	52
NBA on ESPN	Tv network	51
Memphis Grizzlies	Professional sports tea	50
Washington Wizards	Professional sports tea	50
Russell Westbrook	Athlete	48
iHoops	Company	48

(b)

Figure 4. Precise interests screenshots: (a) Visualization of the interests for the description *New York Knicks*; thickness of the edge represents the strength of the connection; size of the geometry of each node represents the predictive confidence; each interest node is clickable and expandable (e.g. *HOT 97* and *New York Rangers*). (b) List view of the precise interests in (a) with assigned category and relative lift. (c) Category-level roll-up lift chart.

and $\tilde{p} = \sup_{p_j^i}\left\{p_j^i < \left|\left\{p_k^i \in P_i : p_k^i \geq p_j^i\right\}\right|\right\}$. (4)

Just as TIME magazine ranks the most influential people on both positive and negative impact, in the Voxsup Influence Score we take the absolute value of the sentiment to accommodate such consideration. We empirically approximate the effect of sentimental strength by scalar multiplication. An alternative approach in our practice is to use power scale: $SC[i] = \tilde{p}^{\bar{s}}$. The scores shown in Figure 3 are normalized between 0 and 100. Figure 3 contains some examples of Voxsup Influence Score.

Precise interests discovery analyzes the entire public social web and extracts the most relevant/interesting items to a given description. A description here means a description of an interest; it could be a brand, a phrase, a group of users, etc. For example, the brand "Mercedes-Benz" is a description of an interest in luxury cars. VOXSUP system would then query its social database and returns a list of relevant interests that share a similar demographic as the chosen interest. Voxsupian precise interests are particularly useful for the behavioral targeting world. The screenshots in Figure 4 can best illustrate the Voxsupian precise interest. Figure 4 (a) and (b) show two different ways to explore the interests: breadth first and depth first. In the interests graph, we apply the same algorithm to each node interest to get a list of interests and sort the output by "lift". This is an atomic operation, which we call *probe*. Each *probe* terminates on a user-set lift threshold. By setting the threshold to just the interest with the highest lift, *probe* becomes depth first; otherwise, it is breadth first. Suppose X is a random variable denoting average social user's interest distribution and if we are given two interest descriptions x_1 and x_2, we define x_1's lift on x_2 as the ratio: $\Pr(X = x_1 | x_2) / \Pr(X = x_1)$. Figure 4 (c) further shows the lift numbers on category level. VOXSUP assigns categories of interests by clustering the interests based on their online demographics [5].

3. CONCLUSION AND FUTURE WORK

In this work, we introduced VOXSUP as a social engagement framework. To support its large-scale data-mining tasks, VOXSUP employs distributed solutions to handle and deliver its enormous magnitude of data. Based on our previous multi-lingual sentiment identification algorithms, we present the Voxsupian Knowledge Discovery as three major components: Theme Canvas® discovery, user profile discovery, and precise interests discovery. We describe the technical aspects and potential applications of the three components. Future research on network sampling techniques will be very helpful in our data mining practice if such techniques can promise good estimates of the original data using much less computing resources.

4. ACKNOWLEDGEMENTS

This research was supported by Voxsup, Inc.

5. REFERENCES

[1] S. Kim, T. Qin, H. Yu, and T.-Y. Liu. Advertiser-centric approach to understand user click behavior in sponsored search. In *CIKM '11*. ACM, 2011

[2] K. Zhang, Y. Cheng, Y. Xie, A. Agrawal, D. Palsetia, K. Lee, and A. Choudhary. SES: Sentiment Elicitation System for Social Media Data, *ICDM-SENTIRE '11*. IEEE, 2011

[3] D. M. Blei and J. D. Lafferty. Dynamic topic models. In *ICML '06*. ACM, 2006

[4] G. Cormode and M. Hadjieleftheriou. Finding frequent items in data streams. In *VLDB*. ACM, 2008

[5] A. Lancichinetti and S Fortunato1. Community detection algorithms: A comparative analysis. *Phys. Rev.* E 80, 056117. 2009

[6] J. E. Hirsch. An index to quantify an individual's scientific research output. In *PNAS* 102 (46). 2005

A System for Extracting Top-K Lists from the Web

Zhixian Zhang
Shanghai Jiao Tong University
Shanghai, China
zzx1989@sjtu.edu.cn

Kenny Q. Zhu *
Shanghai Jiao Tong University
Shanghai, China
kzhu@cs.sjtu.edu.cn

Haixun Wang
Microsoft Research Asia
Beijing, China
haixunw@microsoft.com

ABSTRACT

List data is an important source of structured data on the web. This paper is concerned with "top-k" pages, which are web pages that describe a list of k instances of a particular topic or concept. Examples include "the 10 tallest persons in the world" and "the 50 hits of 2010 you don't want to miss". Compared to normal web list data, "top-k" lists contain richer information and are easier to understand. Therefore the extraction of such lists can help enrich existing knowledge bases about general concepts, or act as a preprocessing step to produce facts for a fact answering engine. We present an efficient system that extracts the target lists from web pages with high accuracy. We have used the system to process up to 160 million, or 1/10 of a high-frequency web snapshot from Bing, and obtained over 140,000 lists with 90.4% precision.

Categories and Subject Descriptors

H.3.3 [**Information Storage and Retrieval**]: Information Search and Retrieval; H.2.8 [**Database Management**]: Database Applications—*Data Mining*

Keywords

Web information extraction, top-k lists, list extraction, web mining

1. INTRODUCTION

The world wide web is by far the largest source of information today. Much of that information contains structured data such as tables and lists which are very valuable for knowledge discovery and data mining. This structured data is valuable not only because of the relational values it contains, but also because it is relatively easier to unlock information from data with some regular patterns than free text which makes up most of the web content. However, when encoded in HTML, structured data becomes *semi-structured*. And because HTML is designed for rendering in a browser, different HTML code segments can give the same visual effect at least to the human eye. As a result, HTML coding is much less stringent than XML, and inconsistencies and errors are abundant in HTML documents. All these pose significant challenges in the extraction of structured data from the web [14].

In this demo, we focus on list data in web pages. In particular, we are interested in extracting from a kind of web pages which present a list of k instances of a topic or a concept. Examples of such topic include "20 Most Influential Scientists Alive Today", "Ten Hollywood Classics You Shouldn't Miss", and "50 Tallest Persons in the World". We call these pages "top-k" pages. Figure 1 shows one such "top-k" page [1]. Figure 1.(a) is a snapshot of the page and Figure 1.(b-d) are some of its segments. The title (Figure 1.(b)) of a "top-k" page usually contains a number k indicating the list size (20), as well as the head word/phrase (e.g., scientist) which best describes the entities in the list. Figure 1.(c) shows one instance (element) in the list, which not only contains the instance name (Timothy J. Berners-Lee), but also optionally additional information like a picture, a textual description and a link to a relevant wikipedia page. The additional information can be treated as the attributes of the instance. A "top-k" page can also contain unwanted lists such as Figure 1.(d) which should be filtered out.

Our system is designed to extract "top-k" lists from web pages. Basically, it performs three tasks: 1) Recognize a "top-k" page; 2) Extract the "top-k" list; 3) Understand and process list content.

The input of the system is any HTML web page and the output is the extracted "top-k" list of the page, if any. Table 1 shows the sample output from the page shown in Figure 1. [1]

There were many previous attempts to extract lists or tables from the web. None of them targets the "top-k" list extraction that is studied in this work. In fact, most of the methods are based on either very specific list-related tags [4] such as `<ul>`, `<li>` and `<table>` or the similarity between DOM trees [9, 10] and ignore the visual aspect of HTML documents. These approaches are likely to be brittle because of the dynamic and inconsistent nature of web pages. More recently, several groups have attempted to utilize visual information in HTML in information extraction. Most notably, Ventex [7] and HyLiEn [6] were designed to correlate the rendered visual model or features with the corresponding DOM structure and achieved remarkable improvements in performance. However, these techniques indiscriminatingly extract *all* elements of *all* lists or tables from a web page, therefore the objective is different from that of this work which is to extract *one* specific list from a page while purging all other lists (e.g. (d) in Figure 1) as noise. The latter poses different challenges such as distinguishing ambiguous list boundaries and identifying unwanted lists.

We target "top-k" list data for information extraction for the following reasons. First, there are *large* amount of "top-k" lists around on the web. We estimate that the total number in Bing's

*This work was partially supported by NSFC Grant 61100050 and MOE New Faculty Award No. 20110073120023.

KDD'12, August 12–16, 2012, Beijing, China.

[1]The actual output is stored in XML format and includes additional information.

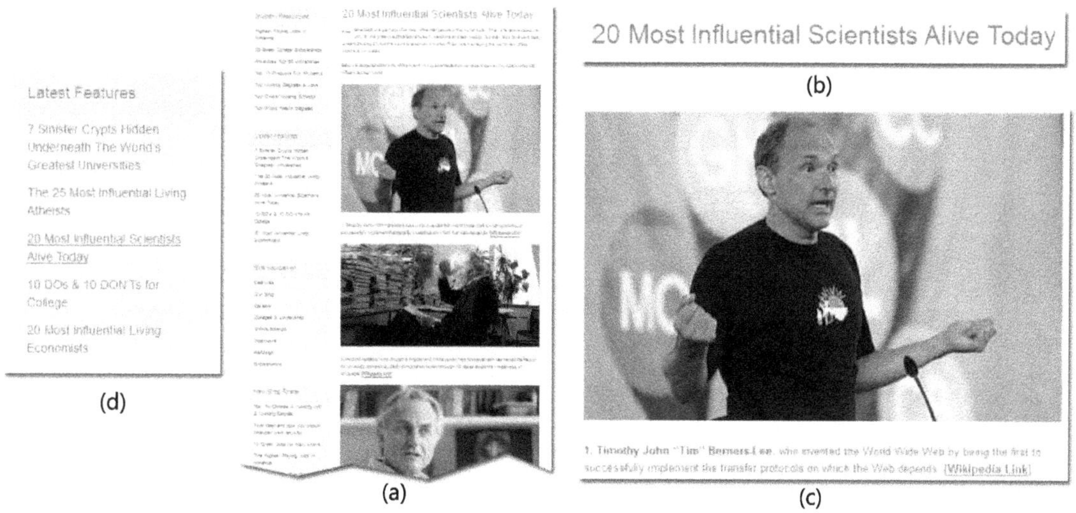

Figure 1: Snapshot of a typical "top-k" page [1] and its page segments

Index	Name	Image	Description	Wiki. Link
1	*Timothy J. Berners-Lee*	tim-berners-lee_1366736c.jpg	who invented the World Wide Web...	[link]
2	*Noam Chomsky*	noam_chomsky.jpg	who, though a linguist and philosopher...	[link]
3	*Richard Dawkins*	richard_dawkins.jpg	whose use of evolutionary biology has shaped...	[link]
...	...	...	...	...
20	*Edward Witten*	edward_witten.jpg	whose work on the mathematical underpinnings...	[link]

Table 1: Sample extraction output of "20 Most Influential Scientists Alive Today" [1]

corpus is around 2.24 million (1.4‰ of total number of pages), and our system can effectively extract up to 75.5% of them. The scale of this data is larger than any manually or automatically extracted lists in the past.

Second, list data is generally *cleaner* than other forms of web data. Free text contains a lot of variation and ambiguity and is known to be hard to understand and extract. General tables, even though structured, can have many different forms (such as row span and column span) and styles, and many of them are not meaningful if we don't know the schema of the table or the meaning of the headers [12]. Lists, on the other hand, have relatively simpler structures and are easier to identify. What's more, "top-k" lists, with their unique semantics, are even cleaner than ordinary lists.

Third, "top-k" lists are relatively *easier* to understand. "top-k" list pages share a common style: the title contains a number and the topic or concept of the list. Each list item can be considered as an instance of the page title. The number of items should be equal to the number mentioned in the title. Besides the name of the instance, each list item may contain additional attributes of the instance.

Finally, "top-k" lists have *interesting* semantics. The fact that the list items are called "top XXX" means that these items are more important, popular or meaningful than an arbitrary list. What's more, people are always fascinated about rankings. Information of this sort is likely to find a large audience.

We deployed our prototype system on a distributed computing platform and performed extraction on up to 1/10 of a high frequency web snapshot crawled by Bing. Our preliminary results showed that the system achieved 90.4% precision and 57.7% recall. That amounts to the correct extraction of 129,169 lists from a total of 160 million randomly selected web pages.

The work described in this paper is an important step in our bigger effort of automatic constructing a universal knowledge base that includes large number of known concepts and their instances. To that end, we have already built one of the largest open-domain taxonomy called Probase [15, 13, 12, 11] which consists of 2.7 million concepts and many more instances. The "top-k" lists we extracted from the web can be an important source for enriching Probase's instance space. Also, our system enables the construction of an effective fact answer engine [16]. With such an engine, we can answer queries such as "Who are the 10 tallest persons in the world", or "What are 50 best-selling books in 2010" directly, instead of referring the users to a set of ranked pages like all search engines do today.

Next we will briefly discuss the framework of our system (Section 2) and the preliminary evaluation results (Section 3), and present a plan for demonstration (Section 4).

2. TECHNICAL SPECIFICATION

Figure 2 shows the block diagram of our system. As the input of the system, the web page is first parsed by a HTML parser[3] to obtain a complete DOM representation. Then the title classifier attempts to recognize the page title. If it is a "top-k like" title, the classifier outputs the list size (the number k) and a set of possible concepts mentioned in the title. With the number k, the candidate picker extracts all lists of size k from the page body as candidate lists. Only one of them will be the actual list of interest. With the concept set, the top-k ranker can score each candidate list and pick the best one as the "top-k" list. Finally the content processor analyzes the list content and extracts the entity names and attributes.

2.1 Title Classifier

The title of a web page (string enclosed in `<title>` tag) helps us identify a "top-k" page. The goal of the classifier is to recognize "top-k like" titles, the likely name of a "top-k" page. In general,

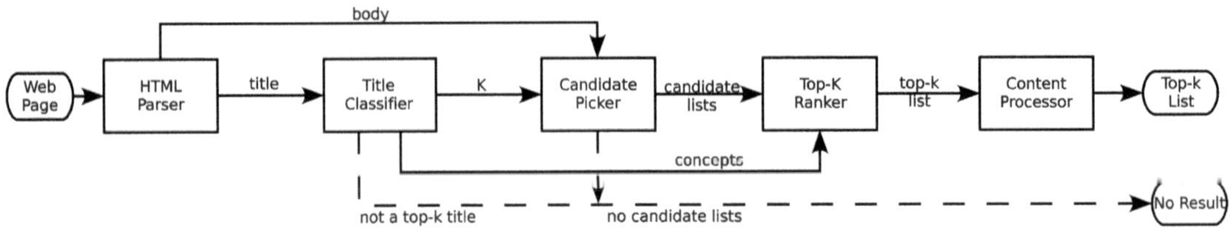

Figure 2: System Overview

a "top-k like" title represents the topic of "top-k" list. Note that a "top-k like" title may contain multiple segments, and usually only one segment describes the topic or concept of the list.

We trained a Conditional Random Fields (CRF) [8] model from both positive and negative sample titles. In addition to recognizing a "top-k like" title, the classifier also transfers the cardinal digit word (word like "ten" or "fifteen") into the number k, and outputs a set of Probase concepts such as "scientists" which are mentioned in the title.

2.2 Candidate Picker

Given an HTML page body and the number k, the candidate picker collects a set of lists as candidates. Each list item is a text node in the page body.

We define a *tag path* of a node as a path from the root to this node in the DOM tree. Items in a "top-k" list usually have similar format and style, and therefore they share an identical tag path. For example, in Table 1, the tag path corresponding to the second column *Name* is `html/body/.../p/strong`. Our *Default* algorithm takes advantage of this observation to identify lists of size k. Note that there might be multiple lists of the same size from a given page.

The *Default* algorithm achieves good recall but may produce noise. In a modified algorithm, known as *Def+Patt*, we introduce filters based on more reliable patterns such as indices and highlighting.

2.3 Top-K Ranker

When there are multiple candidate lists, we select only one of them as the *main list*. Intuitively, the main list is the one that best matches the title. In Subsection 2.1, we extract a set of concepts from the title, and one of them should be the central concept of the "top-k" list. Our key idea is that one or more items from the main list should be instances of one of the concepts extracted from the title. Probase taxonomy is used for this concept-instance matching. We design a scoring function in the ranker that measure the amount of matching as well as the visual features of a given list.

2.4 Content Processor

The content processor takes as input a "top-k" list and extracts the main entities as well as their attributes. Sometimes the text within an HTML text node contains a structure itself, e.g. "Hamlet By William Shakespeare". The content processor infers the structure of the text [5] by building a histogram for all potential separator tokens such as "By", ":" and "," from all the items of the "top-k" list. If we identify a sharp spike in the histogram for a particular token, then we successfully find a separator token, and we use that token to separate the text into multiple fields.

3. PRELIMINARY RESULTS

In this section, we present some preliminary results of the system from three experiments. The first two experiments test the precision and recall of the two main functions, namely title recognition and list extraction, respectively. In the last experiment, we performed large-scale extraction on a massive distributed computing platform.

For title recognition, we build a benchmark with 2000 random web page titles, all of which contains at least one number. 50 of these are "top-k like" and are treated as ground truth. The precision of the classifier is 76.7%, while the recall is 92%. The high recall ensures that most of the real "top-k" pages can pass through this stage.

In the second experiment, the input is the DOM representation of 100 correct "top-k" pages as well as the correct title analysis result (number k and concept set). Both algorithms obtain very high precision, with *Def+Patt* at 97.4%. In terms of recall, *Default* is better at 85% since *Def+Patt* uses stricter patterns.

In the last experiment, we apply the framework on 1/10 of a high-frequency web snapshot from Bing, which are about 160 million. Algorithm *Def+Patt* achieves 90.4% precision and 57.7% recall. We measured the recall by taking a smaller sample of the web corpus, manually checking the pages returned after the title recognition. If applied to the whole web corpus, *Def+Patt* is expected to harness over 1.4 million "top-k list" with over 90% precision.

4. DEMOSTRATION SETUP

At the heart of our demonstration is a web-based "Top-k" list extraction user interface [2]. It contains three main sections: TryItOut, Benchmark and Title. Under the TryItOut section, a user can test our system with an abitrary URL. In the Benchmark section, we present 100 typical "top-k" pages which the user can test either individually or in one go. We obtain these benchmark pages by manually searching through over 5000 web pages with "top-k" like titles. And in the Title section, a user can test an abitrary page title (string) with the title classifier.

A screenshot of the TryItOut section with blow-ups of extracted content is shown in Figure 3. Here, a user can type in the URL in the textbox and click "Extract" button, the system will retrieve the page in real time and attempt to extract a "top-k" list from it. The output result includes the page title, running time (in millisecond), number k, concepts as well as the "top-k list". Both the result and the original page will be presented after extraction.

In Benchmark section, as shown in Figure 4, we list 100 "top-k" pages with their URLs. If a user want to test any one of them, she can click "Test Me" button, the browser will be redirected to TryItOut and show her the result. If the user wants to test the entire benchmark, she can click "Test All" (in the bottom), the system will process through the benchmark and send her a result file in XML format.

In Title section, a user can type a string as input in the textbox, then click "Parse" button, and the system will analyze it as a page title and return detailed result, including time, features, concepts

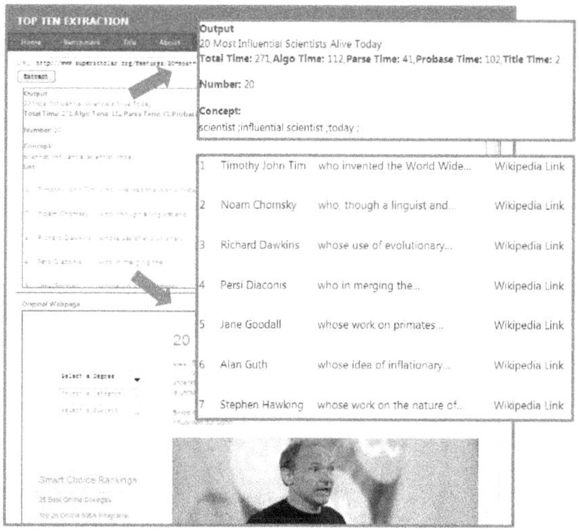

Figure 3: Web Demo GUI: TryItOut

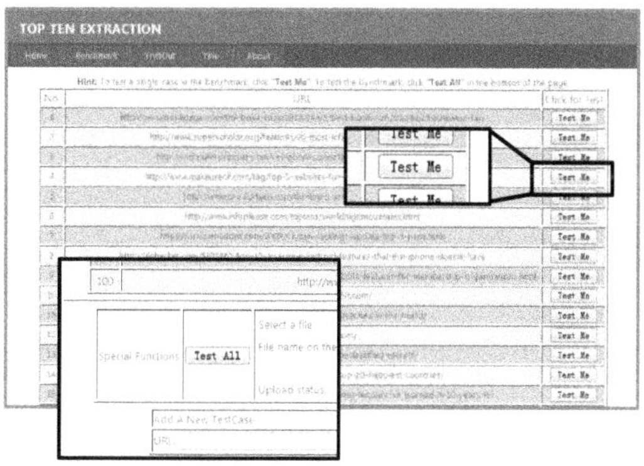

Figure 4: Web Demo GUI: Benchmark

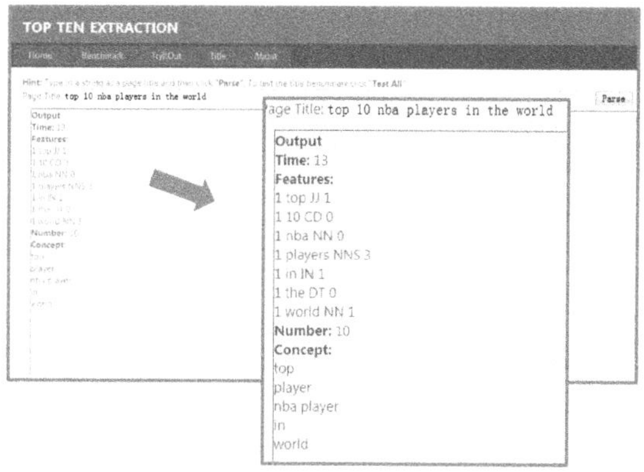

Figure 5: Web Demo GUI: Title

and whether it is a "top-k like" title. A screenshot of this section is shown in Figure 5.

5. CONCLUSION

In this paper, we define a novel list extraction problem, which aims at recognizing, extracting and understanding "top-k" lists from web pages. The problem is distinctive from other data mining tasks, because compared to other structured data, "top-k" lists are clearer, easier to understand and more interesting for readers. Besides these advantages, "top-k" lists are of great importance in knowledge discovery and fact answering simply because there are millions of "top-k" lists around on the web. With the massive knowledge stored in those lists, we can enhance the instance space of a general purpose knowledge base such as Probase. It is also possible to build a search engine for "top-k" lists as an effective fact answering machine. Our proposed 4-stage extraction framework has demonstrated its ability to retrieve large number of "top-k" lists at a very high precision.

6. REFERENCES

[1] 20 most influential scientists alive today. `http://goo.gl/KbB90`.

[2] Top-k web demo. `http://202.120.38.145:8088/TopTenSite/Default.aspx`.

[3] Winista htmlparser. `http://www.netomatix.com`.

[4] M. J. Cafarella, E. Wu, A. Halevy, Y. Zhang, and D. Z. Wang. Webtables: Exploring the power of tables on the web. In *VLDB*, 2008.

[5] K. Fisher, D. Walker, K. Q. Zhu, and P. White. From dirt to shovels: Fully automatic tools generation from ad hoc data. In *ACM POPL*, 2008.

[6] F. Fumarola, T. Weninger, R. Barber, D. Malerba, and J. Han. Extracting general lists from web documents: A hybrid approach. In *IEA/AIE (1)*, pages 285–294, 2011.

[7] W. Gatterbauer, P. Bohunsky, M. Herzog, B. Krüpl, and B. Pollak. Towards domain-independent information extraction from web tables. In *WWW*, pages 71–80. ACM Press, 2007.

[8] J. Lafferty, A. McCallum, and F. Pereira. Conditional random fields: Probabilistic models for segmenting and labeling sequence data. In *ICML*, 2001.

[9] B. Liu, R. L. Grossman, and Y. Zhai. Mining data records in web pages. In *KDD*, pages 601–606, 2003.

[10] G. Miao, J. Tatemura, W.-P. Hsiung, A. Sawires, and L. E. Moser. Extracting data records from the web using tag path clustering. In *WWW*, pages 981–990, 2009.

[11] Y. Song, H. Wang, Z. Wang, H. Li, and W. Chen. Short text conceptualization using a probabilistic knowledgebase. In *IJCAI*, 2011.

[12] J. Wang, H. Wang, Z. Wang, and K. Q. Zhu. Understanding tables on the web. In *ER*, 2012.

[13] Y. Wang, H. Li, H. Wang, and K. Q. Zhu. Toward topic search on the web. In *ER*, 2012.

[14] T. Weninger, F. Fumarola, R. Barber, J. Han, and D. Malerba. Unexpected results in automatic list extraction on the web. *SIGKDD Explorations*, 12(2):26–30, 2010.

[15] W. Wu, H. Li, H. Wang, and K. Q. Zhu. Probase: A probabilistic taxonomy for text understanding. In *SIGMOD*, 2012.

[16] X. Yin, W. Tan, and C. Liu. Facto: a fact lookup engine based on web tables. In *WWW*, pages 507–516, 2011.

EventSearch: A System for Event Discovery and Retrieval on Multi-Type Historical Data

Dongdong Shan[+] Wayne Xin Zhao[+] Rishan Chen[+] Baihan Shu[+] Ziqi Wang[++] Junjie Yao[++]
Hongfei Yan[+*] Xiaoming Li[++]
School of Electronics Engineering and Computer Science, Peking University, Beijing, China
{sdd, zhaoxin, crs, sbh, yhf }[+]@net.pku.edu.cn {wangziqi, junjie.yao, lxm}[++]@pku.edu.cn

ABSTRACT

We present EventSearch, a system for event extraction and retrieval on four types of news-related historical data, i.e., Web news articles, newspapers, TV news program, and micro-blog short messages. The system incorporates over 11 million web pages extracted from "Web InfoMall", the Chinese Web Archive since 2001. The newspaper and TV news video clips also span from 2001 to 2011. The system, upon a user query, returns a list of event snippets from multiple data sources. A novel burst model is used to discover events from time-stamped texts. In addition to offline event extraction, our system also provides online event extraction to further meet the user needs. EventSearch provides meaningful analytics that synthesize an accurate description of events. Users interact with the system by ranking the identified events using different criteria (scale, recency and relevance) and submitting their own information needs in different input fields.

Categories and Subject Descriptors

H.3.3 [**INFORMATION STORAGE AND RETRIEVAL**]: Information Search and Retrieval.

General Terms

Algorithms, Performance.

Keywords

event detection, event search.

1. INTRODUCTION

Along with the rapid growth of the World Wide Web, various news-related Web data is generated in a dramatic rate, and spreads throughout the Internet. Not only limited to traditional text based news, on-line news data usually contains various types of information, including news articles, news videos and micro-blog short messages. In order to facilitate the process of accessing news and revisiting retrospective events, it is essential to analyze and mine the information contained in these data. Thus, there is an emergent need of a comprehensive event extraction and retrieval system, which can help users to manage the overflow of news information and to extract valuable knowledge from on-line news sources.

A significant number of approaches to event mining and news exploration systems have been reported recently[1,4,5]. The most prevalent way is to detect events by grouping topically similar news articles into clusters [5]. However, most of previous studies focus on a single type of textual news data, e.g., either on news articles [1,5] or tweets [4]. Due to the complex nature of news information, a single stream, which only considers textual information, may not be able to form a comprehensive view of events. News- related data often involve various types of information, and it is beneficial to combine different types of information for event discovery and visualization. In fact, mainstream newspaper websites, e.g., New York Times, have extended the traditional text based news by incorporating multimedia information, e.g., videos and photos. Such a mechanism significantly improves user experience and utilities when reading news. In addition, few studies consider mining events within a very long time span, e.g., ten years. In order to obtain a better global view of event evolution and understand the underlying causalities among events, it is necessary to analyze and mine events in a long time period.

To address these problems and challenges using mutli-type news streams with a long time period, this paper gives an overview of our Event Discovery and Retrieval System (EventSearch[1]) developed for facilitating users with better utilities to access news information. EventSearch has two major functions: 1) automatically detect events from multi-type historical data; 2) maintain a two-layer index and provides flexible and efficient retrieval operations to users. Compared with previous event search engines, our system has three significant merits:

- Multi-type data aggregation. We consider a broad aggregation of four type of news streams as our input and provide a very comprehensive perspective of news events.
- Very long news streams. Our system detects and traces events in a very long time period, i.e., ten years, and it provides a better understanding of event evaluation and causalities among events. e.g., Iraq war. Note although our dataset has covered a very long time span, our system is capable to extract event information accurate to days.
- Multi-modality event visualization. Our system provides a multimedia-based visualization for automatically discovered events. Each event snippet in our system consists of mutli-modality data elements, including text, photos and videos. These types of data are combined in a systematic way to enhance the readability of information and improve user utility.

2. SYSTEM ARCHITECTURE

We first introduce the system architecture of our demo EventSearch. It consists of a Back-End and a Front-End layer (Figure 1).

*Corresponding author

KDD'12, August 12–16, 2012, Beijing, China.

[1] Demo address: http://162.105.205.253/eventsearch/

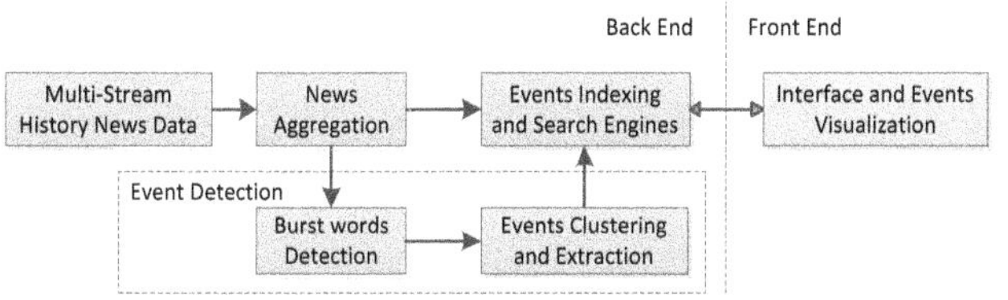

Figure 1: The system architecture.

Back-End module mainly takes charge of data aggregation, data preprocessing, offline event extraction and index building. **1) Data aggregation.** We employ an aggregation engine to collect various news-related data. Our input contains four important sources of news-related data: Web page based, video based, traditional newspaper based and micro-blog based. The Web page based news articles come from InfoMall[2] system, which achieved billions of Chinese Web pages since 2001. Since our major focus is to mine newsworthy events, we extract 11M news articles from 2001 to 2011, by requiring that the URL field should contain the keyword "news". Video based news articles are mainly downloaded from CCTV[3], which is China's national daily news program. We download the videos and their corresponding textual information. For traditional newspapers, we partially downloaded the articles from RMRB[4], which is the official newspaper of the Communist Party of China. We totally extract 59K and 0.89M articles respectively for CCTV and RMRB. Those data also range from 2001 to 2011. For micro-blogs, we use an official API authorized by Sina Weibo[5], which is the largest micro-blog in China, and we can retrieve short micro-blog messages since 2009. We do not download any data from Sina Weibo but get the data by submitting real-time queries when needed. Specifically, we first perform event extraction from news articles and generate event keywords. Then we query Sina Weibo API with event keywords within the event period to generate micro-blog results when presenting the event. **2) Data preprocessing.** After collecting data, the aggregation engine assigns a unique global document ID to each document, and extracts different fields (URL, title, body, score, ID, timestamp, etc). Note that the definition of "document" is very general, not limited to textual articles. For example, one document may contain both videos and text. For each article, we extract its corresponding keywords and location information. For video based documents, we adopt a non-broadcast clips extraction algorithm[6] to extract representative pictures as descriptions of documents. Then we merge all the textual news data (including the text from video based documents) into one unified stream ordered by timestamps for downstream tasks. **3) Offline event extraction.** Our event algorithm consists of three major parts: a) detect bursty feature (A bursty feature comprises a bursty term together with a bursty period) from the unified stream; b) use these bursty features to represent documents for clustering; c) perform clustering based on our proposed text representation. See Section 3 for details. Note that we only perform event extraction on textual data, we map non-textual data to corresponding events by utilizing the relationship between textual data and non-textual data, i.e., they coexist in the same document.. **4) Index building.** When document are clustered into events, we further generate event-dependent features, including event keywords, location and start/end time. We design a two-layer index for the whole data collection, i.e., event-level index and document-level index. See Section 4 for details.

In the Front-End module, EventSearch provides a friendly Web based interface. To help users to flexibly explore the discovered events, we set up three kinds of query fields: keywords, time and location, and each kind of query field can be left as blanks. The search result consists of a set of event snippets. In addition to news titles, each event snippet contains rich event metadata, including event location, time, keyword clouds and photos. The search result interface also allows user to click the returned events to zoom into the event detail page. See Section 5 for details.

3. OFFLINE EVENT EXTRACTION

One standard way for event detection is to cluster news articles as events by following a two-step approach [5]: 1) represent document as vectors and calculate similarities between documents; 2) run the clustering algorithm and determine events. Although it seems very natural and straightforward, event detection in long text streams is very challenging. Traditional Vector Space Model does not consider modeling temporal aspects of documents and it is not suitable for temporal modeling. In addition, we have to face with the scalability problem from our very big news archive for clustering these temporal documents. To effectively and efficiently model temporal document for clustering, we propose a novel burst-based document representation.

Burst based VSM. Inspired by the work [2,3], we select *bursty features* as the basic representation units of documents, which contain both temporal and semantic information. We use *bursty feature* to denote a sudden surge of the frequency of a single term in a text stream, and represent a bursty feature by the term itself together with the time interval during which the burst takes place. For example, (Olympic, Aug-08-2008, Aug-24-2008) can be regarded as a bursty feature. We also call the term in a bursty feature its bursty term. We merged all the text documents as one news stream, and use the two-state machine algorithm [3] to detect a set of bursty features from this news stream, denoted as B. A document $\boldsymbol{d_i(t)}$ with timestamp t is represented as a vector of weights in ***bursty feature dimensions***:

$$d_i(t) = (d_{i,1}(t), d_{i,2}(t), \ldots, d_{i,|B|}(t)) \tag{1}$$

We define the jth weight of $\mathbf{d}_i$ as follows:

$$d_{i,j} = \begin{cases} \text{tf-idf}_{i,w_{B_j}}, & \text{if } t \in bi_{B_j} \\ 0, & \text{otherwise} \end{cases} \tag{2}$$

where B_j is the jth bursty feature in B, w_{Bj} and b_{iBj} are the bursty term of B_j and bursty interval of B_j respectively, $|B|$ is the number of bursty features in B. When the timestamp of $\boldsymbol{d}_i$ is in the bursty interval of B_j and contains term w_{Bj}, we set up the weight using the common used *tf-idf* method.

From the definition above, we can see that one dimension is active only when the document falls in the corresponding bursty interval. BurstVSM considers both semantic and of temporal information: semantics are modeled by the weight of bursty terms while temporal dynamics are modeled by mapping one dimension to one bursty feature. Usually, BurstVSM represents one document as a vector with only a few non-zero entries. It makes computation of document similarities more efficient in a large dataset compared with VSM. See [7] for more details.

Event detection algorithm. Based on the discussions above, each document can be represented as a burst-based vector. We use cosine function to compute document similarities. Our dataset

[2] http://www.infomall.cn/

[3] http://cctv.cntv.cn/lm/xinwenlianbo/

[4] http://paper.people.com.cn/

[5] http://weibo.com/

consists of 11 million documents in a long time span (10 years), and it is infeasible to cluster all the documents together. We develop a heuristic clustering algorithm for event detection, denoted as *split-cluster-merge*. It includes three main steps, namely split, cluster and merge. The idea is that we first split the dataset into small parts, then cluster the documents of each part independently and finally merge similar clusters from two consecutive parts. It has a merit that *cluster* step could be executed in parallel for different parts. In our dataset, we find that most of events last no more than one month, so we split the dataset by months. After splitting, clustering can run in parallel for different parts (we use *CLUTO*[6] as the clustering tool), which significantly reduces total time cost. For *merge*, we empirically set a threshold of 0.5. The final clusters are returned as identified events. See [7] for more details.

4. EVENT INDEXING AND SEARCH ENGINE

For an event retrieval system, a user may submit either event-level queries (by inputting queries to retrieve relevant events) or document-level queries (by zooming into the detailed content of one specific document). To facilitate both types of queries, we build a two-layer index: document-level and event-level index.

Our textual data are indexed in the document-level index, including keywords, bursty features and corresponding event ID (in our system, one article only belongs to one event), timestamp and relevant locations. In our system, since documents may contain non-textual information, to manage them, we set up special fields in document-level index, e.g., photo linking field and video linking field. These fields are filled with internal position pointers on disks where we store non-textual information. To discriminate documents from different source types, we add a source type field in document-level index. In the event-level index, we store information from offline-discovered events, including start/end time, relevant locations and event keywords. One important field in even-level index is the collection of relevant documents in one event. Given a specific event, this field records all the global IDs of relevant documents. We use this field to link event-level index with document-level index. The two-layer index can support various queries flexibly.

Next, we describe how to perform keywords based retrieval using such a two-layer index. Figure 2 shows the general flow of query processing. Firstly, we use a BM25 like retrieval model for keyword-based queries in the document-level index. We keep top ranked 10000 articles and get their corresponding event IDs.

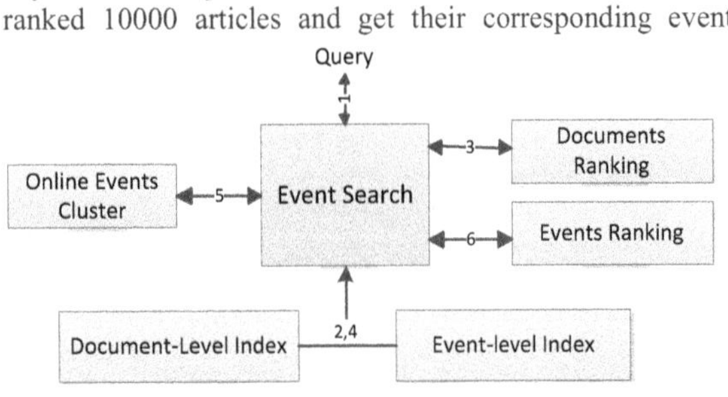

Figure 2: The flow of query processing.

Secondly, we obtain corresponding detailed information of these events from event-level index using retrieved event IDs, and these event details are used as ranking features, including the number of relevant documents (scales), event period (recency and time span), the number of different types and the number of related document in certain source. Thirdly, we compute the divergence of the distribution of relevant documents in different events. If the divergence is too large, in other words, relevant documents appear in quite a lot of offline-discovered events, we employ an online event extraction module to rediscover events from top ranked documents to better satisfy user needs. Otherwise we will combine relevant documents from the same event as an event result set. Finally, we use corresponding relevance scores or other criteria, e.g., recency, to rank events.

For non-keyword queries, we only use event-level index to retrieve events, and rank the candidate events by considering three factors: event static quality score (offline calculated), event period and event locations. In this case, online cluster module will not be triggered. Another important problem is how to incorporate the micro-blog data in the event snippet. Since we have generated event keywords and event period, for a given event, we query Sina Weibo API with the top ranked keywords within the corresponding period, and micro-blog results are generated in an online way.

5. EVENT VISUALIZATION

Our system allows the users to specify the queries by inputting three kinds of information: keywords, start/end time and location. When a user submits a query, the system will return a list of snippets for relevant events (shown in Figure 4). An event snippet consists of news titles, event keyword cloud, event period and relevant event locations, possibly with news photos and videos. Users can slip mouse on photos to select the corresponding videos, and our system will play the clicked video in a separate page (shown in figure 3).

Figure 3: Web page for playing video.

The major merit of our event visualization is that we incorporate multi-modality and multi-type information. Such visualizations can provide a comprehensive view of events and significantly improve user utilities. In addition, we have offered some basic mechanisms for mining and analyzing events. See the top two subfigures in Figure 4, respectively the trend of the number of events and the hottest relevant locations related with the given query. Take the query "Olympics Games" as one example (in Chinese), we can see that there is a significant spike in terms of the number of related events. The major reason is that the hold of "Beijing 2008 Summer Olympics Games". We use Baidu map to present the hottest event locations. In the subfigure on the right, Beijing has been marked as the hottest event location and Shanghai as second. More interestingly, users can click any points in the timeline or map to see the events that happened around that time or location.

Given these returned event snippets, a user may be interested in a specific event. Our system provides a link to event detail page to help users to zoom into the details of one event. Figure 5

[6] www-users.cs.umn.edu/~karypis/cluto/

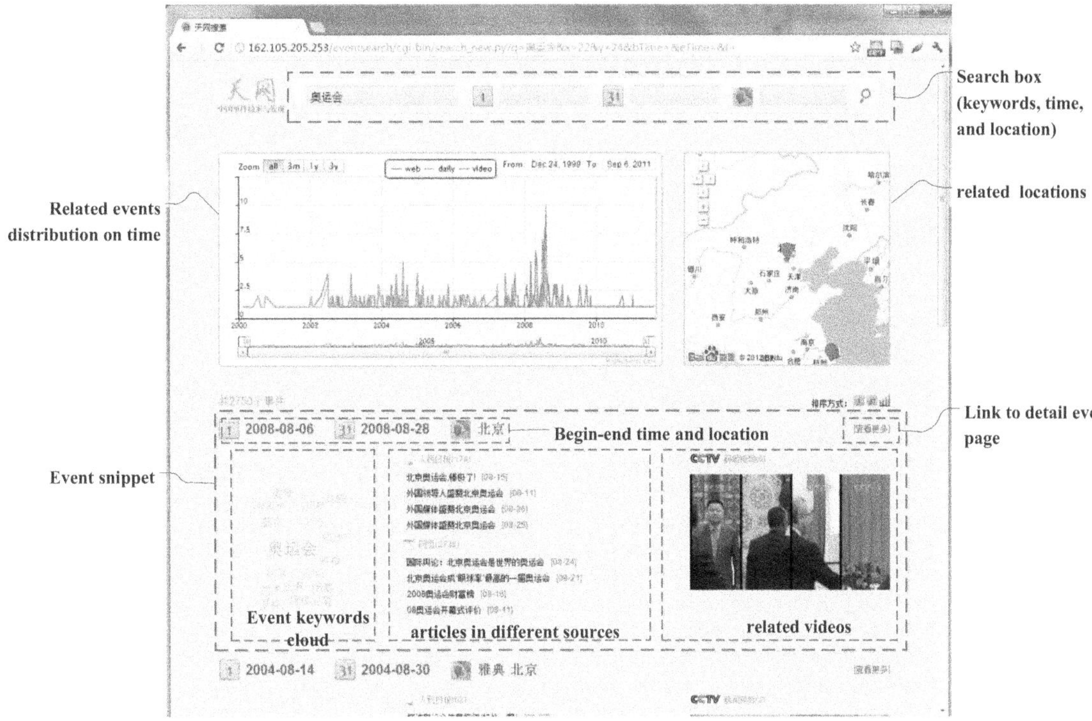

Figure 4: Result page of event searching for query "Olympic Games".

presents an event detail page of "Beijing 2008 Summer Olympics Games". Users can browse articles by selecting different views of by clicking source type tag i.e. in a specific type of news stream. Note that the keyword clouds shown on the left in Figure 5 are source dependent, indicating the system generates different keyword clouds for multiple sources. Relevant articles are returned and presented as document snippets, and we can rank those articles either by relevance or recency. Users can click the link in one document snippet to view the full information and corresponding link in InfoMall for one document (shown in figure 6).

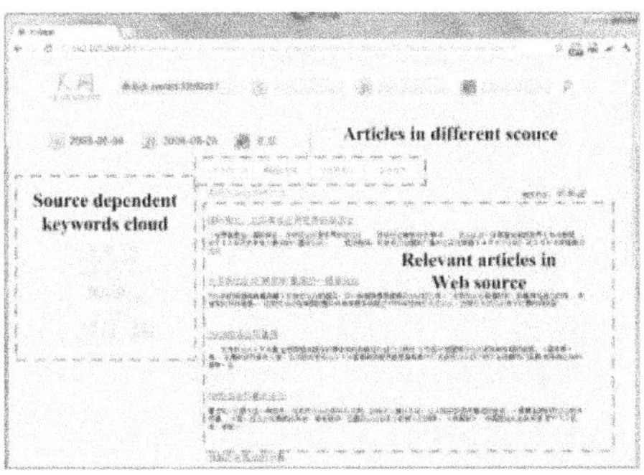

Figure 5: Event detail page for one event for query "Olympic Games".

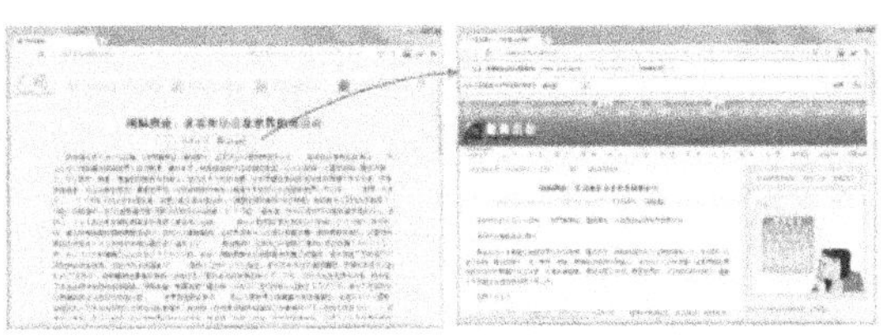

Figure 6: News article's detail page and its archived page in InfoMall.

ACKNOWLEDEMENTS

This work is supported by NSFC Grant (60933004, 70903008, 61073082) and HGJ Grant 2011ZX01042-001-001.

6. REFERENCE

[1] Fung, G.P.C., Yu, J.X., Liu, H., and Yu, P.S. Time-dependent event hierarchy construction. *Proceedings of the 13th ACM SIGKDD international conference on Knowledge discovery and data mining*, ACM (2007), 300-309.

[2] He, Q., Chang, K., Lim, E.P., and Zhang, J. Bursty feature representation for clustering text streams. *Proc. SIAM Conference on Data Mining*, (2007), 26-28.

[3] Kleinberg, J. Bursty and hierarchical structure in streams. *Proceedings of the eighth ACM SIGKDD international conference on Knowledge discovery and data mining*, ACM (2002), 91-101.

[4] Mathioudakis, M. and Koudas, N. TwitterMonitor: trend detection over the twitter stream. *Proceedings of the 2010 international conference on Management of data*, ACM (2010), 1155-1158.

[5] Yang, Y., Pierce, T., and Carbonell, J. A study of retrospective and on-line event detection. *Proceedings of the 21st annual international ACM SIGIR conference on Research and development in information retrieval*, ACM (1998), 28-36.

[6] Ye, Q., Huang, Q., Gao, W., and Jiang, S. Exciting event detection in broadcast soccer video with mid-level description and incremental learning. *Proceedings of the 13th annual ACM international conference on Multimedia*, ACM (2005), 455-458.

[7] Zhao, X., Chen, R., Fan, K., Yan, H., and Li, X. A Novel Burst-based Text Representation Model for Scalable Event Detection. In *ACL*, 2012.

EvaPlanner: An Evacuation Planner with Social-based Flocking Kinetics

Cheng-Te Li
Graduate Institute of Networking and Multimedia,
National Taiwan University, Taipei, Taiwan
d98944005@csie.ntu.edu.tw

Shou-De Lin
Dept. of Computer Science & Information Engineering
National Taiwan University, Taipei, Taiwan
sdlin@csie.ntu.edu.tw

ABSTRACT
This paper demonstrates a system that exploits graph mining, social network analysis, and agent-based crowd simulation techniques to investigate the evacuation dynamics during fire emergency. We create a novel evacuation planning system, *EvaPlanner*, to deal with three tasks. First, the system identifies the preferable locations to establish the exits to facilitate efficient evacuation from the dangerous areas. Second, it determines the most effective positions to place the emergency signs such that panic crowd can quickly find the exits. Third, it faithfully simulates the evacuation dynamics of crowd considering not only the individual movement kinetics but also the social connections between people. *EvaPlanner* provides a flexible experimental platform for investigating the evacuation dynamics under a variety of settings, and can further be utilized for animation and movie production. In addition, it can serve as a tool to assist architects address the safety concern during the planning phase. The demo system can be found in the link: http://mslab.csie.ntu.edu.tw/evaplanner/ .

Categories and Subject Descriptors
H.2.8 [**Database Management**]: Database Applications–*Data mining*.

General Terms
Algorithms, Performance, Design.

Keywords
Social network, crowd simulation, evacuation planning.

1. INTRODUCTION
Pedestrian evacuation and fire safety is an important research area that studies the interactions between pedestrian movement and complex spatial environment under a variety of scenarios (e.g. terrorism, fire, or natural disasters), with the goal to implement a more effective evacuation plan to improve the ultimate survival rate. To perform such study, researchers have to consider the arrangement of objects in a given space, the deployment of exits and signs, and the identification of most direct routes toward the closest exits. Many practical issues, ranging from mental status, spatial cognition, panic factors, and group coordination are discussed from the perspectives of physics, physiology, psychology, and computer simulation (refer to the survey [11]). While most of existing works conduct qualitative studies to explore the evacuation dynamics, agent-based simulation is believed to be one of the most effective approaches to explore the evacuation dynamics based on quantitative models.

Instead of relying completely on agent-based simulation, this paper integrates data mining techniques, in particular graph mining and social network models, with crowd simulation mechanism, to tackle the evacuation planning problem. We present a novel evacuation planning system, *EvaPlanner*, to explore and simulate the escaping dynamics of people in certain emergency situations. More specifically, we concentrate on answering three challenges. (a) Given any room structures and the deployment of interior objects and walls, where should the exits be setup to achieve better evacuation efficiency? (b) Where to put the signs pointing to the exits to optimize the survival rate during fire accident? (c) How to faithfully model, simulate, and visualize the crowd movement during evacuation for animation creation?

(a) Automatic Exit Determination. From the prospect of safety, it is critical to determine where to place the exits in a large room (e.g. exhibition or hall) during the blueprinting stage of the construction. Proper design of the location of the exits can improve the survival rate during fire. This paper proposes a novel idea to transform the exit-location determination task into an optimization problem in a graph and solve it with a graph-based random-walk mechanism.

(b) Automatic Sign Placement. Being able to place exit signs at the proper positions can also lead to more effective and efficient evacuation. In general, the signs have to be established in certain positions that are clearly visible, such that they are on the tracks of the shortest paths to the nearest exits. We transform the sign placement problem into a graph mining problem through exploiting graph-based traversing model, and then take advantage of the centrality measures designed for social networks as heuristics to identify the effective spots to put the signs.

(c) Evacuation Simulation for Fire Accidents. Here the goal is to simulate the realistic movement and evacuation traces of agents during fire emergency. Actually there have been proposals (e.g. [2][4][9]) exploiting techniques of crowd simulation to produce the escaping dynamics of agents in an indoor space. In these models, the persons are assumed to be independent agents and do not possess social relationships with each other. The key novelty of our simulation model is that it considers not only the kinetics of individual movement but also the social impact during evacuation. Naturally when experiencing an emergency such as a fire accident, people do not run away without attempting to rescue their family or friends. In this sense, people who are acquainted with each other tend to move and flock together during evacuation; therefore we believe a faithful simulation model should consider this social factor. Besides the basic movement kinetics proposed by Reynolds [10], we introduce a new steering force to model the acquaintance relationships between individuals. In the simulation, we first execute the exit-placement and sign-placement algorithms

KDD'12, August 12 – 16, 2012, Beijing, China.
Copyright 2012 ACM 978-1-4503-1462-6 /12/08…$15.00.

to find the best locations to place exits and signs, and then perform crowd simulation with the devised social force to model the evacuation of humans during a fire accident.

2. SYSTEM FRAMEWORK

The *EvaPlanner* system framework is shown in Figure 1, which consists of three major components (drawn with dotted rectangles). The first component sets up the environment, which allows users to determine where to deploy the obstacles and agents in the environment. The second component is the core engine of the evacuation planner, which automatically determines the locations of *exits and signs* using graph mining techniques. The final component integrates the above modules to simulate the crowd movement under the *propagation of fire*. The main sub-component in the simulation is the *social-based flocking kinetics*, which aims to combine the flocking behavior and social acquaintance between agents into their collective movement.

Next, we will first describe how to intelligently determine the locations of exits and signs in Section 3, and the simulation module with social-based flocking kinetics in Section 4. We present the system demonstration in Section 5.

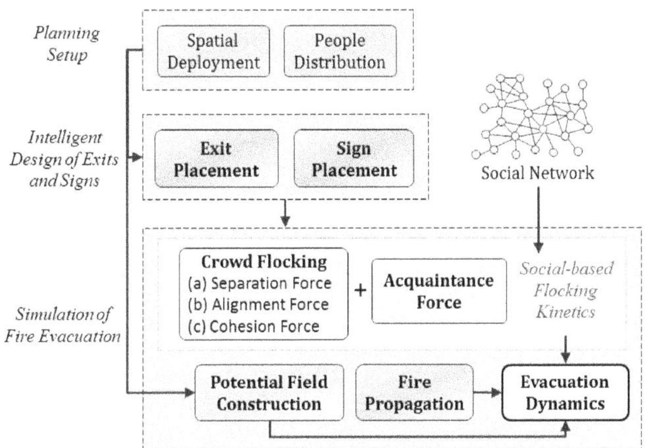

Figure 1: The system framework of *EvaPlanner*.

3. INTELLIGENT DESIGN OF EXIT & SIGN

Given an indoor space with scattered objects representing furniture and walls separating the rooms, our goal is to design an intelligent method to automatically determine the best positions on the border to implement the exits for smoother evacuation. Furthermore, once the locations of the exits are determined, we want to then determine the best spots to put the exit signs to optimize the total number of safely-evacuated persons. We devise graph mining approaches to fulfill these goals.

3.1 Exit Determination

For safety purpose, it is preferable to place exists that maximize the evacuation efficiency. To realize this idea, we propose a random-walk based mechanism for exit deployment. Our method consists of three steps. First, we transform the closed environment into a *navigation graph*. The navigation graph is devised to maintain the connectivity among spatial areas (represented by grids), where some grids are blank (i.e. indicates free-to-move spaces) and others are occupied by obstacles (i.e. impassable). For example, in Figure 4(a), the white grids are free areas while the shadowed grids are impassable areas. In the navigation graph, nodes represent the free grids and edges stand for the eight-directional neighboring relationship between grids (see Figure 4(b)). Second, we apply the *Random Walk* (RW) algorithm [12] on the navigation graph. We randomly select some grids as the initialization nodes to perform RW. Third, as the RW process are executed up to N times (N=100 in our system), we can derive the average reach probability of each grids. Those peripheral grids with highest probabilities are the preferable locations for exits as they are more likely to be reached by agents. In the demo system, we choose one exit for each peripheral side in the space.

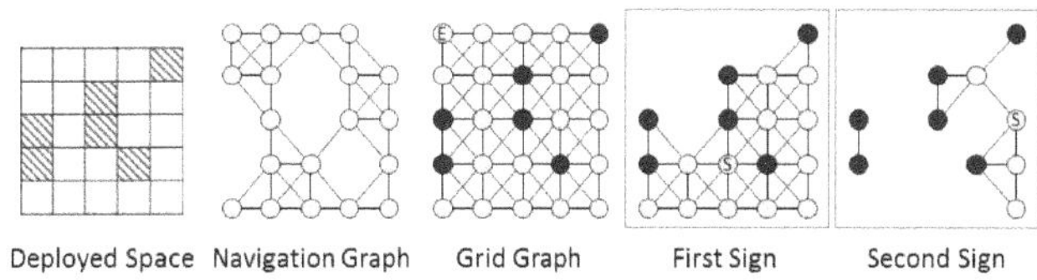

Figure 2: Transforming (a) the deployed space into (b) the *navigation graph* and (c) the *visibility graph*. The running example for (d) the first sign and (e) the second sign placed.

3.2 Sign Placement

The exit signs, which are set up to guide panic people towards the exits during emergency, play a key role in the evacuation process. Consequently, where to put the sign in the indoor environment can affect the evacuation efficiency. A preferable location to place the signs usually follows the following rules: (R1) it should be easily visible in the room, (R2) it indicates the shortest path to the nearest exits, and (R3) it should be placed at the prime locations where most people have to pass through. To incorporate these concepts, we propose to transform this problem into an optimization problem on a graph, and solve it using a greedy method with network analysis techniques.

We propose a three-step approach to greedily identify locations for placing signs pointing towards the exits. First, we transform the deployed space into a *grid graph*, which is a lattice representation of the space with the eight-directional connectivity. The grid graph aims to capture the spatial relationships between free spaces and obstacle spaces. For example, Figure 2(c) is the grid graph of Figure 2(a), in which white nodes are free grids while black nodes are the ones with obstacles. Given the derived exits, the second step aims to remove the free grids which can directly see the exits because they do not need to be guided by a sign. To do so, we first construct the shortest paths of each free grid to each exit. For each free grid, if any of its shortest paths contains no obstacle grid, then such grid (as well as its edges) is removed from the graph because we are sure there is a direct view from it to one of the exits. In other words, every free node that has at least one shortest path to the exit without being blocked will be removed from the grid graph because later we do not need to consider them for sign placement. After removing the visible grids, we then obtain a *visibility graph*. For example, assuming the only exit, marked as "E", is located at the top-left position in a grid graph, as shown in Figure 2(c), the corresponding visibility graph is shown in Figure 2(d), where free nodes that are visible from the exit are removed. The third step is to determine where to put the sign based on the visibility graph. Here we compute the *closeness* centrality [13] and the *betweenness* centrality [13] values of each node in the visibility graph, and choose the grid with the highest average score of closeness and betweeness as the place for the first sign. Then we can go back to step-2, removing all the free-grids that have direct visibility to the first sign to obtain a new visibility graph as Figure 2(e), and then repeat step-3 to pick the place for the second sign. Such process continues until no free grids are left in the visibility graph. For example, the first sign, marked as "S", is placed at the center-bottom position in Figure 2(d), and the second sign is placed at the middle right of Figure 2(e). Note that choosing grids with the highest closeness scores usually satisfies R1 and R2, while choosing the grids with highest betweenness scores generally fit the criteria of R3.

4. SIMULATION OF FIRE EVACUATION

In this section, we aim to integrate the previously discussed evacuation planning engine with an agent-based simulation framework to simulate how crowd moves during an emergency fire accident. The main novelty of this component lies in the introduction of a social-oriented moving kinetics to faithfully model the human's behavior given social ties.

4.1 Social-based Flocking Kinetics

We construct the social-based flocking kinetics of agents by devising the flocking steering forces and a social acquaintance force to jointly drive the movement of agents. First, we exploit Reynolds' flocking model [10] as the basic movement guideline for agents. This model was proposed to model the flocking behavior of humans in a dynamic virtual environment. It consists of three steering rules, (a) *separation force* (f_s) steers each agent to avoid crowding local flockmates, (b) *alignment force* (f_a) steers each agent towards the average heading of local flockmates, and (c) *cohesion force* (f_c) steers each agent to move toward the average position of local flockmates. Besides, each agent is an independent actor and has his own local perception of navigation (see Figure 3).

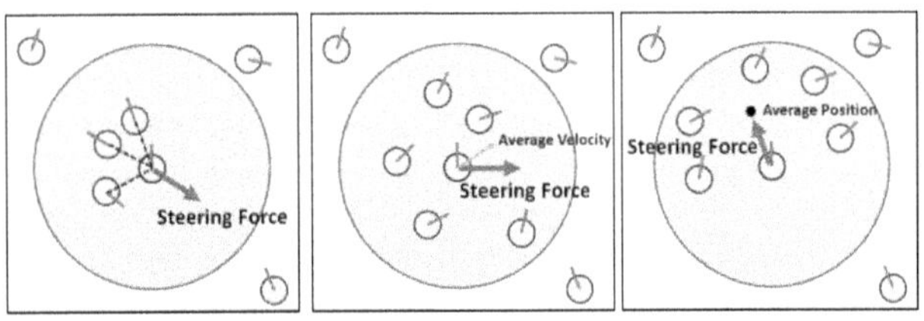

Figure 3: From left to right: illustrations of *separation*, *alignment*, and *cohesion* steering forces.

We also believe that besides these three factors, the movement of a human is also affected by his or her own social ties. That is, people who are acquainted with one another usually have higher chance to flock together in a particular spatial area [7]. Therefore, given a social network, a faithful simulation should provide a mechanism allowing people in the same community to have higher chance to flock together.

To emerge social-based flocking groups in the simulation, we introduce the *acquaintance force* (f_q), into the flocking simulation. While the previous three forces are used to model the flocking behavior by gathering agents that are close enough in the simulating space, the integration of the acquaintance force is expected to produce the following effects: (a) determining the members of each flocking group, (b) steering agents whose corresponding nodes are close enough in the network to flock together, and (c) avoiding agents whose nodes are far apart to flock together. An illustration of the idea of acquaintance force is shown in Figure 4. For an agent/node u, the acquaintance force $f_q(u)$ is computed by

$$\overrightarrow{f_q(u)} = \frac{1}{|R_u|}\sum_{v \in R_u} 1 - \frac{Length(u,v)}{\theta},$$

where R_u is the set of agents under the local perception of agent u, *Length*(u,v) is the length of shortest path between the node u and v in the network, and θ is a constant value that determines the shift border between the attraction and repulsion forces. That says, if *Length*(u,v) $< \theta$, the agent v will exert an attraction force on u. If *Length*(u,v) $> \theta$, v will exert an repulsion force on u. And if *Length*(u,v) $= \theta$, v has no effect on u. In this work, θ is set to be 3. In the end, by integrating our acquaintance force with previous three steering forces, the eventual force $\overrightarrow{f_q(u)}$ to guide agent u is $\overrightarrow{f(u)} = w_s \cdot \overrightarrow{f_s(u)} + w_a \cdot \overrightarrow{f_a(u)} + w_c \cdot \overrightarrow{f_c(u)} + w_q \cdot \overrightarrow{f_q(u)}$, where w_s, w_a, w_c, are w_q are the weights of separation, alignment, cohesion, and acquaintance forces respectively. We set them to be (w_s, w_a, w_c, w_q) = (0.3, 0.3, 0.3, 0.1) in our system.

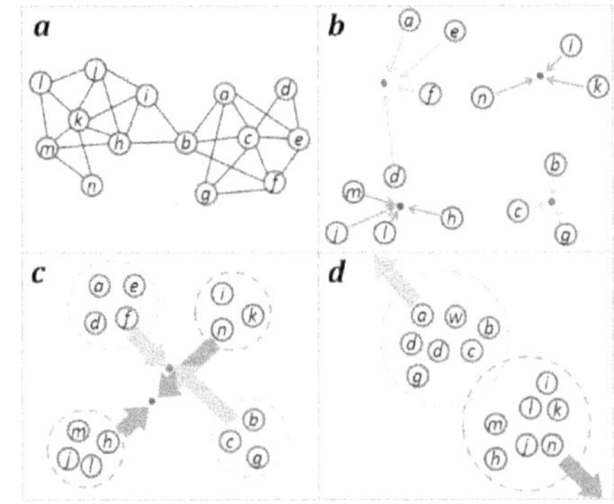

Figure 4: The effects of the acquaintance force. (a) An example social network containing two cohesive subgroups colored by blue and red. (b) The forces gradually gather local flocks together into some small groups whose members tend to be acquainted with each other. (c) The forces attract and merge some local flocks whose members are close enough in terms of graph distance. (d) For small groups whose members are farther apart in the network, repulsive forces will drive them away from one another.

4.2 Potential Field Construction

Besides the mentioned four forces that guild the subtle movements of an agent in normal condition. We further propose to take advantage of the *potential field* [5] to guide the movements of agents in the deployed space during evacuation. The potential field is devised as a high-level force to drive the agents away from the obstacles or fire, and closer to the exits. The potential field we designed consists of two parts, the *guided attractive field*, which directs agents to the exits, and the *obstacle repulsive field*, which steers agents to bypass the obstacles. Figure 5 shows the idea of potential field, in which the exit has lowest potential while the obstacles possess highest potentials. Agents in the space tend to move from positions with higher potentials to positions with lower potentials. More details are described in the literature [3][5].

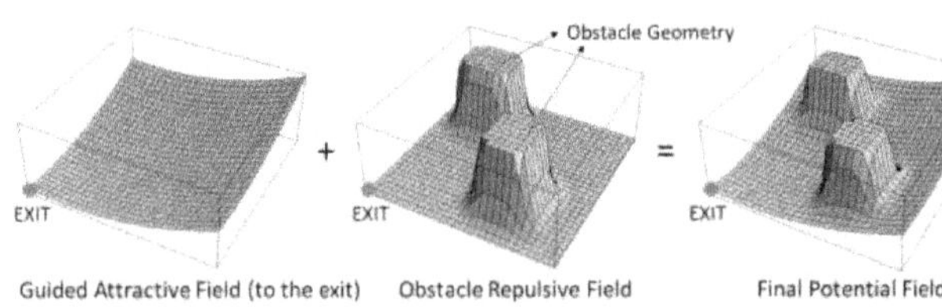

Figure 5: Combining (a) the *guided attractive field* and (b) the *obstacle repulsive field* to generate the final (c) *potential field*. Referred and modified from the material [3].

4.3 Fire Propagation and Evacuation

With the aforementioned mechanism, we can simulate the escaping behavior of agents during the propagation of fire. The fire evacuation simulation is continuously regulated by the following process, as described below. First, the fire events are initialized randomly in the closed space, and then gradually propagate to wider areas. Then the moving agents are notified about the fire events and starting to evacuate. During the evacuation process, family or friends would tend to move together given our flocking kinetics. As agents find the signs, they will learn the directions to the nearest exits. In the meantime, agents could be attacked by the fire and become unmovable (in the injured or dead status). This process continues until no more agents can move in the closed space. That says, agents either escaped or die in the fire. We report the number of evacuated and dead agents.

5. DEMONSTRATION

In addition to the abovementioned mechanism, *EvaPlanner* additionally provides the flexibility for users to setup the environment. To be more precise, given the initial blank/free space, *EvaPlanner* allow users to determine where to place obstacles or objects in the space. Such spatial deployment is fulfilled by allowing users to create some two-dimensional geometric obstacles and placing them onto the desired location in the free space. The remaining unoccupied area is considered as traversing spaces where people are allowed to pass through. Furthermore, users are allowed to determine the initial location of each agent. A random assignment of obstacles and agents in the space by our program can also be performed.

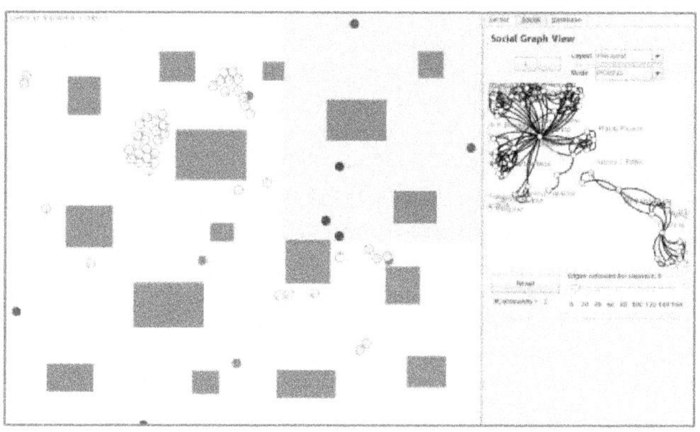

Figure 6: A system snapshot of *EvaPlanner*.

Figure 6 shows a snapshot of the evacuation process in our *EvaPlanner* system. The system consists of two parts, the simulation view on the left panel and the social network view on the right panel. In the simulation view, gray areas represent the obstacles, red circles indicate the emergency signs, and blue circles indicate the exits. The normal agents are the circles with red arrows revealing their current moving directions. A community detection method [8] is performed on the social network and agents in different community will be colored differently (e.g. white and yellow in Figure 6). During the simulation, the light-red area, which represents the fire coverage, propagates gradually. Agents touched by the fire will turn black and cannot move anymore, indicating injured or dead. We can observe that some agents moving in communities, such as the group at the top-left part of the graph. The survival statistics is also shown in the top-left corner as "LIVING: 47, ESCAPED: 1, DIED: 3." Note that to understand the evacuation dynamics using our system, we create a demo video, which can be accessed via http://mslab.csie.ntu.edu.tw/evaplanner/.

6. CONCLUSION

While existing works on evacuation dynamics use mostly qualitative operations, this work presents a novel simulation-based evacuation planning system to model the evacuation dynamics. Systematically, we robustly integrate a series of important functions, especially on realistic social movement, intelligent design of exits and signs, and simulation of fire events. Technically, we exploit the techniques of social network analysis and graph mining [1][13] (from data mining), crowd simulation [10] (from computer animation), and motion planning [5] (from robotics) to develop the evacuation planner. Ongoing work focuses on three directions: designing different heterogeneous roles on agents (e.g. leader, trained, and untrained people), modeling sophisticated behaviors of agents (e.g. arsonist and fireman), and modeling the panic propagation [6] among agents.

7. REFERENCES

[1] D. Chakrabarti and C. Faloutsos. Graph Mining: Laws, Generators, and Algorithms. *ACM Computing Survey*, 38(1), 2006.

[2] S. Chenney. Flow Tiles. *ACM SIGGRAPH/Eurographics Symposium on Computer Animation*. 233-242, 2004.

[3] Howie Choset. Robotic Motion Planning: Potential Functions. Lecture slides of motion planning, Robotics Institute 16-735.

[4] D. Helbing, J. Farkas, and T. Vicsek. Simulating Dynamical Features of Escape Panic. *Nature*, 407, 487-490, 2000.

[5] Y. K. Hwang and N. Ahuja. A Potential Field Approach to Path Planning. *IEEE Transactions on Robotics and Automation*, 8(1), 23-32, 1991.

[6] D. Kempe, J. M. Kleinberg, and E. Tardos. Maximizing the Spread of Influence through a Social Network. *ACM SIGKDD*, 137-146, 2003.

[7] M. McPherson, L. Smith-Lovin, and J. M. Cook. Birds of a Feather: Homophily in Social Networks. *Annual Review of Sociology*, 27:415-444, 2001.

[8] M. E. J. Newman. Fast Algorithm for Detecting Community Structure in Networks. *Physical Review*, E 69, 066133, 2004.

[9] N. Pelechano, J. M. Allbeck, and N. I. Badler. Controlling Individual Agents in High-Density Crowd Simulation. *ACM SIGGRAPH/Eurographics Symposium on Computer Animation*, 99-108, 2007.

[10] C. W. Reynolds. Flocks, Herds and Schools. A Distributed Behavior Model. *ACM SIGGRAPH*, 25-34, 1987.

[11] A. Schadschneider, W. Klingsch, H. Klüpfel, T. Kretz, C. Rogsch, and A. Seyfried. Evacuation Dynamics: Empirical Results, Modeling and Applications. *Encyclopedia of Complexity and Systems Science*, 3142-3176, 2009.

[12] H. Tong, C. Faloutsos, and J.-Y. Pan. Fast Random Walk with Restart and its Applications. *IEEE ICDM*, 613-622, 2006.

[13] S. Wasserman and K. Faust. Social Network Analysis. *Cambridge University Press*, 1994.

PubMed Search and Exploration with Real-Time Semantic Network Construction*

Jinoh Oh, Taehoon Kim, Sun Park, and Hwanjo Yu †
Pohang University of Science and Technology
Pohang, South Korea
{kurin, zyint, dingga, hwanjoyu}@postech.ac.kr

ABSTRACT

Exploring PubMed to find relevant information is challenging and time-consuming because PubMed typically returns a long list of articles as a result of query. Semantic network helps users to explore a large document collection and to capture key concepts and relationships among the concepts. The semantic network also serves to broaden the user's knowledge and extend query keyword by detecting and visualizing new related concepts or relations hidden in the retrieved documents. The problem of existing semantic network techniques is that they typically produce many redundant relationships, which prevents users from quickly capturing the underlying relationships among concepts. This paper develops an online PubMed search system, which displays semantic networks having no redundant relationships in real-time as a result of query. To do so, we propose an efficient semantic network construction algorithm, which prevents producing redundant relationships during the network construction. Our extensive experiments on actual PubMed data show that the proposed method is significantly faster than the method removing redundant relationships afterward. Our method is implemented and integrated into a relevance-feedback PubMed search engine, called RefMed, "http://dm.postech.ac.kr/refmed", and will be demonstrated through the website.

Categories and Subject Descriptors

H.3.3 [**Information Search and Retrieval**]: System

General Terms

Algorithm, Performance

Keywords

Semantic network construction, Information Retrieval, PubMed

*This work is supported by Mid-career Researcher Program through NRF grant funded by the MEST (No. KRF-2011-0016029).

†Corresponding author

1. INTRODUCTION

PubMed-Medline is a biomedical and life science literature repository that contains 18 million articles and keeps growing. It is one of the most important knowledge sources for medical doctors and biomedical researchers. PubMed supports an exact matching search using attributes including title, author, abstract, journal, MeSH terms. However, exploring PubMed to find relevant information is challenging and time-consuming because PubMed typically returns a long list of articles as a result of query.

Semantic network helps users to explore a large document collection and to capture key concepts and relationships among the concepts [8]. The semantic network also serves to broaden the user's knowledge and extend query keyword by detecting and visualizing new related concepts or relations hidden in the retrieved documents. Typical semantic network techniques analyze the relationship between concepts by considering co-occurrence of concepts [7, 3, 1]. For example, one of fundamental relationships among concepts is superset-subset relationship. If the document set showing a certain concept x is included in another document set showing another concept y, we call y is a superset of x, and x is a subset of y.

The problem of existing techniques generating semantic network is that, many of the superset-subset relationships are redundant thus do not provide additional information. Instead, they prevents users from quickly capturing the underlying relation among concepts. For example, in Figure 1, there are six superset-subset relationships. However, among them, three relationships (i.e., relationship ④, ⑤, ⑥) are redundant and thus do not provide meaningful information to user. To deliver information more precisely and clearly, we need to remove redundant relationships. However, identifying and removing such redundant relationships incur non-trivial computational overhead.

This paper proposes an efficient semantic network construction algorithm, which prevents producing redundant relationship during the network construction. Our extensive experiments on actual PubMed data show that the proposed method is significantly faster than the method removing redundant relationships afterward. Our method is implemented and integrated into a relevance-feedback

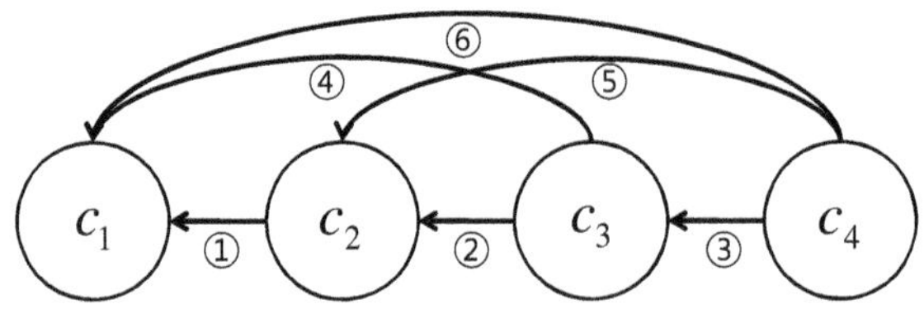

Figure 1: Example of redundant relationships. Nodes are concepts and edges indicate superset-subset relationships

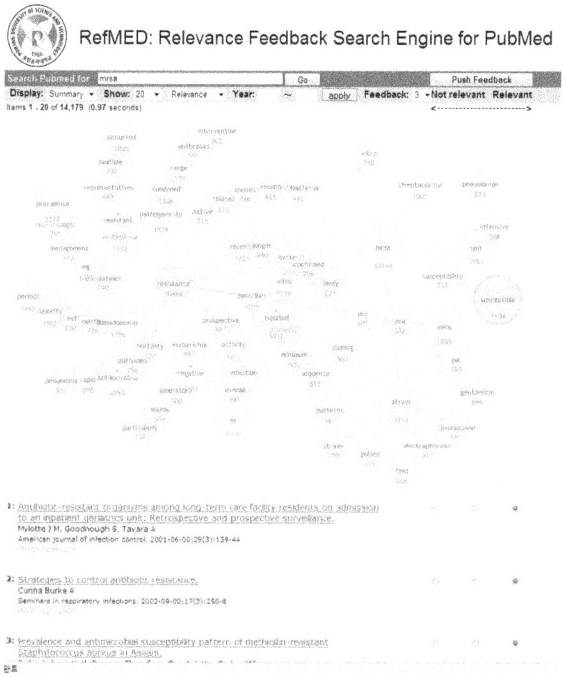

Figure 2: Screen shot of RefMed

PubMed search engine, called RefMed, `http://dm.postech.ac.kr/refmed`, and will be demonstrated through the website.

For example, Figure 2 shows a screenshot of the result of query "mrsa". As a result of a query, 14,179 articles are retrieved, and the semantic network is shown in the middle of the figure. There are several subset concepts of the query concept, some of which have hidden subset concepts that will be expanded when clicked. The user can relocate the nodes by dragging them.

Related Work: Automatic taxonomy generation (ATG) is a technique to improve PubMed search quality and has been researched for a decade [5, 7, 3, 2, 1, 9]. The main goal of ATG is generating the structure of terms from document collection. Among various approaches for ATG, word-clustering-based approaches [4, 5, 7, 2, 3] generate structure of considerable terms in a document collection. Most methods generate the hierarchical structure (e.g., tree) of considerable terms or concepts based on subsumption relationship.

Recently, hierarchical structure of ATG has been expanded to a more complex but flexible structure called *semantic network* [8]. The output of semantic network is a large graph, which is not limited to tree, presenting relatedness among concepts. The output of semantic network is different from that of ATG, but the way of determining relationships among concepts is similar. It also uses subsumption relationship and other variations based on co-occurrence.

2. TECHNICAL SPECIFICATION

2.1 Preliminary: Elements of Semantic Network

Basic structure and construction process of semantic network are introduced in [7, 8]. The semantic network consists of concepts and relationships among concepts. Two concepts may be related to each other as related set or superset-subset in the network.

Concept: A concept means a considerable term in a document collection. A term becomes considerable if (1) it occurs more than a certain threshold in the search results and (2) the fraction of the term's probability in the search results over the total document collection is higher than a threshold [7]. For example, a term becomes a concept when it satisfies the following two conditions.

$$p_D(x_i) = \frac{\text{\# of occurrence of } x_i \text{ in D}}{\text{\# of documents in D}} > \theta_{c_1} \quad (1)$$

and

$$\frac{p_D(x_i)}{p_T(x_i)} > \theta_{c_2} \quad (2)$$

where D and T are the retrieved documents and the total document collection, respectively.

Superset-subset Relationship: The superset-subset relationship is determined in a similar way. If the document set of x_i is almost included in that of x_j but not in the other way, x_j is a superset of x_i.

$$p_D(x_j|x_i)\left(=\frac{p_D(x_i,x_j)}{p_D(x_i)}\right) > \theta_p \quad \text{and} \quad p_D(x_i|x_j) < \theta_p$$

where

$$p_D(x_i,x_j) = \frac{\text{\# of co-occurrence of } x_i, x_j \text{ in D}}{\text{\# of documents in D}}$$

Note that when x_j is a superset of x_i then $|x_j| > |x_i|$ where $|x_i|$ is the size of documents showing x_i. It is clear because $\theta_p * P_D(x_j) > P_D(x_i,x_j) > \theta_p * P_D(x_i)$.

Related term: Relationship *related* is also defined based on the co-occurrence ratio of two concepts. Suppose a term x_j appears in most of the documents having x_i and vice versa. Then, it indicates that there is a strong relationship between x_i and x_j. This is called *related* relationship. For example, concepts x_i and x_j become *related* to each other if they satisfy the following conditions.

$$p_D(x_i|x_j) > \theta_s \quad \text{and} \quad p_D(x_j|x_i) > \theta_s$$

2.2 System framework

Figure 2.2 shows the framework of our system. If user enters a keyword, the system (1) first finds exactly matching documents as done in the original PubMed search engine, and (2) preprocesses the result documents by running stemming and stopwords. After that, the system (3) extracts the concepts, (4) constructs semantic network of concepts by analyzing the relationships among concepts, and (5) visualizes them by drawing an interactive graph. In

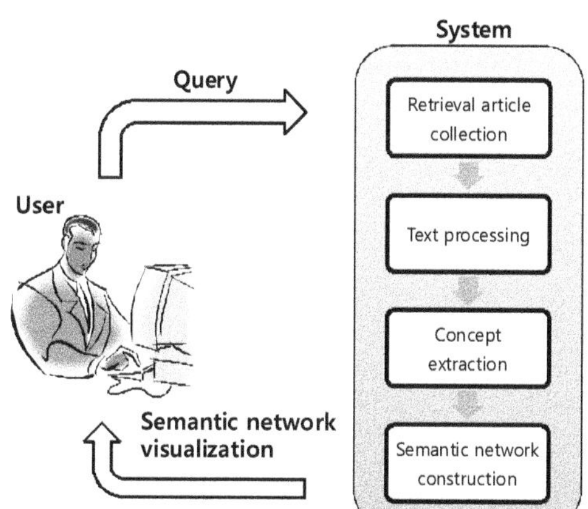

Figure 3: Framework of RefMed

the final query result, a semantic graph is presented with exactly matching documents as shown in Figure 2. This process is done in real-time.

2.3 Efficient Semantic Network Construction

This section presents an efficient semantic network construction method. Further details on the method and experiment results are found in our technical reports [6].

Redundant Relationship: Redundant relationship is the relationship that can be induced by other relationships, thus do not provide additional information and need to be removed. Accordingly we define the redundant relationship as follows.

DEFINITION 1 (REDUNDANT RELATIONSHIP). *Let $c_i \rightarrow c_j$ denote c_i is a superset of c_j. A relationship $c_i \rightarrow c_j$ is redundant if there exists another path $c_i \rightarrow c_k \rightarrow \cdots \rightarrow c_j$ in the semantic network.*

2.3.1 *Removing redundant relationships as post processing*

We can detect and remove the redundant relationships after fully constructing the semantic network as a post processing. Let $R = \{(c_i, c_j, Type)\}$ be the set of extracted relationships and each relationship is expressed by a triplet $(c_i, c_j, Type)$ where c_i and c_j are concepts and "Type" is the relationship type between c_i and c_j. For example, a triplet $(c_i, c_j, Superset)$ indicates "c_i is a *superset* of c_j". The post-processing method first extracts R from the document set, and for each triplet $(c_i, c_j, Superset) \in R$, if there is another path from c_i to c_j, it removes the triplet from R.

Note that the complexity of the post processing method is quadratic to the number of triplets in R because, for each triplet in R, examining the possibility of indirect paths takes an additional scan of R. Thus, at the worst case, when the number of relationships is proportional to the number of pairs of concepts (i.e., $|R| = O(n^2)$ where n is the number of concepts), the complexity becomes $O(n^4)$. The post-processing method is too expensive to run in our applications where the semantic network must be constructed in real-time as a result of query.

2.3.2 *Compact Semantic Network Generation*

This section proposes a novel algorithm for generating the *compact semantic network* that has no redundant relationships and thus does not require removing redundant relationships afterward. The algorithm runs in two phases – (1) building *minimal semantic network* and (2) expanding the *minimal semantic network* to the *compact semantic network*.

Phase 1. Building the minimal semantic network

We first define two new terminologies – *closest superset* and *minimal semantic network*. *Closest superset* is defined to be a superset that has the smallest supporting document size:

DEFINITION 2 (CLOSEST SUPERSET). *Let $\mathcal{C}_x = \{c_1 \ldots c_k\}$ be a set of supersets of c_x. Among them, the smallest concept c_i (i.e., $\arg\min_{c_i} |c_i|$) is the closest superset of c_x.*

The following Lemma shows that the relationship between a concept c_x and its closest superset is always *not redundant*.

LEMMA 1. *For any concept c_x in a semantic network $\mathcal{G}$, a relationship between c_x and its closest superset is not redundant.*

PROOF. We prove this by contradiction. Let c_i be the closest superset of c_j (i.e., $c_i \rightarrow c_j$). In order for $c_i \rightarrow c_j$ to be redundant, there must be a sequence $K = c_1 \rightarrow \cdots \rightarrow c_n$ connecting c_i and c_j (i.e., $c_i \rightarrow K \rightarrow c_j$). Then, one of the concept c_k in K is a superset of c_j and a subset of c_i. That is, $|c_k| > |c_j|$ and $|c_k| < |c_i|$ from the definition of the superset-subset relationship. Thus, c_i cannot be the closest superset of c_j. Therefore, if c_i is the closest superset of c_j, $c_i \rightarrow c_j$ is not redundant. □

Minimal semantic network is defined to be the semantic network in which the nodes have only their closest supersets:

DEFINITION 3 (MINIMAL SEMANTIC NETWORK). *Let graph $\mathcal{G} = (\mathcal{C}, \mathcal{R})$ be a semantic network where $\mathcal{C}$ is a set of concepts and $\mathcal{R}$ is a set of triplets $(c_i, c_j, Type)$. A semantic network $\mathcal{G}'(\subset \mathcal{G}) = (\mathcal{C}, \mathcal{R}'(\subset \mathcal{R}))$ is a minimal semantic network if, for all the superset-subset relationship $R'_k = (c_i, c_j, Superset) \in \mathcal{R}'$, c_i is the closest superset of c_j.*

To construct the minimal semantic network, we first sort the concepts $\mathcal{C} = \{c_1, ..., c_n\}$ according to their sizes in an ascending order. Then, for each concept c_i, we check the superset-subset relationship from c_{i+1} to c_n and stop checking when we find the first superset which will be the closest superset of c_i.

Phase 2. Expanding to compact semantic network

DEFINITION 4 (COMPACT SEMANTIC NETWORK). *Let graph $\mathcal{G} = (\mathcal{C}, \mathcal{R})$ be a semantic network where $\mathcal{C}$ is a set of concepts and $\mathcal{R}$ is a set of triplets $(c_i, c_j, Type)$. A semantic network $\mathcal{G}'(\subset \mathcal{G}) = (\mathcal{C}, \mathcal{R}'(\subset \mathcal{R}))$ is a compact semantic network if, all the superset-subset relationship $R_k = (c_i, c_j, Superset) \in \mathcal{R}'$ is not redundant, and all non-redundant relationship in $\mathcal{R}$ is in $\mathcal{R}'$.*

Once the minimal semantic network is built, we expand it to a compact semantic network by generating additional superset-subset relationships that are not redundant. We first prove by the following Lemma that, given a minimal semantic network $\mathcal{G}$, any additional superset-subset relationship between c_i and its ancestor c_j will be redundant.

LEMMA 2. *Let graph $\mathcal{G}$ be a minimal semantic network. For any concept c_i and its ancestors $c_1, ..., c_k$ in $\mathcal{G}$, any additional superset-subset relationships from one of $c_1, ..., c_k$ to c_i will be redundant.*

Any additional path to c_i from its ancestor c_j is redundant because there exists another path from c_j to c_i since c_j is an ancestor of c_i. From Lemma 2, we can skip examining the superset-subset relationship from c_i to its ancestors. Based on this idea, we used sorted concept list and minimal semantic network. For each concept, we remove all the superset of the concept from the candidate list and test the relationship only between the concept and non-superset concepts. When another relationship is added, we also remove the supersets of the added concepts from the candidate list. We illustrate the expansion algorithm by the following example.

EXAMPLE 1. *Figure 4(a), (b), and (c) respectively show an example of minimal semantic network, compact semantic network, and four lists of concepts sorted according to their sizes. From the minimal semantic network, suppose we examine to find another non-redundant superset of c_7. Then, we can first delete c_7, c_6, c_1 because they are ancestors of c_7 or itself (shown at the second list of Figure 4(c)). After that, we test the relationship between c_5 and c_7 and find new superset-subset relationship from c_5 to c_7. Next, we can delete c_5 and c_2 because c_2 became an ancestor of c_7 (shown at the third list of Figure 4(c)). If we repeat this process until we*

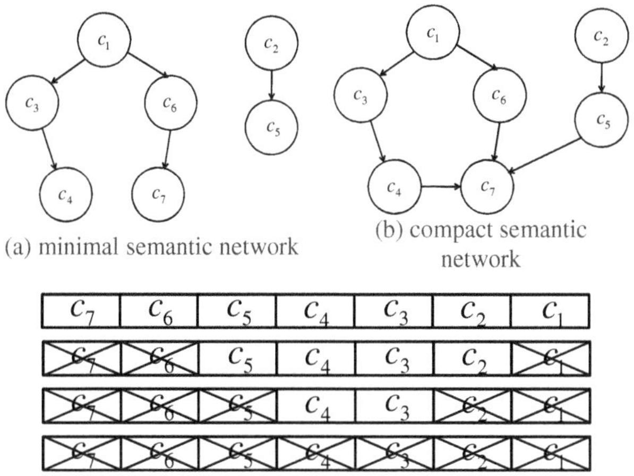

(a) minimal semantic network

(b) compact semantic network

(c) Candidate list for expansion

Figure 4: Example for expanding semantic network

delete all the elements in the list, we will discover all the additional non-redundant supersets of c_7*. After testing this for all the nodes in the minimal semantic network, we finally get the compact semantic network of Figure 4(b).*

3. EVALUATION RESULTS

We evaluate the proposed method against the post processing method that removes redundancy after construction. For evaluation, we implemented the methods in RefMed, an interactive search engine for PubMed.

Implementation: The dynamic construction of semantic network is implemented in the PHP (v5.1.6) and the Adobe Flash CS4. The algorithm is implemented using the PHP and the visualization is implemented using the Flash. The implementation is integrated into our RefMed. The RefMed is implemented using MySQL(v5.1) and C language. We store the entire PubMed data in RefMed. The system currently runs on a server of quadcore 2.87GHz with 46M memory, thus cannot support many simultaneous accesses at this point.

Semantic Network Construction Time Evaluation: We evaluate the time of semantic network construction on queries having results of varying sizes. Table 1 reports the construction time. Our method took less than 0.3 seconds for all queries. On the other hand, in worst case, the naive method took more than 1.5 seconds which is 7 times longer than our method.

Figure 5 illustrates the construction time on an increasing number of concepts. The construction time of POST rapidly increases as the number of concepts increases. On the other hand, our method produces stable construction time.

query	# of doc.	# of concepts	POST (sec.)	COMPACT (sec.)
mrsa	14,345	123	1.0931	**0.0638**
hemophilia	20,039	55	0.0688	**0.0417**
methyltransferase	28,153	99	0.3606	**0.1367**
melanoma	76,274	146	1.0930	**0.1665**
malignant	239,278	171	1.5557	**0.2269**

Table 1: Network construction time. POST: post processing method; COMPACT: proposed method .

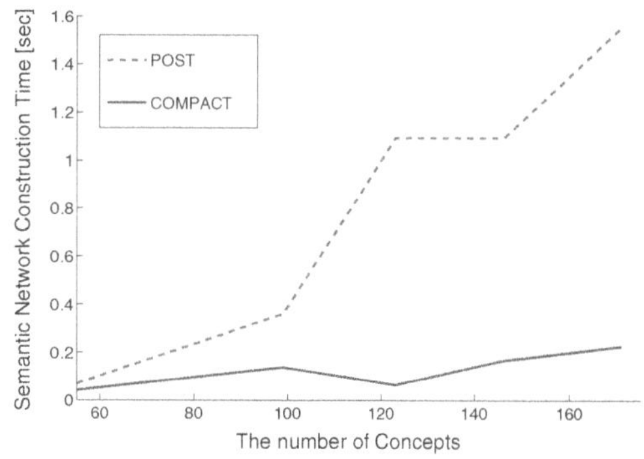

Figure 5: Change of construction time as the number of concept increases

4. DEMONSTRATION PLAN

We will demonstrate our system in the following steps.

1. First, we will use a poster to give an overview of the system including the motivation, algorithm, framework for the system.
2. Next, we will present a video explaining how to explore semantic network and use it to expanding query.
3. Then, we will qualitatively evaluate our system by providing a sample query through demo system.
4. Finally, we will let users freely make a query to our demo system through web, and expand query keyword by exploring presenting semantic graph.

References

[1] C. Carpineto, S. Osiński, G. Romano, and D. Weiss. A survey of Web clustering engines. *ACM Computing Surveys*, 41(3): 1–38, July 2009.

[2] R. Krishnapuram and K. Kummamuru. Automatic taxonomy generation: Issues and possibilities. In *Fuzzy Sets and Systems*, pages 184–184. Springer, 2003.

[3] K. Kummamuru, R. Lotlikar, S. Roy, K. Singal, and R. Krishnapuram. A hierarchical monothetic document clustering algorithm for summarization and browsing search results. In *WWW '04*, page 658, 2004.

[4] D. Lawrie and W. Croft. Discovering and comparing topic hierarchies. In *Proceedings of RIAO 2000 Conference*, 2000.

[5] D. Lawrie, W. B. Croft, and A. Rosenberg. Finding topic words for hierarchical summarization. In *SIGIR '01*, pages 349–357, 2001. ACM Press.

[6] J. Oh, T. Kim, S. Park, and H. Yu. PubMed Search and Exploration with Real-Time Semantic Network Construction. Technical report, 2012. URL `http://dm.postech.ac.kr/techreport/TechReport-POSTECH-2012-03-SemanticNetwork.pdf`.

[7] M. Sanderson and B. Croft. Deriving concept hierarchies from text. In *SIGIR '99*, pages 206–213, 1999. ACM Press.

[8] S. Szumlanski and F. Gomez. Automatically acquiring a semantic network of related concepts. In *CIKM'10*, pages 19–28. ACM, 2010.

[9] X. Wang and M. Bramer. Exploring web search results clustering. In *in intelligent systems XXIII: proceedings of*, 2006.

Author Index

Abe, Yoshihisa 1158
Abrahao, Bruno 624
Agarwal, Pankaj K. 1487
Agarwal, Shivali 1393
Agichtein, Eugene 123
Agrawal, Ankit 1556
Agrawal, Gagan 1113
Agrawal, Rakesh 435, 967
Agüera y Arcas, Blaise 678
Akoglu, Leman 1231, 1516
Al Bawab, Ziad 397
Ali, Kamal 204
Almeida, Virgílio 1014
Alonso, Gustavo 1451
Anderson, Ashton 850
Anerousis, Nikos 1415
Antonini, Gianluca 1460
Ardon, Sebastien 1186
Arlitt, Martin 994
Aufaure, Marie-Aude 1520
Azimi, Javad 777
Baeza-Yates, Ricardo 1014
Bagnall, Anthony 289
Bahmani, Bahman 24
Bailey, James 651
Bailey, Thomas C. 1140
Barford, Paul 886
Bash, Cullen 994
Basu, Sugato 1231
Batal, Iyad 280
Batista, Gustavo 262
Bellala, Gowtham 994
Bellare, Kedar 1131
Benevenuto, Fabrício 1014
Benzi, Michele 123
Berberich, Klaus 1512
Beutel, Alex 426
Bhalgat, Anand 1213
Bharadwaj, Vijay 1195
Biagioni, James 669
Boddeti, Vishnu Naresh 1158
Boden, Brigitte 1258
Boedihardjo, Arnold P. 1375
Böhlen, Michael H. 471
Böhm, Christian 1249
Boley, Mario 69
Bonchi, Francesco 1321
Borghol, Youmna 1186
Brefeld, Ulf 417
Briggs, Forrest 534
Butler, Patrick 1375
Cadonna, Bruno 471
Cai, Deng 723
Campana, Bilson 262
Cao, Jie 985
Cao, Longbing 660, 976
Carin, Lawrence 96, 325
Carlsson, Niklas 1186
Caruana, Rich 150
Cataldi, Mario 1520
Chakrabarti, Kaushik 1384
Chakraborty, Sunandan 967
Chan, Jeffrey 651
Chang, Kevin Chen-Chuan 1023
Chatterjee, Snigdhansu 642
Chattopadhyay, Rita 741
Chau, Duen Horng (Polo) 1516
Chaudhuri, Surajit 1384
Chawla, Nitesh V. 168
Chen, Enhong 570
Chen, Hung-Hsuan 1524
Chen, Lei 1508
Chen, Ming-Syan 949, 1403
Chen, Peiji 1195
Chen, Rishan 1564
Chen, Rui 213
Chen, Shuo 714
Chen, Wenlin 1140
Chen, Xu 96
Chen, Ye 795
Chen, Yixin 1140
Cheng, Haibin 777
Cheng, Hanqiang 552
Cheng, James 1240
Cheng, Tao 1384
Cheng, Yu 1556
Chiang, Kai-Yang 507
Chiarandini, Luca 417
Chiranjeevi, Kunapareddy 1532
Choudhary, Alok 1556
Chu, Shumo 1240
Ciou, Yan-Bin 1524
Clark, Sam 1104
Clifton, Chris 1041
Comarela, Giovanni 1014
Compton, Paul 814
Cong, Gao 114
Connolly, Andrew J. 1478
Correa, Carlos D. 1330
Corso, Jason J. 958
Coscia, Michele 615
Crespo, Jean-Francois 397
Crovella, Mark 832, 886
Dalessandro, Brian 804, 1357
Das, Abhimanyu 1204
Dasdan, Ali 768
Dasgupta, Anirban 235
Datta, Samik 1005
Davidson, Ian 741, 1312
Davis, Luke M. 289
Deng, Alex 786
Deng, Hongbo 1023
Desai, Bipin C. 213
Dhillon, Inderjit S. 507
Di Caro, Luigi 1520
Ding, Qi 886
Ding, Wei 60, 976
Domeniconi, Carlotta 1077
Dong, Li 1528
Douglas, Seymour 1004
Dror, Gideon 1406
Duggal, Geet 42
Duivesteijn, Wouter 868

Eager, Derek 1186
Ebadollahi, Shahram 453
El-Arini, Khalid 678
Eliassi-Rad, Tina 1231
Eriksson, Jakob 669
Etzioni, Oren 1104
Faloutsos, Christos 6, 271, 316
426, 1158, 1231, 1516
Fan, Wei 696, 741
Fan, Xiaoming 561
Färber, Ines 132, 352
Feelders, Ad 868
Fei-Fei, Li 1068
Feldman, Jon 1213
Feng, Jing 1249
Feng, Mengling 1536
Feng, Wei 1276
Fern, Xiaoli Z. 534
Filippova, Darya 42
Forman, George 669
Fradkin, Dmitriy 280
Frasca, Brian 786
Fujiwara, Yasuhiro 15
Fung, Benjamin C. M. 213
Gabrilovich, Evgeniy 1406
Galbrun, Esther 1544
Gallagher, Brian 1231
Gamper, Johann 471
Ganger, Gregory R. 1158
Gao, Bin 1177
Gao, Bo 1366
Gao, Huiji 253
Gao, Jing 859
Gärtner, Thomas 69
Gehrke, Johannes 150
Ghoting, Amol 370, 489
Giannotti, Fosca 615
Giatsidis, Christos 1512
Gionis, Aristides 687, 1321
Gleich, David F. 597
Gollapudi, Sreenivas 967
Gong, Pinghua 895
Goyal, Amit 1294
Gray, Alexander 159, 931, 1478
Großkreutz, Henrik 1442
Guan, Ziyu 1415
Guestrin, Carlos 1122
Gullo, Francesco 1321
Günnemann, Stephan 132,
352, 1258
Gunopulos, Dimitrios 408
Gupta, Manish 859
Gupta, Neha 1204
Haider, Peter 417
Halawi, Guy 1406
Han, Jiawei 2, 444, 723,
859, 1032, 1348, 1500
Han, Lei 114
Han, Richard 552
Harpale, Abhay 316
Harrison, James 280
Hauskrecht, Milos 280
He, Qi 1032
He, Xiao 1249
He, Xiaofei 298, 723
Henderson, Keith 1231
Herbrich, Ralf 678
Hills, Jon 289
Hirai, So 343
Hoens, Thomas Ryan 168
Hoffmann, Holger 1258
Holada, Rich 407
Holmes, Geoff 225
Honbo, Daniel 1556
Hook, Rod 804
Hopcroft, John 624
Horvitz, Eric 1122
Hossain, M. Shahriar 1375
Hsieh, Cho-Jui 507
Hu, Jianying 453
Hu, Po 1366
Hu, Yao 298
Huan, Jun 543
Huang, Minlie 1366
Huang, Sheng-Jun 525
Huang, Sui 552
Huberman, Bernardo A. 244
Huttenlocher, Daniel 850
Ieong, Samuel 435
Iwata, Tomoharu 271
Iyengar, Suresh 1131
Jain, Ashesh 750
Jan, Te-Kang 141
Ji, Ming 723
Ji, Shuiwang 334
Jiao, L. C. 732
Jiao, Limei 570
Jin, Hongxia 388
Jin, Ruoming 1303
Jin, Xiaoming 1086
Joachims, Thorsten 705, 714
Johnson, David 958
Jojic, Nebojsa 1339
Jordan, Michael I. 4, 1339
Kalousis, Alexandros 913
Kang, U 316
Kannan, Anitha 967
Kantarcioglu, Murat 1059
Karras, Panagiotis 1050
Karwath, Andreas 516
Katenka, Natallia 886
Kawale, Jaya 642
Ke, Yiping 1240
Kearns, Michael 5
Kenthapadi, Krishnaram 967
Keogh, Eamonn 262
Kim, Gunhee 1068
Kim, Jinha 1540
Kim, Taehoon 1572
Kim, Youngwoo 1540
Kingsford, Carl 42
Kitsuregawa, Masaru 223
Kleinberg, Jon 850
Kleinberg, Robert 624
Kliot, Gabriel 1222
Knobbe, Arno 868
Kohavi, Ron 786
Kolaczyk, Eric 886
Kollef, Marin 1140
Kong, Xiangnan 1552
Konte, Bettina 1249
Koren, Yehuda 1406
Koutra, Danai 1231
Kramer, Stefan 516
Kuksa, Pavel P. 759

Kumar, Ravi 24, 235
Kumar, Shamanth 1548
Kumar, Vipin 642
Kurihara, Kenichi 105
Labbi, Abderrahim 1460
Lai, Ying-Cheng 922
Lakshmanan, Laks V. S. 1294
Lappas, Theodoros 408, 687, 832
Lebanon, Guy 307
Leckie, Christopher 651
Lee, Jaewoo 1041
Lee, Kuang-chih 768
Lee, Noah 453
Lee, Wang-Chien 949, 1032
Leskovec, Jure 33, 850
Li, Baoxin 1469
Li, Chengkai 1487
Li, Cheng-Te 1568
Li, Cuiping 1405
Li, Deyi 222
Li, Geng 87
Li, Jianzhong 813
Li, Lei 6, 1231
Li, Liangda 307
Li, Lianghao 1086
Li, Robin 1
Li, Rui 1023
Li, Sujian 379
Li, Tao 633
Li, Weichang 1366
Li, Wentong 768
Li, Xiaoming 1564
Li, Yong 696
Li, Zhenhui 444
Liang, Yu-li 552
Liess, Stefan 642
Lin, Binbin 723
Lin, Chih-Jen 1176
Lin, Chi-Hung 141
Lin, Hsuan-Tien 141
Lin, Shou-De 1524, 1568
Lin, Shuyang 823
Lindstrom, Peter 1330
Lines, Jason 289
Liu, Bing 841
Liu, Gang 1552
Liu, Guimei 51, 1536
Liu, Guiquan 570
Liu, Huan 253, 904, 1548
Liu, Jun 298, 334, 1095
Liu, Shixia 1433
Liu, Tantan 1113
Liu, Tie-Yan 1177
Liu, Wei 651
Liu, Xiaohua 379
Liu, Xingjie 1032
Liu, Xue 552
Liu, Xuemei 669
Liu, Xueqing 1433
Liu, Yan 388
Liu, Yong 1267
Longbotham, Roger 786
Lou, Yin 150
Lu, Chenyang 1140
Luo, Ping 570, 1424
Lv, Qin 552
Lyon, Geoff 994
Ma, Haixin 1402
Ma, Wei-Ying 586
Ma, Wenjing 1195
Mahanti, Anirban 1186
Mahdian, Mohammad 24
Majumder, Anirban 1005
Malik, Shahzad Malik 1532
Manavoglu, Eren 777
Mao, Yi 1140
March, William B. 1478
Marshall, Grant 1548
Marwah, Manish 994
Matsubara, Yasuko 6, 271
Matsushima, Shin 177
Mausam 1104
Mayer, Uwe F. 579
McPherson, John 1032
Meng, Xinfan 379
Miao, Gengxin 1415
Miettinen, Pauli 1544
Mills, George H. 397
Mirrokni, Vahab 1213
Mishra, Shivakant 552
Moens, Sandy 69
Moerchen, Fabian 280
Moore, Joshua L. 714
Morstatter, Fred 1548
Moser, Louise 1415
Mueen, Abdullah 262
Mukherjee, Arjun 841
Myers, Seth 33
Nagarajan, Chandrashekhar 1195
Naidu, KVM 1005
Nakagawa, Hiroshi 105
Nakatsuji, Makoto 15
Nambiar, Ullas 1548
Narayan, Vaibhav A. 1095, 1149
Narayanan, Vijay K. 1204
Navalpakkam, Vidhya 777
Ng, See-Kiong 1536
Nguyen, Phong 913
Norick, Brandon 1348
Oh, Jinoh 1572
Olteanu, Dan 1504
Onizuka, Makoto 15
Ormsby, Dominick 642
Orten, Burkay 768
Ouyang, Hua 159
Pagh, Rasmus 877
Pan, Sinno Jialin 1086
Panchanathan, Sethuraman 741
Pandey, Sandeep 1204
Papalexakis, Evangelos 316
Paquet, Ulrich 678
Parameswaran, Aditya 1131
Park, Haesun 307
Park, Sun 1572
Parthasarathy, Srinivasan 370
Patro, Rob 42
Paurat, Daniel 1442
Pavlovic, Vladimir 759
Pedreschi, Dino 615
Peng, Wen-Chih 195
Perlich, Claudia 804, 1357
Pham, Ninh 877
Plant, Claudia 361, 1249
Posse, Christian 587
Prakash, B. Aditya 6, 426

Provost, Foster 804, 1357
Qian, Long 1496
Qian, Weining 1402
Raeder, Troy 804, 1357
Raich, Raviv 534
Raïssi, Chedy 1050
Rakthanmanon, Thanawin 262
Ram, Parikshit 931
Ramakrishnan, Naren 1375
Ramamohanarao, Kotagiri 651
Raman, Karthik 705
Rangwala, Huzefa 1077
Rastogi, Vibhor 1131
Ren, Kai 1158
Ritter, Alan 1104
Rosenfeld, Roni 426
Rossetti, Giulio 615
Roy, Pratanu 1451
Ruan, Yiye 370
Rueping, Stefan 1442
Saez-Trumper, Diego 1014
Sakurai, Yasushi 6, 271
Sanjay, Addicam V. 1532
Sarma, Atish Das 253
Sato, Issei 105
Schifanella, Claudio 1520
Seeland, Madeleine 516
Sefer, Emre 42
Seidl, Thomas 132, 352, 1258
Sengupta, Bikram 1393
Seshadhri, C 597
Shafer, Ilari 1158
Shahaf, Dafna 1122
Shan, Dongdong 1564
Shang, Fanhua 732
Shen, Chih-Ya 949
Shen, Chongwei 1496
Shen, Wei 1424
Shen, Xiaotong 480, 922
Shen, Yelong 1303
Shi, Chuan 1552
Shi, Kent 204
Shi, Xiaoxiao 588
Shi, Yong 406
Shi, Zhongzhi 816
Shie, Bai-En 78
Shiokawa, Hiroaki 15
Shivaswamy, Pannaga 705
Shu, Baihan 1564
Shwartz, Larisa 633
Silva, Jorge 325
Simovici, Dan A. 60
Sindhgatta, Renuka 1393
Sindhwani, Vikas 489
Sivakumar, D 235
Smola, Alexander J. 177
Sondhi, Parikshit 1167
Song, Guojie 114
Song, Yangqiu 1433
Song, Yin 976
Sossou, Nériah M. 213
Soundarajan, Sucheta 624
Speiser, Michel 1460
Stanton, Isabelle 1222
Steck, Harald 1267
Steinhaeuser, Karsten 642
Stitelman, Ori 804, 1357
Su, Hang 1285
Suchitra, Andre 1536
Sun, Gordon 1404
Sun, Jian-Tao 1086
Sun, Jimeng 453, 1167, 1285, 1415
Sun, Yizhou 859, 1348, 1500
Sutanto, Juliana 1460
Tan, Kian-Lee 1050
Tang, Jie 1285, 1366
Tang, Jiliang 253, 904
Tang, Liang 633
Tang, Linpeng 570
Tao, Dacheng 985
Tao, Shu 1415
Tatti, Nikolaj 462
Terzi, Evimaria 687, 832
Teubner, Jens 1451
Thilikos, Dimitrios M. 1512
Thompson, Paul M. 1149
Thuraisingham, Bhavani 1059
Tian, Phil 1532
Tian, Yuandong 226
Tian, Yuanyuan 1032
Tomlin, John 1195
Tong, Hanghang .. 1167, 1231, 1516
Tong, Yongxin 1508
Tseng, Vincent S. 78
Turnbull, Douglas 714
Ueda, Naonori 815
Ukkonen, Antti 1321
Upfal, Eli 24
Usadi, Adam K. 1366
Vaidya, Jaideep 1050
Valkanas, George 408
Van Gael, Jurgen 678
van Schaik, Sebastiaan J. 1504
Varma, Manik 750
Vassilvitskii, Sergei 1195
Vazirgiannis, Michalis 1512
Vee, Erik 1195
Virochsiri, Kittipat 352
Vishwanathan, S. V. N. 177, 750
Vreeken, Jilles 462, 1516
Walker, Toby 786
Wang, Bai 1496, 1552
Wang, Bo 1366
Wang, Chunyan 244
Wang, Da-Wei 141
Wang, Fei 453, 732
Wang, Guan 588, 823
Wang, Haixun 1433, 1560
Wang, Hao 42
Wang, Houfeng 379
Wang, Jianyong 561, 1276, 1424
Wang, Jingjing 444
Wang, Junwei 696
Wang, Min 570, 1424
Wang, Rui 1023
Wang, Shengjie 1023
Wang, Yalin 1149
Wang, Yin 669
Wang, Yu 123
Wang, Zheng 741
Wang, Ziqi 1564
Wauthier, Fabian L. 1339
Wei, Furu 379
Wei, Gang 976

Wei, Ling-Yin 195
Westover, Brandon 262
Williams, Graham 1003
Wong, Limsoon 51, 1536
Wonka, Peter 922
Woznica, Adam 913
Wu, Bin 1496
Wu, Cheng Wei 78
Wu, Junjie 985, 1528
Wu, Sen 1285
Wu, Xindong 60, 976
Wu, You 1487
Wu, Zhiang 985
Xi, Bowei 1059
Xiang, Shuo 480
Xiao, Lei 696
Xie, Kunqing 114
Xie, Sihong 823
Xie, Xing 186
Xie, Yusheng 1556
Xin, Dong 1384
Xing, Eric P. 1068
Xing, Xinyu 552
Xiong, Caiming 958
Xu, Ke 1528
Xu, Peng 1366
Xu, Ran 958
Xu, Ya 786
Xue, Mingqiang 1050
Yamamuro, Takeshi 15
Yamanishi, Kenji 343
Yan, Hongfei 1564
Yan, Tak W. 795
Yan, Xifeng 1348, 1415
Yan, Xinyu 1366
Yang, De-Nian 949
Yang, Jian 1195
Yang, Jun 1487
Yang, Sen 922
Yang, Xintian 370
Yang, Xiwang 1267
Yang, Yang 1366
Yao, Junjie 1564
Ye, Jieping 298, 480, 741, 895, 922, 1095, 1149
Ye, Mao 244
Ye, Wu 976
Yeung, Dit-Yan 606, 940
Yin, Junfu 660
Yoshikawa, Masatoshi 271
Yu, Cong 1487
Yu, Guoxian 1077
Yu, Hwanjo 1540, 1572
Yu, Kui 60
Yu, Le 1496
Yu, Philip S. 78, 588, 823, 1348, 1508, 1552
Yu, Xiao 1348, 1500
Yu, Yang 525
Yu, Yong 1177
Yu, Zhiwen 1077
Yuan, Jing 186
Yuan, Lei 922, 1149
Yuan, Xiaojie 1177
Zakaria, Jesin 262
Zaki, Mohammed J. 87
Zha, Hongyuan 498
Zhai, ChengXiang 1167
Zhang, Bo 224
Zhang, Changshui 895
Zhang, Debing 298
Zhang, Guoji 1077
Zhang, Haojun 51, 1536
Zhang, Jintao 543
Zhang, Jun 561
Zhang, Kunpeng 1556
Zhang, Lei 570
Zhang, Qiang 1469
Zhang, Renbo 1496
Zhang, Ruofei 777
Zhang, Weinan 1177
Zhang, Wenlu 334
Zhang, Ying 1177
Zhang, Yu 606
Zhang, Zhixian 1560
Zhao, Jichang 1528
Zhao, Peixiang 1500
Zhao, Wayne Xin 1564
Zhao, Yanting 1366
Zhao, Yuchen 588
Zhen, Yi 940
Zheng, Jian 1496
Zheng, Yu 186, 195
Zheng, Zhigang 660
Zhong, Erheng 696
Zhou, Aoying 1402
Zhou, Chong 1552
Zhou, Jiayu 1095
Zhou, Ke 498
Zhou, Lizhu 561
Zhou, Ming 379
Zhou, Mingyuan 96
Zhou, Wenjun 388
Zhou, Yan 1059
Zhou, Yang 777
Zhou, Zhi-Hua 525
Zhu, Chenguang 33
Zhu, Jun 226
Zhu, Kenny Q. 1560
Zhu, Linhong 1240
Zhu, Qiang 262
Zhu, Yanmin 669
Zhu, Yi 552
Zhu, Yunzhang 480
Zwol, Roelof van 777

www.ingramcontent.com/pod-product-compliance
Ingram Content Group UK Ltd.
Pitfield, Milton Keynes, MK11 3LW, UK
UKHW051240300926
15471UKWH00015B/1208

9 781450 319478